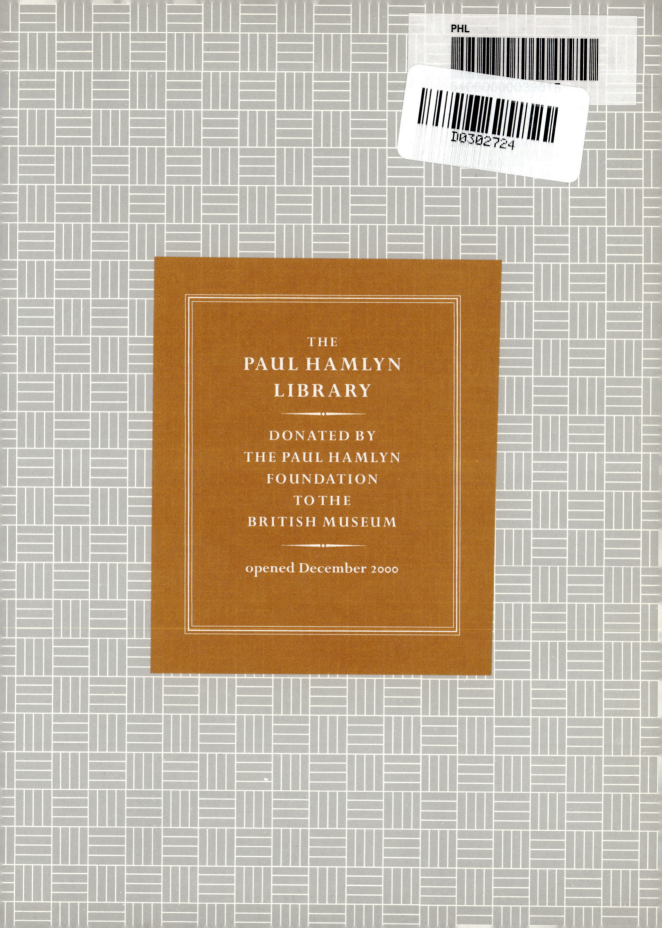

DICTIONARY OF

ISLAMIC ARCHITECTURE

DICTIONARY OF
ISLAMIC ARCHITECTURE

Andrew Petersen

ROUTLEDGE

London and New York

First published 1996
by Routledge
11 New Fetter Lane, London EC4P 4EE

Simultaneously published in the USA and Canada by Routledge
29 West 35th Street, New York, NY 10001

Typeset in Optima and Palatino
Printed and bound in Great Britain by Clays Ltd, St Ives plc

British Library Cataloguing in Publication Data
A catalogue record for this book is available from the British Library

Library of Congress Cataloging in Publication Data
Applied for

ISBN 0–415–06084–2

Contents

Dedication

This book is dedicated to my friend Jamie Cameron (1962-95) historian of James V of Scotland.

Preface

> In one of the quarters of the city is the Muhammadan town, where the Muslims have their cathedral, mosque, hospice and bazar. They have also a qadi and a shaykh, for in every one of the cities of China there must always be a shaykh al-Islam, to whom all matters concerning Muslims are referred.
>
> Ibn Battuta, *Travels in Asia and Africa 1325–1354*, Routledge & Kegan Paul, 1929

Abu Abdallah Mahammad of Tangier, also known as Ibn Battuta, is the most famous of the Arab travellers. His journeys started with a pilgrimage (hajj) to Mecca and afterwards he always tried to travel within a Muslim context whether he was in Timbuktu or China. What is notable about these accounts is that they deal with Muslim communities which are remote from the western stereotype of Muslim society. For example most general works on Islamic architecture tend to confine themselves to the Middle East and North Africa, neglecting the centuries old Islamic heritage of South-East Asia, India, East and West Africa. It is an aim of this book to include as many as possible of these less well known Muslim cultures whose populations now outnumber those of the central Islamic lands.

As a corollary to this approach there has been an attempt to include vernacular architecture rather than dealing exclusively with well known monumental architecture. As well as being important in its own right vernacular architecture provides an architectural context for the more famous monuments. In order to aid the reader's appreciation of this relationship, vernacular architecture has been included in regional summaries, which also discuss the geographical and cultural character of an area. As a balance to the regional approach there are also historical accounts dealing with particular dynasties or historic styles.

The encyclopedic nature of this work has meant that there is little room for theoretical discussions of aesthetics or meaning. This is not because these are unimportant considerations but because these are issues best discussed in a different, more selective format. The main purpose of this book is to provide basic information which includes definitions of architectural terms, descriptions of specific monuments and summaries of regional and historic groups. Attached to each entry there is a short list of books for further reading which refers the user to the principal works on the subject. It is hoped that the information provided will enable the reader to gain some appreciation of the diversity and genius of Muslim culture.

Acknowledgements

First, I must thank my parents who have enabled me to pursue my interest in this subject. Gwendolyn Leick gave me the idea for the book in the first place and subsequently encouraged me in the long process of writing.

The research that I undertook for the book was of two kinds – library based and field work. The library research was carried out in a number of institutions in Europe and the Middle East and I would like to thank everyone who helped me with references or information, in particular: Michael Given, Tony Grey, StJohn Simpson, Benjamin Pickles, Mark Horton, Alistair Northedge, Matt Thompson and Jeremy Johns. The field research was usually carried out as an incidental part of other projects. Several individuals and institutions have been particularly helpful; these are: the British School of Archaeology in Jerusalem, the British School of Archaeology in Iraq, the British Institute at Amman for Archaeology and History, the British Institute in Eastern Africa, the International Merv Project, Dr Julian Reade and the Turkish Government.

Preparation of the manuscript and drawings was helped by a number of people including Heather Nixon, Charles Craske, Crispian Pickles, David Myres and Kate Cheyne. Photographs were provided by a number of people and institutions, in particular I would like to thank Kerry Abbott, Pat and Charles Aithie, Susan Bailey, Rebecca Foote, Cherry Pickles and James Allan. Here I would also like to express my thanks to Mark Barragry and Seth Denbo both of Routledge for their enthusiasm and patience.

Finally, I would like to express my gratitude to my wife Heather Nixon who tolerated and helped with this book for so long.

A

Abbasids

Dynasty which ruled most of the Islamic world between 750 and 945.

In 750 CE there was a revolution against Umayyad rule which began in eastern Iran and rapidly spread over the whole empire. The Umayyads were totally destroyed except for one prince who fled to Spain and established the Umayyad dynasty there. The newly established Abbasids decided to move the capital from Damascus to a city further east, first Raqqa was chosen and then in 762 Baghdad was founded by the Abbasid caliph al-Mansur. Baghdad grew to be one of the biggest and most populous cities in the world based around Mansur's famous round city. In 836 the caliph al-Mu'tassim was unhappy about clashes between the local population and his troops so he established a new capital further north on the Tigris at Samarra. During this period the power of the caliphate began to decline and control over distant provinces was loosened. Several local dynasties grew up including the Tulunids in Egypt, the Aghlabids in Ifriqiyya and the Samanids in Khurassan (eastern Iran). Internal troubles in Samarra caused the caliph al Mu'tamid to move back to Baghdad in 889; at this time Abbasid power outside Iraq was purely nominal. In 945 the Abbasids were replaced by the Shi'a Buwaihid amirs as rulers of Iraq and Iran. For the next two hundred years the Abbasids remained nominal caliphs with no real authority. In the mid-twelfth century the Abbasids were able to reassert some authority when the Seljuk ruler Sultan Muhamad abandoned his siege of Baghdad. During the reign of Caliph al-Nasir (1179–1225) the Abbasids were able to gain control over much of present-day Iraq. The Mongol invasions and sack of Baghdad in 1258 dealt a final blow to the political aspirations of the Abbasids.

Although Abbasid architecture covers a vast area from North Africa to western India, the majority of extant buildings are in the Abbasid homeland of Iraq. Abbasid architecture was influenced by three architectural traditions – Sassanian, Central Asian (Soghdian) and later, during the twelfth and thirteenth centuries, Seljuk. Many early Abbasid structures such as the palace of Ukhaidhir bear a striking resemblance to Sassanian architecture, as they used the same techniques (vaults made without centring) and materials (mud brick, baked brick and roughly hewn stone laid in mortar), and built to similar designs (solid buttress towers). Central Asian influence was already present in Sassanian architecture but it was reinforced by the Islamic conquest of Central Asia and the incorporation of a large number of Turkic troops into the army. Central Asian influence is seen most clearly at Samarra where the wall paintings and some of the stucco work resemble that of the Soghdian palaces at Panjikent. The Abbasid architecture of the twelfth and thirteenth centuries is essentially Seljuk architecture built with Iraqi materials.

In addition to the various influences upon it, early Abbasid architecture can be seen to have developed its own characteristics. One of the most notable features of the Abbasid cities of Baghdad and Samarra is their vast scale. This is most clearly demonstrated at Samarra with its extensive palaces and mosques stretched out for more than 40 km along the banks of the Tigris. The scale of the site led to the development of new forms: thus the great spiral minarets of the Great Mosque and the Abu Dulaf Mosque were never repeated elsewhere (with the possible exception of the Ibn Tulun Mosque). Other developments had far-reaching consequences; for example, the three stucco types developed at Samarra rapidly spread throughout the Islamic world (e.g. the Abbasid mosque at Balkh in Afghanistan) and continued to be used centuries later.

See also: Aghlabids, Baghdad, Balkh, Iraq, Samarra, Tulunids, Ukhaidhir

ablaq

Term used to describe alternating light and dark courses of masonry.

Azzam Palace, Damascus. Eighteenth-century example of ablaq masonry, ©*Rebecca Foote*

It is thought that the origin of this decorative technique may derive from the Byzantine use of alternating courses of white ashlar stone and orange baked brick. The technique of ablaq seems to have originated in southern Syria where volcanic black basalt and white limestone naturally occur in equal quantities. The first recorded use is in repairs to the north wall of the Great Mosque of Damascus which are dated to 1109. In 1266 Sultan Baybars built a palace known as Qasr Ablaq which was built out of bands of light and dark masonry. Although the building has not survived, it demonstrates that the term ablaq was used to describe masonry of this type. In the fourteenth and fifteenth centuries this became a characteristic feature of Mamluk architecture in Egypt, Syria and Palestine. At this stage red stone is also used so that some buildings are striped in three colours, red, black and white. Ablaq continued to be used in the Ottoman period and can be seen in buildings such as the Azzam palace in Damascus. A difference between its use in the Mamluk and the Ottoman periods is that earlier on it was restricted to façades, doorways and windows whereas in the Ottoman period it is used for overall decoration, sometimes including the floors. The technique was also used in Spain and can be seen in the voussoirs of the arcades of the Great Mosque in Córdoba which are red and white.

The technique also seems to have been invented in Europe in the mid-twelfth century although it is not certain whether it was invented independently or copied from Syria. Important European examples are the thirteenth-century churches of Monza, Siena and Orvieto and a four-storey palace in Genoa.

Afghanistan

Mountainous country located between Iran, India and Central Asia.

Most of Afghanistan is either mountain or desert with only 13 per cent of the land under cultivation. The country is dominated by two mountain ranges, the Hindu Kush and the Himalayas. Communication between different areas is difficult and many villages are cut off by snow for half the year. The climate is extreme with temperatures varying from −26 to 50 degrees centigrade. The population is a mixture of ethnic groups including Pushtun, Tajiks, Uzbeks and Turkoman.

Since earliest times Afghanistan's importance has been based on its position between the great civilizations of Iran to the west and India to the south-east. In addition the country formed a route between nomadic Central Asia and the more settled regions to the south. These diverse cultures have all left their mark on the history and archaeology of the country. Before the second century BCE Afghanistan was ruled by the Achaemenids who traced their origins to the conquests of Alexander the Great. From the first century BCE the country was taken over by nomadic groups from Chinese Central Asia, the most significant of which were the Kushans who established a major empire with Buddhism as the official religion. The great Kushan Empire had broken up by the eighth century CE leaving the Sassanians controlling the west and the eastern part in the hands of independent Kushan rulers.

With the fall of the Sassanian Empire the western provinces of Khurassan and Sistan were incorporated into the Islamic Empire although the eastern province of Kabul did not accept Islam until the ninth or tenth century. The first Muslim rulers to control the entire area were the Ghaznavids who seized power from the Samanid rulers of Khurassan in the late tenth century. Under the second ruler, Mahmud, the Ghaznavid Empire was extended to include the Punjab and parts of western Iran. In the late eleventh century the Ghaznavids were threatened by the Seljuks who took over most of Iran and eventually reduced them to the status of vassals. Both the Seljuks and the Ghaznavids were defeated by a local dynasty known as the Ghurids in the late twelfth century. The thirteenth century saw the arrival of the Mongols who incorporated the region into their vast empire. During the fourteenth century the Mongol Empire fragmented and in 1339 Timur established his own empire. Herat was established under the Timurids as capital of the dynasty and became the principal city of the region. A further nomadic invasion at the beginning of the sixteenth century led to the collapse of the Timurid Empire. In 1528 Herat was occupied by the Saffavids whilst the Mughals (descendants of the Timurids) retained control of Kandahar in the south. The decline of these two empires in the eighteenth century led to the establishment of the kingdom of Afghanistan which was able to maintain its independence between the expanding Russian and British empires.

The principal building materials used in Afghanistan are mud brick and pisé, baked brick and stone; wood is fairly rare. The majority of pre-modern buildings in Afghanistan are built of mud brick or pisé and have not survived well the ravages of time. More important buildings are made of baked brick which is often decorated with stucco, painted frescos, tiles or relief brick patterns. There is no tradition of ashlar masonry and stonework usually consists of rubble masonry foundations for mud-brick structures. Exceptions to this usually represent outside influence such as the mosque of Larwand which is Indian in its design and execution.

The oldest identifiable Islamic building in Afghanistan is the ninth-century Abbasid mosque at Balkh. This is a square nine-domed structure with arches resting on four central piers. The north, west and south sides are solid walls whilst the east side opposite the mihrab is an open arcade resting on two round piers. The distinctive feature of the mosque is its stucco decoration which resembles that of Samarra and demonstrates the long distance transmission of ideas and motifs during this period. A more unusual form is the eleventh-century mosque/madrassa at Lashkari Bazar near the modern town of Bust. This is a square mud-brick and pisé structure with external buttress towers and a central courtyard. On the west side of the courtyard there is a small iwan containing a mihrab. The orientation of the building is aligned with the qibla (unlike other buildings on the site) suggesting that it served a religious function, possibly a madrassa. Further east at Ghazni is the palace mosque of Masud III; this is a rectangular structure with a roof supported on six pillars and three doors on the west side. The mihrab is made from marble panels carved with Quranic calligraphy and stylized vegetation. Contemporary descriptions of the city mention a hypostyle mosque supported with wooden columns made of trees imported from India. Unfortunately no mosques of this type have survived although the carved wooden mihrab in the village of Charkh-i Loghar gives an idea of the quality of woodwork of the period.

Mosques of the Ghurid period show a marked Iranian influence which can be seen in buildings such as the mosque and madrassa of Ghiyath al-Din in the village of Ghist. The remains of the building comprise two large domed units made of brick with semi-circular squinches. A better preserved example is the Shahr-i Mashad Madrassa which forms a square courtyard building with domed room. The most notable feature of the building is the decorative brickwork façade which comprises five blind niches and a projecting entrance iwan or pishtaq. The façade is decorated with cut brickwork and stucco which form elaborate patterns and include fifteen bands of inscription. More unusual is the mosque of Larwand which is built entirely of monolithic stone panels and resembles contemporary Indian architecture. The entrance is set within a façade of three arches supported by faceted engaged columns. The doorway itself is decorated with elaborate carving which resembles woodwork. Inside the mosque is covered with a dome which rests on flat corbels.

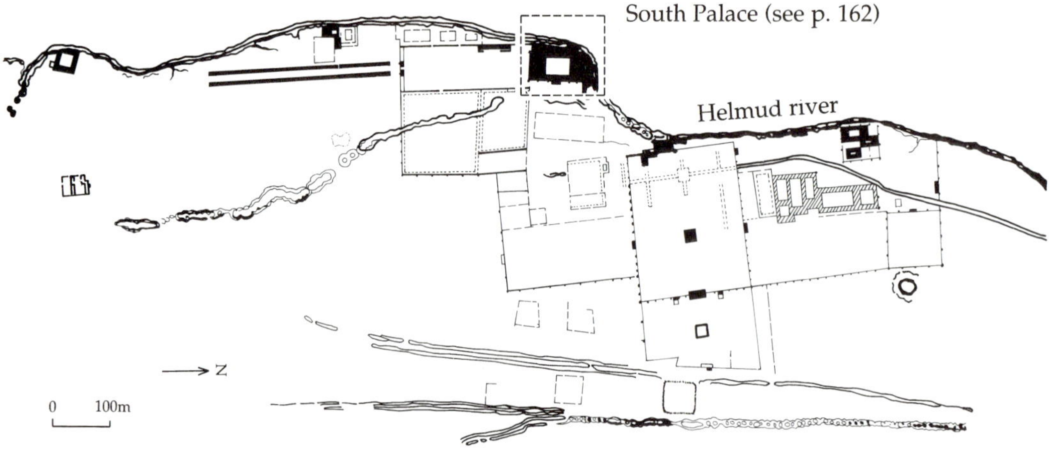

Plan of Lashkari Bazar, Afghanistan (after Allen)

Mosques of the Ilkhanid and Timurid periods continued to use the same Iranian forms although a greater variety of vaults was employed. One of the most important innovations was the double dome which was used for tombs and memorials, this comprised a shallow domed ceiling inside and a tall elongated dome outside. The greatest mosque of the Timurid period is the Great Mosque of Herat which was rebuilt during the reign of the Timurid Sultan Husain Baiqara. The mosque is built around a huge brick-paved courtyard with the principal iwan or prayer hall flanked by twin minarets at the west end. Either side of the main iwan are shallower iwans with doors leading to prayer and teaching rooms. Unfortunately the original glazed tilework of the Great Mosque has mostly been replaced although the smaller mosque of Hauz-i Karboz contains a superb example of a tiled Timurid mihrab.

The minarets or memorial towers first erected by the Ghaznavids in the eleventh century are probably the most distinctive feature of Afghan Islamic architecture. The earliest examples are the minaret of Masud III and the minaret of Bahram Shah both at the capital, Ghazni. Each of these structures consists of a baked brick tower standing on an octagonal or cylindrical stone base or socle. The baked brick shafts have a stellate (eight-pointed, star-shaped) plan and are divided into decorative brick panels. The tower of Masud originally stood more than 44 m high but has now been reduced to 20 m. The upper part of both minarets was a cylindrical shaft but these have now disappeared. Other examples of a related type are the minaret of Zaranj and the minaret of Khwaja Siah Posh, both in Sistan. The Zaranj minaret had an octagonal shaft with a semi-circular flange in the centre of each side whilst the Khwaju Siah Posh minaret comprised sixteen alternating angular and rounded flanges. The culmination of this form is the 65-metre-high minaret of Jam built by the Ghurids in the twelfth century. The height of the structure is further emphasized by its position in a deep valley at the intersection of two rivers. The tower consists of three main sections each in the form of a tapering cylinder. The lowest and largest section is decorated with panels alternating with giant strap-work loops and terminating in a muqarnas corbel balcony. The second and third storeys are each decorated with giant bands of calligraphy.

The first examples of Islamic domestic architecture occur at the site of Lashkari Bazar near the modern town of Bust. The site contains three palaces, the most famous of which is the southern palace which overlooks the Helmud river. This was built around a rectangular courtyard with four iwans (one on each side) leading into separate quarters. The palace was luxuriously decorated with stucco, wall paintings and carved marble panels in a style reminiscent of Abbasid Samarra. In addition to the main palaces there were a number of smaller mansions with a similar design based around a courtyard and iwans. This design was to remain a feature of later Afghan architecture and can be seen in the medieval (thirteenth- to

Twelfth-century minaret, Jam, Afghanistan, ©Ashmolean Museum

fourteenth-century) houses of Dewal-i Khodayda and Gol-i Safed. The village of Dewal-i Khodayda comprises a number of courtyard-iwan houses aligned to protect them from the north-west wind. Gol-i Safed is a walled town with houses of a similar design to Khodayda but more elaborate decoration in the form of blind niches and decorative brickwork.

See also: Herat, Iran, Lashkari Bazar, Mughals, Timurids

Further reading:

F. R. Allcin and N. Hammond (eds), *The Archaeology of Afghanistan from Earliest Times to the Timurid Period*, London, New York, San Francisco 1978.

Agades (also Agadez)

Islamic trading city located in the Aïr region of Niger, West Africa.

The origins of the city are obscure although it is likely that it began as a Tuareg encampment like its western counterpart Timbuktu. The first arrival of Tuareg into the region is not known although Ibn Battuta describes the area as under Tuareg domination in the fourteenth century. In 1405 the Tuareg sultanate of Aïr was inaugurated and it is likely that Agades was founded at this time. Nevertheless, the first Tuareg sultans remained nomads and were not based in the city until the mid-fifteenth century by which time the town was an important entrepôt for the trade between Timbuktu and Cairo. In the early sixteenth century Sonni Ali the emperor of Gao deposed Adil the ruling sultan of Agades and replaced him with a governor. At the same time a Songhay colony was established and Songhay was established as the official language of the city. Although the city was not captured during the Moroccan invasion of 1591, the disruption of the trade routes meant that the city declined and by 1790 it was almost completely deserted. Many of the inhabitants migrated to the Hausa cities of the south. By the mid-nineteenth century the city had recovered and was once more a prosperous trading centre with a mixed population of Berbers from the Algerian Sahara and immigrants from the Hausa cities of Kano and Sokoto.

The main building material in Agades is mud-brick although immediately outside the city in the Tuareg encampments stone is the main material of construction. Most houses are single storey with roofs built from split palm trunks laid diagonally across the corners supporting more beams on top of which are palm frond mats with earth piled on top.

Little remains of the pre-nineteenth-century town although descriptions by early European and Arab travellers give some idea of what the earlier Tuareg city looked like. A sixteenth-century description by Leo Africanus describes the city as built in the 'Barbary mode' (i.e. Berber) which implies that it may have consisted of stone houses like those inhabited by the present-day Tuareg of the region. These houses are simple two-roomed rectangular buildings made of stone and mortar often with mud-brick courtyards and outhouses.

The Tuareg nature of the city is further emphasized by the open prayer place (musalla) and shrine known as Sidi Hamada just outside the south walls of the city. The site consists of an open area of ground with a low bank at the east side against which is built a dry stone wall which rises up to the mihrab in the centre. A nineteenth-century description of the southern part of the city mentions a large mud-brick complex surrounded by a walled enclosure crowned with pinnacles. It seems likely that this may have been the citadel of the Tuareg city although it has also been interpreted as a khan. Also in this area were some well-built (stone?) houses amongst which was a building interpreted as a bath house (hammam).

When the city was resettled in the nineteenth century a large northern extension was added which was enclosed within a city wall (katanga). The houses of this period were built of mud and their interiors resembled those of the Hausa cities of northern Nigeria with moulded mud decoration.

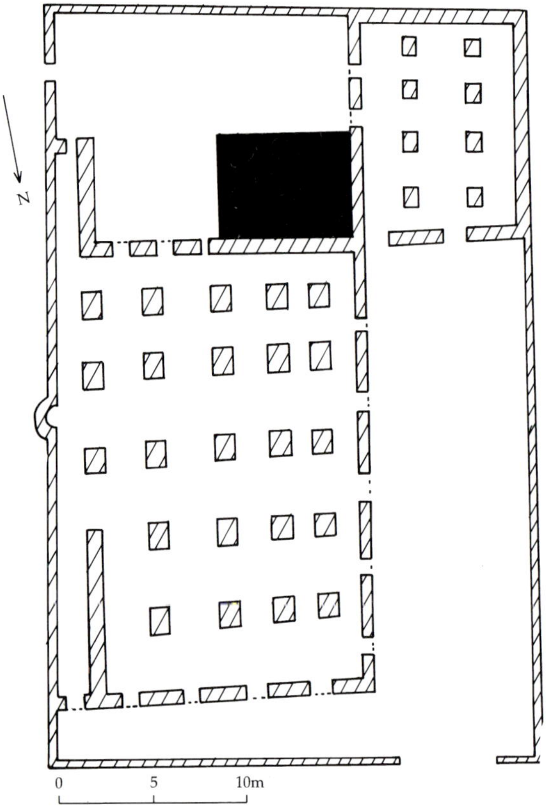

Plan of the Great Mosque, Agades, Niger. Minaret shaded (after Prussin)

The major work of this period was the rebuilding of the minaret of the Great Mosque between 1844 and 1847. The mosque consists of a large rectangular sanctuary with a mihrab in the centre of the east wall and the huge minaret attached to the north-west corner. A nineteenth-century description mentions another ruined minaret to the south of the mosque; this has now entirely disappeared. The present minaret is over 30 m high and tapers from a square base (10 m per side) at the bottom to a square platform (3 m square) at the top. The exterior faces of the minaret are characterized by thirteen layers of projecting palm timbers which act as tie beams for this complex structure. Inside the minaret there is a timber-framed staircase lit by twenty-eight openings (seven on each side). This structure is distinguished from other monumental minarets in the region by its base which consists of four massive earth piers instead of a solid block. The architectural origins of the building are not known although it has been suggested that it bears some similarity to the tapering stone-built minarets of southern Algeria.

See also: Oualata, Timbuktu, West Africa

Aghlabids

Dynasty which ruled the north African province of Ifriqiyya during the ninth century.

Although nominally under Abbasid control, the Aghlabids were able to exercise a great deal of independence. Militarily their great achievement was the conquest of Byzantine Sicily.

The Aghlabids were great patrons of architecture and much of their work has survived. Their work demonstrates a mixture of Byzantine and Abbasid building styles. One of the most important projects was the rebuilding of the Great Mosque of Qairawan and the addition of the huge three-tiered minaret/tower. The Aghlabids were also responsible for major irrigation and water supply systems the most famous example of which are the huge circular cisterns of Qairawan. Much of their effort was also directed towards the development of the coastal towns as bases from which to launch the conquest of Sicily. The military nature of Aghlabid rule is further reflected in the large number of ribats or fortified monasteries which they constructed.

See also: Tunisia

Further reading:

A. Lezine, *Architecture de l'Ifriqiyya: recherche sur les monuments aghlabides*, Paris 1966.

Agra

City in central northern India famous for its Mughal monuments.

Agra is located on the banks of the river Jumna 160 km south of Delhi. Although Agra was an ancient Hindu city the present city was refounded as a capital by Sikander Lodi at the beginning of the sixteenth century. In 1505 Iskander built a mud-brick fortress by the banks of the river at the centre of his new city. However, in 1526 the Lodis were defeated by Babur at the battle of Panipat and Agra was incorporated into the expanding Mughal Empire. Although Agra became one of the principal Mughal cities, little construction took place until 1565 when the third emperor Akbar demolished the old fort of Sikander Lodi and built a new fort faced in red sandstone. For the next eighty years Agra was the imperial capital apart from a brief period between 1571 and 1585 when Akbar moved to nearby Fatehpur Sikri.

The main monuments of Agra are the fort and the Taj Mahal which are located 1.5 km apart on the west bank of the river. The fort consists of a roughly triangular area enclosed by a huge red sandstone wall capped with pointed crenellations. The walls have two main gates (the Delhi Gate and the Amar Singh Gate) and are surrounded by a deep paved moat. The fort is the product of several construction phases the earliest of which belongs to the reign of Akbar. Little of Akbar's original palace survives, except for the enclosure walls and the Jahangari Mahal which is a Hindu-style pavilion in the south part of the building. Most of the interior of the fort may be attributed to the reign of Shah Jahan who also built the Taj Mahal which can be viewed across the water from the private apartments of the palace. Although less rigidly planned, the interior of the Agra Fort bears a striking similarity to the Red Fort in Delhi also built by Shah Jahan. The layout is based around a series of formal gardens and pavilions the most beautiful of which is the Mussaman Burj or octagonal tower which overlooks the river and is capped by an octagonal copper dome. Other important monuments in Agra include the Rambagh, the Chini Ka Rauza and the tomb of Itmad al-Daula. The Rambagh is a formal four-part garden laid out by the first Mughal emperor Babur. In the centre of the garden is an open octagonal domed pavilion standing on thirty-six columns. The Chini Ka Rauza is a Persian-style tiled tomb crowned with a bulbous dome built for the seventeenth-century poet Afzal Khan. The tomb of Iltimad al-Daula is a square structure with octagonal domed minarets at each corner, the outer surface of the tomb is decorated with carved white marble and geometric marble screen. In the centre of the structure is the tomb of Iltimad al-Daula which is lined with yellow marble and has fine pietra dura stone inlay.

See also: Delhi, India, Mughals, Red Fort, Taj Mahal

Further reading:

M. Ashraf Husain, *An Historical Guide to the Agra Fort based on Contemporary Records*, Delhi 1937.
W. G. Klingelhofer, 'The Jahangiri Mahal of the Agra Fort: expression and experience in early Mughal architecture', *Muqarnas* 5: 153–69, 1988.
E. Koch, 'The lost colonnade of Shah Jahan's bath in the Red Fort at Agra', *Burlington Magazine* 124: 331–9, 1982.
—— 'The Zahara Bagh (Bagh-i Jahanara) at Agra', *Environmental Design* 1986: 30–7.

Ahmadabad

Main city of Gujarat in western India with a mixed Hindu, Muslim and Jain population.

The old city is located on the east bank of the Sabarmati river. Ahmadabad was founded by Ahmad Shah I in 1411 near to the old Hindu town of Asaval which it replaced. The Bhadra towers erected by Ahmad Shah to protect the citadel are the oldest surviving part of the city; however, most of the original fortifications have been destroyed. The city contains some of the best examples of medieval Gujarati architecture which is characterized by its integration of Hindu, Jain and Islamic forms.

At the centre of the city is the Jami Masjid built by Ahmad Shah I and completed in 1424. The plan of the building comprises a huge rectangular courtyard with entrances on three sides and a covered sanctuary to the west. The sanctuary is divided into fifteen domed bays (five wide and three deep) supported on 260 columns. In the centre of the sanctuary façade is the huge main entrance flanked by two tall minarets (now partially demolished). At the end of each of the aisles there is a mihrab made of coloured marble. The central

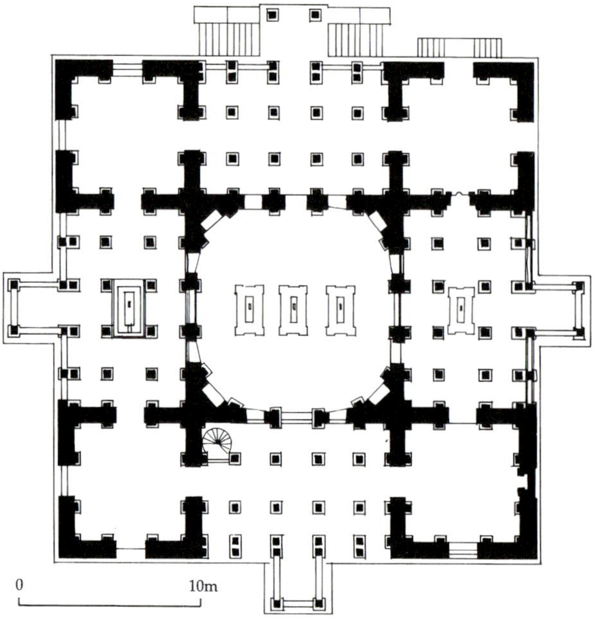

Plan of the tomb of Ahmad Shah, Ahmadabad, India

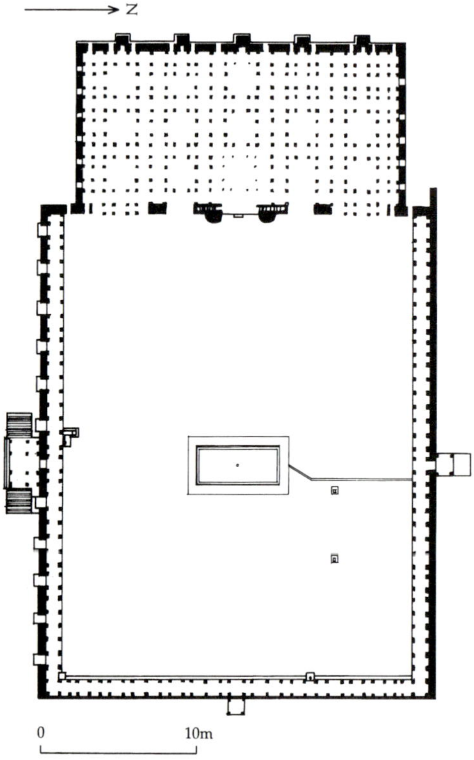

Jami Masjid, Ahmadabad, India

aisle is three times the height of the rest of the building and contains projecting balconies looking in to the central area. To the east of the mosque is the tomb of Ahmad Shah which consists of a square domed mausoleum in the centre with four smaller square domed chambers at the corners and pillared verandas in between.

One of the finest buildings of the city is the Rani Sipri Mosque built in 1514. The building is quite small and has a pronounced Hindu character with elaborate carved decoration and fine perforated jalis or screens.

See also: Gujarat, India

Further reading:

G. Mitchell and S. Shah, *Ahmadabad*, Bombay 1988.

Ajdabiya (Roman Corniclanum)

Prominent Fatimid city in Libiya.

Ajdabiya's owed its importance to its position on the junction of two important routes, the coastal route from Tunisia to Egypt and the desert caravan route from the oases of Jaly and al-Ujlah. Although the site was known in Roman times, it was during the Fatimid period that the city achieved its greatest development.

Several remains of the Fatimid complex have been recovered including a rectangular mud-brick enclosure wall, the qasr or palace and the mosque. The palace is a rectangular stone built structure approximately 22 by 33 m with solid circular corner towers and semi-circular buttress towers. The palace has one entrance in the north wall leading into a courtyard enclosed by apartments. At the opposite end to the corner from the entrance there is a large T-shaped suite of rooms which probably functioned as the royal apartment. The royal apartments were once luxuriously decorated with stucco work.

The most important building at the site is the mosque located in the south-west corner of the complex. Extensive archaeological work on the mosque has defined a Fatimid and pre-Fatimid phase above an earlier Roman site, but only the Fatimid phase has been investigated in any detail. In 912 the Fatimids sacked the town of Ajdabiya and destroyed the mosque building a new one on the site. The Fatimid mosque consists of a rectangular structure (47 by 31 m) built out of mud brick with corners, piers, jambs and other structurally important points built out of stone. There was one entrance in the north-west side opposite the mihrab and several other side entrances, all of which appear to have been plain in contrast to the monumental porches at Mahdiya and Cairo. Inside there is a large courtyard paved with flagstones and a water tank in the middle at the northern end of the mosque. The courtyard is surrounded by arcades and on the south-eastern side is the sanctuary. The latter has a wide central aisle running at right angles to the qibla wall where it meets a transept running parallel to the qibla wall; all the other aisles are aligned at right angles to the qibla.

To the left of the main entrance is a large square block 4 m high which was the base of a minaret with an octagonal shaft. This is the earliest example of this type of minaret which was later developed into the characteristic Cairene minaret form. There are also traces of a staircase built into the wall which have been interpreted as the remains of a staircase minaret used before the erection of the later octagonal one.

Little remains of the mihrab apart from the foundations and some stucco fragments; however, nineteenth-century drawings depict it as a curved recessed niche with a horseshoe arch.

See also: Fatimids, Libiya

Further reading:

A. Abdussaid, 'Early Islamic monuments at Ajdabiyah', *Libiya Antiqua* 1: 115–19, 1964.

—— 'The old Islamic city of Ajdabiyah', in *Some Islamic Sites in Libiya*, Art and Archaeology Research Papers, London 1976, 19–24.

H. Blake, A. Hutt and D. Whitehouse, 'Ajdabiyah and the earliest Fatimid architecture', *Libiya Antiqua* 8: 105–20, 1970.

P. Donaldson, 'Excavations at Ajdabiya, 1976', *Libyan Studies* 7: 9–10, 1976.

D. Whitehouse, 'The excavations at Ajdabiyah: an interim report', *Libyan Studies* 3: 12–21, 1972.

—— 'Excavations at Ajdabiyah: second interim report', *Libyan Studies* 4: 20–7, 1973.

ajimez

Spanish term for pair of windows sharing a central column. This is one of the distinctive features of Islamic buildings in Spain and is especially noticeable on minarets.

Albania

Mountainous country in south-eastern Europe which was incorporated into the Ottoman Empire in the fifteenth century.

The first Ottoman incursions into Albania in the late fourteenth and early part of the fifteenth century were fiercely resisted by the Albanians under their leader Skanderberg who managed to unite the various feudal factions who had previously ruled the country. The resistance of the people together with its mountainous terrain meant that the country was not fully conquered until the late fifteenth century. Few Turks settled in the country which nevertheless converted to Islam. This remained the state religion until the revolution of 1967 when the country became officially atheist. Mosques were converted into museums and minarets were demolished in order to destroy the distinctive Islamic appearance of the cities. In 1991 with the collapse of the authoritarian communist regime Islam has again become the main religion with 72 per cent of the population Muslim and 27 per cent Christian (Greek Orthodox and Catholic). As a result mosques have been reopened with rebuilt minarets. There are substantial numbers of Albanians living abroad particularly in the USA where there are four Albanian mosques (in Detroit, Chicago and Waterbury, Connecticut).

A recent survey has indicated that there may be as many as 800 mosques surviving in Albania along with 300 historical Muslim sites. The mosques in Albania are of two types, the classical Ottoman type derived from Byzantine architecture based on a square domed area with a triple-domed portico and the more common rectangular buildings with wooden painted ceilings which are typical of the Balkans. The oldest Muslim building in the country is the Berat Congregational Mosque built in 1380. Another early mosque is the Ilias Mirahori Mosque in the town of Korçë built in 1494 after the Ottomans had gained control of the whole country. One of the most celebrated mosques in Albania is at Krujë 20 km north of the capital Tiranë. The mosque, located in the grounds of Skanderberg's castle, was built in 1779 and has wooden ceilings painted to look like a dome set on squinches. Another famous building is the Peqin Mosque built in 1822 which incorporates a clock tower into the design of the minaret.

Much of the secular Ottoman architecture in Albania was destroyed in the fierce modernizing programmes of the 1960s and 1970s with the exception of the towns of Gjirokastër and Berat which have been preserved as museum towns. The town of Gjirokastër is built on slopes around the citadel which is located on a high plateau. The town is first mentioned in the twelfth century although the majority of surviving buildings belong to the seventeenth and eighteenth centuries. The typical house in the city consists of a tall stone block structure up to five storeys high with external and internal staircases, a design thought to originate from fortified country houses in southern Albania. The basic form of the house consists of a lower storey containing a cistern and stable with an upper storey reached by a flight of exterior stairs. The upper storey was divided into two units: a guest room, and a winter or family room containing a fireplace. Later on more storeys were added to accommodate extended families; these upper floors were reached by internal staircases. In the seventeenth century houses were built with two wings protecting the lower external staircase.

Berat is a much older city dating back to the Ilyrian period. Initially conquered by the Ottomans in the fourteenth century, it was then recaptured, and not finally occupied by the Turks until 1417. The town is located on the banks of the Osun river and like Gjirokastër is built around a citadel. The citadel was remodelled by the Turks soon after its capture in 1417 and again in the eighteenth and nineteenth centuries to take account of the use of artillery. Like the fortified houses of Gjirokastër the houses of Berat have external staircases and the main living area of the building is on the upper floor. However, at Berat this feature was designed to overcome the hilly nature of the ground rather than for defensive reasons. Thus to avoid dampness and having to excavate hillsides the houses are built on stone substructures which are sometimes used for storage. The upper parts of Berat houses are built out of timber filled in with lath and plaster and then whitewashed. The verandas sometimes extend along the whole front of the house although in many cases part of the veranda is occupied by a separate room. In the nineteenth century many of these verandas were filled in with large glazed windows. Inside the houses are elaborately decorated with carved and painted woodwork.

Further reading:

R. I. Lawless, 'Berat and Gjirokastër: two museum towns in Albania', in *Islam in the Balkans: Persian Art and Culture of the Eighteenth and Nineteenth Centuries*, Edinburgh 1979, 9–18.

P. Ward, *Albania*, Cambridge and New York 1983.

'Albania', *Aramco World* July/August 1992: 38–47.

albarrani

Spanish term for a tower projecting from the walls of a castle or city fortifications and connected by means of a bridge. The earliest example in Spain is at Mérida and is connected to the ninth-century fortress, but most other examples are later.

Further reading:

J. Zozaya, 'Islamic fortifications in Spain: some aspects', in *Papers in Iberian Archaeology*, BAR, *Oxford 1984.*

Aleppo (Arabic Halab)

Syria's second city located on the river Qoueiq in north-west Syria.

Aleppo is often regarded as the oldest inhabited city in the world because of its continous history from at least the twentieth century BCE. Although the city was of great significance in Roman and Byzantine times its importance declined during the first three centuries of Islam in favour of the nearby city of Qinnarisin. Under the Hamdanids Aleppo once more became powerful as capital of a dynasty ruling northern Syria; this was short-

Aleppo (Arabic Halab)

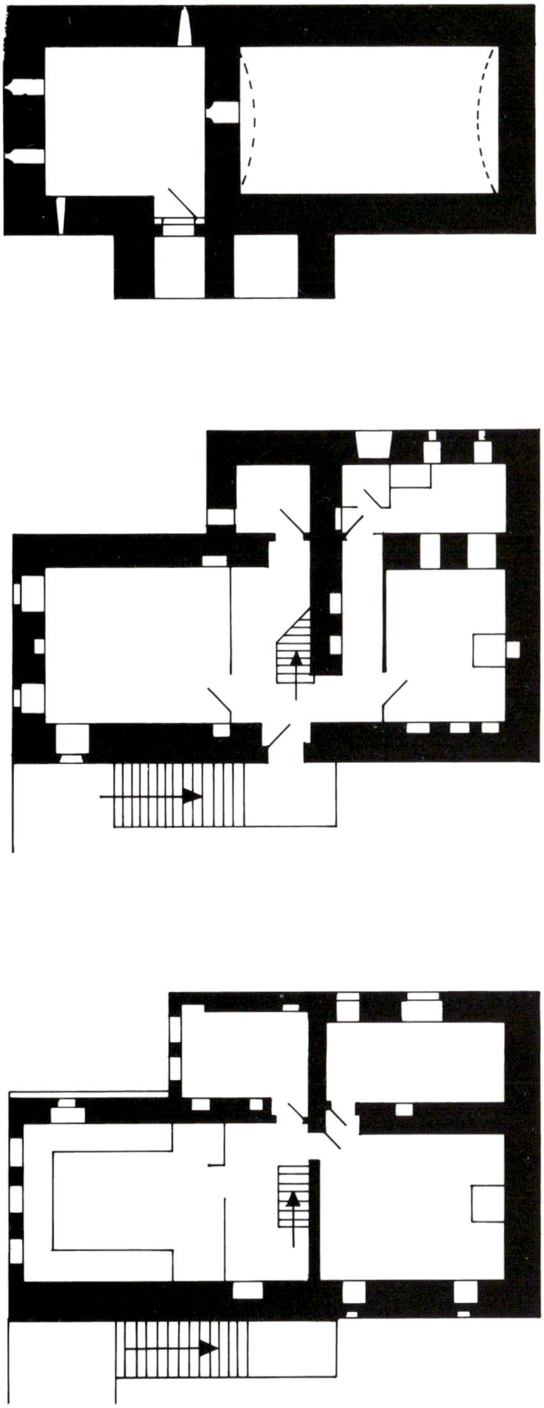

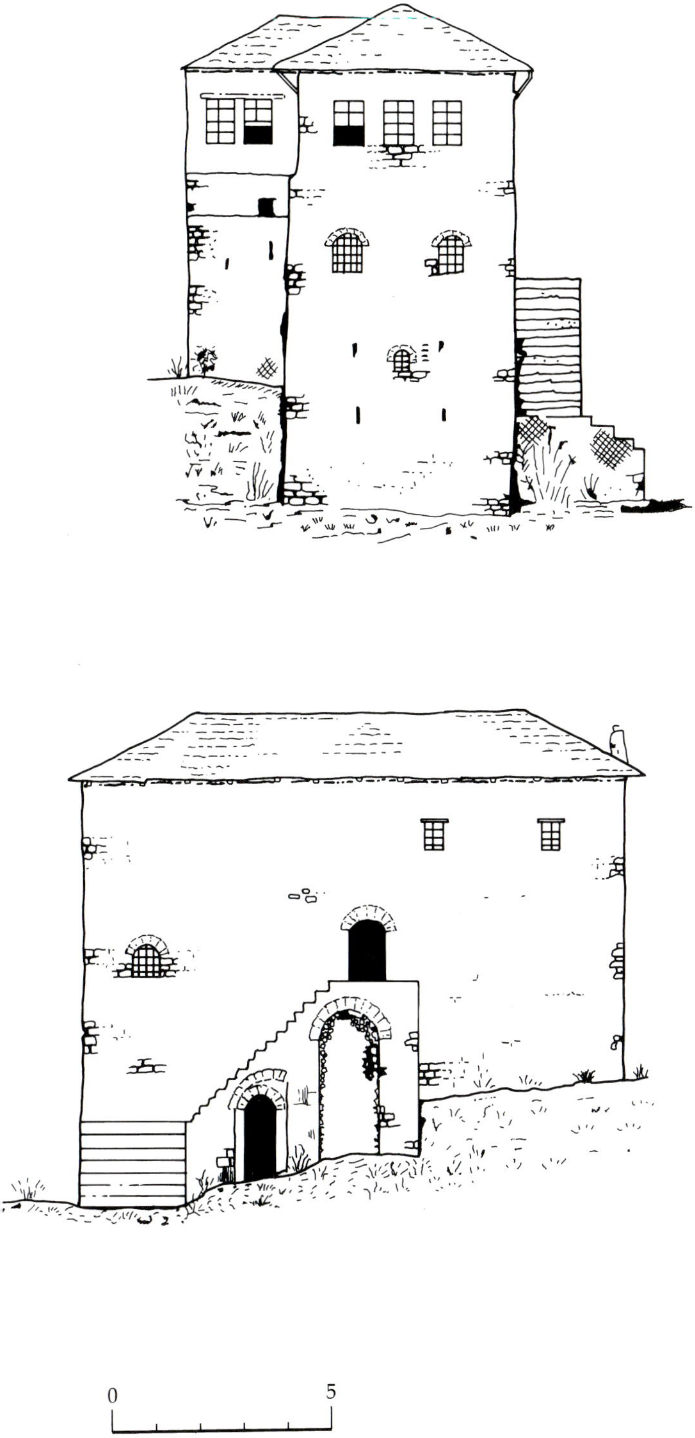

Tower houses in Girokastër, Albania (after Lawless)

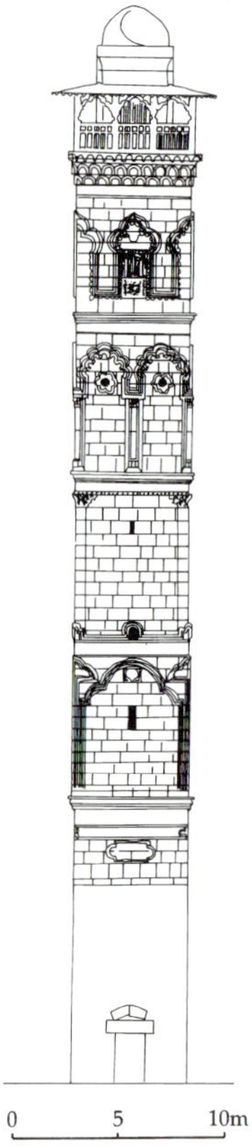

Eleventh-century minaret of the Great Mosque, Aleppo

lived, however, and the city was not able to recover its status until 1129 when Imad al Din Zengi was made governor. Imad al Din was able to consolidate his position through a series of victories against the Crusaders which established him as premier ruler in Syria. Under Imad and his successors the Zangids and later the Ayyubids the city grew to be one of the great cities of Islam. Despite the Mongol invasions of 1260 and 1400 Aleppo remained a major city throughout the Middle Ages and the Ottoman period.

Although there are the remains of an Umayyad mosque enclosed within the Great Mosque, most of the monuments in Aleppo belong to the period after the eleventh century. During the twelfth and early thirteenth centuries a number of important madrassas were built including al-Zahiriyyah (1217), al-Sultaniyyah (1223) and the Madrassa al-Firdaws which includes a mosque, a school and a turbah. Important public buildings from the fourteenth and fifteenth centuries include the Maristan (hospital) Arghuni and the Hammam al-Nasiri (public baths).

In spite of the great beauty of Aleppo's madrassas and mosques the best-known feature of the city is its fortifications, particularly the citadel which dominates the old city. Although fortification on the citadel began as early as the tenth century, the most spectacular work dates from the thirteenth century under Ghazi al Malik al-Zahir. During this period the glacis, triple entrance and most of the towers were built. Characteristic features of this work are the monumental inscriptions, carved animal sculpture and massive masonry. In addition to the citadel the old city is enclosed within a medieval wall and gates.

Whilst the medieval period saw the development of Aleppo's fortifications and religious buildings the Ottoman era produced a large number of commercial and industrial buildings. Prominent amongst these are Khan al-Sabun (early sixteenth century), Khan al-Jumruk, Khan al-Wazir and Bayt Dallal (all seventeenth century). These buildings belong to a complex network of suks which extend for a distance of 15 km.

Further reading:

A. Bahnassi, 'Aleppo', in *The Islamic City*, ed. R. B. Serjeant, Paris 1980. This gives a general overview of the city's monuments.

J. Sauvaget, 'Halab', E. I. IV, gives a general history of the city.

Bulletin des Études orientales, esp. 36, 'Études sur la ville d'Alep', 1984, contains recent research.

Algeria

North African country located between Morocco and Tunisia.

Algeria can be divided into three main regions, the Mediterranean coast known as the Tell, the High Plateaux immediately south of the coast and further south the Sahara desert. The Tell is dominated by coastal mountains, although there are three small sections of coastal plain, one at Algiers, one at Oran and one at Annaba. The High Plateaux are more arid with marginal areas for agriculture. The Sahara desert covers four-fifths of the country and links it to West Africa.

Algeria did not exist as a political unit until the Ottoman occupation of the sixteenth century (the country did not include the Sahara regions until the early twentieth century). Before that period it is difficult to separate the history of this area from the rest of North Africa. The first Arab invasion of Algeria occurred in 681 and by the beginning of the eighth century the Byzantine towns of the coast had all surrendered. The predominantly Berber population was converted to Islam relatively quickly and in the early eighth century took part in the conquest of Spain. A notable feature of Algeria at this point was the rapid development of religious sects the most important of which were the Kharijites who established independent rule in the area. The expansion of the Fatimids in the ninth century attracted Berber support particularly along the coast, although those of the south remained opposed to the Fatimid regime. During the eleventh century Berber groups in the south of the country emerged as a coherent political and military force known as the Almoravids. The Almoravids were able to conquer most of Morocco and Algeria and Spain before the end of the eleventh century. Internal disputes meant that the dynasty lasted only fifty years more before being overthrown by the Almohads, another Berber group with similar origins. Like their predecessors the Almohads too had early successes, but did not last much beyond the twelfth century. The political history of the region from the thirteenth to the sixteenth century is quite confused, with various local dynasties trying to establish control over the whole area. The Spanish took advantage of this situation and invaded in 1510. There was strong local resistance to the Spanish invasion and the Ottoman Turks were called in as allies against the Christians. The Turks formally established their rule in 1587 by appointing a governor and defining the present borders of the country. In the early nineteenth century the French occupied the coastal cities to prevent attacks on their ships. This temporary occupation gradually developed into a virtual annexation with French settlers arriving in the country. The occupation lasted until 1962 when Algeria was established as an independent state.

The principal building materials of Algeria are stone, baked brick and mud brick (toub) with wood used as a roofing material. In the coastal cities the quality of the buildings is of a very high standard with ashlar masonry and ornamental stonework in a style similar to North Africa and Spain. South of the coast dressed stonework is very rare and even palatial buildings such as Qal'at Banu Hammad are built out of roughly squared stone. Baked brick is found mostly in coastal cities such as Tlemcen and Nedroma, although is also used for houses in oasis cities in the east such as Tamelhat where houses have decorative brickwork panels. Roofing tiles made of baked clay are a feature of coastal cities, in particular Tlemcen which is heavily influenced by neighbouring Morocco. Mud brick is used in the High Plateaux regions and in the oasis towns of the desert.

The earliest Islamic architecture which has survived belongs to the Sanhaja Berber dynasties. Excavations at Ashir 170 km due south of Algiers have revealed the remains of a tenth-century palace built by the Zirid dynasty. The palace is a rectangular enclosure (72 by 40 m) with a large central courtyard around which were four separate residences. Across the courtyard from the entrance there was an arcade resting on columns behind which was a domed audience hall. One hundred and fifty kilometres east is the site of Qal'at Banu Hammad capital of the Hammadid dynasty. The city is located high up in the mountains at an altitude of 1,400 m. The city was founded in 1007 by Hammad the father of the dynasty and a relation of the Zirids. Excavations at the site have revealed the Great Mosque and three palaces. In 1015 Hammad broke his allegiance to the Fatimids and pledged his support for the Abbasids. The results of this change of policy can be seen in the architecture of the city; thus a minaret was added to the Great Mosque and the palaces are decorated with carved stone screens reminiscent of contemporary Abbasid stucco work. To the north of Qal'at on the coast is the city of Bougie which became the Hammadid capital from 1060 to 1085, but there are few standing remains of the Hammadid city with the exception of a monumental sea gate.

The south of Algeria was a refuge for Ibadis who rebelled against both the Shi'a orthodoxy of the Fatimids and the Sunni orthodoxy of the Abbasids and their local supporters. In the eleventh century the Ibadis established a capital at the oasis town of Sadrat. Excavations have revealed a number of houses decorated with ornate stucco in the Abbasid style.

The rise of the Almoravids in the eleventh century led to the development of a new mosque form which can be seen in the Great Mosques of Tlemcen, Nedroma, Algiers and Tozeur. This new form preserved the North African tradition of aisles running perpendicular to the qibla with a

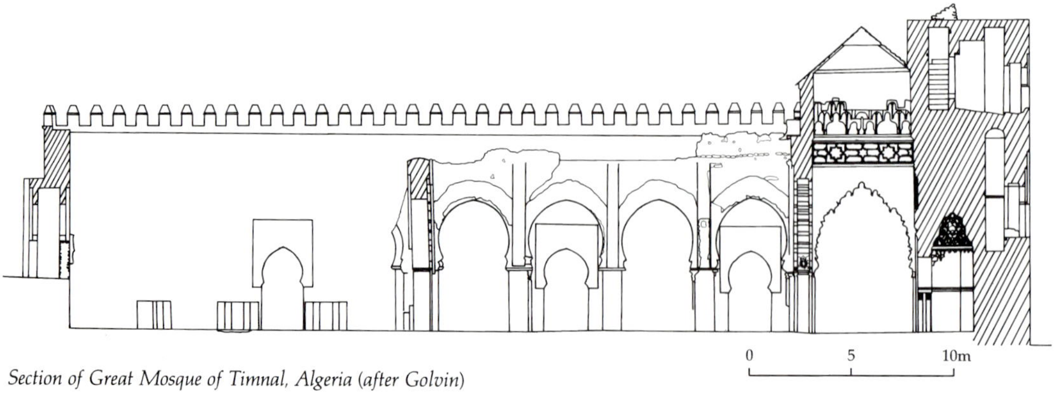

Section of Great Mosque of Timnal, Algeria (after Golvin)

dome in front of the mihrab. The new development was to integrate the lateral arcades into the prayer hall of the mosque and incidentally reduce the size of the courtyard. Another notable feature is that none of the mosques was built with minarets although these were added in later periods.

The breakdown of central political authority after the twelfth century meant that with occasional notable exceptions there were few major architectural projects. In religious architecture this meant the construction of madrassas instead of congregational mosques and in secular architecture it meant the construction of khans/funduqs instead of palaces. A notable exception to this general pattern is the city of Tlemcen which formed the centrepiece of a contest between the Zayyanid and Marinid dynasties. The most ambitious project of the period was the city of al-Mansura outside Tlemcen which was built by the Marinids in 1303 as a base for besieging Tlemcen. After the failure of the first attempt a new siege city was built in 1336. At the centre of this city was the Great Mosque which still survives in its unfinished state. The mosque forms a large rectangle 85 by 60 m and, like the Almoravid mosques, the lateral arcades form an integral part of the prayer hall. The most striking feature of the building is the minaret, at the base of which is the main entrance to the mosque. The minaret is built in a reddish stone decorated with geometric patterns carved into it.

Ottoman architecture was confined principally to the coastal cities with the best examples in Algiers which became the capital at this time. Under French rule Islamic architecture was relegated to a secondary position, although at the beginning of the twentieth century they introduced the West African 'Sudanese Style' to cities such as Ardar in the southern Sahara.

See also: Algiers, Qal'at Banu Hammad

Further reading:

D. Hill and L. Golvin, *The Islamic Architecture of North Africa*, London 1976.

Algiers

Capital city of Algeria.

Algiers is located in the middle of the north coast of Algeria and is built on the site of the Roman town of Icosium. The Muslim city was founded in 944 and rose to prominence under the Almoravids who built the Great Mosque. The city did not become the capital until the Ottoman conquest of the sixteenth century. The city has two seventeenth-century Turkish mosques built in the classical Ottoman style with a large central dome and multiple-domed portico. There are also a number of Turkish mansions in the city built on the wealth derived from attacking Christian ships.

See also: Algeria, Qal'at Banu Hammad

Further reading:

G. Marçais, 'La vie et l'art d'Alger à l'époque Turque', *Communications of the First International Congress of Turkish Art*, Ankara 1986, 251–9.
C. Vincent, 'L'habitation de Grande Kablylie (Algérie)', *Cahiers des Arts et Techniques d'Afrique du Nord* no. 5, 1955, 17–29.

Alhambra

Palace complex in Granada in south-west Spain known for being one of the most beautiful examples of Islamic architecture.

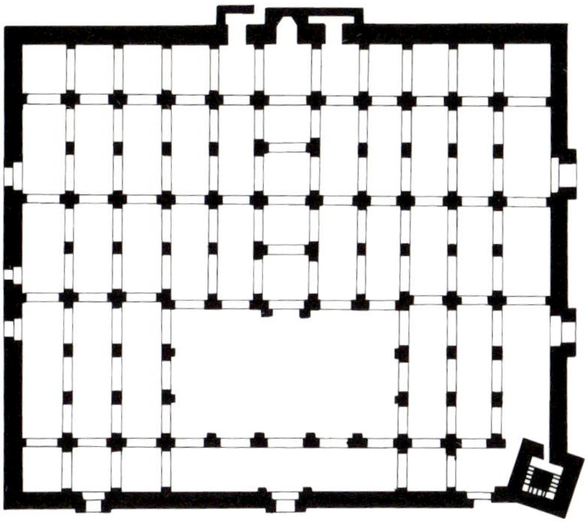

Great Mosque, Algiers (after Golvin)

The name Alhambra, 'The Red Fort', accurately reflects the building's fortified position on a rocky spur in the middle of Granada between the river Darro and the river Genil. The city of Granada first rose to importance in 1012 as capital of the Zirid dynasty who established their base on the site of the Alhambra. Later in 1231 the city was capital of the Nasirid dynasty under Banu al-Ahmar who ruled the province of Andalucía until the final conquest of Ferdinand and Isabella in 1492. As rulers of the last Muslim state in Spain the Nasirids were able to collect some of the most able craftsmen in the peninsula.

The oldest part of the present structure is the Alcazaba which was built in the twelfth century by the Almohads and which protects the western end of the spur on which the Alhambra is built. It is entered through the Puerta de las Armas and enclosed by strong walls which are fortified by rectangular towers. The earliest of these is the Torre Quebrada whilst other early towers are the Torre del Adarguero and the Torre del Homenaje. The Torre del Homenaje was the keep of the Alcazaba and in it the first Nasirid emirs had their apartments. Excavations within the Alcazaba have revealed traces of barracks and a large cistern which date from this early period.

Most of the Alhambra, however, dates from the fourteenth and fifteenth centuries and consists of several palaces built for successive emirs. The earliest of these is known as the Palacio del Partal; built in the early fourteenth century, it now consists of a tower with an arcaded patio on brick piers. There is also a small mosque built for Yusuf I in 1354 with a small mihrab. The largest and most famous of the palaces is the Palacio de Comares which takes much of its present form from Muhammad V's rebuilding in 1365. The palace is entered through a series of patios or arcaded courtyards with central pools or fountains. The main courtyard for the Comares palace is the Patio de los Arrayanes, on either side of which were the private rooms of the emir's wives. On the north-east side is the entrance to the emir's private quarters known as the Sala de la Barca. This room consisted of a long rectangular chamber with alcoves at either end covered in semi-domes decorated with stars; the area between the alcoves is covered by an inverted boat-shaped vault. These quarters lead via a small mosque to the Salón del Trono or throne room. This room is a large square structure with three deep vaulted recesses on each side formed by the artificially thick walls. The recesses open into paired or single arched windows which overlook the city of Granada whilst the interior of the room is decorated in a profusion of coloured tiles, carved stucco and intricate carpentry.

Later, to distinguish between the personal quarters and formal public reception rooms, Muhammad V created the Patio de los Leones leading on to the Sala des Reyes as a centre for ceremonial. These buildings are regarded by many as the culmination of Islamic palace architecture. The centrepiece of the Patio de los Leones is the fountain, consisting of a polygonal basin supported by marble lions. The Sala des Reyes is a long room or series of rooms opening on to a larger vaulted area, which in turn opens on to the Patio de los Leones. Architecturally this room is a complex structure which questions the distinction between internal and external space. Each of the smaller rooms is decorated with painted ceilings depicting scenes of chivalry and the walls are decorated with intricate stucco work.

See also: Granada, Spain

Further reading:

O. Grabar, *The Alhambra*, London 1978.
W. Irving, *The Alhambra*, London 1906.
F. Prieto-Moreno, *Los Jardines de Granada*, Madrid 1952.
E. Sordo and W. Swaan, *Moorish Spain: Córdoba, Seville and Granada*, London 1963.

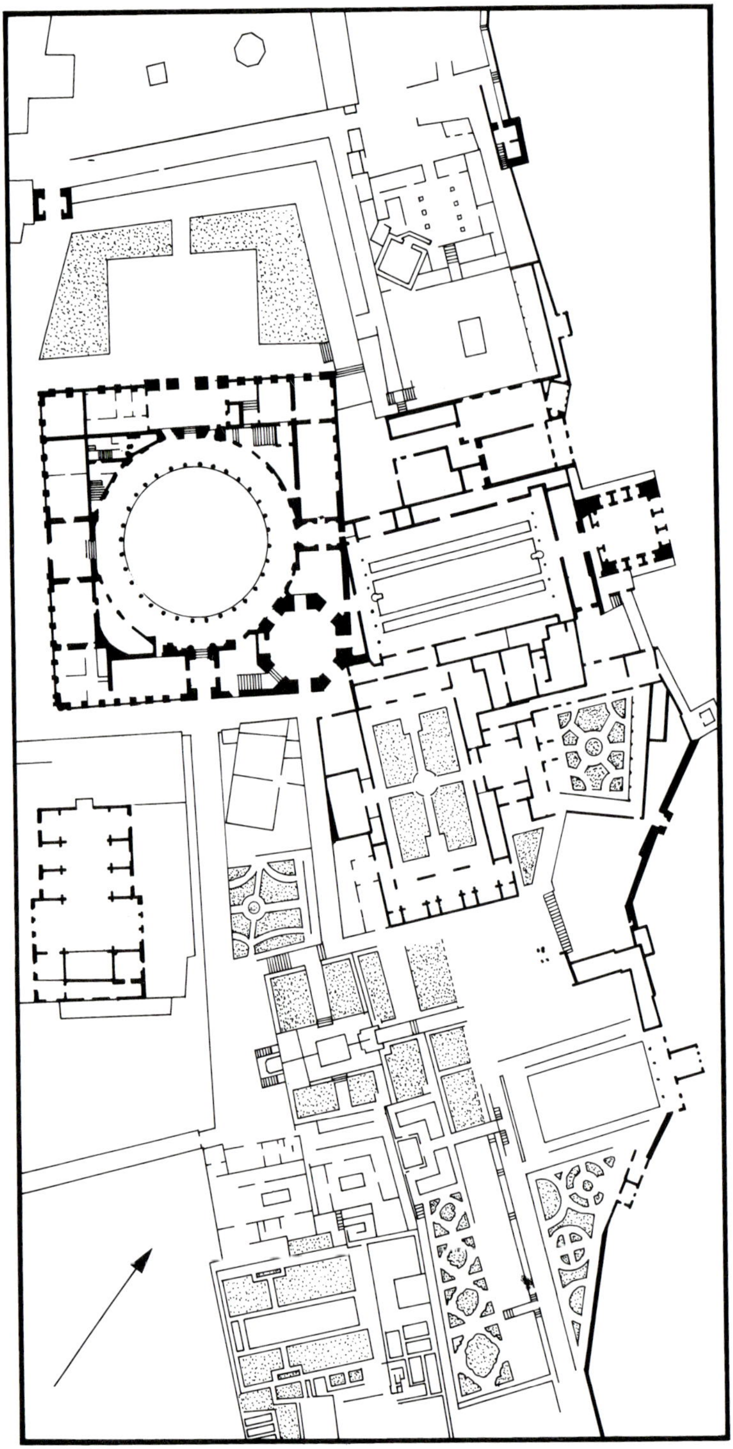

Plan of Alhambra Palace Granada, Spain (after Goodwin)

The Partal Palace Alhambra, © J.W. Allan, Ashmolean Museum

Almohads

North African Berber dynasty which ruled over much of North Africa, Spain and parts of sub-Saharan West Africa.

The Almohads originated from the Atlas mountains of Morocco and were led by a religious leader who preached moral reform. They defeated the ruling dynasty of the Almoravids and established the greatest empire of the western Islamic world. In 1170 the capital was moved to Seville from where resistance to the Christian reconquest could be organized.

Almohad architecture is characterized by its mosques and fortifications. The most notable feature of Almohad mosques are the large minaret towers which dominate the great mosques of Seville, Marakesh and Rabat. Under their predecessors, the Almoravids, minarets were thought to be inappropriate and were left out of mosque designs. The Almohads were responsible for reintroducing the minaret, first in a tentative form, as in the minaret of Timnal where it is a low tower behind the mihrab, and later in a monumental form. The design varied from one tower to another but the basic form was a square shaft containing a central core with a vaulted room on each storey. The exterior was usually decorated with windows set within frames made of cusped arches which formed networks of lozenge shapes. The form of these minarets established a tradition which was followed in mosques of the fourteenth century and later.

City walls are equally demonstrative symbols of Almohad ideology with stepped crenellations and decorated gateway façades. The best examples of Almohad fortifications are the city gates at Rabat with their complex bent entrances and monumental façades decorated with cusped arches.

See also: Marakesh, Morocco, Rabat, Seville

Further reading:

H. Basset and H. Terrasse, *Sanctuaires et fortresses almohades*, Paris 1938.

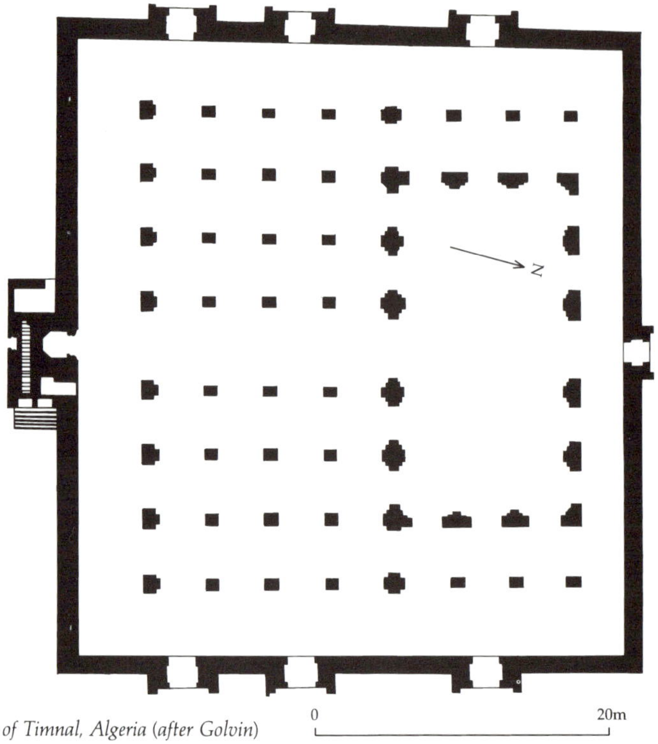

Plan of Great Mosque of Timnal, Algeria (after Golvin)

Amman (Roman Philadelphia)

Capital of Jordan containing palace of Umayyad princes.

The Ummayad palatial complex which probably dates from the early eighth century occupies the ancient citadel area in the centre of modern Amman. The most famous part of the complex is the cruciform reception hall which stood at the entrance to the palace. This building consists of four arched iwans set around a central square space which was probably an open courtyard rather than a roofed space. The interior of the courtyard and iwans are decorated with blind niches which are reminiscent of Sassanian buildings in Iraq and further east. Each iwan comprises a tall slightly pointed arch facing the courtyard with a semi-dome behind. In general the form of the building seems to represent an eastern tradition whilst the materials and method of construction suggest a more local (Roman) ancestry.

The rest of the palatial complex forms a rough parallelogram bisected by a central street or processional way. On either side of the central street there are separate buildings or apartments each built around its own courtyard. At the end of the main street a gateway leads into a large courtyard dominated by a large iwan. A door at the back of the iwan gives access to a cruciform domed chamber which may have served as the throne room.

The other important Umayyad building in Amman was the Friday mosque which was demolished and completely rebuilt in 1923. This was a large rectangular building measuring 60 m by 40 m with three entrances on the north side opposite the mihrab. At some later period, probably during the thirteenth century, a square minaret was built at the north-east corner.

See also: Jordan, Umayyads

Further reading:

A. E. Northedge et. al., *Studies on Roman and Islamic Amman*, Oxford 1993.

ʿAmr, Mosque of

Mosque in Fustat, said to be the oldest mosque in Egypt.

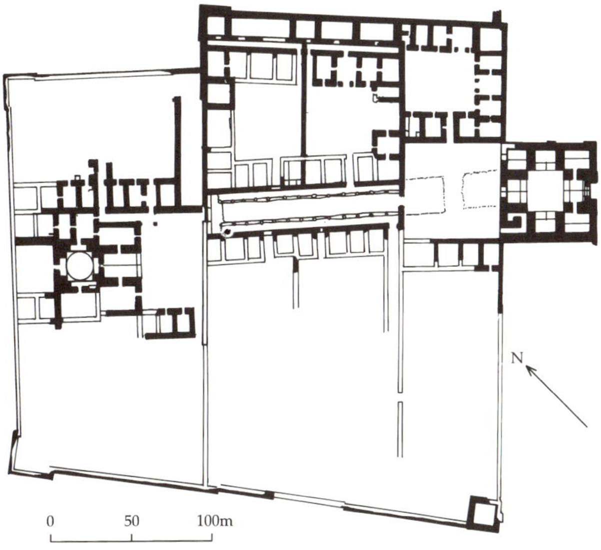

Plan of Umayyad palatial complex, Amman (after Northedge)

The present structure consists of a large roughly square enclosure measuring approximately 120 m on each side. The great variation in the thickness and design of the walls testifies to the building's long history of development and restoration. The first mosque on the site is said to have been built by ʿAmr ibn al–ʿAs in 641–42. ʿAmr was the chief commander of the Arab troops who won Egypt for Islam and so the building has an historical significance beyond the surviving architecture. Although the remains of this earliest mosque have not survived, there are several historical accounts from which the design of the building can be reconstructed. It consisted of a rectangular structure 29 by 17 m without a concave mihrab and was probably built of mud brick and palm trunks.

Thirty-two years later in 673 the first mosque was pulled down and a larger structure built to accommodate the growing number of Muslims. As well as being larger the new mosque was equipped with four towers which could be used for the call to prayer. These have been interpreted as the first minarets although it is likely that they were not much higher than the roof of the mosque.

The earliest mosque from which any remains survive belongs to the reconstruction of 827 carried out by ʿAbd Allah Ibn Tahir. The remains comprise the southern wall of the present mosque which contains blocked-up windows alternating with round-arched niches with shell-like hoods. Both niches and windows are framed by engaged colonettes. Internally there are remains of wooden cornices carved in late Hellenistic style which joined the end columns of the arcades to the wall. Descriptions of the mosque in the tenth century describe it as having glass mosaics on the wall and a bayt al-mal, or treasury, in the centre of the courtyard which together with the four towers suggest a resemblance to the Great Mosque of Damascus.

In later periods several reconstructions and restorations were carried out. The most important changes include those made by Khalif Hakim who added two arcades in the sahn and had the mosaics removed, Sultan Baybars who rebuilt the north wall, the merchants whose restorations were carried out in 1401–2, Murad Bey who strengthened the building and added two minarets in 1797–8. In the restorations of Muhammad Ali in the 1840s the mosque achieved its present form.

Further reading:

D. Berhens-Abouseif, *Islamic Architecture in Cairo: An Introduction,* Supplements to Muqarnas vol. 3, Leiden 1989, 47–50. Contains a general summary and bibliography.

K. A. C. Creswell, *A Short Account of Early Muslim Architecture,* revised and enlarged ed. J. Allan, Aldershot 1989, 8, 15, 17, 46, and chapter 14, 303–14. This gives a detailed account of the building.

Anjar (ʿAyn Jar)

Umayyad city in Lebanon.

Anjar was built by the Umayyad caliph al–Walid in 714–15 CE. The city is contained within a rectangular enclosure (370 m north–south and 310 m east–west) supported by a series of solid semi-circular buttress towers and four hollow corner towers. There are four principal gateways and the walls were originally crowned with stepped merlons (crenellation). Internally the city is built to a regular plan recalling earlier Byzantine and Roman cities. There are four principal colonnaded streets which meet at the centre in a tetrapylon. Many of the buildings are built of alternating courses of ashlar blocks and layers of baked brick. There is a series of shop units (3.5 m wide and 5 m deep) lining the main streets behind the colonnades. In the south-east quadrant of the city is a palace within a rectangular enclosure (about 70 by 60 m). The interior of the palace is divided into four units arranged symmetrically; at the south end there is a building with with a triple aisles and an apse resembling a basilical hall, this is duplicated at the north end. To the north of the palace is the mosque which is entered from the west street. The mosque is a rectangular structure (47 by 30 m) with a small central courtyard surrounded by two aisles on the west, east and qibla (south) sides whilst there is one aisle on the north side. On either side of the mihrab are two entrances which lead into a narrow lane that connects with the palace. There is a small bath house next to the north gate which comprises a square vaulted hall, leading via two intermediate rooms into a hot room.

Ankara (Ancyra)

Capital of Republic of Turkey set in the centre of the Anatolian plain.

During the ninth century Anatolia was subject to a number of Arab raids, the most serious of which occupied Ankara for a short period. However, the city was not finally captured until 1071 when it fell to the Seljuk Turks. The oldest surviving mosque in the city is the Aslan Cami built out of wooden columns and reused classical and Byzantine stones. In 1402 the Ottomans suffered a major setback at Ankara when they were defeated by Timur. During the seventeenth century the city was considered to be one of the more important business centres with its own purpose-built bedestan (now the Museum of Anatolian Civilizations). Ankara has some interesting examples of Ottoman domestic architecture with houses built out of wooden frames filled in with brickwork. However, for most of the Ottoman period the city was of minor importance and only rose to prominence when Mustafa Kemal Attatürk chose the city as the site for Turkey's new capital. As a planned city Ankara has some of the best examples of Turkish Republican architecture which is a heavy monolithic architecture reminiscent of Eastern Europe under Communism. The architecture of this period is tempered by conscious references to a Turkish past which include large overhanging eaves and simplified Seljuk-type stonework. Prominent examples of this architecture are the railway station and the offices of the Turkish historical society.

See also: Ottomans, Seljuks, Turkey

Further reading:

H. M. Akok, *Ankari'nin Eski Evleri*, Ankara 1951.
R. Holod and A. Evin, *Modern Turkish Architecture*, Philadelphia 1984.
G. Öney, *Ankara'da Türk Devri Yapilari* (*Turkish Period Buildings in Ankara*), Ankara 1971.

appadana

A method of construction whereby a flat roof rests directly on columns (i.e. without intervening arches).

al-Aqmar Mosque

Small Fatimid mosque in Cairo noted for its design and the decoration of the façade.

The mosque is known as al-Aqmar, 'the moonlit', and was founded by Ma'mun al-Bata'ihi, vizier of the Fatimid caliph al-Amir in 1125. The building consists of a small 10-metre square courtyard surrounded by an arcade one bay deep on three sides and three bays deep on the qibla side. Most of the building is made from brick except for the front which faces the main street which is faced in dressed stone.

Architecturally the most important feature of the building is the way the façade is set at a different angle from the rest of the mosque to reconcile the need of having the mosque correctly oriented towards Mecca and the façade facing

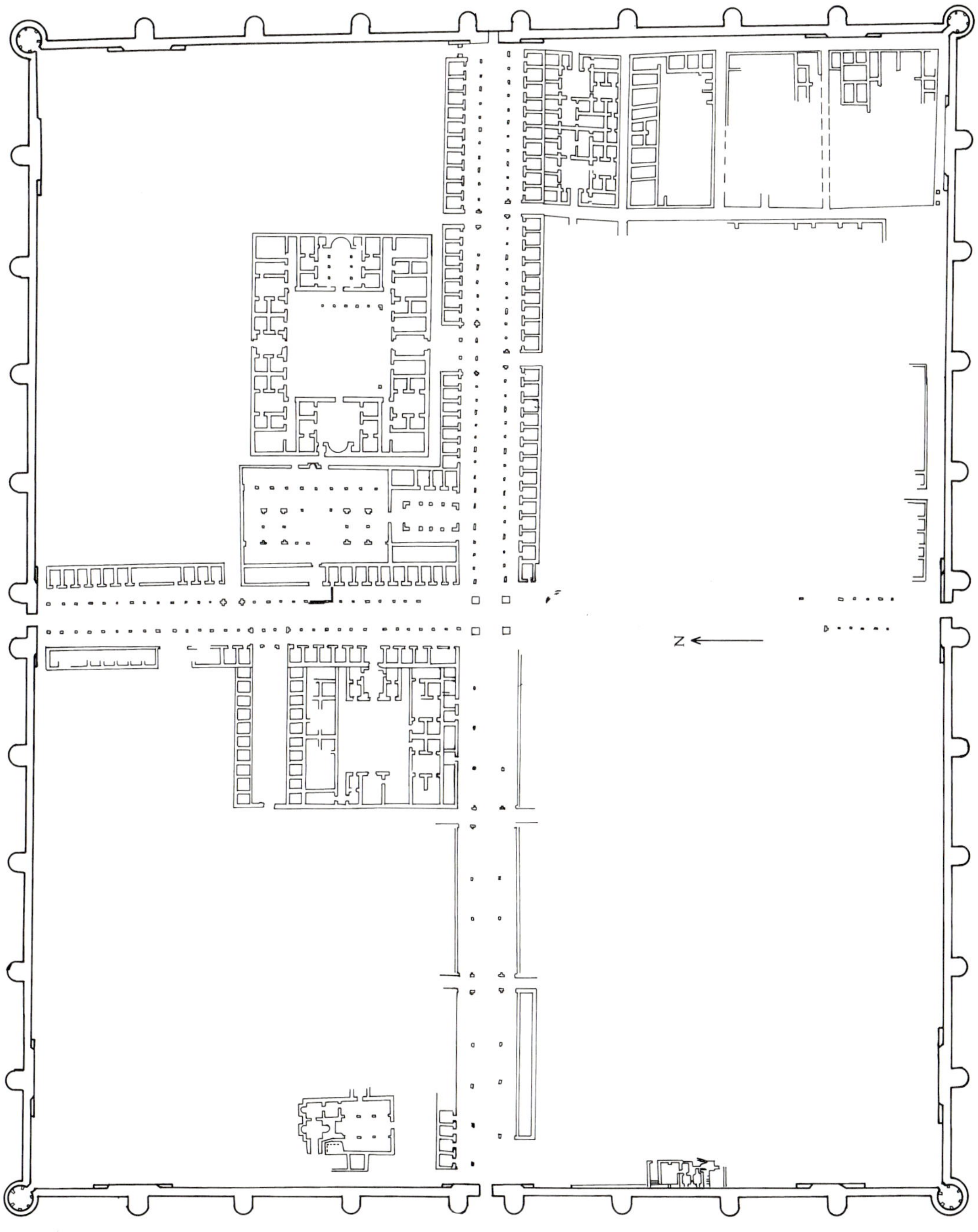

Plan of Umayyad city, Anjar, Lebanon (after Creswell)

Principal street, Anjar, Lebanon

onto the main street. This is the first mosque in Cairo to adopt this arrangement which became common in later mosques. The façade is further emphasized by its decoration and design. It consists of a projecting entrance in the centre flanked by two large niches (only one of these is now visible). The hood of each niche is composed of radiating flutes with a central medallion. The projecting portal consists of a central doorway also with a fluted hood. Either side of the doorway are two smaller niches each with a cusped arch surmounted by a muqarnas moulding. The shape of the arches, the fluted hoods with central medallions and the arrangement of the façade are all features which later become common in Cairene architecture.

Al-Aqmar is also important as it is the first instance of a mosque which incorporates shops into its design. The mosque was originally raised up above street level and the shops were incorporated into the outside walls of the building on a lower level.

See also: Cairo, Fatimids

Further Reading:

D. Berhens-Abouseif, *Islamic Architecture in Cairo: An Introduction*, Supplements to Muqarnas, vol. 3, Leiden 1989, 71–4.

K. A. C. Creswell, *The Muslim Architecture of Egypt*, Oxford 1932–40, 1:241 ff.

C. Williams, 'The Cult of ʻAlid Saints in the Fatimid Monuments of Cairo. Part I: The Mosque of Aqmar', *Muqarnas* 1:37 ff., 1983.

al-Aqsa Mosque

The principal mosque of Jerusalem which forms part of the sacred enclosure (haram) with the Dome of the Rock at the centre.

The Aqsa Mosque is located on the southern part of the Haram al-Sharif on an axis with the south door of the Dome of the Rock. In the time of Umar a mosque is known to have been built on the site although it appears to have been a semi-permanent structure made out of re-used material, hastily put together to form a covered prayer area with a shed roof. During the reign of al-Walid the mosque was rebuilt with its present alignment.

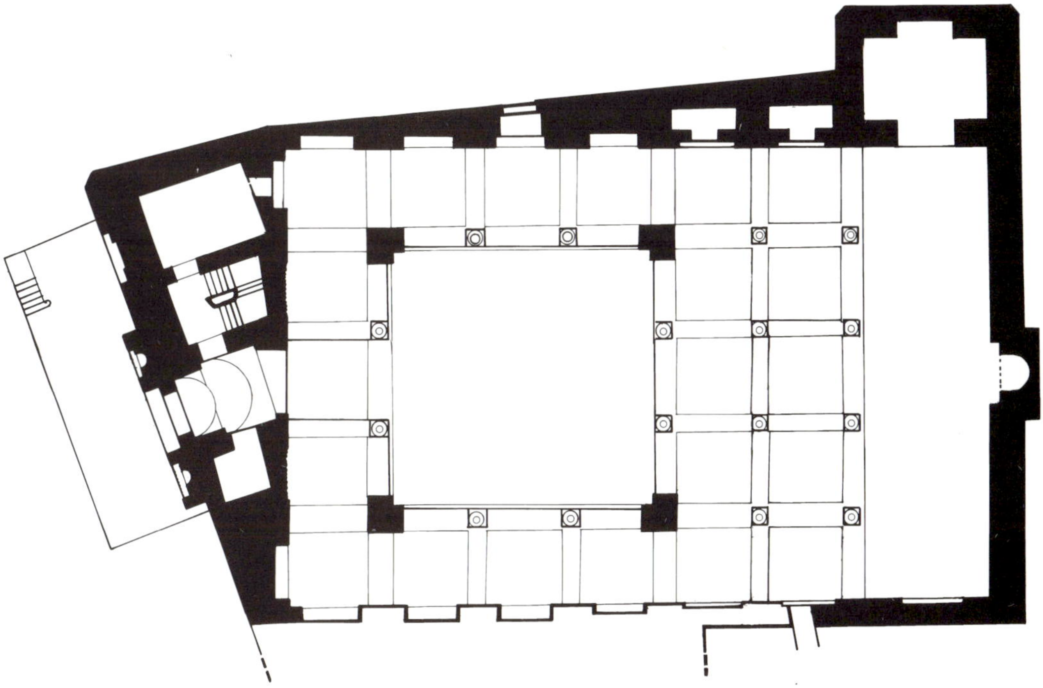

Plan of mosque of al-Aqmar, Cairo (after Williams)

Mosque of al-Aqmar, Cairo, © Creswell Archive, Ashmolean Museum

Only a small part of al-Walid's mosque survives but this indicates that the aisles all ran perpendicular to the qibla wall (as they do today). This arrangement is unusual and recalls the arrangement of Byzantine churches such as the Church of the Nativity in Bethlehem.

The earthquake of 748 severely damaged the mosque which was subsequently rebuilt by the Abbasid caliphs al-Mansur (759) and al-Mahdi (775). The mosque of al-Mahdi had a raised central aisle leading to the mihrab in front of which he built a wooden dome; either side of the central aisle were seven side-aisles. An earthquake of 1033 destroyed the mosque and it was once again rebuilt by the Fatimid caliph al-Zahir in 1035. This mosque had a total of seven aisles, a central aisle with three aisles on either side.

See also: Damascus Great Mosque, Dome of the Rock, Jerusalem, Medina, Palestine, Umayyads

Further reading:

R. W. Hamilton, *The Structural History of the Aqsa Mosque. A Record of Archaeological Gleanings from the Repairs of 1938–42*, Government of Palestine, Jerusalem 1949.

arasta

Turkish term for a street or row of shops whose income is devoted to a charitable endowment or waqf (equivalent to a European shopping arcade).

Arastas are found in most of the regions of the former Ottoman Empire and usually form part of a commercial or religious complex which may include a han (or khan), a mosque and bath house. Many arastas were probably made of wood but these have largely disappeared leaving only those made of more permanent materials. Arastas are often covered over with a barrel vault and have a row of shops either side of a central street, but they can also be open to the sky. Important examples of arastas include the Misir Çarşi in Istanbul, the arasta associated with the Selimiye mosque in Edirne and the arastas at the Sokollu complex at Lüleburgaz and the Selim I complex at Payas both designed by Sinan.

See also: Ottomans

Further reading:

M. Cezar, *Typical Commercial Buildings of the Ottoman Classical Period and the Ottoman Construction System*, Istanbul 1983.

arch

Method of vaulting area between two walls, columns or piers.

Islamic architecture is characterized by arches which are employed in all types of buildings from houses to mosques. One of the most common uses is in arcades where arches span a series of columns or piers to form a gallery open on one side. Arcades are used to line mosque courtyards although they are also used in courtyard houses.

The earliest form of arches employed in Islamic architecture were the semi-circular round arches which were characteristic of Roman and Byzantine architecture. However, fairly soon after the Islamic conquests a new type of pointed arch began to develop. Round arches are formed from a continuous curve which has its centre at a point directly below the apex and level with the springing of the arch on either side. Pointed arches are made by forming each side of the arch from a different centre point, the greater the distance between the two points the sharper the point. In the Dome of the Rock built in 691 the arches supporting the dome are slightly pointed whilst in the cisterns at Ramla built in 759 there is a pronounced point. The arches at Ramla are formed by a separation of the points by a distance of one-fifth the span of the arch; this ratio became standard in many early Islamic buildings.

Another arch form developed during the early Islamic period is the horseshoe arch. Horseshoe arches are those where the arch starts to curve inwards above the level of the capital or impost. Horseshoe arches were developed in Syria in pre-Islamic times and have been recorded as early as the fourth century CE in the Baptistery of Mar Ya'qub at Nisibin. The earliest Islamic monument with horseshoe arches is the Great Mosque of Damascus where the arches of the sanctuary were of slightly horseshoe form. However, the area where horseshoe arches developed their characteristic form was in Spain and North Africa where they can be seen in the Great Mosque of Córdoba. In Tunisia the horseshoe arches of the Great Mosque of Qairawan and the mosque of Muhammad ibn Khairun have a slightly pointed form. Probably the most advanced arch form developed in the early Islamic period is the four-centre arch. This is a pointed arch form composed of four curved sections each with its own centre producing

'Atshan, Khan, Iraq

an arch with steep curves lower down and flattened point at the apex. The earliest occurrence of the four-centred arch is at Samarra at the Qubbat al-Sulaiybiyya. Another arch form which makes its first appearance at Samarra is the cusped arch which is used in the external decoration of the Qasr al-Ashiq. This arch form later became one of the favourite decorative arch forms used throughout the Islamic world from Spain to India.

Arches were not used in India before Islamic times where trabeate construction was the main method of roofing an area. However, arches were regarded as essential by the first Muslim rulers who built arched screens in front of trabeate structures such as the Quwwat al-Islam Mosque in Delhi. Even the screens of the earliest Indian mosques were not composed of true arches but were corbelled structures made to look like arches.

artesonado

Spanish term for wooden panelled ceiling found in Islamic and Mudéjar buildings. Some of the best examples can be found in palaces especially the Alhambra in Granada.

'Atshan, Khan

Small palatial building in the Iraqi western desert between Ukhaidhir and Kufa.

Built of baked brick the design is similar to Ukhaidhir although on a much smaller scale (17 m per side). Externally the building has a simple regular plan consisting of four circular solid corner towers with semi-round towers on three sides and an entrance set between two quarter-round towers on the north side. Internally the building appears to have an irregular plan with long vaulted halls along two sides and a small courtyard decorated with a façade of blind niches. The structure was probably built in the Umayyad period although it has previously been considered an Abbasid (post-750) construction.

See also: Ukhaidhir

Further reading:

B. Finster and J. Schmidt, *Sasaidische und fruhislamische Ruinen im Iraq, Baghdader Mitteilungen* 8, Berlin 1976.

avulu

Turkish term for the courtyard of a mosque which in the summer could be used as an extension of the prayer area.

ayina kari

Mosaic of mirrored glass used in Mughal architecture.

Ayyubids

Medieval dynasty which ruled Syria, Palestine, Iraq, Egypt and Yemen during the twelfth and thirteenth centuries.

The founder of the dynasty was Shirukh, a Kurdish retainer of the Zengid prince Nur al-Din. First Shirukh secured the governorship of Aleppo and later was appointed vizier to the Fatimid ruler of Egypt. Shirukh was succeeded by his nephew Salah al-Din who rapidly extended his position and became ruler of Egypt, Syria and northern Iraq whilst he appointed his brother ruler of Yemen. Salah al-Din's greatest accomplishment was the defeat of the Crusaders and the reconquest of Jerusalem. Salah al-Din died in 1189 and his empire fragmented under his successors who ruled various parts of the empire until the mid-thirteenth century.

Ayyubid architecture was dominated by the need to combat two enemies: the Crusaders in Palestine and the rising threat of Shiʿism and religious dissension. To combat the Crusaders a network of fortresses was built which rivalled those of the Crusaders both in size and technical sophistication. Amongst the best examples of Ayyubid military architecture are Qal'at Rabad at Ajlun in Jordan and Qal'at Nimrud at Banyas in Syria. In addition the fortification of citadels was improved and the famous gateway of the Aleppo Citadel dates from this period. Some of the techniques of fortification were learned from the Crusaders (curtain walls following the natural topography), although many were inherited from the Fatimids (machicolations and round towers) and some were developed simultaneously (concentric planning).

Shiʿism was an equally dangerous threat to the Ayyubids who built a large number of madrassas in both Syria and Egypt. In Egypt the Ayyubids had to reintroduce religious orthodoxy after two centuries of government-imposed Shiʿism. In Syria there was a so a growing threat of Shiʿism in the form of the Assassins who had benefited from the confusion of the Crusader conflict. The Ayyubids tried to promote Sufism as an orthodox alternative and began to build khanqas and Sufi shrines to provide a focus for these activities.

See also: Cairo, Damascus, fortification, Syria, Yemen

Azerbayjan

Country lying south of the Caucasus and east of the Republic of Armenia.

The present Independent Republic of Azerbayjan is the northern part of the Azeri-speaking region which also includes north-western Iran. The capital of the southern part of Azerbayjan is Tabriz whilst the capital of the Independent Republic is Baku. The Independent Republic of Azerbayjan received its name from the Turkish invasion of 1918 although historically it may be identified with the Albania of classical writers. The country lies to the south of the Caucasus and to the east of the Republic of Armenia. More than half of the country is mountainous, though the eastern coastal strip bordering the Caspian Sea is relatively flat. From the twelfth century at least Baku has been known for its natural oil wells which are also the basis of its modern economy. Turkish became the main language of the country after the Seljuk invasions of the eleventh century. Most of the population is Muslim although there are a small number of Zoroastrians with their own fire-temple.

Unlike much of Central Asia and Iran Azerbayjan has its own well-developed, dressed-stone masonry tradition. This can be seen in the tombs, madrassas and mosques of Azerbayjan which have façades carved in relief in a style reminiscent of Seljuk Anatolia. One of the best examples of this stone-working tradition is the palace of the Shirvan Shas in Baku which has monolithic stone columns with austere geometric capitals. Baked brick was also used throughout Azerbayjan, though predominantly in south (now western Iran). One of the most elegant examples of Seljuk brickwork is found in the Gunbad-i-Surkh at Maragha which was built in 1146.

See also: Baku

al-Azhar

One of the main mosques in Cairo and also important as one of the oldest universities.

The name of the mosque, al-Azhar, means 'the flourishing'. The mosque was built in 970 by the Fatimid caliph al-Muciz as the main mosque of the new city of al-Qahira. In 989 the mosque was given the status of theological college to teach the Isma'ili theology. Because of its age and importance the mosque has undergone many alterations and developments although the core of the tenth-century mosque is preserved. The original mosque consisted of a central courtyard with three arcades, two either side of the qibla and the qibla arcade itself. A raised transept runs from the mihrab to the courtyard and there were originally three domes in front of the qibla wall, one above the mihrab and one at either corner.

The plan shares many features with the Fatimid architecture of North Africa, in particular the arrangement of the aisles and the projecting entrance similar to that of Ajdabiya in Libiya.

Later in the Fatimid period the size of the courtyard was reduced by adding four extra arcades around the courtyard. Also a dome was added to the courtyard end of the transept and was hidden by a pishtaq or raised wall above the arcade. Some of the original Fatimid stucco decoration is also preserved, in particular the hood of the prayer niche and on the interior of the arcades. The style is similar to stucco found at Samarra but includes scrolls and palmettes typical of Byzantine decoration.

Further reading:

D. Berhens-Abouseif, *Islamic Architecture in Cairo: An Introduction*, Supplements to Muqarnas, Leiden 1989, 3: 58–63

K. A. C. Creswell, *The Muslim Architecture of Egypt*, Oxford 1952–60, 1: 36 ff.

azulejo

Spanish term for small glazed tiles often used as dadoes in courtyards and palaces.

B

bab

gate.

badgir

Iranian term for wind tower. Tall chimney-like structure which projects above the roof of a building to expel warm air in the day and trap cooler breezes at night.

See also: mulqaf

Badr al-Jamali, Tomb of (also referred to as the Mashhad of al-Juyushi)

Important eleventh-century Fatimid tomb complex in Cairo.

This complex was built by the Armenian general Badr al-Jamali, chief vizier of the Fatimid caliph al-Mustansir, in 1085. Although it is known as a mashhad or tomb complex, the name of the person buried or commemorated is not known (Badr al-Jamali is buried elsewhere).

The complex consists of a prayer room, a small domed room (possibly a tomb) and a tall square minaret built around a small courtyard. The courtyard façade of the prayer room consists of a triple-arched arcade with a large central arch and two smaller side arches. The prayer room is cross vaulted except for the area in front of the mihrab which is covered with a large dome resting on an octagonal drum resting on plain squinches. Both the mihrab and the dome are decorated in stucco work in an Iranian style.

The minaret or tower consists of a tall rectangular shaft with a two-storey structure on the top. This is a square room with a domed octagonal pavilion above it. A significant feature of the design is that at the top of the shaft is a muqarnas cornice which may be one of the first occurrences of this decoration in Egypt. On the roof of the complex are two domed kiosks containing prayer niches. The exact function of these is not known although it has been suggested that they were shelters for the muezzin who would make the call to prayer from the roof similar to the goldasteh found in mosques in Iran.

The exact purpose of this unique building is not known although there have been suggestions that it is a watchtower disguised as a mosque or that it is a victory monument commemorating the victories of Badr al-Jamali.

Further reading:

D. Berhens-Abouseif, *Islamic Architecture in Cairo: An Introduction*, Supplements to Muqarnas, vol. 3, Leiden 1989, 66 ff.

K. A. C. Creswell, *The Muslim Architecture of Egypt*, Oxford 1952–60, 1:155 ff.

F. Shafici, 'The Mashhad of al-Juyushi: Archaeological notes and studies', *Studies in Islamic Art and Architecture in Honour of Professor K. A. C. Creswell*, Cairo 1965, 237 ff.

bagh

Iranian and Mughal term for garden or garden pavilion.

See also: chahar bagh

Baghdad (Madinat al-Salam)

Capital city of Iraq.

Baghdad was founded by the Abbasid caliph al-Mansur in 762. According to historical accounts al-Mansur built a round city with four gates and a palace and mosque at the centre. Leading from the four gates to the centre there were streets lined with shops and markets whilst the area between these streets were quarters reserved for different groups of people. The round shape of the city may be derived from Central Asian ideas of planning or may have some symbolic significance. In any case a round city wall would be both cheaper to build for a given area and would be easier to defend (no weak corner points). The defensive nature of the city is further emphasized by the bent entrances

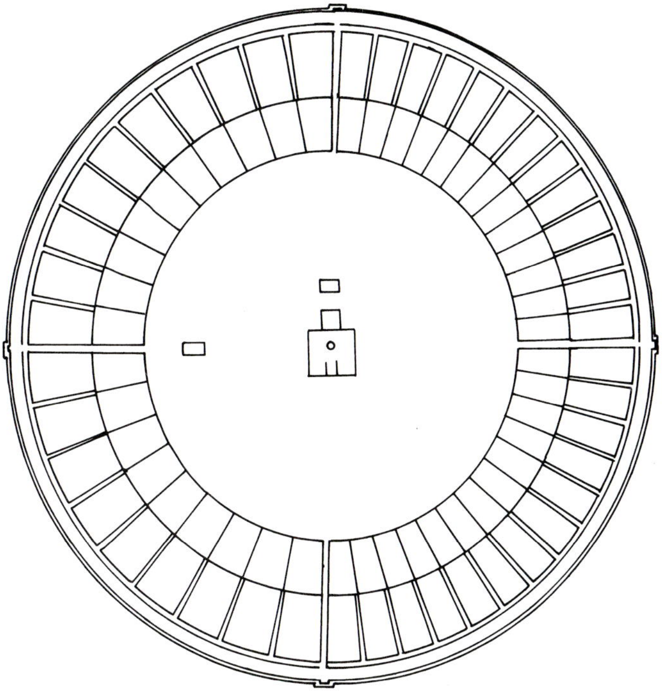

Reconstruction of plan of eighth-century Round City of al-Mansur (Baghdad) (after Creswell)

and the double wall. Unfortunately nothing remains of al-Mansur's city with the possible exception of a mihrab in the Iraq museum. The round city was built on the west bank of the Tigris and shortly afterwards a complementary settlement was founded on the east bank known as Mu'asker al-Mahdi. In 773 al-Mansur moved the markets outside to a place called al-Karkh. From 836 to 892 the capital was transferred to Samarra because of troubles with the caliph's Turkish troops in Baghdad. When Caliph al-Mu'tamid moved back to Baghdad he settled on the east bank of the Tigris which has remained the centre of the city to the present day.

The Buwaihids built a number of important buildings, such as the Bimaristan al-Aduli (hospital) and the Dar al-Alim (house of science) but the Seljuk conquest found the city in a ruinous condition because of the conflict between the Buwaihid amirs and their soldiers. In 1056 Tughril Beg separated his residence from the rest of the city by a broad wall. Although few buildings of the Seljuk period survive, an idea of the appearance of the city in the thirteenth century (before the Mongol invasion) can be gained by looking at the illustrations of al-Wasiti to the Maqamat of al-Harriri (MS Arabe 5874).

During the period of the later Abbasid caliphate (twelfth to thirteenth century) a massive defensive wall was built around east Baghdad which for centuries marked the boundary of the city. The walls had four gates of which only one survives, the Bab al-Wastani. The gate stood in the centre of a moat and was connected to the city wall and the outside by two brick bridges. The arch of the main entrance is decorated with geometric interlace and is flanked by two lions in relief. Other buildings which survive from this period are the Zummurud Khatun Tomb, the Mustansiriya Madrassa, the building known as the Abbasid palace and two minarets. The Zummurud Khatun Tomb built in 1209 consists of a conical muqarnas dome built on an octagonal base. The sides of the base are decorated with decorative brickwork set over a series of blind niches. Until the eighteenth century a ribat and madrassa built at the request of Zummurud Khatun (mother of the Abbasid caliph al-Nasir) were located near the tomb. The Mustansiriya Madrassa was built between 1227 and 1233 and is the most famous surviving building in Baghdad. It was built by the caliph al-Mustansir and contained four Sunni law schools (i.e. Sha'fi, Hanafi, Maliki and Hanbali). The madrassa is a rectangular courtyard building with four large iwans, one for each law school. The courtyards and iwans are faced with ornate hazarbaf brickwork and carved interlace. The building now known as the Abbasid palace was probably originally the madrassa of al-Sharabiyya built by Sharif al-Din Iqbal in 1230. The building is situated within a rectangular enclosure of 430 square metres and is dominated by a vaulted hall over 9 m high. The brickwork decoration of the building is identical to that of the Zummurud Khatun Tomb. The surviving pre-Mongol minarets belong to the Jami' al-Khaffin and the 'Ami Qumuriyya Mosque; both structures comprise a cylindrical shaft resting on a square base with muqarnas corbelling supporting the balcony.

The most important remains of the Ilkhanid period are Khan Mirjan and the Mirjaniya Madrassa. The khan was built in 1359 to support the madrassa which was completed in 1357. The madrassa is mostly destroyed apart from the gateway which is a monumental portal with carved brickwork similar to that of the Abbasid palace. Khan Mirjan is a remarkable building built around a central covered courtyard. The roof of the courtyard is made of giant transverse vaults which in turn are spanned by barrel vaults. This system made it possible to cover a huge interior space as well as providing light to the interior (through windows set between the transverse vaults).

Many buildings survive from the Ottoman period, the most significant being the shrine of al-Kadhimiyya which houses the tombs of the imams Musa al-Kadhim and Muhammad Jawad. The shrine has been successively rebuilt and much of the structure belongs to the eighteenth or nineteenth century. The shrines stand in the middle of a large courtyard lined with two storeys of arcades. The tombs are covered by tall golden domes and flanked by four minarets, a porch runs around three sides of the tomb structure and there is a mosque on the south side.

The traditional houses of Baghdad are built of brick around small central courtyards. Many houses had projecting wooden balconies often with carved wooden screens. Most of the houses had windcatchers (mulqaf) which would keep the houses cool during the oppressive summer heat.

See also: Iraq

Further reading:

J. Lassner, *The Topography of Baghdad in the Middle Ages*, Wayne State University Press, Detroit 1970.

V. Strika and J. Khalil, *The Islamic Architecture of Baghdad*, Naples 1987.

J. Warren and I. Fethi, *Traditional Houses in Baghdad*, Horsham, UK 1982.

Bahrain

The State of Bahrain comprises a small island on the west side of the Persian/Arabian Gulf located between Qatar and Saudi Arabia.

During Antiquity the island may have been known as Dilmun and during the early Islamic period was known as Awal. The Islamic history of the country is closely tied to its Persian and Arabian neighbours, a fact which is reflected in its architecture and culture. The island seems to have been an important trading centre in the Sassanian period but seems to have missed out from the general economic boom of the early Islamic period. In the tenth century the island escaped from the control of the Abbasid dynasty and became one of the main bases of the Ismaili Carmathian state which controlled much of the northern Gulf during this period. With the collapse of the Carmathians in the tenth century the island came under the control of the Uyunids who were another local dynasty. From the twelfth century onwards Bahrain was under the influence of Persian dynasties who used the island as a trading base with pearls as the basic commodity. In 1504 Bahrain was captured by the Portuguese who controlled the island until 1602 when the country again fell under the influence of Iran. In the 1780s the Khalifa family came from Arabia and established themselves as rulers of the island with British protection. In 1860 Bahrain became a British dependency until its independence in 1971.

The building materials on Bahrain are similar to those used elsewhere in the Gulf and include limestone and coral blocks for masonry and palm trees for wood and thatch. The country contains several early Islamic sites the most famous of which is Qal'at Bahrain on the north coast. The Qal'at as revealed by excavation is a small rectangular building with round corner towers, semi-circular buttress towers and a projecting entrance made out of two quarter circles with a gateway between. Next to this fort is a large fortress built in the thirteenth century which is known as the Portuguese fort because of its restoration in the sixteenth century.

Bahrain contains several historical mosques, the most famous of which is the Suq al-Khamis Mosque founded in the eleventh century. The present building has two main phases, an earlier prayer hall with a flat roof supported by wooden columns dated to the fourteenth century and a later section with a flat roof supported on arches resting on thick masonry piers (this has been dated to 1339). Another distinctive building is the Abu Zaidan Mosque built in the eighteenth century which has a long transverse prayer hall with open sides and a triple arched portico.

The typical Bahrain merchant's house is built around several courtyards each of which forms a separate unit opening on to a series of shallow rooms. Upstairs the arrangement of rooms is repeated but instead of the thick stone walls of the ground floor the walls are built of a series of piers alternating with panels made out of thin coral slabs. Sometimes two layers of coral slabs were used with a cavity in between to provide increased thermal insulation. The temperature of the lower rooms is kept low by various ventilation ducts connected to wind catchers. In addition to coral panels plaster screens are used as a means of ensuring privacy in the upper part of the house. These screens are often decorated with geometric patterns, the most common of which is a series of intersecting rectangles producing a stepped pattern. Most of the traditional houses of Bahrain are located in the Muharraq district of the capital Manama. The most famous house is the palace of Sheikh Isa built in 1830 and recently restored as a national monument. The house is built around four courtyards and includes some beautiful incised stucco panels in the upper rooms.

See also: Kuwait, Oman, Qatar, Saudi Arabia, UAE

Further reading:

S. Kay, *Bahrain: Island Heritage*, Dubai 1985.

C. Larsen, *Life and Land Use on the Bahrain Islands*, Chicago 1983.

R. Lewcock, 'The Traditional Architecture of Bahrain', in *Bahrain through the Ages: The Archaeology*, ed. S. H. Ali al-Khalifa and M. Rice, London 1986.

Baku

Capital of the Independent Republic of Azerbayjan.

Baku is located on a peninsula on the west coast of the Caspian Sea. The city has always been famous for its naturally occurring oil wells although it did not achieve political importance until the fifteenth century, when it was established as the capital of a local dynasty known as the Sherwan Shahs. The Sherwan Shahs had established themselves along the west coast of the Caspian Sea as early as the fourteenth century although they did not move to Baku until their previous capital of Shir'wan was captured by the Qara Qoyonulu in 1426. The Sherwan Shahs were effectively destroyed in 1500 when the Saffavid ruler Isma'il killed the reigning shah. Baku remained part of the Iranian Empire from the sixteenth until the early twentieth century when it was annexed by Russia.

One of the earliest Islamic monuments in Baku is the Kiz Kallesi which is a huge round bastion tower built of brick. The tower was probably built in the eleventh century although the precise date has not been agreed. The tower may have formed part of the city walls of Baku although alternatively it may have been an independent castle or watchtower. The majority of monuments in Baku date from the period of the Sherwan Shahs or later. The most important monuments form part of the royal complex which stands on a hill overlooking the Caspian Sea. All of these buildings are made out of large bluish-grey limestone blocks which are carefully squared and dressed. At the centre of the complex is the palace which was built in the mid-fifteenth century. The layout of the palace is based on two interconnected octagons with two storeys. A tall entrance portal opens into an octagonal hall which in turn leads via a passageway into a smaller hall. The palace complex includes a private mosque which has a cruciform plan entered from monumental portal set to one side. One of the other arms contained a separate women's mosque and there was another prayer hall upstairs. The complex also includes a number of mausoleums the most important of which is the tomb of the shahs. This comprises a square central chamber leading on to four barrel-vaulted side rooms. The dome is slightly pointed and decorated with faceting.

See also: Azerbayjan

Balkh, Hajji Piyadi Mosque (also known as Masjid-i Tarikh, Nuh Gunbad or Masjid-i Ka'b al-Akhbar)

Site of a badly damaged mosque, believed to date from the early Islamic period.

The mosque is situated north-east of the city walls

of Balkh in Afghanistan. Most scholars agree that the monument should be dated to the ninth century CE. Although the roof itself has collapsed the building is regarded as one of the earliest examples of a nine-domed mosque.

The mosque is built out of a combination of baked and unbaked brick and pisé. The extant remains include massive round piers and smaller engaged columns typical of Abbasid architecture.

Further reading:

L. Golombeck, 'Abbasid mosque at Balkh', *Oriental Art* NS 15(3): 173–89, Autumn 1969.
J. D. Hoag, *Islamic Architecture*, New York 1977, 48–9.

Banbhore

Major early Islamic site in Pakistan.

Banbhore is located on the north bank of the Gharro Creek near the Indian Ocean coast in the Pakistani state of Sind. Archaeological work at the site has revealed a long-term occupation from the first century to the thirteenth century CE which includes three distinct periods, Scytho–Parthian, Hindu–Buddhist and early Islamic. It seems probable that the site is the ancient city of Debal referred to in early Muslim accounts of the area and conquered by the Arab general Mohammed ibn al-Qasim in 711.

The city comprises a large area enclosed by a stone and mud wall strengthened by solid semi-circular bastions with three main gateways. The walled area is divided into two parts, an eastern and a western section separated by a fortified stone wall. In the middle of the eastern sector is the congregational mosque. The mosque has a roughly square plan, built around a central courtyard, two arcades on each of the sides except the qibla side which is three bays deep. The mosque has been dated by an inscription to 727 CE, two years after the capture of Debal. Significantly there is no trace of a concave or projecting mihrab which confirms the mosque's early date as the first concave mihrab was introduced at Medina between 707 and 709 (see also Wasit and mihrab).

Remains of houses and streets have been found both within the walls and outside to the north and east. Large houses were built of semi-dressed stone or brick, the smaller houses of mud brick.

See also: Pakistan

Further reading:

S. M. Ashfaque, 'The Grand Mosque of Banbhore', *Pakistan Archaeology* 6: 182–209, 1969.
M. A. Ghafur, 'Fourteen Kufic inscriptions of Banbhore, the site of Daybul', *Pakistan Archaeology* 3: 65–90, 1966.
S. Qudratullah, 'The twin ports of Daybul', *in Sind through the Centuries*, Karachi 1981.

bangala

Mughal and Indian term for roof with curved eaves resembling the traditional Bengali hut.

See also: char-chala, do-chala

Bangladesh

See Bengal

Basra

Early Islamic garrison town and Iraq's principal port.

Basra was founded in 635 as a twin garrison town of Kufa. The purpose was to relieve the pressure of the constant immigration into Iraq as well as to provide a base for the opening of a new front against the Arabs of Bahrain. The majority of Arabs in Basra, unlike those of Kufa, had not taken part in the wars of conquest in Iraq. The first mosque was marked out with reeds and people prayed within the enclosed space without any fixed building. In 665 CE a new mosque was built on the site by Ziyad, governor of Iraq. The mosque was built out of baked bricks with a flat roof supported by teak columns. Unfortunately the expansion of modern Basra has meant that no remains of the early period stand above ground.

See also: Iraq, khatta

bayt

Arabic term for house. In Umayyad and Abbasid architecture it is used to describe the living units within palaces and desert residences.

bayt al-mal

Arabic term for treasury (literally 'house of the money'). In Friday mosques usually an octagonal or square room raised up on columns in the centre of the courtyard.

bazar

Market area in Turkish city.

The Turkish word bazar is derived from the Persian 'pazar'. A Turkish bazar will normally contain a number of specialized buildings such as bedestans, bath houses (hammams), hans (khans) and caravanserais as well as private shops, market stalls and a mosque. One of the earliest examples of a Turkish bazar is that of Bursa which was first developed in the fourteenth century. This complex includes six mosques, three baths, seventeen khans, six madrassas and a bedestan.

See also: arasta, bedestan, Ottomans

bedestan

Special closed form of Turkish market where goods of high value were traded. The usual form of bedestan is a long domed or vaulted hall two storeys high with external shop units.

Originally bedestan referred to the area of a market where cloth was sold or traded from the 'bezzaz han' (cloth market). The earliest bedestans were probably specific areas of a general bazar or market. The earliest known bedestan is the Beyşehir Bedestan built in 1297 according to an inscription above the gateway. The building consists of a closed rectangular courtyard covered by six domes supported on two central piers. There are doorways on three sides and on the outside there are small open shop units, six on the east and west sides and nine on the north and south sides.

During the Ottoman period bedestans developed as a specific building type and became the centre of economic life in a city. Because they could be locked they were often used for jewellery or money transactions and came to be regarded as signs of prosperity in a city. Ottoman bedestans were built in a variety of forms and may include features such as external shops, internal cell units and arastas (arcades). The simplest plan consists of a square domed hall with one or two entrances like those at Amasya or Trabzon. More complicated structures like the Rüstem Pasha Bedestan in Erzerum consist of a central enclosed courtyard surrounded by a closed vaulted corridor containing shop units.

Bengal

Low-lying delta area in the north-west corner of the Indian subcontinent.

The character of Bengal is largely determined by the Ganges and Bramaputra rivers which divide into innumerable branches before entering the sea. Although the area is currently divided between the two modern states of India and Bangladesh it retains a certain homogeneity based on its language (Bangli) and culture.

In the thirteenth century the region was conquered by Muslim Turks who occupied the city of Gaur (Lakhnaw) in north-west Bengal. From this base the areas of Satgaon (south-west Bengal) and Sonargaon (east Bengal) were conquered and incorporated into an independent sultanate in 1352 CE by Iliyas Shah. Despite dynastic changes the area remained independent until the sixteenth century when it was incorporated into the Mughal sultanate, and even then it still retained its identity as a separate province.

Lack of suitable building stone in the area meant that the predominant materials of construction were red clay bricks from the alluvial silts and bamboo and thatch. The majority of buildings were made of bamboo and thatch and consist of a rectangular area which is roofed by a curved thatch roof ('char-chala' and 'do-chala'). Most of the more important buildings, however, were made out of brick. In the pre-Mughal period such buildings were faced either with red terracotta plaques or less frequently in stone. From the sixteenth century onwards brick buildings were coated in white plaster.

One of the achievements of Bengali building was its translation of traditional bamboo and thatch architecture into more permanent stone and brick forms. One of the best examples of this is the use of curved roofs from the sixteenth century onwards. There are two main forms of this roof – do-chala and char-chala. A do-chala roof consists of a central curved ridge rising in the middle with curved side eaves and gabled ends. A char-chala roof is made of crossed curved ridges with curved eaves. The earliest surving example of this roof type in a brick building is the tomb of Fath Khan at Gaur dated to the seventeenth century. This form was so successful that it was used elsewhere in the Mughal Empire, at Agra, Fatehpur Sikri, Delhi and Lahore. In addition to its aesthetic appeal curved roofs also have a practical purpose in an area of high rainfall.

Other characteristic features of Bengali architecture adopted by the Mughals and used elsewhere are the two-centre pointed arch and the use of cusped arches for openings.

The predominant form of Islamic architecture in Bengal is the mosque. In pre-Mughal Bengal the mosque was virtually the only form of Islamic building, although after the sixteenth century a

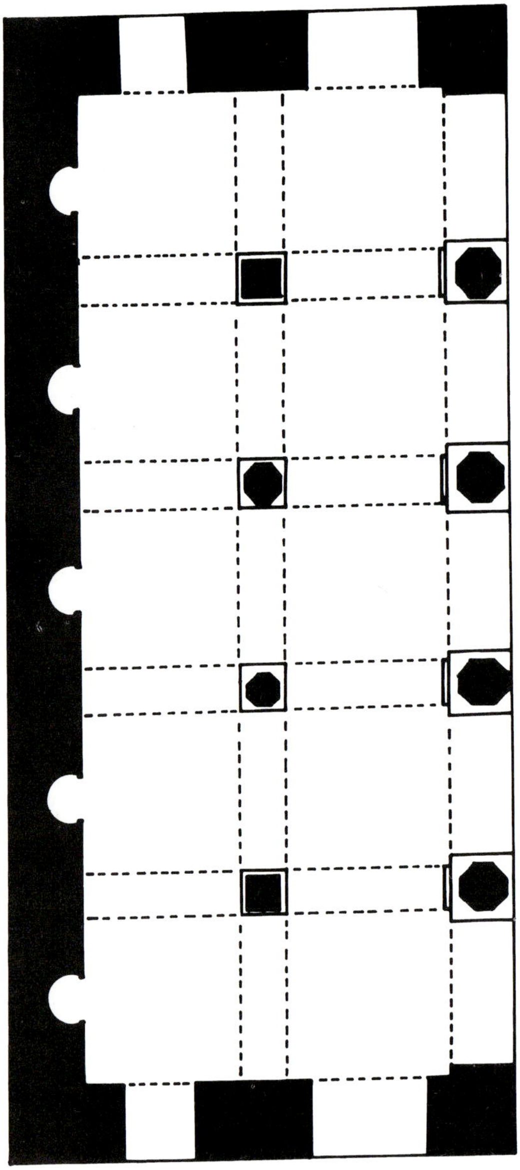

Mosque of Zafar Khan, Ghazi, Bengal. Note multiple mihrabs (after Michell)

wide variety of Islamic building types such as the caravanserai and madrassa were introduced. Characteristic features of Bengali mosques of all periods are multiple mihrabs, engaged corner towers and curved cornices. Although multiple mihrabs sometimes occur in North India, Bengal is the only place where they are a constant feature in mosques. The number of mihrabs is determined by the number of entrances in the east wall. Engaged corner towers are a constant feature of Bengali architecture and may derive from pre-Islamic temples. Curved cornices are probably derived from the curved roofs of bamboo huts; it is possible that they may have a practical function for draining water away from the base of the domes.

During the pre-Mughal sultanate three types of mosque were built, rectangular, square nine-domed and square single-domed.

Mosques built on a rectangular plan are divided into aisles and bays according to the number of domes on the roof. At the east end of each aisle is a doorway and at the west end a mihrab. There are also openings on the south and north sides of the mosque corresponding to the number of bays. The nine-domed mosques are similar to those found elsewhere in the Islamic world, but they differ in having three mihrabs at the west end. The most popular form of mosque in pre-Mughal Bengal was the single-domed chamber. It is likely that this design is developed from the pre-Islamic temple of Bengal.

None of these early mosques was equipped with minarets and sahns as was common in the Middle East but these features were introduced with the Mughal conquest in the sixteenth century. However, the Mughals were also influenced by the local architecture of Bengal and it is from this period that we have the first example of a do-chala roof translated into brick (the Fath Khan Tomb at Gaur, dated to the seventeenth century).

Muslim buildings can be found all over the region of Bengal, although the largest concentrations can be found at Dhaka and Gaur (Lucknow). Calcutta, the capital of Indian Bengal, was founded during the period of British rule in the nineteenth century. As might be expected the early mosques of the city show strong British influence. The descendants of Tipu Sultan built three mosques in the city all with the same double-aisled, multi-domed rectangular plan. The most famous of these buildings, the Tipu Sultan Mosque built by his son Muhammad, is built in the style of a European building with Tuscan colonettes and Ionic columns used for the windows and central piers.

Further reading:

P. Hassan, 'Sultanate mosques and continuity in Bengal architecture', *Muqarnas* 6, 1989. This deals with pre-Mughal architecture.

G. Michell (ed.), *The Islamic Heritage of Bengal*, Paris 1984. This is the best reference book on Islamic architecture in Bengal.

beteng

Indonesian term for enclosure wall, used to refer to the outer walls of palaces in Java.

Bijapur

City in southern India famous for its sixteenth- and seventeenth-century architecture.

Bijapur is located on an arid plateau between the Krishna and Bhima rivers. The city rose to prominence under the Adil Shahi dynasty who ruled the city from the fifteenth century until its conquest by the Mughals in 1686. Traditionally the dynasty was founded in 1490 when the Turkish governor Yusuf Khan declared the independence of Bijapur. By the sixteenth century the Adil Shahi dynasty ruled a huge area which extended as far as Goa on the western coast.

Since the seventeenth century the city has shrunk so that the present town occupies less than half the original area. The original city walls with a circumference of over 10 km survive to give some idea of the city's original importance. These massive walls are surrounded by a moat and protected by ninety-six bastions. There are five main gateways, each of which consists of a bent entrance protected by two large bastions. Within this huge enclosure there is a smaller walled area known as the Arquila or citadel which forms the centre of the modern town. The city is supplied with water by a series of underground water channels interspersed with water towers to regulate the pressure.

Water is perhaps the most distinctive element in the architecture of Bijapur and is used for ornamental tanks, water pavilions, bath houses and ornamental channels. The Mubarak Khan is one of the best surviving examples of a water pavilion; it consists of a three-storey structure with a shower bath on the roof. Other notable examples include the Jal Mandir Palace once located in the centre of a reservoir (now disappeared) and the Sat Manzili which was originally a seven-storey structure enlivened with water tanks and spouting water.

The city contains several mosques, the largest of which is the Jami Masjid founded in the sixteenth century. The mosque has a rectangular central courtyard containing several fountains in the centre. The mosque sanctuary is nine bays wide and is crowned by a large central dome. One of the more unusual features of the mosque is the stone floor which is divided up into 2,250 individual prayer spaces. Other important mosques in the city are the Jhangari Mosque and the Mecca Masjid which is enclosed within huge walls.

The city contains many tomb complexes the best known of which is the mausoleum of Muhamad Adil Shah II, known as the Gol Gumbaz. Other important mausoleums include the Ibrahim Rauza built between 1626 and 1633. The complex consists of a large square area enclosed within a tall wall and entered via a monumental gateway flanked by twin minarets. In the centre of the complex is a raised platform containing two large buildings either side of a sunken rectangular tank. To the east surrounded by a colonnade is the domed tomb chamber which has an extraordinary suspended stone ceiling. To the west of the pool is the the mosque with four thin minarets, one at each corner. The whole complex is decorated with painted, inlaid and carved ornament in the form of flowers and arabic calligraphy.

See also: Deccan, Gol Gumbaz, India

birka

Arabic term for tank, reservoir or cistern.

blazon

Decorative device or symbol used in Mamluk architecture to denote particular amirs or military dignitaries.

The earliest blazons were circular shields containing a simple symbol. Later these became complex designs divided into three fields with a variety of symbols used to denote different offices (i.e. a napkin represents the master of the robes and a pen box represents the secretary). The earliest example of a blazon was found in the tomb of Sheikh Iliyas in Gaza dated to 1272. Blazons are not used after the Ottoman conquest of 1517.

Further reading:

W. Leaf, 'Not trousers but trumpets: a further look at Saracenic heraldry', *Palestine Exploration Quarterly*, 1982.
L. A. Mayer, *Saracenic Heraldry*, Oxford 1933.

Bosnia

Independent state in south-eastern Europe, previously constituting part of the former Republic of Yugoslavia.

Fourteenth-century composite Mamluk blazon used by warrior class (after Mayer)

Islam was introduced to Bosnia by the Ottoman Turks although it later became the religion of a large proportion of the native Bosnian population. The first Turkish invasion of Bosnia was in 1386 and by 1389 after the battle of Kosovo the Bosnian rulers had accepted Turkish suzerainty. In 1463 the Bosnian king Stjepan Tomasevic failed to pay tribute to the Ottomans resulting in a further invasion of Bosnia. By 1512, with the conquest of the district of Sebrenik, all Bosnia had been incorporated into the Ottoman Empire. After the conquest there was large-scale Islamization which appears to have spread from the towns outwards. During the seventeenth century Bosnia served as a base for the conquest of Hungary whilst during the eighteenth century it became a border area between the Austro-Hungarian and Ottoman empires. In 1878 Bosnia was invaded by the Austro-Hungarian army after the Turks had been forced to leave under the terms of the Congress of Berlin. After the First World War Bosnia was incorporated into the Federal Republic of Yugoslavia until 1992 when it became an independent state.

In general Ottoman buildings in Bosnia reflect the imperial architecture of Istanbul, Bursa and Edirne although there are also elements of a local style. This style seems to have been partly developed by Dalmatian builders from Dubrovnik who were hired to construct some of the monumental buildings. One characteristic of Dalmatian building is the use of small cut stones instead of the bricks more commonly used in Ottoman architecture. Another notable feature of Bosnian architecture is the use of squinches instead of the triangular pendentives more common in Turkish architecture.

Four main periods of Islamic architecture have been identified. The first period which begins with the Turkish conquest is characterized by the founding of cities such as the capital Sarajevo, Banja Luka and Mostar. Also during this period many public buildings and mosques were founded by the Turkish governors and aristocracy. Important buildings from the sixteenth century in Sarajevo include Ghazi Khusraw Bey Cami, the ʿAli Pasha Cami and the Brusa Bedestan. During the second period, in the seventeenth century, the patronage of buildings was mostly by local merchants and includes khans, bath houses and mescits although some imperial buildings were erected such as the Ṭekke of Hajji Sinan in Sarajevo (1640). During the eighteenth and nineteenth centuries (the third period) there was increased European influence in the architecture as well as fashions imported from Istanbul. An interesting phenomenon is the development of the town of Trevnik as the official residence of the Ottoman vizier. Under the Austro-Hungarian Empire a fourth period can be distinguished which was characterized by an attempt to build non-Turkish Islamic architecture. Many of the buildings of this period were built in 'Moorish Style', the most famous example of which is Sarajevo Town Hall.

See also: Albania, Bulgaria, Ottomans

Further reading:

M. Kiel, 'Some reflections on the origins of provincial tendencies in the Ottoman architecture of the Balkans', in *Islam in the Balkans: Persian Art and Culture of the 18th & 19th Centuries*, Edinburgh 1979.

brickwork

In many areas of the Islamic world brick is the primary building material.

There is an important distinction to be made between fired or baked brick and mud brick. Fired brick requires fuel to heat the kilns, making it relatively expensive, although the firing makes it more durable and therefore more suitable for monumental building. Architecture of the early Islamic period drew on two distinct building traditions each of which used fired brick as a major component. In the Mediterranean area brickwork derived from Byzantine and ultimately Roman traditions whereas in former Sassanian territories it dated back to the ancient civilizations of Mesopotamia and Iran.

In the Byzantine tradition brick was usually used for specific parts of a building such as the dome or as string courses to level off layers of rubble wall. In the area of Syria and Jordan the availability of good quality stone meant that bricks were little used in the Byzantine architecture of the area and consequently were little used in the early Islamic architecture of the area. In the few examples – Mshatta and Qasr al-Tuba – where brickwork is employed it seems to be an import from the Sassanian east rather than a continuation of a local tradition. It is only with the Ottoman conquest of Anatolia that the Byzantine brickwork tradition becomes fully incorporated into Islamic architecture.

In the east (Iran and Iraq), however, brick was employed in the earliest Islamic buildings (i.e. Khan Atshan) as a direct continuation of Sassanian practice. It was in this area that the techniques of decorative brickwork developed using either standard bricks arranged in patterns or specially shaped bricks. Bricks could be laid vertically, sideways, flat on or in a herringbone pattern and were used to form geometric patterns or even inscriptions. Particularly elaborate brickwork was referred to by the Persian term hazarbaf (qv). Brickwork of the Seljuk period, from the eleventh to thirteenth century, in Iran and Central Asia is particularly elaborate using specially manufactured bricks. A particularly good example is Aisha Bibi Khanum Mausoleum at Djambul, Uzbekistan.

See also: hazarbaf, mud brick

Bukhara

Oasis city in the Republic of Uzbekistan, Central Asia.

Bukhara is located in the valley of the Zeravshan river 200 km west of Samarkand. The city was first mentioned by its present name in a seventh-century Chinese text; however the city itself is probably older. The first Arab raid on Bukhara occurred in 674 although it was not finally conquered until 739. During the ninth and tenth centuries the city was under the rule of the Samanids and from 900 was capital of the province of Khurassan. During this period the city flourished and became established as one of the greatest centres of learning in the Islamic world.

Descriptions of Bukhara in the Samanid period indicate that it consisted of two main parts, the citadel and the town itself. The citadel and the town were separate walled enclosures on a high plateau, with a space between them which was later occupied by a congregational mosque. The citadel had a circumference of 1.5 km and contained, besides the palace, the city's first Friday mosque which was built on a pagan temple. The town itself was approximately twice the size of the citadel and was enclosed by a wall with seven gates. Later the whole area of the city and the citadel was enclosed within a wall with eleven gates (visible until 1938). In addition to the city walls there were outer walls which enclosed the villages around the city to protect them from nomad attacks; traces of these walls still survive.

Little is left of the Samanid city except the tenth-century mausoleum of the Samanid rulers known as the mausoleum of Isma'il the Samanid. This is one of the earliest examples of Islamic funerary architecture and consists of a square chamber with a hemispherical dome and decorative brickwork on both the exterior and the interior. The corners of the building are formed by engaged cylindrical brick piers whilst the corners of the dome are marked by small domed finials. In the centre of each side there is a recessed niche containing a door which acts as a focus for the surface decoration. The main form of decoration is small, flat, tile-like bricks laid alternately in vertical or horizontal groups of three. Another decorative technique is bricks laid horizontally in groups of three with one corner projecting outwards producing a dog-tooth pattern. This dog-tooth pattern is used mainly in the spandrels of the door arch which are also decorated with square terracotta plaques. At the top of the exterior façade there is an arcade of small niches which mask the zone of transition and also provide light to the interior. The decoration of the interior is similar to the exterior façade although here tiles are set vertically on end producing a diaper pattern. The dome rests on arched squinches which alternate with arched grilles which admit light to the interior.

The collapse of the Samanids at the end of the tenth century led to the gradual decline of Bukhara under their successors the Kharakhanids. This decline was reinforced by the Mongol invasions of the thirteenth century which twice destroyed the city. There seems to have been no recovery in the

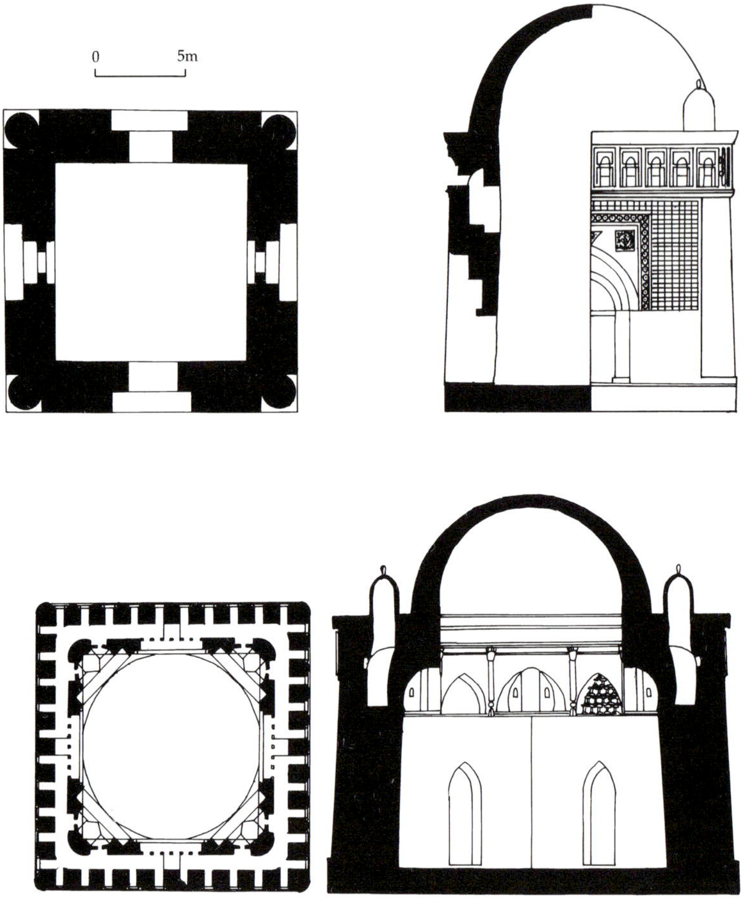

Tenth-century tomb of the Samanids, Bukhara, Uzbekistan (after Creswell)

fifteenth century and it was not until the arrival of the Uzbeks in the sixteenth that the city recovered some of its former splendour. There are few structures which survive from the period between the Samanids and the Uzbeks although there are a few important buildings which date from the twelfth century. The most famous of these is the Kaylan Minaret which is a huge tower over 45 m high and is decorated with bands of decorative brickwork. The tower is a tapering cylinder with an arcaded gallery surmounted by an overhanging muqarnas corbel; its form is similar to that of Seljuk towers in Iran with its band of polychrome tile decoration at the top. Another twelfth-century structure demonstrating Seljuk influence is the shrine of Chasma Ayyub with its conical dome. A few buildings survive from the fifteenth century including the Ulugh Beg Madrassa built in 1417.

Most of the major monuments of Bukhara date from the Uzbek period and include the massive Kukeldash Madrassa, the Divan Begi Mosque and Madrassa and the Kaylan Mosque. The buildings of this period resemble the Timurid buildings of Samarkand which they were clearly intended to imitate in both size and design. Another feature of this period is the grouping of buildings around a focal point or square such as the Lyabi Hauz or the Poi Kaylan in order to increase the visual effect. The Kukeldash Madrassa measures 80 by 60 m and is the largest madrassa in Central Asia although its decoration is surprisingly austere. The Divan Begi Mosque and Madrassa are equally impressive

Tenth-century mausoleum of the Samanids, Bukhara © StJohn Simpson

Minaret of the Kaylan Mosque, Bukhara © StJohn Simpson

with tall pishtaq entrances framed by twin minarets. The largest mosque in the city is the Kaylan Mosque built in the sixteenth century with the twelfth-century minaret nearby. The entrance to the mosque is through a huge entrance iwan or pishtaq decorated with blue glazed tiles covered with yellow flowers and turquoise stars. Within the mosque is a huge courtyard surrounded on three sides by a deep arcaded gallery. At the south-west end is another large iwan which leads to a domed room covered with a mihrab.

During the eighteenth century there was a move away from the monumental architecture of the first Uzbek rulers towards a lighter form of architecture inspired by Saffavid Iran. One of the finest examples of this style is the Masjid-i Jami opposite the Bola Hauz which has a magnificent hypostyle wooden porch supported on twenty wooden columns with painted muqarnas capitals.

See also: Samarkand, Timurids, Uzbekistan

Further reading:

J. Lawton and F. Venturi, *Samarkand and Bukhara*, London 1991.

G. Pugacenkova and L. Rempel, *Bukhara*, Moscow 1949.

L. Rempel, 'The Mausoleum of Isma'il the Samanid', *Bulletin of the American Institute of Persian Art and Archaeology* 4: 199–209, 1936.

Bulgaria

A small country located on the Danube in south-eastern Europe.

Bulgaria borders Turkey, Greece, Serbia, Russia and Romania. The name of the country derives from the Bulgars, a Turkic people who conquered this area in 679 CE and adopted Christianity from the Byzantines in 865. The presence of Islam in Bulgaria is almost exclusively connected with the Ottoman conquest of the region.

The first Ottoman conquest in Bulgaria took place in the mid-fourteenth century when they occupied part of the area now known as Bulgarian

Thrace. In 1396, after Sultan Bayezid's victory at the battle of Nikeboli (Nicopolis), the Danube area of Bulgaria was incorporated into the Ottoman Empire. From the end of the fourteenth century Bulgaria was strongly Ottomanized and new Muslim cities were established especially in the south-east of the country. By the sixteenth century this part of the country was predominantly Muslim and remained so until the nineteenth.

The main building materials used in Bulgaria were similar to those used by the Byzantines and later the Ottomans in Anatolia. These included baked brick on its own, baked brick in combination with ashlar masonry, ashlar masonry, coursed rubble masonry with wood and mud brick and wood. The choice of material depended partly on the area and partly on the status of a particular building.

Bulgaria can be divided into two main regions on the basis of Ottoman architecture: Bulgarian Thrace and the area of the Danube (Danubia). Bulgarian Thrace was the first area conquered by the Ottomans and so has a higher proportion of Ottoman buildings than the rest of the country.

Bulgarian Thrace

One of the oldest Islamic structures in Bulgaria is the turba of Lal Sahin Pasa in Kazanlik, thought to date from the mid-fourteenth century. The turba is an open, domed canopy supported on piers; the entire structure is made out of baked brick.

Most of the surviving Ottoman buildings, however, are in the major cities. Some of the best examples can be found in Plovdiv (Turkish Filibe and Byzantine Philippopolis) in the south-east of Bulgaria near Turkish Thrace. Here the Ottomans founded a new Muslim settlement outside the walls of the Christian one. The focal points of the city were the two mosques located at either end of the city centre. The older of these is the Cumaya Cami or Great Mosque built by Murad II in the 1420s which is reputedly one of the largest and most important mosques in the Balkans. It has nine bays roofed by three central domes and six wooden vaults, and beneath the central dome is a pool or fountain. In general the building resembles that of the Sehadet Cami in Bursa built in 1365. To the south of the Great Mosque is the Zaviye Cami or Imaret Mosque built in 1440 which formed the core of a commercial district with a bedestan and hammam. The Ottoman town of Filibe was developed between these two mosques and a main street was built to link the two.

To the east of Filibe is the city of Yambol which was established after the Ottoman conquests in 1365. Probably the most important monument at Yambol is the Eski Cami built between 1375 and 1385. This consists of a single-domed unit built of brick and ashlar masonry in the Byzantine and early Ottoman style. In the mid-fifteenth century rooms were added on to the sides and a square minaret was also added. At Yambol too is one of the best preserved examples of an early Ottoman bedestan. This consists of a long hall roofed by four domes and entered through the middle of the long sides. On the outside of the building are thirty vaulted rooms or shop units.

North and West Bulgaria (Danubia)

Outside Thrace Ottoman buildings tended to have more local characteristics. In the area of Danubia a particular form of mosque developed consisting of a spacious wooden rectangular hall with a flat roof or wooden ceiling (sometimes with an inset wooden dome), covered by a gently sloping roof. This roofing system was lighter than a brick or stone dome so that walls could be made thinner and could be built out of coursed rubble rather than ashlar masonry. Two examples of such mosques survive at Vidin on the Danube; the mosque of Mustafa Pasa built in the early eighteenth century and the Ak Cami built in 1800. Both are built out of coursed rubble masonry with flat wooden ceilings under tiled roofs. Another such mosque at Belgradcik (Haci Husseyin Aga) has a carved wooden ceiling in the local Bulgarian style.

A characteristic type of building found in north-east Bulgaria is the tekke or dervish lodge. The Kizane Tekkesi near Nikopol on the Danube is characteristic of the Besiktasi order in the sixteenth century. The complex is built of wood and mud brick and was last rebuilt in 1855. The tekke comprises several elements including a kitchen, guesthouse, assembly hall and the mausoleum of the saint.

Further reading:

M. Kiel, 'Early Ottoman monuments in Bulgarian Thrace', *Belleten* 37 no.152, 1974.
—— 'Urban development in Bulgaria in the Turkish

period: the place of architecture in the process', *International Journal of Turkish Studies* 4 no.2: 79–158, Fall/Winter 1989.

burj

Arabic term for a fortified tower.

Bursa (Brousse)

Located on the slopes of the Uludag (Great Mountain) in north-west Anatolia, Bursa became the first capital of the Ottoman state after its capture from the Byzantines in the fourteenth century.

The city first came under Turkish control in 1071 after the battle of Manzikert when it was captured by the Seljuk leader Alp Arslan. In 1107 the city was recaptured by the Byzantines who retained their control until 1326, when it was finally taken by the Ottomans after a ten-year siege. During the remainder of the fourteenth century Bursa was established as the Ottoman capital with imperial mosques, palaces and a flourishing commercial centre. In 1402, after the battle of Ankara, Timur marched westwards where he plundered and burned the city. It quickly recovered and during the subsequent period one of the city's most important monuments, the Yeşil Cami, was built. However, the city never recovered its former importance especially as it had been replaced as capital by Edirne in 1366. In 1429 the city suffered a severe plague, and the fall of Constantinople in 1453 meant that it was no longer the Asian capital of the Ottomans. During the sixteenth century Bursa was merely a provincial city and there are no major monuments of this period in contrast to Edirne and Istanbul. In the early nineteenth century the city was established as the centre of the silk trade with the first silk factory opened in 1837.

Bursa is dominated by the ancient citadel which had proved such an obstacle to early Turkish attacks. The early Ottoman palaces were built of wood on the spurs of the mountain and none has survived. However, the commercial centre of the city, established by Orhan in the fourteenth century, still contains a number of early buildings. The oldest Ottoman building in Bursa is the Alaettin Cami built in 1335 which consists of a square domed prayer hall and vaulted portico. Two years later Orhan built the first of the Bursa T-plan mosques. It consists of a domed central courtyard flanked by two student rooms and with a prayer hall to the south. Orhan's mosque was part of a complex which included two bath houses and a soup kitchen. One of the bath houses, known as the Bey Hammam, has survived in its original form and is the oldest known Ottoman bath house. The building has the same basic form as later hammams and consists of a large domed dressing room leading via an intermediary room to the cruciform domed hot room. Next door on the same street is the Bey Han also built by Orhan in the early fourteenth century. This is a two-storey structure built around a central rectangular courtyard with an entrance on the north side and a stable block at the back. The lower windowless rooms were used for storage whilst the upper floor contained the rooms for travellers each with its own chimney.

To the west of Bursa is an area known as Çekirge which was developed as a royal centre by Orhan's successor Murat between 1366 and 1385. At the centre of the complex was the Hüdavendigâr Cami, or royal mosque, which is a unique example of a madrassa and zawiya in one building. The lower floor is occupied by the zawiya and mosque whilst the upper floor is the madrassa. The zawiya and mosque is built to the same T-plan as was used earlier in Orhan's mosque whilst the upper floor is built as a traditional madrassa modified to the shape of the building below. The arrangement is unusual because the zawiya was used by mystical dervishes hostile to religious orthodoxy and the madrassa by students and teachers of orthodox Islamic law. The combination reflects the political situation of the time when the Ottomans were moving away from their role as leaders of frontier warriors with traditional dervish supporters to a more centralized state system relying on religious orthodoxy for support. Like the Hüdavendigâr Mosque, the Beyazit complex begun in 1490 includes a zawiya mosque and an orthodox madrassa although here the two buildings are separate with the mosque zawiya on a hill and the rectangular madrassa below. The mosque has the same T-plan as Orhan's original mosque although the tall five-domed portico represents an advance in mosque design.

The main mosque of Bursa is the Ulu Cami (Great Mosque) built by Beyazit between 1399 and 1400. The mosque covers a large area (63 by 50 m) and is roofed by twenty domes resting on large square piers. The main entrance and the

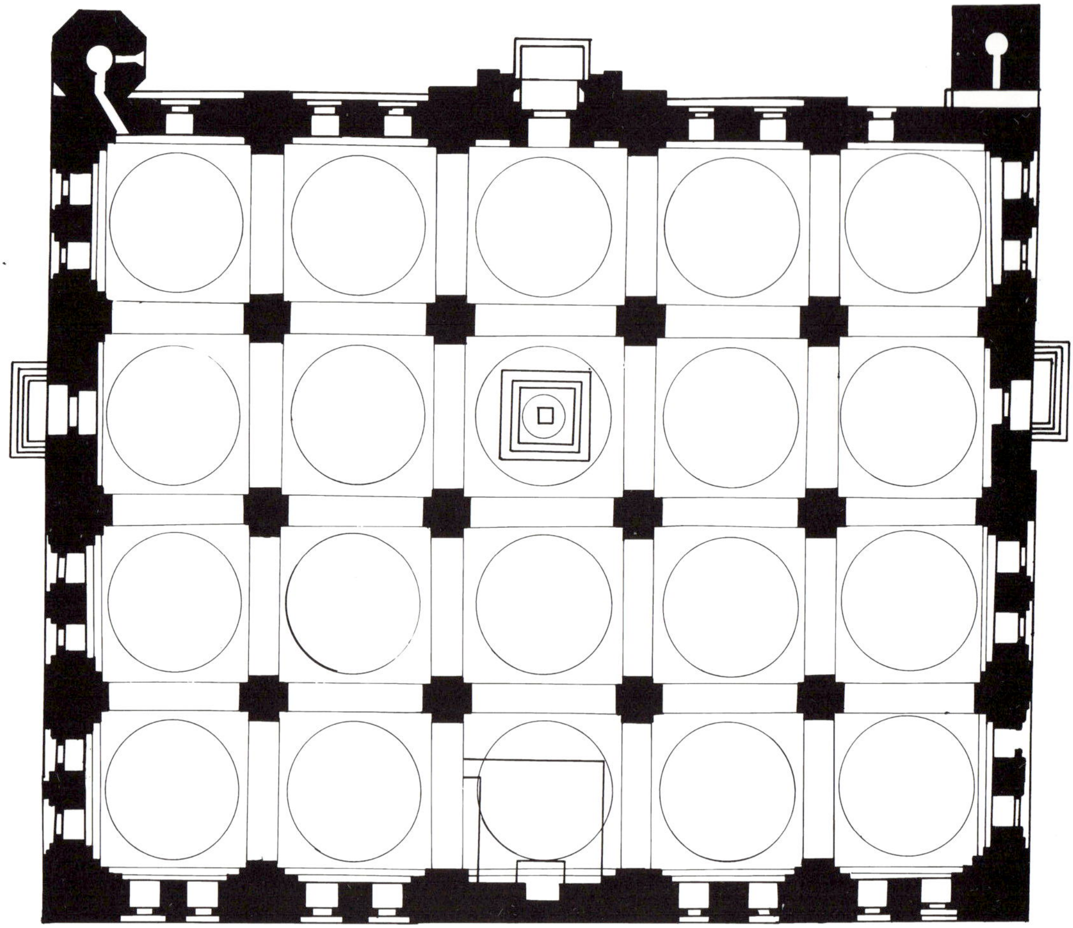

Ulu Cami, Bursa, Turkey (after Goodwin)

mihrab are on the same central axis and there is a sunken pool underneath the second dome in front of the mihrab. The interior is decorated with giant black calligraphy which dates to the nineteenth century but which may be copied from earlier originals.

The culmination of the Bursa T-plan mosques is the Yeşil Cami built by Mehmet I between 1403 and 1421. The building forms the centre of a complex which includes a madrassa, bath house, soup kitchen and the tomb of Mehmet I. The last imperial mosque to be built in Bursa is that of Murat II built in 1447. The building is a simplified version of the T-plan mosque and dispenses with the vestigial entrance vestibules found on the earlier mosques so that the portico leads directly on to the domed courtyard. Although the Muradiye was the last of the Bursa imperial mosques, the Bursa T-plan continued to influence the form of later Ottoman mosques.

Bursa is well known for its bath houses (kapilica) which relied upon naturally occurring warm spring water. The sulphurous spring water occurs naturally at a temperature of 80° which is too hot for human use so that it must be mixed with cold water to achieve a bearable temperature. One of the oldest thermal bath houses is the Eski Kapilica (Old Bath House) rebuilt by Murat I on the site of an earlier Roman bath. Also famous is the Yeni Kapilica built by the grand vizier Rüstem Pasha in the sixteenth century which has a similar plan to the Haseki Hammam in Istanbul built by Sinan.

See also: Ottomans, Yeşil Cami

Further reading:

A. Gabriel, *Une Capitale Turque, Brousse*, Paris 1958.
A. Tuna, *Bursa Yeni Kapilica* (The Yeni Bath House at Bursa), Istanbul 1987.

Byzantine architecture

Architecture characterized by brick and masonry construction, round arches and domes, developed within the Byzantine Empire.

Byzantine architecture was of crucial importance to the development of early Islamic architecture and later the architecture of the Ottoman Empire. At the time of the Islamic conquest of Syria in the seventh century Byzantine was essentially a continuation of Roman architecture. There were, however, a few major differences, the most significant of which was the massive church-building campaign of Justinian (sixth century) which made Christianity the central focus of architecture. Also noticeable in the architecture of this period was the influence of the capital Constantinople on the rest of the empire.

During the ninth to eleventh centuries the Byzantines recovered from the disastrous effects of the Islamic conquests, and in this period there is evidence of Islamic influence on Byzantine architecture, particularly in descriptions of the palaces of Constantinople.

During the fourteenth to fifteenth centuries Byzantine architecture was a major influence on that of the Turkish principalities in Anatolia. In particular the domed basilical church had a formative influence on early Ottoman mosques.

See also: Hagia Sophia, Ottomans, Umayyads

Further reading:

C. Mango, *Byzantine Architecture*, London 1986.

C

Cairo (Arabic: al-Qahira)

Capital of Egypt and one of the most prominent cities of the Islamic world. The English name for the city derives from the French, Le Caire, which in turn is derived from the Arabic al-Qahira. The modern town is composed of the remains of four cities established in this area during the early Islamic period.

At the time of the Islamic conquest the capital of Egypt was Alexandria, although by 641 a new city called Fustat was founded further south on the east bank of the Nile, next to the old Roman fortress town of Babylon. In 750 the newly established Abbasid caliphs established another city or camp known as al-ʿAskar to the east of Fustat. During the ninth century the semi-autonomous Tulunids expanded further north-east with the establishment of the city of al-Qataic which was based around the grand palace of Ibn Tulun. Under the Fatimids Egypt became the seat of the caliphate and to this end in 971 a new city was founded to the north-east. Originally the city was called al-Mansuriyya, but four years later was renamed al-Qahira 'the victorious', after al-Qahir (the planet Mars), which was in the ascendant at the time of its foundation. Although today the whole city is referred to officially as Cairo or al-Qahira, before the eighteenth century only the original Fatimid capital was referred to by this name whilst the whole city was known as Misr or Masr (literally Egypt).

The original al-Qahira of the Fatimids was a luxurious palace city described by contemporary writers as having marble floors grouted with gold and vast treasure houses filled with beautiful golden objects. From the tenth to the twelfth century Cairo was symbolically divided between al-Fustat, the commercial and popular capital, and al-Qahira, the royal city of the caliphs. The devastation and dislocation brought about in Egypt by the Crusaders changed the old order, so that al-Qahira was no longer exclusively a royal enclosure and instead became the true capital whilst al-Fustat became a dying suburb.

Salah al-Din planned to unite the city by enclosing both Fustat and al-Qahira in massive walls. Although unable to complete this project Salah al-Din was able to build the massive citadel on Muqattam hill. During the Mamluk and Ottoman periods the city continued to grow with suburbs growing up around the citadel and al-Qahira and huge cemeteries extending east and west into the desert.

The Fatimid Cairo

The two most important pre-Fatimid buildings to survive in some form are the mosque of Camr at Fustat and the mosque of Ibn Tulun. Little survives of either, nor of the original mosque of Camr ibn al-ʿAs built in 641 and said to be the earliest mosque in Egypt. The most important feature of the present mosque is that it indicates the position of the original settlement of al-Fustat. The mosque of Ibn Tulun on the other hand represents the remains of the city or settlement known as al-Qataic founded by Ahmad ibn Tulun. In many ways the Tulunid capital resembled the contemporary Abbasid capital at Samarra – from the triple-arched gate, the polo ground and the racecourses, to the extensive use of stucco.

The Fatimid Period (969–1171)

This is earliest time from which a significant number of monuments survive. It was during this period that Egypt became centre of the caliphate which ruled from North Africa to Palestine. Although the Fatimids ruled a vast empire, they were to a certain extent strangers in Egypt as the majority of the population remained Sunni. This alienation is reflected in the way al-Qahira was kept as an official city closed to the general population. The caliphs lived in palaces lavishly decorated with gold and jewels and when they died they were also buried within them. Unfortunately nothing survives of these palaces as they were systematically destroyed by later rulers, although detailed descriptions can be found in the writings of Nasiri Khusraw or al-Maqrizi.

The best surviving examples of Fatimid architecture in Cairo are the mosques of al-Azhar (970) and al-Aqmar (1125) which demonstrate a transition from early Islamic to medieval forms. Despite later accretions, the mosque of al-Azhar represents an early Islamic hypostyle form with three arcades around a central courtyard. The sanctuary is composed of five aisles parallel to the qibla and a central transverse aisle which is emphasized by being both higher and wider than the surrounding roof. Originally there were three domes at the qibla end, one in front of the mihrab and one on either side. Three aisles around a central courtyard and the arrangement of three domes are all features common in early North African mosques. Inside the mosque was lavishly decorated with stucco work, only part of which survives (around the mihrab and on parts of the arcades). The stucco has some Abbasid influence although there are also Byzantine and Coptic elements in the designs.

Built some 150 years later, the mosque of al-Aqmar has a much more sophisticated design, reminiscent of the later medieval buildings of Cairo. It was founded by the vizier Ma'mun al Bata'ihi during the reign of Caliph al-Amir. The interior plan consists of a small central courtyard surrounded on four sides by triple arcades. The sanctuary consists of a small area divided into three aisles parallel to the qibla wall. Initially the mosque would have been covered with a flat hypostyle roof but it is now covered with shallow brick domes. Stylistically the most important feature of the plan is the way the entrance is positioned at an angle to the main building. This feature allows the mosque to be incorporated into a pre-existing street plan whilst having the prayer hall correctly aligned for the qibla. This is one of the earliest examples of this type of plan which was to become more pronounced in Mamluk religious buildings. The other important feature of the al-Aqmar Mosque is the decoration of the façade which was developed in later mosques to be a main feature of the design. The façade is made of stone overlying a brick structure. Today the right hand side is hidden by a later building but it is assumed that it was originally symmetrical with a projecting portal in the middle. The decoration of the façade is dominated by decorated niches with fluted conch-like niches, an arrangement used in more complex forms in later mosques. The al-Aqmar Mosque is also significant as the earliest mosque to incorporate shops in its design (these were below the present street level and have been revealed by excavations). Another important mosque of Fatimid Cairo is that of the caliph al-Hakim built between 990 and 1003. The mosque, which has recently been restored, has a large rectangular courtyard surrounded by four arcades. A transept aisle opposite the mihrab indicates the direction of the qibla which is further emphasized by three domes. The entrance to the mosque is via a large projecting portal similar to that of the mosque of Mahdiyya, the Fatimid capital in North Africa. Probably the most famous feature of this mosque are the minarets at either end of the north façade. They were built in 990 and consist of one octagonal and one cylindrical decorated brick tower; at some later date (probably 1110) the lower parts of these minarets were encased in large brick cubes for some unknown reason.

Apart from mosques, various other types of religious building are known to have been built in Fatimid Cairo including many tombs or mashads devoted to religious personalities. However, most of these have not survived or have been altered beyond recognition as they have been in continuous religious use. An exception to this is the mashad of al-Juyushi also known as Mashad Badr al-Jamali.

This structure consists of two main parts, a domed prayer hall opening on to a courtyard and a large minaret. Although there is a side chamber which may have been a tomb, there is no positive identification of the person commemorated. The prayer hall is covered with cross vaults except for the area in front of the mihrab which is covered with a tall dome resting on plain squinches. The minaret is a tall square tower capped by an octagonal lantern covered with a dome. A notable feature of the minaret is the use of a muqarnas cornice which is the first example of this decoration on the exterior of a building. The roof of the complex also houses two small kiosks whose function has not been resolved. Other notable Fatimid mashads are the tombs of Sayyida Ruqayya and Yayha al-Shabih both in the cemetery of Fustat. The first of these was built to commemorate Sayyida Ruqayya, a descendant of Cali even though she never visited Egypt. The layout of this building is similar to that of al-Juyushi except that the dome is larger and is fluted inside and out. Visually the most impressive feature of this building is the mihrab, the hood of which is composed of radiating flutes of stucco set within a large decorated frame.

The best surviving examples of Fatimid secular architecture are the walls and gates built by Badr al-Jamali between 1087 and 1092. The first walls and gates of Cairo were built of brick during the reign of al-Mucizz but were replaced with stone walls by Badr al-Jamali in the eleventh century. The stone for the walls was mostly quarried from ancient Egyptian structures and many of the stones display hieroglyphic inscriptions and ancient motifs. The walls were built on three levels: a lower level raised slightly above the street level containing shops and the entrances to gates, a middle level containing vaulted galleries and pierced with arrow slits, and an upper level consisting of a parapet protected by large rounded crenellations. The gates are set between large semi-circular or rectangular buttress towers, the lower parts of which are made of solid masonry. The surviving gates of Fatimid Cairo are Bab al-Nasr (Gate of Victory), Bab al-Futuh (Gate of Conquest) and Bab Zuwayla (after a North African tribe prominent in the Fatimid armies). The general appearance of the towers and gates seems to be developed from Byzantine military architecture.

The Ayyubid Period (1171–1250)

The Ayyubid period in Cairo represents a return to orthodox Sunni Islam. One of the consequences of this was that there was not allowed to be more than one Friday mosque in any urban area. Instead the Ayyubid period saw the foundation of many madrassas and khanqas as a means of propagating orthodox law and religion. The earliest such madrassa was that of Imam Shafci founded by Salah al-Din. Although the madrassa has not survived, the connected tomb of Imam Shafci still stands. This is much larger than any of the earlier Fatimid tombs measuring approximately 15 m square underneath the central dome. The wooden cenotaph of the imam survives intact and is decorated with carved geometric designs around bands of Kufic and Naskhi script which are dated to 1178.

The best surviving example of an Ayyubid madrassa is that of Sultan al-Salih Najm al-Din Ayyub built in 1243. It is built on the site of one of the great Fatimid palaces. Like the Mustansariyya this madrassa was built for all four of the orthodox Sunni rites of Islamic law with a separate area for each rite; today only the minaret, the entrance complex and part of the east courtyard survive. The original plan consisted of two courtyards either side of a passageway. Each courtyard was flanked on two sides by small barrel-vaulted cells and on the other two sides by large iwans. The minaret of this complex is the only surviving Ayyubid minaret of Cairo and consists of a square brick shaft with an octagonal upper part covered with a ribbed dome. The entrance-way includes a decorated keel-arched niche, in the centre of which is a Naskhi foundation inscription; the whole is encased by a muqarnas frame.

One of the finest buildings attributed to the Ayyubid period is known as the 'Mausoleum of the Abbasid Caliphs' because it was used for this purpose after the Mongol sack of Baghdad. Although there is some dispute about its date of construction, it is generally agreed to have been built between 1240 and 1270. The central dome is supported on two tiers of squinches which alternate with similarly shaped windows and muqarnas stucco niches so that the zone of transition becomes two continuous bands of niches. This pattern was later adopted for most domes resting on squinches.

Other important buildings of the late Ayyubid period are the tomb of Sultan Salah al-Din, the mausoleum of Shajarat al Durr and the minaret of Zawiyat al Hunud all dated to around 1250.

Few remains of secular buildings survive with the exception of the citadel and the fortification walls. The citadel was probably the most substantial building of Ayyubid Cairo, its main function being to strengthen and connect the city's walls. It was built on Muqattam hill in the style of Syrian castles of the Crusader period using material taken from several small pyramids at Giza which were demolished for the purpose. Both square and round towers were used to fortify the walls which may reflect two periods of construction, one under Salah al-Din and one under his son and successor al-Malik al-ʿAdil. Innovations to the fortifications included bent entrances in the gateways and arrowslits which reached the floor.

Bahri Mamluk Period (1250–1382)

The early Mamluk period is architecturally the most prolific period in Cairo with a wide range of major building projects carried out. Many of these buildings have survived demonstrating a diverse range of styles, techniques and designs. During this period some of the major forms of later Cairene architecture were established such as the erection of sabils on street corners often linked to primary schools. During this period there was also considerable foreign influence from Sicily, Iran, North Africa and Spain which was absorbed into the architecture of Cairo.

Congregational mosques were founded during this period after the strict Shafiʿite orthodoxy of the Ayyubid sultans who only permitted one congregational mosque in the city, that of al-Hakim. Under the Mamluks each area had its own Friday mosque and during the fourteenth century madrassas and khanqas were also used as Friday mosques. The earliest and grandest mosque built

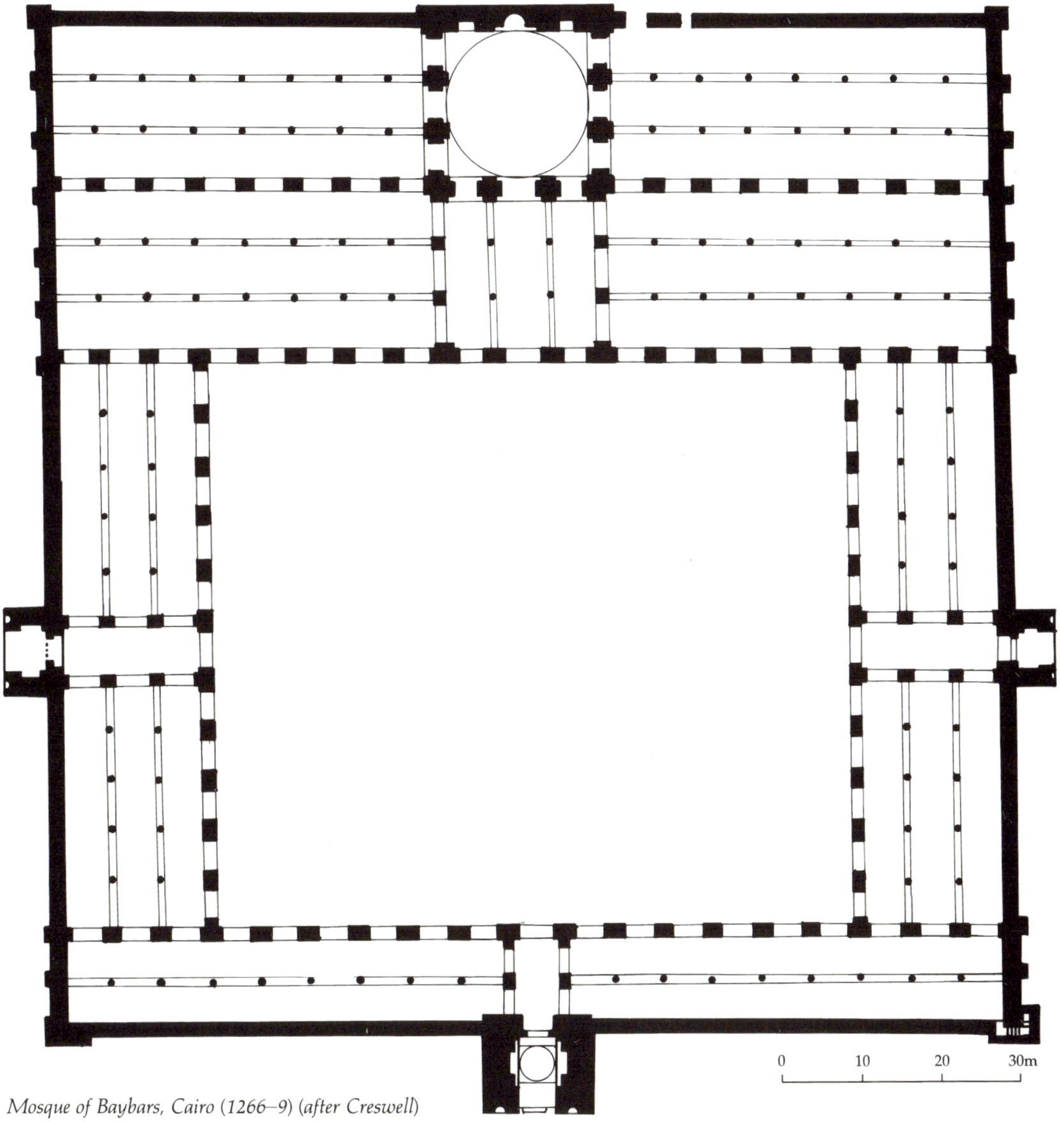

Mosque of Baybars, Cairo (1266–9) (after Creswell)

under the Mamluks was that of Sultan al-Zahir Baybars built between 1266 and 1269. Although partially ruined the general plan of this mosque can be reconstructed – it consists of a large rectangular courtyard with arcades on four sides and projecting entrances on three sides. Most of the arcades rested on columns except for those around the sanctuary which rest on rectangular piers. The outer walls are protected by rectangular buttresses in between which are pointed arched windows with stucco grilles. The walls are built out of stone, and alternate courses are painted to achieve the effect of ablaq masonry; the upper part of the wall is crenellated. There was once a minaret next to the main entrance which has now disappeared. The area in front of the mihrab known as the maqsura was once covered with a large wooden dome decorated in marble; between this and the courtyard was a nine-domed transept.

Another royal mosque of this period is that of Sultan al-Nasir Muhammad at the citadel, built between 1318 and 1385. Like that of Baybars this is a hypostyle mosque built around a rectangular courtyard with a large dome covering the area in front of the mihrab. The most remarkable feature of this mosque are the two cylindrical stone minarets, one opposite the army headquarters and the other opposite the royal palace. The more elaborate of the two faces the palace and is decorated with vertical and horizontal zig-zag patterns with a small solid bulbous dome on the top. The other minaret is similar except that it is less decorated and has a hexagonal pavilion covered by a bulbous dome. The upper portion of each minaret is covered in blue, white and green faience tiles. It seems likely that both the faience decoration and the bulbous domes are copied from similar minarets in Iran, probably Tabriz, where such forms were common at the time.

Other important mosques built during this period were those of Amir Altinbugha al-Maridani built in 1340 and of Amir Aqsunqur built in 1347. Important features of the al-Maridani Mosque include the minaret which is the earliest example of the octagonal minaret with pavilion which was to become typical of later Cairene architecture. The building is also notable for its wooden mashrabiyya screen that separates the maqsura from the rest of the mosque. The mosque of Aqsunqur is a good example of an attempt to use a Syrian building tradition in Egypt. The building was originally roofed with cross-vaults in the Syrian style but later these were replaced with a flat wooden roof.

Probably the most famous building of Mamluk Cairo is the Sultan Hasan Mosque. This was built on a four-iwan plan madrassa and was the first madrassa in Cairo to be accorded the status of a congregational mosque. The building consists of a square central courtyard with four great iwans. The largest of the iwans is a prayer hall behind which is the domed mausoleum. Between the four iwans are four separate courtyards one for each of the orthodox Sunni rites of Islamic law. The building includes several notable architectural features amongst which are the doorway thought to be modelled on that of the Gök Madrassa at Sivas and the floriated stucco inscriptions in the prayer hall.

Mausoleums were a common feature of religious and semi-religious institutions from the early Mamluk period onwards. One of the best examples of this is the mausoleum, madrassa and hospital of Sultan al-Mansur Qalawun built between 1284 and 1285. Today the hospital has disappeared leaving only the madrassa and mausoleum. The madrassa is built on the typical Cairene four-iwan plan with iwans of differing sizes. The largest iwan is that of the prayer hall which is arranged in three aisles like a Byzantine basilica. The most outstanding feature of the complex is the mausoleum itself which consists of a huge rectangular hall with a central dome supported on piers and massive columns arranged in a manner similar to the Dome of the Rock in Jerusalem. The walls are decorated in a wide variety of materials including marble inlay, mother of pearl and coloured stones. The mihrab is one of the largest in Cairo and is decorated with several tiers of blind niches within the niche itself. The importance of the mausoleum is evident from the fact that it had its own madrassa in addition to the madrassa attached.

Although mausoleums did not usually achieve the grandeur of Qalawun's tomb, often the mausoleum was the most impressive part of a complex. Thus the tomb of Sultan Baybars al-Jashankir was an elaborate and richly decorated building in relation to the rather plain khanqa associated with it. Tombs often acted as a focal point for a building and sometimes incorporated foreign features or unusual techniques in order to draw attention to the building and its founder. This can be seen in the madrassa–mausoleum of Amir Sarghitmish built in 1356 where the mausoleum is not placed next to the prayer hall as was usual but instead was built in a position so that its façade and profile were directly on the main street. The mausoleum is covered by a double-shell dome set on an unusually high drum with an exterior moulding of muqarnas marking the transition from drum to dome. This form of dome is not usual in Cairo and may have been copied from similar domes in Samarkand.

Circassian Mamluk Period (1382–1517)

Several developments took place in the fifteenth-century architecture of Cairo which distinguish it from the earlier Mamluk period. These developments were of two basic types: those concerned with the layout and plan of buildings and those concerned with the decoration and construction of buildings.

The biggest factor affecting design and layout was the lack of space in an increasingly crowded area. The most obvious result of this was that mosques tended to be smaller and were designed to fill awkwardly shaped plots. The size of mosques was reduced in a number of ways, the most notable of which was the reduction in size of the central courtyard until it became a small square area in the centre covered by a wooden lantern to admit light. A result of this design change was that the side walls of mosques were now pierced with many windows to make up for the lack of light from the courtyards. Also there was a move away from the hypostyle mosque towards the four-iwan plan used for madrassas. However, the form of the iwans changed from brick or stone vaults to flat wooden roofed units. Another change was that now madrassas did not include accommodation blocks for students who were located outside.

The trend which had begun in the fourteenth century of using madrassas as Friday mosques was extended so that now buildings would fulfil several roles such as khanqa, madrassa and jami. The earliest example of such a combination was the complex of Sultan Barquq built between 1384 and 1386.

One of the exceptions to the decreasing size of mosques is the Khanqah of Sultan Faraj ibn Barquq built between 1400 and 1411. This large complex was deliberately built outside the main urban area in the cemetery on the eastern outskirts of Cairo. The plan adopted for this building was that of a hypostyle mosque, with a spacious central courtyard containing an octagonal central fountain. Despite its traditional Friday mosque layout this structure contained living units for Sufis as well as two domed mausoleums flanking the sanctuary or prayer hall.

Many of the changes in the architecture of the late Mamluk period are concerned with the building and decoration of domes. Among the most famous features of Cairo are the carved stone domes built during this period. These are fairly unique to Cairo although occasional examples can be found elsewhere, such as the Sabil Qaytbay in Jerusalem which is known to be a copy of similar Egyptian domes. Up to the late fourteenth century most domes in Egypt were either built of wood or brick, and stone domes were only used for the tops of minarets. It is thought likely that this was the origin of the larger stone domes used on tombs. The earliest stone domes had ribbed decoration similar to that seen on the tops of minarets; later this was developed into a swirled turban style as can be seen on the mausoleum of Amir Aytimish al-Bajasi built in 1383. The next stage was zig-zag patterns followed by the intricate star patterns which can be seen on the mausoleums built for Sultan Barbays. Under Sultan Qaytbay an important innovation was made where the star pattern would start at the top, whereas previously decoration had started at the bottom. With the increasing sophistication of dome decoration it was natural that domes were set on higher drums so that they could be seen from far away. The increased confidence in stone carving exhibited in domes is also reflected in the decoration of minarets which are now also carved in stone. One of the earliest examples of this is the minaret belonging to the complex of Sultan Barquq built between 1384 and 1386. The minaret is octagonal throughout and has a central section composed of giant intersecting circles.

Another innovation in the architecture of this period was the triangular pendentive. The earliest examples in Cairo were used in the citadel mosque of al-Nasir Muhammad and were made of wood. Later pendentives were used for stone domes although muqarnas squinches continued to be used. A related feature introduced at this time was the groin vault used in complex arrangements for portals. Often doorways would be covered by a complex groin vault with a small dome in the centre forming a half-star shape.

The Ottoman Period (1517–1914)

The Ottoman conquest of Egypt marks a fundamental change in the architecture of Cairo. Most noticeably, new architectural forms were introduced from Istanbul and Anatolia, whilst several types of Mamluk buildings, such as domed mausoleums or khanqahs ceased to be built.

One of the earliest Ottoman buildings of Cairo is the mosque of Sulayman Pasha built in 1528. This building is almost entirely Ottoman in its construction and shows little relationship to the pre-existing Mamluk architecture. The mosque consists of a central prayer hall flanked by three semi-domes and opening on to a central courtyard enclosed by domed arcades.

In addition to new layouts and forms the Ottomans also introduced new types of buildings such as the takiyya which performed a similar function to the khanqa and madrassa.

Unlike the khanqa or madrassa the takiyya was built separate from the mosque. This was characteristic of Ottoman institutions which were built separately from mosques rather than as buildings with several functions like the madrassa, khanqa, jami combination of the late Mamluk period.

Despite the new styles and forms introduced by the Ottomans many buildings continued to be built in Mamluk architectural style. A good example of this is the mosque and mausoleum of Mahmud Pasha built in 1567 which in many ways resembles the mosque of Sultan Hasan, with a large domed mausoleum behind the prayer hall. The minaret, however, is built in the classic Ottoman style with a tall thin fluted shaft.

Probably the most famous building of Ottoman Cairo is the mosque of Muhammad Cali Pasha built between 1830 and 1848. This building has a classical Ottoman design consisting of a large central domed area flanked by semi-domes and a large open courtyard surrounded by arcades covered with shallow domes. On the west wall of the courtyard is a clock tower including a clock presented by Louis Philippe, King of France. The mosque was designed by an Armenian and is said to be based on the Sultan Ahmet Mosque in Istanbul.

Domestic and Secular Architecture

The continuous development of Cairo has meant that apart from the major monuments very few secular buildings have survived from before the Ottoman period. The earliest evidence for Cairo's houses comes from excavations at Fustat where Iraqi-style four-iwan plan houses were discovered. This style consists of four iwans, one on each side of a central courtyard with a fountain. In each house the main iwan was divided into three, a central area and two side rooms. There are also descriptions of early Islamic Cairo which describe multi-storey apartments.

During the Fatimid period we have the first evidence for the living unit known as the qaca which became the typical living unit of Cairo. This consists of a small courtyard area with two iwans opposite each other. The iwans could be closed off with folding doors whilst the courtyard could be covered over with an awning. On the upper floor overlooking the courtyard were wooden galleries. In Mamluk times the qaca was developed so that the central courtyard became smaller and was covered by a wooden dome or lantern. The central hall or courtyard would often be decorated with coloured marble and finely carved mashrabiyya doorways and screens. The central fountain was usually octagonal and was sometimes fed by a stream of water running from the back wall of the main iwan.

In the late Mamluk and early Ottoman period a particular type of sitting room known as the maqad became popular. This consisted of an arcade on the upper floor level which overlooked the main public courtyard of an important residence. From the sixteenth century onwards important residences would also incorporate an extra kitchen for the preparation of coffee.

In addition to private houses there were from a very early period blocks of houses or apartments which would have been rented by the occupiers. These buildings were known as 'rabc' and consisted of rows of two-storey apartments usually built above shops or khans. One of the earliest examples is the rabc of Sultan al-Ghuri at Khan al-Khalili.

It is known that many of the larger houses had private bathrooms although these would not have included all the facilities available in a public bath house or hammam. Cairo is known to have had a large number of hammams although many of these have recently disappeared. In general the rooms of a bath house were fairly plain with the exception of the maslakh (reception hall) which was often domed and sometimes was supported with columns.

Further reading:

D. Berhens-Abouseif, *Islamic Architecture in Cairo: An Introduction*, Supplements to Muquarnas vol. 3, Leiden 1989. This is the best modern summary of Islamic architecture in Cairo.

K. A. C. Creswell, *The Muslim Architecture of Egypt*, Oxford 1952–60. Contains the most comprehensive discussion and treatment of buildings from the beginning of the Fatimid (969) to the end of the Mamluk (1517) periods.

For domestic architecture see:

J. C. Garcin, B. Maury, J. Revault and M. Zakariya, *Palais et Maisons du Caire: I. D'Époque Mamelouke* (XIIIe–XVIe siècles), Paris 1982.

B. Maury, A. Raymond, J. Revault and M. Zakariya, *Palais et Maisons du Caire: II. Époque Ottomane* (XVIe–XVIIIe siècles) vol. 2, Paris 1983.

For modern architecture see:

M. al-Gawhury, *Ex-Royal Palaces of Egypt*, Cairo 1954.

A. D. C. Hyland, A. G. Tipple and N. Wilkinson, *Housing in Egypt*, Newcastle-upon-Tyne 1984.

cami

Turkish term for a congregational or Friday mosque as opposed to the smaller mescit.

caravanserai

Roadside building which provides accomodation and shelter for travellers.

The term caravanserai is a composite Turkish term derived from caravan (i.e. a group of travellers) and serai (palace). Generally it refers to a large structure which would be capable of coping with a large number of travellers, their animals and goods. The term first seems to have been used in the twelfth century under the Seljuks and may indicate a particularly grand form of khan with a monumental entrance. During the Saffavid period in Iran (seventeenth to eighteenth century) caravanserais are often huge structures with four iwans.

See also: khan

çarşi

Turkish term for a market.

Central Asia

Central Asia comprises the modern independent republics of Khazakstan, Turkmenistan, Khirgiziya and Uzbekistan.

In pre-Islamic times Central Asia was the home of several important Turkic dynasties the most important of which were the Kushans who ruled over most of the area in the fifth century CE. By the seventh century the western part of the Kushan Empire had been conquered by the Sassanians whilst the eastern part fractured into a number of independent principalities. One of the most important principalities was that of the Sogdians whose art and architecture seem to have been an important influence on Islamic architecture of the ninth century and after.

During the Islamic period the cities of central Asia continued to control the Silk Route and cities

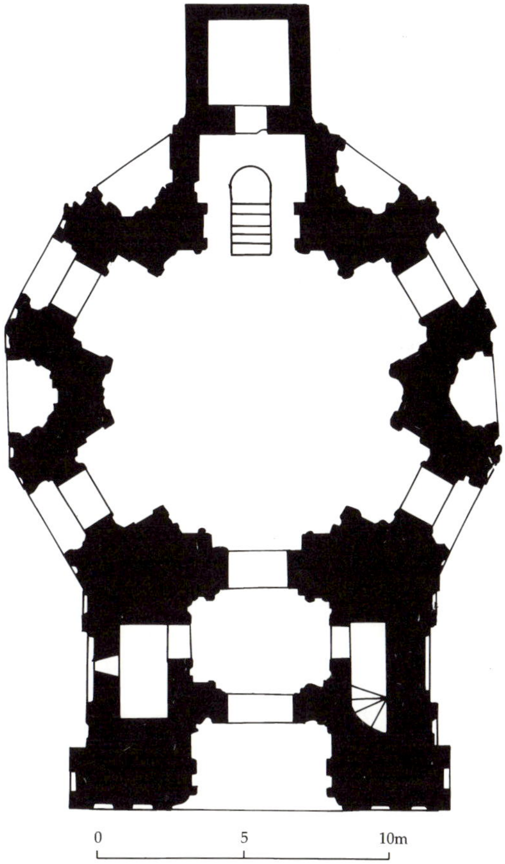

Plan of Tutabeg Khatun Tomb, fourteenth century, Urgench, Uzbekistan

such as Samarkand, Bukhara and Merv rose to great prosperity.

See also: Turkmenistan, Uzbekistan

çeşme

A Turkish term for a fountain or tap used to provide drinking water. These were often attached to Ottoman monuments to fulfil a charitable purpose.

chahar bagh or char bagh

Iranian and Mughal term for a formal garden laid out in four plots of equal size and divided by axial paths.

See also: gardens, Mughals

chajja

Mughal and Hindu term for projecting eaves or cover usually supported on large carved brackets.

char-chala

Indian roof form with curved eaves and curved surfaces. Derived from Bengali architecture.

See also: bangala, Bengal, do-chala

Char Minar

Ceremonial gateway in Hyderabad which is one of the best examples of south Indian Islamic architecture.

When it was built in 1589 the Char Minar (literally four towers) formed the centre of the city and with the charkaman (four gates) was part of the ceremonial approach to the royal palaces (now destroyed). The building is a square structure with arched gateways in the centre of each side which intersect at the centre. At each of the four corners is a tower or minaret nearly 60 m high and crowned with an onion-shaped bulbous dome. The first storey above the arches contains a circular cistern whilst on the second storey there is a small domed mosque.

See also: Deccan, Hyderabad, India

char su or char taq

Iranian and Mughal term for the intersection of two market streets where there is usually an open square with four arched entrances. (Roughly equivalent to the classical tetra pylon.)

chatri

Mughal and Hindu term for a domed kiosk on the roof of a temple, tomb or mosque. The domes are usually supported on four columns.

chauk

Indian term for an open square or courtyard.

China

There are three main Muslim groups within the Republic of China, these are the maritime communities of the great ports, the urban communities of northern China and the predominantly Turkic people of Central Asia.

Maritime Communities

The development of maritime Muslim communities in China is less well documented than the conquests of Central Asia or the inland settlements of northern China. The first coastal settlements seem to have been mostly in southern and eastern ports and include the cities of Canton, Chuan Chou, Hang Chou in Chekiang Province and Yang Chou on the lower Yangtze. The descendants of these early Muslims are known as Hui (a term also applied to the Muslims of the northern inland cities) and through intermarriage have become culturally Sinicized. This was partly as the result of increased intermarriage and also missionary activity. The prominence of the Muslim communities grew under the Yuan and Ming dynasties so that in the fifteenth century the Chinese navy was commanded by Muslims, the most famous of whom was Cheng Ho, who cleared the China sea of pirates and led an expedition to East Africa.

According to Islamic tradition the first mosques in China belong to the maritime community and were located in the coastal ports. Historical sources suggest that they may have been established in the seventh century by Sa'd bin Abi Waqqas and several other companions of the prophet. There is little archaeological evidence for mosques of this period although there are several mosques which may have been founded at an early date. Probably the oldest of these is the Huai-Shang Mosque in Canton which is referred to as early as 1206, although a mosque probably existed on the site in T'ang times (618–906). The oldest part of the building is the 36-m-high minaret with a thick tapering shaft. As minarets are rare in China it has

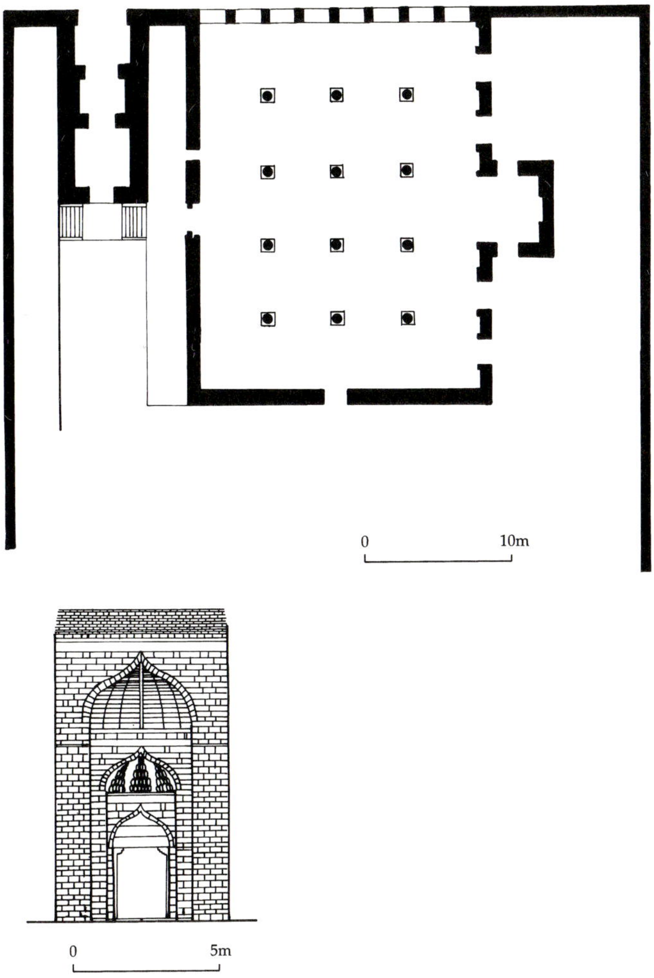

Plan and doorway of the mosque of Chuan Chou, China

been suggested that the minaret functioned as a lighthouse. The rest of the mosque was built in the fourteenth century and is built in Chinese style with green tiled wooden roofs. The Sheng Yu Mosque at Chuan Chou is surrounded by massive granite walls and is the last of seven mosques which once stood in the city. The building was founded in 1009 although most of the building seems to date from the fourteenth century or later. Another early mosque is the Feng-Huan Mosque at Hang Chou which is locally attributed to the T'ang period (according to a seventeenth-century inscription) although it seems more likely that it was established during the Yuan period.

Inland Communities

Away from the coast the Muslims of China may be divided into two main groups, the Turkic- and Persian-speaking peoples of Xinjiang (formerly Chinese Turkestan) and the Chinese-speaking Hui people of Yunnan, Ningxia and Gansu. Initially both these groups were less integrated into Chinese society than their maritime counterparts and their early history is one of conflict rather than acculturation. The first direct confrontation between Arabs and Chinese occurred in 751 at the battle of Talas and resulted in a victory for the Arabs. During the Yuan period (1279–1368) there was increased Muslim presence in central China due to the large numbers of Muslim soldiers introduced by the Mongols. The growth of Muslim communities continued during the Ming period (1368–1644) when there was also a certain amount of Sinicization of the Muslims which is reflected in the architecture. These communities established many of the usual Islamic institutions, including mosques, madrassas and caravanserais although the methods and techniques of construction appear to have been predominantly Chinese.

Traditionally the oldest inland mosque in China is the mosque of Ch'ang-an which is supposed to have been founded in the T'ang period although a Sung or Yuan foundation is now thought more likely. The Great Mosque of Xian at the eastern end of the Silk Route was founded by the Muslim Admiral Cheng Ho in the fourteenth century. Contained within a huge enclosure wall measuring 48 by 246 m this is the largest mosque in China. The layout of this building with its succession of courtyards, green tiled pavilions and tiered pagoda-like minarets resembles a Buddhist temple rather than any traditional mosque form. However, there are many subtle deviations from typical Chinese forms including the east–west orientation (temples were normally oriented east–west) and the wooden dome which is built into the flared pitched roof of the ablutions pavilion. The flat wooden mihrab is contained within a small room which projects from the centre of the west side of the prayer hall. Other historical mosques in central China include the recently renovated Nui Jei Mosque in Beijing which is reputed to have been founded in the tenth century although there is no archaeological evidence for this.

In Central Asia the Muslims retained their ethnic identity so that the Xinjian region has the largest number of Muslims composed of several groups including Uighurs, Khazaks, Khirgiz and Tajiks. The architecture of this region is similar to that of the former Soviet Republics to the west and has little in common with the rest of China. One of the most famous mosques of this region is the Imin Mosque of Turfan built in 1779. The main features of the mosque are the prayer hall and next to it the huge minaret. The minaret is a cylindrical brick-built structure over 44 m tall and decorated with fifteen bands of geometric brickwork. The large prayer hall is built of mud brick and entered through a large iwan flanked by shallow arched niches. Other mosques in Turfan are more modest in scale and usually consist of a rectangular brick prayer hall with arcades supported on wooden columns. In the city of Urumqui there is a mixture of architectural styles reflecting the cosmopolitan nature of a city on the Silk Route. One of the largest mosques in the city is the Beytallah Mosque which has traces of Persian and Mughal influence. The building consists of a rectangular prayer hall with engaged minarets at each corner and a tall bulbous dome in the centre. Perhaps more unusual is the Tartar Mosque which is a small wooden building with a short square minaret capped with a pointed wooden spire.

See also: Central Asia, Indonesia, Java, Malaysia, Philippines, Uzbekistan

Further reading:

China Islamic Association, *The Religious Life of Chinese Muslims*, Peking 1981.
A. D. W. Forbes, 'Masjid V. In China', *Encyclopedia of Islam* 6: 702–3, 1991.
J. Lawton, N. Wheeler *et al.*, 'Muslims in China', *Aramco World Magazine* 36 no. 4: July/August 1985.
D. Leslie, *Islam in Traditional China*, Canberra 1986.
H. Saladin, 'Monuments musulmanes de Chine et d'Extrème Orient', *Manuel d'art musulmans*, Paris 1907.
—— 'Les mosquées de Pékin', *Revue du Monde Musulmans*, 2: 1907.

coral

Coral is used as a building material for coastal settlements throughout the Indian Ocean, Arabian/Persian Gulf and the Red Sea.

Two main types of coral stone are used for construction: fossil coral quarried from the coastal foreshore, and reef coral which is cut live from the sea bed. Fossil corals are more suitable for load-bearing walls whilst reef corals such as porites are more suitable for architectural features such as door-jambs or mihrab niches. Fossil corals are mostly from an order of coral known as Rugosa which is now extinct. When quarried this coral forms rough uneven blocks known as coral rag. Although this can be cut into rough blocks it cannot be dressed to a smooth finish and therefore has to be used in conjunction with another material to produce an even surface.

Living coral from the reef is easier to cut and dress to a smooth finish although it does require hardening by exposure to the air. The preferred type of reef coral for building is porites because of its compact vascular structure which means it is both strong and easy to carve. However, this is

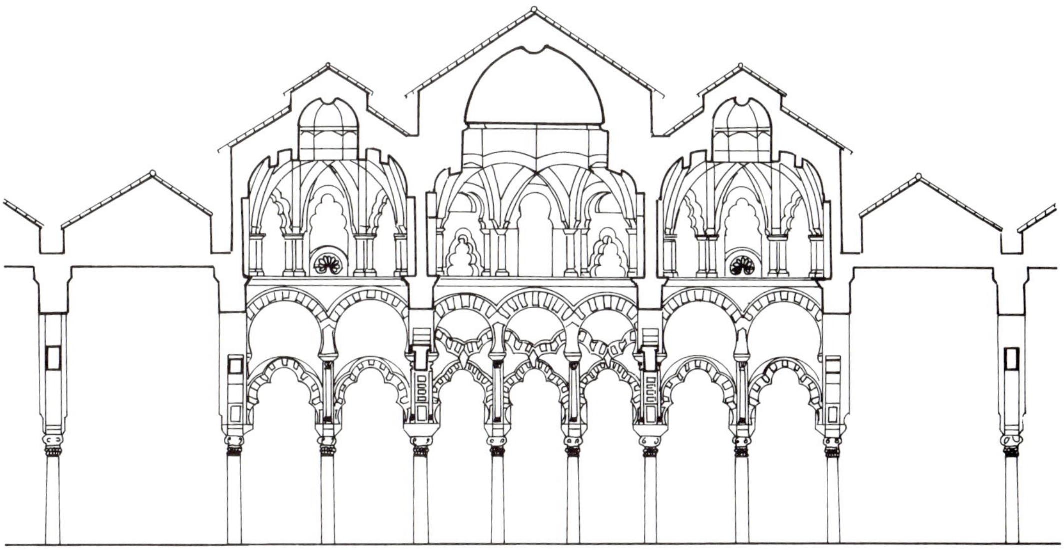

Section through the Great Mosque of Córdoba, Spain (after Barucand)

not the only type used and, at the eleventh-century site of Ras al-Hadd in Oman, at least seven different types were noted. In the Maldives and Bahrain platy corals such as oxypora and montipora are used for partitions.

The origins of coral-building are not well understood although it is generally believed that the technique originated on the coasts of the Red Sea. The earliest example was discovered at the site of al-Rih in the Sudan where a Hellenistic cornice made of coral was found re-used in an Islamic tomb. From the Red Sea the technique spread to the East African coast of the Indian Ocean where its was established as the primary building material for monumental buildings. In the Arabian/Persian Gulf there is another tradition of coral stone construction although the antiquity of this tradition is in doubt as suitable coral has only grown in the area within the last 1,000 years. At the present time the use of coral stone extends over large areas of the Indian Ocean and includes the coastline of India (Gujarat), the Maldives and Sri Lanka. The origins of coral-building in these areas has not been investigated although it generally seems to be associated with Islamic traders.

See also: Bahrain, East Africa, Maldives, Qatar, Saudi Arabia, Sudan, United Arab Emirates

Córdoba

Capital of Islamic Spain (al-Andalus) from 717 until the eleventh century although it continued to be in Muslim hands until its capture by Ferdinand III of Castile.

In Arabic the city was known as Qurtabat al-Wadi al-Kabir and together with Madinat al Zahra' represented the centre of Islamic Spain under the Umayyad dynasty of Spain. It is located on a plateau next to the Guadalquivir river (from Arabic Wadi al-Kabir) which was navigable from the sea in Islamic times. Abd al-Rahman I made it the capital of al-Andalus and laid out the famous Great Mosque of Córdoba (known in Spanish as 'La Mezquita') next to the river. The Great Mosque became the centre of the city which was said to have had fifty mosques in the tenth century. Few of these mosques have survived although the convent of Santa Clara and the church of San Juan are both converted mosques. Santa Clara has fine marble columns and the remains of a minaret whilst San Juan has a minaret which retains its original paired window. In the tenth century Córdoba was famous as the wealthiest city in Europe with paved streets illuminated by street lighting. Some of the atmosphere of the medieval Islamic city can still be recalled in the Jewish quarter to the north of the Great Mosque next to the

Umayyad city walls. Outside the walls Umayyad remains can be seen along the river bank. The bridge known as the Puente Romano was rebuilt in 720 and is 250 m long and rests on sixteen arches. Also alongside the river are remains of water mills which date from Muslim times.

See also: Córdoba Great Mosque, Madinat al-Zahra', Spain.

Further reading:

G. Goodwin, *Islamic Spain: Architectural Guides for Travellers*, London 1990, 39–63.
E. Sordo and W. Swaan, *Moorish Spain: Córdoba, Seville and Granada*, Eng. trans. I. Michael, London 1963.

Córdoba Great Mosque

Principal mosque of Spain under the Umayyads.

The Great Mosque was laid out in 786 by Abd al-Rahman I who built it on the site of a Christian church which the Muslims had previously shared with the Christians. The mosque was supposedly built by a Syrian architect to recall the Great Mosque at Damascus although it has more in common with the Aqsa Mosque in Jerusalem. Less than fifty years later Abd al-Rahman II extended the mosque to the south adding eighty new columns. In 964 al-Hakim II also extended the mosque further south. Towards the end on the tenth century the mosque was once more enlarged by adding fourteen aisles to the east thus balancing the length with the width. Each of these extensions meant building a mihrab further south, each of which was successively more grand. Two of these mihrabs have survived. The earlier, ninth-century mihrab is the size of a large room and has now been converted into the Capilla Villavicosa; it is roofed by a large dome supported on ribs resting on cusped arches. Next to this mihrab is the maqsura or royal enclosure which is equally grand with carved stucco decoration and interlaced cusped horseshoe arches. The tenth-century mihrab consists of an octagonal chamber set into the wall with a massive ribbed dome supported on flying arches. The interior of the dome is decorated with polychrome gold and glass mosaics which may be a gift of the Byzantine emperor. This mihrab suggests the change in status of the Umayyad rulers from amirs to caliphs.

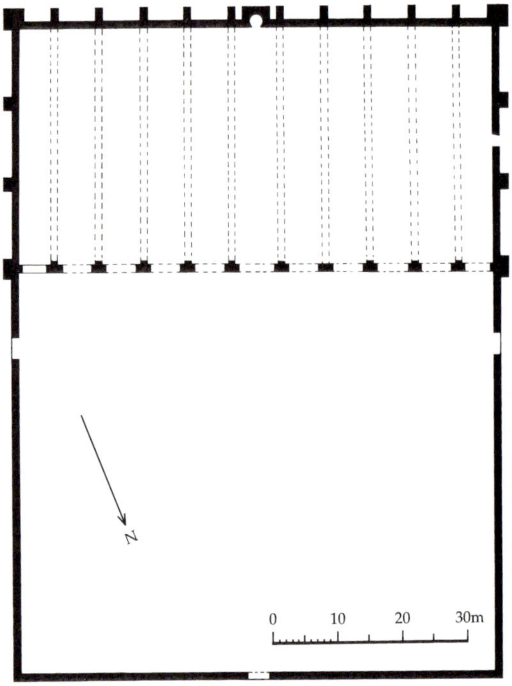

Reconstruction of the Great Mosque, Córdoba (after Creswell)

The most remarkable feature of the Great Mosque are the two-tier free-standing horseshoe arches resting on columns. It is thought that this arrangement is a structural solution to the problem of achieving a high roof with only short columns. The roof of the mosque consists of aisles arranged perpendicular to the quibla wall, a feature elsewhere encountered only in the Aqsa Mosque in Jerusalem.

The appearance of the mosque was ruined in the sixteenth century when a cathedral was built in the middle of the sanctuary, the minaret of the Great Mosque is now encased within the belfry of the cathedral. Diagonally opposite the Great Mosque is the caliph's palace which has now been converted into the archbishop's palace.

See also: Córdoba, Spain

Further reading:

K. A. C. Creswell, *A Short Account of Early Muslim Architecture*, revised and enlarged ed. J. W. Allan, Aldershot 1989, 291–303.
G. Goodwin, *Islamic Spain: Architectural Guides for Travellers*, London 1990, 44–55.

Crusader architecture

European architecture of the Christian states established in Syria and Palestine during the Middle Ages; also architecture associated with those states in other parts of the Middle East or Europe.

The largest concentration of Crusader architecture is to be found in Palestine although Crusader strongholds were also built further afield from the Gulf of Aqaba to Anatolia. The main territories comprising the Crusader dominions were: the kingdom of Jerusalem (roughly equivalent to modern Palestine), the county of Tripoli (centred on the Lebanese port of Tripoli), the principality of Antioch (on the north coast of Syria) and the county of Edessa (with its capital at Urfa).

Although the Crusades continued up until the sixteenth century, the main period of Crusader architecture was from the beginning of the twelfth century to the end of the thirteenth, the period during which the Crusaders occupied Palestine.

Crusader architecture is characterized by high quality ashlar masonry, massive construction and the frequent use of masonry marks. Sculptural decoration and the extensive use of vaulting are other characteristic features. Although the Crusaders built a variety of buildings, including hospices, mills and harbours, their most distinctive work is found in castles and churches.

Generally Crusader castles were a developed form of European fortification with additional features learnt from Byzantine and Islamic military technology. The most common form of fortification was the tower (*tour*) which is equivalent with the Arabic burj. Typically these had two or three vaulted storeys which would provide protection and a good view of the surrounding countryside. The larger castles were all designed for a specific location so that each building has a different plan. Nevertheless each castle would be composed of a number of common features which could include a rock-cut fosse or ditch, a glacis or stone revetment and one or more sets of curtain wall linked by towers, with possibly a keep in the middle. Loopholes tended to be very large with wide reveals.

The churches were often as strongly built as the castles as they were an integral part of Crusader rule. The importance of Jerusalem is notable in the fact that out of 300 churches in Palestine 66 were in Jerusalem. Most Crusader churches were small barrel-vaulted single-cell buildings with an apse at the west end. The larger churches were mainly built on a cross-in-square plan, although it is noticeable that domes were rarely used.

As in other areas it is difficult to assess the relative effects which Crusader, Byzantine and Islamic architecture had on each other. It is, however, possible to see specific areas where there was influence, thus the Muslim castle at Ajlun is obviously similar to Crusader castles. However, the most significant way in which the Crusades influenced Islamic architecture was indirect, through the Venetians who provided the Crusaders with ships.

Further reading:

J. Folda (ed.), *Crusader Art in the Twelfth Century*, Oxford.

T. E. Lawrence, *Crusader Castles*, new edn. with introduction and notes by Denys Pringle, Oxford 1988.

R. C. Smail, *The Crusaders in Syria and the Holy Land*, London 1973.

Cyprus (Turkish: Kibris; Arabic: Qubrus)

Large island off the southern coast of Turkey and east coast of Syria with a mixed Greek- and Turkish-speaking population.

The first Islamic conquest of Cyprus was led by the Arab general Mu'awiya as part of the naval war against the Byzantines who had previously controlled the island. In 653 Abu al-Awar established a garrison on the island which remained until it was withdrawn by the caliph Yazid in 680–83. Cyprus remained nominally under the control of Islam until it was retaken by the Byzantine emperor Nicephorus Phocas in 965. For the next 600 years Cyprus was under a succession of different, mostly Christian rulers, thus in 1189 Isaac Comnenus, governor of the island, seceded from direct Byzantine control. In 1191 the island was captured by Richard I of England and came under western (Frankish) control under the house of Lusignan. Between 1424 and 1426 the island briefly came under the control of the Mamluks of Egypt but was restored to Lusignan control through Venetian intervention. From 1489 to 1570 Cyprus was under direct Venetian rule which was terminated by the Ottoman conquest of 1571. The Ottoman invasion, under Lala Mustapha Pasha, marks the real beginning of Cyprus's long engagement with Islam. However, in many ways the Ottoman conquest had simply replaced one group of rulers with another, leaving the Greek Orthodox population largely intact. This situation was understood by the Ottoman emperor, Selim I, who after the conquest tried to improve the prosperity of the island by populating it with Greek families from the Kayseri region. Ottoman rule ended with the First World War and from 1918 the island was under British rule until it became independent in the 1950s.

The main building material on Cyprus is dressed limestone although baked brick is also used. Also Cyprus differs from its other near-eastern neighbours in having a rich source of high quality timber, enabling buildings to be built with pitched wooden roofs covered with tiles. Although it is known that the early Arab conquerors of Cyprus built several mosques in Nicosia most of these were dismantled or destroyed when Yazid withdrew the garrison in 683. The only Islamic building in Cyprus connected with this period is the tomb of Umm Haram who died near Larnaca during the early Arab invasion. However, the earliest reference to the tomb is 1683 and the main structure on the site today is a tekke (Hala Sultan Tekke) built in 1797. Thus the Islamic architecture of Cyprus is all from the Ottoman period and is closely linked to the Ottoman architecture of Anatolia. There are, however, distinctive features in Cypriot Islamic architecture which may be traced to the fact that the Ottomans converted many of the existing Gothic buildings into mosques or palaces leaving the Greek Orthodox churches untouched. The most spectacular examples of this are the Selimiye Cami in Nicosia and the Lala Mustapha Pasha Cami in Famagusta which are both converted Gothic cathedrals. The Selimiye in Nicosia was a thirteenth-century cathedral (Ayia Sofia) which was converted to a mosque in 1570 by removing the choir and altars and changing the arrangement of windows and doors so that the main entrance was from the north. At some later date a cylindrical Ottoman minaret was built on to the projecting corner buttresses. The Lala Mustapha Mosque on Famagusta was built in the fourteenth century as the cathedral of St Nicholas, it was badly damaged during the conquest of 1570 and converted into a mosque in 1571 after being stripped of all its internal decoration. Like the Selimiye, the Lala Mustapha Mosque had a minaret added to its west end at a later date. The same procedure was adopted with the Lusignan Palace which was converted into the governor's palace by the addition of a new Ottoman reception room (diwan). Some buildings were converted for different uses, thus the fourteenth-century church of St George of the Latins was converted into the Büyük Hammam of Nicosia by adding an Ottoman-style porch with niches and thickening the walls.

In addition to converting Gothic churches the Ottomans constructed new buildings with Gothic details – thus the minaret of the Cami Kebir (Great Mosque) at Larnaca is built with trefoil panels. Elsewhere Gothic influence on Ottoman buildings can be seen in the use of round windows and the dog-tooth pattern on balcony supports.

See also: Ottomans

Further reading:

Association of Cypriot Archaeologists, *Muslim Places of Worship in Cyprus*, Nicosia 1990.
E. C. Aristidou, *The Tekke of Hal Sultan*, Nicosia 1982.
C. Enlart, *The Gothic Art and the Renaissance in Cyprus*, trans. and ed. D. Hunt, London 1987.
A. C. Gazioglu, *The Turks in Cyprus: A Province of the Ottoman Empire (1571–1878)*, London 1990.
G. Jeffrey, *A Description of the Historic Monuments of Cyprus: Studies in the Archaeology and Architecture of the Island*, Nicosia 1918 and London 1983.
—— *The Mosques of Nicosia*, Nicosia 1935.

D

Damascus

Capital city of Syria and one of the chief cities of the Middle East.

Damascus is located in southern Syria on the banks of the Barada river. The area of Damascus forms an oasis on the edge of the Great Syrian desert. The name Damascus is pre-Semitic and is mentioned in Egyptian texts of the second millennium BCE. The oldest standing remains date from the Roman period and include parts of the city wall, columns marking the lines of street, and the enclosure on which the Umayyad mosque is built. During the Umayyad period Damascus was established as capital of the Islamic world which stretched from Spain to Central Asia. With the establishment of the Abbasid caliphate based in Iraq and later the Fatimid caliphate in Egypt the status of the city declined. In 1154 Nur al-Din established it as his capital, and under his successors the Ayyubids it was once again one of the principal cities of the Islamic world. The Mongol raids of the second half of the thirteenth century reduced the city to a secondary role with Cairo established as the Mamluk capital. The Ottoman conquest in 1516 restored the prosperity which was reinforced by its position as starting point of the Ottoman Hajj caravans. During the eighteenth century the city was eclipsed by the commercial prosperity of Aleppo, though Damascus remained the political capital. With the collapse of the Ottoman Empire in 1918 Damascus was re-established as an Arab capital.

Mud brick and wood are the principal materials of construction for traditional houses. The lower parts of houses have thick walls made out of mud brick which are strengthened at the corners with wooden stakes laid horizontally. The upper parts of the houses are often cantilevered over the street on wooden beams. The walls of the upper part are made out of a wooden framework with bricks laid in between often in a herringbone pattern. The more important monuments are made of stone with baked brick or stone rubble used for domes and vaulting. A characteristic of the monumental masonry of Damascus is the use of ablaq (alternating courses of dark and light masonry) made out of white limestone and black basalt.

There are few standing remains from the Umayyad period with the exception of the Great Mosque which is the oldest major mosque still preserved in its original form. Little was done to alter the pre-Islamic plan of the city and many of the Byzantine buildings were simply converted; thus the caliph's palace, behind the Great Mosque, was formerly the residence of the Byzantine governors. The plan of the city at this time formed a roughly rectangular shape along the banks of the Barada river, a shape which was retained until the expansion during the sixteenth century.

In the three centuries following the fall of the Umayyads Damascus suffered a state of near anarchy. In 1076 strong rule was restored by the Turkoman chief Atsiz ibn Uvak and for the next eighty years the city was ruled by Turkish chiefs or Taabegs. During this period a hospital was built and seven madrassas were established.

With Nur al-Din's capture of Damascus in 1154 the city became the centre of activity directed against the Crusaders who had seized Palestine. During this period there was a great deal of military and religious building. The walls of the city were strengthened with new gateways such as the Bab al-Seghir whilst the older gateways were reinforced. The citadel was also remodelled with a new gate and a large mosque. The number of mosques and madrassas were increased in order to promote orthodox Sunni Islam against both Shi'is and the Christianity of the Crusaders. Other important buildings included the maristan, or hospital, of Nur al-Din and the madrassa and tomb of Nur al-Din. The hospital, which also functioned as a medical school, has a magnificent portal which is a mixture of Roman, Iranian and Mesopotamian styles. Directly above the door is a classic Roman pediment above which there is an arch with a

Entrance to the Hospital of Nur al-Din (built 1154), Damascus, ©Rebecca Foote

muqarnas archway. The top of the structure is crowned with an Iraqi-style conical dome. Inside the hospital is built like a madrassa with four iwans opening on to a central courtyard with a fountain in the centre. One of the iwans is a prayer hall whilst the other is a consultation room. The tomb of Nur al-Din is located on the corner of his madrassa and comprises a square chamber covered with a muqarnas dome resembling that of the hospital and ultimately the conical domes of Iraq.

Under the Ayyubids the madrassa became the main form of religious building with more than twenty examples recorded by Ibn Jubayr in 1184. Most of these tombs were commemorative structures which usually had the tomb of the founder attached. The standard form of Ayyubid tomb was a square room covered with an octagonal zone of transition made up of squinches and blind arches; above this there was usually a sixteen-sided drum which was pierced with windows and arches. The domes are usually tall, slightly pointed structures with broad fluting. The interior of the tombs was usually decorated with painted stucco designs. Important examples include the tomb of Badr al-Din Hassan and the mausoleum of Saladin in the Madrassa Aziziya. The cenotaph of Saladin is made of carved wooden panels whilst the walls were covered with polychrome tiles by the Ottomans in the sixteenth century. Another feature of Ayyubid architecture was the introduction of ablaq masonry.

The Mongol invasion of 1260 put an end to the most brilliant period of Damascus's post-Umayyad history. Although the Mamluks continued to develop the city it was no longer the foremost capital in the region. Baybars, the first Mamluk sultan, was particularly fond of the city and refurbished the citadel as a royal residence for himself. To the west of the city he built another palace known as the Qasr Ablaq which was built out of alternating courses of black and ochre-coloured masonry. Madrassas continued to be built although not on the same scale as before. There was a proliferation of mausoleums and to this period may be ascribed the invention of the double mausoleum where two mausoleums were included within a single complex. Examples of this type of building include the tomb of the Mamluk sultan Kit Bugha and the tomb of the Muhajirin commemorating a Mamluk who had fought the Mongols. The form of these double mausoleums was of two symmetrical domed tombs, with a monumental portal between them which would lead to the madrassa or memorial mosque.

In the later Mamluk period there was a development in the outward appearance of buildings characterized by the growth in the number of decorative octagonal minarets. These towers were decorated with blind niches, muqarnas corbelling elaborate finials and stone inlays. There was also a development of the markets outside the city centre and to this period may be ascribed the development of the suqs known as Taht Qal'a (below the citadel).

The Ottoman conquest of the early sixteenth century re-established Damascus as a regional capital, a position which was reinforced by its position at the start of the Hajj (pilgrimage) route to Damascus. New facilities both religious and practical were built to accommodate the vast numbers of pilgrims coming from Anatolia, Syria and even from Iran. The most important monument was the Tekiyya of Sulayman the Magnificent designed by his architect Sinan and completed in 1555. The

Tekiyya is built on the river bank on the site of the old Mamluk palace, Qasr Ablaq. The Tekiyya comprises a mosque, kitchens and a camping ground for pilgrims. The mosque is built in the classical Ottoman style with a prayer hall covered by a large dome and a double arcade running round it on three sides. The twin minarets are tall pencil-like structures with sharp pointed roofs. The pure Ottoman appearance of the building is modified by the use of alternating black and white (ablaq) masonry. Other Ottoman mosques of the period also display a mixture of local and Ottoman features, thus the Sinaniya (after Sinan Pasha the governor of Damascus, not the architect) mosque has a large central dome in the Ottoman style but the use of ablaq masonry and the monumental muqarnas portal resemble earlier Mamluk buildings.

The Ottoman conquest also brought a fresh impetus to the trade of the city with the establishment of numerous khans. One of the earliest Ottoman examples is Khan al-Haria built in 1572 around a square courtyard with stables and store rooms on the ground floor and accomodation above. In eighteenth-century khans the central courtyard was often smaller and covered with domes. The most famous example of this later type is the As'ad Pasha Khan which is a square building covered with eight small domes and a large central dome supported on marble columns. The eighteenth century also saw the development of domestic architecture influenced by buildings such as the Azzam palace which was built around a courtyard in the traditional Syrian manner but with decoration that recalls the mansions of Istanbul.

See also: Aleppo, Ayyubids, Mamluks, Syria

Further reading:

R. S. Humphreys, 'Politics and architectural patronage in Ayyubid Damascus', *Essays in Honour of Bernard Lewis: The Islamic World from Classical to Modern Times*, ed. C. E. Bosworth, C. Issawi, R. Savory and A. L. Udovitch, Princeton, NJ 1989.

J. G. De Maussion, *Damas, Bagdad, capitales et terres des califes*, Beirut 1971.

J. Sauvaget and M. Ecochard, *Les Monuments Ayyubides de Damas*, Damascus 1938–50.

Damascus Great Mosque

Principal mosque of Damascus founded by the Umayyad caliph al-Walid in 706 CE.

The Great Mosque stands in the centre of the old city of Damascus on the site of the Roman temple platform, or *temenos*. The outer walls of the *temenos* still survive and are distinguished as large blocks of dressed masonry with pilasters set at intervals into the side. At the four corners of the *temenos* there are large square towers and around the edge there were arcades which opened into a large rectangular courtyard. There were four axial doorways to the *temenos*, that on the east being the principal entrance. At the time of the Islamic conquest the Byzantine church of St John stood in the middle of this platform. Immediately after the conquest the Muslims shared this space with the Christians with the Christians retaining possession of their church and the Muslims using the southern arcades of the *temenos* as a prayer area.

In 706 al-Walid destroyed the church and built a mosque along the southern wall of the *temenos*. The layout of the mosque comprised three aisles running parallel to the south (qibla) wall cut in the centre by a raised perpendicular aisle or transept. At the south end of this transept there was a mihrab set into one of the blocked doors of the south façade. Walls were inserted on the west and east sides between the corner towers, and new two-storey arcades were built around the east, north and west sides of the courtyard. The arcades and prayer hall were covered with pitched wooden roofs covered with tiles except for the centre of the transept which had a wooden dome. In the north-west of the courtyard there is an octagonal chamber raised up on eight columns with a pool beneath. This structure functioned as the bayt al-mal or treasury and is found in other early mosques such as Harran and Hamma.

Since the Umayyad period the mosque has been rebuilt several times because of fires (1069, 1401 and 1893) although its basic plan has remained the same. Originally the arcade of the sanctuary façade comprised one pier alternating with two columns but this was subsequently changed to piers only. A range of different arch forms is used in the arcades including round, semi-circular horseshoe and slightly pointed arches. The walls of the mosque are decorated with glass mosaics similar to those in the Dome of the Rock, with depictions of palaces and houses next to a river (possibly the Barada river in Damascus). The long rooms in the east and west sides were lit by marble grilles with geometric interlace patterns based on octagons and circles.

The form of the mosque, particularly the sanctuary façade, was probably derived from Byzantine palatial architecture, possibly the Chalci palace in Constantinople. Later mosques in Syria such as the Great Mosques of Aleppo, Hamma, Harran and Córdoba. The Great Mosque of Diyarbakir built in the Seljuk period is also of this form.

See also: Damascus, Diyarbakir, Harran, Syria, Umayyads

Further reading:

K. A. C. Creswell (mosaics by Marguerite Van Berchem), *Early Muslim Architecture*, Oxford 1969, 1 (1): 156–210, 323–72.

dam

Dams have always been an important factor in Islamic civilization as a means of harnessing scarce or fugitive water supplies. Famous examples of pre-Islamic dams in the Middle East include the Macrib dam in Yemen and the Shallalat dam in northern Iraq. The advantages of dams over cisterns or reservoirs is that a large volume of water can be stored with a relatively small amount of construction work. The simplest forms of dam are made of earth with a clay core whilst more imposing masonry dams are built to contain larger volumes of water. Most dams are associated with irrigation works and are sometimes linked to water mills. However, some of the largest dams are built to provide drinking water for cities; one of the best examples is the Birket al-Sultan in Jerusalem which consists of a large masonry dam built across the wadi Hinon in the sixteenth century. On top of the dam in the centre is a drinking fountain or sebil which supplied water to travellers. One of the greatest examples of Ottoman engineering is the Valide Bend, a large masonry dam constructed in the Belgrade forest in 1769 to supply water to Istanbul.

dar

House or residence. Often implies a house of high status and may be roughly equivalent to mansion.

dar al-imara

Governor's palace. In early Islamic architecture this was usually located at the qibla end of the mosque (i.e. behind the mihrab). This was a safety measure to enable the govenor (or caliph) to enter the mosque without having to pass through other worshippers.

See also: Kufa

dargah or dukka

Covered courtyard in traditional Cairene houses.

Deccan

Region of southern India famous for its distinctive pre-Mughal Islamic architecture.

The Deccan includes the modern Indian states of Maharashtra, northern Andhra Pradesh, northern Karnataka and Goa. Physically the Deccan comprises a plateau bordered by the Arabian Sea to the west and the Bay of Bengal to the east. Each of these coasts is bordered by a range of hills known as the western and eastern Ghats. The central plateau is watered by the Krishna and Godavari rivers which flow eastwards into the Bay of Bengal. The region has a long history of monumental religious architecture with Buddhist cave art at Ajanta and numerous medieval Hindu shrines. Although the coastal regions were exposed to Islam from an early period it was not until the thirteenth century that there were any significant Islamic conquests in the area. In the early fourteenth century the Tughluq ruler of Delhi destroyed the power of the Hindu Hoysala kingdom and for the first time a major Muslim presence was established in the area. In 1338 after his victories in the region Muhammad Tughluq Shah II decided to move his capital from Delhi to Daulatabad, and although the transfer was unsuccessful and most of the population returned to Delhi the conquest established permanent Muslim rule in the region.

Muslim rule in the Deccan was complex and fragmentary, with dynasties established at various capitals gaining the upper hand at different times, until the late seventeenth century when the area was brought into the Mughal Empire. From 1347 to 1422 the central Deccan was ruled by the Muslim Bahmani kings from the newly established fortress city of Gulbarga. In 1424 Sultan Ahmad Shah Bahmani moved the capital to another fortress city Bidar. In 1487 the Bahmani kings were overthrown by the Barid Shahi dynasty who ruled the city until the seventeenth century. However, in 1512 real power passed to the Qutb Shahi sultans who ruled from their capital of Golconda. Although the Mughal conquests effectively ended the independence of the Deccani sultans, the city of Hyderabad managed to survive into the twentieth century as an autonomous state.

The earliest Muslim architecture of the region

was derivative of local architecture, thus the mosque of Daulatabad incorporates many of the features of a Hindu temple. However, the architecture of the newly established fortress cities of Bidar, Golconda, Gulbaraga and Bijapur was a distinctive mixture of Indian and Middle Eastern styles. The defensive architecture of the cities was highly sophisticated using concentric planning and bent entrances. Decoration was in the form of coloured tiles imported from Kashan (Iran), and Persian calligraphers were used to decorate the façades of tombs and mosques. The area developed a distinctive bulbous dome form with petals around the base (or drum) and heavy tiered finials rising from a moulded lotus-shaped apex. Other distinctive architectural features are the use of huge decorative battlements and complex stucco forms. The standard tomb form was a domed square with engaged towers or minar at each corner the finest example of which is the Gol Gumbaz at Bijapur.

See also: Bijapur, Char Minar, Firuzabad (India), Gol Gumbaz (India), Hyderabad.

Further reading:

E. S. Merklinger, *Indian Islamic Architecture: The Deccan*, Warminster 1981.

P. Davis, *The Penguin Guide to the Monuments of India, 2: Islamic, Rajput and European*, London 1989.

Delhi

Capital city of India containing some of the finest examples of Indian-Islamic architecture.

Delhi is located approximately in the centre of northern India between the mountains of the Himalayas and the Rajasthan desert. More immediately the city is located on the banks of the Jumna river and near the Aravalli hills.

The modern city of New Delhi is only the latest in a series of eight cities which have occupied the area of Delhi. Although there were earlier settlements on the site the oldest architectural remains can be attributed to the eleventh-century city built by the Rajput Tomar king Anangpal. In 1193 the city (known as Lal Kot) was captured by the Afghan conqueror Muhammad of Ghur who left the city in charge of his deputy, Qutb al-Din Aybak. By the time of Muhammad of Ghur's death in 1206 Qutb al-Din Aybak had declared himself independent and established himself as the first Muslim ruler of Delhi. In 1304 Ala al-Din Khalji founded a second city known as Siri which was

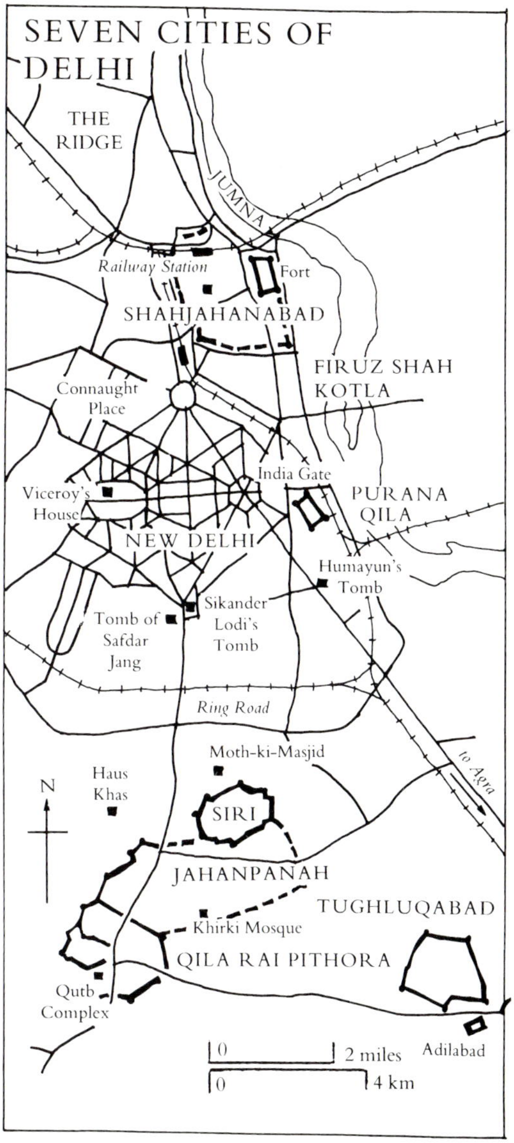

The seven cities of Delhi

located to the north of the first city. Later on, in 1321, a third city known as Tughluqabad after its founder Ghiyath al-Din Tughluq was founded to the east of the first city. However, this city was only used for four years until Muhamd Tughluq founded a fourth city known as Jahanpanah which also only lasted a short time as it was abandoned in 1328 when the ruler moved the capital to Daulatabad in the Deccan. The move to Daulatabad was disastrous and the sultan soon returned to Delhi. In 1354 Firuz Shah Tughluq established Firuzabad as the fifth city located by the river several kilometres to the north. For the next 150 years the area around Firuzabad was developed by successive dynasties although the central area fell into ruin. In 1534 the Bengali ruler Sher Shah founded the sixth city on the ruins of Firuzabad. This remained the centre of the city until 1638 when the Mughal ruler Shah Jahan established the city of Shahjahanabad. This was a huge new development to the north with the Red Fort at its centre. In 1911 Shahjahanabad became Old Delhi when the British laid out the present city of New Delhi.

Remains of all these cities have survived to present a cross-section of the development of Islamic architecture in India. The first city is known as Qila Rai Pithora after the Rajput ruler who built the fortifications. The most significant remains from the first city are the Qutb Minar and Mosque begun by Qutb al-Din Aybak in 1193. The Qutb Mosque complex stands inside the remains of fortification walls which were built by the Rajputs in the twelfth century. Originally the enclosure walls had thirteen gates although only three have survived. Fragments of Hindu temples incorporated into the mosque complex demonstrate the abrupt transition from Hindu to Muslim rule.

Apart from fortifications there are few remains of Siri (the second city of Delhi) because much of the stone was taken in the sixteenth century for use in Sher Shah's city. However, the remains of the third city, Tughluqabad, are remarkably well preserved. The remains consist of a huge irregular four-sided enclosure 1.5 by 2 km which includes a palace area, seven large cisterns, remains of a Friday mosque, the citadel and a tomb complex. The enclosure walls are tapering structures up to 30 m high, pierced with arrow slits and crowned by massive crenellations. Outside the enclosure walls to the south is the tomb of Ghiyath al-Din Tughluq which was originally an island set in an artificial lake and approached via a causeway from the palace complex. The tomb is a square domed building set within its own enclosure

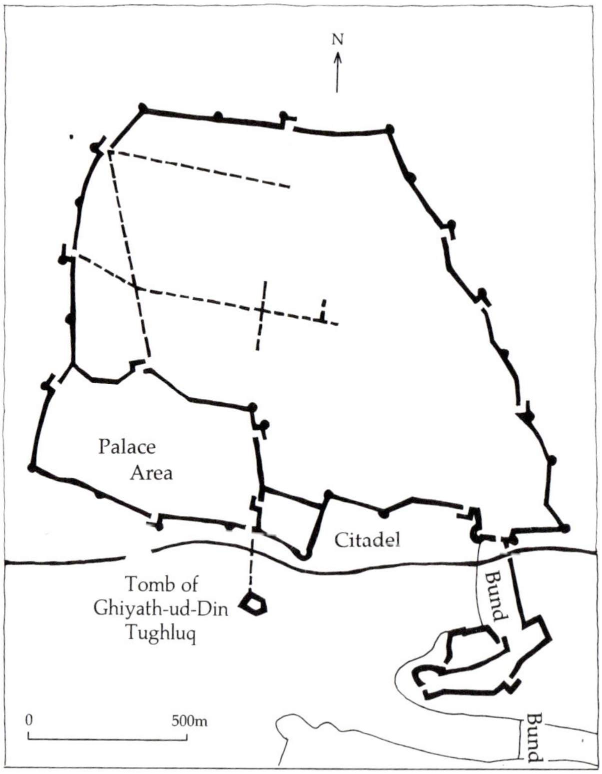

Plan of Tughluqabad, Delhi

and fortified with round bastions. To the east is a similar island structure known as Adilabad. Like the tomb complex this was a fortified area connected to the rest of the city by a causeway; within it was a huge audience hall on pillars built by Muhamad Tughluq.

The remains of the fourth city, Jahanpanah are located to the west of Tughluqabad between Siri and Qila Rai Pithora. Although much of this city has been destroyed the mosque is still standing and has an unusual plan consisting of four open courtyards. There are even fewer remains of the fifth city, Firuzabad, which was later built over by Sher Shah in the construction of the sixth city. The centre of the sixth city is the Purana Qila or 'Old Fort' initially built by the Mughal emperor Humayun and later developed by Sher Shah. The Purana Qila is a rectangular enclosure with huge corner bastions built on the supposed site of the city of Indraprastha mentioned in the Mahabharata. The interior of the fort is largely empty except for the Qala-i-Kuhna Mosque and the octagonal three-storey pavilion known as the Sher Mandal.

The seventh city, Shahjahanabad was founded by Shah Jahan in 1638 and was completed ten years later. Located on the banks of the Jumna river, the new city was dominated by the imperial palace known as the Red Fort. The street plan was based on two main avenues, the Chandni Chowk running east–west and the Faiz Bazar which runs south from the Red Fort. Near the intersection of these streets is the principal mosque of the city. This is one of the largest mosques in India and consists of a huge courtyard over 90 m square with three monumental gateways, a central rectangular cistern and a triple-domed sanctuary flanked by two minarets.

New Delhi is an Anglo–Indian city with few traditional Islamic buildings although the area occupied by the city includes some fine Islamic tombs the most famous of which is that of the second Mughal emperor Humayun.

See also: India, Mughals, Qutb Minar and Mosque, Red Fort

Further reading:

R. E. Frykenberg, *Delhi through the Ages: Essays in Urban History, Culture and Society*, Delhi 1986.

S. A. A. Naqvi, *Delhi: Humayun's Tomb and Adjacent Buildings*, Delhi 1946.

R. Nath, *Monuments of Delhi*, New Delhi 1979.

A. Petruccioli, 'Modelli culturali nell'impianto e nelle transformazioni di Old Delhi', *Storia della città* 31–2: 123–44, 1985.

Y. D. Sharma, *Delhi and its Neighbourhood*, 2nd edn., New Delhi 1974.

desert

The definition of desert varies with different authors, but it is generally agreed that any area with less than 50 mm annual rainfall may be counted as desert. For practical purposes, however, areas with less than 200 mm (the limit of dry farming) may reasonably be regarded as desert. Although deserts are a common feature of the Islamic world, most cities and areas of settlement are either outside this area or located next to large river systems such as the Nile, Tigris, Euphrates and Indus.

Until recently the majority of desert inhabitants have been nomadic pastoralists keeping either sheep and goats or camels and living in some form of tent. Important exceptions to this have been oasis trading settlements, Hajj routes and mining centres which are generally dependent on outside support for their survival. In certain periods, such as the early Islamic, political conditions, or more recently the exploitation of oil in Arabia, have made desert settlements more viable.

The architecture of the desert may be divided into three categories: permanent, semi-permanent and temporary. Temporary structures are either portable tents or made of expendable materials such as palm fronds, requiring minimum input of labour. Semi-permanent structures may be made out of a combination of portable and non-portable materials (e.g. a tent with stone walls) or may be made of perishable materials which need frequent renewal such as the palm-frond huts of the Tihama in Yemen. Permanent structures may be built of pisé, mud brick, baked brick, stone or, more recently, cement blocks and reinforced concrete.

Any desert settlement must make some provision for obtaining and storing water, usually from wells or seasonal rainfall, although occasionally sites are dependent on water brought from elsewhere (this was often the case with Hajj routes). The unpredictability of rain and the high evaporation rates in the desert (in many areas of the Middle East the rate of evaporation can exceed 2,000 mm annually) mean that elaborate water catchment and storage facilities are developed. Sites dependent on seasonal and sometimes erratic rain usually employ a system of dams, cisterns and run-off channels to maximize the catchment area. If water needs to be transported some distance, underground channels (qanats) are built to minimize evaporation.

Further reading:

E. Beazley and M. Howerson, *Living with the Desert: Working Buildings of the Iranian Plateau*, Warminster 1982.

S. Helms (with contributions by A. V. G. Betts, W. and F. Lancaster and C. J. Lenzen), *Early Islamic Architecture of the Desert: A Bedouin Station in Eastern Jordan*, Edinburgh 1990.

dershane

Turkish term for lecture hall or studying room, literally 'room for lessons'. Usually these are larger domed rooms or vaulted iwans on one side of an Ottoman madrassa.

diwan

Term of Iranian origin describing a reception hall, either in a house or a palace. Later on the word is also used to describe a government ministry.

diwan-i amm

Public reception hall.

diwan-i khass

Private reception hall.

Ulu Cami, Diyarbakir, Turkey

Diyarbakir (Amida)

Prominent city on the banks of the Tigris in south-east Turkey famous for its massive black basalt walls which are still largely intact.

Diyarbakir was captured from the Byzantines by Arab armies in 693 and became one of the great Islamic frontier fortresses. On capturing the city the Byzantine cathedral was shared between Muslims and Christians, although by 770 it was again used as a church. Later a Great Mosque was built on the site of the present Ulu Cami which according to a contemporary description (Nasiri Khusraw, 1045) had arcades two tiers high. The Ulu Cami in its present form dates to between 1090 and 1155 according to two inscriptions in the name of the Seljuk leader Malik Shah. The prayer room or sanctuary of the mosque is three aisles wide and covered with a transept in the middle on the axis of the mihrab. This arrangement and the similarity with the Great Mosque in Damascus (once thought to have been a church) has given rise to the assertion that the building was once a church in spite of contradictory evidence. The similarity with the Great Mosque in Damascus is explained by the fact that Malik Shah also carried out work there and may have used this as a model for that of Diyarbakir.

During the fifteenth century Diyarbakir became capital of the Aq-qoyunulu Turkman dynasty which was given control of the city in return for its support of Timur at the battle of Ankara in 1492. Buildings of the Aq-qoyunulu period provided a model for those of the Ottoman period. Several mosques of this period survive, the most famous of which is that of Kasim Padişah with its large central dome. The minaret is detached and consists of a tall square structure raised on four columns.

After its capture from the Aq-qoyunulu the Ottomans developed Diyarbakir as a regional administrative centre with its own mint. There are several notable sixteenth-century Ottoman mosques in Diyarbakir all built in the ablaq style (striped black and white masonry) with tall minarets with square shafts. Several of the mosques have fine tile decoration similar but inferior to that of Iznik which was probably produced within the city. The first of these is the Fatih Cami built between 1518 and 1520 which consists of a large dome supported by four semi-domes in a quatrefoil pattern. This plan, which is also used in the Peygamber Cami built in 1524, was probably the inspiration for Sinan's use of the plan in the Şehzade Cami in Istanbul. One of the more interesting mosques is the Melek Ahmet Pasha Cami which is built on first-floor level and is entered by a passage under the mosque which leads into a courtyard from which a set of stairs leads up into the prayer room.

Several nineteenth-century konaks (palatial houses) survive in Diyarbakir. One of the best examples is the Gevraniler Konak completed in 1819. The house is built around a courtyard on a vaulted sub-structure which contains cisterns, stables and a bath house. The apartments face north and are arranged as separate pavilions with their own terraces.

See also: Ottomans

Further reading:

D. Erginbaş, *Diyarbakir eveleri*, Istanbul 1954.

J. Raby, 'Diyarbakir: A rival to Iznik', *Istanbuler Mitteilungen* 26: 429–59, 1976.

Djenné (Dienné)

City in central Mali known for its unique mud-brick architecture which is a blend of African and Islamic styles.

The city was founded sometime between 767 and 1250 CE and was converted to Islam by Koy Kunboro, the twenty-sixth chief of the city, between 1106 and 1300. The prosperity of the city was based on the long-distance trans-Saharan trade routes, the most important commodities being gold and salt. The city was conquered by the Moroccans in 1591 who ruled the town until 1780. In the nineteenth century it was incorporated into the theocratic state of Macina, and came under French control in 1898, after which it declined in importance.

The main building material used in Djenné is mud brick, locally known as ferey. The mud bricks are plastered with mud plaster giving buildings a smooth rounded organic look which is offset by the use of bundles of palm sticks projecting from the walls (turon). These palm sticks have a dual function providing both decoration and a form of scaffolding for maintenance. Small cylindrical bricks were used until the 1930s when rectangular bricks were introduced. It is thought that the cylindrical bricks provided greater stability than modern ones, which is why so many older buildings have survived.

The city is built on a small hill between creeks and until recently was surrounded by a wall with eleven gates. The city was divided into quarters according to tribal divisions. More wealthy merchants lived in large monumental courtyard-houses, surrounded by open spaces. The houses were divided into male and female areas, with the men's area on the first floor at the front overlooking the street. The women's area by contrast was usually on the ground floor at the back of the courtyard. Traditionally these houses are decorated with a façade known as the 'Sudan Façade' which includes pillars and decorated entrances as its characteristic features.

The most famous building of the city is the Great Mosque which is said to have been originally built by Koy Kunboro who destroyed his palace to build it. The early mosque is known to have survived to the 1830s when it was destroyed. The present Great Mosque was built in 1909 on the foundations of the earlier structure. It stands on a raised platform approximately 75 m square reached six monumental staircases. The mosque consists of a large internal courtyard surrounded by a corridor, and a huge prayer hall, with a wooden roof supported by ninety rectangular piers. All four faces of the mosque are decorated with round pinnacles or cones, engaged pillars and bundles of palm sticks set into the side. The main entrances to the mosque are on the south and north sides (the east side is the qibla wall). The north side is more decorated than that of the south reflecting its proximity to the richer areas of the city. The east side or qibla wall is supported by three large rectangular towers. On the inside of the mosque a deep recessed mihrab is built into each one of these towers, and the central tower contains in addition a staircase to a platform on the roof, whence the speech of the imam could be relayed to the rest of the town.

P. Maas, *Aramco World*, November/December 1990: 18–29, gives the best recent account of Djenné.

L. Prussin, *The Architecture of Djenné: African Synthesis and Transformation*, Yale 1973.

do-chala

Type of roof with curved eaves, derived from Bengali huts (bangala). Used first in Bengali and later in Mughal architecture.

dome

Circular vaulted construction used as a means of roofing. First used in much of the Middle East and North Africa whence it spread to other parts of the Islamic world, because of its distinctive form the dome has, like the minaret, become a symbol of Islamic architecture.

It seems likely that the dome originated as a roofing method where the absence of suitable timber meant that it was impossible to make a flat timber roof. The earliest domes in the Middle East were associated with round buildings and were produced out of mud brick placed in layers which tilt slightly inwards. Another early method of dome construction which can still be seen in northern Syria and Harran in Turkey is the corbelled dome where mud bricks are placed horizontally in circular layers of diminishing circumference producing a corbelled dome. When the Romans conquered the Middle East the dome was incorporated into Roman architecture and under the Byzantines it became the main method of roofing monumental buildings. The chief advantage of domes is that large areas can be roofed without the interference of columns. At this time the wooden dome was developed which combined the space of dome building with the flexibility and lightness of wood. By the seventh century wooden domes were a normal method of roofing churches so that when the Arabs came to build the Dome of the Rock a wooden dome was used as the most appropriate form for this major religious building. Wooden domes were usually covered with sheets of metal, either copper or lead, as protection against the weather. The exact construction of the domes of the Caliph's Mosque in Baghdad is not known although the fact that it was described as green suggests that it was covered in copper.

Most domes, however, continued to be built of less flexible materials such as stone, mud brick and baked brick. One of the main problems of dome construction was the transition from a square space or area into a circular domed area. Usually there was an intermediary octagonal area from which it is easier to convert to a circular area although there is still the problem of converting from square to octagon. Two main methods were adopted, which are the *squinch* and the *pendentive*. The squinch is a mini-arch which is used to bridge a diagonal corner area whilst a pendentive is an inverted cone with its point set low down into the corner and its base at the top providing a platform for the dome. Squinches are the main method of transition in pre-Ottoman architecture whilst pendentives are more common after the sixteenth century. In India, where there was no tradition of arches before the advent of Islam, domes rest on flat corbels which bridge the corners.

During the medieval period Islam developed a wide variety of dome types which reflect dynastic, religious and social distinctions as much as different construction techniques. One of the most extravagant dome forms is the muqarnas or conical dome which appears as early as the eleventh century in Iraq at Imam Dur. A conical dome consists of multiple tiers of muqarnas which blur the distinction between structure and decoration and between circular and square forms. Later on the idea of the double dome was introduced as it was recognized that there was a conflict between the external appearance of the dome and the aesthetics of the interior of the domed space. The result was tall external domes with shallower interior domes. Increasing emphasis on the exterior can be seen in Cairo and Egypt where masonry domes with intricately carved exteriors were developed. In Iran and Central Asia tall domes were covered in coloured (usually blue) glazed tiles, culminating in the huge bulbous fluted domes on a high circular drum which were characteristic of the Timurid period (fifteenth century). In pre-Mughal India the standard dome form was derived from Hindu architecture and consisted of a squat circular form with a lotus design around the apex and a characteristic bulbous finial. Ottoman architecture adopted the Byzantine dome form and developed it to produce vast domed areas such as that of the Selimiye in Edirne.

Dome of the Rock (Qubbat al-Sakhra)

The third most important shrine of Islam. It is located on the Temple Mount in Jerusalem.

The Dome of the Rock was built by the early caliph Abd al-Malik in 691 and is generally agreed to be one of the oldest Islamic monuments. The building consists of a domed octagonal structure set in the middle of a raised plaza or enclosure known as the Haram al-Sharif or holy place. In the immediate vicinity of the Dome of the Rock are two other buildings of similar antiquity, the Qubbat al-Silsila and the Aqsa Mosque. The Qubbat al-Silsila is a smaller structure immediately to the east of the Dome of the Rock; it shares the same basic plan of an octagonal structure covered with a dome, although unlike the larger monument the sides of the structure are open. The purpose of the Qubbat al-Silsila is unknown although it probably had some ritual function. The Aqsa Mosque has been rebuilt several times so that its original form is difficult to determine although its basic form was probably similar to that of today. The Aqsa Mosque serves as the main place of prayer for the Haram and is located to the south of the Dome of the Rock.

The plan of the Dome of the Rock is based around a central dome resting on a circular drum supported by an arcade. This inner arcade is enclosed by an outer octagonal arcade and a solid octagonal wall which supports the shallow pitched roof around the dome. Both sets of arcades are carried on a mixture of piers and columns; the inner arcade is composed of four piers and twelve columns whilst the outer arcade consists of eight piers and sixteen columns. There are four entrances to the building, one on each of the sides facing the four cardinal points. Each of the eight sides of the outer octagon is divided into seven tall arches or bays, five of the arches on each side are open as doors or windows whilst the two nearest the corners are blind arches. There are twelve more windows in the circular drum below the dome. Directly below the dome is an exposed area of natural rock enclosed by a screen or fence, underneath this is a small cave with a mihrab reached by a set of steps.

Several forms of decoration are used including mosaics, marble, repoussé metalwork and coloured glass. The mosaics are particularly important examples of the combination of Sassanian and Byzantine motifs which is a characteristic of early Islamic art. Another important feature of the mosaics is that they carry an inscription dating the building to 691. At present only the interior mosaics survive although originally they also covered the outside.

The building has been restored many times in its 1,300-year history. One of the most important restorations was carried out during the sixteenth-century reign of the Ottoman sultan Suleyman the Magnificent. It was during this restoration that the exterior was covered with glazed ceramic tiles which covered the earlier mosaic coating. The tiles were the forerunners of Iznik tiles (q.v.) which became such a significant feature of Ottoman architecture. The present tiles covering the building were added in 1968. At the same time the Dome was covered with gold for the first time, although the present covering dates from 1993.

The Dome of the Rock is generally regarded as an attempt to provide a Muslim alternative to the Church of the Holy Sepulchre which had previously dominated the city of Jerusalem. The plan and design of the Dome of the Rock reflect this rivalry. In religious terms the building is significant because it commemorates the place where Abraham offered his son Isaac as a sacrifice and the place from which Muhammad made his night journey to heaven.

See also: Jerusalem

Further reading:

K. A. C. Creswell, *A Short Account of Early Islamic Architecture*, ed. J. W. Allan, Aldershot 1989.
O. Grabar, *The Formation of Islamic Art*, Yale 1973.

domical vault

A dome which rises from a square or rectangular base without the intervention of a drum, squinches or pendentives.

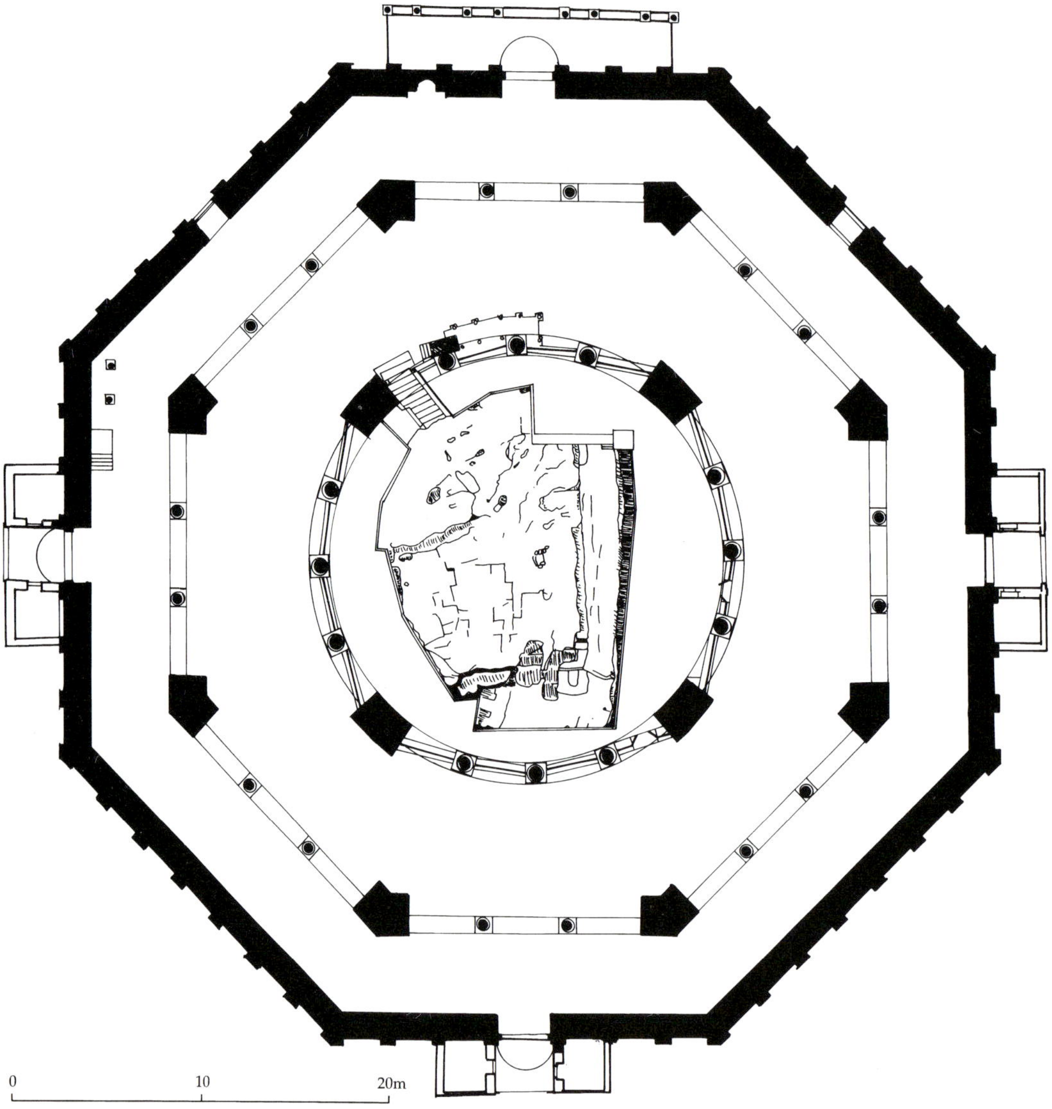

Ground plan of the Dome of the Rock, Jerusalem. Note exposed rock surface in centre (after Creswell)

E

East Africa

Muslim areas of East Africa have traditionally been the coastal strip which extends for over a thousand miles and includes the coasts of Somalia, Kenya, Tanzania (including Zanzibar) and northern Mozambique. This area has a homogeneous culture, known as Swahili, which is distinct from but related to both the Arabic Islamic world and the Bantu-speaking peoples of the interior.

Historical Background

The first documentary evidence concerning the East African coast comes from the first-century CE Periplus of the Erythraen Sea and the fourth-century geography of Ptolemy. The origins and history of Islam on the East African coast are obscure, although historical sources have been supplemented recently by information from archaeological excavations to produce at least an outline picture. Historically the earliest Islamic settlements on the coast took place during the eighth century and this has been confirmed recently by excavations at Shanga in Kenya.

The Swahili culture has traditionally been based on Indian Ocean trade with Arabia, India and the Far East and it is probable that this is how Islam arrived in East Africa rather than by conquest or a policy of colonization. Although it is likely that some Arabs and Persians may have settled on the coast, the overwhelming majority of the population had African origins as is demonstrated by the Swahili language itself which is essentially a Bantu language with many Arabic loan words. There is little documentary evidence of the early period before the arrival of the Portuguese although there are several early buildings which are dated by inscriptions. The earliest of these is a Kufic inscription in the Kizimkazi Mosque in Zanzibar dated to 1107 CE, although the mosque was rebuilt in the eighteenth century according to another inscription in the building. Other early dated monuments are in Somalia, including the Great Mosque of Mogadishu built in 1238 and the mosque of Fakhr al-Din in 1269.

In addition to inscriptions there are also various early accounts by travellers. In 1331 the coast was visited by Ibn Battuta who travelled as far south as Kilwa in southern Tanzania and described the people and buildings of the coast, and also in the early fourteenth century a Chinese embassy visited and described the coast.

Through analysis of trade goods, architectural features and local artefacts, archaeology has provided a more detailed model of how Swahili culture developed in the centuries prior to the Portuguese. In the earliest phase of settlement (eighth–ninth century) the main trading partner seemed to be the Persian Gulf; later on with the collapse of the Abbasid caliphate trade seems to be more connected with the Red Sea and ultimately Egypt. During these two early periods the towns of the Lamu archipelago such Manda and Shanga seem to have risen in wealth and importance. Later in the thirteenth century the area around Kilwa in southern Tanzania seems to have risen rapidly in wealth and importance along with the city of Mogadishu in Somalia. This change can partly be explained through the history of local dynasties and partly through the growth of the gold trade which originated in Zimbabwe and made its way via Sofala, Kilwa, Mogadishu and Yemen to the Middle East.

In the sixteenth century the coast was opened to Europeans when the Portuguese established a base in Mombasa as part of the sea route India. For the next two hundred years until the mid-eighteenth century the Portuguese tried to control the trade of the coast against the rival claims of the Dutch and the Omanis. Whilst the rivalry of the maritime powers disrupted trade, the stability of the coastal towns was threatened by the Galla, a nomadic tribe from Somalia, who sacked and pillaged towns as far south as Mombasa. In the mid-eighteenth century the Omanis at last won the struggle for supremacy on the coast when

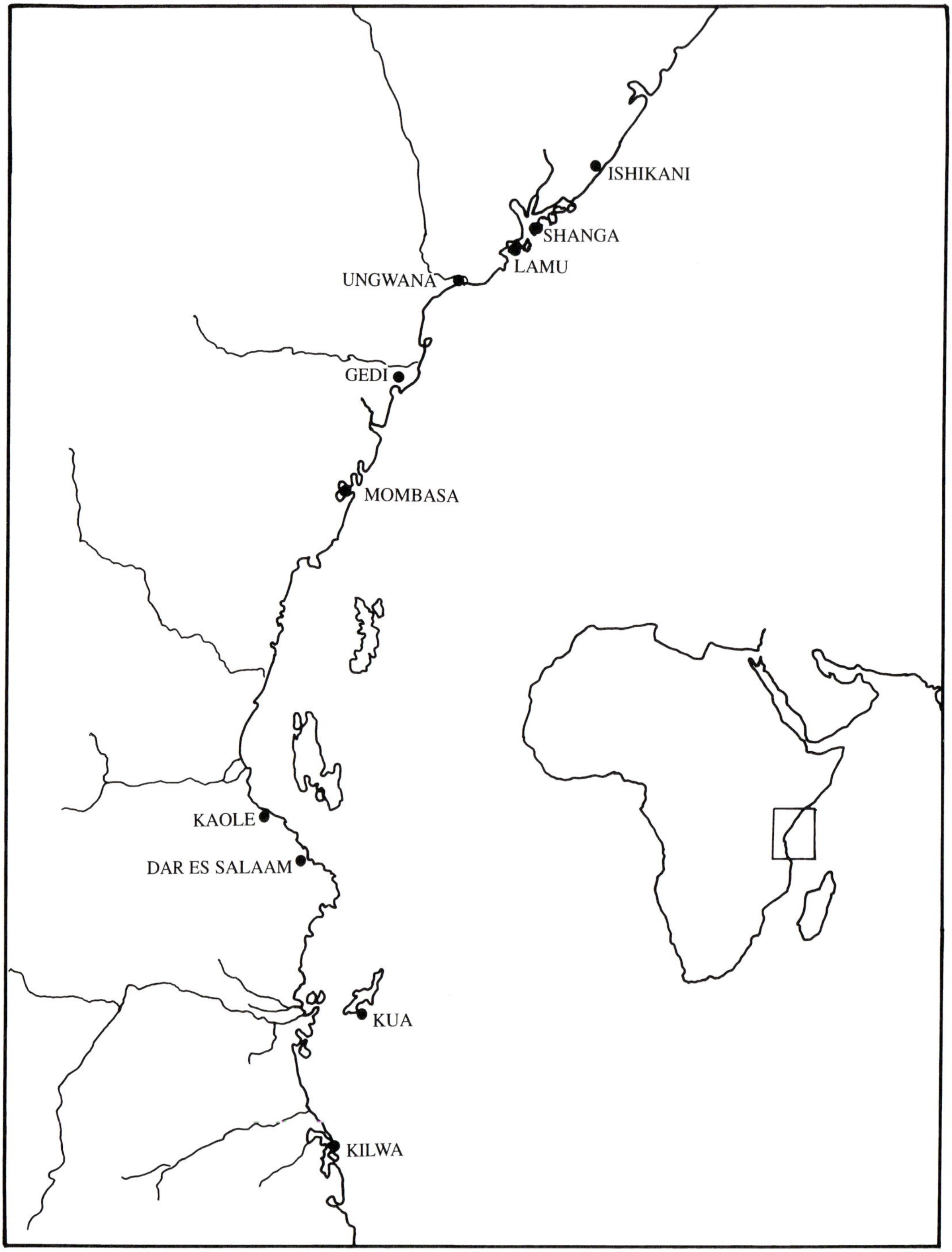

Principal Islamic sites of East Africa

they captured the Portuguese base of Fort Jesus in Mombasa. During the next century Omani power was extended inland and by 1832 their position was so secure that Sultan Sayyid Said moved his capital from Muscat to Zanzibar which remained the capital until the beginning of the twentieth century.

The coast of East Africa is fairly low-lying and is fringed with extensive tracts of mangrove forests intermittently punctuated by inlets and creeks. Occasionally there are groups of islands such as at Kilwa or Lamu forming small archipelagoes and a few larger offshore islands like Zanzibar, Pemba and Mafia. The coast is protected along most of its length by substantial coral reefs which also form the base of most of the coastal foreshore. It is important to note that all the Islamic settlements so far discovered in East Africa are within four miles of the coast and most are considerably nearer. Most sites are located slightly apart from the mainland either on peninsulas which are cut off at high tide or on islands, although many are also located on the shores of creeks or inlets. The main form of communication was by boats with a fairly shallow draught, which could be brought in close to the shore at high tide.

The main building materials were coral, mangrove poles (barriti), coconut thatch (barissti) and mud which were all easily available on the coast. In the absence of any other suitable form of stone on the coast coral was employed as the main building material for stone houses. Two main types were used, reef coral quarried live from the sea and fossil coral which formed the main rock underlying the coast. Usually reef coral was used for the finer decorative elements of a building whilst fossil coral was used for the walls, although there are certain variations on this. Coral was also burnt and used to make lime for plaster and mortar. Mangrove poles were the main type of timber used and were available in considerable quantities as any coastal settlement would involve the clearance of large areas of mangrove. The standard dimensions of mangrove poles are between 1.80 and 2.80 m long which imposes a maximum span on roofs without supports. Barissti or coconut palm was used as a thatch to roof mud-walled houses and to build temporary fishing shelters (bandas). Red mud earth was used either as a building material for walls in wattle-and-daub constructions or as floor make up within stone houses. In most places and at most periods throughout the coast mud wattle-and-daub constructions would have been the predominant form of construction whilst stone was only used for special purposes.

Architecture

Although East Africa has been Islamic for more than 1,000 years the towns or settlements do not contain all the elements usually found in a Muslim town. There are, for example, no public baths or hammams, presumably because of the hot moist climate (although the Omanis built baths on Zanzibar in the nineteenth century). Similarly there are no suqs or open-air markets and no caravanserais or khans. Before the Portuguese period (sixteenth century) there do not seem to have been significant attempts to fortify towns with walls and there are few examples of fortified buildings before this period with the enigmatic exception of Husuni Ndogo (see Kilwa). The reasons for this are presumably connected with the maritime nature of Swahili civilization and its relative remoteness from other Muslim areas. Nevertheless the East African coast does have some outstanding examples of other Islamic building types including mosques, palaces, houses and tombs.

The earliest mosques so far discovered have all been in excavations at Shanga in Kenya where a sequence of five superimposed mosques have been discovered dating from the ninth to the fourteenth centuries. The first three of these mosques (Shanga I–III) are dated to before 900 CE and the earliest appears to have been a small open-air structure surrounded by an enclosure made out of wattle and daub. The structure was rectangular, measuring approximately 5 m north–south by 3.5 m east–west, with rounded corners, an entrance on the south side and a floor made of stamped green earth. No mihrab could be detected in the structure and may not have been thought necessary at this early date in such a small structure, where the orientation of the building and the position of the door opposite the qibla were enough to indicate the direction of Mecca (in East Africa the qibla is due north). The second mosque (Shanga II) was of a similar size and design although it had a more substantial structure with a plaster floor and roof supported on a single central timber post and ten external posts. In the centre of the north wall was a large semi-circular post hole which may have been for a wooden mihrab. The next (Shanga III) to be built on the site was largely destroyed by subsequent rebuilding but was of similar dimensions to the two earlier mosques and had a roof supported by at least eight large posts. The first stone mosque (Shanga IV), dated to between 850 and 890, was built directly on top of the previous wooden building (Shanga III) and consisted of a rectangular structure built out of reef coral (also called porites) with a rectangular antechamber at the south end. The latest mosque on the site (Shanga V) is still standing to roof height and is dated to around 1000 CE. It is also a rectangular structure built out of fossil coral (coral rag) with an antechamber at the south end and four large posts to support the roof in the centre. There are entrances to this building on the east and west sides and no traces of a mihrab in the first phase, although this may have been a portable wooden structure.

Unfortunately there are few examples of early mosques to compare with those at Shanga so it is not possible to say how typical they are. However, comparison shows that many of the features at Shanga were developed in later mosques, in particular the absence of an external courtyard with arcades, the rectangular longitudinal alignment of the plan, the use of side rooms, the arrangement of doors either at the south end or from the sides and the gradual introduction of more permanent materials.

Other early mosques include the Kizimkazi Mosque on Zanzibar, the mosque at Manda, the three thirteenth-century mosques in Mogadishu, and the Great Mosque at Kilwa. The Kizimkazi Mosque on Zanzibar was rebuilt in the eighteenth century but has a twelfth-century foundation inscription confirmed by excavations. The plan consists of a narrow rectangular structure with a row of central columns supporting a roof two aisles wide and four bays deep. Excavations at Manda in Kenya have revealed a mosque with a similar plan which may date to the tenth century. Although more complex, the Great Mosque in Mogadishu (1238) is built around the same basic plan and consists of a simple rectangular structure two aisles wide and five bays deep. This building is also unusual for having a minaret, a feature which does not occur elsewhere in the architecture of East Africa until the nineteenth century.

Of all the mosques on the East African coast the Great Mosque at Kilwa is the most impressive because of its size and antiquity. The mosque basically consists of two parts, an earlier northern part and a much larger southern extension. Beneath the floors of the northern part of the building remains of an earlier mosque have been found which was initially dated to the twelfth century but may well be earlier. Although this mosque was not fully excavated it seems to have had the same design as the twelfth-century mosque which was later built over it. This mosque has a rectangular plan measuring approximately 6 m east–west by 12 m north–south with nine columns arranged in three rows. There is a large deeply recessed mihrab in the centre of the north wall and doorways on the west and east sides. In general this plan conforms to the general type of mosque on the coast although it is much larger than its contemporaries. Sometime in the sixteenth century a massive southern extension (20 m north–south by 15 m east–west) was added with alternating domed and barrel-vaulted chambers supported first on timber columns and later on composite octagonal masonry columns. The whole area was five aisles wide and six bays deep and had entrances on the west and east sides. Attached to the south-east corner of this area was a large masonry dome used as a prayer room by the sultan of Kilwa. The island of Kilwa also contains a nine-domed mosque known as the Small Domed Mosque which is one of the few examples of a Middle Eastern type of mosque in East Africa.

Before the sixteenth century most mosques were rectangular with a single row of columns aligned with the mihrab and a separate room for ablutions to the south. After this time, however, new forms were introduced, including the square-plan mosque as seen in the small mosques at Kua and the main mosque at Songo Mnara. From the fifteenth century onwards it is also possible to see a development of mihrabs from simple recessed niches into much more complex forms with multi-lobed arches recessed several times. From the late eighteenth century onwards carved plaster is used in place of reef coral to decorate the mihrab. Another feature which becomes popular at this period (except in the Lamu area) is the recessed minbar which is set into the north wall of the mosque and is entered either through the mihrab itself or through a separate opening in the wall. Later on, in the nineteenth century, minarets become a feature of mosques for the first time. Previously some mosques had a form of staircase minaret which provided access to the roof from which the call to prayer could be made. The reason for the absence of minarets until this relatively late date is not known, although it is likely that it may have had a religious basis connected with Ibadiism. Certainly the technology for building towers was present as can be seen in the numerous pillar tombs of the coast and structures such as the Mbraaki pillar in Mombasa built in the fourteenth century. Some of the earliest minarets in East Africa were built on the Kenya coast such as at Shella near Lamu and several mosques in Mombasa town.

After the mosques palaces represent some of the best examples of Islamic architecture on the coast. Although not many have survived from the earliest period it is likely that most settlements had some form of palace or great house located next to the main mosque. Excavations at Shanga and Manda (both in Kenya) have revealed early monumental buildings which date to before 1000 CE near the congregational mosque of the settlement. The island of Kilwa contains several palaces, the most famous of which is Husuni Kubwa which may date from the thirteenth century. This is a massive complex over 100 m long which occupies a projecting headland away from the main settlement. The palace has a monumental entrance at the south end which leads into the south court, roughly 40 m square with arcades and rooms arranged on each side. A doorway in the north wall leads on to the central palace area which is in turn divided into four courtyards which have been interpreted as an audience court, a domestic court, a palace court and a courtyard around an octagonal pool. Other palaces on Kilwa include the Makutani Palace (eighteenth century), the Great House next to the Great Mosque (fifteenth century) and Songo Mnara on a nearby island (also fifteenth century).

Husuni Kubwa is certainly the largest pre-nineteenth-century palace on the coast and most subsequent palaces were more like large houses. The fifteenth-century palace at Gedi appears as the largest house amongst several large houses each with similar arrangements of courtyards, storage areas and public and private rooms. The palace was built by the Sheikh of Malindi and was distinguished from other buildings in the town by a royal tomb adjacent to the entrance. The palace consists of a high-walled rectangular enclosure (approximately 35 by 25 m) with a monumental entrance on the east side. The main area of the building is the north courtyard which has been interpreted as an audience hall for the ruler who would have conducted his official business from there. This courtyard leads on to the private quarters of the sultan to the south. The harem courtyard is on the west side of the audience courtyard but separated from it by a wall, and is only accessible by going through the private apartments or by a separate entrance to the palace on the west side which opens directly into the harem area.

At the beginning of the nineteenth century the Omanis introduced a new concept of palace architecture with large multi-storey buildings enclosed within gardens. The earliest of these is the Mtoni Palace built in 1830 around a large square courtyard and with a Persian bath house attached. The largest of the Omani palaces is the Maruhubi Palace which also had a bath house and fort within the gardens which covered 50 hectares.

Houses of the East African coast represent a continuous development of domestic architecture that can be traced back over 1,000 years. Unfortunately most houses were built of impermanent materials such as wattle and daub, so that the surviving stone houses only represent a small proportion of the dwellings in even the wealthiest towns. However, from the available evidence it seems likely that the basic wattle-and-daub house retained a fairly conservative plan through history; thus remains of wattle-and-daub houses at Shanga, Manda and Kilwa seem to be fairly consistent with present-day houses. These consist of a rectangular structure with a pitched roof supported on rafters and posts sunk into the ground. The roofs would be covered in coconut palm thatch (barissti) and the walls made of wattle and daub (thin stakes dug into the ground, interwoven with palm leaves and covered with a protective layer of mud). Wattle-and-daub constructions appear to be the earliest form of housing in Swahili settlements and predate the first stone houses by 200 years.

The earliest coral stone buildings on the coast seem to have been public buildings such as mosques and administrative centres, and the first domestic stone buildings appear to have been palaces. Only in the fifteenth and sixteenth centuries did stone houses become common in the settlements of the coast at places like Songo Mnara and Gedi. At Takwa, a settlement inhabited between the sixteenth and seventeenth centuries, there were over 150 stone houses and one mosque, indicating that stone houses were the norm. However, it was not until the eighteenth and nineteenth centuries that stone houses became common in most of the major settlements. The town of Lamu probably contains the best examples of eighteenth-century domestic architecture on the coast: the typical Swahili house of the period consists of a stone enclosure wall with no outward-facing windows. The entrance to the building is usually a porch with benches either side which forms the only generally accessible part of the house. The porch opens on to a small anteroom which in turn leads out into a courtyard which contains a small bathroom and a well. There is a guest room on one side of the courtyard (usually the north) which is separate from the rest of the house, whilst the private quarters are on the other (south) side of the courtyard. These usually consist of a series of long narrow rooms arranged side by side and opening successively one on to the other. The outer two rooms are the outer and inner living rooms which are both open to receive light from the courtyard. There are usually raised areas at either end of each room which can be curtained off and used for sleeping areas. Behind the inner living room is the harem which is another narrow longitudinal room with wooden doors separating it from the living rooms. Behind this room there is an inner bathroom on one side and a larger room usually with a small blocked doorway to the outside which is used for laying out the dead. The houses are usually decorated with stucco work in the form of niches and large decorative friezes which are mostly concentrated around the harem. Either side of the doorway to the harem are niches, and within the harem itself, set into the wall facing the door, are a large array of niches. The niches were used for displaying valuable imported pottery although their precise significance is a matter for discussion.

Most houses were single storey and if another level was built this was usually for another house or family unit for the children of the family on the ground floor. When an upper storey was added there was usually an extra single room with a thatched roof added at a higher level which functioned as a kitchen (kitchens were usually in the courtyard so that the smoke could escape). Stone houses were only built by people of high status within the community and could not be bought or sold to outsiders.

Monumental stone tombs are one of the characteristic features of Swahili architecture. Like stone houses tombs made of stone were not available to everyone and were probably reserved for people of wealth or rank; the precise status required is not known, although it has been pointed out that the tomb of the Lamu saint Habib Salih bin Alwi was built of wood as he may have been considered an outsider and therefore not eligible for a stone tomb.

Most tombs consist of a rectangular enclosure of varying dimensions with the east side of the tomb decorated in various ways. Monumental tombs are usually built either next to a mosque (usually the north end) or isolated in the open country. Often they are used as shrines where offerings are left and prayers said on specific days. In Somalia and northern Kenya there is a group of tombs consisting of large enclosures with an average size of 30 m square and a maximum of over 75 m square.

Decoration takes several forms, the best known of which is the pillar; other forms include panelled decoration, stepped ends, and a domed or pitched roof. Pillar tombs consist of a cylindrical or square shafted pillar rising out of the wall of the tomb which is usually decorated with panels. The pillars are sometimes decorated with fluting and Chinese bowls set into the top of the pillar. Pillar tombs are widely distributed and the earli est examples are dated to the fourteenth century. Although most tombs have some form of panelled decoration, in some structures this becomes quite complex and is the main form of decoration as in the Ishakani tomb of north Kenya which is decorated with more than thirty panels with various forms of geometric designs consisting of triangles, diamonds, squares, rectangles and

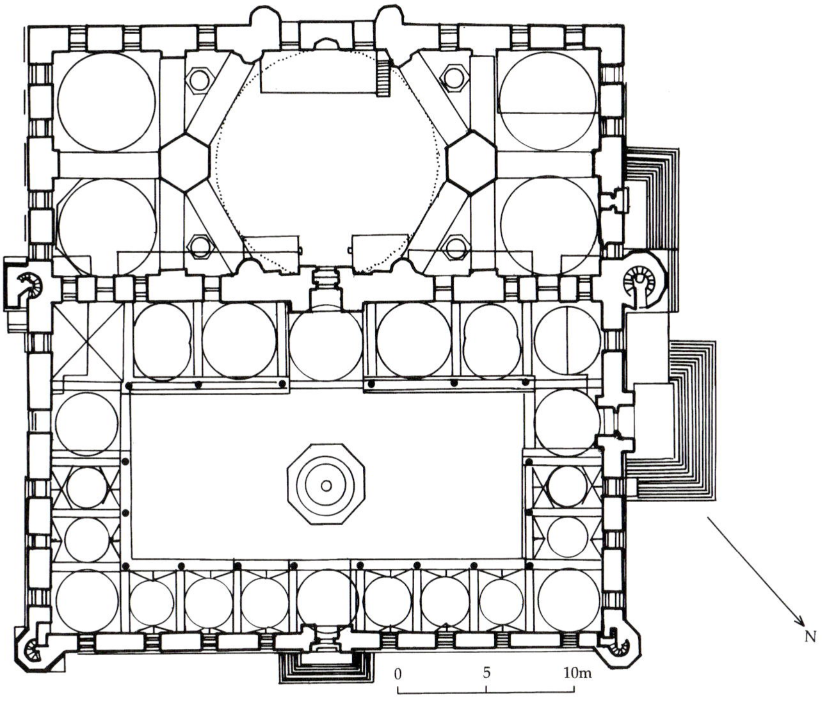

Üç Şerefeli Cami, Edirne, Turkey (after Goodwin)

chevrons. Other panelled tombs are decorated with plain panels alternating with niches. Many tombs are decorated with stepped corners as a main feature of their decoration; this was the predominant form of tomb until the nineteenth century. Although most tombs are open enclosures, occasionally they are covered over either with a dome or a pitched roof. The earliest examples of covered tombs are from Ungwana, where three tombs covered with gabled roofs are dated to the mid-thirteenth century. Domed tombs seem to be much later and only occur after the sixteenth century.

See also: coral, Gedi, Kenya, Kilwa, Lamu, minaret, Somalia, Sudan, Tanzania, Zanzibar

Further reading:

J. de V. Allen and T. H. Wilson, *Swahili Houses and Tombs of the Coast of Kenya*, Art and Archaeology Research Papers, London 1979.

P. Garlake, *The Early Islamic Architecture of the East African Coast*, Memoir no.1 of the British Institute of History and Archaeology in Eastern Africa, Oxford 1966.

M. C. Horton, 'Early Muslim trading settlements on the East African coast: new evidence from Shanga', *Antiquaries Journal* 67: 290–323, 1987.

H. C. Sanservino, 'Archaeological remains on the southern Somali coast', *Azania* 18: 151–64, 1983.

P. Sinclair, 'Chibuene: an early trading site in southern Mozambique', *Paideuma* 28: 148–64.

Edirne (Byzantine: Adrianople)

Major Ottoman city in European Turkey on the main route between the Middle East and Europe.

Edirne was captured in 1362 and rapidly rose to replace Bursa as the Ottoman capital in 1366. During the fifteenth century the city was developed as a major Turkish city with caravanserais, khans and mosques and a royal palace. The capture of Constantinople (later Istanbul) in 1453 meant that Edirne was no longer the capital, although it continued to be one of the first cities of the empire and a country residence for the Ottoman sultans until the nineteenth century. Unfortunately the royal palace which was located on the banks of the Tunca river has disappeared, but photographs and plans show an ancient building considerably altered

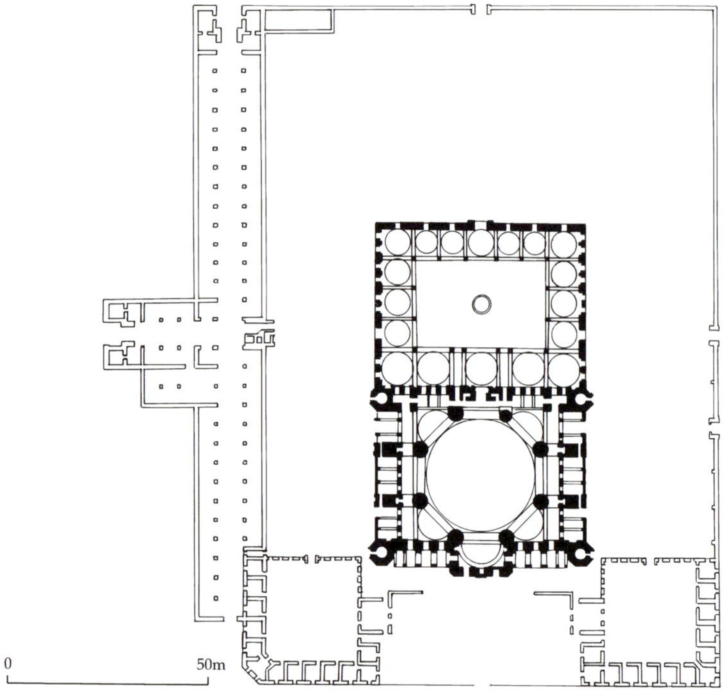

Selimiye Complex, Edirne, Turkey (after Goodwin)

by nineteenth-century additions when it again was used as a residence of the sultans. The best-preserved part of the palace seems to have been the kitchens which provided a model for those of the Topkapisarai.

The oldest surviving mosque in Edirne is known as the Yildirim Cami which is built on the ruins of a church. The date of construction is debated but is believed to be between 1360 and 1390. Other early mosques include the Muradiye Tekke and Mosque built in 1421 which includes both green tiles of the Yeşil Cami (Bursa) type and blue and white Chinese style tiles. Unfortunately the building was heavily damaged in an earthquake of 1751 and much of the original appearance of the mosque has been lost in the eighteenth-century restoration. The largest early mosque at Edirne is the Eski Cami completed during the reign of Mehmet I in 1413. This is a nine-domed building with a portico of five bays on the north side and a minaret at the north-west corner (the second minaret was added twenty years later). The six side domes are hemispherical whilst the central domes on the line of the mihrab are a variety of shapes (polygonal, octagonal and star-shaped vaults).

Of a similar period but very different style is the Üç Şerefeli Cami begun in 1437. Where the Eski Cami was the last great Ottoman mosque to be built in the multi-domed fashion the Üç Şerefeli was the first of the new type of imperial mosque. It consists of a rectangular courtyard and smaller rectangular prayer area covered by one large dome and four subsidiary domes (two either side). The main dome rests on a hexagonal drum supported by two large octagonal piers. This was a revolutionary design when mosques were either a collection of single-domed units or a large area covered by multiple domes of equal size like the Eski Cami. The Üç Şerefeli was also unique for its time because of its four minarets decorated in a variety of patterns; they were placed at the corners of the courtyard and arranged so that the two smallest were at the front and the tallest minarets were at the back. The tallest minaret is in the north-west corner and is distinguished by its three balconies which give the building its name.

In 1484 Beyazit ordered the construction of a major new mosque and hospital by the side of the Tunca river. The complex covers a large area (approx. 300 by 200 m) and includes the mosque, a hospital, sanatorium and medical school. There is a stone bridge next to the complex which was probably built at the same time. The mosque at the centre of the complex consists of a single-domed unit, flanked by two tabhanes (dervish hostels) and approached via a rectangular arcaded courtyard. The most significant architectural feature of the complex is the hexagonal hospital hall which encloses a central domed hexagonal court leading off to vaulted iwans.

Edirne's continued importance during the sixteenth century is proved by Selim II's choice of the city for his imperial mosque the Selimiye, whose central dome was the largest Ottoman dome and was equal to that of Hagia Sophia with a diameter of 32 m. The mosque forms part of a complex which includes a covered market, a madrassa and primary school. Like the Üç Şerefeli Mosque the Selimiye has four minarets although here one is placed at each corner of the domed prayer hall rather than the courtyard.

See also: Ottomans, Selimiye, tekke

Further reading:

A. Kuran, 'Edirne'de Yildirim Camii' (The Mosque of Yildirim in Edirne), *Belletin*, 28(3): 429–38, 1964.
R. M. Meriç, 'Edirne'nin tarihi ve mimari eserleri hakkinda', in *Türk San'ati Tarihi Araştima ve Incelemeleri*, Istanbul 1963.
R. Meyer-Riefstahl, 'Early Turkish tile revetments in Turkey', *Ars Islamica*, 4: 1937.
R. Osman, *Edirne sarayi*, Ankara 1956.
A. S. Ünver, *Edirne Muradiye cami'i*, Istanbul 1953.

Egypt (excluding Cairo)

Located at the north-eastern tip of Africa forming a bridge between Africa and Asia. The population of the Arab Republic of Egypt is 90 per cent Muslim and 10 per cent Coptic Christian. Despite its vast size (1 million square kilometres) most of the population lives in the region of the Nile Delta between Cairo and Alexandria. The other inhabited area is the Nile valley which runs the whole length of the country from Sudan in the south to the Mediterranean in the north. The rest of Egypt is inhospitable desert with a sparse population.

Egypt is fortunate in having a wealth of building materials at its disposal. The main materials are stone, baked brick, mud brick and wood. In the Delta region (which includes Cairo and Alexandria) suitable building stone is not naturally available, although Ancient Egyptian monuments containing stone imported from Upper Egypt provided a plentiful quarry for many Islamic buildings. Even in Upper Egypt ancient structures were often the most accessible source of building stone. Nevertheless, baked brick was often the preferred material because of its relative cheapness (i.e. transport costs), its versatility and standard size. Mud brick is obviously cheaper than baked brick, can be quickly produced and provides excellent thermal insulation. In pre-modern times mud brick formed the basic building material for most of the country but more recently it is confined to southern Egypt. Date palms form the main natural source of wood and palm wood is used for most traditional architecture. More exotic wood could be imported from Europe or Africa for use in the wealthier houses of Cairo.

Several factors have combined to make the Islamic architecture of Egypt outside Cairo virtually unknown: first, the overwhelming wealth of Cairo's architectural heritage; second, the monuments outside Cairo are often made of mud brick and have survived less well; third, monuments of Egypt's pharaonic past have tended to overshadow those of later periods. In this discussion I have concentrated on the architecture of Upper Egypt which generally receives less attention.

The most important monuments of Upper Egypt are the necropolis of Aswan, the al-'Amri Mosque at Qus and a group of five Fatimid minarets. The necropolis of Aswan is located outside the town of Aswan in Upper Egypt. The necropolis consists of a long strip 500 m wide stretching along the side of the road for nearly 2 km. Within the necropolis there are more than 1000 tombs built which originally had inscriptions dating them to the eleventh or early twelfth century. The tombs represent one of the best examples of medieval funerary architecture in the Middle East. There are several forms of tomb, from simple rectangular enclosures open to the sky to elaborate domed structures with mihrabs and a variety of vaults. Mud brick is the main material of construction although baked brick was used for the domes and some of the arches. The outer surfaces of the tombs were originally covered in lime plaster although in most cases this has now worn off. A characteristic feature of the domed tombs were projecting horns at the angles of the drum which supported the dome. The tombs are also significant as some of the earliest examples of muqarnas squinches.

The city of Qus is located on the east bank of the Nile more than 950 km south of Cairo. Qus replaced Qift as the dominant city of Upper Egypt during the ninth to tenth centuries. The city's main role was as a Nile port for goods coming overland from the Red Sea port of Qusayr. The main monument in the city is the al-'Amri Mosque which is a Fatimid building founded in 1083 although it has later Mamluk and Ottoman additions. The only Fatimid remains are part of the qibla wall which includes the original round-arched mihrab. The most famous part of the complex is the tomb from the Ayyubid period built for Mubarak ibn Maqlid in 1172. The mausoleum stands on a square base and is similar to some of the later tombs at Aswan with projecting horns on the drum. However, the design is more advanced and includes developed muqarnas niches and a slightly fluted dome pierced with star- and tear-shaped openings.

The five minarets of Upper Egypt which are usually included in any discussion of Fatimid minarets are also dated to the eleventh century. The mosque of Abu al-Hajjaj in Luxor is the most famous because of its position on the roof of the Temple of Luxor. The mosque is mostly a nineteenth-century construction but one of the two minarets dates to the eleventh century. The minaret is built of mud brick and has a square base 5 m high surmounted by a tapering cylindrical shaft which reaches a height of nearly 15 m. The top of the minaret is a tall domed pavilion with two tiers of windows. The square base is reinforced with three layers of wooden beams and the staircase inside is also made of wood. Eighty kilometres south of Luxor is the small market town of Esna. In the centre of the town is the Ottoman mosque of al-'Amri with a Fatimid minaret similar to those of Aswan and Luxor. The square base of the minaret is built out of baked brick with layers of wood inserted every nine courses. The tapering cylindrical shaft is white-washed and may be built of mud brick. The minaret at Aswan is similar with a square base and a tapering shaft, but lacks

Minaret, Aswan, Egypt, © Hutt Archive, Ashmolean Museum

the domed chamber on the top, although the remains of brackets indicate that there was once a superstructure. Externally this building is built of baked brick although the interior is made of unbaked mud brick. Its notable feature is the two bands of brickwork inscription at the top. This is one of the earliest examples of this type of inscription (hazarbaf) which was later to become a common feature in Islamic architecture. To the south of Aswan near the village of Shellal are two minarets of similar style to the minaret of Aswan and the mosque of Abu al-Hajjaj in Luxor. One of the minarets known as Mashad al-Bahri has a brick inscription similar to that of the minaret in Aswan. The other minaret known as al-Mashad al-Qibli is of interest as it stands next to a mosque of approximately the same date. The mosque is built on to a slope so that at one end it rests on a vaulted substructure which overlooks the valley below. The sanctuary of the mosque is covered by six domes and has three minarets in the qibla wall.

See also: Cairo, Fathy, Fustat, Hassan, mud brick

Further reading:

J. Bloom, 'Five Fatimid minarets in Upper Egypt', *Journal of the Society of Architectural Historians* 43: 162–7, 1984.

—— 'The introduction of the muqarnas in Egypt', *Muqarnas* 5: 1988.

K. A. C. Creswell, *The Muslim Architecture of Egypt*, 2 vols, Oxford 1952; repr. New York 1978.

F

Fatehpur Sikri

Abandoned city in northern India founded by the Mughal emperor Akbar in 1571.

Fatehpur Sikri derives its name from the village of Sikri which occupied the spot before, the prefix Fatehpur, City of Victory, was added in 1573 after Akbar's conquest of Gujerat in that year. Akbar chose this site for a city out of reverence for Sheikh Salim, a religious mystic of the Chisti order who prophesied that he would have three sons. In order to ensure the efficacy of the prophecy Akbar moved his pregnant wife to Sikri where she had two sons. In response Akbar decided to build an imperial mosque and palace at the village of Sikri. The location of the palace and mosque at the site encouraged further settlement by courtiers, noblemen and their attendants so that within a few years a city had grown up which was enclosed by a defensive wall. The city is built on the ridge of a hill next to a lake which has now dried up, giving rise to the theory that the city was abandoned because its water supply had failed. The centre of the city was the palace and mosque, which are located on the top of the ridge overlooking the lake, while the rest of the city was located on the sides of the ridge away from the lake. The city occupies an area of 5 km square with a wall on three sides and a fourth side open to the lake. There are three main gateways in the city wall between which there are semi-circular buttress towers.

The rise of the city from 1571 was very rapid so that after 1573 it was regarded as the capital of the Mughal Empire. However, after the city was abandoned by Akbar in 1585 to fight a campaign in the Punjab, the city seems to have declined just as rapidly so that by 1610 it was completely abandoned. The reason for the sudden decline of the city is usually given as the failure of the water supply, however the real reason may have been the emperor's loss of interest in the place. As the sole reason for the city's existence seems to have been a whim of the emperor, the fact that he was no longer in residence meant that there was no longer any incentive for anybody else to stay. The effect of the emperor's presence on the place may be gauged from an early description of the town which described the road from Agra to Fatehpur Sikri as completely filled with merchants' shops and stalls as if the two cities were one. A useful analogy may be with the Abbasid capital of Samarra which flourished for fifty years until the caliphs moved back to Baghdad when it declined to the level of a market town.

The first major structure built at the site was Jami Masjid (congregational mosque) which was completed in 1571 the year of Sheikh Salim's death. At the time of its construction it was the biggest mosque in India measuring 160 m east–west by 130 m north–south. The central courtyard is surrounded by arcades of pointed arches which lead into small cell-like rooms. The centre of the west of the courtyard is dominated by the sanctuary which has a huge central iwan leading on to a domed area in front of the main mihrab. Either side of the central dome are two smaller domes each covering the area in front of a smaller mihrab. As elsewhere at Fatehpur Sikri the building is covered with Hindu architectural features, thus the arcade of the sanctuary and the central iwan are capped by lines of chatris and internally the roofs are supported on Hindu-style carved columns, whilst the domes are supported on corbels in the tradition of Indian temple architecture. Approximately in the centre of the north side of the courtyard are two tombs, one belonging to Sheikh Salim and another to his grandson Islam Khan. The tomb of Sheikh Salim consists of a square domed chamber with an outer veranda filled in with a pierced marble screen (jali). The outside of the tomb is protected by a sloping canopy (chajja) supported on snake-like brackets. There are two main entrances to the mosque, a small private entrance from the palace on the east side and a monumental public entrance on the south side. The public entrance is known as the Buland Darwaza and was built in 1576 to commemorate Akbar's victory over Gujarat. The gate's name Buland Darwaza, 'Tall Gate', refers to the gate's outstanding height of 40 m. Like most Mughal mosques this building is raised up on a terrace so that the entrances are approached by flights of steps; in the case of the Buland Darwaza the stairs rise up another 12 m from ground level. The gate has an iwan plan with a large, deep central iwan flanked by two pairs of side iwans. In the middle of the back wall is a smaller gateway leading in to the mosque also flanked by two blind arches of equal size. The frame of the central iwan is surrounded by a monumental inscription and is capped by domed chatris.

The largest building complex at Fatehpur Sikri is the palace, covering an area approximately 250 m square. The layout is similar to that of other imperial Mughal palaces with three main areas, the public area, the mardana or men's area, and the zenana or women's area. Visitors approaching the palace first enter through a gateway to a large arcaded courtyard with the Diwan-i Amm (public audience hall) in the centre of the west side. In other Mughal palaces this is usually a grand, highly decorated building, but in this case it is a small rectangular pavilion with a central bay at the front to accommodate the emperor. There is no direct access from the courtyard to the pavilion which is raised at least 2 m above the level of the courtyard. This arrangement suggests a greater degree of security than at other palaces, a theme which is repeated throughout the palace particularly in the women's quarters.

The overwhelming impression within is of a Hindu palace, with few indications of Islamic design. Immediately behind the Diwan-i Amm is a large courtyard in the centre of which a cross is marked out; this is a giant version of a Pachisi board which is an ancient Indian game. To the north of this courtyard is the most intriguing section of the palace, called the Diwan-i Khass. This is a square two-storey building with a balcony supported on heavy corbels above which is a chajja also supported on heavy corbels. On the roof there are domed chatris at each corner. Inside the building consists of a two-storey hall with a gallery at first-floor level. Bridges which run diagonally from the corners of the gallery connect to a balcony supported by a central pillar. The pillar is richly carved in the Hindu tradition with a mass of heavy corbels supporting the circular balcony above. This arrangement does not correspond to any other private audience room in a Mughal palace, nor is it encountered elsewhere in Mughal architecture. However, the arrangement of a square building with a central pillar may reflect some Hindu mandala whereby the central column represents the axis of the world; in this, if this was also the place where the emperor sat, he would be identifying himself as the axis of the world. In the context of his conquest of Gujarat Akbar may have been wishing to describe himself in Hindu terms of power.

The arrangement of a central column approached by four bridges is repeated in a less formal setting in the courtyard known as the Anup Talao where there is a square pool with a central island approached by bridges from each of the four sides. The Anup Talao forms the central area of the private residence of the emperor and the main part of the mardana, or men's area. To the south of the pool is a pavilion known as the khwabagh or bedroom although its exact use is not known.

The area to the east of the Anup Talao is the zenana, or women's area, separated from the rest of the complex by a long wall. This is the most magnificent part of the palace and was decorated with painting and rich carvings. One of the most highly decorated buildings of the palace is the Sunahra Makan which is decorated with both geometric and figurative wall paintings. The most visible building in this area is the Panch Mahal, a five-storey pavilion crowned with a domed chatri which overlooks the men's area. The heart of the women's area, however, is known as Jodh Bai's Palace, a rectangular courtyard enclosure separate from the rest of the palace. The enclosure is entered through a single fortified gateway on the east side which leads into the rectangular courtyard. The courtyard is surrounded by arcades on all four sides and in the middle of each is a two-storey house with staircases to the upper floors and apartments. To the north of Jodh Bai's Palace is the Hawa Mahal or wind palace, which is a raised pavilion designed to catch the breeze. Another of the residential areas for women is a structure known as Birbal's House which is located to the west of Jodh Bai's Palace and is thought to be one of the earliest parts of the palace (it is dated by an inscription to 1571).

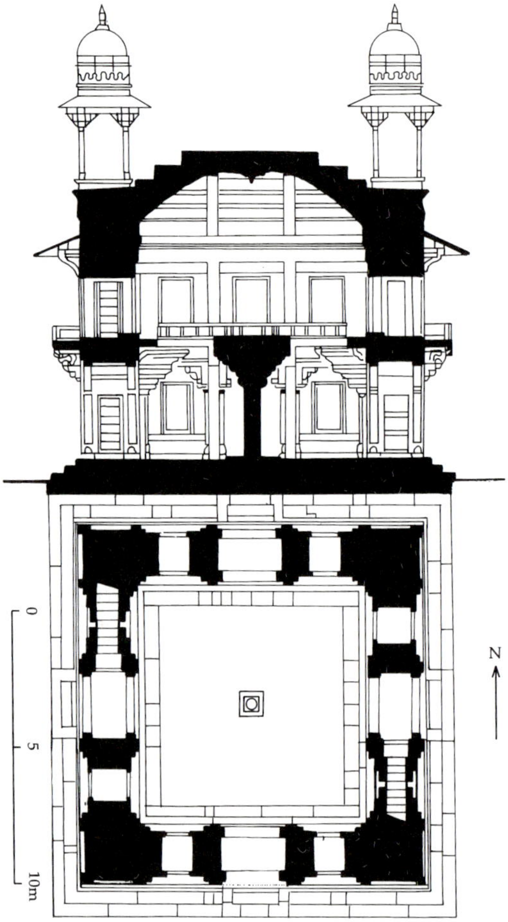

Plan and section of Diwan-i Khass, Fatehpur Sikri

Although the palace and city of Fatehpur Sikri are remarkably well preserved, the design and decoration present a problem of interpretation. First it should be pointed out that, although the city was not inhabited for very long, at least two phases of construction can be discerned. The period during which Fatehpur Sikri was built coincided with two important events, the conquest of Gujarat in 1573 and the convening of an inter-faith conference in 1575. The conquest of Gujarat was one of Akbar's major achievements marking the Mughal domination of all northern India; it is commemorated in the gate of the mosque and in the name of the city. It seems likely that this victory may have been the impetus which changed the city from religious shrine to imperial capital. The conference of 1575 involved participants from the major religions in India at the time and included several Muslim sects, Hindus, Jains, Zoroastrians and Catholic Christians from Goa (Jesuits). The debates took place in a part of the palace known as the Ibadat Khana which is now thought to have disappeared. The end result of the conference was the formulation of a controversial new religion called Din Ilahi of which Akbar was the head. Akbar's interest in other religions may explain why he was prepared to have so much Hindu-style architecture in his palace, in particular the enigmatic form of the Diwan-i-Khass. The design of Fatehpur Sikri is unusual in Mughal architecture as a whole but may be regarded as characteristic of Akbar's reign. Other examples of Akbar's Hindu-style architecture are the Jahangari Mahal in Agra fort, the Ajmer fort in Rajasthan and Akbar's tomb at Sikandara near Agra.

See also: Mughals

Further reading:

M. Brand and G. D. Lowry, *Akbar's India: Art from the Mughal City of Victory*, New York 1985.

—— *Fatehpur Sikri*, Bombay 1987.

S. A. A. Rizvi, *Fatehpur Sikri*, New Delhi 1972.

S. A. A. Rizvi and V. J. Flynn, *Fatehpur Sikri*, Bombay 1975.

G. H. R. Tillotson, *Mughal India*, Architectural Guides for Travellers, London 1990.

Fathy, Hassan

Egyptian architect noted for his use of traditional materials to build modern Islamic structures.

Born in 1900 the son of a wealthy landowner Hassan Fathy was brought up in Cairo, Alexandria and Europe. He studied architecture at the University of Cairo whence he graduated in 1926. In 1927, on his first visit to one of the family estates, he was shocked by the terrible living conditions of the poor and resolved to find a way to house the poor reasonably. He also conceived a love for the Egyptian countryside which was to motivate him for the rest of his life. He realized that imported western material and technology was too expensive and inappropriate for rural housing in Egypt. Instead Fathy thought that mud brick, the traditional building material of Egypt, should be used in modern constructions. Although he realized that traditional designs were sometimes too cramped and dark for modern housing, Fathy argued that this was not the fault of the material.

In 1937 Fathy held exhibitions of his work at Mansoura and Cairo which resulted in several commissions from wealthy patrons. However, these buildings were quite expensive and relied on timber for their flat roofs. With the outbreak of the Second World War and the resulting shortage of timber, he had to find a new method of roofing his houses. On a visit to Upper Egypt Fathy noticed that the Nubian villages were roofed with mud brick vaults produced without wooden centring. The method used was to lean the bricks against an end wall so that all the bricks leant against each other. Fathy employed the local Nubian builders and undertook several projects using these workers. The most important of these projects was the Nasr House in Fayyum and the tourist rest-house at Safaga.

In 1946 Fathy was approached by the Department of Antiquities who wanted to move the people of Gurna in western Luxor out of the ruins of ancient Thebes where they had been living. The Gurnis had been living in the ancient Necropolis for several generations and some lived in the tombs themselves. Nevertheless, the Department of Antiquities issued a decree stating that they wanted the 7,000 people moved to a new settlement which was to be designed by Fathy. The settlement was to contain homes for 1,000 families and include public buildings like a mosque, a covered market, schools and a theatre. The houses were built around courtyards and arranged in neighbourhood groups which had access to the main streets. Although built with traditional materials Fathy made use of earth scientists and structural and mechanical engineers to improve his designs and ensure that they worked. Part of the project was to involve the future inhabitants in the construction, both as a cost-saving measure and so that they were not alienated from their new housing.

However, the project faced considerable difficulties in implementation through the opposition of some of the Gurni Sheikhs and the slow-moving bureaucracy of the Egyptian Antiquities Department.

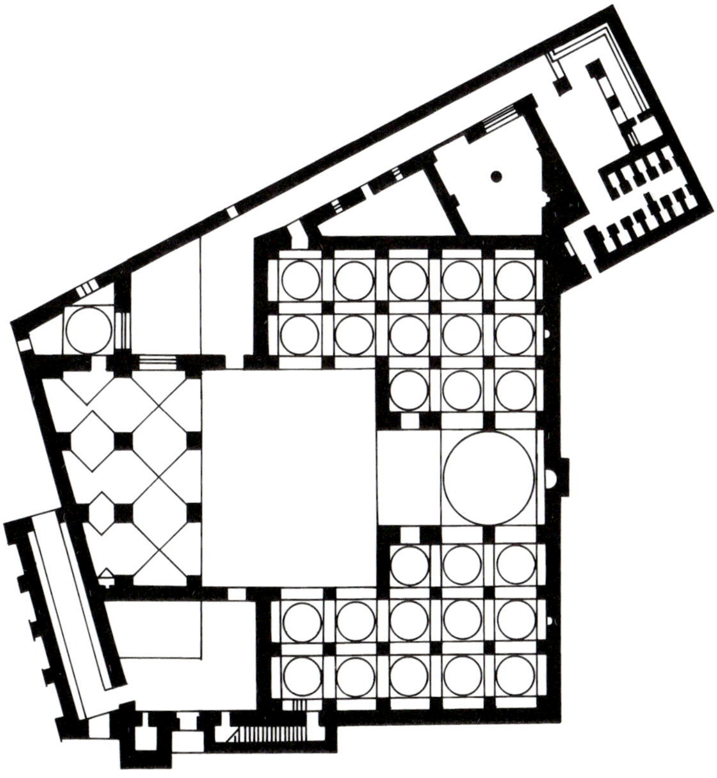

Mosque designed by Hassan Fathy, New Gurna, Egypt

In addition there was general suspicion of a project which involved traditional materials at a time when Modernism was seen as the only way to build. In the end only one-fifth of the project was completed and some parts of the village like the khan and the craft centre remain unused. Nevertheless, the mosque is well used and maintained and the Department of Antiquities has restored the theatre, belatedly realizing the value of Fathy's work. Despite the difficulties New Gurna showed the potential of mud-brick architecture and the value of training people in traditional techniques.

Other important projects carried out by Fathy in the 1950s were at Lu'luat al-Sahara in the Nile Delta and the village schools project. At Lu'lat al-Sahara houses were built in pairs, together with a mosque and a school. The village schools project involved Fathy in designing a school which was to be the prototype for village schools throughout Egypt. The design consisted of domed rooms opening on to courtyards with ventilation shafts to cool the interior during the summer. Unfortunately only two of the schools were built, one at Fares and the other at Edfu.

In 1957 Fathy left Egypt for several years to work for an architectural firm in Athens specializing in the Middle East, and during this time he designed a traditional housing scheme in Iraq. In the early 1960s Fathy returned to Egypt where he undertook two further major projects, a training centre in the Nile Valley and a new town in the Kharga oasis. Unfortunately the training centre was subsequently destroyed because of its bad location and the town known as New Bariz was abandoned because of the 1967 war.

In the 1970s Fathy began writing books about his work which were highly successful in universities throughout the world where the appeal of Modernism was wearing off. He showed that it was possible to design and build desirable residences and functional buildings which respected the traditional values of a culture and were also cheap. Since the 1970s Fathy's work in Egypt was concentrated on private houses and commissions. These buildings were constructed with increasingly sophisticated designs based on harmonic units of measurement derived from the dimensions of the human body. Probably the most important recent commission was for a Muslim community in New Mexico known as Dar al-Salam and built in 1981.

Further reading:

H. Fathy, *The Arab House in the Urban Setting: Past, Present and Future*, Fourth Arab Carreras Lecture, University of Essex, November 1970. London 1972.

—— *Architecture for the Poor*, Chicago and London 1973.

—— *Natural Energy and Vernacular Architecture*, Chicago 1985.

G. Leick, 'Hassan Fathy, architect for the poor', *Egyptian Bulletin* May 1988: 4–8.

J. M Richards, I. Serageldin and D. Rastorfer, *Hassan Fathy*, London 1985.

A. Schkifer, 'Hassan Fathy: a voyage to New Mexico', *Arts and the Islamic World* 1(1): 1982/3.

Fatimids

Caliphs who ruled North Africa, Egypt and Palestine from the tenth to the twelfth century.

The Fatimids were a religious dynasty who claimed descent from the prophet's daughter Fatima. In historical terms the Fatimids belonged to an extreme sect of Shi'a known as Ismailis who emerged as rivals to both the Umayyads of Spain and the Abbasid caliphate in Baghdad. The Fatimids' first successes were amongst the Berber tribes of North Africa who adopted the Fatimids as leaders. Their first conquest destroyed the Aghlabid rulers of Ifriqiyya (Tunisia) in 909 and replaced them with the Fatimid caliph the Mahdi Ubaid Allah. In the following years the Fatimids pursued an aggressive expansionist policy, conquering Tripoli and making raids on the French and Italian coasts. During the reign of the Caliph al-Mu'iz the empire was expanded westwards to include the whole of North Africa to the Atlantic Ocean and eastwards to Egypt and Palestine in 969. The conquest of Egypt began a new phase in Fatimid history with the foundation of Cairo as the imperial capital.

The architecture of the Fatimids can be divided into two periods, the North African period from 909 to 969 and the Egyptian period from 969 to 1171. The North African period was a time of expansion and religious extremism which can be seen in the architecture of the mosques. Examples of early Fatimid mosques are at Ajdabiya in Libiya and Mahdiya in Tunisia. The first of these was the mosque of Mahdiya, which was built like a fortress with two square corner towers flanking a single projecting monumental entrance. The mosque at Ajdabiya had a similar plan but lacks the monumental entrance façade. For ideological reasons neither of these mosques had a minaret, a feature which remained absent until the last years of Fatimid rule in Egypt.

See also: Ajdabiya, Cairo (The Fatimid Period), Libiya, Mahdiya, Tunisia

Fez

Moroccan city noted for its Islamic architecture.

Fez is located in the north-east of Morocco on either side of the Wadi Fez. The city was founded in the late eighth and early ninth century by Moulay Idris the Younger. It was divided into two halves, the east bank representing the late eighth-century city and the west bank representing the city of Moulay Idris. Each of the districts had its own congregational mosque, that on the west bank is known as the Qarawiyyin Mosque and that on the east is known as the mosque of the Andalusians.

The Qarawiyyin Mosque, founded in 859, is the most famous mosque of Morocco and attracted continuous investment by Muslim rulers. There were extensive renovations in 956 by the Umayyad caliph of Spain who also added the minaret. The building did not reach its present form and size (85 by 44 m) until 1135. The prayer hall comprises ten aisles running parallel to the qibla wall and a raised transverse aisle leading to the mihrab. The aisles are covered with gabled wooden roofs covered with roof tiles. There is a dome over the mihrab and the entrance porch in addition to the seven domes which cover the north arcade of the courtyard. The domes are made of elaborate muqarnas vaulting with zig-zag ribbing on the exterior. Inside the mosque is decorated with stucco, the most elaborate being reserved for the area in front of the mihrab. The mosque preserves its twelfth-century minbar which is regarded as one of the finest in the world. The courtyard is decorated with tile mosaic (zilij) dadoes and has a magnificent ablutions pavilion at the west. The pavilion, built in the sixteenth century, rests on eight marble columns and has a tile-covered wooden roof with overhanging eaves. The woodwork of the eaves is of exceptional quality with carved muqarnas mouldings and miniature engaged piers forming blind niches decorated with geometric interlace.

The mosque of the Andalusians has a similar plan to the Qarawiyyin Mosque although it is less well endowed. Like its twin this mosque had a minaret added by the Umayyad caliph Abd al-Rahman, although subsequent restorations were less successful. The other Great Mosque of Fez, the Jama' al-Hamra, was built in 1276 and has aisles aligned perpendicular to the qibla wall in the typical North African style.

From the thirteenth to the seventeenth centuries the madrassa became the principal form of religious architecture. The madrassas of Fez have a standard form of a two-storey courtyard building, with students' cells above and a mosque and teaching rooms below. The courtyards were usually decorated with tile mosaic and had a central pool. The most famous examples are the Saffarin, the Sahrij, the 'Attarin and the Bu 'Inaniya each of which has special features to distinguish it from its neighbours. The Bu 'Inaniya is the most unusual as it has a minaret and an early mechanical clock with gongs.

Most of the houses in Fez date from the seventeenth century or later although they preserve earlier plans. The standard construction material is either rubble stone or baked brick, with wood used for the roofs and decorative details. The usual plan is similar to the madrassas, with a rectangular courtyard and two storeys although the houses are usually less spacious.

See also: Morocco

Further reading:

D. Hill and L. Golvin, *Islamic Architecture in North Africa*, London 1976.
R. Le Tourneau, *Fez in the Age of the Marinides*, tr. B.A.Clement, Norman, USA 1961.
H. Terrasse, *La Mosquée al-Qaraouiyin à Fes*, Paris 1968.
—— *La Mosquée des Andalous à Fes*, Paris (n.d.).

Firuzabad (India)

Deserted fifteenth-century palace city in the Deccan, southern India.

The city was founded in 1400 by the Bahmani ruler Taj-al-Din Firuz Shah. The site is located on the banks of the Bhima river and consists of massive fortification walls which enclose the city on three sides. In the centre of each side are huge vaulted gateways which lead into the ruined central area. There are several buildings still standing within the city, the most impressive being the Jami

Minar i-Zarin, Firuzabad, India

Masjid which includes a huge rectangular courtyard entered via a domed gateway. Next to the Jami Masjid is the main palace area which comprises a series of interconnecting courtyards enclosed within high walls. Other standing monuments include several vaulted chambers, bath houses and a small mosque. The buildings are built in the local Sultanate style with flattened domes, bulbous finials and tapering bartered walls. There is also a notable Central Asian influence in the layout and architecture of the city

See also: Deccan, India

Further reading:

S. Digby, 'Firuzabad: Palace City of the Deccan', in G. Michelle and R. Eaton, *Oxford Studies in Islamic Art VIII*, 1992.

Firuzabad (Iran)

Sassanian capital of Iran near the modern Iranian capital of Tehran. Famous for its royal palace.

fortification

The earliest forms of fortification in Islam were probably towers of a type still seen in Arabia today, of mud brick or dry stone wall, with a tapering profile, built on a circular plan. City walls do not appear to have been common in Muhammad's time and Ta'if is the only city known to have had a wall. The conquest of Syria in the first decades of Islam brought the Arabs into contact with the forts and fortresses of the Roman *limes* (desert border). Many of these fortresses were adapted for residential or official uses, thus Qasr al-Hallabat, Udruh, and Azraq were all remodelled during the Umayyad period. This form was also adapted for new constructions, thus the palaces of Mshatta, Khirbet al-Mafjar and Qasr al-Tuba are all built in the form of fortresses with a square or rectangular enclosure protected with corner and interval towers. The palace of Qasr al-Hayr West was built around the tower of an existing (sixth-century) Byzantine monastery which included a machicolation above the gateway. This feature was later included in the gate of the palace at Qasr al-Hayr East 40 km east of the earlier one.

The influence of Sassanian architecture in this early period should also be noted – thus Qasr Kharana in Jordan is purely Sassanian in form although it is certainly an Umayyad construction. Further east in Iraq is the palace of Ukhaidhir which is the most complete example of early Islamic fortification. The palace forms a large rectangular enclosure with round corner towers and semi-circular buttresses at regular intervals. The area between each buttress comprised two tall arches built flat against the wall, above the arches there is an enclosed parapet containing vertical arrow slits and downward openings between the arches. This is the first example of continuous machicolation, a feature which did not appear in Europe until the fourteenth century.

The eighth-century walls of Baghdad were one of the greatest feats of military engineering in the Islamic world. Although there are no physical remains, descriptions indicate that the city was a vast circle enclosed within a moat and double walls. There were four gates each approached through a bent entrance. The bent entrance and the circular shape of the city are both features which appear to be copied from Central Asian architecture and were not found in contemporary Byzantine architecture.

The best surviving examples of pre-Crusader city fortifications are the wall and gates of Fatimid Cairo built in the eleventh century. There are three gates – the Bab al-Futuh, the Bab Zuwayla and the Bab al-Nasr – each of which is supposed to have been built by a different architect. Each gate consists of two towers either side of a large archway which leads into a vaulted passageway 20 m long with concealed machicolation in the roof. The lower two thirds of each gateway is solid whilst the upper part contains a vaulted room with arrow slits. Another feature of the tenth and eleventh centuries is the development of coastal forts or ribats which were designed to protect the land of Islam from Byzantine attacks. These forts have a similar design to the early Islamic palaces comprising a square or rectangular enclosure with solid buttress towers.

The arrival of the Crusaders at the end of the eleventh century revolutionized military architecture. During this period there is a fusion of European, Byzantine and Islamic principles of fortification which produced castles of enormous size and strength. European introductions were the central keep, curtain walls which follow the contours of a site and massive masonry. Although the majority of castles of the period were built by the Crusaders there are some outstanding examples of twelfth-century Ayyubid castles such as Qal'at Nimrud (Subeibe) and Qal'at Rabad (Ajlun). This new sophistication was also applied to city fortifications, thus the gateway to the citadel of Aleppo has a bent entrance with five right-angle turns approached by a bridge carried on seven arches. Elsewhere in the Islamic world fortifications were also developed in response to the increased Christian threat, thus the Almohads developed sophisticated fortifications with elaborate bent entrances.

With the defeat of the Crusaders in the East the impetus for fortress-building declined and architecture of the Mamluk period was directed mainly to civil purposes. The castles and fortifications which were built tended to be archaic in their military design although elaborate in their decoration and

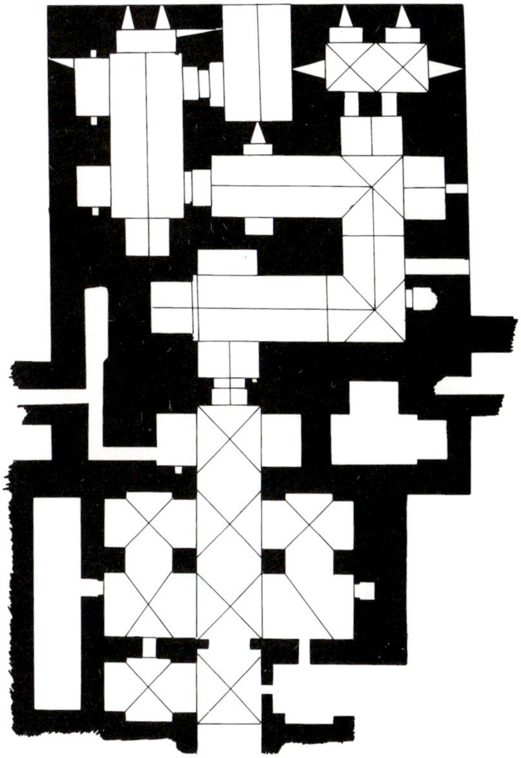

Plan of Ayyubid-period bent entrance to citadel, Aleppo

military imagery. With the introduction of firearms many of the older techniques of fortification were obsolete. From the eighteenth century onwards western techniques were adopted although these were sometimes modified to the local conditions.

See also: Aleppo, Almohads, Crusader architecture, Kharana, Qasr al-Hayr (East), Qasr al-Hayr (West), Ukhaidhir

Further reading:

K. A. C. Creswell, 'Fortification in Islam before AD 1250', *Proceedings of the British Academy* 38: 1953.
T. E. Lawrence, *Crusader Castles*, new edn. ed. R. D. Pringle, Oxford 1988.
R. D. Pringle, 'Crusader castles: the first generation', *Fortress* 1: 1989.
J. Wood, 'The fortifications of Amman citadel', *Fortress* 16: 1993.

France

France's first real contact with Islam was in the eighth century at the battle of Poitiers where the Arab forces were defeated by Charles Martel. The Arab raids into France were not part of a serious attempt to conquer the country and have left few archaeological or architectural remains. However, during the ninth century a series of Muslim Arab forts were established along the Mediterranean coast. The design of these buildings resembled the ribats of North Africa and were intended as bases for naval activity rather than as permanent settlements.

France's first modern encounter with Islam was in the late eighteenth century when Napoleon launched his expedition to Egypt. The military expedition was accompanied by a large team of scholars who introduced the concept of 'Orientalism' to Europe. Conversely, the expedition was also responsible for introducing European ideas and architecture into the region. The colonization of Algeria in the nineteenth century continued France's link with the Islamic world and was also responsible for the introduction of European architecture into North Africa.

Since the Algerian independence in the 1960s there has been a steady flow of North African immigrants to France, which thus now has a large ethnic North African population resident mostly in the larger cities (Paris, Marseilles and Lyons). The earliest mosques in France were converted churches and houses although more recently purpose-built mosques have been erected. The centre of Islamic life in Paris is the Islamic Centre which includes a mosque built in the North African style with horseshoe arches and geometric tile mosaic decoration. The mosque's minaret resembles those of Tlemcen and Marrakesh. The best-known Islamic building in Paris is the Institut du Monde Arabe built in the late 1980s in recognition of the prominent role of Arab culture in France. Although designed by Europeans the building is based on traditional Islamic principles modified for a twentieth-century European setting. The Institut is a rectangular glass building built over a steel frame and located next to the University on the banks of the Seine. One of the more unusual features of the building is the moving metal window grilles, which open and close according to the light. The movements of the window grilles are computer controlled and form geometric Islamic patterns.

Central Mosque, Paris, © *Susan Bailey*

Further reading:

J. Fremeaux, *La France et l'Islam depuis 1789*, Paris 1991.
G. Keppel, *Les Banlieus de l'Islam, Naissance d'une religion en France*, Paris 1991.
J. Novel and H. Tokka, *Institut du Monde Arabe: Une Architecture*, Paris 1990.

Fulbe

Name of West African people speaking Fulbe-related languages.

The Fulbe originated as a nomadic people inhabiting the Sahara areas of West Africa. From the fifteenth century onwards groups of Fulbe began settling in the more fertile regions south of the Sahara and integrating with resident groups. Since the seventeenth century the Fulbe were associated with orthodox Islam and inaugurated jihads in several parts of West Africa. The main areas of Fulbe settlement were the Hausa region of northern Nigeria, the Adamawa region of Cameroon and the Futa-Djallon region of Guinea.

The architectural tradition of the Fulbe originated in the circular wooden-framed tents of their nomadic lifestyle. Elements of this nomadic style are said to have been incorporated into the Hausa architecture of northern Nigeria which is a mixture Fulbe and indigenous Hausa style.

See also: Futa-Djallon, Hausa, West Africa

funduq

North African term for a small, urban shop complex. A typical funduq is a square two-storey structure built around a central courtyard with shops on one floor and store rooms on the other. Equivalent to a khan in the Middle East.

Fustat

The first Islamic capital of Egypt, now within the modern city of Cairo.

Fustat was built on the east bank of the Nile opposite the pre-Islamic Coptic settlement of Babylon. The first permanent settlement on the site was established by the Muslim general ʿAmr ibn al-ʾAs in 643. This first settlement appears to have been a huge encampment of tents arranged into tribal groups separated by open ground. In the centre of the camp was the mosque of ʿAmr which is known as the oldest mosque in Egypt. Little of the original fabric of the mosque survives and in its present form it dates to 827. The settlement was not fortified until 684 when a ditch was dug around the camp in order to defend it against the Umayyad army under Marwan. During the Abbasid period Fustat was no longer the centre of government, although it was still the main commercial centre. The Fatimid conquest and the establishment of Cairo did little to alter this situation and during the tenth century Fustat was known as one of the wealthiest cities of the world. A series of famines and fires during the eleventh and early twelfth century led to the decline of the city. The Crusader siege of 1168 dealt a further blow to the city and in later periods the area of Fustat was redeveloped as a suburb of Cairo within a new wall built on the orders of Salah al-Din.

Excavations in Fustat have revealed complex street and house plans which indicate a high degree of sophistication. The basic unit appears to have been of rooms built around a square or rectangular central courtyard with a central basin. On one or two sides of the courtyard there was an open arcade of three arches, with a wide central arch and two side arches. Behind the central arch there was usually an open iwan flanked by two side rooms. On the other sides of the courtyard there was either an iwan opening directly on to the courtyard or a door to another room. In general there were few connections from one room to another and the courtyard remained the principal means of access.

See also: ʿAmr, Mosque of, Cairo, Egypt

Further reading:

A. Baghat, 'Les Fouilles d'al-Foustat', *Syria* 4: 59–65, 1923.
W. B. Kubiak, *Al-Fustat: Its Foundation and Early Development*, American University in Cairo, 1987.
A. A. Ostrasz, 'The archaeological material for the study of the domestic architecture at Fustat', *African Bulletin* 26: 57–86, 1977.
G. T. Scanlon, 'Fustat expedition preliminary report 1968. Part II', *Journal of the American Research Centre in Egypt* 13: 69–89, 1976.

Futa-Djallon

Islamic region in the highlands of north-west Guinea on border with the Ivory Coast in West Africa.

Before the fifteenth century the primary residents were the Djallonke people who were sedentary agriculturalists. During the fifteenth century various groups of nomadic Fulbe arrived in the area and were absorbed into Djallonke society. During the seventeenth century more Fulbe groups with a strong attachment to Islam arrived from the Muslim state of Macina in the north-east. These newly arrived Fulbe organized themselves into a theocratic state under the direction of the religious leader Karamoko Alfa. During the nineteenth century a jihad was instigated against the non-believers of the area until the whole area was under Islamic control. The new state was divided into nine provinces each under a different leading family with a capital at Timbo.

Despite the strongly orthodox beliefs of the new state, the integration of previous generations of Fulbe into the resident pagan society meant that the architecture was essentially that of the Djallonke modified to fit the requirements of Islam. The essential architectural unit of the pre-Islamic Djallonke is the sudu, or roundhouse, a form which was also adopted for religious shrines and burials. The basic form of the sudu consists of a thatched roundhouse enclosed by concentric walls with two opposed entrances. Each entrance gives access to a semi-circular vestibule and the main central space of the building. Beds consist of moulded mud platforms set against the walls of the central inner space. Several sudu, or house units, form a family compound with a separate one for each wife. The entrance to a compound was through an entrance vestibule which was a round sudu-like construction with a doorway either side. Such vestibules were used to receive visitors in a similar manner to the more familiar entrance rooms of Islamic courtyard houses (compare for example the houses of Timbuktu). The houses of Timbo have the same basic form as traditional Djallonke housing except that the bed is placed opposite the entrance rather than to one side; they also have rectangular storage platforms supported on four posts in the centre of the room. During construction a piece of paper containing a verse of the Quran is buried under each post.

The mosques of Futa-Djallon have the same basic form as the houses although they are built on a larger scale. The earliest mosques were copies of the traditional village meeting-houses which consisted of a raised circular floor enclosed within a low mud wall above which is a steep conical thatched roof made of rafters supported by posts embedded into the wall. When a new mosque is built the older mosque is often converted into a women's area or a Quranic reading room and included within the compound of the new building. As elsewhere in the Islamic world mosques are often associated with the palace of the local ruler, thus at Fougoumba the royal audience hall was directly opposite the mosque. In the mid-nineteenth century a new concept in the architecture of mosques in the region was introduced by al-Hajj Umar who established himself as the ruler of Dingueraye. Educated as a strict Sufi, the new leader attracted a large following which transformed Dingueraye from a small village into a town of 8,000 people. As a result of this huge influx of people a city wall was built to enclose the entire settlement and a new mosque was erected. Although this mosque has not survived, its replacement built on the same site in 1883 is thought to have essentially the same design. Like earlier mosques in the region the Great Mosque at Dingueraye consists of a large thatched roundhouse with a diameter of 30 m and enclosed within a wooden fence. The thatch reaches down almost to the ground so that the ten entrances are only marked by gaps in the wooden fence. The outer wall of the mosque consists of a mud wall containing posts supporting the roof rafters. Immediately inside the outer wall there is circular arrangement of wooden pillars which also supports the roof rafters. The extraordinary arrangement of the interior consists of a square, mud-brick, box-like building in the middle which forms the sanctuary of the mosque. This mud-brick structure has three entrances on each side except for the qibla side where there is only one. The entrance on the qibla side is through an opening in the side of the mihrab and is reserved for the imam. The flat ceiling of the box is supported by rafters resting on sixteen wooden pillars arranged in four rows. In the centre there is a mud-brick pier which protrudes through the roof of the box to support a series of radiating rafters holding up the steep conical thatched roof. This design was later copied in other parts of Futa-Djallon and has now become the typical mosque form of the area. The rationale behind the Dingueraye Mosque design can be deduced from a drawing of the design by al-Hajj Umar. The drawing depicts a magic square and appears to refer only to the central square box and makes no reference to the outer circle of the thatched roof. Local religious leaders also believe that the mosque only consists of the central square

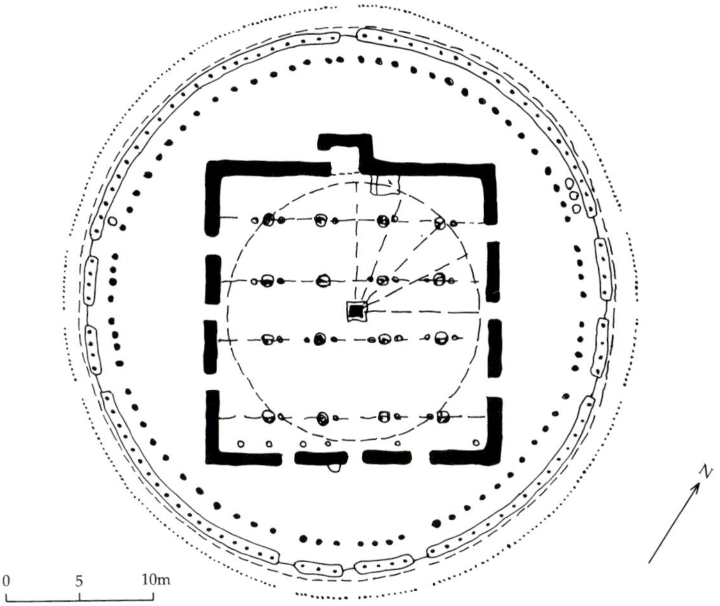

Dingueraye Mosque in Futa-Djallon region, Guinea, West Africa (after Prussin)

and that the conical thatched roof is merely for protection. This suggests the application of a standard Fulbe square mosque in a context where it was environmentally and culturally inappropriate. The thatched superstructure not only protected it from rain but also made it look like an important Djallonke building rather than an alien imposition.

See also: Fulbe, West Africa

G

Gao

West African empire, which flourished in the fifteenth and sixteenth centuries, referred to by contemporary Arabic writers as Kawkaw.

The empire was founded by the Songhay groups who inhabited the banks of the Niger river in the eastern part of the present-day state of Mali. As with the other empires in the region the origin of the kingdom is shrouded in myths and legends, although there seems to be some evidence that the original capital of Gao was 100 km further south. The earliest record of Gao is from the eighth century when it is mentioned as one of the towns in contact with the Algerian city of Tahert. A tenth-century description describes the capital as composed of twin cities like the contemporary capital of Ghana and also describes the ruler as a Muslim.

Despite its strategic position on the trade routes Gao did not achieve imperial status until the fifteenth century when the empire of Mali was in decline. The first ruler to begin the expansion was Ali (1464–92) who conquered Timbuktu from the Berbers and Djenné from the disintegrating empire of Mali. Ali was followed by the most famous ruler of Gao, Askiya Muhammad, who usurped the throne from Ali's son. Askiya Muhammad consolidated the conquests of Ali and centralized the administration of the empire. He was a more convinced Muslim than Ali and made Islam the state religion as well as promoting Timbuktu as a centre of learning. In 1528 at the age of 85 Askia was deposed by his son and died ten years later in 1538. Following Askia there were a succession of short reigns between 1528 and 1591 which ended with the Moroccan invasion and the destruction of the Songhay Empire of Gao.

Fortunately the ancient capital of Gao has survived to provide some of the best examples of medieval architecture in West Africa. Three main groups of remains can be identified, Gao, Old Gao and Gao-Sané. It has been suggested that the twin-city configuration referred to in early accounts of Gao may be confirmed by the location of Gao-Sané 6 km east of the rest of the city. It is believed that Gao-Sané represents the Muslim quarter of the town due to its position facing the trade routes to North Africa. Old Gao probably represents the remains of the fourteenth-century city during the period when it was ruled by the empire of Mali. Excavations in Old Gao have revealed a large rectangular mosque (approximately 40 m wide) built of mud brick which was dated to 1325. In the centre of the west side is a deep circular mihrab (about 3 m in diameter) built of baked brick with a small doorway (a half-metre wide) on the north side. Behind the mihrab on the outside are three rectangular tombs one of which contains a headstone dated 1364. South of Old Gao is the main town which was the city of Askiya Muhhamad with its famous mausoleum contained within the courtyard of the Great Mosque. The Great Mosque is located within an area of cemeteries containing Kufic-inscribed tombstones dating from the early twelfth century. Some of the oldest tombstones were found within a subterranean vault made of baked brick similar to that used in the mihrab of the excavated mosque at Old Gao. The use of baked brick is significant in a context where they would have been very difficult to produce.

Undoubtedly the most important monument in Gao is the Great Mosque containing the tomb of Askiya Muhammad. The mosque consists of a large rectangular enclosure (45 by 50 m) with a sanctuary four bays deep. In the middle of the east wall of the sanctuary is a pair of niches one of which is the mihrab whilst the other contains a fixed minbar. The centre of the courtyard is occupied by the tomb of Askiya Muhammad, a huge pyramidical earth construction resting on a base measuring 14 by 18 m. The tomb consists of three steps or stages reaching a height of just over 10 m above ground level. A stair ramp made of split palms leads up the east side of the structure to reach the top. The appearance of the tomb is enhanced by

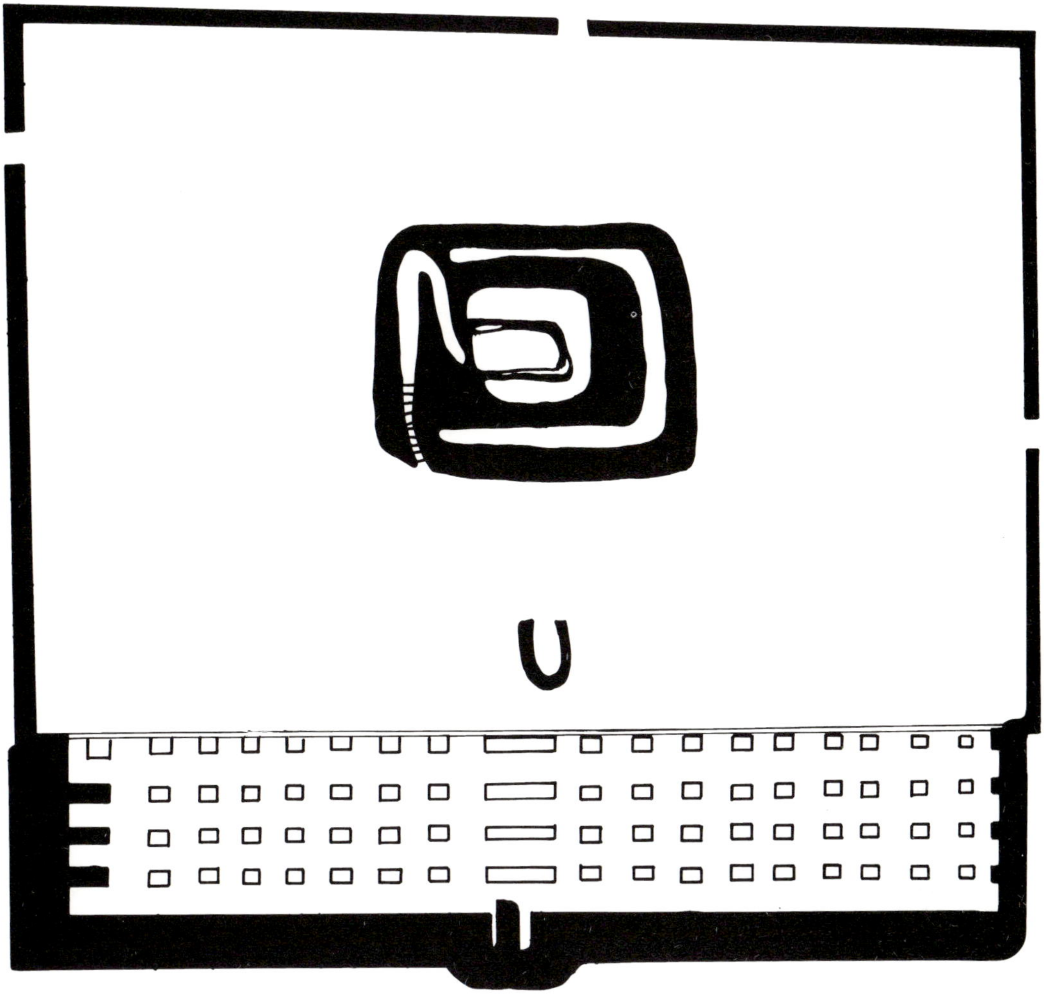

Plan of mosque and tomb of Askiya Muhammad, Gao, West Africa (after Prussin)

the many toron, or stakes, made of acacia wood which project from each side. A description of the monument from 1852 mentioned another eastern tower which was in ruins at the time; this may have been the mihrab tower which also functioned as a minaret. It seems likely that with the collapse of the eastern mihrab/minaret tower stairs were cut into the tomb of Askiya Muhammad so that this could function as the place for the call to prayer. In view of Askiya Muhammad's strong attachment to Ibadi teachings it is thought that the architectural origins of this tomb may be found in various Ibadi zawiyas in the Mzab region of southern Algeria. The design of these three-tier constructions is said to derive ultimately from the minaret of the Great Mosque at Qairawan. One of the best examples is at Tidikelt in southern Algeria and consists of three superimposed stages each with a crenellated parapet. In addition to the orthodox Muslim influences on the design of the tomb, it should be noted that it also resembles the ancestral tumuli of the pre-Islamic Songhay past. This connection is reinforced by the toron projecting from the sides of the tomb.

In addition to Gao itself, there are a number of towns which contain monumental remains of the Songhay Empire. One of the best examples is the city of Tendirma in Mali built for Amar-Komdiago the brother of Askiya Muhammad in 1497. The construction of the city was carried out by Manding craftsmen under the direction of Ouahab Bari. Standing remains at Tendirma include the massive palace walls and the Great Mosque which is substantially unchanged since the Moroccan invasion of the sixteenth century. The mosque is built out of spherical mud bricks with the use of split palm and acacia wood for roof timbers. The most remarkable feature of the mosque is the mihrab tower which consists of a sloping cone with a flat surface on the side facing the mosque. Like the mausoleum of Askiya Muhammad the outer surface of the minaret is covered with projecting toron made of acacia wood. Other examples of Songhay imperial architecture can be seen in the mosques of Katsina and Birni in northern Nigeria. The Katsina minaret is particularly unusual and consists of a central square shaft with stair ramps ascending around the four sides. The minaret bears a striking similarity to the Malwiyya in Samarra although stylistically it is more closely related to the minaret of the Great Mosque in Qairawan.

See also: Songhay, West Africa

Further reading:

T. Insol, 'Looting the antiques of Mali: the story continues at Gao', *Antiquity* 67: 628–32, 1993.
——, 'A preliminary reconnaisance and survey at Gao, the Republic of Mali', *Nyame Akuma* 39; 40–3, 1993.
R. Mauny, 'La Tour et la mosquée de l'Askia Mohammed à Gao', *Notes Africaines* 47: 66–7, 1950.
—— 'Notes archéologiques au sujet de Gao', *Bulletin IFAN* 13: 837–52, 1951.
J. Sauvaget, 'Les Epitaphes royales de Gao', *Bulletin IFAN* 12: 418–40, 1950.
M.–M. Vire, 'Notes sur trois epigraphes royales de Gao', *Bulletin IFAN* 20B (3–4): 459–600, 1958.

gardens

Gardens have often been an integral feature of Islamic architectural design, particularly for palaces.

Several Umayyad palaces seem to have incorporated gardens as part of their design. At Khirbet al-Mafjar in the Jordan valley there is a large square pool with a central pavilion on columns which would have formed the centrepiece of a garden. At Qasr al-Hayr West it is likely that the immediate vicinity of the palace had a garden whilst there was a large walled garden enclosure to the west of the main building. The exact function of some of the early Islamic gardens is not always clear and some may have been purely for producing vegetables. In Islamic Spain the garden was an integral part of the palatial design of Madinat al Zahra and reached its peak in the gardens of Granada. The development of formal gardens became an art form in Iran from at least the fourteenth century as can be seen from their frequent depiction in miniature paintings of the period. Under the Timurids gardens became a priority for royal residences which were often no more than pavilions in large formal gardens. The Mughals of India acquired their interest in gardens from the Timurids and developed the idea of a memorial garden which would surround a tomb.

From the sixteenth century garden cities became fashionable throughout the Islamic world with cities such as Isfahan in Iran or Meknes in Morocco. Further east in Java and Indonesia gardens were an essential part of the pre-Islamic Hindu tradition and continued to be built by the Muslim sultans.

Further reading:

A. Petruccioli (ed.), *The Garden as a City: The City as a Garden*, Journal of the Islamic Environmental Design Research Centre, Rome 1984.
N. Titley and F. Wood, *Oriental Gardens*, BL Humanities, 1991.

Gedi

Ruined Islamic city near Malindi in Kenya, one of the first Islamic settlements in East Africa to be systematically investigated by archaeologists starting in 1945.

Gedi is unusual as it is the only major settlement on the East African coast not to be built directly on the sea-shore – instead it is located 6 km inland and 3 km from the nearest navigable creek. The city seems to have been founded in the thirteenth century although most of the standing remains date from the fifteenth century. By the sixteenth century the city seems to have been abandoned, although it was briefly resettled in the seventeenth only to be finally abandoned after the attacks of the migrating Galla tribesmen.

The site stands on a rocky spur which dominates the surrounding countryside. The city covers an area of 45 acres and was contained within a town wall which enclosed a Great Mosque, seven smaller mosques, a palace and several private mansions, in addition to many smaller houses which must have been made of wattle and daub. The ruins also contain the remains of substantial coral stone tombs one of which carries an inscription dated to 1399.

The Great Mosque is one of the best-preserved examples of its type in East Africa. It is constructed in the typical East African style with a flat concrete roof supported on rectangular stone piers and doorways on the west and east sides. There are three rows of six piers with the middle row aligned on the central axis in line with the mihrab. The mosque has a fairly wide plan achieved by placing transverse beams between piers and spanning the distance between beams by longitudinally placed rafters. This differs from the more usual technique of placing beams longitudinally with transverse rafters as was used in the smaller mosques at Gedi and elsewhere on the coast. The mihrab is a fine example of the developed form of the early type of coastal mihrab. It is built out of dressed undersea or reef coral and set in a rectangular panel surrounded with an architrave carved in a cable pattern. The mihrab is decorated with eleven inset blue and white porcelain bowls, five in the spandrel above the niche, two in the pilasters and six in the niche itself. The edge of the mihrab is recessed five times before the niche itself which is a plain, undecorated semi-circular apse. Immediately to the east is a built-in stone minbar.

Sometime in the sixteenth century a separate area for women was screened off at the back of the mosque. To the east of the prayer hall is a veranda opening onto the ablutions court which contains a tank fed by a well, footscrapers, a latrine and a staircase to the roof. The other mosques at Gedi are all much smaller, narrower structures consisting of a simple prayer room and ablutions area to the east.

The palace of Gedi is a large complex probably built for the Sultan of Malindi. It stands amongst several other grand houses which probably housed ministers or other members of the royal family. The palace essentially consists of two main areas, the original palace and the northern annexe. It has a monumental entrance leading via a small courtyard into the main reception area, which is a long open courtyard aligned east–west. The sultan's private residence was to the south of this whilst the harem was located on the west side, although it only connects with the main palace via a small doorway from a courtyard at the back of the sultan's quarters.

The houses at Gedi are of interest because they show a development in form from the fourteenth to the sixteenth centuries and are the prototype for the more famous Swahili houses of the eighteenth century. The earliest houses consist of entrances into a long, narrow sunken courtyard from which a single entrance would lead into a reception room behind which were bedrooms and a store room. In later houses the courtyards became bigger and often an extra 'domestic' courtyard was added at the back.

See also: coral, East Africa, Kenya, Lamu

Further reading:

J. Kirkman, *The Arab City of Gedi: Excavations at the Great Mosque. Architecture and Finds*, Royal National Parks of Kenya, Oxford 1954.

—— *Gedi: The Tomb of the Dated Inscription H.802/AD 1399*, Royal Anthropological Society of Great Britain and Ireland, Occasional Paper no. 14, London 1960.

—— *Gedi: The Palace*, Studies in African History no.1, The Hague 1963.

Germany

Before the Second World War there were few Muslims in Germany although during the nineteenth century the Ottoman ambassador in Berlin established a mosque and cemetery. There were, however, a number of Islamic-type buildings in Germany influenced by the growing interest in Orientalism. The most famous example is the water-pumping station at Potsdam (1841–5) built in the form of an Egyptian Mamluk mosque. Perhaps a more suprising example is the tobacco factory at Dresden where the minarets are used as factory chimneys.

After the Second World War the German government made an arrangement with Turkey for Turks to come to Germany as temporary 'Guest workers'. By the 1970s many of these Turkish workers had become established as permanent residents although with no official status. Present estimates suggest that Germany has a Turkish minority of two to three million, many of whom live in the industrial towns of the Ruhr valley. The first mosques were usually converted houses and were architecturally indistinct from the surrounding buildings. More recently purpose-built mosques have been erected, usually in a modern Turkish style.

See also: France, Great Britain, USA

Further reading:

S. Koppelkamm, *Der imaginaire Orient: Exotische Bauten des -achtzen und neunzen Jahrhunderts in Europa*, Berlin 1987.

W. A. Barbieri, 'Citizenship and Group Rights: "Guestworkers" in the Federal Republic of Germany', Unpublished PhD. dissertation, Yale University 1992.

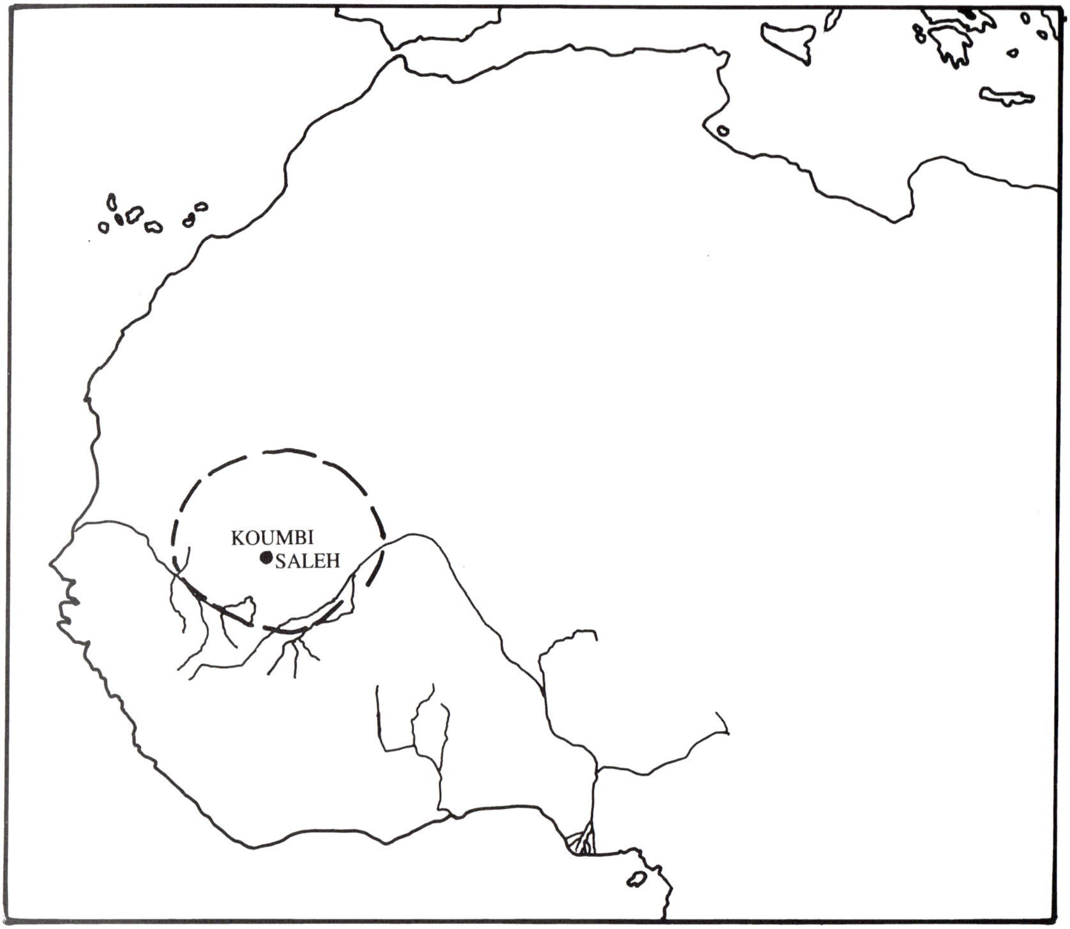

West Africa showing the empire of Ghana in the ninth century CE

Ghana

Medieval West African kingdom heavily influenced by Islam which flourished between the eighth and eleventh centuries.

Like other medieval West African kingdoms the empire of Ghana was not so much a centralized territorial entity as a network of different kinship groups, castes and age sets owing allegiance to the ruler of a powerful dynasty. Despite its rather diffuse nature the empire was well known in North Africa by the end of the eighth century and was marked on a map made before 833. The fame of the city derived from its role as the major supplier of gold which during the eighth and ninth centuries was sent via Sijilmasa and Tahert to North Africa. Although the empire never became Muslim the ruler had a high degree of respect for Islam and many of the more important positions of government were filled by Muslims.

In 990 disruption of the trade routes led the ruler of Ghana to launch an expedition to capture the oasis city of Awdaghast from the Berbers and impose a black governor. However, in 1077 the capital of Ghana was attacked by the Berber Almoravids who massacred many of the inhabitants and forced the remainder to convert to Islam. Whilst this conquest destroyed Ghana as an empire, a reduced kingdom of this name continued to survive into the twelfth century; al-Idrisi writing in 1154 described the capital as the most extensive and thickly populated town of the blacks with the most widespread commerce. However, in 1204 there was another disaster when the town was sacked by the Sonnike ruler Sumaguru Kante. This led to the dispersion of a large number of Ghana's inhabitants and the foundation of a new settlement known as Oualata which replaced Ghana as the main caravan terminal. However, Ghana recovered and continued to function as an important trade centre until 1240 when it was conquered and incorporated into the empire of Mali. Nevertheless, Ghana continued to function as a semi-independent state within the Mali Empire and its ruler even retained the title of king.

An eleventh-century description by the Andalusian writer al-Bakri describes the capital as divided into two cities, a Muslim city and a royal city. The Muslim city had twelve mosques including a Friday mosque each with its own imam and muezzin (one who announces the call to prayer). The royal city was a pagan city containing the palace of the king within a sacred grove or wood. The houses in the city are described as being built with stone and acacia wood. The exact location of the capital is not known and there is some dispute about whether the state had a fixed capital in the modern sense. However, the site of Koumbi Saleh in Mauritania is regarded as one of the principal capitals if not the main capital.

Excavations at Koumbi Saleh, begun in 1914, have revealed a vast set of stone ruins which are still in need of full interpretation although the evidence suggests a period of occupation from the seventh to the seventeenth century. One of the most interesting discoveries is a square tomb chamber measuring just over 5 m on each side with a column recessed into each of the external corners. There were originally four openings into the chamber but three of these were subsequently blocked up leaving a single entrance on the east side. Just inside the entrance are a set of steps made of fired brick which lead down into a subterranean chamber containing spaces for three sarcophagi. Parallels have been suggested with Ibadi tombs in North Africa and the Bab Lalla Rayhana entrance to the Great Mosque of Qairawan which also employs engaged corner columns. Elsewhere excavation has revealed a row of shops connected to houses. The shops are open onto the street front whilst every other unit opens at the back onto an entrance vestibule lined with triangular niches. These vestibules consist of long narrow rooms with a bed platform at one end and stairs to another floor at the opposite end. The rooms (7 to 8 m long and 1.5 to 2 m wide) are placed side by side with two doorways in each side either side of a central pillar. The other Ghanaian city which has been excavated is the oasis city of Awdaghast also in Mauritania. The architecture here is similar to that at Koumbi Saleh with triangular niches and long narrow rooms. Although the evidence from archaeology is limited it appears that Awdaghast was inhabited from the seventh to the thirteenth century.

See also: West Africa

Gok Madrassa

The Gok Madrassa is one of the most famous buildings in the north-east Anatolian city of Sivas. Built in 1271 the building has a cruciform plan with a central open court opening onto two-storey cloisters. The most significant part of the design is the façade which comprises two corner buttress towers with a central entrance flanked by two tall minaret towers. The portal itself is recessed within a tall muqarnas niche which itself is set within a carved stone frame. Both the entrance portal and the corner buttress towers are decorated in deep relief stone carving which is characteristic of the thirteenth-century architecture of the city. The twin minarets above the entrance are built of baked brick with vertical flutes and large muqarnas corbelled balconies.

Gol Gumbaz

Mausoleum of Muhammad Adil Shah II (1627–57), one of the major Islamic monuments of India.

The tomb, located in the city of Bijapur, southern India, was built in 1659 by the famous architect, Yaqut of Dabul. The structure consists of a massive square chamber measuring nearly 50 m on each side and covered by a huge dome 37.9 m in diameter making it the largest dome in the Islamic world. The dome is supported on giant squinches supported by groined pendentives whilst outside the building is supported by domed octagonal corner towers. Each tower consists of seven storeys and the upper floor of each opens on to a round gallery which surrounds the dome.

In the centre of the chamber is a square raised podium approached by steps in the centre of each side. In the centre of the podium are the tombs of Muhammad Adil Shah II and his relations. To the west of the podium in a large apse-like projection is the mosque, also raised slightly above the floor level of the chamber.

See also: Bijapur, Deccan, India

Granada

City in south-west Spain famous as the capital of the last Muslim state in Spain.

Granada is located high up in the mountains near the Sierra Nevada and rose to prominence after the other Muslim states were defeated in the thirteenth century. During this time from 1231 to 1492 Granada was ruled by the Nasirid dynasty who survived by maintaining alliances with Christian dynasties.

Undoubtedly the most famous building in the city is the Alhambra which has a claim to being one of the most beautiful buildings of the Islamic world. The palace is located on a rocky spur which dominates the rest of the city. Although contained within a single enclosure the Alhambra is not a single palace but a complex of palaces built over hundreds of years. The earliest parts of the complex date from the twelfth century although most of the buildings were erected in the fourteenth or fifteenth centuries. On the opposite side of the valley from the Alhambra is the Generalife palace which is sometimes erroneously thought to be part of the Alhambra. Although now covered with gardens the Generalife was originally a country estate for the Nasirids.

Some remains of the eleventh-century walls are still standing together with five of the city gates, the Puerta Nueva, the Puerta de Elvira, the Puerta de Fajalauza and the Puerta Hizna Roman. Architecturally the most interesting of these gates is the Puerta Nueva which combines a bent entrance with an upward sloping ramp to slow down potential attackers. Within the walls several public buildings survive including the hammam (Bañuelo Carrera del Darro) which is one of the best examples remaining in Spain. Also within the city is the Casa del Carbón (coal exchange) formerly known as the Funduq al-Yadida (new market) which is one of the few surviving khans in Spain. It has a monumental portico decorated with plaster and decorative brickwork within which the entrance is set below a set of paired windows. The interior of the building consists of a square courtyard with three storeys of arcades on each of the four sides containing sixty rooms. In addition to public buildings several Muslim houses survive in the Albaicín Quarter of the city.

With the exception of the one in the Alhambra there are few remains of Granada's many mosques, although traces can be found in some of the churches. The church of San Salvador is built over a tenth-century mosque and remains of the ablutions court and the minaret can still be seen. The church of San Sebastian is a converted rabita, or hermitage, and is the only example of its type in Spain. It consists of a square courtyard covered with a ribbed dome supported on squinches.

See also: Alhambra, Spain

Further reading:

F. Prieto-Moreno, *Los Jardines de Granada*, Madrid 1952.

E. Sordo and W. Swaan, *Moorish Spain: Córdoba, Seville and Granada*, London 1963.

Great Britain (United Kingdom)

Britain's main source of contact with the Islamic world has been through the British Empire and in particular the Indian subcontinent. India was acquired by Britain in the eighteenth century and was one of Britain's earliest colonial acquisitions. As with most colonial encounters each side was influenced by the culture and architecture of the other. In India the British built the city of Calcutta as capital complete with Anglo-Indian mosques. In Britain the architecture of India was evoked in several buildings, the most famous of which is the Royal Pavilion at Brighton. Externally the building resembles a late Mughal palace with bulbous domes, chajjas and chatris, although internally it is decorated like a Chinese palace.

With the Independence of India in 1948 and the division of the subcontinent into Pakistan and Bangladesh a large number of immigrants came to Britain. Indians now make up the majority of Britain's Muslim population although they are mostly concentrated in cities and the larger towns. The first mosques in Britain were converted churches or houses although more recently (since 1980) many new mosques have been built, financed partly by British Muslim communities and partly by donations from oil-rich Arab countries. The best-known mosque in Britain is in Regents Park in London although other cities like Bradford also have prominent new mosques. In the typical modern British mosque there is usually an emphasis on the dome which is often covered in metal. Minarets are usually quite small and are often non-functional (i.e not used for the call to prayer).

Greece

Mountainous country in south-eastern Europe which for over 400 years formed a part of the Ottoman Empire.

The position of Greece opposite Libiya and Egypt and its exposure to the east Mediterranean sea meant that it was exposed to Muslim raids from the beginnings of Islam. Crete in particular was open to attack and was briefly occupied by Muslim forces as early as 674. Between 827 and 961 Crete was again captured by Muslim forces who used the island as a base for pirate raids against the rest of Greece. At some time during the tenth century Athens seems to have had an Arabic settlement with its own mosque, traces of which have been excavated.

It was not, however, until the rise of the Ottomans that Greece was fully brought under Islamic rule. Different parts of Greece were incorporated into the Ottoman Empire at different times and for varying degrees of time. Thus the south and central part of the country (Peleponnesus and Ionnia) were conquered in 1460 but lost to the Venetians between 1687 and 1715 after which they were recaptured and remained part of the empire for another 100 years until the Greek War of Independence in 1821–9. Parts of northern Greece, however, were conquered by the Ottomans as early as 1360 and by 1430 the whole of the northern part of the country was under Turkish rule which lasted until 1912. There was little Turkish settlement in Greece with the exception of Thrace where colonists were brought in soon after the conquest.

There are comparatively few remains of Turkish rule in central and southern Greece although Athens contains a few notable examples. The

Fethie Cami, Athens © Cherry Pickles

oldest standing mosque in Athens is the Fethie Cami built in the late fifteenth century; the building is unusual because in plan it closely resembles an Orthodox church. The last Ottoman mosque built in Athens is the Djisdaraki Cami erected in 1759, a building with a distinctive Ottoman form, consisting of a triple-domed portico and a square domed prayer hall. In addition to mosques the Ottomans also built baths and madrassas in Athens none of which has survived although remains of the city wall built in 1788 by Ali Hadeski can still be seen. The islands of Greece, in particular Crete and Rhodes, have traces of the Ottoman occupation although as with southern mainland Greece there was no substantial Turkish settlement.

Northern Greece can be divided into three main areas, Epirus in the west near Albania, Macedonia in the middle and Thrace on the east side bordering Turkey. The area of Epirus has few traces of Turkish rule outside its capital at Ioannina and the city of Arta. At the centre of Ioannina is the fortress of Frourion which was substantially repaired in the eighteenth century by the famous Ottoman governor Ali Pasha. Within the citadel is the mosque of Aslan Pasha built in 1688 which, with its position overlooking the lake, is one of the most romantic Turkish buildings in the Balkans. Whilst Turkish settlement in Ioannina was limited to the governor and his garrison, the town of Arta had a new Muslim suburb added to it. This suburb, now in a state of disrepair, is one of the best examples of Ottoman town planning with its mosque, imaret and hammam.

Macedonia has the highest concentration of Ottoman monuments in Greece in the five cities of Thessaloniki, Seres, Kavalla, Yenice-i Vardar and Verria. In the regional capital, Thessaloniki, the most significant remains are the Hamsa Beg Cami and the Imaret Cami both of which date to the fifteenth century. In addition the city has three large hammams and a bedestan still standing. The other towns of Macedonia are less well known although each contains important monuments such as the aqueduct of Suleyman the Magnificent in Seres.

The oldest Ottoman monuments in Greece are to be found in the region of Thrace where there is still a significant Muslim population. One of the buildings still in use is the Komotini Mosque built in 1610 which is the only Balkan mosque to have large-scale Iznik tile decoration. Other monuments in the area include the Oruc Beg Hammam in Dimetoka built in 1398 and the Munschi Feridun Ahmed Pasha Hammam built in 1571.

See also: Ottomans

Further reading:

K. W. Arafat, 'Ottoman Athens', *Arts and the Islamic World* 4 no. 4: 1987/8.

—— 'Ottoman Ioannina', *Arts and the Islamic World* no. 20: 1991.

E. H. Ayverdi, 'Yunanistan', in *Avrupa'da Osmanli Mimari Eserleri* 4 book 5, Istanbul 1981.

M. Kiel, 'Islamic Architecture in the Balkans', *Arts and the Islamic World* 4 no. 3: 1987.

G. Soteriou, 'Arabic remains in Athens in Byzantine times', *Social Science Abstracts* 2 no. 2360: 1930.

Gujarat

Predominantly Hindu coastal region of western India with distinctive Islamic architecture.

Gujarat is a fertile low-lying region located between Pakistan, Rajasthan and the Indian Ocean. The position of the region on the Indian Ocean has meant that it has always had extensive trading contacts particularly with the Arabian peninsula. It is likely that the first Muslims in Gujarat arrived sometime in the eighth century although there is little published archaeological evidence of this. The oldest standing mosques in the area are located at the old seaport of Bhadresvar in western Gujarat and have been dated to the mid-twelfth century although they may stand on older foundations.

The first Muslim conquest of the area took place at the end of the thirteenth century under the Ala al-Din the Khaliji sultan of Delhi. The earliest monument from this period is the Jami Masjid at Cambay which includes columns taken from ruined Hindu and Jain temples. The form of the mosque resembles that of the Quwwat al-Islam Mosque in Delhi with a rectangular courtyard with gateways on three sides and an arched screen in front of the sanctuary on the west side. Other early mosques built in a similar style include those of Dholka Patan and Broach all of which are located close to the coast. During the fifteenth century many mosques, tombs and other monuments were built in the regional capital Ahmadabad, the most significant of which are the Jami Masjid and the tomb of Ahmad Shah. These buildings incorporate many features from Hindu temple architecture including projecting balconies, perforated jali screens and square decorated columns. Monuments of the sixteenth century contain the same Hindu and Islamic elements combined in a more developed fashion as can be seen in the Jami Masjid of Champaner built in 1550. The Mughal conquest in the mid-sixteenth century brought Gujarat into the mainstream of architectural development. However, the architecture of the region exerted a considerable influence on the Mughal emperor Akbar, who built the city of Fatehpur Sikri in Gujarati style.

The secular architecture of Gujarat is mostly built of wood and characterized by elaborately carved screens and overhanging balconies. Another characteristic feature of the region is the use of step wells, or vavs, which consist of deep vertical shafts, approached via recessed chambers and steps. Sometimes these were very elaborate structures with multiple tiers of steps.

See also: Ahmadabad, India, Mughals, Qutb Minar

Further reading:

Z. A. Desai, 'Some Mughal inscriptions from Gujarat', *Epigraphia Indica: Arabic and Persian Supplement,* 1970, 63–92.

J. Jain-Neubauer, *The Stepwells of Gujarat in Art Historical Perspective,* New Delhi 1981.

E. Koch, '[The] Influence [of Gujarat] on Mughal architecture', in *Ahmadabad,* ed. G. Michell and S. Shah, Bombay 1988, 168–85

M. Shokooy, M. Bayani-Wolpert and N. H. Shokooy, *Bhadresvar: The Oldest Islamic Monuments in India,* part of Studies in Islamic Art and Architecture, Supplements to Muqarnas, vol. 2, Leiden 1988.

guldasta

An ornamental pinnacle in the shape of flowers.

gunbad

An Iranian and Mughal term for dome, usually used for a domed tomb.

H

Hadramawt

A large wadi in Yemen with distinctive mud-brick architecture. It runs from west to east and meets the Indian Ocean at Qishn.

The wadi is exceptionally fertile and has been settled since ancient times. The tall mud-brick tower houses, which from a distance resemble skyscrapers are the most characteristic feature of the architecture. The form of these houses is probably derived from the stone-built tower houses of the highlands adapted into a mud-brick form for the plains at the bottom of the wadi. The best example of this architecture is the city of Shibam which has houses over eight storeys high. The exceptional height of the Shibam houses may partly be due to the wall which encloses the city, for whilst this provides protection it limits the available building land. The houses are usually built on stone foundations with mud-brick walls tapering from one metre at the bottom to a quarter of a metre at the top. The strongest part of the house is the stair-well which is often built of stone to the full height of the house. The exteriors have wooden window screens and ornamental relieving arches, and the upper parts of the houses are generally whitewashed.

The main door for each house has a wooden latch attached to a cord enabling the door to be opened from the apartments above. The ground floors of the houses are either storerooms or shops whilst the first-floor rooms may be used for animal stalls. The second floor was used a reception area for business, and the rooms above were private apartments; the lower parts of the private rooms were functional whilst those at the top were reception rooms and open-air terraces. The reception room or majlis is usually a tall room decorated with carved plaster designs which may include a mihrab niche. At the upper levels there are often doorways to neighbouring houses so that women may visit each other without having to go out on to the streets. There are efficient waste-disposal systems with separate chutes for water and sewage. The age of the houses is difficult to determine although locally they are thought to last 300 years or more after which they will be replaced with another house on the same spot.

See also: Yemen

Further reading:

J. F. Breton, L. Badre, R. Audouin and J. Seigne, 'Le Wadi Hadramout', *Prospections*, 1978–9.

R. Lewcock, *Wadi Hadramawt and the Walled City of Shibam*, UNESCO, Paris 1986.

M. Raemakers, 'Towns and architecture in the Hadramaut', *Journal of the Royal Central Asian Society* (London) 40:246 ff., 1953.

Hagia Sophia (Aya Sophia; Church of Holy Wisdom)

Central church of Constantinople turned into a mosque after the Ottoman conquest and now a museum.

The first Hagia Sophia built in 360 by Constantine II had a timber roof and was burnt down in 404. This was replaced by a second building which was also burnt down a hundred years later. The present structure was founded in 537 although the huge central dome fell down and was replaced by the present construction in 558. The plan of the building consists of a large central dome (32 m diameter) flanked by two huge semi-domes supported by smaller subsidiary domes; the two aisles are separated from the main area by a marble colonnade.

In 1453 the building was converted into a mosque by the addition of a wooden minaret; by the end of the sixteenth century the building was adorned with four tall pointed stone minarets. During the sixteenth century Selim II had his tomb built next to the building and in the seventeenth century Sultan Ahmet added a madrassa. The cathedral is important to Islamic architecture because its grandeur inspired Ottoman architects. The huge dome in particular impressed the Ottomans who, during the sixteenth century, built a number of mosques to rival the church of St Sophia, the most notable of which were the Süleymaniye and the Selimiye.

See also: Istanbul, Ottomans

Further reading:

W. S. George, *The Church of St Eirene at Constantinople*, Oxford 1912.

R. L. Van Nice and W. Emerson, 'Hagia Sophia and the first minaret erected after the conquest of Istanbul', *American Journal of Archaeology* 54, 1950.

Hajj routes

Special roads or routes which are taken by pilgrims on their way to Mecca.

Hajj, or pilgrimage, is one of the five pillars of Islam along with prayer five times a day, fasting, the giving of alms, and bearing witness that there is only one true God. Each Muslim is required to attempt at least once in a lifetime to visit the holy cities of Medina and Mecca. It is well known that Mecca was an important ritual centre before Islam and that it would have been visited as a shrine. Under Islam, however, the importance of visiting Mecca was greatly increased especially as the numbers of Muslims increased around the world.

Until the advent of rail and more recently air travel, the Hajj was a very arduous and risky undertaking requiring considerable preparation. Although coming from diverse locations, most pilgrims would have to make the last part of their journey through Arabia on one of several major Hajj routes. The main routes were Damascus to Mecca, Cairo to Mecca via the Sinai, Basra to Mecca, Sanca to Mecca coastal route, Sanca to Mecca inland route and Oman to Mecca via one of the Yemeni routes. Of these routes the most important were those that led from Damascus, Baghdad and Cairo. Over the centuries each of these routes developed various facilities for travellers which included wells, cisterns and dams, bridges, paved roads, markers and milestones, khans and forts. Of all the routes the Damascus route appears to be the oldest, following pre-Islamic trade routes. One of the most important stations on this route is the city of Humayma in southern Jordan where the Abbasids planned their revolution. Other early sites on this route are Khan al-Zabib, Jize and Macan, all of which contain remains of early Islamic structures associated with the Hajj. At Jise there is a huge Roman reservoir and nearby are the remains of the recently excavated Umayyad palace of Qastal which may have functioned as a royal caravanserai to receive important officials on the Hajj. Khan al-Zabib consists of a large square fortress-like building with a central courtyard and a mosque built to one side. At the oasis town of Macan there is also a huge Roman reservoir and there are signs that the nearby Roman fortress at Udruh was converted into an official Umayyad residence at this time. With the move of the caliphate from Syria to Iraq the Damascus route declined in importance, but the route was still used throughout the Ayyubid and Mamluk periods, as testified by the fourteenth-century pilgrimage itinerary of Ibn Battuta and the existence of several Mamluk forts on the route such as those at Jize and Zerka. With the Ottoman conquest of the Mamluk Empire in the sixteenth century the Hajj route was provided with new facilities and provided with fortified garrisons stationed in small forts along the route. The forts were built not only to protect the water cisterns and wells (which were repaired at the same time) but also to provide an efficient postal service for the Hajj. The forts had a simple square plan based around a central courtyard with a well in the centre. They were mostly two-storey structures with a crenellated parapet above and projecting machicolations (structures protecting openings through which to attack the enemy) on one or more sides. The forts were built to overlook the water reservoirs which were filled each year in preparation for the Hajj. It should, however, be remembered that the pilgrims would have stayed in vast encampments of tents next to the cisterns. By the eighteenth century the facilities had fallen into disrepair and the forts were inadequate protection against increased bedouin raids. In consequence the number of forts was augmented to cover most of the stops between Damascus and Mecca, and new wells, cisterns and bridges were provided. The design of the eighteenth-century forts was slightly different, with square projecting corner turrets and small gun slits. At the beginning of the twentieth century a narrow-gauge railway was built to replace the camel caravans; it used many of the same stops as the caravan route and forts were erected to protect the stations.

The decline of the Syria–Damascus Hajj route in the eighth century was largely a result of the development of a direct desert route between Baghdad and Mecca. The route was provided with

Qal'at Qatrana on the Ottoman Hajj route, Jordan

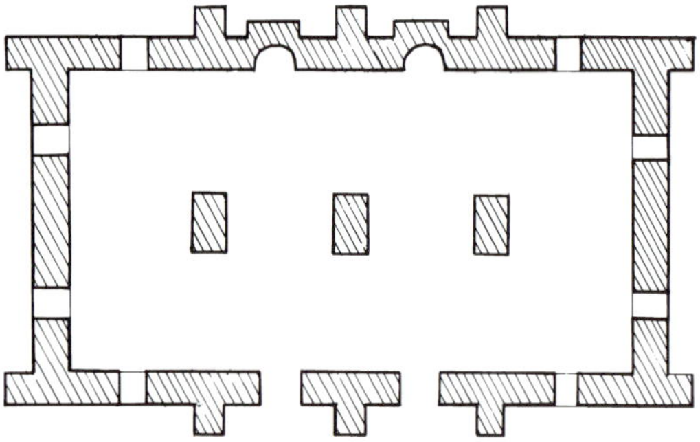

al-Rowdah, eighteenth-century mosque on Syrian Hajj route. Note double mihrab

facilities paid for by Zubayda, wife of Caliph Harun al-Rashid. Over fifty stations have been identified on the route which is marked with milestones. The most important facilities were the cisterns which were either square structures in rocky ground or circular where they were built in sand. The route included a number of stops of varying size, the most important of which was al-Rabadah, which has recently been excavated to reveal a desert city in an area used to raise camels – probably for the Hajj. Facilities at the sites varied but usually included a mosque, a fort or palace and several unfortified residential units. The buildings were mostly built out of coursed stone rubble for foundations and had a mud-brick superstructure, although occasionally buildings were made of fired brick. Several of the mosques have been excavated (at Zubalah, al-Qac and al-Rabadah). They generally have a courtyard leading to the prayer hall which has a projecting mihrab and a fixed minbar, and there is also usually the remains of the base of a minaret. Palaces were found at several sites (al-'Ashar, al-Shihiyat, Zubalah and al-Qac) and consist of large rectangular or square enclosures divided into separate inner courtyards, which in turn may be composed of several residential units. The outer walls of the palace enclosures are supported by solid semi-circular and circular buttresses. On a smaller scale are the small forts discovered on the northern part of the route which are simple square structures built around a central courtyard with circular and semi-circular buttress towers on the outside. The houses on the route resemble the palaces in the variety of their internal arrangements; however, the basic unit seems to consist of a courtyard leading on to one or more groups of three rooms.

In more recent times the Hajj has been made by rail, sea and air and appropriate facilities have been built to accommodate modern pilgrims. One of the more famous recent buildings connected with the Hajj is the Hajj terminal at Jeddah which has won an award from the Agha Khan foundation.

Further reading:

J. S. Birks, *Across the Savannas to Mecca: The Overland Pilgrimage Route from West Africa*, London 1978.
A. D. Petersen, 'Early Ottoman forts on the Darb al-Hajj', *Levant* XXI, 97–118, 1989.
—— 'Two medieval forts on the Hajj route in Jordan', *Annual of the Department of Antiquities of Jordan*, Vol 35, 1991.
S. A. al-Rashid, *Darb Zubaydah*, Riyadh 1980.
J. Sauvaget, 'Les Caravanserais syriens du Hadjdj de Constantinople', *Ars Islamica* 4, 1937.

al-Hakim, Mosque of

One of the principal mosques of Cairo named after the Fatimid Caliph al-Hakim bi Amr Allah.

This mosque, also known as al-Anwar, 'the illuminated', was begun in 990 under the Caliph al-'Aziz but was not completed until 12 years later under the Caliph al-Hakim. At the time of its construction this mosque was outside the city but was later incorporated within the city walls of Badr al-Jamali.

In its general design the mosque resembles those of Ibn Tulun and al-Azhar. It has a central rectangular courtyard surrounded by an arcade of pointed arches resting on brick piers. A raised transept runs from the courtyard to the mihrab. There were three domes on the qibla side, one in front of the mihrab and one in either corner. The front façade has a projecting entrance flanked by two cylindrical minarets decorated with inscriptions and carved bands. Later in 1010 the minarets were enclosed by giant brick cubes possibly because the minarets contravened a long-established Fatimid rule that the call to prayer was not to be made from a place higher than the mosque roof. The present minarets on top of the brick cubes belong to the Mamluk period.

Some of the original decoration has survived, in particular the stucco work with bands of Kufic inscriptions and stylized tree motifs. In the 1020s a ziyada was added to the south side by the caliph al-Zahir. During the Ayyubid period this mosque was the only congregational mosque in the city as the Ayyubids did not permit more than one congregational mosque within the city.

Further reading:

D. Berhens-Abouseif, *Islamic Architecture in Cairo: An Introduction*, Supplements to Muqarnas, vol. 3, Leiden 1989, 63–5.
J. M. Bloom, 'The mosque of al-Hakim in Cairo', *Muqarnas* 1: 15 ff., 1983.
K. A. C. Creswell, *The Muslim Architecture of Egypt*, Oxford 1952–60, 1: 68 ff.

hammam ('Turkish bath'; bath house)

General term used to describe both private and public bath houses. Public hammams are found throughout the Islamic world and together with the mosque are regarded as one of the essential features of an Islamic city. Private bath houses are less well known although it is known that they existed from the early Islamic period where they have been found in palaces such as Qasr al-Hayr and Ukhaidhir.

Hammams developed directly out of Byzantine bath houses such as those discovered at Avdat, and Yotvata in the Negev. One of the earliest and certainly the most famous early Islamic bath house is Qusayr Amra located in the north-eastern Jordanian desert. The building was heated by a hypocaust system supported on short brick pillars and supplied with water raised from a deep well by an animal-powered mechanism. Like other early Islamic baths Qusayr Amra does not have the frigidarium common in Roman baths although it does have an enlarged reception room, or apodyterium, decorated with frescoes in late Antique style. Other early Islamic bath houses such as Hammam al-Sarakh, 'Ayn al-Sinu and Jabal Usays have the same arrangement as Qusayr Amra with no frigidarium. The one exception to this pattern is the bath house at Khirbet al-Mafjar where the heated rooms are approached via a large hall (30 m square) resembling the classical frigidarium, with a long pool approached by steps and a mosaic floor.

There are few remains of bath houses from the period between the ninth and twelfth centuries although excavations at Nishapur have uncovered a bath house with hypocaust heating dated to the tenth/eleventh century. Sometime after the tenth century hypocausts seem to have been abandoned (in Syria at least) in favour of a system where the chimney of the furnace runs under the floor of the rooms to be heated. The effect of this innovation was that the layout of rooms was dictated by the axis of the chimney flue, and led to the warm room becoming the central room of the hammam. The typical Ayyubid hammam as it is known from Syria consists of an entrance room leading to the warm room via an intermediate unheated room. The warm room is usually octagonal with smaller hot rooms leading off at the sides. In baths built after the fifteenth century there is no intermediate room between the warm room and the changing room. As a corollary of this the size of the warm room is increased in later baths, until in eighteenth-century baths it becomes the main room. The octagonal warm room often has a central octagonal platform for massages whilst the smaller warm rooms have stone basins for washing. The warm and hot rooms never have windows but are lit instead by thick glass roundels set into the dome. A further development of the Ottoman period are twin hammams where a bath house for women and a bath house for men were set back to back to avoid the prohibition of mixed bathing. This problem is usually dealt with by having different bathing times for men and women.

See also: Khirbet al-Mafjar, Qusayr Amra

Further reading:

M. Dow, *Hammams of Palestine*, Oxford 1993.

M. Ecochard and C. Le Coeur, *Les Bains de Damas*, Beirut 1943.

E. Pauty, *Les Hammams du Caire*, Cairo 1963.

H. Terrasse, 'Trois Bains marinides du Maroc', *Mélanges*, 311–20, 1950.

haram

The private quarters of a house, sanctuary of a mosque or more generally an area set apart.

Haramayn

Term used to refer to the two holy places of Mecca and Medina. In Mamluk and Ottoman times this term was sometimes also used to refer to Jerusalem and Hebron.

haremlik

Turkish term for the private part of an Ottoman house which is only open to members of the family (from Arabic hareem).

Harran

Ancient city in south-eastern Turkey important as a centre of learning and Umayyad capital.

Harran is located in the flat plain between the Tigris and Euphrates rivers. The city was famous in early Islamic times as the centre of the pagan Sabians who worshipped the stars and achieved protected (dhimini) status in return for their astrological and scientific advice. The last Sabian temples were destroyed by the Mongol invasion of the mid-twelfth century. In 744 Caliph Marwan II established himself at Harran and made it the Umayyad capital.

The site includes the remains of a city wall, a castle and a congregational mosque. The most important monument is the Great Mosque founded by Marwan II between 744 and 750. Major modifications were carried out during the twelfth century under Salah al-Din who also fortified the citadel. The building is badly ruined, so that only the rough outline of the plan can be traced and the date of different phases is not clear. The mosque is roughly square measuring approximately 100 m per side with a rectangular courtyard to the north and the sanctuary to the south. There are two main entrances to the complex, one on the east side and one in the centre of the north side. The façade of the sanctuary consisted of nineteen arches resting on piers with engaged columns. In the centre of the façade is a wide central arch approximately in line with the deeply recessed mihrab in the south wall. Roughly in the centre of the courtyard there is an octagonal basin, above which there may have been a domed chamber supported on columns which functioned as the treasury (bayt al-mal). To the east of the north entrance is a tall square tower or minaret built in two distinct phases, the lower part is built of stone whilst the upper part is made of brick. The destruction of the mosque can be attributed to the Mongol invasion in the mid-twelfth century.

Harran is also noted for its characteristic architecture which consists of houses and storerooms covered with conical mud-brick domes.

haud or hauz

A pool or tank, often in the centre of the courtyard of a mosque.

Hausa

West African people living in northern Nigeria with a long-established distinctive architectural tradition.

Modern Hausa society is a combination of two groups of people, the Hausa themselves and the Fulbe-speaking Fulani people. The Fulani first moved into the area in the fifteenth century although it was not until the nineteenth that large-scale migrations took place. The Fulani constitute a literate Muslim class attached to the ruling élite in Hausa society. In addition to the Muslim urban populations there is also a rural population of non-Muslim Hausa known as Maguzawa. The Hausa civilization is generally agreed to have formed in about 1000 CE and comprised the cities of Daura, Kano, Gobir, Katsina, Zaria, Biram and Rano. In the nineteenth century a Fulani-led jihad established a caliphate in Hausaland with the new city of Sokoto as its capital. The main materials of Hausa architecture are oval mud bricks (tubali) and palm wood (deleb). Walls are built out of mud brick whilst palm trunks split into beams (azarori) are used for roofing. Unlike most other areas of West Africa, Hausa architecture is in the hands of a hereditary group of trained masons who are organized into guilds. These trained masons have been responsible for some of the most celebrated architecture in West Africa.

The traditional layout of a Hausa city consists of narrow winding streets set within a thick outer enclosure wall. In the older cities the outer walls have an irregular/organic shape but the walls of Sokoto, established in the nineteenth century, are square as an expression of Islamic conformity and bordered by houses which consist of courtyard compounds. In the past the street façades of the houses were left unadorned although in recent times there has been a tendency to decorate the outer façade of the entrance vestibule with embossed designs. Circular rooms with two entrances are traditionally used as entrance vestibules and are known as *zaure*. Square or rectangular rooms, called *sigifa*, are usually used for internal reception rooms. In recent times circular rooms have become less common and have been replaced with rectangular rooms with the more complex *daurin guga* dome form.

The characteristic feature of Hausa architecture is the domed room formed by a number of intersecting arches projecting from the walls of the building. The arches are made of lengths of palm wood set into the wall and projecting at increasing angles until they are horizontal at the apex of the arch where they are joined to a similar construction projecting from the opposite wall. The palm-wood frame is then covered with mud to produce smooth free-standing arches which support a ceiling made of palm-wood panels and covered with rush mats and then with a water-resistant layer of plaster, like material made out of the residue of indigo dye pits. Two main types of arch configuration are used depending on the shape of the room to be covered. The simplest form, known as the *kafin laima* vault, is used for a circular room and has all the arches or ribs meeting at a central point which is often decorated with an inset metal or ceramic bowl. The more complex vault form, known as *daurin guga*, is used for rectangular or square rooms and consists of two sets of parallel arches or ribs which intersect at the centre to form square compartments. The soffits of the arches are often decorated with abstract designs which may either be relief mouldings or painted in bright, locally produced colours.

See also: Kano, West Africa

Further reading:

S. B. Aradeon, 'Traditional Hausa architecture: the interface between structure and decoration', *Arts of the Islamic World* 5(1): 19–23, 1988.

A. Leary, 'A decorated palace in Kano', *Art and Archaeology Research Papers* 12: 11–17, 1977.

J. C. Moughtin, 'The traditional settlements of the Hausa people', *Town Planning Review* 35(1): 21–34, 1964.

—— 'The Friday mosque at Zaria city', *Savanah*, 1(2): 143–63, 1972.

L. Prussin, 'Fulani-Hausa architecture', *African Arts* 10(1), 1976.

——, 'Fulani-Hausa architecture: genesis of a style', *African Arts* 13(2): 57–65, 79–82, 85–7, 1976.

F. Schwerdtfeger, 'Housing in Zaria', *Shelter in Africa*, New York 1971.

M. G. Smith, 'The beginnings of Hausa society, AD 1000–1500', in *The Historian in Tropical Africa*, ed. J. Vanisa *et al.*, London 1964.

H. Tukur Saad, *Between Myth and Reality: The Aesthetics of Traditional Architecture in Hausaland*, Ann Arbor University Microfilms.

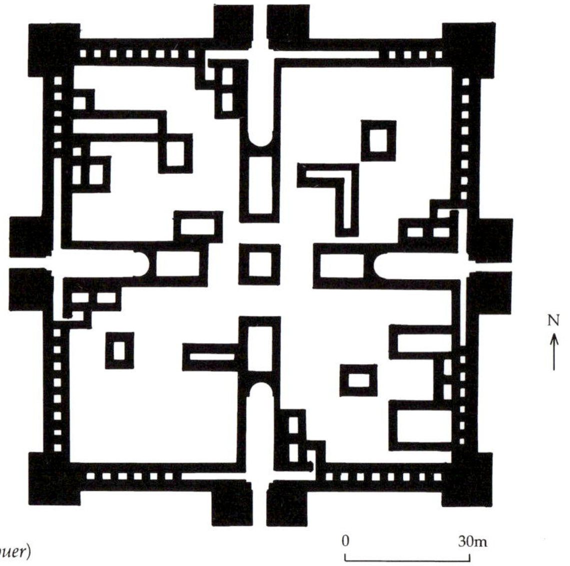

Heraqlah, near Raqqa (after Touer)

hayr (ha'ir)

Walled enclosures often associated with early Islamic palaces. Early examples are the enclosures at Qasr al-Hayr (East and West) and more significantly those of Samarra in Iraq. The exact function of these enclosures may vary; at Samarra they appear to be hunting reserves whereas at Qasr al-Hayr they may have a more utilitarian function.

hazarbaf

Iranian term for decorative brickwork.

hazira

A tomb contained within an enclosure which often includes a mosque. This form of tomb became popular in Timurid Iran.

Heraqlah

A square-shaped terrace-like structure with four corner towers enclosed within a small circular moat and circular wall.

This site is located in north-east Syria, 8 km west of the city of Raqqa near the Euphrates. On historical grounds this monument is reliably dated to the early ninth century, probably between 806 and 808 CE.

The monument is almost entirely built out of stone with the exception of the vaults and paving of the central structure, which are baked brick. The circular outer wall is supported by square buttresses at regular intervals and has gates at the four cardinal points (i.e. north, south, east and west). The entrances to the central building are aligned with those of the outer wall and each leads into a long vaulted hall. To the left of each entrance is a long ramp which gives access to the top of the monument. Although there are structures in the centre of the building, excavations have revealed that these cannot have been built as rooms as they have no doors or other means of access. Instead it is believed that the centre of the structure would have been filled in with earth to provide a monumental platform and that the structures must have fulfilled some symbolic or functional purpose.

The whole complex has been convincingly described as a victory monument to the Abbasid caliph Harun al-Rashid to commemorate his victory over the Byzantines at Herakleon. The size, date and geometric design is comparable with other Abbasid projects such as the octagon at Qadissiya and the Round City of Baghdad.

See also: Abbasids

Further reading:

F. Sarre and E. Herzfeld, *Archäologische Reise im Euphrat und Tigris,* Gebeit I, Berlin 1911, 161–3.

K. Touer, 'Heraqlah: a unique victory monument of Harun al-Rashid', *World Archaeology* 14(3): 1973.

Herat

City in north-west Afghanistan which became capital of the Timurid Empire in the fourteenth and fifteenth centuries.

Herat has existed since ancient times and was referred to in Greek as Aria. It was conquered by the Arabs in the seventh century but does not seem to have been fully subdued until the early eighth century. In the tenth century it was described as having four gates, a strong citadel and extensive suburbs. In the twelfth and early thirteenth century the city was developed by the Ghurids who established the Great Mosque. The city suffered under the Mongols in the thirteenth century although it began to be redeveloped by the fourteenth. In 1380 Timur entered Herat and later expelled the local ruler, this was the beginning of Herat's greatest period which lasted until the Uzbek conquest in 1508.

Timurid buildings in Herat include the Great Mosque, the madrassa and tomb of Gauhar Shad, the mausoleum of Sheikh Zadeh Abdallah and the famous shrine of Gazur Gah. The Great Mosque was established under the Ghurids in the twelfth century and contains the tomb of the Ghurid ruler Sultan Ghiyath al-Din. Although a few traces of twelfth-century stucco decoration remain, the design of the complex is mostly Timurid modified by more recent renovations. The mosque is built on a four-iwan plan with a central courtyard and an enlarged western iwan flanked with twin minarets which serves as the main prayer hall. The whole complex was decorated with polychrome tiles but these have mostly disappeared to be replaced by modern copies. The madrassa and tomb of Gauhar Shad form part of a large complex built around a musalla, or open air prayer area, measuring 106 by 64 m. The inner court had a two-storey arcade built around four iwans. The mausoleum of Gauhar Shad has a cruciform plan with the centre covered by a shallow convex dome supported by a network of pendentives and semi-domes. Above the inner dome there is a tall, ribbed outer dome resting on a cylindrical collar and covered with polychrome tiles on a blue background. Opposite the tomb of Gauhar Shad is the tomb of Sheikh Zadeh Abdallah which has a dome of similar design. The building has an octagonal plan with an large frontal iwan and side iwans added on to the south, west and east sides.

The most celebrated building in Herat is the shrine of Gazur Gah dedicated to an eleventh-century Sufi poet, Khwajeh ʿAbdallah Ansari. The complex is a high-walled enclosure with a large iwan, above which is an arcade of five arches capped with two domes. The brilliance of the shrine is its original tiled decoration which consists of square geometric panels, monumental calligraphy and abstract designs.

See also: Afghanistan, Timurids

Further reading:

T. Allen, *Timurid Herat*, Wiesbaden 1983.
H. Gaube, *Iranian Cities*, New York 1979, 31–64.
F. J. Hecker, 'A fifteenth-century Chinese diplomat in Herat', *Journal of the Royal Asiatic Society*, 3rd series 3 (1): 85–91, 1993.

hosh

The courtyard of a house in Egypt or, in Palestine, used to describe houses built around a courtyard.

hujra

Small chamber or cell.

Hungary

The earliest recorded presence of Muslims in Hungary is during the ninth century of Khazars. Some of these converted to Christianity during the reign of King Stephen in the tenth century although many remained Muslim. Another Muslim (Turkic) group known as the Pecheneg was also present from the tenth century onwards. Many of these were located on the western frontier of Hungary as a defensive force for the Magyar kingdom. During the thirteenth century the Pecheneg seem to have been prosperous with large settlements the size of towns but without walls as these were forbidden to Muslim communities to prevent rebellion. By the end of the fourteenth century most Pecheneg had been forced to convert to Christianity although some remained Muslim until the beginning of the sixteenth century.

The Ottoman victory at the battle of Mohacs in 1526 renewed the Muslim presence in Hungary.

For the next 150 years, until its reconquest at the end of the seventeenth century, Hungary was a province of the Ottoman Empire. There are few buildings remaining from the period of Turkish rule although the reasons for this are unclear. One of the best-known Ottoman monuments is the tomb of Gul Baba in Buda erected between 1543 and 1548. The building is an octagonal mausoleum with a shallow domed roof covered in lead. There was once a mosque associated with the tomb but this has now disappeared. This tomb is now to be the centrepiece of an Islamic cultural centre incorporating a mosque and library.

See also: Albania, Bosnia, Bulgaria, Ottomans

Further reading:

G. Fehevari, 'A centre for Islamic culture in Hungary', *Arts of the Islamic World* 5(2) 18: 46–8, 1990.

hunkar mahfil

A royal lodge or gallery in an Ottoman mosque.

Hyderabad

Fifth largest city in India and capital of the second largest native state in British India.

The state of Hyderabad was ruled over by the Nizams of Hyderabad who were Muslims although the majority of the population was Hindu. Although conquered by the Mughals in the late seventeenth century the Nizams managed to retain their independence until 1947 when the state was taken over by Indian government troops.

The city was founded in 1591 by the fifth ruler of Golconda, Quli Qutb Saha. The city was originally known as Baghnagar (city of gardens) and later acquired the name Hyderabad. It is located on the banks of the river Musi and was laid out on a plan with the two main roads intersecting at the Char Minar at the centre of the city. To the north of the Char Minar were the palaces of the Nizam rulers which were destroyed during the Mughal conquest of 1687. Between 1724 and 1740 Mubariz Khan, the Mughal governor, supervised the construction of the city walls with fourteen gates, only two of which have survived.

Several buildings survive from the pre-Mughal period the most famous of which is the Char Minar which dominates the centre of the city. To the north-east of the Char Minar is the Mecca Masjid built out of local granite between 1614 and 1693. This is one of the largest mosques in India and the main entrance consists of five arches and four minars whilst the interior of the mosque contains two huge domes supported on monolithic columns. Directly to the north of the Char Minar is the Jami Masjid which was built in 1598 and is one of the oldest mosques in the city. This mosque forms part of a complex that included a bath house and madrassa which have survived as ruins. A better preserved complex is the Darush Shifa hospital and medical college (built in 1535) which consists of a two-storey square courtyard building with a mosque attached. Also from this early period is the Badshahi Ashurkhana which was built in 1592 as a royal house of mourning. The building is decorated with Persian-style tile mosaics and has an outer timber porch added in the late eighteenth century. Little remains of the original royal palaces although the Charkaman (Four arches) built in 1594 was originally a monumental gateway opening on to the palace grounds.

See also: Char Minar, Deccan, India

Further reading:

A. Bakshian and G. D. Schad, 'Hyderabad: shadow of empire', *History Today* 39: 19–28, Jan. 1989.

hypostyle

A flat-roofed structure supported by columns.

See also: appadana

I

Ibn Tulun, Mosque of (also referred to as Mosque of al-Maydan)

One of the oldest mosques in Egypt to have survived relatively intact. It was built by Ahmad ibn Tulun the semi-independent ruler of Egypt in 870.

The mosque formed part of the new suburb of al-Qata'ic which ibn Tulun added on to the two towns of Fustat and al-ʿAskar which were later incorporated into the city of Cairo. Ahmad ibn Tulun was born in Iraq and brought up at the caliph's court in Samarra and the new city of al-Qata'ic bore some resemblance to Samarra.

The mosque was begun in 876 and completed in 879. The building consists of a large rectangular enclosure with a central courtyard measuring 92 m square. Arcades two-aisles deep are ranged around three sides of the courtyard whilst on the qibla side (south-east) there are five rows of arcades. The central building is enclosed by an outer enclosure, or ziyada, on the three sides adjoining the qibla. Almost directly opposite the central mihrab is a minaret consisting of a square tower with a spiral section on the top. Access to the top of minaret is by an external staircase. At the top there is a two-storey octagonal kiosk. Whilst the octagonal kiosk and the windows on the side of the square shape appear to be of a later (thirteenth century) date there is some debate about whether the minaret is an original ninth-century structure or a later copy.

Due to its good state of preservation the Ibn Tulun Mosque provides an excellent example of ninth-century decoration and structural techniques. The most notable feature of the outer walls is the decorative openwork crenellations which resemble paper cut-outs. The courtyard façades consist of slightly pointed arches resting on rectangular piers with engaged colonettes, which is an unusual arrangement for Cairo where marble columns were usually used. Between the arches are rectangular arched niches also with engaged colonettes. Either side of each niche is a sunken rosette divided into eight lobes. A band of similar rosettes forms a cornice running around the four faces of the courtyard. Probably the most remarkable feature of the decoration is the carved stucco work which decorates the interior of the mosque. The best examples are in the soffits of the arches of the sanctuary where geometric interlace patterns are filled with stylized leaf ornament similar to Samarra stucco style B. The edges of the arches and the capitals are decorated with stucco resembling Samarra style A.

Many elements of the Ibn Tulun Mosque recall the architecture of Samarra, in particular the ziyadas, the rectangular piers and the stucco work. The minaret recalls the spiral minarets of the Great Mosque and the Abu Dulaf Mosque both because of the spiral shapes used and the positioning of the ziyada opposite the mihrab.

See also: stucco

Further reading:

K. A. C. Creswell, *A Short Account of Early Muslim Architecture*, revised and enlarged edn. J. W. Allan, Aldershot 1989, 392–406.

D. Berhens-Abouseif, *Islamic Architecture in Cairo: An Introduction*, Supplements to Muqarnas vol. 3, Leiden 1989, 51–7.

idgah

Iranian term for an open-air prayer area, particularly used during festivals.

See also: musalla, namazgah

Ilkhanids

Mongol dynasty which ruled much of the eastern Islamic world from the mid-thirteenth to the mid-fourteenth century.

In 1258 Hulagau ibn Kublai Khan sacked Baghdad and killed the last Abbasid caliph al-Mu'tassim making Iraq part of the great Mongol Empire. This empire was divided into four parts of which Hulagau ruled one. Hulagau's dominions included Iran, Khurassan, Azerbayjan, Georgia, Armenia and Iraq.

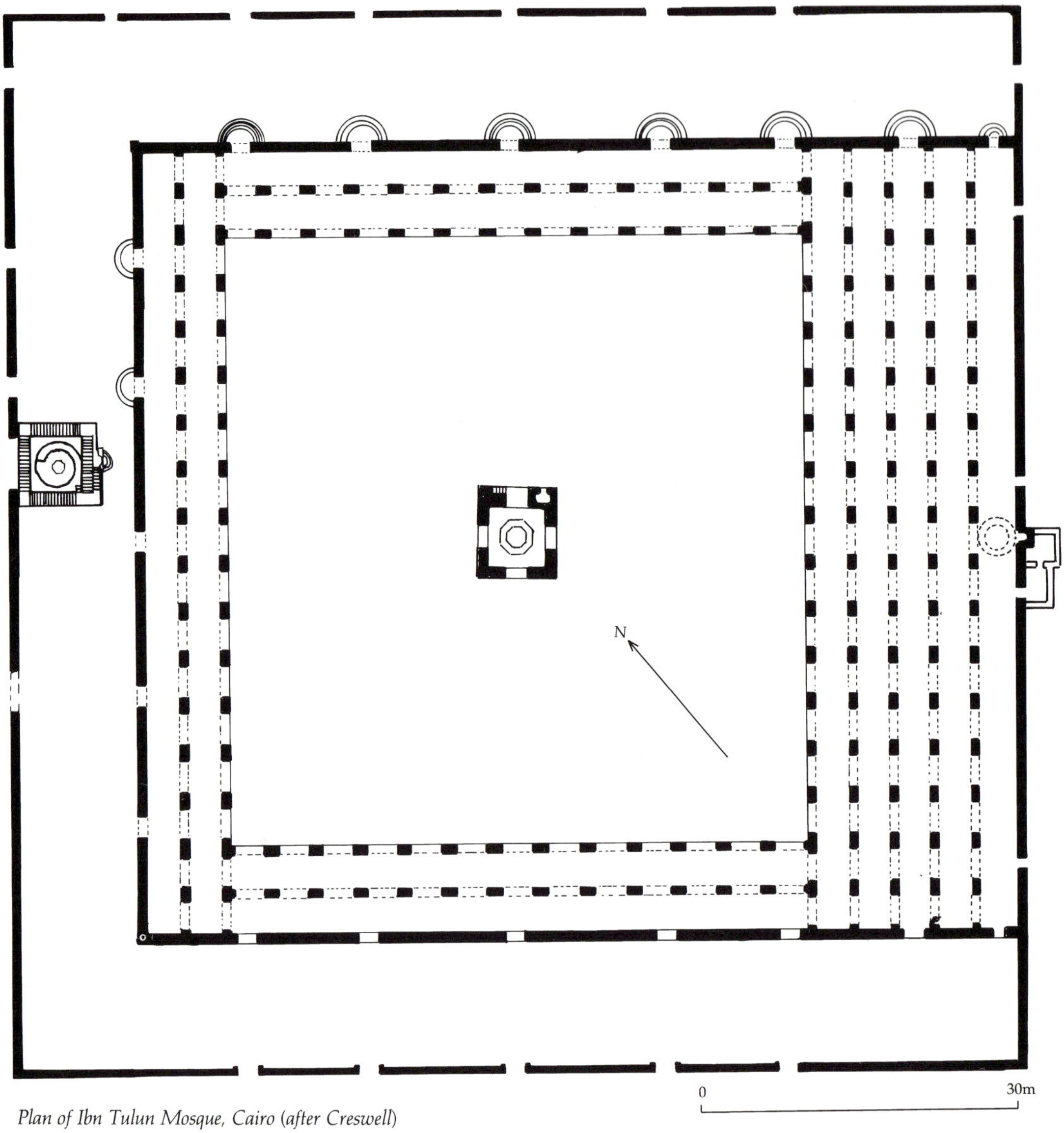

Plan of Ibn Tulun Mosque, Cairo (after Creswell)

Although the Ilkhanids rebuilt much of Baghdad, most imperial building was confined to Iran.

There are few Ilkhanid monuments which survive from before the fourteenth century. Characteristic features of Ilkhanid architecture are the massive size of monuments (which anticipates those of the Timurids), the extensive use of stucco work and the development of the transverse arch. The transverse arch was a method of covering large open areas without the use of piers or columns. The principle of the technique was to have a series of wide arches spanning the short axis of a room, these arches would then form the base for transverse vaults. Although the technique had been used before, this was the first time it was used in baked-brick architecture. One of the best examples is Khan Mirjan (1359) in Baghdad where a two-storey rectangular courtyard is covered with seven huge transverse arches.

The extant examples of imperial Ilkhanid architecture are few, although the ruins of the Mongol capital at Sultaniya give some idea of the scale of their buildings. The city was founded in 1306 and contained a huge citadel surrounded by a stone wall. Little survives of the city with the exception of the massive tomb complex of Oljetu. This is a huge octagonal building with a diameter of more than 30 m, surmounted by a massive dome covered with blue tiles. Other imperial projects were the Great Mosques of Tabriz and Varamin. The Tabriz Mosque was based around a prayer hall consisting of a single massive iwan 40 m wide and more than 80 m deep. In front of the iwan there was a courtyard which contained a madrassa and a khanqa. The Varamin Mosque is equally huge and is dominated by the strict symmetry of its axial iwans.

See also: Iran, Iraq

imamzadeh

Iranian term for venerated tomb of holy man.

imaret

Ottoman Turkish term for a kitchen which dispenses soup and bread free to the poor, students and wandering mystics (dervishes). Imarets usually form part of a larger religious complex which normally includes a mosque, madrassa and bath house (hammam).

India

The Republic of India is the largest country in south Asia and occupies the greater part of the Indian subcontinent which it shares with Pakistan and Bangladesh.

The present population of India is nearly 800 million of which almost 80 million (10 per cent) are Muslim, making it the second largest Muslim country in the world after Indonesia. Geographically India is fairly well defined, with the Himalayas to the north isolating it from the rest of Asia, whilst the Indian Ocean surrounds the country to the south. Within this vast area there are many regions each with its own languages, traditions, climate and environment, varying from the cool mountains of Kashmir to the tropical heat of the Deccan.

India differs from other parts of the Islamic world as it does not share the Roman and Sassanian traditions of the Middle East and North Africa, instead it has its own complex history which includes many different religions, cultures and ethnic groups. The most significant of these is the Hindu religion which was a highly developed culture well before the Muslim conquest and continues to be the major religion of the country. The effect of this on architecture means that Indian buildings have distinct design and building characteristics which distinguish them from Islamic buildings elsewhere. The most significant influence on architecture was the Hindu temple. Initially Hindu temples were destroyed and the remains were used to build mosques, such as the Quwwat al-Islam Mosque in Delhi which was built out of the remains of twenty-seven temples; later, however, Hindu features were copied for use in mosques and have now become characteristic of Indo-Islamic architecture. Examples of Hindu features incorporated into Islamic buildings include domed chatris, projecting chajjas and bulbous dome finials. Later on the influence of India can be seen in the mosques of south-east Asia, many of which are Indian in form.

Islam arrived in India by two routes, the overland route through Central Asia and the maritime coastal route. In general the overland route was used by Turkic and Afghan peoples who arrived in India as warriors and conquerors. These peoples established the first Muslim states in India starting in the north and later expanding to the south and east. The coastal route is less well documented and consists of the gradual development of independent Muslim trading communities along the coast in a similar manner to the establishment of Islam in East Africa. Some of the oldest established coastal communities are in Gujarat and the Malabar coast from where Islam eventually spread to south-east Asia as testified by the Gujarati gravestones found in Malaysia and Indonesia. The coastal communities were usually fairly small with no territorial or dynastic ambitions and consequently produced little monumental architecture apart from small local mosques. Occasionally there was some co-operation between the inland Muslim dynasties and the coastal Muslims as can be seen in Gujarat and the Deccan.

There are few documented remains of early Muslim coastal communities. This is partly because of the lack of archaeological work and partly because the monumental character of inland sites has taken up most of the attention of scholars. There is, however, significant historical information of Muslim coastal communities from as early as the ninth century at Quilon on the Malabar coast.

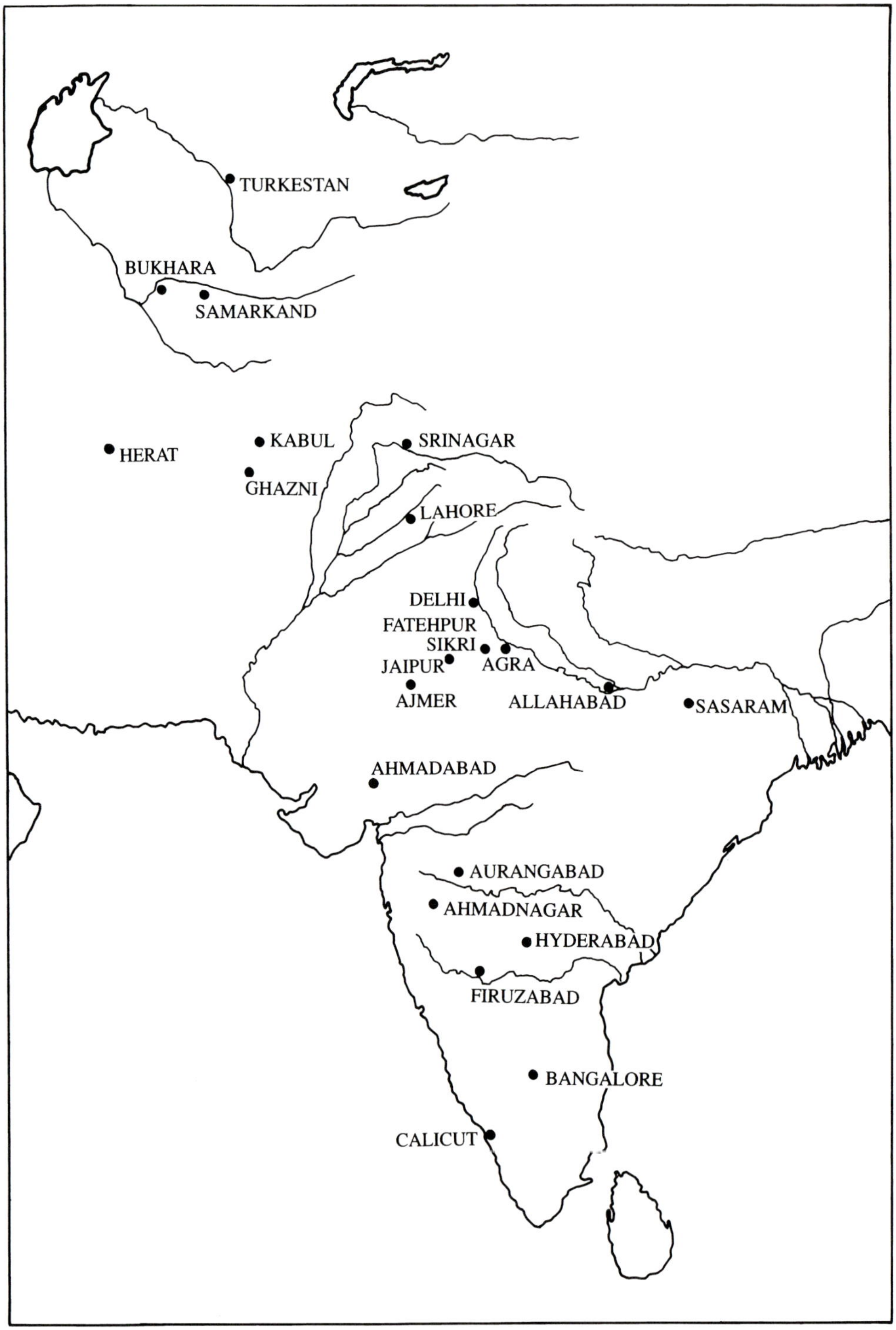

Principal sites and cities of the Islamic period in India

One of the few coastal sites with early standing remains is the old seaport of Bhadresvar which has two mid-twelfth-century mosques which predate the Muslim conquest of Gujarat.

The Muslim conquest of India started in the late twelfth century with the Afghan invasion led by Muhammad of Ghur who captured the Hindu stronghold of Rai Pithora, later known as Delhi (see below Pakistan for the early Islamic conquest of Sind). The death of Muhammad in 1206 left his lieutenant Qutb al-Din Aybak in control of the new Indian Muslim state. During the next 300 years much of northern India and the area of modern Pakistan was ruled by a succession of five dynasties based at Delhi. The first of these dynasties comprised the descendants of Qutb al-Din and collectively was known as the Slave dynasty. In 1290 power was seized by Jalal al-Din Firuz Shah II who was founder of the second dynasty known as the Khaliji sultans. In 1296 Jalal al-Din was murdered by his nephew who replaced him as sultan. The new sultan, Ala al-Din Muhamad Shah, reigned for seventeen years during which time he made extensive conquests in Gujarat, Rajasthan and the Deccan. However, the Khaliji dynasty was short-lived and in 1320 it was replaced by the Tughluq, named after its founder Ghiyath al-Din Tughluq. For a brief period in the mid-fourteenth century Ghiyath al-Din's successor moved the capital to Daulatabad in the Deccan, but famine and disease forced him to return to Delhi. The invasion of Timur at the end of the fourteenth century brought about the destruction of Delhi and dealt a deathly blow to the Tughluqid sultans. The last Tughluqid sultan died in 1414 leaving Delhi under the control of the Sayyid sultans who ruled as Timur's deputies. The Sayyid sultans ruled for less than forty years until 1451 when they were replaced by the Lodi kings. The end of the Delhi sultanate came in 1526 when the last Lodi king was defeated by Babur the first Mughal emperor.

The architecture of the Delhi sultanate represents a gradual evolution from an imported Afghan style using unfamiliar materials to a developed Indo-Islamic style which formed the basis of later Mughal architecture. The first building of the Delhi sultanate was the Quwwat al-Islam Mosque complex built by Qutb al-Din Aybak out of the remains of twenty-seven destroyed Hindu temples. The arcades were supported by two tiers of Hindu temple pillars placed one on top of the other to achieve the desired height. They were built in a trabeate construction and in 1199 an arched façade was added to the east side of the sanctuary to give it the familiar appearance of a mosque. However, the arches of the screen were built out of corbels rather than voussoirs whilst the decoration consisted of Quranic inscriptions contained within dense Hindu-style foliage. In the same year Qutb al-Din began the famous Qutb Minar which has become one of the potent symbols of Islam in India. Other work carried out at this time was the construction of the Great Mosque of Ajmer which like the Delhi Mosque employed re-used Hindu columns and later had an arched screen added to the front. Other notable monuments of the Slave dynasty include the tomb of Iltumish built in 1236 which includes the first use of squinches to support a dome.

Work on the Delhi Mosque continued under the Khaliji dynasty. Ala al-Din in particular devoted a great deal of attention to the mosque by extending the area of the sanctuary as well as beginning a new minaret on the same design as the Qutb Minar but more than twice the size. Unfortunately Ala al-Din was unable to finish his work and the only part completed is a monumental gateway. Other work carried out by Ala al-Din was the foundation of Siri, the second city of Delhi.

The real expansion of Sultanate architecture came during the rule of the Tughluqids in the fourteenth century. Several new cities were founded including Fathabad, Hissar and Jaunpaur as well as the third, fourth and fifth cities of Delhi. Also at this time the influence of Sultanate architecture was felt in the Deccan when Muhammad Tughluq II moved his capital to Daulatabad. Characteristic features of this architecture are massive sloping fortification walls with pointed crenellations and the development of the tomb as the focus of architectural design. One of the more important tombs is that of Khan Jahan built in 1369 which incorporates Hindu features into an Islamic form. The tomb has an octagonal domed form with chajjas, or projecting eaves, on each side and domed chatris on the roof. Another notable feature of Tughluqid architecture is the restrained use of epigraphy unlike earlier Sultanate architecture.

The monuments of the Sayyid and Lodi sultans are distinguished by their severity and lack of decoration. Nevertheless, many of the buildings are sophisticated structures like the tomb of Sikander Lodi which uses a double dome form so that the dome may have a significant form on the outside without disrupting the proportions of the interior (a technique later used in the Taj Mahal). The tomb is also the first Indian tomb to form part of a formal garden which became the established format under the Mughals. In addition to the centralized architectural styles developed during the Delhi sultanate several vigorous regional traditions also developed. The four most significant styles are those of Gujarat, Kashmir, the Deccan and Bengal. The style of Gujarat developed independently for over 200 years from its conquest by the Khaliji sultan Ala al-Din Shah in the early fourteenth century to its incorporation in the Mughal Empire in the late sixteenth century. Characteristic features of Gujarati architecture are the use of Hindu methods of decoration and construction for mosques long after they had ceased to be fashionable in Delhi. After the conquest of Gujarat, the Mughal emperor Akbar adopted this style for his most ambitious architectural project, Fatehpur Sikri. Less well known but equally distinctive is the architecture of Kashmir where the first Islamic conquest was in the mid-fourteenth century. The significant features of Kashmiri architecture are the use of wood as the main building material and tall pyramid-shaped roofs on mosques. The third major regional style is the architecture of the Deccan in southern India. Deccani architecture is characterized by massive monumental stonework, bulbous onion-shaped domes and elaborate stone carving, including vegetal forms, arched niches and medallions. Far to the east, in the region of Bengal and modern Bangladesh, a distinctive architecture developed using baked brick as the main building material. Other characteristic features of Bengal include the use of the curved do-chala and char-chala roofs which were later incorporated into imperial Mughal architecture under Shah Jahan.

See also: Bengal, Deccan, Delhi, Gujarat, Mughals

Further reading:

P. Andrews, 'The architecture and gardens of Islamic India', in *The Arts of India*, ed. B. Gray, Oxford 1981, 95–124.

P. Davies, *The Penguin Guide to the Monuments of India*, vol. 2: *Islamic Rajput and European*, London 1989.

Z. A. Desai, *Indo-Islamic Architecture*, 2nd edn. New Delhi 1986.

S. Grover, *The Architecture of India: Islamic*, New Delhi 1981.

R. Nath, *Islamic Architecture and Culture in India*, Delhi 1982.

M. Shokoohy and N. H. Shokoohy, *Hisar-i Firuza: Sultanate and Early Mughal Architecture in the District of Hisar India*, Monographs on Art and Archaeology, London 1988.

M. Shokoohy, M. Bayani-Walpert and N. H. Shokoohy, *Bhadresvar: The Oldest Islamic Monuments in India*, Studies in Islamic Art and Architecture, Supplements to Muqarnas vol. 2, Leiden 1988.

K. V. Soundara Rajan, *Islam Builds in India: Cultural Study of Islamic Architecture*, Delhi 1983.

F. Watson, *A Concise History of India*, London 1979.

A. Welch and H. Crane, 'The Tughluqs: master-builders of the Delhi Sultanate', *Muqarnas* 1: 123–66, 1983.

A. Volwahsen, *Living Architecture: Islamic Indian*, London 1970.

Indonesia

Large country in south-east Asia comprising an archipelago of over 17,000 islands stretching for over 5,000 km along the equator. The country has a large population of over 180 million of whom more than 80 per cent are Muslim, making it the most populous country in the Islamic world.

Islam reached separate parts of Indonesia at different times; it arrived in Sumatra in the thirteenth century; in the fourteenth century it was established in Java, southern Celebes, northern Moluccas and southern Borneo (Kalimantan). By the fifteenth century; it had reached the smaller islands to the east of Bali (this remained Hindu) including Lombok, Sumbawa and the northern coast of Flores.

With the exception of the mosque at Demak there are few examples of early mosques in Indonesia because they were mostly wooden and were replaced by brick or stone structures in the nineteenth century. What the wooden mosques do demonstrate is a continuity with the pre-Islamic Hindu and Buddhist past and it seems likely that for this reason they were later replaced with buildings which look more traditionally Islamic. The modern Islamic buildings of Indonesia often have more in common with India and Europe than with any indigenous Indonesian architecture. Recently, however, there have been attempts to revive traditional mosque forms by the 'Amal Bakti Muslim Pancasila' foundation which builds wooden mosques similar to the historical mosque at Demak.

See also: Java, Sumatra

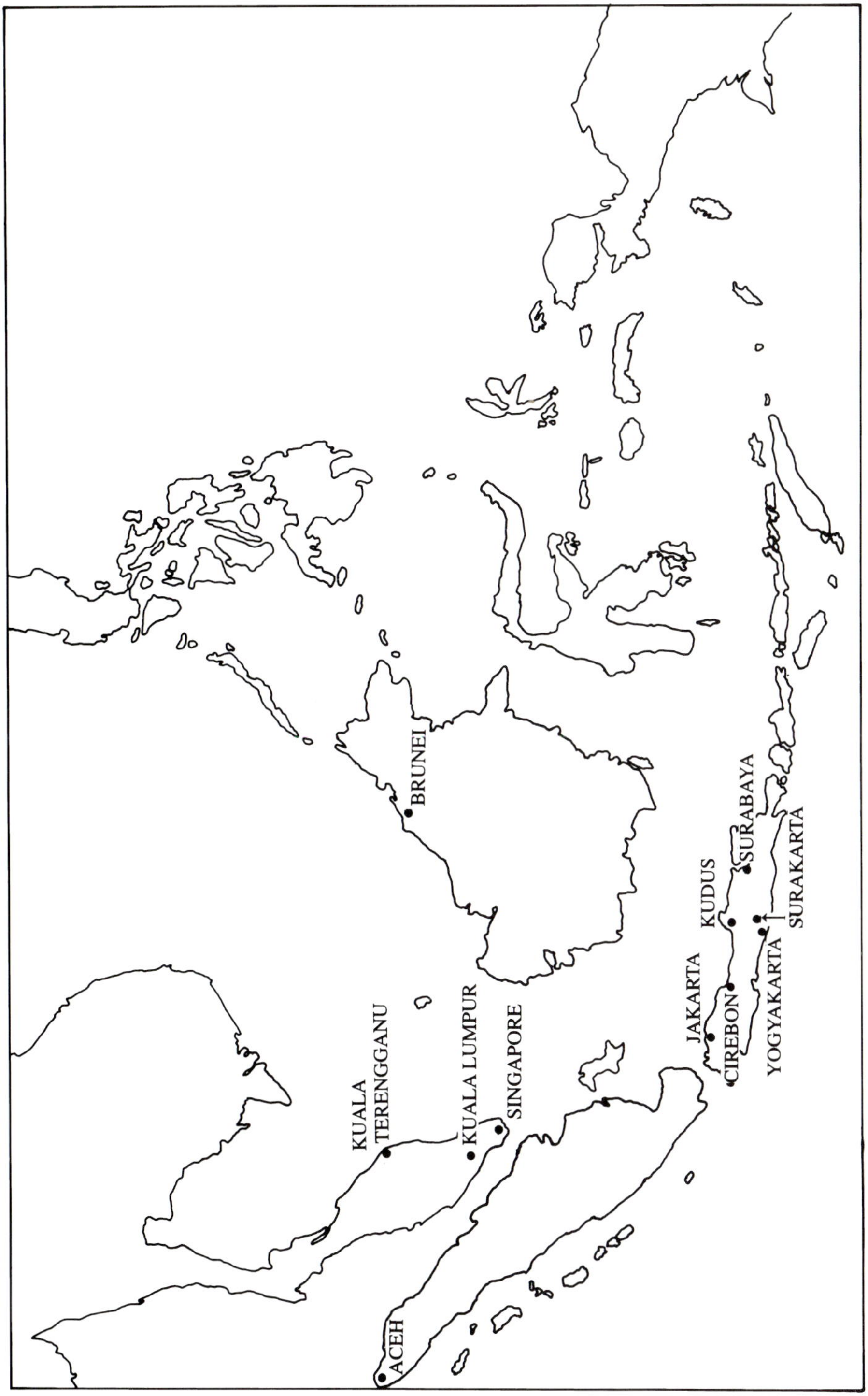

Principal Islamic sites of south-east Asia and Indonesia

Further reading:

H. I. Jessup, 'Princely pavilions: architecture as an index to court and society', *Court Arts of Indonesia*, New York 1990, chap. 3.

A. H. Johns, 'From coastal settlement to Islamic school and city: Islamization in Sumatra, the Malay Peninsula and Java', in *Indonesia: Australian Perspectives. I: Indonesia: The Making of a Culture*, ed. J. J. Fox, Canberra 1980.

N. Madjid, 'Islam on the Indonesian soil: an ongoing process of acculturation and adaptation', *Arts and the Islamic World*, 20: 67–8, 1991.

A. A. Nanji, 'Space and spirit: the contemporary expressions of buildings in Islam', *Arts and the Islamic World* 2: 63–5, 1991.

Y. Saliya, 'Mosque architecture in Indonesia: variations on a theme', *Arts and the Islamic World* 21, 1992.

Iran (Islamic Republic of Iran, formerly Persia)

Large Middle-Eastern country containing some of the most celebrated examples of Islamic architecture.

Iran is bordered on the west by Iraq and Turkey, on the east by Pakistan and Afghanistan and on the north by the former Soviet Republics of Turkmeniya and Azerbayjan. To the south the country is open to the Persian/Arabian Gulf and the Indian Ocean. The centre of the country comprises a high plateau surrounded by mountains, to the south and west are the Zagros mountains whilst to the north along the shores of the Caspian Sea are the Elbruz mountains. The majority of the population lives on the edges of the central plateau as much of the interior is fairly barren, consisting of kavir (salt marsh) and dasht (stony desert). Most of the country is fairly arid except for the north-west on the borders of the Caspian Sea where there are forests.

In addition to the present state of Iran, Iranian culture has traditionally extended into the neighbouring regions comprising the modern states of Afghanistan, Turkmeniya, Uzbekistan and Tajikistan.

History

Iran has a long history as a unified state starting with the conquests of Cyrus the Great, founder of the Achaemenid Empire in the sixth century BCE. By 525 BCE Cyrus's successor Cambyses had captured Egypt and was in control of most of the Middle East. The Achaemenid Empire was eventually destroyed by Alexander the Great in 331 BCE after which Iran was ruled by his successors known as the Seleucids. The Seleucids were in turn overthrown by the Sassanians who ruled an empire which included most of modern Iran as well as Mesopotamia. The earliest Arab attacks on the Sassanian Empire took place in the 630s and by 637 CE the Arabs had won a major victory at the battle of Qadisiyya. Although the Sassanians were decisively defeated at the battle of Nihavand in 642 the Arab conquest was not completed until 651 when the last Sassanian emperor, Yazdigrid, was killed near Murghab in Transoxiana. However, even after the emperor's death, resistance continued whilst many parts of the country conquered by the Arabs remained under the control of Persian princes. The Arab conquest was carried out mostly by troops from the Iraqi garrison cities of Basra and Kufa, a factor which subsequently had profound influence on the politics and religion of early Islamic Iran.

For the next hundred years Iran was ruled by a series of governors appointed by the Umayyad caliphs based in Syria. The rule of the Umayyads was resented by many of the Arab troops in Iran, many of whom were influenced by the emerging Kharjirism (opposition to religious claims of the caliphate) and Shiʿism (supporters of ʿAli) of Basra and Kufa. In addition a large number of Iranian converts to Islam were unhappy about their status in relation to the Arab rulers. The result of the growing opposition to the Umayyads was the Abbasid revolution which began in eastern Iran and eventually spread to most of the Islamic world. One of the consequences of the Abbasid revolution was increased Iranian influence in both the culture and administration of the caliphate. During the ninth century independent local dynasties began to emerge as rulers in several parts of Iran, the most significant of which were the Buwaihids. The Buwaihids were a Shiʿa group originating from the Caspian region who eventually dominated even the Abbasid caliphs. In the ninth century eastern Iran (including the modern states of Afghanistan and Uzbekistan) was under the control of the Samanids based at Bukhara and Samarkand. In 1040 the Seljuk Turks conquered the whole of Iran and established the great Seljuk Empire. For a short period in the eleventh century a huge area from Syria to eastern Iran was nominally under the control of the Seljuks who as a Sunni group were endorsed by the religious orthodoxy and the caliphate in Baghdad. However, the unity of the

Seljuks was short lived and by the end of the eleventh century the empire was divided into a number of independent principalities. In the mid-thirteenth century Iran was conquered by the Mongols who dominated the country for the next hundred years. In the late thirteenth century the Mongol leader Ghazan Khan converted to Islam and broke away from central Mongol control. Between 1381 and 1404 Iran was subjected to another devastating Mongol invasion under the legendary Timur. The Timurid state in western Iran did not last long after Timur's death in 1405 and was replaced by the Turkoman dynasties who ruled until 1501 when they were defeated by the forces of the Saffavids under Shah Isma'il. However, in eastern Iran Timurid rule continued until 1510 when the last Timurid sultan was defeated by the Saffavids.

The Saffavids ruled Iran for more than 200 years establishing it as a unified modern state. Unlike their predecessors, the Saffavids were Shi'a and converted most of Iran to this form of Islam. By the 1730s the Saffavids were no longer able to control large areas of the country which was subjected to increasing Afghan attacks. In the 1740s the Afghans were repulsed by a Nadir Shah, ruler of a local north-eastern dynasty known as the Zands. Nadir Shah's success against the Afghans enabled him to take control of the whole of Iran, though the Saffavids remained nominally in control. In 1779 the Zands were overthrown by the leader of a Turkish dynasty known as the Qajars who ruled the country until 1924 when they were replaced by the modernizing Pahvli dynasty. In 1979 the last Pahvli ruler was overthrown and Iran became an Islamic republic.

Architecture

The building materials vary from place to place and according to the period although certain materials and techniques tend to remain predominant. For most of the Islamic period the shortage of suitable stone has meant that brick (baked or unbaked) has been the main construction material. Unbaked mud brick or pisé is generally the cheapest building material and has been used for most Iranian houses since early times. In many buildings mud brick is used in conjunction with baked brick which is employed for the more important parts of the structure. Baked (or fired) bricks were used for more important monuments in the early Islamic period although later they were adopted for a wider range of building types. In the earliest monuments brickwork is undecorated with large expanses of plain wall in the Sassanian tradition. In later buildings decorative patterns are introduced which reach their culmination under the Seljuks with complex geometric patterns and inscriptions. Two techniques of brickwork decoration (hazarbaf) are used, one employing bricks of standard size arranged in simple patterns and the other using bricks specially cut or manufactured for the purpose. The latter technique was more suitable for inscriptions and complex motifs. Also during the Seljuk period buildings began to be decorated with glazed bricks and coloured ceramic tile inlays. During the Seljuk and Ilkhanid periods the preferred colours were turquoise, light blue and dark blue. In earlier buildings glazed tiles and bricks were set into the exterior walls of buildings to enliven the uniform earth colours of the brick and dark blue; however, during the fourteenth century the technique of tile mosaic was developed whereby large areas would be covered by tiles specially cut or shaped to form geometric and floral designs. Under the Timurids new colours were introduced including green, yellow and terracotta. The technique of tile mosaic was perfected in the fifteenth century under the Timurids who also introduced new colours including green and yellow. During the sixteenth century the Saffavids introduced overglaze painted panels using a technique known as haft-rangi (i.e. seven colours). The advantage of this technique was that it was possible to cover large areas fairly cheaply, although the quality of the colours was inferior to that produced in tile mosaics.

Cut stone architecture is rare in Iran which has no tradition of ashlar masonry to compare with that of the eastern Mediterranean. There are, however, several notable exceptions to this such as the Khuda Khana of the Friday mosque in Shiraz built in 1351. However, most stone buildings in Iran were made out of rubble stones set within a thick mortar and covered with plaster. The lack of a stone carving tradition in Iran led to the development of decorative plasterwork or stucco. The technique of stucco decoration was developed under the Sassanians, but achieved its definitive Islamic form at the Abbasid capital of Samarra in Iraq. Subsequently stucco decoration in Iran developed its own form and was used in particular for decorating mihrabs.

Wood is rarely used in Iran except in the northwest region on the borders of the Caspian Sea. Unfortunately few wooden structures survive from the earlier periods although there are several notable examples from the Saffavid period. The most famous example of wooden architecture is the porch of the Ali Qapu Palace in Isfahan which consists of a flat roof supported on huge wooden columns with muqarnas capitals. Although fairly unique because of its size the porch of the Ali Qapu Palace represents a traditional form in Iranian architecture.

Two types of building are particularly characteristic of Islamic architecture in Iran, these are mosques and tombs. In addition there is a range of secular buildings which gives some idea of the diversity of Iranian architecture. Unfortunately very little survives of Iran's Islamic architecture from before the Seljuk period so that it is difficult to trace the origin of particular building types and their relationship to Islamic architecture elsewhere.

The earliest Iranian mosques were hypostyle structures with the sanctuary located on the southwestern (qibla) side of an open courtyard which was lined by arcades on the other three sides. In the absence of the marble columns used in Syria and Egypt the roof was usually supported by baked-brick piers or wooden columns. Only a few early mosques have been discovered, the most important of which are Siraf, Susa, Isfahan, Fahraj, Damghan and Nayin. The first three buildings were covered by a flat wooden roofs whilst the latter three were roofed with a system of barrel vaults supported on squat octagonal or round brick piers. The walls of these structures were initially built out of mud brick or rubble stone set in mortar and decorated with stucco.

Sometime during the eleventh century a new mosque form was introduced based on the four-iwan plan. The advent of this new building type seems to be associated with the arrival of the Seljuks. Examples of this form are found mostly in western and central Iran and include Isfahan, Basian, Zavareh, Qazvin, Yazd, Kirman and Rayy. One of the clearest examples of this new form is the mosque of Zavareh (dated to 1136) which consists of a square central courtyard with iwans in the centre of each side, behind the qibla iwan is a square domed chamber containing the mihrab. From the Seljuk period onwards the four-iwan plan became the standard format for mosques and later developments took place within the context of this plan. Ilkhanid developments in mosque architecture were concerned with a refinement of the four-iwan plan and the increased use of decorative techniques. The problem of the four-iwan plan is that it detracts from the directional emphasis of the mihrab. One method used to strengthen this axis is the enlargement of the qibla iwan which can be seen in its most exaggerated form in the mosque of Ali Shah in Tabriz built between 1310 and 1320 where the qibla iwan was over 48 m deep and 30 m wide. Another method of strengthening the orientation is the decorative elaboration of the qibla iwan and façade (pishtaq). In the Great Mosque of Varamin built in 1322 the monumental qibla iwan is decorated with giant muqarnas, stucco inscriptions and decorative brickwork.

The collapse of Ilkhanid power in 1335 left Iran under the control of competing dynasties the most important of which was the Muzaffarids who ruled the area of Fars and Kirman. Several innovations in mosque architecture were introduced at this time which collectively have been called the Muzaffarid style. One of the most distinctive features is the use of large transverse arches which support transverse barrel vaults. This system was used in an extra prayer hall added to the Great Mosque at Yazd and the madrassa attached to the Masjid-i Jami at Isfahan. The advantage of this innovation is that large areas can be covered without intervening pillars. This period is also characterized by the growing use of tile mosaic as decoration both for the interior of mosques and for the portal façades.

In 1393 the conquests of Timur brought an abrupt end to Muzaffarid rule and marked the beginning of a period during which monumental building activity was confined to the eastern part of the Iranian world outside the borders of the present state of Iran. However, it is notable that many of the buildings erected by Timur and his successors in Samarkand and Bukhara resemble the earlier buildings of western Iran. One of the reasons for this situation is that Timurids employed craftsmen from western Iran, a fact which may also explain the comparative dearth of building activity in the west. The situation in western Iran later improved under the Qara Qoyunlu dynasty who established their capital at Tabriz. The most significant monument of the period is the Blue Mosque of Tabriz which consists of a domed central courtyard opening on to four iwans. The plan is similar to that of the early T-plan mosques of Bursa and was probably influenced by contemporary Ottoman architecture.

With the exception of Isfahan there were few major new mosques built during the Saffavid period although extensive restorations were carried out to older mosques and shrines. In particular there was an increased emphasis on the shrines of Mashad and Ardabil which were adapted for large numbers of pilgrims. At Isfahan the Saffavids built a new city based on a huge central maidan which functioned as the centre of the city. Opening on to the maidan are two mosques, the Masjid-i Shah and the Masjid-i Sheikh Luft ʻAllah, one on the east and one on the south side. The maidan is aligned north–south whilst the mosques are built on a qibla axis (i.e. north-east–south-west), thus the junction between the mosques and the maidan form entrances bent to an angle of 45 degrees. The Masjid-i Sheikh is the smaller and also the more unusual mosque and comprises a single-domed chamber approached via an L-shaped corridor. The plan of the building lacks the central courtyard found in most earlier mosques and has more in common with domed mausoleums than the typical Iranian mosque. The Masjid-i Shah with its four-iwan plan appears more conventional although it has several unusual features including minarets either side of the qibla iwan, domed halls leading off the side iwans and two eight-domed prayer halls either side of the domed sanctuary area. Perhaps more surprising are the twin madrassas which flank the central prayer area creating a unified religious complex. The architectural unity of the complex is cleverly reinforced by the bent axis which allows a person standing in the maidan to see the entrance portal, the qibla iwan and the large central dome at the same time. The impact of this view is reinforced by the blue and turquoise glazed tilework and the twin sets of minarets flanking the entrance portal and the quibla iwan. Other mosques built under the Saffavids were generally less adventurous in their design and were built on the standard four-iwan plan.

Mosques built during the period of Zand and Qajar rule continued to be built in the classic Saffavid style but with increased emphasis on decoration. The most famous building attributable to the Zands is the Vakil Mosque in Shiraz, which is characterized by its vivid yellow and pink tile decoration. Several nineteenth-century Qajar mosques begin to show variations in the standard format such as entrances placed to one side and multiple minarets.

The development of commemorative tomb structures mirrors that of mosques with few structures from before the eleventh century and a wide range of structures produced before the sixteenth century after which there is little innovation. Two distinct traditions of monumental tombs developed which may be described as domed mausoleums and tomb towers.

Tomb towers were generally reserved for rulers or prominent local princes and were probably a continuation of pre-Islamic Iranian practices. The degree of continuity can be seen in the tomb tower of Lajim where the commemorative inscription is in Arabic and Pahlavi. The earliest and probably the most famous commemorative tomb in Iran is the Gunbad-i Qabus built between 1006 and 1007. The tomb consists of a tall cylindrical tower 55 m high with ten angular buttresses and a conical roof. There is no decoration to relieve the stark simplicity of the brickwork except for two lines of inscription, one near the base and one below the roof. Although unusual, the monument is related to a group of Ghaznavid tomb towers produced further east in Afghanistan. During the Seljuk period the tomb tower became established as the principal type of funerary monument. Other important tomb towers include the Pir-i ʻAlamdar tower (1026–7) and the Chihil Dukhtaran tower (1054–5) both in Damghan. The significance of the Damghan towers is their decorative brickwork which later became one of the standard decorative techniques on tomb towers. Also during the Seljuk period tile inlay and glazed bricks became increasingly popular as a form of decoration. During the Ilkhanid period the standard smooth round form of tomb towers was modified by the addition of semi-circular or angular flanges seen in buildings such as the ʻAla al-Din tomb tower in Varamin (1289). In the ʻAliabad Kishmar tomb tower semi-circular and angular flanges are combined creating a complex interplay of shadows. During the fourteenth and fifteenth century the smooth conical roof form is replaced by a pyramid form in which the conical form is made of a number of flat planes which meet at the apex.

Domed mausoleums are probably the earliest

form of commemorative tomb and can be traced back to structures such as the Qubbat al-Sulaybiyya at Samarra. These structures usually have a square or octagonal base and hemispherical dome, one of the earliest Iranian examples being the Arslan Jadhib tomb built in 1028. Another early example is the Davazdah Imam at Yazd (1036–7) which consists of a massive square chamber covered by a dome resting on an octagonal drum. During the Ilkhanid period the principle of the double dome developed with a tall outer dome concealing a lower inner dome. The purpose of the double dome arrangement was that a tall dome may attract attention to a building from the outside but is unsuitable for the smaller proportions of the interior. Under the Timurids a bulbous dome shape was developed which became characteristic of Iranian architecture and was used on many of the tombs built after the fifteenth century. In addition to the standard dome form a regional variant developed in western Iran which is linked to the Iraqi muqarnas domes.

As well as tomb towers and domed octagonal mausoleums, a third category of tomb is represented by the great shrines of Mashad, Qum and Mahan. Probably the greatest of these is the shrine of Imam Riza at Mashad which was built by the Timurids in 1418 and subsequently adorned by later Iranian dynasties. At the centre of the shrine is a great chamber covered by a bulbous glazed dome. Around the sides of the building are two tiers of glazed iwans and a monumental iwan flanked by twin minarets at the front.

Secular architecture in Iran is represented by a wide range of buildings including palaces, caravanserais, bridges, city walls, bazars, ice houses, pigeon towers and bath houses. Unfortunately most secular buildings date from the fairly recent past and their are few examples from before the Saffavid period. This is particularly true of palaces; thus the Ali Qapu Palace in Isfahan is one of the few imperial palaces to survive. Remains of earlier palaces have been found but these are mostly ruins of buildings destroyed by war or natural disasters. The Ali Qapu forms part of the imperial complex at Isfahan built by Shah Abbas in the seventeenth century. The palace is located on the west side of the central maidan and consists of a tall square building with a monumental porch at the front overlooking the maidan. The porch is more than two storeys high and is raised above the ground on a vaulted substructure so that it functions as a huge covered viewing platform. Behind the main building of the Ali Qapu there are a series of gardens and pavilions which recall the garden palaces depicted in Persian miniature painting. However, most secular buildings such as caravanserais or bazars tend to be of more utilitarian form although sometimes they are enriched by decorative details derived from religious architecture. This process can be seen very early on in Iranian architecture in buildings such as the Seljuk caravanserai of Robat Sharaf where the entrance is decorated with elaborate brickwork and incorporates a mihrab for the use of travellers. This process continued into the nineteenth century as can be seen in the bazar entrance at Yazd which consists of three-storey triple iwans flanked by twin minarets and covered with glazed tiles. However, most caravanserais and bazars contained very little decoration beyond a foundation inscription above the gateway.

See also: badgir, Isfahan, Saffavids, Seljuks, Timurids

Further reading:

T. Allen, 'Notes on Bust', *Iran* 27: 57–66, 1989, and *Iran* 28: 23–30, 1990.

E. Beazley, 'Some vernacular buildings of the Iranian Plateau', *Iran* 15: 89–108, 1977.

—— 'The pigeon towers of Isfahan', *Iran* 4: 1–20, 1966.

L. Bier, 'The Masjid-i Sang near Darab and the Mosque of Shahr-i Ij: rock cut architecture of the Ilkhanid period', *Iran* 24: 117–30, 1986.

S. S. Blair, 'The Mongol capital of Sultaniyya, "The Imperial"', *Iran* 24: 139–52, 1986.

W. M. Clevenger, 'Some minor monuments in Khurassan', *Iran* 4: 57–64, 1966.

H. Gaube, *Iranian Cities*, New York 1979.

O. Grabar, 'The visual arts from the Arab invasions to the Saljuks', in *Cambridge History of Iran*, 1993.

—— 'The visual arts 1050–1350', in *Cambridge History of Iran*, 1993.

R. Hillenbrand, 'Saljuk dome chambers in north-west Iran', *Iran* 14: 93–102, 1976.

—— 'Safavid architecture', in *Cambridge History of Iran* 1993.

—— 'Saljuk monuments in Iran V: the Imamzada Nur Gurgan', *Iran* 25: 55–76, 1987.

L. Horne, 'Reading village plans: architecture and social change in north-eastern Iran', *Expedition* (The University Museum Magazine of Archaeology and Anthropology, University of Pennsylvania) 33(1) 1991.

A. Hutt and L. Harrow, *Islamic Architecture: Iran 1*, London 1977.

—— *Islamic Architecture: Iran 2*, London 1978.

A. K. Lambton and R. M. Savory, 'Iran (v. History)', in *Encyclopedia of Islam* (new edn.), 1954.

C. Melville, 'Historical monuments and earthquakes in Tabriz', *Iran* 19: 1981.
B. O'Kane, 'The Imamzada Husain Rida at Varamin', *Iran* 16: 175–7, 1978.
R. Pinder Wilson, 'Timurid architecture', in *Cambridge History of Iran*, 6: 728–58, 1993
R. Shani, 'On the stylistic idiosyncracies of a Saljuk stucco workshop from the region of Kashan', *Iran*, 27: 67–74, 1989.
O. Watson, 'The Masjid-i Ali Quhrud: an architectural and epigraphic survey', *Iran*, 13: 59–74, 1975.

Iraq

Large country to the north-east of Arabia and west of Iran, dominated by the twin rivers of the Tigris and Euphrates.

The present state of Iraq more or less coincides with the historical term Mesopotamia which refers to the land between the two rivers. The country may be divided into three main geographical regions: the Kurdish areas of the north, the central area between Mosul and Baghdad and the desert areas to the south and west. The Kurdish areas of the north-east are dominated by high mountains which continue into Turkey and Iran. The central area between the rivers is extremely flat, especially the southern areas and it is here that the remains of the ancient civilizations (Sumerians, Babylonians, Assyrians) have been found. The desert areas to the west are sparsely populated and have connections with the Arabic countries to the west and south.

Before the Arab conquests in the seventh century Iraq was ruled by the Sassanians from their capital at al-Mada'in or Ctesiphon. In 633 CE the Muslim Arabs crossed the Euphrates and occupied Hira; four years later at the battle of Qadisiyya the Sassanians were defeated. Initially the Arabs ruled from the old Sassanian capital but later moved to the newly established garrison town of Kufa. Basra, the other garrison city, was later built to cope with the increasing number of immigrants. Under the Umayyads the Islamic empire continued to expand, which led to the continued development of the garrison cities. In order to retain order a third, Wasit, was established midway between Kufa and Basra.

With the Abbasid revolution of 750 Iraq was established as the home of the caliphate. This shift in political power is symbolized by the building of Baghdad as a new capital in 762. Conflict between the caliph's soldiers and the local population in Baghdad resulted in the al-Mu'tassim founding a new capital further north at Samarra. For a little over fifty years Samarra was capital of the Islamic world but in 889 Caliph Mu'tamid moved back to Baghdad. Abbasid power in Iraq was smashed in 946 by the Buwaihids, a Sh'ite Persian dynasty who ruled in the name of the Abbasid caliphs. The Buwaihids spent considerable sums on building activity in Iraq, their most famous construction being the Bimaristan (hospital) built in 978 at a cost of 100,000 dinars. The Buwaihids were replaced as rulers by the Seljuks who ruled until 1154 when the long-dormant Abbasid caliphs were able to reassert their power over much of Iraq. In 1258 the Mongols sacked Baghdad putting an end to further hopes of Abbasid revival. Under the Ilkhanids Iraq was ruled by local governors, a situation which was changed when the Jalairids took over in the fourteenth century and ruled from Baghdad. In the sixteenth century Iraq was conquered by the Ottomans who incorporated it into the Ottoman Empire.

The principal building material of Iraq is mud brick whilst baked brick is used for more permanent or important structures. The abscence of suitable wood led to the development of vaults, arches and domes that could be built without wood. In the Kurdish areas of the north hewn stone set into a thick limey mortar (juss) is used as a building material. This method is also used in the desert areas of the west although mud brick is also used. The only form of wood available is the palm tree and split palm trunks are sometimes used for roofing. In the southern area near the entrance to the Gulf is a unique marshy environment where reeds are the main building material.

Architecturally the most significant time is the early Islamic period up until the tenth century. During this period five major cities were established (Kufa, Basra, Wasit, Baghdad and Samarra) which had an effect on the art and architecture of the whole Islamic world. During the medieval period Iraqi architecture generally follows that of Iran with few innovations or great monuments. One exception to this is the Harba bridge near Samarra which has a long brick inscription which is one of the finest examples of its type. Another exception is a building type known as the conical-domed mausoleum which has its origin in Iraq. The conical dome comprises a tall dome made of interlocking muqarnas vaults which has the

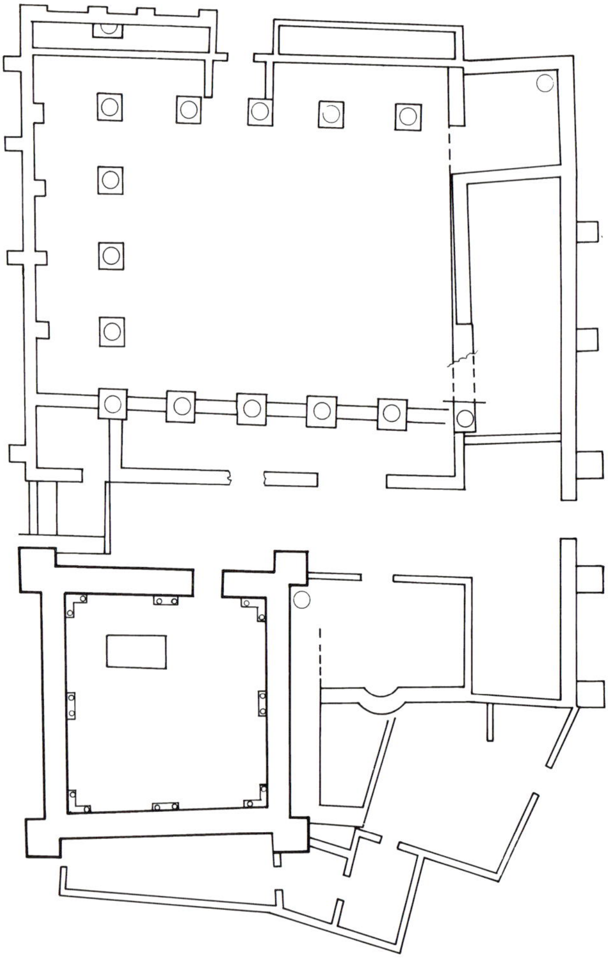

Plan of mosque and tomb of Imam Dur, Samarra, Iraq (after al-Janabi)

appearance of a honeycomb. The earliest example is the tomb of Imam Dur north of Samarra, built by the Seljuk Sharif al-Daula between 1061 and 1065. Other examples in Iraq include the Zumurrud Khatun tomb in Baghdad and the tomb of the prophet Ezekiel in Kifl. From Iraq the form spread to Syria where it was used in Damascus at the tomb and hospital of Nur al-Din.

The main development during the Ottoman period was the development of the shrines at the Shiʿa holy cities of Kerbala, Khadamiya, Najaf and Samarra. The architecture of these shrines is mostly Iranian and much of the work was either paid for or built by the Saffavid shahs of Iran. Saffavid influence can also be seen outside the immediate vicinity of the shrines in the pilgrim caravanserais between Kerbala and Najaf or in some of the bridges in the area.

See also: ʿAtshan, Baghdad, Basra, Kufa, Samarra, Ukhaidhir, Wasit

Further reading:

T. al-Janabi, *Studies in Medieval Iraqi Architecture*, Baghdad 1983.

G. Reitlinger, 'Medieval antiquities west of Mosul', *Iraq* 5: 1938.

Isfahan

Capital city of Iran famous for its city planning under the Saffavids in the sixteenth century.

Isfahan is located in western Iran in an area surrounded by deserts. It is supplied with water by

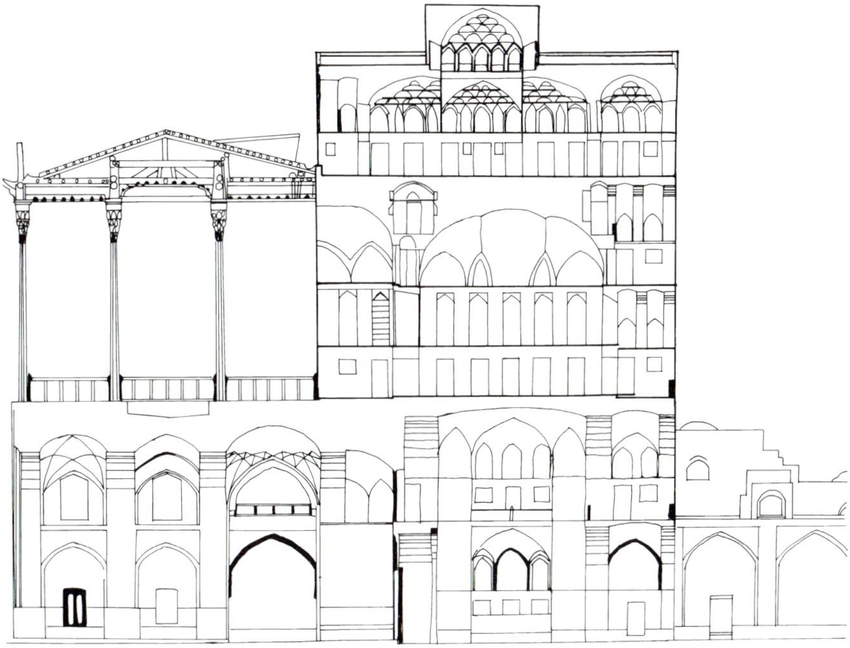

Ali Qapu gateway to palace of Shah Abbas Isfahan, Iran

the Zayandah-Rud which makes settlement in the area possible.

The main building in the city which survives from before the sixteenth century is the Great Mosque. This building was founded in 773 and comprised a prayer hall with a flat roof supported on wooden columns. Nothing remains of this structure, although large parts of the present building, including the north dome and the dome in front of the mihrab, date from the eleventh century. The north dome was built by Terkan Khatun, wife of the Seljuk ruler Malik Shah. Although now incorporated within the mosque it was originally a separate building, possibly another mosque. The most significant feature of the dome is the quality of the brickwork which is the best surviving example of Seljuk brick decoration. The dome in front of the mihrab is of similar quality although this is also decorated with stucco work. In the early twelfth century the Great Mosque was fundamentally redesigned by the creation of four axial iwans making this the earliest example of the four-iwan plan mosque which was later to be the characteristic form for Iranian mosques.

In the sixteenth century the city was completely replanned under the Saffavid ruler Shah Abbas. The centre of this new plan was the famous maidan which is a huge rectangular open space which could be used for recreation and public displays. The principal buildings of the new capital were built around this maidan. At the south end is the Shah Mosque and facing each other near the middle of the maidan are the Luft ʻAllah Mosque and the Ali Qapu or gate to the Shah's palace. At the north end there is a caravanserai and the entrance on to the bazar. To the west of the maidan there was a park area with a long boulevard leading south across the river to a country palace known as the Hazar-Jarib.

See also: Iran

Israel

See Palestine.

Istanbul (Byzantine Constantinople)

Capital city of the Byzantine and Ottoman empires, now the largest city in the modern state of Turkey.

History

Constantinople was founded by the Roman emperor Constantine in 330 CE on the site of an earlier

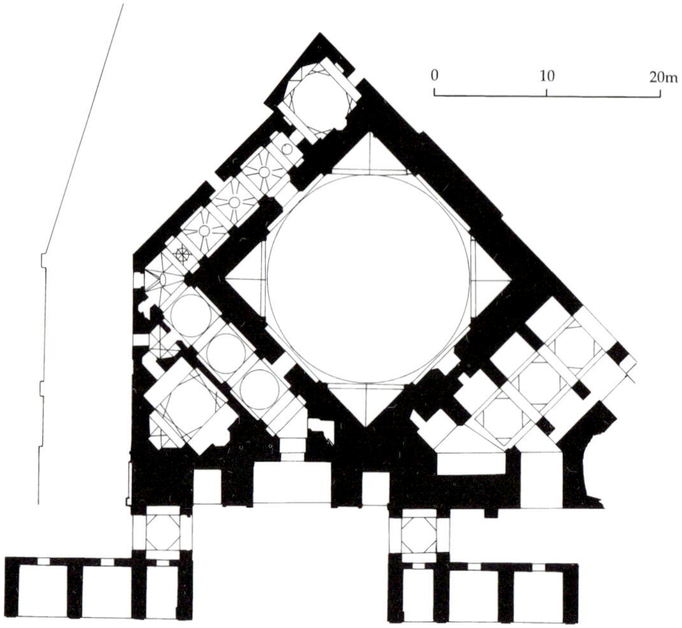

Plan of seventeenth-century mosque of Luft ʻAllah, Isafahan, Iran

town which traced its origins back to the Iron Age. At the centre of Constantine's city was the hippodrome, the imperial palace and the first cathedral of St Sophia (Hagia Sophia). By the fifth century the population of the city had grown so fast that Theodosius expanded the circuit of the city wall to include a large area to the west; these walls remain the boundary of the city. In 1453 the city finally fell to the Ottoman Turks after centuries of gradual Turkish advances. By the time of the final conquest the Ottomans controlled the land on both sides of the city so that it was in effect under permanent siege. The Ottoman conquest was a well-ordered operation which took several years and involved the construction of two large fortresses (Rumeli and Anadolu Hisarlar) on either side of the Bosphorus and two either side of the Dardenelles (Sultan Kale and Kilidbahir Kale) to enforce a blockade of the besieged city. The city which the Ottomans took over was in a dilapidated state with a declining population and and had little of the grandeur associated with the early Byzantine city. Much of the damage had been caused by the Fourth Crusade in the twelfth century which had been diverted from its objective and sacked Constantinople instead.

The city has a unique position on a peninsula at the point where the Bosphorus joins the Sea of Marmara. Surrounded by water on three sides, it has easy access to the Black Sea, the Aegean and the Mediterranean making it ideal as an imperial capital.

During the Ottoman period the city rapidly expanded to include the area of Galta on the opposite side of the Golden Horn and the various towns on the Asian side like Üskudar. Also during this period the banks of the Bosphorus up towards the Black Sea were gradually developed as residential areas and during the eighteenth and nineteenth centuries this became the fashionable area.

After the conquest the hippodrome (Turkish: Atmeydan) and cathedral of St Sophia remained the centre of the city with the cathedral converted into a mosque by the addition of a wooden minaret to one of the turrets. The first Ottoman palace (Eski Sarai) begun in 1454 was built between the old forum and the market area overlooking the Golden Horn. The palace was located in the middle of a park surrounded by high walls and was later abandoned as imperial residence in favour of the Topkapisarai. The new palace built on the site of the former acropolis was completed in 1472 and

Masjid Luft 'Allah, Isfahan, Iran, © J.W.A Allan, Ashmolean Museum

remained the centre of the empire until the twentieth century. In addition to the royal palace there were also a number of smaller palaces for notables, the most important of which is the palace of Ibrahim Pasha (now the Islamic Art Museum) located on the north side of the Atmeydan.

Architecture

The first major mosque, the Fatih Cami, was begun in 1463 although smaller mosques were built before that date and some date from before the conquest. Like the Hagia Sophia some of the earliest mosques were converted churches and those that were not (like the Yarhisar Cami) were mostly square domed units with a portico. Despite the conversion of churches in 1459 the Ottomans encouraged the former Christian inhabitants of the city to return and they were offered land grants as an incentive.

With the completion of the Fatih Cami in 1470 the city had its first imperial mosque which was followed forty years later by the Beyazit complex and sixty years later by Selim I's mosque. For nearly 100 years, until the completion of Sinan's masterpiece, the mosque of Suleyman in 1557, the Fatih Cami remained the largest and most important mosque. The Süleymaniye became most important of the imperial mosques for the rest of the Ottoman period, although the Sultan Ahmet Cami (Blue Mosque) with its position next to the Atmeydan (Hippodrome) and its six minarets attracted a lot of attention. Each of the imperial mosques was accompanied by a complex consisting of madrassas (colleges), hospices, bath houses and shops. The revenue from the shops, hammams and any other endowments was used to pay for the upkeep of the mosque and its charitable dependencies. The revenue from the Süleymaniye foundation was still large enough to pay for the upkeep of over 300 people in 1900.

The key to Istanbul's success was its many markets or bazars which continue to be some of the busiest in the Islamic world. Soon after the conquest the city was provided with two bedestans and later a third at Galata. These formed the centre of commercial life in the city with bazars growing up around each bedestan. The commercial centre of the city during the Byzantine period had been the area around Hagia Sophia but during the Ottoman period it moved to its present position near Eminönü and Sirkeci. The centre of this bazar is the bedestan established by Mehmet II which consists of a central hall covered by fifteen domes. In 1701 the bazaar around this bedestan was roofed over to become the covered bazar.

Throughout its history most of the houses of Istanbul were built of wood with stone or brick foundations and tiled roofs. The houses were built out of a wooden frame and then covered with weather boarding on the outside with shallow double pitched roofs. Houses were usually two storeys high and often had cantilevered windows projecting out over the street. The predominant use of wood caused great danger from fires and there were frequent regulations which tried to make people build in brick or stone. Before the twentieth century the skyline of Istanbul was punctuated with frequent water towers which were to be used in the event of fire.

Since Byzantine times water had come into the city along a network of channels and aqueducts from the Belgrade forest. On taking over the city the Ottomans repaired the water system building

J

jali

An Indian term for a perforated stone screen, usually with an ornamental pattern.

jami or jami masjid

A congregational mosque which can be used by all the community for Friday prayers.

jarokha

A Mughal term for a projecting covered balcony, often used for ceremonial appearances.

Java

Large island in south-east Indonesia located between Sumatra and Borneo, now forming the main island of the State of Indonesia.

The earliest traces of Islam in Java may be from as early as the eleventh century in the form of an inscribed tombstone found at Leran. However, it was not until the late fourteenth century that Islam became a major force in the politics of the island. Before the fourteenth century Islam had been a minority religion spread by Muslim sea traders from Malaysia and India. The predominant religion before the arrival of Islam was Hinduism, though some Buddhism also existed there. Central Java is covered with the remains of Hindu temples from this period, the most famous of which is Borabadur. The most important of the states in pre-Islamic Java was the kingdom of Majapahit (founded in 1293) which in the fourteenth century controlled the greater part of Indonesia and large parts of the Malay Peninsula. After the death of King Rajasanagara in 1389 the Majapahit declined rapidly mostly due to the rising power of the Malaysian state of Malacca which by this time had been converted to Islam. The Majapahit kingdom continued until the early sixteenth century when it was finally replaced by Islamic kingdoms.

Despite the political and religious defeat of the Old Javanese state, the culture of Java continued in the Islamic states that replaced it, including their architecture. The centre of Javanese cult life had always been the mountain, often surrounded by the sea. In architecture this was symbolized by artificial hills surrounded by moats, a feature found in the palaces and mosques of the new Islamic states. Three main types of monument have been identified from the Islamic period, these are palaces (*kraton*), mosques and gardens (*taman*).

Palaces

The palaces of the Islamic states developed from those of their Javanese predecessors although it is likely that the Islamic buildings also drew on some other traditions. The Javanese kratons have particular ritual significance and were built as symbolic representations of the cosmos with the king at the centre. The typical layout of the complexes reflects this symbolism with a central area surrounded by symmetrically arranged courtyards. The design of the palaces was fairly conservative and new palaces were built as copies of older palaces and were called 'putra', sons of the old palace. The palace of a particular dynasty formed the capital of a state – when the palace was abandoned and moved elsewhere the status of capital moved with it, and the former site reverted to the status of village. The Islamic palaces may be classified into two main groups: the six palaces of the Mataram dynasty, who replaced the Majapahit kings in the sixteenth century; and the palaces of the earlier Islamic kingdoms of Banten and Cirebon. In addition there were a few palaces and lesser palatial centres including the rebel palaces at Kediri and Pasuruhan and the courts at Demak and Giri.

The oldest Islamic palace in Java is the Kraton Kasepuhan (Palace of the Senior Sultan) built in 1529 by the Cirebon dynasty. This palace has a circular outer enclosure (*beteng*) which together with its monumental gates and pillar bases shows a marked affinity with the palaces of the pre-Islamic

Majapahit kings. Another early palace is that of the Banten dynasty known as the Kraton Surasowan built between 1552 and 1570. The palace is largely ruined, but remains of the rectangular outer enclosure wall with four corner towers survive, as well as a bathing fountain.

The most impressive palaces were those of the Mataram dynasty built between the seventeenth and eighteenth centuries. Not much survives of the three earliest of these palaces known as Kutha Gedhe, Kerta and Plered, although there are substantial remains of the fourth capital Kartasura abandoned in 1746. Remains at Kartasura include the outer enclosure wall (*beteng*) and the inner kraton wall both of which are made of baked red brick. However, the earliest palace of which there are extensive remains is the kraton of Kasunanan Surakarta built in 1746. This palace consists of an outer enclosure wall (*beteng*) 6 m high enclosing a rectangular area 1.8 km long by 1 km wide. The enclosure contains the inner palace in the centre and around it on either side accommodation for the palace staff and courtiers. The palace is arranged on a north–south axis with a walled courtyard (*alun-alun*) projecting on both the north and south sides. The north courtyard measured 300 m per side and was the main square of the town and centre of royal events. It was entered via a gateway in its north wall, guarded by two monster statues robbed from a nearby Hindu temple; in the centre of the courtyard were two sacred banyan trees. The south courtyard was smaller and of less importance, it contained the palace orchard and its main function seems to have been to preserve the symmetry of the north–south axis. A gateway at the back of the north courtyard (*alun-alun*) led into a smaller courtyard within the palace walls; this was the outer audience hall where the king dealt with the public. A further gateway led into two more courtyards opening on to the central courtyard of the palace which functioned as a private audience court. To the west of this was a large building known as the 'Dalem Prabasuyasa', or inner palace, which contained the ritual symbols of kingship. Either side of the central axis were residential areas: to the west the area for women and children (*kauputren*), to the east the residence of the crown prince and his family.

The palace of Yogyakarta begun in 1756 was built when the Mataram kingdom was divided in two. The basic design is identical with Kasunanan Surakarta although the east–west arrangement was reversed and the southern courtyards were more developed.

Gardens

One of the most sophisticated products of Islamic architecture in Java is the pleasure gardens (*taman*). Like Islamic gardens elsewhere the gardens of Java were an extension of the royal palaces and included architectural elements such as fountains and pavilions besides the usual flowers and trees. However, the symbolism of the Javanese gardens differs from that elsewhere in the Islamic world and is based on the dualist theme of mountain and sea derived from pre-Islamic times. This theme is represented by pavilions standing in water and centrally placed towers or artificial hills.

Although gardens were known in pre-Islamic Java none have survived and the earliest example is the Tasik Ardi in the grounds of the sixteenth-century Surasowan Palace. The gardens, however, are attributed to Sultan Agung who laid them out in the mid-seventeenth century. The garden is badly ruined, apart from the central part which has survived; this consists of a square brick tank with a two-storey stone pavilion in the centre. Other early pleasure gardens dating from the beginning of the eighteenth century can be found at the palaces of Cirebon and are composed mostly of artificial hills with caves set into them. One of the caves at the Kasepuhan garden is guarded by two lion statues and was used by the sultan as a place of meditation. A more complex garden known as Sunya Ragi is located on the outskirts of Cirebon and dates from the 1730s. Like the other gardens at Cirebon the gardens of Sunya Ragi are full of artificial hills covered with small pavilions and caves; however, here the gardens are linked by a complex set of passageways and courtyards. To the west of the mountain area was a large lake known as 'the sea' which contained an island with a central pavilion.

The most remarkable garden of Java is the famous Tamam Sari built between 1758 and 1765 next to the palace of Yogyakarta. This is the largest and most complex of all Javanese gardens, containing some fifty buildings enclosed within more than twelve walled gardens. One of the main features of the gardens is the Pula Kenanga which is a large three-storey building set in the middle of a huge basin. The building can only be reached by raft or sub-aquatic passages. One of the most remarkable buildings in the complex is the Sumur Gumulig which has been variously interpreted as a mosque and place of meditation for the sultan. The building consists of a tall two-storey structure set in the middle of the lake and it can only be reached by a sub-aquatic passage. There are two storeys inside the tower with an open central space; within this area four staircases rise from the ground floor to a central circular platform level with the second storey. A single staircase leads from the platform to the top floor which gives a view over the lake.

Mosques

The earliest mosques in Java were built from the mid-fifteenth century onwards, although there is an earlier reference to mosques in the fourteenth-century Majapahit capital. Unfortunately no early mosques have yet been discovered in Java and the oldest extant structures date from the sixteenth century.

The standard plan of a Javanese congregational mosque consists of a square enclosure with a central platform in the centre on which the main mosque building stands. The enclosure walls are usually fairly low and are decorated with inset bowls and plates from China and elsewhere and in the middle of the east side there is a monumental gate. In many of the early mosques which have survived, the central part of the mosque is further enclosed by a moat. In front of the mosque on the east side is a smaller subsidiary building called the *surambi*, used for social activities, study and the call to prayer. The sanctuary or central building of the mosque is a raised square wooden structure supported by four giant corner posts, between which small pillars take the weight of the wooden walls. The roofs are usually tiered structures made of thatch, with the number of tiers reflecting the importance of the mosque. The minimum number of tiers is two whilst the maximum is five, the top roof usually being crowned with a finial called a *mustaka*. The tiered roof structure is essential to keep these enclosed buildings cool and dry.

Sometimes the roof tiers represent a division into separate floors each of which is used for a different function; thus the lower floor may be used as the prayer room whilst the middle floor is used for study and the top floor for the call to prayer. Minarets were not introduced into Java until the end of the nineteenth century so that in mosques where there is only one storey the call to prayer is made from a veranda or from the attached *surambi*. The *surambi* was not present in the earliest mosques in Java and seems to have been introduced in the seventeenth century.

Inside the mosque there are one or two mihrabs in the west wall and a minbar made of wood, usually teak. The mihrab niches are made of brick or wood and are highly decorated with deep wood-carving derived from the pre-Islamic art of the area. In addition to the congregational mosques there are small neighbourhood mosques (*langgar*) which are small wooden structures raised up on four poles in the manner of typical Javanese houses.

Traditionally the Mesjid Agung at Demak is one of the oldest mosques in Java and is said to have been founded in 1506 although the present structure has been rebuilt and altered many times since, most recently in 1974–5. The mosque has a three-tiered roof and, unusually, a special women's prayer area separated from the main mosque by a narrow corridor. Also of an early date (sixteenth century) is the congregational mosque at Banten which is located to the west of the main square (*alun-alun lor*). The mosque has a five-tiered roof, although within the building has only three storeys. To the south of the mosque is a rectangular structure used as a social centre or meeting place (*surambi*) which was built by the Dutchman Lucas Cardeel in the seventeenth century. Within the enclosure is a tall tower also built in the Dutch style which functions as a minaret for the mosque. Nearby are the remains of another sixteenth-century mosque, also with traces of a stone tower. Both towers date to the mid-sixteenth century, which raises several questions as they pre-date the supposed introduction of minarets into Java by 300 years.

A similar question is posed by the menara and mesjid at Kudus also dated to the mid-sixteenth century. The mosque itself has been rebuilt since its foundation and represents a fairly standard mosque design. The menara or minaret consists of a tower-like brick structure with a split gateway and pottery dishes inlaid into the sides. The design of the menara resembles the lower part of East

Javanese temples and may actually be a re-used pre-Islamic structure. However, it should be pointed out that many of the earliest mosques were built with pre-Islamic features. The remains of the sixteenth-century mosque of Sendhang Dhuwur incorporate many Hindu Indonesian features in its stone- and wood-relief carving. The winged gateways present a particularly striking image of this style.

See also: Indonesia

Further reading:

H. M. Ambary, *Historical Monuments: Cerbon*, Jakarta 1982.

—— 'Laporan penelitian kepurbakalaan di Pajang (Jawa Tengah)', *Archipel* 1983, 75–84.

T. E. Behrend, 'Kraton, taman and mesjid: a brief survey and bibliographic review of Islamic antiquities in Java', *Indonesia Circle* 35: 29–55, Nov. 1984.

L. F. Brakel and H. Massarik, 'A note on the Panjuan Mosque in Cirebon', *Archipel* 23: 119–34, 1982.

K. P. H. Brongtodiningrat, *Arti Kraton Yogyakarta* (trans. R. Murdani), Yogyakarta 1978.

H. D. de Graaf, 'The origin of the Javanese mosque', *Journal of Southeast Asian History* 4(i): 1–5, 1963.

D. Lombard, 'Jardins à Java', *Arts Asiatiques* 20: 135–83, 1969.

—— 'A travers le vieux Djakarta: I. La Mosquée des Balinais', *Archipel* 3: 97–101, 1972.

T. G. T. Pigeaud, *Java in the 14th Century: A Study in Cultural History. The Nagra-Kertagama by Rakawi Prapanca of Majapahit 1365* (3 edn.), 5 vols., The Hague 1960–3.

G. F. Pijper, 'The minaret in Java', in *India Antiqua: A Volume of Studies Presented to J. P. Vogel*, Leiden 1947, 274–83.

M. C. Ricklefs, *Jogyakarta under Sultan Mangkubumi, 1749–1792: A History of Division in Java* (London Oriental Series 30), London 1974.

U. Tjandrasasmita, *Islamic Antiquities of Sendag Duwur*, Jakarta 1975.

—— 'The introduction of Islam and the growth of Moslem coastal cities in the Indonesian Archipelago', in *Dynamics of Indonesian History*, ed. H. Soebadio and M. Sarvas, Amsterdam 1978.

Jerusalem (al Quds)

Major religious city in Palestine sacred to Muslims, Jews and Christians.

Within the Muslim faith Jerusalem is regarded as the third holiest shrine and the second most important place of pilgrimage after Mecca. Muslims know Jerusalem as the city of the prophets and the place of Muhammad's night journey. The importance of the site to the Jews is that it was the site of the Temple built by Solomon in the 10th century BCE, whilst the Christians know it as the place where Christ was crucified and resurrected.

The first walled town on the site dates from the Middle Bronze Age (1800 BCE). The earliest literary reference is also from the same period when the city is mentioned as one of the enemies of Egypt. The next mention of the city is from the Amarna letters in the fourteenth century BCE. The main source for the subsequent history of the city is the Bible which describes its capture from the Jebusites under David, and the building of the Temple under Solomon.

In 70 CE the Romans destroyed the city in response to the Jewish Revolt. The site lay uninhabited for the next seventy-five years until the emperor Hadrian founded a new city known as Aelia Capitolina. Jews were specifically excluded from this new city and the area of the Temple was left undeveloped (and remained so until the Arab conquest). The layout of the present Old City of Jerusalem is approximately the same as that of the Roman town. In 324 Palestine became part of the Christian Eastern Roman Empire (Byzantium) under Constantine who founded the Church of the Holy Sepulchre in 325–6 CE. Constantine's mother took an active part in promoting the building of Christian places of worship during this period. A depiction of the city in the Madaba Mosaic Map shows it in the sixth century before the Muslim conquest. From 614 to 629 the city was in the possession of the Sassanians under Chosroes II who destroyed many Christian buildings. In 629 the city was recaptured by the Byzantines under Heraclius only to be conquered by the Muslim Arab armies ten years later. For the following 1,200 years (with the exception of the Crusader occupation) Jerusalem developed as major Islamic city although it never developed into a great commercial or administrative centre.

The main building material used for Jerusalem was stone, as wood has always been fairly scarce. The main types of stone available were limestone and Dolomite. Four types of limestone can be found in the Jerusalem region, of which two were used for building in the Islamic period. (i) Mizzi, is a hard fine-grained stone sometimes known as 'Palestinan Marble'. This occurs in two varieties, a reddish type known as mizzi ahmar from near Bethlehem and a yellowish variety from Dayr Yasin 5 km east of the city. (ii) Malaki which is less hard than mizzi but is still hard and fine grained. Outcrops were quarried to the north of the city at Solomon's Quarries and in the Kidron valley.

The development of Islamic Jerusalem can be divided into four main periods: (i) the early Islamic period from the Arab conquest to the first Crusade, (ii) the Crusader period, (iii) the Ayyubid and Mamluk periods and (iv) the Ottoman period.

Early Islamic Period

During the early Islamic period the area of the Temple Mount (Haram) was developed for the first time since Hadrian's destruction in 70 CE. The first mosque known to have been built in Jerusalem was erected by the caliph 'Umar and was described by the Christian pilgrim Arculf as 'a rectangular place of prayer . . . roughly built by setting big beams on the remains of some ruins'. However, nothing of this early structure remains so that the earliest surviving structure in the city is the Dome of the Rock built by Abd al-Malik in 691. This is a large, domed octagonal structure built over the bare rock of the Temple platform, below which is a cave. Related to the Dome of the Rock is the Qubbat al-Silsila which was probably built at the same time.

To the south of the Dome of the Rock is the Aqsa Mosque which may have been started under Abd al-Malik although most of the construction was carried out under al-Walid. The mosque has been rebuilt several times subsequently although it is believed that the present structure maintains the basic layout of al-Walid's mosque. It has recently been demonstrated that the walls of the Haram were probably rebuilt at this time and provided with gateways, thus suggesting that the area was systematically developed by the Umayyads probably as a rival to the Church of the Holy Sepulchre. Further evidence for this comes from the excavations to the south of the Haram which have revealed a large Umayyad palace located at the back of the Aqsa Mosque. This follows the pattern established at other early Islamic cities such as Kufa, where the royal palace Dar al Imara is placed behind the mihrab.

Although it is known that many repairs and rebuildings were carried out during the Abbasid and Fatimid periods there was no major building programme similar to that carried out under the Umayyads.

Crusader Period

The capture of Jerusalem by the Crusaders marked an abrupt end to four and a half centuries of Muslim rule. The Crusader occupation completely changed the character of the city as the Muslim inhabitants had either been killed, fled or sold for ransom. Even most of the Christian inhabitants had fled and the Crusaders had problems repopulating the city with Europeans.

One of the first priorities of the Crusaders was to rebuild Christian churches and monuments and convert Islamic buildings to other uses. Thus the Church of the Holy Sepulchre was expanded by adding a Romanesque transept to the east side of the Rotunda. Elsewhere in the city over sixty churches were built or renovated, whilst mosques were converted into churches. The Dome of the Rock was given to the Augustinians who made it into a church whilst in 1104 Baldwin I made the Aqsa Mosque into a royal palace.

Some of the houses built during this period were similar to southern European town houses with two or three storeys above a shop or store room. However, other houses were built with courtyards in a style more familiar to the Middle East. Several suqs were built during this period and the main suq in the centre of the Old City was largely built during this period. This is a covered street with shop units either side and light openings in the roof.

The Crusades influenced the subsequent architecture of Jerusalem in several ways including the introduction of the folded cross vault and the use of cushion-shaped voussoirs.

Ayyubid and Mamluk Period

In 1188 Jerusalem was recaptured by Salah al-Din and reconverted into a Muslim city. The Haram was cleared of its Christian accretions and reconsecrated as Muslim sanctuary. The cross was removed from the top of the Dome of the Rock and replaced with a golden crescent and a wooden screen was placed around the rock below. Also at this time the famous wooden minbar of Salah al-Din was placed next to the new mihrab in the Aqsa Mosque. However, the major building projects of the Ayyubid period date mostly to the time of Salah al-Din's nephew al-Malik al-Mu'azzam Isa. During this period the most important project was rebuilding the city walls. Within the Haram certain restorations were carried out and at least two madrassas were founded, the Nahawiyya and the Mu'azzamiyya. Also the porch of the Aqsa Mosque was built during this period.

In the later Ayyubid period (first half of the thirteenth century) Jerusalem was again subjected to invasions first by the Crusaders and later by the Khwazmian Turks so that no substantial building work was carried out.

The Mamluk period lasted from 1250 to 1516 and has provided Jerusalem with some of its most beautiful and distinctive architecture. Over sixty-four major monuments survive from this period and testify to the city's wealth and confidence. The Haram in particular received a great deal of attention from the Mamluk sultans who regarded the patronage of building in this area as a royal prerogative. During this period the walls of the Haram were repaired and the interior of the west wall was provided with an arcaded portico. Several major buildings were built within the Haram, one of the more important of which is the Ashrafiyya Madrassa built on the west side. Several attempts were made to build this structure although the final attempt only took two years with masons sent from Cairo. The most impressive part is the open-sided porch, roofed with a complex folded cross vault, with alternate stones painted red to resemble ablaq.

Elsewhere within the Haram various sebils, tombs and monuments were erected. One of the most beautiful of these is the Sebil Qaitbay (built in 1482) which consists of a small three-tiered structure. The tallest part is the square base (about 5 m high), above which is a complex zone of transition (about 2 m), surmounted by a tall dome (about 3.5 m high). The exterior of the dome is carved in low relief with arabesque designs and resembles the carved masonry domes of mausoleums in Cairo, although the form of the carving suggests local workmanship.

One of the most productive reigns was that of Sultan al-Nasir Muhammad during which time the Suq al-Qattinin was built. This is the largest Mamluk complex in Jerusalem and consisted of over fifty shops with living quarters above, two bath houses and a khan.

Characteristic features of Mamluk architecture in Jerusalem include ablaq masonry in a variety of colours (black, yellow, white and red), muqarnas used in corbels, squinches and zones of transition, joggled voussoirs used for supporting arches, composite lintels and relieving arches.

Ottoman Period

One of the best-known buildings of Jerusalem is the Damascus Gate with its monumental bent entrance, crenellated parapet, machicolations, arrow slits and inscriptions. It forms part of the city wall erected by Suleyman the Magnificent between 1538 and 1541. This was one of the many building projects begun in Jerusalem at this time to renew the city's infrastructure and demonstrate that Jerusalem was now part of the Ottoman Empire. By the end of Suleyman's reign the population of Jerusalem had grown to three times its size at the beginning. Another project initiated during this period was the covering of the outside of the Dome of the Rock with Iznik tiles. This took a period of at least seven years during which several techniques of tiling were used, including cut tile-work, cuerda seca, polychrome underglaze, and blue and white underglaze. Also during this period the water system of the city was overhauled with repairs carried out to the Birket al-Sultan and Solomon's pools. Within the city this was reflected in the erection of a series of sebils (drinking fountains).

The later Ottoman period in Jerusalem has not been studied in any detail although a number of inscriptions refer to repairs and rebuilding. During the nineteenth century new suburbs grew up around the old city and there was increased European influence in the architecture.

Further reading:

M. Burgoyne, *The Architecture of Islamic Jerusalem*, Jerusalem 1976.

M. Burgoyne and D. Richards, *Mamluk Jerusalem: An Architectural Study*, London 1987.

A. Cohen, 'The walls of Jerusalem', in *Essays in Honour of Bernard Lewis: The Islamic World from Classical to Modern Times*, ed. C. E. Bosworth, C. Issawi, R. Savory and A. Udovitch, Princeton, N.J., 1989, 467–78.

K. Prag, *Jerusalem Blue Guide*, London 1989.

D. Pringle, 'Crusader architecture in Jerusalem', *Bulletin of the Anglo–Israel Archaeological Society* 10: 105–13, 1990–1.

M. Rosen-Ayalon, 'Art and architecture in Ayyubid Jerusalem', *Israel Exploration Journal* 40(4): 305–14, 1990.

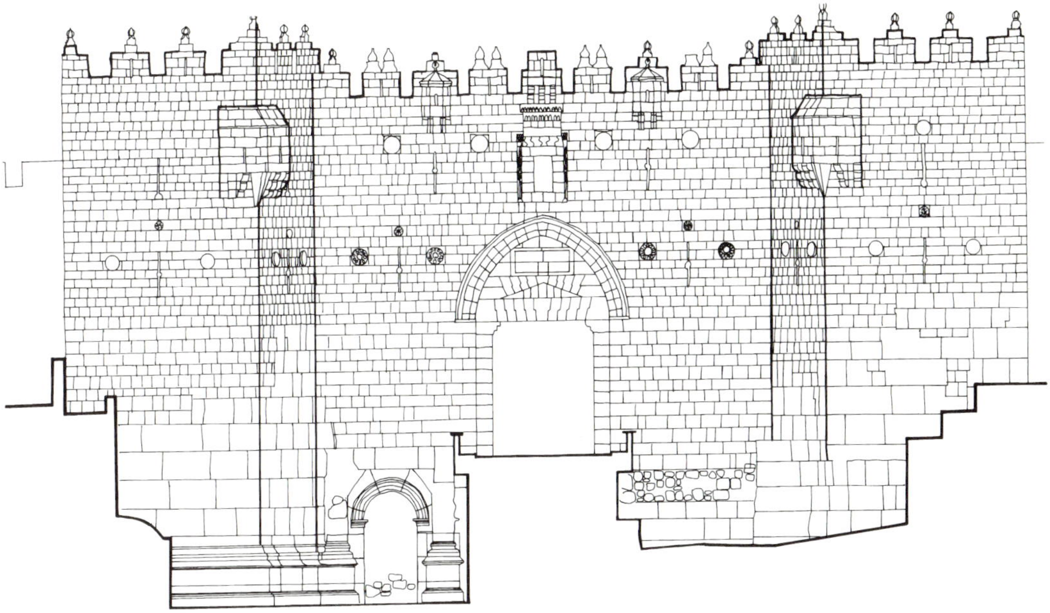

Damascus Gate with remains of Roman gate below, Jerusalem

Joggled string course

joggled voussoirs

Term used to describe a method of construction where stones in an arch or composite lintel are interlocked.

The earliest examples of joggled voussoirs are found in Roman architecture particularly in Spain and France where they are used in bridge construction. It seems that the purpose of this structural device was to strengthen lintels and arches during earthquakes, thus the arch could be pulled apart but would fall back to its original position afterwards.

The first use of joggled voussoirs in Islamic architecture is for the lintel above the entrance to the greater enclosure at Qasr al-Hayr East. Later on (twelfth century) they become characteristic of Ayyubid architecture and stones of alternating colours were used. Under the Mamluks (mid-thirteenth to early sixteenth century) they are one of the main decorative features in architecture and are cut into very complex patterns. At this stage the patterns become more important than the structural design thus the patterns are sometimes achieved by inlaying one type of stone into another or even painting the design on.

Jordan (Hashemite Kingdom of Jordan)

Small country (88,946 square km) located at the east end of the Mediterranean, bordering Palestine, Syria, Iraq and Saudi Arabia.

Jordan can be divided into four main zones, each of which extends into neighbouring countries. In the north of the country the landscape is dominated by black basalt rock which in places forms an almost impenetrable barrier to travel. The oasis of Azraq is located on the southern edge of this region and functions as a station for eastbound traffic to Iraq. The western edge of the country lies within the Jordan valley where it borders Palestine; this area is known locally as the Ghor and includes both the area of the Dead Sea and the east side of the wadi Arabah. The highland area to the east of the Dead Sea and the Jordan river is the most densely populated area of the country and includes the main cities of Amman, Irbid and Zerka. To the south and east of this region is the desert known as the Badiyya; this includes a variety of landscapes ranging from dry steppe in the north to large expanses of sandy desert in the south around Wadi Rum.

Jordan was not a fully independent state until 1946; before this period it formed part of various empires, kingdoms and lordships. Nevertheless, Jordan has one of the longest and richest archaeological sequences in the Middle East, which is reflected in architecture such as the 9,000-year-old Neolithic houses of Beidha. Probably the best-known architecture of Jordan is that of the Nabatean city of Petra which dates mostly from the period between the first century BCE and the third century CE. Here a series of magnificent façades are carved into the rose-coloured rock reflecting the wealth and connections of the Nabatean kingdom. Further north a series of cities known as the Decapolis (including Jerash, Umm Qeis, Umm al-Jemal, Pella and Amman) testify to the prosperity of this area during the Classical and Byzantine period. During the Byzantine period numerous churches with mosaics were built, the most famous of which is one at Madaba which includes a mosaic map of Palestine.

In 631 the first Arab armies invaded the prosperous lands of the Byzantine Empire. After an initial defeat at Mu'tah the Arabs eventually triumphed over the Byzantines at the battle of Yarmouk near the city of Pella. During the next 120 years Jordan was enriched with some of the finest examples of early Islamic architecture found anywhere, including the painted bath house of Qusayr Amra and the palace of Mshatta. Subsequent periods in the history of Jordan are not so well known, with the exception of the Crusader period, when magnificent strongholds were built by both Arabs and Crusaders.

The main building materials in Jordan are basalt in the north, limestone and sandstone in the central highlands and mud brick in the Jordan valley and in areas of the desert. Occasionally in the early Islamic period baked brick was employed for vaulting, although this was not repeated in the later periods. The best examples of basalt construction can be seen at Umm al-Jemal where a system of corbels supporting basalt beams was employed. Limestone was used in some of the finer architecture of Roman and early Islamic Jordan because it can be dressed to a fine finish. Mud brick does not survive well, but representative examples of mud-brick architecture can be seen in the oasis town of Ma'an.

Umayyad architecture in Jordan contains a mixture of eastern and western influences with the result that the surviving buildings represent a variety of different architectural types some of which were never repeated (i.e. the use of baked brick and stone at Mshatta and Tuba). Generally buildings from this period may be grouped into three categories: (i) those which are purely developments of Roman Byzantine architecture, (ii) those which are heavily influenced by Persian (Sassanian) architectural concepts and (iii) buildings which combine both eastern and western traditions.

Roman-Byzantine Influence

Probably the most famous Islamic building in Jordan is the bath house of Qusayr Amra located in the desert approximately 60 km west of Amman. The building stands alone apart from a small fort or caravanserai several kilometres to the north. Inside the building the walls and ceilings are decorated with a remarkable series of frescoes, including depictions of bathing women, a series of royal portraits, a hunting scene and the zodiac. Although the choice of pictures is certainly Umayyad the style of painting and the design of the bath house is purely Byzantine.

Some of the best-known Umayyad castles are re-used Roman forts or fortresses, whilst others are built in the style of Roman forts with more luxurious fittings. Qasr Hallabat is a square Roman fort 44 m per side with square corner towers. It was originally built in the second century CE to protect the Via Nova Traiana and later expanded in 212–215 CE and restored in 529. Careful excavation and analysis of the fort show that it was subsequently changed into an Umayyad residence with mosaics, painted plaster (frescoes), carved and painted wood and finely carved stucco with geometric, floral and animal motifs. To the east of the castle is a tall rectangular mosque with three entrances and a mihrab in the south wall; this building was also decorated with stucco work. Outside the forts, remains of an Umayyad agricultural settlement have been found including small houses. Approximately 3 km to the south of Hallabat is a bath house also of the Umayyad period which probably served Qasr Hallabat. The bath house is similar to that of Qasayr Amra and was decorated with painted plasterwork and stucco. Whilst the particular combination of structures and their design is characteristic of the Umayyad period (a fort converted to palace, bath house and mosque), the individual elements and building style at Hallabat are all Byzantine.

A similar structure to Hallabat is the Umayyad complex at Qastal (25 km south of Amman) which until recently was thought to have been built as a Roman or Byzantine fort. However, recent research has shown that all the main structures date from the Umayyad period. The main structure are a fort-like palace, a mosque, a bath house, reservoir, dams, cisterns, a cemetery and domestic houses. The central palace complex consists of a square fort-like building (about 68 m per side) with four round corner towers and intermediate semi-circular buttress towers. The decoration within the palace is similar to that found at Hallabat and includes mosaics, stucco work and carved stonework. Internally the building consists of a central courtyard opening on to six buyut (pl. of bayt) or houses. Probably the most impressive feature of the building was the large triple-apsed audience hall, located directly above the entrance.

Interior of Qasr Kharana, Jordan

Sassanian Influence ('Eastern')

Structures representing strong Sassanian or eastern influences are less numerous although perhaps more striking because of their obviously foreign derivation. Perhaps the best-known building of this type is Qasr Kharana (located 50 km east of Amman on the present Baghdad–Amman highway). Kharana consists of a two-storey square-plan structure, 35 m per side, with small projecting corner towers and a projecting rounded entrance. The building is remarkable for its superb state of preservation, which includes *in situ* plasterwork on the upper floor. The building is made out of roughly shaped blocks set in a mud-based mortar with decorative courses of flat stones placed in bands running around the outside of the building. There are also small slits set within the wall which were probably for ventilation (their size and positioning means that they could not have been used as arrow slits). Internally the building is decorated with pilasters, blind niches and medallions finished in plaster. The whole appearance of the building is so different from other Umayyad structures in Jordan that scholars have tried to attribute it to the period of Sassanian occupation of the area despite an eighth-century inscription. The best parallels for Kharana are to be found in early Islamic buildings in Iraq such as Khan 'Atshan (similar size and decoration) and Qasr Khubbaz which is built using the same materials (i.e. rough stone blocks set in mud mortar).

Another building erroneously attributed to the Sassanian period is the palace on the citadel in Amman. Like Kharana the Amman citadel building exhibits unmistakable eastern influence in its architecture and layout. The best preserved part of the palace is the building known as the kiosk. This is constructed on a four-iwan plan and decorated with blind niches lined with plaster, a common feature of Sassanian and Umayyad architecture in Iraq (e.g. Ctesiphon and Ukhaidhir). The layout of the palace was huge with at least twelve courtyards arranged on a linear plan. At the opposite end of the complex from the kiosk was a large iwan leading to a cruciform-plan audience hall. All of these features are reminiscent of Mesopotamian palace arcitecture, where palaces are like small cities, containing both administrative and residential areas.

East–West Influence

Two buildings dated to the later Umayyad period (probably the reign of Walid II 743–4) represent a combination of eastern and western influences. The most obvious demonstration of these mixed influences is the use of baked brick for vaults and walls and dressed stone masonry for foundations and architectural details. The most famous of these buildings is Qasr Mshatta located 25 km to the south of Amman. This consists of a large square enclosure with four semi-circular buttress towers. The best-known feature of this palace is the southern façade which consists of a delicately carved stone frieze incorporating animals and plant motifs within a geometric scheme of giant triangles. Internally the building is divided into three longitudinal strips; only the central strip (running north–south) was developed and contains within it the entrance, the central courtyard and the audience hall. The audience hall consists of a triple-apsed room covered by a large brick dome. The layout of the palace immediately recalls that of the Abbasid palaces of Iraq such as Ukhaidhir and has led some scholars to suggest an Abbasid date for the structure. Byzantine elements are also present, however, most notably in the basilical arrangement of the approach to the triple-apsed room and in the motifs of the stonework

Although Qasr al-Tuba is in many respects similar to Mshatta it is much simpler in its decoration and is generally thought to be closer to a caravanserai than a palace. Qasr al-Tuba is the largest of the desert castles and consists of two identical halves, the southern half of which appears never to have been built. Stacks of bricks on the floor testify to the unfinished nature of the building, although it is possible that some of the structure was originally built out of mud brick. Originally there were some fine carved stone lintels at Tuba but these have now disappeared.

Medieval Period

Standing remains of the Abbasid and Fatimid period in Jordan are rare and architectural remains are mostly limited to archaeological excavations. The reasons for this are complex and related to the fall of the Umayyads and Jordan's peripheral position in relation to the Abbasid and Fatimid caliphates. The only place where significant architectural remains from this period have been uncovered are at Aqaba on Jordan's Red Sea coast. This town seems to have reached its peak of prosperity during the Abbasid and Fatimid periods, when it was a trading port in contact with Iraq, Yemen, Egypt and China. Excavations at the site have revealed a walled town (160 by 120 m approximately) with rounded buttress towers and four gateways providing access to the two main streets. Sometime during the Fatimid period mud brick replaced cut stone as the building material for many of the houses.

The Ayyubid and Mamluk periods are marked by the intrusion of the Crusaders who built castles at Karak, Shawbak and Petra to control movement between Egypt and Syria. As a result of the Crusader presence most of the well-known buildings from this period are castles and forts. Examples of Islamic forts can be seen at Azraq, Ajlun, Jise and Qasr Shebib (the Crusader castles at Karak and Shawbak were also remodelled during this period). The best example of medieval fortification can be seen at Qal'at Rabad (Ajlun) built in 1184–5. This consists of several thick walled towers with V-shaped arrow slits linked by curtain walls. The masonry of the castle consists of large blocks similar to those used by the Crusaders at Karak and Shawbak.

In addition to the large castles several smaller forts survive from the medieval period. These

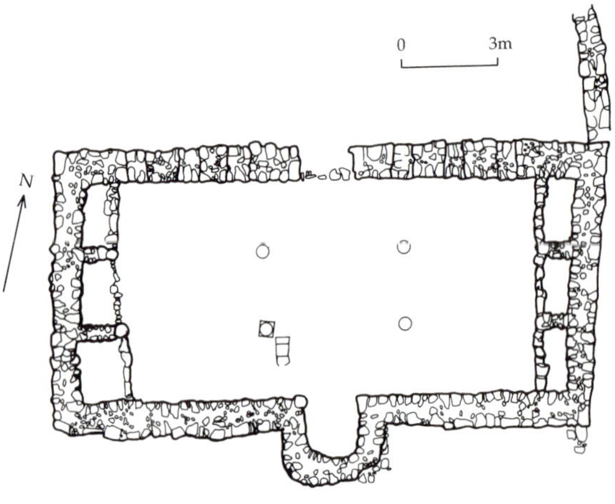

Mamluk mosque at Pella, Jordan (after Bishe)

were either built to protect the road system or as signal posts. Probably the most important route in Jordan was the pilgrimage route from Damascus to Mecca; several forts on this route have survived, notably the forts at Jise and Qasr Shebib in Zerka. Related to these forts is the Mamluk fortified khan at Aqaba. This is a rectangular structure with circular corner towers and a deep protected entrance. The form of the arch above the entrance recalls the architecture of Mamluk Egypt with its ablaq masonry and horseshoe arch.

Later Islamic Architecture

The best-known examples of early Ottoman architecture in Jordan are the Hajj forts which were built to protect the pilgrimage route from Damascus to Mecca. The earliest of the these forts were built in the sixteenth century during the reign of Suleyman the Magnificent. These were small square structures with large decorated arrow slits, projecting machicolations and large crenellated parapets. In the late eighteenth century the fort network was expanded to counter increased bedouin raids. Forts of this period are more functional and have small gun slits instead of large arrow slits, with projecting corner towers to increase the field of fire.

Other early Ottoman buildings in Jordan are difficult to date so precisely, although the fortified farmsteads at Yadudeh and Udruh probably both date from the eighteenth century.

The best examples of nineteenth-century architecture in Jordan can be seen at al-Salt west of Amman and at Umm Qeis north of Irbid. The architecture of both towns shows strong Palestinian influence. Salt in particular shares many features with Nablus. Amman, however, differs from the other cities in north Jordan as it was settled by Circassian refugees. Characteristic features of Circassian houses are the use of wood, the introduction of chimneys and small rooms.

Several mosques of the medieval period are known in Jordan, the finest of which was the twelfth-century structure at Mazar, near Mut'ah (this has now been destroyed). Mamluk mosques can also be seen at Pella and in the fort at Azraq; these are rectangular structures with flat roofs resting on arches supported by columns.

Further reading:

G. L. Harding, *The Antiquities of Jordan*, London 1967.

S. Helms, with A. V. G. Betts, W. and F. Lancaster and C. J. Lenzen, *Early Islamic Architecture of the Desert: A Bedouin Station in Eastern Jordan*, Edinburgh 1990.

A. Khammash, *Notes on the Village Architecture of Jordan*, Louisiana 1986.

R. G. Khoury, *Pella: A Brief Guide to the Antiquities*, Amman and Sydney 1988.

—— *Amman: A Brief Guide to the Antiquities*, Amman 1988.

—— *The Desert Castles: A Brief Guide to the Antiquities*, Amman 1988.

—— *Petra: A Brief Guide to the Antiquities*, Amman 1988.

A. McQuitty, 'An architectural study of the Irbid region with particular reference to a building in Irbid', *Levant* 21: 119–28, 1989.

A. D. Petersen, 'Early Ottoman forts on the Darb al-Hajj', *Levant* 21: 97–117, 1989.

—— 'Two medieval forts on the medieval Hajj route in Jordan', *Annual of the Department of Antiquities of Jordan* 35: 347–89, 1991.

K

Ka'ba

Most sacred building of Islam located in the centre of the Holy Mosque in Mecca.

In its present form the Ka'ba consists of a tall, rectangular, box-like structure 15 m high with sides measuring 10.5 m by 12 m. The building is oriented 30 degrees off the north–south axis so that the corners face the cardinal points. The flat roof has a gentle slope towards the north-west where there is a water spout (mizab al-rahman, or spout of mercy). The Black Stone (possibly derived from a meteorite) is built into the eastern corner of the structure. Also at the east corner is another stone known as Hajar as'ad (the lucky stone) which is touched during the circumambulation. Outside the north-west side there is a low semicircular wall which encloses an area known as the Hijr which is believed to mark the burial place of Ismail and his mother Hajar. The Ka'ba is built of large blue-grey granite blocks set in mortar resting on a base of marble. The entrance is on the north-east side and is 2 m above ground level (it is reached by a portable set of wooden steps). Inside the Ka'ba there are three tall wooden pillars which support the wooden roof which can be reached by a wooden ladder. The floor is made of marble and the ceiling is covered with cloth hangings.

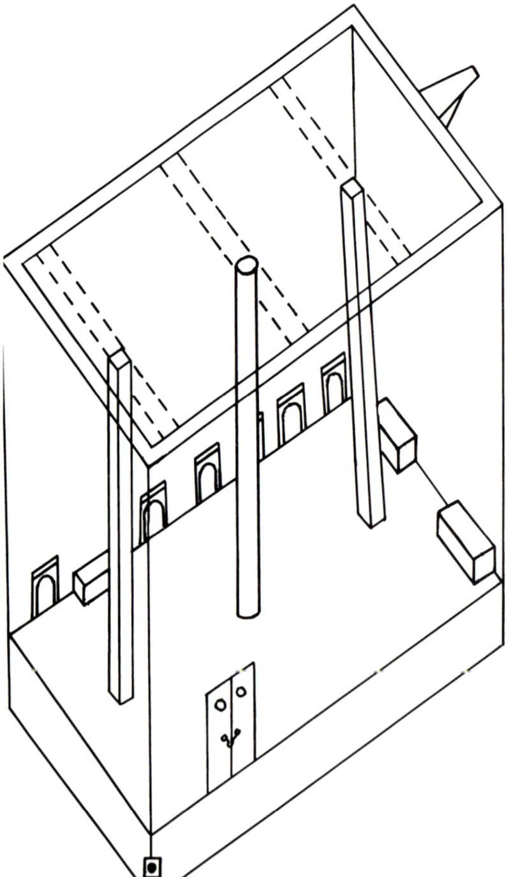

Ka'ba in the eleventh century (after Jairazbhoy)

According to Muslim tradition the Ka'ba was built by Ibrahim and Ismail and was the first sanctuary established on earth. This early building was simply a rectangular unroofed enclosure the height of a man. Idols were housed within the Ka'ba, the most prominent of whom were al-Lat, al-Uzza and al-Manat. Three hundred and sixty idols were arranged in a circle outside the Ka'ba forming a sacred area (Haram) where no blood could be shed. In the time of Muhammad the old Ka'ba was burnt down and it was rebuilt with the help of a man called Baqum. This new Ka'ba was built of alternate layers of stone and wood, possibly in a similar fashion to traditional Meccan houses. The height of the building was doubled and it was covered with a roof. The entrance to the building was some distance from the ground and a ladder was needed to enter it. Muhammad is said to have placed the Black Stone in its position with the help of the main tribal leaders.

In 629 after a period of exile Muhammad conquered Mecca but left the form of the Ka'ba unaltered (except for the removal of idols). In 683 during the conflict between Abd Allah Ibn Zubayr and the Umayyads the Ka'ba was destroyed by stones hurled by catapults. After the Umayyads withdrew the Ka'ba was rebuilt on a larger scale with two doors. This Ka'ba was subsequently destroyed by the Umayyad general Hajjaj bin Yusuf who rebuilt it in its previous form with only one door. This is essentially the form of the present Ka'ba although the Black Stone was removed for a period of twenty years by the Qarmathians in 929. Flood damage in 1611 necessitated its rebuilding in 1630, although the old form of the building was retained. A continuous feature of the Ka'ba's history, at least from Muhammad's time, is that the outside of the structure is covered with a huge cloth of fabric (kiswa) which is replaced annually. During the first years of Islam the old covers were not removed and new covers were placed on top. This practice was stopped in the Umayyad period as the weight of cloths was thought to threaten the stability of the Ka'ba.

See also: Mecca

Further reading:

H. A. A. Ba Salama, *Tarikh al-kab'a al mu'azzama*, 2nd printing, Jeddah 1982.
R. A. Jairazbhoy, 'The architecture of the Holy Shrine in Makkah', in *Hajj in Focus*, ed. Z. I. Khan and Y. Zaki, London 1986.
V. Strika , 'A Ka'bah picture in the Iraq Museum', *Sumer* 32: 195–201, 1976
A. J. Wensinck and J. Jomier, 'Ka'ba', in *Encyclopedia of Islam*, new edn. 4: 317–22, 1978.

Kano

Major Islamic city in the Hausa region, northern Nigeria.

Kano is the most famous of a group of cities including Zaria, Katsina, Gobir, Daura, Biram and Rano which trace their origins back to the eleventh century. At this time Kano was probably pagan, although Muslim traders may have been living there. During the fourteenth century the city was at least superficially Muslim but it was not until the end of the fifteenth century that Kano was firmly established as an Islamic town. The Kano Chronicle records how an Egyptian, Cabd al-Rahman, came to Kano to confirm Islam in the town and build a Friday mosque with a minaret there. During the eighteenth century there was a large migration of people to Kano from the city of Agades in present-day Mali. This influx had a great effect on the culture and architecture of Kano making it into a centre of scholarship and trade.

The city is surrounded by mud-brick walls which at their maximum extent enclose an area more than 15 km in circumference. The area within the walls includes not only the city itself but agricultural and grazing land as well. The city wall is pierced by several monumental gateways, including the massive triple-arched Nasarawa Gate. Inside the city are narrow streets leading on to houses which consist of square or irregular-shaped compounds. A typical compound (or gida) is entered via a circular entrance vestibule that leads into an outer courtyard which may contain huts for unmarried sons and a reception room. At the back of the rectangular reception room is a door leading to the inner courtyard which contains the owner's house, huts for his wives, granaries, a well and a bathroom. The best houses are located within the fifteenth-century palace compound of the emir known as the Gidan Rumfa which is a large area of over 30 acres. This compound is entered via an ancient gatehouse known as the Kofar Kwaru which, with an internal height of 9 m, is the highest internal space in Kano. Within the compound are grazing land for the royal cattle, houses of retainers and public reception rooms, as well as the apartments of the ruler himself. Since the early twentieth century the internal layout of the palace has changed with circular entrance vestibules (zaure) replaced with rectangular rooms (this reflects a wider development in Hausa architecture where rectangular buildings are replacing round constructions). The most elaborately decorated part of the palace is the royal audience chamber which consists of rectangular rooms covered with domed roofs supported on intersecting arches. Both the soffits of the arches and the ceiling panels in between are decorated with brightly painted moulded abstract designs.

The famous Great Mosque of Kano (now destroyed) may be the mosque erected by Cabd al-Rahman in the fifteenth century although little of the structure remains to confirm this. One of the better known mosques of the town is the Yangoro Mosque built by the famous master-mason Bala Gwani. The mosque is divided into a series of small rectangular domed bays (2.75 by 3.35 m) resting on two-tier arches.

See also: Fulbe, Hausa, West Africa

Further reading:

D. Heathecote, 'The Princess's apartments in Kano Old Treasury', *Savanna* 2(1), 1973.

A. Leary, 'A decorated palace in Kano', *Art and Archaeology Research Papers* 12: 1–17, 1977.

H. Palmer, 'The Kano Chronicle', in *Sudanese Memoirs*, vol. 3, 1928.

kapilica

Turkish term for a specialized form of bath house, or hammam, where the building is provided with hot water from a thermal spring. Kapilicas usually have swimming pools unlike the usual Ottoman bath house.

Karaman (Laranda)

City in Konya region of Anatolia noted for its medieval architecture.

In 1071 the Byzantine city of Laranda fell to the Seljuks and remained under Muslim control until the present day, except for a brief period when it was controlled by the German emperor Frederick Barbarossa. In 1256 the city became the capital of the Karaman Oghulu who established many fine buildings in the city. In 1300 the name of the city was changed to Karaman although by 1321 the capital was moved to Konya. In 1397 the city was briefly occupied by the Ottomans but managed to regain its independence after 1402 until it was finally incorporated into the Ottoman Empire in 1415.

Undoubtedly the most famous building in Karaman is the Hatuniye Madrassa built in 1381–2 by Sultan Khatun, the wife of the Karamanid 'Ala al-Din Beg. The building has a projecting entrance portal carved in high relief and flanked by two small domed rooms. The coloured marble doorway is recessed within the portal frame and covered by a tall muqarnas hood in the Seljuk tradition. Inside there is a rectangular courtyard with a vaulted dershane and three cells on each side with an iwan flanked by two domed rooms opposite the entrance. The entrance to the domed rooms flanking the iwan are richly carved with vegetal, epigraphic and abstract motifs. Originally the interior of the madrassa was covered in hexagonal dark turquoise-green tiles although most of these have disappeared.

Other important monuments in the city include the khanqah of Sheikh 'Ala al-Din built in 1460 the imaret of Ibrahim Beg and the turbe of 'Ala al-Din. The citadel and city walls of Karaman seem to have been destroyed in the fifteenth century and the present fortifications were probably erected in the sixteenth. The present Great Mosque has been radically restored and also seems to date from the late sixteenth century.

See also: Konya, Ottomans, Seljuks, Turkey

Further reading:

J. M. Rogers, 'Laranda [Karaman] 2. Monuments', in *Encyclopedia of Islam*, 5: 678–82, 1954.

Kashmir

Isolated region of northern India famous for its wooden architecture.

Islam arrived in Kashmir in the mid-fourteenth century although it did not really become a major force until the Mughal conquest of the late sixteenth century. Wood is the standard building material with deodar (a relation of cedar) being the preferred material for monumental structures. The traditional mosque form consists of a square or rectangular timber hall covered with a pyramid-shaped roof with a pointed spire or finial. The walls are built of logs laid horizontally and intersecting at the corners. Often there was a small gallery or pavilion below the spire which could be used by the muezzin for the call to prayer. This form was also used for saints' shrines which locally are known as ziarat. After the Mughal conquest extensive royal gardens were built around Lake Dal; these were equipped with grey limestone pavilions built in the form of wooden Kashmiri mosques.

See also: India, Mughals

Further reading:

W. H. Nichols, 'Muhammadan architecture in Kashmir', *Archaeological Survey of India Annual Report*, 1906–7: 161–70.

Kenya

Country in East Africa with a significant Muslim population on the coast.

The coastal population of Kenya are part of the Swahili people who occupy the coast from Somalia to Mozambique. The origins of the Swahili culture are problematic although it has recently been shown that the Swahili are an indigenous people who converted to Islam rather than Arab colonists. Most of the settlements have their basis in the Indian Ocean trade to Arabia, India and the Far East and are consequently located next to the sea. There was, however, a strong local economy with connections to the interior which has not yet been investigated in any great detail. For example the walled city of Gedi is 6 km inland and presumably had some contact with inland tribes. It is known, too, that Kenya's fertile coast was attractive to nomadic herders and tribesmen from the north, who periodically raided and migrated southwards into Kenya causing large-scale desertion of mainland sites on the northern coast. The most famous of these nomadic groups were the Galla who raided as far south as Mombasa in the sixteenth and seventeenth centuries.

The Kenya coast contains the remains of many settlements dating from the eighth to the nineteenth century. The remains can be divided into two geographical groups – a northern group based around the Lamu archipelago, and a southern group between Gedi and Mombasa. Between these two areas there are few remains of earlier settlement, probably because there are no useful creeks or anchorages.

The Lamu archipelago is a complex series of islands and creeks which probably represents the remains of the Tana river delta before it moved further south. This heavily indented coastline provided an ideal area for coastal settlement and some of the earliest remains of Islamic trading sites have been found here. The main islands in this group are Pate, Manda and Lamu. Pate is the largest island of the group and contains the walled city of Pate which under the Nabhani kings ruled a large area of the coast during the seventeenth century. Other important sites on Pate are Faza, Siu, Tundwa and Shanga. The ruins at Shanga are mostly fourteenth century, but excavations have revealed a dense continuity of occupation which stretches back to the eighth century and includes the earliest remains of a mosque in sub-Saharan Africa. The nearby island of Manda also contains an early site (known as Manda) which is dated to the ninth century and is one of the only sites on the coast to use baked brick for construction. As well as the important early site of Manda, the island also contains the ruins of Takwa and Kitao. The island of Lamu contains the settlements of Lamu and Shella which have in recent times dominated this area of the coast. To the north there are a few sites on the mainland like Ishikani, Omwe, Mwana, Dondo and Kiunga noted for their monumental tombs. On the mainland to the south, at the mouth of the Tana river, are the sites of Mwana, Shaka and Ungwana. The site of Ungwana is famous for its congregational mosque with two parallel prayer halls which was built in several phases between the fifteenth and sixteenth centuries. The early mosque was built in the fifteenth and later in the same century a second prayer hall with three rows of piers and a domed portico was added.

The southern group of settlements are located south of the Sabaki river and are mostly mainland sites based around creeks. Immediately to the south of the Sabaki river is the town of Malindi which, although largely modern, is built over the remains of one of the main towns on the coast that flourished in the sixteenth century under Portuguese protection. Nearby is the walled city of Gedi where the Sheikh of Malindi had his residence during the fifteenth and sixteenth centuries. To the south of Gedi are the three ruined settlements of Kilifi, Mnaarani and Kitoka which collectively formed the city-state of Kilifi during the sixteenth century. Several other ancient settlements can be found next to creeks further south towards Mombasa. One of the best-known sites is Jumba La Mtwana dating mostly from the fourteenth century. Mombasa itself was an important early settlement with its deep water anchorage at Kilindi although little remains of the early settlement with the exception of a small mosque in the harbour. Mombasa island is dominated by Fort Jesus built by the Portuguese as their base on the coast and later captured and remodelled by the Omanis. One of the most intriguing monuments in Mombasa is the Mbraaki Pillar which has been dated to the eighteenth century. The pillar is a hollow cylindrical structure resembling a minaret, an idea which is reinforced by its position next to a small mosque. However, the pillar has no internal staircase and minarets are unknown in the area before the nineteenth century implying some other function. South of Mombasa towards the Tanzania border there are few early sites although there are ruined early mosques at Tiwi and Diani.

In addition to the pre-colonial Islamic architecture Kenya also contains Muslim buildings dating from the period of British rule and later. Mombasa has the largest community of Muslims on the coast and has several modern mosques which are

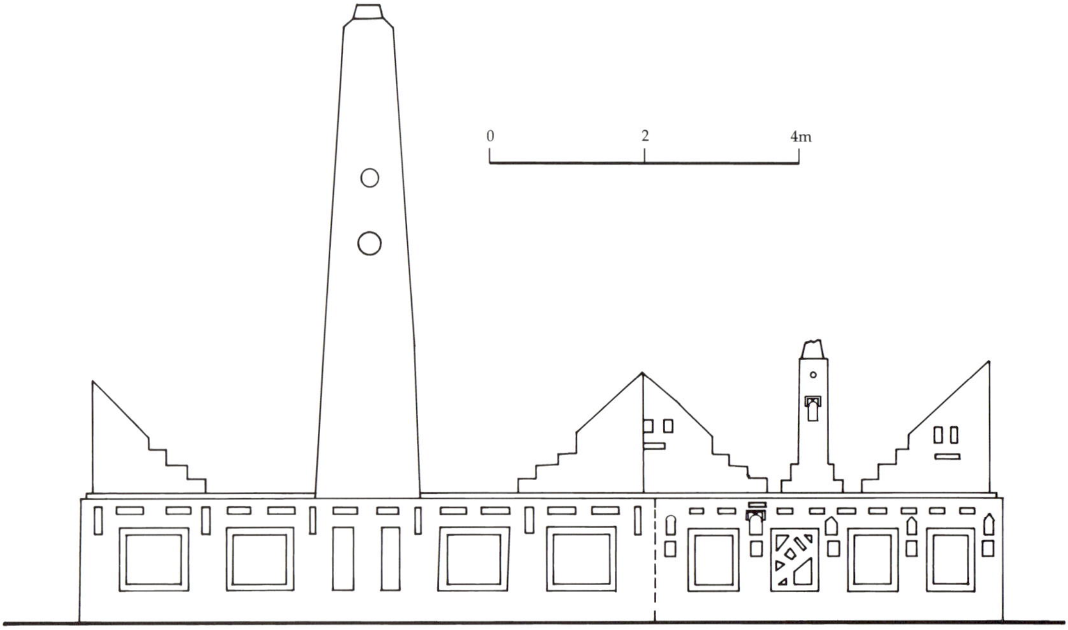

Ishikani pillar tomb, north Kenya coast (after Wilson)

still in use. Also on the main road between Mombasa and Nairobi are a series of small roadside mosques for travellers.

See also: East Africa, Gedi, Lamu

Further reading:

Azania Journal of the British Institute in Eastern Africa, 1965, ff.
J. de V. Allen and T. H. Wilson, *Swahili Houses and Tombs of the Coast of Kenya*, Art and Archaeology Research Papers, London 1979.
H. N. C. Chittick, *Manda: Excavations at an Island Port on the Kenya Coast*, British Institute in Eastern Africa Memoir no. 9, Nairobi 1984.
P. S. Garlake, *Early Islamic Architecture of the East African Coast*, British Institute in Eastern Africa Memoir no. 1, Nairobi and London 1966.
M. C. Horton, 'Early Muslim trading settlements on the East African coast: new evidence from Shanga', *Antiquaries Journal* 67: 290–323, 1987.
H. Sasoon, *Jumba La Mtwana Guide*, Mombasa 1981.
T. Wilson, *The Monumental Architecture and Archaeology North of the Tana River*, Nairobi 1978.
—— *The Monumental Architecture and Archaeology of the Central and Southern Kenyan Coast*, Nairobi, 1980.

keshk

Central Asian term used to describe mud brick buildings with square or rectangular plan and corrugated sides.

khan

Building which combines the function of hostel and trading centre. Standard features which one might expect to find in a khan are stables, store rooms, sleeping accommodation and a mosque.

The word khan is a Persian term, indicating the eastern (non-Roman) origin of this architectural form. Both the Parthians and the Nabateans built khans, the former on the eastward route to India and and the latter on the desert routes in the Negev. The earliest Islamic khans are found in Syria and date from the Umayyad period; examples include Qasr al-Hayr East and West, Khan al-Zabib and the building at Tell al-Sadiyyeh in the Jordan valley. These buildings all have a standard plan comprising a square or rectangular enclosure with rooms built around a central courtyard. During the Abbasid period khans were established on the Darb Zubayda (the pilgrimage route running through Iraq and central Arabia), although the commercial importance of these installations is not known. From the twelfth century onwards khans became a standard feature of Islamic architecture and were particularly popular under the Seljuks. During this period khans began to be established in towns where they would become centres for trade. Also at this time the caravanserai is established as a more specialized form of khan catering specifically for caravans.

During the sixteenth century Ottoman khans developed a variety of forms where the central courtyard is enclosed; some of the best examples are in Damascus and Aleppo. Also at this time khans become part of larger complexes that included a mosque, fort and bath house, as at the village of Payas near Iskenderun in Turkey.

khanqa

A monastery or hostel for sufis or dervishes.

Kharana

Early Islamic or Sassanian building in the Jordanian desert 60 km east of Amman.

Kharana is a remarkably preserved square two-storey structure with solid semi-circular and circular buttress towers. The building is made out of roughly hewn stone blocks laid in courses covered with successive layers of plaster. There are three rows of vertical slits in the walls which have been interpreted as arrow slits, although their height above the inside floor level makes this unlikely. The gateway is set between two quarter-round towers which lead into an entrance passage flanked with two long vaulted rooms that functioned as stables. Inside the building is a square courtyard with a series of undecorated rooms (for storage?) whilst on the upper floor the rooms are decorated with plaster/stucco designs similar to those at Ukhaidhir in Iraq. These include engaged pilasters, blind niches and decorative bosses. Two of the upper rooms have semi-domes resting on wide squinches at the end.

Although it was built before 710 (according to an inscription) and is Sassanian in style, the building is now generally believed to be early Islamic.

Further reading:

S. Urice, *Qasr Kharana in the Transjordan*, Durham, NC: AASDR, 1987.

khatta

An Arabic term meaning marked out (from khatt a line). This term was used by historians of the early Islamic period to describe the process of marking out new settlements or camps (amsar) such as Basra, Kufa and Fustat. The word also conveys a sense of claiming possession of a piece of land by marking out.

Further reading:

J. Akbar, 'Khatta and the territorial structure of early Muslim towns', *Muqarnas* 6: 22–32, 1989.

Khirbet al-Mafjar (Qasr Hisham)

Umayyad palace located in the Jordan valley near the ancient city of Jericho.

The palace at Khirbet al-Mafjar is a large complex comprising three main architectural elements: the mosque, the palace, and the bath house or audience hall. These are all set within a large enclosure entered by a main gateway in the outer enclosure wall. This gateway projects outwards from the enclosure wall and is set between two quarter-circular solid buttress towers. The gateway leads into a long rectangular courtyard which runs the whole length of the western side of the palace. In the centre of the courtyard is a square pool or fountain whilst towards the south end of the west wall there is another gateway leading into the central palace complex. This consists of a roughly square enclosure with solid round corner towers and semi-circular buttress towers in the middle of

Merlon at Khirbet al-Mafjar

the south, west and north walls. In the centre of this palace area is a square colonnaded courtyard with access to the ground-floor rooms. The north range consists of one large rectangular room divided into fourteen bays (two bays wide and seven long). The south range consists of five long rooms oriented north–south; in the south wall of the central room is a large concave niche which may have functioned as a mihrab. Approximately in the middle of the west colonnade is a staircase descending into a small serdab, or cellar.

In the north-west corner of the central palace is a staircase leading to a gateway which gives access to a rectangular courtyard connecting the palace to the bath house or audience hall. In the west wall there is a small opening to the outside, whilst on the east side there is a mosque. The mosque is a fairly simple rectangular structure aligned north–south and entered via a rectangular entrance vestibule on the north side. The sanctuary at the south end is three aisles wide and two bays deep with a concave mihrab niche in the centre of the south wall. In addition there is another entrance to the mosque via a staircase leading down from the upper floor of the palace to a position in the south wall of the mosque next to the mihrab.

Probably the most famous part of the palace is the audience hall or bath house which stands at the north-west corner of the complex. This was a highly sophisticated building consisting of a nine-domed hall supported on sixteen piers and flanked on all four sides by barrel-vaulted exhedrae terminating in semi-circular apses. At the south end of the hall is a pool three aisles wide and filling the three southern apses. In the centre of the east wall is a monumental doorway which leads from a small courtyard in front of the mosque. Directly opposite this doorway in the centre of the west wall is the principal apse distinguished by a huge stone chain which hung down from the arch above. At the end of the chain was a tall conical pendant which has been interpreted as a representation of an imperial

Stone decoration of Khirbet al-Mafjar, near Jericho

Carved stone balustrade next to pool, Khirbet al-Mafjar

Sassanian crown. In the western most apse of the north wall is a doorway into the actual bath complex which is heated by an underfloor hypercaust system. In the north-west corner of the hall is a doorway leading into a small rectangular room with an apse at the end. This room has been interpreted as the caliph's private audience room and is decorated with the famous mosaic of a lion bringing down a gazelle in front of a large tree.

The complex is mostly built out of finely dressed ashlar blocks although baked brick is used occasionally as in the bath complex. One of the most significant features of the palace is its decoration which consists of elaborately carved and painted three-dimensional stucco as well as extensive carpet-like mosaics. The stucco decoration includes representations of semi-naked women as well as male statues which are thought to represent the caliph himself.

There has been much discussion of the purpose of the palace and the function of the various rooms, most of which emphasize the evidently luxurious nature of life in the palace. It is not known exactly when the complex was built and there is no specific identification of it in early Islamic texts. The only historical evidence comes from a piece of graffiti which mentions the caliph Hisham (724–43); however, it is now generally agreed that in its final (unfinished) form the palace represents the tastes and lifestyle of al-Walid II (mid-eighth century). The solution may be that the core of the palace represented by the courtyard palace structure was built during the rule of Hisham whilst the 'bath hall' was added by his more exuberant nephew.

See also: Khirbet al-Minya, Palestine, stucco, Umayyads

Further reading:

R. Ettinghausen, *From Byzantium to Sassanian Iran and the Islamic World*, Leiden 1972.

R. W. Hamilton, *Khirbat al-Mafjar: An Arabian Mansion in the Jordan Valley*, Oxford 1959.

—— 'Who built Khirbet al-Mafjar?', *Levant* 1: 61–7, 1969.
—— 'Khirbet al-Mafjar: the bath hall reconsidered', *Levant* 10: 126–38, 1978.

Khirbet al-Minya (Hebrew: Horvat Minim; ʿAyn Minyat Hisham)

Small Umayyad palace located on the north-western shore of the Sea of Galilee (Lake Tiberias).

The palace is contained within a rectangular enclosure (66 by 73 m) oriented north–south with round corner towers and semi-circular interval towers on the south-west and north sides. In the middle of the east side is the main gate formed by two projecting half-round towers separated by the arch of the gateway. The centre of the building is occupied by a colonnaded courtyard with twin staircases giving access to an upper floor level. In the south-east corner is the mosque which is divided into twelve bays supported on piers. Next to the mosque is a triple-aisled basilical hall, whilst to the north are the residential quarters.

The buildings is built out of finely dressed limestone blocks laid in regular courses with a lower course of black basalt blocks. The top of the walls were decorated with giant stepped merlons whilst the interior was decorated with a variety of glass and stone mosaics as well as marble panels.

The building of the palace is attributed to al-Walid (705–15) on the basis of a re-used inscription set into the gateway. There is evidence that the palace continued in use at least until the end of the Umayyad period and probably, on the basis of Mamluk pottery found at the site, later. Nearby are the remains of the medieval and Ottoman site of Khan Minya which was an important post on the Damascus–Cairo trade route.

See also: Palestine, Umayyads

Further reading:

K. A. C. Creswell, *Early Muslim Architecture*, 1(2), Oxford 1969.
O. Grabar, J. Perrot, B. Ravani and M. Rosen, 'Sondages à Khirbet el-Minyeh', *Israel Exploration Journal* 10(4): 226–43, 1960.

Kilwa

Trading city on the southern coast of Tanzania which has the largest group of pre-colonial ruins in East Africa.

The name Kilwa today is used for three settlements: Kilwa Kiswani, Kilwa Kivinje and Kilwa Masoko. The ruins are confined almost exclusively to Kilwa Kiswani (on the island), whilst Kivinje and Masoko are both later settlements on the mainland.

The history of Kilwa is known from the Kilwa Chronicle which relates the history of the city from its foundation to the beginning of the Portuguese period in the sixteenth century. The earliest settlement at the site seems to have been in the eighth century although there are few standing remains from this period. At some time between the ninth and the twelfth century the settlement was taken over by a new dynasty from Shiraz in Iran who established themselves as sultans of Kilwa. The first sultan was Ali bin al-Hasan who is said to have bought the town from a pagan. The sultans of Kilwa continued to rule the town until the nineteenth century when the last sultan was deported to Zanzibar.

The wealth of the town depended on trade in ivory and other goods, but the most important commodity was gold. Gold was mined in the area of the African city of Great Zimbabwe and taken to the coast at Sofala (present-day Beira), from which it was shipped up the coast via Kilwa. There was also an overland route from Kilwa to Lake Nyasa and the Zambezi but this was always secondary to the sea routes. Sometime in the thirteenth century the sultans of Kilwa seem to have gained direct control of Sofala.

The wealth brought in by the gold trade meant that Kilwa had its own mint and was the only place in sub-Saharan Africa to issue coins. In 1332 the city was visited by Ibn Battuta who decribed it as one of the most beautiful and best-constructed towns he had visited. The wealth of Kilwa was legendary and it was mentioned by Milton in 'Paradise Lost' where it is called 'Quiloa'. However, the arrival of the Portuguese at the beginning of the sixteenth century brought an abrupt end to the prosperity of the city. During the seventeenth century the city seemed to have declined, and to have become a very small settlement, and it was only with the establishment of an Omani base there in the eighteenth century that the city again rose to prosperity. By the nineteenth century the city had again declined to a point where the administrative centre was moved to the mainland settlement of Kilwa Kivinje.

The history of the city is reflected in the surviving buildings, although it should be remembered that the number of stone buildings was small compared to a majority made out of less permanent materials. The main building materials on the island were the same as elsewhere on the coast and included reef and fossil coral used as stone, mangrove poles for wood and coconut palms for roofing. A notable feature of the medieval architecture of Kilwa is the use of domes which is not paralleled anywhere else on the East African coast at this early period. With the exception of some domes in the palace of Husuni Kubwa all of the domes in the Kilwa area are supported on squinches. Elsewhere on Kilwa buildings are covered either with barrel vaults or flat roofs made out of wood and concrete. The Makutani Palace may be an exception to this as it seems to have had a wooden roof covered with palm thatch (makuti).

The main buildings on Kilwa are the Great Mosque and the Great House, the Small Domed Mosque, the Jangwani Mosque, the palace of Husuni Kubwa and the nearby Husuni Ndogo, the Makutani palace and the Gereza fort. There are also important ruins on nearby islands including Songo Mnara, Sanje Majoma and Sanje ya Kate.

The best-known building in Kilwa is the Great Mosque which is a large complex structure dating from several periods. The building consists of two main parts, a small northern part divided into sixteen bays and a larger southern extension divided into thirty bays. The earliest phase evident at the mosque is dated to the tenth century although little survives of this above foundation level. The earliest standing area of the mosque is the northern part which dates to the eleventh or tenth century and was modified at the beginning of the thirteenth. This area was probably covered with a flat roof supported on nine timber columns. The next phase included the addition of a large cloistered courtyard to the south supported on monolithic coral stone columns and a small chamber to the south-west covered by a large dome. This was probably the sultan's personal prayer room and the dome is the largest dome on the East African coast, with a diameter of nearly 5 m. Also belonging to this period is the southern ablutions courtyard which included a well, latrines and at least three water tanks. Sometime in the fifteenth century this arcaded southern courtyard was rebuilt and covered over with the present arrangement of domes and barrel vaults supported on composite octagonal columns, making this the largest pre-nineteenth-century mosque in East Africa.

Adjacent to the Great Mosque on the south side is the Great House which mostly dates to the same period as the latest phase of the mosque (i.e. eighteenth century). The Great House actually consists of three connected residential units each with a sunken central courtyard. Most of the complex would have been a single storey although a second floor was added to some of the central area. The purpose of the Great House is not known, but it is likely that at some stage it served as the sultan's residence judging from a royal tombstone found during excavations.

To the south-west of the Great Mosque is the Small Domed Mosque which together with the Jangwani Mosque are the only two examples of a nine-domed mosque in this area. This building probably dates from the mid-fifteenth century (it is built on an earlier structure) and contains an arrangement of vaults and domes similar to the later phase of the Great Mosque. There are only two entrances, one on the south side opposite the mihrab and one in the centre of the east side. Domes cover most of the area of the mosque except for two bays covered with barrel vaults, one next to the entrance and one in front of the mihrab. The central bays are differentiated from the side bays by being wider and by the use of barrel vaults at either end, emphasizing the north–south axis. The dominant feature of the mosque is the central dome which is crowned with an octagonal pillar and internally contains three concentric circles of Islamic glazed bowls set within the dome. The two vaults to the north and south of the central dome are also decorated with inset bowls of glazed ceramics whilst the two domes either side of it are fluted internally; the other four domes are plain internally.

The other nine-domed mosque is of approximately the same date and is known as the Jangwani Mosque; it is located to the south of the Small Domed Mosque. Although more ruinous, excavation has shown this mosque to be similar, with the same use of fluted and plain domes, and entrances only on the south and east sides.

To the east of the main group of buildings are

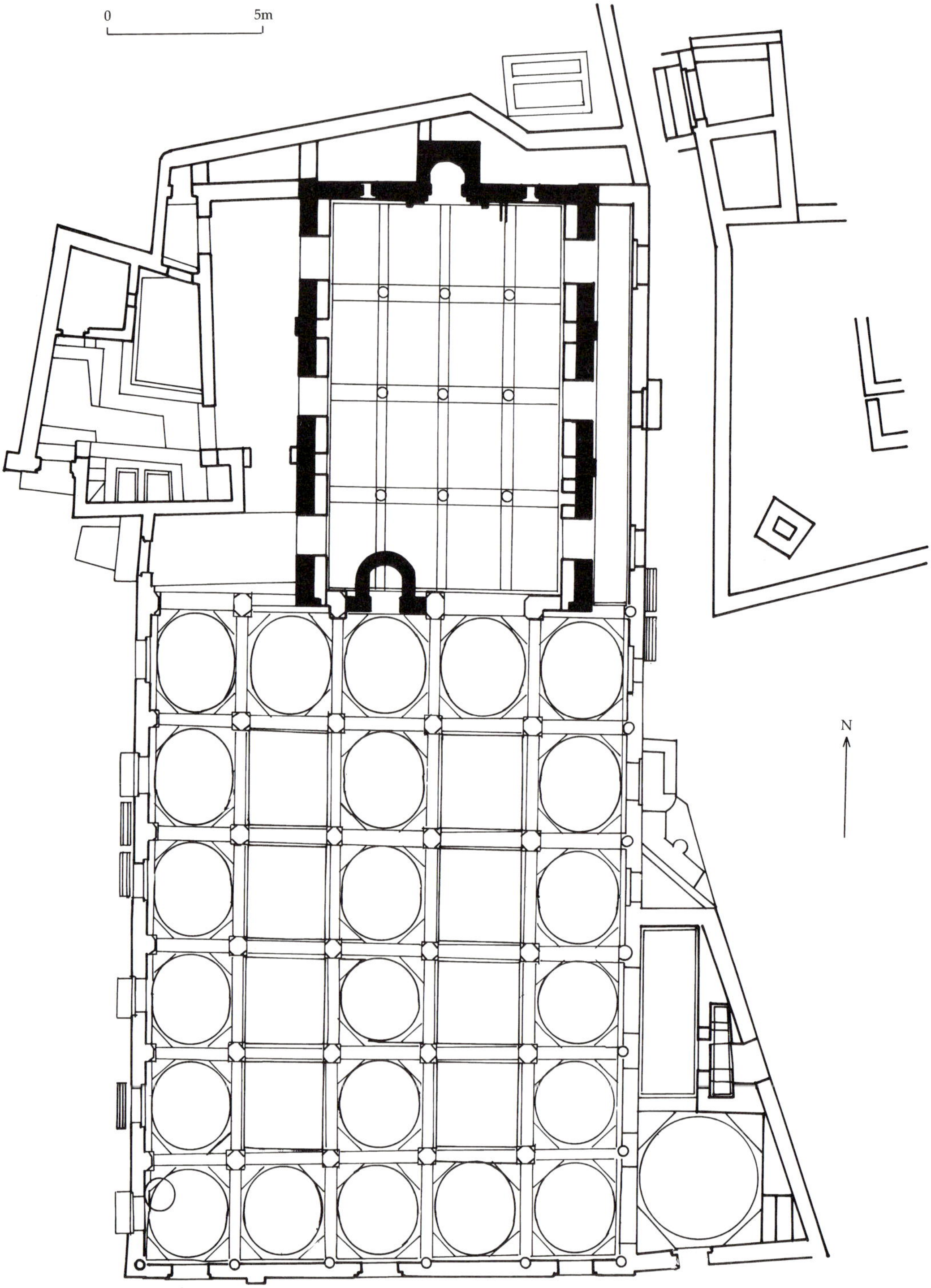

Plan of Great Mosque, Kilwa, Tanzania. Original mosque in black (after Chittick and Garlake)

the remains known as Husuni Kubwa (large Husuni) and Husuni Ndogo (small Husuni). The term Husuni derives from the Arabic term *husn* meaning fortified enclosure or fortress. Whilst this term may be appropriate for the the latter, its application to Husuni Kubwa seems unlikely for a palace complex. Husuni Kubwa is located on a coastal headland overlooking the Indian Ocean. It seems to date mostly from the late thirteenth or early fourteenth century and may well have never been completed. The complex consists of three main elements, the gateway or monumental entrance, the large south court and a complex of four courtyards which form the core of the palace. Also at the northern end of the complex there is a separate private mosque located on rocks next to the sea and reached by a staircase. The four courtyards at the northern end of the complex comprise an audience court, a domestic court, a bathing pool and a palace court. On the east side of the audience court are a flight of steps leading up to a flat-roofed pavilion which has been interpreted as the sultan's throne room. To the east of this is the domestic court which opens on to a complex of residential rooms, or *beyts*. The bathing pool consists of a sunken octagonal structure with steps and lobed recesses on each side. The palace court at the northern end of the palace is a sunken rectangular structure aligned north–south with steps at either end. The north set of steps leads to a further residential unit which overlooks the sea and the small mosque. It is possible that the sea mosque and the staircase represent the sultan's private entry to the palace. The royal nature of the palace is confirmed by a floriated Kufic inscription found during excavations which mentioned Sultan al-Hasn bin Sulayman.

By contrast Husuni Kubwa is a severe-looking building which fits the name Husuni (fort). It consists of a rectangular structure aligned north–south and measuring over 70 m long by more than 50 m wide. Thirteen evenly spaced, solid, semi-circular bastions protect the outside of the wall with one rectangular tower on the west side. The only entrance is in the middle of the south side and consists of a wide gateway leading into a gateway with the exit on the east side thus forming a bent entrance. Excavations have revealed the traces of a few structures inside but these may be later and do not give any indication of the function of the building which is unparalleled elsewhere in East Africa and suggests an outside influence. There is little evidence for dating this structure although it is thought to be contemporary with Husuni Kubwa.

The other two important buildings on Kilwa island are also defensive structures although they seem to date mostly to the eighteenth century. The largest of these is the Makutani palace which was the residence of the sultan in the eighteenth century. This building is contained within a fortified enclosure known as the Makutani, which consists of two curtain walls fortified by square towers with embrasures. The wall was originally approximately 3 m high and crenellated. Although there is no trace of a parapet this could have been built of wood like many other features of the eighteenth-century remains at Kilwa. The palace occupies a position between the two enclosure walls and appears to be built around one of the earlier towers. It is the only building on the island still to have an upper floor which contained the main residential area of the palace.

The Gereza or fort is located between the Makutani palace and the Great Mosque. It consists of a roughly square enclosure with two towers at opposite corners. Although there is some evidence that the original structure was Portuguese, the present form of the building seems to be typical of Omani forts.

In addition to sites on Kilwa island there are important sites on nearby islands. The earliest of these sites is Sanje ya Kate, an island to the south of Kilwa where there are ruins covering an area of 400 acres, including houses and a mosque. The mosque is of an early type with a mihrab niche contained in the thickness of the wall rather than projecting out of the north wall as is usual in later East African mosques. Excavations have shown that the settlement was abandoned before 1200 and most of the ruins date to the tenth century or even earlier.

To the east of Sanje ya Kate is the larger island of Songo Mnara which contains extensive ruins on its northern tip. The remains date to the fourteenth and fifteenth centuries and consist of thirty-three houses and a palace complex, as well as five mosques contained within a defensive enclosure wall. The remains at Songo Mnara are informative as they are one of the few places in East Africa where pre-eighteenth-century houses survive in any numbers. The houses have a standardized design with a monumental entrance approached by a flight of steps leading via an anteroom into a sunken courtyard, to the south of which are the main living quarters of the house.

See also: coral, East Africa, nine-domed mosque, Tanzania

Further reading:

H. N. Chittick, *A Guide to the Ruins of Kilwa with Some Notes on the Other Antiquities of the Region,* Dar es Salaam 1965.

—— *Kilwa: An Islamic City on the East African Coast,* British Institute in Eastern Africa Memoir No. 5, Nairobi 1974.

P. S. Garlake, *The Early Islamic Architecture of the East African Coast,* British Institute in Eastern Africa Memoir No. 1, Nairobi and London 1966.

kiosk (köshk)

Turkish term for a small pavilion not intended for permanent residence.

konak

Palatial Ottoman Turkish house.

The traditional Ottoman konak in western Anatolia and the Balkans is based on a four-iwan plan which is said to derive ultimately from the Çinili Kiosk in Istanbul. The plan consists of a central hall leading off to four iwans between which are enclosed rooms, often the plan is varied from this but the basic principal of a central hall with iwans is retained.

Most konaks are built of wood and have their main rooms on the upper floor with the lower floor used as a basement. The central hall is often covered with a wooden dome or a two-dimensional representation of a dome made of carved wood or paint. Sometimes the central hall is open on one side and functions as a veranda. The walls of the rooms are usually lined with sofas or long benches which are the main form of furniture. The most common form of decoration is painted ceilings, although shallow relief carving is also used. In eastern Anatolia konaks are built of stone and are built around open courtyards in the Syrian fashion; there is also a more strict division between the men's area (selamlik) and the women's area (harem).

See also: Istanbul, Ottomans, Topkapisarai

Further reading:

N. Çakiroglu, *Kayseri Evleri,* Istanbul 1952.

D. Erginbaş, *Diyabakir Evleri,* Istanbul 1954.

L. Eser, *Kütahya Evleri,* Istanbul 1955.

E. Esin, 'An eighteenth century yali', in *Second International Congress of Turkish Art,* Naples 1965.

G. Goodwin, *A History of Ottoman Architecture,* London 1971: chap. 11, 'The Ottoman House', 428–53.

E. Kömürcüoglu, *Ankara Evleri,* Istanbul 1950.

Konya (Arabic: Quniyah; Byzantine: Iconium)

City in southern Anatolia (Turkey) which was the capital of the Anatolian Seljuks now famous as the home of the whirling Dervishes.

Konya was established as capital in 1084 after the defeat of the Byzantines at Myriakefalon and just before the recapture of Iznik from the Crusaders. During the Byzantine period Iconium had been one of the richest Anatolian cities, a prosperity which was continued under Seljuk rule. In 1258 Konya was taken by the Mongols although it was later recaptured by the Karramanli Turks who continued to build in the Seljuk tradition. In the fifteenth century Konya was incorporated into the growing Ottoman Empire and became a regional capital.

The oldest mosque in Konya is the Alaeddin Cami built by the Seljuk sultan Alattin Keykubat between 1219 and 1221. This building stands on a hill in the centre of the city next to the remains of the Alaeddin palace. Within the mosque courtyard is an octagonal mausoleum with a tall conical (pyramid-shaped) dome which contains the remains of eight Seljuk sultans. In common with other Seljuk buildings in Konya, the entrances to the courtyard and prayer hall are surrounded by elaborate marble interlace patterns. The prayer hall is covered with a flat wooden roof supported by over forty Byzantine and classical columns. Other important Seljuk mosques in Konya include the Sahib Ata Mosque, the Iplikçili Mosque and the Ince Minareli. The Ince Minareli Mosque also has a madrassa with one of the most striking entrance façades in Seljuk architecture. This consists of a small pointed-arched doorway recessed within a huge stone frame which is covered with ornamental calligraphy. Two bands of calligraphy start either side of the doorway arch, cross over, run parallel up the centre of the portal and again cross over at

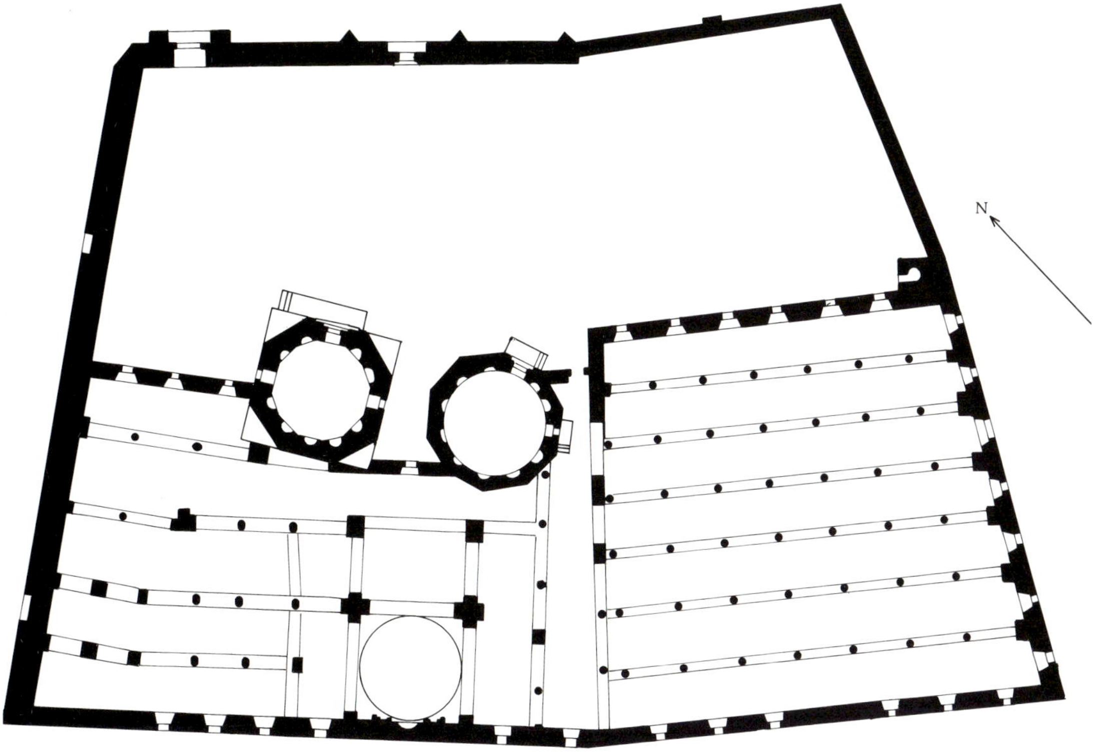

Mosque of Alaeddin, Konya, Turkey

the top. The edges of the frame are also decorated with calligraphic ornament whilst the areas in between are covered with stylized vegetal motifs. The Sahib Ata Cami also has a monumental portal consisting of a small pointed doorway set within a deep recess covered within a fourteen-tier muqarnas hood and flanked by bands of geometric motifs and calligraphic bands. The doorway is set between the bases of two minarets only one of which has survived as a fluted stump decorated with star patterns. Little remains of the Seljuk palaces of Konya although excavations have recovered architectural fragments indicating a rich artistic repertoire, including glazed tiles, stucco work and carved stone ornament. The decoration is noticeable for its rich figural content including depictions of birds, horses, mythical beasts and human figures. The tiles consist of eight-pointed star-shaped panels set between cross-shaped tiles.

The city's religious importance can be traced to the Sufi mystical poet Jalal al-Din Rumi who died in Konya in 1273. Jalal al-Din's tomb is the most famous building in Konya and forms part of a complex known as the Mevlana Masjid which included a mosque, madrassa, kitchen and semahane, or dance hall. The tomb itself is covered with a conical dome resting on a tall fluted cylindrical drum. The outside of the tomb and drum are covered in green tiles which distinguish it from the lead-covered roofs of the rest of the complex. Most of the complex with the exception of the tomb itself dates from the reign of Suleyman the Magnificent who added the mosque and dance hall. Next to the Mevlana complex is the Selimiye Cami commissioned by Sultan Selim II and designed by the famous architect Sinan. The mosque is unusual for the period as it has no courtyard.

See also: Ottomans, Seljuks, Turkey

kraton

General term for Javanese palaces. Derived from the Javanese root *ratu* meaning 'king', the term thus means 'residence of the king'. Sometimes the term *kadhaton* is also used which has a more specialized meaning referring to the royal quarters.

See also: Java

Kubadabad Palace

Seljuk palace famous for its glazed tilework and stucco decoration.

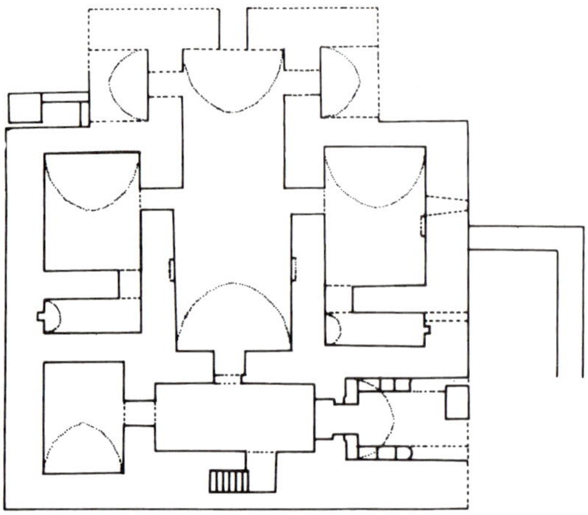

Kubadabad Palace, Beyshehir, Turkey (after Arik)

Kubadabad is located on the south-western shore of Lake Beyshehir in central Turkey. The settlement is dated by an inscription to the first half of the thirteenth century and is known to have been used by the Seljuk sultans Keykavus II and Keyhusrev III. The remains consist of more than sixteen buildings on the mainland and a separate castle or palace on an island known as Maidens' Castle. The tilework included underglaze painted star-shaped tiles with figurative scenes.

See also: Konya, Seljuks, Turkey

Further reading:

R. Arik, 'Kubad-Abad Excavations (1980–91)', *Anatolica* 18: 101–18, 1992.

K. Otto-Dorn, 'Kubadabad Kazilari 1965 On Raporu', *Turk Arkeoloji Degesi* 5.14(1–2): 237–43, 1967.

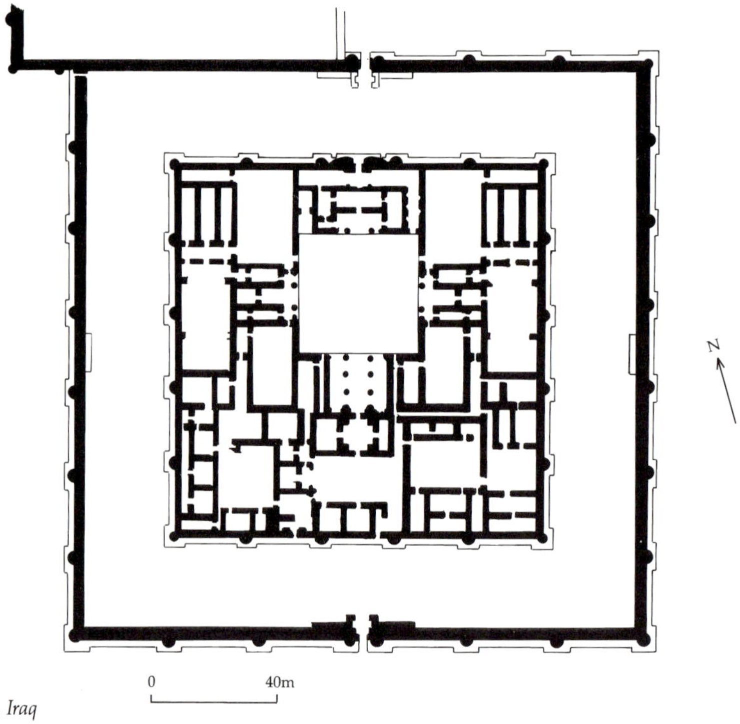

Dar al-Imara, Kufa, Iraq

Kufa

Southern Iraqi city founded in the early Islamic period.

Kufa is located on the west bank of the Eurphrates near the Shiʿa shrine city of Najaf. Like Baghdad, Kufa was a purely Islamic foundation, although it stood close to the Lakhimid capital of al-Hira.

After the battle of Ctesiphon and the capture of al-Mad'ain (Ctesiphon and Seleucia) the Arab armies settled in the old Sassanian capital. Soon afterwards, the armies moved to Kufa because of its pleasanter climate and strategic location on the west bank of the Euphrates (i.e. easy access to Syria and the Hijaz). In 645 Ali transferred the seat of government to Kufa. The assassination of Ali in the Great Mosque of the city in 645 brought an end to the city's role as capital.

The original city had no walls and was simply surrounded by a ditch. The principal monuments in Kufa are the Great Mosque and the Dar al-Imara, or Governor's Palace. The Great Mosque consists of a number of different phases from the early Islamic period to the present day. The first mosque on the site was laid out by a man who threw spears to each of the cardinal points to delineate a square two-spear throws long. The area was enclosed by a ditch and the only permanent architectural feature was a marble colonnade 20 m long. The columns were taken from the nearby city of al-Hira. In 670 CE the mosque was expanded and covered with a flat roof resting on stone columns. The mosque visible today has a beautiful golden dome and contains the tombs of the two saints Muslim ibn Aqeel and Hani ibn Arwa. The golden dome and tilework date to the Saffavid period (seventeenth and eighteenth centuries), although the outer wall of the mosque which is supported by twenty-eight semi-circular buttress towers probably originates in the early Islamic period.

To the south of the Great Mosque is the Dar al-Imara which was excavated by the Iraqi Antiquities Authority. The palace is enclosed by a square enclosure 170 m per side with walls 4 m wide supported by twenty semi-circular buttress towers and four round corner buttresses. In the centre of the palace there is a square (domed?) chamber approached by a vaulted hall which was probably the throne room.

See also: Dar al-Imara, Iraq

Further reading:

S. Ahmad, 'Survey of the Kufa area' (in Arabic), *Sumer* 21:229–252, 1965.

M. A. Mustafa, 'Dar al Imara at Kufa', *Sumer* 21:229–252, 1965.

——, 'Preliminary report on the excavations in Kufa during the third season', *Sumer* 19:36–65, 1963.

kuliyye

Ottoman term used to describe large complexes around mosques, which might include madrassas, libraries, khanqas, bath houses and a kitchen for the poor.

Kuwait

Small desert country located in the northern Arabia/Persian Gulf.

The first Islamic settlements in the Kuwait area were on the island of Failika and at the small port of Kathima near the modern town of Jahra. The present state of Kuwait was founded in the eighteenth century when descendants of the ruling al-Sabah family established themselves as rulers in alliance with local merchants. The prosperity of the town of Kuwait rapidly increased attracting a growing population. In 1793 the British moved their commercial base from Basra to Kuwait and in 1899 Kuwait ended its formal ties to the Ottoman authorities by signing a protection treaty with Britain. In the early part of the nineteenth century Kuwait was relatively poor with an economy reliant on a declining dhow trade and pearl fishing. After the Second World War the economy was transformed by the discovery of oil (it had actually been discovered before the war) and since then the country has seen unprecedented economic growth.

Little has survived of Kuwait's traditional architecture because of its high-speed development. The traditional building materials were rubble stone covered with thick mud plaster, mud brick and some coral stone. With the exception of date palms wood was rare, although mangrove poles imported from East Africa were used for the roofs.

Kuwait city was surrounded by a wall with five gates in the eighteenth century but this has now disappeared. Apart from the city wall Kuwait was protected by two forts, one in the city and the other on the end of the peninsula known as the Red Fort. Within the city there were a number of mosques most of which have been rebuilt several times. The oldest mosques in Kuwait are the Masjid al-Khamis built between 1772 and 1773 and the Masjid Abd al-Razzaq built in 1797. Before the nineteenth century minarets were rare and where they did exist consisted of small square towers covered with a small roof canopy.

A typical Kuwaiti merchant house was built in

the Ottoman style which reached the city from Basra. Ottoman features included projecting wooden balconies enclosed with wooden screens, or mashrabiyya, and carved wooden doorways which sometimes included European motifs. The extreme heat of the city made wind-catchers and ventilators a necessity for most houses.

Modern architecture in Kuwait is mostly in the modern international style, although there are several buildings which demonstrate some relationship to Islamic themes. The best-known example of Kuwaiti modern architecture is the water towers, consisting of tall pointed conical spires on which spherical water tanks are skewered.

See also: Bahrain, Qatar, United Arab Emirates

Further reading:

R. Lewcock and Z. Freeth, *Traditional Architecture in Kuwait and the Northern Gulf*, London 1978.

L

Lahore

Imperial Mughal capital located in the Punjab region of Pakistan.

Lahore is located in the eastern Punjab close to the Indian border and the Sikh city of Amritsar. The origins of the city are obscure although it is known that it existed as early as the tenth century. In 1021 the city was captured by Mahmud of Ghazni who demolished the fort and appointed Malik Ayaz as governor. In 1037 Malik Ayaz began construction of a new fort on the remains of the old one, which was completed in 1040. Excavation of the old fort has recently revealed a section which consists of a mud-brick wall approximately 4 m high. The new fort was also built of mud brick and consisted of a large rectangular enclosure by the banks of the river. In 1556 this fort was demolished by the Mughal emperor Akbar and replaced with a baked-brick enclosure fortified with semi-circular bastions. Akbar extended the area of the fort to the north to enclose the low lying area next to the river which was supported on vaulted sub-structures. Akbar's construction forms the core of the present fort which was added to by later Mughal emperors, as well as Sikh and British rulers of the area. The basic design of the fort is similar to the Red Fort at Delhi and the fort at Agra and consists of a huge public courtyard to the south with the private apartments and gardens to the north overlooking the river. The public courtyard known as Jahangir's Quadrangle contains some of the best examples of Akbar's architecture built in the characteristic red sandstone. The courtyard is lined by pavilions supported by massive brackets resting on twin columns. Most of the fort, however, is attributed to Akbar's successors, in particular Jahangir and Shah Jahan. Jahangir was responsible for the most magnificent example of ceramic art in Pakistan which is the 'Picture Wall'. This is an area of more than 6,000 m square decorated with human and animal figures besides the more usual geometric and figural designs. Areas of the palace built by Shah Jahan are characterized by the use of white marble and intricate decoration. One of the most extravagant rooms in the building is the Sheesh Mahal, is a half-octagonal room decorated with mirror tiles. Outside the fort, Lahore contains a number of important Mughal buildings including the Badshahi Mosque, Jahangir's tomb, the Shalimar Bagh and the Shahdara complex. In addition to the imperial Mughal buildings there are a number of Mughal period buildings which exhibit a mixture of Mughal, Persian and local design. One of the most famous examples is the mosque of Wazir Khan built in 1634 which is profusely decorated with brightly coloured tile mosaic. At each corner of the courtyard is a thick octagonal minaret of a type which later became characteristic of Lahore. Several mosques of the late eighteenth and early nineteenth century exhibit the influence of Sikh architecture from nearby Amritsar. One of the best examples is the Sonehri Masjid (Golden Mosque) built by Bhikari Khan in 1753 which has bulbous gilded copper domes with miniature domed chatris.

See also: Mughals, Pakistan

Further reading:

M. A. Chughtai, *Badshahi Mosque*, Lahore 1972.
—— *Tarikhi Masjid*, Lahore 1974.
—— *The Wazir Khan Mosque*, Lahore 1975.
S. R. Dar, *Historical Gardens of Lahore*, 1972.
M. W. U. Khan, *Lahore and its Important Monuments*, Karachi 1964.
S. M. Latif, *Lahore: Its History, Architectural Remains and Antiquities*, Lahore 1956.

Lamu

Town on an island off the north Kenya coast, noted for its fine eighteenth- and nineteenth-century houses.

The origins of Lamu are uncertain although archaeological evidence suggests that there has been a settlement on the site since well before the sixteenth century. However, the present town of Lamu developed largely in the eighteenth and nineteenth century, eventually taking over from its rival city of Pate. Like all Swahili towns the wealth of Lamu was built on the Indian Ocean dhow trade and the main focus of the town is still the sea front or quay. The town is built on a gentle slope which runs down towards the sea and at its centre is the old fort constructed by the Omanis, who controlled the area from the eighteenth century onwards. Unlike most other towns Lamu has survived as a traditional Swahili town with a dense network of streets between tall stone mansions and over twenty-two mosques. In addition to the stone buildings of the town are suburbs of mud and thatch houses in which many of the population of Lamu live, as was probably the case in the past. The stone houses are built of out of coral stone and mangrove poles in the manner typical of East Africa until the twentieth century. Most were originally single storey, and upper floors were added subsequently as separate living units. The typical eighteenth-century Lamu house has a small entrance porch, or *daka,* with stone benches either side which forms the main reception area of the house. The outer porch opens on to a small inner porch (*tekani*) and at right angles to this is the main courtyard of the house (*kiwanda*) thus forming a bent entrance to ensure privacy. Next to the inner porch, on the same side of the courtyard, is the guest room (*sabule*). Also contained within the courtyard is a bathroom or toilet, stairs to the upper floor and a semi-open kitchen covered with thatch. The main residential part of the house is located on the side of the courtyard away from the entrance and consists of a series of rooms of increasing privacy. Thus next to the courtyard is an outer living room followed by an inner living room behind which is the harem. The inner and outer living rooms are open to each other and the courtyard, whilst access to the women's area or harem (*ndani*) is via a pair of doors. The remarkable feature of these rooms is the use of decorative carved plaster and wall niches on the outward-facing walls of the living rooms and harem. The most elaborately decorated area is the harem, followed by the inner and outer living rooms. The wall niches are usually arranged in tiers and may cover the entire wall of the harem. The purposes of the niches is not fully understood although they are often used to display valuable pottery. Behind

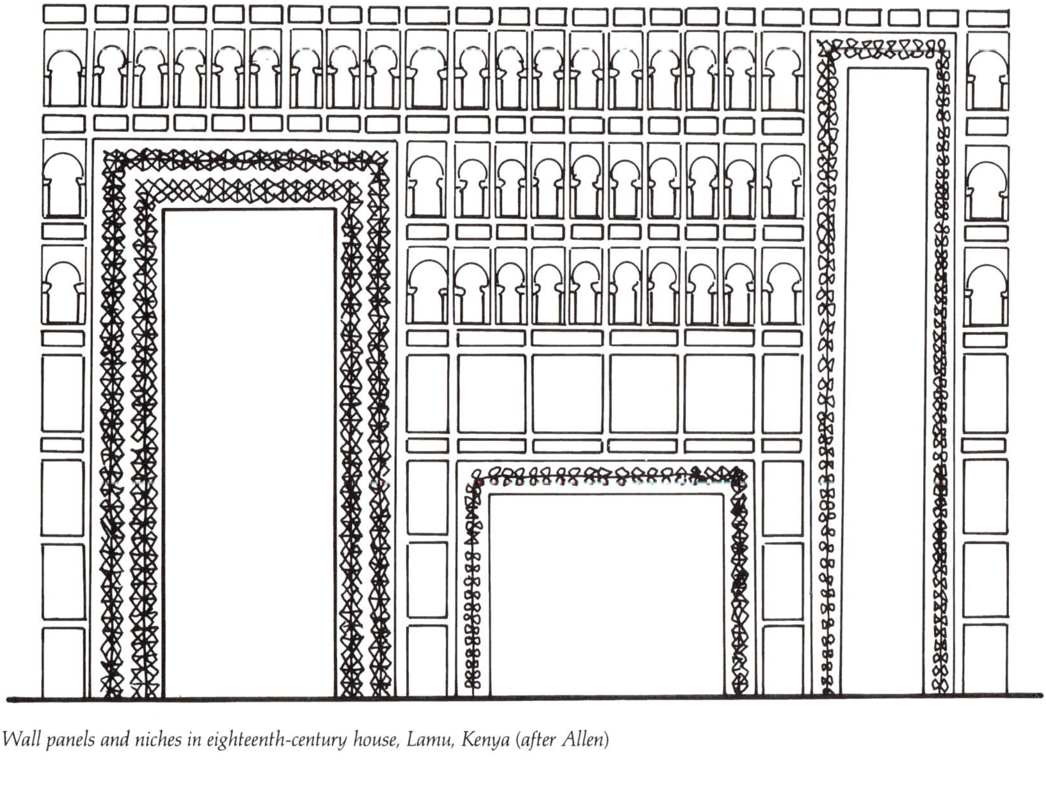

Wall panels and niches in eighteenth-century house, Lamu, Kenya (after Allen)

the harem are the inner bathroom and a room known as *nyumba ya kati* which may be for laying out and washing the dead.

Access to the upper floor is via a staircase which also has its own porch which may be used for receiving visitors. The arrangement of the upper floor is similar to downstairs except that there is no room for the dead and the kitchen is raised above the rest of the building on one side of the courtyard.

See also: coral, East Africa, Kenya

Further reading:

J. de V. Allen, *Lamu Town: A Guide*, Mombasa 1974.

J. de V. Allen and T. H. Wilson, *Swahili Houses and Tombs of Kenya*, Art and Archaeology Research Papers, London 1979.

R. L. Flemming, 'Lamu: a special Islamic townscape with no conservation plan and no policy', *Monumentum* 71–7, 1983.

U. Ghaidan, *Lamu: A Case Study of the Swahili Town*, Nairobi 1975.

U. Ghaidan and H. R. Hughes, 'Lamu, a lesson in townscape', *Architectural Review* Nov. 1973.

M. Ylvisaker, *Lamu in the Nineteenth Century: Land, Trade and Politics*, Boston 1979.

Lashkari Bazar

Ruined eleventh-century city in Afghanistan.

Lashkari Bazar is located to the north of the modern city of Bust on the east side of the Helmud river in south-west Afghanistan. The principal ruins at the city date from the Ghaznavid period in the eleventh century although there are both earlier remains from the Parthian period and later remains from the Ghurid period (twelfth to thirteenth century). In many ways the site resembles the Abbasid site of Samarra with its monumental size, its palaces, its mud-brick architecture and its elongated development alongside the river.

The citadel of Bust to the south seems to have been the first area of settlement and Lashkari Bazar seems to have been developed as a suburb or camp referred to as al–'Askar. The three principal structures at the site are the North, Centre and South palaces. The earliest of these is the Centre Palace which was probably built in the Samanid period. This is a rectangular building (32 by 52 m) with circular buttress towers at the corners. There are two storeys – a ground floor and an upper floor – although it appears that these were not connected. The largest building at the site is the South Palace which has been identified as the palace of Mahmud of Ghazni. This is a huge structure (170 by 100 m) built around a central courtyard which opens on to four main iwans. The building is entered from the south which leads into the courtyard via a cruciform hall. At the opposite end of the courtyard is a large iwan which leads, via a passageway, into a larger one overlooking the river. This iwan which has a staircase leading down to the river has been compared to the Bab al-Amma at Samarra although it has a different form. The private quarters were arranged down the west side of the courtyard and include a small mosque at the south end (this was not accessible from the rest of the palace). The interior of the palace was richly decorated with stucco work, frescoes and carved marble panels. To the east of the palace was a large walled garden which may have contained animals.

In addition to palaces there are remains of smaller private mansions built in the same style, with iwans opening on to a courtyard. One of the more interesting features of the site is the bazar from which the site gets its name. This is a street more than 100 m long lined with small shop units (3.5 by 5 m). On one side of this street, approximately in the middle, there is courtyard building with store rooms, which was probably the office of the market inspector (muhtasib).

See also: Afghanistan, Samarra

Further reading:

T. Allen, 'Notes on Bust', *Iran. Journal of the British Institute of Persian Studies*, 26: 55–68 1988; 27: 57–66, 1989; 28: 23–30, 1990.

D. Schlumberger, M. Le Berre, J. C. Garcin and G. Casal, *Lashkari Bazar, une residence royale ghaznevide et ghoride*, Memoires de la Delegation Archéologique Française en Afghanistan, Part 1A 'L'Architecture', 1978.

Lebanon

The republic of Lebanon is located on the east coast of the Mediterranean between Palestine and Syria.

Lebanon is dominated by two geographical features, the sea and the Lebanon and Anti Lebanon mountains. The principal cities of the country are located on the coast and include the old Phoenician settlements of Tyre, Sidon, Beirut and Tripoli. The history of Lebanon in the Islamic period is similar to that of Syria with some minor variations. The main consideration is that the Lebanon mountains cut off Lebanon from the rest of Syria whilst the sea opened it up to European contact. One of the first indications of Syria's separateness occurred in the eighth century when the Christian Maronites

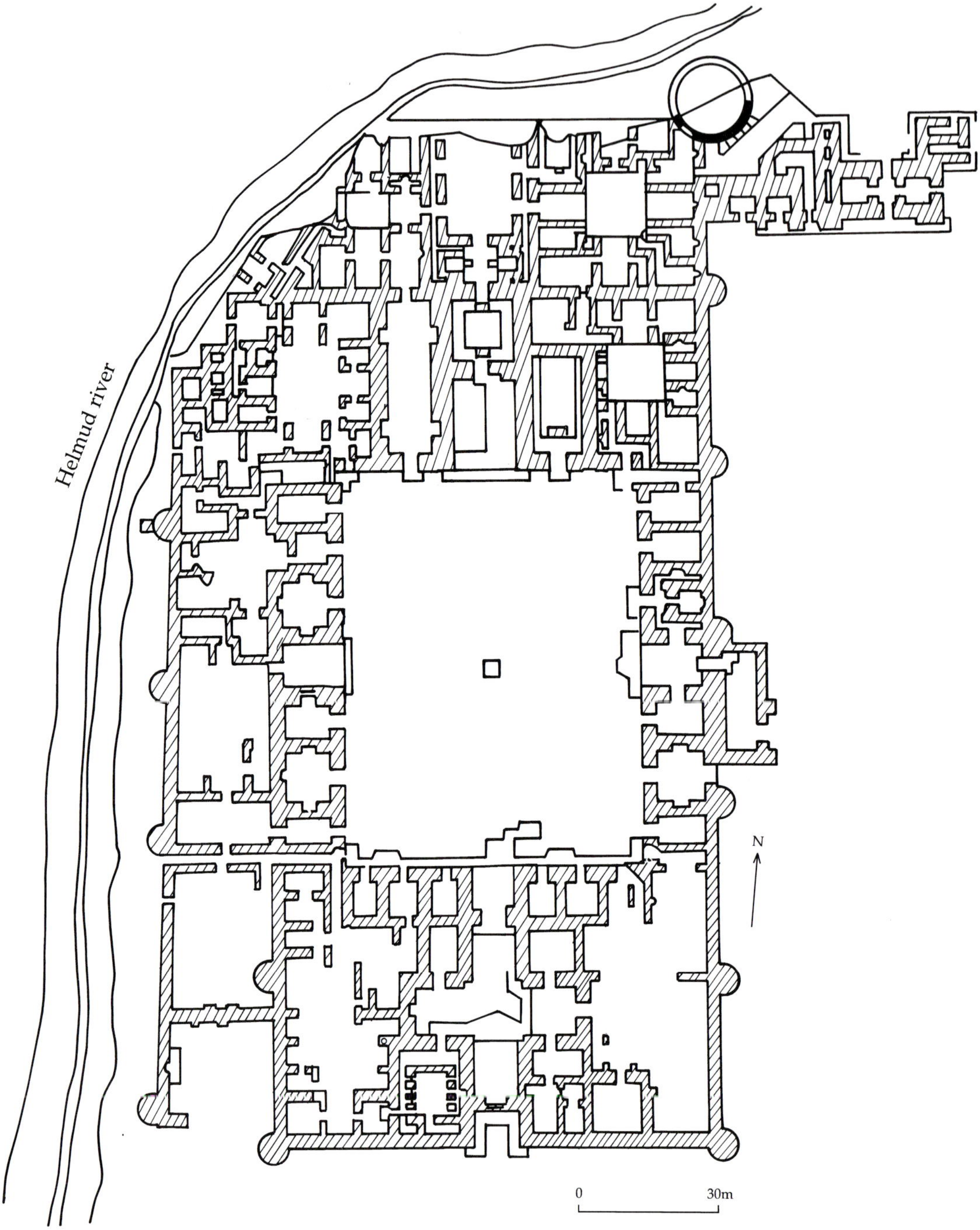

The South Palace, Lashkari Bazar, Afghanistan (after Allen)

established an independent state in the Kadisha valley amongst the mountains of north Lebanon. In the eleventh century dissident followers of the Fatimid caliph al–Hakim settled in the mountains of southern Lebanon and established the Druze community. During the twelfth and thirteenth centuries the country was dominated by the Crusaders who had conquered the coastal cities for use as bases in their conquest of Palestine. With the expulsion of the Crusaders in 1289 the Mamluks rebuilt cities such as Tripoli to remove all trace of the Crusader presence. In 1516 Lebanon was incorporated into the Ottoman Empire although its position enabled it to develop its own trading links with Europe. Contact with Europe was increased throughout the Ottoman period and in the eighteenth century Maronites were placed under the special protection of France. Massacres of Christians in the nineteenth century led France to press for the autonomy of Lebanon within the Ottoman Empire and from 1860 Lebanon has functioned as a semi-independent state. The country achieved full independence in 1944 at the end of the Second World War.

Stone is the principal building material in Lebanon and is used both in a dressed form and as uncut rubble. The presence of black basalt and limestone has made striped (ablaq) masonry a popular form of decoration for important buildings.

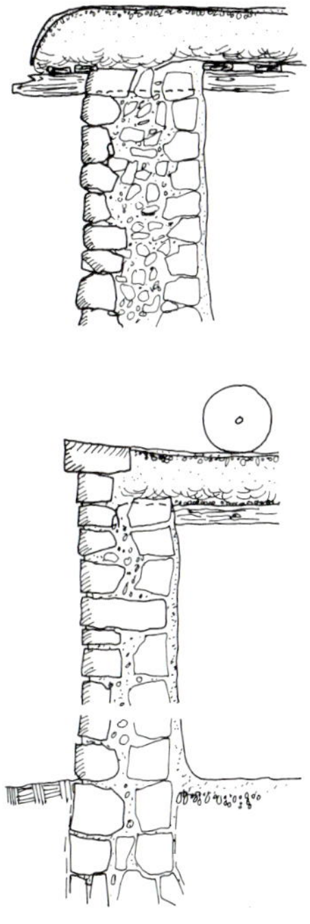

Types of wall construction, Beqʿa Valley, Lebanon (after Ragette)

Wood is used as a roofing material as well as for balconies and projecting windows. Unfortunately the cedar forests of Lebanon were destroyed before the medieval period and the principal types of wood are poplar, walnut, willow and maple. Mud brick is used as a building material in the Beqʿa valley where the climate is dry enough and there is suitable clay.

The only major creation of the Umayyad period was the city of Anjar which like Ramla in Palestine was intended as a new regional centre away from the predominantly Christian cities. The Mamluk period is represented by the city of Tripoli which was completely rebuilt after its conquest. Moreover, the Mamluk period left a great impression on the Christian, Druze and Muslim architecture of the country which can be seen in buildings such as the Bayt al-Din Palace.

The most distinctive feature of Lebanese architecture is seen in the houses of the coast, which display a mixture of Middle Eastern and European influence. European elements include the use of pitched wooden roofs covered with clay tiles, prominent windows and balconies (distinct from the enclosed spaces usual in Islamic domestic architecture). Middle Eastern elements include the use of the vaulted iwan (open arched room), arcades and the occasional use of domes. Mountain-houses are generally less sophisticated and are often built of roughly square blocks held together in a mud mortar. Roofs are usually flat and made of earth resting on mats supported on wooden beams. Inside, the mountain-houses may be decorated with mud plaster mixed with white lime to produce a type of stucco. This material is used to decorate walls and is also used for the construction of storage bins and hearths.

See also: Anjar, Syria, Tripoli (Lebanon)

Further reading:

F. Ragette, *Architecture in Lebanon. The Lebanese House during the 18th and 19th centuries*, New York 1980.

Libiya (Libyan Arab People's Socialist State)

Large North African country located between Tunisia and Egypt, with the Mediterranean to the north and the Sahara desert to the south.

Libiya comprises two main geographic areas, the coast and the Sahara; these areas may be further separated into several regions. The narrow coastal strip is divided into three regions: Cyrenaica in the

Bayt al-Din, Druze mansion, Lebanon © Kerry Abbott

east with its capital of Benghazi, the Gulf of Sirte in the centre and Tripolitania in the west. The interior desert region may be divided into several areas, the most important of which are the Jabal Nafusa in south-eastern Tripolitania, and the Fezzan in the south-east of the Libyan desert.

The present state of Libiya is largely a modern phenomenon created by Italian colonialism in the early twentieth century. Ironically, 2,000 years previously the Romans developed the regions of Cyrenaica and Tripolitania into some of the wealthiest provinces of their empire, providing grain for the Italian peninsula. During the Byzantine era the prosperity of the area continued with a population that was predominantly Christian with a large Jewish minority. The area was first conquered by Islamic forces in the mid-seventh century with the capture of Barqa (modern al-Marj) in 642 under ʿAmr ibn al-As, followed in 643 by the conquest of Tripolitania. After the coastal strip was secured a further force under ʿUqba ibn Nafi was sent to take control of Zuwayla in the Fezzan. In the past it has been generally assumed that the Islamic conquest led to the collapse of the Roman urban network but it has recently been shown that change was more gradual, with a considerable degree of continuity of settlement from the Byzantine to the early Islamic period.

During the early tenth century the power of the Abbasid caliphs in North Africa was destroyed by the radical Shʿite Fatimid dynasty who ruled from their capital of Mahadiyya in Tunisia. During this period the importance of Libiya increased and the best examples of early Islamic architecture in the country are from this period. After the Fatimid conquest of Egypt much of North Africa, including the area of present-day Libiya, came under the control of the Berber Zirid governors. In the eleventh century North Africa was subject to a new influx known as the Banu Hilal who were supposedly dispatched by the Fatimid caliphs to reintroduce Fatimid propaganda to the rebellious Berber tribes. In the past the Hilalian invasions have been seen as the cause of North Africa's comparative backwardness in the Middle Ages. More recently this view has been modified, but the idea of the

Beirut house, Lebanon © Kerry Abbott

political weakness of the area cannot be dispelled. During the twelfth century this weakness was exploited by Roger, the Norman king of Sicily, who established a Norman kingdom in Ifriqiya which included the area of Libiya. After the expulsion of the Normans the history of Libiya is fragmented into successive dynasties controlling individual cities. For a brief period in the early sixteenth century part of Libiya was occupied by the Spanish, but they were soon displaced by the Ottomans who established naval bases on the coast to harass European shipping in the Mediterranean. During the eighteenth century Libiya was briefly ruled by the semi-independent Qarahmanli dynasty. In 1911 Libiya was again brought under European rule when the Italians invaded and established the country as an Italian colony.

The main building materials in Libiya are stone and mud brick. Re-used Roman or Byzantine stone has always been in plentiful supply so that many of the older buildings in Tripoli, Adjdabiyah or elsewhere use Roman columns and capitals. Mud brick was employed as a cheap alternative when dressed stone was not readily available, although baked brick was also sometimes used. In the southern desert areas where Roman material was not so plentiful the main building material is roughly hewn stones set within a mud mortar. This use of material determined architectural forms, thus in the Jabal Nafusa area tall triangular arches were used as there was no suitable material for normal arch construction.

With the exception of the occasional building in the old Byzantine coastal cities, the first distinctive Islamic architecture in Libiya dates from the Fatimid period. During the later tenth century the Fatimids were increasingly interested in Egypt and to this end developed a number of garrison cities or staging posts on the route between Mahdiya and Egypt. Probably the best-known site is the garrison city of Ajdabiya, south-west of Benghazi, which had both a large mosque and a palace. The palace is a rectangular stone-built structure with a central courtyard flanked by suites of rooms. Directly opposite the entrance is a monumental portico which gives access to the principal rooms of the palace which are arranged in a T-plan. The mosque was a mud-brick building with stone used for the corners, piers and jambs. The mosque had a main entrance in the north-west side opposite the mihrab as well as several lateral entrances. The aisles run at right angles to the qibla wall, with the exception of the transept adjacent to the qibla wall which runs parallel (an arrangement frequent in Fatimid mosques). The mosque is important for its early evidence of a minaret which consists of a square base with an octagonal shaft, a design which later became the basis for the Mamluk minarets of Cairo.

Another early Fatimid site is the city of Madinah Sultan (Surt or Sirt) which is approximately midway between Benghazi and Tripoli. The city was enclosed by a large oval-shaped town wall with at least three gateways. One of the larger buildings uncovered during excavations was the Friday mosque which is oriented south–east (an incorrect qibla). The mosque had four gates, the most prominent of which was the monumental north gate which is of double width. Monumental gateways are a characteristic feature of Fatimid mosques and can also be seen at Mahdiya in Tunisia and in Cairo. The Madinah Sultan Mosque has a central aisle running at right angles to the qibla wall, although unusually for North Africa the rest of the aisles run parallel to the qibla wall. Some remains of the original decorative scheme of the mosque have been recovered including stucco frames for coloured glass windows, red and green coloured bricks. There are traces of a subsidiary mihrab in the arcade facing the courtyard which may possibly be the remains of an eighth-century mosque which was rebuilt in 952 by the Fatimid caliph al-Muciz. Several other Fatimid establishments are known but have not yet been investigated in detail; one of the better known examples is Qasr al-Hammam near the ancient site of Leptis Magna.

Few early Islamic remains survive in Tripoli although traces of the rebuilt Umayyad fortification walls have been excavated. These were made of stone and mortar and vary between 6 and 7 m in thickness. The oldest mosque in Tripoli is the al-Naqah Mosque which was probably built by the Fatimid caliph al-Muciz in 973 although some suggest that it may be older. The present shape of the mosque is irregular indicating numerous alterations throughout history although the basic plan consists of a rectangular courtyard and a sanctuary or prayer hall covered with forty-two brick domes. Although many of the other mosques in Tripoli may have medieval origins their remains mostly date from the Ottoman period. Few important monuments of the post Fatimid medieval period in Libiya have survived although many small mosques may date to the medieval period. At the oasis site of Ujlah (Awjlah) 200 km to the south of Ajdabiya is a small twelfth-century mosque built of stone and brick. The mosque consists of at least twelve bays covered with pointed conical domes, although the most interesting feature of the building is the recessed minbar niche to the side of the mihrab (this feature is also found in East Africa and Arabia and may represent an Ibadi tradition). South of Tripoli in the area of Jabal Nafusa is a region with a high concentration of ancient mosques, many of which date from before the thirteenth century. Many of these mosques are built partially underground giving them a low profile and an organic feel accentuated by the absence of minarets. The area is also characterized by fortified store houses, known as qusur (plural of qasr), which consist of agglomerations of barrel-vaulted units contained within a defensive wall. The barrel-vaulted units are often stacked one on top of the other and are reached by ladder or ropes. During peaceful times each qasr functions as a central storage area and in times of attack the population of the village retreats into the qasr where it can withstand a long siege.

See also: Ajdabiya, Fatimids, Tripoli (Libiya)

Further reading:

A. Abdussaid, 'Early Islamic monuments at Ajdabiyah', *Libiya Antiqua* 1: 115–19, 1964.

—— 'An early mosque at Medina Sultan (Ancient Sort)', *Libiya Antiqua* 3–4: 155–60, 1967.

—— 'Barqa, modern al-Merj', *Libiya Antiqua* 8: 121–8, 1971.

J. W. Allan, 'Some mosques on the Jabal Nefusa', *Libiya Antiqua* 9–10: 147–69, 1973.

J. M. Evans, 'The traditional house in the Oasis of Ghadames', *Libyan Studies* 7: 31–40, 1976.

A. Hutt, 'Survey of Islamic sites', *Libyan Studies* 3: 5–6, 1972.

—— *Islamic Architecture: North Africa*, London 1977.

G. R. D. King, 'Islamic archaeology in Libiya 1969–1989', *Libyan Studies* 20: 193–207, 1989.

N. M. Lowick, 'The Arabic inscriptions on the mosque of Abu Macruf at Sharwas (Jebel Nefusa)', *Libyan Studies*, 5: 14–19, 1974.

A. M. Ramadan, *Reflections on Islamic Architecture in Libiya*, Tripoli 1975.

M. Shagluf, 'The Old Mosque of Ujlah', *Some Islamic Sites in Libiya*, Art and Archaeology Research Papers, London 1976, 25–8.

H. Ziegert and A. Abdussalam, 'The White Mosque at Zuila', *Libiya Antiqua* 9–10: 221–2, 1973.

M

ma'adhana

Place for the call to prayer, often identified with the minaret.

machicolation

Downward openings or slits used defending a castle or fortification.

There are three types of machicolation, a box machicolation, concealed machicolation and continuous machicolation.

A box machicolation resembles a projecting window or gallery and may also be used for this purpose. There are usually one or more slits in the floor and the box is normally located over a gate or doorway. Box machicolations were used in Roman times and their first use in Islamic structures is at Qasr al-Hayr (East and West).

Concealed machicolations are usually set into the roof above a vaulted passage leading from a gateway and are often used in conjunction with a portcullis. The first example in Islamic architecture comes from the eighth-century palace of Ukhaidhir in Iraq. These were frequently used in medieval Islamic fortifications.

Continuous machicolation consists of a parapet which is cantilevered over the front face of a wall with a series of downward openings. The earliest example of this is also at Ukhaidhir although it is not used later on in Islamic architecture.

See also: fortification

madafa

Arabic term for guest house, or room for guests.

Madinat al-Zahra'

Tenth-century palace city (now in ruins) 6 km west of Córdoba in southern Spain.

The complex was begun by Abd al-Rahman II and completed by his son al-Hakim II. The complex was named after Abd al-Rahman's favourite wife Zahra' and located near springs at the foot of the Sierra Morena. The complex was founded as a palatial residence and administrative centre away from the crowded capital at Córdoba and had a staff of 20,000 people including guards, officials and families. It was finally destroyed by fire in 1010 by the caliph's vizier al-Mansur who resented the caliph's personal residence. Material from the palace was re-used by Pedro the Cruel to build his palace in Seville.

The complex was built on three terraces surrounded by gardens with pools and water channels. On the lowest terrace is a garden pavilion built for Abd al-Rahman as a formal reception and ceremonial centre. This consisted of four pools and the pavilion itself known as the Salón Rico which has intricate decoration carved in stone to match the stucco work of the maqsura at the Great Mosque in Córdoba. This pavilion is associated with a hammam in an arrangement common to the desert palaces of Syria. Across a bridge from the Salón Rico is the main mosque of the complex with an arcaded courtyard leading on to the sanctuary five aisles deep. Next to the mosque is the Dar al-Yund (army headquarters) which consists of a cruciform basilical hall with triple-arched arcades and a ramp leading out on to the parade ground.

The upper part is occupied by the caliph's personal residence known as the Dar al-Mulk. This consisted of several apartments based around courtyards which in turn enclosed a central hall. It is likely that these apartments were at least four storeys high although they are now much damaged.

The complex is a useful example of how the Spanish Umayyads tried to copy the architecture and protocol of their more powerful ancestors. In particular the complex is thought to recall the country residence of Abd al-Rahman, the first Spanish Umayyad, at Rusafa in Syria.

See also: Córdoba, Córdoba Great Mosque, Spain

Further reading:

F. Hernandez Gimenéz, *Madinat al Zahra': Arquitectura y Decoración*, Granada 1985.
B. Pavon Malddonao, *Memoria de la Excavación de la Mezquita de Medinat al-Zahra*, No. 50 of Excavaciones Arqueologicas en Espagne, Madrid 1966.

madrassa

Building which functions as a teaching institution primarily of Islamic sciences.

It is thought that the earliest madrassas were built by the Seljuks in eleventh-century Iran and that the design was derived either from contemporary house plans or Buddhist teaching structures, known as viharas, which survived in Afghanistan and Central Asia. The oldest extant madrassa is the Gumushtutigin Madrassa in Bosra built in 1136. This is a small structure (20 by 17 m) with a domed courtyard and two lateral iwans. However, the majority of early madrassas are found in Anatolia where two main types occur, based either on an open or a closed courtyard building. The domed madrassas are usually smaller buildings whilst those with an open courtyard are generally larger and have central iwans surrounded by arcades. The first Egyptian madrassas date from after 1160 when Sunni orthodoxy was returned to the country. The significance of the Egyptian madrassas is the four-iwan plan where each iwan represented one of the four orthodox schools of law. This design later spread to other countries and can be seen in the Mustansriya Madrassa in Baghdad. Another significant development which took place in Egypt is the madrassa becoming the dominant architectural form with mosques adopting their four-iwan plan.

Although it is traditionally thought that madrassas provide sleeping and working accommodation for students, the extant examples show that this was not a rule and it is only later on that student facilities became an accepted part of a madrassa.

mahal

Arabic term for place or location. In Mughal architecture it is used to describe the palace pavilion, or more specifically the women's quarters.

Mahdiya

Fatimid capital of North Africa located on the east coast of Tunisia.

The city of Mahdiya occupies a defensive position on the peninsula of Ras Mahdi. The city was established in 913 by the Fatimid Mahdi (leader) 'Ubaid Allah on the site of the destroyed Carthiginian port of Zella. The city functioned as a port from which the Fatimids were able to launch their campaign to conquer Egypt.

Architecturally the most significant building in the town is the Great Mosque built in 916. This is the earliest surviving example of a Fatimid mosque. The design of the mosque differs considerably from earlier North African mosques as it had no minarets and only one monumental entrance giving it the appearance of a fortress rather than a mosque. This view is reinforced by the massive square corner buttresses and the stark simplicity of the design. The internal layout of the mosque is similar to earlier mosques of the region with nine aisles running perpendicular to the qibla wall and a transverse aisle parallel with the qibla wall. In the eleventh century erosion by the sea destroyed the original qibla wall which was subsequently rebuilt further back thus reducing the space of the prayer hall.

See also: Ajdabiya, Fatimids, Tunisia

Further reading:

A. Lezine, *Mahdiyya: Recherches d'Archéologie Islamiques*, Paris 1965.

maidan

A large open space, or square, for ceremonial functions.

Malaysia

Predominantly Muslim country in south-east Asia divided into two parts, the southern half of the Malay peninsula and the northern part of Borneo.

It seems likely that Islam came to Malaysia as early as the ninth century although at present there is no archaeological confirmation of this. The earliest record of Islam in Malaysia is the Trengganu Stone dated to 1303 or 1386. The stone is written in Malay with Arabic script and records various regulations of Islamic law.

Before the fourteenth century the southern half of the Malay peninsula was home to a series of small weak states which were dominated by their northern neighbours of Cambodia and Thailand and later by the Indonesian kingdom of Majapahit. By 1403, however, the first king of Malacca had established himself as ruler of the southern Malay peninsula with the support of the Chinese emperor. The king of Malacca made several friendly visits to the Chinese emperor in return for support against the Thai kingdom of Ayudhya which was encroaching on the northern part of the peninsula. At this time (in the 1420s) the king of Malacca converted from Hinduism to Islam making Malacca the main centre of Islamic culture in south-east Asia. Under Chinese protection the state of Malacca grew to become the most powerful in the area with its control of the strategic straits of Malacca which were the main route for commerce between China and the west. By the end of the fifteenth century Malacca's position was threatened by the Portuguese who saw it as a threat to their further eastward expansion. In the early sixteenth century China withdrew its naval support of Malacca and in 1511 the sultanate of Malacca was finally defeated.

The Portuguese victory was the start of a long period of colonial rule first by the Portuguese, followed by the Dutch after 1641 and finally by the British from 1824 until 1957. Despite the crusading zeal of the Portuguese the Malay inhabitants remained Muslim throughout the colonial period.

Unfortunately there are few architectural remains from the pre-Portuguese period and these are mostly Buddhist or Hindu, although the surviving fortifications of Malacca may be Islamic. Most pre-nineteenth-century mosques in Malaysia were built of wood and have not survived very well. The oldest mosque in Malaysia is generally agreed to be the Masjid Kampaung Laut in the state of Kelantan built in the sixteenth century. The mosque was moved from its original location in 1970 after serious floods damaged its structure. The mosque stands on a square raised platform and has a three-tier pyramid roof with each tier separated by a gap to allow air circulation. A similar mosque was built at Demak in Indonesia by the same group of Muslim traders. Another early mosque is the Masjid Trengkera in Malacca built in the early eighteenth century (1728). This is a four-tier structure on a square base with a polygonal six-storey minaret. The form of the minaret resembles a pagoda and suggests strong Chinese influence. Most early Malaysian mosques have neither minarets nor mihrabs although these were often added in the nineteenth century. The window frames were usually decorated with bands of Quranic calligraphy and there are often elaborately carved minbars and Quran stands.

The colonization of Malaysia by Britain in the nineteenth century introduced a new Anglo–Indian stone- and brick-built mosque form. These mosques are characterized by the use of domes, crenellations and arched windows which locally are characterized as 'Moorish architecture'. One of the best examples of this architecture is the Headquarters of the Malayan Railway Company which is covered with onion domes with arched windows and striped masonry. This architecture which can also be seen in Singapore seems to be derived primarily from south India.

Since Independence in 1957 there have been attempts to move away from this Anglo–Indian architecture to buildings that are more traditionally Malay. The model for such buildings is usually the traditional form of Malay houses – wooden buildings with tall thatched roofs in three or more tiers. One of the earliest examples of this post-colonial architecture is the National Museum at Kuala Lumpur which uses traditional roof forms, although many of the other elements are built in a modern international style. More successful as an evocation of the traditional style is the Bank of Bumipatra which is based on the traditional Kelantan house design. The building has a huge three-tiered roof on a rectangular base.

See also: Indonesia, Java, Singapore

Further reading:

G. Haidar, 'On the crest of the hill: The International Institute of Islamic Thought and Civilization, Kuala Lumpur', *Arts and the Islamic World* 21: 14–18, 1992.

A. Lamb, 'Miscellaneous papers on early Hindu-Buddhist settlement in northern Malaya and southern Thailand', *Federation Museums Journal* NS 6: 1961.

Wan Hussein Azmi, 'Islam di Malaysia-Kedatangan dan Perkembangan (Abad 7–20 m)', *Tamadun Islam di Malaysia*, Kuala Lumpur 1980.

O. bm. Yatim, 'Islamic arts in Malaysia', *Arts and the Islamic World* 1(2): 1993.

Zainal Abidin Wahid (ed.), *Glimpses of Malaysian History*, Kuala Lumpur 1980.

S. S. Zubir, 'Identity and architecture in Malaysia', *Arts and the Islamic World* 5(1): 74–6, 1988.

Maldives

A group of over 2,000 islands off the south–west coast of Sri Lanka which now forms an independent republic with its capital at Male.

The inhabitants of the Maldives have been Muslim

since 1153 when they were converted by a Berber known as Abu al-Barakat. The language of the islands is Dihevi which is related to Sinhalese although it is written in a script based on Arabic numerals.

The houses are made out of coral stone and coconut wood; the stone is used to build a platform and the wood is used for the superstructure. As experienced boat builders the Maldivians were able to build wooden houses without nails and make very tight joints. Ibn Battuta visited the islands twice in 1343 and 1346 and gave an account of the construction of houses. The house was built around a hall which opened on to the reception room, known as the malem, where the owner of the house would receive his male friends. At the back of the malem was another door which opened on to the rest of the house forbidden to guests.

There are many mosques on the islands; at present Male has thirty-three including the main mosque known as the Hukuru Meskit (Great Mosque). The standard mosque plan which seems to have remained the same since the seventeenth century consists of a stone building raised on a rectangular platform with an entrance at the east end and a rectangular recess at the west end. Near the entrance is a well set within a paved area with a path leading to the mosque entrance to keep feet clean after washing. Many of the mosques are built of stone although some are built out of wood like the houses. Each mosque is surrounded by a graveyard on three sides with tombstones made of finely dressed coral blocks (rounded stones represent women and pointed stones represent men). In general Maldivian mosques do not have mihrabs although they are oriented towards Mecca and have a square recess at the qibla end. Minarets are also unusual although the Hukuru Meskit has a thick cylindrical tower which functions as a minaret.

See also: coral

Further reading:

J. Carswell, 'Mosques and tombs in the Maldive Islands', *Art and Archaeology Research Papers* 9: 26–30, 1976.
—— 'China and Islam in the Maldive Islands', *Transactions of the Oriental Ceramic Society* 41: 121–98, 1975–6.

Mali

Islamic West African empire which flourished during the thirteenth and fourteenth centuries.

The date of the first emergence of the kingdom of Mali is not known although there are references to it as early as the ninth century. However, it was not until the thirteenth century that the kingdom achieved the status of empire through the conquest of a number of rival states. The medieval empire of Mali was formed out of the unification of two distinct Manding groups, an established northern group and a more recent southern group. The unification was achieved by the famous Mali hero Sundiata who defeated Sumaguru Kante, lord of Susu in 1234 and then went on to conquer Ghana, Gangaran and the gold-producing area of Bambuko. The ruling clan, from which the king was selected, was the Keita clan of the northern group which traced its ancestry back to Bilal, the first black follower of the prophet. The empire had two distinct capitals: Kangaba, the religious capital, and Niani, capital of the Keita clan and birthplace of Sundiata. Although some branches of the Mali dynasty were Muslim fairly early on, it was not until the thirteenth century that the kings were Muslim.

After Sundiata the most famous king of Mali was Mansa Musa who made a legendary pilgrimage to Mecca in 1324–5. Although previous kings of Mali had made the pilgrimage to Mecca the journey of Mansa Musa made a particularly big impression because he dispersed large quantities of gold on the way. The amount of gold given away was so large that a contemporary account said that the value of gold in Egypt depreciated considerably after his arrival. In consequence of this the fame of Mansa Musa and Mali spread all over the Islamic world and beyond, so that Mali even appeared on contemporary European maps for the first time. When Mansa Musa returned to Mali he was accompanied by several North African travellers amongst whom was Abu Ishaq al-Saheli a poet from Andalusia who is credited with the introduction of a new style into West African architecture.

Mansa Musa was succeeded by Maghan I (1337–41) about whom little is known except that he had acted as regent for Mansa Musa during his absence on pilgrimage. In 1341 Maghan was succeeded by Mansa Musa's brother Sulayman who reorganized the empire and financial system in order to recover from the excessive expenditure of his brother. Sulayman was the ruler at the time of Ibn Battuta's visit in 1353 so that there is quite a detailed description of his rule including the king's friendly relations with the Marinid sultans of Morocco. Ibn Khaldun traced the careers of the next

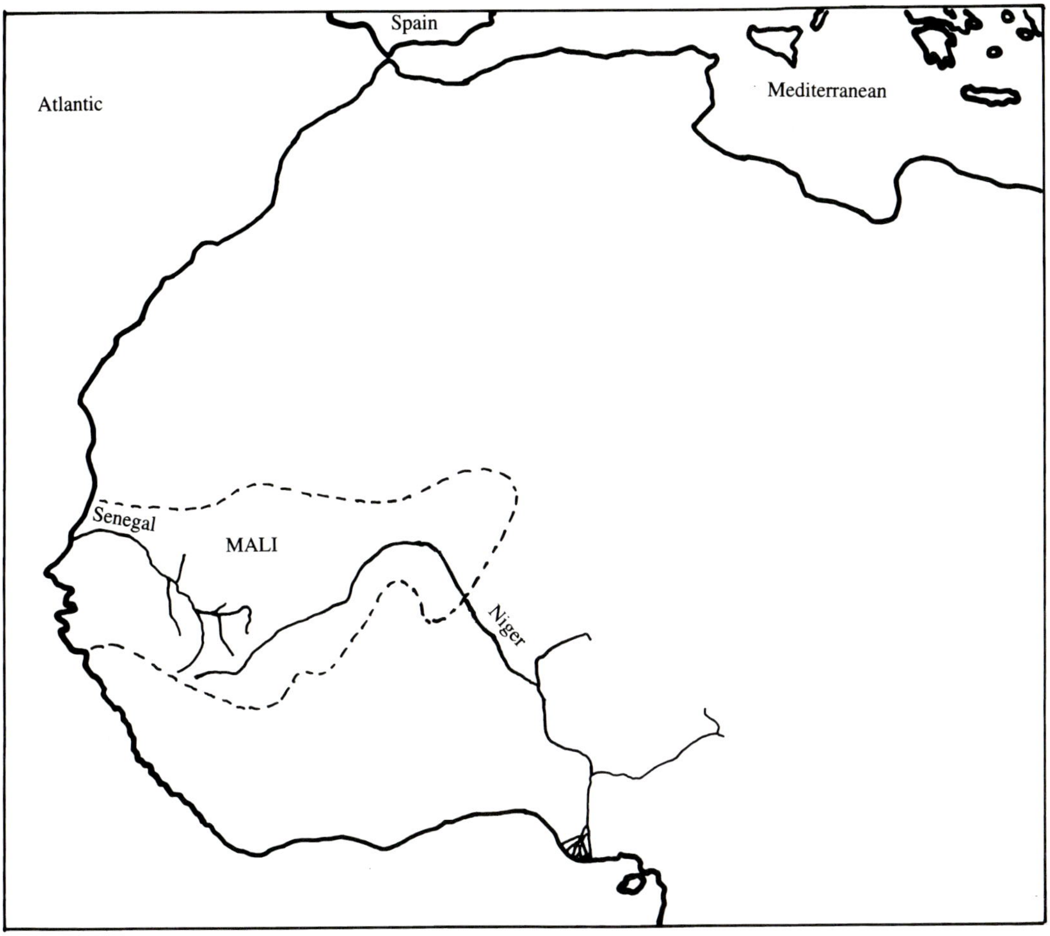

West Africa, showing the empire of Mali in the fourteenth century CE

five kings until the beginning of the fifteenth century, when the kingdom had been seriously weakened by civil wars and was no longer in a position to control all its dependencies which gradually were lost to rival kingdoms. One of the most formidable of these rivals was the Songhay kingdom of Gao or Kawkaw based on the banks of the Niger east of Mali. The arrival of the Portuguese during the fifteenth century introduced another new factor into the politics of the region. The ruler of Mali sought the assistance of these newcomers to fight off African rivals but they were unable to prevent the continuing disintegration of Malian power. In the 1590s the Moroccans occupied Djenné and the rulers of Mali were unable to retake the town. However, the greatly reduced kingdom of Mali continued to survive until 1670 when it was finally destroyed.

Despite its fame there are few architectural remains of the empire of Mali and one is forced to rely mostly on contemporary Arabic descriptions and rather complex oral traditions. At the spiritual capital of Kangaba there is little that remains from the medieval period with the exception of the giant linke (baobab) tree which marks the ancestral centre of the Mali Empire. There are several descriptions of the political capital at Niani, one of the best is that of the fourteenth-century writer al-Umari.

'[The capital] extends in length and breadth to a distance of approximately one barid (postal stage). It is not surrounded by a wall and most of it is scattered .... The town is surrounded on four sides by the "Nile" .... The buildings of this town are made of iwad or clay like the walls of the gardens of Damascus. This consists of building two thirds of a cubit (approximately 30 cm) in clay, then leaving it to dry, then building above it in the same way ... and so on until it is complete. The roofs are of wood and reeds and are generally domed or conical, in the form of cupolas of camel-backs, similar to the arch-shaped openings of vaults.'

Ibn Battuta's description of 1353 is not so full although he does indicate that he reached the city by boat and that it had a separate quarter for white merchants. He then describes the king's palace in some detail, in particular the audience hall which may be the same as that built by Abu Ishaq al–Saheli a decade or two earlier. The audience hall is contained within the palace and consists of a square domed chamber with triple-arched windows in each side. The windows are filled with wooden lattice work or grilles covered in silver and gold leaf (mashrabiyya?). Ibn Khaldun probably describing the same building notes that it was 'solidly built and faced with plaster; because such buildings are unknown in his [the sultan's] country'. Obvious parallels for this building can be found in the architecture of fourteenth-century North Africa and Spain (compare for example the Salón del Trono in the Alhambra). Next to the palace was a large open area used as a mosque or place of prayer.

The location of Mali's capital is unknown although it may be the site of Niani-en-Sankrani in Guinea occupied between the sixth and seventeenth centuries. Archaeological work at the site has revealed a large complex with a fortified royal compound, several residential areas, a metal-working centre and many cemeteries. A possible mosque site and Muslim cemetery have been identified near the royal complex which consists of a large square courtyard (20 m per side) and a smaller circular structure. The residential structures at the site consist of roundhouses built of mud with stone foundations.

See also: Djenné, Manding, West Africa

Further reading:

H. Haselberger, 'Architekturskizzen aus der Republic Mali Ergebnisse der DIAFE 190709 des Frobenius Institut', *International Archives of Ethnography* 50(1): 244–80, 1966.

J. Hunwick, 'The mid-fourteenth-century capital of Mali', *Journal of African History* 14(2): 195–206, 1973.

Mamluks

Term applied to the architecture of Greater Syria and Egypt between 1250 and 1516. During this period the area was ruled by the Mamluk sultans based in Cairo.

The word 'mamluk' is an Arabic term for slave and was applied to soldiers who, although non-Muslim by birth, had been captured as children, converted to Islam and trained to fight on behalf of their owners. The Mamluk sultanate had its origins in such slave soldiers, usually of Turkic or Mongol origin, who were used as guards by the Ayyubid sultans and princes. Gradually the Mamluks increased their power and by 1250 their position was so strong that they were able to depose and appoint sultans. In 1260 one of these soldiers, Baybars, became the first Mamluk sultan starting a tradition that was to endure for the next 250 years.

The Mamluk sultanate can be divided into two periods; the first lasted from 1250 to 1382 and is known as the Bahri (sea-based) Mamluk period because the dominant Mamluks were based on Roda island in the Nile delta. The second period from 1382 to 1517 is known as the Burji Mamluk period because those in power came from the Citadel in Cairo (burj is Arabic for tower). This period is sometimes also called the Circassian period, as most of the sultans were of Circassian origin.

The Mamluks were able to seize and retain power primarily through their superior military organization and training. This was demonstrated in 1260 when Sultan Baybars was able to halt the westward advance of the Mongols at the battle of 'Ayn Jalut in Palestine. Similarly the Mamluks continued to fight the Crusaders who by this time were confined to the coast of Syria. The main battles against the Crusaders took place under Sultan Qalaoun and his son Khalil, who in 1291 captured the cities of Acre, Tyre, Sidon, Beirut and Tripoli ending the Crusader presence in the Levant.

Mamluk architecture reflects the confidence derived from its military successes and is one of the most distinctive Islamic styles of building. The main source for Mamluk architecture was the buildings of the Ayyubids and in some senses the Mamluk style is simply a development of that of the Ayyubids. However, the Mamluks were also influenced by other styles, in particular Italian and Andalusian architecture.

As with Ayyubid architecture there is a significant difference between Syrian and Egyptian Mamluk architecture, which can be explained by the availability of materials and differing traditions of building. In Egypt brick remained an important material of construction up until the fifteenth century, whereas in Syria it was seldom used. Other differences can be detected in decorative details such as the type of arch used in muqarnas mouldings (in Egypt they are angular points whereas in Syria they have a rounded profile). Another factor which created different styles was Cairo's position as capital city which meant that its buildings tended to be grander and more highly decorated than those of Syria. Jerusalem is interesting in this respect as its position midway between Damascus and Cairo made it susceptible to influences from both Syria and Egypt.

There are, however, several features which are characteristic of buildings throughout the area under Mamluk control. These can be considered under three headings: surface decoration, layout and planning, and structural elements.

Surface Decoration

The most characteristic feature of Mamluk architecture (and art in general) is the use of heraldic blazons. These are usually round discs divided into three fields with various emblems (e.g. cup, horn, disc, etc.) set into the middle. Each sultan and group of Mamluks had their own blazon which would be applied to any objects belonging to the group including buildings. As well as providing dating evidence these blazons give a useful insight into how the Mamluk regime operated. Another related decoration employed on buildings was monumental calligraphy in Naskhi script, this would usually state the name and rank of a building's founder.

The usual surface for both blazons and calligraphy is ashlar masonry, although plaster and wood are also sometimes used. Other decorative motifs employed are geometric and floral patterns which are often interlaced. Ceramic tile decoration is rare, although coloured glass mosaics and inlaid marble are occasionally used for mihrabs and other places of special importance. One decorative feature to spread from Syria to Egypt is the use of ablaq (alternating layers of different colours, or shades of masonry); this was used in Syria in Ayyubid times but is not found in Egypt until 1300 (it is possible that this idea may have Italian origins). Mashrabiyya screens of turned wood were also used for interiors.

Structural Elements

In addition to surface decoration many structural elements were developed into decorative features. Openings, in particular doorways, became subjects for elaboration and frequently consisted of a monumental frame or panel and a recessed niche for the door covered with a muqarnas vault. Another example of such elaboration is the joggled voussoir where the stones of an arch were cut so as to interlock and provide increased strength to the arch. Usually the effect is enhanced by using ablaq techniques. Sometimes this becomes purely surface decoration when the actual voussoirs are not intercut and there is simply an interlocking façade. Another decorative effect created with openings was the horsehoe arch which was introduced during this period.

Buildings were generally roofed with cross vaults although sometimes plain barrel vaults were used. In Jerusalem an elaborate form of vault called the folded cross vault was developed from Ayyubid military architecture. This is basically a cross vault with a large circular hole in the roof over which a wooden clerestory or other feature could be added. Domes were common in buildings of this period and could be made from a variety of materials including baked brick, wood and stone. Wooden domes were often used in houses and palaces because they were lighter and easier to build, although mausoleums tended to be covered with brick or stone domes. In fourteenth-century Cairo, masonry domes carved with arabesque designs became a fashionable method of covering tombs.

Layout and Planning

The growth of cities during the Mamluk period meant that most types of building, even palaces, were located within the fabric of a city. The result of this was that buildings were often built on an irregular-shaped plot because of the shortage of space. Many Mamluk buildings which

Doorway of Serai al-Takiyya. Mamluk period, Jerusalem (after Burgoyne)

seem to be square and symmetrical are built on irregular ground plans. The architects were able to make the buildings appear square by a variety of techniques such as horizontal lines (ablaq) and controlled access (passageways) which distort perspective. A related problem was that narrow streets tend to detract from the visual impact of a building façade. This was overcome by use of recessed entrances, domes, and projecting corners which have a cumulative effect of a staggered façade which can be viewed from the side.

The military nature of Mamluk rule affected society in many ways although it did not have much effect on architecture. The main reason for this was that so many fortresses had been built by the Ayyubids and Crusaders that there was generally no need to build new castles when existing fortifications could be repaired. Also with the advance of the Mongols the nature of warfare changed so that speed and communications became more important than the defence and capture of strongholds. As a consequence of this the Mamluks invested instead in an efficient system of communication based on small forts, fire beacons and pigeon lofts. This system was kept separate from the usual trade network of khans and caravanserais and was regarded as part of the Mamluks' military organization.

Building Types

Some of the most distinctive buildings of the Mamluk period are the many religious foundations. Most cities already had Friday mosques so that these were seldom built during this period. The Great Mosque in Tripoli is one exception to this and was built soon after the city was taken from the Crusaders, it has a traditional plan based around a central courtyard with single arcades on three sides and a double arcade on the qibla side. More typical of the period are the many religious institutions such as madrassas, zawiyas and khanqas built to counter the spread of Shiʿism. In Cairo these were often built to a cruciform plan which developed from the four-iwan madrassa where each iwan represents one of the schools of law. Many of these buildings also had some political purpose, thus they were often built as memorials to a particular Sultan or were used as centres for training officials. During this period it was common for the tomb of the founder to be incorporated into the building, this applied to mosques, madrassas and even hospitals.

Madrassas became a common feature in most cities and were used to train administrators. Jerusalem in particular seems to have been developed as a training ground for Mamluk clergy and officials and the area around the Haram was extensively developed (Mecca was too far from Cairo to be developed in this way and in any case was not directly under Mamluk control).

The stability provided by the Mamluk regime was a stimulus to trade and numerous suqs, khans and caravanserais can be dated to this period. The Suq al-Qattanin (Cotton Market) in Jerusalem is one of the best preserved Mamluk city markets. It was built on the orders of Sultan al-Nasir Muhammad in 1336 as a huge complex with over fifty shop units, two bath houses and a khan. Each shop is a small cross-vaulted room opening onto the covered street with another room (for storage or accommodation) located above with a separate access. Although the highest concentration of suqs and khans was in the cities there was also an extensive network of roadside khans and caravanserais. Some of these buildings were quite large as they were not restricted by the competition for space evident in city buildings. Khan Yunis in Ghaza is a huge complex built in 1387 on the main road between Egypt and Syria. The plan comprises a huge central courtyard (perhaps with a building in the centre) with accommodation and storage units around the sides and a domed mosque with a minaret next to the gateway.

See also: ablaq, joggled voussoirs, mashrabiyya

Further reading:

There are several books devoted to Mamluk cities; the most useful of these are:

M. H. Burgoyne and D. Richards, *Mamluk Jerusalem: An Architectural Study*, Essex 1987.

J. C. Garlin, J. Revault, B. Maury and M. Zakariya, *Palais et maisons du Caire: Époque mamelouke*, Paris 1982.

H. Salam-Liebech, *The Architecture of Mamluk Tripoli*, Harvard 1983.

Other useful works are:

M. Abu Khalaf, 'Khan Yunnus and the khans of Palestine', *Levant* 15: 178–86, 1983.

J. C. Kessler, *The Carved Masonry Domes of Cairo*, London 1976.

J. Sauvaget, *La Poste aux Chevaux dans l'empire des Mamlouks*, Paris 1941.

Manda

Island trading port on the north Kenya coast in East Africa.

This is the largest early Islamic complex in the Lamu archipelago and one of the largest on the coast. The earliest occupation seems to have been in the mid-eighth century and to have continued until the sixteenth when it was noted by the Portuguese.

The earliest structures at the site were made with timber posts and walls of wattle and daub. During the tenth century the settlement expanded on to an area of land reclaimed from the sea by sea walls built from huge coral blocks. Sometime in the tenth century the wooden structures were replaced with stone buildings made out of reef coral. Also during the tenth century some buildings were made out of two types of baked brick, a locally made variety and rarer imported brick (possibly from Oman). The only tenth-century building completely excavated is known as the 'House of Cisterns' and consists of a large courtyard building entered via a flight of seven steps.

Buildings erected after the thirteenth century used fossil coral instead of the reef coral of earlier structures. Ruins surviving from the later period of occupation include several houses, a town wall, two mosques and several monumental tombs.

See also: coral, East Africa, Kenya, Shanga

Further reading:

H. N. Chittick, *Manda: Excavations at an Island Port on the Kenya Coast*, British Institute in Eastern Africa Memoir 9, in 2 vols., Nairobi 1984.

M. C. Horton, 'Asiatic colonization of the East African coast: the Manda evidence', *Journal of the Royal Asiatic Society* pt. 2: 201–12, 1986.

mandal

Mughal term for a pavilion or house.

manding (Mande)

West African language group which formed the ruling class of the empire of Mali, now used to describe one of the dominant urban architectural styles of the region.

The current distribution of the Manding peoples covers an area including southern Mali, Burkina Faso and the Ivory Coast. Prominent cities with Manding architecture include Mopti, Djenné, Ségou, Bobo Dioulasso, Wa and Kong.

Characteristic features of Manding architecture are the use of mud brick, conical towers with projecting toron, and elaborate decorated entrance façades. Mud is the traditional building material of the area and is used in several forms, either as spherical hand-rolled lumps or as rectangular or cylindrical bricks. Conical towers may either occur as buttresses or as towers marking the position of a mihrab in a mosque. It is thought that the conical towers derive from the pre-Islamic ancestral pillars of the region whilst the use of toron traditionally suggests continual rebirth. Whilst the façades of mosques and palaces are often decorated with earthen pillars and projecting toron, the decoration of house façades is normally restricted to the entrances. Some of the most elaborate entrance façades can be found at Djenné in Mali which is usually considered the birthplace of the Manding style. A traditional façade will consist of three levels contained within two parallel buttresses. The first two levels correspond to the two storeys inside the house whilst the third level corresponds to the roof level parapet. The first level consists of the doorway covered by a steep sloping sill above which is the second level containing a rectangular panel with a square window in the middle. The third level consists of a line of projecting toron made of split palm, a panel containing four pillared niches and four pointed crenellations on the top.

See also: Djenné, Mali, Sudan, West Africa

Further reading:

L. Prussin, 'Sudanese architecture and the Manding', *African Arts* 3(4): 12–19 and 64–7, 1970.

manzil

Arabic term for house or way station (literally 'a place to stay').

maqʿad

Projecting balcony overlooking a courtyard in Egyptian houses.

maqbara

Graveyard.

maqsura

Screen which encloses the area of the mihrab and minbar in early mosques.

The origin of the screens was to protect the caliph from assassination attempts during praying. There also may have been some spiritual connotation similar to the chancel screen in churches. They were often wooden screens decorated with carvings or interlocking turned pieces of wood (mashrabiyya).

Marakesh

Southern capital of Morocco.

Marakesh is on a wide plain located 40 km from the High Atlas. It was founded by the Almoravid ruler Yusf ibn Tashfin in 1062, although there are few buildings which have survived from this period. The best surviving example is the dome of the Almoravid palace; built of baked brick covered with plaster, the dome rests on a square brick base. The area immediately below the drum is pierced with twenty-four multifoil niches, whilst the dome itself is decorated with interlaced arches in relief and zig-zag patterns on the top. Inside the dome has an entirely different configuration and consists of an eight-pointed star rising to a muqarnas dome.

Remains from the Almohad period (twelfth to thirteenth century) include the Kutubiyya Mosque, the Kasba Mosque and the Bab Agnau. The Kutubiyya Mosque is built in the traditional Almohad style with the lateral arcades of the courtyard forming an integral part of the prayer hall. The mosque has a minaret more than 60 m high, decorated with windows and blind niches with interlaced arches; at the top there is a small kiosk covered with a fluted dome. The parapet is decorated with ceramic tile inlays and stepped merlons. The minaret is ascended by a ramp which is built around a hollow square core. The core contains a series of six vaulted rooms, one on each storey and each with a different form of vault (the design is similar to the Giralda tower in Seville). The Kasba Mosque is a square building containing five courtyards, four subsidiary and one central. The minaret is decorated in a similar style to the Kutubiyya and inside there is a staircase built around a central core. The Bab Agnau is part of the massive Almohad fortifications which stretch around the city for a distance of over 10 km. The gateway is built of brick and comprises a wide opening covered with a pointed horseshoe arch. The inner arch is framed by a magnificent round horseshoe arch decorated with a bold interlaced pattern. The intrados of the arch is decorated with bold stylized flora, and the whole is enclosed within a giant rectangular frame with a Kufic inscription.

The city has three madrassas the oldest of which is the Bin Yusuf Madrassa built as a mosque in the twelfth century and converted in the sixteenth. The town also contains the tombs of various Moroccan rulers, including that of Yusuf ibn Tashfin founder of the Almoravid dynasty, and the tomb of the seven saints which is still the object of an annual pilgrimage.

There are several palaces within the city, the oldest of which is the Dar al Makhzan founded by the Almohads but considerably altered in the sixteenth century. The city also contains historic gardens, the most important being the Mamounia, originally laid out in the seventeenth century.

See also: Morocco

Mardin

City in south-east Anatolia (Turkey) associated with the Artukid dynasty during the medieval period.

Mardin is located in a strategic position on a rocky spur overlooking the crossroads between east–west and north–south routes. The city is dominated by the fortress which has stood on this site since Roman times. During the Islamic period the castle has been extensively repaired several times, first by the Hamdanids in the ninth century, later by the Artukids and more recently by the Ottomans. From 1104 to 1408 the city became the principal stronghold of the Artukids who resisted successive attacks by the Ayyubids, the Mongols and the Timurids.

The buildings of the town are terraced into the hillside and all have magnificent views over the Mesopotamian plain. The main building stone is brilliant white limestone which provides a dazzling contrast to the grey-black basalt which characterizes the surrounding region.

Several important buildings survive from the Artukid period including the Great Mosque, a hammam and several madrassas. The prayer hall of the Great Mosque is a multi-domed unit in the usual Artukid style whilst the minaret is a tall cylindrical tower with elaborately carved cartouches. One of the most striking buildings in the city is the Kasim Pasha Madrassa built in 1445 by the Aq-qoyunulu ruler Kasim b. Jahangir. There are also several important churches and monasteries in the region.

See also: Turkey

maristan

Hospital.

marqad

Tombstone.

mashad

Shrine, or commemorative mosque.

mashrabiyya

Wooden grille or grate used to cover windows or balconies.

The word is derived from the niches used to store vessels of drinking water. The grilles are traditionally made from short lengths of turned wood joined together through polygonal blocks so that

Star-shaped mashrabiyya

they form large areas of lattice-like patterns. The patterns formed by the lattice work vary from place to place although commonly the main lines of the grille are at a 45 degree angle. Mashrabiyya can also be made of metalwork although this is more rare and was usually reserved for the houses of the very rich or public buildings.

masjid

Mosque.

mastaba

Bench or platform.

mathara

Place of ritual ablution.

mazar

Mausoleum or shrine.

Mecca (Makkah)

The most sacred city of Islam located in western Saudi Arabia.

The city of Mecca lies about 70 km inland from the Red Sea port of Jeddah. It is built in a hollow in the mountains known as Batn Mecca. The oldest part of the city contains the Holy Mosque and the Ka'ba and is known as al-Batha. Rainfall is extremely scarce and unpredictable; in ancient times water was supplied by a series of wells, the most important of which is the well of Zamzam within the holy precinct. Despite the aridity of the area the city's position makes it prone to flash floods which are diverted by a series of dams and channels which deflect water away from the city centre.

History

In pre-Islamic times Mecca was known as a sacred site and was referred to as Maccorba in the time of Ptolemy. The first permanent settlements on the site were made in the fifth century CE by the Quraysh tribe. By the sixth century the city appears to have become a great trading centre profiting from the caravan trade between the Mediterranean and the Indian Ocean. In 570 the prophet Muhammad was born in Mecca, by the year 610 he had begun to preach the message revealed to him as Quran. Muhammad's teaching annoyed the prominent merchants of the town so that in 622 he was compelled to leave for the city of Medina. (This event is known as the Hejira or migration and is the starting point for the Muslim calendar.) In Medina Muhammad attracted a large following who were able to attack the Meccan caravans. By 630 Muhammad and his followers (the Muslims) had defeated Mecca and converted most of its inhabitants to Islam. In the following years Medina became capital of the new Islamic state whilst Mecca retained its position as religious centre and centre of pilgrimage.

For a brief period between 680 and 692 Mecca became the capital of a rival caliphate established by Abd Allah Ibn Zubayr who controlled most of Arabia and Iraq. During the Abbasid period huge sums of money were spent on developing the city. In the tenth century the decline of the caliphate allowed the Qarmathians (a radical anti-establishment group) to sack Mecca and carry off the Black Stone to their base in Bahrain. The Black Stone

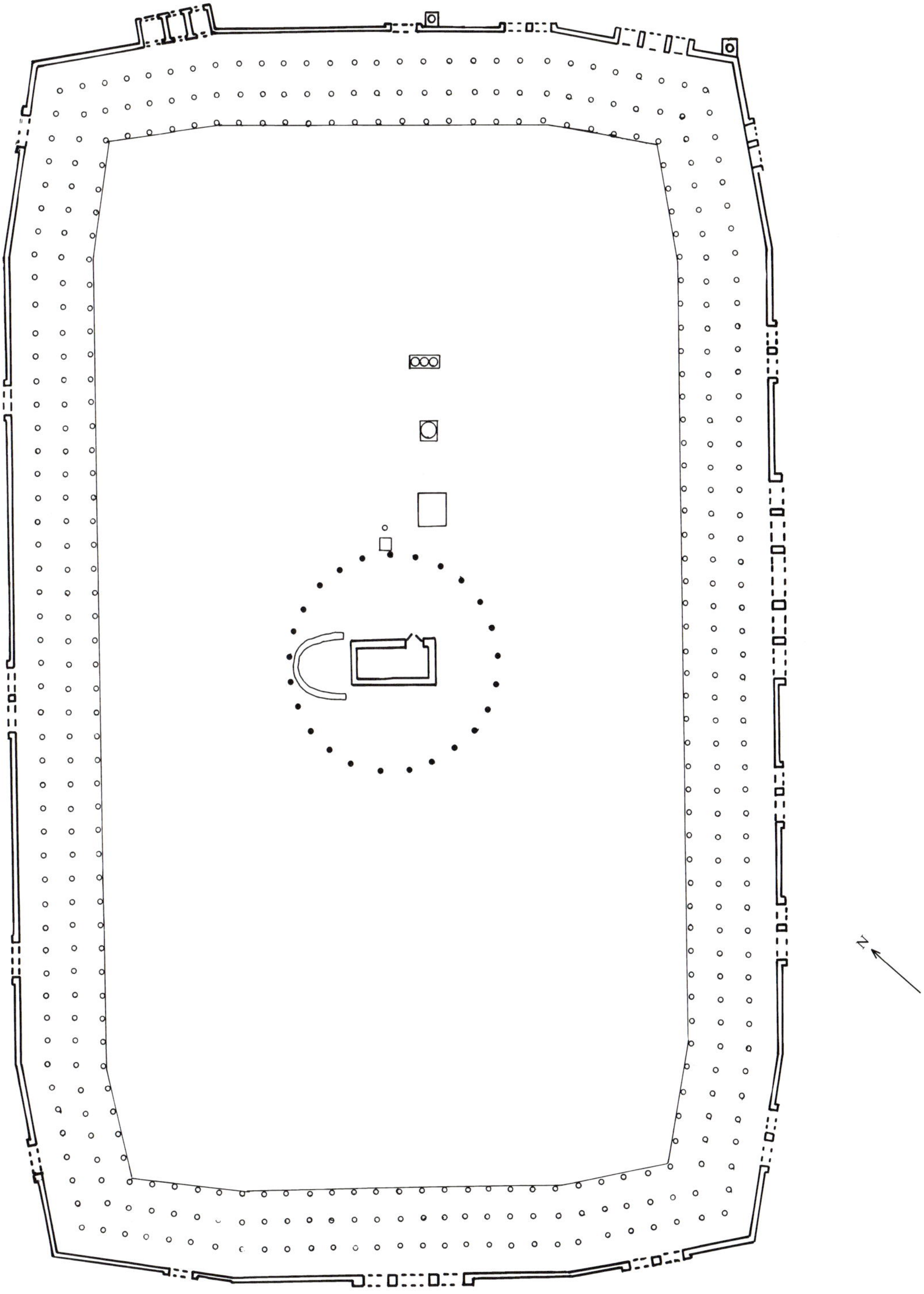

The Haram, Mecca (after Jairazbhoy)

was later returned and Mecca continued to develop as a religious centre.

From the late tenth century to the beginning of the nineteenth century Mecca was ruled by the Sharifs of Mecca who attempted to remain independent of the dominant powers of the time. In 1929 Mecca became part of the Kingdom of Saudi Arabia.

Architecture

The most important building in Mecca is the Holy Mosque of Mecca which contains the Ka'ba, a tall box-like structure which stands in a courtyard in the centre of the mosque. The Ka'ba is pre-Islamic in origin although at the beginning of the Islamic period it became established as the main object of pilgrimages to Mecca.

The area around the Ka'ba was first enclosed by a wall in 638 in order to create an open space for the tawaf (circumambulation). In 646 the area was enlarged with a new enclosure wall with arcades opening on to the courtyard. In 684 under Abd Allah Ibn Zubayr the mosque was further enlarged and decorated with marble and mosaic decoration. In 709 the Umayyad caliph al-Walid covered the arcades of the mosque with a teak roof resting on marble columns. A further enlargement was carried out by the Abbasid caliph al-Mansur between 754 and 757, and it was at this time that the first minaret was built. For the next 700 years numerous modifications were carried out although no major alterations to the form of the building occurred until the Ottoman period in the sixteenth century. The best medieval description of the mosque is by Ibn Jubayr who visited it in 1183. He describes a roofed arcade around a central courtyard decorated with large merlons and stucco decoration.

Major renovations were carried out in 1564 under the direction of the Ottoman sultan Suleyman the Magnificent who replaced the flat roofs of the arcades with stone domes and rebuilt the minarets. The next major rebuilding took place in the twentieth century under Saudi rule and made the Holy Mosque of Mecca the largest mosque in the world. In its present form the mosque has seven minarets, two-storey arcades around the enlarged courtyard and a covered street (Ma'sa) between the hills of al-Safa and al-Marwa (1920s).

Other features within the Holy Mosque include the well of Zamzam and the Maqam Ibrahim. According to Muslim tradition the well of Zamzam sprang up when Hajar (the wife of Ibrahim) was looking for water for her child Ishmael. In the ninth century the well was covered with a vaulted roof by the Abbasid caliph al-Mu'tassim. The form of the building was changed several times in the following centuries the most enduring of which was that built by the Ottomans in the seventeenth century. In addition to its function as a cover of the well the Maqam Zamzam also functioned as a base for Shafi theologians. Hanbali, Hanafi and Malaki theologians each had their own maqam within the courtyard which were also rebuilt at this time. In the 1950s all these maqams were removed by the Saudi authorities to make more space for the circumambulation of the Ka'ba. The Maqam of Zamzam was replaced by two underground ablutions rooms fed by the well of Zamzam. The Maqam Ibrahim contains a stone with two footprints which are thought to be those of Ibrahim. This building was restored by the Saudi authorities in the 1950s.

In its present form Mecca is predominantly a modern city although it does contain a few houses from the Ottoman period (eighteenth century or later). Traditional Meccan houses are generally tall (three to four storeys) with projecting wooden windows (mashrabiyya) and flat roofs enclosed by walls 2 m high. The extreme heat of the city in the summer (50 degrees celsius) means that the houses are equipped with airshafts which allow hot air to escape. Most of the houses in Mecca are dual purpose, serving as family homes and as pilgrim hostels during the season of the Hajj.

The main building materials used in Meccan houses are stone, brick and wood. Two types of stone are used, finely dressed stone and rubble stone. The dressed stone (sandstone or granite) is used for decorative panels around doorways and windows that often incorporate decorative niches. Rubble stone is used for load-bearing walls which are usually two stones wide and laid in rough courses of mud-based mortar. At regular intervals (between 50 and 70 cm) there are layers of wood (usually palm or mangrove) which improves the load-bearing capacity of the walls. The windows are made of hardwood (usually teak) and are highly decorated. Windows may be either flat panels with openings protected by screens or elaborated structures resting on carved brackets. Brick is used in

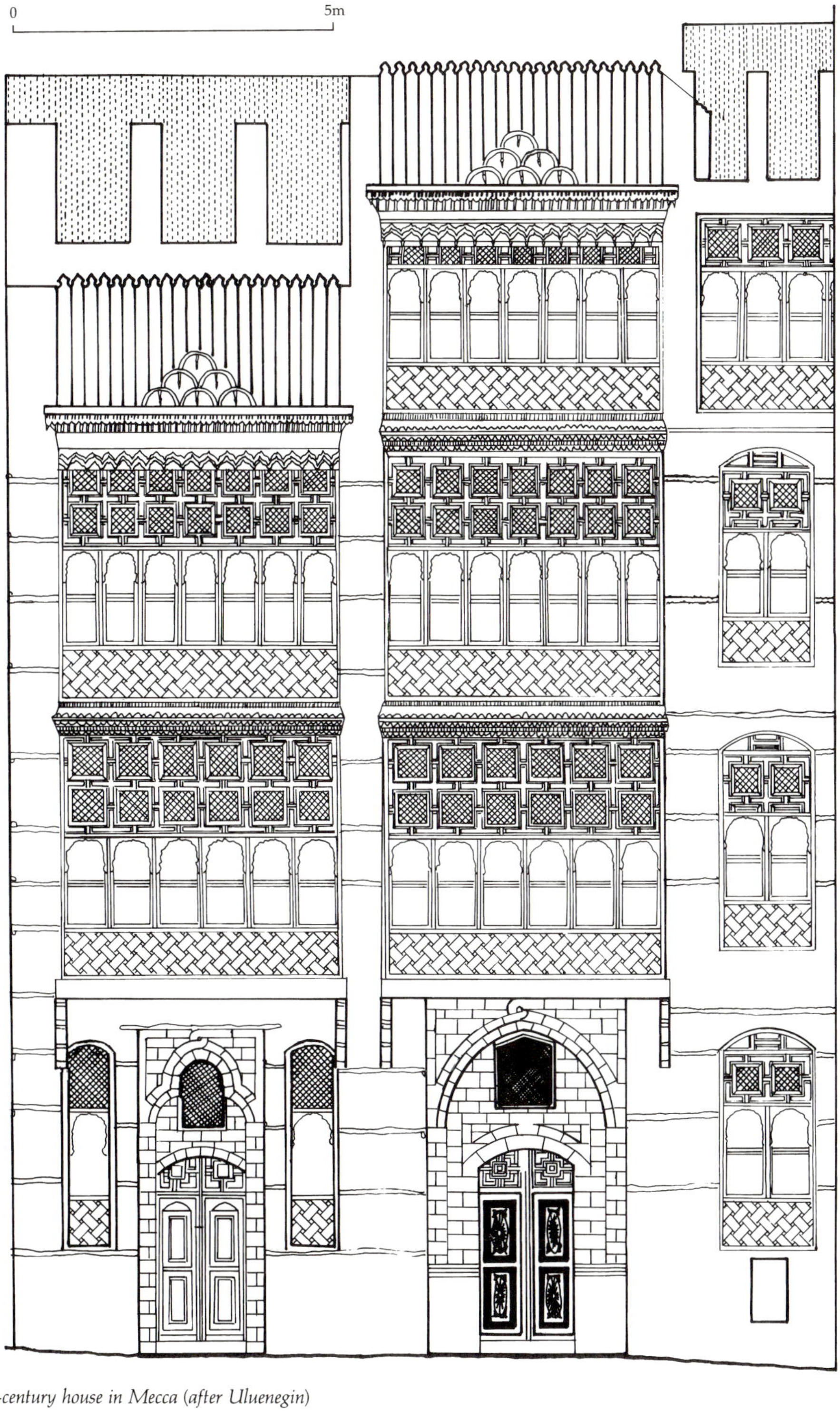

Eighteenth-century house in Mecca (after Uluenegin)

walls which enclose the terraces or roof gardens on the top of each house. The brick is locally made and laid in a decorative pattern which leaves holes for ventilation.

See also: Hajj routes, Ka'ba, Medina, Saudi Arabia

Further reading:

E. Esin, *Mecca the Blessed, Medinah the Radiant*, London 1963.
R. A. Jairazbhoy, 'The architecture of the Holy Shrine in Makkah', in *Hajj in Focus*, ed. Z. I. Khan and Y. Zaki, London 1986, 151–70.
G. R. D. King, *The Historical Mosques of Saudi Arabia*, London and New York 1986, 19–26.
N. and B. Uluenegin, 'Homes of Old Makkah', *Aramco World* 44(4): 20–9, 1993.
M. Watt, A. J. Wensinck, C. E. Bosworth, R. B. Winder and D. King, 'Makka', *Encyclopedia of Islam* 6: 144–87, 1991.
A. Yusef, 'Al-Haramain: a development study', *Hajj in Focus*, ed. Z. I. Khan and Y. Zaki, London 1986, 171–80.

medina

Literally 'city'. This term is often used in North Africa to describe the older part of the city.

Medina (Arabic: Madinah al-Monawarah)

Second most sacred city of Islam located in the Hijaz region of Saudi Arabia.

The city of Medina stands in a fertile oasis 360 km north of Mecca and 160 km east of the Red Sea. In pre-Islamic times the city was known as Yathrib although by the early years of Islam it was also referred to as Medina. The original city of Medina comprised a series of small settlements dispersed over a wide plain. The spaces between the settlements were filled with fruit gardens, fields and date-palm groves. Each settlement was protected by a number of forts or towers which at the beginning of Islam are said to have numbered more than 200. At the time of Muhammad's arrival in Medina (the first year of the Hejira) the town had a large Judaeo-Arabic population in addition to the pagan Arab population. The first Muslim converts in Medina were converted by Muhammad whilst they were on a pilgrimage to Mecca. In 622 Muslim pilgrims from Medina invited Muhammad to come to their city to escape the growing hostility of the Meccan hierarchy. With Muhammad's arrival in Medina the city became the capital of an expanding Muslim Empire. After Muhammad's death Abu Bakr was appointed as caliph and continued to rule from Medina as did his two successors Umar and Uthman. Under Ali the newly established town of Kufa replaced Medina as the capital. Medina remained in a secondary position under the Umayyads although they did develop it as a religious centre.

The first city wall was built around the centre of Medina in 974 in preparation for a Fatimid attack. In 1162 a larger area was enclosed by a wall with towers and gates erected by Nur al-Din Zangi. After the Ottoman conquest of the Hijaz in the sixteenth century the Ottoman sultan Suleyman the Magnificent enclosed the city in a new wall 12 m high made of granite and basalt blocks. Suleyman was also responsible for building an aqueduct which brought water into the city from the south. In the 1860s the Ottoman sultan Abd al-Aziz increased the height of the walls to 25 m. During the twentieth century the walls were gradually removed as they were thought to be of no further use.

The most important building in Medina is the Mosque of the Prophet Muhammad. When Muhammad arrived in 622 he was given a plot of land on which to build his house and prayer area (the first mosque). The mosque was a rectangular enclosure (35 by 30 m) with covered areas at the south and north ends. The house of Muhammad and his wives was built on the outside of the east wall. Originally Muhammad and his followers prayed towards Jerusalem but after a revelation the direction of prayer was changed to Mecca in the south. In 629 the mosque was extended on the north, south and west sides to form a square enclosure. In its earliest form the mosque had no mihrab although there was a wooden minbar of three steps which was used by the prophet for preaching the Quran. After his death Muhammad was buried in his house in the room of one of his wives. Subsequently the caliphs Abu Bakr and Umar were buried in the same place. During the reign of Umar the palm trunks were replaced with stone columns and a new roof of teak was added.

The first major rebuilding of the mosque was carried out during the reign of the Umayyad caliph al-Walid. Walid more than doubled the size of the mosque and incorporated the room contain-

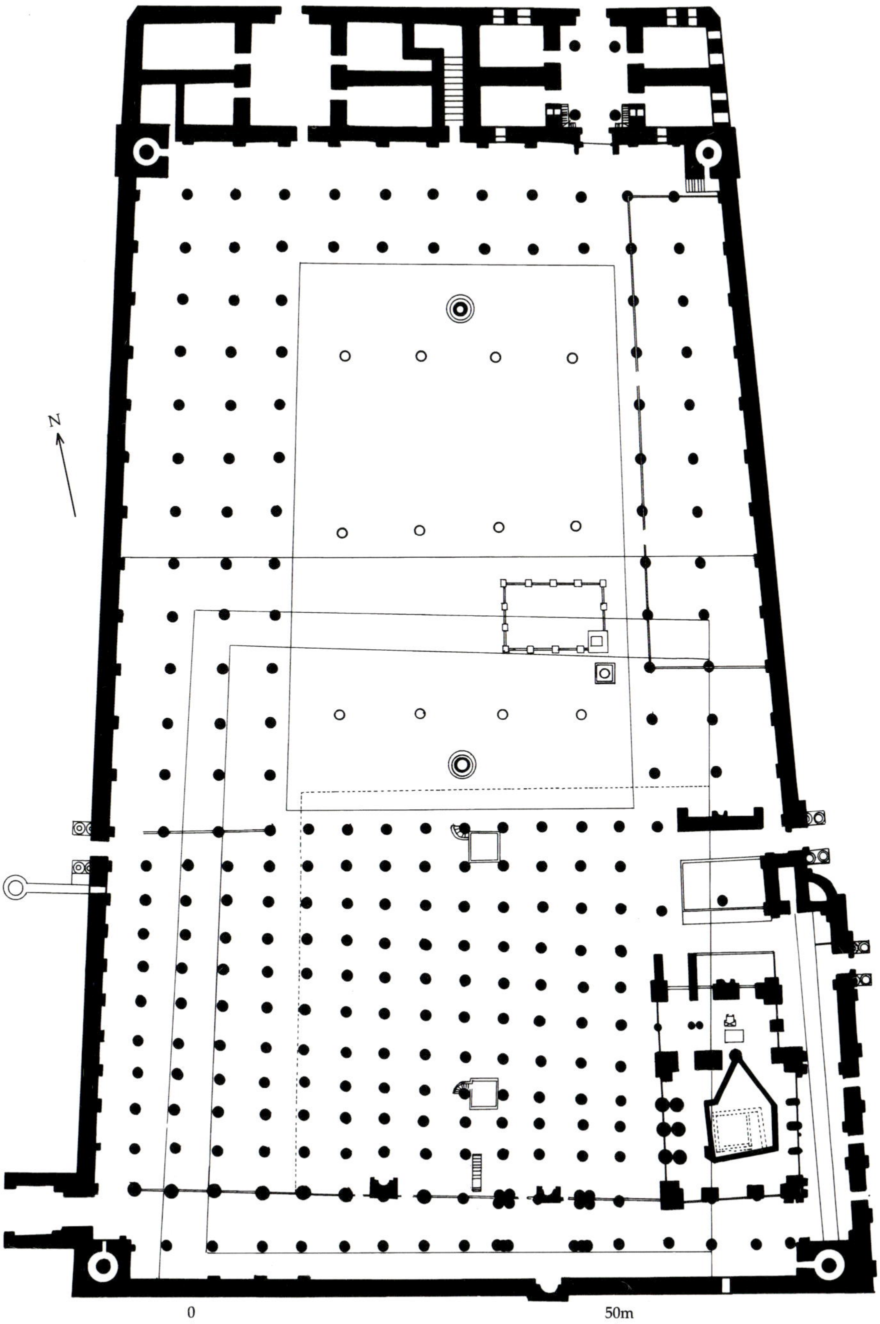

The mosque of the Prophet, Medina; with tomb of Muhammad in lower right-hand corner (after Sauvaget)

ing the graves into the body of the mosque. To prevent any confusion with the Ka'ba in Mecca the enclosure around the graves was of an irregular shape. Walid also added a mihrab and four minarets to the structure of the mosque and embellished the interior of the mosque with mosaic and marble decoration. The mosque was further enlarged under the Abbasid caliphs in 781 by al-Mahdi and in 862 by al-Muawakkil. In 1256 the mosque suffered from a major fire which destroyed the roof, the Quran of Uthman and the minbar of the prophet. The mosque was rebuilt by the Egyptian Mamluk sultan Baybars who established a tradition of Mamluk restoration work on the mosque. In 1279 the Mamluk sultan Qala'un added a wooden dome over the tomb of the prophet. In 1467 this was replaced by a stone dome under the directions of Qayt Bay who also replaced the maqsura.

The Ottoman conquest of the city in the sixteenth century introduced a new architectural style into the Medina Mosque. One of the first modifications was the mihrab Suleymani added by Suleyman the Magnificent. Later on in the sixteenth century the mosque was extended to the west and a new minaret was added. The present green dome over the tomb of the prophet was added in 1818 under the Ottoman sultan Mahmud II. In the 1920s the mosque became the responsibility of the Saudi rulers who undertook various repairs and restorations. In 1951 the Saudi government initiated the largest programme of expansion in the mosque's history making the total mosque area 22,955 m square. In 1973 a huge new court was added on to the west side of the mosque to cope with the increasing number of pilgrims.

Like Mecca, the city of Medina is mostly a modern concrete construction. By analogy with the Prophet's mosque it is known that in the early days of Islam the houses were built of mud brick with palm wood used for roofing and pillars. The advent of Islam brought new wealth to the city and may have encouraged the development of stone architecture. Certainly by the beginning of the Ottoman period stone was in use on a large enough scale to be employed for the city walls. The traditional house form in Mecca appears to have been a courtyard house three or four storeys high built out of granite or basalt. Water was relatively more plentiful than at Mecca and each house had its own well. According to reports, some of the houses had columned halls opening on to bathing pools.

Further reading:

G. R. D. King, *Historical Mosques of Saudi Arabia*, London and New York 1986.

J. Sauvaget, *La Mosquée Omeyyade de Medine. Études sur les origines architecturales de la mosquée et de la basilique*, Paris 1947.

W. M. Watt and R. B. Winder, 'Al-Madina', *Encyclopaedia of Islam*, new edn., 5: 994–1007, 1986.

A. Youssef, 'Al Haramain: a development study', in *Hajj in Focus*, ed. Z. I. Khan and Y. Zaki, London 1986.

Meknes

Former capital of Morocco located on a high plateau between Fez and Rabat.

The city of Meknes was founded by the Almoravids in the eleventh century, before that period the site was occupied by a cluster of small villages. The city suffered from the Almohad conquest in 1150, although it was later restored and in the thirteenth century was provided with an aqueduct, bridges and a madrassa. The city reached its peak under the Sa'adians who adopted it as their capital in the seventeenth century. Under the sultan Moulay Ismail the city was enclosed by a triple wall with a perimeter of more than 30 km pierced by twenty gates. To the south of the city is a huge separate enclosure reserved for the sultan which contains two palaces, one for the sultan and one for his wives and 500 concubines. The palaces were built as a series of gardens connected by pavilions supported on marble columns. There are a total of forty-five separate pavilions within the grounds, as well as four mosques and twenty domed tombs containing the graves of sultans and their families. To support the palace there was a huge granary, store house, stables, an army camp and palatial residences for the officials.

See also: Morocco

Mérida

City in south-west Spain noted for its Roman ruins and early Islamic fortress.

The fortress is located next to the river Guadiana and the famous Roman bridge. It is probably a continuation of an older structure, although it was substantially altered to its present form in 835 according to an inscription found in the fortress (now in the local museum). It is similar to sixth- and seventh-century Byzantine forts of North Africa although the arches above the gateways are horseshoe-shaped indicating their Islamic provenance.

The fortress is essentially a large square enclo-

Tomb of Sultan Sanjar, Merv, Turkmenistan (after Pugachenkara)

sure (130 m per side) with solid rectangular buttress towers and three gateways. The gateway leading from the Roman bridge is in the form of a gatehouse flanked by two massive towers. The only contemporary structure within the fortress is a cistern which took water directly from the river via a tunnel. Entry to the cistern is from a barrel-vaulted corridor with staircases at either end and doorways in the side which lead to the cistern. The jambs of the doorways and other parts of the cistern include re-used Visigothic building stones.

See also: Spain

Further reading:

K. A. C. Creswell, *A Short Account of Early Muslim Architecture*, revised and enlarged ed. J. W. Allan, Aldershot 1989, 302.

G. Goodwin, *Islamic Spain*, Architectural Guides for Travellers, London 1990, 125–6.

Merv (also Marw or Marv)

Ancient city in the Central Asian republic of Turkmenistan. Also called Merv al-Shahijan or Royal Merv to distinguish it from the city of the same name in modern Afghanistan.

The city is located in the Merv oasis on the banks of the Murghab river. During the early Islamic period it functioned as one of the chief cities of Khurassan and under the Abbasids was capital of the east. During the eighth century the centre of the town gradually moved from its old Sassanian site of Gavur Kala to a new site which is now known as Sultan Kala. In 1070 the Seljuk sultan Malik Sha rebuilt the city wall which remains as one of the finest examples of medieval fortification. Other remains from the Seljuk period include the mausoleum of Sultan Sanjar which is a domed structure standing on a square base measuring 27 m per side. The Mongol invasions caused severe damage to the city which never fully

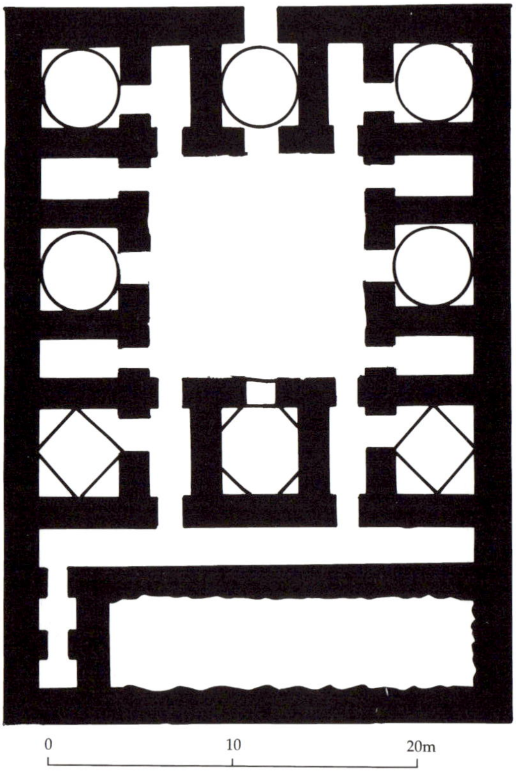

Pre-thirteenth-century house, Merv, Turkmenistan

recovered. Under the Timurid sultan Sha Rukh attempts were made to revive the fortunes of the city. The city dam was rebuilt to restore the irrigation system but this was only partially successful. Also the city of this period was built on a different site known as Abd Allah Khan Kala.

Further reading:

G. Herrman, V. Masson, K. Kurbansakhatov, et. al., 'The International Merv Project, preliminary report on the First Season', *Iran* 31: 39–62, 1993.

E. O'Donovan, *The Merv Oasis and Adventures East of the Caspian During the Years 1879–81*, London 1882.

G. A. Pugachenkava, 'Puti razvitiya arkhitekturi Iuzhnogo Turkmenistana pori rabovladeniya', *Trudi Iuzhno-Turkmenistanskoi Arkheologicheskoi Ekspeditsii* 6: Moscow, 1958.

mescit

Turkish term for a small mosque without a minbar, equivalent to the Arabic term masjid.

Mihrab built in 1227 of dressed limestone, Great Mosque, Silvan

mihrab

Niche or marker used to indicate the direction of prayer usually in a mosque.

A mihrab is usually a niche set into the middle of the qibla wall of a building in order to indicate the direction of Mecca. The earliest mosques do not appear to have had mihrabs and instead the whole qibla wall was used to indicate the direction of Mecca. Sometimes a painted mark or a tree stump would be used to reinforce the direction. In the cave beneath the rock in the Dome of the Rock there is a marble plaque with a blind niche carved into it which, if contemporary with the rest of the structure, may be dated to 692 making it the oldest surviving mihrab. The first concave mihrab appears to have been inserted into the Prophet's Mosque at Medina during some restorations carried out by the Umayyad caliph al-Walid I in 706. Excavations at Wasit in Iraq have confirmed this date for the introduction of the first concave mihrab where there are two superimposed mosques; the lower one datable to the seventh century has no mihrab whilst the upper mosque has a concave mihrab.

Mihrab of mausoleum of Iltumish, Delhi

Mihrab, Kilwa-Kivinje, Tanzania

In addition to its function as a directional indicator it is thought that the first mihrab niches had a ceremonial or ritual function associated with symbols of royalty. Certainly the mihrab became a focus for architectural decoration and was often embellished with the latest artistic techniques (e.g. stucco, polychrome glazed tiles, carved woodwork, glass mosaic, marble inlay). The designs were usually epigraphic and often geometric or vegetal, but never with any suggestion of figurative imagery. The area in front of the mihrab was also emphasized, either by a maqsura immediately in front of the mihrab or a raised aisle leading from the courtyard to the niche. In later mosques, especially in Bengal, multiple mihrabs are set into the qibla wall, thus diffusing any hierarchy of sanctity.

There is also an early association of mihrab and minbar, with the minbar placed next to the mihrab possibly to lend spiritual authority to the sermon. In some areas such as East Africa the mihrab is linked to a recessed minbar niche so that the imam climbs the minbar by entering a door in the side of the mihrab. This arrangement, however, is extremely unusual as the mihrab should be kept free of any mystical connotations.

mimar

Islamic term for architect.

minaret

Tower-like structure usually associated with mosques or other religious buildings.

Although the mosques of Damascus, Fustat and Medina had towers during the Umayyad period it is now generally agreed that the minaret was introduced during the Abbasid period (i.e. after 750 CE). Six mosques dated to the early ninth century all have a single tower or minaret attached to the wall opposite the mihrab. The purpose of the minaret in these mosques was to demonstrate the power of Abbasid religious authority. Those opposed to Abbasid power would not adopt this symbol of conformity, thus Fatimid mosques did not have towers. Although later minarets appear to have become synonymous with Islamic architecture they have never been entirely universal. In parts of Iran, East Africa, Arabia and much of the Far East many mosques were built without them. In such places the call to prayer is either made from the courtyard of the mosque or from the roof.

The form of minarets differs throughout the Islamic world. A brief summary of the form in each area is required.

Egypt

In post-Fatimid Egypt minarets developed into a complex and distinctive form. Each tower is composed of three distinct zones: a square section at the bottom, an octagonal middle section and a dome on the top. The zone of transition between each section is covered with a band of muqarnas decoration. In earlier structures the square shaft was tall and the dome was ornate, later the central octagonal section became longer whilst the square shaft was reduced to a square socle at the base. During the fourteenth century the dome at the top was modified into the form of a stone bulb.

Another feature of the post-Fatimid period (after the twelfth century CE) is the increase in the number of buildings which had minarets. Whereas under the Abbasids minarets had been restricted to congregational mosques, during the Mamluk period all kinds of buildings could have minarets including smaller mosques, tombs, khanqas and madrassas.

Syria

The traditional Syrian minaret consists of a square plan tower built of stone. The form is thought to derive from the traditional Syrian church tower of the Byzantine period. The tower standing opposite the mihrab in the Great Mosque of Damascus is the oldest minaret in Syria, dating from the early ninth century, although the upper part may have been rebuilt several times. Another early Syrian minaret is that of the Great Mosque at Harran (now in modern Turkey) built sometime between the eighth and eleventh centuries. It is built of large dressed ashlar blocks with a cyma reversa moulding at 16 m above ground level. Generally during the Ottoman period the square tower was abandoned in favour of the octagonal or cylindrical minaret.

North Africa and Spain

North Africa and Spain share the square tower form with Syria and are thought to derive from the same source – Syrian church towers. In time this design was adapted by Christians in Spain for use as church bell towers.

The earliest minaret in North Africa is that of the Great Mosque of Qayrawan built in 836. This massive tower with battered walls is over 31 m high with a square base 10.6 m per side. The lower 4 m are built of large re-used stone blocks whilst the upper sections are built of smaller long slabs which resemble baked bricks. The smaller minaret at Sfax also dated to the ninth century was probably modelled on that at Qayrawan.

Several early minarets survive in Spain including that belonging to the congregational mosque in Seville and that of the mosque at Medina al-Zahra. However, the most impressive early minaret is that of Abd al-Rahman of Córdoba completed in 968 and now encased within the church tower. The minaret is 8.5 m square at the base, 47 m high and contains two independent staircases. Related minarets are those of the Qarawiyyin Mosque in Fez (built 955) and the mosque of the Andalusians at Fez (built 956) although both are smaller than that at Córdoba.

The Almoravids and early Almohads followed Fatimid precedent in not building minarets. The earliest Almohad tower is at the mosque of Timnal which is unusual both for its positioning (behind the mihrab) and its relatively short height of 15 m. It appears that the architect sought to make it appear tall from outside without it being visible from the courtyard of the mosque. However, later Almohad minarets were tall, impressive structures such as that of the Kutubiyya Mosque which is 67 m tall and 12.5 m per side at the base. The exterior is decorated with panels of decorative motifs around paired sets of windows. The top is decorated with with serrated crenellations, a band of polychrome tilework and three gilded copper balls.

In the same tradition are the minarets of the

Great Mosque of Seville (built 1184), the unfinished minaret of the mosque of Hassan at Rabat and the minaret of the Qasaba Mosque in Marrakesh.

Iran

The oldest known minaret in Iran is that of the congregational mosque at Siraf dated to the ninth century. It is known that many minarets were built during the tenth century although the only the survivors are the minarets at Fahraj and Nayin. The minaret at Fahraj has a tapering cylindrical form and a projecting balcony. The minaret attached to the Friday mosque at Nayin consists of a tall tapering brick shaft, the lower part of which is octagonal in plan whilst the upper part is cylindrical. The shaft is decorated with a simple chevron pattern using diagonally laid bricks. A similarly ancient miharet is attached to the Tarik-Khana in Damghan built in 1026. Like the minaret at Nayin it is decorated with bricks bonded in different ways, although here the decoration is more complex containing seven bands of diamond patterns.

The cylindrical minaret form, which was developed in Iran, spread over a huge area with the Seljuk conquests of Syria, Anatolia, Iraq, Afghanistan and India. Some of the structures were severe plain brick shafts whilst others were highly decorated with complex brick patterns. A variation of the standard from was the introduction of various forms of cylindrical fluting. The Jar Kurgan minaret has semi-circular fluting whilst the minaret of Ghazna attributed to Masud II has angular flutes. Minarets of this type may be interpreted as victory towers rather than as religious towers in the strict sense. Probably the most surprising example of this type of tower is the Jam minaret. This 60 m high tower stands in a secluded valley in Afghanistan and is decorated with monumental calligraphy celebrating the victory of the Ghurid sultan. It is significant that the Qutb Minar in Delhi was built by a Turkish general who served in the army of the Ghurid sultan who built the Jam minaret.

Iraq

Probably the earliest standing minaret in Iraq is the manar al-Mujida located in the desert northwest of Kufa. This has a cylindrical shaft 7 m high on a square base with a spiral staircase inside. The structure is not associated with any mosque but is dated to the Umayyad period (before 750 CE) on the basis of its plain brick decoration and association with nearby structures.

The most famous minarets in Iraq are the giant spiral minarets of Samarra both of which are dated to the ninth century. The larger of these, known as the Malwiyya, stands away from the rear of the Great Mosque at Samarra. The other minaret stands in the same position near the Abu Dulaf Mosque. Although it is generally believed that the form of these minarets is derived from the ziggurat (e.g. Khorsabad) their relationship to the topography of Samarra is often not considered. As the Great Mosque at Samarra was the largest mosque in the world it would have needed a correspondingly tall minaret. To have built a cylindrical minaret 50 m high would have been both impractical and visually unimpressive within the vast horizontal spaces of Samarra. However, a giant spiral minaret contains enough mass in relation to its height to make a significant visual impact.

The spiral minarets of Samarra were never copied, except in the mosque of Ibn Tulun in Egypt which copies many other features from Samarra. In the Ibn Tulun minaret the top part has a small spiral ramp reminiscent of the minarets of Samarra.

Later minarets in Iraq are versions of Iranian Seljuk minarets although Iraq seems to have developed its own local schools. Thus, the minaret of the Friday mosque in Mosul (known locally as al-Hadba) is decorated with complex geometric patterns and seems to be related to other minarets in the vicinity such as Mardin, Sinjar and Irbil.

India

Minarets were never universally adopted in India and where they were built they were not necessarily used for the call to prayer.

The most famous minaret in India is the Qutb Minar attached to the Kuwwat al-Islam Mosque in Delhi which was begun in 1189. This tower has four storeys marked by balconies supported on bands of muqarnas corbels. The upper storey was rebuilt in 1368. An interesting feature is the alternation of circular and angular flutes which relates it to similar minarets of Jam and Ghazna in Afghanistan.

With the exception of Gujarat and Burhanpur in

Khandesh functional minarets attached to mosques did not become popular until the Mughal period. In Gujarat and Burhanpur minarets were always built in pairs flanking the central iwan as in Iran. These minarets were cylindrical constructions with internal staircases with intermediate balconies leading to conical roofs. Elsewhere before the Mughal period solid tower-like buttresses were attached to the corners of mosques.

The first minarets of the Mughal period are the four seventeenth-century towers flanking Akbar's tomb at Sikandara. These are tapering white marble constructions with two intermediate balconies and an open canopy on top. The lower stages of these towers are fluted. Later Mughal minarets copied this form with some variation in the decoration of the shaft.

Ottoman Minarets

The earliest minarets in Anatolia were built by the Seljuks. Often these were pairs of towers with a stone base and a brick shaft. Some mosques however were built with single minarets such as the Alaeddin Mosque at Konya.

The combination of tall pointed minarets and large lead covered domes gives Ottoman architecture its distinctive form. In most mosques in the Ottoman Empire this was achieved with a single minaret attached to the corner of a mosque. However, in the major cities of the empire mosques were built with two, four or even six minarets. At some point it seems to have been established that only a reigning sultan could erect more than one minaret per mosque. A characteristic feature of these minarets is the use of multiple balconies which was first developed in the Uç Şerefeli Mosque in Edirne which was built in 1447.

Arabia

Outside Mecca and Medina minarets were fairly rare before the nineteenth century. The few minarets that do survive are either square or circular in plan often with a slightly tapering profile. In southern Yemen the larger mosques occasionally have large minarets to distinguish them from the tall tower houses. In northern Yemen minarets are rare outside the capital San'a. The minarets of San'a are similar to those of medieval Cairo although the external decoration is characteristically Yemeni.

East Africa

With the exception of the thirteenth-century mosque of Fakhr al-Din in Mogadishu (Somalia) minarets dating from before the nineteenth century are rare. Nineteenth-century minarets include those of Mombasa and the Shella minaret on Lamu island.

One of the most curious structures in the area is the Mbraaki pillar dated to circa 1700. This 14 m-high structure has no means of access to the interior although it is believed to be hollow. At the foot of the minaret a mosque was excavated which is believed to be of the same period making this the oldest minaret in Kenya.

West Africa

The earliest minarets are those of the ninth- to thirteenth-century settlements at Koumbi Saleh and Tegadoust. Excavated remains indicate that these had large square minarets. During the thirteenth and fourteenth centuries the characteristic West African minaret developed. These minarets have a massive square structure with tapering sides and projecting wooden beams (torons). One of the most famous minarets is that of the Kano Great Mosque (destroyed 1937) which was over 20 m high on a square base with battered sides. The Fulani reformers of the nineteenth century objected to the use of minarets and replaced many of them with staircase minarets.

Far East

Minarets are not a traditional feature of Far Eastern Islamic architecture and have only recently been introduced on a large scale. In western China minarets usually take the form of squat pagoda-like structures, with a few exceptions such as the minaret of the Huaisheng Mosque in Guangzhou which is a tall tapering cylinder 20 m high.

See also: East Africa, Cairo, India, Iran, Iraq, Mosque, Syria, West Africa.

Further reading:

D. Berens-Abouseif, *The Minarets of Cairo*, Cairo 1985.
J. Bloom, *Minaret: Symbol of Islam*, Oxford 1989.

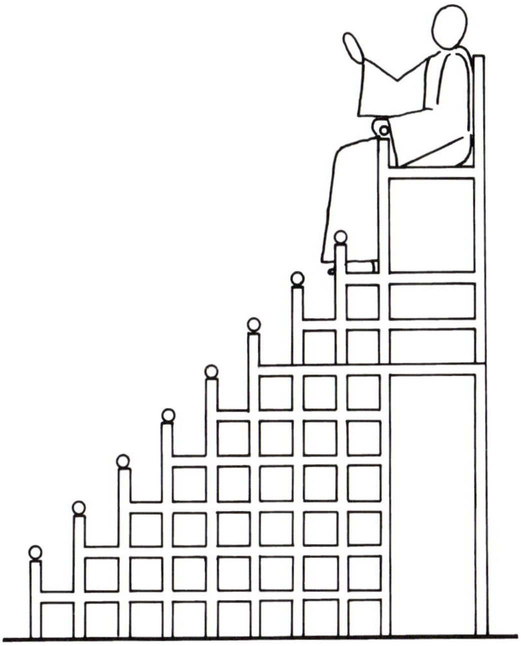

Umayyad minbar in the mosque of the Prophet, Medina (after Sauvaget)

K. A. C. Creswell, 'The evolution of the minaret with special reference to Egypt', *Burlington Magazine* 48, 1926: 134–40, 252–8, 290–8.
R. Hillenbrand, *Islamic Architecture: Form, Function and Meaning*, Edinburgh 1994.
B. O'Kane, 'Seljuk minarets: some new data', *Annales islamologiques* 20, 1994: 85–101.
G. F. Pijper, 'The Minaret in Java', *India Antiqua: A Volume of Essays Presented to Jean Phillipe Vogel*, Leiden 1947.

minbar

Type of pulpit usually found in mosques from which prayers, speeches and religious guidance are given. The minbar is situated to the right of the mihrab and consists of a raised platform reached by a set of steps, often there is a door at the entrance to the steps and a dome or canopy above the platform.

The minbar is one of the earliest architectural features to be identified with Islam. The earliest historical reference to a minbar states that in 629 the Prophet made a minbar from which he used to preach to the people. This minbar consisted of two steps and a seat (mak'ad) and resembled a throne. After the death of the Prophet the minbar was used by caliphs and governors as a symbol of authority. This continued under the last few years of Umayyad rule until in 750 CE the caliph Mu'Awiya ordered that all the mosques of Egypt be provided with minbars. This process was repeated in other Islamic lands so that by the beginning of the Abbasid period the minbar's function as a pulpit was universally established.

Most minbars are made of wood and are highly decorated whilst those made of stone or brick tend to be much simpler and often comprise a bare platform reached by three to five steps. The earliest extant wooden minbar is that in the Great Mosque in Qairawan which is said to have originated in Baghdad. It is a fairly simple design without a gate or canopy and consists of seventeen steps leading up to a platform. This minbar is made of plane tree and decorated with 200 carved panels and strips of unequal size. Although it has been restored several times most of the decoration seems to be Umayyad, consisting of diverse motifs held together within a rigid framework in a manner similar to that used at Mshatta.

In the Fatimid period minbars are built with a doorway at the entrance to the stairway and a domed canopy above the platform. The best example of this type is that in the Aqsa mosque in Jerusalem built for Nur al-Din in 1168. An example of this style in stone is the minbar in the mosque of Sultan Hasan (1356–63). Over the doorway to the minbar and also in the mihrab of this mosque muqarnas carving is used. Later on muqarnas remains an important decorative element in minbar design and is used particularly on minbar domes.

Most early minbars in Persia and Afghanistan were destroyed by the Mongol invasions; however, from the Timurid period we have several examples. One of the most impressive of these is that in the Djawahr Shah Agah in Meshed (constructed between 1436 and 1446). Structural elements in this minbar are subordinated to the covering of pentagonal and star-shaped panels with tendrils in relief, which has the overall effect of a woven carpet.

In Ottoman Turkey although most minbars were made of wood some of the most important were built of marble. Thus in the Selimiye Cami in Edirne there is a tall minbar of Marmara marble which is widely regarded as the finest in Turkey. The form of this minbar with its solid portal, its steep stairs and tall hood are all characteristic Ottoman features.

In India almost all minbars are built of stone and

are often elaborately carved. In Gujarat and Ahmadabad minbars are in the form of pavilions on four piers. In Hyderabad, to the south, the minbars are heavier and plainer, with no canopies or portals.

The Swahili mosques of the East African coast usually have simple stone mihrabs. At Sanje Ya Kate in southern Tanzania there is a sixteenth-century mosque with a unique minbar set into the wall. This is entered through an opening in the qibla wall from which the stairs lead to a niche next to the mihrab.

Mogadishu

Capital of Somalia located on the southern coast.

Mogadishu was established as a trading city sometime before the twelfth century although no early remains have yet been discovered. There are a number of historic mosques in the old quarter of the city which mostly date from the nineteenth century or later. The principal mosque of the town is the mosque of Fakhr al-Din dated to the thirteenth century. This is the most sophisticated example of mosque architecture in East Africa and demonstrates architectural planning. The mosque has a narrow courtyard which opens on to a portico of five bays, the central bay of which is covered with a fluted dome. Entry into the prayer hall is through doorways decorated with marble panels. The prayer hall is divided into nine bays covered with a panelled ceiling with a central dome. The mihrab is carved out of north Indian marble and carries a date of 1269. The mosque also has a minaret which is the earliest occurrence of this feature in East Africa (minarets only become widespread from the nineteenth century).

See also: East Africa, Somalia

Monastir

Important medieval city on the east coast of Tunisia.

At present Monastir is on the coast, but in early Islamic times it was probably a peninsula or island. Monastir was one of the coastal cities developed by the Aghlabids during the ninth century. The city contains the remains of three ribats or fortified monasteries the earliest of which is the great ribat of Harthma ibn A'iyan founded in 796. The Great Mosque of the city was built in the ninth century although most of the structure dates to the tenth century or later.

See also: Aghlabids, Tunisia

Morocco (Arabic: Maghrib)

Country at the north-west corner of Africa with an Atlantic and Mediterranean coast.

The country may be divided into three main regions, the coastal plains, the Atlas mountains and the Sahara desert. The majority of the population lives on the plains with a smaller, more rural population in the mountains. The Sahara is sparsely inhabited.

Traditionally Islam first reached Morocco during the conquest of the Arab general 'Uqba who reached the shores of the Atlantic in 684. However, it seems likely that the first real conquest, as opposed to a temporary raid, took place at the beginning of the eighth century under the general Musa ibn Nusayr. The predominantly Berber population was quickly converted to Islam and took part in the Muslim conquest of Spain. After the initial success of the Spanish conquest the Berbers were disappointed with their share of the land allocations, in addition many were affected by the doctrines of Kharijism which represented a deviation from orthodox Islam. By 740 the situation had become critical and there was a rebellion against the Umayyads. A Syrian army sent to restore order was defeated in 742 leaving Morocco independent of central control. For the next forty years there was a period of anarchy with several Berber groups vying for power. In 788 the Idrissids emerged as the victors and were able to establish an independent monarchy which lasted until the end of the tenth century when it became a victim of Fatimid and Umayyad (Spanish) rivalry. During the eleventh century the country was taken over by the Almoravids who ruled an empire which included southern Spain and much of north-west Africa. In the mid-twelfth century the Almoravids were displaced by the Almohads who conquered a vast territory from the southern Sahara to central Spain. The Almohad Empire collapsed in the mid-thirteenth century to be replaced by the Marinids who ruled an area roughly equivalent to modern Morocco although there were constant attempts to expand eastward. Local unrest and increasing European interest in Morocco led to the collapse of the Marinids in the fifteenth century. A period of anarchy was followed by a reaction against Christian occupation of the coast which was embod-

Dome of Baru Din, Great Mosque, Marakesh, Morocco

ied in the Sa'dian dynasty. The Sa'dians who claimed descent from the Idrisids lasted until the mid-seventeenth century when they were defeated by the 'Alawids. The 'Alawids also had a semi-religious basis claiming their descent from 'Ali, members of this dynasty still rule the country.

A large variety of materials are used in historic and traditional Moroccan architecture. This partly reflects the variety of the natural landscape which includes extremely high mountains, fertile plains and arid desert. Another important factor is the influence of Spanish architecture which was reinforced by the Christian reconquest which drove Muslims southwards into Morocco. The coastal cities of the north inherited the Byzantine system of construction in stone and baked brick. In the Atlas mountains mud pisé and rubble stone construction were the predominant materials although these were often covered with plaster. Overlapping gutter-shaped tiles with a characteristic blue-green colour were used for the roofs of important buildings and may represent Spanish influence. Small monochrome tiles were used for floors, as dadoes for courtyards and sometimes as decoration for whole façades. Wood was relatively plentiful, cedar, cork and oak from the Atlas mountains was used for a variety of functions including roofing timber, supports for projecting windows, panelled ceilings and decorative mashrabiyya screens. The quality of wood carving is extremely high and resembles that of Muslim Spain. Stucco was extensively used for decorative features such as multifoil arches and decorative panels.

There are few examples of Moroccan Islamic architecture from before the eleventh century and those which do survive have been extensively altered. The most important city for the early period is Fez which was established as a capital in 807 by Moulay Idris the Younger. Very little survives of the early city although it is known that it had an advanced water system which supplied water for domestic use. Architecturally the most significant buildings in the town are the Qarawiyyin and the Andalusian mosques which were both built in the ninth century. The form of these mosques with aisles running parallel to the qibla wall cut by an axial aisle is a Syrian–Umayyad plan. Later mosques in Morocco follow the more usual North African practice of aisles perpendicular to the qibla. No mosques of the Almoravid period have survived with the exception of the Great Mosque of Taza which was considerably remodelled in later periods.

Remains of the Almohad period are more plentiful and include the Kutubiya and Kasba mosques in Marakesh, the Hassan Mosque in Rabat and the Great Mosque of Timnal. The earliest of these is the mosque of Timnal which is built out of mud pisé and baked brick. The prayer hall has nine aisles perpendicular to the qibla wall and one aisle parallel to the qibla wall, an arrangement which was to become standard. The unusual feature of the building is the incorporation of the mihrab into the base of the minaret. This arrangement was not used in subsequent mosques although huge decorative minarets became one of the characteristic features of Almohad architecture. The most impressive example is the unfinished mosque of Hassan in Rabat begun in 1196. This vast mosque measures 140 by 185 m and includes three rectangular courtyards. The minaret, at the north end of the building (opposite the mihrab), has a massive square base measuring 16 m per side containing a ramp which rises around a square core. Although the tower is only 44 m high its is known that its projected

Khirbet al-Mafjar, mosaic in diwan

the Great Mosque of Al-Mansura in Tlemcen (Algeria), within Morocco their chief concern was the building of madrassas in which they excelled. Fez in particular contains a large number of Marinid madrassas the most famous of which are the 'Attarin, the Sahrij and the Bu 'Inaniya. The standard plan comprises rooms arranged around a rectangular courtyard with a central pool and decorated with tile mosaic and stucco work. The main focus of each madrassa is the prayer room which opens on to one of the shorter sides of the courtyard.

Another development of the Marinid period is the funerary complex which sees its first expression in the necropolis of Challa near Rabat built in the

Khirbet al-Mafjar, mosaic in diwan (detail)

height would have been approximately 70 m. The exterior of the tower is decorated with a variety of blind niches with cusped arches and a network of lozenges.

Although the Marinids were responsible for

fourteenth century. The complex is a large garden enclosed by a high wall fortified with buttress towers and an Almohad-style gateway. Within the complex there are tombs set within extensive areas of vegetation. There are two funerary mosques within the complex both with square decorated minarets in the Almohad style. In the sixteenth and seventeenth centuries the Sa'adians built a similar type of complex but on a grander scale with decoration of unparalleled ornateness. A different type of funerary–memorial complex is represented by the city of Moulay Idriss built by the Sa'adian ruler Moulay Ismail in the seventeenth century. Here the tomb of Idris I forms the centre of a sacred city which is restricted to Muslims.

The domestic architecture of Morocco represents a wide variety of architectural forms from semi-permanent camps to the luxurious courtyard villas of Fez, Rabat, Marakesh and Meknes. The simplest form of dwelling is the thatched hut or gourbi which may either be rectangular with a pitched roof or circular in plan with a conical roof. In the Atlas mountains there are villages of semi-permanent huts built around a central keep, or kasba. Sometimes these are purely for storage (tiremt) and have no accommodation although there is usually a guard's house. Some of the more developed villages formed walled enclosures with the keep functioning as a residence for the ruling family. City houses were enclosed courtyard structures with little external decoration. Inside the wealthier houses contain some of the most eloquent examples of Islamic decoration and recall the splendour of Muslim Spain.

See also: Almohads, Fez, Marakesh, Meknes, Rabat

Further reading:

R. Landau, *The Kasbas of Southern Morocco*, London 1969.

mosaics

Inlay of small tiles or stones used for decoration of walls or floors.

The use of mosaics in Islam is derived directly from Roman and Byzantine architecture where their most common function was to decorate churches and public buildings. It is known that many mosaics in the early Islamic period were carried out by Byzantine craftsmen and artists. Two main types of mosaic can be distinguished, those used for floors and those used for walls. Floor mosaics were made out of coloured fragments of stone or marble and were often arranged as patterns. Wall mosaics were often made out of specially manufactured tesserae of glass and were usually arranged as illustrative scenes.

Examples of floor mosaics have been found in excavations of the earliest Islamic structures in Syria and Palestine which were often converted Byzantine buildings. Floor mosaics usually lack any figural depictions of animals or humans and it is noticeable that many churches had the figural parts of the mosaics removed or scrambled during the Islamic period. Nevertheless, private palaces such as Qasr al-Hayr in Syria and Khirbet al-Mafjar had figural mosaics on the floor. It has been argued that figural representation on the floor was permitted as it was not in a respectful situation and could be walked over. The most famous example is the apse of the audience hall at Khirbet al-Mafjar which has a depiction of a lion attacking a deer in front of a tree.

Wall mosaics are more elaborate than those on the floor and are often gilded with gold leaf. The oldest example of wall mosaics in Islamic architecture is the decoration of the Dome of the Rock in Jerusalem, dated by an inscription to 691 CE. The motifs used include both Sassanian (winged crowns) and Byzantine (jewelled vases) themes held together within an arabesque foliage. Other early Islamic wall mosaics are those of the Great Mosque in Damascus which depict houses and gardens next to a river but significantly no people or animals. Although mosaic was primarily a technique employed in the Mediterranean area it was occasionally used further east in Iraq and Iran. Some of the best examples have been found at the palace of al-Quwair in Samarra. Generally mosaics declined in importance after the tenth century, although in Egypt glass mosaics were used for the decoration of mihrabs as late as the thirteenth century (see for example the mausoleum of Shajar-at al Durr in Cairo). From the eleventh century onwards mosaics were replaced by glazed tilework in most parts of the Islamic world.

See also: pietra dura, tilework, Umayyads

mosque

Building used for Muslim prayer, the principal unit of Islamic architecture.

The first mosque was the house of the Prophet Muhammad in Medina. This was a simple rectangular (53 by 56 m) enclosure containing rooms for the Prophet and his wives and a shaded area on the south side of the courtyard which could be used for prayer in the direction of Mecca. This building became the model for subsequent mosques which had the same basic courtyard layout with a prayer area against the qibla wall. An early development of this basic plan was the provision of shade on the other three sides of the courtyard, forming a basic plan which has become known as the Arab-plan mosque. The roofs of the prayer area (sanctuary or musalla) were supported by columns which were either made of wood (palm trunks in the Medina Mosque) or later on of re-used columns. From the ninth century onwards columns began to replace piers as the main form of roof support and domes were introduced as a roofing method.

Several features which were later to become standard features of mosques were introduced at an early stage. The first of these is the minbar, or pulpit, which was used by Muhammad to give sermons. A later introduction was the mihrab or prayer niche which was first introduced by the Umayyad caliph al-Walid in the eighth century. Other features include the ablutions facilities and a central pool or fountain and the minaret which

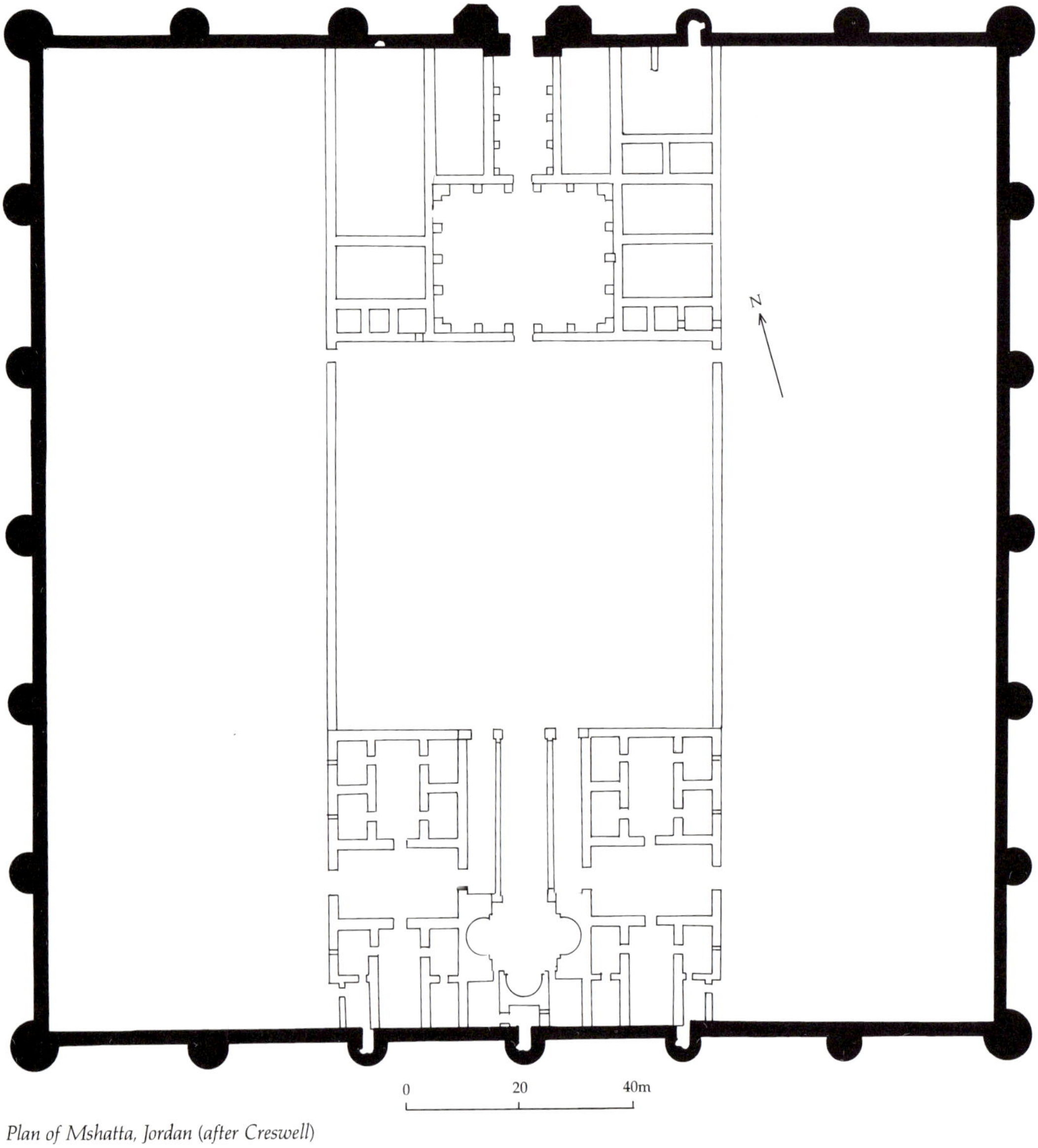

Plan of Mshatta, Jordan (after Creswell)

seems to make its first appearance in the Abbasid period. Also during this formative period the maqsura was introduced which was designed to provide privacy and protection to the ruler and also possibly to give him added mystery. This sense of mystery may have been reinforced by the placing of the royal palace or Dar al-Imara at the back of the mosque behind the qibla wall often with a connecting door.

The details of mosques in different areas of the Islamic world were dictated by local building traditions and materials, although the basic form remained the same until the eleventh century when the Seljuks introduced new architectural forms based specifically on the dome and the iwan. Although these had been known in Sassanian times and had been used in mosque architecture, they had not been used to alter the basic plan of the mosque. However, the Seljuks introduced the idea of four iwans set into the middle of each courtyard façade, as seen in the twelfth-century mosques of Isfahan, Zawara and Simnan. This arrangement became the standard form for the Iranian mosque and was later adopted for madrassas.

See also: Aqsa, Cairo, China, Damascus, East Africa, Fatimids, India, Indonesia, Iran, Iraq, Java, Malaysia, Mughals, nine-domed mosques, Ottomans, Spain, Turkey, West Africa

Mshatta

One of the most famous desert castles of the early Islamic period.

The palace of Mshatta is located on the border of the desert in Jordan (about 25 km south-west of Amman). It is generally dated to the late Umayyad period (the reign of Walid II) although an Abbasid date has also been suggested.

The palace consists of a large square enclosure with four semi-circular buttress towers. Outside the enclosure are the remains of a large bath house which has recently been excavated. The best-known feature of this palace is the southern façade which consists of a delicately carved stone frieze incorporating animal and plant motifs within a geometric scheme of twenty giant triangles (this façade is now in Berlin). Internally the building is divided into three longitudinal strips of equal size; only the central strip (running north–south) was developed, and contains within it the entrance, the central courtyard and the audience hall. The area immediately inside the entrance has only foundations to mark the positions of rooms which were arranged symmetrically on either side of a central axis. This consists of a narrow vaulted passageway leading to a small square courtyard, on one side of which is the small palace mosque. This courtyard opens on to a large central courtyard (including a rectangular pond) at the other side of which is the heart of the palace. This consists of three iwans, the central iwan leading to the throne room (audience hall) and the side iwans leading to housing units (buyut – pl. of bayt) either side of the audience hall. The audience hall consists of a triple-apsed room covered by a large brick dome.

The importance of the palace for architectural historians is that it combines western (Roman and Byzantine) elements with features derived from the art of the Sassanians. The decorative frieze at the front of the building is one of the best examples of this combination. The vine leaves and naturalistic depictions of animals resembles Byzantine art although the decoration also includes popular Sassanian motifs such as the senmurv, a dragon-like mythological beast, and griffin. The most significant eastern feature of the design is thought to be the way the geometric pattern of giant triangles dictates the nature and space of the more naturalistic ornament.

Other eastern features found at Mshatta include the use of brickwork for vaults and the layout of the palace which resembles that of early Islamic buildings in Iraq (cf. Abbasid palaces at Ukaidhir and Samarra). However, Byzantine elements are also present, most notably in the basilical arrangement of the approach to the triple-apsed room and in the motifs of the stonework.

Further reading:

K. A. C. Creswell, E. M. A. Vol 1 Part 2, 578–622

O. Grabar, 'The date and meaning of Mshatta', *Dumbarton Oaks Papers*, 41: 243–8, 1987.

R. Hillenbrand, 'Islamic art at the crossroads; East versus West at Mshatta', in *Essays in Honour of Katharina Otto-Dorn*, Malibu 1981, 63–86.

mud brick

Traditional building material in much of the Middle East, India and North Africa. It is likely that in the past the majority of buildings in an Islamic city were made of this material. Mud brick has only recently been superseded by concrete as a cheap and versatile building material and is still used in many areas.

The traditional form of a mud brick is a large flat square slab produced by filling a wooden mould with mud or clay of the preferred type. In some areas the shape of the bricks is varied; thus in Djenné, West Africa, conical bricks were used until quite recently. Often some additional material (temper) such as straw is added to the brick to give it increased strength. The brick is then left to bake in the sun for several days until it is very hard and can be used for building. The bricks are laid in the normal manner, with layers of mud mortar used to bind the bricks together. When a mud-brick wall is completed it is usually coated with a layer of water-resistant mud plaster. In order to avoid the problems of water erosion mud-brick buildings are often built on stone footings or have overhanging roofs with water run-off directed into special channels. Mud brick also requires a certain amount of maintenance usually in the form of annual replastering.

Mud brick has several advantages over more modern materials: it has better thermal insulation (warmer in winter and cooler in summer), it is cheaper, it can be produced locally and it is environmentally less harmful. Recently there have been attempts to revive the use of mud brick through special projects such as those instigated by Hassan Fathy in Egypt.

See also: Djenné; Fathy, Hassan

Mughals

The Mughals were an Indian Islamic dynasty which ruled most of northern India (including the area of present-day Pakistan) from the beginning of the sixteenth to the mid-eighteenth century. As patrons of architecture the Mughals commissioned some of the finest buildings known to the world including the Red Fort at Delhi and the Taj Mahal.

History

The earliest Muslim presence in India dates from 712 with the Arab conquest of Sind which was a part of the original eastward expansion of Islam. However, it was not until the eleventh century that Muslim warriors first penetrated to the Indian heartland under the leadership of Mahmud of Ghazni. For the next 150 years the Punjab and Lahore were part of the Ghaznavid Empire although the Rajput princes of Rajasthan prevented further penetration into the subcontinent. In 1192 an Afghan sultan, Mahmud of Ghur, defeated an alliance of Rajput princes and captured Delhi, one of their principal cities. Although Mahmud soon left India he made his Mamluk (slave) general Qutb al-Din Aibak governor of Delhi. For the next 300 years this part of India was ruled by various competing Islamic dynasties including the Timurids.

The first Mughal ruler was Babur who traced his descent on his mother's side from Chengiz Khan and on his father's side from Timur (Tamuralne). Babur was a Central Asian prince who ruled the area of Fargahna but had some claim to Samarkand which he repeatedly tried to capture. In addition to his dream of taking Samarkand Babur also believed he had some claim to the Delhi sultanate through his Timurid ancestors. At the battle of Paniput in 1526 Babur defeated Ibrahim Lodi, the Muslim sultan of Delhi, with a small force which had, however, the additional advantage of artillery and gunpowder. A year later this victory was consolidated by Babur's defeat of the combined forces of the Rajput princes at Khanuna. Three years later, in 1530, Babur died at Agra leaving the sultanate to his son Humayun. Despite the enormous advantages bequeathed by his father Humayun did not have his father's ruthlessness and in 1540 lost the throne to the Bengali ruler Sher Khan. For the next fifteen years Delhi was ruled by Sher Khan and after his death by his son Islam Sher Sur. Humayun had lost the throne mostly through the treachery of his brothers and it was only after he had defeated them by recapturing Kabul and Kandahar in 1545 that he was in a position to retake Delhi which he did in 1555 defeating Sher Sur. Unfortunately Humayun was only able to enjoy his position for a year as he died in 1556 falling down a stairway in his library in Delhi.

Humayun left the empire to his 13-year-old son Akbar and his Turcoman guardian Bairam Khan. For the next four years the prince and his guardian had to fight off rival claims to the throne whilst securing the boundaries of the kingdom. Akbar's first concern on assuming full power was the pacification of the Rajput princes who constantly threatened the Delhi sultanate. In 1562 Akbar married the daughter of the Raja of Amber (the nearest Rajput state to Delhi later known as Jaipur) who became the mother of the Sultan's heir Jahangir. This was the beginning of a policy that he continued with other Rajput princes so that by the end of his reign all were under his overlordship although with varying degrees of independence. In addition to marital alliances and diplomacy Akbar also gained territory by force conquering Gujarat in 1573, Bengal in 1576, Kashmir in the 1586, Sind and Baluchistan between 1591 and 1595. The southern part of India was added in the latter part of his reign and included Berar and part of Ahmadnagar.

Akbar's territorial victories were consolidated by an efficient system of government with a paid non-hereditary civil service. In addition Akbar abolished the 'jizya', poll tax payable by Hindus and other non-Muslims, in order to integrate and unify the differing peoples of his expanding empire in the same way that the Rajput dominions had been incorporated. Religious toleration became a central principle of Akbar's government to the extent that in 1570 he convened a conference between the different religions at his newly established city of Fatehpur Sikri. The conference included scholars from Hindu and Muslim sects as well as Jains, Zoroastrians and Catholic Jesuits from Goa. The result was a new religion conceived by Akbar himself and known as Din Ilahi (Divine Faith) which drew elements from all the sects. Although the religion was not successful it shows Akbar's concern to create an empire free from religious divisions. Akbar died in 1605 leaving the empire to his son Jahangir who had recently been in open revolt of his father. On his accession to the throne Jahangir left his son Shah Jahan in charge of the military campaigns, a pattern which was later repeated when as emperor Shah Jahan delegated control of the south to his son Aurangzeb. Both Jahangir and later Shah Jahan continued the policies of Akbar so that the empire remained relatively stable despite more or less constant warfare in the south of the country. Shah Jahan failed in his attempt to create a united Sunni state incorporating India with Central Asia, but managed to keep the empire more or less intact for his son Aurangzeb.

The last of the great Mughals, Aurangzeb, departed from the pattern of government set by Akbar and precipitated the decline of the empire. Aurangzeb devoted a great deal of energy and manpower to continuing the conquest of the south of India at the expense of all other policies. The empire reached its greatest extent during this period and included the whole subcontinent with the exception of the southern tip. However, this brought increased problems of communication and military control which the empire was not able to manage. These problems were exacerbated by Aurangzeb's fanatical Muslim zeal which meant that he reversed the policy of religious tolerance exercised by his great-grandfather by introducing the poll tax (jizya) for non-Muslims. Similarly he encouraged the destruction of Hindu temples and other religious shrines and his southern conquests became one of the greatest iconoclastic excursions in India's history. Although Aurangzeb may have been a pious Muslim, this policy was not successful in an empire which depended on the co-operation and toleration of different ethnic and religious groups. Perhaps the best example of Aurangzeb's policy was the Great Mosque built to tower over the Hindu holy city of Banares.

With Aurangzeb's death at the age of 90 in 1707 the empire passed to his son Bahadur Shah who only lived another five years. During the next half-century the rapidly disintegrating empire was ruled by eight sultans. The weakness of the empire was shown in 1739 when Delhi was sacked by the Persian emperor Nadir Shah who carried off the peacock throne along with countless other treasures. The latter part of the century witnessed the conflict between a variety of forces including the Mughals, the Hindu Marathas and the British East India Company. In 1803 the East India company occupied Delhi and Agra thus ending Mughal power in India. For the next half-century the powerless Mughals were retained by the British as 'Kings of Delhi'. Finally in 1857 the last Mughal Bahadur Shah II was stripped of even this title and was removed from Delhi for his part in the sepoy mutiny.

Architecture

Mughal architecture was derived from three main sources: native Indian Islamic, Persian Central Asian and local Hindu architecture. It is difficult to determine the extent to which any feature or building type used by the Mughals derives from any of these particular sources, partly because earlier Indian Islamic architecture contains both Hindu and Islamic elements. What is clear, however, is that Mughal architecture does incorporate many elements from local Hindu architecture, in particular the art of the Rajput palaces. Distinctive Hindu features incorporated into Mughal architecture include trabeate stone construction, richly ornamented carved piers and columns, and shallow arches made out of corbels rather than voussoirs. In addition there are particular constructions usually associated with Hindu buildings, including chatris, chajjas and jarokhas, which became characteristic of Mughal architecture. A chatri is a domed kiosk resting on pillars which in Hindu architecture is used as a cenotaph but in Islamic architecture is placed as decoration on top of mosques, palaces and tombs. A chatri is a sloping stone overhang at roof level, used to deflect rain water away from the walls of a building and usually supported on heavy carved corbels. A jarokha is a projecting balcony supported on corbels with a hood resting on columns. Whilst all of these features may be paralleled elsewhere in Islam, the particular form which they assume in Mughal architecture shows a clear derivation from local Hindu architecture. In addition to Hindu features there are some elements derived from the pre-existing Islamic architecture of India. The best example is the curved do-chala roof derived from Bengali huts which was first used in this stone form in the sultanate architecture of Bengal. Another Indo-Islamic feature is the cusped arch which can be found in the pre-Mughal architecture of Delhi and Gujarat.

Obvious Persian influences in Mughal architecture are the extensive use of tilework, the iwan as a central feature in mosques, the use of domes, the charbagh, or garden, divided into four and the four-centrepoint arch. The form of buildings and some of the decorative motifs also suggests obvious Persian influence.

The materials used for Mughal architecture varies widely depending on the region and the type of construction. As with most other areas, many of the original buildings have not survived because they were made of less permanent materials such as wood, as well as having been subject to deliberate destruction as a result of wars or rebuilding. However, the material which stands out as characteristic of Mughal architecture is the use of a hard, deep-red sandstone. This material is very strong under compression and so can be used for trabeate construction where roofs are made of flat stone slabs supported on stone columns. When domes were built these were sometimes constructed in the Persian tradition using squinches or pendentives, but more commonly they rested on horizontal flat beams laid over the corners of the structure. Despite its strength and hardness the Indian masons trained in the Hindu tradition of building ornate temples were able to carve this sandstone with intricate details as seen in the columns of the Jami Masjid in Delhi. White marble is the other type of stone often associated with Mughal architecture. It is first used in conjunction with red sandstone as a stone cladding for the front of monumental buildings such as the tomb of Humayun in Delhi where it is used as an inlay and outline for the red sandstone ground. Later, during the reign of Shah Jahan in the seventeenth century, white marble facing was used to cover entire buildings, the best-known example of which is the Taj Mahal. In addition to the fine-cut stone masonry used for façades coursed rubble stone construction was used for the majority of walls. Baked brick was also used for some elements of the construction like domes and arches although this was usually covered with plaster or facing stones.

Decoration of buildings was carried out using a variety of techniques including ceramic tilework, carved and inlaid stonework, pietra dura inlay with coloured and semi-precious stones. Tilework was applied to the exterior of buildings in the Persian manner using Chinese, Persian and Indian tiles. Two main types of tile were used – cuerda sec using coloured glazes, and tile mosaic which used cut pieces of monochrome tiles to produce a pattern. Mughal architecture excels in the quality of its carved stonework, from shallow relief depictions of flowers to intricate pierced-marble screens known as jalis. It has previously been thought that the pietra dura work in Mughal architecture was an Italian introduction because Shah Jahan used some Italian examples of the technique in his palace in Delhi, however this technique had an independent development in India which is obvious when the Italian panels are compared with Indian examples. The main types of building designed for the sultans included palaces and forts, mosques, tombs and gardens. The range of buildings indicates the image the emperors wished to project of themselves as all-powerful rulers close to heaven. One of the most important types of building was the fortified palace as seen at Delhi, Agra, Ajmer,

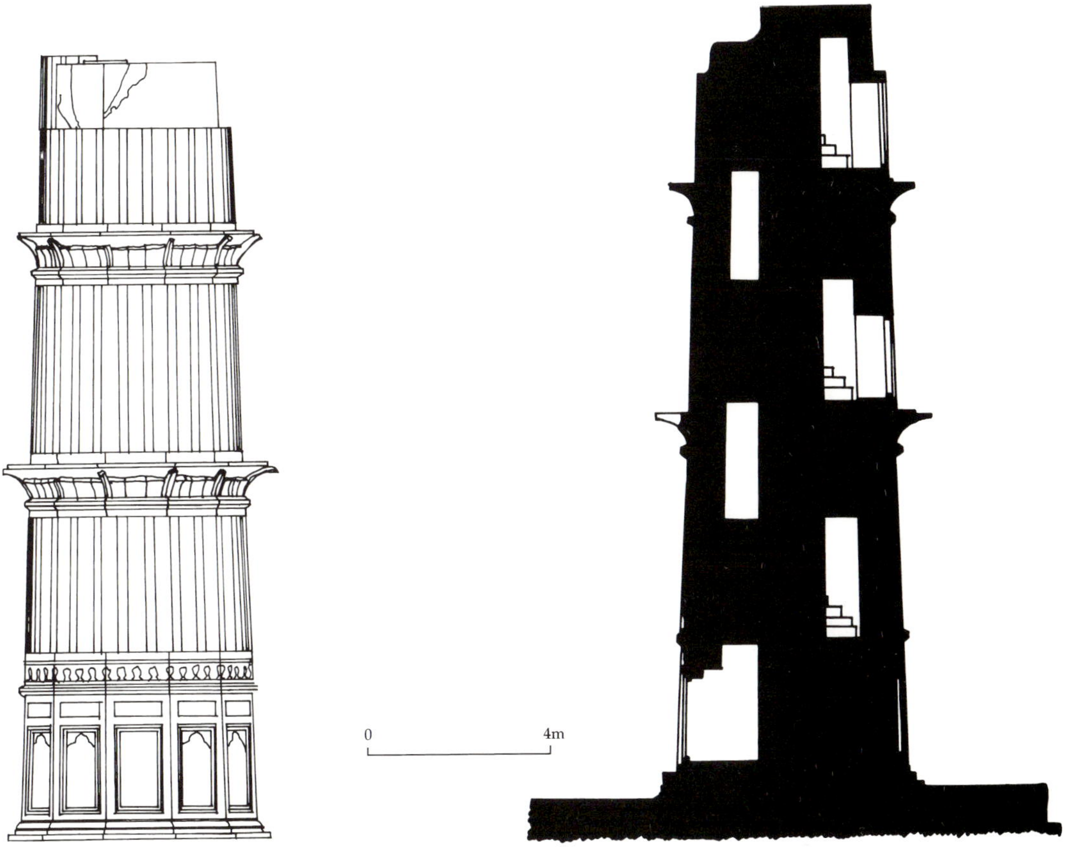

Elevation *Section*

Elevation and section of Hashtsal Minar (1634), India (after Koch)

Fatehpur Sikri and Lahore. Although differing substantially in details the palaces share a common overall design where severe external walls conceal a series of courtyards, pavilions and gardens which convey an impression of paradise on earth. The standard plan was of a monumental outer gate which leads inside to another gate known as the 'Hathai Pol' where visitors dismount from elephants. From here there was access to the Diwan-i Amm or public audience hall behind which were the private areas of the palace. The private areas of the palace were usually raised up above the rest of the complex for increased privacy and to catch any breezes in the summer heat. This part of the palace usually included a private audience hall, a bath house, several courtyards with pavilions based around pools and a separate area for the women, known as the zenana. On one side of this private area was a tower projecting from the outer walls known as the Mussaman Burj (octagonal tower) from which the emperor appeared once a day to show that he was still alive.

Babur, the first Mughal emperor, only reigned for four years, during which time he was too busy securing his empire to spend time on major building projects like palaces and instead governed from tented encampments. The earliest Mughal palace is the Purana Qila in Delhi built by Humayun and continued by the Bengali usurpers Sher Sur and Islam Sur. The palace is surrounded by a huge wall 1.5 km long with three huge gateways. Each gateway consists of an arched opening flanked by two huge semi-circular bastion towers with battered walls, arrow slits and pointed crenellations. Little remains of the original structures inside the fort with the exception of the mosque and a domed octagonal pavilion known as the Sher Mandal so that it is not possible to tell much about the building's layout. The next imperial palace to be built was Akbar's fort at Agra where enough remains to show that it was the basic model for subsequent Mughal palaces. The palace is built next to the river Jumna and is surrounded by huge walls fortified with semi-circular towers. There are two gates, an outer gate with a drawbridge and complex bent entrance leading to an inner gate called the Hathai Pol where visitors were required to dismount from their elephants. Most of the buildings inside the complex belong to Akbar's successor Shah Jahan with the exception of the court known as the Jahangiri Mahal. This structure was built in the style of a Hindu Rajput palace with carved stone beams and giant corbels supporting chajjas. This tendency is carried further in Akbar's new city of Fatehpur Sikri founded in 1570 where the whole palace is overwhelmingly Hindu in its form with Islamic elements reduced to a minimum. Of the same period is the fort at Ajmer in Rajasthan, this is much smaller than the imperial palaces and consists of a rectangular courtyard enclosure measuring 85 by 75 m with four octagonal corner towers and a half-octagonal gateway. In the centre of the courtyard is a rectangular pavilion built of yellow stone and divided into nine chambers in the form of a Hindu mandala. Hindu elements were also predominant in Akbar's other palaces at Allahabad and Lahore although little of Akbar's original work survives at either of these palaces.

The palaces of Shah Jahan by contrast have a more familiar Islamic appearance as can be seen in his modifications to Akbar's fort at Agra where he added several new courtyards, the most famous of which is the Anguri Bagh (grape garden). This is a square garden divided into four sections with a central rectangular pool with lobed sides which provides water for the garden. The garden is surrounded by various pavilions the most prominent of which are the Khas Mahal (private audience hall) and the Sheesh Mahal (glass pavilion). Although these pavilions have many of the same Hindu features seen in Akbar's architecture (i.e domed chatris and chajjas) they are less prominent and tempered with more Islamic forms like lobed arches and the curved Bengali do-chala roofs. In addition the white marble facing of the buildings produces a new lighter appearance which is not found in the earlier buildings of Akbar or in Hindu architecture. The most lavishly decorated building of the palace is the Mussaman Burj which overlooks the river at the east side of the palace. The tower has an octagonal copper dome and inside is lined with carved marble dadoes, pietra dura inlay, pierced screens above the doorways and decorative rows of niches. From inside there is an uninterrupted view of the river and the Taj Mahal built by Shah Jahan for his wife Mumtaz Mahal.

In 1638 Shah Jahan chose the site of his new city at Delhi based around his palace which became known as the Red Fort. By 1648 the fort was completed at a cost of ten million rupees. The layout and design of the Red Fort bears a striking resemblance to the Agra Fort on which it was probably based. Like the Agra Fort, the Red Fort has rectangular open pavilions with cusped arches, white marble dadoes carved in relief and pietra dura work. However, the Red Fort has a more regular symmetrical design, reflecting the fact that it was planned and built mostly by one patron (with a few additions by Aurangzeb) unlike the Agra Fort which gradually developed under two emperors. The most magnificent of the rooms at the Red Fort is the Diwan-i Amm or public reception room where the enthroned emperor would receive audiences. This room was approached from the main gate via an arcaded passageway, a large courtyard, another gateway and an even larger courtyard so that visitors were suitably awed by the time they reached the emperor. The room consists of a hypostyle hall nine bays wide and three bays deep supported by twelve-sided columns spanned by cusped arches. The throne occupies a special position in the middle of the back wall and consists of a raised platform covered by a dome supported on columns. The area behind the throne is decorated by pietra dura panels imported from Italy. Within the palace is the Diwan-i Khass or private audience hall which is equally lavishly decorated and originally had a silver-clad ceiling inlaid with gold.

Unlike the palaces, the mosques of the Mughals were built to accommodate the public and were thus more restrained in their decoration although equally monumental. Delhi contains some of the earliest examples of Mughal mosques in India which clearly show their derivation from earlier Sultanate mosques. The Mahdi Masjid is one of the earliest examples of a Mughal mosque and its architecture resembles that of the Lodi sultanate which preceded the Mughals. The mosque is built like a small fort with corner turrets and a monumental gateway built in the style of Lodi tombs. The arrangement inside is unique and consists of a rectangular courtyard with two prayer halls at the qibla end either side of a central piece of blank wall. Nearby is the Jamali Kamali Masjid built between 1528 and 1536 which has a more distinctively Mughal appearance. The building is faced in red sandstone with white stone outlining the details to relieve the intensity of the red. The sanctuary façade consists of an arcade of four centrepoint arches resting on thick piers; the heaviness of the façade is relieved by rosettes in the spandrels of the arches, two-tier blind arches on the piers and a row of smaller blind arches running in a line above the arches. The central arch leading on to the mihrab is the same size as the other arches but is emphasized by a tall pishtak-like façade with engaged columns. The area behind this arch is covered by a squat masonry dome typical of Rajput and earlier Sultanate architecture.

The earliest surviving imperial Mughal mosque is the Qala-i-Kuhna Masjid in the Old Fort (Purana Qila) in Delhi although ironically it was begun in 1541 during the Shah Sur period. Like the Jamali Kamali Masjid the sanctuary of this mosque consists of five bays running north–south parallel to the qibla with the central bay emphasized by a dome. The arrangement of the arcade is the same although here the arches are set within taller pointed arches of differing sizes to lighten the appearance of the façade. The next imperial mosque is attributable to Akbar's reign and rather surprisingly shows more signs of Hindu influence than mosques of the earlier period. This is the mosque of Fatehpur Sikri, the palace city built by Akbar in the 1570s, where Hindu influence was at its most pronounced. The basic plan of the mosque conforms to the established pattern of Mughal mosques with a large courtyard surrounded by an arcade and a centrally placed iwan set into the arcade of the sanctuary on the west side of the courtyard. However, the details of the mosque are mostly Hindu in their associations, from the richly carved columns and corbelled arches in the arcades and the sanctuary to the domed chatris lining the roof. With the reign of Jahangir and later Shah Jahan the appearance of mosques returns to a more overtly Islamic form. In the Jami Masjid of Shahjahanabad built in 1650 the use of Hindu elements is drastically reduced to two chatris on the roof whilst other more Islamic feature such as the minarets, the central iwan and cusped arches assume a higher prominence. The domes have a taller pointed appearance familiar in Islamic buildings elsewhere instead of the squat Hindu style domes used in earlier Mughal mosques. The design of the Shahjahanabad Jami Masjid was a major influence on later Indian mosque architecture with its use of three domes over the sanctuary in conjunction with a raised central arch, or iwan, and engaged minarets. During the reign of Aurangzeb this form was developed as the standard mosque form. The Moti Masjid (Pearl Mosque) built by Aurangzeb in the Red Fort at Delhi was too small to incorporate all the features found at the Jami Masjid but incorporated a three-domed sanctuary with a raised central arch and mini-domed pillars projecting out of the roof to resemble minarets. In the Badshahi Mosque in Lahore built by Aurangzeb in 1674 the pattern of the Jami Masjid was copied with the addition of more minarets making a total of eight.

An important function of imperial Mughal architecture was to overawe people with the power, wealth and sophistication of the sultans; in no area was this more effective than in the design and construction of the sultans' tombs. The earliest tombs of the Mughal period resemble those of the previous Muslim sultans of Delhi and typically consist of an octagonal domed structure sometimes surrounded by an open veranda. One of the first Mughal examples is the tomb of Adham Khan built by Akbar for his wet nurse and her son who was killed in a palace dispute. Another example of this tomb type is the mausoleum of Sher Shah Sur at Sasaram built before 1540. This has the same basic plan as the Adham Khan tomb with a central domed octagonal chamber surrounded by an octagonal arcade with three arches per side. The tomb is made more elaborate, however, by its location in the middle of a specially made moat and its use of domed chatris to mark the corners of each side of the octagon. Other related tombs with a similar design include the tomb of Sayyid Lodi (1517), the tomb of Isa Khan in Delhi.

Later Mughal tombs were also based on an octagonal form but instead of sides of equal length four of the sides were shortened thus producing a square shape with cut off corners. An early example of this type is the Afsarwala tomb in

Delhi, situated in the garden of the Arab serai near the tomb of Humayun. Humayun's tomb built in the 1560s is the first example of the imperial Mughal tomb complexes which came to characterize the splendour of the dynasty (Babur was buried in a simple garden grave and later his remains were transferred to Kabul). Humayun's tomb is composed of four-square octagonal shapes built on two storeys around an octagonal domed space. Between each octagon is a deep iwan giving access to the central domed space which contains the tomb of Humayun. The central structure is surrounded with arcades forming a low square with chamfered corners. In turn this central structure is set in the middle of a square garden divided into quarters which are further subdivided into thirty-two separate sections. The tomb of Humayun was a model for later Mughal tombs, although the tomb of his immediate successor Akbar differs greatly from this model. Akbar's tomb, located in the district of Sikandara (8 km outside Agra) was begun in 1605 and completed seven years later. It is not known whether Akbar took any part in the design of the tomb although it is known that his son Jahangir may have altered the original design. The outer part of the building is a rectangular structure with engaged octagonal towers at each corner and a tall iwan in the centre of each side. The central part of the complex is very different from any other tomb as it lacks a central dome. It consists of a five-storey pavilion with an open rectangular courtyard at the top containing a tomb-like cenotaph. This architecture is characteristic of Akbar's reign and can be compared with the Panch Mahal in the palace at Fatehpur Sikri where there is also a conglomeration of pavilions five storeys high. The outer form of the complex can be compared with the tomb of Itimad-ud-Daulah's tomb completed in 1628 which consists of a low building with a square plan and short engaged octagonal corner towers. In the centre, raised one storey above the rest of the structure, is a vaulted pavilion.

The classic form of tomb was returned to for the Taj Mahal built by Shah Jahan for his wife Mumtaz Mahal who died in 1631. The basic form of the tomb recalls that of Humayun's tomb at Delhi and consists of four octagonal structures joined together by iwans and grouped around a central domed area. As in Humayun's tomb the central building is two storeys high, but here the central dome is more than double the height of the rest of the structure. Instead of being surrounded by arcades the lower part of the structure is raised on a terrace, the sides of which are marked by blind arcades. At each corner of the square terrace is a tapering cylindrical minaret on an octagonal base. The basic forms used in the Taj Mahal were re-used in later tombs but never with the same success. The Bibi ka Maqbara tomb, built less than forty years later, has the same design as the Taj Mahal but the octagonal minarets are thicker and higher in proportion to the central complex which consequently loses some of its significance. A later tomb in this tradition is that built for Safdar Jang in 1753. In this building the minarets are incorporated into the central structure as engaged corner turrets whilst the terrace becomes an arcaded substructure.

One of the most important aspects of Mughal architecture was the design of gardens which provided the setting for tombs and palaces or stood on their own as places for relaxation. Babur, author of the first Mughal architecture, was a lover of gardens and laid out several after his conquest of Delhi. One of the earliest Mughal gardens is known as the Rambagh or Aram Bagh in Agra and was planned by Babur. Although the original form of the garden may have been altered the narrow water channels are indicative of its early date. The usual form of Mughal gardens was derived from the Persian char bagh which consists of a square walled garden divided into four equal units around a central feature usually a pool or fountain. The geometric form of gardens meant that the plant borders assumed a certain importance as can be seen at the Anguri Bagh in Agra Fort where the flower beds are made of interlocking cusped squares like a jigsaw puzzle. Also the form of gardens meant that the plants were usually kept quite low so that the shape of the arrangement was visible. In Kashmir Mughal gardens assumed a less formal and more natural appearance, with tall trees and shrubs and architecture hidden within the garden rather than dominating it as was the case with the more formal gardens of Delhi and Agra. At Srinagar there were once several hundred gardens built around the Dal Lake although only a few still remain. One of the most famous of these is the Shalimar Bagh laid out during the reign of Jahangir in 1619. The form of the garden echoed that of palace architecture and consisted of a terraced system where the garden was divided into three parts; the lowest part was accessible to the public, the middle section was for the emperor and his friends, whilst the highest part (which was totally out of view) contained the zenana, or women's private area. In the centre of the women's area, in the middle of a formal pool, is the Black Pavilion built by Shah Jahan. The building has a three-tiered tiled roof and is built in the style of local Kashmiri wooden mosques.

Like his ancestor Babur, Aurangzeb was more concerned with garden architecture than the construction of palaces. One of the most impressive of these gardens was that of Fatehbad near Agra which although now largely derelict contains a central arcaded pavilion surrounded by a crenellated wall with a monumental entrance.

Public buildings of the Mughal period were usually of a utilitarian design with very little embellishment. The roads were one of the primary concerns of the Mughal administration and during the 1570s Akbar initiated a programme of road improvements including the provision of milestones, wells, reservoirs and caravanserais. The best examples of this are the caravanserais built at Chata near Mathura and Chaparghat. These buildings have a fairly uniform design consisting of a large rectangular enclosure with octagonal corner towers. Inside there are iwans leading on to cells along the side of the walls. The cells are usually arranged in pairs with a connecting door in between, thus forming units of four (two iwans and two closed rooms). In addition to the standard rooms there are usually at least two larger sets of rooms for more important travellers. Most caravanserais have one entrance; where there are two these are usually opposite each other. Sometimes the central axis of the caravanserais are built as bazars for the visiting merchants. The only areas of architectural elaboration are the gates or mosques which were attached to the buildings. One of the most magnificently decorated gateways is that of the Nur Mahal caravanserai by Nur Jahan between 1618 and 1620. Its design resembles funerary and mosque architecture of the period, with a central iwan flanked by three tiers of side iwans; however, the decoration, which consists of carved human, animal and mythical figures, is more reminiscent of palatial architecture of the period.

Milestones, known as kos minar (small towers), were used to mark the roads. These are usually very plain structures with an octagonal base and a tapering cylindrical shaft. One of the main routes which received attention during Akbar's reign was the Agra to Ajmer pilgrimage route which was provided with road markers and small resthouses. Under Jahangir the improvement of roads continued with trees planted on the road from Agra to Bengal, the construction of wells and kos minar on the road from Agra to Lahore and the provision of small stations on the Pir Panjal pass into Kashmir. During the reign of Aurangzeb the roadside facilities were extended and improved, with particular attention paid to the roads between Agra and Aurangbad and Lahore to Kabul. Repairs carried out on bridges, caravanserais and roadside mosques were paid for out of the emperor's private income.

See also: Fatehpur Sikri, Taj Mahal

Further reading:

C. Ascher, 'The Mughal and post-Mughal periods', in *The Islamic Heritage of Bengal*, G. Michell, Paris 1984.

H. Crane, 'The patronage of Zahir al-Din Babur and the origins of Mughal architecture', *Bulletin of the Asia Institute* NS 1: 95–110, 1987.

S. Crowe, S. Haywood and S. Jelicoe, *The Gardens of Mughal India*, London 1972.

Z. A. Dessai, 'Mughal architecture in the Deccan', in *History of Medieval Deccan: 1295–1724* 2, ed. H. K. Sherwani and P. M. Joshi, Hyderabad 1974, 305–14.

J. Dickie, 'The Mughal garden: gateway to paradise', *Muqarnas* 3: 128–37, 1985.

A. N. Khan, *The Hiran Minar and Baradari Shaikhpura: A Hunting Resort of the Mughal Emperors*, Lahore 1980.

I. A. Khan, 'New light on the history of two early Mughal monuments of Bayana', *Muqarnas* 6: 55–82, 1990.

W. G. Klingelhofer, 'The Jahangari Mahal of the Agra Fort: expression and experience in early Mughal architecture', *Muqarnas* 5: 153–69, 1988.

E. Koch, *Mughal Architecture*, Munich 1991.

—— *The Hunting Palaces of Shah Jahan* (forthcoming).

G. D. Lowry, 'Humayun's Tomb: form, function and meaning in early Mughal architecture', *Muqarnas* 4: 133–48, 1987.

K. K. Muhammad, 'The houses of the nobility in Mughal India', *Islamic Culture* 60(3): 81–104, 1986.

R. Nath, *History of Mughal Architecture* (*i*) (*Babur to Humayun*), New Delhi 1982.

—— *History of Mughal Architecture* (*ii*) (*Akbar*), New Delhi 1982.

S. Parihar, *Mughal Monuments in the Punjab and the Haryana*, New Delhi 1985.

G. H. R. Tillotson, *The Rajput Palaces; The Development of an Architectural Style 1450–1750*, New Haven, Conn., and London 1987.

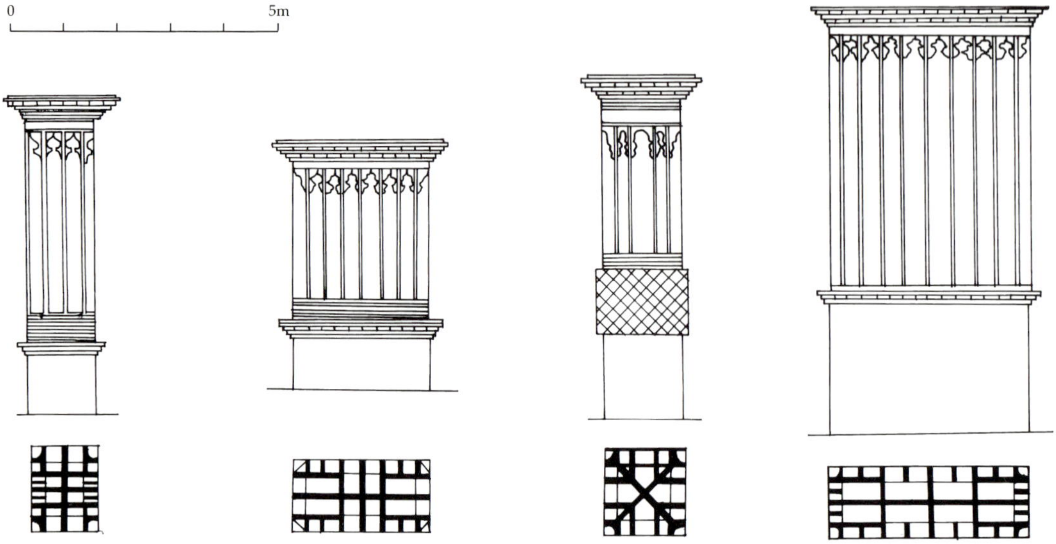

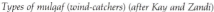

Types of mulqaf (wind-catchers) (after Kay and Zandi)

—— *Mughal India*, Architectural Guides for Travellers, London 1990.
F. Watson, *A Concise History of India*, London 1979.

muhtasib

A municipal officer responsible for public morals and regulation of markets.

An important duty of the muhtasib was the supervision of building construction which involved regulation and inspection of materials. The uniform size of materials used in construction was ensured by the use of wooden templates which were kept in the mosque. The muhtasib was also responsible for checking mould boxes used for baked bricks and mud bricks to check that these were not distorted. Raw mud bricks were not allowed to be used until they had whitened. Also the muhtasib ensured that builders kept stockpiles of the correct spare materials such as bricks for lining wells, floor bricks, and fire bricks for ovens.

mulqaf

Arabic term for wind-catcher.

See also: badgir

muqarnas

System of projecting niches used for zones of transition and for architectural decoration.

Muqarnas is one of the most characteristic features of Islamic architecture and is used throughout most of the Muslim world (in North Africa a related system known as muqarbaras is also used). Muqarnas is usually associated with domes, doorways and niches, although it is often applied to other architectural features and is sometimes used as an ornamental band on a flat surface.

The earliest examples of muqarnas so far discovered were found at Nishapur in eastern Iran and date to the late ninth or early tenth century. These consist of fragments of stucco niches with carved and painted decoration which were found within domestic buildings. Of a similarly early date are fragments of painted stucco muqarnas belonging to a bath house of the Abbasid or Fatimid period at Fustat in Egypt. The wide dispersion of muqarnas at this early date (ninth–tenth century) suggests that its origin was somewhere in the centre of the Islamic world, probably Baghdad.

During the eleventh century muqarnas spread to most parts of the Middle East (from Egypt to Central Asia) whilst in the western Islamic World a similar device called muqarbaras was also used. The earliest use of muqarnas seems to have been on the inside of buildings in association with domes and vaults. The first use of muqarnas on the exterior of a building is on the tomb of Ladjin in Mazandaran built in 1022 where two superimposed rows are used as decoration. Some of the most

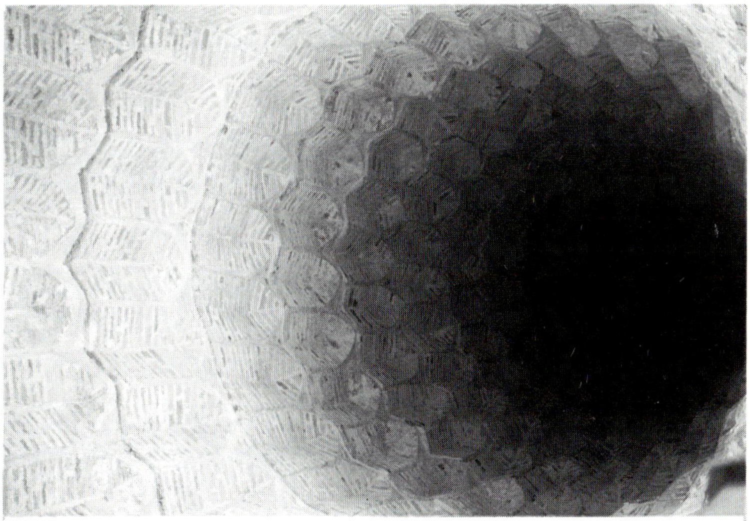

Interior of muqarnas dome, Mashad al-Shams, Hilla, Iraq

Exterior of muqarnas dome, Mashad al-Shams, Hilla, Iraq

impressive examples of muqarnas on the exterior of buildings are where it is used as corbelling for balconies on minarets. One of the best examples of such muqarnas corbelling is found on the minaret of Suq al-Ghazzal in Baghdad dated to the thirteenth century. The base of the minaret is encased in a thick sleeve of muqarnas corbelling above which there is a short shaft which supports a giant six-tiered band of muqarnas corbelling which forms a platform for the balcony.

Generally, however, the most elaborate muqarnas are associated with domes. Some of the earliest and simplest forms of muqarnas can be found in the eleventh-century mausoleums at Aswan in Egypt. One example consists of an arched squinch divided into three lobes on the bottom with a small single niche on top. In Iraq the same device was taken to its most extreme form with the development of conical domes made of muqarnas. The oldest surviving example is the mausoleum of Imam Dur north of Samarra. This dome is extraordinary both for its height (over 25 m) and its profuse, almost organic, muqarnas plaster decoration.

One of the most common uses of muqarnas was for column capitals. Before the eleventh century Islamic buildings would rely on re-used classical and Byzantine capitals or copies of these forms. Muqarnas was particularly suited for use in capitals as it lends itself to the transition from circular column to the square section of an arch and was uniquely Islamic in form. In Ottoman architecture, where Turkish triangles performed the same function as muqarnas pendentives and squinches, muqarnas was still employed for portals, niches, column capitals and other decorative features.

It is in its use for domes and vaults that muqarnas was to have its most significant impact. By providing a diffused method of transition from flat to curved, muqarnas zones of transition were able to break down the distinction between vertical and curved, domed and horizontal. The best examples of this can be seen in conical domes such as that at Natanz in Iran where the roof emerges not as a hemispherical dome but as a multi-faceted prism-like series of surfaces.

The almost universal adoption of muqarnas as architectural decoration meant that it was also adapted for woodwork such as mosque furniture. The minbar of Nur al-Din built for the Aqsa Mosque in Jerusalem had three bands of tiered muqarnas on a canopy above the foot of the stairs.

In Iraq, Iran and the eastern Islamic world the most suitable materials for muqarnas construction were plaster and baked brick. Both materials have the advantage of being light whilst bricks have the additional advantage of being made to a standard dimension which is useful when repeating the complex geometric alignments necessary for muqarnas. Plaster also has the advantage that it can easily be decorated by carving or painting. In Syria and Egypt the first muqarnas domes were made from plaster suspended from a wooden frame within an outer dome made out of stone. The most famous example of this technique is the dome in Nur al-Din's maristan built in 1154. Later muqarnas stone domes were made, the best examples of which belong to fifteenth-century Egypt.

The first muqarnas was made purely out of interlocking cut niches but fairly early on 'dripping' stalactites were developed. These are thin downward projections from the cut side of the niche which give the illusion of arches suspended in mid-air. These stalactite niches are some of the most elaborate form of muqarnas which defy attempts at two-dimensional representation.

There are several theories about the origins of muqarnas. Generally the decorative origin and function is favoured over the suggestion that muqarnas was the solution to a particular structural problem. The reason for this conclusion is that some of the earliest examples of muqarnas found were decorative plaster bands, although equally early are examples of muqarnas squinches from Egypt. Whilst certainly muqarnas did have a decorative function, from the beginning its early and frequent association with domes and pendentives suggests that the form had structural associations. The tiered form of muqarnas means that the thrust of the dome could be directed downwards into the corner of a building without adding the extra weight of a pendentive. On the other hand muqarnas squinches are a way of providing a greater span without having to build large heavy arches. In general muqarnas tends to blur the distinction between squinch and pendentive and provides a more subtle transition from square to octagon. A view which combines both decorative and structural functions suggests that the origins of muqarnas may be found in Islamic theology which promotes an occasionalist view of the universe whereby the continued existence of anything is dependent on the will of God. Muqarnas is then a way of expressing this view of the universe where the dome appears to stand without visible support.

Further reading:

J. Bloom, 'The introduction of the muqarnas in Egypt', *Muqarnas* 5, 1988.

O. Grabar, *The Formation of Islamic Art* (revised and enlarged edition), Yale University Press: New Haven and London 1987.

musalla

Literally a place where prayer is performed, although in practice it has come to refer to large open spaces outside cities for that purpose.

The prime function of a musalla is to provide additional space for prayer during festivals such as Ramadhan. Sometimes they are referred to as 'Festival Mosques', and in India, Iran and Ottoman Turkey they are referred to by the term *namazgah*. Sometimes a musalla is no more than an open space marked out with a line which indicates the direction of Mecca (the qibla), although more often it will include a long wall on the qibla side which may include a mihrab. Sometimes musalla reached advanced stages of building with an arcade covering the qibla wall (as recorded at Bahrain) and elaborately decorated mihrabs such as that of Mashad. The usual position of a musalla was outside the city gates although they are occasionally within the city as in Abbasid Samarra.

N

nahr

Canal or river.

namazgah

Turkish and Persian term for an open-air prayer place often used by the army. Sometimes these are quite elaborately built with a minbar and a standing mihrab.

naqqar khana

Mughal term for a drum house or place for an orchestra during ceremonies.

Natanz, shrine of Abd al-Samad

Sufi funerary complex at Natanz in western Iran.

Natanz is located on the edge of the Dasht-i Kavir desert 60 km south-east of Kashan. This is a large funerary complex which has grown up organically around the tomb of Abd al-Samad, a follower of the famous Sufi saint Abu Said who died in 1049. The central feature of the site is the octagonal tomb around which is built a four-iwan congregational mosque dated to 1309. Internally the tomb is a cruciform chamber which is converted to an octagon at roof level. The roof is a blue-tiled octagonal pyramid dome outside and internally comprises a tall muqarnas vault. Another important structure at the site is the khanqa or dervish hostel built in 1317 which is located to the south-west of the tomb. Only the portal of this structure survives with a large muqarnas semi-dome.

Nilometer

Device located on Roda island, Egypt for measuring the rise of the Nile during the period of inundation.

This structure was built in 861–2 CE during the reign of Caliph al-Mutawakil. The purpose of the device is to measure the level of the flood to work out the amount of tax due to the government (a higher flood level indicates a higher yield). The structure consists of a ·2 m square stone-lined pit 13.14 m deep connected to the Nile by three tunnels. In the centre of the square pit is a tall octagonal column divided into cubits each of which is subdivided into twenty-four smaller units. A staircase runs down the four sides so that the central column could be read. The floor at the bottom was made of cedar beams. Approximately halfway up there are four pointed relieving arches, one on each side of the pit. The arches are of a two-centred type used in Gothic architecture in Europe during the fourteenth century. The curves of the arches are emphasized by two bands of moulding whilst above there are foliated kufic inscriptions which contain Quranic passages referring to crops and harvests.

Further reading:

K. A. C. Creswell, *A Short Account of Early Muslim Architecture*, revised and enlarged edn. J. W. Allan, Aldershot 1989, 383–5.

nine-domed mosque (also known as nine-bay domed mosque)

This is a type of mosque roofed by nine domes of equal size.

Although the distribution of this building type is very wide (it is found as far apart as East Africa, Bangladesh, Central Asia and North Africa) it does not occur in great numbers in any one area. The earliest extant examples date from the ninth century CE, whilst there are few buildings of this type later than the sixteenth century.

Most nine-domed mosques are fairly small (usually 10–15 m square) though substantially built. It is common for these buildings to be open on two, three or even four sides but it is rare for them to have a sahn or minaret. Sometimes the central row of domes is raised to emphasize the mihrab axis.

There are two theories about the origin of this type of mosque. The older theory originated by Creswell asserts that the mosque is derived from the earliest forms of Islamic funerary monuments,

nine-domed mosque (also known as nine-bay domed mosque)

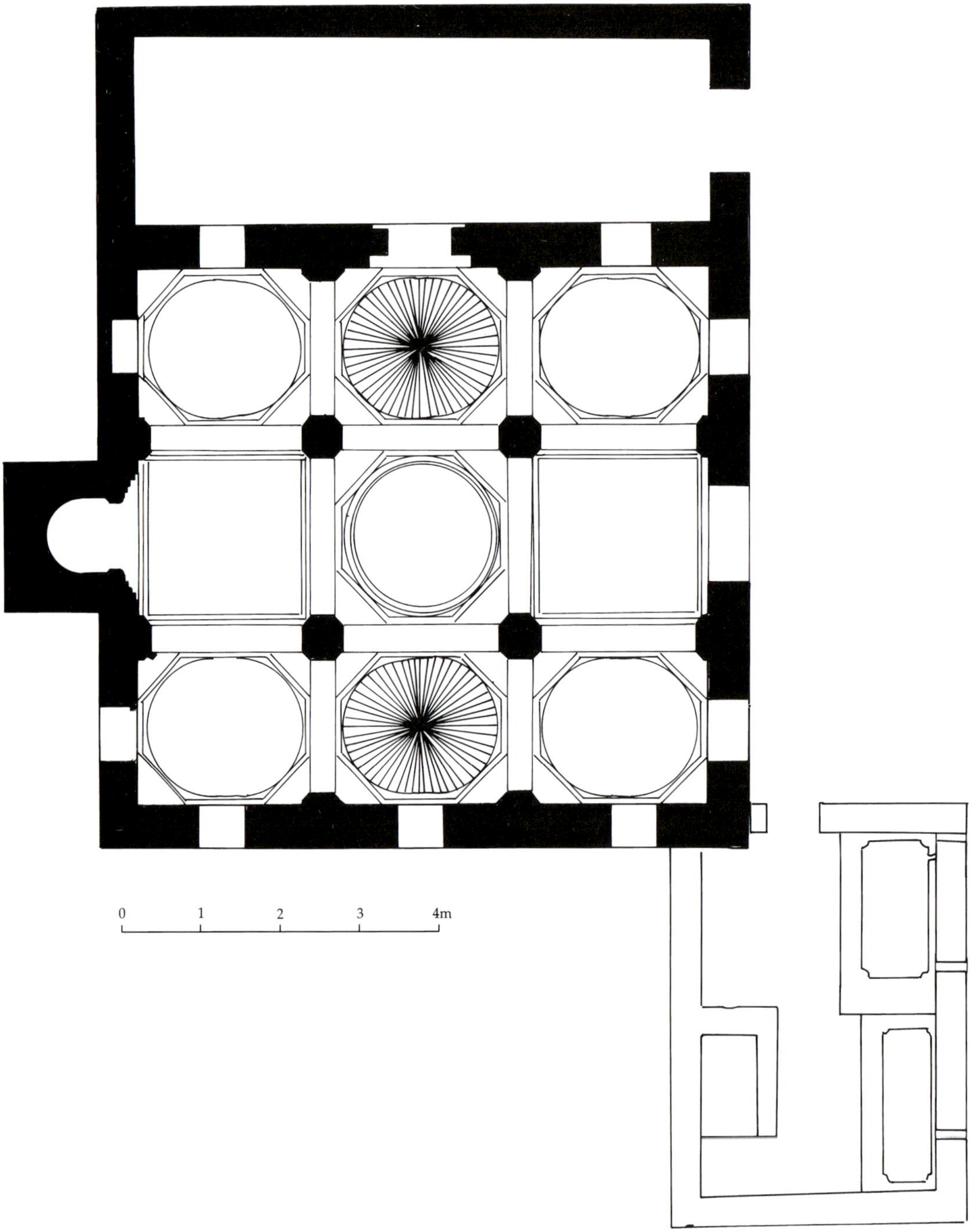

Nine-domed mosque, Kilwa (after Garlake)

such as the Qubbat al-Sulaybiyya at Samarra, which were domed and had open sides. More recently it has been suggested that the type derives from honorific buildings such as Khirbet al-Mafjar.

Whilst the origin of the design may be disputed it is clear that many of the mosques were associated with tombs or burials so that it is reasonable to suggest that they should be regarded as memorial mosques. Important examples can be found at Kilwa, Fustat, and Toledo.

Further reading:

K. A. C. Creswell, *Muslim Architecture of Egypt I*, Oxford 1952, 11–13.

R. Ettinghausen, *From Byzantium to Sassanian Iran and the Islamic World*, London 1972, 57–8.

G. R. H. King, 'The nine bay domed mosque in Islam', *Madrider Mitteilungen* 30: 1989.

Nishapur

Famous medieval city located in the Khurassan region of eastern Iran.

Nishapur was founded in Sassanian times as 'New Shapur' and rose to prominence in early Islamic times as capital of the Tahirid dynasty in the ninth century. The city was at the height of its prosperity and importance under the Samanid dynasty in the tenth century. In 1037 the city was captured by the Seljuks and remained a part of that empire until 1153 when it was sacked by the Ghuzz. Despite the sacking and several earthquakes the city continued to function until 1221 when it was sacked by the Mongols. A modern city of the same name has grown up near the site based around an eighteenth-century shrine.

Although no standing architecture remains at the site, excavation has revealed extensive architectural remains together with a large number of finds making this one of the best examples of a medieval Islamic city. The remains were found mostly within three mounds known as Tepe Madrasseh, Sabz Pushan and Qanat Tepe. There is no evidence of occupation at any of the sites before the eighth century indicating that the Sassanian city may have been elsewhere. The main materials of construction were mud brick (*khist*) and trodden earth or pisé (*chineh*) and baked brick. Wood was used as a strengthening material in walls as well as for columns. Many of the walls were covered with stucco and painted plaster panels (frescoes). The remains of several mosques were found on the site all with rectangular recessed mihrabs. At Tepe Madrasseh remains of a prayer-hall iwan were found together with the base of a minaret. The minaret had an octagonal shaft and was built of yellow fired bricks with decorated with shallow vertical slots. Elsewhere on the site columns built of baked brick were also decorated with slots. At Qanat Tepe remains of a mosque were found close to the remains of a bath house. The bath house had hypocaust heating, a plunge pool and a nine-sided octagonal basin in the centre. The most remarkable feature of the bath house was the frescoes which included representations of human figures. At Sabz Pushan remains of small houses were found which included centrally placed sunken fireplaces made from earthenware jars set into the ground. Among the most important finds at the site were the remains of eleven muqarnas panels excavated from a cellar. These were prefabricated plaster panels which would have been attached to the zone of transition in the roof of the cellar and are some of the earliest evidence for the use of muqarnas.

O

ocak

Turkish word for a chimney hood, also used to designate a unit of Ottoman troops of Janissaries. The typical Ottoman ocak consists of a tall conical hood set against the inside wall of a building. Some of the best examples can be found in the kitchens in the Topkapisarai.

See also: Ottomans

Oman

The sultanate of Oman is located in the south-east corner of the Arabian peninsula and borders on the Indian Ocean.

It is the third largest country in Arabia after Saudi Arabia and Yemen and comprises five distinct geographical regions, the Musandam peninsula, the Batinah coastal strip, the Hajjar mountains, the Naj desert and Dhofar. The Musandam peninsula is separate from the rest of the country and comprises a rocky headland adjacent to the straits of Hormuz. The Batinah coastal strip is located between the sea and the mountains in the northern part of the country and varies between 20 and 25 km wide, this is the most densely populated region of Oman. The Hajjar mountains are a very distinctive feature; running in a belt parallel to the coast in the northern part of the country, they are the source of most of Oman's water. The Naj desert, comprising several areas including the Wahiba sands, separates the northern mountains from those of the south and its population is mostly nomadic. Dhofar is a mountainous region in the south of the country with a tropical climate and is the only part of Arabia to experience a summer monsoon.

Until the discovery of oil Oman's economy was based upon a number of natural resources, the most important of which were copper from the mountains in the north and frankincense from Dhofar. Also Oman's position on the Indian Ocean meant that it was able to establish a long-distance maritime trade based on the monsoons of the Indian Ocean. In addition, fishing and dates have remained important components of Oman's economy even after the discovery of oil.

The earliest settled communities in Oman have been dated to 3000 BCE and by 2000 BCE copper was being exported to Mesopotamia. In the fourth century BCE Oman was occupied by the Persians who remained in control of the country until the advent of Islam in 630 CE. Under Islam Oman's trading network flourished and included East Africa, India and the Far East. During this period various coastal towns grew up, the most important of which were Sohar, Qalhat and Dhofar (al-Balid). In 1503 the coastal towns were captured and occupied by the Portuguese. As a result the towns of the interior, the most important of which were Nizwa and Bahla, grew in power and influence. By 1650 the Portuguese had been expelled by the Ya'ariba leader, Sultan bin Sayf, who rebuilt the fort at Nizwa. Internal conflicts allowed a Persian invasion in 1743 but this was brought to an end by Ahmad ibn Sa'id governor of Sohar who was elected imam in 1743. He was the founder of the Al Bu Sa'id dynasty which continues to rule Oman today.

In 1730 Oman had acquired the island of Zanzibar and by the 1830s Sultan Sa'id ibn Sultan had built a new capital in Zanzibar. From 1856 Oman and Zanzibar were ruled by two branches of the same family.

For various reasons Oman was not modernized until the 1970s, which has meant that traditional architecture has survived here better than in most of the other Gulf states. The main building materials employed in Oman are mud brick, baked brick, stone, mangrove poles, palm trees and lime (used for mortar and plaster). The particular combination of materials employed depends on the region and type of building.

Baked brick is used fairly infrequently in Oman and is confined mostly to the port of Sohar. Baked bricks were first used in the early Islamic city and were also used in houses of the nineteenth century although it is not certain if bricks were still made in nineteenth-century Oman or imported from elsewhere. Occasionally baked bricks are found incorporated into buildings outside Sohar such as the arches of the Great Mosque in Bahla or in the columns of the mosque of the Samad quarter in Nizwa. Mud brick on the other hand is more common and is frequently used in the oasis towns of the interior. It is usually used in conjunction with mud mortar and plaster sometimes mixed with lime. Mangrove poles imported from East Africa are frequently used for roofing in the houses of the coast. Palm trunks are also used for roofing there and for inland parts of the country. Palm fronds and trunks are also used for less permanent structures on the coast. Several types of stone are used for building in Oman; amongst the more common types are coral blocks on the north coast, coastal limestone in Dhofar and roughly hewn blocks of igneous rock in the mountains. Lime for use in mortars is either made from burning limestone or coral blocks.

The architecture of Oman can be divided into several types based on the type of building, the materials used and the location. The main groups are houses, mosques, forts and mansions.

Until recently the most common form of architecture on the coast was the palm-frond house which may take several forms from a single-room temporary dwelling used for the date harvest to a large enclosure incorporating winter and summer rooms. The basic unit of construction is a rectangular room measuring approximately 3 by 5.5 m. The walls are made from stems (zur) tied together to form a panel whilst the main form of support are palm trunks placed externally. The winter houses have flat roofs whereas the summer houses have pitched roofs and are called Khaymah (tent). Often houses made of other materials have palm-frond roofs or verandas.

Mud-brick houses are found throughout Oman, although they are most common in oasis towns. They are usually built with very shallow foundations or directly on to the ground, and the first metre or so is often built out of irregular stones to serve as a base for the mud-brick superstructure. Simple mud-brick houses have pitched palm-frond (barristi) roofs whilst the larger houses have flat earth roofs supported by palm trunks or mangrove poles. Some of the larger mud-brick houses are three storeys high.

Stone-built houses are common on the coast or in the mountains. One of the simplest forms is a type of coral house found in the Batinah. These are built out of rough lumps of coral rag which are plastered over with mud; the roofs are usually made of palm fronds; locally these are called kerin. In Salalah and the Dhofar coast houses are made out of roughly squared limestone blocks which are laid in courses and interspersed with wooden tie-beams. Usually, however, stone buildings in Oman are made out of rough-hewn stones laid in successive bands approximately half a metre high and covered with a plaster surface, producing walls with layers of overlapping plaster coats.

Mosques are mostly built out of stone or mud brick with flat roofs. Minarets are rare in Oman before the nineteenth century. A fairly common feature in Omani mosques is the combination of mihrab and minbar, where the minbar is entered through an opening in the mihrab (this feature is also found in other parts of the Indian Ocean littoral such as East Africa and Yemen). In the north of Oman mosque roofs are usually supported by arches resting on cylindrical columns, in Dhofar the columns are usually octagonal. Built shrines do not occur in the Ibadi region of the north but are fairly common in the predominantly Sunni region of Dhofar where they usually have pointed domes.

Fortified buildings are one of the most noticeable features of Omani architecture. Most settlements, however small, have some form of fortified structure. There are two main types of fortified building in Oman, the sur or fortified enclosure and the citadel. A sur is a fortified enclosure which is used on a temporary basis during raids or other disturbances, consequently the design of such enclosures is fairly simple and consists of a roughly square enclosure which may or may not have a tower. On the other hand the citadels or forts of the main towns are fairly sophisticated structures designed for use with artillery. The most famous forts in Oman are at Nizwa, Ibra, Izki, Mudhairib and al-Rustaq. These buildings were influenced by the Portuguese forts of the sixteenth and seventeenth centuries, although they also included local developments such as the use of two diagonally opposed towers linked by thick curtain walls.

One of the consequences of Oman's vast trading links was the growth of a wealthy mercantile class who were able to build mansions. Some of these are located within coastal cities such as Sur or

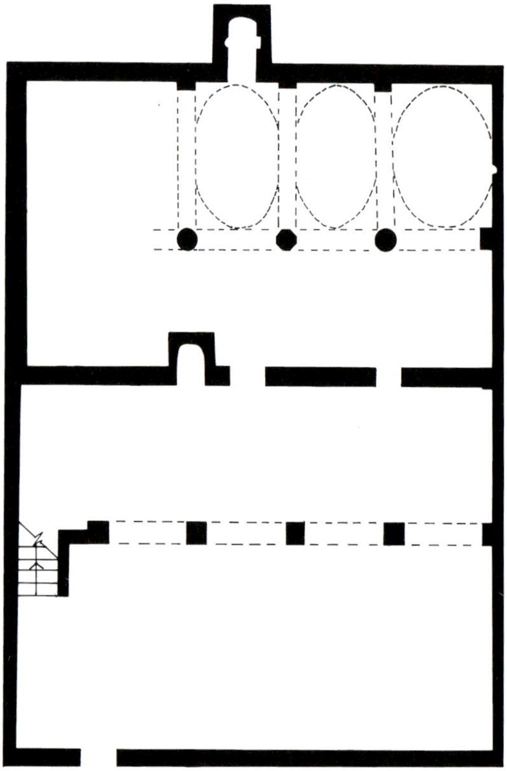

Traditional mosque, Banu Bu Ali, Oman

Muscat, whilst others are rural dwellings set in their own grounds such as Bayt Na'man on the Batinah plain. Common features found in mansions and in more important houses include elaborately carved doorways, pre-cast stucco mouldings around doorways and recesses, and painted wooden ceilings. Such buildings often have a private prayer room, a light well (shamsiya) and ventilation slits above the windows.

Further reading:

The most useful works on the architecture and archaeology of Oman can be found in the *Journal of Oman Studies*, including those listed below.

P. and G. Bonnenfant and Salim ibn Hamad ibn Sulaiman al-Hathri, 'Architecture and social history at Mudayrib', 3: 107–35, 1977.

P. M. Costa, 'The study of the city of Zafar (al-Balid)', 5: 111–50, 1979.

—— 'Studies on the built environment of the Batinah', 8(2): 1985.

—— 'Bayt Na'man, a seventeenth-century mansion of the Batinah', 8(2): 195–210, 1985.

P. M. Costa and S. Kite, 'The architecture of Salalah and the Dhofar littoral', 7: 131–53, 1985.

E. Enrico, 'Introduction to Omani architecture of the sixteenth, seventeenth and eighteenth centuries', 6(2): 291–306, 1983.

E. Galdieri, 'A masterpiece of Omani 17th-century architecture. The palace of Imam Bilarab Sultan al-Yaariba at Jabrin', 1: 167–79, 1975.

M. Kerveran, C. LeCouer-Grandmaison, M. Soubeyran and A. Vialatte de Pemille, 'Suhari houses', 6(2): 307–16, 1983.

Ottomans (Turkish: Osmanli)

Major Islamic dynasty based in Turkey which at its height controlled a vast area including all of modern Turkey, the Balkans and much of the Middle East and North Africa.

The origins of the Ottoman dynasty can be traced back as far as their thirteenth-century founder Othman (Osman). Othman was a leader of a branch of the Qayïgh clan which was part of the Turkic Öghuz tribe originally from Central Asia. The Öghuz was amongst those Turkic groups who had fled west with the Mongol invasions of the thirteenth century and now threatened the ailing Byzantine Empire. Originally the Ottomans had been based around the southern city of Konya but later moved north-west to the area of Bursa later known in Turkish as the Hüdavendigâr (royal) region. The position of the Ottomans on the border with Byzantine territory meant that they constantly attracted fresh Turkic warriors (ghazis) willing to fight the Christians. The constant warfare and arrival of new soldiers meant that the emerging Ottoman state developed a strong military organization and tradition which enabled it gradually to take over rival Turkish states in the vicinity. In 1357 a new phase in Ottoman expansion was achieved by crossing the Dardanelles into Europe and fighting the divided Balkan Christians. By 1366 the Balkan provinces had become so important to the Ottoman state that the capital was moved from Bursa to Edirne. Another result of the move into Europe was that instead of relying on the Turkic warriors the army was now formed by Christians who had been captured as children and converted to Islam. The advantage of this new method was that the religious orthodoxy and absolute allegiance of the soldiers could be ensured. The new troops known as Janissaries were the élite force of the growing empire; at the same time a system of feudal land grants was adopted for the Ottoman cavalry. In 1394 Ottoman control of the

Open-air mosque, Ras al-Junayz, Oman

Balkan provinces was recognized when Bayazit was granted the title Sultan of Rum by the Abbasid caliph in Cairo. A major setback occurred in 1402 when a second Mongol invasion led by Timur (Tamurlane) conquered much of Anatolia and defeated the Ottoman sultan at Ankara. However, Timurid success was short lived and soon the Ottomans were able to regain control of much of their territory in Anatolia. The major event of the fifteenth century was the capture of Constantinople (later known as Istanbul) and the defeat of the Byzantine Empire by Mehmet the Conqueror in 1453.

Having consolidated their position in Anatolia during the fifteenth century by the beginning of the sixteenth century the Ottomans were able to launch a major offensive in Europe and the Middle East. In 1517 the defeat of the Mamluks brought Syria and Egypt into the Ottoman Empire and in 1526 Hungary was brought under Ottoman control. For the next century and a half the Ottomans were the world's foremost Islamic power and undisputed rulers of most of the eastern Mediterranean. As orthodox Sunnis the Ottomans established contacts with their co-religionists the Mughals of India although the distance was too great for any meaningful co-operation beyond sending a few Turkish ships against the Portuguese in the Indian Ocean.

The siege of Vienna in 1683 marked the high point of their military power in Europe and their defeat marked the beginning of an irreversible decline which continued into the eighteenth century. Nevertheless, Turkey remained a major power during the nineteenth century despite the loss of large amounts of territory to local leaders in Europe

Bibi Miriyam, domed thirteenth-century mausoleum, Qalhat, Oman

and the Middle East. Turkey's disastrous participation in the First World War led to the loss of its remaining Arab provinces and a European attempt to take control of Anatolia. European expansionism in turn prompted a reaction in Turkey which led to the rise of the Young Turks and the abolition of the Ottoman sultanate in 1922.

For over 500 years the Ottomans ruled an area now occupied by more than fifteen modern states so that Ottoman buildings now represent a sizeable proportion of the historic architecture of the region. The Ottoman presence in these areas was marked by the erection of imperial structures such as fortresses, mosques and khans which preserve a remarkable degree of uniformity despite the large distances involved. However this picture must be modified by two observations, first that direct Ottoman control over some areas was limited to relatively short periods and second that Ottoman architecture was subject to local influences. The first observation may be illustrated by the case of Iraq where constant warfare with the Saffavids meant that Ottoman control fluctuated throughout the sixteenth, seventeenth and eighteenth centuries and was only firmly established in the nineteenth century. The consequence of this is that Iraq contains few distinctively Ottoman buildings from before the nineteenth century. The second observation is important as it calls for a distinction between buildings in the imperial style and locally derived buildings – thus an imperial mosque in Damascus (e.g. the Tekkiye) may differ from a local mosque in the Syrian style. Even in the case of imperial Ottoman buildings concessions were made to local taste; thus the Sinan Pasha Cami in Cairo is Ottoman in plan but has distinct Egyptian features like the use of muqarnas above the windows, the short minaret and the use of ablaq masonry. Sometimes local styles affected the imperial style – thus the tall domes of Syria and Egypt influenced the 'baroque' buildings of seventeenth-century Istanbul.

The heartland of the Ottoman Empire was western Anatolia and Thrace and it was in this area that the imperial style developed out of Byzantine and Seljuk architectural traditions. The Byzantine tradition is characterized by domes, baked brick and tiles, the Seljuk by iwans, carved stonework and the use of spolia. The main building materials used in Ottoman architecture were baked bricks and tiles, cut limestone, marble and wood, whilst glazed tiles and glass (coloured and plain) were used for decoration.

The use of baked brick in Ottoman architecture was inherited directly from Byzantine practice which in turn was copied from earlier Roman work. Brick is used on a much greater scale in early Ottoman buildings than those of the later period possibly in imitation of contemporary Byzantine practice which used bricks until the beginning of the fourteenth century when they were no longer available. The usual brick form was a flat square of varying dimensions, the Ottomans had a much wider range of brick sizes than the Byzantines whose bricks were of a standard size although better in quality. The standard Byzantine construction technique, copied in early Ottoman buildings, was rubble and brick construction where the size of bricks determined the thickness of the walls. Often layers of brick alternate with layers of cut stone thus the Haci Özbek Cami at Iznik is built of triple layers of brick alternating with layers of individual cut stone blocks separated by single vertically laid bricks. The ratio of layers of brick to layers of stone does not seem to have been standard for every building and in some cases the thickness of layers varies in the same building. In general, however, three layers of brick to one of stone was fairly usual during most periods. The standardized size of bricks and their lightness compared with stone also made them ideal material for the construction of domes, barrel vaults and arches. When stone replaced brick and stone as the main facing material, bricks continued to be used for arches, domes and vaults. In early Ottoman buildings tiles were used to cover the outside of the dome although from the sixteenth century onwards lead was increasingly used.

The walls of Ottoman buildings were built with a rubble stone core enclosed by a facing of stone or brick and stone. In some of the earlier buildings rubble stone was used on the exterior of buildings either contained within layers of brick or plastered over. Later on the use of cut limestone became more usual, first in conjunction with brick and later on its own. Immediately after the conquest of Constantinople there seems to have been a reversion to brick and stone due to a shortage of cut limestone. However, from the beginning of the sixteenth century onwards most important buildings were faced in cut stone, although subsidiary structures continued to use brick and stone. The quality of masonry in Ottoman buildings is extraordinary due to its precision and smoothness which gave buildings a monumentality not easily achieved with brick and stone.

In addition to limestone Ottoman buildings used large quantities of antique and Byzantine marble both as columns and for decoration. During the sixteenth century there were large numbers of disused Byzantine churches which were used as quarries for marble columns thus the Ottoman buildings of this period tend to use more columns than earlier or later periods. The hardest form of marble available was porphyry, which is twice as hard as granite, although this was only used rarely as it tended to crack. New marble seems only to have been available from the quarries at Marmara although there was enough ancient marble available to fulfil most needs. Sometimes, however, there seems to have been an acute shortage of marble; thus the tomb of Suleyman was built using fake red and green marble. Fake marble was often used for voussoirs of arches where the weight of real marble would cause structural problems. Fake marble voussoirs were usually made of brick and covered with plaster which was then painted.

Wood was essential in the construction of Ottoman buildings and was used for the centring of vaults and domes, for tie-beams and as scaffolding. In addition wood was used for projecting galleries and also for pitched wooden roofs, although these were less common than brick domes in monumental buildings. In domestic architecture, however, wood was the predominant material and most of the houses of Istanbul were built entirely out of wood.

One of the most distinctive features of imperial Ottoman architecture is its use of polychrome glazed tiles as wall decoration. Glazed tiles were used by the Ottomans as early as thirteenth century at the Yeşil Cami at Iznik although it was not until the fifteenth century that the first of the famous Iznik tiles were produced. During the sixteenth century Iznik tiles replaced marble as the main form of decoration in mosques thus in the Ivaz Efendi Cami in Istanbul tilework columns are placed either side of the mihrab instead of the usual marble columns.

The windows of mosques were often decorated with stained glass set into thick plasterwork frames. Coloured glass made with a high proportion of lead was mostly imported from Europe and clipped to the sizes required. Although coloured glass was used more often, the architect Sinan preferred to use clear glass and altered the structural arrangement of buildings to introduce the maximum amount of light into the interior.

Sixteenth-century Ottoman fortress at Ras al-ʿAyn, Israel/Palestine

Ottoman architecture can be divided into three major periods which roughly correspond to historical developments. The early period between the thirteenth and mid-fifteenth century was the period before the capture of Constantinople in 1453 and characterized by the transition from a small principality to a sultanate. The second period from the capture of Constantinople (Istanbul) to the mid-sixteenth century is regarded as the classical Ottoman period and saw the most brilliant developments in arts and technology to match the spectacular Ottoman victories in Europe, North Africa and the Middle East. The third period from the end of the sixteenth century to the twentieth century is known for political and economic decline, matched in architecture by weaker forms on a smaller scale and the increasing influence of Europe.

Early Period

Possibly the oldest Ottoman building is the Etrugrul Mescit in Sögüt 40 km south-east of Iznik which dates from the first years of the fourteenth century. The mosque has been significantly altered by the addition of a minaret and tall arched windows although its essential form of a tall cube capped by a dome remains unchanged. More authentic and better dated is the Haci Özbek Cami at Iznik which is dated to 1333, two years after the capture of the city from the Byzantines. Like the mosque at Sögüt the Haci Özbek Cami is a small cube covered with an almost hemispherical dome (radius 4 m) resting on a zone of Turkish triangles. The original portico was on the west side (i.e. at right angles to the qibla) and consisted of three bays resting on two marble columns. Two of the bays were covered by barrel vaults, whilst that above the entrance was covered with a cross vault; the north and south sides of the portico were walled in as protection against the wind. Other early Ottoman mosques include the Alaettin Cami at Bursa and the Orhan Ghazi Cami at Bilecik. The Aleattin Cami was built in 1335 after the Ottoman capture of Bursa and is of a similar form and size to the Haci Özbek Cami except that the portico and entrance is on the north side in line with the mihrab. The Orhan Ghazi also has a similar plan but here the size of the prayer hall is increased by four large (approximately 9 by 2.5 m) arched recesses which make it twice as large as the Haci Özbek Cami whose dome is approximately the same size. The walls are pierced with windows and the mihrab is flanked by two large windows in an arrangement which became standard in later Ottoman mosques. The Orhan Ghazi Mosque also has a detached minaret which may be the oldest surviving Ottoman minaret.

The next major development in Ottoman mosque architecture is the Yeşil Cami at Iznik built in the late fourteenth century (1378–92). This is one of the first buildings for which the name of the architect is known (Haci bin Musa). The portico consists of three long bays set side by side with a high fluted dome in the central bay. The portico is open on three sides with the entrance in the middle of the north side formed by a stone door frame. The portico leads into the main part of the mosque which contains a rectangular vestibule and a prayer hall. The vestibule is an arcade of three bays resting on two thick columns and opening into the main prayer hall. The central bay of the arcade is covered by a fluted dome and is flanked by two flat-topped cross vaults. The prayer hall is the usual square domed unit although its diameter is slightly larger (11 m) and the vestibule on the north side appears to increase its floor area. The Seljuk-style brick minaret is set on the north-west side of the mosque, a position which became traditional in Ottoman mosques.

The capture of Bursa in 1325 led to its growth as the Ottoman capital city with mosques, khans, public baths and madrassas. A result of this centralizing process was the development of new, more specialized, architectural forms. The most remarkable changes occurred in mosque architecture with Orhan's royal mosque which is an adaptation of the Ottoman square domed unit to a Seljuk madrassa plan. The building consists of a central domed courtyard opening on to three domed chambers one either side on the east and west and a larger one on the south side. The building is entered via a five-bay portico and a small vestibule. The plan is ultimately derived from the Iranian four-iwan plan although the northern iwan has been reduced to a shallow vestibule. The side rooms were used as teaching areas as the building was also a zawiya, or convent, and the main room to the south is the prayer hall. The courtyard dome is higher than that of the prayer hall and originally had an occulus or hole at the apex to let in light and air. This plan was later used by Orhan's successor Murat for the famous Hüdavendigâr Mosque which he built just outside Bursa at Çekirge. This extraordinary two-storey building combines two functions, a zawiya on the ground floor and a madrassa on top. The combination seems particularly surprising when it is realized that the zawiya represents a mystical form of Islam and the madrassa represents orthodox Sunni Islam which would generally have been opposed to mystical sects. This combination suggests a royal attempt to incorporate reconciled mystical and orthodox forces in the service of the Ottoman state.

The zawiya on the ground floor has the same basic T-plan as Orhan's mosque with a central domed courtyard leading off to iwans; however, in this building the iwans are vaults instead of domes and the mihrab projects out of the south wall of the southern iwan. The walls of the central courtyard and the prayer hall are raised up above the upper floor thus forming a two-storey courtyard. The upper floor is reached by twin staircases either side of the main entrance which lead upwards to a five-bay portico directly above that on the ground floor. Five entrances lead off the portico into the body of the madrassa which also has a four-iwan plan around a central courtyard. The centre of the courtyard is occupied by the prayer hall and courtyard from the ground floor and so is reduced to a vaulted walkway with windows opening on to the courtyard below. To the north of the upper courtyard between the staircases is a vaulted iwan which is the main entrance to the upper floor. Either side of the courtyard are six vaulted cells whilst at the south end there is a domed room directly above the mihrab on the ground floor. The same T-plan is used for the mosque of Murat's successor Beyazit, built between 1391 and 1395. Modifications in this mosque include the positioning of the lateral iwans along the side of the prayer hall, or in other words the prayer hall is brought into the body of the mosque instead of projecting beyond it. This building is also noted for its portico which is regarded as the first monumental Ottoman portico because of its height and the use of wide stilted arches to create an elevated and open space separate from the mosque inside. The Yeşil Cami built in 1412 has essentially the same plan although the portico was not completed.

In addition to the royal mosque Beyazit also built the first great Ottoman congregational mosque or Ulu Cami at Bursa. The building was begun in 1396 and completed four years later in 1400. Before this period congregational mosques had usually been re-used Byzantine churches. The Ulu Cami represents a different design concept from either the square domed unit or the Bursa T-plan mosques and is more closely related to the ancient mosques of Syria, Egypt and Iraq. The Ulu Cami consists of a large rectangular enclosure five bays wide by four bays deep (63 by 50 m) and roofed by twenty domes resting on twelve massive central piers. The mihrab is centrally placed and is on the same axis as the main doorway. In the second bay in front of the mihrab is the courtyard represented by an open dome above a sunken pool. The mosque has two minarets, one on the north-east and one on the north-west corner of the mosque; the north-east minaret was added later by Mehmet I, some time after 1413. Mehmet also built a smaller version of the Bursa Ulu Cami at Edirne known as the Eski (old) Cami which consists of nine domes.

The climax of the first period of Ottoman architecture was the Yeşil Cami at Bursa which was part of a complex built for Mehmet I. The complex consists of a mosque, madrassa, bath house (hammam), an imaret, or kitchen, and the turba (tomb) of Mehmet. Earlier sultans had built complexes such as that of Beyazit or Orhan, but this is the best preserved example of its type. The madrassa has a standard form consisting of cells on three sides and a domed prayer hall on the south side. The kitchen and bath house are both rectangular domed structures whilst the turba is an octagonal domed building located high up above the rest of the complex. The mosque is of the familiar Bursa T-plan design and closely resembles that of the Beyazit complex. The chief differences are the use of brilliant green tiles to decorate the interior and royal boxes or loggias which overlook the internal domed courtyard.

The development of mosques and religious buildings is paralleled in secular architecture by the evolution of classical Ottoman forms from the Seljuk period. The clearest examples of this are bridges, which in the early period are graceful structures with a high central arch flanked by two lower arches, whereas those of the later period are more heavily built in the Roman style, with a succession of evenly spaced arches resting on massive piers. Several bath houses survive from this period particularly in Bursa which contains simple structures like the Çekige Hammam and complex double-domed structures like the Bey Hammam. The plan of these bath houses develops from a single-domed area leading off to two or three smaller domed or vaulted chambers to a building consisting of one or two large domed areas which open on to a series of small cells arranged around a cruciform covered courtyard.

Classical Period

The second period of Ottoman architecture, often referred to as the 'Classical' period, has its origins in the Üç Şerefeli Cami in Edirne built by Murat II and completed in 1447 six years before the conquest of Constantinople. The Üç Şerefeli Mosque had its origins in the fourteenth-century Ulu Cami of Manisa which was visited by Murat II sometime before 1437. The Ulu Cami of Manisa differs from others of the time in having a large central dome in front of the mihrab covering a space equivalent to nine bays. The Manisa Ulu Cami is also unusual because the central courtyard is separated from the main body of the mosque and is not covered by a dome as in the Bursa tradition. Both of these features were found in the Üç Şerefeli Mosque built over seventy years later. However, the dome of the Edirne mosque is much larger and measures over 24 m in diameter, more than double that of its Manisa prototype. Also in the Edirne mosque, the size of the central courtyard is increased so that it resembles those of Syria and Egypt rather than the internal courtyards of the Bursa tradition. However, the arcade on the south side of the courtyard adjacent to the sanctuary of the mosque is raised up in the manner of earlier Ottoman porticoes (e.g. Beyazit Cami in Bursa). The exterior of the building is distinguished by four minarets placed outside each corner of the courtyard. The two north minarets have one balcony (şeref) each whilst the south-east minaret has two balconies and the massive north-west minaret (from which the mosque gets its name) has three balconies each with its own spiral staircase.

The conquest of Constantinople in 1453 exposed Ottoman architects to a whole new range of buildings, the most important of which is the Hagia Sophia (Aya Sophia) which was immediately converted into a mosque by the addition of a wooden minaret to one of the corner turrets. The new concepts introduced by the Üç Şerefeli were not immediately incorporated into Ottoman buildings, and the first mosques were either converted churches or single-domed units in the traditional style. The first major complex to include these features was the Mehmet Fatih Cami built for Murat II between 1463 and 1470. Unfortunately the complex suffered an earthquake in 1766 and the main part of the mosque collapsed so that the present building is an eighteenth-century replica built on the same foundations. The most notable feature of the Fatih Cami was its 26 m dome which for the next hundred years was the largest dome in the empire with the exception of the Hagia Sophia dome of 32 m. The internal arrangement of the Fatih Cami consisted of a large central dome combined with a semi-dome of similar diameter flanked on two sides by three smaller domes and a half dome. This huge area (approximately 40 by 58 m) is entirely open except for two massive piers either side of the semi-dome and two smaller piers either side of the main dome. Outside the mosque is the original rectangular courtyard built to the same design as the Üç Şerefeli Cami courtyard although here there are only two minarets placed against the north wall of the mosque. In addition to the mosque itself the Fatih Cami is remarkable for the ordered geometry of the vast complex which surrounds it. The complex is located on an artificially levelled terrace with the western part of the complex raised up on a vaulted substructure. To the west and east of the mosque are eight orthodox madrassas, four on the west and four on the east side. The design of the madrassas is uniform and consists of nineteen cells arranged around three sides of a rectangular arcaded courtyard with a domed teaching room (dershane) on the fourth side. The complex also includes a hospital and a hostel for travellers and dervishes built on a similar plan to the madrassas.

The next major imperial complex was built by Beyazit II at Edirne in 1484. This complex is the major monument to Beyazit's reign and significantly is not in Istanbul, which was dominated by Mehmet's complex, but at Edirne the former capital. The mosque at the centre of the complex combined the new concepts of courtyard and large domes with older ideas of the single-domed unit and the incorporation of tabhanes (hostels for dervishes). The central area of the mosque is a single square unit covered with a dome of 20 m diameter. Flanking this central area but separate from it are two square nine-domed tabhanes (one on either side). Although separate from the central area the tabhanes are definitely part of the mosque as they are both incorporated into the south side of the courtyard and each has a minaret attached on the exposed north corner. The rest of the complex includes the elements found in earlier structures, although here the buildings are specifically directed towards medical facilities, thus there is a hospital, asylum and medical college as well as the usual kitchen, bath house and bakery. The main hospital building is hexagonal and consists of series of iwans opening on to a central hexagonal hall covered by a dome. Another complex built by Beyazit at Amasya also contains a building which departs from the traditional square form of Ottoman architecture. This is the Kapiaga Madrassa which is an octagonal building built around a central arcaded courtyard.

Although Beyazit's complex at Edirne is the largest monument to his reign, probably the finest is his mosque in Istanbul begun in 1491. The building has a cruciform plan consisting of the square domed sanctuary, a square courtyard of equal size and two small rectangular wings projecting out of the sides. Like the Edirne mosque these wings were officially tabhanes although unlike Edirne they are not separated from the main area of the mosque by walls suggesting resting rooms rather than hostels. The architectural achievement of this mosque is the incorporation of a second semi-dome so that the large central dome (in this case only 17 m diameter) is balanced by a semi-dome either side, one above the door and the other above the mihrab. Either side of this central domed area are rows of four domes balancing the space of the central area. Like other imperial mosques before it with the exception of the Üç Şerefeli Mosque, this building has two minarets placed at the northern corners of the covered area. The next major mosque to be erected in Istanbul was the Selim I Cami completed in 1522 during the reign of Suleyman the Magnificent. The building comprised a single-domed space flanked by tabhanes and opening on to a rectangular arcaded courtyard. The main dome has a diameter of 24.5 m and was the largest Ottoman dome of the time. However, the design of the building with its single dome covering a square area recalled earlier Ottoman mosques and represented no significant architectural advance. The real advance came with Sinan, whose designs ensured him a place as the foremost of Ottoman architects.

Sinan's first major project was the mosque of Şehzade built for Suleyman the Magnificent in memory of his son Şehzade who died at the age of 22. The mosque was begun in 1543 and completed five years later. The main feature of the design was the quatrefoil arrangement of domes based on the use of a single central dome flanked by four semi-domes, one on each side. The idea was not entirely new and had been used before in the Fatih Pasha Cami at Diyarbakir and Piri Pasha Mosque at Hasköy. Sinan's achievement was to translate this plan into a large scale and reduce to a minimum the obstruction of piers to create an open space horizontally and vertically. The domes rest on four huge central piers and sixteen wall piers and four major corner piers which also functioned as buttresses for the outward thrust of the domes. The size and proportions of the domed area are matched by those of the courtyard, a symmetry which is improved by the absence of the tabhane rooms of the Beyazit and Selim mosques.

Sinan's next major work was the mosque of Suleyman the Magnificent begun in 1550 and known as the Süleymaniye. This building and its associated complex was Sinan's largest commission and took seven years to build. Like the Fatih complex the Süleymaniye is located on a large artificially levelled terrace and has foundations which reach 12 m into the ground. At the centre the complex consists of the mosque in the middle with a courtyard to the north and a tomb garden to the south all enclosed within a wall defining the mosque precincts (cf. ziyada). Outside this enclosure are the usual buildings of an imperial complex including a hospital, medical college, hospice, advanced religious college, primary school, soup kitchen and bath house. In the north-east corner of the complex there is a small garden containing the tomb of Sinan who was buried there thirty years after the completion of this complex. The mosque at the centre of the complex was covered by a large central dome (26 m diameter) contained within two semi-domes instead of the four used at Şehazade's complex. Either side of the central dome are a series smaller domes alternating in size from 5 to 10 m in diameter. The same principal of four massive central piers and several external piers is used here as in the Şehzade Mosque although here the arrangement of the outer piers is more complex – on the south (qibla) side they are on the outside as buttresses whilst on the north side abutting the courtyard they are inside the mosque to enable a neat join with the courtyard portico.

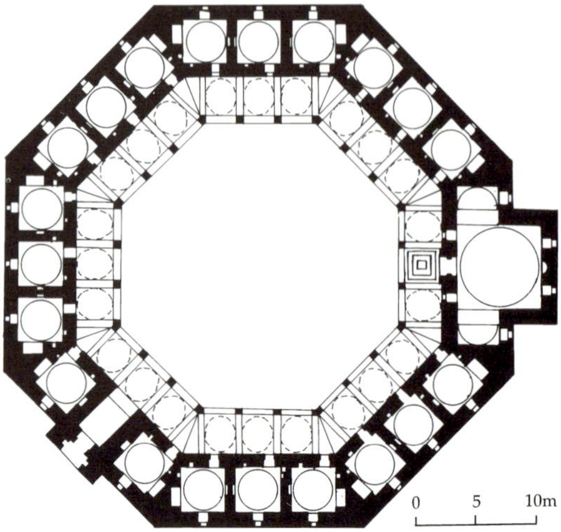

Kapiaga Madrassa, Amasya, Turkey (sixteenth century)

Several other of Sinan's buildings stand out including the Rüstem Pasha Cami noted for its profusion of Iznik tilework, the Mirimah Pasha Cami and the Zal Mahmut Pasha complex. However, undoubtedly Sinan's greatest achievement is the Selimiye Cami in Edirne built between 1569 and 1575. This building, with a dome of equal dimensions to that of Hagia Sophia, is regarded as the supreme achievement of Ottoman architecture. The brilliance of the building relies on the enormous size of the dome which is emphasized by the use of giant squinches or exhedra instead of the semi-domes used earlier at the Süleymaniye or the Şehzade Mosque. In the earlier buildings the semi-domes tended to break up the interior space whereas the giant squinches emphasize the circular space. The central dome and its supporting domes rest on eight huge circular piers which are detached from the exterior walls and appear as free-standing columns although they are actually tied to huge external piers of buttresses. The mihrab space is emphasized by placing it in an apse-like half-dome which projects out of the mosque between the two southern piers. Like the Üç Şerefeli Cami the Selimiye is equipped with four minarets, two on the north side of the dome and two at the north end of the courtyard. Although Sinan continued for another thirteen years after the completion of the Selimiye, his most important work had already been done.

In contrast to the advances of religious architecture, secular buildings of the period are fairly conservative and tend to stick to established forms. Where there is development this is often influenced by mosque architecture; thus the Haseki Hürrem Hammam in Istanbul designed by Sinan owes much of its grandeur to its tall domes inspired by contemporary mosques. Civil engineering, including bridges and forts, is characterized by solid construction and austere design reminiscent of Roman architecture. This can be seen in Rumeli Hisar, the fortress built by Mehmet II to control the Bosphorus before the conquest of Constantinople. The building consists of a huge enclosure (approximately 220 by 100 m) formed by three huge towers (two semicircular and one polygonal) linked by a tall crenellated wall strengthened by interval towers or bastions. The interior was filled with a mosque and a large number of wooden buildings which have now disappeared. The bastions and towers represent a variety of different shapes and designs which suggest that the fortress was built by a number of individuals working to a broad general design rather than a detailed architect's plan. Bridges on the other hand tended to be built to a standard plan which was applied to a variety of situations. The most famous bridge of the period is that of Büyükçekmice to the west of Istanbul; built by Sinan in 1566, it consists of a series of four humped bridges resting on three artificial islands. At the west end of the bridge there is a rectangular caravanserai covered with a wooden gabled roof. Other important caravanserais of the period include the Sokollu Mehmed Pasha Caravanserai at Lüleburgaz and the Selim II complex at Payas in eastern Anatolia both built by Sinan. One area where secular architecture was innovative and influential was in the imperial palace or Topkapisarai. This building was established as the centre of imperial power soon after Mehmed II entered Istanbul and remained the centre until the collapse of Ottoman power in the twentieth century. Several parts of the fifteenth-century palace remain, the most important of which is the Çinili Kiosk built in 1473. This pavilion, based on a four-iwan plan, was designed by a Persian architect and decorated with blue glazed bricks in Timurid style. The building influenced much of the subsequent domestic architecture of Istanbul, in particular some of the Bosphorus mansions.

Later Period

In the last years of the sixteenth century and the first years of the seventeenth century Ottoman architecture continued to use the forms and style developed by Sinan during the Classical period. Thus the Yeni Valide complex built by Sinan's successor Davut is a copy of the Şehzade Mosque with a few alterations to the size and shape of the courtyard. The most famous building in this late classical style is the Sultan Ahmet Cami in Istanbul also known as the Blue Mosque begun in 1609 and completed in 1617. The most distinctive feature of this building is the use of six minarets instead of the previous maximum of four. It is roofed with the quatrefoil design used in the Şehzade Cami with four huge cylindrical fluted piers supporting the 23.5 m dome (considerably smaller than the Selimiye). The plan has several weaknesses, the most notable of which is the way the mihrab is placed in the middle of a flat wall without any architectural emphasis. Also the portico is not raised to the level of the central domed area thus making the mosque and courtyard seem like two independent units rather than a gradual development of mass.

From the end of the sixteenth century slavish copying of the Classical style was gradually replaced; characteristic features of the new style are flamboyant decoration, increased use of windows and curves, and growing European influences. The most famous example is the Nuruosmaniye Cami in Istanbul completed in 1755. The plan of this building is still based on the square covered by a dome but the strict geometry of the Classical period is modified, thus there are small projecting wings either end of the qibla wall and the mihrab is located in a curved apse in a manner similar to that of the Selimiye in Edirne although here the apse is curved. The recessed porches, which in earlier mosques would have been filled with muqarnas mouldings, are here filled with carved acanthus leaves. The most striking feature of the building is the courtyard which is built in a curved D-shape with the straight side forming the portico of the mosque. The courtyard is also unusual because the domes above the two north entrances are pierced with a series of arched windows which add to the light coming from the trefoil arched windows at the sides. The absence of a central fountain and the positioning of the mosque on an irregular-shaped terrace add to the surprise of this building. Other eighteenth- and nineteenth-century mosques, however, retained the strict square geometry which was now prescribed by the religious orthodoxy as the necessary form for a mosque. Thus the Laleli Cami and complex built ten years later in 1783 has a conventional plan, although this is modified by making the prayer hall rectangular instead of square, by cutting off the two side aisles either side of the main dome and making them into external arcades. The apse form of the mihrab area used in the Nuruosmaniye is retained although here it has a square form similar to the Selimiye in Edirne instead of the curved form of the Nuruosmaniye. The Laleli is also noticeable for its use of Ionic capitals instead of the muqarnas capitals preferred in the Classical period.

Several methods were used to break away from the enforced geometry of the square domed unit; one method was to give an undulating curved form to the outer edges of domes. This was a technique which was first used on the wooden roofs of sebils (fountains) and kiosks such as that on the tomb of Mehmet II rebuilt in 1784. The use of this technique on mosque domes can be seen on the Beylerbey Cami of 1778 and in an extravagant form at the Iliyas Bey Cami built in 1812. Similar techniques were used for windows and arches which had undulating curves hung as drapery in the European manner. Outside the strict boundaries of orthodoxy there was more room for experimentation, thus the Küçük Efendi complex in Istanbul was built for dervishes and has a radical plan. The building, completed in 1825, consists of an oval structure which combines a mosque and dervish dance hall.

The nineteenth century saw the emergence of new building forms and types influenced by Europe. The most successful of these new forms was the clock tower which by the beginning of the First World War had been established in Ottoman cities throughout the empire. The earliest example was a three-storey wooden tower outside the Nusretiye Cami in Istanbul, other early examples are at Yozgat and Adana. The extent of European influence can be seen in the decision to move the royal residence from the Topkapisarai in old Istanbul to the newly fashionable banks of the Bosphorus. The new residence known as the Dolmabahçe Palace was built in 1853 in the European Classical style with a colonnaded façade looking out over the water. The palace stretches out along the side of the Bosphorus in a series of blocks or wings, the most famous of which is the throne room measuring 44 by 46 m.

Increased European interest in Ottoman and Seljuk architecture also stimulated an interest in revivalist architecture. One of the earliest examples of revivalism in Turkish architecture is the palace of Ishak Pasha at Dogubayazit in eastern Anatolia completed in 1784. This imposing building, set against the backdrop of Mount Ararat, recalls the Seljuk architecture of eastern Anatolia with carved animals and huge monumental doorways. However, this building is exceptional and it is not until the late nineteenth and early twentieth centuries that revivalism becomes established as a style in Ottoman art. Notable examples are the Vakif Han built by Kemalettin in 1914 and the Istanbul main post office built in 1909. Both these buildings incorporate medieval and early Ottoman features in buildings made using modern methods and materials.

See also: Albania, Bosnia, Bulgaria, Bursa, Byzantine architecture, Cairo, Cyprus, Edirne, Greece, Iraq, Istanbul, Iznik, Jordan, Lebanon, Palestine, Sinan, Syria, Turkey

Further reading:

O. Aslanapa, *Turkish Art and Architecture,* London 1971.

Y. Bingöl, *Der Ishak Pascha Palast in Dogubayazit am Berg Ararat,* Berlin 1982.

M. Cezar, *Typical Commercial Buildings of the Ottoman Classical Period and the Ottoman Construction System,* Istanbul 1983.

A. Gabriel, *Les Monuments turcs d'anatolie,* 2 vols., Paris 1931–4.

—— *Châteaux turcs du Bosphore,* Paris 1943.

—— *Une Capitale turque, Brousse,* Paris 1958.

G. Goodwin, *A History of Ottoman Architecture,* London 1971.

—— *Ottoman Turkey,* London 1977.

A. Kuran, *The Mosque in Early Ottoman Architecture,* Chicago 1968.

J. M. Rogers and R. M. Ward, *Suleyman the Magnificent,* London 1988.

I. Utkular, *Çanakkale Bogazinda Fatih Keleleri,* Istanbul 1954.

Oualata (also known as Walata, Iwalatan and Birou)

Important trading city in south-west Mauritania.

The collapse of the empire of Ghana in 1224 led refugees from Awdaghast to found a new city in the small village of Birou. The new city was called Oualata and contained immigrants from several ethnic groups including Berbers, Islamized Soninke and Massufa nomads. The Berbers were the religious leaders as well as the merchants whilst the Soninke provided craftsmen and the Massufa nomads acted as caravan leaders and guides. The rise of the empire of Mali and the subsequent shift of political power to the south strengthened the position of Oualata as a regional centre and as a terminus for trans-Saharan caravans. The main partner for this desert trade was the city of Sijimassa from which goods would be traded to Fez and Tlemcen in Morocco.

During the fourteenth century Mansa Musa started his famous pilgrimage from Oualata and on his return brought with him the famous architect and poet al-Saheli who built an audience hall there. In 1352 the city was visited by Ibn Battuta who stayed there for seven weeks. He described the city as a cosmopolitan trading and intellectual centre under the administration of the empire of Mali. In the sixteenth century a new component was added to the city's ethnic composition with the arrival of the Arabic Beni Hassan tribe. The lasting result of this was the adoption of Hassaniya, a mixed Arabic Berber language which became the main language of commerce in the city. The other main language of Oualata is the Soninke language of Azer.

The buildings of Oualata are made of stone with roofs made of split-palm beams and palm-frond matting overlaid with earth. The houses consist of a central courtyard entered through an inner and outer vestibule. There are often two storeys in the houses with the upper floor reached by an external staircase in the courtyard. All the rooms lead directly off from the courtyard which is the centre of activity and contains beds for the servants. The stone walls of the houses are covered with a thick layer of mud plaster (banco) on both the outside and the inside. This technique is unique to Oualata and distinguishes it from other Berber towns of Mauritania suggesting the influence of non-Berber architecture from further south. This idea is strengthened by the fact that the mud rendering is carried out by the women of the society. The most remarkable feature of the earthen rendering is the application of striking white-painted designs around the doorways, windows and niches of the courtyard. It is noticeable that the designs are restricted to the interior of the courtyards and are not visible from the outside, consisting of arabesque medallions and chain motifs executed in thick but precise white lines. The most elaborate decoration is reserved for the doorway of the senior wife's room where a number of different motifs are used to produce a highly ornate design. The doorways are made of wooden planks with wooden locks and are decorated with Moroccan brass medallions. Either side of the doorway are elaborately carved wooden pillars, or asnads, which are used as calabash supports. The pillars are set into an earthen base made in the shape of a small stepped pyramid but at the top divide into three branches. Similar pillars are found in Berber tents and their presence in these houses are reminders of a nomadic past. Inside, the rooms are fairly bare except for a large canopied platform bed hung with tapestries and mats.

See also: Agades, Timbuktu, West Africa

Further reading:

G. J. Duchemin, 'A propos des decorations murales des habitations de Oualata (Mauretanie)', *Bulletin IFAN* 12(4): 1095–110, 1950.

O. Du Puigaudeau, 'Contribution à l'étude du symbolisme dans le décor mural et l'artisanat de Walat', *Bulletin IFAN* 19(1–2): 137–83, 1957.

P

Pakistan

Predominantly Muslim country in the north-west corner of the Indian subcontinent.

Pakistan is located in a strategic position with Afghanistan and Iran to the west, India to the east, the Sinkiang region of China to the north and the Indian Ocean to the south. Running down the centre of the country from the Chinese border to the Indian Ocean is the Indus river which unites the diverse regions and cultures through which it passes. In the north and west the country is dominated by the highest mountains in the world and includes parts of Himalayas, the Hindu Kush and the Karakoram mountain ranges. Officially the country is divided into five regions, the Northern Areas, the North-West Frontier, the Punjab, Baluchistan and Sind. Each region has its own languages and cultures reflecting a complex historical development. Most of the population lives in the Indus valley which comprises the states of Punjab and Sind. The valley is home to one of the world's oldest civilizations based on the cities of Mohenjodaro and Harrapa which flourished more than 4,000 years ago. During the fourth century BCE the northern part of the country was conquered by Alexander the Great who established a Macedonian garrison at Taxilla. The Greeks were soon defeated by the Mauryans who later introduced Buddhism as the state religion. For the next 400 years or more the region was the centre of a Graeco-Indian Buddhist culture illustrated by the great stupas of Taxilla. During the fifth century CE there was a period of Hindu revival under the Gupta dynasty, remains of which can be seen in Hindu and Jain stone shrines.

The first Muslims in Pakistan were probably Arab seafarers taking part in the extensive Indian Ocean trade network. However, the first Muslim conquest of the area was by Mohammad ibn al-Qasim who captured the region of Sind in 711. For the next one and a half centuries Sind was ruled by Umayyad and later Abbasid governors until 873 when the province broke away from the caliphate. The province was now divided into several independent city states the most important of which were Multan and Mansurah. During the tenth century Sind developed as an important centre of Ismaili and Khariji thought which was brought to an abrupt end by the invasions of Mahmud of Ghazni between 1004 and 1008. Several years later the province of Punjab, then under Hindu control, was captured by Mahmud who established a fort and mint at Lahore. For the next 150 years much of the present area of Pakistan was under Ghaznavid control, until the invasions of Mahmud of Ghur at the end of the twelfth century. Mahmud's deputy Qutb al-Din Aybak soon took over and ruled the Punjab from his Indian capital of Delhi. For the following 300 years with a few exceptions Pakistan was under the control of the various dynasties ruling from Delhi the most significant of which was the Tughluqs. In the sixteenth century the Punjab was incorporated into the Mughal Empire and Lahore became one of the three main cities of the empire. For a period of about fifty years in the early nineteenth century the Punjab was under the control of the Sikhs although by the end of the century it was firmly incorporated into British India. In 1947 the Muslim parts of India comprising the modern states of Pakistan and Bangladesh were made independent as one country despite the great distances separating them. In 1970 the country separated into two independent states, Pakistan and Bangladesh.

The range of building materials and techniques used in Pakistan reflects both the variety of its natural environment and its long cultural history. The scarcity of suitable building stone in the Indus valley has meant that mud or clay has always been the main building material. Mud may be used in several forms: as mud brick, baked brick or pisé. Mud brick was first used in the cities of Harrapa and Mohenjodaro over 4,000 years ago and continues to be used in many of the villages of the

Punjab today. Baked brick is used for more permanent structures such as wells, important houses or mosques whilst pisé is used for structures which need to be built cheaply and quickly. On the coast of Sind mud is used as a thick plaster over a wooden frame to produce wattle-and-daub constructions. In the mountains of the North-West Frontier the typical form of construction consists of rubble stone walls set in mud mortar and covered over with a mud-plaster finish. These buildings are covered with flat roofs made of timber branches overlaid with matting and then covered with earth. The only region where timber is plentiful is in the northern region of the Swat valley where there are dense pine forests. The architecture of this region is similar to its Indian neighbour, Kashmir with finely carved wooden mosques covered by pagoda-style roofs.

Archaeological work in Sind has revealed the remains of several early Islamic sites, the most significant of which is Bhambore, thought to be the ancient city of Debal. The city was divided into two parts and enclosed with a defensive wall fortified with semi-circular buttress towers. Probably the most important discovery is the congregational mosque with a large central courtyard and no mihrab. The absence of a mihrab confirms the early date of the building given by an inscription dated to 727.

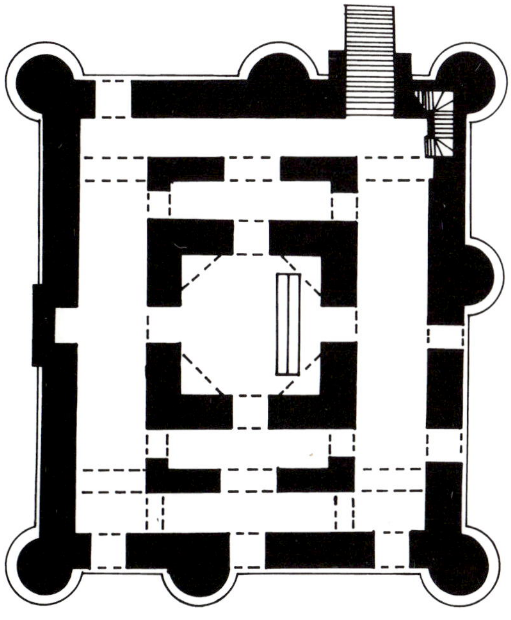

Plan of tomb of Khalid Walid at Kabriwala, Pakistan (after Mumtaz)

Medieval architecture in Pakistan is best represented by the funerary and religious buildings of Multan and Uchch in the Punjab. There are few remains from the Ghaznavid period apart from the twelfth-century tomb of Khaliq Walid or Khalid Walid near Multan. The tomb consists of a rectangular baked-brick enclosure containing a square domed chamber. The outer enclosure wall is strengthened with semi-circular buttress towers and includes a rectangular projection marking the position of the mihrab in the west wall. Inside, the mihrab consists of a rectangular recess covered with an arched hood and framed by bands of inscriptions cut into the brickwork. In the centre of the recess is a blind niche set between pilasters and crowned with a trefoil arch. The design of this mausoleum represents the first stage in the evolution of the medieval tombs of Multan which culminated in the tomb of Shah Rukn-i Alam built during the reign of Ghiyas al-Din Tughluq. In the latter tomb the outer walls no longer form an enclosure but are wrapped around the central octagonal tomb. Externally the walls slope inward and are strengthened at the corners by tapering domed turrets providing a counter thrust to the weight of the dome. The distinctive sloping walls and corner turrets of this tomb were later repeated in the Tughluqid architecture of Delhi.

Another architectural tradition is represented by the flat-roofed tombs and mosques of Uchch a small city to the south of Multan. A typical Uchch mosque consists of a rectangular hall with wooden pillars supporting beams resting on carved brackets. The areas between the beams are covered with wooden boards which are usually painted in yellow or white against a bright orange or red ground. The walls of the buildings are usually made of baked brick covered in decorative cut plaster. Most buildings of this type are entered via a projecting wooden porch also supported on wooden columns. Prominent buildings of this type are the tombs of Jalal Din Surkh Bukhari, Abu Hanifa and Rajan Qattal.

During the sixteenth century most of the area of modern Pakistan was brought under Mughal rule. In general imperial Mughal architecture was restricted to Lahore, whilst the rest of the country developed its own regional style. One exception to this general rule is the fort at Attock in the

North-West Province built by Akbar as a defence against invasion from the west. The fort is built on a hillside between the Indus and Kabul rivers and consists of a huge enclosure wall fortified by projecting machicolations and large round bastions. Other buildings at Attock include the garden and palace of Akbar which are small structures hidden amongst the hills. Certainly the most developed expression of Mughal architecture in Pakistan is the fort at Lahore built by Akbar in 1556 on the banks of the river Ravi. The plan of the Lahore fort resembles those of Agra and Delhi with its riverside position and its arrangement of gardens and pavilions. The fort is entered via a main gateway leading into a large rectangular courtyard with the imperial reception hall (diwan-i amm) in the centre of the wall opposite the entrance. Behind the reception hall is the private area of the palace divided into courtyards and gardens overlooking the river. Apart from the fort the most important imperial building in the city is the Badshahi Mosque built by Aurangzeb in 1674. The mosque has the same general plan as that of the Jami Masjid in Delhi although the Badshahi Mosque is much larger. Other imperial Mughal buildings in Lahore include the tomb of Jahangir, the Shahdara complex and the Shalamar Bagh.

In addition to the imperial Mughal complexes, Lahore also contains some of the finest examples of the regional Mughal style which is a mixture of Mughal forms with local and Persian modifications. Characteristic features of this style are the use of brightly coloured tile mosaics, thick octagonal minarets, wide flattened domes and arches. Probably the finest example of tile mosaic (kashi) is the Picture Wall in the fort at Lahore which includes both animal and human figures. Probably more representative of the local style is the tilework of the Wazir Khan Mosque, where all surfaces are covered with floral and geometric designs in coloured tiles. This mosque also has the earliest examples of the thick octagonal minarets which later became characteristic features of Lahore architecture.

Outside Lahore, Mughal-period architecture may be divided into a number of local styles, the most significant of which is that of Sind. The architecture of Sind was heavily influenced by the neighbouring state of Gujarat in India which consists of heavily carved trabeate stone buildings. Some of the finest examples can be found in the Makli cemetery in

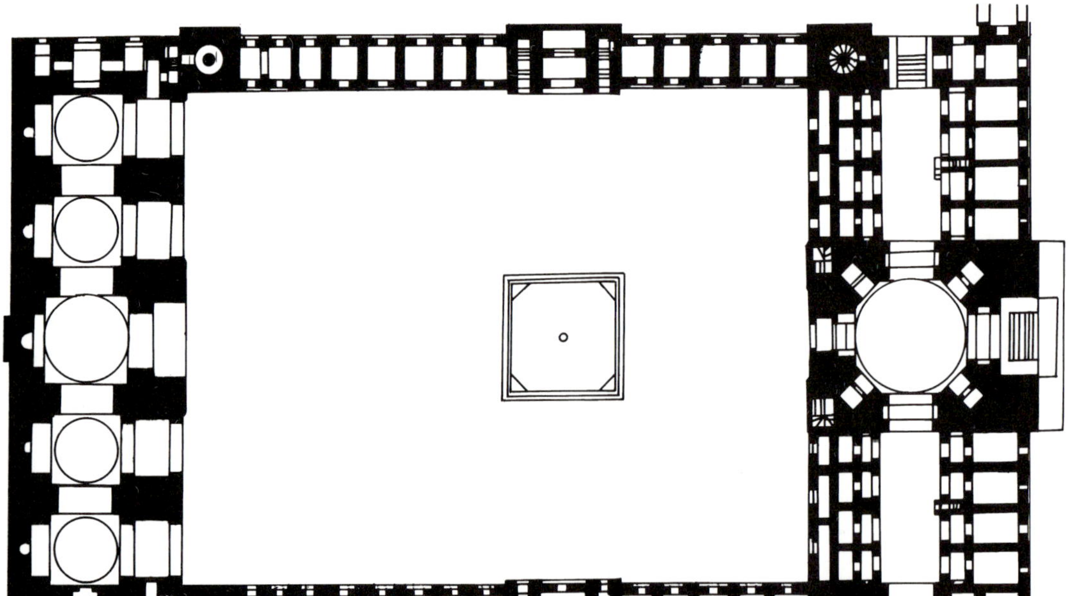

Seventeenth-century Mosque of Wazir Khan, Lahore, Pakistan (after Mumtaz)

lower Sind, where exuberantly carved tombs are covered by corbelled domed canopies resting on square carved monolithic columns. Sind is also noted for its geometric tile mosaics which may have been the inspiration for the more naturalistic tilework of Lahore. Some of the best examples of tilework can be seen in the monuments of Hyderabad and Thatta in upper Sind. Other characteristic features of architecture in this region are the use of multiple blind niches on outer walls and elaborately shaped crenellations. During the period of British rule the architecture of Pakistan was represented by an eclectic mixture of European, Hindu and Mughal styles. Immediately after Independence, Pakistani architecture developed under the influence of Modernism which saw its culmination in the establishment of a new capital at Islamabad in 1960. Although the design of Islamabad was based on religious and national criteria it did not include provision for a national mosque. This situation was rectified in 1970 when work began on the Shah Faisal Masjid which is a huge structure covered with a roof in the form of a truncated pyramid flanked by four tall pointed minarets.

See also: Banbhore, India, Lahore, mihrab, Mughals

Further reading:

A. H. Dani, *Thatta-Islamic Architecture*, Islamabad 1982.
J. Kalter, *The Arts and Crafts of the Swat Valley: Living Traditions in the Hindu Kush*, London 1991.
A. N. Khan, *Uchch History and Architecture*, Islamabad 1983.
F. A. Khan, *Architecture and Art Treasures in Pakistan*, Karachi.
K. K. Mumtaz, *Architecture in Pakistan*, London 1985.
A. B. Rajput, *Architecture in Pakistan*, Karachi 1963.
N. I. Siddiqui, *Thatta*, Karachi 1963.

Palestine

Small country on the eastern shore of the Mediterranean comprising an area of 26,650 square km.

Physically it is divided into four main regions; a low-lying coastal strip along the Mediterranean, a central hilly or mountainous area running north to south through the centre of the country, the Jordan Rift Valley containing the Sea of Galilee and the Dead Sea, and the Negev desert which covers most of the southern part of the country.

Until 1918, when it was conquered by Britain, the country was part of the Ottoman Empire. At present the land is divided between the state of Israel and the occupied territories of Gaza and the West Bank. Israel is a new state created in 1948 with a largely immigrant population, whose architecture is alien to the region. However the people of Gaza and the West Bank are mostly the indigenous inhabitants of the country, whose architecture has developed within the landscape for at least the last two thousand years.

Palestine was one of the first areas to be conquered by the Arab armies of Islam in 637 and from that point onwards has remained one of the main centres of Islamic culture. For some time during the seventh century Muslims were expected to pray towards Jerusalem rather than Mecca, thus establishing Jerusalem's position as one of the holiest sites of Islam. However, throughout the Umayyad period the culture of the area remained predominantly Byzantine and there was only gradual change to a new Islamic culture. With the Abbasid revolution in 750 Palestine was no longer near the centre of the empire and consequently was exposed to a number of competing forces including the Tulunids and Ikhshids. In the tenth century Palestine came under the control of the Fatimids who ruled the area from their newly founded capital at Cairo. During the following century the country was fought over by Byzantines and the Fatimids, but it was eventually conquered by the European Crusaders at the end of the eleventh century. For the next two hundred years, parts of Palestine were ruled by a series of Crusader kings. The Crusaders were gradually expelled through a series of wars conducted first by the Ayyubids under Nur al-Din and Salah al-Din, and later by the Mamluks under Baybars and his successors. Cultural, spiritual and commercial life flourished under the Mamluks until the late fifteenth century when internal problems and external pressures allowed the conquest of the area by the Ottoman Turks in 1516. For the next four hundred years Palestine was part of the Ottoman province of Damascus. However, during this period various local governors were able to achieve semi-independent status. During the eighteenth century Dhahir al 'Umar ruled a large area of northern Palestine and amassed a great deal of wealth from the cotton trade. Dhahir was succeeded by Ahmad al-Jazzar Pasha the governor of Sidon who re-established the city of Acre as one of the major ports of the Mediterranean. During the nineteenth century the country was subjected to increasing European influence with colonies established in Haifa and Jerusalem. The British defeat of the Ottomans in 1918 led to the establishment of the British Mandate which ruled the country until 1948. In 1948 Palestine was divided between Jordan, Israel and Egypt; in 1968 Israel occupied the entire country.

The main building materials in Palestine are stone and unbaked mud brick. Wood and baked brick are hardly ever used. Three main types of stone are used, depending on the region of the country. Along the Mediterranean coast kurkar, a silicous limestone, is used for building. This has the property that it can easily be cut from the outcrops near the seashore, although it also weathers easily and is difficult to dress to a fine finish. Both the cities of Acre and Jaffa are built of this material. In the northern part of the Jordan Rift Valley and around the Sea of Galilee, basalt blocks are used in construction. Basalt is extremely hard and is consequently difficult to cut or carve, although once shaped it does not weather much. As a consequence basalt is often used in combination with limestone which is used for architectural details. The cities of Tiberias and Beisan (Bet Shean) have the best examples of basalt architecture. The best-quality building stone comes from the central hilly region. In this area various types of limestone can be found. Limestone is fairly easy to cut and does not erode as much as kurkar stone. Limestone cut and dressed to a fine finish is known as ashlar masonry and is used in some of the finest buildings in the country. Limestone occurs in a variety of colours from white to honey yellow and pink; some of the best examples can be found in Jerusalem, Hebron and Ramla. In addition various types of marble are obtained from the hills around Jerusalem, whilst Dolomite (hard limestone with magnesium) is used in areas of Galilee.

Until recently a large number of buildings were made out of mud brick and pisé particularly in the Jordan valley and the coastal plain where building stone was not so readily available as in the hills. Mud brick has the advantages of being cheap, easy to work with good thermal insulating properties. Unfortunately mud brick also requires a high degree of maintenance and it has mostly been replaced with reinforced concrete which has some of the same plastic qualities. The best examples of mud-brick architecture still surviving are in Jericho, where a wide variety of buildings, including mosques and cinemas, are built out of this material.

Early Islamic Period

Undoubtedly the most famous building in Palestine is the Dome of the Rock built by the caliph Abd al-Malik in 691. The significance of this building extends beyond its immediate architectural design to its symbolic function of demonstrating the presence of Islam and its status as a major religion in Jerusalem, home to both Christianity and Judaism. Together with the Aqsa Mosque and the Royal Palace to the south of the Haram, Jerusalem's place as a religious and cultural centre of Islam was established.

However, the capital of Palestine during the Umayyad and Abbasid periods was not Jerusalem but Ramla. Like Basra, Kufa and Wasit, Ramla was one of the new towns established in the first years of the Arab conquests. Today little survives of the early Islamic city with the exception of two large underground cisterns, one below the congregational mosque (Jami' al-Abiyad) and one outside the city to the west. Generally, however, the major cities of the Byzantine period continued to be the major settlements; thus archaeology has demonstrated the continued occupation of Lydda, Beisan, Tiberias Gaza, Caesarea and Acre into the Umayyad and Abbasid periods. As much of the population remained Christian, churches continued to be built during the period.

Outside the cities and in the Negev a number of new settlements were built in the early Islamic period. Some of these were agricultural centres, whilst others were palaces and mansions for the new élite. The best known of these is the Umayyad palace of Khirbet al-Mafjar near Jericho in the Jordan valley (known locally as Hisham's palace although it has now been reliably attributed to Walid II). This building was modelled on a Roman bath house and was lavishly decorated with mosaics and stucco. The stucco includes representations of semi-naked women and is unique in Islamic art. A similar but smaller structure was built at the south end of Lake Tiberias (the Sea of Galilee) in an area of hot springs. The original building was a Roman fort although this was substantially rebuilt during the Umayyad period to resemble a palace, with mosaics etc.

In the Negev large numbers of early Islamic sites have been found, which indicate a growth in the settlement of the area. This parallels the increased building activity in the deserts of Jordan, Iraq and Saudi Arabia and may be linked to a shift in emphasis towards Arabia in the early Islamic period.

Increasing political tension and fragmentation in the later Abbasid and Fatimid periods meant that few major monuments can be dated to this period. Significantly two large monuments in Palestine which can be dated to this period (tenth and eleventh centuries) are fortified structures built to guard against an impending Byzantine invasion. One of these buildings, Kefar Lam is built on the north coast south of Haifa and the other, Mina al-Qal'a (now known as Ashdod Yam) is located on the southern coast near Ashdod. Both are built of thin slabs of kurkar stone (laid in a manner resembling brick construction) forming large rectangular enclosures with solid corner towers and semi-circular buttresses. The fort at Ashdod was fairly luxurious and includes a line of marble columns in the centre re-used from the classical site of Ashdod. Outside the fort at Ashdod there are the remains of a domed building which has been interpreted as a bath house. The domes are supported on shell-like squinches (characteristic of the Fatimid period) with pierced holes for light.

Crusader Period

The Crusader conquest of Palestine had a profound influence on the appearance of the country. In Jerusalem the Aqsa Mosque was converted into a palace by Baldwin I and the Dome of the Rock was converted into an Augustinian church. In the countryside numerous castles, tower houses and churches testify to the Crusader presence. The castles guarding prominent positions are perhaps the best-known architectural legacy of the Crusades. The most famous in Palestine are Monfort and Belvoir, although there are numerous smaller fortresses throughout the area. Typically a Crusader castle consisted of a square or rectangular tower surrounded by thick enclosing walls. The enclosure walls would follow the shape of the land unlike the regular shapes of the earlier Islamic forts. Many of the features found in Crusader fortification were later re-used in Arab castles such as Ajlun (Qal'at Rabad) and Nimrud.

Whilst the Crusader castles controlled the land physically, the spiritual possession of the holy land was marked by the construction of hundreds of churches. In Jerusalem alone there were sixty, some of which were built on the ruins of Byzantine churches. The churches were distinguished with fine carved capitals and sculptures.

With the Muslim reconquest of Jerusalem in 1187 the Crusader presence was reduced to the area around Acre, which for the next hundred years (until it too fell in 1191) was the centre of the Crusader kingdoms, and was enriched with some of the finest Crusader architecture in the Middle East.

The Crusades influenced the architecture of Palestine in two ways: directly through the copying of techniques and the re-use of buildings, and indirectly through the development of the counter-Crusade. The direct influence is seen in the adaptation of certain techniques for Islamic buildings such as cushion-shaped voussoirs and folded cross vaults, all of which can be found in the Mamluk buildings of Jerusalem. One of the best examples of this influence can be seen in the minaret of the Great Mosque of Ramla, which resembles a Crusader church tower. The indirect influence can be seen in the development of a propaganda expressed through monumental inscriptions and carved devices. One of the most famous examples of the latter, of the lion of Baybars catching a mouse, is depicted on the Lion Gate in Jerusalem (this can also be seen at Jisr Jindas between Ramla and Lydda).

Mamluk Era

Mamluk rule in Palestine produced some of the best examples of medieval architecture in the Middle East, with a proliferation of religious buildings including mosques, madrassas, khanqas and commemorative mausoleums. Jerusalem in particular was provided with a large number of religious buildings as befitted Islam's holiest shrine after Mecca and Medina. Mamluk architecture in Jerusalem was characterized by the use of joggled voussoirs, ablaq masonry, muqarnas mouldings and coloured marble inlays. In Ramla, the Great Mosque was rebuilt and the Crusader church was converted into a mosque.

One of the more beautiful Mamluk buildings of Palestine is the tomb of Abu Hoeira near Yabne (modern Yavne). This consists of a triple-domed portico and a central area covered by a large dome set on squinches. The decoration is restrained and restricted to the areas around the doorway and mihrab which are decorated with inlaid marble and inscriptions.

A characteristic feature of the Mamluk period was the revitalization of the road systems which were provided with khans, mosques and bridges. Examples of Mamluk khans include Khan al-Tujjar, Khan al-Minya, Jaljuliyya, Ramla and Lydda. Probably the most impressive of these is Khan Yunis at Ghaza built out of ablaq masonry with a mosque and minaret included in its design. Several Mamluk bridges survive in Palestine, the most impressive of which is Jisr Jindas, decorated with an inscription flanked by two lions (other bridges include Jisr Banat Yaqub and a bridge at Beisan).

Ottoman Conquest

The Ottoman conquest of Palestine in 1516 introduced new architectural concepts, although these were only gradually adopted and never became universal. The most obvious symbol of the Ottoman conquest was the redevelopment of Jerusalem; this included rebuilding the walls, tiling the Dome of the Rock and renovating the city's water supply.

The city of Acre, rebuilt in the eighteenth century, is the best example of a complete Ottoman city in Palestine. It has several khans, at least two bath houses, three main suqs, at least ten mosques and a citadel. The wealth of the city was expressed in the mosque of al-Jazzar Pasha and the large bath complex known as Hammam al-Basha. The mosque was modelled on those of Istanbul with a large central dome and a pencil-like minaret. The baths were extensively decorated with Armenian tiles and inlaid marble floors. The houses of Acre were two, three- or even four-storeyed structures with painted wooden ceilings.

Important cities during the Ottoman period included Hebron, Nablus, Ramla, Jaffa, Safed, Tiberias and Acre (from the eighteenth century onwards). Most of the cities were surrounded by walls, the best surviving example of which are the walls of Tiberias rebuilt by Dhahir al 'Umar. The walls of Acre date mostly from the late eighteenth century and are of Italian design.

The houses of Ottoman Palestine varied depending on the region in which they were located. There are few or no remains of the mud-brick houses of the coastal plain although the stone houses of the villages have survived well until recent times. The predominant form of roofing for stone houses was the dome made by filling a room with earth, covering this with a reed mat and then building the dome over the top. During the eighteenth century domes were often decorated with carved plaster usually in the form of swirls, rosettes and semi-circles. In Galilee, buildings were roofed by using transverse stone arches to support short beams over which a roof could be laid.

Outside Jerusalem Ottoman control was established through a series of forts garrisoned by Janissaries (imperial Ottoman troops). These fortresses were large square or rectangular structures with square corner towers; surviving examples can be seen at Ras al-Ain near Tel Aviv, Khan al-Tujjar near Kefar Kanna and Qal'at Burak south of Jerusalem.

See also: Abbasids, al-Aqsa Mosque, Dome of the Rock, Fatimids, Jersalem, Khirbet al-Mafjar, Khirbet al-Minya, Mamluks, Ottomans, Ramla, Umayyads

Further reading:

S. Amiry and V. Tamari, *Palestinian Village Architecture*, London 1990.

T. Canaan, *Mohammedan Saints and Santuaries in Palestine*, Jerusalem 1927.

—— *The Palestinian Arab House*, Jerusalem 1933.

L. Mayer, *Some Principal Muslim Religious Buildings in Israel*, Jerusalem 1950.

Persia

See Iran.

Philippines

Country composed of a group of islands on the east side of the South China Sea between Taiwan, Indonesia and Malaysia.

The country consists of two main islands, Mindanao in the south and Luzon in the north and more than twenty smaller islands. The south-western islands have a large Muslim population whereas the northern ones are predominantly Roman Catholic. Filipino Muslims share much in common with their Indonesian and Malaysian neighbours who first introduced Islam to the Philippines. The first areas to be converted to Islam were the islands of the Sulu archipelago between the fourteenth and fifteenth centuries. By the mid-sixteenth century Muslim missionaries from Borneo were working on the island of Luzon. However, earlier in 1522 the islands were discovered by the Spanish who established their first permanent settlement in 1565 and in 1571 founded the capital of Manila. There was some conflict with the newly established Muslim sultanates of Luzon but the Spanish won with their superior firepower. Nevertheless, the south-western part of the Philippines remained Muslim despite constant attempts to defeat them by the Spanish. The Muslims of the islands were given the name Moros by the Spanish who associated them with the Muslims of North Africa. Throughout the seventeenth, eighteenth and nineteenth centuries the Spanish tried unsuccessfully to conquer the Moro people. When the Philippines passed into American control in 1898 the Americans continued the Spanish policy of trying to subdue the Muslims of the south-west. In 1913 the Moros were finally defeated by superior American arms and a peace treaty was signed. The peace treaty was a success as it allowed the Muslims complete control over their own affairs and equality with the Catholic Filipinos.

The earliest physical evidence of Islam in the Philippines is a tombstone on the island of Jolo which has been provisionally dated to 1310. Oral history recounts how Islam was brought to the island of Jolo by Tuan ul Makdum (later called Sharif Aulia) who built 'a house for religious worship'. Later, in 1380 he built another mosque at Tubig Indangan on Simunul island south of Jolo. This mosque, considerably altered, is now known as the oldest mosque in the Philippines. A photograph of the building taken in 1923 shows a square wooden structure open on one side with remains of a two-tier coconut-palm thatch roof. The mosque was comprehensively rebuilt in the 1970s with concrete walls and a two-tier tin roof.

Islam came to the island of Mindanao in the fifteenth century and several mosques on the shores of Lake Lanao may have been founded in this early period, although no early remains seem to have survived. One of the oldest mosques is the Taraka Mosque in Lanao del Sur which is a square structure with a three-tier tin roof and painted abstract designs on the walls. Another early mosque is the Ranggar in Karigongan which consists of a simple square room with bamboo walls and a pyramid roof. A later development is represented by the insertion of an onion-shaped dome on an octagonal drum in the centre of the roof also found in one of the Lake Lanao mosques. This design reaches its climax in one of the Lanao mosques where there is a central onion dome flanked by four pagoda-like minarets. It is generally assumed that the use of domes reflects Indian influence via Malaysia and Indonesia, although it may also be through Chinese influence. After the Second World War, since Filipinos have been able to travel to Mecca, a new Middle-Eastern mosque style is noticeable in the Philippines. One of the more notable examples is the mosque of Jolo town on Jolo island which consists of a large rectangular prayer hall with a central dome and four flanking minarets. Probably the most famous mosque in the Philippines is the Quiapo Mosque in Manila which has an arcaded courtyard containing a fountain and a domed prayer hall.

Other examples of Islamic architecture in the Maranao area include royal residences and fortifications. Royal residences are known as 'torogan' and consist of raised platforms with tall sloping roofs. Inside, a torogan consists of one room with the king's bed in the centre and a small bedroom for the royal daughters. Sometimes the daughters' room (known as a lamin) is located in a separate room above the main roof of the torogan. Islamic forts (kota) were used to resist the Spanish and later American attempts to convert the Maranao Muslims to Christianity. Kotas consist of earthworks reinforced with wooden stakes.

See also: Indonesia, Java, Malaysia, Sumatra

Further reading:

A. Abbahil, 'The Maranao Mosque: its origins, structure and community role', *Danslan Quarterly* 1(20):85–103, 1980.

E. G. Giron, 'A mosque in Quiapo', in *Philippine Panorama*, 1977, 5–6.

P. Gowing, *Muslim Filipinos: Heritage and Horizon*, Quezon City, Philippines 1979.

W. Klassen, *Architecture in the Philippines*, Cebu, Philippines 1986, 125–52.

pisé

A form of mud brick where the brick is moulded in situ on a wall.

This technique is quicker than usual mud-brick construction because larger bricks can be produced which would not be able to be transported under normal circumstances. Because pisé allows high-speed (and therefore cheaper) construction it was often used for large-scale works such as enclosures or city walls.

pishtaq

Iranian term for a portal projecting from the façade of a building.

This device is most common in Anatolian and Iranian architecture although it also occurs in India. In its most characteristic form this consists of a high arch set within a rectangular frame, which may be decorated with bands of calligraphy, glazed tilework, geometric and vegetal designs.

Q

qa'a

A reception hall in Cairene houses.

qabr

A grave. It may also refer to the structure erected above the grave.

qabrstan

An Iranian term for a cemetery, equivalent to maqbara.

Qairawan

City in north-west Tunisia which functioned as the capital of the province of Ifriqiyya (roughly equivalent to modern Tunisia) during the early Islamic period.

Qairawan was founded in 670 by 'Uqba ibn Nafi, the Arab general in command of the Muslim conquest of North Africa. The principal monument in the city is the Great Mosque also known as the mosque of Sidi 'Uqba after the general who founded it. The first mosque on the site was begun immediately after the Arab conquest and consisted of a square enclosure containing a courtyard and prayer hall or sanctuary. This first building was made of mud brick and had to be restored in 695. There was another major reconstruction in 724–43 when a minaret was added. The present minaret was

Great Mosque, Qairawan, Tunisia, © Creswell Archive; Ashmolean Museum

added by the Aghlabids in 836. It is a giant three-tier structure built of baked bricks on a base of re-used ashlar blocks. At present the minaret stands on the north wall of the courtyard but in the ninth century it would have been outside the mosque courtyard in a manner similar to the contemporary Abbasid mosques of Samarra.

The mosque took its present form from the major rebuilding which took place under the Aghlabids which was completed in 862. The present mosque enclosure forms a large rectangle measuring 125 by 85 m. The prayer hall is one third of the mosque area and comprises seventeen aisles perpendicular to the qibla wall with another aisle parallel to the wall. Aghlabid modifications included the present mihrab, the dome in front of the mihrab and the minbar. The mihrab niche is lined with perforated marble panels decorated with vegetal designs. Surrounding the mihrab are a series of polychrome lustre tiles which are believed to have been imported from Baghdad. The dome covering the area in front of the mihrab is built of stone and rests on a drum supported by large shell-shaped squinches. The dome has a gadrooned form which internally takes the form of thin radiating ribs. The inside of the drum is circular and decorated with a series of sixteen blind niches and eight arched windows. The minbar is the oldest in existence and consists of a high staircase with a series of intricately carved panels on the side decorated with geometric and stylized vegetal designs. The present maqsura (screen) was added in restorations of the eleventh century. Further restorations were carried out in 1294 when the arches of the arcades were remodelled and the projecting portal of Bab Lalla Rayhana was added. Other Aghlabid monuments at Qairawan include the Mosque of the Three Gates, and the famous polygonal cisterns or artificial lakes. Outside Qairawan three satellite cities were established known as al-Abbasiya, Raqqada and Sabra al-Mansuriyya. Nothing remains of Abasiyya, although at Raqqada there are huge reservoirs and the remains of a large palace built of baked brick. Other cities with Aghlabid monuments include Tunis, Susa, Sfax and Monastir. In 1052 the city was enclosed with a crenellated brick wall which was extensively restored in the eighteenth century.

See also: Aghlabids, Monastir, Sfax, Susa, Tunis, Tunisia

Further reading:

L. W. Boothe, 'The Great Mosque of Qirouan', *Oriental Art New Series* 16:321–36, 1970.

L. Golvin, 'Quelques réflexions sur la Grande Mosquée de Kairouan à la période des Aghlabides', *Revue de l'Occident musulmans et de la Méditerranée*, 1968.

qal'a

Castle, fortress or citadel.

Qal'at Banu Hammad

Eleventh-century capital of the Hammadids located in the mountains to the south of Algiers.

The city was founded in 1007 by Hammad ibn Buluggin, although it did not become capital until 1015 when Hammad withdrew his allegiance from the Fatimids. Excavations at the site have revealed the plan of the Great Mosque and three palaces. The buildings were constructed of roughly squared stones laid in courses which were originally covered in plaster. The Great Mosque was built in the North African style with its aisle running perpendicular to the qibla wall. Opposite the qibla wall is a square minaret 25 m high, with large blind niches which were originally decorated with coloured glazed tiles. The remains of the palaces indicate a high degree of wealth and probably an elaborate ceremonial function. One of the palaces is built around a cruciform tower containing ramps which led to a domed pavilion on the top. Another palace was built around a rectangular pond or lake measuring 65 by 45 m. The palaces were decorated with stucco which included early examples of muqarnas decoration.

See also: Algeria

Further reading:

L. Golvin, *Recherches Archéologiques à la Qal'a des Banu Hammad*, CNRS, Paris 1965.

A. Lezine, 'Le Minaret de la Qal'a des Banu Hammad', *Bulletin d'Archéologie Algérienne* 2:261–70, 1966–7.

qanat

Subterranean canal system usually used to bring water some distance from a river or mountains. Access to the qanat is by vertical shafts at regular distances.

qasaba

Central part of a town or citadel.

qasr

Palace or mansion.

Qasr al-Hayr East (Qasr al-Hayr al-Sharqi)

Settlement in the Syrian desert built by the Umayyads in 730 CE.

Qasr al-Hayr East is located 80 km east of Palmyra and 80 km south of Dayr al-Zor on the Euphrates. The Qasr represents a large complex which may be divided into four main groups: the small enclosure, the large enclosure, the bath house and the outer enclosure.

The small enclosure is a square building, approximately 70 m per side, with two solid semi-circular buttress towers on each side and four round towers at the corners. The entrance is on the western side through a monumental gateway flanked by two half-round towers. The lintel of the gateway is made of joggled voussoirs above which there is a relieving arch outlined by a continous moulding which also runs along the front of the towers. Either side of the relieving arch there are shallow recessed niches with engaged side columns. At the top of the gateway is a panelled frieze, in the centre of which there is a projecting machicolation. Inside there is a courtyard with a central pool around which there is a columned arcade or portico. On the north, east and south sides the rooms are arranged in groups of three with a central room and two rooms either side. At the north- and south-east corners there are small rooms with latrines set into the wall. On the west side there are two long vaulted rooms either side of the gateway which includes a mihrab in its south wall. The pattern of the upper floor is similar to the ground floor. The building probably funtioned as a khan.

The large enclosure has a similar plan to the small enclosure but is much larger, measuring 167 m per side. This building also differs in having four axial entrances leading into a large central courtyard lined with an arcade. The internal plan comprises twelve structural units, eight of which (two per side) are courtyard buildings. Three of the four corner units seem to have been open areas, whilst the south-east corner contains a small mosque with a raised central aisle. One of the courtyard buildings on the east side appears to have been an industrial building for the production of olive oil (i.e. presses and vats). The function of the building is not clear although it may have been a governor's residence.

The bath house comprises a triple-aisled hall with cold plunge pools, a series of three hot rooms and a warm room with a heated pool. The complex included a furnace, latrines and two service rooms. There were two separate sets of latrines and two entrances which implies there may have been some sexual segregation.

The outer enclosure from which the complex derives its name (Hayr) is a vast wall of irregular shape which stretches for more than 15 km. The wall is approximately 1 m wide and is buttressed internally and externally with solid semi-circular buttresses. Four gates were discovered, each contained within pairs of circular buttress towers. The purpose of the enclosure is debated, although it may have been partially for water conservation, for agriculture and animals (domestic or wild?).

See also: Qasr al-Hayr West, Syria, Ummayads

Further reading:

O. Grabar, R. Holod, J. Knutstad and W. Trousdale, *A City in the Desert: Qasr al-Hayr East*, Harvard Middle Eastern Monographs 22/24, 1978.

Qasr al-Hayr West (Qasr al-Hayr al-Gharbi)

Umayyad palace and settlement in the Syrian desert.

Qasr al-Hayr was built by the Umayyad caliph al-Walid in 728. It is located in the Syrian desert 40 km east of Palmyra and 40 km west of Qasr al-Hayr East. The complex comprises a khan, a palace, a bath house, mills and various hydraulic installations.

The khan is a square courtyard structure with two projecting wings to the east, on the side of the entrance. The foundations of the building were of stone but the upper parts (with the exception of the stone doorway) were of mud brick and have not survived. The southern wing on the outside is a small mosque with the mihrab in the centre of the south wall; the north wing has a water trough against the wall and may have been a stable or place for watering animals. The entrance to the khan is through a large rectangular doorway above which is an Arabic inscription with the date of construction 727. Internally the khan comprises a series of rooms around a colonnaded central courtyard.

The palace is one of the most luxurious examples

Qasr al-Hayr West (Qasr al-Hayr al-Gharbi)

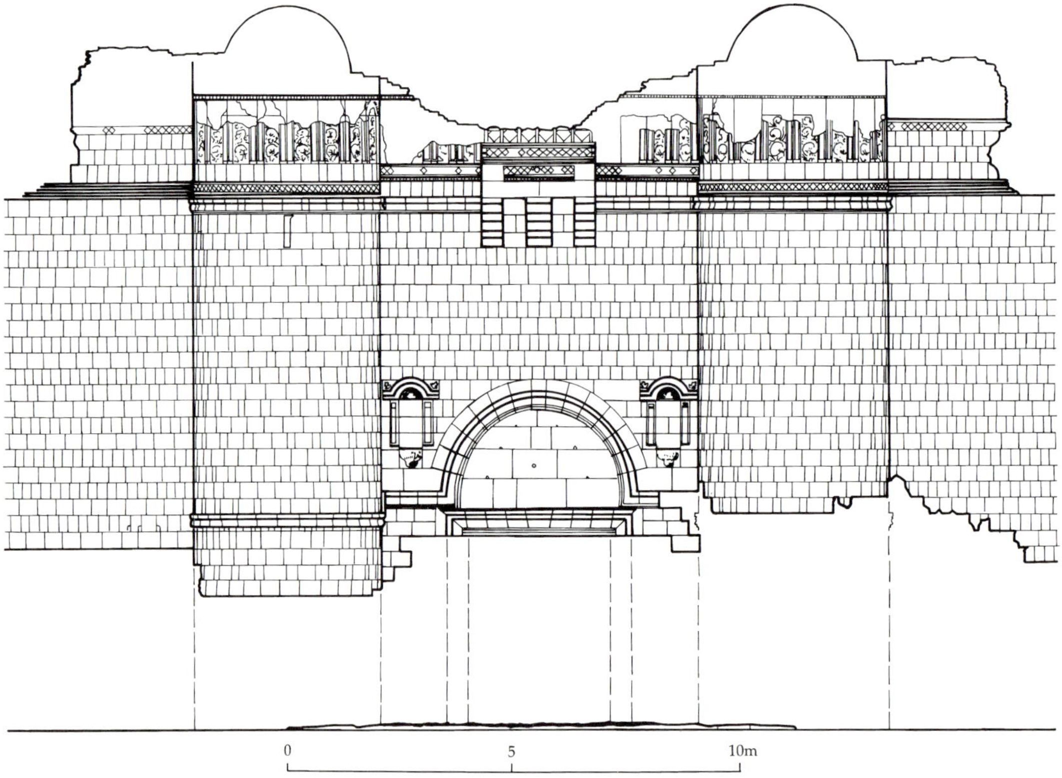

Gateway to lesser enclosure, Qasr al-Hayr al-Gharbi, Syria (after Grabar). Note machicolation above gate

of Umayyad palatial architecture. The structure, which is approximately square, is built on to a pre-existing Byzantine monastic tower dating from the sixth century. The tower is built of massive dressed masonry whereas the rest of the palace is built of mud brick on stone foundation. Above the entrance to the tower are the remains of a box machicolation which may have been the example for the gateway at Qasr al-Hayr East. The main part of the palace comprises a square enclosure with solid semi-circular buttress towers and round corner towers built around a paved courtyard. There are eight living-units, or bayts (two per side), each comprising a central hall leading out on either side to a set of side rooms including a latrine. The most impressive feature of the building is the arched gateway set between two half-round towers. The outer façade was decorated with panels of elaborate stucco which are now in the Damascus museum. The lower part of the decoration is large panels of vegetation arranged in geometric patterns, above which is a smaller set of panels containing vegetal ornament within squares, circles and diamonds. Above the panels is a row of blind niches with alternating round and pointed arches; the top was made up of stepped merlons or crenelations. The interior of the gatehouse above the entrance was probably a palatial domed reception hall decorated with frescoes. Inside the palace the arcade around the courtyard was decorated with carved stucco animals whilst at the base of the staircase there were frescoes containing naked women and hunting scenes.

Immediately to the north of the palace there is a bath house, a fairly small building containing a vaulted hall with benches around the side and three warm rooms. An unusual feature is that a mosque was attached to the south side of the dressing hall.

The entire complex of Qasr al-Hayr al-Gharbi relied on a water system ultimately derived from a dam 15 km distant. There are two main canals, one leading to the palace and bath house and the other leading via a cistern to the khan, some mills and then a huge rectangular enclosure containing a network of small irrigation channels. The irrigation channels are also fed by a large semi-circular barrage which collects water from the hill.

See also: Qasr al-Hayr East, Syria, Umayyads

Further reading:

D. Schlumberger (ed.), *Qasr el-Heir el Gharbi*, Paris 1986.

Qasr al-Tuba

Unfinished Umayyad complex in south-east Jordan.

Qasr al-Tuba is a large rectangular enclosure divided into three strips; only the west wing appears to have been completed, although there are traces of mud-brick structures elsewhere in the complex. Like Mshatta the remaining parts of the building are made of ashlar masonry with baked brick used for the barrel-vaulted roofs. There is a dam and several wells associated with the qasr but no other

Stone and brick construction, Qasr al-Tuba, Jordan

Slightly pointed doorway arches, Qasr al-Tuba, Jordan

Qasr al-Tuba, Jordan

structures have been identified. The purpose of the building is not clear but it may have been connected with the Wadi Sirhan caravan route.

Qatar

A peninsula on the east coast of Arabia projecting northwards into the Gulf.

Although it used to be dependent on pearl diving and fishing, today the main economy of the State of Qatar is oil. The country is predominantly desert with few natural water resources. It is ruled by the Amir of Qatar from the capital Doha.

Until recently permanent architecture has been confined to one or two towns and several semi-permanent encampments. Archaeological excavations at Ras Abrak has revealed the presence of several semi-permanent seasonal encampments. One of these has been interpreted as a fish-curing complex and consisted of two roughly rectangular rooms linked by a sheltered courtyard containing fireplaces and a cairn. The entire complex was built out of thin limestone slabs laid without mortar although there may have been a superstructure built out of some less durable material.

On the northern tip of the country are the remains of a small town, al-Huwailah. At present the site is largely in ruins but the main features can be distinguished, including a fort surrounded by several stone houses. Around this central complex are the remains of further structures which were probably huts built of palm fronds and were the main form of accommodation in the town.

Recent development has meant that little survives of the traditional town of Doha with the exception of the Old Amiri Palace which has recently been restored and is now used as a museum. This is a large complex containing quarters for several families. There are three gatehouses and two public reception rooms (an inner and outer majlis). The main material for construction is coral blocks (both in the form of lumps and thin slabs) used in conjunction with mangrove poles in a panel--and-frame construction. For ornamental purposes carved teak and mahogany from India were used.

Further reading:

B. DeCardi, *Qatar Archaeological Report: Excavations*, Oxford 1973.

G. R. H. Wright, *The Old Amiri Palace Doha, Qatar*, Qatar 1975.

qibla

Direction of Mecca which determines the direction of prayer.

The qibla is the prime factor in the orientation of mosques and is usually marked by a mihrab (or more in India). Many early mosques were not built to a correct qibla orientation, as has been demonstrated in the excavations of the Great Mosque of Wasit, where three different qibla orientations are recorded. It is believed that idea of qibla orientation is derived from the Jewish practice of indicating the direction of Jerusalem in synagogues.

qubba

Literally 'dome', often used to refer to a domed mausoleum which contains the grave of a saint or some important personage.

The earliest surviving example of this type of structure is the Qubbat al-Sulaybiyya at Samarra which is octagonal. Another early example is the tomb of Ismail the Samanid in Balkh which is a square structure with a hemispherical dome. Also dated to the ninth century are large numbers of domed mausoleums at Aswan in southern Egypt. From the eleventh century this type of structure becomes widespread in the Islamic world and is now one of the most common building types.

Qusayr Amra

Umayyad bath house complex in the eastern desert of Jordan famous for its painted frescoes.

The building was probably built by the Umayyad caliph al-Walid between 712 and 715. It comprises three main parts, a hall or undressing room, three heated rooms and a well-house to the north. The hall is divided into four parts, the main hall, an alcove and two small rooms either side. The entire hall (including the two side rooms) is roofed by three barrel vaults resting on transverse arches. The walls of both the main hall and the two side rooms are covered in frescoes whilst the floors were covered with marble, except in the side rooms where there were floor mosaics. The subjects of the frescoes differ according to their position; thus the main hall is decorated with hunting scenes and semi-naked women on the soffits of the arches. The alcove is decorated with six figures representing the defeated enemies of Islam. The two rooms leading to the hot room are decorated

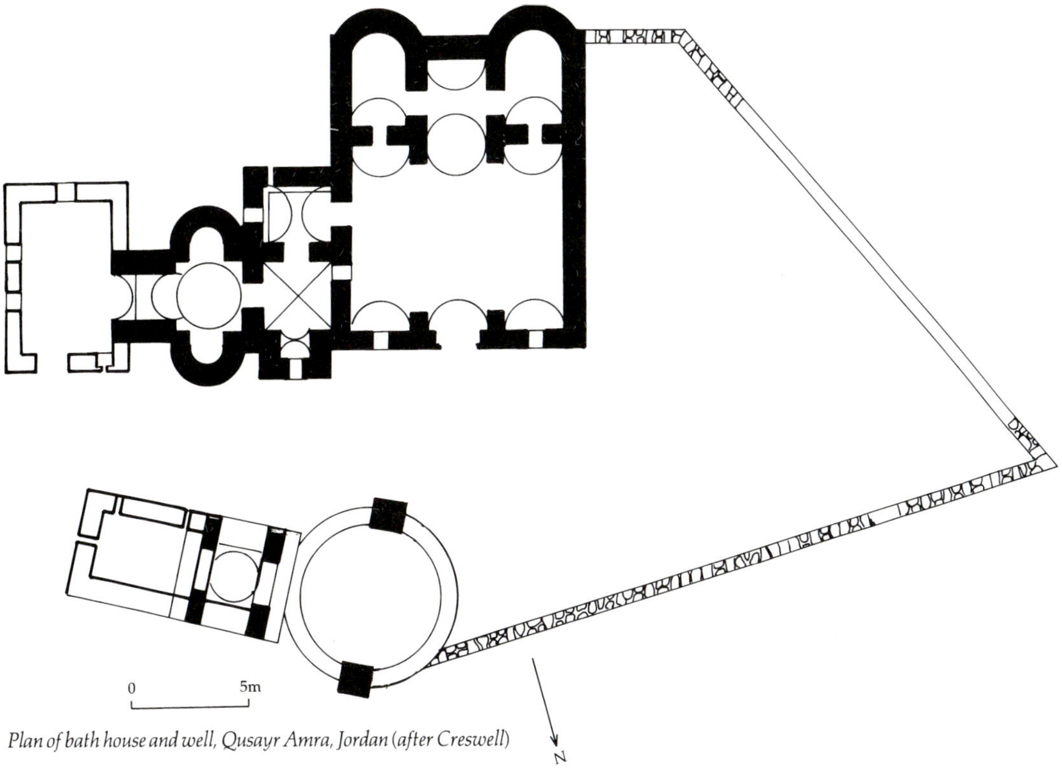

Plan of bath house and well, Qusayr Amra, Jordan (after Creswell)

with bathing women whilst the dome of the hot room is painted with a representation of the zodiac. The zodiac representation is the earliest surviving example of a domed representation of the stars and is of fundamental importance to the history of science.

The exact function of Qusayr Amra is not known although it seems to have been a princely desert retreat with formal associations (e.g. the audience hall).

See also: hammam, Jordan, Umayyads

Qutb Minar and Mosque

Famous twelfth-century minaret and mosque complex in Delhi, northern India.

The complex commemorates the first Islamic conquest of Delhi by Muhammad of Ghur in 1193. The mosque was built in the centre of the Hindu fort of Rai Pithora built earlier in the twelfth century by the Chauhan Rajputs. The area occupied by the mosque in the centre of the citadel is known as Lal Kot and was built by the Tomar Rajputs in the eleventh century. The mosque was begun by Qutb al-Din the first Islamic sultan of Delhi and is all that remains of the first Islamic city.

The Mosque

The present buildings are contained within a large, partially ruined, rectangular enclosure approximately 225 by 125 m. The enclosure is a multi-period complex containing three major phases of Islamic building, the earliest of which is dated to between 1193 and 1198. Twenty-seven Hindu and Jain temples were demolished to make room for the first mosque, which was called 'The Might of Islam' (Quwwatu'l Islam); however, the remains of the temples were used to provide building materials for the mosque, in particular the columns used in the arcades of the courtyard. This consists of a rectangular enclosure built on an east–west axis with the qibla pointing west towards Mecca. The courtyard is entered from two entrances on the north–south sides and a larger domed entrance to the east. Inside, the courtyard is bordered on three sides by arcades whilst on the west side is the sanctuary separated from the courtyard by a screen. The screen contains five arches, of which the central arch is the highest; it is framed by a decorative border which combines Quranic inscriptions with dense vegetal carving and the spandrels of the arches are decorated with interlocking pierced discs. Standing in the courtyard directly in front of the central arch is an iron pillar 12 m high which was made for the Hindu god Vishnu in the fourth century CE. The columns supporting the arcades are made of finely carved red sandstone and consist of alternate square and round sections carved with various Hindu motifs, such as the bell and chain, as well as some figural sculpture. Because the columns were not sufficiently tall for the mosque they were placed one on top of the other to double the height. The arcades and sanctuary are covered with a trabeate roof where the columns support flat beams resting on brackets. The area immediately in front of the mihrab was covered by a large dome although this has now disappeared. The first stage of the Qutb Minar can also be attributed to this initial phase of construction.

The second stage of the mosque was carried out in the early thirteenth century by Iltumish, who extended the mosque laterally and completed the work of his father on the Qutb Minar. The lateral extension of the mosque was carried out by extending the screen north and south and adding an outer enclosure, or courtyard, which included the Qutb Minar in the south-east corner. The arcades of the extension were built in the same way as the inner enclosure and used columns which were specially carved to resemble the two-tier Hindu temple columns used in the first mosque. Iltumish was also responsible for commissioning his own tomb, which was begun the year before his death. The tomb is located outside the mosque to the west and consists of a square chamber covered with a dome, now collapsed. The interior is extravagantly decorated with carvings in red sandstone which included Hindu motifs intertwined with passages of Quranic calligraphy. In the centre of the building is Iltumish's tomb whilst to the west are three mihrab niches.

The third major phase of the mosque complex was carried out by Ala al-Din Khaliji, the fourteenth sultan of Delhi, between 1296 and 1316. Like his predecessor Ala al-Din decided to increase the area of the original mosque by extending the length of the screen to the north thus enclosing an area more than double the size of the previous extension. At the same time Ala al-Din also began work on another minaret on the same pattern as the Qutb Minar which is known as the Alai Minar. For various reasons Ala al-Din was not able to complete either of these ambitious projects leaving the stump of a minaret and in the north part of the unfinished new courtyard. However, in 1311 he was able to complete a new monumental gateway to the complex known as the Alai Darwaza which linked the west wall of Iltumish's complex with the completed west wall of his new courtyard. The gateway consists of a large square domed chamber with a tall pointed arch in the north and south sides. The gateway is faced in red sandstone inlaid with bands of white marble and is completely covered in carved designs and epigraphic bands. The south façade of the chamber consists of a tall pointed arch in the centre, flanked on each side by a window covered with a pierced stone screen (jalis) and a blind arch of similar design. Above the two arches either side of the main arch are two flat rectangular panels each divided in two and containing a small square blind niche. The arches of the façade are decorated with spiky projecting tassels whilst the jambs of the arches are made up of engaged columns similar to those used to support the arcades.

East of the Alai Darwaza is a small square domed tomb built by the Turkestani Imam Zamin. This is the latest building at the site dating to 1538.

The Minar

Although subsequently copied in various ways, the Qutb Minar is a unique building which announces the arrival of Islam in India. The minar comprises a tall tapering cylindrical tower standing on a circular base with five storeys which together reach a height of 72.5 m. Each of the storeys is reached by an internal spiral staircase which leads to the balconies which are supported on muqarnas corbels. The most characteristic feature of the building is the corrugated angular and rounded fluting on the shaft which forms the basis for many later imitations. The first part of the tower was built by Qutb al-Din who died in 1210 leaving only one storey completed. This is the thickest part of the tower with a base diameter of 14 m tapering to 9 m at the first balcony. This part of the minaret is built with alternating sharp-angled and rounded fluting (twelve of each type) which are decorated with bands of inscriptions. Between 1211 and 1236 the tower was completed by Iltumish with three more storeys, each with a different pattern of fluting. The second storey added by Iltumish has rounded flutes, the third storey has angular flutes and the fourth storey was plain. During the fourteenth century the top of the building was damaged by lightning and in 1369 Firuz Shah repaired the damage to the top and added an extra storey. The diameter at the fifth storey is only 2.7 m making a reduction from an area of 44 square metres at the base to 8.5 m at the top.

The design of the Qutb Minar and in particular the fluting have clear antecedents and parallels in Afghan architecture; thus the first storey built by Qutb al-Din may be compared to the twelfth-century tower at Khwaja Siyah Push in Sistan which has eight semi-circular flutes alternating with eight shallow-angled flutes. Similarly the round flutes of the second storey may be compared with those of the early twelfth-century Jar Kurgan tower in Uzbekistan.

The effect of the tower on later Indian architecture is significant, influencing not only towers but the decoration of columns and domes. The earliest known direct copy is the Alai Minar in the same complex which was begun by Ala al-Din Khaliji in the early fourteenth century; it had twice the base area of the Qutb Minar and was projected to be twice the height. Although it was never completed, the base can still be seen and is circular, with square flutes and a tapering cylindrical shaft with sharp-angled flutes. An earlier example of the influence of the Qutb Minar can be found in the paired minarets on top of the early thirteenth-century gateway of Araha-i-Din Mosque at Ajmer. However, the most complete copy is the Hashtsal Minar near Palam built for Shar Jahan and completed in 1634. The top of the building has been damaged, as have the two collar-like balconies of which only the projecting supports remain, so that its present height is 17 m. Like its ancient model the Hashtsal Minaret is decorated with alternating round and angled flutes although there is no attempt to recreate the muqarnas mouldings which support the balconies of the Qutb Minar. There is no mosque associated with the tower and it seems likely that this was a hunting monument consciously recalling the victory connotations of the Qutb Minar.

See also: Delhi, India, minaret

Further reading:

T. W. Arnold and K. Fischer, 'Kutb Minar', *Encyclopedia of Islam*, 1954.

A. B. M. Hussain, *The Manara in Indo-Muslim Architecture*, Dacca 1970.

E. Koch, 'The copies of the Qutb Minar', *Iran* 29: 95–108, 1991.

J. A. Page, *An Historical Memoir on the Qutb, Delhi* (originally published in *Memoirs of the Archaeological Survey of India* 22. 1926), reprinted New Delhi, Delhi 1970.

R

Rabat

Capital of Morocco located on the Atlantic coast.

The city of Rabat is located at the mouth of the Bou Regreg river. Rabat stands on the south side of the river and the twin city of Sale occupies the north bank. Although there was probably a Roman settlement on the site, the present city of Rabat was founded in the twelfth century by the Almohad ruler Sultan Abd al-Mumin as a depot and launching point for the Almohad conquest of Spain. The city still retains parts of its twelfth-century walls including two monumental Almohad gateways. The façade of the gateways consists of a central entrance with a slightly pointed horseshoe arch with spandrels decorated with bold interlace designs. Both gateways form bent entrances, the Udayya gate has a passage which runs along the side of the wall before opening into the town, whilst the Bab Ruwah has a complicated zig-zag pattern with blind passages.

The most famous monument in Rabat is the mosque of Hassan begun in 1196 after the Almohad victory over Alfonso VIII at Alarcos in Spain. The mosque would have been one of the largest in the Islamic world but construction ceased after the death of Ya'qub al-Mansur in 1199. The plan of the mosque can still be discerned and consists of a huge rectangle 140 by 185 m with three courtyards and a huge minaret in the middle of the north side opposite the qibla wall. The unfinished minaret is 40 m high, but if completed it would have reached a height of over 70 m. The tower is built in the characteristic Almohad style with a square central core around which a ramp rises to reach the top. Within the central core are a series of vaulted rooms, one on each storey, each with a different form of vault. The exterior of the tower is decorated with windows set within blind niches with multi-foil and cusped arches, the upper part of the tower is covered with a network of interlaced arches.

The current main mosque of the city was built by the Marinids in the thirteenth century and stands opposite a madrassa built in the same period. The Kasba des Ouadias forms an enclosure within the city which contains houses and a twelfth-century mosque. To the south of the city is the fortified necropolis of Challa built by the Marinids in the fourteenth century.

See also: Almohads, Morocco

Ramla

Capital of Palestine in the early Islamic period.

Ramla is located in the southern coastal plain of Palestine roughly equidistant between Gaza and

Tower of White Mosque, Ramla, Israel/Palestine

Jerusalem. The city was founded in 712 by the Umayyad caliph Sulayman as an alternative to nearby Lydda which had a predominantly Christian population.

Little remains from the early Islamic period, although the White Mosque to the north-east of the modern town preserves the shape of the Umayyad mosque, whilst the cistern known as Birket al-ʾAnaziya was built during the reign of the Abbasid caliph Harun al-Rashid. The city suffered from a series of earthquakes and the Crusader occupation of the twelfth century so that by the Mamluk period (1250s) it was at least a quarter of its former size. Although the White Mosque was rebuilt by Sultan Baybars, this area of the town never recovered. Instead, the south-east part of the city became the centre of the town with the Crusader church of St John functioning as the Great Mosque. This has remained the town centre to the present day and contains a number of interesting Mamluk and Ottoman buildings.

See also: Mamluks, Palestine

Further reading:

M. Ben-Dov and M. Rosen Ayalon, 'Ramla', in *New Encyclopaedia of Excavations in the Holy Land*, Jerusalem 1993.

A. D. Petersen, 'A preliminary report on a survey of historic buildings in Ramla', *Levant* 25: 1995, 75–101.

Raqqa

Prominent Abbasid and medieval city located on the Euphrates river in Syria.

Raqqa was founded by Alexander the Great and was known as Leontopolis in the Byzantine period. In 639 the town was captured by the Arabs and renamed Raqqa. In 772 the Abbasid caliph al-Mansur founded a new city, west of the old one, which he enclosed with a wall similar to that of Baghdad, with an inner and an outer wall and a moat or ditch. The remains of the walls can still be seen and form a rounded enclosure with a straight wall on the south side. The inner wall still survives to a height of 10 m in places and is studded with half-round towers at regular intervals. There is a gap of 20 m between this and the outer wall of which little survives. In the middle of the enclosure are the remains of the Great Mosque which was built in 772. This is a huge rectangular enclosure measuring 90 by 110 m, with a large central courtyard containing a minaret of later date (twelfth century). The outer walls of the mosque are made of mud brick supported by solid semi-circular buttress towers. The prayer hall consisted of three arcades supported on cylindrical piers, whilst the other three sides were lined with double arcades. The building was decorated with stucco, traces of which survive.

The famous Baghdad gate which stands at the south-east corner of the city is now thought to date to the twelfth century. It is a baked-brick construction with a main gateway set below a row of two-tier blind niches separated by engaged columns. The gateway itself and the upper tier of arches are of a four-centrepoint design which makes its first appearance in the late ninth century at Samarra.

See also: Abbasids, Baghdad, Samarra, Syria

Further reading:

J.-C. Heusch and M. Meinecke, 'Grabungen im abbasidischen Palastareal von ar-Raqqa/ar-Rafiqa', *Damaszener Mitteilungen* 2: 85-105, 1985.

M. al-Khalaf, 'Die abbasidische Stadtmauer von ar-Raqqa/ ar Rafiqa', *Damaszener Mitteilungen* 2: 122–31, 1985.

J. Warren, 'The date of the Baghdad Gate at Raqqa', *Art and Archaeology Research Papers* XIII: 22–3, 1978.

rauza

Persian term for mausoleum.

Red Fort (Lal Qila)

Mughal palace in Delhi built by the Mughal emperor Shah Jahan between 1638 and 1648.

The building derives its name from the use of red sandstone as the main building material. The palace forms the core of Shah Jahan's new city of Shahjahanabad. The fort is located next to the Jumna river and surrounded on all four sides by a high crenellated wall which on the landward side is enclosed within a moat. The two main entrances to the palace are the Lahore and Delhi gates both of which were enlarged by Jahan's successor Aurangzeb. The internal layout of the palace is symmetrical and was probably based on that of the Agra fort. The Lahore gate was the main form of public access and leads into a large square with the imperial audience hall on the opposite side. The private apartments were made up of a series of pavilions and gardens arranged in a rigid geometry. The decoration of the palace is of outstanding quality and refinement and with the Alhambra is one of the finest examples of Islamic palatial architecture. Decorative techniques include painting, gilding, pietra dura (stone inlay) gilding and white marble carved in shallow relief.

See also: Agra, Delhi, India, Lahore, Mughals, Taj Mahal

riad

North African term for a walled garden.

ribat

Fortified enclosure for religious warriors, common in North Africa in the early Islamic period.

A typical ribat is located near the coast and partially functions as a look-out post. Usually ribats are square or rectangular courtyard structures, two storeys high, with storage rooms and stables on the ground floor and sleeping accomodation and a mosque on the upper floor. Later ribats seem to have lost their military function. Important examples are at Sfax, Monastir and Sousse in Tunisia.

See also: Tunisia

riwaq

Arcade or portico open on at least one side.

Robat Sharaf

Royal Seljuk caravanserai on the road between Nishapur and Merv.

This building was founded in 1114 as a royal caravanserai and expanded in 1156 when it was used as a semi-permanent residence for Sultan Sanjar and his wife who were held under house arrest by the Öghuz Turks. The first part of the structure is a square enclosure built around a central courtyard with a central iwan in each side leading to a domed room. The extension is half the size and is built on to the front of the original structure. The building was decorated with elaborate stucco work and a monumental entrance pishtaq flanked with twin blind niches.

S

sabil

See sebil.

Saffavid

Dynasty of Kurdish origin which ruled Iran during the sixteenth and seventeenth centuries.

Although the founder of the dynasty was probably a Sunni, the Saffavids later became Shiʿa and adopted this as a state religion. Little remains of the early architecture of the Saffavids who established capitals first at Tabriz and later at Qazvin. The little that does survive indicates that they continued the architectural forms established by their predecessors the Timurids. Thus the Saffavids continued to use the complex vaulting forms, with networks of arches, squinches and pendentives, developed under the Timurids. An early example of a Saffavid building is the tomb of Harun-i Vilayat which although Timurid in form has an emphasis on exterior tile decoration. This was a feature which was developed in later Saffavid architecture where the architectural form seems to be subordinated to the tile patterns.

The most productive period of Saffavid architecture began in 1598 with Shah Tahmasp's decision to redesign Isfahan as an imperial capital. The centre of the new developments was the Maidan-i-Shah which is a rectangular square or park around which was built the palace, the principal mosques and the principal bazar of the city. The main characteristics of this architecture was the layout and planning with the mosques built at a deliberate angle to the maidan to show off both their monumental portals (pishtaq iwans) and their glazed domes. Similarly the main gate of the palace, the Ali Qapu, was made into a pavilion overlooking the Maidan-i-Shah from which the shah's palace could be seen. The emphasis on accessibility is also demonstrated in the tomb complexes, where the outside faces are pierced with arches instead of forbidding walls. This is also seen on utilitarian structures such as the famous Pol-i-Khaju bridge built in 1650. This bridge, which links Isfahan to the southern palace, is 110 m long and has two tiers of arcades which provide shelter from the summer heat. Another characteristic of the architecture is the use of lighter materials such as wood, stucco, paint and tiles, and an increasing emphasis on gardens. However, this may appear to be a development simply because earlier structures of this type have not survived.

Outside Isfahan buildings such as caravanserais are generally larger and plainer than their predecessors indicating the growth of commercial traffic.

See also: Iran, Isfahan

sahn

Courtyard of a mosque.

Samarkand

Timurid capital located in the Central Asian state of Uzbekistan.

Samarkand is located on the banks of the Zeravshan river approximately 200 km east of Bukhara. Next to the present city are the ruins of Afrasiyab which was the site of the city from 500 BCE until the Mongol destruction of 1220 CE. In the eighth century the city was sacked by the Arab general Qutaiba bin Muslim. After the Arab conquest a new city was built to the south-west with Afrasiyab remaining as an industrial quarter specializing in the production of paper for which it was famous. Excavations have revealed workshops for pottery and glass in addition to a large mosque which was burnt during the Mongol invasion.

Samarkand once again rose to international prominence in 1369 when it was captured by the Mongol emperor Timur and chosen as his capital. Timur enclosed the city with a wall 7 km long and established his citadel and palace in the western part of the city. There are few monuments which survive from the reign of Timur partly because he was more concerned with conquest than architecture and partly because he was more interested in a more ephemeral type of architecture represented by gardens, pavilions and tents. Contemporary accounts describe a series of magnificent gardens with three-storey pavilions made of wood and decorated with porcelain and marble. One of the most splendid examples of this type of architecture must have been the tented encampment erected to celebrate the wedding of Timur's grandsons. It comprised 20,000 tents arranged into streets in a meadow on the banks of the Zeravshan river. The most magnificent tent was that of Timur which was 100 m square with a central dome supported on twelve giant tent poles above which was a square wooden turret.

Two major monuments have survived from Timur's reign, however; these are the Bibi Khanum Mosque and the mausoleum of Gur-i Amir. The Bibi Khanum Mosque is a massive building begun in 1399, after Timur's conquest of India. It forms a rectangle 160 by 200 m built around a huge central courtyard, entered via a monumental portal iwan flanked by twin towers. Either side of the central courtyard there were shallow iwans leading into prayer halls roofed with fluted domes covered in blue glazed tiles. The main prayer hall/sanctuary with its massive tiled dome is hidden behind a huge pishtaq iwan 40 m high and flanked with twin towers more than 50 m high. Unfortunately the speed of construction together with the massive size of the mosque combined to make it unstable and it started to disintegrate as soon as it was built. The other major monument surviving from Timur's time is the mausoleum of Gur-i Amir built by Timur for his grandson Muhamad Sultan between 1403 and 1404. This tomb eventually housed Timur himself after his death on campaign in 1405. The tomb is built on an octagonal plan and is crowned with a bulbous dome resting on a muqarnas band set on an octagonal drum. The interior of the tomb is square with deeply recessed arches set into the middle of each side. The dome is supported on a network of eight intersecting arches supported by corner squinches. On the floor of the tomb are the cenotaphs of Timur's descendants, the tomb of Timur is marked by a huge green jade slab.

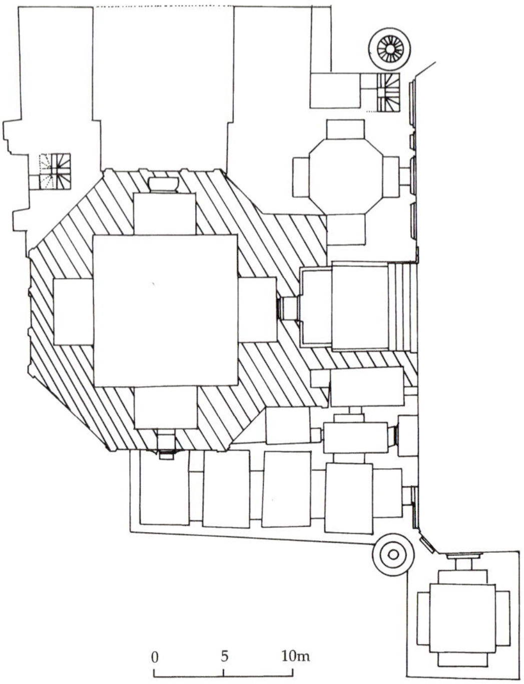

Mausoleum of Gur-i Amir, Samarkand, Uzbekistan

Other funerary monuments erected by Timur were part of a mausoleum complex known as the Shah i-Zinda. The complex was built around the shrine of Quthman ibn Abbas whose tomb stood at the end of a narrow lane approached by a set of thirty-six stone steps. The shrine of Quthman is approached through a series of anterooms decorated with stucco and covered with a roof resting on carved wooden columns. Either side of the lane leading to the shrine there are a total of sixteen tombs representing the development of tomb architecture. The royal tombs are of two types: a square type with a main façade and polygonal type with two or more entrances. The oldest tomb, that of Timur's niece, Shad i Mulk, is of the first type with a large screen which hides the ribbed dome behind. The screen is contained within two engaged columns and frames a large recessed portal decorated with muqarnas mouldings and glazed tiles inset within carved mouldings. The tomb of Shihrin Bika Aka was built some ten years later and also has a screen façade although this is decorated with tile mosaic, a new technique imported from Persia. This tomb also has a more advanced dome design which has a slightly bulbous form resting on a sixteen-sided drum.

The centre of the city was the Registan, although no buildings of Timur's period survive in this square, considered the finest in Central Asia. The oldest building in the Registan is the madrassa of Ulugh Beg built between 1417 and 1420. The madrassa has the typical Timurid form with a huge entrance iwan (pishtaq) set into an entrance façade flanked with twin minarets. The entire surface of the façade and minarets is decorated with blue, turquoise and yellow tile mosaic against a background of yellow/buff baked brick. One of the notable features of the decoration is the use of giant calligraphic patterns in complex geometric arrangements. The interior of the madrassa consisted of a courtyard surrounded by two storeys of cells and teaching rooms designed to accommodate 100 students. Ulugh Beg's love of learning is further demonstrated by his observatory which was a three-storey tiled structure nearly 50 m in diameter cut into the hillside. In the middle of the building was a deep slit 40 m long which contained a sextant with an arc of 63 m. With this instrument Ulugh Beg was able to produce the first precise map of the stars and planets.

Opposite the Ulugh Beg Madrassa in the Registan is the Shirdar Madrassa which has the same general form even though it was built 200 years later in the seventeenth century. On the third side of the square is the Tilakar Mosque and Madrassa also built in the seventeenth century. This building has the largest façade, which is over 120 m long with a massive entrance iwan (pishtaq) flanked on either side by two storeys of open arches facing on to the square and domed cylindrical corner turrets. Inside, the mosque is decorated with multiple layers of gold painted on to a blue background.

See also: Bukhara, Timurids, Uzbekistan

Further reading:

J. Lawton and F. Venturi, *Samarkand and Bukhara*, London 1991.

A. L. Mongait, *Archaeology in the U.S.S.R.*, trans. M. W. Thomson, Pelican, London 1961.

N. B. Nemtseva, 'The origins and architectural development of the Shah i Zinda', trans. with additions by J. M. Rogers and A. Yasin, *Iran* 15: 51–74, 1977.

R. Pinder-Wilson, 'Timurid architecture', in *Cambridge History of Iran* 6, 1993.

D. N. Wilber, 'The Timurid court: life in gardens and tents', *Iran* 27: 127–134, 1979.

Samarra

Abbasid capital in central Iraq.

Samarra is now recognized as the largest archaeological site in the world and stretches for over 40 km along the banks of the Tigris. Although there were settlements in the area of Samarra before the Abbasid period, it was not established as capital until 836 CE when the Abbasid caliph al-Mu'tassim decided to set up a new city following clashes between his troops and the local population of Baghdad. The city remained capital for fifty-six years and was home to eight caliphs, until 892 when the capital was moved back to Baghdad.

The predominant building material in Samarra was mud brick and pisé with baked brick reserved for more important structures (i.e. the Great Mosque and the Bab al-Amma). Houses and palaces were decorated with carved and moulded stucco panels, and Samarra provides the earliest examples of bevelled stucco decoration. Some of the palaces were also decorated with wall paintings and glass mosaic although none of this remains in situ.

The modern town of Samarra is located approximately in the centre of the Abbasid city. Immediately to the north-west of the city, on the west bank of the Tigris, is the Jausaq al-Khaqani which for most of the time was the caliph's palace and was always his official residence. It was built by one of al-Mu'tasim's Turkish generals and reflects features of Central Asian influence such as wall paintings with Bactrian camels. The palace is a vast complex, including a mosque, a polo ground and a horse-racing track. On the west side of the palace, facing the river, there is a monumental gateway or portal known as the Bab al-Amma, or public gate. This structure was probably an official entrance and a place for public audiences. Directly to the east of the palace is the Great Mosque of Samarra with its spiral minaret (the Malwiyya). Measuring over 240 by 160 m this is one of the largest mosques in the world. It is built entirely of baked brick although marble columns on brick piles originally supported the roof. The outer wall of the mosque is supported by four corner towers and twenty semi-circular bastions resting on square bases. The curtain wall is entirely plain except for a frieze which runs between the bastions, each section consisting of six bevelled squares with shallow concave discs in the centre. The Malwiyya,

Qubbat al-Sulaybiyya, Samarra, Iraq

Great Mosque above and smaller mosque in foreground, Samarra, Iraq

or spiral minaret, is 52 m high and may have been influenced by earlier Mesopotamian ziggurats.

In the north of Samarra are the remains of an extension to the city built by Caliph al-Mutawakkil in an attempt to found a new city. This new area had a palace, garrisons and a congregational mosque known as the Abu Dulaf. The Abu Dulaf Mosque is a smaller version of the Great Mosque and has a spiral minaret 19 m high. On the west bank of the Tigris is the Ashiq Palace, one of the last buildings made before the capital was relocated in Baghdad. The palace is built on a vaulted substructure or terrace so that it can overlook the Tigris. The building forms a high rectangle with the outer walls decorated by a series of blind niches. One of the distinctive features of the palace is the use of the four-centrepoint arch for the first time in Islamic architecture.

South of the modern town of Samarra are a number of major structures, including the palaces of al-Istabulat, al-Balkuwara and Musharrahat. In addition, there is a huge octagonal enclosure, each side of which is half a kilometre long, known as the octagon of Qadisiyya. This probably represents the remains of an unfinished city started by Harun al-Rashid in the eighth century.

See also: Abbasids, Baghdad, Iraq

Further reading:

A. Northedge, 'Planning Samarra', *Iraq* 47: 109–28, 1985.
—— 'The Palace of Istabulat', *Archéologie islamique* 4: 1993.
A. Northedge and R. Falkner, 'The 1986 survey season at Samarra', *Iraq* 49: 143–74, 1987.
A. Northedge, T. J. Wilkinson and R. Falkner, 'Survey and excavations at Samarra 1989', *Iraq* 52: 121–48.

San'a

Capital city of Yemen.

The city is located on a high plateau 2,200 m above sea level. Above the city is Jabal Nuqum which acts as a collecting point for clouds and consequently precipitation. San'a seems to have risen to prominence in the third century CE although an earlier settlement probably existed on the site.

San'a has thirty-four historic mosques, the oldest of which is the Great Mosque which is said to have been founded on the orders of Muhammad during his lifetime. This early mosque was extended northwards during the Umayyad period on the orders of Caliph al-Walid. Subsequent restorations were carried out in the twelfth, thirteenth and sixteenth centuries, although the basic form of the building appears to have remained the same. In its present form the mosque consists of a large rectangle measuring 66 by 78 m with six gateways, one at the south, four on the east and west sides and one in the north wall next to the mihrab. The external walls are built of large blocks of squared basalt with a central core of rubble. The courses of the wall are marked by narrow ridges (approximately 0.5 cm wide) formed by the faces of the stones leaning outwards. This is a masonry technique characteristic of pre-Islamic Yemeni architecture. In the centre of the mosque there is a square courtyard surrounded by arcades, four on the south side, three on the east and west sides and five on the north (qibla) side. The arcades have a flat wooden roof supported by arches resting either on columns or on circular stone piers. In the centre of the courtyard is a square box-shaped structure covered with a dome known as Sinan Pashas Qubbah. Although it was built in the early seventeenth century, its form and position suggest it may have earlier antecedents. There are two minarets, one in the south-east corner of the courtyard and the other at the east side of the mosque next to the outer wall. They both seem to date from the thirteenth century but may have been restored later. The mosque has four mihrabs, three subsidiary ones at its south end and a main mihrab to the left of centre in the north wall. The area above the mihrab is roofed by five corbelled wooden domes, a central dome and four smaller side domes. In the centre of each dome is a block of alabaster which would have functioned as a skylight.

Other early mosques in San'a include the Jabbanah Musalla, the Tawus Mosque, the mosque of al-Jala and the Jami al-Tawashi. The Jabbanah Musalla is an open-air prayer area which is said to date from the time of Muhammad, although it has been extended in later times. The other early mosques are rectangular box-like structures with hypostyle roofs and recall pre-Islamic Yemeni temples. Mosques of the twelfth century and later are influenced by the architecture of Egypt and Syria. This influence can be seen in the use of arches and domes, which are rare features in the traditional architecture of Yemen. After the Ottoman occupation of the sixteenth century, mosques were built with large central domes and domed arcades.

The domestic architecture of San'a is represented by tall tower houses built of stone and decorated with white plasterwork around the windows and coloured glass in the reception rooms (mafraj) at the top of the house.

See also: Yemen

Further reading:

R. B. Serjeant and R. Lewcock (eds.), *San'a. An Arabian*

Mosque, San'a, Yemen, © *Charles Aithie*

Islamic City, World of Islam Festival Trust, London 1983.

saqaqa

Water tank for ritual ablutions.

sardivan

Fountain in the centre of a mosque courtyard.

Sassanians

Iranian dynasty which ruled from 226 CE to the Arab conquest in 651.

The Sassanians controlled the eastern half of what became the Umayyad and Abbasid empires. Unlike their Byzantine rivals, the Sassanians were completely destroyed by the Arab invasions. Nevertheless, Sassanian traditions continued to have great importance, particularly during the Abbasid period in the eighth and ninth centuries. This influence is symbolized by the great arched iwan (Taq i Khusrau) at Ctesiphon which, like the Hagia Sophia in Constantinople, provided an example for Islamic architects. The influence of the Sassanians on Islamic architecture can even be seen in Syria Palestine in the Umayyad period thus the mosaics of the Dome of the Rock are decorated with Sassanian symbols of royalty. More tangible evidence is found at Qasr Kharana which is purely Sassanian in design although it appears to date from the Islamic period. Other examples of Sassanian influence are the stepped merlons found at Umayyad palaces such as Khirbet al-Minya or the stucco work of Khirbet al-Mafjar.

The architecture of Iraq at this period is a continuation of Sassanian practice with baked brick and roughly coursed stone set in thick mortar as the main building materials. Buildings such as Khan ʿAtshan and Ukhaidhir are very similar to Sassanian buildings in their design, although constructional details such as the development of the pointed arch and the use of machicolations indicates new developments. In eastern Iran the influence of Sassanian culture remained longer, thus some ninth-century buildings have inscriptions in Pahlavi (Sassanian script) and Arabic.

See also: Abbasids, ʿAtshan, Byzantine architecture, Samarra, Ukhaidhir, Umayyads

Saudi Arabia

One of the largest countries in the Middle East occupying the greater part of the Arabian peninsula.

To the north the country is bordered by the states of Jordan, Iraq and Kuwait, whilst to the south are Yemen and Oman. On the west side is the Red Sea and on the east the coast of the Arabian Gulf, with the Gulf states of Bahrain, Qatar and the United Arab Emirates. The country is divided into three provinces: Western Province comprising the Hijaz and the Tihama, Central Province comprising Najd and the Empty Quarter, and Eastern Province comprising the oasis of al-Hassa and the towns of the Arabian Gulf.

Before Islam the principal settlements were the trading cities of the Hijaz which included Yathrib (Medina), Medain Saleh and Mecca. The establishment of Islam guaranteed Mecca's position as both a trading city and centre of the Muslim world. For a period of approximately 300 years after the death of Muhammad Arabia enjoyed an unprecedented economic growth and settlements like al-Rabadah grew from small settlements into major towns. During this time Arabia had the largest area of settlement until modern times. During the Middle Ages (1000–1500) the lack of central authority meant that Arabia was again a marginal area, only enlivened by pilgrim routes and secondary trade routes. With the growth of the Ottoman Empire in the sixteenth century Arabia became strategically important both for religious reasons (Mecca and Medina) and strategic reasons (growing European presence in the Indian Ocean). The increasing involvement of the Turks in the area provoked a reaction both within Arabia and from outside. The reaction from within Arabia led to the creation of the first Saudi state by Muhammad ibn Saud and Muhammad ibn Abd al-Wahhab. The state began in Najd in the 1740s and gradually expanded so that by the beginning of the nineteenth century successful attacks had been mounted against Kerbala in Iraq and Mecca in the Hijaz. The growing power of the Saudis was viewed with alarm by the Ottomans, who launched a campaign which led to the execution of the Saudi ruler. During the nineteenth century the Saudis gradually reasserted themselves spreading over large areas of Arabia. With the defeat of the Turks in the First World War the Saudis were able to make great gains and in the 1920s were able to take control of the Hijaz. Oil wealth has added to the strength of the kingdom which is now one of the oldest monarchies in the Middle East.

A variety of materials are employed in the traditional architecture of Saudi Arabia, these may be divided into three groups, stone, wood and mud. Mud is the commonest building material and may either be used as mud brick, pisé or as mud plaster for stone walls. Mud brick is the principal construction material in central Arabia as well as in the oasis towns of the eastern and western provinces. In northern Najd mud brick has recently replaced stone as the principal material of construction; the reasons for this are not known, although mud brick may be more versatile.

Stone is predominantly used in the mountainous regions of the Hijaz and 'Asir province and formerly in the northern Najd. Dressed stonework and ashlar masonry are uncommon in most of Saudi Arabia with the exception of the older cities of the Hijaz. The usual method of stone construction in most of the country is stone slabs laid in rough courses without mortar. True arches are rare in traditional stone architecture and the usual means of covering an opening are with a lintel or corbelled arch. Sometimes the outer surfaces are plastered with mud plaster or lime plaster where it is available. In the mountains of 'Asir layers of projecting flat stones are set into the walls to deflect rainfall away from their coating of mud plaster.

On the east and west coasts coral forms the principal building material. This may either be fossil or reef coral depending on preference and availability. Coral walls are usually coated with a hard white lime plaster, which is sometimes carved into elaborate stucco patterns.

Wood is an essential component of traditional architecture despite its natural scarcity in the arid desert environment. The date palm is the main source of wood in much of the country and is used for roofing and lintels. Tamarisk wood is also used but is more scarce and difficult to find in suitable lengths. On the coasts imported mangrove wood is used for roofs and strengthening in walls.

Hijaz

Historically the cities of the Hijaz have been the main cultural centres of Arabia, but recently Riyadh has grown in significance. The principal towns of the Hijaz are Mecca, Medina and Jeddah, in addition there are a number of smaller towns such as Tabuk and al-'Ula. As religious cities Mecca and Medina are responsible for bringing a large number of pilgrims to the area and have a cosmopolitan population. However, Jeddah as the port of Mecca has grown to be the main city of the Hijaz and until recently has been the main commercial centre of Saudi Arabia. The architecture of the Hijaz is particularly subject to outside influences, thus settlements of al-'Ula, Tabuk and al-Wajh developed as a result of the pilgrim routes. The medieval khan of Qasr Zurayb near al-Wajh is a clear example of this external influence.

Tihama and 'Asir

The Tihama is located in the south-west corner of Saudi Arabia and comprises two distinct regions, the hot humid coastal plain and the high mountains of 'Asir. The architecture of the coastal plain is of two types, town houses and rural houses. The town houses are built of coral and are usually rectangular single-storey buildings with a courtyard. Rural houses are made of wood and thatch and are related to the architecture of nearby East Africa. The architecture of the mountains is built of stone and is related to the mountain architecture of Yemen.

Najd

The Najd is a plateau in the centre of Arabia south of the Nafud desert. The principal areas of occupation are clustered around the Jabal Tuwayq and include Riyadh, the present capital of the country as well as Ha'il, the nineteenth-century capital. North of the Nafud desert is the oasis town of Dumat al-Jandal which has a mosque attributed to the second caliph, 'Umar ibn al-Khattab (634–44).

Al-Hassa

The great oasis of al-Hassa stands about 60 km from the coast of the Arabian Gulf. The architecture of the area is predominantly stone and mud, although its position near the coast means that it is open to outside influences, the most obvious of which is the white plaster decoration used to create stucco panels and decorative arches. During the sixteenth century the oasis was occupied by the Ottoman Turks in an attempt to curb Saffavid or Portuguese ambitions in the area, and Ottoman influence may still be seen in Hufuf, the principal town of the oasis. The mosque of Ibrahim has a large central dome resting on four large squinches and a domed portico similar to classical Ottoman mosques. Nevertheless, the mosque is not Ottoman in details such as the muqarnas hood of the mihrab or the use of polylobed arches.

The Gulf Coast

The Gulf coast includes the towns of al-Jubayl, al-Qatif and the modern city of Dhahran. As on the west coast coral is the traditional building material although it is used in a different form. One of the notable features of this architecture is the use of thin coral panels held between piers. Also the buildings of this region are distinguished by their use of decorative arches and ornamental plasterwork.

See also: Ka'ba, Mecca, Medina

Further reading:

G. R. D. King, 'Traditional architecture in Najd, Saudi Arabia', *Proceedings of the Tenth Seminar for Arabian Studies*, London 1976, 90–100.

—— 'Islamic architecture in Eastern Arabia', *Proceedings of the Eleventh Seminar for Arabian Studies*, London 1977, 15–28.

—— *Historical Mosques of Saudi Arabia*, London and New York 1986.

—— 'Building methods and materials in western Saudi Arabia', *Proceedings of the Seminar for Arabian Studies*, vol. 19 1989.

T. Prochazka, 'The architecture of the Saudi Arabian south west', *Proceedings of the Tenth Seminar for Arabian Studies*, London 1976, 120–33.

Sawma'a

Minaret.

sebil

Turkish term for a drinking fountain. Also used to refer to a small kiosk with attendant who dispenses water, or sherbet, from behind a grille.

Selimiye

Ottoman mosque at Edirne in European Turkey considered to be the culmination of Ottoman architecture.

The mosque forms the centre of a complex which includes a madrassa (college), a Quran reading room and a huge covered market, the proceeds of which paid for the upkeep of the mosque. This complex, built by the famous architect Sinan, is generally considered to be his greatest work. The mosque consists of two rectangular areas of equal size placed side by side; the northern area is the courtyard and portico and the southern area comprises the prayer hall of the mosque covered by a huge dome, 32 m in diameter. The dome is the same size as that of the Hagia Sophia, thus achieving the Ottoman ambition of building a mosque of equal size and brilliance to the Ottoman masterpiece. Instead of using half-domes of the same radius placed at the sides of the central dome as was usual in earlier mosques, Sinan used smaller corner domes which function as giant squinches. The dome rests on an octagon formed by eight massive cylindrical fluted piers which project through the roof to act as stabilizing turrets for the fenestrated drum. The significance of the design is that it breaks away from the square domed area which had remained the dominant principal in Ottoman mosque architecture.

Like the Süleymaniye and the Üç Şerefeli Mosque, the Selimiye has four minarets, but here they are placed at each corner of the mosque rather than at the corners of the courtyard as had happened previously. At 68 m these are the tallest Ottoman minarets and with their central positioning emphasize the pyramid-like mass of the dome.

The mosque is built mainly of yellow sandstone although red sandstone is also used for voussoirs in arches and for outlining architectural details. The interior of the building is provided with traditional mosque furniture, the most impressive of which is the tall marble minbar. The sides of the minbar are decorated with a carved geometric interlace pattern based on a twelve-pointed star and circle. Directly below the dome is the square muezzin's gallery resting on an arcade of wide-lobed arches, and below this is a small marble fountain emphasizing the central axis of the dome. The mihrab is contained within a square, apse-like area and covered by a small semi-dome which emphasizes its position. The royal prayer room is located on an upper gallery in the north-west corner of the mosque as was traditional in Ottoman architecture. The royal area is heavily decorated with Iznik tile panels and stained-glass windows, whilst the south window forms the mihrab niche.

See also: Edirne, Ottomans, Sinan, Süleymaniye

Seljuks

Turkish dynasty which ruled much of Anatolia, Syria, Iraq, Iran and Central Asia during the eleventh century.

The Seljuks were a division of the Kiniq clan of Öghuz Turks who originated in the steppes north of the Aral Sea. Originally they were hired as soldiers to take part in the internal feuding of Khurassan and eastern Iran. In 1038 the leader Tughril Beg gained control of all Khurassan and had himself proclaimed sultan at Nishapur. As Sunni Muslims the Seljuks wanted to restore orthodoxy to the central Islamic lands and in 1055 Tughril defeated the Sh'ia Buwaihids who ruled from Baghdad. Further victories followed with the defeat of the Byzantines at Manzikert in 1071 and the defeat of the Qarakhanids in Central Asia in the late eleventh century. The unified Seljuk state did not last much beyond the beginning of the twelfth century, partly owing to its pattern of inheritance and partly because the areas covered were too diverse.

During the twelfth century the empire broke up into a number of independent principalities which can be classified into three main groups: a western group comprising Anatolia, a central group covering Syria and Iraq, and an eastern group including Iran and and Central Asia.

Seljuk architecture is characterized by the rapid transmission of ideas and forms. During this period many of the characteristic forms of Islamic architecture become common everywhere, thus madrassas, memorial tombs and khans were built from Central Asia to western Anatolia. Iwans became one of the principal architectural units and were used both for religious and secular buildings. In Iran and the eastern areas decorative brickwork and elaborate stucco ornamentation are common, whilst in Anatolia these decorative themes were translated into stone.

The homeland of Seljuk architecture was Iran, where the first permanent Seljuk structures were built. Unfortunately the Mongol invasions destroyed most of these buildings and only a few remain. In 1063 Isfahan was established as capital of the Great Seljuk Empire under Alp Arslan and parts of the Great Mosque date to this period. The most significant alteration carried out in the early twelfth century was the conversion of the building into a four-iwan plan mosque. Another mosque-type introduced at this time was the kiosk mosque, consisting of a domed space with three open sides and wall containing a mihrab on the qibla side. The architecture of this period was also characterized by memorial tombs which were usually octagonal structures with domed roofs. The most impressive example of tomb architecture is the mausoleum of Sultan Sanjar at Merv, a massive building measuring 27 m square with a huge double dome resting on squinches and muqarnas pendentives.

In Syria and Iraq the surviving monuments are represented by madrassas and tombs. The madrassas such as the Mustansiriya in Baghdad or the Muristan in Damascus were built to a four-iwan plan, while the tombs were characterized by conical muqarnas domes.

The greatest number of surviving Seljuk monuments are in Anatolia. Characteristic features of

Seljuk architecture in the region are elaborate stone portal façades carved in deep relief, small courtyards which are sometimes covered (to cope with the cold climate), and the introduction of tiles as architectural decoration.

The first mosques built in Anatolia copied the layout of Syrian mosques thus the mosques of Diyarbakir (1091), Dunaysir (1204) and Silvan (1152) have a design based in that of the Great Mosque in Damascus. Later on the design changes, so that in buildings such as the Great Mosque at Harout and the Kolluk Mosque at Kayseri the courtyard is reduced to a small area in the centre of a large prayer hall. Other mosques were built with an iwan on the qibla side of the courtyard which leads into a domed prayer hall. Another development of the period is the introduction of wooden mosques which may have been common in Central Asia at the time (no examples survive from there). These are large halls with flat roofs supported on wooden columns with muqarnas capitals. The Eshrefoglu Mosque at Beyshehir has this form but has a separate brick dome resting on columns in front of the mihrab and an open bay in the centre recalling the courtyard of earlier mosques.

Like the mosques, the Seljuk madrassas of Anatolia were built around small courtyards which were sometimes roofed with domes or vaults. The central court was often surrounded with arcades, with an iwan on the qibla side functioning as the prayer hall. The mausoleums were like those of Central Asia with an octagonal plan and conical roofs.

See also: Baghdad, Damascus, Iran, Iraq, Isfahan, Merv, Nishapur, Syria

semahane

Literally 'dance hall'; an Ottoman Turkish term for a room used for dervishes to dance. The typical Ottoman semahane was an octagonal domed room often attached to a mosque. The most famous is the Mevlana dervish centre in Konya.

serai

Turkish term for a palace.

serdab

Sunken courtyard opening on to underground rooms used to escape the heat of the day. Serdabs are of pre-Islamic Iranian origin but were rapidly incorporated into Islamic architecture. One of the earliest examples is in the palace of Khirbet al-Mafjar.

şeref

Ottoman term for the balcony on a minaret. Most minarets only have one balcony, although some of the more important mosques have minarets with up to three, the most famous example being the Üç Şerefeli Mosque in Edirne.

Seville (Arabic: Ishbiliyya)

City in south-west Spain originally capital of the Muslim province of al-Andalus (Spain) and later one of main centres of Islamic culture in Spain.

Before the coming of Islam, Seville was the first capital of the Visigoths until they moved to Toledo. It was captured by the Arabs in the eighth century and remained a Muslim city until the early thirteenth century when it was taken by the Christian armies of Ferdinand III. Despite this change Seville remained an important centre of Mudéjar architecture throughout the Middle Ages.

During the Islamic period the city was known for silk weaving and scholarship and was the home to the famous physician and philosopher Averroës. Unfortunately little remains of the early Islamic city, although traces of the Almohad and Almoravid city remain along with fine examples of Mudéjar craftsmanship.

Parts of the first Umayyad mosque founded in 859 can be found in the church of San Salvador. These remains include arcades resting on columns (now sunk deep into the ground) and the minaret which may be the oldest surviving Muslim building in Spain. The present cathedral of Santa Maria de la Sede is built on the site of the Almohad Great Mosque built in 1172. The mosque itself no longer exists but the minaret known as La Giralda still dominates the city's main square. The tower took fourteen years to build and is over 50 m high. The tower has a square base and shaft (like all minarets in Spain) and has ramps inside instead of staircases. The interior contains seven chambers, one on each storey, each with a different type of vault. Each face of the exterior is divided into three vertical strips or decorative panels. Each floor has a centrally placed pair of windows with a single column in the middle and either side of the windows are paired niches of similar design. Above the windows and niches is a delicate net-like diamond pattern executed in elaborate brickwork. The tower bears a strong resemblance to the Kutubiyya minaret in Marakesh also built by the Almohads.

Little remains of the original defences of the city which contained twelve gates and 116 interval towers, although the remaining parts have been recently restored. The Torre del Oro, a twelve-sided tower, represents the latest phase of Muslim fortifications. The best example of Mudéjar architecture in Seville is the Alcazar which was rebuilt as the palace of Pedro the Cruel in the fourteenth century. Many of the masons and carpenters were hired from Granada thus explaining some of the similarity between the lavish decoration and intricate design of this palace and the Alhambra. The palace also re-used some of the columns and other building materials taken from Madinat al-Zahra' after its destruction in 1010. The palace contains a series of courtyards or patios which are decorated with intricate carved stonework arcades and polychrome tile dadoes. The most famous of these courtyards is the Patio de las Doncellas which has an arcade composed of multi-lobed arches resting on twin columns, above which is a diaper pattern similar to that of the Giralda Minaret. The highlight of the palace is the Salón de los Embajadores which is covered with an amazing wooden dome decorated with star patterns and supported on intricate wooden muqarnas squinches.

See also: Alhambra, Córdoba, Mudéjar, Spain

Sfax

Walled city located on the east coast of Tunisia.

Sfax rose to prominence under the Aghlabids in the ninth century. The city walls, built in the late seventh century, were renewed in the ninth and provided with huge square and polygonal towers. The Great Mosque is similar to that of Qairawan and is the only mosque to have the same arrangement of a square minaret on the north side aligned with the mihrab.

See also: Aghlabids, Tunisia

Shanga

Islamic trading city in the Lamu archipelago off the north Kenya coast, East Africa.

Shanga is one of the most intensively investigated early Islamic sites in East Africa with an occupation stretching from the mid-eighth to the fourteenth century. It is not mentioned in any major historical sources except for a passing reference in the Pate Chronicle, so that all information comes from excavations carried out in recent years.

The earliest phase, dated to the eighth century, is represented by a large rectangular wooden enclosure containing a well and surrounded by roundhouses made of wattle and daub on timber frames. In the second period (ninth–tenth century) a rectangular wooden mosque was built in the central area. Whilst roundhouses continued to be built on the west, on the east side the houses were now rectangular. In the third phase (tenth–eleventh century) the enclosure and mosque were rebuilt in coral stone and a monumental stone building was erected in the centre. At this same time many of the houses outside were also built out of coral stone. The fourth and fifth periods, lasting from the eleventh to the end of the twelfth century, is marked by the decline of the settlement and the

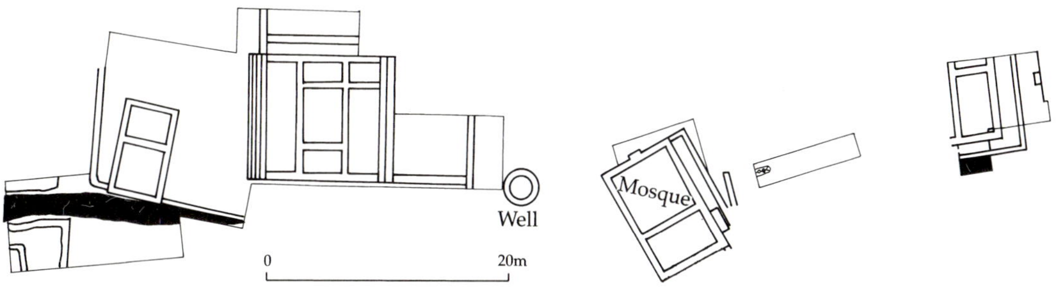

Plan of ninth-century monumental buildings, Shanga, Kenya (after Horton)

reintroduction of wooden architecture in the centre of the site. The sixth phase of occupation (early fourteenth to fifteenth centuries) is represented by the reintroduction of stone buildings using a new technique of fossil coral instead of the previous reef coral. Many of the ruins of this period still survive, and consist of remains of over 200 houses, three mosques and a large number of tombs.

See also: coral, East Africa, Kenya, Manda

Further reading:

M. C. Horton, *Shanga: An Interim Report*, National Museums of Kenya, Nairobi 1981.

—— 'Early Muslim trading settlements on the East African coast: new evidence from Shanga', *Antiquaries Journal* 67: 290–323, 1987.

Shar-i Sabz

Town in Uzbekistan, Central Asia, which Timur tried to make his capital in the fourteenth century.

The city or town forms a rectangular enclosure surrounded by a wall approximately 4 km in circumference and in places up to 5 m thick. The main ruins at the site are the monumental entrance to Timur's palace (the Ak Saray, 'White Palace') and the Dar al-Siyadat. Although incomplete it can be seen that the entrance arch would have been more than 50 m high and 22 m wide, making it one of the largest archways in the Islamic world. The interior of the iwan and the towers flanking it are decorated with light and dark blue-glazed bricks forming a geometric carpet-like pattern which includes the names Allah, Muhammad, Ali and Othman in large square calligraphy. An archaeological analysis of the site has shown that the portal would have been preceded by a huge open space 70–80 m long which would have emphasized the massive proportions of the building. Inside the entrance, the palace would have comprised a large courtyard with a central pool and audience hall on the same axis as the entrance. The royal cemetery known as the Dar al-Siyadat contained the tomb of Jahangir (with a tall domed roof) and the tomb intended for Timur himself (this had a conical roof on a cruciform plan). Other buildings preserved at the site include the baths and the bazar. The bazar comprises four main streets which converge on a central crossroads covered with a dome.

shish mahal

Mughal term for a room decorated with mirror mosaics.

Sicily

Large island south of Italy, occupied by Muslim Arabs for 200 years.

The first Arab conquest in Sicily was the capture of Mazara in 827 by the Aghlabid governors of Ifriqiyya (roughly equivalent to modern Tunisia). The conquest of the island was not complete until 75 years later, although immigration began immediately. In 1061 the island was captured by the Normans and became the centre of a flourishing Byzantine, Islamic and Norman culture.

There are few architectural remains of the Islamic period because most buildings were rebuilt or remodelled later under the Normans. Indeed, many of the most important Arab buildings were themselves converted Byzantine structures; thus the cathedral of the capital at Palermo was converted into the Great Mosque by the Arabs and subsequently became a Norman cathedral. There are only two entirely Muslim structures which have survived. These are La Favara Castle (Arabic al-Fawwara) and the eleventh-century baths of Cefala 30 km outside Palermo.

Probably the most significant traces of Islamic architecture are found in the buildings of the Norman kingdom, when Arab craftsmen and designs continued to be used. Probably the most striking example of this is the Cappella Palatina with its painted wooden ceiling. To the south of Palermo the Norman king built a royal park in the Islamic style, with palaces and hunting lodges. One of the best preserved palaces is the Ziza Palace built by William II (1166–89). This rectangular structure is built in the form of an Islamic reception hall with a central cruciform reception room flanked by smaller rooms. The building is decorated with muqarnas corbels, rows of blind niches and a fountain which runs in a narrow channel through the palace.

See also: Aghlabids

Further reading:

G. Marçais, *L'architecture musulmane d'Occident: Tunisie, Algerie, Maroc, Espagne et Sicile*, Paris 1955.

Sinan (Koca Sinan; 1491–1588)

Famous Ottoman architect responsible for transforming Ottoman architecture from a traditional discipline into a conscious art form.

Sinan was born a Christian in the Karaman region of south-east Anatolia and at the age of 21 was recruited into the Janissaries (special Ottoman force selected from subject Christian populations). As part of his training Sinan worked as a carpenter and engineer on building sites in Istanbul. As a soldier Sinan fought for the emperor in Rhodes, Belgrade, Baghdad and Moldavia, rising rapidly to the position of Commander of the Royal Guard. During this period Sinan may have worked as a military engineer converting churches into mosques and building bridges. Sinan's first recorded building is the Hüsrev Pasha Cami in Aleppo built between 1536 and 1537. This complex consists of a single-domed mosque with a small rectangular courtyard and two madrassas located on an irregular-shaped site. The mosque's tall dome is pierced by sixteen windows and supported by buttresses. In order to compensate for the height of the dome Sinan built the portico wider than the mosque adding an extra bay at each end. This solution causes problems for the positioning of the windows and the pendentives of the portico domes which clash.

In 1538 at the age of 47 Sinan was appointed as the chief architect of Istanbul by Suleyman the Magnificent. During the next fifty years Sinan built over 300 buildings, recorded by his friend and biographer Mustafa Sâ'i. Sinan's first task as chief architect was the construction of a women's hospital for Suleyman's Russian wife. The complex known as the Haseki Hürrem was built on an irregular site and consisted of a hospital, hostel, mosque and medical school (Tip medrese). Although the building may not have been started by Sinan and has been subsequently altered, it conveys an impression of his ability to manage a difficult site and produce an impressive, functioning building. This ability is more clearly expressed in the tomb of the Grand Admiral Hayrettin Barbaros built in 1541. This is a tall octagonal chamber covered with a dome and pierced by two sets of windows, an upper level and a lower level. The lower-level windows are rectangular, covered with lintels under relieving arches, whilst those of the upper level are covered with shallow four-pointed arches. The exterior of the building is very plain, except for the windows and two plain mouldings marking the transition from wall to drum and from drum to dome. The severe impression created is modified by the high quality of workmanship and the harmonic proportions.

Sinan's first major work is the Şehzade Cami in Istanbul built in memory of Suleyman's son and the heir to the throne who died at the age of 22. The complex, begun in 1543 and completed five years later, contains a madrassa, an imaret (hospice) and a Quran school besides the mosque and the tomb of Şehzade. The mosque consists of two equal squares comprising a courtyard and domed prayer room. The most notable feature of the design is the use of four semi-domes to expand the interior space, for although this plan had been used earlier at Diyarbakir this was the first time it had been used in an imperial mosque. The arches carrying the large central dome rest on four giant piers which rise up above roof level to act as buttresses for the drum of the dome. This design later became a standard solution to the limitations imposed by the size of domes in Ottoman mosques. Another important innovation was the development of the façades at the side of the mosque and courtyard. This was achieved by placing doorways at the side of the building thus giving the it a cross-axial arrangement. This was important in large complexes where the north façade was not necessarily the most important and certainly not the longest side of the building. The tomb of Şehzade stands alone in a garden to the south of the mosque. This tomb has the same basic form as the Admiral Barbaros tomb although here the austerity is replaced with intense beauty. The dome is composed of fluted ribs, whilst the top of the octagon is marked by ornate crenellations supported on muqarnas corbelling. The interior of the tomb is covered with yellow, blue and green Iznik tiles and light is filtered through stained-glass windows.

Sinan's next important commission was the mosque of Suleyman's daughter Mirimah at Üsküdar known as the Iskele Cami (Harbour Mosque). This was the first of three commissions for Mirimah and her husband Rüstem Pasha the Grand Vizier. The Iskele Cami is built on a raised platform to protect it from the water and has a double portico instead of a courtyard because of lack of space. The double portico is an idea which was also used at the Rüstem Pasha mosques at Tekirdag and Eminönü, both in Istanbul, and later became a standard format for lesser mosques.

Sinan's largest project at this time was the mosque complex of Suleyman which was to be the largest purpose-built mosque in Istanbul. This building known as the Süleymaniye established Sinan's reputation as the foremost of Ottoman architects and is the place which he chose for his own tomb. The complex covers a huge area (about 330 by 200 m) of sloping ground overlooking the Bosphorus with the mosque at the centre. Characteristically Sinan was able to turn the difficulties of the terrain to his advantage by building the complex on several levels. Thus the two madrassas on the east side of the complex are built in steps down the hillside, whilst the mosque itself is built on a huge artificial platform with vaulted substructures on the east side. The mosque itself uses many of the features of the Şehzade Cami such as the lateral entrances, but in place of the cruciform plan there is a central dome between two semi-domes. The mass of the central dome is emphasized by the four minarets, a feature only previously seen at the Üç Şerefeli Cami in Edirne.

Although the Süleymaniye was probably Sinan's largest building complex, it was not his greatest work; this was the Selimiye Cami in Edirne begun nearly twenty years later. The Selimiye built between 1569 and 1575 incorporates many of the features of the Süleymaniye but abandons the system of large semi-domes at the side of the dome in favour of giant squinches placed at the corners. Also the system of four central piers is replaced by eight piers arranged in an octagon with the result that the building has an airiness and space unparalleled in Islamic or Western architecture. The main dome has the same diameter as that of Hagia Sophia and thus achieves the Ottoman ambition of constructing a building equal to the highest achievement of the Byzantines.

Whilst working on the Selimiye Sinan continued to produce a variety of smaller buildings, for example the Sokollu Mehmet Pasha Cami in Istanbul which, like many of his other famous works, was built on a steep hillside. Again Sinan was able to exploit the site by building the courtyard out on to an artificial terrace with an entrance from below. This technique had been used before at the Iskele Cami and the Rüstem Pasha Cami, but not as effectively as here, where a wide staircase leads up into the middle of the courtyard facing the sardivan (fountain).

After the completion of the Selimiye in 1575 Sinan lived for a further thirteen years and continued to design buildings, though is likely that many of these were not visited by him. When he died at the age of 97 Sinan was interred in the tomb he had built for himself next to the Süleymaniye. This is an open canopy covered by a vault set in a garden which originally contained his house. At the end of the garden is a small octagonal domed fountain which had earlier been the cause of a dispute. Sinan's epitaph was written by his friend Mustapha Sâ'i and only mentions one of his works, the four-humped bridge at Büyükçekmice.

Art historians have spent a considerable amount of time discussing Sinan's contribution to architecture and particular his relationship to the Renaissance. There was a considerable amount of contact between Italy and the Ottoman Empire at this stage, as can be seen from invitations to Leonardo da Vinci and later Michelangelo to build a bridge across the Golden Horn. Despite this contact and the similarities between the work of Alberti and Sinan it should be noted that their objectives were different. In Renaissance buildings there was a tension between humanity and God; in those of Sinan there was a single purpose – to mirror a single and infinite Divinity.

See also: Ottomans, Selimiye, Süleymaniye

Further reading:

Ahmet Refik, *Mimar Sinan*, Istanbul 1931.

A. Gabriel, 'Le maître-architecte Sinan', in *La Turquie Kemaliste* 16, Ankara 1936.

G. Goodwin, *A History of Ottoman Architecture*, London 1971.

—— *Sinan*, London 1992.

A. Güler, J. Freely and A. R. Burrelli, *Sinan: Architect of Süleyman the Magnificent and the Ottoman Golden Age*, London 1992.

A. Kuran, M. Niksarli and A. Güler, *Sinan: The Grand Old Master of Ottoman Architecture*, Istanbul 1987.

A. Petruccioli (ed.), *Mimar Sinan: The Urban Vision* (Journal of the Islamic Environmental Design Research Centre), Rome 1988.

A. Stratton, *Sinan*, London 1972.

Singapore

City-state on southern tip of the Malay peninsular with a mixed population of Malays, Chinese and Indians, as well as a small Arab minority.

The earliest mosques in Singapore were built of wood and thatch; during the nineteenth century these were replaced with brick structures. The most important mosque in Singapore is known as the Sultan Mosque and was originally built between 1823 and 1824 with a grant of $3,000 from the British East India Company. The original mosque was demolished in the 1920s to make way for the present structure built by the British firm Swan and Maclaren in 1928. The building has two large onion-shaped domes, a polygonal minaret and crenellations to enliven the façade. Either side of the prayer hall are separate areas for women.

The oldest surviving mosque in Singapore is the Jamae Mosque, which was built on the site of an earlier structure between 1826 and 1835. Its main feature is the façade, which is flanked by two square towers. Each tower is divided into seven mini-storeys linked by decorative crenellations in the form of a mini-gateway. Of similar design is the Nagore Durgha shrine built between 1828 and 1830 which also has two miniature towers either side of a miniaturized entrance façade located on top of the real entrance. It seems likely that these mosque façades may derive from the Char Minar in Hyderabad, south India. A simpler design is represented by the Tamil al Abrar Mosque built in the 1850s where the entrance is flanked by two pillars. Other early mosques include the Abdul Gafoor Mosque (1850s) and the Hajjah Fatimah Mosque (1930) both of which combine European (British) elements with Indian design.

See also: India, Indonesia, Malaysia

Further reading:

J. Beamish and J. Ferguson, *A History of Singapore Architecture: The Making of a City*, Singapore 1985.
Monuments Board of Singapore, *Preservation of Singapore National Monuments*, Singapore 1985.

Siraf

Major early Islamic port city located on the Iranian side of the Arabian/Persian Gulf.

The city contains some of the earliest examples of Islamic architecture excavated in Iran. The most significant discovery is the congregational mosque, a huge rectangular structure with a central courtyard set on a raised podium. There is a single entrance reached by a set of steps on the east side opposite the qibla, next to which is the square base of a mihrab. The first phase of the mosque, dated to the early ninth century, has three arcades parallel to the qibla wall forming the prayer hall, and a single arcade on the other three sides. In the second phase (dated to 850) two more arcades were added to the prayer hall and the single arcades on the other three sides were made double. In both phases the mihrab was a simple rectangular niche set into the middle of the qibla wall. Several smaller mosques were also discovered, each with a rectangular mihrab projecting on to the outside of the building.

See also: Abbasids, Iran, Iraq, Samarra

Further reading:

D. Whitehouse, *Siraf II. The Congregational Mosque and Other Mosques from the Ninth to the Twelfth Centuries*, The British Institute for Persian Studies.

Somalia

Somalia is located on the coast of East Africa directly below the Arabian peninsula.

The landscape of the country is predominantly semi-arid bush with mountains in the north near the border with Ethiopia. The coastal plain is similar to that of Kenya further south, with mangroves and coastal reefs.

Islam seems to have spread to Somalia through Muslim traders who established trading stations and urban centres along the coast between the seventh and the twelfth centuries CE. From the twelfth century the coastal towns had become independent Muslim sultanates fighting the Ethiopian Christians who controlled the interior. From the tenth century the Somalis of the interior gradually adopted Islam and became attached to the coastal towns. During the nineteenth and twentieth centuries Somalia was divided between Italian, British and French administrations before achieving independence in 1960.

The Islamic architecture of Somalia is similar to that of Kenya, with coral used as the main material for permanent buildings. The principal urban centre is Mogadishu which also has some of the oldest mosques, the most famous of which is the mosque of Fakhr al-Din built in the thirteenth century. Further south are a number of ancient urban settlements, the most important of which are Merka, Munghia, Barawa and Bur Gao. Most of the mosques of Merka are eighteenth century or later, although the tomb of Sheikh Uthman Hassan may date to the thirteenth century. Munghia consists of a large roughly square enclosure (about 200 m per side) built of earth with a facing of stone. Approximately in the centre there is a raised mound with the remains of a mosque on

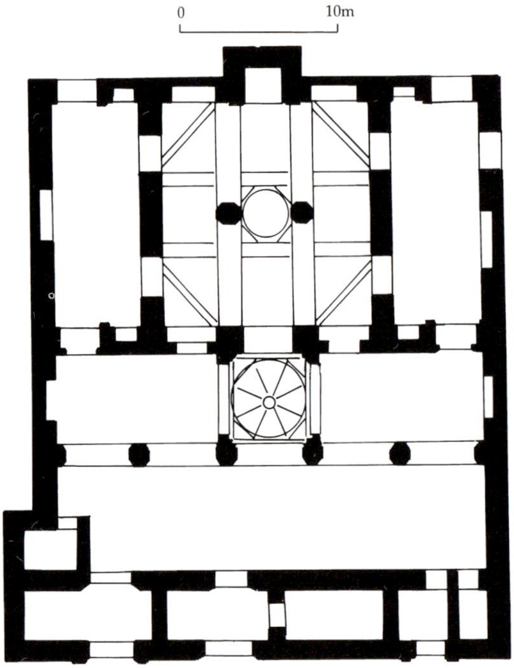

Mosque of Fakhr al-Din, Mogadishu, Somalia (after Garlake)

top. Although the mosque is badly damaged, it seems to consist of a central rectangular hall flanked by two side aisles. The mihrab in the centre of the north wall has a fluted semi-dome and, together with the pottery found there, suggests a twelfth-century foundation for the site. Although Barawa was probably founded at a similar date, the earliest buildings in the town date from the eighteenth century. One of these, a mosque, has a square minaret with elaborate carved woodwork. Probably the largest early site on the coast is Bur Gao whose are contained within a huge enclosure similar to that of Munghia. The principal standing structure on the site is a square building covered with a low domical vault. The site also contains a number of pillar tombs similar to those of north Kenya.

See also: East Africa, Kenya

Further reading:

N. Chittick, 'An archaeological reconnaissance of the southern Somali coast', *Azania* 4: 115–30, 1969.

H. C. Sanservino, 'Archaeological remains on the southern Somali coast', *Azania* 18: 151–64, 1983.

Songhay

The people who inhabit the banks of the Niger river between Gao and Dendi in West Africa.

The Songhay people were the ruling population of the empire of Gao during the fifteenth and sixteenth centuries. Some of them were Muslim before the eleventh century but some have remained pagan to the present day. Little is known of early Songhay architecture, although ancestor-worship seems to have been expressed through earthen burial mounds. Elements of this tradition seem to have been incorporated in Islamic monuments where prominent people are buried within solid-earth pyramid-like constructions, the most famous of which is the tomb of Askiya Muhammad at Gao.

See also: Gao, West Africa

South Africa

The Muslim community of South Africa seems to have originated from south-east Asia, mostly Malaysia. The Malays were mostly brought to South Africa as slaves in the eighteenth century, although some came freely as political exiles Although they were allowed to remain Muslim they were not able to worship publicly until 1804. Before that time prayer was carried out within houses or in the open air. The first purpose-built mosque was the Auwal Mosque in Cape Town built at the beginning of the eighteenth century. In its earliest form the mosque lacked a minaret and resembled a chapel from the exterior. Inside, there were two courtyards, a kitchen and storage rooms as well as a prayer hall. For planning reasons the building was not oriented to face Mecca; instead the mihrab inside was built at an angle to the rest of the building to correct this.

Further reading:

F. R. Bradlow and M. C. Cairns, *The Early Cape Muslims: A Study of their Mosques, Genealogy and Origins*, Cape Town 1978.

Spain (Arabic: al-Andalus)

Large country in south-western Europe occupying the greater part of the Iberian peninsula and known in Arabic as al-Andalus.

Large parts of this country were Muslim from the arrival of the Arab armies in 711 to the fall of the amirate of Granada in 1492. Before the arrival of the first Arab armies Spain was ruled by the

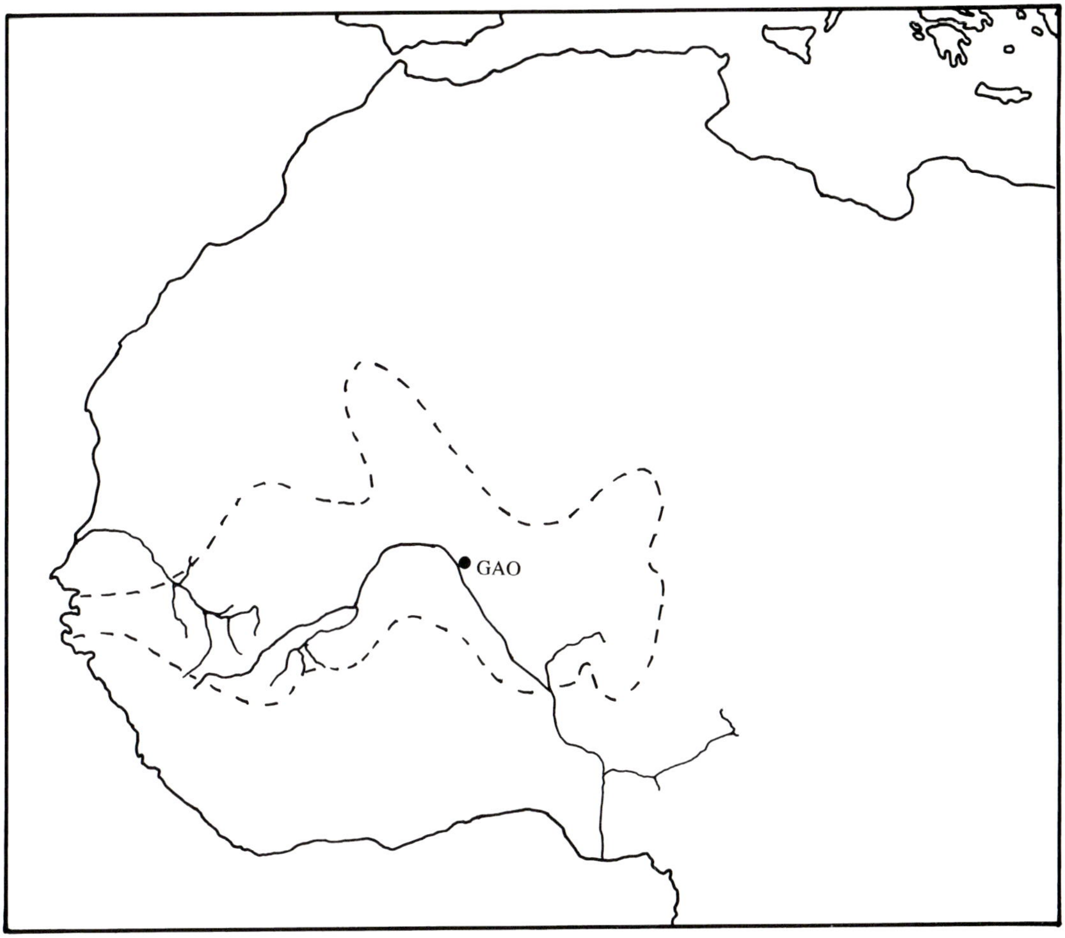

West Africa showing extent of Songhay empire in the sixteenth century

Visigoths, warrior nomads from east of Europe who had recently been converted to Christianity. They in turn had taken over the country after the collapse of the Byzantine rule which was a direct continuation of Roman suzerainty in the country. At the time of the Arab invasions the Visigothic kingdom was weak and their king Roderick was not universally acknowledged.

The Arab conquest was carried out by Musa the commander of North Africa and his semilegendary lieutenant Tariq. Within a year Toledo, the Visigothic capital, had been captured. The speed of the conquest alarmed the caliph who in 716 summoned the commander and his general to return. Nevertheless, the conquest continued northwards and by the 730s had reached central France where it was finally checked by Charles Martel at a battle between Poitiers and Tours. The only area of Spain which withstood the invasion was the region of Asturias in the Cantabrian mountains of the north-west. Until the 750s the province was ruled by governors sent by the Umayyad caliphs. The Abbasid revolution had led to the killing of all members of the Umayyad dynasty with the exception of Abd al-Rahman who escaped via North Africa to Spain where he defeated the resident governor Yusuf in a battle near Toledo. For the next 270 years the country was ruled by the Umayyad descendants of Abd al-Rahman. The most famous member of this dynasty was Abd al-Rahman III who reigned for fifty years between 912 and 961. It was during this reign that the title of the ruler

Islamic Spain in the eighth century

was changed from amir to caliph and 'Commander of the Faithful' in order to counter the claims of the Fatimid caliphate. During this period the capital was Córdoba which became one of the brightest centres of culture in the Islamic world. Despite this high level of sophistication, the dynasty itself was prone to internal divisions and finally collapsed in 1031.

For the next half century Spain was divided into at least twenty-three independent principalities, known as the Muluk al-Tawaif, each with its own court and ruler. The size of these principalities varied greatly, with some ruling a single city whilst others like the Aftasids in south-west Spain ruled large areas of the country. Despite political disunity the Islamic culture of Spain thrived during this period. Nevertheless, the Christians of the north-west were able to exploit divisions amongst the Muslims to conquer extensive territories. The capture of Toledo by Alfonso VI of Castile in 1085 showed the weakness of these principalities and encouraged the conquest of the Almoravids in 1090.

The Almoravids were a dynasty of fanatical fundamentalist Berbers from North Africa. Under their leader Yusuf, the Almoravids invaded Spain and stemmed the tide of Christian conquest. From their newly established capital of Marakesh the Almoravids now ruled a huge area from present-day Senegal to Spain.

In 1145 the Almoravids, weakened by disunity, were replaced by the Almohads, another fanatical Berber group who managed to challenge the Christian advance. By 1212, however, the Almohads were driven from Spain by a coalition of Christian rulers. This left Granada as the only Muslim province to survive the Christian invasions. Granada was ruled by the Nasirid dynasty which maintained the area as a centre of cultural and scientific excellence with the Alhambra at its centre. The Nasirids were finally ousted from their position in 1492 by the united forces of Castile and Aragon under Ferdinand and Isabella.

Despite the political defeat of Islam in Spain Muslims continued to live in the country until the seventeenth century when they were all expelled. Nevertheless, traces of Islamic presence survive in the culture and architecture of Spain.

In many ways the landscape of Spain is similar to that of North Africa with its aridity, high mountains and endless desert-like plains. Communication from one part to another is hindered by precipitous valleys, high mountains and the three major rivers of the Ebro, Tagus and the Duero.

The building materials of Islamic Spain reflect the availability of natural resources and the diversity of cultural influences. The main materials used are wood, stone and baked brick, although mud brick was also used. Unlike many parts of the Middle East, Spain had plentiful supplies of timber suitable for building including both pine and oak. Wood was usually used for roofs which were normally gabled and covered with baked clay tiles, although occasionally wooden domes were also used. The pine roofs of the Great Mosque in Córdoba reflect the plentiful supplies of wood in medieval Spain. Stone was used for walls either in the form of ashlar masonry or in the form of coursed rubble. Often masonry was re-used from earlier Roman or Visigothic structures, although fine stone carving continued. One of the most distinctive features of Spanish Islamic architecture is the use of brick which, like ashlar masonry, was a direct continuation of Roman building methods. Sometimes stone was encased in brick in the same manner as Byzantine fortifications.

Notable features of Spanish Islamic architecture include horseshoe arches, paired windows with a central column, construction in brick and stone, polychrome tiles, intricate carved stucco work and overlapping arches. Several terms are used to describe Islamic-type architecture in Spain each of which has a particular meaning. The best-known term is 'Moorish' which is often used to refer to Islamic architecture in general although it more properly should be used to describe the architecture of the Moors or Berbers of North Africa. The less well-known term Mudéjar refers to architecture carried out for Christian patrons by Muslim craftsmen. Mudéjar architecture uses many of the most characteristic features of Islamic architecture including Arabic calligraphy and the horseshoe arch. Many of Christian Spain's most beautiful churches and palaces were built by Mudéjar craftsmen and the tradition was carried on into the new world. A related style is known as Mozarabic which refers to the architecture of Christian buildings under Muslim rule. In addition to its influence on Christian buildings, Islamic architecture also influenced the substantial Jewish community in Spain so that many synagogues in Spain were built in an Islamic style (the best examples are in Toledo, see below).

The range of buildings surviving from the Islamic period in Spain is quite large and includes castles, fortifications, mosques, churches and synagogues, palaces, bridges, hammams, mills, villages and towns. The most numerous remains are castles and fortifications which can be found throughout the country and from all periods from the eighth to the fifteenth century. These are often difficult to date precisely and most were subsequently re-used after the Christian reconquest. One of the best examples of early fortification are the walls and square battered towers of the castle known as Baños de la Encina near Jaén in Andalusía. Here the gate is sandwiched between two towers and protected by machicolation and a portcullis. Later on fortifications were protected by bent entrances where the gateway was perpendicular to the walls, thus exposing attackers to fire from three sides. A later development of fortifications was the albarrani tower which was located outside the city walls but connected to it by a bridge so that defenders were able to outflank their attackers. Often albarrani towers were built to protect buildings outside the walls without the added expense and inconvenience of changing the line of the city wall; thus at Calatrava la Vieja the tower was built to protect a nearby watermill. In addition to the major fortifications hundreds of small towers and forts were built all over the peninsula to defend borders and coasts. These were often small isolated towers built of cheap local materials such as mud brick or coursed rubble, although sometimes they were sophisticated structures dominating the countryside like the castle of Belmez near Córdoba.

Most of the mosques of Spain were converted into churches after the reconquest, some with very little alteration and others where the architecture was profoundly damaged as in the case of the Great Mosque of Córdoba where a cathedral was built in the middle of the structure in the sixteenth century. Characteristic features of Spanish mosques are square minarets and large mihrabs which are sometimes like a separate room. Where decoration has survived intact it is usually very elaborate and includes carved plaster and woodwork.

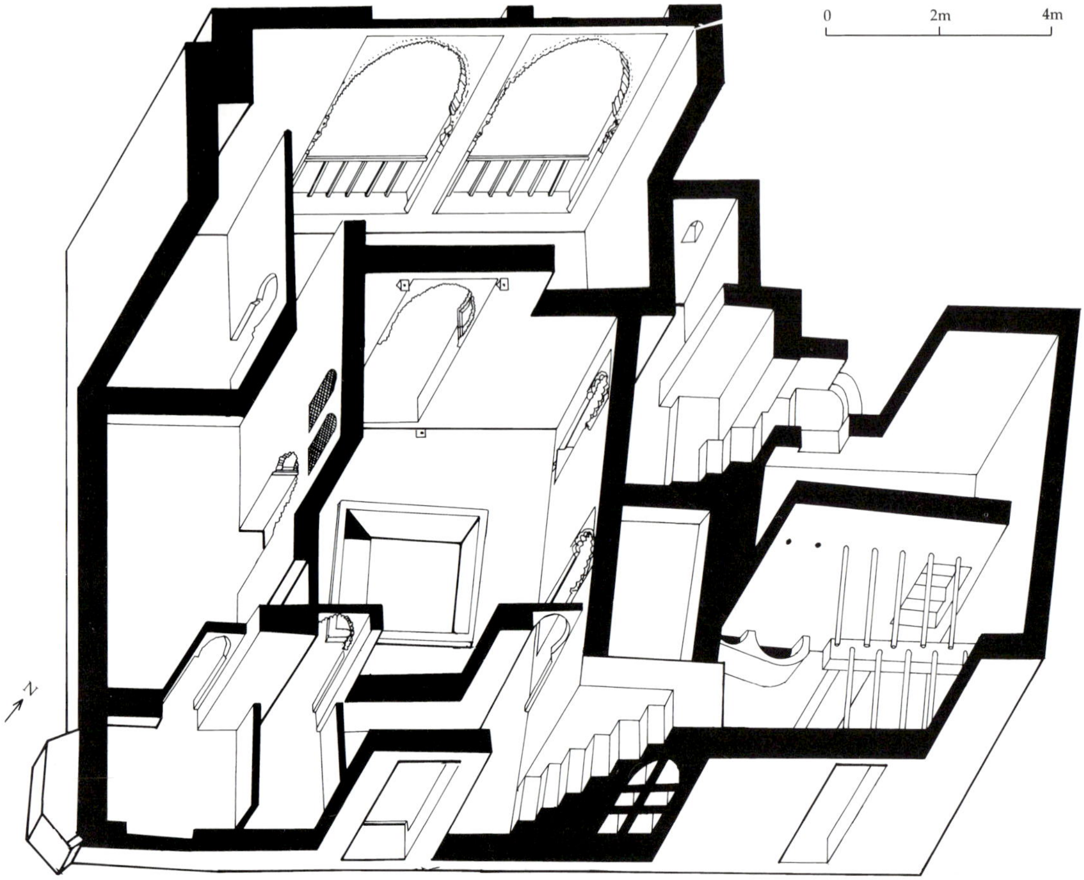

Thirteenth-century house at Siyasa (after Palazon)

Palaces fared better after the reconquest and some of the finest examples of Islamic palaces can be found in Spain such as the Alhambra and the Generalife. The Islamic palatial tradition was continued after the reconquest with palaces which are almost entirely Islamic in conception, like that of Pedro the Cruel in the Alcazar at Seville. Another type of Islamic building often associated with palaces is the hammam. Few of these have survived in Spain although fine examples can be seen at Ronda and Granada. Bridges and mills are less easy to distinguish as Muslim work, although many examples survive. It is thought that some of the water mills near Córdoba may be related to the great water wheels of Syria. In addition to specific buildings and monuments many towns and villages retain the layout and appearance of Islamic times. Some of the more important cities with substantial traces of Islamic architecture are Córdoba, Seville, Granada, Toledo and Zaragoza, but many other towns and cities contain traces of Islamic buildings including Madrid and Asturias (starting-point of the reconquest).

The area conquered by the Arabs in the eighth century still contained many remains of the Roman and Byzantine civilizations which proceeded the Visigothic conquest, and many of the basic techniques of construction remained the same throughout the Islamic period. The contribution of the Visigoths to Islamic architecture is poorly documented although it is thought that the ubiquitous horseshoe arch may be derived from Visigothic architecture. The distinctive features of Islamic buildings in Spain may in part reflect its early incorporation into the Islamic caliphate and its distance from the centre of the empire. The most notable influences from within Islam are from North Africa and Syria. The North African influence is easy to explain through its proximity and the successive invasions of Berber tribes under the Almohads and the Almoravids, the most famous example being the Giralda tower in Seville. Syrian architecture, however, influenced Spain through the Umayyad dynasty who sought to recall their homeland and assert their legitimacy through copying Syrian buildings and hiring Syrian architects. The most striking example of this is the city of Madinat al-Zahra' near Córdoba which is meant to recall the desert palaces of the Umayyads and in particular Rusafa.

Other notable influences were Byzantine architecture, both through remains of Byzantine structures in Spain and through the friendship between the Byzantine emperors and the Umayyad rulers, born out of a mutual dislike of the Fatimids.

See also: Alhambra, Córdoba, Córdoba Great Mosque, Granada, Seville, Toledo, Zaragoza

Further reading:

G. Goodwin, *Islamic Spain*, Architectural Guides for Travellers, London 1990. (This is the best available general guide in English.)

M. Asin, *Guadalajara Medieval, Arte y Arqueología Arabe y Mudéjar*, C.S.I.C. Madrid 1984.

C. Esco, J. Giraut and P. Senac, *Arqueología Islamica de la Marca Superior de al-Andalus*, Huesca 1988.

C. Ewart, 'Tipología de la mezquita en Occidente de los Amayas a los Almohades', Congresso de Arqueología Medieval Española, 1: 180–204, Madrid 1987.

E. Lambert, *Art Musulman et Art Chrétien dans la Péninsule Ibérique*, Paris and Toulouse 1958.

B. Pavón-Maldoado, *Les Almenas Decorativas Hispano Musulmanas*, Madrid 1967.

F. Prieto-Moreno, *Los Jardines de Granada*, Madrid 1952.

E. Sordo and W. Swaan, *Moorish Spain: Córdoba, Seville and Granada*, trans. I. Michael, London 1963.

J. Zozaya, 'Islamic fortifications in Spain; some aspects', Papers in Iberian Archaeology, B.A.R. 193, Oxford 1984.

squinch

Small arch in the corner of a building that converts a square space to an octagonal area which may then be covered with a dome.

stucco

Decorative plasterwork used in architecture.

Stucco is primarily an invention of the Iranian world where it was used in the absence of suitable stone for carving. It has a long history which can be traced back as far as Parthian times, when it was used to cover rubble masonry. During the Sassanian period stucco continued to be used to enliven surfaces on buildings made of baked brick or mud brick. By the sixth century stucco was used in the eastern Mediterranean although it was mostly a characteristic of Iranian architecture. The advent of Islam led to an unparalleled growth in its use throughout the Middle East and North Africa. Many of the earliest Islamic monuments employ stucco as the main form of decoration, as dadoes, ceiling decoration or sculpture. Usually the stucco was carved or moulded, although it was often painted as well.

The most adventurous uses of stucco can be found in the Umayyad palaces of Syria and Palestine. At Khirbet al-Mafjar in the Jordan valley the lavish decoration includes painted stucco statues of semi-naked bathing girls and stucco representation of the caliph himself. However, usually stucco was

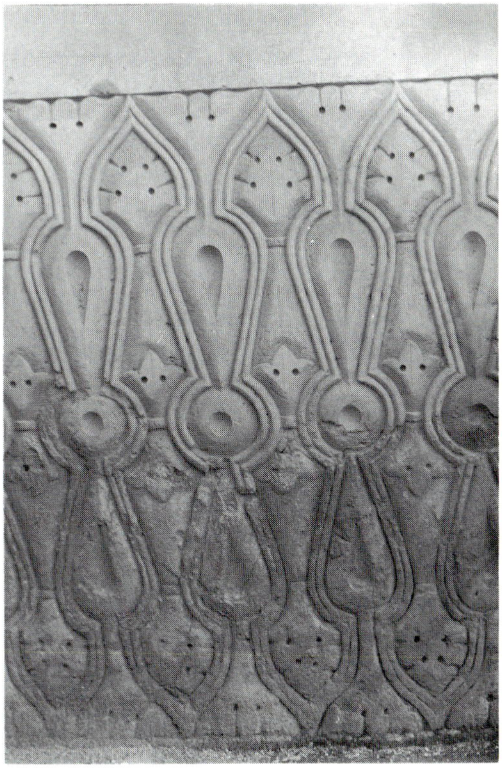

Stucco in serdab of main palace at Samarra

restricted to its original function of covering walls and ceilings with carved or moulded patterns. The largest corpus of stucco work from the early Islamic period has been found at the Abbasid capital of Samarra in Iraq. The stucco from this site has been divided into three groups or styles which may represent a chronological development. Style 'A' consists of vine leaves and vegetal forms derived from the Byzantine architecture of Syria–Palestine; style 'B' is a more abstract version of this; and style 'C' is entirely abstract with no recognizable representational forms. The first two styles appear to be carved, but the third style was produced by wooden moulds. The Samarra styles are significant as they reappear later in buildings such as the Ibn Tulun Mosque where the soffits of the arches are decorated with style 'B' ornament. After the collapse of the Abbasid caliphate stucco continued to be one of the main forms of decoration and spread throughout the Islamic world to India, Anatolia and Spain.

See also: Khirbet al-Mafjar, Samarra

Sudan

The Republic of Sudan is the largest country in Africa and spans the area between North Africa and sub-Saharan Africa.

Like Egypt, Sudan owes its existence to the Nile, which flows through the country from Kenya in the south to Egypt in the north. The western part of the country forms part of the Sahara desert whilst the area east of the Nile is divided between the Ethiopian Highlands and the Red Sea.

Although Islam is the official religion, Muslims only make up two-thirds of the population, the rest of whom are either Christian (4 per cent) or have tribal religions. Historically northern Sudan has always been dominated by its Egyptian neighbour to the north, nevertheless, throughout the medieval period (seventh to sixteenth centuries) a number of Christian urban centres such as Meroe and Kush have flourished. Islam became the principal religion of north Sudan in the early nineteenth century after the invasions of the Egyptian ruler Muhammad Ali. In the late nineteenth century there was a revolt against Turkish Egyptian rule which led to the establishment of a quasi-religious state ruled by the Mahdi. This state lasted for sixteen years until 1898 when the country was incorporated into the British Empire.

The materials of construction used in the Sudan vary greatly depending on the region and the people. On the Red Sea coast in the north of the country coral is the traditional material for permanent buildings, whereas in those parts bordering on the Nile, including Khartoum, mud is principally used.

There are few Islamic buildings in Sudan which date from before the nineteenth century, except in the Red Sea port of Suakin. This city which lies to the south of Port Sudan flourished under the Ottomans from the sixteenth century. Now almost entirely abandoned, Suakin provides a useful indication of the historic urban architecture of the Red Sea coast which has elsewhere mostly disappeared. The houses, many of them up to three storeys high, are built of coral slabs taken from the coastal foreshore.

In the Nile valley houses are traditionally built around two or three sides of a large central courtyard or compound. The standard method of construction is horizontal courses of mud and dung mixed with small stones and later covered with a plaster of smooth mud (jalus). The most striking feature of traditional houses in the area is the painted decoration made of mud- and lime-based pigments. Usually the outer façades of the houses are decorated with particular emphasis on the doors, whilst inside a principal reception room is also decorated.

See also: East Africa, Egypt, Somalia

Süleymaniye

Ottoman mosque complex in Istanbul built for Suleyman the Magnificent between 1550 and 1557.

The complex consisted of a hospital, medical school, hospice, soup kitchen, primary school, four madrassas (colleges), shops and coffee houses in addition to the mosque itself. The complex is built on an artificial platform on top of a hill that overlooks the Bosphorus; to the east the ground slopes away rapidly. The mosque precinct contains three main areas, the mosque itself in the centre, a courtyard to the north and a tomb garden to the south which contains the tomb of Suleyman and his wife. The mosque is covered with a large central dome (25 m diameter) with two large semi-domes of equal radius, one above the north entrance and one above the mihrab. The central area is flanked by side aisles covered by small domes of alternating size. Like that of its predecessor the Şehzade Cami, the central dome rests on four huge central piers placed in a square. The whole building is illuminated with more than a hundred windows and grilles, many of which are filled with stained glass made by the celebrated Ottoman glass-maker Ibrahim Şarhoş. Outside at each corner of the courtyard are four minarets with balconies supported on muqarnas corbels. This is the first Ottoman building in Istanbul to have four minarets, although previously the Üç Şerefeli in Edirne also had four. The sides of the building are enlivened with several entrances (three on each side) approached by steps and two-tier arcaded galleries placed between the outer corner buttresses.

The tomb garden behind the mosque contains a large cemetery which has grown up around the tombs of Suleyman and Roxelane. Both tombs are octagonal structures in the traditional Ottoman fashion, although Suleyman's tomb unusually faces east instead of north. Roxelane's tomb is smaller and placed to one side of Suleyman's tomb which stands in the middle of the garden. The interiors of both tombs are decorated with Iznik tiles, although Roxelane's tomb is significantly less grand. Suleyman's tomb is surrounded by a colonnaded veranda with a porch on the east side. This arrangement is echoed internally where Suleyman's sarcophagus is surrounded by a circular colonnade.

The arrangement of the complex outside the mosque precinct consists of an L-shaped arrangement of buildings on the north-west side and a smaller group to the east. The eastern complex is built on a steep hill so the madrassas are stepped into the hillside. On the north-west corner of the complex is the tomb of the architect Sinan.

See also: Istanbul, Ottomans, Sinan

Sultan Hasan Mosque

Large madrassa, mosque and tomb complex in Cairo built by the Mamluk sultan Hasan.

This building was erected between 1356 and 1361 next to the Citadel of Cairo. The cost of the project was so high that it was never fully completed and Sultan Hasan himself was murdered and his body hidden, so that he was never buried in the mausoleum. It is a huge complex, measuring 65 by 140 m, and four storeys high, making it one of the largest mosques in Cairo. The main function of the building was as a madrassa with tomb attached but its size and the beauty of its prayer hall meant that it was recognized as a congregational mosque as well.

The basic plan of the building consists of a central courtyard leading off into four large iwans. The largest iwan is the prayer hall and behind this is the domed mausoleum. As this was a madrassa for the four rites of Sunni law there were four separate courtyards, one for each of the rites. Around each of these courtyards were the students' rooms arranged in four tiers. Many of the rooms were equipped with latrines and those facing the street had large windows.

The arch of the main iwan, or prayer hall, is very large and certainly the largest of its kind in Cairo. An inscription runs around the three walls of the iwan in an ornate Kufic on a background of floral scrolls which includes Chinese lotus flowers. The mausoleum is entered through a doorway to one side of the mihrab and consists of a domed chamber 21 m square and 30 m high. The original dome was wooden and has not survived, although the muqarnas wooden pendentives which carried it remain.

One of the most important aspects of the Sultan Hasan complex is the treatment of the external façades. Given its prominent position next to the citadel and the size of the complex it was important that its exterior reflected this. Each of the three sides of the mausoleum which projects on the south-east side of the complex consists of a central medallion around which are ranged four sets of windows, two above and two below. The most famous façade of the structure is that containing the entrance on the north side. The entrance-way itself consists of a large recess covered with an extravagant muqarnas vault which is comparable with that of the Gök Madrassa in Turkey. The doorway is set at an angle to the rest of the façade so that it can be seen when approaching along the street. The façade to the right of the doorway consists of long rectangular recesses extending four storeys from the base of the building to the top, each recess containing windows from the students' rooms. The height of this arrangement and its simplicity give this façade a strangely modern appearance.

Further reading:

D. Berhens-Abouseif, *Islamic Architecture in Cairo: An Introduction*, Supplements to Muqarnas, 3: 122–8, Leiden 1989.

J. M. Rogers, 'Seljuk influence in the monuments of Cairo', *Kunst des Orients* 7: 40 ff., 1970–1.

Sumatra

Most westerly large Indonesian island located west of the Malay peninsula and east of Java.

The first evidence for Islam in Indonesia comes from late thirteenth-century accounts of Marco Polo and Chinese documents which state that the region of Aceh on the northern tip of Sumatra was ruled by Muslim kingdoms. At this time the southern part of Sumatra was ruled by the Javanese kingdom of Majpahit which came to control most of the area of present-day Indonesia. Nevertheless, the Muslim states in the north of Sumatra began to spread, converting first the coastal peoples and only later the central area of Melayu. It was from Sumatra that Islam reached the Malay peninsula and gradually spread into Java itself. The Portuguese victory over Malacca in the early sixteenth century meant that Aceh once again became the main centre of Islam in the area. During the seventeenth century Sumatra was dominated by the ruler of Aceh, Iskandar Muda (1607–36) who had artillery, elephant and horse cavalry and a navy capable of carrying 700 men. The rule of Iskandar Muda's successor Iskandar Thani Alauddin Mughayat Syah (1636–41) was a period of cultural renaissance with several books written about the life of the court.

Unfortunately few early Islamic buildings survive in Sumatra probably because they were built of wood and frequently replaced. The earliest mosque of which records survive is the Masjid Agung Baiturrahman at Banda Aceh on the northern tip of Sumatra. It is likely that the present building stands on the site of one of the earliest mosques in Indonesia; however, the first records of the building (1612) describe an Indo-Islamic structure designed with the help of Dutch engineers. The building had three domes which were increased to five after a fire. However, it is likely that most early mosque forms were related to the traditional Sumatran house design. A recent example is the Rao-Rao Mosque in Batu Sangkar (west Sumatra) with an Indo-Islamic façade behind which is wooden mosque with a complex Sumatran roof-type known as rumah-adhat. This consists of a three-tiered pyramid roof construction with a small kiosk on top crowned with a tall finial.

The houses of Sumatra are one of the most distinctive features of the island and are world famous as examples of vernacular architecture. There are many regional house forms representing different cultural traditions, many of which predate Islam. The basic form of a Sumatran house consists of a building, set on upright piles driven into the ground, above which is a huge pitched roof. Wood is used for the piles and framework of the house, bamboo poles for the roof and the walls. Distinctively Islamic house types include the houses of Aceh, Minangkabu, Batak Mandailing and Lampung regions. The traditional Aceh house has a fairly basic design consisting of a rectangular platform resting on piles with a longitudinal gabled roof. Aceh houses are usually divided into three with the central area reserved for sleeping. The entrance is usually in the middle of one of the long sides and the gable ends are often decorated with geometric or other non-representational designs. The designs are either painted or carved, sometimes as fretwork panels. The most celebrated Sumatran house type is that of Minangkabu which has the entrance set in the middle of the long side. The roofs of the house are made up of a succession of pointed gables resembling the prow of a ship; the decoration is similar to that of the Aceh houses but may also include inset mirror work. The Batak Mandailing houses are similar to those of Minangkabu with roof ridges that sag in the middle and point upwards at the ends. The southern part of Sumatra, the Lampung area, is heavily influenced by neighbouring Java and Malaysia, and its houses are mostly of the coastal type.

Several palaces survive on Sumatra, the oldest of which is the seventeenth-century Aceh palace known as Dar al-Dunya. The building shares many characteristics with the Javanese palaces, or kratons, with many references to Hindu cosmology and little relationship to Islamic design. The Dar al-Dunya palace has the same north–south axis and three successive courtyards found in Java and, like the palaces of Yogyakarta and Surakarta, has a large formal garden. In the centre of the garden is a mountain-shaped structure with caves and ledges for meditation similar to the mountain representations of Java (e.g. Sunya Ragi). Nineteenth-century palaces show increasing Islamic and European influence, although there is still little relationship to the traditional wooden architecture of the island. The palace of Istana Maimun at Medan is laid out in a formal European style enlivened with arcades of horseshoe arches and crenellations.

See also: Indonesia, Java

Further reading:

E. M. Loeb, *Sumatra its History and People*, Oxford 1935.

D. Lombard, *Le Sultunat d'atjéh au temps d'iskandar Muda 1607–1636*, Publications de l'École Française d'extrême-Orient, 51, Paris 1967.

G. Serjeant, 'House form and decoration in Sumatra', *Art and Archaeology Research Papers* no. 12, 1977.

Susa

Tunisian coastal city noted for its ninth-century Aghlabid buildings.

Under the Byzantines the city was known as Justinianopolis in honour of Justinian who rebuilt it after the Vandal destruction. In 689 CE it was captured by the Arabs and became one of the principal ports for the Aghlabid conquest of Sicily. In 827 the city was refortified with ramparts and walls built in the Byzantine style. Important Aghlabid buildings within the city include the ribat built or restored by Ziyadat Allah in 821, the Bu Fatata Mosque built in 840 and the Great Mosque established in 859.

See also: Aghlabids, Tunisia

Syria (Arabic: al-Sham)

Geographically Syria may be defined as the northern part of Arabia between the Mediterranean and the Euphrates river. This area includes Lebanon, Palestine and Jordan as well as the modern state of Syria. Politically Syria refers to the modern state of Syria which roughly corresponds to the northern part of the geographical area of Syria excluding the mountains of Lebanon and including parts of the Jazira between the Euphrates and the Tigris. (Here the term Syria will be used to identify the area of the modern Arab Republic.) The majority of Syria's population lives within 100 km of the Mediterranean whilst there is lesser concentration of people along the Euphrates river valley. The area between the coastal strip and the Euphrates is sparsely populated semi-desert.

Syria was relatively densely populated in Roman and Byzantine times, with large cities such as

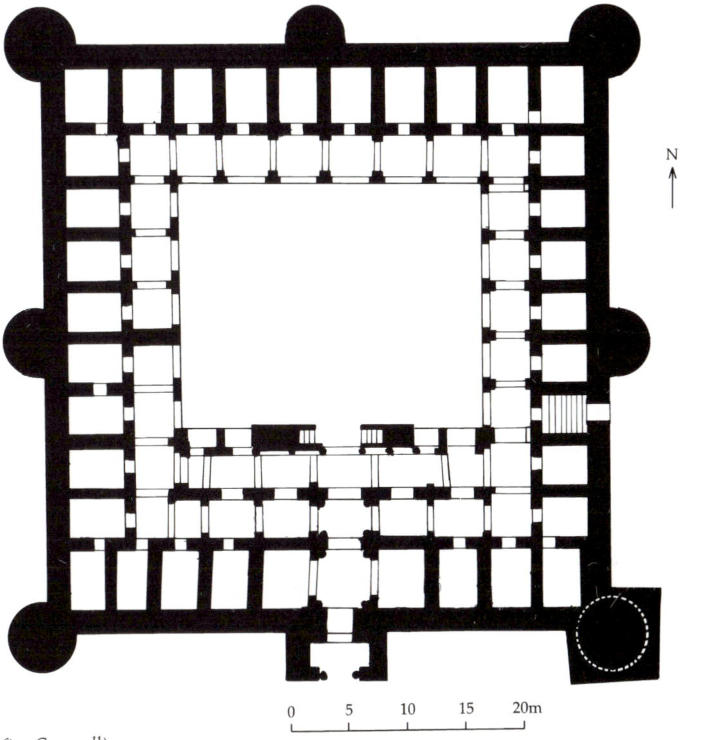

Ribat at Susa, Tunisia (after Creswell)

Muqarnas dome, Hospital of Nur al-Din, Damascus, Syria, © *Rebecca Foote*

Palmyra, Rusafa and Sergiopolis developing in the eastern part of the country. Traditionally it has been thought that the Arab conquest of the seventh century bought an end to this wealthy urbanization. Recent studies, however, have shown that there was a more complex sequence of events, which led to the growth of different parts of the country and different areas of cities. What is certain is that the eastern part of the country, in particular Damascus and Raqqa were developed in the Umayyad and early Abbasid periods. Damascus flourished under the Umayyads who established it as the capital of their vast empire. The topography of Damascus changed very little from late Byzantine times and the only major addition was the construction of the Great Mosque. Elsewhere cities such as Palmyra, Bostra and Raqqa continued to be inhabited with few changes from the Byzantine plan. However, a major change in the Umayyad period was the development of desert settlements such as Qasr al-Hayr (East and West). These settlements relied on the increased trade and mobility offered by a situation where both eastern and western parts of the desert were united under Islamic rule. The Abbasid revolution in the mid-eighth century brought about a radical change in the orientation of the Islamic world, where the lands of the former Sassanian Empire became central and the west declined in importance. The result in Syria was a decline in wealth and urbanization exacerbated by the growth of a rival caliphate (the Fatimids) in Egypt. During the ninth and tenth centuries Syria was in the middle of a three-way conflict between the Abbasids and their successors, the Fatimids and the Byzantines.

During the eleventh century the Seljuk Turks established themselves in the north of the country. By the end of the eleventh century the Great Seljuk Empire had divided into a number of independent principalities, or Atabegs. The arrival of the Crusaders in the early twelfth century imposed a sense of unity on the Muslim principalities which made itself felt under Salah al-Din and his Ayyubid successors. During the thirteenth century Syria was subjected to a series of Mongol invasions which were repulsed by the Mamluks who had replaced the Ayyubids as rulers of Syria. There were further Mongol raids in the fifteenth century led by the Central Asian ruler Timur. Despite the successive waves of invaders Syria seems to have been prosperous in the Middle Ages and some of the finest artistic and architectural works were carried out during this period.

In 1516 the Mamluks were defeated and Syria was incorporated into the Ottoman Empire. The country thrived during the first century of Ottoman rule with many khans established in the major cities as well in the countryside. The Ottoman Hajj (pilgrimage) route to Mecca was of great importance during this period with Damascus established as the starting-point. During the eighteenth century Europeans seem to have become increasingly involved in the commerce of the region. Cotton was of particular importance and many Europeans established consulates in the coastal cities in order to control this trade. In the nineteenth century there seems to have been an economic decline with less European trade and increasing interference from Egypt, culminating in the invasion of 1831. Administrative reforms were introduced in the latter part of the nineteenth century which led to Syria being regarded as one of the most advanced parts of the Ottoman Empire. The collapse of Turkish rule in 1918 led to the creation of a French protectorate which formed the basis of the modern independent republic.

The building materials used in Syria vary depending on the area and type of settlement. On the Mediterranean coast houses are generally stone built, often of ashlar masonry; their general appearance is that of Lebanese houses. In the mountains buildings are made out of rubble stone with mud mortar, their roofs made of wooden beams covered with matting and an exterior coating of earth. The region of the Hauran in the south-east is predominantly basalt desert with no trees. Basalt has been the main material of construction since ancient times and many traditional houses re-use ancient material because of its indestructibility and the difficulty of carving new basalt blocks. One of the principal forms of house construction is to have transverse arches carrying short basalt beams which form the roof. Houses in the Aleppo region are built of mud brick with conical mud domes resembling beehives. Several buildings joined together within a courtyard form a single house. In central Syria the traditional house is a rectangular mud-brick building with a flat roof. These houses are usually surrounded by a courtyard wall which may also include animal pens. In addition to permanent settlements many people are traditionally nomadic or semi-nomadic. Black goat-hair tents are the principal form of bedouin tent used in the region. The main cities also have their own methods of construction which differ from those of the countryside.

See also: Aleppo, Basra, Damascus, Lebanon, Qasr al-Hayr East, Qasr al-Hayr West, Raqqa

T

tabhane

Turkish term for the hostel attached to a mosque where travellers (usually dervishes and mystics) could live free for three days. In early Ottoman mosques these formed separate chambers although they were later incorporated into the main body of the mosque.

Taj Mahal

Major Islamic tomb complex built by the Mughal emperor at Agra in India.

The Taj Mahal was begun by Shah Jahan in 1631 and took over twenty years to build. The tomb was built for Shah Jahan's wife Arjumand Banu Begam (also known as Mumtaz Mahal) who he married in 1612 before he was made emperor. She was the niece of Jahangir's wife Nur Jahan and granddaughter of his famous Persian minister Ilti-mad al-Daulah. Mumtaz Mahal was the emperor's favourite wife and during nineteen years of marriage she bore him fourteen children. Her death whilst accompanying him on a campaign in the Deccan caused the emperor great sorrow and inspired him to build the most beautiful tomb complex in the world.

Although unique in its size and beauty, the Taj Mahal forms part of a series of imperial Mughal tombs of which it is undoubtedly the greatest. The earliest Mughal tombs copied those of their Islamic predecessors the Lodi sultans of Delhi and were octagonal domed structures surrounded by arcades. Another popular tomb form in the early Mughal period was the square chamber-tomb as seen in the 'Barber's tomb' in Delhi. Later on in the Mughal period the two forms were combined to produce octagonal tombs with four sides shorter than the others, thus producing a square with the corners cut off. In the tomb of Humayun at Delhi four of these 'square' octagons were assembled around a central octagonal space which was then covered with a dome. The area between the octagons was bridged by iwans which formed the main access points to the central domed area. This is essentially the same design that was used in the Taj Mahal. In Humayun's tomb, however, the central area is surrounded on four sides by an arcade of pointed arches at ground level and is made of red sandstone with marble inlay, neither of which features are found in the Taj Mahal. Similarly the dome on the roof is lower set than in the Taj Mahal so that it does not produce a dominant upright form but rather a pyramidal one.

The Taj Mahal is located on a terrace on the banks of the Jumna river and can be seen from the emperor's palace in the Agra Fort. The building is part of a complex which included many buildings beside the central tomb and garden; to the south is a complex known as the 'chauk-i jilau khana', or ceremonial forecourt, which was flanked by four courtyards (two on each side) containing apartments for the tomb attendants; directly south of these is a further area divided into four caravanserais by two intersecting streets, and south of this are two more caravanserais and a bazar built around a square. A residential area grew up around this complex which was known as Mumtazabad. The revenue of this village together with that of thirty other villages in the vicinity was devoted to the upkeep of the building.

Like many other Mughal memorial tombs the Taj Mahal was incorporated into a formal garden of the Persian char bagh form where a square garden wall encloses a garden divided equally into four. In most tomb complexes the tomb forms the centre of the garden with the four parts arranged equally around it. In the case of the Taj Mahal, however, a square pool forms the centre of the garden whilst the tomb building was located at the far end of it, overlooking the river. The walls of the garden tomb complex are strengthened by six octagonal towers capped with domed chatris. The gate to the complex consists of a large rectangular structure with engaged corner turrets placed in the middle of a tall wall which effectively screens the

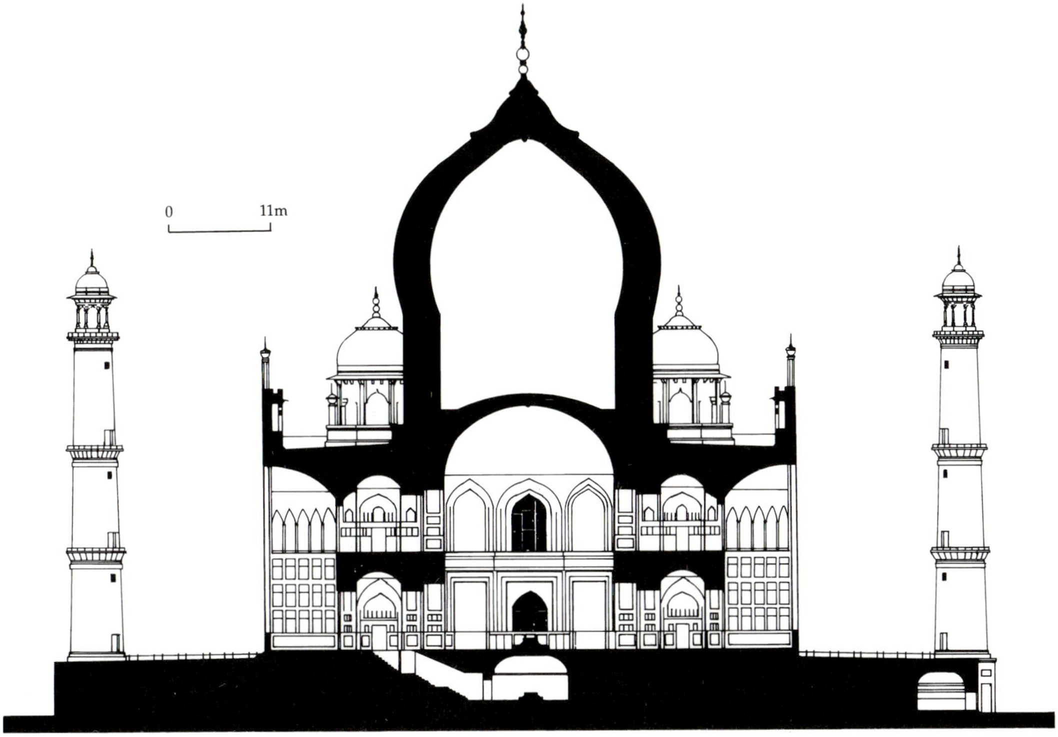

Section through Taj Mahal (after Tillotson)

Taj Mahal from view until the visitor has passed through the gate. The effect of this is enhanced by the fact that the outer buildings of the complex and the gateway are built and faced in red sandstone whereas the tomb and minarets are faced in white marble.

The central part of the complex is raised on a rectangular podium decorated with arcades of blind niches. At each corner of the podium is an octagonal base for a minaret whilst the tomb stands in the centre. The gate is directly in line with the centre of the dome on the tomb, a symmetry which is emphasized by the minarets, two either side of the tomb. Each minaret is a tall (42 m), slightly tapering, cylindrical structure with two intermediate balconies and an open domed pavilion (chatri) on the top. Long pools divide the garden into four parts, one running east–west and the other running north–south from the gate to the Taj Mahal. At either end of the east–west axis are large triple-domed buildings with a central iwan. The building on the west side is a mosque whilst that to the east is known as the 'jawab', or echo, as it has no other function than to balance the view with the mosque on the other side. The north–south pools further emphasize the central axis of the gateway and dome.

The Taj Mahal has the same basic form as Humayun's tomb and consists of four octagons arranged around a central domed space. The façade of the tomb consists of a tall central iwan framed by a pishtaq which contains a frame of Quranic calligraphy flanked on each side by four smaller iwans, two on each storey. The iwans are all composed of four centre-pointed arches with pietra dura decoration in the spandrels. The corners of the building are cut off or chamfered with projecting pillars marking the change from one face to another. The central dome is flanked by four large domed chatris supported on piers between lobed arches. The domes on the chatris and the central dome represent a synthesis of Persian and Indian architecture where the bulbous form of the dome is derived from Persian Timurid architecture and the finial and its lotus base derive ultimately from Hindu temple architecture.

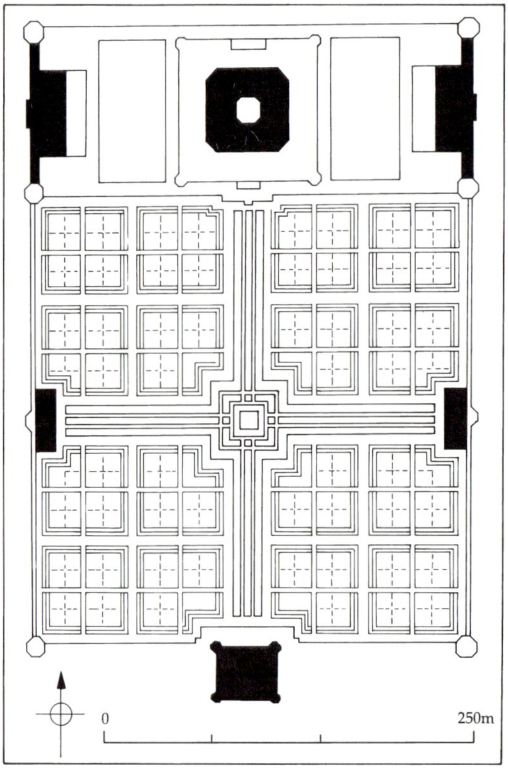

Plan of Taj Mahal and gardens (after Tillotson)

The central dome of the Taj Mahal is very tall (the finial is 73 m above ground level) and is raised up above the pishtaqs of the surrounding iwans by a tall circular drum about 15 m high. The dome is composed of two parts, an inner dome and an outer shell. The inner dome is approximately the same height as the iwans whilst the outer dome towers above. The use of an inner dome keeps the height of the inner space in proportion whilst the outer dome makes the height of the building correspond to its mass and with the minarets makes building stand out visually. Directly below the centre of the dome is the cenotaph of Mumtaz Mahal and next to it that of her husband Shah Jahan. The actual tombs, however, are in a vault or cave directly beneath the cenotaphs. The cenotaphs in the main chamber are surrounded by an octagonal pierced screen with two gates with pietra dura inlay on the posts. The walls of the interior are divided into blind arches alternating with arched doorways which give access to the four circular side chambers. Around each of the arches is a frame of Quranic inscriptions whilst the marble dadoes are also lavishly decorated with naturalistic depictions of flowers in low relief. The whole arrangement of the tomb, in particular the octagonal screen and the cave beneath, recalls the arrangement of the Dome of the Rock in Jerusalem. The reasons for this are probably coincidental and may simply reflect the fact that whilst octagonal mausoleums are rare in the Middle East they were common in India and there was no religious awareness of its significance.

As the finest example of Mughal funerary architecture it is not surprising that the design of the Taj Mahal was subsequently copied and developed in later tombs. The most obvious copy is the tomb of Rabiʿa Daurani in Aurangabad built in 1660 which has the same arrangement of a central tomb on a podium with minarets at each corner. The Aurangabad tomb, however, is different because the central building is square instead of octagonal and the minarets are thicker and taller in proportion to the central structure. A more interesting version of this design is the tomb of Safdar Jang in Delhi built in 1753. This building is also square like the tomb at Aurangabad, but here the minarets are attached to the central structure instead of standing apart at the corners of the terrace. Instead of white marble the building is faced in red sandstone with white marble inlay.

See also: Mughals

Further reading:

W. F. Begley, 'Amanat Khan and the calligraphy on the Taj Mahal', *Kunst des Orients* 12: 5–39, 1978–9.

—— 'The myth of the Taj Mahal and a new theory about its symbolic meaning', *The Art Bulletin* 61: 7–37, 1979.

W. E. Begley and Z. A. Desai, *Taj Mahal: The Illumined Tomb: An Anthology of Seventeenth Century Mughal and European Documentary Sources*, The Agha Khan Program for Islamic Architecture, Cambridge, Mass. 1989.

D. Brandenburg, *Der Taj Mahal in Agra*, Berlin 1969.

S. Gole, 'From Tamerlane to the Taj Mahal', in *Islamic Art and Architecture: Essays in Honour of of Katherina Otto-Dorn* 1, ed. A. Daneshavari, 1981, 43–50.

R. A. Jairazbhoy, 'The Taj Mahal in the context of East and West: a study in comparative method', *Journal of the Warburg and Courtauld Institutes* 24: 59–88, 1961.

R. Nath, *The Immortal Taj Mahal: The Evolution of the Tomb in Mughal Architecture*, New Delhi 1972.

talar

Iranian term for a hypostyle wooden hall which proceeds through the main part of a building.

taman

Indonesian term for a pleasure garden, usually associated with the royal palaces, or kraton. Taman gardens usually have a central tower, or artificial mountain, surrounded or approached by water, which in pre-Islamic tradition symbolizes mountain and sea.

See also: Java, kraton

Tanzania

Country in East Africa bordering on the Indian Ocean with a substantial Swahili-speaking Muslim population on the coast.

Tanzania forms part of the Islamic coast of East Africa which stretches from Somalia in the north to Mozambique in the south. Before 1970 the country was known as Tanganyika but following independence it united with Zanzibar to form the present state of Tanzania with its capital at Dar es Salaam. However, the two former countries retain autonomy and only the former territory of Tanganyika will be dealt with here (see separate entry for Zanzibar).

The earliest Islamic settlements in Tanzania can be traced back to at least the eighth century CE and appear to be related to the Indian Ocean dhow trade. The famous site of Kilwa on an island off the south coast contains traces of ninth-century Islamic structures, but unfortunately these are too fragmentary to reconstruct their form beyond establishing that they were built of mud over wooden frames. However, from the tenth-century levels of the site remains were found of an early stone mosque which, although not fully excavated, appears to conform to the same plan as early mosques elsewhere on the coast (e.g. the use of coursed coral blocks). Apart from archaeological sites the majority of Islamic monuments on the coast date from the period before 1200. The earliest standing monuments on the coast are the early mosque at Kaole and the mosque at Sanje ya Kati.

The ruins at Kaole consist of about fifteen tombs, two of which have pillars, and two mosques. The early mosque dates from the thirteenth century whilst the later one was probably built sometime in the sixteenth century. The early mosque has several unusual features not found later. It consists of a rectangular hall approximately 4 by 6 m north–south. Originally there was a set of masonry columns running down the centre of the structure which would have supported a flat roof. Access to the flat roof is by means of a staircase at the south end of the building. Either side of the central prayer hall were narrow side aisles (about 1 m wide) which were later enlarged. Architecturally the most interesting feature of the building is the mihrab. The mihrab arch consists of a plain border approximately 20 cm wide with a round arch containing a pointed niche at the apex. The panelled apse of the mihrab which projects out of the wall is probably a later fourteenth-century addition and it is likely that the original mihrab was set within the thickness of the wall. The mihrab arch is built out of roughly squared blocks covered with plaster to produce a smooth finish. This is an unusual technique which is not found in later mosques where the mihrab is usually made out of dressed coral blocks. The ablution area of the mosque is situated to the south of the prayer hall rather than to the east which became more usual later. The ablution area consists of a square well next to a rectangular tank covered with a barrel vault and a rectangular foot scraping area. Both the barrel vault and the footscraper consist of raw blocks of coral set in mortar, features which are unusual and may be a sign of early mosques.

The later mosque of Kaole is larger than its earlier neighbour and consisted of a central prayer hall supported by two rows of wooden columns. Each column was sunk deep into the ground and was encased in an octagonal masonry collar where it met the plastered floor of the mosque. Like the early mosque, the ablutions area is at the south end of the building which is unusual in mosques of this date and may well result from the influence of the earlier structure.

Other important medieval sites in Tanzania include the ruins at Kilwa, Tongoni, Kunduchi and Mafia island. The ruins of Kilwa form a group on their own noted for the dense concentration of buildings and independent architectural development. Kilwa is the only place on the coast where dome construction was widespread and the only place where a significant continuity of occupation can be traced from the thirteenth to the sixteenth century.

Tongoni (from Swahili meaning 'ruins') is located on the north coast of Tanzania near the mouth of the Pangani river. The settlement, originally known as Mtangata, was founded in the fourteenth century and flourished until the arrival of the Portuguese in the sixteenth century, although it continued to be inhabited until the eighteenth, when it was finally abandoned. Remains at the site include a mosque and over forty tombs, of which nearly half are pillar tombs, which makes it the largest concentration of this form of monument on the coast. Only one of these pillars is still standing, although the size and shapes of fallen pillars can be worked out. Most of the pillars are cylindrical, although some have square and octagonal sections and nearly all have concave recesses or indentations which contained imported ceramic bowls (usually Chinese celadon ware). The mosque consists of a narrow central prayer hall, with a roof supported on a central row of four columns and two side aisles. Accessible through open archways at the south end is a transverse room which may have been used as a separate area for women.

The ruins of Kunduchi are located next to a creek 20 km north of Dar es Salaam. The earliest remains at the site date from the fourteenth century which continued in use until the nineteenth century. The standing remains consist of a mosque and cemetery containing pillar tombs. The mosque was built in the fifteenth century, although most of the pillar tombs are from the eighteenth, which represents one of the latest groups of pillar tombs.

The island of Mafia is located at the end of the Rufiji delta about 15 km offshore. There are extensive remains of several eighteenth- and nineteenth-century settlements on the island. The most famous of these, known as Kua, contains five mosques (at least) and the remains of many eighteenth-century houses. The mosques have a variety of mihrab types which were developed in later nineteenth-century mosques. The mihrabs at Kua include apses decorated with blind arcades and an early example of a recessed stepped minbar in the Friday mosque. The houses at Kua are unique on the East African coast and consist of two identical halves with a single entrance. A typical house is entered through

Nine-domed mosque, Kilwa, Tanzania. Note pillar above central dome

a single gateway leading into a long transverse room; behind this is a doorway leading to two separate L-shaped passages which lead into a long reception room that opens on to a courtyard on one side and a small private room (harem) on the inner side. Sometimes there are additional buildings in the courtyard and sometimes there are two separate entrances. It is thought that the two identical halves may represent the family houses of two wives rather than a men's and a women's section. Nineteenth- and twentieth-century Islamic architecture in Tanzania is best represented in the cities of Bagamoyo and Dar es Salaam. Bagamoyo was the capital of German East Africa before the First World War and contains the various elements associated with a small colonial capital. The architecture is an interesting mixture of styles including Omani Arab, German, German Orientalist (i.e. Ottoman) and Swahili. Many of the more important government buildings are built in the style of Omani palaces with external verandas and carved wooden doors – the important addition of steel girders enabling larger spaces to be covered without support. After the defeat of the Germans in the First World War, Dar es Salaam replaced Bagamoyo as capital. Like the Germans in Bagamoyo the British in Dar es Salaam built official buildings in an Oriental style with modern materials; some of the more notable ones are the National Museum with its Turkish tiles and the old hospital.

See also: East Africa, Kilwa, Zanzibar

Further reading:

H. N. Chittick, *Annual Reports of the Department of Antiquities*, Dar es Salaam 1958–64.

G. S. P. Freeman-Grenville, *The Medieval History of the Coast of Tanganyika*, London 1962.

P. S. Garlake, *The Early Islamic Architecture of the East African Coast*, Memoir No. 1 of the British Institute in Eastern Africa, London and Nairobi 1966.

Tanganyika Notes and Records, Dar es Salaam 1959 onwards.

taq

Iranian term for an arch.

tekke

Also known as a dergah, a tekke is a lodge for dervishes. Tekkes are a frequent occurrence in Turkish architecture and are usually part of a complex which includes a mosque and memorial tomb. They may be regarded as the counterpart of the more orthodox madrassa. A tekke often consists of a number of individual cells which are used as shelters for the dervishes.

See also: Edirne, Ottomans, Turkey

tilework

Glazed tiles are one of the most characteristic features of Islamic architecture.

Three distinct tile formats were developed which may be characterized as single tiles, composite tile panels and tile mosaics. Single tiles are complete compositions which may include abstract designs or figural representation but are independent of other tiles. Composite tile panels consist of several tiles carrying a design or picture which together form a complete composition. Tile mosaics are made of many pieces of monochrome coloured tile which are joined together to form a picture. There is also a fourth category which consists of three-dimensional glazed ceramics which are used to form architectural features such as mihrabs. The decoration of tiles may be classified according to the various techniques used, which are similar to those used on pottery. The simplest technique is to paint a tile with a monochrome glaze before firing. Extra colours may be added by coating the glaze with lustre after the first firing and then firing the tile a second time at a lower temperature. More complex polychrome tiles may be produced by using a technique known as 'cuerda seca' which uses coloured glazes separated by outlines made of a greasy substance which burns away after firing. Other techniques include overglaze painting (known as 'minai'), underglaze painting and relief moulded designs.

The earliest dated examples of Islamic tiles are those around the mihrab of the Great Mosque of Qairawan which were produced in Iraq sometime before 862 CE. These are square tiles (21 cm per side) decorated with abstract and vegetal forms in polychrome and monochrome lustre on a white ground. From the eleventh century onwards tiles replaced mosaics as the main form of wall decoration in many parts of the Islamic world. Three main tile-making traditions can be distinguished: these are Spain and North Africa, Turkey and Iran.

In Seljuk Iran the exterior surfaces of brick buildings were enlivened by blue-green glazed bricks or tiles whilst alternating star- and cross-shaped minai tiles were used to decorate interiors. Other techniques developed during the Seljuk period include tile mosaics and decorative inscriptions which were generally restricted to blue, black, turquoise and green as the main pigments. In the fourteenth century potters working in Tabriz developed the cuerda seca technique which enabled them to adopt complex Chinese patterns. This technique continued to be used during the Saffavid period and it was not until the nineteenth century that underglaze painting was introduced to Iranian tilework. The tilework of Iran also influenced the architecture of India to the east, in particular the area of present-day Pakistan. Generally Indian glazed tilework was restricted to tile mosaics and can be seen in the magnificent 'Picture Wall' at Lahore Fort. Indian craftsmen took the tile mosaic one stage further when they developed the technique of mirror mosaics which was later adopted in Iran.

In Spain and North Africa a technique of tile mosaic, known as zilij, was developed using yellow, green, blue and turquoise tiles. In the eighteenth century the Ottomans introduced the techniques of polychrome panels made of square or rectangular tiles. One of the main centres of production was Tunis, where tiles were decorated with green, yellow and blue designs. Before the fifteenth century several different formats of tile decoration were used in Anatolia which included tile mosaic, hexagonal, octagonal, star- and cross-shaped tiles. In the fourteenth century the Ottomans adopted the Persian technique of cuerda seca for the brilliant green tiles which characterize early Ottoman mosques such as the Yeşil Cami in Bursa. However, the most significant development came in the sixteenth century when the potteries of Iznik began producing tilework for imperial use. The achievement of Iznik potters was to produce tiles with underglaze colours which remained stable under the glaze. Characteristic colours of Iznik tiles are blue, turquoise and red against a white background.

See also: Iznik, tilework

Further reading:

J. Hedgecoe and S. S. Damulji, *Zillij: The Art of Moroccan Ceramics*, New York, NY 1993.

J. M. Scarce, 'Function and decoration in Qajar tilework', *Persian Art and Culture of the 18th and 19th Centuries*, Edinburgh 1979.

Timbuktu (also known as Tombouctou)

Famous Islamic trading city in Mali, West Africa.

Timbuktu is located on the southern edge of the Sahara several kilometres north of the Niger river. According to tradition the city originated as a nomadic Tuareg encampment in the twelfth century. The encampment would have consisted of tents made out of acacia wood frames covered over with mats and animal-skin canopies. In 1325 the city was conquered by Mansa Musa who incorporated it into the empire of Mali. During this period the famous Andalusian poet and architect Abu Ishaq al-Saheli visited the city and built a mosque there. Several years later in 1333 the city was burnt and pillaged in an attack by Mossi tribesmen from Yatenga (present-day Upper Volta) although it was later rebuilt by Sulayman the emperor of Mali. The rule of Mali ended in the fifteenth century and for the next forty years the city was controlled by Tuareg nomads until its annexation by Ali the ruler of Gao in 1468. During this time Timbuktu became the main centre for the trade with North Africa and enjoyed its greatest period of prosperity. This was brought to an abrupt end with the Moroccan invasion of 1591, although the city managed to remain more or less independent until 1787 when it passed into the control of the Tuareg. In the nineteenth century the city was incorporated into the Fulbe state of Massina and remained under nominal Fulbe control until the advent of French colonialism in the late nineteenth century. Despite these conquests by various groups and dynasties, Timbuktu remained substantially independent for most of its history due to its position on the border of the desert.

The first known European visitor was Caillié who wrote the following description of the city in 1828: 'The city of Timbuktu forms a sort of triangle, measuring about three miles in circuit. The houses are large, but not high, consisting entirely of a ground floor. In some a sort of water closet is constructed above the entrance.' The city has retained this triangular configuration into recent times although new houses have been built around the central core. The city is divided into five districts, or quarters, traditionally inhabited by different ethnic groups – the Ba Dinde, the Saré-kaina, the Bella Faraji, the Sankoré and the Dijingueré Ber. The Dijingueré Ber quarter is generally thought to be the oldest Muslim part of the city and in earlier times may have been separated from the rest of the town with its own city wall. The Saré-kaina quarter, also known as the Sané-gungu quarter, is the area inhabited by the rulers and political élite; in this area are the largest houses and also the remains of the Moroccan kasbah built on the site of the Songhay royal palace. The Sankoré quarter in the north-west tip of the city is the area formerly inhabited by the Berber tribes and is said to have been founded by Sidi Mahmoud a sixteenth-century immigrant from Oualata. The main material of construction in Timbuktu is mud brick, although stone is used for strengthening the walls and in important places such as doorways. Early nineteenth-century descriptions of the city describe the making of hand-rolled round bricks which are then baked in the sun. Roofs are made of split palm beams and palm-frond matting which is then covered with earth. Construction is in the hands of a group of Songhay-speaking people known as the 'gabibi' who are also responsible for gravedigging.

The major monuments of the city are the three ancient mosques each located in a different quarter of the city. Reputedly the oldest building is the Sankoré Mosque, which was founded by a woman during one of the periods of Tuareg rule, possibly during the thirteenth century. The building was subsequently repaired, rebuilt and developed so that in its present form it consists of an irregular form based around a square central courtyard. This courtyard seems to represent an early phase of the mosque's development as it conforms to the dimensions of the courtyard built by Qadi al-Aqib in 1581. On the south-east corner of the mosque is a small, square, entrance vestibule built during Fulbe rule in the nineteenth century to serve as a Shar'ia court. The mosque contains two mihrabs, a small one in the east wall of the interior courtyard and a larger one in the east wall of the sanctuary. The larger mihrab is located north of the centre of the

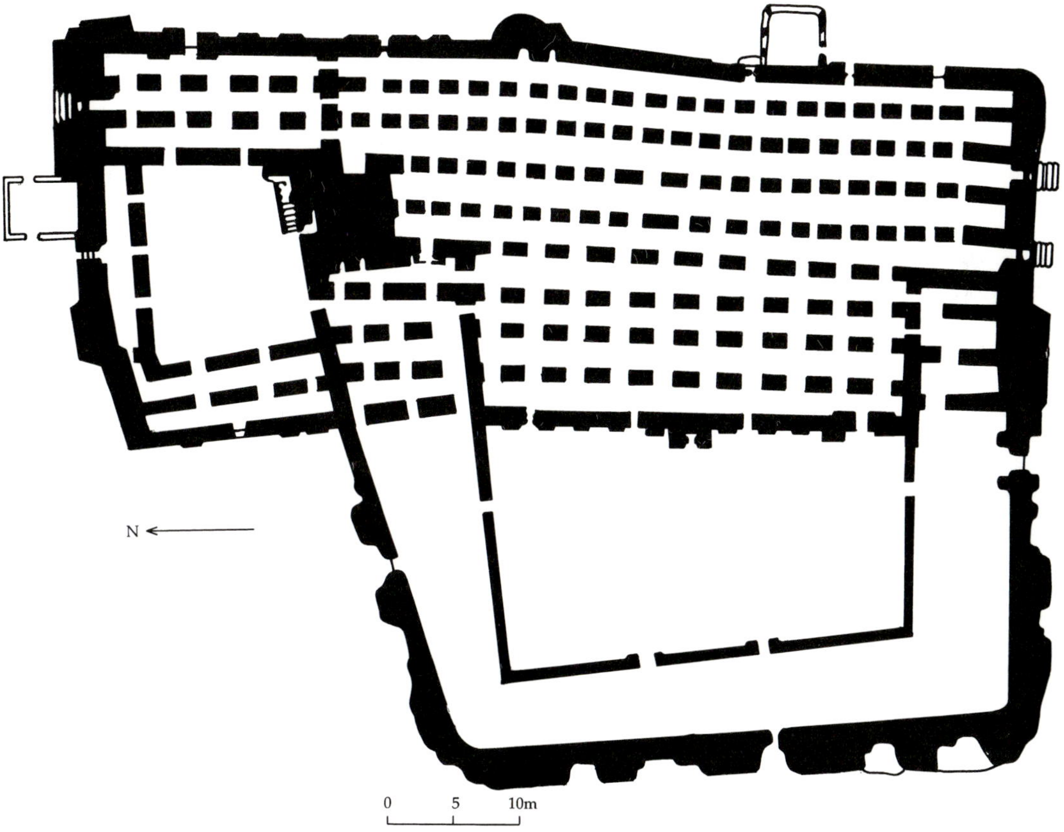

Great Mosque, Timbuktu, Mali (after Prussin)

east wall and externally consists of a tower-like conical projection similar to that of the Dijingueré Ber Mosque. The dominant feature of the building is the minaret on the south side of the courtyard, consisting of a large stepped pyramid similar to that of the mausoleum of Askiya Muhammad at Gao. However, the Sankoré minaret is slightly smaller and has an internal staircase instead of external stair ramps as at Gao.

The most famous mosque in Timbuktu is the Dijingueré Ber Mosque, which was built between 1324 and 1327 by Mansa Musa emperor of Mali after his return from the Hajj. The mosque is attributed to the architect Abu Isahq al-Saheli who built a royal audience chamber at the same time. Today there is no trace of the audience chamber which may have resembled that of the capital at Niani described by contemporary Arab travellers. Like most other ancient buildings in the city the mosque underwent several successive stages of construction and repairs. As it stands at present the plan of mosque consists of a roughly rectangular sanctuary with a small internal courtyard at the northern end and a large double-walled external courtyard on the western side. The oldest part of the mosque is generally agreed to be the western part of the sanctuary. In this part there are round arches made of dressed limestone supporting the roof, a feature not found elsewhere in West Africa until the colonial period. Like the Sankoré Mosque the Dijingueré Ber has two towers, a conical mihrab tower with projecting toron (acacia wood stakes) and a tapering square minaret adjacent to the interior courtyard.

The third ancient mosque in Timbuktu is the small complex in the centre of the city known as the mosque of Sidi Yahyia built in the mid-fifteenth century. This consists of a rectangular sanctuary attached to a short, square, tapering minaret enclosed within a large outer courtyard. The sanctuary is four bays deep and has three entrances on the short northern side and two entrances in the eastern wall either side of the wide shallow central mihrab. According to tradition, the first imam of the mosque is buried under the minaret, a concept that parallels the stepped pyramid minarets of the Gao and Sankoré mosques.

The houses of Timbuktu are either single-storey or two-storey courtyard houses. The two-storey houses tend to be more elaborate and are mostly confined to the Sané-gungu quarter inhabited by the chief merchants. From the outside the houses are generally quite plain with shallow square buttresses dividing the wall into panels. The doorways are fairly simple with wooden doors decorated with Moroccan brass bosses, although this has been superseded by snipped tin decoration. Above the main doorway is a single window, decorated, containing a Moroccan-style hardwood grille. Each grille consists of two parts, opening shutters recessed within a horseshoe arch on the top and the wooden grille below made of intersecting wooden strips (cf. mashrabiyya). The houses are entered via an outer and inner vestibule which leads out on to a square courtyard from which the other rooms of the house can be reached. In a two-storey building there are men's rooms either side of the courtyard, whilst in a single-storey house the single men's room is to the right of the entrance. In larger houses there is usually a secondary courtyard for women behind the main courtyard. In two-storey houses latrines are usually on the upper floor above a sealed latrine shaft (sekudar).

See also: Agades, Oualata, West Africa

Further reading:

R. J. and S. K. McIntosh, 'Archaeological reconnaisance in the region of Timbuktu, Mali', *National Geographic Research* 2: 302–19, 1986.

L. Prussin, *Hatumere: Islamic Design in West Africa*, Berkeley 1986.

Timurids

Central Asian dynasty founded by Timur which flourished from the end of the fourteenth century to the end of the fifteenth.

Timur was born a member of the Barlas tribe and claimed descent from the Mongol Khan Chatagay. By 1370 Timur had gained control of Samarkand and Balkh after which he spent ten years consolidating his control of Central Asia. From 1381 Timur extended the range of his operations and managed to gain control of Iran, Iraq, Syria, the Caucasus and Delhi. In 1402 Timur's excursions into Anatolia brought him into conflict with the Ottoman sultan Bayazit whom he defeated and captured at the battle of Ankara. One of the results of these wide-ranging conquests was the collection of skilled craftsmen from all over the Middle East who were used to enrich the new capital at Samarkand. Timur died in 1405 and was succeeded by his son Shah Rukh who ruled the empire from Herat where he had been governor during the reign of Timur.

Samarkand was ruled by Shah Rukh's son Ulugh Beg whilst Fars was ruled first by his nephew Ibrahim. By the mid-fifteenth century the western provinces were mostly lost to the Turkmans leaving Herat as capital of a much diminished empire which continued until 1507 when it was taken over by the Turkmans.

The main building material employed for imperial monuments was baked brick although dressed stone was used in Azerbayjan. The standard brick form was square (24–27 cm per side and 4–7 cm thick) whilst cut or moulded bricks were relatively rare compared with earlier periods. Mortar was usually quick-setting gypsum plaster rather than the more common lime plaster. The standard method of exterior decoration was tile revetments which were on a larger scale than in previous periods. Two main forms of tilework were used, tile mosaic, with individual coloured pieces cut to form patterns, and underglaze-painted tiles known as 'haft rangi' (seven colours). The underglaze-painted tiles tended to be of a lower quality but were useful for covering large areas. A large variety of arch forms were used including round, two-, three-, and four-centre arches, although the most common was the three-centred arch with a high crown, where the height of the arch was more than half the height of the entire opening. A large variety of domes and vaults were employed which displays the wide range of influences in Timurid architecture. One of the most significant vaulting forms employed was based on the use of wide transverse arches spanning between parallel walls. Vaults of various forms were then built to cover the area between each transverse arch to produce a large vaulted area. The vaults used to span the arches included tunnel or barrel vaults, stellar vaults and cross vaults, all of which produce characteristic humps on the roofs of buildings.

Dome forms became increasingly distinctive under the Timurids with the development of double-shell domes where there is an outer dome and a shallower inner dome. The characteristic outer dome form consists of a tall 'melon-shaped' structure set on a high drum and decorated with ribs covered in decorative tilework.

The most characteristic feature of Timurid imperial buildings is their massive scale, emphasized by huge entrance portals and thick minarets covered in tile decoration. Internally the buildings are slightly less well organized and they often have a large variety of smaller rooms whose relationship to the overall plan is not always evident. The most famous of the Timurid monuments are the shrine of Ahmed Yasavi at Turkestan (Yasi) in Khazakstan and the Masjid Jami' at Samarkand. The monuments are quite similar in their scale and conception with huge portal iwans behind which rise characteristic melon-shaped domes on high collars or drums. The Ahmed Yasavi tomb was built by Timur for his son Jahangir whilst the Masjid Jami' at Samarkand was built to commemorate the Timurid capture of Delhi. Other monumental projects carried out by Timur include the mausoleums at Shahrisbaz (his first capital) for his father Taraghay and the Gur-i-Amir for his son Muhammad Sultan at Samarkand. In addition Timur undertook massive civil engineering projects including building the towns of Baylaqan, Shahrukhiya and Iryah, the citadels and walls of Ghazui, Balkh and Samarkand.

The later Timurid buildings of Herat in Afghanistan mirror those of the early Timurid Empire, although many were destroyed in the nineteenth century. One of the most celebrated buildings in Herat was the mosque and madrassa built by the architect Qavam al-Din for the wife of Shah Rukh. Little is left of the complex except for two minarets at diagonally opposite corners of the mosque and a minaret and iwan from the madrassa. The best preserved Timurid structure in Herat is the shrine of the mystic of Khwajeh 'Abdallah Ansari at Gazur Gah. The complex is built on the plan of a four-iwan madrassa and oriented to the qibla (i.e. east–west) with the entrance in the centre of the west façade. The entrance portal consists of a large iwan, half-octagonal in plan, leading into the rectangular central courtyard. There is a mosque and cells for mystics at the western end, whilst at the eastern end is a shallow iwan set into a tall pishtaq.

See also: Herat, Iran, Samarkand

Further reading:

L. Golombek and D. L. Wilber, *The Timurid Architecture of Iran and Turan*, Princeton, NJ 1988.

B. O'Kane, *Timurid Architecture in Khurassan*, Costa Mesa, CA 1987.

Tlemcen

City in western Algeria noted for its medieval architecture.

Tlemcen was founded in the eighth century on the ruins of the Roman city of Pomaria although it did not rise to prominence until the Almoravid period in the eleventh century. The most important Almoravid contribution to the city was the Great Mosque which survives in the centre of the town. The prayer hall consists of thirteen aisles running perpendicular to the qibla wall and covered with pitched tile roofs. Like other Almoravid mosques the courtyard arcades of the Great Mosque open directly into the prayer hall. The minaret which stands opposite the qibla was added in 1136. The most astonishing feature of the mosque is the lavish decoration in the area of the mihrab which includes stone panels with intricately carved stylized flora. Covering the area in front of the mihrab is a magnificent perforated dome carried on sixteen brick ribs and four small squinches. Between the ribs there is an intricate stucco latticework of stylized floral motifs whilst at the apex of the dome is a small muqarnas cupola. The entire dome is covered by a tiled roof on the exterior.

The other important mosque in Tlemcen is the al-'Ubbad Mosque built by the Marinid sultan Abu al-Hasan in 1339. The mosque is raised on a plinth and approached by a monumental staircase leading to a ceremonial projecting porch with an entrance hall behind it. The entrance hall leads on to a small courtyard behind which is the prayer hall. The whole structure is covered with opulent decoration in the form of carved stucco work, glazed tiles and delicately carved stone.

See also: Algeria

Toledo

City in central Spain famous as first Arab capital of Spain and later major Islamic and Christian city.

Toledo was the capital of the Visigoths until its capture in 712 CE by the Arabs, who used the city as their capital until they moved to Córdoba in 717. The city remained an important frontier city until its capture by the Christians in 1085, and even after this Muslims and Jews continued to make important contributions to the intellectual life of the city with translations of scientific treatises.

Despite its fairly early conquest by the Christians, substantial remains of the Islamic period are still standing, together with some notable examples of Mudéjar architecture. The walls of the city contain many early sections including the Bab al-Qantara (*c.* 850) which is thought to be the earliest use of a bent entrance in Spanish fortifications. Access to this gate is via a bridge known as the Puente de Alcantara (866–71) which has a magnificent high-sprung central arch similar to those of Seljuk bridges in Anatolia. Probably the most famous gate of the city is the Old Bisagra Gate (also known as Puerta de Alfonso VI) through which El Cid entered the city in 1085. The gate is a monumental structure built out of huge uneven blocks near the ground and smaller pieces of coursed rubble near the top. The gateway is flanked by two blind niches with pointed horseshoe arches resting on engaged columns. The gateway itself is recessed behind a wide arched machicolation and consists of a round horseshoe arch with a huge stone lintel spanning the width between the two imposts.

Within the city there are several important religious buildings which are Cristo de la Luz (mosque of Bab al-Mardum), Santa María La Blanca (a former synagogue), the Sinagoga del Transito and the cathedral. The mosque of Bab al-Mardum is a nine-domed mosque with a raised central dome built in 999. Originally there were triple entrances on three sides with a mihrab on the south side. Three of the outer faces are made of brick and decorated with a band of Kufic inscriptions, below which is a geometric panel above decorative intersecting round horseshoe arches.

The church of Santa María La Blanca was built as a synagogue in 1250 and contains four rows of arches supported on octagonal brick piers with capitals decorated with fir cones and punctuate scrolls. More well known is the Sinagoga del Transito built in 1357 during the reign of Pedro the Cruel. The building is lavishly decorated with carved plaster and woodwork, with Arabic and Hebrew inscriptions and coloured tiles. The cathedral of Toledo was once the Great Mosque of the city and possibly contains the remains of a large Córdoba-style mihrab, now the octagonal chapel of Ildefonso.

See also: Córdoba, Granada, Mudéjar, Seville, Spain, Zaragoza

Tomb of the Abbasid caliphs (Cairo)

Mid-thirteenth-century tomb in Cairo containing tombs of the Abbasid caliphs who were taken there after the Mongol sack of Baghdad.

The date of the tomb is not known; some attribute it to the Ayyubid period whilst others believe it was built by the Mamluk sultan Baybars in the 1260s. The complex is one of the most highly decorated buildings to have survived in Cairo with finely carved stucco and painted Kufic inscriptions. The mihrab is a keel-arched niche, with a central medallion from which lines radiated to form a muqarnas frame to the opening. The dome is supported on two-tier muqarnas squinches between which are carved niches and windows.

Topkapisarai (literally: 'Gun-Gate Palace')

Imperial Ottoman palace in Istanbul founded by Mehmet II in 1459.

The Topkapi replaces an early royal palace that was established between the old forum and the Golden Horn. This early palace was built predominantly of wood and surrounded by a high wall.

The Topkapi Palace is located on the old Byzantine acropolis and overlooks the Sea of Marmara and the Bosphorus. The building consists of four great courtyards built over a period of four hundred years. Most of the early buildings in the palace were probably built of wood and have not survived the great fires of 1574 and 1665. Fifteenth-century buildings which have survived include the kitchens, the treasury, the physician's building and the Çinili Kiosk. The kitchens on the south side of the second court consist of a long building covered with huge domed chimneys and ventilators. There are several other kitchens in the palace including a separate women's kitchen, a hospital kitchen and several smaller private ones. The treasury is built as a long six-domed hall in the form of a small bedestan and is located in the second court. One of the most unusual buildings of this period is the Physician's Tower, a square building with extremely thick walls and a small chamber on the top. It has been suggested that the lower building was a drug store whilst the upper room was the doctor's office. Outside the main area of the palace but within the outer walls is the celebrated Cinili Kiosk. Designed by a Persian architect, this has many Persian features such as the wide arches. It is set on a raised platform reached by external steps and has a four-iwan plan with a tall dome above the centre.

During the sixteenth century the architect Sinan carried out extensive work at the palace including building (or rebuilding) the vaults supporting the east end. Other work carried out at this period was the building of Murat III's bedchamber next to a heated outdoor pool. Unfortunately another fire in 1574 destroyed large areas of the palace which had to be rebuilt. This was taken as a chance to remodel much of the palace including the kitchens and the wooden quarters of the Halberdiers (halberd carriers) which were completely rebuilt at this time. A second fire in 1665 led to another period of rebuilding and refurbishment particularly of the harem area. Important buildings from the seventeenth century include the Baghdad Kiosk erected to celebrate the reconquest of that city.

During the early eighteenth century the palace was redecorated in the Ottoman baroque style. A new bath house for the sultan and a palace school were built at this time, both of which include lavish decoration in the European style. In 1789 Selim III became sultan and instituted a series of apartments or salons in the French Rococo style. These buildings had large European glazed windows and were decorated in ornate painted plasterwork. In the mid-nineteenth century the sultans moved to a new palace (the Dolmabahçe) on the banks of the Bosphorus which was more fashionable and not cluttered with associations of the past.

See also: Istanbul, Ottomans

Further reading:

F. Davis, *The Palace of Topkapi in Istanbul*, New York 1971.

B. Miller, *Beyond the Sublime Porte; The Grand Seraglio of Stamboul*, New York 1970.

toron

West African term for projecting wooden stakes used in mud-brick architecture especially in minarets.

The preferred material is acacia wood although split palm is sometimes also used. It is generally agreed that toron have a practical purpose as fixed scaffolding for mud-brick structures which need constant maintenance, although they may also have a symbolic and aesthetic function. Symbolically the use of projecting wooden branches relates the structure to a tree which in West African tradition is a symbol of renewal and rebirth, an idea strengthened by the fact that toron are primarily associated with religious structures. Aesthetically toron may be compared to the horns used in hunting towers (as in e.g. Manara Umm al-Qaroun in Iraq, or the Hiran Manar at Fatehpur Sikri).

See also: Manding, West Africa

Tripoli (Lebanon)

Tripoli is located on the north coast of Lebanon and in the medieval period was the principal port.

Tripoli has a long history of settlement although it first became a city in 358 BCE under the Phoenicians. The city was captured by the Muslim Arabs in the early seventh century CE and became a flourishing Arab seaport until 1109, when it was captured by the Crusaders. For nearly 200 years Tripoli was one of the principal Crusader ports and was one of the last Crusader cities to be recaptured by the Muslims. The city was finally retaken in 1289 and an ambitious programme of reconstruction was initiated. The Mamluk city was built on a new site slightly inland from the Crusader city. Tripoli flourished during this period with a series of nine mosques, sixteen madrassas and five khans constructed before the Ottoman conquest of the sixteenth century. The principal mosque of the city (the Great Mosque) was built in 1294 and includes a Crusader tower which was converted into a minaret. The city remains one of the best examples of Mamluk planning and architecture outside Egypt.

See also: Lebanon, Mamluks

Further reading:

H. Salam-Liebich, *The Architecture of the Mamluk City of Tripoli*, Cambridge, Mass. 1983.

Tripoli (Libiya)

Capital city of Libiya located on the Mediterranean coast.

The name Tripoli derives from the Roman term for the three cities of Tripolitania, which were Leptis Magna, Oea and Sabratha. The present city of Tripoli is built on the site of Oea.

Tripoli was first conquered by the Arab armies of Camr ibn al-As in 643 CE. The captured Byzantine city had a wall which was pulled down by the Arab conquerors and later rebuilt at the end of the Umayyad period. The remains of the Umayyad wall have recently been discovered by archaeologists who have identified a stone wall 6–7 m wide.

Apart from the Umayyad wall there are few remains of the early Islamic period in the city. The oldest mosque is the al-Naqah Mosque which has been interpreted as the mosque of Camr ibn al-As, although it is more likely that it was built by the Fatimid caliph al-Muciz in 973. The al-Naqah Mosque is roughly rectangular, measuring approximately 20 by 40 m, and divided between the courtyard and the sanctuary. The sanctuary is covered by forty-two brick domes supported on columns, some of which have Roman capitals. The mihrab is in the middle of south-east side of the courtyard and has a slight turn to the east to correct the misalignment of the original building.

Most of the other remains in Tripoli date from the Ottoman period when the city was the most westerly Turkish port. The present city walls date from the sixteenth century as testified by Turkish inscriptions on some of the gates. One of the oldest Ottoman buildings is the mosque of Darghut, governor of Tripoli and Turkish commander, who died in 1564 during the siege of Malta. The mosque has a T-shaped plan with a central area divided into fifteen domed bays flanked by two six-bay annexes recalling the tabhanes of Ottoman mosques elsewhere. Behind the qibla wall is a square domed room which contains the tomb of Darghut Pasha. To the south-west of the mosque is a bath house which is built on the remains of Darghut's palace. The most celebrated Turkish mosque is that of Ahmad Pasha al-Qarahmanli built by the semi-independent Turkish governor in 1736. The mosque is located in the middle of a square complex which includes a madrassa, graveyard and the tomb of Ahmad Pasha. The sanctuary consists of a square area covered with twenty-five domes (i.e. five arcades of five bays). There is no courtyard but there is an L-shaped ambulatory on the north-west and south-west sides. In addition there is a raised gallery at first floor level opening on to a wooden balcony which runs around three sides of the sanctuary. The whole building is decorated with fine green, yellow and blue tiles imported from Tunis.

In addition to mosques Tripoli contains many examples of Ottoman houses and funduqs. The houses are usually two-storey structures built around a central colonnaded courtyard and are decorated with polychrome tile and stucco decoration. A typical funduq has a similar design, consisting of a two-storey structure built around a central courtyard. The lower floors are usually used for storage and the upper floor for shop units. There also used to be many bath houses, but only three of these have survived.

See also: Libiya, Ottomans, Tunis

Further reading:

M. Brett, 'Tripoli at the beginning of the fourteenth century AD/ eighth century A.H.', *Libyan Studies* 9: 55–9, 1978.
K. McLachlan, 'Tripoli – city, oasis and hinterland – reflections on the old city 1551 to the present', *Libyan Studies* 9: 53–4, 1978.
M. Warfelli, 'The old city of Tripoli', in *Some Islamic Sites in Libiya: Tripoli Ajdabiyah and Uljah*, Art and Archaeology Research Papers, London 1976.

Tulunids

Dynasty which ruled over Egypt and Syria in the late ninth and early tenth century.

The dynasty was founded by Ahmed ibn Tulun the son of a Turkic soldier from Bukhara who was based at the Abbasid capital of Samarra. Ahmed was originally sent to Egypt as deputy to the governor but soon acquired the governorship himself. As governor of Egypt Ahmed soon extended his power to Syria and Palestine whilst the Abbasids were distracted by rebellions in lower Iraq.

Ahmed's son and successor Khumarawayah received official recognition of his position from the caliph when he was granted Syria and Egypt in return for an annual tribute of 300,000 dinars. By the time of Khumarawayah's death in 896 the empire was weakened by extravagance and internal revolts. Three more Tulunid rulers followed but in the next ten years their situation was so weakened that in 906 an Abbasid general was able to take over Egypt and put an end to Tulunid rule.

Architecturally the most significant member of the dynasty is Ahmed ibn Tulun who established a new city as his capital in Egypt. This city was known as al-Qat'ic and was effectively an addition to Fustat. The city was famous for its similarity to the great Abbasid capital of Samarra. Not much remains of Ahmed's city but it is known to have had a triple-arched public entrance like the Bab al-Amma at Samarra, a polo ground, race track and park for wild animals. Ahmed also built structures useful to the general population such as a 60,000-dinar hospital. However, the only monuments remaining are the congregational mosque of Ibn Tulun and an aqueduct. The mosque displays certain similarities to the congregational mosques of Samarra, in particular the minarets. The aqueduct is built of brick and has a large inlet tower at the village of Basatin about two miles south of the citadel.

Ahmed's son Khumarawayah is known to have built a beautiful palace with a golden hall decorated with sheets of gold carrying representations of himself and his wife. Not surprisingly the palace has not survived.

Further reading:

K. A. C. Creswell, *A Short Account of Early Muslim Architecture*, ed. by J. Allen, Aldershot 1989.
P. K. Hitti, *History of the Arabs*, 10th edn., London 1970, 452–5.
C. E. Bosworth, *The Islamic Dynasties*, revised paperback edn., Edinburgh 1980, 43–4.

Tunis

Capital city of Tunisia since the thirteenth century.

Although smaller than that of Qairawan, the Great Mosque of Tunis (known as the Zaituna Mosque) has a similar history and design. The first mosque on the site was built in 732 to be replaced in 863 with the Aghlabid structure which forms the core of the present mosque. The prayer hall consists of fifteen aisles running east–west (i.e. perpendicular to the qibla wall) with the mihrab at the end of the central aisle, which is both wider and taller than the other aisles and surmounted by a dome at the end next to the mihrab; there is also a dome over the entrance, but this was added later, in the eleventh century. Both domes are ribbed and rest on shell squinches like the domes of the Great Mosque of Qairawan. The Tunis mosque is also famous for its role as a university. Next to it is an ablutions courtyard constructed by the Hafisid rulers in the fourteenth century which is one of the best examples of Tunisian decorative architecture. In the centre of the courtyard is an octagonal fountain and the whole area is decorated with white marble with black marble inlay.

Other important mosques in Tunis are the Qasr Mosque built in the twelfth century and the mosque of the Kasba built in the thirteenth century. The latter is interesting as one of the best examples of Andalusian influence in Tunisian architecture with its decorated minaret and ornate stucco decoration.

Tunis also contains a number of eighteenth-century palaces.

See also: Aghlabids, Tunisia

Further reading:

J. Revault, *Palais et demeurres de Tunis (XVIe et XVIIe siècles)*, Paris 1967.
—— *Palais et demeurres de Tunis (XVIIIe et XIXe siècles)*, Paris 1971.

Tunisia

North African country named after its capital Tunis.

Tunisia is a predominantly coastal country located between Algeria and Libiya. Northwards, a short distance across the sea, is the island of Sicily. Physically the country can be divided into three regions, a forested mountainous area to the north, a central plain watered by the Wadi Mejerda and a drier mountainous region to the south.

Tunisia has a long history of settlement starting with the Phoenician ports of the ninth century BCE. The greatest of these ports developed into the city of Carthage which dominated the trade of the Mediterranean until it was destroyed by the Romans in 146 CE. For a short period after the collapse of Roman rule the country was taken over by the Vandals until they were expelled by the Byzantines who ruled the country up to the time of the Arab conquest in 640. During the early Islamic period the country was known as Ifriqiyya with its capital at Qairawan. In the ninth century the country was ruled by the semi-autonomous Aghlabid dynasty who undertook the conquest of Sicily. During the tenth century the country became a base for the Fatimids before they moved to Egypt in 969. Tunisia's prominent position in Islamic history was brought to an end in the mid-eleventh century by the invasions of the Banu Hilal from northern Egypt. In a reversal of history the Normans of Sicily occupied the country for a short period in the mid-twelfth century until they were expelled by the Almohads. Following the Almohad victory Tunisia was ruled by a local dynasty known as the Hafisids who remained in power until the sixteenth century. In 1574, after a struggle between the Turks and the Spanish, the Turks gained the upper hand and Tunisia was incorporated into the Ottoman Empire. During the eighteenth century the country was ruled by a local dynasty known as the Husseinis, who, with increasing French help, ruled the country up to 1945 when Tunisia became an independent republic.

The main building material in Tunisia is stone which may either be finely dressed ashlar or smaller squared blocks. Baked brick was used, particularly in the early Islamic period for buildings like the Great Mosque at Qairawan. Roman and Byzantine material, in particular columns, formed one of the major building materials for early Islamic buildings. As elsewhere in North Africa the horshoe arch was the dominant arch form in monumental architecture. A certain amount of wood was available for roofs although generally buildings were covered with stone vaults. From the fifteenth century onwards glazed tiles became a common architectural feature which has survived until the twentieth century.

Tunisia is noted for the large number of religious buildings surviving from before the tenth century. The oldest Islamic monument in Tunisia is the Great Mosque of Qairawan which was built in 670 by ʿUqba ibn Nafi. Little remains of this early mosque which was rebuilt more than three times until 862 when it reached its present form under

Ribal of Susa, Tunisia © Creswell Archive, Ashmolean Museum

the Aghlabid ruler Abu Ibrahim Ahmad. The plan of this building became a model for later Tunisian mosques. The standard form comprises aisles running perpendicular to the qibla wall with a raised aisle in the centre leading to a domed cupola in front of the mihrab. In addition there is usually one (or more) aisle running parallel to the qibla wall forming a T-plan. Examples of this style include the Great Mosques of Tunis, Susa, Mahadiya, Monastir and Sfax – only the Great Mosque of Tozeur differs from it, with aisles running parallel to the qibla wall. This mosque form remained remarkably constant and even continued after the Ottoman conquest although there are examples of mosques of pure Ottoman form such as the Sidi Mahriz Mosque in Tunis.

Other religious structures include the ribat or fortified convent, an architectural form particularly characteristic of Tunisia. One of the best examples is the Ribat of Susa which was built by the Aghlabid ruler Ziyadat Allah in 821. This consists of a square building (95 m per side) with a central courtyard, towers at the corners and a monumental entrance. Three of the corner towers are circular whilst the fourth is square and forms a base for a cylindrical watchtower. The ground floor contains numerous rooms opening from the courtyard whilst on the first floor above the entrance there is a large prayer hall covered with barrel-vaulted aisles perpendicular to the mihrab. Other examples include the three ribats of Monastir, the oldest of which was founded in 796.

There is a wide variety of traditional house types in Tunisia from the bedouin tent to sophisticated courtyard villas. In southern Tunisia there are fortified settlements (qusur) which contain several tiers of barrel-vaulted rooms (ghorfas) arranged around a courtyard. The appearance of these structures is quite organic and resembles a beehive. Most of the time they are used for storage, but they could be used as dwellings in times of trouble. The standard form of village house is a windowless, flat-roofed structure, with a central courtyard used for animals. Town houses are a developed form of the village house; they are often two storeys high and decorated with polychrome glazed tiles. The houses of Tozeur are noted for their decorative brickwork façades. In Tunis there are a number of eighteenth-century Ottoman palaces and mansions. These are usually multiple courtyard structures with extravagant decoration which is a mixture of Islamic and European style.

See also: Aghlabids, Qairawan, Tunis

Further reading:

A. Lezine, *Architecture de l'Ifriqiyya: recherche sur les monuments aghlabides*, CNRS, Paris 1966.

G. Marçais, 'Recherches d'archéologie musulmane en Tunisie', *Bulletin de la Société Française des Fouilles Archéologiques* 5: 38–46, 1923–4.

turba (or turbe)

Mausoleum.

Turkey

The Republic of Turkey occupies a position between Asia and Europe and comprises Anatolia and Turkish Thrace.

Turkey is a large country open to the sea on three sides with the land route to the Middle East and Asia on the fourth side. The country may be divided roughly into five areas, each with a different environment and culture. West of Istanbul is Turkish Thrace, a green area with many connections with the Balkans. The northern part of the country stretching along the Black Sea coast is heavily wooded, with a high rainfall and cultural connections with Russia, Ukraine and other former Soviet Republics. The central area, where the capital Ankara is situated, is known as the Anatolian plain and has an extreme climate which produces snow in the winter and very hot summers. This area is largely inhabited by rural farmers although there are also Turkish nomads with tents. To the south and west is the Aegean and Mediterranean coast which has a mild climate and rich classical heritage. To the east, on the borders of Iraq and Iran, is a harsh mountainous area with a mixed population of Kurds, Armenians and Turks. Historically Turkey's position has meant that it has often been the scene of conflict between East and West, although the corollary of this is that it has also become extremely wealthy through East–West trade. Until the eleventh century most of Turkey was controlled by the Byzantine Empire which ruled from its capital at Constantinople (later Istanbul). During the ninth century there were regular Muslim raids which were sometimes quite successful. One of the largest raids was that of 838 when the city of Amorium was occupied and marble columns were taken back and used at Samarra. However, not until the eleventh century did the Byzantines, who had already lost the Middle East and North Africa to Islam, begin to lose large amounts of territory to the recently converted Seljuk Turks. In the early thirteenth century the Byzantines suffered a further blow when Constantinople was sacked by the soldiers of the Fourth Crusade. By the beginning of the fourteenth century Byzantine control was reduced to the area around Constantinople and Trabzon to the east on the Black Sea. In 1453 Constantinople was taken by the Ottomans who by the early sixteenth century controlled all of modern Turkey as well as large areas beyond its borders. In 1922 the Ottoman sultanate was abolished and replaced by the Turkish Republic under Mustafa Kemal Attaturk who instituted a policy of modernization and secularism.

The traditional architecture of Turkey reflects this varied landscape and rich history with many regional styles. A large range of building materials are employed including mud and baked brick, wood, stone and nomad tents.

The traditional Turkic nomad tent is known as a yurt and consists of a round wooden frame covered with a skin or hair tent. In south-western Anatolia the traditional Arabic type is found, comprising a black goat-hair tent which is supported with wooden poles and long ropes anchored with pegs. Mud brick is employed predominantly in the south-east of the country and in central Anatolia. At the town of Harran near the Syrian border houses are built out of one or more square mud-brick units, capped with flat-topped or pointed conical domes. In central Anatolia rectangular houses are built out of mud brick with stone foundations and roofs of wood and mud. The houses have thick walls with few windows to conserve heat in the winter and remain cool in the summer. Rooms are heated by open dung fires with a hole in the roof or an earthenware jar as a chimney. The roofs are built with roughly shaped timber branches up to 4 m long laid perpendicular to the walls of the house and covered with a layer of thatch which is then covered with mud. The mud on the roof is kept flat and waterproof with a section of column or other cylindrical stone which is rolled over the roof.

Baked brick in Turkey derives from two independent traditions, the Byzantine and the Persian Seljuk tradition. During the Byzantine era baked brick was one of the main building materials, especially in the cities of western Anatolia. This tradition continued into the Ottoman period and bricks are still one of the main building materials alongside the ubiquitous concrete. The usual method of using the flat tile-like bricks was in combination with rubble stone or dressed stone construction in alternate layers. Seljuk Persian brickwork was restricted in its impact on eastern Anatolia because of the strong stone-carving tradition already prevalent there. However, baked brick was often used in minarets in the west where it was sometimes arranged in decorative patterns in a manner alien to Byzantine practice. Glazed bricks are another technique imported into Anatolia by the Seljuks, although the most famous example is the Çinili Kiosk in the Topkapi Palace which was built by a Timurid architect.

In north-western Turkey and on the coast of the Black Sea wood is fairly plentiful and is the main building material. It is used in a number of ways from all-timber constructions to buildings with stone or brick walls and a wooden superstructure. Some of the oldest surviving wooden structures are Seljuk-period mosques which have been preserved because of their religious importance. A good example is the Aslan Cami in Ankara which has walls built of re-used stone and brick and an interior made of wooden columns supporting a flat roof made of wooden beams. However, most wooden structures are not more than 250 years old so that a large part of the architectural tradition is lost. The standard form of a traditional wooden town house consists of a stone basement, on top of which is built a rectangular platform cantilevered to project out above the street. Although the basement may be irregular, this is corrected on the upper floors where the cantilevering is used to produce a rectangular shape. Windows are often built to project an extra half-metre or more beyond the façade to give views along the street. Many houses are three storeys high including the basement, although it is likely that in the past most were one or two storeys high. In Istanbul many of the houses are clad in external weather-boarding, but elsewhere the walls of the houses are made of lath and plaster. Inside the grander houses the ceilings are often decorated with painted scenes on plaster or wood.

Stone buildings represent the largest group of

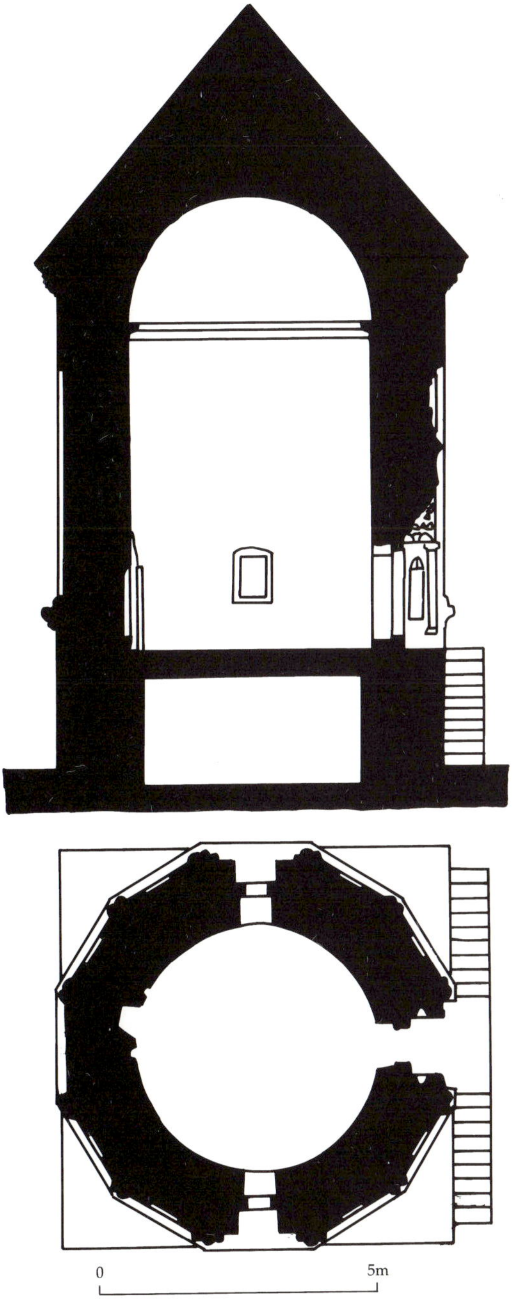

Donner Kumbet, Kayseri, Turkey

historical buildings in Turkey from the eighth-century mosque at Harran to the eighteenth-century baroque mosques of Istanbul. The material used

Donner Kumbet, Kayseri, Turkey

varies according to the region; thus in Diyarbakir black basalt is used whereas in Edirne red sandstone is employed in conjunction with yellow limestone. The most basic form of stone construction can be found in the Gourami region near Kayseri where houses are built out of the abandoned caves previously used by Christians. The houses may either consists of a cave on its own or a cave with a stone-built arched porch. Some of the most sophisticated stonework is found in the carved doorways of the Seljuk period in Konya, Nigde, Erzerum, Kayseri and Sivas. Probably the most spectacular example is the doorway of the Gök Madrassa in Sivas which combines intricate calligraphy and floral designs with bold carved borders. Ottoman stonework by contrast tends to be fairly austere with a restrained use of carved decoration relying instead on the form and mass of the building.

See also: Bursa, Byzantine architecture, Diyarbakir, Edirne, Istanbul, Konyo, Seljuks, Ottomans

Mausoleum Kounia Urgench, Turkmenistan © StJohn Simpson

Further reading:

K. A. Aru, *Türk Hamamlari Etüdü*, Istanbul 1949.
Ö. Bakirer, *Selçuklu Öncesi ve Selçuklu Dönemi Anadolu Mimarisinde Tugla Kullani*, Ankara 1981.
G. Goodwin, *A History of Ottoman Architecture*, London 1971.
R. Holod and A. Evin, *Modern Turkish Architecture*, Philadelphia 1984.
F. Seton Lloyd and D. Storm Rice, *Alanya ('Alaiyya)*, London 1958.
S. Ögel, *Anadolu Selçuklulari'nin Taş Tezyinati (Anatolian Seljuk Stone Ornamentation)*, Ankara 1987.
R. M. Riefstahl, *Turkish Architecture in South Western Anatolia*, Cambridge, Mass. 1931.
M. Sözen, *Anadolu Medreseleri Selçuklular ve Beylikler Devri*, vols. Istanbul 1970–2.
—— *Anadolu'da Akkoyonulu Mimarisi (Anatolian Aqqounulu Architecture)* Istanbul 1981.
M. Sözen and M. Tapan, *50 Yilin Türk Mimarisi (50 Years of Turkish Architecture)*, Istanbul 1973.
B. Ünsal, *Turkish Islamic Architecture in Seljuk and Ottoman Times 1071–1923*, London 1973.

Turkmenistan

Former Soviet Central Asian Republic which lies to the east of the Caspian Sea and to the north of Afghanistan and Iran.

Geographically Turkmenistan is defined by the Koppet Dag mountains along its southern border with Iran and to the north by the Amu Darya (Oxus) river which separates it from Uzbekistan.

Mausoleum, Kouria-Urgeuch, Turkmenistan

The Kara Kum desert covers the central part of Turkmenistan dividing the country into north and south. Before the construction of the Kara Kum canal at the beginning of this century habitation in southern Turkmenistan was only possible at oases where rivers from the Koppet Dag mountains disappeared into the sands of the Kara Kum. The most famous of these desert oases was the ancient city of Merv (qv) fed by the Murghab river.

Mud brick is the principal construction material although fired brick is used for monumental architecture. To the north along the Amu Darya wood is often used for columns and roofs.

Buildings of the early Islamic period, from the eighth to eleventh centuries CE, are mostly found in the area around Merv although there may also be isolated buildings of the period in the Kara Kum desert. Many buildings of the eleventh to thirteenth century Seljuk period have survived in particular at Serakhs on the border with Afghanistan, at Mestorian in the south-west and at Urgench on the border with Uzbekistan. These are mostly religious buildings characterized by elaborate brick decoration, epigraphic bands, the use of stucco, and the combination of mud brick with fired brick. Buildings of the later medieval period are more difficult to identify, although the city of Bairam Ali near Merv preserves the layout and walls of a fifteenth- to sixteenth-century Timurid city. Probably the most significant Islamic building of later periods is the Great Mosque of Anau, destroyed by an earthquake in 1948, most of which dates to the seventeenth century. The mosque comprises a huge domed iwan flanked by twin minarets and two smaller domed chambers on either side of the courtyard. The façade of the iwan was decorated with polychrome tiles depicting dragons and elaborate decorative brickwork.

After the Russian conquest in the nineteenth century Islamic forms were used in buildings of Russian design such as the Tsar's hunting lodge at Bairam Ali which employs domes, crenellations and minaret-like pinnacles. This tradition was continued into the Soviet period with buildings such as the Academy of Sciences where the arcades are decorated with pseudo-epigraphic brickwork.

See also: Central Asia, Merv

Further reading:

G. A. Pugachenkava, 'Puti razvitiya arkhitekturi Iuzhnogo Turkmenistana pori rabovladeniya', *Trudi Iuzhno-Turkmenistanskoi Arkheologicheskoi Ekspeditsii* 6, 1958.

U

Ukhaidhir

Early Abbasid palace in the desert of south-western Iraq.

The palace stands in the desert west of the city of Kerbala and east of the oasis of Shithatha. The building is made out of rough-hewn limestone blocks and mud plaster with baked brick used for roofing vaults, resembling earlier Sassanian structures (cf. Kharana in Jordan). The palace may be divided into two structural phases, a central palace core and an outer enclosure wall added slightly later. The exterior curtain wall is composed of tall blind niches alternating with solid semi-circular buttress towers. On top of the wall there was a parapet which was cantilevered over the niches allowing a continuous series of slits (machicolation) which could protect the lower parts of the wall from attack. The main gateway is set between two quarter-round towers and contains a slot for a portcullis. To the right of the entrance on the outside there is a large stable block. The central core of the palace contains a mosque, a bath house and a main reception hall. The upper floor is reached by ramps running up at right angles to the axis of the main gateway. There are small tunnels running over the main vaults which provided cooling and ventilation.

Recent survey work in the vicinity of Ukhaidhir has demonstrated the development of the area during the early Isalmic period, starting with the small palace at Tulul Ukhaidhir several kilometres to the north of the main palace. In addition there is an outer mud-brick enclosure containing a variety of mud-brick buildings which are now only visible as humps.

See also: Abbasids: Atshan, Khan; Iraq; Sassanians

Further reading:

G. Bell, *Palace and Mosque at Ukhaidhir: A Study in Early Muhammadan Architecture*, Oxford 1914.

B. Finnster and J. Schmidt, *Sasaidische und fruhislamische Ruinem im Iraq, Baghdader Mitteilungen* 8, Berlin 1976.

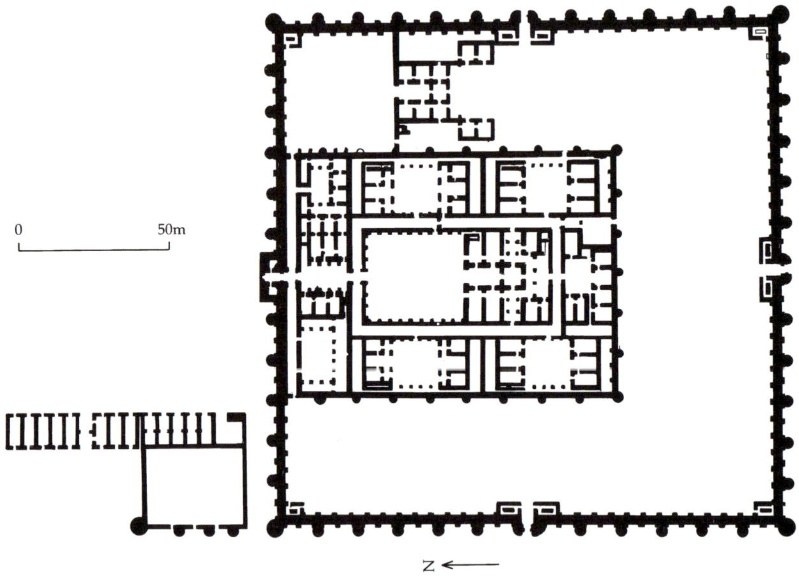

Plan of Ukhaidhir Palace, Iraq (after Mehdi)

ulu cami

Turkish term for a congregational or Friday mosque.

Umayyads

The dynasty of Umayyad caliphs was based in Syria and ruled the Islamic world from 660 to 750 CE.

Under the Umayyads the Islamic state was transformed from a theocracy to an Arab monarchy. In 661 Ali, the last Orthodox caliph was murdered and Muʿawiya, the governor of Syria, became the first Umayyad caliph. Muʿawiya provided the centralization essential for the survival and continuing expansion of the Arab Empire. At its height Umayyad rule extended from the Atlantic coast of North Africa to India and from Central Asia to the Yemen. The administration of conquered provinces was usually left intact, so that the tax accounts for Syria, for example, continued to be kept in Greek. Socially, however, Umayyad rule was characterized by the domination of Arabs.

The success of the Umayyad caliphate carried within it the seeds of its own destruction. Because the economic and social structure of the empire was dependent on the conquest of new lands, any setbacks or reverses caused resentment and dissatisfaction throughout the regime. Similarly the secular nature of the dynasty aroused opposition amongst those in favour of a more theocratic state. In 747 a revolution against the Umayyads began in Khurassan and soon spread throughout the eastern part of the empire. By 750 the Umayyad regime had been defeated to be replaced by the Abbasids who ruled from Iraq. Only one branch of the Umayyads survived by fleeing to Spain where the dynasty continued to rule until 1051 CE.

Almost all surviving Umayyad monuments are in Syria and Palestine whence the dynasty derived most of its support. As the Arabs did not have an architectural tradition suited to the needs of a great empire, they adopted the building methods of the defeated Sassanian and Byzantine empires. Because they ruled from Syria, Byzantine influence was stronger, although Sassanian elements became increasingly important. In many cases Byzantine or even Roman buildings were simply taken over with little or no modification. However, the conquests did provide some innovation both in terms of building types and in the prominence given to decoration.

The most important building projects undertaken during the Umayyad era included mosques, palaces and cities. Mosques were obviously an important element in the expansion of the Islamic state although the speed of the conquests meant that these were often temporary structures or converted churches. New cities were built in answer to specific requirements, such as the need for an administrative centre rather than for dynastic propaganda as in the Abbasid period. The most characteristic type of building is the 'Desert Palace' built as a residence for the ruling élite.

The earliest Islamic cities were garrison towns such as Basra and Kufa, built as centres for the conquest of Khurassan and Central Asia. The Umayyads continued this policy of building cities which were little more than giant military camps, although significantly these were unfortified. The most important city of this type was Wasit built in 701 by Yussuf ibn al-Hajjaj the Umayyad governor of Iraq. Architecturally these cities were important because they were divided according to tribal groups, each with its own masjid, which prefigures similar divisions in later Arab cities. Trade was also a powerful stimulus for the foundation and growth of cities in the early Islamic period. The frontiers of the Islamic state were particularly conducive to the growth of cities in North Africa and in eastern Iran military camps quickly grew into trading cities.

Mosques were an essential part of early Islamic government as they provided a meeting place at which important announcements could be made. Early on two separate mosque-building traditions developed; in Syria this was based on the conversion of churches whilst in Iraq mosques developed out of square enclosures used for prayer. The earliest Iraqi mosque for which we have archaeological evidence is the Friday mosque at Wasit built to a square plan with a hypostyle roof. The oldest Islamic building in the west is the Dome of the Rock built by Abd al-Malik in 691. However, this building is a sanctuary rather than a mosque and its influence on later Islamic architecture is limited.

More important in terms of mosque development is the Great Mosque in Damascus built by the caliph al-Walid in 705 CE. This building is modelled on Syrian churches, which after the conquest were used as mosques. Churches were converted to mosques by blocking up the west door and piercing the north wall with doorways, creating a building with a lateral axis perpendicular to the direction of prayer. Mosques built in the same style as Damascus include Qasr al-Hayr, Qusayr Hallabat, Raqqa, Balis, Diyarbakir and Der'a. Other developments in religious architecture in the Umayyad period include the introduction of the mihrab and the minaret.

In secular building the most important constructions of the Umayyad period were the desert palaces of Syria and Palestine. Some of these buildings were new foundations, whilst others were Roman or Byzantine forts converted to meet the needs of the new Arab rulers. Significantly, most of these buildings were abandoned soon after the fall of the Umayyad regime and they remain as monuments to the wealth and tastes of the dynasty. Their size and scale vary enormously, from the small and lavishly decorated bath house of Qusayr Amrah to the great fortified city–palace of Qasr al-Hayr al-Sharqi. From the outside most of these buildings resemble fortresses; thus the main entrance of Qasr al-Hayr al-Sharqi is protected by two tall semi-circular towers and a machicolice. In some of the palaces the effect of the fortifications is softened by great decorative friezes, as at Mshatta, Qasr al-Hayr al-Gharbi and Khirbet al-Mafjar. Most of these palaces include a bath house and a mosque as well as living accommodation arranged according to the bayt system. Each palace comprised a number of bayts, each of which would house a family or tribal unit. There is very little differentiation between the rooms within each bayt, so they were probably used simply as shelters in a similar manner to a bedouin tent with no permanent fixtures.

The building techniques employed by the Umayyads were as diverse as the regions they conquered, so that major projects would employ workmen of several different nationalities. At its most conservative Umayyad architecture is indistinguishable from either Byzantine or Sassanian work but usually there is a combination of eastern and western elements which produce an unmistakably Islamic building. One of the best examples of this mixture is to be found at Mshatta where the walls are of cut stone in the Syrian tradition, the vaults are constructed in the Mesopotamian fashion and the decorative carving is a mixture of Byzantine and Coptic motifs.

The most common building materials used in this period were stone, wood and brick. In Syria the majority of buildings were constructed out of cut stone or ashlar masonry. The quality of Umayyad masonry is generally very high with sharp edges, tight joins and large blocks producing buildings with a monumentality unsurpassed in later Islamic building. Ashlar masonry is particularly suited to the construction of large vertical surfaces which can be enlivened by carving, as on the entrance façade at Mshatta. With the exception of basalt most stone is unsuitable for roofing large areas and only small spans could be roofed with barrel vaulting. In general Umayyad architecture avoided the problem of intersecting vaults so that most buildings were either made up of small units or roofed in wood.

In Syria, timber from the forests of Lebanon was often used for roofing. Roofs were either shallow, pitched structures supported by wooden trusses, as in the Great Mosque of Damascus, or occasionally wooden domes, as in the Dome of the Rock or the Aqsa Mosque. Timber was also used for centring, scaffolding, tie-beams and mosque furniture such as minbars.

Although brick architecture was common to both the Byzantine and Sassanian empires its use in Umayyad architecture was limited to the eastern part of the empire. The availability of suitable stone in Syria meant that bricks were rarely used there even in Byzantine times. When bricks were used in Syria it is significant that the Mesopotamian style was used with thin joints, rather than the thick layers of mortar used in the Byzantine tradition. Examples of this are found at Qasr al-Tuba and Mshatta. In Iraq both baked brick and mud brick were used extensively. Often baked brick was used for pillars, vaults and the lower courses of walls whilst mud brick was used for the upper parts. Examples can be seen at Wasit and Usqaf Bani Junayd.

Umayyad architecture can be distinguished from that of earlier periods by its use of decorative techniques. None of these was new but the variety and scale of decorative effects was far greater than ever before. The most important decorative methods employed were mosaic, wall painting, sculpture and relief carving.

Although it is probable that most Umayyad mosaics were made by Byzantine craftsmen, the motifs used and the choice of designs usually indicate an Islamic influence. The earliest Islamic mosaics are those in the Dome of the Rock, which consist of gold and polychrome tesserae in representations of Byzantine and Sassanian royal jewels. The Great Mosque in Damascus contains a very important group of mosaics depicting an ideal city which, significantly, is devoid of people. This is due to the ban on figural representation in mosques and is a good example of Byzantine art adapted for Islamic purposes. Even in the desert palaces mosaics usually avoided figures, although occasionally, as at Khirbet al-Mafjar, there are representations of animals.

In addition to floor mosaics most Umayyad palaces were decorated with frescoes, usually on walls, although occasionally on floors, as at Qasr al-Hayr al-Gharbi. The best preserved paintings are those at Qusayr Amrah which include representations of a great hunt, half-naked dancing girls and a famous portrait of six rulers of the world.

Sculptures are found at a number of desert palaces, most notably Khirbet al-Mafjar and Qasr al-Hayr al-Gharbi. Both eastern and western sculptural traditions were used, although the medium was usually stucco rather than stone. Because stucco is not free-standing, sculptures were usually incorporated into some structural feature of a building such as the entrance.

See also: bayt, masjid, mihrab, minaret

Further reading:

K. A. C. Creswell, *A Short Account of Early Muslim Architecture*, ed. by J. Allen, Aldershot 1989.

R. Ettinghausen, *From Byzantium to Sassanian Iran and the Islamic World*, Leiden 1976.

R. Hillenbrand, 'La dolce vita in Early Islamic Syria: the evidence of later Umayyad palaces', *Art History* 5(1): 1–35, 1982.

H. N. Kennedy, *The Prophet and the Age of the Caliphates: The Islamic Near East from the Sixth to the Eleventh Century*, London and New York 1986.

United Arab Emirates (UAE)

Federation composed of the seven emirates of Fujairah, Ajman, Ras al-Khaimah, Abu Dhabi, Dubai, Umm al-Quwain and Sharjah. The country previously known as the Trucial Coast is located on the Arabian side of the Gulf between Qatar and Oman. The eastern part of the country bordering on Oman is mountainous whilst the western part is flat sandy coastal plain.

The traditional materials of construction in the emirates are coral, mud brick, dry stone and wood and thatch. Coral obtained from the coastal reefs is the prime building material on the coast. Two forms are used, irregular rubble blocks set into a thick mortar known as 'sarooj' and thin coral slabs used as panels between load-bearing pillars. Mangrove wood obtained from East Africa is used both as strengthening for walls and for roof beams. The maximum length of mangrove poles is 3.5 m which imposes a rigid geometry on the coastal houses. Ceilings resting on the mangrove beams are made of planks of date-palm wood and are sometimes painted.

In oasis towns, such as al-Cain on the Omani border, houses are built out of mud brick with split-palm beams used for roofing in a manner common throughout the Arabian peninsula. Often the lower parts of the walls are built from large stone blocks to strengthen the buildings against water and wind erosion. The most ephemeral buildings are those built of palm fronds and wood, although it is likely that in the past these may have been the commonest form of dwelling. Palm-frond, or barasti, houses are usually built on a wooden frame made out of mangrove poles, split-palm trunk or any other available wood. The palm fronds are used in two forms, either as straight poles (approximately 1 m long) stripped of their leaves used for creating screens or with the leaves still on for roof thatch. The shape of palm-frond houses varies from square or rectangular flat-roofed buildings to triangular tent-like structures.

In the mountains in the east of the country houses are built out of irregular-shaped blocks laid without mortar; inside, the walls of the houses may be plastered with mud. The flat roofs are made out of palm fronds or any other locally available wood. Sometimes the houses are built into the ground, with triangular pitched roofs made of palm wood. Most of the stone houses are rectangular, although in the central mountains of the UAE round stone houses are also found, with roofs made of mountain bushes.

Before the twentieth century the emirates depended on trade and fishing for their primary income. Each town was located on a creek or peninsula with easy access to the sea and a hinterland used for agriculture. The most famous of these towns (now disappeared) is Julfar which had extensive trade links with East Africa, India and the Far East during the seventeenth and eighteenth centuries. The location of the emirates on the coast

Traditional house, UAE. Note wind-tower (mulqaf) (after Kay and Zandi)

of the Gulf has also meant that the country was heavily influenced by it neighbour Iran. This influence can be seen in the Bastakia quarter of Dubai which developed as an outpost of the Iranian city of Bastak. Today the Bastakiya quarter is notable for its wind-towers, which are a characteristic feature of central Iranian towns.

There are few old mosques standing in the UAE and those that do survive are mostly in the smaller villages. This is because the larger mosques of the towns have undergone constant renovation and renewal so that the main mosques are now dazzling new structures. Reputedly the oldest mosque in the emirates is the mosque of Bidiya on the east coast, near the site of the battle of Dibba which established Islam in the area. This mosque is a rectangular building with a large central pillar supporting four flat-topped domes with pointed finials. The deep-set mihrab projects out of the back of the mosque and is flanked by a fixed minbar of four steps. Until recently minarets were fairly unusual in the UAE although in the east there are a number of small coastal mosques with squat minarets capped with unusual pointed domes.

Like many of the other countries of the Arabian peninsula the emirates have a number of forts and watch-towers built to protect the urban populations. Each of the seven emirates had its own forts which are now in varying states of repair. The oldest of these is the Husn of Abu Dhabi originally built in the eighteenth century to protect the city's well. The emirate of al-Cain has six forts built by the Nahyan family around the Buraimi oasis between 1830 and 1910. Most of the forts have now been restored and converted into museums.

The most sophisticated houses in the UAE are found in the coastal towns where there was enough wealth and outside influence to build on a large scale. The typical house of a wealthy coastal family consists of a two-storey structure built around a central courtyard. From the outside the houses are generally quite plain, although sometimes the upper parts of the walls were decorated with crenellations and the wind-towers were decorated with elaborate arches. Inside, the rooms opening on to the courtyard were decorated with carved stucco panels or grilles, sometimes containing stained glass.

The phenomenal growth of the emirates since

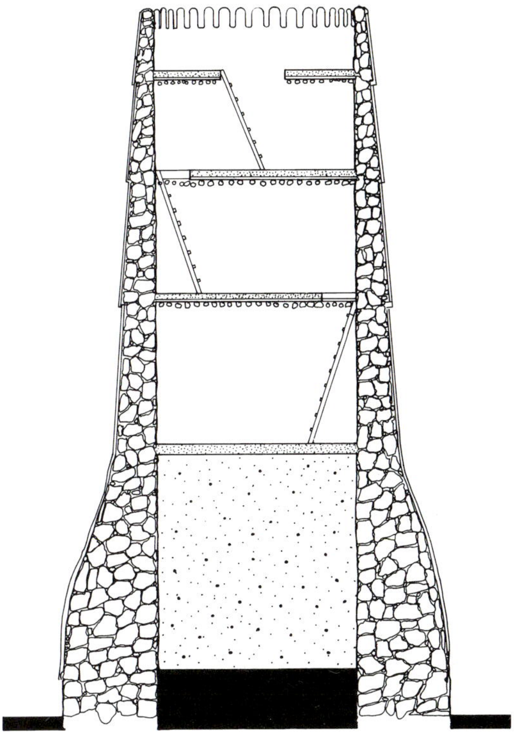

Defensive tower, UAE. Note lower part of tower is filled with sand (after Kay and Zandi)

the Second World War has meant that many of the older historical and traditional buildings were destroyed. In recent times, however (since the 1970s), there has been a concerted effort to protect and restore historical buildings. One of the most successful projects has been the restoration of the abandoned nineteenth-century palace of Sheikh Saeed, ruler of Dubai from 1912 to 1958. The present architecture of the UAE represents a wide variety of Islamic styles indicating both the wealth and cosmopolitan nature of the country.

See also: Bahrain, Oman, Qatar

Further reading:

A. Coles and J. Jackson, 'A windtower house in Dubai', *Art and Archaeology Research Papers*, 1975.

W. Dostal, *The Traditional Architecture of Ras al-Khaimah*, Dubai 1983.

S. Kay, 'Richness of style in UAE mosques', *Arts and the Islamic World*, 3(4), 1985–6.

S. Kay and D. Zandi, *Architectural Heritage of the Gulf*, Dubai 1991.

A. al-Tajir, 'Traditional architecture of the UAE', *Arts and the Islamic World* 3(4): 68ff., 1985–6.

United States of America (USA)

Islamic architecture in America can be divided into three distinct types, buildings for Muslim Americans, Orientalist buildings built by non-Muslims to evoke the spirit of the Orient, and buildings in the Spanish-American style which recalls the Mudéjar architecture of Spain.

American cities with large Muslim populations include New York, Chicago, Detroit and Los Angeles, all of which have several mosques. The architecture of these mosques generally reflects the ethnic origin of the main Muslim group in the area, thus there are Albanian mosques in the four cities with large Albanian populations. In recent times the influx of students from oil-rich countries into colleges in the United States has led to a number of mosques being built on campuses. One of the most ambitious projects is the headquarters of the Islamic Society of North America (ISNA) at Plainfields, Indiana, begun in 1975. Although not yet complete, the centre will eventually include a mosque, accommodation for 500 students, a refectory, a library for 100,000 volumes and recreational facilities. Another notable Islamic student centre is that of the University of Arkansas at Johesboro financed by a patron from Saudi Arabia. The main building of the centre is a mosque with a small courtyard and a square-shafted minaret. There is a separate women's section or gallery on the upper floor which is reached by external and internal staircases. The building is faced in dark and light coloured brick and the façade is decorated with a calligraphic brick frieze. Both the Arkansas and the Indiana centres are undoubtedly modern buildings which reflect traditional Islamic architecture. By contrast the Dar al-Salam centre at Abiquiu in New Mexico, designed by the Egyptian architect Hassan Fathy, is built with traditional materials and techniques. The complex consists of a mosque, madrassa and several accommodation blocks, all built out of mud brick known locally as adobe (from the Arabic al-toub). The building is covered with barrel vaults and domes and decorated with crenellations and carved woodwork. As well as being a religious centre Dar al-Salam will also function as a centre for traditional architecture and technology.

Orientalist architecture in the USA is primarily a feature of the early twentieth century and is a product of the incredible wealth of America combined with cinema-inspired fantasy (e.g. *The Thief of Baghdad*). This can be seen in the numerous cinemas built in the Moorish palace style with names like the Alhambra. The most complete examples of this Islamic fantasy architecture is the city of Opa-Locka conceived as 'the Baghdad of south Florida'. The buildings have horseshoe-shaped windows, minarets, domes and crenellations. The most important building is the city hall, built as a fortified citadel with thick crenellated enclosure walls. This building is covered with five large domes and framed by four minarets (three small cylindrical towers and one huge octagonal tower). Other Islamic-style buildings in the city include the railway station, the archery club, the archaeological museum and the Opa Locka hotel.

The discovery of the New World and the expulsion of Muslims from Spain occurred in the same year, 1492. The result was that a large number of Muslims converted to Christianity and emigrated to the New World where their skills were used in the development of New Spain. Mudéjar (forced Muslim converts to Christianity) style architecture in America is found mostly in Mexico and Central America, although it can also be seen in the south and west of the USA in Texas, New Mexico and California.

See also: Mudéjar, Spain

Further reading:

N. Ardalan, 'Architects in America design for Islamic cultures', *Arts and the Islamic World* 3(3): 46–50, 1985.
F. S. Fitzgerald Bush, *A Dream of Araby* (n.d.).
C. Hotchkiss Malt, 'Opa–Locka: American city with Islamic design', *Arts and the Islamic World*, 1(3): 33–6, 1983.
A. Schleifer, 'Hassan Fathy: a voyage to New Mexico', *Arts and the Islamic World* 1(1): 1982/3.

Urgench

Ancient capital of Khorezm in western Uzbekistan.

Urgench was established as the Mongol capital in the early fourteenth century. The most prominent remains at the site is the tomb of Turabek Khanum dated to 1320. This has a massive portal with a muqarnas vault. Outside, the tomb has a polygonal plan whilst the interior is hexagonal.

Uzbekistan

Independent Central Asian Republic with a predominantly Muslim population.

Uzbekistan occupies a vast area between Afghanistan, Turkmenistan and Khazakstan; most of this area is desert, semi-desert or steppe. The main areas of occupation are the western area of Khorezm, where the river Amu Dar'ya enters the Aral Sea, and the cities of Bukhara and Samarkand on the Zeravshan river. The population of the Republic is predominantly Uzbek (Turkic) although Persian was the main language in the early Islamic period.

The main source of prosperity for this region is the trans-continental trade route between China, India, the Middle East and Europe known as the Silk Route. The trade led to the establishment of urban centres on the edge of the deserts of Central Asia. From the second century this trade was controlled by the Kushans, a semi-nomadic people from Chinese Central Asia. The Kushans built up a vast empire which controlled most of the trade passing through Central Asia. In the fourth century the Sassanians took control of the western part of the trade routes and reduced the Kushans to a series of independent principalities. The central part of the route was controlled by the Soghdians who occupied Samarkand and Bukhara. The first Arab raids occurred in the mid-seventh century, although it was not until the beginning of the eighth century that any real conquests were made with the capture of Bukhara and Samarkand. By the mid-eighth century most of the region was under Arab control. By the ninth century a Persian dynasty known as the Samanids was in control of both Bukhara and Samarkand. The Samanids were nominally vassals of the Abbasids although they acted independently. During this period Islam gradually replaced Buddhism, Manichaeism and Zorastrianism as the main religion of the area. At the end of the tenth century the Samanids were replaced by the Karakhanid Turks who established Samarkand as their capital. During the eleventh century the Seljuk Turks rapidly expanded westwards from their base in the region of Khorezm in western Uzbekistan. The region of Khorezm was left under the rule of the Khorezmshas who were vassals of the Seljuks. In 1077 the Khorezmshas declared themselves independent, establishing their capital at Urgench. By the twelfth century the Khorezmshas had gained control of most of Central

Asia. This period of great prosperity was interrupted by the Mongol invasions of the early thirteenth century. The earliest period of Mongol rule in the region was not characterized as successful, although under the Timurids in the fourteenth and fifteenth centuries it entered one of the most brilliant periods of history. In the sixteenth century the region was conquered by the Uzbeks who now form the majority of the population.

The main building materials are mud brick and pisé, baked brick and wood. Stone is generally not available for use as a building material. In addition to the fixed buildings temporary or mobile dwellings (yurt) are made of felt over a wooden frame. For traditional houses throughout the region mud brick and pisé are most commonly used. Some of the best examples of mud architecture are the fortified walls which surround most settlements from small villages to major cities such as Bukhara. Important buildings such as mosques, madrassas and mausoleums were sometimes built of baked brick. In premodern times the standard brick form was a square tile 5–7 cm thick. These were used in a variety of decorative patterns produced by placing bricks in alternating groups vertically and horizontally. From the twelfth century glazed bricks were used and eventually became common in the fifteenth century under the Timurids. Although wood has always been rare, especially in the eastern parts of Uzbekistan, it was used for roofs and occasionally for columns, especially in mosques and palaces. Some of the best examples of wooden architecture are in Khiva and include carved wooden columns with muqarnas capitals and bulbous lotus bases resembling lotus buds. Wooden ceilings are often painted.

The majority of Islamic monuments in Uzbekistan are found in Bukhara and Samarkand whilst Khiva is a good example of traditional nineteenth-century architecture. Outside these cities the most important monuments in the country are at Shar-i Sabz, the village which Timur tried to make his capital.

See also: Bukhara, Samarkand, Shar-i Sabz, Timurids

W

wakala

Urban building combining the functions of khan, warehouse and market.

waqf

A charitable endowment often intended for the upkeep of a religious building, educational establishment or hospital.

Wasit

Capital of Iraq during the Umayyad period.

Wasit lies south-east of the modern town of Kut in southern Iraq. It was founded in 701 CE by al-Hajjaj, governor of Iraq, as a garrison town to replace Kufa and Basra which had been demilitarized after a revolt against the Umayyads. In 874 another Friday mosque was built by the Turkish general Musa ibn Bugha in the eastern part of the city. The devastation wrought by the Mongols in the thirteenth century and by Timur in the fourteenth hastened the decline of a city that was no longer on the main trade routes due to a change in the course of the Tigris.

The first mosque on the site was built by al-Hajjaj in 703; measuring 100 m per side, it was located next to the governor's residence. Iraqi excavations revealed two superimposed mosques, the earlier of which had no mihrab. This confirms the early date of the mosque, as the first concave mihrab was introduced by al-Walid in 707–9 in the mosque of Medina.

There are also the remains of a thirteenth-century madrassa on the site, consisting of a monumental portal flanked by twin minarets with fluted brick decoration.

West Africa

Region of Africa comprising the modern states of Mali, Mauritania, Senegal, Niger, Nigeria, Cameroon, Burkina Faso, Guinea and Ghana.

Known to medieval geographers as the Sudan, this area extends from the Sahara desert in the north to the mouth of the Niger river in the south, and from Atlantic in the west to Lake Chad in the east. The region was subject to the influence of Islam from the eighth or ninth century onwards and by the nineteenth century large areas were Islamicized.

West Africa can be divided into four main zones, the Sahara, the Sahel, the Savannah and the rain forests. The largest zone is the Sahara desert which extends from the Atlas mountains in Morocco and Algeria to the Senegal river. Until recent times the vast dunes and extreme temperatures of this desert have formed an impenetrable barrier to all except the nomadic tribes which inhabit the area. South of the desert is band of semi-arid country known as the Sahel (Arabic for 'coast') where there is an intermittent vegetation of scrub and occasional small trees. Below this is the Savannah region characterized by a rich growth of grass and plentiful seasonal rainfall. Further south near the coast, especially in Nigeria, Benin, Togo and Ghana, are the dense rain-forests. In recent times the area of the Sahara and the Sahel have been increasing at the expense of the Savannah, probably due to human activity. The best example of this phenomenon is the area occupied by the empire of Ghana which in medieval times was rich grassland and is now desert.

History

The means by which Islam penetrated into West Africa was via the trade routes from North Africa. The main goods involved in the trade included gold, slaves, ivory and gum from West Africa and manufactured goods from the Mediterranean area. This trade was a continuation of pre-Islamic Roman and Byzantine trade routes and was in the hands of the Berber tribes of the Sahara. Already by the end of the seventh century there are accounts of Muslim traders from North Africa and Egypt in the markets of the Sudan. By the end of the eighth

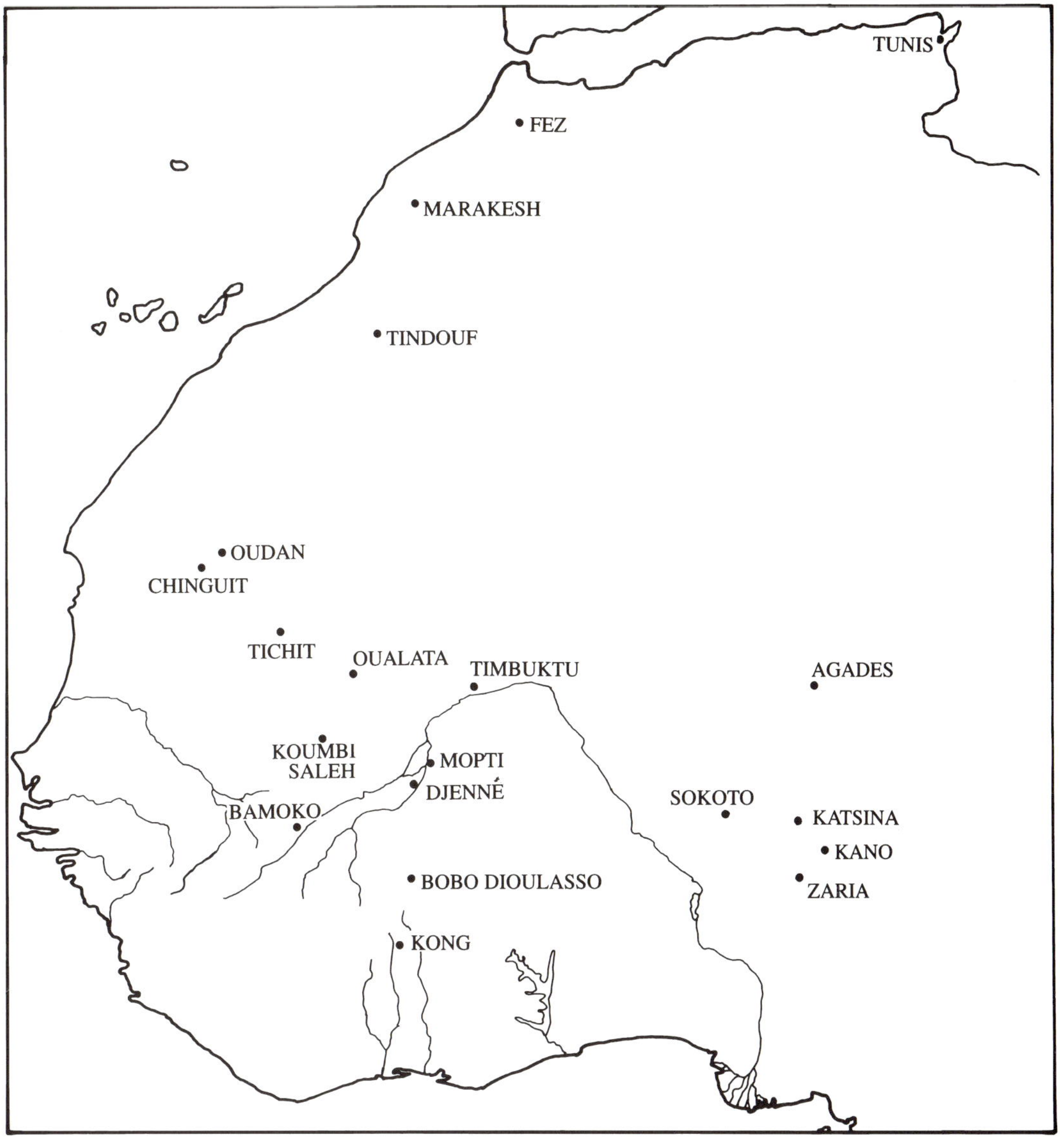

Principal Islamic sites of West Africa

century the northern part of the trade was controlled by the semi-independent Berber dynasties of the Rustamids in Morocco and the Idrisids in western Algeria. These dynasties controlled the northern termini of the West African routes at Sijimassa and Tahert and were able to collect taxes from this lucrative trade. It was this trade which was one of the motivating forces behind the rise of the Fatimids in North Africa. With the support of Berber tribes the Fatimids gained control of most of North Africa in the ninth century and by the tenth century were in a strong enough position to take control of Egypt, Africa's wealthiest province.

The role of the Berbers in the dissemination of Islam amongst the peoples of the Sudan was critical, particularly in the area of present-day Mauritania. The Berbers in this area are known as the Sanhadja or Muthalamin and were the ancestors of

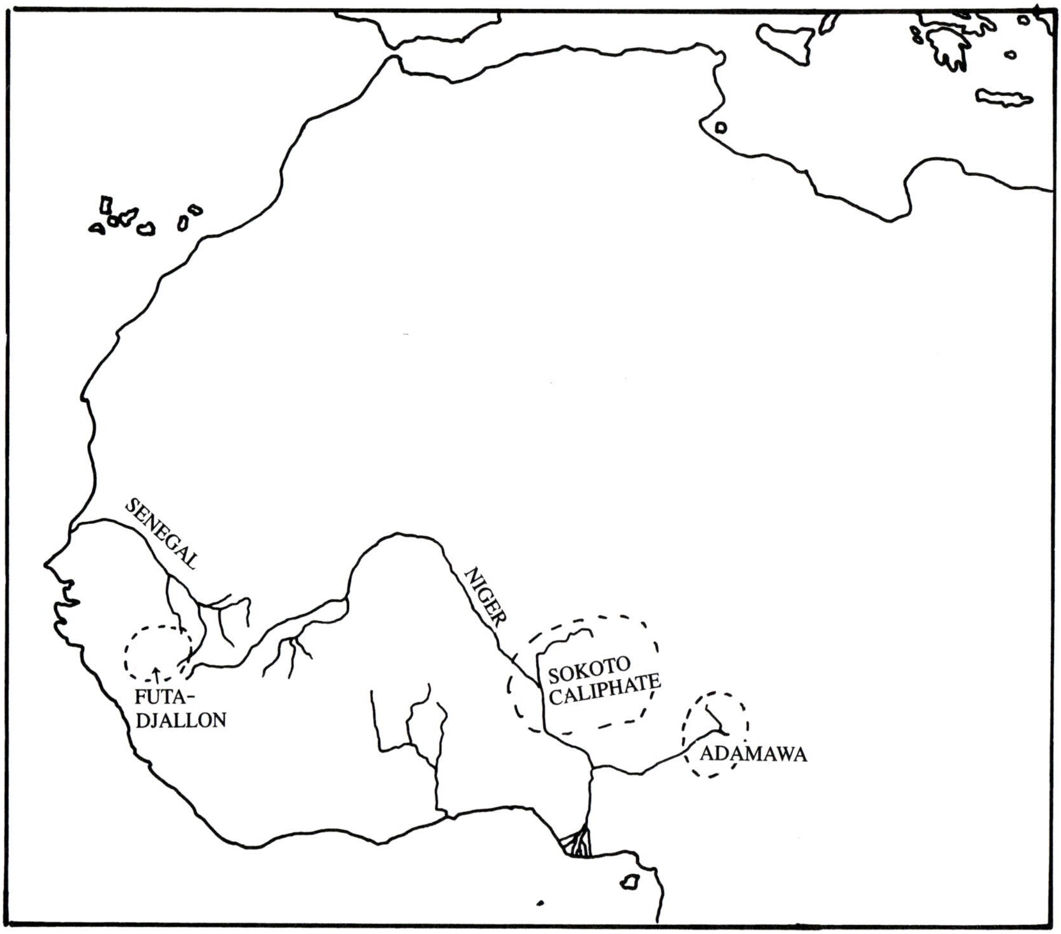

West Africa showing Fulbe areas of Futa-Djallon, Sokoto and Adamawa

the Almoravids who invaded Spain in the eleventh century. They comprised three main tribal groups, the Lamtuna, Massufa and Godala, who were allied into a loose confederation. The most prominent of these groups was the Lamtuna who arrived in the area in the eighth century and captured the oasis city of Awdaghast in Mauritania. By the tenth century most of the Sanhadja leaders had adopted Islam which they used to wage a jihad against the southern kingdoms.

The southern part of West Africa below the Sahel was dominated by the three great empires of Ghana, Mali and Gao. Each of these empires was composed of a particular language group; thus Ghana was controlled by Soninke-speaking peoples, Mali by Manding peoples and Gao by Songhay people. These were not empires in the modern sense but rather confederations of language and kinship groups which owed allegiance to a central ruler whose capital was often mobile. The empires are difficult to define in territorial terms as they had differing degrees of control over different peoples over a wide area. The key to the rise and fall of these empires was the control of the gold trade with North Africa.

Ghana controlled an area roughly equivalent to south-eastern Mauritania and south-western Mali and flourished between the ninth and eleventh centuries. During this period Ghana was the main opposition to the Sanhadja Berbers of western Mauritania and in 990 captured the Berber city of Awdaghast. Although it was a pagan country there were large numbers of Muslims in Ghana's administration and by the eleventh century the capital was divided into two cities, a Muslim city and a pagan royal city. In spite of this the Almoravid Berbers launched a jihad against the empire and in 1077 destroyed the capital and forced the survivors to convert to Islam. A reconstituted kingdom of Ghana managed to survive until 1240 when it was incorporated into the empire of Mali.

The rise of Mali was due to a number of factors including the decline of the empire of Ghana and the discovery of a new oriferous (gold producing) region on the Niger river. The Mali Empire was formed by the unification of two groups of Manding peoples in the thirteenth century, and was located south of Ghana on the banks of the Niger, although it later took control of much of the former empire of Ghana. Unlike Ghana's, the ruler of Mali was a Muslim although most of the people within the empire remained pagan. The most famous of Mali's rulers was Mansa Musa who made a pilgrimage to Mecca in 1324 during which he gave away large quantities of gold. By the end of the fifteenth century Mali was in decline due to the devastating effects of rival claimants to the throne, a shift in trade patterns and increasing attacks from the Tuareg and Mossi. The empire which grew to replace the power of Mali was the Songhay Empire of Gao, with its centre on the banks of the Niger in the east of the modern state of Mali. Gao had a long history stretching back to the ninth century when it was an important kingdom on the route to Tahert in Algeria and Ghana and Silgilmasa to the west. By the ninth century the ruler of Gao was Muslim, although it is probable that this was merely one of the king's religions. During the thirteenth and fourteenth centuries Gao became subject to the empire of Mali; when this declined at the end of the fourteenth century Gao began taking over some of the outer dependencies of Mali. By the end of the 1460s Ali, the founder of the Songhay Empire, had taken Djenné and Timbuktu thus gaining control of some of the principal trading towns of the Sahel. Ali was succeeded by Askiya Muhammad who consolidated his territorial conquests and introduced Islam as the state religion. The empire flourished for the next hundred years until the Moroccan conquest of 1591.

In addition to the medieval empires which dominated West Africa there are a number of trading cities on the border of the Sahara desert which, although sometimes incorporated into empires, were essentially independent. The most important of these cities were, from east to west, Oualata, Timbuktu and Agades. Oualata in western Mauritania rose to prominence in the thirteenth century after the collapse of Ghana when it was populated by refugees from Awdaghast and other cities. The city was predominantly Ibadi with a mixed Arab Berber population and was one of the principal towns trading with Sijilmasa in Morocco. Further west, in the modern state of Mali, is the famous city of Timbuktu, established as a nomadic Tuareg encampment in the twelfth century. During the fifteenth century under Songhay rule the city became the principal intellectual and religious centre in West Africa. The city has a mixed population of predominantly Berber origin although there are significant numbers of Soninke and Manding.

Whilst the medieval period in West Africa was dominated by the great empires the period after the sixteenth century was characterized by the emergence of smaller independent cities and kingdoms. The post-medieval period is also notable for the integration of Islam into local culture. Whereas Islam had previously been the religion of foreign traders and local rulers who adopted Islam as another attribute of kingship, it now became the religion of whole groups and villages. In the nineteenth century this was partially achieved through jihads or holy wars, but the more common method of diffusion was through the urbanized trade networks. The widespread adoption of Islam throughout West Africa meant that the nature of the religion itself was modified to conform to local ritual requirements. In most cases this meant that local rituals and cultures were adapted to serve Islamic requirements, although in other cases (such as among the Ashante) this meant the adaptation of Islamic forms for use in essentially pagan societies.

Islamic West Africa south of the Sahel can be divided into two main language groups, the Mande-speaking peoples of Mali, Burkina Faso, Ivory Coast and Ghana, and the Fulbe-speaking peoples of northern Nigeria and Futa-Djallon in Guinea. The Mande-speaking peoples occupy roughly the same area as the empire of Mali, although the main cities of the post-medieval era are further east than the old capitals of Kangaba and Niani. The main Manding cities are Mopti, Djenné, Ségou, Bobo Dioulasso, Wa and Kong, each of which functioned as independent or semi-independent states in the eighteenth and nineteenth centuries. The most famous of these cities is Djenné whose origins may be traced back to the thirteenth century. Although the city did not rise to prominence until the sixteenth century, by the nineteenth century it was one of the main towns in West Africa. Less well known but equally important in the propagation of Islam was the city of Kong established by immigrants from Ségou and Djenné in the eighteenth century. Kong was located further south on the edges of the equatorial forest (present-day Ivory Coast) and developed as a centre of Islamic scholarship and commerce for the surrounding area.

The Fulbe-speaking people occupy two distinct areas either side of the area dominated by the Mande peoples. First to be settled by Fulbe-speaking people was the Hausa area of north Nigeria where they arrived as Muslim clerics in the fifteenth century. Hausaland already had an established, partially Muslim, society dating from the beginning of the eleventh century, comprising seven independent city-states. These cities, known as bakwoi, were Dauro, Kano, Gobir, Katsina, Zaria, Biram and Rano. Kano and Katsina already had an Islamic tradition and it was these cities that the Fulbe developed into a seat of Islamic learning and culture. Although Hausaland was subjected to subsequent waves of influence, most notably Songhay rule in the sixteenth century and large-scale immigration from Agades in the eighteenth, the Fulbe continued to arrive both as clerics and pastoralists. In the nineteenth century the urbanized Fulbe instigated a jihad for Islamic reform in the Hausa states. The result was a new state based on the recently founded capital of Sokoto, known as the Sokoto caliphate. The success of the Sokoto caliphate encouraged Fulbe in the neighbouring region of Adamawa (present-day Cameroon) to carry out a similar jihad from their newly established capital of Yolo. The jihad was similarly successful and Adamawa was eventually included within the Sokoto caliphate.

Two thousand kilometres further west is the other area of Fulbe domination in the Futa-Djallon region of Guinea. The early Fulbe migrations into this area were peaceful and were accompanied with intermarriage with the native Djallonke people. From the late seventeenth century onwards there was an intensification of the immigration until the eighteenth century when it was organized into a jihad. By the end of the eighteenth century Fulbe control of the area was complete with a capital established at Timbo.

Architecture

The Islamic architecture of West Africa reflects the complexities and diversities of its history as well as the differing natural environments. In the past, analysis of the architecture of the area has tended to concentrate on the influence of North Africa and the Middle East rather than to examine the indigenous cultures and architecture of the area. Three main sources of influence were identified each of which ignored the possibility of local invention or development. The most far-fetched idea was that the monumental architecture of the region was developed from the dynastic architecture of Egypt and was transmitted by the migration of Songhay people from the upper Nile to the Niger. The second explanation attributes the entire West African architectural tradition to the Andalusian poet and architect al-Saheli who accompanied Mansa Musa on his return from the Hajj in 1324. Whilst there is some information that al-Saheli did design an audience hall it is unlikely that this or any other work he may have carried out created an architectural style for the whole region. The third suggestion is that the Moroccan invasion of 1591 was the primary influence on the subsequent architecture of the region. Whilst the Moroccan invasion was certainly accompanied by builders and craftsmen and may have had some influence this was not sufficient to create a complex and distinct architectural style. More recently scholars have emphasized the architectural styles and beliefs of indigenous pagan cultures as influences on the later Islamic architecture of the region.

A wide variety of building materials and techniques are used over this vast region. The techniques are largely defined by the material, which may be grouped into three basic types, stone, mud and wood. Stone predominates in the western Sahara and Sahel and tends to be associated with Berber architecture. The best examples of stone cities are found in Mauritania at sites like Chinguit, Oudan, Tijika, Qasr el Barka and Tichit. Excavation has shown that Koumbi Saleh, the capital of ancient Ghana, and its sister city Awdaghast were also built of stone. Many of these sites were originally founded as ribats, although they later grew into large trading cities. The commonest method of building in stone in the area uses split limestone in dry-stone wall constructions. The limestone used in the buildings comes in several colours from green and yellow to rose, depending on local availability. The outer faces are usually left unplastered although at Tichit the inner surfaces are coated in clay and a mud mortar is used for some of the walls (at Oualata both the inner and outer surfaces are covered in mud plaster). A characteristic feature of this masonry is the use of triangular niches sometimes arranged to form composite triangular features. Also common are projecting corbels, bands of triangular niches forming chevron patterns and battered walls. The roof and ceilings are usually built of split date-palm trunks arranged diagonally over the corners, forming a square shape in the centre which is then covered by further split-palm beams arranged longitudinally. Above the beams, is placed a woven matting of split palm fronds, on top of which a layer of earth is spread. Although in the cities the buildings are built to a rectangular or square plan, many of the buildings in villages are built with a round plan or with rounded corners. Even in Chinguit itself many of the houses are built with the external corners rounded off.

Whilst stone is the building material of the western Sahara, mud is the characteristic building material of the southern Sahel and the Savannah areas. Sometimes mud is used in combination with stone as at Timbuktu and Oualata, suggesting either the integration of two cultural traditions or the interface between two different environments. At Oualata the buildings are essentially dry-stone constructions covered with layers of mud plaster which serve no structural function. The effect of the mud-plaster coverings is to make the buildings look like mud-brick structures suggesting a cultural tradition originating from the southern Savannah regions grafted on to an existing Berber architecture. This suggestion is strengthened by the make-up of the population, a mixture of Berber and Soninke people. Inside the houses of Oualata, the areas around doorways and niches are decorated with brilliant white wall paintings in the form of arabesque medallions. The use of the mixture of mud and stone at Timbuktu is very different from the practice at Oualata; thus the buildings have a rubble-stone core held together by mud mortar and plaster. The quality of the stones used at Timbuktu mean that it would not be possible to build houses solely out of stone, thus the mud plaster and mortar here perform a structural function whilst the stone is used for strength. In many Timbuktu houses exposed limestone is used for corner quoins and door jambs and the building of any house starts with the laying out of four corner stones. The decoration of buildings at Timbuktu suggests a close relationship with the stone-built Berber cities of Mauritania; thus the triangular niches and chevron bands are here executed in mud brick. This architectural similarity is paralleled in the ceilings and roofs which employ the same method of diagonally split palm beams. The preference for stone architecture is most clearly expressed on the interior of the oldest part of the Djingueré Ber Mosque where round 'Roman' arches made of dressed limestone are used to support the roof. The distinction between stone and mud-brick architecture in Timbuktu is observed by the builders who are divided into two castes depending on which material they use. It seems likely that there was a pre-existing mud-architecture tradition in the area which was developed by the incoming Berber population who were unable to find their normal building materials. The city of Agades was founded as a Berber city and one might expect it to be built of stone especially as the surrounding Berber villages consist of rectangular stone structures with Oualata-style ceilings. However, the city itself is made almost entirely of mud and resembles the Hausa architecture of north Nigeria. The reason for this could perhaps be attributed to the city's abandonment in the eighteenth century and it should be noted that a sixteenth-century traveller described the city as built in the Berber style. The subsequent rebuilding of the city in the nineteenth century was by people from north Nigeria which may explain its close relationship to Hausa architecture.

Mud either as brick or as pisé is associated with the greatest examples of West Africa's monumental architecture such as the mosque of Djenné or the minaret of Agades. The area most suited to mud-brick architecture is the Savannah region where there is enough water to make bricks, plaster and pisé yet not too much rain to dissolve the dried mud walls. Mud architecture lends itself to the creation of plastic sculptural forms on fairly simple structures, thus a simple rectangular façade can be enlivened by the addition of crenellations, engaged pillars and decorative panels. The traditional methods of mud architecture vary from one town to another; thus in Djenné cylindrical mud-bricks are used whereas in other towns simple dried-earth lumps will be used as the building material. Stylistically there are two main groups of mud architecture, a western tradition originating in the Manding cities of modern Mali and a more easterly tradition in the Hausa cities of north Nigeria.

The western style, often referred to as the 'Sudan style', can trace its origins to the city of Djenné in Mali. This architecture is characterized by the elaborate decorated façades of houses which emphasize verticality by the use of crenellations, engaged pillars and division into several registers. Mosques are distinguished by large minaret-like towers above the mihrab and tapering buttresses terminating in cone-shaped pinnacles. The mihrab towers are usually covered with projecting wooden stakes, known as 'toron'. These stakes were often found all around the walls of a mosque and functioned as scaffolding although they may also have some ritual significance. The most famous building in Djenné is the Great Mosque built in 1909 on the ruins of the previous mosque. It was meant to be a replica but differed considerably from the ruined original which had been recorded before its destruction. The new mosque was built with French funding and guidance from French military engineers and was used by the French as a basis for a neo-Sudanese style. Thus in 1935 the French Administration at Mopti built a new Friday mosque, using the new Great Mosque of Djenné as a model. Although the new Sudan style was based on the pre-colonial style it emphasized symmetry and monumentality at the expense of tradition and ritual.

Like the western tradition of mud architecture the origin of the eastern tradition can be traced to one main town, which in the case of Hausa architecture is Kano. Externally Hausa architecture is plainer than its western counterpart, although inside it displays a wide variety of decorative motifs. Hausa buildings are distinguished by their extensive use of wood and may be regarded as timber-frame buildings as opposed to the more pure mud-brick architecture in the west. The origins of this style are thought to derive from mat-frame tents where the mat-walls are gradually replaced with earth walls. The advantages of this can be seen in the use of one of the most characteristic features of Hausa architecture, the ribbed dome. This consists of a number of ribs converging in the centre and covered over with palm-frond matting. These domes may be set on a square or circular base producing either a single central point or a central square at the intersection of the ribs. The wooden ribs (usually acacia wood) are then plastered with mud to produce free-standing arches which are decorated with abstract designs. Flat roofs are achieved by building light mud walls on top of the ribs between the centre and the outer wall, making the ribs into giant armatures or brackets with a curved inner profile. South of the Hausa area in the region of Adamawa the concept of mud-brick architecture with flat roofs is modified by the use of conical thatched roofs. This adaptation is necessary in a region where high rainfall makes flat roofs impracticable. One of the more interesting results of this is that in order to preserve the appearance of an Islamic rectangular or square house façades are built on to the front of thatched buildings. These stage-like façades built of mud are enlivened by the use of elaborate arabesque designs above projecting doorways.

Further west, in the Futa-Djallon region of Guinea, wood and thatch replaces mud as the main building material. The buildings of this region consist of circular huts covered with huge conical thatched roofs supported by large central poles. The lower part of the roof is supported by shorter poles contained within a circular outer wall. The eaves of the thatched roof project beyond the line of the outer wall so that from the outside the walls and entrances are barely visible. Mosques in the region are built in the same manner as the houses, but inside the hut there is a flat-roofed rectangular mud-walled building with a mihrab in the east wall. According to local tradition the mosque is only the square building inside whilst the outer thatched building is merely for protection. This arrangement further strengthens the idea that in West Africa Islam can only be represented by rectangular or square architecture of mud or stone.

Further reading:

R. M. A. Bedaux, 'Tellem, reconnaissance d'une culture de l'ouest african au moyen âge: recherches architectoniques', *Journal de la Société des Africanistes* 42: 103–85, 1972.

R. Bravmann, *Islam and Tribal Art in West Africa*, Cambridge 1974.

N. David, 'The Fulani compound and the archaeologist', *World Archaeology* 3: 111–31, 1971.
S. Denyer, *African Traditional Architecture*, New York 1978.
A. D. Hyland, *Traditional Forms of Architecture in Ghana*, Kumasi 1975.
D. Jacques–Meunie, *Cités anciennes de Mauritanie*, Paris 1961.
R. J. McIntosh, 'Archaeology and mud wall decay in a West African village', *World Archaeology* 6: 154–71, 1974.
B. Mallen and C. Benedetti, 'Afro-Brazilian mosques', *Mimar* 29: 1988.
L. Prussin, 'The architecture of Islam in West Africa', *African Arts* 1(2): 32–25 and 70–4, 1968.
—— 'Sudanese architecture and the Manding', *African Arts* 3(4): 12–19 and 64–7, 1970.
—— 'Contribution à l'étude du cadre historique de la technologie de la construction dans l'Ouest africain', *Journal de la Société des Africanistes* 40: 175–8, 1970.
—— 'West African mud granaries', *Paideuma* 18: 144–69, 1972.
—— 'Building technologies in the West African savannah', *Le Sol, la parole et l'écrit, mélanges en hommage à Raymond Maury*, Paris 1981.
—— *Hatumere: Islamic Design in West Africa*, Berkeley 1986.
J. Sacht, 'Sur la diffusion des formes d'architecture religieuse musulmane à travers le Sahara', *Travaux de l'Institut de Recherches Sahariennes* 11(1): 11–27, 1954.
M.-M. Vire, 'Stèles funéraires musulmanes soudano-sahariennes', *Bulletin IFAN* 21 B (3–4): 459–600, 1959.

Y

Yasavi (Shrine of Ahmed Yasavi)

Shrine built by Timur for his son Jahangir between 1397 and 1399.

The shrine is located in the city of Turkestan (modern Yasi) in the Republic of Kazakhstan. The building is oriented north–south on a rectangular ground plan (65.5 by 46.5 m) with portals at the south and north ends. The main doorway is the magnificent south portal which is flanked by huge cylindrical corner towers or minarets over 20 m high. Behind the portal is the dome of the prayer hall rising to a height of over 37 m. At the other end of the structure is the north façade in the centre of which is the entrance to the mausoleum. The mausoleum is capped by a tall 'melon-shaped' ribbed dome set on a high cylindrical drum. Externally the building is well articulated with its two entrance façades, domes and an extensive covering of tilework. Internally, however, there is less feeling of unity beyond the principal rooms: leading off from the prayer hall and mausoleum are many smaller rooms with different vaulting systems which do not seem integrated in an overall design.

Yemen

Second largest country in Arabia located in the south-west of the Arabian peninsula.

The country comprises three main inhabited regions, the highlands, the coastal plain and the Wadi Hadramat. The mountains of the highlands are extremely high (up to 4,000 m) giving the region a moderate temperature and relatively high rainfall. The favourable climate makes this the most fertile part of southern Arabia with intensive cultivation of tropical plants in the wadis and in steep mountain terraces. The coastal plain is extremely hot and fairly arid, with little potential for agriculture; traditionally the main occupations have been fishing and trade. The Wadi Hadramat is a wide valley 160 km long which runs from west to east, roughly parallel with Gulf of Aden. The valley is very fertile with a system of dams and terraces which catch the water from the twice-yearly monsoon.

In pre-Islamic times Yemen was the home to advanced cultures which traded with the great civilizations of Mesopotamia, Egypt and Syria. The best known are the Sabeans who flourished between the tenth and the first centuries BCE. The Sabeans were responsible for the Marib Dam, one of the greatest engineering feats of the ancient world. In the first century BCE the Sabeans were replaced by the Himyarite clan who ruled the area until the sixth century CE. By the early sixth century Judaism had become established as the official religion as a counter to the missionary activity of the Byzantines. In 575 Sassanian interest in the country culminated in its conquest and annexation as a Persian satrapy.

The history of Yemen under the first caliphs is confused but it is clear that there was some conversion to Islam during the seventh century. During the Abbasid period (eighth to ninth centuries) there appears to have been a division with Shafi orthodox Sunnis on the coast and Zayidi Shiʿa in the highlands. This division reflected older tribal rivalries and does not exactly mirror similar movements elsewhere in the caliphate. During the ninth century Yemen was ruled by a number of competing dynasties the most prominent of which were the Zayidis, the Rassids and the Yafurids. The Rassids were a dynasty of imams claiming descent from the prophet and they continued to rule parts of the country until 1962. In 1174 Yemen was conquered by the Ayyubids seeking a haven from the turmoil of northern Arabia brought about by the Crusaders. In 1230 Nur al-Din 'Umar the deputy of the Ayyubid ruler declared himself independent and started a new dynasty known as the Rasulids, who ruled until the mid-fifteenth century when they were replaced by the Tahirids.

The Tahirids remained in power till the early sixteenth century when increasing European interest in the area resulted in two successive invasions

Mosque near Ta'iz, Yemen, ©Charles Aithie

by Muslim powers determined to prevent a Christian presence in the land of Islam. The first invasion by the Mamluks was of short duration and achieved little. A year later after their defeat of the Mamluks the Ottomans launched an invasion and by 1547 they were established in the capital, San'a. Ottoman rule lasted until 1602 when the Zayidi imams once again established themselves as rulers of San'a. The Ottomans invaded for a second time in 1872 and remained in at least partial control until their defeat at the end of the First World War. With the defeat of the Turks the Zayidi imams once again took power until they were deposed in 1962. The post-sixteenth-century history of south Yemen is slightly different and is dominated by the rivalry of two tribal groups, the Kathiris and the Qu'aitis.

The traditional building materials in Yemen are stone, coral, mud brick, baked brick, wood and stucco. Stone is the principal building material in the highland regions, although mud brick and baked brick are also used for the upper parts of the tall houses. The quality of stonework varies from massive dressed sandstone blocks used in the more important buildings of San'a to roughly squared blocks of stone laid in rough courses for village houses. Coral is the principal building material in coastal towns where it is used in conjunction with hard white lime plaster. Mud brick is used throughout the country but is employed to its greatest effect in the Wadi Hadramat where structures over eight storeys high are built of mud brick. Baked brick is comparatively more rare and is used for the upper parts of buildings in the principal cities of San'a and Zabid. Decorative brickwork appears to have been introduced to Yemen during the Ayyubid period (twelfth century) as can be seen from the brick minaret of the Great Mosque in Zabid. As in the rest of Arabia suitable building wood is very scarce and is usually imported from Africa or India. Yemeni woodwork is of extremely high quality and the panelled ceilings are some of the best in the Islamic world. Stucco work is also highly developed with elaborate arches, decorative panels and delicate calligraphy all executed in fine white stucco. One of the most important uses of stucco is for the elaborate windows of coloured glass which characterize Yemeni houses.

The religious architecture of Yemen may be divided into three types of building, mosques, madrassas and tombs. The earliest mosques in Yemen are cubical mosques and hypostyle halls, both of which may be directly related to pre-Islamic temple architecture in the country. The typical cubical mosque consists of a tall rectangular chamber with a flat wooden roof supported by two rows of three columns. These mosques are usually windowless, although they may have windows placed high up near the ceiling. Some of the earliest examples of this type of mosque may actually be converted temples, as seems to be the case with the mosque of Tamur restored in 1089. Hypostyle halls also appear in Yemeni temple architecture and appear to form an early mosque type. Early examples include the Great Mosque of Zabid and the mosque of Sulayman ibn Daud in Marib. These buildings differ from the early mosques of the Hijaz and Syria–Palestine which opened on to large open courtyards. The earliest example of the courtyard mosque in Yemen is the Great Mosque of San'a which traditionally was planned by Muhammad although in its present form seems to date from the time of Abd al-Malik (early eighth century).

The Ayyubid invasion of the twelfth century introduced many new features into Yemeni architecture, the most significant of which was the dome. The earliest domed mosques had a large central

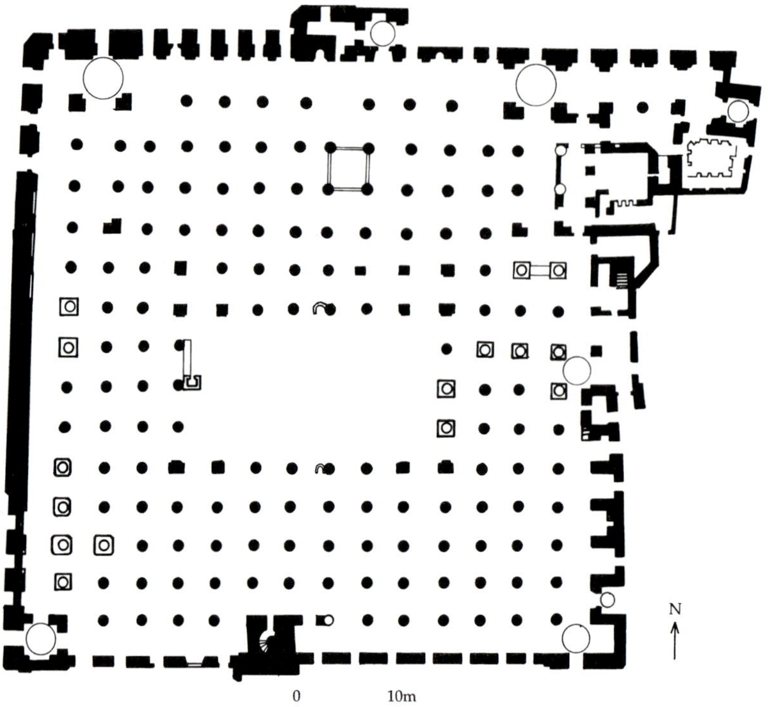

Great Mosque of Zabid, Yemen (after Finster)

dome flanked by smaller domed bays either side. Another innovation of this period is the decorative brick minaret such as that of al-Mahjam which consists of a square socle with an octagonal shaft which is faceted lower down and has a large diaper pattern on the upper shaft. A characteristic feature of Yemeni mosques of this period (twelfth to fifteenth centuries) is a domed tower-like structure marking the position of the mihrab. The Ottoman conquest of the sixteenth century introduced a new form of domed mosque comprising a large domed area with a multiple-domed portico. One of the best examples of this type is the mosque of Mustafa Pasha in Ta'iz built in 1554. Despite the Ottoman form of this building the execution is entirely Yemeni with stucco decoration and a thick cylindrical minaret.

The Ayyubids were responsible for introducing the madrassa as an architectural type, although the form in Yemen differed from that found elsewhere in the Islamic world. The main distinguishing feature is that Yemeni madrassas had no accommodation for students and teachers. Many Yemeni madrassas simply comprised a mosque with a teaching hall opposite. One of the finest examples of Yemeni Islamic architecture is the Ashrafiyya Madrassa in Ta'iz which comprises a mosque, a teaching hall, a Quran school and a library arranged around an internal courtyard. Another innovation of the Ayyubid period was the domed mausoleum which was used to commemorate deceased imams and rulers. The earliest examples date from the thirteenth century and comprise square domed structures open on three sides, the fourth side containing the mihrab. Probably the most elaborately decorated structures are the tombs of Sa'da which have extravagantly decorated domes covered with calligraphic and geometric designs executed in painted stucco.

The richness of Yemeni religious architecture is matched in the domestic architecture of the towns and some of the villages. One of the most characteristic building forms is that of the tower houses which in San'a and the highlands are built of stone and brick but in the Wadi Hadramat are extravagantly tall mud-brick structures. The external walls of these houses are normally battered, with their thickness decreasing with height. The windows are usually decorated with wooden grilles which are often plain but can become quite elaborate. In

Al-mudhafar Mosque with Ashrafiyya Mosque in the background, Ta'iz, Yemen, ©*Charles Aithie*

San'a and the highlands the exterior of the buildings are also decorated with geometric brickwork and white stucco borders around the windows. The design of these buildings varies with regions and the date of construction, although they have the same basic plan. Each house has a single door which opens on to the street. Inside there is a passageway or hall opening on to various rooms of utilitarian function (storage, animal pens etc.). At the end of the hallway there is a staircase leading up to the first floor. Depending on the height of the house the living quarters may start at the first or the third floor. In the upper storeys there are bedrooms, bathrooms and pillared reception rooms which often open on to terraces. The room at the top of the house is usually a large reception hall (mufraj) with two tiers of windows. The upper row of windows in the mufraj usually comprise elaborate stucco tracery filled in with coloured glass (green, blue, red and yellow). At the top of the house are parapets, sometimes with arrow slits for defence.

See also: Hadramawt, San'a

Further reading:

P. Costa, 'Islamic religious buildings in Yemen', *Proceedings of the 8th Seminar for Arabian Studies 1974*, London 1975.

B. Finster, 'An outline of the history of Islamic religious architecture in Yemen', *Muqarnas: An Annual on Islamic Art and Architecture* 9: 124–47, 1992.

L. Golvin and M. C. Fromont, *Architecture et urbanisme d'une cité de haute montagne en République arabe du Yemen*, Éditions de Recherche sur les Civilisations, Mémoire no. 30, Paris 1984.

R. B. Lewcock and G. R. Smith, 'Two early mosques in

A funduq in Thula, Yemen (after Golvin and Fromont)

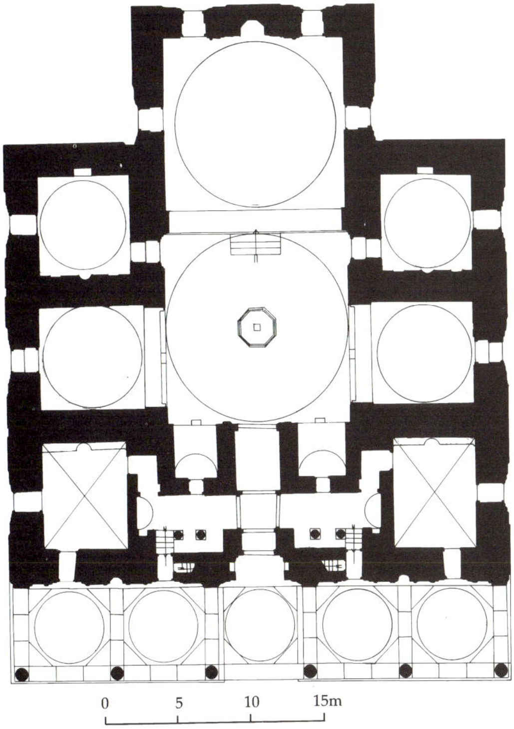

Yeşil Cami, Bursa, Turkey

the Yemen, a preliminary report', *Art and Archaeology Research Papers*, 1973.
—— 'Three early mosques in the Yemen', *Oriental Art*, NS 20: 1974.
Naval Intelligence Division, *Western Arabia and the Red Sea*, Geographical Handbook Series, BR 527, Oxford 1946.
U. Scerrato, G. Ventrane and P. Cuneo, 'Report on the third campaign for the typological survey of the Islamic religious architecture of the Yemen', *East and West*, 36(4): 1986

Yeşil Cami (The Green Mosque)

Imperial Ottoman mosque in Bursa famed for its green tile decoration.

The Yeşil Cami is part of a large complex built by Sultan Mehmet and completed in 1420. The complex is one of the last in a series of royal mosque complexes in Bursa starting with the Orhaniya in the fourteenth century and ending with the Muradiye completed in 1447. The complex includes a mosque, madrassa, bath house, soup kitchen and the tomb of Mehmet.

The mosque is built in the Bursa T-plan style which is based on the four-iwan plan of Seljuk madrassas. In Bursa mosques the entrance iwan becomes reduced to a small entrance vestibule leaving a T-shaped building with a central courtyard flanked by side rooms (iwans) and with a large prayer hall in front. The central courtyard is covered with a dome which has an oculus, or round hole, in the roof to let in light and air. In most of the Bursa T-plan mosques the entrance is preceded by a three- or five-domed portico, which is a feature borrowed from the usual Ottoman single-domed mosque. In the Yeşil Cami, however, the portico is missing as Mehmet died before this could be added. The entrance façade of the mosque contains eight windows, one pair either side of the door on the ground floor and four on the upper floor. Each of the ground-floor windows consists of a rectangular grilled opening inset into a richly carved arched frame which itself is set into a recessed panel. Between each pair of windows there is a deeply recessed minbar with a muqarnas hood. The upper windows are set into rectangular panels and are entirely open except for a low carved balustrade. Only the two central windows are real; the other two serve no purpose except to balance the composition of the façade. The entrance opens into a small vestibule from which stairs lead up to the celebrated royal gallery. On the ground floor the vestibule opens into the domed central courtyard which is flanked on either side by small domed alcoves. To the south of the courtyard under a large arch is the domed prayer hall with its magnificent muqarnas hooded mihrab surrounded by a tilework frame.

The most noticeable feature of the interior is the extensive use of polychrome glazed tiles. Until the seventeenth century the outer surface of the domes were covered in green tiles giving the mosque its name. The tiles carry a variety of patterns including flowers, calligraphic inscriptions, geometric interlace as well as motifs executed in three dimensions like the tile bosses in the royal gallery. The tilework of the mosque is reproduced in Mehmet's tomb, which is located on a hill above the mosque.

See also: Bursa, Ottomans

yurt

Circular tent used in Turkey and Central Asia. It is made out of a portable wooden frame covered with skin or felt.

Z

zanana

Mughal term used to describe the women's quarters in a palace or house.

Zanzibar

Large island off the east coast of Africa; together with the island of Pemba it forms an autonomous part of Tanzania. The capital of Zanzibar is Zanzibar town and the capital of Pemba is Chake.

Zanzibar is a low-lying coral island covered with coconut palms and famed for its cultivation of spices, in particular cloves. Pemba on the other hand is a true island lying on rock away from the continental shelf. The island rises much higher out of the water and has a deeply indented coastline with many remains of ancient settlement. Remains of pre-Islamic sites have been found on both Zanzibar and Pemba although the nature of settlement at these sites has yet to be clarified.

Zanzibar

Zanzibar has a long history of Islamic settlement starting in the eighth century at the trading site of Unguja Ukuu on the southern part of the island where a hoard of gold Abbasid coins was found. Unfortunately no traces of early structures have been discovered at this site although there is a later mosque there. The earliest known structure on the island is the Kizimkazi Mosque which is dated by an inscription to 1107 CE and consists of a rectangular structure with three columns running down the centre to support the roof, which would have been flat. Although it was restored in the eighteenth century, excavations have shown that the basic form of the mosque dates back to the twelfth. South of the mosque are traces of domestic occupation and a stone tomb within an enclosure wall. Jongowe on Tumbatu island north-west of Zanzibar island contains one of the largest groups of remains on the island, covering an area of 25 hectares. The site has a long history with its own chronicle and was mentioned by Yakut. The present remains consist of a mosque and a group of houses dated to the twelfth and thirteenth centuries. The best-preserved building is the mosque which stands in an irregular enclosure next to the sea. It has a rectangular shape with a deep mihrab projecting from the north end and eight arched doorways, four on the west and four on east side. On the east side there is a side aisle next to the sea with its own mihrab. Both mihrabs are fairly plain structures built of cut reef coral. Also on Tumbatu island is the site of Gomani which has important examples of local tombs dated to 1400 CE. In the sixteenth century Zanzibar was occupied by the Portuguese who established farmsteads on the island and built a church in Zanzibar town which was later converted into an Omani fort. There are a few remains of Islamic buildings from the eighteenth century with the exception of some of the Kizimkazi ruins and the mosque and tombs of Shakani. From the beginning of the eighteenth century Portuguese power in the area declined in favour of the Omanis who took over many of the former Portuguese bases. By 1832 the Omani position in Zanzibar was so secure that Sultan Sayyid Saʿid moved his capital from Muscat to Zanzibar. This move meant that a whole new series of buildings were erected to house the new sultans and their administration. One of the first Omani buildings in Zanzibar was the Mtoni Palace built for Sayyid Saʿid in 1830 which is about 5 km north of Zanzibar town. Although the palace is much ruined, substantial remains are still standing including the harem, the domed bath block containing hot and cold water plunges and the sultan's personal mosque on the beach. Nearby is the Marhubi Palace, built in 1880 by Sayyid Barghash and enclosed in over 50 hectares of gardens. Although the palace was burnt down in 1890 the bath complex still stands which includes domed baths, pavilions, water storage tanks and an aqueduct. Other buildings with bath complexes are the country houses of Kidichi and Kizimbai – the Kidichi baths have beautiful examples of Persian stucco work on the interior. Approximately 10 km north of Zanzibar town are the ruins of Chuini Palace also built by Sayyid Barghash. The building is several storeys high and consists of a central core containing rooms opening out to balconies on each side which are supported with massive cylindrical columns. Other Omani palaces on Zanzibar are Beit al-Ras and the Dunga Palace both built around 1850.

The town of Zanzibar is known as the 'Stone Town' to distinguish it from the newer suburbs. Most of the buildings in the old town date to the nineteenth century and are notable for their highly decorative wooden doorways. The centre of the town contains the various ministries of the sultanate built in the eighteenth and nineteenth centuries. These buildings have the same form of some of the palaces with a multi-storey central block surrounded on all sides by extensive verandas. One of the more recent palaces, the Beit al-Ajcib, is built in the same style but the verandas are supported with imported iron columns. The Portuguese church in the centre was converted into a fort with four towers by the Omanis in 1800. One of the more unusual buildings is the public baths (Hamani) built out of brick and coral stone by Sayyid Barghash in 1880 which are the only known public baths of this type in East Africa. Another notable building in Zanzibar town is the National Museum completed in 1925 to the design of a British architect working in the Oriental style, which resembles the Hagia Sophia in Istanbul.

Pemba

Pemba has many more archaeological sites than Zanzibar and even today it is more populous than its neighbour. The earliest site so far discovered is at Mtambwe Mkuu dated to the eleventh century, although this has no early standing structures. Some of the earliest structures on the island are found at Ras Mkumbuu which is one of the largest sites on the East African coast. The remains date to the fourteenth century and consist of a mosque, a number of pillar tombs and many houses, of which four are still standing. The mosque is a large structure four aisles wide and five bays deep, supported on three rows of four rectangular piers. The mihrab is centrally placed and aligned with the central row of columns and there is a tower entered from a doorway to the east of the mihrab. This is one of the few pre-nineteenth-century examples of a minaret in East Africa, although it seems likely that the tower was not very tall. (Other fourteenth-century mosques on Pemba include Shamiani, Mtangani, Mduni and Mkia wa Ngombe.) On the east coast of Pemba are the remains of Pujini which are famous as the only pre-Portuguese fortifications on the East African coast. The fortifications date to approximately 1400 CE and comprise a square area enclosed by walls and ramparts containing houses and a barrack block.

The capital, Chake, contains a nineteenth-century Swahili fort and the Bohra Mosque. The Bohra Mosque dates to the early twentieth century and was built by the Bohra Indians of Pemba. The mosque is a two-storey structure containing a prayer hall below and a Quran school above and is one of the few examples of Indian Muslim architecture in East Africa.

See also: coral, East Africa, Tanzania

Further Reading:

F. Aalund, 'Zanzibar old stone town', *Monumentum* 143–59, 1983.
M. C. Horton and C. M. Clark, *Zanzibar Archaeological Survey 1984–5*, Zanzibar 1985.
M. C. Horton, C. M. Clarke and Y. Staelens, *Zanzibar Museums Project 1986*, Zanzibar 1986.
J. S. Kirkman, 'Excavations at Ras Mkumbuu on the island of Pemba', *Tanjanyika Notes and Records* 1: 94–101, 1959.
A. Prins, *The Swahili-Speaking Peoples of Zanzibar and the East African Coast*, London 1964.

Zaragoza

City in north-west Spain which was Muslim from the eighth to the twelfth century and which continued as a centre of Mudéjar culture.

During the Islamic period the town was settled by Berbers from North Africa who in the eleventh century were ruled over by their own Dhu Nunid amirs. The city finally fell to Alfonso VI of León and Castile in 1085.

Few remains of the Islamic period survive with the exception of Parts of the city walls and parts of the Aljafería palace. The Islamic parts of the city walls have been dated to the late ninth century whilst the most visible parts are Mudéjar work.

The most well-known part of Zaragoza is the fortified palace complex known as the Aljafería.

The outer walls of this structure have recently been restored and may be Islamic, the main gate is a round horseshoe arch between two semi-circular bastions. Remains of the mosque can be found incorporated into a later church. Inside, there is a square room covered by a dome and a mihrab with a horseshoe arch covered by a semi-dome as in the mosque at Córdoba.

Within the palace most of the building is Mudéjar and consists of a series of courtyards decorated with arches and pools leading to the royal hall. The arches are cusped and rest on pairs of columns with re-used Islamic capitals. Between the arches the building is decorated with ornate interlacing strapwork and vegetal motifs.

Many of the churches of the city also contain much Mudéjar work. The cathedral, known as La Seo, has an interesting mixture of Islamic-style blind niches and diaper-patterned brickwork with Gothic windows.

See also: Córdoba, Granada, Seville, Spain

Further reading:

G. Goodwin, *Islamic Spain*, Architectural Guides for Travellers, London 1990, 131–7.

zawiya

Literally 'a corner': often the place where a holy man both lived and was buried.

zigara

Mausoleum (literally 'place of visitation').

zilij

North African term for glazed tiles, usually applied to tile mosaics used for dadoes in houses and mosques. Predominant colours are orange, green and white.

ziyada

Outer enclosure or extension of mosque common to congregational mosques in the early Islamic period.

The name is derived from an Arabic term meaning an addition or increase in size. The best surviving examples of ziyadas can be found in Samarra at the Great Mosque (847) and the Abu Dulaf Mosque (861) and also at the mosque of Ibn Tulun in Cairo. The earliest example is at the Great Mosque at Samarra where an outer enclosure surrounds the mosque on the east, north and west sides (i.e. not on the qibla side). This enclosure is surrounded by an even larger rectangle which encloses all four sides of the mosque although the south side is narrower than the other sides. The area covered by the mosque and its ziyadas amounts to 17 hectares. Likewise the mosque of Abu Dulaf which copies the Great Mosque in many ways also has two ziyadas or enclosures.

The mosque of Ibn Tulun provides the best-preserved example of a ziyada. Like the mosques at Samarra the ziyada encloses the mosque on the three sides away from the qibla. The enclosure wall resembles that of the mosque itself with its niches and crenellations. Each wall is pierced with several doorways which led from adjoining markets. Although no remains have been traced, four historical sources imply that latrines and places for ablution were located within the ziyada.

The origin of the ziyada is likely to have been the outer *temenos* of pre-Islamic shrines or sanctuaries where the temple was separated from the secular city by an outer enclosure. Ziyadas are not usually found on the qibla side of a mosque as this position was reserved for the Dar al-Imara.

Further reading:

K. A. C. Creswell, *A Short Account of Early Muslim Architecture*, revised and enlarged edn. J. W. Allan, Aldershot 1989, 395–6.

ziyaret

Venerated shrine or mausoleum.

zulla

Arabic term for shaded area. Used to refer to sanctuary or covered part of mosque.

Appendix

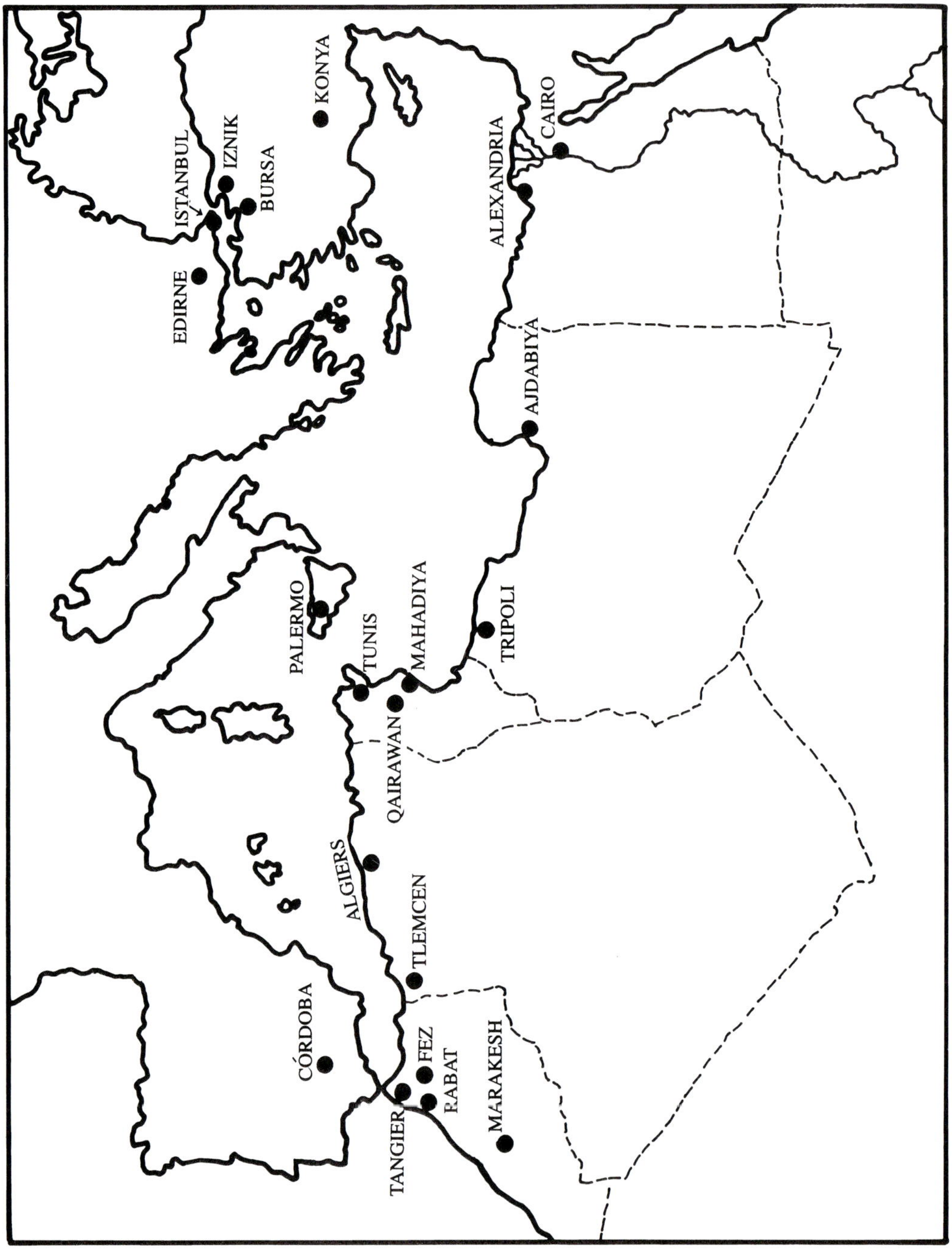

The Mediterranean World showing principal historic cities and sites

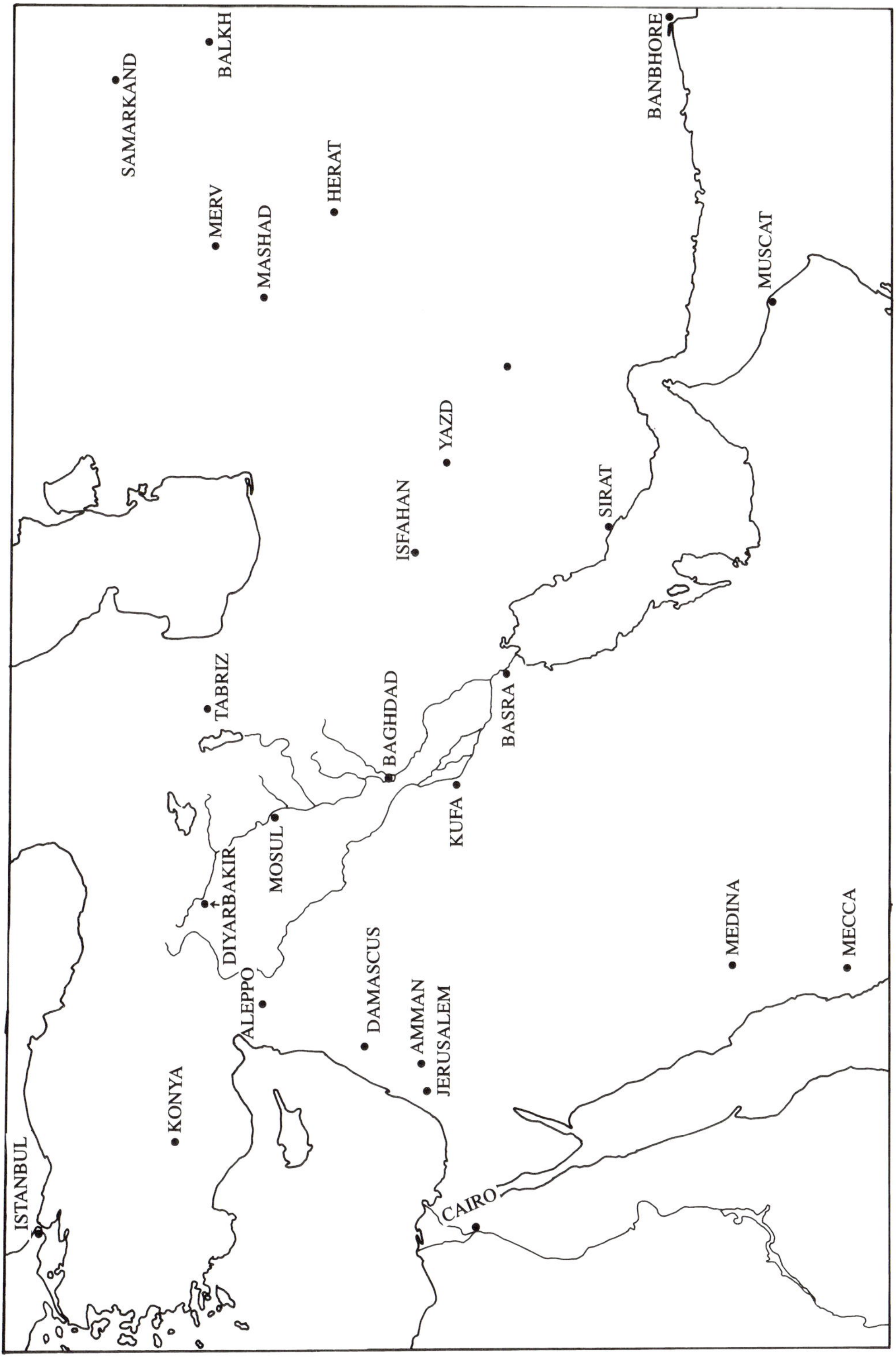

The Middle East and Central Asia showing principal historic cities and sites

Index

Index

Index

Index

Index

Index

Index

FOURTH EDITION

Engineering Mechanics

Statics and Dynamics

Irving H. Shames

Professor
Dept. of Civil, Mechanical and Environmental Engineering
The George Washington University

Prentice Hall, Upper Saddle River, New Jersey 07458

Library of Congress Cataloging-in-Publication Data
Shames, Irving Herman.
Engineering mechanics. Statics and dynamics / Irving H. Shames.—4th ed.
p. cm.
Includes bibliographical references and index.
ISBN 0–13–356924–1
1. Mechanics, Applied. I. Title
TA350.S492 1996
620.1—dc20 96–631
CIP

Acquisitions Editor: William Stenquist
Editor in Chief: Marcia Horton
Production Editor: Rose Kernan
Text Designer: Christine Wolf
Cover Designer: Amy Rosen
Editorial Assistant: Meg Weist
Manufacturing Buyer: Donna Sullivan

Simon & Schuster/A Viacom Company
Upper Saddle River, New Jersey 07458

Printed in the United States of America

10 9 8 7 6 5 4 3 2 1

ISBN 0-13-356924-1

Prentice-Hall International (UK) Limited, London
Prentice-Hall of Australia Pty. Limited, Sydney
Prentice-Hall Canada Inc., Toronto
Prentice-Hall Hispanoamericana, S.A., Mexico
Prentice-Hall of India Private Limited, New Delhi
Prentice-Hall of Japan, Inc., Tokyo
Simon & Schuster Asia Pte. Ltd., Singapore
Editora Prentice Hall do Brasil, Ltda., Rio de Janeiro

SELECTED DIMENSIONAL EQUIVALENTS

LENGTH	1 m ≡ 3.281 ft ≡ 39.37 in. 1 mi ≡ 5280 ft ≡ 1.609 km 1 km ≡ .6214 mi
TIME	1 hr ≡ 60 min ≡ 3600 sec
MASS	1 kg ≡ 2.2046 lbm ≡ .068521 slug
FORCE	1 N ≡ .2248 lbf 1 dyne ≡ 10 μN
SPEED	1 mi/hr ≡ 1.609 km/hr ≡ 1.467 ft/sec 1 km/hr = .6214 mi/hr 1 knot = 1.152 mi/hr ≡ 1.853 km/hr ≡ 1.689 ft/sec
ENERGY	1 J ≡ 1 N-m 1 Btu ≡ 778.16 ft-lbf ≡ 1.055 kJ 1 watt-hour ≡ 2.778×10^{-4} J
VOLUME	1 gal ≡ .16054 ft^3 ≡ .0045461 m^3 1 liter ≡ .03531 ft^3 = .2642 gal
POWER	1 w ≡ 1 J/S 1 hp ≡ 550 ft-lb/sec ≡ .7068 Btu/sec ≡ 746 w

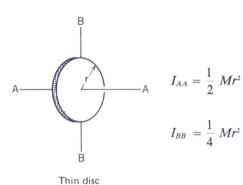

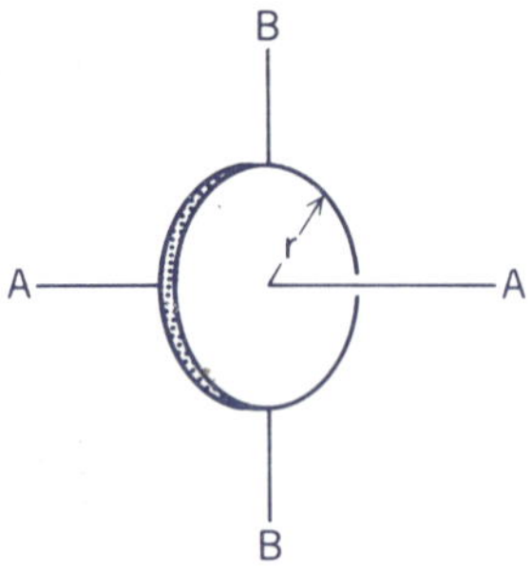

$$I_{AA} = \frac{1}{2} Mr^2$$

$$I_{BB} = \frac{1}{4} Mr^2$$

Thin disc

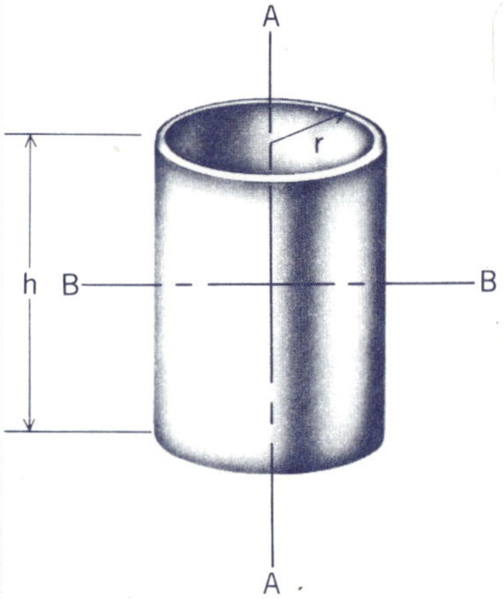

$$I_{BB} = \frac{M}{2}\left(r^2 + \frac{h^2}{6}\right)$$

Thin-walled cylinder

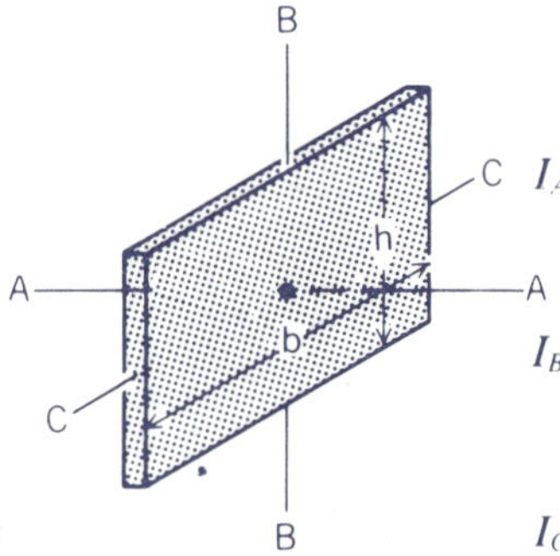

$$I_{AA} = \frac{1}{12} M(b^2 + h^2)$$

$$I_{BB} = \frac{1}{12} Mb^2$$

$$I_{CC} = \frac{1}{12} Mh^2$$

Thin rectangular plate

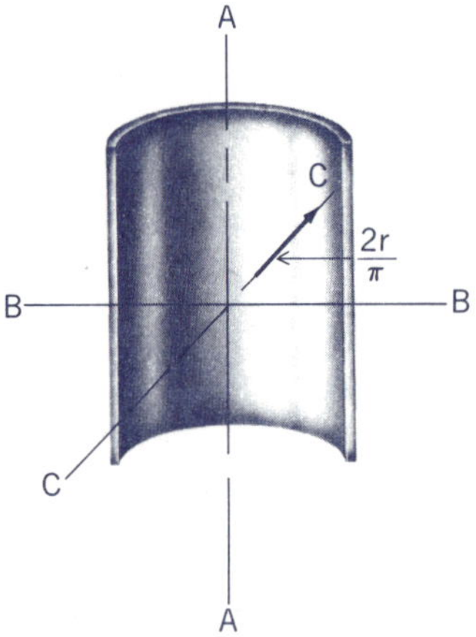

$$I_{BB} = \frac{1}{2} M\left(\frac{r^2 + h^2}{6}\right)$$

$$I_{AA} = Mr^2$$

$$I_{CC} = \frac{1}{2} M\left(\frac{r^2 + h^2}{6}\right)$$

Thin half cylinder

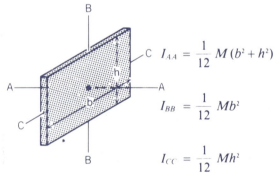

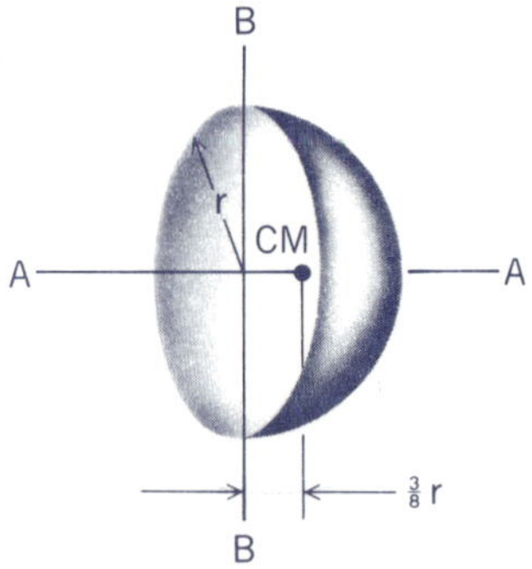

$$V = \frac{2}{3}\pi r^3$$

$$I_{AA} = \frac{2}{5} Mr^2$$

$$I_{BB} = \frac{2}{5} Mr^2$$

Hemisphere

Contents

Preface

With the publication of the fourth edition, this text moves into the fourth decade of its existence. In the spirit of the times, the first edition introduced a number of "firsts" in an introductory engineering mechanics textbook. These "firsts" included

a) the first treatment of space mechanics
b) the first use of the control volume for linear momentum considerations of fluids
c) the first introduction to the concept of the tensor

Users of the earlier editions will be glad to know that the 4th edition continues with the same approach to engineering mechanics. The goal has always been to aim toward working problems as soon as possible from first principles. Thus, examples are carefully chosen during the development of a series of related areas to instill continuity in the evolving theory and then, after these areas have been carefully discussed with rigor, come the problems. Furthermore at the ends of each chapter, there are many problems that have not been arranged by text section. The instructor is encouraged as soon as he/she is well along in the chapter to use these problems. The instructors manual will indicate the nature of each of these problems as well as the degree of difficulty. The text is not chopped up into many methodologies each with an abbreviated discussion followed by many examples for using the specific methodology and finally a set of problems carefully tailored for the methodology. The nature of the format in this and preceding editions is more than ever first to discourage excessive mapping of homework problems from the examples. And second, it is to lessen the memorization of specific, specialized methodologies in lieu of absorbing basic principles.

A new feature in the fourth edition is a series of starred sections called "Looking Ahead . . . ." These are simplified discussions of topics that appear in later engineering courses and tie in directly or indirectly to the topic under study. For instance, after discussing free body diagrams, there is a short "Looking Ahead" section in which the concept and use of the control volume is presented as well as the system concepts that appear in fluid mechanics and thermodynamics. In the chapter on virtual work for particles and rigid bodies, there is a simplified discussion of the displacement methods and force methods for deformable bodies that will show up later in solids courses. After finding the forces for simple trusses, there is a "Looking Ahead" section discussing briefly what has to be done to get displacements. There are quite a few others in the text. It has been found that many students find these interesting and later when they come across these topics in other courses or work, they report that the connections so formed coming out of their sophomore mechanics courses have been most valuable.

Over 400 new problems have been added to the fourth edition equally divided between the statics and dynamics books. A complete word-processed solutions manual accompanies the text. The illustrations needed for problem statement and solution are taken as enlargements from the text. Generally, each problem is on a separate page. The instructor will be able conveniently to select problems in order to post solutions or to form transparencies as desired. Also, there are 30 computer projects in which, for a number of cases, the student prepares his/her own software or engages in design. As an added bonus, the student will be able to maintain his/her proficiency in programming. Carefully prepared computer programs as well as computer outputs will be included in the manual. I normally assign one or two such projects during a semester over and above the usual course material. Also included in the manual is a disk that has the aforementioned programs for each of the computer projects. The computer programs for these projects generally run about 30 lines of FORTRAN and run on a personal computer. The programming required involves skills developed in the freshman course on FORTRAN.

Another important new feature of the fourth edition is an organization that allows one to go directly to the three dimensional chapter on dynamics of rigid bodies (Chapter 18) and then to easily return to plane motion (Chapter 16). Or one can go the opposite way. Footnotes indicate how this can be done, and complimentary problems are noted in the Solutions Manual.

Another change is Chapter 16 on plane motion. It has been reworked with the aim of attaining greater rigor and clarity particularly in the solving of problems.

There has also been an increase in the coverage and problems for hydrostatics as well as examples and problems that will preview problems coming in the solids course that utilize principles from statics.

It should also be noted that the notation used has been chosen to correspond to that which will be used in more advanced courses in order to improve continuity with upper division courses. Thus, for moments and products of inertia I use I_{xx}, I_{yy}, I_{xz} *etc. rather than* I_x, I_y, P_{xy} etc. The same notation is used for second moments and products of area to emphasize the direct relation between these and the preceding quantities. Experience indicates that there need be no difficulty on the student's part in distinguishing between these quantities; the context of the discussion suffices for this purpose. The concept of the tensor is presented in a way that for years we have found to be readily understood by sophomores even when presented in large classes. This saves time and makes for continuity in all mechanics courses, particularly in the solid mechanics course. For bending moment, shear force, and stress use is made of a common convention for the sign—namely the convention involving the normal to the area element and the direction of the quantity involved be it bending moment, shear force or stress component. All this and indeed other steps taken in the book will make for smooth transition to upper division course work.

In overall summary, two main goals have been pursued in this edition. They are

1. To encourage working problems from first principles and thus to minimize excessive mapping from examples and to discourage rote learning of specific methodologies for solving various and sundry kinds of specific problems.
2. To "open-end" the material to later course work in other engineering sciences with the view toward making smoother transitions and to provide for greater continuity. Also, the purpose is to engage the interest and curiosity of students for further study of mechanics.

During the 13 years after the third edition, I have been teaching sophomore mechanics to very large classes at SUNY, Buffalo, and, after that, to regular sections of students at The George Washington University, the latter involving an international student body with very diverse backgrounds. During this time, I have been working on improving the clarity and strength of this book under classroom conditions giving it the most severe test as a text. I believe the fourth edition as a result will be a distinct improvement over the previous editions and will offer a real choice for schools desiring a more mature treatment of engineering mechanics.

I believe sophomore mechanics is probably the most important course taken by engineers in that much of the later curriculum depends heavily on this course. And for **all** engineering programs, this is usually the first real engineering course where students can and must be creative and inventive in solving problems. Their old habits of mapping and rote learning of specific problem methodologies will not suffice and they must learn to see mechanics as an integral science. The student must "bite the bullet" and work in the way he/she will have to work later in the curriculum and even later when getting out of school altogether. No other subject so richly involves mathematics, physics, computers, and down to earth common sense simultaneously in such an interesting and challenging way. We should take maximum advantage of the students exposure to this beautiful subject to get him/her on the right track now so as to be ready for upper division work.

At this stage of my career, I will risk impropriety by presenting now an extended section of acknowledgments. I want to give thanks to SUNY at Buffalo where I spent 31 happy years and where I wrote many of my books. And I want to salute the thousands (about 5000) of fine students who took my courses during this long stretch. I wish to thank my eminent friend and colleague Professor Shahid Ahmad who among other things taught the sophomore mechanics sequence with me and who continues to teach it. He gave me a very thorough review of the fourth edition with many valuable suggestions. I thank him profusely. I want particularly to thank Professor Michael Symans, from Washington State University, Pullman for his superb contributions to the entire manuscript. I came to The George Washington University at the invitation of my longtime friend and former Buffalo colleague Dean Gideon Frieder and the faculty in the Civil, Mechanical and Environmental Engineering Department. Here, I came back into contact with two well-known scholars that I knew from the early days of my career, namely Professor Hal Liebowitz (president-elect of the National Academy of Engineering) and Professor Ali Cambel (author of recent well-received book on chaos). I must give profound thanks to the chairman of my new department at G.W., Professor Sharam Sarkani. He has allowed me to play a vital role in the academic program of the department. I will be able to continue my writing at full speed as a result. I shall always be grateful to him. Let me not forget the two dear ladies in the front office of the department. Mrs. Zephra Coles in her decisive efficient way took care of all my needs even before I was aware of them. And Ms. Joyce Jeffress was no less helpful and always had a humorous comment to make.

I was extremely fortunate in having the following professors as reviewers.

Professor Shahid Ahmad, SUNY at Buffalo
Professor Ravinder Chona, Texas A&M University
Professor Bruce H. Karnopp. University of Michigan
Professor Richard F. Keltie, North Carolina State University
Professor Stephen Malkin, University of Massachusetts
Professor Sudhakar Nair, Illinois Institute of Technology
Professor Jonathan Wickert, Carnegie Mellon University

I wish to thank these gentlemen for their valuable assistance and encouragement.

I have two people left. One is my good friend Professor Bob Jones from V.P.I. who assisted me in the third edition with several hundred excellent statics problems and who went over the entire manuscript with me with able assistance and advice. I continue to benefit in the new edition from his input of the third edition. And now, finally, the most important person of all, my dear wife Sheila. She has put up all these years with the author of this book, an absent-minded, hopeless workaholic. Whatever I have accomplished of any value in a long and ongoing career, I owe to her.

To my Dear, Wonderful Wife Sheila

About the Author

Irving Shames presently serves as a Professor in the Department of Civil, Mechanical, and Environmental Engineering at The George Washington University. Prior to this appointment Professor Shames was a Distinguished Teaching Professor and Faculty Professor at The State University of New York—Buffalo, where he spent 31 years.

Professor Shames has written up to this point in time 10 textbooks. His first book *Engineering Mechanics, Statics and Dynamics* was originally published in 1958, and it is going into its fourth edition in 1996. All of the books written by Professor Shames have been characterized by innovations that have become mainstays of how engineering principles are taught to students. *Engineering Mechanics, Statics and Dynamics* was the first widely used Mechanics book based on vector principles. It ushered in the almost universal use of vector principles in teaching engineering mechanics courses today.

Other textbooks written by Professor Shames include:

- *Mechanics of Deformable Solids*, Prentice-Hall, Inc.
- *Mechanics of Fluids*, McGraw-Hill
- *Introduction to Solid Mechanics*, Prentice-Hall, Inc.
- *Introduction to Statics*, Prentice-Hall, Inc.
- *Solid Mechanics—A Variational Approach* (with C.L. Dym), McGraw-Hill
- *Energy and Finite Element Methods in Structural Mechanics*, (with C.L. Dym), Hemisphere Corp., of Taylor and Francis
- *Elastic and Inelastic Stress Analysis* (with F. Cozzarelli), Prentice-Hall, Inc.

In recent years, Professor Shames has expanded his teaching activities and has held two summer faculty workshops in mechanics sponsored by the State of New York, and one national workshop sponsored by the National Science Foundation. The programs involved the integration both conceptually and pedagogically of mechanics from the sophomore year on through graduate school.

Statics

CHAPTER 1

REVIEW I*

Fundamentals of Mechanics

†1.1 Introduction

Mechanics is the physical science concerned with the dynamical behavior (as opposed to chemical and thermal behavior) of bodies that are acted on by mechanical disturbances. Since such behavior is involved in virtually all the situations that confront an engineer, mechanics lies at the core of much engineering analysis. In fact, no physical science plays a greater role in engineering than does mechanics, and it is the oldest of all the physical sciences. The writings of Archimedes covering buoyancy and the lever were recorded before 200 B.C. Our modern knowledge of gravity and motion was established by Isaac Newton (1642–1727), whose laws founded Newtonian mechanics, the subject matter of this text.

In 1905, Einstein placed limitations on Newton's formulations with his theory of relativity and thus set the stage for the development of relativistic mechanics. The newer theories, however, give results that depart from those of Newton's formulations only when the speed of a body approaches the speed of light (186,000 miles/sec). These speeds are encountered in the large-scale phenomena of dynamical astronomy. Furthermore for small-scale phenomena involving subatomic particles, quantum mechanics must be used rather than Newtonian mechanics. Despite these limitations, it remains nevertheless true that, in the great bulk of engineering problems, Newtonian mechanics still applies.

*The reader is urged to be sure that Section 1.9 is thoroughly understood since this section is vital for a good understanding of statics in particular and mechanics in general.

Also, the notation † before the titles of certain sections indicates that specific questions concerning the contents of these sections requiring verbal answers are presented at the end of the chapter. The instructor may wish to assign these sections as a reading assignment along with the requirement to answer the aforestated associated questions as the author routinely does himself.

†1.2 Basic Dimensions and Units of Mechanics

To study mechanics, we must establish abstractions to describe those characteristics of a body that interest us. These abstractions are called *dimensions*. The dimensions that we pick, which are independent of all other dimensions, are termed *primary* or *basic dimensions*, and the ones that are then developed in terms of the basic dimensions we call *secondary dimensions*. Of the many possible sets of basic dimensions that we could use, we will confine ourselves at present to the set that includes the dimensions of length, time, and mass. Another convenient set will be examined later.

Length—A Concept for Describing Size Quantitatively. In order to determine the size of an object, we must place a second object of known size next to it. Thus, in pictures of machinery, a man often appears standing disinterestedly beside the apparatus. Without him, it would be difficult to gage the size of the unfamiliar machine. Although the man has served as some sort of standard measure, we can, of course, only get an approximate idea of the machine's size. Men's heights vary, and, what is even worse, the shape of a man is too complicated to be of much help in acquiring a precise measurement of the machine's size. What we need, obviously, is an object that is constant in shape and, moreover, simple in concept. Thus, instead of a three-dimensional object, we choose a one-dimensional object.[1] Then, we can use the known mathematical concepts of geometry to extend the measure of size in one dimension to the three dimensions necessary to characterize a general body. A straight line scratched on a metal bar that is kept at uniform thermal and physical conditions (as, e.g., the meter bar kept at Sèvres, France) serves as this simple invariant standard in one dimension. We can now readily calculate and communicate the distance along a certain direction of an object by counting the number of standards and fractions thereof that can be marked off along this direction. We commonly refer to this distance as length, although the term "length" could also apply to the more general concept of size. Other aspects of size, such as volume and area, can then be formulated in terms of the standard by the methods of plane, spherical, and solid geometry.

A *unit* is the name we give an accepted measure of a dimension. Many systems of units are actually employed around the world, but we shall only use the two major systems, the American system and the SI system. The basic unit of length in the American system is the foot, whereas the basic unit of length in the SI system is the meter.

Time—A Concept for Ordering the Flow of Events. In observing the picture of the machine with the man standing close by, we can sometimes tell approximately when the picture was taken by the style of clothes the man is

[1] We are using the word "dimensional" here in its everyday sense and not as defined above.

wearing. But how do we determine this? We may say to ourselves: "During the thirties, people wore the type of straw hat that the fellow in the picture is wearing." In other words, the "when" is tied to certain events that are experienced by, or otherwise known to, the observer. For a more accurate description of "when," we must find an action that appears to be completely repeatable. Then, we can order the events under study by counting the number of these repeatable actions and fractions thereof that occur while the events transpire. The rotation of the earth gives rise to an event that serves as a good measure of time—the day. But we need smaller units in most of our work in engineering, and thus, generally, we tie events to the second, which is an interval repeatable 86,400 times a day.

Mass—A Property of Matter. The student ordinarily has no trouble understanding the concepts of length and time because he/she is constantly aware of the size of things through his/her senses of sight and touch, and is always conscious of time by observing the flow of events in his/her daily life. The concept of mass, however, is not as easily grasped since it does not impinge as directly on our daily experience.

Mass is a property of matter that can be determined from *two* different actions on bodies. To study the first action, suppose that we consider two hard bodies of entirely different composition, size, shape, color, and so on. If we attach the bodies to identical springs, as shown in Fig. 1.1, each spring will extend some distance as a result of the attraction of gravity for the bodies. By grinding off some of the material on the body that causes the greater extension, we can make the deflections that are induced on both springs equal. Even if we raise the springs to a new height above the earth's surface, thus lessening the deformation of the springs, the extensions induced by the pull of gravity will be the same for both bodies. And since they are, we can conclude that the bodies have an equivalent innate property. This property of each body that manifests itself in the *amount of gravitational attraction* we call *mass*.

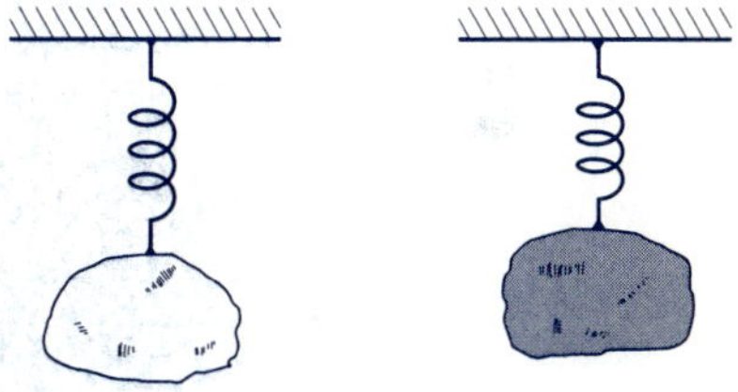

Figure 1.1. Bodies restrained by identical springs.

The equivalence of these bodies, after the aforementioned grinding operation, can be indicated in yet a second action. If we move both bodies an equal distance downward, by stretching each spring, and then release them at the same time, they will begin to move in an identical manner (except for small variations due to differences in wind friction and local deformations of the bodies). We have imposed, in effect, the same mechanical disturbance on each body and we have elicited the same dynamical response. Hence, despite many obvious differences, the two bodies again show an equivalence.

The property of mass, then, characterizes a body both in the action of gravitational attraction and in the response to a mechanical disturbance.

To communicate this property quantitatively, we may choose some convenient body and compare other bodies to it in either of the two abovementioned actions. The two basic units commonly used in much American engineering practice to measure mass are the *pound mass*, which is defined in terms of the attraction of gravity for a standard body at a standard location, and the *slug*, which is defined in terms of the dynamical response of a standard body to a standard mechanical disturbance. A similar duality of mass units does not exist in the SI system. There only the *kilogram* is used as the basic measure of mass. The kilogram is measured in terms of response of a body to a mechanical disturbance. Both systems of units will be discussed further in a subsequent section.

We have now established three basic independent dimensions to describe certain physical phenomena. It is convenient to identify these dimensions in the following manner:

$$\begin{array}{ll} \text{length} & [L] \\ \text{time} & [t] \\ \text{mass} & [M] \end{array}$$

These formal expressions of identification for basic dimensions and the more complicated groupings to be presented in Section 1.3 for secondary dimensions are called "dimensional representations."

Often, there are occasions when we want to change units during computations. For instance, we may wish to change feet into inches or millimeters. In such a case, we must replace the unit in question by a *physically equivalent* number of new units. Thus, a foot is replaced by 12 inches or 305 millimeters. A listing of common systems of units is given in Table 1.1, and a table of equivalences between these and other units is given on the inside covers. Such relations between units will be expressed in this way:

$$1 \text{ ft} \equiv 12 \text{ in.} \equiv 305 \text{ mm}$$

The three horizontal bars are not used to denote *algebraic* equivalence; instead, they are used to indicate physical equivalence. Here is another way of expressing the relations above:

Table 1.1 Common Systems of Units

cgs		*SI*	
Mass	Gram	Mass	Kilogram
Length	Centimeter	Length	Meter
Time	Second	Time	Second
Force	Dyne	Force	Newton
English		*American Practice*	
Mass	Pound mass	Mass	Slug or pound mass
Length	Foot	Length	Foot
Time	Second	Time	Second
Force	Poundal	Force	Pound force

$$\left(\frac{1\text{ ft}}{12\text{ in.}}\right) \equiv 1, \quad \left(\frac{1\text{ ft}}{305\text{ mm}}\right) \equiv 1$$
$$\left(\frac{12\text{ in.}}{1\text{ ft}}\right) \equiv 1, \quad \left(\frac{305\text{ mm}}{1\text{ ft}}\right) \equiv 1 \qquad (1.1)$$

The unity on the right side of these relations indicates that the numerator and denominator on the left side are physically equivalent, and thus have a 1:1 relation. This notation will prove convenient when we consider the change of units for secondary dimensions in the next section.

†1.3 Secondary Dimensional Quantities

When physical characteristics are described in terms of basic dimensions by the use of suitable definitions (e.g., velocity is defined[2] as a distance divided by a time interval), such quantities are called *secondary dimensional quantities*. In Section 1.4, we will see that these quantities may also be established as a consequence of natural laws. The dimensional representation of secondary quantities is given in terms of the basic dimensions that enter into the formulation of the concept. For example, the dimensional representation of velocity is

$$[\text{velocity}] \equiv \frac{[L]}{[t]}$$

That is, the dimensional representation of velocity is the dimension length divided by the dimension time. The units for a secondary quantity are then given in terms of the units of the constituent basic dimensions. Thus,

$$[\text{velocity units}] \equiv \frac{[\text{ft}]}{[\text{sec}]}$$

A *change* of units from one system into another usually involves a change in the scale of measure of the secondary quantities involved in the problem. Thus, one scale unit of velocity in the American system is 1 foot per second, while in the SI system it is 1 meter per second. How may these scale units be correctly related for complicated secondary quantities? That is, for our simple case, how many meters per second are equivalent to 1 foot per second? The formal expressions of dimensional representation may be put to good use for such an evaluation. The procedure is as follows. Express the dependent quantity dimensionally; substitute existing units for the basic dimensions; and finally, change these units to the equivalent numbers of units in the new system. The result gives the number of scale units of the quantity in the new system of units that is equivalent to 1 scale unit of the quantity in the old system. Performing these operations for velocity, we would thus have

$$1\left(\frac{\text{ft}}{\text{sec}}\right) \equiv 1\left(\frac{.305\text{ m}}{\text{sec}}\right) \equiv .305\left(\frac{\text{m}}{\text{sec}}\right)$$

[2]A more precise definition will be given in the chapters on dynamics.

which means that .305 scale unit of velocity in the SI system is equivalent to 1 scale unit in the American system.

Another way of changing units when secondary dimensions are present is to make use of the formalism illustrated in relations 1.1. To change a unit in an expression, multiply this unit by a ratio physically equivalent to unity, as we discussed earlier, so that the old unit is canceled out, leaving the desired unit with the proper numerical coefficient. In the example of velocity used above, we may replace ft/sec by m/sec in the following manner:

$$1\left(\frac{\text{ft}}{\text{sec}}\right) \equiv \left(\frac{1\cancel{\text{ft}}}{\text{sec}}\right)\bullet\left(\frac{.305\text{m}}{1\cancel{\text{ft}}}\right) \equiv .305\left(\frac{\text{m}}{\text{sec}}\right)$$

It should be clear that, when we multiply by such ratios to accomplish a change of units as shown above, we do not alter the magnitude of the *actual physical quantity* represented by the expression. Students are strongly urged to employ the above technique in their work, for the use of less formal methods is generally an invitation to error.

†1.4 Law of Dimensional Homogeneity

Now that we can describe certain aspects of nature in a quantitative manner through basic and secondary dimensions, we can by careful observation and experimentation learn to relate certain of the quantities in the form of equations. In this regard, there is an important law, the law of *dimensional homogeneity*, which imposes a restriction on the formulation of such equations. This law states that, because natural phenomena proceed with no regard for man-made units, *basic equations representing physical phenomena must be valid for all systems of units.* Thus, the equation for the period of a pendulum, $t = 2\pi\sqrt{L/g}$, must be valid for all systems of units, and is accordingly said to be *dimensionally homogeneous.* It then follows that the fundamental equations of physics are dimensionally homogeneous; and all equations derived analytically from these fundamental laws must also be dimensionally homogeneous.

What restriction does this condition place on an equation? To answer this, let us examine the following arbitrary equation:

$$x = ygd + k$$

For this equation to be dimensionally homogeneous, the numerical equality between both sides of the equation must be maintained for all systems of units. To accomplish this, the change in the scale of measure of each group of terms must be the same when there is a change of units. That is, if the numerical measure of one group such as ygd is doubled for a new system of units, so must that of the quantities x and k. *For this to occur under all systems of units, it is necessary that every grouping in the equation have the same dimensional representation.*

In this regard, consider the dimensional representation of the above equation expressed in the following manner:

$$[x] = [ygd] + [k]$$

From the previous conclusion for dimensional homogeneity, we require that

$$[x] \equiv [ygd] \equiv [k]$$

As a further illustration, consider the dimensional representation of an equation that is *not* dimensionally homogeneous:

$$[L] = [t]^2 + [t]$$

When we change units from the American to the SI system, the units of feet give way to units of meters, but there is no change in the unit of time, and it becomes clear that the numerical value of the left side of the equation changes while that of the right side does not. The equation, then, becomes invalid in the new system of units and hence is not derived from the basic laws of physics. Throughout this book, we shall invariably be concerned with dimensionally homogeneous equations. Therefore, we should dimensionally analyze our equations to help spot errors.

†1.5 Dimensional Relation Between Force and Mass

We shall now employ the law of dimensional homogeneity to establish a new secondary dimension—namely *force*. A superficial use of Newton's law will be employed for this purpose. In a later section, this law will be presented in greater detail, but it will suffice at this time to state that the acceleration of a particle[3] is inversely proportional to its mass for a given disturbance. Mathematically, this becomes

$$a \propto \frac{1}{m} \tag{1.2}$$

where $\propto$ is the proportionality symbol. Inserting the constant of proportionality, F, we have, on rearranging the equation,

$$F = ma \tag{1.3}$$

The mechanical disturbance, represented by F and called *force*, must have the following dimensional representation, according to the law of dimensional homogeneity:

$$[F] \equiv [M]\frac{[L]}{[t]^2} \tag{1.4}$$

The type of disturbance for which relation 1.2 is valid is usually the action of one body on another by direct contact. However, other actions, such as magnetic, electrostatic, and gravitational actions of one body on another involving no contact, also create mechanical effects that are valid in Newton's equation.

[3]We shall define particles in Section 1.7.

We could have initiated the study of mechanics by considering *force* as a basic dimension, the manifestation of which can be measured by the elongation of a standard spring at a prescribed temperature. Experiment would then indicate that for a given body the acceleration is directly proportional to the applied force. Mathematically,

$$F \propto a; \text{ therefore, } F = ma$$

from which we see that the proportionality constant now represents the property of mass. Here, mass is now a secondary quantity whose dimensional representation is determined from Newton's law:

$$M \equiv [F]\frac{[t]^2}{[L]} \tag{1.5}$$

As was mentioned earlier, we now have a choice between two systems of basic dimensions—the *MLt* or the *FLt* system of basic dimensions. Physicists prefer the former, whereas engineers usually prefer the latter.

1.6 Units of Mass

As we have already seen, the concept of mass arose from two types of actions —those of motion and gravitational attraction. In American engineering practice, units of mass are based on both actions, and this sometimes leads to confusion. Let us consider the *FLt* system of basic dimensions for the following discussion. The unit of force may be taken to be the pound-force (lbf), which is defined as a force that extends a standard spring a certain distance at a given temperature. Using Newton's law, we then define the *slug* as the amount of mass that a 1-pound force will cause to accelerate at the rate of 1 foot per second per second.

On the other hand, another unit of mass can be stipulated if we use the gravitational effect as a criterion. Here, the *pound mass* (lbm) is defined as the amount of matter that is drawn by gravity toward the earth by a force of 1 pound-force (lbf) at a specified position on the earth's surface.

We have formulated two units of mass by two different actions, and to relate these units we must subject them to the *same* action. Thus, we can take 1 pound mass and see what fraction or multiple of it will be accelerated 1 ft/sec^2 under the action of 1 pound of force. This fraction or multiple will then represent the number of units of pound mass that are equivalent to 1 slug. It turns out that this coefficient is g_0, where g_0 has the value corresponding to the acceleration of gravity at a position on the earth's surface where the pound mass was standardized. To three significant figures, the value of g_0 is 32.2. We may then make the statement of equivalence that

$$1 \text{ slug} \equiv 32.2 \text{ pounds mass}$$

To use the pound-mass unit in Newton's law, it is necessary to divide by g_0 to form units of mass, that have been derived from Newton's law. Thus,

$$F = \frac{m}{g_0} a \tag{1.6}$$

where m has the units of pound mass and m/g_0 has units of slugs. Having properly introduced into Newton's law the pound-mass unit from the viewpoint of physical equivalence, let us now consider the dimensional homogeneity of the resulting equation. The right side of Eq. 1.6 must have the dimensional representation of F and, since the unit here for F is the pound force, the right side must then have this unit. Examination of the units on the right side of the equation then indicates that the units of g_0 must be

$$\left[g_0\right] \equiv \frac{[\text{lbm}][\text{ft}]}{[\text{lbf}][\text{sec}]^2} \tag{1.7}$$

How does *weight* fit into this picture? Weight is defined as *the force of gravity on a body*. Its value will depend on the position of the body relative to the earth's surface. At a location on the earth's surface where the pound mass is standardized, a mass of 1 pound (lbm) has the weight of 1 pound (lbf), but with increasing altitude the weight will become smaller than 1 pound (lbf). The mass, however, remains at all times a 1-pound mass (lbm). If the altitude is not exceedingly large, the measure of weight, in lbf, will practically equal the measure of mass, in lbm. Therefore, it is unfortunately the practice in engineering to think erroneously of weight at positions other than on the earth's surface as the measure of mass, and consequently to use the symbol W to represent either lbm or lbf. In this age of rockets and missiles, it behooves us to be careful about the proper usage of units of mass and weight throughout the entire text.

If we know the weight of a body at some point, we can determine its mass in slugs very easily, provided that we know the acceleration of gravity, g, at that point. Thus, according to Newton's law,

$$W(\text{lbf}) = m(\text{slugs}) \times g(\text{ft/sec}^2)$$

Therefore,

$$m(\text{slugs}) = \frac{W(\text{lbf})}{g(\text{ft/sec}^2)} \tag{1.8}$$

Up to this point, we have only considered the American system of units. In the SI system of units, a *kilogram* is the amount of mass that will accelerate 1 m/sec^2 under the action of a force of 1 newton. Here we do not have the problem of 2 units of mass; the kilogram is the basic unit of mass. However, we do have another kind of problem—that the kilogram is unfortunately also used as a measure of force, as is the newton. One kilogram of force is the weight of 1 kilogram of mass at the earth's surface, where the acceleration of gravity (i.e., the acceleration due to the force of gravity) is

9.81 m/sec^2. A newton, on the other hand, is the force that causes 1 kilogram of mass to have an acceleration of 1 m/sec^2. Hence, 9.81 newtons are equivalent to 1 kilogram of force. That is,

$$9.81 \text{ newtons} \equiv 1 \text{ kilogram(force)} \equiv 2.205 \text{ lbf}$$

Note from the above that the newton is a comparatively small force, equaling approximately one-fifth of a pound. A kilonewton (1000 newtons), which will be used often, is about 200 lb. In this text, we shall *not* use the kilogram as a unit of force. However, you should be aware that many people do.[4]

Note that at the earth's surface the weight W of a mass M is:

$$W(\text{newtons}) = [M(\text{kilograms})](9.81)(\text{m/s}^2) \tag{1.9}$$

Hence:

$$M(\text{kilograms}) = \frac{W(\text{newtons})}{9.81\ (\text{m/s}^2)} \tag{1.10}$$

Away from the earth's surface, use the acceleration of gravity g rather than 9.81 in the above equations.

1.7 Idealizations of Mechanics

As we have pointed out, basic and secondary dimensions may sometimes be related in equations to represent a physical action that we are interested in. We want to represent an action using the known laws of physics, and also to be able to form equations simple enough to be susceptible to mathematical computational techniques. Invariably in our deliberations, we must replace the actual physical action and the participating bodies with hypothetical, highly simplified substitutes. We must be sure, of course, that the results of our substitutions have some reasonable correlation with reality. All analytical physical sciences must resort to this technique, and, consequently, their computations are not cut-and-dried but involve a considerable amount of imagination, ingenuity, and insight into physical behavior. We shall, at this time, set forth the most fundamental idealizations of mechanics and a bit of the philosophy involved in scientific analysis.

Continuum. Even the simplification of matter into molecules, atoms, electrons, and so on, is too complex a picture for many problems of engineering mechanics. In most problems, we are interested only in the average measurable manifestations of these elementary bodies. Pressure, density, and temperature are actually the gross effects of the actions of the many molecules and atoms, and they can be conveniently assumed to arise from a hypothetically continuous distribution of matter, which we shall call the *continuum*, instead of from a conglomeration of discrete, tiny bodies. Without such an

[4]This is particularly true in the marketplace where the word "kilos" is often heard.

artifice, we would have to consider the action of each of these elementary bodies—a virtual impossibility for most problems.

Rigid Body. In many cases involving the action on a body by a force, we simplify the continuum concept even further. The most elemental case is that of a rigid body, which is a continuum that undergoes theoretically no deformation whatever. Actually, every body must deform to a certain degree under the actions of forces, but in many cases the deformation is too small to affect the desired analysis. It is then preferable to consider the body as rigid, and proceed with simplified computations. For example, assume that we are to determine the forces transmitted by a beam to the earth as the result of a load P (Fig. 1.2). If P is small enough, the beam will undergo little deflection, and we can carry out a straightforward simple analysis using the *undeformed geometry* as if the body were indeed rigid. If we were to attempt a more accurate analysis—even though a slight increase in accuracy is not required—we would then need to know the exact position that the load assumes relative to the beam *after* the beam has ceased to deform, as shown in an exaggerated manner in Fig. 1.3. To do this accurately is a hopelessly difficult task, especially when we consider that the support must also "give" in a certain way. Although the alternative to a rigid-body analysis here leads us to a virtually impossible calculation, situations do arise in which more realistic models must be employed to yield the required accuracy. For example, when determining the internal force distribution in a body, we must often take the deformation into account, however small it might be. Other cases will be presented later. *The guiding principle is to make such simplifications as are consistent with the required accuracy of the results.*

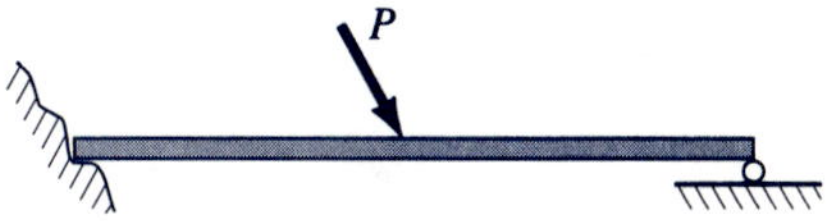

Figure 1.2. Rigid-body assumption—use original geometry.

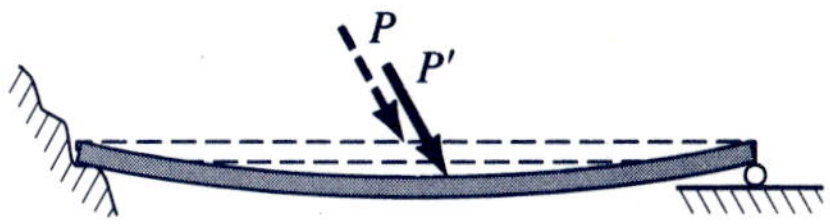

Figure 1.3. Deformable body.

Point Force. A finite force exerted on one body by another must cause a finite amount of local deformation, and always creates a finite area of contact between the bodies through which the force is transmitted. However, since we have formulated the concept of the rigid body, we should also be able to imagine a finite force to be transmitted through an infinitesimal area or point. This simplification of a force distribution is called a *point force*. In many cases where the actual area of contact in a problem is very small but is not known exactly, the use of the concept of the point force results in little sacrifice in accuracy. In Figs. 1.2 and 1.3, we actually employed the graphical representation of the point force.

Particle. The *particle* is defined as an object that has no size but that has a mass. Perhaps this does not sound like a very helpful definition for engineers to employ, but it is actually one of the most useful in mechanics. For the trajectory of a planet, for example, it is the mass of the planet and not its size that is significant. Hence, we can consider planets as particles for such computations. On the other hand, take a figure skater spinning on the ice. Her revolutions are controlled beautifully by the orientation of the body. In this motion, the size and distribution of the body are significant, and since a particle, by definition, can have no distribution, it is patently clear that a particle cannot represent the skater in this case. If, however, the skater should be billed as the "human cannonball on skates" and be shot out of a large air gun, it would be possible to consider her as a single particle in ascertaining her trajectory, since arm and leg movements that were significant while she was spinning on the ice would have little effect on the arc traversed by the main portion of her body.

You will learn later that the *center of mass* or *mass center* is a hypothetical point at which one can concentrate the mass of the body for certain dynamics calculations. Actually in the previous examples of the planet and the "human cannonball on skates," the particle we refer to is actually the mass center whose motion is sufficient for the desired information. Thus, when the motion of the mass center of a body suffices for the information desired, we can replace the body by a particle, namely the mass center.

Many other simplifications pervade mechanics. The perfectly elastic body, the frictionless fluid, and so on, will become familiar as you study various phases of mechanics.

†1.8 Vector and Scalar Quantities

We have now proposed sets of basic dimensions and secondary dimensions to describe certain aspects of nature. However, more than just the dimensional identification and the number of units are often needed to convey adequately the desired information. For instance, to specify fully the motion of a car, which we may represent as a particle at this time, we must answer the following questions:

1. How fast?
2. Which way?

The concept of velocity entails the information desired in questions 1 and 2. The first question, "How fast?", is answered by the speedometer reading, which gives the value of the velocity in miles per hour or kilometers per hour. The second question, "Which way?", is more complicated, because two separate factors are involved. First, we must specify the angular orientation of the velocity relative to a reference frame. Second, we must specify the sense of the velocity, which tells us whether we are moving *toward or away from* a given point. The concepts of angular orientation of the velocity and sense of the velocity are often collectively denoted as the *direction* of the velocity. Graphically, we may use a *directed line segment* (an arrow) to describe the velocity of the car. The *length* of the directed line segment gives information as to "how fast" and is the *magnitude* of the velocity. The angular orientation of the directed line segment and the position of the arrowhead give information as to "which way"—that is, as to the *direction* of the velocity. The directed line segment itself is called the *velocity*, whereas the length of the directed line segment—that is, the magnitude—is called the *speed*.

There are many physical quantities that are represented by a directed line segment and thus are describable by specifying a magnitude and a direction. The most common example is force, where the magnitude is a measure of the intensity of the force and the direction is evident from how the force is applied. Another example is the *displacement vector* between two points on the path of a particle. The magnitude of the displacement vector corresponds to the distance moved along a *straight line* between two points, and the direction is defined by the orientation of this line relative to a reference, with the sense corresponding to which point is being approached. Thus, $\boldsymbol{\rho}_{AB}$ (see Fig. 1.4) is the displacement vector from A to B (while $\boldsymbol{\rho}_{BA}$ goes from B to A).

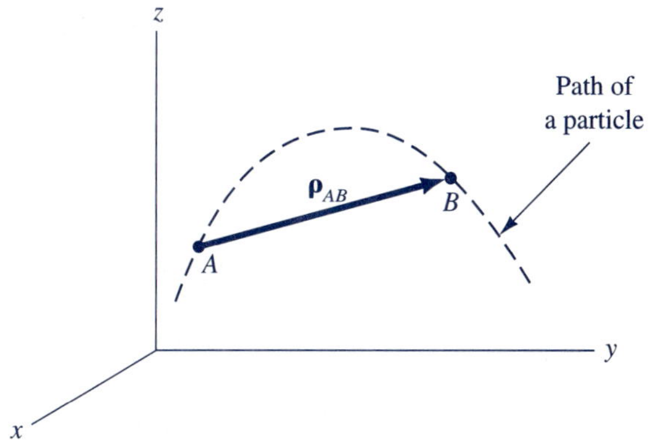

Figure 1.4. Displacement vector $\boldsymbol{\rho}_{AB}$.

Certain quantities having magnitude and direction combine their effects in a special way. Thus, the combined effect of two forces acting on a particle, as shown in Fig. 1.5, corresponds to a single force that may be shown by experiment to be equal to the diagonal of a parallelogram formed by the graphical representation of the forces. That is, the quantities add according to the *parallelogram law*. All quantities that have magnitude and direction and that add according to the parallelogram law are called *vector quantities*. Other quantities that have only magnitude, such as temperature and work, are called *scalar quantities*. A vector quantity will be denoted with a boldface italic letter, which in the case of force becomes $\boldsymbol{F}$.[5]

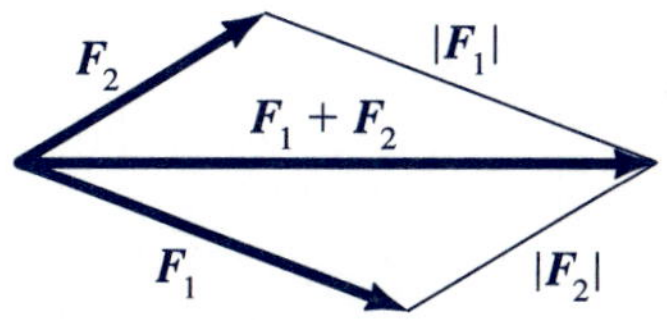

Figure 1.5. Parallelogram law.

The reader may ask: Don't all quantities having magnitude and direction combine according to the parallelogram law and, therefore, become

[5]Your instructor on the blackboard and you in your homework will not be able to use boldface notation for vectors. Accordingly, you may choose to use a superscript arrow or bar, e.g., $\vec{F}$ or $\bar{F}$ ($\underline{F}$ or $\underset{\sim}{F}$ are other possibilities).

vector quantities? No, not all of them do. One very important example will be pointed out after we reconsider Fig. 1.5. In the construction of the parallelogram it matters not which force is laid out first. In other words, "$\boldsymbol{F}_1$ combined with $\boldsymbol{F}_2$" gives the same result as "$\boldsymbol{F}_2$ combined with $\boldsymbol{F}_1$." In short, the combination is *commutative*. If a combination is not commutative, it cannot in general be represented by a parallelogram operation and is thus not a vector. With this in mind, consider the *finite* angle of rotation of a body about an axis. We can associate a magnitude (degrees or radians) and a direction (the axis and a stipulation of clockwise or counterclockwise) with this quantity. However, the finite angle of rotation cannot be considered a vector because in general two finite rotations about different axes cannot be replaced by a single

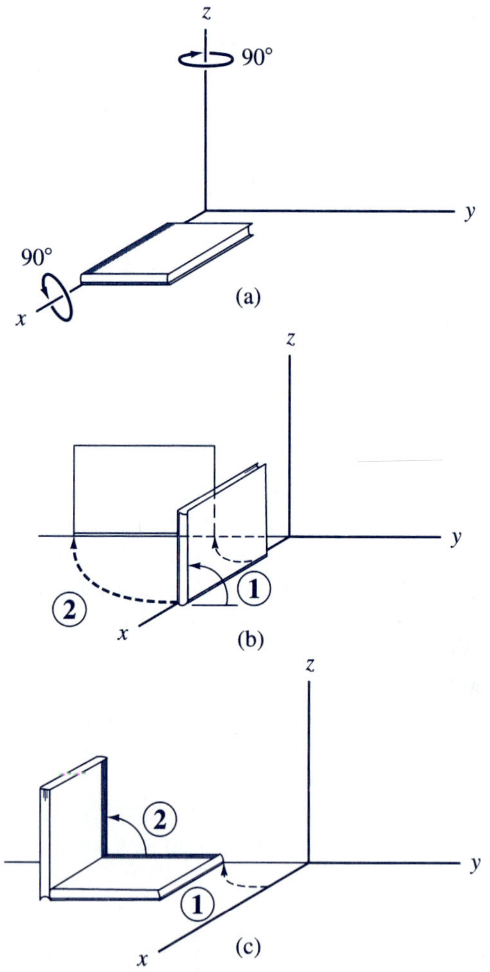

Figure 1.6. Successive rotations are not commutative.

finite rotation consistent with the parallelogram law. The easiest way to show this is to demonstrate that the combination of such rotations is not commutative. In Fig. 1.6(a) a book is to be given two rotations—a 90° counterclockwise rotation about the x axis and a 90° clockwise rotation about the z axis, both looking in toward the origin. This is carried out in Figs. 1.6(b) and (c). In Fig. 1.6(c), the sequence of combination is reversed from that in Fig. 1.6(b), and you can see how it alters the final orientation of the book. Finite angular rotation, therefore, is not a vector quantity, since the parallelogram law is not valid for such a combination.[6]

You may now wonder why we tacked on the parallelogram law for the definition of a vector and thereby excluded finite rotations from this category. The answer to this query is as follows. In the next chapter, we will present certain sets of very useful operations termed *vector algebra*. These operations are valid in general *only* if the parallelogram law is satisfied as you will see when we get to Chapter 2. Therefore, we had to restrict the definition of a vector in order to be able to use this kind of algebra for these quantities. Also, it is to be pointed out that later in the text we will present yet a third definition consistent with our latest definition. This next definition will have certain advantages as we will see later.

Before closing the section, we will set forth one more definition. The *line of action* of a vector is a hypothetical infinite straight line collinear with the vector (see Fig. 1.7). Thus, the velocities of two cars moving on different lanes of a straight highway have different lines of action. Keep in mind that the line of action involves no connotation as to sense. Thus, a vector $\boldsymbol{V}'$ collinear with $\boldsymbol{V}$ in Fig. 1.7 and with opposite sense would nevertheless have the same line of action.

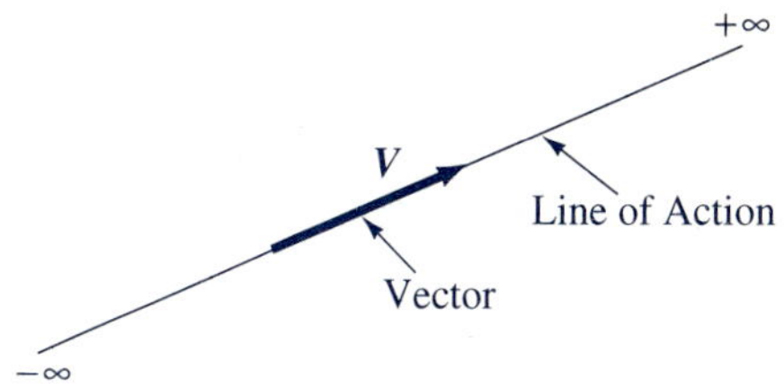

Figure 1.7. Line of action of a vector.

1.9 Equality and Equivalence of Vectors

We shall avoid many pitfalls in the study of mechanics if we clearly make a distinction between the equality and the equivalence of vectors.

Two vectors are equal if they have the same dimensions, magnitude, and direction. In Fig. 1.8, the velocity vectors of three particles have equal length, are identically inclined toward the reference xyz, and have the same sense. Although they have different lines of action, they are nevertheless equal according to the definition.

Two vectors are equivalent in a certain capacity if each produces the very same effect in this capacity. If the criterion in Fig. 1.8 is change of elevation of the particles or total distance traveled by the particles, all three vectors give the same result. They are, in addition to being equal, also

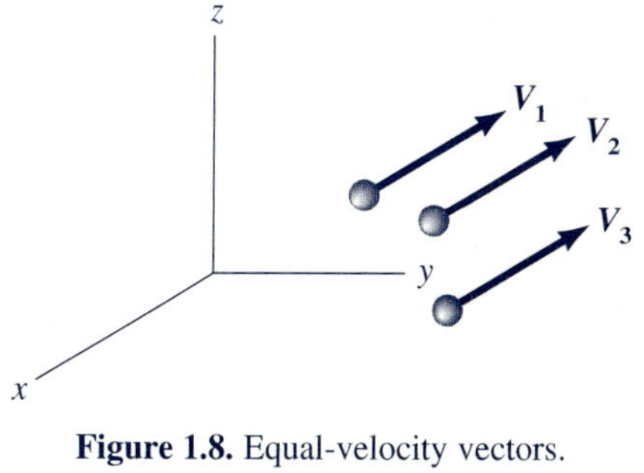

Figure 1.8. Equal-velocity vectors.

[6]However, *vanishingly small* rotations can be considered as vectors since the commutative law applies for the combination of such rotations. A proof of this assertion is presented in Appendix IV. The fact that infinitesimal rotations are vectors in accordance with our definition will be an important consideration when we discuss angular velocity in Chapter 15.

equivalent for these capacities. If the absolute height of the particles above the *xy* plane is the question in point, these vectors will not be equivalent despite their equality. Thus, it must be emphasized that *equal vectors need not always be equivalent; it depends entirely on the situation at hand.* Furthermore, vectors that are not equal may still be equivalent in some capacity. Thus, in the beam in Fig. 1.9, forces F_1 and F_2 are unequal, since their magnitudes are 10 lb and 20 lb, respectively. However, it is clear from elementary physics that their moments about the base of the beam are equal, and so the forces have the same "turning" action at the fixed end of the beam. In that capacity, the forces are equivalent. If, however, we are interested in the deflection of the free end of the beam resulting from each force, there is no longer an equivalence between the forces, since each will give a different deflection.

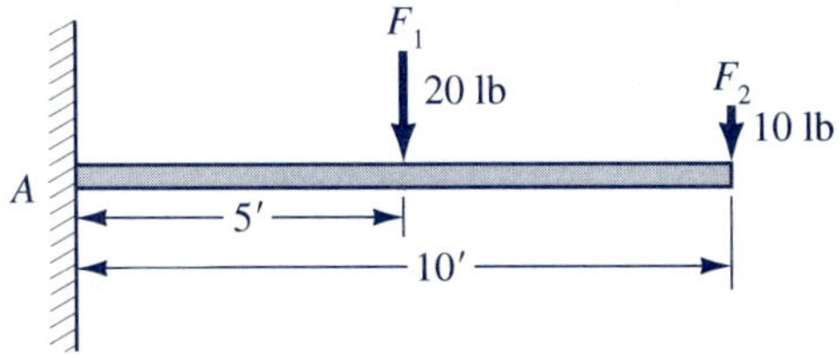

Figure 1.9. F_1 and F_2 equivalent for moment about *A*.

To sum up, the *equality* of two vectors is determined by the vectors themselves, and the *equivalence* between two vectors is determined by the task involving the vectors.

In problems of mechanics, we can profitably delineate three classes of situations concerning equivalence of vectors:

1. *Situations in which vectors may be positioned anywhere in space without loss or change of meaning provided that magnitude and direction are kept intact.* Under such circumstances the vectors are called *free vectors.* For example, the velocity vectors in Fig. 1.8 are free vectors as far as total distance traveled is concerned.
2. *Situations in which vectors may be moved along their lines of action without change of meaning.* Under such circumstances the vectors are called *transmissible vectors.* For example, in towing the object in Fig. 1.10, we may apply the force anywhere along the rope *AB* or may push at point *C*. The resulting motion is the same in all cases, so the force is a transmissible vector for this purpose.
3. *Situations in which the vectors must be applied at definite points.* The point may be represented as the tail or head of the arrow in the graphical representation. For this case, no other position of application leads to

equivalence. Under such circumstances, the vector is called a *bound vector*. For example, if we are interested in the deformation induced by forces in the body in Fig. 1.10, we must be more selective in our actions than we were when all we wanted to know was the motion of the body. Clearly, force $\boldsymbol{F}$ will cause a different deformation when applied at point C than it will when applied at point A. The force is thus a bound vector for this problem.

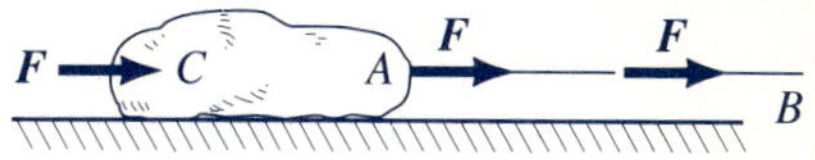

Figure 1.10. F is transmissible for towing.

We shall be concerned throughout this text with considerations of equivalence.

†1.10 Laws of Mechanics

The entire structure of mechanics rests on relatively few basic laws. Nevertheless, for the student to comprehend these laws sufficiently to undertake novel and varied problems, much study will be required.

We shall now discuss briefly the following laws, which are considered to be the foundation of mechanics:

1. Newton's first and second laws of motion.
2. Newton's third law.
3. The gravitational law of attraction.
4. The parallelogram law.

Newton's First and Second Laws of Motion. These laws were first stated by Newton as

Every particle continues in a state of rest or uniform motion in a straight line unless it is compelled to change that state by forces imposed on it.

The change of motion is proportional to the natural force impressed and is made in a direction of the straight line in which the force is impressed.

Notice that the words "rest," "uniform motion," and "change of motion" appear in the statements above. For such information to be meaningful, we must have some frame of reference relative to which these states of motion can be described. We may then ask: relative to what reference in space does every particle remain at "rest" or "move uniformly along a straight line" in the absence of any forces? Or, in the case of a force acting on the particle, relative to what reference in space is the "change in motion proportional to the force"? Experiment indicates that the "fixed" stars act as a reference for which the first and second laws of Newton are highly accurate. Later, we will see that any other system that moves uniformly and without rotation relative to the fixed stars may be used as a reference with equal accuracy. All such references are called *inertial references*. The earth's surface is usually employed as a reference in engineering work. Because of the rotation of the earth and the variations in its motion around the sun, it is not, strictly speaking, an inertial reference. However, the departure is so small for most situations (exceptions are the motion of guided missiles and spacecraft) that the error incurred is very slight. We shall, therefore, usually consider the earth's surface as an inertial reference, but will keep in mind the somewhat approximate nature of this step.

As a result of the preceding discussion, we may define *equilibrium* as *that state of a body in which all its constituent particles are at rest or moving uniformly along a straight line relative to an inertial reference.* The converse of Newton's first law, then, stipulates for the equilibrium state that there must be no force (or equivalent action of no force) acting on the body. Many situations fall into this category. The study of bodies in equilibrium is called *statics*, and it will be an important consideration in this text.

In addition to the reference limitations explained above, a serious limitation was brought to light at the turn of this century. As pointed out earlier, the pioneering work of Einstein revealed that the laws of Newton become increasingly more approximate as the speed of a body increases. Near the speed of light, they are untenable. In the vast majority of engineering computations, the speed of a body is so small compared to the speed of light that these departures from Newtonian mechanics, called *relativistic effects*, may be entirely disregarded with little sacrifice in accuracy. In considering the motion of high-energy elementary particles occurring in nuclear phenomena, however, we cannot ignore relativistic effects. Finally, when we get down to very small distances, such as those between the protons and neutrons in the nucleus of an atom, we find that Newtonian mechanics cannot explain many observed phenomena. In this case, we must resort to quantum mechanics, and then Newton's laws give way to the Schrödinger equation as the key equation.

Newton's Third Law. Newton stated in his third law:

To every action there is always opposed an equal reaction, or the mutual actions of two bodies upon each other are always equal and directed to contrary points.

This is illustrated graphically in Fig. 1.11, where the action and reaction between two bodies arise from direct contact. Other important actions in which Newton's third law holds are gravitational attractions (to be discussed next) and electrostatic forces between charged particles. It should be pointed out that there are actions that do not follow this law, notably the electromagnetic forces between charged moving bodies.[7]

Law of Gravitational Attraction. It has already been pointed out that there is an attraction between the earth and the bodies at its surface, such as A and B

[7]Electromagnetic forces between charged moving particles are equal and opposite but are not collinear and hence are not "directed to contrary points."

in Fig. 1.11. This attraction is mutual and Newton's third law applies. There is also an attraction between the two bodies A and B themselves, but this force because of the small size of both bodies is extremely weak. However, the mechanism for the mutual attraction between the earth and each body is the same as that for the mutual attraction between the bodies. These forces of attraction may be given by the *law of gravitational attraction*:

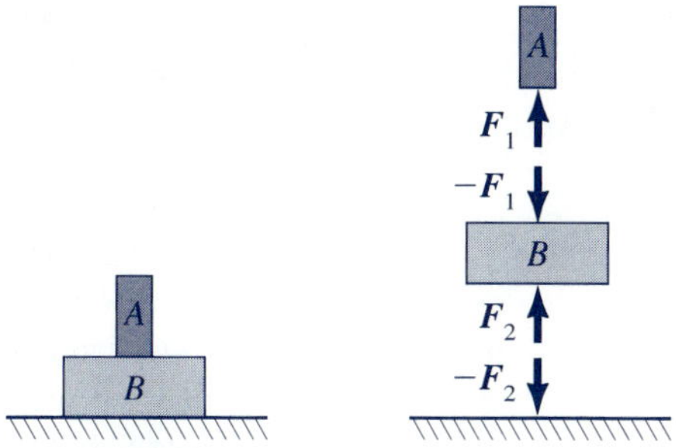

Figure 1.11. Newton's third law.

Two particles will be attracted toward each other along their connecting line with a force whose magnitude is directly proportional to the product of the masses and inversely proportional to the distance squared between the particles.

Avoiding vector notation for now, we may thus say that

$$F = G\frac{m_1 m_2}{r^2} \tag{1.11}$$

where G is called the *universal gravitational constant.* In the actions involving the earth and the bodies discussed above, we may consider each body as a particle, with its entire mass concentrated at its center of gravity.[8] Hence, if we know the various constants in formula 1.11, we can compute the weight of a given mass at different altitudes above the earth.

Parallelogram Law. Stevinius (1548–1620) was the first to demonstrate that forces could be combined by representing them by arrows to some suitable scale, and then forming a parallelogram in which the diagonal represents the sum of the two forces. As we pointed out, all vectors must combine in this manner.

[8]To be studied in detail in Chapter 4.

1.11 Closure

In this chapter, we have introduced the basic dimensions by which we can describe in a quantitative manner certain aspects of nature. These basic, and from them secondary, dimensions may be related by dimensionally homogeneous equations which, with suitable idealizations, can represent certain actions in nature. The basic laws of mechanics were thus introduced. Since the equations of these laws relate vector quantities, we shall introduce a useful and highly descriptive set of vector operations in Chapter 2 in order to learn to handle these laws effectively and to gain more insight into mechanics in general. These operations are generally called *vector algebra.*

Check-Out for Sections with †

1.1. What are two kinds of limitations on Newtonian mechanics?

1.2. What are the two phenomena wherein mass plays a key role?

1.3. If a pound force is defined by the extension of a standard spring, define the pound mass and the slug.

1.4. Express mass density dimensionally. How many scale units of mass density (mass per unit volume) in the SI units are equivalent to 1 scale unit in the American system using (a) slugs, ft, sec and (b) lbm, ft, sec?

1.5. **(a)** What is a necessary condition for *dimensional homogeneity* in an equation?

(b) In the Newtonian viscosity law, the frictional resistance τ (force per unit area) in a fluid is proportional to the distance rate of change of velocity dV/dy. The proportionality constant μ is called the *coefficient of viscosity.* What is its dimensional representation?

1.6. Define a vector and a scalar.

1.7. What is meant by *line of action* of a vector?

1.8. What is a *displacement* vector?

1.9. What is an *inertial reference*?

CHAPTER 2

REVIEW II*

Elements of Vector Algebra

†2.1 Introduction

In Chapter 1, we saw that a scalar quantity is adequately given by a magnitude, while a vector quantity requires the additional specification of a direction. The basic algebraic operations for the handling of scalar quantities are those familiar ones studied in grade school, so familiar that you now wonder even that you had to be "introduced" to them. For vector quantities, these methods may be cumbersome since the directional aspects must be taken into account. Therefore, an algebra has evolved that clearly and concisely allows for certain very useful manipulations of vectors. It is not merely for elegance or sophistication that we employ vector algebra. Indeed, we can achieve greater insight into the subject matter—particularly into dynamics—by employing the more powerful and descriptive methods introduced in this chapter.

†2.2 Magnitude and Multiplication of a Vector by a Scalar

The magnitude of a quantity, in strict mathematical parlance, is always a *positive* number of units whose value corresponds to the numerical measure of the quantity. Thus, the magnitude of a quantity of measure −50 units is +50 units. Note that the magnitude of a quantity is its absolute value. The mathematical symbol for indicating the magnitude of a quantity is a set of vertical lines enclosing the quantity. That is,

$$|-50 \text{ units}| = \text{absolute value } (-50 \text{ units}) = +50 \text{ units}$$

*The reader is urged to pay particular attention to Section 2.4 on **Resolution of Vectors** and Section 2.6 on **Useful Ways of Representing Vectors**.

†Again, as in Chapter 1, we have used the symbol † for certain section headings to indicate that at the end of the chapter there are questions to be answered in writing pertaining to these sections. The instructer may wish to assign the reading of these sections along with the aforementioned questions.

Similarly, the magnitude of a vector quantity is a positive number of units corresponding to the length of the vector in those units. Using our vector symbols, we can say that

$$\text{magnitude of vector } \boldsymbol{A} = |\boldsymbol{A}| \equiv A$$

Thus, A is a positive scalar quantity. We may now discuss the multiplication of a vector by a scalar.

The definition of the product of vector $\boldsymbol{A}$ by scalar m, written simply as $m\boldsymbol{A}$, is given in the following manner:

> *$m\boldsymbol{A}$ is a vector having the same direction as $\boldsymbol{A}$ and a magnitude equal to the ordinary scalar product between the magnitudes of m and $\boldsymbol{A}$. If m is negative, it means simply that the vector $m\boldsymbol{A}$ has a direction directly opposite to that of $\boldsymbol{A}$.*

The vector $-\boldsymbol{A}$ may be considered as the product of the scalar -1 and the vector $\boldsymbol{A}$. Thus, from the statement above we see that $-\boldsymbol{A}$ differs from $\boldsymbol{A}$ in that it has an opposite sense. Furthermore, these operations have nothing to do with the line of action of a vector, so $\boldsymbol{A}$ and $-\boldsymbol{A}$ may have different lines of action. This will be the case of the couple to be studied in Chapter 3.

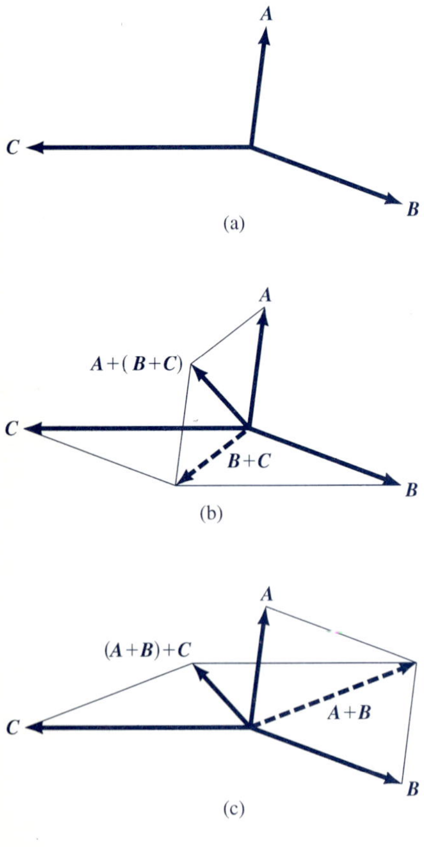

Figure 2.1. Addition by parallelogram law.

†2.3 Addition and Subtraction of Vectors

In adding a number of vectors, we may repeatedly employ the parallelogram construction. We can do this graphically by scaling the lengths of the arrows according to the magnitudes of the vector quantities they represent. The magnitude of the final arrow can then be interpreted in terms of its length by employing the chosen scale factor. As an example, consider the coplanar[1] vectors $\boldsymbol{A}$, $\boldsymbol{B}$, and $\boldsymbol{C}$ shown in Fig. 2.1(a). The addition of the vectors $\boldsymbol{A}$, $\boldsymbol{B}$, and $\boldsymbol{C}$ has been accomplished in two ways. In Fig. 2.1(b) we first add $\boldsymbol{B}$ and $\boldsymbol{C}$ and then add the resulting vector (shown dashed) to $\boldsymbol{A}$. This combination can be represented by the notation $\boldsymbol{A} + (\boldsymbol{B} + \boldsymbol{C})$. In Fig. 2.1(c), we add $\boldsymbol{A}$ and $\boldsymbol{B}$, and then add the resulting vector (shown dashed) to $\boldsymbol{C}$. The representation of this combination is given as $(\boldsymbol{A} + \boldsymbol{B}) + \boldsymbol{C}$. Note that the final vector is identical for both procedures. Thus,

$$\boldsymbol{A} + (\boldsymbol{B} + \boldsymbol{C}) = (\boldsymbol{A} + \boldsymbol{B}) + \boldsymbol{C} \tag{2.1}$$

When the quantities involved in an algebraic operation can be grouped without restriction, the operation is said to be *associative*. Thus, the addition of vectors is both commutative, as explained earlier, and associative.

To determine a summation of, let us say, two vectors without recourse to graphics, we need only make a simple sketch of the vectors approximately to scale. By using familiar trigonometric relations, we can get a direct evaluation of the result. This is illustrated in the following examples.

[1]Coplanar, meaning "same plane," is a word used often in mechanics.

Example 2.1

Add the forces acting on a particle situated at the origin of a two-dimensional reference frame (Fig. 2.2). One force has a magnitude of 10 lb acting in the positive x direction, whereas the other has a magnitude of 5 lb acting at an angle of 135° with a sense directed away from the origin.

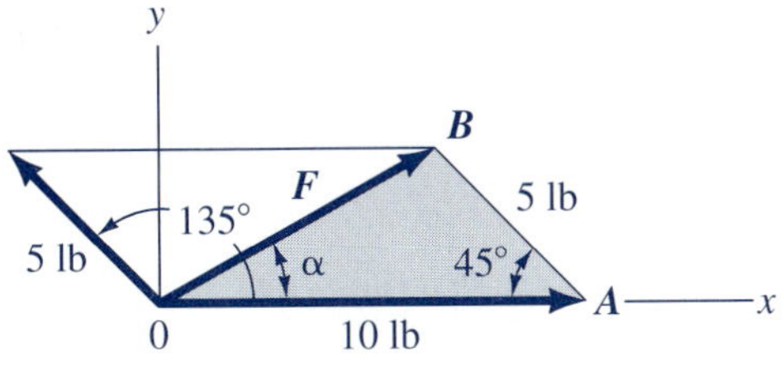

Figure 2.2. Find F and α using trigonometry.

To get the sum (shown as $\boldsymbol{F}$), we may use the law of cosines[2] for one of the triangular portions of the sketched parallelogram. Thus, using triangle OBA,

$$|\boldsymbol{F}| = \left[10^2 + 5^2 - (2)(10)(5)\cos 45°\right]^{1/2}$$
$$= (100 + 25 - 70.7)^{1/2} = \sqrt{54.3} = 7.37 \text{ lb}$$

The direction of the vector may be described by giving the angle and the sense. The angle is determined by employing the law of sines for triangle OBA.[3]

$$\frac{5}{\sin\alpha} = \frac{7.37}{\sin 45°}$$

$$\sin\alpha = \frac{(5)(0.707)}{7.37} = 0.480$$

Therefore,

$$\boldsymbol{F} = 7.37 \text{ lb}$$
$$\alpha = 28.6°$$

The sense is shown using the directed line segment.

[2]

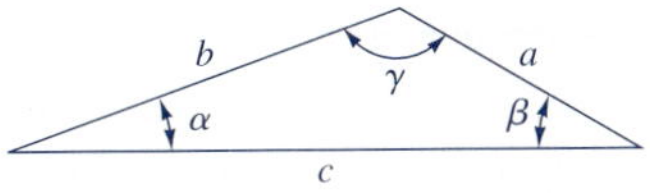

You will recall from trigonometry that the *law of cosines* for side b of a triangle is given as

$$b^2 = a^2 + c^2 - 2ac\cos\beta$$

[3]The *law of sines* is given as follows for a triangle:

$$\frac{a}{\sin\alpha} = \frac{b}{\sin\beta} = \frac{c}{\sin\gamma}$$

Example 2.2

A simple slingshot (see Fig. 2.3) is about to be "fired." If the entire rubber band requires 3 lb per inch of elongation, what force does the band exert on the hand? The total unstretched length of the rubber band is 5 in.

The top view of the slingshot is shown in Fig. 2.4. The change in overall length of the rubber band ΔL from its unstretched length is

$$\Delta L = 2\left(1.5^2 + 8^2\right)^{1/2} - 5 = 11.28 \text{ in.}$$

The tension in the entire extended rubber band is then (11.28)(3) lb. Consequently, the force F transmitted by *each leg* of the slingshot is

$$F = (11.28)(3) = \boxed{33.84 \text{ lb}}$$

and the value of θ

$$\theta = \tan^{-1}\frac{1.5}{8} = 10.62°$$

In Fig. 2.5, we show a parallelogram involving the forces F and their sum R where R is the force that the band exerts on the hand. We can use the law of cosines on either of the triangles to get R. Thus

$$R^2 = 33.84^2 + 33.84^2 - (2)(33.84)(33.84)\cos\alpha$$

Noting that $\alpha = 180° - (2)(10.62°) = 158.8°$ we have

$$R = \left[(2)(33.84)^2(1 - \cos 158.8°)\right]^{1/2} = \boxed{66.52 \text{ lb}}$$

A more direct calculation can be used by considering two right triangles within the chosen triangle. Then using elementary trigonometry we have

$$R = (2)(33.84)\cos(10.62)° = 66.52 \text{ lb}$$

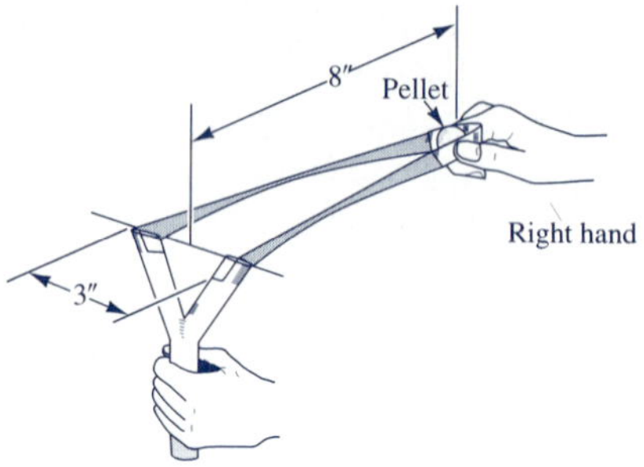

Figure 2.3. Simple slingshot.

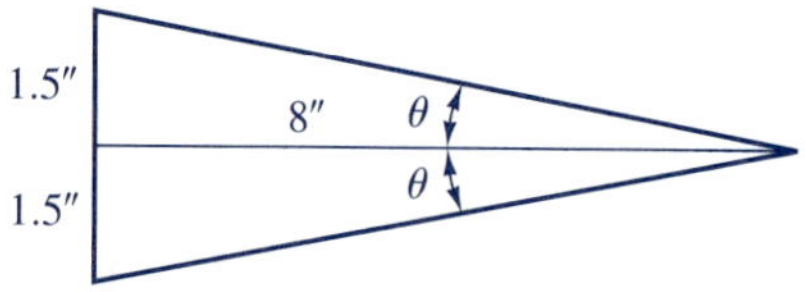

Figure 2.4. Top view of the slingshot.

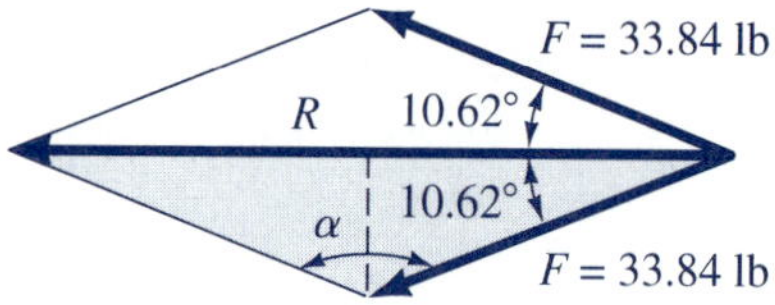

Figure 2.5. Parallelogram of forces.

It must be emphatically pointed out that the addition of vectors $\boldsymbol{A}$ and $\boldsymbol{B}$ only involves the vectors themselves and *not* their lines of actions or their positions along their respective lines of action. That is, we can change their lines of action and move them along their respective lines of action so as to form two sides of a parallelogram. For the additional vector algebra that we will develop in this chapter, we can take similar liberties with the vectors involved.

We may also add the vectors by moving them successively to parallel positions so that the head of one vector connects to the tail of the next vector, and so on. The sum of the vectors will then be a vector whose tail connects to the tail of the first vector and whose head connects to the head of the last vector. This last step will form a polygon from the vectors, and we say that the vector sum then "closes the polygon." Thus, adding the 10-lb vector to the

5-lb vector in Fig. 2.2, we would form the sides *OA* and *AB* of a triangle. The sum $\boldsymbol{F}$ then closes the triangle and is *OB*. Also, in Fig. 2.6(a), we have shown three coplanar vectors $\boldsymbol{F}_1$, $\boldsymbol{F}_2$, and $\boldsymbol{F}_3$. The vectors are connected in Fig. 2.6(b) as described. The sum of the vectors then is the dashed vector that closes the polygon. In Fig. 2.6(c), we have laid off the vectors $\boldsymbol{F}_1$, $\boldsymbol{F}_2$, and $\boldsymbol{F}_3$ in a different sequence. Nevertheless, it is seen that the sum is the same vector as in Fig. 2.6(b). Clearly, the *order* of laying off the vectors is not significant.

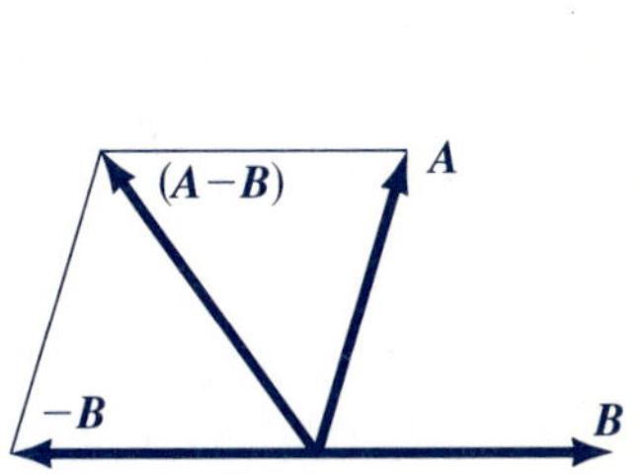

Figure 2.7. Subtraction of vectors.

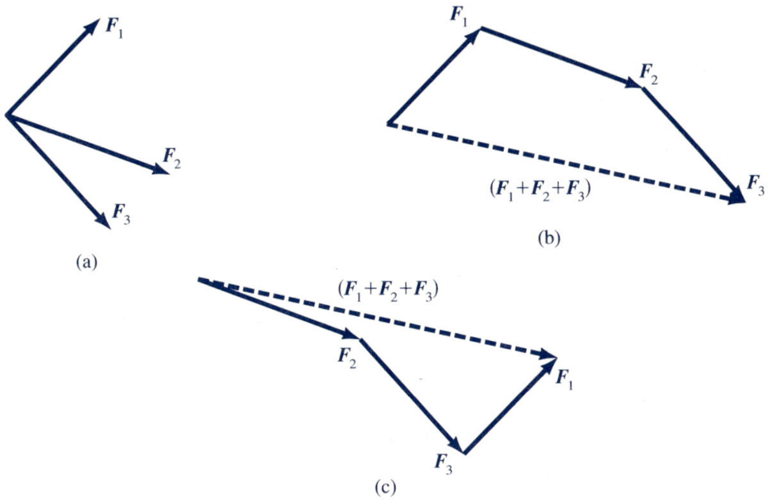

Figure 2.6. Addition by "closing the polygon."

A simple physical interpretation of the above vector sum can be formed for vectors each of which represents a movement of a certain distance and direction (i.e., a *displacement* vector). Then, traveling along the system of given vectors you start from one point (the tail of the first vector) and end at another point (the head of the last vector). The vector *sum* that closes the polygon is equivalent to the system of given vectors, in that it takes you from the same initial to the same final point.

The polygon summation process, like the parallelogram of addition, can be used as a graphical process, or, still better, can be used to generate analytical computations with the aid of trigonometry. The extension of this procedure to any number of vectors is obvious.

The process of *subtraction* of vectors is defined in the following manner: to subtract vector $\boldsymbol{B}$ from vector $\boldsymbol{A}$, we reverse the direction of $\boldsymbol{B}$ (i.e., multiply by -1) and then add this new vector to $\boldsymbol{A}$ (Fig. 2.7).

This process may also be used in the polygon construction. Thus, consider coplanar vectors $\boldsymbol{A}$, $\boldsymbol{B}$, $\boldsymbol{C}$, and $\boldsymbol{D}$ in Fig. 2.8(a). To form $\boldsymbol{A} + \boldsymbol{B} - \boldsymbol{C} - \boldsymbol{D}$, we proceed as shown in Fig. 2.8(b). Again, the order of the process is not significant, as can be seen in Fig. 2.8(c).

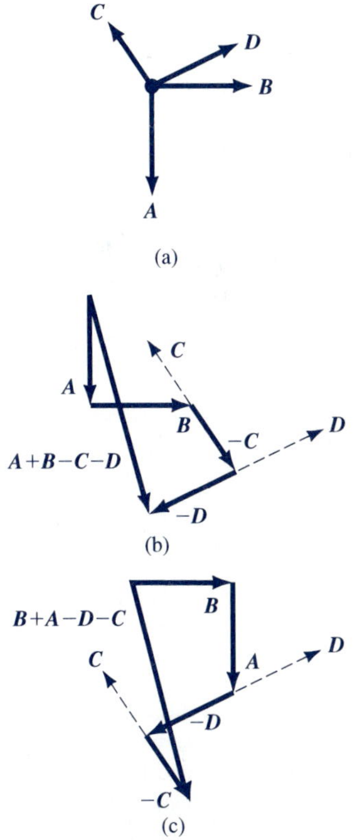

Figure 2.8. Addition and subtraction using polygon construction.

PROBLEMS

2.1. Add a 20-N force pointing in the positive x direction to a 50-N force at an angle 45° to the x axis in the first quadrant and directed away from the origin.

2.2. Subtract the 20-N force in Problem 2.1 from the 50-N force.

2.3. Add the vectors in the xy plane. Do this first graphically, using the force polygon, and then do it analytically.

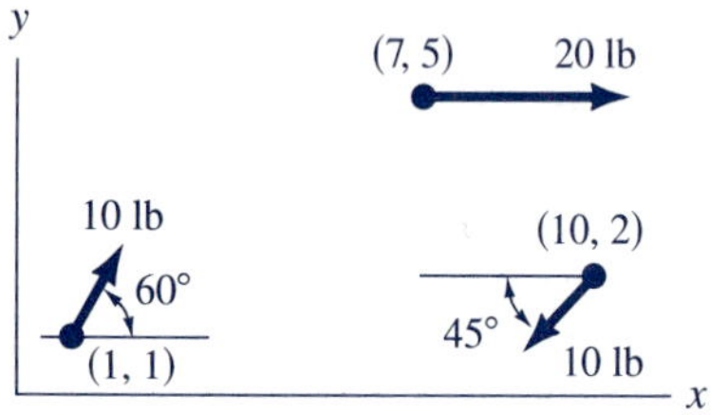

Figure P.2.3

2.4. A lightweight homemade plane is being observed as it flies at constant altitude but in a series of separate constant directions. At the outset, it goes due east for 5 km, then due north for 7 km, then southeast for 4 km, and finally, southwest for 8 km. Graphically determine the shortest distance from the starting point to the end point of the previous observations. See Fig. P.2.4.

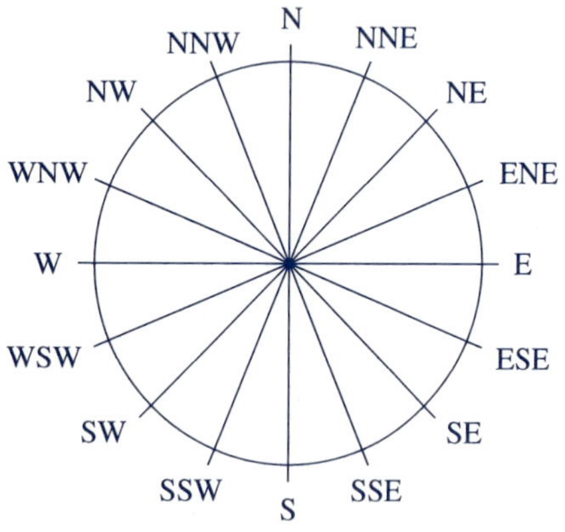

Figure P.2.4

2.5. A homing pigeon is released at point A and is observed. It flies 10 km due south, then goes due east for 15 km. Next it goes southeast for 10 km and finally goes due south 5 km to reach its destination B. Graphically determine the shortest distance between A and B. Neglect the earth's curvature.

2.6. Force $\boldsymbol{A}$ (given as a horizontal 10-N force) and $\boldsymbol{B}$ (vertical) add up to a force $\boldsymbol{C}$ that has a magnitude of 20 N. What is the magnitude of force $\boldsymbol{B}$ and the direction of force $\boldsymbol{C}$? (For the simplest results, use the force polygon, which for this case is a right triangle, and perform analytical computations.)

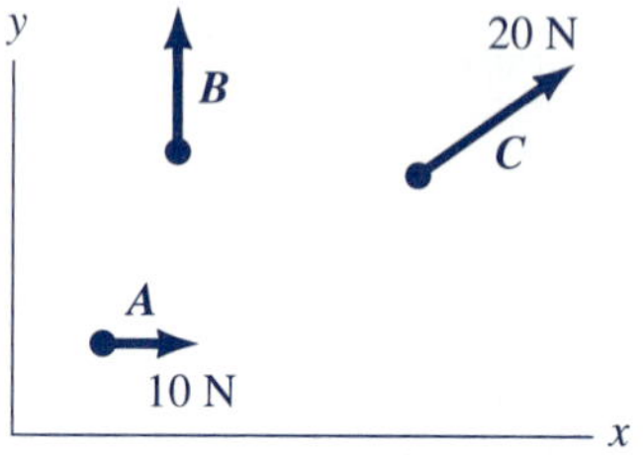

Figure P.2.6

2.7. A light cable from a Jeep is tied to the peak of an A-frame and exerts a force of 450 N along the cable. A 1,000-kg log is suspended from a second cable, which is fastened to the peak. What is the total force from the cables on the A-frame?

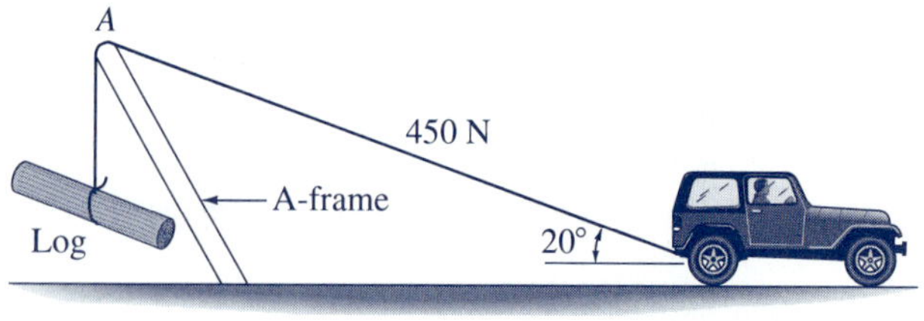

Figure P.2.7

2.8. Find the total force and its direction from the cable acting on each of the three pulleys, each of which is free to turn. The 100-N weight is stationary.

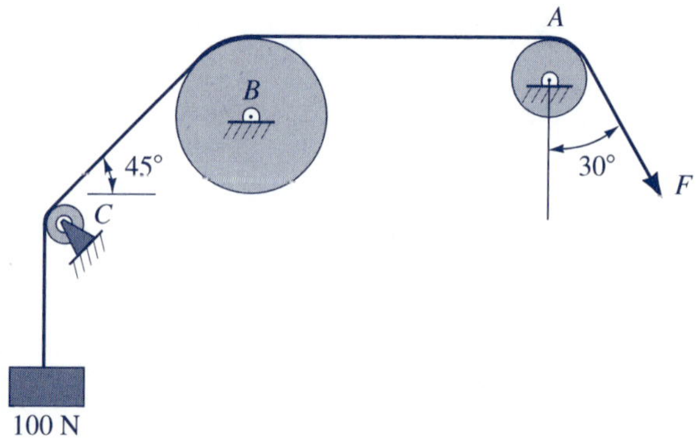

Figure P.2.8

2.9. If the difference between forces ***B*** and ***A*** in Fig. P.2.6 is a force ***D*** having a magnitude of 25 N, what is the magnitude of ***B*** and the direction of ***D***?

2.10. What is the sum of the forces transmitted by the structural rods to the pin at A?

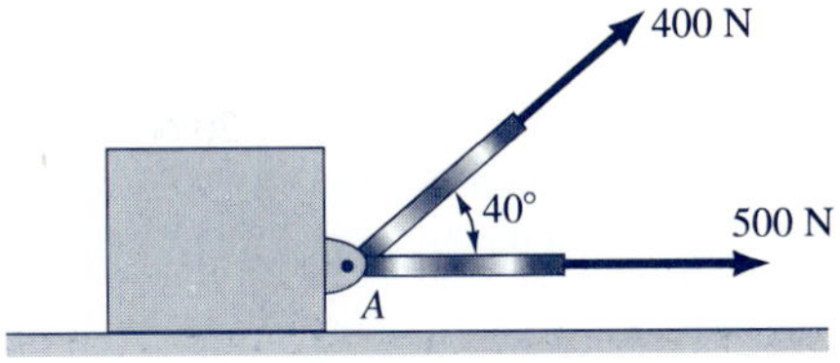

Figure P.2.10

2.11. Suppose in Problem 2.10 we require that the total force transmitted by the members to pin A be inclined 12° to the horizontal. If we do not change the force transmitted by the horizontal member, what must be the new force for the other member whose direction remains at 40°? What is the total force?

2.12. Using the parallelogram law, find the tensile force in cable AC, T_{AC}, and the angle α. (We will do this problem differently in Example 5.4.)

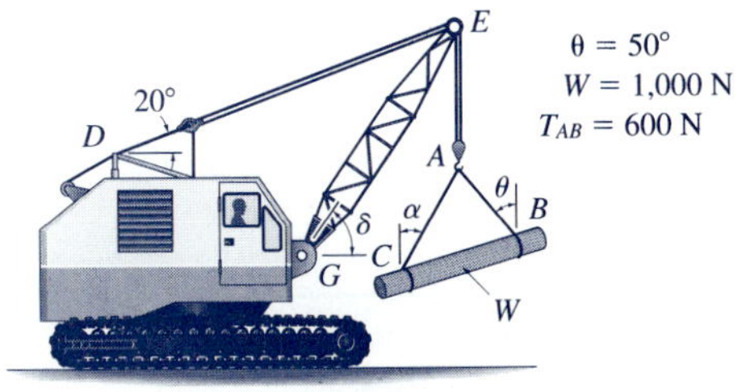

Figure P.2.12

2.13. In the preceding problem, what should the angle δ be so that the sum of the forces from cable DE and cable EA is colinear with the boom GE? Verify that $\delta = 55°$.

2.14. Three forces act on the block. The 500-N and the 600-N forces act, respectively, on the upper and lower faces of the block, while the 1,000-N force acts along the edge. Give the magnitude of the sum of these forces using the parallelogram law twice.

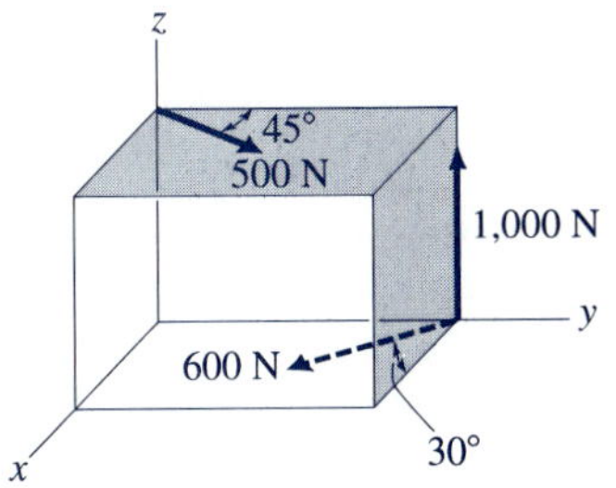

Figure P.2.14

2.15. A man pulls with force W on a rope through a simple frictionless pulley to raise a weight W. What total force is exerted on the pulley?

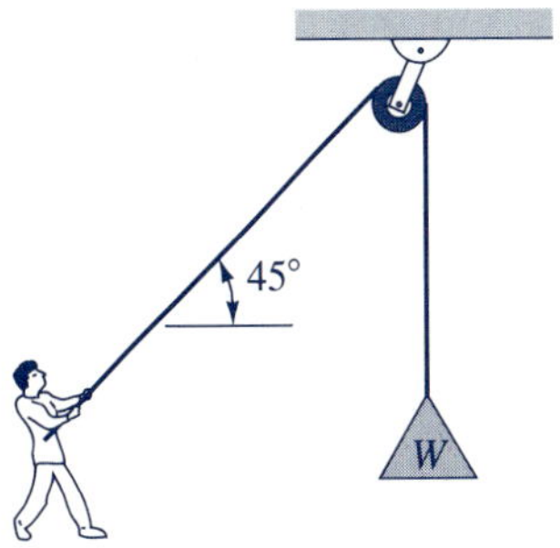

Figure P.2.15

2.16. Add the three vectors using the parallelogram law twice. The 100-N force is in the xz plane, while the other two forces are parallel to the yz plane and do not intersect. Give the magnitude of the sum and the angle it forms with the x axis.

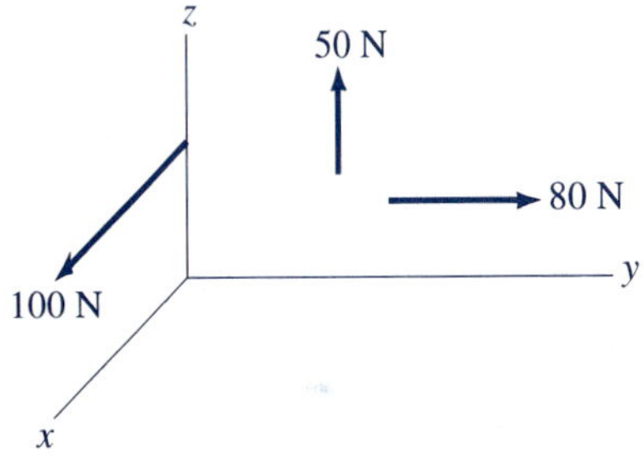

Figure P.2.16

2.17. A mass M is supported by cables (1) and (2). The tension in cable (1) is 200 N, whereas the tension in (2) is such as to maintain the configuration shown. What is the mass of M in kilograms? (You will learn very shortly that the weight of M must be equal and opposite to the vector sum of the supporting forces for equilibrium.)

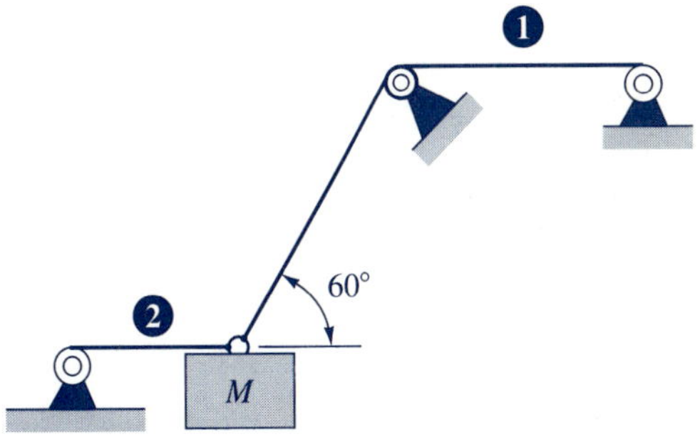

Figure P.2.17

2.18. Two football players are pushing a blocking dummy. Player A pushes with 100-lb force while player B pushes with 150-lb force toward bow C of the dummy. What is the total force exerted on the dummy by the players?

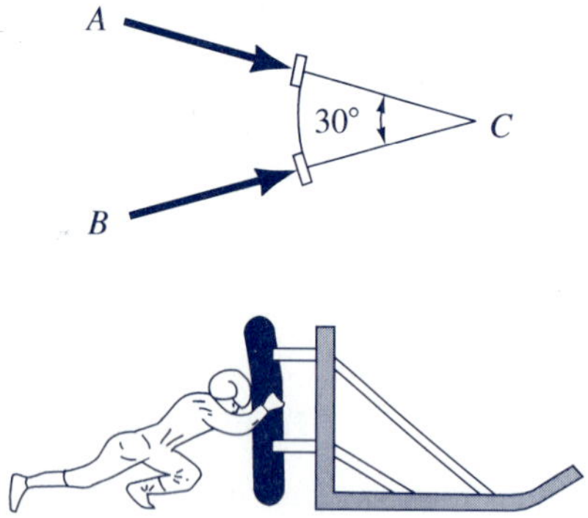

Figure P.2.18

2.19. What are the forces F_1 and F_2 and the angle β for any given angle α to relieve the force of gravity W from the horizontal support of the block at A? The rollers on the side of the block do not contribute to the vertical support of the block. The wires connect to the geometric center of the block C. The weight W is 500 N. Form three independent equations for any given α involving the unknowns F_1, F_2, and β.

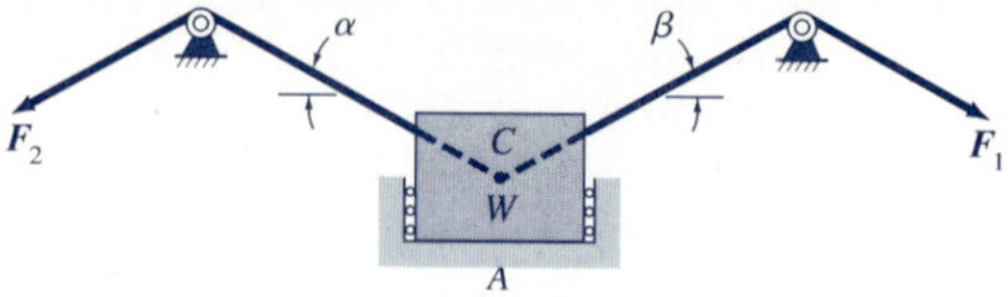

Figure P.2.19

***2.20.** Do problem 2.19 and then form an interactive computer program so that the user at a prompt is asked to insert an angle α in radians for which the program will deliver the correct values of F_1, F_2, and β.

2.21. Two soccer players approach a stationary ball 10 ft away from the goal. Simultaneously, a player on team O (offense) kicks the ball with force 100 lb for a split second while a player on team D (defense) kicks with force 70 lb during the same time interval. Does the offense score (assuming that the goalie is asleep)?

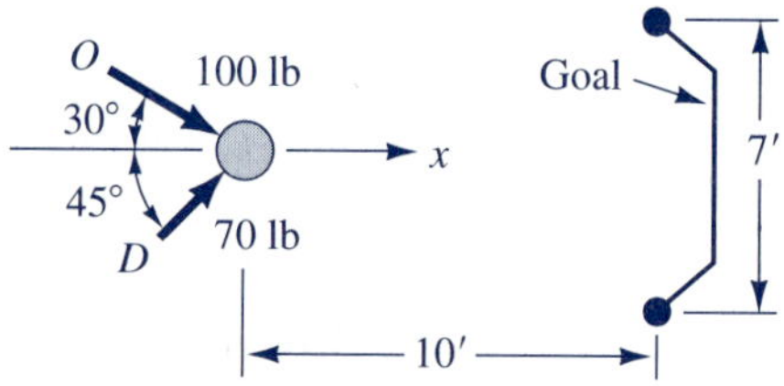

Figure P.2.21

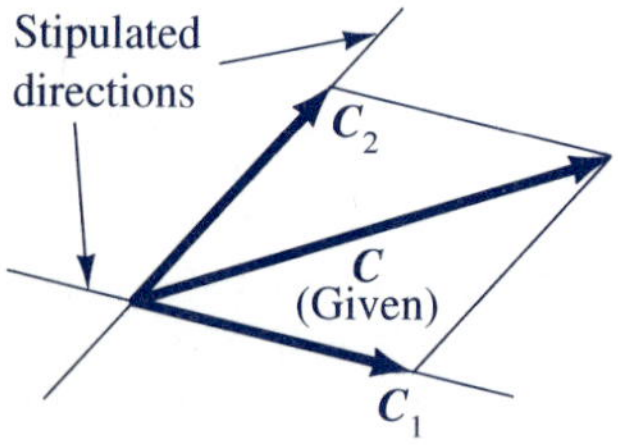

Figure 2.9. Two-dimensional resolution of vector $\boldsymbol{C}$.

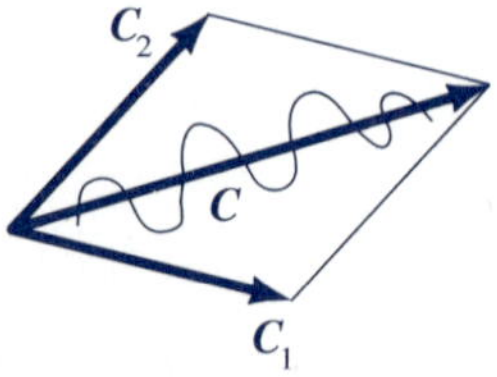

Figure 2.10. Vector $\boldsymbol{C}$ is replaced by its components and is no longer operative.

2.4 Resolution of Vectors; Scalar Components

The opposite action of addition of vectors is called *resolution*. Thus, for a given vector $\boldsymbol{C}$, we may find a pair of vectors in any two stipulated directions coplanar with $\boldsymbol{C}$ such that the two vectors, called *components*, sum to the original vector. This is a *two-dimensional* resolution involving two component vectors *coplanar* with the original vector. We shall discuss three-dimensional resolution involving three noncoplanar component vectors later in the section. The two-dimensional resolution can be accomplished by graphical construction of the parallelogram, or by using simple helpful sketches and then employing trigonometric relations. An example of two-dimensional resolution is shown in Fig. 2.9. The two vectors $\boldsymbol{C}_1$ and $\boldsymbol{C}_2$ formed in this way are the *component* vectors. We often replace a vector by its components since the components are always equivalent in rigid-body mechanics to the original vector. When this is done, it is often helpful to indicate that the original vector is no longer operative by drawing a wavy line through the original vector as shown in Fig. 2.10.

Example 2.3

A sailboat cannot go directly into the wind, but must *tack* from side to side as shown in Fig. 2.11 wherein a sailboat is going from marker A to marker $\boldsymbol{B}$ 5,000 meters apart. What is the additional distance ΔL beyond 5,000 m that the sailboat must travel to get from A to B?

Clearly the displacement vector[4] $\boldsymbol{\rho}_{AB}$ is equivalent to the vector sum of displacement vectors $\boldsymbol{\rho}_{AC}$ plus $\boldsymbol{\rho}_{CB}$ in that the same starting points $\boldsymbol{A}$, and the same destination points B, are involved in each case. Thus, vectors $\boldsymbol{\rho}_{AC}$ and $\boldsymbol{\rho}_{CB}$ are two-dimensional components of vector $\boldsymbol{\rho}_{AB}$. Accordingly, we can show a parallelogram for those vectors for which triangle ABC forms half of the parallelogram (see Fig. 2.12). We leave it for you to justify the various angles indicated in the diagram. Now we first use the *law of sines*.

$$\frac{AC}{\sin\beta} = \frac{5,000}{\sin\alpha}$$

$$\therefore\ AC = \frac{5,000 \sin 20°}{\sin 135°} = 2,418.4 \text{ m}$$

And

$$\frac{BC}{\sin\gamma} = \frac{5,000}{\sin\alpha}$$

$$\therefore\ BC = \frac{5,000 \sin 25°}{\sin 135°} = 2,988.4 \text{ m}$$

Hence the increase in distance ΔL is

$$\Delta L = (2,418.4 + 2,988.4) - 5,000 = \boxed{406.8 \text{ m}}$$

[4]A *displacement vector*, we remind you, connects two points A and B in space and is often denoted as $\boldsymbol{\rho}_{AB}$. The order of the subscripts gives the sense of the vector—here going from A to B.

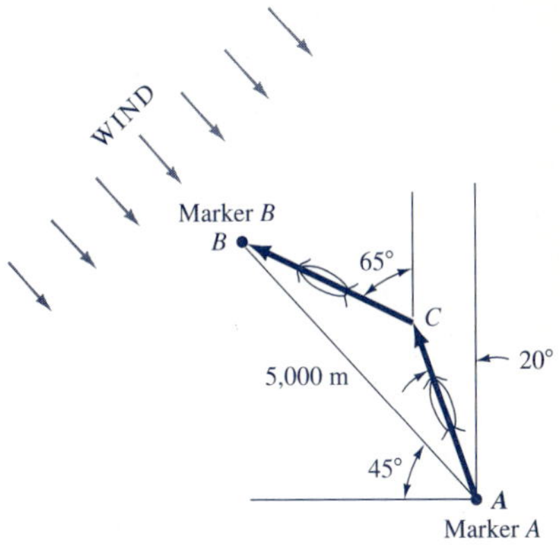

Figure 2.11. Sailboat tacking.

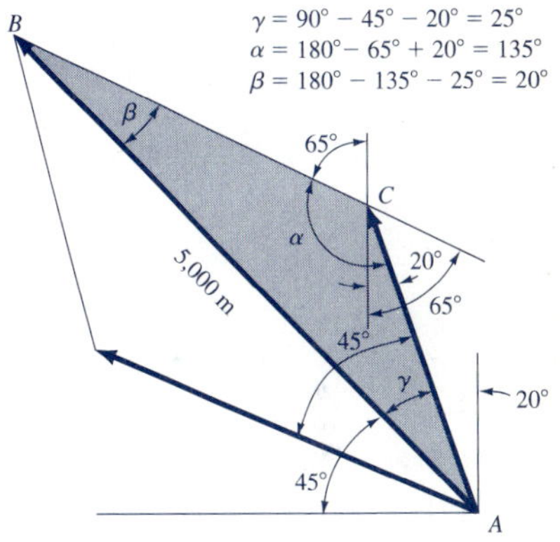

Figure 2.12. Enlarged parallelogram.

It is also readily possible to find *three* components *not in the same plane as* $\boldsymbol{C}$ that add up to $\boldsymbol{C}$. This is the aforementioned three-dimensional resolution. Consider the specification of three *orthogonal* directions[5] for the resolution of $\boldsymbol{C}$ positioned in the first quadrant, as is shown in Fig. 2.13. The resolution may be accomplished in two steps. Resolve $\boldsymbol{C}$ along the z direction, and along the

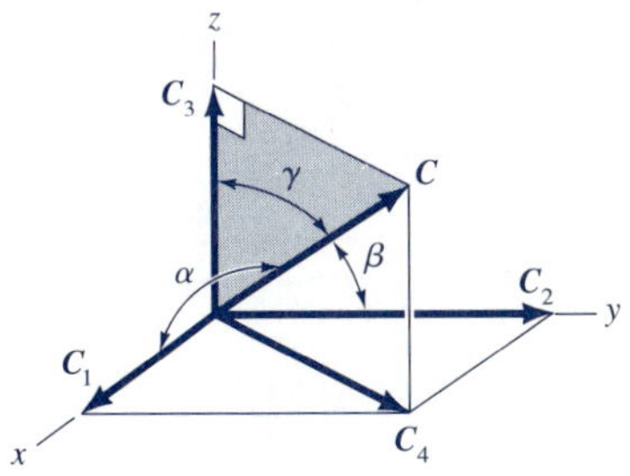

Figure 2.13. Orthogonal or rectangular components.

[5]Although the vector can be resolved along three *skew* directions (hence nonorthogonal), the orthogonal directions are used most often in engineering practice.

intersection of the xy plane and the plane formed by $\boldsymbol{C}$ and the z axis. This is a two-dimensional resolution with the parallelogram becoming a rectangle because of the normalcy of the z axis to the xy plane. This gives orthogonal vectors $\boldsymbol{C}_3$ and $\boldsymbol{C}_4$ that replace original vector $\boldsymbol{C}$. Next take vector $\boldsymbol{C}_4$ and resolve it along axes x and y by a second two-dimensional resolution involving a rectangle once again thus forming orthogonal vectors $\boldsymbol{C}_1$ and $\boldsymbol{C}_2$ that may replace vector $\boldsymbol{C}_4$. Clearly orthogonal vectors $\boldsymbol{C}_1$, $\boldsymbol{C}_2$, and $\boldsymbol{C}_3$ add up to $\boldsymbol{C}$ and accordingly can replace $\boldsymbol{C}$ under any and all circumstances. Hence $\boldsymbol{C}_1$, $\boldsymbol{C}_2$, and $\boldsymbol{C}_3$ are called *orthogonal* or *rectangular component vectors* of vector $\boldsymbol{C}$.

The direction of a vector $\boldsymbol{C}$ relative to an orthogonal reference is given by the cosines of the angles formed by the vector and the respective coordinate axes. These are called *direction cosines* and are denoted as

$$\begin{aligned} \cos(\boldsymbol{C}, x) &= \cos\alpha \equiv l \\ \cos(\boldsymbol{C}, y) &= \cos\beta \equiv m \\ \cos(\boldsymbol{C}, z) &= \cos\gamma \equiv n \end{aligned} \tag{2.2}$$

where α, β, and γ are associated with the x, y, and z axes, respectively. Now let us consider the right triangle, whose sides are $\boldsymbol{C}$ and the component vector, $\boldsymbol{C}_3$, shown shaded in Fig. 2.13. It then becomes clear, from trigonometric considerations of the right triangle, that for the first quadrant

$$|\boldsymbol{C}_3| = |\boldsymbol{C}| \cos\gamma = |\boldsymbol{C}|\, n \tag{2.3}$$

If we had decided to resolve $\boldsymbol{C}$ first in the y direction instead of the z direction, we would have produced a geometry from which we could conclude that $|\boldsymbol{C}_2| = |\boldsymbol{C}|m$. Similarly, we can say that $|\boldsymbol{C}_1| = |\boldsymbol{C}|l$. We can then express $|\boldsymbol{C}|$ in terms of its orthogonal components in the following manner, using the Pythagorean theorem.[6]

$$|\boldsymbol{C}| = \left[(|\boldsymbol{C}|l)^2 + (|\boldsymbol{C}|m)^2 + (|\boldsymbol{C}|n)^2\right]^{1/2} \tag{2.4}$$

From this equation we can define the *orthogonal* or *rectangular scalar components* of the vector $\boldsymbol{C}$ having *any* orientation as

$$C_x = |\boldsymbol{C}|l, \qquad C_y = |\boldsymbol{C}|m, \qquad C_z = |\boldsymbol{C}|n \tag{2.5}$$

Note that C_x, C_y, and C_z may be negative, depending on the sign of the direction cosines. Finally, it must be pointed out that *although C_x, C_y, and C_z are associated with certain axes and hence certain directions, they have been developed as scalars and must be handled as scalars.* Thus, an equation such as $10\boldsymbol{V} = V_x \cos\beta$ is not correct, because the left side is a vector and the right side is a scalar. This should spur you to observe care in your notation.

Sometimes only *one* of the scalar orthogonal components of a vector (often called a rectangular scalar component) is desired. Then, just one direction is prescribed, as shown in Fig. 2.14. Thus, the scalar rectangular component C_s is $|\boldsymbol{C}| \cos\delta$. Note we have shown a pair of other rectangular

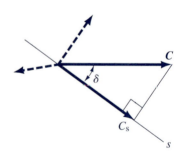

Figure 2.14. Rectangular component of ***C***.

[6]From Eq. 2.4 one readily can conclude that $l^2 + m^2 + n^2 = 1$, which is a well-known geometric relation.

components as dashed vectors in Fig. 2.14. However, it is only the single component C_s that we often use, disregarding other rectangular components. It is always the case that the triangle formed by the vector and its scalar rectangular component is a right triangle. In establishing C_s we therefore speak of "dropping a perpendicular from **C** to *s*" or of "projecting along *s*."

The scalar rectangular component C_s could also be the result of a *two-dimensional* orthogonal resolution wherein the other component is in the plane of **C** and C_s and is *normal* to C_s. It is important to remember, however, that a component of a *nonorthogonal* two-dimensional resolution is *not* a rectangular component.

As a final consideration, let us examine vectors **A** and **B**, which, along with direction *s*, form a plane as is shown in Fig. 2.15. The sum of the vectors **A** and **B** is found by the parallelogram law to be **C**. We shall now show that the projection of **C** along *s* is the same as the sum of the projections of the two-dimensional components of **A** and **B**, taken along *s*. That is,

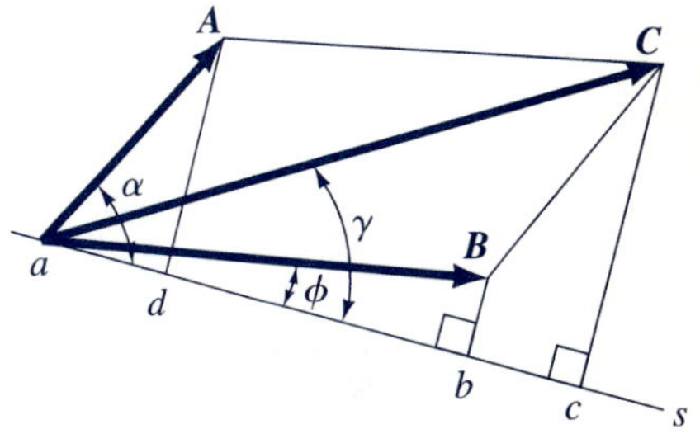

Figure 2.15. $C_s = A_s + B_s$.

$$C_s = A_s + B_s$$

On the diagram, then, the following relation must be verified:

$$ac = ad + ab \tag{a}$$

But

$$ac = ab + bc \tag{b}$$

Also, it is clear that

$$ad = bc \tag{c}$$

By substituting from Eqs. (b) and (c) into Eq. (a), we reduce Eq. (a) to an identity which shows that the projection of the sum of two vectors is the same as the sum of the projections of the two vectors.

2.5 Unit Vectors

It is sometimes convenient to express a vector **C** as the product of its magnitude and a vector **a** of unit magnitude and having direction corresponding to the vector **C**. The vector **a** is called a *unit vector*. The unit vector is also at times denoted as $\hat{\boldsymbol{a}}$. (You will write it as $\hat{a}$.) It has no dimensions. We formulate this vector as follows:

$$\boldsymbol{a}(\text{unit vector in direction } \boldsymbol{C}) = \frac{\boldsymbol{C}}{|\boldsymbol{C}|} \tag{2.6}$$

Clearly, this development fulfills the requirements that have been set forth for this vector. We can then express the vector **C** in the form

$$\boldsymbol{C} = |\boldsymbol{C}|\boldsymbol{a} \tag{2.7}$$

The unit vector, once established, does not have, per se, an inherent line of action. This will be determined entirely by its use. In the preceding equation,

Figure 2.16. Unit vector ***a***.

the unit vector ***a*** might be considered collinear with the vector ***C***. However, we can represent the vector ***D***, shown in Fig. 2.16 parallel to ***C***, by using the unit vector ***a*** as follows:

$$\boldsymbol{D} = |\boldsymbol{D}|\boldsymbol{a} \tag{2.7a}$$

It thus acts as a free vector. Occasionally, it is useful to label a unit vector meant to have the line of action of a certain vector with the lowercase letter of the capital letter associated with that vector. Thus, in Eqs. 2.7 and 2.7(a) for this purpose we might have employed in the place of ***a*** the letters ***c*** and ***d*** (in your case $\hat{c}$ and $\hat{d}$), respectively. Next, if a given vector is represented using a lowercase letter, such as the vector ***r***, then we often make use of the circumflex mark to indicate the associated unit vector. Thus,

$$\boldsymbol{r} = |\boldsymbol{r}|\hat{\boldsymbol{r}} \tag{2.7b}$$

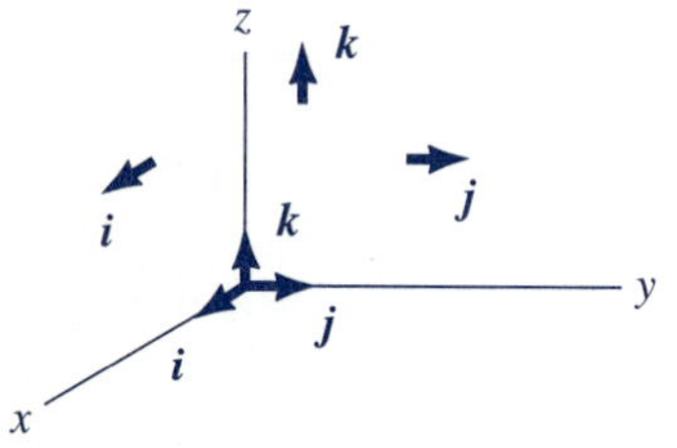

Figure 2.17. Unit vectors for *xyz* axes.

Unit vectors that are of particular use are those directed along the directions of coordinate axes of a rectangular reference, where ***i***, ***j***, and ***k*** (your instructor will probably use the notation $\hat{\imath}$, $\hat{\jmath}$, and $\hat{k}$) correspond to the *x*, *y*, and *z* directions, as shown in Fig. 2.17.[7]

Since the sum of a set of concurrent vectors is equivalent in all situations to the original vector, we can always replace the vector ***C*** by its rectangular scalar components in the following manner:

$$\boldsymbol{C} = C_x\boldsymbol{i} + C_y\boldsymbol{j} + C_z\boldsymbol{k} \tag{2.8}$$

In Chapter 1, we saw that vectors that are equal have the same magnitude and direction. Hence, if ***A*** = ***B***, we can say that

$$A_x\boldsymbol{i} + A_y\boldsymbol{j} + A_z\boldsymbol{k} = B_x\boldsymbol{i} + B_y\boldsymbol{j} + B_z\boldsymbol{k} \tag{2.9}$$

Then, since the unit vectors have mutually different directions, we conclude from above that

$$A_x\boldsymbol{i} = B_x\boldsymbol{i}$$
$$A_y\boldsymbol{j} = B_y\boldsymbol{j}$$
$$A_z\boldsymbol{k} = B_z\boldsymbol{k}$$

It then follows that

$$A_x = B_x$$
$$A_y = B_y$$
$$A_z = B_z$$

[7]Curvilinear coordinate systems have associated sets of unit vectors just as do the rectangular coordinate systems. As will be seen later, however, certain of these unit vectors do not all have fixed directions in space for a given reference as do the vectors ***i***, ***j***, and ***k***.

Hence, the vector equation, $\boldsymbol{A} = \boldsymbol{B}$, has resulted in three scalar equations that in totality are equivalent in every way to the vector statement of equality. Thus, in Newton's law we would have

$$\boldsymbol{F} = m\boldsymbol{a} \tag{2.10a}$$

as the vector equation, and

$$F_x = ma_x, \quad F_y = ma_y, \quad F_z = ma_z \tag{2.10b}$$

as the corresponding scalar equations.

2.6 Useful Ways of Representing Vectors

Quite often, we show a rectangular parallelepiped with sides oriented parallel to the coordinate axes and positioned somewhere along the line of action of a vector (see Fig. 2.18) such that this line of action coincides with an inside diagonal of the rectangular parallelepiped. The purpose of this rectangular parallelepiped and diagonal is to allow for the easy determination of the orientation of the line of action and hence the orientation of a vector. AB in the diagram is such a diagonal used for the determination of the line of action of vector $\boldsymbol{F}$. Numbers for this purpose are shown along the sides of the rectangular parallelepiped without units. *Any* set of numbers can be used as long as the *ratios* of these numbers remain the ones required for the proper determination of the orientation of the vector. That determination proceeds by first replacing the *displacement vector* $\boldsymbol{\rho}_{AB}$ from corner A to corner B by a set of three vector displacements going from A to B along the sides of the rectangular parallelepiped. We thereby can replace the vector $\boldsymbol{\rho}_{AB}$ by the sum of its rectangular components. Thus, for the case shown in Fig. 2.18 we can say[8]

$$\boldsymbol{\rho}_{AB} = 10\boldsymbol{j} - 4\boldsymbol{i} + 6\boldsymbol{k} = -4\boldsymbol{i} + 10\boldsymbol{j} + 6\boldsymbol{k}$$

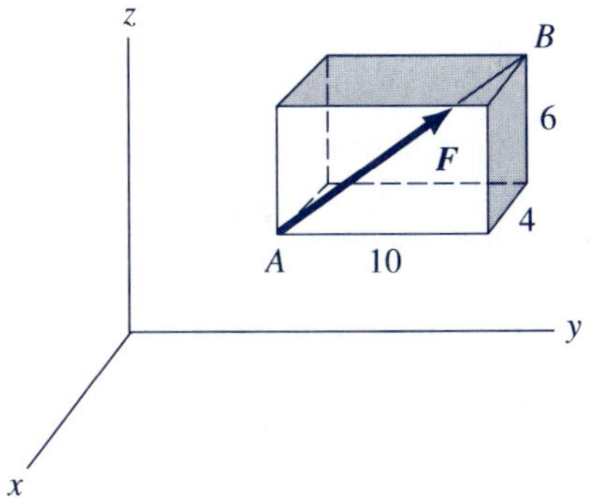

Figure 2.18. Rectangular parallelepiped used for specifying the direction of a vector.

[8]Imagine you are "walking" from A to B but restricting your movements to be along the coordinate directions. This movement is equivalent to going directly from A to B in that the same endpoints result.

Now using the Pythagorean theorem, divide $\boldsymbol{\rho}_{AB}$ by its magnitude, namely: $\sqrt{4^2 + 10^2 + 6^2}$. We thus form the unit vector $\hat{\boldsymbol{\rho}}_{AB}$. That is,

$$\hat{\boldsymbol{\rho}}_{AB} = \frac{\boldsymbol{\rho}_{AB}}{|\boldsymbol{\rho}_{AB}|} = \frac{-4\boldsymbol{i} + 10\boldsymbol{j} + 6\boldsymbol{k}}{\sqrt{4^2 + 10^2 + 6^2}} = -.3244\boldsymbol{i} + .8111\boldsymbol{j} + .4867\boldsymbol{k}$$

As a final step we can give vector $\boldsymbol{F}$ as follows:

$$\boldsymbol{F} = F(-.3244\boldsymbol{i} + .8111\boldsymbol{j} + .4867\boldsymbol{k})$$

If $F = 100$ N we then can say:

$$\boldsymbol{F} = -32.44\boldsymbol{i} + 81.11\boldsymbol{j} + 48.67\boldsymbol{k} \text{ N}$$

Note that the rectangular parallelepiped can be anywhere along the line of action of $\boldsymbol{F}$ including cases where $\boldsymbol{F}$ is not inside of the parallelepiped or extends beyond the parallelepiped (see Fig. 2.19). In the two-dimensional case, a right triangle serves the same purpose as the rectangular parallelepiped in three dimensions. This is shown in Fig. 2.20 where vector $\boldsymbol{V}$ is in the xy plane. Here we can say,

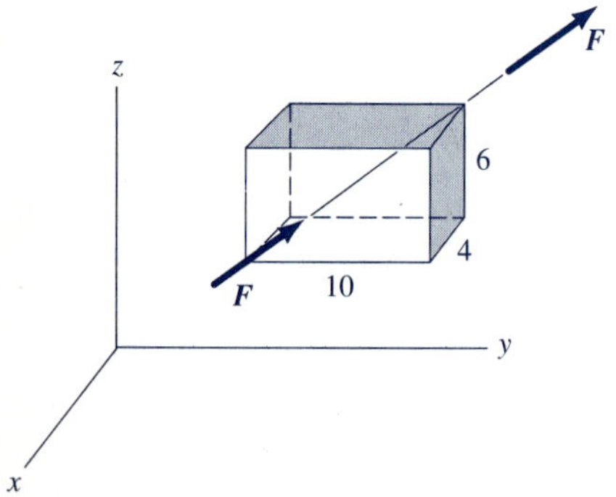

Figure 2.19. Other ways to use the rectangular parallelepiped.

$$\boldsymbol{V} = V\left[\frac{9}{\sqrt{2^2 + 9^2}}\boldsymbol{i} + \frac{2}{\sqrt{2^2 + 9^2}}\boldsymbol{j}\right] = V(.9762\boldsymbol{i} + .2169\boldsymbol{j})$$

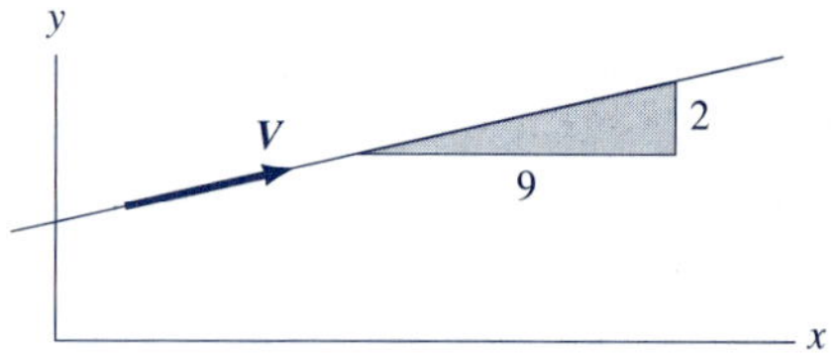

Figure 2.20. Right triangle used for specifying the direction of a vector in two dimensions.

There are times when the rectangular parallelpiped is not shown explicitly. However, the length of the sides of one having the proper diagonal may be available so that the replacement of the diagonal displacement vector into rectangular components can be readily achieved. The simplest procedure is to mentally move from the beginning point of the diagonal to the final point always moving along coordinate directions, or, in other words, always moving along the sides of the hypothetical rectangular parallelepiped. Thus, in Fig. 2.21, for the vector $\boldsymbol{F}_1$ we can consider AB to be the diagonal and in going from A to B we could first move in the minus x direction by an amount -1, then move in the plus y direction by the amount 1.5, and finally in the z direction by an amount 3. This would take us from initial point A to final point B. The corresponding displacement vector would then be

$$\boldsymbol{\rho}_{AB} = -1\boldsymbol{i} + 1.5\boldsymbol{j} + 3\boldsymbol{j}$$

The following example will illustrate the use of orthogonal resolution as well as the use of rectangular components of vectors.

Example 2.4

A crane (not shown) is supporting a 2,000-N crate (see Fig. 2.21) through three cables: *AB*, *CB*, and *DB*. Note that *D* is at the center of the outer edge of the crate; *C* is 1.6 m from the corner of this edge; and *B* is directly above the center of the crate. What are the forces F_1, F_2, and F_3 transmitted by the cables?

We will soon learn formally what our common sense tells us, namely that the vector sum of force F_1, force F_2, and force F_3 must equal 2,000$\boldsymbol{k}$ N. We first express these three forces in terms of rectangular components. Thus,

$$\boldsymbol{F}_{AB} = F_1\left(\frac{\boldsymbol{\rho}_{AB}}{|\boldsymbol{\rho}_{AB}|}\right) = F_1\left[\frac{-1\boldsymbol{i} + 1.5\boldsymbol{j} + 3\boldsymbol{k}}{\sqrt{1^2 + 1.5^2 + 3^2}}\right]$$
$$= F_1(-.2857\boldsymbol{i} + .4286\boldsymbol{j} + .8571\boldsymbol{k})\text{ N}$$

$$\boldsymbol{F}_{DB} = F_2\left(\frac{\boldsymbol{\rho}_{DB}}{|\boldsymbol{\rho}_{DB}|}\right) = F_2\left[\frac{1\boldsymbol{i} + 0\boldsymbol{j} + 3\boldsymbol{k}}{\sqrt{1^2 + 3^2}}\right] = F_2(.3162\boldsymbol{i} + .9487\boldsymbol{k})\text{ N}$$

$$\boldsymbol{F}_{CB} = F_3\left(\frac{\boldsymbol{\rho}_{CB}}{|\boldsymbol{\rho}_{CB}|}\right) = F_3\left[\frac{-.6\boldsymbol{i} - 1.5\boldsymbol{j} + 3\boldsymbol{k}}{\sqrt{.6^2 + 1.5^2 + 3^2}}\right]$$
$$= F_3(-.1761\boldsymbol{i} - .4402\boldsymbol{j} + .8805\boldsymbol{k})\text{ N}$$

We now sum the three forces to equal 2,000$\boldsymbol{k}$ N.

$$F_1(-.2857\boldsymbol{i} + .4286\boldsymbol{j} + .8571\boldsymbol{k}) + F_2(.3162\boldsymbol{i} + .9487\boldsymbol{k})$$
$$+ F_3(-.1761\boldsymbol{i} - .4402\boldsymbol{j} + .8805\boldsymbol{k}) = 2{,}000\boldsymbol{k}$$

We have three scalar equations from the previous equation.

$$-.2857\,F_1 + .3162\,F_2 - .1761\,F_3 = 0$$
$$.4286\,F_1 + 0 - .4402\,F_3 = 0$$
$$.8571\,F_1 + .9487\,F_2 + .8805\,F_3 = 2{,}000$$

Solving simultaneously, we get the following results:

$$F_1 = 648.1\text{ N}$$
$$F_2 = 937.1\text{ N}$$
$$F_3 = 631.1\text{ N}$$

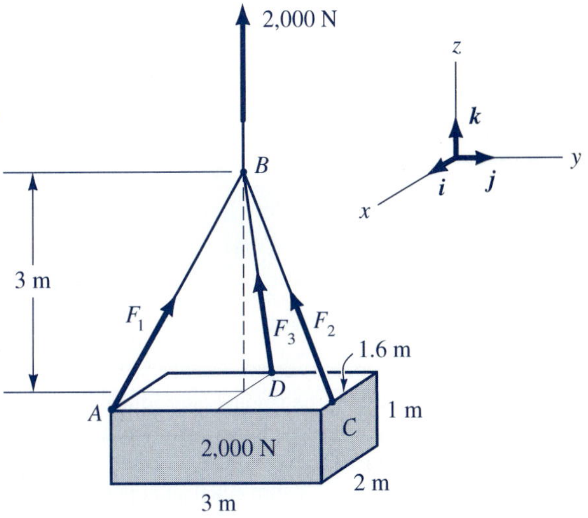

Figure 2.21. A crate is supported by three forces.

PROBLEMS

2.22. Resolve the 100-lb force into a set of components along the slot shown and in the vertical direction.

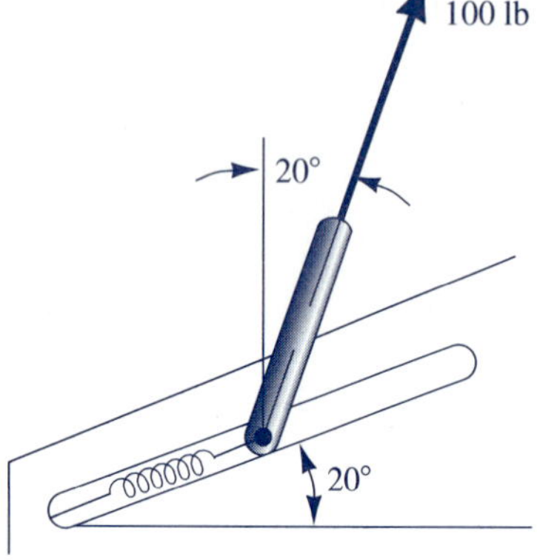

Figure P.2.22

2.23. A farmer needs to build a fence from the corner of his barn to the corner of his chicken house 30 m away in the NE direction. However, he wants to enclose as much of the barnyard as possible. Thus, he runs the fence east, from the corner of his barn to the property line and then NNE to the corner of his chicken house. How long is the fence?

2.24. Resolve the force $\boldsymbol{F}$ into a component perpendicular to AB and a component parallel to BC.

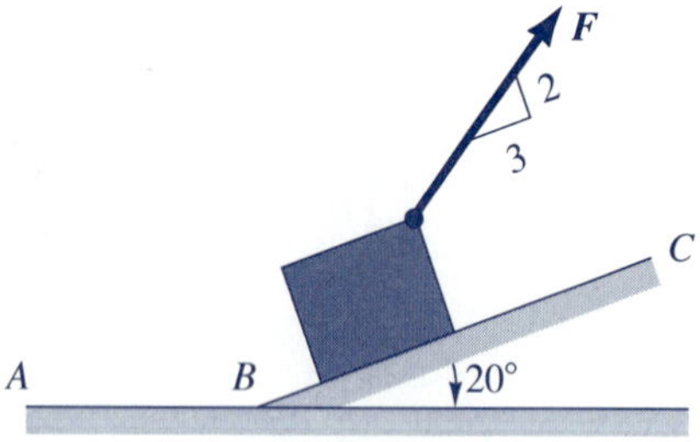

Figure P.2.24

2.25. A simple truss (to be studied later in detail) supports two forces. If the forces in the members are colinear with the members, what are the forces in the members? *Hint:* The forces in the members must have a vector sum equal and opposite to the vector sum of F_1 and F_2. The entire system is coplanar.

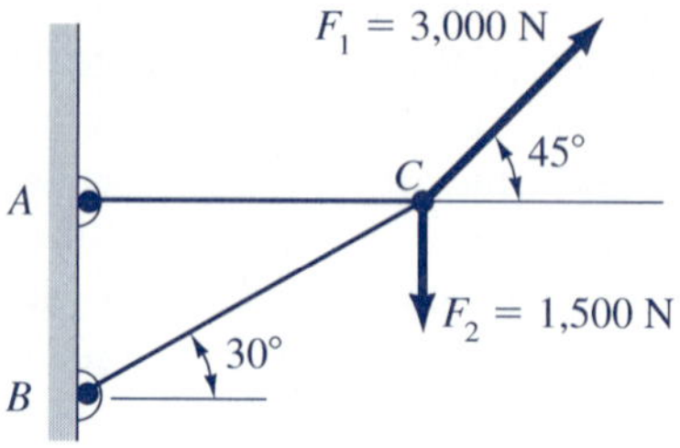

Figure P.2.25

2.26. Two tugboats are maneuvering an ocean liner. The desired total force is 3,000 lb at an angle of 15° as shown in the diagram. If the tugboat forces have directions as shown, what must the forces F_1 and F_2 be?

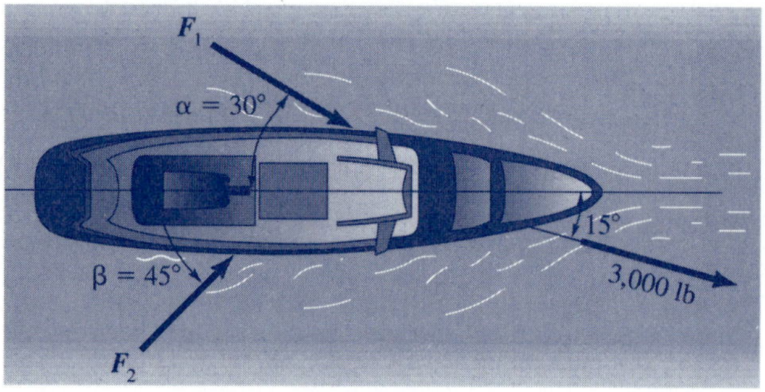

Figure P.2.26

2.27. In the previous problem, if $F_2 = 1{,}000$ lb and $\beta = 40°$, what should F_1 and α be so that $\boldsymbol{F}_1 + \boldsymbol{F}_2$ yields the indicated 3,000-lb force?

2.28. A 1,000-N force is resolved into components along AB and AC. If the component along AB is 700 N, determine the angle α and the value of the component along AC.

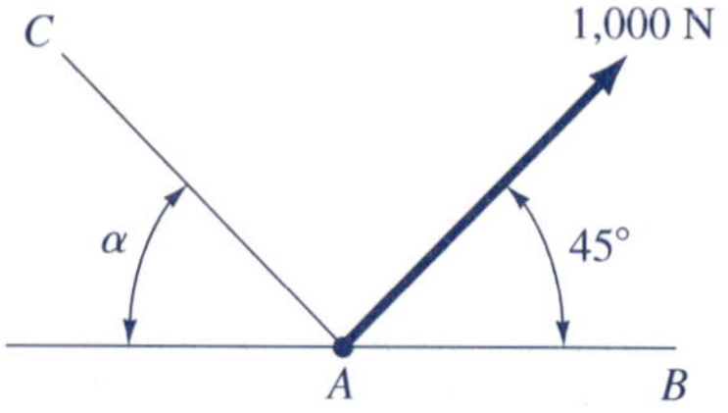

Figure P.2.28

2.29. Two men are trying to pull a crate which will not move until a 150-lb total force is applied in any one direction. Man *A* can pull only at 45° to the desired direction of crate motion, whereas man *B* can pull only at 60° to the desired motion. What force must each man exert to start the box moving as shown?

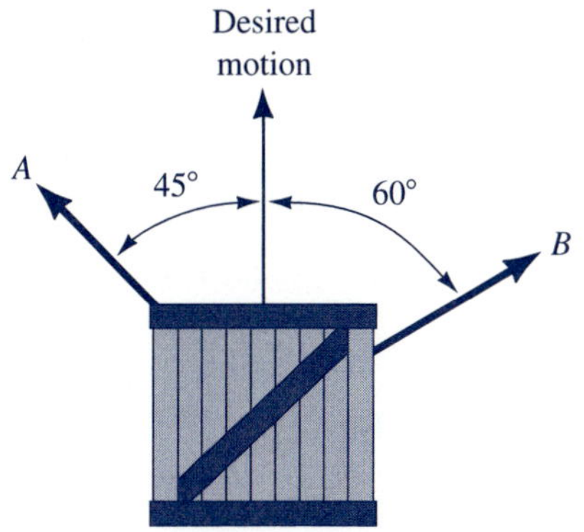

Figure P.2.29

2.30. What is the sum of the three forces? The 2,000-N force is in the *yz* plane.

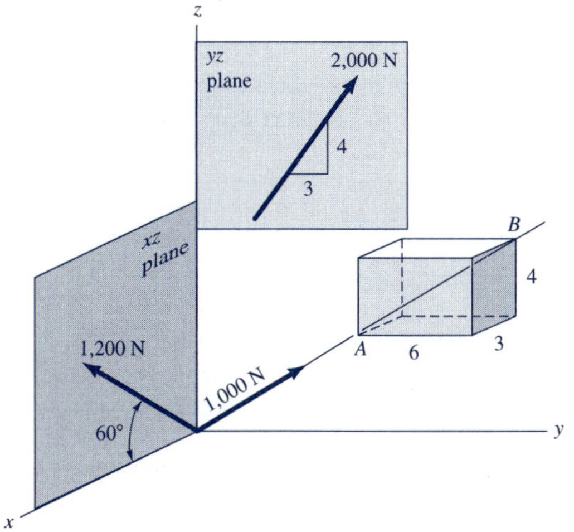

Figure P.2.30

2.31. The 500-N force is to be resolved into components along the *AC* and *AB* directions in the *xy* plane measured by the angles α and β. If the component along *AC* is to be 1,000 N and the component along *AB* is to be 800 N, compute α and β.

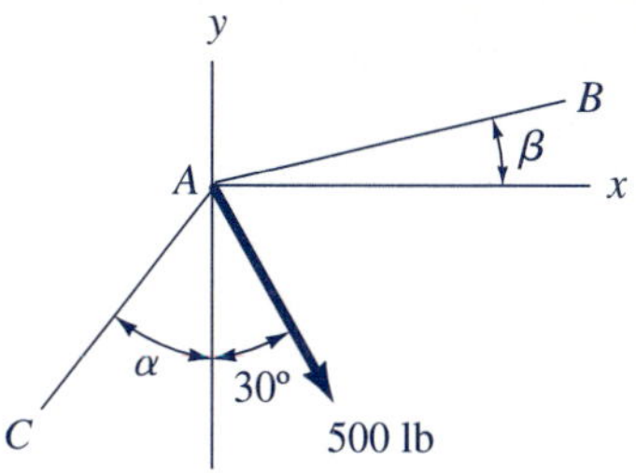

Figure P.2.31

2.32. The orthogonal components of a force are:
x component 10 lb in positive *x* direction
y component 20 lb in positive *y* direction
z component 30 lb in negative *z* direction
(a) What is the magnitude of the force itself?
(b) What are the direction cosines of the force?

2.33. What are the rectangular components of the 100-lb force? What are the direction cosines for this force?

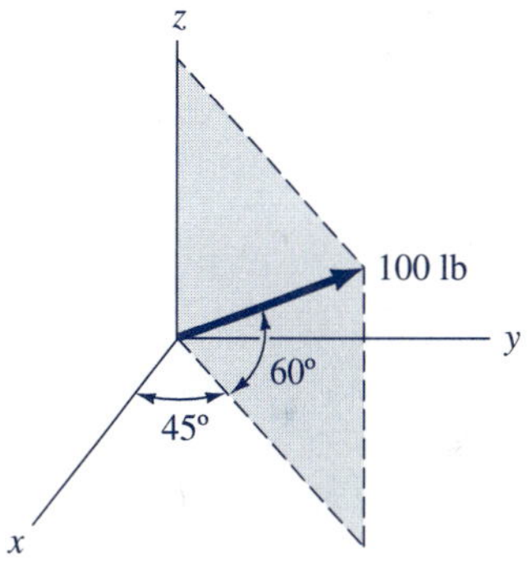

Figure P.2.33

2.34. The 1,000-N force is parallel to the displacement vector $\vec{OA}$ while the 2,000-N force is parallel to the displacement vector $\vec{CB}$. What is the vector sum of these forces?

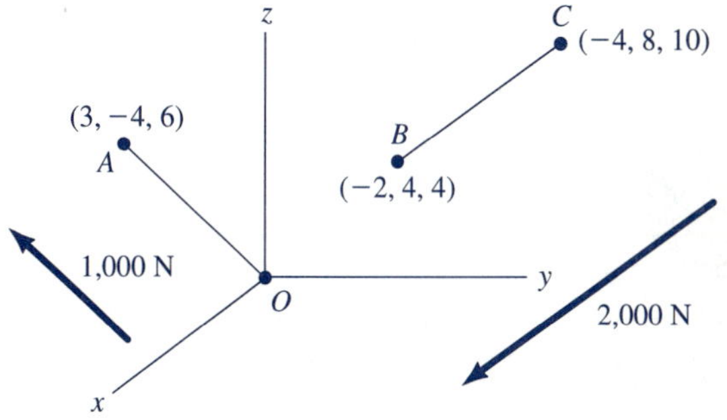

Figure P.2.34

2.35. A 50-m-long diagonal member OE in a space frame is inclined at $\alpha = 70°$ and $\beta = 30°$ to the x and y axes, respectively. What is γ? How long must members OA, AC, OB, BC, and CE be to support end E of OE?

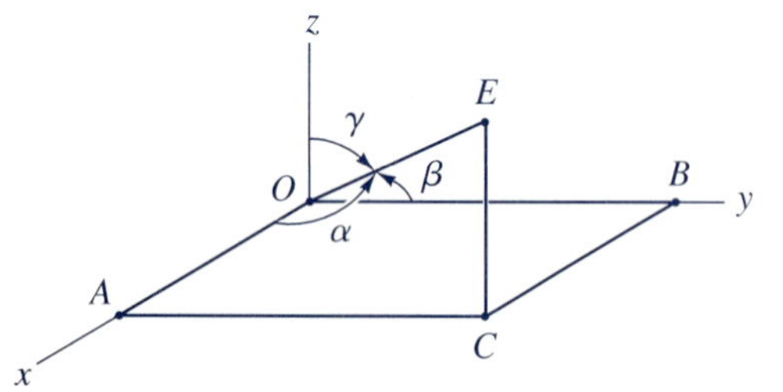

Figure P.2.35

2.36. What is the orthogonal total force component in the x direction of the force transmitted to pin A of a roof truss by the four members? What is the total component in the y direction?

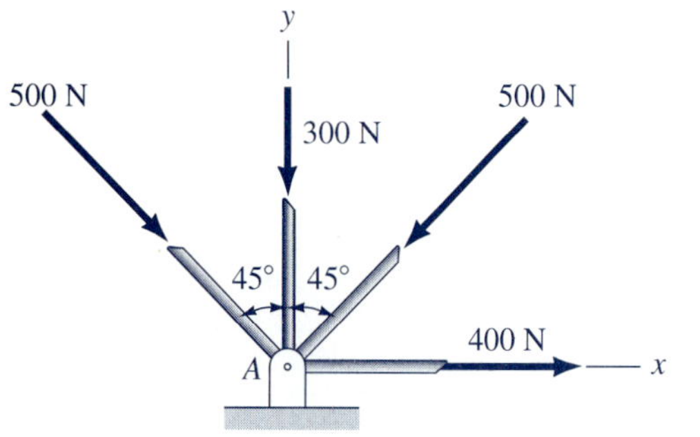

Figure P.2.36

2.37. A 30-ton light tank is being lowered from a ship using two cables AB and BC. What are the forces in these cables? Use a parallelogram sketch. Also, do this problem using rectangular components.

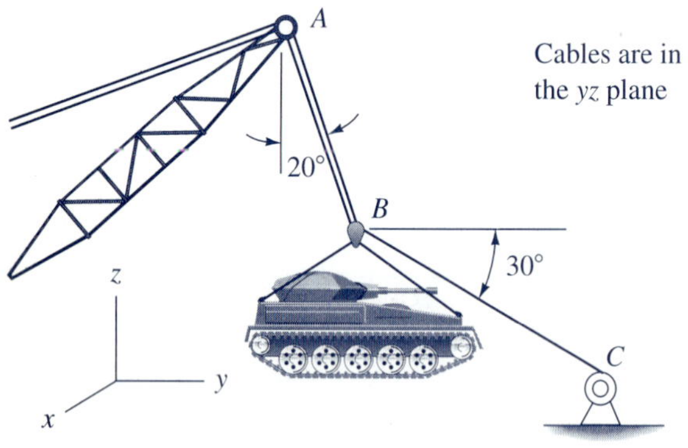

Figure P.2.37

2.38. Suppose two points A and B in space are designated and a velocity vector $\boldsymbol{V}$ is colinear with the line of action of the displacement vector $\boldsymbol{\rho}_{AB}$ as has been shown. Express $\boldsymbol{V}$ in terms of its rectangular components.

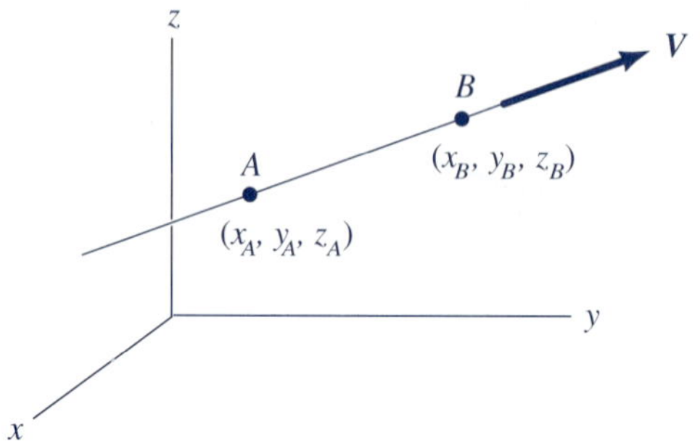

Figure P.2.38

2.39. Given the following force expressed as a function of position:

$$\boldsymbol{F} = (10x - 6)\boldsymbol{i} + x^2z\boldsymbol{j} + xy\boldsymbol{k}$$

What are the direction cosines of the force at position (1, 2, 2)? What is the position along the x coordinate where $F_x = 0$? Plot F_y versus the x coordinate for an elevation $z = 1$.

2.40. What is the sum of the following set of three vectors?

$\boldsymbol{A} = 6\boldsymbol{i} + 10\boldsymbol{j} + 16\boldsymbol{k}$ lb

$\boldsymbol{B} = 2\boldsymbol{i} - 3\boldsymbol{j}$ lb

$\boldsymbol{C}$ is a vector in the xy plane at an inclination of 45° to the positive x axis and directed away from the origin; it has a magnitude of 25 lb.

2.41. What is the unit vector for the displacement vector from point (2, 1, 9) to point (7, 4, 2)? Express a 10-m displacement vector in the same direction in terms of $\boldsymbol{i}, \boldsymbol{j}$, and $\boldsymbol{k}$.

2.42. A vector $\boldsymbol{A}$ has a line of action that goes through the coordinates (0, 2, 3) and (−1, 2, 4). If the magnitude of this vector is 10 units, express the vector in terms of the unit vectors $\boldsymbol{i}, \boldsymbol{j}$, and $\boldsymbol{k}$.

2.43. Express the force $\boldsymbol{F}$ in terms of the unit vectors $\boldsymbol{i}, \boldsymbol{j}$, and $\boldsymbol{k}$.

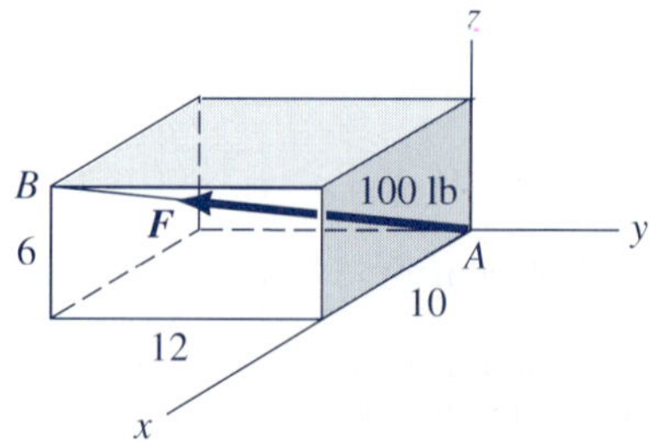

Figure P.2.43

2.44. Express the 100-N force in terms of the unit vectors $\boldsymbol{i}, \boldsymbol{j}$, and $\boldsymbol{k}$. What is the unit vector in the direction of the 100-N force? The force lies along diagonal *AB*.

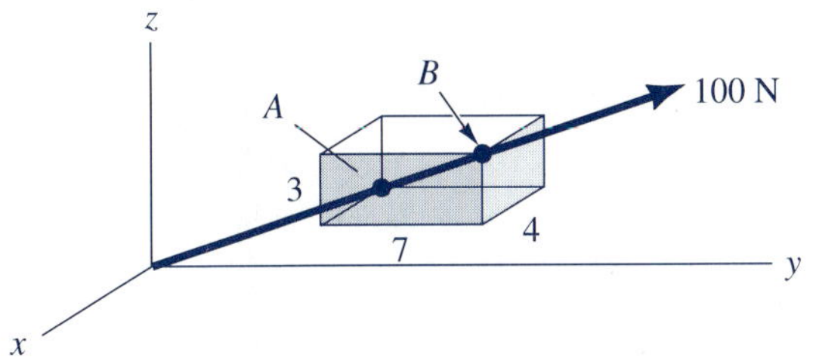

Figure P.2.44

2.45. Express the unit vectors $\boldsymbol{i}, \boldsymbol{j}$, and $\boldsymbol{k}$ in terms of unit vectors $\boldsymbol{\epsilon}_{\bar{r}}$, $\boldsymbol{\epsilon}_\theta$, and $\boldsymbol{\epsilon}_z$. (These are unit vectors for *cylindrical coordinates*.) Express the 1,000-lb force going through the origin and through point (2, 4, 4) in terms of the unit vectors $\boldsymbol{i}, \boldsymbol{j}, \boldsymbol{k}$ and $\boldsymbol{\epsilon}_{\bar{r}}$, $\boldsymbol{\epsilon}_\theta$, $\boldsymbol{\epsilon}_z$ with $\theta = 60°$. (See the footnote on p. 34.)

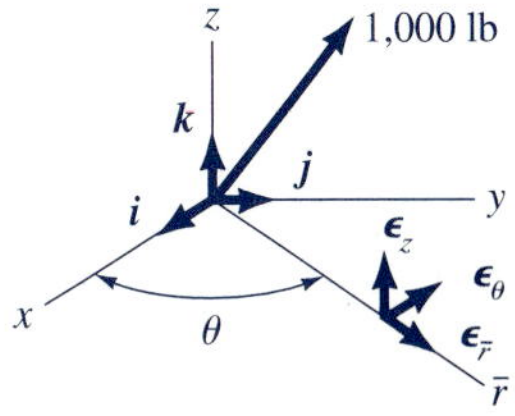

Figure P.2.45

2.7 Scalar or Dot Product of Two Vectors

In elementary physics, work was defined as the product of the force component, in the direction of a displacement, times the displacement. In effect, two vectors, force and displacement, are employed to give a scalar, work. In other physical problems, vectors are associated in this same manner so as to result in a scalar quantity. A vector operation that represents such operations concisely is the scalar product (or dot product), which, for the vector $\boldsymbol{A}$ and $\boldsymbol{B}$ in Fig. 2.22, is defined as[9]

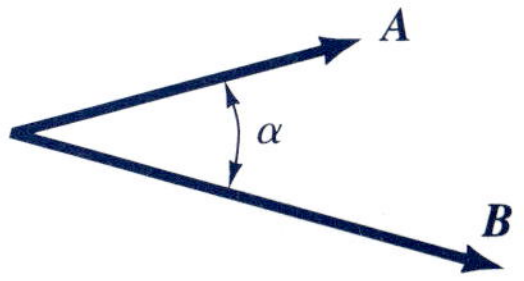

Figure 2.22. α is smallest angle between $\boldsymbol{A}$ and $\boldsymbol{B}$.

$$\boldsymbol{A} \cdot \boldsymbol{B} = |\boldsymbol{A}|\,|\boldsymbol{B}| \cos \alpha \tag{2.11}$$

where α is the smaller angle between the two vectors. Note that the dot product may involve vectors of different dimensional representation, and may be positive or negative, depending on whether the smaller included angle α is less than or greater than 90°. Note also that $\boldsymbol{A} \cdot \boldsymbol{B}$ is equivalent to first projecting vector $\boldsymbol{A}$ onto the line of action of vector $\boldsymbol{B}$ (this gives us $|\boldsymbol{A}| \cos \alpha$), and then multiplying by the magnitude of vector $\boldsymbol{B}$ (or vice versa). The appropriate sign must, of course, be assigned positive if the projected component of vector $\boldsymbol{A}$ and vector $\boldsymbol{B}$ point in the same direction; negative, if not.

The work concept for a force $\boldsymbol{F}$ acting on a particle moving along a path described by s can now be given as

$$W = \int \boldsymbol{F} \cdot d\boldsymbol{s}$$

where $d\boldsymbol{s}$ is a displacement on the path along which the particle is moved.

[9] To ensure that there is no confusion between the dot product of two vectors and the ordinary product of two scalars that you have used up to now, we urge you to read $\boldsymbol{A} \cdot \boldsymbol{B} = \boldsymbol{C}$ as "$\boldsymbol{A}$ dotted into $\boldsymbol{B}$ yields $\boldsymbol{C}$."

As with addition and subtraction of vectors, the dot product operation involves only the vectors themselves and not their respective lines of action. Accordingly, for a dot product of two vectors, we can move the vectors so as to intersect at their tails as in Fig. 2.22. Remember in so doing we must not alter the magnitudes and directions of the vectors.

Let us next consider the scalar product of $m\boldsymbol{A}$ and $n\boldsymbol{B}$. If we carry it out according to our definitions:

$$\begin{aligned}(m\boldsymbol{A}) \cdot (n\boldsymbol{B}) &= |m\boldsymbol{A}|\,|n\boldsymbol{B}| \cos (m\boldsymbol{A}, n\boldsymbol{B}) \\ &= (mn)\,|\boldsymbol{A}|\,|\boldsymbol{B}| \cos (\boldsymbol{A}, \boldsymbol{B}) = (mn)\,(\boldsymbol{A} \cdot \boldsymbol{B})\end{aligned} \tag{2.13}$$

Hence, the scalar coefficients in the dot product of two vectors multiply in the ordinary way, while only the vectors themselves undergo the vectorial operation as we have defined it.

From the definition, clearly the dot product is *commutative,* since the number $|\boldsymbol{A}|\,|\boldsymbol{B}| \cos (\boldsymbol{A}, \boldsymbol{B})$ is independent of the order of multiplication of its terms. Thus,

$$\boldsymbol{A} \cdot \boldsymbol{B} = \boldsymbol{B} \cdot \boldsymbol{A} \tag{2.14}$$

Let us now consider $\boldsymbol{A} \cdot (\boldsymbol{B} + \boldsymbol{C})$. By definition, we may project the vector $(\boldsymbol{B} + \boldsymbol{C})$ onto the line of action of $\boldsymbol{A}$ and then, assigning the appropriate sign, multiply the magnitude of $\boldsymbol{A}$ times the projection of $\boldsymbol{B} + \boldsymbol{C}$. However, in Section 2.4 we showed that the projection of the sum of two vectors is the same as the sum of the projections of the vectors, which means that

$$\boldsymbol{A} \cdot (\boldsymbol{B} + \boldsymbol{C}) = \boldsymbol{A} \cdot \boldsymbol{B} + \boldsymbol{A} \cdot \boldsymbol{C} \tag{2.15}$$

An operation on a sum of quantities that is the same as the sum of the operations on the quantities is called a *distributive operation*. Thus, the dot product is distributive.

The scalar product between unit vectors will now be carried out. The product $\boldsymbol{i} \cdot \boldsymbol{j}$ is 0, since the angle α in Eq. 2.11 is 90°, which makes $\cos \alpha = 0$. On the other hand, $\boldsymbol{i} \cdot \boldsymbol{i} = 1$. We can thus conclude that the dot product of equal orthogonal unit vectors for a given reference is unity and that of unequal orthogonal unit vectors is zero.

If we express the vectors $\boldsymbol{A}$ and $\boldsymbol{B}$ in Cartesian components when taking the dot product, we get

$$\begin{aligned}\boldsymbol{A} \cdot \boldsymbol{B} &= (A_x\boldsymbol{i} + A_y\boldsymbol{j} + A_z\boldsymbol{k}) \cdot (B_x\boldsymbol{i} + B_y\boldsymbol{j} + B_z\boldsymbol{k}) \\ &= A_xB_x + A_yB_y + A_zB_z\end{aligned} \tag{2.16}$$

Thus, we see that a scalar product of two vectors is the sum of the ordinary products of the respective components.[10]

[10]Thus the ordinary grade school product of two numbers, i.e. $(a)(b)$, is a special case of the dot product $\boldsymbol{a} \cdot \boldsymbol{b}$ where the the vectors have the same direction. Thus

$$a\boldsymbol{i} \cdot b\boldsymbol{i} = (a)(b)$$

If a vector is multiplied by itself as a dot product, the result is the square of the magnitude of the vector. That is,

$$\boldsymbol{A} \cdot \boldsymbol{A} = |\boldsymbol{A}|\,|\boldsymbol{A}| = A^2 \tag{2.17}$$

Conversely, the square of a number may be considered to be the dot product of two equal vectors having a magnitude equal to the number. Note also that

$$\boldsymbol{A} \cdot \boldsymbol{A} = A_x^2 + A_y^2 + A_z^2 = A^2 \tag{2.18}$$

We can conclude from Eq. 2.18 that

$$A = \sqrt{A_x^2 + A_y^2 + A_z^2}$$

which checks with the Pythagorean theorem.

The dot product may be of immediate use in expressing the scalar rectangular component of a vector along a given direction as discussed in Section 2.4. If you refer back to Fig. 2.14, you will recall that the component of $\boldsymbol{C}$ along the direction s is given as

$$C_s = |\boldsymbol{C}| \cos \delta$$

Now let us consider a unit vector $\boldsymbol{s}$ along the direction of the line s. If we carry out the dot product of $\boldsymbol{C}$ and $\boldsymbol{s}$ according to our fundamental definition, the result is

$$\boldsymbol{C} \cdot \boldsymbol{s} = |\boldsymbol{C}|\,|\boldsymbol{s}| \cos \delta$$

But since $|\boldsymbol{s}|$ is unity, when we compare the preceding two equations, it is apparent that

$$C_s = \boldsymbol{C} \cdot \boldsymbol{s}$$

Similarly, the following useful relations are valid:

$$C_x = \boldsymbol{C} \cdot \boldsymbol{i}, \qquad C_y = \boldsymbol{C} \cdot \boldsymbol{j}, \qquad C_z = \boldsymbol{C} \cdot \boldsymbol{k}$$

Finally, express the unit vector $\hat{\boldsymbol{r}}$ directed out from the origin (see Fig. 2.23) in terms of the orthogonal scalar components:

$$\hat{\boldsymbol{r}} = (\hat{\boldsymbol{r}} \cdot \boldsymbol{i})\boldsymbol{i} + (\hat{\boldsymbol{r}} \cdot \boldsymbol{j})\boldsymbol{j} + (\hat{\boldsymbol{r}} \cdot \boldsymbol{k})\boldsymbol{k}$$

But

$$\hat{\boldsymbol{r}} \cdot \boldsymbol{i} = |\hat{\boldsymbol{r}}|\,|\boldsymbol{i}| \cos (\hat{\boldsymbol{r}}, x) = l$$

Similarly, $\hat{\boldsymbol{r}} \cdot \boldsymbol{j} = m$ and $\hat{\boldsymbol{r}} \cdot \boldsymbol{k} = n$. Hence, we can say that

$$\hat{\boldsymbol{r}} = l\boldsymbol{i} + m\boldsymbol{j} + n\boldsymbol{k} \tag{2.19}$$

Thus, *the orthogonal scalar components of a unit vector are the direction cosines of the direction of the unit vector.* Now, computing the square of the magnitude of $\hat{\boldsymbol{r}}$, we have

$$|\hat{\boldsymbol{r}}|^2 = 1 = l^2 + m^2 + n^2 \tag{2.20}$$

We thus arrive at the familiar geometrical relation that the sum of the squares of the direction cosines of a vector is unity.

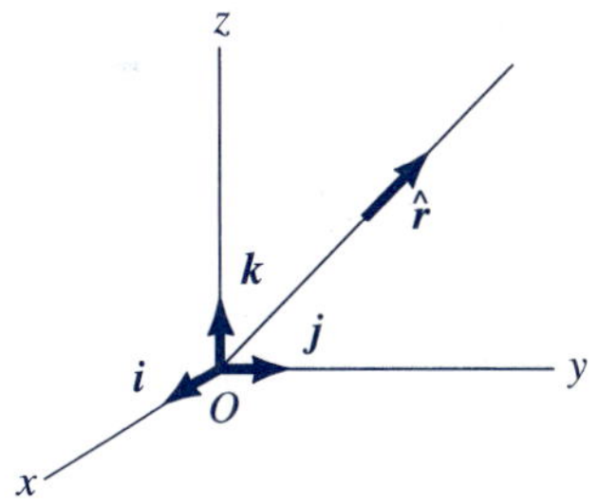

Figure 2.23. Unit vector $\hat{\boldsymbol{r}}$ directed from O.

Example 2.5

Cables *GA* and *GB* (see Fig. 2.24) are part of a guy-wire system supporting two radio transmission towers. What are the lengths of *GA* and *GB* and the angle α between them?

We may directly set up the vectors $\vec{GA}$ and $\vec{GB}$ by inspecting the diagram. Thus on moving along the coordinate directions, it is easy to see that

$$\vec{GA} = 300\boldsymbol{j} - 400\boldsymbol{i} + 500\boldsymbol{k} \text{ m}$$
$$\vec{GB} = 300\boldsymbol{j} + 100\boldsymbol{i} + 500\boldsymbol{k} \text{ m}$$

Using the Pythagorean theorem, we can say for the lengths of $\vec{GA}$ and $\vec{GB}$:

$$GA = (300^2 + 400^2 + 500^2)^{1/2} = 707 \text{ m}$$
$$GB = (300^2 + 100^2 + 500^2)^{1/2} = 592 \text{ m}$$

Now we use the dot product definition to find the angle.

$$\vec{GA} \bullet \vec{GB} = (GA)(GB) \cos \alpha$$

Therefore,

$$\cos\alpha = \frac{\vec{GA} \bullet \vec{GB}}{(GA)(GB)} = \frac{90{,}000 - 40{,}000 + 250{,}000}{(707)(592)}$$
$$= .717$$

Hence,

$$\alpha = 44.18°$$

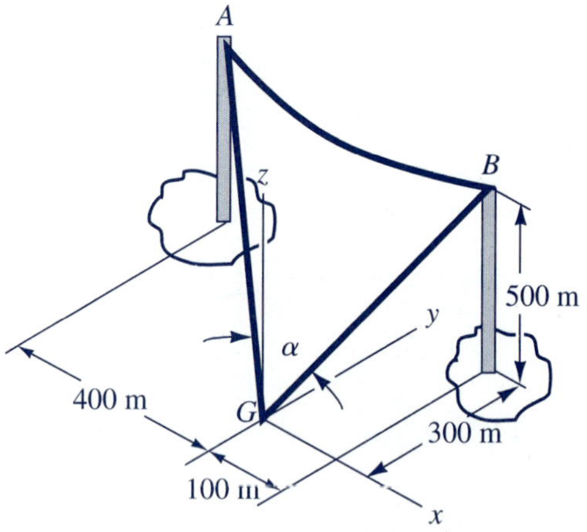

Figure 2.24. Radio transmission towers.

PROBLEMS

2.46. Given the vectors

$$A = 10i + 20j + 3k$$
$$B = -10j + 12k$$

what is $A \cdot B$? What is $\cos(A, B)$? What is the projection of A along B?

2.47. Given the vectors

$$A = 16i + 3j, \quad B = 10k - 6i, \quad C = 4j$$

compute

(a) $C(A \cdot C) + B$
(b) $-C + [B \cdot (-A)]C$

2.48. Given the vectors

$$A = 6i + 3j + 10k$$
$$B = 2i - 5j + 5k$$
$$C = 5i - 2j + 7k$$

what vector D gives the following results?

$$D \cdot A = 20$$
$$D \cdot B = 5$$
$$D \cdot i = 10$$

2.49. A sailboat is tacking into a 20-knot wind. The boat has a velocity component along its axis of 6 kn but because of side slip and water currents, it has a speed a speed of .2 kn at right angles to its axis. What are the x and y components of the wind velocity and the boat velocity? What is the angle between the wind velocity and the sailboat velocity?

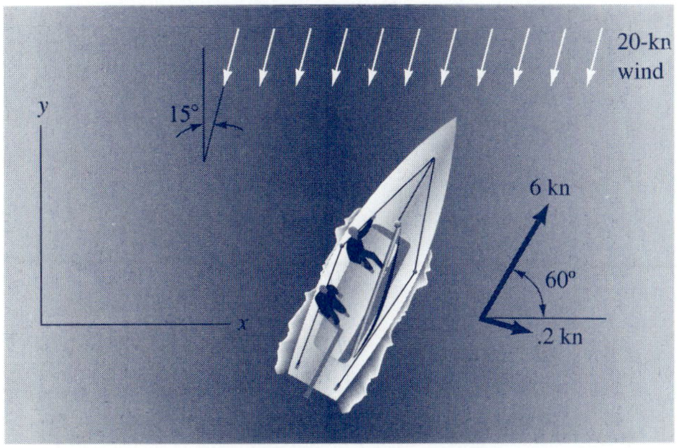

Figure P.2.49

2.50. Show that

$$\cos(A, B) = ll' + mm' + nn'$$

where l, m, n and l', m', n' are direction cosines of A and B, respectively, with respect to the given xyz reference.

2.51. Explain why the following operations are meaningless:

(a) $(A \cdot B) \cdot C$
(b) $(A \cdot B) + C$

2.52. A block A is constrained to move along a 20° incline in the yz plane. How far does the block have to move if the force F is to do 10 ft-lb of work?

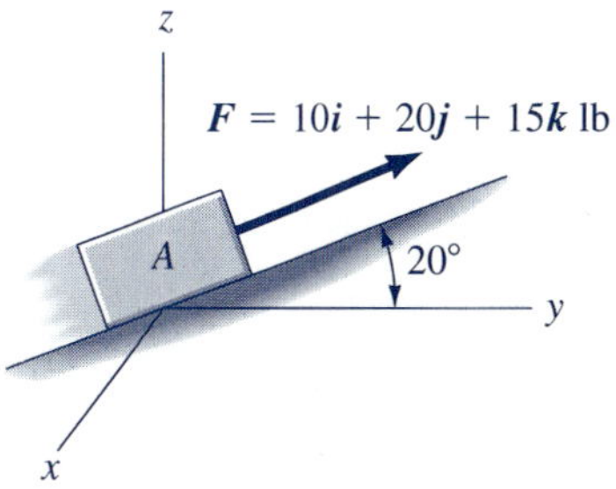

Figure P.2.52

2.53. An electrostatic field E exerts a force on a charged particle of qE, where q is the charge of the particle. If we have for E:

$$E = 6i + 3j + 2k \text{ dynes/coulomb}$$

what work is done by the field on a particle with a unit charge moving along a straight line from the origin to position $x = 20$ mm, $y = 40$ mm, $z = -40$ mm?

2.54. A force vector of magnitude 100 N has a line of action with direction cosines $l = .7$, $m = .2$, $n = .59$ relative to a reference xyz. The vector points away from the origin. What is the component of the force vector along a direction a having direction cosines $l = -.3$, $m = .1$, and $n = .95$ for the xyz reference? (*Hint:* Whenever simply a component is asked for, it is virtually always the *rectangular* component that is desired.)

2.55. What is the angle between the 1,000-N force and the axis *AB*? The force is in the diagonal plane *GCDE*.

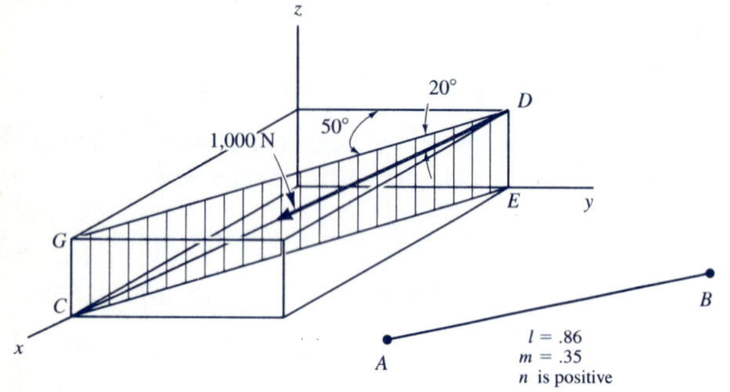

Figure P.2.55

2.56. Given a force $\boldsymbol{F} = 10\boldsymbol{i} + 5\boldsymbol{j} + A\boldsymbol{k}$ N. If this force is to have a rectangular component of 8 N along a line having a unit vector $\hat{\boldsymbol{r}} = .6\boldsymbol{i} + .8\boldsymbol{k}$, what should A be? What is the angle between $\boldsymbol{F}$ and $\hat{\boldsymbol{r}}$?

2.57. Given a force $A\boldsymbol{i} + B\boldsymbol{j} + 20\boldsymbol{k}$ N, what must A and B be to give a rectangular component of 10 N in the direction

$$\hat{\boldsymbol{r}}_1 = .3\boldsymbol{i} + .6\boldsymbol{j} + .742\boldsymbol{k}$$

as well as a component of 18 N in the direction

$$\hat{\boldsymbol{r}}_2 = .4\boldsymbol{i} + .9\boldsymbol{j} + .1732\boldsymbol{k}?$$

2.58. Find the dot product of the vectors represented by the diagonals from *A* to *F* and from *D* to *G*. What is the angle between them?

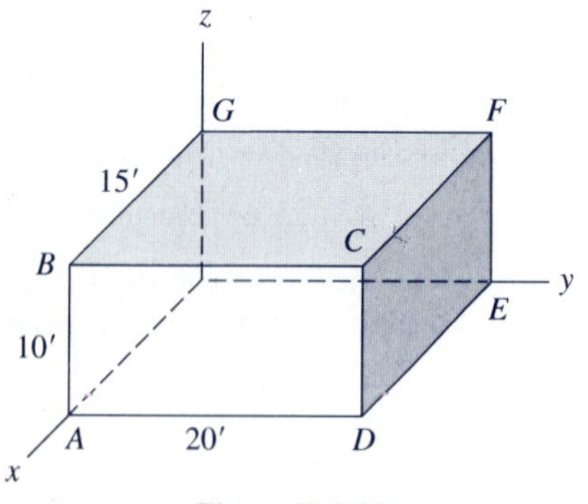

Figure P.2.58

2.59. A force $\boldsymbol{F}$ is given as

$$\boldsymbol{F} = 800\boldsymbol{i} + 600\boldsymbol{j} - 1{,}000\boldsymbol{k} \text{ N}$$

What is the *rectangular component* along an axis *A-A* equally inclined to the positive *x*, *y*, and *z* axes?

2.60. What is the rectangular component of the 500-N force along the diagonal from *B* to *A*?

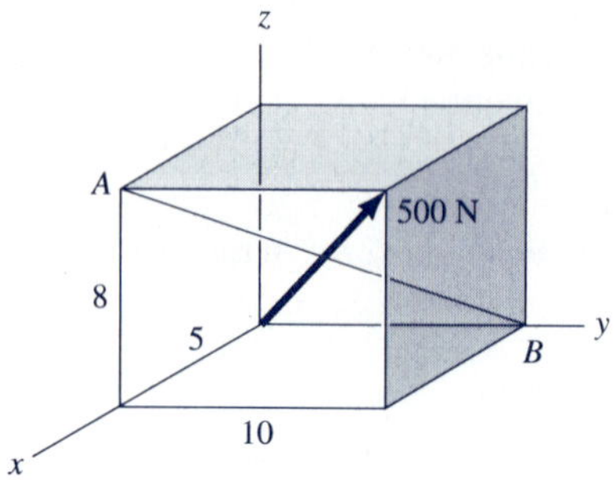

Figure P.2.60

2.61. A radio tower is held by guy wires. If *AB* were to be moved to intersect *CD* while remaining parallel to its original position, what is the angle between *AB* and *CD*?

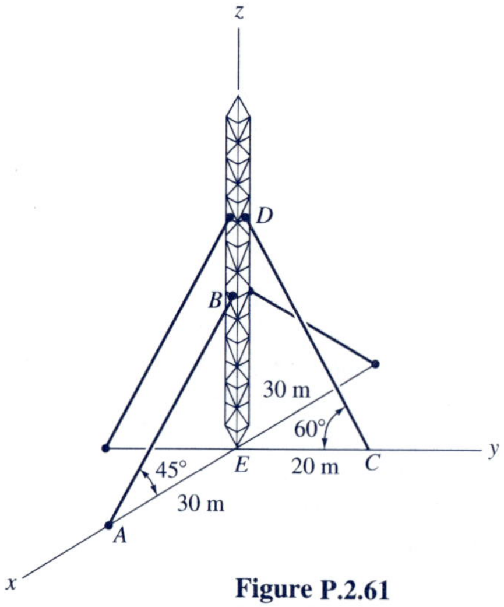

Figure P.2.61

2.62. What is the angle between the 1,000-N force and the position vector $\boldsymbol{r}$?

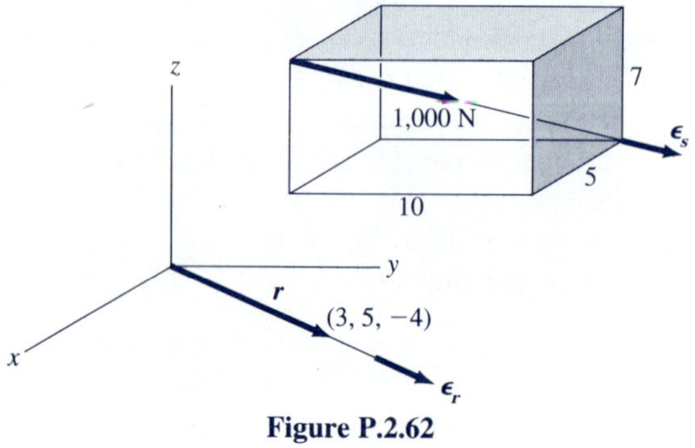

Figure P.2.62

2.8 Cross Product of Two Vectors

There are interactions between vector quantities that result in vector quantities. One such interaction is the moment of a force, which involves a special product of the force and a position vector (to be studied in Chapter 3). To set up a convenient operation for these situations, the *vector cross product* has been established. For the two vectors (having possibly different dimensions) shown in Fig. 2.25 as $\boldsymbol{A}$ and $\boldsymbol{B}$, the operation[11] is defined as

$$\boldsymbol{A} \times \boldsymbol{B} = \boldsymbol{C} \tag{2.21}$$

where $\boldsymbol{C}$ has a magnitude that is given as

$$|\boldsymbol{C}| = |\boldsymbol{A}|\,|\boldsymbol{B}| \sin \alpha \tag{2.22}$$

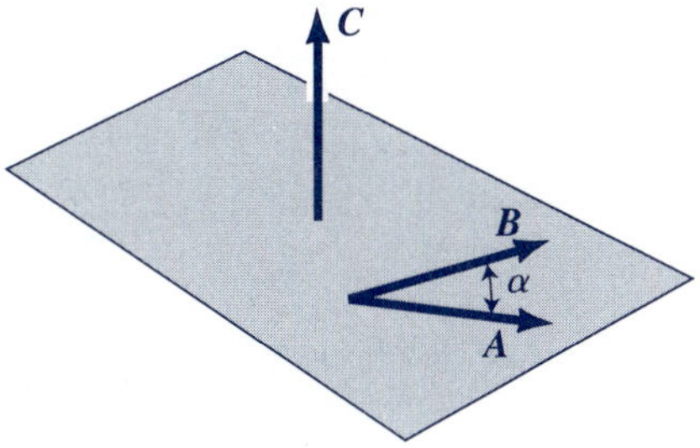

Figure 2.25. $\boldsymbol{A} \times \boldsymbol{B} = \boldsymbol{C}$.

The angle α is the smaller of the two angles between the vectors, thus making $\sin \alpha$ always positive. The vector $\boldsymbol{C}$ has an orientation normal to the plane of the vectors $\boldsymbol{A}$ and $\boldsymbol{B}$. The sense, furthermore, corresponds to the advance of a right-hand screw rotated about $\boldsymbol{C}$ as an axis while turning from $\boldsymbol{A}$ to $\boldsymbol{B}$ through α—that is, from the first stated vector to the second stated vector through the smaller angle between them. In Fig. 2.25, the screw would advance upward in rotating from $\boldsymbol{A}$ to $\boldsymbol{B}$, whether the procedure is viewed from above or below the plane formed by $\boldsymbol{A}$ and $\boldsymbol{B}$. The reader can easily verify this. The description of vector $\boldsymbol{C}$ is now complete, since the magnitude and direction are fully established. The line of action of $\boldsymbol{C}$ is not determined by the cross product; it depends on the use of the vector $\boldsymbol{C}$.

Again we remind you that the cross product, like the other vector algebraic operations, does not involve lines of action, so in taking a cross product we can move the vectors so as to come together at their tails as in Fig. 2.25.

As in the previous case, the coefficients of the vectors will multiply as ordinary scalars. This may be deduced from the nature of the definition. However, the *commutative* law breaks down for this product. We can verify, by carefully considering the definition of the cross product, that

$$(\boldsymbol{A} \times \boldsymbol{B}) = -(\boldsymbol{B} \times \boldsymbol{A}) \tag{2.23}$$

[11]Again, we urge you to read $\boldsymbol{A} \times \boldsymbol{B} = \boldsymbol{C}$ as "$\boldsymbol{A}$ crossed into $\boldsymbol{B}$ yields $\boldsymbol{C}$."

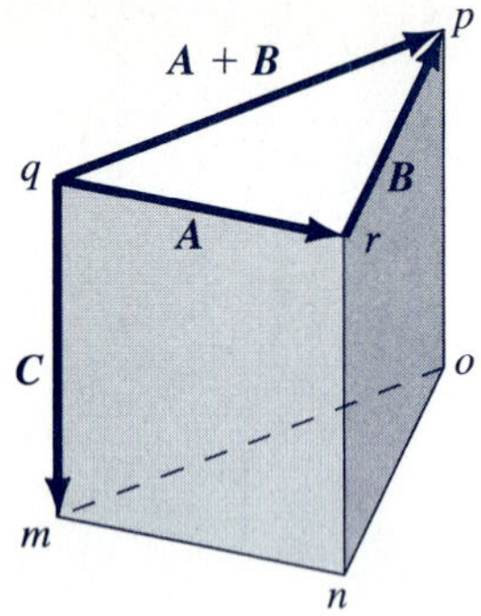

Figure 2.26. Prism using $\boldsymbol{A}$, $\boldsymbol{B}$, and $\boldsymbol{C}$.

We can readily show that the cross product, like the dot product, is a distributive operation. To do this, consider in Fig. 2.26 a prism *mnopqr* with edges coinciding with the vectors $\boldsymbol{A}$, $\boldsymbol{B}$, $\boldsymbol{C}$, and $(\boldsymbol{A} + \boldsymbol{B})$. We can represent the area of each face of the prism as a vector whose magnitude equals the area of the face and whose direction is normal to the face with a sense pointing out (by convention) from the body. It will be left to the student to justify the given formulation for each of the vectors in Fig. 2.27. Since the prism is a closed surface, the net projected area in any direction must be zero, and this, in turn, means that the total area vector must be zero. We then get

$$(\boldsymbol{A} + \boldsymbol{B}) \times \boldsymbol{C} + \tfrac{1}{2}\boldsymbol{A} \times \boldsymbol{B} + \tfrac{1}{2}\boldsymbol{B} \times \boldsymbol{A} + \boldsymbol{C} \times \boldsymbol{A} + \boldsymbol{C} \times \boldsymbol{B} = \boldsymbol{0}$$

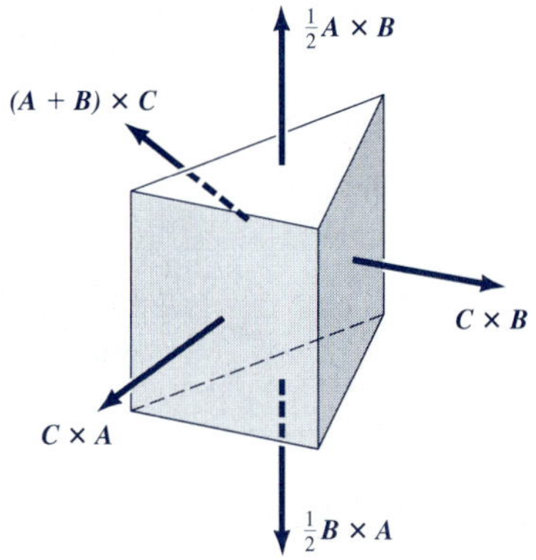

Figure 2.27. Area vectors for prism faces.

Noting that the second and third expressions cancel each other, we get, on rearranging the terms,

$$\boldsymbol{C} \times (\boldsymbol{A} + \boldsymbol{B}) = \boldsymbol{C} \times \boldsymbol{A} + \boldsymbol{C} \times \boldsymbol{B} \tag{2.24}$$

We have thus demonstrated the *distributive* property of the cross product.

Next, consider the cross product of rectangular unit vectors. Here, the product of equal vectors is zero because α and, consequently, $\sin \alpha$ are zero. The product $\boldsymbol{i} \times \boldsymbol{j}$ is unity in magnitude, and because of the right-hand-screw rule must be parallel to the z axis. If the z axis has been erected in a sense con-

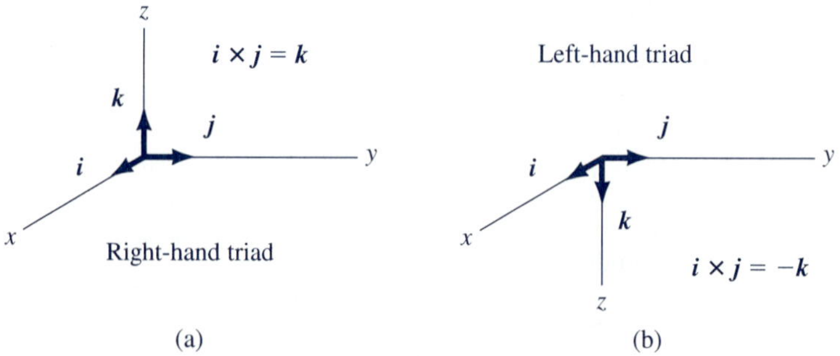

Figure 2.28. Different kinds of references.

sistent with the right-hand-screw rule when rotating from the x to the y direction, the reference is called a *right-hand triad* [see Fig. 2.28(a)] and we can write

$$\boldsymbol{i} \times \boldsymbol{j} = \boldsymbol{k}$$

If a left-hand triad is used, the result is a $-\boldsymbol{k}$ for the cross product above [see Fig. 2.28(b)]. In this text, we will use a right-hand triad as a reference. For ease in evaluation of unit cross products for such references, a simple permutation scheme is helpful. In Fig. 2.29, the unit vectors $\boldsymbol{i}, \boldsymbol{j}$, and $\boldsymbol{k}$ are indicated on a circle in a clockwise sequence. Any cross product of a pair of unit vectors results in a positive third unit vector if going from the first vector to the second vector involves a clockwise motion on this circle. Otherwise, the vector is negative. Thus,

$$\boldsymbol{k} \times \boldsymbol{j} = -\boldsymbol{i}, \qquad \boldsymbol{k} \times \boldsymbol{i} = \boldsymbol{j}, \qquad \text{etc.}$$

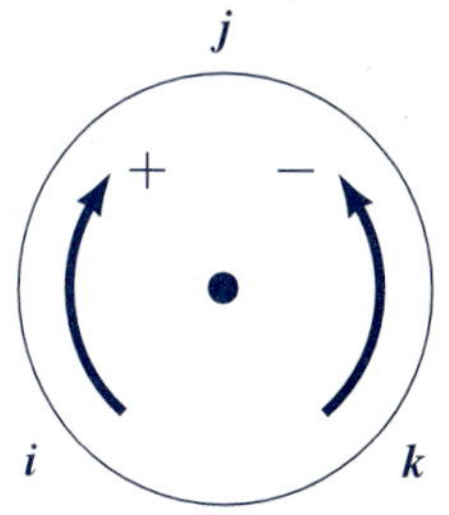

Figure 2.29. Permutation scheme.

Next, the cross product of two vectors in terms of their rectangular components is

$$\begin{aligned} \boldsymbol{A} \times \boldsymbol{B} &= (A_x\boldsymbol{i} + A_y\boldsymbol{j} + A_z\boldsymbol{k}) \times (B_x\boldsymbol{i} + B_y\boldsymbol{j} + B_z\boldsymbol{k}) \\ &= (A_yB_z - A_zB_y)\boldsymbol{i} + (A_zB_x - A_xB_z)\boldsymbol{j} + (A_xB_y - A_yB_x)\boldsymbol{k} \end{aligned} \tag{2.25}$$

Another method of carrying out this long computation is to evaluate the following determinant:

$$\begin{vmatrix} A_x & A_y & A_z \\ B_x & B_y & B_z \\ \boldsymbol{i} & \boldsymbol{j} & \boldsymbol{k} \end{vmatrix} \tag{2.26}$$

The determinant may easily be evaluated in the following manner. Repeat the first two rows below the determinant, and then form products along diagonals.

$$\begin{array}{ccc} A_x & A_y & A_z \\ B_x & B_y & B_z \\ \boldsymbol{i} & \boldsymbol{j} & \boldsymbol{k} \\ A_x & A_y & A_z \\ B_x & B_y & B_z \end{array} \tag{2.27}$$

For the products along the dashed diagonals, we must remember in this method to multiply by -1. We then add all six products as follows:

$$\begin{aligned} &A_xB_y\boldsymbol{k} + B_xA_z\boldsymbol{j} + A_yB_z\boldsymbol{i} - A_zB_y\boldsymbol{i} - B_zA_x\boldsymbol{j} - A_yB_x\boldsymbol{k} \\ &\qquad = (A_yB_z - A_zB_y)\boldsymbol{i} + (A_zB_x - A_xB_z)\boldsymbol{j} + (A_xB_y - A_yB_x)\boldsymbol{k} \end{aligned}$$

Clearly, this is the same result as in Eq. 2.25. It must be cautioned that this method of evaluating a determinant is correct only for 3×3 determinants. If the cross product of two vectors involves less than six nonzero components, such as in the cross product

$$(6\boldsymbol{i} + 10\boldsymbol{j}) \times (5\boldsymbol{j} - 3\boldsymbol{k})$$

then it is advisable to multiply the components directly and collect terms, as in Eq. 2.25.

Example 2.6

A pyramid is shown in Fig. 2.30. If the height of the pyramid is 300 ft, find the angle between the outward normals to planes *ADB* and *BDC*.[12]

We shall first find the unit normals to the aforestated planes. Then, using the dot product between these normals, we can easily find the desired angle.

To get the unit normal $\boldsymbol{n}_1$ to plane *ABD*, we first compute the area vector $\boldsymbol{A}_1$ for this plane. Thus, from simple trigonometry and the definition of the cross product,

$$\boldsymbol{A}_1 = \tfrac{1}{2}\vec{AB} \times \vec{AD}$$

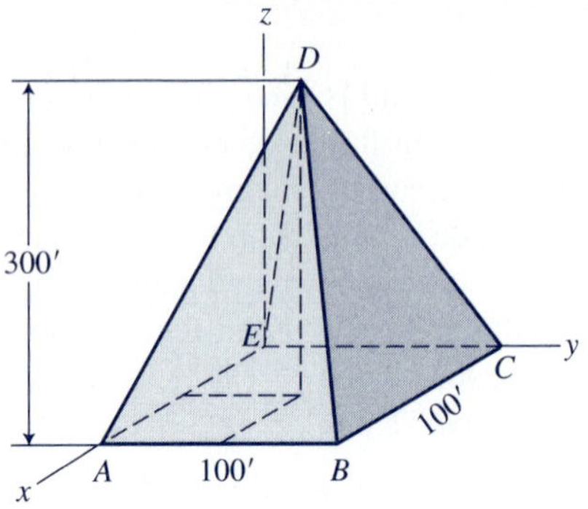

Figure 2.30. Pyramid.

Note next that

$$\vec{AB} = 100\boldsymbol{j} \text{ ft}$$

Furthermore, we can express $\vec{AD}$ in rectangular components by moving from *A* to *D* along coordinate directions as follows:

$$\vec{AD} = 50\boldsymbol{j} - 50\boldsymbol{i} + 300\boldsymbol{k} \text{ ft}$$

Hence,

$$\begin{aligned}\boldsymbol{A}_1 &= \tfrac{1}{2}(100\boldsymbol{j}) \times (-50\boldsymbol{i} + 50\boldsymbol{j} + 300\boldsymbol{k}) \\ &= 15{,}000\boldsymbol{i} + 2{,}500\boldsymbol{k} \text{ ft}^2\end{aligned}$$

Accordingly,

$$\begin{aligned}\boldsymbol{n}_1 &= \frac{\boldsymbol{A}_1}{|\boldsymbol{A}_1|} = \frac{15{,}000\boldsymbol{i} + 2{,}500\boldsymbol{k}}{\sqrt{15{,}000^2 + 2{,}500^2}} \\ &= .9864\boldsymbol{i} + .1644\boldsymbol{k}\end{aligned} \qquad \text{(a)}$$

As for unit normal $\boldsymbol{n}_2$ corresponding to plane *BDC*, whose area vector we denote as $\boldsymbol{A}_2$, we have

$$\boldsymbol{A}_2 = \tfrac{1}{2}\vec{BC} \times \vec{BD}$$

Note that

$$\vec{BC} = -100\boldsymbol{i} \text{ ft}$$

And once again, moving along coordinate directions, we have for $\vec{BD}$

$$\vec{BD} = -50\boldsymbol{j} - 50\boldsymbol{i} + 300\boldsymbol{k} \text{ ft}$$

[12] π minus this angle is the angle between these planes.

Example 2.6 (Continued)

Hence,

$$A_2 = \tfrac{1}{2}(-100\boldsymbol{i}) \times (-50\boldsymbol{i} - 50\boldsymbol{j} + 300\boldsymbol{k})$$
$$= 15{,}000\boldsymbol{j} + 2{,}500\boldsymbol{k} \text{ ft}^2$$

Accordingly,

$$\boldsymbol{n}_2 = \frac{A_2}{|A_2|} = \frac{15{,}000\boldsymbol{j} + 2{,}500\boldsymbol{k}}{\sqrt{15{,}000^2 + 2{,}500^2}} \tag{b}$$
$$= .9864\boldsymbol{j} + .1644\boldsymbol{k}$$

Now, we use the dot product of $\boldsymbol{n}_1$ and $\boldsymbol{n}_2$. Thus,

$$\boldsymbol{n}_1 \cdot \boldsymbol{n}_2 = \cos\beta \tag{c}$$

where β is the angle between the normals to the planes. Substituting from Eqs. (a) and (b) into (c), we get

$$\cos\beta = .0270$$

Therefore,

$$\beta = 88.5°$$

We see from this example that a plane surface can be represented as a vector, and if that plane surface is part of a closed surface, by convention the area vector is in the direction of the outward normal.

2.9 Scalar Triple Product

A very useful quantity is the *scalar triple product,* which for a set of vectors $\boldsymbol{A}$, $\boldsymbol{B}$, and $\boldsymbol{C}$ is defined as

$$(\boldsymbol{A} \times \boldsymbol{B}) \cdot \boldsymbol{C} \tag{2.28}$$

This clearly is a scalar quantity.

A simple geometric meaning can be associated with this operation. In Fig. 2.31, we have shown $\boldsymbol{A}$, $\boldsymbol{B}$, and $\boldsymbol{C}$ as an arbitrary set of concurrent vectors. We have set up an xyz reference such that the $\boldsymbol{A}$ and $\boldsymbol{B}$ vectors are in the xy plane. Further, a parallelogram *abcd* in the xy plane is shown in the diagram. We can say that

$$|\boldsymbol{A} \times \boldsymbol{B}| = |\boldsymbol{A}|\,|\boldsymbol{B}| \sin\alpha = \text{area of } abcd$$

Furthermore, the direction of $\boldsymbol{A} \times \boldsymbol{B}$ is in the z direction. Clearly, when we carry out Eq. 2.28, we are thus multiplying the scalar component of $\boldsymbol{C}$ in the z direction by the area of the aforementioned parallelogram. Thus, we have, for Eq. 2.28:

$$(\boldsymbol{A} \times \boldsymbol{B}) \cdot \boldsymbol{C} = (\text{area of } abcd)(C_z)$$

But C_z is the altitude of the parallelepiped formed by vectors $\boldsymbol{A}$, $\boldsymbol{B}$, and $\boldsymbol{C}$ (see Fig. 2.31). We then conclude from solid geometry that *the scalar triple product is the volume of the parallelepiped formed by the concurrent vectors of the scalar triple product.*

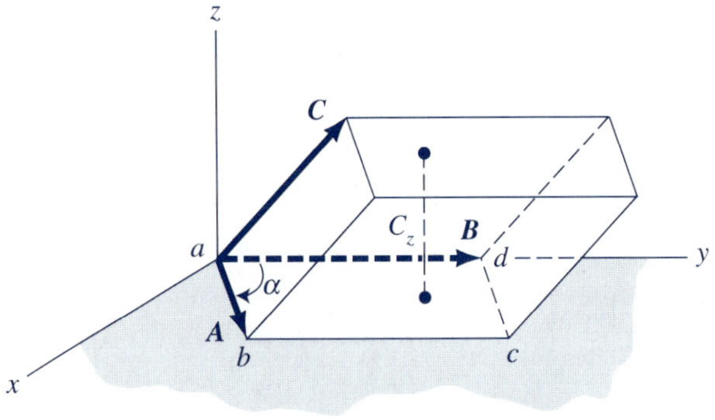

Figure 2.31. ***A*** and ***B*** in *xy* plane.

Using this geometrical interpretation of the scalar triple product, the reader can easily conclude that

$$(\boldsymbol{A} \times \boldsymbol{B}) \cdot \boldsymbol{C} = -(\boldsymbol{A} \times \boldsymbol{C}) \cdot \boldsymbol{B} = -(\boldsymbol{C} \times \boldsymbol{B}) \cdot \boldsymbol{A} \qquad (2.29)$$

The computation of the scalar triple product is a very straightforward process. It will be left as an exercise (Problem 2.72) for you to demonstrate that

$$(\boldsymbol{A} \times \boldsymbol{B}) \cdot \boldsymbol{C} = \begin{vmatrix} A_x & A_y & A_z \\ B_x & B_y & B_z \\ C_x & C_y & C_z \end{vmatrix} \qquad (2.30)$$

In later chapters, we shall employ the scalar triple product, although we shall not always want to associate the preceding geometric interpretation of this product.

Another operation involving three vectors is the *vector triple product* defined for vectors $\boldsymbol{A}$, $\boldsymbol{B}$, and $\boldsymbol{C}$ as $\boldsymbol{A} \times (\boldsymbol{B} \times \boldsymbol{C})$. The vector triple product is a vector quantity and will appear quite often in studies of dynamics. It will be left for you to demonstrate that

$$\boldsymbol{A} \times (\boldsymbol{B} \times \boldsymbol{C}) = \boldsymbol{B}(\boldsymbol{A} \cdot \boldsymbol{C}) - \boldsymbol{C}(\boldsymbol{A} \cdot \boldsymbol{B}) \qquad (2.31)$$

Notice here that the vector triple product can be carried out by using only dot products.

Example 2.7

In Example 2.6, what is the area projected by plane *ADE* onto an infinite plane that is inclined equally to the x, y, and z axes?

The normal $\boldsymbol{n}$ to the infinite plane must have three equal direction cosines. Hence, noting Eq. 2.20 for the sum of the squares of a set of direction cosines, we can say that

$$l^2 = m^2 = n^2 = \tfrac{1}{3}$$

Therefore,

$$l = m = n = \frac{1}{\sqrt{3}}$$

Hence,

$$\boldsymbol{n} = \frac{1}{\sqrt{3}}\boldsymbol{i} + \frac{1}{\sqrt{3}}\boldsymbol{j} + \frac{1}{\sqrt{3}}\boldsymbol{k}$$

The projected area then is given as

$$\begin{aligned} A_n &= \left(\tfrac{1}{2}\,\overrightarrow{AD} \times \overrightarrow{AE}\right) \bullet \boldsymbol{n} \\ &= \left[\tfrac{1}{2}(-50\boldsymbol{i} + 50\boldsymbol{j} + 300\boldsymbol{k}) \times (-100\boldsymbol{i})\right] \bullet \frac{1}{\sqrt{3}}(\boldsymbol{i} + \boldsymbol{j} + \boldsymbol{k}) \end{aligned}$$

The preceding result is a scalar triple product that can readily be solved as follows (disregarding the final sign):

$$A_n = \frac{1}{2\sqrt{3}} \begin{array}{|ccc|} -50 & 50 & 300 \\ -100 & 0 & 0 \\ 1 & 1 & 1 \\ \end{array} = 7{,}217 \text{ ft}^2$$
$$\begin{array}{ccc} -50 & 50 & 300 \\ -100 & 0 & 0 \end{array}$$

2.10 A Note on Vector Notation

When expressing *equations,* we must at all times clearly denote scalar and vector quantities and handle them accordingly. When we are simply identifying quantities in a *discussion* or in a *diagram,* however, instead of using the vector representation, $\boldsymbol{F}$, we can just use F. On the other hand, F will be understood to represent in an equation the magnitude of the vector $\boldsymbol{F}$. Thus, using $\boldsymbol{f}$ as the unit vector in the direction of $\boldsymbol{F}$, we can then say:

$$\begin{aligned}\boldsymbol{F} &= F\boldsymbol{f}\\ &= F[\cos(\boldsymbol{F}, x)\boldsymbol{i} + \cos(\boldsymbol{F}, y)\boldsymbol{j} + \cos(\boldsymbol{F}, z)\boldsymbol{k}]\end{aligned}$$

As another example, we might want to employ the force F, which is shown in the coplanar diagram of Fig. 2.32(a) at a known inclination and acting at a point a. A correct representation of this force in a vector equation would be $F(-\cos\alpha\boldsymbol{i} + \sin\alpha\boldsymbol{j})$.

As for scalar components of any vector $\boldsymbol{F}$, we shall adopt the following understanding. The notation F_x, F_y, or F_z labeling some vector component in a *diagram* will be understood to represent the *magnitude* of that particular component. Thus, in Fig. 2.32(b) the two components shown are equal in magnitude but opposite in sense. Nevertheless, they are both labeled F_x. However, in an equation involving these quantities, the sense must properly be accounted for by the appropriate use of signs.

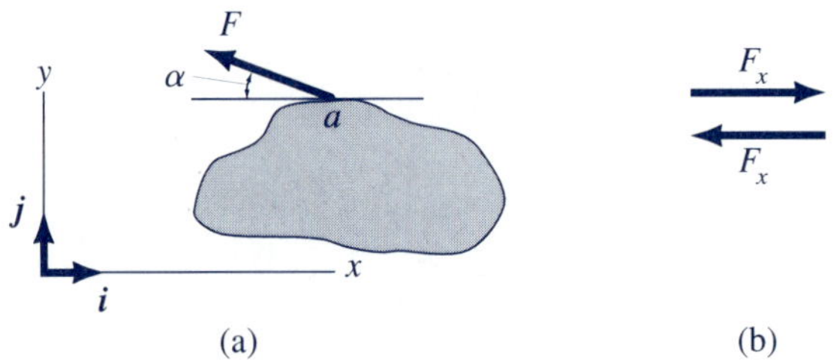

Figure 2.32. Notation in diagrams.

PROBLEMS

2.63. If $\boldsymbol{A} = 10\boldsymbol{i} + 6\boldsymbol{j} - 3\boldsymbol{k}$ and $\boldsymbol{B} = 6\boldsymbol{i}$, find $\boldsymbol{A} \times \boldsymbol{B}$ and $\boldsymbol{B} \times \boldsymbol{A}$. What is the magnitude of the resulting vector? What are its direction cosines relative to the xyz reference in which $\boldsymbol{A}$ and $\boldsymbol{B}$ are expressed?

2.64. What are the cross and dot products for the vectors $\boldsymbol{A}$ and $\boldsymbol{B}$ given as:

$$\boldsymbol{A} = 6\boldsymbol{i} + 3\boldsymbol{j} + 4\boldsymbol{k}$$
$$\boldsymbol{B} = 8\boldsymbol{i} - 3\boldsymbol{j} + 2\boldsymbol{k}?$$

2.65. If vectors $\boldsymbol{A}$ and $\boldsymbol{B}$ in the xy plane have a dot product of 50 units, and if the magnitudes of these vectors are 10 units and 8 units, respectively, what is $\boldsymbol{A} \times \boldsymbol{B}$?

2.66. (a) If $\boldsymbol{A} \cdot \boldsymbol{B} = \boldsymbol{A} \cdot \boldsymbol{B}'$, does $\boldsymbol{B}$ necessarily equal $\boldsymbol{B}'$? Explain.
(b) If $\boldsymbol{A} \times \boldsymbol{B} = \boldsymbol{A} \times \boldsymbol{B}'$, does $\boldsymbol{B}$ necessarily equal $\boldsymbol{B}'$? Explain.

2.67. What is the cross product of the displacement vector from A to B times the displacement vector from C to D?

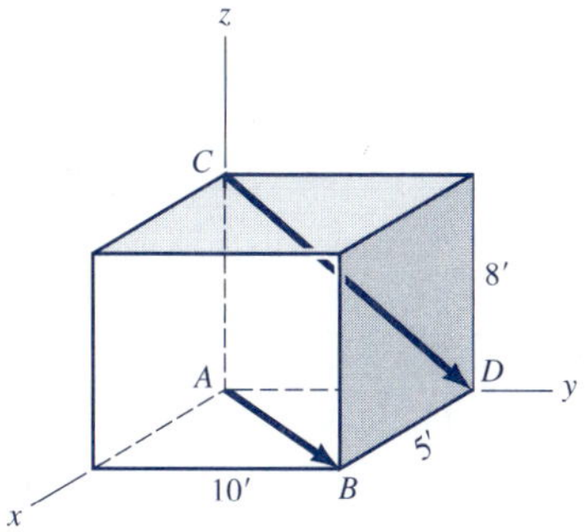

Figure P.2.67

2.68. Making use of the cross product, give the unit vector $\boldsymbol{n}$ normal to the inclined surface ABC.

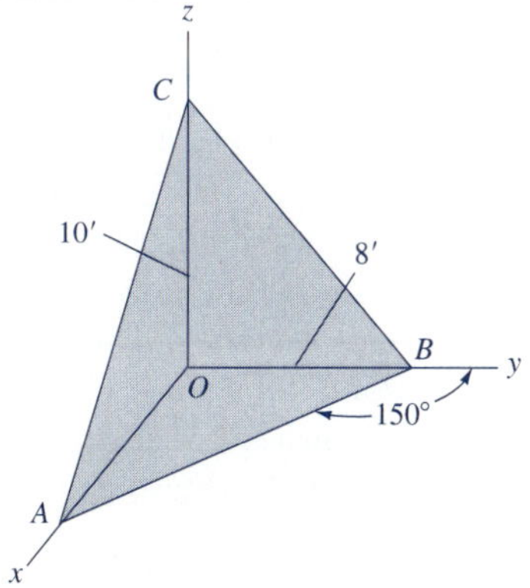

Figure P.2.68

2.69. If the coordinates of vertex E of the inclined pyramid are (5, 50, 80) m, what is the angle between outward normals to faces ADE and BCE?

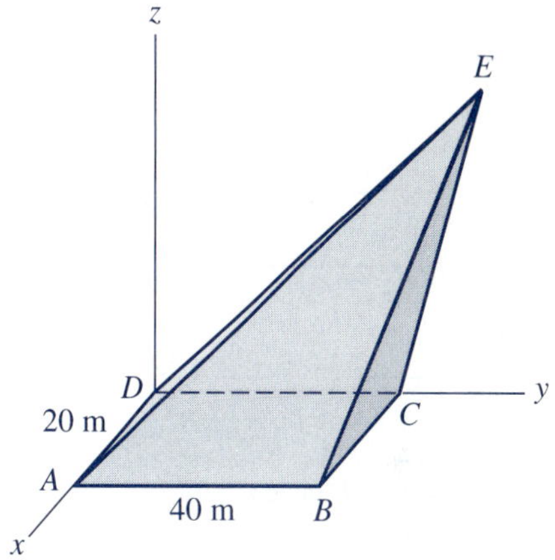

Figure P.2.69

2.70. In Problem 2.69, what is the area of face ADE of the pyramid? What is the projection of the area of face ADE onto a plane whose normal is along the direction $\boldsymbol{\epsilon}$ where:

$$\boldsymbol{\epsilon} = 0.6\boldsymbol{i} - 0.8\boldsymbol{j}$$

2.71. (a) Compute the product

$$(\boldsymbol{A} \times \boldsymbol{B}) \cdot \boldsymbol{C}$$

in terms of orthogonal components.
(b) Compute $(\boldsymbol{C} \times \boldsymbol{A}) \cdot \boldsymbol{B}$ and compare with the result in part (a).

2.72. Compute the determinant

$$\begin{vmatrix} A_x & A_y & A_z \\ B_x & B_y & B_z \\ C_x & C_y & C_z \end{vmatrix}$$

where each row represents, respectively, the scalar components of $\boldsymbol{A}$, $\boldsymbol{B}$, and $\boldsymbol{C}$. Compare the result with the computation of $(\boldsymbol{A} \times \boldsymbol{B}) \cdot \boldsymbol{C}$ by using the dot-product and cross-product operations.

2.73. In Example 2.5, what is the area vector for GAB assuming a straight line connects points A and B? Give the results in kilometers squared.

2.74. What is the component of the cross product $\boldsymbol{A} \times \boldsymbol{B}$ along the direction $\boldsymbol{n}$, where

$$\boldsymbol{A} = 10\boldsymbol{i} + 16\boldsymbol{j} + 3\boldsymbol{k}$$
$$\boldsymbol{B} = 5\boldsymbol{i} - 2\boldsymbol{j} + 2\boldsymbol{k}$$
$$\boldsymbol{n} = 0.8\boldsymbol{i} + 0.6\boldsymbol{k}$$

2.75. The surface *abcd* of the parallelepiped is in the *xz* plane. Compute the volume using vector analysis.

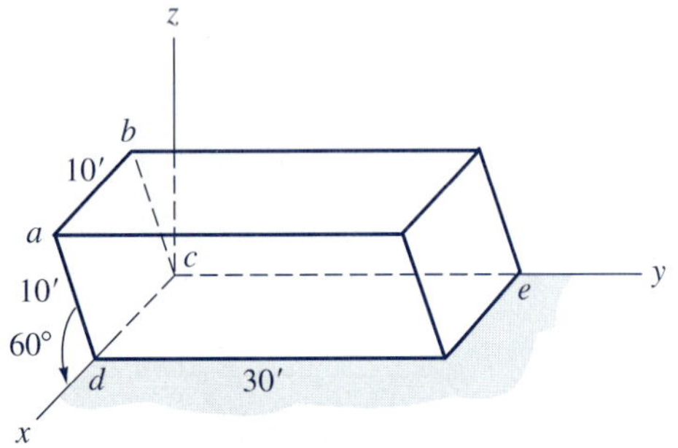

Figure P.2.75

2.76. Given the vectors

$$\boldsymbol{A} = 10\boldsymbol{i} + 6\boldsymbol{j}$$
$$\boldsymbol{B} = 3\boldsymbol{i} + 5\boldsymbol{j} + 10\boldsymbol{k}$$
$$\boldsymbol{C} = \boldsymbol{i} + \boldsymbol{j} - 3\boldsymbol{k}$$

find

(a) $(\boldsymbol{A} + \boldsymbol{B}) \times \boldsymbol{C}$
(b) $(\boldsymbol{A} \times \boldsymbol{B}) \cdot \boldsymbol{C}$
(c) $\boldsymbol{A} \cdot (\boldsymbol{B} \times \boldsymbol{C})$

***2.77.** A mirror system is used to relay a laser-beam signal from mountain *M* to hill *H*. The mountain is 5,000 m high and 20,000 m NW from the mirror site *S*, while the hill is 200 m high and 15,000 m ENE from the mirror site *S*. Set up, but do not necessarily solve, the equations to find the direction of the mirror to properly relay the signal. Recall that the angle of reflection for a mirror equals the angle of incidence and that the incident ray, reflecting ray, and normal to the mirror are coplanar.

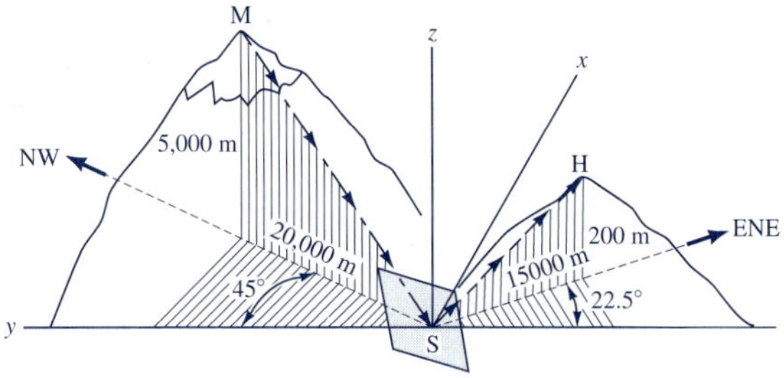

Figure P.2.77

2.11 Closure

In this chapter, we have presented symbols and notations that are associated with vectors. Also, various vector operations have been set forth that enable us to represent certain actions in nature mathematically. With this background, we shall now be able to study certain vector quantities that are of essential importance in mechanics. Some of these vectors will be formulated in terms of the operations contained in this chapter.

Check-Out for Sections with †

2.1 What is meant by the *magnitude* of a vector? What sign must it have?
2.2 Can you multiply a vector **C** by a scalar *s*? If so, describe the result.
2.3 What are the *law of cosines* and the *law of sines*?
2.4 What is meant by the *associative* law of addition?
2.5 Describe two ways to add any three vectors graphically.
2.6 How do you subtract vector **D** from vector **F**?
2.7 Given a vector **D**, how would you form a *unit* vector collinear with **D**?
2.8 What are the scalar equations of the following vector equation?

$$D\boldsymbol{i} + E\boldsymbol{j} - 16\boldsymbol{k} = 20\boldsymbol{i} + (15 + G)\boldsymbol{k}$$

PROBLEMS

2.78. Flight 304 from Dallas is flying NE to Chicago 900 miles away. To avoid a massive storm front, the pilot decides instead to fly due north to Topeka, Kansas, and then ENE (see Fig. P.2.4 for compass settings) to Chicago. What are the distances that he must travel from Dallas to Topeka and from Topeka to Chicago?

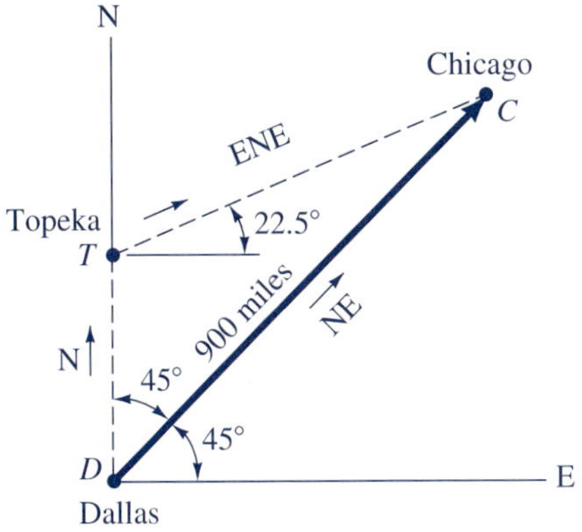

Figure P.2.78

2.79. What is the cross product between the 1,000-N force and the displacement vector $\boldsymbol{\rho}_{AB}$?

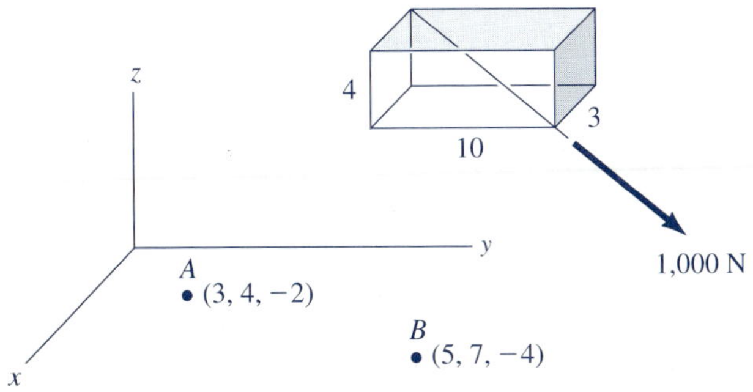

Figure P.2.79

2.80. Four members of a space frame are loaded as shown. What are the orthogonal scalar components of the forces on the ball joint at O? The 1,000-N force goes through points D and E of the rectangular parallelepiped.

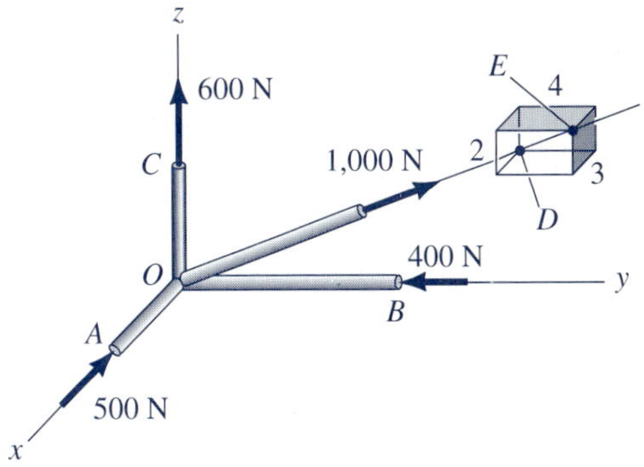

Figure P.2.80

2.81. Contractors encountered an impassable swamp while building a road from town T to city C 50 km SE. To avoid the swamp, they built the road SSW from T and then ENE to C. How long is the road? (*Hint:* See the compass-settings diagram, Fig. P.2.4.)

2.82. Sum all forces acting on the block. Plane A is parallel to the xy plane. We will later study the special properties of two parallel forces (called a *couple*) that are opposite in direction and equal in magnitude.

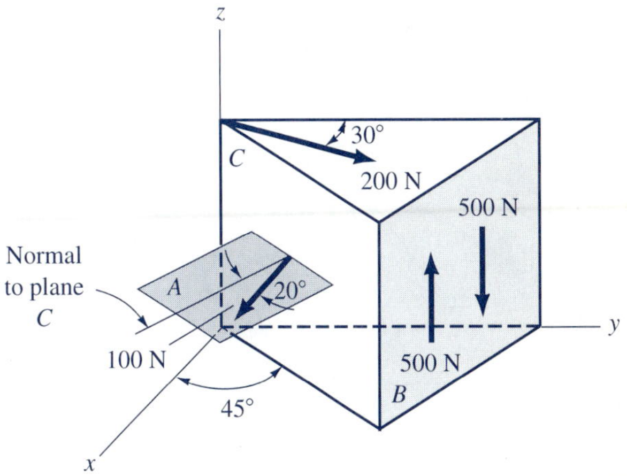

Figure P.2.82

2.83. The x and z components of the force F are known to be 100 lb and –30 lb, respectively. What is the force F and what are its direction cosines?

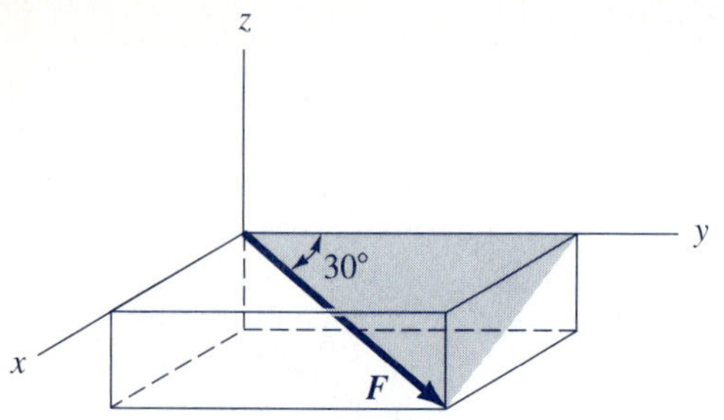

Figure P.2.83

2.84. A constant force given as $2\boldsymbol{i} + 3\boldsymbol{k}$ N moves a particle along a straight line from position $x = 10$, $y = 20$, $z = 0$ to position $x = 3$, $y = 0$, $z = -10$. If the coordinates of the xyz reference are given in meter units, how much work does the force do in ft-lb?

2.85. Rain is falling on a ferris wheel. The velocity of the rain is constant having reached a terminal velocity of 5 ft/sec. The angular speed of the ferris wheel is constant at 0.5 RPM. At what position θ will the angle between the velocity of the occupant at A and that of the rain drops be 158°? You will recall from freshman physics that the speed of a particle in circular motion is $r\omega$ with ω in radians per unit time. First use the dot-product approach and then check your result using a common sense approach.

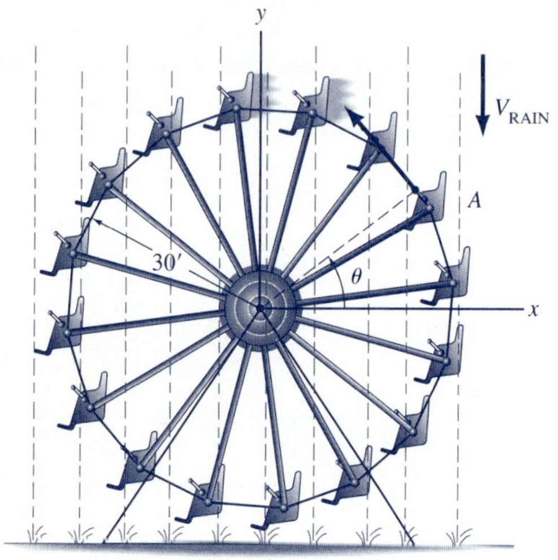

Figure P.2.85

2.86. A force $F = 500$ lb has a line of action that goes through points A and B. What is the angle δ between $\boldsymbol{F}$ and the displacement vector $\boldsymbol{\rho}_{CD}$. What is the scalar *rectangular component* of the force along axis CD?

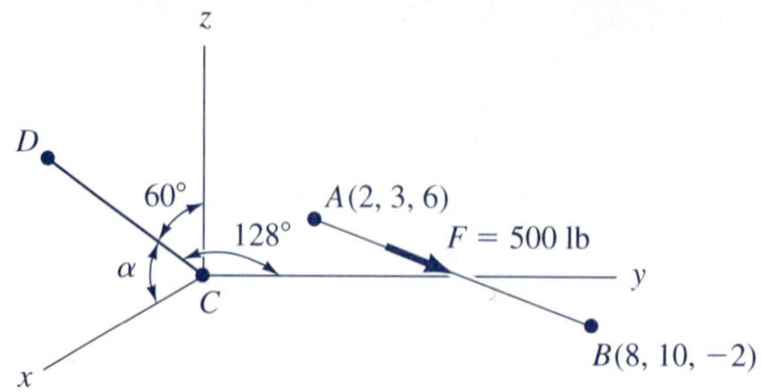

Figure P.2.86

2.87. The velocity of a particle of flow is given as

$$\boldsymbol{V} = 10\boldsymbol{i} + 16\boldsymbol{j} + 2\boldsymbol{k} \text{ m/sec}$$

What is the cross product $\boldsymbol{r} \times \boldsymbol{V}$, where $\boldsymbol{r}$ is given as

$$\boldsymbol{r} = 3\boldsymbol{i} + 2\boldsymbol{j} + 10\boldsymbol{k} \text{ m}$$

Give the proper units.

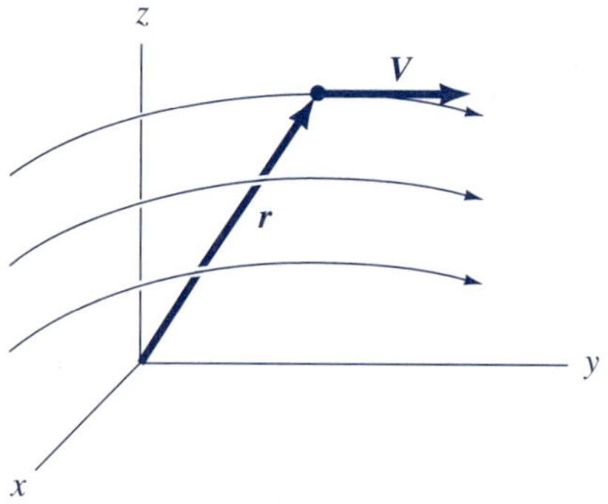

Figure P.2.87

2.88. A bridge truss has bar forces as shown in the cutaway sketch. What is the total force on the supporting pin at point A from the members?

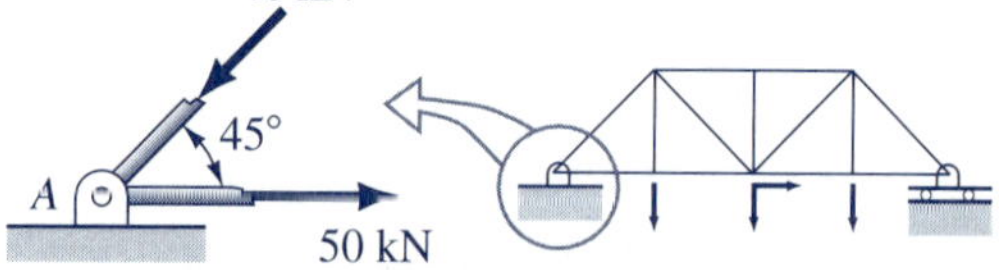

Figure P.2.88

2.89. Forces are transmitted by two members to pin A. If the sum of these forces is 700 lb directed vertically, what are the angles α and β?

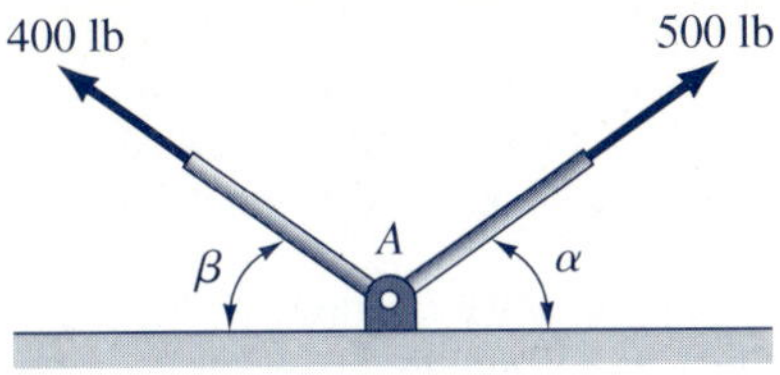

Figure P.2.89

2.90. A skeet shooter is aiming his gun at point A. What is the height z of point A?

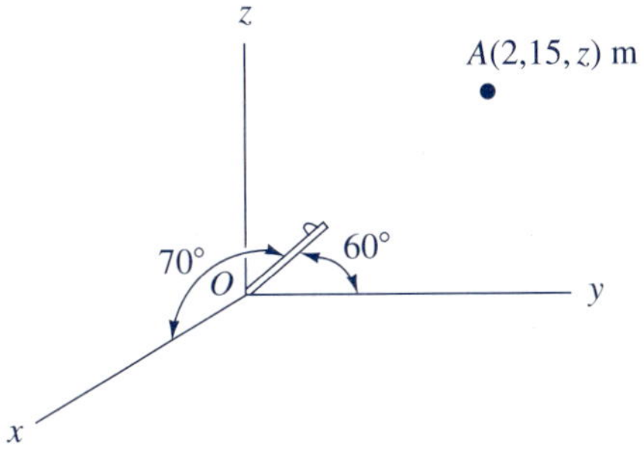

Figure P.2.90

2.91. If F_1 and the 500-N force sum vectorially to F_T, determine F_1 and F_T.

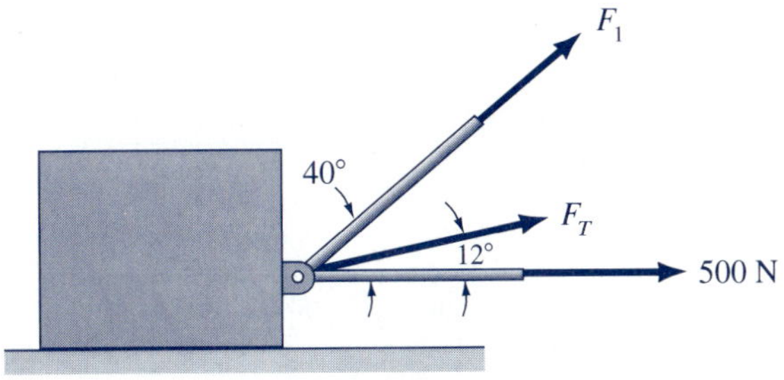

Figure P.2.91

2.92. The force on a charge moving through a magnetic field $\boldsymbol{B}$ is given as

$$\boldsymbol{F} = q\boldsymbol{V} \times \boldsymbol{B}$$

where q = magnitude of the charge, coulombs
$\boldsymbol{F}$ = force on the body, newtons
$\boldsymbol{V}$ = velocity vector of the particle, meters per second
$\boldsymbol{B}$ = magnetic flux density, webers per meter^2

Suppose that an electron moves through a uniform magnetic field of 10^6 Wb/m^2 in a direction inclined 30° to the field, as shown, with a speed of 100 m/sec. What are the force components on the electron? The charge of the electron is 1.6018×10^{-19} coulombs.

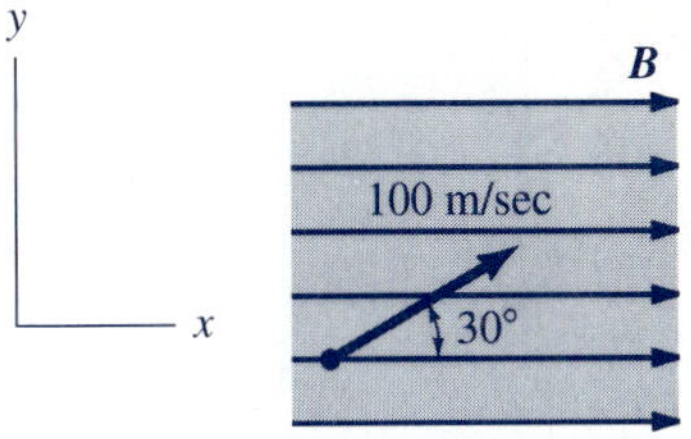

Figure P.2.92

2.93. For the line segment AB, determine z_B and direction cosines m and n.

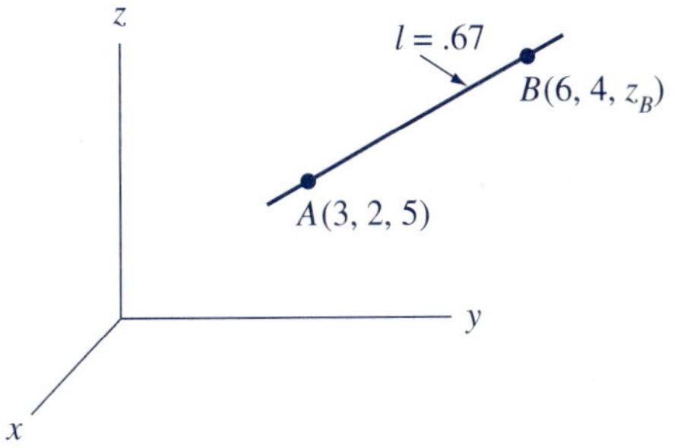

Figure P.2.93

2.94. Using the scalar triple product, find the area projected onto the plane N from the surface ABC. Plane N is infinite and is normal to the vector

$$\boldsymbol{r} = 50\boldsymbol{i} + 40\boldsymbol{j} + 30\boldsymbol{k} \text{ ft}$$

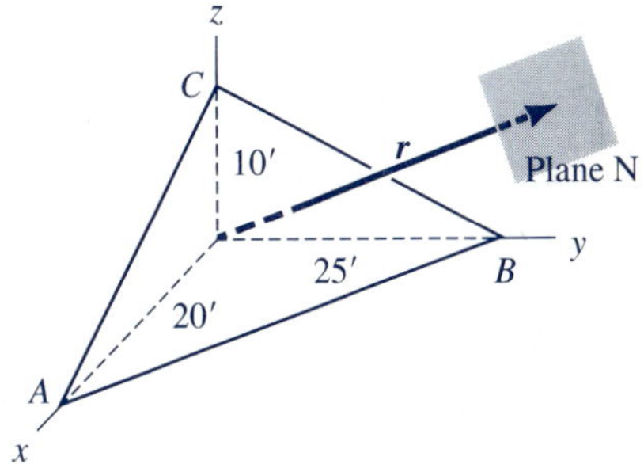

Figure P.2.94

2.95. A 500-lb crate is held up by three forces. Clearly the three forces should add up to a force of 500 lb going upward. What should forces F_1 and F_3 be for this condition? All forces are coplanar (in the same plane).

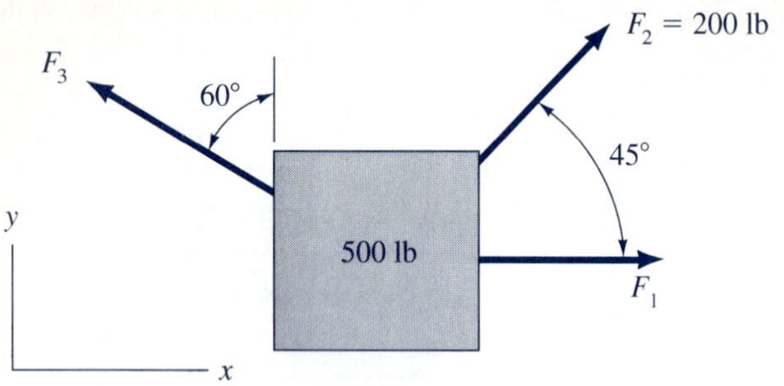

Figure P.2.95

2.96. A balloon on a gusty day goes from *A* to *B*, then is seen at *D* and finally is seen at *C*.

(a) If the balloon moves along straight lines, how far has it moved?

(b) If a bee-bee gun is to shoot down the balloon, assuming it is momentarily stationary at *C*, what are the direction cosines of the proper line of sight?

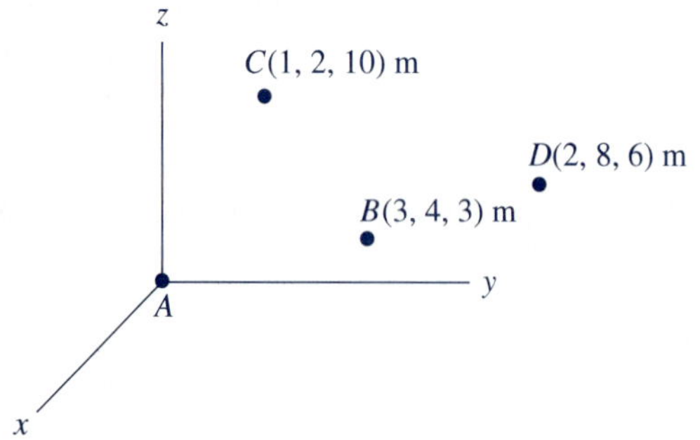

Figure P.2.96

2.97. In Problem 2.12 what should T_{AC}, T_{AB}, and the acute angle θ between T_{AB} and the vertical to minimize the tension T_{AB}? Take $\alpha = 36.5°$ and $W = 1{,}000$ N. *Hint:* Consider various possible force triangles and decide on inspection how to minimize T_{AB}.

2.98. In Problem 2.12, what should tensions T_{AC}, T_{AB}, and angle α be to minimize T_{AC}? Assume the angle between T_{AB} and the vertical is equal to 60°. See previous problem.

2.99. To illustrate the random motion of molecules in a liquid, a very small particle placed on the surface of the liquid is observed. The particle, if it is small enough, will jump around in a random manner giving rise to the *random walk* phenomenon described in your physics course. Suppose such a particle jumps from position (0,0) mm in the *xy* plane to (.01, −.03) mm to (−.01, −.02) mm to (.01, −.01) mm and finally to (.02, .01) mm. What is the shortest distance between end points of this movement? Solve this graphically.

2.100. What is the angle δ between F and the displacement vector $\boldsymbol{\rho}_{AB}$?

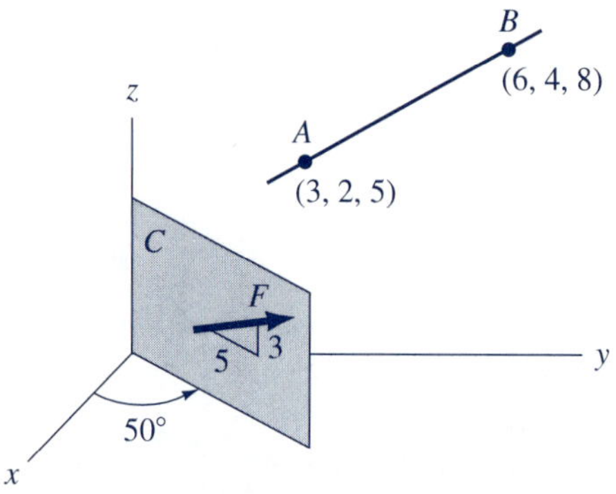

Figure P.2.100

CHAPTER 3

Important Vector Quantities

3.1 Position Vector

In this chapter, we shall discuss a number of useful vector quantities. Consider first the path of motion of a particle shown dashed in Fig. 3.1. As indicated in Chapter 1, the *displacement vector* $\boldsymbol{\rho}$ is a directed line segment connecting any two points on the path of motion, such as points 1 and 2 in Fig. 3.1. The displacement vector thus represents the shortest movement of the particle to get from one position on the path of motion to another. The purpose of the rectangular parallelepiped shown in the diagram is to convey the magnitude and direction of $\boldsymbol{\rho}$ as explained earlier. We can readily express $\boldsymbol{\rho}$ between points 1 and 2 in terms of rectangular components by noting the distance in the coordinate directions needed to go from 1 to 2. Thus, in Fig. 3.1, $\boldsymbol{\rho}_{12} = -2\boldsymbol{i} + 6\boldsymbol{j} + 3\boldsymbol{k}$ m.

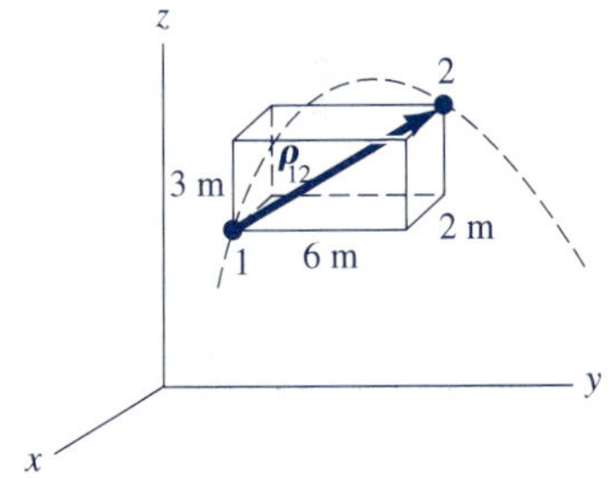

Figure 3.1. Displacement vector $\boldsymbol{\rho}$ between points 1 and 2.

The directed line segment $\boldsymbol{r}$ from the origin of a coordinate system to a point P in space (Fig. 3.2) is called the *position vector.* The notations $\boldsymbol{R}$ and $\boldsymbol{\rho}$ are also used for position vectors. You can conclude from Chapter 2 that the magnitude of the position vector is the distance between the origin O and point P. The scalar components of a position vector are simply the coordinates of the point P. To express $\boldsymbol{r}$ in Cartesian components, we then have

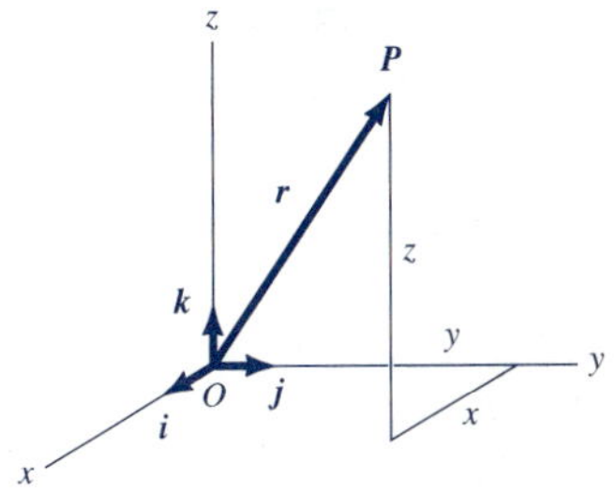

Figure 3.2. Position vector.

$$\boldsymbol{r} = x\boldsymbol{i} + y\boldsymbol{j} + z\boldsymbol{k} \tag{3.1}$$

We can obviously express a displacement vector $\boldsymbol{\rho}$ between points 1 and 2 (see Fig. 3.3) in terms of position vectors for points 1 and 2 (i.e., $\boldsymbol{r}_1$ and $\boldsymbol{r}_2$) as follows:

$$\boldsymbol{\rho} = \boldsymbol{r}_2 - \boldsymbol{r}_1 = (x_2 - x_1)\boldsymbol{i} + (y_2 - y_1)\boldsymbol{j} + (z_2 - z_1)\boldsymbol{k} \tag{3.2}$$

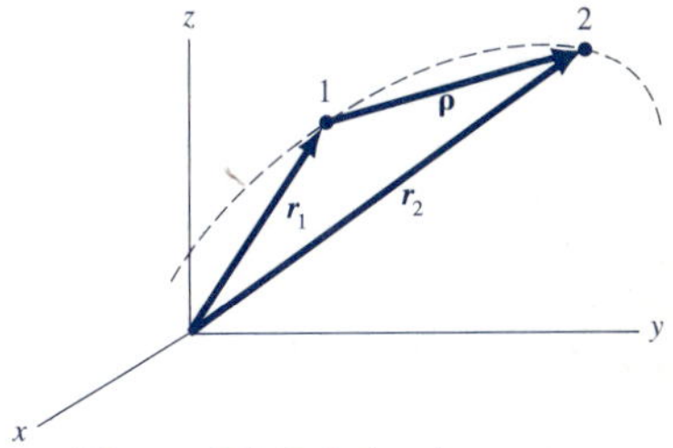

Figure 3.3. Relation between a displacement vector and position vectors.

Example 3.1

Two sets of references, xyz and XYZ, are shown in Fig. 3.4. The position vector of the origin O of xyz relative to XYZ is given as

$$\boldsymbol{R} = 10\boldsymbol{i} + 6\boldsymbol{j} + 5\boldsymbol{k} \text{ m} \quad \text{(a)}$$

The position vector, $\boldsymbol{r}'$, of a point P relative to XYZ is

$$\boldsymbol{r}' = 3\boldsymbol{i} + 2\boldsymbol{j} - 6\boldsymbol{k} \text{ m} \quad \text{(b)}$$

What is the position vector $\boldsymbol{r}$ of point P relative to xyz? What are the coordinates x, y, and z of P?

From Fig. 3.4, it is clear that

$$\boldsymbol{r}' = \boldsymbol{R} + \boldsymbol{r} \quad \text{(c)}$$

Therefore,

$$\begin{aligned} \boldsymbol{r} = \boldsymbol{r}' - \boldsymbol{R} &= (3\boldsymbol{i} + 2\boldsymbol{j} - 6\boldsymbol{k}) - (10\boldsymbol{i} + 6\boldsymbol{j} + 5\boldsymbol{k}) \\ \boldsymbol{r} &= -7\boldsymbol{i} - 4\boldsymbol{j} - 11\boldsymbol{k} \text{ m} \end{aligned} \quad \text{(d)}$$

We can then conclude that

$$\begin{aligned} x &= -7 \text{ m} \\ y &= -4 \text{ m} \\ z &= -11 \text{ m} \end{aligned} \quad \text{(e)}$$

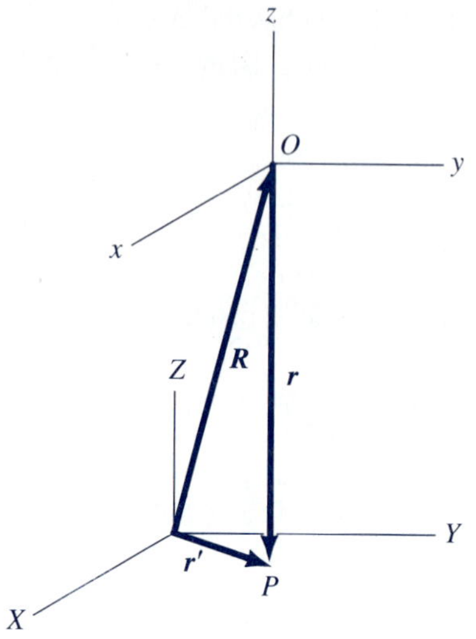

Figure 3.4. References xyz and XYZ separated by position vector $\boldsymbol{R}$.

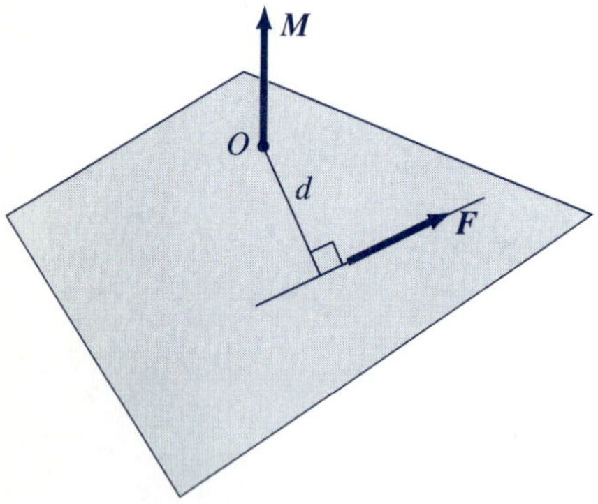

Figure 3.5. Moment of force $\boldsymbol{F}$ about O is Fd.

3.2 Moment of a Force About a Point

Case A. For Simple Cases. The moment of a force about a point O (see Fig. 3.5), you will recall from physics, is a vector $\boldsymbol{M}$ whose magnitude equals the product of the force magnitude times the perpendicular distance d from O to the line of action of the force. And the direction of this vector is perpendicular to the plane of the point and the force, with a sense determined from the familiar right-hand-screw rule.[1] The line of action of $\boldsymbol{M}$ is determined by the problem at hand. In Fig. 3.5, the line of action of $\boldsymbol{M}$ is taken for simplicity through point O.

Case B. For Complex Cases. Another approach is to employ a position vector $\boldsymbol{r}$ from point O to *any point* P along the line of action of force $\boldsymbol{F}$ as shown in Fig. 3.6. The moment $\boldsymbol{M}$ of $\boldsymbol{F}$ about point O will be shown to be given as[2]

$$\boldsymbol{M} = \boldsymbol{r} \times \boldsymbol{F} \quad (3.3)$$

[1]The sense of $\boldsymbol{M}$ would be that of the direction of advance of an ordinary right-hand screw at O, oriented normal to the plane of O and $\boldsymbol{F}$, when this screw is turned with a sense of rotation corresponding to that of $\boldsymbol{F}$ around O.

[2]It is worth pointing out again that in determining the moment of force $\boldsymbol{F}$ about any point O, we must always take the position vector $\boldsymbol{r}$ going *from* point O to *any point along the line of action of the force* $\boldsymbol{F}$. It is easy to make errors here.

For the purpose of forming the cross product, the vectors in Fig. 3.6 can be moved to the configuration shown in Fig. 3.7. Then the cross product between $\boldsymbol{r}$ and $\boldsymbol{F}$ obviously has the magnitude

$$|\boldsymbol{r} \times \boldsymbol{F}| = |\boldsymbol{r}|\,|\boldsymbol{F}| \sin\alpha = |\boldsymbol{F}|\,|\boldsymbol{r}| \sin\beta = |\boldsymbol{F}|\, r \sin\beta = Fd$$

where $r \sin\beta = d$, the perpendicular distance from O to the line of action of $\boldsymbol{F}$, as can readily be seen in Fig. 3.7. Thus, we get the same *magnitude* of $\boldsymbol{M}$ as with the elementary definition. Also, note that the *direction* of $\boldsymbol{M}$ here is identical to that of the elementary definition. Thus we have the same result as for the elementary definition in all pertinent respects. We shall use either of these formulations depending on the situation at hand.

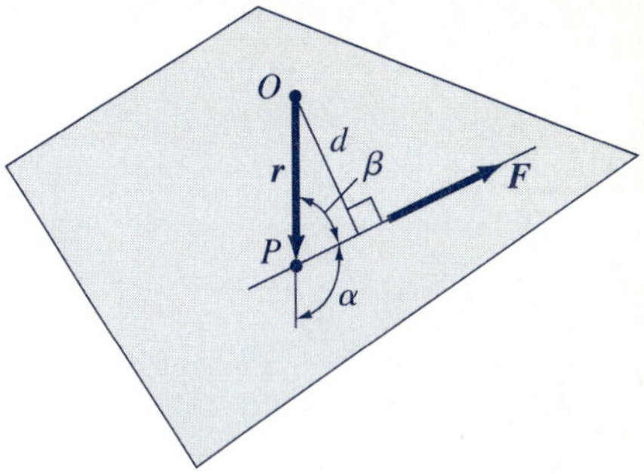

Figure 3.6. Put $\boldsymbol{r}$ from O to any point along the line of action of $\boldsymbol{F}$.

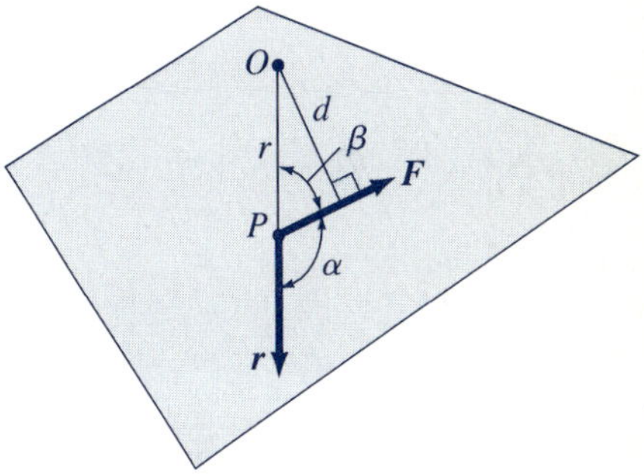

Figure 3.7. Move vector $\boldsymbol{r}$ end $\boldsymbol{F}$.

The first of these formulations will be used generally for cases where the force and point are in a convenient plane, and where the perpendicular distance between the point and the line of action of the force is easily measured. As an example, we have shown in Fig. 3.8 a system of coplanar forces acting on a beam. The moment of the forces about point $\boldsymbol{A}$ is then[3]

$$\begin{aligned}\boldsymbol{M}_A &= -(5)(1{,}000)\boldsymbol{k} - (4)(600)\boldsymbol{k} + (11)R_B\boldsymbol{k} \text{ ft-lb}\\ &= (11R_B - 7{,}400)\boldsymbol{k} \text{ ft-lb}\end{aligned}$$

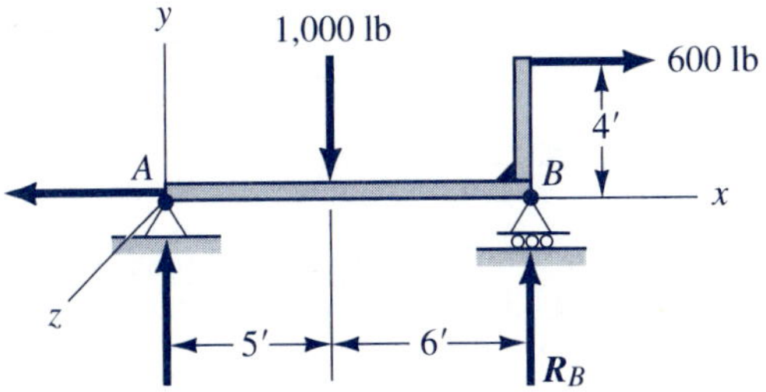

Figure 3.8. Coplanar forces on a beam.

For a coplanar force system such as this, we may simply give the scalar form of the equation above, as follows:

$$M_A = 11R_B - 7{,}400 \text{ ft-lb}$$

The second formulation of the moment about a point, namely $\boldsymbol{r} \times \boldsymbol{F}$, is used for complicated coplanar cases and for three-dimensional cases. We shall illustrate such a case in Example 3.2 after we discuss the rectangular components of $\boldsymbol{M}$.

Consider next a system of n concurrent forces in Fig. 3.9 whose total moment about point O (where we have established reference xyz) is desired. We can say that

$$\begin{aligned}\boldsymbol{M} &= \boldsymbol{M}_1 + \boldsymbol{M}_2 + \boldsymbol{M}_3 + \ldots + \boldsymbol{M}_n\\ &= \boldsymbol{r} \times \boldsymbol{F}_1 + \boldsymbol{r} \times \boldsymbol{F}_2 + \boldsymbol{r} \times \boldsymbol{F}_3\\ &\quad + \ldots + \boldsymbol{r} \times \boldsymbol{F}_n\end{aligned} \tag{3.5}$$

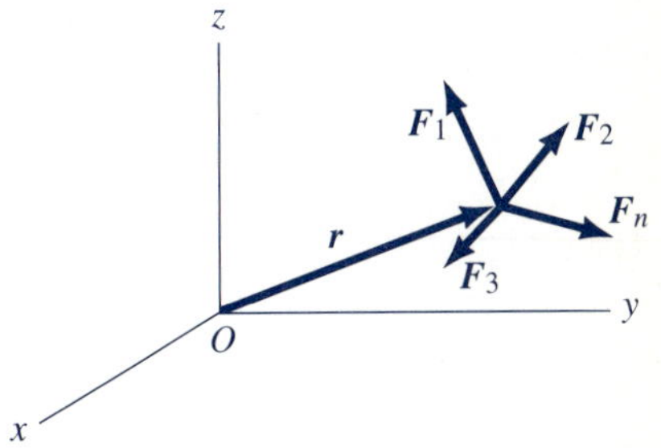

Figure 3.9. Concurrent forces.

[3]Please note that we still use the right-hand-screw rule in determining the signs of the respective moments.

Now, because of the distributive property of the cross product, Eq. 3.5 can be written

$$M = r \times (F_1 + F_2 + F_3 + \ldots + F_n) \tag{3.6}$$

We can conclude from the preceding equations that the sum of the moments about a point of a system of concurrent forces is the same as the moment about the point of the sum of the forces. This result is known as *Varignon's theorem,* which you may well recall from physics.

As a special case of Varignon's theorem, we may find it convenient to decompose a force $\boldsymbol{F}$ into its rectangular components (Fig. 3.10), and then to use these components for taking moments about a point. We can then say that

$$\boldsymbol{M} = \boldsymbol{r} \times \boldsymbol{F} = \boldsymbol{r} \times (F_x\boldsymbol{i} + F_y\boldsymbol{j} + F_z\boldsymbol{k}) \tag{3.7}$$

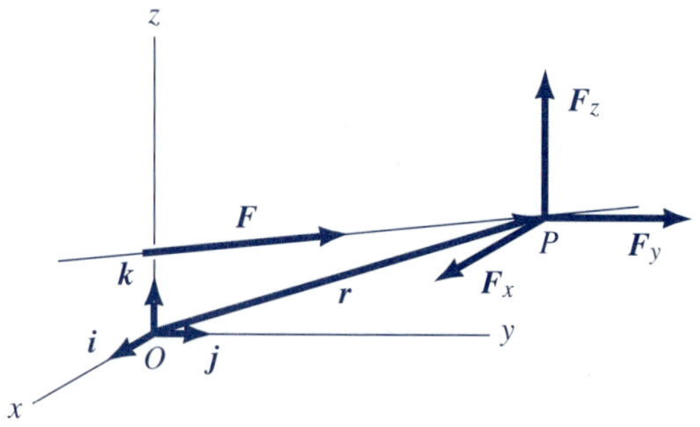

Figure 3.10. Decompose $\boldsymbol{F}$ into components.

Now, replacing $\boldsymbol{r}$ by its components, we get

$$\begin{aligned} \boldsymbol{M} &= (x\boldsymbol{i} + y\boldsymbol{j} + z\boldsymbol{k}) \times (F_x\boldsymbol{i} + F_y\boldsymbol{j} + F_z\boldsymbol{k}) \\ &= (yF_z - zF_y)\boldsymbol{i} + (zF_x - xF_z)\boldsymbol{j} + (xF_y - yF_x)\boldsymbol{k} \end{aligned} \tag{3.8}$$

The scalar rectangular components of $\boldsymbol{M}$ are then

$$M_x = yF_z - zF_y \tag{3.9a}$$
$$M_y = zF_x - xF_z \tag{3.9b}$$
$$M_z = xF_y - yF_x \tag{3.9c}$$

As a final note, it should be apparent that, because we can choose $\boldsymbol{r}$ so as to terminate anywhere along the line of action of $\boldsymbol{F}$ in computing $\boldsymbol{M}$, we are, in effect, stipulating that $\boldsymbol{F}$ is a *transmissible* vector (defined in Chapter 1) in the computation of $\boldsymbol{M}$. However, it must be emphasized that we cannot change the line of action of $\boldsymbol{F}$ here.

We are now ready for the example involving the direct vectorial computation of $\boldsymbol{M}$ promised just before the above discussion.

Example 3.2

Determine the moment of the 100-lb force F, shown in Fig. 3.11, about points A and B, respectively.

As a first step, let us express force F vectorially. Note that the force is collinear with the vector $\boldsymbol{\rho}_{DE}$ from D_{DE} to E, where

$$\boldsymbol{\rho}_{DE} = 8\boldsymbol{i} + 4\boldsymbol{j} - 4\boldsymbol{k} \tag{a}$$

To get a unit vector $\hat{\boldsymbol{\rho}}$ in the direction of $\boldsymbol{\rho}_{DE}$, we proceed as follows:

$$\hat{\boldsymbol{\rho}}_{DE} = \frac{\boldsymbol{\rho}_{DE}}{|\boldsymbol{\rho}_{DE}|} = \frac{8\boldsymbol{i} + 4\boldsymbol{j} - 4\boldsymbol{k}}{\sqrt{8^2 + 4^2 + 4^2}} \tag{b}$$

$$= .816\boldsymbol{i} + .408\boldsymbol{j} - .408\boldsymbol{k}$$

We can then express the force $\boldsymbol{F}$ in the following manner:

$$\boldsymbol{F} = F\hat{\boldsymbol{\rho}}_{DE} = (100)(.816\boldsymbol{i} + .408\boldsymbol{j} - .408\boldsymbol{k})$$

$$= 81.6\boldsymbol{i} + 40.8\boldsymbol{j} - 40.8\boldsymbol{k} \tag{c}$$

To get the moment $\boldsymbol{M}_A$ about point A, we choose a position vector from point A to point D which is on the line of action of force F. Thus, we have, for $\boldsymbol{r}_{AD}$,

$$\boldsymbol{r}_{AD} = 10\boldsymbol{i} + 4\boldsymbol{j} - 8\boldsymbol{k} \text{ ft} \tag{d}$$

and for $\boldsymbol{M}_A$, we than get

$$\boldsymbol{M}_A = \boldsymbol{r}_{AD} \times \boldsymbol{F} = (10\boldsymbol{i} + 4\boldsymbol{j} - 8\boldsymbol{k}) \times (81.6\boldsymbol{i} + 40.8\boldsymbol{j} - 40.8\boldsymbol{k})$$

$$= \left|\begin{array}{ccc} 10 & 4 & -8 \\ 81.6 & 40.8 & -40.8 \\ \boldsymbol{i} & \boldsymbol{j} & \boldsymbol{k} \end{array}\right| \begin{array}{ccc} 10 & 4 & -8 \\ 81.6 & 40.8 & -40.8 \end{array}$$

$$= (10)(40.8)\boldsymbol{k} + (81.6)(-8)\boldsymbol{j} + (4)(-40.8)\boldsymbol{i}$$

$$-(-8)(40.8)\boldsymbol{i} - (-40.8)(10)\boldsymbol{j} - (4)(81.6)\boldsymbol{k}$$

Therefore,

$$\boldsymbol{M}_A = 163.2\boldsymbol{i} - 245\boldsymbol{j} + 81.6\boldsymbol{k} \text{ ft-lb} \tag{e}$$

As for the moment about reference point B, we employ the position vector $\boldsymbol{r}_{BD}$ from B to position D, again on the line of action of force $\boldsymbol{F}$. Thus, we have

$$\boldsymbol{r}_{BD} = 4\boldsymbol{j} - 8\boldsymbol{k} \text{ ft}$$

Accordingly,

$$\boldsymbol{M}_B = \boldsymbol{r}_{BD} \times \boldsymbol{F} = (4\boldsymbol{j} - 8\boldsymbol{k}) \times (81.6\boldsymbol{i} + 40.8\boldsymbol{j} - 40.8\boldsymbol{k})$$

$$= (4)(81.6)(-\boldsymbol{k}) + (4)(-40.8)(\boldsymbol{i}) + (-8)(81.6)(\boldsymbol{j}) + (-8)(40.8)(-\boldsymbol{i}) \tag{f}$$

$$\boldsymbol{M}_B = 163.2\boldsymbol{i} - 653\boldsymbol{j} - 326\boldsymbol{k} \text{ ft-lb}$$

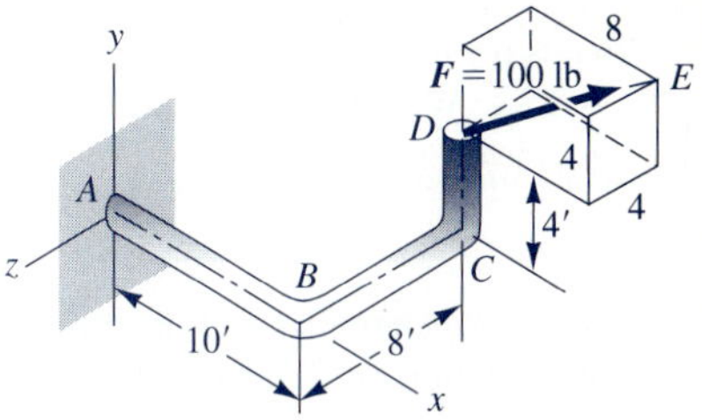

Figure 3.11. Find moments at A and B.

PROBLEMS

3.1. What is the position vector $\boldsymbol{r}$ from the origin (0, 0, 0) to the point (3, 4, 5) ft? What are its magnitude and direction cosines?

3.2. What is the displacement vector from position (6, 13, 7) ft to position (10, –3, 4) ft?

3.3. A surveyor determines that the top of a radio transmission tower is at position $\boldsymbol{r}_1 = (1{,}000\boldsymbol{i} + 1{,}000\boldsymbol{j} + 1{,}000\boldsymbol{k})$ m relative to her position. Similarly, the top of a second tower is located by $\boldsymbol{r}_2 = (2{,}000\boldsymbol{i} + 500\boldsymbol{j} + 700\boldsymbol{k})$ m. What is the distance between the two tower tops?

3.4. Reference xyz is rotated 30° counterclockwise about its x axis to form reference XYZ. What is the position vector $\boldsymbol{r}$ for reference xyz of a point having a position vector $\boldsymbol{r}'$ for reference XYZ given as

$$\boldsymbol{r}' = 6\boldsymbol{i}' + 10\boldsymbol{j}' + 3\boldsymbol{k}' \text{ m?}$$

Use $\boldsymbol{i}, \boldsymbol{j}$, and $\boldsymbol{k}$ (no primes) for unit vectors associated with reference xyz.

3.5. Find the moment of the 50-lb force about the support at A and about support B of the simply supported beam.

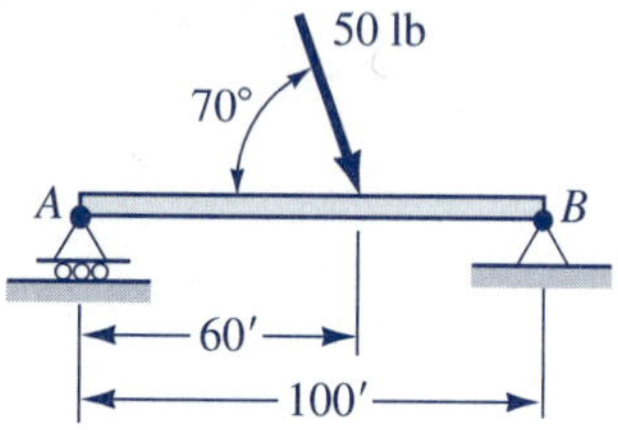

Figure P.3.5.

3.6. Find the moment of the two forces first about point A and then about point B.

(a) Do not use $\boldsymbol{r} \times \boldsymbol{F}$ format—only scalar products.

(b) Use vector approach.

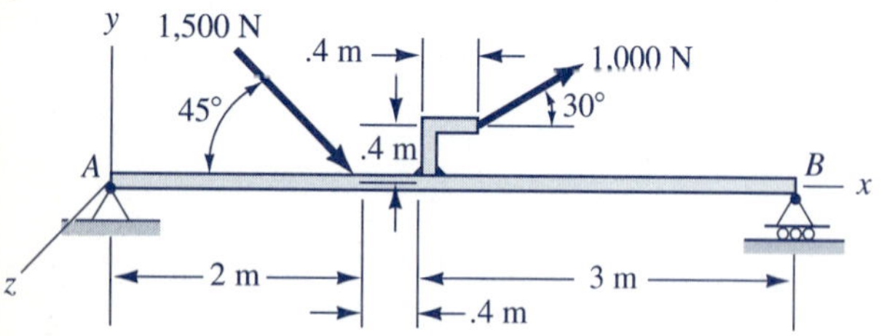

Figure P.3.6.

3.7. A particle moves along a circular path in the xy plane. What is the position vector $\boldsymbol{r}$ of this particle as a function of the coordinate x?

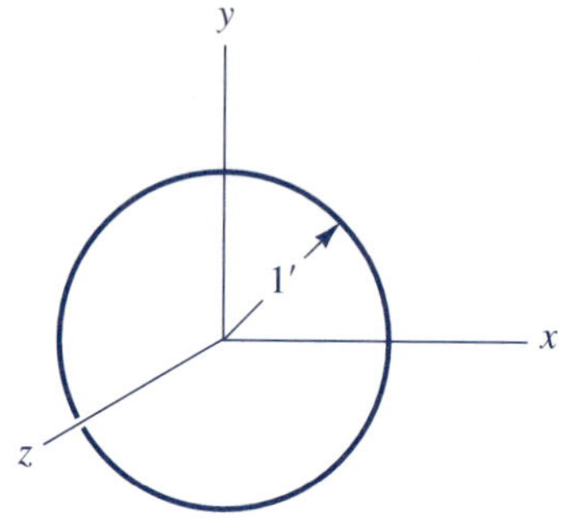

Figure P.3.7.

3.8. A particle moves along a parabolic path in the yz plane. If the particle has at one point a position vector $\boldsymbol{r} = 4\boldsymbol{j} + 2\boldsymbol{k}$, give the position vector at any point on the path as a function of the z coordinate.

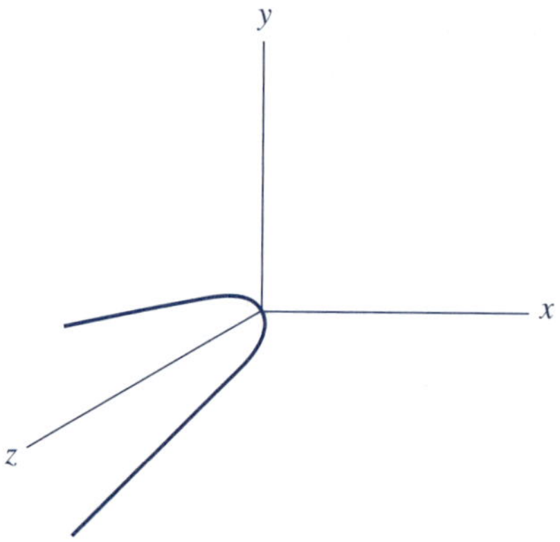

Figure P.3.8.

3.9. An artillery spotter on Hill 350 (350 m high) estimates the position of an enemy tank as 3,000 m NE of him at an elevation 200 m below his position. A 105-mm howitzer unit with a range of 11,000 m is 10,000 m due south of the spotter, and a 155-mm howitzer unit with a range of 15,000 m is 13,000 m SSE of the spotter (see Fig. P.2.4). Both gun units are located at an elevation of 150 m. Can either or both gun units hit the tank, or must an air strike be called in?

3.10. Find the moment of the forces about points A and B.
(a) Use scalar approach.
(b) Use vector approach.

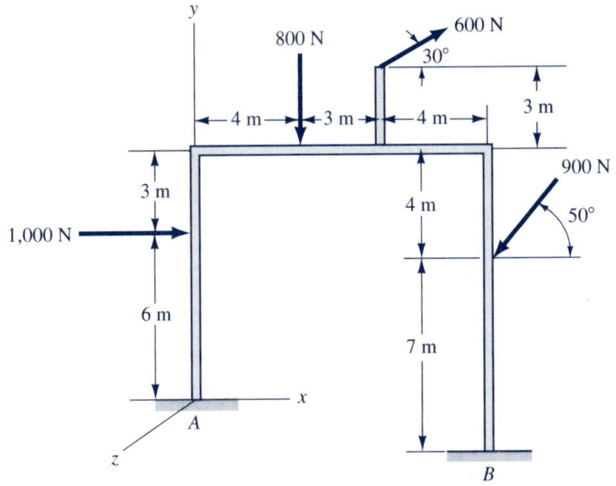

Figure P.3.10.

3.11. The crew of a submarine patrol plane, with three-dimensional radar, sights a surfaced submarine 10,000 yards north and 5,000 yards east while flying at an elevation of 3,000 ft above sea level. Where should the pilot instruct a second patrol plane flying at an elevation of 4,000 ft at a position 40,000 yards east of the first plane to look for confirmation of the sighting?

3.12. A power company lineman can comfortably trim branches 1 m from his waist at an angle of 45° above the horizontal. His waist coincides with the pivot of the work capsule. How high a branch can he trim if the maximum elevation angle of the arm is 75° and the maximum extended length is 12 m?

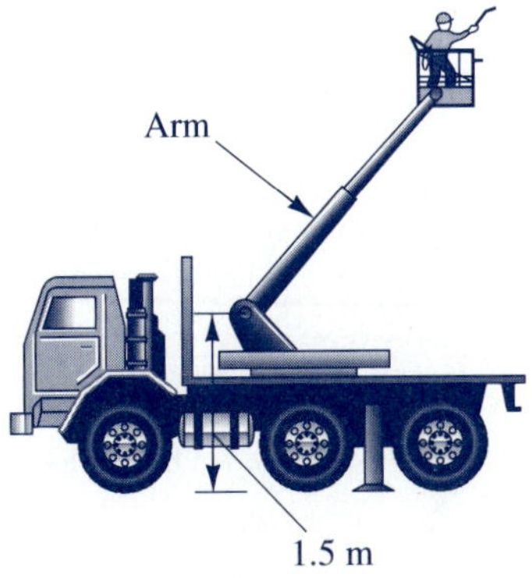

Figure P.3.12.

3.13. The total equivalent forces from water and gravity are shown on the dam. (We will soon be able to compute such equivalents.) Compute the moment of these forces about the toe of the dam in the right-hand corner.

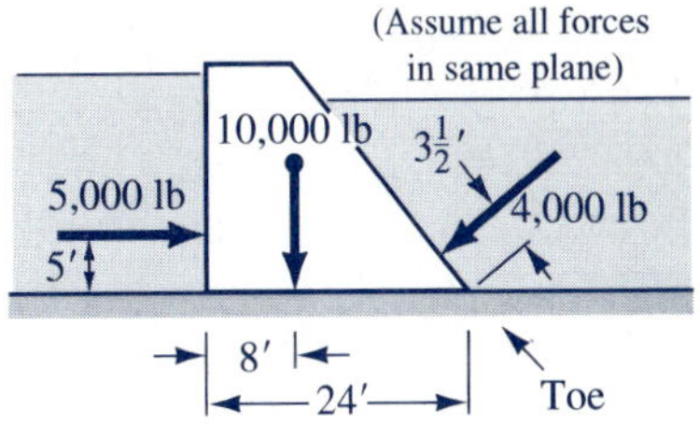

Figure P.3.13.

3.14. In an underwater "village" for research, an American flag is in place as shown. It is of plastic material and can rotate so as to be oriented parallel to the flow of water. A uniform friction force distribution from the flow is present on both faces of the flag having the value of 10 N per square meter. Also the flagpole has a uniform force from the flow of 20 N per meter of length of the flagpole. Finally there is an upward buoyant force on the flag of 30 N and on the flagpole of 8 N. What is the moment vector of these forces at the base of the flagpole?

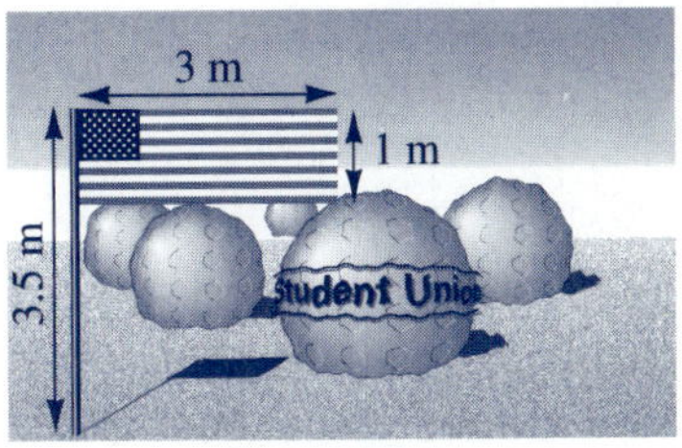

Figure P.3.14.

3.15. Three transmission lines are placed unsymmetrically on a power-line pole. For each pole, the weight of a single line when covered with ice is 2,000 N. What is the moment at the base of a pole?

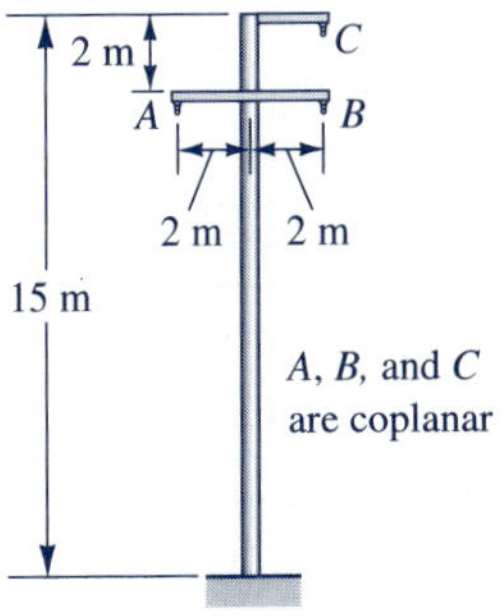

Figure P.3.15.

3.16. Compute the moment of the 1,000-lb force about points A, B, and C. Use the transmissibility property of force and rectangular components to make the computations simplest.

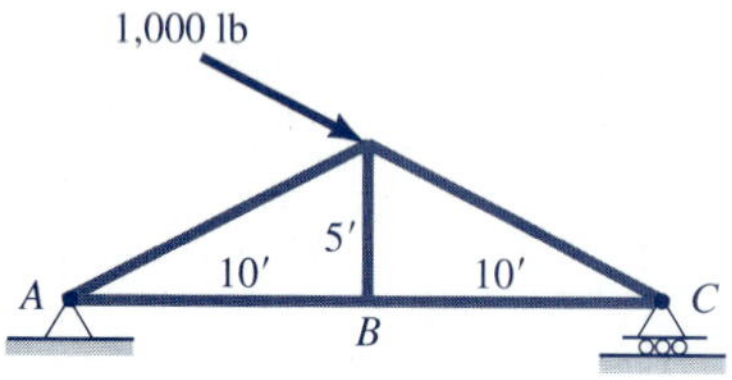

Figure P.3.16.

3.17. A truck-mounted crane has a 20-m boom inclined at 60° to the horizontal. What is the moment about the boom pivot due to a lifted weight of 30 kN? Do by vector and by scalar methods.

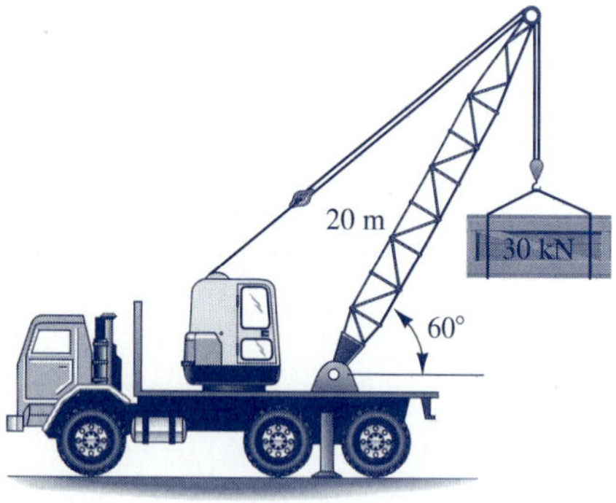

Figure P.3.17.

3.18. A small blimp is temporarily moored as shown in the diagram wherein DC and the centerline of AB are coplanar. A force $\boldsymbol{F}$ from wind, weight, and buoyancy is shown acting at the centerline of the blimp. If

$$\boldsymbol{F} = 5\boldsymbol{i} + 10\boldsymbol{j} + 18\boldsymbol{k} \text{ kN}$$

what are the moment vectors from $\boldsymbol{F}$ about A, B, and C?

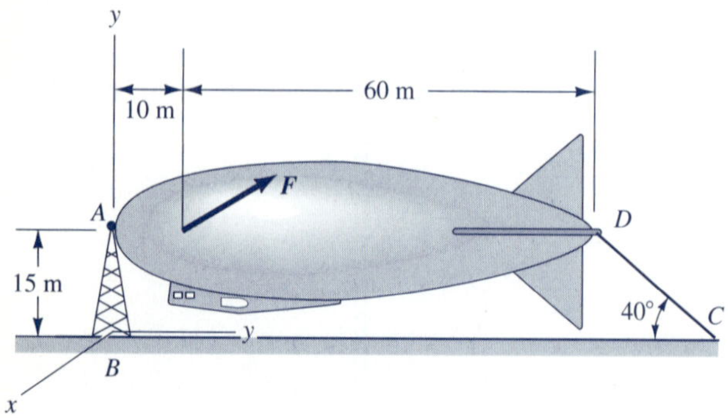

Figure P.3.18.

3.19. A force $\boldsymbol{F} = 10\boldsymbol{i} + 6\boldsymbol{j} - 6\boldsymbol{k}$ N acts at position (10, 3, 4) m relative to a coordinate system. What is the moment of the force about the origin?

3.20. What is the moment of the force in Problem 3.19 about the point (6, −4, −3) m?

3.21. Two forces $\boldsymbol{F}_1$ and $\boldsymbol{F}_2$ have magnitudes of 10 lb and 20 lb, respectively. $\boldsymbol{F}_1$ has a set of direction cosines $l = 0.5$, $m = 0.707$, $n = -0.5$. $\boldsymbol{F}_2$ has a set of direction cosines $l = 0$, $m = 0.6$, $n = 0.8$. If $\boldsymbol{F}_1$ acts at point (3, 2, 2) and $\boldsymbol{F}_2$ acts at (1, 0, −3), what is the sum of the moments about the origin?

3.22. What is the moment of a 10-lb force $\boldsymbol{F}$ directed along the diagonal of a cube about the corners of the cube? The side of the cube is a ft.

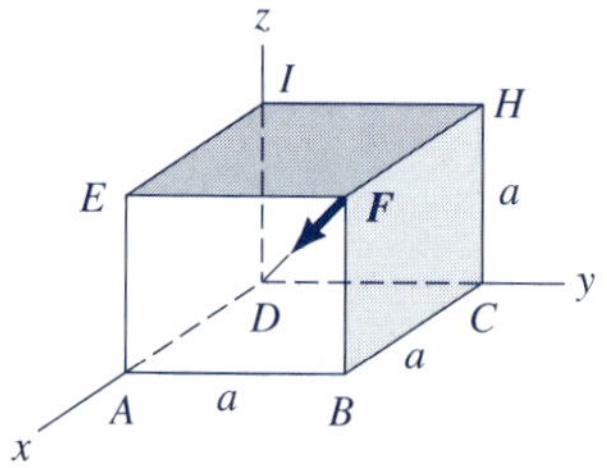

Figure P.3.22.

3.23. Three guy wires are used in the support system for a television transmission tower that is 600 m tall. Wires A and B are tightened to a tension of 60 kN, whereas wire C has only 30 kN of tension. What is the moment of the wire forces about the base O of the tower? The y axis is collinear with AO.

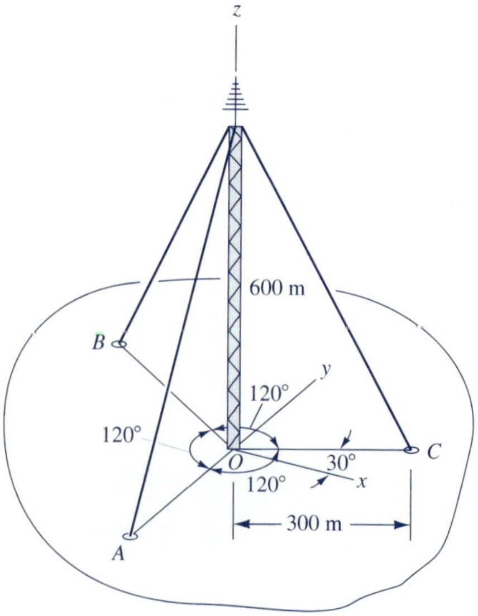

Figure P.3.23.

3.24. Cables CD and AB help support member ED and the 1,000-lb load at D. At E there is a ball-and-socket joint which also supports the member. Denoting the forces from the cables as F_{CD} and F_{AB}, respectively, compute moments of the three forces about point E. Plane EGD is perpendicular to the wall. Get results in terms of F_{CD} and F_{AB}.

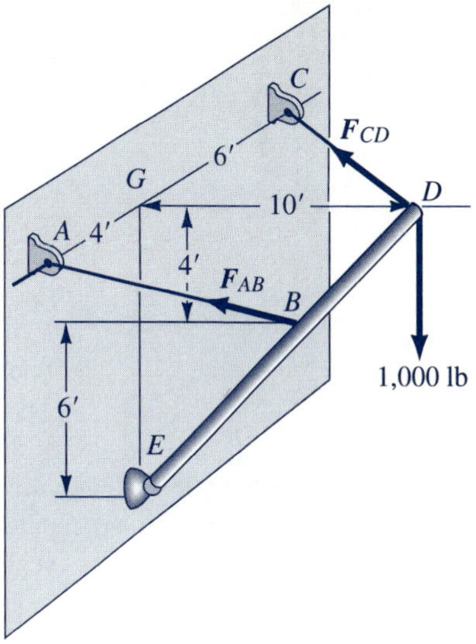

Figure P.3.24.

3.3 Moment of a Force About an Axis

Case A. For Simple Cases. By means of a simple situation, we shall set forth a definition of the moment of a force about an axis. Suppose that a disc is mounted on a shaft that is free to rotate in a set of bearings, as shown in Fig. 3.12. A force $\boldsymbol{F}$, inclined to the plane A of the disc, acts on the disc. We decompose the force into two coplanar rectangular components, one normal to plane A of the disc and one tangent to plane A of the disc, that is, into forces F_B and F_A, respectively, so as to form a plane shown tinted, normal to plane A.

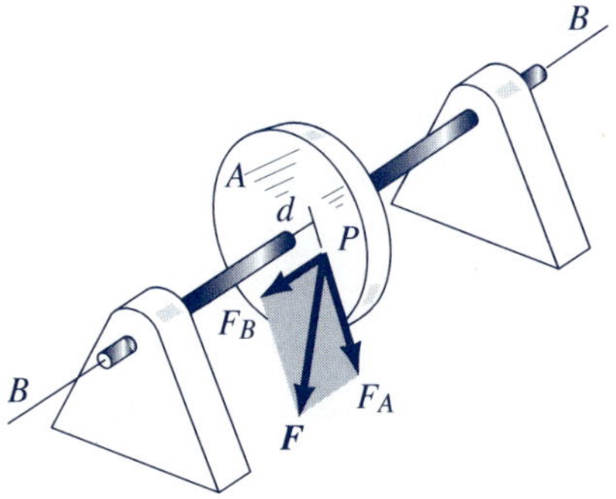

Figure 3.12. F_A turns disc.

We know from experience that F_B does not cause the disc to rotate. And we know from physics and intuition that the rotational motion of the disc is determined by the product of F_A and the perpendicular distance d from the centerline of the shaft to the line of action of F_A. You will remember from physics, this product is nothing more than the moment of force $\boldsymbol{F}$ about the axis of the shaft. We shall next generalize from this simple case to the general case of taking the moment of *any* force $\boldsymbol{F}$ about *any* axis.

To compute the moment (or torque) of a force $\boldsymbol{F}$ in a plane perpendicular to plane A about an axis B–B (Fig. 3.13), we pass any plane A perpendicular to the axis. This plane cuts B–B at a and the line of action of force $\boldsymbol{F}$ at some point P. The force $\boldsymbol{F}$ is then projected to form a rectangular component F_B along a line at P normal to plane A and thus parallel to B–B, as shown in the diagram. The intersection of plane A with the plane of forces F_B and $\boldsymbol{F}$ (the latter plane is shown shaded and is a plane through $\boldsymbol{F}$ and perpendicular to plane A) gives a direction C–C along which the other rectangular component of $\boldsymbol{F}$, denoted as F_A, can be projected.[4] The moment of $\boldsymbol{F}$ about the line B–B is then defined as the scalar representation of the moment of F_A about point a with a magnitude equal to $F_A d$—a problem discussed at the beginning of the previous section (Case A). Thus in accordance with the definition, the component F_B, which is parallel to the axis B–B, contributes no moment about the axis, and we may say:

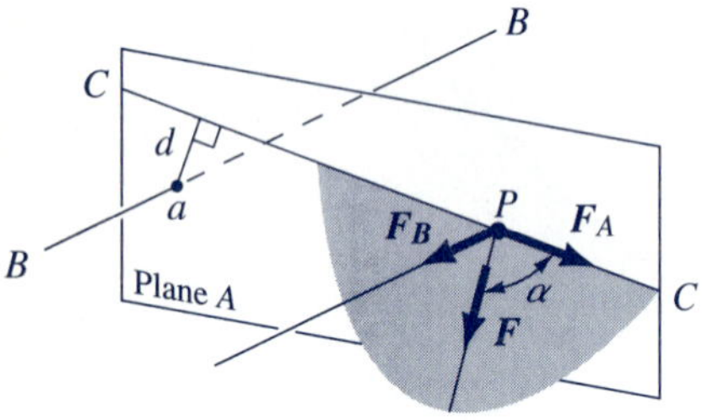

Figure 3.13. Formulating the moment about an axis B–B.

$$\text{Moment about axis } B\text{–}B = (F_A)(d) = |\boldsymbol{F}|(\cos\alpha)(d)$$

with an appropriate sign. The moment about an axis clearly is a scalar, even though this moment is associated with a particular axis that has a distinct direction. The situation is the same as it is with the scalar components V_x, V_y, V_z, etc., which are associated with certain directions but which are scalars. The reader will be quick to note that Fig. 3.13 represents a generalization of Fig. 3.12 having an axis B–B, a plane A normal to this axis and finally an arbitrary force $\boldsymbol{F}$. To explain further, we have redrawn Fig. 3.13 [see Fig. 3.14(a)] showing only plane A, axes B–B and C–C, and the force F_A. In Fig. 3.14(b), we have also included the moment vector $\boldsymbol{M}$. This latter diagram then takes us back to Fig. 3.5 where we first defined the moment vector of a force about a point in a most simple manner. Accordingly, we note, on the one hand, for the moment about point a [see Fig. 3.14(b)], we can get the vector $\boldsymbol{M}$, whereas on the other hand in Fig. 3.14(a) we can get the scalar moment M about an axis B–B at point a and perpendicular to plane A. Thus, by taking the scalar value of $\boldsymbol{M}$ in Fig. 3.14(b), we get the moment about the axis at point a normal to plane A as formulated in the development of Fig. 3.13.

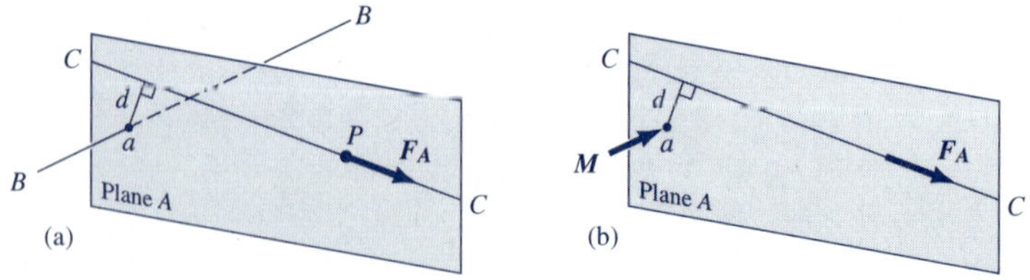

Figure 3.14. Comparison of Figs. 3.13 and 3.5.

[4]Notice that we are decomposing $\boldsymbol{F}$ into only *two* rectangular components, which, to replace $\boldsymbol{F}$, must be coplanar with $\boldsymbol{F}$.

We can thus conclude, on considering Fig. 3.15, that the moment of $\boldsymbol{F}$ about point C can be considered in two ways as follows:

Moment vector about point C = $-Fd\,\mathbf{k}$
Torque (or moment) about z axis at point C = $-Fd$

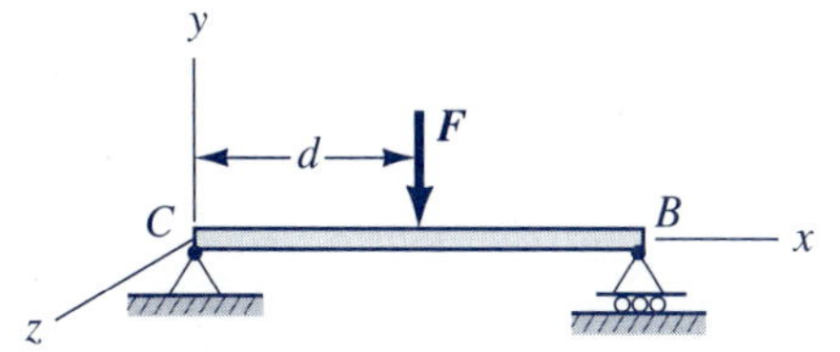

Figure 3.15. Consideration of the moment of $\boldsymbol{F}$ about point A.

Before continuing, we wish to point out that F_A in Fig. 3.13 can be decomposed into pairs of components in plane A. From Varignon's theorem we can employ these components instead of F_A in computing the moment about the B–B axis. For each force component, we multiply the force times the perpendicular distance from a to the line of action of the force component using the right-hand-screw rule to determine the sense and thus the sign.

Case B. For Complex Cases. When we discussed the moment of a force about a *point*, we presented a formulation useful for simple cases (i.e., a vector of magnitude Fd) as well as a more powerful formulation that would be needed for more complex situations (i.e., $\boldsymbol{r} \times \boldsymbol{F}$). Thus far, for moments about an *axis*, we have presented a formulation Fd that is useful for simple cases,[5] and now we shall present a formulation that is needed for more complex cases. For this purpose, we have redrawn Fig. 13.13 as Fig. 13.16(a). In Fig. 13.16(b), we have shown axis B–B of Fig. 13.16(a) as an x axis and have set up coordinate axes y and z at *any* point O anywhere on axis B–B. The coordinate distances x, y, and z for the point P are shown for this reference. The position vector $\boldsymbol{r}$ to P is also shown. The force component F_B of Fig. 3.16(a) now becomes force component F_x. And, instead of using F_A, we shall decompose it into components F_y and F_z in plane A as shown in Fig. 3.16(b). We now compute the moment about the x axis for force $\boldsymbol{F}$ using this new arrangement which does not require $\boldsymbol{F}$ to be in a plane perpendicular to plane A. Clearly, F_x contributes no moment, as before. The force components F_y and F_z are in plane A that is perpendicular to the axis of interest and so, as before in the case of F_A, we multiply each of these forces by the perpendicular distance of point a to the respective lines of action of these forces.

[5]That is, for cases where the *force* and *point* in question are in a plane easily seen to be normal to the *axis* in question, thus allowing for an easy determination of the perpendicular distance between the point and the line of action of the force.

For force F_z, this perpendicular distance is clearly y, as can readily be seen from the diagram, and, for force F_y, this perpendicular distance is z. Using the right-hand-screw rule for ascertaining the sense of each of the moments, we can say:

$$\text{moment about } x \text{ axis} = (yF_z - zF_y) \tag{3.10}$$

Were we to take moments of $\boldsymbol{F}$ about the origin O, we would get (see Eq. 3.8)

$$\begin{aligned} \boldsymbol{M} &= M_x\boldsymbol{i} + M_y\boldsymbol{j} + M_z\boldsymbol{k} = \boldsymbol{r} \times \boldsymbol{F} \\ &= (yF_z - zF_y)\boldsymbol{i} + (zF_x - xF_z)\boldsymbol{j} + (xF_y - yF_x)\boldsymbol{k} \end{aligned} \tag{3.11}$$

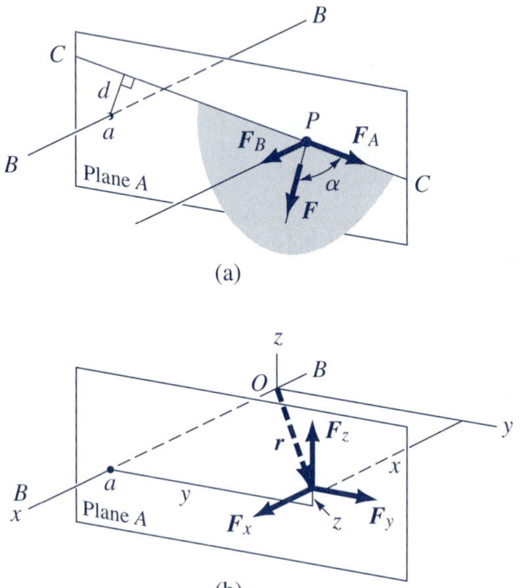

Figure 3.16. Moment about an axis.

Comparing Eqs. 3.10 and 3.11, we can conclude that the moment about the x axis is simply M_x, the x component of $\boldsymbol{M}$ about O. We can thus conclude that the moment about the x axis of the force $\boldsymbol{F}$ is the component in the x direction of the moment of $\boldsymbol{F}$ about a point O positioned *anywhere* along the x axis. That is,

$$\text{moment about } x \text{ axis} = M_x = M_o \cdot \boldsymbol{i} = (\boldsymbol{r} \times \boldsymbol{F}) \cdot \boldsymbol{i} \tag{3.12}$$

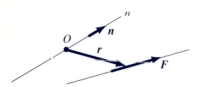

Figure 3.17. $M_n = (\boldsymbol{r} \times \boldsymbol{F}) \cdot \boldsymbol{n}$.

We may generalize the preceding discussion as follows. Consider an arbitrary axis n–n to which we have assigned a unit vector $\boldsymbol{n}$ (Fig. 3.17). An arbitrary force $\boldsymbol{F}$ is also shown. To get the moment M_n of force $\boldsymbol{F}$ about axis n–n, we choose any point O along n–n. Then draw a position vector $\boldsymbol{r}$ from point O to any point along the line of action of $\boldsymbol{F}$. This has been shown in the diagram. We can then say, from our previous discussion,

$$M_n = (\boldsymbol{r} \times \boldsymbol{F}) \cdot \boldsymbol{n} \tag{3.13}$$

(Notice from Eqs. 3.12 and 3.13 that the moment of a force about an axis involves a scalar triple product.) Equation 3.13 stipulates in words that:

The moment of a force about an axis equals the scalar component in the direction of the axis of the moment vector taken about any point along the axis.

This is the more powerful formulation that can be used for complex cases.

Note that the unit vector $\boldsymbol{n}$ can have two opposite senses along the axis n, in contrast to the usual unit vectors $\boldsymbol{i}$, $\boldsymbol{j}$, and $\boldsymbol{k}$ associated with the coordinate axes. A moment M_n about the n axis determined from $\boldsymbol{M} \cdot \boldsymbol{n}$ has a sense consistent with the sense chosen for $\boldsymbol{n}$. That is, a positive moment M_n has a sense corresponding to that of $\boldsymbol{n}$, and a negative moment M_n has a sense opposite to that of $\boldsymbol{n}$. If the opposite sense had been chosen for $\boldsymbol{n}$, the sign of $\boldsymbol{M} \cdot \boldsymbol{n}$ would be opposite to that found in the first case. However, the same physical moment is obtained in both cases.

If we specify the moments of a force about *three* orthogonal concurrent axes, we then single out *one* possible point in space for O along the axes. Point O, of course, is the origin of the axes. These three moments about orthogonal axes then become the orthogonal scalar components of the moment of $\boldsymbol{F}$ about point O, and we can say:

$$\begin{aligned}\boldsymbol{M} = &\text{(moment about the } x \text{ axis)}\boldsymbol{i} + \\ &\text{(moment about the } y \text{ axis)}\boldsymbol{j} + \\ &\text{(moment about the } z \text{ axis)}\boldsymbol{k} = M_x\boldsymbol{i} + M_y\boldsymbol{j} + M_z\boldsymbol{k}\end{aligned} \tag{3.14}$$

From this relation, we can conclude that:

The three orthogonal components of the moment of a force about a point are the moments of this force about the three orthogonal axes that have the point as an origin.

You may now ask what the physical differences are in applications of moments about an axis and moments about a point. The simplest example is in the dynamics of rigid bodies. If a body is constrained so it can only spin about its axis, as in Fig. 3.12, the rotary motion will depend on the moment of the forces about the axis of rotation, as related by a scalar equation. The less familiar concept of moment about a point is illustrated in the motion of bodies that have no constraints, such as missiles and rockets. In these cases, the rotational motion of the body is related by a vector equation to the moment of forces acting on the body about a point called the *center of mass*. (The center of mass will be defined completely later.)

Example 3.3

Compute the moment of a force $\boldsymbol{F} = 10\boldsymbol{i} + 6\boldsymbol{j}$ N, which goes through position $\boldsymbol{r}_a = 2\boldsymbol{i} + 6\boldsymbol{j}$ m (see Fig. 3.18), about a line going through points 1 and 2 having the respective position vectors

$$\boldsymbol{r}_1 = 6\boldsymbol{i} + 10\boldsymbol{j} - 3\boldsymbol{k} \text{ m}$$
$$\boldsymbol{r}_2 = -3\boldsymbol{i} - 12\boldsymbol{j} + 6\boldsymbol{k} \text{ m}$$

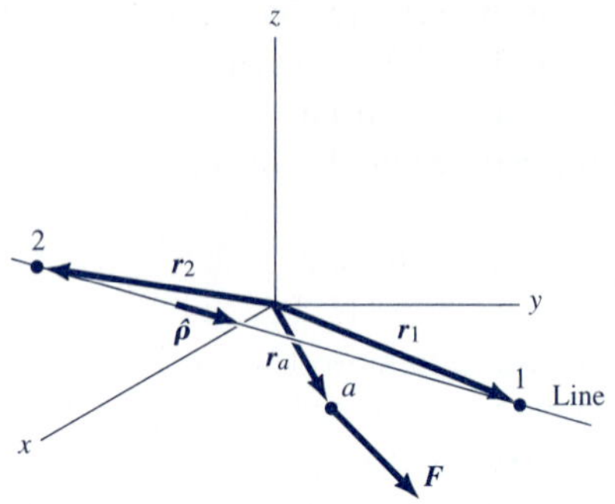

Figure 3.18. Find moment of $\boldsymbol{F}$ about line.

To compute this moment, we can take the moment of $\boldsymbol{F}$ about either point 1 or point 2, and then find the component of this vector along the direction of the displacement vector between 1 and 2 or between 2 and 1. Mathematically, we have, using a displacement vector from point 1 to point a, namely $(\boldsymbol{r}_a - \boldsymbol{r}_1)$,

$$M_\rho = [(\boldsymbol{r}_a - \boldsymbol{r}_1) \times \boldsymbol{F}] \cdot \hat{\boldsymbol{\rho}} \qquad \text{(a)}$$

where $\hat{\boldsymbol{\rho}}$ is the unit vector along the line chosen to have a sense going from point 2 to point 1. The formulation above is the scalar triple product examined in Chapter 2 and we can use the determinant approach for the calculation once the components of the vectors $(\boldsymbol{r}_a - \boldsymbol{r}_1)$, $\boldsymbol{F}$, and $\hat{\boldsymbol{\rho}}$ have been determined. Thus, we have

$$\begin{aligned}
\boldsymbol{r}_a - \boldsymbol{r}_1 &= (2\boldsymbol{i} + 6\boldsymbol{j}) - (6\boldsymbol{i} + 10\boldsymbol{j} - 3\boldsymbol{k}) \\
&= -4\boldsymbol{i} - 4\boldsymbol{j} + 3\boldsymbol{k} \text{ m} \\
\boldsymbol{F} &= 10\boldsymbol{i} + 6\boldsymbol{j} \text{ N} \\
\hat{\boldsymbol{\rho}} &= \frac{\boldsymbol{r}_1 - \boldsymbol{r}_2}{|\boldsymbol{r}_1 - \boldsymbol{r}_2|} = \frac{9\boldsymbol{i} + 22\boldsymbol{j} - 9\boldsymbol{k}}{\sqrt{81 + 484 + 81}} \\
&= .354\boldsymbol{i} + .866\boldsymbol{j} - .354\boldsymbol{k}
\end{aligned}$$

We then have, for M_ρ:

$$M_\rho = \begin{vmatrix} -4 & -4 & 3 \\ 10 & 6 & 0 \\ .354 & .866 & -.354 \end{vmatrix} = \boxed{13.94 \text{ N-m}} \qquad \text{(b)}$$

Because M_ρ is positive, we have a clockwise moment about the line as we look from point 2 to point 1. If we had chosen $\hat{\boldsymbol{\rho}}$ to have an opposite sense, then M_ρ would have been computed as −13.94 N-m. Then, we would conclude that M_ρ is a counterclockwise moment about the line as one looks from point 1 to point 2. Note that the same physical moment is determined in both cases.

Example 3.4

A deep submergence vessel is connected to its mother ship by a cable (Fig. 3.19). The vessel becomes snagged on some rocks and the mother ship steams ahead in a forward direction in an attempt to free the submerged vessel. The connecting cable is suspended from a crane directed up over the water 20 m above the center of mass of the mother ship and 15 m out from the longitudinal axis of the mother ship. The cable transmits a force of 200 kN. It is inclined 50° from the vertical in a vertical plane which, in turn, is oriented 20° from the longitudinal axis of the ship. What is the moment tending to cause the mother ship to roll about its longitudinal axis (i.e., the x-axis)?

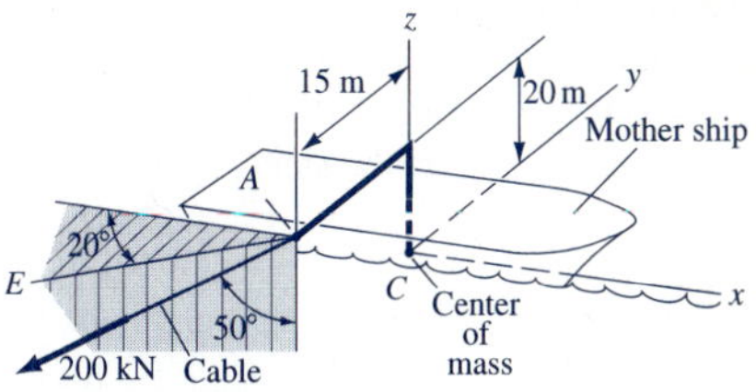

Figure 3.19. Torque on a ship about a horizontal axis through the center of mass.

The position vector from the center of mass C to point A is

$$\boldsymbol{r} = -15\boldsymbol{j} + 20\boldsymbol{k} \text{ m}$$

Next consider the 200-kN force on the cable. Notice that the cable is in a plane which was rotated 20° counterclockwise from an orientation parallel to the xz plane and in this rotated plane, the cable is at an angle of 50° from the vertical. We first decompose the 200-kN force into two coplanar rectangular components, one along the vertical and one along AE. We have then

$$\boldsymbol{F}_{CABLE} = -200 \cos 50° \,\boldsymbol{k} + \boldsymbol{F}_{AE} = -128.6\boldsymbol{k} + \boldsymbol{F}_{AE} \text{ kN}$$

Next, decompose $\boldsymbol{F}_{AE}$ into two coplanar rectangular components, one parallel to the y axis, and the other parallel to the x axis. We then get, noting that $|\boldsymbol{F}_{AE}| = 200 \sin 50°$ kN,

$$\boldsymbol{F}_{AE} = (200 \sin 50°)[-\cos 20°\boldsymbol{i} - \sin 20°\boldsymbol{j}] = -144\boldsymbol{i} - 52.4\boldsymbol{j} \text{ kN}$$

Hence,

$$\boldsymbol{F}_{CABLE} = -144\boldsymbol{i} - 52.4\boldsymbol{j} - 128.6\boldsymbol{k} \text{ kN}$$

To get the desired moment, we have the following formulation:

$$\boldsymbol{M}_x = \left[\mathbf{r} \times \boldsymbol{F}_{CABLE}\right] \bullet \mathbf{i}$$
$$\boldsymbol{M}_x = \left[(-15\mathbf{j} + 20\mathbf{k}) \times (-144\mathbf{i} - 52.4\mathbf{j} - 128.6\mathbf{k})\right] \bullet \mathbf{i}$$

Using the determinant format for the triple scalar product we get

$$\boldsymbol{M}_x = \begin{vmatrix} 0 & -15 & 20 \\ -144 & -52.4 & -128.6 \\ 1 & 0 & 0 \end{vmatrix} \text{ kN-m}$$

We get on carrying out the determinant

$$\boldsymbol{M}_x = 2{,}977 \text{ kN–m}$$

PROBLEMS

3.25. Disc A has a radius of 600 mm. What is the moment of the forces about the center of the disc? What is the torque of these forces about the axis of the shaft?

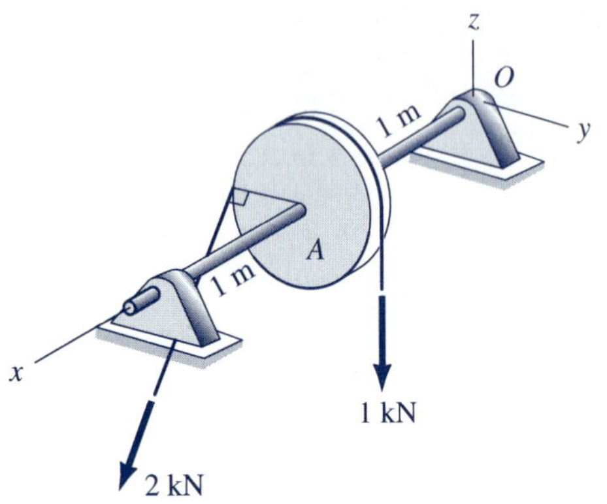

Figure P.3.25.

3.26. A force $\boldsymbol{F}$ acts at position (3, 2, 0) ft. It is in the xy plane and is inclined at 30° from the x axis with a sense directed away from the origin. What is the moment of this force about an axis going through the points (6, 2, 5) ft and (0, −2, −3) ft?

3.27. A force $\boldsymbol{F} = 10\boldsymbol{i} + 6\boldsymbol{j}$ N goes through the origin of the coordinate system. What is the moment of this force $\boldsymbol{F}$ about an axis going through points 1 and 2 with position vectors?

$$\boldsymbol{r}_1 = 6\boldsymbol{i} + 3\boldsymbol{k} \text{ m}$$
$$\boldsymbol{r}_2 = 16\boldsymbol{j} - 4\boldsymbol{k} \text{ m}$$

3.28. Given a force $\boldsymbol{F} = 10\boldsymbol{i} + 3\boldsymbol{j}$ N acting at position $\boldsymbol{r} = 5\boldsymbol{j} + 10\boldsymbol{k}$ m, what is the torque about the diagonal shown in the diagram? What is the moment about point E?

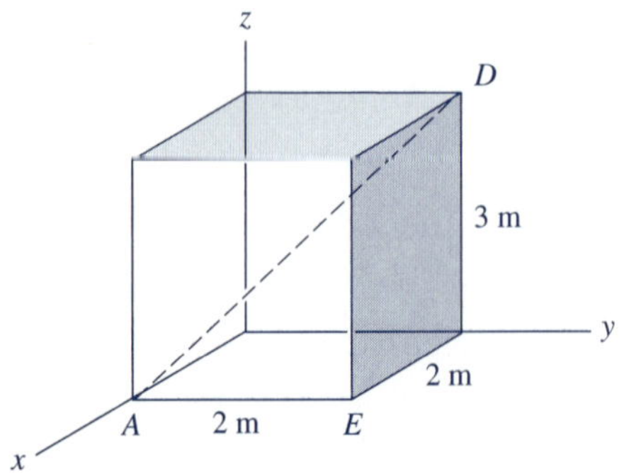

Figure P.3.28.

3.29. A blimp is moored to a tower at A. A force on A from this blimp is

$$\boldsymbol{F} = 5\boldsymbol{i} + 3\boldsymbol{j} + 1.8\boldsymbol{k} \text{ kN}$$

What is the moment about axis C on the ground? Knowledge of this moment and other moments at the base is needed to properly design the foundation of the tower.

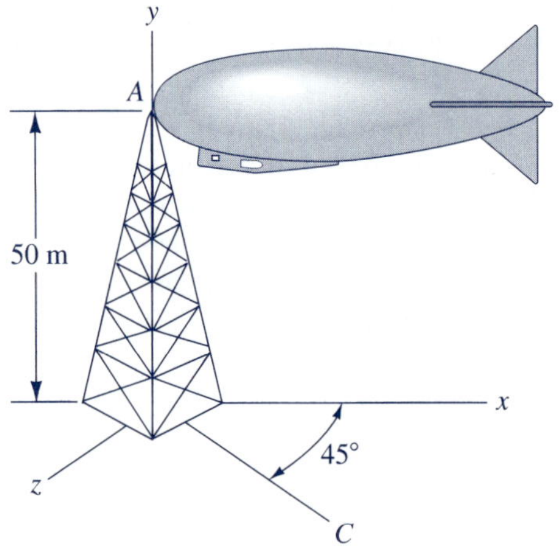

Figure P.3.29.

3.30. Compute the thrust of the applied forces shown along the axis of the shaft and the torque of the forces about the axis of the shaft.

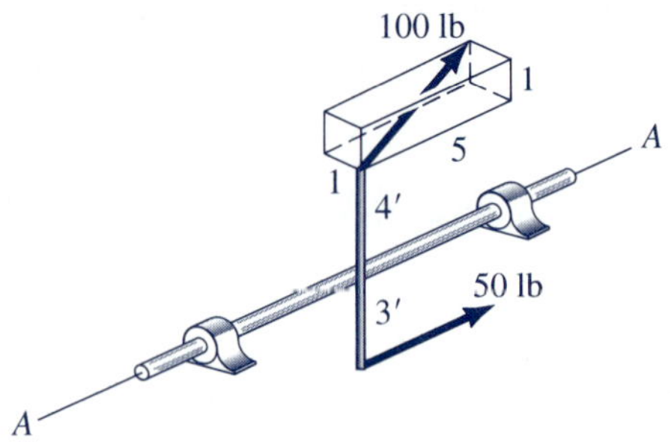

Figure P.3.30.

3.31. What is the maximum load W that the crane can lift without tipping about A? *Hint:* when tipping is impending, what is the supporting force at the wheel at B?

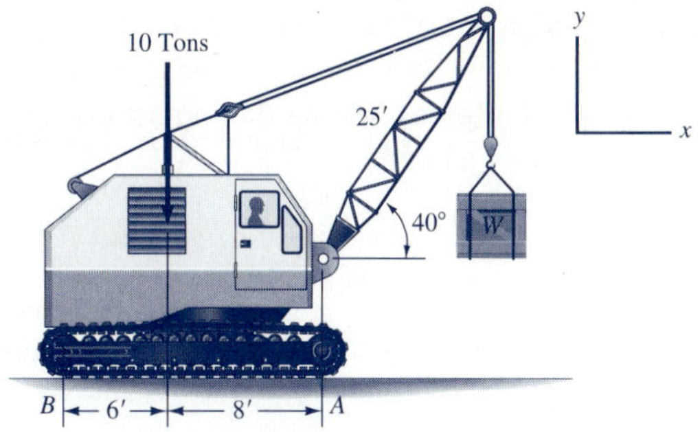

Figure P.3.31.

3.32. Find the moment of the 1,000-lb force about an axis going between points D and C.

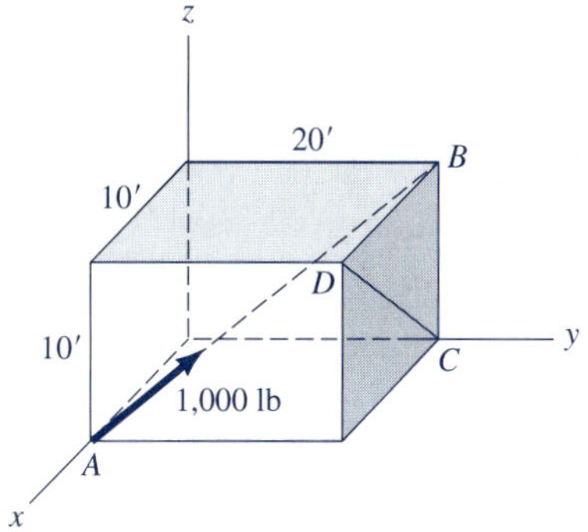

Figure P.3.32.

3.33. In Problem 3.24, what is the moment of the three indicated forces about axis GD?

3.34. The base of a fire truck extension ladder is rotated 75° counter-clockwise. The 25-m ladder is elevated 60° from the horizontal. The ladder weight is 20 kN and is regarded as concentrated at a point 10 m up from the base (the lower part of the ladder weighs much more than the upper part). A 900-N fireman and the 500-N young lady he is rescuing are at the top of the ladder. (a) What is the moment at the base of the ladder tending to tip over the fire truck? (b) What is the moment about the horizontal axis having unit vector $\hat{\boldsymbol{\rho}}$ shown in the diagram?

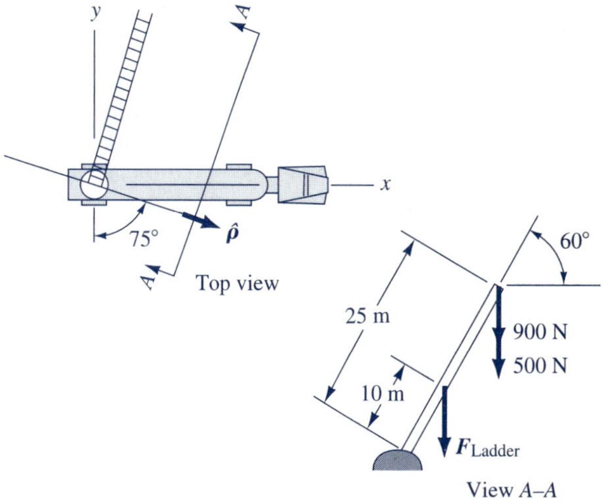

Figure P.3.34.

3.4 The Couple and Couple Moment

A special arrangement of forces that is of great importance is the *couple. The couple is formed by any two equal parallel forces that have opposite senses* (Fig. 3.20). On a rigid body, a couple has only *one* effect, a "turning" action. Individual forces or combinations of forces that do not constitute couples may "push" or "pull" as well as "turn" a body. The turning action is given quantitatively by the moment of forces about a point or an axis. We shall, accordingly, be most concerned with the moment of a couple, or what we shall call the *couple moment.*

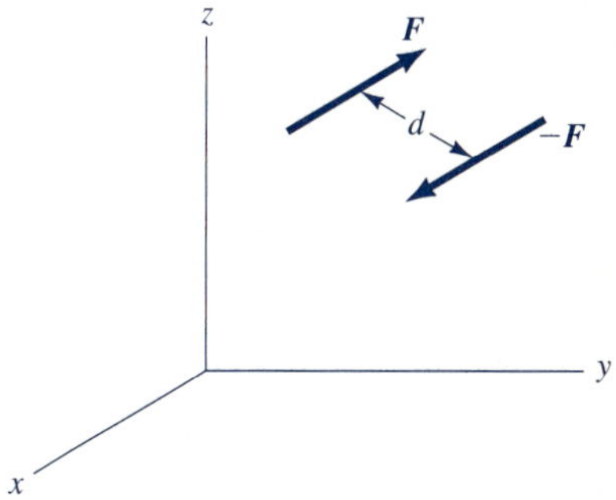

Figure 3.20. A couple.

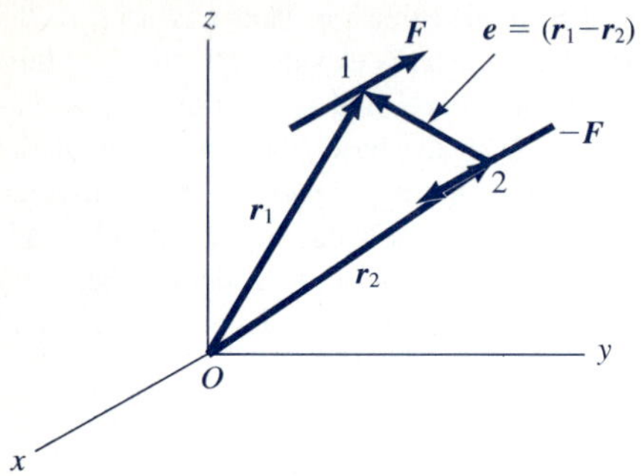

Figure 3.21. Compute moment of couple about O.

Let us now evaluate the moment of the couple about the origin. Position vectors have been drawn in Fig. 3.21 to points 1 and 2 anywhere along the respective line of action of each force. Adding the moment of each force about O, we have for the couple moment $\boldsymbol{M}$

$$\begin{aligned} \boldsymbol{M} &= \boldsymbol{r}_1 \times \boldsymbol{F} + \boldsymbol{r}_2 \times (-\boldsymbol{F}) \\ &= (\boldsymbol{r}_1 - \boldsymbol{r}_2) \times \boldsymbol{F} \end{aligned} \tag{3.15}$$

We can see that $(\boldsymbol{r}_1 - \boldsymbol{r}_2)$ is a displacement vector between points 2 and 1, and if we call this vector $\boldsymbol{e}$, the formulation above becomes

$$\boldsymbol{M} = \boldsymbol{e} \times \boldsymbol{F} \tag{3.16}$$

Since $\boldsymbol{e}$ is in the plane of the couple, it is clear from the definition of a cross product that $\boldsymbol{M}$ is in an orientation normal to the plane of the couple. The sense in this case may be seen in Fig. 3.22 to be directed downward, in accordance with the right-hand-screw rule. Note the use of the double arrow to represent the couple moment. Note also that the rotation of $\boldsymbol{e}$ to $\boldsymbol{F}$, as stipulated in the cross-product formulation, is in the same direction as the "turning" action of the two force vectors, and from now on we shall use the latter criterion for determining the sense of rotation to be used with the right-hand-screw rule.

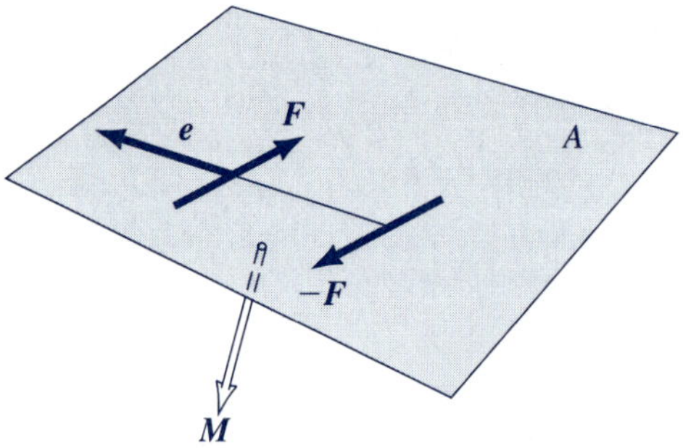

Figure 3.22. The couple moment $\boldsymbol{M}$.

Now that the direction of couple moment $\boldsymbol{M}$ has been established for the couple, we need only compute the magnitude for a complete description. Points 1 and 2 may be chosen anywhere along the lines of action of the forces without changing the resulting moment, since the forces are transmissible for taking moments. Therefore, to compute the magnitude of the couple moment vector it will be simplest to choose positions 1 and 2 so that $\boldsymbol{e}$ is *perpendicular* to the lines of action of the forces ($\boldsymbol{e}$ is then denoted as $\boldsymbol{e}_\perp$). From the definition of the cross product, we can then say:

$$|\boldsymbol{M}| = |\boldsymbol{e}_\perp|\,|\boldsymbol{F}| \sin 90^\circ = |\boldsymbol{e}_\perp|\,|\boldsymbol{F}| = |\boldsymbol{F}|d \tag{3.17}$$

where the more familiar notation, d, has been used in place of $|\boldsymbol{e}_\perp|$ as the perpendicular distance between the lines of action of the forces.

To summarize the preceding discussions, we may say that: The moment of a couple is a vector whose orientation is normal to the plane of the couple and whose sense is determined in accordance with the right-hand-screw rule, using the "turning" action of the forces to give the proper rotation. The magnitude of the couple moment equals the product of either force magnitude comprising the couple times the perpendicular distance between the forces.

Note that in the computation of the moment of the couple about origin O, the final result in no way involved the position of point O. Thus, we can assume immediately that the couple has the *same* moment about every point in space. More about this in the next section.

3.5 The Couple Moment as a Free Vector

Had we chosen any other position in space as the origin, and had we computed the moment of the couple about it, we would have formed the same moment vector. To understand this, note that although the position vectors to points 1 and 2 will change for a new origin O', the *difference* between these vectors (which has been termed $\boldsymbol{e}$) does *not* change, as can readily be observed in Fig. 3.23. Since $\boldsymbol{M} = \boldsymbol{e} \times \boldsymbol{F}$, we can conclude that *the couple has the same moment about every point in space.* The particular line of action of the vector representation of the couple moment that is illustrated in Fig. 3.24 is then of little significance and can be moved anywhere. In short, the *couple moment is a free vector.* That is, we may move this vector anywhere in space without changing its meaning, provided that we keep the direction and magnitude intact. Consequently, *for the purpose of taking moments,* we may move the couple itself anywhere in its own or a parallel plane, provided that the direction of turning is not altered—i.e., we cannot "flip" the couple over. In any of these possible planes, we can also change the magnitude of the forces of the couple to other equal values, provided that the distance d is simultaneously changed so that the product $|\boldsymbol{F}|d$ remains the same. Since none of these steps changes the direction or magnitude of the couple moment, all of them are permissible.

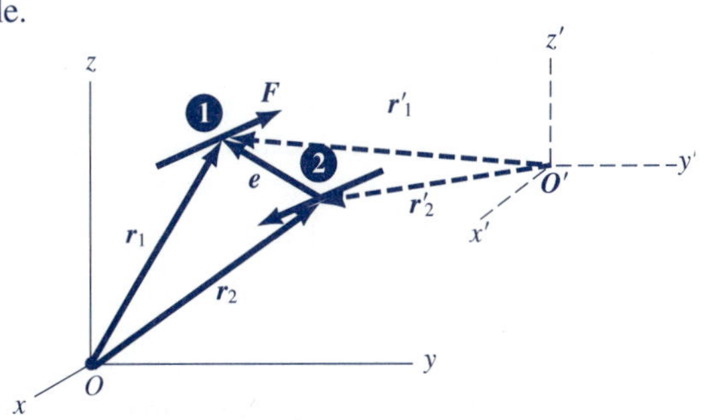

Figure 3.23. Vector $\boldsymbol{e}$ is the same for both references.

As we pointed out earlier, the only effect of a couple on a rigid body is its turning action, which is represented quantitatively by the moment of the couple—i.e., the couple moment. Since this is its sole effect, it is only natural to represent the couple by specifications of its moment; its magnitude, then, becomes $|\boldsymbol{F}|d$ and its direction that of its moment. This is the same as identifying a person by her/his job (i.e., as a teacher, plumber, etc.). Thus, in Fig. 3.24, the couple moment $\boldsymbol{C}$ may be used to represent the indicated couple.

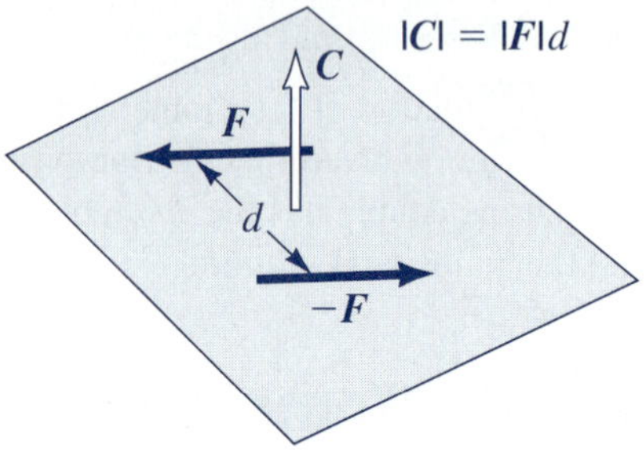

Figure 3.24. *C* represents couple.

3.6 Addition and Subtraction of Couples

Since couples themselves have zero net forces, addition per se of couples always yields zero force. For this reason, the addition and subtraction of couples is interpreted to mean addition and subtraction of the *moments* of the couples. Since couple moments are free vectors, we can always arrange to have a concurrent system of vectors. We shall now take the opportunity to illustrate many of the earlier remarks about couples by adding the two couples shown on the face of the cube in Fig. 3.25. Notice that the couple moment vectors of the couples have been drawn. Since these vectors are free, they may be moved to a convenient position and then added. The total couple moment then becomes 103.2 lb-ft at an angle of 76° with the horizontal, as shown in Fig. 3.26. The couple that creates this turning action is in a plane at right angles to this orientation with a clockwise sense as observed from below.

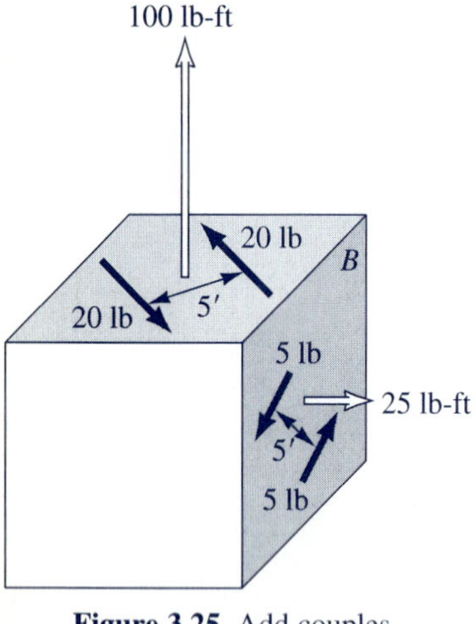

Figure 3.25. Add couples.

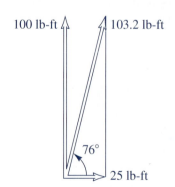

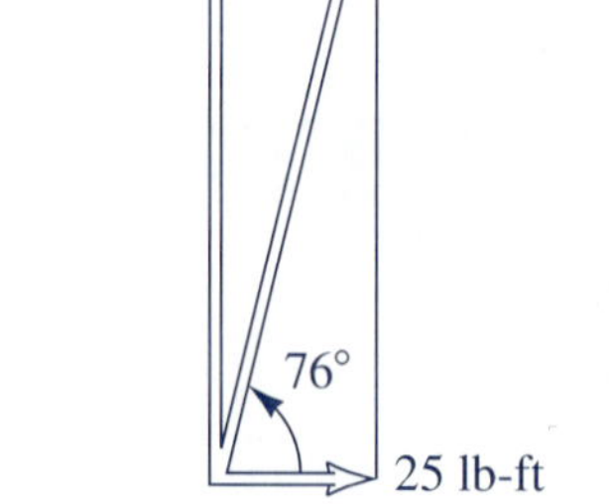

Figure 3.26. Add couple moments.

This addition may be shown to be valid by the following more elementary procedure. The couples of the cube are moved in their respective planes to the positions shown in Fig. 3.27, which does not alter the moment of the couples, as pointed out in Section 3.5. If the couple on plane B is adjusted to have a force magnitude of 20 lb and if the separating distance is decreased to 5/4 ft, the couple moment is not changed (Fig. 3.28). We thus form a system of forces in which two of the forces are equal, opposite, and collinear and, since these two forces together cannot contribute moment, they may be deleted, leaving a single couple on a plane inclined to the original planes (Fig. 3.29). The distance between the remaining forces is

$$\sqrt{25 + \tfrac{25}{16}}\ \text{ft} = 5.16\ \text{ft}$$

and so the magnitude of the couple moment may then be computed to be 103.2 lb-ft. The orientation of the normal to the plane of the couple is readily evaluated as 76° with the horizontal, making the total couple moment identical to our preceding result.

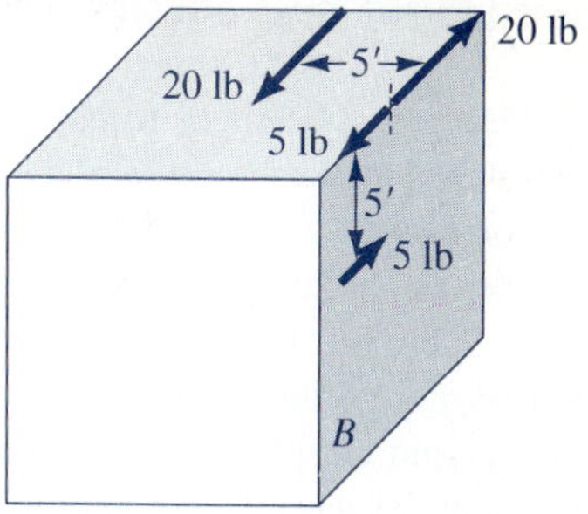

Figure 3.27. Move couples.

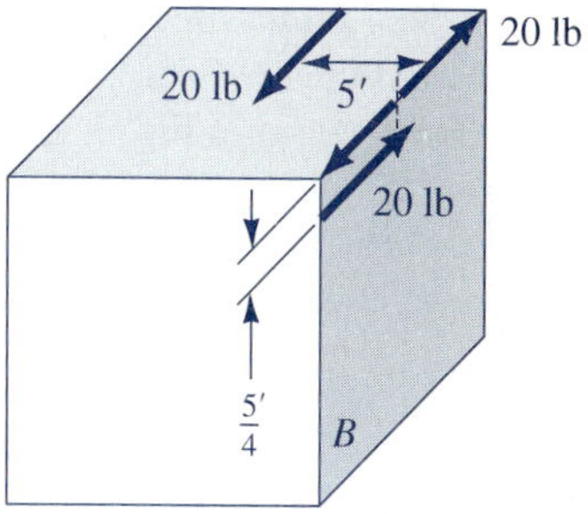

Figure 3.28. Change values of two forces.

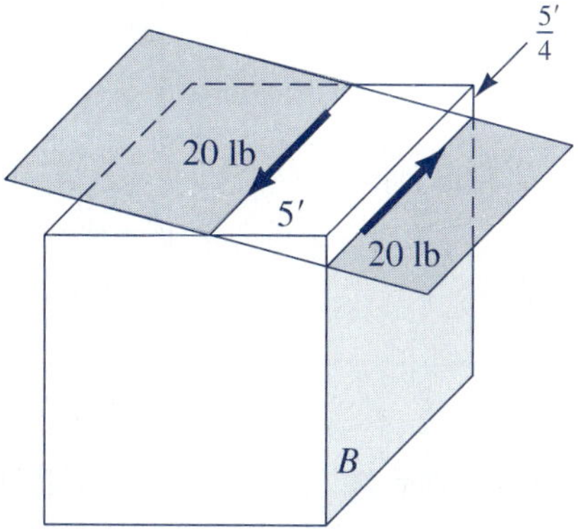

Figure 3.29. Eliminate collinear 20-lb forces.

A common notation for couples in a plane is shown in Fig. 3.30. The values given will be that of the couple moments.

Figure 3.30. Representation of couple moments in a plane.

Example 3.5

Replace the system of forces and couple shown in Fig. 3.31 by a single couple moment. Note that the 1,000-N-m couple moment is in the diagonal plane *ABCD*. As a first step in the problem, identify a second couple moment in addition to the couple moment in the diagonal plane.

Examine the vertical forces. There is an upward sum of 1,700 N clearly not colinear with the downward 1,700-N force. These forces form the second couple. To get the couple moment for these forces, we take moments of these forces about the origin as follows:

$$\begin{aligned} \boldsymbol{C}_1 &= 3\boldsymbol{k} \times 800\boldsymbol{j} + (3\boldsymbol{k} + 2\boldsymbol{i}) \times (700 - 1700)\boldsymbol{j} + 2\boldsymbol{i} \times 200\boldsymbol{j} \\ &= 600\boldsymbol{i} - 1{,}600\boldsymbol{k} \text{ N-m} \end{aligned}$$

As for the 1,000-N-m couple moment, we look in a direction along the x axis toward the origin as shown in Fig. 3.32.

The angle α in Fig. 3.32 is given as follows:

$$\tan \alpha = 3/4 \qquad \therefore\ \alpha = 36.87°$$

Hence we have for the second couple moment $\boldsymbol{C}_2$.

$$\begin{aligned} \boldsymbol{C}_2 &= -1{,}000 \cos 36.87°\boldsymbol{k} + 1{,}000 \sin 36.87°\boldsymbol{j} \\ &= -800\boldsymbol{k} + 600\boldsymbol{j} \text{ N-m} \end{aligned}$$

Now we can add the two couple moments to get $\boldsymbol{C}_{TOTAL}$.

$$\boldsymbol{C}_{TOTAL} = \boldsymbol{C}_1 + \boldsymbol{C}_2 = (600\boldsymbol{i} - 1{,}600\boldsymbol{k}) + (-800\boldsymbol{k} + 600\boldsymbol{j})$$

$$\boldsymbol{C}_{TOTAL} = 600\boldsymbol{i} + 600\boldsymbol{j} - 2{,}400\boldsymbol{k} \text{ N-m}$$

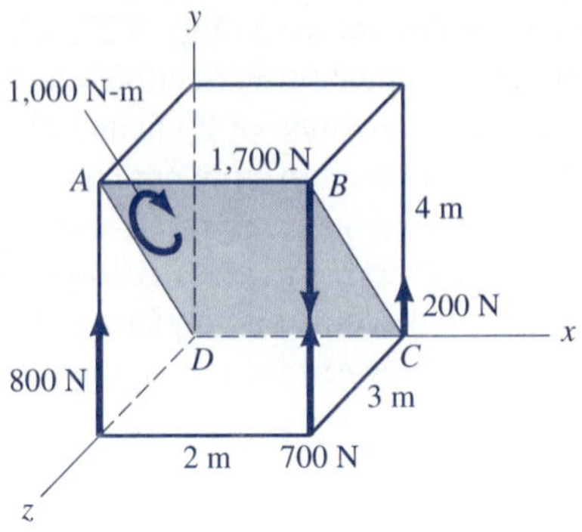

Figure 3.31. Replace system of forces by a single couple moment.

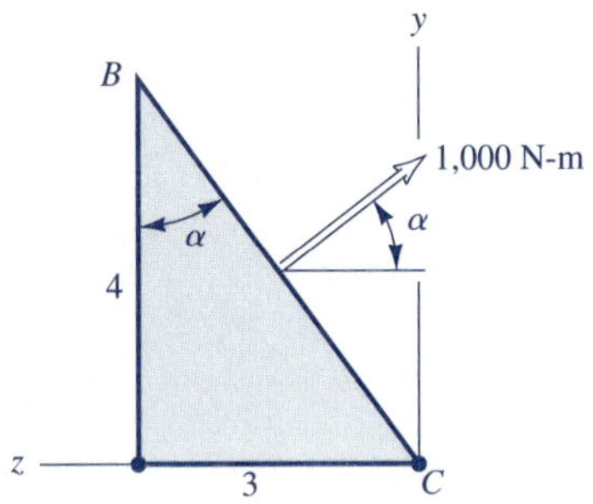

Figure 3.32. View along the x axis.

3.7 Moment of a Couple About a Line

In section 3.3, we pointed out that the moment of a force $\boldsymbol{F}$ about a line A–A (see Fig. 3.33) is found by first taking the moment of $\boldsymbol{F}$ about *any* point P on A-A and then dotting this vector into $\boldsymbol{a}$, the unit vector along the line. That is,

$$M_{AA} = (\boldsymbol{r} \times \boldsymbol{F}) \cdot \boldsymbol{a} \qquad (3.18)$$

Consider now the moment of a couple about a line. For this purpose, we show a couple moment $\boldsymbol{C}$ and line A–A in Fig. 3.34. As before, we first want the moment of the couple about any point P along A–A. But the moment of $\boldsymbol{C}$ about *every* point in space is simply $\boldsymbol{C}$ itself. Therefore, to get the moment about the line A–A all we need to do is dot $\boldsymbol{C}$ into $\boldsymbol{a}$. Thus,

$$M_{AA} = \boldsymbol{C} \cdot \boldsymbol{a} \qquad (3.19)$$

Since $\boldsymbol{C}$ is a free vector, the moments of $\boldsymbol{C}$ about all lines parallel to A–A must have the same value.

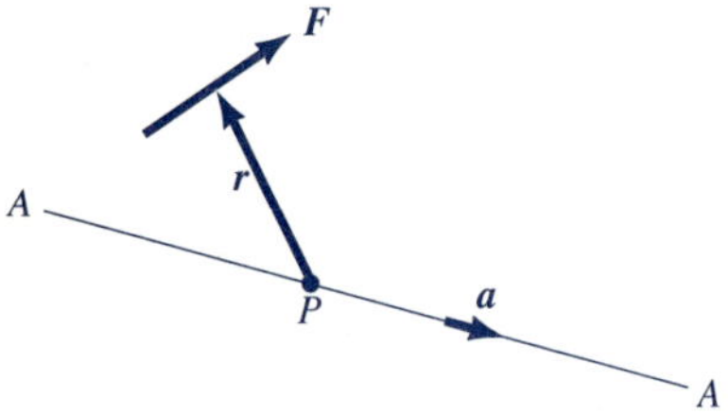

Figure 3.33. To find moment of $\boldsymbol{F}$ about A–A.

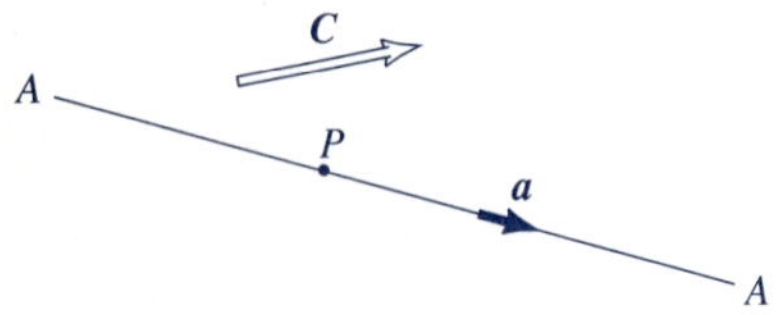

Figure 3.34. To find moment of couple about A–A.

Example 3.6

Consider the steering mechanism for a go-cart in Fig. 3.35. The linkages are all in a plane oriented at 45° to the horizontal. This plane is perpendicular to the steering column. In a hard turn, the driver exerts oppositely directed forces of 30 lb with each hand in order to turn the 12-in. diameter steering wheel clockwise as the driver looks at the steering wheel. What is the moment applied to each wheel about an axis normal to the ground? Assume half the transmitted torque goes to each wheel.

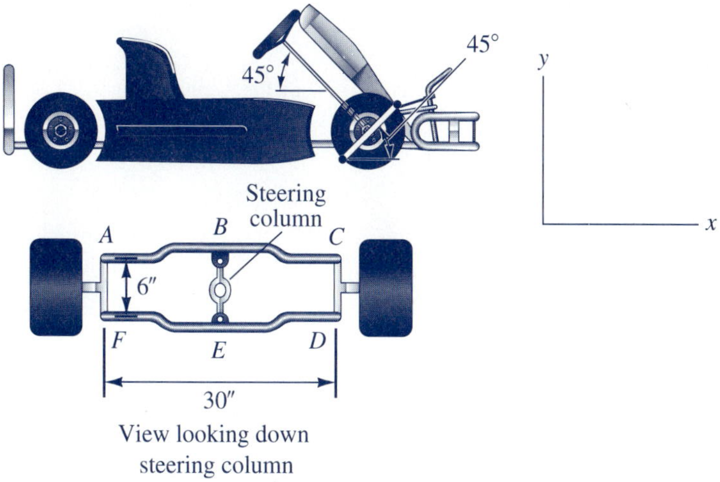

Figure 3.35. Steering mechanism of a go-cart.

The couple moment applied to the steering wheel is readily determined as

$$\boldsymbol{C} = (30)(12)(.707\boldsymbol{i} - .707\boldsymbol{j}) = 254.5\boldsymbol{i} - 254.5\boldsymbol{j} \text{ in-lb}$$

The torque about the vertical axis for each wheel is now easily evaluated. Thus

$$Torque = \frac{1}{2}(254.5\boldsymbol{i} - 254.5\boldsymbol{j}) \bullet \boldsymbol{j} = \boxed{-127.3 \text{ in-lb}}$$

Example 3.7

In Fig. 3.36, find

(a) the sum of the forces
(b) the sum of the couples
(c) the torque of the entire system about axis C–C having direction cosines $l = .46$ and $m = .63$ and going through point A.

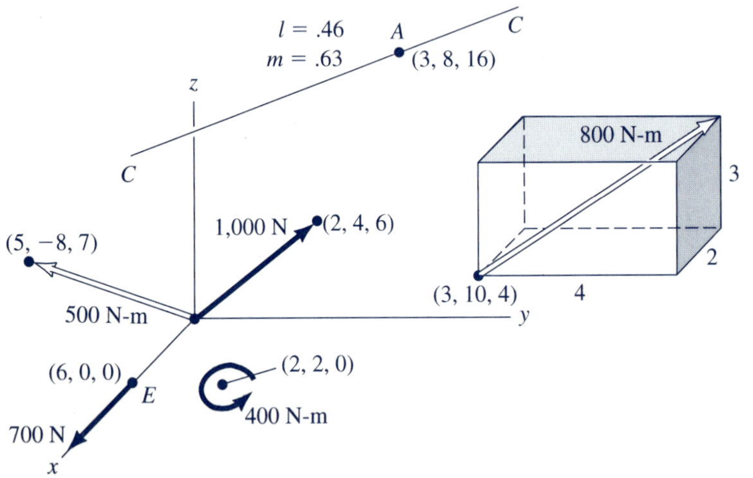

Figure 3.36. Force system in space.

(a)

$$\sum F = 700\boldsymbol{i} + 1,000\left[\frac{2\boldsymbol{i} + 4\boldsymbol{j} + 6\boldsymbol{k}}{\sqrt{2^2 + 4^2 + 6^2}}\right]$$
$$= 700\boldsymbol{i} + 267.3\boldsymbol{i} + 534.5\boldsymbol{j} + 801.8\boldsymbol{k}$$

$$\sum \boldsymbol{F} = 967.3\boldsymbol{i} + 534.5\boldsymbol{j} + 801.8\boldsymbol{k}\ \text{N}$$

(b)

$$\sum \boldsymbol{C} = 400\boldsymbol{k} + 500\left[\frac{5\boldsymbol{i} - 8\boldsymbol{j} + 7\boldsymbol{k}}{\sqrt{5^2 + 8^2 + 7^2}}\right]$$
$$+ 800\frac{4\boldsymbol{j} - 2\boldsymbol{i} + 3\boldsymbol{k}}{\sqrt{4^2 + 2^2 + 3^2}}\ \text{N-m}$$

Example 3.7 (Continued)

$$\sum C = 400\boldsymbol{k} + 212.8\boldsymbol{i} - 340.5\boldsymbol{j} + 297.9\boldsymbol{k} + 594.2\boldsymbol{j} - 297.1\boldsymbol{i} + 445.7\boldsymbol{k}$$

$$\sum C = -84.3\boldsymbol{i} + 253.7\boldsymbol{j} + 1{,}144\boldsymbol{k} \text{ N-m}$$

(c) To find M_{CC} we proceed by first finding the unit vector along C–C, which we denote as $\hat{\boldsymbol{c}}$. Thus from geometry

$$l^2 + m^2 + n^2 = 1$$
$$\therefore\ .46^2 + .63^2 + n^2 = 1$$
$$n = .6257$$

Hence,

$$\hat{\boldsymbol{c}} = .46\boldsymbol{i} + .63\boldsymbol{j} + .6257\boldsymbol{k}$$

We now get M_{CC}.

$$M_{CC} = \left[(\boldsymbol{r}_E - \boldsymbol{r}_A) \times (700\boldsymbol{i})\right] \bullet \hat{\boldsymbol{c}} + \left[(\boldsymbol{O} - \boldsymbol{r}_A) \times (1{,}000)\frac{2\boldsymbol{i} + 4\boldsymbol{j} + 6\boldsymbol{k}}{\sqrt{2^2 + 4^2 + 6^2}}\right] \bullet \hat{\boldsymbol{c}}$$
$$+ \left[500\frac{5\boldsymbol{i} - 8\boldsymbol{j} + 7\boldsymbol{k}}{\sqrt{5^2 + 8^2 + 7^2}}\right] \bullet \hat{\boldsymbol{c}} + \left[800\frac{4\boldsymbol{j} - 2\boldsymbol{i} + 3\boldsymbol{k}}{\sqrt{4^2 + 2^2 + 3^2}}\right] \bullet \hat{\boldsymbol{c}} + 400\boldsymbol{k} \bullet \hat{\boldsymbol{c}}$$

$$M_{CC} = \{(6\boldsymbol{i} - 3\boldsymbol{i} - 8\boldsymbol{j} - 16\boldsymbol{k}) \times (700\boldsymbol{i}) + (-3\boldsymbol{i} - 8\boldsymbol{j} - 16\boldsymbol{k})$$
$$\times (267.3\boldsymbol{i} + 534.5\boldsymbol{j} + 801.8\boldsymbol{k}) + (212.8\boldsymbol{i} - 340.5\boldsymbol{j} + 297.9\boldsymbol{k})$$
$$+ (594.2\boldsymbol{j} - 297.1\boldsymbol{i} + 445.7\boldsymbol{k}) + 400\boldsymbol{k}\} \bullet (.46\boldsymbol{i} + .63\boldsymbol{j} + .6257\boldsymbol{k})$$

Carrying out calculations in the large bracket, we get:

$$M_{CC} = \{(5{,}600\boldsymbol{k} - 11{,}200\boldsymbol{j}) + (2{,}138\boldsymbol{i} - 1{,}872\boldsymbol{j} + 534.9\boldsymbol{k})$$
$$+ (212.8\boldsymbol{i} - 340.5\boldsymbol{j} + 297.9\boldsymbol{k}) + (594.2\boldsymbol{j} - 297.1\boldsymbol{i} + 445.7\boldsymbol{k})$$
$$+ 400\boldsymbol{k}\} \bullet (.46\boldsymbol{i} + .63\boldsymbol{j} + .6257\boldsymbol{k})$$

$$M_{CC} = 944.7 - 8{,}075 + 4{,}554 = -2{,}576 \text{ N-m}$$

PROBLEMS

3.35. A truck driver, while changing a tire, must tighten the nuts holding on the wheel using a torque of 80 lb-ft. If his tire tool has a length such that the forces from his hand are 22 in. apart, how much force must he exert with each hand? To remove the nuts, he exerted 70 lb with each hand. What torque did he apply?

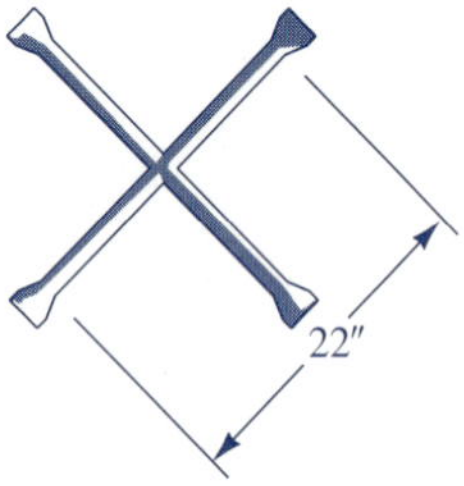

Figure P.3.35.

3.36. Equal couples in the plane of a wheel are shown in Fig. P.3.36. Explain why they are equivalent for the purpose of turning the wheel. Are they equivalent from the viewpoint of the deformation of the wheel? Explain.

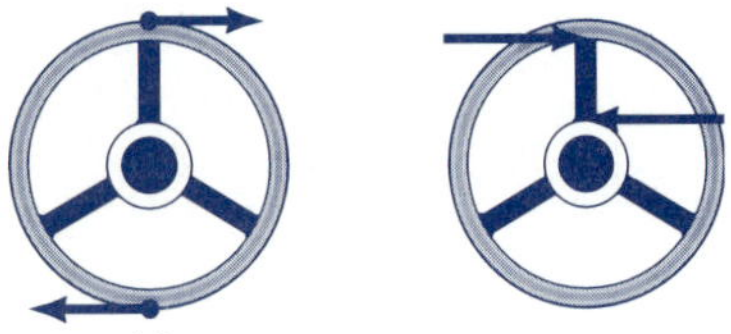

Figure P.3.36.

3.37. Oil-field workers can exert between 50 lb and 125 lb with each hand on a valve wheel (one hand on each side). If a couple moment of 100 lb-ft is required to close the valve, what diameter d must the wheel have?

Figure P.3.37.

3.38. Two children push with 30 lb of force each on the rail of a 10-ft-diameter merry-go-round. What couple moment do they produce? They fasten a 20-ft-long 2-in. by 4-in. board to the merry-go-round so that the middle of the board is at the middle of the merry-go-round. What is the resulting couple moment if they push on the ends of the board? What moment about the merry-go-round axis would they generate by fastening one end of the board to the middle of the merry-go-round and both pushing in the same direction on the other end?

3.39. A posthole digger has a 2-ft-long handle on a 5-ft-long shaft fastened to the digging (scraping) base. From tests, we know that a couple moment of 100 lb-ft is required to dig a posthole in clay, but only 65 lb-ft is needed in sandy soil. What force $\boldsymbol{F}$ must be applied in each case to dig a hole if the distance between the forces from a person's hands is 20 in.?

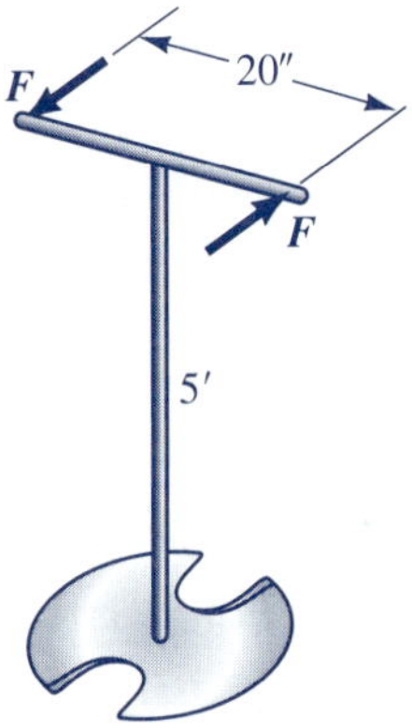

Figure P.3.39.

3.40. While stopping, a truck develops 350 N-m of torque at the rear axle due to the action of the brake drum on the axle. What forces are generated at the front and rear supports of the springs to which the axle is attached?

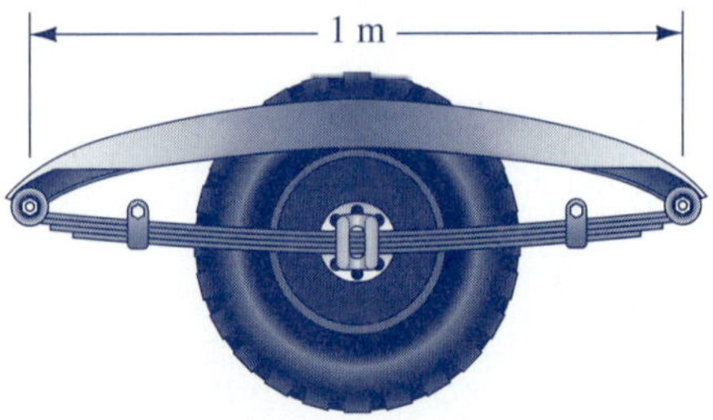

Figure P.3.40.

3.41. A couple is shown in the yz plane. What is the moment of this couple about the origin? About point (6, 3, 4) m? What is the moment of the couple about a line through the origin with direction cosines $l = 0$, $m = .8$, $n = -.6$? If this line is shifted to a parallel position so that it goes through point (6, 3, 4) m, what is the moment of the couple about this line?

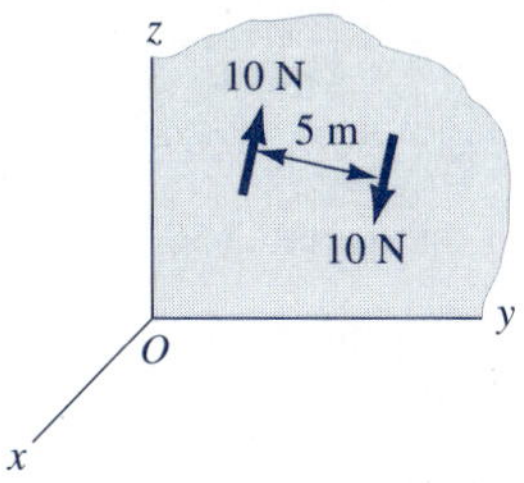

Figure P.3.41.

3.42. Given the indicated forces, what is the moment of these forces about points A and B?

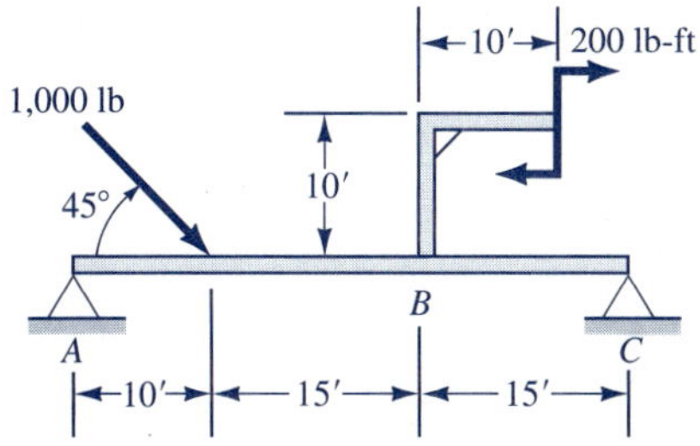

Figure P.3.42.

3.43. An eight-bladed windmill used for power generation and pumping water stops turning because a bearing on the blade shaft has "frozen up." However, the wind still blows, so each blade is subjected to a 25-lb force perpendicular to the (flat) blade surface. The force effectively acts at 2 ft from the centerline of the shaft to which the blades are attached. The blades are inclined at 60° to the axis of rotation. What is the total thrust of all the blade forces on the windmill shaft? What is the moment on the stalled shaft?

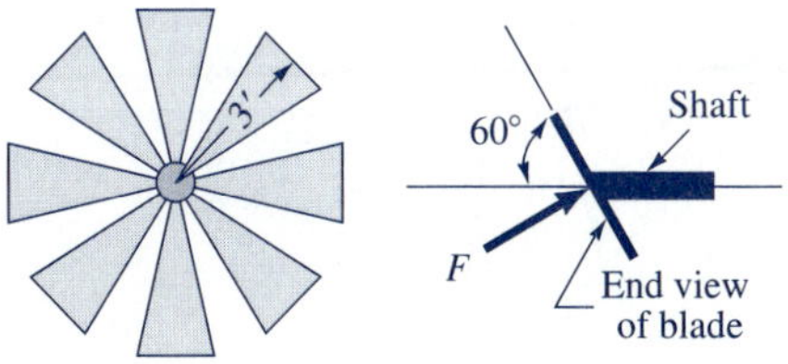

Figure P.3.43.

3.44. What is the moment of the forces shown about point A and about a point P having a position vector

$$\boldsymbol{r}_p = 10\boldsymbol{i} + 7\boldsymbol{j} + 15\boldsymbol{k} \text{ m?}$$

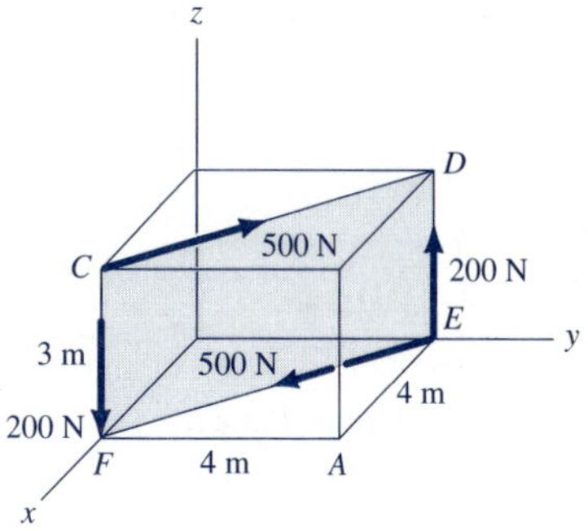

Figure P.3.44.

3.45. Find the torque about axis A–A developed by the 100-lb force and the 3,000-ft-lb couple moment. The position vector $\boldsymbol{r}_1$ is:

$$\boldsymbol{r}_1 = 10\boldsymbol{i} + 8\boldsymbol{j} + 12\boldsymbol{k} \text{ ft}$$

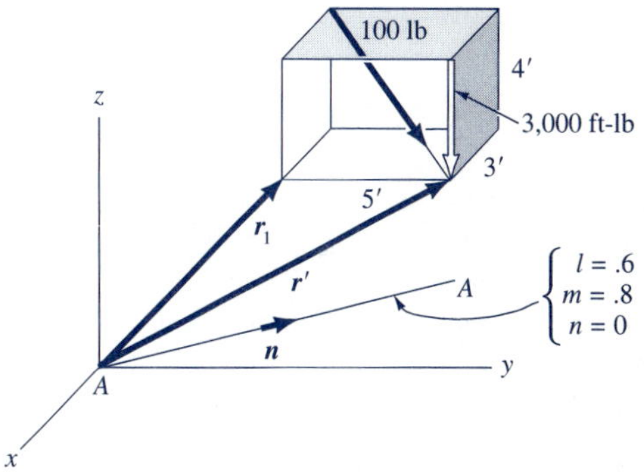

Figure P.3.45.

3.46. Find M_{CD}. Note that the 400-ft-lb couple moment is along the diagonal from point A to point B.

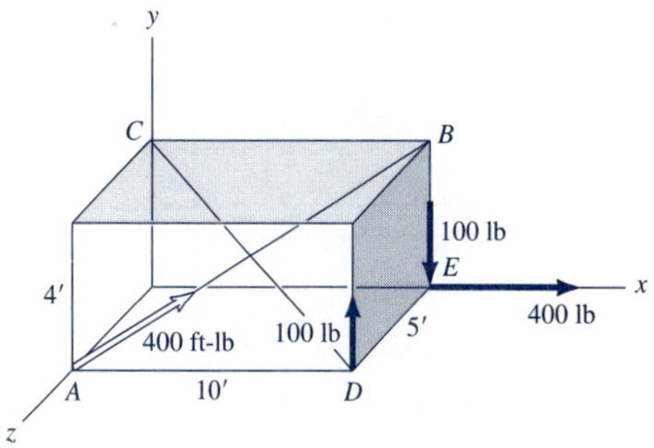

Figure P.3.46.

3.47. Find the torque about an axis going from A to B.

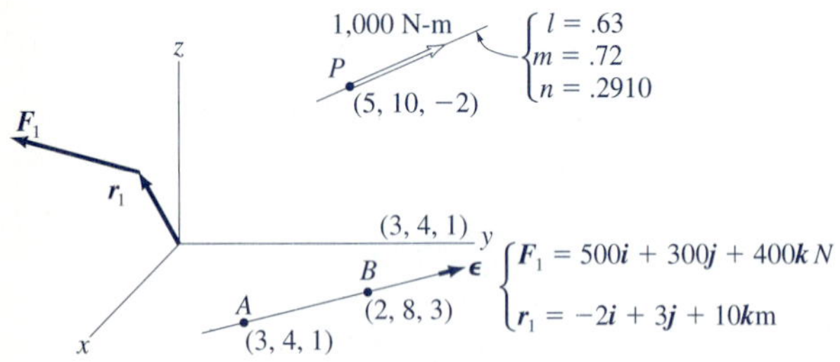

Figure P.3.47.

3.48. Given the couple moments

$$\begin{aligned} \boldsymbol{C}_1 &= 100\boldsymbol{i} + 30\boldsymbol{j} + 82\boldsymbol{k} \text{ lb-ft} \\ \boldsymbol{C}_2 &= -16\boldsymbol{i} + 42\boldsymbol{j} \text{ lb-ft} \\ \boldsymbol{C}_3 &= 15\boldsymbol{k} \text{ lb-ft} \end{aligned}$$

what couple will restrain the twisting action of this system about an axis going from

$$\boldsymbol{r}_1 = 6\boldsymbol{i} + 3\boldsymbol{j} + 2\boldsymbol{k} \text{ ft}$$

to

$$\boldsymbol{r}_2 = 10\boldsymbol{i} - 2\boldsymbol{j} + 3\boldsymbol{k} \text{ ft}$$

while giving a moment of 100 lb-ft about the x axis and 50 lb-ft about the y axis?

3.49. Equal and opposite forces are directed along diagonals on the faces of a cube. What is the couple moment if $a = 3$ m and $F = 10$ N? What is the moment of this couple about a diagonal from A to D?

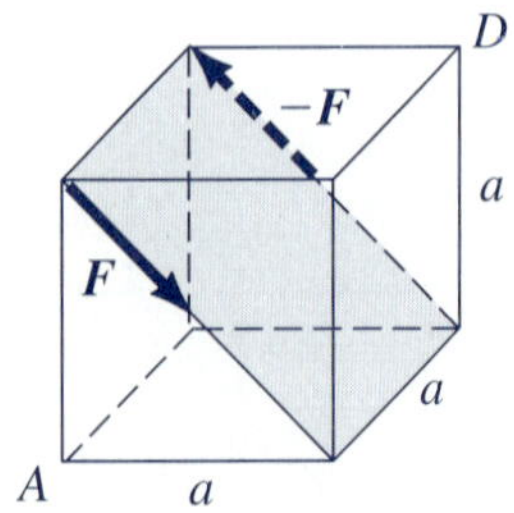

Figure P.3.49.

3.50. Find the torque about an axis going through points A and B.

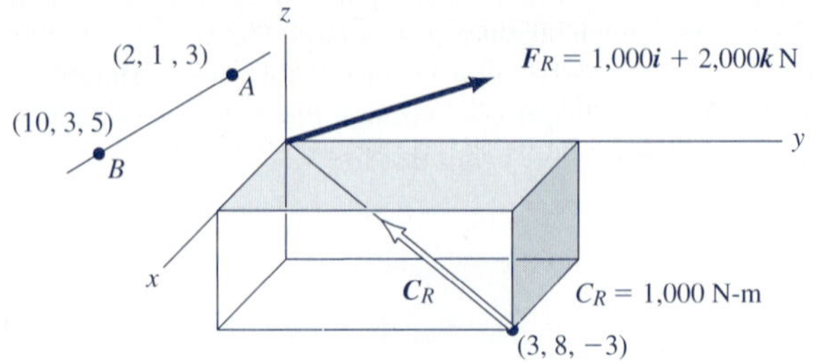

Figure P.3.50.

3.51. A force $\boldsymbol{F}_1 = 10\boldsymbol{i} + 6\boldsymbol{j} + 3\boldsymbol{k}$ N acts at position (3, 0, 2) m. At point (0, 2, −3) m, an equal but opposite force $-\boldsymbol{F}_1$ acts. What is the couple moment? What are the direction cosines of the normal to the plane of the couple?

3.52. Force $\boldsymbol{F}_1 = -16\boldsymbol{i} + 10\boldsymbol{j} - 5\boldsymbol{k}$ N acts at the origin while $\boldsymbol{F}_2 = -\boldsymbol{F}_1$ acts at the end of a rod of length 12 m protruding from the origin with direction cosines $l = .6$, $m = .8$. What is the moment about point P at

$$\boldsymbol{r}_p = 3\boldsymbol{i} + 10\boldsymbol{j} + 15\boldsymbol{k} \text{ m?}$$

What is the twist about an axis going through P and having the unit vector

$$\boldsymbol{\epsilon} = .2\boldsymbol{i} + .8\boldsymbol{j} + .566\boldsymbol{k}?$$

3.53. Given the following data:

$$\begin{aligned} \boldsymbol{F} &= 100\boldsymbol{i} + 300\boldsymbol{j} \text{ N} \\ \boldsymbol{C} &= 200\boldsymbol{j} + 300\boldsymbol{k} \text{ N-m} \\ \boldsymbol{r}_1 &= 3\boldsymbol{i} - 6\boldsymbol{j} + 4\boldsymbol{k} \text{ m} \\ \boldsymbol{r}_2 &= 8\boldsymbol{i} + 3\boldsymbol{j} \text{ m} \end{aligned}$$

Find the torque about axis A–A from $\boldsymbol{F}$ and $\boldsymbol{C}$.

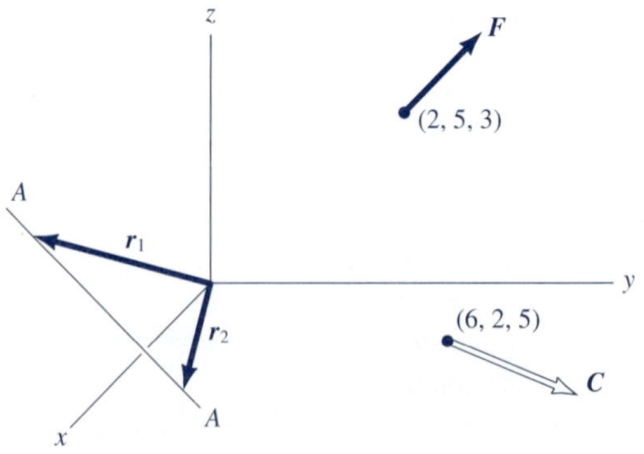

Figure P.3.53.

3.54. An oil-field pump has two valves, one on top and one on the side, that must be closed simultaneously. The valve wheels are each 27 in. in diameter and are turned with both hands by workers who can exert between 50 lb and 125 lb with each hand. If a weak worker turns the side wheel and a strong worker turns the top wheel, what is the total twisting moment (couple moment) on the pump?

3.55. What is the total moment about the origin of the force system shown?

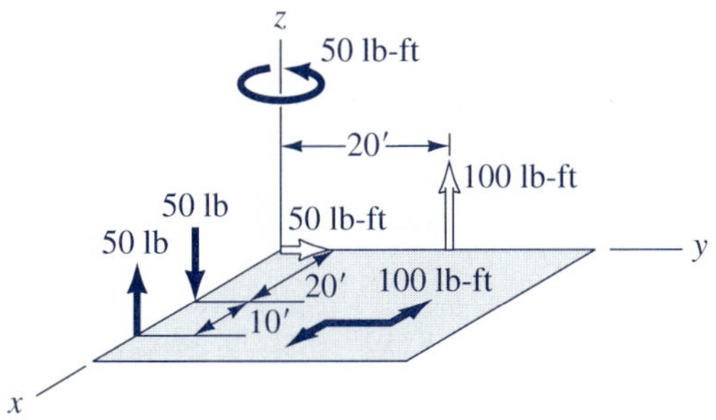

Figure P.3.55.

3.56. Add the couples whose forces act along diagonals of the sides of the rectangular parallelepiped.

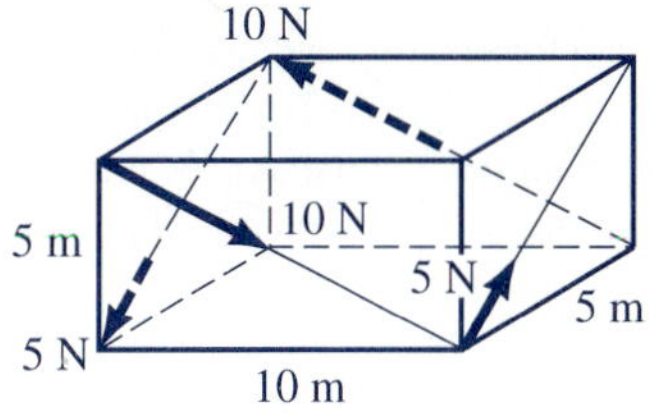

Figure P.3.56.

3.8 Closure

In this chapter, we have considered several important vector quantities and their properties. In particular, for rigid bodies we found we could take certain liberties with a couple without invalidating the results.

Note in particular that in the chapter on vector algebra, the line of action was of no significance. However, it should now be abundantly clear that in taking moments we *cannot* change the line of action of the force. *Only* the line of action of a *couple moment* can be changed to any parallel position for rigid bodies. Moreover, it is important to remember that we can always move a force along its line of action any time we are computing moments.

We are now ready to pursue in greater detail the important subject of equivalence of force systems for rigid body considerations. We will see that in equivalence considerations of rigid bodies, we again must be careful about what to do with lines of action. They will play a vital role in our deliberations.

PROBLEMS

3.57. An A-frame for hoisting and dragging equipment is held in the position shown by a cable *C*. To determine the cable force, the moment of the applied force about axis *B–B* must be known. What is that moment when a 1,000-N force is applied as shown?

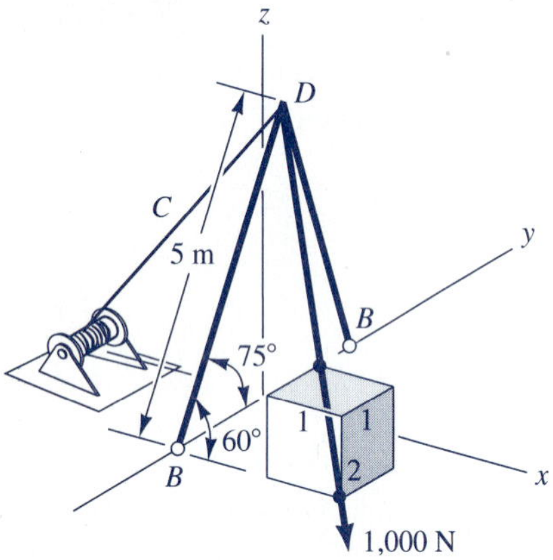

Figure P.3.57.

3.58. A plumber places his hands 18 in. apart on a pipe threader and can push (and pull) with 80 lb of force. What couple moment does he exert? How much could he exert if he moved his hands to the ends so that his hands are 24 in. apart? What force must he apply at the ends to achieve the same couple moment as when he held his hands 18 in. apart?

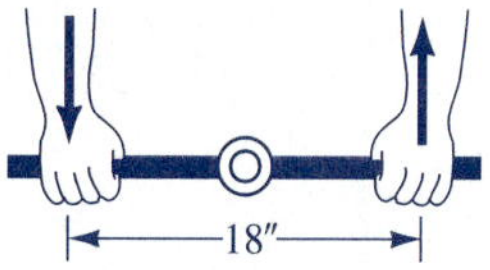

Figure P.3.58.

3.59. Find the torque about a line going from point 1 to point 2.

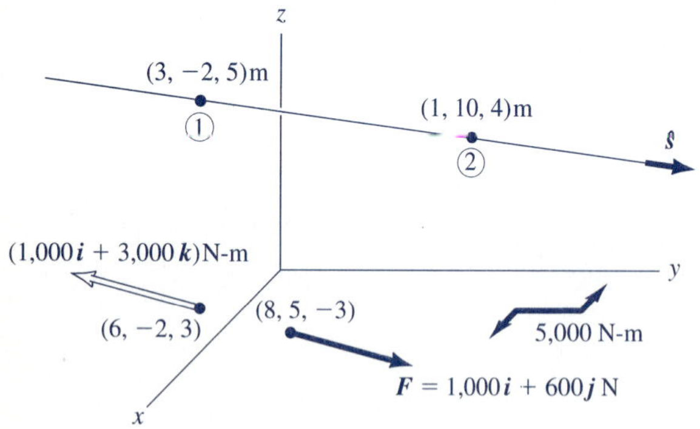

Figure P.3.59.

3.60. What is the moment about *A* of the 500-N force and the 3,000-N-m couple acting on the cantilever beam?

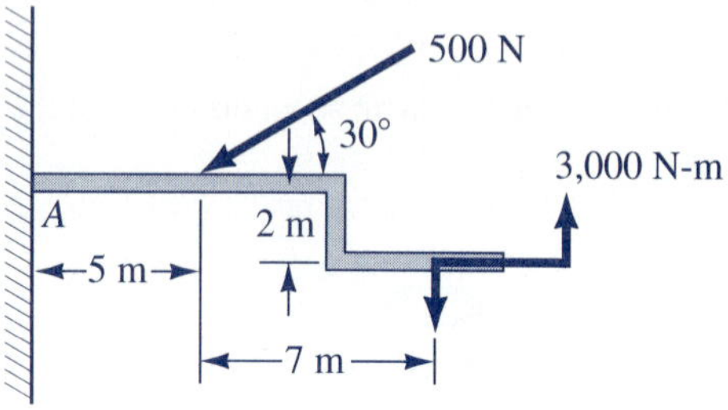

Figure P.3.60.

3.61. A force $\boldsymbol{F} = 16\boldsymbol{i} + 10\boldsymbol{j} - 3\boldsymbol{k}$ lb goes through point *a* having a position vector $\boldsymbol{r}_a = 16\boldsymbol{i} - 3\boldsymbol{j} + 12\boldsymbol{k}$ ft. What is the moment about an axis going through points 1 and 2 having respective position vectors given as

$$\boldsymbol{r}_1 = 6\boldsymbol{i} + 3\boldsymbol{j} - 2\boldsymbol{k} \text{ ft}$$
$$\boldsymbol{r}_2 = 3\boldsymbol{i} - 4\boldsymbol{j} + 12\boldsymbol{k} \text{ ft?}$$

3.62. Compute the torque about axis *C–C* from the entire force system shown. The axis goes through the origin.

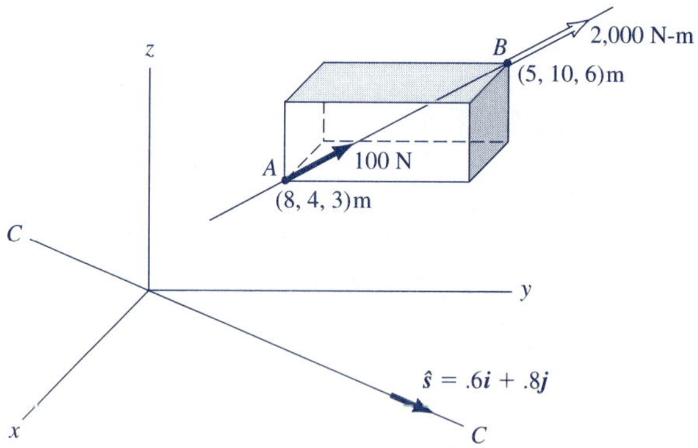

Figure P.3.62.

3.63. What is the total couple moment of the three couples shown? What is the moment of this force system about point (3, 4, 2) ft? What is the moment of this force system about the position vector $\boldsymbol{r} = 3\boldsymbol{i} + 4\boldsymbol{j} + 2\boldsymbol{k}$ ft taken as an axis? What is the total force of this system?

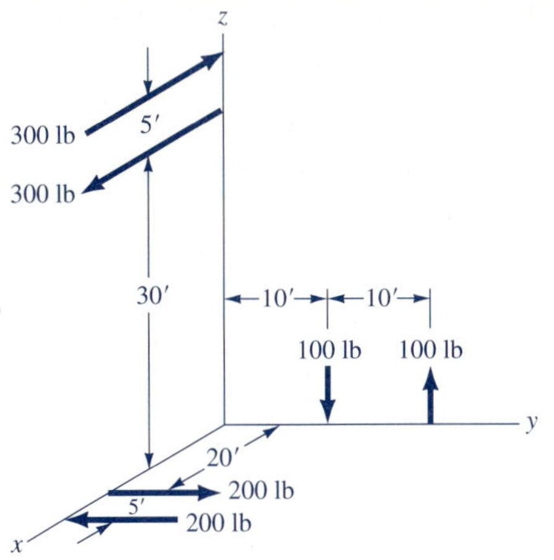

Figure P.3.63.

3.64. Find the torque about axis *AB*.

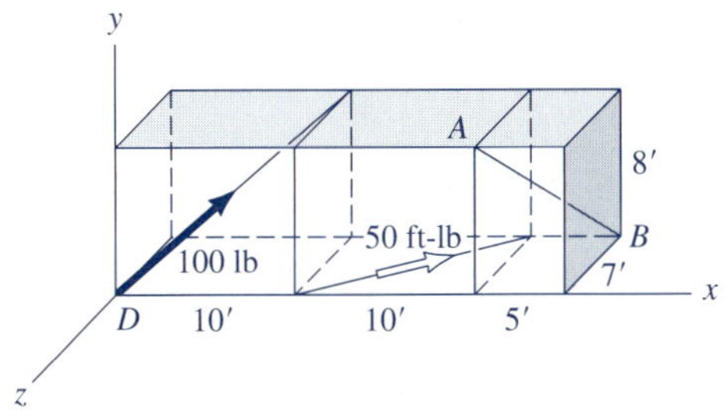

Figure P.3.64.

3.65. A force is developed by a liquid on a pipe any time the pipe changes the direction or the speed of flow as a result of an elbow or a nozzle. Such forces can be of considerable magnitude and must be taken into account in building design. We have shown three such forces. What moment stemming from these forces must be counteracted by the support at *O*?

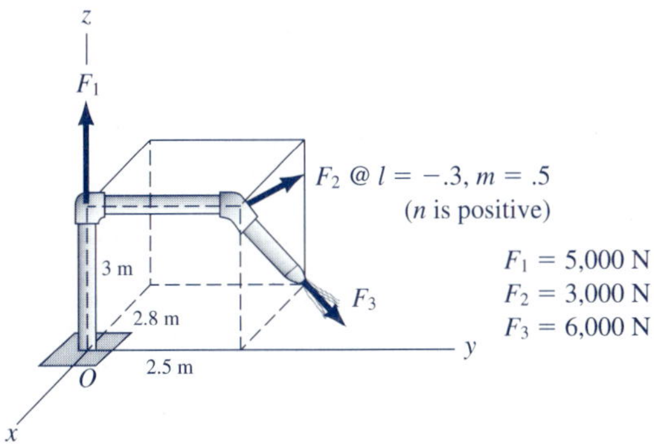

Figure P.3.65.

3.66. Compute the moment of the 300-lb force about points P_1 and P_2.

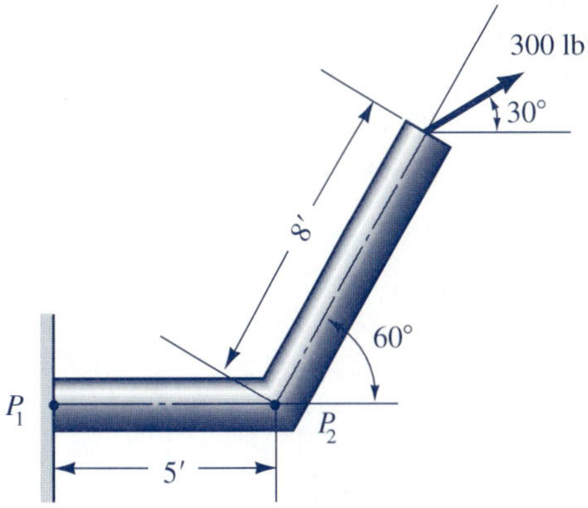

Figure P.3.66.

3.67. A tow truck is inclined at 45° to the edge *A-A* of a ravine with sides sloping at 45° to the vertical. The operator attaches a cable to a wrecked car in the ravine and starts the winch. The cable is oriented normal to *A-A* and develops a force of 15 kN. What are the moments tending to tip over the tow truck about the rear wheels (rocking backward). (*Hint:* Use the position vector from *C* to *B* in Fig. P.3.67(c).) Note that view *D–D* is normal to *A–A* and parallel to the incline.

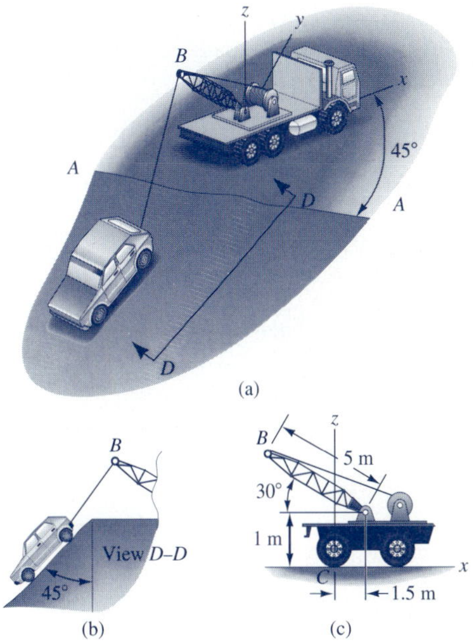

Figure P.3.67.

3.68. A surveyor on a 100-m-high hill determines that the corner of a building at the base of the hill is 600 m east and 1,500 m north of her position. What is the position of the building corner relative to another surveyor on top of a 5,000-m-high mountain that is 10,000 m west and 3,000 m south of the hill? What is the distance from the second surveyor to the building corner?

3.69. Compute the moment of the 1,000-lb force about supporting points *A* and *B*.

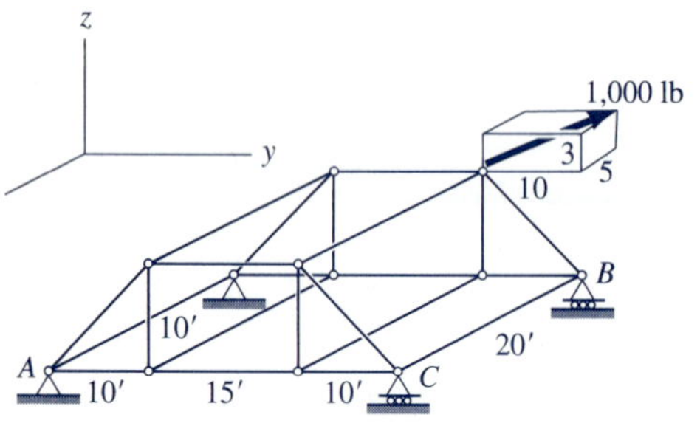

Figure P.3.69.

3.70. What is the turning action of the forces shown about the diagonal *A–D*?

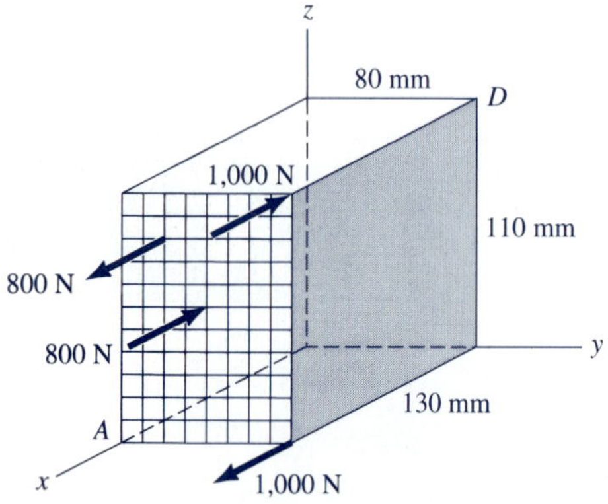

Figure P.3.70.

3.71. Find the torque of the force system about axis *A–B*.

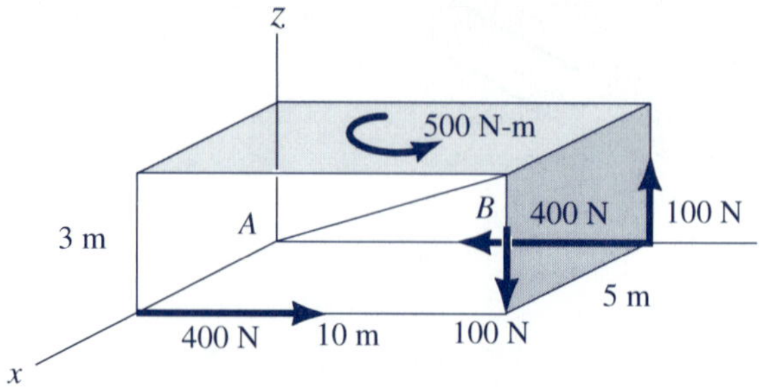

Figure P.3.71.

3.72. For the system of forces shown, what is the torque about axis *A–B*? *Note:* The 100-N and 50-N forces are in the *xz* plane and are perpendicular to line *AC*.

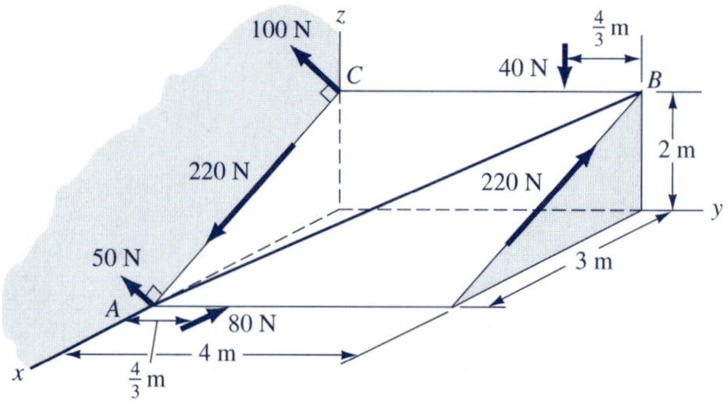

Figure P.3.72.

CHAPTER 4

Equivalent Force Systems

4.1 Introduction

In Chapter 1, we defined equivalent vectors as those that have the same capacity in some given situation. We shall now investigate an important class of situations, namely those in which a rigid-body model can be employed. Specifically, we will be concerned with equivalence requirements for force systems acting on a rigid body. Parenthetically, we will begin to see that the line of action plays a vital role in the mechanics of rigid bodies.

The effect that forces have on a rigid body is only manifested in the motion (or lack of motion) of the body induced by the forces. Two force systems, then, are equivalent if they are capable of *initiating* the same motion of the rigid body. The conditions required to give two force systems this equal capacity are:

1. Each force system must exert an equal "push" or "pull" on the body in any direction. For two systems, this requirement is satisfied if the addition of the forces in each system results in equal force vectors.
2. Each force system must exert an equal "turning" action about any point in space. This means that the moment vectors of the force systems for any chosen point must be equal.

Although these conditions will most likely be intuitively acceptable to the reader, we shall later prove them to be necessary and, for certain situations, sufficient for equivalence when we study dynamics.

As a beginning here, we shall reiterate several basic force equivalences for rigid bodies that will serve as a foundation for more complex cases. You should subject them to the tests listed above.

1. The sum of a set of concurrent forces is a single force that is equivalent to the original system. Conversely, a single force is equivalent to any complete set of its components.
2. A force may be moved along its line of action (i.e., forces are transmissible vectors).
3. The only effect that a couple develops on a rigid body is embodied in the couple moment. Since the couple moment is always a free vector, for our purposes at present the couple may be altered in any way as long as the couple moment is not changed.

Note for (1) and (2) above, we cannot change the line of action alone while maintaining equivalence.

In succeeding sections, we shall present other equivalence relations for rigid bodies and then examine perfectly general force systems with a view to replacing them with more convenient and simpler equivalent force systems. These simple replacements are often called *resultants* of the more general systems.

4.2 Translation of a Force to a Parallel Position

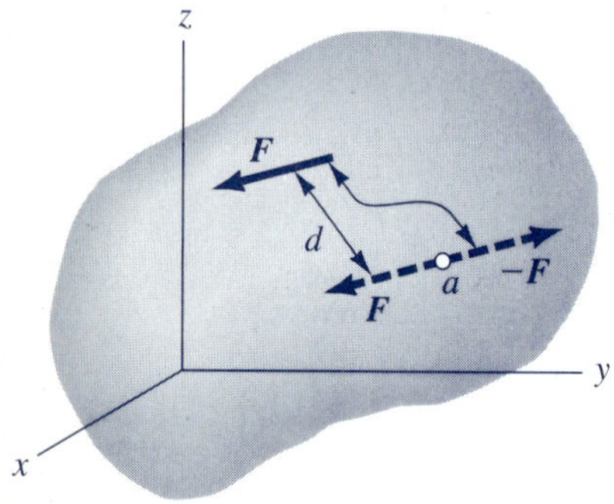

Figure 4.1. Insert equal and opposite forces at a.

In Fig. 4.1, let us consider the possibility of moving a force $\boldsymbol{F}$ (solid arrow) acting on a rigid body to a parallel position at point a while maintaining rigid-body equivalence. If at position a we apply equal and opposite forces, one of which is $\boldsymbol{F}$ and the other $-\boldsymbol{F}$, a system of three forces is formed that is clearly equivalent to the original single force $\boldsymbol{F}$. Note that the original force $\boldsymbol{F}$ and the new force in the opposite sense form a couple (the pair is identified by a wavy connecting line). As usual, we represent the couple by its moment $\boldsymbol{C}$, as shown in Fig. 4.2, normal to the plane A of point a and the original force $\boldsymbol{F}$. The magnitude of the couple moment $\boldsymbol{C}$ is $|\boldsymbol{F}|d$, where d is the perpendicular distance between point a and the original line of action of the force. The couple moment may be moved to any parallel position, including the origin, as indicated in Fig. 4.2.

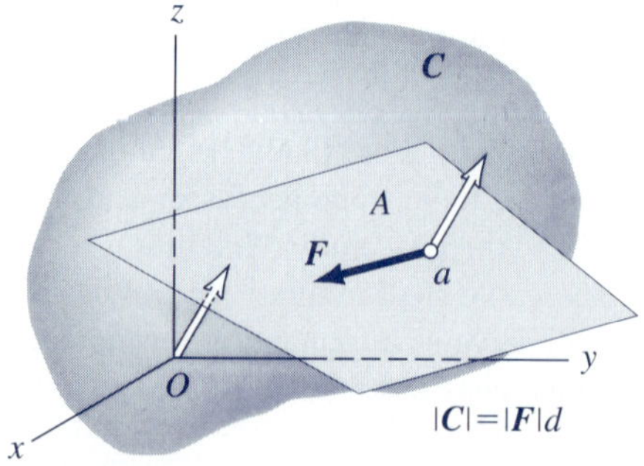

Figure 4.2. Equivalent system at a.

Thus, we see that *a force may be moved to any parallel position, provided that a couple moment of the correct orientation and magnitude is simultaneously provided.* There are, then, an infinite number of arrangements possible to get the equivalent effects of a single force on a rigid body.[1]

We now present a simple method for computing the couple moment developed on moving a force to a parallel position. Return to Fig. 4.1 and compute the moment $\boldsymbol{M}$ of the original force $\boldsymbol{F}$ about point a. We can express this as [see Fig. 4.3 (a)]

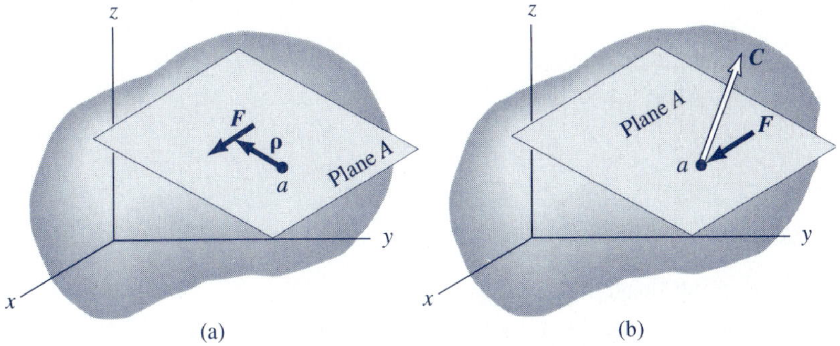

Figure 4.3. Couple moment on moving $\boldsymbol{F}$ is $\boldsymbol{\rho} \times \boldsymbol{F}$.

$$\boldsymbol{M} = \boldsymbol{\rho} \times \boldsymbol{F} \tag{4.1}$$

where $\boldsymbol{\rho}$ is a position vector from a to any point along the line of action of $\boldsymbol{F}$. Now the equivalent force system, shown in Fig. 4.3 (b), must have the *same moment,* $\boldsymbol{M}$, about point a as the original system. Clearly, the moment about point a in Fig 4.3 (b) is due only to the couple moment $\boldsymbol{C}$. That is,

$$\boldsymbol{M} = \boldsymbol{C} \tag{4.2}$$

Accordingly, we conclude, on comparing the previous two equations, that

$$\boldsymbol{C} = \boldsymbol{\rho} \times \boldsymbol{F}$$

Thus, in shifting a force to pass through some new point, *we introduce a couple whose couple moment equals the moment of the force about this new point.*

We illustrate this in the following examples.

[1]A moment of thought will give credence to the above procedure of maintaining rigid body equivalence while moving a force to a different line of action. By moving $\boldsymbol{F}$ to go through point a, you are eliminating the moment about a that existed before the move. The couple moment inserted at the time of the move restores this lost moment.

Example 4.1

A force $\boldsymbol{F} = 6\boldsymbol{i} + 3\boldsymbol{j} + 6\boldsymbol{k}$ lb goes through a point whose position vector is $\boldsymbol{r}_1 = 2\boldsymbol{i} + \boldsymbol{j} + 10\boldsymbol{k}$ ft (see Fig. 4.4). Replace this force by an equivalent force system, for purposes of rigid-body mechanics, going through position P, whose position vector is $\boldsymbol{r}_2 = 6\boldsymbol{i} + 10\boldsymbol{j} + 12\boldsymbol{k}$ ft.

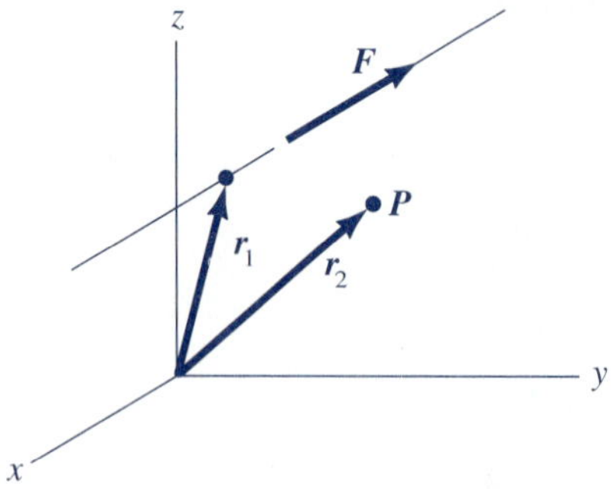

Figure 4.4. Move $\boldsymbol{F}$ to point P.

The new system will consist of the force $\boldsymbol{F}$ going through the position $\boldsymbol{r}_2$ and, in addition, there will be a couple moment $\boldsymbol{C}$ given as

$$\boldsymbol{C} = \boldsymbol{\rho} \times \boldsymbol{F} = (\boldsymbol{r}_1 - \boldsymbol{r}_2) \times \boldsymbol{F}$$

Inserting values, we have

$$\begin{aligned}\boldsymbol{C} &= [(2\boldsymbol{i} + \boldsymbol{j} + 10\boldsymbol{k}) - (6\boldsymbol{i} + 10\boldsymbol{j} + 12\boldsymbol{k})] \\ &\quad \times (6\boldsymbol{i} + 3\boldsymbol{j} + 6\boldsymbol{k}) \\ &= (-4\boldsymbol{i} - 9\boldsymbol{j} - 2\boldsymbol{k}) \times (6\boldsymbol{i} + 3\boldsymbol{j} + 6\boldsymbol{k}) \\ &= \begin{vmatrix} -4 & -9 & -2 \\ 6 & 3 & 6 \\ \boldsymbol{i} & \boldsymbol{j} & \boldsymbol{k} \end{vmatrix} \\ &\qquad \begin{matrix} -4 & -9 & -2 \\ 6 & 3 & 6 \end{matrix}\end{aligned}$$

Therefore,

$$\boldsymbol{C} = -12\boldsymbol{k} - 12\boldsymbol{j} - 54\boldsymbol{i} + 6\boldsymbol{i} + 24\boldsymbol{j} + 54\boldsymbol{k}$$

$$\boldsymbol{C} = -48\boldsymbol{i} + 12\boldsymbol{j} + 42\boldsymbol{k} \text{ ft-lb}$$

Note that if the position vector $\boldsymbol{r}_1$ to a point along the line of action of $\boldsymbol{F}$ had not been given thus permitting us to get $\boldsymbol{\rho} = (\boldsymbol{r}_1 - \boldsymbol{r}_2)$, we could have used *any* positon vector $\boldsymbol{\rho}$ going from point P to *anywhere* along the line of action of $\boldsymbol{F}$.

Example 4.2

What is the equivalent force system at position A for the 100-N force shown in Fig. 4.5?

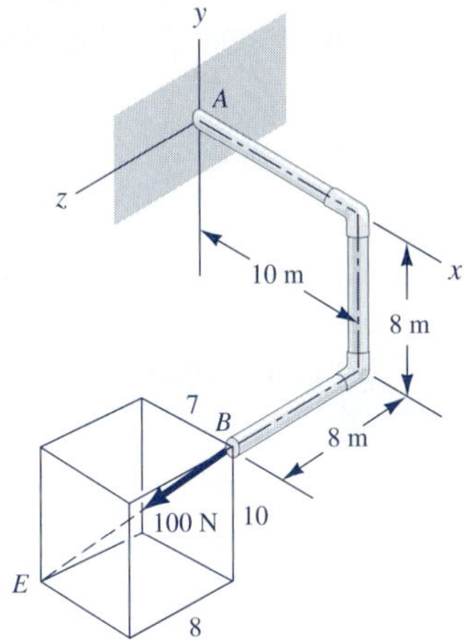

Figure 4.5. Find equivalent force system at A.

The 100-N force can be expressed vectorially as follows:

$$\boldsymbol{F} = F\frac{\overrightarrow{BE}}{\left|\overrightarrow{BE}\right|} = 100\left(\frac{-7\boldsymbol{i} - 10\boldsymbol{j} + 8\boldsymbol{k}}{\sqrt{7^2 + 10^2 + 8^2}}\right) \tag{a}$$

$$\boldsymbol{F} = -48.0\boldsymbol{i} - 68.5\boldsymbol{j} + 54.8\boldsymbol{k} \text{ N}$$

We then have the force given above at A. In addition, we have a couple moment, $\boldsymbol{C}$, found using a position vector, $\boldsymbol{r}$, from A to any point along the line of action of the 100-N force. Thus, choosing point B for $\boldsymbol{r}$, we have

$$\boldsymbol{C} = (10\boldsymbol{i} - 8\boldsymbol{j} + 8\boldsymbol{k}) \times (-48.0\boldsymbol{i} - 68.5\boldsymbol{j} + 54.8\boldsymbol{k})$$

$$= \begin{vmatrix} 10 & -8 & 8 \\ -48.0 & -68.5 & 54.8 \\ \boldsymbol{i} & \boldsymbol{j} & \boldsymbol{k} \end{vmatrix} \begin{matrix} 10 & -8 & 8 \\ -48.0 & -68.5 & 54.8 \end{matrix}$$

$$= (10)(-68.5)\boldsymbol{k} + (-48)(8)\boldsymbol{j} + (-8)(54.8)\boldsymbol{i} - (8)(-68.5)\boldsymbol{i} - (54.8)(10)\boldsymbol{j} - (-8)(-48.0)\boldsymbol{k}$$

Therefore,

$$\boldsymbol{C} = 109.6\boldsymbol{i} - 932\boldsymbol{j} - 1{,}069\boldsymbol{k} \text{ N-m} \tag{b}$$

The reverse of the procedure just presented may be instituted in reducing a force and a couple *in the same plane* to a *single* equivalent force. This is illustrated in Fig. 4.6 (a) where a couple composed of forces $\boldsymbol{B}$ and $-\boldsymbol{B}$ a distance d_1 apart and a force $\boldsymbol{A}$ are shown in plane N. The moment representation of the couple is shown with force $\boldsymbol{A}$ in Fig. 4.6 (b).

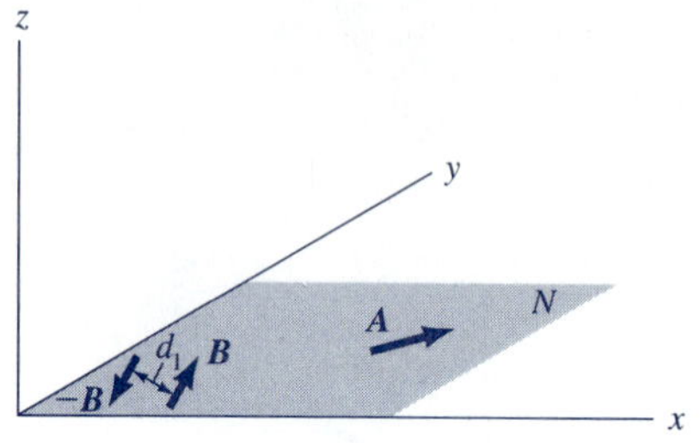

(a) Force A and couple in same plane.

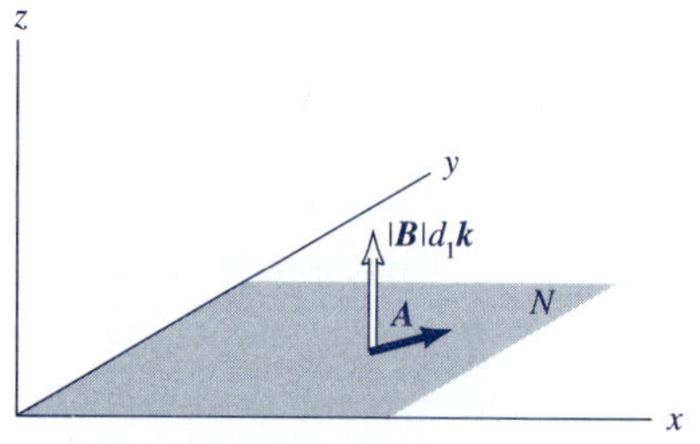

(b) Force A and couple moment.

Figure 4.6. A coplanar force and couple.

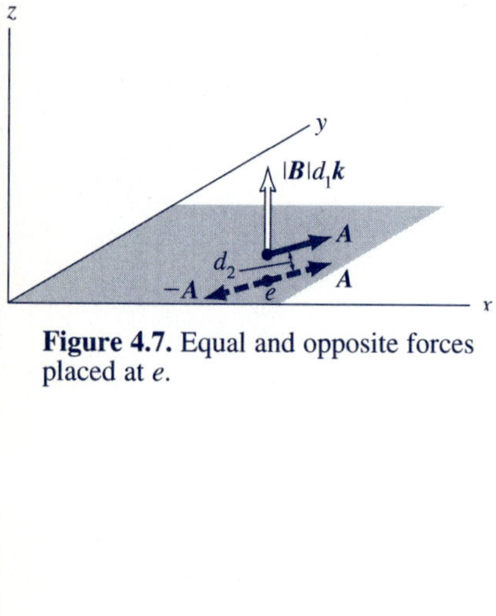

Figure 4.7. Equal and opposite forces placed at e.

Equal and opposite forces $\boldsymbol{A}$ and $-\boldsymbol{A}$ may next be added to the system at a specific position e (see Fig. 4.7). The purpose of this step is to form another couple moment with a magnitude $|\boldsymbol{A}|d_2$ equal to $|\boldsymbol{B}|d_1$ and with a directon of turning opposite to the original couple moment (see Fig. 4.8) and this dictates the position of e. The couple moments then cancel each other out and we are left with only a single force $\boldsymbol{A}$ going through point e. Therefore, we can always reduce a force and a couple in the same plane to a single force which clearly must have a *specific line of action* for the case at hand.

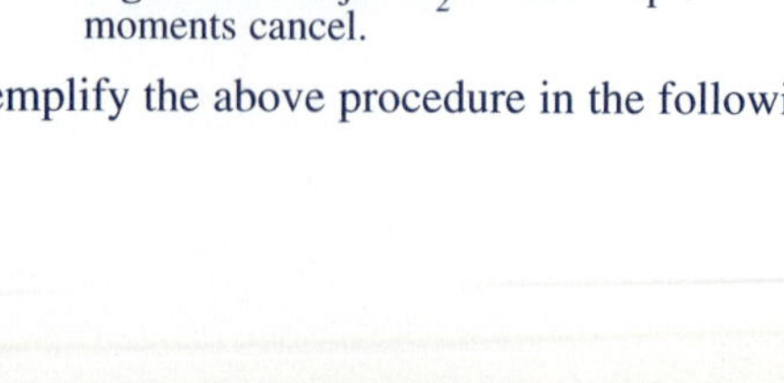

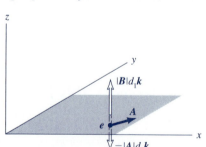

Figure 4.8. Adjust d_2 so that couple moments cancel.

We now exemplify the above procedure in the following example.

Example 4.3

In Fig. 4.9(a), we have shown a cantilever beam supporting a single force and a couple in the *xy* plane. We wish to reduce this system to a single force equivalent to the given system for purposes of rigid-body mechanics.

In Fig. 4.9(b), we have shown the couple moment and a point *e* to which we shall shift the 1,000-N force. It should be clear on inspection that the couple moment accompanying this shift will have a sign opposite to the original couple moment. Our task now is to get the correct distance *d* so as to effect a cancellation of the couple moments. Thus we require that

$$d\mathbf{i} \times (1{,}000)\,(.707\mathbf{i} - .707\mathbf{j}) + 550\mathbf{k} = \mathbf{0}$$

$$\therefore\ -(707d)\mathbf{k} + 550\mathbf{k} = \mathbf{0} \qquad d = .778 \text{ m}$$

Note we could have reached the above result more simply if we had resolved the force into rectangular components first. Only the vertical component has nonzero moment about *e* and so dispensing with vectors, we can directly say

$$-707d + 550 = 0 \qquad d = .778 \text{ m}$$

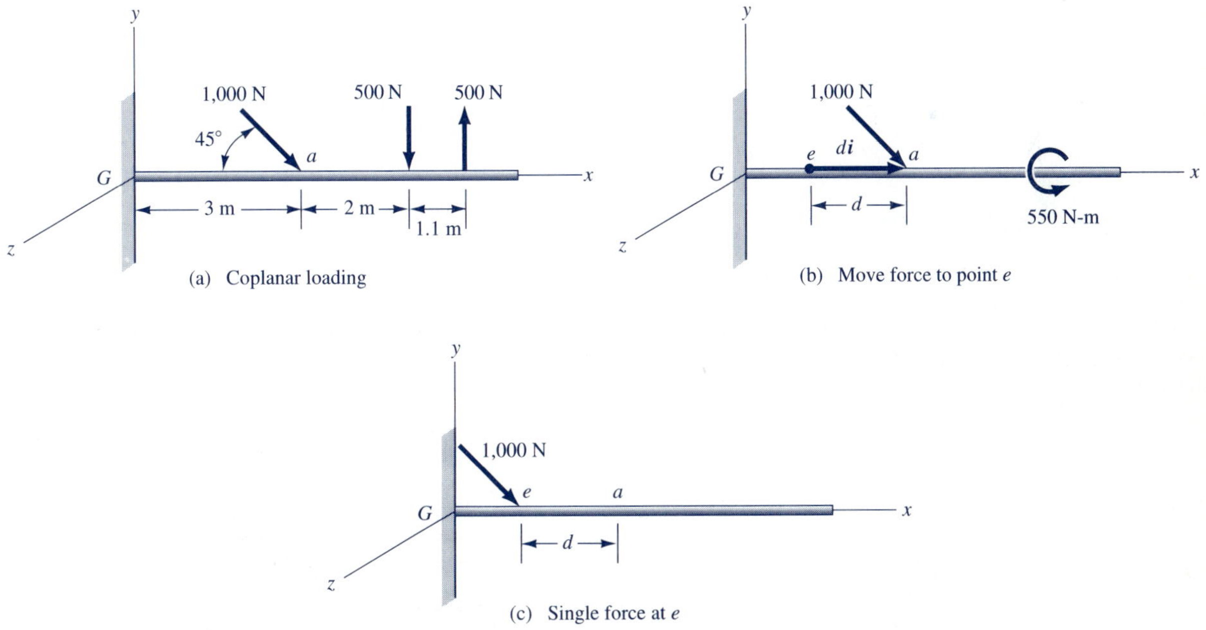

Figure 4.9. Reduction of a coplanar force and couple to a single force with a specific line of action.

PROBLEMS

In several of the problems of this set we shall concentrate the weight of a body at its center of gravity. Most likely you are used to doing this from an earlier physics course. In Section 4.5 we shall justify this procedure.

4.1. Replace the 100-lb force by an equivalent system, from a rigid-body point of view, at *A*. Do the same for point *B*. Do this problem by the technique of adding equal and opposite collinear forces and also by using the cross product.

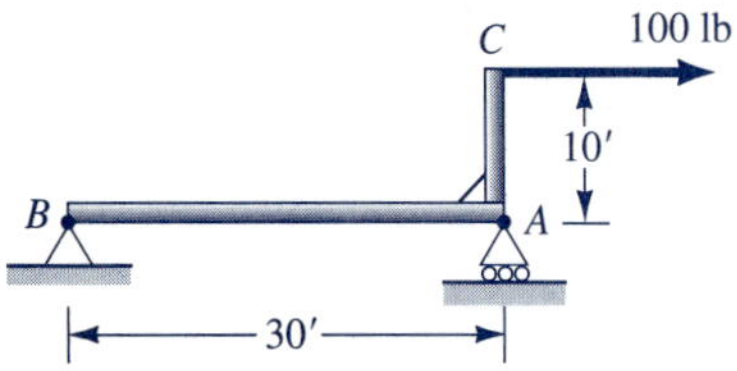

Figure P.4.1.

4.2. To back an airplane away from the boarding gate, a tractor pushes with a force of 15 kN on the nose wheels. What is the equivalent force system on the landing-gear pivot point, which is 2 m above the point where the tractor pushes?

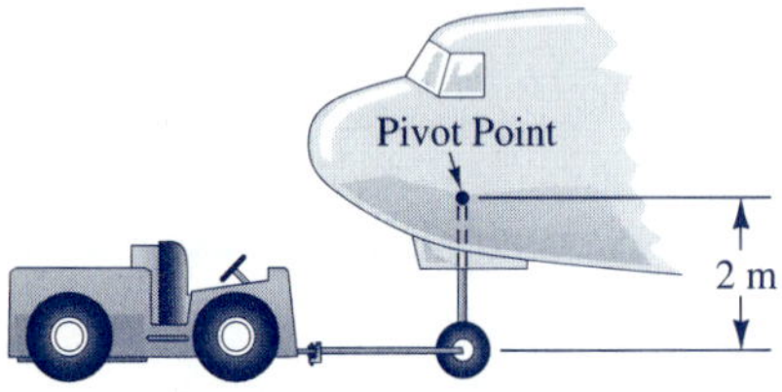

Figure P.4.2.

4.3. Replace the 1,000-lb force by equivalent systems at points *A* and *B*. Do so by using the addition of equal and opposite collinear force components and by using the cross product.

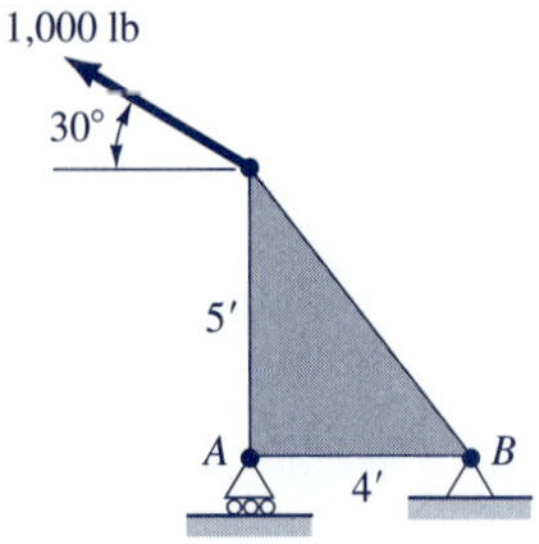

Figure P.4.3.

4.4. A parking-lot gate arms weighs 150 N. Because of the taper, the weight is concentrated at a point $1\frac{1}{4}$ m from the pivot point. What is the equivalent force system at the pivot point?

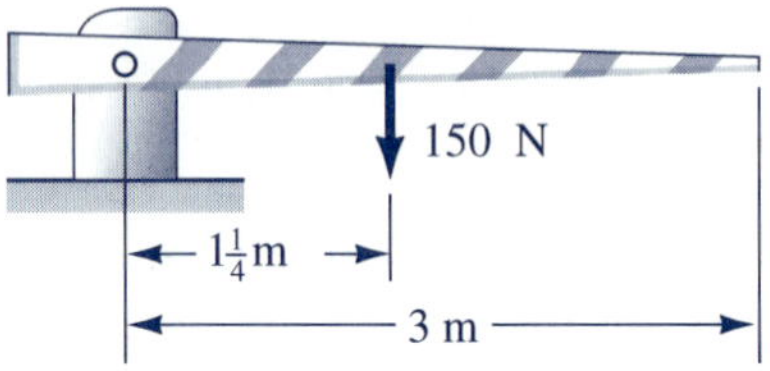

Figure P.4.4.

4.5. A plumber exerts a vertical 60-lb force on a pipe wrench inclined at 30° to the horizontal. What force and couple moment on the pipe are equivalent to the plumber's action?

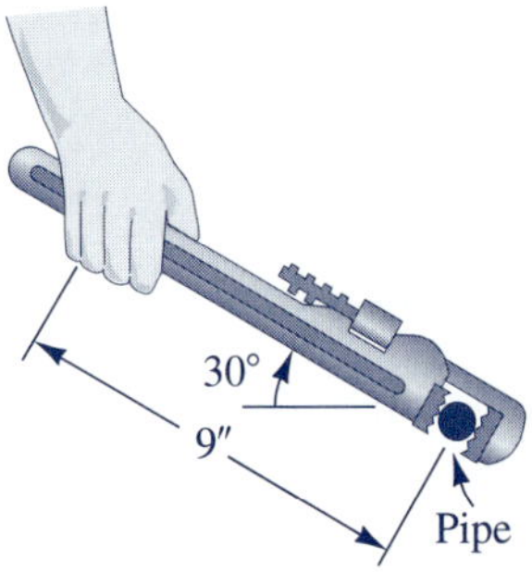

Figure P.4.5.

4.6. A tractor operator is attempting to lift a 10-kN boulder. What are the equivalent force systems at *A* and at *B* from the boulder?

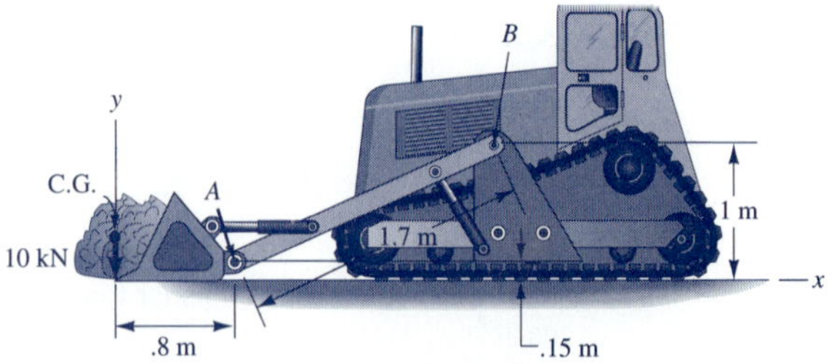

Figure P.4.6.

4.7. A small hoist has a lifting capacity of 20 kN. What are the largest and smallest equivalent force systems at *A* for the rated maximum capacity?

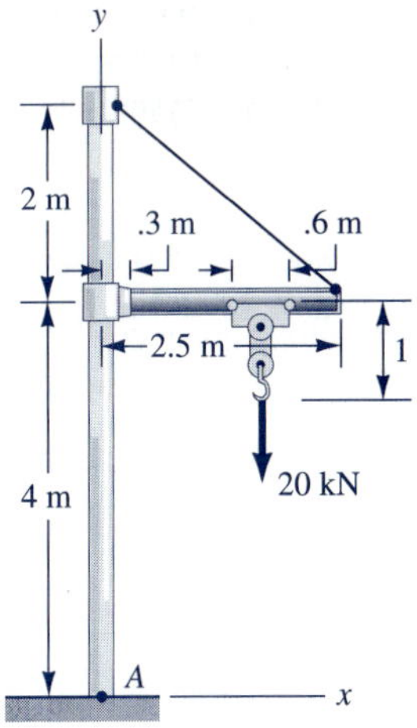

Figure P.4.7.

4.8. Replace the forces by a single equivalent force.

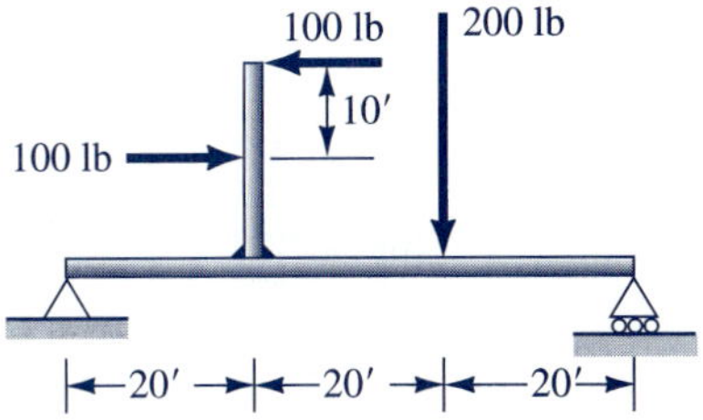

Figure P.4.8.

4.9. Replace the forces and torques shown acting on the apparatus by a single force. Carefully give the line of action of this force.

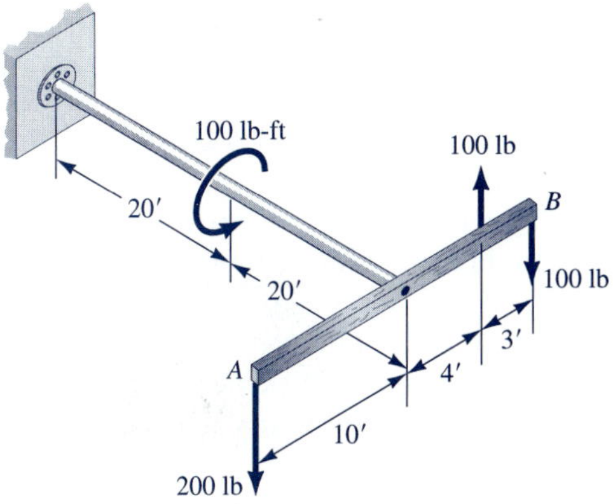

Figure P.4.9.

4.10. A carpenter presses down on a brace-and-bit with a 150-N force while turning the brace with a 200-N force oriented for maximum twist. What is the equivalent force system on the end of the bit at *A*?

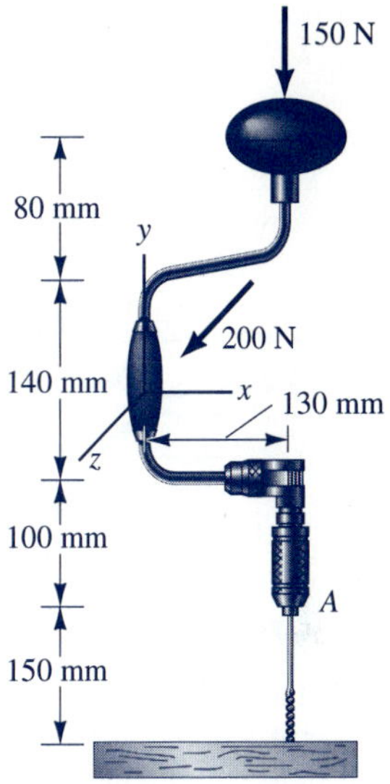

Figure P.4.10.

4.11. A force $\boldsymbol{F} = 3\boldsymbol{i} - 6\boldsymbol{j} + 4\boldsymbol{k}$ lb goes through point (6, 3, 2) ft. Replace this force by an equivalent system where the force goes through point (2, –5, 10) ft.

4.12. A force $\boldsymbol{F} = 20\boldsymbol{i} - 60\boldsymbol{j} + 30\boldsymbol{k}$ N goes through a point (10, – 5, 4) m. What is the equivalent system at point *A* having position vector $\boldsymbol{r}_A = 20\boldsymbol{i} + 3\boldsymbol{j} - 15\boldsymbol{k}$ m?

4.13. Find the equivalent force system at the base of the cantilever pipe system stemming from force $\boldsymbol{F}$ = 1,000 lb.

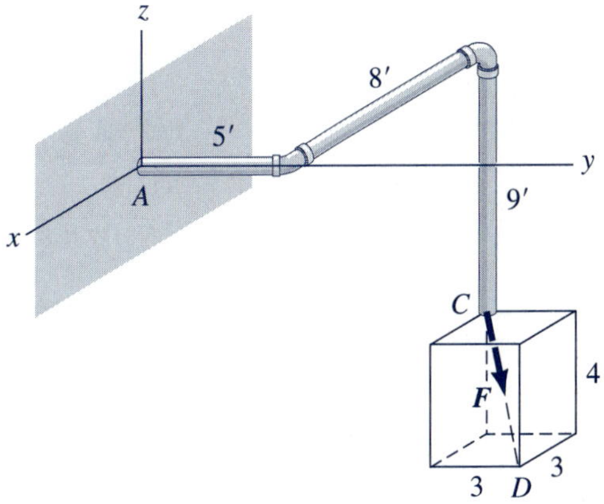

Figure P.4.13.

4.14. Replace the 6,000-N force and the 10,000-N-m couple moment by a single force. Where does this force cross the x axis?

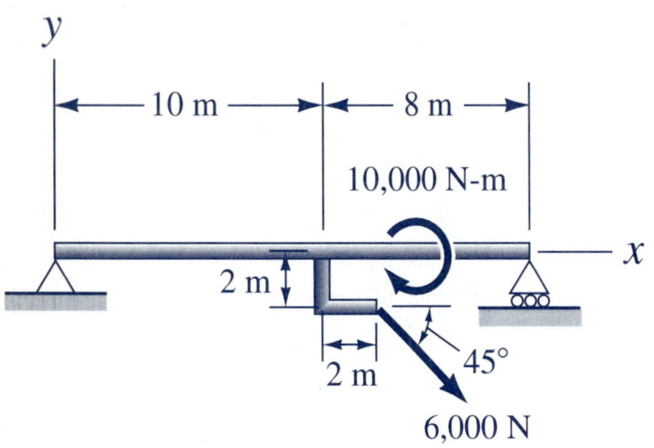

Figure P.4.14.

4.15. In Problem 4.13, the pipe weighs 20 lb/ft. What is the equivalent force system at A from the weight of the pipe? [*Hint:* Concentrate the weights of the pipe sections at the respective centers of gravity (geometric centers in this case).]

4.16. The operator of a small boom-type crane is trying to drag a chunk of concrete. The boom is 10° above the horizontal and rotated 30° clockwise as seen from above. The cable is directed as shown in the diagram and has 60 kN of tension. What is the equivalent force system at the boom pivot point?

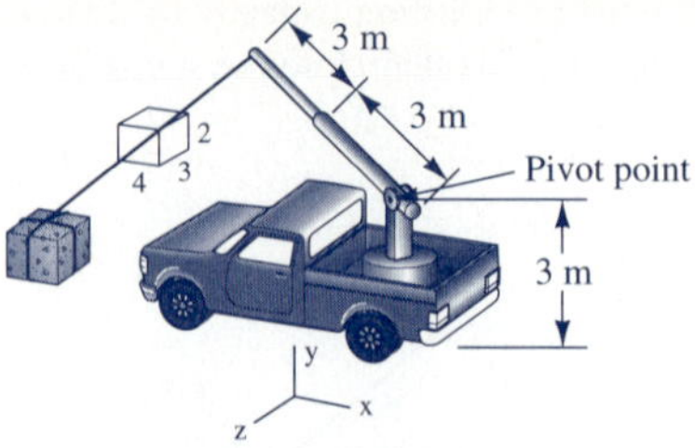

Figure P.4.16.

4.17. A supplementary supporting guy-wire system for a 200-m-tall tower is tightened. The cables are fastened to the ground at points 120° apart and 100 m from the tower base. What is the equivalent force system acting on the tower base when the tension is 50 kN in cable AT, 75 kN in BT, and 25 kN in CT?

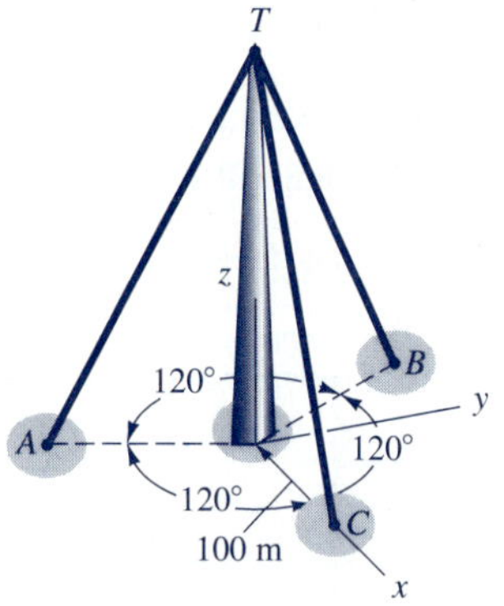

Figure P.4.17.

4.3 Resultant of a Force System

As defined at the beginning of the chapter, a *resultant of a force system* is a simpler equivalent force system. In many computations it is desirable first to establish a resultant before entering into other computations.

For a general arrangement of forces, no matter how complex, we can always move all forces and couple moments, the latter including both those given and those formed from the movement of forces, to proceed through any single point. The result is then a system of concurrent forces at the point and a system of concurrent couple moments. These systems may then be combined into a single force and a single couple moment. Thus, in Fig. 4.10 we have shown some arbitrary system of forces and couples using full lines. The resultant force and couple moment combination at the origin of a rectangular reference is shown as dashed lines.

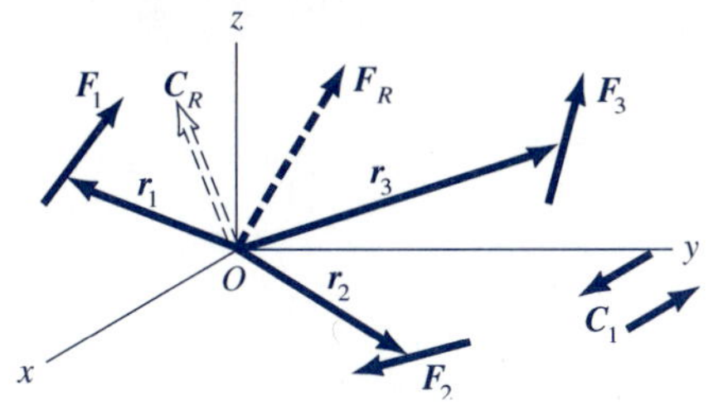

Figure 4.10. Resultant of general force system.

Thus, *any force system can be replaced at any point by equivalents no more complex than a single force and a single couple moment.* In special cases, which we shall examine shortly, we may have simpler equivalents such as a single force or a single couple moment. Finally, for *equilibrium of a body*, it is necessary that at any chosen point the simplest resultant system of force and couple moment acting on the body be zero vectors—a fact that will be discussed in dynamics.[2]

The methods of finding a resultant of forces involve nothing new. In moving to any new point, you will recall, there is no change in the force itself other than a shift of line of action; thus, any component of the *resultant* force, such as the x component, can simply be taken as the sum of the respective x components of all the forces in the system. We may then say for the resultant force

$$\boldsymbol{F}_R = \left[\sum_p (F_p)_x\right]\boldsymbol{i} + \left[\sum_p (F_p)_y\right]\boldsymbol{j} + \left[\sum_p (F_p)_z\right]\boldsymbol{k} \tag{4.3}$$

The couple moment accompanying $\boldsymbol{F}_R$ for a chosen point a may then be given as

$$\boldsymbol{C}_R = [\boldsymbol{r}_1 \times \boldsymbol{F}_1 + \boldsymbol{r}_2 \times \boldsymbol{F}_2 + \dots] + [\boldsymbol{C}_1 + \boldsymbol{C}_2 + \dots] \tag{4.4}$$

where the first bracketed quantities result from moving the noncouple forces to a, and the second are simply the sum of the given couple moments. The vectors $\boldsymbol{r}$ are from a to arbitrary points along the lines of action of the forces. In more compact form, the equation above becomes

$$\boldsymbol{C}_R = \sum_p \boldsymbol{r}_p \times \boldsymbol{F}_p + \sum_q \boldsymbol{C}_q \tag{4.5}$$

The following example is an illustration of the procedure.

[2]When we refer hereafter to a resultant, we shall mean the simplest resultant.

Example 4.4

Two forces and a couple are shown in Fig. 4.11, the couple being positioned in the zy plane. We shall find the resultant of the system at the origin O.

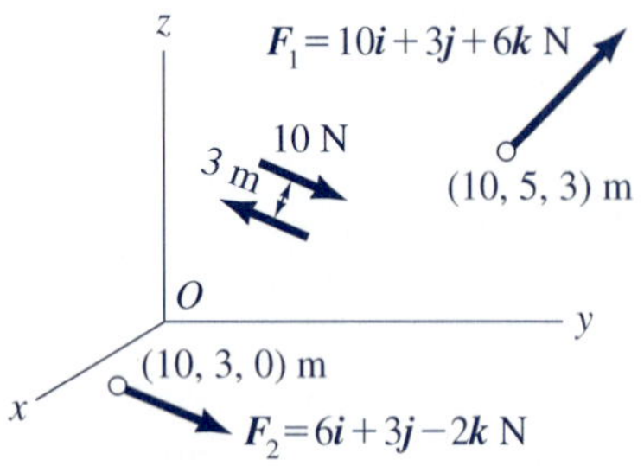

Figure 4.11. Find resultant at O.

At O we will have a set of two concurrent forces, which may be added to give $\boldsymbol{F}_R$:

$$\boldsymbol{F}_R = (10 + 6)\boldsymbol{i} + (3 + 3)\boldsymbol{j} + (6 - 2)\boldsymbol{k}$$

$$\boldsymbol{F}_R = 16\boldsymbol{i} + 6\boldsymbol{j} + 4\boldsymbol{k} \text{ N}$$

The resultant couple moment at point O is the vector sum of the couple-moment vectors developed by moving the two forces, plus the couple moment of the couple in the zy plane. Thus,

$$\boldsymbol{C}_R = \boldsymbol{r}_1 \times \boldsymbol{F}_1 + \boldsymbol{r}_2 \times \boldsymbol{F}_2 - 30\boldsymbol{i} \text{ N-m}$$

Now

$$\begin{aligned}\boldsymbol{r}_1 \times \boldsymbol{F}_1 &= (10\boldsymbol{i} + 5\boldsymbol{j} + 3\boldsymbol{k}) \times (10\boldsymbol{i} + 3\boldsymbol{j} + 6\boldsymbol{k}) \\ &= 21\boldsymbol{i} - 30\boldsymbol{j} - 20\boldsymbol{k} \text{ N-m} \\ \boldsymbol{r}_2 \times \boldsymbol{F}_2 &= (10\boldsymbol{i} + 3\boldsymbol{j}) \times (6\boldsymbol{i} + 3\boldsymbol{j} - 2\boldsymbol{k}) \\ &= -6\boldsymbol{i} + 20\boldsymbol{j} + 12\boldsymbol{k} \text{ N-m}\end{aligned}$$

Hence,

$$\boldsymbol{C}_R = -15\boldsymbol{i} - 10\boldsymbol{j} - 8\boldsymbol{k} \text{ N-m}$$

The resultant is shown in Fig. 4.12.

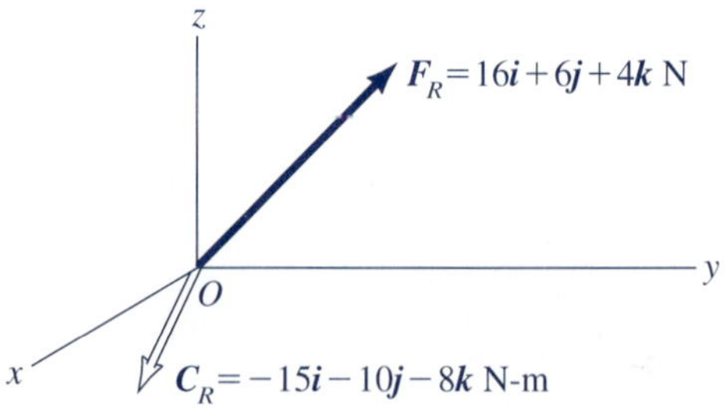

Figure 4.12. Resultant at O.

Example 4.5

What is the resultant at A of the applied loads acting in Fig. 4.13? The forces are directed to intersect the centerline of the shaft along which we

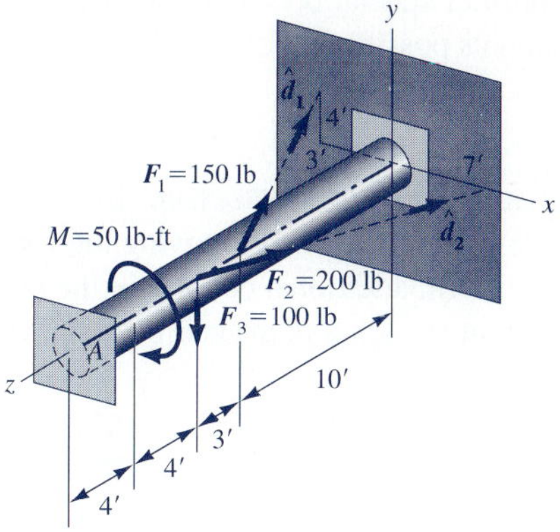

Figure 4.13. Find resultant at A; $\boldsymbol{F}_1$ and $\boldsymbol{F}_3$ are concurrent.

have placed the z axis. We first express the loads vectorially. Thus,

$$\boldsymbol{F}_1 = F_1\hat{\boldsymbol{d}}_1 = 150\left(\frac{-10\boldsymbol{k} - 3\boldsymbol{i} + 4\boldsymbol{j}}{\sqrt{10^2 + 3^2 + 4^2}}\right)$$
$$= -40.2\boldsymbol{i} + 53.7\boldsymbol{j} - 134.1\boldsymbol{k} \text{ lb}$$

$$\boldsymbol{F}_2 = F_2\hat{\boldsymbol{d}}_2 = 200\left(\frac{-13\boldsymbol{k} + 7\boldsymbol{i}}{\sqrt{13^2 + 7^2}}\right)$$
$$= 94.8\boldsymbol{i} - 176\boldsymbol{k} \text{ lb}$$
$$\boldsymbol{F}_3 = -100\boldsymbol{j} \text{ lb}$$
$$\boldsymbol{C} = -50\boldsymbol{k} \text{ ft-lb}$$

We can now readily find the resultant force system at A. Thus,[3]

$$\boldsymbol{F}_R = (-40.2 + 94.8)\boldsymbol{i} + (53.7 - 100)\boldsymbol{j} + (-134.1 - 176.0)\boldsymbol{k}$$

$$\boldsymbol{F}_R = 54.6\boldsymbol{i} - 46.3\boldsymbol{j} - 310\boldsymbol{k} \text{ lb}$$

$$\boldsymbol{C}_R = (-11\boldsymbol{k}) \times \boldsymbol{F}_1 + (-8\boldsymbol{k}) \times (\boldsymbol{F}_2 + \boldsymbol{F}_3) + (-50\boldsymbol{k})$$
$$= -11\boldsymbol{k} \times (-40.2\boldsymbol{i} + 53.7\boldsymbol{j} - 134.1\boldsymbol{k}) + (-8\boldsymbol{k})$$
$$\times (94.8\boldsymbol{i} - 176.0\boldsymbol{k} - 100\boldsymbol{j}) - 50\boldsymbol{k}$$

$$\boldsymbol{C}_R = -209\boldsymbol{i} - 316\boldsymbol{j} - 50\boldsymbol{k} \text{ ft-lb}$$

[3]Remember that for $\boldsymbol{C}$ resulting from a movement of a force, the position vector goes from the point (in this case point A) to the line of action of the force.

4.4 Simplest Resultants of Special Force Systems

We shall now consider special but important force systems and will establish the *simplest* resultants possible for each case. Examples will serve to illustrate the method of procedure.

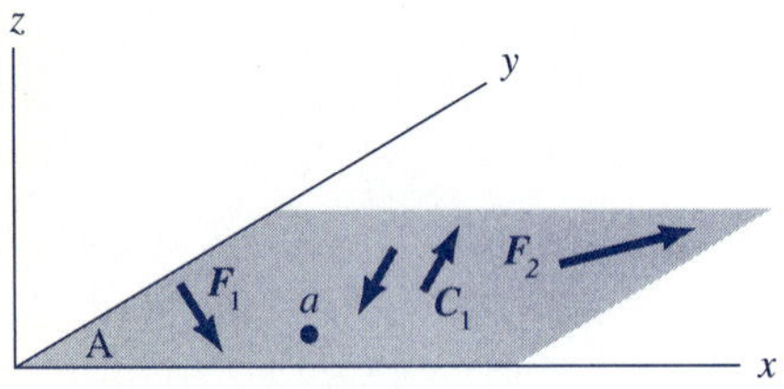

Figure 4.14. Coplanar force system.

Case A. Coplanar Force Systems. In Fig. 4.14, a system of forces and couples is shown in plane A. By moving the forces to a common point a in plane A, we will form additional couples in the plane. The force portion of the equivalent system at such a point will be given as

$$\boldsymbol{F}_R = \left[\sum_p (F_p)_x\right]\boldsymbol{i} + \left[\sum_p (F_p)_y\right]\boldsymbol{j} \tag{4.6}$$

The couple moment portion of the equivalent system can be given as (using the right hand rule for proper signs):

$$\boldsymbol{C}_R = (F_1 d_1 + F_2 d_2 + \ldots)\boldsymbol{k} + (C_1 + C_2 + \ldots)\boldsymbol{k} \tag{4.7}$$

where d_1, d_2, etc., are perpendicular distances from point a to the lines of action of the noncouple forces, and C_1, C_2, etc., are the values of the given couple moments. The resultant at a is shown in Fig. 4.15.

If $\boldsymbol{F}_R \neq \boldsymbol{0}$, (i.e., if $\sum_p F_x \neq 0$ and/or $\sum_p F_y \neq 0$) we can move the force from a to yet a new parallel position so as to introduce a second couple moment to cancel $\boldsymbol{C}_R$ of Fig. 4.15 in the manner described earlier in Section 4.2. Since the x and y directions used are arbitrary, except for the condition that they be in the plane of the forces, we can make the following conclusion. *If the force components in any direction in the plane add to other than zero, we may replace the entire coplanar system by a single force with a specific line of action.*

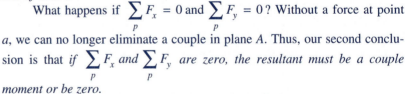

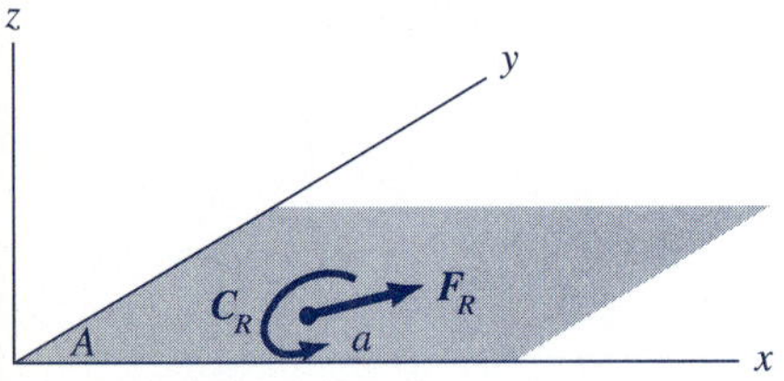

Figure 4.15. Resultant at point a.

What happens if $\sum_p F_x = 0$ and $\sum_p F_y = 0$? Without a force at point a, we can no longer eliminate a couple in plane A. Thus, our second conclusion is that *if $\sum_p F_x$ and $\sum_p F_y$ are zero, the resultant must be a couple moment or be zero.*

In the coplanar case, therefore, the simplest equivalent force system must be a single force along a specific line of action, a single couple moment, or a null vector. The following example is used to illustrate the method of determining such a resultant directly without the intermediate steps followed in this discussion.

Example 4.6

Consider a coplanar force system shown in Fig. 4.16. The *simplest* resultant is to be found. Since $\sum_p F_x$ and $\sum_p F_y$ are not zero, we know that we can replace the system by a single force, which is

$$\boldsymbol{F}_R = 6\boldsymbol{i} + 13\boldsymbol{j} \text{ N} \tag{a}$$

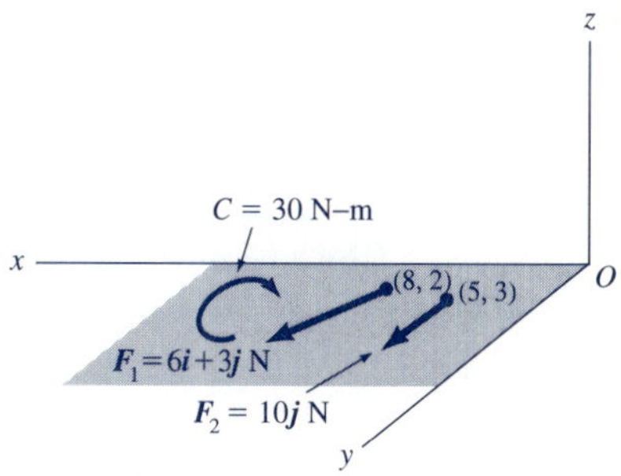

Figure 4.16. Find simplest resultant.

We now need to find the line of action in the plane that will make this single force equivalent to the given system. To be equivalent for rigid-body mechanics, this force without a couple moment must have the same turning action about any point or axis in space as that of the given system. Now the simplest resultant force must intercept the x axis at some point $\bar{x}$.[4] We can determine $\bar{x}$ by equating the moment of the resultant force without a couple moment about the origin with that of the original system of forces and couples. Using the vector $\bar{x}\boldsymbol{i}$ as a position vector from the origin to the line of action of $\boldsymbol{F}_R$ (see Fig. 4.17), we accordingly have

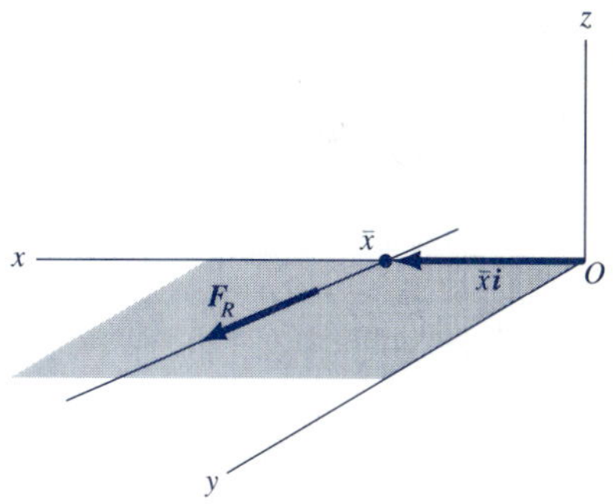

Figure 4.17. Simplest resultant.

$$\bar{x}\boldsymbol{i} \times (6\boldsymbol{i} + 13\boldsymbol{j}) = (8\boldsymbol{i} + 2\boldsymbol{j}) \times (6\boldsymbol{i} + 3\boldsymbol{j}) + (5\boldsymbol{i} + 3\boldsymbol{j}) \times (10\boldsymbol{j}) - 30\boldsymbol{k} \tag{b}$$

Carrying out the cross products,

$$24\boldsymbol{k} - 12\boldsymbol{k} + 50\boldsymbol{k} - 30\boldsymbol{k} = 13\bar{x}\boldsymbol{k} \tag{c}$$

Hence,

$$\bar{x} = 2.46 \text{ m}$$

By specifying the x intercept, $\bar{x}$, we fully determine the line of action of the simplest resultant force. We could have also used the intercept with the y axis, $\bar{y}$, for this purpose. In that case, the position vector from the origin out to the line of action is $\bar{y}\boldsymbol{j}$, and we have, on equating moments about O of the resultant without a couple moment with that of the original system:

$$\bar{y}\boldsymbol{j} \times (6\boldsymbol{i} + 13\boldsymbol{j}) = (8\boldsymbol{i} + 2\boldsymbol{j}) \times (6\boldsymbol{i} + 3\boldsymbol{j}) + (5\boldsymbol{i} + 3\boldsymbol{j}) \times (10\boldsymbol{j}) - 30\boldsymbol{k}$$

$$\bar{y} = -5.35 \text{ m}$$

[4] If the resultant force is parallel to the x axis, the intercept will be at infinity.

Example 4.7

Compute the *simplest* resultant for the loads shown acting on the beam in Fig. 4.18(a). Give the intercept with the x axis.

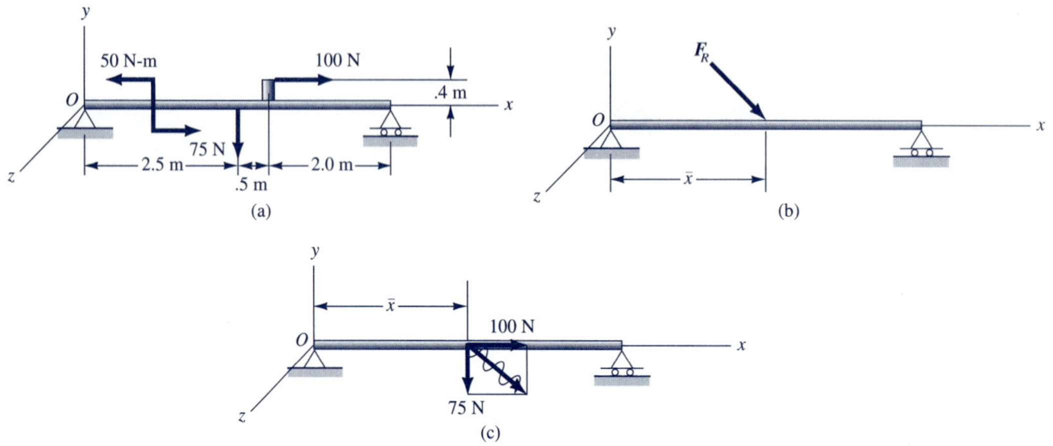

Figure 4.18. Find simplest resultant.

It is immediately apparent on inspection of the diagram that

$$F_R = 100\boldsymbol{i} - 75\boldsymbol{j} \text{ N} \qquad \text{(a)}$$

Let $\bar{x}$ be the intercept with the x axis of the line of action of $\boldsymbol{F}_R$ when this line of action corresponds to zero couple moment $\boldsymbol{C}_R$ [see Fig. 4.18(b)]. In Fig. 4.18(c), we have decomposed $\boldsymbol{F}_R$ along this line of action into rectangular components so as to permit simple calculations of moments about the origin O (here we mean moments about the z axis). Accordingly, equating moments about the z axis of $\boldsymbol{F}_R$ without a couple moment, with that of the original system of loads, we get,

$$-(75)(\bar{x}) = 50 - (2.5)(75) - (.4)(100)$$

$$\bar{x} = 2.37 \text{ m}$$

Thus, the simplest resultant is a force $100\boldsymbol{i} - 75\boldsymbol{j}$ N intercepting the beam axis at a position $\bar{x} = 2.37$ m.

As pointed out earlier, in the instance wherein $\boldsymbol{F}_R = \boldsymbol{0}$, we then possibly have as the simplest resultant a couple moment normal to the plane of the coplanar force system. There is also the possibility that there is zero couple moment, in which case the forces of the coplanar force system *completely cancel* each other's effects on a rigid body. To find the couple moment for the case where $\boldsymbol{F}_R = \boldsymbol{0}$, we simply take moments of the coplanar force system about *any point* in space. This moment, if it is not equal to zero, is clearly the couple-moment vector sought.

Example 4.8

What is the simplest resultant for the forces shown acting on beam *AB* in Fig. 4.19?

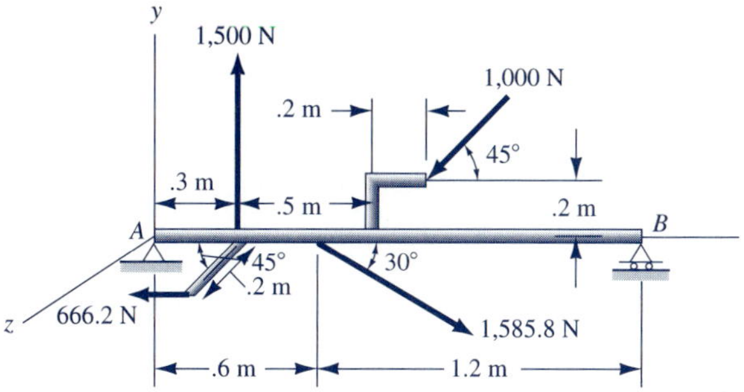

Figure 4.19. Coplanar loading on a simply supported beam.

Our first step will be to compute the resultant force by adding up the force vectors. Thus

$$\boldsymbol{F}_R = 1{,}500\boldsymbol{j} - 666.2\boldsymbol{i} - (1{,}585.8)(.5)\boldsymbol{j} + (1{,}585.8)(.866)\boldsymbol{i} - 707.1\boldsymbol{i} - 707.1\boldsymbol{j}$$

Collecting terms, we have

$$\boldsymbol{F}_R = (-666.2 + 1{,}373.3 - 707.1)\boldsymbol{i} + (1{,}500 - 792.9 - 701.1)\boldsymbol{j} = \boldsymbol{0}$$

The simplest resultant clearly must be either a couple moment or be a null vector. For this information, we shall take moments about point *A*.

$$\boldsymbol{C}_R = \{[.3 - (.2)(.707)]\boldsymbol{i} - (.2)(.707)\boldsymbol{j}\} \times (-666.2\boldsymbol{i}) + (.3)(1{,}500)\boldsymbol{k} - (.6)(1{,}585.8)(.5)\boldsymbol{k} + (1\boldsymbol{i} + .2\boldsymbol{j}) \times (-707.1\boldsymbol{i} - 707.1\boldsymbol{j})$$

$$\boldsymbol{C}_R = -94.20\boldsymbol{k} + 450\boldsymbol{k} - 475.7\boldsymbol{k} - 707.1\boldsymbol{k} + 141.4\boldsymbol{k} = -685.6\boldsymbol{k} \text{ N-m}$$

We have a couple moment in the minus *z* direction having any arbitrary line of action as the simplest resultant.

It is important that the nature of the equivalence just instituted be clearly understood. Thus, for finding the supporting force system, we can use the undeformed geometry and hence the single force replacement. However, for finding the deflection of the beam, it should be obvious that the replacement is invalid. Note, finally, that there is only one point on the beam that will allow for a single force to be equivalent to the original system for purposes of rigid-body considerations.

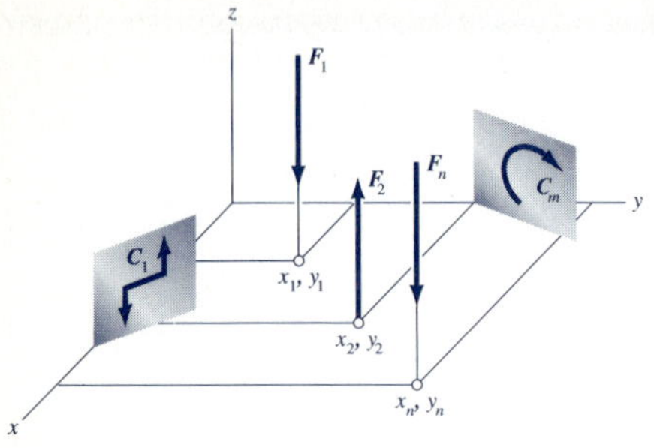

Figure 4.20. Parallel system of forces.

Case B. Parallel Force Systems in Space. Now, consider the system of n parallel forces in Fig. 4.20, where the z direction has been selected parallel to the forces. We also include m couples whose planes are parallel to the z direction because such couples can be considered to be composed of equal and opposite forces parallel to the z direction. We can move the forces so that they all pass through the origin of the xyz axes; the force portion of the equivalent system is then

$$\boldsymbol{F}_R = \left(\sum_{p=1}^{n} (F_p)\right)\boldsymbol{k} \tag{4.8}$$

The couple moment portion of the equivalent system is found by applying Eq. 4.5 to this case:

$$\boldsymbol{C}_R = \sum_{p=1}^{n}\left[\left(x_p\boldsymbol{i} + y_p\boldsymbol{j}\right)\times F_p\boldsymbol{k}\right] + \sum_{p=1}^{m}\left[\left(C_p\right)_x\boldsymbol{i} + \left(C_p\right)_y\boldsymbol{j}\right] \tag{4.9}$$

where $\boldsymbol{F}_p$ represents the noncouple forces. Carrying out the cross product, we get

$$\boldsymbol{C}_R = \sum_{p=1}^{n}\left[\left(F_p y_p\right)\boldsymbol{i} - \left(F_p x_p\right)\right]\boldsymbol{j} + \sum_{p=1}^{m}\left[\left(C_p\right)_x\boldsymbol{i} + \left(C_p\right)_y\boldsymbol{j}\right] \tag{4.10}$$

From this, we see that the couple moment must always be parallel to the xy plane (i.e., perpendicular to the direction of the forces). We then have at the origin a single force and a single couple moment at right angles to each other [see Fig. 4.21(a)]. If $\boldsymbol{F}_R \neq \boldsymbol{0}$, we can move $\boldsymbol{F}_R$ again to another line of action in a plane A perpendicular to $\boldsymbol{C}_R$ [see Fig. 4.21(b)] and, choosing the proper value of d, ensure that $F_R d = |\boldsymbol{C}_R|$ with a sense opposite to $\boldsymbol{C}_R$[5] such that we eliminate the couple moment. We thus end up with a *single* force having a particular line of action specified by the intercept $\bar{x}, \bar{y}$ of the line of action of the force with the xy plane. If the summation of forces should happen to be zero, the equivalent system must then be a couple moment or a null vector.

Thus, *the simplest resultant system of a parallel force system is either a force with a specific line of action, a single couple moment, or a null vector.* The following example will illustrate how we can directly determine the simplest resultant.

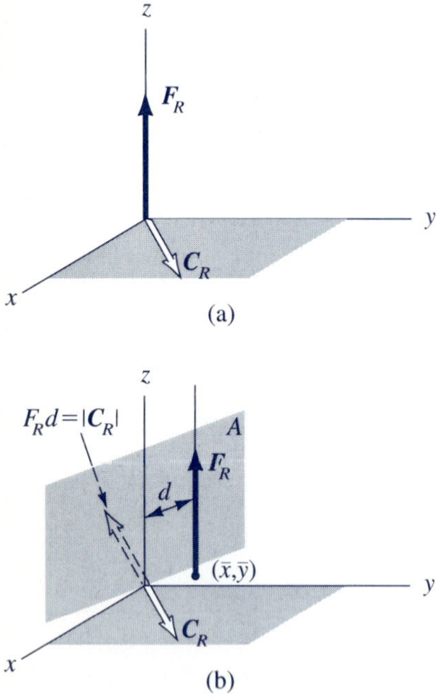

Figure 4.21. Simplest resultant for parallel force system.

[5]Here we urge some caution! The proper displacement vector to be used in computing the moment induced by moving $\boldsymbol{F}$ is found by going from the *new* position to the *original* position. The displacement vector here accordingly must go from right to left a distance d. Recall in this regard that when moving a force to a line of action through a point a, the position vector used in computing the induced couple moment always goes *from the point to the force* [see Fig. 4.3(a)].

Example 4.9

Find the simplest resultant of the parallel force system in Fig. 4.22(a).

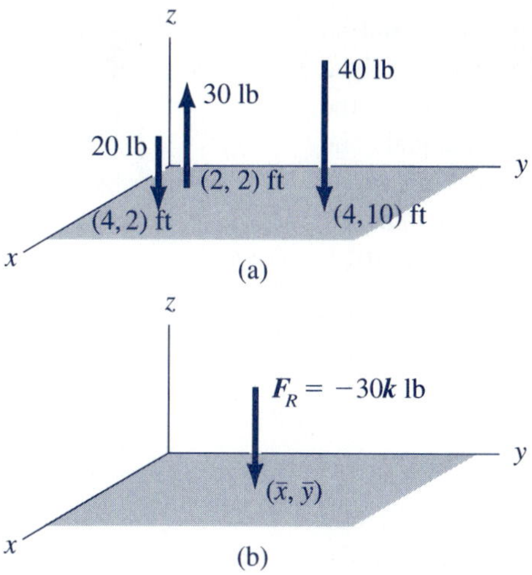

Figure 4.22. Find simplest resultant.

The sum of the forces is 30 lb in the negative z direction. Hence, a position can be found in which a single force is equivalent to the original system. Assume that this resultant force without a couple moment proceeds through the point $\bar{x}$, $\bar{y}$ [Fig. 4.22(b)]. We can equate the moment of this resultant force about the x and y axes with the corresponding moments of the original system and thus form the scalar equations that yield the proper value of $\bar{x}$ and $\bar{y}$. Equating moments about the x axis, we get

$$(30)(2) - (20)(2) - (40)(10) = -30\bar{y}$$

Therefore,

$$\bar{y} = 12.7 \text{ ft}$$

Equating moments about the y axis, we have

$$-(30)(2) + (20)(4) + (40)(4) = 30\bar{x}$$

Therefore,

$$\bar{x} = 6 \text{ ft}$$

You can also show, as an exercise, that the same result can be reached for $\bar{x}$, $\bar{y}$ by equating moments of the resultant force without a couple moment about the origin with that of the original system about the origin.

Example 4.10

Consider the parallel force system in Fig. 4.23(a). What is the simplest resultant?

Here we have a case where the sum of the forces is zero and so $\boldsymbol{F}_R = \boldsymbol{0}$. Therefore, the simplest resultant must be a couple moment or be a null vector. To get this couple moment, $\boldsymbol{C}_R$, we can take moments of the forces about *any point* in space. This moment vector then equals the desired couple moment $\boldsymbol{C}_R$. One procedure is to use the origin of the reference as the point about which to take moments. Then we can say that

$$\boldsymbol{C}_R = (4\boldsymbol{i} + 2\boldsymbol{j}) \times (-30\boldsymbol{k}) + (3\boldsymbol{i} + 2\boldsymbol{j}) \times (40\boldsymbol{k}) + (2\boldsymbol{i} + 4\boldsymbol{j}) \times (-10\boldsymbol{k})$$
$$= -20\boldsymbol{i} + 20\boldsymbol{j} \text{ N-m} \quad \text{(a)}$$

The rectangular components of $\boldsymbol{C}_R$ along the x and y axes are the moments of the force system about these axes. Thus,

$$(\boldsymbol{C}_R)_x = -20 \text{ N-m}$$
$$(\boldsymbol{C}_R)_y = 20 \text{ N-m} \quad \text{(b)}$$

We can get the moments of the forces about the x and y axes directly and thus generate the components of the desired couple moment $\boldsymbol{C}_R$. Accordingly, using the elementary definition of the moment of a force about a line as presented earlier, we have

$$(\boldsymbol{C}_R)_x = -(10)(4) + (40)(2) - (30)(2) = -20 \text{ N-m}$$
$$(\boldsymbol{C}_R)_y = (10)(2) - (40)(3) + (30)(4) = 20 \text{ N-m}$$

Thus, the moment of the force system about the origin, and hence about any point, is then the desired couple moment (Fig. 4.23(b))

$$\boldsymbol{C}_R = -20\boldsymbol{i} + 20\boldsymbol{j} \text{ N-m}$$

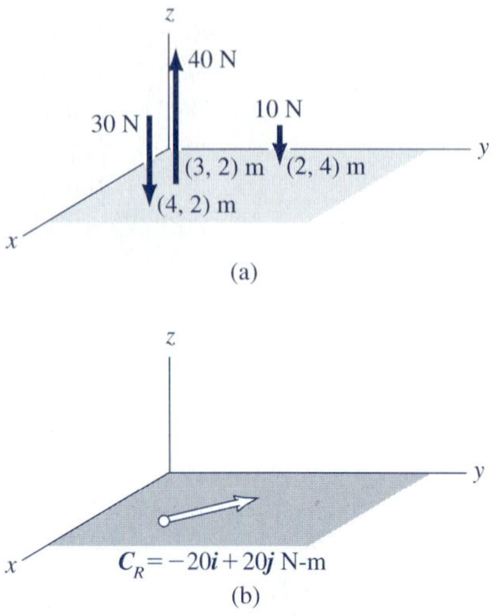

Figure 4.23. Parallel force system.

Now that we have considered the concept of the simplest resultant for coplanar and parallel force systems, we wish to go back to the *general force* systems for a moment. We learned earlier that we can always replace such a system in rigid-body mechanics by a single force $\boldsymbol{F}_R$ and a single couple moment $\boldsymbol{C}_R$ at any chosen point. Is this always the very simplest system for rigid-body mechanics? No, it is not. To show this, decompose the couple moment $\boldsymbol{C}_R$ into two rectangular components $C_\perp$ and $C_\parallel$, perpendicular to the force and collinear with the force, respectively. We can now conceivably move the force to a specific parallel position and can eliminate $C_\perp$, the component of couple moment normal to the force. However, there is nothing that we can do about the $C_\parallel$ component of couple moment collinear (or parallel) to the force. The reason for this is that any movement of the force to a parallel position *always* introduces a couple moment *perpendicular* to the force. Thus the component $C_\parallel$ cannot be affected. By eliminating $C_\perp$ we end up with the force $\boldsymbol{F}_R$ and $\boldsymbol{C}_\parallel$ collinear with $\boldsymbol{F}_R$. This system is the simplest in the general case and it is called a *wrench* (see Fig. 4.24). However, we shall not generally use the wrench concept in this text and will work instead with the resultant force $\boldsymbol{F}_R$ and the couple moment $\boldsymbol{C}_R$ at any chosen point.

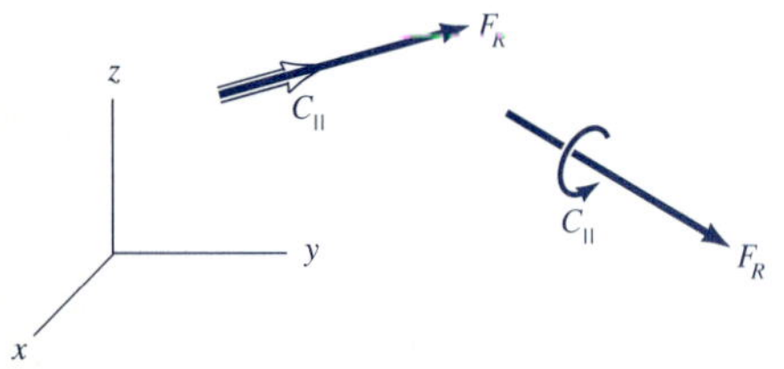

Figure 4.24. Examples of the so-called wrench. This is the simplest representation of a general force system.

PROBLEMS

In several of the problems of this set we shall concentrate the weight of a body at its center of gravity. Most likely you are used to doing this from your previous physics course. In Section 4.5 we shall justify this procedure.

4.18. Compute the resultant force system of the applied loads at positions *A* and *B*.

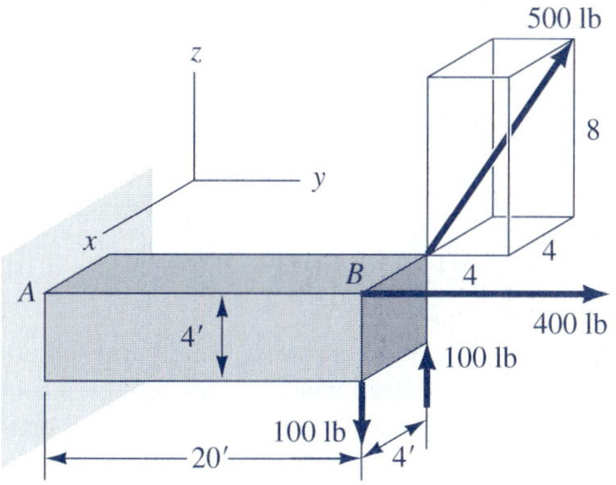

Figure P.4.18.

4.19. Compute the resultant force system at *A* stemming from the indicated 50-lb force. What is the twist developed about the axis of the shaft at *A*? The 50-lb force is normal to the wrench.

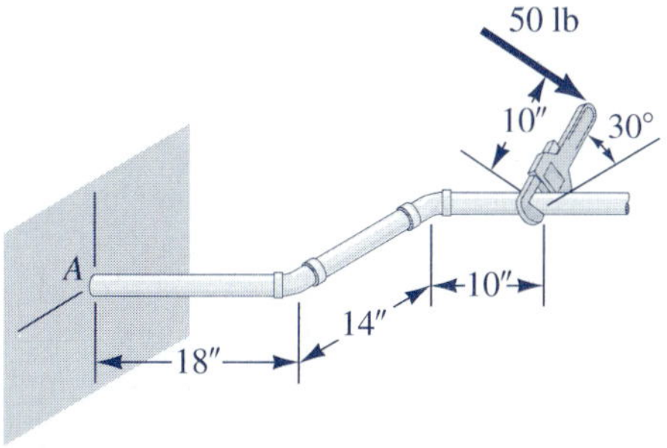

Figure P.4.19.

4.20. Find the resultant of the force system at point *A*. The 300-N, 200-N, and 900-N loads are at the centers of the pipe sections.

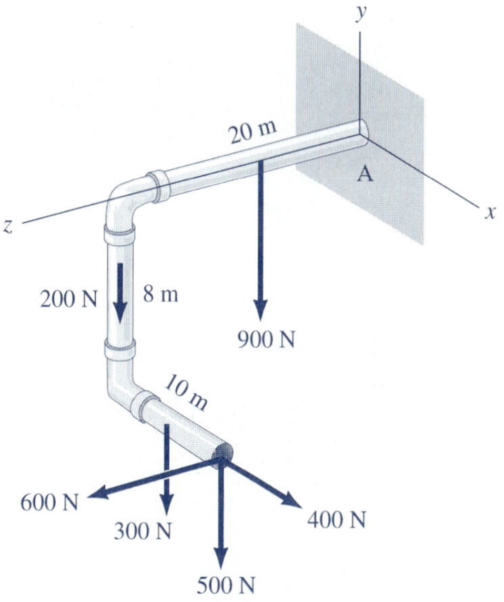

Figure P.4.20.

4.21. A 20-kN car and an 80-kN truck are stopped on a bridge. What is the resultant force system of these vehicles at the center of the bridge? At the center of the left end of the bridge? The distances given to truck and car are to respective centers of gravity where we can concentrate the weights.

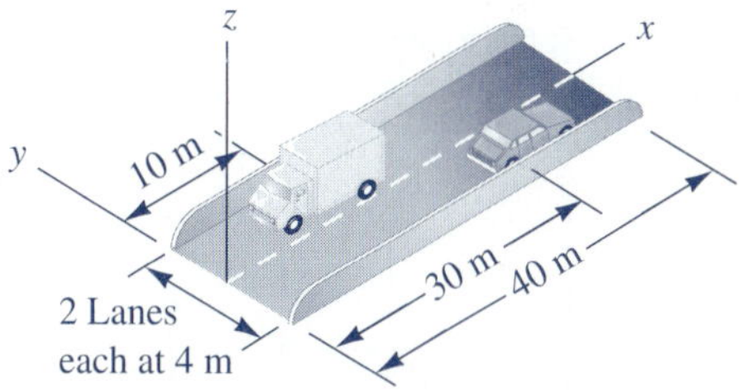

Figure P.4.21.

4.22. Two heavy machinery crates (*A* weighs 20 kN and *B* weighs 30 kN) are placed on a truck. What is the resultant force system at the center of the rear axle? The centers of gravity of the crates, where we can concentrate the weights, are at the geometric centers.

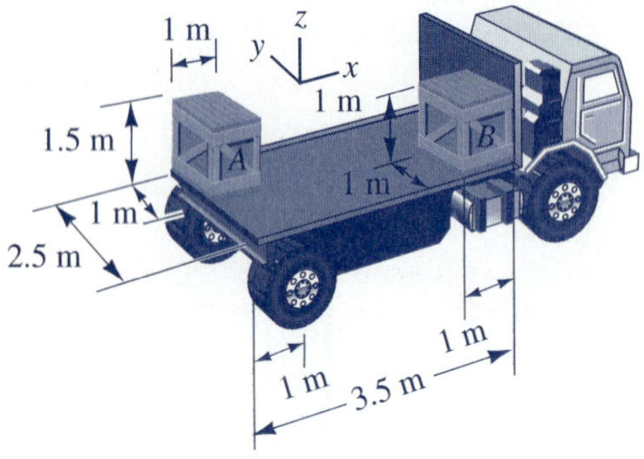

Figure P.4.22.

4.23. Replace the system of forces by a resultant at *A*.

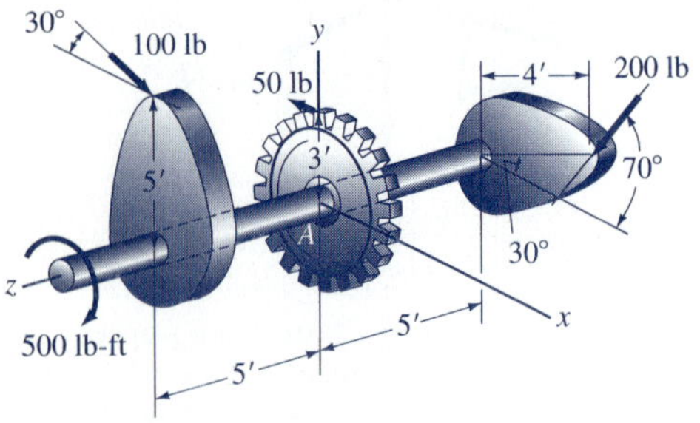

Figure P.4.23.

4.24. Evaluate Forces F_1, F_2, and F_3 so that the resultant of the forces and torque acting on the plate is zero in both force and couple moment. (*Hint:* If the resultant is zero for one point, will it not be zero for any point? Explain why.)

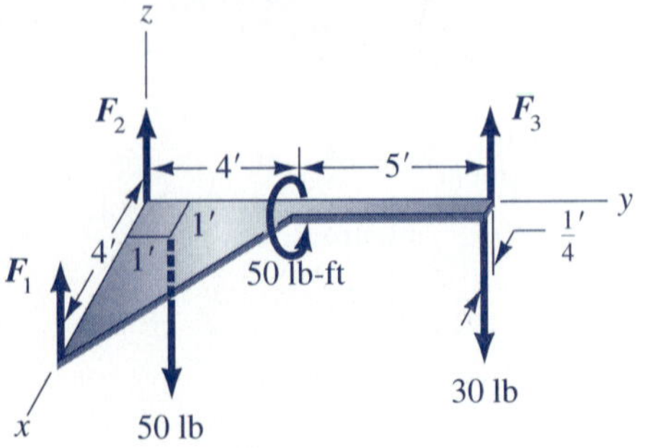

Figure P.4.24.

4.25. Find the *simplest* resultant of the forces shown acting on the beam. Give the intercept with the axis of the beam.

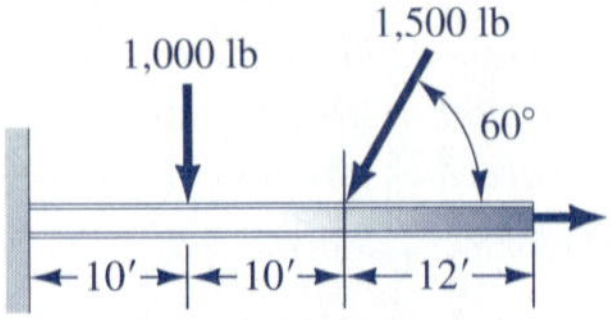

Figure P.4.25.

4.26. Find the *simplest* resultant of the forces shown acting on the pulley. Give the intercept with the *x* axis.

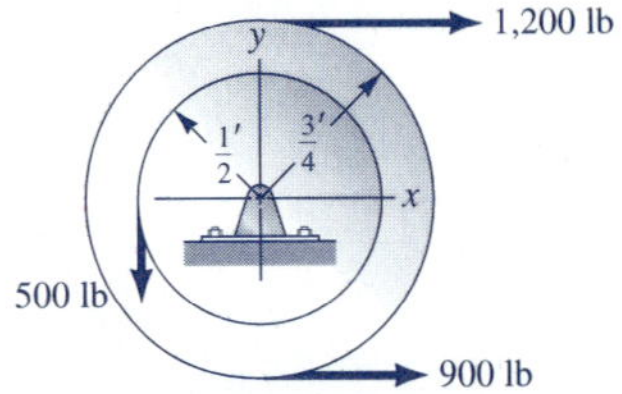

Figure P.4.26.

4.27. A man raises a 50-lb bucket of water to the top of a bricklayer's scaffold. Also, a Jeep winch is used to raise a 200-lb load of bricks. What is the *simplest* resultant force system on the scaffold? Give the *x* intercept. Consider the pulleys to be frictionless so that the 50-lb force and the 200-lb force are transmitted respectively to the man and to the Jeep.

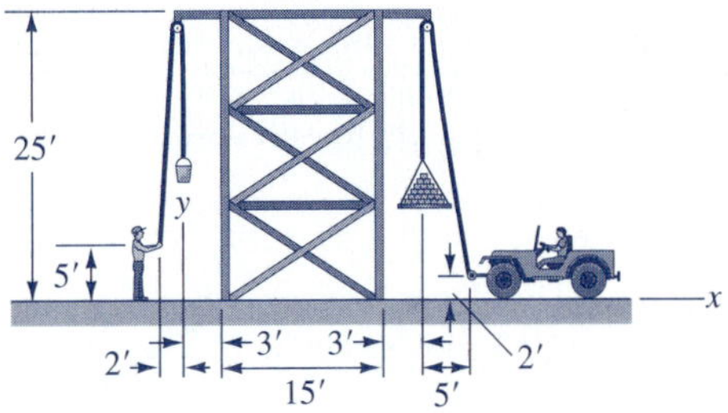

Figure P.4.27.

4.28. Find the resultant at *A*.

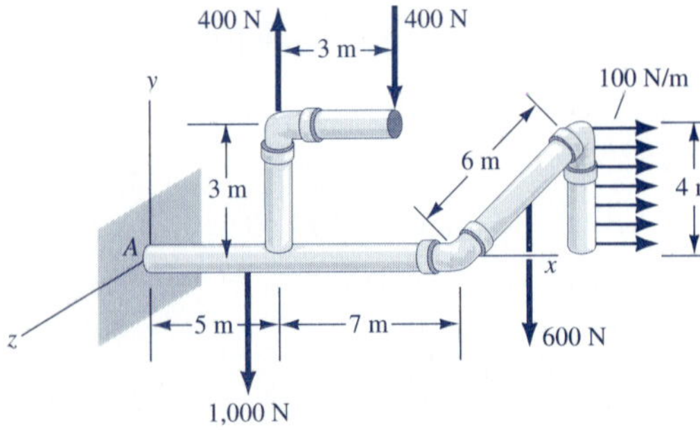

Figure P.4.28.

4.29. Compute the *simplest* resultant for the loads acting on the beam. Give the intercept with the axis of the beam.

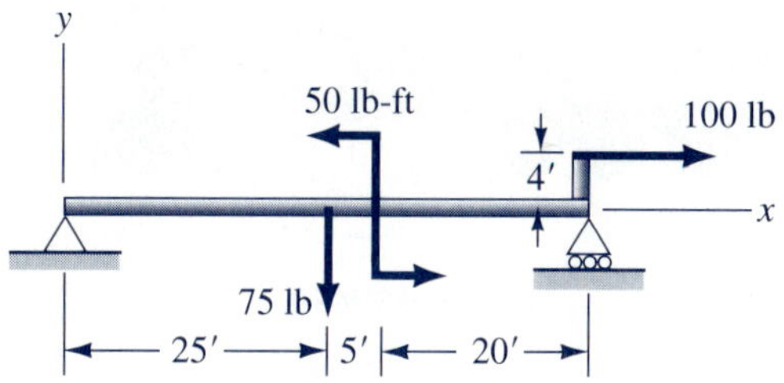

Figure P.4.29.

4.30. Find the *simplest* resultant for the forces. Give the location of this resultant clearly.

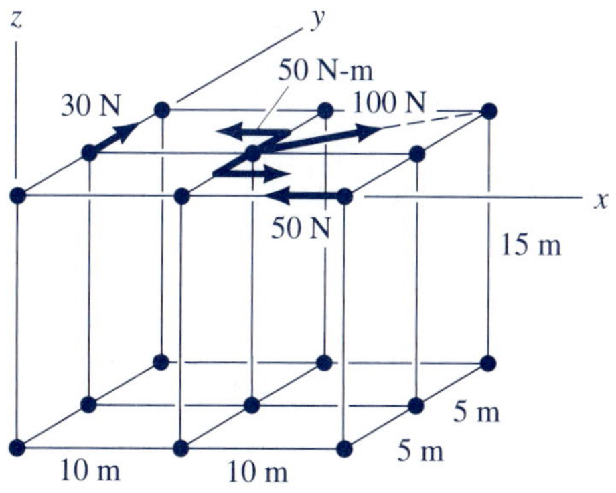

Figure P.4.30.

4.31. Replace the system of forces acting on the rivets of the plate by the *simplest* resultant. Give the intercept of this resultant with the x axis.

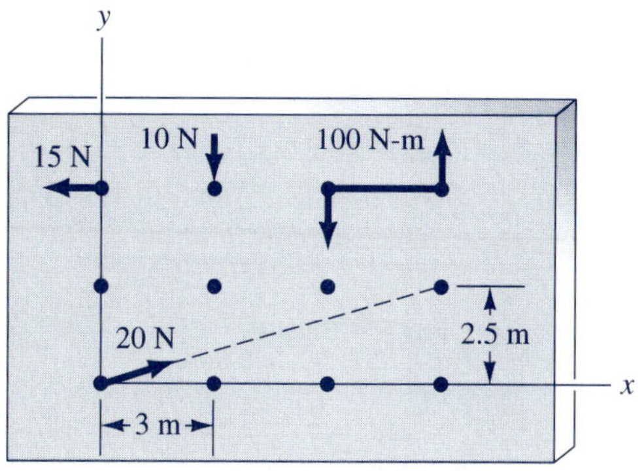

Figure P.4.31.

4.32. A parallel system of forces is such that: a 20-N force acts at position $x = 10$ m, $y = 3$ m; a 30-N force acts at position $x = 5$ m, $y = -3$m; a 50-N force acts at position $x = -2$ m, $y = 5$ m.

(a) If all forces point in the negative z direction, give the *simplest* resultant force and its line of action.

(b) If the 50-N force points in the plus z direction and the others in the negative z direction, what is the *simplest* resultant?

4.33. What is the *simplest* resultant of the three forces and couple shown acting on the shaft and disc? The disc radius is 5 ft.

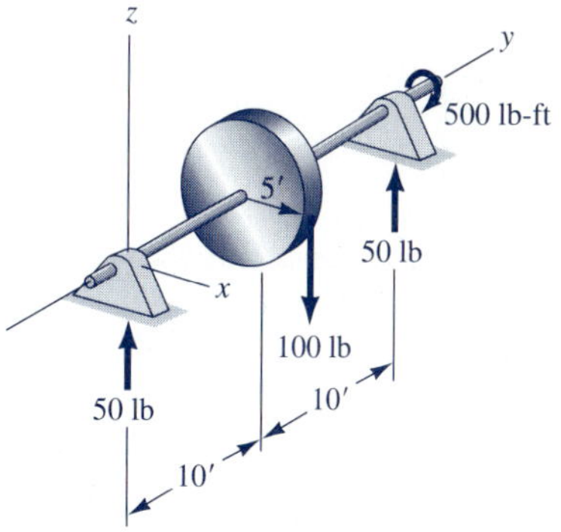

Figure P.4.33.

4.34. What is the *simplest* resultant for the system of forces? Each square is 10 mm on edge.

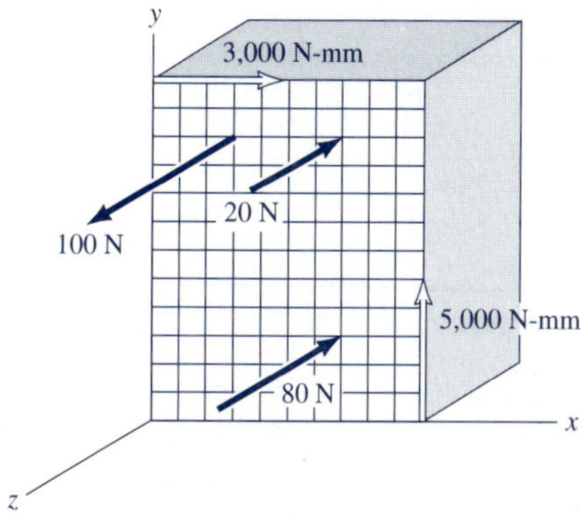

Figure P.4.34.

4.35. What is the simplest resultant? Where does its line of action cross the *x* axis?

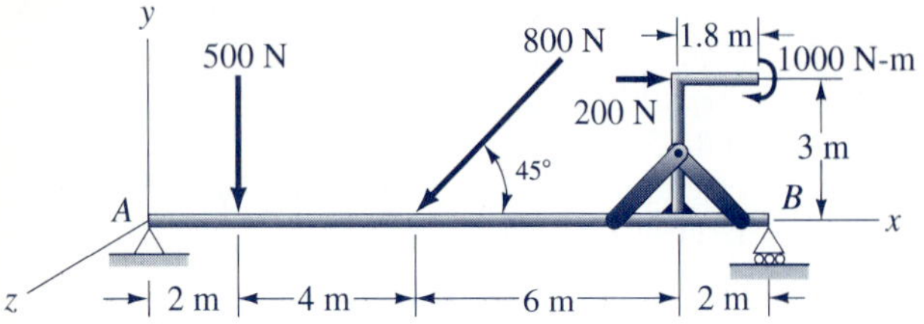

Figure P.4.35.

4.36. What is the simplest resultant of the loadings shown? Be sure to give its line of action.

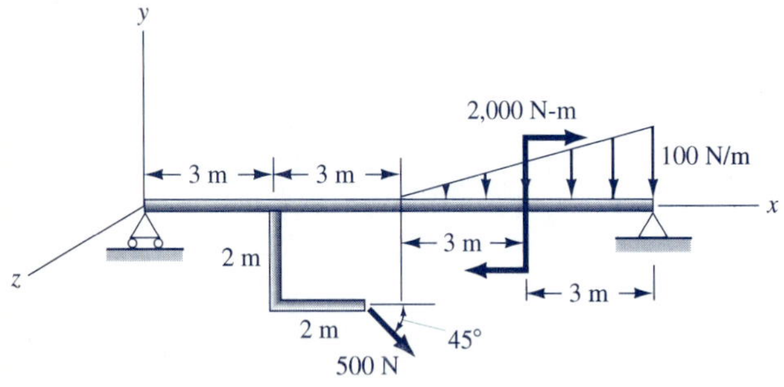

Figure P.4.36.

4.37. Two hoists are operated on the same overhead track. Hoist *A* has a 3,000-kN load, and hoist *B* has a 4,000-kN load. What is the resultant force system at the left end *O* of the track? Where does the *simplest* resultant force act?

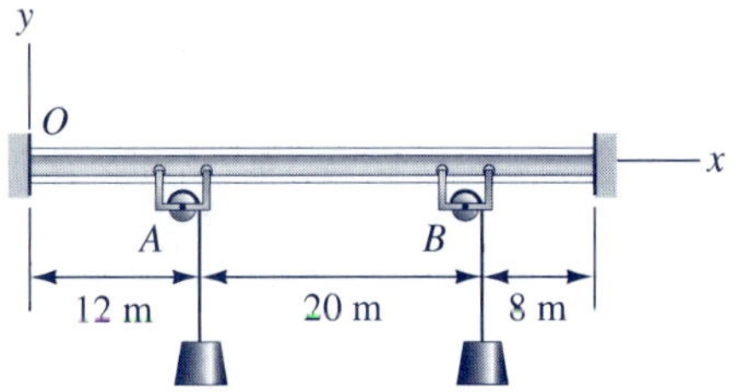

Figure P.4.37.

4.38. A lo-boy trailer weighs 16,000 lb and is loaded with a 15,000-lb bulldozer *A* and a 12,000-lb front-end loader *B*. What is the simplest resultant force and where does it act? The weights of the machines and trailer act at their respective centers of gravity (C.G.).

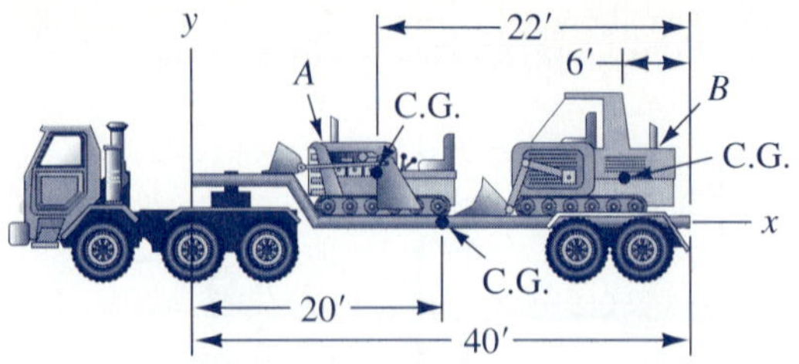

Figure P.4.38.

4.39. Where should a 100-N force in a downward direction be placed for the *simplest* resultant of all shown forces to be at position (5, 5) m?

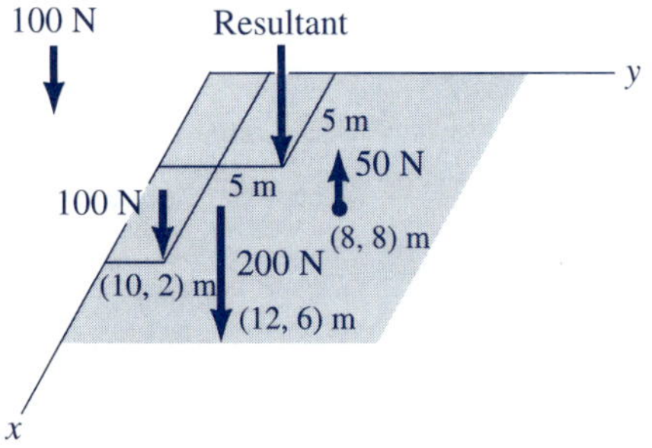

Figure P.4.39.

4.40. A barge must be evenly loaded so it does not list in any direction. Where can the three large machinery crates be placed (without either hanging over the edge, stacking, or standing on end)? Each crate is as tall as it is wide. Is there only one solution to this problem? Centers of gravity of crates correspond to geometric centers.

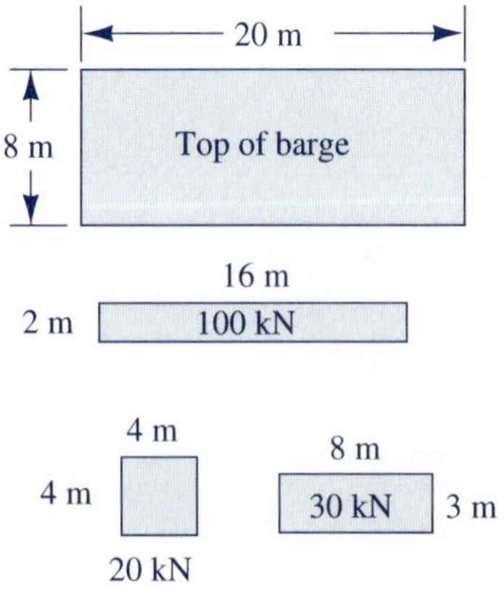

Figure P.4.40.

4.5 Distributed Force Systems

Our discussions up to now have been restricted to discrete vectors—in particular, to point forces. Vectors as well as scalars, may also be continuously distributed throughout a finite volume. Such distributions are called *vector* and *scalar fields*, respectively. A simple example of a scalar field is the temperature distribution, expressed as $T(x, y, z, t)$, where the variable t indicates that the field may be changing with time. Thus, if a position x_0, y_0, z_0 and a time t_0 are specified, we can determine the temperature at this position and time provided that we know the temperature distribution function (i.e., how T depends on the independent variables x, y, z, and t). A vector field is sometimes expressed in the form $\boldsymbol{F}(x, y, z, t)$. A common example of a vector field is the gravitational force field of the earth—a field that is known to vary with elevation above sea level, among other factors. Note, however, that the gravitational field is virtually constant with time.

In place of the vector field, it is more convenient at times to employ three scalar fields that represent the orthogonal scalar components of a vector field at all points. Thus, for a force field we can say:

$$\begin{aligned}\text{force component in } x \text{ direction} &= g(x, y, z, t)\\ \text{force component in } y \text{ direction} &= h(x, y, z, t)\\ \text{force component in } z \text{ direction} &= l(x, y, z, t)\end{aligned}$$

where g, h, and l represent functions of the coordinates and time. If we substitute coordinates of a special position and the time into these functions, we get the force components F_x, F_y, and F_z for that position and time. The force field and its component scalar fields are then related in this way:

$$\boldsymbol{F}(x, y, z, t) = g(x, y, z, t)\boldsymbol{i} + h(x, y, z, t)\boldsymbol{j} + l(x, y, z, t)\boldsymbol{k}$$

More often, the notation for the equation above is written

$$\boldsymbol{F}(x, y, z, t) = F_x(x, y, z, t)\boldsymbol{i} + F_y(x, y, z, t)\boldsymbol{j} + F_z(x, y, z, t)\boldsymbol{k} \quad (4.11)$$

Vector fields are not restricted to forces but include other quantities such as velocity fields and heat-flow fields.

Force distributions, such as gravitational force, that exert influence directly on the elements of mass distributed throughout the body are termed *body force distributions* and are usually given per unit of mass that they directly influence. Thus, if $\boldsymbol{B}(x, y, z, t)$ is such a body force distribution, the force on an element dm would be $\boldsymbol{B}(x, y, z, t)dm$.

Force distributions over a *surface* are called *surface force distributions*[6] $\boldsymbol{T}(x, y, z, t)$ and are given per unit area of the surface directly influenced. A simple example is the force distribution on the surface of a body submerged in a fluid. In the case of a static fluid or of a frictionless fluid, the force from the fluid on an area element is always normal to the area element and directed

[6]Surface forces are often called *surface tractions* in solid mechanics.

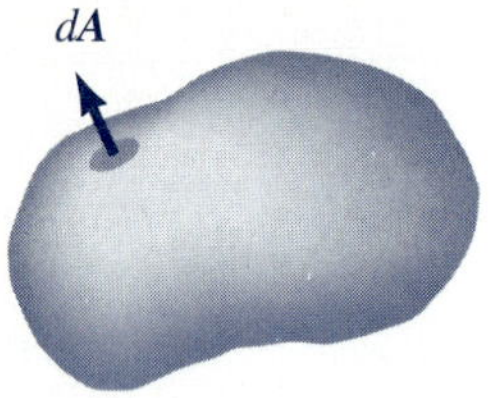

Figure 4.25. Area vector.

in toward the body. The force per unit area stemming from such fluid action is called *pressure* and is denoted as p. Pressure is a scalar quantity. The direction of the force resulting from a pressure on a surface is given by the orientation of the surface. [You will recall from Chapter 2 that an area element can be considered as a vector which is normal to the area element and directed outward from the enclosed body (Fig. 4.25).] The infinitesimal force on the area element is then given as

$$d\mathbf{f} = -p\, d\mathbf{A}$$

A more specialized, but nevertheless common, force distribution is that of a continuous load on a beam. This is often a parallel loading distribution that is symmetrical about the center plane xy of a beam, as illustrated in Fig. 4.26. Various heights of bricks stacked on a beam would be an example of this kind of loading. We can replace such a loading by an equivalent coplanar distribution that acts at the center plane. The loading is given per unit length and is denoted as w, the *intensity of loading*. The force on an element dx of the beam, then, is $w\, dx$.

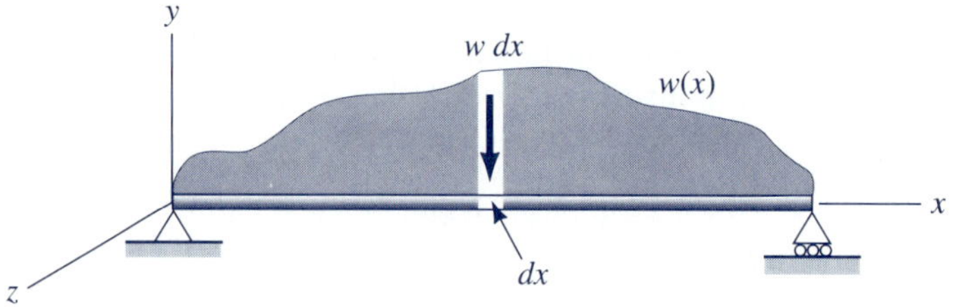

Figure 4.26. Loading on a beam.

We have thus presented force systems distributed throughout volumes (body forces), over surfaces (surface forces or tractions), and over lines. The conclusions about resultants that were reached earlier for general, parallel, and coplanar point force systems are also valid for these distributed force systems. These conclusions are true because each distributed force system can be considered as an infinite number of infinitesimal point forces of the type used heretofore. We shall illustrate the handling of force distributions in the following examples.

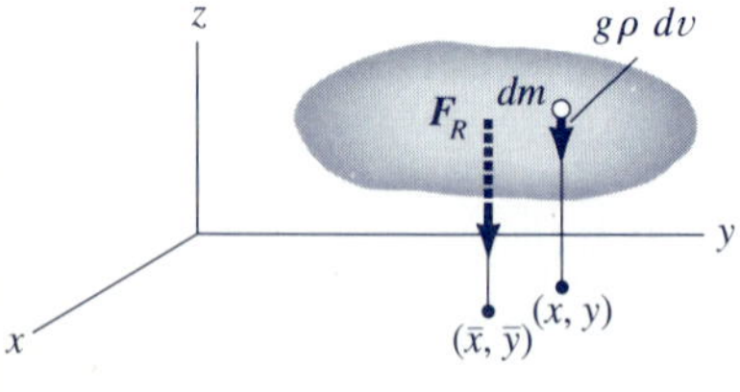

Figure 4.27. Gravity body force distribution.

Case A. Parallel Body Force System—Center of Gravity.

Consider a rigid body (Fig. 4.27) whose density (mass/unit volume) is given as $\rho(x, y, z)$. It is acted on by gravity, which, for a small body, may be considered to result in a distributed parallel force field.

Since we have here a parallel system of forces in space with the same sense, we know that a single force without a couple moment along a certain line of action will be equivalent to the distribution. The gravity body force

$\boldsymbol{B}(x, y, z)$ given per unit mass is $-g\boldsymbol{k}$. The infinitesimal force on a differential mass element dm, then , is $-g(\rho\, dv)\boldsymbol{k}$, where dv is the volume of the element.[7] We find the resultant force on the system by replacing the summation in Eq. 4.8 with an integration, Thus,

$$\boldsymbol{F}_R = -\int_V g(\rho\, dv)\boldsymbol{k} = -g\boldsymbol{k}\int_V \rho\, dv = -gM\boldsymbol{k}$$

where, with g as a constant, the second integral becomes simply the entire mass of the body M.

Next, we must find the line of action of this single equivalent force without a couple moment. Let us denote the intercept of this line of action with the xy plane as $\bar{x}$, $\bar{y}$ (see Fig. 4.27). The resultant at this position must have the same moments as the distribution about the x and y axes:

$$-F_R\bar{y} = -g\int_V y\rho\, dv \qquad F_R\bar{x} = -g\int_V x\rho\, dv,$$

Hence, we have

$$\bar{x} = \frac{\int x\rho\, dv}{M} \qquad \bar{y} = \frac{\int y\rho\, dv}{M}$$

Thus, we have fully established the simplest resultant. Now, the body is reoriented in space, keeping with it the line of action of the resultant as shown in Fig. 4.28. A new computation of the line of action of the simplest resultant for the second orientation yields a line that intersects the original line at a point C. It can be shown that lines of action for simplest resultants for all other orientations of the body must intersect at the same point C. We call this point the *center of gravity*. Effectively, we can say for rigid-body considerations that all the weight of the body can be assumed to be concentrated at the center of gravity.

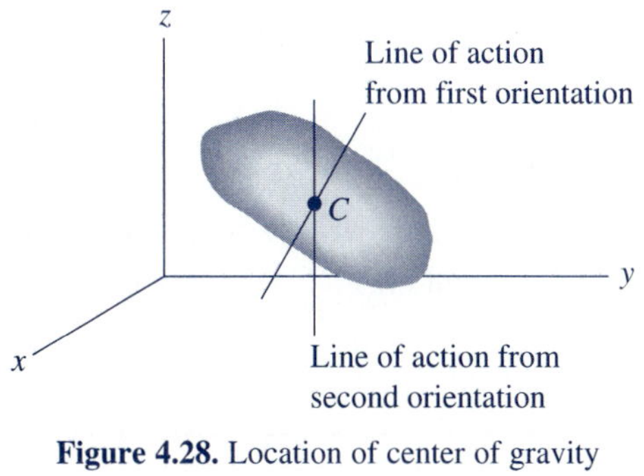

Figure 4.28. Location of center of gravity

[7]Note that $g\rho$ is the weight per unit volume, which is often given as γ, the so-called specific weight.

Example 4.11

Find the center of gravity of the triangular block having a uniform density ρ shown in Fig. 4.29.

The total weight of the body is easily evaluated as

$$F_R = g\rho\left(abc/2\right) \quad \text{(a)}$$

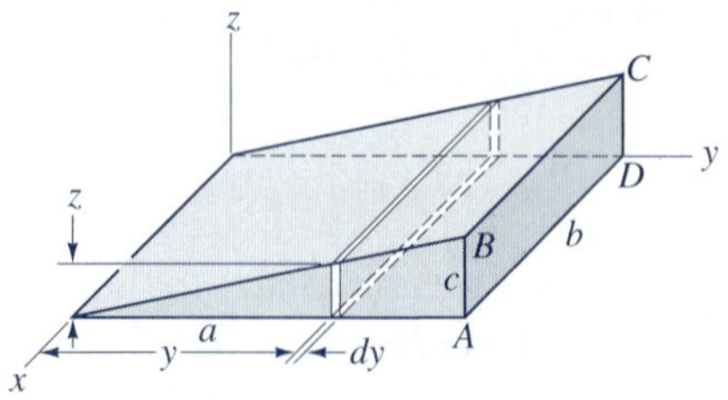

Figure 4.29. Find center of gravity.

To find $\bar{y}$, we will equate the moment of F_R about the x axis with that of the weight distribution of the block. To facilitate the latter, we shall choose within the block *infinitesimal* elements whose weights are easily computed. Also, the moment of the weight of each element about the x axis is to be likewise easily computed. Infinitesimal slices of thickness dy parallel to the xz plane fulfill our requirements nicely. The weight of such a slice is simply $(zb\,dy)\rho g$, where z is the height of the slice (see Fig. 4.29). Because all points of the slice are at the same coordinate distance y from the x axis, clearly the moment of the weight of the slice is easily computed as $-y(zb\,dy)\rho g$. By letting y run from 0 to a during an integration, we can account for all the slices in the body. Thus, we have

$$-F_R\bar{y} = -\int_0^a y(zb\,dy)\rho g \quad \text{(b)}$$

The term z can be expressed with the aid of similar triangles in terms of the integration variable y as follows:

$$\frac{z}{c} = \frac{y}{a}$$

$$z = \left(\frac{y}{a}\right)c \quad \text{(c)}$$

We then have for Eq. (b), on replacing F_R using Eq. (a),

$$\bar{y} = \frac{1}{g\rho(abc\,/\,2)}g\int_0^a \rho y^2 \frac{bc}{a}\,dy = \frac{2}{3}a \quad \text{(d)}$$

To find the coordinate in the z direction to the center of gravity, we could reorient the body as shown in Fig 4.30. A computation similar to the preceding one would give the result that $\bar{z} = \frac{2}{3}c$. You are urged to verify this yourself.

Finally, it should be clear by inspection of Fig. 4.28 that $\bar{x} = \frac{1}{2}b$.

Thus we have $\bar{x} = \dfrac{b}{2}$, $\bar{y} = \dfrac{2}{3}$a, and $\bar{z} = \dfrac{2}{3}$c

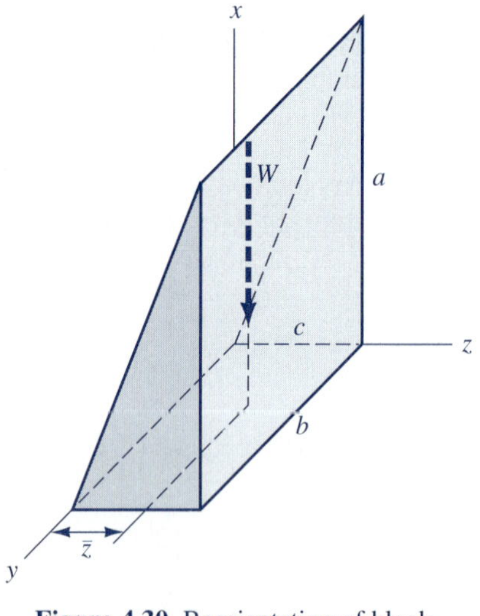

Figure 4.30. Reorientation of block.

Example 4.12

Find the center of gravity for the body of revolution shown in Fig. 4.31. The radial distance of the surface from the y axis is given as

$$r = \frac{1}{20} y^2 \text{ ft} \tag{a}$$

The body has constant density ρ, is 10 ft long, and has a cylindrical hole at the right end of length 2 ft and diameter 1 ft.

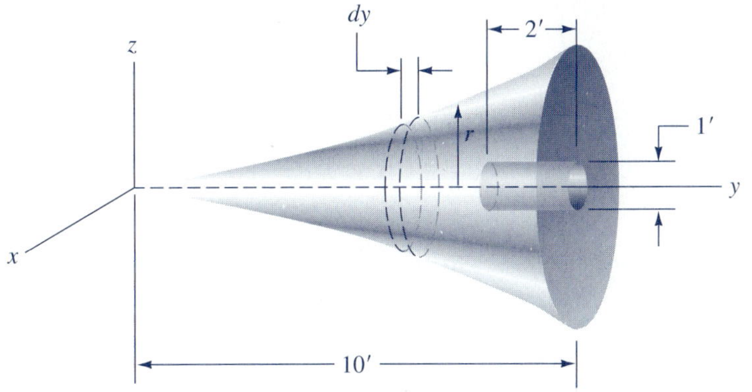

Figure 4.31. Body of revolution. Find center of gravity.

We need only compute $\bar{y}$, since it is clear that $\bar{z} = \bar{x} = 0$, owing to symmetry. We first compute the weight of the body. Using slices of thickness dy, as shown in the diagram, we sum the weight of all slices in the body assuming it is whole by letting y run from 0 to 10 in an integration. We then subtract the weight of a 2-ft cylinder of diameter 1 ft to take into account the cylindrical cavity inside the body. Thus, we have, noting that the area of a circle is πr^2 or $\pi D^2/4$

$$W = \int_0^{10} \left(\pi r^2\right) dy\, \rho g - \frac{\pi\left(1^2\right)}{4}(2)(\rho g) \tag{b}$$

Using Eq. (a) to replace r^2 in terms of y, we get

$$W = \rho g\left(\pi \int_0^{10} \frac{y^4}{400} dy - \frac{\pi}{2}\right) = g\rho\pi\left(50 - \frac{1}{2}\right) \tag{c}$$

$$= 49.5\pi\rho g \text{ lb}$$

Example 4.12 (Continued)

To get $\bar{y}$, we equate the moment of W about the x axis with that of the weight distribution. For the latter, we sum the moments about the x axis of the weight of all slices, assuming first no inside cavity. Then, we subtract from this the moment about the x axis of the weight of a cylinder corresponding to the cavity in the body. Because ρ is constant, the center of gravity of this latter cylinder is at its geometric center so that the moment arm from the x axis for the weight of the cylinder is clearly 9 ft. Thus, we have

$$-(49.5\pi\rho g)\bar{y} = -\rho g\left\{\int_0^{10} y\left(\pi r^2\, dy\right) - \left[\frac{\pi\left(1^2\right)}{4}(2)\right]9\right\}$$

$$\bar{y} = \frac{1}{49.5}\left(\int_0^{10} \frac{y^5}{400}\, dy - 4.5\right) = \boxed{8.33 \text{ ft}}$$

Suppose as will be the case in Problem 4.43 that γ (= ρg), which is the *specific weight* (weight per unit volume), varies with y. That is, $\gamma = \gamma(y)$. Then for this problem, note that

$$W = \int_0^{10} \pi r^2 \gamma\, dy - \int_8^{10} \pi\left(\frac{1}{2}\right)^2 \gamma\, dy$$

also

$$-W\bar{y} = -\left[\int_0^{10} y\pi r^2 \gamma\, dy - \int_8^{10} y\pi\left(\frac{1}{2}\right)^2 \gamma\, dy\right]$$

Note here we cannot take the short cuts used in the original problem where γ was a constant.

Example 4.13

A plate is shown in Fig. 4.32 lying flat on the ground. The plate is 60 mm thick and has a uniform density. The curved edge is that of a parabola with zero slope at the origin. Find the coordinates of the center of gravity.

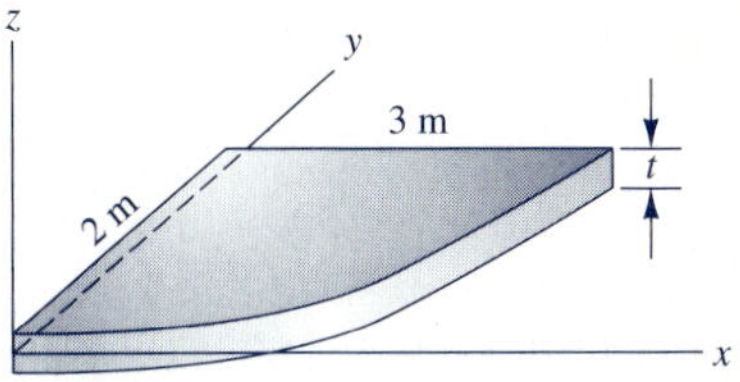

Figure 4.32. Find center of gravity of plate.

The equation of a parabola oriented like that of the curved edge of the plate is

$$y = Cx^2 \tag{a}$$

We can determine C by noting that $y = 2\ m$ when $x = 3\ m$. Hence,

$$2 = C \cdot 9 \tag{b}$$

Therefore,

$$C = \frac{2}{9}$$

The desired curve then is

$$y = \frac{2}{9}x^2$$

Therefore,

$$x = \frac{3}{\sqrt{2}}y^{1/2} \tag{c}$$

We shall consider horizontal strips of the plate of width dy (see Fig. 4.33). Using the specific weight, γ, which is weight per volume and is equal to ρg, we have for the total weight W of the plate:

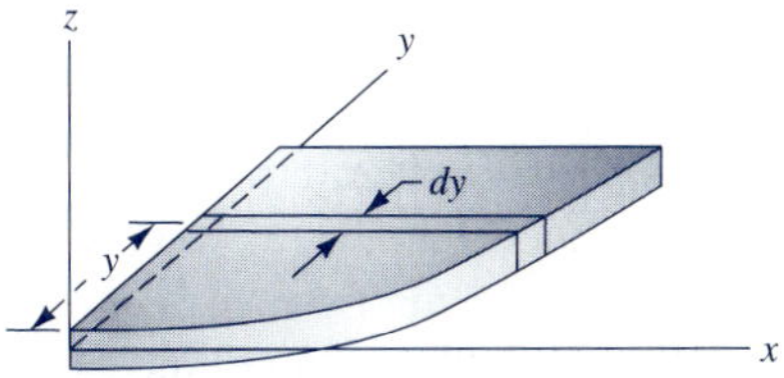

Figure 4.33. Use of horizontal strips.

$$W = \int_0^2 (t\,x\,dy)\gamma$$

where t is the thickness. We replace x using Eq. (c) to get

$$W = t\gamma\int_0^2 \left(\frac{3}{\sqrt{2}}y^{1/2}\right)dy$$

Integrating, we get

$$W = t\gamma\frac{3}{\sqrt{2}}\left(y^{3/2}\right)\left(\frac{2}{3}\right)\Bigg|_0^2 = t\gamma\sqrt{2}(2)^{3/2} = 4t\gamma\ \text{N} \tag{d}$$

We next take moments about the x axis in order to get $\bar{y}$. Thus,

$$\begin{aligned} -W\bar{y} &= -\int_0^2 y(t\,x\,dy)\gamma \\ &= -\gamma t\int_0^2 (y)\left(\frac{3}{\sqrt{2}}y^{1/2}\right)dy \\ &= -\gamma t\frac{3}{\sqrt{2}}\left(y^{5/2}\right)\left(\frac{2}{5}\right)\Bigg|_0^2 \qquad (e) \\ &= -\gamma t\left(\frac{3}{\sqrt{2}}\right)\left(\frac{2}{5}\right)[(2^2)(2^{1/2})] \\ &= -\frac{24}{5}\gamma t \end{aligned}$$

Example 4.13 (Continued)

Using $4t\gamma$ for W from Eq. (d), we get, for $\bar{y}$:

$$\bar{y} = \tfrac{6}{5} \text{ m} \tag{f}$$

To get $\bar{x}$, we take moments about the y axis, still utilizing the horizontal strips of Fig. 4.33. The center of gravity of a strip is at its center since γ is constant and so the moment arm for a strip about the y axis is $x/2$.

$$W\bar{x} = \int_0^2 \frac{x}{2}(t\,x\,dy)\gamma \tag{g}$$

Continuing with the calculations, we have

$$W\bar{x} = \frac{t\gamma}{2}\int_0^2 x^2\,dy = \frac{t\gamma}{2}\int_0^2\left(\frac{9}{2}y\right)dy$$

$$= \frac{t\gamma}{2}\frac{9}{2}\frac{y^2}{2}\bigg|_0^2 = \frac{9t\gamma}{2}$$

On replacing W according to Eq. (d), we get for $\bar{x}$:

$$\bar{x} = \tfrac{9}{8} \text{ m} \tag{h}$$

Next, we proceed to get $\bar{x}$ using vertical strips as shown in Fig. 4.34. Equating moments of the weights of these vertical strips about the y axis with that of the total weight W at its center of gravity $\bar{x}$, we get on noting that $(2 - y)$ is the length of the strip

$$W\bar{x} = \int_0^3 x\gamma(2-y)t\,dx = \int_0^3 x\gamma\left(2 - \frac{2}{9}x^2\right)t\,dx \tag{i}$$

$$= 2\gamma t\int_0^3\left(x - \frac{1}{9}x^3\right)dx = 2\gamma t\left(\frac{3^2}{2} - \frac{1}{9}\frac{3^4}{4}\right) = \gamma t\frac{9}{2}$$

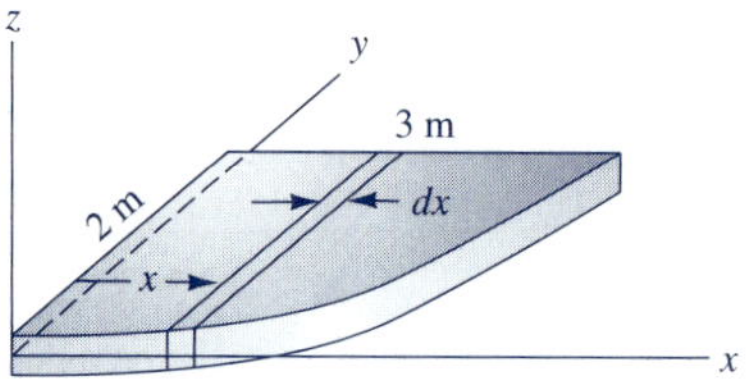

Figure 4.34. Use of vertical strips.

Using $W = 4\gamma t$, we can now solve for $\bar{x}$. Thus, we again get

$$\bar{x} = \tfrac{9}{8} \text{ m}$$

Finally, it is clear that the $\bar{z}$ coordinate is zero for reference xy at the center plane of the plate.

In the previous problems, we used slices of the body having a thicknesses dy or dx. If the specific weight were a function of position, $\gamma(x, y, z)$, we could not readily use such slices, since we cannot easily express the weight of such slices in a simple manner. The reason for this is that in the x and z directions the dimensions of the element are finite, and so γ would vary in these directions throughout the element. If, however, we choose an element that is infinitesimal in *all directions*, such as an infinitesimal rectangular parallelepiped having volume $dx\,dy\,dz$, then γ can be assumed to be constant throughout the element. The weight of the element is then easily seen to be $\gamma(dx\,dy\,dz)$, where the coordinates of γ correspond to the position of the element. We now illustrate a simple case.

Example 4.14

Consider a block (see Fig. 4.35) wherein the specific weight γ at corner A is 200 lbf/ft^3. The specific weight in the block does not change in the x direction. However, it decreases linearly by 50 lbf/ft^3 in 10 ft in the y direction, and increases linearly by 50 lbf/ft^3 in 8 ft in the z direction, as has been shown in the diagram. What are the coordinates $\bar{x}$, $\bar{y}$ of the center of gravity for this block?

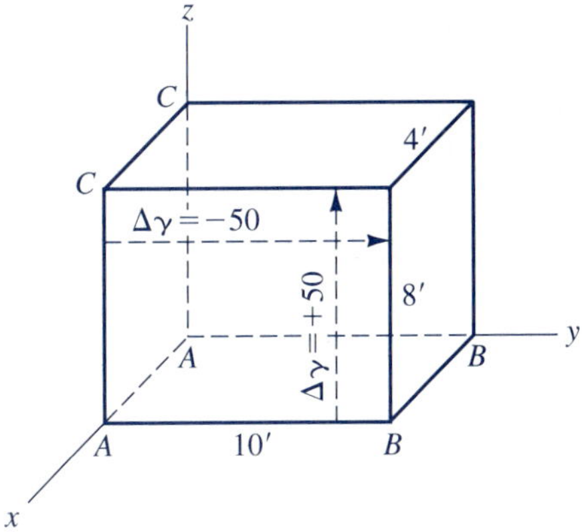

Figure 4.35. Block with varying γ.

We must first express γ at any position $P(x, y, z)$. Using simple proportions, we can say

$$\begin{aligned}\gamma &= 200 - \frac{y}{10}(50) + \frac{z}{8}(50) \qquad \text{(a)}\\ &= 200 - 5y + 6.25z \text{ lbf/ft}^3\end{aligned}$$

We shall first compute the weight of the block (i.e., the resultant force of gravity). We do not use an infinitesimal slice or rectangular rod of the block, as we have done heretofore. With the specific weight varying with both y and z, it would not be an easy matter to compute the weight and moment of a slice or a rod. Instead, we shall use an infinitesimal rectangular parallelepiped having volume $dx\, dy\, dz$, located at a position having coordinates x, y, and z as has been shown in Fig. 4.36(a). Because of the vanishingly small size of this element, the specific weight γ can be considered constant inside the element, and so the weight dW of the element can be given as[8]

$$dW = \gamma(dx\, dy\, dz) = (200 - 5y + 6.25z)\, dx\, dy\, dz$$

[8]We are deleting higher order quantities.

Example 4.14 (Continued)

To include the weight of *all* such elements in the block, we first let x "run" from 0 to 4 ft while holding y and z fixed. The rectangular parallelepiped of Fig. 4.36(a) then becomes a rectangular rod as shown in Fig. 4.36(b). Having run its course, x is no longer a variable in this summation process. Next, let y "run" from 0 to 10 while holding z constant. The rectangular rod of Fig. 4.36(b) then becomes an infinitesimal slice, as shown in Fig. 4.36(c). The variable y has thus run its course and is no longer a variable. This leaves only the variable z, and now we let z "run" from 0 to 8. Clearly, we cover the entire block by this process.

We can do this mathematically by a process called *multiple integration.* We perform three integrations, paralleling the three steps outlined in the previous paragraph. Thus, we can formulate W as follows:

$$-W\mathbf{k} = \int_0^8\int_0^{10}\int_0^4 (200 - 5y + 6.25z)\,dx\,dy\,dz\,(-\mathbf{k})$$

We first consider integration with respect to x holding y and z constant. That is

$$\int_0^4 (200 - 5y + 6.25z)\,dx$$

As in the first step set forth in the previous paragraph, to go from a rectangular parallelepiped to a rectangular rod, we integrate with respect to x from $x = 0$ to $x = 4$ while holding y and z constant. Thus,

$$\int_0^4 (200 - 5y + 6.25z)\,dx = (200x - 5yx + 6.25z\,x)\Big|_0^4$$
$$= 800 - 20y + 25z$$

With x no longer a variable (since it has run its course), the equation for W becomes

$$W = \int_0^8\int_0^{10} (800 - 20y + 25z)\,dy\,dz$$

Now, we hold z constant and integrate with respect to y from 0 to 10. (This takes us from a rectangular rod to a slice.) Thus,

$$\int_0^{10} (800 - 20y + 25z)\,dy = \left(800y - 20\frac{y^2}{2} + 25zy\right)\Bigg|_0^{10}$$
$$= 8{,}000 - 1{,}000 + 250z$$

Now y has run its course, and we have

$$W = \int_0^8 (7{,}000 + 250z)\,dz$$

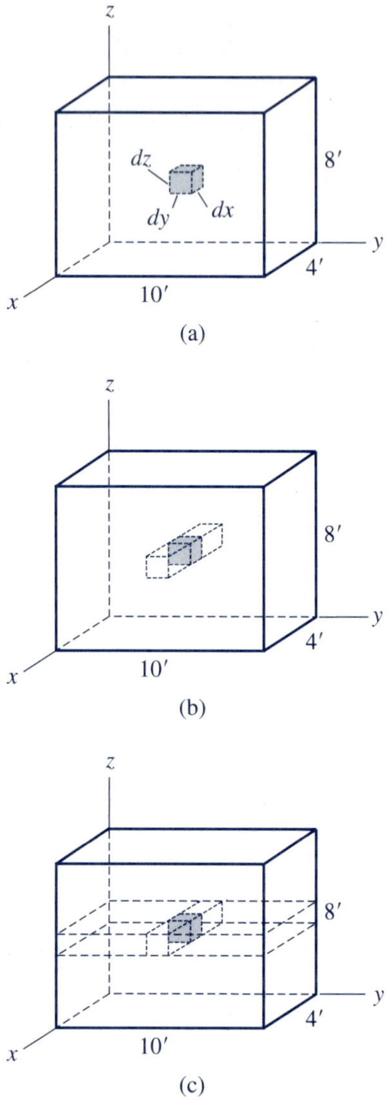

Figure 4.36. (a) Infinitesimal element at $P(x, y, z)$; (b) x runs from 0 to 4, while z and y are fixed, to form rectangular rod; (c) y runs from 0 to 10, while holding z fixed, to form slice.

Example 4.14 (Continued)

By integrating with respect to z, we sum up all the slices, and we have covered the entire block. Thus,

$$W = \left(7{,}000z + 250\frac{z^2}{2}\right)\Bigg|_0^8 = 64{,}000 \text{ lb}$$

To get $\bar{y}$, we equate the moment about the x axis of the resultant force without a couple moment with the moment of the distribution. Thus, using multiple integration as described above:

$$-(64{,}000)\bar{y} = -\int_0^8\int_0^{10}\int_0^4 y(200 - 5y + 6.25z)\,dx\,dy\,dz$$

Therefore, integrating with respect to x, then y, and then z as before, we have

$$\begin{aligned}
64{,}000\bar{y} &= \int_0^8\int_0^{10} (200yx - 5y^2x + 6.25yzx)\Big|_0^4\,dy\,dz \\
&= \int_0^8\int_0^{10} (800y - 20y^2 + 25yz)\,dy\,dz \\
&= \int_0^8\left(800\frac{y^2}{2} - \frac{20y^3}{3}x + \frac{25y^2}{2}z\right)\Bigg|_0^{10} dz \\
&= \int_0^8 (40{,}000 - 6{,}667 + 1{,}250z)\,dz \\
&= \left(33{,}333z + 1{,}250\frac{z^2}{2}\right)\Bigg|_0^8 = 307{,}000
\end{aligned}$$

and

$$\bar{y} = 4.79 \text{ ft}$$

Because γ does not depend on x, we can directly conclude by inspection that $\bar{x} = 2$ ft.

Next, in the case of a body made up of simple shapes (subbodies) such as cones, spheres, cylinders, and cubes, we can find the center of gravity of the body by using the centers of gravity of the known subbody shapes. Thus, we can say on taking moments about the y axis that

$$W_{\text{total}}(\bar{x}) = \sum_i W_i(\bar{x})_i \qquad (4.12)$$

where W_i is the weight of the ith subbody and where $(\bar{x})_i$ is the x coordinate to the center of gravity of the ith subbody. Bodies made up of simple subbodies are called *composite bodies*.

Example 4.15

Find the weight and center of gravity of a large steam turbine for power generation (Fig. 4.37) needed for earthquake safety calculations. The specific weights of each turbine component are shown. Cylinder 2 has a radius of 5 m and is 14 m long. Half of this cylinder is embedded in the block 1.

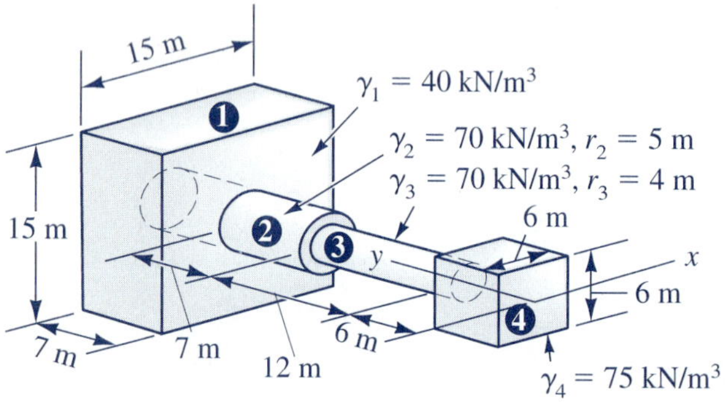

Figure 4.37. A composite body.

The weights of each component of this model are first calculated.

$$W_1 = \gamma_1 V_1 = [40][(7)(15)(15) - (7)(\pi)(5^2)] = 41 \text{ MN}$$

$$W_2 = \gamma_2 V_2 = [70][(14)(\pi)(5^2)] = 77 \text{ MN}$$

$$W_3 = \gamma_3 V_3 = [70][(12)(\pi)(4^2)] = 42.2 \text{ MN}$$

$$W_4 = \gamma_4 V_4 = [75][(6)(6)(6)] = 16.2 \text{ MN}$$

$$W_{TOTAL} = \Sigma W_i = 41 + 77 + 42.2 + 16.2 = \boxed{176.4 \text{ MN}}$$

The center of gravity lies along the axis of the shaft. Taking moments about the x axis we have

$$176.4\bar{y} = (41)(28.5) + (77)(25) + (42.2)(12) + (16.2)(3) = 3{,}648.5 \text{ MN}$$

$$\boxed{\bar{y} = 20.68 \text{ m}}$$

Case B. Parallel Force Distribution over a Plane Surface—Center of Pressure. Let us now consider a normal pressure distribution over a *plane* surface A in the xy plane in Fig. 4.38. The vertical ordinate is taken as a pressure ordinate, so that over the area A we have a pressure distribution $p(x, y)$ represented by the pressure surface. Since in this case there is a parallel force system with one sense of direction, we know that the simplest resultant is a single force, which is given as

$$\boldsymbol{F}_R = -\int p\, d\boldsymbol{A} = -\left(\int p\, dA\right)\boldsymbol{k} \tag{4.13}$$

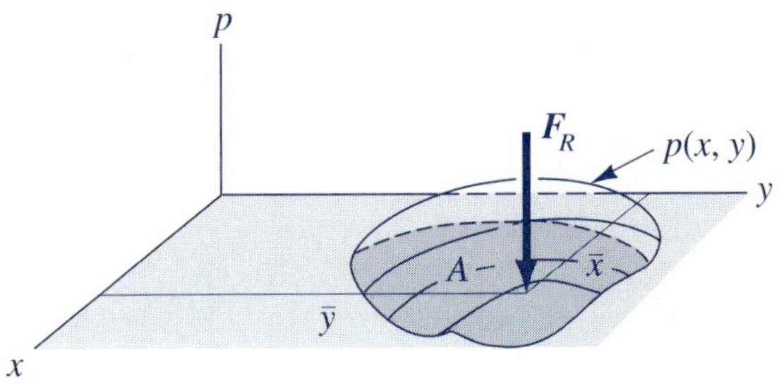

Figure 4.38. Pressure distribution.

The position $\bar{x}$, $\bar{y}$ can be computed by equating the moments about the y and x axes of the resultant force without a couple moment with the corresponding moments of the distribution. Solving for $\bar{x}$ and $\bar{y}$,

$$\bar{x} = \frac{\int px\, dA}{\int p\, dA}$$

$$\bar{y} = \frac{\int py\, dA}{\int p\, dA}$$

Since we know that p is a function of x and y over the surface, we can carry out the preceding integrations either analytically or numerically. The point thus determined is called the *center of pressure.*

(In later chapters, we shall consider distributed frictional forces over plane and curved surfaces. In these cases, the simplest resultant is not necessarily a single force as it was in the special case above.)

Example 4.16

A plate *ABCD* on which both distributed and point force systems act is shown in Fig. 4.39. The pressure distribution is given as

$$p = -4y^2 + 100 \text{ psf} \qquad \text{(a)}$$

Find the simplest resultant for the system.

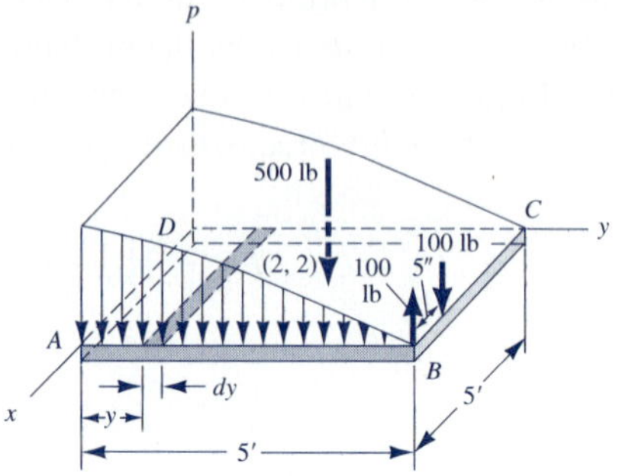

Figure 4.39. Find simplest resultant.

To get the resultant force, we consider a strip *dy* along the plate as shown in Fig. 4.39. The reason for using such a strip is that the pressure *p* is uniform along this strip, as can be seen from the diagram. Hence, the force from the pressure on the strip is simply $p\,dA = p(dy)(5)$. Thus, we can say that

$$F_R = -\int_0^5 p(5)(dy) - 500$$

$$= -\int_0^5 (-4y^2 + 100)(5)\,dy - 500 \qquad \text{(b)}$$

$$F_R = \left(20\frac{y^3}{3} - 500y\right)\Big|_0^5 - 500 = -2{,}167 \text{ lb}$$

To get the position $\bar{x}$, $\bar{y}$ of the resultant force F_R without a couple moment, we equate moments of F_R about the *x* and *y* axes with that of the original system. Thus, starting with the *x* axis, we have using strip *dy* as before:

$$-2{,}167\bar{y} = -\int_0^5 yp(5dy) - (500)(2)$$

$$= -\int_0^5 5y(-4y^2 + 100)\,dy - 1{,}000$$

$$= \left(20\frac{y^4}{4} - 500\frac{y^2}{2}\right)\Big|_0^5 - 1{,}000 = -4{,}125$$

Therefore,

$$\bar{y} = 1.904 \text{ ft}$$

Now, considering the *y* axis, we still use the strips *dy* because *p* is uniform along such strips. However, the force $df = p\,dA = p(5)(dy)$ may be considered acting at the center of the strip, and accordingly has a moment arm about the *y* axis equal to 5/2 for each strip. Hence, we can say that

$$2{,}167\bar{x} = \int_0^5 \frac{5}{2}p(5dy) + (500)(2) - \frac{500}{12}$$

$$= \frac{25}{2}\int_0^5 (-4y^2 + 100)\,dy + 1{,}000 - 41.7 = 5{,}125$$

Therefore,

$$x = 2.36 \text{ ft}$$

In a stationary liquid, the pressure at the surface of the liquid is transmitted uniformly throughout the liquid. In addition, there is superposed a linearly increasing pressure with depth resulting from gravity acting on the liquid. Thus, if we have p_{atm} at the surface (often called the free surface), the pressure in the liquid is

$$p = p_{atm} + \gamma y$$

where γ is the specific weight of the liquid and *y* is the depth below the surface. Thus, for a given liquid the pressure is uniform at any constant distance below the free surface. With this in mind, examine the following example.

Example 4.17

In Fig. 4.40 find the force on the door AB from water whose specific weight is 9,806 N/m^3 and on whose free surface there is atmospheric pressure equal to 101,325 N/m^2 ($\equiv$ 101,325 Pa).[9] Also find the center of pressure.

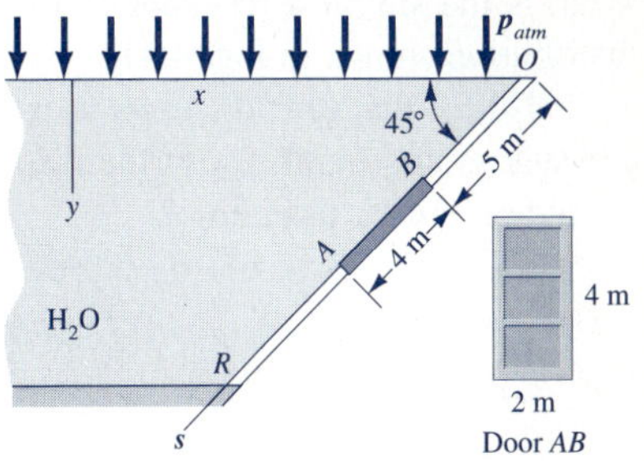

Figure 4.40. Door AB is exposed on one side to water and on the other side to air.

The pressure on the door AB is then

$$p = p_{atm} + (\gamma)(y) = p_{atm} + (\gamma)(s)(\sin 45°)$$

where s is the distance from O along the inclined wall OR. The resultant force is then

$$F = \int_5^9 \left[p_{atm} + (\gamma)(s)(\sin 45°)\right](2)(ds)$$

$$= \int_5^9 [101{,}325 + (9{,}806)(.707)s](2)ds$$

$$= (2)\left[101{,}325s + (9{,}806)(.707)\frac{s^2}{2}\right]_5^9$$

$$\therefore \quad F = 1.199 \times 10^6 \text{ N}$$

To get the center of pressure equate moments about O with that of the resultant. Thus using the notation $\bar{s}$ to locate the center of pressure we have

$$1.199 \times 10^6\, \bar{s} = \int_5^9 s\left[p_{atm} + (\gamma)(s)(\sin 45°)\right](2)\, ds$$

$$= \left[101{,}325\frac{s^2}{2} + (9{,}806)(.707)\frac{s^3}{3}\right]_5^9 (2)$$

$$\therefore \quad \bar{s} = 7.061 \text{ m}$$

Clearly the *total* force on the door from inside and outside would include the contribution of the atmospheric pressure on the outside. We can easily determine this force by deleting p_{atm} in the preceding calculations.[10]

[9]The unit of pressure in the SI system is the *pascal*, where 1 pascal = 1 Pa = 1 N/m^2.

[10]We have touched here on the subject of *hydrostatics*. For a treatment of this subject that may be similar to what you will study in your upcoming course in fluid mechanics, see Shames, I.H., *Mechanics of Fluids*, 3rd Edition, 1992, McGraw-Hill, Inc., Chapter 3

We finish this series of examples with a multiple integration problem.

*Example 4.18

What is the simplest resultant and the center of pressure for the pressure distribution shown in Fig. 4.41?

Notice that the pressure varies linearly in the x and y directions. The pressure at any point x, y in the distribution can be given as follows with the aid of similar triangles:

$$p = \left(\frac{y}{10}\right)(20) + \left(\frac{x}{5}\right)(30) \qquad \text{(a)}$$
$$= 2y + 6x \text{ Pa}$$

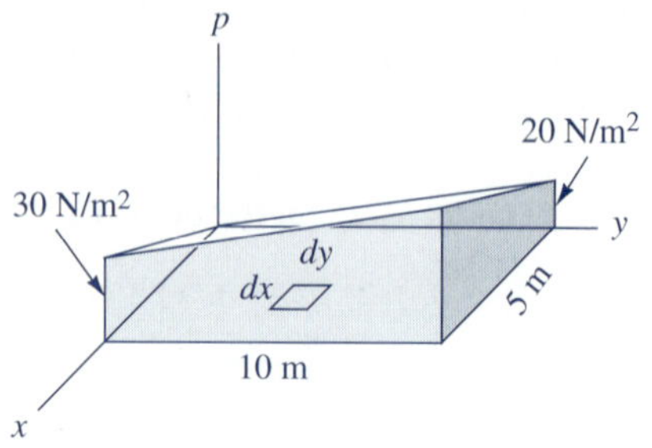

Figure 4.41. Nonuniform pressure distribution.

We cannot employ a convenient strip here along which the pressure is uniform, as in Example 4.16. For this reason we consider rectangular area element $dx\,dy$ to work with (see Fig. 4.41). For such a small area, we can assume the pressure as constant so that $p\,dx\,dy$ is the force on the element. To find the resultant force, we must integrate over the 10×5 rectangle. This integration involves two variables and is again a case of *multiple integration*. Thus, we can say that

$$F_R = -\int_0^{10}\int_0^5 p\,dx\,dy$$

wherein we first integrate with respect to x while holding y constant and then integrate with respect to y (in this way we cover the entire 10×5 rectangular area). Thus, we have

$$F_R = -\int_0^{10}\int_0^5 (2y + 6x)\,dx\,dy$$
$$= -\int_0^{10}\left(2yx + \frac{6x^2}{2}\right)\Bigg|_0^5 dy$$
$$= -\int_0^{10}(10y + 75)\,dy$$
$$= -\left[\frac{10y^2}{2} + 75y\right]_0^{10} = -1{,}250 \text{ N}$$

$$F_R = \quad 1{,}250 \text{ N}$$

To find $\bar{y}$ for F_R without a couple moment, we equate moments of F_R about the x axis with that of the distribution. Thus,

$$-\bar{y}(1{,}250) = -\int_0^{10}\int_0^5 py\,dx\,dy$$

Example 4.18 (Continued)

Therefore,

$$\bar{y} = \frac{1}{1{,}250}\int_0^{10}\int_0^5 (2y + 6x)y\,dx\,dy$$

$$= \frac{1}{1{,}250}\int_0^{10}\left(2y^2x + \frac{6x^2}{2}y\right)\Bigg|_0^5 dy$$

$$= \frac{1}{1{,}250}\int_0^{10}(10y^2 + 75y)\,dy$$

$$= \frac{1}{1{,}250}\left(\frac{10y^3}{3} + 75\frac{y^2}{2}\right)\Bigg|_0^{10}$$

$$\bar{y} = 5.67 \text{ m}$$

As for $\bar{x}$, we proceed as follows:

$$\bar{x}(1{,}250) = \int_5^{10}\int_0^5 px\,dx\,dy$$

Therefore,

$$\bar{x} = \frac{1}{1{,}250}\int_0^{10}\int_0^5 (2y + 6x)x\,dx\,dy$$

$$= \frac{1}{1{,}250}\int_0^{10}\left(2y\frac{x^2}{2} + \frac{6x^3}{3}\right)\Bigg|_0^5 dy$$

$$= \frac{1}{1{,}250}\int_0^{10}(25y + 250)\,dy$$

$$= \frac{1}{1{,}250}\left(25\frac{y^2}{2} + 250y\right)\Bigg|_0^{10}$$

$$\bar{x} = 3.00 \text{ m}$$

The center of pressure is thus at (3.00, 5.67) m.

Case C. Coplanar Parallel Force Distribution. As we pointed out earlier, this type of loading may be considered for beams loaded symmetrically over the longitudinal midplane of the beam. The loading is represented by an intensity function $w(x)$ as shown in Fig. 4.26. This coplanar parallel force distribution can be replaced by a single force given as

$$\boldsymbol{F}_R = -\int w(x)\,dx\boldsymbol{j}$$

We find the position of $\boldsymbol{F}_R$ without a couple moment by equating moments of $\boldsymbol{F}_R$ and the distribution w about a convenient point of the beam, usually one of the ends. Solving for $\bar{x}$, we get

$$\bar{x} = \frac{\int xw(x)\,dx}{\int w(x)\,dx}$$

Example 4.19

A simply supported beam is shown in Fig. 4.42 supporting a 1,000-lb point force, a 500 lb-ft couple, and a coplanar, parabolic, distributed load w lb/ft. Find the simplest resultant of this force system.

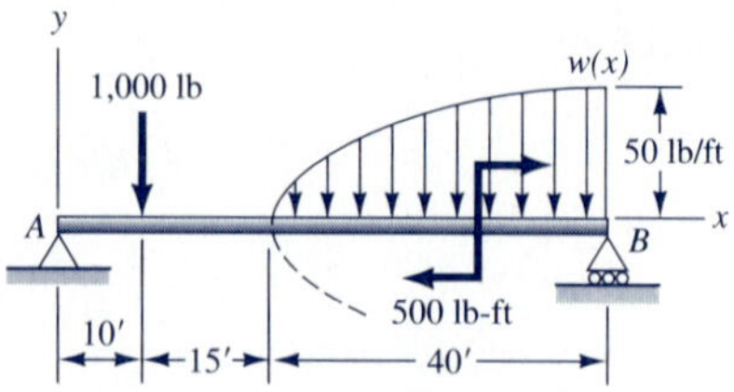

Figure 4.42. Find simplest resultant.

To express the intensity of loading for the coordinate system shown in the diagram, we begin with the general formulation

$$w^2 = ax + b \tag{a}$$

Note from the diagram that when $x = 25$ we have $w = 0$, and when $x = 65$, we have $w = 50$. Subjecting Eq. (a) to these conditions, we can determine a and b. Thus,

$$0 = a(25) + b \tag{b}$$

$$2{,}500 = a(65) + b \tag{c}$$

Subtracting, we can get a as follows:

$$-2{,}500 = -40a$$

Therefore,

$$a = 62.5$$

From Eq. (b), we get

$$b = -(25)(62.5) = -1{,}562.5$$

Thus, we have

$$w^2 = 62.5x - 1{,}562.5 \tag{d}$$

Summing forces, we get for F_R,

$$F_R = -1{,}000 - \int_{25}^{65} \sqrt{62.5x - 1{,}562.5}\, dx \tag{e}$$

To integrate this, we may change variables as follows:

$$\mu = 62.5x - 1{,}562.5 \tag{f}$$

Therefore,

$$d\mu = 62.5\, dx$$

Substituting into the integral in Eq. (e), we have[11]

$$F_R = -1{,}000 - \int_0^{2{,}500} \mu^{1/2} \frac{d\mu}{62.5}$$
$$= -1{,}000 - \frac{1}{62.5}\mu^{3/2}\left(\frac{2}{3}\right)\bigg|_0^{2{,}500}$$

[11]Do not forget to change the limits for μ. Thus, from Eq. (f), the upper limit is $(62.5)(65) - 1{,}562.5 = 2{,}500$, whereas the lower limit is $(62.5)(25) - 1{,}562.5 = 0$.

Example 4.19 (Continued)

$$= -1{,}000 - \frac{1}{62.5}(2{,}500)^{3/2}\left(\frac{2}{3}\right)$$

$$F_R = -2{,}333 \text{ lb}$$

We now compute $\bar{x}$ for the resultant without a couple as follows:

$$-2{,}333\bar{x} = -(10)(1{,}000) - \int_{25}^{65} x\sqrt{62.5x - 1{,}562.5}\,dx - 500 \qquad \text{(g)}$$

We can evaluate the integral most readily by consulting the mathematical formulas in Appendix I. We find the following formula (No 6):

$$\int x\sqrt{a + bx}\,dx = -\frac{2(2a - 3bx)\sqrt{(bx + a)^3}}{15b^2}$$

In our case $b = 62.5$ and $a = -1{,}562.5$, so the indefinite integral for our case is

$$\int x\sqrt{62.5x - 1{,}562.5}\,dx = -\frac{(2)(-3{,}125 - 187.5x)\sqrt{(62.5x - 1{,}562.5)^3}}{(15)(3{,}906)}$$

Putting in limits, we have

$$\int_{25}^{65} x\sqrt{62.5x - 1{,}562.5}\,dx = -\left.\frac{(2)(-3{,}125 - 187.5x)\sqrt{(62.5x - 1{,}562.5)^3}}{(15)(3{,}906)}\right|_{25}^{65}$$

$$= 65{,}333 - 0 = 65{,}333$$

Going back to Eq. (g), we can now solve easily for $\bar{x}$. Thus,

$$\bar{x} = -\frac{1}{2{,}330}\left[-(10)(1{,}000) - 65{,}300 - 500\right]$$

$$\bar{x} = 32.5 \text{ ft}$$

Before closing, it will be pointed out that, for a loading function $w(x)$, the resultant $\int_0^x w\,dx$, equals the *area* under the loading curve. This fact is particularly useful for the case of a triangular loading function such as is shown in Fig. 4.43. Hence, we can say on inspection that the resultant force has the value

$$F_R = \tfrac{1}{2}(5)(1{,}000) = 2{,}500 \text{ N}$$

Furthermore, you can readily show that the *simplest* resultant has a line of action that is (2/3) × (length of loading) from the toe of the loading.[12] Thus, F_R without a couple moment is at a position (2/3)(5) to the right of a (see Fig. 4.43). You are urged to use this information when needed.

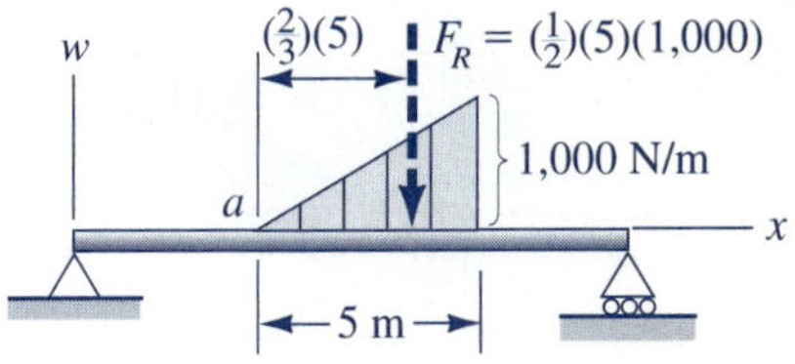

Figure 4.43. Triangular loading resultant.

[12]In Chapter 8, you will learn that the simplest resultant force for a distribution $w(x)$ goes through the *centroid* of the area under $w(x)$. The centroid will be carefully defined at that time.

PROBLEMS

4.41. A force field is given as

$$\boldsymbol{F}(x, y, z, t) = (10x + 5)\boldsymbol{i} + (16x^2 + 2z)\boldsymbol{j} + 15\boldsymbol{k} \text{ N}$$

What is the force at position (3, 6, 7) m? What is the difference between the force at this position and that at the origin?

4.42. A magnetic field is developed such that the body force on the rectangular parallelepiped of metal is given as

$$f = (.01x + \tfrac{1}{8})\boldsymbol{k} \text{ oz/lbm}$$

If the mass density of the metal is 450 lbm/ft³, what is the *simplest* resultant body force from such a field? Note that at the earth's surface the number of pounds mass equals the number of pounds force of weight.

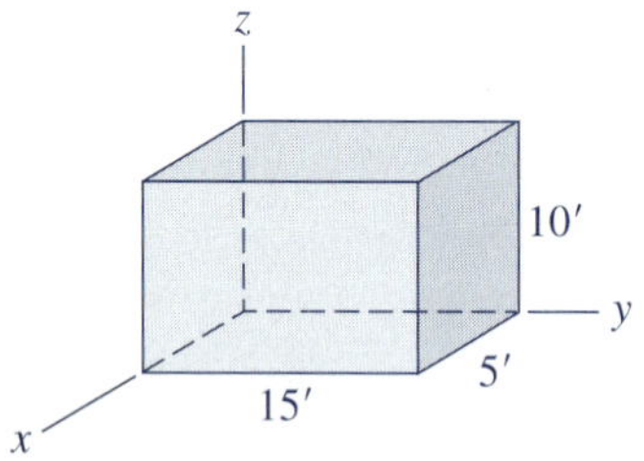

Figure P.4.42.

4.43. A body of revolution has a variable specific weight such that $\gamma = (36 + .01x^2)$ kN/m³ with x in meters. A hole of diameter 3 m and length 6 m is cut from the body as shown. Where is the center of gravity?

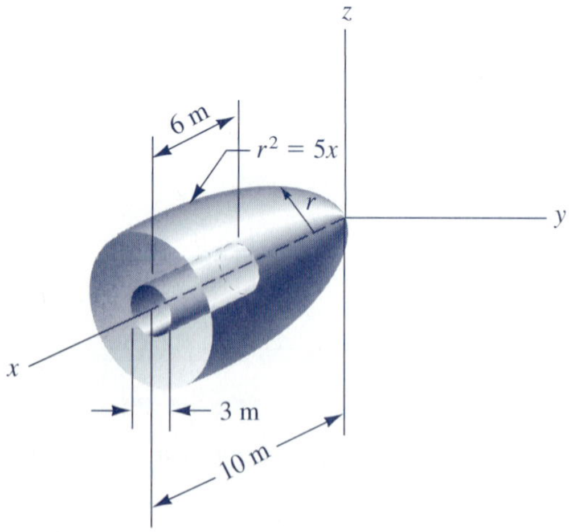

Figure P.4.43.

4.44. The specific weight γ of the material in the solid cylinder varies linearly as one goes from face A to face B. If

$$\gamma_A = 400 \text{ lbf/ft}^3, \qquad \gamma_B = 500 \text{ lbf/ft}^3$$

what is the position of the center of gravity of the cylinder?

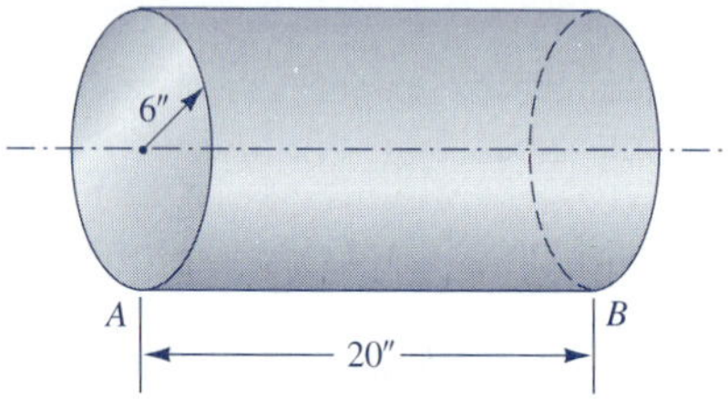

Figure P.4.44.

4.45. The specific weight of the material in a right circular cone is constant. Where is the center of gravity of the cone? *Hint:* Rotate cone 90° so that gravity is perpendicular to the z axis. Use concept of similar triangles to show that $r/R = (h - z)/h$ and solve for r needed for the integration.

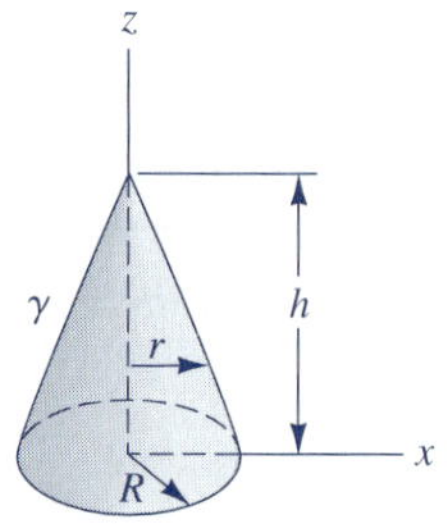

Figure P.4.45.

4.46. Show that the center of gravity of the right triangular plate of thickness t is at $x = a/3$ and $y = b/3$.

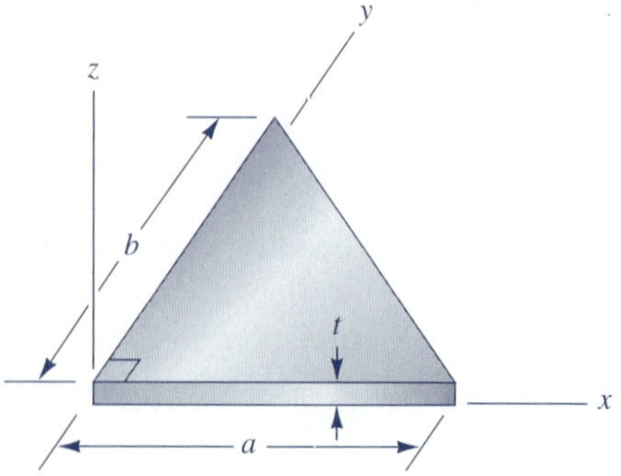

Figure P.4.46.

4.47. Show that the volume and center of gravity of the conical frustum are, respectively,

$$V = \frac{\pi h}{3}\left(r_2^2 + r_1 r_2 + r_1^2\right)$$

and

$$\bar{z} = \frac{h}{4}\,\frac{3r_2^2 + r_1^2 + 2r_1 r_2}{r_2^2 + r_1^2 + r_1 r_2}$$

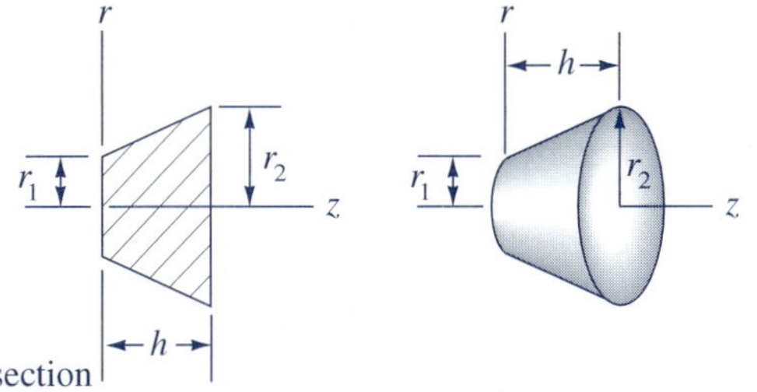

Figure P.4.47.

4.48. Find the center of gravity of the plate bounded by a straight line and a parabola.

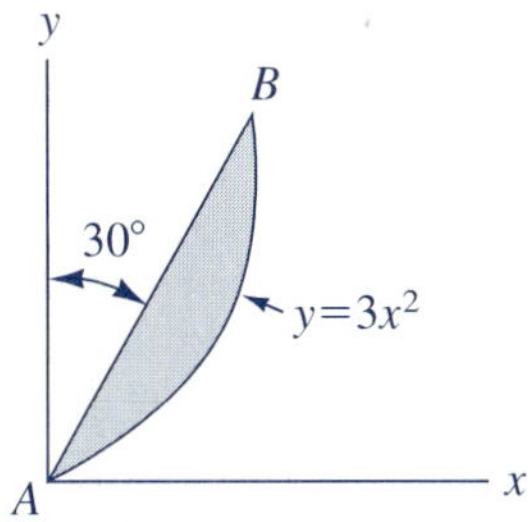

Figure P.4.48.

4.49. A massive radio-wave antenna for detection of signals from outer space is a body of revolution with a parabolic face (see the diagram). These antennas may be carved from rock in a valley away from other disturbing signals. What would the antenna weigh if made from concrete (23.6 kN/m³) for location in a remote desert area?

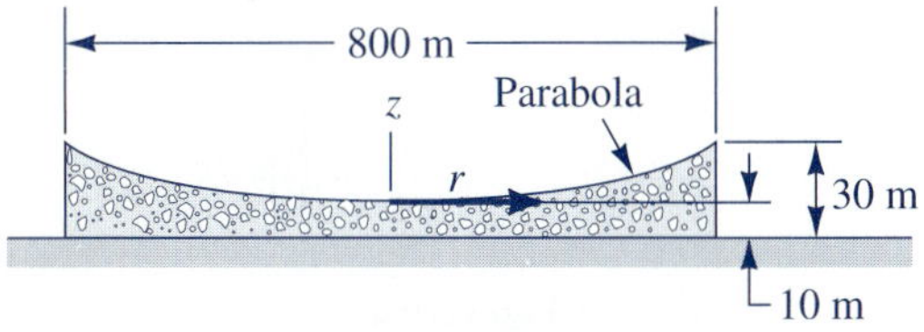

Figure P.4.49.

4.50. In Problem 4.49 find the distance from the ground to the center of gravity if the total weight is 2.37×10^8 kN.

***4.51.** A plate of thickness 30 mm has a specific weight γ that varies linearly in the x direction from 26 kN/m³ at A to 36 kN/m³ at B, and varies in the y direction as the square of y from 26 kN/m³ at A to 40 kN/m³ at C. Where is the center of gravity of the plate?

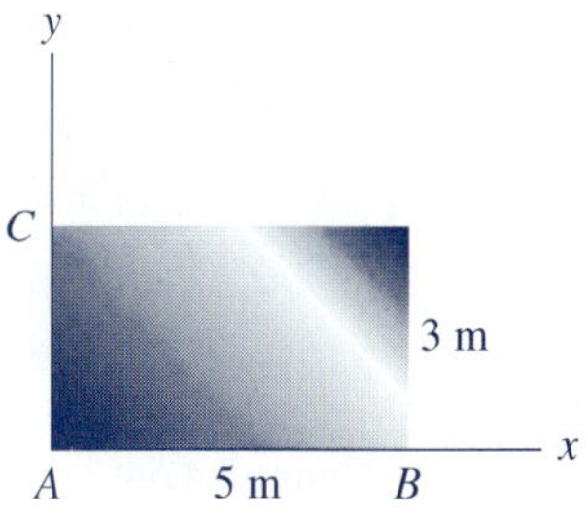

Figure P.4.51.

4.52. You are looking down on a plate with a hole in it as shown. The thickness has a constant value equal to t and the specific weight γ is constant. Find the coordinates $\bar{x}$, $\bar{y}$ of the *center of gravity*.

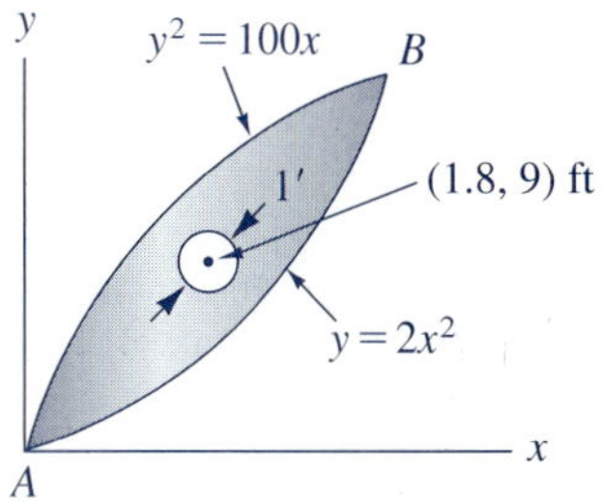

Figure P.4.52.

4.53. Find the center of gravity of the plate having uniform thickness and uniform specific weight. You are looking down onto the top of the plate.

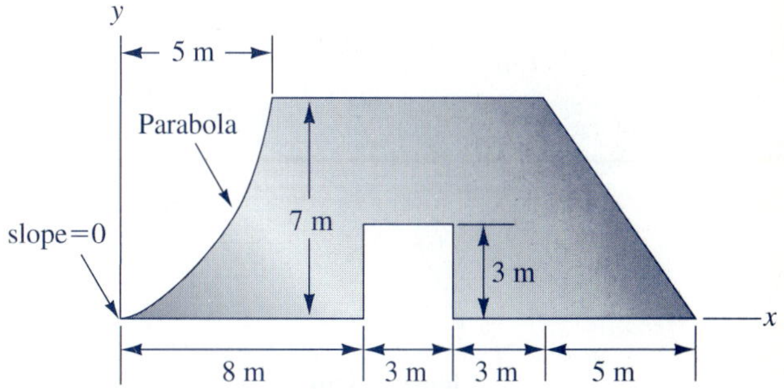

Figure P.4.53.

4.54. The top view of a plate is shown. Find center of gravity coordinates $\bar{x}$, $\bar{y}$.

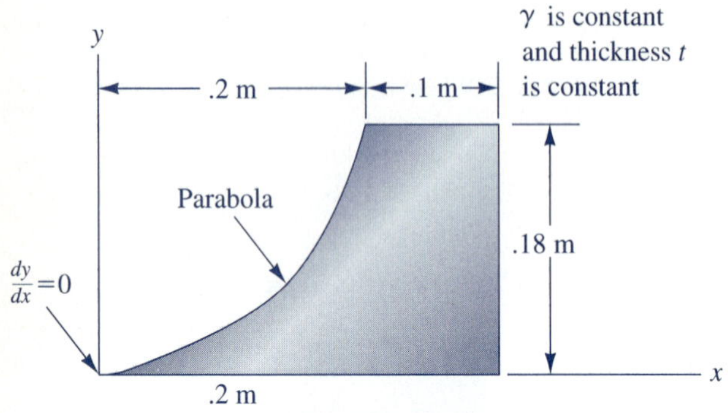

Figure P.4.54.

4.55. The thin circular rod has a weight of w N/m. What is the y coordinate of its center of gravity? The rod forms one-half of a circle.

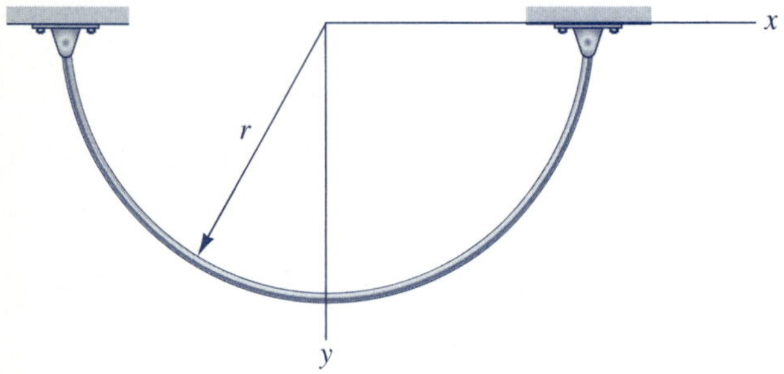

Figure P.4.55.

4.56. Find $\bar{y}$ for the center of gravity of the horizontal plate with a hole in it.

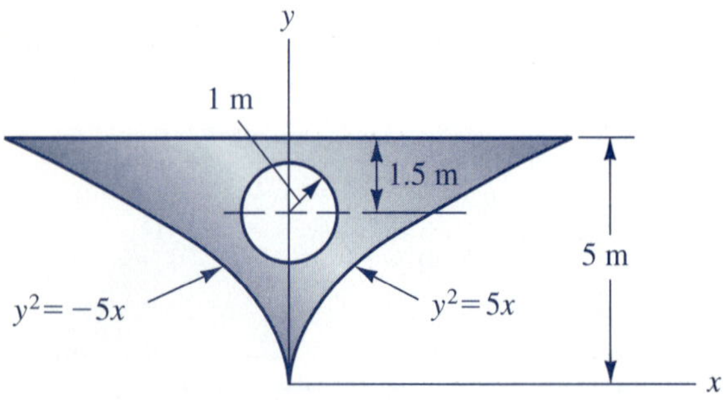

Figure P.4.56.

***4.57.** Suppose in Problem 4.42 that

$$\boldsymbol{f} = (.01x + .2y + .3z)\boldsymbol{k} \text{ oz/lbm}$$

Find the *simplest* resultant for $\boldsymbol{\rho} = 450$ lbm/ft^3. Find the proper line of action.

4.58. After a fast stop and swerve to the left, the load of sand (specific weight = 15 kN/m^3) in a dump truck is in the position shown. What is the simplest resultant force on the truck from the sand and where does it act? If the truck was full (with a level top) before the stop, how much sand spilled? Use the results of Problem 4.46.

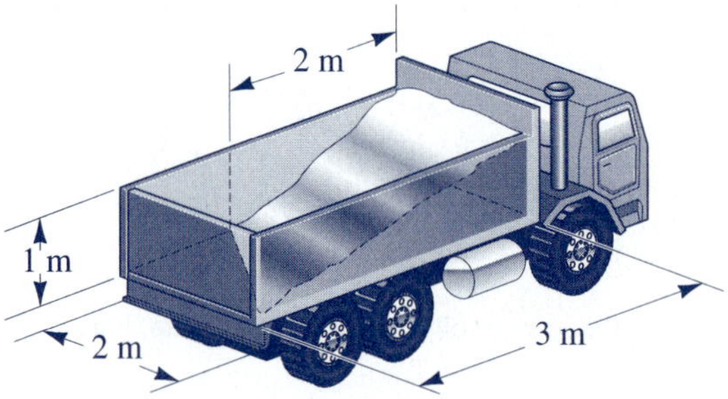

Figure P.4.58.

In Problems 4.59 through 4.62 use the known positions of centers of gravity of simple shapes.

4.59. An I-beam cantilevered out from a wall weighs 30 lb/ft and supports a 300-lb hoist. Steel (487 lb/ft^3) cover plates 1 in. thick are welded on the beam near the wall to increase the carrying capacity of the beam. What is the moment at the wall due to the weight of the reinforced beam and the hoisted load of 4,000 lb at the outermost position of the hoist? What is the *simplest* resultant force and its location?

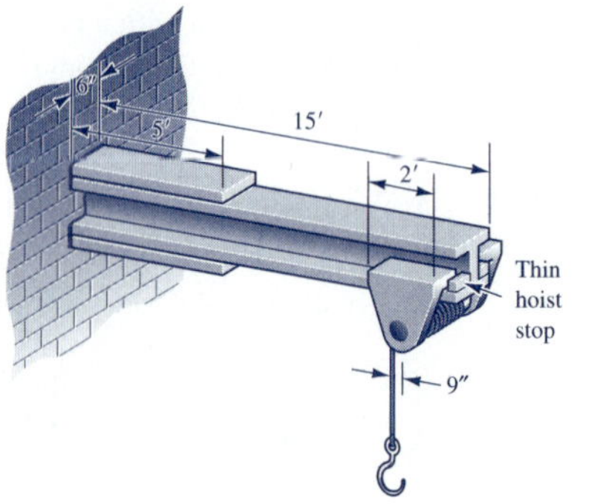

Figure P.4.59.

4.60. The bulk materials trailer weighs 10,000 lb and is filled with cement (γ = 94 lb/ft^3) in the front compartment (sections 1 and 2), and half-filled with water (γ = 62.5 lb/ft^3) in the rear compartment (sections 3 and 4). What is the *simplest* resultant force, and where does it act? What is the resultant when the water is drained? Use the center of gravity and volume results from Problem 4.47 (conical frustum).

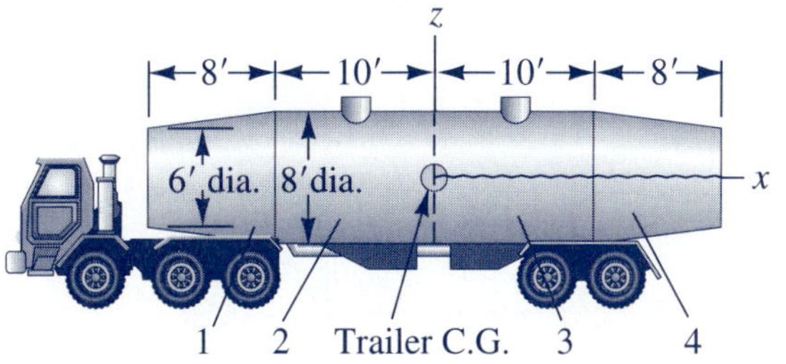

Figure P.4.60.

4.61. Find the coordinates $(x, y)_{CG}$ of the center of gravity of the loaded conveyor system. The centers of gravity of the crates C and D are at their geometric centers. W_E is the weight of the frame whose C.G. is at its geometric center.

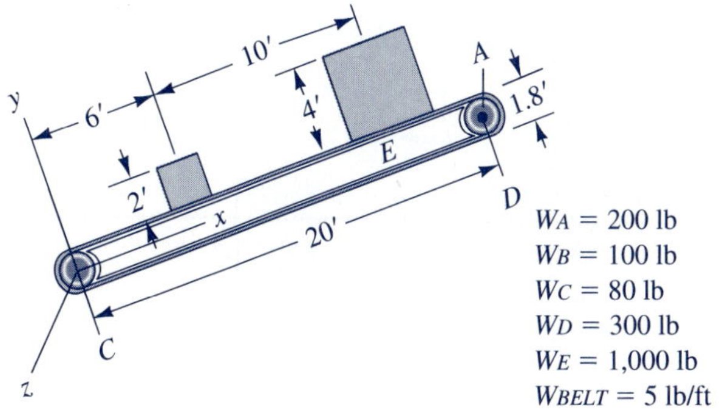

Figure P.4.61.

4.62. Find the center of gravity of the body shown. It has a constant specific weight throughout. Cone and cylinder are on block surfaces.

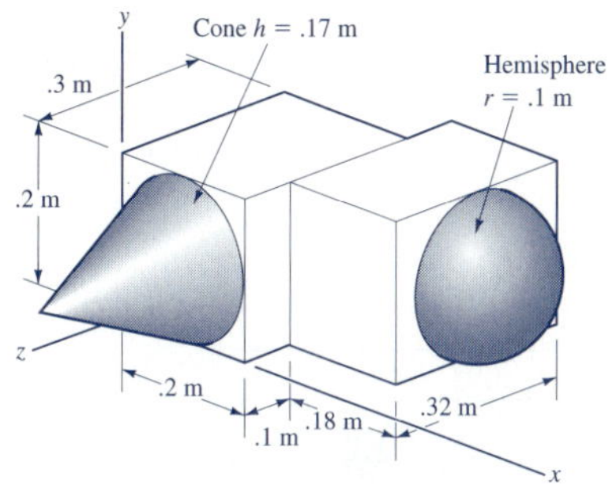

Figure P.4.62.

4.63. Find the *simplest* resultant of a normal pressure distribution over the rectangular area with sides a and b. Give the coordinates of the center of pressure.

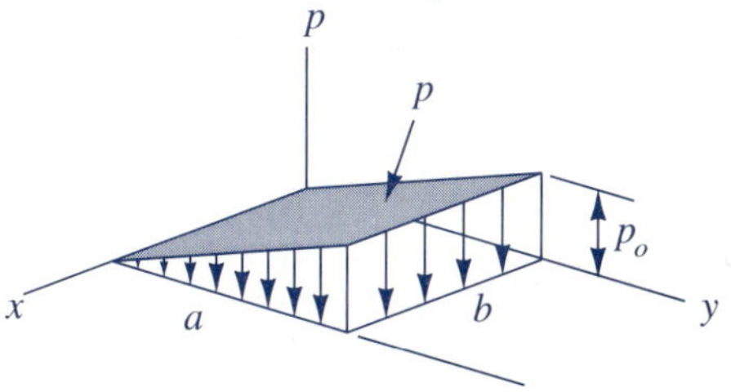

Figure P.4.63.

4.64. Find the *simplest* resultant acting on the vertical wall $ABCD$. Give the coordinates of the center of pressure. The pressure varies such that p = E/(y + 1) + F psi, with y in feet, from 10 psi to 50 psi, as indicated in the diagram. E and F are constants.

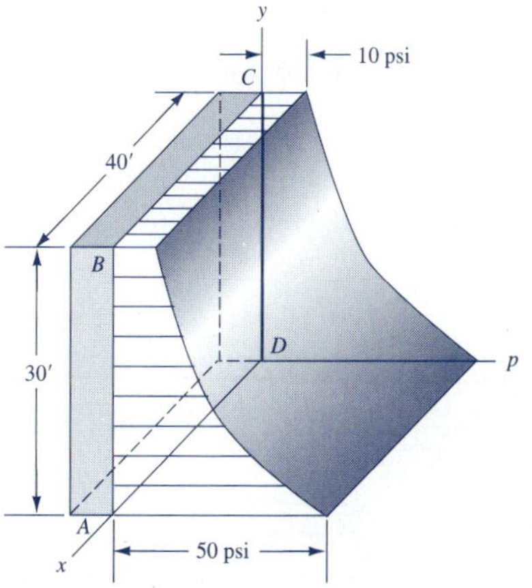

Figure P.4.64.

4.65. One floor of a warehouse is divided into four areas. Area 1 is stacked high with TV sets such that the distributed load is $p = 120$ lb/ft^2. Area 2 has refrigerators with $p = 65$ lb/ft^2. Area 3 has stereos stacked so that $p = 80$ lb/ft^2. Area 4 has washing machines with $p = 50$ lb/ft^2. What is the simplest resultant force and where does it act?

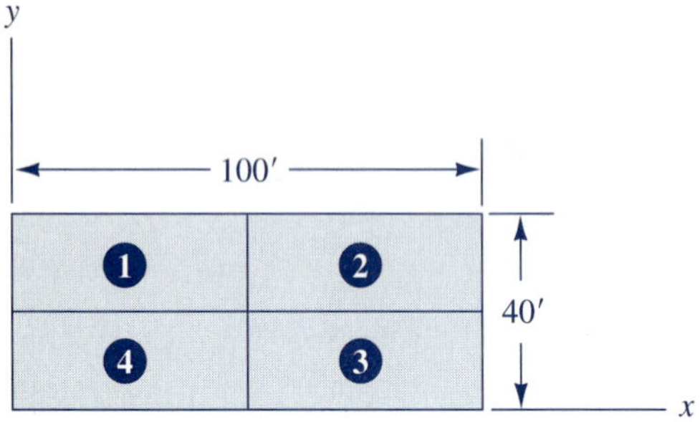

Figure P.4.65.

4.66. Consider a pressure distribution p forming a hemispherical surface over a domain of radius 5 m. If the maximum pressure is 5 Pa, what is the *simplest* resultant from this pressure distribution?

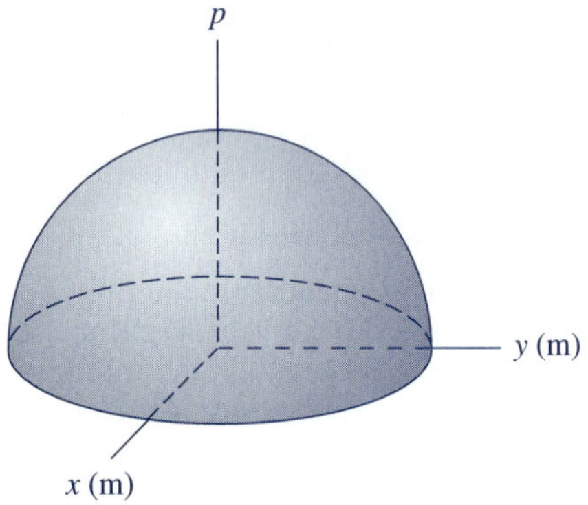

Figure P.4.66.

4.67. A rectangular tank contains water. If the tank is rotated clockwise 10° about an axis normal to the page, what torque is required to maintain the configuration? Width of tank is 1 ft.

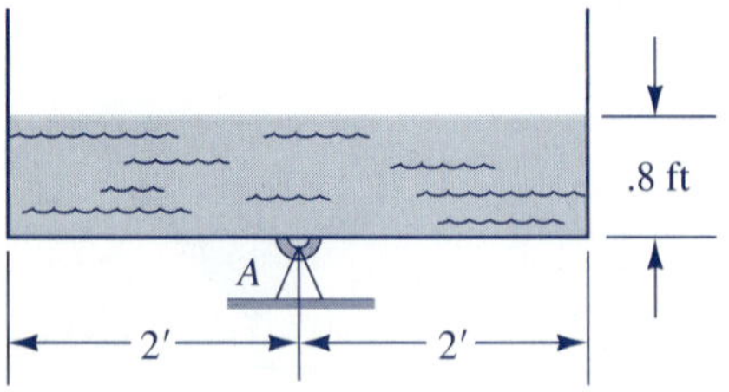

Figure P.4.67.

4.68. (a) Find the torque about axis $\overline{AB}$ from the wrench.

(b) Find the torque about axis $\overline{AB}$ from the distributed loads. (*Hint:* Look down from above to help view problem.)

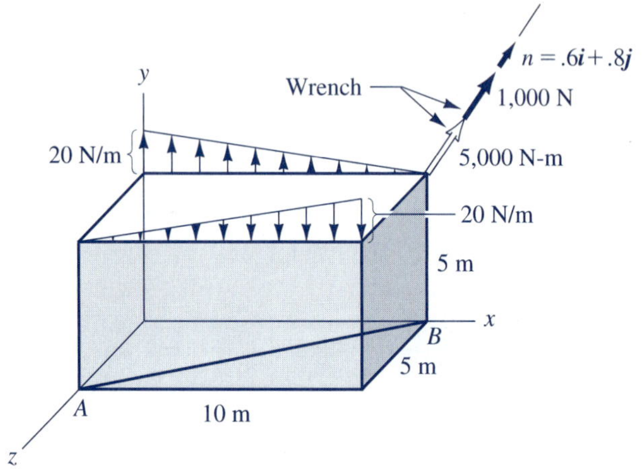

Figure P.4.68.

4.69. For the system of forces shown, determine the torque about the axis going from A to B. *Note:* The 100-N force and the triangular load distribution are in the yz plane and the 300-N-m couple is on the top face of the rectangular box.

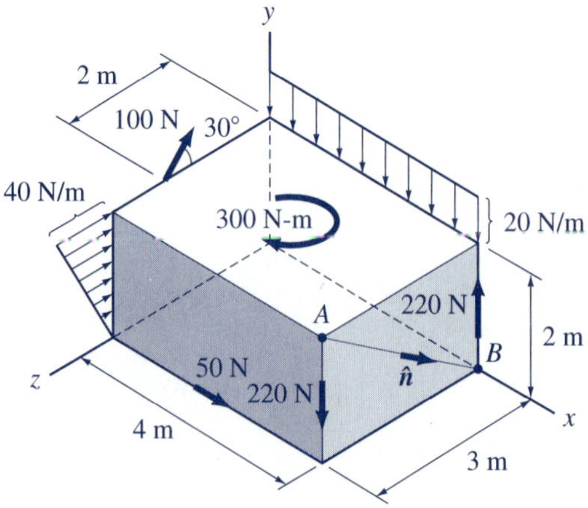

Figure P.4.69.

4.70. A *manometer* is a simple pressure measuring device. One such manometer called a *U tube* is shown in the diagram. The tank contains water including the tube to level M where mercury is present. M and N are at the same level. What is the gage pressure (i.e., the pressure above atmosphere) at point a in the tank for the following data:

$$d_1 = .2 \text{ m} \quad d_2 = .6 \text{ m} \quad \gamma_{H_2O} = 9{,}806 \text{ N/m}^3$$
$$\gamma_{Hg} = (13.7)(\gamma_{H_2O}) \text{ N/m}^3$$

[*Hint:* M and N are at the same level and are joined by the same fluid, namely mercury. Hence, the pressures there are equal.]

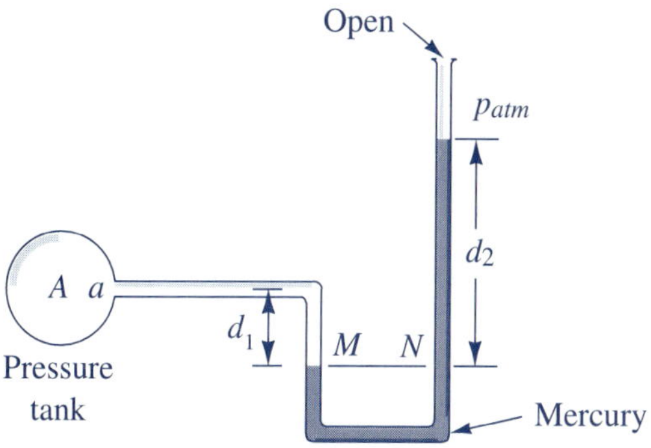

Figure P.4.70.

4.71. Imagine a liquid which when stationary stratifies in such a way that the specific weight is proportional to the square root of the pressure. At the free surface, the specific weight is known and has the value γ_0. What is the pressure as a function of depth from the free surface? What is the resultant force on one face AB of a rectangular plate submerged in the liquid? The width of the plate is b.

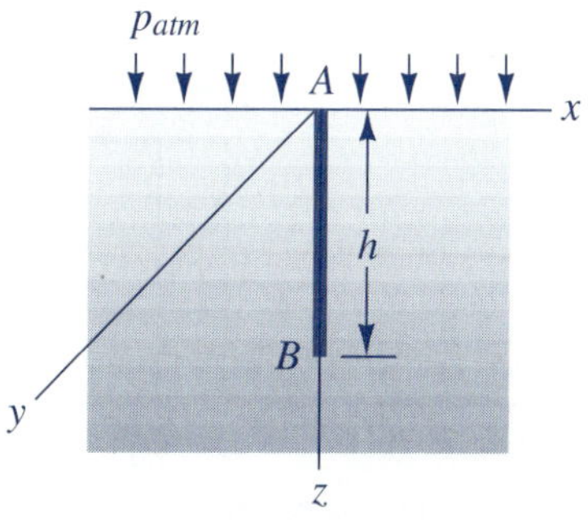

Figure P.4.71.

4.72. (a) Calculate the force on the door from all fluids inside and outside. The specific gravity of the oil is 0.8. This means that the oil has a specific weight γ which is 0.8 times that of water ($\gamma_{water} = 62.4$ lb/ft^3). Note that a uniform pressure on the surface of a liquid extends undiminished throughout the depth of the liquid.

(b) Determine the distance from the surface of the oil to the *simplest* resultant force on the door from all fluids.

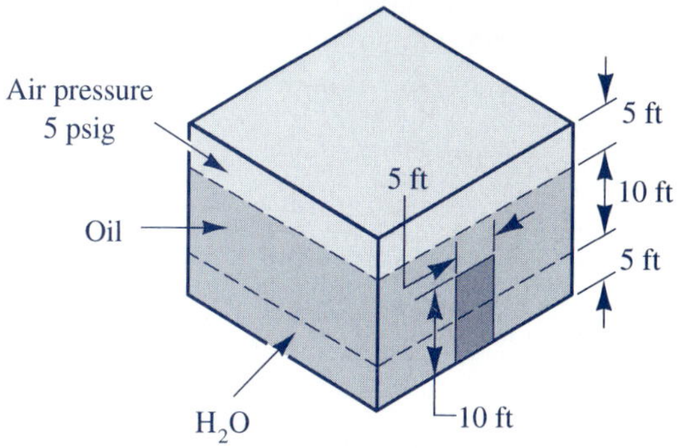

Figure P.4.72.

4.73. At what height h will the water cause the door to rotate clockwise? The door is 3 m wide. Neglect friction and the weight of the door.

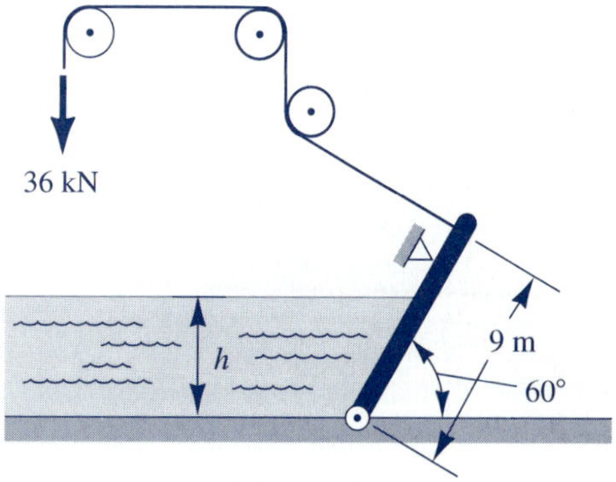

Figure P.4.73.

4.74. Find the force on the door from the inside and outside pressures. Give the position of the resultant force above the base of the door. The specific gravity S of the oil is 0.7, i.e., $\gamma_{oil} = (0.7)\gamma_{H_2O}$.

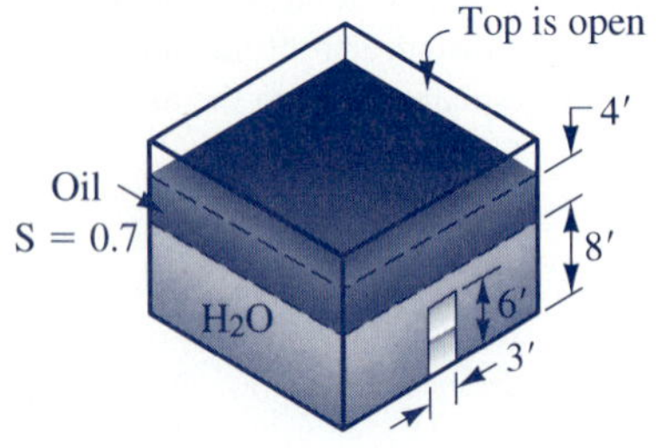

Figure P.4.74.

4.75. Find the total force on door AB from fluids. The specific gravity S of a fluid is $\gamma_{fluid}/\gamma_{H_2O}$. Take $S_{oil} = 0.6$. Find the position of this force from the bottom of the door.

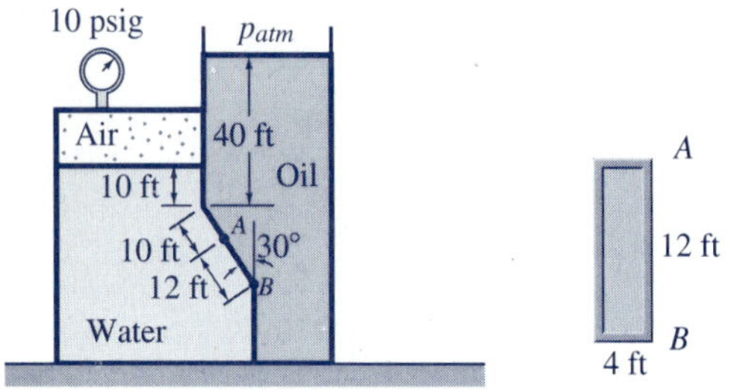

Figure P.4.75.

4.76. What is the simplest resultant force from the water and where does it act on the 60-m-high 800-m-long straight earthfill dam? (Water weighs 9,806 N/m³.)

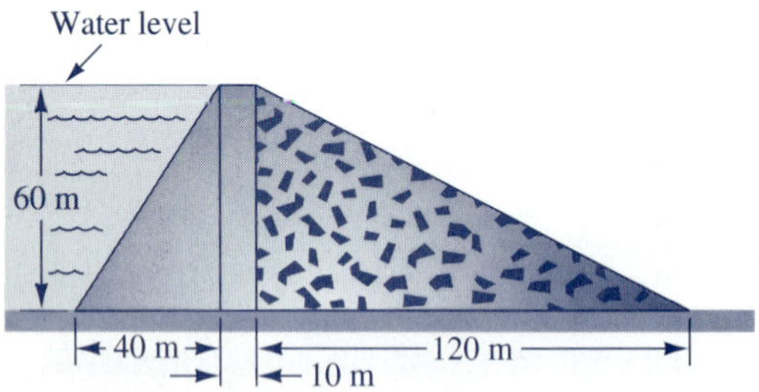

Figure P.4.76.

4.77. A block 1 ft thick is submerged in water. Compute the simplest resultant force and the center of pressure on the bottom surface. Take $\gamma = 62.4$ lb/ft³.

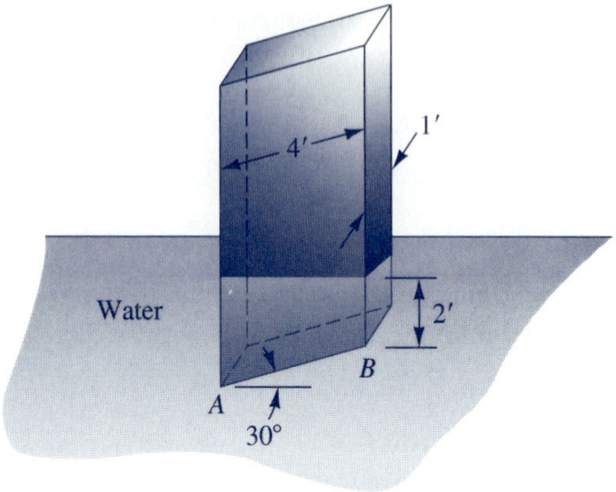

Figure P.4.77.

***4.78.** What is the resultant force from water and where does it act on the 40-m-high circular concrete dam between two walls of a rocky gorge? (Water weighs 9,806 N/m³.)

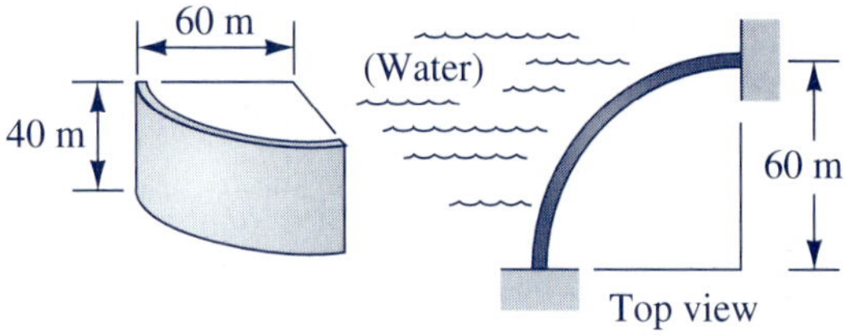

Figure P.4.78.

4.79. The weight of the wire $ABCD$ per unit length, w, increases linearly from 4 oz/ft at A to 20 oz/ft at D. Where is the center of gravity of the wire?

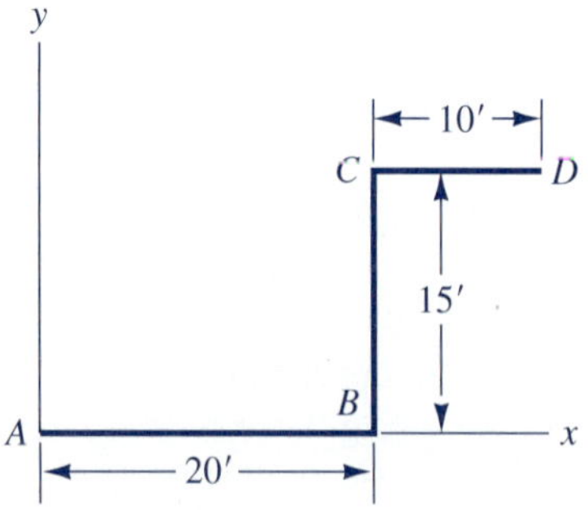

Figure P.4.79.

4.80. Find the center of gravity of the wire. The weight per unit length increases as the square of the length of wire from a value of 3 oz/ft at A until it reaches the value of 8 oz/ft at C. It then decreases 1 oz/ft for every 10 ft of length.

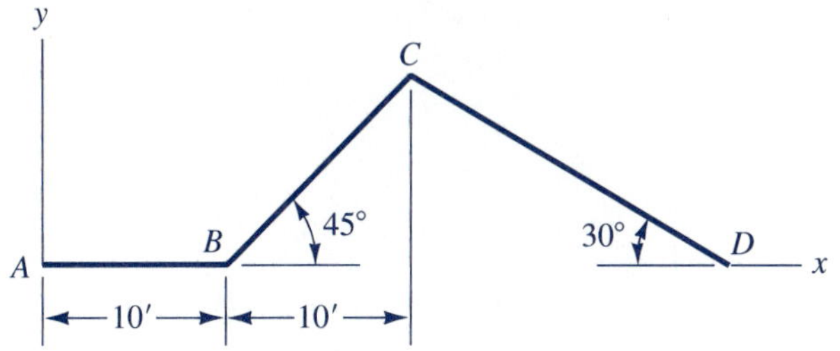

Figure P.4.80.

4.81. What is the center of gravity coordinate y_c for a thin circular rod shown in the diagram? It has a weight of w N/m. The rod is placed symmetrically about the y axis. The angle ϕ is in degrees.

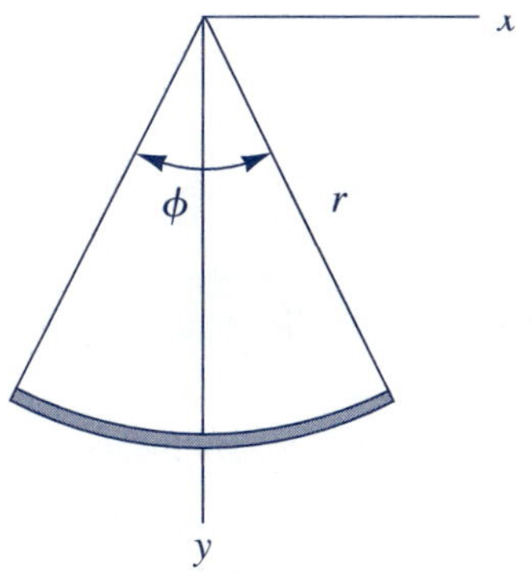

Figure P.4.81.

4.82. At what distance $\bar{x}$ from point A can the system of thin rods be suspended so that it will just balance? Use the formula developed in the previous problem for the radial distance to the center of gravity of a thin circular rod, namely $\dfrac{360r}{\pi\phi}\sin\dfrac{\phi}{2}$.

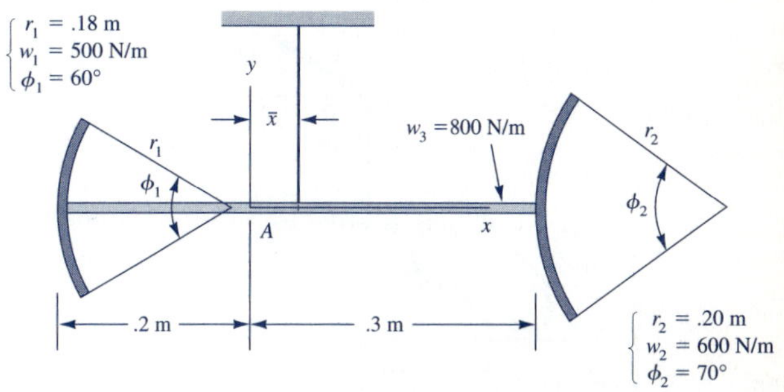

Figure P.4.82.

4.6 Closure

We now have the tools that enable us to replace, for purposes of rigid body mechanics, any system of forces by a resultant consisting of a force and a couple moment. These tools will prove very helpful in our computations. More important at this time, however, is the fact that in considering conditions of equilibrium for rigid bodies we need only concern ourselves with this resultant to reach conclusions valid for any force system, no matter how complex. From this viewpoint, we shall develop the fundamental equations of statics in Chapter 5 and then employ them to solve a large variety of problems.

PROBLEMS

4.83. Replace the force and couples acting on the plate by a single force. Give the intercept of the line of action of this force with the vertical edge BC of the plate.

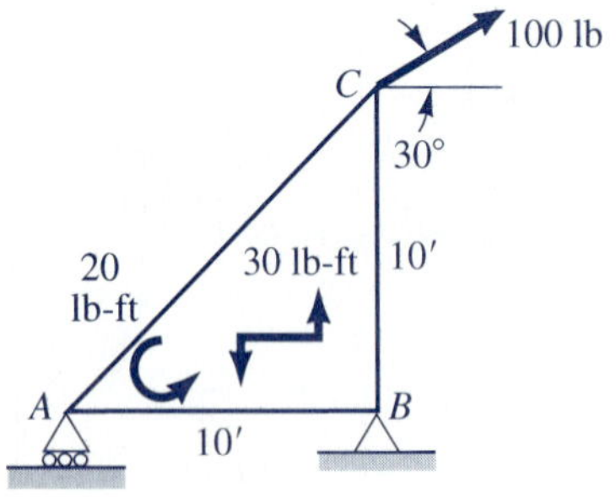

Figure P.4.83.

4.84. A 100-kN bridge pier supports a 10-m segment length of roadway weighing 150 kN and a 150-kN truck. The truck is located at the same position along the roadway as the pier. What is the equivalent force system acting on the base of the bridge pier when the truck is (a) in the center of the outside lane and (b) in the center of the inside lane?

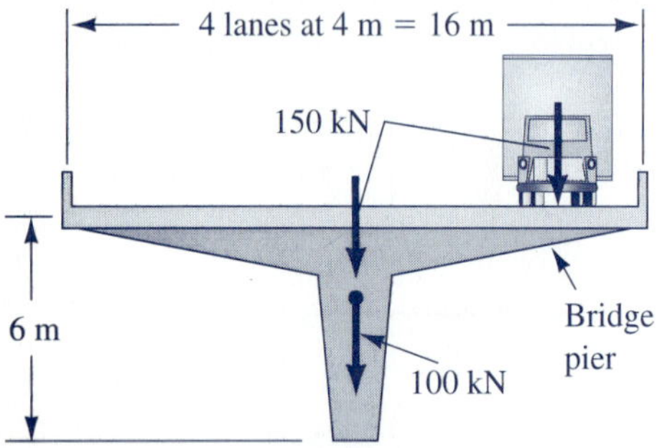

Figure P.4.84.

4.85. Find the center of gravity of a flat plate having constant specific weight γ and thickness t. You are looking down on the plate from above. Proceed as follows:

(a) Give weight of plate in terms of γt.
(b) Determine $\bar{y}$.
(c) Determine $\bar{x}$. Use vertical strips and be careful with integration limits.

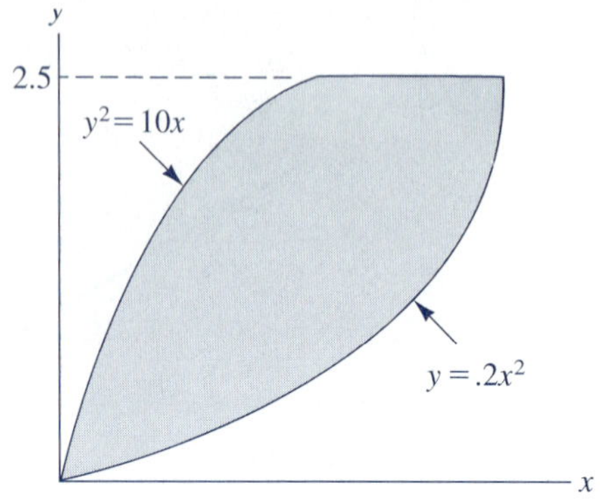

Figure P.4.85.

4.86. A heavy duty off-the-road dump truck is loaded with iron ore that weighs 51 kN/m^3. What is the *simplest* resultant force on the truck and where does it act?

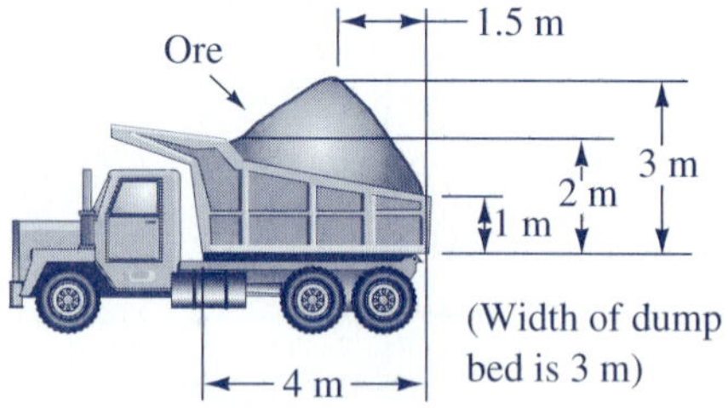

Figure P.4.86.

4.87. Find the *center of gravity* of the *system* of two plates shown (not separately) in terms of the specific weight γ and thickness t, both of which are uniform and the same for both plates. You are looking down on the plates.

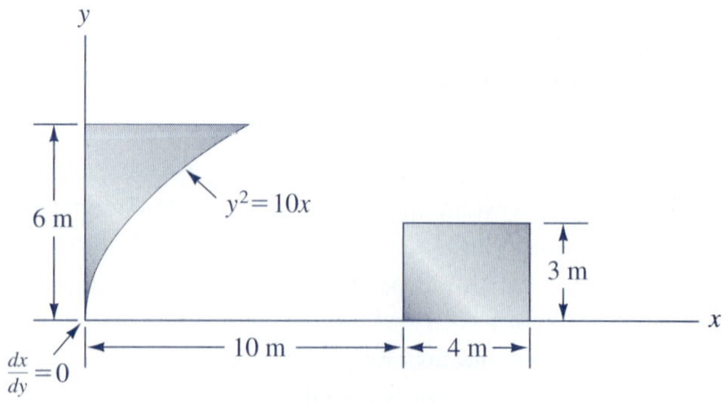

Figure P.4.87.

4.88. A Jeep weighs 11 kN and has both a front winch and a rear power take-off. The tension in the winch cable is 5 kN. The power take-off develops 300 N-m of torque T about an axis parallel to the x axis. If the driver weighs 800 N, what is the resultant force system at the indicated center of gravity of the Jeep where we can consider the weight of the Jeep to be concentrated?

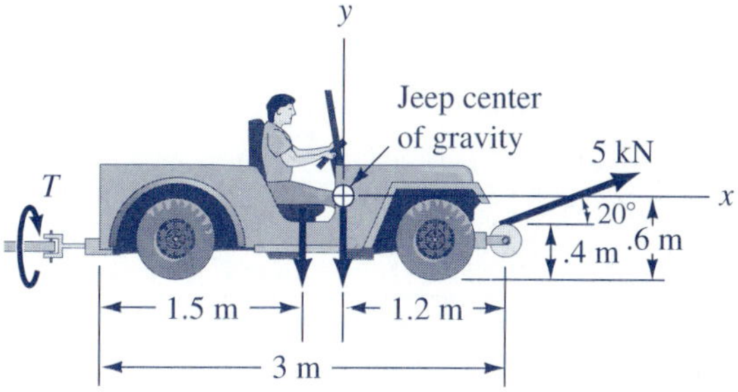

Figure P.4.88.

4.89. What is the *simplest* resultant for the forces and couple acting on the beam?

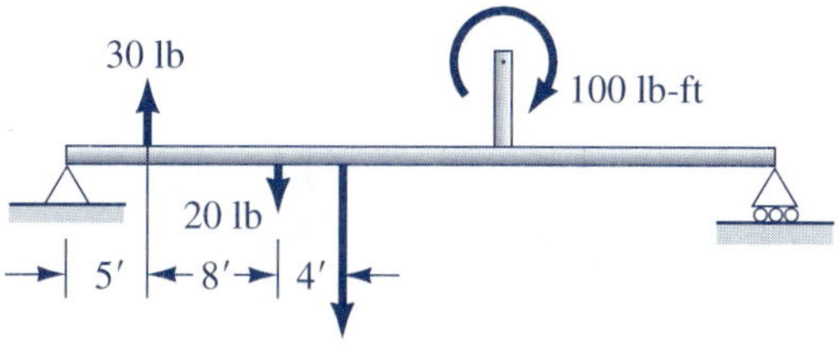

Figure P.4.89.

4.90. A parabolic body of revolution has cut out of it a second parabolic body of revolution starting at A and forming a sharp edge at B with zero slope at A.

(a) What is r' as a function of x for the cut-out body of revolution?

(b) Set up an integral for computing W (weight) and then the center of gravity coordinate $\bar{x}$.

Note: γ varies with x. Do not solve the integral.

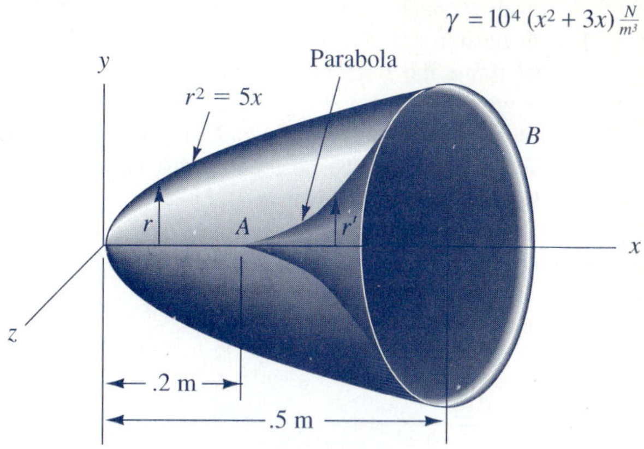

Figure P.4.90.

4.91. Find the torque about axis OB from the system of forces.

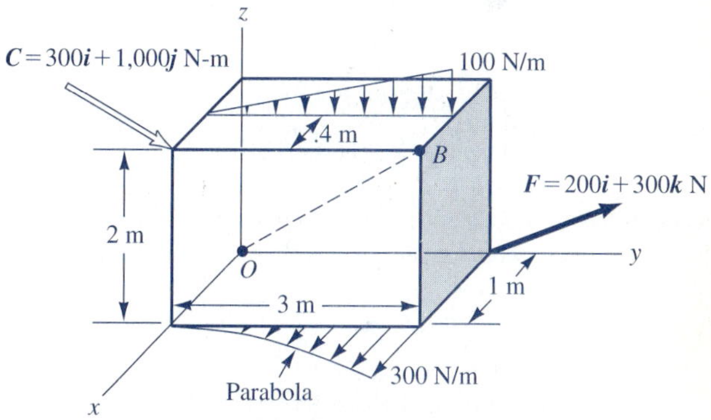

Figure P.4.91.

4.92. A rectangular plate shown as ABC can rotate about hinge B. What length l should BC be so there is zero torque about B from the water, air, and weight of the plate? Take this weight as 1,000 N/m of length. The width is 1 m. γ_{H_2O} = 9,806 N/m^3.

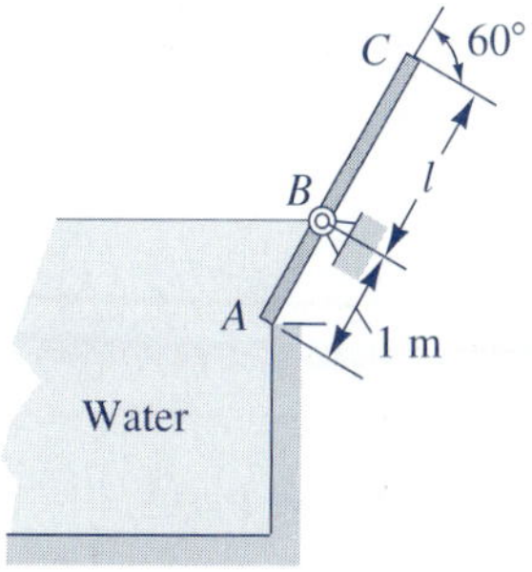

Figure P.4.92.

4.93. An open rectangular tank of water is partially filled with water. The dimensions are shown.

(a) Determine the force on the bottom of the tank from the water.

(b) Determine the force on the door shown at the side of the tank. Indicate the position of this force from the bottom of the tank.

Note that the atmospheric pressure develops equal and opposite forces on both sides of the door and hence yields no net force.

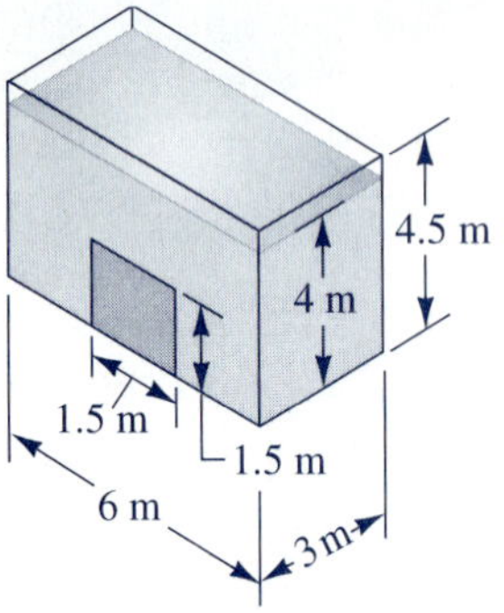

Figure P.4.93.

4.94. Sandbags are piled on a beam. Each bag is 1 ft wide and weighs 100 lb. What is the simplest resultant force and where does it act? What linear mathematical function of the distributed load can be used to represent the sandbags over the left 3 ft of the beam?

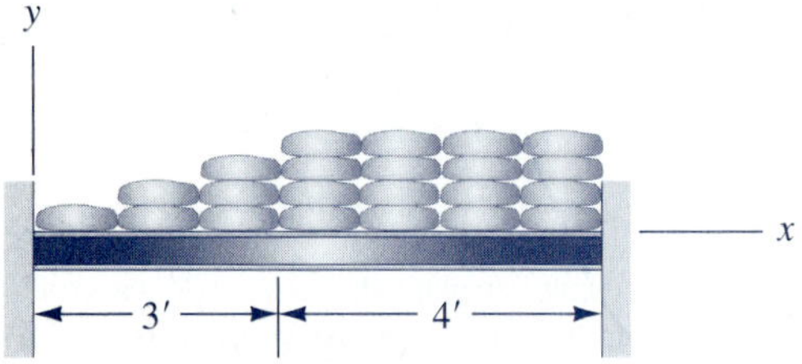

Figure P.4.94.

4.95. A cantilever beam is subjected to a linearly varying load over part of its length. What is the *simplest* resultant force, and where does it act? What is the moment at the supported end?

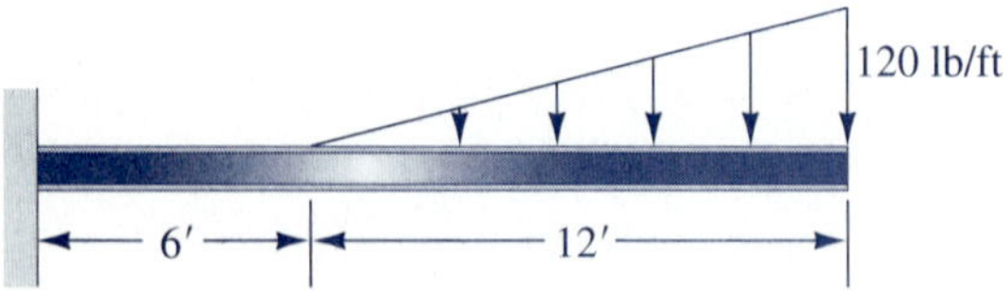

Figure P.4.95.

4.96. Find the torque about an axis along position vector $\boldsymbol{r} = 3\boldsymbol{i} + 4\boldsymbol{j} + 2\boldsymbol{k}$ m. Note we have a pressure distribution on *ABED* and a coplanar loading in the *yz* plane along the *y* axis.

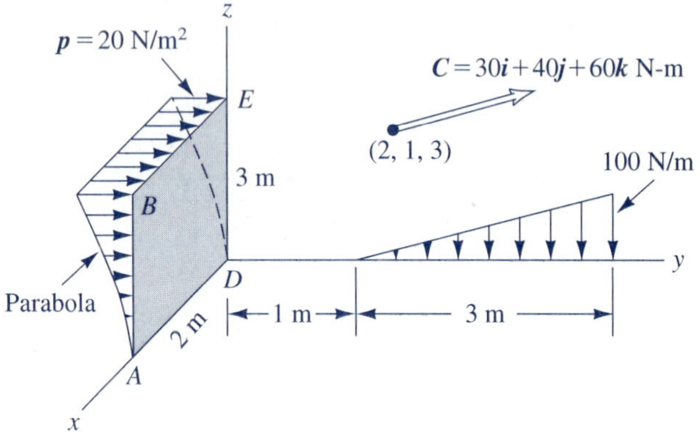

Figure P.4.96.

4.97. Compute the *simplest* resultant force for the loads acting on the cantilever beam.

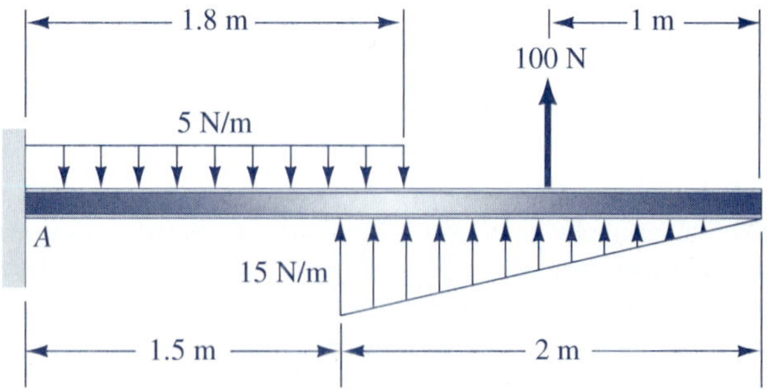

Figure P.4.97.

4.98. Find the resultant force system at A for the forces on the bent cantilever beam. BC is parallel to z axis.

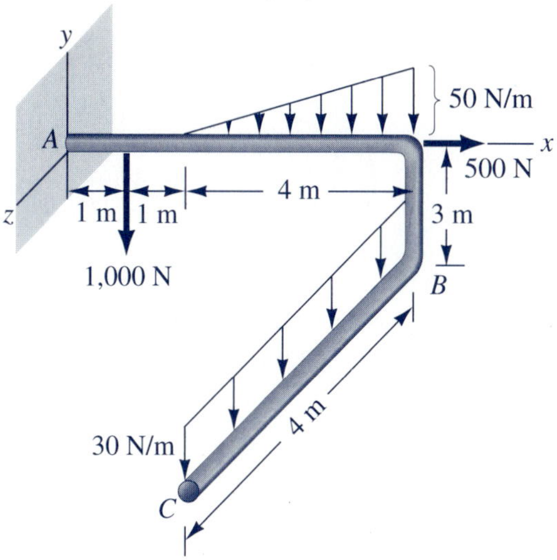

Figure P.4.98.

4.99. (a) Find equations describing both parabolas.
(b) Using *vertical* strips (and a composite body approach), find weight of plate in terms of γt.
(c) Using vertical strips, find $\bar{x}$ of C.G.

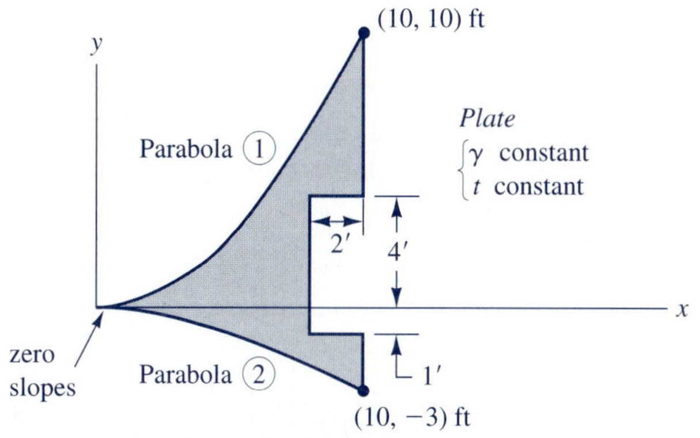

Figure P.4.99.

4.100. The L-shaped concrete post supports an elevated railroad. The concrete weighs 150 lb/ft^3. What is the simplest resultant force from the weight and the load and where does it act? Load acts at center of top surface.

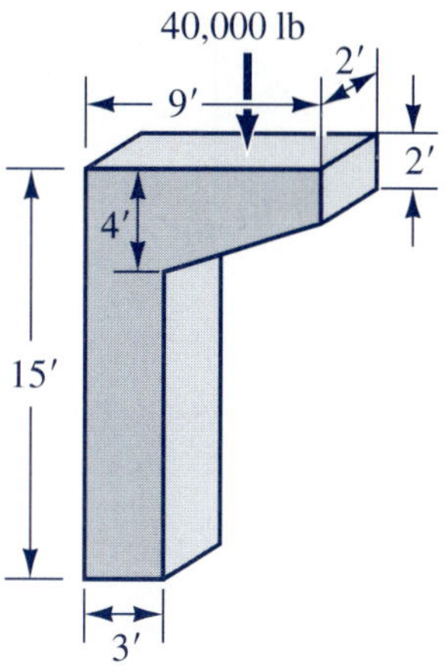

Figure P.4.100.

4.101. Explain why the system shown can be considered a system of parallel forces. Find the *simplest* resultant for this system. The grid is composed of 1-m squares.

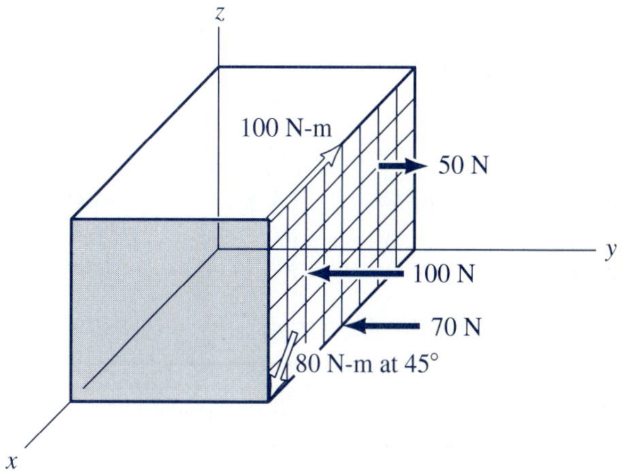

Figure P.4.101.

4.102. A plate of thickness t has as the upper edge a parabolic curve with infinite slope at the origin. Find the x, y coordinates of the center of gravity for this plate.

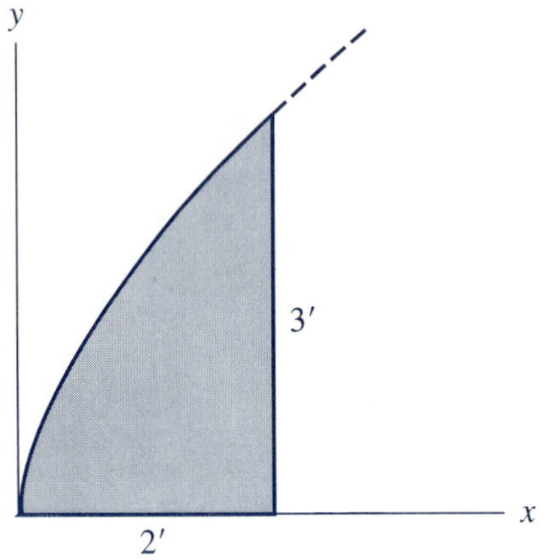

Figure P.4.102.

4.103. A rectangular tank contains a liquid. At the top of the liquid there is a pressure of .1380 N/mm^2 absolute. What is the simplest resultant force in the inside surface of the door AB? Where is the center of pressure relative to the bottom of the door? Take $\gamma = 8{,}190$ N/m^3 for the liquid.

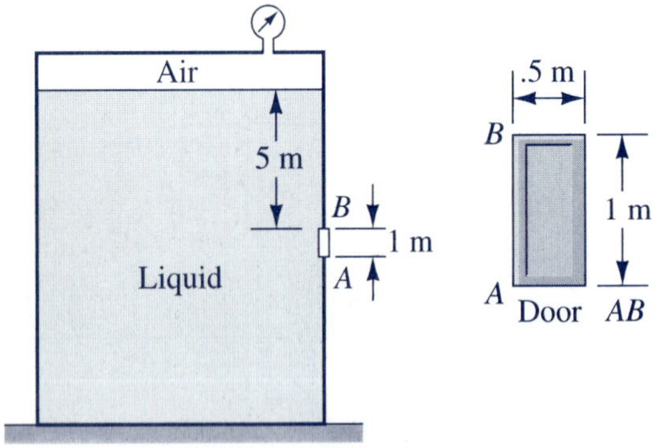

Figure P.4.103.

4.104. The specific weight of the material in a right circular cone varies directly as the square of the distance y from the base. If $\gamma_0 = 50$ lb/ft^3 is the specific weight at the base, and if $\gamma' = 70$ lb/ft^3 is the specific weight at the tip, where is the center of gravity of the cone? (See hint in Problem 4.45.)

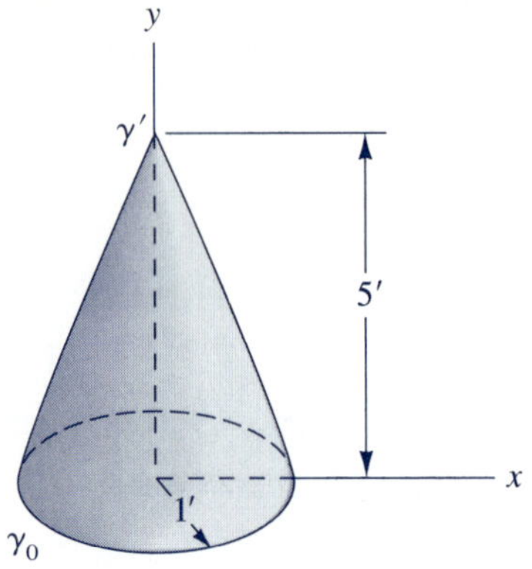

Figure P.4.104.

***4.105.** A block has a rectangular portion removed (darkened region). If the specific weight is given as

$$\gamma = (2.0x + y + 3xyz) \text{ kN/m}^3$$

find $\bar{x}$ for the center of gravity.

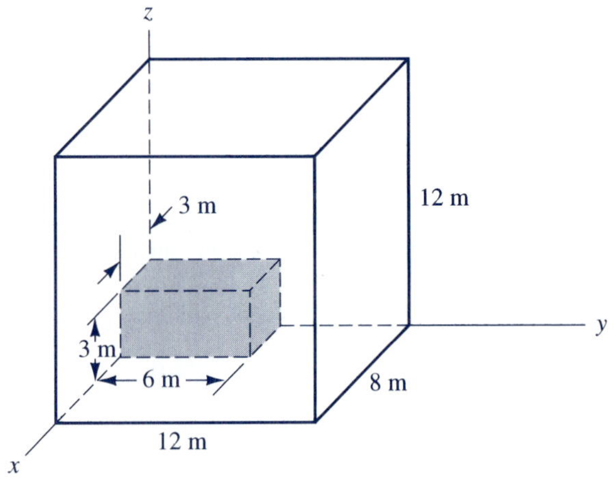

Figure P.4.105.

4.106. Compute the *simplest* resultant for the loads shown acting on the simply supported beam. Give the line of action.

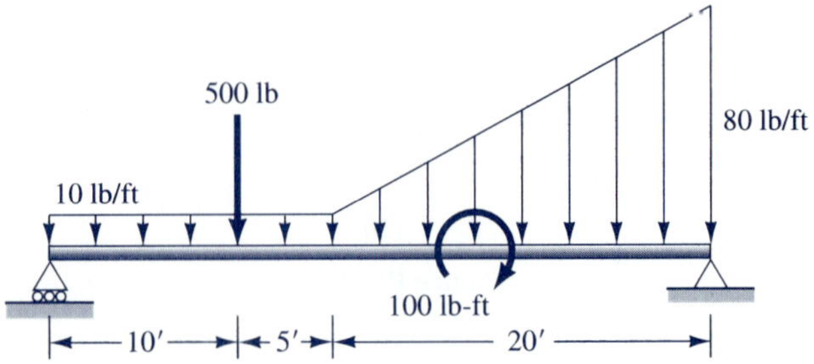

Figure P.4.106.

4.107. Find the center of gravity of the plate.

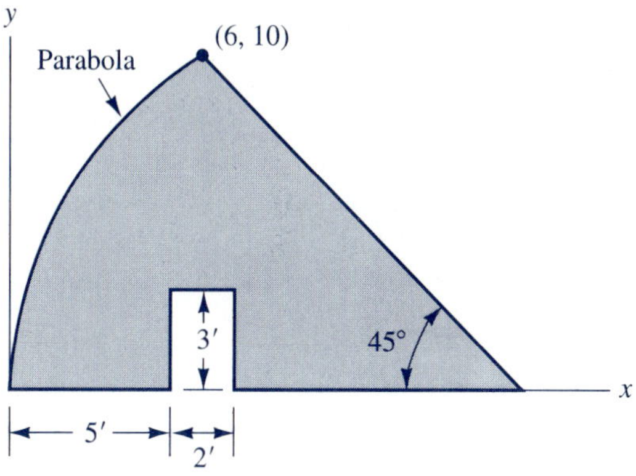

Figure P.4.107.

4.108. Find the center of gravity of the truss. All members have the same weight per unit length.

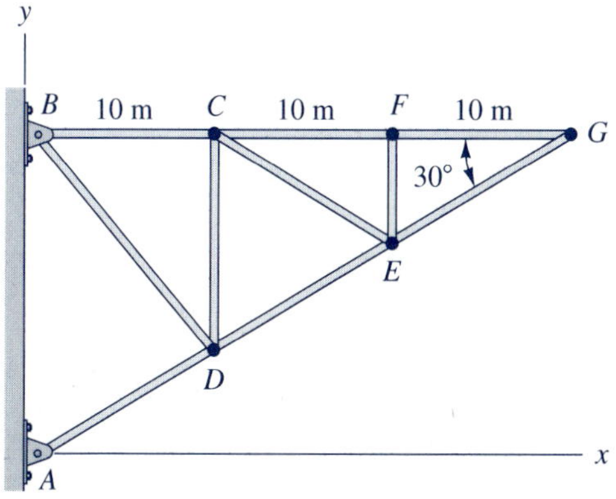

Figure P.4.108.

***4.109.** The pressure p_0 at the corner O of the plate is 50 Pa and increases linearly in the y direction by 5 Pa/m. In the x direction, it increases parabolically starting with zero slope so that in 20 m the pressure has gone from 50 Pa to 500 Pa. What is the simplest resultant for this distribution? Give the coordinates of the center of pressure.

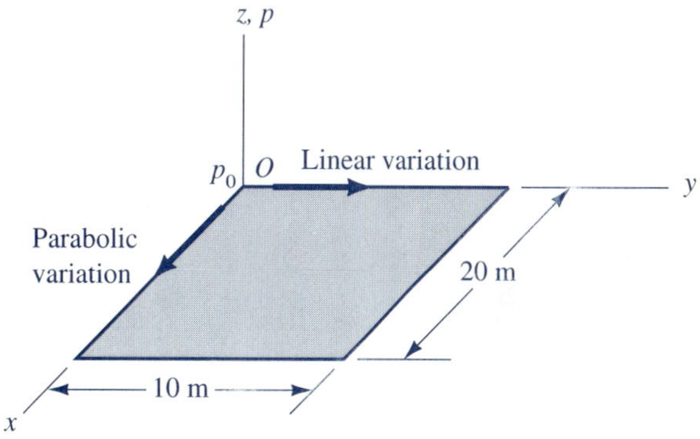

Figure P.4.109.

4.110. A sluice-gate door in a dam is 3 m wide and 3 m high. The water level in the dam is 4 m above the top of the door. The gate is opened until the water level falls 4 m. What is the simplest resultant force on the closed door at both water levels? Where do the forces act (i.e., where is the "center of pressure" in each case)? Water weighs 9,806 N/m^3.

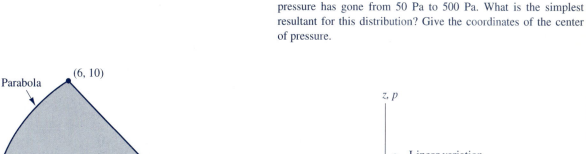

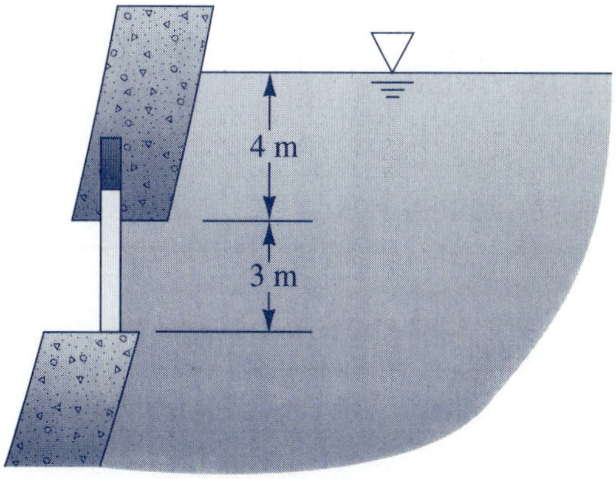

Figure P.4.110.

4.111. A cylindrical tank of water is rotated at constant angular speed ω until the water ceases to change shape. The result is a free surface which, from fluid mechanics considerations, is that of a paraboloid. If the pressure varies directly as the depth below the free surface, what is the resultant force on a quadrant of the base of the cylinder? Take $\gamma = 62.4$ lb/ft^3. [*Hint:* Use circular strip in quadrant having area $1/4(2\pi r\, dr)$.]

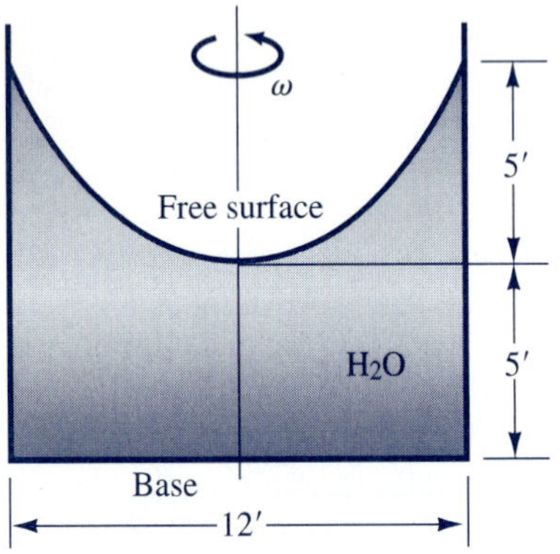

Figure P.4.111.

4.112. Find the x and y coordinates of the center of gravity of the bodies shown. These consist of:

(a) A plate ABC whose thickness $t = 50$ mm.
(b) A rod D of diameter .3 m and length 3 m.
(c) A block F whose thickness (not shown) is .3 m.

The density of the three bodies is the same.

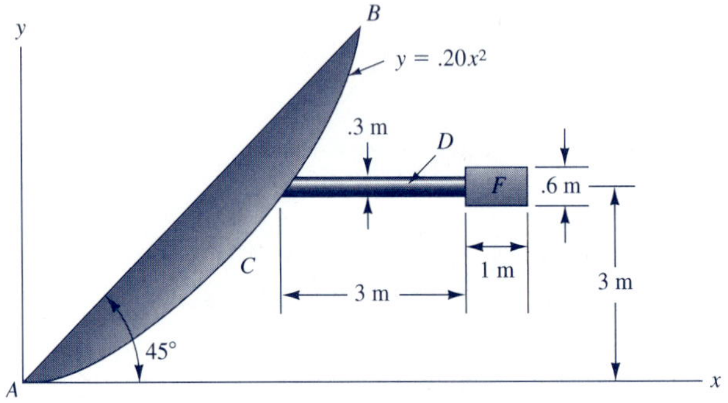

Figure P.4.112.

CHAPTER 5

Equations of Equilibrium

5.1 Introduction

You will recall from Section 1.10 that a *particle* in equilibrium is one that is stationary or that moves uniformly relative to an inertial reference. A *body* is in equilibrium if all the particles that may be considered to comprise the body are in equilibrium. It follows, then, that a rigid body in equilibrium cannot be rotating relative to an inertial reference. In this chapter, we shall consider bodies in equilibrium for which the rigid-body model is valid. For these bodies, there are certain simple equations that relate all the surface and body forces, or their equivalents, that act on the body. With these equations, we can sometimes ascertain the value of a certain number of unknown forces. For instance, in the beam shown in Fig. 5.1, we know the loads F_1 and F_2 and also the weight W of the beam, and we want to determine the forces transmitted to the earth so that we can design a foundation to support the structure properly. Knowing that the beam is in equilibrium and that the small deflection of the beam will not appreciably affect the forces transmitted to the earth, we can write rigid-body equations of equilibrium involving the unknown and known forces acting on the beam and thus arrive at the desired information.

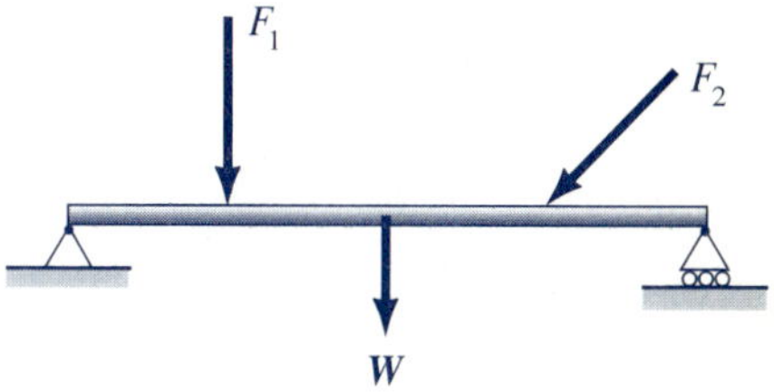

Figure 5.1. Loaded beam.

Note in the beam problem above that a number of steps are implied. First, there is the singling out of the beam itself for discussion. Then, we express certain equations of equilibrium for the beam, which we take as a rigid body. Finally, there is the evaluation of the unknowns and interpretation of the results. In this chapter, we will carefully examine each of these steps.

Of critical importance is the need to be able to isolate a body or part of a body for analysis. Such a body is called a *free body*. We will first carefully investigate the development of free-body diagrams. We urge you to pay special heed to this topic, since *it is the most important step in the solving of mechanics problems*. An incorrect free-body diagram means that all ensuing

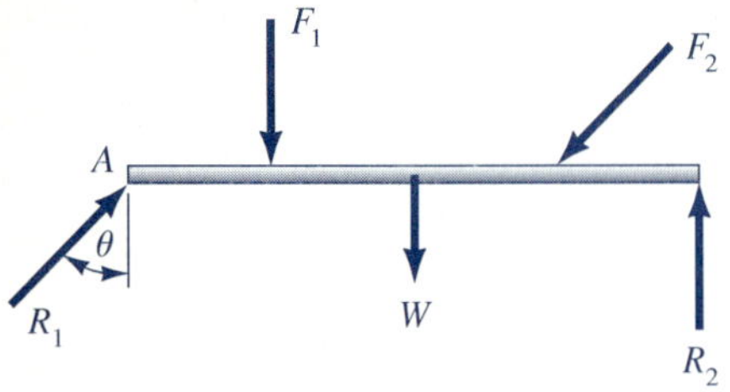

Figure 5.2. Free-body diagram of beam.

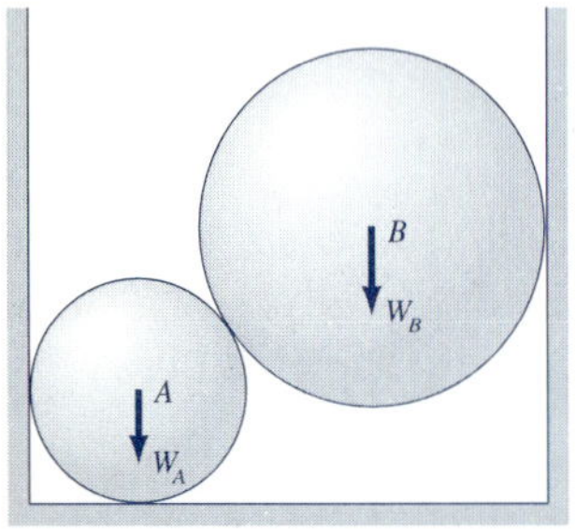

Figure 5.3. Smooth spheres in equilibrium.

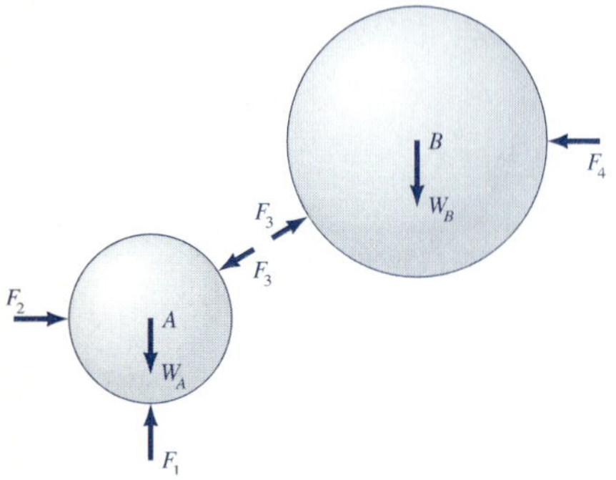

Figure 5.4. Free-body diagrams.

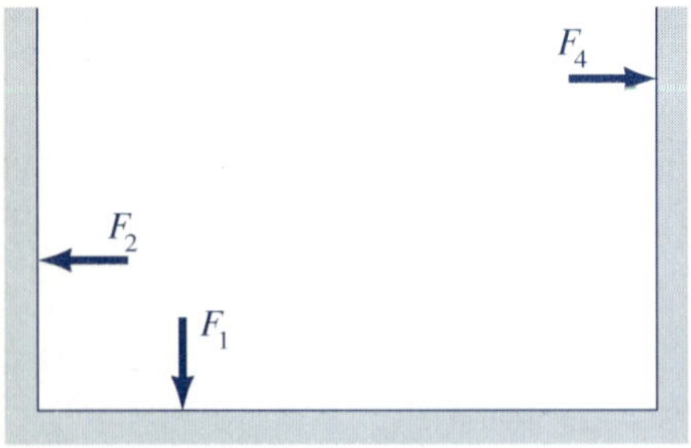

Figure 5.5. This is *not* a free-body diagram.

work, no matter how brilliant, will lead to wrong results. More than just a means of attacking statics problems, the free-body concept is your first exposure to the overridingly important topic of *engineering analysis* in general.[1] We now examine this critical step.

5.2 The Free-Body Diagram

Since the equations of equilibrium for a particular body actually stem from the dynamic considerations of the body, we must be sure to include *all* the forces (or their equivalents) acting *on* this body, because they all affect the motion of the body and must be accounted for. To help identify all the forces and so ensure the correct use of the equations of equilibrium, we isolate the body in a simple diagram and show *all* the forces from the *surroundings* that act *on* the body. Such a diagram is called a *free-body diagram*. When we isolate the beam in our problem from its surroundings, we get Fig. 5.2. On the left end, there is an unknown force from the ground that has a magnitude denoted as R_1 and a direction denoted as θ, with a line of action going through a known point A. [We may also use components $(R_1)_x$ and $(R_1)_y$ as unknowns rather than R_1 and θ.] The right side involves a force in the vertical direction with an unknown magnitude denoted as R_2. The direction is vertical because the beam is on rollers to allow for thermal expansion or thermal contraction and to thus allow unhindered stretching or shrinking of the beam in the axial direction. As a result, the ground exerts a negligibly small horizontal force there. Once all the forces acting on the beam have been identified, including the three unknown quantities R_1, R_2, and θ, we can solve for these unknowns by using three equations of equilibrium.

Consider now the hard spheres shown in Fig. 5.3 in a condition of equilibrium with surfaces smooth enough to permit us to neglect friction completely. The contact forces thus must be in a direction normal to the surface of contact. The free bodies of the spheres are shown in Fig. 5.4. Notice that F_3 is the magnitude of the force from sphere B on sphere A, while the reaction, also shown as F_3 according to Newton's third law, is the magnitude of the force from sphere A on sphere B.

You might be tempted to consider a portion of the container as a free body in the manner shown in Fig. 5.5. But even if this diagram did clearly depict a body (which it does not!), it would not qualify as a free body, since all the forces acting on the body have not been shown.

In engineering problems, bodies are often in contact in a number of standard ways. In Fig. 5.6, you will find the types of forces transmitted from body M to body N for body connections that are often found in practice. (These are not free-body diagrams, since all the forces on any given body have not been shown.)

[1] The author has found through many years of experience that the absence of a free-body diagram in a student's work on a particular problem signifies that:

1. There will most likely be errors in the analysis of the problem, or
2. Even worse, the student does not have a good grasp of the problem.

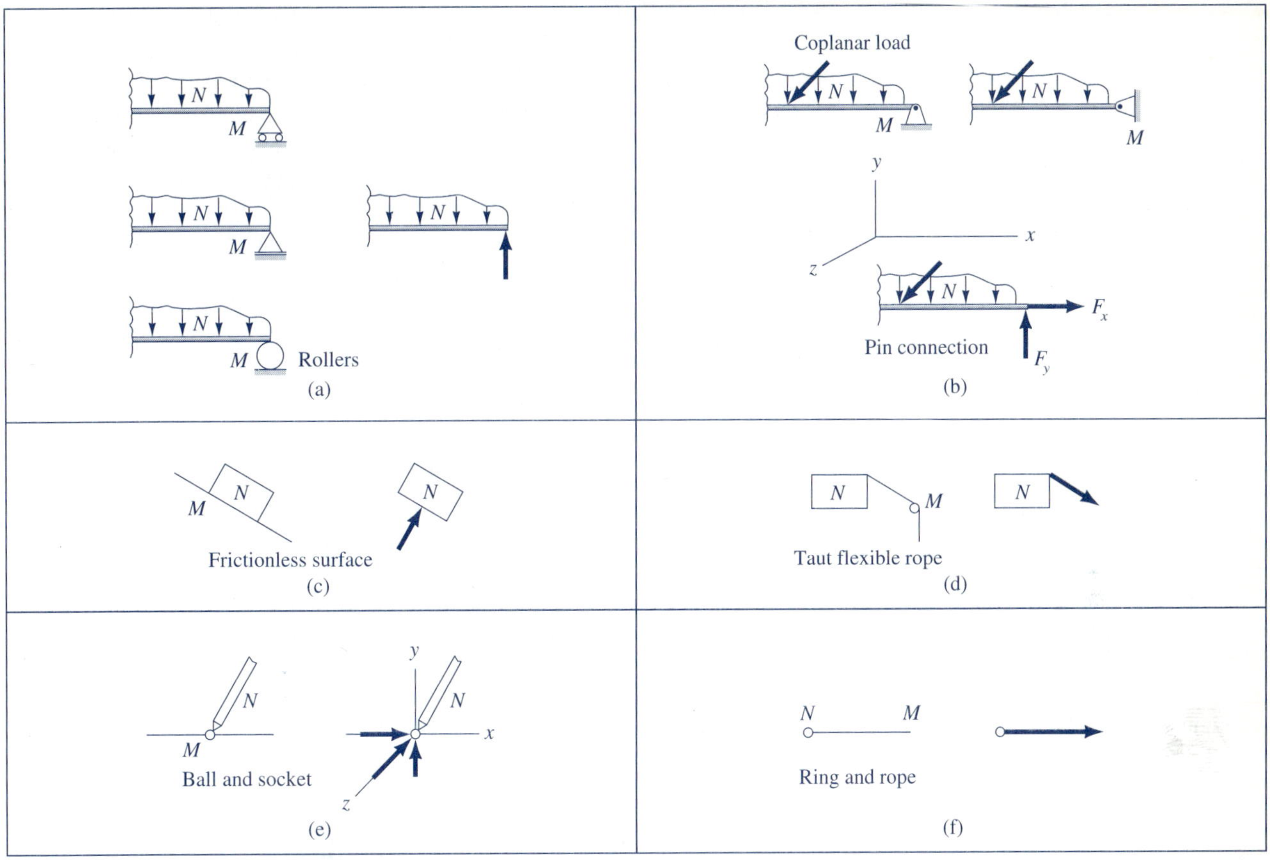

Figure 5.6. Standard connections.

In general, to ascertain the nature of the force system that a body M is capable of transmitting to a second body N through some connector or support, we may proceed in the following manner. Mentally move the bodies relative to each other in each of three orthogonal directions. In those directions where relative motion is impeded or prevented by the connector or support, there can be a force component at this connector or support in a free-body diagram of either body M or N. Next, mentally rotate bodies M and N relative to each other about the orthogonal axes. In each direction about which relative rotation is impeded or prevented by the connector or support, there can be a couple-moment component at this connector or support in a free-body diagram of body M or N. Now as a result of equilibrium considerations of body M or N, certain force and couple-moment components that are capable of being generated at a support or connector will be zero for the particular loadings at hand. Indeed, one can often readily recognize this by inspection. For instance, consider the pin-connected beam loaded in a coplanar manner shown partially in Fig. 5.7. If we mentally move the beam relative to the ground in the x, y, and z directions, we get resistance from the pin for each direction, and so the ground at A can transmit force components A_x, A_y, and

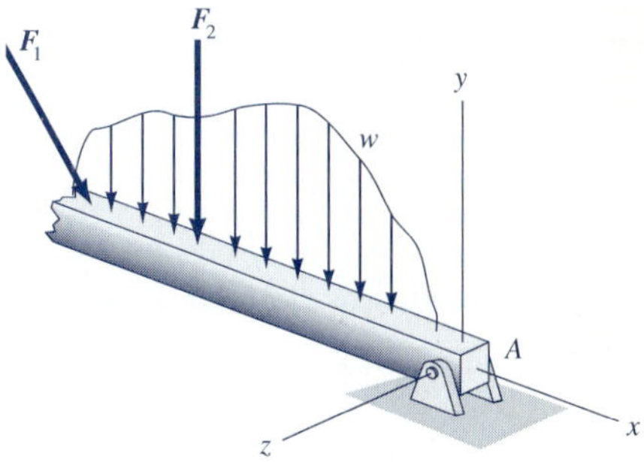

Figure 5.7. Pin connection.

A_z. However, because the loading is coplanar in the xy plane, the force component A_z must be zero and can be deleted. Next, mentally rotate the beam relative to the ground at A about the three orthogonal axes. Because of the smooth pin connection, there is no resistance about the z axis and so $M_z = 0$. But there is resistance about the x and y axes. However, the coplanar loading in the xy plane cannot exert moments about the x and y axes, and so the couple moments M_x and M_y are zero. All told, then, we just have force components A_x and A_y at the pin connection, as has been shown earlier in Fig. 5.6(b), wherein we relied on physical reasoning for this result.

5.3 Free Bodies Involving Interior Sections

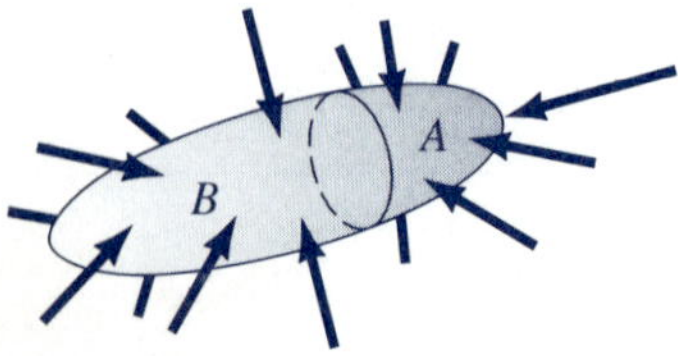

Figure 5.8. Rigid body in equilibrium.

Let us consider a rigid body in equilibrium as shown in Fig. 5.8. Clearly, every portion of this body must also be in equilibrium. If we consider the body as two parts A and B, we can present either part in a free-body diagram. To do this, we must include on the portion chosen to be the free body the forces *from the other part* that arise at the common section (Fig. 5.9). The surface between both sections may be any curved or plane surface, and over it there will be a continuous force distribution. In the general case, we know that such a distribution can be replaced by a single force and a single couple moment (at any chosen point) and this has been done in the free-body diagram of parts A and B in Fig. 5.9. Notice that Newton's third law has been observed.

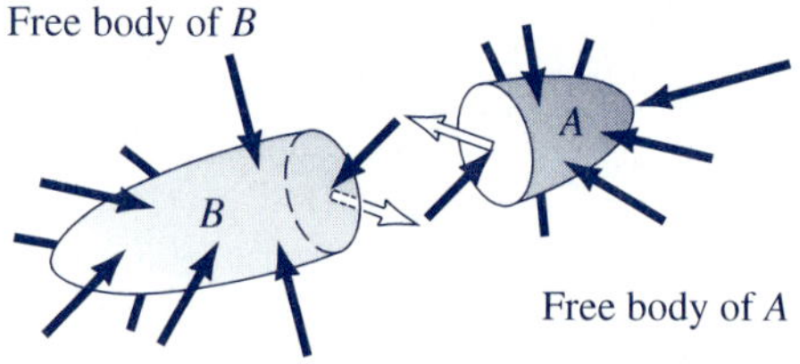

Figure 5.9. Free bodies of parts A and B.

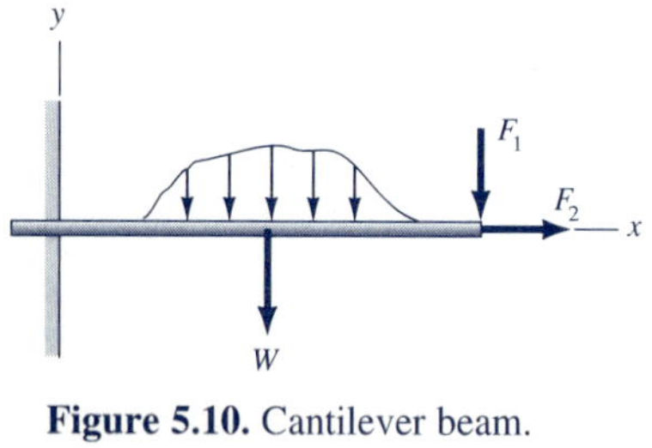

Figure 5.10. Cantilever beam.

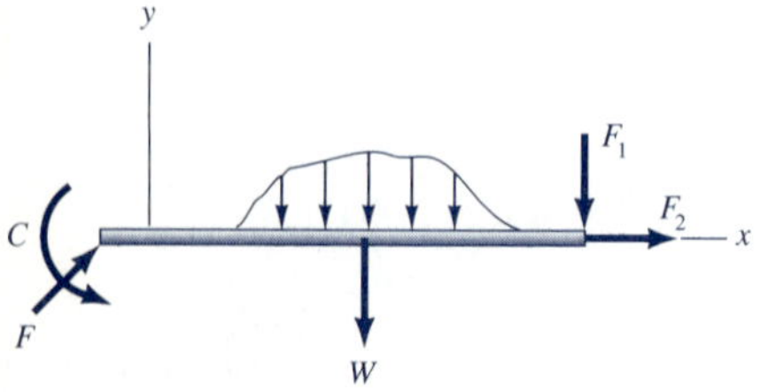

Figure 5.11. Free-body diagram of cantilever beam.

As a special case, consider a beam with one end embedded in a massive wall (cantilever beam) and loaded within the xy plane (Fig. 5.10). A free body of the portion of the beam extending from the wall is shown in Fig. 5.11. Because of the geometric symmetry of the beam about the xy plane and the fact that the loads are in this plane, the exposed forces in the cut section can be considered coplanar. Hence, these exposed forces can be replaced by a single force and a single couple moment in the center plane, and it is the usual practice to decompose the force into components F_y and F_x. Although a line of action for the force can be found that would enable us to eliminate the couple moment, it is desirable in structural problems to work with an equivalent system that has the force passing through the center of the beam cross section, and thus to have a couple moment. In the next section, we will see how F and C can be ascertained.

Example 5.1

As a further illustration of a free-body diagram, we shall now consider the frame[2] shown in Fig. 5.12, which consists of members connected by frictionless pins. The force systems acting on the assembly and its parts will be taken as coplanar. We shall now sketch free-body diagrams of the assembly and its parts.

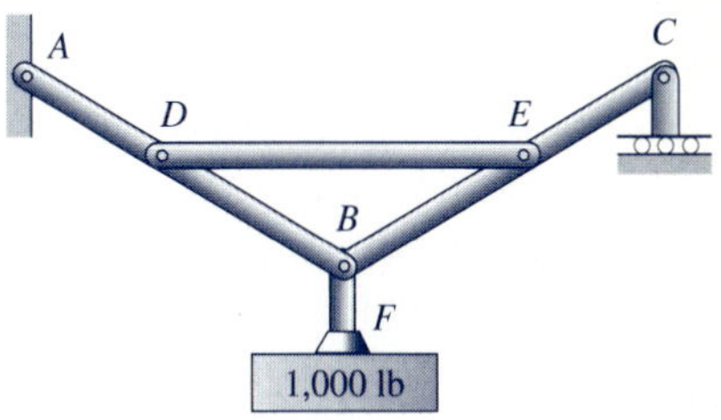

Figure 5.12. A frame.

Free-body diagram of the entire assembly. The magnitude and direction of the force at A from the wall onto the assembly is not known. However, we know that this force is in the plane of the system. Therefore, two components are shown at this point (Fig. 5.13). Since the direction of the force C is known, there are then three unknown scalar quantities, A_y, A_x, and C, for the free body.

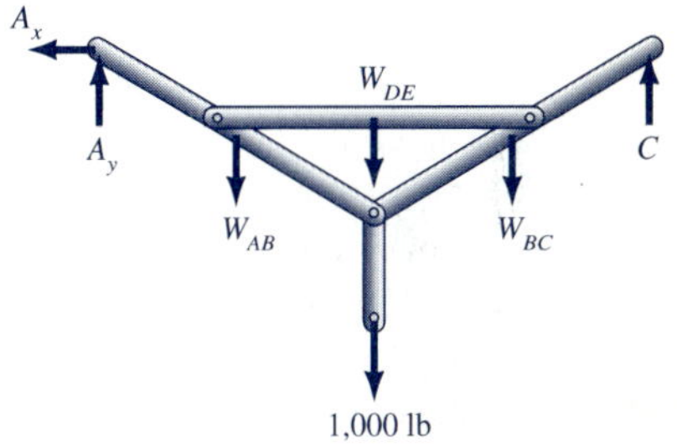

Figure 5.13. Free-body diagram of frame.

Free-body diagram of the component parts. When two members are pinned together, such as members DE and AB or DE and BC, we usually consider the pin to be part of one of the bodies. However, when more than two members are connected at a pin, such as members AB, BC, and BF at B, we often isolate the pin and consider that all members act on the pin rather than directly on each other, as illustrated in Fig. 5.14. Notice four sets of forces that form pairs of reactions have been enclosed with dashed lines. The fifth set is the 1,000-lb force on the pin and on the member BF.

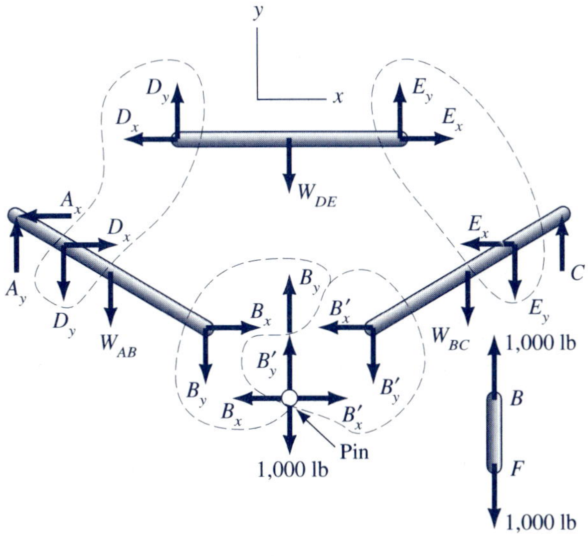

Figure 5.14. Free-body diagrams of parts.

[2]A *frame* is a system of connected straight or bent, long, slender members where some of the connecting pins are not at the ends of the members as is the case for structures that we will study later called *trusses*.

Example 5.1 (Continued)

Do not be concerned about the proper *sense* of an unknown force component that you draw on the free-body diagram, for you may choose either a positive or negative sense for these components. When the values of these quantities are ascertained by methods of statics, the proper sense for each component can then be established; but, having chosen a sense for a component, you must be sure that the *reaction* to this component has the *opposite* sense—else you will violate Newton's third law.

Free-body diagram of portion of the assembly to the right of M–M. In making a free body of the portion to the right of section *M–M* (see Fig. 5.15a), we must remember to put in the weight of the portions of the members remaining *after* the cut has been made. At the two cuts made by *M–M* we must replace coplanar force distributions by resultants, as in the case of the previously considered cantilever beam. This is accomplished by inserting two force components usually normal and tangential to the cross section and a couple moment as was done for the cantilever beam. Note in Fig. 5.15(b) that there are seven unknown scalar quantities for this free-body diagram. They are C_1, C_2, F_1, F_2, F_3, and F_4. Apparently, the number of unknowns varies widely for the various free bodies that may be drawn for the system. For this reason, you must choose the free-body diagram that is suitable for your needs with some discretion in order to effectively solve for the desired unknowns.

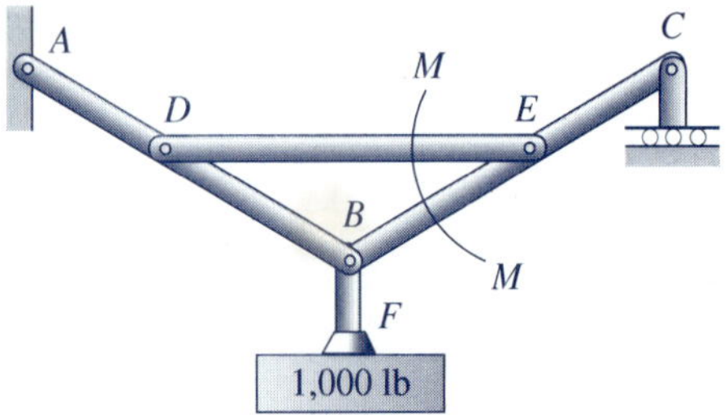

(a)

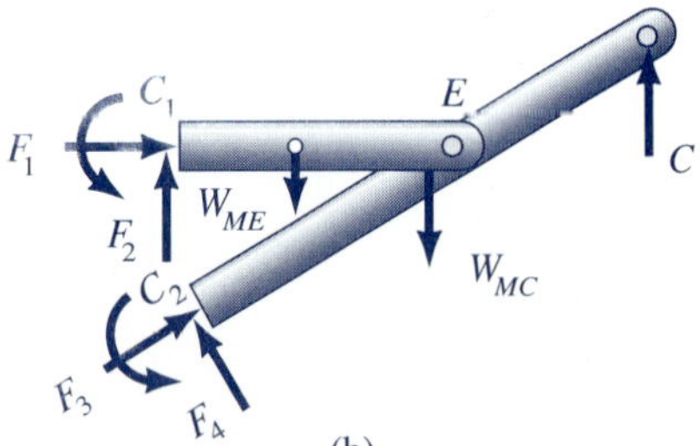

(b)

Figure 5.15. Cutting a frame to expose forces in certain members.

Example 5.2

Draw a free-body diagram of the beam *AB* and the frictionless pulley in Fig. 5.16 (a). The weight of the pulley is W_D, and the weight of the beam is W_{AB}.

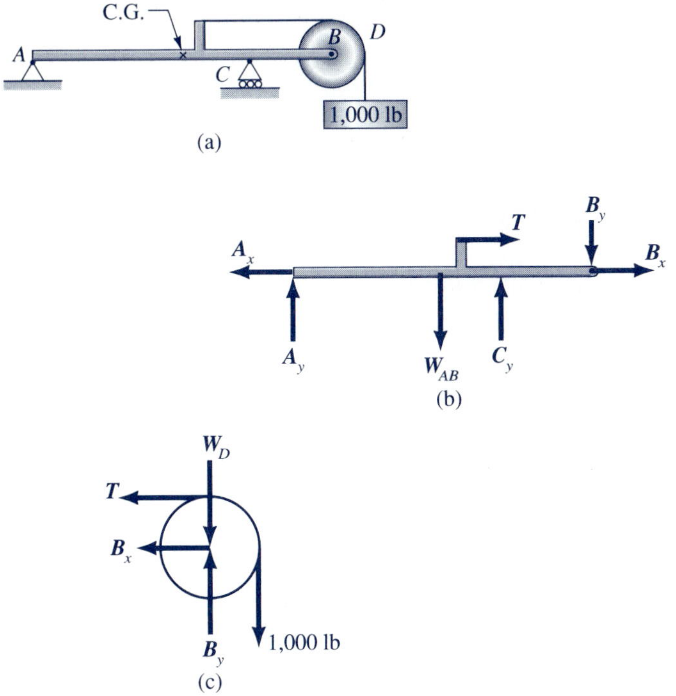

Figure 5.16. (a) Beam AB: (b) Free-body diagram of AB; (c) Free-body diagram of Pulley D

The free-body diagram of beam *AB* is shown in Fig. 5.16(b). The weight of the beam has been shown at its center of gravity. Components B_x and B_y are forces from the pulley *D* acting on the beam through the pin at *B*. The free-body diagram of the pulley is shown in Fig. 5.16(c).

Some students may be tempted to put the weight of the pulley at *B* in the free-body diagram of beam *AB*. The argument given is that this weight "goes through *B*." To put the pulley weight at *B* on free body *AB* is strictly speaking an error! The fact is that the weight of the pulley is a body force acting throughout the *pulley* and *does not* act on the *beam BD*. It so happens that the simplest resultant of this body force distribution on *D* goes through a *position* corresponding to pin *B*. This does not alter the fact that this weight acts *on the pulley* and *not on the beam*. The beam can only feel forces B_x and B_y transmitted from the pulley to the beam through pin *B*. These forces are related to the pulley weight as well as the tension in the cord around the pulley through equations of equilibrium for the free body

Example 5.3

We finish this series of free-body diagrams with a three-dimensional case. In Fig. 5.17(a) we show a structure having ball-joint connections at A and D, a fixed-end support at B and, finally, at C the column B resting directly on the foundation. Draw the free-body diagram for the structure.

We show the free body diagram for this case in Fig. 5.17(b).

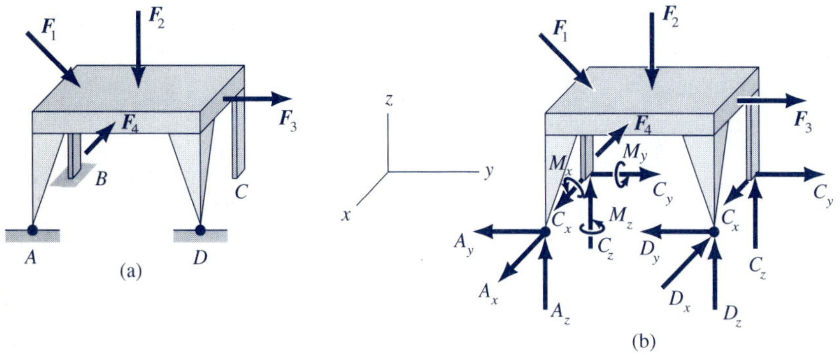

Figure 5.17. Three-dimensional structure with a free-body diagram.

*5.4 Looking Ahead—Control Volumes

In *rigid-body mechanics* we use the free body wherein we isolate a body or a portion of a body and we identify all the external forces acting on the body so that we can employ Newton's law.

In *fluid mechanics*, we may either make a free body of some chosen chunk of fluid (here it is called a system), but more likely it will be more profitable to identify some volume in space involving fluid flow through the volume. Such a volume is called a *control volume*. Here, as in the case of a free body, we must specify *all* the *external forces* such as tractions on the bounding surfaces of the control volume and, in addition, body forces on the material inside the control volume. This identification and force specification is needed to ensure, in appropriate equations, that Newton's law and other laws are satisfied for the fluid and other bodies inside the control volume at any time t.

Thus, you must develop sensitivity at this early stage of your studies in depicting external forces for a free body. The same care will be needed in your upcoming courses in fluid mechanics.

PROBLEMS

5.1. Draw the free-body diagram of the gas-grill lid when it is lifted at the handle to a 45° open position.

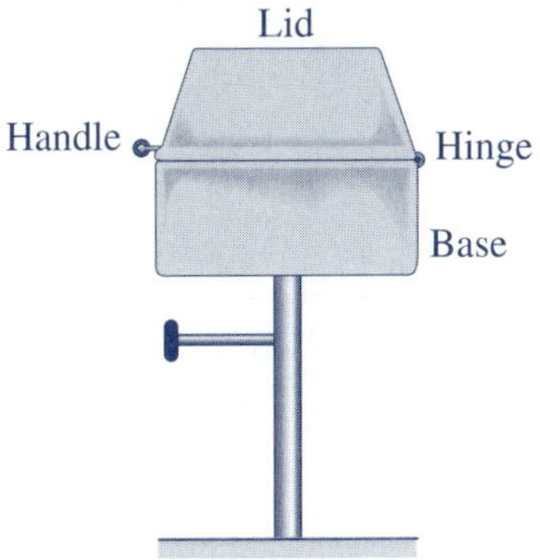

Figure P.5.1.

5.2. A large antenna is supported by three guy wires and rests on a large spherical ball joint. Draw the free-body diagram of the antenna.

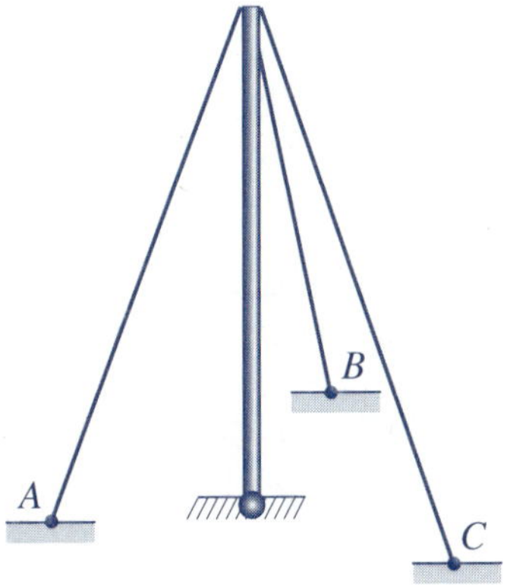

Figure P.5.2.

5.3. Draw a free-body diagram of the A-frame.

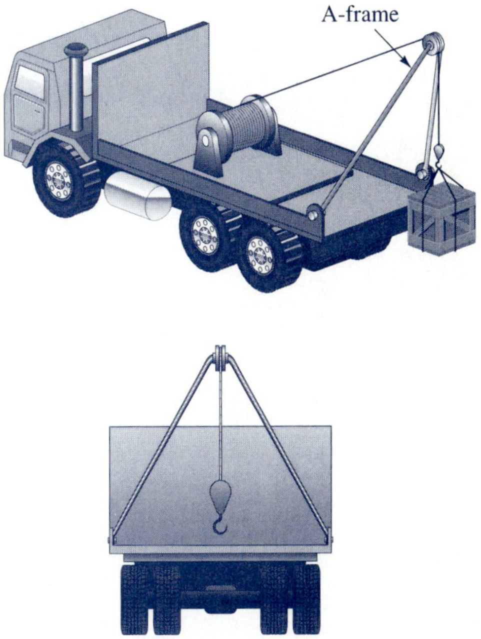

Figure P.5.3.

5.4. Draw complete free-body diagrams for the member *AB* and for cylinder *D*. Neglect friction at the contact surfaces of the cylinder. The weights of the cylinder and the member are denoted as W_D and W_{AB}, respectively.

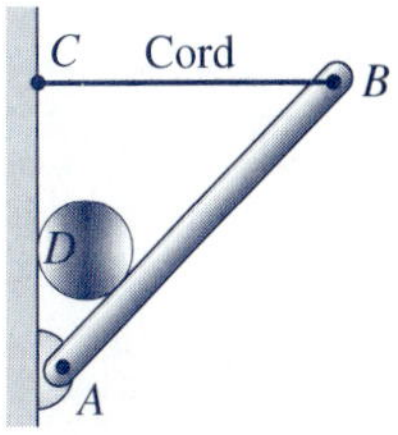

Figure P.5.4.

5.5. Draw free-body diagrams of the plate *ABCD* and the bar *EG*. Assume that there is no friction at the pulley *H* or at the contact surface *C*.

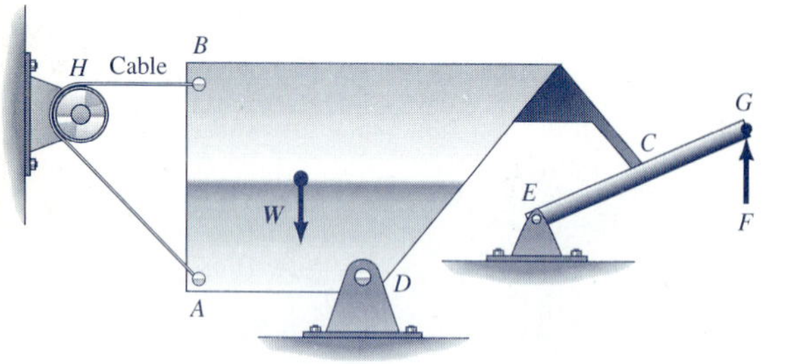

Figure P.5.5.

5.6. Draw the free-body diagram of one part of the two-piece posthole digger.

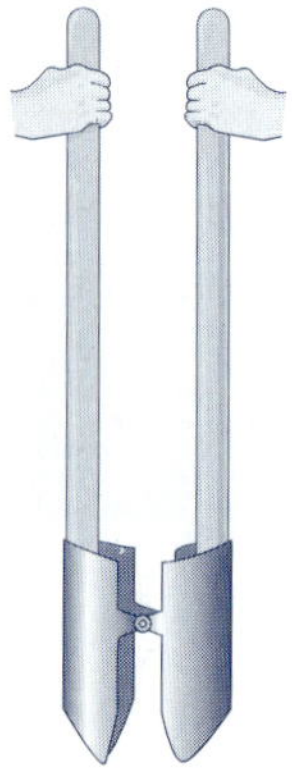

Figure P.5.6.

5.7. Draw a free-body diagram for each member of the system. Neglect the weights of the members. Replace the distributed load by a resultant.

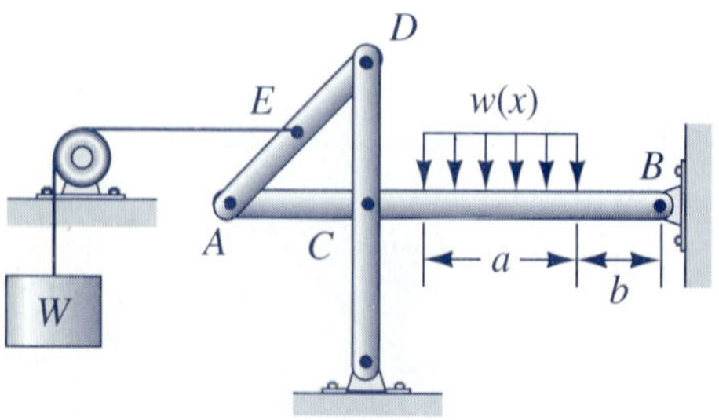

Figure P.5.7.

5.8. Draw the free-body diagrams for the oars of a rowboat when the rower pushes with one hand and pulls with the other (i.e., turns the boat).

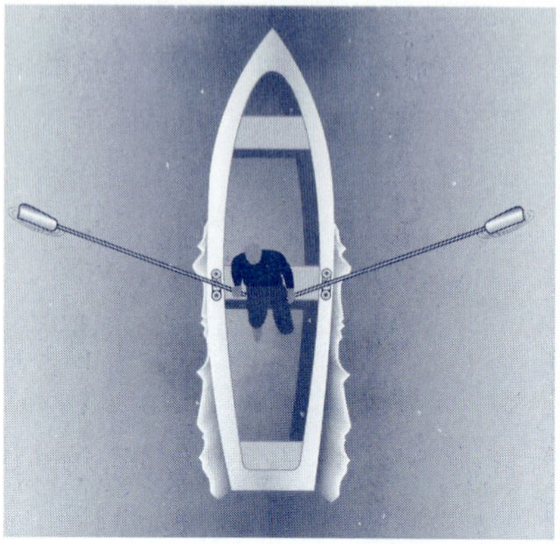

Figure P.5.8.

5.9. Draw a free-body diagram of the beam. Replace all distributions by simplest equivalent force systems. Neglect the weight of the beam.

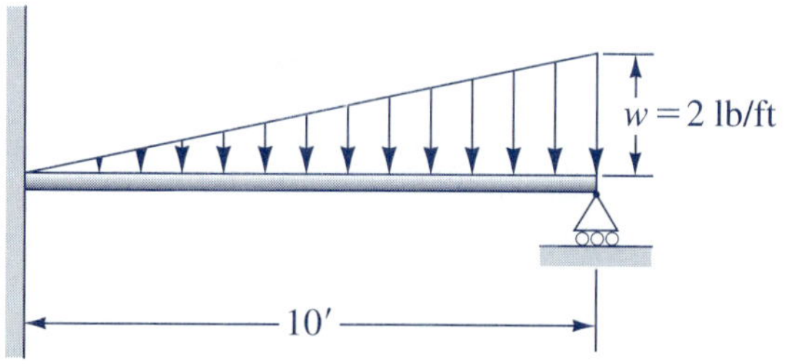

Figure P.5.9.

5.10. Two cantilever beams are pinned together at *A*. Draw free-body diagrams of each cantilever beam.

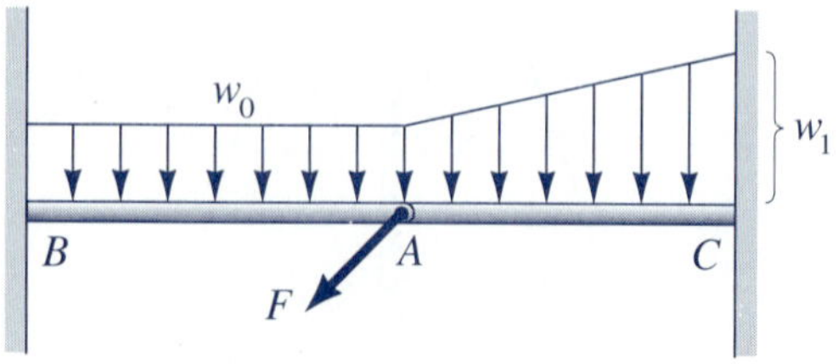

Figure P.5.10.

5.11. Draw free-body diagrams of each part of the tree-branch trimmer.

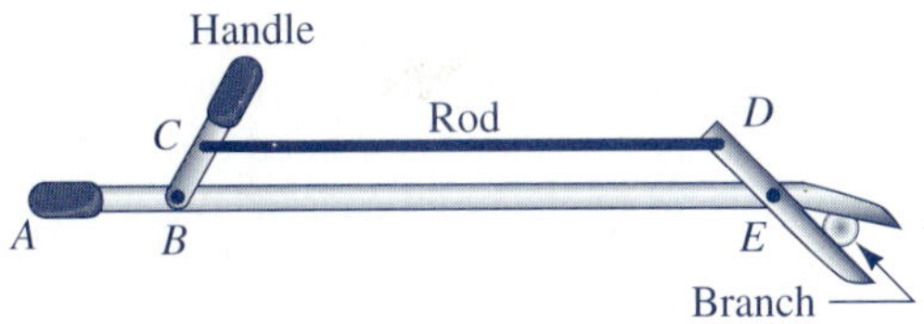

Figure P.5.11.

5.12. Draw free-body diagrams for the two booms and the body E of the power shovel. Consider the weight of each part to act at a central location. (Regard the shovel and payload as concentrated forces, W_S and W_{PL}, respectively.)

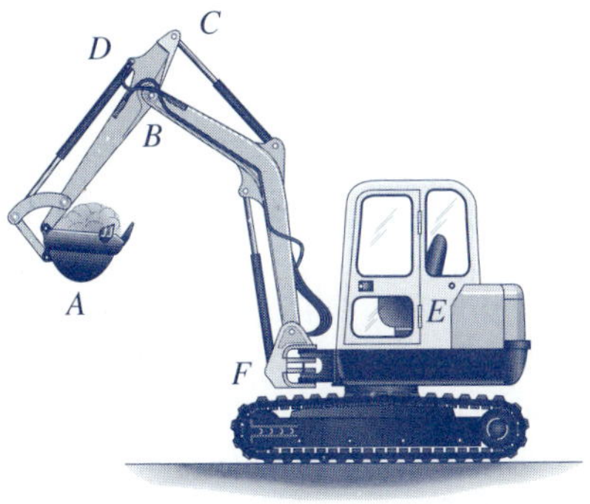

Figure P.5.12.

5.13. Draw the free-body diagram for the bulldozer, B, hydraulic ram, R, and tractor, T. Consider the weight of each part, B, R, and T.

Figure P.5.13.

5.14. Draw a free-body diagram of the whole apparatus and of each of its parts: AB, AC, BC, and D. Include the weights of all bodies. Label forces.

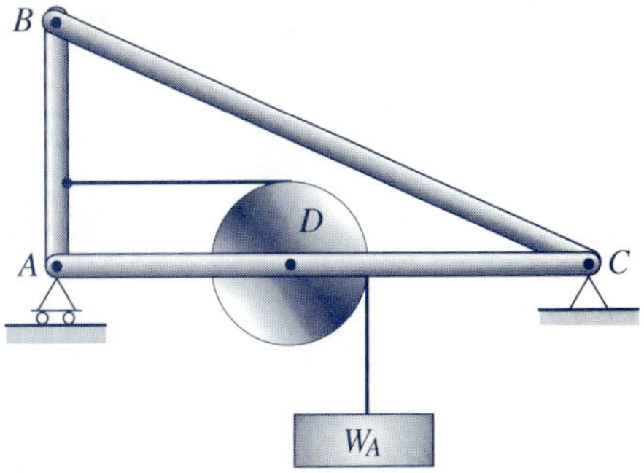

Figure P.5.14.

5.15. Draw a free-body diagram of members CG, AG, and the disc B. Include as the only weight that of disc B. Label all forces. (*Hint:* Consider the pin at G as a separate free body.)

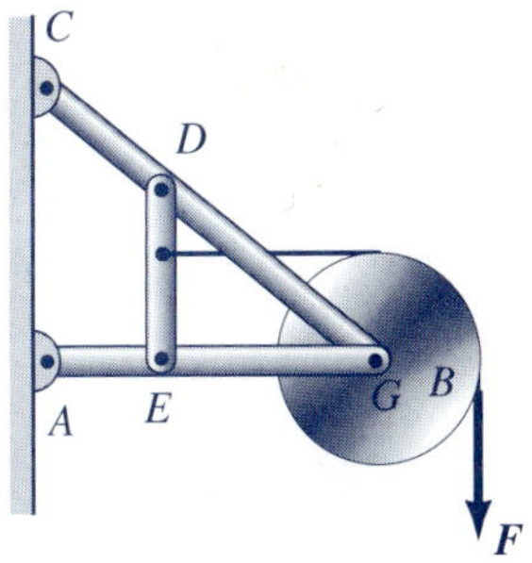

Figure P.5.15.

5.16. Draw the free-body diagram of the horizontally bent cantilevered beam. Use only xyz components of all vectors drawn.

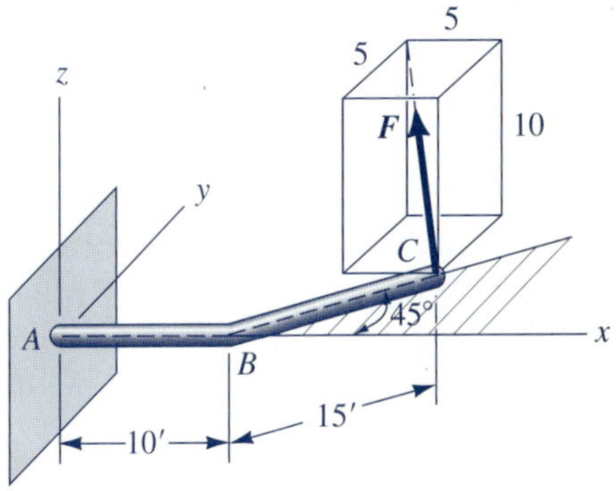

Figure P.5.16.

5.5 General Equations of Equilibrium

For every free-body diagram, we can replace the system of forces and couples acting on the body by a single force and a single couple moment at a point a. The force will have the same magnitude and direction, no matter where point a is chosen to move the entire system by methods discussed earlier. However, the couple-moment vector will depend on the point chosen. We will prove in dynamics that:

The necessary conditions for a rigid body to be in equilibrium are that the resultant force $\boldsymbol{F}_R$ and the resultant couple moment $\boldsymbol{C}_R$ for any point a be zero vectors.

That is,

$$\boldsymbol{F}_R = \boldsymbol{0} \tag{5.1a}$$
$$\boldsymbol{C}_R = \boldsymbol{0} \tag{5.1b}$$

We shall prove in dynamics, furthermore, that the conditions above are *sufficient* to maintain an *initially stationary* body in a state of equilibrium. These are the fundamental equations of statics. You will remember from Section 4.3 that the resultant $\boldsymbol{F}_R$ is the sum of the forces moved to the common point, and that the couple moment $\boldsymbol{C}_R$ is equal to the sum of the moments of all the original forces and couples taken about this point. Hence, the equations above can be written

$$\sum_i \boldsymbol{F}_i = \boldsymbol{0} \tag{5.2a}$$
$$\sum_i \boldsymbol{\rho}_i \times \boldsymbol{F}_i + \sum_i \boldsymbol{C}_i = \boldsymbol{0} \tag{5.2b}$$

where the $\boldsymbol{\rho}_i$'s are displacement vectors from the common point a to any point on the lines of action of the respective forces. From this form of the equations of statics, we can conclude that for equilibrium to exist, *the vector sum of the forces must be zero and the moment of the system of forces and couples about any point in space must be zero*.

Now that we have summed forces and have taken moments about a point a, we will demonstrate that we cannot find another *independent* equation by taking moments about a *different* point b. For the body in Fig. 5.18, we have initially the following equations of equilibrium using point a:

$$\boldsymbol{F}_1 + \boldsymbol{F}_2 + \boldsymbol{F}_3 + \boldsymbol{F}_4 = \boldsymbol{0} \tag{5.3}$$

$$\boldsymbol{\rho}_1 \times \boldsymbol{F}_1 + \boldsymbol{\rho}_2 \times \boldsymbol{F}_2 + \boldsymbol{\rho}_3 \times \boldsymbol{F}_3 + \boldsymbol{\rho}_4 \times \boldsymbol{F}_4 = \boldsymbol{0} \tag{5.4}$$

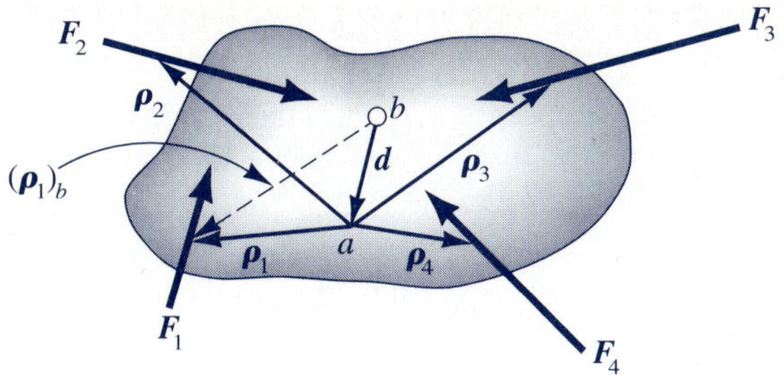

Figure 5.18. Consider moments about point b.

The new point b is separated from a by the position vector $\boldsymbol{d}$. The position vector (shown dashed) from b to the line of action of the force F_1 can be given in terms of $\boldsymbol{d}$ and the displacement vector $\boldsymbol{\rho}_1$ as follows. Similarly for $(\boldsymbol{\rho}_2)_b$, which is not shown, and others.

$$(\boldsymbol{\rho}_1)_b = (\boldsymbol{d} + \boldsymbol{\rho}_1)$$
$$(\boldsymbol{\rho}_2)_b = (\boldsymbol{d} + \boldsymbol{\rho}_2), \quad \text{etc.}$$

The moment equation for point b can then be given as

$$(\boldsymbol{\rho}_1 + \boldsymbol{d}) \times \boldsymbol{F}_1 + (\boldsymbol{\rho}_2 + \boldsymbol{d}) \times \boldsymbol{F}_2 + (\boldsymbol{\rho}_3 + \boldsymbol{d}) \times \boldsymbol{F}_3 + (\boldsymbol{\rho}_4 + \boldsymbol{d}) \times \boldsymbol{F}_4 = \boldsymbol{0}$$

Using the distributive rule for cross products, we can restate this equation as

$$\begin{aligned}(\boldsymbol{\rho}_1 \times \boldsymbol{F}_1 + \boldsymbol{\rho}_2 \times \boldsymbol{F}_2 + \boldsymbol{\rho}_3 \times \boldsymbol{F}_3 + \boldsymbol{\rho}_4 \times \boldsymbol{F}_4)\\ + \boldsymbol{d} \times (\boldsymbol{F}_1 + \boldsymbol{F}_2 + \boldsymbol{F}_3 + \boldsymbol{F}_4) = \boldsymbol{0}\end{aligned} \tag{5.5}$$

Since the expression in the second set of parentheses is zero, in accordance with Eq. 5.3, the remaining portion degenerates to Eq. 5.4, and thus we have not introduced a new equation. Therefore, *there are only two independent vector equations of equilibrium for any single free body.*

We shall now show that instead of using Eqs. 5.3 and 5.4 as the equations of equilibrium, we can instead use Eqs. 5.4 and 5.5. That is, instead of summing forces and then taking moments about a point for equilibrium, we can instead take moments about *two* points. Thus, if Eq. 5.4 is satisfied for point a, then for point b we end up in Eq. 5.5 with

$$\boldsymbol{d} \times (\boldsymbol{F}_1 + \boldsymbol{F}_2 + \boldsymbol{F}_3 + \boldsymbol{F}_4) = \boldsymbol{0} \tag{5.6}$$

If point b can be any point in space making $\boldsymbol{d}$ arbitrary, then the above equation indicates that the vector sum of forces is zero. If a point b happens to be chosen making Eq. (5.6) identically $0 = 0$, (and hence useless), choose another point b. We then have equilibrium since $\boldsymbol{F}_R = \boldsymbol{0}$ and $\boldsymbol{C}_R = \boldsymbol{0}$.

Using the vector Eqs. 5.2, we can now express the scalar equations of equilibrium. Since, as you will recall, the rectangular components of the moment of a force about a point are the moments of the force about the orthogonal axes at the point, we may state these equations in the following manner:

$$\sum_i (F_x)_i = 0 \quad \text{(a)} \qquad \sum_i (M_x)_i = 0 \quad \text{(d)}$$
$$\sum_i (F_y)_i = 0 \quad \text{(b)} \qquad \sum_i (M_y)_i = 0 \quad \text{(e)} \qquad (5.7)$$
$$\sum_i (F_z)_i = 0 \quad \text{(c)} \qquad \sum_i (M_z)_i = 0 \quad \text{(f)}$$

From this set of equations, it is clear that *no more than six unknown scalar quantities in the general case can be solved by methods of statics for a single free body.*[3]

We can easily express *any number* of scalar equations of equilibrium for a free body by selecting references that have different axis directions, along which we can sum forces and about which we can take moments. However, in choosing six *independent* equations, we will find that the remaining equations will be dependent on these six. That is, these equations will be sums, differences, etc., of the independent set and so will be of no use in solving for desired unknowns other than for purposes of checking calculations.

5.6 Problems of Equilibrium I

We shall now examine problems of equilibrium in which the rigid-body assumption is valid. To solve such problems, we must find the value of certain unknown forces and couple moments. We first draw a free-body diagram of the entire system or portions thereof to clearly *expose* pertinent unknowns for analysis. We then write the equilibrium equations in terms of the unknowns along with the known forces and geometry. As we have seen, for any free body there is a limited number of independent scalar equations of equilibrium. Thus, at times we must employ several free-body diagrams for portions of the system to produce enough independent equations to solve all the unknowns.

For any free body, we may proceed by expressing two basic vector equations of statics. After carrying out such vector operations as cross products and additions in the equations, we form scalar equations. These scalar equations are then solved simultaneously (together with scalar equations from other free-body diagrams that may be needed) to find the unknown forces and

[3]Keep in mind that we can also take moments about two sets of axes just as we could take moments about two points for the vector equations of equilibrium. The two sets of axes like the two points must be chosen properly so as to yield *independent* scalar equations. This can readily be done. If your second point and associated axes do not yield three additional independent equations, select another point and axes until you have your six independent equations of equilibrium.

couple moments. We can also express the scalar equations immediately by using the alternative scalar equilibrium relations that we formulated in previous sections. In the first case, we start with more compact vector equations and arrive at the expanded scalar equations by the formal procedures of vector algebra. In the latter case, we evaluate the expanded scalar equations by carrying out arithmetic operations on the free-body diagram as we write the equations. Which procedure is more desirable? It all depends on the problem and the investigator's skill in vector manipulation. It is true that many statics problems submit easily to a direct scalar approach, but the more challenging problems of statics and dynamics definitely favor an initial vector approach. In this text, we shall employ the particular procedure that the occasion warrants.

In statics problems, we must assign a sense to each component of an unknown force or couple moment in order to write the equations. If, on solving the equations, *we obtain a negative sign for a component, then we have guessed the wrong sense for that component*. Nothing need be redone should this occur. Continue with the remainder of the problem, retaining the minus sign (or signs). At the end of the problem, report the correct sense of your force components and couple-moment components.

We shall now solve and discuss a number of problems of equilibrium. These problems are divided into four classes of force systems:

1. Concurrent.
2. Coplanar.
3. Parallel.
4. General.

The type of *simplest* resultant for each special system of forces is most useful in determining the number of scalar equations available in a given problem. The procedure is to classify the force system, note what simplest resultant force system is associated with the classification, and then consider the number of scalar equations necessary and sufficient to guarantee this resultant to be zero. The following cases exemplify this procedure.

Case A. Concurrent System of Forces. In this case, since the simplest resultant is a single force at the point of concurrency, the only requirement for equilibrium is that this force be zero. We can ensure this condition if the orthogonal components of this force are separately equal to zero. Thus, we have *three* equations of equilibrium of the form

$$\sum_i (F_x)_i = 0, \qquad \sum_i (F_y)_i = 0, \qquad \sum_i (F_z)_i = 0 \qquad (5.8)$$

As was pointed out in the general vector discussion, there are other ways of ensuring a zero resultant. Suppose that the moments of the concurrent force system are zero about three nonparallel axes: α, β, and γ. That is,

$$\sum_i (M_\alpha)_i = 0, \qquad \sum_i (M_\beta)_i = 0, \qquad \sum_i (M_\gamma)_i = 0 \qquad (5.9)$$

Any one of the following three conditions must then be true:

1. The resultant force F_R is zero.
2. F_R cuts all three axes (see Fig. 5.19).
3. F_R cuts two axes and is parallel to the third (see Fig. 5.20).

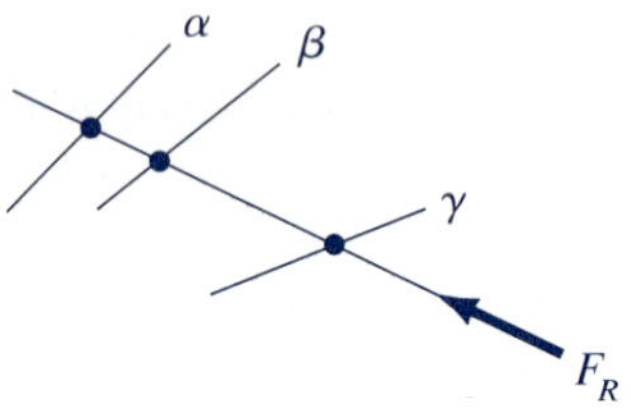

Figure 5.19. F_R cuts three axes.

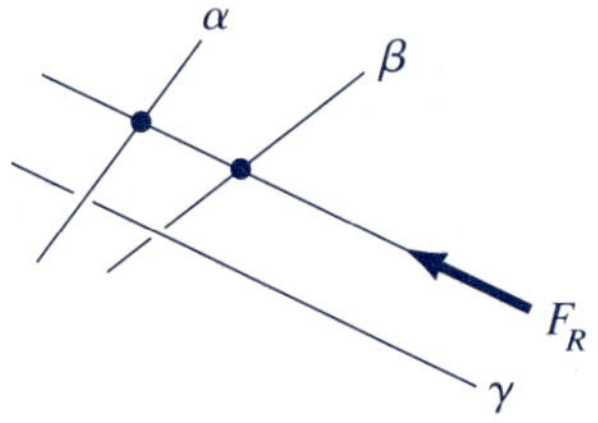

Figure 5.20. F_R cuts two axes and is parallel to third.

We can guarantee condition 1 and thus equilibrium if we select axes α, β, and γ so that no straight line can intersect all three axes or can cut two axes and be parallel to the third. Then we can use Eqs. 5.9 as the equations of equilibrium under the aforestated conditions rather than using Eqs. 5.8. What happens if an axis used violates these conditions? The resulting equation will either be an *identity* $0 = 0$ or will be dependent on a previous independent equation of equilibrium for one of the axes. No harm is done. One should use other axes until three independent equations are found.

Similarly, one can sum forces in one direction and take moments about two axes. Setting these equal to zero can yield three independent equations of equilibrium. If not, use other axes.

The essential conclusion to be drawn is that *there are three independent scalar equations of equilibrium for a concurrent force system.* For such systems it is most likely that you will always sum forces rather than take moments. However, for other force systems that we shall undertake, there will be ample opportunity to profitably employ alternate forms of equations other than those that we shall at first prescribe. The important thing to remember is that, just as in the concurrent force systems, only a definite number of equations for a given free body will be independent. Simply writing more equations beyond this number will only lead to identities and equations that will be of no use for solving for the desired unknowns.

Example 5.4

What are the tensions in cables AC and AB in Fig. 5.21? The system is in equilibrium. The following data apply:

$$W = 1{,}000 \text{ N} \qquad \beta = 50° \qquad \alpha = 37°$$

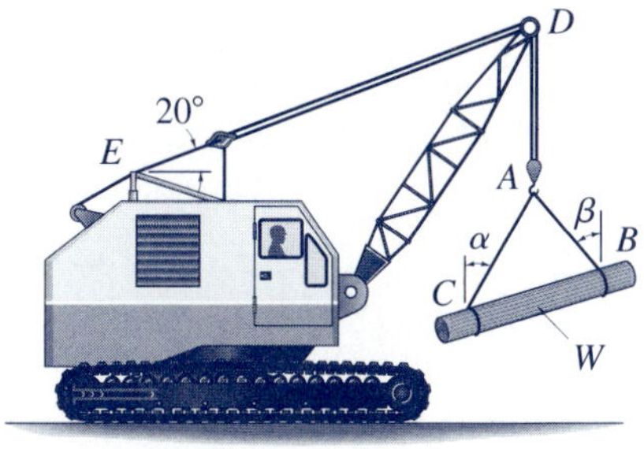

Figure 5.21. Derrick holding a beam.

Immediately it should be clear from observation of the diagram that

$$T_{AD} = 1{,}000 \text{ N (tension)}$$

A suitable free body that exposes the desired unknowns is the ring A, which may be considered as a particle for this computation because of its comparatively small size (Fig. 5.22). Physical intuition indicates that the cables are in tension and hence pulling away from A as we have indicated in the diagram although, as mentioned previously, it is *not* necessary to recognize at the outset the correct sense of an unknown force. The force system acting on the particle must be a concurrent system. Here it is also coplanar as well, and therefore we may solve for only two unknowns. Hence, we can proceed to the scalar equations of equilibrium. Thus,

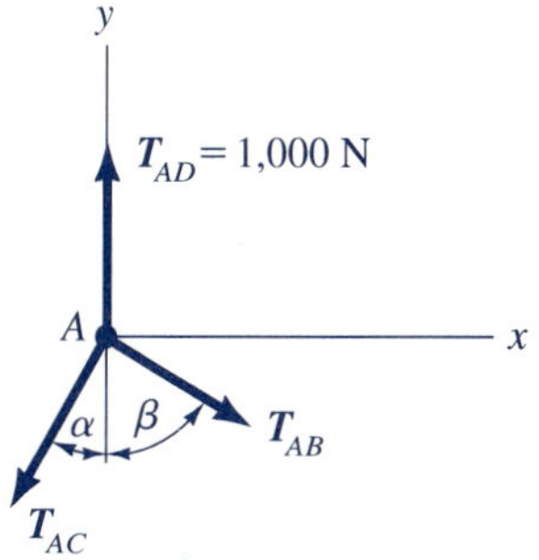

Figure 5.22. Free-body diagram of pin A.

$$\underline{\sum F_y = 0} \qquad 1{,}000 - T_{AC}\cos 37° - T_{AB}\cos 50° = 0$$

$$\therefore\ .7986T_{AC} + .6428T_{AB} = 1{,}000 \qquad \text{(a)}$$

$$\underline{\sum F_x = 0} \qquad -T_{AC}\sin\alpha - T_{AB}\sin\beta = 0$$

$$\therefore\ T_{AC} = 1.2729T_{AB} \qquad \text{(b)}$$

Solving for T_{AC} and T_{AB} from Eqs. (a) and (b), we get

$$T_{AB} = 602.6 \text{ N} \qquad T_{AC} = 767.1 \text{ N}$$

Since the signs for T_{AC} and T_{AB} are positive, we have chosen the correct senses for the forces in the free-body diagram.

Example 5.4 (Continued)

Another way of arriving at the solution, is to consider the *force polygon* that was discussed in Section 2.3. Because the forces are in equilibrium, the polygon must close; that is, the head of the final force must coincide with the tail of the initial force. In this case, we have a triangle, as shown in Fig. 5.23 approximately to scale. We can now use the law of sines.

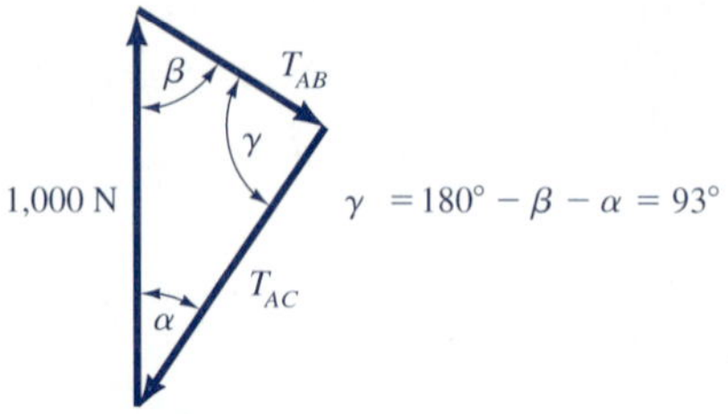

Figure 5.23. Force polygon.

$$\frac{T_{AB}}{\sin 37°} = \frac{1{,}000}{\sin 93°} \qquad T_{AB} = 602.6 \text{ N}$$

$$\frac{T_{AC}}{\sin 50°} = \frac{1{,}000}{\sin 93°} \qquad T_{AC} = 767.1 \text{ N}$$

The force polygon may thus be used to good advantage when three concurrent coplanar forces are in equilibrium.

As a final alternative, let us now initiate the computation for the unknown tensions from the basic *vector* equations of statics. First, we must express all forces in vector notation.

$$\boldsymbol{T}_{AC} = T_{AC}\,(-\sin 37°\,\boldsymbol{i} - \cos 37°\,\boldsymbol{j})$$

$$\boldsymbol{T}_{AB} = T_{AB}\,(\sin 50°\,\boldsymbol{i} - \cos 50°\,\boldsymbol{j})$$

We get the following equation when the vector sum of the forces is set equal to zero:

$$T_{AC}\,(-.6018\boldsymbol{i} - .7986\boldsymbol{j}) + T_{AB}\,(.7660\boldsymbol{i} - .6428\boldsymbol{j}) + 1{,}000\boldsymbol{j} = \boldsymbol{0}$$

Choosing point *A*, the point of concurrency, we clearly see that the sum of moments of the forces about this point is zero, so the second basic equation of equilibrium is intrinsically satisfied. We now regroup the terms of the preceding equation in the following manner:

$$(-.6018T_{AC} + .7660T_{AB})\boldsymbol{i} + (-.7986T_{AC} - .6428T_{AB} + 1{,}000)\boldsymbol{j} = \boldsymbol{0}$$

To satisfy this equation, each of the quantities in parentheses must be zero. This gives the scalar equations (a) and (b) stated earlier, from which the scalar quantities T_{AB} and T_{AC} can be solved.

The three alternative methods of solution are apparently of equal usefulness in this simple problem. However, the force polygon is only of practical use for three concurrent coplanar forces, where the trigonometric properties of a triangle can be directly used. The other methods can be readily extended to more complex concurrent problems.

Example 5.5

Find the forces in cables *DB* and *CB* in Fig. 5.24. The 500-N force is parallel to the *y* axis. Consider *B* to be a ball joint located in the *xz* plane. Rod *AB* is a compression member, with a ball joint at *A*.

In Fig. 5.25 we have indicated the forces acting on joint *B*. Clearly we have a three-dimensional concurrent force system with three unknowns. We can readily determine the unknown forces here by simply setting the sum of the forces equal to zero. However, since we only want the forces in the two cables, we shall proceed by setting the moment of the forces about point *A* of rod *AB* equal to zero, thereby not including the force in member *AB*.

Denoting the force in *BC* as T_C and the force in *BD* as T_D, we proceed now to establish the rectangular components of these forces.

$$\boldsymbol{T}_C = T_C\left(\frac{-15\boldsymbol{i} + 9\boldsymbol{j} + 5\boldsymbol{k}}{\sqrt{15^2 + 9^2 + 5^2}}\right) = T_C(-.824\boldsymbol{i} + .495\boldsymbol{j} + .275\boldsymbol{k})\text{ N}$$

$$\boldsymbol{T}_D = T_D\left(\frac{-15\boldsymbol{i} + 5\boldsymbol{j} + 13\boldsymbol{k}}{\sqrt{15^2 + 5^2 + 13^2}}\right) = T_D(-.733\boldsymbol{i} + .244\boldsymbol{j} + .635\boldsymbol{k})\text{ N}$$

The position vector that we shall use for the moment about point *A* is $\boldsymbol{r}_{AB}$, which is

$$\boldsymbol{r}_{AB} = 15\boldsymbol{i} + 5\boldsymbol{j} - 5\boldsymbol{k}\text{ m}$$

We now set the moments about point *A* equal to zero.

$$\sum M_A = \boldsymbol{0}$$

$$(15\boldsymbol{i} + 5\boldsymbol{j} - 5\boldsymbol{k}) \times [T_C(-.824\boldsymbol{i} + .495\boldsymbol{j} + .275\boldsymbol{k}) +$$
$$T_D(-.733\boldsymbol{i} + .244\boldsymbol{j} + .635\boldsymbol{k}) - 500\boldsymbol{j}] = \boldsymbol{0}$$

We simplify the calculations further by noting that cable *BD* has a direction inclined to the plane *ACB* in which the other three forces lie. This can only mean that the force T_D must have a zero value. Hence, deleting this force in the above equation and carrying out the cross products, it is easy to get the remaining nonzero force. We thus have

$$T_C = 649\text{ N} \qquad T_D = 0\text{ N}$$

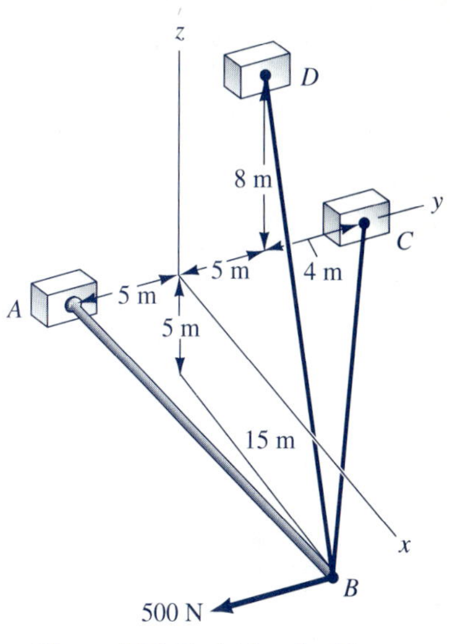

Figure 5.24. Rod *AB* and cables *CB* and *DB* support a 500-lb force.

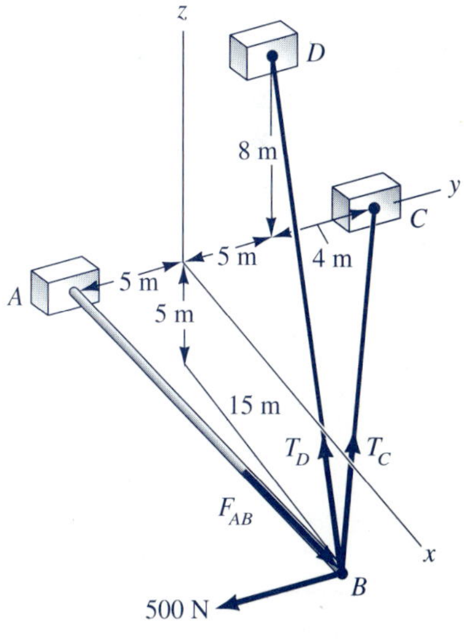

Figure 5.25. Free-body diagram of joint *B*.

Example 5.5 (Continued)

Finally, as indicated at the outset, we could proceed by summing forces in the coordinate directions. The resulting scalar equations for all three unknown forces are

$$\begin{aligned} -0.824T_C - 0.733T_D + 0.905T_A &= 0 \\ 0.495T_C + 0.244T_D + 0.302T_A &= 500 \\ 0.275T_C + 0.635T_D - 0.302T_A &= 0 \end{aligned}$$

We may now solve the simultaneous equations using *Cramer's rule*. Thus we calculate first the determinant of the coefficients of the unknowns. Thus

$$\begin{vmatrix} -0.824 & -0.733 & 0.905 \\ 0.495 & 0.244 & 0.302 \\ 0.275 & 0.635 & -0.302 \end{vmatrix} = 0.272$$

To calculate T_C we proceed as follows:

$$T_C = \frac{\begin{vmatrix} 0 & -0.733 & 0.905 \\ 500 & 0.244 & 0.302 \\ 0 & 0.635 & 0.302 \end{vmatrix}}{0.272} = 649 \text{ N}$$

Note that the first column of the determinant consists of the right side terms of the set of simultaneous equations in place of the coefficients of the desired unknown. We can solve for the other unknowns similarly. We then would have the compressive force in member *AB* which is 591 N.

Case B. Coplanar Forces System. We have shown that the simplest resultant for a coplanar force system (see Fig. 4.14) is a single force or a single couple moment normal to the plane. Thus, to ensure that the resultant force is zero, we require for a coplanar system in which all forces are in the *xy* plane:

$$\sum_i (F_x)_i = 0, \qquad \sum_i (F_y)_i = 0 \tag{5.10}$$

To ensure that the resultant couple moment is zero, we require for moments about any axis parallel to the *z* axis:

$$\sum_i (M_z)_i = 0 \tag{5.11}$$

We conclude that there are *three* scalar equations of equilibrium for a coplanar force system. Other combinations, such as two moment equations for two axes parallel to the *z* axis and a single force summation, if properly chosen, may be employed to give the three independent scalar equations of equilibrium, as was discussed in case A.

Example 5.6

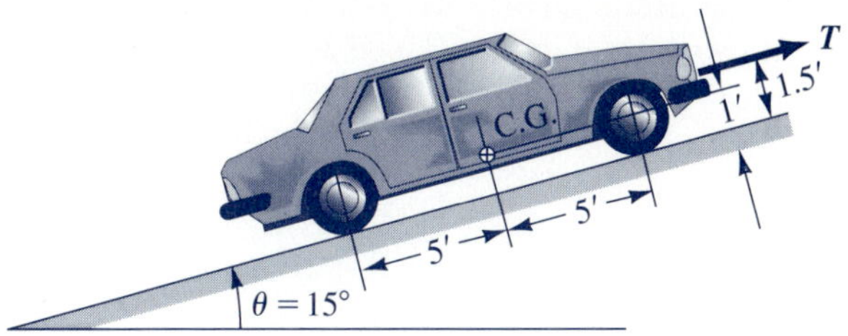

Figure 5.26. A car is being towed up an incline at a constant speed.

A car shown in Fig. 5.26 is being towed at a steady speed up an incline having an angle of 15°. The car weighs 3,600 lb. The center of gravity is located as is shown in the diagram. Calculate the supporting force on each wheel and force *T*.

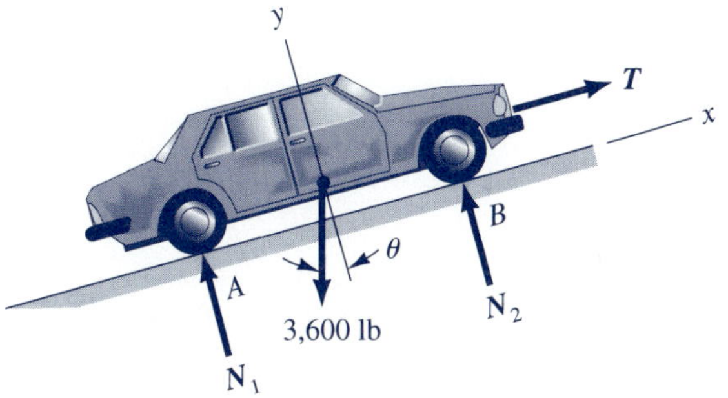

Figure 5.27. Free-body diagram of the car.

A free-body diagram of the car is shown in Fig. 5.27. The forces N_1 and N_2 are the total forces, respectively, for the rear wheels and the front wheels. Note, because the wheels are rotating at constant speed, there are no friction forces present. We have thus formed on this free body a *coplanar* force system involving three unknowns and hence the unknowns are solvable by rigid-body statics. Using axes tangent and normal to the incline we have

Example 5.6 (Continued)

$\underline{\sum F_x = 0}$ $\quad T - W\sin\theta = 0$

$$\therefore T = (3{,}600)(\sin 15°) = 931.7 \text{ lb}$$

$$\boxed{\text{T} = 931.7 \text{ lb}}$$

$\underline{\sum F_y = 0}$ $\quad N_1 + N_2 - W\cos\theta = 0$

$$\therefore N_1 + N_2 = (3{,}600)(\cos 15°) = 3{,}477 \text{ lb} \qquad (1)$$

$\underline{\sum M_A = 0}$ $\quad (N_2)(10) + (W\sin\theta)(1) - (W\cos\theta)(5) - (T)(1.5) = 0$

$$\therefore N_2 = \frac{1}{10}[-(3{,}600)(\sin 15°)(1) + (3{,}600)(\cos 15°)(5)$$

$$+(931.7)(1.5)] = 1{,}785 \text{ lb}$$

From Eq.(1), we can now get N_1. Thus

$$N_1 = 3{,}477 - N_2 = 3{,}477 - 1{,}785 = 1{,}692 \text{ lb}$$

Clearly each rear wheel has acting on it a normal force of $N_1/2 = 846.1$ lb and each front wheel has a normal force of $N_2/2 = 892.5$ lb.

∴ Rear wheel support force = 846.1 lb
Front wheel support force = 892.5 lb

We may now check this solution by using a redundant equation of equilibrium. Thus

$\underline{\sum M_B \overset{?}{=} 0}$

$$-(N_1)(10) + (W\sin\theta)(1) - (W\cos\theta)(5) - (T)(1.5) = 0$$

$$\therefore -(1{,}692)(10) + (3{,}600)(\sin 15°)(1) +$$

$$(3{,}600)(\cos 15°)(5) - (931.7)(1.5)] = 0$$

$$.8634 \approx 0$$

We have here a roundoff error, which we can accept for the accuracy of the calculations taken in this problem.

Example 5.7

A frame is shown in Fig. 5.28 in which the frictionless pulley at D has a mass of 200 kg. Neglecting the weights of the bars, find the force transmitted from one bar to the other at joint C.

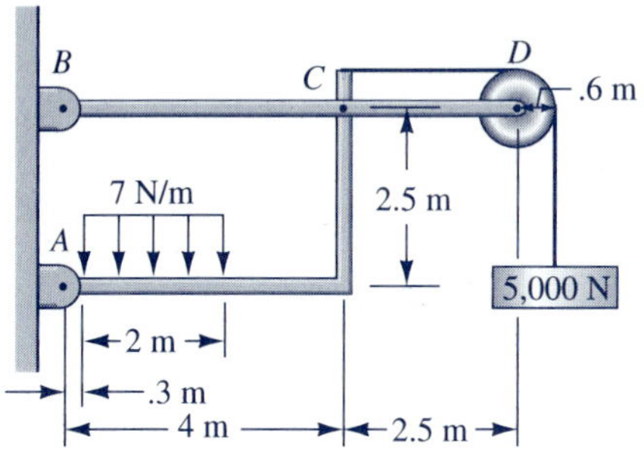

Figure 5.28. Loaded frame.

To expose force components C_x and C_y, we form the free body of bar BD. This is shown as F.B.D. I in Fig. 5.29. It is clear that for this free body we have six unknowns and only three independent equations of equilibrium.[4] The free-body diagram of the bent bar AC is then drawn (F.B.D. II in Fig. 5.29). Here, we have three more equations but we bring in three

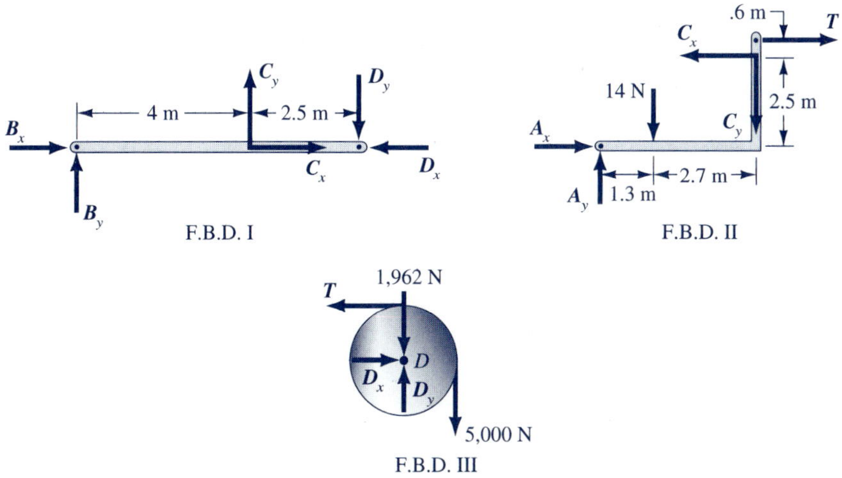

Figure 5.29. Free-body diagrams of frame parts.

[4]It should be noted that it is possible to have situations wherein there are more unknowns than independent equations of equilibrium for a given free body, but wherein some of the unknowns—perhaps the desired ones—can be still determined by the equations available. However, not all the unknowns of the free body can be solved. Accordingly, be alert for such situations, so as to minimize the work involved. In this case, we must consider other free-body diagrams.

Example 5.7 (Continued)

more unknowns. Finally, the free-body diagram of the pulley (F.B.D. III in Fig. 5.29) gives three more equations with no additional unknowns. We now have nine equations available and nine unknowns and can proceed with confidence. Since only two of the unknowns are desired, we shall take select scalar equations from each of the free-body diagrams to arrive at the components C_x and C_y most quickly.

From F.B.D. III:

$\sum M_D = 0$:

$$(T)(.6) - (5{,}000)(.6) = 0$$

Therefore,

$$T = 5{,}000 \text{ N}$$

$\sum F_x = 0$:

$$-T + D_x = 0$$

Therefore,

$$D_x = 5{,}000 \text{ N}$$

$\sum F_y = 0$:

$$-1{,}962 - 5{,}000 + D_y = 0$$

Therefore,

$$D_y = 6{,}962 \text{ N}$$

From F.B.D. I:

$\sum M_B = 0$:

$$(4)(C_y) - (6.5)(D_y) = 0$$

Therefore,

$$C_y = 11{,}313 \text{ N}$$

From F.B.D. II:

$\sum M_A = 0$:

$$-(1.3)(14) - (T)(3.1) - C_y(4) + C_x(2.5) = 0$$

Therefore,

$$C_x = 24{,}300 \text{ N}$$

We can give the force at C (transmitted from bar AC to bar BD) as

$$C = 24{,}300\boldsymbol{i} + 11.313\boldsymbol{j} \text{ N}$$

PROBLEMS

5.17. In a tug of war, when team *B* pulls with a 400-lb force, how much force must team *C* exert for a draw? With what force does team *A* pull?

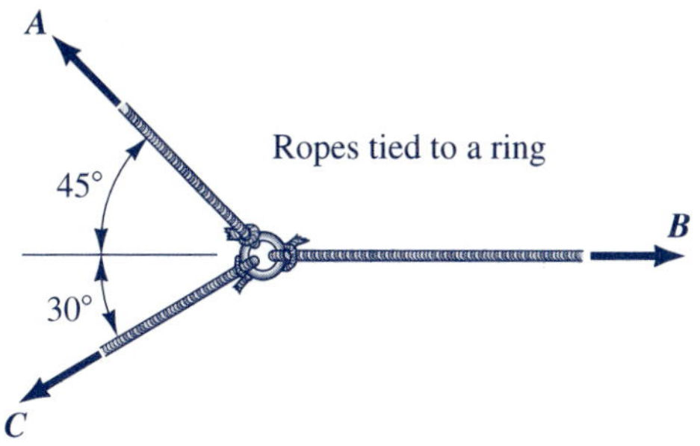

Figure P.5.17.

5.18. Find the tensile force in cables *AB* and *CB*. The remaining cables ride over frictionless pulleys *E* and *F*.

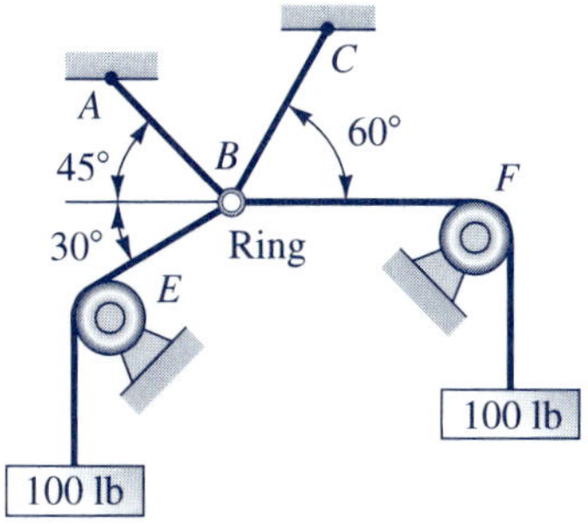

Figure P.5.18.

5.19. Find the force transmitted by wire *BC*. The pulley *E* can be assumed to be frictionless in this problem.

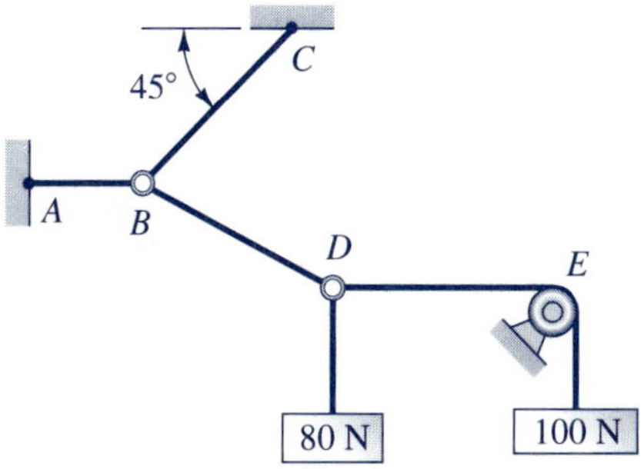

Figure P.5.19.

5.20. Find the tensions in the three cables connected to *B*. The entire system of cables is coplanar. The roller at *E* is free to turn without resistance.

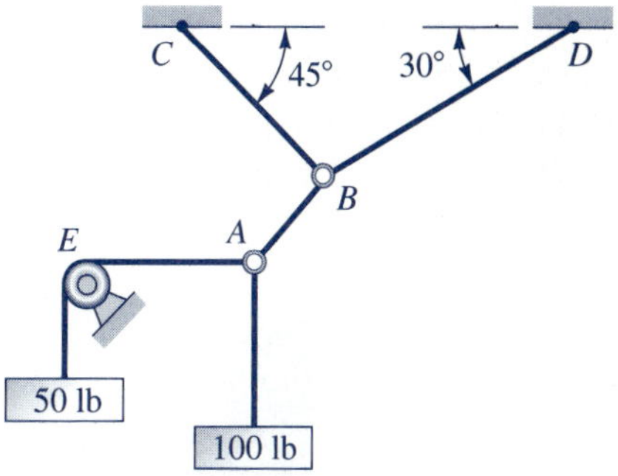

Figure P.5.20.

5.21. A 700-N circus performer causes a .15-m sag in the middle of a 12-m tightrope with a 5,000-N initial tension. What additional tension is induced in the cable? What is the cable tension when the performer is 3 m from the end and the sag is .12 m?

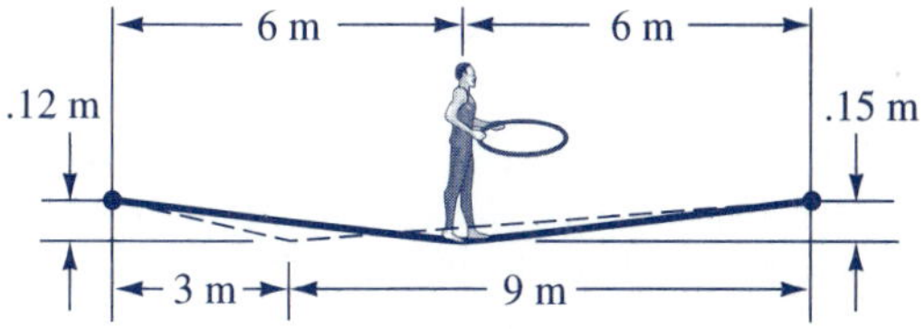

Figure P.5.21.

5.22. A 27-lb mirror is held up by a wire fastened to two hooks on the mirror frame. (a) What is the force on the wall hook and the tension in the wire? (b) If the wire will break at a tension of 32 lb, must the wall hook be moved (i.e., the wire lengthened or shortened and the 4-in. rise distance changed)? If so, to what point?

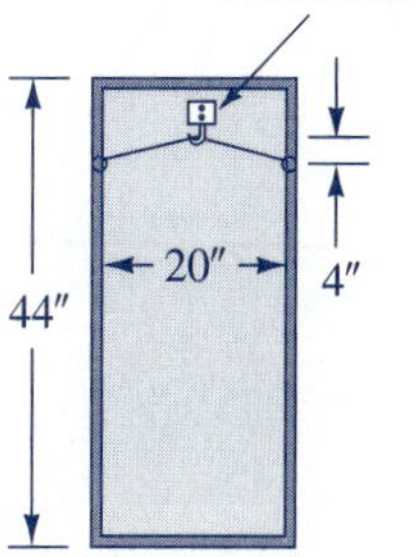

Figure P.5.22.

5.23. Explain why equilibrium of a concurrent force system is guaranteed by having $\sum_i (F_y)_i = 0$, $\sum_i (M_d)_i = 0$, and $\sum_i (M_e)_i = 0$. Axes d and e are not parallel to the xz plane. Moreover, the axes are oriented so that the line of action of the resultant force cannot intersect both axes.

5.24. Cylinders A and B weigh 500 N each and cylinder C weighs 1,000 N. Compute all contact forces.

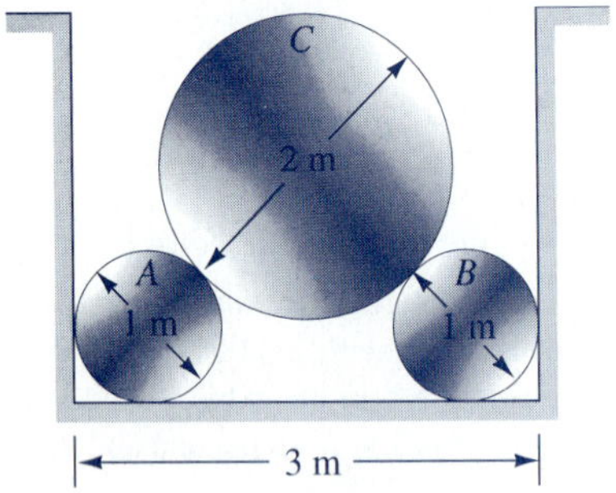

Figure P.5.24.

5.25. A block having a mass of 500 kg is held by five cables. What are the tensions in these cables? Lower cables are identical and are identically connected at ends.

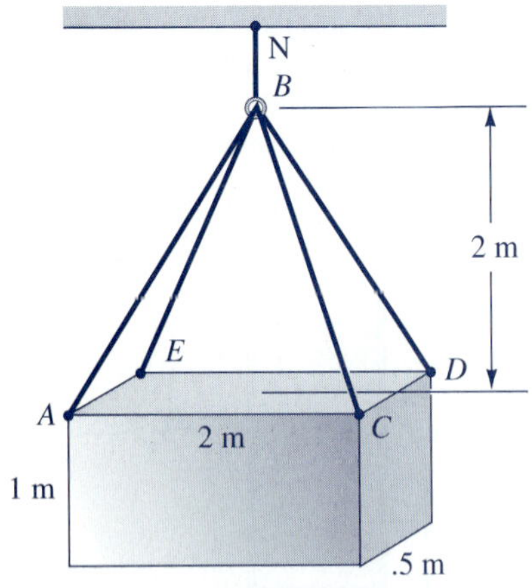

Figure P.5.25.

5.26. Gear D has a weight of 300 N while members AB and BC are light. What torque T is necessary for equilibrium?

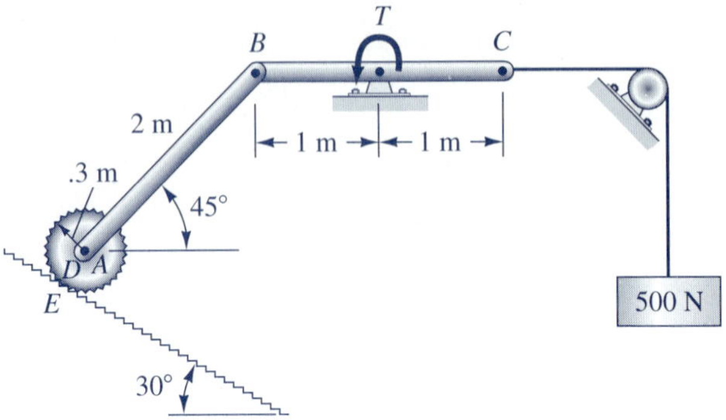

Figure P.5.26.

5.27. Find the supporting forces at A.

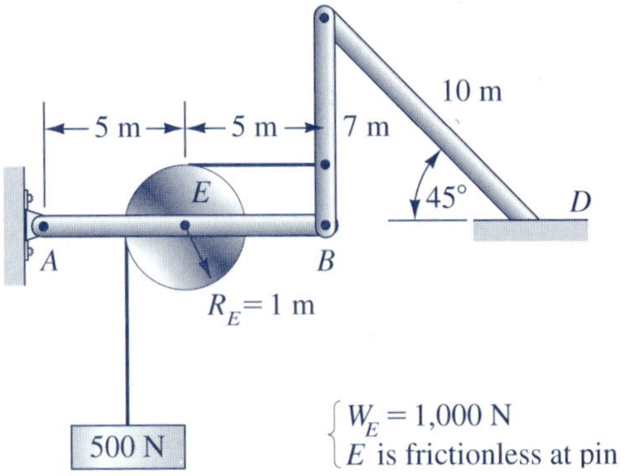

Figure P.5.27.

5.28. Find the supporting forces at A and B. At D there is a cylinder weighing 300 N.

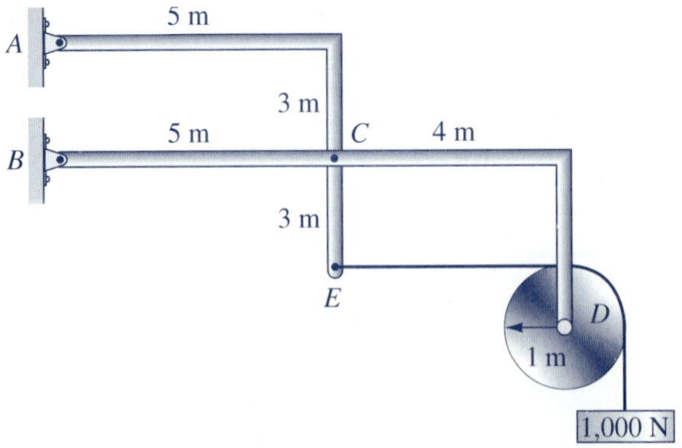

Figure P.5.28.

5.29. Find the supporting force systems for the beams shown. Note that there is a *pin connection* at *C*. Neglect the weights of the beams.

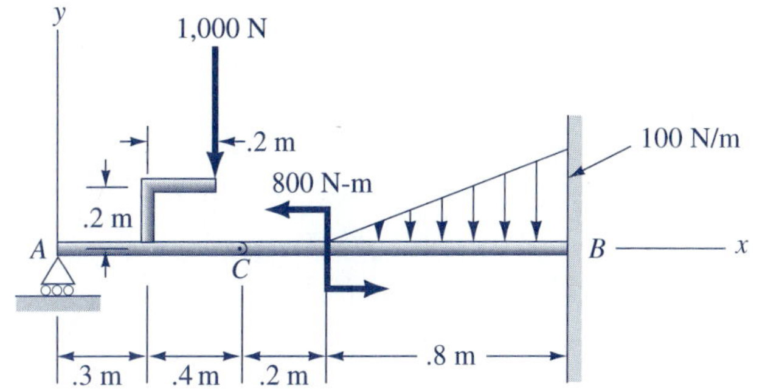

Figure P.5.29.

5.30. Find the supporting force systems at *A* and *B*. The length of *CB* is 8 m.

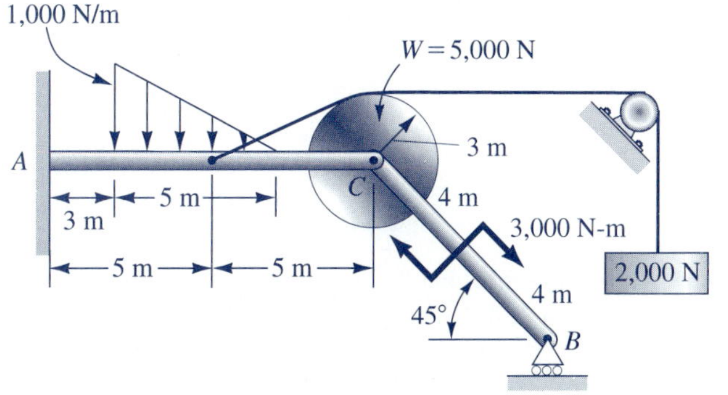

Figure P.5.30.

5.31. What are the supporting forces at *A* and *D* for the frame shown? What are the forces in members *AB*, *BE*, and *BC*?

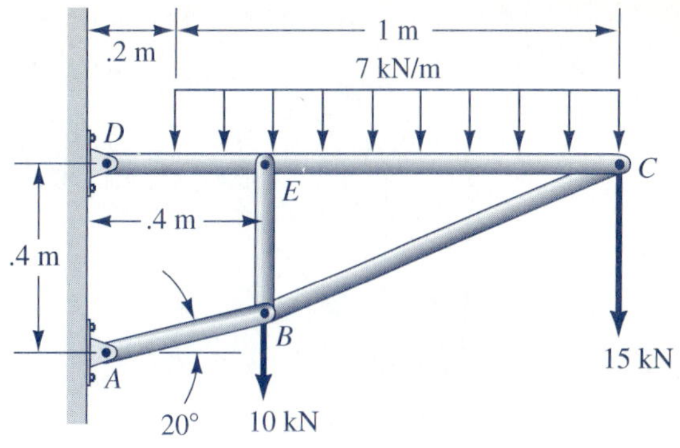

Figure P.5.31.

5.32. What are the supporting forces for the frame? Neglect all weights except the 10-kN weight. Disregard friction.

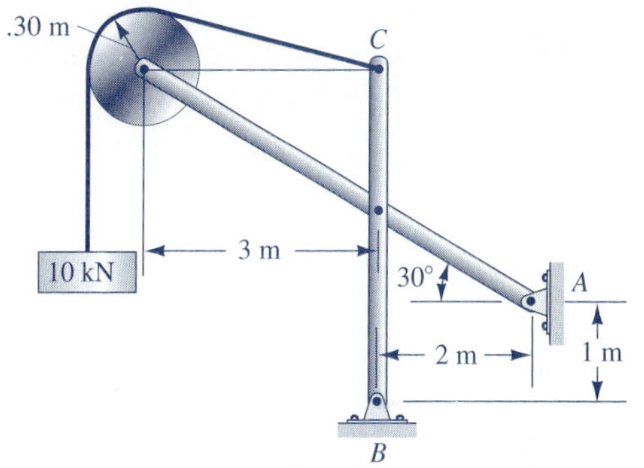

Figure P.5.32.

5.33. Find the supporting forces at *E* and *F*. Pulleys *A* and *B* offer no rotational resistance from friction at the bearings.

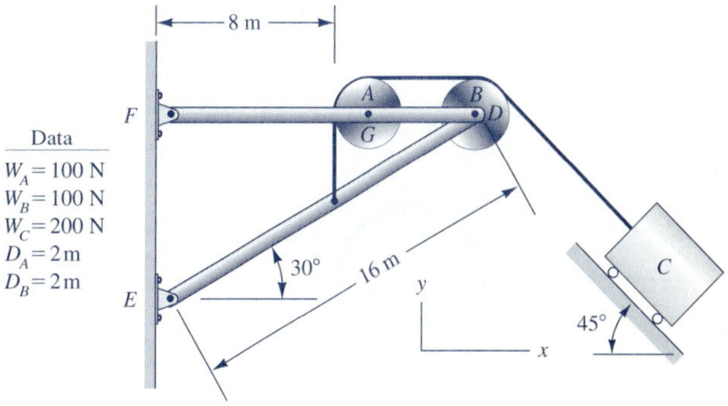

Figure P.5.33.

5.34. What are the tensions in cables AB, BC, and BD? Points A and B are in the yz plane.

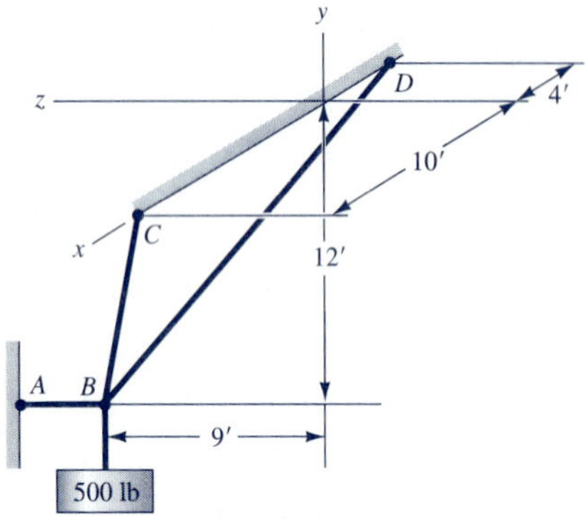

Figure P.5.34.

5.35. An elastic cord AB is just taut before the 1,000-N force is applied. If it takes 5.0 N/mm of elongation of the cord, what is the tension T in the cord after the 1,000-N force is applied? Set up the equation for T but do not solve.

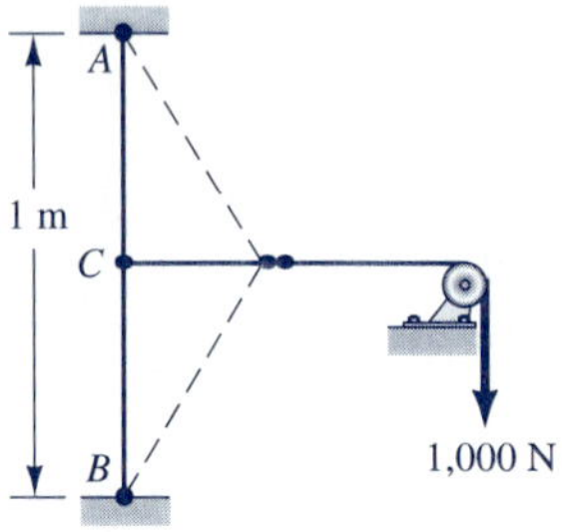

Figure P.5.35.

5.36. A thin hoop of radius 1 m and weight 500 N rests on an incline. What friction force f at A is needed for this configuration? What is the tension in wire CB?

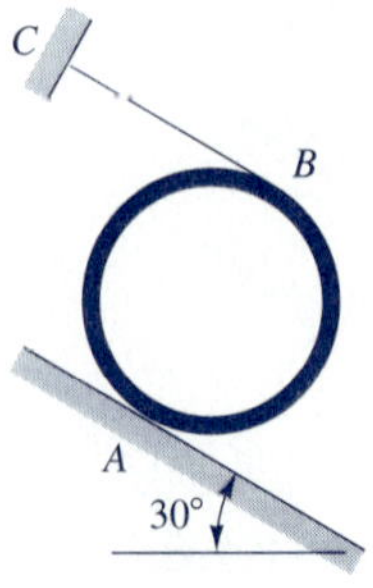

Figure P.5.36.

5.37. A stepped cylinder is pulled down an incline by a force F, which is increased from zero to 20 N very slowly while always maintaining the 30° inclination shown. If the cylinder is in equilibrium when $F = 0$, how far does O move as a result of F after equilibrium has been established with $F = 20$ N? The stepped cylinder has a mass of 10 kg. There is no slipping at the base. The force from the spring is K times the extension of the spring. For this spring, $K = 5$ N/mm. F remains parallel to the position shown.

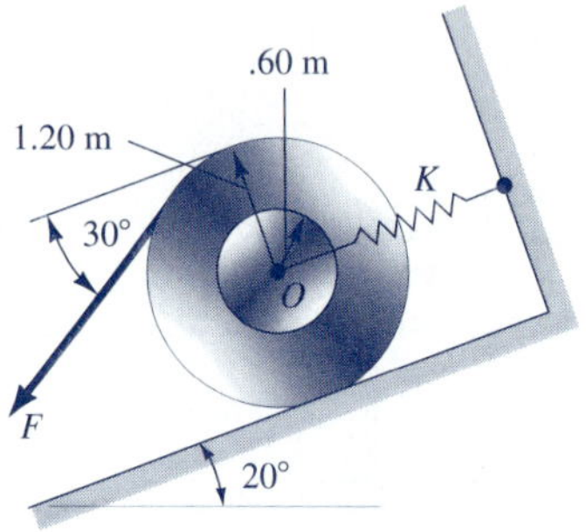

Figure P.5.37.

5.38. A 10-kg ring is supported by a smooth surface E and a wire AB. A body D having a mass of 3 kg is fixed to the ring at the orientation shown. What is the tension in the wire AB? What is its orientation α? Point A is directly above point O.

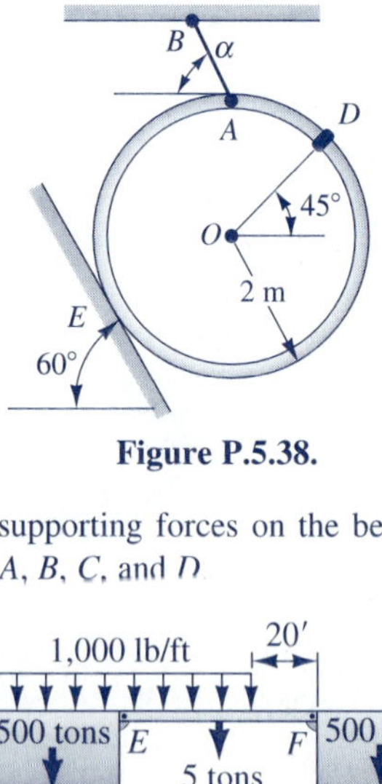

Figure P.5.38.

5.39. Find the supporting forces on the beam EF and the supporting forces at A, B, C, and D.

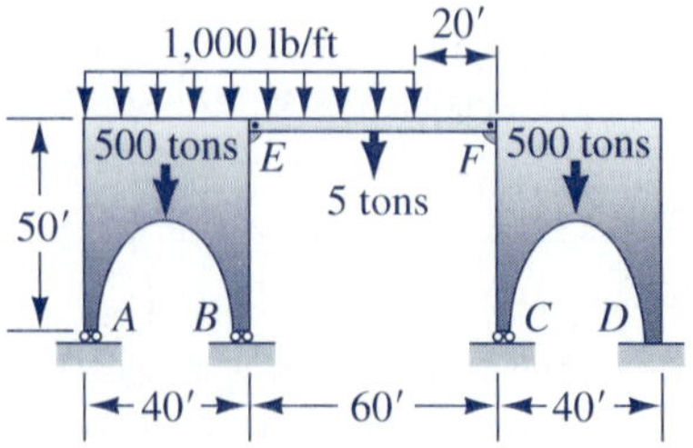

Figure P.5.39.

5.40. What is the supporting force system at A for the cantilever beam? Neglect the weight of the beam.

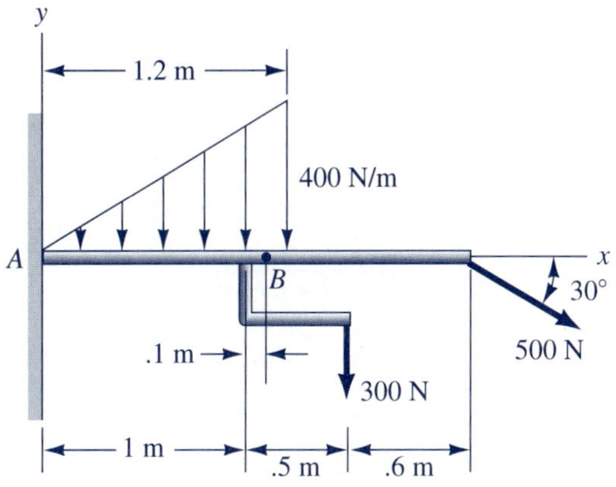

Figure P.5.40.

5.41. In Problem 5.40, find the force system transmitted through the cross section at B.

5.42. A cantilever beam AB is pinned at B to a simply supported beam BC. For the loads given, find the supporting force system at A. Determine force components that are normal and tangential to the cross-section of beam AB. Neglect the weights of the beams.

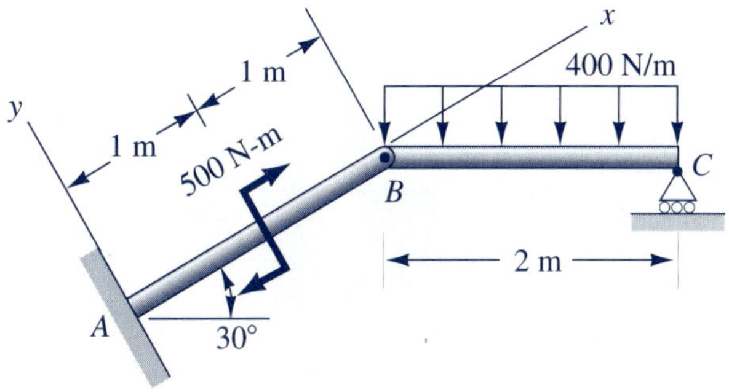

Figure P.5.42.

5.43. Find the supporting force system at A.

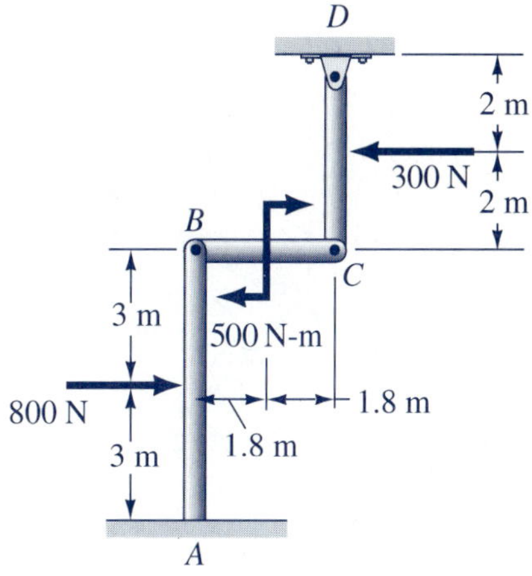

Figure P.5.43.

5.44. A light bent rod AD is pinned to a straight light rod CB at C. The bent rod supports a uniform load. A spring is stretched to connect the two rods. The spring has a spring constant of 10^4 N/m, and its unstretched length is .8 m. Find the supporting forces at A and B. The force in the spring is 10^4 times the elongation in meters.

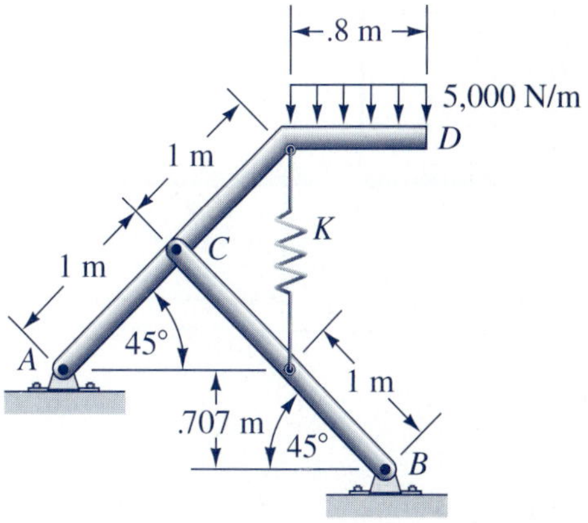

Figure P.5.44.

5.45. Light rods AD and BC are pinned together at C and support a 300-N and a 100-N load. What are the supporting forces at A and B?

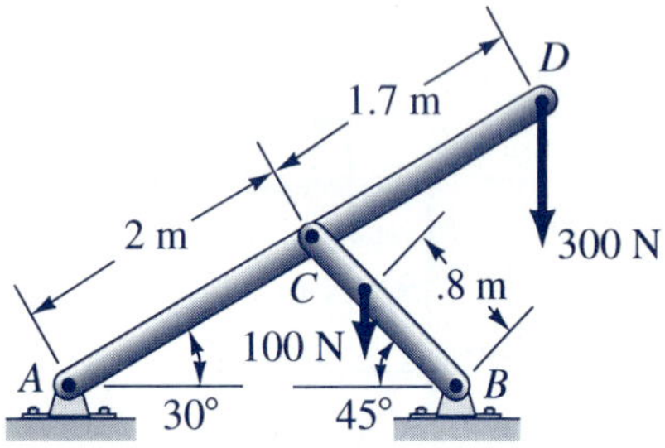

Figure P.5.45.

5.46. A light rod CD is held in a horizontal position by a strong elastic band AB (shock cord), which acts like a spring in that it takes 10^3 N per meter of elongation of the band. The upper part of the band is connected to a small wheel free to roll on a horizontal surface. What is the angle α needed to support a 200-N load as shown?

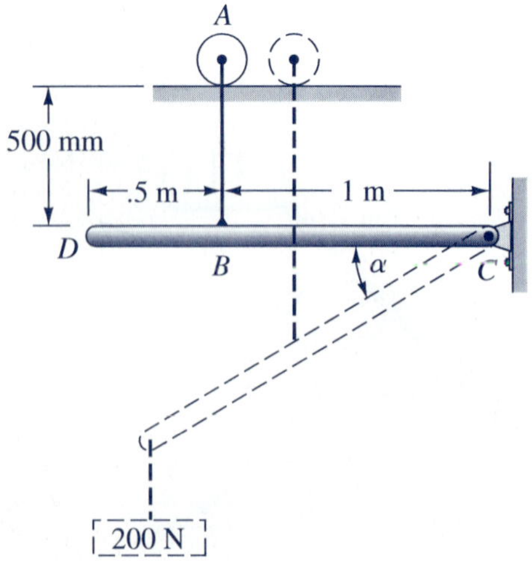

Figure P.5.46.

5.47. Solve for the supporting forces at A and C. AB weighs 100 lb, and BC weighs 150 lb.

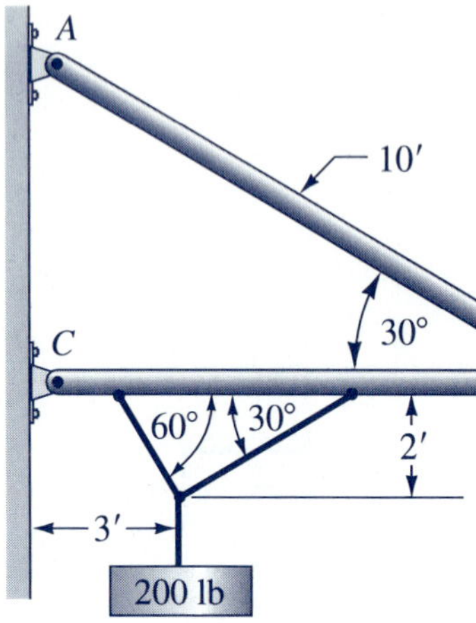

Figure P.5.47.

5.48. What torque T is needed to maintain the configuration shown for the compressor if p_1 = 5 psig? The system lies horizontally.

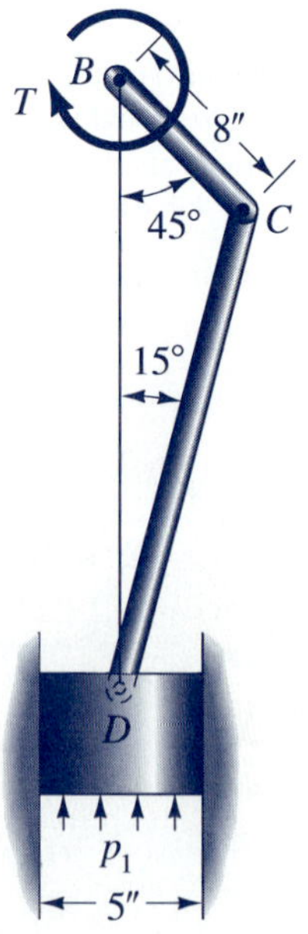

Figure P.5.48.

5.49. Work Problem 5.48 for the system oriented vertically with BC weighing 3 lb and CD weighing 5 lb.

5.50. Neglecting friction, find the angle β of line AB for equilibrium in terms of α_1, α_2 W_1, and W_2.

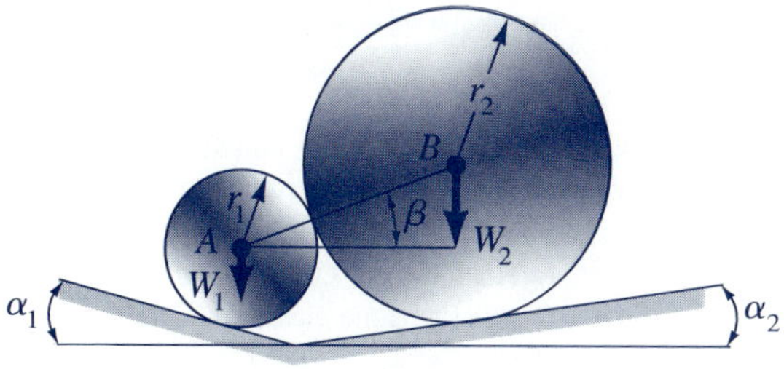

Figure P.5.50.

5.51. If the rod CD weighs 20 lb, what torque T is needed to maintain equilibrium? The system is in a vertical plane. Cylinder A weighs 10 lb and cylinder B weighs 5 lb. Disregard friction. At D there is a slot.

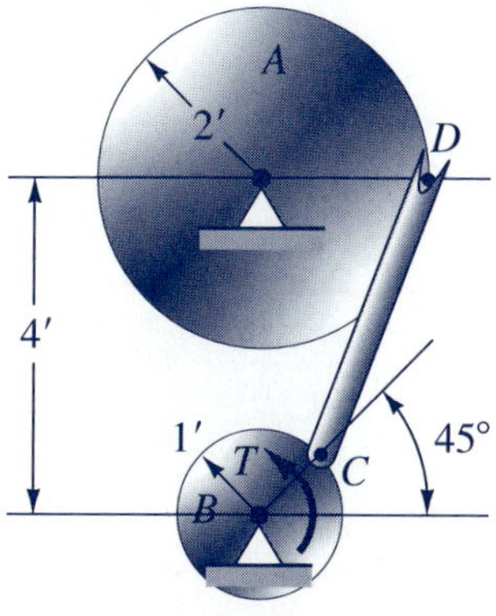

Figure P.5.51.

5.52. Find the supporting forces at A and G. The weight of W is 500 N and the weight of C is 200 N. Neglect all other weights. The cord connecting C and D is vertical.

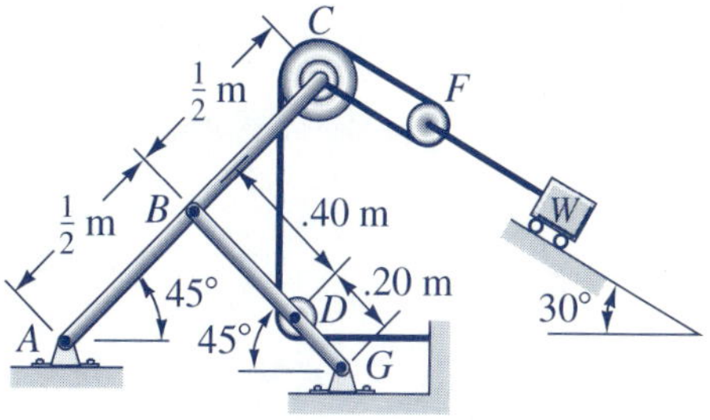

Figure P.5.52.

5.53. What torque T is needed for equilibrium if cylinder B weighs 500 N and CD weighs 300 N?

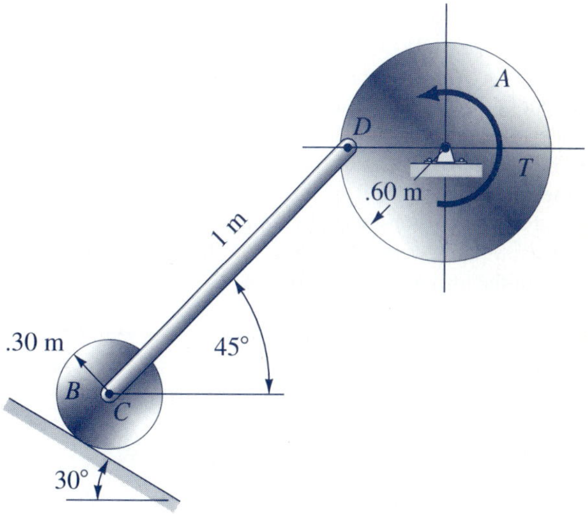

Figure P.5.53.

5.54. A bar AB is pinned to two identical planetary gears each of diameter .30 m. Gear E is pinned to bar AB and meshes with the two planetary gears, which in turn mesh with stationary gear D. If a torque T of 100 N-m is applied to bar AB, what external torque is needed to be applied to the upper planetary gear to maintain equilibrium? The system is horizontal.

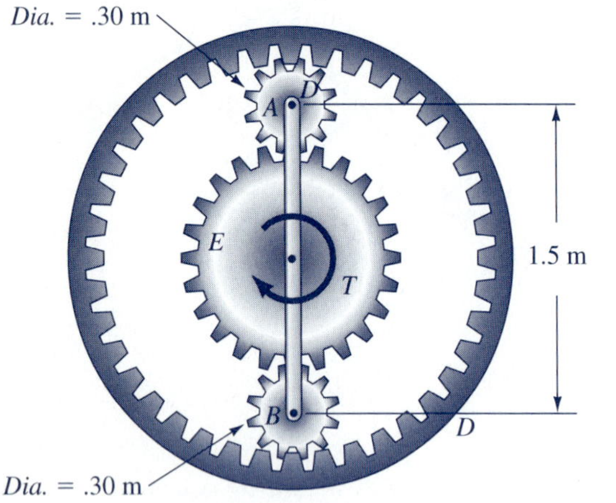

Figure P.5.54.

5.55. In Problem 5.54, equilibrium is maintained by applying a torque on gear E rather than the upper planetary gear. What is this torque?

5.56. A Bucyrus–Erie transit crane is holding a chimney having a weight of 20 kN. The chimney is held by a cable that goes over a pulley at A, then goes over a second pulley at D, and then to a winch at K. The position of boom AH (on top) is maintained by two separate cables, one from A to B, and the other from B to pulley C. Find the tensions in cables AB and BC. Note that BC is oriented 30° from the vertical for the setup shown. Consider only the weight of the load and neglect friction.

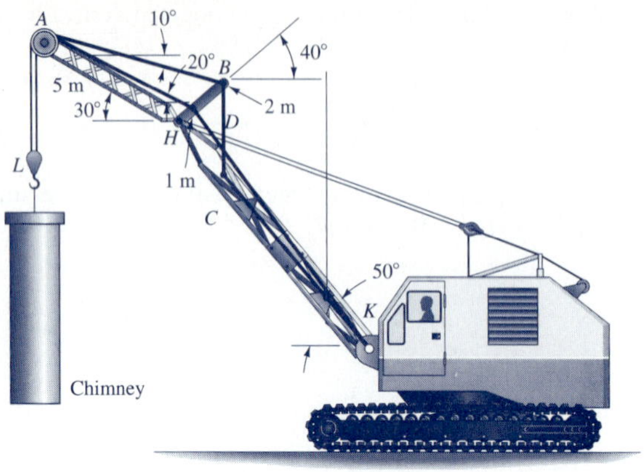

Figure P.5.56.

5.57. What are the forces at the arm connection at B and the cable tensions when the power shovel is in the position shown? Arm AC weighs 13,000 N, arm DF weighs 11,000 N, and the shovel and payload together weigh 9,000 N and act at the center of gravity as shown. B is at the same elevation as G.

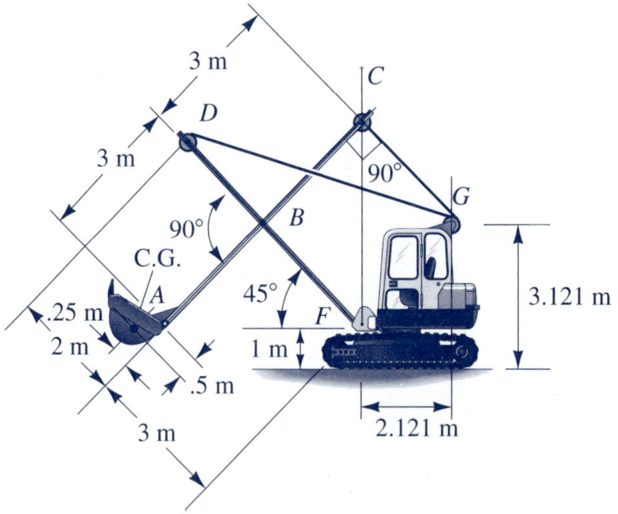

Figure P.5.57.

5.7 Problems of Equilibrium II

Case C. Parallel Forces in Space. In the case of parallel forces in space (see Fig. 4.20), we already know that the simplest resultant can be either a single force or a couple moment. If the forces are in the z direction, then

$$\sum_i (F_z)_i = 0 \tag{5.12}$$

ensures that the resultant force is zero. Also,

$$\sum_i (M_x)_i = 0, \qquad \sum_i (M_y)_i = 0 \tag{5.13}$$

guarantees that the resultant couple moment is zero, where the x and y axes may be chosen in any plane perpendicular to the direction of the forces.[5] Thus, three independent scalar equations are available for equilibrium of parallel forces in space.

A summary of the special cases discussed thus far is given below. For even simpler systems such as the concurrent-coplanar and the parallel-coplanar systems, clearly, there is one less equation of equilibrium.

Summary for Special Cases

System	*Simplest Resultant*	*Number of Equations for Equilibrium*
Concurrent (three-dimensional)	Single force	3
Coplanar single couple moment	Single force or	3
Parallel (three-dimensional)	Single force or single couple moment	3

[5]For parallel forces in the z direction, a simplest resultant consisting of a couple moment only must have this couple moment parallel to the xy plane (see diagram). Recall from Chapter 3 that the orthogonal xyz components of $\boldsymbol{C}_R$ equals the torque of the system about these axes. Hence, by setting $\sum_i (M_x)_i = \sum_i (M_y)_i = 0$, we are ensuring that $\boldsymbol{C}_R = \boldsymbol{0}$.

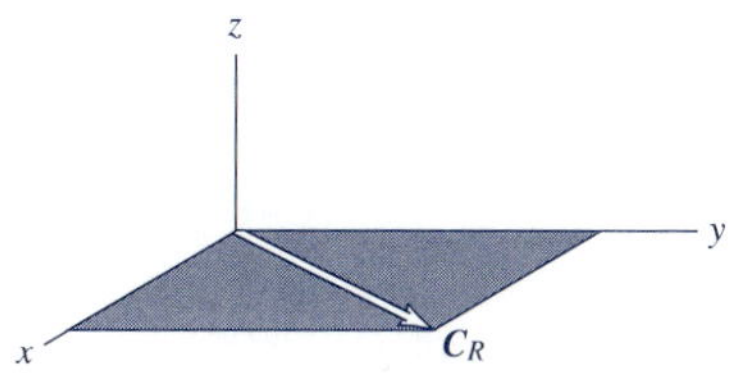

Example 5.8

Determine the forces required to support the uniform beam in Fig. 5.30 shown loaded with a couple, a point force, and a downward parabolic distribution of load having zero slope at the origin. The weight of the beam is 100 lb.

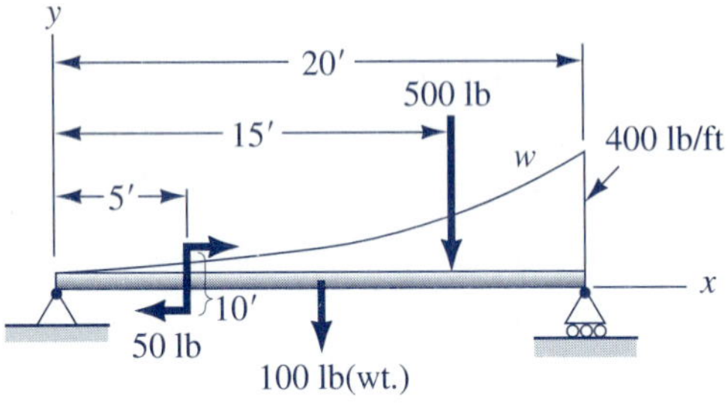

Figure 5.30. Find supporting forces.

Since a couple can be rotated without affecting the equilibrium of the body, we can orient the couple so that the forces are vertical. Accordingly, we have here a beam loaded by a system of parallel coplanar loads. Clearly, the supporting forces must be vertical, as shown in Fig. 5.31, where we have a free-body diagram of the beam. Since there are only two unknown quantities, we can handle the problem by statical consideration of this free body.

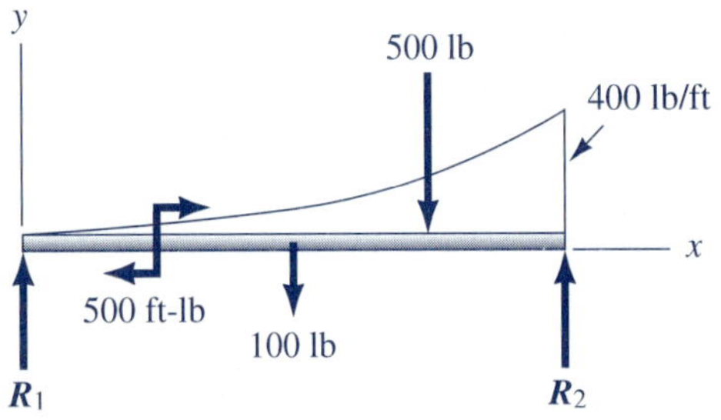

Figure 5.31. Free-body diagram.

The equation for the loading curve must be $w = ax^2 + b$, where a and b are to be determined from the loading data and the choice of reference. With an xy reference at the left end, as shown, we then have the conditions:

1. When $x = 0$, $w = 0$.
2. When $x = 20$, $w = 400$.

To satisfy these conditions, b must be zero and a must be unity; the loading function is thus given as

$$w = x^2 \text{ lb/ft}$$

Example 5.8 (Continued)

In this problem, we shall again work directly with the scalar equations. By summing moments about the left and right ends of the beam, we can then solve for the unknowns directly:

$\sum M_1 = 0$:

$$-500 - (10)(100) - (15)(500) - \int_0^{20} xy\ dx + 20R_2 = 0$$

Replacing y by x^2, then integrating and canceling terms, we get

$$-9,000 - \left.\frac{x^4}{4}\right|_0^{20} + 20R_2 = 0$$

By inserting limits and solving, we get one of the unknowns:

$$R_2 = 2{,}450 \text{ lb}$$

Next,

$\sum M_2 = 0$:

$$-20R_1 - 500 + (10)(100) + (5)(500) + \int_0^{20} (20 - x)y\,dx = 0$$

Replacing y by x^2, integrating and then solving for R_1, we have

$$R_1 = 817 \text{ lb}$$

As a check on these computations, we can sum forces in the vertical direction. The result must be zero (or as close to zero as the accuracy of our calculations permits):

$\sum F_y = 0$:

$$R_1 + R_2 - 100 - 500 - \int_0^{20} x^2\ dx = 0$$

$$3{,}267 - 600 - \left.\frac{x^3}{3}\right|_0^{20} = 0$$

Therefore,

$$2{,}667 - 2{,}667 = 0$$

Always take the opportunity to check a solution in this manner (i.e., by using a redundant equilibrium equation). In later problems, we shall rely heavily on calculated reactions (supporting forces); thus, we must make sure they are correct.

Example 5.9

In Fig. 5.32, find the supporting forces at *A, B,* and *D*. Note the pin connection at *C*. Also note that at *E* we have a welded connection.

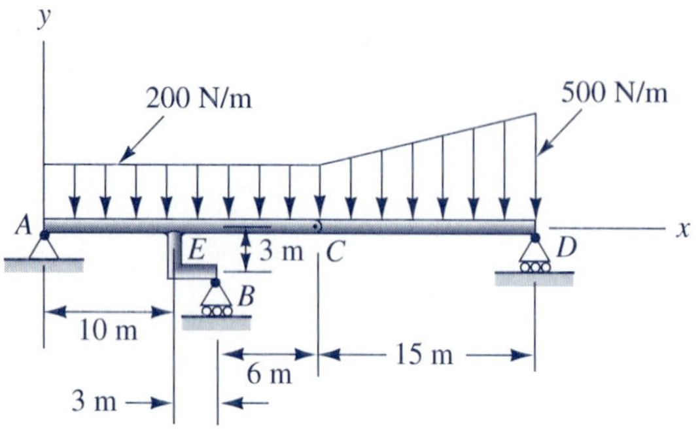

Figure 5.32. Members *AC* and *CD* are pinned at *C*.

The free-body diagram for the entire system is shown in Fig. 5.33. We have a coplanar system of forces for this free body and so we have only three independent equations of equilibrium. However we have here four unknowns. One of the unknowns, namely A_x, can be seen by inspection to be zero leaving now a coplanar parallel system with three unknowns but with only two equations of equilibrium.

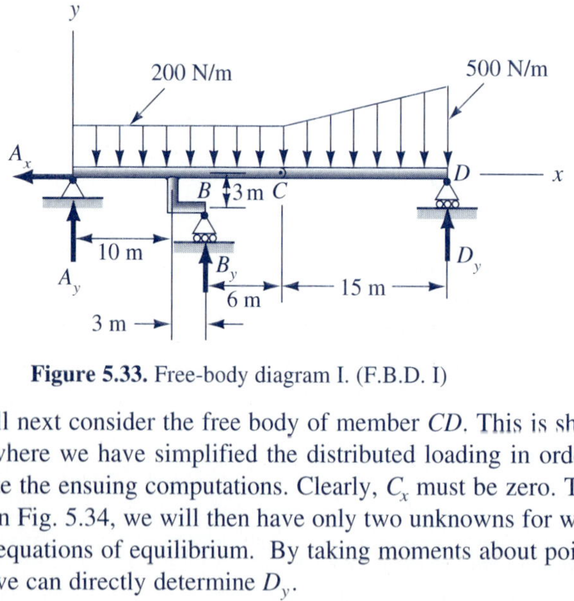

Figure 5.33. Free-body diagram I. (F.B.D. I)

We shall next consider the free body of member *CD*. This is shown in Fig. 5.34 where we have simplified the distributed loading in order to better facilitate the ensuing computations. Clearly, C_x must be zero. Thus, for F.B.D. II in Fig. 5.34, we will then have only two unknowns for which we have two equations of equilibrium. By taking moments about point *C* in Fig. 5.34, we can directly determine D_y.

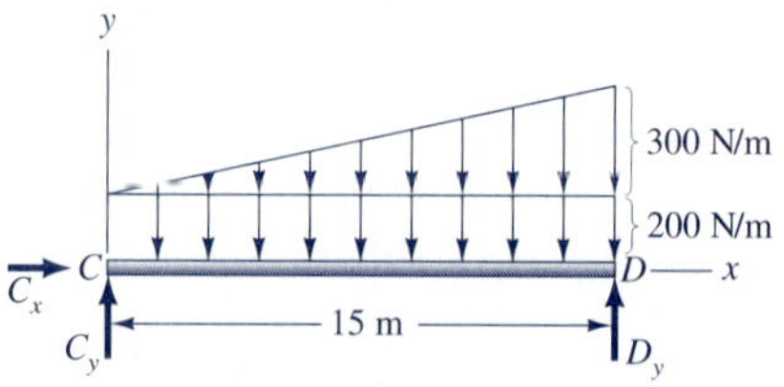

Figure 5.34. Free-body diagram II. (F.B.D. II)

Example 5.9 (Continued)

$\underline{\sum M_C = 0:}$

$$(D_y)(15) - (200)(15)\left(\frac{15}{2}\right) - \left(\frac{1}{2}\right)(15)(300)\left[\left(\frac{2}{3}\right)(15)\right] = 0$$

$$D_y = 3{,}000 \text{ N}$$

We may now go back to Fig. 5.33 to solve for the remaining two unknowns. Thus, simplifying the loading between C and D as we have done in Fig. 5.34, we have

$\underline{\sum F_y = 0:}$

$$A_y + B_y + 3{,}000 - (200)(34) - \frac{1}{2}(300)(15) = 0 \qquad \text{(a)}$$

$\underline{\sum M_B = 0:}$

$$-A_y(13) + (3{,}000)(21) - (200)(34)\left(\frac{34}{2} - 13\right) - \frac{1}{2}(300)(15)\left[6 + \left(\frac{2}{3}\right)(15)\right] = 0 \qquad \text{(b)}$$

From Eq. (b), we get

$$A_y = -15.38 \text{ N} \qquad \text{(c)}$$

And from Eq. (a), we have

$$B_y = 6{,}065 \text{ N}$$

Note that A_y was negative indicating that we had inserted the wrong sense for this force in F.B.D. I. We did not make any changes in the ensuing calculations while going to Eq. (a) (valid for F.B.D. I) to calculate B_y (i.e., we used the result from Eq. (c) with the negative sign of A_y intact).

Also, if you were tempted in F.B.D. I to include the force C_y at pin C in this diagram you were flirting with the prime error in the statics of rigid bodies—namely, including a force which is *internal* to the particular *free body* drawn.

Case D. General Force Systems. The simplest resultant in the general case is a force and a couple moment. Six equations of equilibrium can be given for each free-body diagram. We now examine two examples for this case.

Example 5.10

A derrick is shown in Fig. 5.35 supporting a 1,000-lb load. The vertical beam has a ball-and-socket connection into the ground at *d* and is held by guy wires *ac* and *bc*. Neglect the weight of the members and guy wires, and find the tensions in the guy wires *ac, bc*, and *ce*.

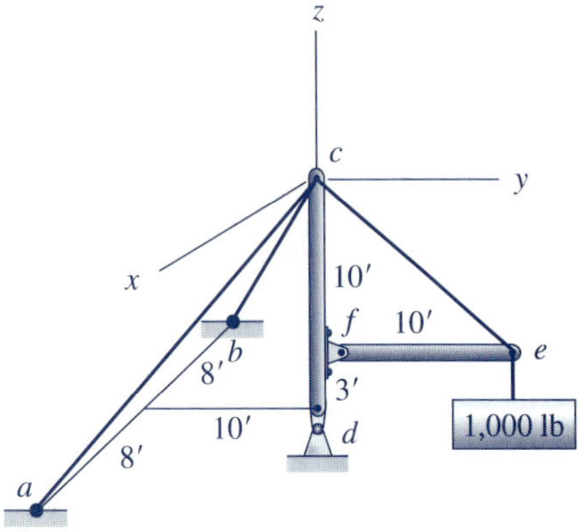

Figure 5.35. Loaded derrick.

If we select as a free body both members and the interconnecting guy wire *ce*, we shall expose two of the desired unknowns (Fig. 5.36). Note that this is a general three-dimensional force system with only five unknowns.[6] Although all these unknowns can be solved by statical considerations of this free body, you will notice that, if we take moments about point *d*, we will involve in a vector equation only the desired unknowns T_{bc} and T_{ac}. Accordingly, all unknown forces need not be computed for this free-body diagram. You should always look for such short cuts in situations such as this.

To determine the unknown tension T_{ce}, we must employ another free-body diagram. Either the vertical or horizontal member will expose this unknown in a manner susceptible to solution. The latter has been selected and is shown in Fig. 5.37. Note that we have here a coplanar force system with three unknowns. Again, you can see that, by taking moments about point *f*, we will involve only the desired unknown.

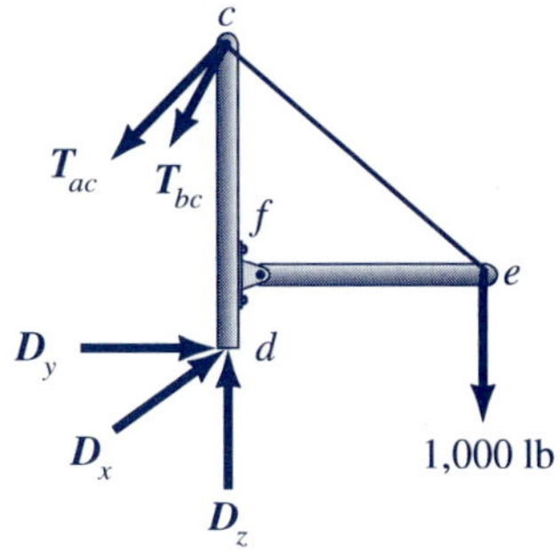

Figure 5.36. Free-body diagram 1.

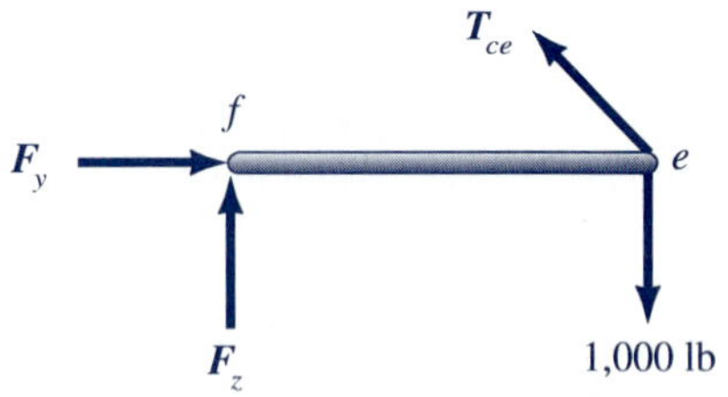

Figure 5.37. Free-body diagram 2.

[6]It should be clear on inspection of Fig. 5.35 that, due to symmetry, forces in the two supporting cables must be equal. Using this information is tantamount to using one of the equations of equilibrium. However, for practice we will not use this information and we will solve for both of these cables and demonstrate their equality. Also, note that there is a sixth equation of equilibrium that is identically satisfied. To see this, look at moments of the forces about axis *cd* in Fig. 5.36. Why is the total moment identically equal to zero about this axis, thus denying us an equation to help solve for unknowns? Is the derrick completely constrained? Explain.

Example 5.10 (Continued)

The vector $\boldsymbol{T}_{ac}$ may then be given as

$$\boldsymbol{T}_{ac} = T_{ac}\left[\frac{1}{\sqrt{333}}(8\boldsymbol{i} - 10\boldsymbol{j} - 13\boldsymbol{k})\right] \qquad \text{(a)}$$

Similarly, we have for $\boldsymbol{T}_{bc}$,

$$\boldsymbol{T}_{bc} = T_{bc}\left[\frac{1}{\sqrt{333}}(-8\boldsymbol{i} - 10\boldsymbol{j} - 13\boldsymbol{k})\right] \qquad \text{(b)}$$

Using the free-body diagram in Fig. 5.36, we now set the sum of moments about point d equal to zero. Thus, employing the relations above, we get

$$13\boldsymbol{k} \times \frac{T_{ac}}{\sqrt{333}}(8\boldsymbol{i} - 10\boldsymbol{j} - 13\boldsymbol{k}) + 13\boldsymbol{k} \times \frac{T_{bc}}{\sqrt{333}}(-8\boldsymbol{i} - 10\boldsymbol{j} - 13\boldsymbol{k})$$
$$+10\boldsymbol{j} \times (-1,000\boldsymbol{k}) = \boldsymbol{0} \qquad \text{(c)}$$

When we make the substitution of variable $t_1 = T_{ac}/\sqrt{333}$ and $t_2 = T_{bc}/\sqrt{333}$, the preceding equation becomes

$$[130(t_1 + t_2) - 10{,}000]\boldsymbol{i} + [104(t_1 - t_2]\boldsymbol{j} = \boldsymbol{0} \qquad \text{(d)}$$

The scalar equations,

$$130(t_1 + t_2) - 10{,}000 = 0$$
$$104(t_1 - t_2) = 0$$

can now be readily solved to give $t_1 = t_2 = 38.5$. Hence, we get $T_{ac} = 38.5\sqrt{333} = 702$ lb and $T_{bc} = 38.5\sqrt{333} = 702$ lb.[7]

$$\therefore \quad T_{ac} = 702 \text{ lb} \qquad T_{bc} = 702 \text{ lb}$$

Turning finally to free-body diagram 2 in Fig. 5.37, we see that, in summing moments about f, the horizontal component of the tension T_{ce} has a zero-moment arm. Thus,

$$(10)(0.707)T_{ce} - (10)(1{,}000) = 0$$

Hence,

$$T_{ce} = 1{,}414 \text{ lb}$$

[7]By taking moments in Fig. 5.36 about the line connecting points a and d (see Fig. 5.35), we could get T_{bc} directly using the scalar triple product. We suggest that you try this.

Example 5.11

A blimp is shown in Fig. 5.38 fixed at the mooring tower D by a ball-joint connection, and held by cables AB and AC. The blimp has a mass of 1,500 kg. The simplest resultant force $\boldsymbol{F}$ from air pressure (including the effects of wind) is

$$\boldsymbol{F} = 17{,}500\boldsymbol{i} + 1{,}000\boldsymbol{j} + 1{,}500\mathbf{k} \text{ N}$$

at a position shown in the diagram. Compute the tension in the cables as well as the force transmitted to the ball joint at the top of the tower at D. Also, what force system is transmitted to the ground at G through the mooring tower? The tower weighs 5,000 N.

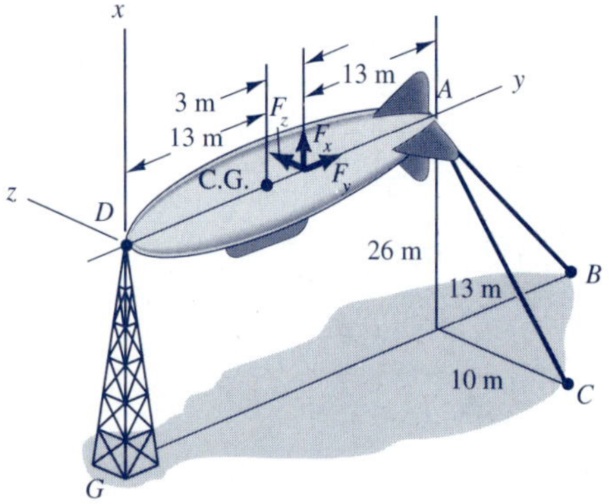

Figure 5.38. Tethered blimp.

We shall first consider a free-body diagram of the blimp, as shown in Fig. 5.39. We have five unknown forces here, and we can solve all of them by using equations of equilibrium for this free body.[8] As a first step, we express the cable tensions vectorially. That is,

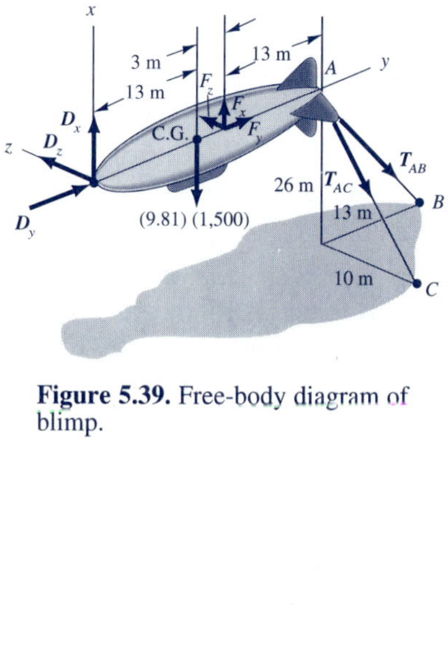

Figure 5.39. Free-body diagram of blimp.

$$\boldsymbol{T}_{AC} = T_{AC}\left(\frac{-26\boldsymbol{i} - 10\boldsymbol{k}}{\sqrt{26^2 + 10^2}}\right) = T_{AC}(-.933\boldsymbol{i} - .359\boldsymbol{k})$$

$$\boldsymbol{T}_{AB} = T_{AB}\left(\frac{-26\boldsymbol{i} + 13\boldsymbol{j}}{\sqrt{26^2 + 13^2}}\right) = T_{AB}(-.894\boldsymbol{i} + .447\boldsymbol{j})$$

We now go back to the basic vector equation of equilibrium. Thus

$\underline{\sum \boldsymbol{F}_i = \boldsymbol{0}}$:

$$D_x\boldsymbol{i} + D_y\boldsymbol{j} + D_z\boldsymbol{k} - (1{,}500)(9.81)\boldsymbol{i} + 17{,}500\boldsymbol{i} + 1{,}000\boldsymbol{j} + 1{,}500\boldsymbol{k}$$
$$+ T_{AC}(-.933\boldsymbol{i} - .359\boldsymbol{k}) + T_{AB}(-.894\boldsymbol{i} + .447\boldsymbol{j}) = \boldsymbol{0}$$

[8] What equation is identically satisfied (thus forming the sixth equation of equilibrium) and thus not helpful in solving for the desired unknowns? What does this say about how the blimp can begin to move with the constraints present? See footnote 6 for the previous example.

Example 5.11 (Continued)

The scalar equations are

$$D_x + 2{,}785 - .933T_{AC} - .894T_{AB} = 0 \qquad \text{(a)}$$
$$D_y + 1{,}000 + .447T_{AB} = 0 \qquad \text{(b)}$$
$$D_z + 1{,}500 - .359T_{AC} = 0 \qquad \text{(c)}$$

Next take moments about point D.

$\underline{\sum (\boldsymbol{M}_i)_D = \boldsymbol{0}}$:

$$13\boldsymbol{j} \times (9.81)(1{,}500)(-\boldsymbol{i}) + 16\boldsymbol{j} \times (17{,}500\boldsymbol{i} + 1{,}000\boldsymbol{j} + 1{,}500\boldsymbol{k})$$
$$+ 29\boldsymbol{j} \times T_{AC}(-.933\boldsymbol{i} - .359\boldsymbol{k}) + 29\boldsymbol{j} \times T_{AB}(-.894\boldsymbol{i} + .447\boldsymbol{j}) = \boldsymbol{0}$$

Carrying out the various cross products, we end up only with $\boldsymbol{k}$ and $\boldsymbol{i}$ components, thus generating two scalar equations.[9] They are

$$-10.41T_{AC} + 24{,}000 = 0 \qquad \text{(d)}$$

$$25.9T_{AB} + 27.1T_{AC} - 88{,}700 = 0 \qquad \text{(e)}$$

We now have five independent equations for five unknowns. We can thus solve these equations simultaneously. From Eq.(d), we have

$$T_{AC} = 2{,}305 \text{ N}$$

From Eq. (e), we have

$$T_{AB} = 1{,}012 \text{ N}$$

From Eq. (c), we have

$$D_z = -673 \text{ N}$$

From Eq. (b), we have

$$D_y = -1{,}452 \text{ N}$$

[9]The third equation is $0 = 0$. That is, there are no moments about the y axis, because all forces pass through the y axis.

Example 5.11 (Continued)

From Eq. (a), we have

$$D_x = 270 \text{ N}$$

Next, consider the mooring tower as a free body (Fig. 5.40). Notice that in showing the forces at the ball joint D, we have taken into account *both* of the negative signs shown above for D_y and D_z as well as Newton's third law.

Again, using the basic vector equations of statics, we have on summing forces

$$-270\boldsymbol{i} + 1{,}452\boldsymbol{j} + 672\boldsymbol{k} + F_x\boldsymbol{i} + F_y\boldsymbol{j} + F_z\boldsymbol{k} - 5{,}000\boldsymbol{i} = \boldsymbol{0}$$

Hence,

$$\begin{aligned} F_x &= 5{,}270 \text{ N} \\ F_y &= -1{,}452 \text{ N} \\ F_z &= -672 \text{ N} \end{aligned}$$

Now take moments about the base at F. We get

$$26\boldsymbol{i} \times (-270\boldsymbol{i} + 1{,}452\boldsymbol{j} + 672\boldsymbol{k}) + M_x\boldsymbol{i} + M_y\boldsymbol{j} + M_z\boldsymbol{k} = \boldsymbol{0}$$

From this, we get

$$\begin{aligned} M_x &= 0 \\ M_y &= 17{,}470 \text{ N-m} \\ M_z &= -37{,}800 \text{ N-m} \end{aligned}$$

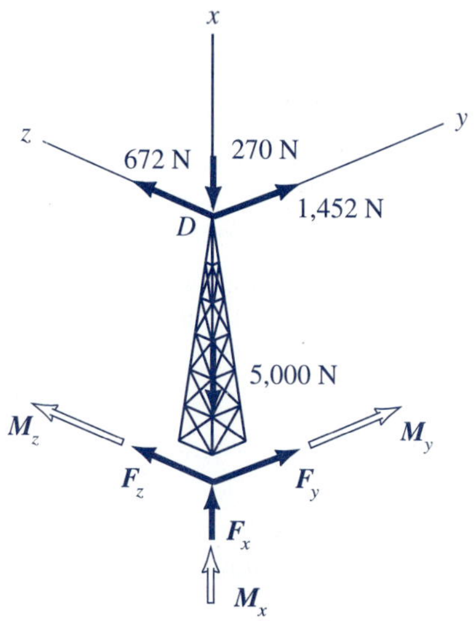

Figure 5.40. Free-body diagram of mooring tower.

We can conclude that, at the center of the base, the force system from the ground is

$$\boldsymbol{F} = 5{,}270\boldsymbol{i} - 1{,}452\boldsymbol{j} - 672\boldsymbol{k} \text{ N}$$

$$\boldsymbol{C} = 17{,}470\boldsymbol{j} - 37{,}800\boldsymbol{k} \text{ N-m}$$

The force system acting on the ground at the center of the base is the reaction to the system above. Thus,

$$\boldsymbol{F}_{\text{ground}} = -5{,}270\boldsymbol{i} + 1{,}452\boldsymbol{j} + 672\boldsymbol{k} \text{ N}$$

$$\boldsymbol{C}_{\text{ground}} = -17{,}470\boldsymbol{j} + 37{,}800\boldsymbol{k} \text{ N-m}$$

5.58. The triple pulley sheave and the double pulley sheave weigh 15 lb and 10 lb, respectively. What rope force is necessary to lift a 350-lb engine? What is the force on the ceiling hook?

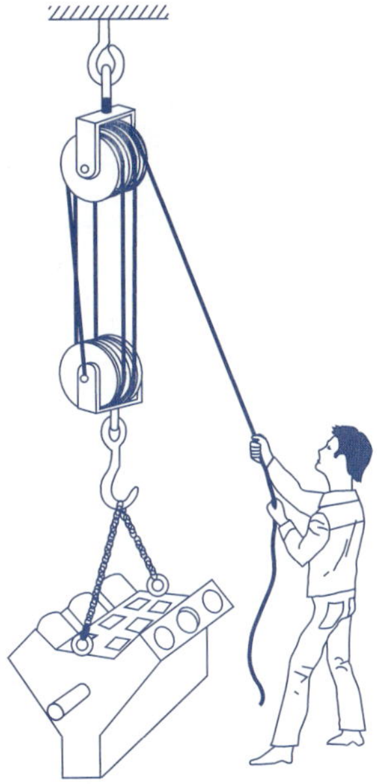

Figure P.5.58.

5.59. A multipurpose pry bar can be used to pull nails in the three positions. If a force of 400 lb is required to remove a nail and a carpenter can exert 50 lb, which position(s) must he use?

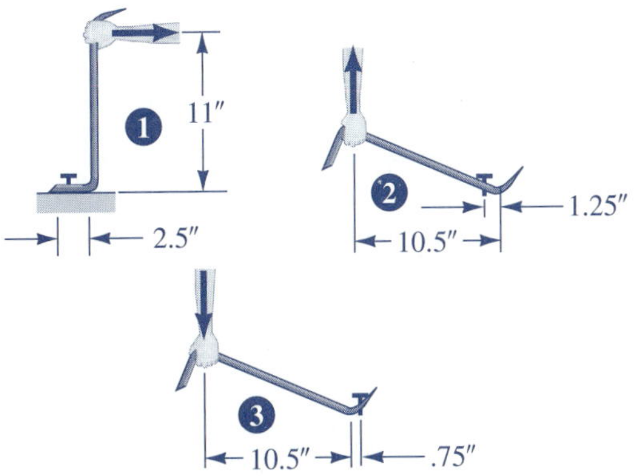

Figure P.5.59.

5.60. At what position must the operator of the counterweight crane locate the 50-kN counterweight when he lifts a 10-kN load of steel?

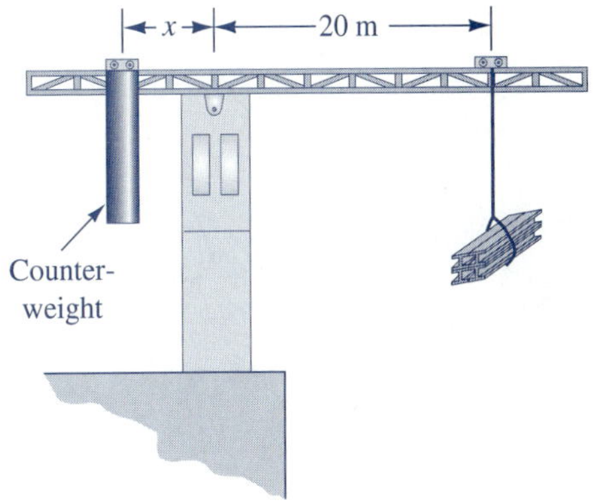

Figure P.5.60.

5.61. A Jeep winch is used to raise itself by a force of 2 kN. What are the reactions at the Jeep tires with and without the winch load? The driver weighs 800 N, and the Jeep weighs 11 kN. The center of gravity of the Jeep is shown.

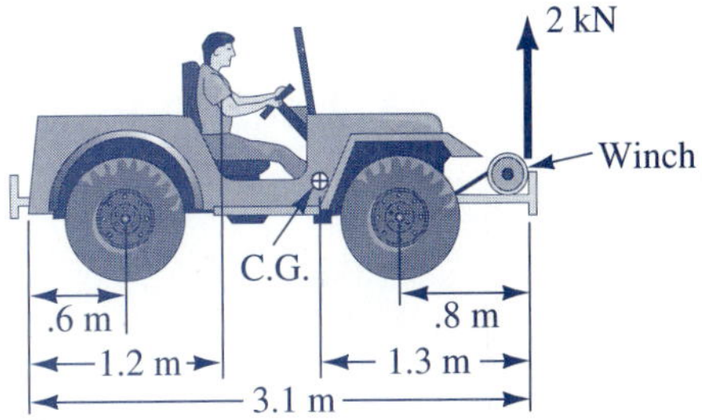

Figure P.5.61.

5.62. A *differential pulley* is shown. Compute F in terms of W, r_1, and r_2.

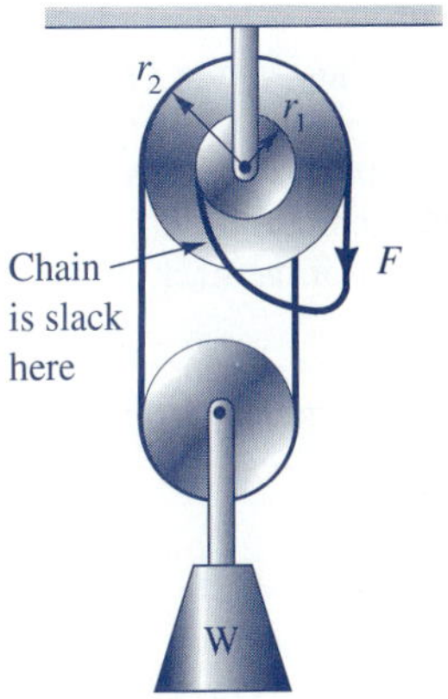

Figure P.5.62.

5.63. What is the longest portion of pipe weighing 400 lb/ft that can be lifted without tipping the 12,000-lb tractor? Take the center of gravity of the tractor at the geometric center.

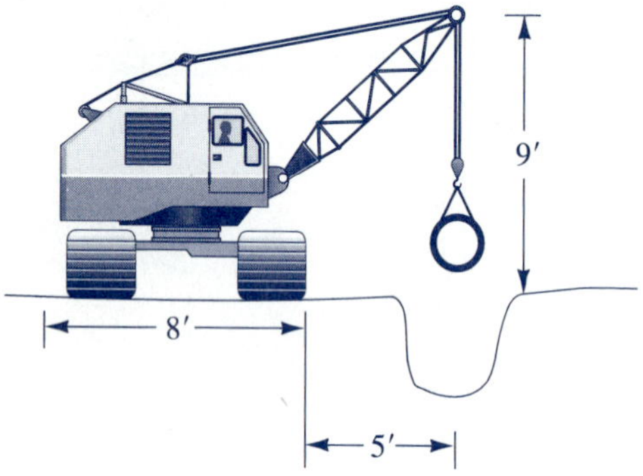

Figure P.5.63.

5.64. The L-shaped concrete post supports an elevated railroad. The concrete weighs 150 lb/ft^3. What are the reactions at the base of the post?

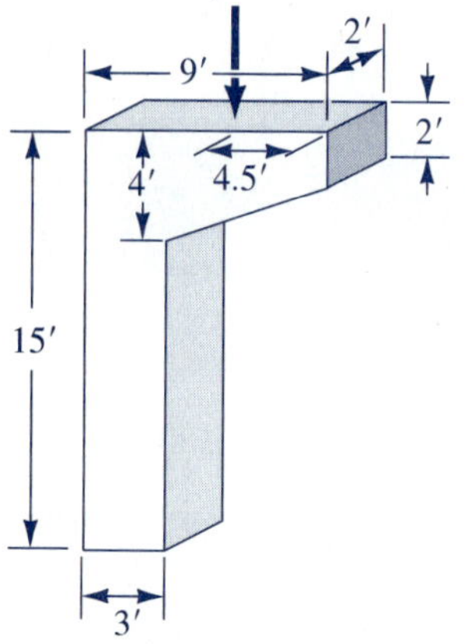

Figure P.5.64.

5.65. Two hoists are operated on the same overhead track. Hoist *A* has a 3,000-lb load, and hoist *B* has a 4,000-lb load. What are the reactions at the ends of the track when the hoists are in the position shown?

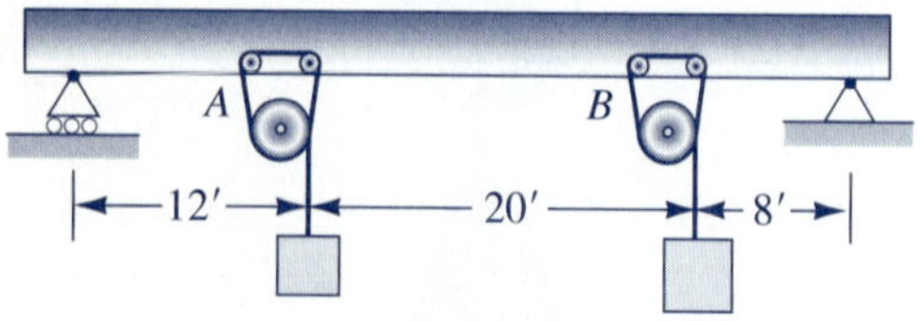

Figure P.5.65.

5.66. An I-beam cantilevered out from a wall weighs 30 lb/ft and supports a 300-lb hoist. Steel (487 lb/ft^3) cover plates 1 in. thick are welded on the beam near the wall to increase the moment-carrying capacity of the beam. What are the reactions at the wall when a 400-lb load is hoisted at the outermost position of the hoist?

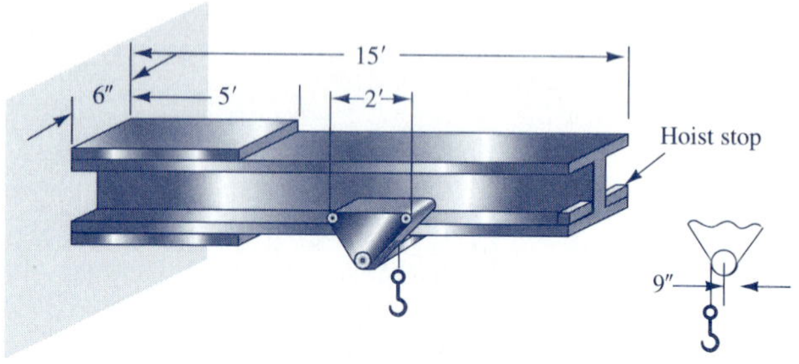

Figure P.5.66.

5.67. Find the supporting force system for the cantilever beam shown pinned at *C*.

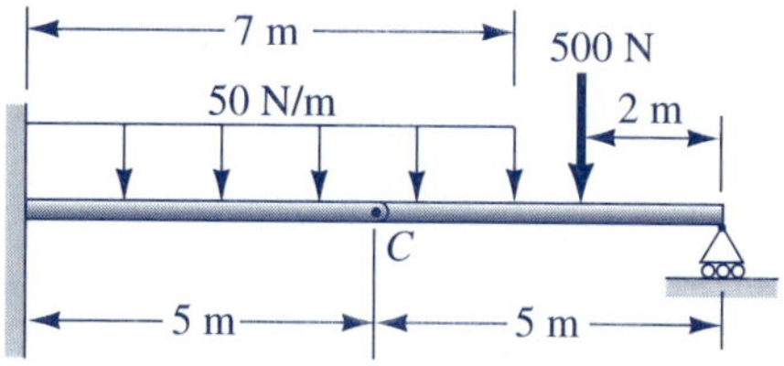

Figure P.5.67.

5.68. Find the supporting force system for the cantilever beams connected to bar *AB* by pins.

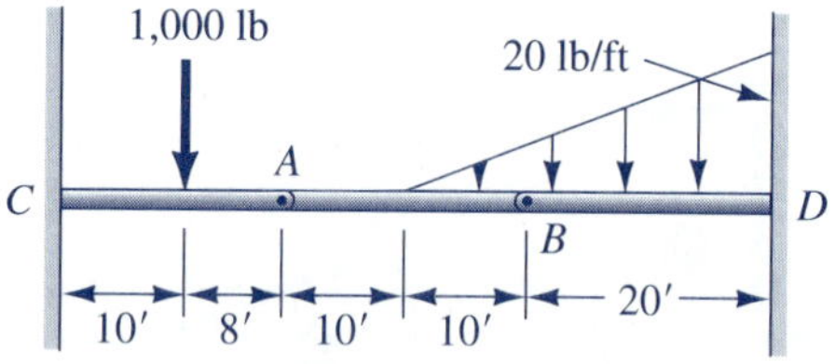

Figure P.5.68.

5.69. The trailer weighs 50 kN and is loaded with crates weighing 90 kN and 40 kN. What are the reactions at the rear wheel and on the tractor at *A*?

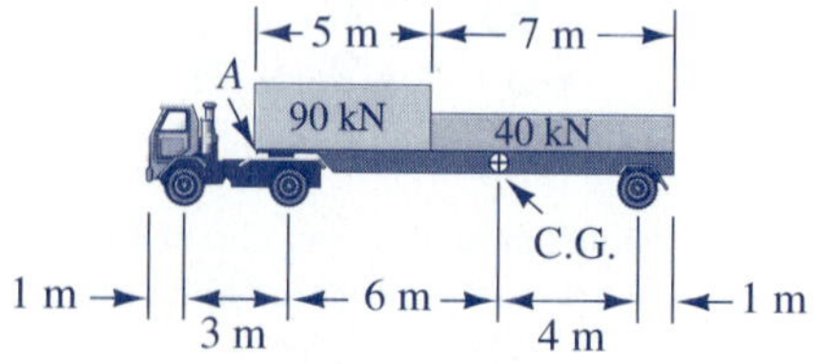

Figure P.5.69.

5.70. What load W will a pull P of 100 lb lift in the pulley system? Sheaves A, B, and C weigh 20 lb, 15 lb, and 30 lb, respectively. Assume first that the three sheaves are frictionless and find W. Then, calculate W that can be raised at constant speed for the case where the resisting torque in each of sheaves A and B is .01 times the total force at the bearing of each of sheaves A and B.

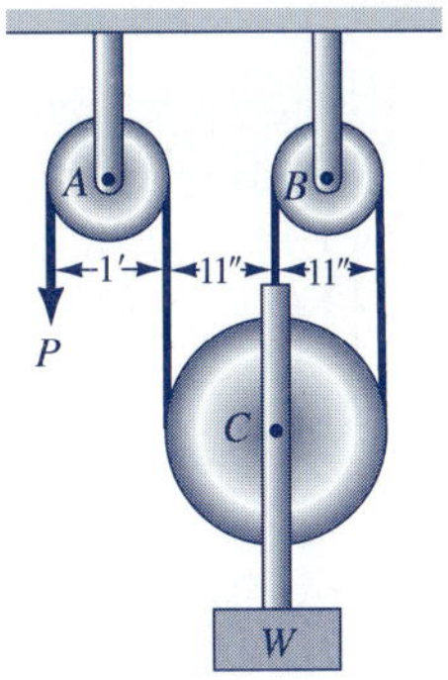

Figure P.5.70.

5.71. A piece of pop art is being developed. The weight of the body enclosed by the full lines is 2 kN. What is the smallest distance d that the artist can use for cutting a .5-m-diameter hole and still avoid tipping? The body is uniform in thickness.

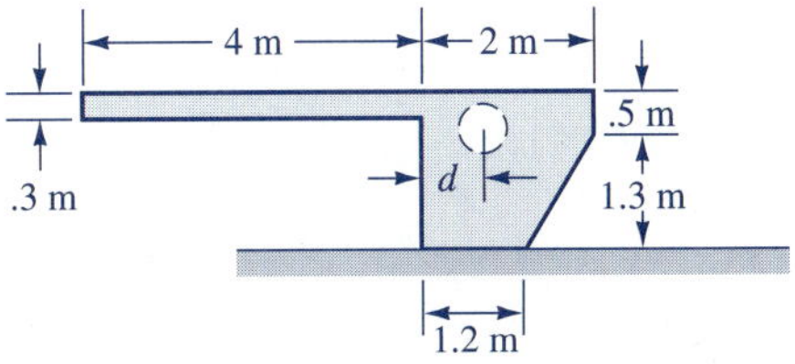

Figure P.5.71.

5.72. What is the largest weight W that the crane can lift without tipping? What are the supporting forces when the crane lifts this load? What is the force and couple-moment system transmitted through section C of the beam? Compute the force and couple-moment system transmitted through section D. The crane weighs 10 tons, having a center of gravity as shown in the diagram.

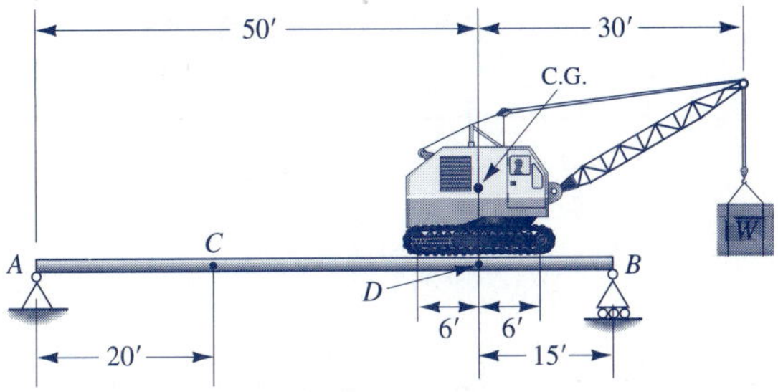

Figure P.5.72.

5.73. A 20-kN block is being raised at constant speed. If there is no friction in the three pulleys, what are forces F_1, F_2, and F_3 needed for the job? The block is not rotating in any way. The line of action of the weight vector passes through point C as shown.

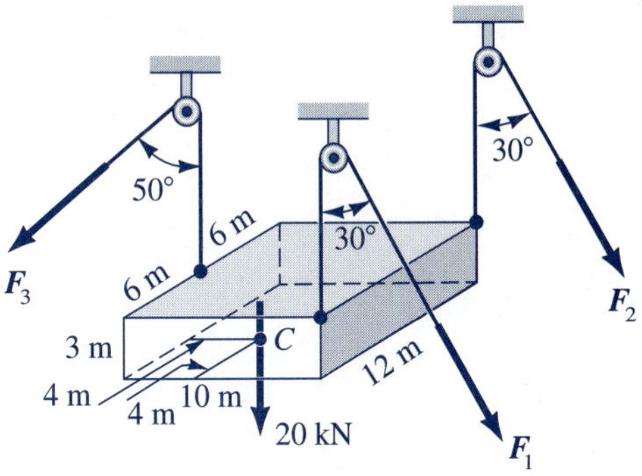

Figure P.5.73.

5.74. A 10-ton sounding rocket (used for exploring outer space) has a center of gravity shown as C.G.$_1$. It is mounted on a launcher whose weight is 50 tons with a center of gravity at C.G.$_2$. The launcher has three identical legs separated 120° from each other. Leg AB is in the same plane as the rocket and supporting arms CDE. What are the supporting forces from the ground? What torque is transmitted from the horizontal arm CD to the ramp ED by the rack and pinion at hinge D to counteract the weight of the rocket?

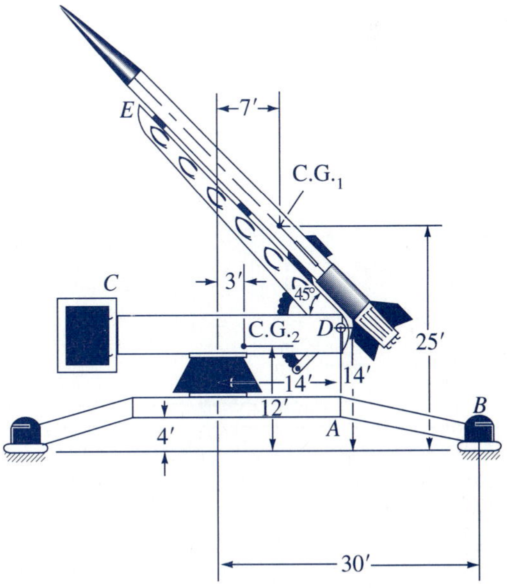

Figure P.5.74.

5.75. A door is hinged at A and B and contains water whose specific weight γ is 62.5 lb/ft^3. A force F normal to the door keeps the door closed. What are the forces on the hinges A and B and the force F to counteract the water? As noted in Chapter 4, the pressure in the water above atmosphere is given as γd, where d is the perpendicular distance from the free surface of the water.

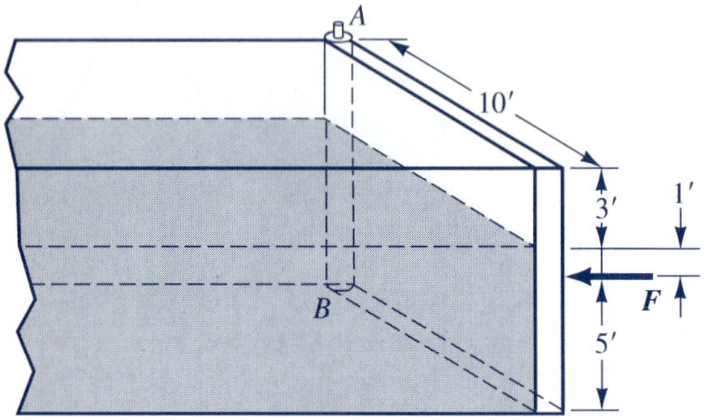

Figure P.5.75.

5.76. A row of books of length 750 mm and weighing 200 N sits on a three-legged table as shown. The legs are equidistant from each other with one leg B coinciding with the y axis. The other two legs lie along a line parallel to the x axis. If the table weighs 400 N, will it tip? If not, what are the forces on the legs?

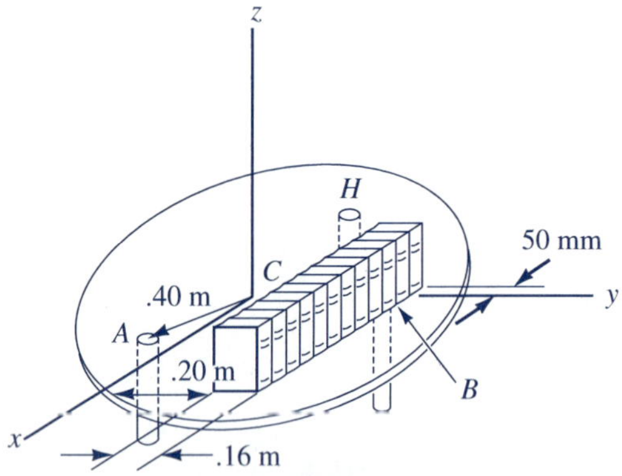

Figure P.5.76.

5.77. A small helicopter is in a hovering maneuver. The helicopter rotor blades give a lifting force F_1 but there results from the air forces on the blades a torque C_1. The rear rotor prevents the helicopter from rotating about the z axis but develops a torque C_2. Compute the force F_1 and couple C_2 in terms of the weight W. How are F_3 and C_1 related?

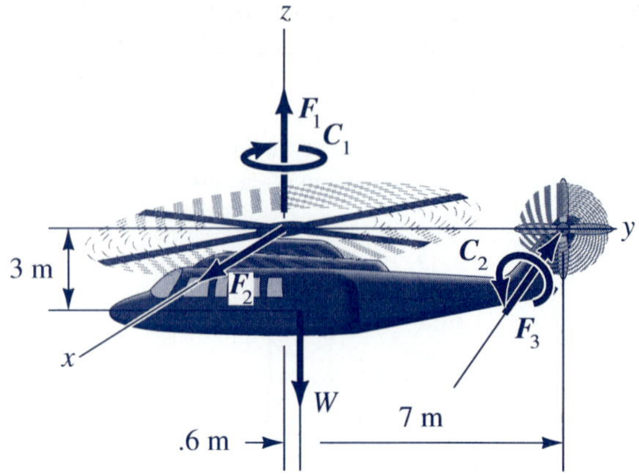

Figure P.5.77.

5.78. Find the supporting force and couple-moment system for the cantilever beam. What is the force and couple-moment system transmitted through a cross section of the beam at B?

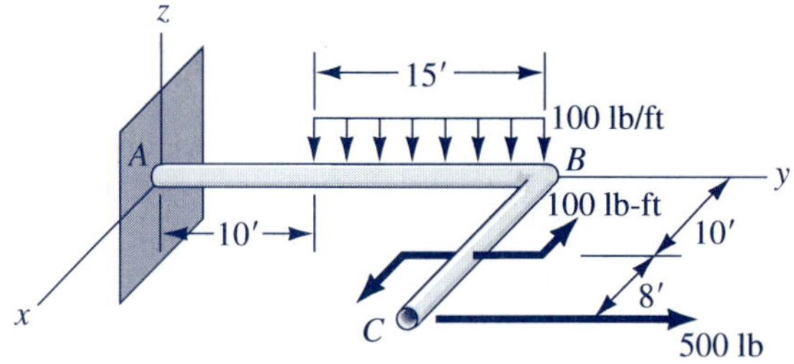

Figure P.5.78.

5.79. A structure is supported by a ball-and-socket joint at A, a pin connection at B offering no resistance in the direction AB, and a simple roller support at C. What are the supporting forces for the loads shown?

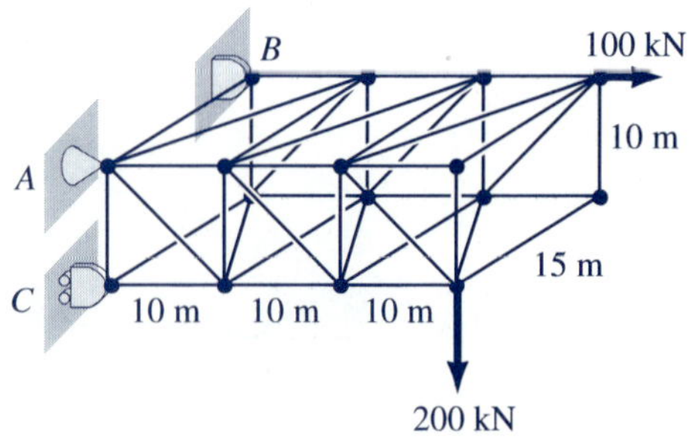

Figure P.5.79.

5.80. Compute the value of F to maintain the 200-lb weight shown. Assume that the bearings are frictionless, and determine the forces from the bearings on the shaft at A and B.

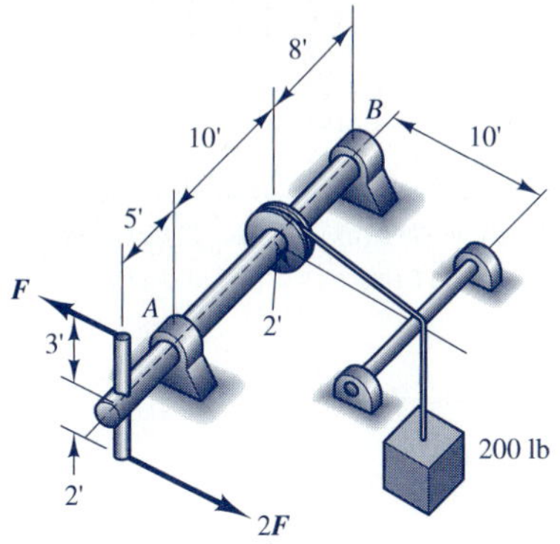

Figure P.5.80.

5.81. A bar with two right-angle bends supports a force $\boldsymbol{F}$ given as

$$\boldsymbol{F} = 10\boldsymbol{i} + 3\boldsymbol{j} + 100\boldsymbol{k} \text{ N}$$

If the bar has a weight of 10 N/m, what is the supporting force system at A?

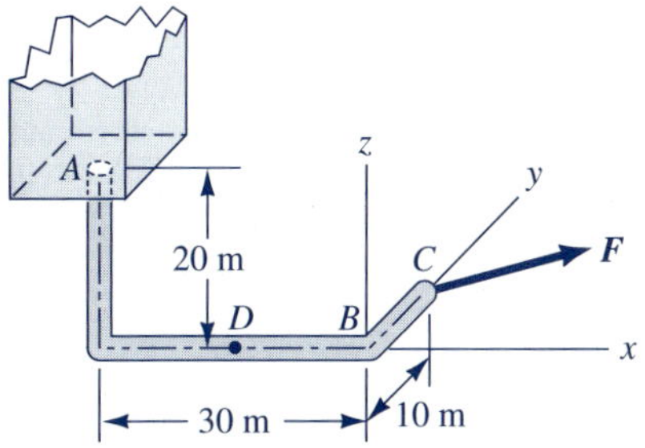

Figure P.5.81.

5.82. What is the resultant of the force system transmitted across the section at A? The couple is parallel to plane M.

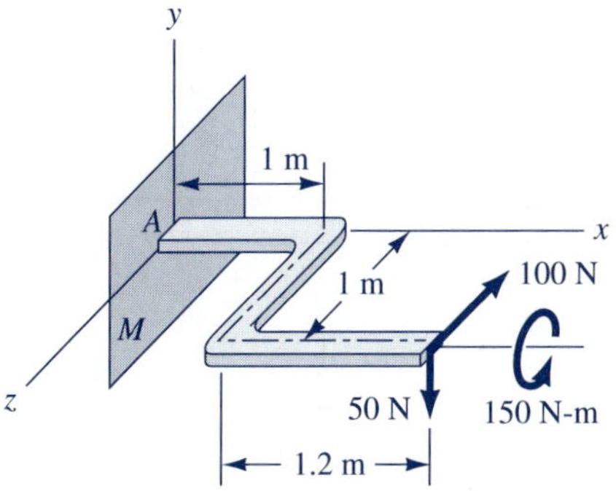

Figure P.5.82.

5.83. Determine the vertical force F that must be applied to the windlass to maintain the 100-lb weight. Also, determine the supporting forces from the bearings onto the shaft. The handle DE on which the force is applied is in the indicated xz plane.

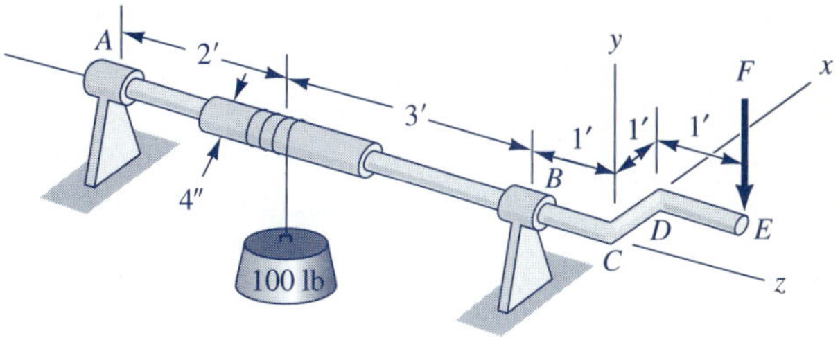

Figure P.5.83.

5.84. A transport plane has a gross weight of 70,000 lb with a center of gravity as shown. Wheels A and B are locked by the braking system while an engine is being tested under load prior to take off. A thrust T of 3,000 lb is developed by this engine. What are the supporting forces?

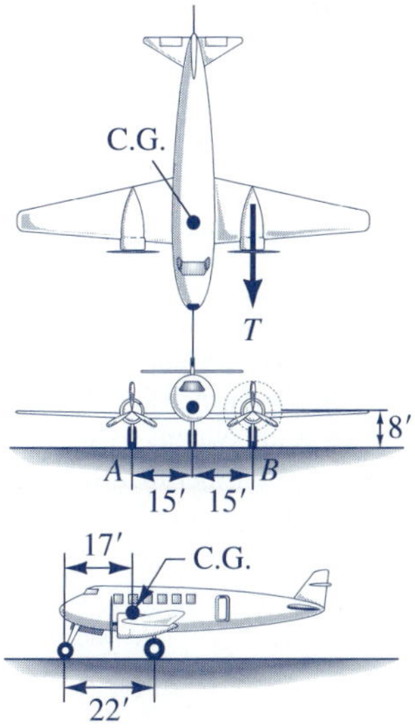

Figure P.5.84.

5.85. Two cables *GH* and *KN* support a rod *AB* which connects to a ball-and-socket joint support at *A* and supports a 500-kg body *C* at *B*. What are the tensions in the cable and the supporting forces at *A*?

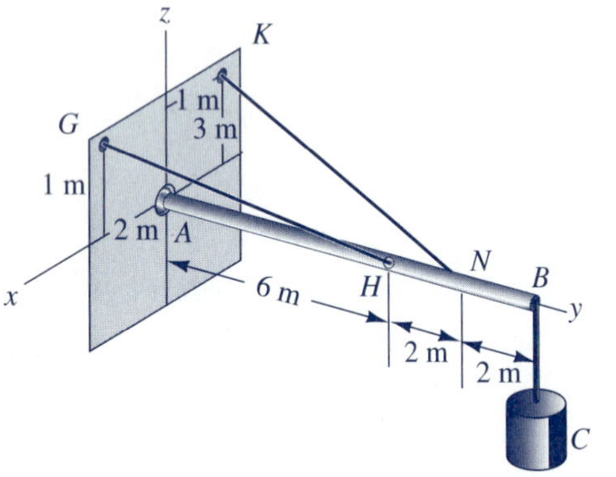

Figure P.5.85.

5.86. What change in elevation for the 100-lb weight will a couple of 300 lb-ft support if we neglect friction in the bearings at *A* and *B*? Also, determine the supporting force components at the bearings for this configuration.

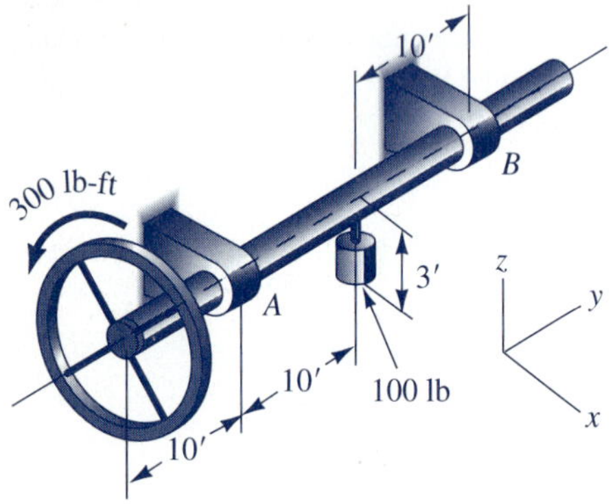

Figure P.5.86.

5.87. Determine the force *P* required to keep the 150-N door of an airplane open 30° while in flight. The force *P* is exerted in a direction normal to the fuselage. There is a net pressure increase on the outside surface of .02 N/mm^2. Also, determine the supporting forces at the hinges. Consider that the top hinge supports any vertical force on the door.

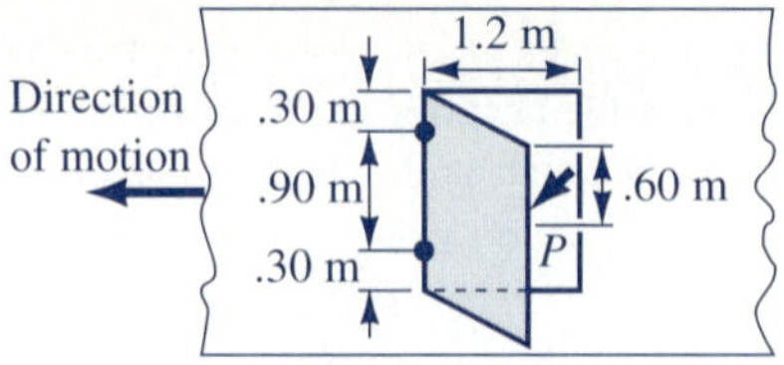

Figure P.5.87.

5.88. What force *P* is needed to hold the door in a horizontal position? The door weighs 50 lb. Determine the supporting forces at *A* and *B*. At *A* there is a pin and at *B* there is a ball-and-socket joint.

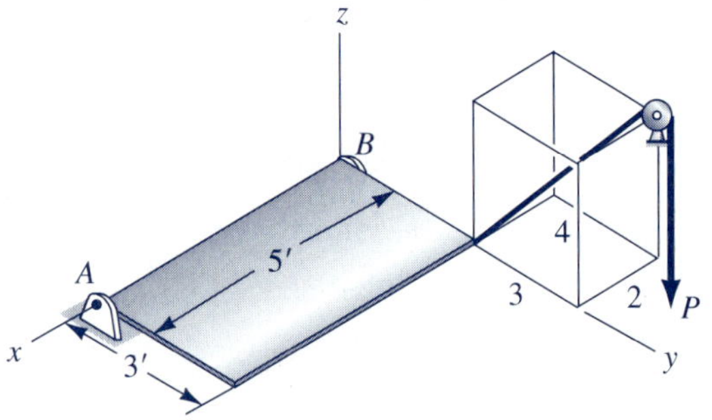

Figure P.5.88.

***5.89.** A uniform bar of length *l* and weight *W* is connected to the ground by a ball-and-socket joint, and rests on a semicylinder from which it is not allowed to slip down by a wall at *B*. If we consider the wall and cylinder to be frictionless, determine the supporting forces at *A* for the following data:

$l = 1$ m
$c = .30$ m
$r = .20$ m
$b = .40$ m
$W = 100$ N

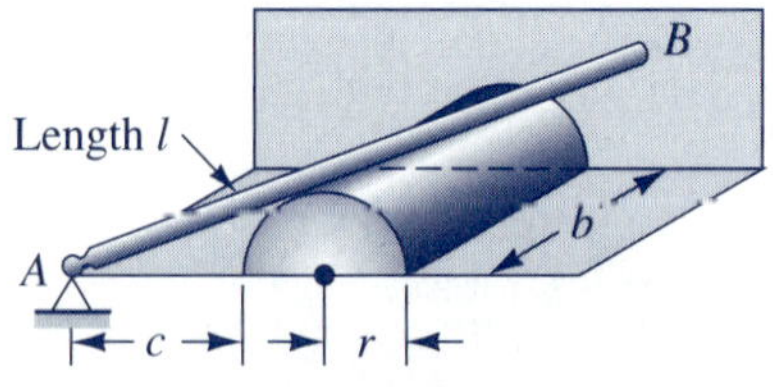

Figure P.5.89.

5.8 Two Point Equivalent Loadings

We shall now consider a simple case of equilibrium that occurs often and from which simple useful conclusions may readily be drawn.

Consider a rigid body on which the *equivalent* systems of two separate forces are respectively applied at two points a and b as shown in Fig. 5.41. If the body is in equilibrium, the first basic equation of statics, 5.1(a), stipulates that $\boldsymbol{F}_1 = -\boldsymbol{F}_2$; that is, the forces must be *equal and opposite*. The second fundamental equation of statics, 5.1(b), requires that $\boldsymbol{C} = \boldsymbol{0}$, indicating that the forces be *collinear* so as not to form a nonzero couple. With points a and b given as points of application for the two forces in Fig. 5.41, clearly the *common line of action for the forces must coincide with the line segment ab*. Such bodies, where there are only *two points of loading*, are sometimes called "two-force" members. Such members occur often in structural mechanics problems. Furthermore, there is considerable saving of time and labor if the student recognizes them at the outset of any problem.

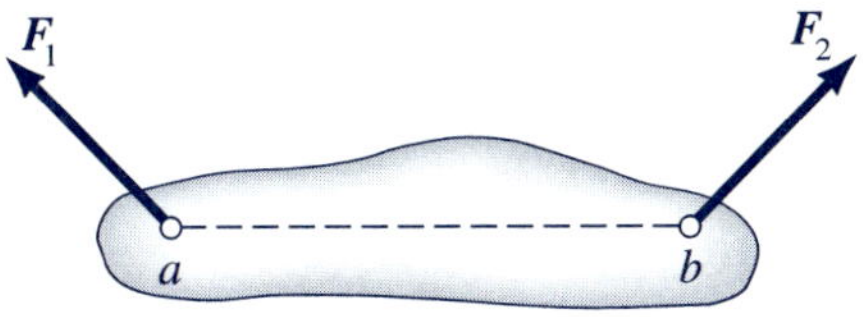

Figure 5.41. Two-force member.

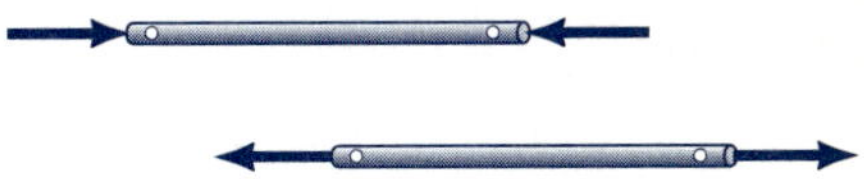

Figure 5.42. Compression and tension members.

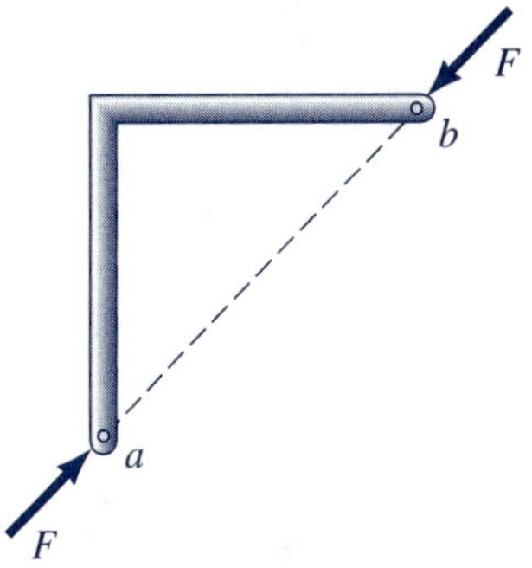

Figure 5.43. Line of action of F collinear with ab.

We often have to deal with pin-connected structural members with loads applied at the pins. If we neglect friction at the pins and also the weight of the members, we can conclude that the equivalent of only two forces act on each member. These forces, then, must be equal and opposite and must have lines of action that are collinear, with the line joining the points of application of the forces. If the member is straight (see Fig. 5.42), the common line of action of the two forces coincides with the centerline of the member. The top member in Fig. 5.42 is a *compression* member, the one below a *tensile* member. Note that the bent member in Fig. 5.43, if weightless, is also a two point loaded member. The line of action of the forces must coincide with the line ab connecting the two points of loading. However, the beam in Fig. 5.44 is not a two point loaded member since at the left end there will be a couple moment. And, clearly, such a loading must entail two points of loading to accommodate the two equal and opposite forces comprising the couple. There are then in effect three points of loading for this member. Accordingly, use caution here when dealing with a cantilever beam.

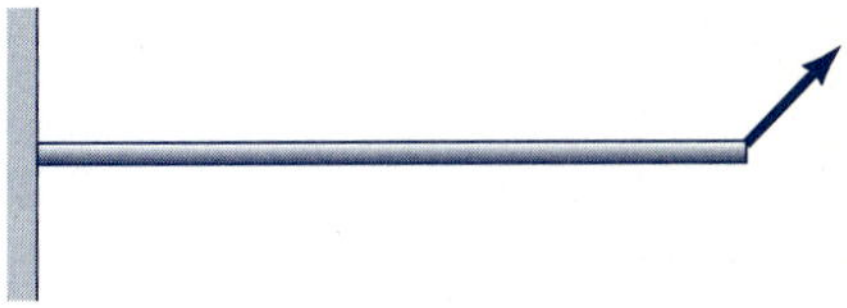

Figure 5.44. Cantilever beam is not an example of a two point loaded member.

Before considering an example, it should be emphasized that the forces F_1 and F_2 in Fig. 5.41 may be the resultants of systems of concurrent forces at a and b, respectively. Since concurrent forces are always equivalent to their resultant at the point of concurrency, the member in Fig. 5.41 is still a two-force member with the resulting restrictions on the resultants F_1 and F_2.

Example 5.12

A device for crushing rocks is shown in Fig. 5.45. A piston D having an 8-in. diameter is activated by a pressure p of 50 psig (pounds per square inch above that of the atmosphere). Rods AB, BC, and BD can be considered weightless for this problem. What is the horizontal force transmitted at A to the trapped rock shown in the diagram?

We have here three two-force members coming together at B. Accordingly, if we isolate pin B as a free body, we will have three forces acting on the pin. These forces must be collinear with the centerlines of the respective members, as explained earlier (Fig. 5.42).

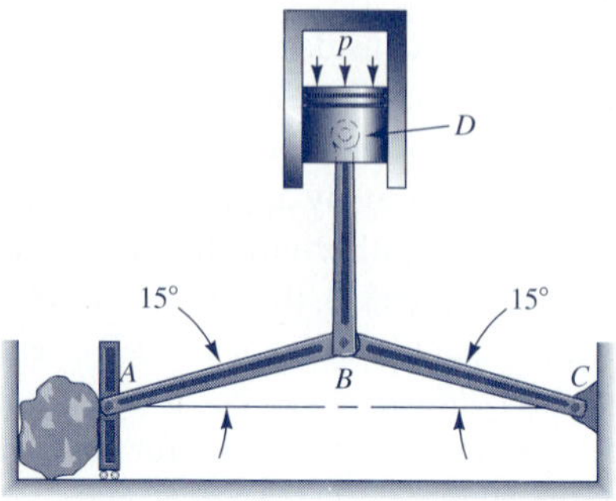

Figure 5.45. Rock crusher.

The force F_D is easily computed by considering the action of the piston. Thus, we get

$$F_D = (50)\frac{\pi 8^2}{4} = 2,510 \text{ lb}$$

Summing forces at pin B:

$\sum F_x = 0$:

$$F_A \cos 15° - F_C \cos 15° = 0$$

$$F_A = F_C$$

$\sum F_y = 0$:

$$2F_A \sin 15° - 2{,}510 = 0$$

$$F_A = \frac{2,510}{(2)(0.259)} = 4{,}850 \text{ lb}$$

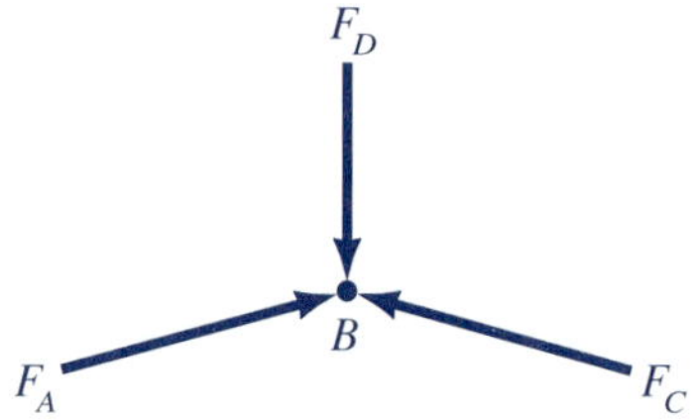

Figure 5.46. Free-body diagram of pin B.

The force transmitted to the rock in the horizontal direction is then 4,850 cos 15° = 4,690 lb.

∴ Horizontal force transmitted to the rock = 4,690 lb

Of less direct use is the *three-force* theorem. It states that a system of three forces in equilibrium must be *coplanar* and either be *concurrent* or be *parallel*.[10]

5.9 Problems Arising From Structures

We will now examine some interesting problems that arise in studies of structural mechanics. Primarily, these problems involve procedures and theory that we have presented in this chapter with some simple additions, (which will be described in the examples to follow), and some use of freshman physics.

[10]To prove this, assume that two of the forces intersect at a point A. Show from the basic equations of equilibrium that the forces must be coplanar and concurrent. Now assume the forces do *not* intersect. Setting moments of the system equal to zero about two points along the line of action of one of the forces, show that the system must be coplanar. Now since the forces do not intersect, they must be parallel. The theorem will thus have been proved.

Example 5.13

Rod *C* shown in Fig. 5.47 is welded to a rigid drum *A*, which is rotating about its axis at a steady angular speed ω of 500 RPM. This rod has a mass per unit length *w*, which varies linearly from the base to the tip starting with the value of 20 kg/m at the base to 28 kg/m at the tip. If *normal stress* is defined as the normal force at a section divided by the area of the section (similar to pressure except that the force can be pulling away from the section rather than always pushing against the section), what is the normal stress at any cross section of the cylinder at a distance *r* from the centerline *B–B* of the drum due only to the motion?

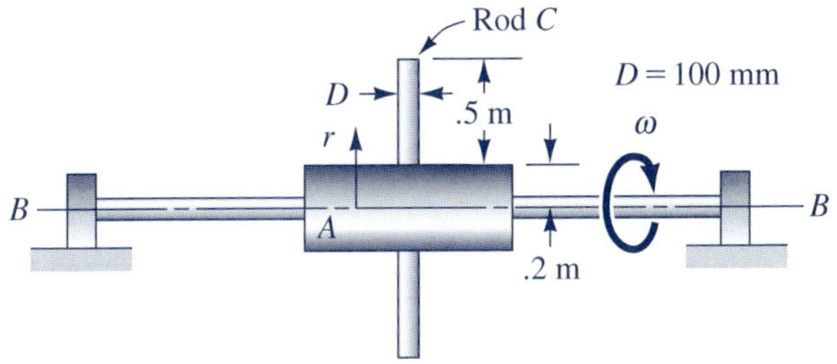

Figure 5.47. Rods attached to a rotating rigid drum.

First we expose a section of the rod at a distance *r* from *B–B* in a *free-body diagram* as shown in Fig. 5.48 in which we denote the normal stress acting on this section as τ_{rr}. The force from this section must restrain the centrifugal force stemming from the angular motion of the portion of the rod beyond position *r*. For this purpose, we consider an infinitesimal slice of the rod (see Fig. 5.48). We shall use the variable η to denote the distance to the slice from the centerline *B–B*. Furthermore, the thickness of the slice shall be $d\eta$. We shall use η to position slices between end position *r* of the free-body diagram and the tip of the rod. We are using this approach for bookkeeping purposes. Now you will recall from freshman physics that the centrifugal force on this slice is given by

$$df_{cent.} = (dm)(\eta)(\omega^2) = (w\,d\eta)(\eta)(\omega^2) \tag{a}$$

Example 5.13 (Continued)

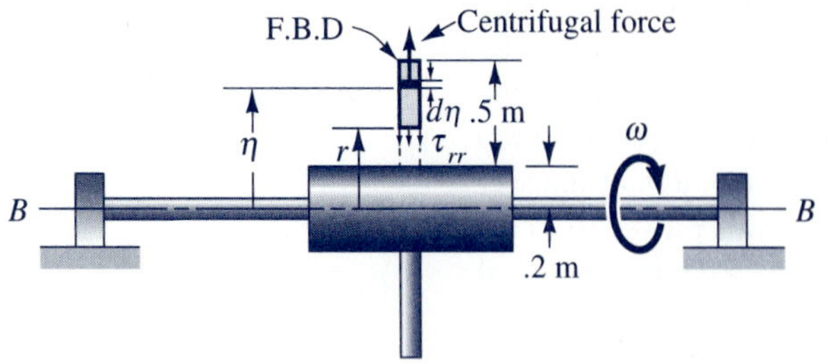

Figure 5.48. Free body exposes τ_{rr} at section r. Note that η is a dummy variable.

Consequently, the total centrifugal force for the material beyond position r in the free body of Fig. 5.48 will be found by integration to be

$$f_{cent.} = \int_r^{.7} w\eta \, d\eta \, \omega^2 \qquad \text{(b)}$$

Next, note that the term w varies linearly with η as follows:

$$w = 20 + \frac{\eta - .2}{.5} 8 \text{ kg/m}$$

Clearly from this equation we see that when $\eta = .2$, we get $w = 20$ kg/m and when $\eta = .7$, we get $w = 28$ kg/m. Also, the variation is linear. Now, going back to Eq. (b), we have

$$f_{cent.} = \int_r^{.7} \left(20 + \frac{\eta - .2}{.5} 8\right)\eta\left(\frac{(500)(2\pi)}{60}\right)^2 d\eta$$

Integrating

$$f_{cent.} = 2.742 \times 10^3 \left[(20 - 3.2)\frac{\eta^2}{2} + 16\frac{\eta^3}{3}\right]_r^{.7}$$

$$= 2.742 \times 10^3 \left[4.116 + 1.829 - 8.40r^2 - 5.333r^3\right]$$

We can give the desired stress τ_{rr} by dividing by the cross-sectional area $\pi D^2/4 = 7.854 \times 10^{-3} m^2$. We thus have the desired normal stress distribution for sections of the rod as follows:

$$\tau_{rr} = 3.491 \times 10^5 \left[5.945 - 8.40r^2 - 5.333r^3\right] \text{ N/m}^2$$

Example 5.14

Consider a *thin-walled* tank containing air at a pressure of 100 psi above that of the atmosphere [see Fig. 5.49(a)]. The outside diameter D of the tank is 2 ft and the wall thickness t is 1/4 in. We consider as a free body from the tank wall a vanishingly small element such as $ABCE$ in the diagram having the shape of a rectangular parallelepiped. What are the stresses on the cut surfaces of the element? Neglect the weight of the cylinder.

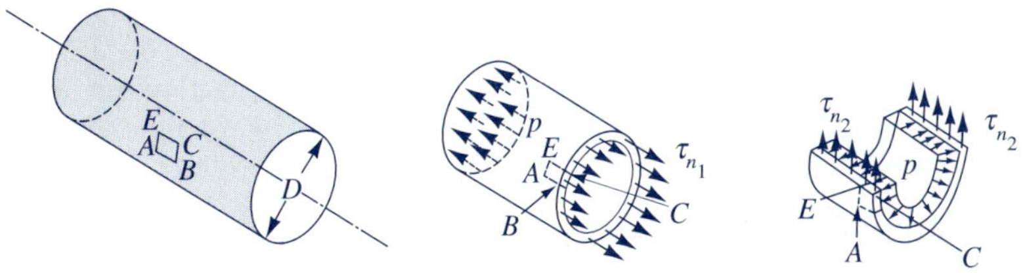

Figure 5.49. Thin-walled tank with inside gauge pressure p.

We can examine face BC by considering a free body of part of the tank, as shown in Fig. 5.49(b) exposing BC. (Note that we have not included the pressure on the inside wall). Because there is a net force from the air pressure only in the *axial* direction of the cylinder, we can expect normal stress τ_{n_1} (like pressure except that it is tensile rather than compressive) over the cut section of the cylinder, as has been indicated in the diagram. Furthermore, because the wall of the tank is *thin* compared to the diameter, we can assume that the stress τ_{n_1} is *uniform* across the thickness. Finally, for reasons of *axial symmetry* of geometry and loading, we can expect this stress to be uniform around the entire cross section. Now we may say from considerations of *equilibrium* in the axial direction that

$$\tau_{n_1}\pi\left[\frac{D^2}{4} - \frac{(D-2t)^2}{4}\right] - p\pi\frac{(D-2t)^2}{4} = 0$$

$$\therefore\ \tau_{n_1} = \frac{p(D-2t)^2}{D^2-(D-2t)^2} = \frac{(100)(24-\frac{1}{2})^2}{24^2-23.5^2} = \boxed{2{,}325 \text{ psi}} \qquad \text{(a)}$$

Hence, on face BC we have a uniform stress of 2,325 psi. Clearly, this must also be true for face AE. This is called an *axial stress.*

To expose face EC next, we consider a half-cylinder of unit length such as is shown in Fig. 5.49(c). Because it is *far* from the ends and because the wall is *thin*, we can assume as an approximation that the stress τ_{n_2} shown is uniform over the cut section.[11] A pressure p is shown acting

[11]Near the ends of the tank the stress distribution *varies* in value because of the proximity of the *complicated geometry* and the contributions toward equilibrium of the end plates.

Example 5.14 (Continued)

normal to the inside wall surface. (The stress τ_{n_1} computed earlier is not shown, to avoid cluttering the diagram.) Now we consider an end view of this body in Fig. 5.50 for equilibrium in the vertical direction. We have

$$2\left[(\tau_{n_2})(t)(1)\right] - \int_0^{\pi} p\left(\frac{D}{2} - t\right) d\theta(1)\sin\theta = 0 \qquad \text{(b)}$$

$$\therefore\ \tau_{n_2} = \frac{1}{2t}\left[p\left(\frac{D}{2} - t\right)\right](-\cos\theta)\Big|_0^{\pi}$$

$$\tau_{n_2} = \frac{p\left(\frac{D}{2} - t\right)}{t} = \boxed{4{,}700 \text{ psi}}$$

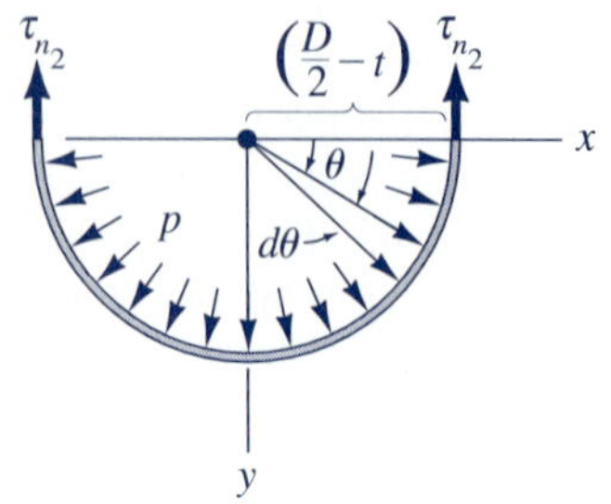

Figure 5.50. Free body of part of cylinder.

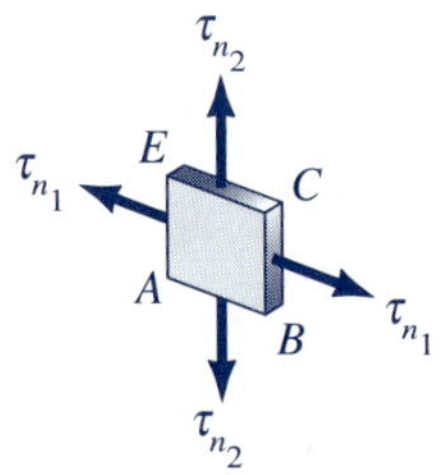

Figure 5.51. Free body of an element of the cylinder.

We point out now that the force in a particular direction from a uniform pressure on a curved surface equals the pressure times the projected area of this surface in the direction of the desired force. (You will learn this in your studies of hydrostatics.) Thus for the case at hand the projected area is that of a rectangle $1 \times (D - 2t)$, so that the second expression of Eq. (b) becomes $p(D - 2t)$. You may readily verify that this gives the same result as above.

The stress τ_{n_2} is called the *hoop stress*; it is about twice the *axial stress* τ_{n_1}. We show element *ABCE* with the stresses present in Fig. 5.51.

5.10 Static Indeterminacy

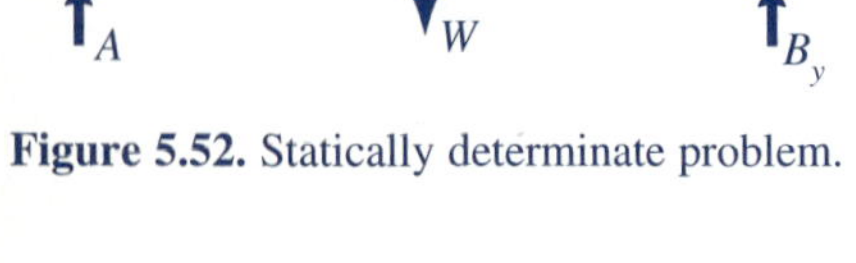

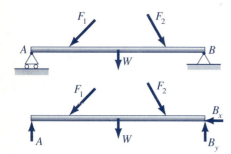

Figure 5.52. Statically determinate problem.

Examine the simple beam in Fig. 5.52, with known external loads and weight. If the deformation of the beam is small, and the final positions of the external loads after deformation differ only slightly from their initial positions, we can assume the beam to be rigid and, using the undeformed geometry, we can solve the supporting forces A, B_x, and B_y. This is possible since we have three equations of equilibrium available. Suppose, now, that an additional support is made available to the beam, as indicated in Fig. 5.53. The beam can still be considered a rigid body, since the applied load will shift even less because of deformation. Therefore, the resultant force coming from the ground to counteract the applied loads and weight of the beam must be the *same* as before. In the first case, in which two supports were given, however, a unique set of values for the forces A, B_x, and B_y gave us the required resultant. In other words, we were able to solve for these forces by statics alone, without further considerations. In the second case, rigid-body statics will give the required *same* resultant supporting force system, but now there are an infinite number of possible combinations of values of the supporting forces that will give us the resultant system demanded by equilibrium of rigid bodies. To decide on the proper combination of supporting forces requires additional computation. Although the deformation properties of the beam were unimportant up to this point, they now become the all-important criterion in apportioning the supporting forces. These problems are termed *statically indeterminate*, in contrast to the statically determinate type, in which statics and the rigid-body assumption suffice. For a given system of loads and masses, two models—the rigid-body model and models taught in other courses involving elastic behavior—are accordingly both employed to achieve a desired end. In summary:

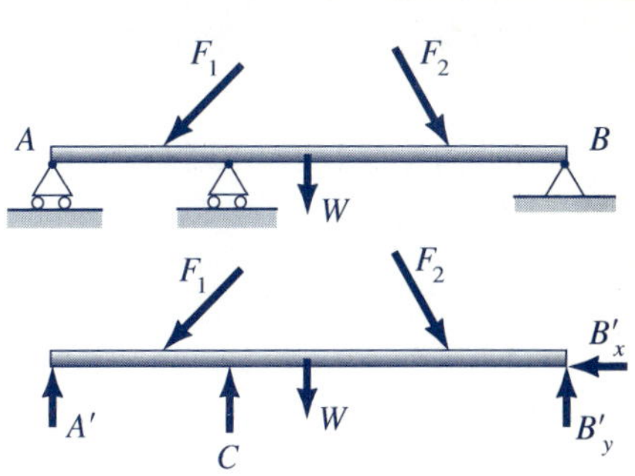

Figure 5.53. Statically indeterminate problem.

In statically indeterminate problems, we must satisfy both the equations of equilibrium for rigid bodies and the equations that stem from deformation considerations. In statically determinate problems, we need only satisfy the equations of equilibrium.

In the discussion thus far, we used a beam as the rigid body and discussed the statical determinacy of the supporting system. Clearly, the same conclusions apply to any structure that, without the aid of the external constraints, can be taken as a rigid body. If, for such a structure as a free body, there are as many unknown supporting force and couple-moment components as there are equations of equilibrium, and if these equations can be solved for these unknowns, we say that the structure is *externally statically determinate*.

On the other hand, should we desire to know the forces transmitted *between* internal members of this kind of structure (i.e., one that does not depend on the external constraints for rigidity), we then examine free bodies of these members. When all the unknown force and couple-moment components can be found by the equations of equilibrium for these free bodies, we then say that the structure is *internally statically determinate*.

There are structures that depend on the external constraints for rigidity (see the structure shown in Fig. 5.54). Mathematically speaking, we can say for such structures that the supporting force system always depends on both the internal forces and the external loads. (This is in contrast to the previous case, where the supporting forces could, for the externally statically determinate case, be related directly with the external loads without consideration of the internal forces.) In this case, we do not distinguish between internal and external statical determinacy, since the evaluation of supporting forces will involve free bodies of some or all of the internal members of the structure; hence, some or all of the internal forces and moments will be involved. For such cases, we simply state that the structure is statically determinate if, for all the unknown force and couple-moment components, we have enough equations of equilibrium that can be solved for these unknowns.

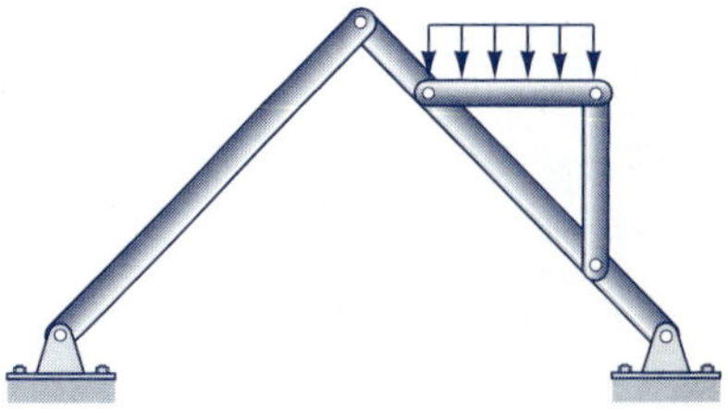

Figure 5.54. Nonrigid structure.

PROBLEMS

5.90. Draw free-body diagrams for the hoe, arms, and tractor of the backhoe. Consider the weight of each part to act at a central location. The backhoe is not digging at the instant shown. Neglect the weights of the hydraulic systems *CE*, *AB*, and *FH*.

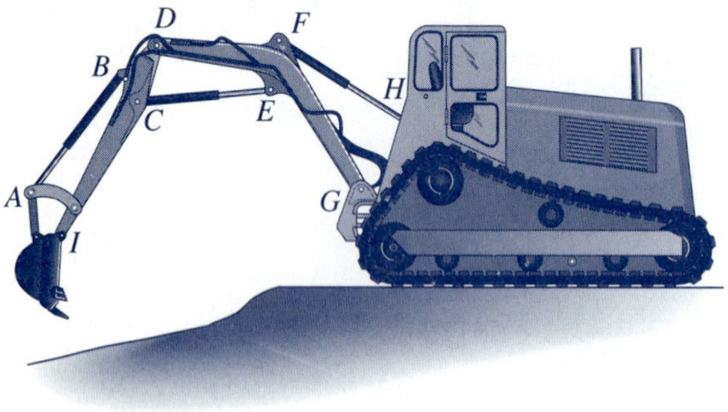

Figure P.5.90.

5.91. A parking-lot gate arm weighs 150 N. Because of the taper, the weight can be regarded as concentrated at a point 1.25 m from the pivot point. What force must be exerted by the solenoid to lift the gate? What solenoid force is necessary if a 300-N counterweight is placed .25 m to the left of the pivot point?

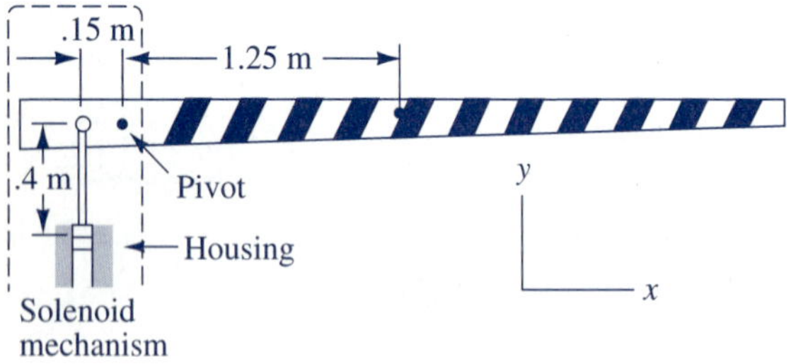

Figure P.5.91.

5.92. Find the force delivered at *C* in a horizontal direction to crush the rock. Pressure p_1 = 100 psig and p_2 = 60 psig (pressures measured above atmospheric pressure). The diameters of the pistons are 6 in. each. Neglect the weight of the rods.

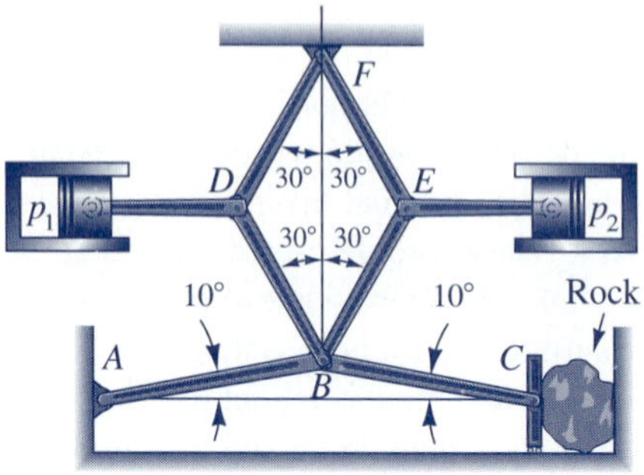

Figure P.5.92.

5.93. A Broyt X-20 digger carries a 20-kN load as shown. If hydraulic ram *CB* is normal to *BA*, where *A* is the axis of rotation for member *E*, find the force needed by ram *CB*. Do not consider the weights of the members.

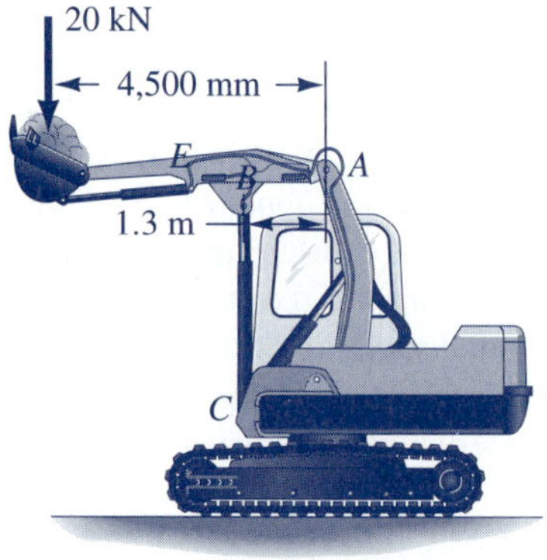

Figure P.5.93.

5.94. What force F_1 is needed for equilibrium? Neglect friction. The design is symmetrical about vertical axis. Horizontal members are pinned at *E*.

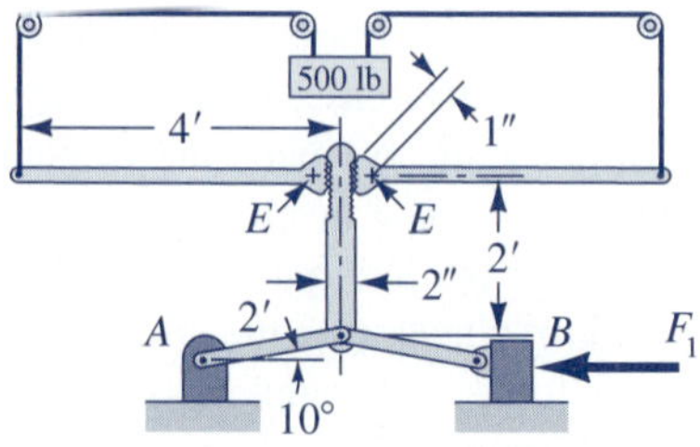

Figure P.5.94.

5.95. Find the values of F and C so that members AB and CD fail simultaneously. The maximum load for AB is 15 kN and for CD is 22 kN. Neglect the weight of the members.

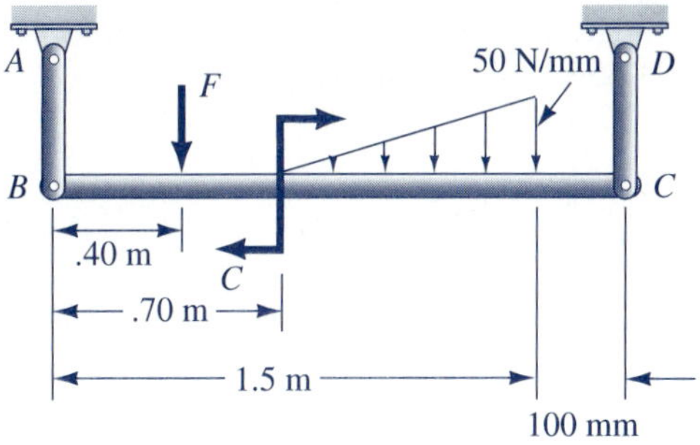

Figure P.5.95.

5.96. The landing carriage of a transport plane supports a stationary total vertical load of 200 kN. There are two wheels on each side of shock strut AB. Find the force in member EC, and the forces transmitted to the fuselage at A, if the brakes are locked and the engines are tested resulting in a thrust of 5 kN, 40% of which is resisted by this landing gear.

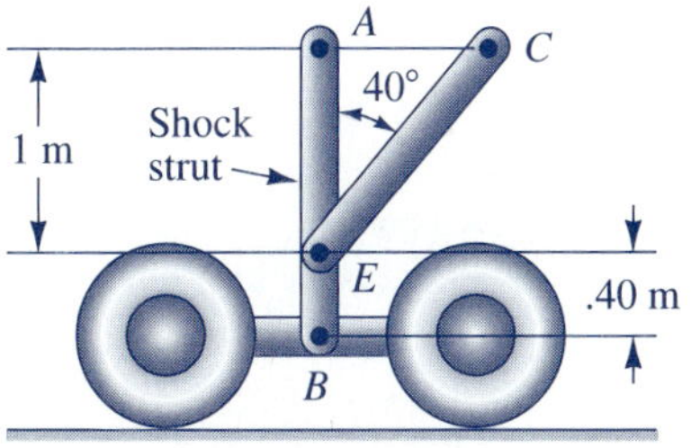

Figure P.5.96.

5.97. Find the magnitudes of the supporting forces for the frame shown. You may only use *two* free-body diagrams for this problem. Set forth a complete system of equations for solving the desired unknowns but do not carry out the algebra for actually solving these equations for the desired unknowns.

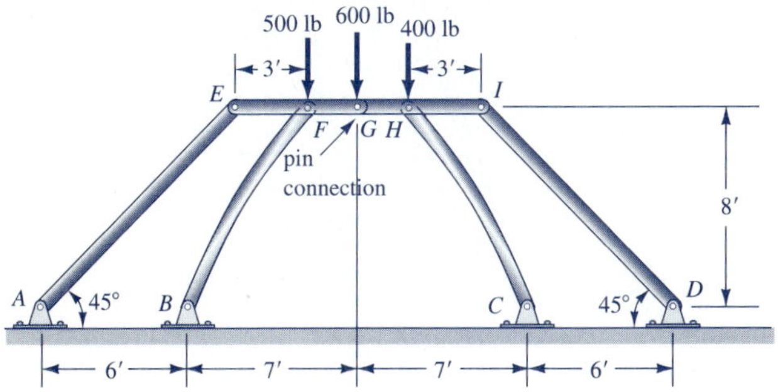

Figure P.5.97.

5.98. (a) Find the supporting forces at B. Neglect the weights of the members.

(b) What is the force in the member CB?

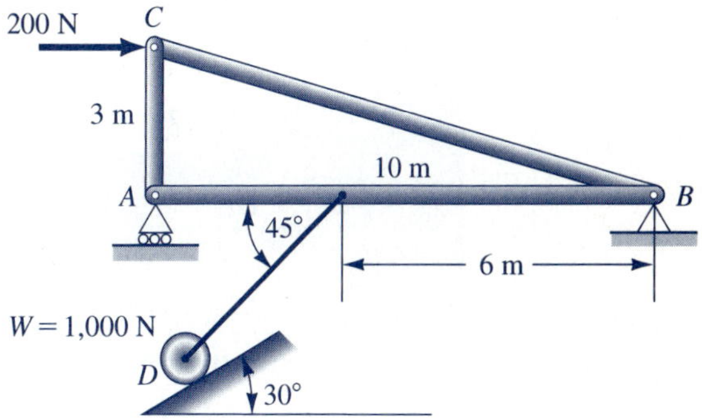

Figure P.5.98.

5.99. Find the supporting forces at B and C. Disc A weighs 200 N. Neglect the weights of the members as well as friction.

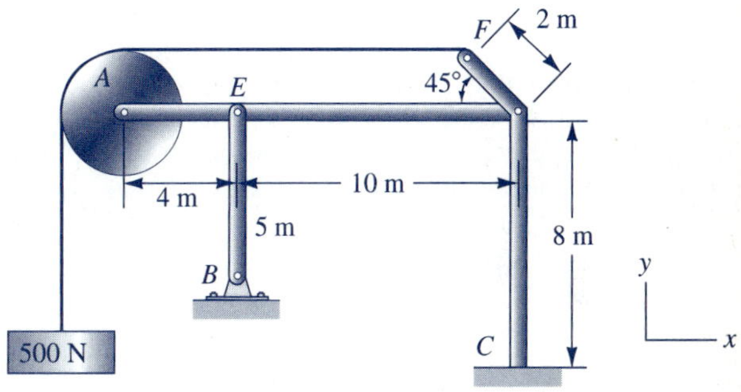

Figure P.5.99.

5.100. Find the supporting force system at C. Neglect friction.

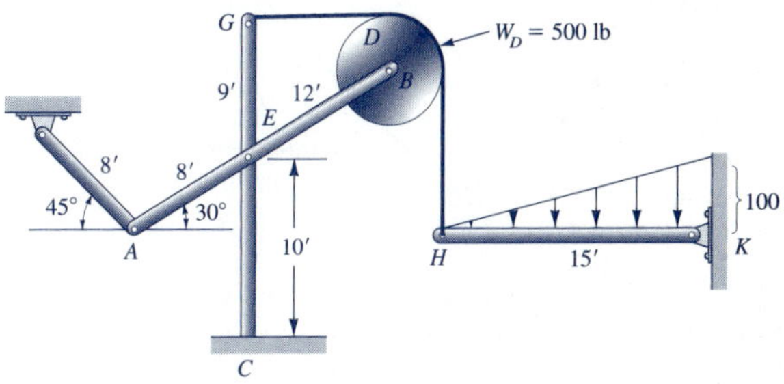

Figure P.5.100.

5.101. The pavement exerts a force of 1,000 lb on the tire. The tire, brakes, and so on, weigh 100 lb; the center of gravity is taken at the center plane of the tire. Determine the force from the spring and the compression force in *CD*.

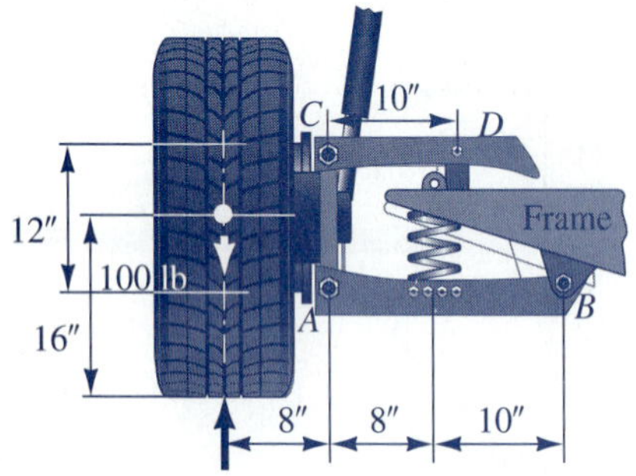

Figure P.5.101.

5.102. A *flyball governor* is shown rotating at a constant speed ω of 500 rpm. The weights *C* and *D* are each of mass 500 g and are pin-connected to light rods. The centrifugal force on the weights, you will recall from physics, is given as $mr\omega^2$, where r is the radial distance to the particle from the axis of rotation and ω is in rad/sec. Using this centrifugal force, and, imagining that we are rotating with the system, we can consider that we have equilibrium. (This is the D'Alembert principle that you learned in physics.) What is the tension in the rods and the downward force *F* at *B* needed to maintain the configuration shown for the given ω?

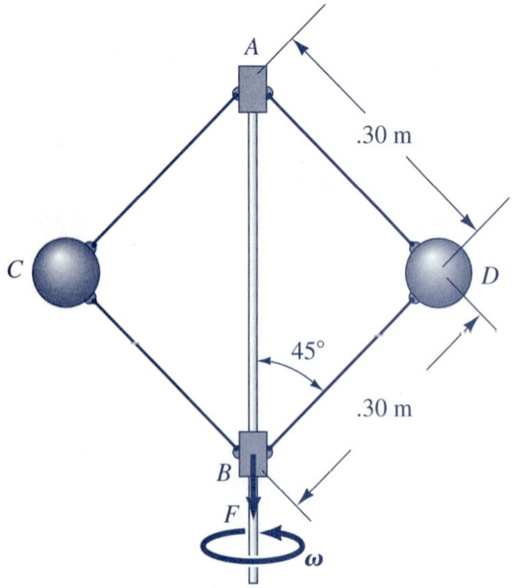

Figure P.5.102.

5.103. A flyball governor is shown below. If $\omega_1 = 3$ rad/sec, compute the tension in *AG* and *AE*. Neglect the weights of the members but assume that *HC* and *HB* are stiff. The weights *C* and *B* each have a mass of 200 g. What is the force *F* needed to maintain the configuration? (*Hint:* Read the discussion of centrifugal force and D'Alembert's principle in Problem 5.102.)

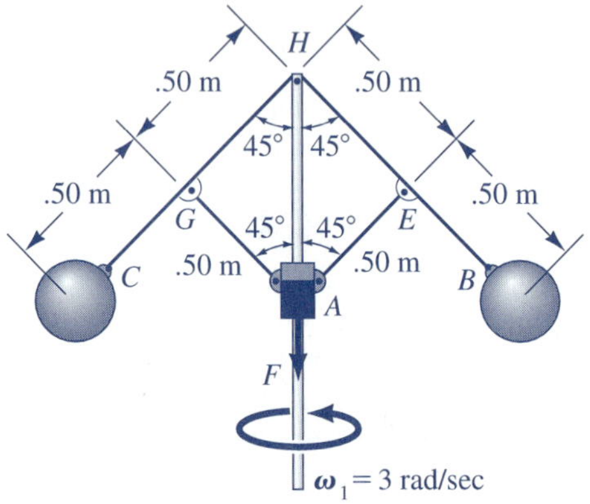

Figure P.5.103.

5.104. Determine the supporting forces at *A*, *C*, *D*, *G*, *F*, and *H* for the structure. *C*, *D*, *H* and *G* are ball joint connections.

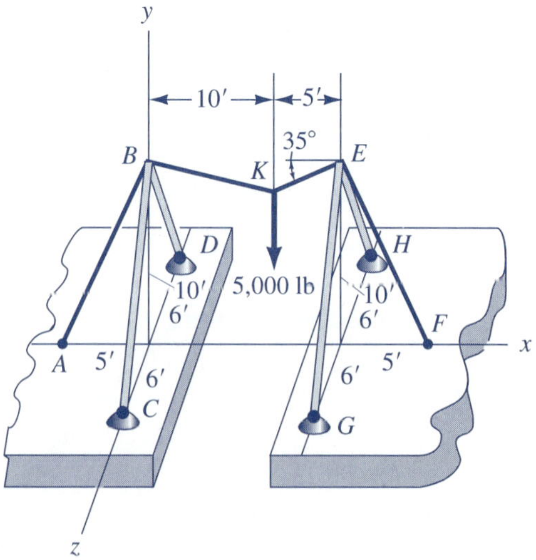

Figure P.5.104.

5.105. A trap door is kept open by a rod *CD*, whose weight we shall neglect. The door has hinges at *A* and *B* and has a weight of 200 lb. A wind blowing against the outside surface of the door creates a pressure increase of 2 lb/ft^2. Find the force in the rod, assuming that it cannot slip from the position shown. Also determine the forces transmitted to the hinges. Only hinge *B* can resist motion along direction *AB*.

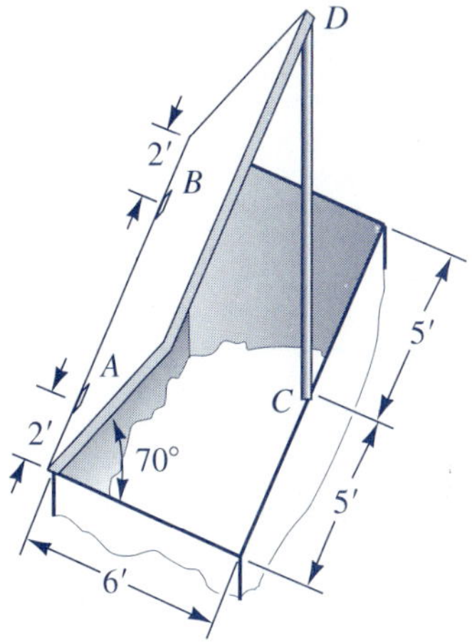

Figure P.5.105.

5.106. Find the force *BD*. All connections are ball-and-socket joints. Neglect the weights of all the members. Member *AB* has two 90° bends. Member *BD* is in the *yz* plane.

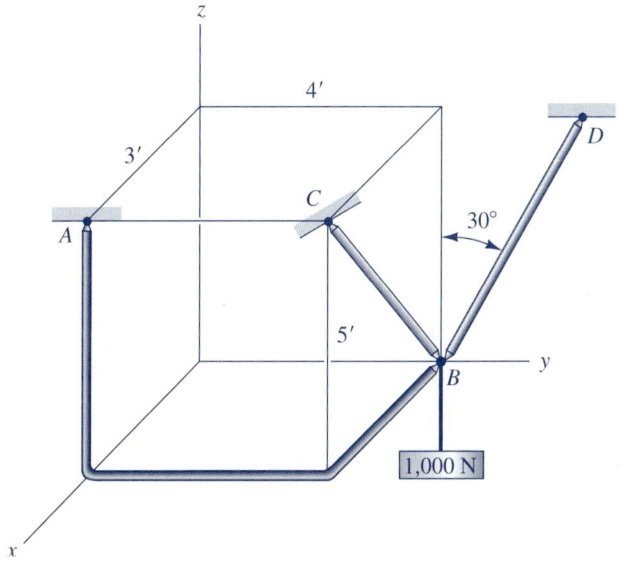

Figure P.5.106.

5.107. Find the supporting forces at *A* and *C*. You must show and use only one free-body diagram.

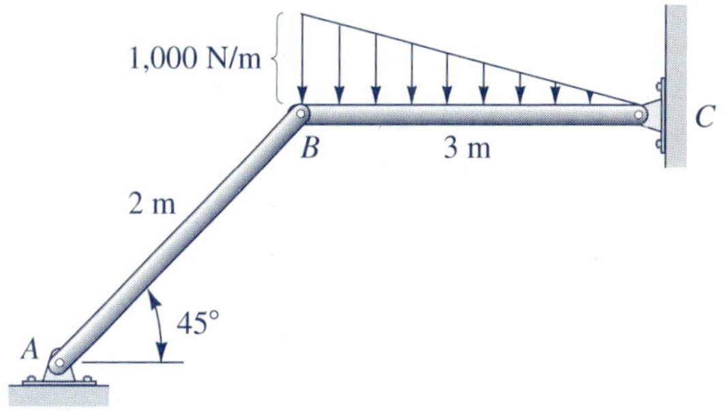

Figure P.5.107.

5.108. A coupling between two shafts transmits an axial load of 5,000 N. Four bolts having a diameter each of 13 mm, connects the two units. Before loading of the shafts, these bolts have only negligible tensile forces. Assuming that each bolt carries the same load, what is the average normal stress in each bolt stemming from the 5,000 N load?

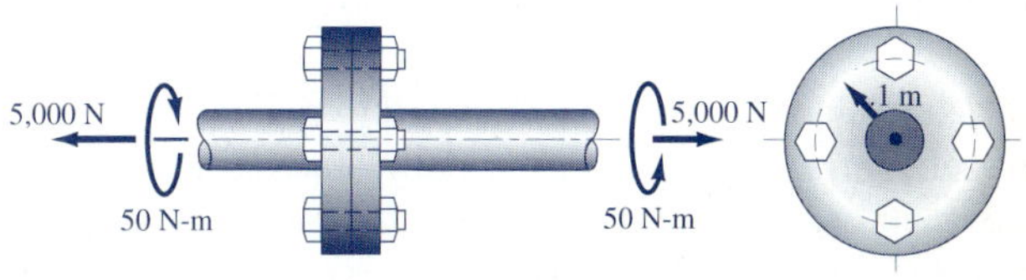

Figure P.5.108.

5.109. A circular shaft is suspended from above. The specific weight of the shaft material is 7.22×10^4 N/m^3. What is the tensile stress τ_{zz} on cross sections of the shaft as a function of z?

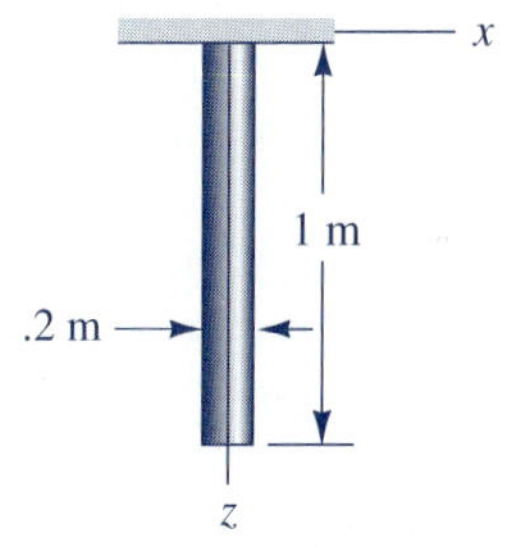

Figure P.5.109.

5.110. Do the previous problem for the case where the specific weight γ varies with the *square* of z starting with the value of 6.50×10^4 N/m^3 at the top and reaching a value of 7.50×10^4 N/m^3 at the bottom.

5.111. A cone is suspended from above. The specific weight γ of the material is 460 lb/ft^3. What is the average normal stress denoted as τ_{zz} for cross-sections of the cone as a function of z?

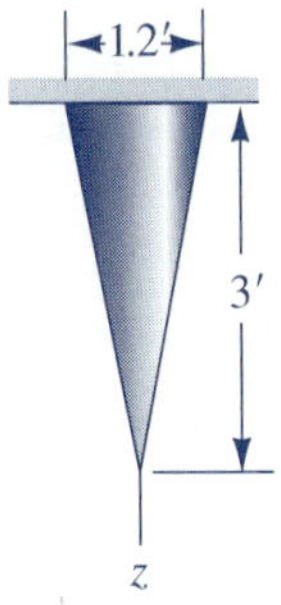

Figure P.5.111.

5.112. Solve the preceding problem for the case where the specific weight γ varies linearly from the top of the cone (γ = 460 lb/ft^3) the bottom (γ = 385 lb/ft^3). Get the normal stress τ_{zz} at cross sections of the cone as a function of z but do not bother to collect terms coming out of the integration. Finally, compute from your function the stress τ_{zz} at a position one foot from the top.

5.11 Closure

We have presented in this chapter the *free-body* concept. We hope that the importance of drawing correct free bodies has been made abundantly clear. Do not proceed in your work on a problem until correct, clearly drawn free bodies have been formed. This is the most critical step in problem solving! If you do not master this capability, you will be plagued throughout your future courses with difficulties and frustrations arising from this inadequacy. Also vital, is to know how many *independent equations of equilibrium* you can write for any free-body diagram you draw. Recall, we reached this capability by considering simplest resultants for various categories of force systems and reasoned what was necessary in terms of equations to render the particular simplest resultant system a null vector system and thus to generate the appropriate number of independent equations of equilibrium.

At the end of the chapter, we considered the case of the *statically indeterminate* problem pointing out that in addition to satisfying the rigid-body equations of equilibrium, we also had to consider the deformation of the body, however small the deformation. These considerations are beyond this course and will be studied in the solid mechanics course which you will take soon after the completion of your statics course.[12]

In Chapter 6, we shall consider certain types of bodies that are of great engineering interest. The problems will be statically determinate and will involve nothing that is fundamentally new. We devote a separate chapter to these problems because they contain sign conventions and techniques that are important and complex enough to warrant such a study. We therefore proceed to an introduction of statically determinate structural mechanics problems.

[12]For such problems, see I. H. Shames, *Introduction to Solid Mechanics*, 2nd edition, Prentice-Hall, Inc., Englewood Cliffs, N.J., 1989.

PROBLEMS

5.113. Determine the tensions in all the cables. Block A has a mass of 600 kg. Note that GH is in the yz plane.

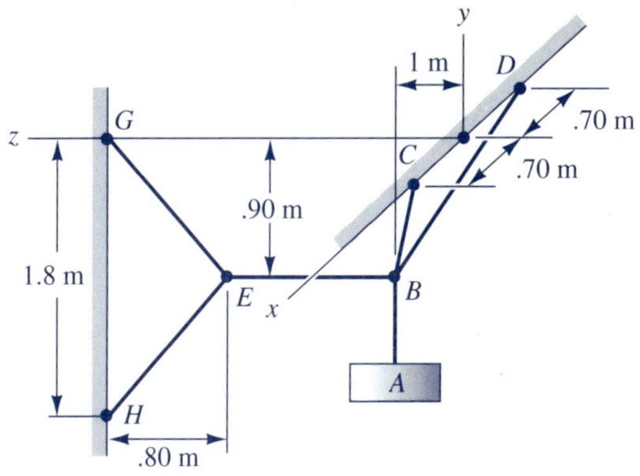

Figure P.5.113.

5.114. Determine the force components at G. E weighs 300 lb.

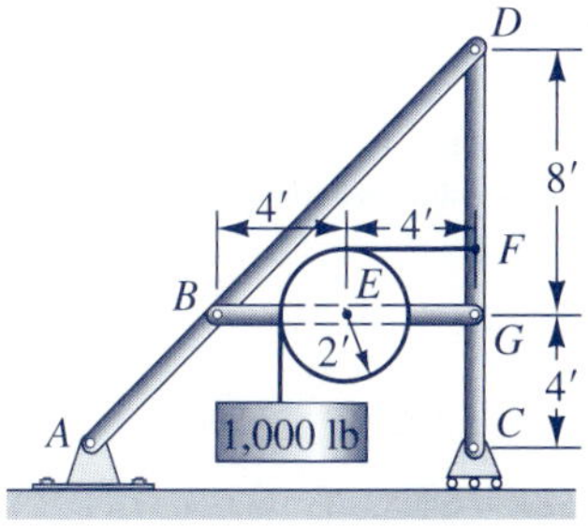

Figure P.5.114.

5.115. A scenic excursion train with cog wheels for steep inclines weighs 30 tons when fully loaded. If the cog wheels have a mean radius to the contact points of the teeth of 2 ft, what torque must be applied to the driver wheels A if wheels B run free? What force do wheels B transmit to the ground?

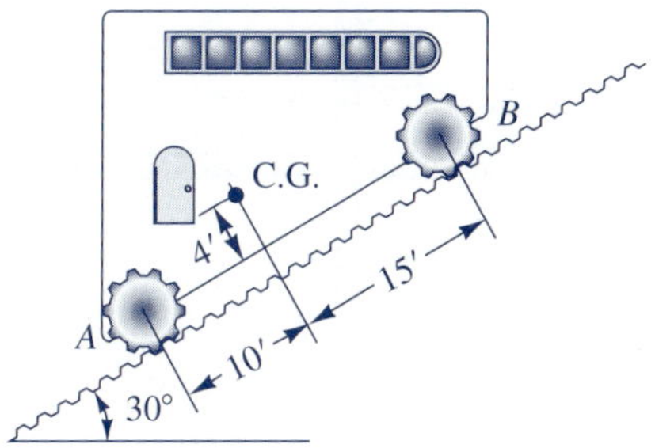

Figure P.5.115.

5.116. Find the forces on the block of ice from the hooks at A and F.

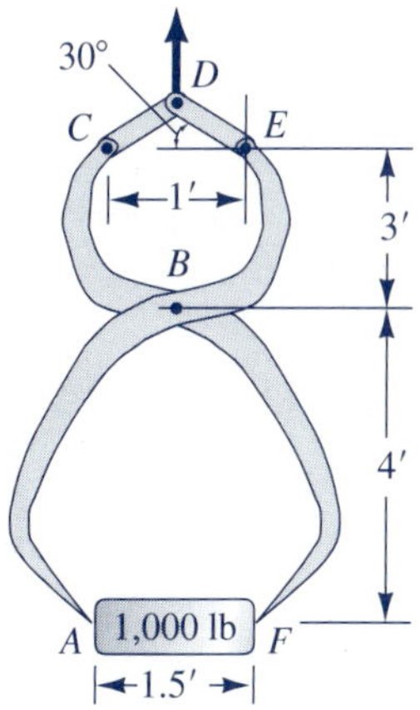

Figure P.5.116.

5.117. Members AB and BC weighing, respectively, 50 N and 200 N are connected to each other by a pin. BC connects to a disc K on which a torque T_K = 200 N-m is applied. What torque T is needed on AB to keep the system in equilibrium at the configuration shown?

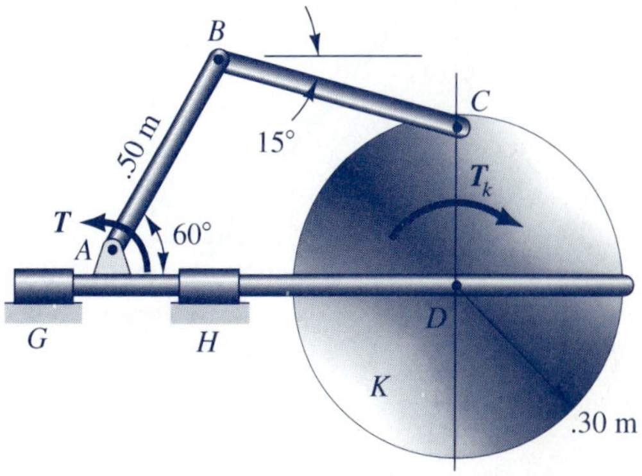

Figure P.5.117.

5.118. A transport jet plane has a weight without fuel of 220 kN. If one wing is loaded with 50 kN of fuel, what are the forces in each of the three landing gear?

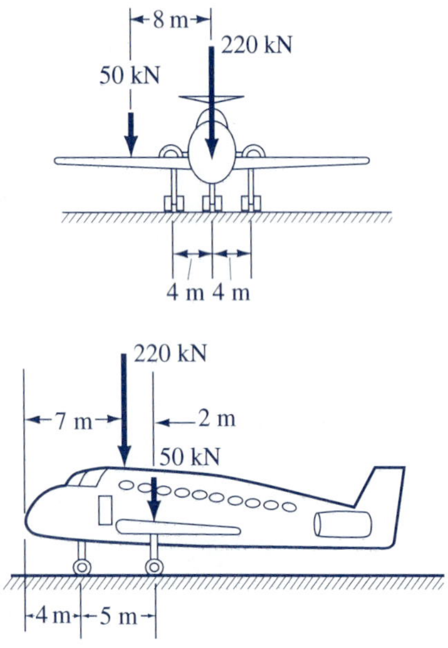

Figure P.5.118.

5.119. A rod *AB* is connected by a ball-and-socket joint to a frictionless sleeve at *A*, and by a ball-and-socket joint to a fixed position at *B*. What are the supporting forces at *B* and at *A* if we neglect the weight of *AB*? The 100-lb load is connected to the center of *AB*.

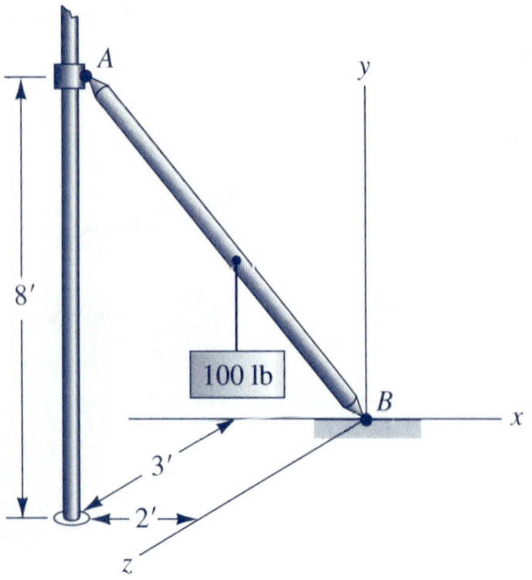

Figure P.5.119.

5.120. A beam weighing 400 lb is held by a ball-and-socket joint at *A* and by two cables *CD* and *EF*. Find the tension in the cables. They are attached to blocks at opposite ends of the beam as shown.

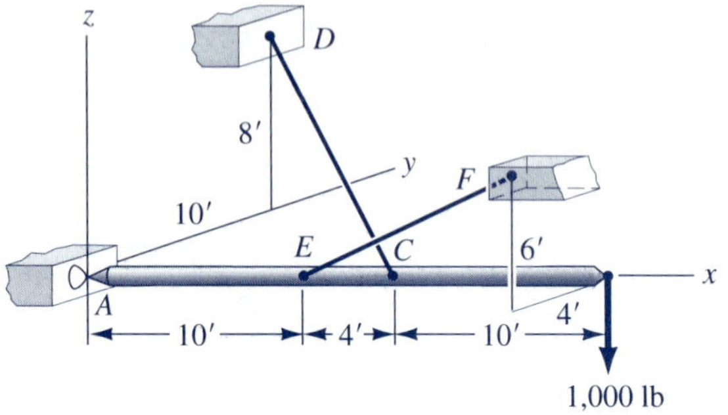

Figure P.5.120.

5.121. What should the values of *R* and *M* be if the supporting rods *AB* and *CD* are to fail simultaneously? Rod *AB* can withstand a 5,000-lb force, and rod *CD* can withstand an 8,000-lb force. Neglect the weights of the members.

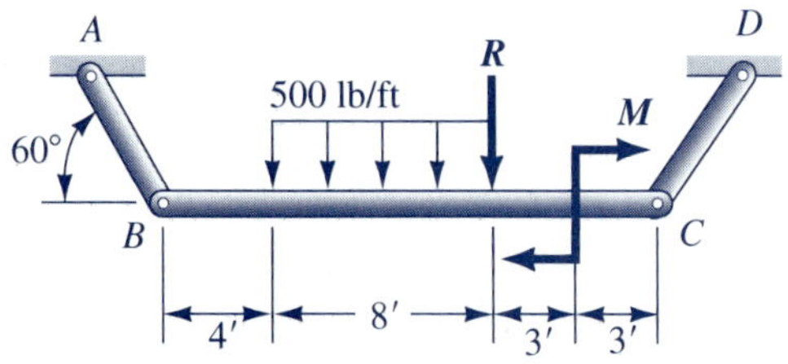

Figure P.5.121.

5.122. Find A_x and A_y at the bottom support. Do *not* determine any other unknowns. Do this using only *two* free-body diagrams and only *two* equations. Disc *D* weighs 30 lb and has a diameter of 2 ft. Neglect the weight of the members. Neglect friction everywhere.

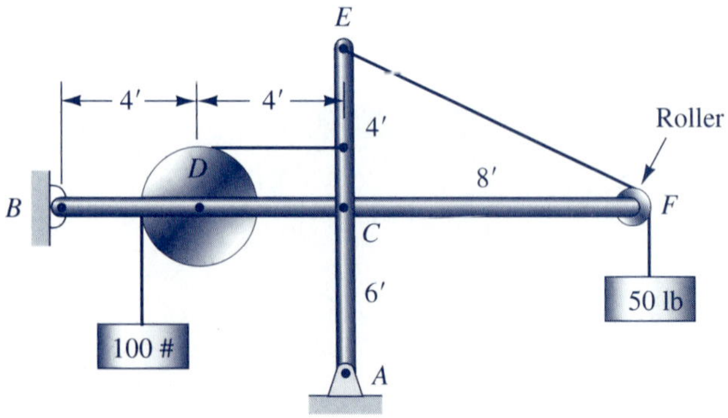

Figure P.5.122.

5.123. Light rods *BC* and *AC* are pinned together at *C* and support a 300-N load and a 500-N-m couple moment. What are the supporting forces at *A* and *B*?

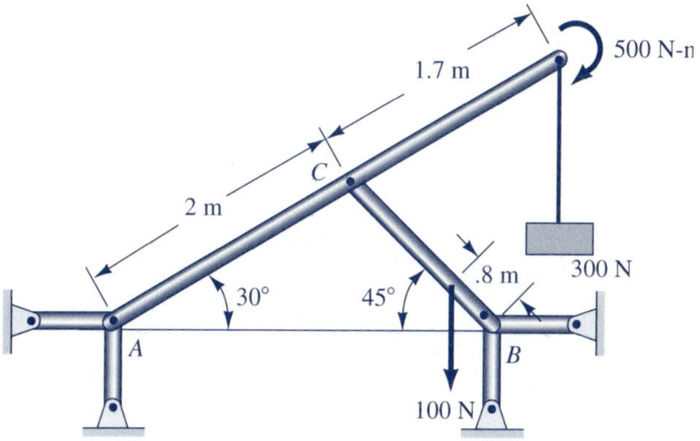

Figure P.5.123.

5.124. A rod *AB* is held by a ball-and-socket joint at *A* and supports a 100-kg mass *C* at *B*. This rod is in the *zy* plane and is inclined to the *y* axis by an angle of 15°. The rod is 16 m long and *F* is at its midpoint. Find the forces in cables *DF* and *EB*. Cross-hatching indicates part of the *yz* plane.

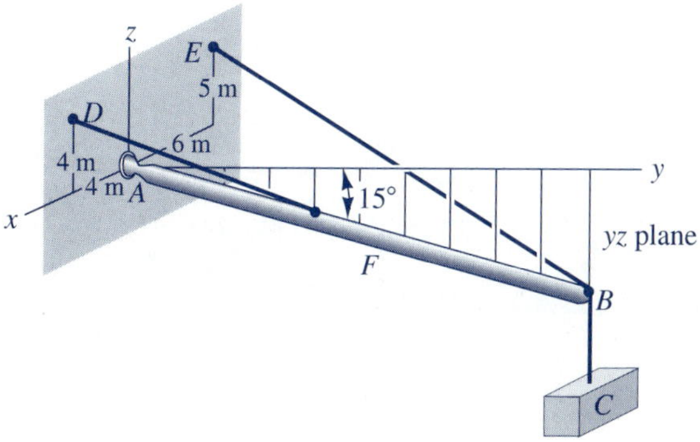

Figure P.5.124.

5.125. A bent rod *ADGB* supports two weights—one at the center of *AD* and one at the center of *DG*. There are ball-and-socket joint supports at *A* and *B*. With one scalar equation using the triple scalar product, determine the tension in cable *DC*.

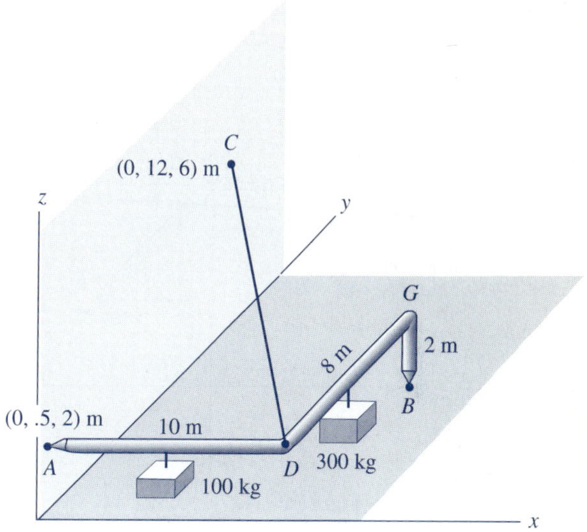

Figure P.5.125.

5.126. Find the tension in cable *FH*. The disc *G* weighs 500 lb. Use only one free body.

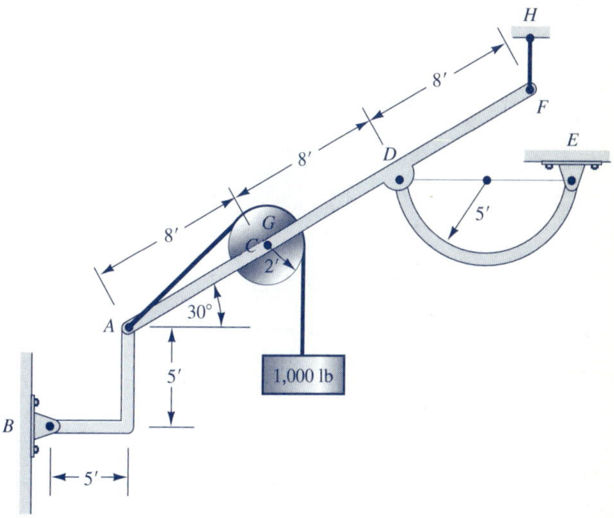

Figure P.5.126.

5.127. (a) Find the supporting force components at A using only one free-body diagram.

(b) Find the force system transmitted through the cross section at E of the beam CD. Again, use only one free-body diagram for this calculation. ACD is a bent member.

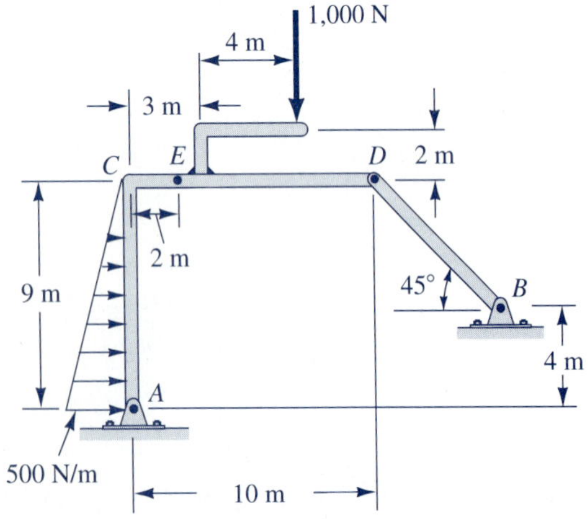

Figure P.5.127.

5.128. A wind is creating a uniform pressure of 0.3 psig on the left side of the door E and causes a uniform suction on the right side of the door of –.02 psig. A wire AB constrains the door. If hinge D allows for movement in the y direction, but hinge C does not, what are the supporting forces from the hinges? The weight of the door is 200 lb with a center of gravity at the geometric center of the door. The position of end A of the supporting wire has coordinates (–6, 5, 15) ft.

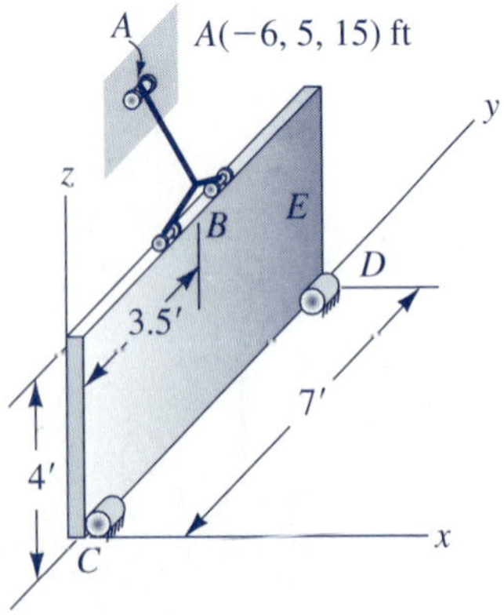

Figure P.5.128.

5.129. Find the supporting forces. Use no more than two free-body diagrams.

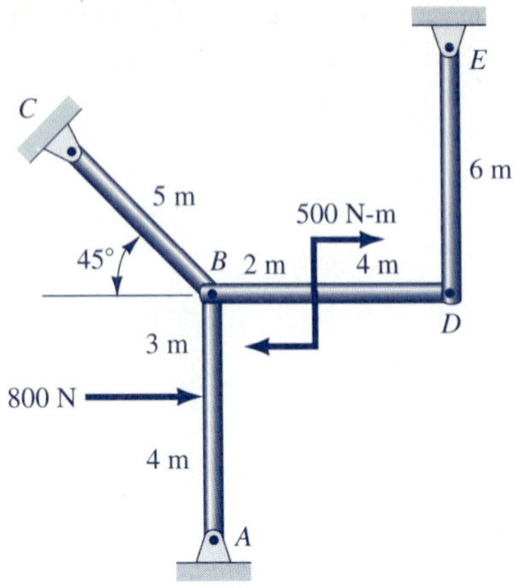

Figure P.5.129.

5.130. What is the tension in the cables of a 10-ft-wide 12-ft-long 6,000-lb castle drawbridge when the bridge is first raised? When the bridge is at 45°? What are the reactions at the hinge pin?

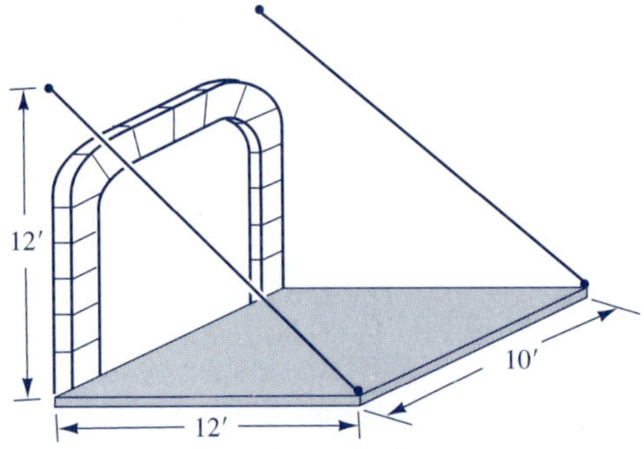

Figure P.5.130.

5.131. A small hoist has a lifting capacity of 20 kN. What is the maximum cable tension and the corresponding reactions at C? Do not consider weight of beam. At C there is a pin connection.

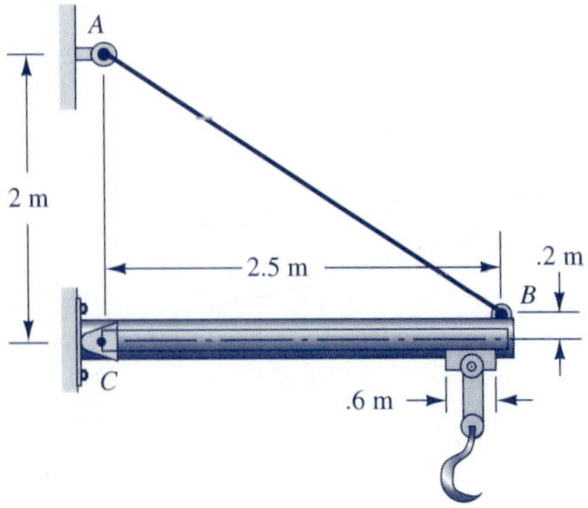

Figure P.5.131.

5.132. A uniform block weighing 500 lb is constrained by three wires. What are the tensions in these wires?

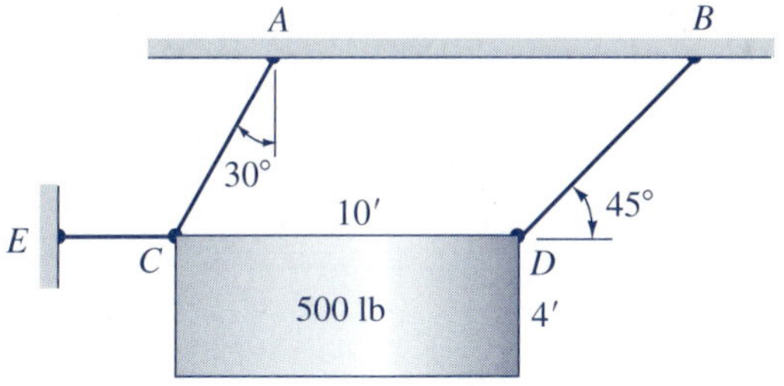

Figure P.5.132.

5.133. Find the supporting forces for the frame shown.

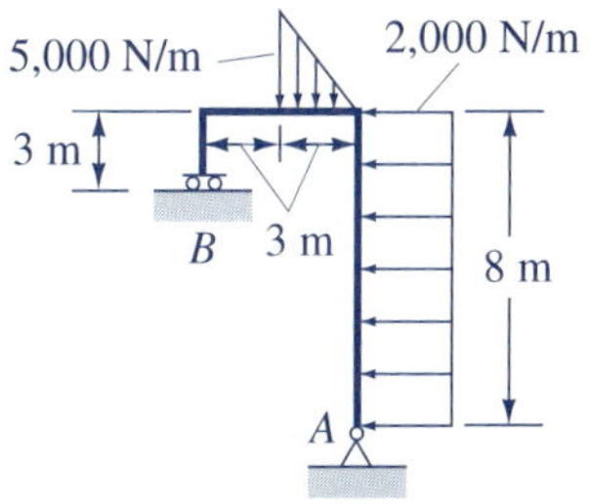

Figure P.5.133.

5.134. Four cables support a block of weight 5,000 N. The edges of the block are parallel to the coordinate axes. Point B is at (7, 7, −15). What are the forces in the cables and the direction cosines for cable CD?

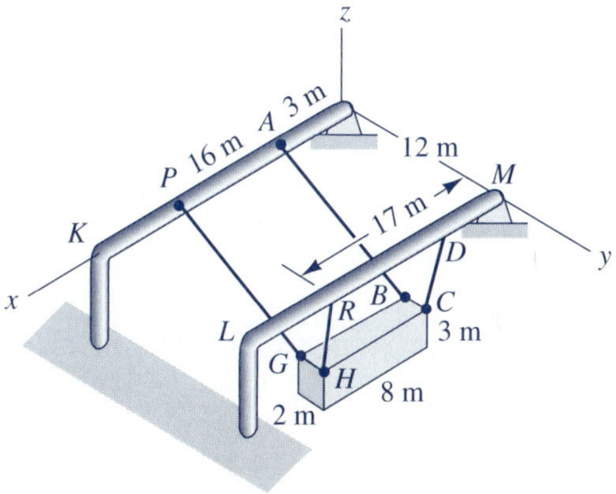

Figure P.5.134.

5.135. A mechanism consists of two weights W each of weight 50 N, four light linkage rods each of length a equal to 200 mm, and a spring K whose spring constant is 8 N/mm. The spring is unextended when $\theta = 45°$. If held vertically, what is the angle θ for equilibrium? Neglect friction. The force from the spring equals K times the compression of the spring.

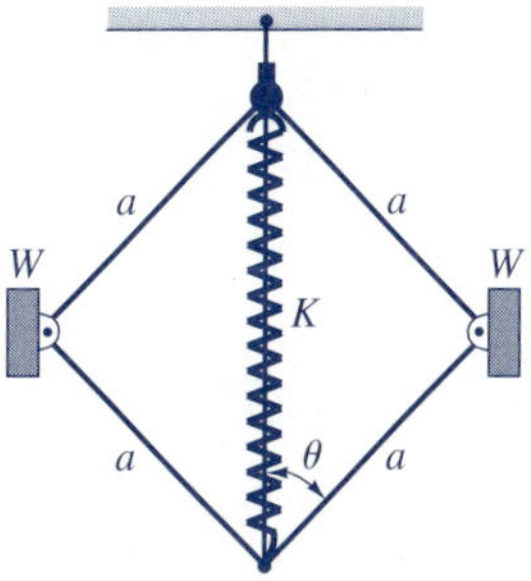

Figure P.5.135.

5.136. Find the compressive force in pawl AB. What is the resultant supporting force system at E?

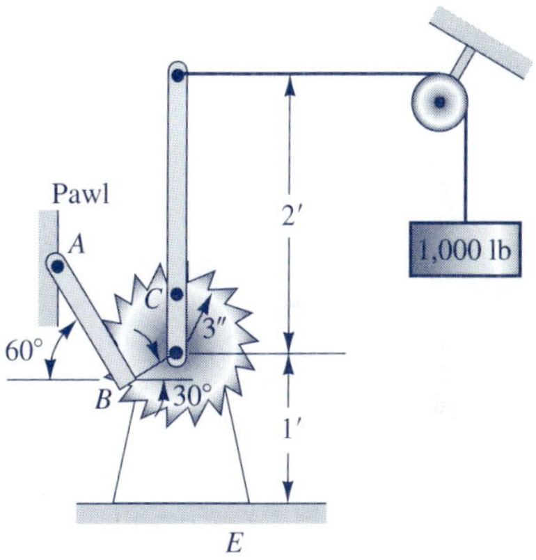

Figure P.5.136.

5.137. A 10-kN load is lifted in the front loader bucket. What are the forces at the connections to the bucket and to arm AE? Hydraulic ram DF is perpendicular to arm AE, and BC is horizontal. Points A and F are at the same height above the ground.

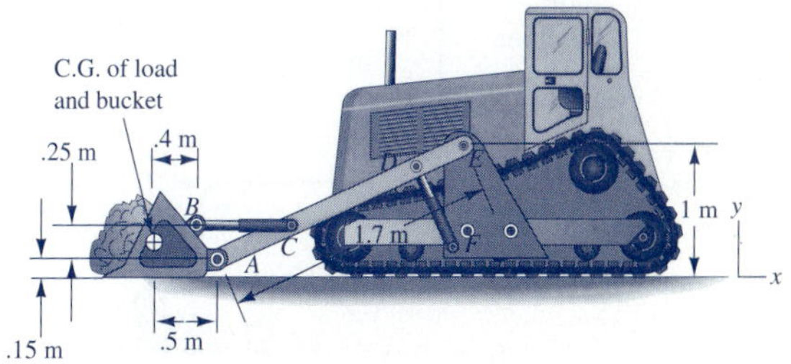

Figure P.5.137.

5.138. Determine the supporting forces at A and B.

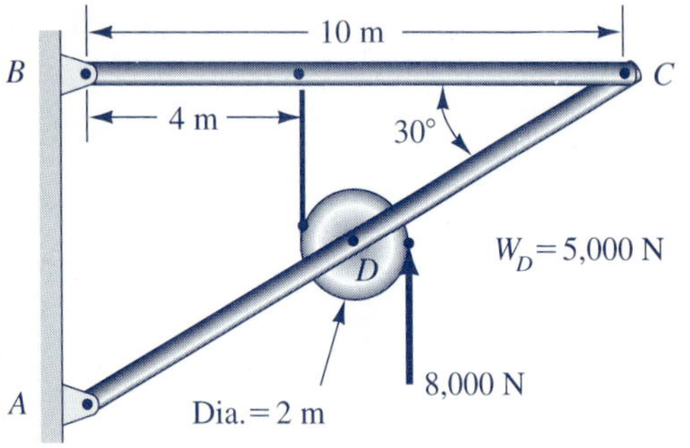

Figure P.5.138.

5.139. Find the force components on the pin C of the frame shown. Neglect friction everywhere as well as the weights of the members.

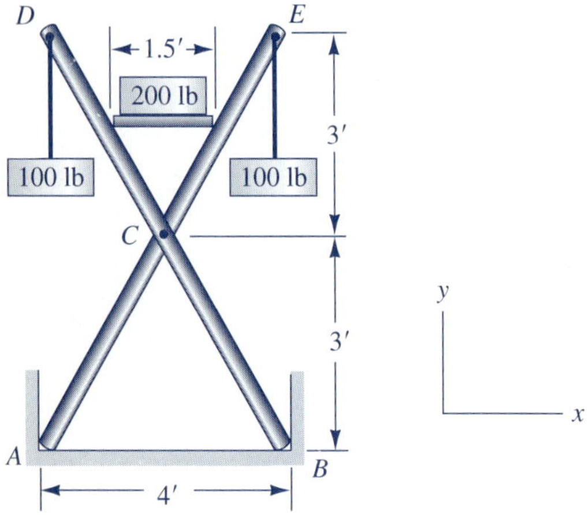

Figure P.5.139.

5.140. Find the supporting force system at A. Use only one free-body diagram.

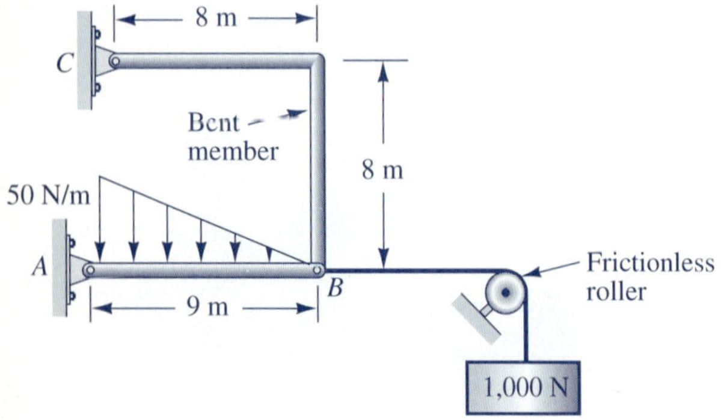

Figure P.5.140.

5.141. Find the supporting force systems at A and B. Note the pin connection at C.

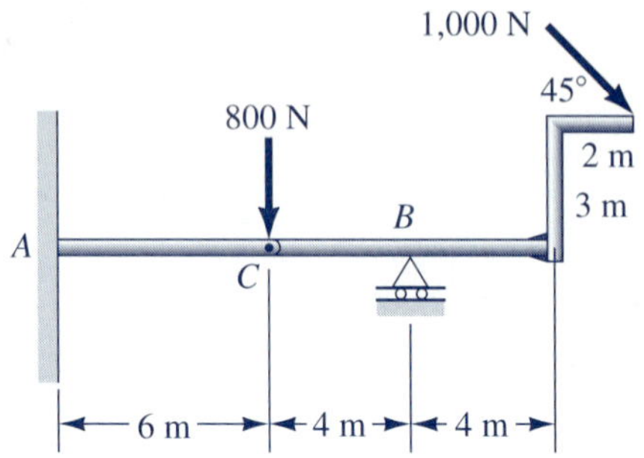

Figure P.5.141.

5.142. A 300-kN tank is climbing up a 30° incline at constant speed. What is the torque developed on the rear drive wheels to accomplish this? Assume that all other wheels are free-turning.

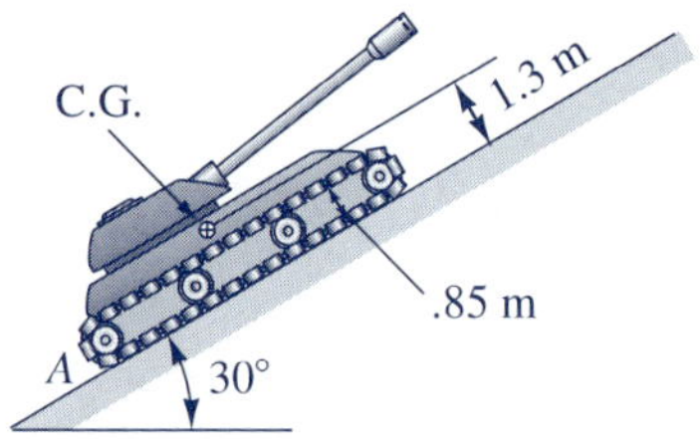

Figure P.5.142.

5.143. Find the components of the forces acting on pins A, B, and C connecting and supporting the blocks shown. Block I weighs 10 kN, and block II weighs 30 kN.

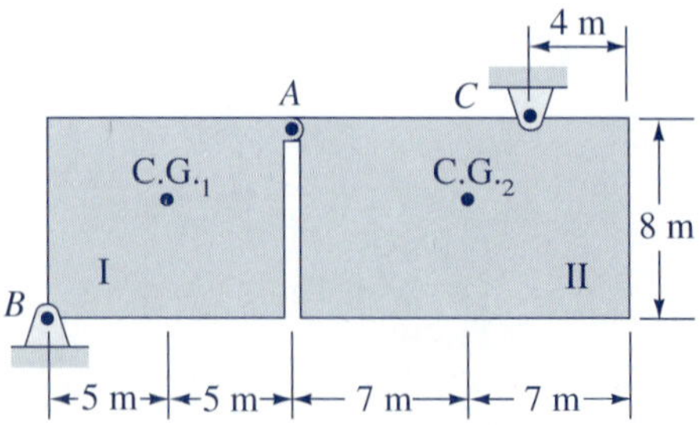

Figure P.5.143.

5.144. What force F do the pliers develop on the pipe section D? Neglect friction.

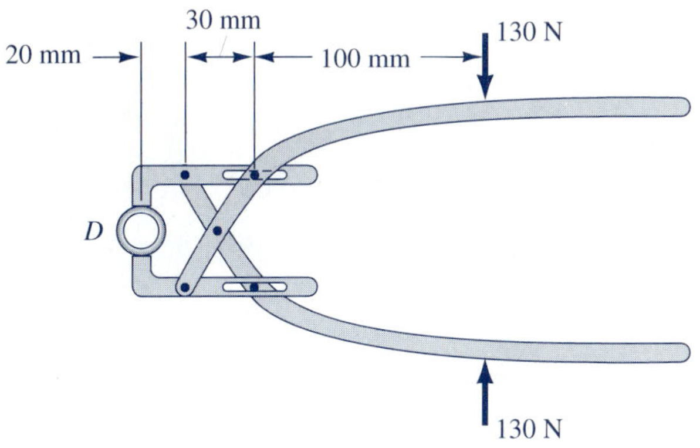

Figure P.5.144.

5.145. What are the supporting forces for the frame? Neglect all weights except the 10-kN weight.

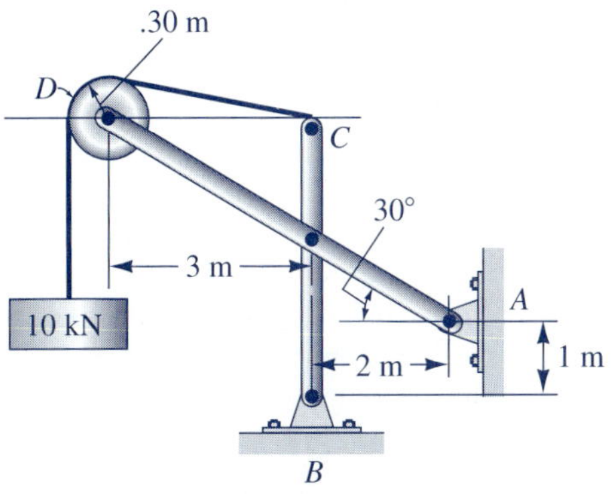

Figure P.5.145.

5.146. A 20-m circular arch must withstand a wind load given for $0 < \theta < \pi/2$ as

$$f = 5{,}000\left(1 - \frac{\theta}{\pi/2}\right) \text{ N/m}$$

where θ is measured in radians. Note that for $\theta > \pi/2$, there is no loading. What are the supporting forces? (*Hint:* What is the point for which taking moments is simplest?)

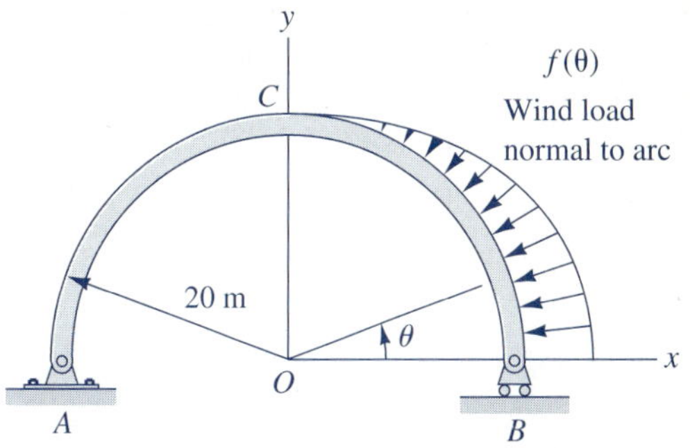

Figure P.5.146.

5.147. An arch is formed by uniform plates A and B. Plate A weighs 5 kN and plate B weighs 2 kN. What are the supporting forces at C, D, and E?

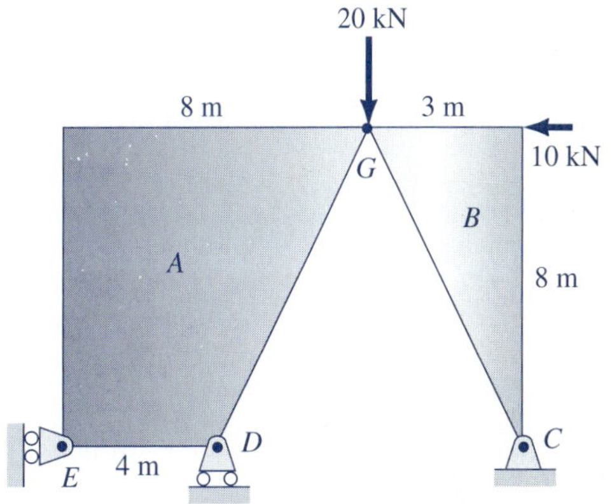

Figure P.5.147.

5.148. Find the supporting forces at the ball-and-socket connections A, D, and C. Members AB and DB are pinned together through member EC at B.

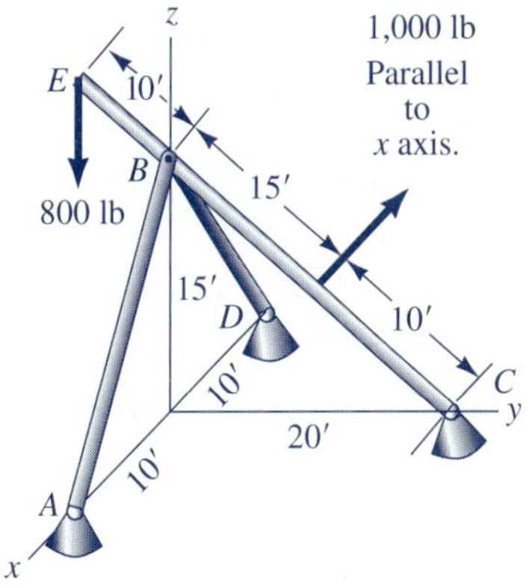

Figure P.5.148.

5.149. A tractor with a bulldozer is used to push an earthmover picking up dirt. If the tractor force on the earthmover is 150 kN in a horizontal direction, what are the reactions of the bulldozer on the tractor at *B* and *A*?

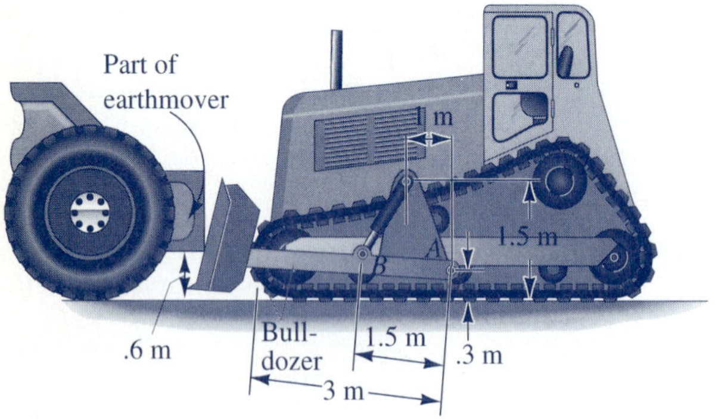

Figure P.5.149.

5.150. A hydraulic-lift platform for loading trucks supports a weight *W* of 5,000 lb. Only one side of the system has been shown; the other side is identical. If the diameter of the pistons in the cylinders is 4 in., what pressure *p* is needed to support *W* when $\theta = 60°$? The following data apply.

$$l = 24 \text{ in.}, \quad d = 60 \text{ in.}, \quad e = 10 \text{ in.}$$

Neglect friction everywhere. (Hint: Only two free-body diagrams need be drawn.)

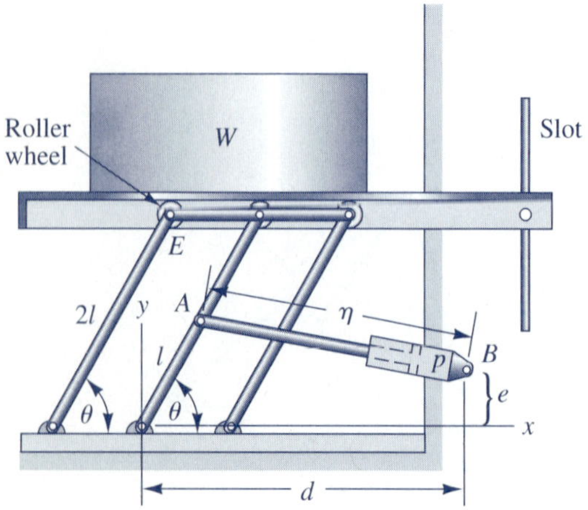

Figure P.5.150.

5.151. A Bucyrus–Erie Dynahoe digger is partially shown. To develop the indicated forces in the bucket, what forces must hydraulic cylinders *HB* and *CD* develop? Consider only the 3-kN and 5-kN loads and not the weights of the members.

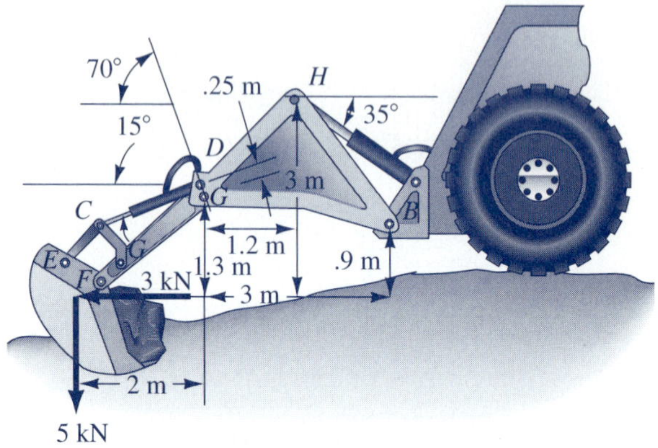

Figure P.5.151.

5.152. A block of material weighing 200-lb is supported by members *KC* and *HB*, whose weight we neglect, a ball-and-socket-joint support at *A*, and a smooth, frictionless support at *E*. Members *KC* and *HB* have directions collinear with diagonals of the block as shown. What are the supporting forces for this block?

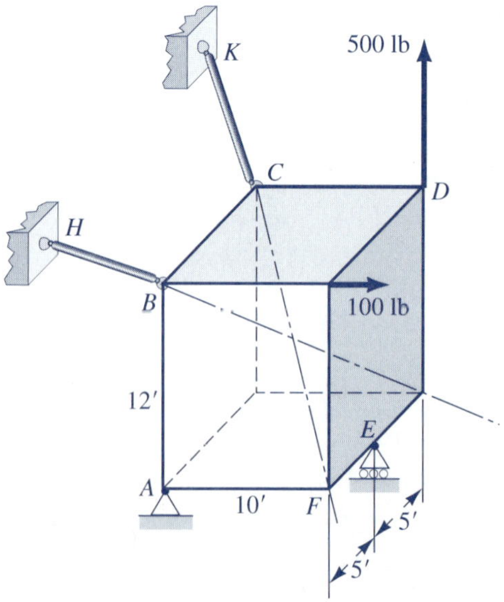

Figure P.5.152.

***5.153.** A bar can rotate parallel to plane A about an axis of rotation normal to the plane at O. A weight W is held by a cord that is attached to the bar over a small pulley that can rotate freely as the bar rotates. Find the value of C for equilibrium if $h = 300$ mm, $W = 30$ N, $\phi = 30°$, $l = 700$ mm, and $d = 500$ mm.

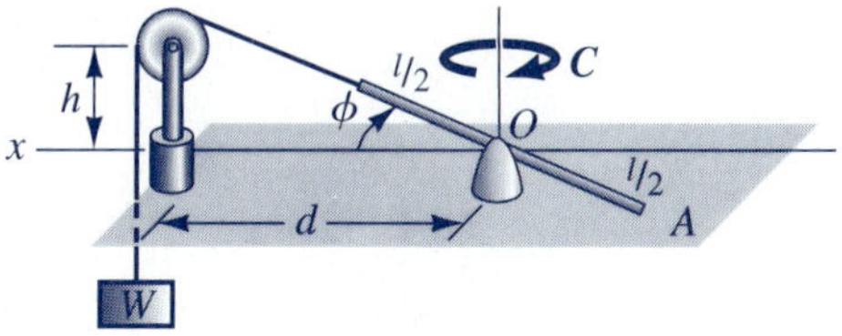

Figure P.5.153.

5.154. Find the supporting forces at A and B in the frame. Neglect weights of members.

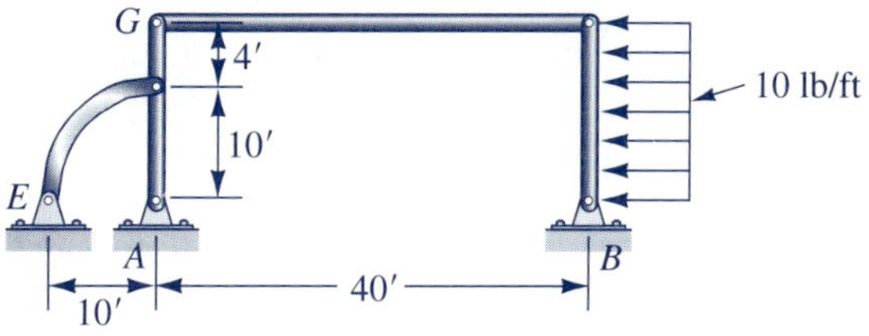

Figure P.5.154.

5.155. A bolt cutter has a force of 130 N applied at each handle. What is the force on the bolt from the cutter edge?

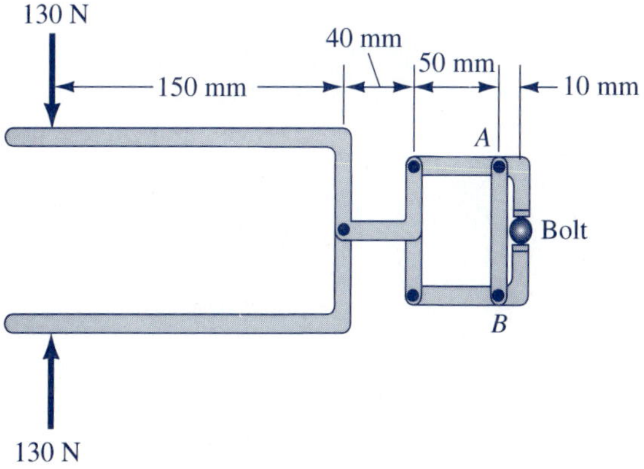

Figure P.5.155.

5.156. A steam locomotive is developing a pressure of .20 N/mm^2 gage. If the train is stationary, what is the total traction force from the two wheels shown? Neglect the weight of the various connecting rods. Neglect friction in piston system and connecting rod pins.

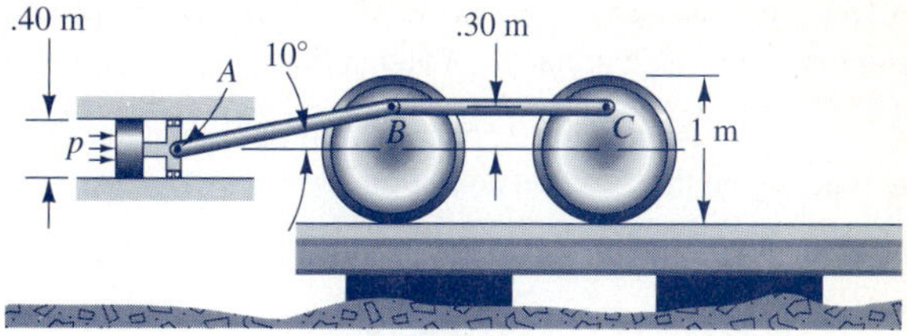

Figure P.5.156.

5.157. Find the supporting forces at A, B, and C. Neglect the weight of the rod. Use only one free-body diagram.

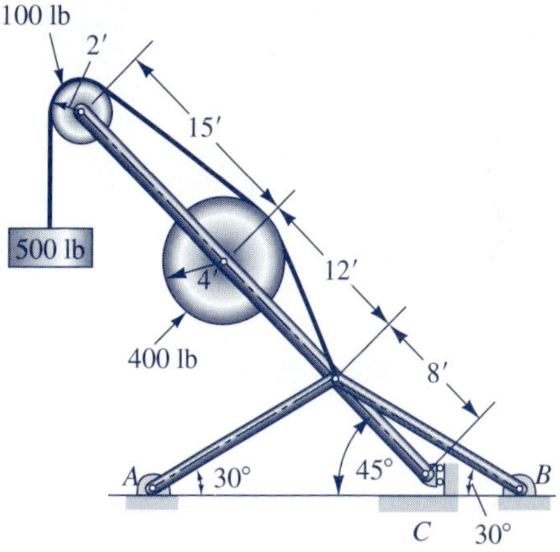

Figure P.5.157.

5.158. The 5,000 lb van A of an airline food catering truck rises straight up until its floor is level with the airplane floor. A hydraulic ram pulls on the right bottom support of the lift mechanism at which we have rollers to prevent friction. The two members of the lift mechanism are pinned at their center. The center of gravity of the van is its geometric center. What is the ram force for this position?

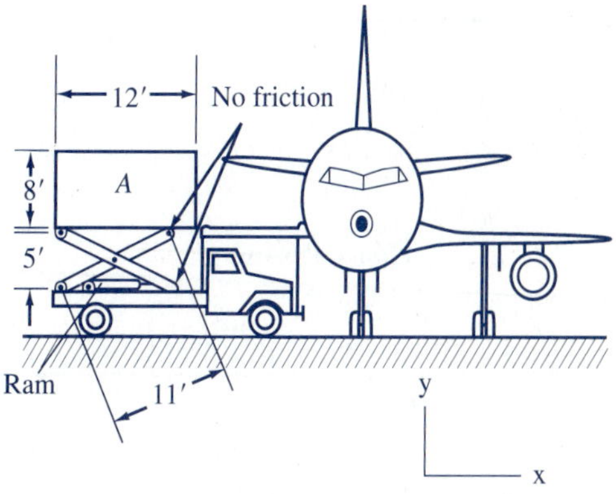

Figure P.5.158.

5.159. (a) Using only one free-body diagram, find the supporting forces from the ground at *A* and at *B*.

(b) At a position 2.5 ft to the left of *D*, find the force system acting on the cross-section of the member *CD*.

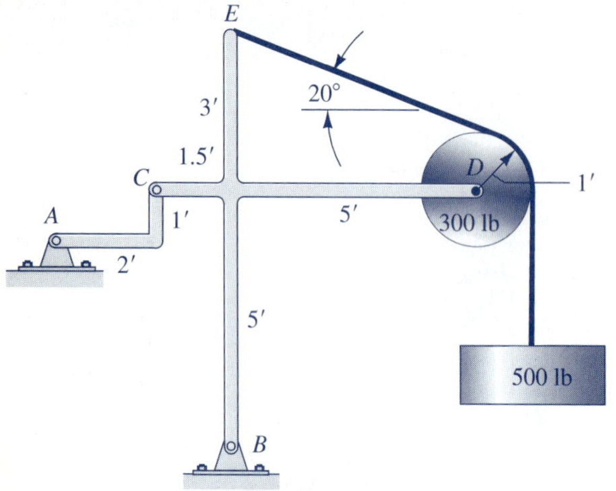

Figure P.5.159.

5.160. For the structure shown, determine the force in the cable *EF*.

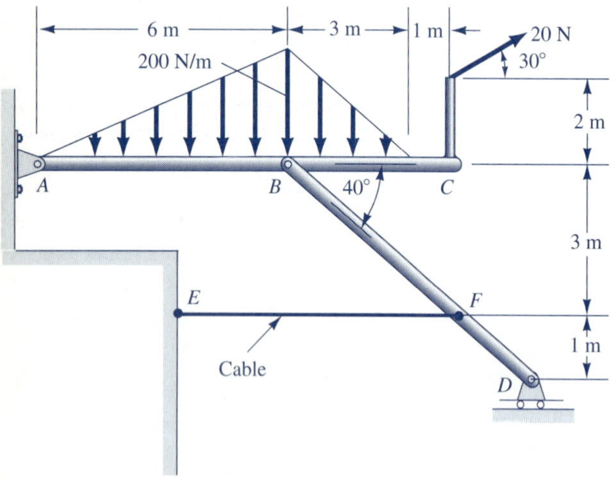

Figure P.5.160.

5.161. Find the supporting forces at *A* and *B*. The cylinder can turn freely.

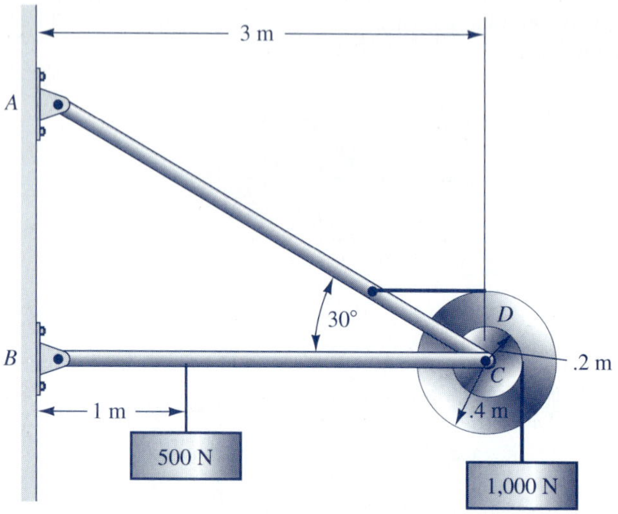

Figure P.5.161.

5.162. Find the supporting force system at *A* and *B*. Cylinder *C* weighs 4,000 N and is free to rotate without friction.

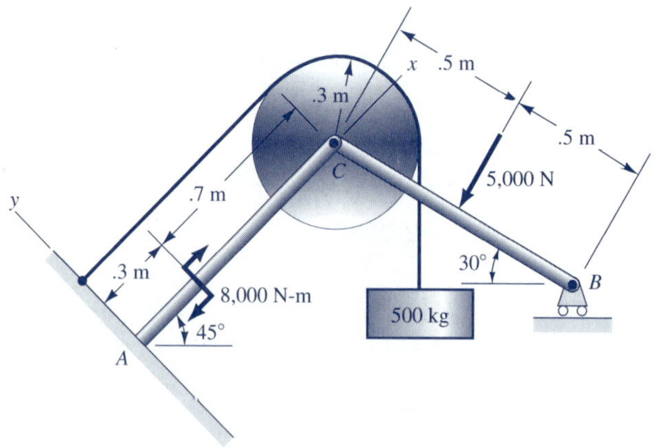

Figure P.5.162.

CHAPTER 6

Introduction to Structural Mechanics

Part A: Trusses

6.1 The Structural Model

A *truss* is a system of members that are fastened together at their ends to support stationary and moving loads.[1] Everyday examples of trusses are shown in Figs. 6.1 and 6.2. Each member of a truss is usually of uniform cross-section along its length; however, the various members typically have different cross-sectional areas because they must transmit different forces. Our purpose in Part A of this chapter is to set forth methods for determining forces in members of an elementary class of trusses.

As a first step, we shall divide trusses into two main categories according to geometry. A truss consisting of a coplanar system of members is called a *plane truss*. Examples of plane trusses are the sides of a bridge (see Fig. 6.1) and a roof truss (see Fig. 6.2). A three-dimensional system of members, on the other hand, is called a *space truss*. A common example of a space truss is the tower from an electric power transmission system (see Fig. 6.3). Both plane trusses and space trusses consist of members having cross-sections resembling the letters H, I, and L. Such members are commonly used in many structural applications. These members are fastened together to form a truss by being welded, riveted, or bolted to intermediate structural elements called *gusset plates* such as has been shown in Fig. 6.4(a) for the case of a plane truss. The analysis of forces and moments in such connections is clearly quite complicated. Fortunately, there is a way of simplifying these connections

[1]A *truss* is different than a *frame* (see the footnote on p. 157) in that the members of a truss are always connected together at the ends of the members, as will soon become evident, whereas a frame has some members with connections not at the ends of the member.

Figure 6.1. Foot bridge near author's former home. Sides of structure are plane trusses.

Figure 6.2. Roof trusses that are plane trusses.

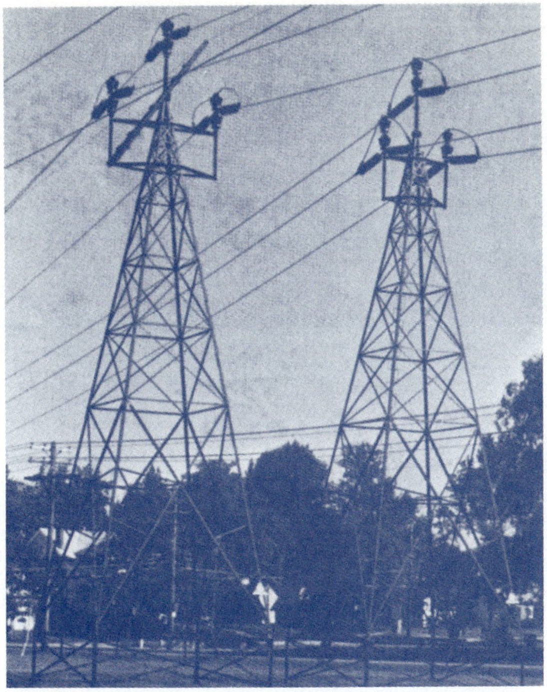

Figure 6.3. Space trusses supporting transmission lines sending power into the northeast grid of the United States.

such as to incur very little loss in accuracy in determining forces in the members. Specifically, if the centerlines of the members are *concurrent* at the connections, such as is shown in Fig. 6.4(a) for the coplanar case, then we can replace the complex connection at the points of concurrency by a simple pin connection in the coplanar truss and a simple ball-and-socket connection for the space truss. Such a replacement is called an *idealization* of the system. This is illustrated for a plane truss in Fig. 6.4, where the actual connector or joint is shown in (a) and the idealization as a pinned joint is shown in (b).

In order to maximize the load-carrying capacity of a truss, the external loads must be applied at the joints. The prime reason for this rule is the fact that the members of a truss are long and slender, thus rendering compression members less able to carry loads transverse to their centerlines away from the ends.[2] If the weights of the members are neglected, as is sometimes the case, it should be apparent that each member is a *two-force member*, and accordingly is either a tensile member or a compression member. If the weight is not negligible, the common practice as an approximation is to apply half the weight of a member to each of its two joints. Thus, the idealization of a member as a two-force member is still valid.

[2]You will understand these limitations more clearly when you study buckling in your strength of materials course.

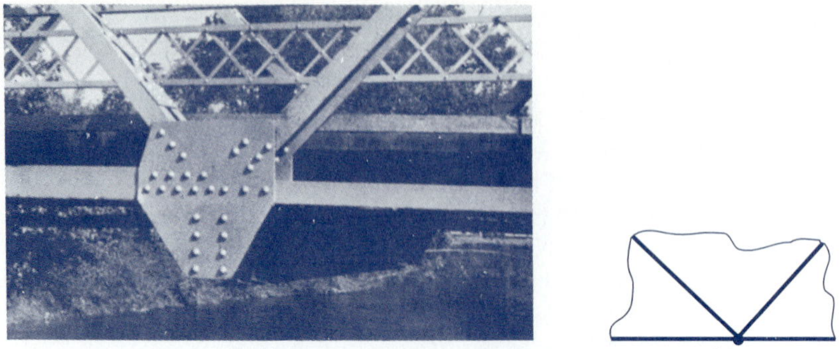

(a) (b)

Figure 6.4. (a) Gusset plate; (b) idealization.

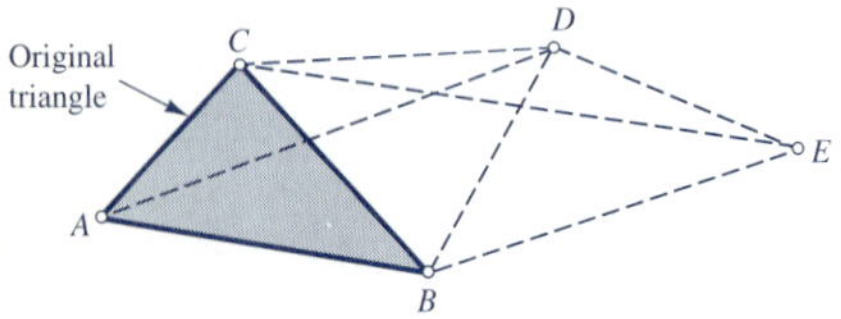

Figure 6.5. (a) Simple space truss.

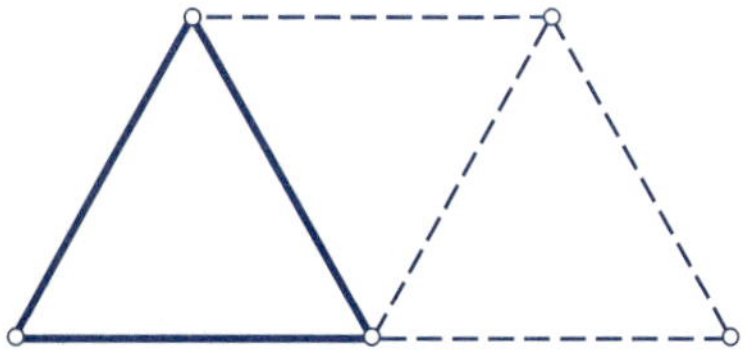

Figure 6.6. Simple plane truss.

6.2 The Simple Truss

An idealized truss as described in Section 6.1 is termed *just-rigid* if the removal of any of its members destroys its rigidity. If removing a member does not destroy rigidity, the structure is said to be *over-rigid*. We shall be concerned with just-rigid trusses in Part A of this chapter.[3]

The most elementary just-rigid truss is one with three members connected to form a triangle. Just-rigid space trusses may be built up from this triangle by adding for each new joint three new members, as is shown *in Fig. 6.5.* Trusses constructed in this manner are called *simple space trusses.* The *simple plane truss* is built up from an elementary triangle by adding two new members for each new pin as shown in Fig. 6.6. Clearly, the simple plane truss is just-rigid.

A simple relationship exists between the number of joints j and the number of members m in a simple truss. You can directly verify by examining the simple space truss in Fig. 6.5 that m is related to j as follows:

$$m = 3j - 6 \qquad (6.1a)$$

Similarly, for the simple plane truss in Fig. 6.6 you can verify that

$$m = 2j - 3 \qquad (6.1b)$$

You will learn in more advanced structures courses that Eqs. 6.1 (a) and 6.1 (b) hold generally for just-rigid space trusses and for just-rigid plane trusses, respectively.

We now show that if the supporting force system is statically determinate, we can compute the forces in all the members of simple trusses. Specifically, in examining the ball joints of simple space trusses, we can see that in the general three-dimensional case, a ball joint with only three unknown

[3]Over-rigid structures are studied in courses of strength of materials and structural mechanics. They are internally statically indeterminate and deformation must be taken into account when computing forces in the members.

forces acting on it from the members can always be found. (One such joint is the last joint formed.) Each unknown force from a member onto this joint must have a direction collinear with that member, and hence has a known direction. There are, then, only three unknown scalars, and since we have a concurrent force system they can be determined by statics alone. We then find another joint with only three unknowns and so carry on the computations until the forces in the entire structure have been evaluated. For the simple plane truss, a similar procedure can be followed. The free body of at least one joint has only two unknown forces. We have a concurrent, coplanar force system, and we accordingly can solve the corresponding two equilibrium equations in two unknowns at that joint. We then proceed to the other joints, thereby evaluating all member forces by the use of statics alone.

6.3 Solution of Simple Trusses

Generally, the first step in a truss analysis is to compute the supporting forces in the overall truss. This calculation of the external forces or reactions that must exist to keep the truss in equilibrium is independent of whether the truss, internally, is statically determinate or statically indeterminate. Simply regard the truss as a rigid body to which forces are applied, some known (given applied forces) and some unknown (reactions),[4] and solve for the reactions as we did in Chapter 5. We have shown a simple plane truss in Fig. 6.7(a) and have shown the features of the truss in Fig. 6.7(b) that are essential for the calculations of the reactions. Note that members such as *CB, DB,* and *DE* need not be shown in the free body since they provide *internal* forces for the body.

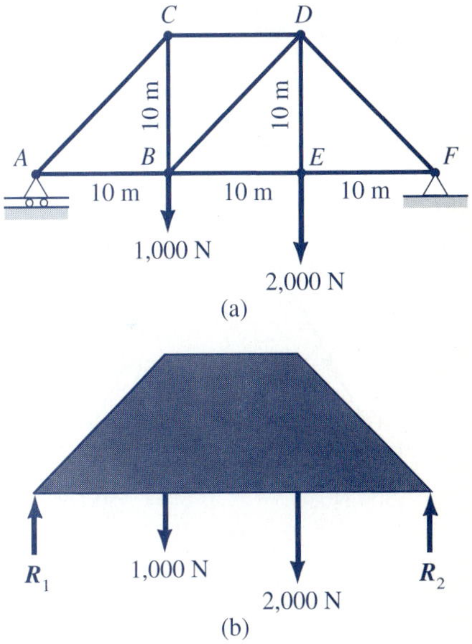

Figure 6.7. Free-body analysis of truss.

Once the free-body diagram has been carefully drawn, use three equations of equilibrium to determine the reactions of a plane truss (six equations for a space truss). It is highly advisable to then check your results by using another (dependent) equation of equilibrium. You will be using the computed reactions for many subsequent calculations involving forces in internal members. Accordingly, with much work at stake, it is important to start off with a correct set of reactions.

We shall present two methods for determining the forces in the members of the truss. One is called the *method of joints* and the other is called the *method of sections.* As will be seen in the following sections, the prime difference between these methods lies in the choice of the free bodies to be used.

6.4 Method of Joints

In the method of joints, the free-body diagrams to be used, once the reactions are determined, are the pins or ball joints and the forces applied to them by the attached members and external loads. Note that we have already alluded

[4]Supporting forces are often called *reactions* in structural mechanics.

to this method in Section 6.2. Consider first the triangular plane truss shown in Fig. 6.8(a). Notice we have already determined the reactions.

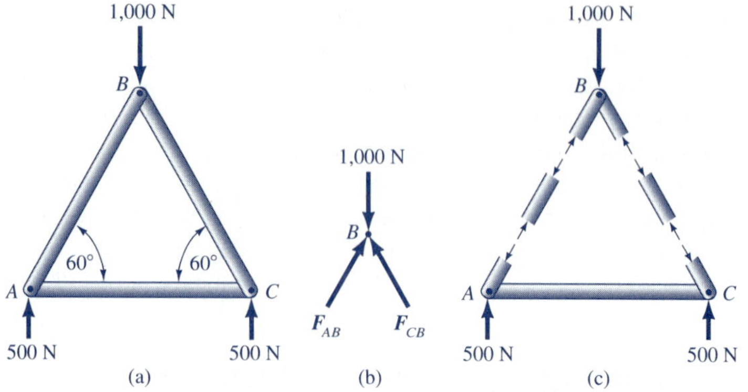

Figure 6.8. Method of joints—joint B.

Next, consider the free body of pin B [Fig. 6.8(b)]. The unknown forces from the members are shown collinear with the centerlines of these members since they are two-force members. We can solve for these forces by setting the sum of forces equal to zero in the horizontal and vertical directions, to get

$$F_{AB} = F_{CB} = 577 \text{ N}$$

Because both forces are *pushing* against pin B, the corresponding members are *compressive* rather than tension members. We can most readily see this fact by considering Fig. 6.8(c), where members AB and CB have been cut at various places. Notice that AB is also pushing against pin A as does CB against pin C. Thus, once having decided that the members are compressive members as a result of considerations at a pin at one end of the member, we can conclude that the member is pushing with equal force against the pin at the other end. To make for speed and accuracy as we go from one joint to another, we recommend that, once the nature of the loading in a member has been established by considerations at a pin, we mark down this value using a T for tension or a C for compression after it on the truss diagram, as shown in Fig. 6.9(a). Note also that appropriate arrows are drawn in the members. These arrows represent forces developed by the *members on the pins*. Hence, for *compression* the arrows point *toward* the pins, and for *tension* they point *away* from the pins. Accordingly, if we now consider the free body of pin A as shown in Fig. 6.9(b), we know the direction and value of the force on A from member AB.

If a negative value is found for a force at a pin, the sense of the force has been taken incorrectly at the outset. With this in mind, we decide whether the member associated with the force is a tension or compression member and we label the member accordingly, as shown in Fig. 6.9(a) for use later in examining the pin at the other end of the member as a free body.

We now consider the solution of a plane truss problem by the method of joints in greater detail.

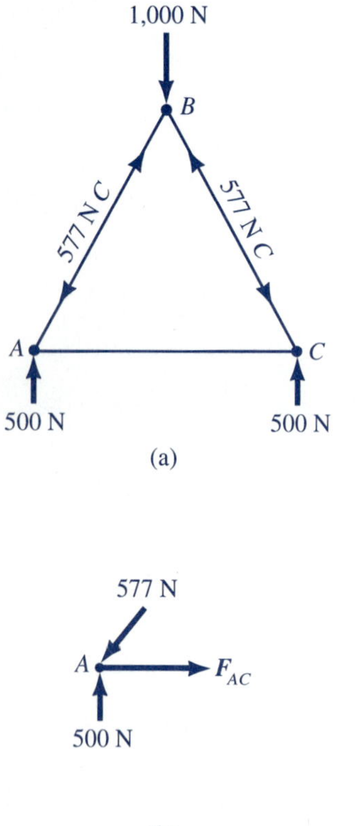

Figure 6.9. Procedure for method of joints. (a) Notation for members AB and CB; (b) free-body diagram of A.

Example 6.1

A simple plane truss is shown in Fig. 6.10. Two 1,000-lb loads are shown acting on pins C and E. We are to determine the force transmitted by each member. Neglect the weight of the members.

In this simple loading, we see by inspection that there are 1,000-lb vertical forces at each support. We shall begin, then, by studying pin A, for which there are only two unknowns.

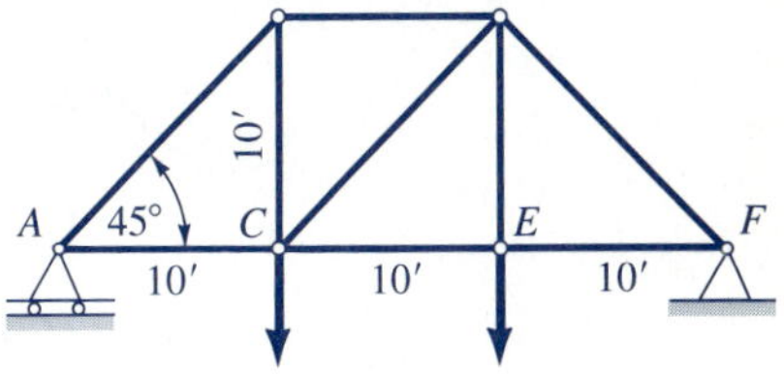

Figure 6.10. Plane truss.

Pin A. The forces on pin A are the known 1,000-lb supporting force and two unknown forces from the members AB and AC. The orientation of these forces is known from the geometry of the truss, but the magnitude and sense must be determined. To help in interpreting the results, put the forces in the same position as the corresponding members in the truss diagram as is shown in Fig. 6.11. That is, avoid the force diagram in Fig. 6.12, which is equivalent to the one in Fig. 6.11 but which may lead to errors in interpretation. There are two unknowns for the concurrent coplanar force system in Fig. 6.11 and thus, if we use the scalar equations of equilibrium, we may evaluate F_{AB} and F_{AC}:

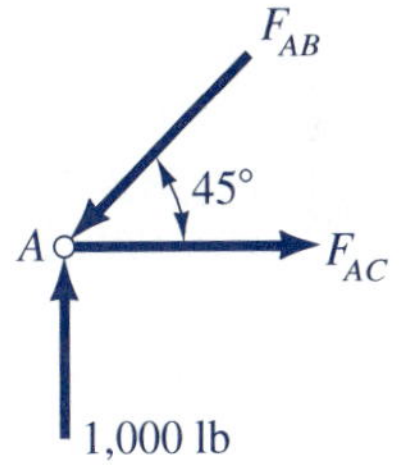

Figure 6.11. Pin A.

$\sum F_x = 0$:

$$F_{AC} - 0.707 F_{AB} = 0$$

$\sum F_y = 0$:

$$-0.707 F_{AB} + 1{,}000 = 0$$

Therefore,

$$F_{AB} = 1{,}414 \text{ lb} \quad ; \quad F_{AC} = 1{,}000 \text{ lb}$$

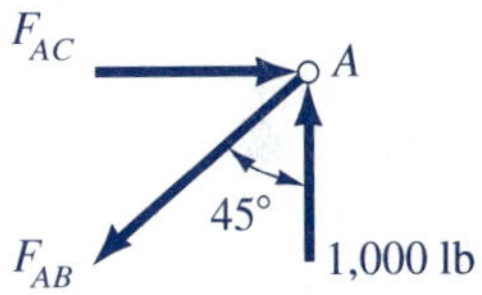

Figure 6.12. Pin A—avoid this diagram.

Since both results are positive, we have chosen the proper senses for the forces. We can then conclude on examining Fig. 6.11 that AB is a compression member, whereas AC is a tension member.[5] In Fig. 6.13, we have labeled the members accordingly.

If we next examine pin C, clearly since there are three unknowns involved for this pin, we cannot solve for the forces by equilibrium equations at this time. However, pin B can be handled, and once F_{BC} is known, the forces on pin C can be determined.

Pin B. Since AB is a compression member (see Fig. 6.13) we know that it exerts a force of 1,414 lb directed against pin B as has been shown in Fig. 6.14. As for members BC and BD, we assign senses as shown.

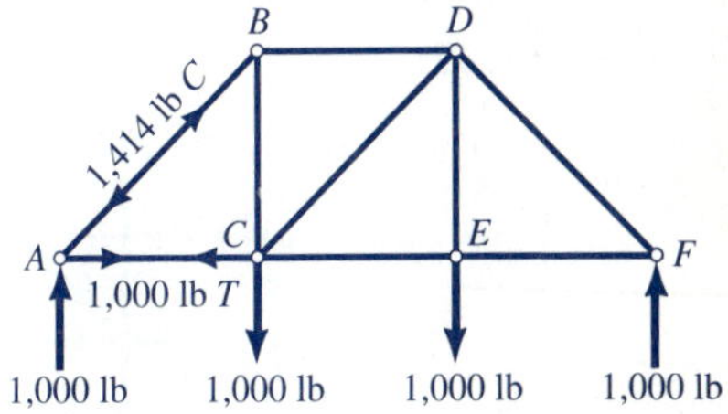

Figure 6.13. Notation for members AB and AC.

[5]Had we used Fig. 6.12 as a free body, the state of loading in the members (i.e., tension or compression) would not be clear. Therefore, we strongly recommend putting forces representing members in positions coinciding with the members.

Example 6.1 (Continued)

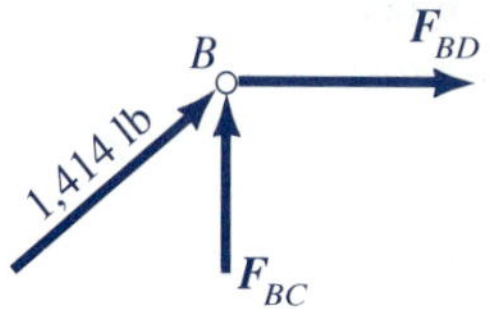

Figure 6.14. Pin *B*.

Summing forces on pin *B* (Fig. 6.14), we get

$\sum F_x = 0$:

$$(1{,}414)(0.707) + F_{BD} = 0$$

$$F_{BD} = -1{,}000 \text{ lb}$$

$\sum F_y = 0$:

$$(1{,}414)(0.707) + F_{BC} = 0$$

$$F_{BC} = -1{,}000 \text{ lb}$$

Here we have obtained two negative quantities, indicating that we have made incorrect choices of sense. Keeping this in mind, we can conclude that member *BD* is a compression member, whereas member *BC* is a tension member. Notice that we have shown these forces properly in Fig. 6.15.

We can proceed in this manner from joint to joint. At the last joint all the forces will have been computed without using it as a free body. Thus, it is available to be used as a check on the solution. That is, the sum of the known forces for the last joint in the *x* and *y* directions should be zero or close to zero, depending on the accuracy of your calculations. We urge you to take advantage of this check. The final solution is shown in Fig. 6.15. Notice that member *CD* has zero load. This does not mean that we can get rid of this member. Other loadings expected for the truss will result in nonzero force for *CD*. Furthermore, without *CD* the truss will not be rigid.

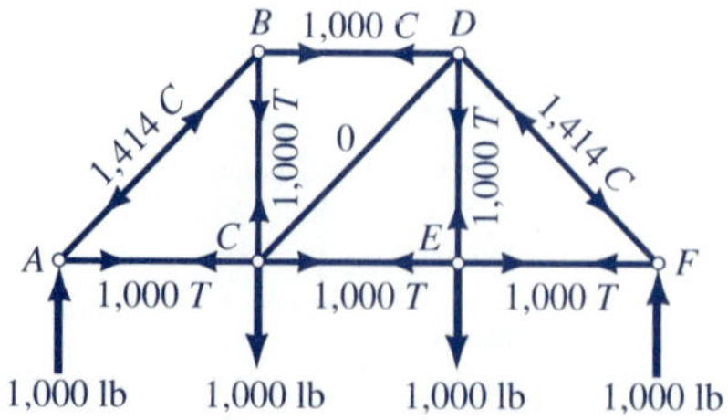

Figure 6.15. Solution for truss.

Example 6.2

A bridge truss is shown in Fig. 6.16 supporting at its pins half of a roadbed weighing 1,000 lb per foot. A truck is shown on the bridge having estimated loads on pins E, G, and I of the truss equaling, respectively, 1 ton, 1.5 tons, and 2.5 tons. The members weigh 45 lb/ft. Include the weight of the members by putting half the weight of a member at each of its two supporting pins. Find the supporting forces.

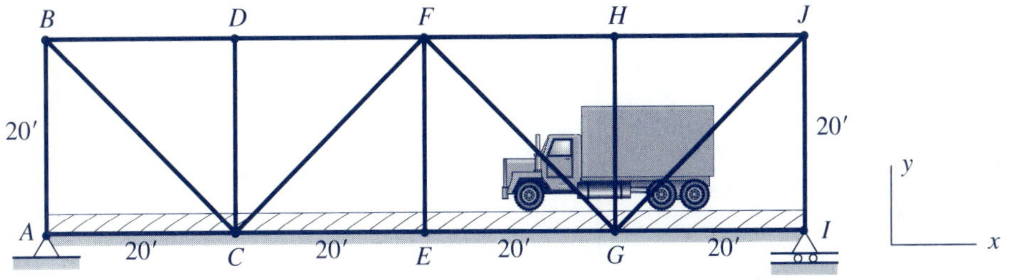

Figure 6.16. A bridge truss supporting a roadbed and a truck.

We first determine the forces on the pins from the weight of the members denoting them as $(W_1)_i$. Thus we have

Loads 1: Weights of members

$$(W_1)_A = (W_1)_I = 2\left[\frac{1}{2}(20)(45)\right] = 900 \text{ lb}$$

$$(W_1)_B = (W_1)_J = 2\left[\frac{1}{2}(20)(45)\right] + \frac{1}{2}\left(\frac{20}{.707}\right)(45) = 1{,}536.5 \text{ lb}$$

$$(W_1)_C = (W_1)_F = (W_1)_G = 3\left[\frac{1}{2}(20)(45)\right] + 2\left[\frac{1}{2}\left(\frac{20}{.707}\right)(45)\right] = 2{,}623 \text{ lb}$$

$$(W_1)_D = (W_1)_H = (W_1)_E = 3\left[\frac{1}{2}(20)(45)\right] = 1{,}350 \text{ lb}$$

Next we get to the roadbed.

Loads 2: Weights from the roadbed

$$(W_2)_A = (W_2)_I = \frac{1}{2}(500)(20) = 5{,}000 \text{ lb}$$

$$(W_2)_C = (W_2)_E = (W_2)_G = (500)(20) = 10{,}000 \text{ lb}$$

Finally, we list the loads from the truck.

Loads 3: Weights from the truck

$$(W_3)_E = 2{,}000 \text{ lb}$$
$$(W_3)_G = 3{,}000 \text{ lb}$$
$$(W_3)_I = 5{,}000 \text{ lb}$$

Example 6.2 (Continued)

We are now ready to determine the supporting forces for the truss. Taking the entire truss as a free body we first take moments about joint *I* (see Fig. 6.17).

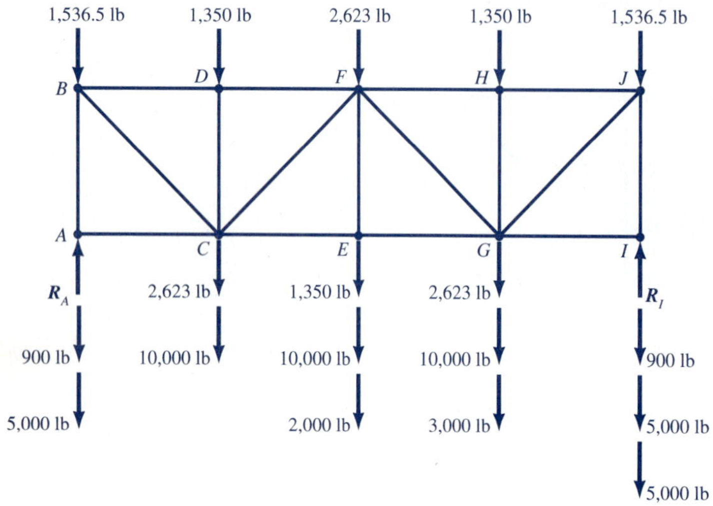

Figure 6.17. Free-body diagram of the bridge truss.

$\sum M_I = 0$:

$$-R_A(80) + (1{,}536.5 + 900 + 5{,}000)(80) + (1{,}350 + 2{,}623 + 10{,}000)(60) + (2{,}623 + 1{,}350 + 10{,}000 + 2{,}000)(40) + (1{,}350 + 2{,}623 + 10{,}000 + 3{,}000)(20) = 0$$

$$R_A = 30{,}146 \text{ lb}$$

$\sum M_A = 0$:

$$R_I(80) - (1{,}536.5 + 900 + 5{,}000 + 5{,}000)(80) - (1{,}350 + 2{,}623 + 10{,}000 + 3{,}000)(60) - (2{,}623 + 1{,}350 + 10{,}000 + 2{,}000)(40) - (1{,}350 + 2{,}623 + 10{,}000)(20) = 0$$

$$R_I = 36{,}646 \text{ lb}$$

Check:

$\sum F_y = 0$:

$$30{,}146 + 36{,}646 - (2)(900) - (2)(1{,}536.5) - (3)(2{,}623) - (3)(1{,}350) - (2)(5{,}000) - (3)(10{,}000) - 2{,}000 - 3{,}000 - 5{,}000 = 0$$

$$0 = 0$$

Example 6.3

Ascertain the forces transmitted by each member of the three-dimensional truss [Fig. 6.18(a)].

We can readily find the supporting forces for this simple structure by considering the whole structure as a free body and by making use of the symmetry of the loading and geometry. The results are shown in Fig. 6.18(b).

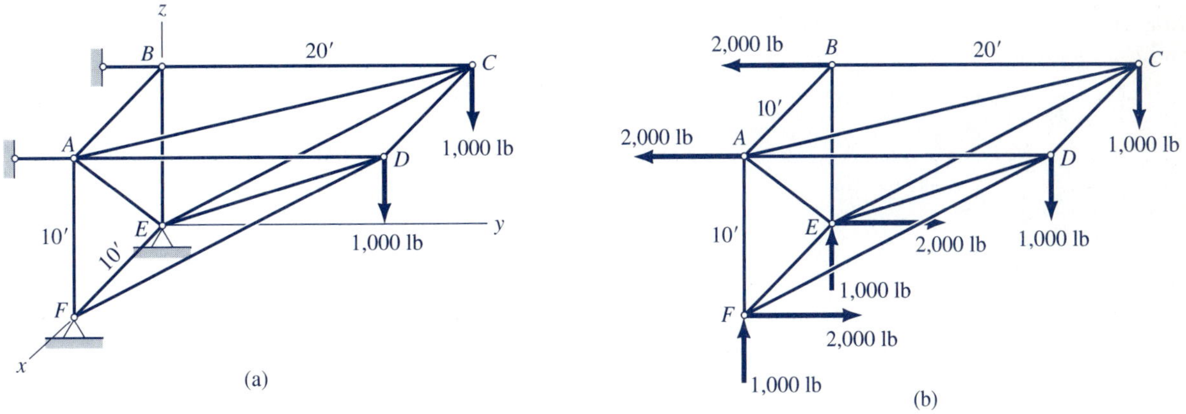

Figure 6.18. (a) Space truss and (b) free-body diagram.

Joint F. It is clear, on an inspection of the forces in the x direction acting on joint F, that $F_{FE} = 0$, since all other forces are in a plane at right angles to it. These other forces are shown in Fig. 6.19. Summing forces in the y and z directions, we get

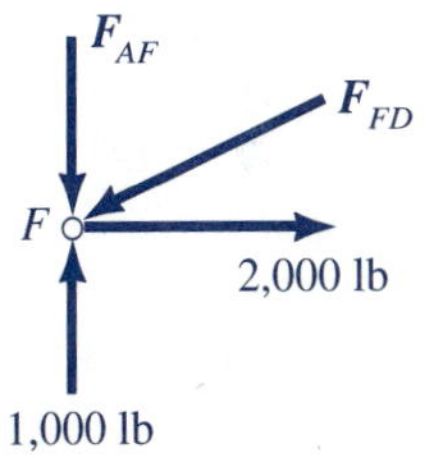

Figure 6.19. Free-body diagram of joint F.

$\sum F_y = 0$:

$$-F_{FD}\frac{20}{\sqrt{20^2 + 10^2}} + 2{,}000 = 0$$

Therefore,

$$F_{FD} = 2{,}240 \text{ lb compression}$$

$\sum F_z = 0$:

$$-F_{AF} + 1{,}000 - 2{,}240\frac{10}{\sqrt{500}} = 0$$

Therefore,

$$F_{AF} = 1{,}000 - 1{,}000 = 0$$

$$F_{AF} = 0$$

Example 6.3 (Continued)

Joint B. Going to joint *B*, we see [Fig. 6.18(b)] that $F_{AB} = 0$ and $F_{BE} = 0$, since there are no other force components on pin *B* in the directions of these members. Finally, F_{BC} = 2,000 lb tension.

Joint A. Let us next consider joint *A* (Fig. 6.20). We can express force $\boldsymbol{F}_{AC}$ and $\boldsymbol{F}_{AE}$ vectorially. Thus,

$$\boldsymbol{F}_{AC} = F_{AC}\frac{-10\boldsymbol{i} + 20\boldsymbol{j}}{\sqrt{10^2 + 20^2}} = F_{AC}(-.447\boldsymbol{i} + .894\boldsymbol{j})\ \text{lb}$$

$$\boldsymbol{F}_{AE} = F_{AE}\frac{-10\boldsymbol{i} - 10\boldsymbol{k}}{\sqrt{10^2 + 10^2}} = F_{AE}(-.707\boldsymbol{i} - .704\boldsymbol{k})\ \text{lb}$$

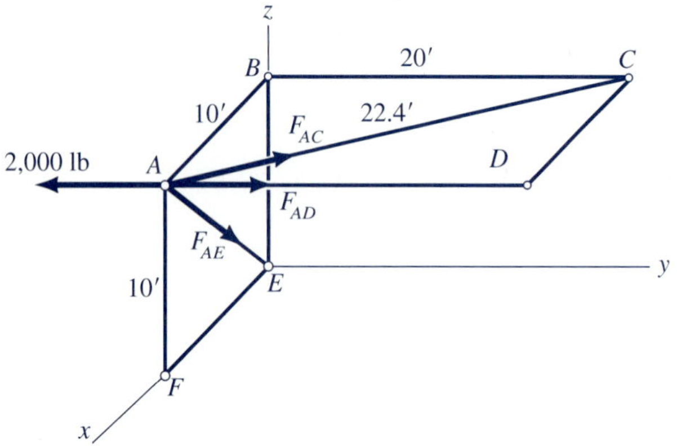

Figure 6.20. Free-body diagram of joint *A*.

Summing forces, we have

$$-2{,}000\boldsymbol{j} + F_{AD}\boldsymbol{j} + F_{AC}(-.447\boldsymbol{i} + .894\boldsymbol{j}) + F_{AE}(-.707\boldsymbol{i} - .707\boldsymbol{k}) = \boldsymbol{0}$$

Hence,

$$.894F_{AC} + F_{AD} = 2{,}000 \qquad \text{(a)}$$

$$-.447F_{AC} - .707F_{AE} = 0 \qquad \text{(b)}$$

$$-.707F_{AE} = 0 \qquad \text{(c)}$$

We see that $F_{AE} = F_{AC} = 0$ and F_{AD} = 2,000 lb tension.

Joint D. We now consider joint *D* (Fig. 6.21). Forces $\boldsymbol{F}_{FD}$ and $\boldsymbol{F}_{ED}$ are expressed as follows:

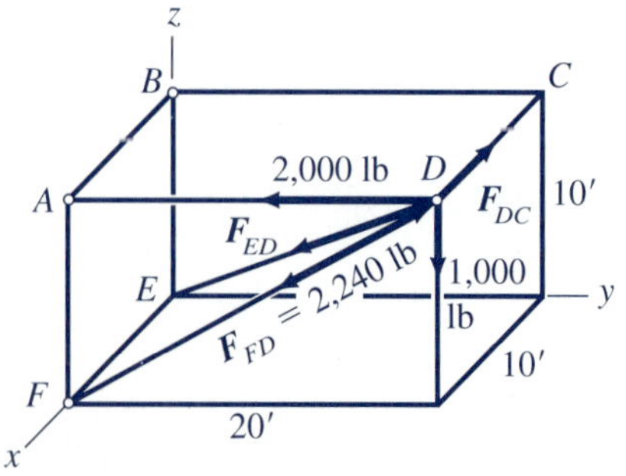

Figure 6.21. Free-body diagram of joint *D*.

Example 6.3 (Continued)

$$\boldsymbol{F}_{ED} = F_{ED}\frac{-10\boldsymbol{i} - 20\boldsymbol{j} - 10\boldsymbol{k}}{\sqrt{10^2 + 20^2 + 10^2}} = F_{ED}(-.408\boldsymbol{i} - .816\boldsymbol{j} - .408\boldsymbol{k})\text{ lb}$$

$$\boldsymbol{F}_{FD} = F_{FD}\frac{20\boldsymbol{j} + 10\boldsymbol{k}}{\sqrt{20^2 + 10^2}} = 2{,}240(.894\boldsymbol{i} + .447\boldsymbol{k})\text{ lb}$$

Hence, summing forces, we get

$$-2{,}000\boldsymbol{j} - 1{,}000\boldsymbol{k} - F_{DC}\boldsymbol{i} + 2{,}240(.894\boldsymbol{j} + .447\boldsymbol{k}) + F_{ED}(-.408\boldsymbol{i} - .816\boldsymbol{j} - .408\boldsymbol{k}) = \boldsymbol{0} \qquad \text{(d)}$$

Thus,

$$-2{,}000 + 2{,}000 - .816F_{ED} = 0 \qquad \text{(e)}$$

$$F_{DC} + .408F_{ED} = 0 \qquad \text{(f)}$$

$$-1{,}000 + 1{,}000 - .408F_{ED} = 0 \qquad \text{(g)}$$

We see here that $F_{ED} = 0$ and $F_{DC} = 0$.

Joint E. The only nonzero forces on joint E are the supporting forces and F_{CE}, as shown in Fig. 6.22(a). We solve $F_{CE} = 2{,}240$ lb compression.

Joint C. As a check on our problem, we can examine joint C. The only nonzero forces are shown on the joint [Fig. 6.22(b)]. The reader may readily verify that the solution checks.

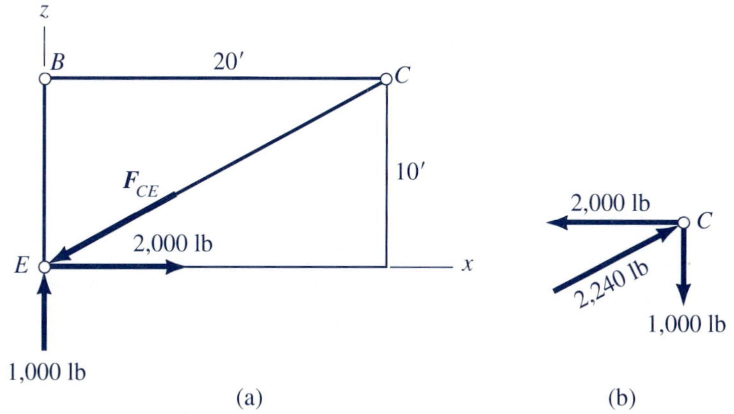

Figure 6.22. (a) Free-body diagram of joint E and (b) joint C.

Before proceeding with the problems, it will be well to comment on the loading of plane roof trusses. Usually there will be a series of separated parallel trusses supporting the loading from the roof such as is shown in Fig. 6.23, where a wind pressure is shown on a roof as p. Now the *inside* truss can be considered to support the loading over a region extending halfway to each neighboring truss (shown as distance d). Furthermore, pins A and B support the force exerted on area $lhmk$ while pins B and C support the forces exerted on area $lrvh$. When dealing with the entire inside truss as a free body, you can use the resultant force from pressure over $krvm$. However, when dealing with the pins as a free body you must use the forces coming on to each pin as described above and *not* the total resultant, which was used for the free body of the entire internal truss. Clearly, the outside trusses support half the loads described above.

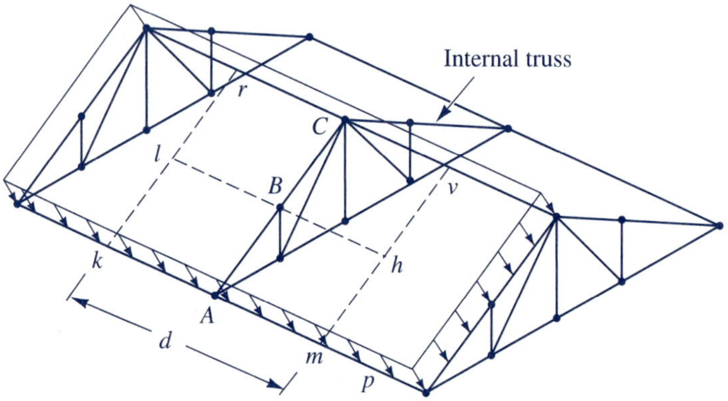

Figure 6.23. Roof trusses supporting a wind load.

Finally, we wish to remind you that a curved member in a truss, such as appears in Problems 6.5 and 6.8, is a two-force member with forces coming only from the pins. Recall that, for such members, the force transmitted to the pins must be collinear with the line connecting the pins, such as is shown in Fig. 6.24.

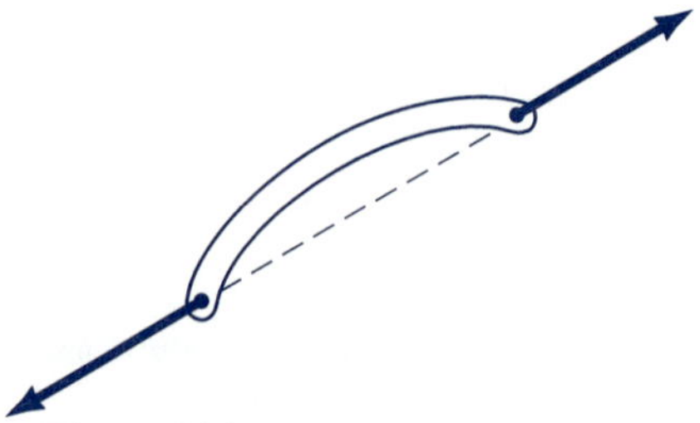

Figure 6.24. Curved two-force member.

PROBLEMS

6.1. State which of the trusses shown are simple trusses and which are not.

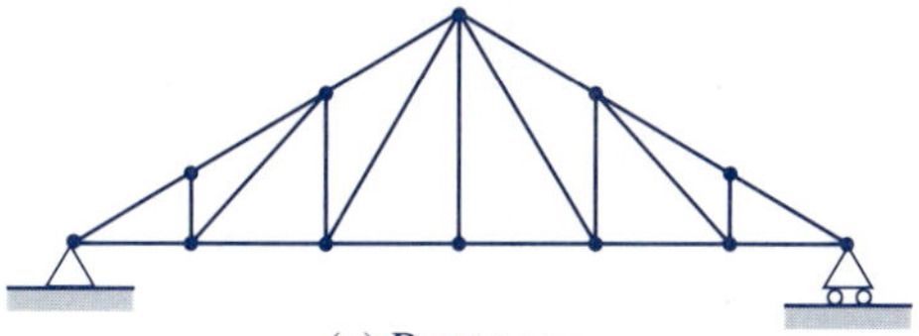

(a) Pratt truss

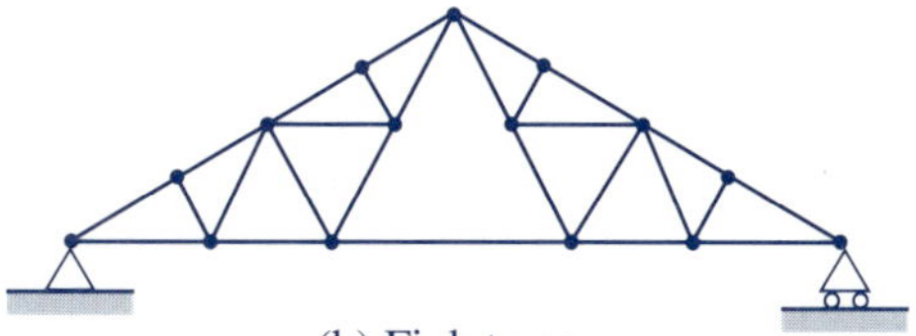

(b) Fink truss

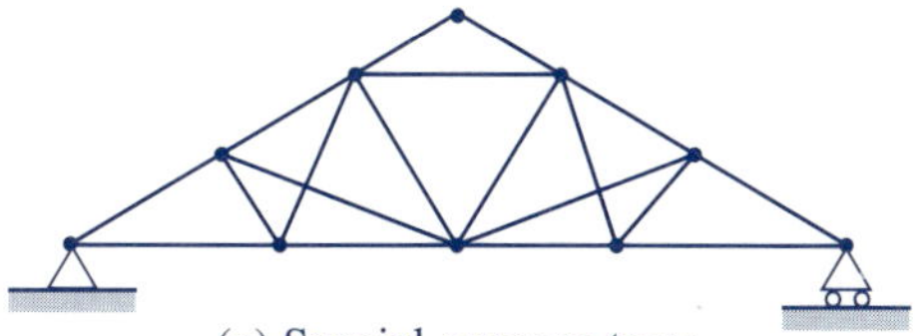

(c) Special-purpose truss

Figure P.6.1.

6.2. Find the forces transmitted by each member of the truss.

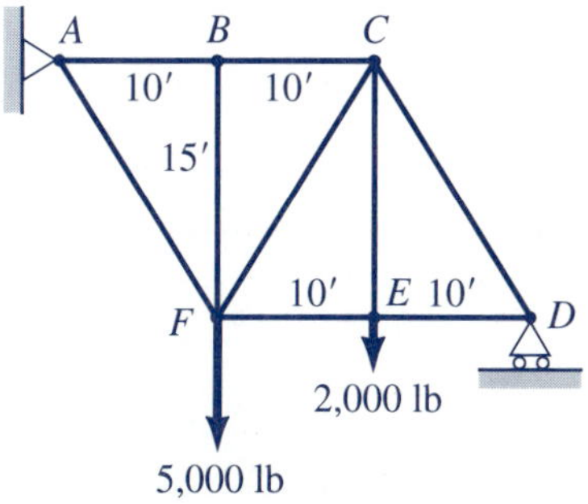

Figure P.6.2.

6.3. The simple country-road bridge has floor beams to carry vehicle loads to the truss joints. Find the forces in all members for a truck-loaded weight of 160 kN. Floor beams 1 are supported by pins A and B, while floor beams 2 are supported by pins B and C.

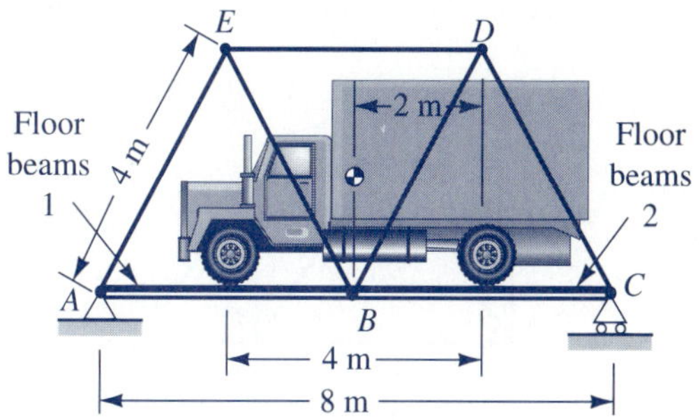

Figure P.6.3.

6.4. A rooftop pond is filled with cooling water from an air conditioner and is supported by a series of parallel plane trusses. What are the forces in each member of an inside truss? The roof trusses are spaced at 10 ft apart. Water weights 62.4 lb/ft.[3]

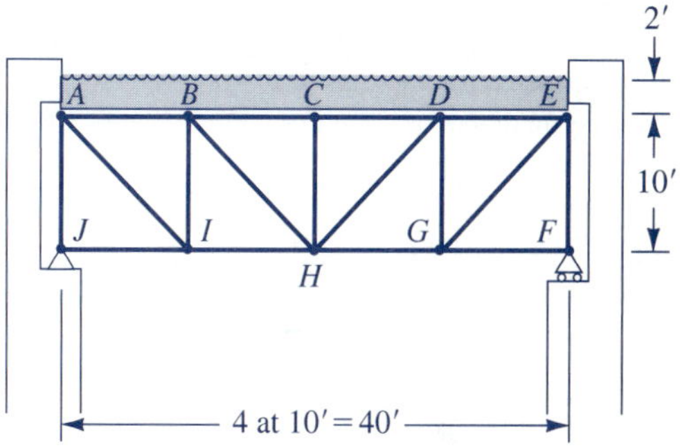

Figure P.6.4.

6.5. Find the forces transmitted by the straight members of the truss. DC is circular.

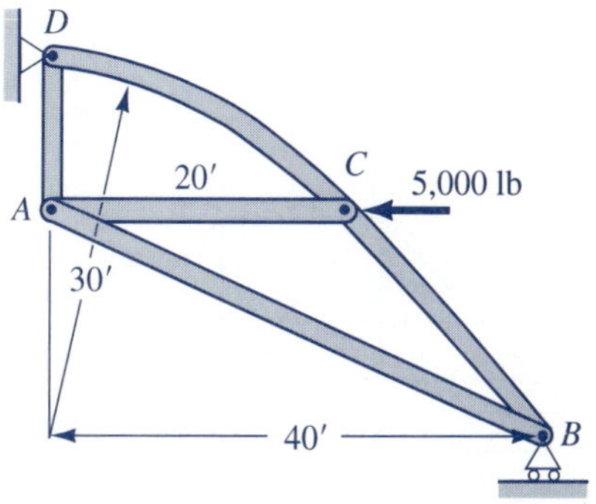

Figure P.6.5.

6.6. Roof trusses such as the one shown are spaced 6 m apart in a long, rectangular building. During the winter, snow loads of up to 1 kN/m^2 (or 1 kPa) accumulate on the central portion of the roof. Find the force in each member for a truss not at the ends of the building.

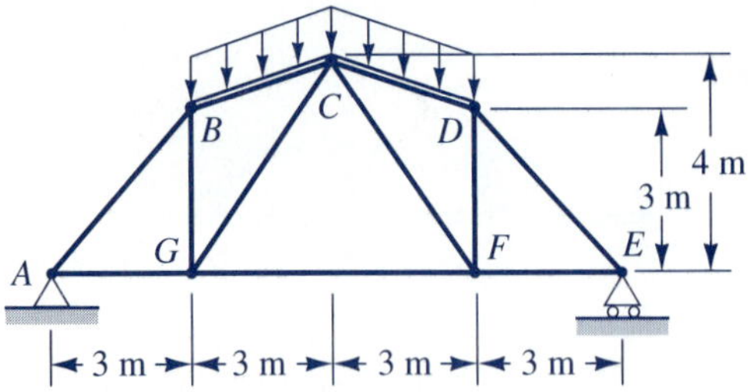

Figure P.6.6.

6.7. The bridge supports a roadway load of 1,000 lb/ft for each of the two trusses. Each member weighs 30 lb/ft. Compute the forces in the members, accounting approximately for the weight of the members.

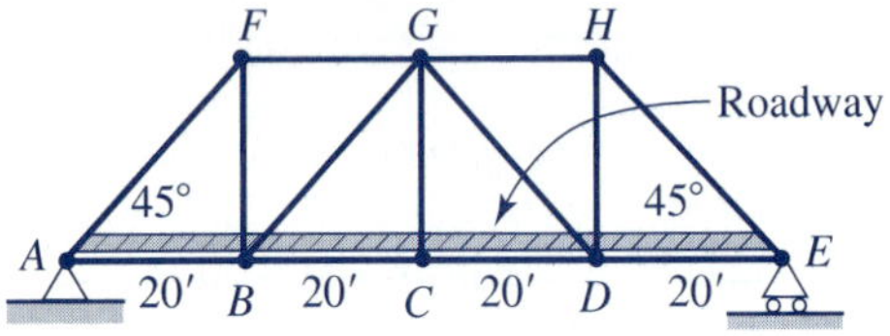

Figure P.6.7.

6.8. Find the forces in the straight members of the truss.

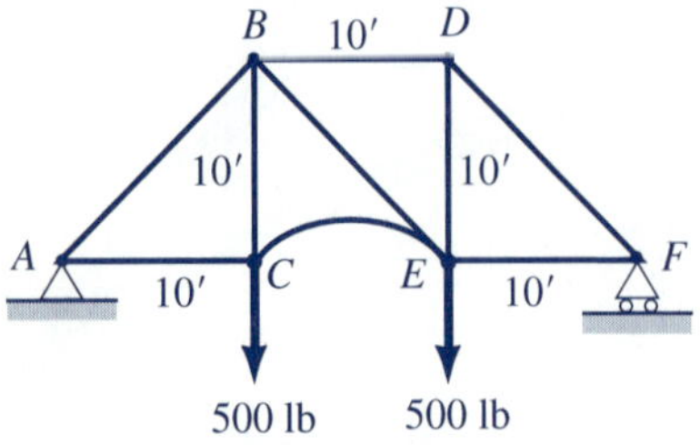

Figure P.6.8.

6.9. Find the forces in the members of the truss.

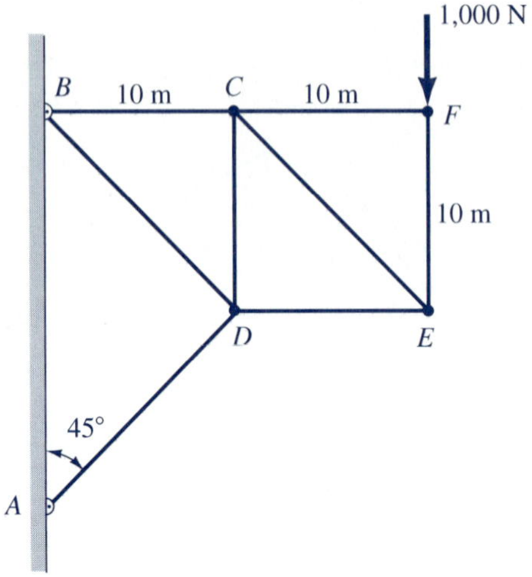

Figure P.6.9.

6.10. In Example 6.1, include the weights of the members approximately. The members each weigh 100 lb/ft.

6.11. Determine the forces in the members. The pulleys at C and F each weigh 300 N. Neglect all other weights. Be sure you have a check on your solution.

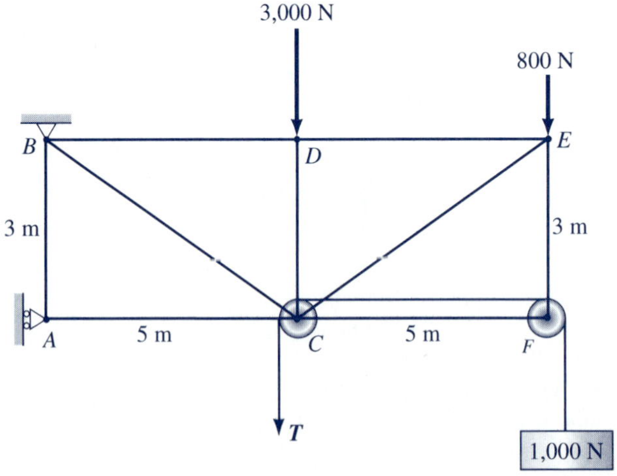

Figure P.6.11.

6.12 Roadway and vehicle loads are transmitted to the highway bridge truss as the idealized forces shown. Each load is 100 kN. What are the forces in the members?

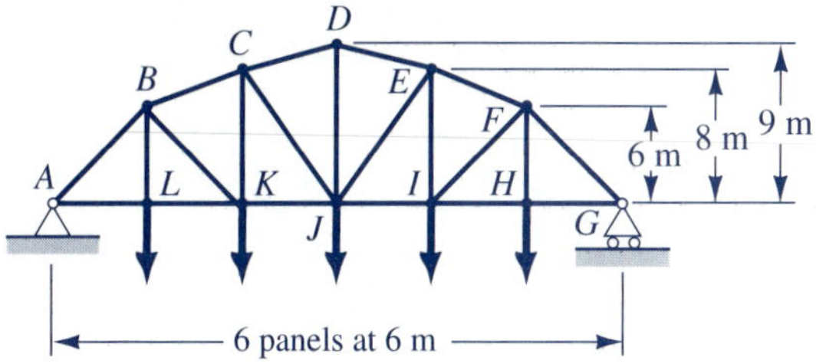

Figure P.6.12.

6.13. A hoist weighing 5 kN lifts railroad cars for truck repair. The hoist has a 150-kN capacity and hangs from a truss with an L-shaped member to clear boxcars. What are the forces in the straight members for full capacity of the hoist?

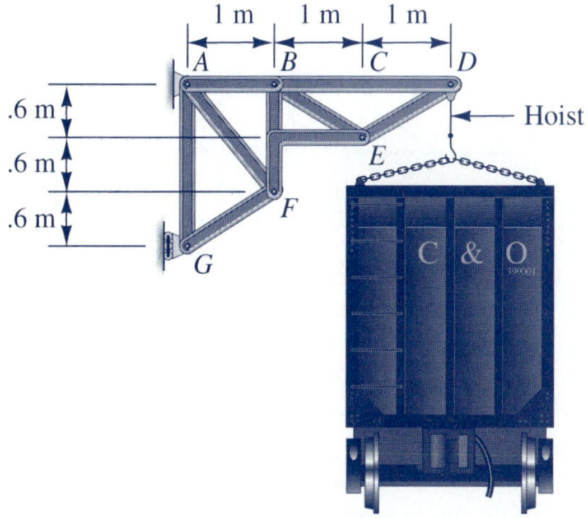

Figure P.6.13.

6.14. A 5-kN traveling hoist has a 50-kN capacity and is suspended from a beam weighing 1 kN/m, which, in turn, is fastened to the roof truss at *I* and *G* as shown. In addition, wind pressures of up to 2 kN/m^2 (or 2 kPA) act on the side of the roof. The resulting force is transmitted to pins *A* and *J*. If the trusses are spaced 5 m apart, what are the forces in each member of the truss when the hoist is in the middle of the span?

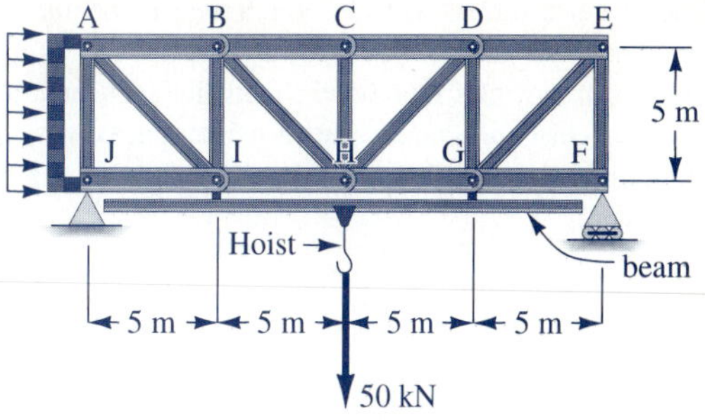

Figure P.6.14.

6.15. Find the forces in the members of the truss. The 1,000-lb force is parallel to the *y* axis, and the 500-lb force is parallel to the *z* axis.

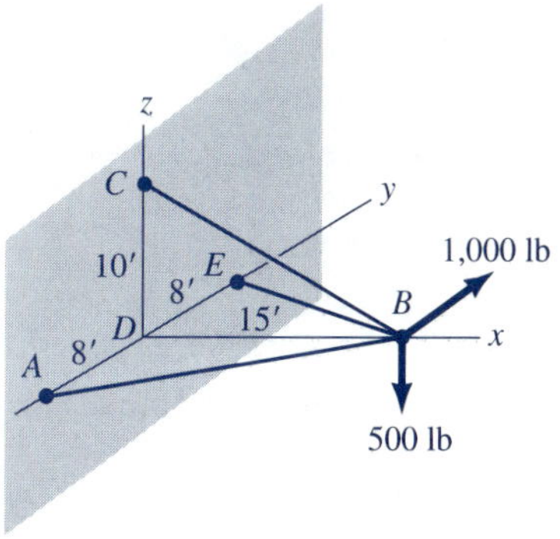

Figure P.6.15.

6.16. Find the forces in the members and the supporting forces for the space truss *ABCD*. Note that *BDC* is in the *xz* plane.

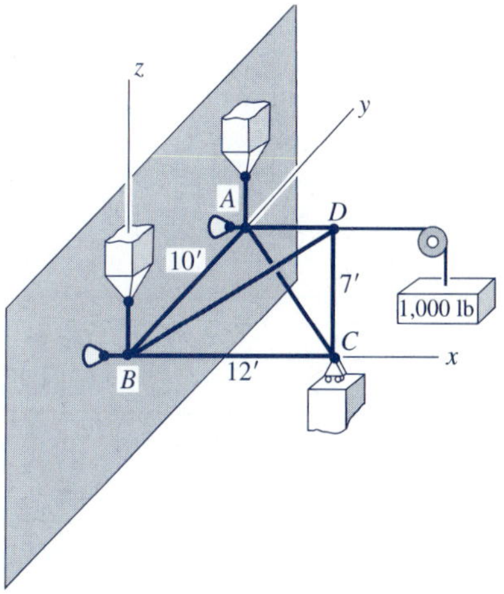

Figure P.6.16.

6.17. A steel space truss *ABCDE* with members having identical cross-sections supports a 50-kN vertical load as well as a 10-kN horizontal load and rests on smooth, mutually perpendicular surfaces. Assume that the contact between the space truss and the smooth surface is at the ball joints. What are the forces in the members at *D*?

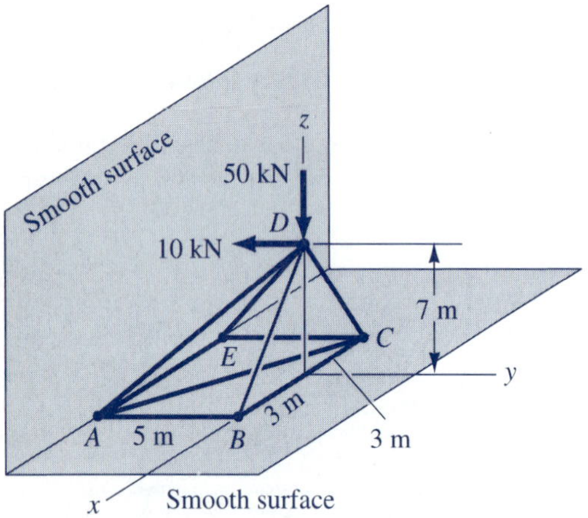

Figure P.6.17.

6.18. Find the forces in the members of the space truss under the action of a force $\boldsymbol{F}$ given as

$$\boldsymbol{F} = 10\boldsymbol{i} - 6\boldsymbol{j} - 12\boldsymbol{k} \text{ kN}$$

Note that *C* is a ball-and-socket joint while *A*, *F*, and *E* are on rollers.

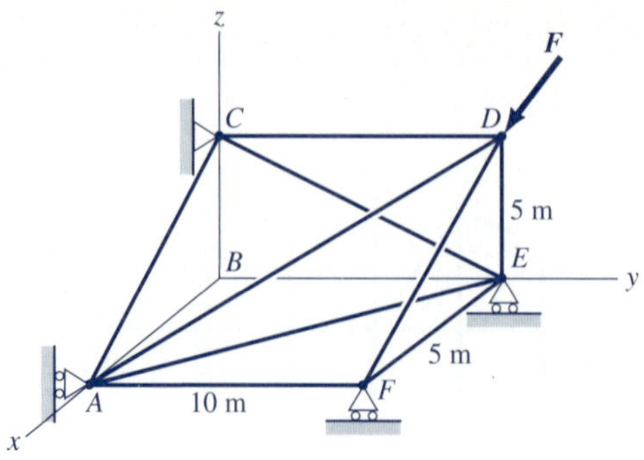

Figure P.6.18.

6.19. The plane of ball-and-socket joints *CDHE* of the space truss is in the *zy* plane, while the plane of *FGDE* is parallel to the *xz* plane. Note that this is *not* a simple space truss. Nevertheless, the forces in the members can be ascertained by choosing a desirable starting joint and proceeding by statics from joint to joint. Determine the forces in all the members and then determine the supporting forces. At *A* and *H* we have ball and socket joints.

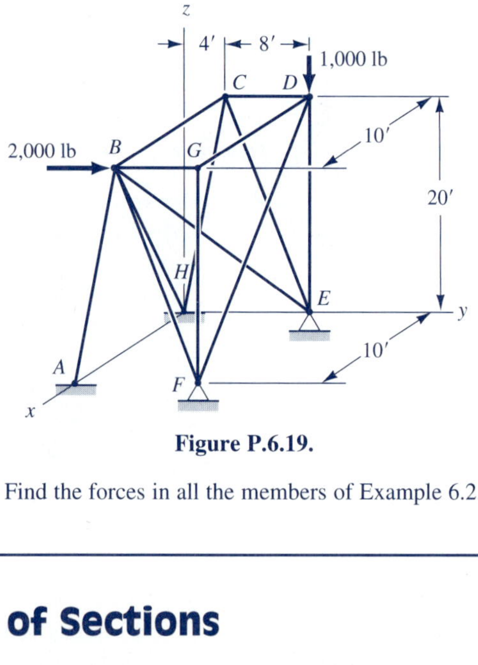

Figure P.6.19.

6.20. Find the forces in all the members of Example 6.2.

6.5 Method of Sections

In the method of sections that we shall use for plane trusses, we employ free-body diagrams that are generally different than that of the method of joints, as was pointed out earlier. *A free body in this method is formed by cutting away a portion of a truss and including at the cut sections the forces that are transmitted across these sections.* We then use the equations of equilibrium for these free bodies. In this way, we can expose for calculation individual members well inside a truss and avoid the laborious process of proceeding joint by joint until reaching a joint on which the desired unknown force acts.

Generally a free body is created by passing a section (or cut) through the truss such as section *A–A* or section *B–B* in Fig 6.25(a). Note that the section can be straight or curved. The corresponding right hand free-body diagrams [see Fig. 6.25(b) for cut *A–A* and Fig. 6.25(c) for cut *B–B*] involve

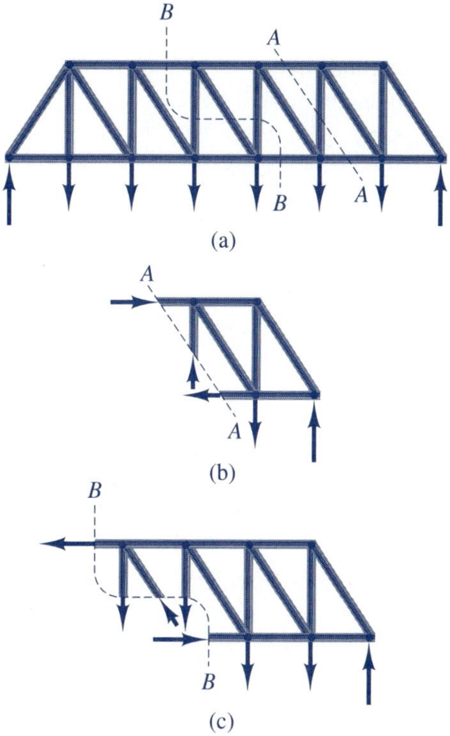

Figure 6.25. Section cuts.

coplanar force systems. We have, accordingly, three equations of equilibrium available for each free body. One can also choose to use left-hand free-body diagrams for these cuts. Note that in contrast to the method of joints, one or more equilibrium equations can most profitably be moment equations. The choice of the section (or sections) to find the desired unknowns inside a truss involves ingenuity on the part of the engineer. He/she will want the fewest and simplest sections to find desired forces for one or more members inside the truss. The method of sections is used for efficiently finding limited information. The method of joints for such problems is by contrast one of "brute force."

We now illustrate the method of sections in the following examples.

Example 6.4

In Example 6.1 suppose that we wish to know the force in member *CE* only.

To avoid the laborious joint-by-joint procedure, we employ a portion of the truss to the left of cut *K–K*, as shown in Fig. 6.26. Notice that the forces from the other part of the truss acting on this part through the cut members have been included, and in this way the desired force has been exposed. The sense of these exposed forces is not known, but we do know the orientations, as explained in our earlier discussions. Using the equations of equilibrium and taking advantage of the fact that the lines of action of some of the exposed unknown forces are concurrent at the location of certain joints, we may readily solve for the unknowns if they number three or less. To determine F_{CE}, we take moments about a point corresponding to joint *D* through which the lines of action of forces F_{BD} and F_{CD} pass:

$$\underline{\sum M_D = 0:}$$

$$-(1{,}000)(20) + (1{,}000)(10) + 10F_{CE} = 0$$

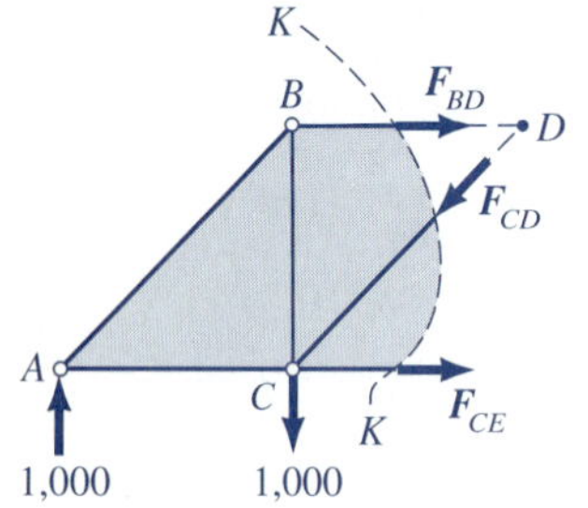

Figure 6.26. Cut *K–K*.

Therefore,

$$F_{CE} = 1{,}000 \text{ lb}$$

Our ingenuity here has led us to one equation with only one unknown, the desired force F_{CE}. By observing the free-body diagram in Fig. 6.26, we can clearly see that *CE* is a tension member.

If we desire F_{BD} also, we can take moments about point *C* through which the lines of action of F_{CE} and F_{CD} pass. However, F_{BD} now comes out negative, indicating that we have made an incorrect choice of sense. With this in mind, we can conclude that *BD* is in compression.

Perhaps a suitable single section with sufficient unknowns for a solution cannot be found. We may then have to take several sections before we can expose the desired force in a free body with enough simultaneous equations to effect a solution. These problems are no different from the ones we studied in Chapter 5, where several free-body diagrams were needed to generate a complete set of equations containing the unknown quantity. We now consider such a problem.

Example 6.5

A plane truss is shown in Fig. 6.27 for which only the force in member *AB* is desired. The supporting forces have been determined and are shown in the diagram.

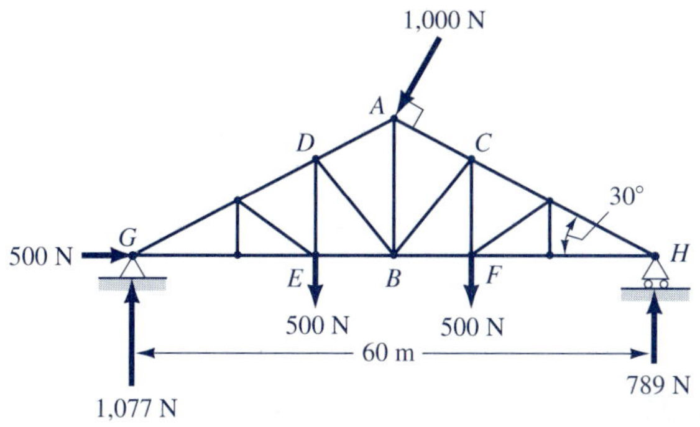

Figure 6.27. Plane truss.

In Fig. 6.28(a) we have shown a cut *J–J* of the truss exposing force F_{AB}. (This is the same force diagram as that which results from the free-body diagram of pin *A*.) We have here three unknown forces for which only two equations of equilibrium are available. We must use an additional free body.

Thus, in Fig. 6.28(b) we have shown a second cut *K–K*. Note that by taking moments about joint *B*, we can solve for F_{AC} directly. With this information we can then return to the first cut to get the desired unknown F_{AB}. Accordingly, we have, for free body II:

$$\underline{\sum M_B = 0:}$$

$$-(10)(500) + (30)(789) - (F_{AC})(\sin\ 30°)(30) = 0$$

(Note we have transmitted F_{AC} to joint *H* in evaluating its moment contribution.) Solving for F_{AC} we get

$$F_{AC} = 1{,}245\ \text{N}$$

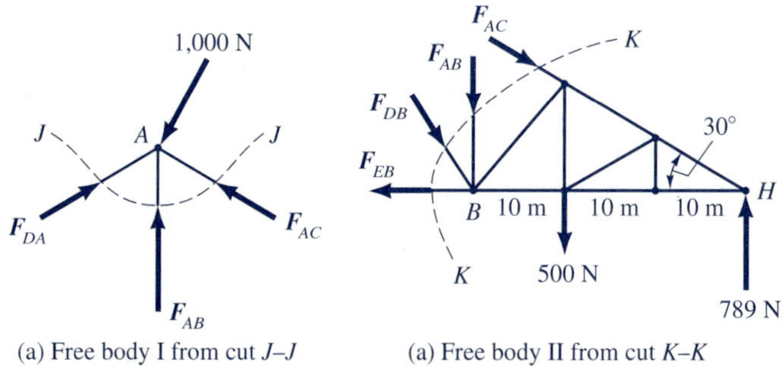

Figure 6.28. Free bodies needed for the computation of force F_{AB}.

Example 6.5 (Continued)

Summing forces for free body I, we have[6]

$$\underline{\sum F_x = 0:}$$

$$F_{DA} \cos 30° - F_{AC} \cos 30° - 1{,}000 \sin 30° = 0$$

Therefore,

$$F_{DA} = 1{,}822\text{N}$$

$$\underline{\sum F_y = 0:}$$

$$F_{DA} \sin 30° + F_{AC} \sin 30° + F_{AB} - 1{,}000 \cos 30° = 0$$

Therefore,

$$F_{AB} = -667 \text{ N}$$

We see that member *AB* is a tension member rather than a compression member as was our initial guess in drawing the free-body diagrams.

[6]What now follows is the same as the method of joints applied to pin *A*.

In retrospect, you will note that, in the method of joints, errors made early will of necessity propagate through the calculations. There is, on the other hand, much less likelihood of this occurring in the method of sections. However, for simple trusses with many members, we may profitably use the method of joints in conjunction with a computer for which the brute-force approach of the method of joints is ideally suited. It is to be pointed out that there is computer software available which makes this kind of computation routine and quick.

*6.6 Looking Ahead—Deflection of a Simple, Linearly Elastic Truss

In the solids or structures courses you will soon be taking, you will be given instruction for determining the movement of the pins of a linearly elastic, simple truss stemming from the external loads. It is true that you can now determine the forces in a simple truss and from this you can determine the change in length of each member. However, using this data as well as the accompanying changes of orientation of the members, you will find it next to impossible to get the movements of the pins for all but the most trivial trusses.

You will learn later of a neat method of doing this. In this method, each movable (unconstrained) pin is imagined to be given first a hypothetical movement[7] δ_1 in one of two orthogonal directions, say the x direction here, while no movement is allowed for that pin in the y direction. All other pins are held fixed for the preceding action. We now evaluate via geometry the changes in length stemming from δ_1 of all members affected by this hypothetical displacement. Also, the energy of deformation[8] for these members is computed. The aforementioned displacement is shown in Fig. 6.29 for δ_1. In addition to the energy of deformation of the affected members, we compute the work done by external forces that undergo movement from δ_1, keeping the forces constant during this movement. Here the work is $F(\cos\alpha)\delta_1$. This procedure is carried out for each such x and y displacement for all of the movable pins. We then add up all the energy terms and all the work terms, multiplying the latter by -1. We then have a function of all of the n δ's comprising the x and y components of all movable pins. This function, which is commonly denoted as π, is then extremized with respect to the n δ's. We then form n simultaneous equations from

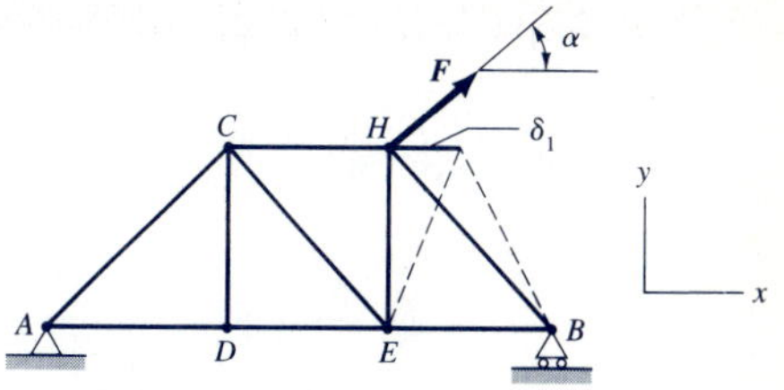

Figure 6.29. A simple truss has its free pin H given a hypothetical displacement δ_1 while keeping all other displacement components fixed. Note that only members CH, EH, and HB are involved. Work done is $F(\cos\alpha)\delta_1$.

$$\left(\frac{\partial \pi}{\partial \delta}\right)_i = 0 \qquad i = 1, 2, \ldots n \qquad (6.2)$$

Solving for the δ's gives the deflection of each pin. This formulation is a form of the method of *total potential energy*. You will later realize that Eqs. (6.2) are possibly the most powerful equations in solid mechanics.

What is particularly interesting here is that Eqs. (6.2), set up properly, are equivalent to equations of *equilibrium*. That is, we have here the strange situation whereby the extremization of a function is, among other things, equivalent to a most important equation.

The same shift can take place in other engineering sciences where we can sometimes shift from a key differential equation with certain boundary conditions to the process of extremizing a function (or some related quantity called a *functional* which, simply speaking, is a function of a function). Notice that for our simple truss we are going from physically obvious equations of equilibrium to a more obscure, more mathematical approach of extremizing a function. Yet (note this carefully) the latter approach yields more useful information of a very practical nature despite its more obscure, more mathematical nature.

In Chapter 10, we shall see a limited form of the total potential energy principle which is applicable for rigid bodies. In the present chapter for the truss, the members were deformable and we mentioned that we needed the energy of deformation for the use of the total potential energy principle.

[7]This is called a *virtual displacement* and will be discussed further in Chapter 10 when we discuss the method of virtual work.

[8]You will learn to calculate the energy of deformation in your solid mechanics or your structures course. The formula is $\frac{EA\delta^2}{2L}$ where δ is the axial change in length of the member, A is the cross-sectional area, E is the modulus of elasticity, and L is the length of the member.

PROBLEMS

6.21. Find the forces in members *CB* and *BE* of the plane truss.

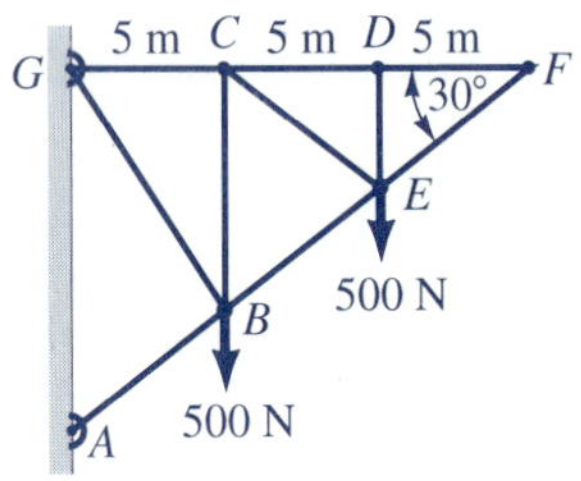

Figure P.6.21.

6.22. For the roof truss: (a) Find the forces transmitted by member *DC*. (b) What is the force transmitted by *DE*?

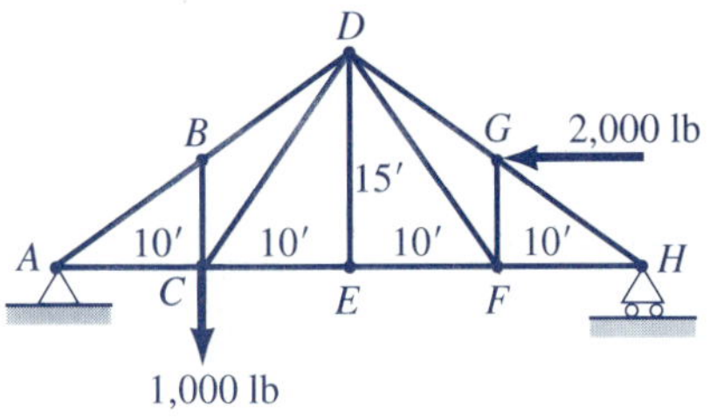

Figure P.6.22.

6.23. Determine the force transmitted by member *KU* in the plane truss. The vertical members are 9m apart.

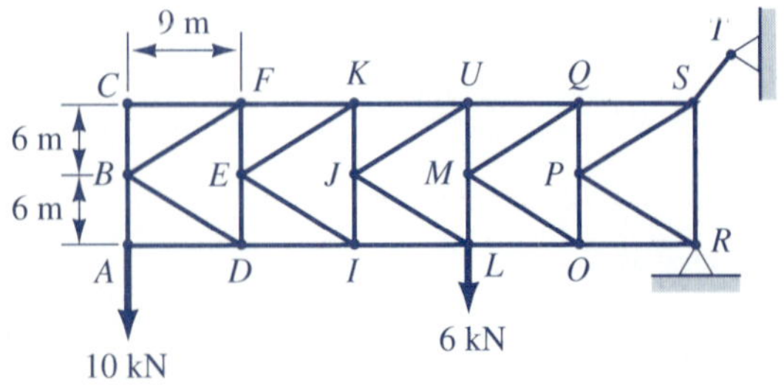

Figure P.6.23.

6.24. In the roof truss of Problem 6.6, find the force in member *GF*. Remember loads are applied to the pins.

6.25. Find the forces in members *CD*, *DG*, and *HG* in the plane truss.

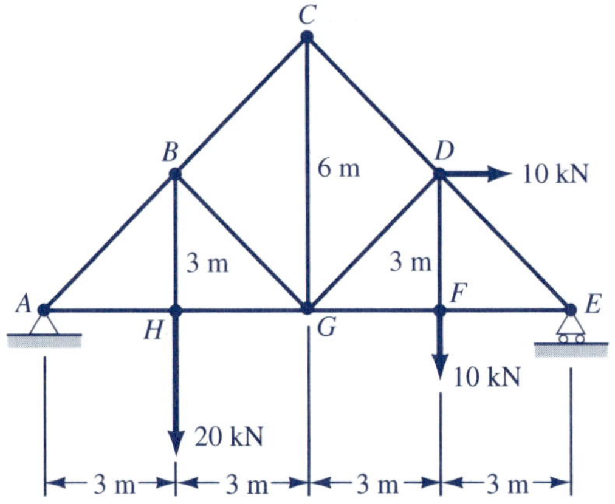

Figure P.6.25.

6.26. In Problem 6.13 find the force in members *BF* and *AB*.

6.27. The roof is subjected to a wind loading of 20 lb/ft². Find the forces in members *LK* and *KJ* of an interior truss if the trusses are spaced 10 ft apart.

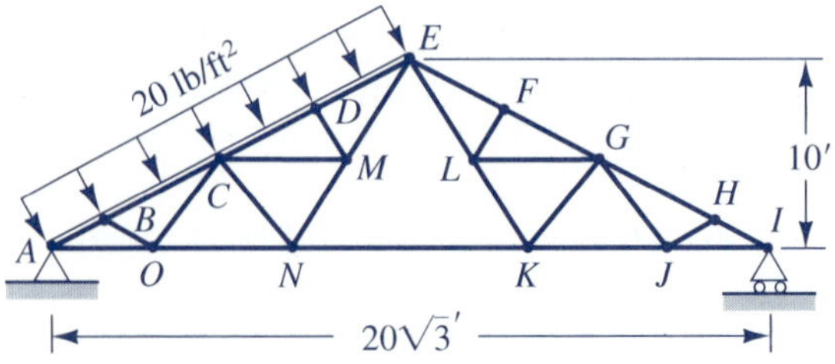

Figure P.6.27.

6.28. The guideways for a large overhanging crane are suspended from certain joints of the truss (*M, K, J,* and *G*). Find the forces in members *BC*, *BK*, *DE*, *DI*, and *EF*. Neglect the truss and guideway weights. Guideways only transmit supported loads to pins and are not considered part of the truss structurally.

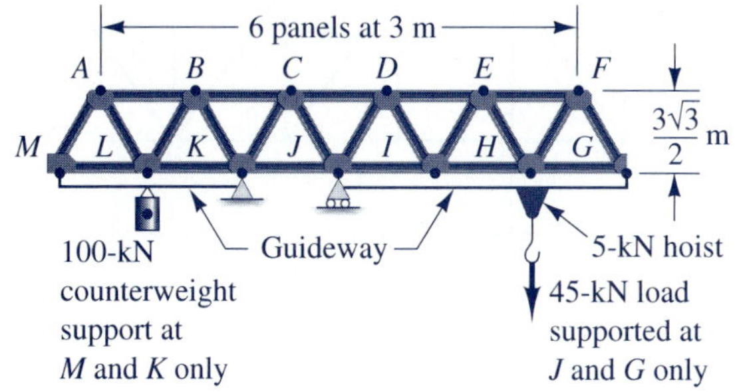

Figure P.6.28.

6.29. In Example 6.2, determine the forces in members *FG* and *CE*.

6.30. (a) Find the forces in members *DG* and *DF* by the method of *sections*. State whether the members are tension or compression members.

(b) Determine the forces in members *AC*, *AB*, *CB*, and *CD* by the method of *joints*. Label the diagram in an appropriate manner and indicate whether members are in tension or compression.

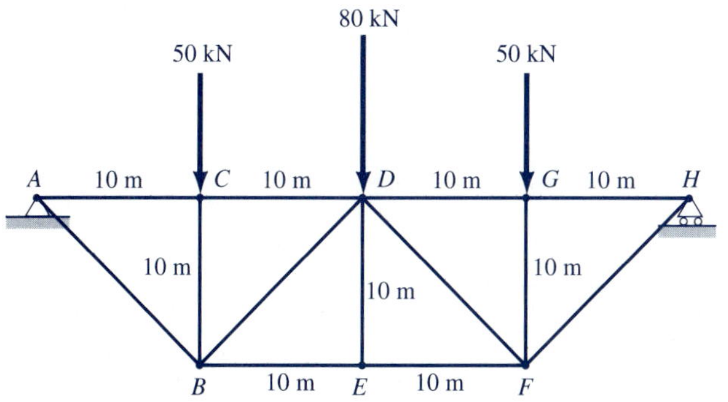

Figure P.6.30.

6.31. A pair of trusses supports a roadway weighing 500 lb/ft. By method of sections, find the forces in *DF* and *DE*. The roadway is supported at pins *A*, *D*, *F*, and *H* on the two trusses.

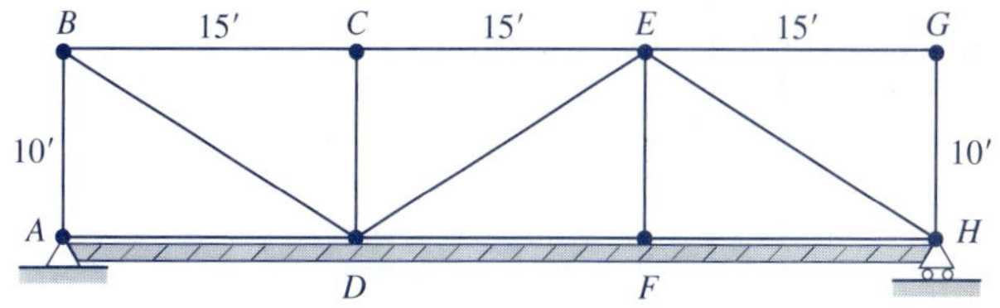

Figure P.6.31.

6.32. Find the force in members *HE*, *FH*, *FE*, and *FC* of the truss.

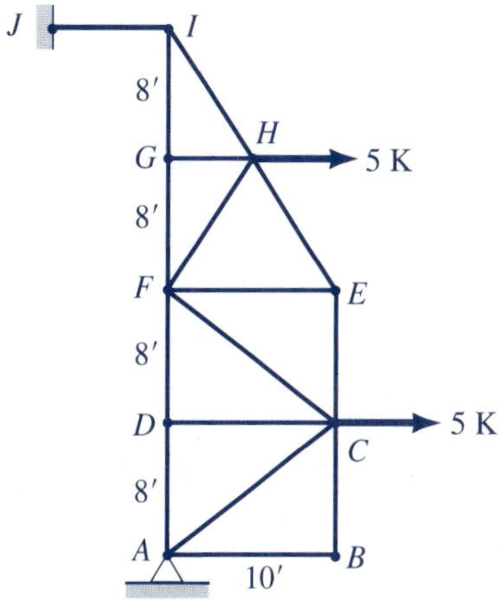

Figure P.6.32.

6.33. Find the force in member JF in the truss.

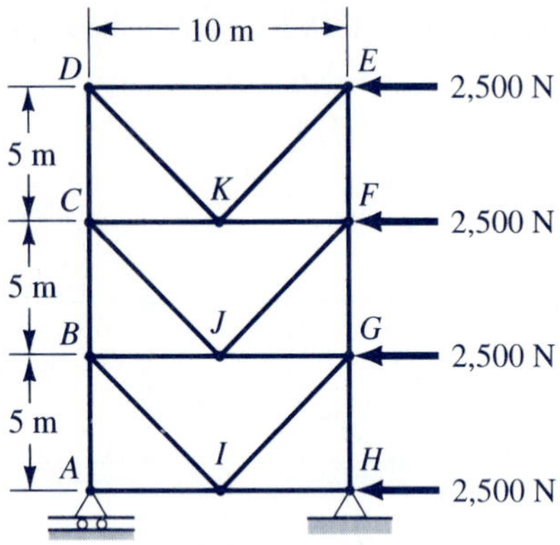

Figure P.6.33.

6.34. Find the force in members FI, EF, and DH in the truss. Neglect the weight of the pulleys.

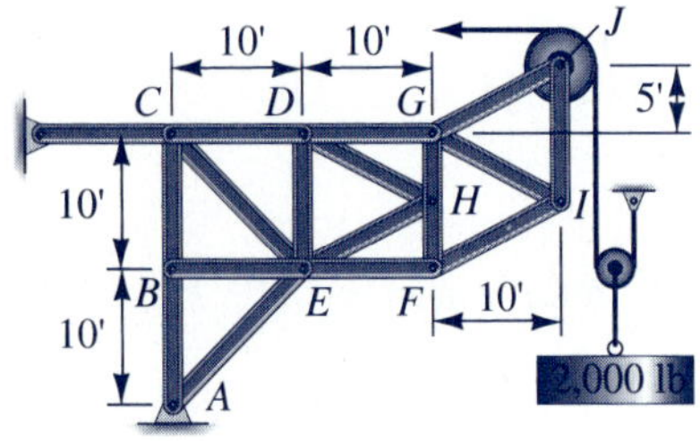

Figure P.6.34.

6.35. A railroad engine is starting to cross the deck-type truss bridge shown. If the weight of the engine is idealized by the four 50-kip loads,[9] find the forces in members AB, BL, CK, CL, LK, DK, KJ, and DJ.

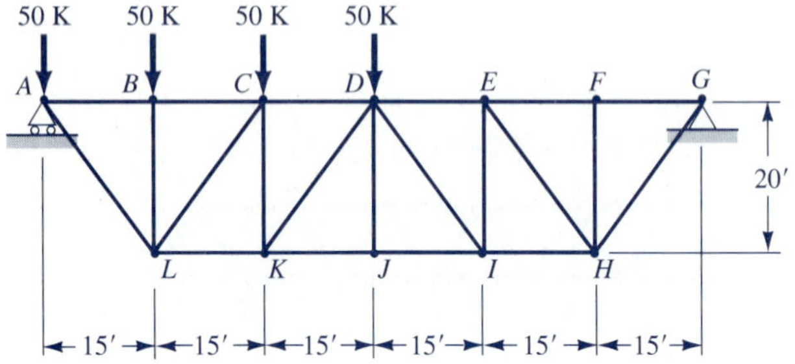

Figure P.6.35.

6.36. A diesel train engine is moving along a deck-type truss which is part of a bridge. If the loads on positions A, B, C, and D are estimated to be 50 kips each,[9] find the forces in members LC, KL, FG, and HG.

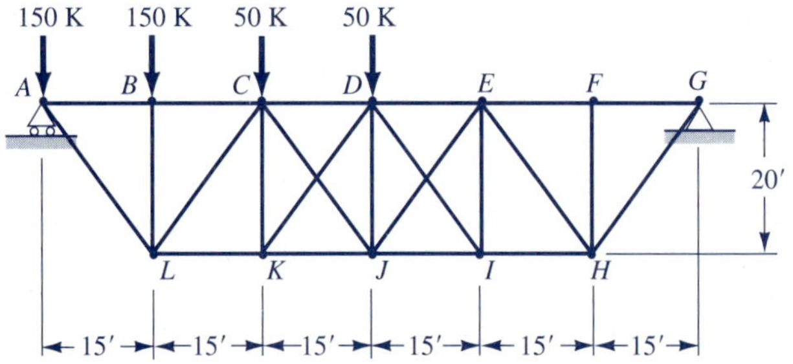

Figure P.6.36.

[9]A kip is a kilopound, or 1,000 lb.

Part B: Section Forces in Beams[10]

6.7 Introduction

In Part A, we considered a number of problems involving members loaded axially along the axes of the members. The resultant force at any section was established easily as a single axial force. We shall now consider thin prismatic members that are loaded *transversely* as well as axially. Generally, when such members are loaded transversely, we call them *beams*. Of considerable use will be certain components of the resultant force system acting on *cross-sections* of the beams. We shall set forth methods in this section for computing these quantities. We consider beams with a vertical plane of symmetry along the axis of the beam.

6.8 Shear Force, Axial Force, and Bending Moment

Consider first a beam with an arbitrary intensity of loading $w(x)$ in the plane of symmetry and a load P along the direction of the beam applied at the end A as shown in Fig. 6.30(a). It will be assumed that the supporting forces have been determined. To find the force transmitted across the cross-sectional interface at position x, we take a portion of the beam as a free body so as to "expose" the section of the beam at x as shown in Fig. 6.30(b). Since we have a coplanar-loading distribution, we know from rigid-body mechanics that, depending on the problem, we can replace the distribution at section x most simply by a single force or a single couple in the plane of the external loads. If the resultant is most simply a single force, we know that it must have a particular line of action. This line of action does not usually go through the center of the cross-section. Since the actual position of the intersection of this force with the cross-section is of little interest in beam theory, we deliberately take the position of the resultant force to be at the center of the cross-section at all times and include the proper couple moment M_z to accompany the force. Furthermore, we decompose the force in orthogonal components—in this case, a vertical force V_y, and a horizontal force H. These quantities are shown in Fig. 6.30(b). Since these quantities are used to such a great extent in structural work, we have associated names with them. They are $V_y \equiv$ *shear-force* component, $H \equiv$ *axial-force* component, $M_z \equiv$ *bending-moment* component.[11] If we had a three-dimensional load, there would have been one

[10]In many engineering programs, this topic is considered in the solid mechanics or strength of materials course which follows the statics course. There, the results are used abundantly throughout the course. It is entirely feasible then to bypass Part B without penalty in this book. For a more detailed treatment along the same lines as in this chapter, see I.H. Shames, *Introduction to Solid Mechanics,* 2nd Ed., Prentice-Hall Inc., Englewood Cliffs, NJ, 1985.

[11]For curved beams, shear forces V are always tangent to the cross-section, whereas axial force H is always normal to the cross-section.

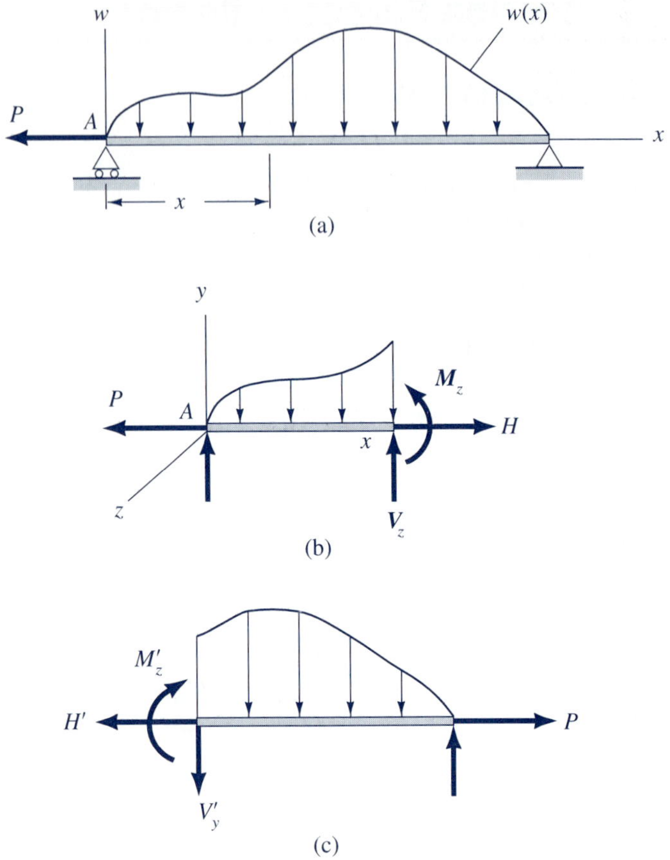

Figure 6.30. Resultant at a section.

additional shear component V_z (see Fig. 6.31), one additional bending-moment component M_y, and a couple moment along the axis of the beam M_x, which we shall call the *twisting moment*.

Notice in Fig. 6.30(c) that a second free-body diagram has been drawn which exposes the "other side" of the cross-section at position x. The shear force, axial force, and bending moment for this section have been primed in the diagram. We know from Newton's third law that they should be equal and opposite to the corresponding unprimed quantities in part (b) of the diagram. We can thus choose for our computations either a left-hand or a right-hand free-body diagram. But this poses somewhat of a problem for us when we come to reporting the signs of the transmitted forces and couple moments at a section. We cannot use the direction of a force or couple moment at the section. Clearly, this would be inadequate since the sense of the force or couple moment at a section would depend on whether a left-hand or a right-hand free-body diagram was used. To associate an unambiguous sign for shear force, axial force, and bending moment at a section, we adopt the following convention:

A force component for a section is positive if the area vector of the cross-section and the force component both have senses either in the positive or in the negative directions of any one or two of the references axes.[12]

The same is true for the bending moment.

Thus, consider Fig. 6.30. For the left-hand free-body diagram, the area vector for section x points in the positive x direction. Note also that H, V_y, and the vectorial representation of M_z also point in positive directions of the xyz axes. Hence, according to our convention we have drawn a positive shear force, a positive axial force, and a positive bending moment at the section at x. For the right-hand free-body diagram, the cross-sectional area vector points in the negative x direction. And, since H', V_y', and M_z' point in negative directions of the x, y, and z axes, these components are again positive for the section at x according to our convention. Clearly, by employing this convention, we can easily and effectively specify the force system at a section without the danger of ambiguity.

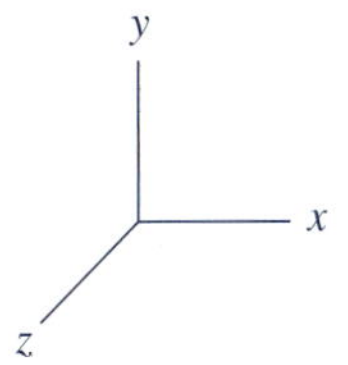

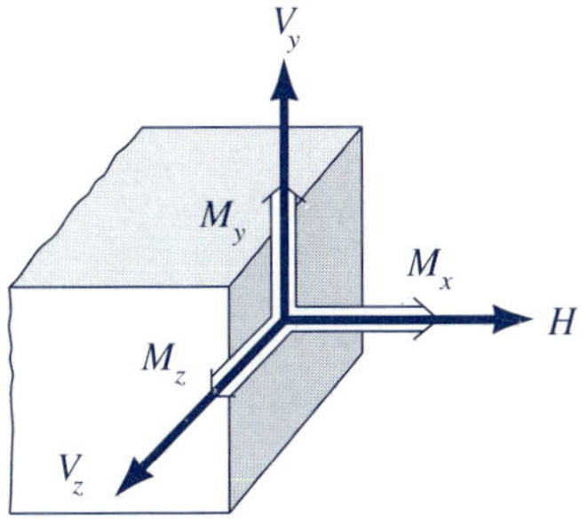

Figure 6.31. Section resultant for three-dimensional loading.

As pointed out earlier, we can solve for V_y, H, and M_z at section x using rigid-body mechanics for either a left-hand or a right-hand free-body diagram provided that we know all the external forces. The quantities V_y, H, and M_z will depend on x, and for this reason, it is the practice to sketch shear-force and bending-moment diagrams to convey this information for the entire beam.

We now illustrate the computation of V and M.

[12]Some authors employ the reverse convention for shear force from the one that we have proposed. Our convention is consistent with the usual convention used in the theory of elasticity for the sign of stress at a point, and it is for this reason that we have employed this convention rather than the other one.

Example 6.6

We shall express the shear-force and bending-moment equations for the simply supported beam shown in Fig. 6.32(a), whose weight we shall neglect. The support forces obtained from equilibrium are 500 N each.

To get the shear force at a section x, we isolate either the left or right side of the beam at x and employ the equations of equilibrium on the resulting free body. If x lies between A and C of the beam, the only noninternal force present for a left-hand free body is the left supporting force [see Fig. 6.32(b)]. Notice that we have used directions for V and M (there is no need for subscripts in the simple problem) corresponding to the *positive* states from the point of view of our convention. Clearly, the *algebraic* sign we get for these quantities from equilibrium calculations will then correspond to the *convention* sign. If x is between C and B for such a free body, two external forces appear [see Fig. 6.32(c)]. Therefore, if the shear force is to be expressed as a function of x, clearly separate equations covering the two ranges, $0 < x < l/2$ and $l/2 < x < l$, are necessary. Summing forces we then get

$\underline{0 < x < l/2:}$

$$500 + V = 0; \quad \text{therefore,} \quad V = -500 \text{ N} \tag{a}$$

$\underline{l/2 < x < l:}$

$$500 - 1{,}000 + V = 0; \quad \text{therefore,} \quad V = 500 \text{ N} \tag{b}$$

Notice from the above results that there is a sudden change of the shear force from –500 N to +500 N as we pass the position of the concentrated 1,000-N load. Clearly then, the value of shear must perforce be *indeterminate* at the position of this concentrated load. It is for this very reason that, in the ranges of applicability of Eqs. (a) and (b), we have excluded the positions of the three concentrated loads of the problem. Note further that if there were only a distributed load starting at point C, there would not be discontinuity in shear and so we would not have to delete the position of point C in the range applicability of the shear equations.

Now let us turn to the bending-moment equations. Again, we must consider two discrete regions. Taking moments about position x, we get

$\underline{0 \leq x \leq l/2:}$

$$-500x + \text{M} = 0; \quad \text{therefore,} \quad M = 500x \text{ N-m} \tag{c}$$

$\underline{l/2 \leq x \leq l:}$

$$-500x + 1{,}000\left(x - \tfrac{l}{2}\right) + M = 0;$$

$$\text{therefore,} \quad M = 500(l - x) \text{ N-m} \tag{d}$$

Example 6.6 (Continued)

If there were a point couple present in the loading, there obviously would be a discontinuity in the bending-moment equation at the position of the point couple exactly as there were discontinuities at the point loads in the shear equations above. We would then not include such points in the bending-moment equations. In the present problem there are no point couples and so, in Eqs. (c) and (d), we include the entire beam in the combined ranges of these equations.

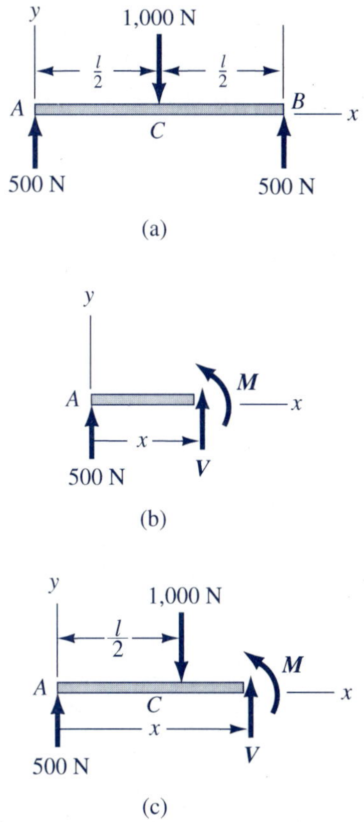

Figure 6.32. Simply supported beam.

It is generally the practice to express the shear and bending-moment equations successively under common ranges of applicability. In such cirumstances, we shall adopt the practice of excluding from any range of applicability *any* points of discontinuity for *either* the shear or the bending-moment equations.

Example 6.7

Determine the shear-force and bending-moment equations for the simply supported beam shown in Fig. 6.33. Neglect the weight of the beam.

We must first find the supporting forces for the beam. Hence, we have using the right-hand rule

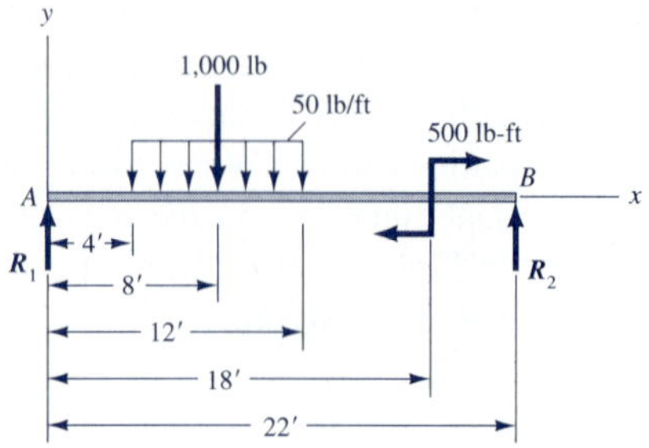

Figure 6.33. Simply supported beam.

$\underline{\sum M_B = 0:}$

$$-R_1(22) + (50)(8)(14) + (1{,}000)(14) - 500 = 0$$

Therefore,

$$R_1 = 868 \text{ lb}$$

$\underline{\sum M_A = 0:}$

$$R_2(22) - 500 - (50)(8)(8) - (1{,}000)(8) = 0$$

Therefore,

$$R_2 = 532 \text{ lb}$$

In Fig. 6.34(a) we have shown a free-body diagram exposing sections between the left support and the uniform load. Summing forces and taking moments about a point in the section, where we have drawn V and M as positive according to our convention, we get

$\underline{0 < x \leq 4:}$

$$868 + V = 0; \quad \text{therefore,} \quad V = -868 \text{ lb}$$
$$-868x + M = 0; \quad \text{therefore,} \quad M = 868x \text{ ft-lb}$$

The next interval is between the beginning of the uniform load and the point force. Thus, observing Fig. 6.34(b):

$\underline{4 \leq x < 8:}$

for V,

$$868 - 50(x - 4) + V = 0$$
$$\therefore V = 50x - 1{,}068 \text{ lb}$$

and for M,

$$-868x + \frac{50(x-4)^2}{2} + M = 0$$
$$\therefore M = -25x^2 + 1{,}068x - 400 \text{ ft-lb}$$

We now consider the interval between the point force and the end of the uniform load. Thus, observing Fig. 6.34(c):

$\underline{8 < x \leq 12:}$

for V,

$$868 - 50(x - 4) - 1{,}000 + V = 0$$
$$\therefore V = 50x - 68 \text{ lb}$$

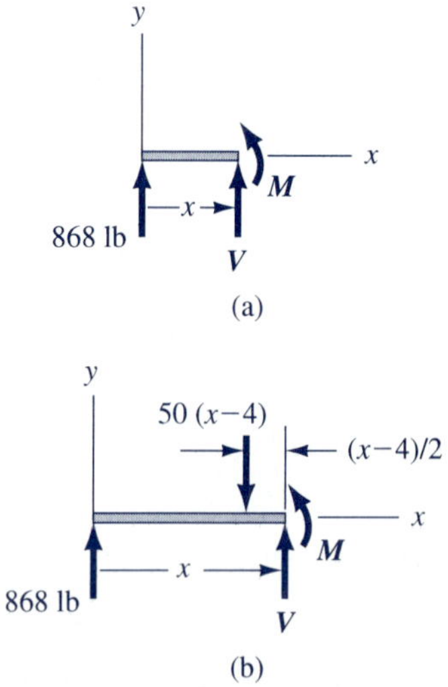

Figure 6.34. Free-body diagrams for various ranges.

Example 6.7 (Continued)

and for M,

$$-868x + \frac{50(x-4)^2}{2} + 1{,}000(x-8) + M = 0$$
$$\therefore\ M = -25x^2 + 68x + 7{,}600 \text{ ft-lb}$$

The next interval is between the end of uniform loading and the point couple. We can now replace the uniform loading by its resultant of 400 lb, as shown in Fig. 6.34(d). Thus,

$12 \le x < 18$:

for V,

$$868 - 400 - 1{,}000 + V = 0$$
$$\therefore\ V = 532 \text{ lb}$$

and for M,

$$-868x + 1{,}400(x-8) + M = 0$$
$$\therefore\ M = -532x + 11{,}200 \text{ ft-lb}$$

The last interval goes from the point couple to the right support. It is to be pointed out that the point couple *does not* contribute directly to the shear force and we could have used the above formulation for V for interval $18 < x < 22$. However, the couple *does* contribute directly to the bending moment, thus requiring the additional interval. Accordingly, using Fig. 6.34(e), we get

$18 < x < 22$:

$$V = 532 \text{ lb} \quad \text{(as in previous interval)}$$

Whereas for M we have

$$-868x + 1{,}400(x-8) - 500 + M = 0$$
$$\therefore\ M = -532x + 11{,}700 \text{ ft-lb}$$

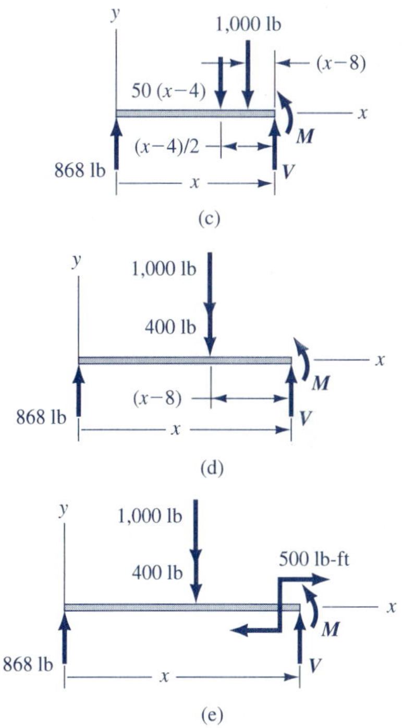

Figure 6.34. *(continued)* Free-body diagrams for various ranges.

We wish to point out now that we can determine shear-force and bending-moment equations in a less formal manner than what has been shown thus far. In this connection, it will be useful to note that from a consideration of equilibrium a downward force P, as shown in Fig. 6.35(a), induces on sections to the right a positive shear force (see insert) of value $+P$, whereas an upward force of P induces on sections to the right of it a negative shear force $-P$ [see Fig. 6.35(b)}. Also, an upward force P induces on sections at a distance ξ to the right of it a positive bending moment $P\xi$ [see Fig. 6.36(a)], whereas a downward force P induces on sections ξ to the right of it a negative bending moment $-P\xi$ [Fig. 6.36(b)]. Finally, as can be seen in Fig. 6.37(a), a clockwise couple moment C requires from equilibrium a positive bending moment $+C$ on the sections to the right of it (it does not require from equilibrium a shear force), whereas a counterclockwise couple moment C [Fig. 6.37(b)] requires a negative bending moment $-C$ on sections to the right of it. In the following example, we shall show how by this reasoning we may more directly formulate the shear-force and bending-moment equations.

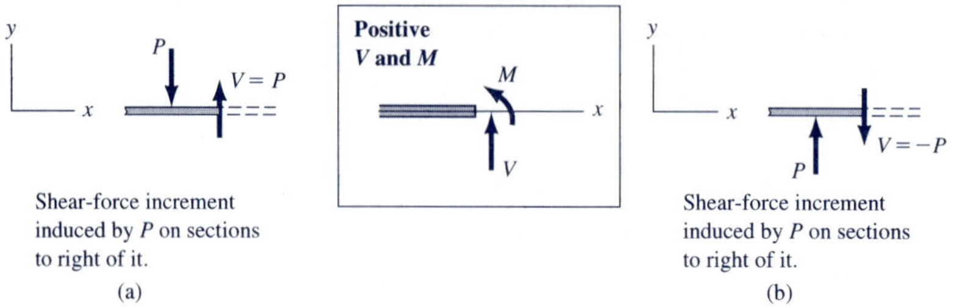

Figure 6.35. Shear induced by ***P***.

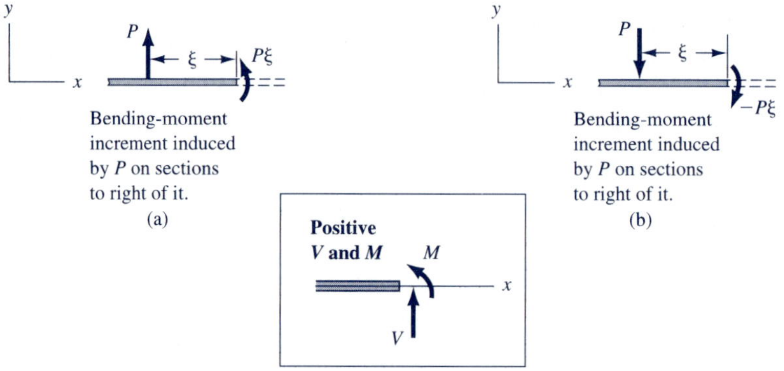

Figure 6.36. Bending moment induced by ***P***.

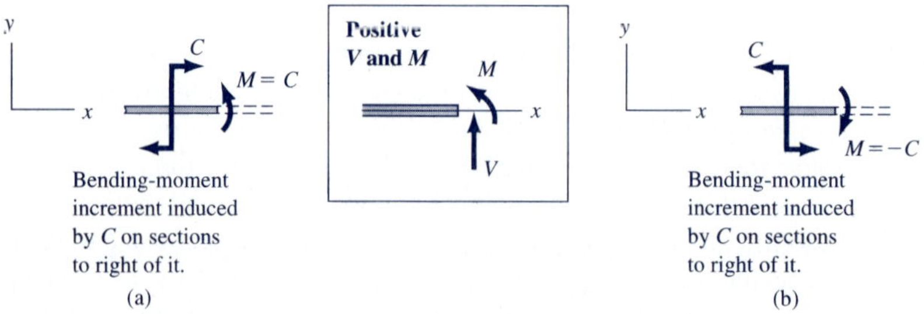

Figure 6.37. Bending moment induced by C.

Example 6.8

Evaluate the shear-force and bending-moment equations for the beam shown in Fig. 6.38.

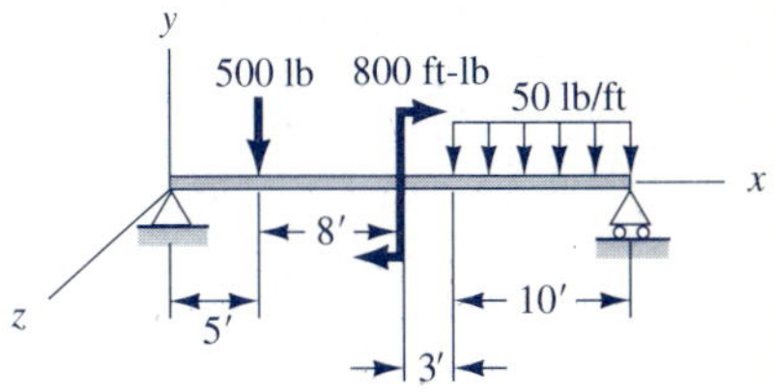

Figure 6.38. Simply supported beam.

A free-body diagram of the beam is shown in Fig. 6.39. We can immediately compute the supporting forces as follows, remembering to use the right-hand rule.

$\underline{\sum M_2 = 0:}$

$$-R_1(26) + (500)(21) - 800 + (500)(5) = 0$$

Therefore,

$$R_1 = 469 \text{ lb}$$

$\underline{\sum M_1 = 0:}$

$$R_2(26) - (500)(21) - 800 - (500)(5) = 0$$

Therefore,

$$R_2 = 531 \text{ lb}$$

We shall now directly give the shear force V and bending moment M while viewing Fig. 6.39. Thus,

$\underline{0 < x < 5:}$

$$V = -469 \text{ lb}$$

$$M = 469x \text{ ft-lb}$$

$\underline{5 < x < 13:}$

$$V = -469 + 500 = 31 \text{ lb}$$

$$M = 469x - 500(x - 5) = -31x + 2{,}500 \text{ ft-lb}$$

$\underline{13 < x \le 16:}$

$$V = 31 \text{ lb} \quad \text{(same as previous interval)}$$

$$M = 469x - 500(x - 5) + 800 = -31x + 3{,}300 \text{ ft-lb}$$

$\underline{16 \le x < 26:}$

$$V = -469 + 500 + 50(x - 16) = -769 + 50x \text{ lb}$$

$$M = 469x - 500(x - 5) + 800 - \frac{50(x - 16)^2}{2}$$

$$= -25x^2 + 769x - 3{,}100 \text{ ft-lb}$$

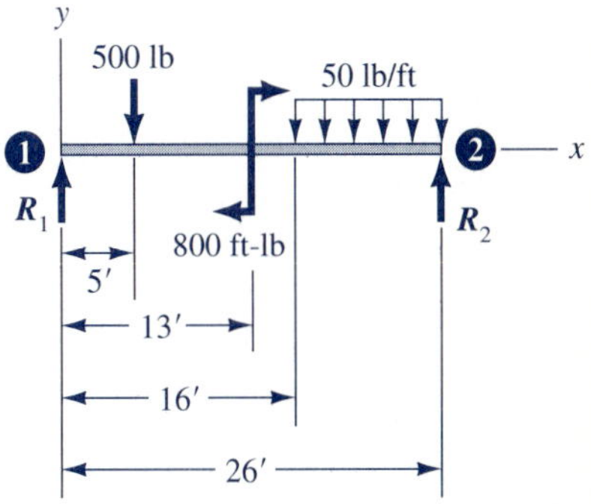

Figure 6.39. Free-body diagram of beam.

We shall present effective methods of sketching the shear-force and bending-moment diagrams in Section 6.9.

Before we proceed further, it must be carefully pointed out that the replacement of a distributed load by a single resultant force is only meaningful for the particular free body on which the force distribution acts. Thus, to compute the reactions for the entire beam taken as a free body (Fig. 6.40), we can

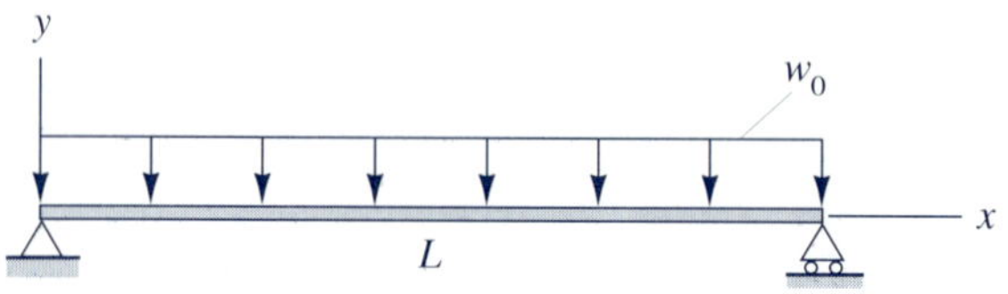

Figure 6.40. Uniform loading.

replace the weight distribution w_0 by the total weight at position $L/2$ (Fig. 6.41). For the bending moment at x, the resultant of the loading for the free

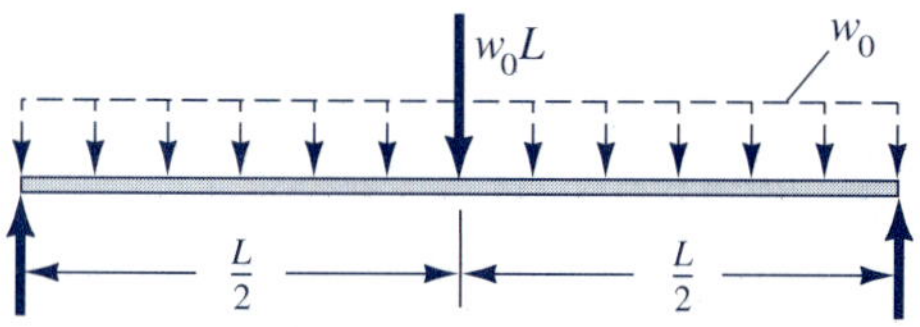

Figure 6.41. Resultant for w_0 for entire beam.

body shown in Fig. 6.42 becomes w_0x and is midway at position $x/2$. In other words, *in making shear-force and bending-moment equations and diagrams, we cannot replace loading distributions over the entire beam by a resultant and then proceed*; there is inherent in these equations an infinite number of free bodies, each shorter than the beam itself, which makes the above-mentioned replacements invalid for shear-force and bending-moment considerations.

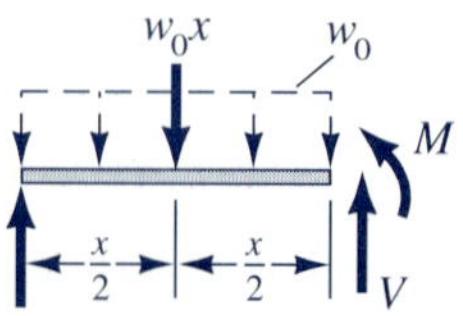

Figure 6.42. Resultant for w_0 for portion x of beam.

PROBLEMS

In Problems 6.37 through 6.48 make use of free-body diagrams.

6.37. Formulate the shear-force and bending-moment equations for the simply supported beam. Do not include the weight of the beam.

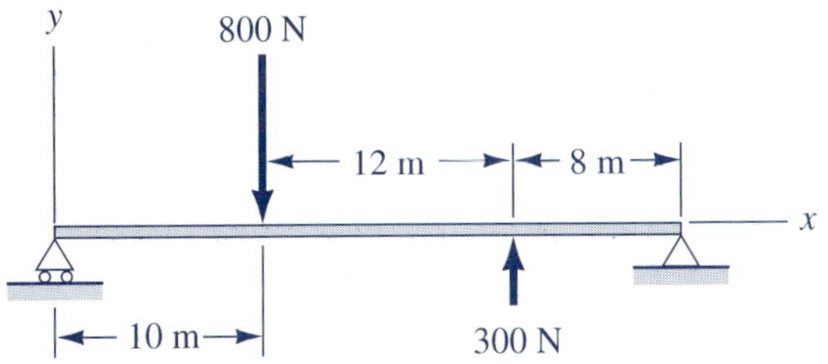

Figure P.6.37.

6.38. Formulate the shear-force and bending-moment equations for the cantilever beam. Do not include the weight of the beam.

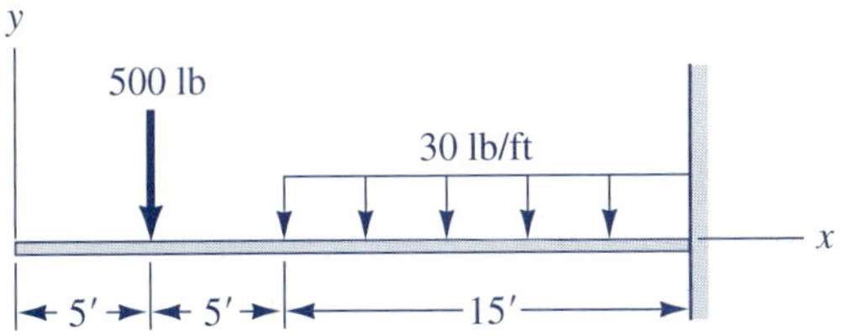

Figure P.6.38.

6.39. Determine the shear-force and bending-moment equations for the simply supported beam.

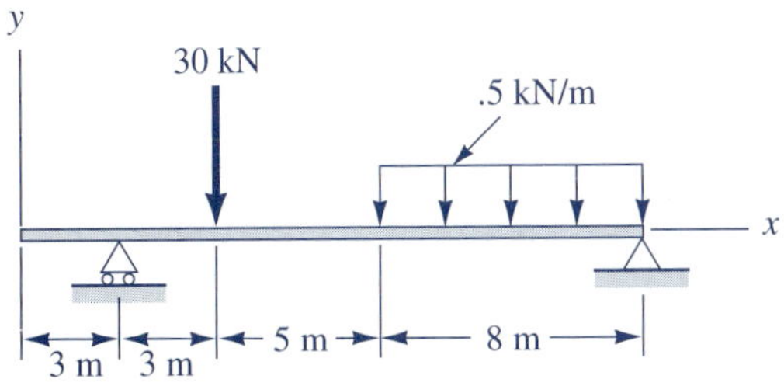

Figure P.6.39.

6.40. For the beam shown, what is the shear force and bending-moment at the following positions?

(a) 5 ft from the left end

(b) 12 ft from the left end

(c) 5 ft from the right end

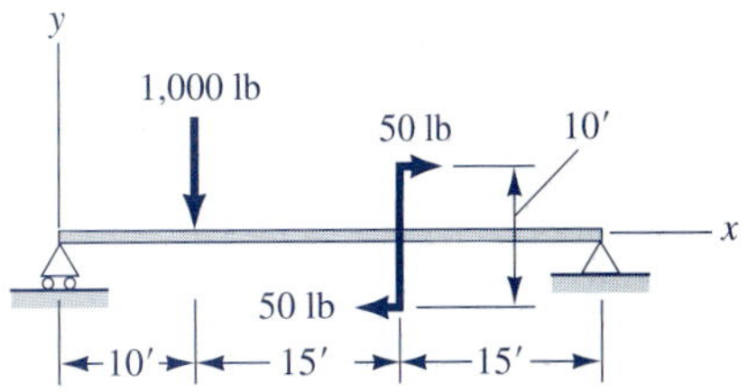

Figure P.6.40.

6.41. Formulate the shear-force and bending-moment equations for the simply supported beam.

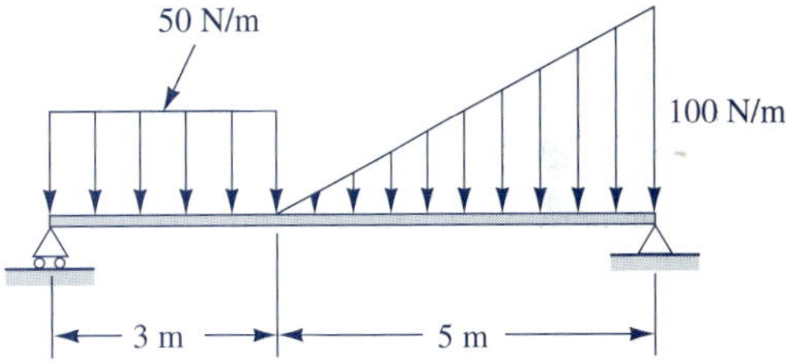

Figure P.6.41.

6.42. Compute shear force and bending moments for the bent beam as functions of s along the centerline of the beam.

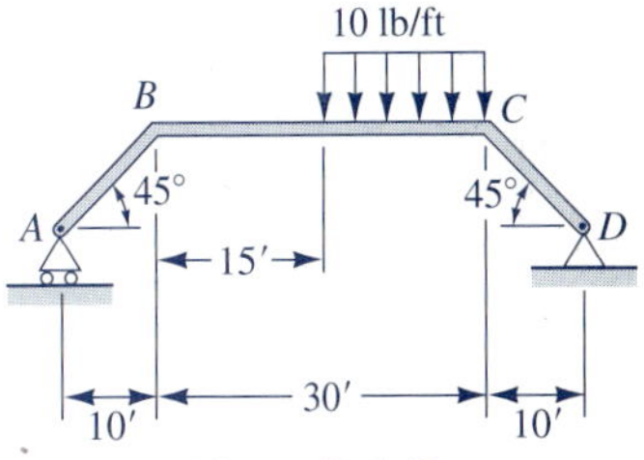

Figure P.6.42.

6.43. A simply supported beam is loaded in two planes. This means there will be shear-force components V_y and V_z and bending-moment components M_z and M_y. Compute these as functions of x. The beam is 40 ft in length.

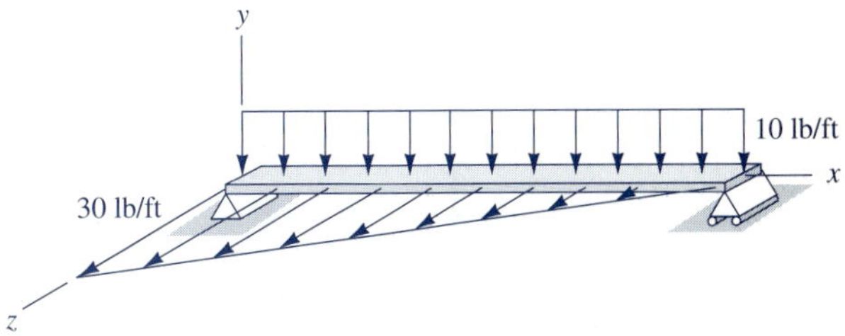

Figure P.6.43.

6.44. What are the shear force, bending moment, and axial force for the three-dimensional cantilever beam? Give your results separately for the three portions *AB*, *BC*, and *CD*. Neglect the weight of the member. Use *s* as the distance along the centerline from *D*.

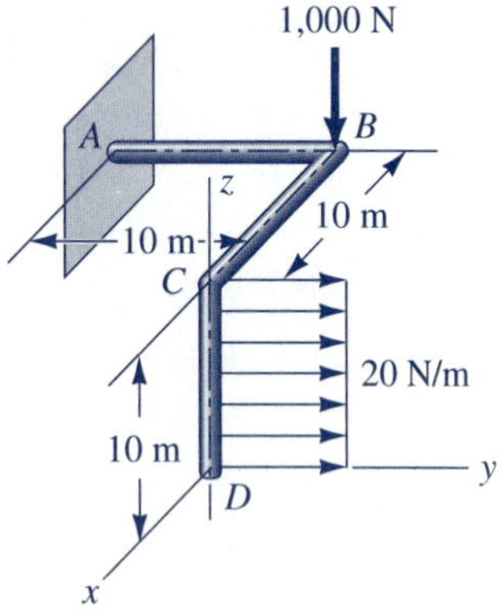

Figure P.6.44.

6.45. Oil flows from a tank through a pipe *AB*. The oil weighs 40 lb/ft^3 and, in flowing, develops a drag on the pipe of 1 lb/ft. The pipe has an inside diameter of 3 in. and a length of 20 ft. Flow conditions are assumed to be the same along the entire length of the pipe. What are the shear force, bending moment, and axial force along the pipe? The pipe weighs 10 lb/ft.

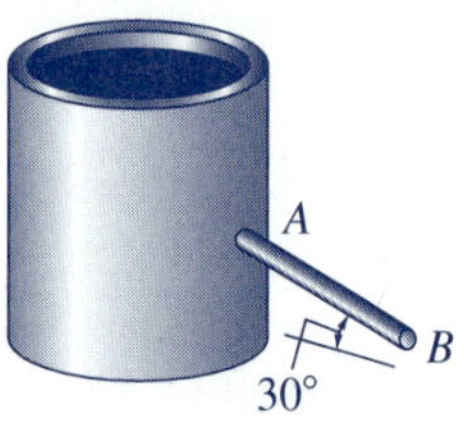

Figure P.6.45.

6.46. Determine the shear force, bending moment, and axial force as functions of θ for the circular beam.

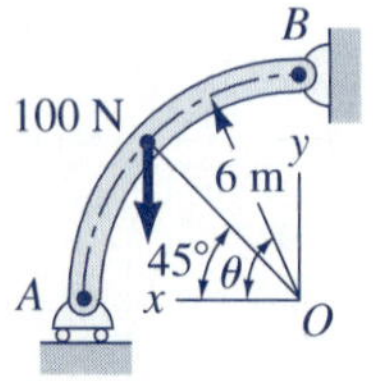

Figure P.6.46.

6.47. A hoist can move along a beam while supporting a 10,000-lb load. If the hoist starts at the left and moves from $\bar{x} = 3$ to $\bar{x} = 12$, determine the shear force and bending moment at *A* in terms of $\bar{x}$. At what position $\bar{x}$ do we get the maximum shear force at *A* and the maximum bending moment at *A*? What are their values?

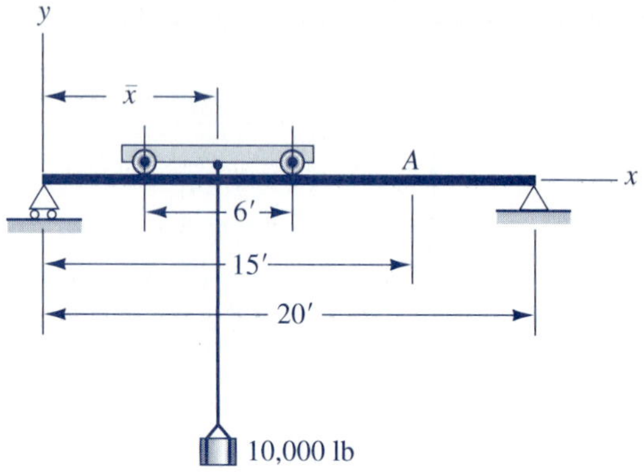

Figure P.6.47.

6.48. A pipe weighs 10 lb/ft and has an inside diameter of 2 in. If it is full of water and the pressure of the water is that of the atmosphere at the entrance *A*, compute the shear force, axial force, and bending moment of the pipe from *A* to *D*. Use coordinate *s* measured from *A* along the centerline of the pipe.

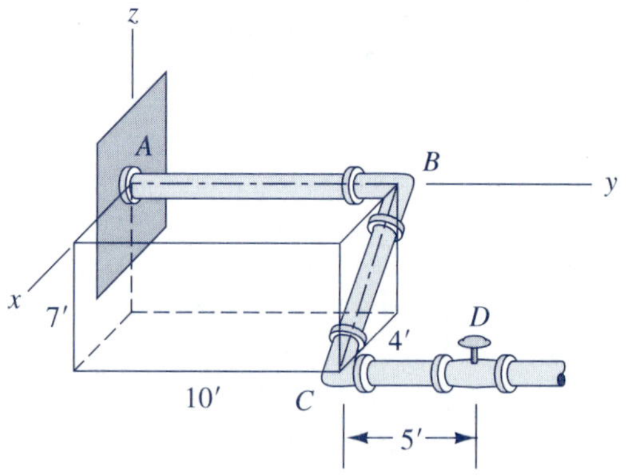

Figure P.6.48.

6.49. After finding the supporting forces, determine for Problem 6.37 the shear-force and bending-moment equations without the further aid of free-body diagrams.

6.50. Determine the shear-force and bending-moment equations for Problem 6.38 without the aid of free-body diagrams.

6.51. In Problem 6.39, after determining the supporting forces, determine the shear-force and bending-moment equations without the aid of free-body diagrams.

6.52. In Problem 6.40, after finding the supporting forces, write the shear force and bending moment as a function of x for the beam without the aid of free-body diagrams.

6.53. Give the shear-force and bending-moment equations for the cantilever beam. Except for determining the supporting forces, do not use free-body diagrams.

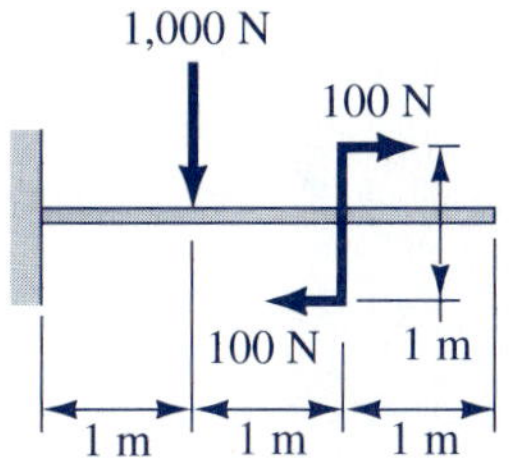

Figure P.6.53.

6.54. Formulate the shear-force and bending-moment equations for the simply supported beam. [*Suggestion:* For the domain $5 < x < 15$, it is simplest to replace the indicated downward triangular load, going from 400 N/m to zero, by a uniform 400-N/m uniform downward load from $x = 5$ to $x = 15$ plus a triangular upward load going from zero to 400 N/m in the interval.]

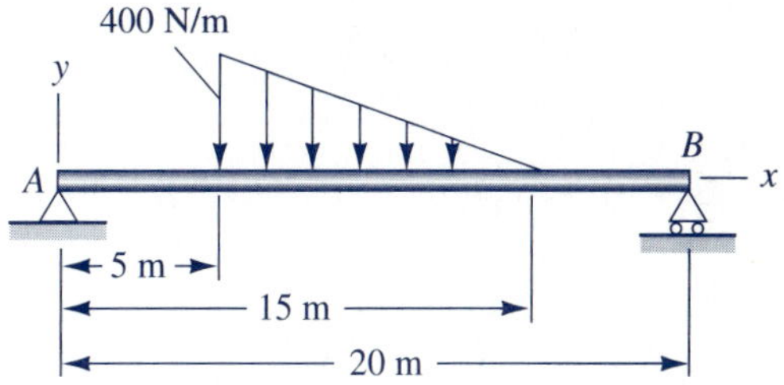

Figure P.6.54.

6.9 Differential Relations for Equilibrium

In Section 6.8, we considered free bodies of *finite size* comprising variable portions of a beam in order to ascertain the resultant force system at sections along the beam. We shall now proceed in a different manner by examining an *infinitesimal slice* of the beam. Equations of equilibrium for this slice will then yield *differential equations* rather than algebraic equations for the variables V and M.

Consider a slice Δx of the beam shown in Fig. 6.43. We adopt the convention that intensity of loading w in the positive coordinate direction is positive. We shall assume here that the weight of the beam has been included in the intensity of loading so that all forces acting on the element have been shown on the free-body diagram of the element in Fig. 6.44. Note we have employed positive shear-force and bending-moment convention as presented in Section 6.9. We now apply the equations of equilibrium. Thus, summing forces:

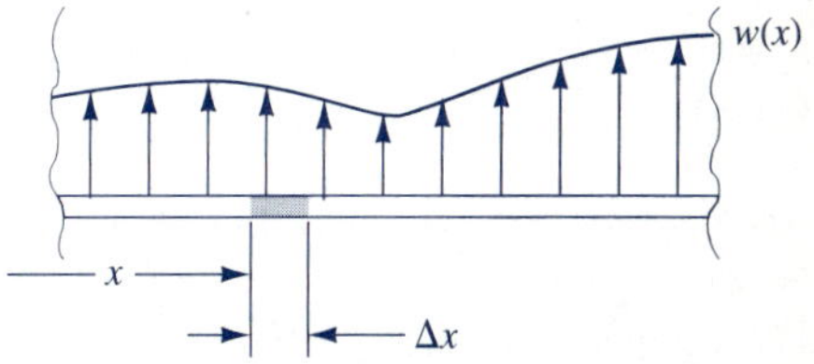

Figure 6.43. Element Δx of beam.

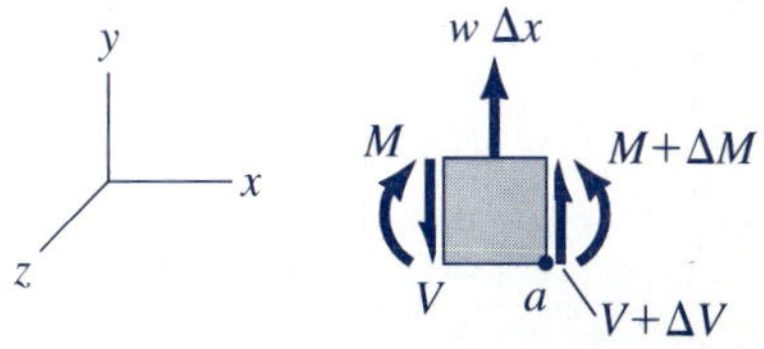

Figure 6.44. Free-body diagram of element.

$$\underline{\sum F_y = 0:}$$

$$-V + (V + \Delta V) + w\,\Delta x = 0$$

Taking moments about corner a of the element, we get

$$\underline{\sum M_a = 0:}$$

$$-M + V\Delta x - (w\Delta x)(\beta\Delta x) + (M + \Delta M) = 0$$

where β is some fraction which, when multiplied by Δx, gives the proper moment arm of the force $w\,\Delta x$ about corner a. These equations can be written in the following manner after we cancel terms and divide through by Δx:

$$\frac{\Delta V}{\Delta x} = -w$$

$$\frac{\Delta M}{\Delta x} = -V + w\beta\,\Delta x$$

In the limit as $\Delta x \to 0$, we get the following differential equations:

$$\frac{dV}{dx} = -w \qquad (6.3a)$$

$$\frac{dM}{dx} = -V \qquad (6.3b)$$

We may next integrate Eqs. 6.3(a) and 6.3(b) from position 1 along the beam to position 2. Thus, we have

$$(V)_2 - (V)_1 = -\int_1^2 w\,dx$$

Therefore,

$$(V)_2 = (V)_1 - \int_1^2 w\,dx \qquad (6.4)$$

and

$$(M)_2 - (M)_1 = -\int_1^2 V\,dx$$

Therefore,

$$(M)_2 = (M)_1 - \int_1^2 V\,dx \qquad (6.5)$$

Equation (6.4) means that the change in the shear force between two points on a beam equals minus the area under the loading curve between these points provided that there is no point force present in the interval.[13] Note that, if $w(x)$ is positive in an interval, the area under this curve is positive in this interval; if $w(x)$ is negative in an interval, the area under this curve is negative in this interval. Similarly, Eq. 6.5 indicates that the change in bending moment between two points on a beam equals minus the area of the shear-force diagram between these points provided that there are no point couple moments applied in the interval. If $V(x)$ is positive in an interval, the area under this curve is positive in this interval; if $V(x)$ is negative in an interval, the area under the curve is negative for this interval. In sketching the diagram, we shall make use of Eq. 6.4 and 6.5 as well as the differential equations 6.3.

[13]The differential equation 6.3(a) is only meaningful with a continuous loading present, while Eq. 6.3(b) is only valid in the absence of point couple moments.

Example 6.9

Sketch the shear-force and bending-moment distributions for the simply supported beam shown in Fig. 6.45 and label the key points.

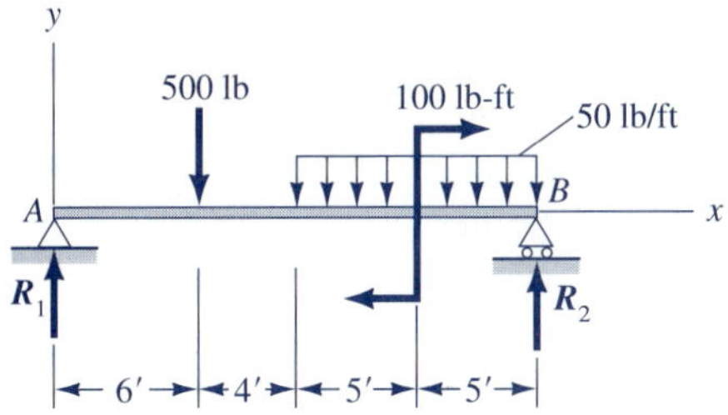

Figure 6.45. Simply supported beam.

The supporting forces R_1 and R_2 are found by rules of statics. Thus,

$\sum M_B = 0$:

$$-R_1(20) + (500)(14) + (50)(10)(10/2) - 100 = 0$$

Therefore,

$$R_1 = 470 \text{ lb}$$

$\sum M_A = 0$:

$$R_2(20) - (500)(6) - (50)(10)(15) - 100 = 0$$

Therefore,

$$R_2 = 530 \text{ lb}$$

In sketching the diagrams, we shall employ Eqs. 6.3, 6.4, and 6.5—i.e., the differential equations of equilibrium and their integrals. Accordingly, we first draw the loading diagram in Fig. 6.46(a), and we shall then sketch the shear-force and bending-moment diagrams directly below without the aid of the shear-force and bending-moment equations, evaluating key points as we go.

Note as we start on the shear diagram that the 470-lb supporting force induces a negative shear of −470 lb just to the right of the support. Now from *A* to *C*, the area under the loading curve is zero and so, in accordance with Eq. 6.4, there is no change in the value of shear between *A* and *C*. Hence, $V_C = -470$ lb, as shown in Fig 6.46(b). Also, since $w = 0$ between *A* and *C*, the slope of the shear curve should be zero, in accordance with Eq. 6.3(a). And so we have a horizontal line for *V* between *A* and *C*. Now as we cross *C*, the 500-lb downward force will induce a positive increment of shear of value 500 on sections to the right of it. Accordingly, *V jumps* from −470 lb to +30 lb as we cross *C*. Between *C* and *D* there is no loading *w*, so $V_D = V_C$ and we have a 30-lb shear force at point *D*. Again, since $w = 0$ in this interval, the slope of the shear curve is zero and we have a horizontal line for the shear curve between *C* and *D*. Since there is no concentrated

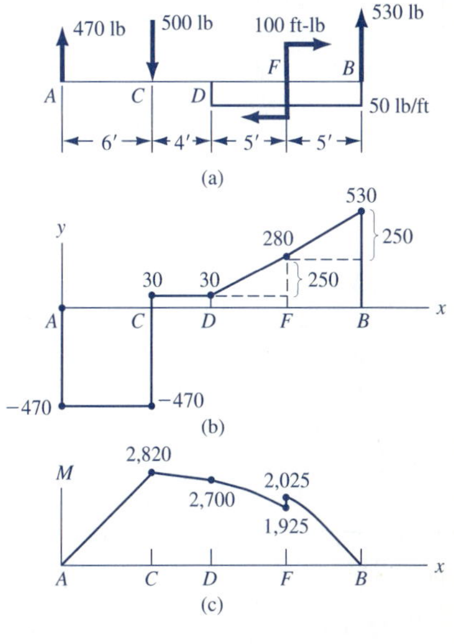

Figure 6.46. Shear-force and bending-moment diagrams.

Example 6.9 (Continued)

load at D, there is no sudden change in shear as we cross this point. Next, the change in shear between D and B is minus the area of the loading curve[14] in this interval in accordance with Eq. 6.4. But this area is (–50)(10) = –500. Hence, from Eq. 6.4 the value of V_B (just to the left of the support) is $V_D - (-500) = 530$ lb. Also, since w is negative and constant between D and B, the slope of the shear curve should be positive and constant, in accordance with Eq. 6.3(a). Hence, we can draw a straight line between $V_D = 30$ lb and $V_B = 530$ lb. As we now cross the right support force, we see that it induces a negative shear of 530 lb on sections to the right of the support, and so at B the shear curve comes back to zero.

We now proceed with the bending-moment curve. With no point couple moment present at A, the value of M_A must be zero. The change in moment between A and C is then minus the area underneath the shear curve in this interval. We can then say from Eq. 6.5 that $M_C = M_A - (-470)(6) = 0 + 2{,}820 = 2{,}820$ ft-lb, and we denote this in the moment diagram. Furthermore the value of V is a negative constant in the interval and, accordingly [see Eq. 6.3(b)], the slope of the moment curve is positive and constant. We can then draw a straight line between M_A and M_C. Between C and D the area for the shear diagram is 120 lb-ft, and so we can say that $M_D = M_C - (120) = 2{,}820 - 120 = 2{,}700$ ft-lb. Again, with V constant and positive in the interval, the slope of the moment curve must be negative and constant in the interval and has been so drawn. Between D and F the area under the shear curve is readily seen to be $(30)(5) + \frac{1}{2}(5)(250) = 775$ ft-lb. Hence, the bending moment goes from 2,700 ft-lb at D to 1,925 ft-lb at F. Now the shear curve is positive and *increasing* in value as we go from D to F. This means that the slope of the bending-moment curve is negative and becoming *steeper* as we go from D to F. As we go by F we encounter the 100-ft-lb point couple moment and we can say that this point couple moment induces a positive 100-ft-lb moment on sections to the right of point F. Accordingly, there is a sudden increase in bending moment of 100 ft-lb at F, as has been shown in the diagram. The area of the shear diagram between F and B is readily seen from Fig. 6.46(b) to be $(280)(5) + \frac{1}{2}(5)(250) = 2{,}025$ ft-lb. We see then that the bending moment goes to zero at B. Since the shear force is positive and *increasing* between F and B, we conclude that the slope of the bending-moment curve is negative and becoming *steeper* as we approach B. We have thus drawn the shear-force and bending-moment diagram and have labeled all key points.

Note that to be correct, both the shear-force and bending-moment curves must go to zero at the end of the beam to the right of the right support. This serves as a check on the correctness of the calculations.

[14]Note that the point couple moment has a zero net force and so need not be of concern in the interval from D to B as far as shear is concerned. However, it will be a point where sudden change occurs in the bending-moment diagram.

In Example 6.9, we can get equations and diagrams of shear force and bending moment independently of each other. With simple loadings such as point forces, point couples, and uniform distributions, this can readily be done. Indeed, this covers many problems that occur in practice. Usually, all that is needed are the labeled diagrams of the kind that we set forth in the previous problem. In problems with more complex loadings, we usually set forth the equations in the customary manner and then sketch the curves using the *equations* to give key values of V and M (the areas for the various curves are no longer the simple familiar ones, thus precluding advantageous use of Eqs. 6.4 and 6.5); the key points are then connected by curves sketched by making use of the slope relations as in Example 6.9.

It will be helpful to remember that if a curve has *increasing* magnitude (absolute value), the subsequent curve must have a *steepening* slope over the corresponding range. On the other hand, if a curve has *decreasing* magnitude (absolutely value), the subsequent curve must have a *flattening* slope over the corresponding range.

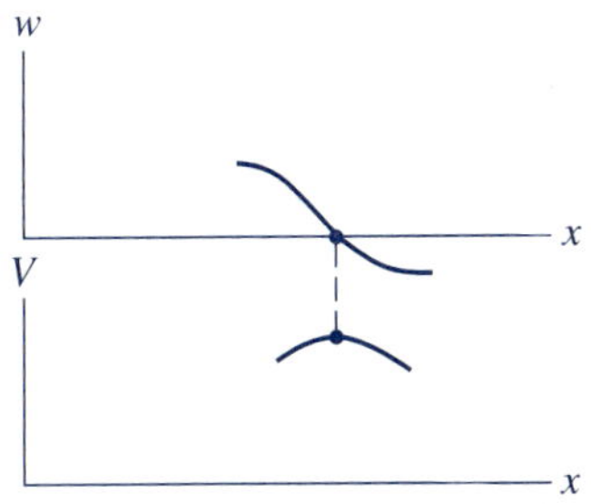

Figure 6.47. At $w = 0$, possible maximum for V.

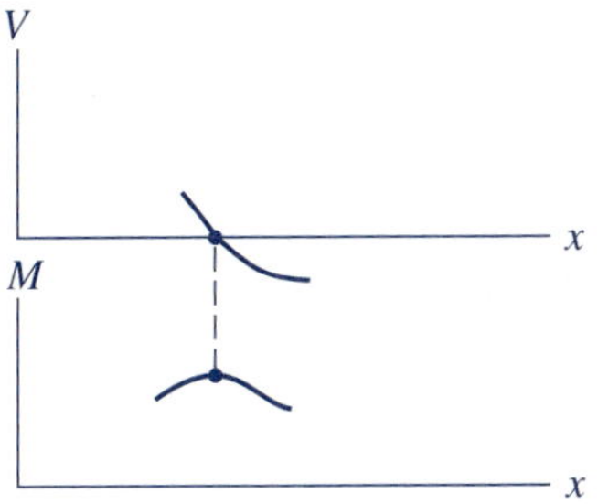

Figure 6.48. At $V = 0$, possible maximum for M.

You will note in the preceding examples that the key points of the shear-force and bending-moment diagrams were evaluated and marked. The maximum value of both the shear force and bending moment were easily depicted from these diagrams. We wish to note, in this regard, that at points on shear-force and bending-moment curves where there is zero value of slope, there may be possible maximum values of shear force and bending moment, respectively, for the beam. This is illustrated for shear force in Fig. 6.47 and for bending moment in Fig. 6.48. Note that where the loading curve w crosses the x axis, we accordingly have the position of a possible maximum shear force; similarly, where the shear curve V crosses the x axis, we accordingly have the position of a possible maximum bending moment. These respective positions and corresponding values of shear force and bending moment should be evaluated and marked in the diagram. Note however, that these are *local maximums* and that elsewhere there may be shears or bending moments exceeding these local maxima.

PROBLEMS

6.55. After finding the supporting forces of the cantilever beam, sketch the shear-force and bending-moment diagrams labeling key points.

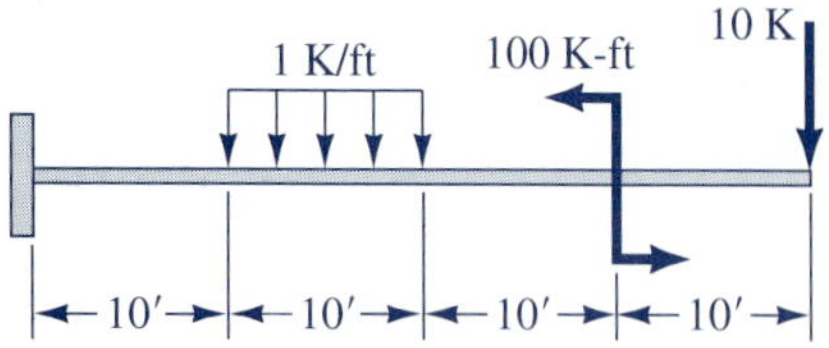

Figure P.6.55.

6.56. What is the maximum negative bending moment in the region between the supports for the simply supported beam?

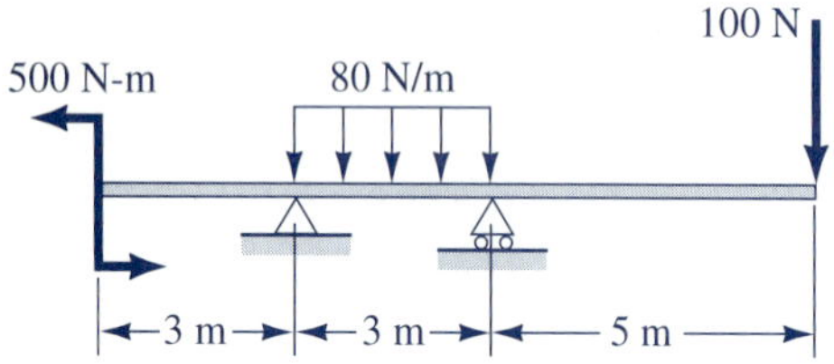

Figure P.6.56.

6.57. Find the supporting forces for the simply supported beam. Then sketch the shear-force and bending-moment diagrams, labeling key points.

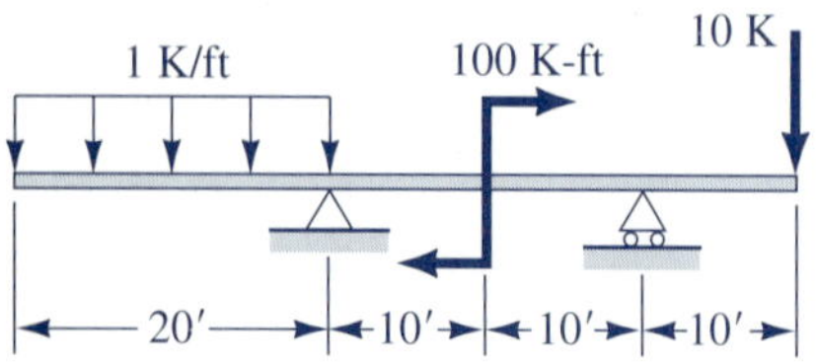

Figure P.6.57.

6.58. Sketch the shear-force and bending-moment diagrams and compute key points for the overhanging beam.

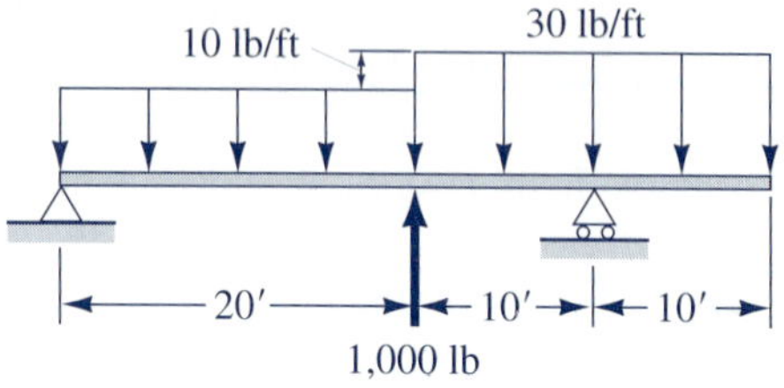

Figure P.6.58.

6.59. A simply supported beam AB is shown. A bar CD is welded to the beam. After determining the supporting forces, sketch the shear-force and bending-moment diagram and determine the maximum bending moment. [*Hint:* Find the position for $V = 0$ using similar triangles.]

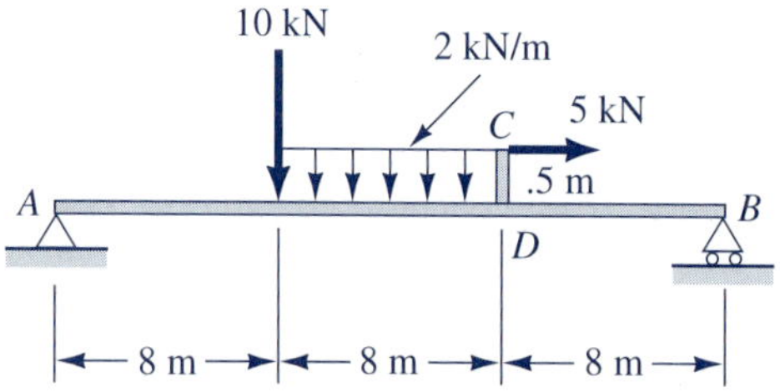

Figure P.6.59.

6.60. For the cantilever beam, sketch the shear-force and bending-moment diagrams evaluating key points only.

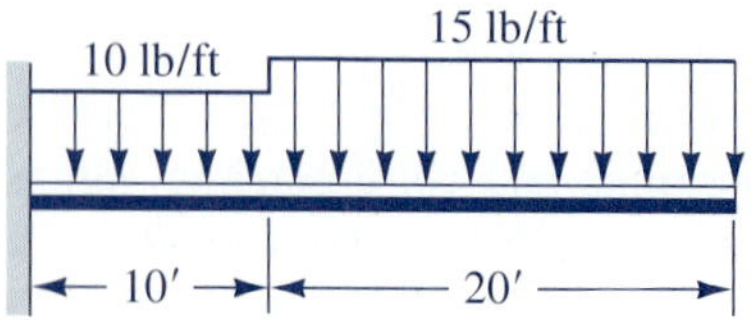

Figure P.6.60.

6.61. Sketch the shear-force and bending-moment diagrams for the sinusoidally loaded beam. What is the maximum bending moment?

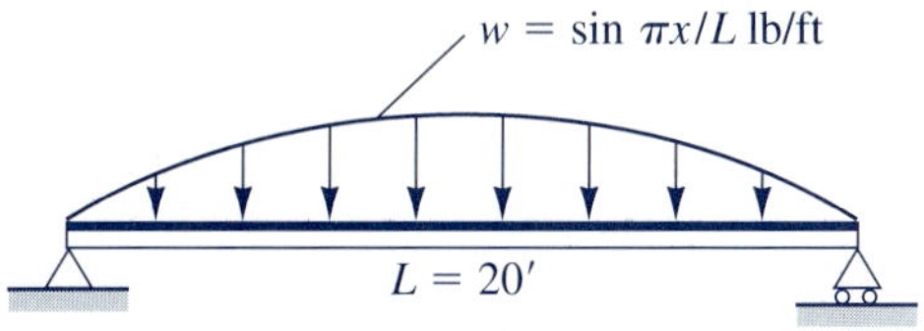

Figure P.6.61.

6.62. Formulate the shear-force and bending-moment equations for the beam. Sketch the shear and moment diagrams.

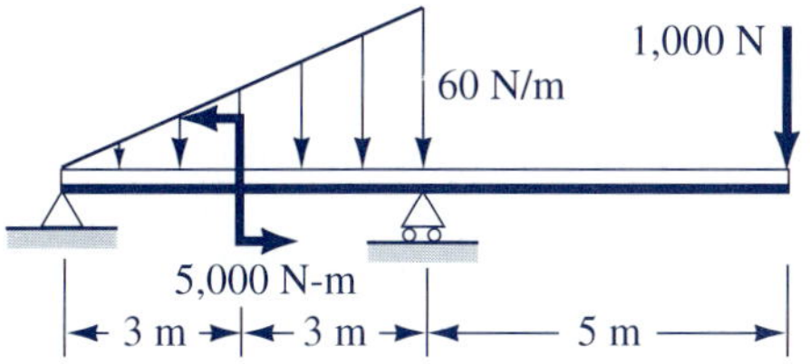

Figure P.6.62.

6.63. A simply supported I-beam is shown. A hole must be cut through the web to allow passage of a pipe that runs horizontally at right angles to the beam.

(a) Where, within the marked 24-ft section, would the hole least affect the moment-carrying capacity of the beam?

(b) In the same marked section, where should the hole go to least affect the shear-carrying capacity of the beam?

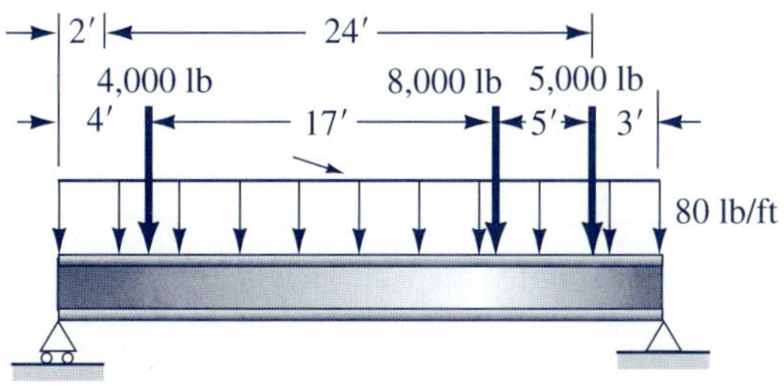

Figure P.6.63.

6.64. A cantilever beam supports a parabolic and a triangular load. What are the shear-force and bending-moment equations? Sketch the shear-force and bending-moment diagrams. See the suggestion in Problem 6.54 regarding the triangular load.

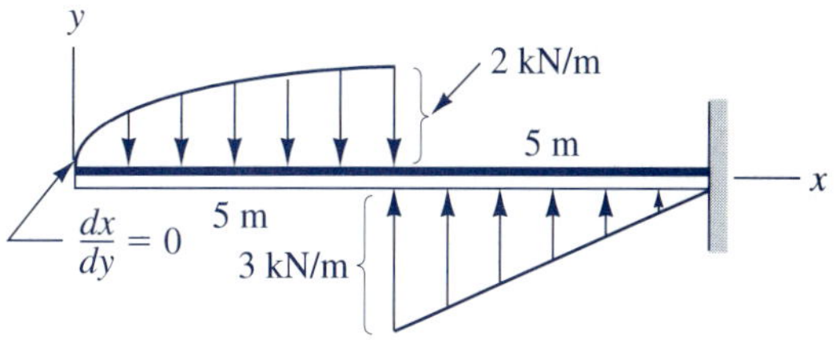

Figure P.6.64.

6.65. Determine the shear-force and bending-moment equations for the beam. Then sketch the diagrams using the aforementioned equations if necessary to ascertain key points in the diagrams, such as the position between the supports where $V = 0$. What is the bending moment there?

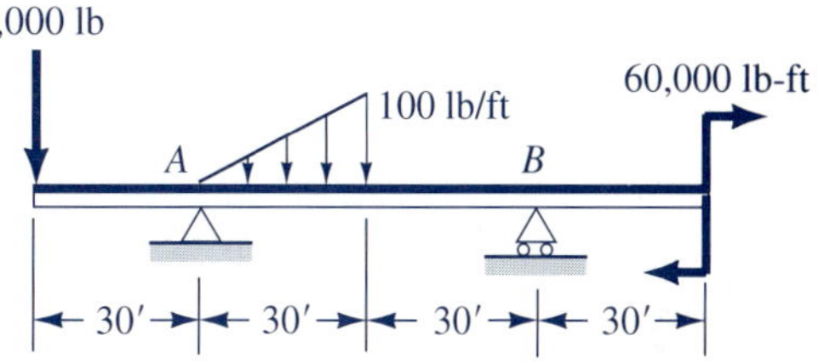

Figure P.6.65.

Part C: Chains and Cables

6.10 Introduction

We often encounter relatively flexible cables or chains that are used to support loads. In suspension bridges, for example, we find a coplanar arrangement in which a cable supports a large load. The weight of the cable itself in such cases may often be considered negligible. In transmission lines, on the other hand, the principal force is the weight of the cable itself. In Part C, we shall evaluate the shape of and the tension in the cables for both these cases.

To facilitate computations, the model of the structural system will be assumed to be perfectly flexible and inextensible. The flexibility assumption means that at the center of any cross section of the cable only a tensile force is transmitted and there can be no bending moment there. The force transmitted through the cable must, under these conditions, be tangent to the cable at all positions along the cable. The inextensibility assumption means that the length of the cable is constant.

6.11 Coplanar Cables; Loading is a Function of x

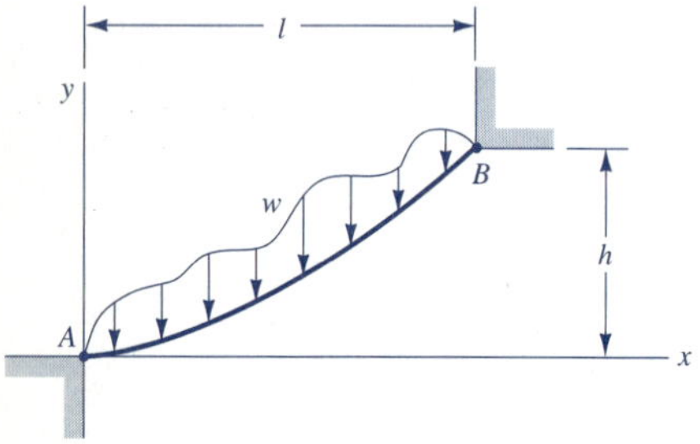

Figure 6.49. Coplanar cable; $w = w(x)$.

We shall now consider the case of a cable suspended between two rigid supports A and B under the action of a loading function $w(x)$ given per unit length as measured in the *horizontal* direction. This loading will be considered to be coplanar with the cable and directed vertically, as shown in Fig. 6.49. Consider an element of the cable of length Δs as a free body (Fig. 6.50).

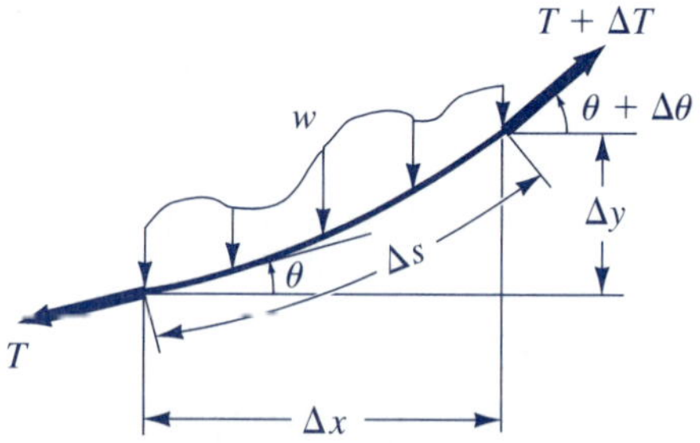

Figure 6.50. Element of cable.

Summing forces in the x and y directions, respectively, we get

$$-T\cos\theta + (T + \Delta T)\cos(\theta + \Delta\theta) = 0 \tag{6.6a}$$

$$-T\sin\theta + (T + \Delta T)\sin(\theta + \Delta\theta) - w_{av}\,\Delta x = 0 \tag{6.6b}$$

where w_{av} is the average loading over the interval Δx. Dividing by Δx and taking the limit as $\Delta x \to 0$, we have

$$\lim_{\Delta x \to 0}\left[\frac{(T + \Delta T)\cos(\theta + \Delta\theta) - T\cos\theta}{\Delta x}\right] = 0$$

$$\lim_{\Delta x \to 0}\left[\frac{(T + \Delta T)\sin(\theta + \Delta\theta) - T\sin\theta}{\Delta x}\right] = w$$

The term w is now the loading at position x. The left sides of the equations above are derivatives in accordance with elementary calculus, and so we can say for these equations:

$$\frac{d(T\cos\theta)}{dx} = 0 \qquad (6.7a)$$

$$\frac{d(T\sin\theta)}{dx} = w \qquad (6.7b)$$

From Eq. 6.7(a), we conclude that

$$T\cos\theta = \text{constant} = H \qquad (6.8)$$

where clearly the constant H represents the *horizontal* component of the tensile force anywhere along the cable. Integrating Eq. 6.7(b), we get

$$T\sin\theta = \int w(x)\,dx + C_1' \qquad (6.9)$$

where C_1' is a constant of integration. Solving for T in Eq. 6.8 and substituting into Eq. 6.9, we get

$$\frac{\sin\theta}{\cos\theta} = \frac{1}{H}\int w(x)\,dx + C_1$$

Noting that $\sin\theta/\cos\theta = \tan\theta = dy/dx$, we have, on carrying out a second integration:

$$y = \frac{1}{H}\int\left[\int w(x)\,dx\right]dx + C_1x + C_2 \qquad (6.10)$$

Equation 6.10 is the deflection curve for the cable in terms of H, $w(x)$, and the constants of integration. The constants of integration must be determined by the boundary conditions at the supports A and B.

Example 6.10

A cable is shown in Fig. 6.51 terminating at points at the same elevation. The loading distribution is uniform, given by constant w. Other known data are the span, l, and the sag, h. The maximum force in the cable, the shape of the cable, and the length of the cable are desired. Neglect the weight of the cable itself.

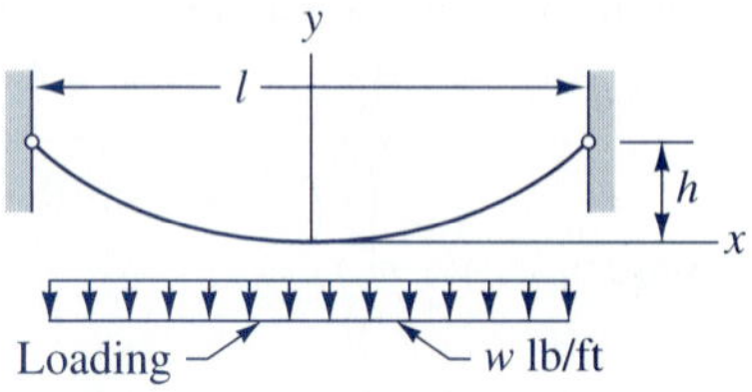

Figure 6.51. Cable with sag h.

We have placed the reference at the center of the cable for simplicity as shown in the diagram. Noting that $w(x) = w =$ constant for this problem, we can proceed directly with the integrations in Eq. 6.10. Thus, we have

$$y = \frac{1}{H}\int\left[\int w\,dx\right]dx + C_1x + C_2 = \frac{1}{H}\int wx\,dx + C_1x + C_2$$

Therefore,

$$y = \frac{1}{H}\frac{wx^2}{2} + C_1x + C_2 \qquad \text{(a)}$$

The deflection curve is thus a *parabola*. We now require that $y = dy/dx = 0$, when $x = 0$. Thus, the constants $C_1 = C_2 = 0$. The deflection curve then is simply

$$y = \frac{w}{2H}x^2 \qquad \text{(b)}$$

To get the constant H, we set $y = h$ for $x = l/2$. Thus,

$$h = \frac{w}{2H}\frac{l^2}{4}$$

Therefore,

$$H = \frac{wl^2}{8h} \qquad \text{(c)}$$

The deflection curve is now fully established in terms of the data of the problem in the form

$$y = \frac{w}{2(wl^2/8h)}x^2 = 4\frac{hx^2}{l^2} \qquad \text{(d)}$$

$$\therefore \quad \boxed{y = 4\frac{hx^2}{l^2}}$$

We next compute the *maximum tension* in the cable. Equation 6.8 can be used for this purpose. Solving for T, we get

$$T = \frac{H}{\cos\theta} \qquad \text{(e)}$$

from which it is apparent that the maximum value of T occurs where θ is greatest. Examining the slope of the deflection curve using Eq. (b),

$$\frac{dy}{dx} = \frac{w}{H}x \qquad \text{(f)}$$

Example 6.10 (Continued)

it is apparent that the largest θ occurs at $x = l/2$ (i.e., at the supports). Hence, from above we have, for θ_{max}:

$$\theta_{max} = \tan^{-1}\left(\frac{dy}{dx}\right)_{x=l/2} = \tan^{-1}\left(\frac{w}{H}\frac{l}{2}\right) \qquad \text{(g)}$$

Consequently, we get for T_{max}:

$$T_{max} = \frac{H}{\cos\left[\tan^{-1}(wl/2H)\right]} \qquad \text{(h)}$$

From trigonometric consideration of the denominator,

$$T_{max} = \frac{H(4H^2 + w^2l^2)^{1/2}}{2H} = H\left[1 + \left(\frac{wl}{2H}\right)^2\right]^{1/2} \qquad \text{(i)}$$

Substituting for H using Eq. (c), we then get, on rearranging the terms,

$$T_{max} = \frac{wl}{2}\sqrt{1 + \left(\frac{l}{4h}\right)^2} \qquad \text{(j)}$$

Finally, to determine the *length of the cable* for the given conditions, we must perform the following integration:

$$L = 2\int_0^{s_{max}} ds = 2\int_0^{s_{max}} \sqrt{dx^2 + dy^2} = 2\int_0^{l/2} \sqrt{1 + \left(\frac{dy}{dx}\right)^2}\, dx \qquad \text{(k)}$$

Now the slope, dy/dx, equals wx/H [see Eq. (f)], which on substituting for H [see Eq. (c)] becomes $8hx/l.^2$ Therefore,

$$L = 2\int_0^{l/2} \sqrt{1 + \left(\frac{8hx}{l^2}\right)^2}\, dx$$

This may be integrated using a formula to be found in Appendix I to give

$$L = \left[x\sqrt{1 + \left(\frac{8hx}{l^2}\right)^2} + \frac{l^2}{8h}\sinh^{-1}\frac{8hx}{l^2}\right]_0^{l/2}$$

Substituting limits, we have

$$L = \left[\frac{l}{2}\sqrt{1 + \left(\frac{4h}{l}\right)^2} + \frac{l^2}{8h}\sinh^{-1}\frac{4h}{l}\right]$$

Rearranging so that the result is given as a function of the sag ratio h/l and the span l, we get finally

Example 6.10 (Continued)

$$L = \frac{l}{2}\left[\sqrt{1 + 16\left(\frac{h}{l}\right)^2} + \frac{1}{4h/l}\sinh^{-1}\frac{4h}{l}\right] \tag{l}$$

Another possible approach to determining the length of the cable is to expand the integrand in Eq. (k) as a power series using the *binomial theorem.* Thus we have

$$L = 2\int_0^{l/2}\left[1 + \frac{1}{2}\left(\frac{dy}{dx}\right)^2 - \frac{1}{8}\left(\frac{dy}{dx}\right)^4 + \dots\right]dx \tag{m}$$

provided that $|dy/dx| < 1$ at all positions along the interval.[15] Now, employ Eq. (f) and Eq. (c) to replace dy/dx in Eq. (m) to get

$$L = 2\int_0^{l/2}\left(1 + \frac{1}{2}\left(\frac{8h}{l^2}\right)^2 x^2 - \frac{1}{8}\left(\frac{8h}{l^2}\right)^4 x^4 + \dots\right)dx \tag{n}$$

We can integrate a power series term by term and so we have, for L:

$$L = l\left[1 + \frac{8}{3}\left(\frac{h}{l}\right)^2 - \frac{32}{5}\left(\frac{h}{l}\right)^4 + \dots\right] \tag{o}$$

For cables having small slopes (i.e., small sag ratio h/l), the series converges rapidly and only the first few terms need generally be employed.

[15]Otherwise, the series diverges. Hence, this approach is limited to cases where the slope of the cable is less than 45°.

In Example 6.10, the supports are at the same level and consequently the position of zero slope is known (i.e., it is at the midpoint). We found it simplest to set our reference xy at this point. In problems at the end of this section, the supports may not be at the same level. For such cases, the reference is best taken at one of the supports. Also, the slope of the cable is often known at some point, and the problem may then be solved in much the same way as Example 6.10.

6.12 Coplanar Cables; Loading is the Weight of the Cable Itself

In the previous development, the loading was given as a function of x. Let us now consider the case of a cable loaded only by its own weight. The loading function is now most easily expressed as a function of s, the position along the cable. Equations 6.6 apply to this case provided that we replace Δx by Δs.

Dividing through by Δs and taking the limit as $\Delta s \rightarrow$ zero, we get equations analogous to Eqs. 6.7.

$$\frac{d(T\cos\theta)}{ds} = 0$$

$$\frac{d(T\sin\theta)}{ds} = w(s)$$

Integrating, we have

$$T\cos\theta = H \tag{6.11a}$$

$$T\sin\theta = \int w(s)\,ds + C_1' \tag{6.11b}$$

Eliminating T from Eqs. 6.11, we get, as in the previous development:

$$\frac{dy}{dx} = \frac{1}{H}\int w(s)ds + C_1$$

The right side of the equation is a function of s. Thus, we cannot directly integrate as a next step. Accordingly, note that

$$dy = (ds^2 - dx^2)^{1/2}$$

Hence, from this equation,

$$\frac{dy}{dx} = \left[\left(\frac{ds}{dx}\right)^2 - 1\right]^{1/2} \tag{6.13}$$

Substituting for dy/dx in Eq. 6.12 using the preceding result, we get

$$\left[\left(\frac{ds}{dx}\right)^2 - 1\right]^{1/2} = \frac{1}{H}\int w(s)\,ds + C_1$$

Solving for ds/dx, we have

$$\frac{ds}{dx} = \left\{1 + \left[\frac{1}{H}\int w(s)\,ds + C_1\right]^2\right\}^{1/2}$$

Separating variables and integrating, we get

$$x = \int \frac{ds}{\left\{1 + \left[\frac{1}{H}\int w(s)\,ds + C_1\right]^2\right\}^{1/2}} + C_2 \tag{6.14}$$

As a first step, if possible determine the constant C_1 by applying a slope-boundary condition to Eq. 6.12. With this C_1 in Eq. 6.14, solve for s as a function of x. Next, substitute for s in Eq. 6.12 using this relation. Finally, integrate Eq. 6.12 with respect to x to get y as a function of x. Boundary conditions must then be used to determine H as well as the remaining constant of the integration. The following examples will illustrate how these steps are carried out.

Example 6.11

Consider a uniform cable having a span l and a sag h as shown in Fig. 6.52. The weight per unit length w of the cable is a constant. Determine the shape of the cable when it is loaded only by its own weight.

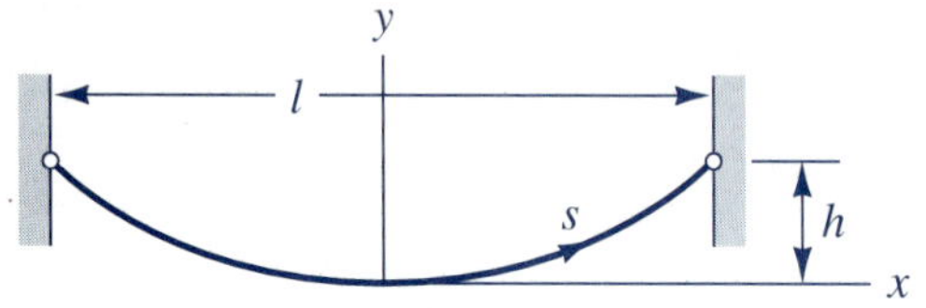

Figure 6.52. Uniform cable loaded by its own weight.

For simplicity, we have placed a reference at the center of the span where the slope of the cable is zero. Accordingly, consider Eq. 6.12 for this case:

$$\frac{dy}{dx} = \frac{1}{H}\int w(s)\,ds + C_1 = \frac{w}{H}s + C_1 \tag{a}$$

When $s = 0$ we require that $dy/dx = 0$, whereupon C_1 is zero. Now consider Eq. 6.14:

$$\begin{aligned} x &= \int \frac{ds}{\left\{1 + \left[(1/H)\int w\,ds + C_1\right]^2\right\}^{1/2}} + C_2 \\ &= \int \frac{ds}{\left\{1 + \left[(w/H)s\right]^2\right\}^{1/2}} + C_2 \end{aligned} \tag{b}$$

Integrating the right side of the equation using integration formula 10 from Appendix I, we get

$$x = \frac{H}{w}\sinh^{-1}\frac{sw}{H} + C_2 \tag{c}$$

Example 6.11 (Continued)

The constant C_2 must also be zero, since $x = 0$ at $s = 0$. Solving for s from Eq. (c), we get

$$s = \frac{H}{w}\sinh\frac{xw}{H} \tag{d}$$

Substituting for s in Eq. (a) using the preceding result, we have

$$\frac{dy}{dx} = \sinh\frac{w}{H}x \tag{e}$$

Integrating, we get

$$y = \frac{H}{w}\cosh\frac{w}{H}x + C_3$$

Since $y = 0$ at $x = 0$, the constant C_3 becomes $-H/w$. We then have the deflection curve:

$$y = \frac{H}{w}\left(\cosh\frac{w}{H}x - 1\right) \tag{f}$$

This curve is called a *catenary curve.*[16]

To determine H, we set $y = h$ when $x = l/2$. Thus,

$$h = \frac{H}{w}\left(\cosh\frac{wl}{2H} - 1\right) \tag{g}$$

This equation can be solved by trial and error by the student or by a computer. We may then proceed to determine the maximum force in the cable as well as the length of the cable in the manner followed in Example 6.10.

[16]The Latin for chain is *catena*.

Example 6.12

A water skier is shown in Fig. 6.53 dangling from a kite that is towed by a powerboat at a speed of 30 mph. The boat develops a thrust of 200 lb. The drag on the boat from the water is estimated as 100 lb. At the support A, the rope has a tangent of 30°. If the man weighs 150 lb, find the height and the lift of the kite as well as the maximum tension in the rope. The kite weighs 25 lb. The uniform rope is 50 ft long and weighs .5 lb/ft. Neglect aerodynamic effects on the rope.

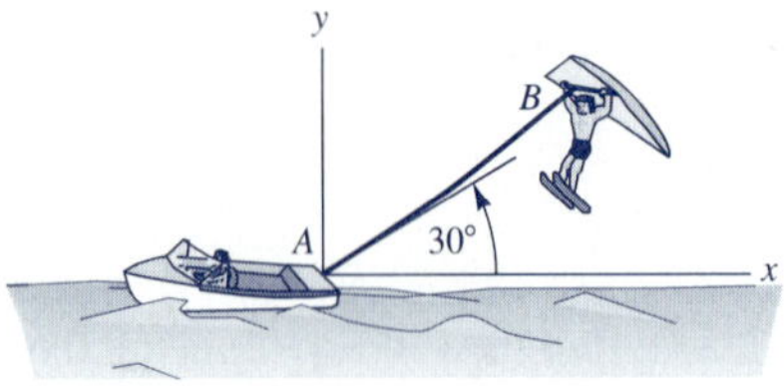

Figure 6.53. Analyze tow rope *AB*.

We start with Eq. 6.12, which becomes for this case:

$$\frac{dy}{dx} = \frac{w}{H}s + C_1 \tag{a}$$

Using a reference at A as shown in the diagram, we know that dy/dx = tan 30° = .577 when $s = 0$. Thus, we get for C_1,

$$C_1 = .577$$

Equation 6.14 is considered next. We have

$$x = \int \frac{ds}{\left\{1 + \left[(w/H)s + .577\right]^2\right\}^{1/2}} + C_2$$

Integrating by making a change in variable to replace $[(w/H)s + .577]$ and using the integration formula 10 in Appendix I, we get

$$x = \frac{H}{w}\sinh^{-1}\left(\frac{w}{H}s + .577\right) + C_2 \tag{b}$$

Solving for s, we have

$$s = \frac{H}{w}\left\{\sinh\left[(x - C_2)\frac{w}{H}\right] - .577\right\} \tag{c}$$

Substituting for s in Eq. (a) using Eq. (c), we get

$$\frac{dy}{dx} = \sinh\left[(x - C_2)\frac{w}{H}\right] \tag{d}$$

Integrating again, we have

$$y = \frac{H}{w}\cosh\left[(x - C_2)\frac{w}{H}\right] + C_3 \tag{e}$$

We must now evaluate the unknown constants C_2, C_3, and H using the boundary conditions and data of the problem. First, since H is the horizontal component of force transmitted by the rope, we know that H is the thrust of the boat minus the drag of the water. Thus,

$$H = 100 \text{ lb}$$

Also, $x = 0$ when $s = 0$, so that from Eq. (c), we get C_2 as follows:

$$\sinh\left(-\frac{.5}{100}C_2\right) = .577$$

Example 6.12 (Continued)

Therefore,

$$-\frac{.5}{100}C_2 = \sinh^{-1} .577 = .549$$

Hence,

$$C_2 = -109.8$$

Finally, note that $x = 0$ when $y = 0$. From Eq. (e), we can then get constant C_3 in the following manner:

$$C_3 = -\frac{100}{.5}\cosh\left[\frac{-.5}{100}(-109.8)\right]$$
$$= -200\cosh .548 = -231$$

We may now evaluate the position x', y' of point B of the kite. To get x', we insert for s in Eq. (b) the value of 50 ft. Thus,

$$x' = \frac{100}{.5}\sinh^{-1}\left[\frac{.5}{100}50 + .577\right] - 109.8 = 40.9 \text{ ft}$$

Now from Eq. (e) we can get y' and consequently the desired height.

$$y' = \frac{100}{.5}\cosh\left[(40.9 + 109.8)\frac{.5}{100}\right] - 231$$

$$y' = 28.6 \text{ ft} \qquad \text{(f)}$$

The maximum tension in the rope occurs at point B, where θ is greatest. To get θ_{max}, we go back to Eq. (a). Thus,

$$\left(\frac{dy}{dx}\right)_{max} = \tan\theta_{max} = \frac{.5}{100}(50) + .577 = .827$$

Therefore,

$$\theta_{max} = 39.6° \qquad \text{(g)}$$

Hence, from Eq. 6.11(a) we have for T_{max}:

$$T_{max} = \frac{100}{\cos 39.6°} = 130 \text{ lb} \qquad \text{(h)}$$

To get the lifting force of the kite, we draw a free-body diagram of point B of the kite as shown in Fig. 6.54. Note that F_y and F_x are, respectively, the aerodynamic lift and drag forces on the kite. The lift force F_y of the kite then becomes

$$F_y = 175 + T_{max}\sin 39.6° = 258 \text{ lb} \qquad \text{(i)}$$

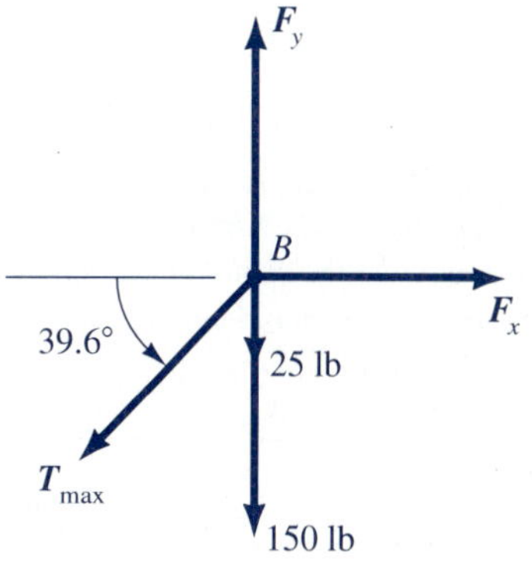

Figure 6.54. Free-body diagram of kite support.

PROBLEMS

6.66. Find the length of a cable stretched between two supports at the same elevation with span l = 200 ft and sag h = 50 ft, if it is subjected to a vertical load of 4 lb/ft uniformly distributed in the horizontal direction. (Assume that the weight of the cable is either negligible or included in the 4-lb/ft distribution.) Find the maximum tension.

6.67. A cable supports an 8000-kg uniform bar. What is the equation describing the shape of the cable and what is the maximum tension in the cable?

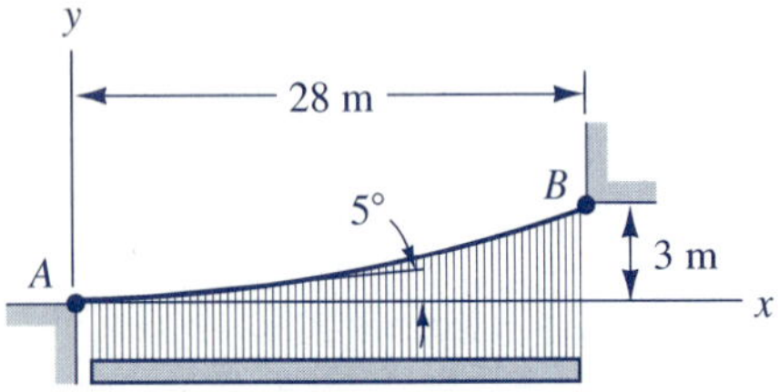

Figure P.6.67.

6.68. A cable supports a uniform loading of 100 lb/ft. If the lowest point of the cable occurs 20 ft from point A as shown, what is the maximum tension in the cable and its length? Use A as the origin of reference.

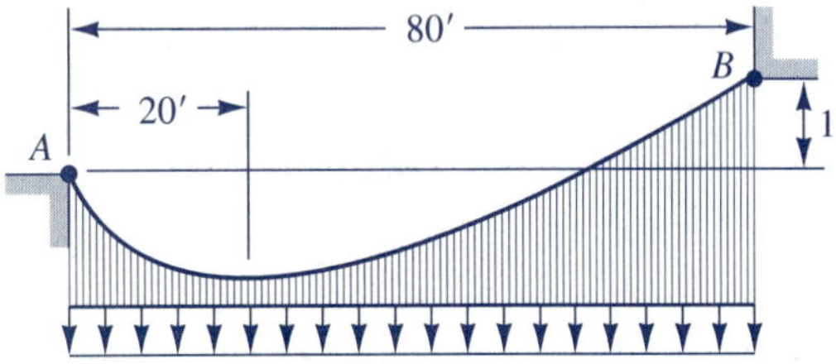

Figure P.6.68.

6.69. A uniform cable is shown whose weight we shall neglect. If a loading given as $5x$ N/m is imposed on the cable, what is the deflection curve of the cable if there is a zero slope of the curve at point A? What is the maximum tension?

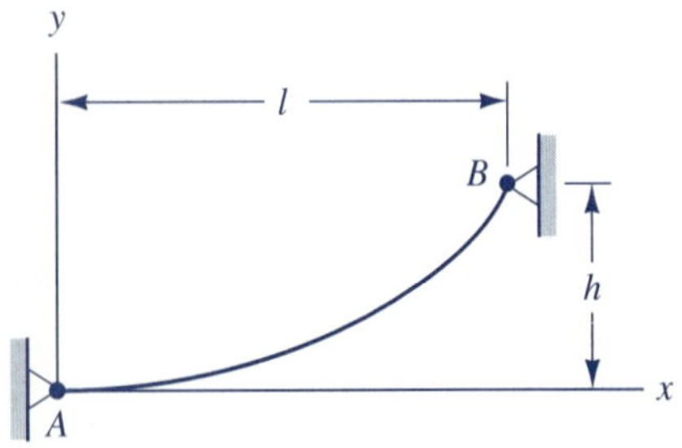

Figure P.6.69.

6.70. The left side of a cable is mounted at an elevation 7 m below the right side. The sag, measured from the left support, is 7 m. Find the maximum tension if the cable has a *uniform* loading in the vertical direction of 1500 N/m. [*Suggestion:* Place reference at position of zero slope and determine the location of this point from the boundary conditions.]

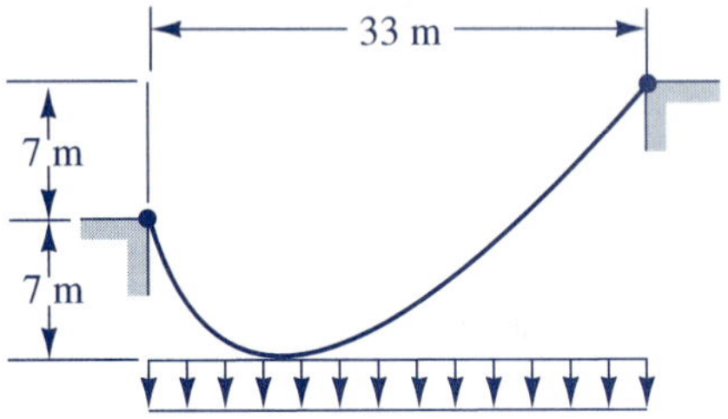

Figure P.6.70.

6.71. A blimp is dragging a chain of length 400 ft and weight 10 lb/ft. A thrust of 300 lb is developed by the blimp as it moves against an air resistance of 200 lb. How much chain is on the ground and how high is the blimp? The vertical lift of the blimp on the cable is taken as 1,000 lb.

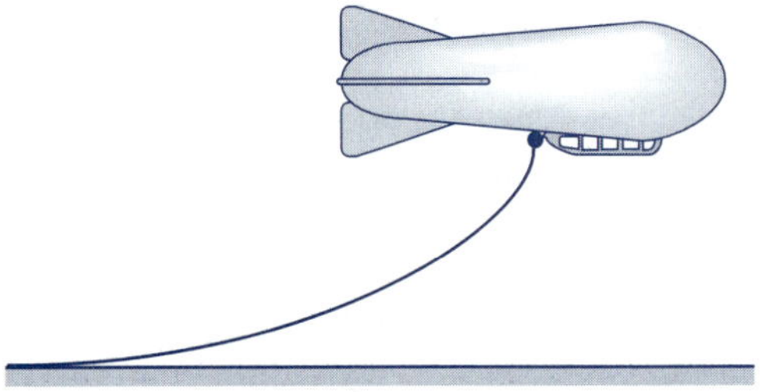

Figure P.6.71.

6.72. A large balloon has a buoyant force of 100 lb. It is held by a 150-ft cable whose weight is .5 lb/ft. What is the height h of the balloon above the ground when a steady wind causes it to assume the position shown? What is the maximum tension in the cable?

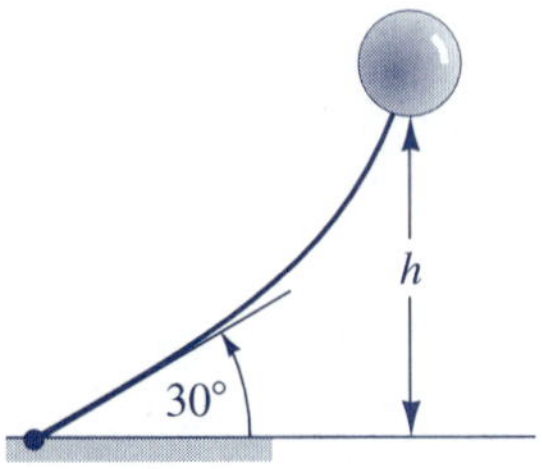

Figure P.6.72.

6.73. What is the deflection curve for the uniform cable shown weighing 30 N/m? Find the maximum tension. Compute the height h of the support B.

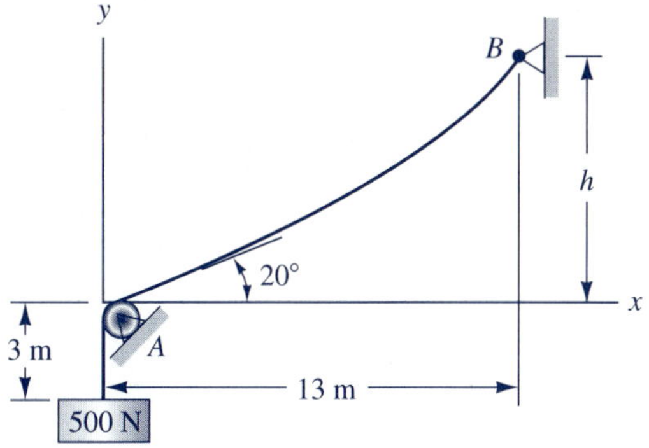

Figure P.6.73.

6.74. A search boat is dragging the lake floor for stolen merchandise using a 100-m chain weighing 100 N/m. The tension of the chain at support point B is 5,000 N and the chain makes an angle of 50° there. What is the height of point B above the lake bed? Also, what length of chain is dragging along on the bottom? Do not consider buoyant effects.

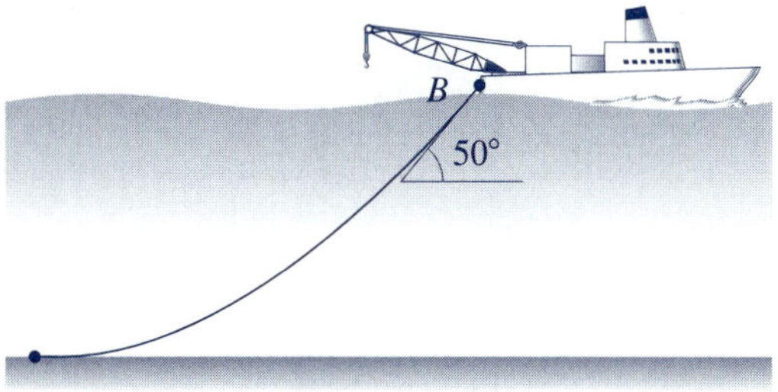

Figure P.6.74.

6.75. A cable weighing 3 lb/ft is stretched between two points on the same level. If the length of the cable is 450 ft and the tension at the points of support is 1,500 lb, find the sag and the distance between the points of support. Put reference at left support.

6.76. A flexible, inextensible cable is loaded by concentrated forces. If we neglect the weight of the cable, what are the supporting forces at A and B? What are the tensions in the chord AC and the angle α? [*Hint:* Proceed by using finite free bodies and working from first principles.]

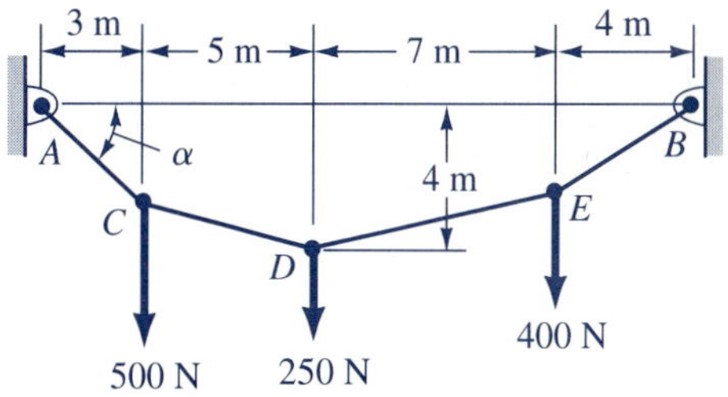

Figure P.6.76.

6.77. A system of two inextensible, flexible cables is shown supporting a 2,000-lb platform in a horizontal position. What are the inclinations of the cable segments AB, BC, and DE to accomplish this and what lengths should they be? Neglect the weight of the segments and note the hint in Problem 6.76.

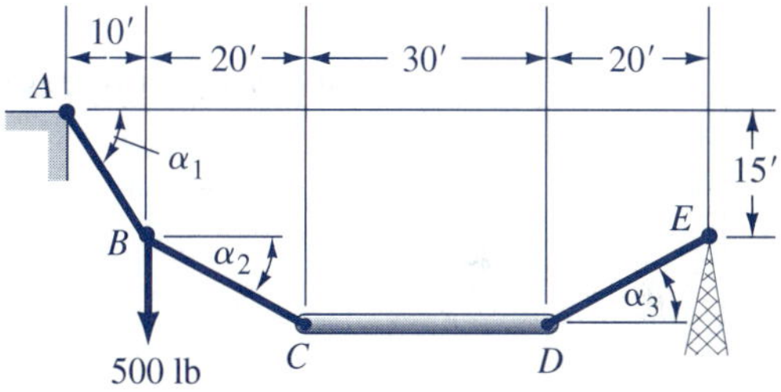

Figure P.6.77.

6.13 Closure

Essentially what we have done in this chapter is to apply previously developed material to situations of singular importance in engineering. Further information on structures can be found in books on strength of materials and structural mechanics. We turn again to new material in Chapter 7, where we will discuss the Coulomb laws of friction.

PROBLEMS

6.78. A 3-kN traveling hoist has a 27-kN capacity and is suspended from a beam weighing .5 kN/m. The beam is fastened to several trusses spaced 4 m apart. What are the forces in each truss member when the fully loaded hoist is located at point *C* directly under the truss shown? Assume that the hoist acts on pin *C* and that pin *C* also supports half of the I-beam *G* between each of the adjacent trusses.

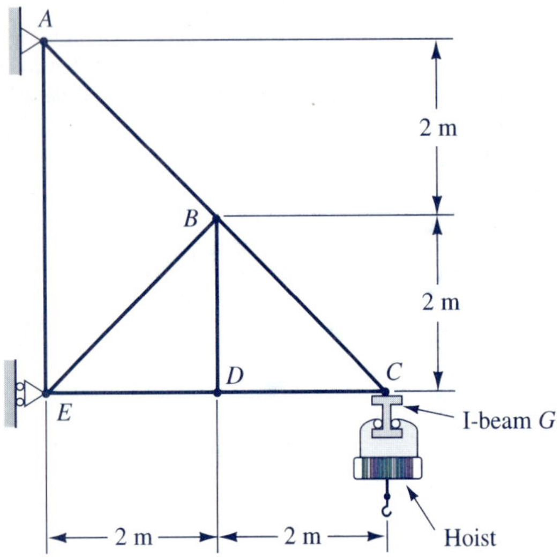

Figure P.6.78.

6.79. The truss is used to support the roof of a low-clearance train-car repair shed (hence the curved members). The roof is subjected to a snow load of 1 kN/m.² What are the forces in the straight members if the trusses are 10 m apart? Consider an inner truss.

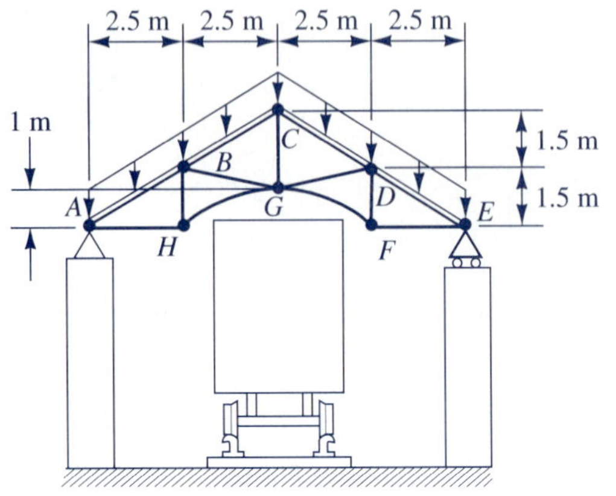

Figure P.6.79.

6.80. Find forces in all the members of the space truss. Note that *ACE* is in the *xz* plane (shaded).

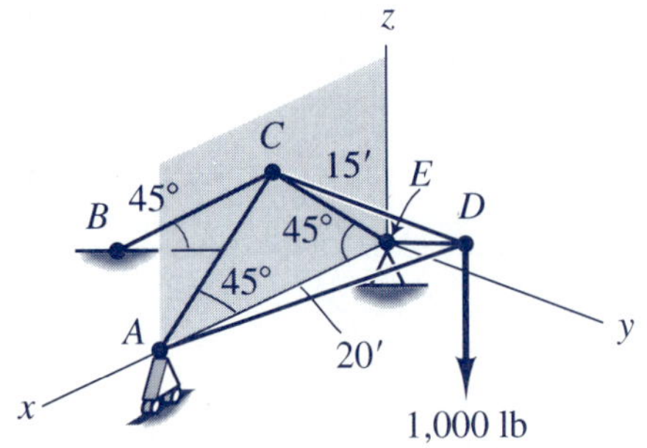

Figure P.6.80.

6.81. Determine the forces in members *BG*, *BF*, and *CE* for the plane truss.

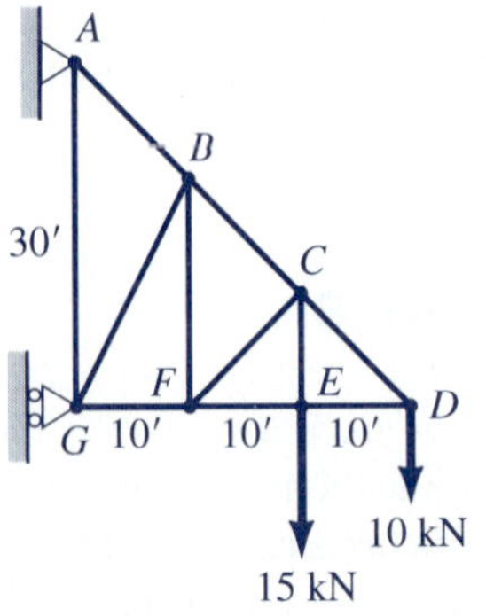

Figure P.6.81.

6.82. Express the shear-force and bending-moment equations with the aid of free-body diagrams. Then express V and M without the diagrams.

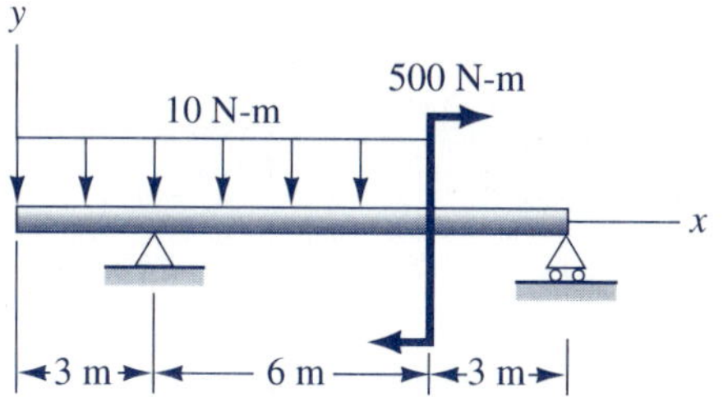

Figure P.6.82.

6.83. Express the shear-force and bending-moment equations without the aid of free-body diagrams.

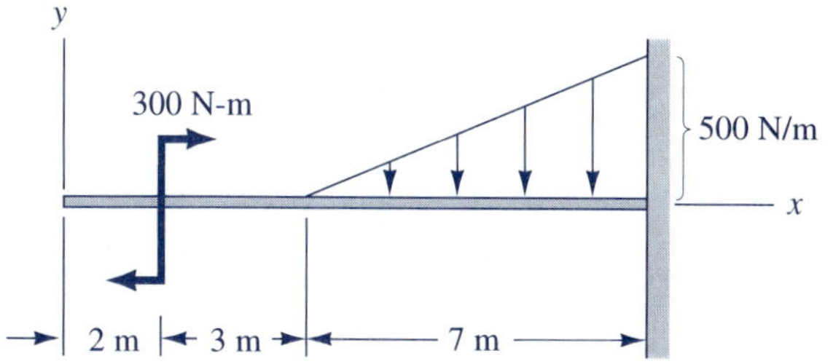

Figure P.6.83.

6.84. Give the shear-force and bending-moment equations for the beam, and sketch shear-force and bending-moment diagrams. At what position between supports is the bending moment equal to zero?

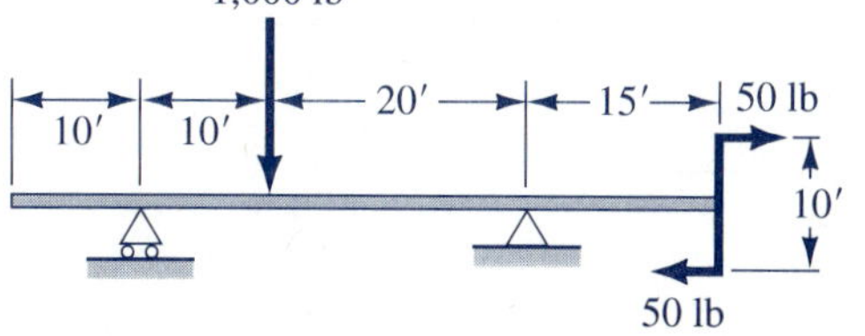

Figure P.6.84.

6.85. Sketch the shear-force and bending-moment diagrams labeling key points.

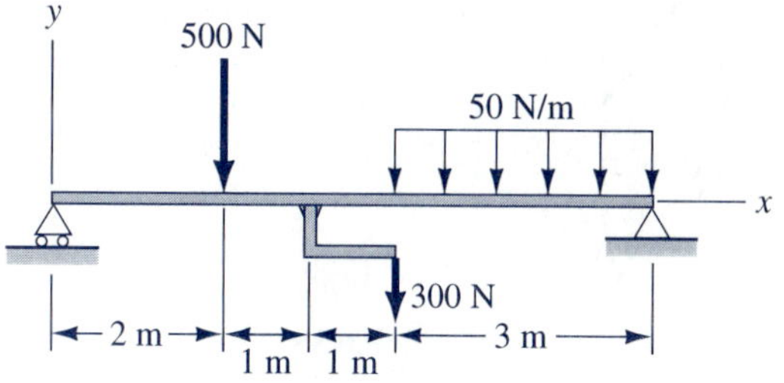

Figure P.6.85.

6.86. Find the shape of a cable stretched between two points on the same level, l units apart with sag h, and subjected to a vertical loading of

$$w(x) = 5 \cos \frac{\pi x}{l} \quad \text{N/m}$$

distributed in the horizontal direction. The coordinate x is measured from the zero slope position of the cable.

6.87. (a) By inspection, which members in the truss shown have a zero force for the given loads?

(b) For the Fink truss in Fig. P.6.1, with vertical loads on the bottom pins, which members will carry a zero force?

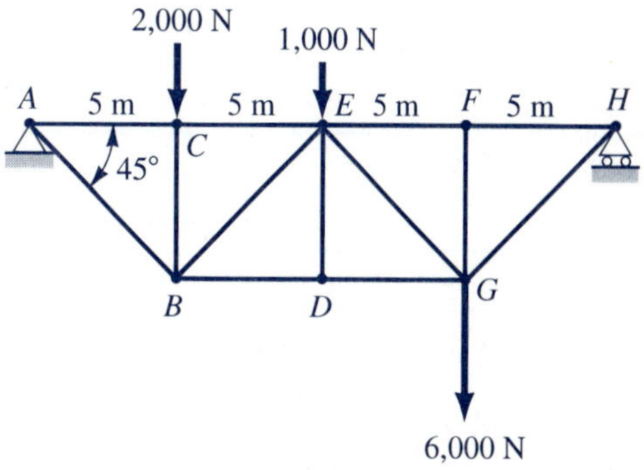

Figure P.6.87.

6.88. A 4,000-N load is being raised at constant speed. What are the forces in the truss?

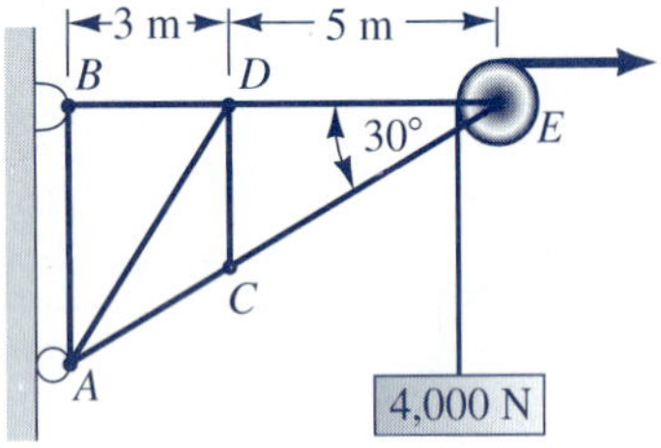

Figure P.6.88.

6.89. A truss supports a roadway load of 800 lb/ft per truss. Concentrated loads have been shown representing approximations of vehicle loading for each truss at some instant of time. The bridge has six 20-ft panels. Determine the forces in members *EG*, *FH*, and *IJ*.

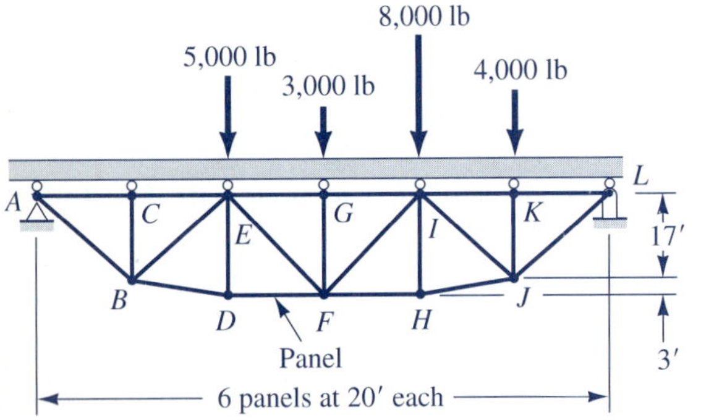

Figure P.6.89.

6.90. After finding the supporting forces for the simply supported beam *AB*, express the shear-force and bending-moment equations without the aid of free-body diagrams. The 10-kN load is applied to a bracket welded to the beam *AB*.

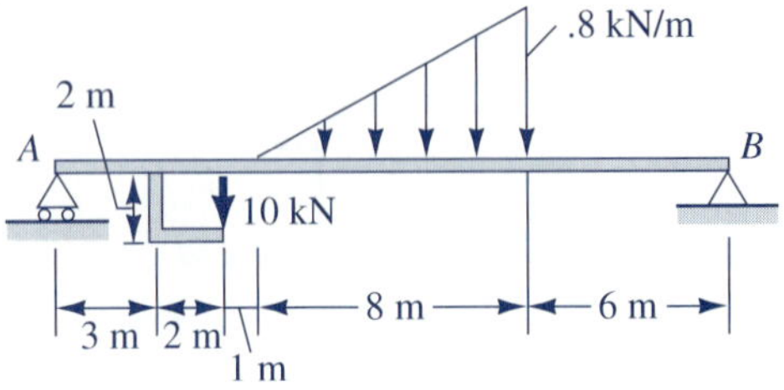

Figure P.6.90.

6.91. A uniform cable weighs 1 lb/ft. It is connected to a uniform rod at *B*. This rod is free to swing about hinge *C*. If a force component F_x of 200 lb is exerted at *A* as shown, what is the resulting angle of inclination α? The cable is 50 ft long and the rod is 20 ft long. What is the weight of the rod?

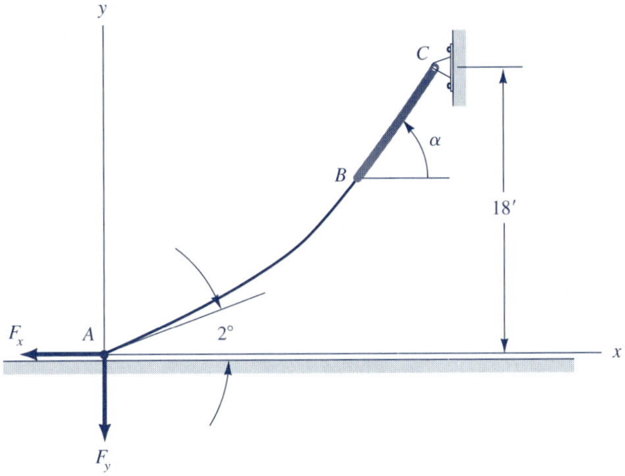

Figure P.6.91.

CHAPTER 7

Friction Forces

7.1 Introduction

Friction is the force distribution at the surface of contact between two bodies that prevents or impedes sliding motion of one body relative to the other. This force distribution is tangent to the contact surface and has, for the body under consideration, a direction at every point in the contact surface that is in opposition to the possible or existing slipping motion of the body at that point.

Frictional effects are associated with energy dissipation and are therefore sometimes considered undesirable. At other times, however, this means of changing mechanical energy to heat is a beneficial one, as for example in brakes, where the kinetic energy of a vehicle is dissipated into heat. In statics applications, frictional forces are often necessary to maintain equilibrium.

Coulomb friction is that friction which occurs between bodies having dry contact surfaces, and is not to be confused with the action of one body on another separated by a film of fluid such as oil. These latter problems are termed *lubrication problems* and are studied in the fluid mechanics courses. Coulomb, or *dry*, friction is a complicated phenomenon, and actually not much is known about its true nature.[1] The major cause of dry friction is believed to be the microscopic roughness of the surfaces of contact. Interlocking microscopic protuberances oppose the relative motion between the surfaces. When sliding is present between the surfaces, some of these protuberances either are sheared off or are melted by high local temperatures. This is the reason for the high rate of "wear" for dry-body contact and indicates why it is desirable to separate the surfaces by a film of fluid.

[1]For a more complete discussion of friction, see F. P. Bowden and D. Tabor, *The Friction and Lubrication of Solids*, Oxford University Press, New York, 1950.

We have previously employed the terms "smooth" and "rough" surfaces of contact. A "smooth" surface can only support a normal force. On the other hand, a "rough" surface in addition can support a force tangent to the contact surface (i.e., a friction force). In this chapter, we shall consider certain situations whereby the friction force can be directly related to the normal force at a surface of contact. Other than including this new relationship, we use only the usual static equilibrium equations.

7.2 Laws of Coulomb Friction

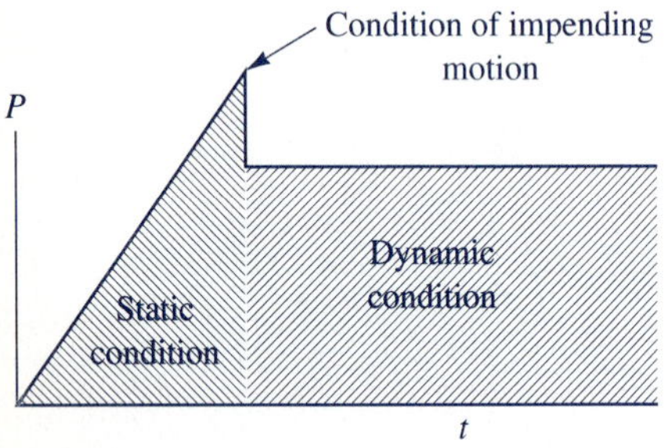

Figure 7.1. Idealized plot of applied force P.

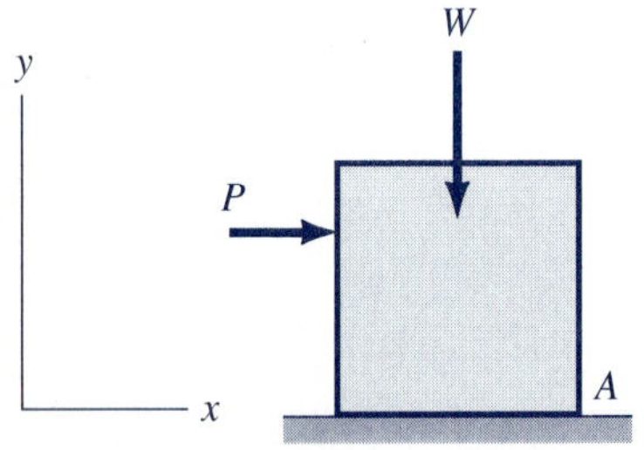

Figure 7.2. Idealization of furniture.

Everybody has gone through the experience of sliding furniture along a floor. We exert a continuously increasing force which is completely resisted by friction until the object begins to move—usually with a lurch. The lurch occurs because once the object begins to move, there is a decrease in frictional force from the maximum force attained under static conditions. An idealized plot of this force as a function of time is shown in Fig. 7.1 where the force P applied to the furniture, idealized as a block in Fig. 7.2, is shown to drop from the highest or limiting value to a lower value which is constant with time. This latter constant value is independent of the velocity of the object. The condition corresponding to the maximum value is termed the condition of *impending motion* or *impending slippage.*

By carrying out experiments on blocks tending to move without rotation or actually moving without rotation on flat surfaces, Coulomb in 1781 presented certain conclusions which are applicable at the condition of *impending slippage* or once *slippage has begun.* These have since become known as Coulomb's laws of friction. For block problems, he reported that:

1. The total force of friction that can be developed is independent of the magnitude of the area of contact.
2. For low relative velocities between sliding objects, the frictional force is practically independent of velocity. However, the sliding frictional force is less than the frictional force corresponding to impending slippage.
3. The total frictional force that can be developed is proportional to the normal force transmitted across the surface of contact.

Conclusions 1 and 2 may come as a surprise to most of you and be contrary to your "intuition." Nevertheless, they are accurate enough statements for many engineering applications. More precise studies of friction, as was pointed out earlier, are complicated and involved. We can express conclusion 3 mathematically as:

$$f \propto N$$

Therefore,

$$f = \mu N \tag{7.1}$$

where μ is called the *coefficient of friction.*

Equation 7.1 is valid *only at conditions of impending slippage or while the body is slipping*. Since the limiting static friction force exceeds the dynamic friction force, we differentiate between coefficients of friction for those conditions. Thus, we have coefficients of *static* friction and coefficients of *dynamic* friction, μ_s and μ_d, respectively. The accompanying table is a small list of static coefficients that are commonly used. The corresponding coefficients of friction for dynamic conditions are about 25% less.

Static Coefficients of Friction[2]

Steel on cast iron	.40
Copper on steel	.36
Hard steel on hard steel	.42
Mild steel on mild steel	.57
Rope on wood	.70
Wood on wood	.20–.75

Let us consider carefully the simple block problem used to develop the laws of Coulomb. Note that we have:

1. A plane surface of contact.
2. An impending or actual motion which is in the same direction for all area elements of the contact surface. Thus, there is no impending or actual rotation between the bodies in contact.
3. The further implication that the properties of the respective bodies are uniform at the contact surface. Thus, the coefficient of friction μ is constant for all area elements of the contact surface.

What do we do if any of these conditions is violated? We can always choose an *infinitesimal* part of the area of contact between the bodies. Such an infinitesimal area can be considered plane even though the general surface of contact of which it is an infinitesimal part is not. Furthermore, the relative motion at this infinitesimal contact surface may be considered as along a straight line even though the finite surface of which it is a part may not have such a simple straight motion. Finally, for the infinitesimal area of contact, we may consider the materials to be uniform even though the properties of the material vary over the finite area of contact. In short, when conditions 1 through 3 do not prevail, we can still use Coulomb's law *in the small* (i.e., at infinitesimal contact areas) and then integrate the results. We shall call such problems *complex* surface contact problems and we shall examine a series of such problems in Section 7.4.

[2]F. P. Bowden and D. Tabor, *The Friction and Lubrication of Solids*, Oxford University Press, New York, 1950.

*7.3 A Comment Concerning the Use of Coulomb's Law

As a simple illustration of why curvature of the surface of contact is second order and hence negligible, consider yourself at a location on the earth where it is perfectly round as a planet. As you look around you over a small area compared to a significant portion of the earth's surface, there is no evidence to your observation or in what you normally do that indicates the presence of curvature of the earth. In the same way, an infinitesimal area can be considered flat even if is part of a finite curved surface when considering Coulomb's law.

Furthermore, a stationary, nonrotating observer in inertial space looking at a similar small area on the earth's surface at the equator sees the velocity of the area essentially as given by $R\omega$ where R is the radius of the earth and ω is its angular velocity. All parts of this small area will have this same velocity up to only second-order variation as seen by this observer. And, so from this viewpoint, all points within the area are essentially translating with the aforementioned speed. To explain further, we will now say that this small area has a maximum dimension given by the length r. The *rotational* speed of any point seen by an inertial and hence nonrotating observer at the area and translating *with* the area must be no greater than $r\omega$. Clearly then, this rotational speed is *negligibly small* when compared with $R\omega$. Hence, an infinitesimal area at a finite distance from the axis of rotation of a rotating surface can be considered as having primarily a translational velocity and so permits the use of Coulomb's law "in the small."

7.4 Simple Contact Friction Problems

We now examine simple contact problems where Coulomb's laws apply to the contact surface *as a whole* without requiring integration procedures. We shall thus consider uniform blocklike bodies akin to those used by Coulomb. Also, we shall consider bodies which however complex have very *small* contact surfaces, such as in Fig. 7.3(a). Clearly, the whole contact surface can then be considered an infinitesimal plane area and for reasons set forth earlier, we shall directly use Coulomb's laws when appropriate as has been shown in Fig. 7.3(b).

Before proceeding to the examples, we have one additional point to make. For a finite simple surface of contact, such as the block shown in Fig. 7.2, we must note that we do not generally know the line of action for the simplest resultant supporting force N, since we do not generally know the normal force distribution between the two bodies. Hence, we cannot take moments for such free-body diagrams without introducing additional unknown distances in the equation. Consequently, for such problems we limit ourselves to summing forces only. This is not true, however, when we have a *point* contact such as in Fig. 7.3(a). The line of action of the supporting force must be at the point of contact, and we can thus take moments without introducing additional unknown distances.

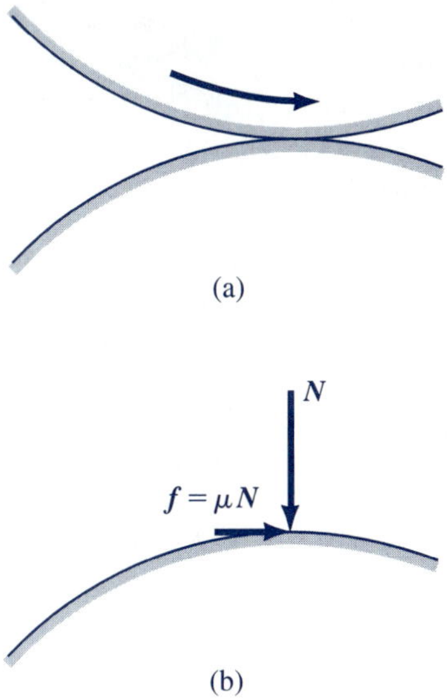

Figure 7.3. (a) Small contact surface; (b) Coulomb's laws applied.

Two common classes of statics problems involve dry friction. In one class, we know that motion is impending, or has been established and is uniform, and we desire information about certain forces that are present. We can then express friction forces at surfaces of contact where there is impending or actual slippage as μN according to Coulomb's law and, using f_i for other friction forces, proceed by methods of statics. However, the proper direction must be given to *all* friction forces. That is, *they must oppose possible, impending, or actual relative motion at the contact surfaces.* In the second class of problems, external loads on a body are given, and we desire to determine whether the friction forces present are sufficient to maintain equilibrium. One way to attack this latter type of problem is to assume that impending motion exists in the various possible directions, and to solve for the external forces required for such conditions. By comparing the actual external forces present with those required for the various impending motions, we can then deduce whether the body can be restrained by frictional forces from sliding.

The following examples are used to illustrate the two classes of problems.

Example 7.1

An automobile is shown in Fig. 7.4(a) on a roadway inclined at an angle θ with the horizontal. If the coefficients of static and dynamic friction between the tires and the road are taken as 0.6 and 0.5, respectively, what is the maximum inclination θ_{max} that the car can climb at uniform speed? It has rear-wheel drive and has a total loaded weight of 3,600 lb. The center of gravity for this loaded condition has been shown in the diagram.

Let us assume that the drive wheels do not "spin"; that is, there is zero relative velocity between the tire surface and the road surface at the point of contact. Then, clearly, the maximum friction force possible is μ_s times the normal force at this contact surface, as has been indicated in Fig. 7.4(b).[3]

We can consider this to be a *coplanar* problem with three unknowns, N_1, N_2, and θ_{max}. Accordingly, since the friction force is restricted to a point, three equations of equilibrium are available. Using the reference xy shown in the diagram, we have:

$\underline{\sum F_x = 0:}$

$$.6N_1 - 3{,}600 \sin\theta_{max} = 0 \quad \text{(a)}$$

$\underline{\sum F_y = 0:}$

$$N_1 + N_2 - 3{,}600 \cos\theta_{max} = 0 \quad \text{(b)}$$

$\underline{\sum M_A = 0:}$

$$10N_2 - (3{,}600 \cos\theta_{max})(5) + (3{,}600 \sin\theta_{max})(1) = 0 \quad \text{(c)}$$

To solve for θ_{max}, we eliminate N_1 from Eqs. (a) and (b), getting as a result the equation

$$N_2 = 3{,}600 \cos\theta_{max} - 6{,}000 \sin\theta_{max} \quad \text{(d)}$$

Now, eliminating N_2 from Eq. (c) using Eq. (d), we get

$$18{,}000 \cos\theta_{max} - 56{,}400 \sin\theta_{max} = 0$$

Therefore,

$$\tan\theta_{max} = .320 \quad \text{(e)}$$

Hence,

$$\boxed{\theta_{max} = 17.7°} \quad \text{(f)}$$

If the drive wheels were caused to spin, we would have to use μ_d in place of μ_s for this problem. We would then arrive at a smaller θ_{max}, which for this problem would be 14.7°.

[3]You will notice that there is no friction force on the front wheels. This is so because there is no torque coming from the automobile's transmission onto these wheels, while at the same time the wheels are rotating at constant speed. Note we are neglecting "rolling" resistance stemming from the deformation of the road surface and the tire, a small force to be considered in Section 7.8, a starred section.

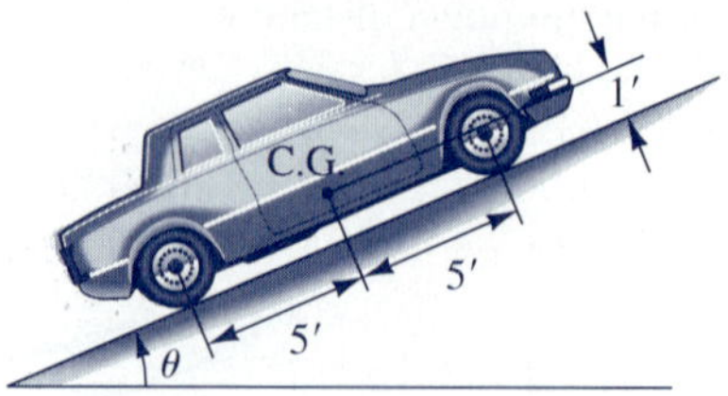

(a)

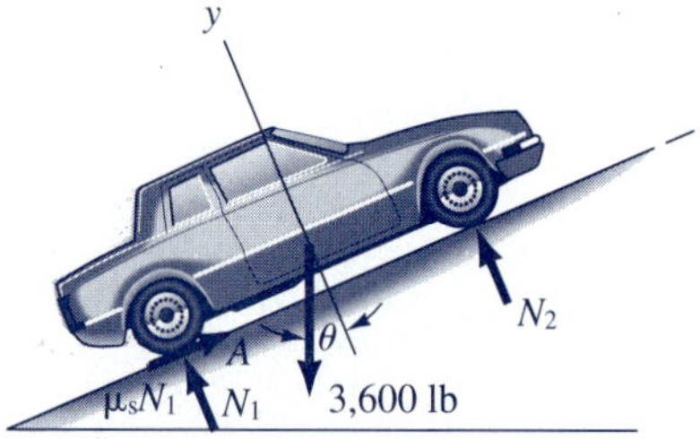

(b)

Figure 7.4. (a) Find maximum θ; (b) free-body diagram using Coulomb's law.

Example 7.2

Using the data of Example 7.1, compute the torque needed by the drive wheels to move the car at a uniform speed up an incline where $\theta = 15°$. Also, assume that the brakes have "locked" while the car is in a parked position on the incline. What force is then needed to tow the car either up the incline or down the incline with the brakes in this condition? The diameter of the tire is 25 in.

A free-body diagram for the first part of the problem is shown in Fig. 7.5(a). Note that the friction force f will now be determined by Newton's law and not by Coulomb's law, since we do not have impending slippage between the wheel and the road for this case. Accordingly, we have, for f:

$\sum F_x = 0$:

$$f - 3{,}600 \sin 15° = 0$$

Therefore,

$$f = 932 \text{ lb}$$

The torque needed is then computed using the rear wheels as a free body [see Fig. 7.5(a)]. Taking moments about A, we have

$$\text{torque} = (f)(r) = (932)\left(\frac{25/2}{12}\right) = \boxed{971 \text{ ft-lb}}$$

For the second part of the problem, we have shown the required free body in Fig. 7.5(b). Note that we have used Coulomb's law for the friction forces with the *dynamic* friction coefficient μ_d on all wheels. We now write the equations of equilibrium for this free body.

$\sum F_x = 0$:

$$T_{up} - .5(N_1 + N_2) - 3{,}600 \sin 15° = 0 \qquad \text{(a)}$$

$\sum F_y = 0$:

$$(N_1 + N_2) - 3{,}600 \cos 15° = 0 \qquad \text{(b)}$$

Solving for $N_1 + N_2$ from Eq. (b), and substituting into Eq. (a), we can now solve for T_{up}. Hence,

$$T_{up} = (.5)(3{,}600)(.966) + 932 = \boxed{2{,}670 \text{ lb}} \qquad \text{(c)}$$

Example 7.2 (Continued)

For towing the car down the incline we must reverse the direction of the friction forces as shown in Fig. 7.5(c). Solving for T_{down} as in the previous calculation, we get

$$T_{\text{down}} = (.5)(3{,}600)(.966) - 932 = \boxed{807\ \text{lb}} \qquad \text{(d)}$$

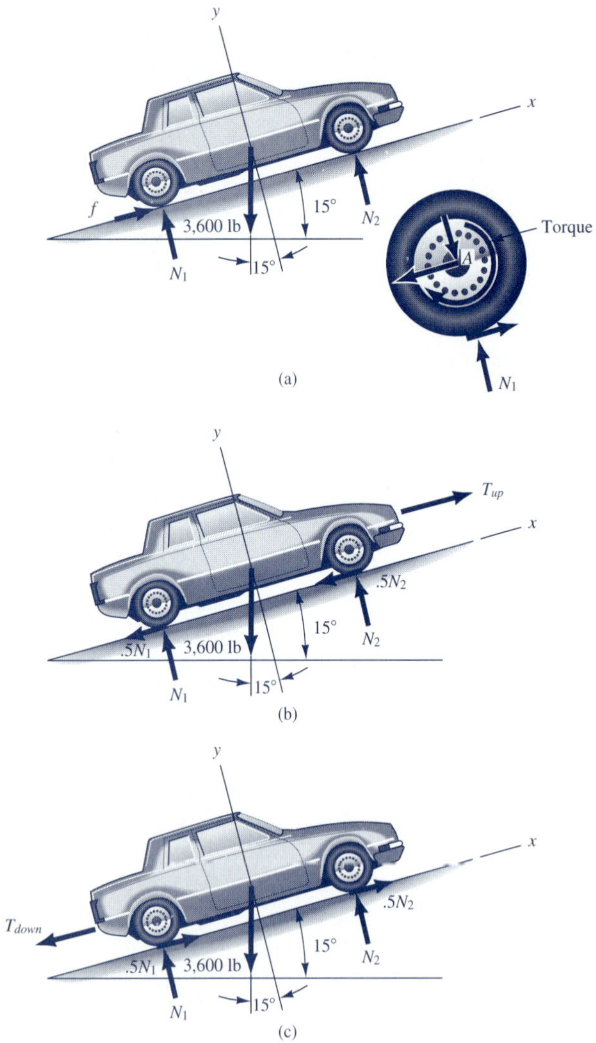

Figure 7.5. Free-body diagrams: (a) climbing at uniform speed; (b) under tow upward; (c) under tow downward.

Example 7.3

In Fig. 7.6 a strongbox of mass 75 kg rests on a floor. The static coefficient of friction for the contact surface is .20. What is the largest force P and what is the highest position h for applying this force that will not allow the strongbox to either slip on the floor or to tip ?

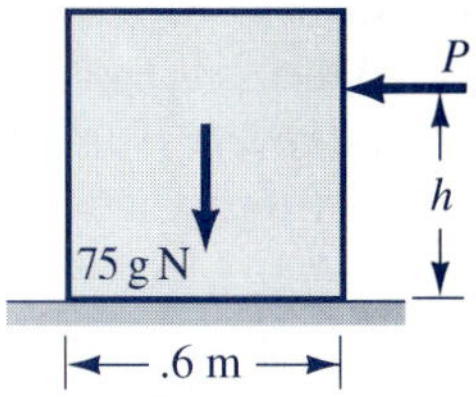

Figure 7.6. Strongbox being pushed.

The free-body diagram for the strongbox is shown in Fig. 7.7. The condition of *impending* motion has been recognized by the use of Coulomb's law. Furthermore, by concentrating the supporting and friction forces at the left corner, we are stipulating *impending tipping* for the problem. These two impending conditions impose the largest possible values of P and h that we are seeking.

The pertinent forces constitute a coplanar system of forces at the midplane of the strongbox. We proceed with the scalar equations of equilibrium:

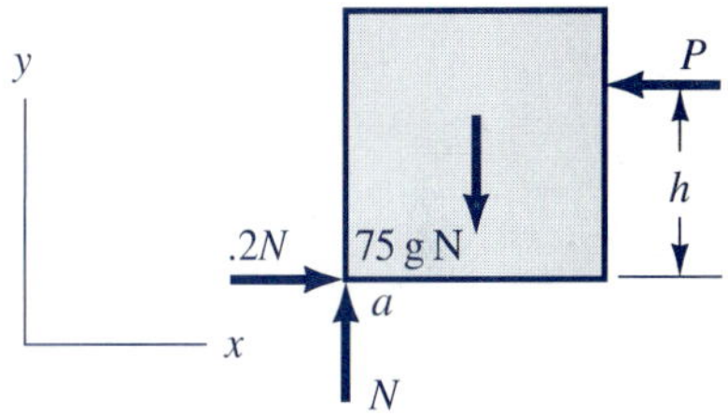

Figure 7.7. Impending tipping and slipping.

$\sum F_y = 0$:

$$N = 75g = 736 \text{ N}$$

$\sum F_x = 0$:

$$P = .2N = 147.15 \text{ N}$$

$\sum M_a = 0$:

$$-(75g)(.3) + (147.15)h = 0$$

Therefore, we get for the largest P and the largest h the following results:

$$P_{max} = 147.15 \text{ N} \qquad h_{max} = 1.50 \text{ m}$$

Thus, the height of the applied load must be less than or equal to 1.50 m in order to avoid tipping.

The three examples presented illustrated the *first* type of friction problem wherein we know the nature of the motion or impending motion present in the system and we determine certain forces or positions of certain forces. In the last example of this series, we illustrate the *second* type of friction problem set forth earlier—namely the problem of deciding whether bodies will move or not move under prescribed external forces.

Example 7.4

The coefficient of static friction for all contact surfaces in Fig. 7.8 is .2. Does the 50-lb force move the block A up, hold it in equilibrium, or is it too small to prevent A from coming down and B from moving out? The 50-lb force is exerted at the midplane of the blocks so that we can consider this a coplanar problem.

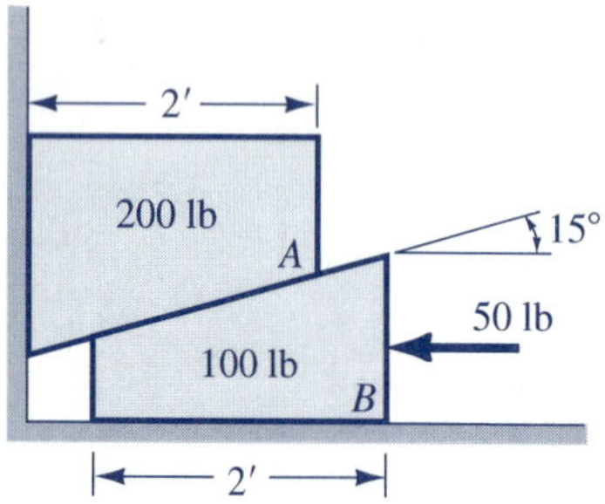

Figure 7.8. Do blocks move?

We can compute a force P in place of the 50-lb force to cause impending motion of block B to the left, and a force P for impending motion of block B to the right. In this way, we can judge by comparison the action that the 50-lb force will cause.

The free-body diagrams for impending motion of block B to the left have been shown in Fig. 7.9, which contains the unknown force P mentioned above. We need not be concerned about the correct location of the centers of gravity of the blocks, since we shall only add forces in the analysis. (We do not know the line of action of the normal forces at the contact surfaces and therefore cannot take moments.) Summing forces on block A, we get

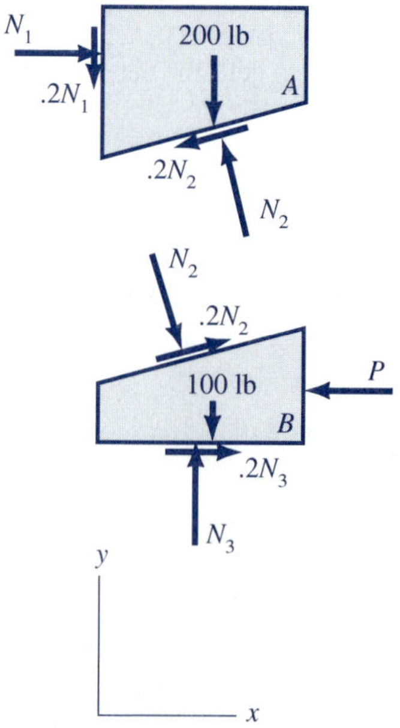

Figure 7.9. Impending motion of B to the left.

$$N_2 \cos 15°\boldsymbol{j} - N_2 \sin 15°\boldsymbol{i} - .2N_1\boldsymbol{j} - 200\boldsymbol{j}$$
$$+ N_1\boldsymbol{i} - .2N_2 \cos 15°\boldsymbol{i} - .2N_2 \sin 15°\boldsymbol{j} = \boldsymbol{0}$$

The scalar equations are:

$$N_1 - .259N_2 - .1932N_2 = 0$$
$$.966N_2 - .2N_1 - 200 - .0518N_2 = 0$$

Solving simultaneously, we get

$$N_2 = 243 \text{ lb}, \qquad N_1 = 109.8 \text{ lb}$$

Example 7.4 (Continued)

For the free-body diagram of *B*, we have, on summing forces,

$$-N_2 \cos 15°\boldsymbol{j} + N_2 \sin 15°\boldsymbol{i} - P\boldsymbol{i} + .2N_3\boldsymbol{i} + N_3\boldsymbol{j}$$
$$- 100\boldsymbol{j} + .2N_2 \cos 15°\boldsymbol{i} + .2N_2 \sin 15°\boldsymbol{j} = \boldsymbol{0}$$

This yields the following scalar equations:

$$-P + 62.9 + .2N_3 + 46.9 = 0$$
$$-235 + N_3 - 100 + 12.6 = 0$$

Solving simultaneously, we have

$$P = 174 \text{ lb}$$

Clearly, the stipulated force of 50 lb is insufficient to induce a motion of block *B* to the left, so further computation is necessary.

Next, we reverse the direction of force *P* and compute what its value must be to move the block *B* to the right. The frictional forces in Fig. 7.9 are all reversed, and the vector equation of equilibrium for block *A* becomes

$$N_2 \cos 15°\boldsymbol{j} - N_2 \sin 15°\boldsymbol{i} + .2N_1\boldsymbol{j} - 200\boldsymbol{j}$$
$$+ N_1\boldsymbol{i} + .2N_2 \cos 15°\boldsymbol{i} + .2N_2 \sin 15°\boldsymbol{j} = \boldsymbol{0}$$

The scalar equations are:

$$N_1 - .259N_2 + .1932N_2 = 0$$
$$.966N_2 + .2N_1 - 200 + .0518N_2 = 0$$

Solving simultaneously, we get

$$N_2 = 194.1 \text{ lb}, \qquad N_1 = 12.80 \text{ lb}$$

For free body *B* we have, on summing forces,

$$-N_2 \cos 15°\boldsymbol{j} + N_2 \sin 15°\boldsymbol{i} + P\boldsymbol{i} - .2N_3\boldsymbol{i} + N_3\boldsymbol{j}$$
$$- 100\boldsymbol{j} - .2N_2 \cos 15°\boldsymbol{i} - .2N_2 \sin 15°\boldsymbol{j} = \boldsymbol{0}$$

The following are the scalar equations:

$$P - .2N_3 + 50.3 - 37.5 = 0$$
$$-100 + N_3 - 187.5 - 10.05 = 0$$

Solving, we get $P = 46.7$ lb. Thus, we would have to *pull to the right* to get block *B* to move in this direction. We can now conclude from this study that the blocks are in equilibrium.

PROBLEMS

7.1. A block has a force F applied to it. If this force has a time variation as shown in the diagram, draw a simple sketch showing the friction force variation with time. Take $\mu_s = .3$ and $\mu_d = .2$ for the problem.

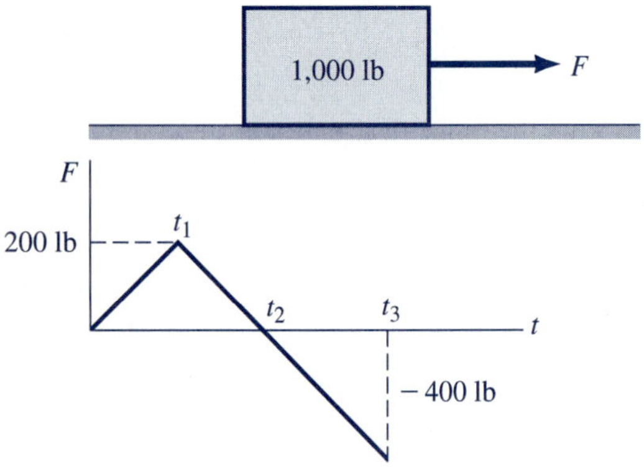

Figure P.7.1.

7.2. Show by increasing the inclination ϕ on an inclined surface until there is impending slippage of supported bodies, we reach the *angle of repose* ϕ_s so that $\tan \phi_s = \mu_s$.

7.3. To what minimum angle must the driver elevate the dump bed of the truck to cause the wooden crate of weight W to slide out? For wood on steel, $\mu_s = .6$ and $\mu_d = .4$.

Figure P.7.3.

7.4. A platform is suspended by two ropes which are attached to blocks that can slide horizontally. At what value of W does the platform begin to descend? Will W start tipping?

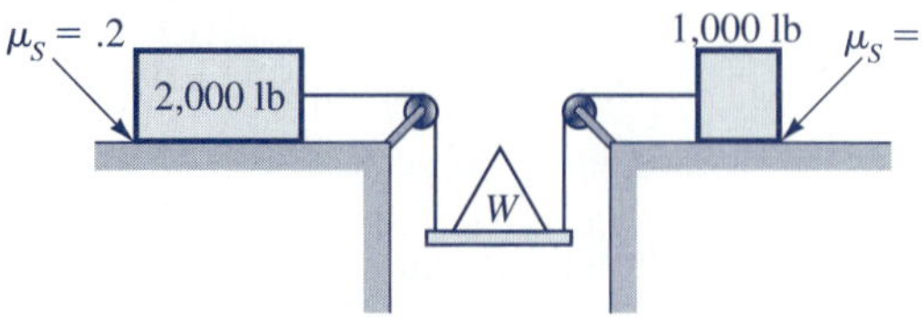

Figure P.7.4.

7.5. Explain how a violin bow, when drawn over a string, maintains the vibration of the string. Put this in terms of friction forces and the difference in static and dynamic coefficients of friction.

7.6. What is the value of the force F, inclined at 30° to the horizontal, needed to get the block just started up the incline? What is the force F needed to keep it just moving up at a constant speed? The coefficients of static and dynamic friction are .3 and .275, respectively.

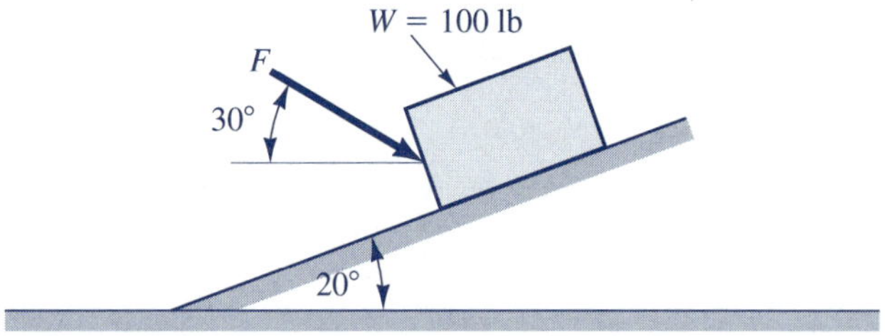

Figure P.7.6.

7.7. Bodies A and B weigh 500 N and 300 N, respectively. The platform on which they are placed is raised from the horizontal position to an angle θ. What is the *maximum* angle that can be reached before the bodies slip down the incline? Take μ_s for body B and the plane as .2 and μ_s for body A and the plane as .3.

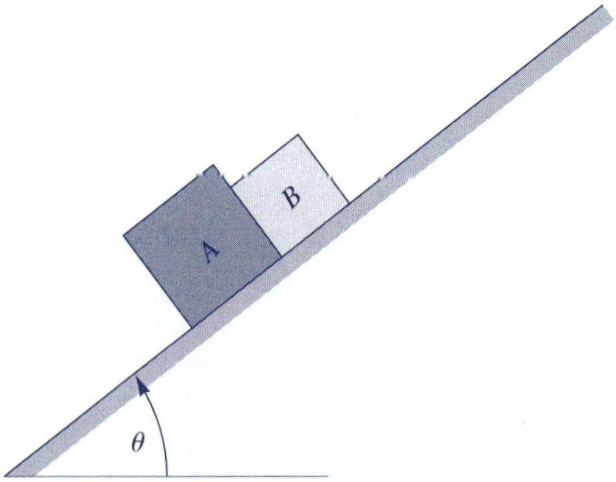

Figure P.7.7.

7.8. What is the minimum value of μ_s that will allow the rod AB to remain in place? The rod has a length of 3.3 m and it has a weight of 200 N.

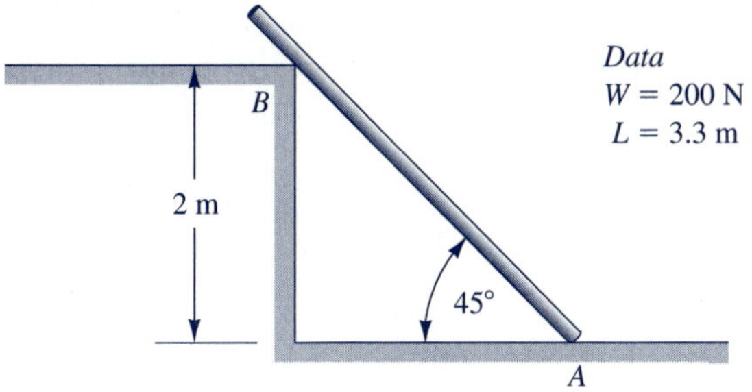

Figure P.7.8.

7.9. Find the minimum force P to get block A moving.

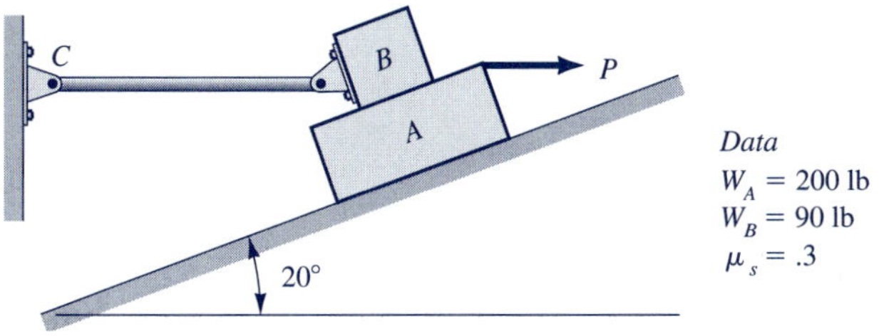

Figure P.7.9.

7.10. What minimum force F is needed to start body A moving to the right if $\mu_s = .25$ for all surfaces? The following weights are given:

$W_A = 125$ N $\qquad W_B = 50$ N $\qquad W_{AB} = 100$ N

The length of AB is 2.5 m.

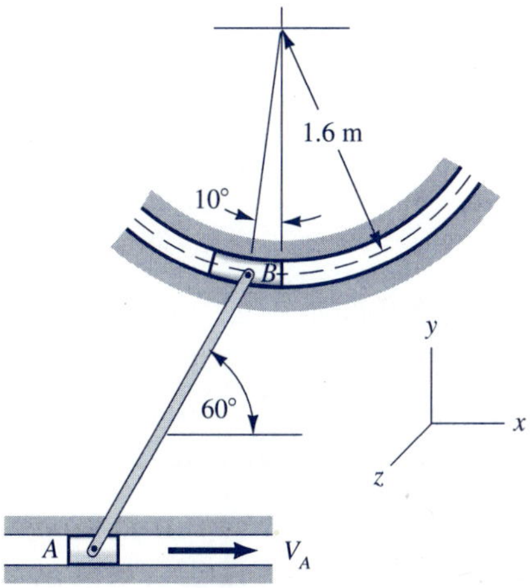

Figure P.7.10.

7.11. A 30-ton tank is moving up a 30° incline. If $\mu_s = .6$ for the contact surface between tread and ground, what *maximum* torque can be developed at the rear drive sprocket with no slipping? What maximum towing force F can the tank develop? Take the mean diameter of the rear sprocket as 2 ft.

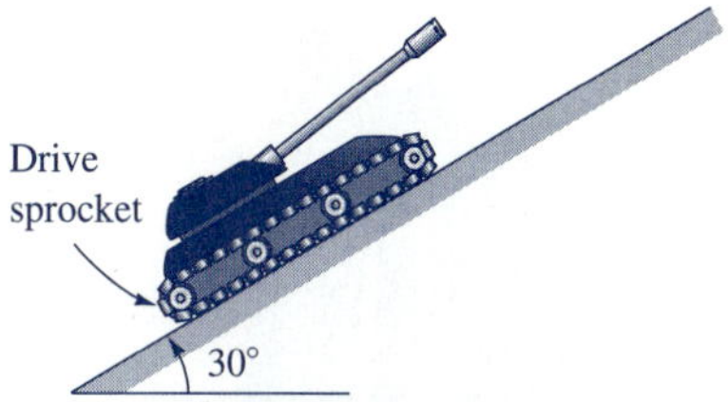

Figure P.7.11.

7.12. A 500-lb crate A rests on a 1,000-lb crate B. The centers of gravity of the crates are at the geometric centers. The coefficients of static friction between contact surfaces are shown in the diagram. The force T is increased from zero. What is the first action to occur?

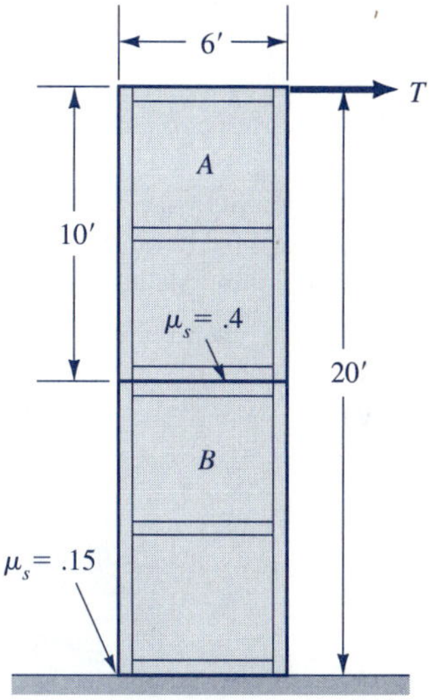

Figure P.7.12.

7.13. What force F is needed to get the 300-kg block moving to the right? The coefficient of static friction for all surfaces is .3.

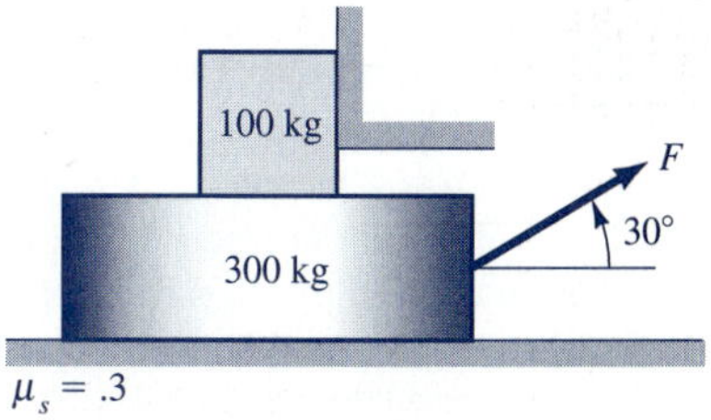

Figure P.7.13.

7.14. A chute is shown having sides that are at right angles to each other. The chute is 30 ft in length with end A 10 ft higher than end B. Cylinders weighing 200 lb are to slide down the chute. What is the *maximum* allowable static coefficient of friction so there cannot be sticking of the cylinders along the chute?

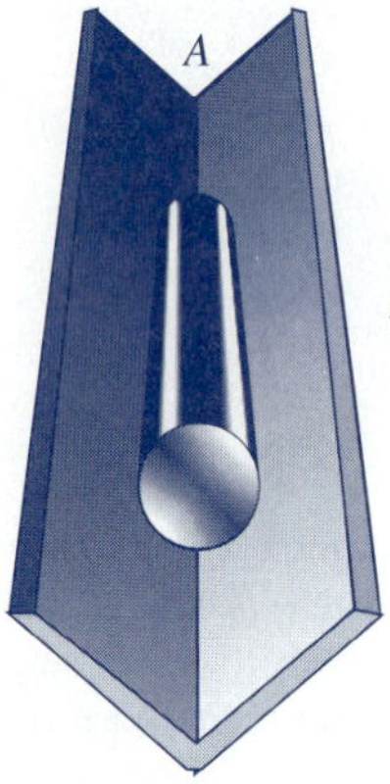

Figure P.7.14.

7.15. (a) Can the tractor move the 60-kN weight? (Prove this in some way)
(b) What is the tension in the connecting chain if the tractor moves the weight at constant speed?
(c) What is the torque for this action from the engine on one of the .8-m-diameter drive sprockets?

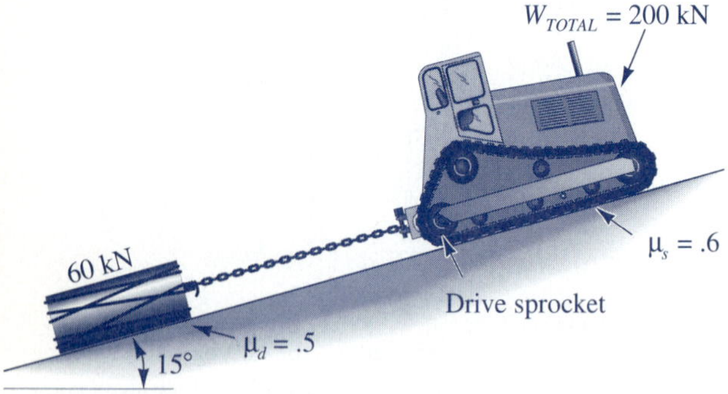

Figure P.7.15.

7.16. In Example 5.12, the wheels at A have rusted so as not to rotate at all, and so there can only be sliding on the floor. The coefficients of friction are $\mu_s = .4$ and $\mu_d = .2$. Using the same data as in the Example, compute the horizontal force on the rock for impending crushing action and then compute the horizontal force at the instant crushing starts. Assume that the action is slow so that we do not need to consider inertial effects. The plate A weighs 100 lb.

7.17. In Problem 5.92, the rollers on the block C have rusted and can no longer roll at all along the floor. There is then a dry friction at the contact surface between the block C and the floor. For this surface, the static coefficient of friction $\mu_s = .4$. If $p_1 = \frac{1}{2} p_2$, what pressures in the cylinders must be reached for the impending crushing action on the rock, which requires from the block at C a force of 7,000 lb in the horizontal direction? Block C weighs 200 lb.

7.18. A frame can slide up or down along the vertical guide rods or can remain stationary depending on the loads. What force P will cause impending slippage downward for the given applied loads? Member GA has a loose fit with circular rod EC, and member BH has a loose fit with circular rod JD. The coefficient of friction everywhere is $\mu_s = .3$. Neglect the weights of the members.

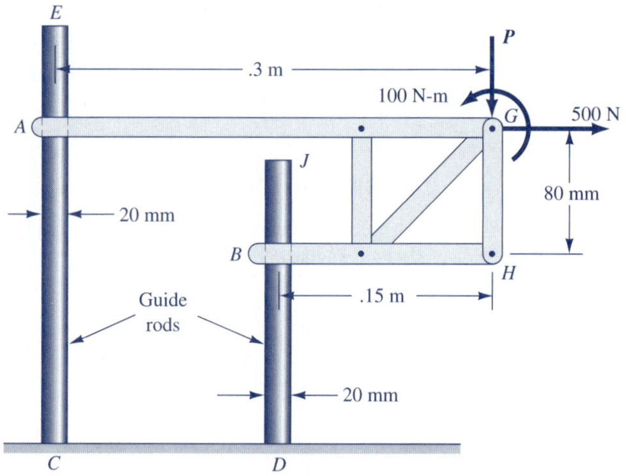

Figure P.7.18.

7.19. Given that $\mu_s = .2$ for all surfaces, find the force P needed to start the block A to the right.

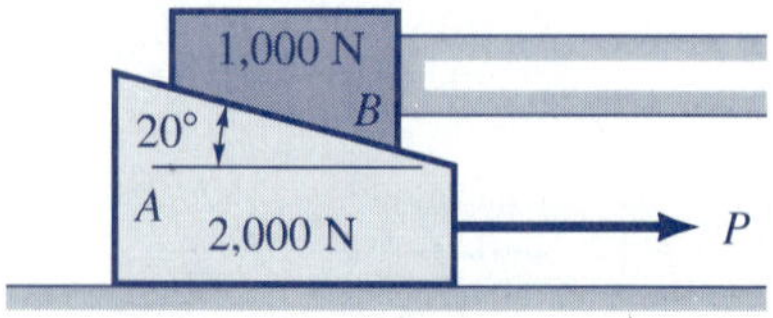

Figure P.7.19.

7.20. The cylinder shown weighs 200 N and is at rest. What is the friction force at A? If there is impending slippage, what is the static coefficient of friction? The supporting plane is inclined at 60° to the horizontal.

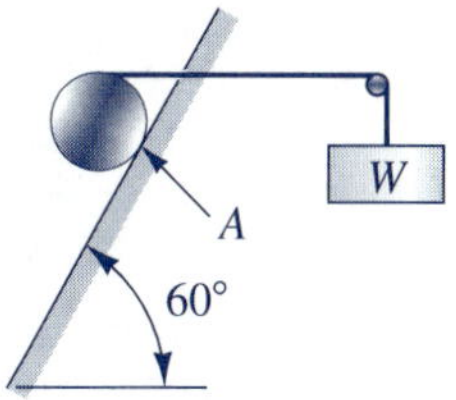

Figure P.7.20.

7.21. Armature B is stationary while rotor A rotates with angular speed ω. In armature B there is a braking system. If $\mu_d = .4$, what is the braking torque on A for a force F of 300 N? Note that the rod on which F is applied is pinned at C to the armature B. Neglect friction between B and the brake pads G and H.

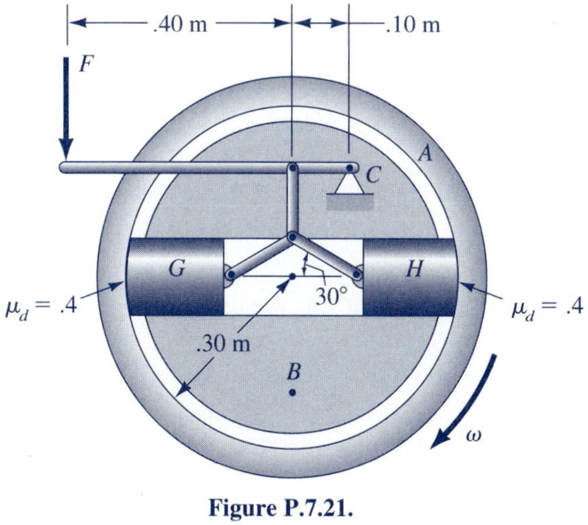

Figure P.7.21.

7.22. A 200-lb load is placed on the luggage rack of the 4,500-lb station wagon. Will the station wagon climb the hill more easily or with greater difficulty with the luggage than without? Explain. The static coefficient of friction is .55.

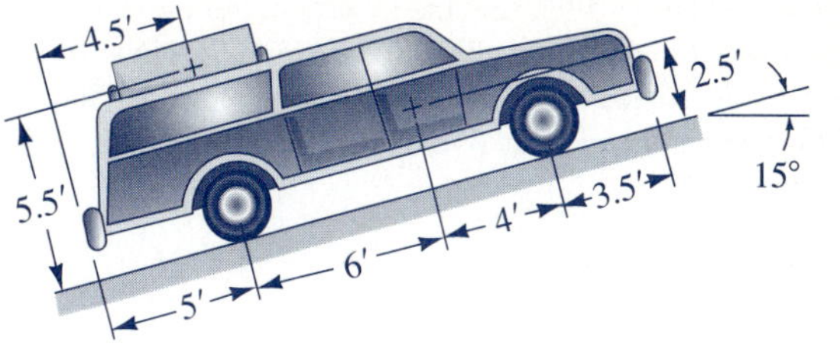

Figure P.7.22.

7.23. An insect tries to climb out of a hemispherical bowl of radius 600 mm. If the coefficient of static friction between insect and bowl is .4, how high up does the insect go? If the bowl is spun about a vertical axis, the bug gets pushed out in a radial direction by the force $mr\omega^2$, as you learned in physics. At what speed ω will the bug just be able to get out of the bowl?

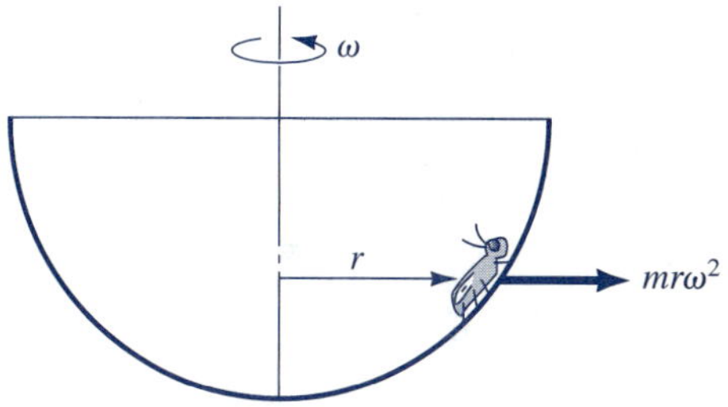

Figure P.7.23.

7.24. A block A of mass 500 kg rests on a stationary support B where the static coefficient of friction $\mu_s = .4$. On the right side, support C is on rollers. The dynamic coefficient of friction μ_d of the support C with body A is .2. If C is moved at constant speed to the left, how far does it move before body A begins to move?

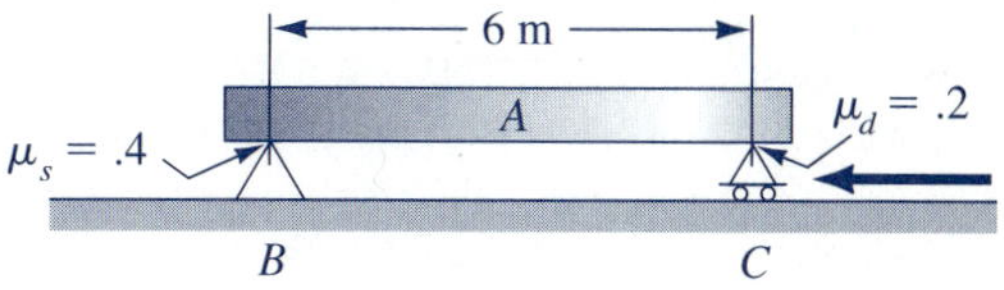

Figure P.7.24.

7.25. In Problem 5.94, find the minimum force F_1 acting on the block needed to maintain equilibrium. Block B weighs 100 lb and the static coefficient of friction between the block and the floor is 0.276. Neglect the weights of the other members of the system.

7.26. If the static coefficient of friction at C is .4, what is the minimum torque T needed to start a counterclockwise rotation of BA about hinge A? The following are the weights of the bodies involved:

$AB = 3$ lb $\quad BC = 4$ lb $\quad C = 2$ lb

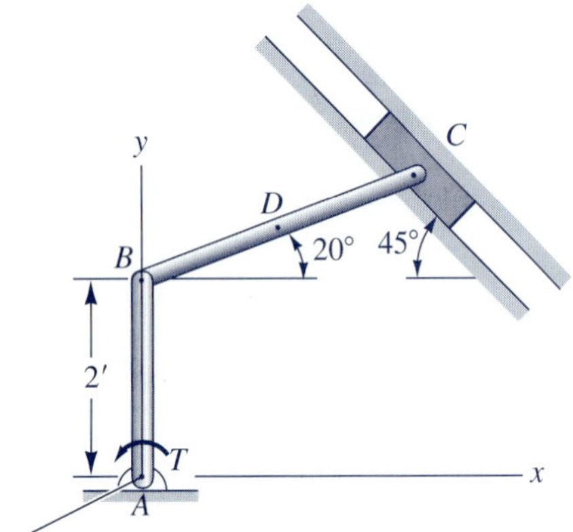

Figure P.7.26.

7.27. What will ensue if the weights are released from a state of rest? Examine all possibilities to justify your result.

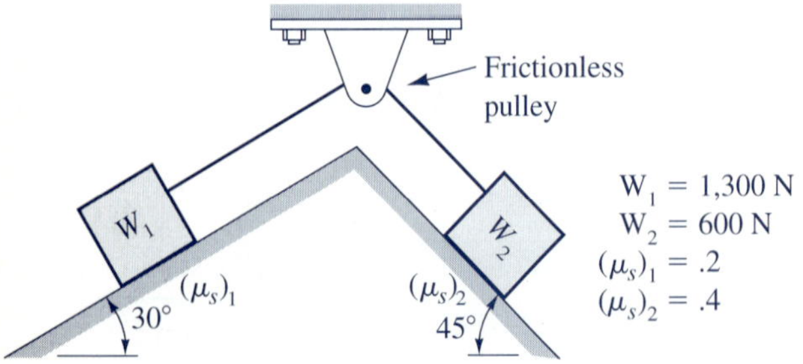

Figure P.7.27.

7.28. In a preliminary grinding operation for a 1,500-N car engine block, the grinding wheel is pushed against the block with a 500-N force. What force must be exerted by the hydraulic ram to move the block to the right if (a) the wheel rotates clockwise and (b) the wheel rotates counterclockwise? The static coefficient of friction between the grinding wheel and the block is .7 and between the table and the block is .2.

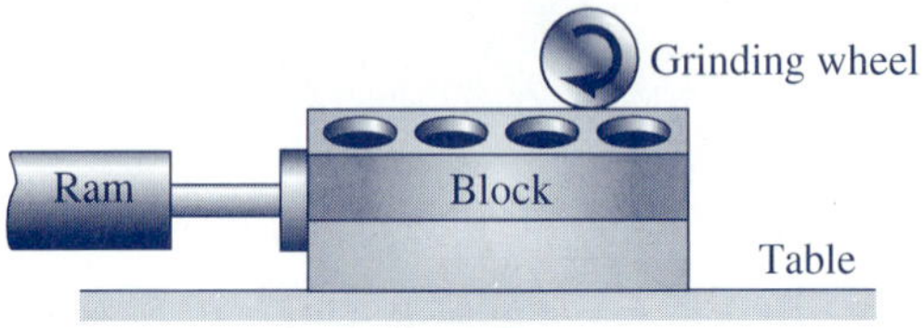

Figure P.7.28.

7.29. An 8,000-lb tow truck with four-wheel drive and 36 in. diameter tires develops a torque of 750 lb-ft at each axle. What is the *heaviest* car that can be towed up a 10° slope if $\mu_s = .3$?

7.30. A 7-m ladder weighing 250 N is being pushed by force F. What is the *minimum* force needed to get the ladder to move? The static coefficient of friction for all contact surfaces is .4.

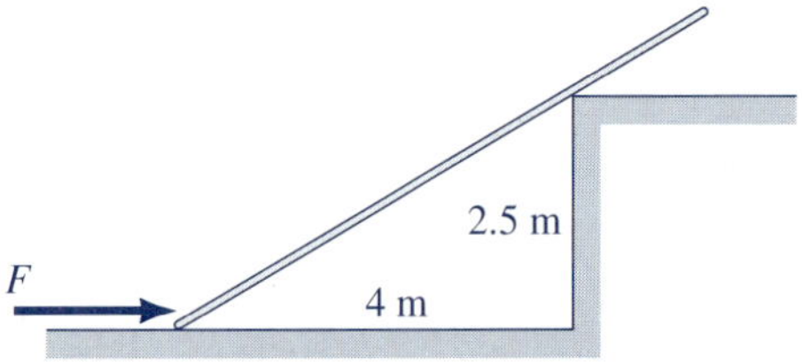

Figure P.7.30.

7.31. In Problem 7.30 if F is released will the ladder begin to slide down?

7.32. Can a force P roll the 50-lb cylinder over the step? The static coefficient of friction is .4. What is the value of P if this can be done?

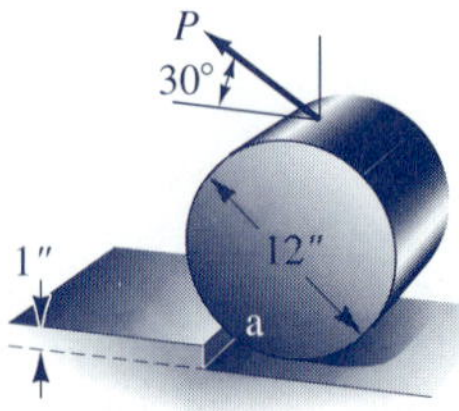

Figure P.7.32.

7.33. The block of weight W is to be moved up an inclined plane. A rod of length c with negligible weight is attached to the block and the force F is applied to the top of this rod. If the coefficient of static friction is μ_s, determine in terms of a, d, and μ_s the *maximum* length c for which the block will begin to slide rather than tip.

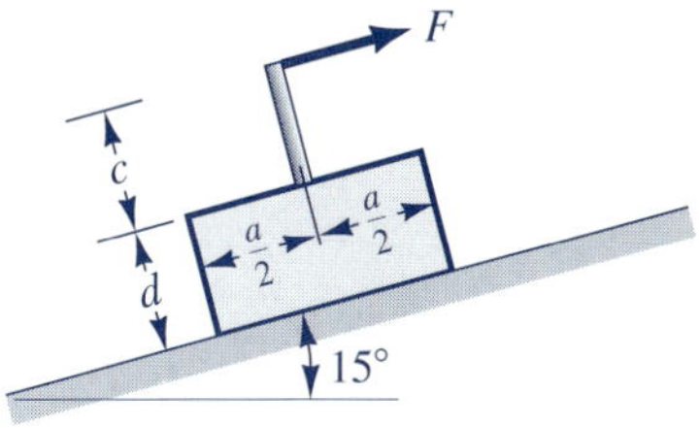

Figure P.7.33.

7.34. Determine the range of values of W_1 for which the block will either slide up the plane or slide down the plane. At what value of W_1 is the friction force zero? $W_2 = 100$ lb.

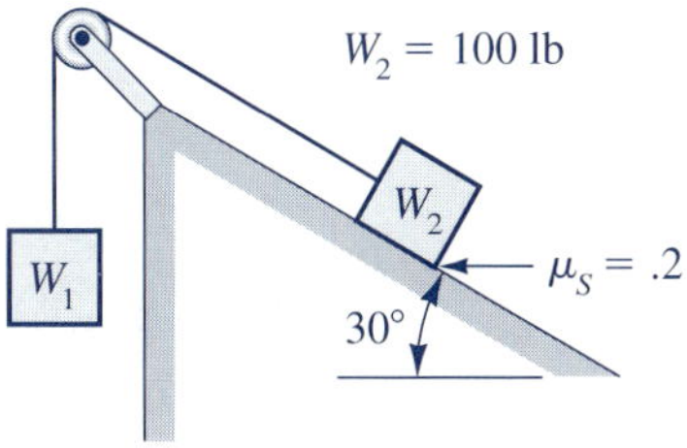

Figure P.7.34.

7.35. A 200-kN tractor is to push a 60-kN concrete beam up a 15° incline at a construction site. If $\mu_d = .5$ between beam and dirt and if μ_s is .6 between tractor tread and dirt, can the tractor do the job? If so, what torque must be developed on the tractor drive sprocket which is .8 m in diameter? What force P is then developed to push the beam?

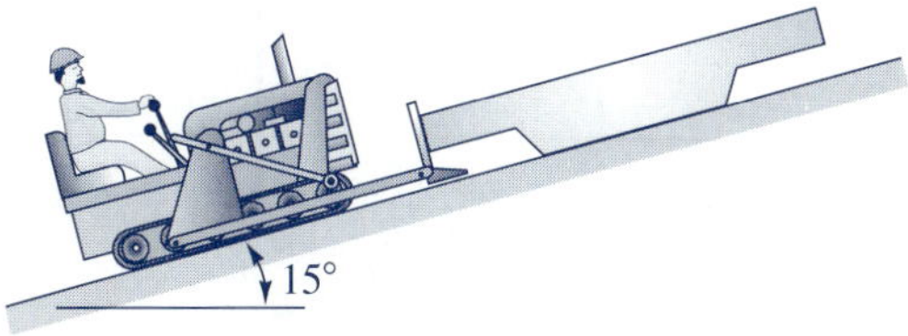

Figure P.7.35.

7.36. What is the *minimum* static coefficient of friction required to maintain the bracket and its 500-lb load in a static position? (Assume point contacts at the horizontal centerlines of the arms.) The center of gravity is 7 in. from the shaft centerline. Hint: Note that there is clearance between the vertical shaft and the horizontal arms.

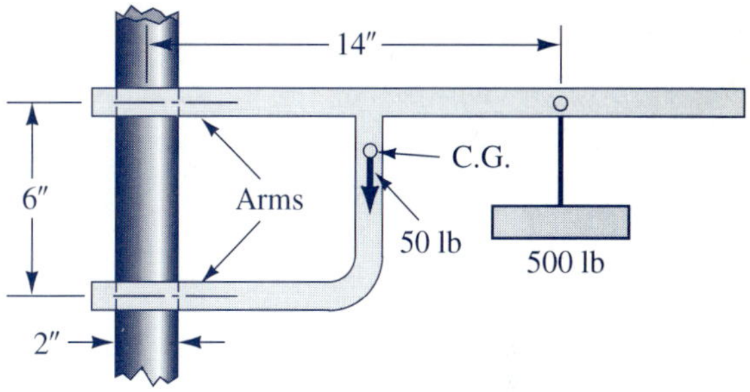

Figure P.7.36.

7.37. If the static coefficient of friction in Problem 7.36 is .2, at what *minimum* distance from the centerline of the vertical shaft can we support the 500-lb load without slipping?

7.38. A rod is held by a cord at one end. If the force $F = 200$ N, and if the rod weighs 450 N, what is the *maximum* angle α that the rod can be placed for μ_s between the rod and the floor equal to .4? The rod is 1 m in length.

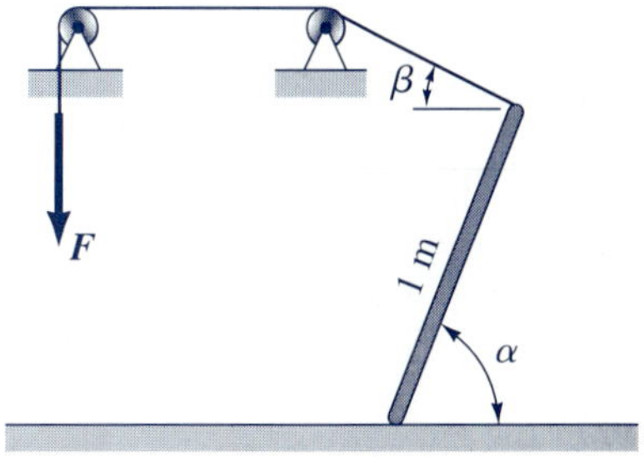

Figure P.7.38.

7.39. Suppose that an ice lifter is used to support a hard block of material by friction only. What is the *minimum* coefficient of static friction, μ_s, to accomplish this for any weight W and for the geometry shown in the diagram?

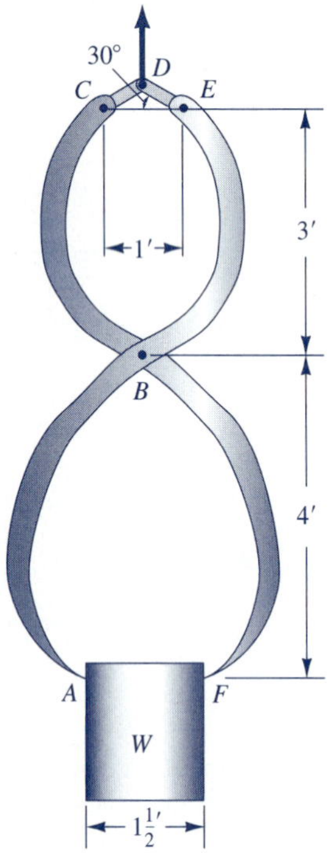

Figure P.7.39.

7.40. A rectangular case is loaded with uniform vertical thin rods such that when it is full, as shown in (a), the case has a total weight of 1,000 lb. The case weighs 100 lb when empty and has a coefficient of static friction of .3 with the floor as shown in the diagram. A force T of 200 lb is maintained on the case. If the rods are unloaded as shown in (b), what is the limiting value of x for equilibrium to be maintained?

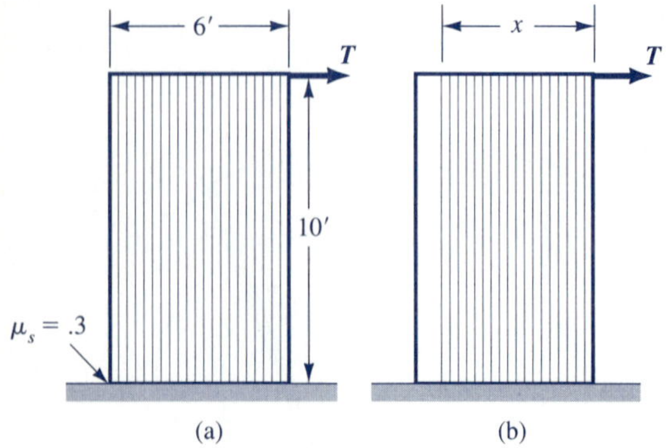

Figure P.7.40.

7.41. A beam supports load C weighing 500 N. At supports A and B, the static coefficient of friction is .2. At the contact surface between load C and the beam, the dynamic coefficient of friction is .75. If force F moves C steadily to the left, how far does it move before the beam begins to move? The beam weighs 200 N. Neglect the height t of the beam in your calculations.

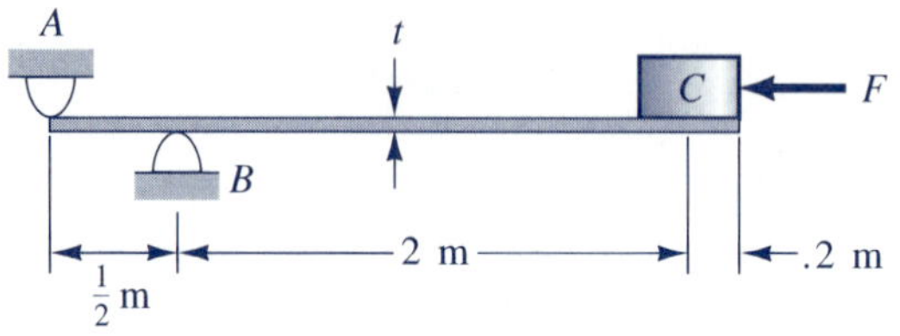

Figure P.7.41.

7.42. Do Problem 7.41 for the case where the height t is taken into account. Take $t = 120$ mm.

7.43. A rod is supported by two wheels spinning in opposite directions. If the wheels were horizontal, the rod would be placed centrally over the wheels for equilibrium. However, the wheels have an inclination of 20° as shown, and the rod must be placed at a position off center for equilibrium. If the coefficient of friction is $\mu_d = .8$, how many feet off center must the rod be placed?

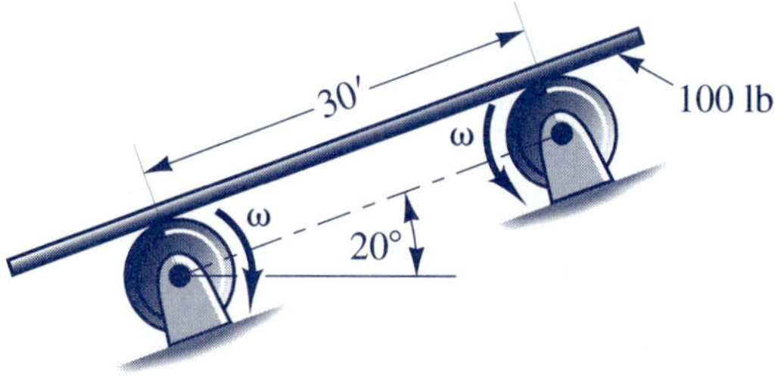

Figure P.7.43.

P.7.44. How much force F must be applied to the wedge to begin to raise the crate? Neglect changes in geometry. What force must the stopper block provide to prevent the crate from moving to the left? The static coefficient of friction between all surfaces is .3.

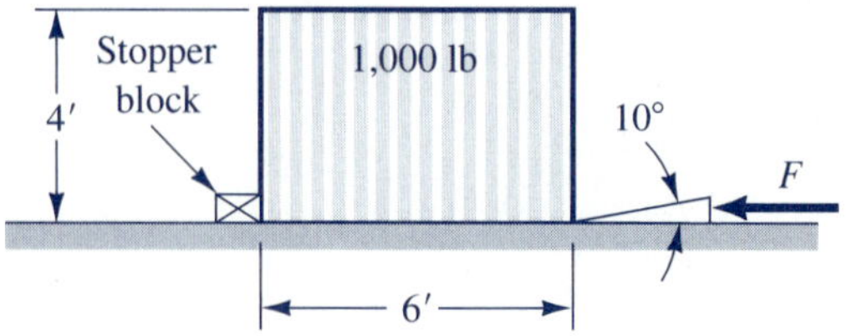

Figure P.7.44.

7.45. What is the *maximum* height x of a step so that the force P will roll the 50-lb cylinder over the step with no slipping at a? Take $\mu_s = .3$.

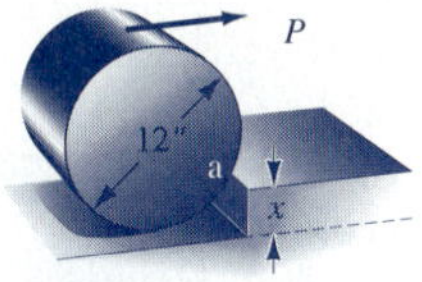

Figure P.7.45.

7.46. The rod AD is pulled at A and it moves to the left. If the coefficient of dynamic friction for the rod at A and B is .4, what must the *minimum* value of W_2 be to prevent the block from tipping when $\alpha = 20°$? With this value of W_2, determine the minimum coefficient of static friction between the block and the supporting plane needed to just prevent the block from sliding. W_1 is 100 N.

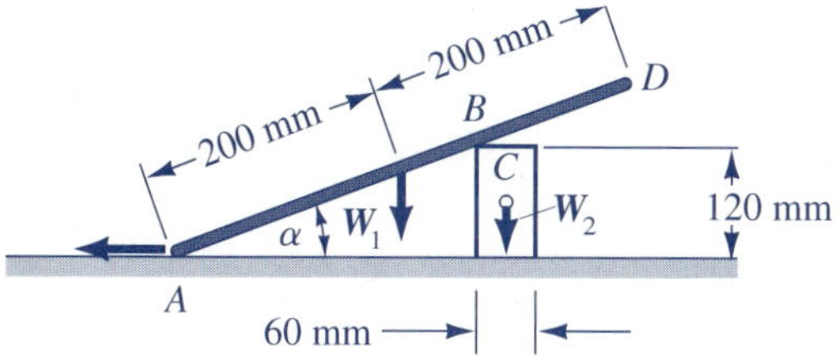

Figure P.7.46.

7.47. If we neglect friction at the rollers, and the coefficient of static friction is .2 for all surfaces, ascertain whether the 5,000-lb weight will go up, go down, or stay stationary.

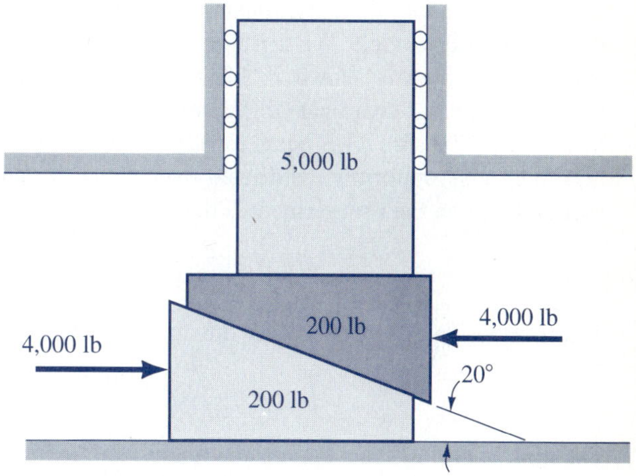

Figure P.7.47.

7.5 Complex Surface Contact Friction Problems

In the examples undertaken heretofore, the nature of the relative impending or actual motion between the plane surfaces of contact was quite simple—that of motion without rotation. We shall now examine more general types of contacts between bodies. In Example 7.5, we have a plane contact surface but with varying direction of impending or slipping motion for the area elements as a result of rotation. In such problems we shall have to apply Coulomb's laws locally to infinitesimal areas of contact and to integrate the results, for reasons explained in Section 7.2. To do this, we must ascertain the distribution of the normal force at the contact surface, an undertaking that is usually difficult and well beyond the capabilities of rigid-body statics, as explained in Chapter 5. However, we can at times *approximately* compute frictional effects by *estimating* the manner of distribution of the normal force at the surface of contact. We now illustrate this.

Example 7.5

Compute the frictional resistance to rotation of a rotating solid cylinder with an attached pad A pressing against a flat dry surface with a force P (see Fig. 7.10). The pad A and the stationary flat dry surface constitute a dry *thrust bearing*.

The direction of the frictional forces distributed over the contact surface is no longer simple. We therefore take an infinitesimal area for examination. This area is shown in Fig. 7.10, where the element has been formed from polar-coordinate differentials so as to be related simply to the boundaries. The area dA is equal to $r\,d\theta\,dr$. We shall *assume* that the normal force P is uniformly distributed over the entire area of contact. The normal force on the area element is then

$$dN = \frac{P}{\pi D^2/4} r\,d\theta\,dr \qquad \text{(a)}$$

The friction force associated with this force during motion is

$$df = \mu_d \frac{P}{\pi D^2/4} r\,d\theta\,dr \qquad \text{(b)}$$

The direction of df must oppose the relative motion between the surfaces. The relative motion is rotation of concentric circles about the centerline, so the direction of a force df_1 (Fig. 7.11) must lie tangent to a circle of radius r. At 180° from the position of the area element for df_1, we may carry out a similar calculation for a force df_2, which for the same r must be equal and opposite to df_1, thus forming a couple. Since the entire area may be decomposed in this way, we can conclude that there are only couples in the plane of contact. If we take moments of all infinitesimal forces about the center, we get the magnitude of the total frictional couple moment. The direction of the couple moment is along the shaft axis. First, consider area elements on the ring of radius r:

$$dM = \int_0^{2\pi} r\mu_d \frac{P}{\pi D^2/4} r\,d\theta\,dr \qquad \text{(c)}$$

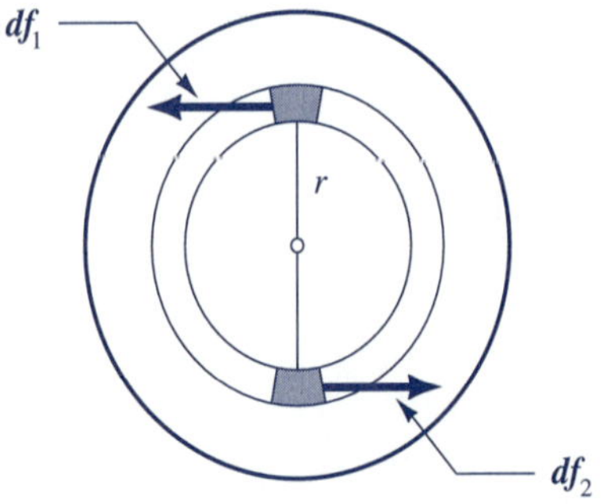

Figure 7.11. Friction forces form couples.

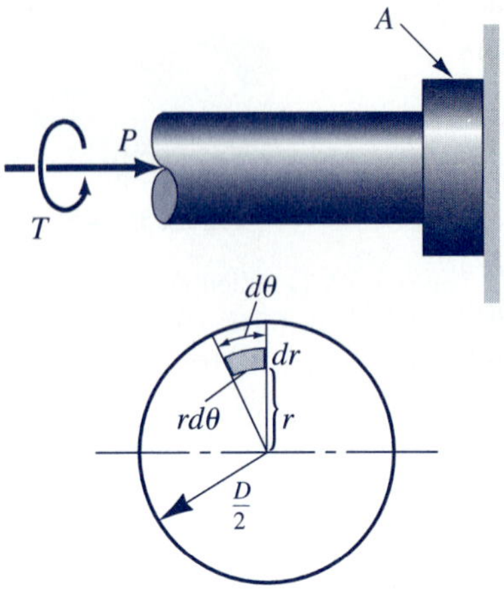

Figure 7.10. Dry thrust bearing.

Example 7.5 (Continued)

Taking μ_d as constant and holding r constant, we have on integration with respect to θ:

$$dM = \mu_d \frac{P}{\pi D^2/4} 2\pi r^2 \, dr$$

We thus account for all area elements on the ring of radius r. To account for all the rings of the contact surface, we next integrate with respect to r from zero to $D/2$. Clearly, this gives us the total resisting torque M. Thus,

$$M = \mu_d \frac{8P}{D^2} \int_0^{D/2} r^2 \, dr = \frac{PD\mu_d}{3} \qquad \text{(d)}$$

What we have performed in the last three steps is *multiple integration*, which we introduced in Chapter 4 when dealing with rectangular coordinates.

7.6 Belt Friction

A flexible belt is shown in Fig. 7.12 wrapped around a portion of a drum, with the amount of wrap indicated by angle β. The angle β is called the *angle of wrap*. Assume that the drum is stationary and tensions T_1 and T_2 are such that motion is impending between the belt and the drum. We shall take the impending motion of the belt to be clockwise relative to the drum, and therefore the tension T_1 exceeds tension T_2.

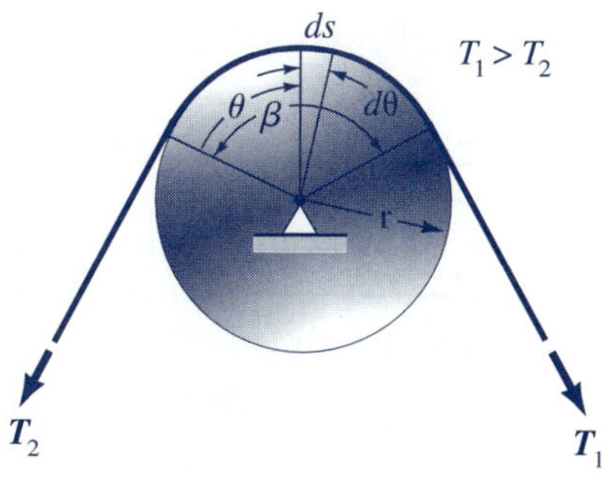

Figure 7.12. Belt wrapped around drum.

Consider an infinitesimal segment of the belt as a free body. This segment subtends an angle $d\theta$ at the drum center as shown in Fig. 7.13. Summing force components in the radial and transverse directions and equating them to zero as per *equilibrium*, we get the following scalar equations:

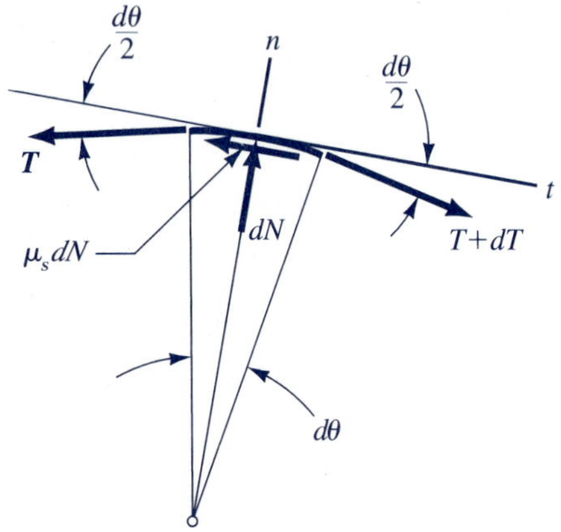

Figure 7.13. Free-body diagram of segment of belt; impending slippage.

$\underline{\sum F_t = 0:}$

$$-T\cos\frac{d\theta}{2} + (T + dT)\cos\frac{d\theta}{2} - \mu_s dN = 0$$

Therefore,

$$dT\cos\frac{d\theta}{2} = \mu_s\, dN$$

$\underline{\sum F_n = 0:}$

$$-T\sin\frac{d\theta}{2} - (T + dT)\sin\frac{d\theta}{2} + dN = 0$$

Therefore,

$$-2T\sin\frac{d\theta}{2} - dT\sin\frac{d\theta}{2} + dN - 0$$

The sine of a very small angle approximately equals the angle itself in radians. Furthermore, to the same degree of accuracy, the cosine of a small angle approaches unity. (That these relations are true may be seen by expanding the sine and cosine in a power series and then retaining only the first terms.) The preceding equilibrium equations then become

$$dT = \mu_s\, dN \tag{7.2a}$$

$$-Td\theta - dT\frac{d\theta}{2} + dN = 0 \tag{7.2b}$$

In the last equation, we have an expression involving the product of two infinitesimals. This quantity may be considered negligible compared to the other terms of the equation involving only one differential. Thus, we have for this equation:

$$T\,d\theta = dN \tag{7.3}$$

From Eqs. 7.2a and 7.3, we may form an equation involving T and θ. Thus, by eliminating dN from the equations, we have

$$dT = \mu_s T\,d\theta$$

Hence,

$$\frac{dT}{T} = \mu_s\,d\theta$$

Integrating both sides around the portion of the belt in contact with the drum,

$$\int_{T_2}^{T_1} \frac{dT}{T} = \int_0^{\beta} \mu_s\,d\theta$$

we get

$$\ln\frac{T_1}{T_2} = \mu_s\beta$$

or

$$\frac{T_1}{T_2} = e^{\mu_s\beta} \tag{7.4}$$

We therefore have established a relation between the tensions on each part of the belt at a condition of impending motion between the belt and the drum. The same relation can be reached for a *rotating* drum with impending slippage between the belt and the drum *if we neglect centrifugal effects on the belt*. Furthermore, by using the *dynamic* coefficient of friction in the formula above, we have the case of the belt slipping at constant speed over either a rotating or stationary drum (again neglecting centrifugal effects on the belt). Thus, for all such cases, we have

$$\frac{T_1}{T_2} = e^{\mu\beta} \tag{7.5}$$

where the proper coefficient of friction must be used to suit the problem, and the angle β must be expressed in *radians*. Note that *the ratio of tensions depends only on the angle of wrap* β and the coefficient of friction μ. Thus, if the drum A is forced to the right, as shown in Fig. 7.14, the tensions will increase, but if β is not affected by the action, the ratio of T_1/T_2 for impending or actual constant speed slippage is *not* affected by this action. However, the *torque* developed by the belt on the drum as a result of friction *is* affected by the force F. The torque is easily determined by using the drum and the portion of the belt in contact with the drum as a free body, as is shown in Fig. 7.14.

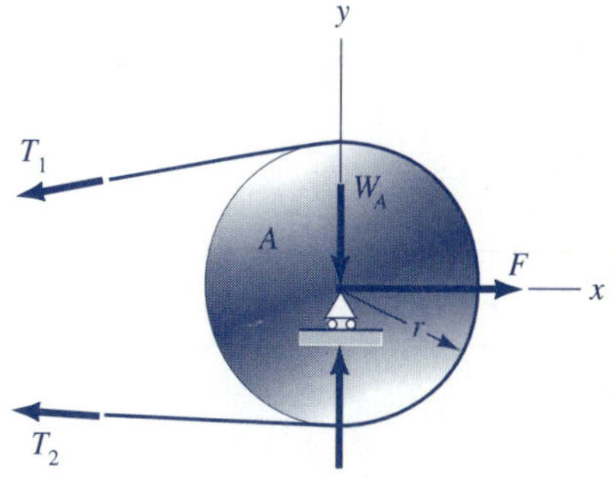

Figure 7.14. Force F affects T_1 and T_2 but not T_1/T_2.

Thus,

$$\text{torque} = T_1 r - T_2 r = (T_1 - T_2)r \tag{7.6}$$

If we pull the drum to the right without disturbing the angle of wrap, we can see from Eq. 7.5 that the tensions T_1 and T_2 must increase by the same factor to maintain the condition of impending or actual constant speed slippage. And if we call this factor H, the new tensions become HT_1 and HT_2, respectively. Substituting into Eq. 7.6, we see that the frictional torque is also increased by the same factor:

$$\text{torque} = H(T_1 - T_2)r = H(\text{torque})_{\text{original}}$$

If we sum forces on the free body diagram in Fig. 7.14, we can determine the force F needed to maintain the tensions T_1 and T_2 as follows:

$$(T_1)_x + (T_2)_x = F \tag{7.7}$$

At impending slippage or at constant speed slippage, Eq. 7.5 is valid, and with Eq. 7.7 and knowing F, we can solve for T_1 and T_2. With Eq. 7.6, the torque that the belt is capable of developing on the drum now becomes a simple computation.

Accordingly, we have three equations at our disposal. Thus, there is the geometry determining for us the angle of wrap and there is the coefficient of friction. These can be combined and used in the *first* equation [Eq. (7.5)] to get the correct *ratio* of tensions for the conditions of impending slippage or for actual slippage. Note, because of the use of *equilibrium* in the derivation of this equation, both of these conditions (impending slippage and actual slippage) require that the belt be stationary or be moving at constant speed in inertial space. These results serve as benchmarks for the design engineer, particularly the impending slippage condition. If the ratio of the belt tensions is less than $e^{\mu_s \beta}$ and the belt has not started to slip, we can say that there will be no slipping until this ratio of the belt tensions is exceeded,[4] at which time for steady speed of the belt, the ratio of the belt tensions will have to become equal to the value $e^{\mu_d \beta}$. In the *second* of the three equations [Eq. (7.6)], the torque on or from the drum is related to the belt tensions via equilibrium. Finally, the *third* equation [Eq. (7.7)], again from equilibrium, gives us the required force F on the drum needed for the aforestated torque. Note that it is desirable to get the ratio of the tensions close to the condition of impending slippage since this means a smaller F and hence a longer life for the belt. This also will mean fewer expensive stoppages for assembly lines.

[4]This is like the example given at the outset of moving a piece of furniture where, as the driving force is increased from zero, no movement occurs until the maximum static friction force has been exceeded.

Example 7.6

A drum (see Fig. 7.15) requires a torque of 200 N-m to get it to start rotating. If the static coefficient of friction μ_s between the belt and the drum is .35, what is the *minimum* axial force F on the drum required to create enough tension in the belt to start the rotation of the drum?

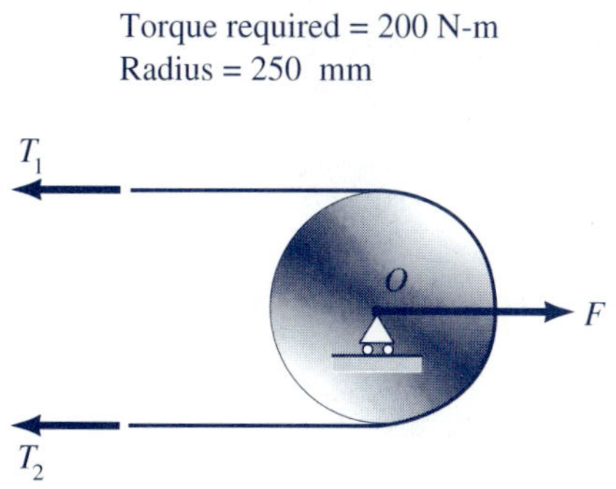

Figure 7.15. Drum is driven by a belt.

The angle of wrap β clearly is π radians. To get the minimum force F, we use the condition of impending slippage between belt and drum so that we can say

$$\frac{T_1}{T_2} = e^{.35\pi} = 3.00 \qquad \text{(a)}$$

For the condition of starting rotation we have

$$\underline{\sum M_0 = \text{torque required} = 200 \text{ N-m}}$$

$$\therefore (T_1 - T_2)(.25) = 200 \qquad \text{(b)}$$

It is now a simple matter to solve the previous two equations simultaneously to get

$$T_1 = 1{,}200 \text{ N} \qquad T_2 = 400 \text{ N}$$

Finally we can determine the minimum value of F for this problem by summing forces in the x direction as follows:

$$\underline{\sum F_x = 0:}$$

$$F_{min} = 1{,}200 + 400 = \boxed{1{,}600 \text{ N}}$$

Example 7.7

A conveyor is moving ten 50-lb boxes at a constant speed at a 45° setting (Fig. 7.16). The dynamic coefficient of friction between the belt and the bed of the conveyor is .05. Furthermore, the static coefficient of friction between the driving pulley and the belt is .4. The idler pulley is moved along the direction of the conveyor by a crank mechanism so that the idler pulley is subject to a force F of 500 lb. Compute the maximum tension found in the belt and ascertain if there will be slipping on the driving pulley. Neglect the weight of the belt.

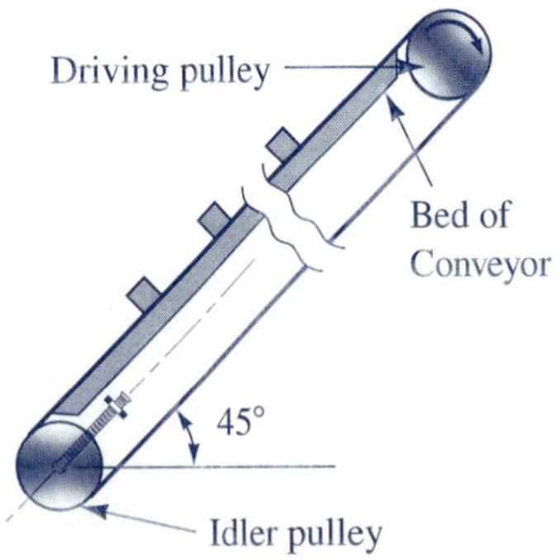

Figure 7.16. Conveyor.

In Fig. 7.17, we have shown free-body diagrams of various parts of the conveyor.[5] Consider the portion of the belt on the conveyor frame. From *equilibrium* we set the sums of forces normal and tangent to the belt equal to zero. Thus

$\underline{\sum F_n = 0:}$

$$N - (10)(50)(.707) = 0$$

Therefore,

$$N = 354 \text{ lb} \tag{a}$$

$\underline{\sum F_t = 0:}$

$$T_1 - T_3 - (10)(50)(.707) - (.05)(354) = 0$$

Therefore,

$$T_1 - T_3 = 371 \text{ lb} \tag{b}$$

[5]The weights of the pulleys have been counteracted by supporting forces at the axles and have not been shown.

Example 7.7 (Continued)

For the idler pulley (no resisting or applied torques), we have

$\underline{\sum M_0 = 0:}$

$$T_3 = T_2 \qquad \text{(c)}$$

$\underline{\sum F_t = 0:}$

$$T_3 + T_2 = 500 \qquad \text{(d)}$$

From Eqs. (c) and (d), we conclude that

$$T_2 = T_3 = 250 \text{ lb} \qquad \text{(e)}$$

From Eq. (b) we now get for the maximum tension T_1:

$$T_1 = T_3 + 371 = \boxed{621 \text{ lb}} \qquad \text{(f)}$$

We must next check the driving pulley to ensure that there is no slippage occurring. For the condition of impending slippage, we have, using as T_2 the value of 250 lb and solving for T_1

$$T_1 = T_2 e^{.4\pi} = (250)(3.51) = 878 \text{ lb}$$

Clearly, since the T_1 needed is only 621 lb (see Eq.(f)), we do not have slippage at the driving pulley, and we conclude that the maximum tension is indeed 621 lb.

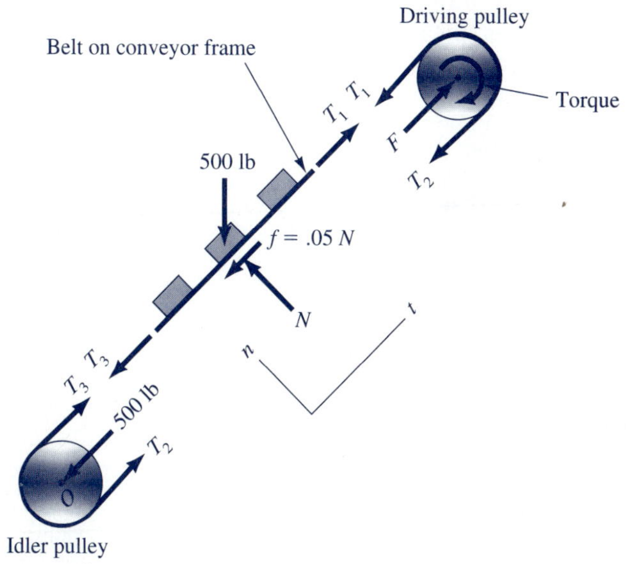

Figure 7.17. Various free-body diagrams of parts of conveyor.

Example 7.8

An electric motor (not shown) in Fig. 7.18 drives at constant speed the pulley B, which connects to pulley A by a belt. Pulley A is connected to a compressor (not shown) which requires 700 N-m torque to drive it at constant speed ω_A. If μ_s for the belt and either pulley is .4, what minimum value of the indicated force F is required to have no slipping anywhere?

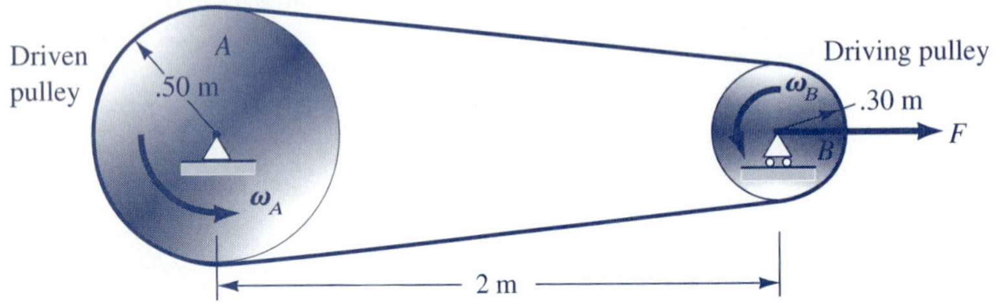

Figure 7.18. Belt-driven compressor.

As a first step, we determine the angles of wrap β for the respective pulleys. For this purpose, we first compute α (Fig. 7.19). Note that the radii O_AD and O_BE, being perpendicular to the same line DE, are therefore parallel to each other. Drawing EC parallel to O_AO_B, we then form α in the shaded triangle. Hence, we can say:

$$\alpha = \sin^{-1}\frac{CD}{CE} = \sin^{-1}\frac{r_A - r_B}{O_AO_B} = \sin^{-1}\frac{.50 - .30}{2} = 5.74°$$

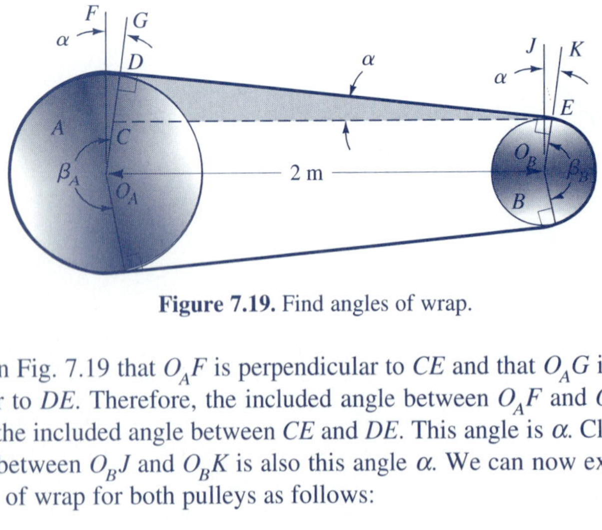

Figure 7.19. Find angles of wrap.

Note in Fig. 7.19 that O_AF is perpendicular to CE and that O_AG is perpendicular to DE. Therefore, the included angle between O_AF and O_AG must equal the included angle between CE and DE. This angle is α. Clearly, the angle between O_BJ and O_BK is also this angle α. We can now express the angles of wrap for both pulleys as follows:

$$\beta_A = 180° + 2(5.74) = 191.5°$$
$$\beta_B = 180° - 2(5.74) = 168.5°$$

Example 7.8 (Continued)

Now consider pulley A as a free body in Fig. 7.20. Note that the minimum force F corresponds to the condition of impending slippage. Accordingly, for this condition at A, we have

$$\frac{(T_1)_A}{(T_2)_A} = e^{\mu_s \beta_A} = e^{(.4)[(191.5/360)2\pi]} = 3.81 \qquad \text{(a)}$$

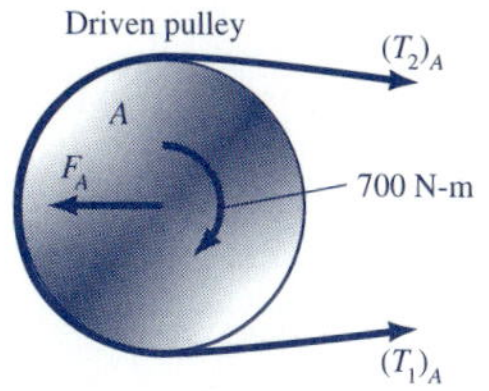

Figure 7.20. Free-body diagram of A.

Also, summing moments about the center of the pulley, we have

$$[(T_1)_A - (T_2)_A](.50) - 700 = 0 \qquad \text{(b)}$$

Therefore,

$$(T_1)_A - (T_2)_A = 1{,}400$$

Solving Eqs. (a) and (b) simultaneously, we get

$$(T_1)_A = 1{,}898 \text{ N}; \qquad (T_2)_A = 498 \text{ N}$$

From *equilibrium*, we can compute force F_A as follows:

$$(1{,}898 + 498) \cos 5.74° - F_A = 0 \qquad \text{(c)}$$

Therefore,

$$F_A = 2{,}384 \text{ N}$$

Now go to pulley B to see what minimum force F_B is needed so that the belt does not slip on it during operations. Consider in *Fig. 7.21* the free-body diagram of pulley B. For impending slipping on pulley B, we have

$$\frac{(T_1)_B}{(T_2)_B} = e^{\mu_s \beta_B} = e^{(.4)[(168.5/360)2\pi]} = 3.24 \qquad \text{(d)}$$

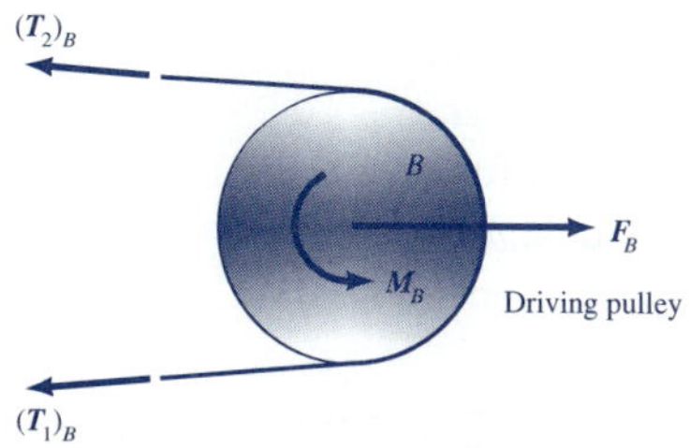

Figure 7.21. Free-body diagram of B.

Example 7.8 (Continued)

The torque for pulley B needed to develop 700 N-m on pulley A is next computed. Thus,[6]

$$M_B = \frac{r_B}{r_A} M_A = \frac{.30}{.50} M_A = \frac{.30}{.50}(700)$$

Therefore,

$$M_B = 420 \text{ N-m}$$

Summing moments in Fig. 7.21 about the center of B, we then have on using the above result

$$-[(T_1)_B - (T_2)_B](.30) + 420 = 0$$

Therefore,

$$(T_1)_B - (T_2)_B = 1{,}400 \qquad \text{(e)}$$

Solving Eqs. (d) and (e) simultaneously, we get

$$(T_1)_B = 2{,}025 \text{ N}; \qquad (T_2)_B = 625 \text{ N}$$

Hence, the minimum F_B needed for pulley B is

$$F_B = (2{,}025 + 625) \cos 5.74° = \boxed{2{,}637 \text{ N}}$$

Note that the ratios of the tensions for *impending slippage* for the two cylinders are

Driven cylinder A	$\frac{T_1}{T_2} = 3.81$	$F_A = 2{,}384$ N
Driving cylinder B	$\frac{T_1}{T_2} = 3.24$	$F_B = 2{,}637$ N

If we use impending slippage for driven cylinder A, we will have slipping for driving cylinder B, which we cannot tolerate. Thus, if we use the larger force of 2,637 N, we will be well under the impending slippage condition of the driven cylinder A. Clearly, the optimum result to *avoid slippage* and to *minimize the belt tension* for greater life of the belt is to have a force somewhere above 2,637 N. Here is a place for good engineering judgement and experience.

[6]Note that the ratio of transmitted torques M_2/M_1 between directly connected pulleys and gears will equal r_2/r_1 or D_2/D_1 of the pulleys or gears. Can you verify this yourself?

PROBLEMS

7.48. Compute the frictional resisting torque for the concentric dry thrust bearing. The coefficient of friction is taken as μ_d.

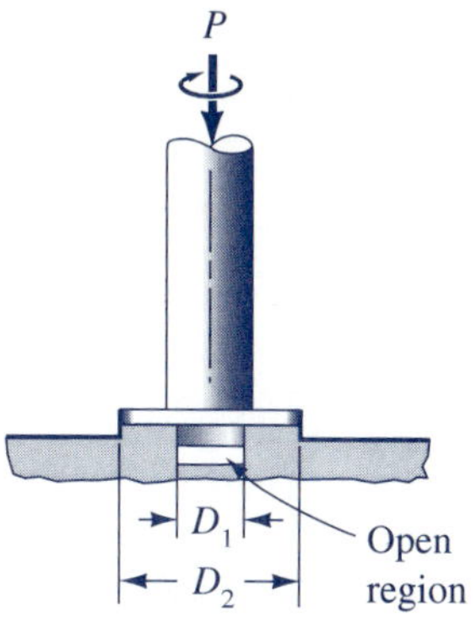

Figure P.7.48.

7.49. The support end of a dry thrust bearing is shown. Four pads form the contact surface. If a shaft creates a 100-N thrust uniformly distributed over the pads, what is the resisting torque for a dynamic coefficient of friction of .1?

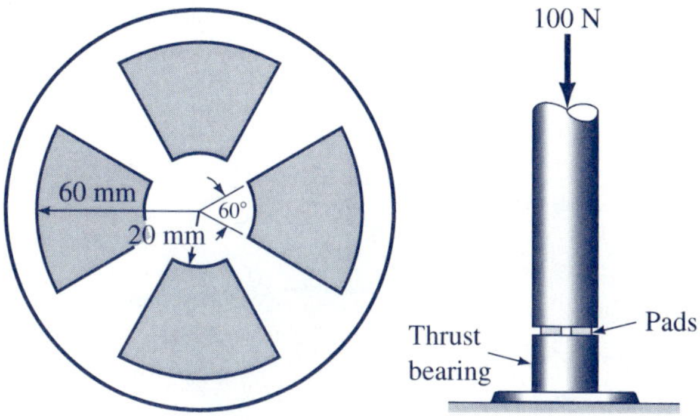

Figure P.7.49.

7.50. In Example 7.5, the normal force distribution at the contact surface is not uniform but, as a result of wear, is inversely proportional to the radius r. What, then, is the resisting torque M?

7.51. Compute the frictional torque needed to rotate the truncated cone relative to the fixed member. The cone has a 20-mm-diameter base and a 60° cone angle and is cut off 3 mm from the cone tip. The dynamic coefficient of friction is .2.

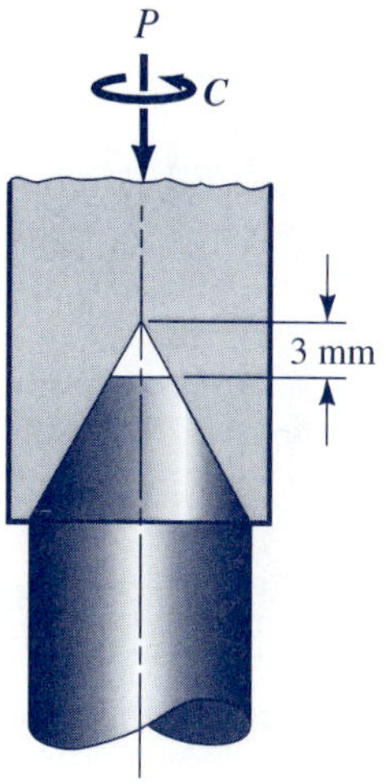

Figure P.7.51.

7.52. A 1,000-N block is being lowered down an inclined surface. The block is pinned to the incline at C, and at B a cord is played out so as to cause the body to rotate at uniform speed about C. Taking μ_d to be .3 and assuming the contact pressure is uniform along the base of the block, compute T for the configuration shown in the diagram.

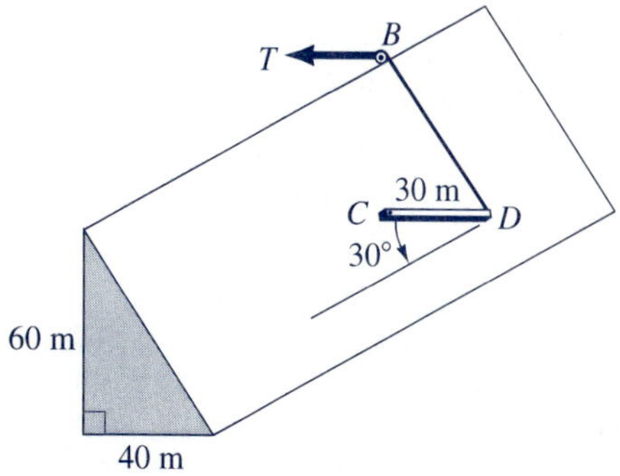

Figure P.7.52.

7.53. A thrust-bearing supports a force P of 1,000 N. Two rings of the system are in contact with the base of the system. The larger ring has a uniform pressure which is half the value of the uniform pressure on the inner ring. The shaft is rotating with an angular speed ω. If the dynamic coefficient of friction μ_d is 0.3, what is the resisting torque generated by this thrust bearing? Consider P to include the weights of the shaft and the pads attached to it.

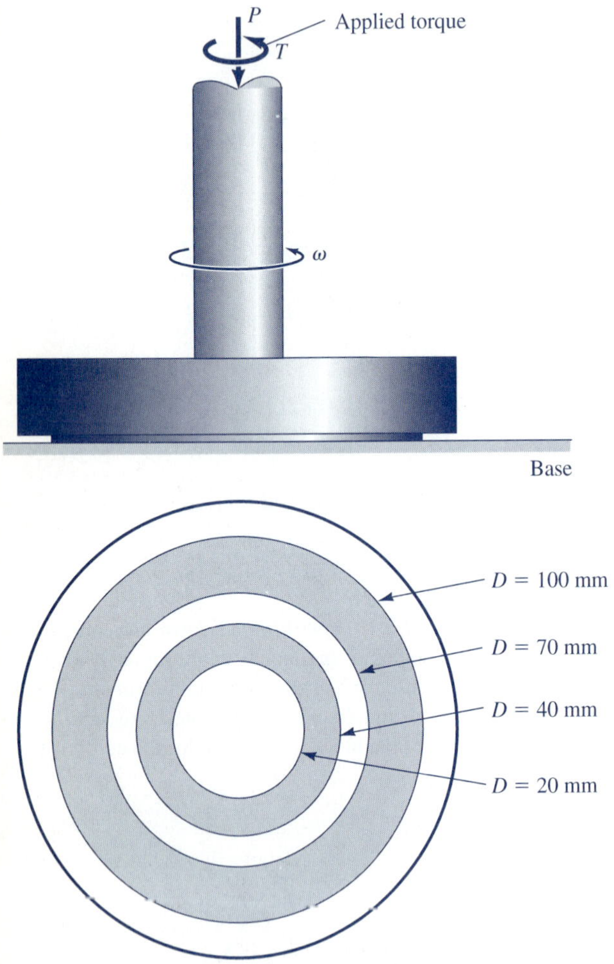

Figure P.7.53.

7.54. A shaft has three dry thrust-bearing surfaces which push, respectively, on three stationary rigid surfaces, namely rigid plates A and B and the rigid base C. The total load P coming onto the shaft including weights of all parts is 6,000 N. What is the minimal torque T needed to start rotation if the pressure on each disc contact surface is uniform for each disc but is proportional to the outside diameter squared of the disc? The static coefficient of friction between the bearing surfaces and the plates A and B as well as the base C is 0.2. The proportionality constant for pressure is the *same value* for all 3 discs. The shaft passes through A and B but is welded to the top surface of C.

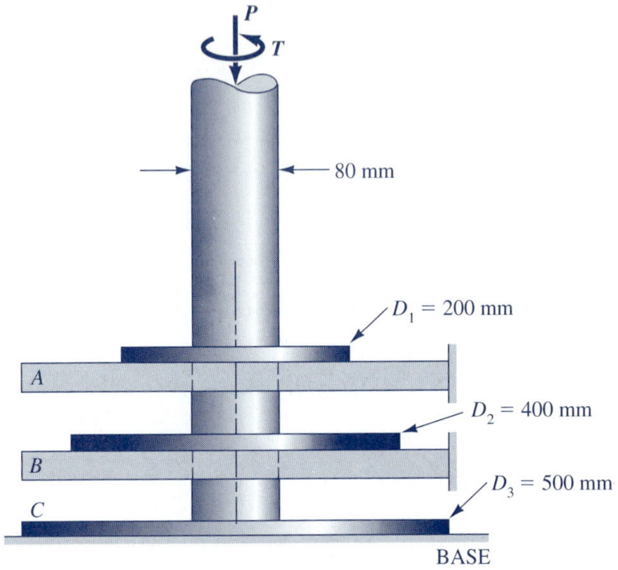

Figure P.7.54.

7.55. A pulley requires 200 N-m torque to get it rotating. μ_s is known to be .25. What is the *minimum* horizontal force F required to create enough tension in the belt so that it can rotate the pulley?

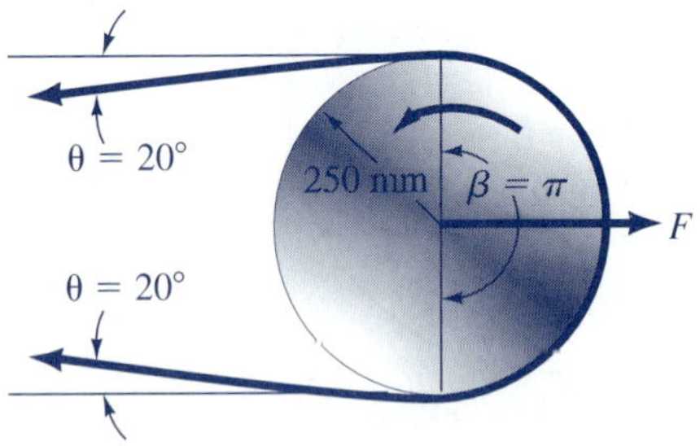

Figure P.7.55.

7.56. If in Problem 7.55, $\theta = 0$ and the belt is wrapped $2\frac{1}{2}$ times around the pulley, what is the *minimum* horizontal force F needed to rotate the pulley?

7.57. The seaman pulls with 100-N force and wants to stop the motorboat from moving away from the dock under power. How few wraps n of the rope must he make around the post if the motorboat develops 3,500 N of thrust and the static coefficient of friction between the rope and the post is .2?

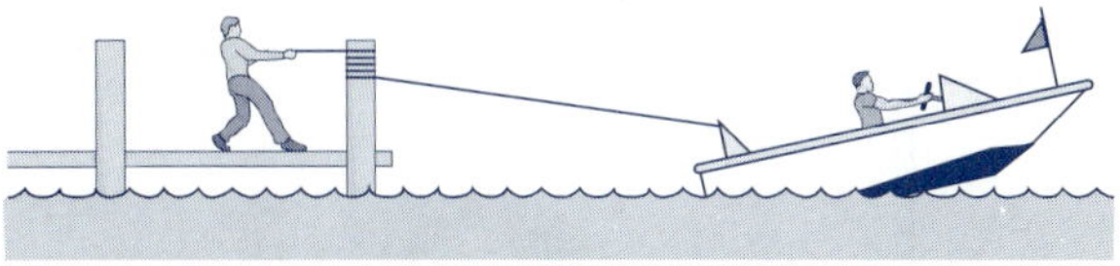

Figure P.7.57.

7.58. A length of belt rests on a flat surface and runs over a quarter of the drum. A load W rests on the horizontal portion of the belt, which in turn is supported by a table. If the static coefficient of friction for all surfaces is .3, compute the *maximum* weight W that can be moved by rotating the drum.

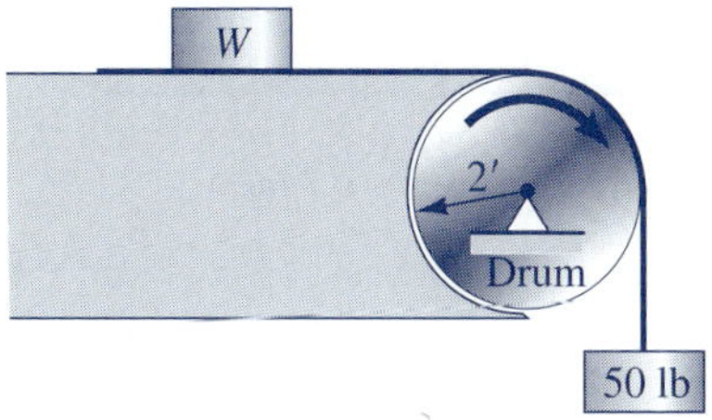

Figure P.7.58.

7.59. The rope holding the 50-lb weight E passes over the drum and is attached at A. The weight of C is 60 lb. What is the *minimum* static coefficient of friction between the rope and the drum to maintain equilibrium of the drum?

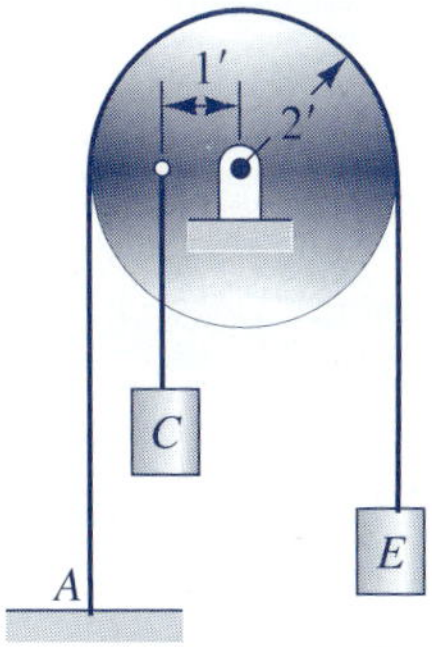

Figure P.7.59.

7.60. What is the *maximum* weight that can be supported by the system in the position shown? Pulley B *cannot* turn. Bar AC is fixed to cylinder A, which weighs 500 N. The coefficient of static friction for all contact surfaces is .3.

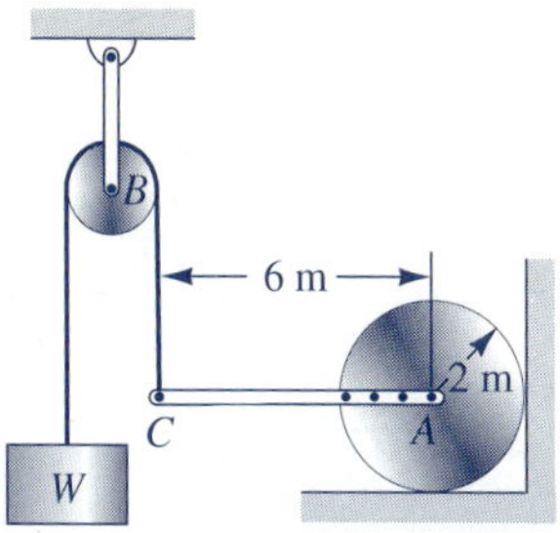

Figure P.7.60.

7.61. A mountain climber of weight W hangs freely suspended by one rope that is fastened at one end to his waist, wrapped one-half turn about a rock with μ_s = .2, and held at the other end in his hand. What *minimum* force in terms of W must he pull with to maintain his position? What minimum force must he pull the rope into himself with to gain altitude?

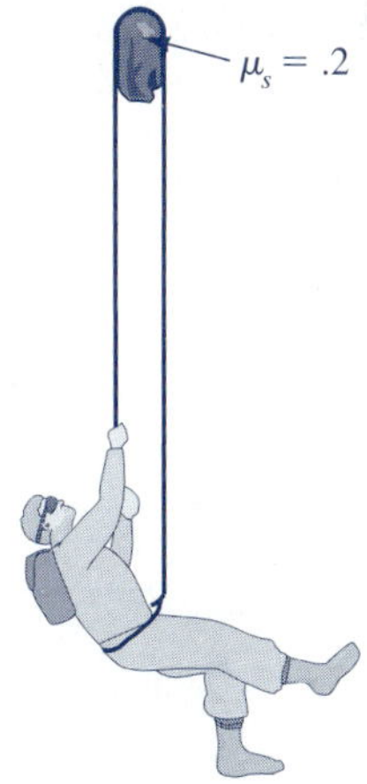

Figure P.7.61.

7.62. Pulley B is turned by a diesel engine and drives pulley A connected to a generator. If the torque that A must transmit to the generator is 500 N-m, what is the *minimum* static coefficient of friction between the belt and pulleys for the case where the force F is 2,000 N?

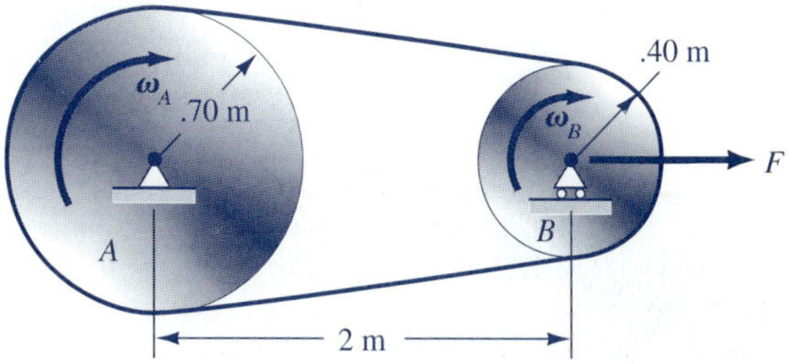

Figure P.7.62.

7.63. A hand brake is shown. If $\mu_d = .4$, what is the resisting torque when the shaft is rotating? What are the supporting forces on the rod AB.

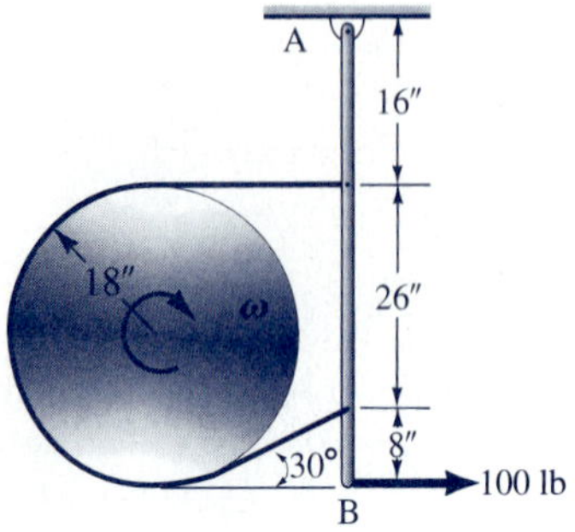

Figure P.7.63.

7.64. A conveyor is shown with two driving pulleys *A* and *B*. Driver *A* has an angle of wrap of 330°, whereas *B* has a wrap of 180°. If the dynamic coefficient of friction between the belt and the bed of the conveyor is .1, and the total weight to be transported is 10,000 N, what is the *smallest* static coefficient of friction between the belt and the driving pulleys? One-fifth of the load can be assumed to be between the two pulleys at all times, and the tension in the slack side (underneath) is 2,000 N. There is a free-wheeling pulley at the left end of the conveyor. You will have to solve an equation by trial and error.

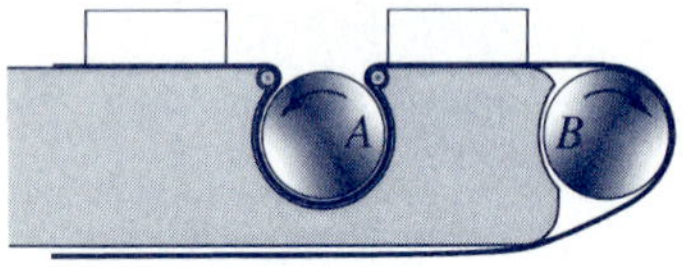

Figure P.7.64.

7.65. A freely turning idler pulley is used to increase the angle of wrap for the pulleys shown. If the tension in the slack side above is 200 lb, find the *maximum* torque that can be transmitted by the pulleys for a static coefficient of friction of .3.

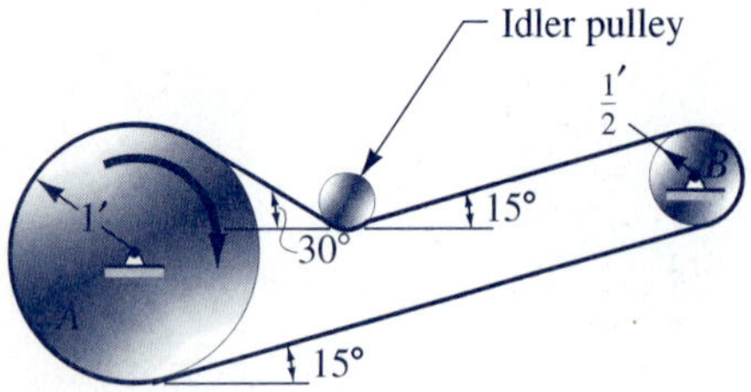

Figure P.7.65.

7.66. (a) What force *P* is needed to develop a resisting torque of 65 N-m on the rotating drum? The dynamic coefficient of friction μ_d is 0.4.

(b) With the same force *P* from part (a), what must the value of μ_d be in order to increase the resisting torque by 10 N-m?

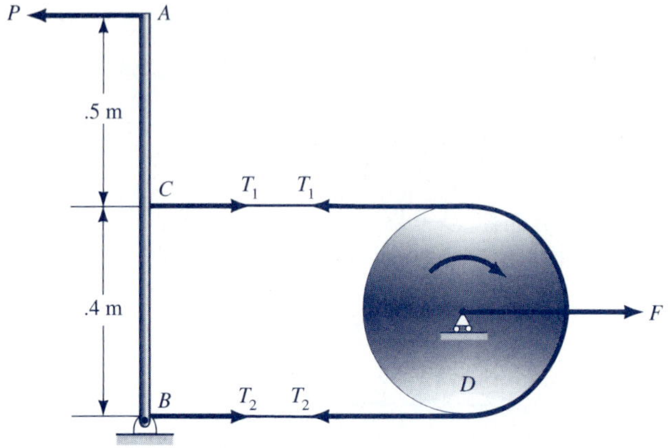

Figure P.7.66.

7.67. What is the maximum value of axial load *P* to maintain a rotational speed $\omega = 5$ rad/s of the dry thrust bearing? The sum of the belt forces is 200 N. The contact surface between the belt and drum and between the dry thrust bearing and base have the same μ_s and μ_d of .4 and .3, respectively.

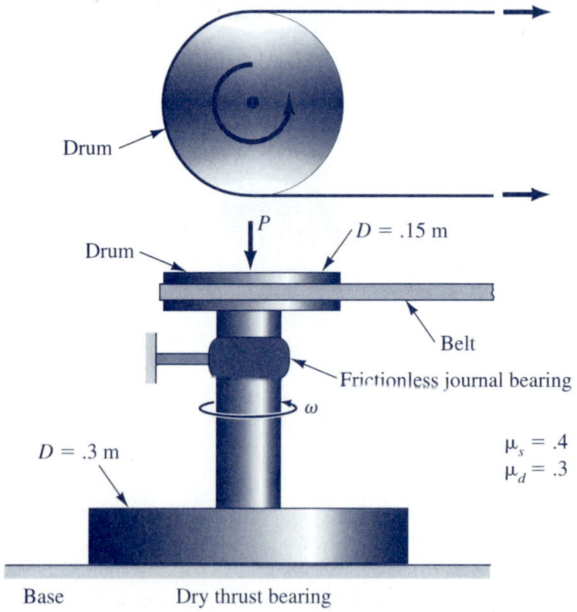

Figure P.7.67.

7.68. Rod *AB* weighing 200 N is supported by a cable wrapped around a semicylinder having a coefficient of friction μ_s equal to .2. A weight *C* having a mass of 10 kg can slide on rod *AB*. What is the maximum range *x* from the centerline that the center of *C* can be placed without causing slippage?

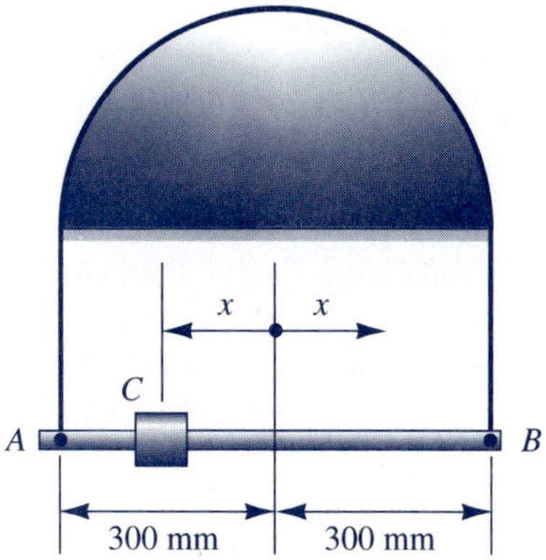

Figure P.7.68.

7.69. The cable mechanism shown is similar to that used to move the station indicator on a radio. If the indicator jams, what force is developed at the indicator base to free the jam when the required torque applied to the turning nob is 10 lb-in? Also, what are the forces in the various regions of the cable? The static coefficient of friction is .15.

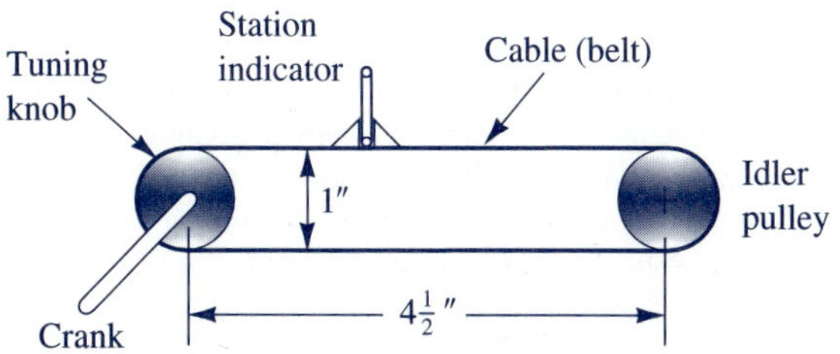

Figure P.7.69.

7.70. What are the *minimum* possible supporting force components needed for pulley *B* as a result of the action of the belt? The static coefficient of friction between the belt and pulley *B* is .3 and between the belt and pulley *A* is .4. The torque that the belt delivers to *A* is 200 N-m.

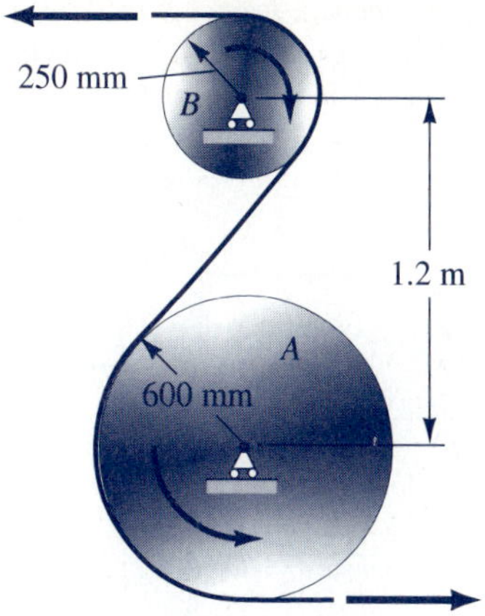

Figure P.7.70.

7.71. From first principles, show that the normal force per unit length, *w*, acting on a drum from a belt is given as

$$w = \frac{T_2}{r} e^{\mu\theta}$$

Use the indicated diagram as an aid. [*Hint:* Start with Eq. 7.2(a) and use Eq. 7.4 for any point *a*.]

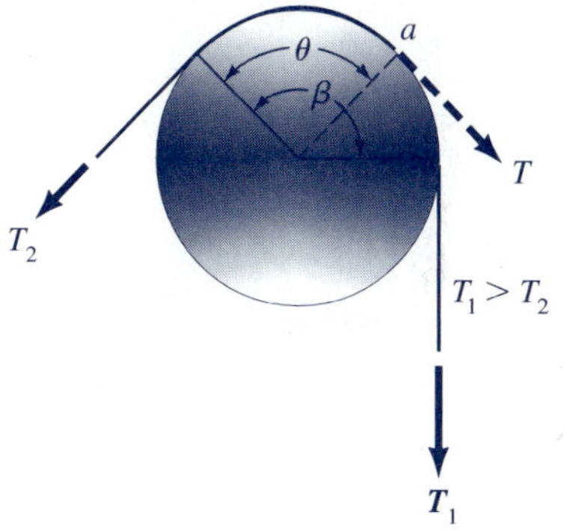

Figure P.7.71.

7.72. What *minimum* force *F* is needed so that drum *A* can transmit a clockwise torque of 500 N-m without slipping? The coefficient of friction, μ_s, between *A* and the belt is .4. What *minimum* coefficient of static friction is needed between drum *B* and belt for no slipping?

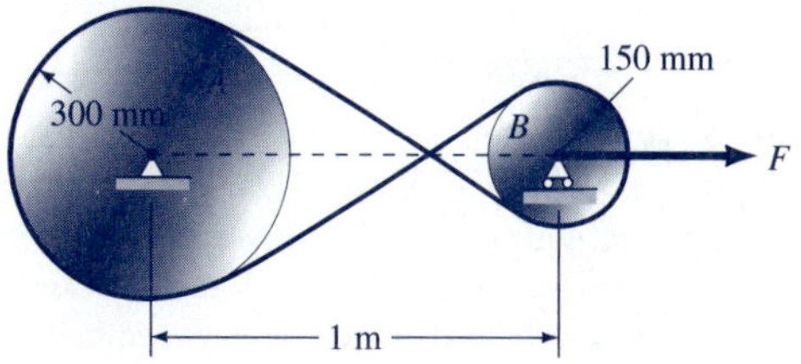

Figure P.7.72.

7.73. What is the *minimum* weight B that will prevent rotation induced by body C weighing 500 N? The weight of A is 100 N. The static coefficient of friction between the belts and A is .4, and between A and the walls is .1. Neglect friction at pulley G.

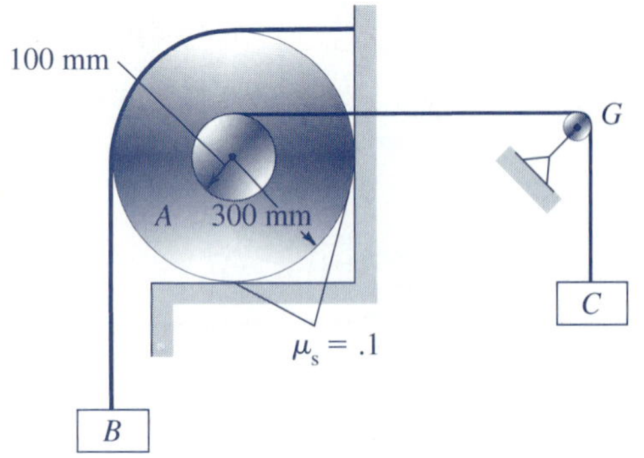

Figure P.7.73.

7.74. A V-belt is shown. Show that

$$\frac{T_1}{T_2} = e^{\mu_s \beta / \sin(\alpha/2)}$$

for impending slippage. Use a development analogous to that of the flat belt in Section 7.6.

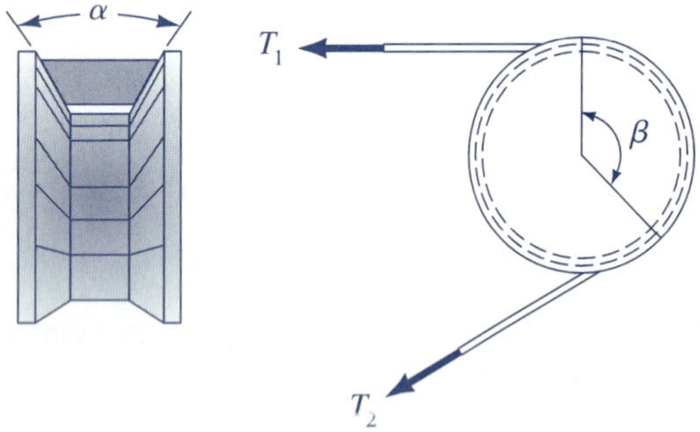

Figure P.7.74.

7.75. An electric motor drives a pulley B, which drives three V-belts having the cross-section shown. These V-belts then drive a compressor through pulley A. If the torque needed to drive the compressor is 1,000 N-m, what *minimum* force F is needed to do the job? The static coefficient of friction between belts and pulleys is .5. See Problem 7.74 before doing this problem.

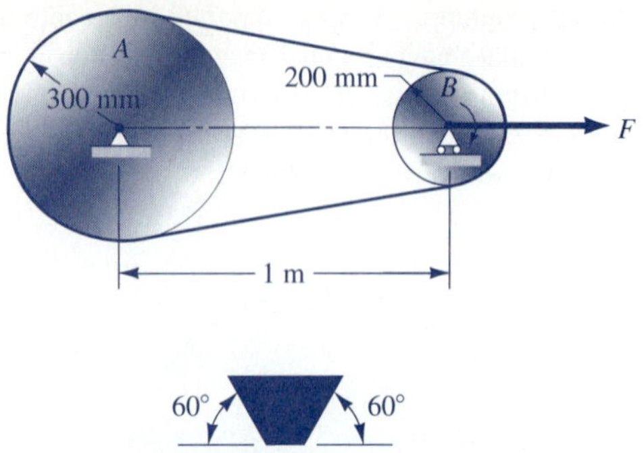

Figure P.7.75.

7.76. A drum of radius r is rotated by a belt with a constant speed ω rad/sec. What is the relation between T_1 and T_2 for the case of impending slipping between drum and belt if *centrifugal* effects are accounted for? The belt has a mass per unit length of m kg/m. Recall from physics that the centrifugal force of a particle of mass M is $Mr\omega^2$, where r is the distance from the axis of rotation. Assume the belt is thin compared to the radius of the drum. The desired result is

$$\frac{T_1 - r^2\omega^2 m}{T_2 - r^2\omega^2 m} = e^{\mu_s \beta}$$

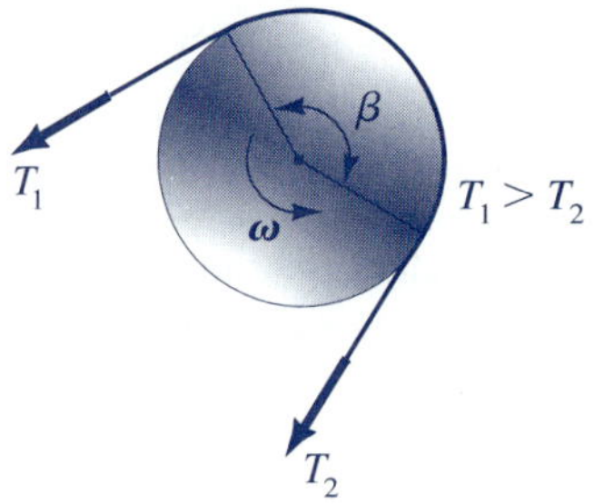

Figure P.7.76.

7.77. A pulley A is driven by an outside agent at a speed ω of 100 rpm. A belt weighing 30 N/m is driven by the pulley. If $T_2 = 200$ N, what is the *maximum* possible tension T_1 computed without considering centrifugal effects? Compute T_1 accounting for centrifugal effects, and give the percentage error incurred by not including centrifugal effects. The static coefficient of friction between the belt and the pulley is .3. See Problem 7.76 before doing this problem.

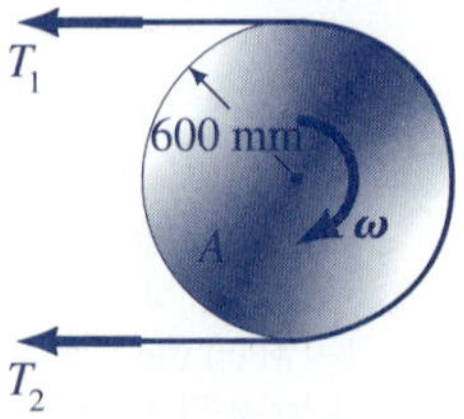

Figure P.7.77.

7.7 The Square Screw Thread

We shall now consider the action of a nut on a screw that has square threads (Fig. 7.22). Let us take r as the mean radius from the centerline of the screw to the thread. The *pitch*, p, is the distance along the screw between adjacent threads, and the *lead*, L, is the distance that a nut will advance in the direction of the axis of the screw in one revolution. For screw threads that are single-threaded, L equals p. For an n-threaded screw, the lead L is np.

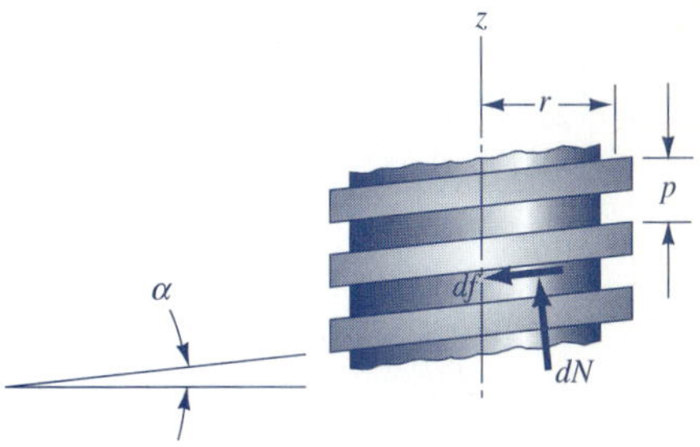

Figure 7.22. Square screw thread.

Forces are transmitted from screw to nut over several revolutions of thread, and hence we have a distribution of normal and friction forces. However, because of the narrow width of the thread, we may consider the distribution to be confined at a distance r from the centerline, thus forming a "loading" strip winding around the centerline of the screw. Figure 7.22 illustrates infinitesimal normal and frictional forces on an infinitesimal part of the strip. The local slope $\tan\alpha$ as one looks in radially is determined by considering the definition of L, the lead. Thus,

$$\text{slope} = \tan\alpha = \frac{L}{2\pi r} = \frac{np}{2\pi r}$$

All elements of the proposed distribution have the same inclination (direction cosine) relative to the z direction. In the summation of forces in this direction, therefore, we can consider the distribution to be replaced by a single normal force N and a single friction force f at the inclinations shown in Fig. 7.23 at a position anywhere along the thread. And, since the elements of the distribution have the same moment arm about the centerline in addition to the common inclination, we may use the concentrated forces mentioned above in taking moments about the centerline. There is thus a "limited equivalence" between N and f and the force distribution from the nut onto the screw. The other forces on the screw will be considered as an axial load P and a torque M_z collinear with P (Fig. 7.23). For equilibrium at a condition of *impending motion* to raise the screw, we then have the following scalar equations:[7]

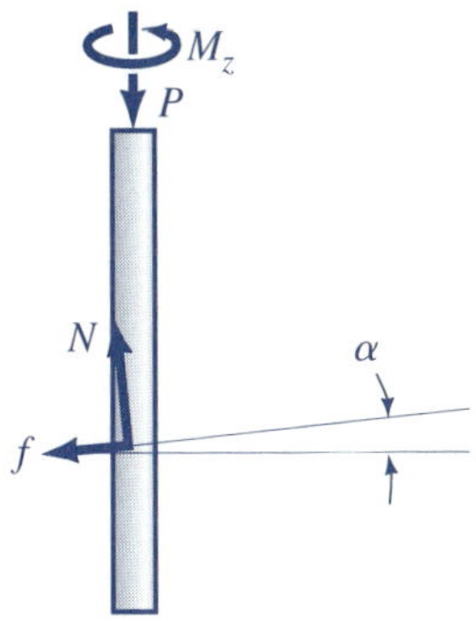

Figure 7.23. Free-body diagram.

$\underline{\sum F_z = 0:}$

$$-P + N\cos\alpha - \mu_s N\sin\alpha = 0 \qquad \text{(a)}$$

$\underline{\sum M_z = 0:}$

$$-\mu_s N\cos\alpha\, r - N\sin\alpha\, r + M_z = 0 \qquad \text{(b)}$$

[7]The equations also apply to *steady rotation* of the nut on the screw, in which case one uses the dynamic coefficient of friction μ_d in the equations.

These equations may be used to eliminate the force N and so get a relation between P and M_z that will be of practical significance. This may readily be done by solving for N in (a) and substituting into (b). The result is

$$M_z = \frac{Pr(\mu_s \cos\alpha + \sin\alpha)}{\cos\alpha - \mu_s \sin\alpha} \tag{7.8}$$

An important question arises when we employ the screw and nut in the form of a jack as shown in Fig. 7.24. Once having raised a load P by applying the torque M_z to the jackscrew, does the device maintain the load at the raised position when the applied torque is released, or does the screw unwind under the action of the load and thus lower the load? In other words, is this a *self-locking* device? To examine this, we go back to the equations of equilibrium. Setting $M_z = 0$ and changing the direction of the friction forces, we have the condition for impending "unwinding" of the screw. Eliminating N from the equations, we get

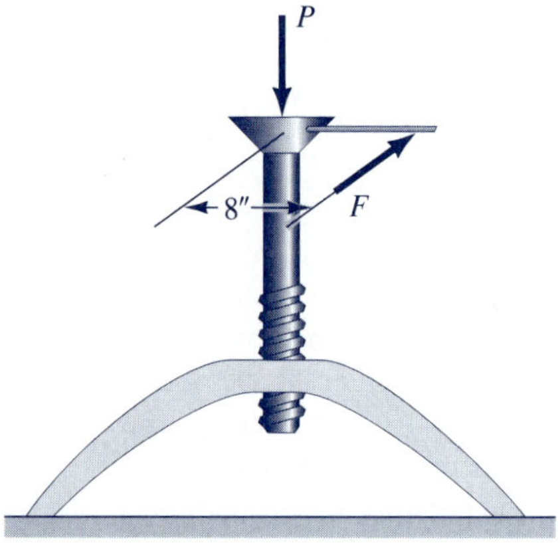

Figure 7.24. Jackscrew.

$$\frac{Pr(-\mu_s \cos\alpha + \sin\alpha)}{\cos\alpha + \mu_s \sin\alpha} = 0$$

This requires that

$$-\mu_s \cos\alpha + \sin\alpha = 0$$

Therefore,

$$\mu_s = \tan\alpha \tag{7.9}$$

We can conclude that, if the coefficient of friction μ_s equals or exceeds $\tan\alpha$, we will have a self-locking condition. If μ_s is less than $\tan\alpha$, the screw will unwind and will not support a load P without the proper external torque.

Example 7.9

A jackscrew with a double thread of mean diameter 2 in. is shown in Fig. 7.24. The pitch is .2 in. If a force F of 40 lb is applied to the device, what load W can be raised? With this load on the device, what will happen if the applied force F is released? Take $\mu_s = .3$ for the surfaces of contact.

The applied torque M_z is clearly:

$$M_z = \tfrac{8}{12}(40) = 26.7 \text{ lb-ft} \tag{a}$$

The angle α for this screw is given as

$$\tan\alpha = \frac{(2)(.2)}{(2\pi)(1)} = .0636 \tag{b}$$

Therefore,

$$\alpha = 3.64°$$

Using Eq. 7.8 we can solve for P. Thus,

$$\begin{aligned} P &= \frac{M_z(\cos\alpha - \mu_s \sin\alpha)}{r(\mu_s\cos\alpha + \sin\alpha)} \\ &= \frac{(26.7)[.998 - (.3)(.0635)]}{\frac{1}{12}[(.3)(.998) + .0635]} = \boxed{864 \text{ lb}} \end{aligned} \tag{c}$$

The load W is 864 lb. The device is self-locking since μ_s exceeds $\tan\alpha = .0636$.

$$\boxed{\mu_s > \tan\alpha \quad \therefore \text{ self-locking}}$$

To lower the load requires a reverse torque. We may readily compute this torque by using Eq. 7.8 with the friction forces reversed. Thus,

$$(M_z)_{\text{down}} = \frac{864(\frac{1}{12})[-(.3)(.998) + .0635]}{.998 + (.3)(.0635)} = -16.71 \text{ lb-ft} \tag{d}$$

*7.8 Rolling Resistance

Let us now consider the situation where a hard roller moves without slipping along a horizontal surface while supporting a load W at the center. Since we know from experience that a horizontal force P is required to maintain uniform motion, some sort of resistance must be present. We can understand this resistance if we examine the deformation shown in an exaggerated manner in

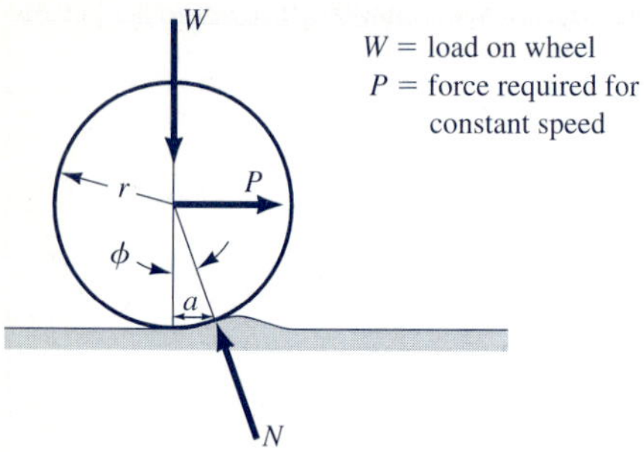

Figure 7.25. Rolling resistance model.

Fig. 7.25. If force P is along the centerline as shown, the equivalent force system coming onto the roller from the region of contact must be that of a force N whose line of action also goes through the center of the roller since, you will recall from Chapter 5, three nonparallel forces must be concurrent for equilibrium. In order to develop a resistance to motion, clearly N must be oriented at an angle ϕ with the vertical direction, as is shown in Fig. 7.25. The scalar equations of *equilibrium* become

$$W = N \cos \phi; \qquad P = N \sin \phi$$

Therefore,

$$\frac{P}{W} = \tan \phi \tag{7.10}$$

Since the area of contact is small, we note that ϕ is a small angle and that $\tan \phi \approx \sin \phi$. The $\sin \phi$ is seen to be a/r from Fig. 7.25. Therefore, we may say that

$$\frac{P}{W} = \frac{a}{r} \tag{7.11a}$$

Solving for P, we get

$$P = \frac{Wa}{r} \tag{7.11b}$$

The distance a in these equations is called the *coefficient of rolling resistance*.

Coulomb suggested that for *variable* loads W, the ratio P/W is constant for given materials and a given geometry (r = constant). Looking at Eq. 7.11a, we see that a must then be a constant for given geometry and materials. Coulomb added that, for given materials and *variable* radius, the ratio P/W varies inversely as r; that is, as the radius of the cylinder is increased, the resistance to uniform motion for a given load W decreases. Thus, considering Eq. 7.11a again, we may conclude that, for given materials, a is also constant for all sizes of rollers and loads. However, other investigators have contested both statements, particularly the latter one, and there is a need for further investigation in this area. Lacking better data, we present the following list of rolling coefficients for your use, but we must caution that you should not expect great accuracy from this general procedure.

Coefficients of Rolling Resistance

	a (in.)
Steel on steel	.007 – .015
Steel on wood	.06 – .10
Pneumatic tires on smooth road	.02 – .03
Pneumatic tires on mud road	.04 – .06
Hardened steel on hardened steel	.0002 – .0005

Example 7.10

What is the rolling resistance of a railroad freight car weighing 100 tons? The wheels have a diameter of 30 in. The coefficient of rolling resistance between wheel and track is .001 in. Compare the resistance to that of a truck and trailer having the same total weight and with tires having a diameter of 4 ft. The coefficient of rolling resistance *a* between the truck tires and road is .025 in.

We can use Eq. 7.11b directly for the desired results. Thus, for the railroad freight car, we have[8]

$$P_1 = \frac{(100)(2{,}000)(.001)}{15} = \boxed{13.33 \text{ lb}} \qquad \text{(a)}$$

For the truck, we get

$$P_2 = \frac{(100)(2{,}000)(.025)}{24} = \boxed{208 \text{ lb}} \qquad \text{(b)}$$

We see a decided differences between the two vehicles, with clear advantage toward the railroad freight car.

[8]The number of wheels n plays no role here since we divide the load by n to get the load per wheel and then multiply by n to get the total resistance.

PROBLEMS

7.78. A simple C-clamp is used to hold two pieces of metal together. The clamp has a single square thread with a pitch of . 12 in. and a mean diameter of .75 in. The static coefficient of friction is .30. Find the torque required if a 1,000-lb compressive load is required on the blocks. If the thread is a double thread, what is the required torque?

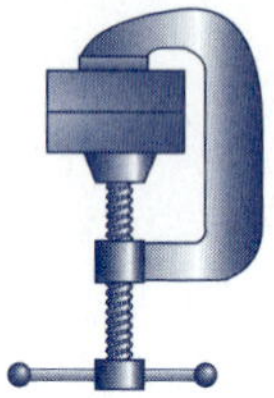

Figure P.7.78.

7.79. The mast of a sailboat is held by wires called shrouds, as shown in the diagram. Racing sailors are careful to get the proper tension in the shrouds by adjusting the turnbuckle at the bottom of the shrouds. When we do this we say we are "tuning" the boat. If a tension of 150 N exists in the shroud, what torque is needed to start tightening further by turning the turnbuckle? The pitch of the single threaded screw is 1.5 mm and the mean diameter is 8.0 mm. The static coefficient of friction is .2.

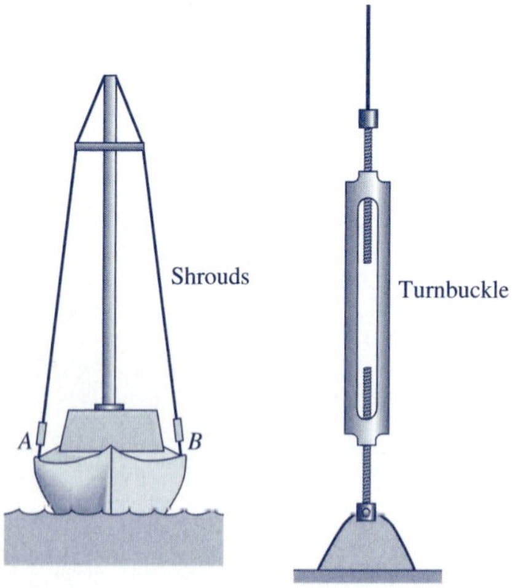

Figure P.7.79.

7.80. Forces F of 50 lb are applied to the jackscrew shown. The thread diameter is 2 in. and the pitch is $\frac{1}{2}$ in. The static coefficient of friction for the thread is .05. The weight W and collar are not permitted to rotate and so the collar must rotate on the shaft of the screw. If the static coefficient of friction between the collar and shaft is .1, determine the weight W that can be lifted by this system.

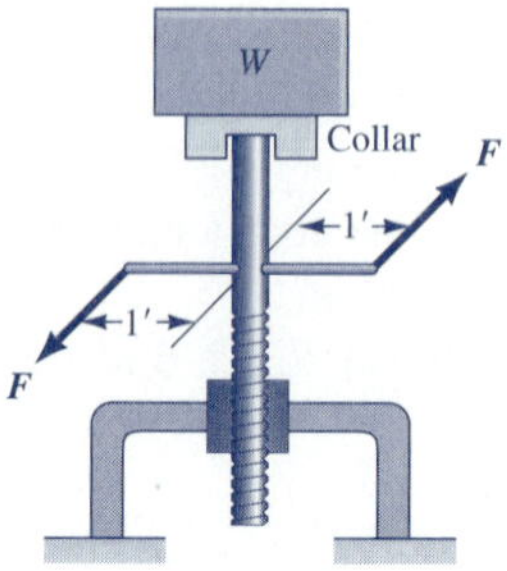

Figure P.7.80.

7.81. A brake is shown. Force is developed at the brake shoes by turning A, which has a single right-handed square screw thread at B and a single left-handed screw thread at C. The diameter of the screw thread is $1\frac{1}{2}$ in. and the pitch is .3 in. If the static coefficient of friction is .1 for the thread and the dynamic coefficient of friction is .4 for the brake shoes, what resisting torque is developed on the wheel by a 100 in.-lb torque at A?

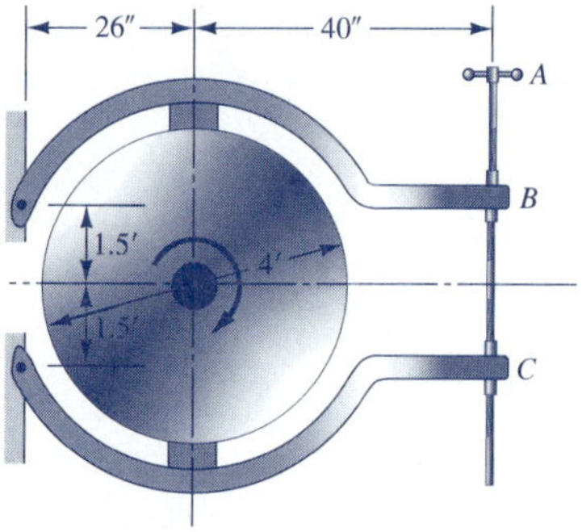

Figure P.7.81.

7.82. A triangular-threaded screw is shown. In a manner paralleling the development of the square-thread formulation in Section 7.7, show that

$$M_z = \frac{rP(\mu_s \cos\alpha + \cos\theta \tan\alpha)}{\cos\theta - \mu_s \sin\alpha}$$

where

$$\cos\theta = \frac{1}{\sqrt{\tan^2\alpha + \tan^2\gamma + 1}}$$

and

$$\gamma = \beta - \alpha$$

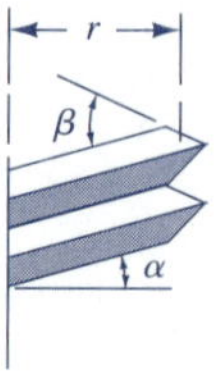

Figure P.7.82.

7.83. Consider a single-threaded screw where the pitch $p = 4.5$ mm and the mean radius is 20 mm. For a coefficient of friction $\mu_s = .3$, what torque is needed on the nut for it to turn under a load of 1,000 N? Compute this for a square thread and then do it for a triangular thread where the angle β is 30°. See Problem 7.82 before doing this problem.

7.84. If the coefficient of rolling resistance of a cylinder on a flat surface is .05 in., at what inclination of the surface will the cylinder of radius $r = 1$ ft roll with uniform velocity?

7.85. A 65-kN vehicle designed for polar expeditions is on a very slippery ice surface for which the static coefficient of friction between tires and ice is .005. Also, the coefficient of rolling resistance is known to be .8 mm. Will the vehicle be able to move? The vehicle has four-wheel drive.

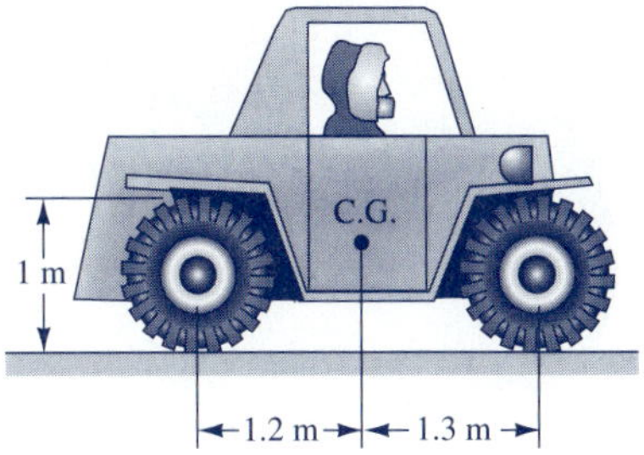

Figure P.7.85.

7.86. In Problem 7.85, suppose there is only rear-wheel drive available. What is the minimum static coefficient of friction needed between tires and ground for the vehicle to move?

7.87. A roller thrust bearing is shown supporting a force P of 2.5 kN. What torque T is need to turn the shaft A at constant speed if the only resistance is that from the ball bearings? The coefficient of rolling resistance for the balls and the bearing surfaces is .01270 mm. The mean radius from the centerline of the shaft to the balls is 30 mm.

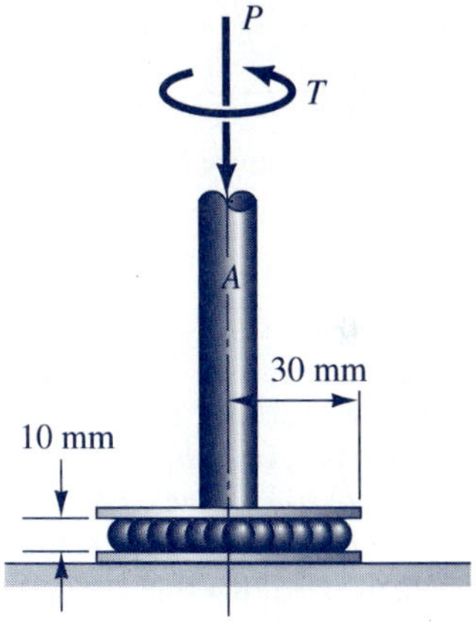

Figure P.7.87.

7.9 Closure

In this chapter, we have examined the results of two independent experiments: that of impending or actual sliding of one body over another and that of a cylinder or sphere rolling at constant speed over a flat surface. Without any theoretical basis, the results of such experiments must be used in situations that closely parallel the experiments themselves.

In the case of a rolling cylinder, both rolling resistance and sliding resistance are present. However, for a cylinder accelerating with any appreciable magnitude, only sliding friction need be accounted for. With no acceleration on a horizontal surface, only rolling resistance need be considered. Most situations fall into these categories. For very small accelerations, both effects are present and must be taken into account. We can then expect only a crude result for such computations.

Before going further, we must carefully define certain properties of plane surfaces in order to facilitate later computations in mechanics where such properties are most useful. These plane surface properties and other related topics will be studied in Chapter 8.

PROBLEMS

7.88. If the static coefficient of friction for all surfaces is .35, find the force F needed to start the 200-N weight moving to the right.

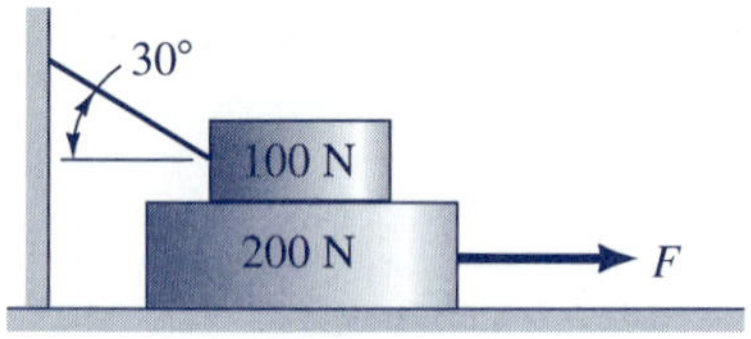

Figure P.7.88.

7.89. A loaded crate is shown. The crate weighs 500 lb with a center of gravity at its geometric center. The contact surface between crate and floor has a static coefficient of friction of .2. If $\theta = 90°$, show that the crate will slide before one can increase T enough for tipping to occur. If a stop is to be inserted in the floor at A to prevent slipping so that the crate could be tipped, what *minimum* horizontal force will be exerted on the stop?

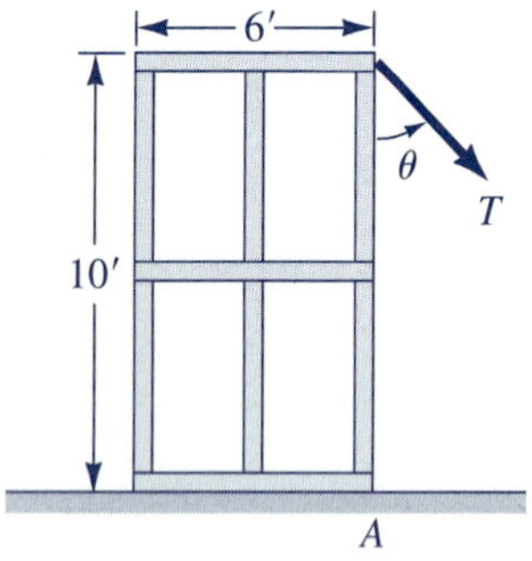

Figure P.7.89.

7.90. In Problem 7.89, compute a value of θ and T where slipping and tipping will occur simultaneously. If the actual angle θ is smaller than this value of θ, is there any further need of the stop at A to prevent slipping?

7.91. A friction drive is shown with A the driver disc and B the driven disc. If force F pressing B onto A is 150 N, what is the *maximum* torque M_2 that can be developed? For this torque, what is the torque M_1 needed for the drive disc A? The static coefficient of friction between A and B is .7. What vertical force must rod G withstand for the action described above?

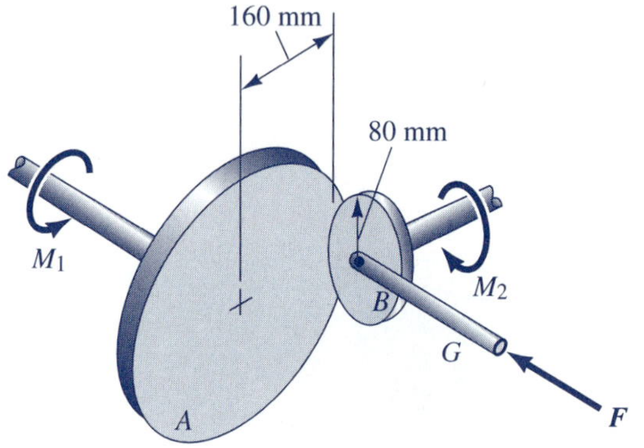

Figure P.7.91.

7.92. Determine the weight of block A for impending motion to the right. The static coefficient of friction between the cable and the surfaces which it contacts is 0.2. The static coefficient of friction between block A and the surface upon which it rests is 0.4. The two posts are circular with a diameter of 0.25 m.

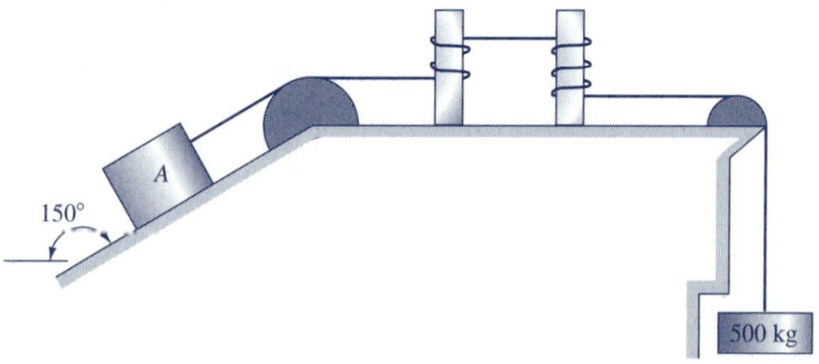

Figure P.7.92.

7.93. Do Problem 7.92 for impending slippage of body A to the left.

7.94. A tug is pushing a barge into a berth. After the barge turns clockwise and touches the sides of the pilings, what thrust must the tug develop to move it at uniform speed of 2 knots farther into the berth? The dynamic coefficient of friction between the barge and the sides of the berth is .4. The drag from the water is 3,000 N along the centerline of the barge.

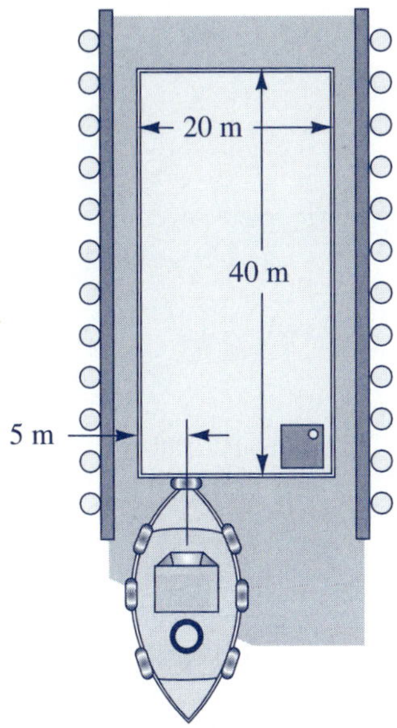

Figure P.7.94.

7.95. The static and dynamic coefficients of friction for the upper surface of contact A of the cylinder are $\mu_s = .4$, $\mu_d = .3$, and for the lower surface of contact B are $\mu_s = .1$ and $\mu_d = .08$. What is the *minimum* force P needed to just get the cylinder moving?

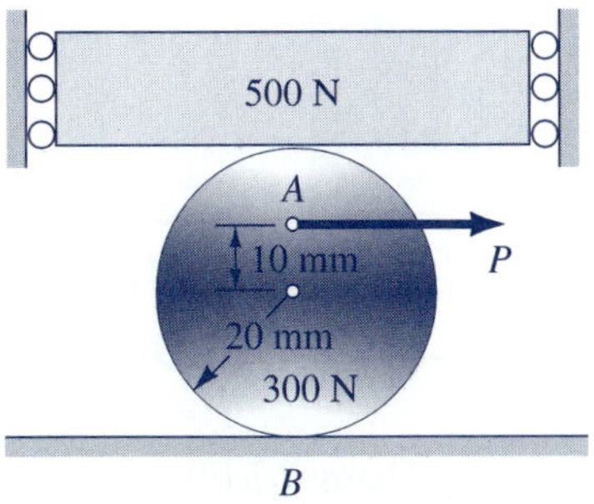

Figure P.7.95.

7.96. The drum is driven by a motor with a maximum torque capability of 500 lb-ft. The static coefficient of friction between the drum and the braking strap (belt) is .4. How much force P must an operator exert to stop the drum if it rotates (1) clockwise and (2) counterclockwise? What are the belt forces in each case?

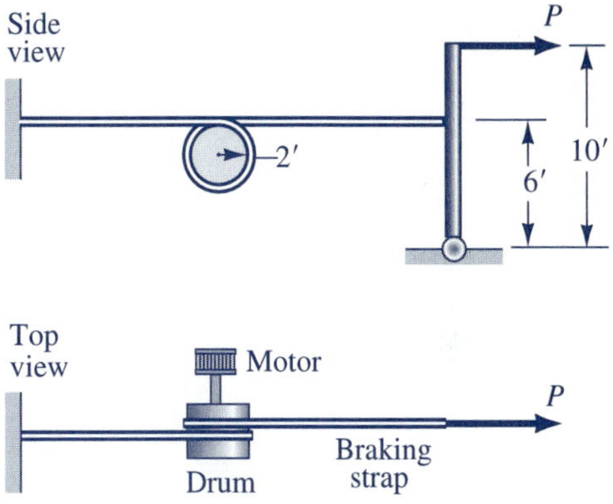

Figure P.7.96.

7.97. The four drive pulleys shown are used to transmit a torque from pulley A to pulley D on an electric typewriter. If the static coefficient of friction between the belts and the pulleys is .3, what is the torque available at pulley D if 10 lb-in. of torque is input to the shaft of pulley A? What are the belt forces?

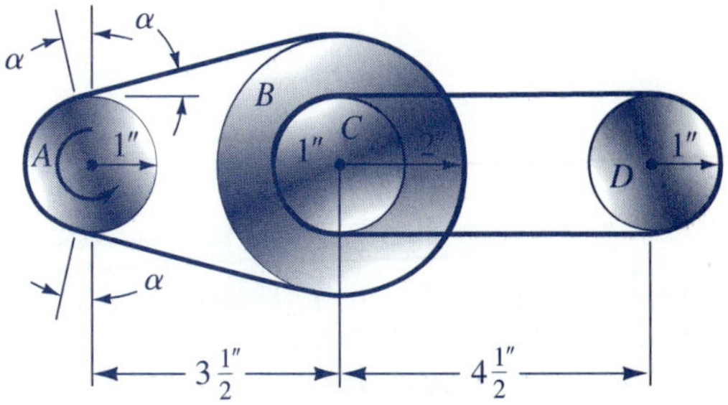

Figure P.7.97.

7.98. A scissors jack is shown lifting the end of a car so that R = 6.67 kN. What torque T is needed for this operation? Note that A is merely a bearing and at B we have a nut. The screw is single-threaded with a pitch of 3 mm and a mean diameter of 20 mm. The static coefficient of friction between the screw and nut at B is .3. Neglect the weight of the members and evaluate T for $\theta = 45°$ and for $\theta = 60°$.

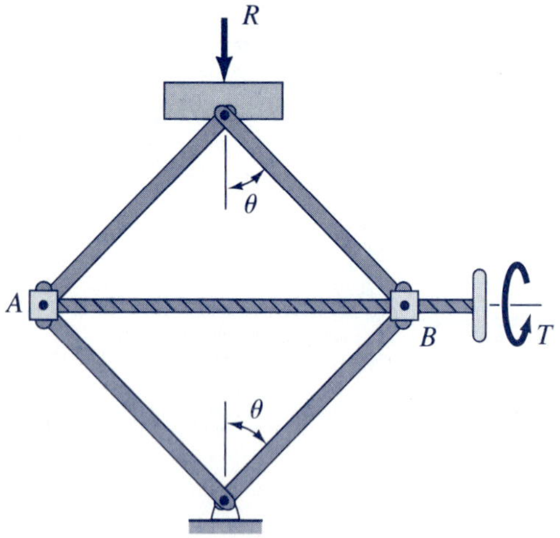

Figure P.7.98.

7.99. A block C weighing 10 kN is being moved on rollers A and B each weighing 1 kN. What force P is needed to maintain steady motion? Take the coefficient of rolling resistance between the rollers and the ground to be .6 mm and between block C and the rollers to be .4 mm.

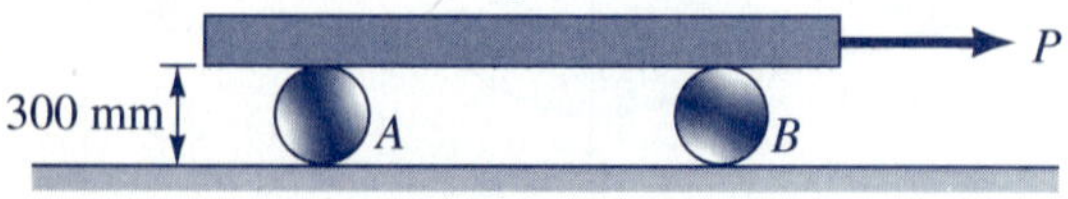

Figure P.7.99.

7.100. A hot rectangular metal ingot is to be flattened by passing through cylindrical rollers. If the ingot is to be drawn into the rollers by friction once it touches the rollers, what is the *minimum* thickness t of the ingot that can be achieved by this process on one pass? The static coefficient of friction for the contact between ingot and cylinder is .3. The cylinders rotate as shown with angular speed ω.

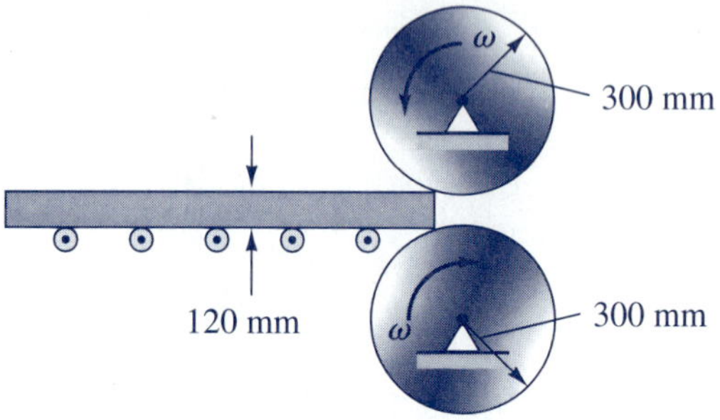

Figure P.7.100.

7.101. A cone clutch is shown. Assuming that uniform pressures exist between the contact surfaces, compute the *maximum* torque that can be transmitted. The static coefficient of friction is .30 and the activating force F is 100 lb. [*Hint:* Assume that the moving cone transmits its 100-lb axial force to the stationary cone by pressure primarily. That is, we will neglect the friction-force component on the cone surface normal to the transverse direction.]

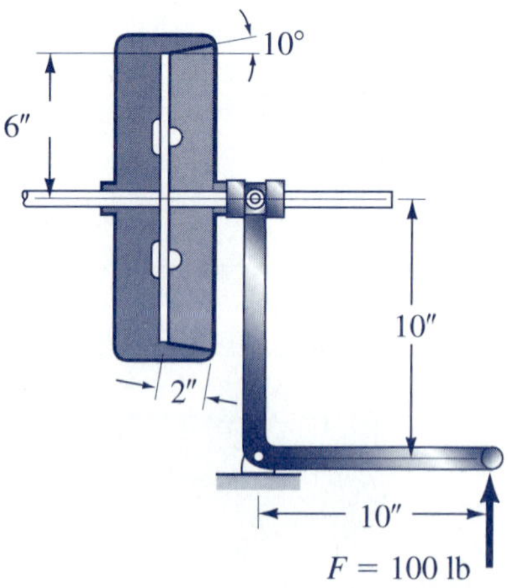

Figure P.7.101.

7.102. In Fig. P.7.18, delete the external forces and couple at point G, and replace with a force of 6,000 N at point G at an angle α with the horizontal going from left to right. For the condition of impending slippage in the downward direction, what should the angle α be?

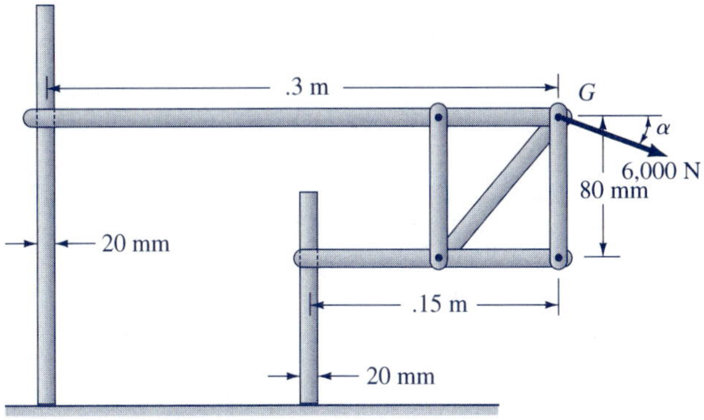

Figure P.7.102.

7.103. In Problem 7.39, what is the minimum angle between the supporting links CD and ED to support any weight W if the static coefficient of friction is $\mu_s = .4$?

7.104. A shaft AB rotates at constant angular speed in a pair of *dry* journal bearings. The total weight of the shaft and the cylinder it is supporting is W. A torque T is needed to maintain the steady angular motion. There is a small clearance between the shaft and the journal, resulting in a *point contact* between these bodies at some position E as shown. Form a two-dimensional force system acting on the shaft by moving W, the total friction force, the total normal force on the shaft surface, and the torque to a plane normal to the centerline of the shaft and at a location at the center of the system. View this system along the centerline.

(a) From considerations of equilibrium, what and where is the resultant force vector from the friction force and the normal force onto the shaft?

(b) If the angle ϕ in the diagram is very small and if the coefficient of dynamic friction is μ_d, explain how we can give the following approximate equation

$$T = W\mu_d r$$

where r is the radius of the shaft.

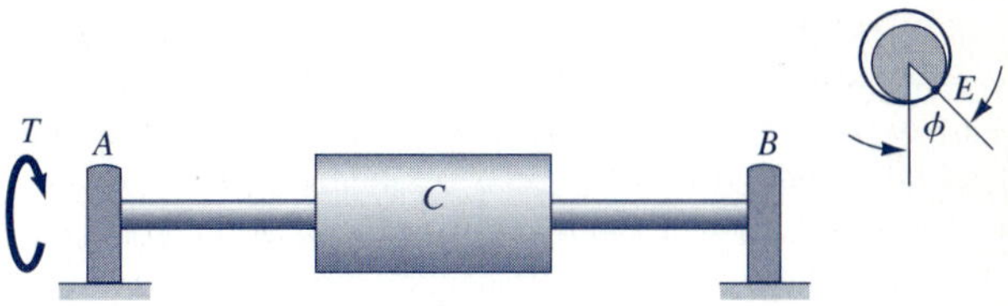

Figure P.7.104.

7.105. Shaft CD rotates at constant angular speed in a set of dry journal bearings (as a result of poor maintenance). Approximately what torque is needed to maintain the angular motion for the following data?

$M_A = 50$ kg $\quad M_B = 80$ kg $\quad$ Shaft $CD = 40$ kg $\quad \mu_d = .2$

See Problem 7.104 before doing this problem.

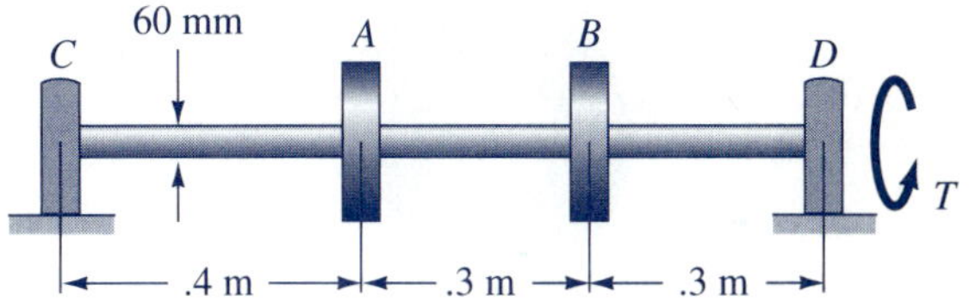

Figure P.7.105.

7.106. Two identical light rods are pinned together at B. End C of rod BC is pinned while end A of rod AB rests on a rough floor having a coefficient of friction with the rod of $\mu_d = .5$. The spring requires a force of 5 N/mm of stretch. A load is applied slowly at B and then maintained constant at $F = 300$ N. What is the angle θ when the system ceases to move? The spring is unstretched when $\theta = 45°$. [*Hint:* You will have to solve an equation by trial and error.]

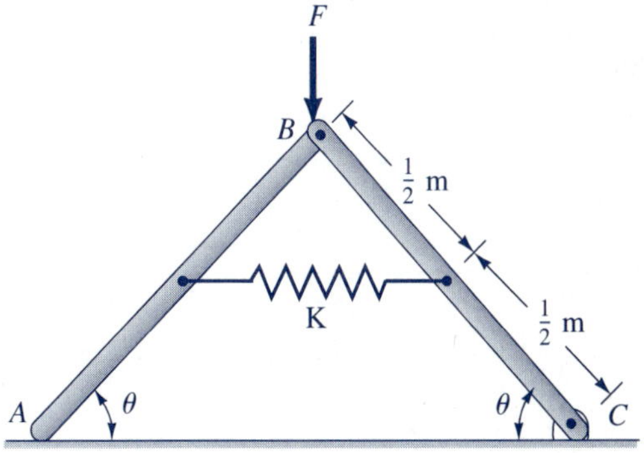

Figure P.7.106.

7.107. A device for "throwing" baseballs is shown. This device is to be found in amusement parks for batting practice. The two wheels are inflated automobile tires that rotate as shown with a constant speed ω. A baseball is fed to a point where it is touching the wheels. What is the *minimum* separation d of the wheels if the ball is to be drawn into the slot and then ejected on the other side as a pitched ball? The coefficient of static friction at the contact surfaces is .4.

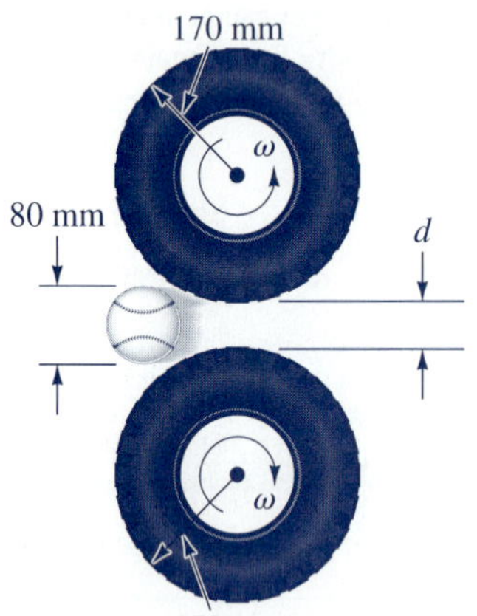

Figure P.7.107.

7.108. What is the *maximum* angle α for which there will be equilibrium if A has a mass of 50 kg. The static coefficient of friction between the supports and the horizontal rod is equal to .3. What is the force in each of the supporting members?

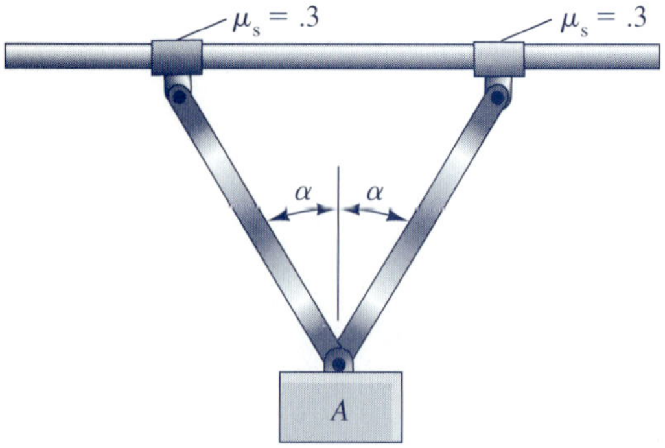

Figure P.7.108.

7.109. What is the *maximum* angle α for which there will be equilibrium if A weighs 1,000 N and if μ_s between the supports and the curved rod is .3? The rods are each 1.3 m long. You will have to solve a transcendental equation by trial and error.

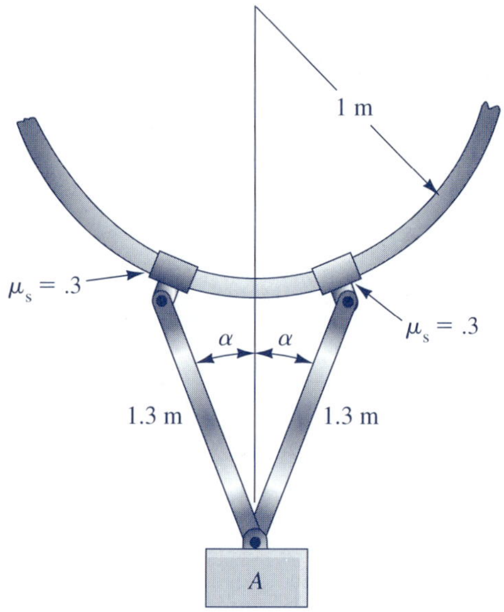

Figure P.7.109.

7.110. A 500-kN crate is being lowered slowly down an elevator shaft, which as shown is slightly wider than the crate. The cord wraps around a freely turning pulley and then has 2 rotations around a capstan. Find the tension T needed for the operation. The center of gravity of the crate is at its geometric center. [*Hint:* The crate will rotate so as to rub against the elevator shaft at points A and B.]

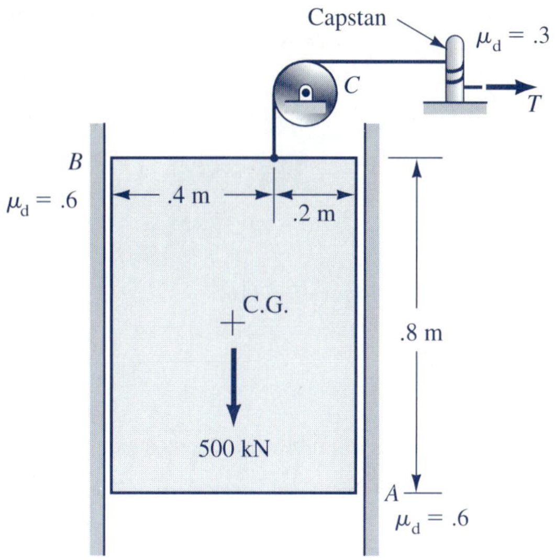

Figure P.7.110.

7.111. A triangular pile of width 1 ft is being driven into the ground slowly by a force P of 50,000 lb. There is pressure on the lateral surfaces of the pile. This pressure varies linearly from 0 at A to p_0 at B, as has been shown in the diagram. If the coefficient of dynamic friction between the pile and the soil is 0.6, what is the maximum pressure p_0?

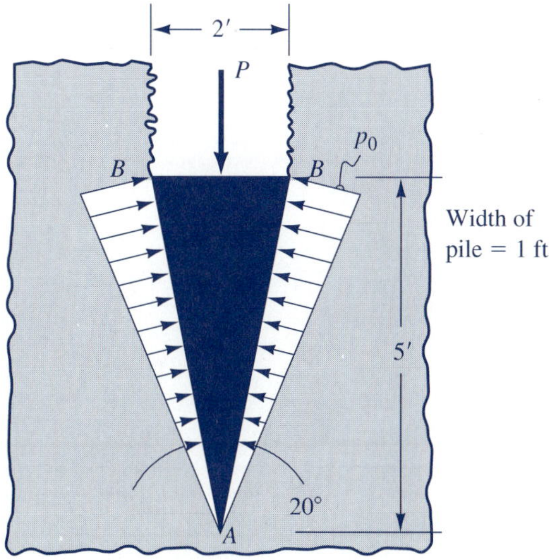

Figure P.7.111.

7.112. In Problem 7.27, what maximum value should W_2 be in order to start moving the system to the left? All other data are unchanged.

7.113. A block rests on a surface for which there is a coefficient of friction $\mu_s = .2$. Over what range of angle β will there be no movement of the block for the 150-N force? (You will have to solve an equation by trial and error.)

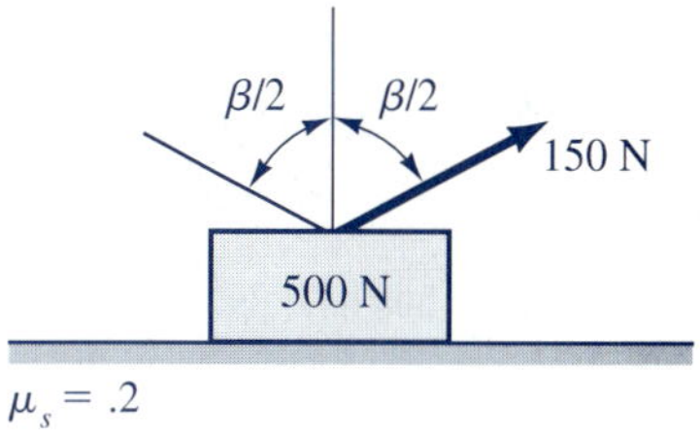

Figure P.7.113.

7.114. What is the *largest* load that can be suspended without moving blocks A and B? The static coefficient of friction for all plane surfaces of contact is .3. Block A weighs 500 N and block B weighs 700 N. Neglect friction in the pulley system.

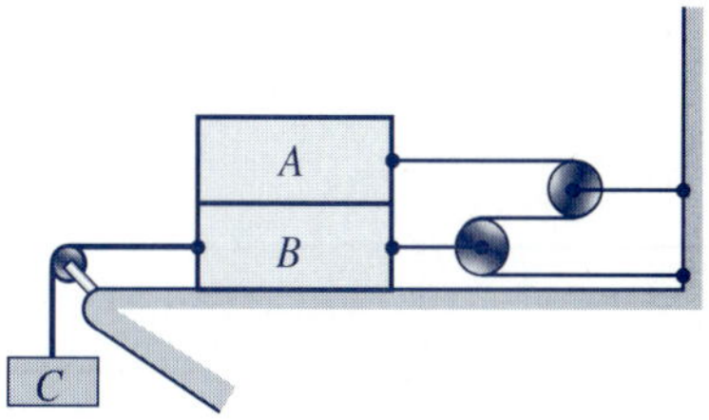

Figure P.7.114.

7.115. What is the *minimum* force F to hold the cylinders, each weighing 100 lb? Take $\mu_s = .2$ for all surfaces of contact.

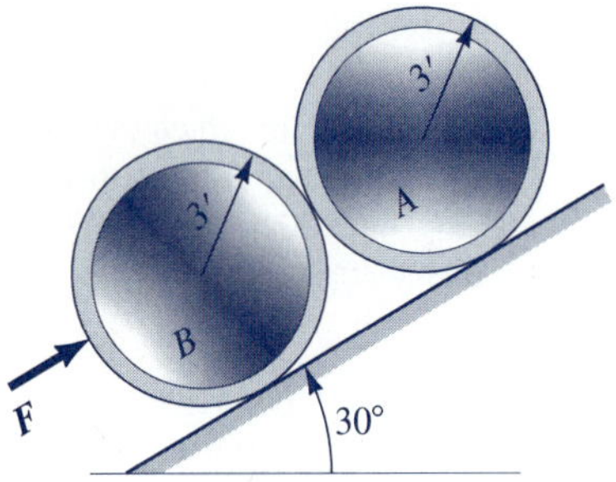

Figure P.7.115.

7.116. A compressor is shown. If the pressure in the cylinder is 1.40 N/mm² above atmosphere (gage), what *minimum* torque T is needed to initiate motion in the system? Neglect the weight of the crank and connecting rod as far as their contribution toward moving the system. Consider friction only between the piston and cylinder walls where the coefficient of friction $\mu_s = .15$.

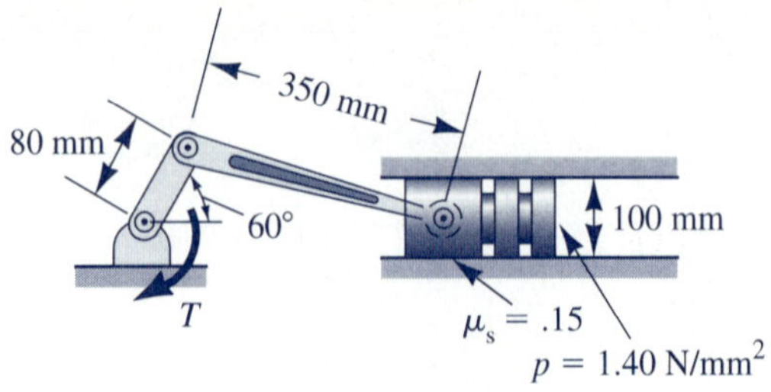

Figure P.7.116.

7.117. Find the cord tension if block 1 attains maximum friction.

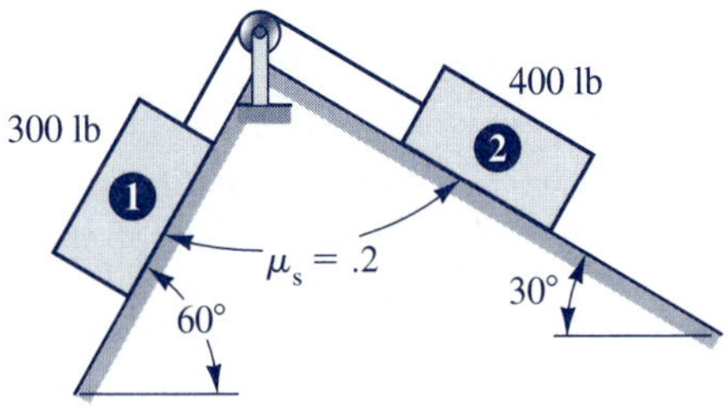

Figure P.7.117.

CHAPTER 8

Properties of Surfaces

8.1 Introduction

If we are buying a tract of land, we certainly want to consider the size and, with equal interest, the shape and orientation of the earth's surface, and possibly its agricultural, geological, or aesthetic potentials. The size of a surface (i.e., the area) is a familiar concept and has been used in the previous section. Certain aspects of the shape and orientation of a surface will be examined in this chapter. There are a number of formulations that convey meaning about the shape and disposition of a surface relative to some reference. To be sure, these formulations are not used by real estate people, but in engineering work, where a variety of quantitative descriptions are necessary, these formulations will prove most useful. In general, we shall restrict our attention to coplanar surfaces.

8.2 First Moment of an Area and the Centroid

A coplanar surface of area A and a reference xy in the plane of the surface are shown in Fig. 8.1. We define the *first moment of area A* about the x axis as

$$M_x = \int_A y\,dA \tag{8.1}$$

and the first moment about the y axis as

$$M_y = \int_A x\,dA \tag{8.2}$$

These two quantities convey a certain knowledge of the shape, size, and orientation of the area, which we can use in many analyses of mechanics.

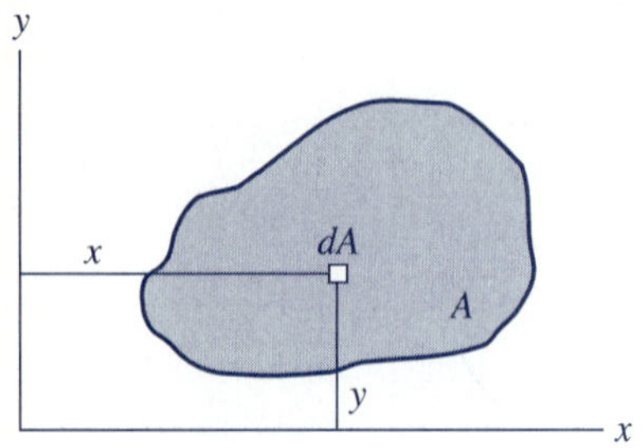

Figure 8.1. Plane area.

You will no doubt notice the similarity of the preceding integrals to those which would occur for computing moments about the x and y axes from a parallel force distribution oriented normal to the area A in Fig. 8.1. The moment of such a force distribution has been shown for the purposes of rigid-body calculations to be equivalent to that of a single resultant force located at a particular point $\bar{x}$, $\bar{y}$. Similarly, we can concentrate the entire area A at a position x_c, y_c, called the *centroid,*[1] where, for computations of first moments, this new arrangement is equivalent to the original distribution (Fig. 8.2). The coordinates x_c and y_c are usually called the *centroidal coordinates.* To compute these coordinates, we simply equate moments of the distributed area with that of the concentrated area about both axes:

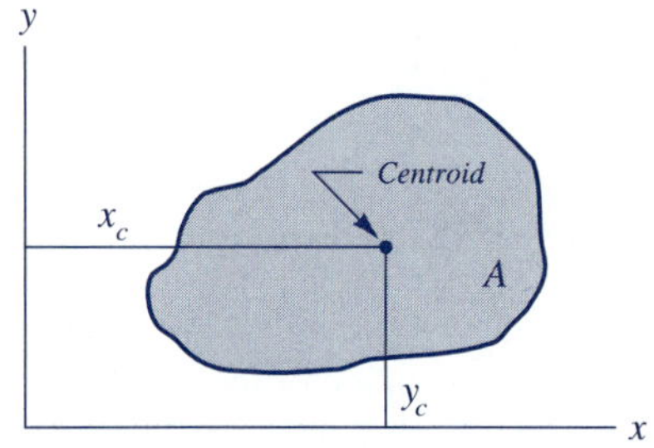

Figure 8.2. Centroidal coordinates.

$$Ay_c = \int_A y\,dA; \qquad \text{therefore, } y_c = \frac{\int_A y\,dA}{A} = \frac{M_x}{A} \tag{8.3a}$$

$$Ax_c = \int_A x\,dA; \qquad \text{therefore, } x_c = \frac{\int_A x\,dA}{A} = \frac{M_y}{A} \tag{8.3b}$$

The location of the centroid of an area can readily be shown to be *independent* of the *reference axes* employed. That is, the centroid is a *property* only of the *area* itself. We have asked the reader to prove this in Problem 8.1.

If the axes xy have their origin at the centroid, then these axes are called *centroidal axes* and clearly the first moments about these axes must be zero.

Finally, we point out that *all* axes going through the centroid of an area are called *centroidal axes* for that area. Clearly, the *first moments of an area about any of its centroidal axes must be zero*. This must be true since the perpendicular distance from the centroid to the centroidal axis must be zero.

[1]The concept of the centroid can be used for any geometric quantity. In the next section, we shall consider centroids of volumes and arcs.

Example 8.1

A plane surface is shown in Fig. 8.3 bounded by the x axis, the curve $y^2 = 25x$, and a line parallel to the y axis. What are the first moments of the area about the x and y axes and what are the centroidal coordinates?

We shall first compute M_x and M_y for this area. Using vertical infinitesimal area elements of width dx and height y, we have noting that $y = 5\sqrt{x}$

$$M_y = \int_0^{10} x(y\,dx) = \int_0^{10} x(5\sqrt{x})\,dx$$

$$= \left.\frac{5x^{5/2}}{\frac{5}{2}}\right|_0^{10} = \boxed{632 \text{ ft}^3}$$

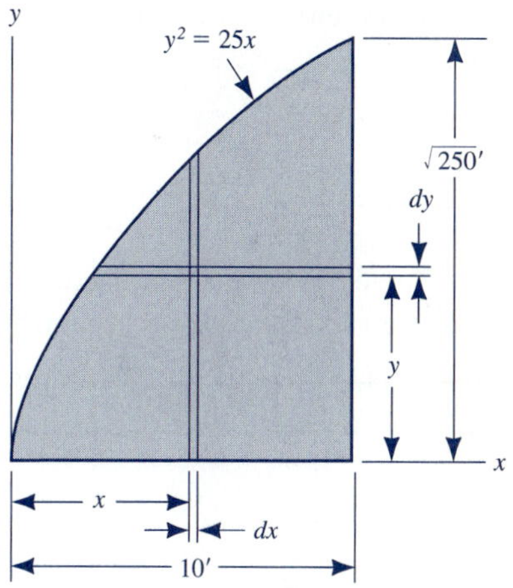

Figure 8.3. Find centroid.

To compute M_x, we use horizontal area elements of width dy and length $(10-x)$ as shown in the diagram. Thus

$$M_x = \int_0^{\sqrt{250}} y[(10 - x)dy]$$
$$= \int_0^{\sqrt{250}} \left(10y - \frac{y^3}{25}\right)dy$$

$$= \left.\left(5y^2 - \frac{y^4}{100}\right)\right|_0^{\sqrt{250}} = \boxed{625 \text{ ft}^3}$$

We could also have used vertical strips for computing M_x as follows using centroids of the vertical strips:

$$M_x = \int_0^{10} \frac{y}{2}(y\,dx) = \int_0^{10} \frac{25x}{2}\,dx$$
$$= (12.5)\left.\left(\frac{x^2}{2}\right)\right|_0^{10} = 625 \text{ ft}^3$$

To compute the position of the centroid (x_c, y_c), we will need the area A of the surface. Thus, using vertical strips:

$$A = \int_0^{10} y\,dx = \int_0^{10} 5\sqrt{x}\,dx = \left.\frac{5x^{3/2}}{\frac{3}{2}}\right|_0^{10}$$
$$= 105.4 \text{ ft}^2$$

Example 8.1 (Continued)

The centroidal coordinates are, accordingly,

$$x_c = \frac{M_y}{A} = \frac{632}{105.4} = \boxed{6.00 \text{ ft}}$$

$$y_c = \frac{M_x}{A} = \frac{625}{105.4} = \boxed{5.93 \text{ ft}}$$

To get the moment of the area about an axis y', which is 15 ft to the left of the y axis, simply proceed as follows:

$$M_{y'} = (A)(x_c + 15) = 105.4(6.00 + 15) = 2{,}213 \text{ ft}^3$$

Consider now a plane area with an *axis of symmetry* such as is shown in Fig. 8.4, where the y axis is collinear with the axis of symmetry. In computing x_c for this area, we have

$$x_c = \frac{1}{A}\int_A x\, dA$$

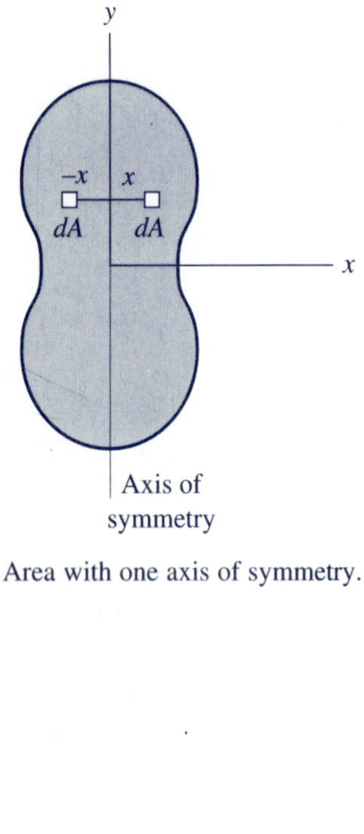

Figure 8.4. Area with one axis of symmetry.

In evaluating the integral above, we can consider area elements in symmetric pairs such as shown in Fig. 8.4, where we have shown a pair of area elements which are mirror images of each other about the axis of symmetry. Clearly, the first moment of such a pair about the axis of symmetry is zero. And, since the entire area can be considered as composed of such pairs, we can conclude that $x_c = 0$. Thus, the centroid of an area with one axis of symmetry must therefore lie somewhere along this axis of symmetry. The axis of symmetry then is a centroidal axis, which is another indication that the first moment of area must be zero about such an axis. With two orthogonal axes of symmetry, the centroid must lie at the intersection of these axes. Thus, for such areas as circles and rectangles, the centroid is easily determined by inspection.

In many problems, the area of interest can be considered formed by the addition or subtraction of simple familiar areas whose centroids are known by inspection as well as by other familiar areas, such as triangles and sectors of circles whose centroids and areas are given in handbooks. We call areas made up of such simple areas *composite* areas. (A listing of familiar areas is given for your convenience on the inside back cover of this text.) For such problems, we can say that

$$x_c = \frac{\sum_i A_i \bar{x}_i}{A}$$

$$y_c = \frac{\sum_i A_i \bar{y}_i}{A}$$

where $\bar{x}_i$ and $\bar{y}_i$, (with proper signs) are the centroidal coordinates to simple area A_i, and where A is the total area.

Example 8.2

Find the centroid of the shaded section shown in Fig. 8.5.

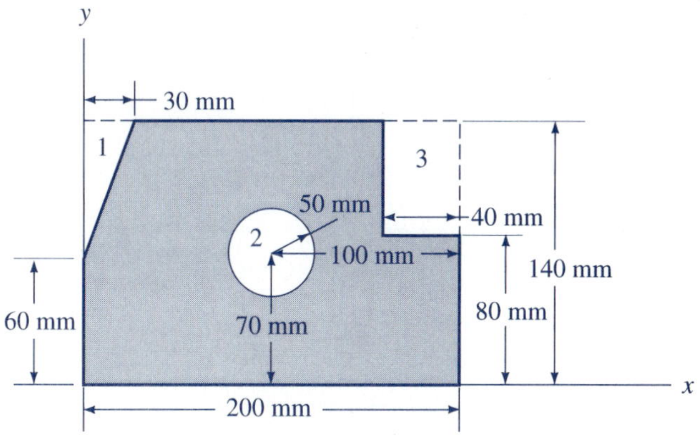

Figure 8.5. Composite area.

We may consider four separate areas. These are the triangle (1), the circle (2), and the rectangle (3) all cut from an original rectangular 200 × 140 mm^2 area which we denote as area (4). In composite-area problems, we urge you to set up a format of the kind we shall now illustrate. Using the positions of the centroid of a right triangle as given in the inside covers of this text, we have:

A_i		$\bar{x}_i$	$A_i\bar{x}_i$	$\bar{y}_i$	$A_i\bar{y}_i$
$A_1 = -\frac{1}{2}(30)(80)$	$= -1{,}200$	10	−12,000	113.3	−136,000
$A_2 = -\pi 50^2$	$= -7{,}850$	100	−785,000	70	−549,780
$A_3 = -(40)(60)$	$= -2{,}400$	180	−432,000	110	−264,000
$A_4 = (200)(140)$	$= 28{,}000$	100	2,800,000	70	1,960,000
	$A = 16{,}550\ \text{mm}^2$		$\sum_i A_i\bar{x}_i = 1.571 \times 10^6\ \text{mm}^3$		$\sum_i A_i\bar{y}_i = 1.011 \times 10^6\ \text{mm}^3$

Therefore,

$$x_c = \frac{\sum A_i\bar{x}_i}{A} = \frac{1.571 \times 10^6}{16{,}550} = \boxed{94.9\ \text{mm}}$$

$$y_c = \frac{\sum A_i\bar{y}_i}{A} = \frac{1.011 \times 10^6}{16{,}550} = \boxed{61.1\ \text{mm}}$$

We now illustrate how we can use the composite-area approach for finding the centroid of an area composed of familiar parts as just described.

In closing, we would like to point out that the centroid concept can be of use in finding the simplest resultant of a distributed loading. Thus, consider the distributed loading $w(x)$ shown in Fig. 8.6. The resultant force F_R of this loading, also shown in the diagram, is given as

$$F_R = \int_0^L w(x)\,dx \tag{8.4}$$

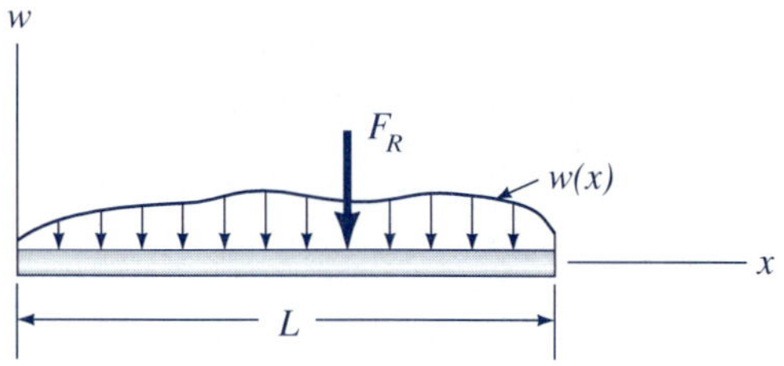

Figure 8.6. Loading curve $w(x)$ and its resultant F_R.

From the equation above, we can readily see that the *resultant force equals the area under the loading curve*. To get the position of the *simplest* resultant for the loading, we then say that

$$F_R\bar{x} = \int_0^L xw(x)\,dx$$

Therefore,

$$\bar{x} = \frac{\int_0^L xw(x)\,dx}{F_R} \tag{8.5}$$

The preceding result shows that $\bar{x}$ is actually the centroidal coordinate of the loading curve area from reference xy. Thus, the *simplest resultant force of a distributed load acts at the centroid of the area under the loading curve.* Accordingly, for a triangular load such as is shown in Fig. 8.7, we can replace the loading for free bodies on which the entire loading acts by a force F equal to $(\frac{1}{2})(w_0)(b-a)$ at a position $\frac{2}{3}(b-a)$ from the left end of the loading. You will recall that we pointed this out in Chapter 4.

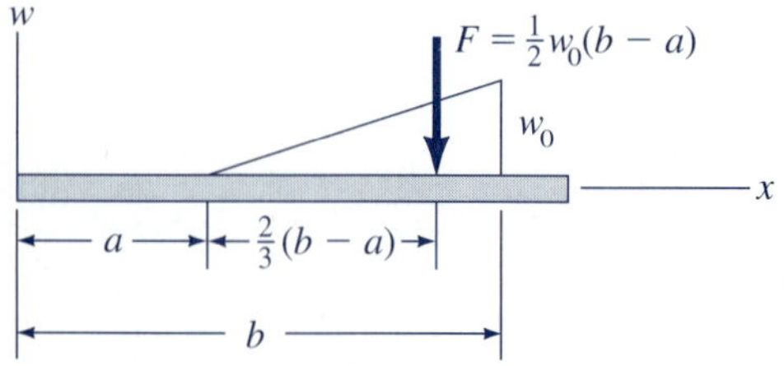

Figure 8.7. Triangular loading with simplest resultant.

PROBLEMS

8.1. Show that the centroid of area A is the same point for axes xy and $x'y'$. Thus, the position of the centroid of an area is a property only of the area.

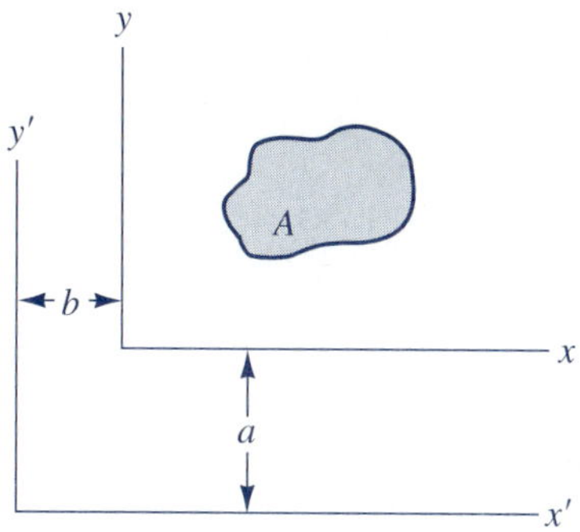

Figure P.8.1.

8.2. Show that the centroid of the right triangle is $x_c = 2a/3$, $y_c = b/3$.

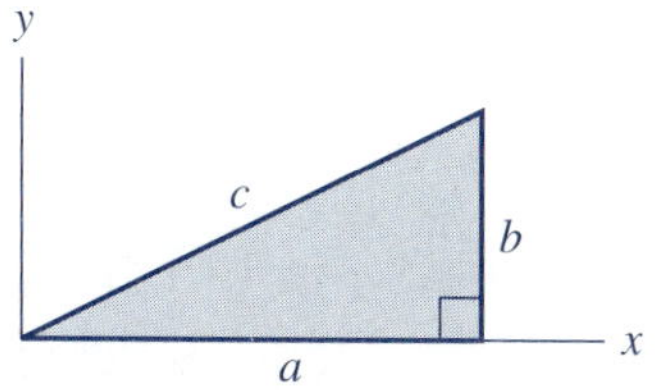

Figure P.8.2.

8.3. Find the centroid of the area under the half-sine wave. What is the first moment of this area about axis A–A?

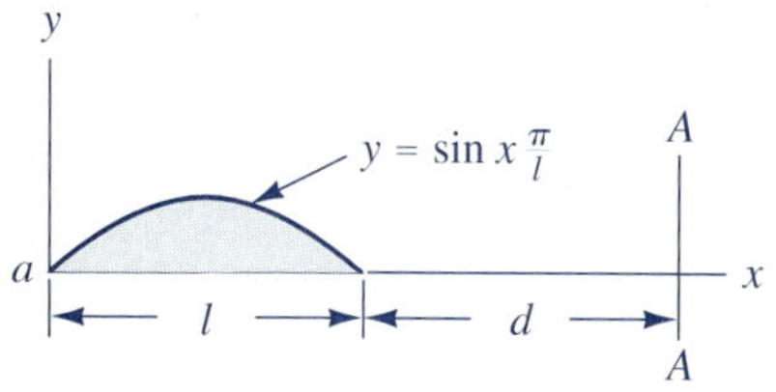

Figure P.8.3.

8.4. What are the first moments of the area about the x and y axes? The curved boundary is that of a parabola. [*Hint:* The general equation for parabolas of the shape shown is $y^2 = ax + b$.]

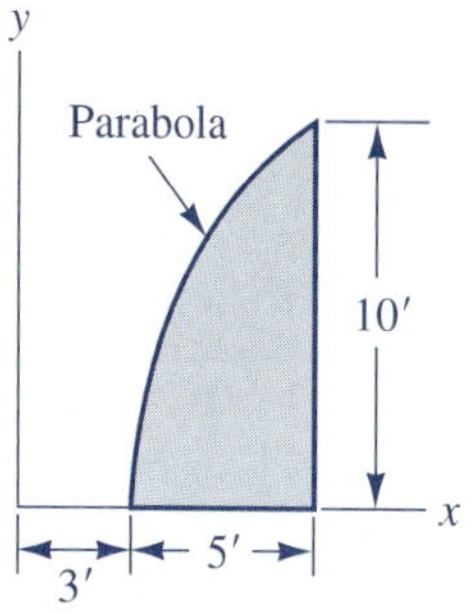

Figure P.8.4.

8.5. What are the centroidal coordinates for the shaded area? The curved boundary is that of a parabola. [*Hint:* The general equation for parabolas of the shape shown is $y = ax^2 + b$.]

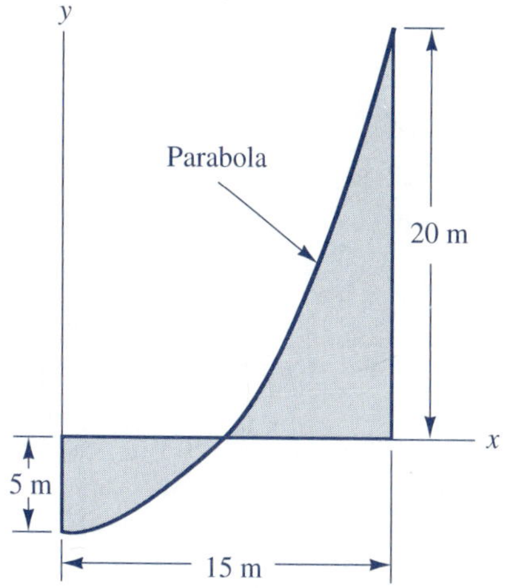

Figure P.8.5.

8.6. Show that the centroid of the area under a semicircle is as shown in the diagram.

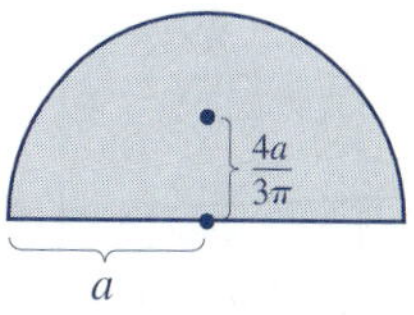

Figure P.8.6.

8.7. What is the first moment of the area under the parabola about an axis through the origin and going through point $\boldsymbol{r} = 6\boldsymbol{i} + 7\boldsymbol{j}$ m. Take $l = 10$ m.

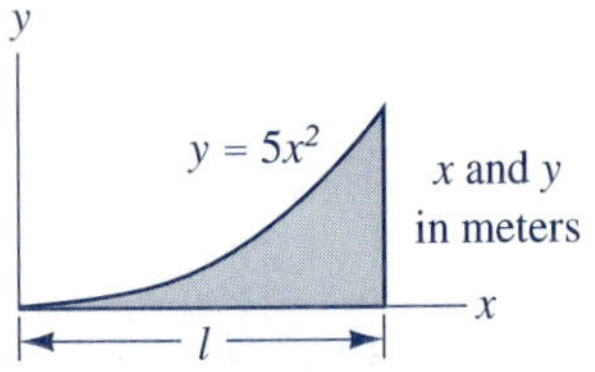

Figure P.8.7.

8.8. Find the centroidal coordinates of the shaded area.

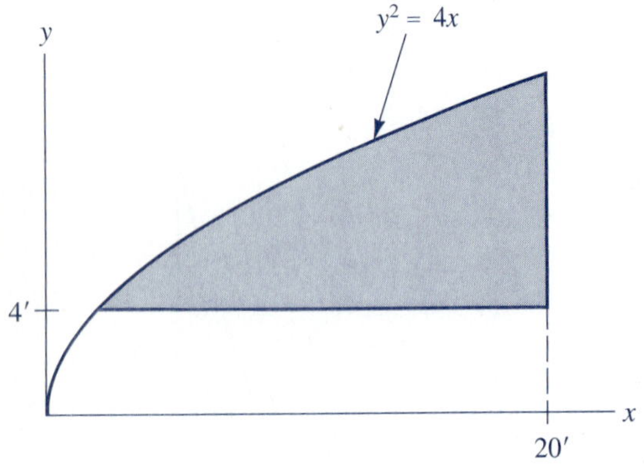

Figure P.8.8.

8.9. Express the first moment of area of the shaded area as a function of y, b, and h for y ranging from the top of the rectangle to the bottom.

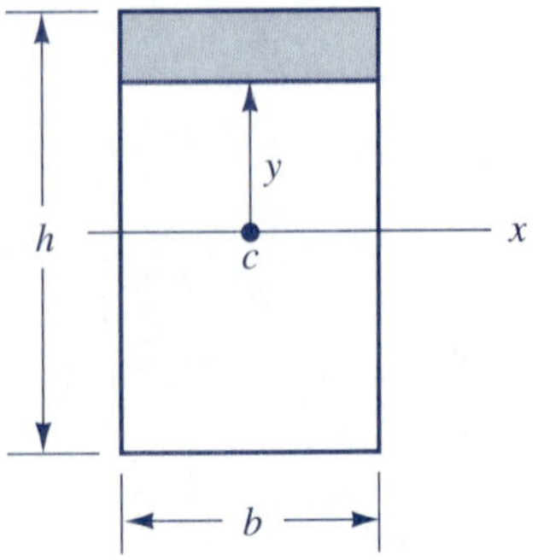

Figure P.8.9.

8.10. Suppose you had an irregular area and you had to *approximate* the location of the centroid. How could you accomplish this using only a straight edge, a ruler, and a pencil?

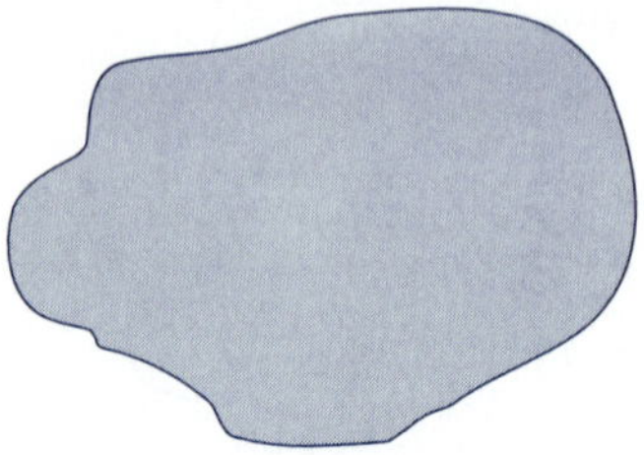

Figure P.8.10.

8.11. Show that the centroid of the triangle is at $x_c = (a + b)/3$, $y_c = h/3$. [*Hint:* Break the triangle into two right triangles for which the centroids are known from Problem 8.2.]

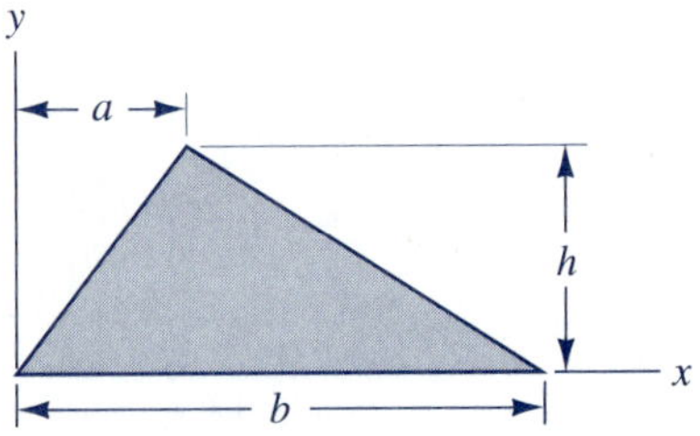

Figure P.8.11.

8.12. What are the centroidal coordinates for the shaded area? The outer boundary is that of a circle having a radius of 1 m.

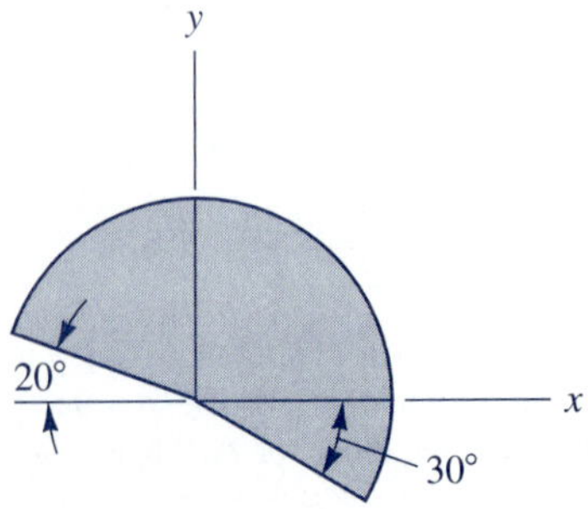

Figure P.8.12.

8.13. What are the coordinates of the centroid of the shaded area? The parabola is given as $y^2 = 2x$ with y and x in millimeters.

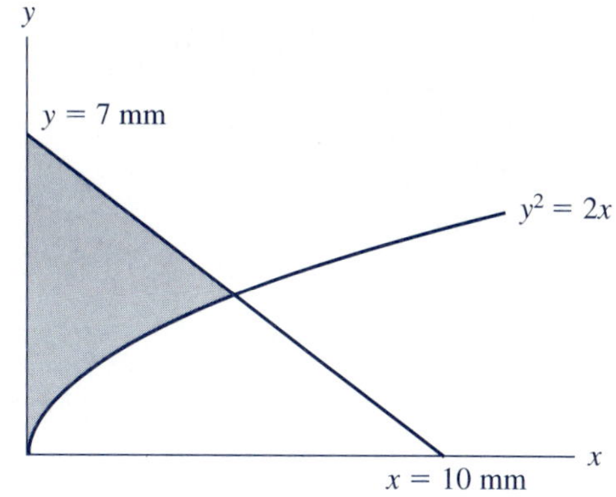

Figure P.8.13.

8.14. Find the centroid of the shaded area. The equation of the curve is $y = 5x^2$ with x and y in millimeters. What is the first moment of the area about line AB?

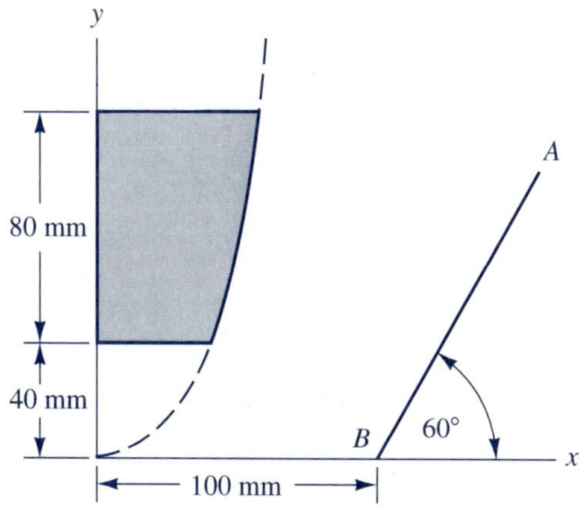

Figure P.8.14.

8.15. Find the centroid of the shaded area. What is the first moment of this area about line A–A. The upper boundary is a parabola $y^2 = 50x$ with x and y in millimeters.

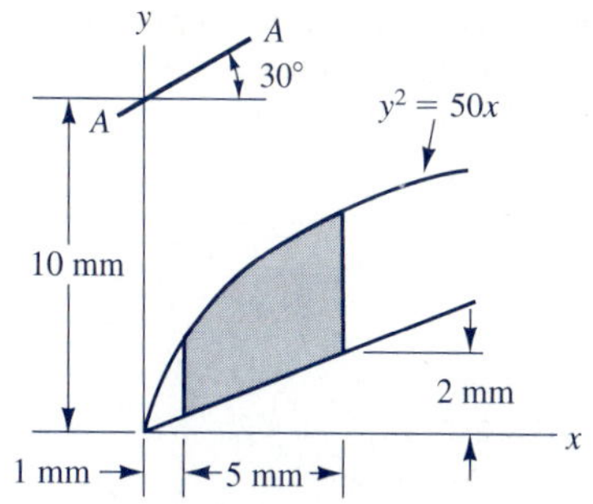

Figure P.8.15.

In the remaining problems of this section, use centroidal positions of simple areas as found in the inside covers.

8.16. Find the centroid of the end shield of a bulldozer blade.

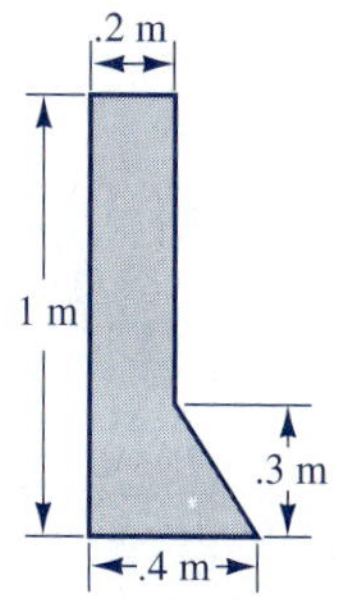

Figure P.8.16.

8.17. In Example 2.6, determine z_C for the centroid of the triangular faces of the pyramid plus the base area $ABCE$. The height of the pyramid is 300 ft.

8.18. A parallelogram and an ellipse have been cut from a rectangular plate, What are the centroidal coordinates of what is left of the plate? What is $M_{x'}$ for this area? Use formulas given on the inside of the back covers.

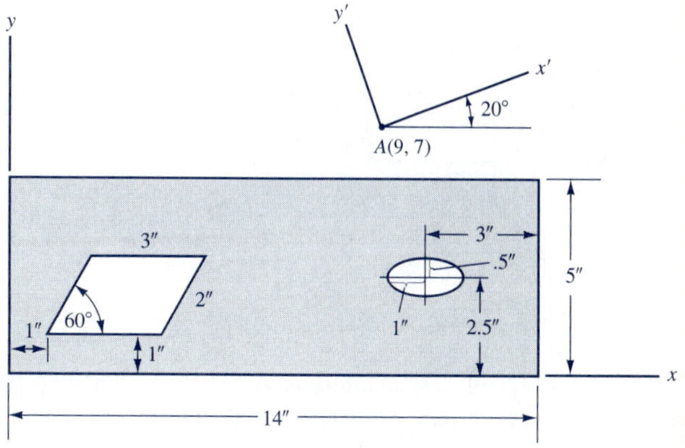

Figure P.8.18.

8.19. A *median* axis has the same area on one side of the axis as it does on the other side. Find the distance between the horizontal median line and a parallel centroidal axis.

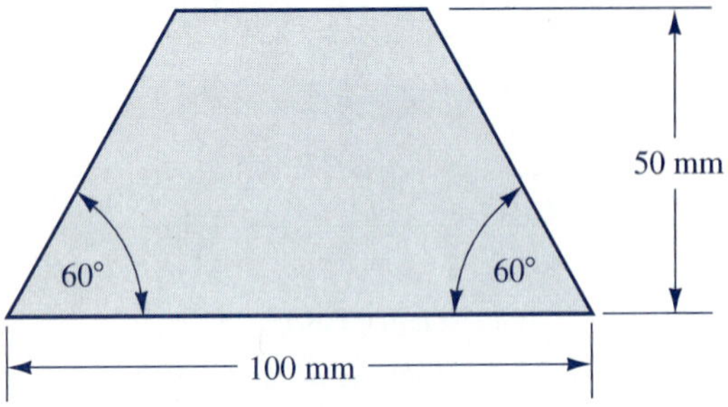

Figure P.8.19.

8.20. Find the centroid of the truss gusset plate.

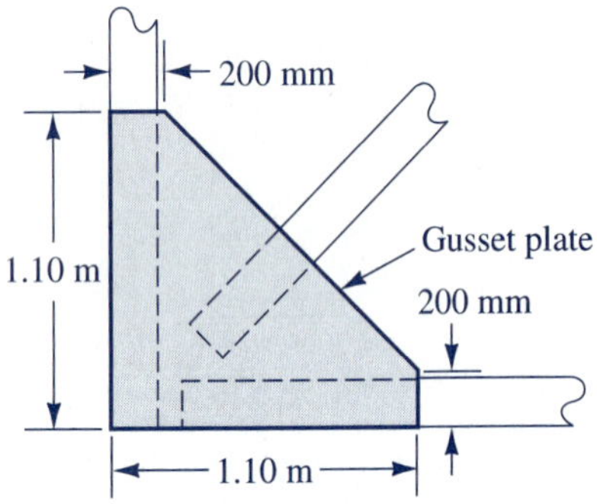

Figure P.8.20.

8.21. Find the centroid of the indicated area.

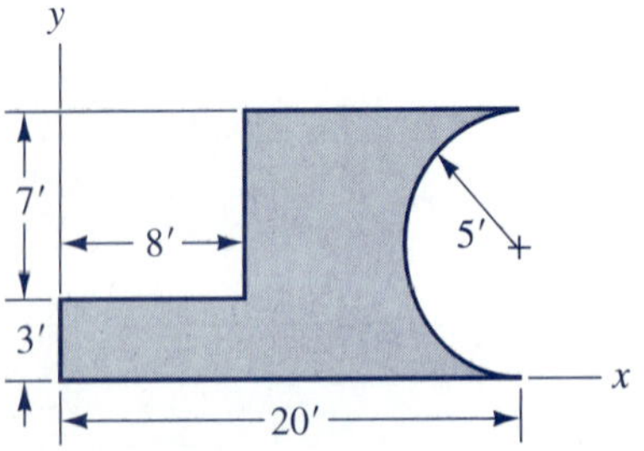

Figure P.8.21.

8.22. Find the centroidal coordinates for the shaded area shown. Give the results in meters. [*Hint:* See Fig. P.8.6.]

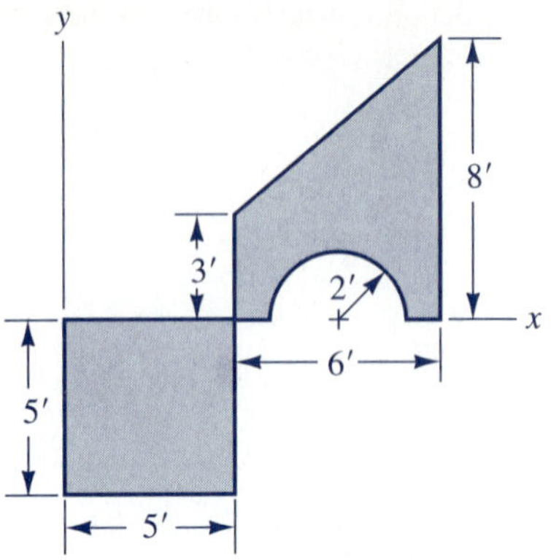

Figure P.8.22.

8.23. Find the centroid of the end of the bucket of a small front-end loader.

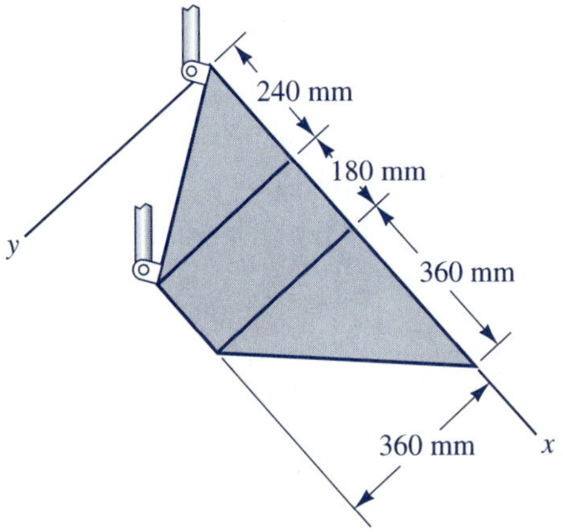

Figure P.8.23.

8.24. Where is the centroid of the airplane's vertical stabilizer (whole area)?

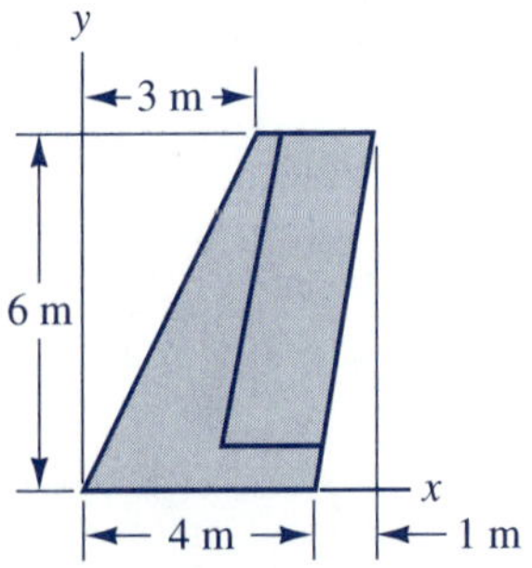

Figure P.8.24.

8.25. What is the first moment of the shaded area about the diagonal *A–A*? [*Hint:* Consider symmetry.]

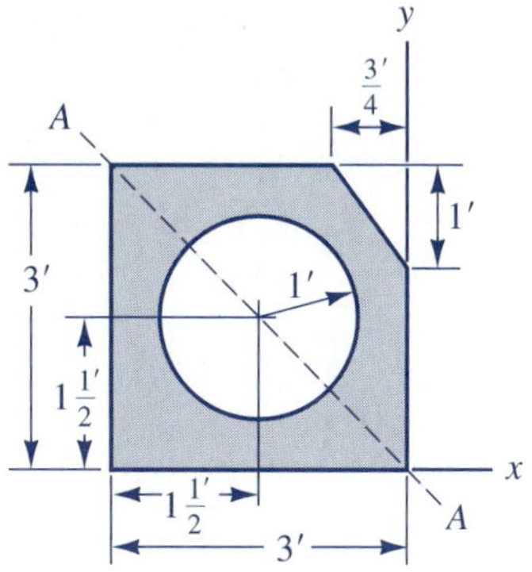

Figure P.8.25.

8.26. A built-up beam is shown with four 120-mm by 120-mm by 20-mm angles. Find the vertical distance above the base for the centroid of the cross-section.

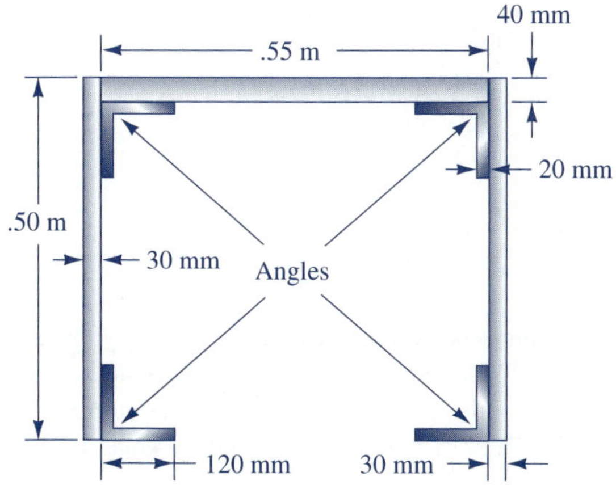

Figure P.8.26.

8.27. A wide-flange I beam (identified as 14WF202 I beam) is shown with two reinforcing plates on top. At what height above the bottom is the centroid of the beam located?

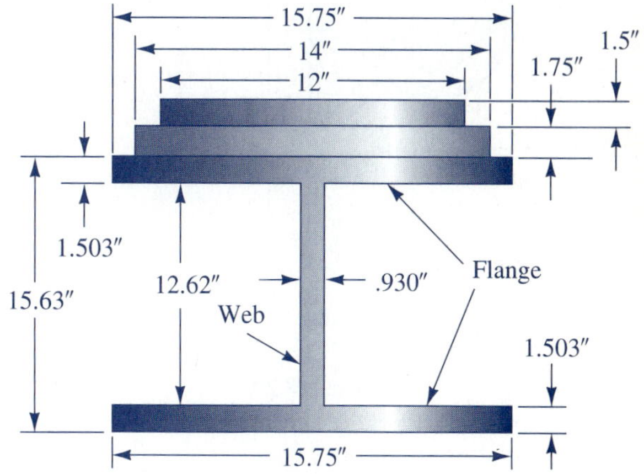

Figure P.8.27.

8.28. Compute the position of the centroid of the shaded area. [*Hint:* See Fig. P.8.6.]

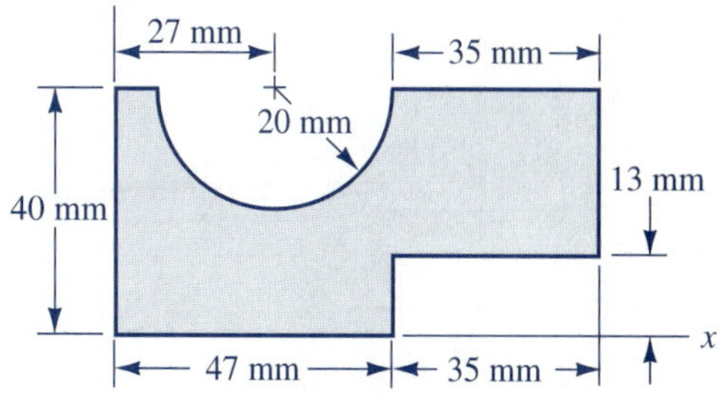

Figure P.8.28.

8.29. Find the centroid of the sheet metal cover of a centrifugal blower (shown shaded).

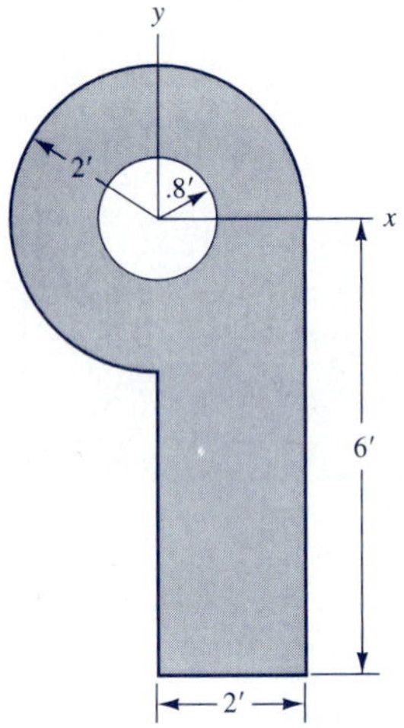

Figure P.8.29.

8.30. What is the position from the left end of the simplest resultant force of the distribution shown?

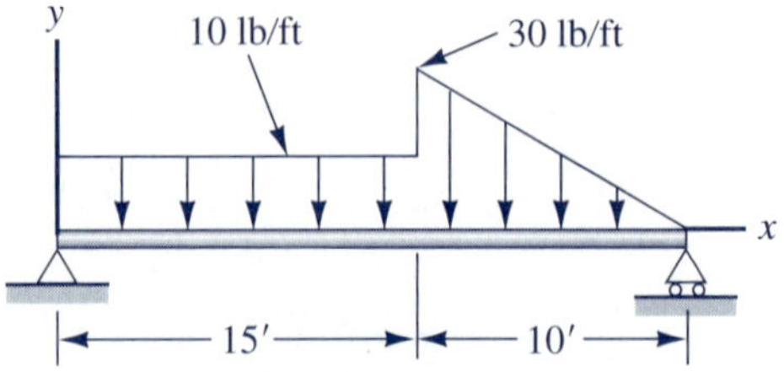

Figure P.8.30.

8.3 Other Centers

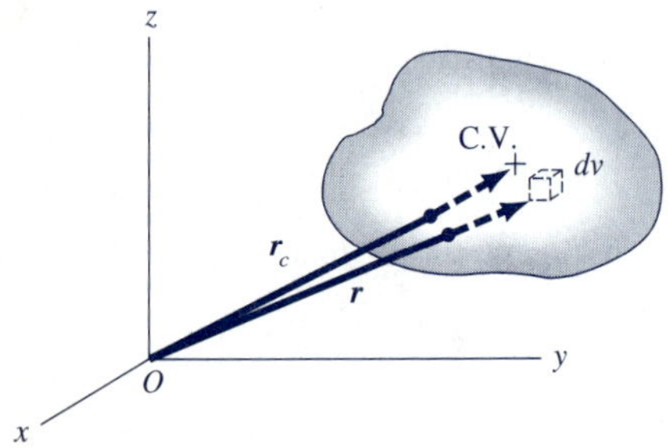

Figure 8.8. Center of volume, C.V., of a body.

We employ the concepts of moments and centroids in mechanics for three-dimensional bodies as well as for plane areas. Thus, we introduce now the first moment of a volume, V, of a body (see Fig. 8.8) about a point O where we have shown a reference xyz. We say that the first *moment of volume V* about O is

$$\text{moment vector of volume} \equiv \iiint_V \boldsymbol{r}\, dv \tag{8.6}$$

The *center of volume*, $\boldsymbol{r}_c$, is then defined as follows:

$$V\boldsymbol{r}_c = \iiint_V \boldsymbol{r}\, dv$$

Therefore,

$$\boldsymbol{r}_c = \frac{1}{V}\iiint_V \boldsymbol{r}\, dv \tag{8.7}$$

We see that the center of volume is the point where we could hypothetically concentrate the entire volume of a body for purposes of computing the first moment of the volume of the body about some point O. The components of Eq. 8.7 give the *centroid distances* of volume x_c, y_c, and z_c. Thus, we have

$$x_c = \frac{\iiint x\, dv}{\iiint dv}, \quad y_c = \frac{\iiint y\, dv}{\iiint dv}, \quad z_c = \frac{\iiint z\, dv}{\iiint dv} \tag{8.8}$$

The integral $\iiint x\,dv$, it should be noted, gives the first moment of volume about the yz plane, etc.

If we replace dv by $dm = \rho\,dv$ in Eq. 8.6, where ρ is the mass *density*, we get the *first moment of mass* about O. That is,

$$\text{moment vector of mass} \equiv \iiint_V \boldsymbol{r}\,\rho\,dv \tag{8.9}$$

The *center of mass* $\boldsymbol{r}_c$ is then given as

$$\boldsymbol{r}_c = \frac{1}{M}\iiint_V \boldsymbol{r}\,\rho\,dv \tag{8.10}$$

where M is the total mass of the body. The center of mass is the point in space where hypothetically we could concentrate the entire mass for purposes of computing the first moment of mass about a point O. Using the components of Eq. 8.10, we can say that

$$x_c = \frac{\iiint x\rho\,dv}{\iiint \rho\,dv}, \quad y_c = \frac{\iiint y\rho\,dv}{\iiint \rho\,dv}, \quad z_c = \frac{\iiint z\rho\,dv}{\iiint \rho\,dv}$$

In our work in dynamics, we shall consider the center of mass of a system of n particles (see Fig. 8.9). We will then say:

$$\left(\sum_{i=1}^{n} m_i\right)\boldsymbol{r}_c = \sum_{i=1}^{n} m_i\boldsymbol{r}_i$$

Therefore,

$$\boldsymbol{r}_c = \frac{\sum_{i=1}^{n} m_i\boldsymbol{r}_i}{M} \tag{8.11}$$

where M is the total mass of the system. Clearly, if the particles are of infinitesimal mass and constitute a continuous body, we get back Eq. 8.10.

Finally, if we replace dv by $\gamma\,dv$, where $\gamma(= \rho g)$ is the *specific weight*, we arrive at the concept of *center of gravity* discussed in Chapter 4. We have used the center of gravity of a body in many calculations thus far as a point to concentrate the entire weight of a body.

You should have no trouble in concluding from Eq. 8.10 that if ρ is constant throughout a body, the center of mass coincides with the center of volume. Furthermore, if $\gamma(= \rho g)$ is constant throughout a body, the center of gravity of the body corresponds to the center of volume of the body. If, finally, ρ and g are each constant for a body, all three points coincide for the body.

We now illustrate the computation of the center of volume. Computation for the center of mass follows similar lines, and we have already computed centers of gravity in Chapter 4.

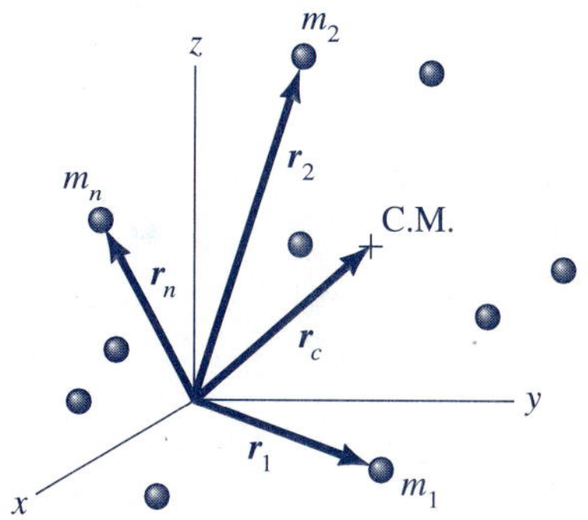

Figure 8.9. System of n particles showing center of mass, C.M.

Example 8.3

Consider a volume of revolution formed by revolving the area shown in Fig. 8.3 about the x axis. This volume has been shown in Fig. 8.10. Clearly, the centroid of this volume must lie somewhere along the x axis. Determine the centroidal distance x_c.

Using r, θ, and x as coordinates (cylindrical coordinates), we then have, using slices of thickness dx as volume elements:

$$V = \int_0^{10} (\pi r^2)\, dx = \int_0^{10} (\pi)(25x)\, dx$$

where we have replaced r^2 with $25x$ according to the equation for the boundary of the generating area. Integrating, we get

$$V = 25\pi \left. \frac{x^2}{2} \right|_0^{10} = 3{,}927 \text{ ft}^3$$

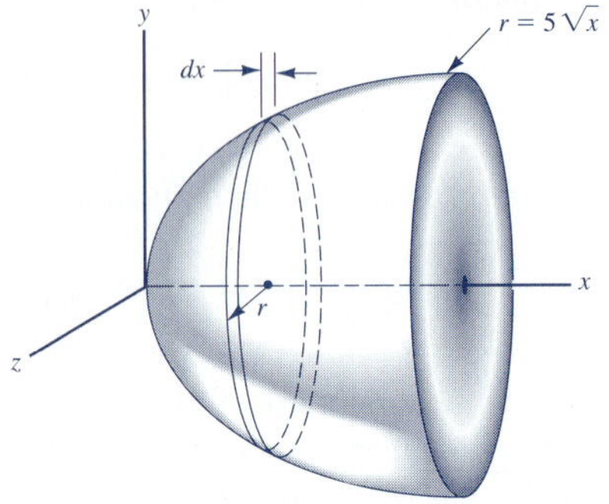

Figure 8.10. Body of revolution.

Now we compute x_c by using infinitesimal slices of the body of the kind employed for the computation of V. The centroid of each such slice is at the intercept of the slice with the x axis. Thus, we have

$$x_c = \frac{1}{V}\int_0^{10} x(\pi r^2\, dx) = \frac{1}{3,927}\int_0^{10} x(\pi)(25x)\, dx$$

$$= \frac{25\pi}{3,927} \left. \frac{x^3}{3} \right|_0^{10} = \boxed{6.67 \text{ ft}}$$

Many volumes are composed of a number of simple familiar shapes whose centers of volume are either known by inspection or can be found in handbooks (also see the inside front cover page). Such volumes may be called *composite volumes*. To find the centroid of such a volume, we use the known centroids of the composite parts. Thus, for x_c of the composite body whose total volume is V, we have

$$x_c = \frac{\sum_i \bar{x}_i V_i}{V}$$

where $\bar{x}_i$ is the x coordinate to the centroid of the ith composite body of volume V_i. Similarly,

$$y_c = \frac{\sum_i \bar{y}_i V_i}{V}$$

$$z_c = \frac{\sum_i \bar{z}_i V_i}{V}$$

We now illustrate the use of these formulas.

Example 8.4

What is the coordinate x_c for the center of volume of the body of revolution shown in Fig. 8.11? Note that a cone has been cut away from the left end while, at the right end, we have a hemispherical region.

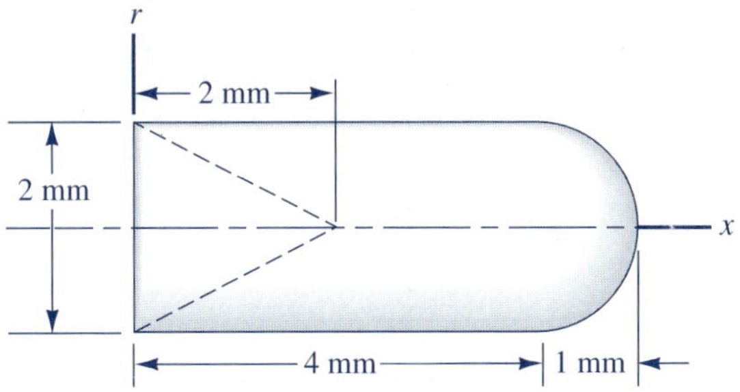

Figure 8.11. Composite volume.

We have a composite body consisting of three simple domains—a cone (body 1), a cylinder (body 2), and a hemisphere (body 3). Using formulas from the inside covers, we have:

V_i (mm^3)		$\bar{x}_i$ (mm)	$V_i\bar{x}_i$ (mm^4)
1. $-(\frac{1}{3})(\pi)(1^2)(2)$	$= -2.09$	$\frac{2}{4}$	-1.047
2. $(\pi)(1^2)(4)$	$= 12.57$	2	25.14
3. $\frac{2}{3}(\pi)(1^3)$	$= 2.09$	$4 + \frac{3}{8}(1) = 4.38$	9.15
	$V = 12.57$		$\sum_i V_i\bar{x}_i = 33.24$

Therefore,

$$x_c = \frac{\sum_i V_i\bar{x}_i}{V} = \frac{33.24}{12.57} = \boxed{2.64 \text{ mm}}$$

We have presented a number of three-dimensional problems for determining the center of volume, center of mass, and the center of gravity of composite bodies. We will leave it to the student to work his/her way through these problems, working from first principles, without the need of examples. However, we ask that you follow the following format, which clearly is an extension of what we have been doing up to this point.

Area, Volume, Mass, or Weight **No.**	*Area, Volume, Mass, or Weight* **Value**	$(r_c)_i$	$(r_c)_i \begin{Bmatrix} A_i \\ V_i \\ M_i \\ W_i \end{Bmatrix}$
1	•	•	•
2	•	•	•
•	•	•	•
•	•	•	•
•	•	•	•
•	•	•	•
•	•	•	•
•	•	•	•
•	•	•	•

$$\sum_i \begin{Bmatrix} A_i \\ V_i \\ M_i \\ W_i \end{Bmatrix} = \qquad \sum_i (r_c)_i \begin{Bmatrix} A_i \\ V_i \\ M_i \\ W_i \end{Bmatrix} =$$

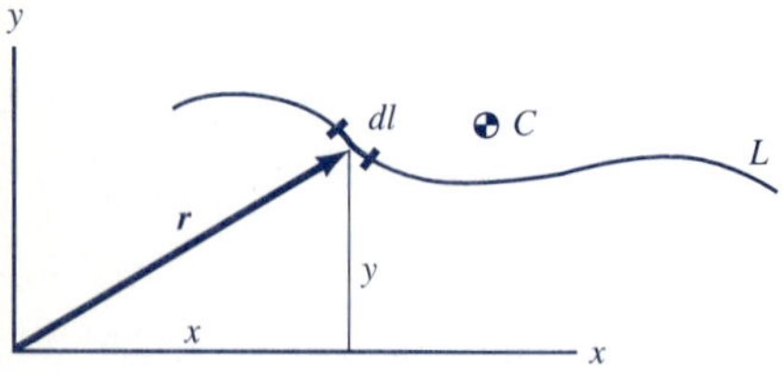

Figure 8.12. Centroid for curved line.

In closing, we wish to point out further that curved surfaces and lines have centroids. Since we shall have occasion in the next section to consider the centroid of a line, we simply point out now (see Fig. 8.12) that

$$x_c = \frac{\int x\,dl}{L} \tag{8.12a}$$

$$y_c = \frac{\int y\,dl}{L} \tag{8.12b}$$

where L is the length of the line. Note that the centroid C will not generally lie along the line.

Consider next a curve made up of simple curves each of whose centroids is known. Such is the case shown in Fig. 8.13, made up of straight lines. The line segment L_1, has for instance centroid C_1 with coordinates $\bar{x}_1, \bar{y}_1$, as has been shown in the diagram. We can then say for the entire curve that

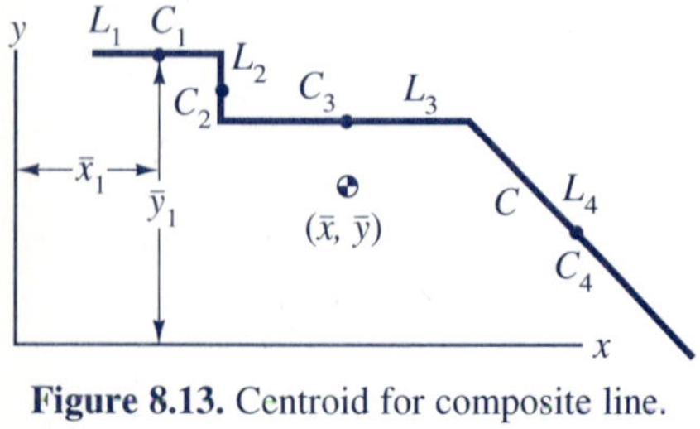

Figure 8.13. Centroid for composite line.

$$x_c = \frac{\sum_i \bar{x}_i L_i}{L}$$

$$y_c = \frac{\sum_i \bar{y}_i L_i}{L} \tag{8.13}$$

*8.4 Theorems of Pappus–Guldinus

The theorems of Pappus–Guldinus were first set forth by Pappus about 300 A.D. and then restated by the Swiss mathematician Paul Guldinus about 1640. These theorems are concerned with the relation of a surface of revolution to its generating curve, and the relation of a volume of revolution to its generating area.

The first of the theorems may be stated as follows:

Consider a coplanar generating curve and an axis of revolution in the plane of this curve (see Fig. 8.14). The generating curve can touch but must not cross the axis of revolution. The surface of revolution developed by revolving the generating curve about the axis of revolution has an area *equal to the product of the* length *of the* generating curve *times the* circumference *of the* circle *formed by the* centroid *of the* generating curve *in the process of generating a surface of revolution.*

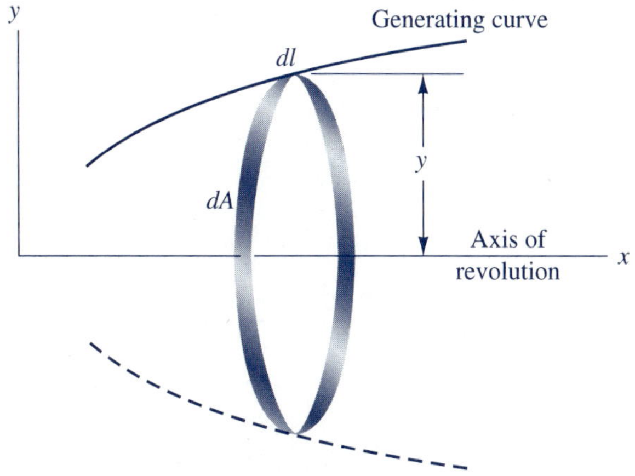

Figure 8.14. Coplanar generating curve.

To prove this theorem, consider first an element dl of the generating curve shown in Fig. 8.14. For a single revolution of the generating curve about the x axis, the line segment dl traces an area

$$dA = 2\pi y\ dl$$

For the entire curve this area becomes the surface of revolution given as

$$A = 2\pi \int y\,dl = 2\pi y_c L \tag{8.14}$$

where L is the length of the curve and y_c is the centroidal coordinate of the curve. But $2\pi y_c$ is the circumferential length of the circle formed by having the centroid of the curve rotate about the x axis. The first theorem is thus proved.

Another way of interpreting Eq. 8.14 is to note that the area of the body of revolution is equal to 2π times the *first moment* of the generating curve about the axis of revolution. If the generating curve is composed of simple curves, L_i, whose centroids are known, such as the case shown in Fig. 8.13, then we can express A as follows:

$$A = 2\pi\left(\sum_i L_i\bar{y}_i\right) \tag{8.15}$$

where $\bar{y}_i$ is the centroidal coordinate to the ith line segment L_i.

The second theorem may be stated as follows:

Consider a plane surface and an axis of revolution coplanar with the surface but oriented such that the axis can intersect the surface only as a tangent at the boundary or have no intersection at all. The volume of the body of revolution developed by rotating the plane surface about the axis of revolution equals the product of the area *of the surface times the* circumference *of the circle formed by the* centroid *of the surface in the process of generating the body of revolution.*

To prove the second theorem, consider a plane surface A as shown in Fig. 8.15. The volume generated by revolving dA of this surface about the x axis is

$$dV = 2\pi y\ dA$$

The volume of the body of revolution formed from A is then

$$V = 2\pi\int_A y\,dA = 2\pi y_c A \tag{8.16}$$

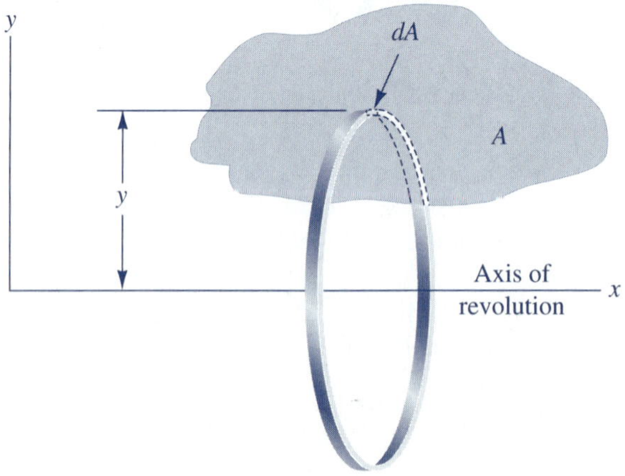

Figure 8.15. Plane surface A coplanarwith xy plane.

Thus, the volume V equals the area of the generating surface A times the circumferential length of the circle of radius y_c. The second theorem is thus also proved.[2]

Another way to interpret Eq. 8.16 is to note that V equals 2π times the *first moment* of the generating area A about the axis of revolution. If this area A is made up of simple areas A_i, we can say that

$$V = 2\pi\left(\sum_i A_i\bar{y}_i\right) \tag{8.17}$$

where $\bar{y}_i$, is the centroidal coordinate to the ith area A_i.

We now illustrate the use of the theorems of Pappus and Guldinus. As we proceed, it will be helpful to remember the theorems by noting that you multiply a length (or area) of the generator by the distance moved by the centroid of the generator.

[2]It is to be pointed out that the centroid of a volume of revolution will not be coincident with the centroid of a longitudinal cross-section taken along the axis of the volume. Example: a cone and its triangular, longitudinal cross-section.

Example 8.5

Determine the surface area and volume of the bulk materials trailer shown in Fig. 8.16.

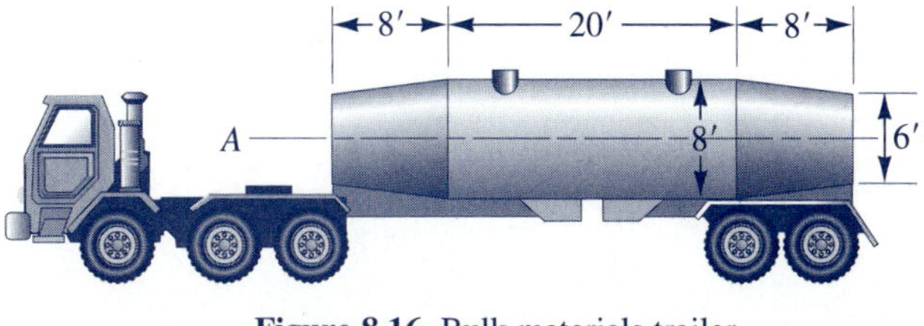

Figure 8.16. Bulk materials trailer.

We shall first determine the surface area by considering the first moment about the centerline A–A (see Fig. 8.17) of the generating curve of

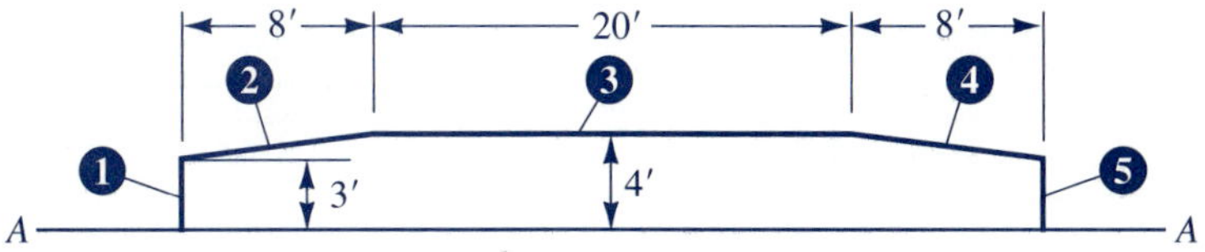

Figure 8.17. Generating curve for surface of revolution.

Example 8.5 (Continued)

the surface of revolution. This curve is a set of 5 straight lines each of whose centroids is easily known by inspection. Accordingly we may use Eq. 8.15. For clarity, we use a column format for the data as follows:

L_i (ft)	$\bar{y}_i$ (ft)	$L_i\bar{y}_i$ (ft^2)
1. 3	1.5	4.5
2. $\sqrt{8^2+1^2} = 8.06$	3.5	28.21
3. 20	4	80
4. 8.06	3.5	28.21
5. 3	1.5	4.5
		$\sum_i L_i\bar{y}_i = 145.43$

Therefore,

$$A = (2\pi)(145.43) = \boxed{914 \text{ ft}^2}$$

To get the volume, we next show in Fig. 8.18 the generating area for the body of revolution. Notice it has been decomposed into simple composite areas. We shall employ Eq. 8.17 and hence we shall need the first moment of area about the axis *A–A* of the composite areas. Again, we shall employ a column format for the data.

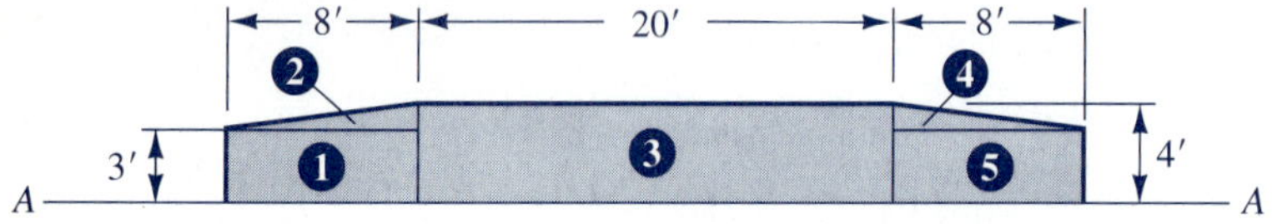

Figure 8.18. Generating area for body of revolution.

A_i (ft^2)	$\bar{y}_i$ (ft)	$A_i\bar{y}_i$ (ft^3)
1. 24	1.5	36
2. $\frac{1}{2}(8)(1) = 4$	$3 + \frac{1}{3} = 3.33$	13.33
3. 80	2	160
4. 4	3.333	13.33
5. 24	1.5	36
		$\sum_i A_i\bar{y}_i = 258.7$

Therefore,

$$V = 2\pi\sum_i A_i\bar{y}_i = (2\pi)(258.7) = \boxed{1{,}625 \text{ft}^3}$$

The theorems of Pappus and Guldinus have enabled us to compute the surface area and the volume of the bulk materials trailer quickly and easily.

PROBLEMS

8.31. If $r^2 = ax$ in the body of revolution shown, compute the centroidal distance x_c of the body.

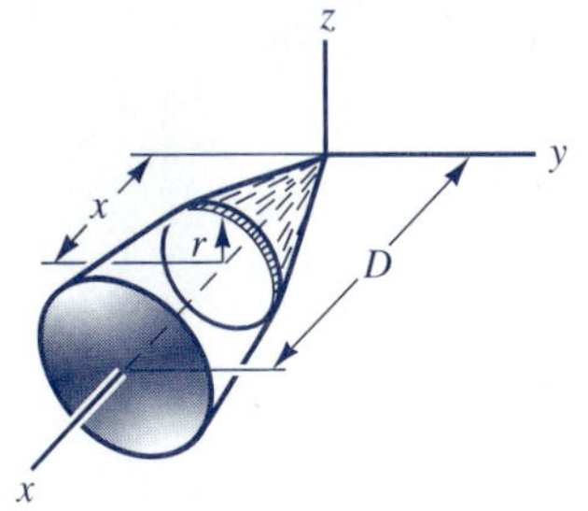

Figure P.8.31.

8.32. Using vertical elements of volume as shown, compute the centroidal coordinates x_c, y_c of the body. Then, using horizontal elements, compute z_c.

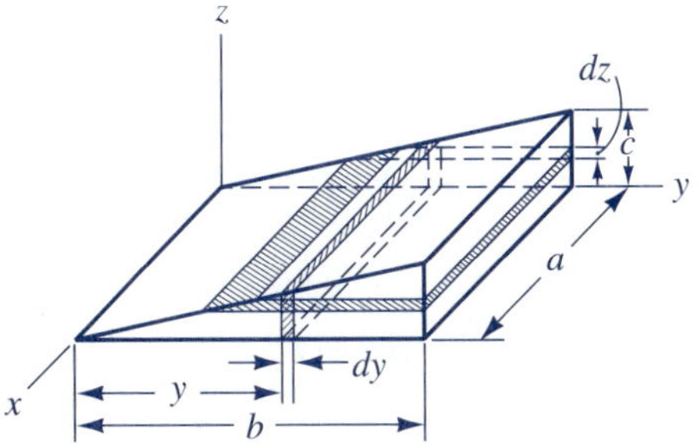

Figure P.8.32.

8.33. Compute the center of volume of a right circular cylinder of height h and radius at the base r.

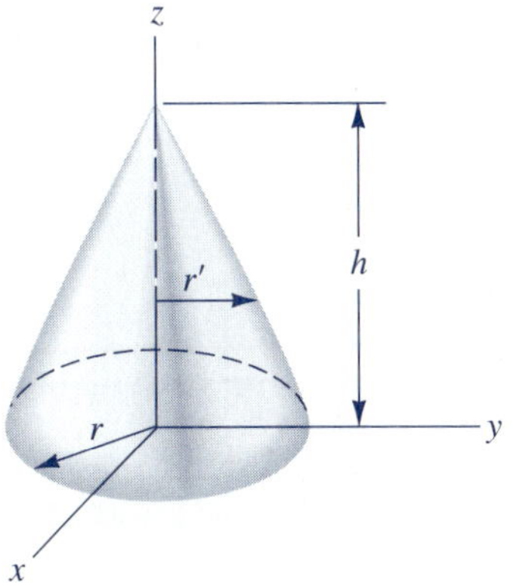

Figure P.8.33.

8.34. Determine the position of the center of mass of the solid hemisphere having a uniform mass density ρ and with a radius a.

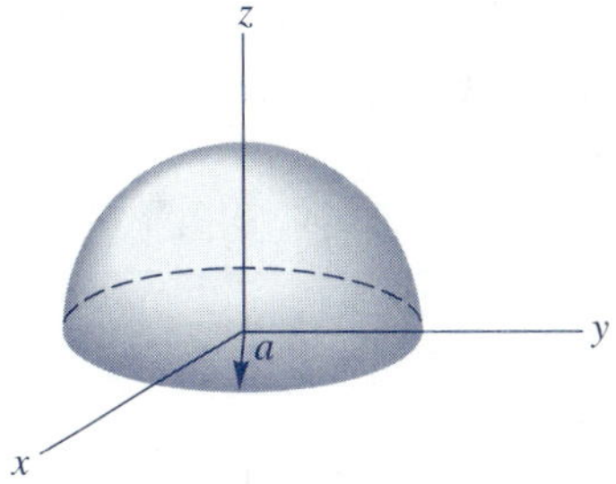

Figure P.8.34.

8.35. Find the center of mass for the paraboloid of revolution having a uniform density ρ.

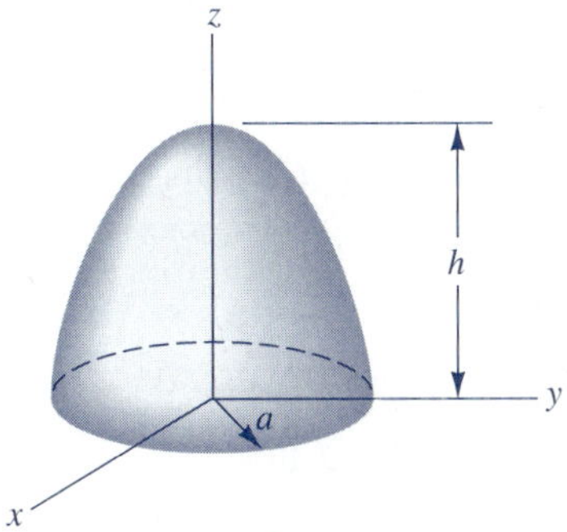

Figure P.8.35.

8.36. A small bomb has exploded at position O. Four pieces of the bomb move off at high speed. At $t = 3$ sec, the following data apply:

m	(kg)	$\mathbf{r}$ (m)
1.	.2	$2\mathbf{i} + 3\mathbf{j} + 4\mathbf{k}$
2.	.1	$4\mathbf{i} + 4\mathbf{j} - 6\mathbf{k}$
3.	.15	$-3\mathbf{i} + 2\mathbf{j} - 3\mathbf{k}$
4.	.22	$2\mathbf{i} - 3\mathbf{j} + 2\mathbf{k}$

What is the position of the center of mass?

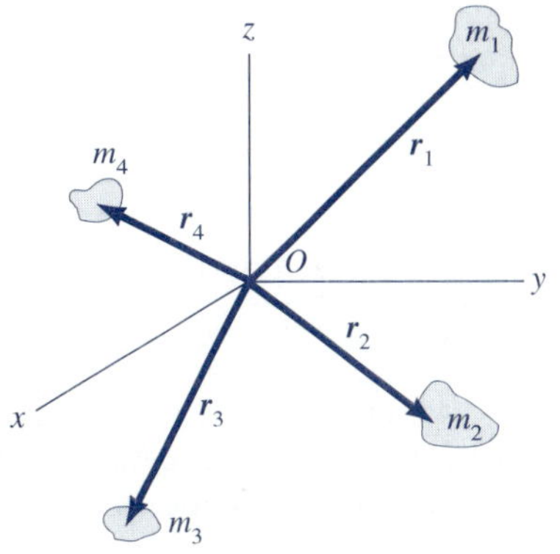

Figure P.8.36.

8.37. A plate of uniform thickness and density has for its curved edge a rectangular hyperbola (xy = constant). Find the centroid of the upper surface. Find the centers of mass, volume, and gravity for the plate.

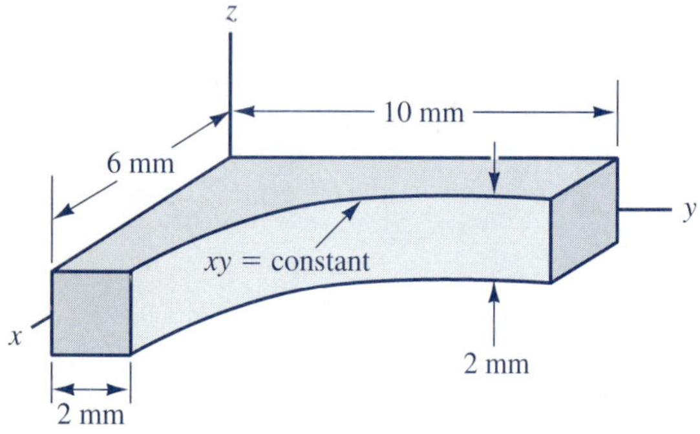

Figure P.8.37.

In Problems 8.38 through 8.46, use the formulas on the inside covers for simple shapes.

8.38. Where must a lifting hook be cast in a tapered concrete beam so that the beam always stays horizontal when lifted?

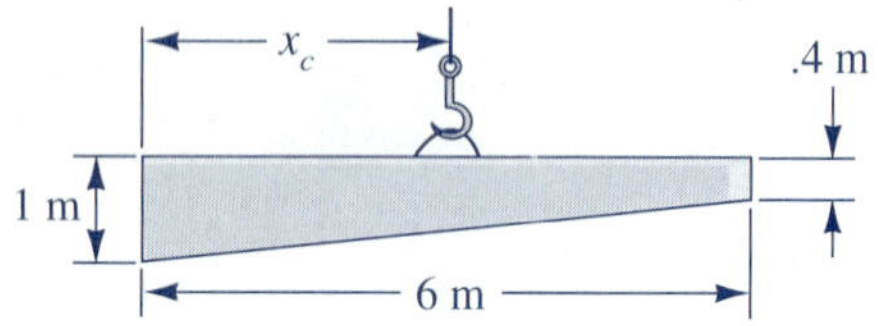

Figure P.8.38.

8.39. Two solid semicylinders are glued together. Body A has a uniform mass density of 6.54 kN/m^3, while body B has a uniform mass density of 10 kN/m^3. Determine:

(a) Center of volume
(b) Center of mass
(c) Center of gravity

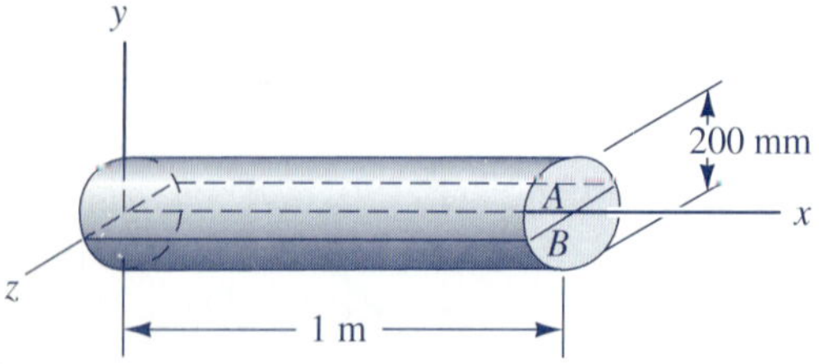

Figure P.8.39.

8.40. What is the centroid of the body shown? It consists of a cylinder A of length 2 m and diameter 6 m, a shaft B of diameter 2 m and length 8 m, and a block C of length 4 m and height and width of 7 m. The x axis is a centerline for the arrangement. Origin O is at the geometric center of cylinder A.

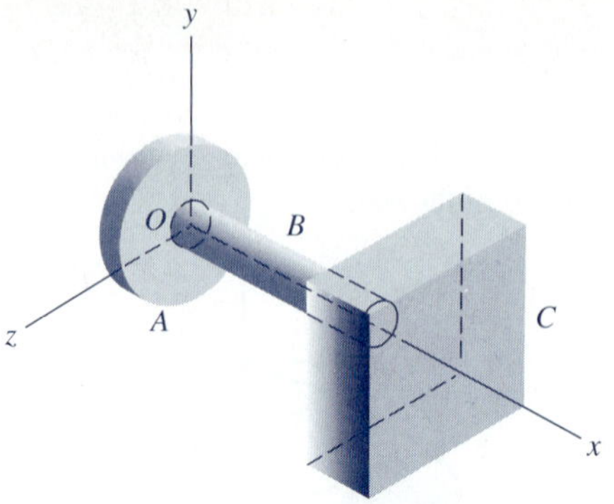

Figure P.8.40.

8.41. Find the center of volume for the cone–cylinder shown. Note that there is a cylindrical hole of length 16 ft and diameter 4 ft cut into the body.

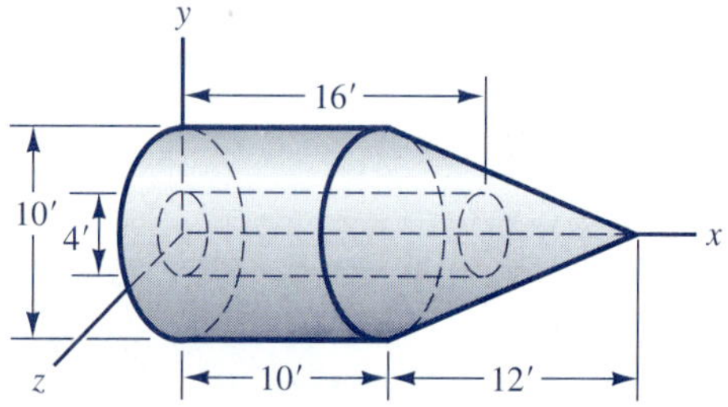

Figure P.8.41.

8.42. A cylinder has cut out of it a cone; a small cylinder directed through the centerline; and a half-sphere as has been shown in the diagram. Determine the center of gravity.

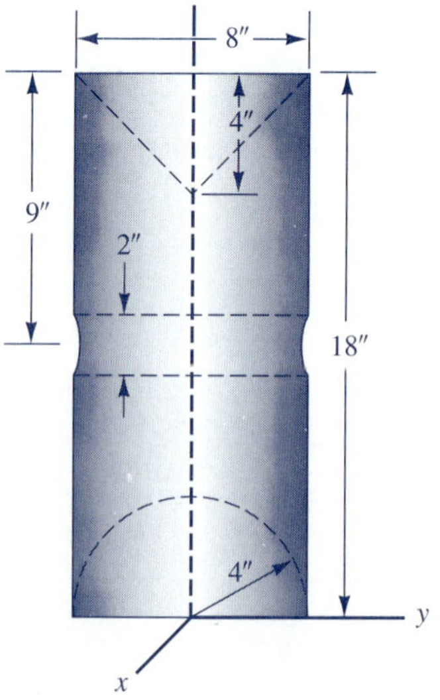

Figure P.8.42.

8.43. Find the center of gravity of the bent plate. The rectangular cutout occurs at the geometric center of the surface in the xz plane.

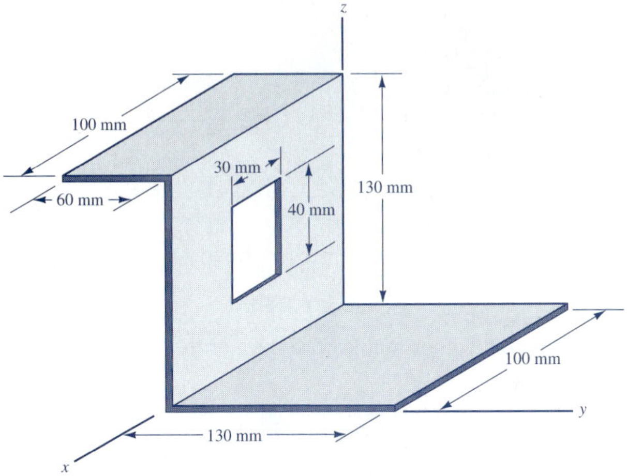

Figure P.8.43.

8.44. A bent aluminum rod weighing 30 N/m is fitted into a plastic cylinder weighing 200 N, as shown. What are the centers of volume, mass, and gravity?

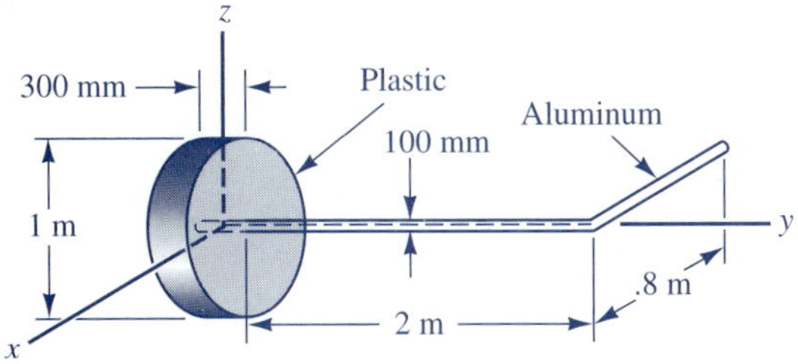

Figure P.8.44.

8.45. An aluminum cylinder fits snugly into a brass block. The brass weighs 43.2 kN/m^3 and the aluminum weighs 30 kN/m^3. Find the center of volume, the center of mass, and the center of gravity.

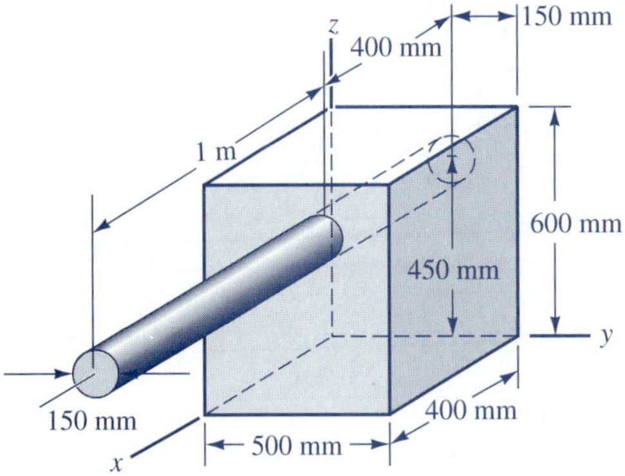

Figure P.8.45.

8.46. Two thin plates are welded together. One has a circle of radius 200 mm cut out as shown. If each plate weighs 450 N/m^2, what is the position of the center of mass?

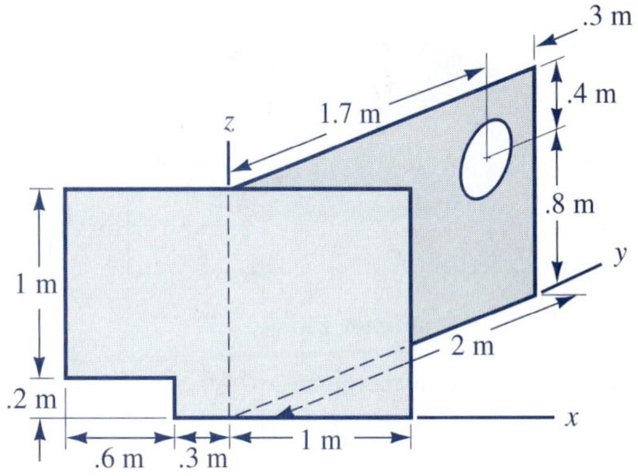

Figure P.8.46.

8.47. Where is the center of mass of the bent wire if it weighs 10 N/m?

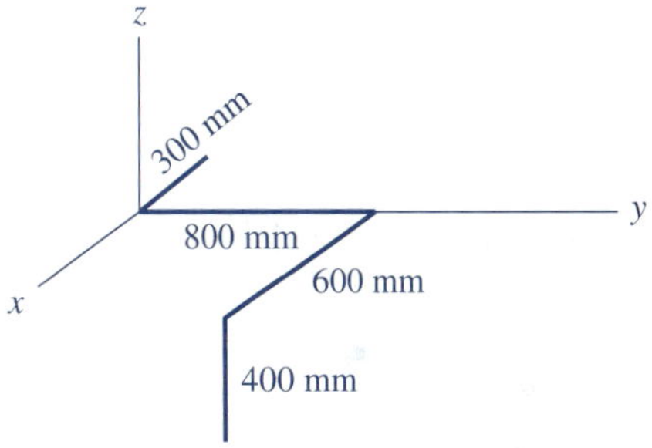

Figure P.8.47.

8.48. Find the center of mass of the bent wire shown in the zy plane. The wire weighs 15 N/m.

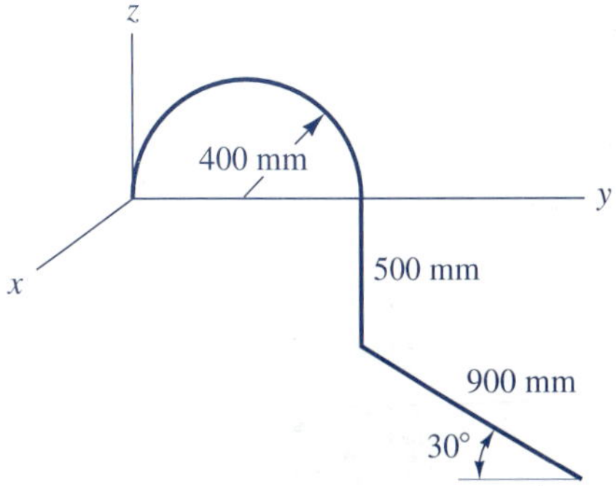

Figure P.8.48.

8.49. In Problem 8.41, involving a wooden cone–cylinder with a cylindrical hole, find the center of mass for the case where the cylinder has a density of 46.0 lbm/ft^3 and the cone has a density of 30.0 lbm/ft^3.

8.50. The volume of an ellipsoidal body of revolution is known from calculus to be $\frac{1}{6}\pi ab^2$. If the area of an ellipse is $\pi ab/4$, find the centroid of the area for a semiellipse.

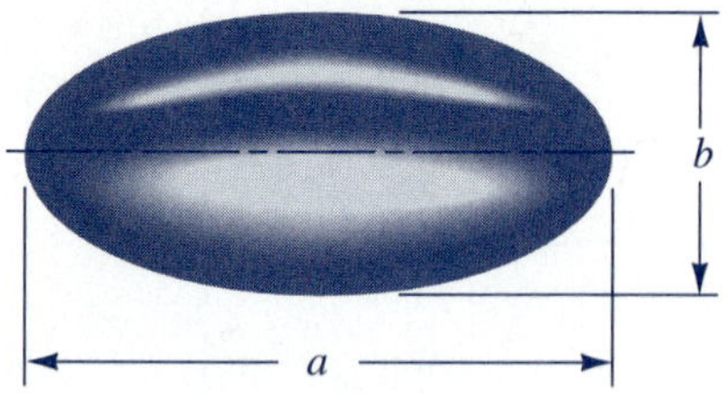

Figure P.8.50.

8.51. Find the centroidal coordinate y_c of the shaded area shown, using the theorems of Pappus and Guldinus.

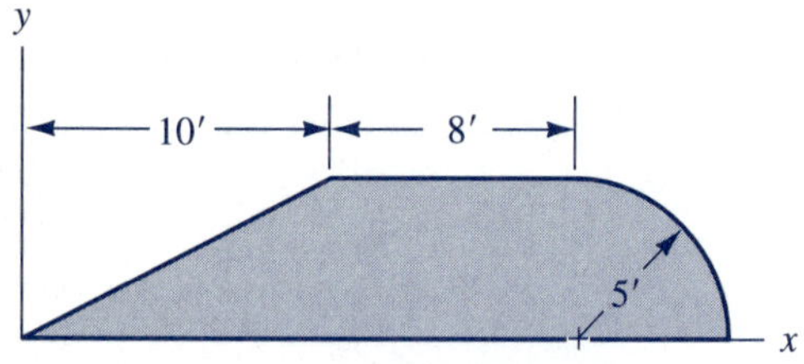

Figure P.8.51.

8.52. The cutting tool of a lathe is programmed to cut along the dashed line as shown. What are the volume and the area of the body of revolution formed on the lathe?

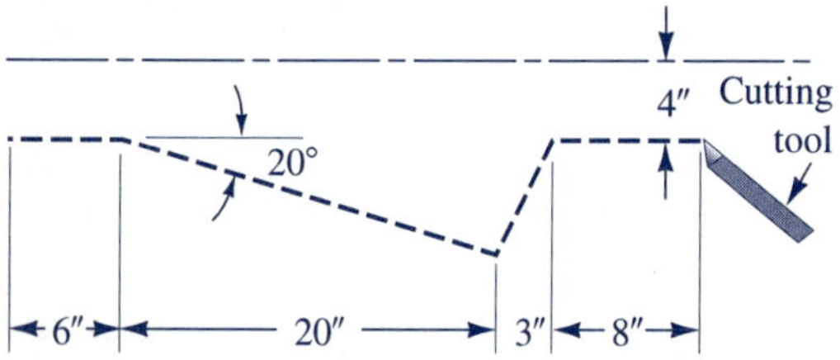

Figure P.8.52.

8.53. Find the surface area and volume of the right conical frustum.

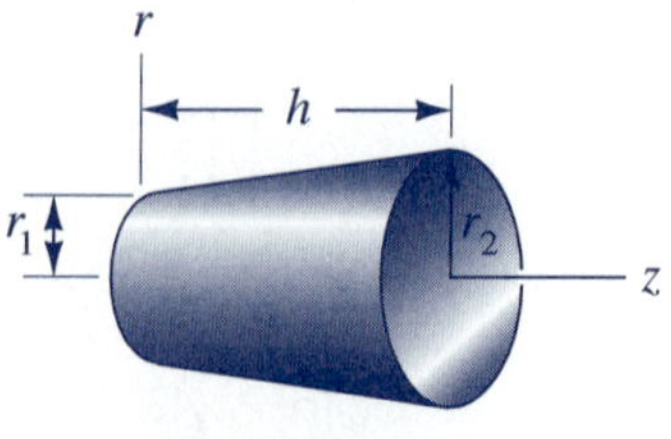

Figure P.8.53.

8.54. Find the surface area and volume of the Earth entry capsule for an unmanned Mars sampling mission. Approximate the rounded nose with a pointed nose as shown with the dashed lines.

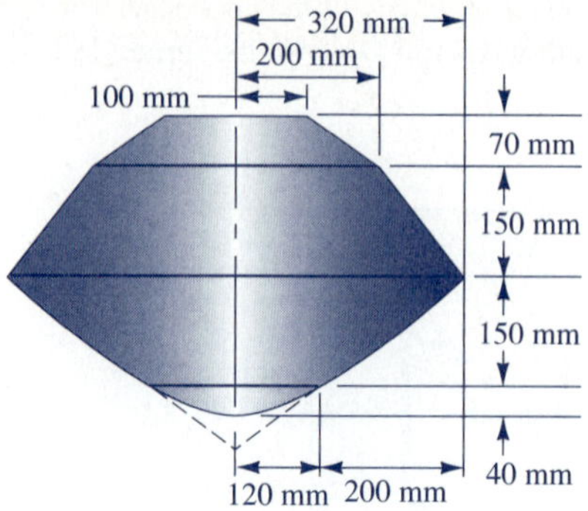

Figure P.8.54.

8.55. Find the volume and surface area of the Apollo spaceship used for lunar exploration.

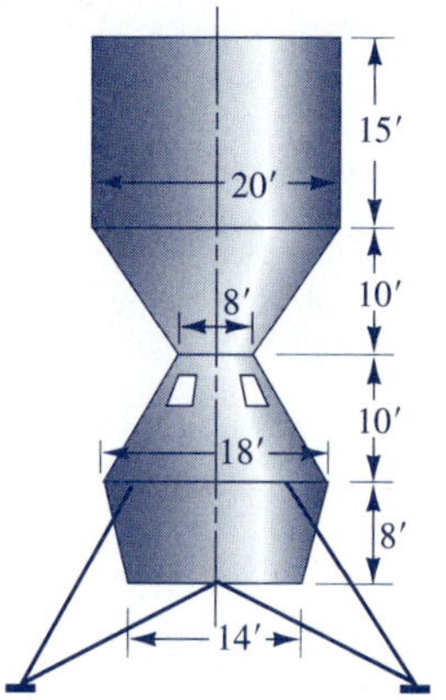

Figure P.8.55.

8.56. Find the center of volume r_c for the machine element shown.

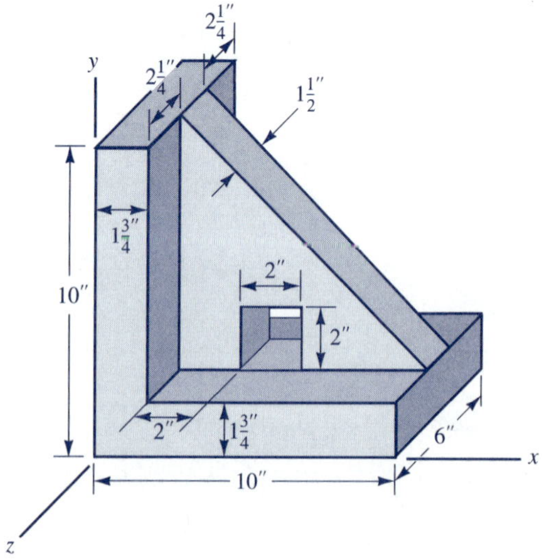

Figure P.8.56.

8.5 Second Moments and the Product of Area[3] of a Plane Area

We shall now consider other properties of a plane area relative to a given reference. The *second moments* of the area A about the x and y axes (Fig. 8.19), denoted as I_{xx} and I_{yy}, respectively, are defined as

$$I_{xx} = \int_A y^2 \, dA \tag{8.18a}$$

$$I_{yy} = \int_A x^2 \, dA \tag{8.18b}$$

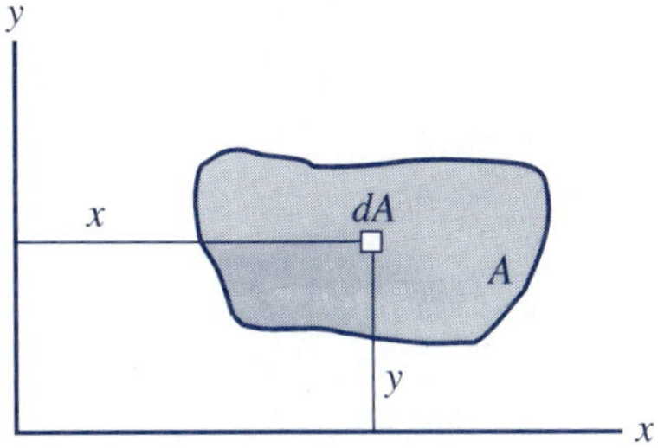

Figure 8.19. Plane surface.

The second moment of area cannot be negative, in contrast to the first moment. Furthermore, because the square of the distance from the axis is used, elements of area that are farthest from the axis contribute most to the second moment of area.

In an analogy to the centroid, the entire area may be concentrated at a single point (k_x, k_y) to give the same second moment of area for a given reference. Thus,

$$Ak_x^2 = I_{xx} = \int_A y^2 \, dA; \qquad \text{therefore, } k_x^2 = \frac{\int_A y^2 \, dA}{A}$$
$$Ak_y^2 = I_{yy} = \int_A x^2 \, dA; \qquad \text{therefore, } k_y^2 = \frac{\int_A x^2 \, dA}{A} \tag{8.19}$$

The distances k_x and k_y are called the *radii of gyration. This point will have a position that depends not only on the shape of the area but also on the position of the reference.* This situation is unlike the centroid, whose location is independent of the reference position.

The *product of area* relates an area directly to a set of axes and is defined as

$$I_{xy} = \int_A xy \, dA \tag{8.20}$$

[3]We often use the expressions *moment* and *product of inertia* for second moment and product of area, respectively. However, we shall also use the former expressions in Chapter 9 in connection with mass distributions.

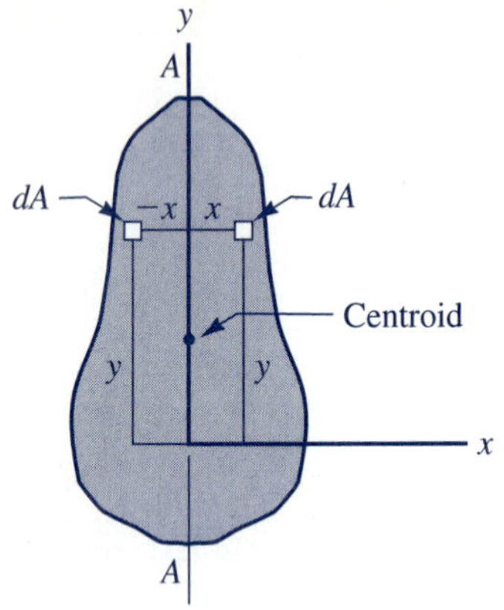

Figure 8.20. Area symmetric about y axis.

This quantity may be negative.

If the area under consideration has an axis of symmetry, the product of area for this axis and any axis orthogonal to this axis must be zero. You can readily reach this conclusion by considering the area in Fig. 8.20, which is symmetrical about the axis A–A. Notice that the centroid is somewhere along this axis. (Why ?) The axis of symmetry has been indicated as the y axis, and an arbitrary x axis coplanar with the area has been shown. Also indicated are two elemental areas that are positioned as mirror images about the y axis. The contribution to the product of area of each element is $xy\,dA$, but with opposite signs, and so the net result is zero. Since the entire area can be considered to be composed of such pairs, it becomes evident that the product of area for such cases is zero. This *should not* be taken to mean that a nonsymmetric area cannot have a zero product of area about a set of axes. We shall discuss this last condition in more detail later.

8.6 Transfer Theorems

We shall now set forth a theorem that will be of great use in computing second moments and products of area for areas that can be decomposed into simple parts (composite areas). With this theorem, we can find second moments or products of area about any axis in terms of second moments or products of area about a *parallel* set of axes going through the *centroid* of the area in question.

An x axis is shown in Fig. 8.21 parallel to and at a distance d from an axis x' going through the centroid of the area. The latter axis you will recall is a *centroidal axis*. The second moment of area about the x axis is

$$I_{xx} = \int_A y^2\,dA = \int_A (y' + d)^2\,dA$$

where the distance y has been replaced by $(y' + d)$. Carrying out the squaring operation and integrating, leads to the result

$$I_{xx} = \int_A y'^2\,dA + 2d\int_A y'\,dA + Ad^2$$

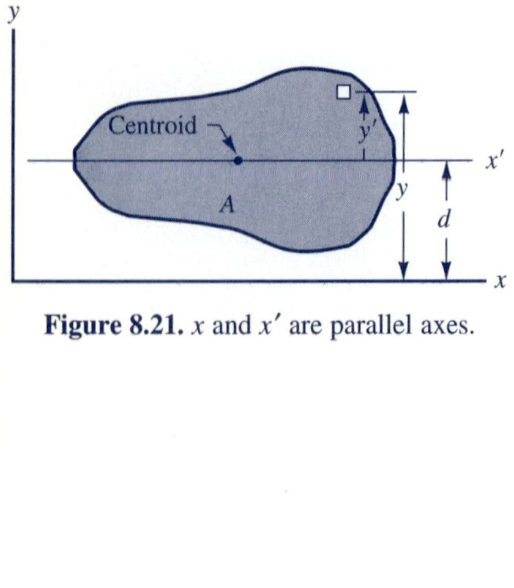

Figure 8.21. x and x' are parallel axes.

The first term on the right-hand side is by definition $I_{x'x'}$. The second term involves the first moment of area about the x' axis. But the x' axis here is a centroidal axis, and so the second term is zero. We can now state the transfer theorem (frequently called the parallel-axis theorem):

$$I_{\text{about any axis}} = I_{\substack{\text{about a parallel}\\ \text{axis at centroid}}} + Ad^2 \tag{8.21}$$

where d is the perpendicular distance between the axis for which I is being computed and the parallel centroidal axis.

In strength of materials, a course generally following statics, second moments of area about noncentroidal axes are commonly used. The areas involved are complicated and not subject to simple integration. Accordingly, in structural handbooks, the areas and second moments about various centroidal axes are listed for many of the practical configurations with the understanding that designers will use the parallel-axis theorem for axes not at the centroid.

Let us now examine the product of area in order to establish a parallel-axis theorem for this quantity. Accordingly, two references are shown in Fig. 8.22, one (x', y') at the centroid and the other (x, y) positioned arbitrarily but *parallel* relative to $x'y'$. Note that c and d are the x and y *coordinates*, respectively, of the centroid of A as measured from reference xy. These coordinates accordingly must have the proper signs, dependent on what quadrant the centroid of A is in relative to xy. The product of area about the noncentroidal axes xy can then be given as

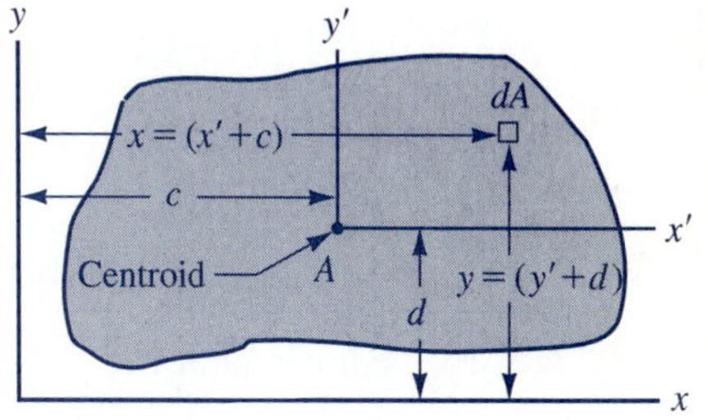

Figure 8.22. c and d measured from xy.

$$I_{xy} = \int_A xy\, dA = \int_A (x' + c)(y' + d)\, dA$$

Carrying out the multiplication, we get

$$I_{xy} = \int_A x'y'\, dA + c\int_A y'\, dA + d\int_A x'\, dA + Adc$$

Clearly, the first term on the right side by definition is $I_{x'y'}$, whereas the next two terms are zero since x' and y' are centroidal axes. Thus, we arrive at a parallel-axis theorem for products of area of the form:

$$I_{xy \text{ for any set of axes}} = I_{x'y' \text{ for a parallel set of axes at centroid}} + Adc \tag{8.22}$$

It is important to remember that c and d are measured *from the xy axes to the centroid* and must have the appropriate sign. This will be carefully pointed out again in the examples of Section 8.7.

8.7 Computations Involving Second Moments and Products of Area

We shall examine examples for the computation of second moments and products of an area.

Example 8.6

A rectangle is shown in Fig. 8.23. Compute the second moments and products of area about the centroidal $x'y'$ axes as well as about the xy axes.

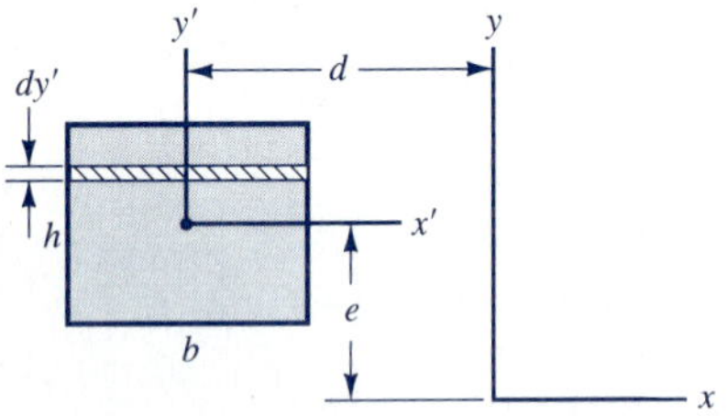

Figure 8.23. Rectangle: base b, height h.

$I_{x'x'}$, $I_{y'y'}$, $I_{x'y'}$. For computing $I_{x'x'}$, we can use a strip of width dy' at a distance y' from the x' axis. The area dA then becomes $b\,dy'$. Hence, we have

$$I_{x'x'} = \int_{-h/2}^{+h/2} y'^2 b\,dy' = b\left.\frac{y'^3}{3}\right|_{-h/2}^{+h/2} = \frac{b}{3}\left(\frac{h^3}{8} + \frac{h^3}{8}\right) = \frac{1}{12}bh^3 \qquad \text{(a)}$$

This is a common result and should well be remembered since it occurs so often. Verbally, for such an axis, the second moment of area is equal to 1/12 the base b times the height h cubed. The second moment of area for the y' axis can immediately be written as

$$I_{y'y'} = \tfrac{1}{12}hb^3 \qquad \text{(b)}$$

where the base and height have simply been interchanged.

As a result of the previous statements on symmetry, we immediately note that

$$I_{x'y'} = 0 \qquad \text{(c)}$$

I_{xx}, I_{yy}, I_{xy}. Employing the transfer theorems, we get

$$I_{xx} = \tfrac{1}{12}bh^3 + bhe^2 \qquad \text{(d)}$$

$$I_{yy} = \tfrac{1}{12}hb^3 + bhd^2 \qquad \text{(e)}$$

In computing the product of area, we must be careful to employ the proper signs for the transfer distances. In checking the derivation of the transfer theorem, we see that these distances are measured from the noncentroidal axes to the centroid C. Therefore, in this problem the transfer distances are $(+e)$ and $(-d)$. Hence, the computation of I_{xy} becomes

$$I_{xy} = 0 + (bh)(+e)(-d) = -bhed \qquad \text{(f)}$$

and is thus a negative quantity.

Example 8.7

What are I_{xx}, I_{yy}, and I_{xy} for the area under the parabolic curve shown in Fig. 8.24?

To find I_{xx}, we may use horizontal strips of width dy as shown in Fig. 8.25. We can then say for I_{xx}:

$$I_{xx} = \int_0^{10} y^2[dy(10 - x)]$$

But

$$x = \sqrt{10}y^{1/2}$$

Therefore,

$$I_{xx} = \int_0^{10} y^2(10 - \sqrt{10}y^{1/2})\,dy$$

$$= \left[10\frac{y^3}{3} - \sqrt{10}y^{7/2}\left(\frac{2}{7}\right)\right]_0^{10}$$

$$= \frac{10(10^3)}{3} - \sqrt{10}(10^{7/2})\left(\frac{2}{7}\right) = 476.2 \text{ mm}^4$$

As for I_{yy}, we use vertical infinitesimal strips as shown in Fig. 8.26. We can, accordingly, say:

$$I_{yy} = \int_0^{10} x^2(y\,dx) = \int_0^{10} \frac{x^4}{10}\,dx$$

$$= \left.\frac{x^5}{50}\right|_0^{10} = 2{,}000 \text{ mm}^4$$

Finally, for I_{xy} we use an infinitesimal area element $dx\,dy$ shown in Fig. 8.27. We must now perform multiple integration.[4] Thus, we have

$$I_{xy} = \int_0^{10}\int_{y=0}^{y=x^2/10} xy\,dy\,dx$$

Notice by holding x constant and letting y first run from $y = 0$ to the curve $y = x^2/10$ we cover the vertical strip of thickness dx at position x such as is shown in Fig. 8.26. Then by letting x run from zero to 10, we cover the entire area. Accordingly, we first integrate with respect to y holding x constant. Thus,

$$I_{xy} = \int_0^{10} x\left(\frac{y^2}{2}\right)\Bigg|_0^{x^2/10} dx = \int_0^{10} \frac{x^5}{200}\,dx$$

Next, integrating with respect to x, we have

$$I_{xy} = \left.\frac{x^6}{1{,}200}\right|_0^{10} = 833 \text{ mm}^4$$

[4]This multiple integration involves boundaries requiring some *variable* limits, in contrast to previous multiple integrations.

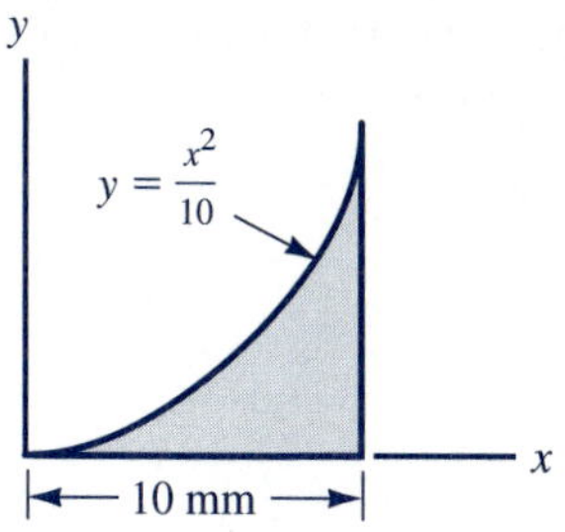

Figure 8.24. Plane area.

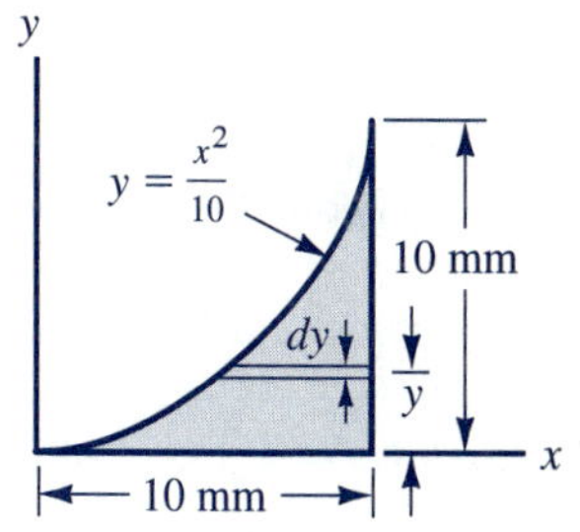

Figure 8.25. Horizontal strip.

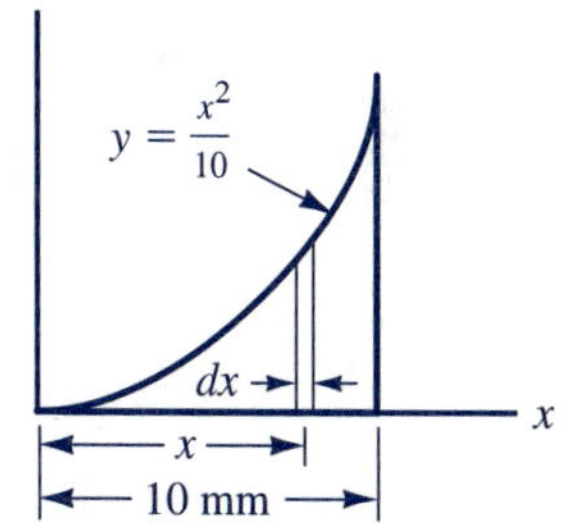

Figure 8.26. Vertical strip.

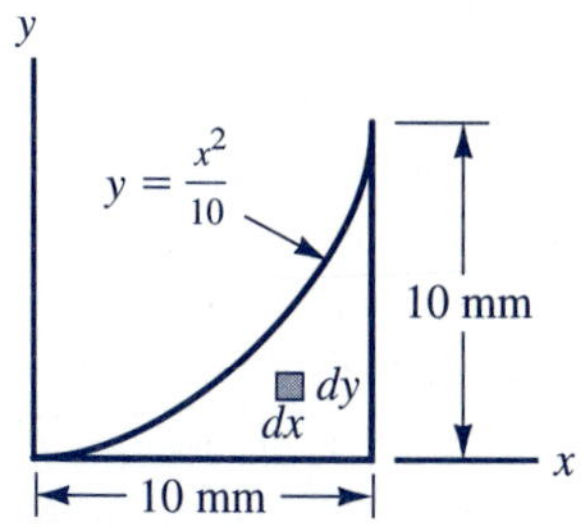

Figure 8.27. Element for multiple integration

Example 8.8

Compute the second moment of area of a circular area about a diameter (Fig. 8.28).

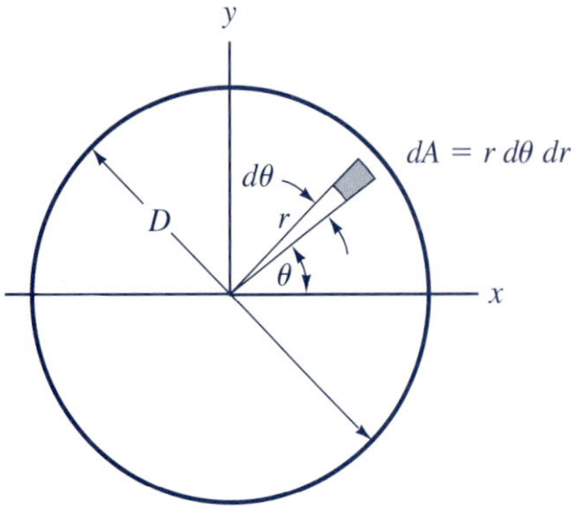

Figure 8.28. Circular area with polar coordinates.

Using polar coordinates, we have[5] for I_{xx}:

$$I_{xx} = \int_0^{D/2}\int_0^{2\pi} (r\sin\theta)^2 r\,d\theta\,dr = \int_0^{D/2} \pi r^3\,dr$$

Completing the integration, we have

$$I_{xx} = \frac{r^4}{4}\pi\Big|_0^{D/2} = \boxed{\pi\frac{D^4}{64}}$$

The product of area I_{xy} must be zero, owing to symmetry of the area about the xy axes.

[5]The integral $\int_0^{2\pi}\sin^2\theta\,d\theta$ may be evaluated by methods of substitution or may readily be seen in the following manner. $\int_0^{2\pi}\sin^2\theta\,d\theta$ equals the area under the curve shown, which is half the area of the dashed rectangle. Hence, this integral equals π.

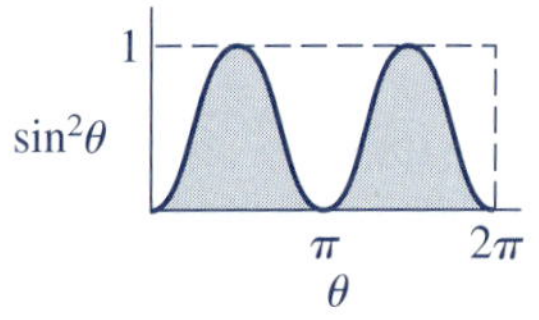

In the previous examples, we computed second moments and products of area using the calculus. Many problems of interest involve an area that may be subdivided into simpler *component* areas. Such an area has been referred to in earlier discussions as a composite area. The second moments and products of area for certain centroidal axes of many simple areas may be found in engineering handbooks (also see the inside covers). Using these formulas combined with the parallel-axis theorems, we can easily compute desired second moments and products of area for composite areas as we have done earlier for first moments of area. The following example illustrates this procedure.

Example 8.9

Find the centroid of the area of the unequal-leg Z section shown in Fig. 8.29. Next, determine the second moment of area about the centroidal axes parallel to the sides of the Z section. Finally, determine the product of area for the aforementioned centroidal axes.

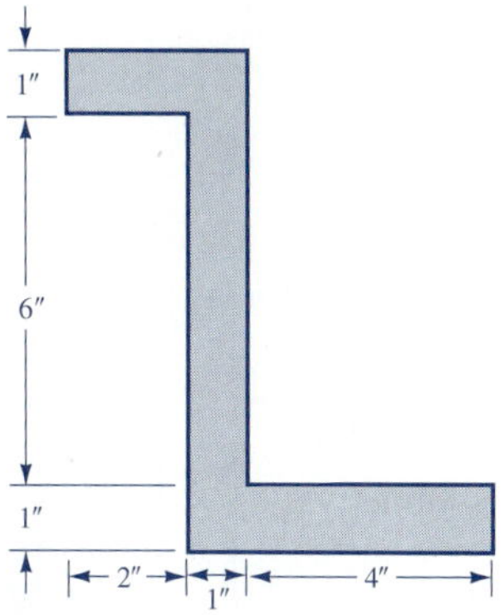

Figure 8.29. Unequal-leg Z section.

We shall subdivide the Z section into three rectangular areas, as shown in Fig. 8.30. Also, we shall insert a convenient reference xy, as shown in the diagram. To find the centroid, we proceed in the following manner:

A_i (in.^{2})	$\bar{x}_i$ (in.)	$\bar{y}_i$ (in.)	$A_i\bar{x}_i$ (in.^{3})	$A_i\bar{y}_i$ (in.^{3})
1. (2)(1) = 2	1	7.50	2	15
2. (8)(1) = 8	2.50	4	20	32
3. (4)(1) = 4	5	.50	20	2
$\sum_i A_i = 14$			$\sum_i A_i\bar{x}_i = 42$	$\sum_i A_i\bar{y}_i = 49$

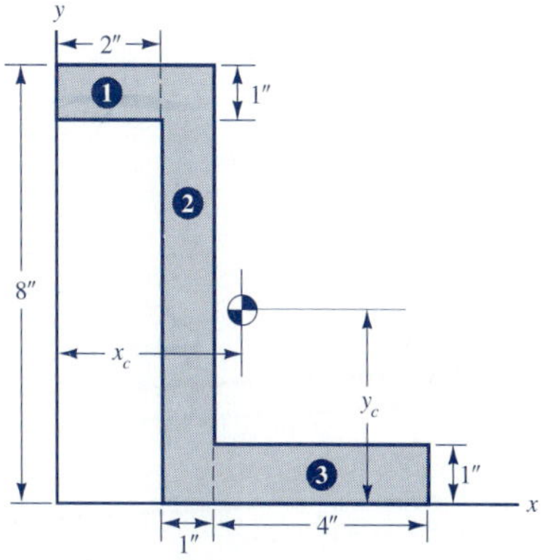

Figure 8.30. Composite area.

Example 8.9 (Continued)

Therefore,

$$x_c = \frac{\sum_i A_i \bar{x}_i}{\sum_i A_i} = \frac{42}{14} = \boxed{3 \text{ in.}}$$

$$y_c = \frac{\sum_i A_i \bar{y}_i}{\sum_i A_i} = \frac{49}{14} = \boxed{3.5 \text{ in.}}$$

We have shown the centroidal axes $x_c y_c$ in Fig. 8.31. We now find $I_{x_c x_c}$ and $I_{y_c y_c}$ using the parallel-axis theorem and the formulas $\frac{1}{12}bh^3$ and $\frac{1}{12}hb^3$ for the second moments of area about centroidal axes of symmetry of a rectangle.

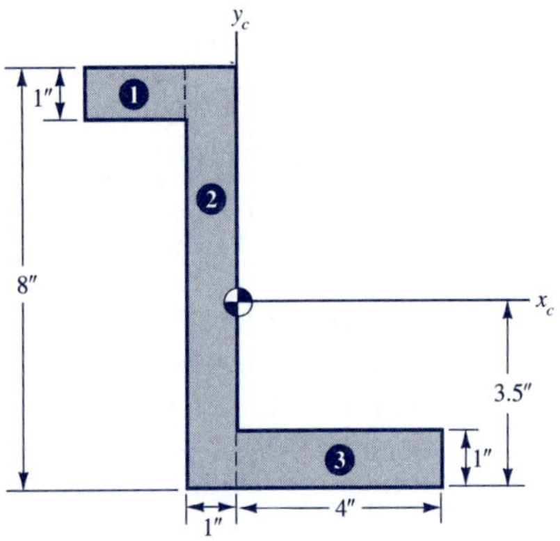

Figure 8.31. Centroidal axes $x_c y_c$.

$$I_{x_c x_c} = \underbrace{\left[(\tfrac{1}{12})(2)(1^3) + (2)(4^2)\right]}_{①} + \underbrace{\left[(\tfrac{1}{12})(1)(8^3) + (8)(\tfrac{1}{12})^2\right]}_{②} + \underbrace{\left[(\tfrac{1}{12})(4)(1^3) + (4)(3^2)\right]}_{③} = \boxed{113.2 \text{ in.}^4}$$

$$I_{y_c y_c} = \underbrace{\left[(\tfrac{1}{12})(1)(2^3) + (2)(2^2)\right]}_{①} + \underbrace{\left[(\tfrac{1}{12})(8)(1^3) + (8)(\tfrac{1}{2})^2\right]}_{②} + \underbrace{\left[(\tfrac{1}{12})(1)(4^3) + (4)(2^2)\right]}_{③} = \boxed{32.67 \text{ in.}^4}$$

Finally, we consider the product of area $I_{x_c y_c}$. Here we must be cautious in using the parallel-axis theorem. Remember that $x_c y_c$ are centroidal axes for the *entire* area of the Z section. In using the parallel-axis theorem for a *subarea*, we must note that $x_c y_c$ are not centroidal axes for the subarea. The centroidal axes to be used in this problem for subareas are the axes of symmetry of each subarea. In short, $x_c y_c$ are simply axes about which we are computing the product of area of each subarea. Therefore, in the parallel-axis theorem, the transfer distances c and d are measured *from the $x_c y_c$ axes to the centroid* in each subarea, as noted in the development of the parallel-axis theorem. The proper sign must be assigned each time to the transfer distances with this in mind. We have for $I_{x_c y_c}$:

$$I_{x_c y_c} = \underbrace{[0 + (2)(-2)(4)]}_{①} + \underbrace{[0 + (8)(-\tfrac{1}{2})(\tfrac{1}{2})]}_{②} + \underbrace{[0 + (4)(2)(-3)]}_{③} = \boxed{-42 \text{ in.}^4}$$

PROBLEMS

8.57. Find I_{xx}, I_{yy}, and I_{xy} for the triangle shown. Give the results in feet.

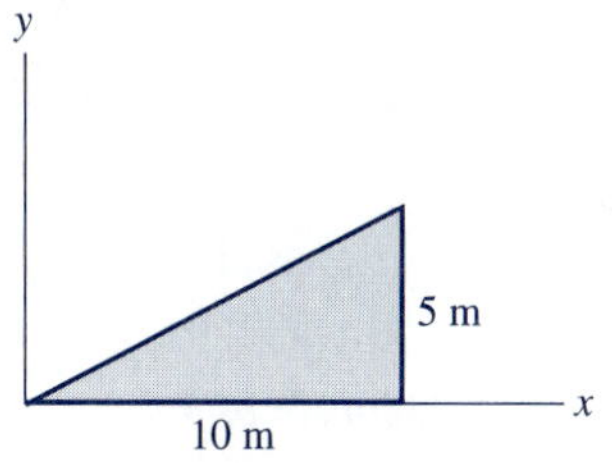

Figure P.8.57.

8.58. What are the second moments and products of area of the ellipse for reference xy? [*Hint:* Can you work with one quadrant and then multiply by 4 for the second moments?]

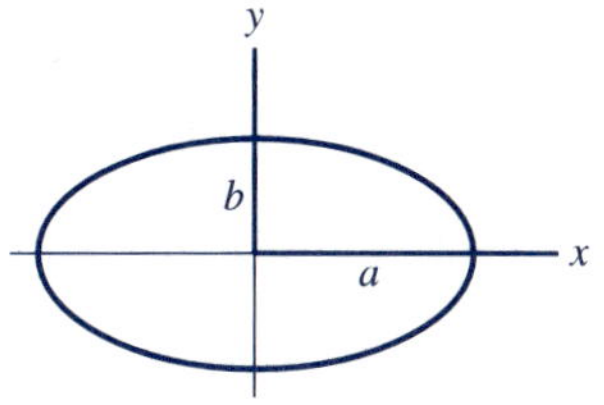

Figure P.8.58.

8.59. Find I_{xx} and I_{yy} for the quarter circle of radius 5 m.

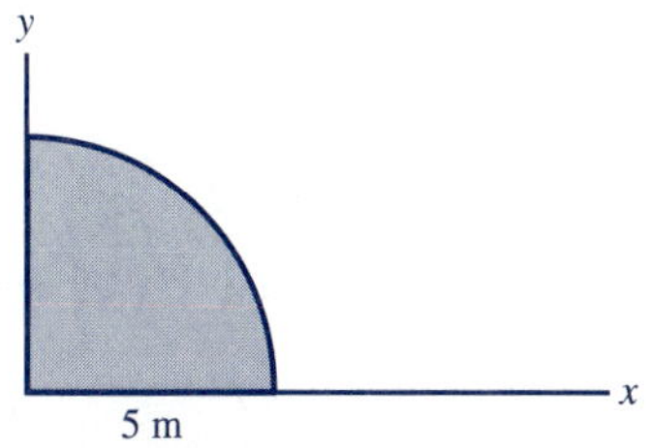

Figure P.8.59.

8.60. Find I_{xx}, I_{yy}, and I_{xy} for the shaded area.

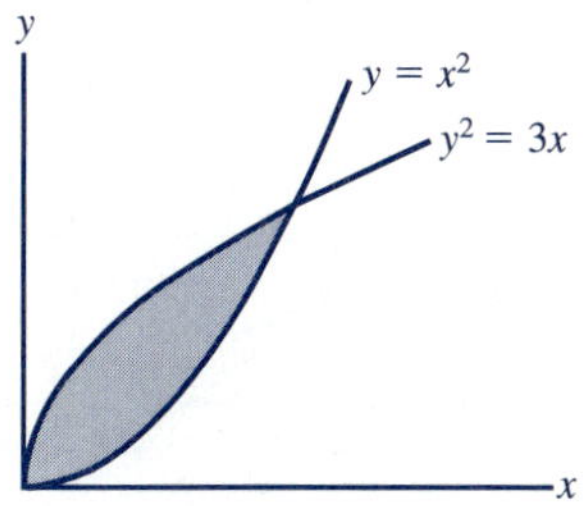

Figure P.8.60.

8.61. Find I_{yy} for the shaded area. You must first determine the constant c.

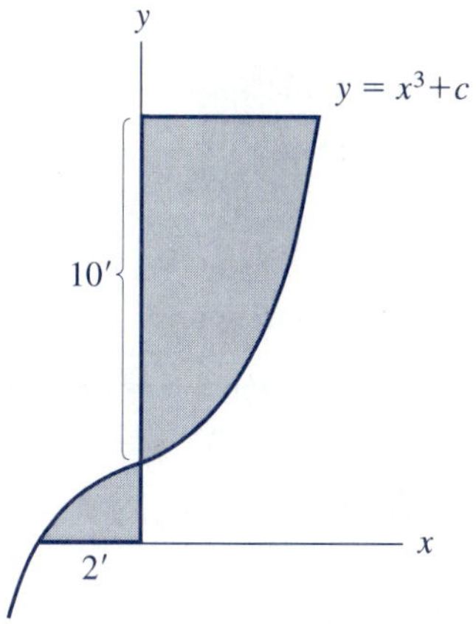

Figure P.8.61.

8.62. Find I_{yy} for the area between the curves

$$y = 2 \sin x \text{ ft}$$
$$y = \sin 2x \text{ ft}$$

from $x = 0$ to $x = \pi$ ft.

8.63. Find I_{yy} for the areas enclosed between curves $y = \cos x$ and $y = \sin x$ and the lines $x = 0$ and $x = \pi/2$.

8.64. Show that $I_{xx} = bh^3/12$, $I_{yy} = b^3h/12$, and $I_{xy} = b^2h^2/24$ for the right triangle.

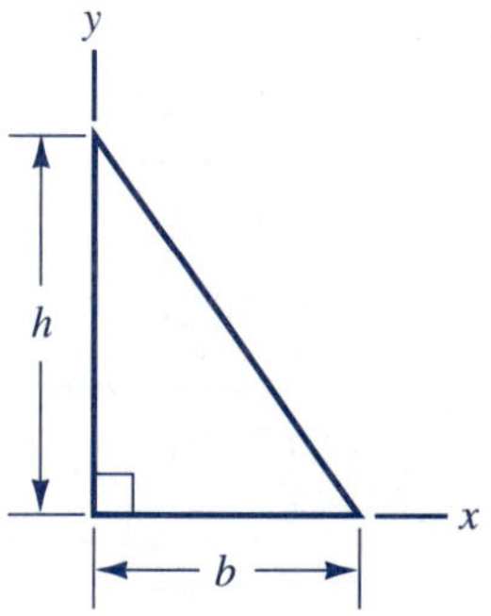

Figure P.8.64.

8.65. Find I_{xx}, I_{yy}, and I_{xy} for the shaded area.

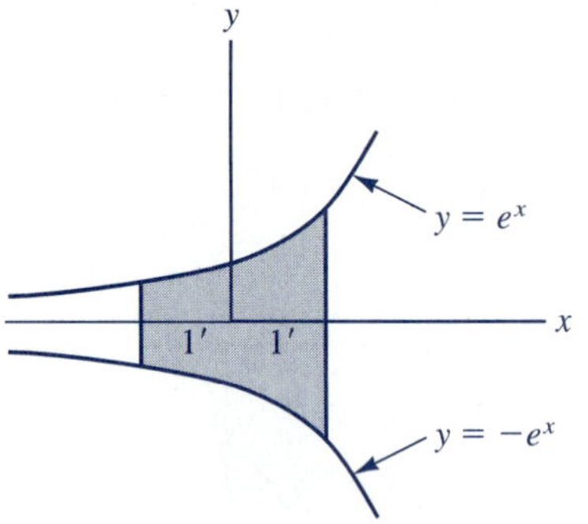

Figure P.8.65.

8.66. Find I_{xx}, I_{yy}, and I_{xy} for the area of Problem 8.4. The equation of the curve is $y^2 = 20x - 60$.

8.67. Find I_{xx}, I_{yy}, and I_{xy} for the cross-section shown.

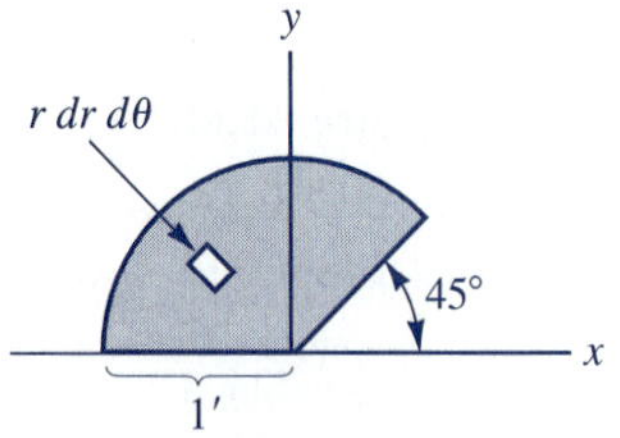

Figure P.8.67.

8.68. Find I_{xx} and I_{yy} for the area of Problem 8.5. The equation of the parabola is $y = (x^2/9) - 5$. [*Hint:* The area of a vertical element in the region below the x axis is $(0 - y)\,dx$.]

8.69. In Problem 8.68 determine I_{xy} using multiple integration.

8.70. Find the second moments of area about axes xy for the shaded area shown.

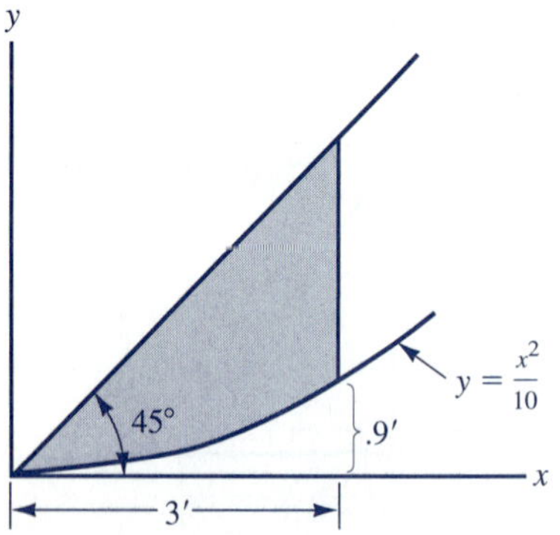

Figure P.8.70.

8.71. If the second moment of area about axis A–A is known to be 600 ft^4, what is the second moment of area about a parallel axis B–B a distance 3 ft from A–A, for an area of 10 ft^2? The centroid of this area is 4 ft from B–B.

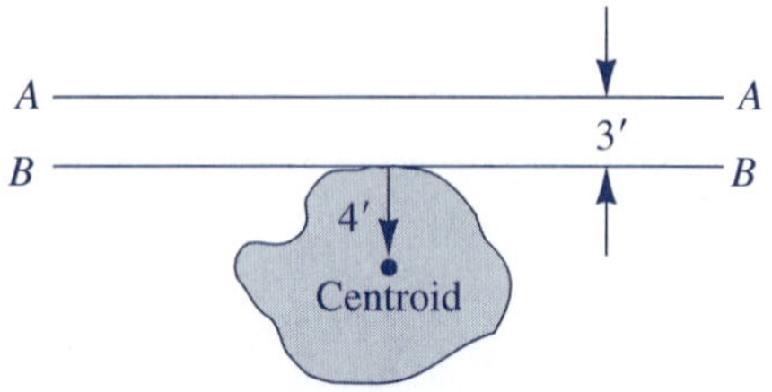

Figure P.8.71.

8.72. Using the results of Problem 8.64, show that $I_{x_cx_c} = bh^3/36$, $I_{y_cy_c} = hb^3/36$, and $I_{x_cy_c} = -b^2h^2/72$ for the right triangle shown.

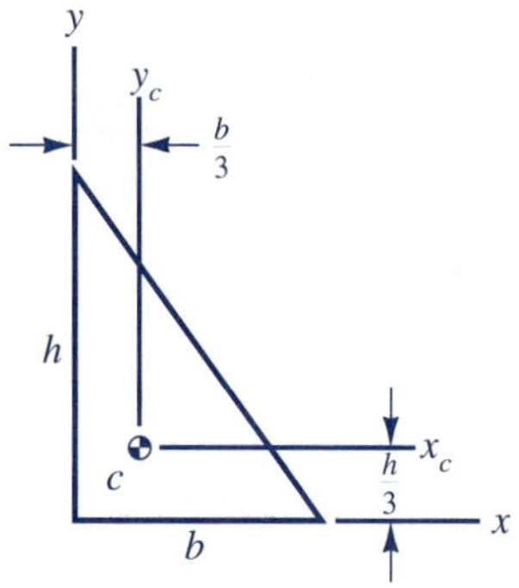

Figure P.8.72.

8.73. Show that $I_{xx} = bh^3/12$, $I_{yy} = (hb/12)(b^2 + ab + a^2)$, and $I_{xy} = (h^2b/24)(2a + b)$ for the triangle. [*Hint:* Break the triangle into two right triangles for which the various moments are known. (See Problem 8.72.)]

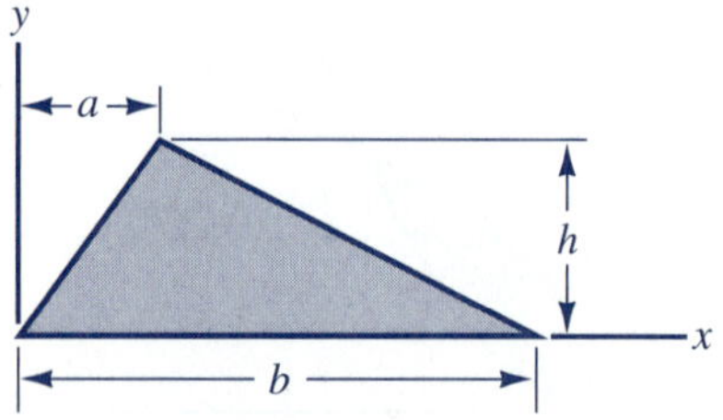

Figure P.8.73.

8.74. In Problem 8.73, show that $I_{x_cx_c} = bh^3/36$, $I_{y_cy_c} = (bh/36)(b2 - ab + a^2)$, and $I_{x_cy_c} = (h^2b/72)(2a - b)$ for the triangle. [*Hint:* Use the results of Problems 8.11 and 8.73 and the parallel-axis theorem.]

8.75. Find I_{xx}, I_{yy}, and I_{xy} of the extruded section. Disregard all rounded edges. Do this problem using 4 areas. Check using 2 areas.

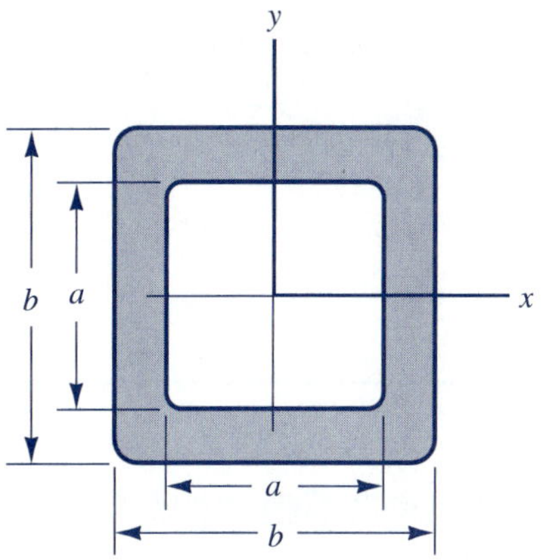

Figure P.8.75.

8.76. Find the second moment of area of the rectangle (with a hole) about the base of the rectangle. Also, determine the product of area about the base and left side.

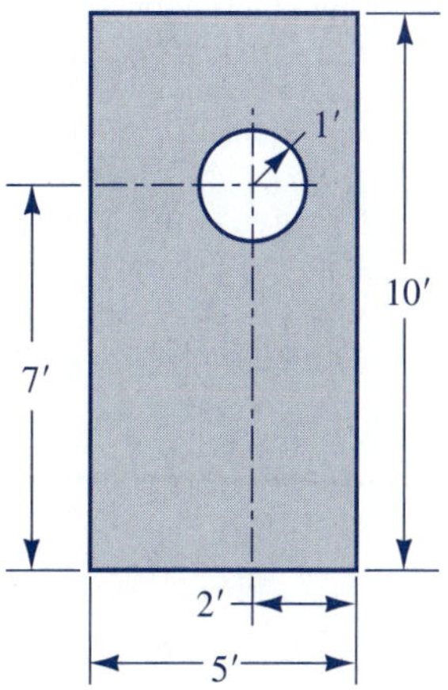

Figure P.8.76.

8.77. Find I_{xx}, I_{yy}, $I_{x_cx_c}$, and $I_{y_cy_c}$ for the structural "hat" section. Disregard all rounded edges.

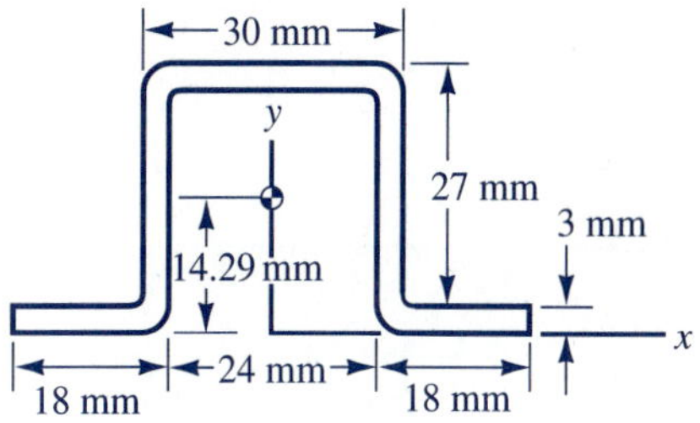

Figure P.8.77.

8.78. Find I_{xx}, I_{yy}, and I_{xy} of the hexagon.

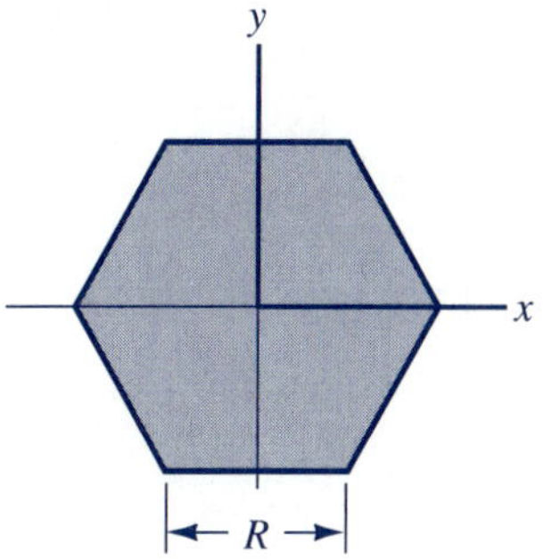

Figure P.8.78.

8.79. A beam cross-section is made up of an I-shaped section with an additional thick plate welded on. Find the second moments of area for the centroidal axes x_cy_c of the beam cross-section. What is $I_{x_cy_c}$? Give the results in millimeters.

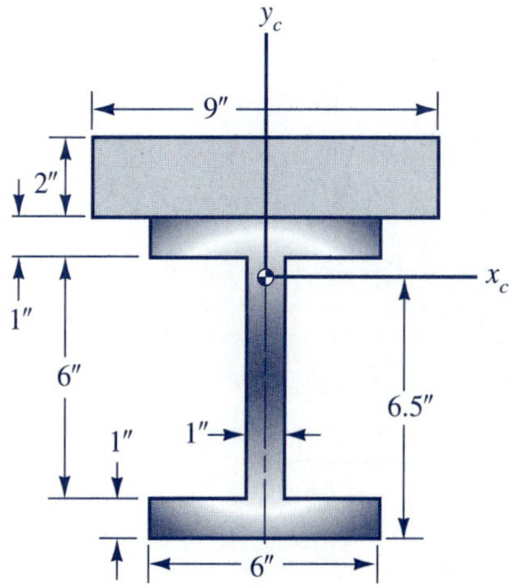

Figure P.8.79.

8.80. Find the second moments of the area shown about centroidal axes parallel to the x and y axes. That is, find $I_{x_c x_c}$ and $I_{y_c y_c}$. Give the results in millimeters.

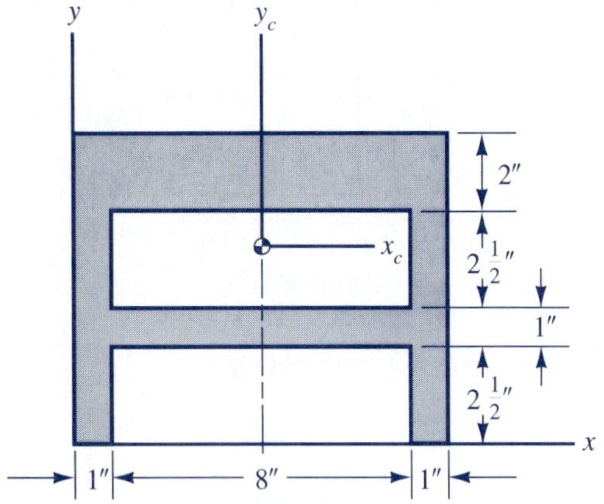

Figure P.8.80.

8.81. The following configuration is given for a plane area.

(a) Find the first moments of area about the x and y axes.

(b) Find the second moments of area for these axes.

(c) Find the product of area for these axes.

(d) What are the radii of gyration, k_x and k_y, for this area?

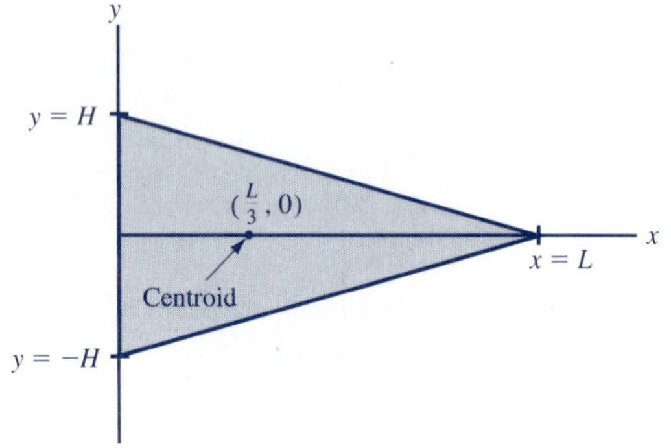

Figure P.8.81.

8.8 Relation Between Second Moments and Products of Area

We shall now show that we can ascertain second moments and product of area relative to a rotated reference $x'y'$ if we know these quantities for reference xy that has the *same origin.* Such a reference $x'y'$ rotated an angle α from xy (counterclockwise as positive) is shown in Fig. 8.32. We shall assume that the second moments and product of area for the unprimed reference are known.

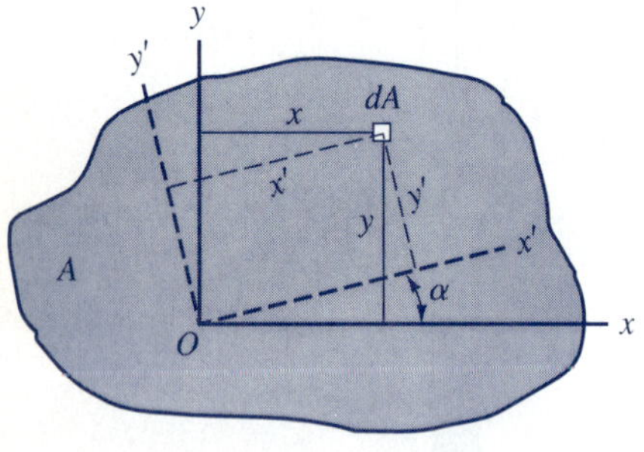

Figure 8.32. Rotation of axes.

Before proceeding, we must know the relation between the coordinates of the area elements dA for the two references. From Fig. 8.32, you may show that

$$x' = x \cos \alpha + y \sin \alpha \tag{8.23a}$$

$$y' = -x \sin \alpha + y \cos \alpha \tag{8.23b}$$

With relation 8.23b, we can express $I_{x'x'}$ in the following manner:

$$I_{x'x'} = \int_A (y')^2 \, dA = \int_A (-x \sin \alpha + y \cos \alpha)^2 \, dA \tag{8.24}$$

Carrying out the square, we have

$$I_{x'x'} = \sin^2 \alpha \int_A x^2 \, dA - 2 \sin \alpha \cos \alpha \int_A xy \, dA + \cos^2 \alpha \int_A y^2 \, dA$$

Therefore,

$$I_{x'x'} = I_{yy} \sin^2 \alpha + I_{xx} \cos^2 \alpha - 2I_{xy} \sin \alpha \cos \alpha \tag{8.25}$$

A more common form of the desired relation can be formed by using the following trigonometric identities:

$$\cos^2\alpha = \tfrac{1}{2}(1+\cos 2\alpha) \quad \text{(a)}$$
$$\sin^2\alpha = \tfrac{1}{2}(1-\cos 2\alpha) \quad \text{(b)}$$
$$2\sin\alpha\cos\alpha = \sin 2\alpha \quad \text{(c)}$$

We then have[6]

$$I_{x'x'} = \frac{I_{xx}+I_{yy}}{2} + \frac{I_{xx}-I_{yy}}{2}\cos 2\alpha - I_{xy}\sin 2\alpha \quad (8.26)$$

To determine $I_{y'y'}$, we need only replace the α in the preceding result by $(\alpha + \pi/2)$. Thus,

$$I_{y'y'} = \frac{I_{xx}+I_{yy}}{2} + \frac{I_{xx}-I_{yy}}{2}\cos(2\alpha+\pi) - I_{xy}\sin(2\alpha+\pi)$$

Note that $\cos(2\alpha+\pi) = -\cos 2\alpha$ and $\sin(2\alpha+\pi) = -\sin 2\alpha$. Hence, the equation above becomes

$$I_{y'y'} = \frac{I_{xx}+I_{yy}}{2} - \frac{I_{xx}-I_{yy}}{2}\cos 2\alpha + I_{xy}\sin 2\alpha \quad (8.27)$$

Next, the product of area $I_{x'y'}$ can be computed in a similar manner:

$$I_{x'y'} = \int_A x'y'\,dA = \int_A (x\cos\alpha + y\sin\alpha)(-x\sin\alpha + y\cos\alpha)\,dA$$

This becomes

$$I_{x'y'} = \sin\alpha\cos\alpha\,(I_{xx} - I_{yy}) + (\cos^2\alpha - \sin^2\alpha)I_{xy}$$

Utilizing the previously defined trigonometric identities, we get

$$I_{x'y'} = \frac{I_{xx}-I_{yy}}{2}\sin 2\alpha + I_{xy}\cos 2\alpha \quad (8.28)$$

Thus, we see that, if we know the quantities I_{xx}, I_{yy}, and I_{xy} for some reference xy at point O, the second moments and products of area for every set of axes at point O can be computed. And if, in addition, we employ the transfer theorems, we can compute second moments and products of area for *any* reference in the plane of the area.

[6]Equations 8.26, 8.27, and 8.28 are called *transformation* equations. They will appear in the next chapter and in your upcoming solid mechanics course for variables other than second moments and products of area. In the remaining portions of this chapter, you will see that a number of important properties of second moments and products of area are deducible *directly* from these transformation equations. This primarily accounts for the importance of the transformation equations. Chapter 9 will give you additional insight into this topic.

Example 8.10

Find $I_{x'x'}$, $I_{y'y'}$ and $I_{x'y'}$ for the cross section of the beam shown in Fig. 8.33. The origin of $x'y'$ is at the centroid of the cross-section.

We shall consider three rectangles labeled in Fig. 8.34. The dimensions of these rectangles are listed below.

Rect. (1)	100 mm × 40 mm (outside outline)
Rect. (2)	20 mm × 30 mm
Rect. (3)	20 mm × 30 mm

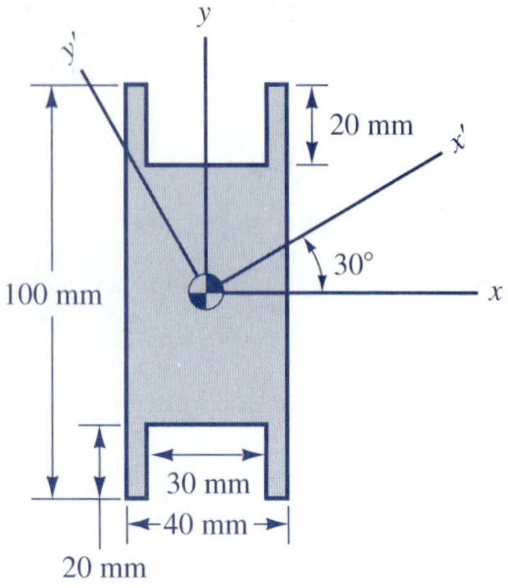

Figure 8.33. A composite area.

We shall find I_{xx}, I_{yy}, and I_{xy} as a first step. Thus

$$I_{xx} = \left(\tfrac{1}{12}\right)(40)(100)^3 - 2\left[\tfrac{1}{12}(30)(20)^3 + (20)(30)(40)^2\right] = 1.373 \times 10^6 \text{ mm}^4$$

$$I_{yy} = \left(\tfrac{1}{12}\right)(100)(40)^3 - 2\left[\tfrac{1}{12}(20)(30)^3\right] = 4.43 \times 10^5 \text{ mm}^4$$

$$I_{xy} = 0 \quad \text{(symmetry)}$$

Hence, we can now go to the transformation equations for the desired information.[7]

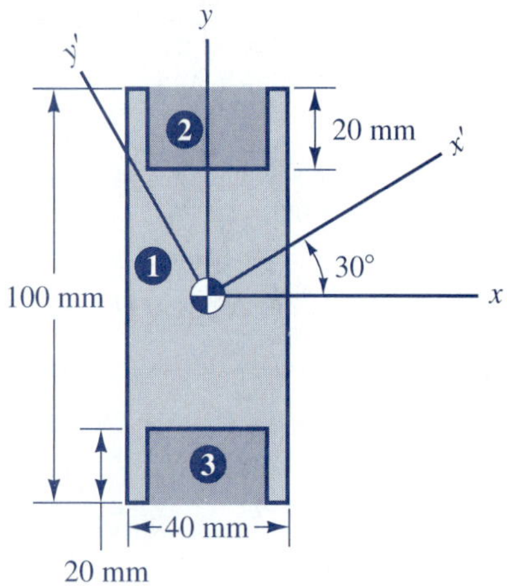

Figure 8.34. Composite area with three subareas.

$$I_{x'x'} = \frac{1.373 \times 10^6 + 4.43 \times 10^5}{2} + \frac{1.373 \times 10^6 - 4.43 \times 10^5}{2} \cos 60° + 0$$

$$= 1.141 \times 10^6 \text{ mm}^4$$

$$I_{y'y'} = \frac{1.373 \times 10^6 + 4.43 \times 10^5}{2} - \frac{1.373 \times 10^6 - 4.43 \times 10^5}{2} \cos 60° + 0$$

$$= 6.76 \times 10^5 \text{ mm}^4$$

$$I_{x'y'} = \frac{1.373 \times 10^6 - 4.43 \times 10^5}{2} \sin 60° = 4.03 \times 10^5 \text{ mm}^4$$

[7]It will be helpful to note that in going from the computation of $I_{x'x'}$ to the computation of $I_{y'y'}$, one needs only to change the sign associated with the second and third expressions for $I_{x'x'}$.

8.9 Polar Moment of Area

In the previous section, we saw that the second moments and product of area for an orthogonal reference determined all such quantities for *any* orthogonal reference having the same origin. We shall now show that the sum of the pairs of second moments of area is a constant for all such references at a point. Thus, in Fig. 8.35 we have a reference xy associated with point a. Summing I_{xx} and I_{yy} we have

$$I_{xx} + I_{yy} = \int_A y^2\, dA + \int_A x^2\, dA$$
$$= \int_A (x^2 + y^2)\, dA = \int_A r^2\, dA$$

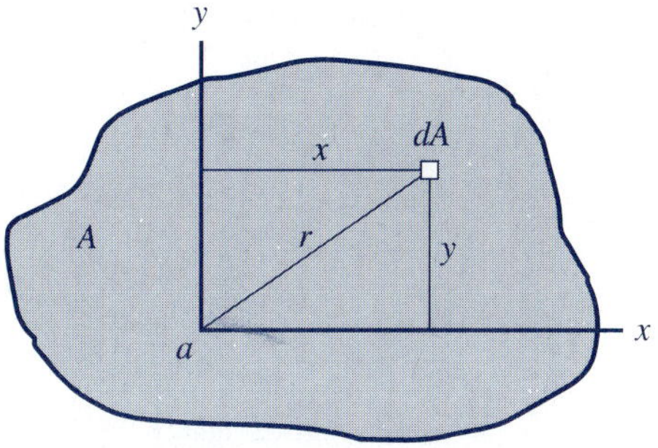

Figure 8.35. $J = I_{xx} + I_{yy}$.

Since r^2 is independent of the orientation of the coordinate system, the sum $I_{xx} + I_{yy}$ is independent of the orientation of the reference. Therefore, the sum of second moments of area about orthogonal axes is a function only of the position of the origin a for the axes. This sum is termed the *polar moment of area*, J.[8] We can then consider J to be a scalar field. Mathematically, this statement is expressed as

$$J = J(x', y') \tag{8.29}$$

where x' and y' are the coordinates as measured from some convenient reference $x'y'$ for the point of interest.

That the quantity $(I_{xx} + I_{yy})$ does not change on rotation of axes can also be deduced by summing transformation equations 8.26 and 8.27 as we suggest you do. This group of terms is accordingly termed an *invariant*. Parenthetically, we can similarly show that $(I_{xx}I_{yy} - I_{xy}^2)$ is also invariant under a rotation of axes.

[8]Quite often I_p is used for the polar moment of area.

8.10 Principal Axes

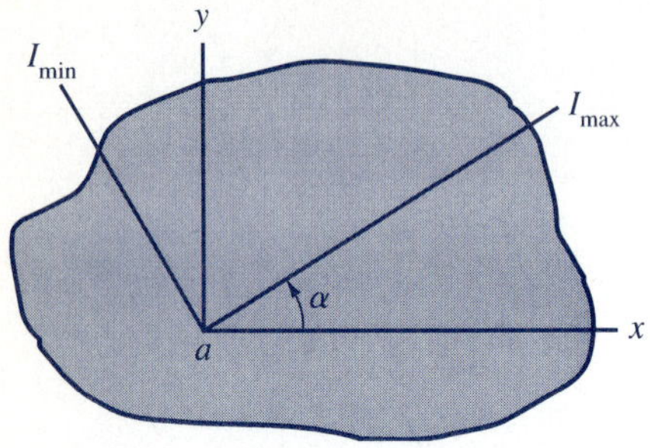

Figure 8.36. Principal axes.

Still other conclusions may be drawn about second moments and products of area associated with a point in an area. In Fig. 8.36 an area is shown with a reference xy having its origin at point a. We shall assume that I_{xx}, I_{yy}, and I_{xy} are known for this reference, and shall ask at what angle α we shall find an axis having the *maximum* second moment of area. Since the sum of the second moments of area is constant for any reference with origin at a, the *minimum* second moment of area must then correspond to an axis at *right angles* to the axis having the maximum second moment. Since second moments of area have been expressed in Eqs. 8.26 and 8.27 as functions of the variable α at a point, these extremes may readily be determined by setting the partial derivative of $I_{x'x'}$ with respect to α equal to zero. Thus,

$$\frac{\partial I_{x'x'}}{\partial \alpha} = (I_{xx} - I_{yy})(-\sin 2\alpha) - 2I_{xy}\cos 2\alpha = 0$$

If we denote the value of α that satisfies the equation above as $\tilde{\alpha}$, we have

$$(I_{yy} - I_{xx})\sin 2\tilde{\alpha} - 2I_{xy}\cos 2\tilde{\alpha} = 0$$

Hence,

$$\tan 2\tilde{\alpha} = \frac{2I_{xy}}{I_{yy} - I_{xx}} \tag{8.30}$$

This formulation gives us the angle $\tilde{\alpha}$, which corresponds to an extreme value of $I_{x'x'}$ (i.e., to a maximum or minimum value). Actually, there are two possible values of $2\tilde{\alpha}$ which are π radians apart that will satisfy the equation above. Thus,

$$2\tilde{\alpha} = \beta \qquad \text{where } \beta = \tan^{-1}\frac{2I_{xy}}{I_{yy} - I_{xx}}$$

or

$$2\tilde{\alpha} = \beta + \pi$$

This means that we have two values of $\tilde{\alpha}$, given as

$$\tilde{\alpha}_1 = \frac{\beta}{2}, \qquad \tilde{\alpha}_2 = \frac{\beta}{2} + \frac{\pi}{2}$$

Thus, there are two axes orthogonal to each other having extreme values for the second moment of area at a. On one of these axes is the maximum second moment of area and, as pointed out earlier, the minimum second moment of area must appear on the other axis. These axes are called the *principal axes.*

Let us now substitute the angle $\tilde{\alpha}$ into Eq. 8.28 for $I_{x'y'}$:

$$I_{x'y'} = \frac{I_{xx} - I_{yy}}{2} \sin 2\tilde{\alpha} + I_{xy} \cos 2\tilde{\alpha} \tag{8.31}$$

If we now form a right triangle with legs $2I_{xy}$ and $(I_{yy} - I_{xx})$ and angle $2\tilde{\alpha}$ such that Eq. (8.30) is satisfied we can readily express the sine and cosine expressions needed in the preceding equation. Thus

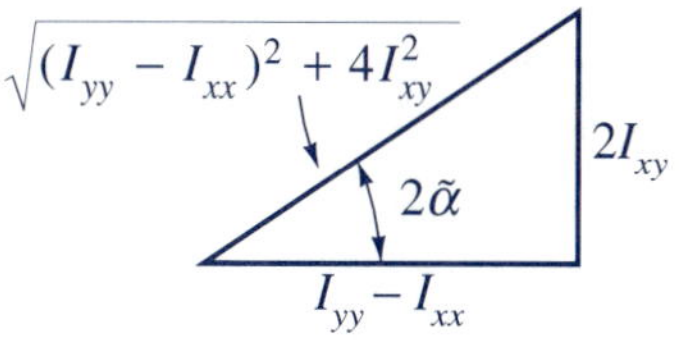

$$\sin 2\tilde{\alpha} = \frac{2I_{xy}}{\sqrt{\left(I_{yy} - I_{xx}\right)^2 + 4I_{xy}^2}}$$

$$\cos 2\tilde{\alpha} = \frac{I_{yy} - I_{xx}}{\sqrt{\left(I_{yy} - I_{xx}\right)^2 + 4I_{xy}^2}}$$

By substituting these results into Eq. 8.31, we get

$$I_{x'y'} = -\left(I_{yy} - I_{xx}\right) \frac{I_{xy}}{\left[\left(I_{yy} - I_{xx}\right)^2 + 4I_{xy}^2\right]^{1/2}} + I_{xy} \frac{I_{yy} - I_{xx}}{\left[\left(I_{yy} - I_{xx}\right)^2 + 4I_{xy}^2\right]^{1/2}}$$

Hence,

$$I_{x'y'} = 0$$

Thus, we see that the *product of area corresponding to the principal axes is zero*. If we set $I_{x'y'}$ equal to zero in Eq. 8.28, you can demonstrate the converse of the preceding statement by solving for α and comparing the result with Eq. 8.30. That is, if the product of area is zero for a set of axes at a point, these axes must be the principal axes at that point. Consequently, if one axis of a set of axes at a point is symmetrical for the area, the axes are principal axes at that point.

The concept of principal axes will appear again in the following chapter in connection with the inertia tensor. Thus, the concept is not an isolated occurrence but is characteristic of a whole family of quantities. We shall, then, have further occasion to examine some of the topics introduced in this chapter from a more general viewpoint.

Example 8.11

Find the principal second moments of area at the centroid of the Z section of Example 8.9.

We have from this example the following results that will be of use to us:

$$I_{x_c x_c} = 113.2 \text{ in.}^4$$
$$I_{y_c y_c} = 32.67 \text{ in.}^4$$
$$I_{x_c y_c} = -42.0 \text{ in.}^4$$

Hence, we have

$$\tan 2\tilde{\alpha} = \frac{2I_{x_c y_c}}{I_{y_c y_c} - I_{x_c x_c}} = \frac{(2)(-42.0)}{32.67 - 113.2} = 1.043$$

$$2\tilde{\alpha} = 46.21°;\ 226.2°$$

For $2\tilde{\alpha} = 46.21°$:

$$I_1 = \frac{113.2 + 32.67}{2} + \frac{113.2 - 32.67}{2}\cos(46.21°) - (-42)\sin 46.21°$$
$$= 72.9 + 27.9 + 30.3 = \boxed{131.1 \text{ in.}^4}$$

For $2\tilde{\alpha} = 226.2°$:

$$I_2 = 72.9 - 27.9 - 30.3 = \boxed{14.75 \text{ in.}^4}$$

As a check on our work, we note that the sum of the second moments of area are invariant at a point for a rotation of axes. This means that

$$I_{x_c x_c} + I_{y_c y_c} = I_1 + I_2$$
$$113.2 + 32.7 = 131.1 + 14.75$$

Therefore,

$$145.9 = 145.9$$

We thus have a check on our work.

Before closing, we wish to point out that there is a graphical construction called *Mohr's circle* relating second moments and products of area for all possible axes at a point. However, in this text we shall use the analytical relations thus far presented rather than Mohr's circle. You will see Mohr circle construction in your strength of materials course where its use in conjunction with the important topics of plane stress and plane strain is very helpful.[9]

[9]See I. H. Shames, *Introduction to Solid Mechanics*, Second Edition, Prentice-Hall, Inc., Englewood Cliffs, N.J., 1989.

PROBLEMS

8.82. It is known that area A is 10 ft^2 and has the following moments and products of area for the centroidal axes shown:

$$I_{xx} = 40 \text{ ft}^4, \qquad I_{yy} = 20 \text{ ft}^4, \qquad I_{xy} = -4 \text{ ft}^4$$

Find the moments and products of area for the $x'y'$ reference at point a.

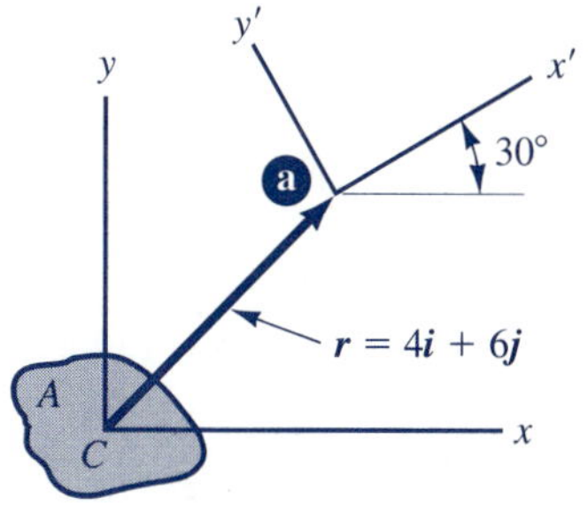

Figure P.8.82.

8.83. The cross-section of a beam is shown. Compute $I_{x'x'}$, $I_{y'y'}$, and $I_{x'y'}$ in the simplest way without using formulas for second moments and products of area for a triangle.

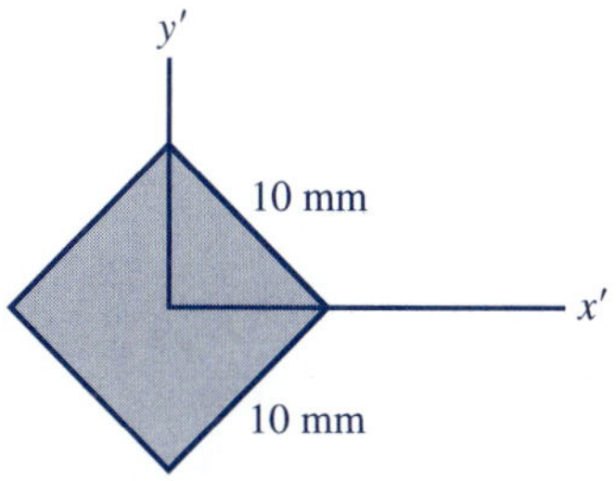

Figure P.8.83.

8.84. Find I_{xx}, I_{yy}, and I_{xy} for the rectangle. Also, compute the polar moment of area at points a and b.

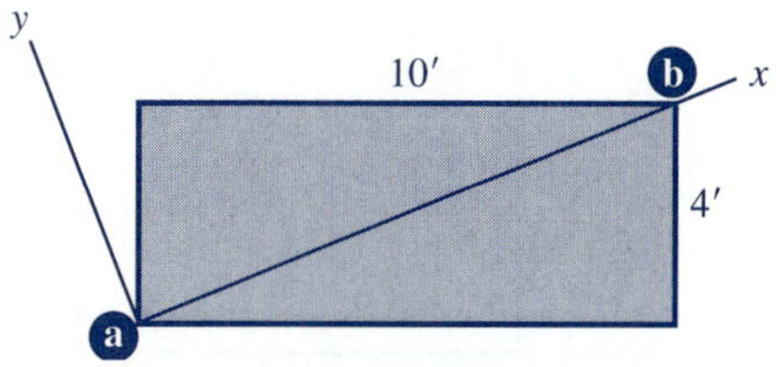

Figure P.8.84.

8.85. Express the polar moment of area of the square as a function of x, y, the coordinates of points about which the polar moment is taken.

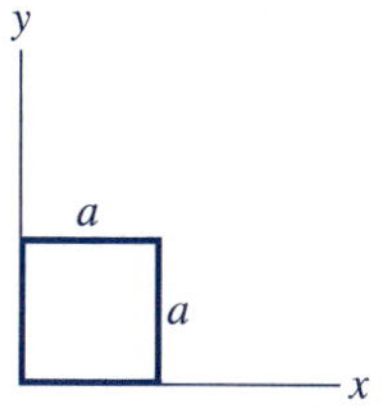

Figure P.8.85.

8.86. Use the calculus to show that the polar moment of area of a circular area of radius r is $\pi r^4/2$ at the center.

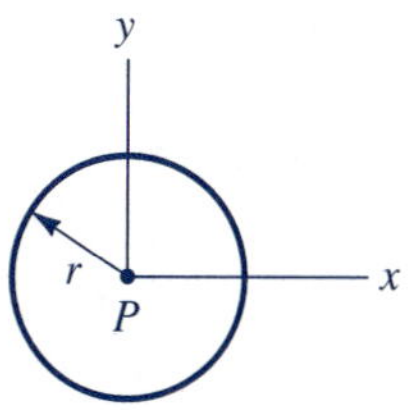

Figure P.8.86.

8.87. Find the direction of the principal axes for the angle section at point A.

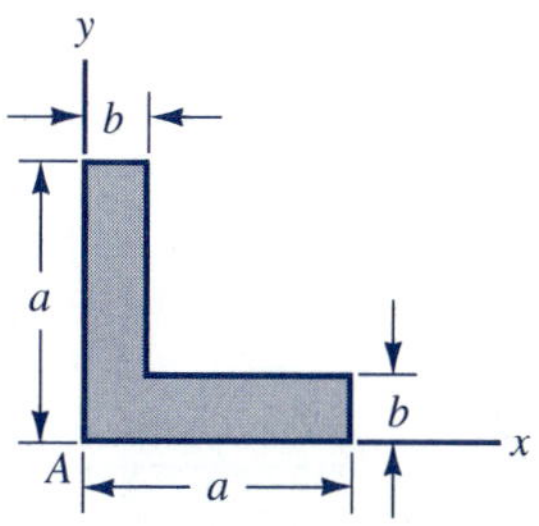

Figure P.8.87.

8.88. What are the principal second moments of area at the origin for the area of Example 8.7?

8.89. Find the principal second moments of area at the centroid for the area shown.

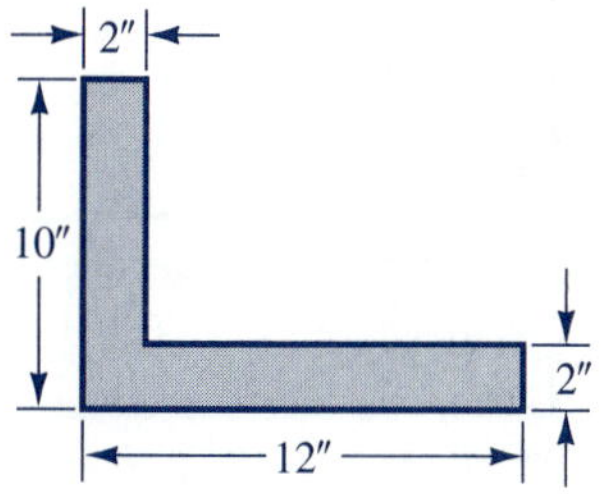

Figure P.8.89.

8.90. Determine the principal second moments of area at point A.

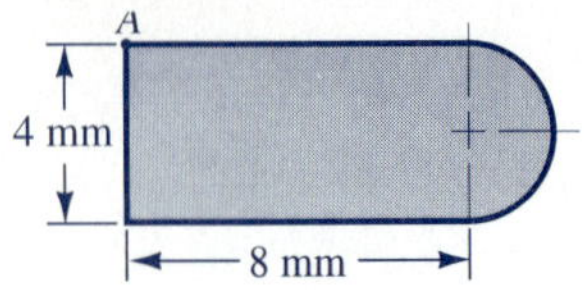

Figure P.8.90.

8.91. A rectangular area has two holes cut out. What is the maximum second moment of area at A? What is it at B halfway between the holes?

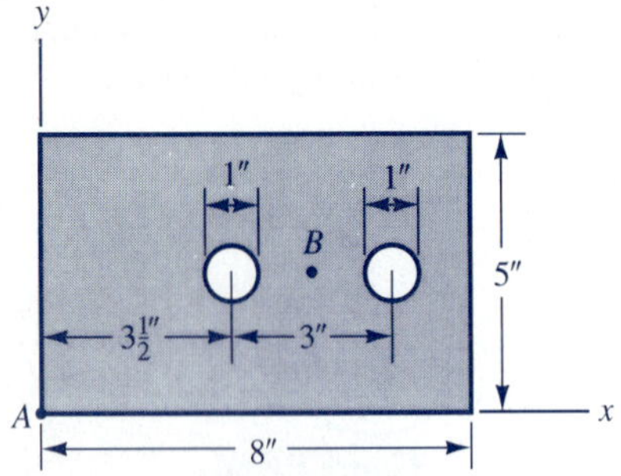

Figure P.8.91.

8.92. Show that the axes for which the product of area is a maximum are rotated from xy by an angle α so that

$$\tan 2\alpha = \frac{I_{xx} - I_{yy}}{2I_{xy}}$$

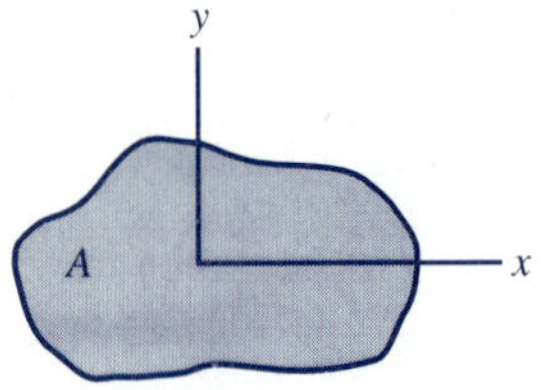

Figure P.8.92.

8.93. What is the value of the angle α for the principal axes at A.

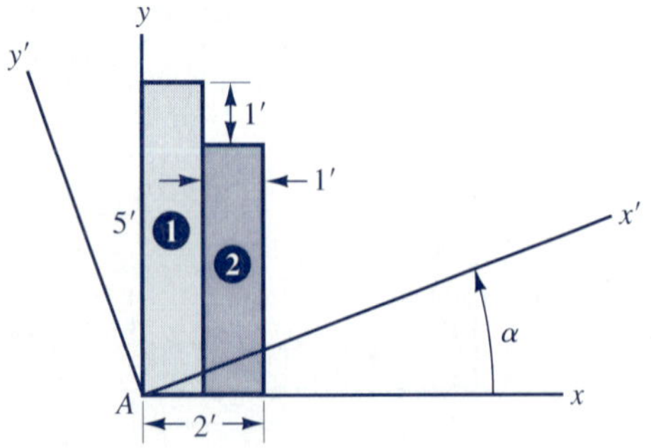

Figure P.8.93.

8.94. Find the principal second moments of area at A.

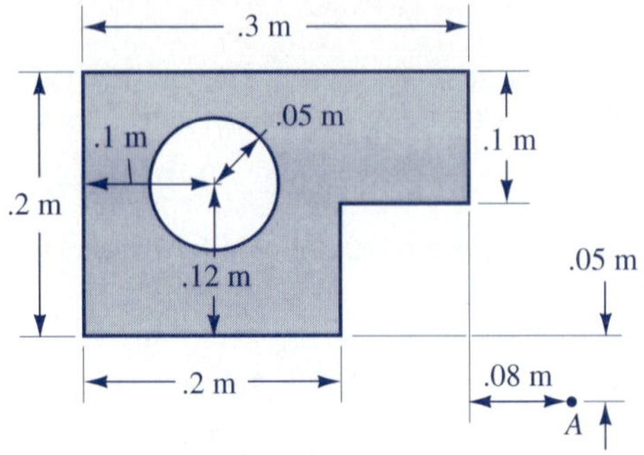

Figure P.8.94.

8.95. (a) Find I_{xx}, I_{yy}, and I_{xy} for the xy axes shown.

(b) What are the algebraically largest and smallest second moments of area at position A? What are the orientations of the corresponding axes? What is the product of area for these axes?

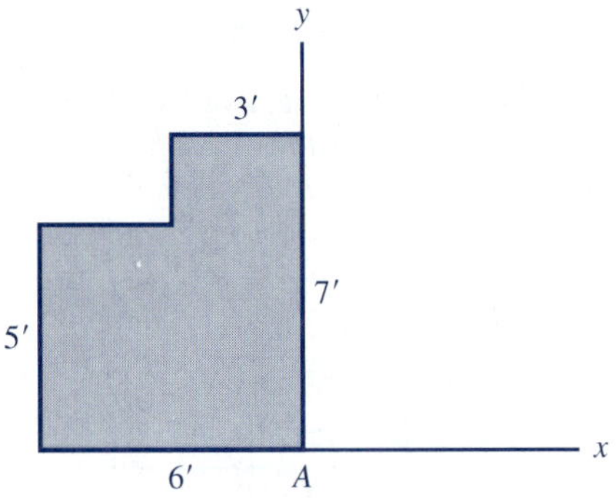

Figure P.8.95.

8.96. (a) Find the centroidal coordinates relative to axes xy.

(b) Find the principal axes and the corresponding maximum and minimum second moments of area at A.

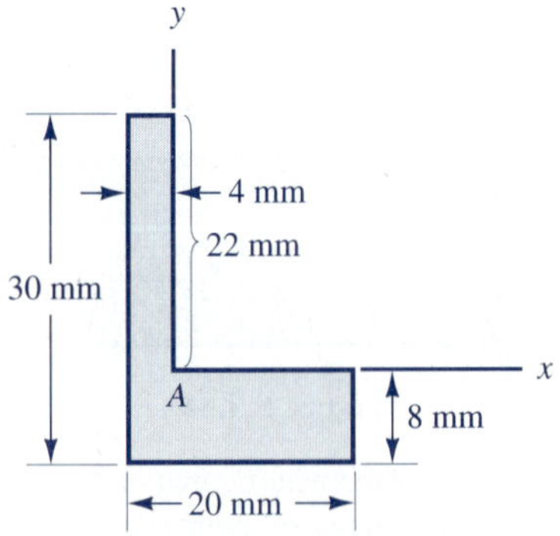

Figure P.8.96.

8.11 Closure

In this chapter, we discussed primarily the first and second moments of plane areas as well as the product of plane areas. These formulations give certain kinds of evaluations of the distribution of area relative to a plane reference *xy*. You will most certainly make much use of these quantities in your later courses in strength of materials.

In this chapter, we have touched on subject matter that you will encounter in the next chapter and also, most assuredly, in later courses. Specifically, in Chapter 9 you will be introduced to the so-called second-order inertia tensor having nine terms which change (or transform) in a certain particular way when we rotate coordinate axes at a point. These particular transformation equations define the inertia tensor. Any other set of nine symmetric terms that transform via the same form of equations, are symmetric second-order tensors. You will also learn that the second moments and products of *area* form a two-dimensional simplification of the inertia tensor. The transformation equations 8.26 through 8.28 are thus special cases of the three-dimensional defining equations of the inertia tensor. Take note that certain vital results emerged from these simplified two-dimensional transformation equations. They included

1. Invariant property at a point for the sum $(I_{xx} + I_{yy})$ on rotation of axes.
2. Principal axes and principal moments of area at a point.
3. A graphical construction called Mohr's circle that depicts the transformation equations. This topic has been omitted in this chapter but will be described in your solids course where you will study the two-dimensional simplifications of the stress and strain tensors. At that time one can make much use of the Mohr's circle construction and it is a simple matter then to describe Mohr's circle for second moments and products of area.

We will emphasize in the next chapter that there are many symmetric sets of nine terms that transform exactly like the terms of the inertia tensor and we classify all of them as second-order tensors. Identifying these sets as second-order tensors immediately yields vital properties common to all of them such as those presented above for the two-dimensional moments and products of area.

There will be more to be said on tensors in a "looking ahead" section of the next chapter which we invite you to examine.

PROBLEMS

8.97. Find the position of the centroid of the shaded area under the curve $y = \sin^2 x$ m. Find $M_{x'}$ and $M_{y'}$ of this area.

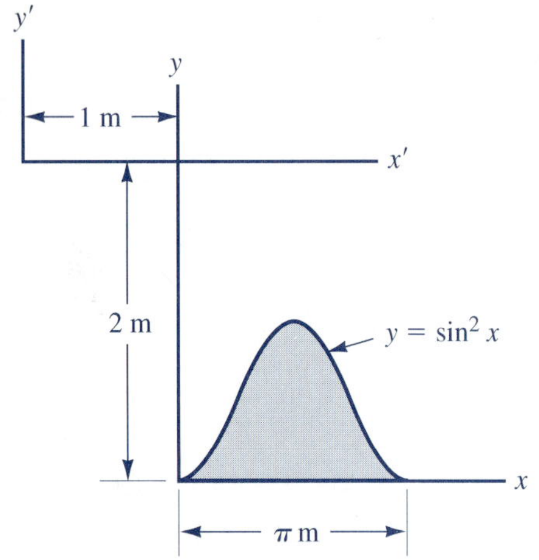

Figure P.8.97.

8.98. Find the center of volume of the body of revolution with a cylindrical cavity.

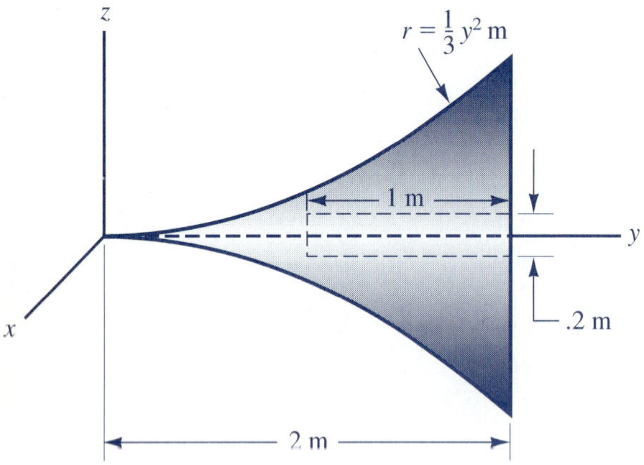

Figure P.8.98.

8.99. Locate the center of volume, center of mass, and center of gravity of the wooden rectangular block and the plastic semicylinder. The wood weighs .0003 N/mm^3 and the plastic weighs .0005 N/mm^3.

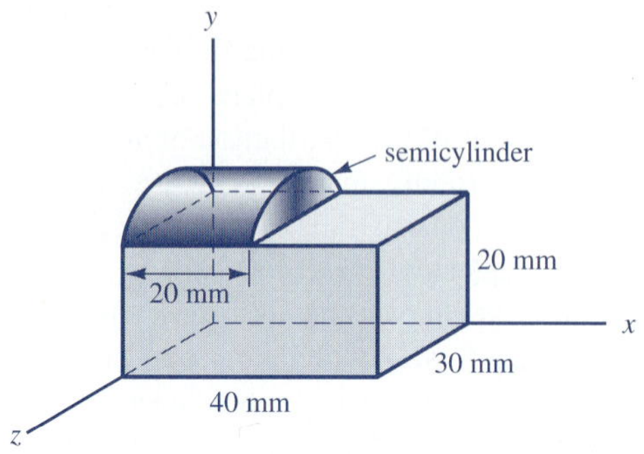

Figure P.8.99.

8.100. Find I_{xx}, I_{yy}, I_{xy}, $I_{x_c x_c}$, $I_{y_c y_c}$, and $I_{x_c y_c}$ of the unequal-leg rolled channel section.

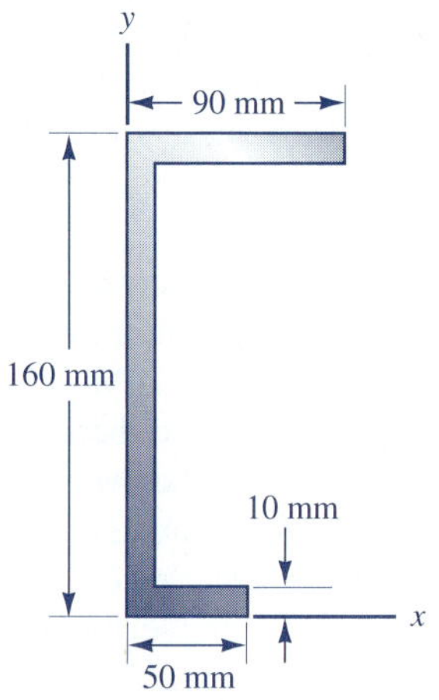

Figure P.8.100.

8.101. Find the centroid of the half cone. Use the known formula for the volume of a half cone, $V = (1/6)\ \pi r^2 h$.

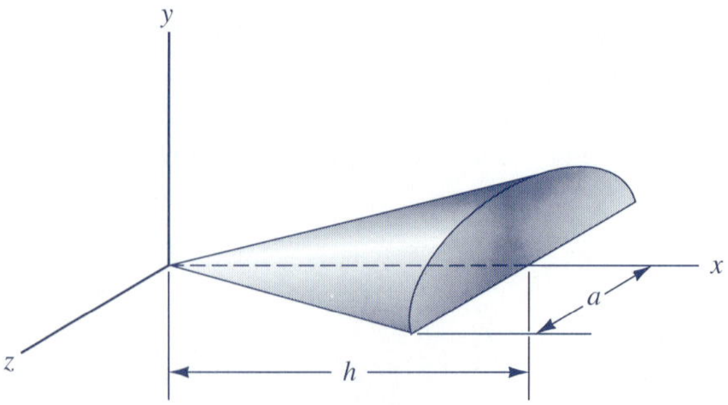

Figure P.8.101.

8.102. A half body of revolution is shown with the xz plane as a plane of symmetry. Determine the centroidal coordinates. The radius at any section x varies as the square of x.

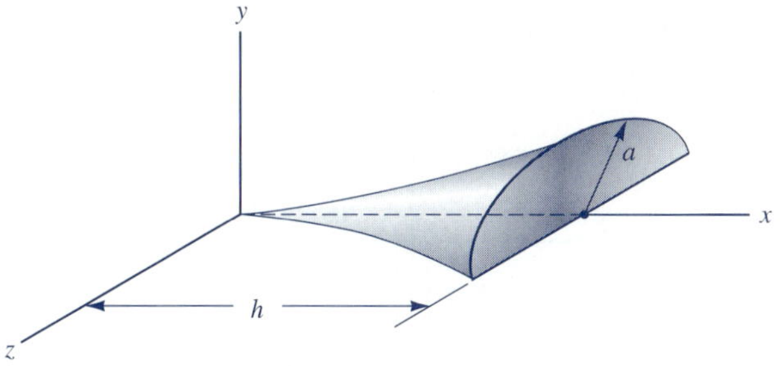

Figure P.8.102.

8.103. (a) Find I_{xx}, I_{yy}, and I_{xy} for the xy axes at position A.

(b) Find the principal second moments of area at point A.

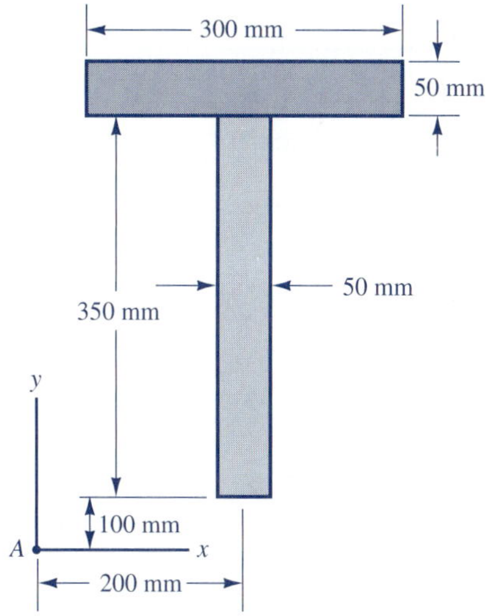

Figure P.8.103.

8.104. What are the directions of the principal axes at point A?

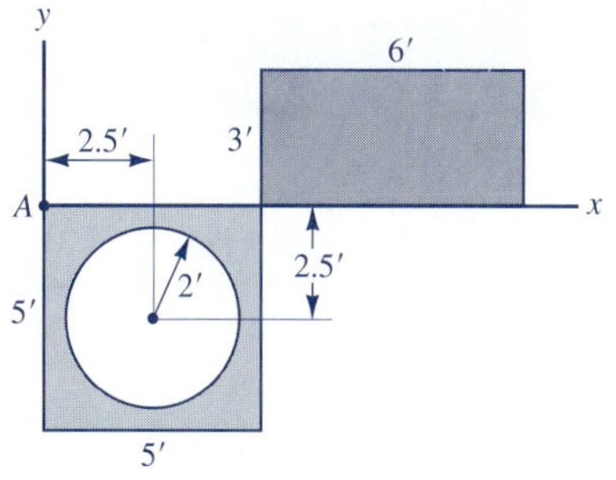

Figure P.8.104.

8.105. Using the theorems of Pappus and Guldinus, find the centroid of the area of a quarter-circle.

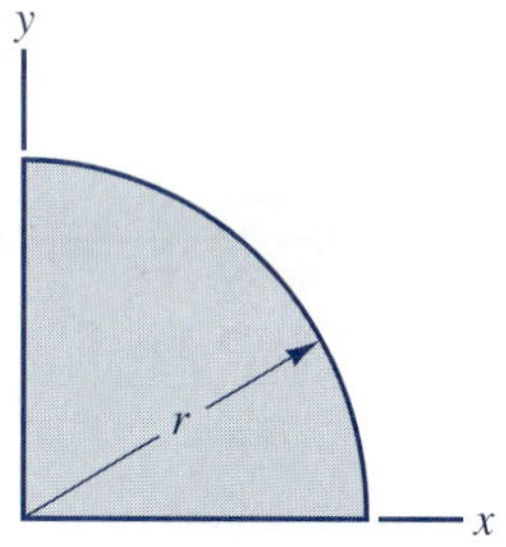

Figure P.8.105.

8.106. A tank has a semispherical dome at the left end. Using the theorems of Pappus and Guldinus, compute the surface and volume of the tank. Give the results in meters.

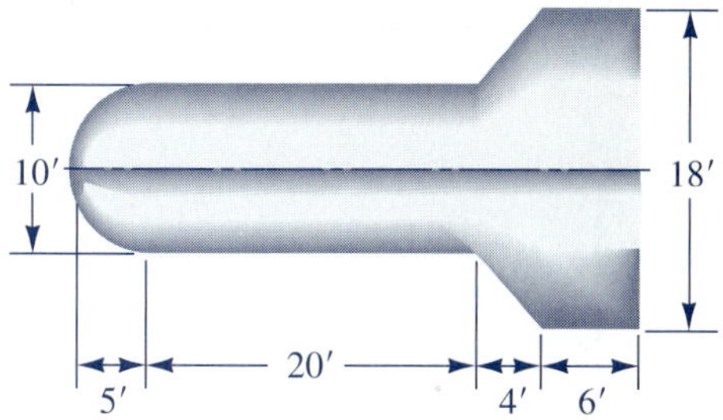

Figure P.8.106.

8.107. Find $I_{x'x'}$, $I_{y'y'}$, and $I_{x'y'}$ for the set of axes at point A for the rectangular area.

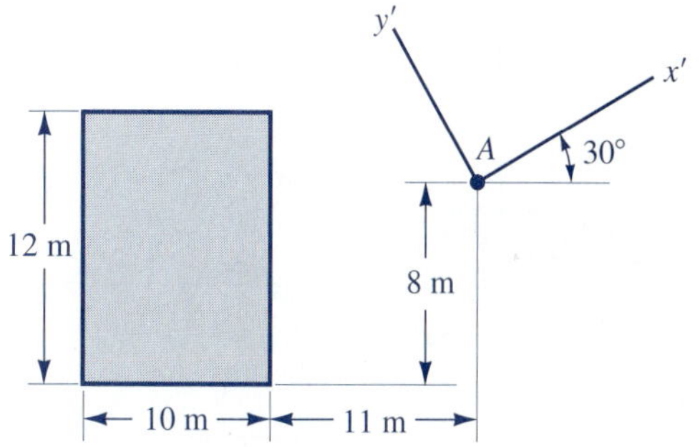

Figure P.8.107.

8.108. Find the centroid of the area, and then find the second moments of the area about centroidal axes parallel to the sides of the area.

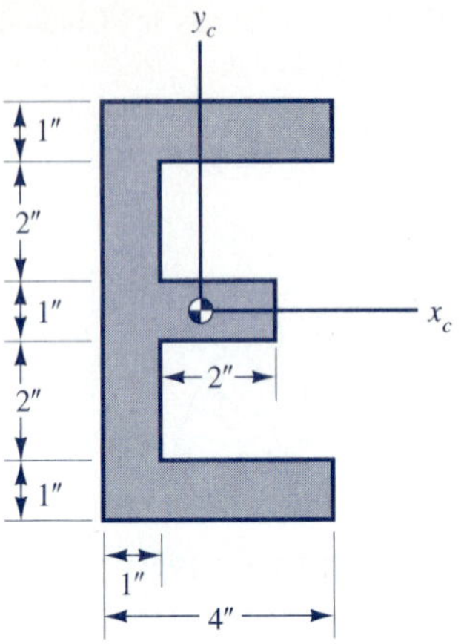

Figure P.8.108.

8.109. Find the principal second moments of area at a point where I_{xy} = 321 in.^{4}, I_{xx} = 118.4 in.^{4}, and I_{yy} = 1,028 in.^{4}.

8.110. Find the polar moment of area at point O for the shaded area.

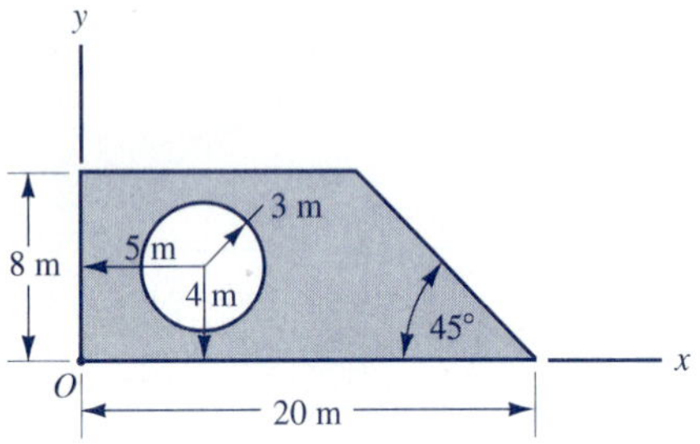

Figure P.8.110.

8.111. (a) What are the centroidal coordinates of the shaded area?

(b) What are $M_{x'}$, and $M_{y'}$ for axes $x'y'$ at A? [*Hint:* Use formulas for the sector of a circle given on the inside back cover.]

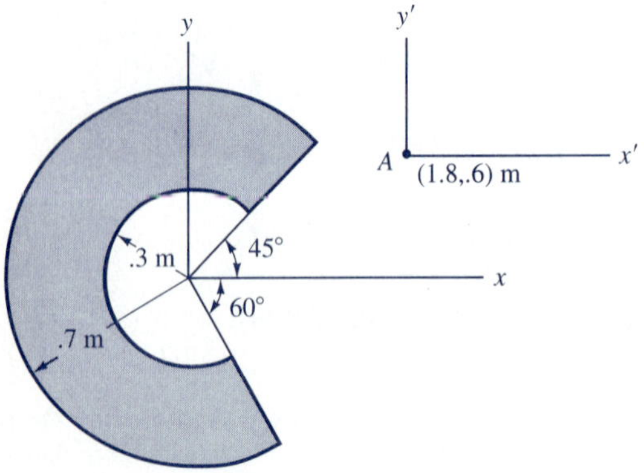

Figure P.8.111.

8.112. A wide-flanged I beam is shown.[10] For the upper flange, what is the first moment of the shaded area as a function of s measured from $s = 0$ at the right end to where s approaches the web? Next get M_x for the entire area above the position shown as y in the web. Let y go from C to the top of the web.

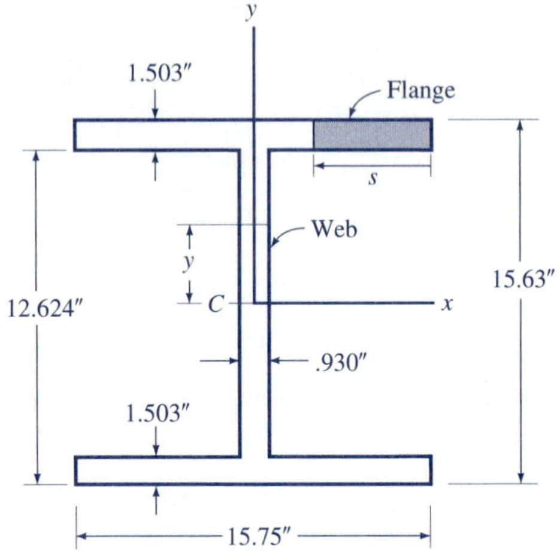

Figure P.8.112.

8.113. Find the center of volume of the machine element with a circular hole as shown.

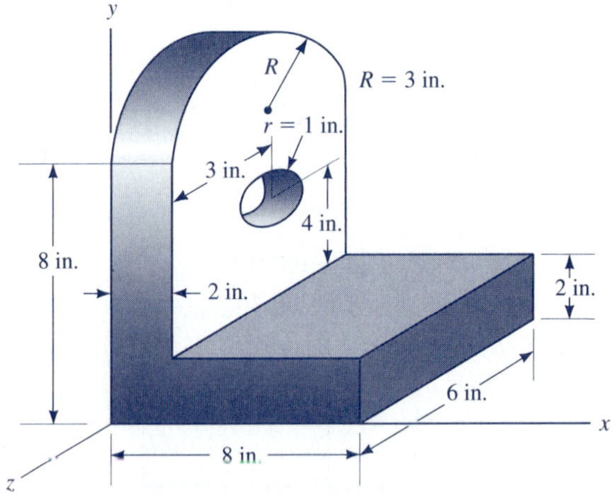

Figure P.8.113.

[10]Actually, it is a 14WF202 I beam, wherein the weight is 202 lb/ft.

CHAPTER 9

Moments and Products of Inertia[1]

9.1 Introduction

In this chapter, we shall consider certain measures of mass distribution relative to a reference. These quantities are vital for the study of the dynamics of rigid bodies. Because these quantities are so closely related to second moments and products of area, we shall consider them at this early stage rather than wait for dynamics. We shall also discuss the fact that these measures of mass distribution—the second moments of inertia of mass and the products of inertia of mass—are components of what we call a second-order tensor. Recognizing this fact early will make more simple and understandable your future studies of stress and strain, since these quantities also happen to be components of second-order tensors.

9.2 Formal Definition of Inertia Quantities

We shall now formally define a set of quantities that give information about the distribution of mass of a body relative to a Cartesian reference. For this purpose, a body of mass M and a reference xyz are presented in Fig. 9.1. This reference and the body may have any motion whatever relative to each other. The ensuing discussion then holds for the instantaneous orientation shown at time t. We shall consider that the body is composed of a continuum of particles, each of which has a mass given by $\rho\, dv$. We now present the following definitions:

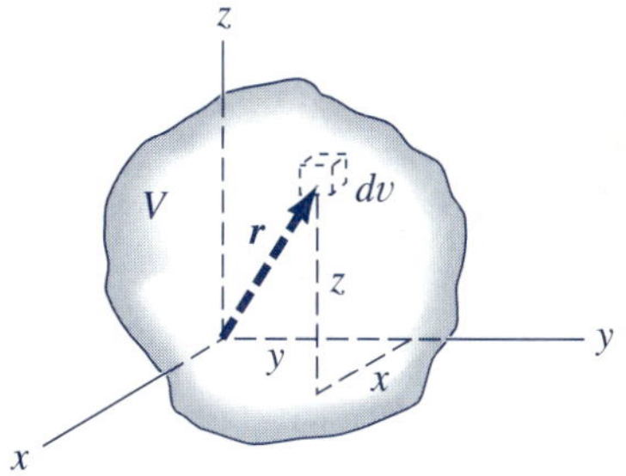

Figure 9.1. Body and reference at time t.

[1]This chapter may be covered at a later stage when studying dynamics. In that case, it should be covered directly after Chapter 15.

$$I_{xx} = \iiint_V (y^2 + z^2)\rho\, dv \tag{9.1a}$$

$$I_{yy} = \iiint_V (x^2 + z^2)\rho\, dv \tag{9.1b}$$

$$I_{zz} = \iiint_V (x^2 + y^2)\rho\, dv \tag{9.1c}$$

$$I_{xy} = \iiint_V xy\, \rho\, dv \tag{9.1d}$$

$$I_{xz} = \iiint_V xz\, \rho\, dv \tag{9.1e}$$

$$I_{yz} = \iiint_V yz\, \rho\, dv \tag{9.1f}$$

The terms I_{xx}, I_{yy}, and I_{zz} in the set above are called the *mass moments of inertia* of the body about the $x,y,$ and z axes, respectively.[2] Note that in each such case we are integrating the mass elements $\rho\, dv$, times the *perpendicular distance squared* from the mass elements to the coordinate axis about which we are computing the moment of inertia. Thus, if we look along the x axis toward the origin in Fig. 9.1, we would have the view shown in Fig. 9.2. The quantity $y^2 + z^2$ used in Eq. 9.1a for I_{xx} is clearly d^2, the perpendicular distance squared from dv to the x axis (now seen as a dot). Each of the terms with mixed indices is called the *mass product of inertia* about the pair of axes given by the indices. Clearly, from the definition of the product of inertia, we could reverse indices and thereby form three additional products of inertia for a reference. The additional three quantities formed in this way, however, are equal to the corresponding quantities of the original set. That is,

$$I_{xy} = I_{yx}, \quad I_{xz} = I_{zx}, \quad I_{yz} = I_{zy}$$

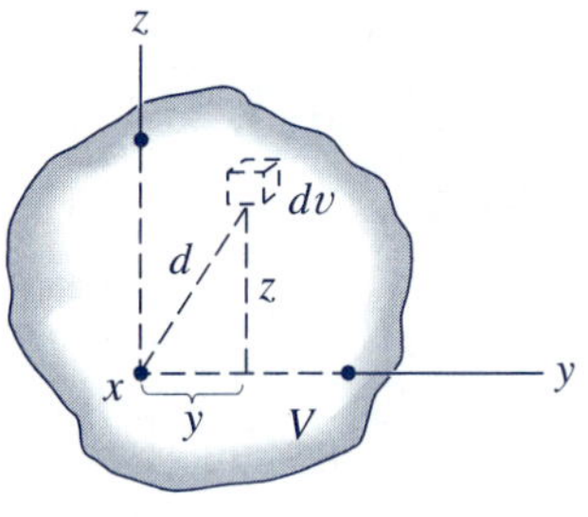

Figure 9.2. View of body along x axis.

We now have nine inertia terms at a point for a given reference at this point. The values of the set of six independent quantities will, for a given body,

[2]We use the same notation as was used for second moments and products of area, which are also sometimes called moments and products of inertia. This is standard practice in mechanics. There need be no confusion in using these quantities if we keep the context of discussions clearly in mind.

depend on the *position* and *inclination* of the reference relative to the body. You should also understand that the reference may be established anywhere in space and *need not* be situated in the rigid body of interest. Thus there will be nine inertia terms for reference xyz at point O outside the body (Fig. 9.3) computed using Eqs. 9.1, where the domain of integration is the volume V of the body. As will be explained later, the nine moments and products of inertia are components of the inertia tensor.

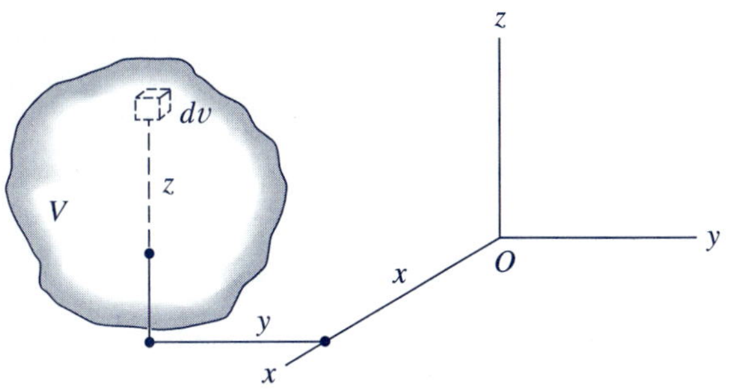

Figure 9.3. Origin of xyz outside body.

It will be convenient, when referring to the nine moments and products of inertia for reference xyz at a point, to list them in a matrix array, as follows:

$$I_{ij} = \begin{pmatrix} I_{xx} & I_{xy} & I_{xz} \\ I_{yx} & I_{yy} & I_{yz} \\ I_{zx} & I_{zy} & I_{zz} \end{pmatrix}$$

Notice that the first subscript gives the row and the second subscript gives the column in the array. Furthermore, the left-to-right downward diagonal in the array is composed of mass moment of inertia terms while the products of inertia, oriented at mirror-image positions about this diagonal, are equal. For this reason we say that the array is *symmetric*.

We shall now show that the sum of the mass moments of inertia for a set of orthogonal axes is independent of the orientation of the axes and depends only on the position of the origin. Examine the sum of such a set of terms:

$$I_{xx} + I_{yy} + I_{zz} = \iiint_V (y^2 + z^2)\rho\, dv + \iiint_V (x^2 + z^2)\rho\, dv + \iiint_V (x^2 + y^2)\rho\, dv$$

Combining the integrals and rearranging, we get

$$I_{xx} + I_{yy} + I_{zz} = \iiint_V 2(x^2 + y^2 + z^2)\rho\, dv = \iiint_V 2|\mathbf{r}|^2 \rho\, dv \qquad (9.2)$$

But the magnitude of the position vector from the origin to a particle is *independent* of the inclination of the reference at the origin. Thus, *the sum of the moments of inertia at a point in space for a given body clearly is an invariant with respect to rotation of axes.*

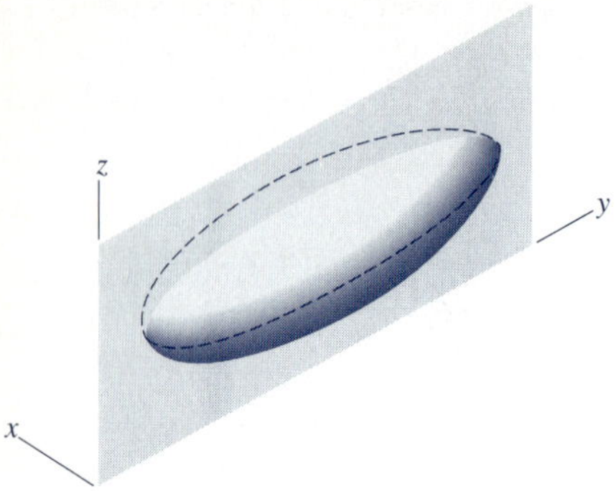

Figure 9.4. zy is plane of symmetry.

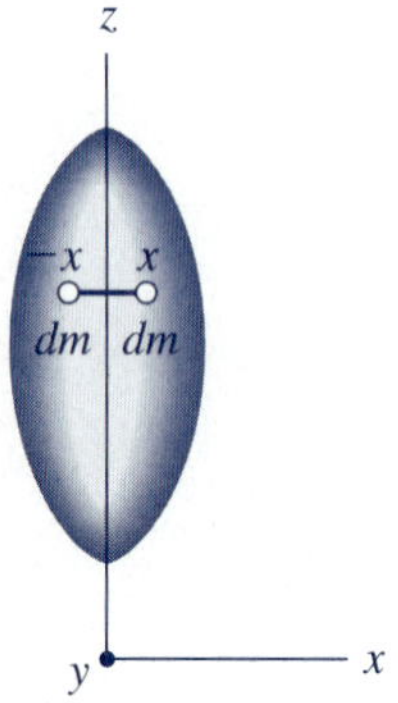

Figure 9.5. View along y axis.

Clearly, on inspection of the equations 9.1, it is clear that the moments of inertia must always be positive, while the products of inertia may be positive or negative. Of interest is the case where one of the coordinate planes is a *plane of symmetry* for the mass distribution of the body. Such a plane is the zy plane shown in Fig. 9.4 cutting a body into two parts, which, by definition of symmetry, are mirror images of each other. For the computation of I_{xz}, each half will give a contribution of the same magnitude but of opposite sign. We can most readily see that this is so by looking along the y axis toward the origin. The plane of symmetry then appears as a line coinciding with the z axis (see Fig. 9.5). We can consider the body to be composed of pairs of mass elements dm which are mirror images of each other with respect to position and shape about the plane of symmetry. The product of inertia I_{xz} for such a pair is then

$$xz\,dm - xz\,dm = 0$$

Thus, we can conclude that

$$I_{xz} = \underbrace{\int xz\,dm}_{\text{right domain}} - \underbrace{\int xz\,dm}_{\text{left domain}} = 0$$

This conclusion is also true for I_{xy}. We can say that $I_{xy} = I_{xz} = 0$. But on consulting Fig. 9.4, you should be able to readily decide that the term I_{zy} will have a positive value. Note that those products of inertia having x as an index are zero and that the x coordinate axis is normal to the plane of symmetry. Thus, we can conclude that *if two axes form a plane of symmetry for the mass distribution of a body, the products of inertia having as an index the coordinate that is normal to the plane of symmetry will be zero.*

Consider next a body of *revolution*. Take the z axis to coincide with the axis of symmetry. It is easy to conclude for the origin O of xyz anywhere along the axis of symmetry that

$$I_{xz} = I_{yz} = I_{xy} = 0$$
$$I_{xx} = I_{yy} = \text{constant}$$

for all possible xy axes formed by rotating about the z axis at O. Can you justify these conclusions?

Finally, we define *radii of gyration* in a manner analogous to that used for second moments of area in Chapter 8. Thus:

$$I_{xx} = k_x^2 M$$
$$I_{yy} = k_y^2 M$$
$$I_{zz} = k_z^2 M$$

where k_x, k_y, and k_z are the radii of gyration and M is the total mass.

Example 9.1

Find the nine components of the inertia tensor of a rectangular body of uniform density ρ about point O for a reference xyz coincident with the edges of the block as shown in Fig. 9.6.

We first compute I_{xx}. Using volume elements $dv = dx\,dy\,dz$, we get on using simple multiple integration:

$$\begin{aligned} I_{xx} &= \int_0^a \int_0^b \int_0^c (y^2 + z^2)\rho\,dx\,dy\,dz \\ &= \int_0^a \int_0^b (y^2 + z^2)c\rho\,dy\,dz = \int_0^a \left(\frac{b^3}{3} + z^2 b\right)c\rho\,dz \qquad \text{(a)} \\ &= \left(\frac{ab^3c}{3} + \frac{a^3bc}{3}\right)\rho = \frac{\rho V}{3}(b^2 + a^2) \end{aligned}$$

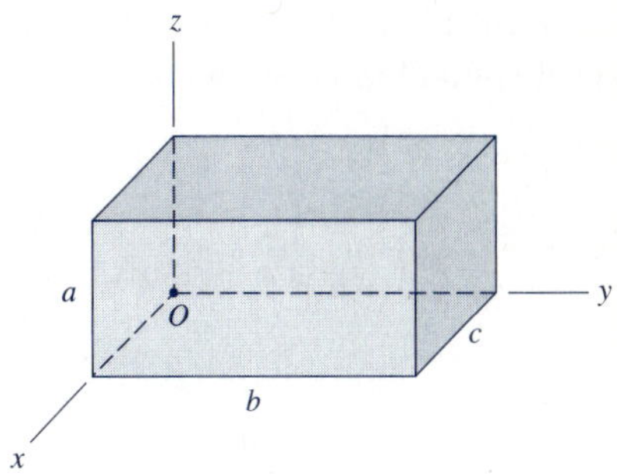

Figure 9.6. Find I_{ij} at O.

where V is the volume of the body. Note that the x axis about which we are computing the moment of inertia I_{xx} is *normal* to the plane having sides of length a and b, i.e., along the z and y axes. Similarly:

$$I_{yy} = \frac{\rho V}{3}(c^2 + a^2) \qquad \text{(b)}$$

$$I_{zz} = \frac{\rho V}{3}(b^2 + c^2) \qquad \text{(c)}$$

We next compute I_{xy}.

$$\begin{aligned} I_{xy} &= \int_0^a \int_0^b \int_0^c xy\,\rho\,dx\,dy\,dz = \int_0^a \int_0^b \frac{c^2}{2} y\rho\,dy\,dz \\ &= \int_0^a \frac{c^2b^2}{4}\rho\,dz = \frac{ac^2b^2}{4}\rho = \frac{\rho V}{4}cb \qquad \text{(d)} \end{aligned}$$

Note for I_{xy}, we use the lengths of the sides along the x and y axes.

$$I_{xz} = \frac{\rho V}{4}ac \qquad \text{(e)}$$

$$I_{yz} = \frac{\rho V}{4}ab \qquad \text{(f)}$$

We accordingly have, for the inertia tensor:

$$I_{ij} = \begin{pmatrix} \frac{\rho V}{3}(b^2 + a^2) & \frac{\rho V}{4}cb & \frac{\rho V}{4}ac \\ \frac{\rho V}{4}cb & \frac{\rho V}{3}(c^2 + a^2) & \frac{\rho V}{4}ab \\ \frac{\rho V}{4}ac & \frac{\rho V}{4}ab & \frac{\rho V}{3}(b^2 + c^2) \end{pmatrix} \qquad \text{(g)}$$

Example 9.2

Compute the components of the inertia tensor at the center of a solid sphere of uniform density ρ as shown in Fig. 9.7.

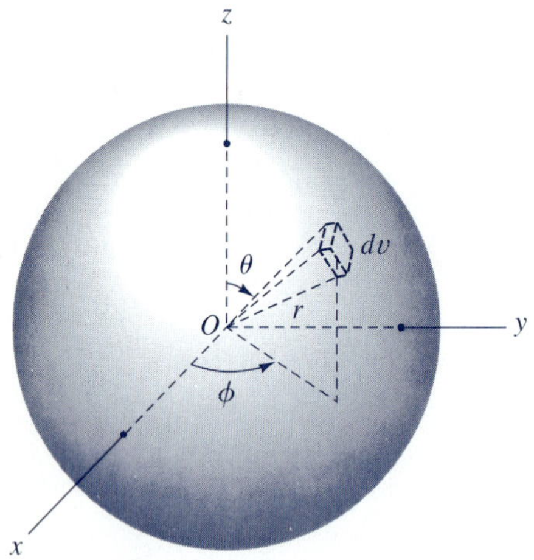

Figure 9.7. Find I_{ij} at O.

We shall first compute I_{yy}. Using spherical coordinates, we have[3]

$$I_{yy} = \iiint_V (x^2 + z^2)\rho\, dv$$

$$= \int_0^R \int_0^{2\pi} \int_0^{\pi} \left[(r \sin\theta \cos\phi)^2 + (r\cos\theta)^2 \right] \rho \left(r^2 \sin\theta \, d\theta \, d\phi \, dr \right)$$

$$= \int_0^R \int_0^{2\pi} \int_0^{\pi} \left(r^4 \sin^3\theta \cos^2\phi \right) \rho \, d\theta \, d\phi \, dr$$

$$+ \int_0^R \int_0^{2\pi} \int_0^{\pi} \left(r^4 \cos^2\theta \sin\theta \right) \rho \, d\theta \, d\phi \, dr$$

$$= \rho \int_0^R \int_0^{2\pi} \left(r^4 \cos^2\phi \right) \left(\int_0^{\pi} \sin^3\theta \, d\theta \right) d\phi \, dr$$

$$+ \rho \int_0^R \int_0^{2\pi} r^4 \left(\int_0^{\pi} \cos^2\theta \sin\theta \, d\theta \right) d\phi \, dr$$

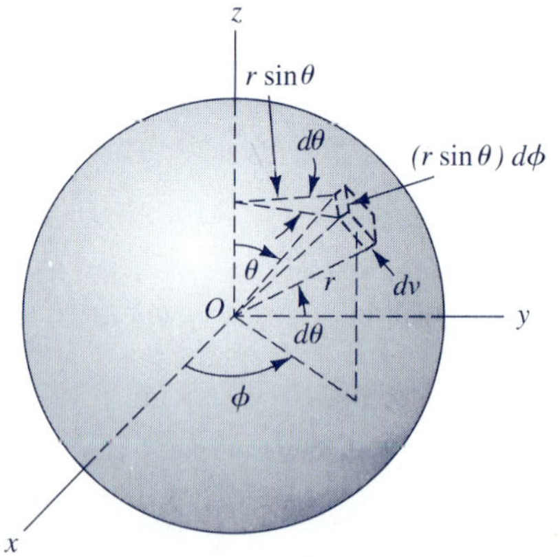

Figure 9.8. $dv = (r \sin\theta \, d\phi)(dr)(r\, d\theta) = r^2 \sin\theta \, d\theta \, d\phi \, dr$.

[3]For those unfamiliar with spherical coordinates, we have shown in Fig. 9.8 a more detailed study of the volume element used. The volume dv is simply the product of the three edges of the element shown in the diagram.

Example 9.2 (Continued)

With the aid of integration formulas from Appendix I, we have

$$I_{yy} = \rho\int_0^R\int_0^{2\pi} r^4\cos^2\phi\left[-\tfrac{1}{3}\cos\theta(\sin^2\theta+2)\right]\Big|_0^{\pi} d\phi\, dr$$

$$+\rho\int_0^R\int_0^{2\pi} r^4\left(-\frac{\cos^3\theta}{3}\right)\Bigg|_0^{\pi} d\phi\, dr$$

$$= \rho\int_0^R\int_0^{2\pi} r^4\cos^2\phi\,\tfrac{4}{3}\,d\phi\, dr + \rho\int_0^R\int_0^{2\pi}(r^4)\tfrac{2}{3}\,d\phi\, dr$$

Integrating next with respect to ϕ, we get

$$I_{yy} = \rho\int_0^R (r^4)\left(\tfrac{4}{3}\right)(\pi)\,dr + \rho\int_0^R (r^4)\left(\tfrac{2}{3}\right)(2\pi)\,dr$$

Finally, we get

$$I_{yy} = \rho\frac{R^5}{5}\frac{4}{3}\pi + \rho\frac{R^5}{5}\frac{4}{3}\pi$$

$$\therefore I_{yy} = \frac{8}{15}\rho\pi R^5$$

But

$$M = \rho\tfrac{4}{3}\pi R^3$$

Hence,

$$I_{yy} = \tfrac{2}{5}MR^2$$

Because of the point symmetry about point O, we can also say that

$$I_{xx} = I_{zz} = \tfrac{2}{5}MR^2$$

Because the coordinate planes are all planes of symmetry for the mass distribution, the products of inertia are zero. Thus, the inertia tensor can be given as

$$I_{ij} = \begin{pmatrix} \tfrac{2}{5}MR^2 & 0 & 0 \\ 0 & \tfrac{2}{5}MR^2 & 0 \\ 0 & 0 & \tfrac{2}{5}MR^2 \end{pmatrix}$$

9.3 Relation Between Mass-Inertia Terms and Area-Inertia Terms

We now relate the second moment and product of area studied in Chapter 8 with the inertia tensor. To do this, consider a plate of constant thickness t and uniform density ρ (Fig. 9.9) A reference is selected so that the xy plane is in the midplane of this plate. The components of the inertia tensor are rewritten for convenience as

$$\begin{aligned} I_{xx} &= \rho \iiint_V (y^2 + z^2)\,dv, & I_{xy} &= \rho \iiint_V xy\,dv \\ I_{yy} &= \rho \iiint_V (x^2 + z^2)\,dv, & I_{xz} &= \rho \iiint_V xz\,dv \\ I_{zz} &= \rho \iiint_V (x^2 + y^2)\,dv, & I_{yz} &= \rho \iiint_V yz\,dv \end{aligned} \tag{9.3}$$

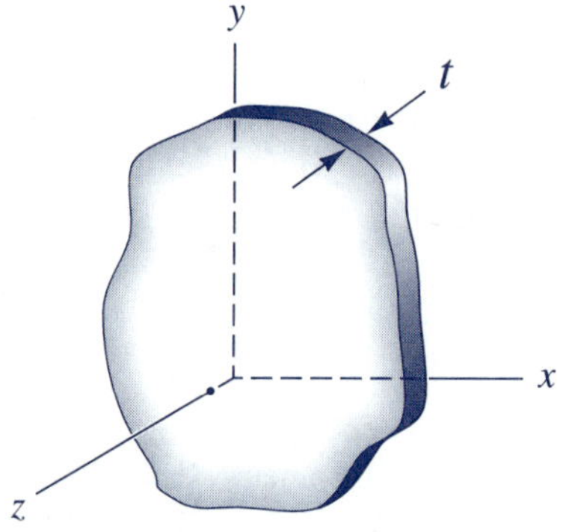

Figure 9.9. Plate of thickness t

Now consider that the thickness t is *small* compared to the lateral dimensions of the plate. This means that z is restricted to a range of values having a small magnitude. As a result, we can make two simplifications in the equations above. First, we shall set z equal to zero whenever it appears on the right side of the equations above. Second, we shall express dv as

$$dv = t\,dA$$

where dA is an area element on the *surface* of the plate, as shown in Fig. 9.10. Equations 9.3 then become

$$I_{xx} = \rho t \iint_A y^2 \, dA, \qquad I_{xy} = \rho t \iint_A xy \, dA$$
$$I_{yy} = \rho t \iint_A x^2 \, dA, \qquad I_{xz} = 0$$
$$I_{zz} = \rho t \iint_A (x^2 + y^2) \, dA, \qquad I_{yz} = 0$$

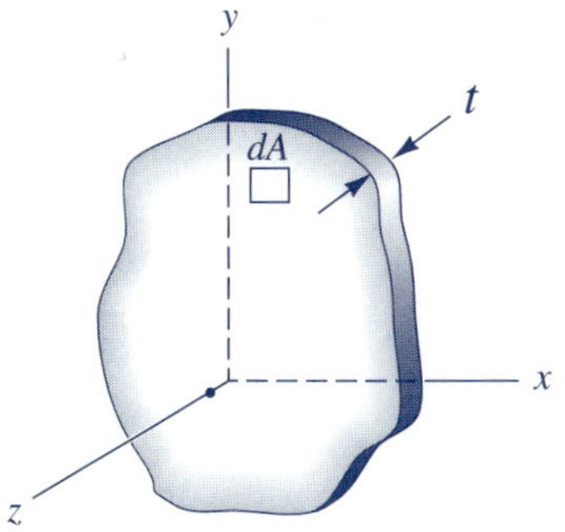

Figure 9.10. Use volume elements $t\,dA$.

Notice, now, that the integrals on the right sides of the equations above are moments and products of *area* as presented in Chapter 8. Denoting mass-moment and product of inertia terms with a subscript M and second moment and product of area terms with a subscript A, we can then say for the nonzero expressions:

$$(I_{xx})_M = \rho t (I_{xx})_A$$
$$(I_{yy})_M = \rho t (I_{yy})_A$$
$$(I_{zz})_M = \rho t (J)_A$$
$$(I_{xy})_M = \rho t (I_{xy})_A$$

Thus, for a thin plate with a constant product ρt throughout, we can compute the inertia tensor components for reference xyz (see Fig. 9.9) by using the second moments and product of area of the surface of the plate relative to axes xy.

It is important to point out that ρt is the *mass per unit area* of the plate. Imagine next that t goes to zero and simultaneously ρ goes to infinity at rates such that the product ρt becomes unity in the limit. One might think of the resulting body to be a *plane area*. By this approach, we have thus formed a plane area from a plate and in this way we can think of a plane area as a special mass. This explains why we use the same notation for mass moments and products of inertia as we use for second moments and products of area. However the units clearly will be different. We now examine a plate problem.

Example 9.3

Determine the inertia tensor components for the thin plate (Fig. 9.11) relative to the indicated axes xyz. The weight of the plate is .002 N/mm.[2] For the top edge, $y = 2\sqrt{x}$ with x and y in millimeters.

It is clear that for ρt we have, remembering that this product represents mass per unit area:

$$\rho t = \frac{.002}{9.81} = .000204 \text{ kg/mm}^2 \tag{a}$$

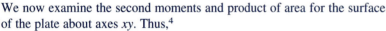

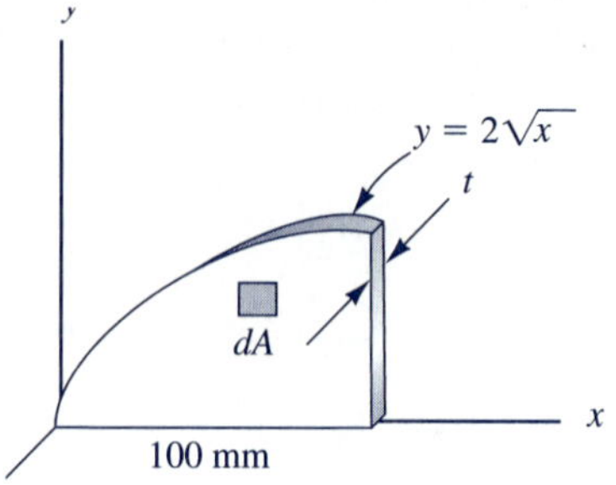

Figure 9.11. Plate of thickness t.

We now examine the second moments and product of area for the surface of the plate about axes xy. Thus,[4]

$$\begin{aligned}
(I_{xx})_A &= \int_0^{100}\int_{y=0}^{y=2\sqrt{x}} y^2\,dy\,dx \\
&= \int_0^{100} \left.\frac{y^3}{3}\right|_0^{2\sqrt{x}} dx = \int_0^{100} \frac{8}{3}x^{3/2}dx \\
&= \left.\frac{8}{3}\frac{x^{5/2}}{\frac{5}{2}}\right|_0^{100} = \left(\tfrac{8}{3}\right)\left(\tfrac{2}{5}\right)\left(100^{5/2}\right) \\
&= 1.067 \times 10^5 \text{ mm}^4
\end{aligned}$$

$$\begin{aligned}
(I_{yy})_A &= \int_0^{100}\int_{y=0}^{y=2\sqrt{x}} x^2\,dy\,dx \\
&= \int_0^{100} x^2 y\Big|_0^{2\sqrt{x}} dx = \int_0^{100} x^2\left(2\sqrt{x}\right)dx \\
&= 2\left.\frac{x^{7/2}}{\frac{7}{2}}\right|_0^{100} = 2\left(\tfrac{2}{7}\right)\left(100^{7/2}\right) \\
&= 5.71 \times 10^6 \text{ mm}^4
\end{aligned}$$

$$\begin{aligned}
(I_{xy})_A &= \int_0^{100}\int_{y=0}^{y=2\sqrt{x}} xy\,dy\,dx \\
&= \int_0^{100} x\left.\frac{y^2}{2}\right|_0^{2\sqrt{x}} dx = \int_0^{100} 2x^2\,dx \\
&= 2\left(\frac{100^3}{3}\right) = 6.67 \times 10^5 \text{ mm}^4
\end{aligned}$$

[4]Note we have multiple integration where one of the boundaries is variable. The procedure to follow should be evident from the example.

Example 9.3 (Continued)

Using Eq. (a), we can then say for the nonzero inertia tensor components:

$$(I_{xx})_M = (.000204)(1.067 \times 10^5) = 21.76 \text{ kg-mm}^2$$
$$(I_{yy})_M = (.000204)(5.71 \times 10^6) = 1{,}165 \text{ kg-mm}^2$$
$$(I_{xy})_M = (.000204)(6.67 \times 10^5) = 136.1 \text{ kg-mm}^2$$

Note that the nonzero inertia tensor components for a reference *xyz* on a plate (see Fig. 9.9) are *proportional* through ρt to the corresponding area-inertia terms for the plate surface. This means that all the formulations of Chapter 8 apply to the aforementioned nonzero inertia tensor components. Thus, on rotating the axes about the *z* axis we may use the transformation equations of Chapter 8. Consequently, the concept of *principal axes* in the midplane of the plate at a point applies. For such axes, the product of inertia is zero. One such axis then gives the maximum moment of inertia for all axes in the midplane at the point, the other the minimum moment of inertia. We have presented such problems at the end of this section.

What about principal axes for the inertia tensor at a point in a general three-dimensional body? Those students who have time to study Section 9.7 will learn that there are *three principal axes* at a point in the general case. These axes are *mutually orthogonal* and the *products of inertia are all zero* for such a set of axes at a point.[5] Furthermore, one of the axes will have a maximum moment of inertia, another axis will have a minimum moment of inertia, while the third axis will have an intermediate value. The sum of these three inertia terms must have a value that is common for all sets of axes at the point.

If, perchance, a set of axes *xyz* at a point is such that *xy* and *xz* form *two planes of symmetry* for the mass distribution of the body, then, as we learned earlier, since the *z* axis and the *y* axis are normal to the planes of symmetry, $I_{xy} = I_{xz} = I_{yz} = 0$. Thus, all products of inertia are zero. This would also be true for *any* two sets of axes of *xyz* forming two planes of symmetry. Clearly, axes forming two planes of symmetry must be *principal axes*. This information will suffice in most instances when we have to identify principal axes. On the other hand, consider the case where there is only *one plane of symmetry* for the mass distribution of a body at some point *A*. Let the *xy* plane at *A* form this plane of symmetry. Then, clearly, the products of inertia between the *z* axis that is normal to the plane of symmetry *xy* and *any axis* in the *xy* plane at *A* must be zero, as pointed out earlier. Obviously, the *z* axis must be a principal axis. The other two principal axes must be in the plane of symmetry, but generally cannot be located by inspection.

[5]The third principal axis for a plate at a point in the midplane is the *z* axis normal to the plate. Note that $(I_{zz})_M$ must always equal $(I_{xx})_M + (I_{yy})_M$. Why?

PROBLEMS

9.1. A uniform homogeneous slender rod of mass M is shown. Compute I_{xx} and $I_{x'x'}$.

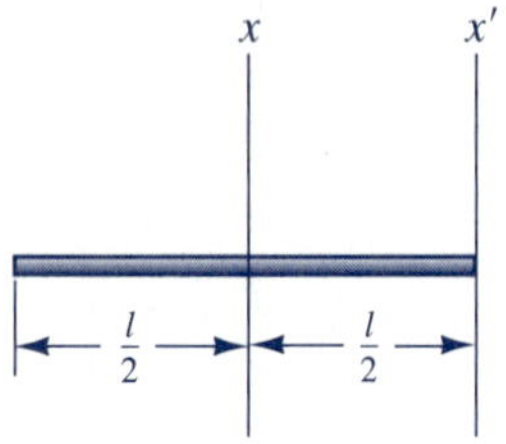

Figure P.9.1.

9.2. Find I_{xx} and $I_{x'x'}$ for the thin rod of Problem 9.1 for the case where the mass per unit length at the left end is 5 lbm/ft and increases linearly so that at the right end it is 8 lbm/ft. The rod is 20 ft in length.

9.3. Compute I_{xy} for the thin homogeneous hoop of mass M.

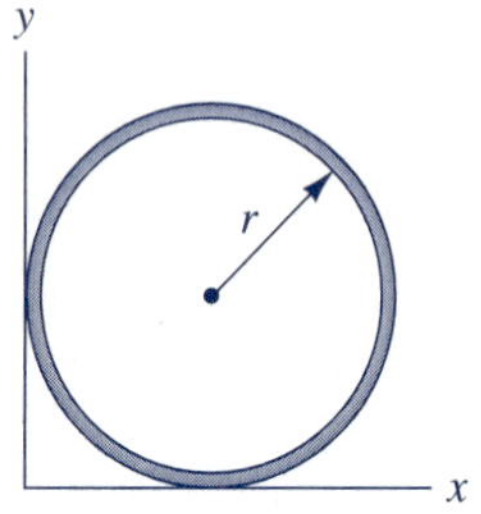

Figure P.9.3.

9.4. Compute I_{xx}, I_{yy}, I_{zz}, and I_{xy} for the homogeneous rectangular parallelepiped.

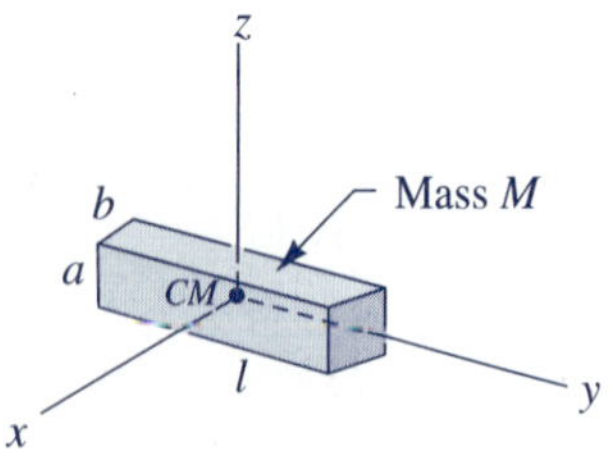

Figure P.9.4.

9.5. A wire having the shape of a parabola is shown. The curve is in the yz plane. If the mass of the wire is .3 N/m, what are I_{yy} and I_{xz}? [*Hint:* Replace ds along the wire by $\sqrt{(dy/dz)^2+1}\,dz$.]

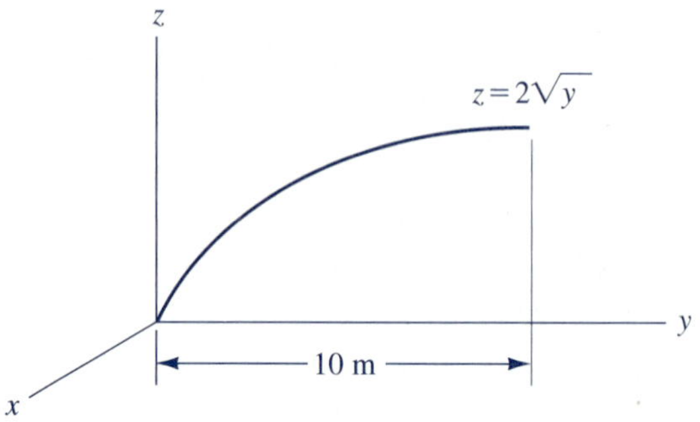

Figure P.9.5.

9.6. Compute the moment of inertia, $I_{BB'}$, for the half-cylinder shown. The body is homogeneous and has a mass M.

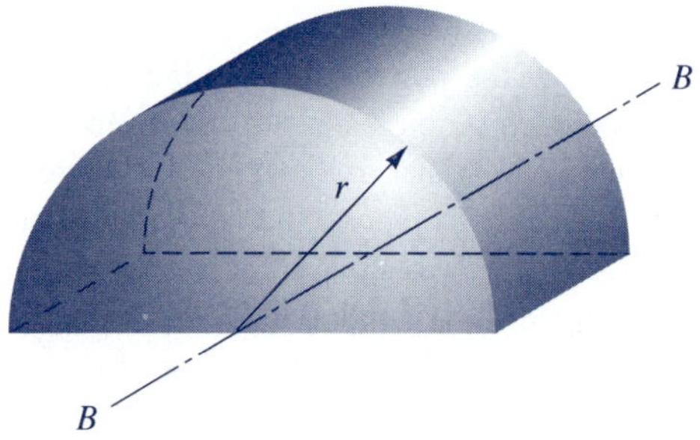

Figure P.9.6.

9.7. Find I_{zz} and I_{xx} for the homogeneous right circular cylinder of mass M.

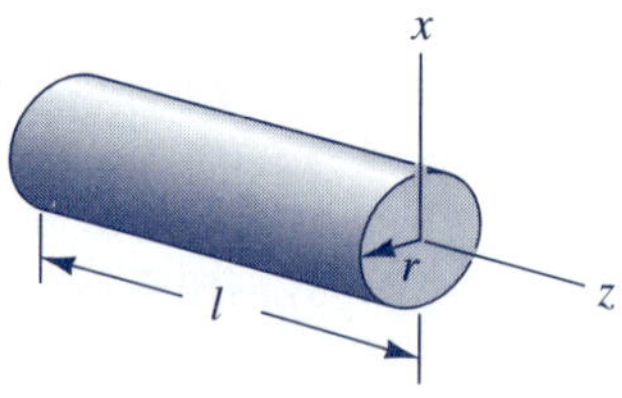

Figure P.9.7.

9.8. For the cylinder in Problem 9.7, the density increases linearly in the z direction from a value of .100 grams/mm^3 at the left end to a value of .180 grams/mm^3 at the right end. Take $r = 30$ mm and $l = 150$ mm. Find I_{xx} and I_{zz}.

9.9. Show that I_{zz} for the homogeneous right circular cone is $\frac{3}{10}MR^2$.

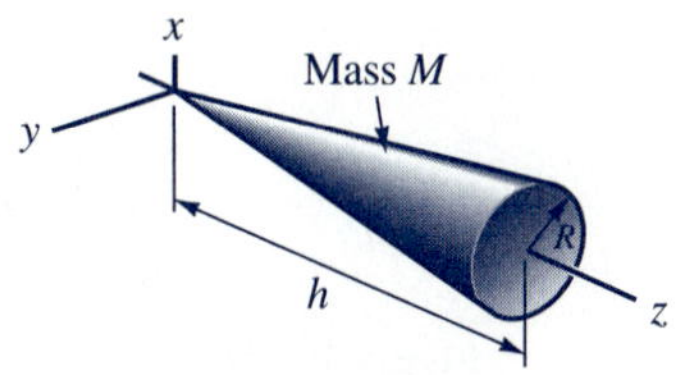

Figure P.9.9.

9.10. In Problem 9.9, the density increases as the square of z in the z direction from a value of .200 grams/mm^3 at the left end to a value of .400 grams/mm^3 at the right end. If $r = 20$ mm and the cone is 100 mm in length, find I_{zz}.

9.11. A body of revolution is shown. The radial distance r of the boundary from the x axis is given as $r = .2x^2$ m. What is I_{xx} for a uniform density of 1,600 kg/m^3?

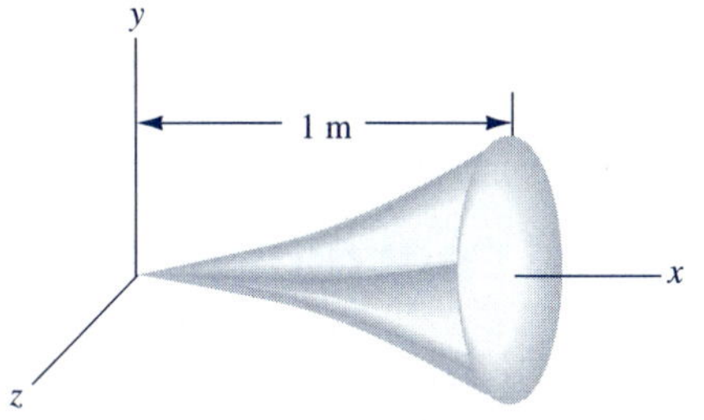

Figure P.9.11.

9.12. A thick hemispherical shell is shown with an inside radius of 40 mm and an outside radius of 60 mm. If the density ρ is 7,000 kg/m,^{3} what is I_{yy}?

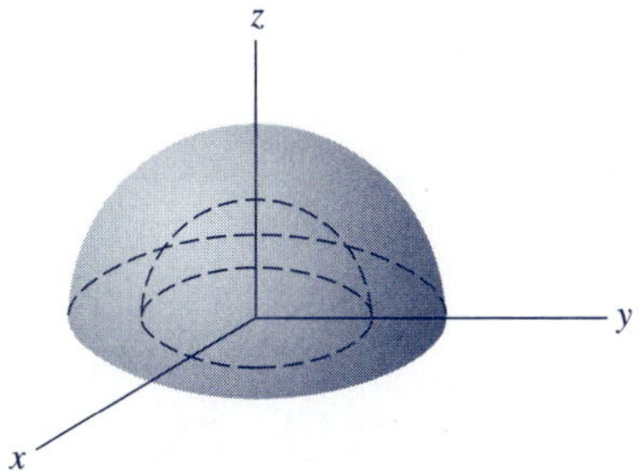

Figure P.9.12.

9.13. Find the mass moment of inertia I_{xx} for a very thin plate forming a quarter-sector of a circle. The plate weighs .4 N. What is the second moment of area about the x axis? What is the product of inertia? Axes are in the midplane of the plate.

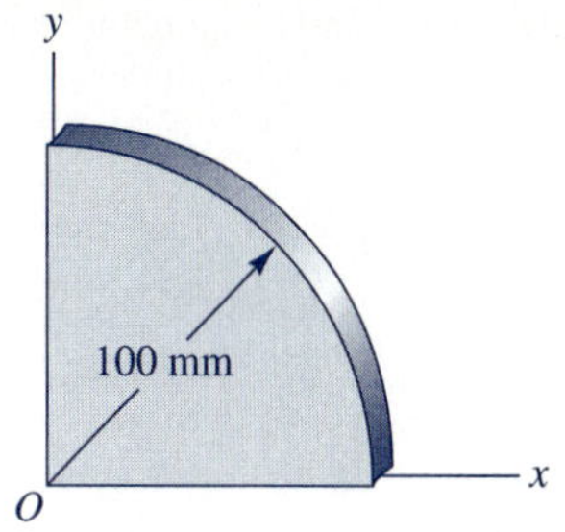

Figure P.9.13.

9.14. Find the second moment of area about the x axis for the front surface of a very thin plate. If the weight of the plate is .02 N/mm^2, find the mass moments of inertia about the x and y axes. What is the mass product of inertia I_{xy}?

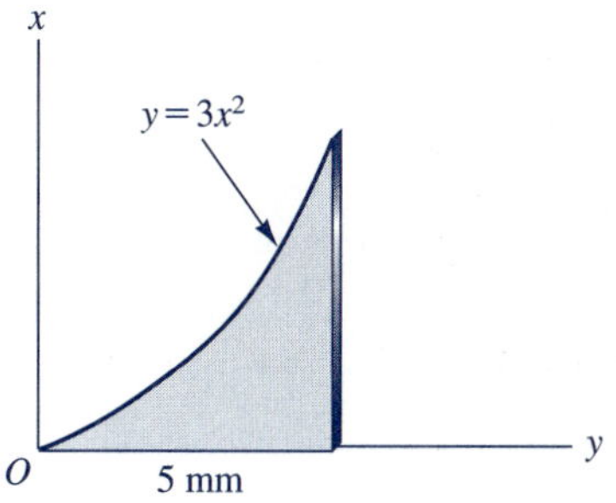

Figure P.9.14.

***9.15.** A uniform tetrahedron is shown having sides of length a, b, and c, respectively, and a mass M. Show that $I_{yz} = \frac{1}{20}Mac$. (*Suggestion:* Let z run from zero to surface ABC. Let x run from zero to line AB. Finally, let y run from zero to B. Note that the equation of a plane surface is $z = \alpha x + \beta y + \gamma$, where α, β, and γ are constants. The mass of the tetrahedron is $\rho abc/6$. It will be simplest in expanding $(1 - x/b - y/c)^2$ to proceed in the form $[(1 - y/c) - (x/b)]^2$, keeping $(1 - y/c)$ intact. In the last integration replace y by $[-c(1 - y/c) + c]$, etc.)

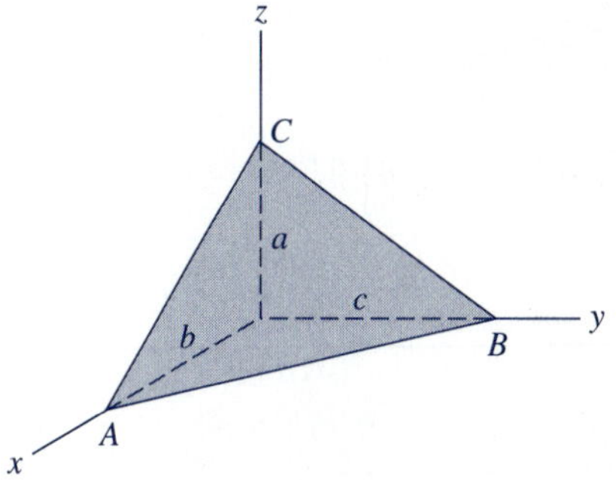

Figure P.9.15.

9.16. In Problem 9.13, find the three principal mass moments of inertia at O. Use the following results from problem 9.13

$$(I_{xx})_M = 101.9 \text{ kg-mm}^2$$
$$(I_{xy})_M = 64.9 \text{ kg-mm}^2$$

9.17. In Problem 9.14, compute the values of the three principal mass moments of inertia at O. From Problem 9.14 we have the results

$$(I_{xx})_M = 205 \text{ kg-mm}^2$$
$$(I_{yy})_M = 3.82 \text{ kg-mm}^2$$
$$(I_{xy})_M = 23.9 \text{ kg-mm}^2$$

9.18. Can you identify by inspection any of the principal axes of inertia at A? At B? Explain. The density of the material is uniform.

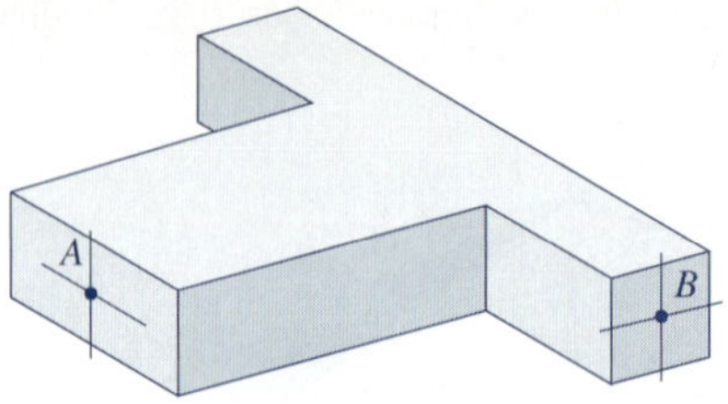

Figure P.9.18.

9.19. By inspection, identify as many principal axes as you can for mass moments of inertia at positions A, B, and C. Explain your choices. The mass density of the material is uniform throughout.

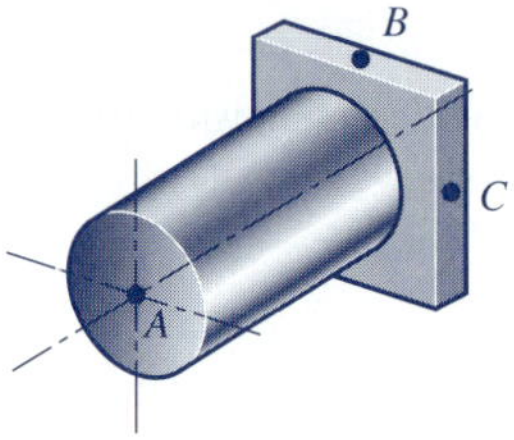

Figure P.9.19.

9.4 Translation of Coordinate Axes

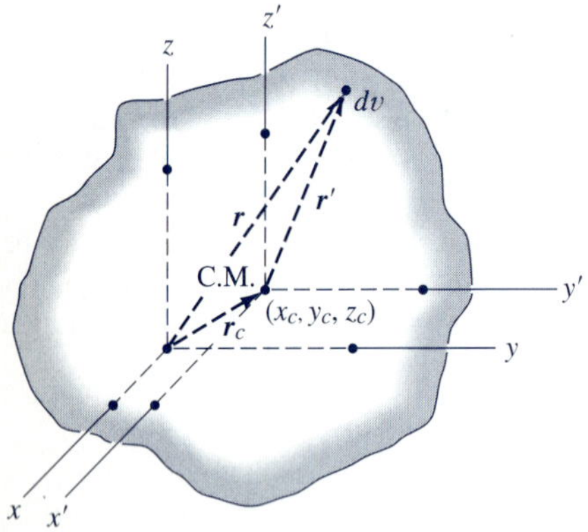

Figure 9.12. *xyz* translated from $x'y'z'$ at C.M.

In this section, we will compute mass moment and product of inertia quantities for a reference xyz that is displaced under a translation (no rotation) from a reference $x'y'z'$ at the center of mass (Fig. 9.12) for which the inertia terms are presumed known. Let us first compute the mass moment of inertia I_{zz}.

Observing Fig. 9.12, we see that

$$\boldsymbol{r} = \boldsymbol{r}_c + \boldsymbol{r}'$$

Hence,

$$x = x_c + x'$$
$$y = y_c + y'$$
$$z = z_c + z'$$

We can now formulate I_{zz} in the following way:

$$I_{zz} = \iiint_V (x^2 + y^2)\rho\, dv = \iiint_V \left[\left(x_c + x'\right)^2 + \left(y_c + y'\right)^2\right]\rho\, dv \qquad (9.4)$$

Carrying out the squares and rearranging, we have

$$I_{zz} = \iiint_V (x_c^2 + y_c^2)\rho\, dv + 2\iiint_V x_c x'\rho\, dv$$
$$+2\iiint_V y_c y'\rho\, dv + \iiint_V (x'^2 + y'^2)\rho\, dv \qquad (9.5)$$

Note that the quantities bearing the subscript c are constant for the integration and can be extracted from under the integral sign. Thus,

$$I_{zz} = M(x_c^2 + y_c^2) + 2x_c \iiint_V x'\,dm + 2y_c \iiint_V y'\,dm + \iiint_V (x'^2 + y'^2)\rho\,dv \quad (9.6)$$

where $\rho\,dv$ has been replaced in some terms by dm, and the integration $\iiint_V \rho\,dv$ in the first integral has been evaluated as M, the total mass of the body. The origin of the primed reference being at the center of mass requires of the first moments of mass that $\iiint x'\,dm = \iiint y'\,dm = \iiint z'\,dm = 0$. The middle two terms accordingly drop out of the expression above, and we recognize the last expression to be $I_{z'z'}$. Thus, the desired relation is

$$I_{zz} = I_{z'z'} + M(x_c^2 + y_c^2) \quad (9.7)$$

By observing the body in Fig. 9.12 along the z and z' axes (i.e., from directly above), we get a view as is shown in Fig 9.13. From this diagram, we can see that $y_c^2 + x_c^2 = d,^2$ where d is the perpendicular distance between the z' axis through the center of mass and the z axis about which we are taking moments of inertia. We may then give the result above as

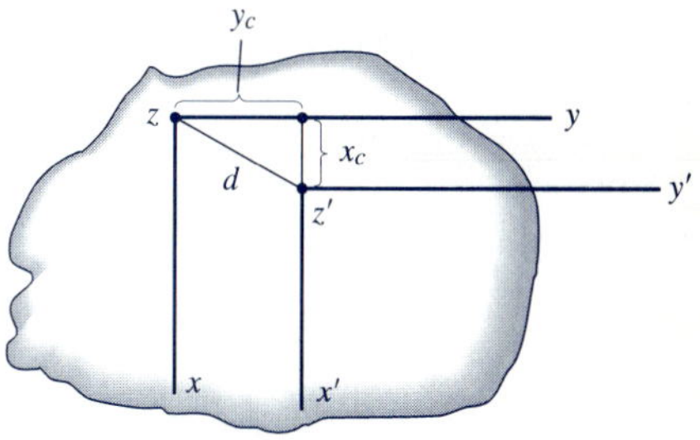

Figure 9.13. View along z direction (from above).

$$I_{zz} = I_{z'z'} + Md^2 \quad (9.8)$$

Let us generalize from the previous statement.

The moment of inertia of a body about any axis equals the moment of inertia of the body about a parallel axis that goes through the center of mass, plus the total mass times the perpendicular distance between the axes squared.

We leave it to you to show that for products of inertia a similar relation can be reached. For I_{xy}, for example, we have

$$I_{xy} = I_{x'y'} + Mx_cy_c \quad (9.9)$$

Here, we must take care to put in the proper signs of x_c and y_c as measured *from* the xyz reference. Equations 9.8 and 9.9 comprise the well-known *parallel-axis theorems* analogous to those formed in Chapter 8 for areas. You can use them to advantage for bodies composed of simple familiar shapes, as we now illustrate.

Example 9.4

Find I_{xx} and I_{xy} for the body shown in Fig. 9.14. Take ρ as constant for the body. Use the formulations for moments and products of inertia at the center of mass as given on the inside front cover page.

We shall consider first a solid rectangular prism having the outer dimensions given in Fig. 9.14, and we shall then subtract the contribution of the cylinder and the rectangular block that have been cut away. Thus, we have, for the overall rectangular block which we consider as body 1,

$$(I_{xx})_1 = (I_{xx})_c + Md^2 = \tfrac{1}{12}M(a^2+b^2) + Md^2$$
$$= \tfrac{1}{12}[(\rho)(20)(8)(15)](8^2+15^2) + [(\rho)(20)(8)(15)](4^2+7.5^2) \quad \text{(a)}$$
$$= 231{,}200\rho$$

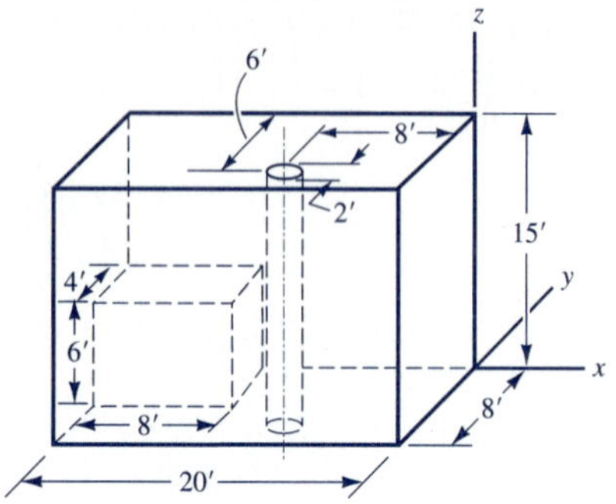

Figure 9.14. Find I_{xx} and I_{xy}.

From this, we shall take away the contribution of the cylinder, which we denote as body 2. Using the formulas from the inside front cover page,

$$(I_{xx})_2 = \tfrac{1}{12}M(3r^2+h^2) + Md^2$$
$$= \tfrac{1}{12}[\rho\pi(1)^2(15)][3(1^2)+15^2] + [\rho\pi(1)^2(15)][6^2+7.5^2] \quad \text{(b)}$$
$$= 5{,}243\rho$$

Also, we shall take away the contribution of the rectangular cutout (body 3):

$$(I_{xx})_3 = \tfrac{1}{12}M(a^2+b^2) + Md^2$$
$$= \tfrac{1}{12}[\rho(8)(6)(4)](4^2+6^2) + [\rho(8)(6)(4)](2^2+3^2) \quad \text{(c)}$$
$$= 3{,}328\rho$$

The quantity I_{xx} for the body with the rectangular and cylindrical cavities is then

$$I_{xx} = (231{,}200 - 5{,}243 - 3{,}328)\rho$$

$$I_{xx} = 223{,}000\rho \quad \text{(d)}$$

We follow the same procedure to obtain I_{xy}. Thus, for the block as a whole, we have

$$(I_{xy})_1 = (I_{xy})_c + Mx_c y_c$$

At the center of mass of the block, both the $(x')_1$ and $(y')_1$ axes are normal to planes of symmetry. Accordingly, $(I_{xy})_c = 0$. Hence,

$$(I_{xy})_1 = 0 + [\rho(20)(8)(15)](-4)(-10)$$
$$= 96{,}000\rho \quad \text{(e)}$$

For the cylinder, we note that both the $(x')_2$ and $(y')_2$ axes at the center of mass are normal to planes of symmetry. Hence, we can say that

$$(I_{xy})_2 = 0 + [\rho(\pi)(1^2)(15)](-8)(-6)$$
$$= 2{,}262\rho \quad \text{(f)}$$

Example 9.4 (Continued)

Finally, for the small cutout rectangular parallelepiped, we note that the $(x')_3$ and $(y')_3$ axes at the center of mass are perpendicular to planes of symmetry. Hence, we have

$$\begin{aligned}(I_{xy})_3 &= 0 + [\rho(8)(6)(4)](-2)(-16) \\ &= 6{,}144\rho \end{aligned} \qquad \text{(g)}$$

The quantity I_{xy} for the body with the rectangular and cylindrical cavities is then

$$I_{xy} = (96{,}000 - 2{,}262 - 6{,}144)\rho = \boxed{87{,}600\rho} \qquad \text{(h)}$$

If ρ is given in units of lbm/ft,^{3} the inertia terms have units of lbm-ft.^{2}

*9.5 Transformation Properties of the Inertia Terms

Let us assume that the six independent inertia terms are known at the origin of a given reference. What is the mass moment of inertia for an axis going through the origin of the reference and having the direction cosines l, m, and n relative to the axes of this reference? The axis about which we are interested in obtaining the mass moment of inertia is designated as kk in Fig. 9.15.

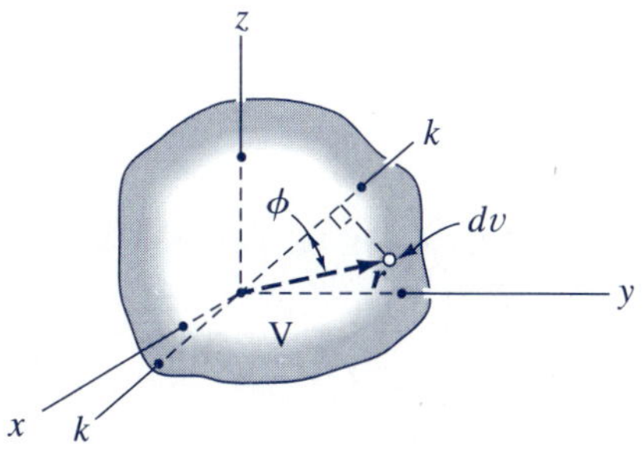

Figure 9.15. Find I_{kk}.

From previous conclusions, we can say that

$$I_{kk} = \iiint\limits_V [|\boldsymbol{r}|(\sin\phi)]^2 \rho\, dv \qquad (9.10)$$

where ϕ is the angle between kk and $\boldsymbol{r}$. We shall now put $\sin^2\phi$ into a more useful form by considering the right triangle formed by the position vector $\boldsymbol{r}$ and the axis kk. This triangle is shown enlarged in Fig. 9.16. The side a of the triangle has a magnitude that can be given by the dot product of $\boldsymbol{r}$ and the unit vector $\boldsymbol{\epsilon}_k$ along kk. Thus,

$$a = \boldsymbol{r} \cdot \boldsymbol{\epsilon}_k = (x\boldsymbol{i} + y\boldsymbol{j} + z\boldsymbol{k}) \cdot (l\boldsymbol{i} + m\boldsymbol{j} + n\boldsymbol{k}) \tag{9.11}$$

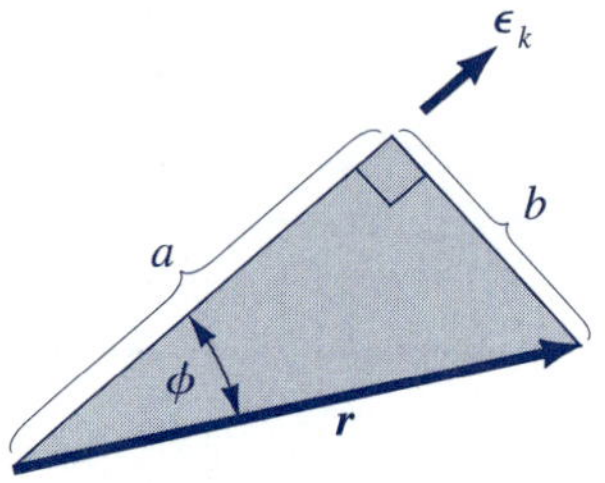

Figure 9.16. Right triangle formed by $\boldsymbol{r}$ and kk.

Hence

$$a = lx + my + nz$$

Using the Pythagorean theorem, we can now give side b as

$$b^2 = |\boldsymbol{r}|^2 - a^2 = (x^2 + y^2 + z^2) - (l^2x^2 + m^2y^2 + n^2z^2 + 2lmxy + 2lnxz + 2mnyz)$$

The term $\sin^2\phi$ may next be given as

$$\sin^2\phi = \frac{b^2}{r^2} = \frac{(x^2 + y^2 + z^2) - (l^2x^2 + m^2y^2 + n^2z^2 + 2lmxy + 2lnxz + 2mnyz)}{x^2 + y^2 + z^2} \tag{9.12}$$

Substituting back into Eq. 9.10, we get, on canceling terms,

$$I_{kk} = \iiint_V \left[(x^2 + y^2 + z^2) - (l^2x^2 + m^2y^2 + n^2z^2 + 2lmxy + 2lnxz + 2mnyz)\right]\rho\, dv$$

Since $l^2 + m^2 + n^2 = 1$, we can multiply the first bracketed expression in the integral by this sum:

$$I_{kk} = \iiint_V [(x^2 + y^2 + z^2)(l^2 + m^2 + n^2) - (l^2x^2 + m^2y^2 + n^2z^2 + 2lmxy + 2lnxz + 2mnyz)]\rho\, dv$$

Carrying out the multiplication and collecting terms, we get the relation

$$I_{kk} = l^2 \iiint_V (y^2 + z^2)\rho\, dv + m^2 \iiint_V (x^2 + z^2)\rho\, dv + n^2 \iiint_V (x^2 + y^2)\rho\, dv$$
$$- 2lm \iiint_V (xy)\rho\, dv - 2ln \iiint_V (xz)\rho\, dv - 2mn \iiint_V (yz)\rho\, dv$$

Referring back to the definitions presented by Eqs. 9.1, we reach the desired transformation equation:

$$I_{kk} = l^2 I_{xx} + m^2 I_{yy} + n^2 I_{zz} - 2lmI_{xy} - 2lnI_{xz} - 2mnI_{yz} \tag{9.13}$$

We next put this in a more useful form of the kind you will see in later courses in mechanics. Note first that l is the direction cosine between the k axis and the x axis. It is common practice to identify this cosine as a_{kx} instead of l. Note that the subscripts identify the axes involved. Similarly, $m = a_{ky}$ and $n = a_{kz}$. We can now express Eq. 9.13 in a form similar to a matrix array as follows on noting that $I_{xy} = I_{yx}$, etc.

$$\begin{aligned} I_{kk} = \;& I_{xx}a_{kx}^2 - I_{xy}a_{kx}a_{ky} - I_{xz}a_{kx}a_{kz} \\ & - I_{yx}a_{ky}a_{kx} + I_{yy}a_{ky}^2 - I_{yz}a_{ky}a_{kz} \\ & - I_{zx}a_{kz}a_{kx} - I_{zy}a_{kz}a_{ky} + I_{zz}a_{kz}^2 \end{aligned} \tag{9.14}$$

This format is easily written by first writing the matrix array of I's on the right side and then inserting the a's remembering to insert minus signs for off-diagonal terms.

Let us next compute the product of inertia for a pair of mutually perpendicular axes, Ok and Oq, as shown in Fig. 9.17. The direction cosines of Ok we shall take as l, m, and n, whereas the direction cosines of Oq we shall take as l', m', and n'. Since the axes are at right angles to each other, we know that

$$\boldsymbol{\epsilon}_k \cdot \boldsymbol{\epsilon}_q = 0$$

Therefore,

$$ll' + mm' + nn' = 0 \tag{9.15}$$

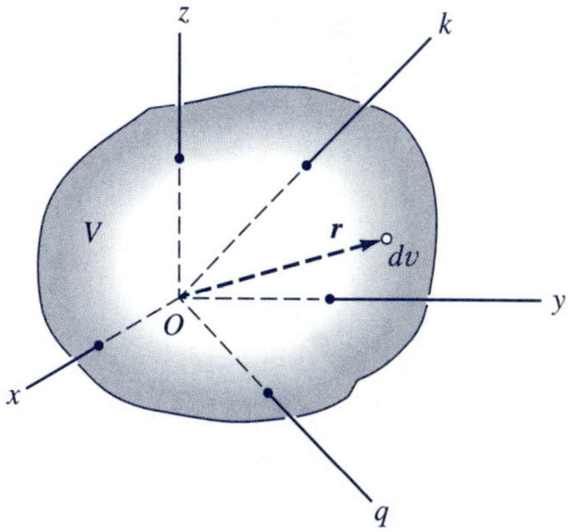

Figure 9.17. Find I_{kq}.

Noting that the coordinates of the mass element $\rho\, dv$ along the axes Ok and Oq are $\boldsymbol{r} \cdot \boldsymbol{\epsilon}_k$ and $\boldsymbol{r} \cdot \boldsymbol{\epsilon}_q$, respectively, we have, for I_{kq}:

$$I_{kq} = \iiint_V (\boldsymbol{r} \cdot \boldsymbol{\epsilon}_k)(\boldsymbol{r} \cdot \boldsymbol{\epsilon}_q)\rho\, dv$$

Using xyz components of $\boldsymbol{r}$ and the unit vectors, we have

$$I_{kq} = \iiint_V [(x\boldsymbol{i} + y\boldsymbol{j} + z\boldsymbol{k}) \cdot (l\boldsymbol{i} + m\boldsymbol{j} + n\boldsymbol{k})]$$
$$\times [(x\boldsymbol{i} + y\boldsymbol{j} + z\boldsymbol{k}) \cdot (l'\boldsymbol{i} + m'\boldsymbol{j} + n'\boldsymbol{k})]\rho\, dv \tag{9.16}$$

Carrying out the dot products in the integrand above, we get the following result:

$$I_{kq} = \iiint_V (xl + ym + zn)(xl' + ym' + zn')\rho\, dv$$

Hence,

$$I_{kq} = \iiint_V (x^2ll' + y^2mm' + z^2nn' + xylm' + xzln' + yxml' + yzmn' + zxnl' + zynm')\rho\, dv \tag{9.17}$$

Noting from Eq. 9.15 that $(ll' + mm' + nn')$ is zero, we may for convenience add the term, $(-x^2 - y^2 - z^2)(ll' + mm' + nn')$, to the integrand in the equation above. After canceling some terms, we have

$$I_{kq} = \iiint_V (-x^2mm' - x^2nn' - y^2ll' - y^2nn' - z^2ll' - z^2mm' + xylm' + xzln' + yxml' + yzmn' + zxnl' + zynm')\rho\, dv$$

Collecting terms and bringing the direction cosines outside the integrations, we get

$$\begin{aligned} I_{kq} = {} & -ll'\iiint_V (y^2 + z^2)\rho\, dv - mm'\iiint_V (x^2 + z^2)\rho\, dv \\ & - nn'\iiint_V (y^2 + x^2)\rho\, dv + (lm' + ml')\iiint_V xy\rho\, dv \\ & + (ln' + nl')\iiint_V xz\rho\, dv + (mn' + nm')\iiint_V yz\rho\, dv \end{aligned} \tag{9.18}$$

Noting the definitions in Eq. 9.1, we can state the desired transformation:

$$I_{kq} = -ll'I_{xx} - mm'I_{yy} - nn'I_{zz} + (lm' + ml')I_{xy} + (ln' + nl')I_{xz} + (mn' + nm')I_{yz} \tag{9.19}$$

We can now rewrite the previous equation in a more useful and simple form using a's as direction cosines. Thus, noting that $l' = a_{qx}$, etc., we proceed as in Eq. 9.14 to obtain

$$\begin{aligned} -I_{kq} = {} & I_{xx}a_{kx}a_{qx} - I_{xy}a_{kx}a_{qy} - I_{xz}a_{kx}a_{qz} \\ & - I_{yx}a_{ky}a_{qx} + I_{yy}a_{ky}a_{qy} - I_{yz}a_{ky}a_{qz} \\ & - I_{zx}a_{kz}a_{qx} - I_{zy}a_{kz}a_{qy} + I_{zz}a_{kz}a_{qz} \end{aligned} \tag{9.20}$$

Again you will note that the right side can easily be set forth by first putting down the matrix array of I_{ij} and then inserting the a's with easily determined subscripts while remembering to insert minus signs for off-diagonal terms.

Example 9.5

Find $I_{z'z'}$ and $I_{x'z'}$ for the solid cylinder shown in Fig. 9.18. The reference $x'y'z'$ is found by rotating about the y axis an amount 30°, as shown in the diagram. The mass of the cylinder is 100 kg.

It is simplest to first get the inertia tensor components for reference xyz. Thus, using formulas from the inside front cover page we have

$$I_{zz} = \frac{1}{2}Mr^2 = \frac{1}{2}(100)\left(\frac{1.3}{2}\right)^2 = 21.13 \text{ kg-m}^2$$

$$I_{xx} = I_{yy} = \frac{1}{12}M(3r^2 + h^2)$$

$$= \frac{1}{12}(100)\left[(3)\left(\frac{1.3}{2}\right)^2 + 3^2\right]$$

$$= 85.56 \text{ kg-m}^2$$

Noting that the xyz coordinate planes are planes of symmetry, we can conclude that

$$I_{xz} = I_{yx} = I_{yz} = 0$$

Next, evaluate the direction cosines of the z' and the x' axes relative to xyz. Thus,

For z' axis:

$$a_{z'x} = \cos 60° = .500$$
$$a_{z'y} = \cos 90° = 0$$
$$a_{z'z} = \cos 30° = .866$$

For x' axis:

$$a_{x'x} = \cos 30° = .866$$
$$a_{x'y} = \cos 90° = 0$$
$$a_{x'z} = \cos 120° = -.500$$

First, we employ Eq. 9.14 to get $I_{z'z'}$.

$$I_{z'z'} = (85.56)(.500)^2 + (21.13)(.866)^2$$

$$= \boxed{37.24 \text{ kg-m}^2}$$

Finally, we employ Eq. 9.20 to get $I_{x'z'}$.

$$-I_{x'z'} = (85.56)(.500)(.866) + (21.13)(.866)(-.500)$$

Therefore,

$$\boxed{I_{x'z'} = -27.90 \text{ kg-m}^2}$$

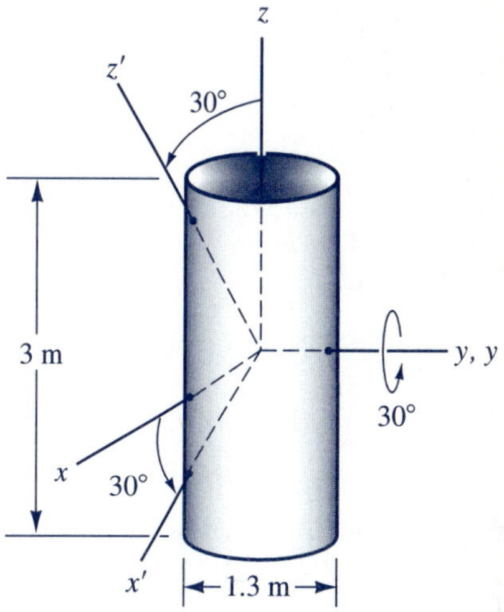

Figure 9.18. Find $I_{z'z'}$ and $I_{x'z'}$.

*9.6 Looking Ahead: Tensors

By making the axis Ok in Fig. 9.17 an x' axis at O and using the direction cosines for this axis ($a_{x'x}$, $a_{x'y}$, $a_{x'z}$), we can formulate $I_{x'x'}$ from Eq. 9.14. By a similar procedure, we can consider axis Ok to be a y' axis at O and we can formulate $I_{y'y'}$ using for this axis direction cosines $a_{y'x}$, $a_{y'y}$, $a_{y'z}$ from Eq. 9.14. Similarly, for $I_{z'z'}$. We can thus get the mass moments of inertia for reference x', y', z' at O rotated arbitrarily relative to xyz. Also by considering the Ok and Oq axes to be x' and y' axes, respectively, with $a_{x'x}$, $a_{x'y}$, and $a_{x'z}$ as direction cosines for the x' axis and $a_{y'x}$, $a_{y'y}$, and $a_{y'z}$ as direction cosines for the y' axis, we can evaluate $I_{x'y'}$ at O using Eq. 9.20. This approach can similarly be followed to find $I_{x'z'}$ and $I_{y'z'}$. Thus, employing Eqs. 9.14 and 9.20 as parent equations, we can develop equations for computing the nine inertia quantities for a reference $x'y'z'$ rotated arbitrarily relative to xyz at O in terms of the nine known inertia quantities for reference xyz at O. Thus, once the nine inertia quantities are known for one reference at some point, they can be determined for *any* reference at that point. We say that the inertia terms *transform* from one set of components for xyz at some point O to another set of components for $x'y'z'$ at point O by means of certain transformations formed from Eqs. 9.14 and 9.20.

We now define a symmetric,[6] *second-order tensor as a set of nine components*

$$\begin{pmatrix} A_{xx} & A_{xy} & A_{xz} \\ A_{yx} & A_{yy} & A_{yz} \\ A_{zx} & A_{zy} & A_{zz} \end{pmatrix}$$

which transforms with a rotation of axes according to the following parent equations. For the diagonal terms,

$$\begin{aligned} A_{kk} = \; & A_{xx}a_{kx}^2 + A_{xy}a_{kx}a_{ky} + A_{xz}a_{kx}a_{kz} \\ & + A_{yx}a_{ky}a_{kx} + A_{yy}a_{ky}^2 + A_{yz}a_{ky}a_{kz} \\ & + A_{zx}a_{kz}a_{kx} + A_{zy}a_{kz}a_{ky} + A_{zz}a_{kz}^2 \end{aligned} \tag{9.21}$$

For the off-diagonal terms,

$$\begin{aligned} A_{kq} = \; & A_{xx}a_{kx}a_{qx} + A_{xy}a_{kx}a_{qy} + A_{xz}a_{kx}a_{kz} \\ & + A_{yx}a_{ky}a_{qx} + A_{yy}a_{ky}a_{qy} + A_{yz}a_{ky}a_{kz} \\ & + A_{zx}a_{kz}a_{qx} + A_{zy}a_{kz}a_{qy} + A_{zz}a_{kz}a_{qz} \end{aligned} \tag{9.22}$$

On comparing Eqs. 9.21 and 9.22, respectively, with Eqs. 9.14 and 9.20, we can conclude that the array of terms

$$I_{ij} = \begin{pmatrix} I_{xx} & -I_{xy} & -I_{xz} \\ -I_{yx} & I_{yy} & -I_{yz} \\ -I_{zx} & -I_{zy} & I_{zz} \end{pmatrix} \tag{9.23}$$

is a second-order tensor.

[6]The word "symmetric" refers to the condition $A_{12} = A_{21}$, etc., that is required if the transformation equation is to have the form given. We can have nonsymmetric second-order tensors, but since they are less common in engineering work, we shall not concern ourselves here with such possibilities.

You will learn that because of the common transformation law identifying certain quantities as tensors, there will be extremely important common characteristics for these quantities which set them apart from other quantities. Thus, in order to learn these common characteristics in an efficient way and to understand them better, we become involved with tensors as an entity in the engineering sciences, physics, and applied mathematics. You will soon be confronted with the stress and strain tensors in your courses in strength of materials.

To explore this point further, we have shown an infinitesimal rectangular parallelepiped extracted from a solid under load. On three orthogonal faces we have shown nine force intensities (i.e., forces per unit area). Those with repeated indices are called *normal stresses* while those with different pairs of indices are called *shear stresses*. You will learn, that knowing nine such stresses, you can readily find three stresses, one normal and two orthogonal shear stresses, on *any* interface at any orientation inside the rectangular parallelepiped. To find such stresses on an interface knowing the stresses shown in Fig. 9.19, we have the *same transformation equations* given by Eqs. 9.21 and 9.22. Thus stress is a *second-order tensor*.

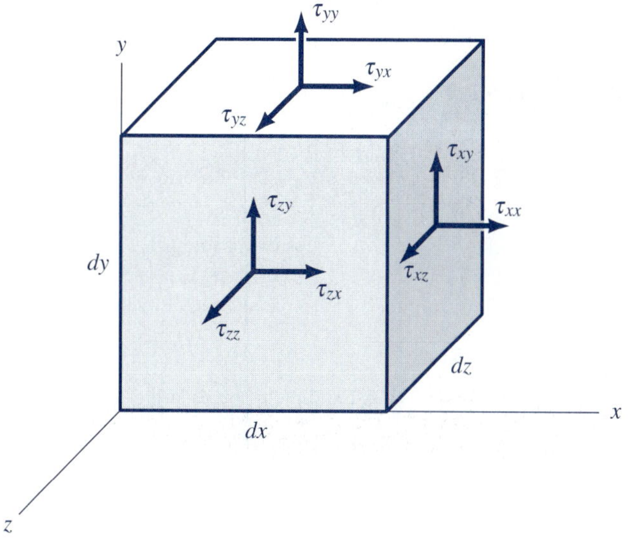

Figure 9.19. Nine stresses on three orthogonal interfaces at a point.

A *two-dimensional* simplification of τ_{ij} involving the quantities τ_{xx}, τ_{yy}, and τ_{xy} $(= \tau_{yx})$ as the only nonzero stresses is called *plane stress*. This occurs in a thin plate loaded in the plane of symmetry as shown in Fig. 9.20. Plane stress is the direct analog of *second moments and products of area*, which is a two-dimensional simplification of the inertia tensor. Clearly, plane stress and second moments and products of area have the same transformation equations, which are Eqs. 8.26 through 8.28 with τ_{xx}, τ_{yy}, τ_{xy}, $\tau_{x'y'}$ replacing I_{xx}, I_{yy}, $-I_{xy}$, $-I_{x'y'}$ respectively.

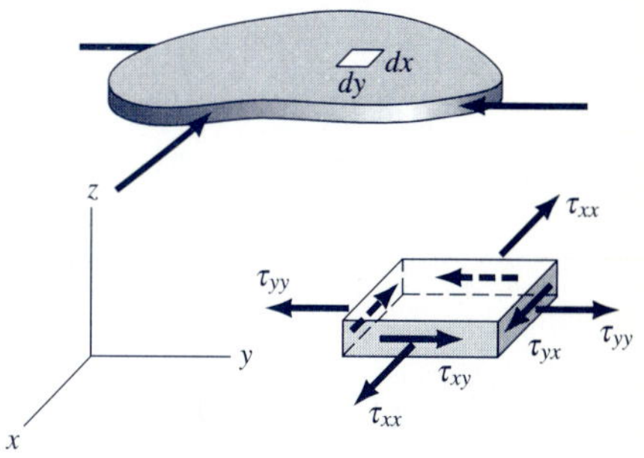

Figure 9.20. The case of plane stress.

In solid mechanics, you will also learn that there are nine terms ϵ_{ij} that describe deformation at a point. Thus consider the undeformed an infinitesimal

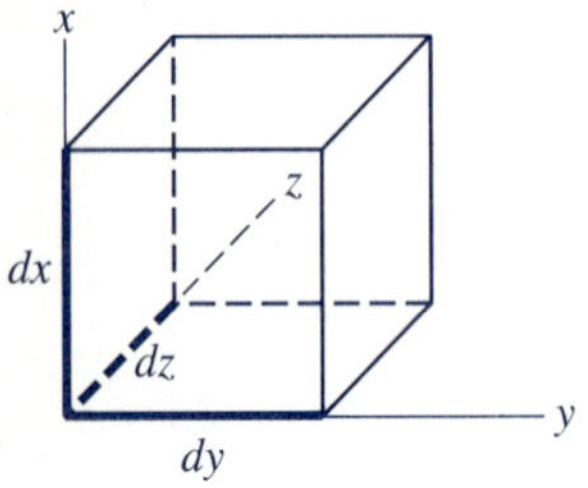

Figure 9.21. An infinitesimal rectangular parallelepiped with three edges highlighted.

rectangular parallelepiped in Fig. 9.21. When there is a deformation there are *normal strains* ϵ_{xx}, ϵ_{yy}, ϵ_{zz} along the direction of the darkened edges which give the changes of length per unit original length of these edges. Furthermore, when there is a deformation, there are six *shear strains* $\epsilon_{xy} = \epsilon_{yx}$, $\epsilon_{xz} = \epsilon_{zx}$, $\epsilon_{yz} = \epsilon_{zy}$ that give the change in angle in radians from that of the right angles of the three darkened edges. Knowing these quantities, we can find any other strains in the rectangular parallelepiped. These other strains can be found by using transformation Eqs. 9.21 and 9.22 and so *strain* is also a *second-order tensor.*

The two-dimensional simplification of ϵ_{ij} involving the quantities, ϵ_{xx}, ϵ_{yy}, and ϵ_{xy} (= ϵ_{yx}) as the only nonzero strains is called *plane strain* and represents the strains in a prismatic body constrained at the ends with loading normal to the centerline in which the loading does not vary with z (see Fig. 9.22). Also, the prismatic body must not be subject to bending. Plane strain is an analogous mathematically to plane stress and second moments and products of area. All three are two-dimensional simplifications of second-order symmetric tensors and have the *same transformation equations* as well as other mathematical properties. Finally, in electromagnetic theory and nuclear physics, you will be introduced to the quadruple tensor.[7]

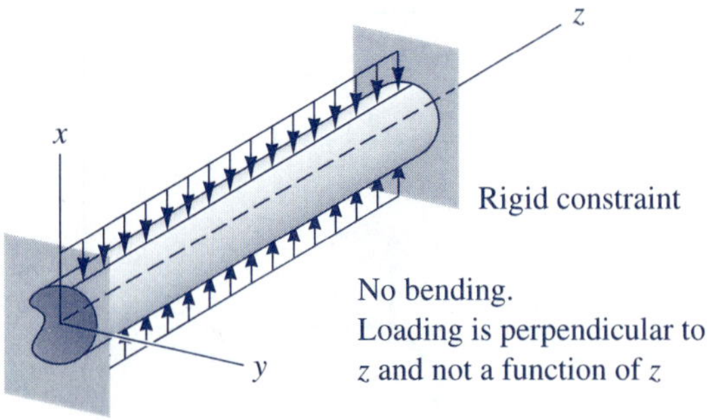

Figure 9.22. Example of plane strain.

[7]Vectors may be defined in terms of the way components of the vector for a new reference are related to the components of the old reference at a point. Thus, for any direction n, we have for component A_n:

$$A_n = A_x a_{nx} + A_y a_{ny} + A_z a_{nz} \tag{a}$$

Using Eq. (a), we can find components of vector $\mathbf{A}$ with respect to $x'y'z'$ rotated arbitrarily relative to xyz. Thus, all vectors must transform in accordance with Eq. (a) on rotation of the reference. Obviously, the vector, as seen from this point of view, is a special, simple case of the second-order tensor. We say, accordingly, that vectors are *first-order tensors.*

As for scalars, there is clearly no change in value when there is a rotation of axes at a point. Thus,

$$T(x', y', z') = T(x, y, z) \tag{b}$$

for $x'y'z'$ rotated relative to xyz. Scalars are a special form of tensor when considered from a transformation point of view. In fact, they are called *zero-order tensors.*

PROBLEMS

In the following problems, use the formulas for moments and products of inertia at the mass center to be found in the inside front cover page.

9.20. What are the moments and products of inertia for the xyz and $x'y'z'$ axes for the cylinder?

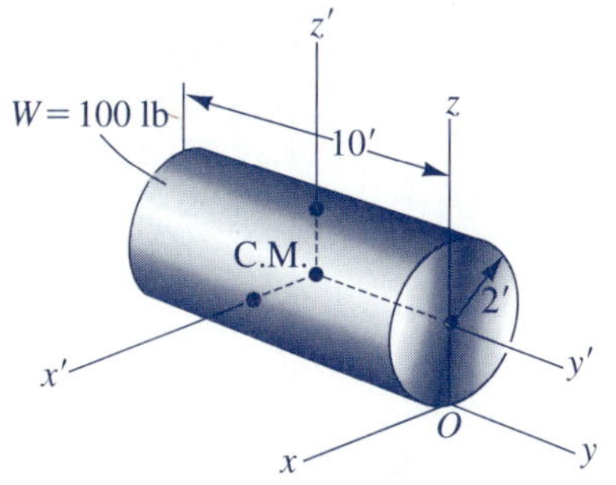

Figure P.9.20.

9.21. For the uniform block, compute the inertia tensor at the center of mass, at point a, and at point b for axes parallel to the xyz reference. Take the mass of the body as M kg.

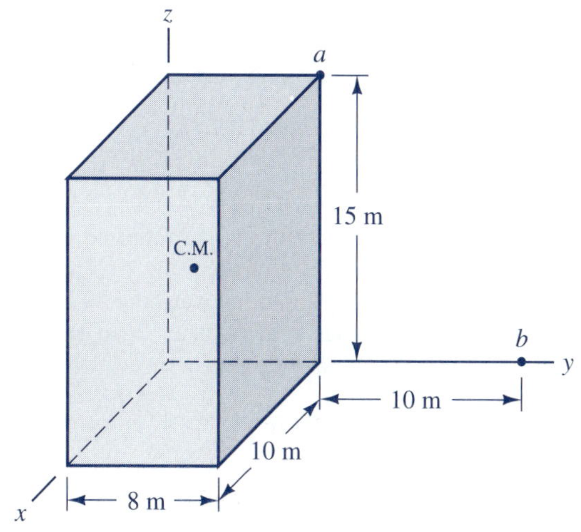

Figure P.9.21.

9.22. Determine $I_{xx} + I_{yy} + I_{zz}$ as a function of x, y, and z for all points in space for the uniform rectangular parallelepiped. Note that xyz has its origin at the center of mass and is parallel to the sides.

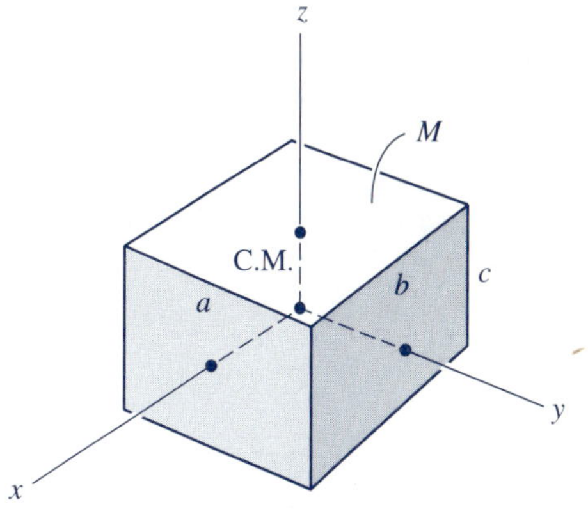

Figure P.9.22.

9.23. A thin plate weighing 100 N has the following mass moments of inertia at mass center O:

$$I_{xx} = 15 \text{ kg-m}^2$$
$$I_{yy} = 13 \text{ kg-m}^2$$
$$I_{xy} = -10 \text{ kg-m}^2$$

What are the moments of inertia $I_{x'x'}$, $I_{y'y'}$, and $I_{z'z'}$ at point P having the position vector:

$$\boldsymbol{r} = .5\boldsymbol{i} + .2\boldsymbol{j} + .6\boldsymbol{k} \text{ m}$$

Also determine $I_{x'z'}$ at P.

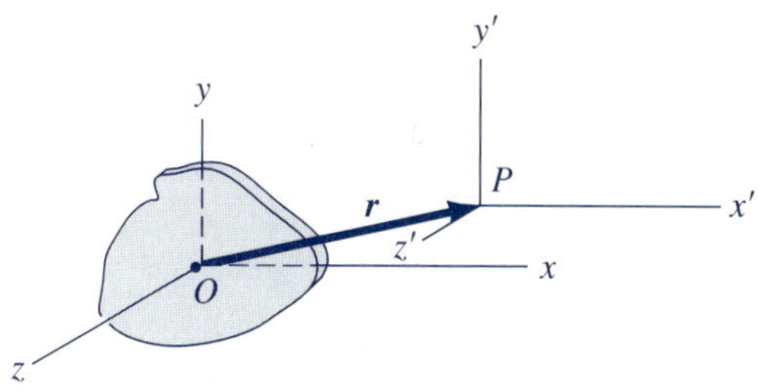

Figure P.9.23.

9.24. A crate with its contents weighs 20 kN and has its center of mass at

$$r_c = 1.3\boldsymbol{i} + 3\boldsymbol{j} + .8\boldsymbol{k} \text{ m}$$

It is known that at corner A,

$$I_{x'x'} = 5{,}500 \text{ kg-m}^2$$
$$I_{x'y'} = -1{,}500 \text{ kg-m}^2$$

for primed axes parallel to xyz. At point B, find $I_{x''x''}$ and $I_{x''y''}$ for double-primed axes parallel to xyz.

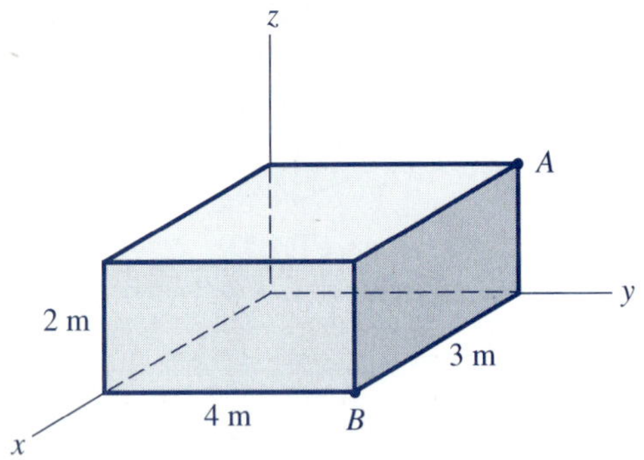

Figure P.9.24.

9.25 A cylindrical crate and its contents weigh 500 N. The center of mass is at

$$r_c = .6\boldsymbol{i} + .7\boldsymbol{j} + 2\boldsymbol{k} \text{ m}$$

It is known that at A,

$$(I_{yy})_A = 85 \text{ kg-m}^2$$
$$(I_{yz})_A = -22 \text{ kg-m}^2$$

Find I_{yy} and I_{zy} at B.

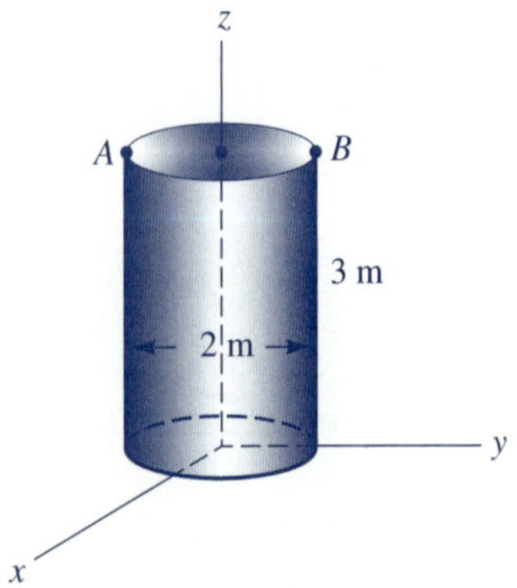

Figure P.9.25.

9.26. A block having a uniform density of 5 grams/cm³ has a hole of diameter 40 mm cut out. What are the principal moments of inertia at point A at the centroid of the right face of the block?

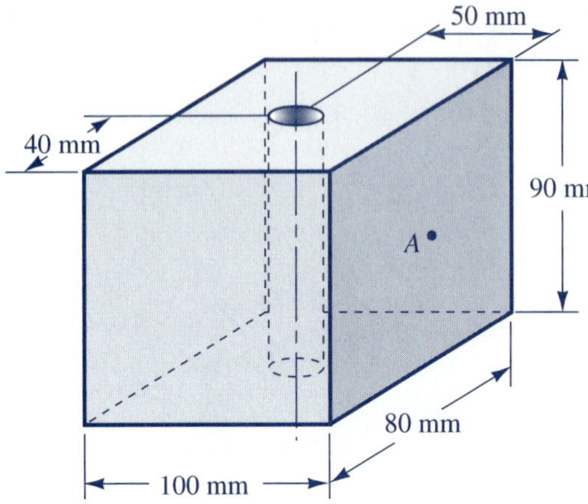

Figure P.9.26.

9.27. Find maximum and minimum moments of inertia at point A. The block weighs 20 N and the cone weighs 14 N.

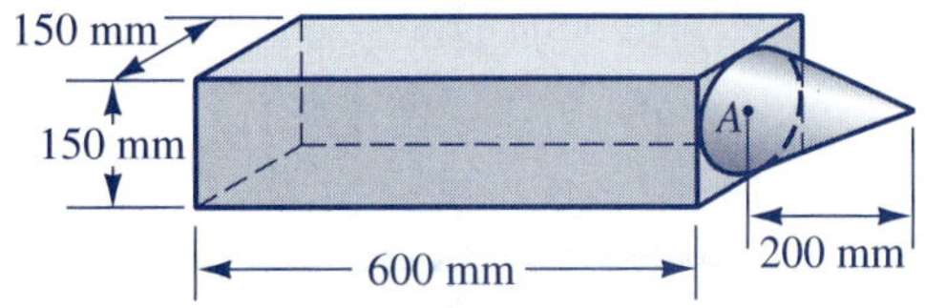

Figure P.9.27.

9.28. Solid spheres C and D each weighing 25 N and having radius of 50 mm are attached to a thin solid rod weighing 30 N. Also, solid spheres E and G each weighing 20 N and having radii of 30 mm are attached to a thin rod weighing 20 N. The rods are attached to be orthogonal to each other. What are the principal moments of inertia at point A?

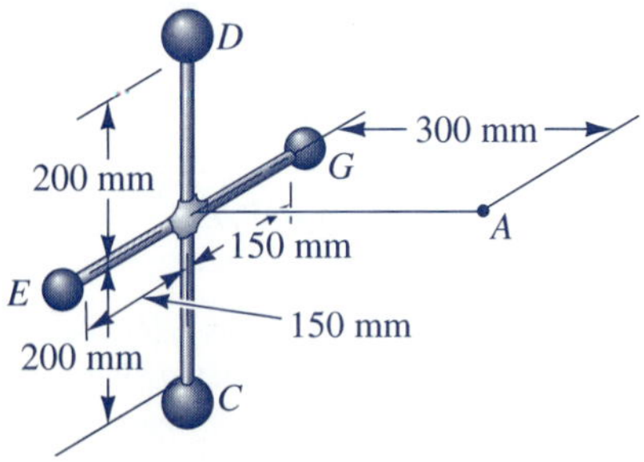

Figure P.9.28.

9.29. A cylinder is shown having a conical cavity oriented along the axis *A–A* and a cylindrical cavity oriented normal to *A–A*. If the density of the material is 7,200 kg/m^3, what is I_{AA}?

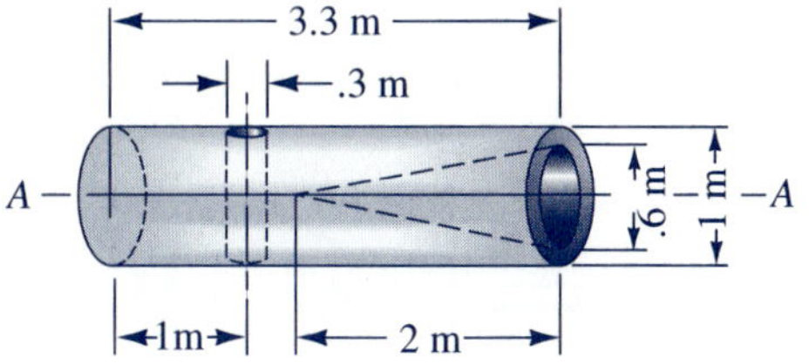

Figure P.9.29.

9.30. A flywheel is made of steel having a specific weight of 490 lb/ft.^{3} What is the moment of inertia about its geometric axis? What is the radius of gyration?

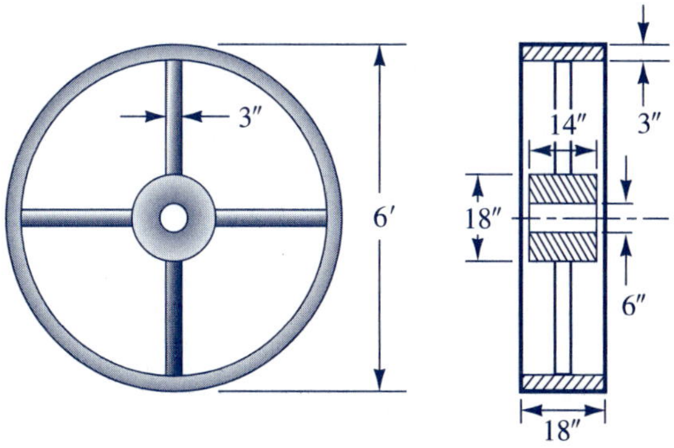

Figure P.9.30.

9.31. Compute I_{yy} and I_{xy} for the right circular cylinder, which has a mass of 50 kg, and the square rod, which has a mass of 10 kg, when the two are joined together so that the rod is radial to the cylinder. The *x* axis lies along the bottom of the square rod.

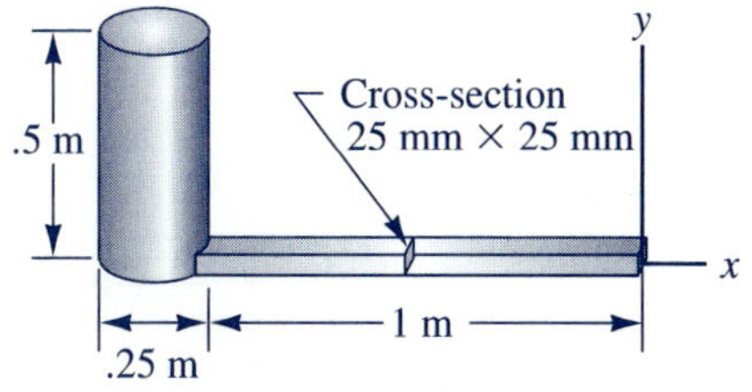

Figure P.9.31.

9.32. Compute the moments and products of inertia for the *xy* axes. The specific weight is 490 lb/ft^3 throughout.

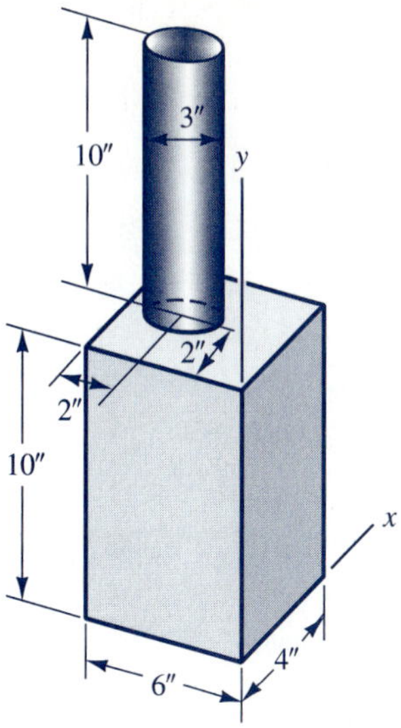

Figure P.9.32.

9.33. A disc *A* is mounted on a shaft such that its normal is oriented 10° from the centerline of the shaft. The disc has a diameter of 2 ft, is 1 in. in thickness, and weighs 100 lb. Compute the moment of inertia of the disc about the centerline of the shaft.

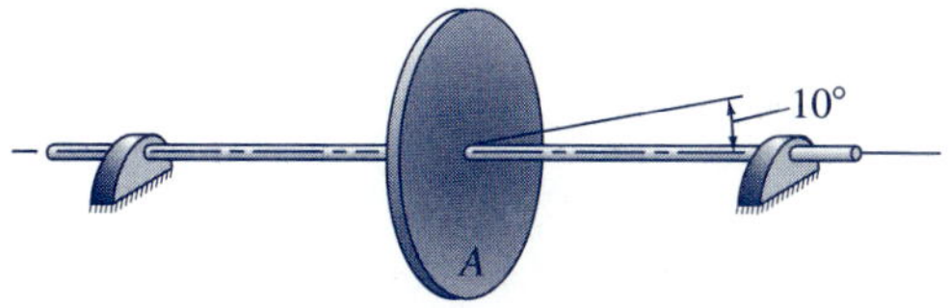

Figure P.9.33.

9.34. A gear *B* having a mass of 25 kg rotates about axis *C–C*. If the rod *A* has a mass distribution of 7.5 kg/m, compute the moment of inertia of *A* and *B* about the axis *C–C*.

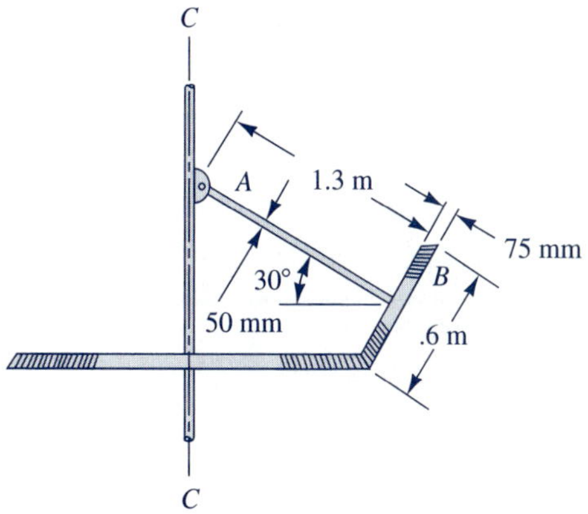

Figure P.9.34.

9.35. A block weighing 100 N is shown. Compute the moment of inertia about the diagonal D–D.

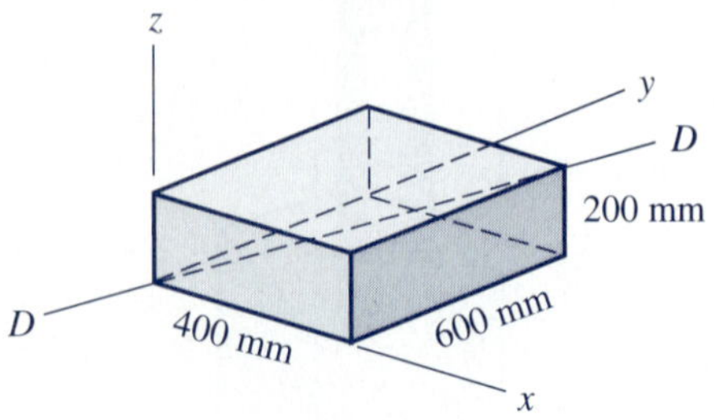

Figure P.9.35.

9.36. A solid sphere A of diameter 1 ft and weight 100 lb is connected to the shaft B–B by a solid rod weighing 2 lb/ft and having a diameter of 1 in. Compute $I_{z'z'}$ for the rod and ball.

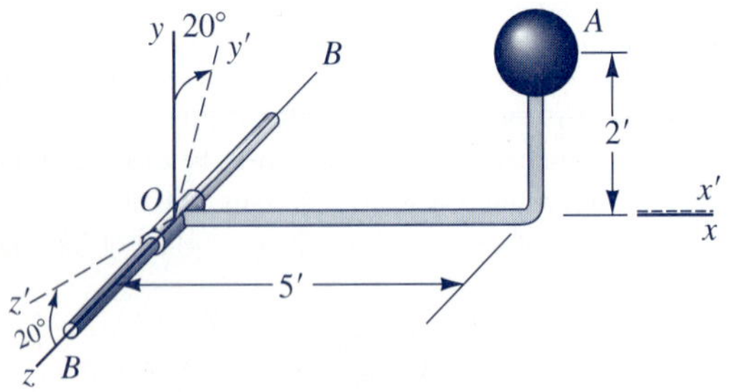

Figure P.9.36.

9.37. In Problem 9.13, we found the following results for the thin plate:

$$I_{xx} = I_{yy} = .1019 \text{ grams-m}^2$$

$$I_{xy} = .0649 \text{ grams-m}^2$$

Find all components for the inertia tensor for reference $x'y'z'$. Axes $x'y'$ lie in the midplane of the plate.

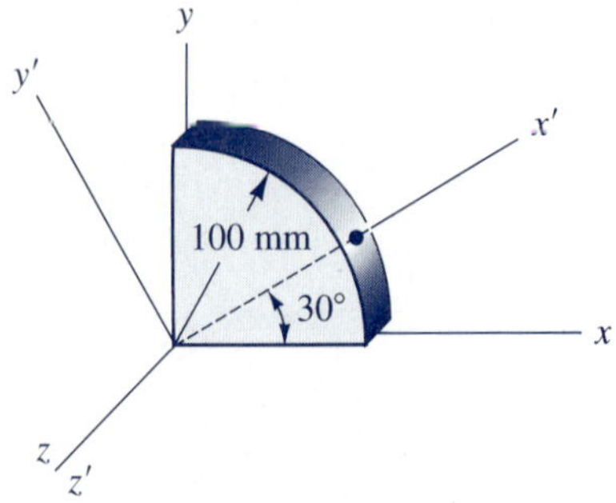

Figure P.9.37.

9.38. A bent rod weighs .1 N/mm. What is I_{nn} for

$$\boldsymbol{\epsilon}_n = .30\boldsymbol{i} + .45\boldsymbol{j} + .841\boldsymbol{k}?$$

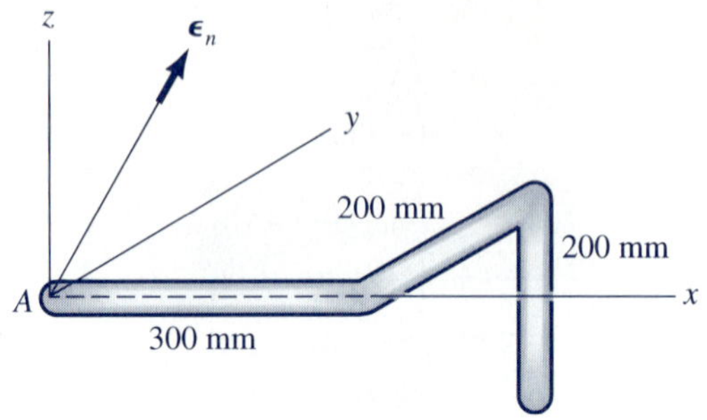

Figure P.9.38.

9.39. Evaluate the matrix of direction cosines for the primed axes relative to the unprimed axes.

$$a_{ij} = \begin{pmatrix} a_{x'x} & a_{x'y} & a_{x'z} \\ a_{y'x} & a_{y'y} & a_{y'z} \\ a_{z'x} & a_{z'y} & a_{z'z} \end{pmatrix}$$

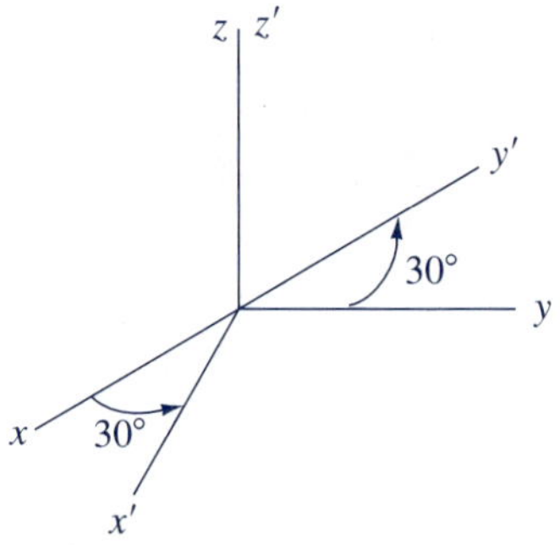

Figure P.9.39.

9.40. The block is uniform in density and weighs 10 N. Find $I_{y'z'}$.

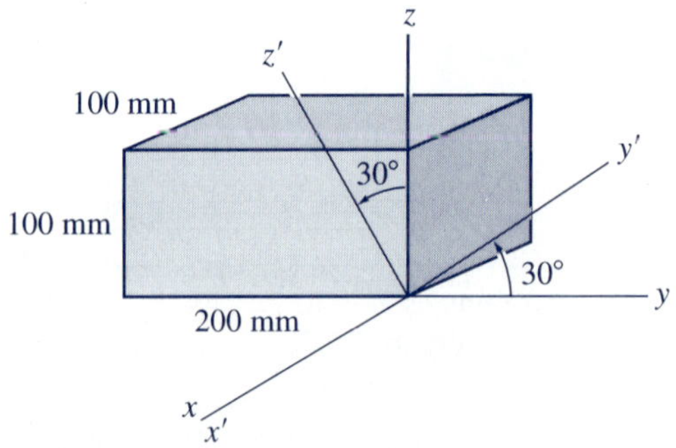

Figure P.9.40.

***9.41.** A thin rod of length 300 mm and weight 12 N is oriented relative to $x'y'z'$ such that

$$\boldsymbol{\epsilon}_n = .4\mathbf{i}' + .3\mathbf{j}' + .866\mathbf{k}'$$

What is $I_{x'y'}$?

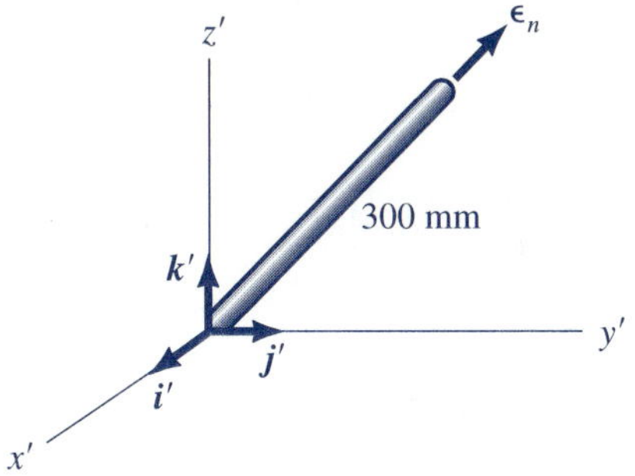

Figure P.9.41.

***9.42.** Show that the transformation equation for the inertia tensor components at a point when there is a rotation of axes (i.e., Eqs. 9.14 and 9.20) can be given as follows:

$$I_{kq} = \sum_j \sum_i a_{ki} a_{qj} I_{ij}$$

where k can be x', y', or z' and q can be x', y', or z', and where i and j go from x to y to z. The equation above is a compact definition of *second-order tensors*. Remember that in the inertia tensor you must have a minus sign in front of each product of inertia term (i.e., $-I_{xy}$, $-I_{yz}$, etc.). [*Hint:* Let $i = x$; then sum over j; then let $i = y$ and sum again over j; etc.]

***9.43.** In Problem 9.42, express the transformation equation to get $I_{y'z'}$ in terms of the inertia tensor components for reference xyz having the same origin as $x'y'z'$.

*9.7 The Inertia Ellipsoid and Principal Moments of Inertia

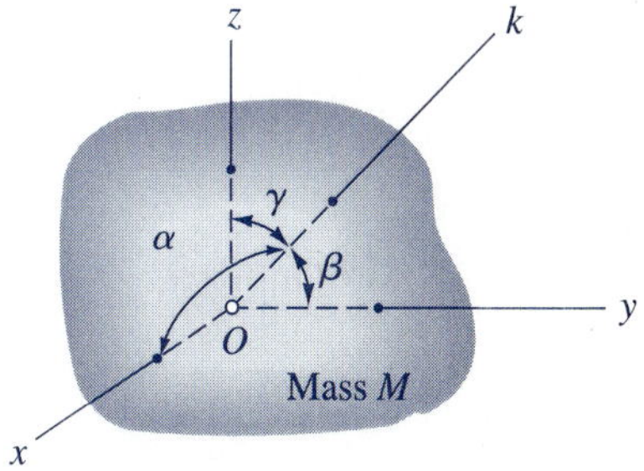

Figure 9.23. Physical diagram.

Equation 9.14 gives the moment of inertia of a body about an axis k in terms of the direction cosines of that axis measured from an orthogonal reference with an origin O on the axis, and in terms of six independent inertia quantities for this reference. We wish to explore the nature of the variation of I_{kk} at a point O in space as the direction of k is changed. (The k axis and the body are shown in Fig. 9.23, which we shall call the physical diagram.) To do this, we will employ a geometric representation of moment of inertia at a point that is developed in the following manner. Along the axis k, we lay off as a distance the quantity OA given by the relation

$$OA = \frac{d}{\sqrt{I_{kk}/M}} \tag{9.24}$$

where d is an arbitrary constant that has a dimension of length that will render OA dimensionless, as the reader can verify. The term $\sqrt{I_{kk}/M}$ is the *radius of gyration* and was presented earlier. To avoid confusion, this operation is shown in another diagram, called the inertia diagram (Fig. 9.24), where the new ξ, η, and ζ axes are *parallel* to the x, y, and z axes of the physical diagram. Considering all possible directions of k, we observe that some surface will be formed about the point O', and this surface is related to the shape of the body through Eq. 9.14. We can express the equation of this surface quite

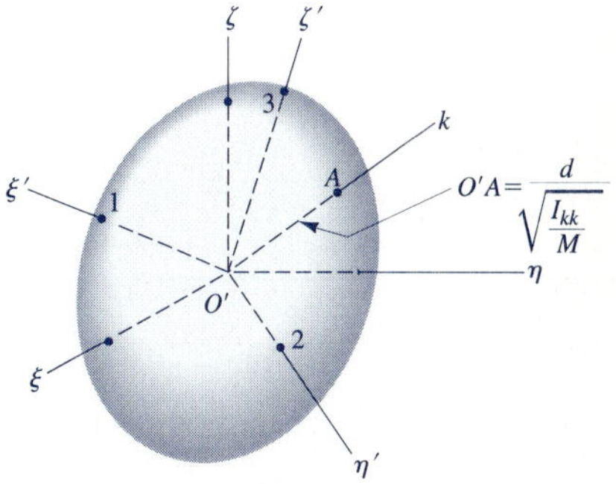

Figure 9.24. Inertia diagram.

readily. Suppose that we call ξ, η, and ζ the coordinates of point A. Since $O'A$ is parallel to the line k and thus has the direction cosines a_{kx}, a_{ky}, and a_{kz} that are associated with this line, we can say that

$$
\begin{aligned}
a_{kx} &= \frac{\xi}{O'A} = \frac{\xi}{d\sqrt{M/I_{kk}}} \\
a_{ky} &= \frac{\eta}{O'A} = \frac{\eta}{d\sqrt{M/I_{kk}}} \\
a_{kz} &= \frac{\zeta}{O'A} = \frac{\zeta}{d\sqrt{M/I_{kk}}}
\end{aligned}
\tag{9.25}
$$

Now replace the direction cosines in Eq. 9.13, using the relations above:

$$
\begin{aligned}
I_{kk} = {} & \frac{\xi^2}{Md^2/I_{kk}} I_{xx} + \frac{\eta^2}{Md^2/I_{kk}} I_{yy} + \frac{\zeta^2}{Md^2/I_{kk}} I_{zz} \\
& + 2\frac{\xi\eta}{Md^2/I_{kk}}(-I_{xy}) + 2\frac{\xi\zeta}{Md^2/I_{kk}}(-I_{xz}) + 2\frac{\eta\zeta}{Md^2/I_{kk}}(-I_{yz})
\end{aligned}
\tag{9.26}
$$

We can see that I_{kk} cancels out of the preceding equation, leaving an equation involving the coordinates ξ, η, and ζ of the surface and the inertia terms of the body itself. Rearranging the terms, we then have

$$
\begin{aligned}
& \frac{\xi^2}{Md^2/I_{xx}} + \frac{\eta^2}{Md^2/I_{yy}} + \frac{\zeta^2}{Md^2/I_{zz}} \\
& \quad + \frac{2\xi\eta}{Md^2}(-I_{xy}) + \frac{2\xi\zeta}{Md^2}(-I_{xz}) + \frac{2\eta\zeta}{Md^2}(-I_{yz}) = 1
\end{aligned}
\tag{9.27}
$$

Considering analytic geometry, we know that the surface is that of an ellipsoid (see Fig. 9.24), and is thus called the *ellipsoid of inertia*. The distance squared from O' to any point A on the ellipsoid is inversely proportional to the moment of inertia (see Eq. 9.24) about an axis in the body at O having the same direction as $O'A$. We can conclude that the inertia tensor for any point of a body can be represented geometrically by such a second-order surface, and this surface may be thought of as analogous to the arrow used to represent a vector graphically. The size, shape, and inclination of the ellipsoid will vary for each point in space for a given body. (Since all second-order tensors may be represented by second-order surfaces, you will, if you study elasticity, also encounter the ellipsoids of stress and strain.)[8]

An ellipsoid has three orthogonal axes of symmetry, which have a common point at the center, O' (see Fig. 9.24). In the figure, these axes are shown as $O'1$, $O'2$, and $O'3$. We pointed out that the shape and inclination of the ellipsoid of inertia depend on the mass distribution of the body about the *origin* of the xyz reference, and they have nothing to do with the choice of *the orientation of the* xyz (and hence the $\xi\eta\zeta$) reference at the point. We can

[8]See I. H. Shames, *Mechanics of Deformable Solids*, Prentice-Hall, Inc., Englewood Cliffs, N.J., 1964, Chap. 2. Also, Krieger Publishing Co., N.Y., 1979.

therefore imagine that the xyz reference (and hence the $\xi\eta\zeta$ reference) can be chosen to have directions that coincide with the aforementioned symmetric axes, $O'1$, $O'2$, and $O'3$. If we call such references $x'y'z'$ and $\xi'\eta'\zeta'$, respectively, we know from analytic geometry that Eq. 9.27 becomes

$$\frac{(\xi')^2}{Md^2/I_{x'x'}} + \frac{(\eta')^2}{Md^2/I_{y'y'}} + \frac{(\zeta')^2}{Md^2/I_{z'z'}} = 1 \tag{9.28}$$

where ξ', η', and ζ' are coordinates of the ellipsoidal surface relative to the new reference, and $I_{x'x'}$, $I_{y'y'}$, and $I_{z'z'}$ are mass moments of inertia of the body about the new axes. We can now draw several important conclusions from this geometrical construction and the accompanying equations. One of the symmetrical axes of the ellipsoid above is the longest distance from the origin to the surface of the ellipsoid, and another axis is the smallest distance from the origin to the ellipsoidal surface. Examining the definition in Eq. 9.24, we must conclude that the minimum moment of inertia for the point O must correspond to the axis having the maximum length, and the maximum moment of inertia must correspond to the axis having the minimum length. The third axis has an intermediate value that makes the sum of the moment of inertia terms equal to the sum of the moment of inertia terms for all orthogonal axes at point O, in accordance with Eq. 9.2. In addition, Eq. 9.28 leads us to conclude that $I_{x'y'} = I_{y'z'} = I_{x'z'} = 0$. That is, the products of inertia of the mass about these axes must be zero. Clearly, these axes are the *principal axes* of inertia at the point O.

Since the preceding operations could be carried out at any point in space for the body, we can conclude that:

At each point there is a set of principal axes having the extreme values of moments of inertia for that point and having zero products of inertia.[9] *The orientation of these axes will vary continuously from point to point throughout space for the given body.*

All symmetric second-order tensor quantities have the properties discussed above for the inertia tensor. By transforming from the original reference to the principal reference, we change the inertia tensor representation from

$$\begin{pmatrix} I_{xx} & (-I_{xy}) & (-I_{xz}) \\ (-I_{yx}) & I_{yy} & (-I_{yz}) \\ (-I_{zx}) & (-I_{zy}) & I_{zz} \end{pmatrix} \quad \text{to} \quad \begin{pmatrix} I_{x'x'} & 0 & 0 \\ 0 & I_{y'y'} & 0 \\ 0 & 0 & I_{z'z'} \end{pmatrix} \tag{9.29}$$

In mathematical parlance, we have "diagonalized" the tensor by the preceding operations.

[9]A general procedure for computing principal moments of inertia is set forth in Appendix II.

9.8 Closure

In this chapter, we first introduced the nine components comprising the inertia tensor. Next, we considered the case of the very thin flat plate in which the xy axes form the midplane of the plate. We found that the mass moments and products of inertia terms $(I_{xx})_M$, $(I_{yy})_M$, and $(I_{xy})_M$ for the plate are proportional, respectively, to $(I_{xx})_A$, $(I_{yy})_A$, and $(I_{xy})_A$, the second moments and product of area of the plate surface. As a result, we could set forth the concept of principal axes for the inertia tensor as an extension of the work in Chapter 8. Thus, we pointed out that for these axes the products of inertia will be zero. Furthermore, one principal axis corresponds to the maximum moment of inertia at the point while another of the principal axes corresponds to the minimum moment of inertia at the point. We pointed out that for bodies with two orthogonal planes of symmetry, the principal axes at any point on the line of intersection of the planes of symmetry must be along this line of intersection and normal to this line in the planes of symmetry.

Those readers who studied the starred sections from Section 9.5 onward will have found proofs of the extensions set forth earlier about principal axes from Chapter 8. Even more important is the disclosure that the inertia tensor components change their values when the axes are rotated at a point in exactly the same way as many other physical quantities having nine components. Such quantities are called second-order tensors. Because of the common transformation equation for such quantities, they have many important identical properties, such as principal axes. In your course in strength of materials you should learn that stress and strain are second-order tensors and hence have principal axes.[10] Additionally, you will find that a two-dimensional stress distribution called *plane stress* is related to the stress tensor exactly as the moments and products of area are related to the inertia tensor. The same situation exists with strain. Consequently, there are similar mathematical formulations for plane stress and the corresponding case for strain (plane strain). Thus, by taking the extra time to consider the mathematical considerations of Sections 9.5 through 9.7, you will find unity between Chapter 9 and some very important aspects of strength of materials to be studied later in your program.

In Chapter 10, we shall introduce another approach to studying equilibrium beyond what we have used thus far. This approach is valuable for certain important classes of statics problems and at the same time forms the groundwork for a number of advanced techniques that many students will study later in their programs.

[10]See I.H. Shames, *Introduction to Solid Mechanics*, 2nd ed., Prentice-Hall, Inc., Englewood Cliffs, New Jersey, 1989.

PROBLEMS

9.44. Find I_{zz} for the body of revolution having uniform density of .2 kg/mm^3. The radial distance out from the z axis to the surface is given as

$$r^2 = -4\,z \text{ mm}^2$$

where z is in millimeters. [*Hint:* Make use of the formula for the moment of inertia about the axis of a disc, $\frac{1}{2}Mr^2$.]

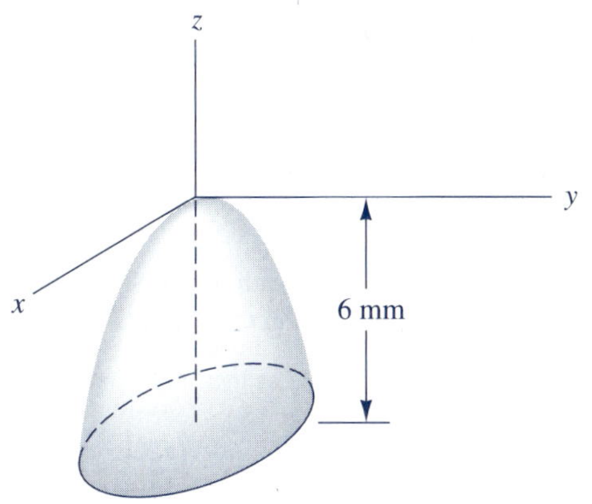

Figure P.9.44.

9.45. In Problem 9.44, determine I_{zz} without using the disc formula but using multiple integration instead.

9.46. What are the inertia tensor components for the thin plate about axes xyz? The plate weighs 2 N.

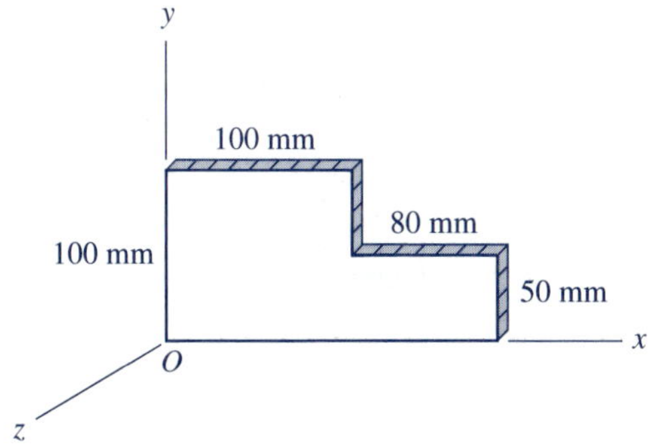

Figure P.9.46.

9.47. In Problem 9.46, what are the principal axes and the principal moments of inertia for the inertia tensor at O?

9.48. What are the principal mass moments of inertia at point O? Block A weighs 15 N. Rod B weighs 6 N and solid sphere C weighs 10 N. The density in each body is uniform. The diameter of the sphere is 50 mm.

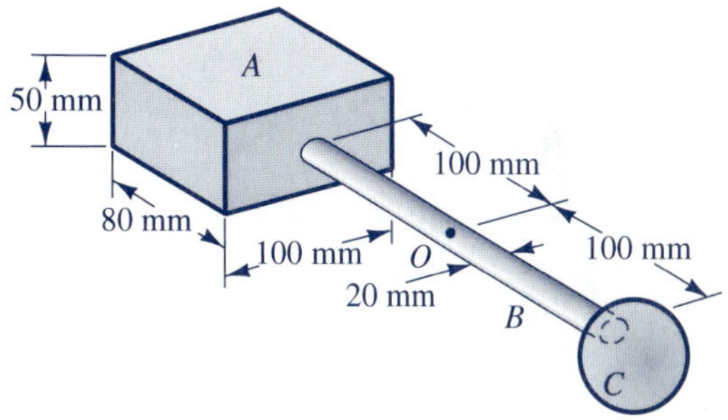

Figure P.9.48.

9.49. The block has a density of 15 kg/m.[3] Find the moment of inertia about axis AB.

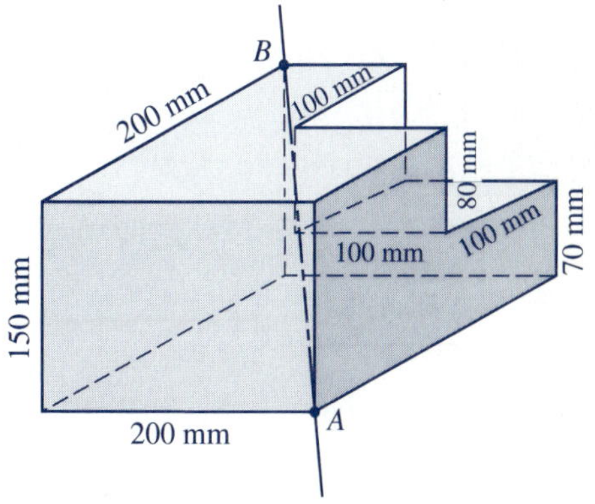

Figure P.9.49.

9.50. A crate and its contents weighs 10 kN. The center of mass of the crate and its contents is at

$$\boldsymbol{r}_c = .40\boldsymbol{i} + .30\boldsymbol{j} + .60\boldsymbol{k} \text{ m}$$

If at A we know that

$$I_{yy} = 800 \text{ kg-m}^2$$
$$I_{yz} = 500 \text{ kg-m}^2$$

find I_{yy} and I_{yz} at B.

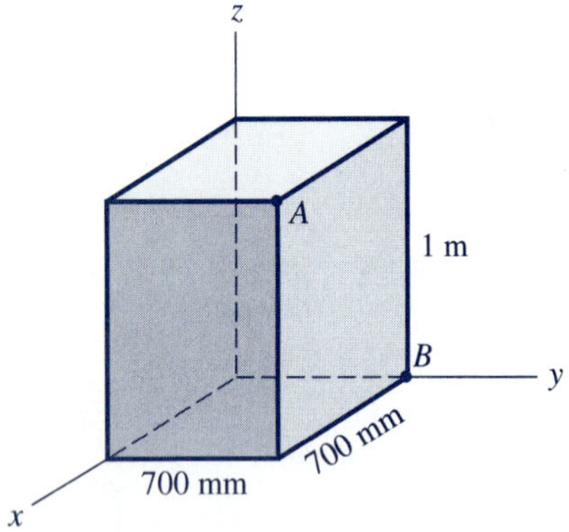

Figure P.9.50.

9.51. A semicylinder weighs 50 N. What are the principal moments of inertia at O? What is the product of inertia $I_{y'z'}$? What conclusion can you draw about the direction of principal axes at O?

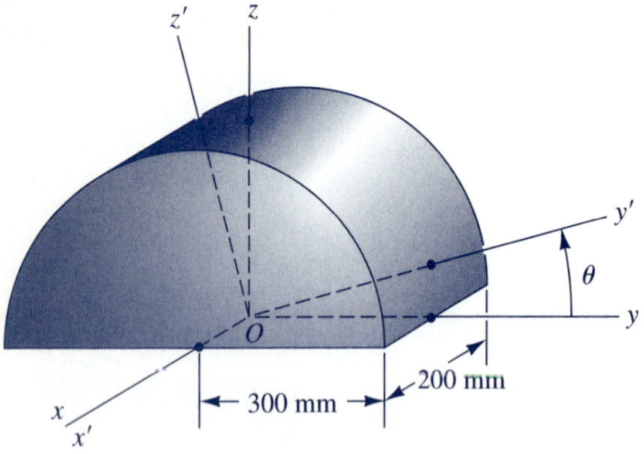

Figure P.9.51.

9.52. Find I_{yy} and I_{yz}. The diameter of A is 0.3 m. B is the center of the right face of the block. Take $\rho = \rho_0$ kg/m.³

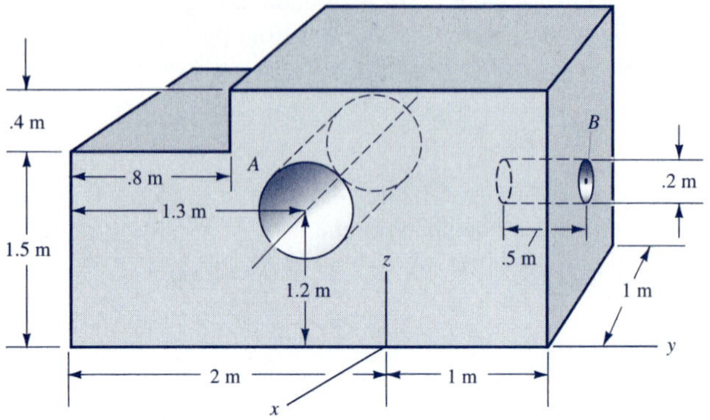

Figure P.9.52.

9.53. A body is composed of two adjoining blocks. Both blocks have a uniform mass density ρ equal to 10 kg/m.³

(a) Find the mass moments of inertia, I_{xx} and I_{zz}

(b) Find the product of inertia I_{xy}.

(c) Is the product of inertia $I_{yz} = 0$ (yes or no)? Why?

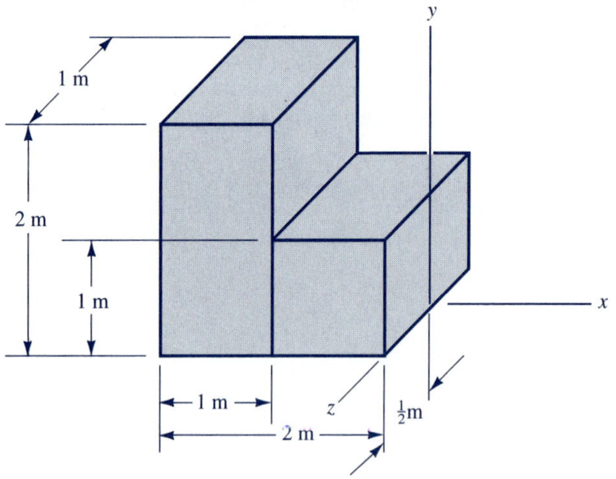

Figure P.9.53.

CHAPTER 10

*Methods of Virtual Work and Stationary Potential Energy

10.1 Introduction

In the study of statics thus far, we have followed the procedure of isolating a body to expose certain unknown forces and then formulating either scalar or vector equations of equilibrium that include *all* the forces acting on the body. At this time, alternative methods of expressing conditions of equilibrium, called the *method of virtual work* and, derived from it, the *method of stationary potential energy*, will be presented. These methods will yield equilibrium equations equivalent to those of preceding sections. Furthermore, these new equations include only certain forces on a body, and accordingly in some problems will provide a more simple means of solving for desired unknowns.

Actually, we are making a very modest beginning into a vast field of endeavor called *variational mechanics* or *energy methods* with important applications to both rigid-body and deformable-body solid mechanics. Indeed, more advanced studies in these fields will surely center around these methods.[1]

A central concept for energy methods is the work of a force. A differential amount of work $d\mathcal{W}_k$ due to a force $\boldsymbol{F}$ acting on a particle equals the component of this force in the direction of movement of the particle times the differential displacement of the particle:

$$d\mathcal{W}_k = \boldsymbol{F} \cdot d\boldsymbol{r} \tag{10.1}$$

And the work $\mathcal{W}_k$ on a particle by force $\boldsymbol{F}$ when the particle moves along some path (see Fig. 10.1) from point 1 to point 2 is then

$$\mathcal{W}_k = \int_{\boldsymbol{r}_1}^{\boldsymbol{r}_2} \boldsymbol{F} \cdot d\boldsymbol{r} \tag{10.2}$$

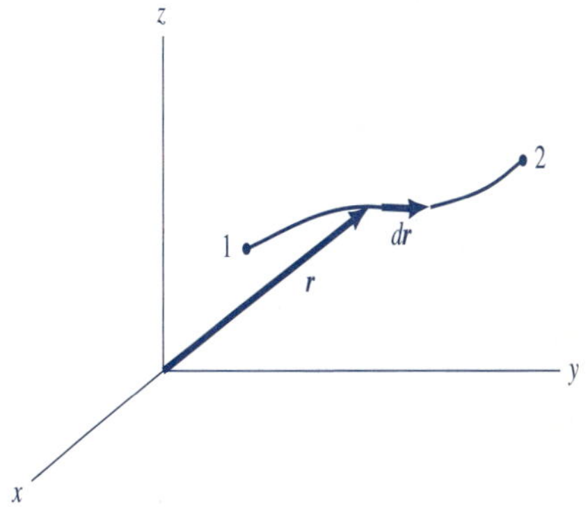

Figure 10.1. Path of particle on which $\boldsymbol{F}$ does work.

[1]For a treatment of energy methods for deformable solids, see I. H. Shames and C. Dym, *Energy and Finite Element Methods in Structural Mechanics*, Taylor and Francis Publishers, 1985.

Note that the value and direction of $\boldsymbol{F}$ can vary along the path. This fact must be taken into account during the integration. We shall have more to say about the concept of work in later sections.[2]

Part A: Method of Virtual Work

10.2 Principle of Virtual Work for a Particle

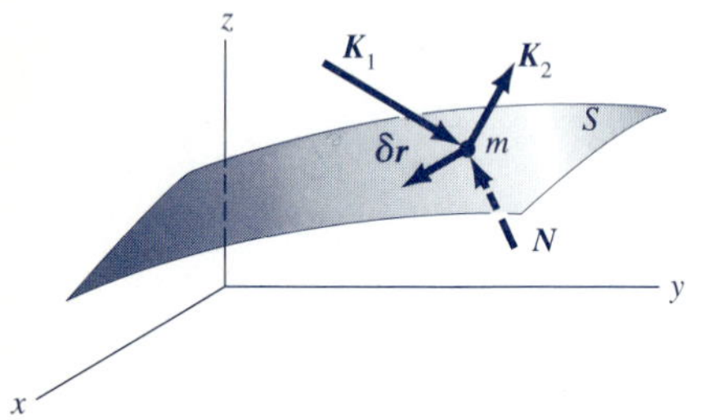

Figure 10.2. Particle on a frictionless surface.

For our introduction to the principle of virtual work, we will first consider a particle acted on by external loads $\boldsymbol{K}_1, \boldsymbol{K}_2, \ldots, \boldsymbol{K}_n$, whose resultant force pushes the particle against a rigid constraining surface S in space (Fig. 10.2). This surface S is assumed to be frictionless and will thus exert a constraining force $\boldsymbol{N}$ on the particle which is normal to S. The forces $\boldsymbol{K}_i$ are called *active forces* in connection with the method of virtual work, while $\boldsymbol{N}$ retains the identification of a *constraining force* as used previously. Employing the resultant active force $\boldsymbol{K}_R$, we can give the necessary and sufficient[3] conditions for equilibrium for the particle as

$$\boldsymbol{K}_R + \boldsymbol{N} = \boldsymbol{0} \tag{10.3}$$

We shall now prove that we can express the necessary and sufficient conditions of equilibrium in yet another way. Let us imagine that we give the particle an infinitesimal hypothetical arbitrary displacement that is consistent with the constraints (i.e., along the surface), while keeping the forces $\boldsymbol{K}_R$ and $\boldsymbol{N}$ constant. Such a displacement is termed a *virtual displacement*, and will be denoted by $\delta\boldsymbol{r}$, in contrast to a real infinitesimal displacement, $d\boldsymbol{r}$, which might actually occur during a time interval dt. We can then take the dot product of the vector $\delta\boldsymbol{r}$ with the force vectors in the equation above:

$$\boldsymbol{K}_R \cdot \delta\boldsymbol{r} + \boldsymbol{N} \cdot \delta\boldsymbol{r} = 0 \tag{10.4}$$

Since $\boldsymbol{N}$ is normal to the surface and $\delta\boldsymbol{r}$ is tangential to the surface, the corresponding scalar product must be zero, leaving

$$\boldsymbol{K}_R \cdot \delta\boldsymbol{r} = 0 \tag{10.5}$$

The expression $\boldsymbol{K}_R \cdot \delta\boldsymbol{r}$ is called the *virtual work* of the system of forces and is denoted as $\delta\mathcal{W}_{\text{Virt}}$. Thus, the virtual work by the active forces on a particle

[2]We could have defined work as

$$\mathcal{W}_k = \int_{t_1}^{t_2} \boldsymbol{F} \cdot \boldsymbol{V}\, dt$$

where $\boldsymbol{V}$ is the velocity of the point of application of the force. When the force acts on a particular particle, the result above becomes $\int_{r_1}^{r_2} \boldsymbol{F} \cdot d\boldsymbol{r}$, (with $\boldsymbol{V}dt$ replaced by $d\boldsymbol{r}$) where $\boldsymbol{r}$ is the position vector of the particle. There are times when the force acts on continually *changing* particles as time passes. The more general formulation above can then be used effectively.

[3]The sufficiency condition applies to an initially stationary particle.

with frictionless constraints is *necessarily* zero for a particle in equilibrium for any virtual displacement consistent with the frictionless constraints.

We shall now show that this statement is also *sufficient* to ensure equilibrium for the case of a particle initially at rest (relative to an inertial reference) at the time of application of the active loads. To demonstrate this, *assume that Eq. 10.5 holds but that the particle is not in equilibrium.* If the particle is not in equilibrium, it must move in a direction that corresponds to the direction of the resultant of all forces acting on the particle. Consider that $\boldsymbol{dr}$ represents the initial displacement during the time interval dt. The work done by the forces must exceed zero for this movement. Since the normal force $\boldsymbol{N}$ cannot do work for this displacement,

$$\boldsymbol{K}_R \cdot \boldsymbol{dr} > 0 \tag{10.6}$$

However, we can choose a *virtual* displacement $\boldsymbol{\delta r}$ to be used in Eq. 10.5 that is *exactly* equal to the proposed $\boldsymbol{dr}$ stated above, and so we see that, by admitting nonequilibrium, we arrive at a result (10.6) that is in *contradiction to the starting known condition* (Eq. 10.5). We can then conclude that the conjecture that the particle is not in equilibrium is false. Thus, Eq. 10.3 is not only a necessary condition of equilibrium, but, for an initially stationary particle, is in itself sufficient for equilibrium. Thus, Eq. 10.5 is completely equivalent to the equation of equilibrium, 10.3.

We can now state the principle of virtual work for a particle.

The necessary and sufficient condition for equilibrium of an initially stationary particle with frictionless constraints requires that the virtual work for all virtual displacements consistent with the constraints be zero.[4]

The case of a particle that is not constrained is a special case of the situation discussed above. Here $\boldsymbol{N} = \boldsymbol{0}$, so that Eq. 10.5 is applicable for *all* infinitesimal displacements as a criterion for equilibrium.

10.3 Principle of Virtual Work for Rigid Bodies

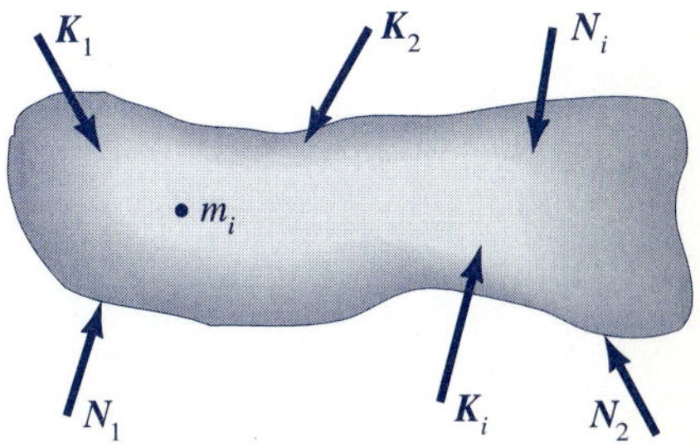

Figure 10.3. Rigid body with active forces and ideal constraining forces.

We now examine a rigid body in equilibrium acted on by active forces $\boldsymbol{K}_i$ and constrained without the aid of friction (Fig. 10.3). The constraining forces $\boldsymbol{N}_i$ arise from direct contact with other immovable bodies (in which case the con-

[4]This test breaks down for a particle that is moving. Consider a particle constrained to move in a circular path in a horizontal plane, as shown in the diagram. The particle is moving with constant speed. There are no active forces, and we consider the constraints as frictionless. The work for a virtual displacement consistent with the constraints at any time t gives us a zero result. Nevertheless, the particle is not in equilibrium, since clearly there is at time t an acceleration toward the center of curvature. Thus, we had to restrict the sufficiency condition to particles that are initially stationary.

straining forces are oriented normal to the contact surface) or from contact with immovable bodies through pin and ball-joint connections. We shall consider the body to be made up of elementary particles for the purposes of discussion.

Now consider a particle of mass m_i. Active loads, external constraining forces, and forces from other particles may possibly be acting on the particle. The forces from other particles are internal forces $\boldsymbol{S}_i$ which maintain the rigidity of the body. Using the resultants of these various forces on the particle, we may state from Newton's law that the necessary and sufficient[5] condition for equilibrium of the ith particle is

$$(\boldsymbol{K}_R)_i + (\boldsymbol{N}_R)_i + (\boldsymbol{S}_R)_i = \boldsymbol{0} \tag{10.7}$$

Now, we give the particle a virtual displacement $\delta \boldsymbol{r}_i$ that is consistent with the exterior constraints and with the condition that the body is rigid. Taking the dot product of the vectors in the equation above with $\delta \boldsymbol{r}_i$, we get

$$(\boldsymbol{K}_R)_i \cdot \delta \boldsymbol{r}_i + (\boldsymbol{N}_R)_i \cdot \delta \boldsymbol{r}_i + (\boldsymbol{S}_R)_i \cdot \delta \boldsymbol{r}_i = 0 \tag{10.8}$$

Clearly, $(\boldsymbol{N_R})_i \cdot \delta \boldsymbol{r}_i$ must be zero, because $\delta \boldsymbol{r}_i$ is normal for $\boldsymbol{N}_i$ for constraint stemming from direct contact with immovable bodies or because $\delta \boldsymbol{r}_i = \boldsymbol{0}$ for constraint stemming from pin and ball-joint connections with immovable bodies. Let us then sum the resulting equations of the form 10.8 for all the particles that are considered to make up the body. We have, for n particles,

$$\sum_{i=1}^{n} (\boldsymbol{K}_R)_i \cdot \delta \boldsymbol{r}_i + \sum_{i=1}^{n} (\boldsymbol{S}_R)_i \cdot \delta \boldsymbol{r}_i = 0 \tag{10.9}$$

Let us now consider in more detail the internal forces in order to show that the second quantity on the left-hand side of the equation above is zero. The force on m_i from particle m_j will be equal and opposite to the force on particle m_j from particle m_i, according to Newton's third law. The internal forces on these particles are shown as $\boldsymbol{S}_{ij}$ and $\boldsymbol{S}_{ji}$ in Fig. 10.4. The first subscript identifies the particle on which a force acts, while the second subscript identifies the particle exerting this force. We can then say that

$$\boldsymbol{S}_{ij} = -\boldsymbol{S}_{ji} \tag{10.10}$$

Any virtual motion we give to any pair of particles must maintain a constant distance between the particles. This requirement stems from the rigid-body condition and will be true if:

1. Both particles are given the same displacement $\delta \boldsymbol{R}$.
2. The particles are rotated $\delta \boldsymbol{\phi}$ relative to each other.[6]

We now consider the general case where both motions are present: that is, both m_i and m_j are given a virtual displacement $\delta \boldsymbol{R}$, and furthermore, m_j is

[5]The sufficiency requirement again applies to an initially stationary particle.

[6]The virtual displacements $\delta \boldsymbol{r}_i$ of each of the two particles must then be the result of the superposition of $\delta \boldsymbol{R}$ and $\delta \boldsymbol{\phi}$.

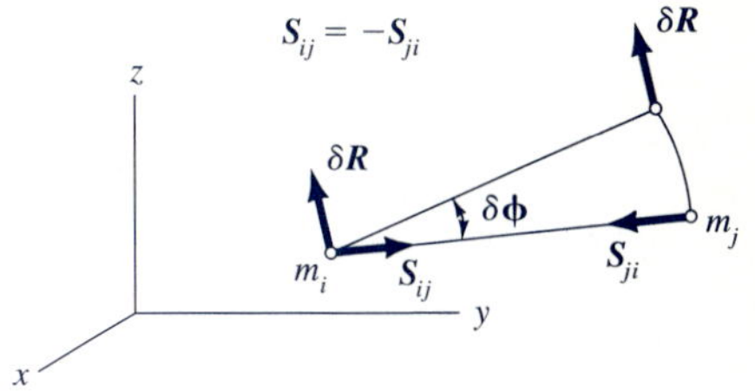

Figure 10.4. Two particles of a body undergoing displacement $\delta\boldsymbol{R}$ and rotation $\delta\boldsymbol{\phi}$.

rotated through some angle $\delta\boldsymbol{\phi}$ about m_i (Fig. 10.4). The work done during the rotation must be zero, since $\boldsymbol{S}_{ji}$ is at right angles to the motion of the mass m_j. Also, the work done on each particle during the equal displacement of both masses must be equal in value and opposite in sign since the forces move through equal displacements and are themselves equal and opposite. The mutual effect of all particles of the body is of the type described. Thus, we can conclude that the internal work done for a rigid body during a virtual displacement is zero. Hence, a *necessary* condition for equilibrium is

$$\sum_{i=1}^{n} (\boldsymbol{K}_R)_i \bullet \delta\boldsymbol{r}_i = \delta\mathcal{W}_{\text{Virt}} = 0 \qquad (10.11)$$

Thus, the virtual work done by active forces on a rigid body having frictionless constraints during virtual displacements consistent with the constraints is zero if the body is in equilibrium.

We can readily prove that Eq. 10.11 is a *sufficient* condition for equilibrium of an initially stationary body by reasoning in the same manner that we did in the case of the single particle. We shall *state first that Eq. 10.11 is valid for a body*. If the body is not in equilibrium, it must begin to move. Let us say that each particle m_i moves a distance $d\boldsymbol{r}_i$ consistent with the constraints under the action of the forces. The work done on particle m_i is

$$(\boldsymbol{K}_R)_i \bullet d\boldsymbol{r}_i + (\boldsymbol{N}_R)_i \bullet d\boldsymbol{r}_i + (\boldsymbol{S}_R)_i \bullet d\boldsymbol{r}_i > 0 \qquad (10.12)$$

But $(\boldsymbol{N}_R)_i \bullet d\boldsymbol{r}_i$ is necessarily zero because of the nature of the constraints. When we sum the terms in the equation above for all particles, $\sum_i (\boldsymbol{S}_R)_i \bullet d\boldsymbol{r}_i$ must also be zero because of the condition of rigidity of the body as previously explained. Therefore, we may state that the supposition of no equilibrium leads to the following inequality:

$$\sum_{i=1}^{n} (\boldsymbol{K}_R)_i \bullet d\boldsymbol{r}_i > 0 \qquad (10.13)$$

But we can conceive a virtual displacement $\delta\boldsymbol{r}_i$ *equal* to $d\boldsymbol{r}_i$ for each particle to be used in Eq. 10.11, thus bringing us to a contradiction between this equation and Eq. 10.13. Since we have taken Eq. 10.11 to apply, we conclude that the supposition of nonequilibrium which led to Eq. 10.13 must be invalid, and so the body must be in equilibrium. This logic proves the sufficiency condition for the principle of virtual work in the case of a rigid body with ideal constraints that is initially stationary at the time of application of the active forces.

Consider now *several* movable rigid bodies that are interconnected by smooth pins and ball joints or that are in direct frictionless contact with each other (Fig. 10.5). Some of these bodies are also ideally constrained by immovable rigid bodies in the manner described above. Again, we may examine the system of particles m_i making up the various rigid bodies. The only new kind of force to be considered is a force at the connecting point between bodies. The force on one such particle on body A will be equal and opposite to the force on the corresponding particle in body B at the contact point; and so on. Since such

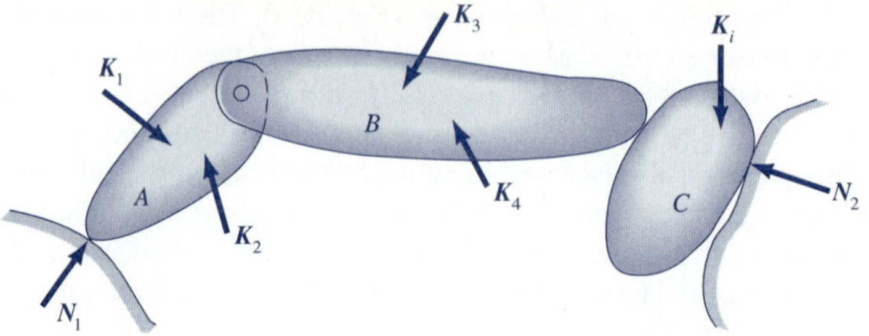

Figure 10.5. System of ideally constrained rigid bodies acted on by forces $\boldsymbol{K}_i$.

pairs of contiguous particles have the same virtual displacement, clearly the virtual work at all connecting points between bodies is zero for any virtual displacement of the system consistent with the constraints. Hence, using the same reasoning as before, we can say *for a system of initially stationary rigid bodies, the necessary and sufficient condition of equilibrium is that the virtual work of the active forces be zero for all possible virtual displacements consistent with the constraints.* We may then use the following equation instead of equilibrium:

$$\sum_i^n (\boldsymbol{K}_R)_i \bullet \delta \boldsymbol{r}_i = \delta \mathcal{W}_{\text{Virt}} = 0 \tag{10.14}$$

where $(\boldsymbol{K}_R)_i$ are the active forces on the system of rigid bodies and $\delta \boldsymbol{r}_i$ are the movements of the point of application of these forces during a virtual displacement of the system consistent with the constraints.

10.4 Degrees of Freedom and the Solution of Problems

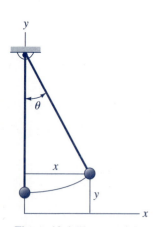

Figure 10.6. Plane pendulum.

We have developed equations sufficient for equilibrium of initially stationary systems of bodies by using the concept of virtual work for virtual displacements consistent with the constraints. These equations do not involve reactions or connecting forces, and when these forces are not of interest, the method is quite useful. Thus, we may solve for as many unknown *active* forces as there are *independent* equations stemming from virtual displacements. Then our prime interest is to know how many independent equations can be written for a system stemming from virtual displacements.

For this purpose, we define *the number of degrees of freedom of a system as the number of generalized coordinates*[7] *which is required to fully specify the configuration of the system.* Thus, for the pendulum in Fig. 10.6, which is restricted to move in a plane, one *independent* coordinate θ locates the pendulum. Hence, this system has but one degree of freedom. We may ask: Can't we specify x and y of the bob, and thus aren't there two degrees of

[7]*Generalized coordinates* are any set of *independent variables* that can fully specify the configuration of a system. Generalized coordinates can include any of the usual coordinates, such as cartesian coordinates or cylindrical coordinates, but need not. We shall only consider those cases where the usual coordinates serve as the generalized coordinates.

freedom? The answer is no, because when we specify x or y, the other coordinate is *determined* since the pendulum support, being inextensible, must sweep out a known circle as shown in the diagram. In Fig. 10.7, the piston and crank arrangement, the four-bar linkage,[8] and the balance require only one coordinate and thus have but one degree of freedom. On the other hand, the double pendulum has two degrees of freedom and a particle in space has three degrees of freedom. The number of degrees of freedom may usually be readily determined by inspection.

Since each degree of freedom represents an independent coordinate, we can, for an n-degree-of-freedom system, institute n unique virtual displacements by varying each coordinate separately. This procedure will then give n independent equations of equilibrium from which n unknowns related to the active forces can be determined. We shall examine several problems to illustrate the method of virtual work and its advantages.

Before considering the examples, we wish to point out that a torque $\boldsymbol{M}$ undergoing a virtual displacement $\delta\boldsymbol{\phi}$ in radians does an amount of virtual work $\delta\mathcal{W}_k$ equal to

$$\delta\mathcal{W}_k = \boldsymbol{M} \cdot \delta\boldsymbol{\phi} \tag{10.15}$$

The proof of this is asked for in Problem 10.30.

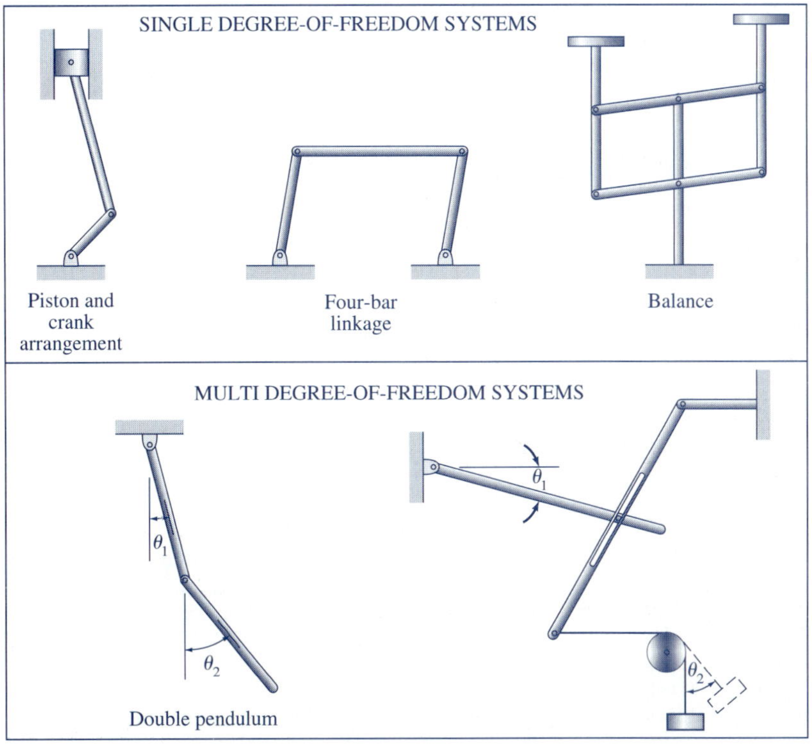

Figure 10.7. Various systems illustrating degrees of freedom.

[8]The fourth bar is the base.

Example 10.1

A device for compressing metal scrap (a compactor) is shown in Fig. 10.8. A horizontal force P is exerted on joint B. The piston at C then compresses the scrap material. For a given force P and a given angle θ, what is the force F developed on the scrap by the piston C? Neglect the friction between the piston and the cylinder wall, and consider the pin joints to be ideal.

We see by inspection that one coordinate θ describes the configuration of the system. The device therefore has one degree of freedom. We shall neglect the weight of the members, and so only two active forces are present, P and F. By assuming a virtual displacement $\delta\theta$, we will involve in the principle of virtual work only those quantities that are of interest to us, P, F, and θ.[9] Let us then compute the virtual work of the active forces.

Force P. The virtual displacement $\delta\theta$ is such that force P has a motion in the horizontal direction of $(l\,\delta\theta\cos\theta)$ as can readily be deduced from Fig. 10.9 by elementary trigonometric considerations. There is yet another way of deducing this horizontal motion, which, sometimes, is more desirable. Using an xy coordinate system at A as shown in Figs. 10.8 and 10.9, we can say for the position of joint B:

$$y_B = l\sin\theta \tag{a}$$

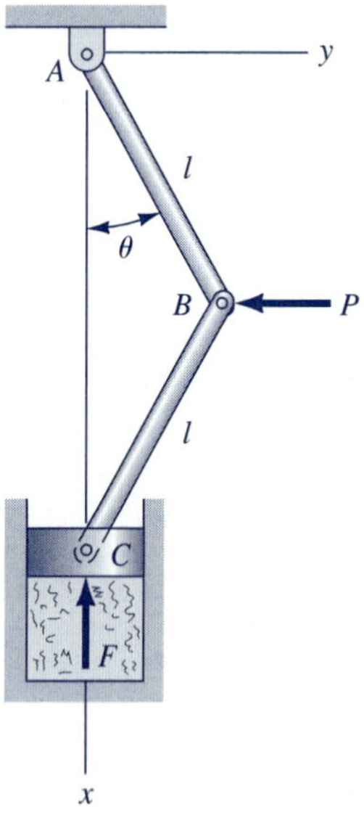

Figure 10.8. Compacting device.

[9]If we had used a free-body approach, we would have had to bring in force components at A and at C, and we would have had to dismember the system. To appreciate the method of virtual work even for this simple problem, we urge you to at least set up the problem by the use of free-body diagrams.

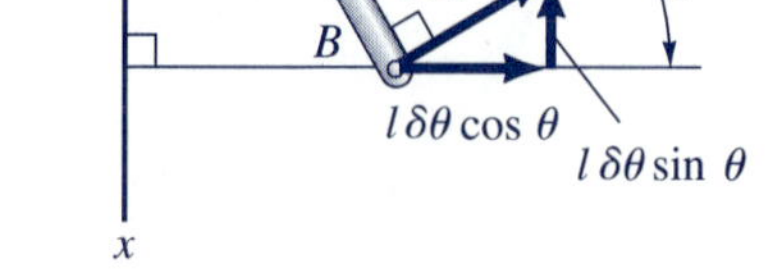

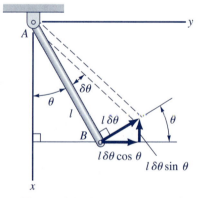

Figure 10.9. Virtual movement of leg AB.

Example 10.1 (Continued)

Now take the differential of both sides of the equation to get

$$dy_B = l \cos\theta \, d\theta \qquad \text{(b)}$$

A differential of a quantity A, namely dA, is very similar to a variation of the quantity, δA. The former might actually take place in a process; the latter takes place in the mind of the engineer. Nevertheless, the relation between differential quantities should be the same as the relation between varied quantities. Accordingly, from Eq. (b), we can say:

$$\delta y_B = l \cos\theta \, \delta\theta \qquad \text{(c)}$$

Note that the same horizontal movement of B for $\delta\theta$ is thus computed as at the outset using trigonometry.

For the variation $\delta\theta$ chosen, the force P acts in the opposite direction of δy_B, and so the virtual work done by force P is negative. Thus, we have

$$\delta(\mathcal{W}_{\text{Virt}})_P = -Pl \cos\theta \, \delta\theta \qquad \text{(d)}$$

Force F. We can use the differential approach to get the virtual displacement of piston C. That is,

$$x_C = l\cos\theta + l\cos\theta = 2l\cos\theta$$
$$dx_C = -2l\sin\theta \, d\theta$$

Therefore,

$$\delta x_C = -2l \sin\theta \, \delta\theta \qquad \text{(e)}$$

Since the force F is in the same direction as δx_C, we should have a positive result for the work done by force F. Accordingly, we have

$$\delta(\mathcal{W}_{\text{Virt}})_F = F(2l\sin\theta)\,\delta\theta \qquad \text{(f)}$$

We may now employ the principle of virtual work, which is sufficient here for ensuring equilibrium. Thus, we can say that

$$-Pl\cos\theta\,\delta\theta + F(2l\sin\theta)\,\delta\theta = 0 \qquad \text{(g)}$$

Canceling $l\,\delta\theta$ and solving for F, we get

$$F = \frac{P}{2\tan\theta}$$

For any given values of P and θ, we now know the amount of compressive force that the compactor can develop.

Example 10.2

A hydraulic-lift platform for loading trucks is shown in Fig. 10.10(a). Only one side of the system is shown; the other side is identical. If the diameter of the piston in the hydraulic ram is 4 in., what pressure p is needed to support a load W of 5,000 lb when $\theta = 60°$? The following additional data apply:

$$l = 24 \text{ in.}$$
$$d = 60 \text{ in.}$$
$$e = 10 \text{ in.}$$

Pin A is at the center of the rod.

We have here a system with one degree of freedom characterized by the angle θ. The active forces that do work during a virtual displacement $\delta\theta$ are the weight W and the force from the hydraulic ram. Accordingly, the virtual movements of both the platform E and joint A of the hydraulic ram must be found. Using reference xy:

$$y_E = 2l \sin\theta$$

Therefore,

$$\delta y_E = 2l \cos\theta\, \delta\theta \qquad \text{(a)}$$

For the ram force, we want the movement of pin A in the direction of the axis of the pump, namely $\delta\eta$ where η is shown in Fig. 10.10(a). Observing Fig. 10.10(b) we can say for η:

$$\begin{aligned}\eta^2 &= \overline{AC}^2 + \overline{CB}^2 \\ &= [l \sin\theta - e]^2 + (d - l\cos\theta)^2 \end{aligned} \qquad \text{(b)}$$

Hence, we have

$$2\eta\, \delta\eta = 2(l\sin\theta - e)(l\cos\theta)\delta\theta + 2(d - l\cos\theta)(l\sin\theta)\,\delta\theta \qquad \text{(c)}$$

Solving for $\delta\eta$, we get

$$\begin{aligned}\delta\eta &= \frac{l}{\eta}[(l\sin\theta - e)\cos\theta + (d - l\cos\theta)\sin\theta]\,\delta\theta \\ &= \frac{l}{\eta}(l\sin\theta\cos\theta - e\cos\theta + d\sin\theta - l\sin\theta\cos\theta)\,\delta\theta \\ &= \frac{l}{\eta}(d\sin\theta - e\cos\theta)\,\delta\theta \end{aligned} \qquad \text{(d)}$$

The principle of virtual work is now applied to ensure equilibrium. Thus, considering one side of the system and using half the load, we have

$$-\frac{W}{2}(\delta y_E) + \left[p\frac{\pi(4^2)}{4}\right]\delta\eta = 0$$

Example 10.2 (Continued)

Hence,

$$-(2,500)(2l\cos\theta\,\delta\theta) + p(4\pi)\left[\frac{l}{\eta}(d\sin\theta - e\cos\theta)\right]\delta\theta = 0 \qquad \text{(e)}$$

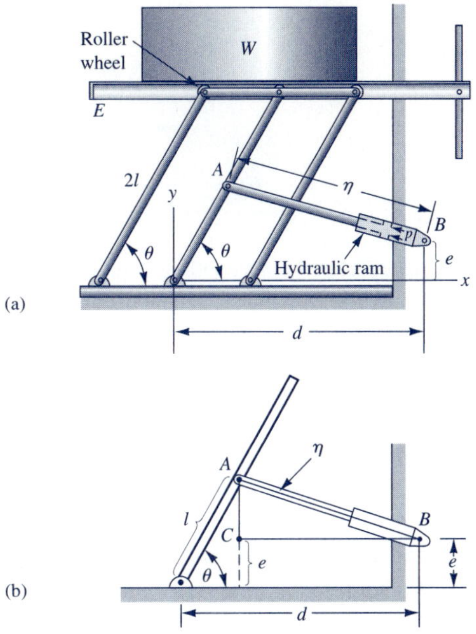

Figure 10.10. Pneumatic loading platform.

The value of η at the configuration of interest may be determined from Eq. (b). Thus,

$$\eta^2 = [(24)(.866) - 10]^2 + [60 - (24)(.5)]^2$$

Therefore,

$$\eta = 49.2 \text{ in.}$$

Now canceling $\delta\theta$ and substituting known data into Eq. (e), we may then determine p for equilibrium:

$$-(2{,}500)(2)(24)(.5) + p(4\pi)\left\{\frac{24}{49.2}[(60)(.866) - (10)(.5)]\right\} = 0$$

Therefore,

$$p = 208 \text{ psi} \qquad \text{(f)}$$

In a few of the homework problems, you have to use simple kinematics of a cylinder rolling without slipping (see Fig. 10.11). You will recall from physics that the cylinder is actually rotating about the point of contact A. If the cylinder rotates an angle $\delta\theta$ then $\delta C = -r\ \delta\theta$. We shall consider kinematics of rigid bodies in detail later in the text.

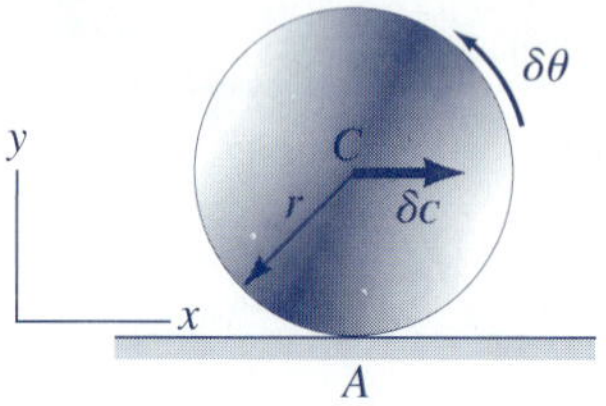

Figure 10.11. Cylinder rolling without slipping.

In concluding this section, we wish to point out that the method of virtual work is actually *not* restricted to ideal systems. Furthermore, it is permissible to give virtual displacements that *violate* one or more constraints. We then proceed by considering those friction forces that perform virtual work as active forces. And, where a constraint is violated, we consider the corresponding constraining force or torque to be active. We point out that the method of virtual work generally offers no advantage in situations where there is friction and where constraints are violated. Furthermore, the extensions of virtual work to other useful theories are primarily restricted to ideal systems. Accordingly we shall consider only ideal systems and shall take virtual displacements that do not violate constraints.

10.5 Looking Ahead: Deformable Solids

Let us now reconsider the virtual displacement concept. Recall that $d\mathbf{r}$ represents *a small change in the spatial coordinates of a particle arbitrary up to the point of not violating constraints.* The change in the spatial coordinates is in no way linked to a change in time. (Such a link would normally exist through Newton's laws when we are working in the field of mechanics.) This has been shown in Fig. 10.12, where we have a virtual displacement $\delta\mathbf{r}$ from point $P(x, y, z)$ to point P', which has coordinates $(x + \delta x)$, $(y + \delta y)$, and $(z + \delta z)$. We call the position vector to point P', the *varied position* vector $\tilde{\mathbf{r}}$. We can then say that

$$\delta\mathbf{r} = \tilde{\mathbf{r}} - \mathbf{r} \tag{10.16}$$

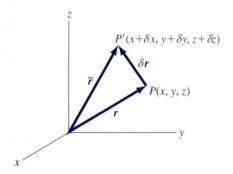

Figure 10.12. Virtual displacement vector.

We may at this stage consider δ above to be an *operator* acting on $\mathbf{r}$ so as to generate the difference vector between the varied position vector $\tilde{\mathbf{r}}$ and the position vector $\mathbf{r}$ itself .

We may also introduce the concept of the *varied function* $\tilde{G}$ such that given a function $G(x, y, z)$ we may form

$$\tilde{G} = G(x + \delta x, y + \delta y, z + \delta z,) \tag{10.17}$$

where δx, δy, and δz are components of $\delta \boldsymbol{r}$[10]. We now define the *variation* of G, denoted as δG, as

$$\delta G = \tilde{G} - G \tag{10.18}$$

In a deformable body we can give the movement of each point in the body when deformation occurs by using the *displacement field* $\boldsymbol{u}(x, y, z)$. Specifically, when coordinates of a specific point in the underformed geometry are substituted into the particular vector function $\boldsymbol{u}(x, y, z)$ depicting a specific deformation, we get the displacement of that point resulting from this deformation.

We now extend the concept of a virtual displacement of a point to that of a virtual displacement *field*, which is a single-valued, continuous vector field representing a *hypothetical deformable body movement consistent with the constraints present*. We shall restrict ourselves here to virtual displacement fields, which result only in infinitesimal deformation.[11] We have shown the gross exaggeration of a virtual displacement field in Fig. 10.13, wherein you will notice that the constraints have not been violated. It should now be clear that we can conveniently set forth a virtual displacement field by employing the so-called variational operator δ. Thus $\delta \boldsymbol{u}$ may be considered as a virtual displacement field from a given configuration to a varied configuration; the constraints present being taken into account by imposing proper conditions on the variation.

The *virtual work* concept can now be extended to the case of a deformable body. We compute the work of the *external* forces during a virtual displacement of the body with the proviso that these external forces be maintained constant. With a total body force distribution $\boldsymbol{B}(x, y, z)$ and a total traction force distribution $\boldsymbol{T}(x, y, z)$, we can then give the virtual work, denoted as δW_{Virt}, as follows:

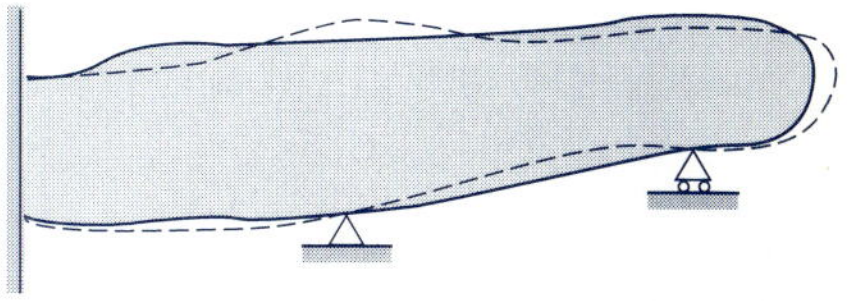

Figure 10.13. Virtual displacement field consistent with constraints.

$$\delta W_{\text{Virt}} = \iiint_V \boldsymbol{B} \cdot \delta \boldsymbol{u}\, dv + \oint\!\!\oint_S \boldsymbol{T} \cdot \delta \boldsymbol{u}\, dA \tag{10.19}$$

For rigid bodies, *the virtual work had to be zero for equilibrium. For deformable bodies this is no longer true*. Instead, for equilibrium the external virtual work δW_{Virt} given above must be equal to *internal* virtual work, which

[10]The changes in the coordinates x, y, and z are not linked to time through the basic laws of physics as would be the case if we were considering G to represent some physical quantity in some real process.

[11]One need not so restrict oneself. That is, we can work with virtual displacement fields for *finite* deformation and formulate a principle of virtual work. This would take us beyond the scope of this book, however.

must be zero for rigid bodies but which is not necessarily zero for deformable solids. In your solid mechanics course you will learn that the internal work for a deformable body is given by $\iiint_V \sum_i \sum_j \tau_{ij}\delta\epsilon_{ij}\,dv$, where the indices i and j range over x, y, and z forming terms in the integrand such as $\tau_{xx}\delta\epsilon_{xx}$, $\tau_{xy}\,\delta\epsilon_{xy}$, etc., (nine expressions). The satisfaction of the resulting formulation is a necessary and sufficient condition for equilibrium and can be used in place of the familiar equations of equilibrium.[12] Why would one want to do this? Actually, as we pointed in the Looking Ahead section in the chapter on structural mechanics, we can readily solve certain types of problems using virtual work, and the theorems derived from virtual work, whereas the approach for these problems using the equilibrium equations is extremely cumbersome. One important case is the solution of indeterminate truss problems. You will come to these problems later in your studies of structures and in your studies of machine design.

Virtual work and two other theorems derivable from it are called *energy displacement methods* because of the use of the virtual displacement.[13] There is an equally useful set of three formulations analogous to the three energy displacement methods and they are called *energy force methods,* wherein we hypothetically vary the forces instead of hypothetically varying the deformation.

Before moving on, the author would like to share a philosophical thought with you. In science we often physically disturb certain surroundings in the laboratory and carefully observe resulting behavior to learn to understand natural phenomena. We perhaps unwittingly mimic this approach here in the study of mechanics. That is, we have instituted mathematical "disturbances" and evaluated the results in order to understand certain vital analytically useful consequences. Thus, we instituted the mathematical "disturbance" of the virtual displacement field to arrive at extremely useful conclusions which form the basis of a considerable amount of structural mechanics. Also, we pointed out that we can institute varied force fields as our mathematical disturbances. Again, vital and useful conclusions follow.

[12]Thus, the virtual work equation is $\iiint_V \boldsymbol{B}\cdot\delta\boldsymbol{u}\,dv + \oiint_S \boldsymbol{T}\cdot\delta\boldsymbol{u}\,dA = \iiint_V \sum_i \sum_j \tau_{ij}\,\delta\epsilon_{ij}dv$

[13]The second energy displacement method is called the method of *total potential energy*. It was this principal that was presented in the "Looking Ahead" Section 6.5 for determining the pin deflections of simple trusses. The special case of this principle for conservative force fields acting on *particles* and *rigid bodies* is developed in Part B of this chapter. The third energy displacement method derivable from the second is the *First Castigliano Theorem*.

For a thorough development of these six principles with many applications and which is within reach of students who have absorbed the key contents of the statics portion of this text, see Shames, I.H., *Introduction to Solid Mechanics,* second ed., Prentice-Hall, Inc., Englewood Cliffs, N.J., Chapters 18 and 19. A good grasp of these six principles is vital for more advanced work in solid and structural mechanics, not to speak of machine design.

PROBLEMS

10.1. How many degrees of freedom do the following systems possess? What coordinates can be used to locate the system?

(a) A rigid body not constrained in space.

(b) A rigid body constrained to move along a plane surface.

(c) The board *AB* in the diagram (a).

(d) The spherical bodies shown in diagram (b) may slide along shaft *C–C*, which in turn rotates about axis *E–E*. Shaft *C–C* may also slide along *E–E*. The spindle *E–E* is on a rotating platform. Give the number of degrees of freedom and coordinates for a sphere, shaft *C–C*, and spindle *E–E*.

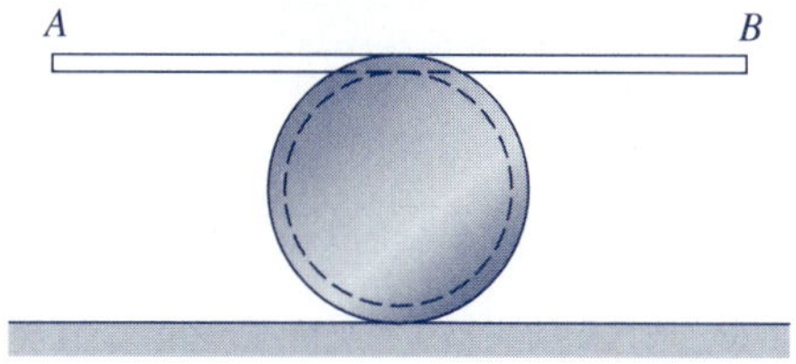

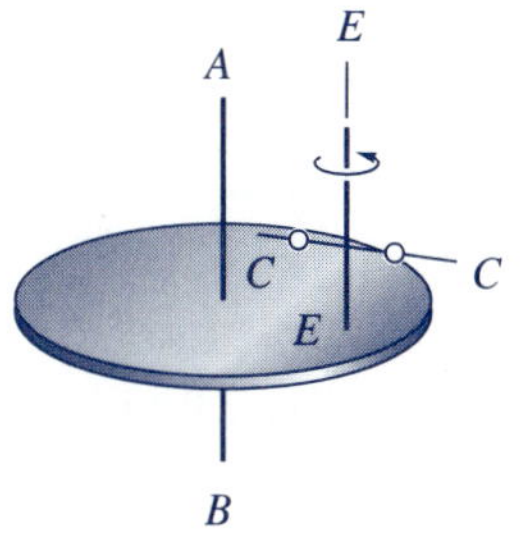

Figure P.10.1.

10.2. A parking-lot gate arm weighs 150 N. Because of the taper, the weight can be regarded as concentrated at a point 1.25 m from the pivot point. What is the solenoid force to lift the gate? What is the solenoid force if a 300-N counterweight is placed .25 m to left of the pivot point?

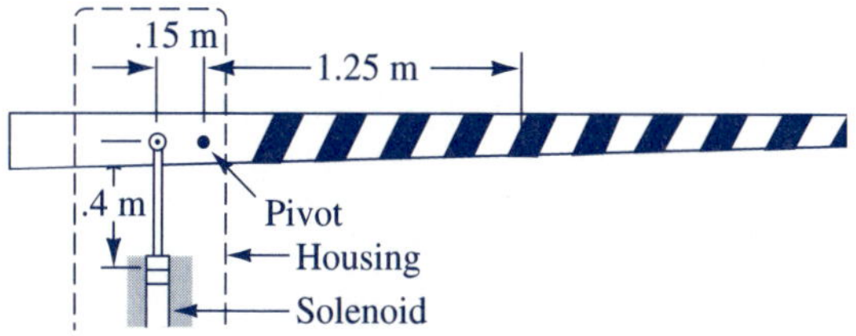

Figure P.10.2.

10.3. What is the longest portion of pipe weighing 400 lb/ft that can be lifted without tipping the 12,000-lb tractor?

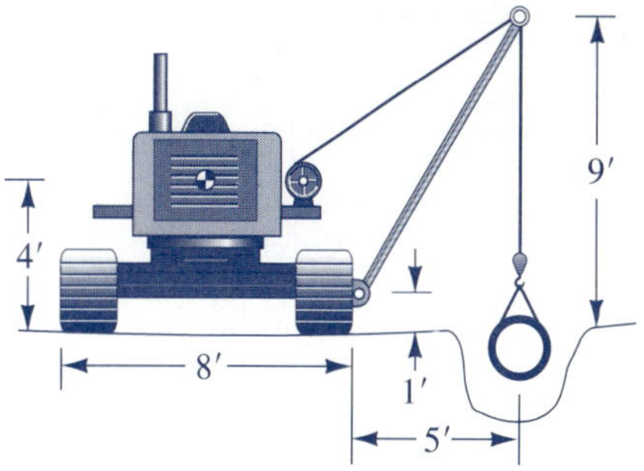

Figure P.10.3.

10.4. If W_1 = 100 N and W_2 = 150 N, find the angle θ for equilibrium.

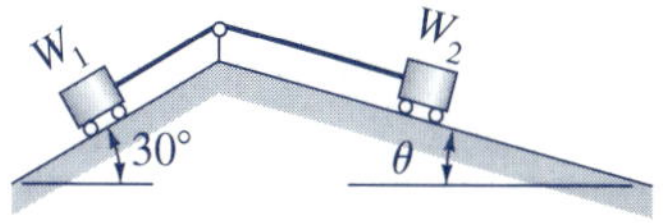

Figure P.10.4.

10.5. The triple pulley sheave and the double pulley sheave weigh 150 N and 100 N, respectively. What rope force is necessary to lift a 3,500-N engine?

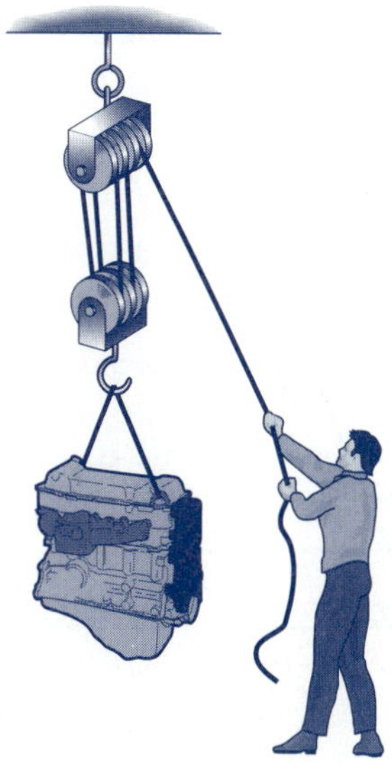

Figure P.10.5.

10.6. What weight W can be lifted with the A-frame hoist in the position shown if the cable tension is T?

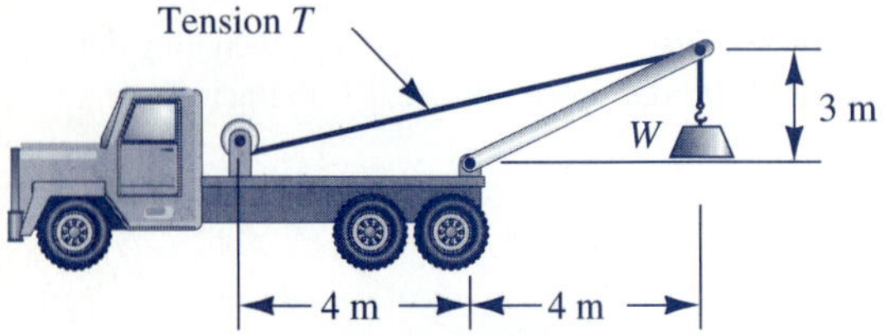

Figure P.10.6.

10.7. A small hoist has a lifting capacity of 20 kN. What is the maximum possible cable tension load?

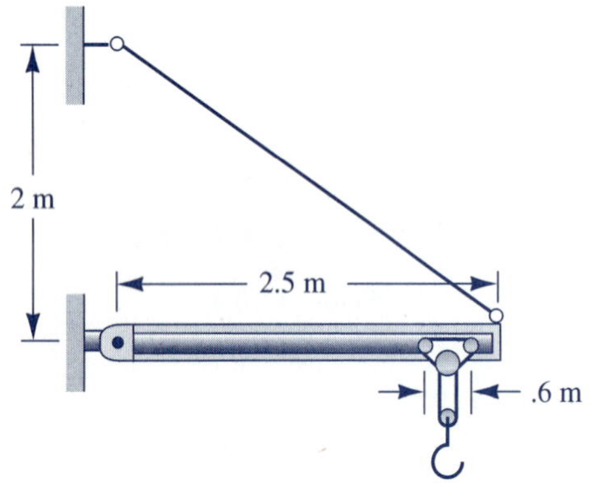

Figure P.10.7.

10.8. If W = 1,000 N and P = 300 N, find the angle θ for equilibrium.

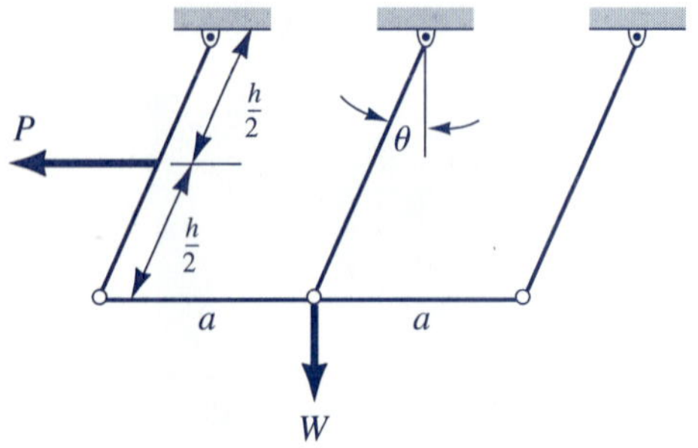

Figure P.10.8.

10.9. What is the tension in the cables of a 10-ft-wide 12-ft-long 6000-lb drawbridge when the bridge is first raised? When the bridge is at 45°?

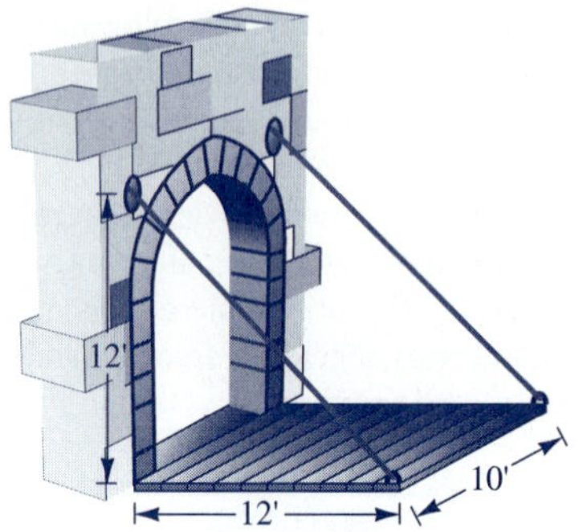

Figure P.10.9.

10.10. Assuming frictionless contacts, determine the magnitude of P for equilibrium.

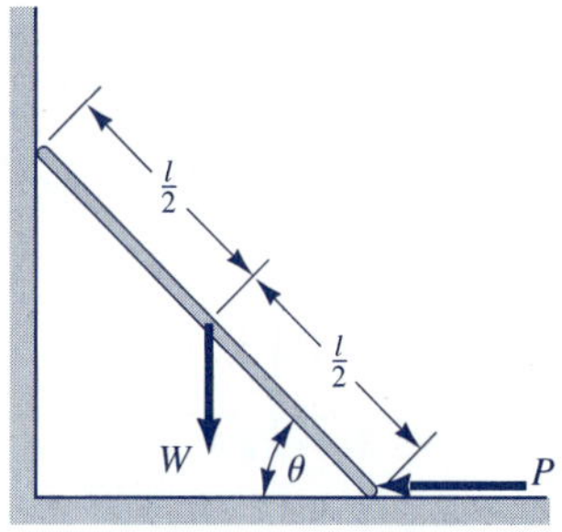

Figure P.10.10.

10.11. A rock crusher is shown in action. If p_1 = 50 psig and p_2 = 100 psig, what is the force on the rock at the configuration shown? The diameter of the pistons is 4 in.

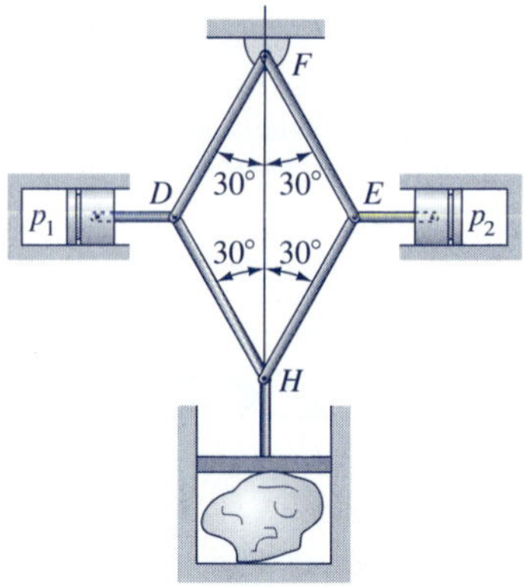

Figure P.10.11.

10.12. A 20-lb-ft torque is applied to a scissor jack. If friction is disregarded throughout, what weight can be maintained in equilibrium? Take the pitch of the screw threads to be .3 in. in opposite senses. All links are of equal length, 1 ft.

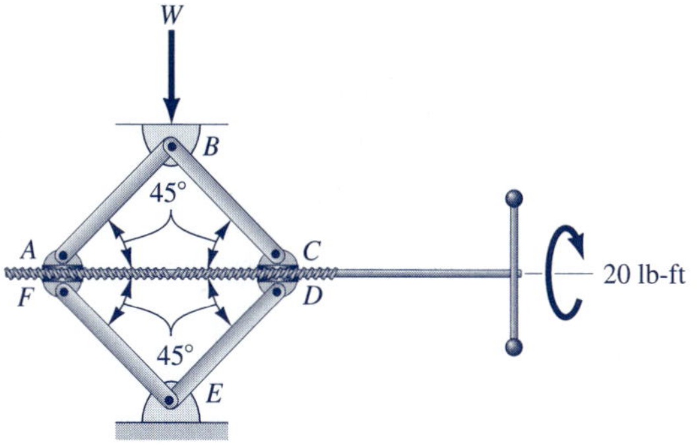

Figure P.10.12.

10.13. The 5,000-lb van of an airline food catering truck rises straight up until its floor is level with the airplane floor. What is the ram force in that position?

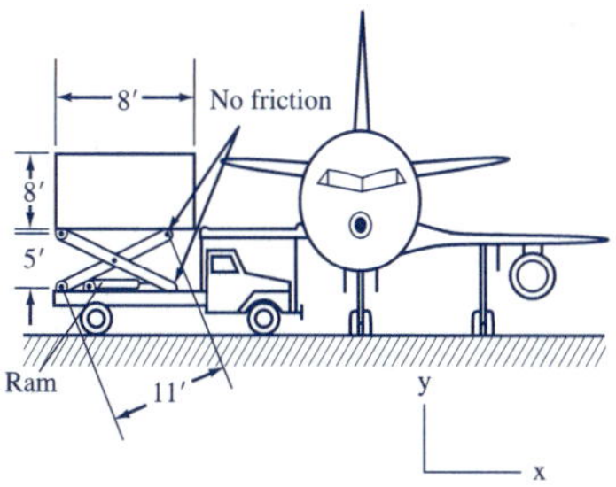

Figure P.10.13.

10.14. What are the cable tensions when the arms of the power shovel are in the position shown? Arm AC weighs 13 kN, arm DF weights 11 kN, and the shovel plus the payload weigh 9 kN.

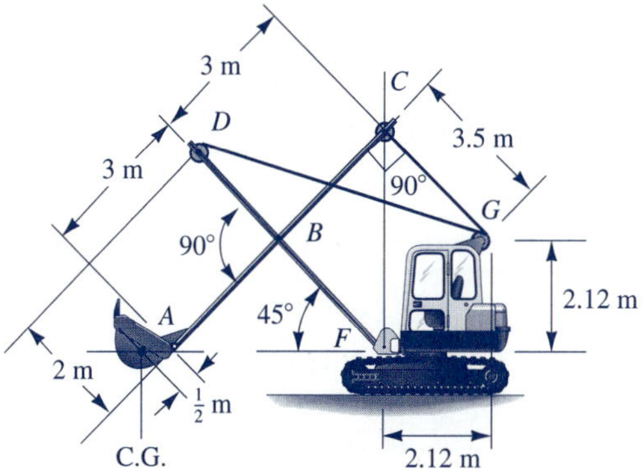

Figure P.10.14.

10.15. A hydraulically actuated gate in a 2-m-square water-carrying tunnel under a dam is held in place with a vertical beam AC. What is the force in the hydraulic ram if the specific weight of water is 9818 N/m³?

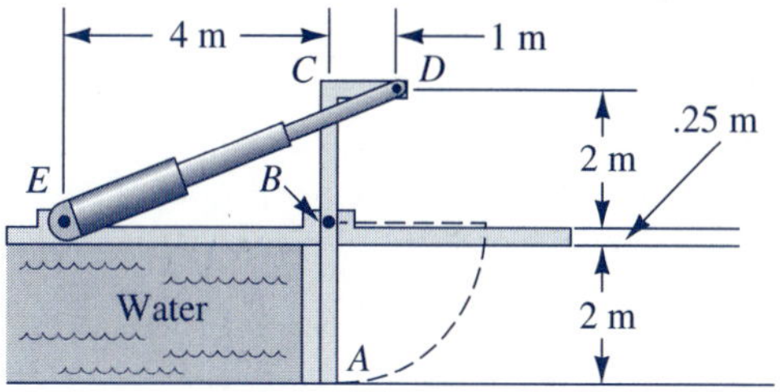

Figure P.10.15.

10.16. Find the angle β for equilibrium in terms of the parameters given in the diagram. Neglect friction and the weight of the beam.

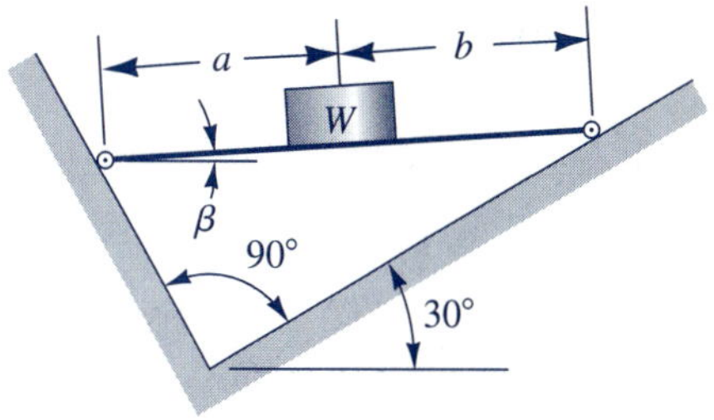

Figure P.10.16.

10.17. Do Problem 5.54 by the method of virtual work.

10.18. Do Problem 5.55 by the method of virtual work.

10.19. What is the relation among P, Q, and θ for equilibrium?

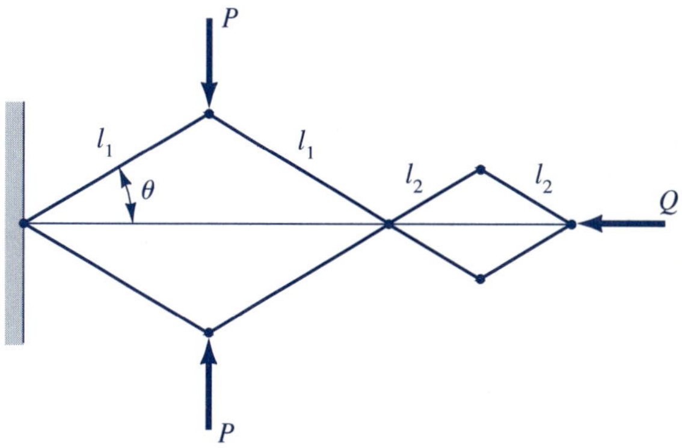

Figure P.10.19.

10.20. A paper collator is shown with the weight Q of the collated papers equal to .2 N. The collator rests on a smooth surface and, accordingly, can slide on this surface with no resistance. What force P is needed to keep the system in equilibrium for the position shown?

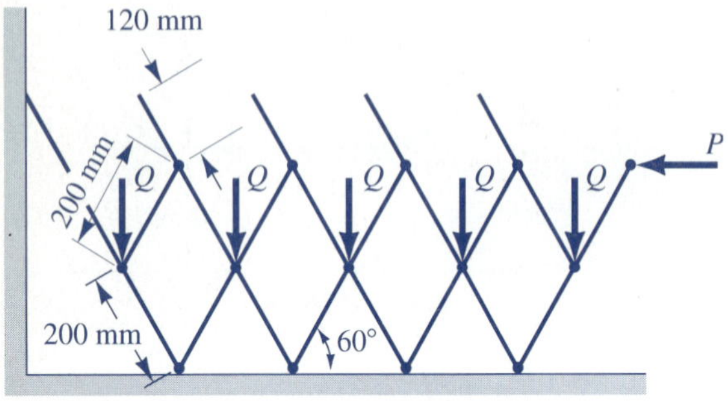

Figure P.10.20.

10.21. A stepped cylinder of weight 500 lb is connected to vehicle A weighing 300 lb and to sheave B weighing 50 lb. Sheave B supports a weight C. What is the value of the weight of C for equilibrium? Neglect friction.

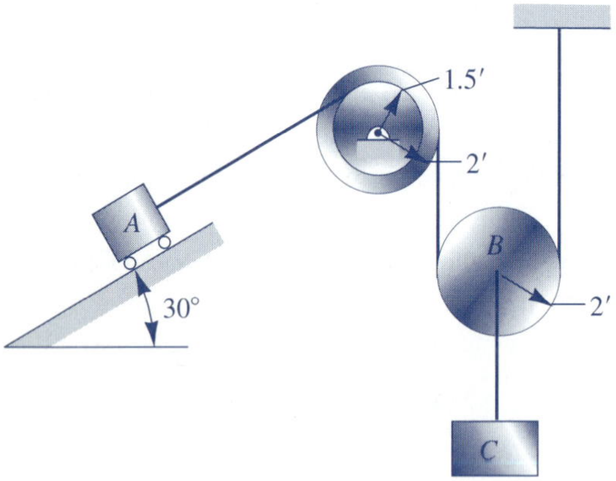

Figure P.10.21.

10.22. Do the first part of Problem 5.70 by the method of virtual work.

10.23. Compute the weight W that can be lifted by the *differential pulley* system for an applied force F. Neglect the weight of the lower pulley.

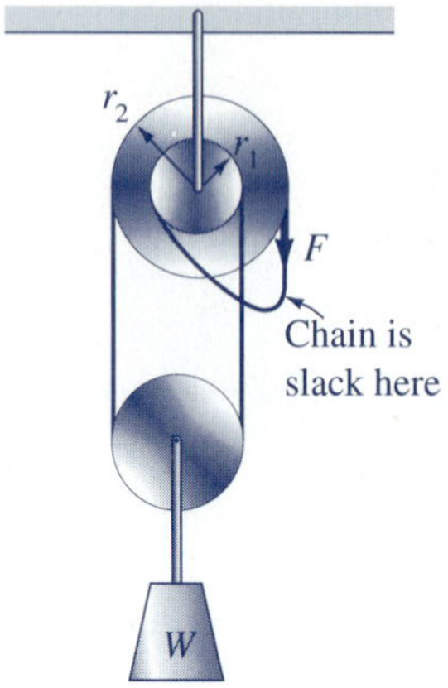

Figure P.10.23.

10.24. The pressure p driving a piston of diameter 100 mm is 1 N/mm². At the configuration shown, what weight W will the system hold if we neglect friction?

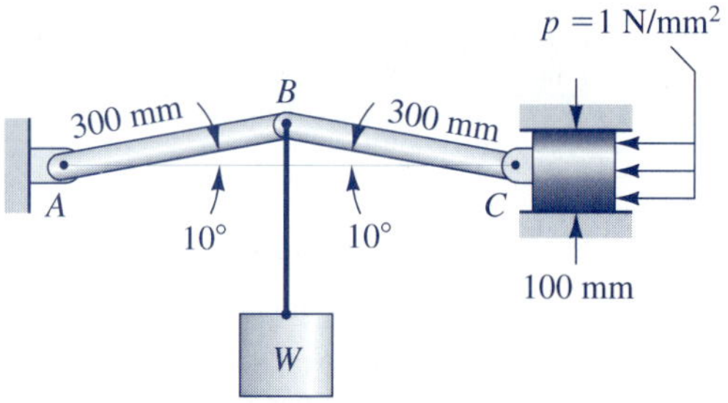

Figure P.10.24.

10.25. Blocks A and B weigh 200 N and 150 N, respectively. They are connected at their base by a light cord. At what position θ is there equilibrium if we disregard friction?

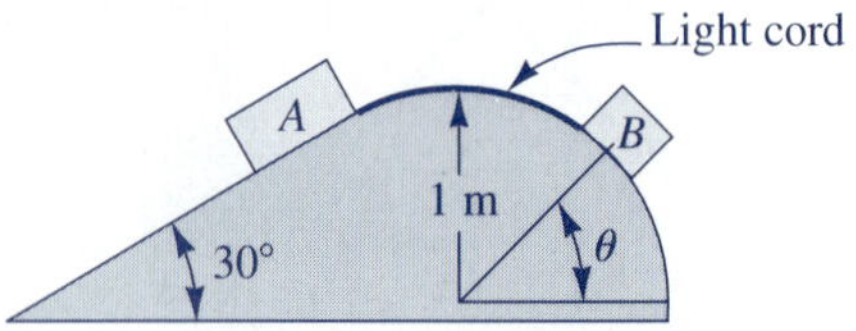

Figure P.10.25.

10.26. If A weighs 500 N, and if B weighs 100 N, determine the weight of C for equilibrium.

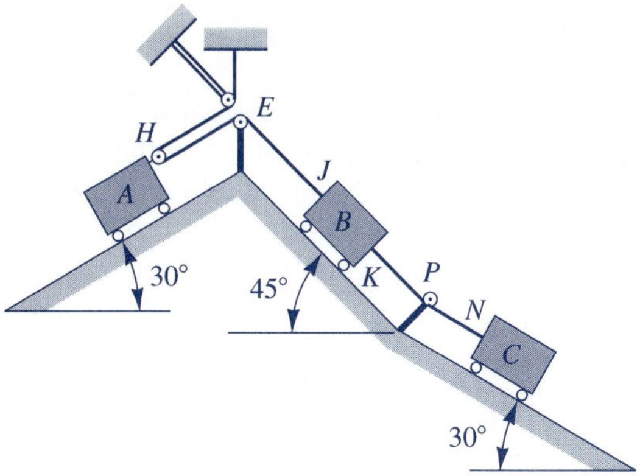

Figure P.10.26.

10.27. An embossing device imprints an image at D on metal stock. If a force F of 200 N is exerted by the operator, what is the force at D on the stock? The lengths of AB and BC are each 150 mm.

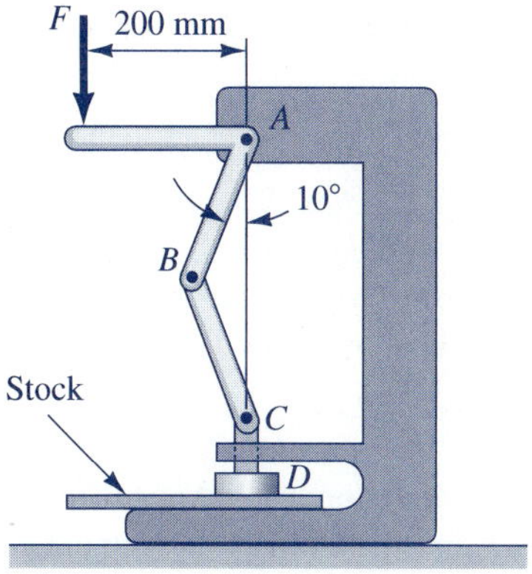

Figure P.10.27.

10.28. A support system holds a 500-N load. Without the load, $\theta = 45^\circ$ and the spring is not compressed. If K for the spring is 10,000 N/m, how far down d will the 500-N load depress the upper platform if the load is applied slowly and carefully? Neglect all other weights. $DB = BE = AB = CB = 400$ mm. (*Note:* The force from the spring is K times its contraction.)

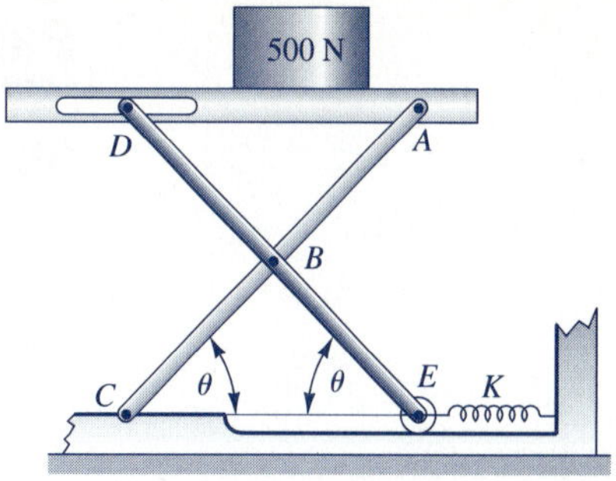

Figure P.10.28.

10.29. Rod ABC is connected through a pin and slot to a sleeve which slides on a vertical rod. Before the weight W of 100 N is applied at C, the rod is inclined at an angle of 45°. If K of the spring is 8,000 N/m, what is the angle θ for equilibrium? The length of AB is 300 mm and the length of BC is 200 mm when $\theta = 45^\circ$. Neglect friction and all weights other than W. (*Note:* The force from the spring is K times its contraction.)

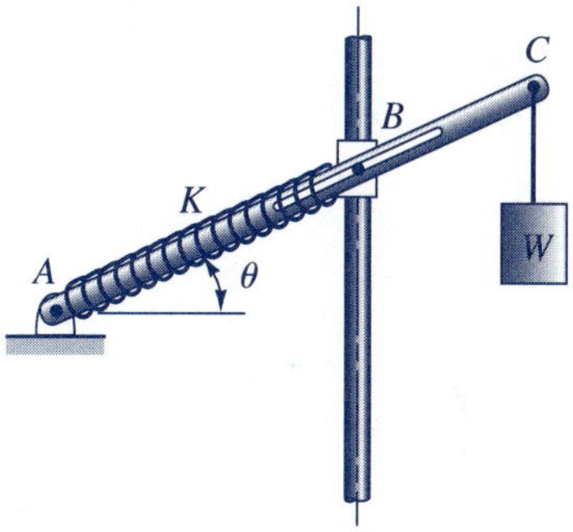

Figure P.10.29.

10.30. Show that the virtual work of a couple moment $\boldsymbol{M}$ for a rotation $\delta\boldsymbol{\phi}$ is given as

$$\delta \mathcal{W} = \boldsymbol{M} \cdot \delta\boldsymbol{\phi}$$

[*Hint:* Decompose $\boldsymbol{M}$ into components normal to and collinear with $\delta\boldsymbol{\phi}$.]

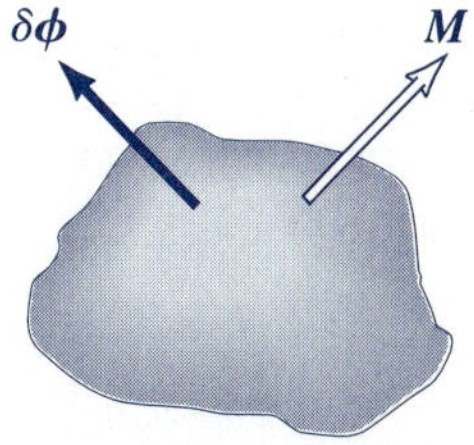

Figure P.10.30.

Part B: Method of Total Potential Energy

10.6 Conservative Systems

We shall restrict ourselves in this section to certain types of active forces. This restriction will permit us to arrive at some additional very useful relations.

Consider first a body acted on only by gravity force W as an active force and moving along a frictionless path from position 1 to position 2, as shown in Fig. 10.14. The work done by gravity, $\mathcal{W}_{1\text{-}2}$, is then

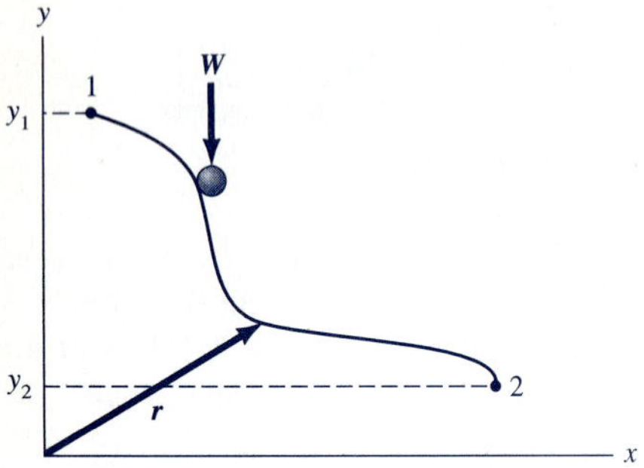

Figure 10.14. Particle moving along frictionless path

$$\begin{aligned}\mathcal{W}_{1-2} = \int_1^2 \boldsymbol{F} \cdot d\boldsymbol{r} = \int_1^2 (-W\boldsymbol{j}) \cdot d\boldsymbol{r} = -W\int_1^2 dy \\ = -W(y_2 - y_1) = W(y_1 - y_2)\end{aligned} \tag{10.20}$$

Note that the work done *does not depend* on the path, but depends only on the positions of the *end points* of the path. *Force fields which are functions of position and whose work like gravity is independent of the path are called conservative force fields.* In general, we can say for a conservative force field $\boldsymbol{F}(x, y, z)$ that, along a path between positions 1 and 2, the work is analogous to that in Eq. 10.20. That is,

$$\mathcal{W}_{1-2} = \int_1^2 \boldsymbol{F} \cdot d\boldsymbol{r} = V_1(x, y, z) - V_2(x, y, z) \tag{10.21}$$

where V, a scalar function evaluated at the end points, is called the *potential energy function.*[14] We may rewrite the equation above as follows:

$$-\int_1^2 \boldsymbol{F} \cdot d\boldsymbol{r} = V_2(x, y, z) - V_1(x, y, z) = \Delta V \tag{10.22}$$

From the result above we can say that *the change in potential energy* ΔV, (equal to the final V minus the initial V), associated with a force field is *the negative of the work done by this force field in going from position 1 to position 2 along any path.* For any *closed* path, the work done by a conservative force field $\boldsymbol{F}$ is then

$$\oint \boldsymbol{F} \cdot d\boldsymbol{r} = 0 \tag{10.23}$$

How is the potential energy function V related to $\boldsymbol{F}$? To answer this query, consider that an arbitrary infinitesimal path segment $d\boldsymbol{r}$ starts from point 1. We can then give Eq. 10.22 as

$$\boldsymbol{F} \cdot d\boldsymbol{r} = -dV \tag{10.24}$$

$$\therefore F_x dx + F_y dy + F_z dz = -\left(\frac{\partial V}{\partial x} dx + \frac{\partial V}{\partial y} dy + \frac{\partial V}{\partial z} dz\right) \tag{10.25}$$

We can conclude from the equation above that since $d\boldsymbol{r}$ is arbitrary

[14]The context of any discussion should make clear whether V refers to potential energy, or to speed, or to volume. V is also denoted here as *P.E.*

$$F_x = -\frac{\partial V}{\partial x}$$
$$F_y = -\frac{\partial V}{\partial y} \tag{10.26}$$
$$F_z = -\frac{\partial V}{\partial z}$$

Or, in other words,

$$\begin{aligned} \boldsymbol{F} &= -\left(\frac{\partial V}{\partial x}\boldsymbol{i} + \frac{\partial V}{\partial y}\boldsymbol{j} + \frac{\partial V}{\partial z}\boldsymbol{k}\right) \\ &= -\left(\frac{\partial}{\partial x}\boldsymbol{i} + \frac{\partial}{\partial y}\boldsymbol{j} + \frac{\partial}{\partial z}\boldsymbol{k}\right)V \\ &= -\mathbf{grad}\, V = -\boldsymbol{\nabla} V \end{aligned} \tag{10.27}$$

The operator we have introduced is called the *gradient* operator and is given as follows for rectangular coordinates:

$$\mathbf{grad} \equiv \boldsymbol{\nabla} \equiv \frac{\partial}{\partial x}\boldsymbol{i} + \frac{\partial}{\partial y}\boldsymbol{j} + \frac{\partial}{\partial z}\boldsymbol{k} \tag{10.28}$$

We can now say, as an alternative definition, that *a conservative force field must be a function of position and expressible as the gradient of a scalar field function*. The inverse to this statement is also valid. *That is, if a force field is a function of position and the gradient of a scalar field, it must then be a conservative force field.* Such are the following two force fields.

Constant Force Field. If the force field is constant at all positions, it can always be expressed as the gradient of a scalar function of the form $V = -(ax + by + cz)$, where a, b, and c are constants. The constant force field, then, is $\boldsymbol{F} = a\boldsymbol{i} + b\boldsymbol{j} + c\boldsymbol{k}$.

In limited changes of position near the Earth's surface (a common situation), we can consider the gravitational force on a particle of mass, m, as a constant force field given by $-mg\boldsymbol{k}$. Thus, the constants for the general force field given above are $a = b = 0$ and $c = -mg$. Clearly, $V \equiv P.E. = mgz$ for this case.

Force Proportional to Linear Displacements. Consider a body limited by constraints to move along a straight line. Along this line a force is developed directly proportional to the displacement of the body from some point on the line. If this line is the x axis, we give this force as

$$\boldsymbol{F} = -Kx\boldsymbol{i} \tag{10.29}$$

where x is the displacement from the point. The constant K is a positive number, so that, with the minus sign in this equation, a positive displacement x from the origin means that the force is negative and is then directed back to the origin. A displacement in the negative direction from the origin (negative x) means that the force is positive and is directed again toward the origin. Thus, the force given above is a *restoring* force about the origin. An example of this force is that resulting from the extension of a linear spring (Fig. 10.15). The force that the spring exerts will be directly proportional to the amount of elongation or compression in the x direction beyond the unextended configuration. This movement is measured from the origin of the x axis. The constant K in this situation is called the *spring constant*. The change in potential energy due to the displacements from the origin to some position x, therefore, is

$$P.E. = \frac{Kx^2}{2} \tag{10.30}$$

since $-\nabla\left(\frac{Kx^2}{2}\right) = -Kx\boldsymbol{i}$.

The *change* in potential energy has been defined as the *negative* of the work done by a conservative force as we go from one position to another. Clearly, the potential energy change is then *directly equal* to the work done by the *reaction* to the conservative force during this displacement. In the case of the spring, the reaction force would be the force *from* the surroundings acting *on* the spring at point A (Fig. 10.15). During extension or compression of the spring from the undeformed position, this force (from the surroundings) clearly must do a positive amount of work. This work must, as noted above, equal the potential energy change. We now note that we can consider this work (or in other words the change in potential energy) to be a measure of the energy *stored* in the spring. That is, when allowed to return to its original position, the spring will do this amount of positive work *on* the surroundings at A, provided that the return motion is slow enough to prevent oscillations, etc.

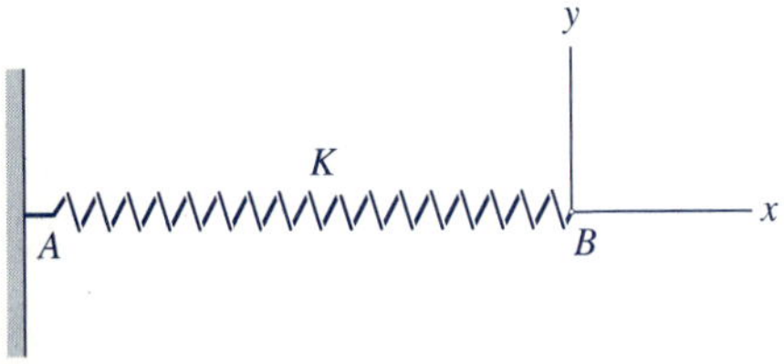

Figure 10.15. Linear spring

10.7 Condition of Equilibrium for a Conservative System

Let us now consider a system of rigid bodies that is ideally constrained and acted on by conservative active forces. For a virtual displacement from a configuration of equilibrium, the virtual work done by the active forces, which are maintained constant during the virtual displacement, must be zero. We shall now show that the condition of equilibrium can be stated in yet another way for this system.

Specifically, suppose that we have n conservative forces acting on the system of bodies. The increment of work for a real infinitesimal movement of the system can be given as follows:

$$\begin{aligned} d\mathcal{W} &= \sum_{p=1}^{n} \boldsymbol{F}_p \cdot d\boldsymbol{r}_p \\ &= \sum_{p=1}^{n}\left[-\left(\frac{\partial V_p}{\partial x_p}\boldsymbol{i} + \frac{\partial V_p}{\partial y_p}\boldsymbol{j} + \frac{\partial V_p}{\partial z_p}\boldsymbol{k}\right)\right] \cdot \left(dx_p\boldsymbol{i} + dy_p\boldsymbol{j} + dz_p\boldsymbol{k}\right) \\ &= \sum_{p=1}^{n}\left[-\left(\frac{\partial V_p}{\partial x_p}dx_p + \frac{\partial V_p}{\partial y_p}dy_p + \frac{\partial V_p}{\partial z_p}dz_p\right)\right] \\ &= -\sum_{p=1}^{n} dV_p = -d\left(\sum_{p=1}^{n} V_p\right) = -dV \end{aligned}$$

where V without subscripts refers to *total* potential energy. By treating $\delta\boldsymbol{r}_p$ like $d\boldsymbol{r}_p$ in the equations above, we can express the virtual work $\delta\mathcal{W}_{\text{Virt}}$ as

$$
\begin{aligned}
\delta \mathcal{W}_{\text{Virt}} &= \sum_{p=1}^{n} \boldsymbol{F}_p \cdot \delta \boldsymbol{r}_p \\
&= \sum_{p=1}^{n} \left[-\left(\frac{\partial V_p}{\partial x_p} \boldsymbol{i} + \frac{\partial V_p}{\partial y_p} \boldsymbol{j} + \frac{\partial V_p}{\partial z_p} \boldsymbol{k} \right) \right] \cdot \left(\delta x_p \boldsymbol{i} + \delta y_p \boldsymbol{j} + \delta z_p \boldsymbol{k} \right) \\
&= \sum_{p=1}^{n} \left[-\left(\frac{\partial V_p}{\partial x_p} \delta x_p + \frac{\partial V_p}{\partial y_p} \delta y_p + \frac{\partial V_p}{\partial z_p} \delta z_p \right) \right] \\
&= -\sum_{p=1}^{n} \delta V_p = -\delta \left(\sum_{p=1}^{n} V_p \right) = -\delta V
\end{aligned}
$$

But we know that for equilibrium $\delta \mathcal{W}_{\text{Virt}} = 0$, and so we can similarly say for equilibrium:

$$
\delta V = 0 \tag{10.31}
$$

Mathematically, this means that *the potential energy has a stationary or an extremum value at a configuration of equilibrium*, or, putting it another way, *the variation of V is zero at a configuration of equilibrium.*[15] Thus, we have another criterion which we may use to solve problems of equilibrium for conservative force systems with ideal constraints.

For solving problems, determine the potential energy using a set of independent coordinates. Then, take the variation, δ, of the potential energy. For example, suppose that V is a function of independent variables $q_1, q_2, \ldots, q_n$, thereby having n degrees of freedom. The variation of V then becomes

$$
\delta V = \frac{\partial V}{\partial q_1} \delta q_1 + \frac{\partial V}{\partial q_2} \delta q_2 + \cdots + \frac{\partial V}{\partial q_n} \delta q_n \tag{10.32}
$$

For equilibrium, we set this variation equal to zero according to Eq. 10.31. For the right side of the equation above to be zero, the coefficient of each δq_i must be zero, since the δq_i are independent of each other. Thus,

$$
\begin{aligned}
\frac{\partial V}{\partial q_1} &= 0 \\
\frac{\partial V}{\partial q_2} &= 0 \\
&\vdots \\
\frac{\partial V}{\partial q_n} &= 0
\end{aligned} \tag{10.33}
$$

We now have n independent equations, which we can now solve for n unknowns. This method of approach is illustrated in the following examples.

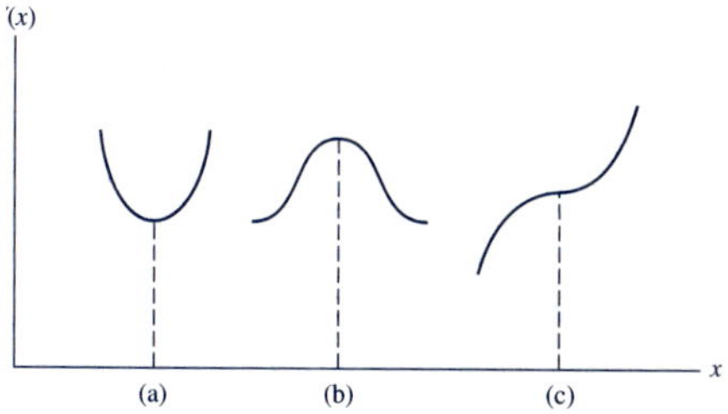

Figure 10.16. Stationary or extremum points.

[15] To further understand this, consider V as a function of only one variable, x. A *stationary* value (or, as we may say, an extremum) might be a local minimum (a in Fig. 10.16), a local maximum (b in the figure), or an inflection point (c in the figure). Note for these points that for a differential movement, δx, there is zero first-order change in V (i.e., $\delta V = 0$).

Example 10.3

A block weighing W lb is placed slowly on a spring having a spring constant of K lb/ft (see Fig. 10.17). Calculate how much the spring is compressed at the equilibrium configuration.

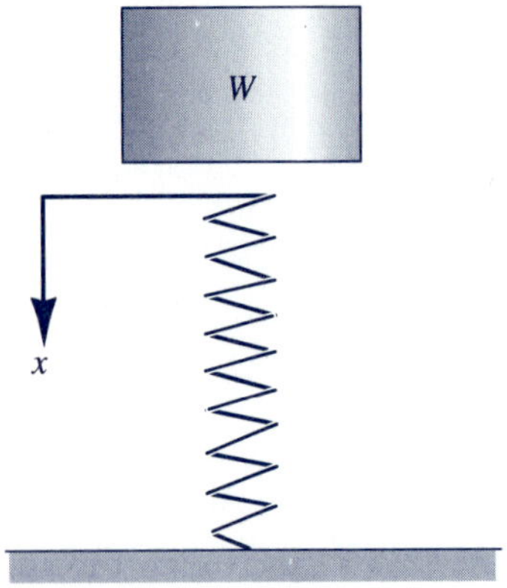

Figure 10.17. Mass placed on a linear spring.

This is a simple problem and could be solved by using the definition of the spring constant, but we shall take advantage of the simplicity to illustrate the preceding comments. Note that only conservative forces act on the block, namely the weight and the spring force. Using the unextended top position of the spring as the datum for gravitational potential energy and measuring x from this position we have, for the potential energy of the system:

$$V = -Wx + \frac{1}{2}Kx^2$$

Consequently, for equilibrium, we have since there is only one degree of freedom

$$\frac{dV}{dx} = -W + Kx = 0$$

Solving for x, we have

$$x = \frac{W}{K}$$

Example 10.4

A mechanism shown in Fig. 10.18 consists of two weights W, four pinned linkage rods of length a, and a spring K connecting the linkage rods and which rides along a stationary vertical rod. The spring is unextended when $\theta = 45^\circ$. If friction and the weights of the linkage rods are negligible, what are the equilibrium configurations for the system of linkage rods and weights?

Only conservative forces can perform work on the system, and so we may use the stationary potential-energy criterion for equilibrium. We shall compute the potential energy as a function of θ (clearly, there is but one degree of freedom) using the configuration $\theta = 45^\circ$ as the source of datum levels for the various energies. Observing Fig. 10.19, we can say that

$$V = -2Wd + \tfrac{1}{2}K(2d)^2 \tag{a}$$

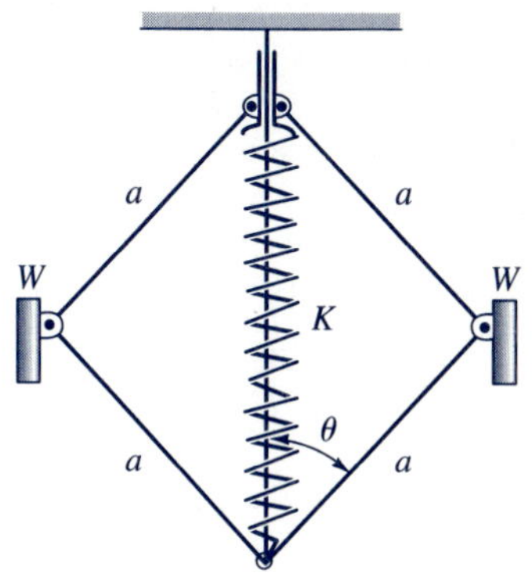

Figure 10.18. A mechanism.

As for the distance d, we can say (see Fig. 10.19)

$$d = a\cos 45^\circ - a\cos\theta \tag{b}$$

Hence, we have, for Eq. (a),

$$V = -2Wa(\cos 45^\circ - \cos\theta) + \tfrac{1}{2}K4a^2(\cos 45^\circ - \cos\theta)^2$$

For equilibrium, we require that

$$\frac{dV}{d\theta} = 0 = -2Wa\sin\theta + 4Ka^2(\cos 45^\circ - \cos\theta)(\sin\theta) \tag{c}$$

We can then say

$$\sin\theta\left[-W - 2Ka\left(\cos\theta - \frac{1}{\sqrt{2}}\right)\right] = 0 \tag{d}$$

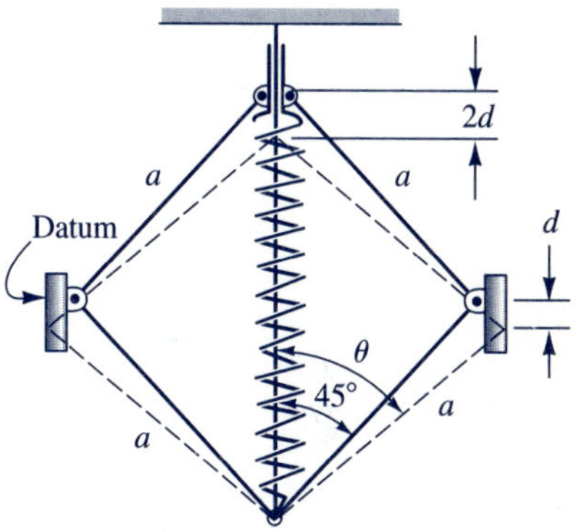

Figure 10.19. Movement of mechanism as determined by θ.

We have here two possibilities for satisfying the equation. First, $\sin\theta = 0$ is a solution, so we may say that $\theta_1 = 0$ (this may not be mechanically possible) is a configuration of equilibrium. Clearly, another solution can be reached by setting the bracketed terms equal to zero:

$$-W - 2Ka\left(\cos\theta - \frac{1}{\sqrt{2}}\right) = 0$$

Therefore,

$$\cos\theta = \frac{1}{\sqrt{2}} - \frac{W}{2Ka} \tag{e}$$

The solutions for θ then are

$$\theta_1 = 0$$
$$\theta_2 = \cos^{-1}\left(\frac{1}{\sqrt{2}} - \frac{W}{2Ka}\right) \tag{f}$$

We have here two possible equilibrium configurations.

PROBLEMS

10.31. A 50-kg block is placed carefully on a spring. The spring is nonlinear. The force to deflect the spring a distance x mm is proportional to the square of x. Also, we know that 5 N deflects the spring 1 mm. By the method of stationary potential energy, what will be the compression of the spring? Check the result using a simple calculation based on the behavior of the spring.

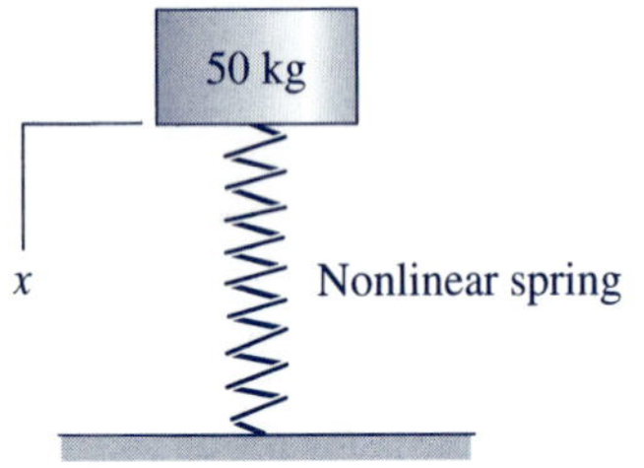

Figure P.10.31.

10.32. A cylinder of radius 2 ft has wrapped around it a light, inextensible cord which is tied to a 100-lb block B on a 30° inclined surface. The cylinder A is connected to a *torsional spring*. This spring requires a torque of 1,000 ft-lb/rad of rotation and it is linear and, of course, restoring. If B is connected to A when the torsional spring is unstrained, and if B is allowed to move slowly down the incline, what distance d do you allow it to move to reach an equilibrium configuration? Use the method of stationary potential energy and then check the result by more elementary reasoning.

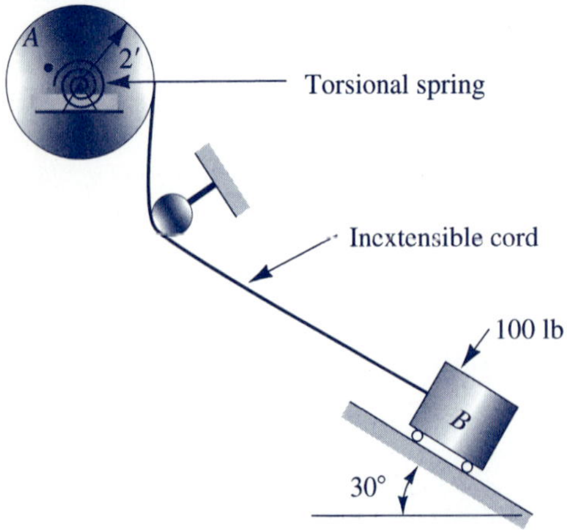

Figure P.10.32.

10.33. Find the equilibrium configurations for the system. The bars are indentical and each has a weight W, a length of 3 m, and a mass of 25 kg. The spring is unstretched when the bars are horizontal and has a spring constant of 1,500 N/m.

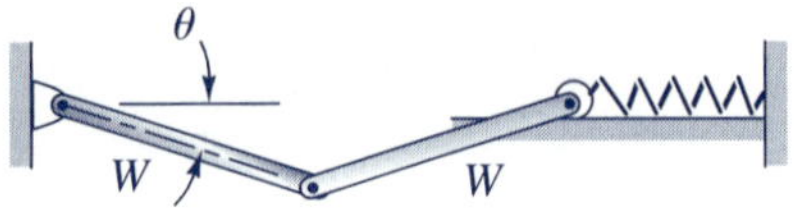

Figure P.10.33.

10.34. The springs of the mechanism are unstretched when $\theta = \theta_0$. Show that $\theta = 25.90°$ when the weight W is added. Take $W = 500$ N, $a = .3$ m, $K_1 = 1$ N/mm, $K_2 = 2$ N/mm, and $\theta_0 = 45°$. Neglect the weight of the members.

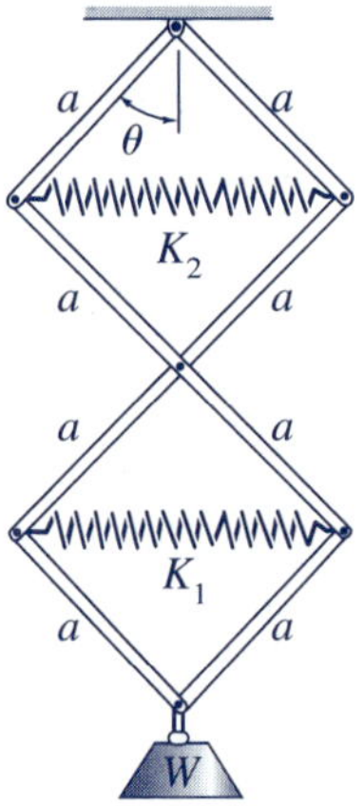

Figure P.10.34.

10.35. At what elevation h must body A be for equilibrium? Neglect friction. [*Hint:* What is the differential relation between θ and l defining the positions of the blocks along the surface? Integrate to get the relation itself.]

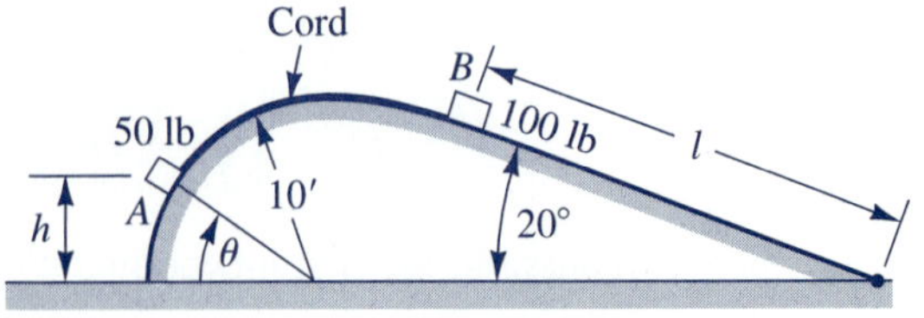

Figure P.10.35.

10.36. Show that the position of equilibrium is $\theta = 77.3^\circ$ for the 20-kg rod *AB*. Neglect friction.

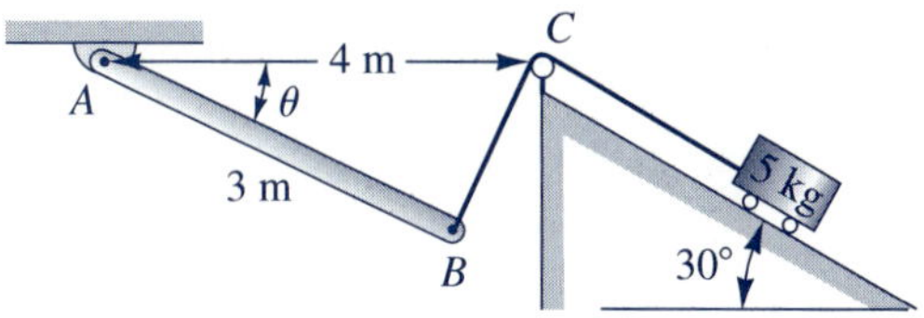

Figure P.10.36.

10.37. A beam *BC* of length 15 ft and weight 500 lb is placed against a spring (which has a spring constant of 10 lb/in.) and smooth walls and allowed to come to rest. If the end of the spring is 5 ft away from the vertical wall when it is not compressed, show by energy methods that the amount that the spring will be compressed is .889 ft.

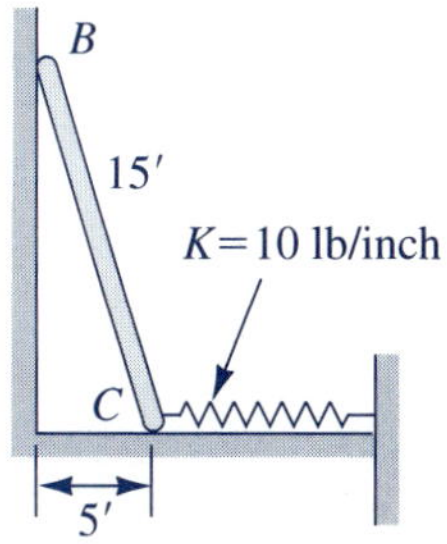

Figure P.10.37.

10.38. Light rods *AB* and *BC* support a 500-N load. End *A* of rod *AB* is pinned, whereas end *C* is on a roller. A spring having a spring constant of 1,000 N/m is connected to *A* and *C*. The spring is unstretched when $\theta = 45^\circ$. Show that the force in the spring is 1,066 N when the 500-N load is being supported.

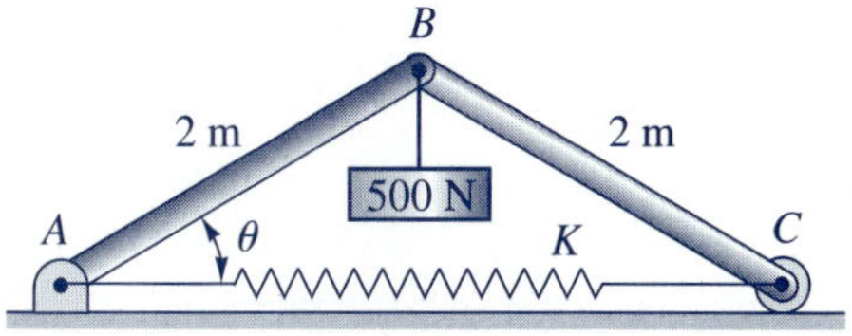

Figure P.10.38.

10.39. Work Problem 10.28 using the method of total potential energy.

10.40. Work Problem 10.29 using the method of total potential energy.

10.41. Do Problem 10.25 by the method of total potential energy. [*Hint:* Consider a length of cord on a circular surface. Use the top part of the surface as a datum.]

10.42. If member *AB* is 10 ft long and member *BC* is 13 ft long, show that the angle θ corresponding to equilibrium is 34.5° if the spring constant *K* is 10 lb/in. Neglect the weight of the members and friction everywhere. Take $\theta = 30^\circ$ for the configuration where the spring is unstretched.

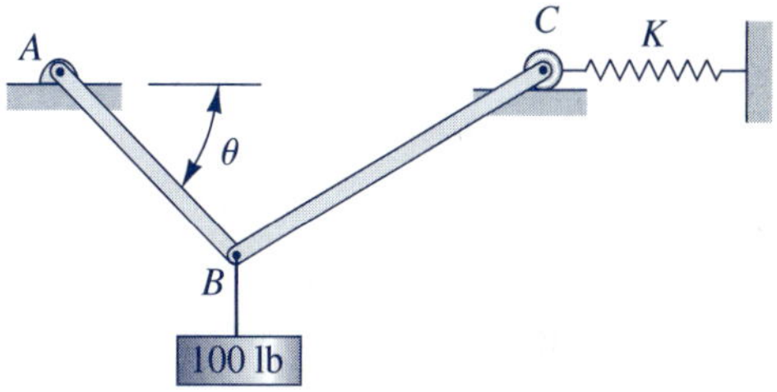

Figure P.10.42.

10.43. A combination of spring and torsion-bar suspension is shown. The spring has a spring constant of 150 N/mm. The torsion bar is shown on end at *A* and has a torsional resistance to rotation of rod *AB* of 5,000 N-m/rad. If the vertical load is zero, the vertical spring is of length 450 mm, and rod *AB* is horizontal. What is the angle α when the suspension supports a weight of 5 kN? Rod *AB* is 400 mm in length.

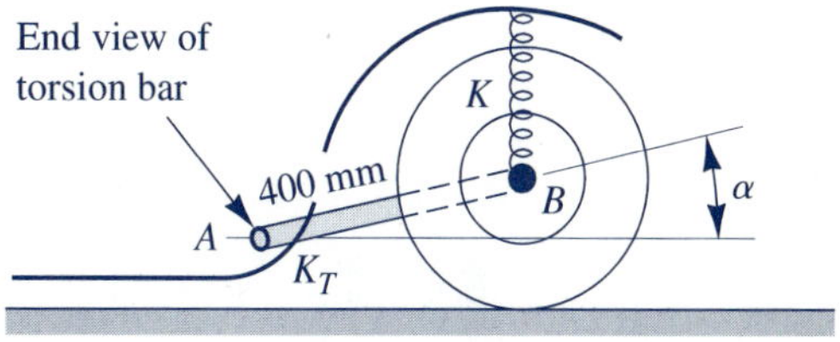

Figure P.10.43.

10.44. Light rods AB and CB are pinned together at B and pass through frictionless bearings D and E. These bearings are connected to the ground by ball-and-socket connections and are free to rotate about these joints. Springs, each having a spring constant K = 800 N/m, restrain the rods as shown. The springs are unstretched when θ = 45°. Show that the deflection of B is .440 m when a 500-N load is attached slowly to pin B. The rods are each 1 m in length, and each unstretched spring is .250 m in length. Neglect the weight of the rods. Rods are welded to small plates at A and C

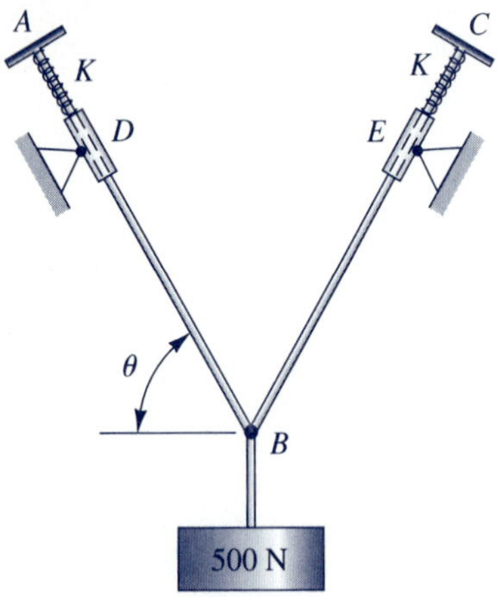

Figure P.10.44.

10.45. Do Problem 10.26 by the method of total potential energy. [*Hint:* Use E as a datum and get lengths EJ, KP, and PN in terms of length HE, including unknown constants.]

10.46. An elastic band is originally 1 m long. Applying a tension force of 30 N, the band will stretch .8 m in length. What deflection a does a 10-N load induce on the band when the load is applied slowly at the center of the band? Consider the force vs. elongation of the band to be linear like a spring. [*Hint:* If you consider half of the band, you double the "spring constant."]

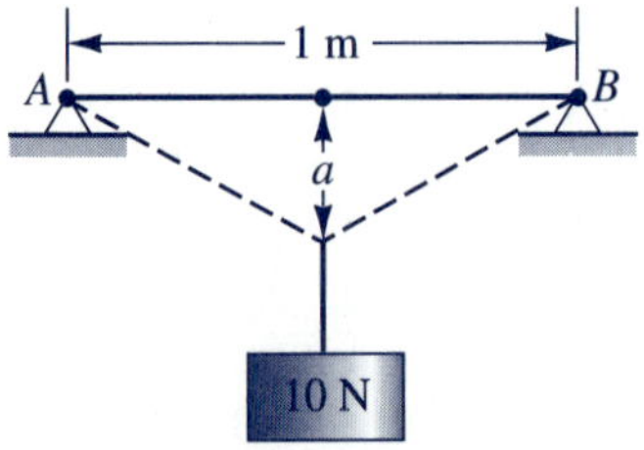

Figure P.10.46.

10.47. In Problem 10.46, the band is first stretched and then tied while stretched to supports A and B so that there is an initial tension in the band of 15 N. What is then the deflection a caused by the 10-N load?

10.48. A rubber band of length .7 m is stretched to connect to points A and B. A tension force of 40 N is thereby developed in the band. A 20-N weight is then attached to the band at C. Find the distance a that point C moves downward if the 20-N weight is constrained to move vertically downward along a frictionless rod. [*Hint:* If you consider part of the band, the "spring constant" for it will be greater than that of the whole band.]

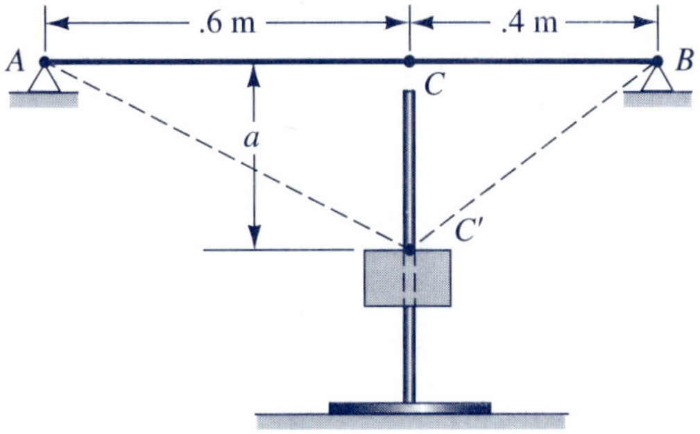

Figure P.10.48.

10.49. The spring connecting bodies A and B has a spring constant K of 3 N/mm. The unstretched length of the spring is 450 mm. If body A weighs 60 N and body B weighs 90 N, what is the stretched length of the spring for equilibrium? [*Hint:* V will be a function of two variables.]

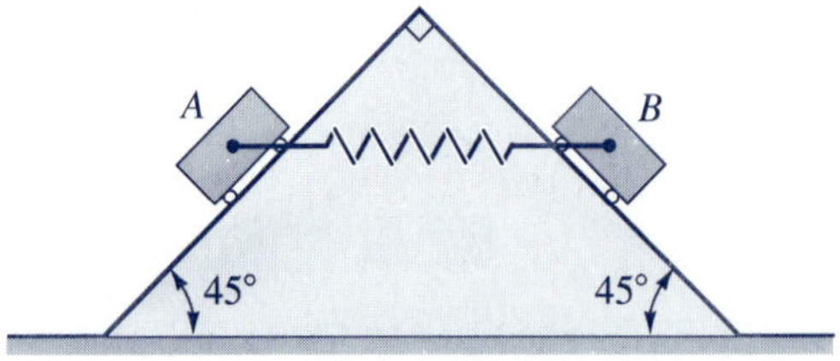

Figure P.10.49

10.8 Stability

Consider a cylinder resting on various surfaces (Fig. 10.20). If we neglect friction, the only active force is that of gravity. Thus, we have here conservative systems for which Eq. 10.31 is valid. The only virtual displacement for which contact with the surfaces is maintained is along the path. In each case, dy/dx is zero. Thus, for an infinitesimal virtual displacement, the first-order change in elevation is zero. Hence, the change in potential energy is zero for the first-order considerations. The bodies, therefore, are in *equilibrium*, according to the previous section. However, distinct physical differences exist between the states of equilibrium of the four cases.

Case A. The equilibrium here is said to be *stable* in that an actual displacement from this configuration is such that the forces tend to return the body to its equilibrium configuration. Notice that the potential energy is at a *minimum* for this condition.

Case B. The equilibrium here is said to be *unstable* in that an actual displacement from the configuration is such that the forces aid in increasing the departure from the equilibrium configuration. The potential energy is at a *maximum* for this condition.

Case C. The equilibrium here is said to be *neutral*. Any displacement means that another equilibrium configuration is established. The potential energy is a constant for all possible positions of the body.

Case D. This equilibrium state is considered *unstable* since any displacement to the left of the equilibrium configuration will result in an increasing departure from this position.

How can we tell whether a system is stable or unstable at its equilibrium configuration other than by physical inspection, as was done above? Consider again a simple situation where the potential energy is a function of only one space coordinate x. That is, $V = V(x)$. We can expand the potential energy in the form of a Maclaurin series about the position of equilibrium.[16] Thus,

$$V = V_{\text{eq}} + \left(\frac{dV}{dx}\right)_{\text{eq}} x + \frac{1}{2!}\left(\frac{d^2V}{d^2x}\right)_{\text{eq}} x^2 + \cdots \tag{10.34}$$

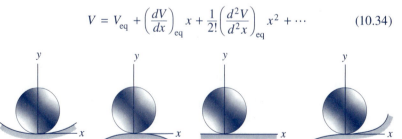

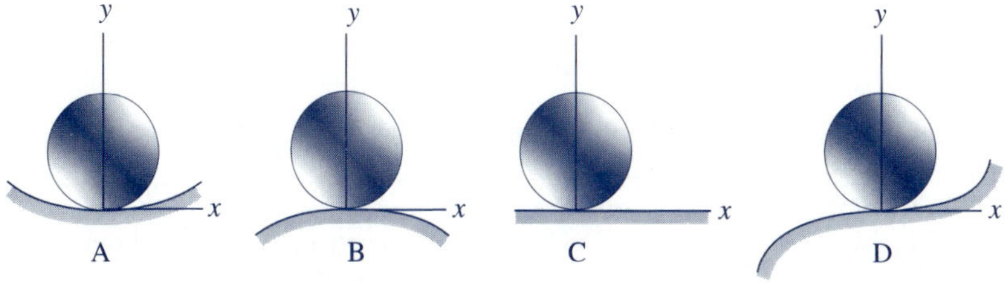

Figure 10.20. Different equilibrium configurations.

[16]Note that in a Maclaurin series the coefficients of the independent variable x are evaluated at $x = 0$, which for us is the equilibrium position. We denote this position with the subscript eq.

We know from Eq. 10.33 applied to one variable that at the equilibrium configuration $(dV/dx)_{eq} = 0$. Hence, we can restate the equation above:

$$V - V_{eq} = \Delta V = \frac{1}{2!}\left(\frac{d^2V}{dx^2}\right)_{eq} x^2 + \frac{1}{3!}\left(\frac{d^3V}{dx^3}\right)_{eq} x^3 + \cdots \qquad (10.35)$$

For small enough x, say x_0, the sign of ΔV will be determined by the sign of the first term in the series, $(1/2!)(d^2V/dx^2)_{eq}\, x^2$.[17] For this reason this term is called the dominant term in the series. Hence, the sign of $(d^2V/dx^2)_{eq}$ is vital in determining the sign of ΔV for small enough x. If $(d^2V/dx^2)_{eq}$ is positive, then ΔV is positive for any value of x smaller than x_0. This means that V is a local minimum at the equilibrium configuration as can be deduced from Fig. 10.20a, and we have *stable equilibrium*.[18] If $(d^2V/dx^2)_{eq}$ is negative, then V is a local maximum at the equilibrium configuration and from Fig. 10.20 we have *unstable equilibrium*. Finally, if $(d^2V/dx^2)_{eq}$ is zero, we must investigate the next higher-order derivative in the expansion, and so forth.

For cases where the potential energy is known in terms of several variables, the determination of the kind of equilibrium for the system is correspondingly more complex. For example, if the function V is known in terms of x and y, we have from the calculus of several variables the following.

For minimum potential energy and therefore for stability:

$$\frac{\partial V}{\partial x} = \frac{\partial V}{\partial y} = 0 \qquad (10.36a)$$

$$\left(\frac{\partial^2 V}{\partial x \partial y}\right)^2 - \frac{\partial^2 V}{\partial x^2}\frac{\partial^2 V}{\partial y^2} < 0 \qquad (10.36b)$$

$$\frac{\partial^2 V}{\partial x^2} + \frac{\partial^2 V}{\partial y^2} > 0 \qquad (10.36c)$$

For maximum potential energy and therefore for instability:

$$\frac{\partial V}{\partial x} = \frac{\partial V}{\partial y} = 0 \qquad (10.37a)$$

$$\left(\frac{\partial^2 V}{\partial x \partial y}\right)^2 - \frac{\partial^2 V}{\partial x^2}\frac{\partial^2 V}{\partial y^2} < 0 \qquad (10.37b)$$

$$\frac{\partial^2 V}{\partial x^2} + \frac{\partial^2 V}{\partial y^2} < 0 \qquad (10.37c)$$

The criteria become increasingly more complex for three or more independent variables.

[17]As x gets smaller than unity, x^2 will become increasingly larger than x^3 and powers of x higher than 3. Hence, depending on the values of derivatives of V at equilibrium, there will be a value of x—say x_0—for which the first term in the series will be larger than the sum of all other terms for values of $x < x_0$.

[18]That is, if the body is displaced a distance $x < x_0$, the body will return to equilibrium on release.

Example 10.5

A thick plate whose bottom edge is that of a circular arc of radius R is shown in Fig. 10.21. The center of gravity of the plate is a distance h above the ground when the plate is in the vertical position as shown in the diagram. What relation must be satisfied by h and R for stable equilibrium?

The plate has one degree of freedom under the action of gravity and we can use the angle θ (Fig. 10.22) as the independent coordinate. We can express the potential energy V of the system relative to the ground as a function of θ in the following manner (see Fig. 10.23):

$$V = W[R - (R - h) \cos \theta] \qquad \text{(a)}$$

where W is the weight of the plate. Clearly, $\theta = 0$ is a position of equilibrium since

$$\left(\frac{dV}{d\theta}\right)_{\theta=0} = [W(R-h)\sin\theta]_{\theta=0} = 0 \qquad \text{(b)}$$

Now consider $d^2V/d\theta^2$ at $\theta = 0$. We have

$$\left(\frac{d^2V}{d\theta^2}\right)_{\theta=0} = W(R-h) \qquad \text{(c)}$$

Clearly, when $R > h$, $(d^2V/d\theta^2)_{\theta = 0}$ is positive, and so this is the desired requirement for stable equilibrium. Thus for stable equilibrium, $R > h$.

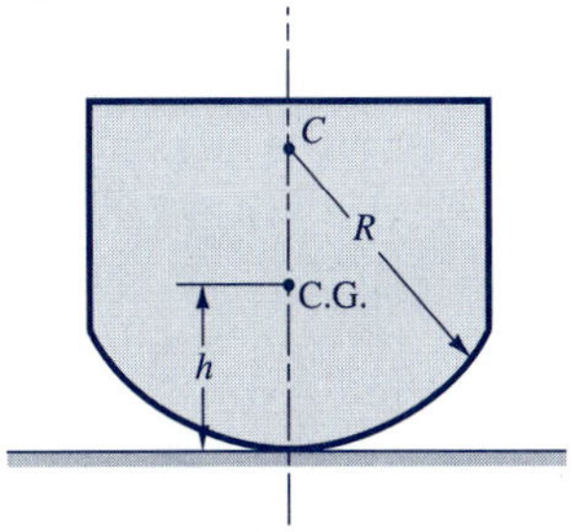

Figure 10.21. Plate with circular bottom edge.

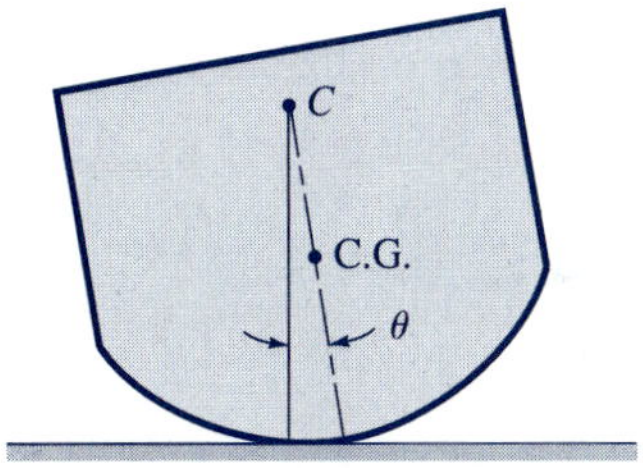

Figure 10.22. One degree of freedom.

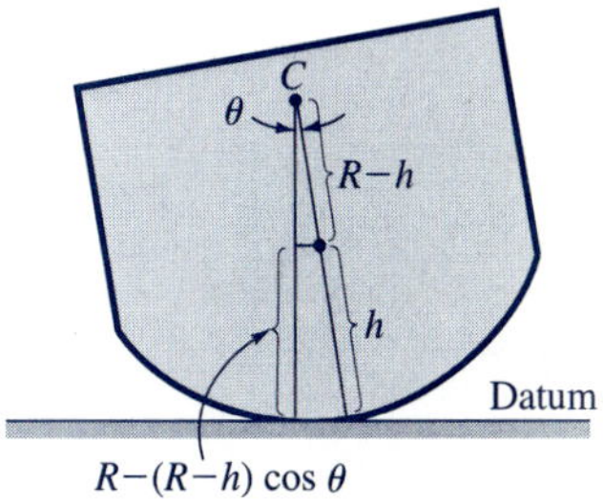

Figure 10.23. Position of C.G.

10.9 Looking Ahead: More on Total Potential Energy

When we have conservative forces acting on particles and rigid bodies, we found earlier that for establishing necessary and sufficient conditions of equilibrium we could extremize the potential energy V associated with the forces. That is, we could set

$$\delta V = 0$$

to satisfy equilibrium. Recall that this result was derived from the method of virtual work. We have a similar formulation for the case of an elastic (not necessarily linearly elastic) body whereby we can guarantee equilibrium. This more-general principle is derivable from the more-general virtual work principle mentioned earlier in section 10.5. Here, we must extremize an expression more complicated (as you might expect) than V. This expression is denoted as π with no relation to the number 3.1416. . . . The expression π is what we call a *functional*, wherein for the substitution of each function, such as $y(x)$, into the functional a number is established. A simple example of a functional I is as follows:

$$I = \int_{x_1}^{x_2} F\left(x, y, \frac{dy}{dx}\right) dx$$

where F is a function of x (the so-called independent variable), y, and dy/dx. Substitution of a function $y(x)$ into F followed by an integration between the fixed limits, yields for this function $y(x)$ a number for I. Functionals pervade the field of mechanics and most other analytic fields of knowledge. A vital step is to find the function $y(x)$ that will extremize I. This function then becomes known as the *extremal function*. The calculus for doing this is called the *calculus of variations*. The particular functional for the method of total potential energy is given as

$$\pi = -\iiint_V \boldsymbol{B} \cdot \boldsymbol{u}\, dv - \oint\!\!\oint_S \boldsymbol{T} \cdot \boldsymbol{u}\, dA + U$$

The function to be adjusted to extremize π is $\boldsymbol{u}(x, y, z)$ taking the place of $y(x)$ in the preceding functional, and now the independent variables are x, y, and z in place of just x in the preceding functional. The expression U is the energy of deformation that you will study later in your solids course and presented earlier in Section 10.5 as $\iiint_V \sum_i \sum_j \tau_{ij} \delta\epsilon_{ij}\, dv$. The principle of total potential energy for the case of elastic bodies is written in the following deceivingly simple looking formulation:

$$\delta\pi = 0$$

What is most intriguing about this innocent looking equation is that it is often considered to be the **most powerful equation in solid mechanics**!

We have touched on a broad area of study, namely variational methods, parts of which you will encounter in many of your studies. For example, just the method of total potential energy has the following major uses:

1. It plays an important role in *optimization theory*.
2. It can be used profitably to derive the *proper equations* and the *boundary conditions* for many areas of vital importance such as plate theory, elastic stability theory, dynamics of plates and beams, torsion theory, etc.
3. From it we can develop a number of vital approximation methods. The most prominent of these methods is the method of *finite elements*.

Clearly this is an impressive list.[19]

[19]You can study in some detail the contents of the two Looking Ahead sections of this chapter in I.H. Shames, *Introduction to Solid Mechanics*, 2nd ed., 1989, Prentice-Hall, Inc., Englewood Cliffs, N.J. This material should be within the reach of bright second-semester sophomores and certainly of juniors. The author has taught this material for many years to second-semester sophomores out of the aforementioned book. See Chapters 18 and 19.

PROBLEMS

10.50. A rod AB is connected to the ground by a frictionless ball-and-socket connection at A. The rod is free to rest on the inside edge of a horizontal plate as shown in the diagram. The square $abcd$ has its center directly over A. The curve efg is a semicircle. Without resorting to mathematical calculations, identify positions on this inside edge where equilibrium is possible for the rod AB. Describe the nature of the equilibrium and supply supporting arguments. Assume the edge of plate is frictionless.

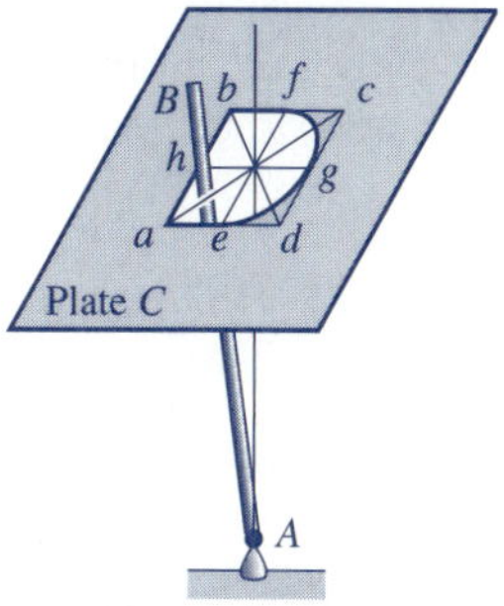

Figure P.10.50.

10.51. In Problem 10.50, show mathematically that position h is a position of unstable equilibrium for the rod.

10.52. Rod AB is supported by a frictionless ball-and-socket joint at A and leans against the inside edge of a horizontal plate. What is the nature of the equilibrium position a for the rod? Assume that the edge of the plate is frictionless.

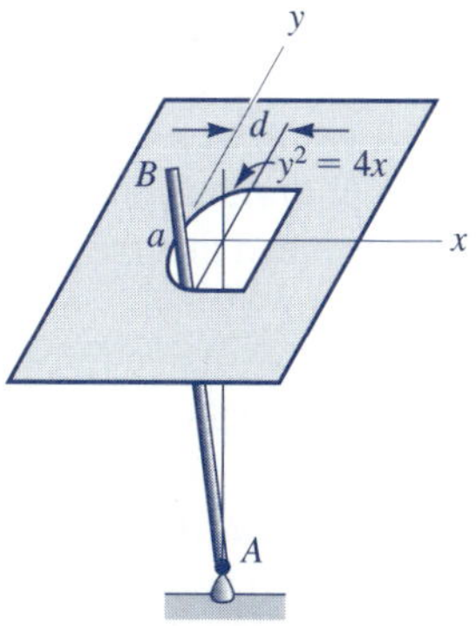

Figure P.10.52.

10.53. Consider that the potential energy of a system is given by the formulation: $V = 8x^3 + 6x^2 - 7x$. What are the equilibrium positions? Indicate whether these positions are stable or not.

10.54. A section of a cylinder is free to roll on a horizontal surface. If γ of the triangular portion of the cylinder is 180 lb/ft^3 and that of the semicircular portion of the cylinder is 100 lb/ft^3, is the configuration shown in the diagram in stable equilibrium?

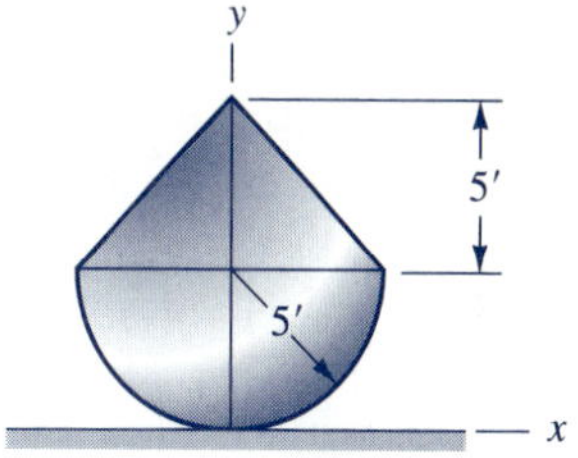

Figure P.10.54.

10.55. A system of springs and rigid bodies AB and BC is acted on by a weight W through a pin connection at A. If K is 50 N/mm, what is the range of the value of W so that the system has an unstable equilibrium configuration when the rods AB and BC are collinear? Neglect the weight of the rods.

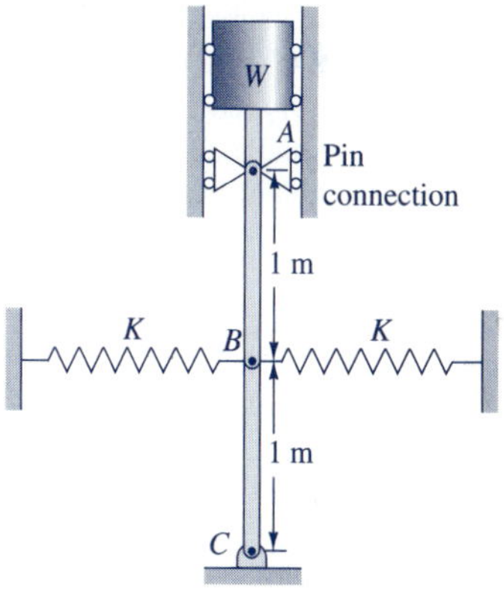

Figure P.10.55.

10.56. A weight W is welded to a light rod AB. At B there is a torsional spring for which it takes 500 ft-lb to rotate 1 rad. The torsional spring is linear and restoring and is, for rotation, the analog of the ordinary linear spring for extension or contraction. If the torsional spring is unstrained when the rod is vertical, what is the largest value of W for which we have stable equilibrium in the vertical direction?

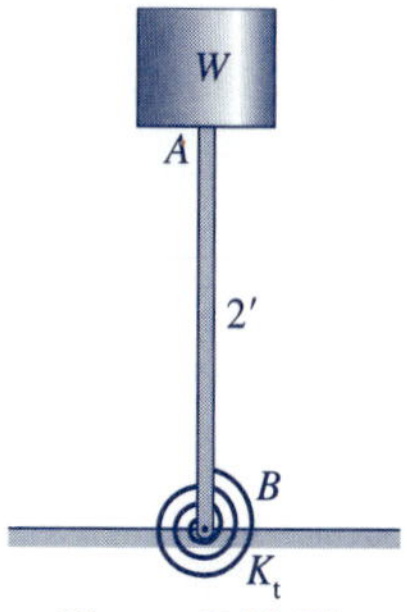

Figure P.10.56.

10.57. A light rod AB is pinned to a block of weight W at A. Also at A are two identical springs K. Show that, for W less than $2Kl$, we have stable equilibrium in the vertical position and, for $W > 2Kl$, we have unstable equilibrium. The value $W = 2Kl$ is called a *critical load* for reasons that are explained in Problem 10.58.

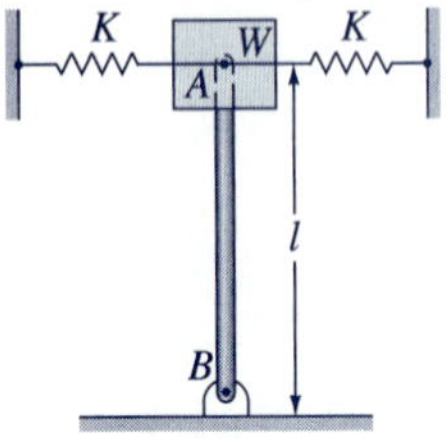

Figure P.10.57.

10.58. In Problem 10.57, apply a small transverse force F to body A as shown. Compute the horizontal deflection δ of point A for a position of equilibrium by using ordinary statics as developed in earlier chapters. Now show that when $W = 2Kl$ (i.e., the critical weight), the deflection δ mathematically blows up to infinity. This shows that, even if $W < 2Kl$ and we have stable equilibrium with $F = 0$, we get increasingly very large deflections as the weight W approaches its critical value and a side load F, however small, is introduced. The study of stability of equilibrium configuration therefore is an important area of study in mechanics. Most of you will encounter this topic in your strength of materials course.

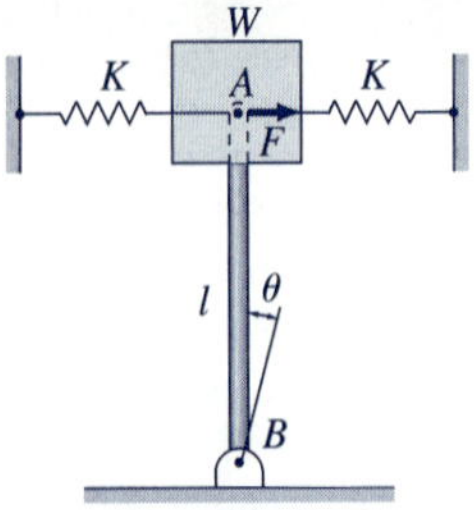

Figure P.10.58.

10.59. Cylinders A and B have semicircular cross-sections. Cylinder A supports a rectangular solid shown as C. If $\rho_A = 1{,}600 \text{ kg/m}^3$ and $\rho_c = 800 \text{ kg/m}^3$, ascertain whether the arrangement shown is in stable equilibrium. [*Hint:* Make use of point O in computing V.]

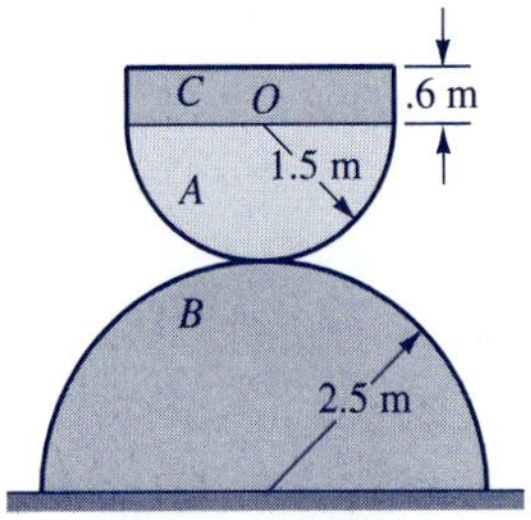

Figure P.10.59.

10.10 Closure

In this chapter, we have taken an approach that differs radically from the approach used earlier in the text. In earlier chapters, we isolated a body for the purpose of writing equilibrium equations using all the forces acting on the body. This is the approach we often call *vectorial mechanics*. In this chapter, we have mathematically compared the equilibrium configuration with admissible neighboring configurations. We concluded that the equilibrium configuration was one from which there is zero virtual work under a virtual displacement. Or, equivalently for conservative active forces, the equilibrium configuration was the configuration having stationary (actually minimum) potential energy when compared to admissible configurations in the neighborhood. We call such an approach *variational mechanics*. The variational mechanics point of view is no doubt strange to you at this stage of study and far more subtle and mathematical than the vectorial mechanics approach.

Shifts like the one from the more physically acceptable vectorial mechanics to the more abstract variational mechanics take place in other engineering sciences. Variational methods and techniques are used in the study of plates and shells, elasticity, quantum mechanics, orbital mechanics, statistical thermodynamics, and electromagnetic theory. The variational methods and viewpoints thus are important and even vital in more advanced studies in the engineering sciences, physics, and applied mathematics.

PROBLEMS

10.60. At what position must the operator of the counterweight crane locate the 50-kN counterweight when he lifts the 10-kN load of steel?

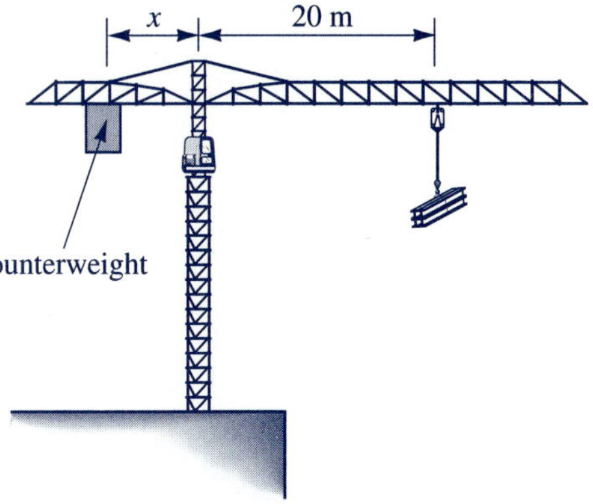

Figure P.10.60.

10.61. What is the relation between P and Q for equilibrium?

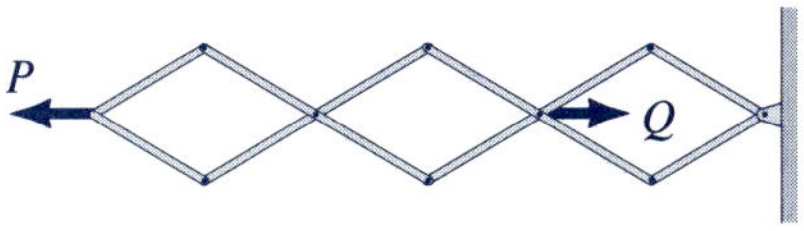

Figure P.10.61.

10.62. A 50 lb-ft torque is applied to a press. The pitch of the screw is .5 in. If there is no friction on the screw, and if the base of the screw can rotate frictionlessly in a base plate A, what is the force P imposed by the base plate on body B?

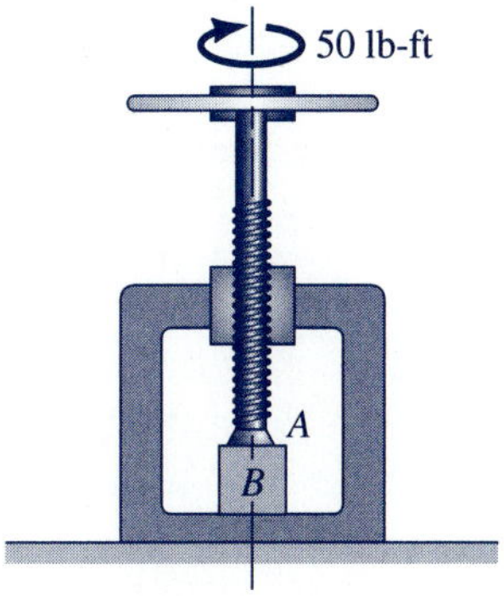

Figure P.10.62.

10.63. The spring is unstretched when $\theta = 30°$. At any position of the pendulum, the spring remains horizontal. If the spring constant is 50 lb/in., at what position will the system be in equilibrium?

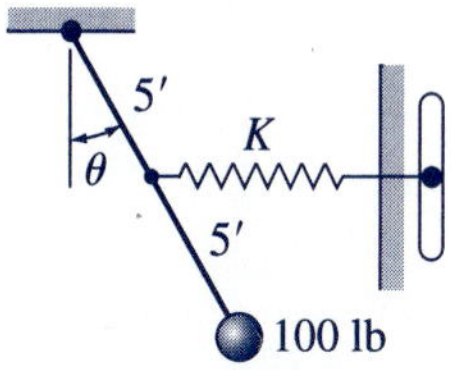

Figure P.10.63.

10.64. If the springs are unstretched when $\theta = \theta_0$, find the angle θ when the weight W is placed on the system. Use the method of stationary potential energy.

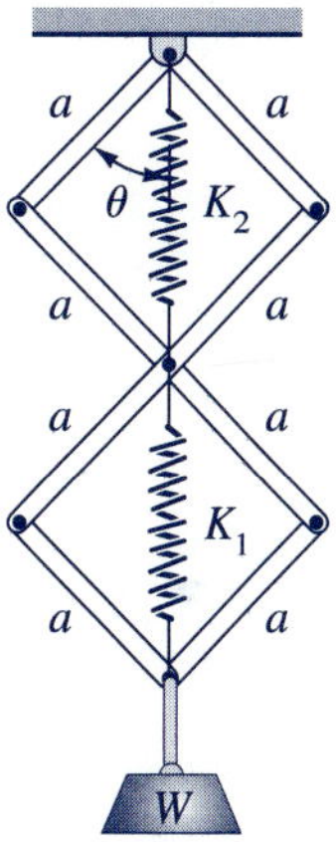

Figure P.10.64.

10.65. A mass M of 20 kg slides with no friction along a vertical rod. Two internal springs K_1 of spring constant 2 N/mm and an external spring K_2 of spring constant 3 N/mm restrain the weight W. If all springs are unstrained at $\theta = 30°$, show that the equilibrium configuration corresponds to $\theta = 27.8°$.

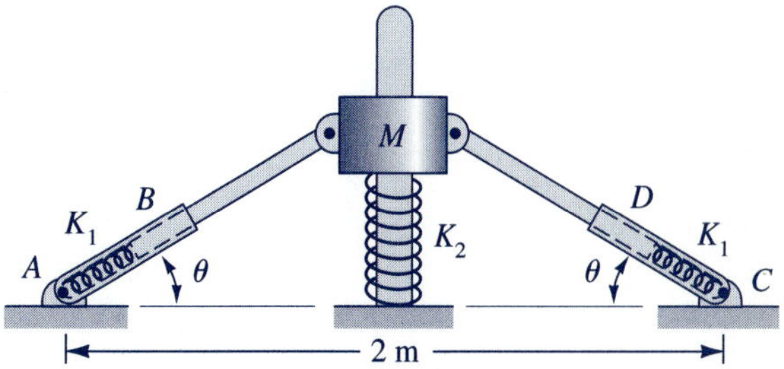

Figure P.10.65.

10.66. When rod AB is in the vertical position, the spring attached to the wheel by a flexible cord is unstretched. Determine all the possible angles θ for equilibrium. Show which are stable and which are not stable. The spring has a spring constant of 8 lb/in.

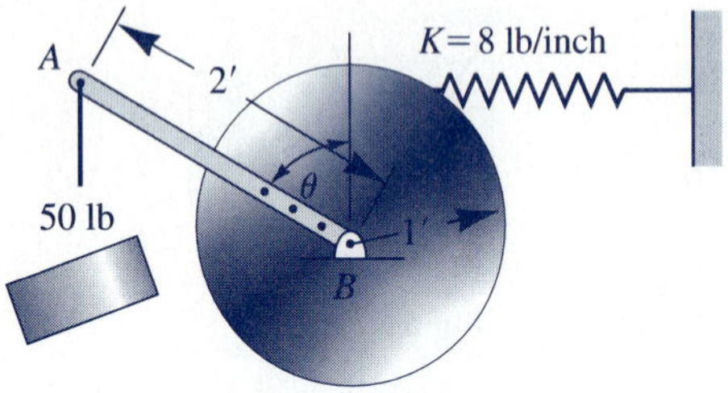

Figure P.10.66.

10.67. Two identical rods are pinned together at B and are pinned at A and C. At B there is a torsional spring requiring 500 N-m/rad of rotation. What is the maximum weight W that each rod can have for a case of stable equilibrium when the rods are collinear?

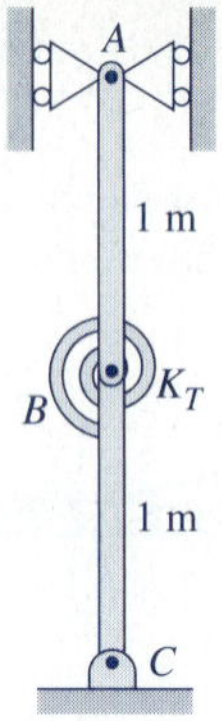

Figure P.10.67.

10.68. A rectangular solid body of height h rests on a cylinder with a semicircular section. Set up criteria for stable and unstable equilibrium in terms of h and R for the position shown.

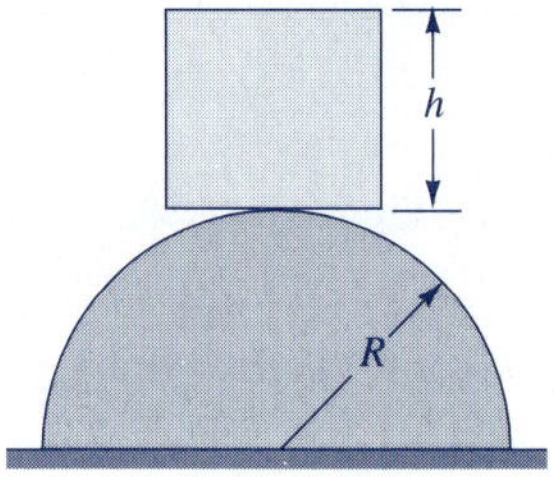

Figure P.10.68.

Dynamics

CHAPTER 11

Kinematics of a Particle—Simple Relative Motion

11.1 Introduction

Kinematics is that phase of mechanics concerned with the study of the motion of particles and rigid bodies without consideration of what has caused the motion. We can consider kinematics as the geometry of motion. Once kinematics is mastered, we can smoothly proceed to the relations between the factors causing the motion and the motion itself. The latter area of study is called *dynamics*. Dynamics can be conveniently separated into the following divisions, most of which we shall study in this text:

1. Dynamics of a single particle. (You will remember from our chapters on statics that a particle is an idealization having no volume but having mass.)
2. Dynamics of a system of particles. This follows division 1 logically and forms the basis for the motion of continuous media such as fluid flow and rigid-body motion.
3. Dynamics of a rigid body. A large portion of this text is concerned with this important part of mechanics.
4. Dynamics of a system of rigid bodies.
5. Dynamics of a continuous deformable medium.

Clearly, from our opening statements, the particle plays a vital role in the study of dynamics. What is the connection between the particle, which is a completely hypothetical concept, and the finite bodies encountered in physical problems? Briefly the relation is this: In many problems, the size and shape of a body are not relevant in the discussion of certain aspects of its motion; only the mass of the object is significant for such computations. For example, in towing a truck up a hill, as shown in Fig. 11.1, we would only be concerned

Figure 11.1. Truck considered as a particle.

with the mass of the truck and not with its shape or size (if we neglect forces from the wind, etc., and the rotational effects of the wheels). The truck can just as well be considered a particle in computing the necessary towing force.

We can present this relationship more precisely in the following manner. As will be learned in the next chapter (Section 12.10), the equation of motion of the center of mass of any body can be formed by:

1. Concentrating the entire mass at the mass center of the body.
2. Applying the total resultant force acting on the body to this hypothetical particle.

When the motion of the mass center characterizes all we need to know about the motion of the body, we employ the particle concept (i.e., we find the motion of the mass center). Thus, if all points of a body have the same velocity at any time t (this is called *translatory motion*), we need only know the motion of the mass center to fully characterize the motion. (This was the case for the truck, where the rotational inertia of the wheels was neglected.) If, additionally, the size of a body is small compared to its trajectory (as in planetary motion, for example), the motion of the center of mass is all that might be needed, and so again we can use the particle concept for such bodies.

Part A: General Notions

11.2 Differentiation of a Vector with Respect to Time

In the study of statics, we dealt with vector quantities. We found it convenient to incorporate the directional nature of these quantities in a certain notation and set of operations. We called the totality of these very useful formulations "vector algebra." We shall again expand our thinking from scalars to vectors—this time for the operations of differentiation and integration with respect to any scalar variable t (such as time).

For scalars, we are concerned only with the variation in magnitude of some quantity that is changing with time. The scalar definition of the time derivative, then, is given as

$$\frac{df(t)}{dt} = \lim_{\Delta t \to 0}\left[\frac{f(t+\Delta t) - f(t)}{\Delta t}\right] \tag{11.1}$$

This operation leads to another function of time, which can once more be differentiated in this manner. The process can be repeated again and again, for suitable functions, to give higher derivatives.

In the case of a vector, the variation in time may be a change in magnitude, a change in direction, or both. The formal definition of the derivative of a vector $\boldsymbol{F}$ with respect to time has the same form as Eq. 11.1:

$$\frac{d\boldsymbol{F}}{dt} = \lim_{\Delta t \to 0}\left[\frac{\boldsymbol{F}(t+\Delta t) - \boldsymbol{F}(t)}{\Delta t}\right] \tag{11.2}$$

If $\boldsymbol{F}$ has no change in direction during the time interval, this operation differs little from the scalar case. However, when $\boldsymbol{F}$ changes in direction, we find for the derivative of $\boldsymbol{F}$ a new vector, having a magnitude as well as a direction, that is different from $\boldsymbol{F}$ itself. This directional consideration can be somewhat troublesome.

Let us consider the rate of change of the position vector for a reference xyz of a particle with respect to time; this rate is defined as the *velocity vector*, $\boldsymbol{V}$, of the particle relative to xyz. Following the definition given by Eq. 11.2, we have

$$\frac{d\boldsymbol{r}}{dt} = \lim_{\Delta t \to 0}\left[\frac{\boldsymbol{r}(t+\Delta t) - \boldsymbol{r}(t)}{\Delta t}\right]$$

The position vectors given in brackets are shown in Fig. 11.2. The subtraction

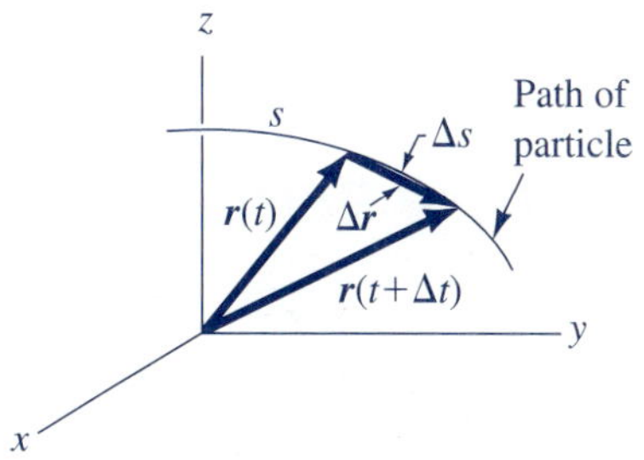

Figure 11.2. Particle at times t and $t + \Delta t$.

between the two vectors gives rise to the displacement vector $\Delta\boldsymbol{r}$, which is shown as a chord connecting two points Δs apart along the trajectory of the particle. Hence, we can say (using the chain rule) that

$$\frac{d\boldsymbol{r}}{dt} = \lim_{\Delta t \to 0}\left(\frac{\Delta\boldsymbol{r}}{\Delta t}\right) = \lim_{\Delta t \to 0}\left(\frac{\Delta\boldsymbol{r}}{\Delta s}\frac{\Delta s}{\Delta t}\right)$$

where we have multiplied and divided by Δs in the last expression. As Δt goes to zero, the direction of $\Delta \boldsymbol{r}$ approaches tangency to the trajectory at position $\boldsymbol{r}(t)$ and approaches Δs in magnitude. Consequently, in the limit, $\Delta \boldsymbol{r}/\Delta s$ becomes a unit vector $\boldsymbol{\epsilon}_t$, tangent to the trajectory. That is

$$\frac{\Delta \boldsymbol{r}}{\Delta s} \rightarrow \frac{\Delta s \boldsymbol{\epsilon}_t}{\Delta s} = \boldsymbol{\epsilon}_t \qquad \therefore \frac{d\boldsymbol{r}}{ds} = \boldsymbol{\epsilon}_t \tag{11.3}$$

We can then say

$$\frac{d\boldsymbol{r}}{dt} = \boldsymbol{V} = \lim_{\Delta t \to 0}\left[\left(\frac{\Delta s}{\Delta t}\right)\left(\frac{\Delta \boldsymbol{r}}{\Delta s}\right)\right] = \frac{ds}{dt}\boldsymbol{\epsilon}_t \tag{11.4}$$

Therefore, $d\boldsymbol{r}/dt$ leads to a vector having a magnitude equal to the speed of the particle and a direction tangent to the trajectory. Keep in mind that there can be any angle between the position vector and the velocity vector. Students seem to want to limit this angle to 90°, which actually restricts you to a circular path. The acceleration vector of a particle can then be given as

$$\boldsymbol{a} = \frac{d\boldsymbol{V}}{dt} = \frac{d^2\boldsymbol{r}}{dt^2} \tag{11.5}$$

The differentiation and integration of vectors $\boldsymbol{r}$, $\boldsymbol{V}$, and $\boldsymbol{a}$ will concern us throughout the text.

Part B: Velocity and Acceleration Calculations

11.3 Introductory Remark

As you know from statics, we can express a vector in many ways. For instance, we can use rectangular components, or, as we will shortly explain, we can use cylindrical components. In evaluating derivatives of vectors with respect to time, we must proceed in accordance with the manner in which the vector has been expressed. In Part B of this chapter, we will therefore examine certain differentiation processes that are used extensively in mechanics. Other differentiation processes will be examined later at appropriate times.

We have already carried out a derivative operation in Section 11.2 directly on the vector $\boldsymbol{r}$. You will see in Section 11.5 that the approach used gives the derivative in terms of *path variables*. This approach will be one of several that we shall now examine with some care.

11.4 Rectangular Components

Consider first the case where the position vector $\boldsymbol{r}$ of a moving particle is expressed for a given reference in terms of rectangular components in the following manner:

$$\boldsymbol{r}(t) = x(t)\boldsymbol{i} + y(t)\boldsymbol{j} + z(t)\boldsymbol{k} \tag{11.6}$$

where $x(t)$, $y(t)$, and $z(t)$ are scalar functions of time. The unit vectors $\boldsymbol{i}, \boldsymbol{j}$, and $\boldsymbol{k}$ are fixed in magnitude and direction at all times, and so we can obtain $d\boldsymbol{r}/dt$ in the following straightforward manner:

$$\frac{d\boldsymbol{r}}{dt} = \boldsymbol{V}(t) = \frac{dx(t)}{dt}\boldsymbol{i} + \frac{dy(t)}{dt}\boldsymbol{j} + \frac{dz(t)}{dt}\boldsymbol{k} = \dot{x}(t)\boldsymbol{i} + \dot{y}(t)\boldsymbol{j} + \dot{z}(t)\boldsymbol{k} \tag{11.7}$$

A second differentiation with respect to time leads to the acceleration vector:

$$\frac{d^2\boldsymbol{r}}{dt^2} = \boldsymbol{a} = \ddot{x}(t)\boldsymbol{i} + \ddot{y}(t)\boldsymbol{j} + \ddot{z}(t)\boldsymbol{k} \tag{11.8}$$

By such a procedure, we have formulated velocity and acceleration vectors in terms of components parallel to the coordinate axes.

Up to this point, we have formulated the rectangular velocity components and the rectangular acceleration components, respectively, by differentiating the position vector once and twice with respect to time. Quite often, we know the acceleration vector of a particle as a function of time in the form

$$\boldsymbol{a}(t) = \ddot{x}(t)\boldsymbol{i} + \ddot{y}(t)\boldsymbol{j} + \ddot{z}(t)\boldsymbol{k} \tag{11.9}$$

and wish to have for this particle the velocity vector or the position vector or any of their components at any time. We then integrate the time function $\ddot{x}(t)$, $\ddot{y}(t)$, and $\ddot{z}(t)$, remembering to include a constant of integration for each integration. For example, consider $\ddot{x}(t)$. Integrating once, we obtain the velocity component $V_x(t)$ as follows:

$$V_x(t) = \int \ddot{x}(t)\,dt + C_1 \tag{11.10}$$

where C_1 is the constant of integration. Knowing V_x at some time t_0, we can determine C_1 by substituting t_0 and $(V_x)_0$ into the equation above and determining C_1. Similarly, for $x(t)$ we obtain from the above:

$$x(t) = \int\left[\int \ddot{x}(t)\,dt\right]dt + C_1t + C_2 \tag{11.11}$$

where C_2 is the second constant of integration. Knowing x at some time t, we can determine C_2 from Eq. 11.11. The same procedure involving additional constants applies to the other acceleration components.

We now illustrate the procedures described above in the following series of examples.

Example 11.1

Pins A and B must always remain in the vertical slot of yoke C, which moves to the right at a constant speed of 6 ft/sec in Fig. 11.3. Furthermore, the pins cannot leave the elliptic slot. (a) What is the speed at which the pins approach each other when the yoke slot is at $x = 5$ ft? (b) What is the rate of change of speed toward each other when the yoke slot is at $x = 5$ ft?

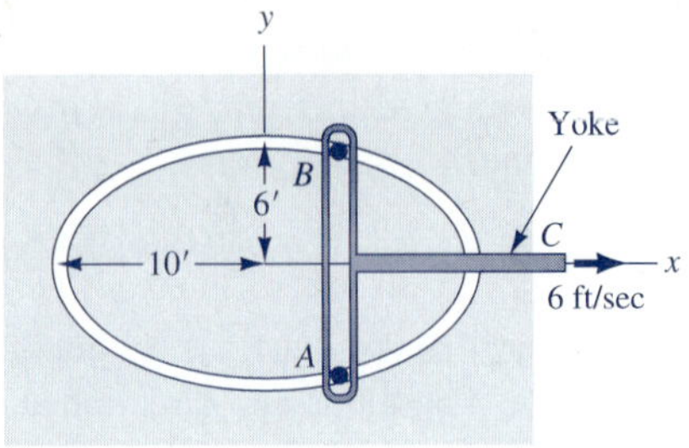

Figure 11.3. Pin slides in slot and yoke.

The equation of the elliptic path in which the pins must move is seen by inspection to be

$$\frac{x^2}{10^2} + \frac{y^2}{6^2} = 1 \qquad \text{(a)}$$

Clearly, if coordinates (x, y) are to represent the coordinates of pin B, they must be time functions such that for any time t the values $x(t)$ and $y(t)$ satisfy Eq. (a). Also, $\dot{x}(t)$ and $\dot{y}(t)$ must be such that pin B moves at all times in the elliptic path. We can satisfy these requirements by first differentiating Eq. (a) with respect to time. Canceling the factor 2, we obtain

$$\frac{x\dot{x}}{10^2} + \frac{y\dot{y}}{6^2} = 0 \qquad \text{(b)}$$

Now $x(t)$, $y(t)$, $\dot{x}(t)$, and $\dot{y}(t)$ must satisfy Eq. (b) for all values of t to ensure that B remains in the elliptic path.

We can now proceed to solve part (a) of this problem. We know that pin B must have a velocity $\dot{x} = 6$ ft/sec because of the yoke. Furthermore, when $x = 5$ ft, we know from Eq. (a) that

$$\frac{5^2}{10^2} + \frac{y^2}{6^2} = 1 \qquad \text{(c)}$$

$$\therefore\ y = 5.20 \text{ ft}$$

Now going to Eq. (b), we can solve for $\dot{y}$ at the instant of interest.

$$\frac{(5)(6)}{10^2} + \frac{(5.20)(\dot{y})}{6^2} = 0$$

Therefore,

$$\dot{y} = -2.08 \text{ ft/sec}$$

Thus, pin B moves downward with a speed of 2.08 ft/sec. Clearly, pin A must move upward with the same speed of 2.08 ft/sec. The pins approach each other at the instant of interest at a speed of 4.16 ft/sec.

Example 11.3

Ballistics Problem 2. A gun empl
The muzzle velocity of the gun is
gun point in order to hit target A sh

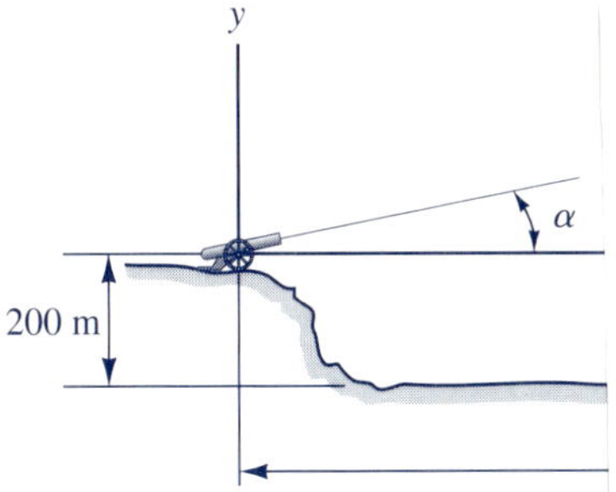

Figure 11.6.

Newton's law for the shell
having its origin at the gun.

$$\ddot{y}(t) =$$
$$\ddot{x}(t) =$$

Integrating, we get

$$\dot{y}(t) = V_y(t)$$
$$\dot{x}(t) = V_x(t)$$

When $t = 0$, we have $\dot{y} = 1{,}000 \sin$
conditions to Eqs. (a) and (b), we sc

$$1{,}000 \sin$$

Therefore,

$$C_1 =$$

Also,

$$1{,}000$$

Therefore,

$$C_2 =$$

Hence, we have

$$\dot{y}(t) = -9.81$$
$$\dot{x}(t) = 1{,}000$$

Integrating again, we get

$$y(t) = -9.81\frac{t^2}{2} +$$
$$x(t) = 1{,}000 \cos$$

Example 11.1 (Continued)

To get the acceleration $\ddot{y}$ of pin B, we first differentiate Eq. (b) with respect to time.

$$\frac{x\ddot{x} + \dot{x}^2}{10^2} + \frac{y\ddot{y} + \dot{y}^2}{6^2} = 0 \qquad \text{(d)}$$

The accelerations $\ddot{x}$ and $\ddot{y}$ must satisfy the equation above. Since the yoke moves at constant speed, we can say immediately that $\ddot{x} = 0$. And using for x, y, $\dot{x}$, and $\dot{y}$ known quantities for the configuration of interest, we can solve for $\ddot{y}$ from Eq. (d). Thus,

$$\frac{0 + 6^2}{10^2} + \frac{5.20\ddot{y} + 2.08^2}{6^2} = 0$$

Therefore,

$$\ddot{y} = -3.32 \text{ ft/sec}^2$$

Pin B must be accelerating downward at a rate of 3.32 ft/sec^2 while pin A accelerates upward at the same rate. The pins accelerate toward each other, then, at a rate of 6.64 ft/sec^2 at the configuration of interest.

In the motion of particles near the earth's surface, such as the motion of shells or ballistic missiles, we can often simplify the problem by neglecting air resistance and taking the acceleration of gravity g as constant (32.2 ft/sec^2 or 9.81 m/sec^2). For such a case (see Fig. 11.4), we know immediately that $\ddot{y}(t) = -g$ and $\ddot{x}(t) = \ddot{z}(t) = 0$. On integrating these accelerations, we can often determine for the particle useful information as to velocities or positions at certain times of interest in the problem. We illustrate this procedure in the following examples.

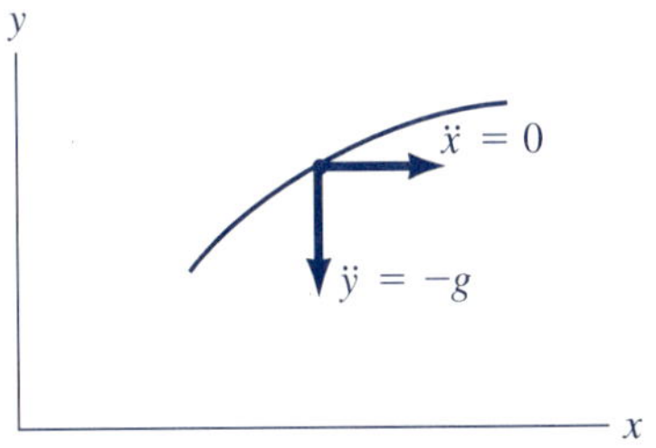

Figure 11.4. Simple ballistic motion of a shell.

Example 11.2 (Continued)

Therefore,

$16.1t^2 - 7$

Using the quadratic formula, we ge

$t = $

Substituting this value of t into Eq.

$d = (2{,}900)(48.$

To get the *maximum height* y_{max}, f
from Eq. (c) we get

$0 = -3$

Therefore,

$t =$

Now substitute $t = 24.1$ sec into Eq.

$y_{max} = -(16.1)(2$

$\therefore\ y_{max} = 9,$

Finally, to get the *trajectory* c
solve for t in Eq. (h) and substitute t

$y = -(16.1)\left(\frac{x}{2{,}90}\right.$

Therefore,

$y = -1.917 \times$

Clearly, the trajectory is that of a *pa*

Since we have not formally carried out the differentiation of a vector with respect to a spatial coordinate, we shall carry out the derivative $d\boldsymbol{\epsilon}_t/ds$ needed in Eq. 11.14 from the basic definition. Thus,

$$\frac{d\boldsymbol{\epsilon}_t}{ds} = \lim_{\Delta s \to 0}\left[\frac{\boldsymbol{\epsilon}_t(s + \Delta s) - \boldsymbol{\epsilon}_t(s)}{\Delta s}\right] = \lim_{\Delta s \to 0}\left(\frac{\Delta\boldsymbol{\epsilon}_t}{\Delta s}\right) \tag{11.15}$$

The vectors $\boldsymbol{\epsilon}_t(s)$ and $\boldsymbol{\epsilon}_t(s + \Delta s)$ are shown in Fig. 11.11(a) along the path and are also shown (enlarged) with $\Delta\boldsymbol{\epsilon}_t$ as a vector triangle in Fig. 11.11(b). As pointed out earlier, for small enough Δs the lines of action of the unit vectors $\boldsymbol{\epsilon}_t(s)$ and $\boldsymbol{\epsilon}_t(s + \Delta s)$ will intersect to form a plane as shown in Fig. 11.11(a). Now in this plane, draw normal lines to the aforementioned vectors at the respective positions s and $s + \Delta s$. These lines will intersect at some point O, as shown in the diagram. Next, consider what happens to the plane and to point O as $\Delta s \to 0$. Clearly, the limiting plane is our osculating plane at s [see Fig. 11.11(c)]. Furthermore, the limiting position arrived at for point O is *in the osculating plane* and is called the *center of curvature* for the path at s. The distance between O and s is denoted as R and is called the *radius of curvature*. Finally, the vector $\Delta\boldsymbol{\epsilon}_t$ (see Fig. 11.11 (b)), in the limit as $\Delta s \to 0$, ends up in the osculating plane normal to the path at s and directed toward the center of curvature. The unit vector collinear with the limiting vector for $\Delta\boldsymbol{\epsilon}_t$ is denoted as $\boldsymbol{\epsilon}_n$ and is called the *principal normal vector*.

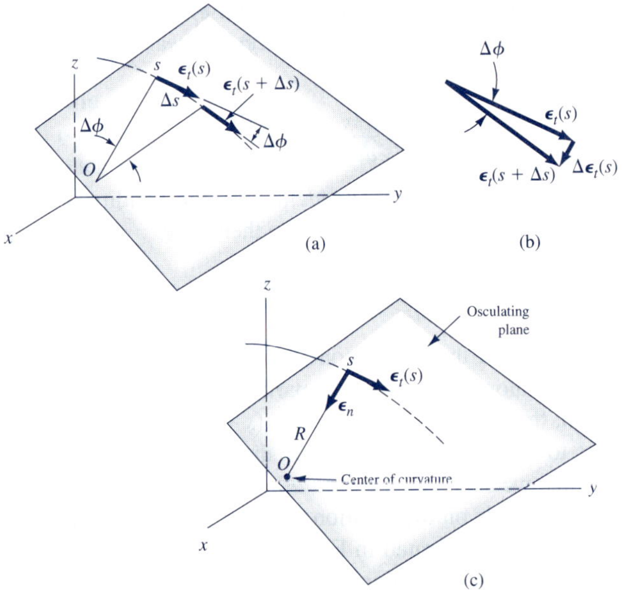

Figure 11.11. Development of the osculating plane and the center of curvature.

With the limiting *direction* of $\Delta\boldsymbol{\epsilon}_t$ established, we next evaluate the *magnitude* of $\Delta\boldsymbol{\epsilon}_t$ as an approximate value that becomes correct as $\Delta s \to 0$. Observing the vector triangle in Fig. 11.11(b), we can accordingly say:

$$|\Delta\boldsymbol{\epsilon}_t| \approx |\boldsymbol{\epsilon}_t|\Delta\phi = \Delta\phi \tag{11.16}$$

Example 11.1 (Continued)

To get the acceleration $\ddot{y}$ of pin B, we first differentiate Eq. (b) with respect to time.

$$\frac{x\ddot{x} + \dot{x}^2}{10^2} + \frac{y\ddot{y} + \dot{y}^2}{6^2} = 0 \tag{d}$$

The accelerations $\ddot{x}$ and $\ddot{y}$ must satisfy the equation above. Since the yoke moves at constant speed, we can say immediately that $\ddot{x} = 0$. And using for x, y, $\dot{x}$, and $\dot{y}$ known quantities for the configuration of interest, we can solve for $\ddot{y}$ from Eq. (d). Thus,

$$\frac{0 + 6^2}{10^2} + \frac{5.20\ddot{y} + 2.08^2}{6^2} = 0$$

Therefore,

$$\ddot{y} = -3.32 \text{ ft/sec}^2$$

Pin B must be accelerating downward at a rate of 3.32 ft/sec^2 while pin A accelerates upward at the same rate. The pins accelerate toward each other, then, at a rate of 6.64 ft/sec^2 at the configuration of interest.

In the motion of particles near the earth's surface, such as the motion of shells or ballistic missiles, we can often simplify the problem by neglecting air resistance and taking the acceleration of gravity g as constant (32.2 ft/sec^2 or 9.81 m/sec^2). For such a case (see Fig. 11.4), we know immediately that $\ddot{y}(t) = -g$ and $\ddot{x}(t) = \ddot{z}(t) = 0$. On integrating these accelerations, we can often determine for the particle useful information as to velocities or positions at certain times of interest in the problem. We illustrate this procedure in the following examples.

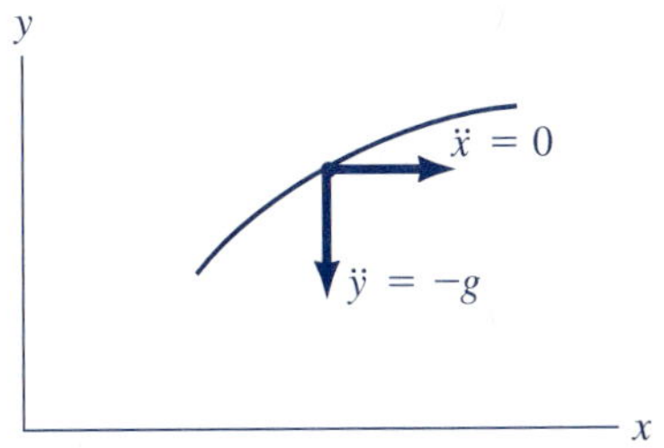

Figure 11.4. Simple ballistic motion of a shell.

Example 11.2

Ballistics Problem 1. A shell is fired from a hill 500 ft above a plain. The angle α of firing (see Fig. 11.5) is 15° above the horizontal, and the muzzle velocity V_0 is 3,000 ft/sec. At what horizontal distance, d, will the shell hit the plain if we neglect friction of the air? What is the maximum height of the shell above the plain? Finally, determine the trajectory of the shell [i.e., find $y = f(x)$].

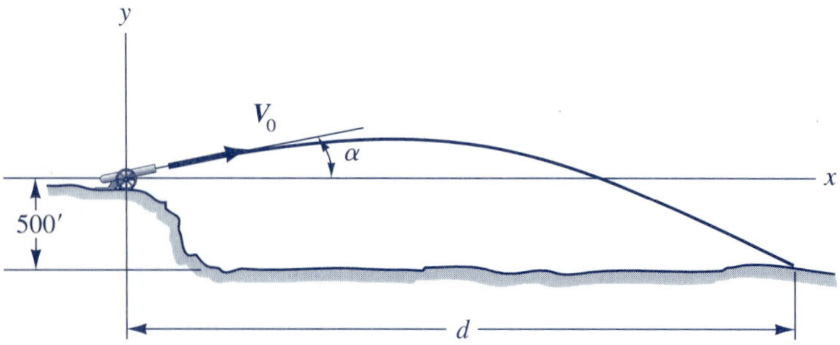

Figure 11.5 Ballistics problem: find *d*.

We know immediately that

$$\ddot{y}(t) = \frac{dV_y}{dt} = -32.2 \text{ ft/sec}^2 \quad \text{(a)}$$

$$\ddot{x}(t) = \frac{dV_x}{dt} = 0 \quad \text{(b)}$$

We need not bother with $\ddot{z}(t)$, since the motion is coplanar with $\dot{z}(t) = z = 0$ at all times. We next separate the velocity variables from the time variables by bringing dt to the right sides of the previous equations. Thus

$$dV_y = -32.2\, dt$$
$$dV_x = 0\, dt$$

Integrating the above equations, we get

$$V_y(t) = -32.2t + C_1$$
$$V_x(t) = C_2$$

We shall take $t = 0$ at the instant the cannon is fired. At this instant, we know V_y and V_x and can determine C_1 and C_2. Thus,

$$V_y(0) = 3{,}000 \sin 15° = (-32.2)(0) + C_1$$

Example 11.2 (Continued)

Therefore,

$$C_1 = V_y(0) = 776 \text{ ft/sec}$$

Also

$$V_x(0) = 3{,}000 \cos 15° = C_2$$

Therefore,

$$C_2 = V_x(0) = 2{,}900 \text{ ft/sec}$$

We can give the velocity components of the shell now as follows:

$$V_y(t) = \frac{dy}{dt} = -32.2t + 776 \text{ ft/sec} \qquad \text{(c)}$$

$$V_x(t) = \frac{dx}{dt} = 2{,}900 \text{ ft/sec} \qquad \text{(d)}$$

Thus, the horizontal velocity is constant. Separating the position and time variables and then integrating, we get the x and y coordinates of the shell.

$$y(t) = -32.2\frac{t^2}{2} + 776t + C_3 \qquad \text{(e)}$$

$$x(t) = 2{,}900t + C_4 \qquad \text{(f)}$$

When $t = 0$, $y = x = 0$. Thus, from Eqs. (e) and (f), we clearly see that $C_3 = C_4 = 0$. The coordinates of the shell are then

$$y(t) = -16.1t^2 + 776t \qquad \text{(g)}$$

$$x(t) = 2{,}900t \qquad \text{(h)}$$

To determine *distance d*, first find the time t for the impact of the shell on the plain. That is, set $y = -500$ in Eq. (g) and solve for the time t. Thus,

$$-500 = -16.1t^2 + 776t$$

Example 11.2 (Continued)

Therefore,

$$16.1t^2 - 776t - 500 = 0$$

Using the quadratic formula, we get for t:

$$t = 48.8 \text{ sec}$$

Substituting this value of t into Eq. (h), we get

$$d = (2{,}900)(48.8) = \boxed{141{,}500 \text{ ft}}$$

To get the *maximum height* y_{max}, first find the time t when $V_y = 0$. Thus, from Eq. (c) we get

$$0 = -32.2t + 776$$

Therefore,

$$t = 24.1 \text{ sec}$$

Now substitute $t = 24.1$ sec into Eq. (g). This gives us y_{max}.

$$y_{max} = -(16.1)(24.1)^2 + (776)(24.1)$$

$$\therefore \boxed{y_{max} = 9{,}350 \text{ ft}}$$

Finally, to get the *trajectory* of the shell (i.e., y as a function of x), solve for t in Eq. (h) and substitute this into Eq. (g). We then have

$$y = -(16.1)\left(\frac{x}{2{,}900}\right)^2 + (776)\left(\frac{x}{2{,}900}\right)$$

Therefore,

$$\boxed{y = -1.917 \times 10^{-6} x^2 + .268x}$$

Clearly, the trajectory is that of a *parabola*.

Example 11.3

Ballistics Problem 2. A gun emplacement is shown on a cliff in Fig. 11.6. The muzzle velocity of the gun is 1,000 m/sec. At what angle α must the gun point in order to hit target A shown in the diagram? Neglect friction.

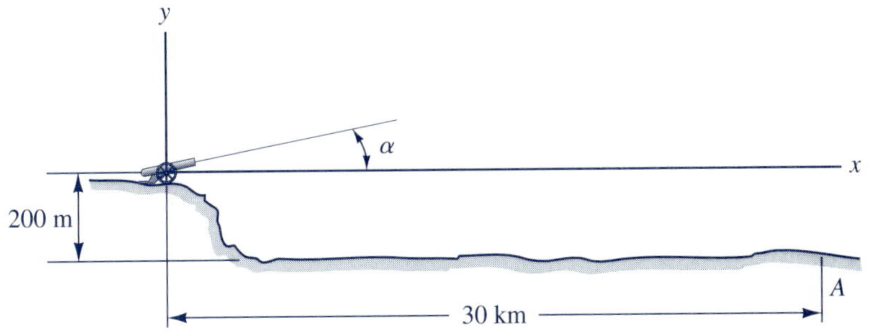

Figure 11.6. Find α to hit A.

Newton's law for the shell is given as follows for a reference xy having its origin at the gun.

$$\ddot{y}(t) = -9.81$$
$$\ddot{x}(t) = 0$$

Integrating, we get

$$\dot{y}(t) = V_y(t) = -9.81t + C_1 \tag{a}$$
$$\dot{x}(t) = V_x(t) = C_2 \tag{b}$$

When $t = 0$, we have $\dot{y} = 1{,}000 \sin \alpha$ and $\dot{x} = 1{,}000 \cos \alpha$. Applying these conditions to Eqs. (a) and (b), we solve for C_1 and C_2. Thus,

$$1{,}000 \sin \alpha = 0 + C_1$$

Therefore,

$$C_1 = 1{,}000 \sin \alpha$$

Also,

$$1{,}000 \cos \alpha = C_2$$

Therefore,

$$C_2 = 1{,}000 \cos \alpha$$

Hence, we have

$$\dot{y}(t) = -9.81t + 1{,}000 \sin \alpha$$
$$\dot{x}(t) = 1{,}000 \cos \alpha$$

Integrating again, we get

$$y(t) = -9.81\frac{t^2}{2} + 1{,}000 \sin \alpha\, t + C_3$$
$$x(t) = 1{,}000 \cos \alpha\, t + C_4$$

Example 11.3 (Continued)

When $t = 0$, $x = y = 0$. Hence, it is clear that $C_3 = C_4 = 0$. Thus, we have

$$y = -4.095t^2 + 1{,}000 \sin \alpha\, t \qquad \text{(c)}$$

$$x = 1{,}000 \cos \alpha\, t \qquad \text{(d)}$$

To get the *trajectory*, we solve for t in Eq. (d) and substitute into Eq. (c).

$$\begin{aligned} y &= -4.095 \frac{x^2}{(1{,}000 \cos \alpha)^2} + 1{,}000 \sin \alpha \frac{x}{(1{,}000 \cos \alpha)} \\ &= -4.095 \times 10^{-6} \frac{x^2}{\cos^2 \alpha} + x \tan \alpha \end{aligned} \qquad \text{(e)}$$

where we have replaced $\sin \alpha / \cos \alpha$ by $\tan \alpha$. When $x = 30$ km (i.e., 30,000 m), $y = -200$ m. Hence, we have on substituting these data into Eq. (e):

$$-200 = -4.095 \times 10^{-6} \frac{(30{,}000)^2}{\cos^2 \alpha} + 30{,}000 \tan \alpha$$

Replace $1/\cos^2 \alpha$ by $\sec^2 \alpha = \left(1 + \tan^2 \alpha\right)$:

$$-200 = -4.095 \times 10^{-6} (30{,}000)^2 (1 + \tan^2 \alpha) + 30{,}000 \tan \alpha$$

Therefore,

$$\tan^2 \alpha - 6.796 \tan \alpha + .955 = 0 \qquad \text{(f)}$$

Using the quadratic formula, we find the following angles:

$$\alpha_1 = 8.17^\circ$$
$$\alpha_2 = 81.44^\circ$$

There are thus *two* possible firing angles that will permit the shell to hit the target, as shown in Fig. 11.7.

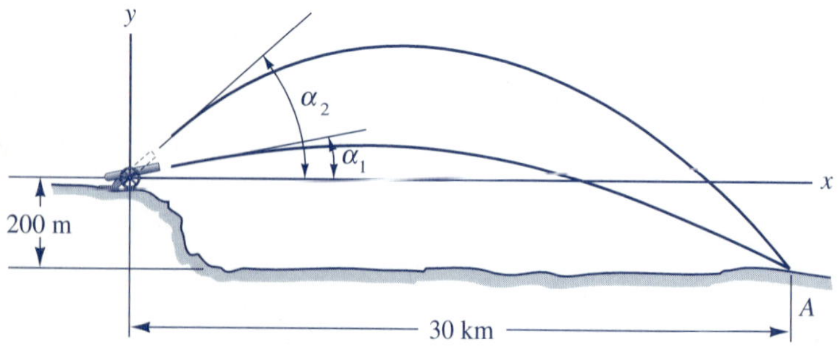

Figure 11.7. Two firing angles are possible.

Example 11.4

The engine room of a freighter is on fire. A fire-fighting tugboat has drawn alongside and is directing a stream of water to enter the stack of the freighter as shown in Fig. 11.8. If the initial speed of the jet of water is 70 ft/sec, is there a value of α of the issuing jet of water that will do the job? If so, what should α be?

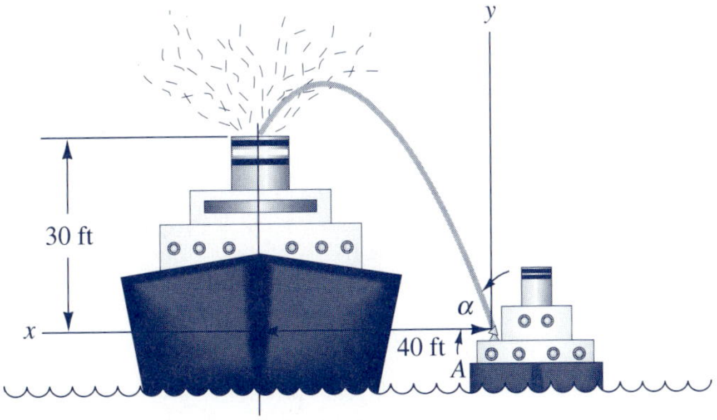

Figure 11.8. Fire-fighting tugboat directing a jet of water into the stack of a freighter.

Consider a particle within the stream of water. Neglecting friction, **Newton's law** for the particle is given as follows:

$$\ddot{y} = -32.2 \text{ ft/sec}^2 \qquad \ddot{x} = 0 \text{ ft/sec}^2$$

Integrating twice, and using initial conditions at A, we get

$$\dot{y} = -32.2t + 70 \sin\alpha \text{ ft/sec} \quad \text{(a)} \qquad \dot{x} = 70\cos\alpha \text{ ft/sec} \quad \text{(c)}$$

$$y = -16.1t^2 + 70\sin\alpha\, t \text{ ft} \quad \text{(b)} \qquad x = 70\cos\alpha\, t \text{ ft} \quad \text{(d)}$$

Solve for t from Eq. (d) and substitute into Eq. (b) to get

$$y = -16.1\left[\frac{x}{70\cos\alpha}\right]^2 + 70\sin\alpha\left[\frac{x}{70\cos\alpha}\right]$$

Replace $\cos^2\alpha$ by $1/(1+\tan^2\alpha)$ and $(\sin\alpha/\cos\alpha)$ by $\tan\alpha$ in the previous equation and then substitute the coordinates of point B at the stack where the water is supposed to reach. That is, set $x = 40$ ft and $y = 30$ ft. We then get

$$30 = -(3.29\times10^{-3})(40^2)(1+\tan^2\alpha) + 40\tan\alpha$$
$$\therefore\ \tan^2\alpha - 7.61\tan\alpha + 6.71 = 0$$

Using the quadratic formula we get

$$\tan\alpha = \frac{7.61 \pm \sqrt{7.61^2 - (4)(6.71)}}{2} = 1.017;\ 6.59$$

Example 11.4 (Continued)

We thus have two angles for α, each of which will theoretically cause the stream to go to point B of the stack. These angles are

$$\alpha_1 = 45.50° \qquad \alpha_2 = 81.37°$$

Does one, none, or both angles above yield a stream of water that will come down at B so as to enter the stack? We can determine this by finding the maximum value of y and locating the position x for this maximum value. To do this, we set $\dot{y} = 0$ and solve for t using each α. Thus we have

$$0 = -32.2t + 70\sin\begin{Bmatrix}45.50°\\81.37°\end{Bmatrix}$$

$$\therefore t = \begin{Bmatrix}1.551\\2.149\end{Bmatrix}\text{ sec}$$

Now get the position x for maximum elevation for each case as well as the elevation maximum, y_{max}.

For $\alpha = 45.50°$:

$$x = (70)(\cos 45.50°)(1.551) = 76.1\text{ ft}$$

$$y_{max} = -(16.1)(1.551)^2 + (70)(\sin 45.50°)(1.551) = 38.7\text{ ft}$$

For $\alpha = 81.37°$:

$$x = (70)(\cos 81.37°)(2.149) = 22.6\text{ ft}$$

$$y_{max} = -(16.1)(2.149)^2 + (70)(\sin 81.37°)(2.149) = 74.4\text{ ft}$$

A sketch of the two possible trajectories is shown in Fig. 11.9. Clearly the shallow trajectory will hit the side of the stack and is unacceptable, while the high trajectory will deposit water inside the stack and is thus the desired trajectory. Thus,

$$\alpha = 81.37°$$

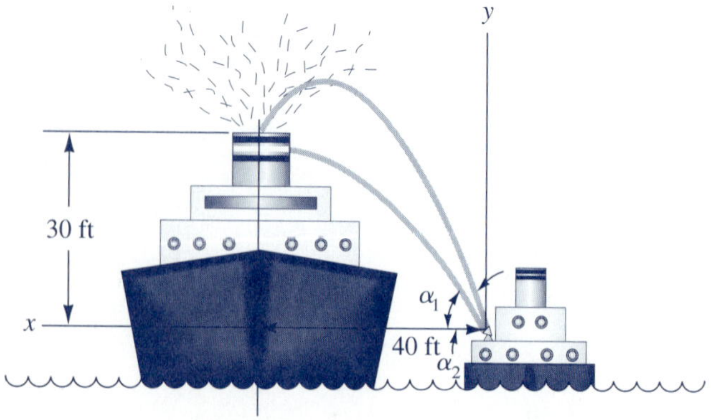

Figure 11.9. Two possible trajectories of the jet.

We do not always know the variation of the position vector with time in the form of Eq. 11.6. Furthermore, it may be that the components of velocity and acceleration that we desire are not those parallel to a fixed Cartesian reference. The evaluation of $\boldsymbol{V}$ and $\boldsymbol{a}$ for certain other circumstances will be considered in the following sections.

11.5 Velocity and Acceleration in Terms of Path Variables

We have formulated velocity and acceleration for the case where the rectangular coordinates of a particle are known as functions of time. We now explore another approach in which the formulations are carried out in terms of the path variables of the particle, that is, in terms of geometrical parameters of the path and the speed and the rate of change of speed of the particle along the path. These results are particularly useful when a particle moves along a path that we know apriori (such as the case of a roller coaster).

As a matter of fact, in Section 11.2 (Eq. 11.4) we expressed the velocity vector in terms of path variables in the following form:

$$\boldsymbol{V} = \frac{ds}{dt}\boldsymbol{\epsilon}_t \tag{11.12}$$

where ds/dt represents the speed along the path and $\boldsymbol{\epsilon}_t = d\boldsymbol{r}/ds$ (see Eq. 11.3) is the unit vector tangent to the path (and hence collinear with the velocity vector). The acceleration becomes

$$\frac{d\mathbf{V}}{dt} = \boldsymbol{a} = \frac{d^2s}{dt^2}\boldsymbol{\epsilon}_t + \frac{ds}{dt}\frac{d\boldsymbol{\epsilon}_t}{dt} \tag{11.13}$$

Replace $d\boldsymbol{\epsilon}_t/dt$ in this expression by $(d\boldsymbol{\epsilon}_t/ds)(ds/dt)$, the validity of which is assured by the chain rule of differentiation. We then have

$$\boldsymbol{a} = \frac{d^2s}{dt^2}\boldsymbol{\epsilon}_t + \left(\frac{ds}{dt}\right)^2\frac{d\boldsymbol{\epsilon}_t}{ds} \tag{11.14}$$

Before proceeding further, let us consider the unit vector $\boldsymbol{\epsilon}_t$ at two positions that are Δs apart along the path of the particle as shown in Fig. 11.10. If Δs is small enough, the unit vectors $\boldsymbol{\epsilon}_t(s)$ and $\boldsymbol{\epsilon}_t(s + \Delta s)$ can be considered to intersect and thus to form a plane. If $\Delta s \to 0$, these unit vectors then form a *limiting plane*, which we shall call the *osculating plane*.[1] The plane will have an orientation that depends on the position s on the path of the particle. The osculating plane at $\boldsymbol{r}(t)$ is illustrated in Fig. 11.10. Having defined the osculating plane, let us continue discussion of Eq. 11.14.

Figure 11.10. Osculating plane at $\boldsymbol{r}(t)$.

[1]From the definition, it should be apparent that the osculating plane at position s along a curve is actually *tangent* to the curve at position s. Since osculate means to kiss, the plane "kisses" the curve, as it were, at s.

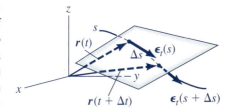

Since we have not formally carried out the differentiation of a vector with respect to a spatial coordinate, we shall carry out the derivative $d\boldsymbol{\epsilon}_t/ds$ needed in Eq. 11.14 from the basic definition. Thus,

$$\frac{d\boldsymbol{\epsilon}_t}{ds} = \lim_{\Delta s \to 0}\left[\frac{\boldsymbol{\epsilon}_t(s+\Delta s) - \boldsymbol{\epsilon}_t(s)}{\Delta s}\right] = \lim_{\Delta s \to 0}\left(\frac{\Delta\boldsymbol{\epsilon}_t}{\Delta s}\right) \tag{11.15}$$

The vectors $\boldsymbol{\epsilon}_t(s)$ and $\boldsymbol{\epsilon}_t(s + \Delta s)$ are shown in Fig. 11.11(a) along the path and are also shown (enlarged) with $\Delta\boldsymbol{\epsilon}_t$ as a vector triangle in Fig. 11.11(b). As pointed out earlier, for small enough Δs the lines of action of the unit vectors $\boldsymbol{\epsilon}_t(s)$ and $\boldsymbol{\epsilon}_t(s + \Delta s)$ will intersect to form a plane as shown in Fig. 11.11(a). Now in this plane, draw normal lines to the aforementioned vectors at the respective positions s and $s + \Delta s$. These lines will intersect at some point O, as shown in the diagram. Next, consider what happens to the plane and to point O as $\Delta s \to 0$. Clearly, the limiting plane is our osculating plane at s [see Fig. 11.11(c)]. Furthermore, the limiting position arrived at for point O is *in the osculating plane* and is called the *center of curvature* for the path at s. The distance between O and s is denoted as R and is called the *radius of curvature*. Finally, the vector $\Delta\boldsymbol{\epsilon}_t$ (see Fig. 11.11 (b)), in the limit as $\Delta s \to 0$, ends up in the osculating plane normal to the path at s and directed toward the center of curvature. The unit vector collinear with the limiting vector for $\Delta\boldsymbol{\epsilon}_t$ is denoted as $\boldsymbol{\epsilon}_n$ and is called the *principal normal vector*.

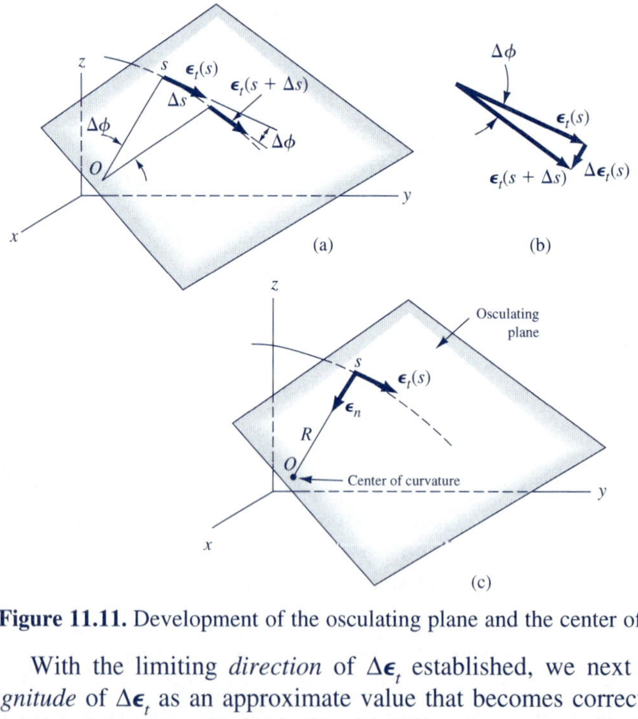

Figure 11.11. Development of the osculating plane and the center of curvature.

With the limiting *direction* of $\Delta\boldsymbol{\epsilon}_t$ established, we next evaluate the *magnitude* of $\Delta\boldsymbol{\epsilon}_t$ as an approximate value that becomes correct as $\Delta s \to 0$. Observing the vector triangle in Fig. 11.11(b), we can accordingly say:

$$|\Delta\boldsymbol{\epsilon}_t| \approx |\boldsymbol{\epsilon}_t|\Delta\phi = \Delta\phi \tag{11.16}$$

Next, we note in Fig. 11.11(a) that the lines from point O to the points s and $s + \Delta s$ along the trajectory form the same angle $\Delta\phi$ as is between the vectors $\boldsymbol{\epsilon}_t(s)$ and $\boldsymbol{\epsilon}_t(s + \Delta s)$ in the vector triangle, and so we can say:

$$\Delta\phi = \frac{\Delta s}{Os} \approx \frac{\Delta s}{R} \tag{11.17}$$

Hence, we have for Eq. 11.16:

$$|\Delta\boldsymbol{\epsilon}_t| \approx \frac{\Delta s}{R} \tag{11.18}$$

We thus have the magnitude of $\Delta\boldsymbol{\epsilon}_t$ established in an approximate manner. Using $\boldsymbol{\epsilon}_n$, the principal normal at s, to approximate the direction of $\Delta\boldsymbol{\epsilon}_t$ we can write

$$\Delta\boldsymbol{\epsilon}_t \approx \frac{\Delta s}{R}\boldsymbol{\epsilon}_n$$

If we use this result in the limiting process of Eq. 11.15 (where it becomes exact), the evaluation of $d\boldsymbol{\epsilon}_t/ds$ becomes

$$\frac{d\boldsymbol{\epsilon}_t}{ds} = \lim_{\Delta s\to 0}\left(\frac{\Delta\boldsymbol{\epsilon}_t}{\Delta s}\right) = \lim_{\Delta s\to 0}\left[\frac{(\Delta s/R)\boldsymbol{\epsilon}_n}{\Delta s}\right] = \frac{\boldsymbol{\epsilon}_n}{R} \tag{11.19}$$

When we substitute Eq. 11.19 into Eq. 11.14, the acceleration vector becomes

$$\boldsymbol{a} = \frac{d^2 s}{dt^2}\boldsymbol{\epsilon}_t + \frac{(ds/dt)^2}{R}\boldsymbol{\epsilon}_n \tag{11.20}$$

We thus have two components of acceleration: *one component in a direction tangent to the path and one component in the osculating plane at right angles to the path and pointing toward the center of curvature*. These components are of great importance in certain problems.

For the special case of a *plane curve*, we learned in analytic geometry that the radius of curvature R is given by the relation

$$R = \frac{\left[1 + \left(\frac{dy}{dx}\right)^2\right]^{3/2}}{\left|\frac{d^2y}{dx^2}\right|} \tag{11.21}$$

Furthermore, in the case of a plane curve, the osculating plane at every point clearly must correspond to the plane of the curve, and the computation of unit vectors $\boldsymbol{\epsilon}_n$ and $\boldsymbol{\epsilon}_t$ is quite simple, as will be illustrated in Example 11.5.

How do we get the principal normal vector $\boldsymbol{\epsilon}_n$, the radius of curvature R, and the direction of the osculating plane for a three-dimensional curve? One procedure is to evaluate $\boldsymbol{\epsilon}_t$ as a function of s and then differentiate this vector with respect to s. Accordingly, from Eq. 11.19 we can then determine $\boldsymbol{\epsilon}_n$ as well as R. We establish the direction of the osculating plane by taking the cross product $\boldsymbol{\epsilon}_n \times \boldsymbol{\epsilon}_t$, to get a unit vector normal to the osculating plane. This vector is called the *binormal vector*. This is illustrated in starred problem 11.7.

Example 11.5

A particle is moving along a circular path in the xy plane (Fig. 11.12). When the particle crosses the x axis, it has an acceleration along the path of 5 ft/sec^2 and is moving with the speed of 20 ft/sec in the negative y direction. What is the total acceleration of the particle?

Clearly, the osculating plane must be the plane of the path. Hence, R is 2 ft, as is shown in the diagram. We need simply to employ Eq. 11.20 for the desired result. Thus,

$$\boldsymbol{a} = 5\boldsymbol{\epsilon}_t + \frac{20^2}{2}\boldsymbol{\epsilon}_n \text{ ft/sec}^2$$

For the xy reference, the acceleration is

$$\boldsymbol{a} = -5\boldsymbol{j} - 200\boldsymbol{i} \text{ ft/sec}^2$$

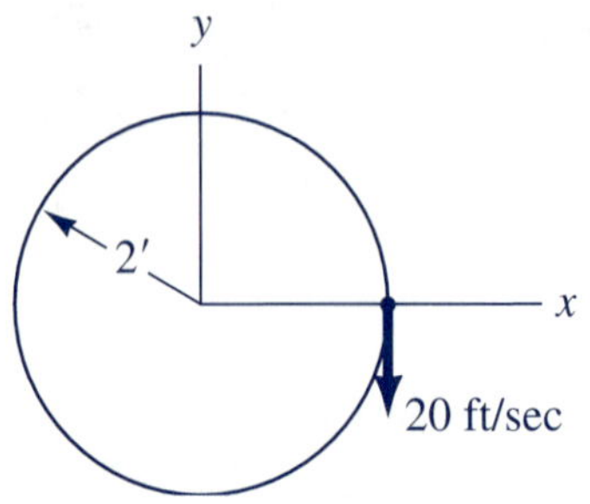

Figure 11.12. Particle on circular path.

Example 11.6

A particle is moving in the xy plane along a parabolic path given as $y = 1.22\sqrt{x}$ (see Fig. 11.13) with x and y in meters. At position A, the particle has a speed of 3 m/sec and has a rate of change of speed of 3 m/sec^2 along the path. What is the acceleration vector of the particle at this position?

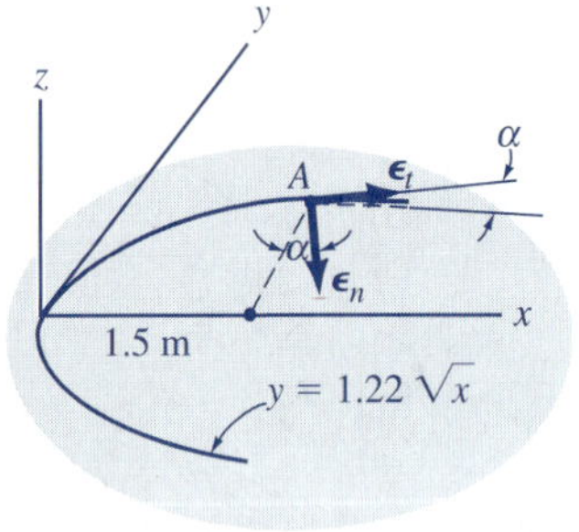

Figure 11.13. Particle on a parabolic path.

We first find $\boldsymbol{\epsilon}_t$ by noting from the diagram that

$$\boldsymbol{\epsilon}_t = \cos\alpha\,\boldsymbol{i} + \sin\alpha\,\boldsymbol{j} \tag{a}$$

Example 11.6 (Continued)

where

$$\tan\alpha = \frac{dy}{dx} = \frac{d}{dx}\left(1.22\sqrt{x}\right) = \frac{.610}{\sqrt{x}} \qquad \text{(b)}$$

At the position of interest ($x = 1.5$ m) we have

$$\tan\alpha = \frac{.610}{\sqrt{1.5}} = \frac{1}{2}$$

Therefore,

$$\alpha = 26.5°$$

Hence,

$$\boldsymbol{\epsilon}_t = .895\boldsymbol{i} + .446\boldsymbol{j} \qquad \text{(c)}$$

As for $\boldsymbol{\epsilon}_n$, we see from the diagram that

$$\boldsymbol{\epsilon}_n = \sin\alpha\,\boldsymbol{i} - \cos\alpha\,\boldsymbol{j}$$

Therefore,

$$\boldsymbol{\epsilon}_n = .446\boldsymbol{i} - .895\boldsymbol{j} \qquad \text{(d)}$$

Next, employing Eq. 11.21, we can find R. We shall need the following results for this step:

$$\frac{dy}{dx} = .610x^{-1/2} \qquad \text{(e)}$$

$$\frac{d^2y}{dx^2} = -.305x^{-3/2} \qquad \text{(f)}$$

Substituting Eqs. (e) and (f) into Eq. 11.21, we have for R:

$$R = \frac{\left[1 + \left(.610x^{-1/2}\right)^2\right]^{3/2}}{.305x^{-3/2}} \qquad \text{(g)}$$

At the position of interest, $x = 1.5$, we get

$$R = 8.40 \text{ m} \qquad \text{(h)}$$

We can now give the desired acceleration vector. Thus, from Eq. 11.20, we have

$$\boldsymbol{a} = 3(.895\boldsymbol{i} + .446\boldsymbol{j}) + \frac{9}{8.40}(.446\boldsymbol{i} - .895\boldsymbol{j}) \qquad \text{(i)}$$

$$\therefore \quad \boldsymbol{a} = 3.16\boldsymbol{i} + .379\boldsymbol{j} \text{ m/sec}^2$$

*Example 11.7

A particle is made to move along a spiral path, as is shown in Fig. 11.14.

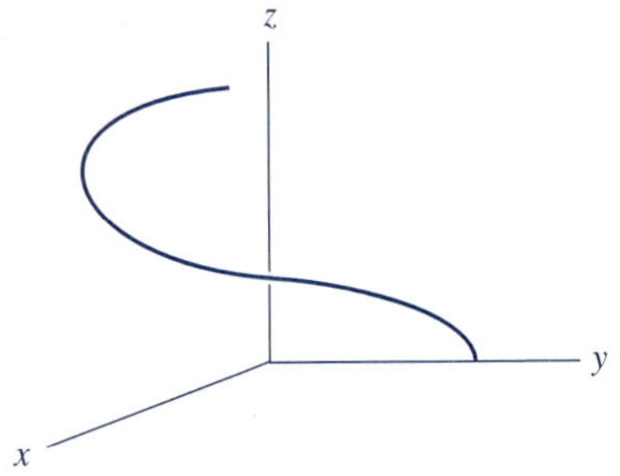

Figure 11.14.

The equations representing the *path* are given parametrically in terms of the variable τ in the following manner:

$$x_p = A \sin \eta\tau$$
$$y_p = A \cos \eta\tau \quad (A,\ \eta,\ C \text{ are known constants}) \qquad \text{(a)}$$
$$z_p = C\tau$$

where the subscript p is to remind the reader that these relations refer to a fixed path. When the particle is at the xy plane ($z = 0$), it has a speed of V_0 ft/sec and a rate of change of speed of N ft/sec^2. What is the acceleration of the particle at this position?

To answer this, we must ascertain $\boldsymbol{\epsilon}_t$, $\boldsymbol{\epsilon}_n$, and R. To get $\boldsymbol{\epsilon}_t$ we write:

$$\boldsymbol{\epsilon}_t = \frac{d\boldsymbol{r}_p}{ds} = \frac{dx_p}{ds}\boldsymbol{i} + \frac{dy_p}{ds}\boldsymbol{j} + \frac{dz_p}{ds}\boldsymbol{k} \qquad \text{(b)}$$

But:

$$\frac{dx_p}{ds} = \frac{dx_p}{d\tau}\frac{d\tau}{ds} \quad \text{and} \quad \frac{dy_p}{ds} = \frac{dy_p}{d\tau}\frac{d\tau}{ds}, \quad \text{etc.}$$

Solving for $dx_p/d\tau$, $dy_p/d\tau$, and $dz_p/d\tau$ from Eq. (a), we can express Eq. (b) as:

$$\boldsymbol{\epsilon}_t = (A\eta \cos \eta\tau \boldsymbol{i} - A\eta \sin \eta\tau \boldsymbol{j} + C\boldsymbol{k})\frac{d\tau}{ds} \qquad \text{(c)}$$

But:

$$ds = \sqrt{(dx_p)^2 + (dy_p)^2 + (dx_p)^2} \qquad \text{(d)}$$

Solving for the differentials dx_p, dy_p, and dz_p from Eq. (a) and substituting into Eq. (d), we get:

$$ds = \left[(A\eta \cos \eta\tau)^2 + (A\eta \sin \eta\tau)^2 + C^2\right]^{1/2} d\tau \qquad \text{(e)}$$

Solving for $d\tau/ds$ from the above equation, we have:

$$\frac{d\tau}{ds} = \frac{1}{\left[(A\eta)^2(\cos^2 \eta\tau + \sin^2 \eta\tau) + C^2\right]^{1/2}} = \frac{1}{(A^2\eta^2 + C^2)^{1/2}} \qquad \text{(f)}$$

Example 11.7 (Continued)

in which we replaced $(\cos^2 \eta\tau + \sin^2 \eta\tau)$ by unity. Returning to Eq. (c), we can thus say:

$$\boldsymbol{\epsilon}_t = \frac{1}{(A^2\eta^2 + C^2)^{1/2}}\left[A\eta(\cos\eta\tau\,\boldsymbol{i} - \sin\eta\tau\,\boldsymbol{j}) + C\boldsymbol{k}\right] \qquad \text{(g)}$$

To get $\boldsymbol{\epsilon}_n$ and R we employ Eq. 11.19, but in the following manner:

$$\boldsymbol{\epsilon}_n = R\frac{d\boldsymbol{\epsilon}_t}{ds} = R\frac{d\boldsymbol{\epsilon}_t/d\tau}{ds/d\tau} = \frac{R}{(A^2\eta^2 + C^2)^{1/2}}\frac{d\boldsymbol{\epsilon}_t}{d\tau} \qquad \text{(h)}$$

in which we have replaced $ds/d\tau$ using Eq. (f). We can now employ Eq. (g) to find $d\boldsymbol{\epsilon}_t/d\tau$:

$$\frac{d\boldsymbol{\epsilon}_t}{d\tau} = -\frac{A\eta^2}{(A^2\eta^2 + C^2)^{1/2}}(\sin\eta\tau\,\boldsymbol{i} + \cos\eta\tau\,\boldsymbol{j}) \qquad \text{(i)}$$

When we substitute this relation for $d\boldsymbol{\epsilon}_t/d\tau$ in Eq. (h), the principal normal vector $\boldsymbol{\epsilon}_n$ becomes:

$$\boldsymbol{\epsilon}_n = -\frac{RA\eta^2}{A^2\eta^2 + C^2}(\sin\eta\tau\,\boldsymbol{i} + \cos\eta\tau\,\boldsymbol{j}) \qquad \text{(j)}$$

If we take the magnitude of each side, we can solve for R:

$$R = \frac{A^2\eta^2 + C^2}{A\eta^2} \qquad \text{(k)}$$

We now have $\boldsymbol{\epsilon}_t$ and $\boldsymbol{\epsilon}_n$ at any point of the curve in terms of the parameter τ. As the particle goes through the xy plane, this means that the z coordinate of the position of the particle is zero and z_p of the path corresponding to the position of the particle is zero. When we note the last of Eqs. (a), it is clear, that τ must be zero for this position. Thus $\boldsymbol{\epsilon}_n$ and $\boldsymbol{\epsilon}_t$ for the point of interest are:

$$\boldsymbol{\epsilon}_t = \frac{1}{(A^2\eta^2 + C^2)^{1/2}}(A\eta\,\boldsymbol{i} + C\boldsymbol{k}) \qquad \text{(l)}$$

$$\boldsymbol{\epsilon}_n = -\frac{RA\eta^2}{A^2\eta^2 + C^2}\boldsymbol{j} = -\boldsymbol{j} \qquad \text{(m)}$$

where we have used Eq. (k) to replace R in Eq. (m). We can now express the acceleration vector using Eq. 11.20. Thus:

$$\boldsymbol{a} = \frac{N}{(A^2\eta^2 + C^2)^{1/2}}(A\eta\,\boldsymbol{i} + C\boldsymbol{k}) - \frac{V_0^2A\eta^2}{A^2\eta^2 + C^2}\boldsymbol{j} \qquad \text{(n)}$$

The direction of the osculating plane can be found by taking the cross product of $\boldsymbol{\epsilon}_t$ and $\boldsymbol{\epsilon}_n$.

PROBLEMS

11.1. A mass is supported by four springs. The mass is given a vibratory movement in the horizontal (x) direction and simultaneously a vibratory movement in the vertical (y) direction. These motions are given as follows:

$$x = 2 \sin 2t \text{ mm}$$
$$y = 2 \cos (2t + .3) \text{ mm}$$

What is the value of the acceleration vector at $t = 4$ sec? How many g's of acceleration does this correspond to?

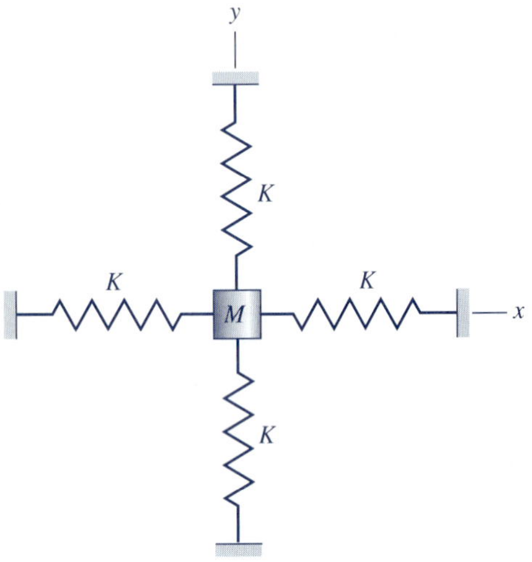

Figure P.11.1.

11.2. A particle moves along a plane circular path of radius r equal to 1 ft. The position OA is given as a function of time as follows:

$$\theta = 6 \sin 5t \text{ rad}$$

where t is in seconds. What are the rectangular components of velocity for the particle at time $t = \frac{1}{5}$ sec?

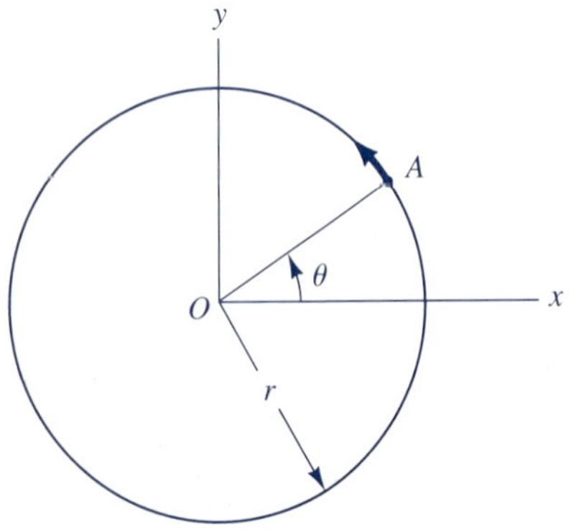

Figure P.11.2.

11.3. A particle with an initial position vector $\boldsymbol{r} = 5\boldsymbol{i} + 6\boldsymbol{j} + \boldsymbol{k}$ m has an acceleration imposed on it, given as

$$\boldsymbol{a} = 6t\boldsymbol{i} + 5t^2\boldsymbol{j} + 10\boldsymbol{k} \text{ m/sec}^2$$

If the particle has zero velocity initially, what are the acceleration, velocity, and position of the particle when $t = 10$ sec?

11.4. The position of a particle at times $t = 10$ sec, $t = 5$ sec, and $t = 2$ sec is known to be, respectively:

$$\boldsymbol{r}(10) = 10\boldsymbol{i} + 5\boldsymbol{j} - 10\boldsymbol{k} \text{ ft}$$
$$\boldsymbol{r}(5) = 3\boldsymbol{i} + 2\boldsymbol{j} + 5\boldsymbol{k} \text{ ft}$$
$$\boldsymbol{r}(2) = 8\boldsymbol{i} - 20\boldsymbol{j} + 10\boldsymbol{k} \text{ ft}$$

What is the acceleration of the particle at time $t = 5$ sec if the acceleration vector has the form

$$\boldsymbol{a} = C_1 t\boldsymbol{i} + C_2 t^2\boldsymbol{j} + C_3 \ln t\boldsymbol{k} \text{ ft/sec}^2$$

where C_1, C_2, and C_3 are constants and t is in seconds?

11.5. A highly idealizeÏam is shown of an *accelerometer*, a device for measuring the acceleration component of motion along a certain direction—in this case the indicated x direction. A mass B is constrained in the accelerometer case so that it can only move against linear springs in the x direction. When the accelerometer case accelerates in this direction, the mass assumes a displaced position, shown dashed, at a distance δ from its original position. This configuration is such that the force in the springs gives the mass B the acceleration corresponding to that of the accelerometer case. The shift δ of the mass in the case is picked up by an electrical sensor device and is plotted as a function of time. The damping fluid present eliminates extraneous oscillations of the mass. If a plot of a_x versus time has the form shown, what is the speed of the body after 10 sec, 30 sec, and 45 sec? The acceleration a_x is measured in g's—i.e., in units of 32.2 ft/sec^2 or 9.81 m/sec^2. Assume that the body starts from rest at $x = 0$.

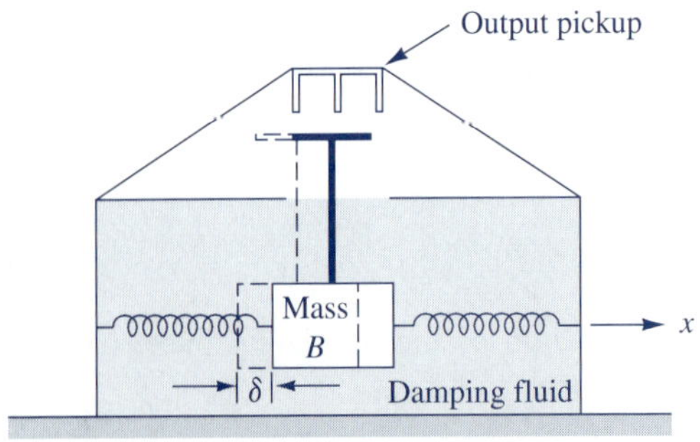

Figure P.11.5 *(Continued)*

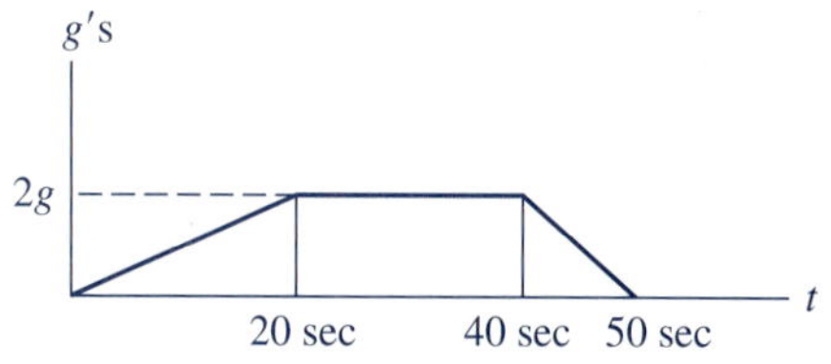

Figure P.11.5.

11.6. The position vector of a particle is given as

$$\boldsymbol{r} = 6t\boldsymbol{i} + (5t + 10)\boldsymbol{j} + 6t^2\boldsymbol{k} \text{ m}$$

What is the acceleration of the particle at $t = 3$ sec? What distance has been traveled by the particle during this time? [*Hint:* Let $dr = \sqrt{dx^2 + dy^2 + dz^2}$ and divide and multiply by dt in second half of problem. Look up integration form $\int \sqrt{a^2 + t^2}\,dt$ in Appendix I.]

11.7. In Example 11.1, what is the acceleration vector for pin B if the yoke C is accelerating at the rate of 10 ft/sec^2 at the instant of interest?

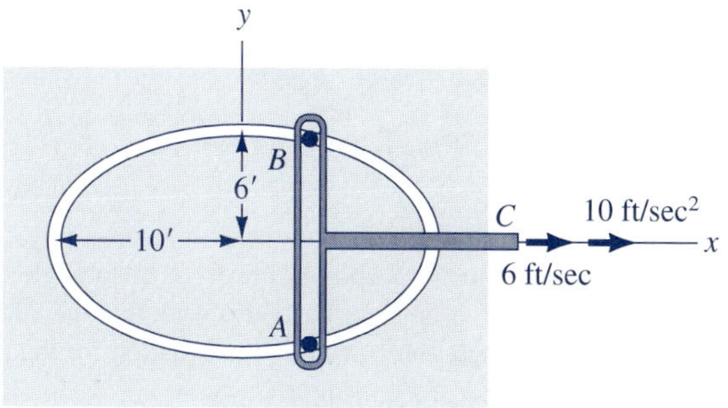

Figure P.11.7.

11.8. Particles A and B are confined to always be in a circular groove of radius 5 ft. At the same time, these particles must also be in a slot that has the shape of a parabola. The slot is shown dashed at time $t = 0$. If the slot moves to the right at a constant speed of 3 ft/sec, what are the speed and rate of change of speed of particles toward each other at $t = 1$ sec?

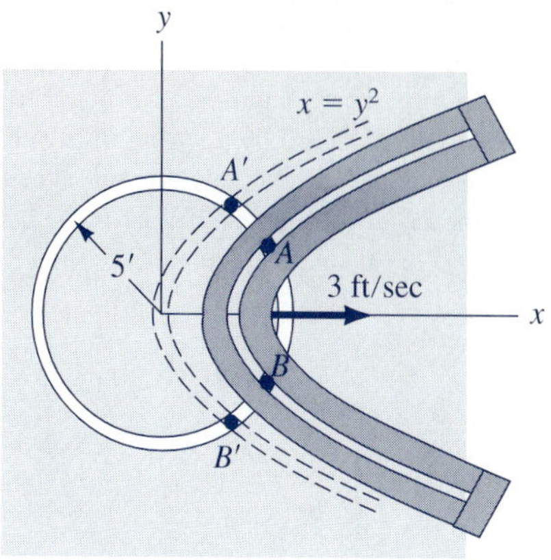

Figure P.11.8.

11.9. The face of a cathode ray tube is shown. An electron is made to move in the horizontal (x) direction due to electric fields in the cathode tube with the following motion:

$$x = A \sin \omega t \text{ mm}$$

Also, the electron is made to move in the vertical direction with the following motion:

$$y = A \sin\ (\omega t + \alpha) \text{ mm}$$

Show that for $\alpha = \pi/2$, the trajectory on the screen is that of a *circle* of radius A mm. If $\alpha = \pi$, show that the trajectory is that of a *straight line* inclined at $-45°$ to the xy axes. Finally, give the formulations for the directions of velocity and acceleration of the electron in the xy plane.

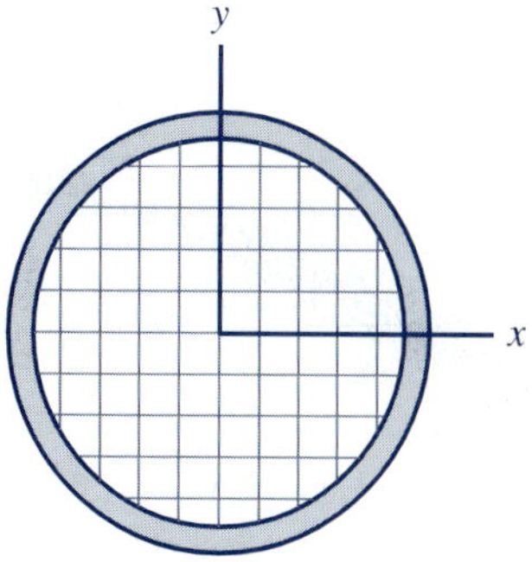

Figure P.11.9.

11.10. A yoke A moves to the right at a speed $V = 2$ m/s and a rate of change of speed $\dot{V} = .6$ m/s^2 when the yoke is at a position $d = .27$ m from the y axis. A pin is constrained to move inside a slot in the yoke and is forced by a spring in the slot to slide on a parabolic surface. What are the velocity and acceleration vectors for the pin at the instant of interest? What is the acceleration normal to the parabolic surface at the position shown?

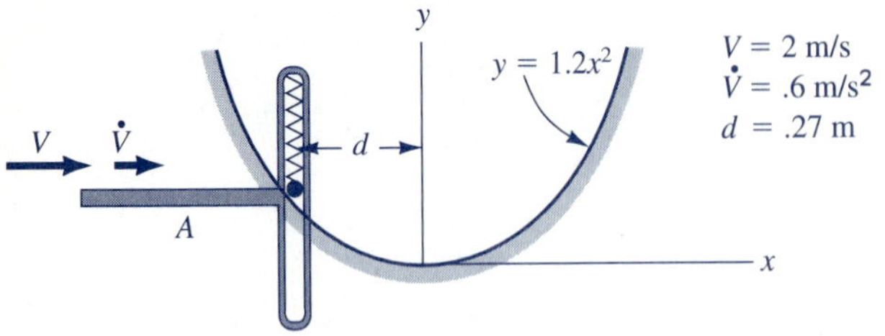

Figure P.11.10.

11.11. A flexible inextensible cord restrains mass M. Both pins A acting on top of the cord move downward at a constant speed V_2 while pin B acting on the bottom of the cord moves upward at a constant speed V_1. The cord is free to slide along the pins without friction. Starting from the horizontal orientation of the cord, what is the velocity of the mass M as a function of time?

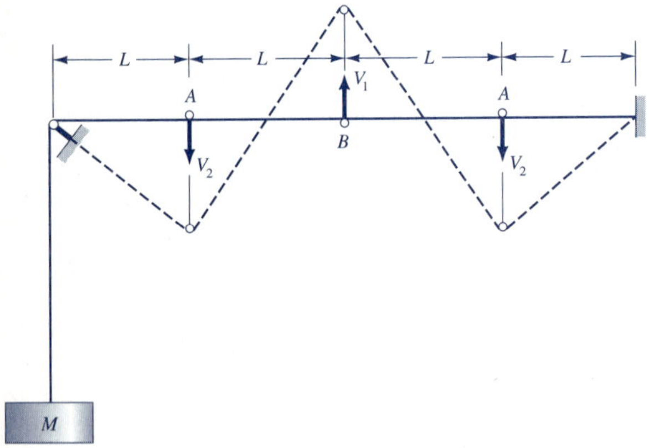

Figure P.11.11.

11.12. Mass M is held by an inextensible cord. What is the velocity of M as a function of α; the time t; the constant velocities V_A and V_C; and the distance h? Disc G is free to turn.

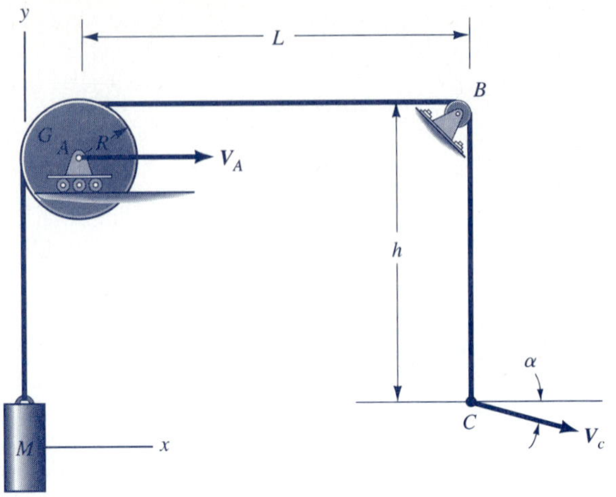

Figure P.11.12.

11.13. A stunt motorcyclist is to attempt a "jump" over a deep chasm. The distance between jump-off point and landing is 100 m. As technical advisor to this stunt man, what minimum speed do you tell him to exceed at the jump-off point A? The cycle is highly streamlined to minimize wind resistance. Give the result in km/hr.

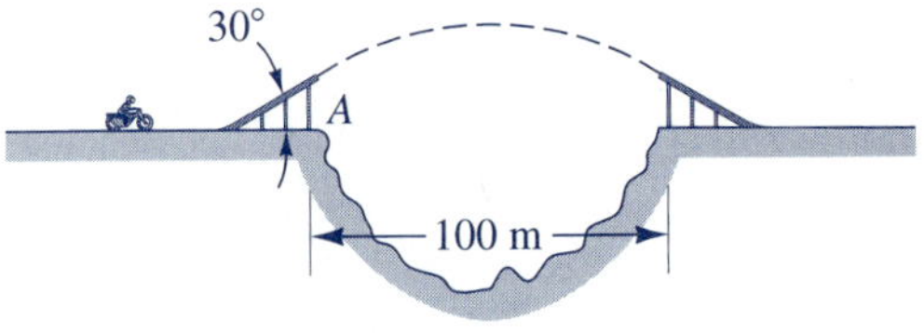

Figure P.11.13.

11.14. A charged particle is shot at time $t = 0$ at an angle of 45° with a speed 10 ft/sec. If an electric field is such that the body has an acceleration $-200t^2\boldsymbol{j}$ ft/sec^2, what is the equation for the trajectory? What is the value of d for impact?

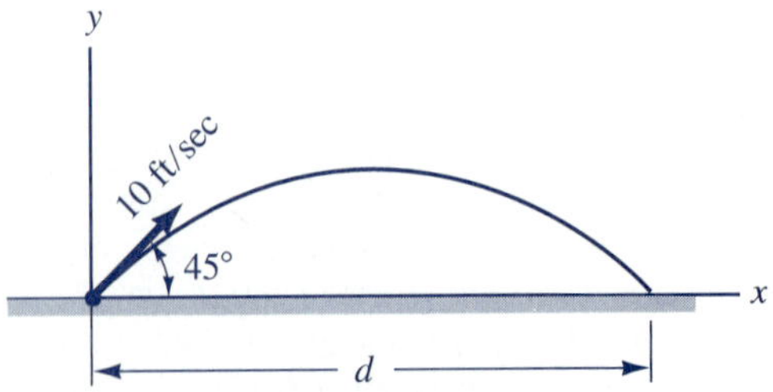

Figure P.11.14.

11.15. A projectile is fired at a speed of 1,000 m/sec at an angle ϵ of 40° measured from an inclined surface, which is at an angle ϕ of 20° from the horizontal. If we neglect friction, at what distance along the incline does the projectile hit the incline?

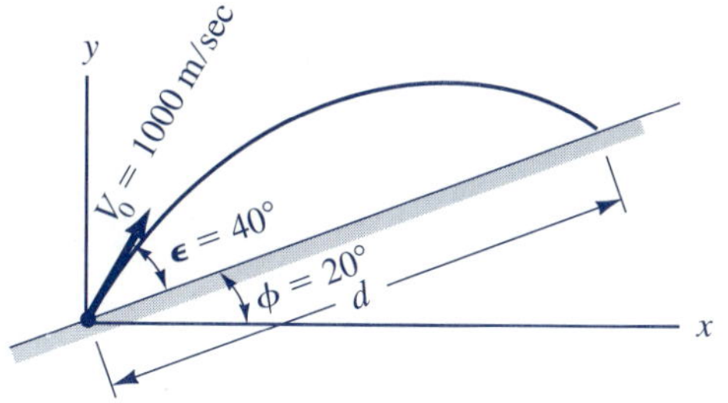

Figure P.11.15.

11.16. Grain is being blown into an open train container at a speed V_0 of 20 ft/sec. What should the minimum and maximum elevations d be to ensure that all the grain gets into the train? Neglect friction and winds.

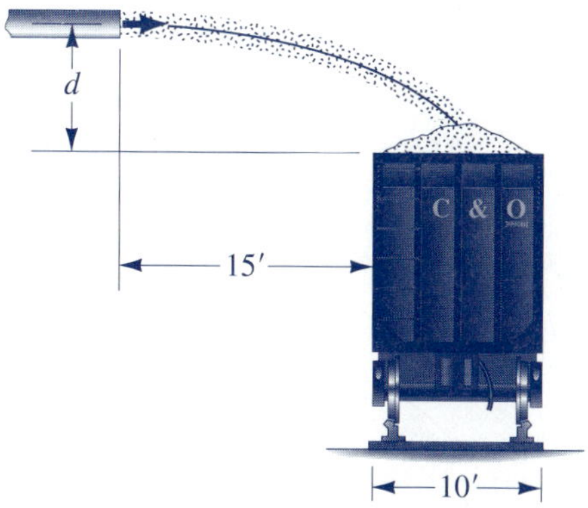

Figure P.11.16.

11.17. A rocket-powered test sled slides over rails. This test sled is used for experimentation on the ability of man to undergo large persistent accelerations. To brake the sled from high speeds, small scoops are lowered to deflect water from a stationary tank of water placed near the end of the run. If the sled is moving at a speed of 100 km/hr at the instant of interest, compute h and d of the deflected stream of water as seen from the sled. Assume no loss in speed of the water relative to the scoop. Consider the sled as an inertial reference at the instant of interest and attach xy reference to the sled.

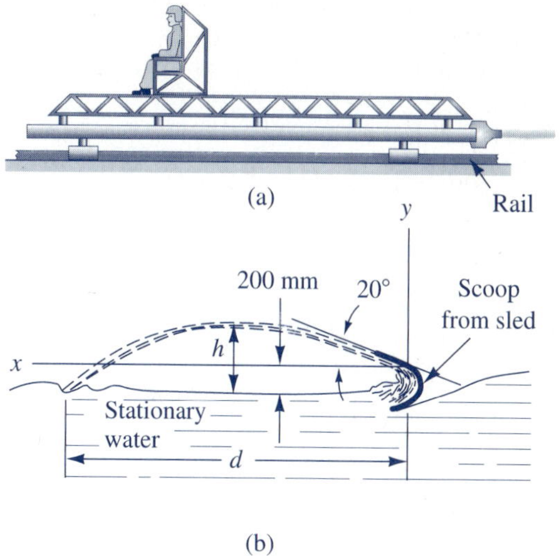

Figure P.11.17.

11.18. In the previous problem, the vane has a velocity given relative to the ground reference XY as

$$V = -5t^2 + 27.8 \text{ m/s}$$

What is the distance δ between the vane and the position of impact of the water that left the vane at time $t = 0$. Use the trajectory of the preceding problem, which relates x and y for a reference xy attached to the vane and moving to the left at $t = 0$ at a speed of 100 km/hr = 27.8 m/s. The trajectory of the water after leaving the vane at $t = 0$ is

$$y = -.00721x^2 + .364x \; m$$

with x in meters.

11.19. A fighter-bomber is moving at a constant speed of 500 m/s when it fires its cannon at a target at B. The cannon has a muzzle velocity of 1,000 m/s (relative to the gun barrel).

(a) Determine the distance d. Use reference shown.

(b) What is the horizontal distance between the plane and position B at the time of impact?

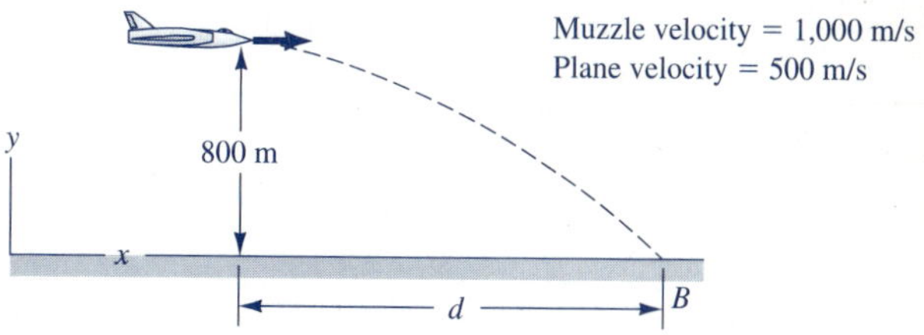

Figure P.11.19.

11.20. A golfer has the bad luck of having his golf ball strike a nearby tree while having a shallow trajectory. The ball bounces off at a speed that is 60 percent of the preimpact speed. If it moves in the same plane as the initial trajectory, compute the distance d at which the ball hits the ground with respect to the tee at A.

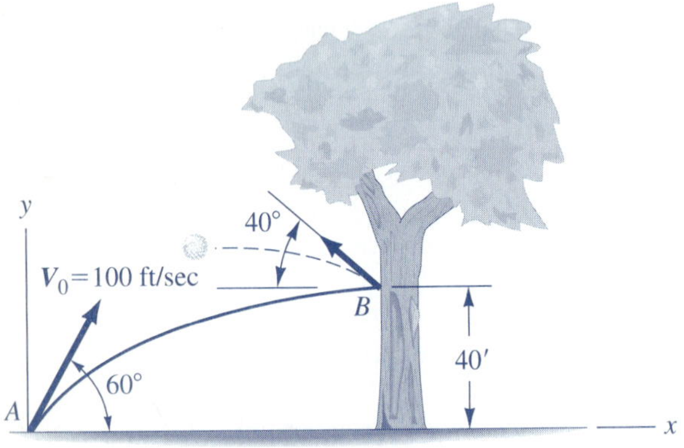

Figure P.11.20.

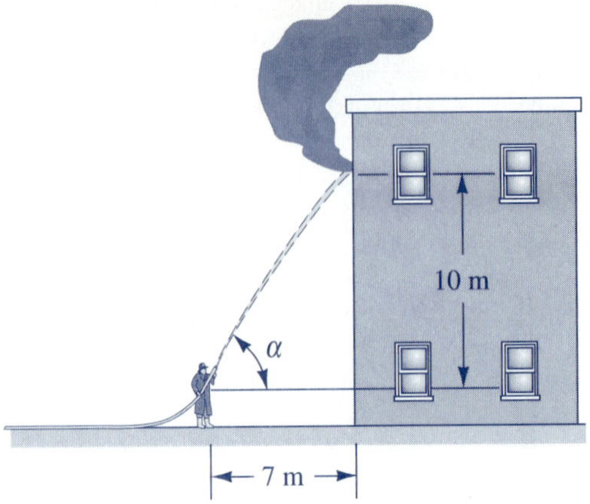

Figure P.11.23.

11.21. What angle α will result in the longest distance d at impact? The muzzle velocity is V_0. The surface is flat.

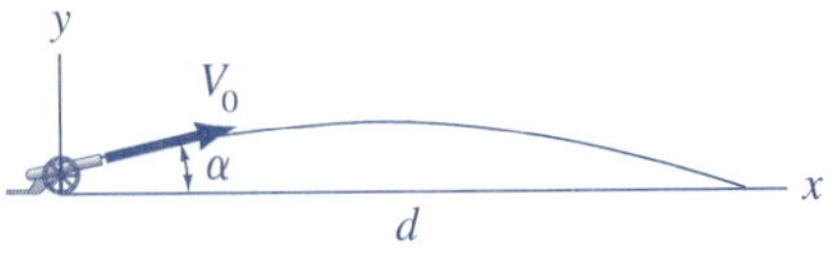

Figure P.11.21.

11.22. A sportsman in a valley is trying to shoot a deer on a hill. He quickly estimates the distance of the deer along his line of sight as 500 yd and the height of the hill as 100 yd. His gun has a muzzle velocity of 3,000 ft/sec. If he has no graduated sight, how many feet above the deer should he aim his rifle in order to hit it? (Neglect friction.)

11.23. A fireman is directing water from a hose into the broken window of a burning house. The velocity of the water is 15 m/sec as it leaves the hose. What are the angles α needed to do the job?

11.24. A long range gun is shown for which the muzzle velocity is 1,000 m/s. If we neglect friction, at what position $\bar{x}$, $\bar{y}$ does the shell hit the ground?

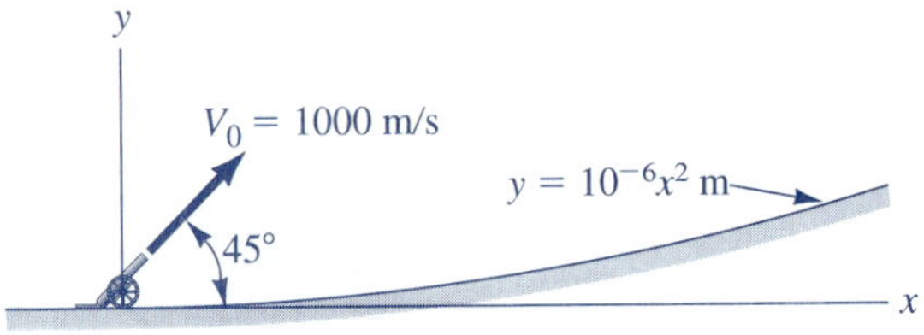

Figure P.11.24.

11.25. An archer in a Jeep is chasing a deer. The Jeep moves at 30 mi/hr and the deer moves at 15 mi/hr along the same direction. At what inclination must the arrow be shot if the deer is 100 yd ahead of the Jeep and if the initial speed of the arrow is 200 ft/sec relative to archer? (Neglect friction.)

11.26. A fighter plane is directly over an antiaircraft gun at time $t = 0$. The plane has a speed V_1 of 500 km/hour. A shell is fired at $t = 0$ in an attempt to hit the plane. If the muzzle velocity V_0 is 1,000 m/sec, how many meters d should the gun be aimed ahead of the plane to hit it? What is the time of impact?

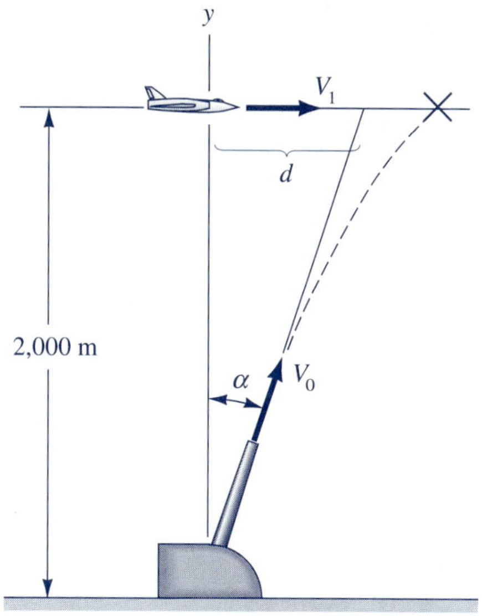

Figure P.11.26.

11.27. A destroyer is making a run at full speed of 75 km/hr. When abreast of a missile site target, it fires two shells. The target is 12,000 m from the destroyer. If the muzzle velocity is 400 m/sec, what is the angle of firing α with the horizontal that the computer must set the guns? Also, what angle β must the turret be rotated relative to the line of sight at the instant of firing? [*Hint:* To hit target, what must V_y of the shell be? Result: $\alpha = 23.7°$ and $\beta = 3.26°$.]

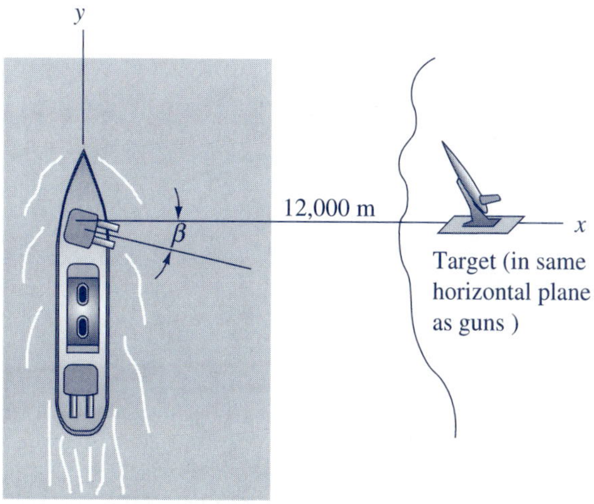

Figure P.11.27.

11.28. In the preceding problem, a second smaller destroyer is firing at the target as shown in the diagram. The data of the preceding problem applies with the following additional data. Due to strong wind and current, the destroyer has a drift velocity of 6 km/hr in a northeast direction in addition to its full speed of 75 km/hr. Form two simultaneous transcendental equations for α and β and verify that $\alpha = 21.39°$ and that $\beta = 10.727°$.

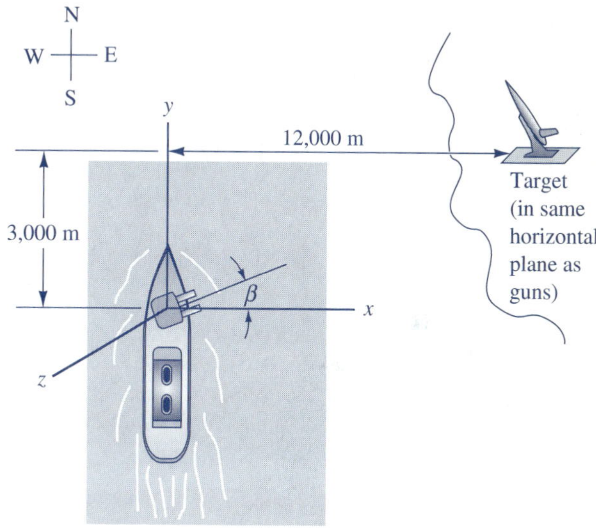

Figure P.11.28.

***11.29.** A Jeep with an archer is moving at a speed of 30 mi/hr. At 100-yd distance and moving at right angles to the Jeep is a deer running at a speed of 15 mi/hr. If the initial speed of the arrow shot by the archer to bag the deer is 200 ft/sec, what inclination α must the shot have with the horizontal and what angle β must the vertical projection of the shot onto the ground have relative to the line *AB*?

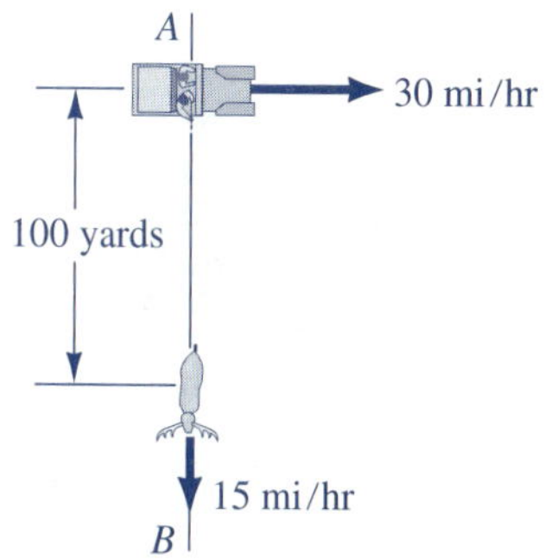

Figure P.11.29.

11.30. A particle moves with a constant speed of 5 ft/sec along the path. Compute the acceleration at points 1, 2, and 3.

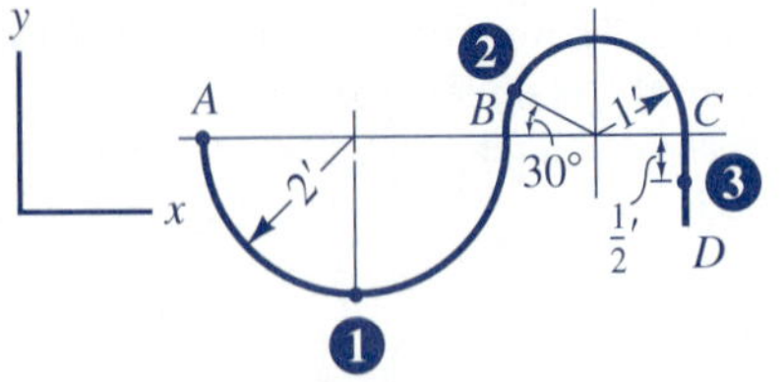

Figure P.11.30.

11.31. If, in Problem 11.30 the speed is 5 ft/sec only at point A, and it increases 5 ft/sec for each foot traveled, compute the acceleration at points 1, 2, and 3.

11.32. A car is moving at a speed of 88 km/hr along a highway. At a curve in the highway, the radius of curvature is 1,300 m. What is the acceleration of the car? To decrease this acceleration by 30%, what must its speed be?

11.33. A high-speed train is running at 100 km/hr. It goes into a curve having a minimum radius of curvature of 2,000 m. What is the acceleration that sitting passengers are subjected to? If the radius of curvature were to be doubled, at what constant speed could the train then go with the same acceleration?

11.34. An amusement park ride consists of a cockpit in which a passenger is strapped in a seated position. The cockpit rotates about A with angular speed ω. The average person's head is 10 ft from the axis of rotation at A. We know that if a person's head is subjected to an acceleration of 3 g's or more in a direction from shoulders to head for any length of time, he/she will be uncomfortable and perhaps black out. What, then, is the maximum value of ω in rpm to prevent these effects, using a safety factor of 3? [*Hint:* You will soon learn that the speed in a circular path is $R\omega$.]

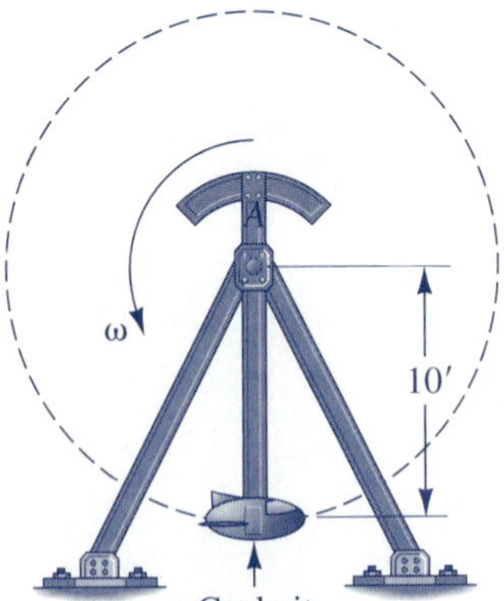

Figure P.11.34.

11.35. A motorcyclist is moving along a circular path having a radius of curvature of 400 m. He is increasing his speed along the path at the rate of 5 km/hr/sec. If he enters the curve at a speed of 48 km/hr, what is his total acceleration after traveling 10 sec along this path?

11.36. What is the direction of the normal vector and the value of the radius of curvature at a position a of the curve?

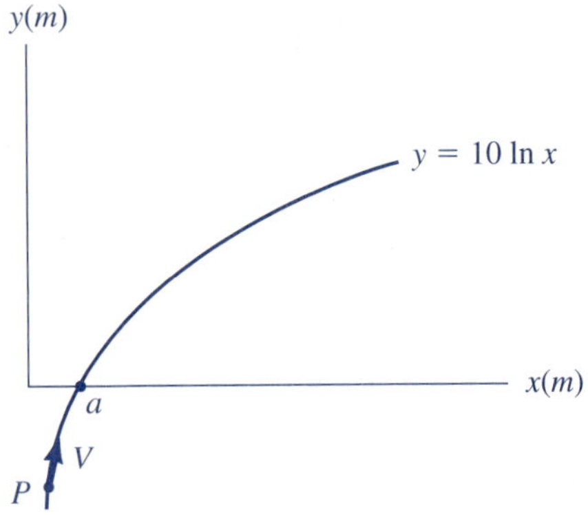

Figure P.11.36.

11.37. A particle P moves with constant speed V along the curve $y = 10 \ln x$ m. At what position x does the particle have the maximum acceleration? What is the value of this acceleration if $V = 1$ m/sec?

11.38. A car is moving along a circularly curved road of radius 2,000 ft so as to merge with traffic on a highway. If the car accelerates at a constant rate of 7 mi/hr/sec, what will be the total acceleration of the car when it is going 50 mph?

11.39. A motorcycle is moving along a circular flat road and is accelerating at a uniform rate of 5 m/s^2. At what speed will the total acceleration be 6 m/s^2? The radius of the path of the motorcycle is 220 m.

11.40. A fighter plane is in a diving maneuver along a trajectory that is approximately a parabola. If the maximum number of g's that the pilot can withstand is 5 g's from shoulder to head from the dynamics of the plane, what is the maximum allowable speed for this maneuver when the plane reaches A?

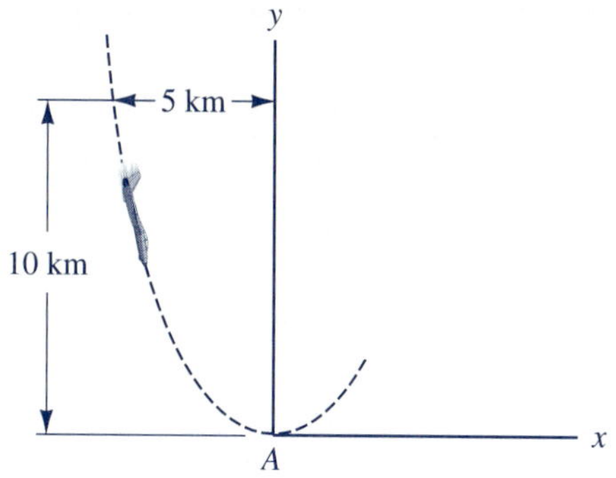

Figure P.11.40.

11.41. A particle moves with a constant speed of 3 m/sec along the path. What is the acceleration $\boldsymbol{a}$ at position $x = 1.5$ m? Give the rectangular components of $\boldsymbol{a}$.

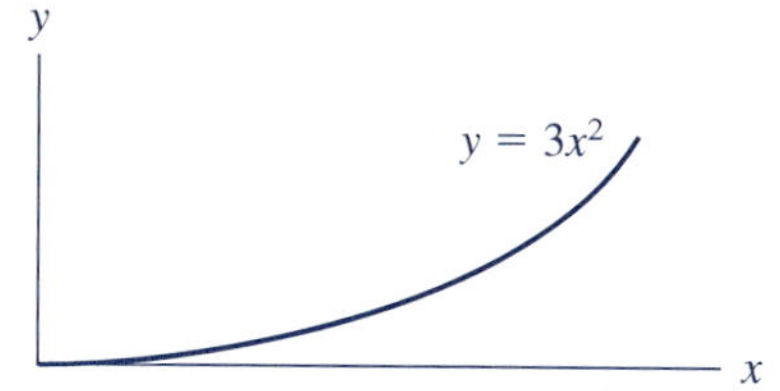

Figure P.11.41.

11.42. A particle moves along a sinusoidal path. If the particle has a speed of 10 ft/sec and a rate of change of speed of 5 ft/sec^2 at A, what is the *magnitude* of the acceleration? What is the magnitude and direction of the acceleration of the particle at B, if it has a speed of 20 ft/sec and a rate of change of speed of 3 ft/sec^2 at this point?

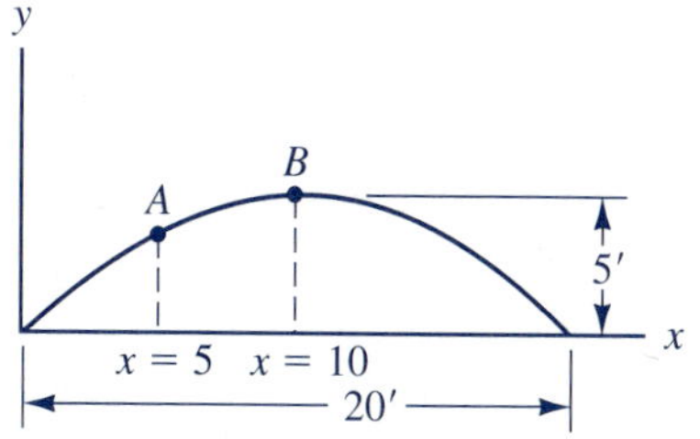

Figure P.11.42.

11.43. A passenger plane is moving at a constant speed of 200 km/hr in a holding pattern at a constant elevation. At the instant of interest, the angle β between the velocity vector and the x axis is 30°. The vector is known through on-board gyroscopic instrumentation to be changing at the rate $\dot{\beta}$ of $-5°$/sec. What is the radius of curvature of the path at this instant? $\left[\textit{Hint}: \boldsymbol{a} = \frac{d(V\boldsymbol{\epsilon}_t)}{dt} = \frac{V^2}{R}\boldsymbol{\epsilon}_n.\right]$

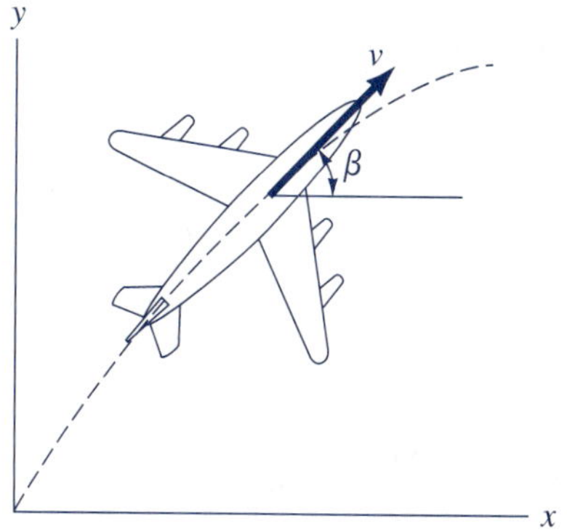

Figure P.11.43.

11.44. At what position along the ellipse shown does the normal vector have a set of direction cosines (.707, .707, 0)? Recall that the equation for an ellipse in the position shown is $x^2/a^2 + y^2/b^2 = 1$.

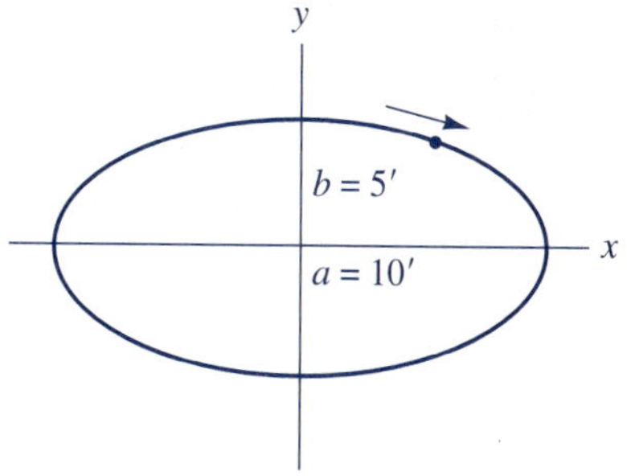

Figure P.11.44.

11.45. A particle moves along a path given as

$$y = 3x^2 \text{ ft}$$

The projection of the particle along the x axis varies as $\sqrt{.2t^2}$ ft (where t is in seconds) starting at the origin at $t = 0$. What are the acceleration components normal and tangential to the path at $t = 2$ sec? What is the radius of curvature at this point?

11.46. A particle moves along a path $y^2 = 10x$ with x and y in meters. The distance traversed along this path starting from the origin is given by S such that

$$S = \frac{t}{2} + \frac{t^2}{100} \text{ m}$$

where t is measured in units of seconds. What are the normal and tangential acceleration components of the particle when $y = 10$ m? [*Hint:* $\int \sqrt{y^2 + a^2}\, dy$ is presented in Appendix I.] Also, note that

$$ds = \sqrt{dx^2 + dy^2} = \sqrt{\left(\frac{dx}{dy}\right)^2 + 1}\, dy.$$

11.47. Show by arguments similar to those used in the text for deriving the relation $d\boldsymbol{\epsilon}_t/ds = (1/R)\boldsymbol{\epsilon}_n$ that $d\boldsymbol{\epsilon}_n/ds = -(1/R)\boldsymbol{\epsilon}_t$.

11.48. **(a)** For coplanar paths in the xy plane, find the formula for $\dot{\boldsymbol{a}}$, that is, the "jerk."

(b) If a particle moves on a plane circular path of radius 5 m at a speed of 5 m/sec, and if the rate of change of speed is 2 m/sec^2, what is $\dot{\boldsymbol{a}}$ for the particle if the second derivative of its speed along the path is 10 m/sec^3? [*Hint:* Use the result of Problem 11.47.]

11.49. A beebee gun shoots a pellet as shown. Determine the radius of curvature of the trajectory as a function of x.

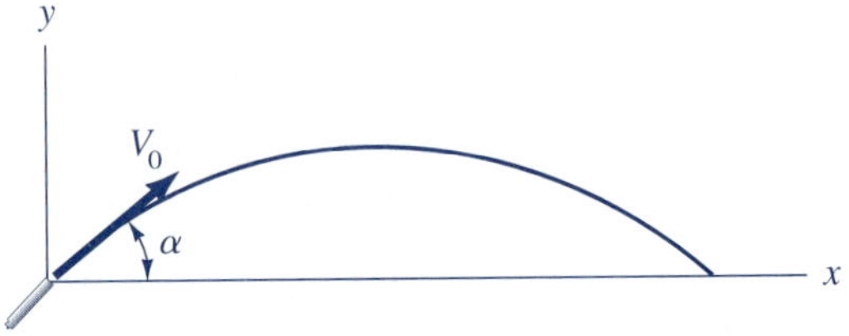

$V_0 = 30$ m/s
$\alpha = 40°$

Figure P.11.49.

11.6 Cylindrical Coordinates

The final method we shall consider for evaluating the velocity and acceleration of a particle brings us back to considering coordinates of the particle as time functions, as we did at the outset of this study. Now we shall employ cylindrical coordinates, and we shall evaluate velocity and acceleration with components having certain directions that are associated with the cylindrical coordinates of the particle. Thus, particle P in Fig. 11.15 is located by specifying cylindrical coordinates θ, $\bar{r}$, and z.[2] The transformation equations between Cartesian and cylindrical coordinates are

$$\begin{aligned} x &= \bar{r}\cos\theta, \qquad & \bar{r} &= (x^2 + y^2)^{1/2} \\ y &= \bar{r}\sin\theta, \qquad & \theta &= \tan^{-1}\frac{y}{x} \end{aligned} \tag{11.22}$$

[2]The notation $\bar{r}$ is used to distinguish it from r, which, according to previous definitions in statics, is the magnitude of $\boldsymbol{r}$, the position vector.

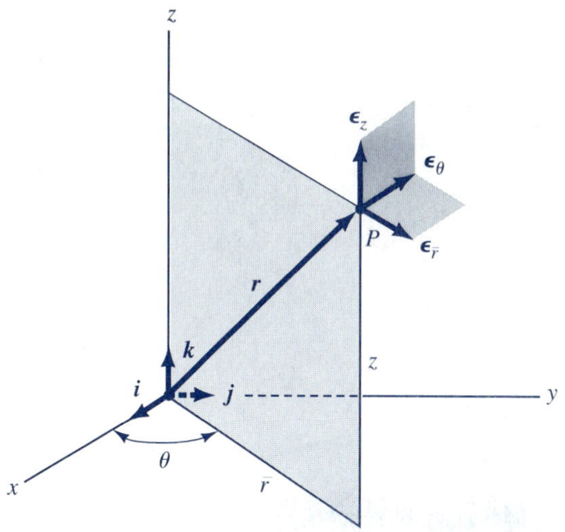

Figure 11.15. Cylindrical coordinates.

Unit vectors are associated with these coordinates and are given as:

$\boldsymbol{\epsilon}_z$, which is parallel to the z axis and, for practical purposes, is the same as $\boldsymbol{k}$. This is considered to be the *axial direction.*

$\boldsymbol{\epsilon}_{\bar{r}}$, which is normal to the z axis, pointing out from the axis, and is identified as the *radial direction* from z.

$\boldsymbol{\epsilon}_\theta$, which is normal to the plane formed by $\boldsymbol{\epsilon}_z$ and $\boldsymbol{\epsilon}_{\bar{r}}$ and has a sense in accordance with the right-hand-screw rule for the permutation $z, \bar{r}, \theta$. We call this the *transverse direction.*

Note that $\boldsymbol{\epsilon}_{\bar{r}}$ *and* $\boldsymbol{\epsilon}_\theta$ *will change direction as the particle moves relative to the xyz reference.* Thus, these unit vectors are generally *functions of time*, whereas $\boldsymbol{\epsilon}_z$ is a constant vector.

Using previously developed concepts, we can express the velocity and acceleration of the particle relative to the xyz reference *in terms of components always in the transverse, radial, and axial directions and can use cylindrical coordinates exclusively in the process.* This information is most useful, for instance, in turbomachine studies (i.e., for centrifugal pumps, compressors, jet engines, etc.), where, if we take the z axis as the axis of rotation, the axial components of fluid acceleration are used for thrust computation while the transverse components are important for torque considerations. It is these components that are meaningful for such computations and not components parallel to some xyz reference.

The position vector $\boldsymbol{r}$ of the particle determines the direction of the unit vectors $\boldsymbol{\epsilon}_{\bar{r}}$ and $\boldsymbol{\epsilon}_\theta$ at any time t and can be expressed as

$$\boldsymbol{r} = \bar{r}\boldsymbol{\epsilon}_{\bar{r}} + z\boldsymbol{\epsilon}_z \tag{11.23}$$

To get the desired velocity, we differentiate $\boldsymbol{r}$ with respect to time:

$$\frac{d\boldsymbol{r}}{dt} = \boldsymbol{V} = \bar{r}\dot{\boldsymbol{\epsilon}}_{\bar{r}} + \dot{\bar{r}}\boldsymbol{\epsilon}_{\bar{r}} + \dot{z}\boldsymbol{\epsilon}_z$$

Our task here is to evaluate $\dot{\boldsymbol{\epsilon}}_{\bar{r}}$. On consulting Fig. 11.16, we see clearly that changes in direction of $\boldsymbol{\epsilon}_{\bar{r}}$ occur only when the θ coordinate of the particle changes. Hence, remembering that the magnitude of $\boldsymbol{\epsilon}_{\bar{r}}$ is always constant, we have for $\dot{\boldsymbol{\epsilon}}_{\bar{r}}$ using the chain rule:

$$\dot{\boldsymbol{\epsilon}}_{\bar{r}} = \frac{d\boldsymbol{\epsilon}_{\bar{r}}}{dt} = \frac{d\boldsymbol{\epsilon}_{\bar{r}}}{d\theta}\frac{d\theta}{dt} = \frac{d\boldsymbol{\epsilon}_{\bar{r}}}{d\theta}\dot{\theta} \tag{11.24}$$

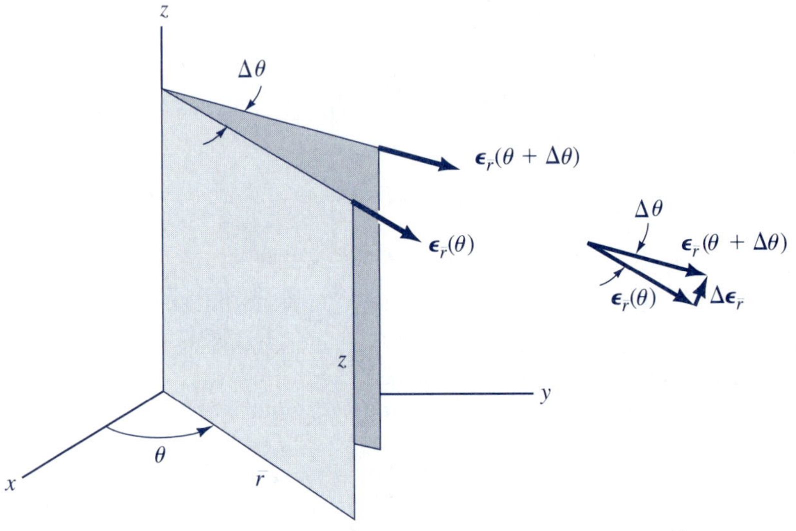

Figure 11.16. Change of unit vector $\boldsymbol{\epsilon}_{\bar{r}}$.

To evaluate $d\boldsymbol{\epsilon}_{\bar{r}}/d\theta$, we have shown in Fig. 11.16(a) the vector $\boldsymbol{\epsilon}_{\bar{r}}$ for a given $\bar{r}$ and z at positions corresponding to θ and $(\theta + \Delta\theta)$. In Fig. 11.16(b), furthermore, we have formed an enlarged vector triangle from these vectors and, in this way, we have shown the vector $\Delta\boldsymbol{\epsilon}_{\bar{r}}$ (i.e., the change in $\boldsymbol{\epsilon}_{\bar{r}}$ during a change in the coordinate θ). From the vector triangle, we see that

$$\left|\Delta\boldsymbol{\epsilon}_{\bar{r}}\right| \approx \left|\boldsymbol{\epsilon}_{\bar{r}}\right|\Delta\theta = \Delta\theta \tag{11.25}$$

Furthermore, as $\Delta\theta \to 0$ we see, on consulting Fig. 11.16, that the *direction* of $\Delta\boldsymbol{\epsilon}_{\bar{r}}$ approaches that of the unit vector $\boldsymbol{\epsilon}_\theta$ and so we can approximate $\Delta\boldsymbol{\epsilon}_r$ as

$$\Delta\boldsymbol{\epsilon}_{\bar{r}} \approx \left|\Delta\boldsymbol{\epsilon}_{\bar{r}}\right|\boldsymbol{\epsilon}_\theta \approx \Delta\theta\,\boldsymbol{\epsilon}_\theta \tag{11.26}$$

where we have used Eq. 11.25 in the last step. Going back to Eq. 11.24, we utilize the preceding result to write

$$\frac{d\boldsymbol{\epsilon}_{\bar{r}}}{dt} = \left(\frac{d\boldsymbol{\epsilon}_{\bar{r}}}{d\theta}\right)\dot{\theta} \approx \left(\frac{\Delta\boldsymbol{\epsilon}_{\bar{r}}}{\Delta\theta}\right)\dot{\theta} \approx \left(\frac{(\Delta\theta)\boldsymbol{\epsilon}_\theta}{\Delta\theta}\right)\dot{\theta} = \dot{\theta}\boldsymbol{\epsilon}_\theta \tag{11.27}$$

In the limit, as $\Delta\theta \rightarrow 0$, all the previously made approximations become exact statements and we accordingly have

$$\frac{d\boldsymbol{\epsilon}_{\bar{r}}}{dt} = \dot{\theta}\boldsymbol{\epsilon}_{\theta} \tag{11.28}$$

The velocity of particle P is, then,

$$\boldsymbol{V} = \dot{\bar{r}}\boldsymbol{\epsilon}_{\bar{r}} + \bar{r}\dot{\theta}\boldsymbol{\epsilon}_{\theta} + \dot{z}\boldsymbol{\epsilon}_{z} \tag{11.29}$$

To get the acceleration relative to xyz in terms of cylindrical coordinates and radial, transverse, and axial components, we simply take the time derivative of the velocity vector above:

$$\boldsymbol{a} = \frac{d\boldsymbol{V}}{dt} = \ddot{\bar{r}}\boldsymbol{\epsilon}_{\bar{r}} + \dot{\bar{r}}\dot{\boldsymbol{\epsilon}}_{\bar{r}} + \dot{\bar{r}}\dot{\theta}\boldsymbol{\epsilon}_{\theta} + \bar{r}\ddot{\theta}\boldsymbol{\epsilon}_{\theta} + \bar{r}\dot{\theta}\dot{\boldsymbol{\epsilon}}_{\theta} + \ddot{z}\boldsymbol{\epsilon}_{z} \tag{11.30}$$

We must next evaluate $\dot{\boldsymbol{\epsilon}}_{\theta}$. Like $\boldsymbol{\epsilon}_{\bar{r}}$, the vector $\boldsymbol{\epsilon}_{\theta}$ can vary only when a change in the coordinate θ causes a change in direction of this vector, as has been shown in Fig. 11.17(a). The vectors $\boldsymbol{\epsilon}_{\theta}(\theta)$ and $\boldsymbol{\epsilon}_{\theta}(\theta + \Delta\theta)$ have been shown in an enlarged vector triangle in Fig. 11.17(b) and here we have shown $\Delta\boldsymbol{\epsilon}_{\theta}$, the change of the vector $\boldsymbol{\epsilon}_{\theta}$ as a result of the change in coordinate θ. We can then say, using the chain rule,

$$\dot{\boldsymbol{\epsilon}}_{\theta} = \frac{d\boldsymbol{\epsilon}_{\theta}}{dt} = \frac{d\boldsymbol{\epsilon}_{\theta}}{d\theta}\dot{\theta} \approx \frac{\Delta\boldsymbol{\epsilon}_{\theta}}{\Delta\theta}\dot{\theta} \tag{11.31}$$

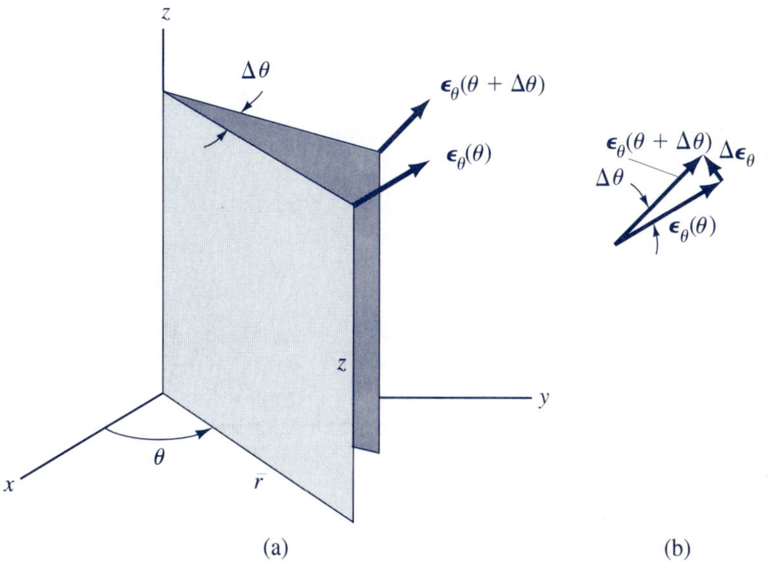

Figure 11.17. Change of unit vector $\boldsymbol{\epsilon}_{\theta}$.

As $\Delta\theta \to 0$, the direction of $\Delta\boldsymbol{\epsilon}_\theta$ becomes that of $-\boldsymbol{\epsilon}_{\bar{r}}$ and the magnitude of $\Delta\boldsymbol{\epsilon}_\theta$, on consulting the vector triangle, clearly approaches $|\boldsymbol{\epsilon}_\theta|\Delta\theta = \Delta\theta$. Thus, the vector $\Delta\boldsymbol{\epsilon}_\theta$ becomes approximately $-\Delta\theta\ \boldsymbol{\epsilon}_{\bar{r}}$. In the limit, we then get for Eq. 11.31:

$$\dot{\boldsymbol{\epsilon}}_\theta = -\dot{\theta}\boldsymbol{\epsilon}_{\bar{r}} \tag{11.32}$$

Using Eqs. 11.28 and 11.32, we find that Eq. 11.30 now becomes

$$\boldsymbol{a} = \ddot{\bar{r}}\boldsymbol{\epsilon}_{\bar{r}} + \dot{\bar{r}}\dot{\theta}\boldsymbol{\epsilon}_\theta + \dot{\bar{r}}\dot{\theta}\boldsymbol{\epsilon}_\theta + \bar{r}\ddot{\theta}\boldsymbol{\epsilon}_\theta - \bar{r}\dot{\theta}^2\boldsymbol{\epsilon}_{\bar{r}} + \ddot{z}\boldsymbol{\epsilon}_z$$

Collecting components, we write

$$\boldsymbol{a} = \left(\ddot{\bar{r}} - \bar{r}\dot{\theta}^2\right)\boldsymbol{\epsilon}_{\bar{r}} + \left(\bar{r}\ddot{\theta} + 2\dot{\bar{r}}\dot{\theta}\right)\boldsymbol{\epsilon}_\theta + \ddot{z}\boldsymbol{\epsilon}_z \tag{11.33}$$

Thus, we have accomplished the desired task. A similar procedure can be followed to reach corresponding formulations for spherical coordinates. By now you should be able to produce the preceding equations readily from the foregoing basic principles.

For motion in a *circle* in the *xy* plane, note that $\dot{\bar{r}} = \dot{z} = 0$, and $\bar{r} = r$. We get the following simplifications:

$$\boldsymbol{V} = r\dot{\theta}\boldsymbol{\epsilon}_\theta \tag{11.34a}$$

$$\boldsymbol{a} = r\ddot{\theta}\boldsymbol{\epsilon}_\theta - r\dot{\theta}^2\boldsymbol{\epsilon}_r \tag{11.34b}$$

Furthermore, the unit vector $\boldsymbol{\epsilon}_\theta$ is tangent to the path, and the unit vector $\boldsymbol{\epsilon}_r$ is normal to the path and points away from the center. Therefore, when we compare Eq. 11.34b with those stemming from considerations of path variables (Section 11.5), clearly for circular motion in the *xy* coordinate plane of a right-hand triad:

$$|r\ddot{\theta}| = \left|\frac{d^2s}{dt^2}\right| \qquad |r\dot{\theta}^2| = \left|\frac{V^2}{r}\right| \qquad \begin{cases} \boldsymbol{\epsilon}_\theta = \boldsymbol{\epsilon}_t & \text{(for counterclockwise motion as seen from } +z)^3 \\ \boldsymbol{\epsilon}_\theta = -\boldsymbol{\epsilon}_t & \text{(for clockwise motion as seen from } +z) \\ \boldsymbol{\epsilon}_r = -\boldsymbol{\epsilon}_n & \end{cases} \tag{11.35}$$

Thus, Eqs. 11.34b and 11.20 are equally useful for quickly expressing the acceleration of a particle moving in a circular path. You probably remember these formulas from earlier physics courses and may want to use them in the ensuing work of this chapter.

[3] The sense of $\boldsymbol{\epsilon}_t$ is that of the velocity of the particle, whereas the sense of $\boldsymbol{\epsilon}_\theta$ is determined by the reference *xyz*. For this reason a multiplicity of relations between these unit vectors exists.

Example 11.8

A *towing tank* is a device used for evaluating the drag and stability of ship hulls. Scaled models are moved by a rig along the water at carefully controlled speeds and attitudes while measurements are being made. Usually, the water is contained in a long narrow tank with the rig moving overhead along the length of the tank. However, another useful setup consists of a rotating radial arm (see Fig. 11.18), which gives the model a transverse motion. A radial motion along the arm is another degree of freedom possible for the model in this system.

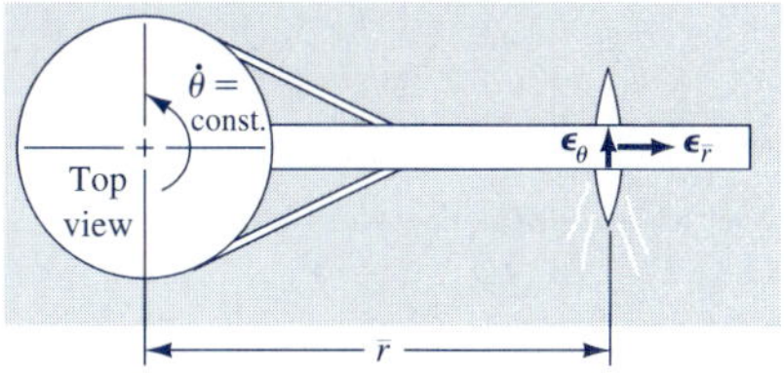

Figure 11.18. Circular towing tank.

Consider the case where a model is being moved out radially so that in one revolution of the main beam it has gone, at constant speed relative to the main beam, from position $\bar{r} = 3.3$ m to $\bar{r} = 4$ m. The angular speed of the beam is 3 rpm. What is the acceleration of the hull model relative to the water when $\bar{r} = 4$ m?

In order to find the radial speed of the model, note that one revolution of the arm corresponds to a time τ evaluated as:

$$\tau = \frac{1}{\frac{3}{60}} = 20 \text{ sec}$$

Hence, we can say for $\dot{\bar{r}}$:

$$\dot{\bar{r}} = \frac{4 - 3.3}{\tau} = .035 \text{ m/sec}$$

We can now readily describe the motion of the system at the instant of interest with cylindrical coordinates as follows:

$$\bar{r} = 4 \text{ m}, \qquad \dot{\theta} = 3\left(\frac{2\pi}{60}\right) = .314 \text{ rad/sec}$$

$$\dot{\bar{r}} = .035 \text{ m/sec}, \qquad \ddot{\theta} = 0$$

$$\ddot{\bar{r}} = 0, \qquad \ddot{z} = 0$$

Using Eq. 11.33, we may now evaluate the acceleration vector,

$$\begin{aligned} \boldsymbol{a} &= \left[0 - (4)(.314)^2\right]\boldsymbol{\epsilon}_{\bar{r}} + \left[0 + (2)(.035)(.314)\right]\boldsymbol{\epsilon}_\theta + [0]\boldsymbol{\epsilon}_z \\ &= -.394\boldsymbol{\epsilon}_{\bar{r}} + .022\boldsymbol{\epsilon}_\theta \text{ m/sec}^2 \end{aligned}$$

Finally,

$$|\boldsymbol{a}| = .395 \text{ m/sec}^2$$

Note that we could have used notation r instead of $\bar{r}$ here. (Why?)

Example 11.9

A firetruck has a telescoping boom holding a firefighter as shown in Fig. 11.19. At time t, the boom is extending at the rate of 6 m/s and increasing its rate of extension at .3 m/s^2. Also at time t, $r = 10$ m and $\beta = 30°$. If a velocity component of the firefighter in the vertical direction is to be 3.3 m/sec at this instant, what should $\dot{\beta}$ be? Also, if at this instant the vertical acceleration of the firefighter is to be 1.7 m/s^2, what should $\ddot{\beta}$ be? Note that the motion of the firefighter is that of joint A.

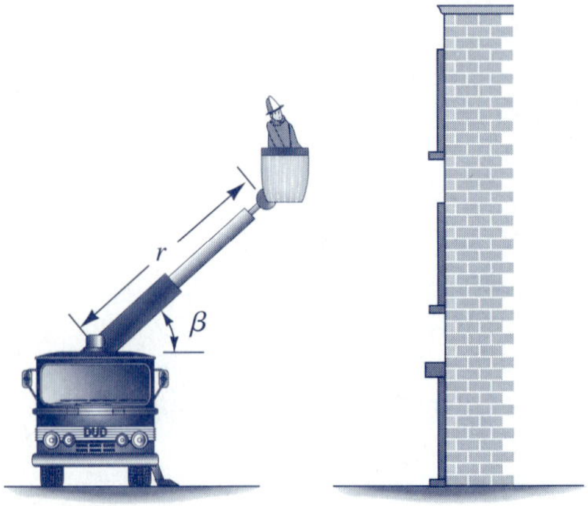

Figure 11.19. A firetruck with a telescoping boom.

We first insert stationary reference xyz at the base of the boom with the boom in the xy plane as shown in Fig. 11.20. Clearly, the boom is rotating

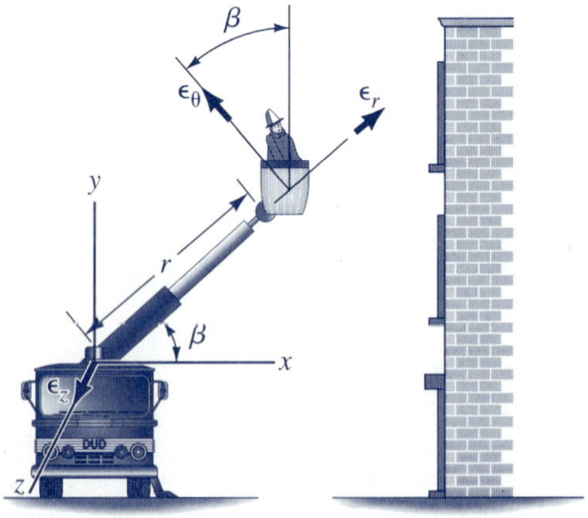

Figure 11.20. System with cylindrical coordinates.

Example 11.9 (Continued)

about the z axis and so this axis is the *axial* direction for the system. Furthermore, the boom being normal to the z axis must then be in the *radial* direction. It should be obvious that there is no motion of the firefighter in the axial direction. We now give the velocity vector as follows, noting that $\theta \equiv \beta$ here.

$$\begin{aligned} \boldsymbol{V} &= \dot{\bar{r}}\boldsymbol{\epsilon}_{\bar{r}} + \bar{r}\dot{\theta}\boldsymbol{\epsilon}_{\theta} + \dot{z}\boldsymbol{\epsilon}_{z} \\ &= (.6)\boldsymbol{\epsilon}_{\bar{r}} + (10)(\dot{\beta})\boldsymbol{\epsilon}_{\theta} + 0\boldsymbol{\epsilon}_{z} \text{ m/s} \end{aligned}$$

We require that $\boldsymbol{V} \cdot \boldsymbol{j} = 3.3$ m/s. We thus have for this purpose

$$3.3 = (.6)(\boldsymbol{\epsilon}_{\bar{r}} \cdot \boldsymbol{j}) + (10)(\dot{\beta})(\boldsymbol{\epsilon}_{\theta} \cdot \boldsymbol{j}) = .6 \sin \beta + 10\dot{\beta} \cos \beta$$

where we have used the fact that the dot product between two unit vectors is simply the cosine of the angle between the unit vectors. Noting that at the instant of interest $\beta = 30°$, we can readily solve for $\dot{\beta}$. We get

$$\dot{\beta} = .346 \text{ rad/s}$$

Now we write the equation for the acceleration.

$$\begin{aligned} \boldsymbol{a} &= \left(\ddot{\bar{r}} - \bar{r}\dot{\theta}^2\right)\boldsymbol{\epsilon}_{\bar{r}} + \left(\bar{r}\ddot{\theta} + 2\dot{\bar{r}}\dot{\theta}\right)\boldsymbol{\epsilon}_{\theta} + 0\boldsymbol{\epsilon}_{z} \\ &= \left(.3 - (10)(.346)^2\right)\boldsymbol{\epsilon}_{\bar{r}} + \left(10\ddot{\beta} + (2)(.6)(.346)\right)\boldsymbol{\epsilon}_{\theta} \\ &= -.900\boldsymbol{\epsilon}_{\bar{r}} + \left(10\ddot{\beta} + .416\right)\boldsymbol{\epsilon}_{\theta} \text{ m/s}^2 \end{aligned}$$

We require that $\boldsymbol{a} \cdot \boldsymbol{j} = 1.7$ m/s^2. Hence

$$\begin{aligned} 1.7 &= -.900(\boldsymbol{\epsilon}_{\bar{r}} \cdot \boldsymbol{j}) + \left(10\ddot{\beta} + .416\right)(\boldsymbol{\epsilon}_{\theta} \cdot \boldsymbol{j}) \\ &= -.900 \sin 30° + \left(10\ddot{\beta} + .416\right) \cos 30° \end{aligned}$$

We then have the following desired information:

$$\ddot{\beta} = .207 \text{ rad/s}^2$$

Again, as in the preceding example, we could have used r instead of $\bar{r}$.

PROBLEMS

11.50. A car is moving along a circular track of radius 40 ft. The position S along the path is given as

$$S = 3t^2 + \frac{t^3}{6} \text{ ft}$$

The time t is given in seconds. What are the angular velocity and angular acceleration of the car at $t = 5$ sec?

11.51. A point P fixed on a rotating plate has an acceleration in the x direction of -10 m/sec^2. If r for the point is 1 m, what is the angular acceleration of the plate? The angular speed at the instant of interest is 2 rad/sec counterclockwise.

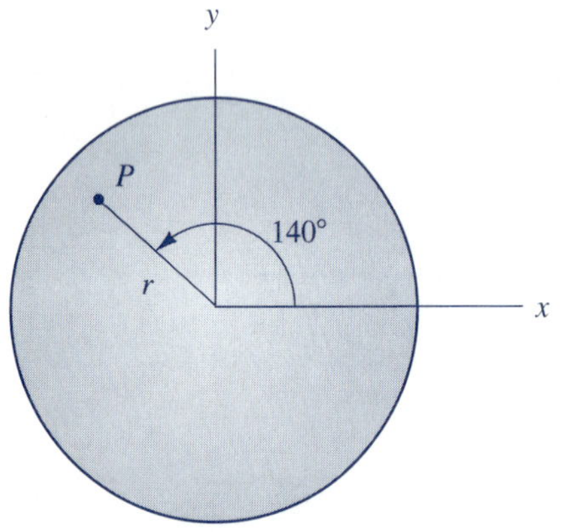

Figure P.11.51.

11.52. A flat disc A with a rubber surface is driven by bevel gears having diameters $D_1 = 8$ in. and $D_2 = 3$ in. A second rubber disc B of diameter $D_3 = 2$ in. is turned by the friction contact with A. We thus have a *friction drive* system. At the instant of interest, $\omega = 5$ rad/sec and $\dot{\omega} = 3$ rad/sec^2. If wheel B is moved downward at a speed $V_B = 3$ in./sec at the instant of interest, what is the rotational speed Ω and the rate of change of rotational speed $\dot{\Omega}$ of the small disc B? Slipping between B and A occurs only in the radial direction of disc A. The distance r is 4 in. at the instant of interest.

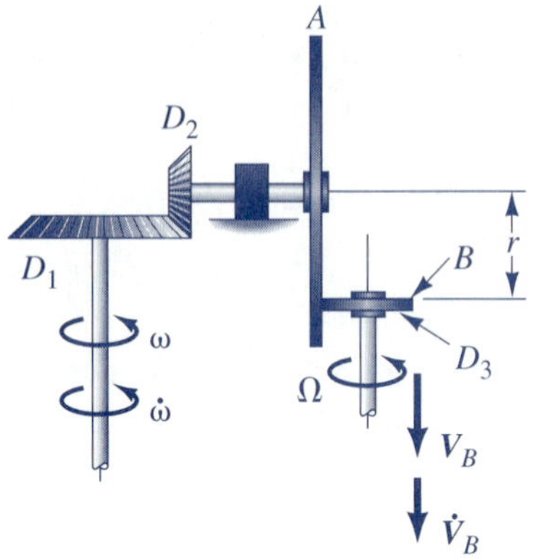

Figure P.11.52.

11.53. What are the velocity and acceleration components in the axial, transverse, and radial directions for a particle moving relative to xyz in the following way:

$$\bar{r} = 10e^{-2t} \text{ m} \qquad \theta = .2t \text{ rad} \qquad z = .6t \text{ m}$$

with t in seconds. Make a rough sketch of the early portion of the path of the particle.

11.54. A vertical member rotates in accordance with:

$$\omega = 3\sin(.1t) \text{ rad/sec}$$

with t in seconds. Attached to CD is a system of rods HI and FG each of length 200 mm and pinned together at their midpoints K. Also, GA and IA of length 100 mm, are pinned together as shown. At the end of A is a stylus which scribes a curve on plate J. The angle β of the system is given as

$$\beta = 1.3 - \frac{t}{10} \text{ rad}$$

with t in seconds. What are the radial and transverse velocity and acceleration components of the stylus at time $t = 5$ sec about axis N–N? (*Note:* Pin F is fixed but pin H moves vertically in a slot as shown.)

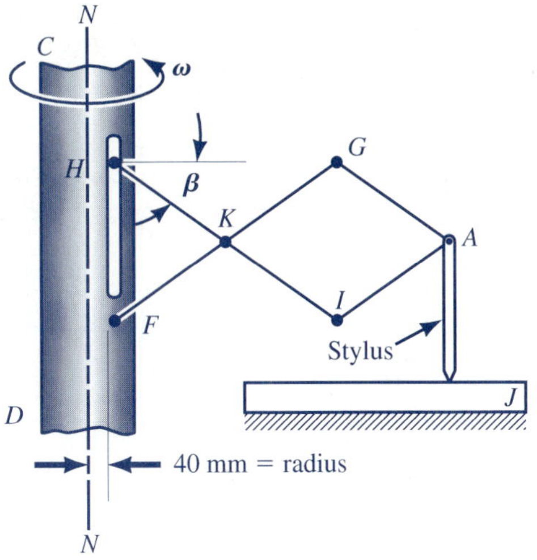

Figure P.11.54.

11.55. A particle moves with a constant speed of 5 ft/sec along a straight line having direction cosines $l = .5$, $m = .3$. What are the cylindrical coordinates when $|\boldsymbol{r}| = 20$ ft? What are the axial and transverse velocities of the particle at this position?

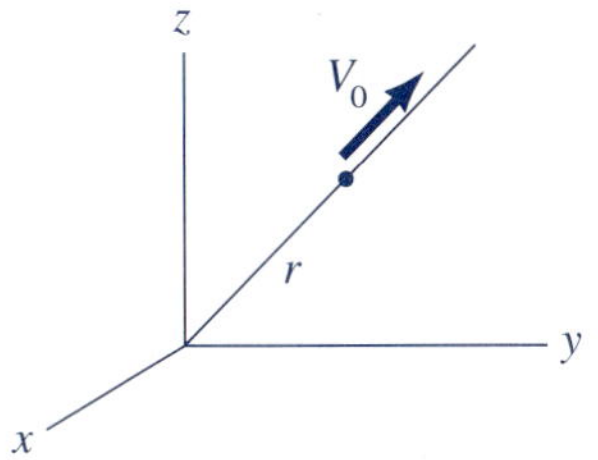

Figure P.11.55.

11.56. A wheel is rotating at time t with an angular speed ω of 5 rad/sec. At this instant, the wheel also has a rate of change of angular speed of 2 rad/sec^2. A body B is moving along a spoke at this instant with a speed of 3 m/sec relative to the spoke and is increasing in its speed at the rate of 1.6 m/sec^2. These data are given when the spoke, on which B is moving, is vertical and when B is .6 m from the center of the wheel, as shown in the diagram. What are the velocity and acceleration of B at this instant relative to the fixed reference xyz?

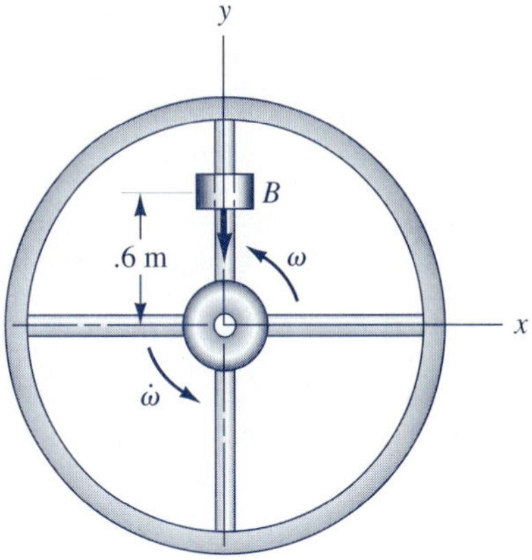

Figure P.11.56.

11.57. A plane is shown in a dive-bombing mission. It has at the instant of interest a speed of 485 km/hr and is increasing its speed downward at a rate of 81 km/hr/sec. The propeller is rotating at 150 rpm and has a diameter of 4 m. What is the velocity of the tip of the propeller shown at A and its acceleration at the instant of interest? Use cylindrical velocity components.

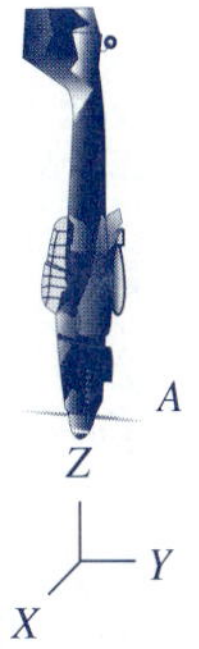

Figure P.11.57.

11.58. The motion of a particle relative to a reference xyz is given as follows:

$$\bar{r} = .2 \sinh t \text{ m} \qquad \theta = .5 \sin \pi t \text{ rad} \qquad z = 6t^2 \text{ m}$$

with t in seconds. What are the magnitudes of the velocity and acceleration vectors at time $t = 2$ sec? Note that sinh 2 = 3.6269 and cosh 2 = 3.7622.

11.59. Given the following cylindrical coordinates for the motion of a particle:

$$\bar{r} = 20 \text{ m} \qquad \theta = 2\pi t \text{ rad} \qquad z = 5t \text{ m}$$

with t in seconds. Sketch the path. What is this curve? Determine the velocity and acceleration vectors.

11.60. A grain of plutonium is being tracked in a turbulent atmosphere. Relative to reference xyz, the displacement components are

$$x = 6t \text{ ft} \qquad y = 10t \text{ ft} \qquad z = t^3 + 10 \text{ ft}$$

Express the position, velocity, and acceleration vectors of the particle using cylindrical coordinates with components in the axial, transverse, and radial directions.

11.61. The motion of a particle in cylindrical coordinates is given by the following parametric equations:

$$\bar{r} = 3 \sin \pi t \text{ m}$$
$$\theta = 6t + 3t^2 \text{ rad}$$
$$z = 5 \cos \pi t + 3 \text{ m} \quad (t \text{ in seconds})$$

Determine the velocity and acceleration of the particle at $t = .35$ sec.

11.62. A flyball governor has the following data at the instant of interest:

$$\omega = .2 \text{ rad/s} \quad \dot{\omega} = .04 \text{ rad/s}^2 \quad \alpha = 45°$$
$$\dot{\alpha} = 5 \text{ rad/s} \quad \ddot{\alpha} = .2 \text{ rad/s}^2$$

If at this instant, the arms are in the xz plane, give the velocity and acceleration vectors of the spheres using cylindrical coordinates for the axial, transverse, and radial directions.

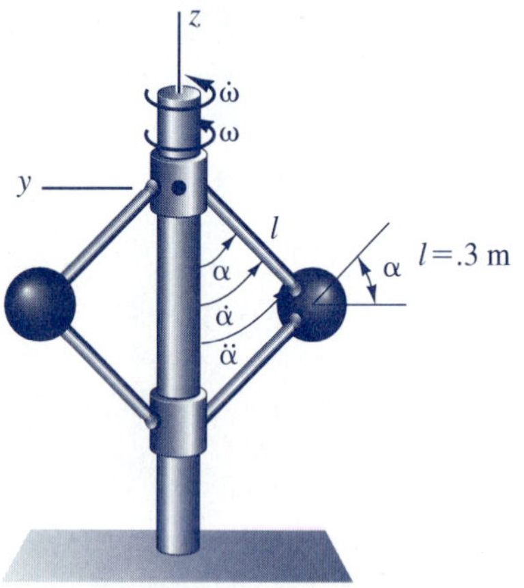

Figure P.11.62.

11.63. A stray tomahawk missile is being tracked. It is moving at a constant speed of 500 mph along a straight path having direction cosines $l = .23$ and $m = .64$. When

$$\boldsymbol{r} = 10\boldsymbol{i} + 6\boldsymbol{j} + 8\boldsymbol{k} \text{ mi}$$

express the position in cylindrical coordinates. Also, give the velocity vector and the acceleration vector using axial, transverse, and radial components.

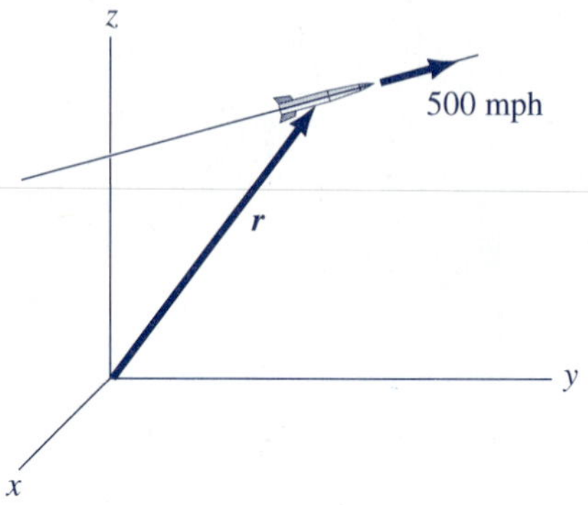

Figure P.11.63.

11.64. A wheel of diameter 2 ft is rotated at a speed of 2 rad/sec and is increasing its rotational speed at the rate of 3 rad/sec^2. It advances along a screw having a pitch of .5 in.[4] What is the acceleration of elements on the rim in terms of cylindrical components?

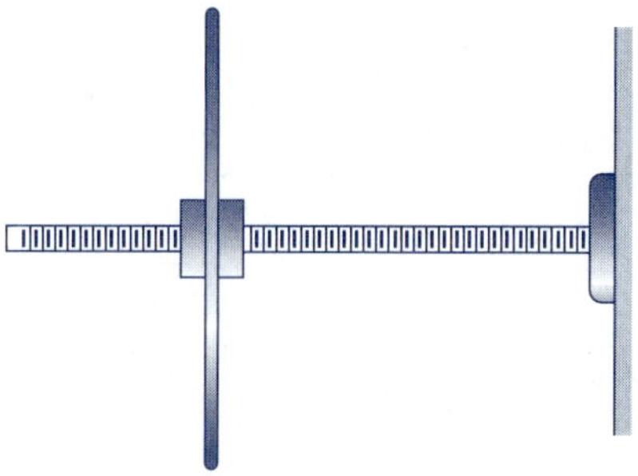

Figure P.11.64.

11.65. A wheel with a threaded hub is rotating at an angular speed of 80 rpm on a right-hand screw having a pitch of .5 in. At the instant of interest, the rate of change of angular speed is 20 rpm/sec. A sleeve A is advancing along a spoke at this instant with a speed of 5 ft/sec and a rate of increase of speed of 5 ft/sec^2. The sleeve is 2 ft from the centerline at O at the instant of interest. What are the velocity vector and the acceleration vector of the sleeve at this instant? Use cylindrical coordinates. (See footnote for definition of pitch.)

[4]Pitch is the distance advanced along a screw for one revolution.

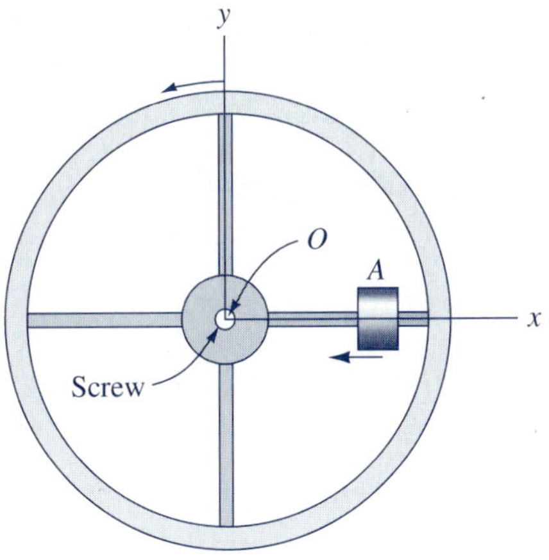

Figure P.11.65.

11.66. A simple garden sprinkler is shown. Water enters at the base and leaves at the end at a speed of 3 m/sec as seen from the rotor of the sprinkler. Furthermore, it leaves upward relative to the rotor at an angle of 60° as shown in the diagram. The rotor has an angular speed ω of 2 rad/sec. As seen from the ground, what are the axial, transverse, and radial velocity and acceleration components of the water just as it leaves the rotor?

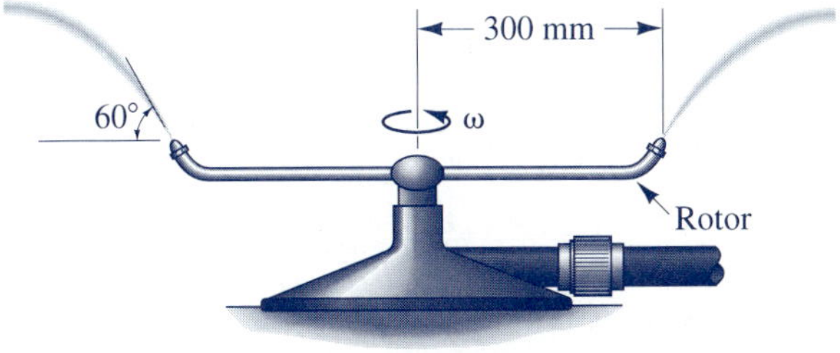

Figure P.11.66.

11.67. The acceleration of gravity on the surface of Mars is .385 times the acceleration of gravity on earth. The radius R of Mars is about .532 times that of the earth. What is the time of flight of one cycle for a satellite in a circular parking orbit 803 miles from the surface of Mars? [*Note:* $GM = gR^2$.]

11.68. A threaded rod rotates with angular position $\theta = .315t^2$ rad. On the rod is a nut which rotates relative to the rod at the rate $\omega = .4t$ rad/sec. When $t = 0$, the nut is at a distance 2 ft from A. What is the velocity and acceleration of the nut at $t = 10$ sec? The thread has a pitch of .2 in (see footnote 4). Give results in radial and transverse directions.

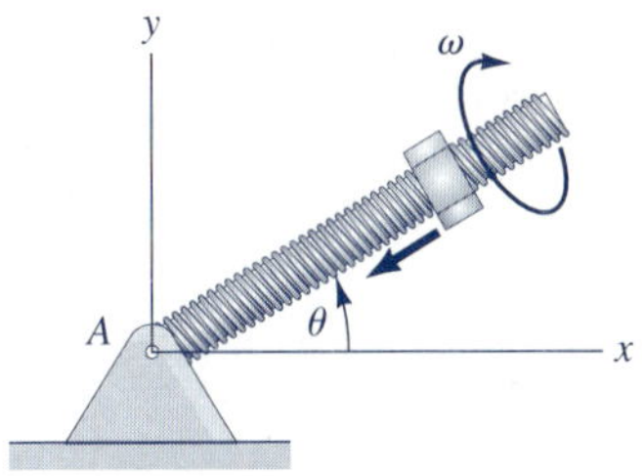

Figure P.11.68.

11.69. Underwater cable is being laid from an ocean-going ship. The cable is unwound from a large spool A at the rear of the ship. The cable must be laid so that is *not dragged* on the ocean bottom. If the ship is moving at a speed of 3 knots, what is the necessary angular speed ω of the spool A when the cable is coming off at a radius of 3.2 m? What is the average rate of change of ω for the spool required for proper operation? The cable has a diameter of 150 mm.

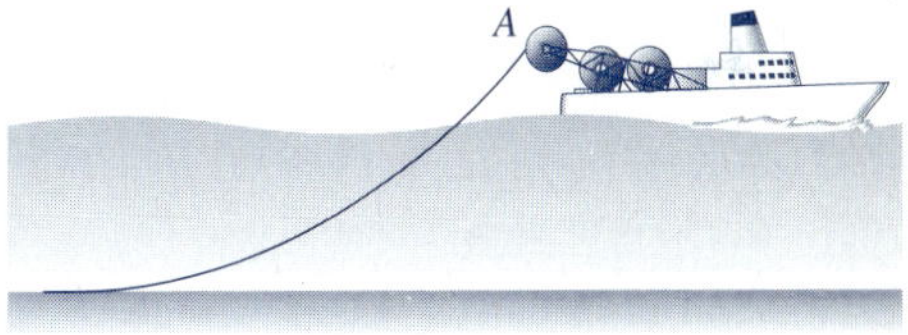

Figure P.11.69.

11.70. A variable diameter drum is rotated by a motor at a constant speed ω of 10 rpm. A rope of diameter d of .5 in. wraps around this drum and pulls up a weight W. It is desired that the velocity of the weight's *upward* movement be given as

$$\dot{X} = .4 + \frac{t^2}{8{,}000} \text{ ft/sec}$$

where for $t = 0$ the rope is just about to start wrapping around the drum at $Z = 0$. What should the radius $\bar{r}$ of the drum be as a function of Z to accomplish this? What are the velocity components $\dot{Y}$ and $\dot{Z}$ of the weight W when $t = 100$ sec?

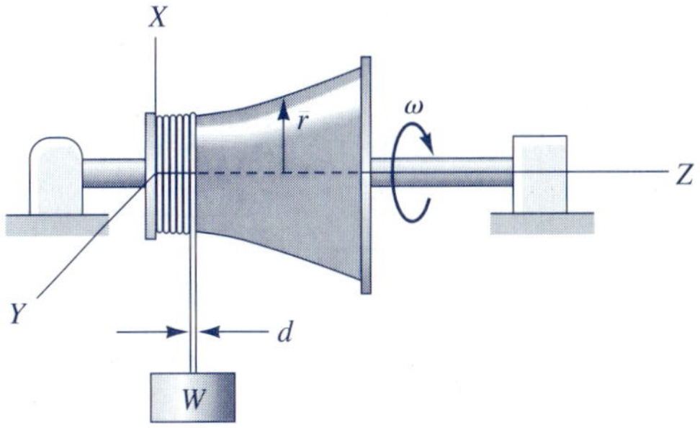

Figure P.11.70.

Part C: Simple Kinematical Relations and Applications

11.7 Simple Relative Motion

Up to now, we have considered only a single reference in our kinematical considerations. There are times when two or more references may be profitably employed in describing the motion of a particle. We shall consider in this section a very simple case that will fulfill our needs in the early portion of the text.

As a first step, consider two references *xyz* and *XYZ* (Fig. 11.21) moving in such a way that the direction of the axes of *xyz* always retain the same orientation relative to *XYZ* such as has been suggested by the dashed references giving successive positions of *xyz*. Such a motion of *xyz* relative to *XYZ* is called *translation*.

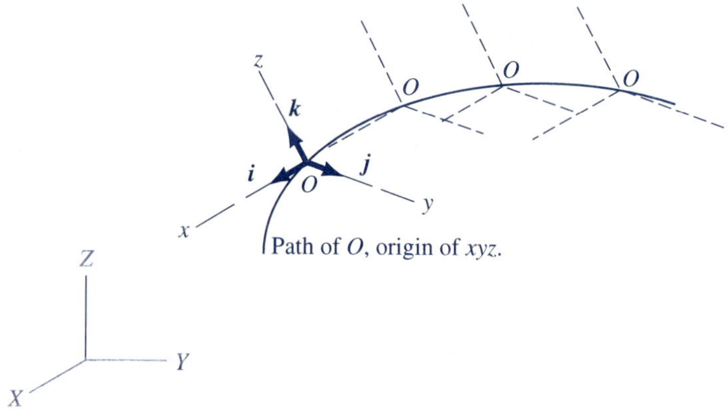

Figure 11.21. Axes *xyz* are translating relative to *XYZ*.

Suppose now that we have a vector $\boldsymbol{A}(t)$ which varies with time. Now in the general case, the time variation of $\boldsymbol{A}$ will depend on from which reference we are observing the time variation. For this reason, we often include subscripts to identify the reference relative to which the time variation is taken. Thus, we have $(d\boldsymbol{A}/dt)_{xyz}$ and $(d\boldsymbol{A}/dt)_{XYZ}$ as time derivatives of $\boldsymbol{A}$ as seen from the *xyz* and *XYZ* axes, respectively. How are these derivatives related for axes *xyz* and *XYZ* that are translating relative to each other? For this purpose, consider $(d\boldsymbol{A}/dt)_{XYZ}$. We will decompose $\boldsymbol{A}$ into components parallel to the *xyz* axes and so we have

$$\left(\frac{d\boldsymbol{A}}{dt}\right)_{XYZ} = \left[\frac{d}{dt}(A_x\boldsymbol{i} + A_y\boldsymbol{j} + A_z\boldsymbol{k}\right]_{XYZ} \tag{11.36}$$

where A_x, A_y, and A_z are the scalar components of $\boldsymbol{A}$ along the *xyz* axes. Because *xyz* translates relative to *XYZ* (see Fig. 11.21), the unit vectors of *xyz*, which we have denoted as $\boldsymbol{i}, \boldsymbol{j}$, and $\boldsymbol{k}$, are *constant vectors* as seen from XYZ. That is, whereas these vectors may change their lines of action, they *do not* change *magnitude* and *direction* as seen from XYZ and are thus constant vectors as seen from XYZ. We then have, for the equation above:

$$\left(\frac{d\boldsymbol{A}}{dt}\right)_{XYZ} = \left(\frac{dA_x}{dt}\right)_{XYZ} \boldsymbol{i} + \left(\frac{dA_y}{dt}\right)_{XYZ} \boldsymbol{j} + \left(\frac{dA_z}{dt}\right)_{XYZ} \boldsymbol{k} \tag{11.37}$$

But A_x, A_y, and A_z are *scalars* and a time derivative of a scalar, as you may remember from the calculus, is not dependent on a reference of observation.[5] We could readily replace $(dA_x/dt)_{XYZ}$ by $(dA_x/dt)_{xyz}$, etc., with no change in meaning—or we could leave off the subscripts entirely for these terms. Thus, we can say now:

$$\left(\frac{d\boldsymbol{A}}{dt}\right)_{XYZ} = \left(\frac{dA_x}{dt}\right)\boldsymbol{i} + \left(\frac{dA_y}{dt}\right)\boldsymbol{j} + \left(\frac{dA_z}{dt}\right)\boldsymbol{k} \tag{11.38}$$

Now consider $(d\boldsymbol{A}/dt)_{xyz}$. Again, decomposing $\boldsymbol{A}$ into components along the xyz axes and noting that $\boldsymbol{i}, \boldsymbol{j}$, and $\boldsymbol{k}$ are constant vectors as seen from xyz, we can conclude that

$$\begin{aligned}\left(\frac{d\boldsymbol{A}}{dt}\right)_{xyz} &= \left(\frac{dA_x}{dt}\right)_{xyz} \boldsymbol{i} + \left(\frac{dA_y}{dt}\right)_{xyz} \boldsymbol{j} + \left(\frac{dA_z}{dt}\right)_{xyz} \boldsymbol{k} \\ &= \left(\frac{dA_x}{dt}\right)\boldsymbol{i} + \left(\frac{dA_y}{dt}\right)\boldsymbol{j} + \left(\frac{dA_z}{dt}\right)\boldsymbol{k}\end{aligned} \tag{11.39}$$

where as discussed earlier we have dropped the xyz subscripts. Observing Eqs. 11.38 and 11.39, we conclude that

$$\left(\frac{d\boldsymbol{A}}{dt}\right)_{XYZ} = \left(\frac{d\boldsymbol{A}}{dt}\right)_{xyz} \tag{11.40}$$

We can conclude that

$$\left(\frac{d}{dt}\right)_{XYZ} = \left(\frac{d}{dt}\right)_{xyz} \tag{11.41}$$

That is, the *time derivative of a vector is the same for all reference axes that are translating relative to each other.*

Note in the discussion that the fact that the unit vectors of xyz were *constant* relative to XYZ resulted in the simple relation 11.41. If xyz were *rotating* relative to XYZ, the unit vectors of xyz would not be constant as seen from XYZ and a more complex relationship would exist between $(d\boldsymbol{A}/dt)_{XYZ}$ and $(d\boldsymbol{A}/dt)_{xyz}$. We shall develop this relationship later in the text.

[5]Clearly, the time variation of the temperature $T(x,y,z)$, a scalar, at any position in the classroom does not depend on the motion of an observer in the classroom who might be interested in the temperature at a particular position at a particular time.

11.8 Motion of a Particle Relative to a Pair of Translating Axes

A pair of references xyz and XYZ are shown now in Fig. 11.22 moving in translation relative to each other. The *velocity vector* of any particle P depends on the reference from which the motion is observed. More precisely, we say that the velocity of particle P relative to reference XYZ is the time rate of change of the position vector $\boldsymbol{r}$ for this reference, where this rate of change is viewed from the XYZ reference. This can be stated mathematically as

$$\boldsymbol{V}_{XYZ} = \left(\frac{d\boldsymbol{r}}{dt}\right)_{XYZ} \tag{11.42}$$

Similarly, for the velocity of particle P as seen from reference xyz, we have

$$\boldsymbol{V}_{xyz} = \left(\frac{d\boldsymbol{\rho}}{dt}\right)_{xyz} \tag{11.43}$$

where we now use position vector $\boldsymbol{\rho}$ for reference xyz and view the change from the xyz reference (see Fig. 11.22). By the same token, $(d\boldsymbol{R}/dt)_{XYZ}$ is the velocity of the origin of the xyz reference as seen from XYZ. Since all points of the xyz reference have the same velocity relative to XYZ at any time t for this case (translation of xyz), we can say that $(d\boldsymbol{R}/dt)_{XYZ}$ is the velocity of reference xyz as seen from XYZ.

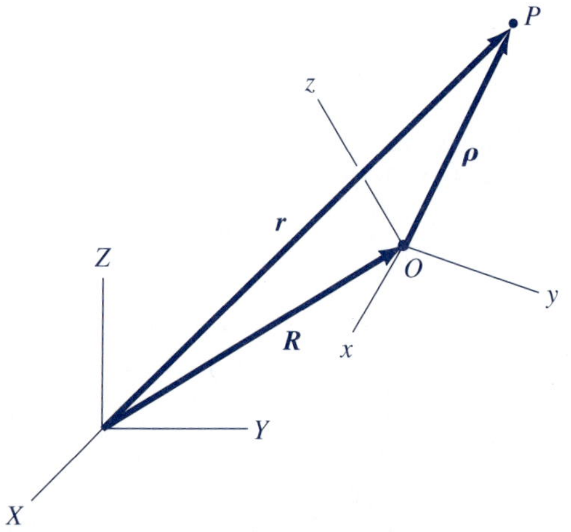

Figure 11.22. Axes xyz are translating relative to XYZ.

From Fig. 11.22 we can relate position vectors $\boldsymbol{\rho}$ and $\boldsymbol{r}$ by the equation

$$\boldsymbol{r} = \boldsymbol{R} + \boldsymbol{\rho} \tag{11.44}$$

Now take the time rate of change of these vectors as seen from XYZ. We get

$$\left(\frac{d\boldsymbol{r}}{dt}\right)_{XYZ} = \left(\frac{d\boldsymbol{R}}{dt}\right)_{XYZ} + \left(\frac{d\boldsymbol{\rho}}{dt}\right)_{XYZ} \tag{11.45}$$

The term on the left side of this equation is $\boldsymbol{V}_{XYZ}$, as indicated earlier, and we shall use the notation $\dot{\boldsymbol{R}}$ for $(d\boldsymbol{R}/dt)_{XYZ}$. We can replace the last term by the derivative $(d\boldsymbol{\rho}/dt)_{xyz}$ in accordance with Eq. 11.41 since the axes are in translation relative to each other. But $(d\boldsymbol{\rho}/dt)_{xyz}$ is simply $\boldsymbol{V}_{xyz}$, the velocity of P relative to xyz. Thus, we have

$$\boldsymbol{V}_{XYZ} = \boldsymbol{V}_{xyz} + \dot{\boldsymbol{R}} \tag{11.46}$$

By the same reasoning, we can show that the acceleration of particle P is related to references XYZ and xyz as follows[6]:

$$\boldsymbol{a}_{XYZ} = \boldsymbol{a}_{xyz} + \ddot{\boldsymbol{R}} \tag{11.47}$$

Equations 11.46 and 11.47 convey the physically simple picture that the motion of a particle relative to XYZ is the sum of the motion of the particle relative to xyz plus the motion of xyz relative to XYZ.

It must be kept clearly in mind that the equations which we have developed apply only to references which have a *translatory* motion relative to each other. In Chapter 15 we shall consider references which have arbitrary motion relative to each other. (Since a reference is a rigid system, we shall need to examine at that time the kinematics of rigid bodies in order to develop these general considerations of relative motion.) The equations presented here will then be special cases.

How can we make use of multiple references? In many problems the motion of a particle is known relative to a given rigid body, and the motion of this body is known relative to the ground or other convenient reference. We can fix a reference xyz to the body, and if the body is in translation relative to the ground, we can then employ the given relations presented in this section to express the motion of the particle relative to the ground.

If, in ensuing chapters, we talk about the "motion of particles relative to a point," such as, for example, the center of mass of the system, then it will be understood that this motion is relative to a *hypothetical reference* moving with the center of mass in a *translatory manner* or, in other words, relative to a nonrotating observer moving with the center of mass.[7]

We illustrate these remarks in the following examples.

[6]As you no doubt will anticipate, the acceleration of a particle as seen from reference XYZ is

$$\boldsymbol{a}_{XYZ} = \left(\frac{d\boldsymbol{V}_{XYZ}}{dt}\right)_{XYZ}$$

Similarly, we have for $\boldsymbol{a}_{xyz}$,

$$\boldsymbol{a}_{xyz} = \left(\frac{d\boldsymbol{V}_{xyz}}{dt}\right)_{xyz}$$

[7]Using a point to convey information about relative motion of a particle only allows you to convey information as to how far or how near the particle is to the point and also as to the speed and rate of change of speed of the particle toward or away from the point. The important information regarding *direction* is entirely left out, requiring a reference frame in order to give this kind of information.

Example 11.10

A jet airliner is shown in Fig. 11.23 flying at a speed of 600 mi/hr in a translatory manner relative to the ground reference *XYZ*. At the instant of interest, a downdraft causes the plane to accelerate downward at a rate of 50 mi/hr/sec. While this is happening, the pilot cuts back on the throttle so that the plane is decelerating in the *Y* direction at the rate of 30 mi/hr/sec. Thus, the plane has an acceleration given as

$$\boldsymbol{a} = -50\boldsymbol{k} - 30\boldsymbol{j} \text{ mi/hr/sec} \tag{a}$$

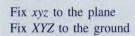

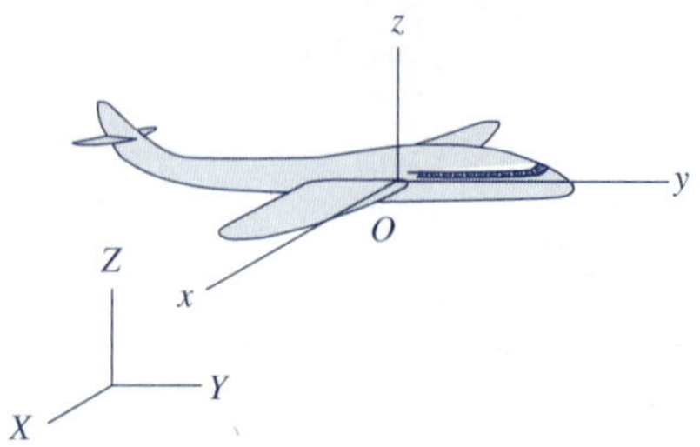

Figure 11.23. Plane translates relative to *XYZ*.

while maintaining a translatory attitude. While this is happening, a solenoid is operated to close a valve gate that weighs $\frac{1}{2}$ lb. What is the force on the valve gate from the plane at the instant when the valve gate is moving downward relative to the airplane at a speed of 10 ft/sec and accelerating downward relative to the plane at a rate of 16.1 ft/sec^2?

We must find the acceleration of the valve relative to the ground reference *XYZ*, which may be taken in the problem to be an *inertial reference*. This information will permit us to use the familiar form of Newton's law. It will be convenient in this undertaking to *fix* a reference *xyz*, having the same unit vectors as reference *XYZ*, to the airplane at any convenient location (see Fig. 11.23). Thus

Fix *xyz* to the plane
Fix *XYZ* to the ground

We can then say for the motion of the valve gate relative to *xyz*:

$$\boldsymbol{a}_{xyz} = -16.1\boldsymbol{k} \text{ ft/sec}^2 \tag{b}$$

The acceleration of *O*, the origin of *xyz* relative to *XYZ*, is

$$\ddot{\boldsymbol{R}} = -50\boldsymbol{k} - 30\boldsymbol{j} \text{ mi/hr/sec} \tag{c}$$

Since the references are translating relative to each other, we can employ Eq. 11.47 to get $\boldsymbol{a}_{XYZ}$, the acceleration of the valve gate relative to inertial space. Thus,

$$\begin{aligned}\boldsymbol{a}_{XYZ} &= (-50\boldsymbol{k} - 30\boldsymbol{j})\left(\frac{5{,}280}{3{,}600}\right) + (-16.1\boldsymbol{k})\\ &= -44\boldsymbol{j} - 89.5\boldsymbol{k} \text{ ft/sec}^2\end{aligned}$$

We can now employ **Newton's law** in the form

$$\boldsymbol{F} = m\boldsymbol{a}_{XYZ} \tag{d}$$

Example 11.10 (Continued)

Thus, denoting the total force from the airplane as $\boldsymbol{F}_{\text{plane}}$, and remembering that the gate valve weighs $\frac{1}{2}$ lb, we have

$$\boldsymbol{F}_{\text{plane}} - \tfrac{1}{2}\boldsymbol{k} = \frac{\frac{1}{2}}{g}(-44\boldsymbol{j} - 89.5\boldsymbol{k}) \tag{e}$$

where $-\frac{1}{2}\boldsymbol{k}$ is the force of gravity. Solving for $\boldsymbol{F}_{\text{plane}}$ we get

$$\boldsymbol{F}_{\text{plane}} = -.684\boldsymbol{j} - .890\boldsymbol{k} \text{ lb} \tag{f}$$

Example 11.11

The freighter in Fig. 11.24 is moving at a steady speed V_1 of 15 km/hr relative to the water. The freighter is 200 m long at the waterline with point A at midship. A stalking submerged submarine fires a torpedo when the submarine and freighter are at the positions shown in the diagram. The torpedo maintains a steady speed V_2 of 40 km/hr relative to the water. Will the torpedo hit the freighter?

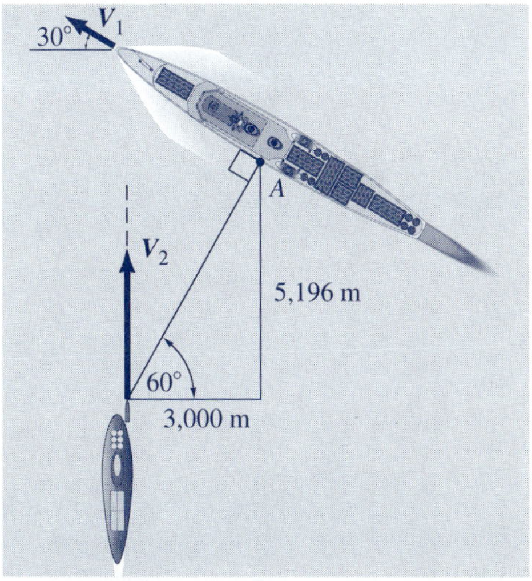

$\boldsymbol{V}_1 = 15$ km/hr
$\boldsymbol{V}_2 = 40$ km/hr
Freighter length = 200 m

Figure 11.24. A torpedo is fired toward a freighter. Does it hit or miss?

A key feature in solving this problem (and others like it) is that we can readily tell whether there is a hit or a miss and, if there is a hit, exactly where this takes place. This is done by simply observing the torpedo from a vantage point of the freighter. The torpedo velocity *relative to the freighter* (i.e., the motion seen by an on-board observer) will point directly to the position of potential contact with the freighter or will indicate a miss.

Example 11.11 (Continued)

We accordingly make the following reference fixes:

Fix xyz to the freighter
Fix XYZ to the water

This is shown in Fig. 11.25. The velocity of xyz, and, hence the freighter, relative to XYZ (i.e., $\dot{\boldsymbol{R}}$) is $(-15 \cos 30° \boldsymbol{i} + 15 \sin 30° \boldsymbol{j})$ km/hr. The velocity of the torpedo relative to XYZ is $40\boldsymbol{j}$ km/hr. We can then say

$$\boldsymbol{V}_{XYZ} = \boldsymbol{V}_{xyz} + \dot{\boldsymbol{R}}$$

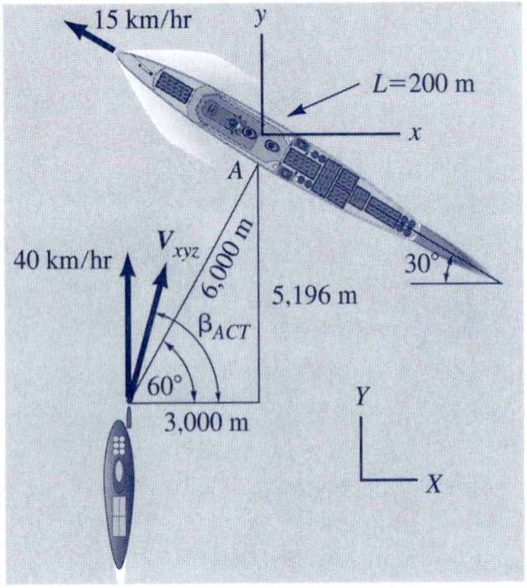

Figure 11.25. Velocity vectors and references for the engagement.

Hence,

$$40\boldsymbol{j} = \boldsymbol{V}_{xyz} - 15\cos 30°\boldsymbol{i} + 15\sin 30°\boldsymbol{j}$$

$$\therefore \boldsymbol{V}_{xyz} = 12.99\boldsymbol{i} + 32.5\boldsymbol{j} \text{ km/hr} \qquad \text{(a)}$$

To just miss the freighter, the velocity vector of the torpedo relative to the freighter, $\boldsymbol{V}_{xyz}$, must have a course such that this vector forms an angle β_0 with the horizontal axis given as (see Fig. 11.26)

$$\beta_0 = \alpha + 60° = \tan^{-1}\frac{100}{6{,}000} + 60° = 60.95° \qquad \text{(b)}$$

Now go back to Eq. (a) to obtain the actual angle, β_{ACT} (see Fig. 11.25), for the actual relative velocity vector $\boldsymbol{V}_{xyz}$.

$$\beta_{ACT} = \tan^{-1}\frac{\left(\boldsymbol{V}_{xyz}\right)_y}{\left(\boldsymbol{V}_{xyz}\right)_x} = \tan^{-1}\frac{32.5}{12.99} = 68.21°$$

Thus we may all relax; the torpedo just misses the freighter since $\beta_{ACT} > \beta_0$.

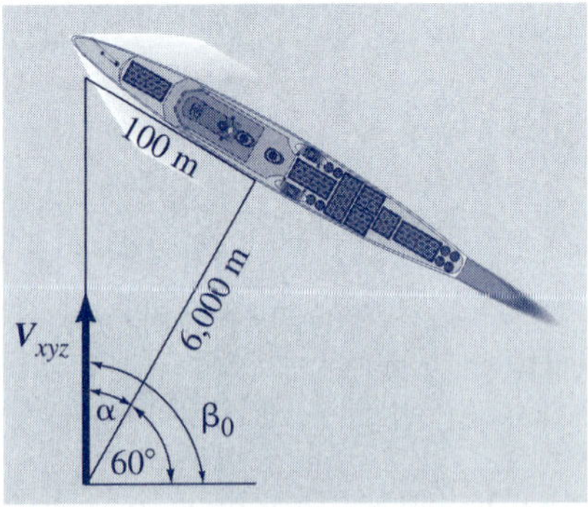

Figure 11.26. Relative velocity vector $\boldsymbol{V}_{xyz}$ for just missing the freighter.

PROBLEMS

11.71. Two wheels rotate about stationary axes each at the same angular velocity, $\dot{\theta} = 5$ rad/sec. A particle A moves along the spoke of the larger wheel at the speed V_1 of 5 ft/sec relative to the spoke and at the instant shown is decelerating at the rate of 3 ft/sec^2 relative to the spoke. What are the velocity and acceleration of particle A as seen by an observer on the hub of the smaller wheel? What are the velocity and acceleration of particle A as seen by an observer on the hub of the smaller wheel if the axis of the larger wheel moves at the instant of interest to the left with a speed of 10 ft/sec while decelerating at the rate of 2 ft/sec^2? Both wheels maintain equal angular speeds.

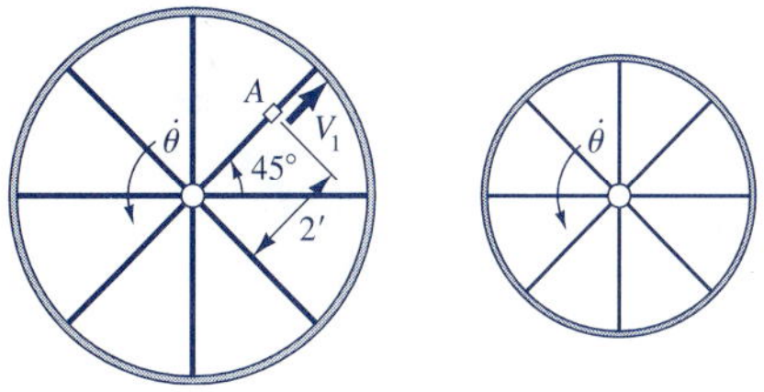

Figure P.11.71.

11.72. Four particles of equal mass undergo coplanar motion in the xy plane with the following velocities:

$$V_1 = 2 \text{ m/sec}$$
$$V_2 = 3 \text{ m/sec}$$
$$V_3 = 2 \text{ m/sec}$$
$$V_4 = 5 \text{ m/sec}$$

We showed in Section 8.3 that the velocity of the center of mass can be found as follows:

$$\left(\sum_i m_i\right)\mathbf{V}_c = \sum_i m_i \mathbf{V}_i$$

where $\mathbf{V}_c$ is the velocity of the center of mass. What are the velocities of the particles relative to the center of mass?

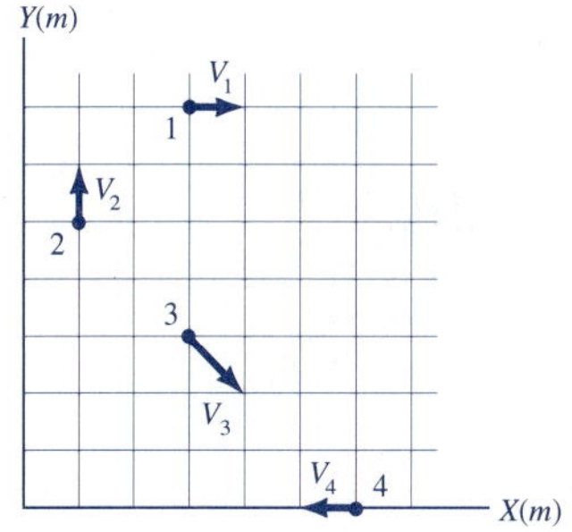

Figure P.11.72.

11.73. A sled, used by researchers to test man's ability to perform during large accelerations over extended periods of time, is powered by a small rocket engine in the rear and slides on lubricated tracks. If the sled is accelerating at 6g, what force does the man need to exert on a 3-ounce body to give it an acceleration relative to the sled of

$$30\boldsymbol{i} + 20\boldsymbol{j} \text{ ft/sec}^2$$

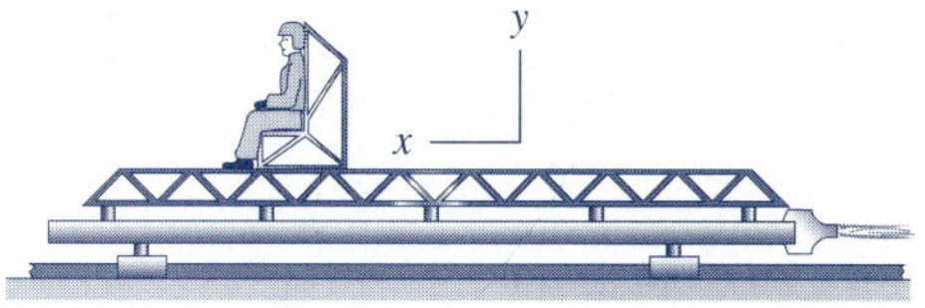

Figure P.11.73.

11.74. On the sled of Problem 11.73 is a device (see the diagram) on which mass M rotates about a horizontal axis at an angular speed ω of 5,000 rpm. If the inclination θ of the arm BM is maintained at 30° with the vertical plane C–C, what is the total force on the mass M at the instant it is in its uppermost position? The sled is undergoing an acceleration of 5g. Take M as having a mass of .15 kg.

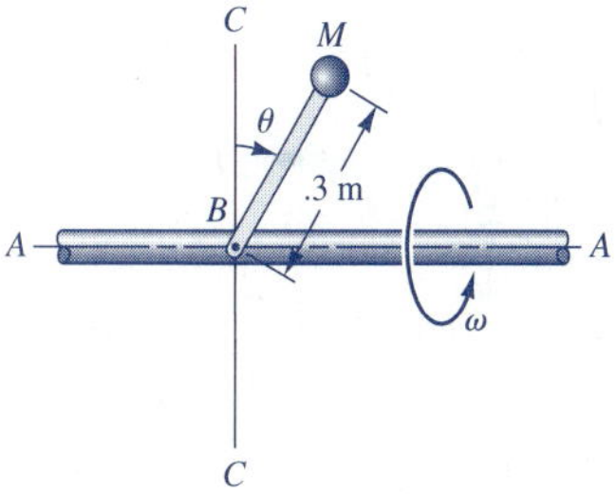

Figure P.11.74.

11.75. A vehicle, wherein a mass M of 1 lbm rotates with an angular speed ω equal to 5 rad/sec, moves with a speed V given as $V = 5 \sin \Omega t$ ft/sec relative to the ground with t in seconds. When $t = 1$ sec, the rod AM is in the position shown. At this instant, what is the dynamic force exerted by the mass M along the axis of rod AM if $\Omega = 3$ rad/sec?

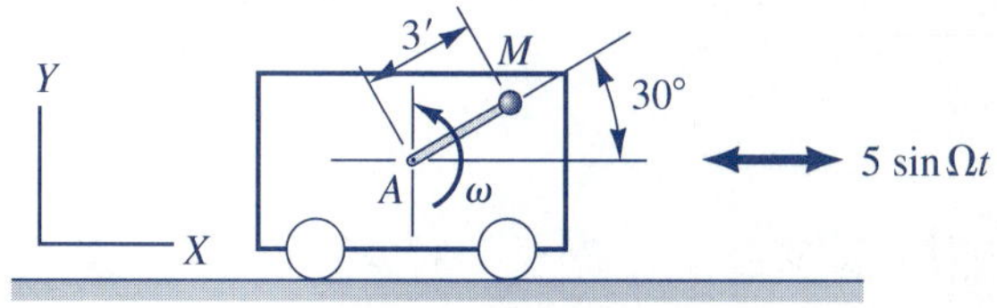

Figure P.11.75.

11.76. In Problem 11.75, what is the frequency of oscillation, Ω, of the vehicle and the value of ω if, at the instant shown, there is a force on the mass M given as

$$\boldsymbol{F} = 25\boldsymbol{i} - 35\boldsymbol{j} \text{ lb}$$

11.77. A cockpit C is used to carry a worker for service work on road lighting systems. The cockpit is moved always in a translatory manner relative to the ground. If the angular speed ω of arm AB is 1 rad/min when $\theta = 30°$, what are the velocity and acceleration of any point in the cockpit body relative to the truck? At this instant, what are the velocity and acceleration, relative to the truck, of a particle moving with a horizontal speed V of .5 ft/sec and with a rate of increase of speed of .02 ft/sec^2, both relative to the cockpit?

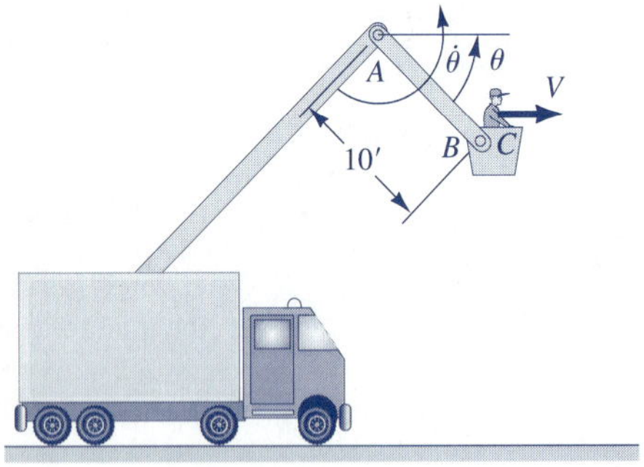

Figure P.11.77.

11.78. A Ferris wheel rotates at the instant of interest with an angular speed $\dot{\theta}$ of .5 rad/sec and is increasing its angular speed at the rate of .1 rad/sec^2. A ball is thrown from the ground to an occupant at A. The ball arrives at the instant of interest with a speed relative to the ground given as

$$\boldsymbol{V}_{XYZ} = -10\boldsymbol{j} - 2\boldsymbol{k} \text{ ft/sec}$$

What are the velocity and the acceleration of the ball relative to the occupant at seat A provided that this seat is not "swinging?" The radius of the wheel is 20 ft.

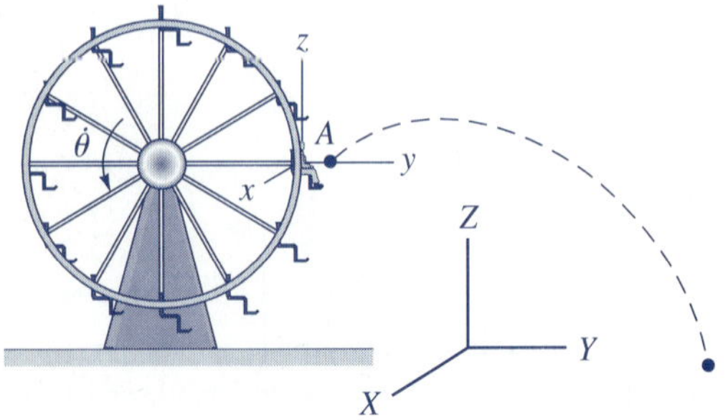

Figure P.11.78.

11.79. A rocket moves at a speed of 700 m/sec and accelerates at a rate of $5g$ relative to the ground reference XYZ. The products of combustion at A leave the rocket at a speed of 1,700 m/sec relative to the rocket and are accelerating at the rate of 30 m/sec^2 relative to the rocket. What are the speed and acceleration of an element of the combustion products as seen from the ground? The rocket moves along a straight-line path whose direction cosines for the XYZ reference are $l = .6$ and $m = .6$.

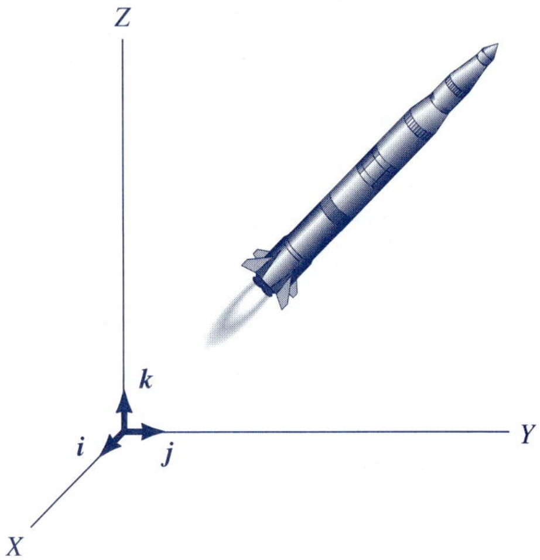

Figure P.11.79.

11.80. Two 10-m international-class sailboats are racing. They are on different tacks. If there is no change in course, will A hit B? If so, where from the center of B does this happen?

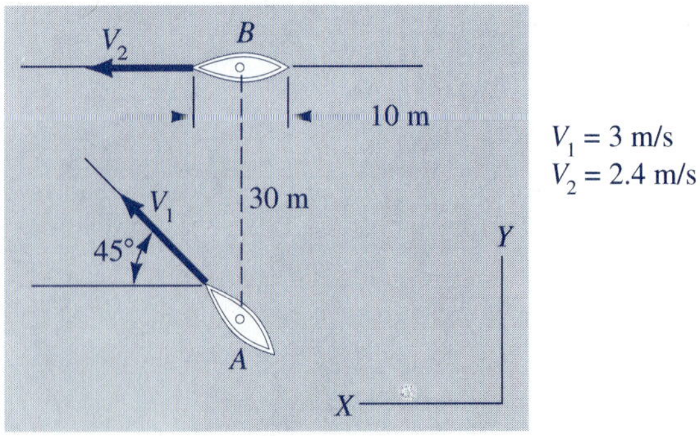

Figure P.11.80.

11.81. A train is moving at a speed of 10 km/hr. What speed should car *A* have to just barely miss the front of the train? How long does it take to reach this position? Use a multireference approach only.

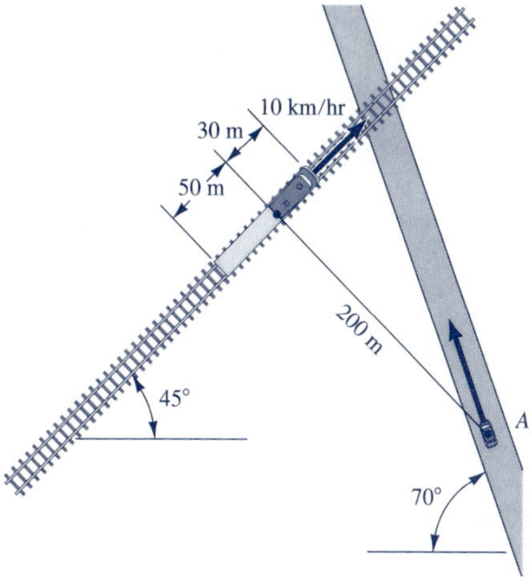

Figure P.11.81.

11.82. A Tomahawk missile is being tested for its effect on a naval vessel. A destroyer is towing an old expendable naval frigate at a speed of 15 knots. The missile is shown at time *t* moving along a straight line at a constant speed of 500 mi/hr, the guidance system having been shut off to avoid an accident involving the towing destroyer. Does the missile hit the target and if so where does the impact occur? The missile moves at a constant elevation of 10 ft above the surface of the water.

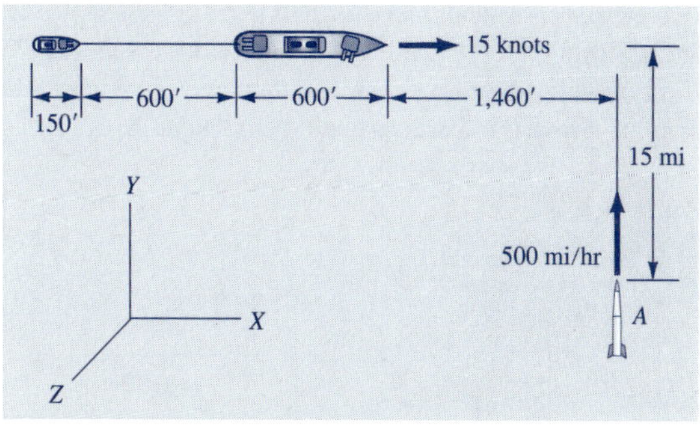

Figure P.11.82.

11.83. On a windy day, a hot air balloon is moving in a translatory manner relative to the ground with the following acceleration:

$$\boldsymbol{a} = 2\boldsymbol{i} - 5\boldsymbol{j} + 3\boldsymbol{k} \text{ m/s}^2$$

Simultaneously, a man in the balloon basket is swinging a small device for measuring the dew point. The device of mass 5 kg is connected to a massless rod. At the instant shown, $\omega = 2$ rad/sec and $\dot{\omega} = 3$ rad/sec^2 both relative to the balloon. What force does the rod exert on the device at this instant? Give the result in vector and scalar form. The rod is in a horizontal position (see elevation view) at the instant shown and has a length of .5 m.

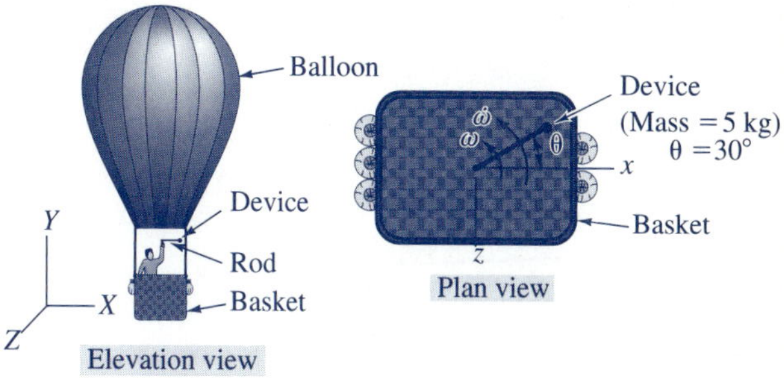

Figure P.11.83.

11.84. A submarine is moving at a constant horizontal speed of 15 knots below the surface of the ocean. At the same time, the sub is descending downward by discharging air with an acceleration of .023g's while remaining horizontal. In the submarine, a flyball governor operates with weights having a mass of 500 g each. The governor is rotating with speed ω of 5 rad/sec. If at time t, $\theta = 30°$, $\dot{\theta} = .2$ rad/sec, and $\ddot{\theta} = 1$ rad/sec^2, what is the force developed on the support of the governor system as a result solely of the motion of the weights at this instant? [*Hint:* What is the *acceleration* of the *center of mass* of the spheres relative to *inertial* space?]

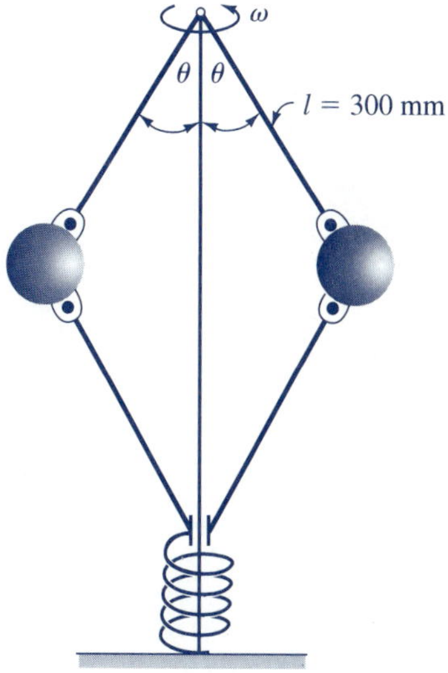

Figure P.11.84.

11.85. A fighter plane is landing and has the following acceleration relative to the ground while moving in a translatory manner:

$$\boldsymbol{a} = -.2g\boldsymbol{k} - .1g\boldsymbol{j} \text{ m/s}^2$$

The wheels are being let down as shown. What is the dynamic force acting at the center of the wheel at the instant shown? The following data apply:

$\omega = .3$ rad/sec $\qquad \dot{\omega} = .4$ rad/sec^2

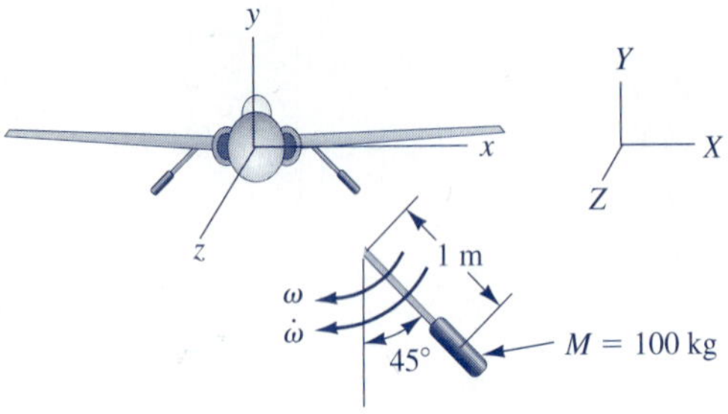

Figure P.11.85.

11.86. In a steam turbine, steam is expended through a stationary nozzle at a speed V_0 of 3,000 m/sec at an angle of 30°. The steam impinges on a series of blades mounted all around the periphery of a cylinder, which is rotating at a speed Ω of 5,000 rpm. The steam impinges on the blades at a radial distance of 1.20 m from the axis of rotation of the cylinder. What angle α should the left side of the blades have for the steam to enter the region between blades most smoothly? [*Hint:* Let *xyz* move with a blade in a translatory manner relative to the ground (*xyz* is thus not entirely fixed to the blade and hence does not rotate).]

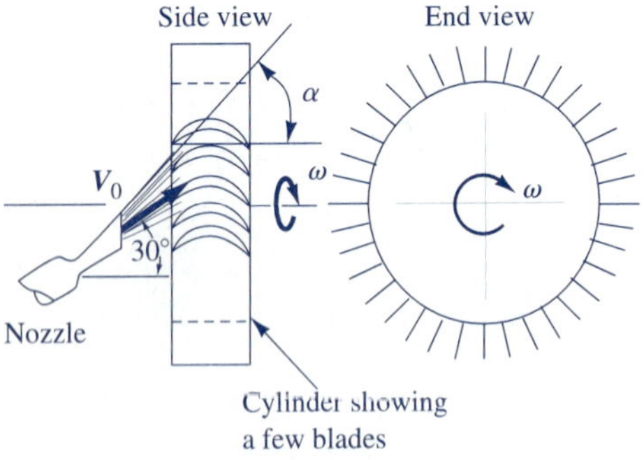

Figure P.11.86.

11.87. A sailboat moves at a speed V_0 of 8 mi/hr relative to a stationary reference *XY*. The wind is moving uniformly at a speed V_1 relative to *XY* in the direction shown. On top of the mast is a direction vane responding to the wind relative to the boat. If this vane points in a direction of 170° from the *X* axis, what is the velocity V_1 of the wind?

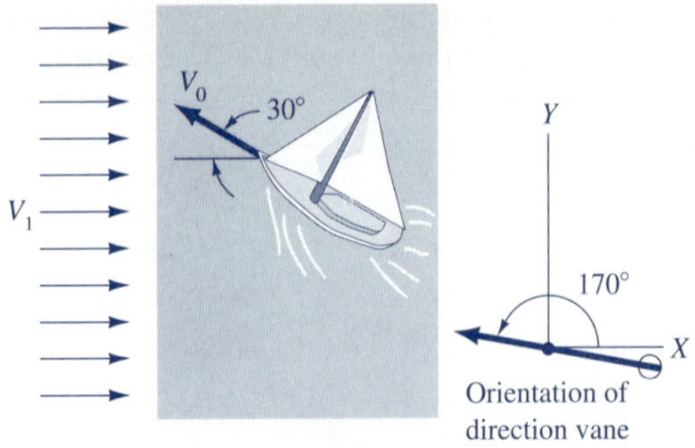

Figure P.11.87.

11.88. A boat is about to depart from point *A* on the shore of a river that has a uniform velocity V_0 of 5 ft/sec. If the boat can move at the rate of 15 ft/sec relative to the water, and if we want to move along a straight path from *A* to *B*, how long will it take to go from *A* to *B*? At what angle β should the boat be aimed relative to the water?

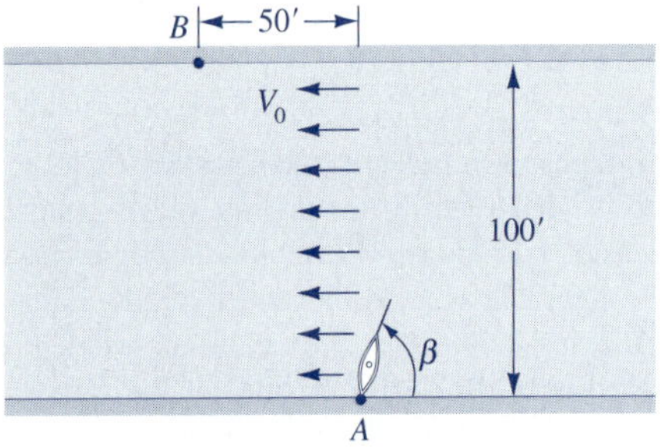

Figure P.11.88.

11.89. A jet passenger plane is moving at a speed V_0 of 800 km/hr. A storm region extending 4 km in width is reported 15 km due East of its position. The region is moving NW at a speed V_1 of 100 km/hr. At what maximum angle α from due N can the plane fly to just miss the storm front?

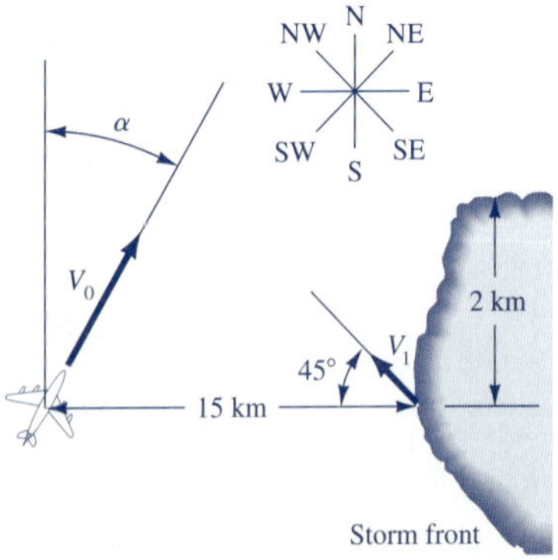

Figure P.11.89.

11.90. Mass M of 3 kg rotates about point O in an accelerating rocket in the xy plane. At the instant shown, what is the force from the rod onto the mass? Include the effects of gravity if $g = 7.00$ m/s^2 at the elevation of the rocket.

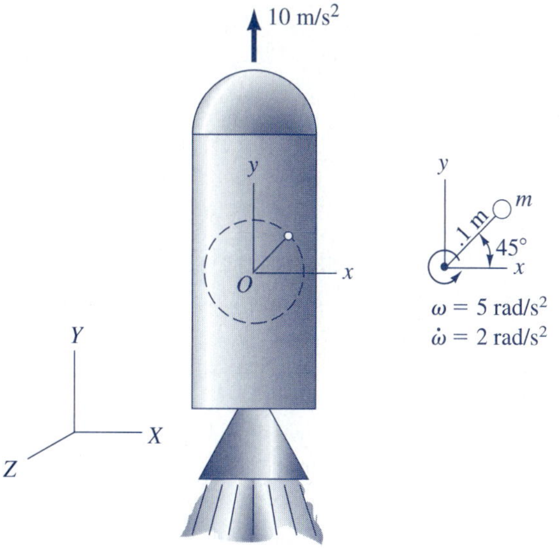

Figure P.11.90.

11.91. A light plane is approaching a runway in a cross-wind. This cross-wind has a uniform speed V_0 of 33 mi/hr. The plane has a velocity component V_1 parallel to the ground of 70 mi/hr relative to the wind at an angle β of 30°. The rate of descent is such that the plane will touch down somewhere along A–A. Will this touchdown occur on the runway or off the runway for the data given?

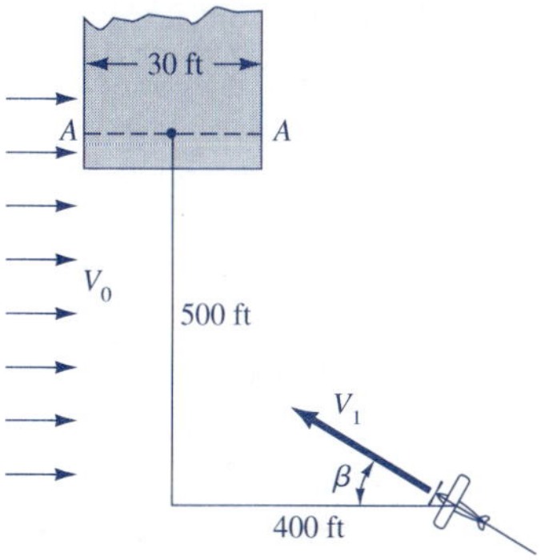

Figure P.11.91.

11.92. A helicopter is shown moving relative to the ground with the following motion:

$$V = 130\boldsymbol{i} + 70\boldsymbol{j} + 20\boldsymbol{k} \text{ km/hr}$$
$$\boldsymbol{a} = 10\boldsymbol{i} + 16\boldsymbol{j} + 7\boldsymbol{k} \text{ km/hr/s}$$

The helicopter blade is rotating relative to the helicopter in the following manner at the instant of interest:

$$\omega_1 = 100 \text{ rpm} \qquad \dot{\omega}_1 = 10.3 \text{ rpm/sec}$$

The blade is 10 m long. What is the velocity and the acceleration of the tip B relative to the ground reference XYZ? Give your results in meters and seconds. The blade is parallel to the X axis at the instant of interest.

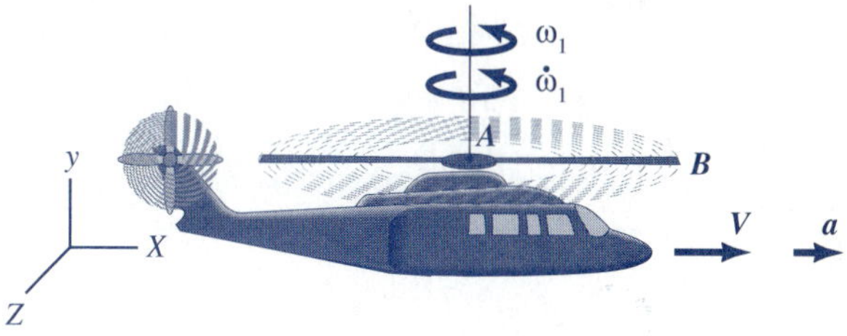

Figure P.11.92.

11.93. A destroyer in rough seas has the following translational acceleration as seen from inertial reference XYZ when it is firing its main battery in the YZ plane:

$$\boldsymbol{a} = 5\boldsymbol{j} + 2\boldsymbol{k} \text{ m/s}^2$$

What must ω_1 and $\dot{\omega}_1$ of the gun barrel be relative to the ship at this instant so that tip A of the barrel has zero acceleration relative to XYZ?

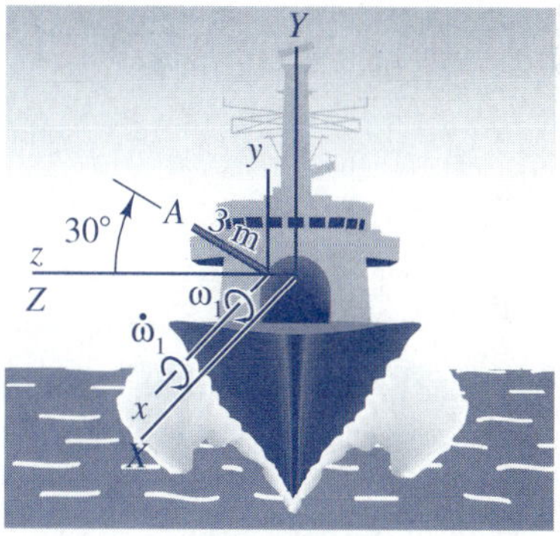

Figure P.11.93.

11.94. A small elevator E in an ocean-going vessel has the following motion relative to the ship:

$$\boldsymbol{a}_{Elev.} = .2g\boldsymbol{k} \text{ m/s}^2$$

The ship has the following motion relative to nearby land:

$$\boldsymbol{a}_{Ship} = .2\boldsymbol{i} + 3\boldsymbol{j} + .6\boldsymbol{k} \text{ m/s}^2$$

If the weight of the elevator including passengers is 8,000 N, what is the force on the ship from the elevator?

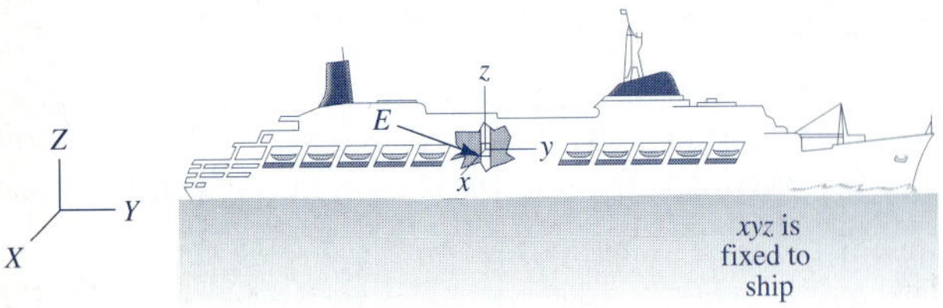

Figure P.11.94.

11.95. You are a court expert consultant. At what distance from point C, the front of the moving train, do you testify that car A collides with train B? Use a multireference approach.

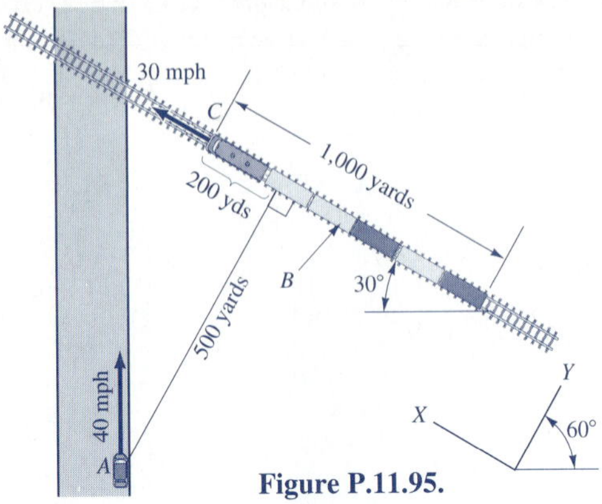

Figure P.11.95.

11.9 Closure

In this chapter, we have presented, first, a few general comments on differentiation and integration of vectors. We then carried out differentiations in a variety of ways. In the first case, the vector $\boldsymbol{r}$ was expressed in terms of rectangular scalar components and the fixed unit vectors $\boldsymbol{i}$, $\boldsymbol{j}$, and $\boldsymbol{k}$. The procedure for finding $\dot{\boldsymbol{r}}$ and $\ddot{\boldsymbol{r}}$ in terms of rectangular scalar components is straightforward and involves only the familiar differentiation operations of scalar calculus. We next considered the kinematics of a particle moving along some given path. Here, we obtained $\dot{\boldsymbol{r}}$ and $\ddot{\boldsymbol{r}}$ in terms of speeds and rates of changes of speeds of the particle along the path with component directions no longer fixed in space but instead related at each point along the path to the geometry of the path. For this reason, we brought in certain concepts of differential geometry such as the osculating plane, the normal vector, etc. Finally, we computed $\dot{\boldsymbol{r}}$ and $\ddot{\boldsymbol{r}}$ in terms of cylindrical coordinates with component directions always in the radial, transverse, and axial directions. Clearly, the radial and transverse directions are not fixed in space and change as the particle moves about.

In carrying out various derivatives of unit vectors that are not fixed in space, such as $\boldsymbol{\epsilon}_{\bar{r}}$ and $\boldsymbol{\epsilon}_{\theta}$, we went through a limiting process in arriving at the desired results. Later, in the study of kinematics of a rigid body, we present simple straightforward formal procedures for this purpose.

We next investigated the relations between velocities and accelerations of a particle, as seen from different references, which are translating relative to each other. We called such motions simple relative motion. Later, when we undertake rigid-body motion, we shall consider the case involving references moving arbitrarily relative to each other. It is vital to remember that we must measure $\boldsymbol{a}$ relative to an *inertial reference* when we employ **Newton's law** in the form $\boldsymbol{F} = m\boldsymbol{a}$. We may at times find it convenient to employ two references in this connection where one reference is the inertial reference needed for the desired acceleration vector. This situation is illustrated in Example 11.10.

In Chapter 12, we shall consider the *dynamics* of motion of a particle. We shall then have ample opportunity to employ the kinematics of Chapter 11.

11.107. Pilots of figh
prevent blackouts durir
keep the blood from d
accelerated in a directic
flier can take $5g$'s of ac
If a flier is diving at a s
radius of curvature that
ing bad physiological e

11.108. A particle mo
a path given as $x = y^2 -$
particle in terms of rect
position $y = 3$ m. Do th
niques and then by Car
g's of acceleration is th

11.109. A submarine
the following velocity a
ence:

$$V = 6i + 7.5j + 2k \; \text{k}$$

A device inside the subr
end of the arm. At the i
vertical plane with the f
eration:

$$\omega = 10 \; \text{r}$$

The arm is vertical at th
may be considered to b
are the velocity and acce
ticle at this instant relat
meters and seconds. Wh
onto the particle at this i

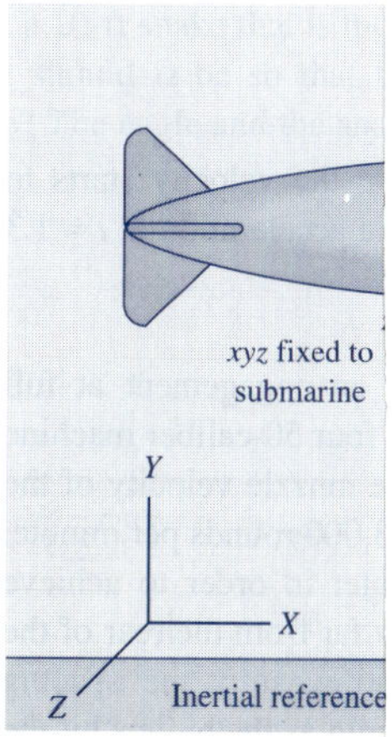

PROBLEMS

11.96. A particle at position (3, 4, 6) ft at time $t_0 = 1$ sec is given a constant acceleration having the value $6i + 3j$ ft/sec^2. If the velocity at the time t_0 is $16i + 20j + 5k$ ft/sec, what is the velocity of the particle 20 sec later? Also give the position of the particle.

11.97. A pin is confined to slide in a circular slot of radius 6 m. The pin must also slide in a straight slot that moves to the right at a constant speed, V, of 3 m/sec while maintaining a constant angle of 30° with the horizontal. What are the velocity and acceleration of the pin A at the instant shown?

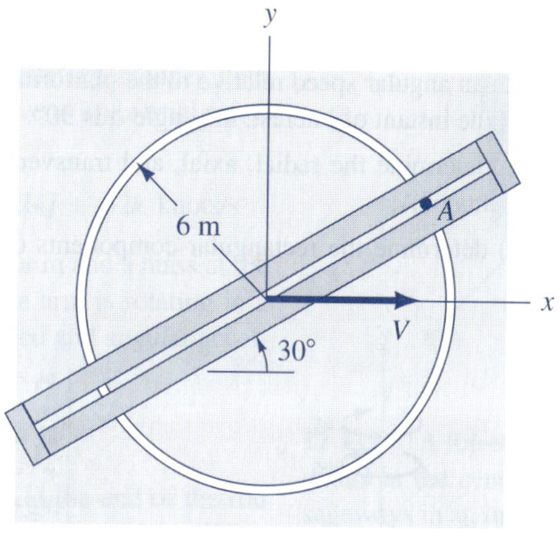

Figure P.11.97.

11.98. A freighter is moving in a river at a speed of 5 knots relative to the water. A small boat A is moving relative to the water at a speed of 3 knots in a direction as shown in the diagram. The river is moving at a uniform speed of .6 knots relative to the ground. Will the boat hit the freighter and, if so, where will the impact occur?

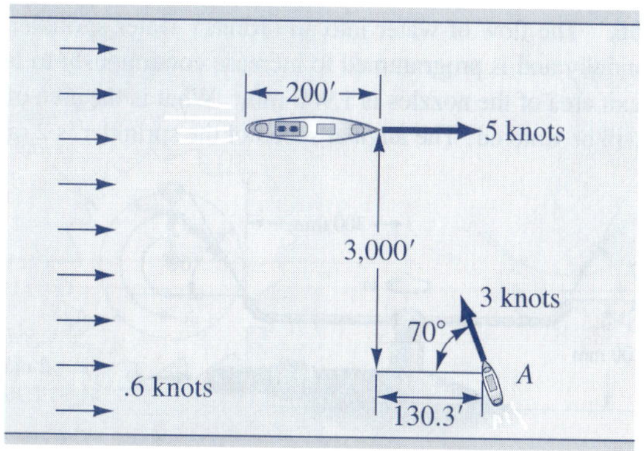

Figure P.11.98.

11.99. A light line attached to a streamlined weight A is "shot" by a line rifle from a small boat C to a large boat D in heavy seas. The weight must travel a distance of 20 yd horizontally and reach the larger boat's deck, which is 20 ft higher than the deck of boat C. If the angle α of firing is 40°, what minimum velocity V_0 is needed? At the instant of firing, boat C is dipping down into the water at a speed of 5 ft/sec. Assume that the larger boat remains essentially fixed at constant level.

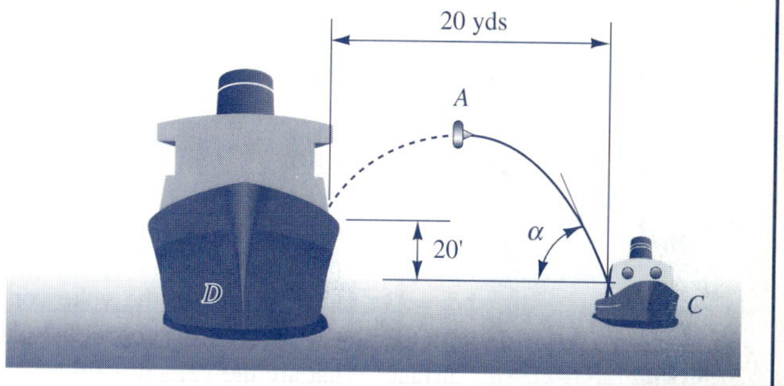

Figure P.11.99.

11.100. A projectile is fired at an angle of 60° as shown. At what elevation y does it strike the hill whose equation has been estimated as $y = 10^{-5}x^2$ m? Neglect air friction and take the muzzle velocity as 1,000 m/sec.

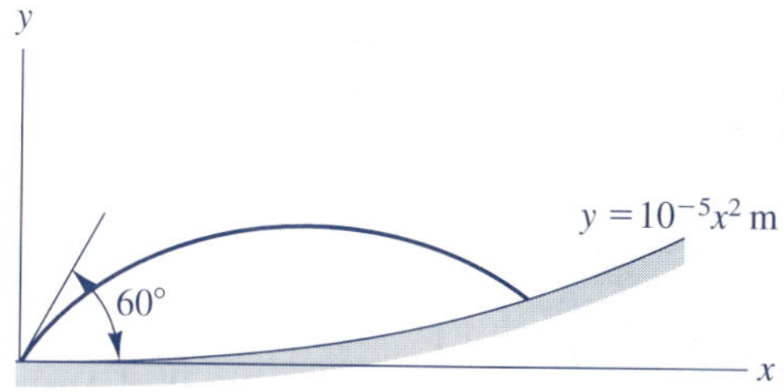

Figure P.11.100.

11.101. A proposed space laboratory, in order to simulate gravity, rotates relative to an inertial reference XYZ at a rate ω_1. For occupant A in the living quarters to be comfortable, what should the approximate value of ω_1 be? Clearly, at the center, there is close to zero gravity for zero-g experiments. A conveyor connects the living quarters with the zero-g laboratory. At the instant of interest, a package D has a speed of 5 m/s and a rate of change of speed of 3 m/s^2 relative to the space station, both toward the laboratory. What are the axial, transverse, and radial velocity and acceleration components at the instant of interest relative to the inertial reference? What are the rectangular components of the acceleration vector?

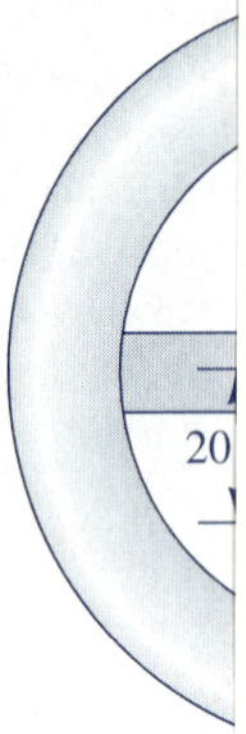

11.102. A yoke *AB* r
equal to $\pi/6$ rad, it has
change of angular spee
strains a pin *C* to move
to slide on the paraboli
eration vectors at the in

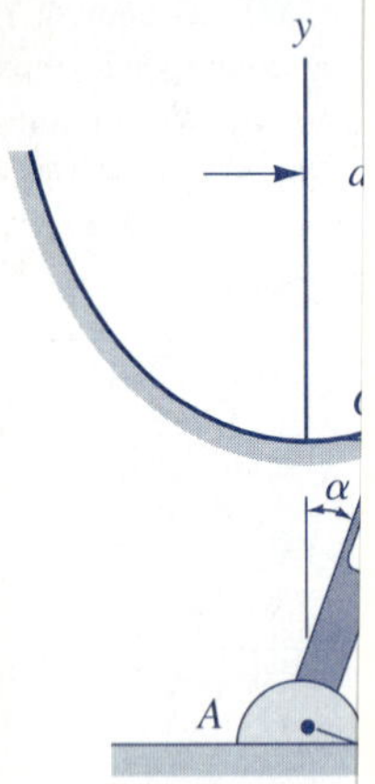

11.103. In Problem 1
ture of a stream of w
radius .30 m into free
radius of curvature?

11.104. A batter ha
fence. It has a line dr
ball. Neglecting frictio
attempts to catch it?

11.121. A space device has a velocity of $.500\boldsymbol{i} + .200\boldsymbol{j}$ m/s and an acceleration of $.200\boldsymbol{i} + .300\boldsymbol{k}$ m/s^2, both relative to the ground reference *XYZ*. Rod *CD* has an angular motion relative to the space device equal to $\omega = 2$ rad/s and $\dot{\omega} = 3$ rad/s^2. What are the velocity and the acceleration of mass *M* relative to the ground? *CD* is in the vertical *zy* plane at the instant of interest. Reference *xyz* shown is fixed to rod *AB*. *CD* is at 60° from *AB*.

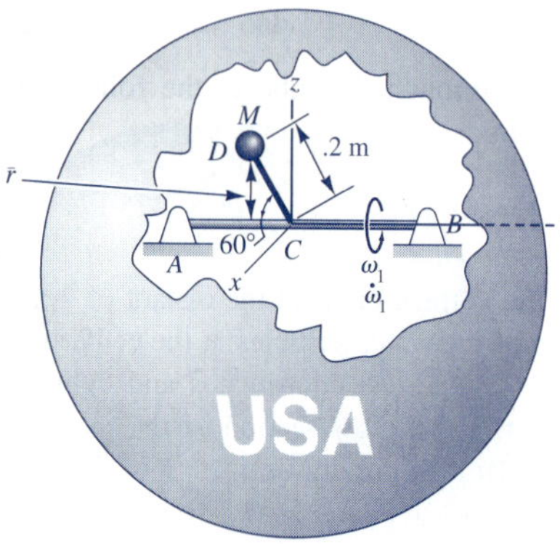

Figure P.11.121.

11.122. A weather balloon has the following motion relative to the inertial reference *XYZ*:

$$\boldsymbol{V} = 150\boldsymbol{i} + 200\boldsymbol{j} + 60\boldsymbol{k} \text{ m/s}$$
$$\boldsymbol{a} = 20\boldsymbol{i} - 40\boldsymbol{j} + 38\boldsymbol{k} \text{ m/s}^2$$

A light rod at *A* is connected to particle *D* and is rotating relative to the balloon at the instant of interest with angular speed $\omega_1 = 5$ rad/s and rate of change of speed $\dot{\omega}_1 = 2$ rad/s^2. What is the velocity of the particle at *D* relative to *XYZ* at the instant of interest? The distance $AD = .2$ m. What is the tensile force on the rod in the direction of *AD*? The mass of the particle at *D* is 1 kg.

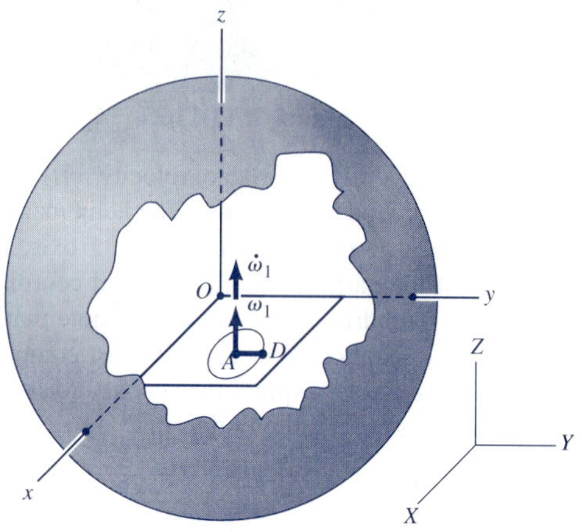

Figure P.11.122.

***11.123.** A particle is made to move along a path given in terms of the parameter τ in the following manner:

$$(x)_p = -\sin 2\tau \qquad (y)_p = \cos 2\tau \qquad (z)_p = e^{-\tau}$$

Give a simple sketch of the path. When the particle is at an elevation $z = 1$, the speed along the path is 5 ft/sec and the rate of change of speed along the path is 10 ft/sec^2. Find the acceleration vector at $z = 1$ in components for path coordinates.

***11.124.** Determine the direction of the osculating plane at position $z = 1$ for the three-dimensional curve of Problem 11.123. We got the following results from the previous problem:

$$\boldsymbol{\epsilon}_n = R(.08\boldsymbol{i} - .80\boldsymbol{j} + .16\boldsymbol{k})$$
$$\boldsymbol{\epsilon}_t = .894\boldsymbol{i} - .447\boldsymbol{k}$$
$$R = .8198 \text{ ft}$$

PROBLEMS

11.96. A particle at position (3, 4, 6) ft at time $t_0 = 1$ sec is given a constant acceleration having the value $6\boldsymbol{i} + 3\boldsymbol{j}$ ft/sec^2. If the velocity at the time t_0 is $16\boldsymbol{i} + 20\boldsymbol{j} + 5\boldsymbol{k}$ ft/sec, what is the velocity of the particle 20 sec later? Also give the position of the particle.

11.97. A pin is confined to slide in a circular slot of radius 6 m. The pin must also slide in a straight slot that moves to the right at a constant speed, V, of 3 m/sec while maintaining a constant angle of 30° with the horizontal. What are the velocity and acceleration of the pin A at the instant shown?

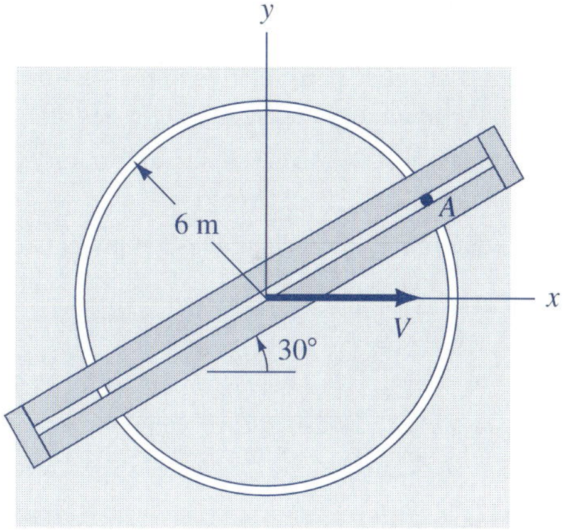

Figure P.11.97.

11.98. A freighter is moving in a river at a speed of 5 knots relative to the water. A small boat A is moving relative to the water at a speed of 3 knots in a direction as shown in the diagram. The river is moving at a uniform speed of .6 knots relative to the ground. Will the boat hit the freighter and, if so, where will the impact occur?

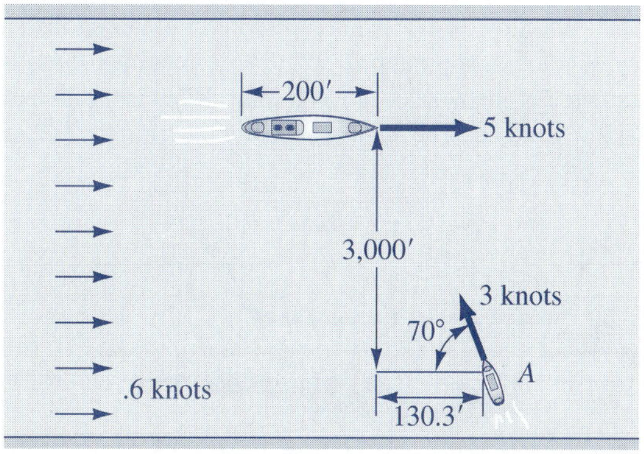

Figure P.11.98.

11.99. A light line attached to a streamlined weight A is "shot" by a line rifle from a small boat C to a large boat D in heavy seas. The weight must travel a distance of 20 yd horizontally and reach the larger boat's deck, which is 20 ft higher than the deck of boat C. If the angle α of firing is 40°, what minimum velocity V_0 is needed? At the instant of firing, boat C is dipping down into the water at a speed of 5 ft/sec. Assume that the larger boat remains essentially fixed at constant level.

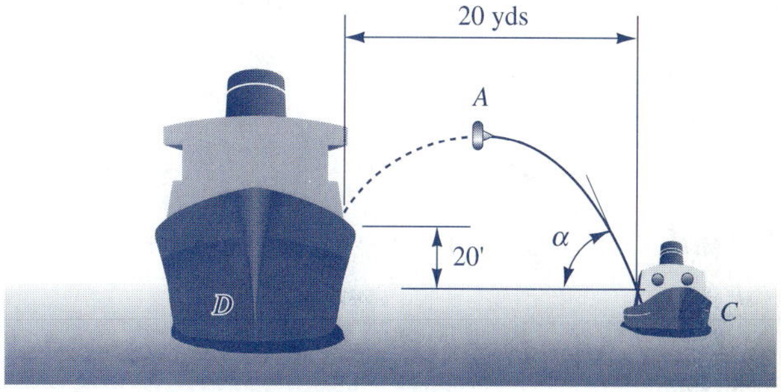

Figure P.11.99.

11.100. A projectile is fired at an angle of 60° as shown. At what elevation y does it strike the hill whose equation has been estimated as $y = 10^{-5}x^2$ m? Neglect air friction and take the muzzle velocity as 1,000 m/sec.

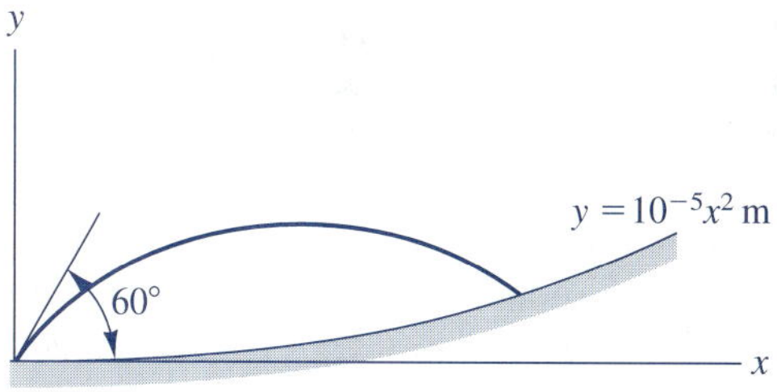

Figure P.11.100.

11.101. A proposed space laboratory, in order to simulate gravity, rotates relative to an inertial reference XYZ at a rate ω_1. For occupant A in the living quarters to be comfortable, what should the approximate value of ω_1 be? Clearly, at the center, there is close to zero gravity for zero-g experiments. A conveyor connects the living quarters with the zero-g laboratory. At the instant of interest, a package D has a speed of 5 m/s and a rate of change of speed of 3 m/s^2 relative to the space station, both toward the laboratory. What are the axial, transverse, and radial velocity and acceleration components at the instant of interest relative to the inertial reference? What are the rectangular components of the acceleration vector?

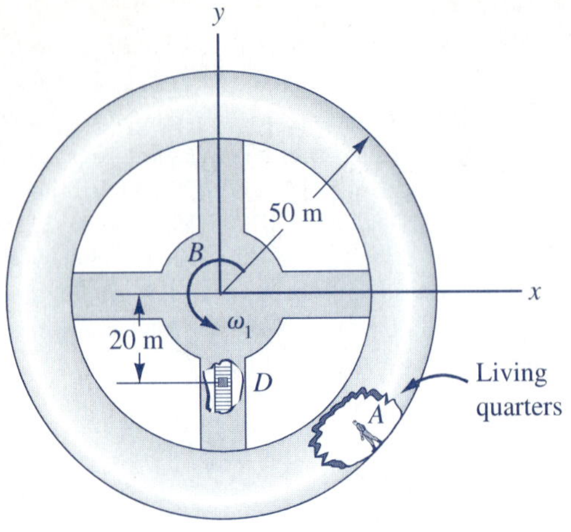

Figure P.11.101.

11.102. A yoke AB rotates about pin A. When the angle α is equal to $\pi/6$ rad, it has an angular speed $\dot{\alpha} = \pi$ rad/s and a rate of change of angular speed $\ddot{\alpha} = .3\pi$ rad/s^2. A slot in the yoke constrains a pin C to move with the slot while a spring forces the pin to slide on the parabolic surface. What are the velocity and acceleration vectors at the instant of interest?

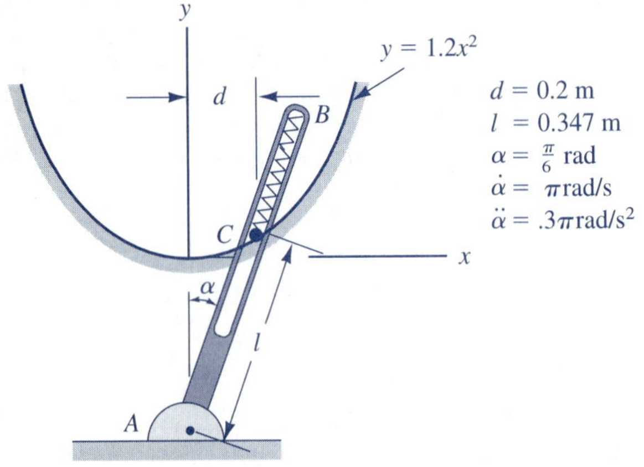

Figure P.11.102.

11.103. In Problem 11.17, what is the change of radius of curvature of a stream of water as it goes out from a circular vane of radius .30 m into free flight? What and where is the minimum radius of curvature?

11.104. A batter has hit a home run ball that just clears the fence. It has a line drive trajectory. A fan attempts to catch the ball. Neglecting friction, what is the speed of the ball as the fan attempts to catch it?

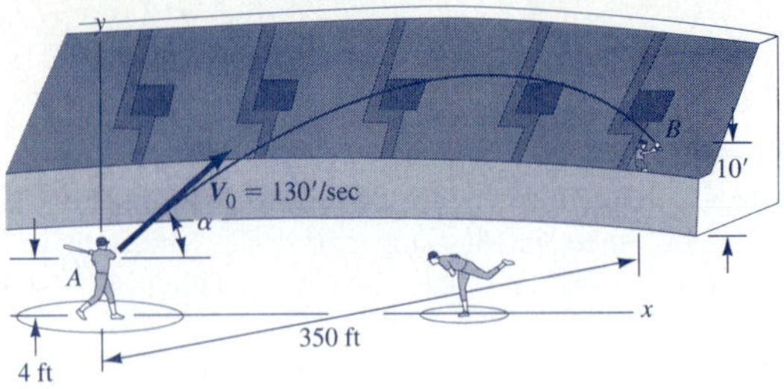

Figure P.11.104.

11.105. A platform is rotating relative to a stationary reference xyz with angular speed $\omega_1 = 1$ rad/s and a rate of change of angular speed $\dot{\omega}_1 = .2$ rad/s^2 at the instant of interest. Also at this instant, the platform is being raised at a speed $V_z = .47$ m/s with a rate of change of speed of $\dot{V}_z = .26$ m/s^2. A rod and mass A rotate on the platform with an angular speed relative to the platform equal to $\omega_2 = .4$ rad/s. At the instant of interest, the angle α is 30°. If $r = .03$ m,

(a) determine the radial, axial, and transverse acceleration components of A;

(b) determine the rectangular components of the acceleration of A.

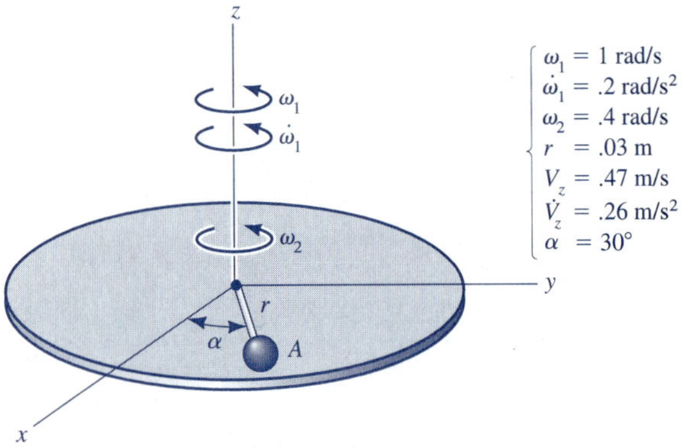

Figure P.11.105.

11.106. The flow of water into an ordinary water sprinkler is 25 L/s initially and is programmed to increase continuously to 50 L/s. The exit area of the nozzles is 1,960 mm^2. What is the area of lawn that will be watered? The angular speed of the sprinkler is 2 rad/sec.

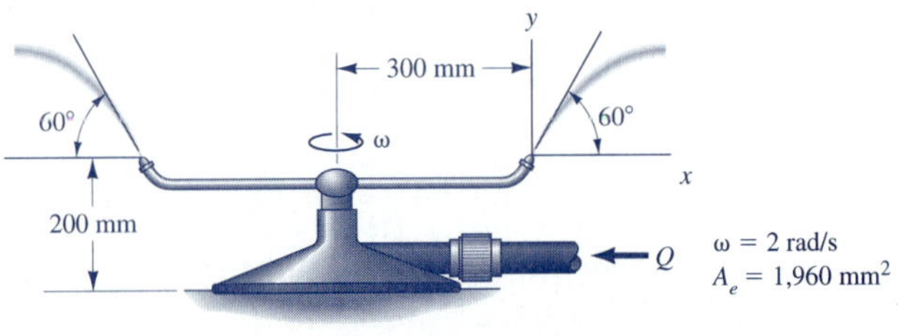

Figure P.11.106.

11.107. Pilots of fighter planes wear special suits designed to prevent blackouts during a severe maneuver. These suits tend to keep the blood from draining out of the head when the head is accelerated in a direction from shoulders to head. With this suit, a flier can take $5g$'s of acceleration in the aforementioned direction. If a flier is diving at a speed of 1,000 km/hr, what is the minimum radius of curvature that he can manage at pullout without suffering bad physiological effects?

11.108. A particle moves with constant speed of 1.5 m/sec along a path given as $x = y^2 - \ln y$ m. Give the acceleration vector of the particle in terms of rectangular components when the particle is at position $y = 3$ m. Do the problem by using path coordinate techniques and then by Cartesian-component techniques. How many g's of acceleration is the particle subject to?

11.109. A submarine is moving in a translatory manner with the following velocity and acceleration relative to an inertial reference:

$$\boldsymbol{V} = 6\boldsymbol{i} + 7.5\boldsymbol{j} + 2\boldsymbol{k} \text{ knots} \qquad \boldsymbol{a} = .2\boldsymbol{i} - .24\boldsymbol{j} + .52\boldsymbol{k} \text{ knots/s}$$

A device inside the submarine consists of an arm and a mass at the end of the arm. At the instant of interest, the arm is rotating in a vertical plane with the following angular speed and angular acceleration:

$$\omega = 10 \text{ rad/s} \qquad \dot{\omega} = 3 \text{ rad/s}^2$$

The arm is vertical at this instant. The mass at the end of the rod may be considered to be a particle having a mass of 5 kg. What are the velocity and acceleration vectors for the motion of the particle at this instant relative to the inertial reference? Use units of meters and seconds. What must be the force vector from the arm onto the particle at this instant?

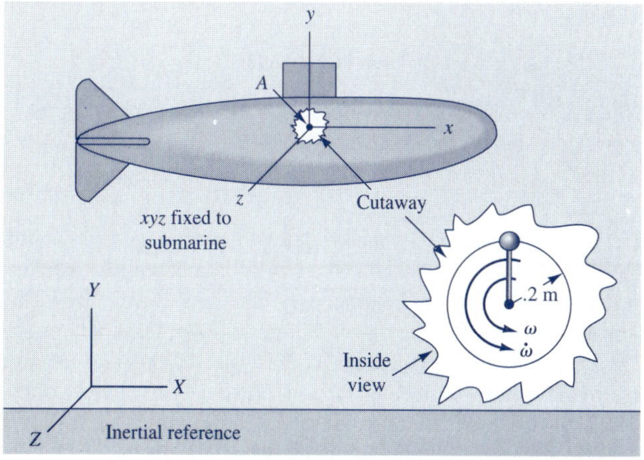

Figure P.11.109.

11.110. A mechanical "arm" for handling radioactive materials is shown. The distance $\bar{r}$ can be varied by telescoping action of the arm. The arm can be rotated about the vertical axis A–A. Finally, the arm can be raised or lowered by a worm gear drive (not shown). What is the velocity and acceleration of the object C if the end of the arm moves out radially at a rate of 1 ft/sec while the arm turns at a speed ω of 2 rad/sec? Finally, the arm is raised at a rate of 2 ft/sec. The distance $\bar{r}$ at the instant of interest is 5 ft. What is the acceleration in the direction $\boldsymbol{\epsilon} = .8\boldsymbol{i} + .6\boldsymbol{j}$?

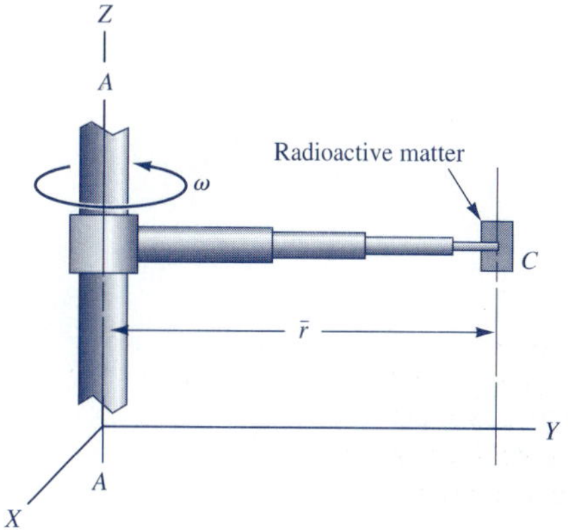

Figure P.11.110.

11.111. A top-section view of a water sprinkler is shown. Water enters at the center from below and then goes through four passageways in an impeller. The impeller is rotating at constant speed ω of 8 rpm. As seen from the impeller, the water leaves at a speed of 10 ft/sec at an angle of 30° relative to r. What is the velocity and acceleration as seen from the ground of the water as it leaves the impeller and becomes free of the impeller? Give results in the radial, axial, and transverse directions. Use one reference only.

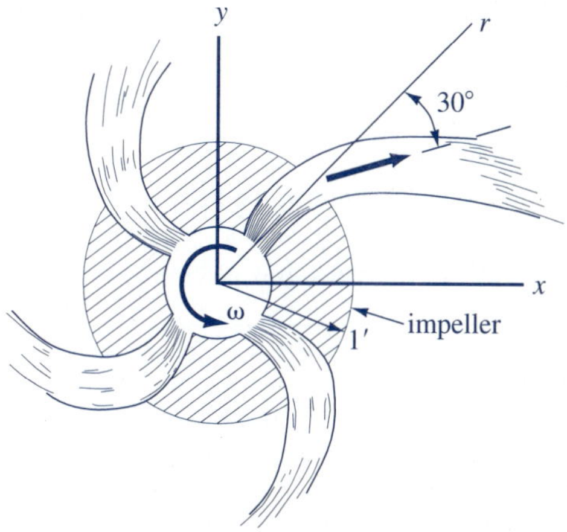

Figure P.11.111.

11.112. A luggage dispenser at an airport resembles a pyramid with six flat segments as sides as shown in the diagram. The system rotates with an angular speed ω of 2 rpm. Luggage is dropped from above and slides down the faces to be picked up by travelers at the base.

A piece of luggage is shown on a face. It has just been dropped at the position indicated. It has at this instant zero velocity as seen from the rotating face but has at this instant and thereafter an acceleration of $.2g$ along the face. What is the total acceleration, as seen from the ground, of the luggage as it reaches the base at B? Use one reference only.

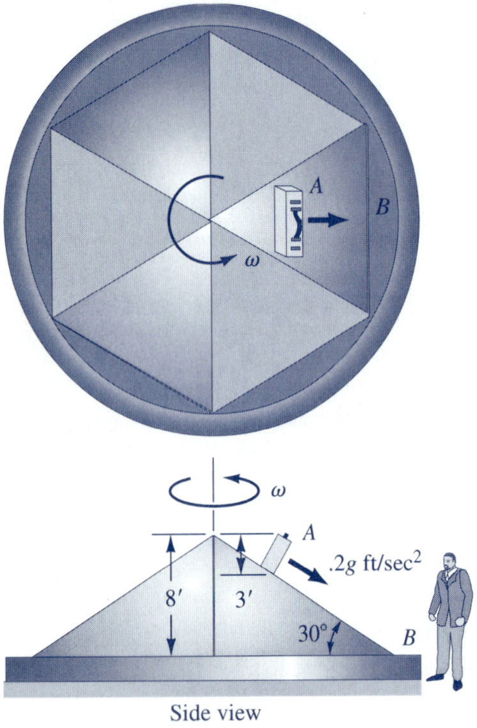

Figure P.11.112.

11.113. A landing craft is in the process of landing on Mars, where the acceleration of gravity is .385 times that of the earth. The craft has the following acceleration relative to the landing surface at the instant of interest:

$$\boldsymbol{a} = .2g\boldsymbol{i} + .4g\boldsymbol{j} - 2g\boldsymbol{k} \text{ m/sec}^2$$

where g is the acceleration of gravity on the earth. At this instant, an astronaut is raising a hand camera weighing 3 N on the earth. If he is giving the camera an upward acceleration of 3 m/sec^2 relative to the landing craft, what force must the astronaut exert on the camera at the instant of interest?

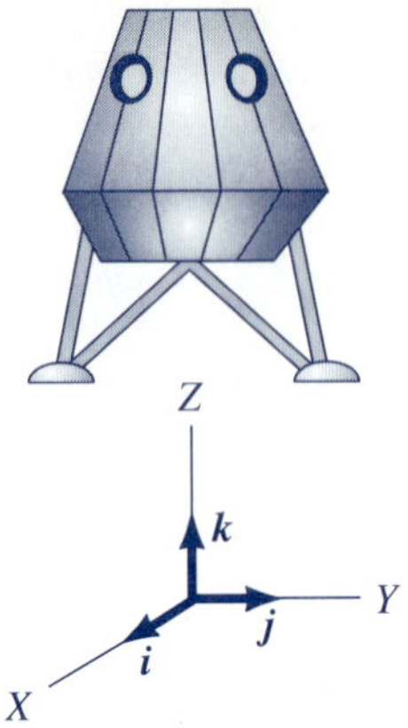

Figure P.11.113.

11.114. A jet of water has a speed at the nozzle of 20 m/s. At what position does it hit the parabolic hill? What is its speed at that point? Do not include friction.

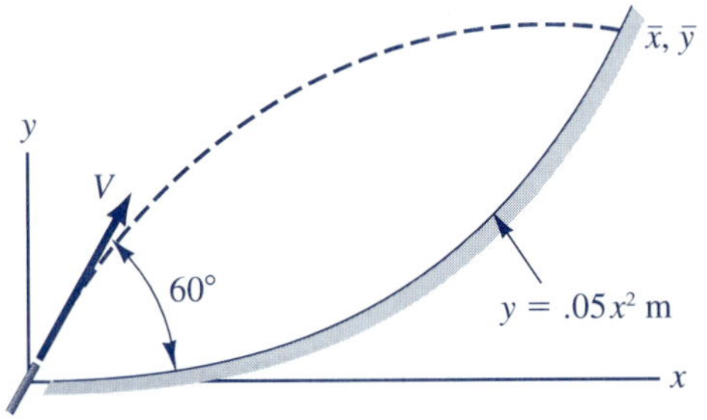

Figure P.11.114.

11.115. A particle moves along a circular path of diameter 10 m such that

$$V = 3t + 6 \text{ m/s}$$

When it has traveled a distance of 15 m, the velocity starts to decrease at the rate of .2 m/s/s. What is the acceleration at $t = 1.3$ sec and at $t = 18$ sec?

11.116. A light attack boat is leaving an engagement at full speed. To help in the process, a battery of four 50-caliber machine guns is fired to the rear continuously. The muzzle velocity of the guns is 1,000 m/s and the rate of firing is 3,000 rounds per minute. The guns are oriented parallel to the water in order to achieve maximum thrust. Neglecting friction, how far from the rear of the boat does each bullet hit the water and what is the spacing between successive bullets from any one gun as the bullets hit the water? The boat is moving at a constant speed of 45 knots.

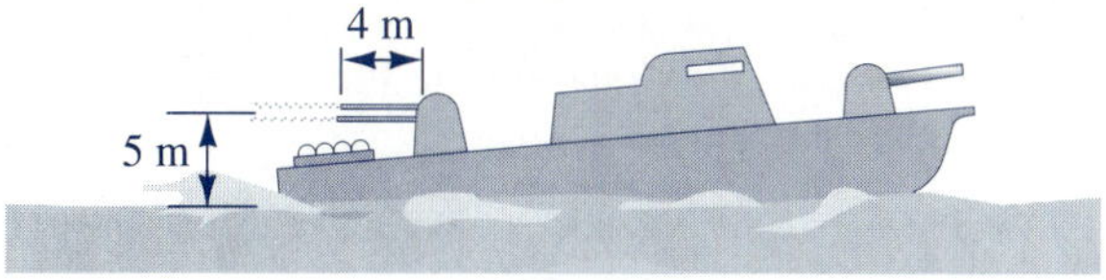

Figure P.11.116.

***11.117.** A particle has a variable velocity $V(t)$ along a helix wrapped around a cylinder of radius e. The helix makes a constant angle α with plane A perpendicular to the z axis. Express the acceleration $\boldsymbol{a}$ of the particle using cylindrical coordinates. Next, express $\boldsymbol{\epsilon}_t$ using cylindrical unit vectors and note that the sum of the transverse and axial components of $\boldsymbol{a}$ (just computed) can be given simply as $\dot{V}\boldsymbol{\epsilon}_t$. Next, express the acceleration of the particle using path coordinates. Finally, noting that $\boldsymbol{\epsilon}_n = -\boldsymbol{\epsilon}_{\bar{r}}$, show that the radius of curvature is given as $R = \dfrac{e}{\cos^2 \alpha}$.

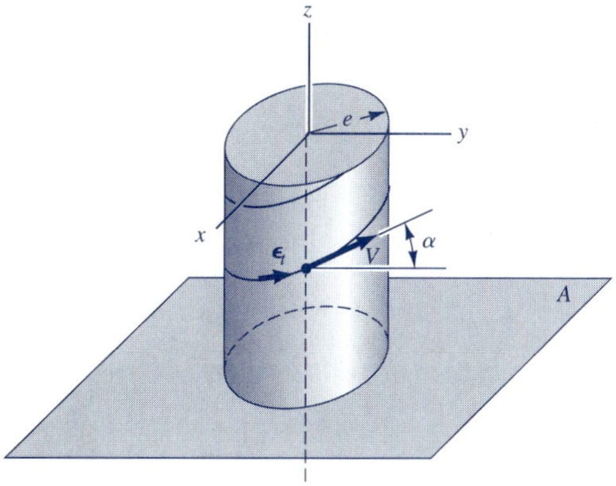

Figure P.11.117.

11.118. An eagle is diving at a constant speed of 40 ft/sec to catch a 10-ft snake that is moving at a constant speed of 15 ft/sec. What should α be so that the eagle hits the small head of the snake? The eagle and the snake are moving in a vertical plane.

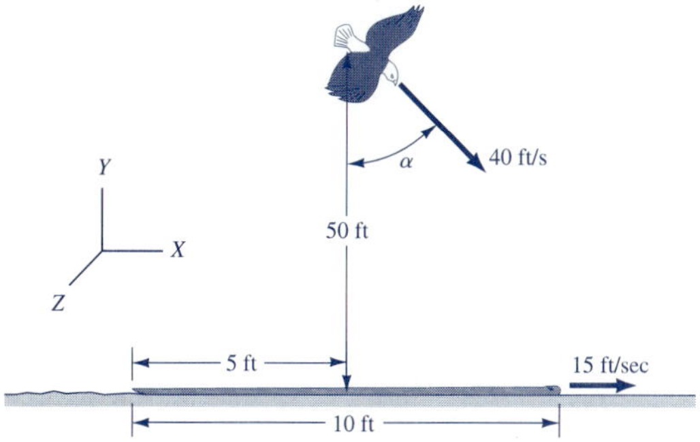

Figure P.11.118.

11.119. A tube, most of whose centerline is that of an ellipse given as

$$\frac{z^2}{1.8^2} + \frac{\bar{r}^2}{.32^2} = 1$$

has a cross-sectional diameter $D = 100$ mm. The tube has the following rotational motion at the instant of interest:

$$\omega = .15 \text{ rad/s} \qquad \dot{\omega} = .036 \text{ rad/s}^2$$

Water is flowing through the tube at the following rate at the instant of interest:

$$Q = .18 \text{ L/s} \qquad \dot{Q} = .025 \text{ L/s}^2$$

The tube is in the vertical plane at the instant of interest. What is the acceleration of the water particles at the centerline of the tube at point C using cylindrical coordinates and cylindrical components? Assume over the cross-section of the tube that the water velocity and acceleration are uniform.

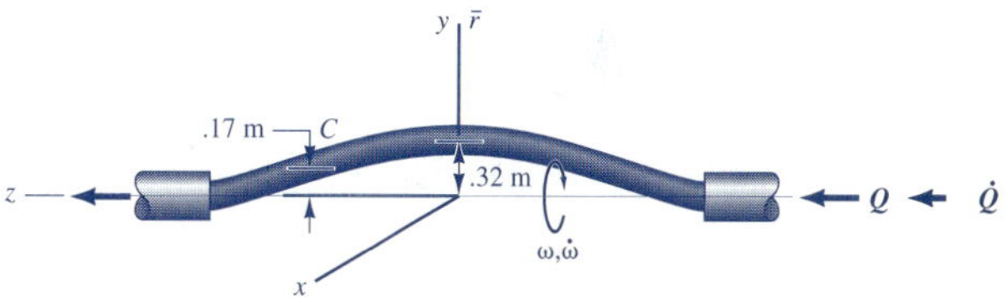

Figure P.11.119.

11.120. A World War I fighter plane is in level flight moving at a speed of 60 km/hr. At time t_0 it has an acceleration given as:

$$\boldsymbol{a} = .2g\boldsymbol{i} - .3g\boldsymbol{j} + 2g\boldsymbol{k} \text{ m/s}^2$$

Also at this time, the co-pilot is raising a camera upward with an acceleration of $0.1g$ relative to the plane. If the camera has a mass of .01 kg, what force must the co-pilot exert on the camera to give it the desired motion at time t_0? Note that the plane never rotates during this action. Take $g = 9.81$ m/s^2.

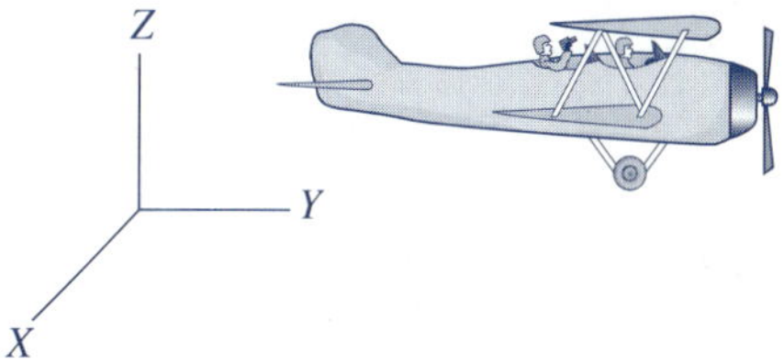

Figure P.11.120.

11.121. A space device has a velocity of $.500\boldsymbol{i} + .200\boldsymbol{j}$ m/s and an acceleration of $.200\boldsymbol{i} + .300\boldsymbol{k}$ m/s^2, both relative to the ground reference XYZ. Rod CD has an angular motion relative to the space device equal to $\omega = 2$ rad/s and $\dot{\omega} = 3$ rad/s^2. What are the velocity and the acceleration of mass M relative to the ground? CD is in the vertical zy plane at the instant of interest. Reference xyz shown is fixed to rod AB. CD is at 60° from AB.

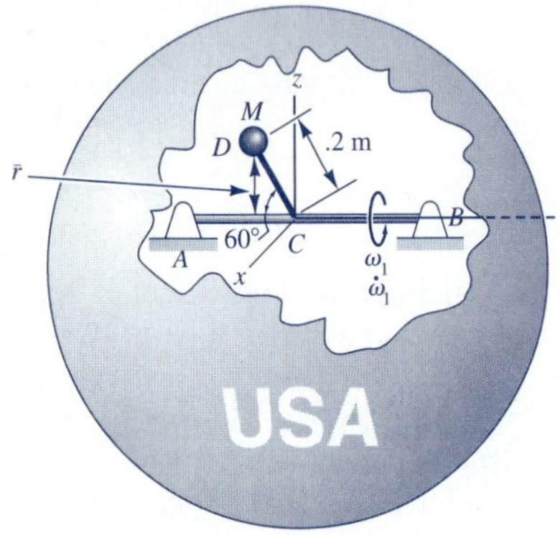

Figure P.11.121.

11.122. A weather balloon has the following motion relative to the inertial reference XYZ:

$$\boldsymbol{V} = 150\boldsymbol{i} + 200\boldsymbol{j} + 60\boldsymbol{k} \text{ m/s}$$
$$\boldsymbol{a} = 20\boldsymbol{i} - 40\boldsymbol{j} + 38\boldsymbol{k} \text{ m/s}^2$$

A light rod at A is connected to particle D and is rotating relative to the balloon at the instant of interest with angular speed $\omega_1 = 5$ rad/s and rate of change of speed $\dot{\omega}_1 = 2$ rad/s^2. What is the velocity of the particle at D relative to XYZ at the instant of interest? The distance $AD = .2$ m. What is the tensile force on the rod in the direction of AD? The mass of the particle at D is 1 kg.

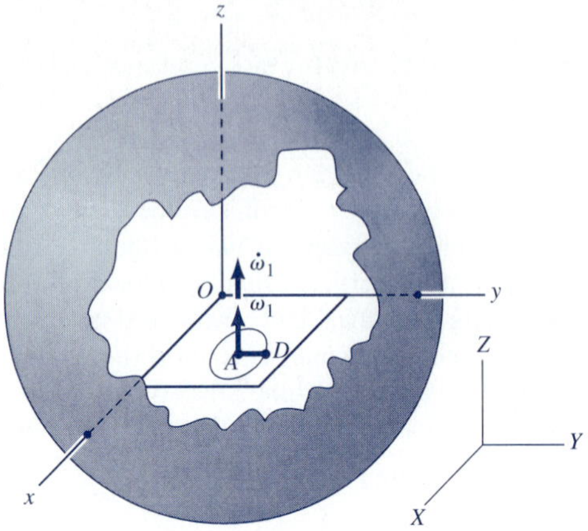

Figure P.11.122.

***11.123.** A particle is made to move along a path given in terms of the parameter τ in the following manner:

$$(x)_p = -\sin 2\tau \qquad (y)_p = \cos 2\tau \qquad (z)_p = e^{-\tau}$$

Give a simple sketch of the path. When the particle is at an elevation $z = 1$, the speed along the path is 5 ft/sec and the rate of change of speed along the path is 10 ft/sec^2. Find the acceleration vector at $z = 1$ in components for path coordinates.

***11.124.** Determine the direction of the osculating plane at position $z = 1$ for the three-dimensional curve of Problem 11.123. We got the following results from the previous problem:

$$\boldsymbol{\epsilon}_n = R(.08\boldsymbol{i} - .80\boldsymbol{j} + .16\boldsymbol{k})$$
$$\boldsymbol{\epsilon}_t = .894\boldsymbol{i} - .447\boldsymbol{k}$$
$$R = .8198 \text{ ft}$$

CHAPTER 12

Particle Dynamics

12.1 Introduction

In Chapter 11, we examined the geometry of motion—the kinematics of motion. In particular, we considered various kinds of coordinate systems: rectangular coordinates, cylindrical coordinates, and path coordinates. In this chapter, we shall consider Newton's law for the three coordinate systems mentioned above, as applied to the motion of a particle.

Before embarking on this study, we shall review notions concerning units of mass presented earlier in Chapter 1. Recall that a pound mass (lbm) is the amount of matter attracted by gravity at a specified location on the earth's surface by a force of 1 pound (lbf). A slug, on the other hand, is the amount of matter that will accelerate relative to an inertial reference at the rate of 1 ft/sec^2 when acted on by a force of 1 lbf. Note that the slug is defined via Newton's law, and therefore the slug is the proper unit to be used in Newton's law. The relation between the pound mass (lbm) and the slug is

$$M\text{ (slugs)} = \frac{M\text{ (lbm)}}{32.2} \tag{12.1}$$

Note also that the weight of a body in pounds force near the earth's surface will numerically equal the mass of the body in pounds mass. It is vital in using Newton's law that the mass of the body in pounds mass be properly converted into slugs via Eq. 12.1.

In SI units, recall that a kilogram is the mass that accelerates relative to an inertial reference at the rate of 1 meter/sec^2 when acted on by a force of 1 newton (which is about one-fifth of a pound). If the weight W of a body is given in terms of newtons, we must divide by 9.81 to get the mass in kilograms needed for Newton's law. That is,

$$M\text{ (kg)} = \frac{W\text{ (N)}}{9.81} \tag{12.2}$$

We are now ready to consider Newton's law in rectangular coordinates.

Part A: Rectangular Coordinates; Rectilinear Translation

12.2 Newton's Law for Rectangular Coordinates

In rectangular coordinates, we can express Newton's law as follows:

$$\begin{aligned} F_x &= ma_x = m\frac{dV_x}{dt} = m\frac{d^2x}{dt^2} \\ F_y &= ma_y = m\frac{dV_y}{dt} = m\frac{d^2y}{dt^2} \\ F_z &= ma_z = m\frac{dV_z}{dt} = m\frac{d^2z}{dt^2} \end{aligned} \tag{12.3}$$

If the motion is known relative to an inertial reference, we can easily solve for the rectangular components of the resultant force on the particle. The equations to be solved are just algebraic equations. The *inverse* of this problem, wherein the forces are known over a time interval and the motion is desired during this interval, is not so simple. For the inverse case, we must get involved generally with integration procedures.

In the next section, we shall consider situations in which the resultant force on a particle has the same direction and line of action at all times. The resulting motion is then confined to a straight line and is usually called *rectilinear translation.*

12.3 Rectilinear Translation

For rectilinear translation, we may consider the line of action of the motion to be collinear with one axis of a rectilinear coordinate system. Newton's law is then one of the equations of the set 12.3. We shall use the x axis to coincide with the line of action of the motion. The resultant force F (we shall not bother with the x subscript here) can be a constant, a function of time, a function of speed, a function of position, or any combination of these. At this time, we shall examine some of these cases, leaving others to Chapter 19, where, with the aid of the students' knowledge of differential equations,[1] we shall be more prepared to consider them.

Case 1. Force Is a Function of Time or a Constant. A particle of mass m acted on by a time-varying force $F(t)$ is shown in Fig. 12.1. The plane on which the body moves is frictionless. The force of gravity is equal and opposite

[1]Most students studying dynamics will concurrently be taking a course in differential equations.

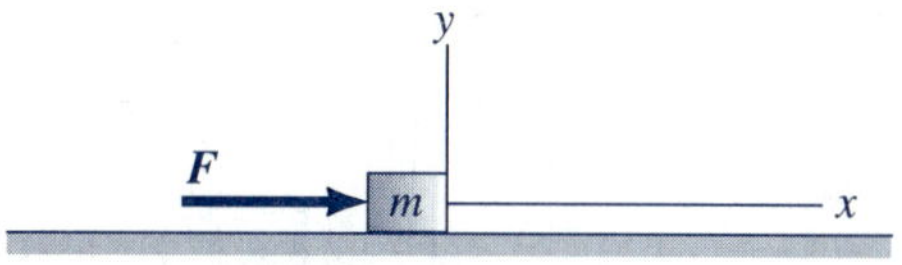

Figure 12.1. Rectilinear translation.

to the normal force from the plane so that $F(t)$ is the resultant force acting on the mass. Newton's law can then be given as follows:

$$F(t) = m\frac{d^2x}{dt^2}$$

Therefore,

$$\frac{d^2x}{dt^2} = \frac{F(t)}{m} \tag{12.4}$$

Knowing the acceleration in the x direction, we can readily solve for $F(t)$.

The inverse problem, where we know $F(t)$ and wish to determine the motion, requires integration. For this operation, the function $F(t)$ must be piecewise continuous.[2] To integrate, we rewrite Eq. 12.4 as follows:

$$\frac{d}{dt}\left(\frac{dx}{dt}\right) = \frac{F(t)}{m}$$

$$d\left(\frac{dx}{dt}\right) = \frac{F(t)}{m}\,dt$$

Now integrating both sides we get

$$\frac{dx}{dt} = V = \int \frac{F(t)}{m}\,dt + C_1 \tag{12.5}$$

where C_1 is a constant of integration. Integrating once again after bringing dt from the left side of the equation to the right side, we get

$$x = \int\left[\int \frac{F(t)}{m}\,dt\right]dt + C_1 t + C_2 \tag{12.6}$$

We have thus found the velocity of the particle and its position as functions of time to within two arbitrary constants. These constants can be readily determined by having the solutions yield a certain velocity and position at given times. Usually, these conditions are specified at time $t = 0$ and are then termed initial conditions. That is, when $t = 0$,

$$V = V_0 \quad \text{and} \quad x = x_0 \tag{12.7}$$

These equations can be satisfied by substituting the initial conditions into Eqs. 12.5 and 12.6 and solving for the constants C_1 and C_2.

Although the preceding discussion centered about a force that is a function of time, the procedures apply directly to a force that is a constant. The following examples illustrate the procedures set forth.

[2]That is, the function has only a finite number of finite discontinuities.

Example 12.1

A 100-lb body is initially stationary on a 45° incline as shown in Fig. 12.2(a). The coefficient of dynamic friction μ_d between the block and incline is .5. What distance along the incline must the weight slide before it reaches a speed of 40 ft/sec?

A free-body diagram is shown in Fig. 12.2(b). Since the acceleration is zero in the direction normal to the incline, we have from **equilibrium** that

$$100 \cos 45° = N = 70.7 \text{ lb} \qquad \text{(a)}$$

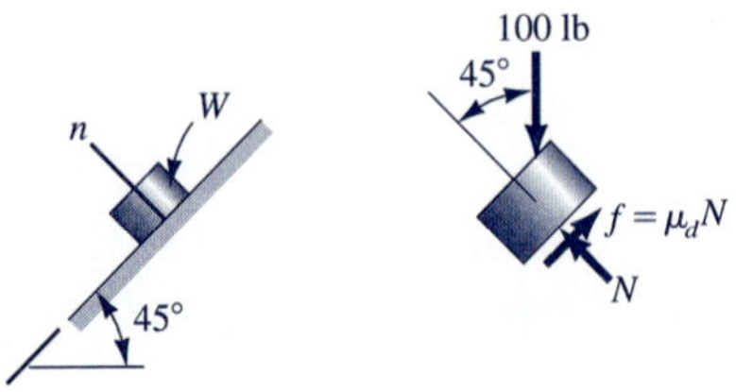

Figure 12.2. Body slides on an incline.

Now applying **Newton's law** in a direction along the incline, we have

$$\frac{100}{g}\frac{d^2s}{dt^2} = 100 \sin 45° - \mu_d N$$

Therefore,

$$\frac{d^2s}{dt^2} = 11.38 \qquad \text{(b)}$$

Rewriting Eq. (b) we have

$$d\left(\frac{ds}{dt}\right) = 11.38\, dt$$

Integrating, we get

$$\frac{ds}{dt} = 11.38t + C_1 \qquad \text{(c)}$$

$$s = 11.38\frac{t^2}{2} + C_1 t + C_2 \qquad \text{(d)}$$

When $t = 0$, $s = ds/dt = 0$, and thus $C_1 = C_2 = 0$. When $ds/dt = 40$ ft/sec, we have for t from Eq. (c) the result

$$40 = 11.38t$$

Therefore,

$$t = 3.51 \text{ sec}$$

Substituting this value of t in Eq. (d), we can get the distance traveled to reach the speed of 40 ft/sec as follows:

$$s = 11.38\frac{(3.51)^2}{2} = \boxed{70.4 \text{ ft}}$$

Example 12.2

A charged particle is shown in Fig. 12.3 at time $t = 0$ between large parallel condenser plates separated by a distance d in a vacuum. A time-varying voltage V (notation not to be confused with velocity) given as

$$V = 6 \sin \omega t \tag{a}$$

is applied to the plates. What is the motion of the particle if it has a charge q coulombs and if we do not consider gravity?

As we learned in physics, the electric field E becomes for this case

$$E = \frac{V}{d} \tag{b}$$

The force on the particle is qE and the resulting motion is that of rectilinear translation. Using **Newton's law** we accordingly have

$$\frac{d^2x}{dt^2} = q\frac{6 \sin \omega t}{md} \tag{c}$$

Rewriting Eq. (c), we have

$$d\left(\frac{dx}{dt}\right) = q\frac{6 \sin \omega t}{md}\,dt$$

Integrating, we get

$$\frac{dx}{dt} = -\frac{6q}{\omega md}\cos \omega t + C_1 \tag{d}$$

$$x = -\frac{6q}{\omega^2 md}\sin \omega t + C_1 t + C_2 \tag{e}$$

Applying the initial conditions $x = b$ and $dx/dt = 0$ when $t = 0$, we see that $C_1 = 6q/m\omega d$ and $C_2 = b$. Thus, we get

$$x = -\frac{6q}{\omega^2 md}\sin \omega t + \frac{6q}{m\omega d}t + b$$

The motion of the charged particle will be that of sinusoidal oscillation in which the center of the oscillation drifts from left to right.

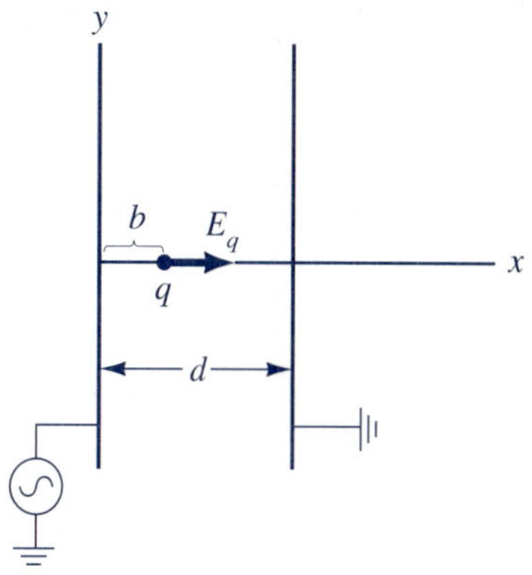

Figure 12.3. Charged particle between condenser plates.

Case 2. Force Is a Function of Speed. We next consider the case where the resultant force on the particle depends only on the value of the speed of the particle. An example of such a force is the aerodynamic drag force on an airplane or missile.

We can express *Newton's law* in the following form:

$$\frac{dV}{dt} = \frac{F(V)}{m} \tag{12.8}$$

where $F(V)$ is a piecewise continuous function representing the force in the positive x direction. If we rearrange the equation in the following manner (this is called *separation* of *variables*):

$$\frac{dV}{F(V)} = \frac{1}{m}\,dt$$

we can integrate to obtain

$$\int \frac{dV}{F(V)} = \frac{1}{m}t + C_1 \qquad (12.9)$$

The result will give t as a function of V. However, we will generally prefer to solve for V in terms of t. The result will then have the form

$$V = H(t, C_1)$$

where H is a function of t and the constant of integration C_1. A second integration may now be performed by first replacing V by dx/dt and bringing dt over to the right side of the equation. We then get on integration

$$x = \int H(t, C_1)\,dt + C_2 \qquad (12.10)$$

The constants of integration are determined from the initial conditions of the problem.

Example 12.3

A high-speed land racer (Fig. 12.4) is moving at a speed of 100 m/sec. The resistance to motion of the vehicle is primarily due to aerodynamic drag, which for this speed can be approximated as $.2V^2$ N with V in m/sec. If the vehicle has a mass of 4,000 kg, what distance will it coast before its speed is reduced to 70 m/sec?

We have, using **Newton's law** for this case,

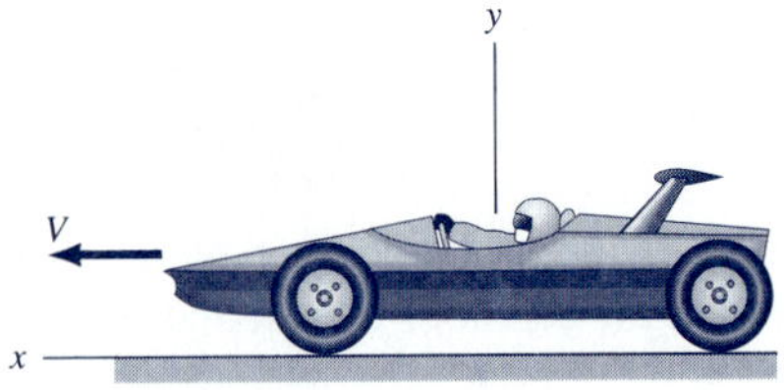

Figure 12.4. High-speed racer.

$$\frac{dV}{dt} = -\frac{.2V^2}{4{,}000} = -5 \times 10^{-5}V^2 \qquad \text{(a)}$$

Separating the variables, we get

$$\frac{dV}{V^2} = -5 \times 10^{-5}\,dt \qquad \text{(b)}$$

Example 12.3 (Continued)

Integrating, we have

$$-\frac{1}{V} = -5 \times 10^{-5}t + C_1 \qquad \text{(c)}$$

Taking $t = 0$ when $V = 100$, we get $C_1 = -1/100$. Replacing V by dx/dt, we have next

$$\frac{1}{V} = \frac{dt}{dx} = 5 \times 10^{-5}t + \frac{1}{100} \qquad \text{(d)}$$

Separating variables once again, we get

$$\frac{dt}{5 \times 10^{-5}t + (1/100)} = dx$$

To integrate, we perform a change of variable. Thus

$$\eta = 5 \times 10^{-5}t + (1/100)$$

$$\therefore\ d\eta = 5 \times 10^{-5}\,dt$$

We then have as a replacement for our equation

$$\frac{d\eta}{\eta} = 5 \times 10^{-5}\,dx$$

Now integrating and replacing η, we get

$$\ln\left(5 \times 10^{-5}t + \frac{1}{100}\right) = 5 \times 10^{-5}x + C_2$$

When $t = 0$, we take $x = 0$ and so $C_2 = \ln(1/100)$. We then have on combining the logarithmic terms:

$$\ln\left(5 \times 10^{-3}t + 1\right) = 5 \times 10^{-5}x \qquad \text{(e)}$$

Substitute $V = 70$ in Eq. (d); solve for t. We get $t = 85.7$ sec. Finally, find x for this time from Eq. (e). Thus,

$$\ln\left[(5 \times 10^{-3})(85.7) + 1\right] = 5 \times 10^{-5}x$$

Therefore,

$$x = 7.13 \text{ km}$$

The distance traveled is then 7.13 km.

Example 12.4

A conveyor is inclined 20° from the horizontal as shown in Fig. 12.5. As a result of spillage of oil on the belt, there is a viscous friction force between body D and the belt. This force equals 0.1 lbf per unit relative velocity between body D and the belt. The belt moves at a constant speed V_B up the conveyor while initially body D has a speed $(V_D)_0 = 2$ ft/sec relative to the ground in a direction down the conveyor. What speed V_B^* should the belt have in order for body D to be able to eventually approach a zero velocity relative to the ground? For belt speed V_B^*, and for the given initial speed of body D, namely $(V_D)_0 = 2$ ft/sec, determine the time when body D attains a speed of 1 ft/sec relative to the ground. The mass of D is 5 lbm.

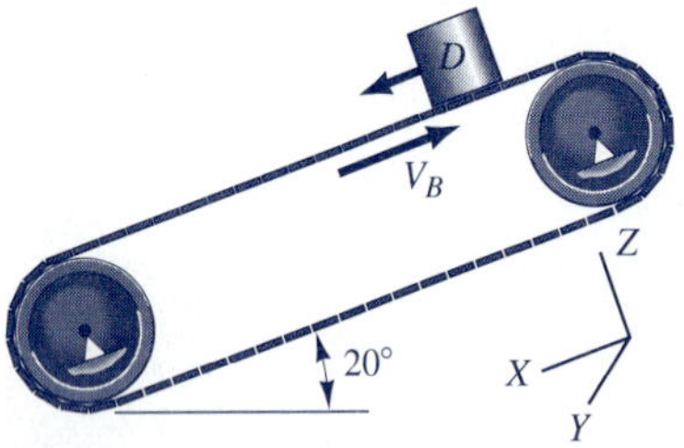

Figure 12.5. A body slides down a conveyor belt wet with oil.

We begin by assigning axes for the problem as follows (see Fig. 12.6):

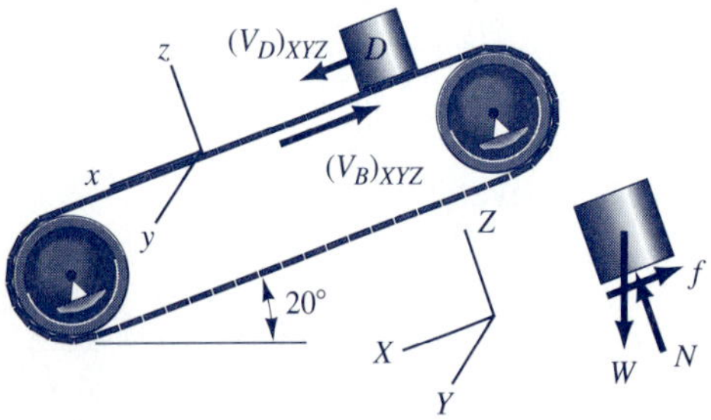

Figure 12.6. Friction force f is 0.1 times the relative velocity between body D and the belt.

Fix xyz to the belt
Fix XYZ to the ground

From **kinematics** we can say

$$(\boldsymbol{V}_D)_{XYZ} = (\boldsymbol{V}_D)_{xyz} + \dot{\boldsymbol{R}} \qquad \text{Note that } \dot{\boldsymbol{R}} = -(V_B)_{XYZ}\boldsymbol{i}$$

$$\therefore (\boldsymbol{V}_D)_{xyz} = (\boldsymbol{V}_D)_{XYZ} - \dot{\boldsymbol{R}} = \left[V_D - (-V_B)\right]_{XYZ}\boldsymbol{i} = (V_D + V_B)_{XYZ}\boldsymbol{i}$$

Example 12.4 (Continued)

For the friction force f we have

$$f = -(.1)(V_D)_{xyz} = -(.1)(V_D + V_B)_{XYZ}\boldsymbol{i}$$

We may now use **Newton's law** for body D in the x direction. Since all velocities from here on will be relative to the ground, we can dispense with the reference subscripts. Thus

$$\frac{5}{g}\frac{dV_D}{dt} = -(.1)(V_D + V_B) + 5\sin 20° \qquad \text{(a)}$$

When body D attains a theoretical permanent zero velocity relative to the ground, V_D and $\frac{dV_D}{dt}$ are equal to zero. This gives us (noting that V_B now becomes V_B^*)

$$0 = -(.1)(0 + V_B^*) + 5\sin 20° \qquad \therefore \quad \boxed{V_B^* = 17.10 \text{ ft./sec}}$$

Now determine the time for body D to attain a velocity of 1 ft/sec relative to the ground for a belt speed of 17.10 ft/sec. For this we go back to Eq. (a).

$$\frac{5}{g}\frac{dV_D}{dt} = (-.1)(V_D + 17.10) + 5\sin 20° = -.1V_D$$

$$\frac{dV_D}{V_D} = -\left(\frac{g}{5}\right)(.1)\,dt = -\frac{3.22}{5}\,dt$$

$$\therefore \ln V_D = -\frac{3.22}{5}t + C_1$$

When

$$t = 0, \qquad V_D = 2 \text{ ft/sec}, \qquad \therefore C_1 = \ln 2$$

Hence, on combining log terms[3]

$$\ln\left(\frac{V_D}{2}\right) = -.644t$$

Set $V_D = 1$ ft/sec. Solve for t.

$$t = -\frac{1}{.644}\ln(.500) = \boxed{1.076 \text{ sec}}$$

[3]Note from this equation that $V_D = 2e^{-0.644t}$ and that $\dot{V}_D = -1.288e^{-0.644t}$ and so we see that as t approaches infinity both of these quantities approach zero. Thus, theoretically body D could approach a permanent zero velocity relative to the ground.

Case 3. Force Is a Function of Position. As the final case of this series, we now consider the rectilinear motion of a body under the action of a force that is expressible as a function of position. Perhaps the simplest example of such a case is the frictionless mass–spring system shown in Fig. 12.7. The body is shown at a position where the spring is unstrained. The horizontal force from the spring at all positions of the body clearly will be a function of position x.

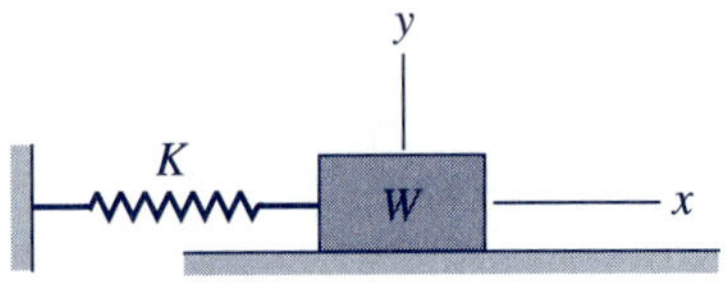

Figure 12.7. Mass–spring system.

Newton's law for position-dependent forces can be given as

$$m\frac{dV}{dt} = F(x) \tag{12.11}$$

We cannot separate the variables for this form of the equation as in previous cases since there are three variables (V, t, and x). However, by using the chain rule of differentiation, we can change the left side of the equation to a more desirable form in the following manner:

$$m\frac{dV}{dt} = m\frac{dV}{dx}\frac{dx}{dt} = mV\frac{dV}{dx}$$

We can now separate the variables in Eq. 12.11 as follows:

$$mV\,dV = F(x)\,dx$$

Integrating, we get

$$\frac{mV^2}{2} = \int F(x)\,dx + C_1 \tag{12.12}$$

Solving for V and using dx/dt in its place, we get

$$\frac{dx}{dt} = \left[\frac{2}{m}\int F(x)\,dx + C_1\right]^{1/2}$$

Separating variables and integrating again, we get

$$t = \int \frac{dx}{\left[\frac{2}{m}\int F(x)\,dx + C_1\right]^{1/2}} + C_2 \tag{12.13}$$

For a given $F(x)$, V and x can accordingly be evaluated as functions of time from Eqs. 12.12 and 12.13. The constants of integration C_1 and C_2 are determined from the initial conditions.

A very common force that occurs in many problems is the *linear restoring force*. Such a force occurs when a body W is constrained by a linear spring (see Fig. 12.7). The force from such a spring will be proportional to x measured from a position of W corresponding to the *undeformed configuration* of the system. Consequently, the force will have a magnitude of $|Kx|$, where K, called the *spring constant*, is the force needed on the spring per unit elongation or compression of the spring. Furthermore, when x has a positive value, the spring force points in the negative direction, and when x is negative, the spring force points in the positive direction. That is, it always points toward the position $x = 0$ for which the spring is undeformed. The spring force is for this reason called a *restoring* force and must be expressed as $-Kx$ to give the proper direction for all values of x.

For a *nonlinear* spring, K will not be constant but will be a function of the elongation or shortening of the spring. The spring force is then given as

$$F_{\text{spring}} = -\int_0^x K(x)\,dx \tag{12.14}$$

In the following example and in the homework problems, we examine certain limited aspects of spring–mass systems to illustrate the formulations of case 3 and to familiarize us with springs in dynamic systems. A more complete study of spring–mass systems will be made in Chapter 19. The motion of such systems, we shall later learn, centers about some stationary point. That is, the motion is *vibratory* in nature. We shall study vibrations in Chapter 19, wherein time-dependent and velocity-dependent forces are present simultaneously with the linear restoring force. We are deferring this topic so as to make maximal use of your course in differential equations that you are most likely studying concurrently with dynamics. It is important to understand, however, that even though we defer vibration studies until later, such studies are not something apart from the general particle dynamics undertaken in this chapter.

Example 12.5

A cart A (see Fig. 12.8) having a mass of 200 kg is held on an incline so as to just touch an undeformed spring whose spring constant K is 50 N/mm. If body A is released very slowly, what distance down the incline must A move to reach an equilibrium configuration? If body A is released suddenly, what is its speed when it reaches the aforementioned equilibrium configuration for a slow release?

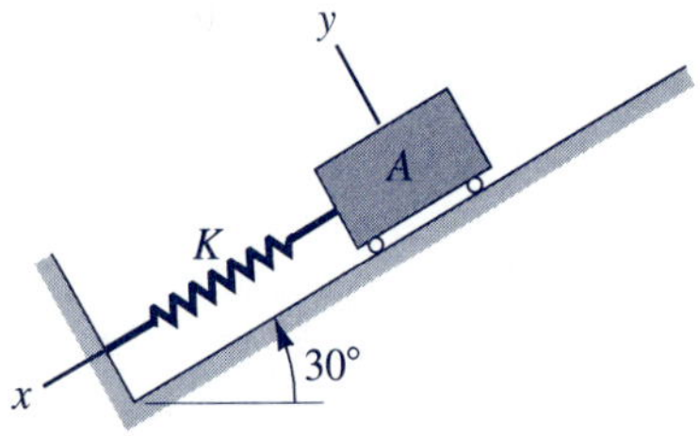

Figure 12.8. Cart–spring system.

As a first step, we have shown a free body of the vehicle in Fig. 12.9. To do the first part of the problem, all we need do is utilize the

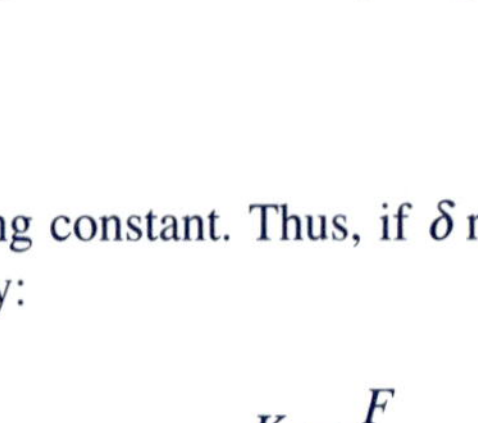

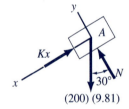

Figure 12.9. Free-body diagram of cart.

definition of the spring constant. Thus, if δ represents the compression of the spring, we can say:

$$K = \frac{F}{\delta}$$

Example 12.5 (Continued)

Therefore,

$$\delta = \frac{F}{K} = \frac{(200)(9.81)\sin 30^\circ}{50}$$

$$\delta = 19.62 \text{ mm}$$

Thus, the spring will be compressed .01962 m by the cart if it is allowed to move down the incline very slowly.

For the case of the quick release, we use **Newton's law**. Thus, using x in meters so that K is (50)(1,000) N/m:

$$200\ddot{x} = (200)(9.81)\sin 30^\circ - (50)(1{,}000)(x)$$

Therefore,

$$\ddot{x} = 4.905 - 250x$$

Rewriting $\ddot{x}$, we have

$$V\frac{dV}{dx} = 4.905 - 250x$$

Separating variables and integrating,

$$\frac{V^2}{2} = 4.905x - 125x^2 + C_1$$

To determine the constant of integration C_1, we set $x = 0$ when $V = 0$. Clearly, $C_1 = 0$. As a final step, we set $x = .01962$ m and solve for V.

$$V = \left\{2\left[(4.905)(.01962) - (125)(.01962)^2\right]\right\}^{1/2}$$

$$V = .310 \text{ m/sec}$$

The following example illustrates an interesting device used by the U.S. Navy to test small devices for high, prolonged acceleration. Hopefully, the length of the problem will not intimidate you. Use is made of the gas laws presented in your elementary chemistry courses.

Example 12.6

An *air gun* is used to test the ability of small devices to withstand high prolonged accelerations. A "floating piston" A (Fig. 12.10), on which the device to be tested is mounted, is held at position C while region D is filled with highly compressed air. Region E is initially at atmospheric pressure but is entirely sealed from the outside. When "fired," a quick-release mechanism releases the piston and it accelerates rapidly toward the other end of the gun, where the trapped air in E "cushions" the motion so that the piston will begin eventually to return. However, as it starts back, the high pressure developed in E is released through valve F and the piston only returns a short distance.

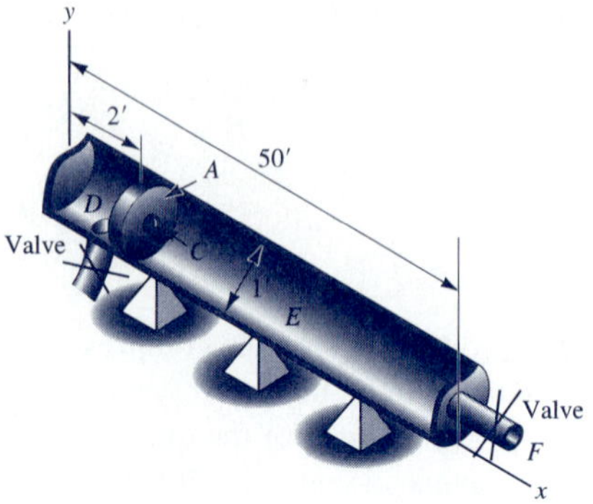

Figure 12.10. Air gun.

Suppose that the piston and its test specimen have a combined mass of 2 lbm and the pressure initially in the chamber D is 1,000 psig (above atmosphere). Compute the speed of the piston at the halfway point of the air gun if we make the simple assumption that the air in D expands according to pv = constant and the air in E is compressed also according to pv = constant.[4] Note that v is the specific volume (i.e., the volume per unit mass). Take v of this fluid at D to be initially .207 ft³/lbm and v in E to be initially 13.10 ft³/lbm. Neglect the inertia of the air.

The force on the piston results from the pressures on each face, and we can show that this force is a function of x (see Fig. 12.10 for reference axes). Thus, examining the pressure p_D first for region D, we have, from initial conditions,

$$(p_D v_D)_0 = [(1{,}000 + 14.7)(144)](.207) = 30{,}300 \qquad \text{(a)}$$

Furthermore, the mass of air D given as M_D is determined from initial data as

$$M_D = \frac{(V_D)_0}{(v_D)_0} = \frac{(2)\left(\frac{\pi}{4}\right)(1^2)}{.207} = 7.58 \text{ lbm} \qquad \text{(b)}$$

where $(V_D)_0$ is the volume of the air in D initially. Noting that pv = const. and then using the right side of Eq. (a) for $p_D v_D$ as well as the first part of Eq. (b) for v_D, we can determine p_D at any position x of the piston:

$$p_D = \frac{30{,}300}{v_D} = \frac{30{,}300}{V_D/M_D} = \frac{30{,}300}{(\pi/4)(1^2)(x)/7.58}$$

Therefore,

$$p_D = \frac{293{,}000}{x} \qquad \text{(c)}$$

[4]You should recall from your earlier work in physics and chemistry that we are using here the isothermal form of the equation of state for a perfect gas. Two factors of caution should be pointed out relative to the use of this expression. First, at the high pressures involved in part of the expansion, the perfect gas model is only an approximation for the gas, and so the equation of state of a perfect gas that gives us pv = constant is only approximate. Furthermore, the assumption of isothermal expansion gives only an approximation of the actual process. Perhaps a better approximation is to assume an adiabatic expansion (i.e, no heat transfer). This is done in Problem 12.130.

Example 12.6 (Continued)

We can similarly get p_E as a function of x for region E. Thus,

$$(p_E v_E)_0 = (14.7)(144)(13.10) = 27{,}700$$

and

$$M_E = \frac{(V_E)_0}{(v_E)_0} = \frac{(48)\left(\frac{\pi}{4}\right)(1^2)}{13.10} = 2.88 \text{ lbm}$$

Hence, at position x of the piston

$$p_E = \frac{27{,}700}{v_E} = \frac{27{,}700}{V_E/M_E} = \frac{27{,}700}{(\pi/4)(1^2)(50-x)/2.88}$$

Therefore,

$$p_E = \frac{101{,}600}{50-x}$$

Now we can write **Newton's law** for this case. Noting that V without subscripts is velocity and not volume,

$$MV\frac{dV}{dx} = \frac{\pi 1^2}{4}\left(p_D - p_E\right) = \frac{\pi}{4}\left(\frac{293{,}000}{x} - \frac{101{,}600}{50-x}\right) \qquad \text{(d)}$$

where M is the mass of piston and load. Separating variables and integrating, we get

$$\frac{MV^2}{2} = \frac{\pi}{4}\left[293{,}000 \ln x + 101{,}600 \ln(50-x)\right] + C_1 \qquad \text{(e)}$$

To get the constant C_1, set $V = 0$ when $x = 2$ ft. Hence,

$$C_1 = -\frac{\pi}{4}\left(293{,}000 \ln 2 + 101{,}600 \ln 48\right)$$

Therefore,

$$C_1 = -468{,}000$$

Substituting C_1 in Eq. (e), we get

$$V = \left(\frac{2}{M}\right)^{1/2}\left\{\frac{\pi}{4}\left[293{,}000 \ln x + 101{,}600 \ln(50-x)\right] - 468{,}000\right\}^{1/2}$$

We may rewrite this as follows noting that $M = 2$ lbm/g:

$$V = 566\left[23 \ln x + 7.98 \ln(50-x) - 46.8\right]^{1/2}$$

At $x = 25$ ft, we then have for V the desired result:

$$V = 566(23 \ln 25 + 7.98 \ln 25 - 46.8)^{1/2}$$

$$V = 4{,}120 \text{ ft/sec}$$

*Example 12.7

A light stiff rod is pinned at A and is constrained by two linear springs, $K_1 = 1{,}000$ N/m and $K_2 = 1{,}200$ N/m. The springs are unstretched when the rod is horizontal. At the right end of the rod, a mass $M = 5$ kg is attached. If the rod is rotated 12° *clockwise* from a horizontal configuration and then released, what is the speed of the mass when the rod returns to a position corresponding to the *static equilibrium* position with mass M attached?

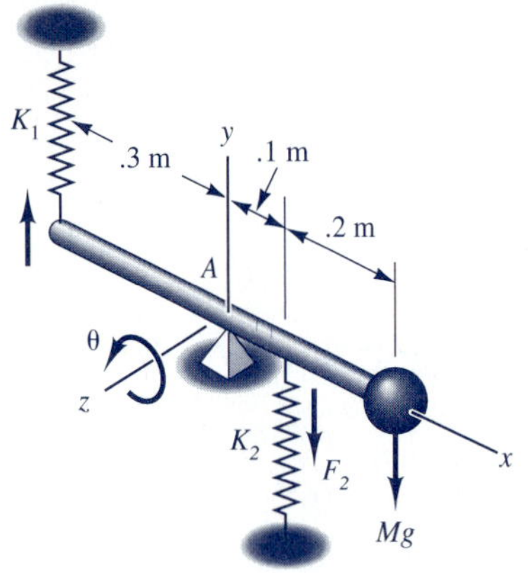

Figure 12.11. Two linear springs and a particle on a weightless rigid rod. Spring forces shown for positive θ.

A free-body diagram of the system for *positive* θ is shown in Fig. 12.12(a) and a free-body diagram of the particle M is shown in

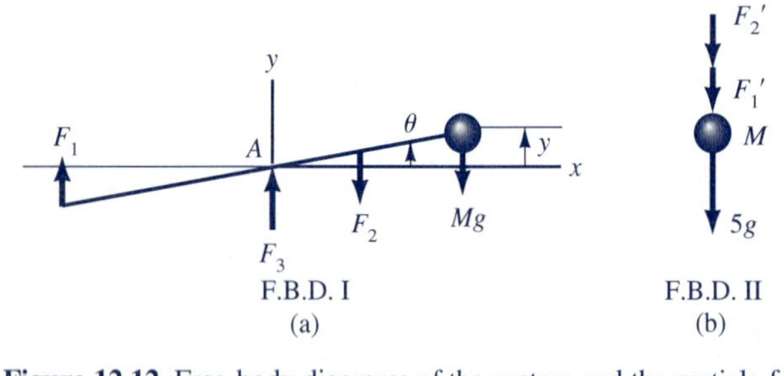

Figure 12.12. Free-body diagrams of the system and the particle for positive θ.

Fig. 12.12(b). The spring forces F_1 and F_2 on the rod are given as follows for small positive rotations θ:

$$F_1 = (.3)(\theta)(K_1) = 300\,\theta\text{ N}$$

$$F_2 = -(.1)(\theta)(K_2) = -120\,\theta\text{ N} \qquad \text{(a)}$$

where θ is in radians. In the first free body, we will think of the rod as a massless perfectly rigid lever as studied in high school or perhaps even

Example 12.7 (Continued)

earlier. Then we can say for the forces on the second of our free bodies stemming from the springs[5]

$$F_1' \quad (\text{from } F_1) = -F_1 = -300\,\theta\,\text{N}$$

$$F_2' \quad (\text{from } F_2) = \frac{.1}{.3}(F_2) = -40\,\theta\,\text{N}$$

We can now give **Newton's law** for M as follows using y for the vertical coordinate of the particle:

$$5\ddot{y} = -5g - 300\,\theta - 40\,\theta$$

$$\therefore\ \ddot{y} = -g - \frac{340}{5}\,\theta \qquad \text{(b)}$$

Next, from **kinematics**, we can say for small rotation

$$\theta = \frac{y}{.3}$$

Now going back to Eq.(b) we replace $\ddot{y}$ by

$$\frac{d\dot{y}}{dt} = \left(\frac{d\dot{y}}{dy}\right)\left(\frac{dy}{dt}\right) = \dot{y}\left(\frac{d\dot{y}}{dy}\right)$$

in order to be able to separate variables. Also replace θ by $y/.3$. We then may say

$$\dot{y}\,d\dot{y} = (-227y - g)\,dy$$

Integrating

$$\frac{\dot{y}^2}{2} = (-227)\left(\frac{y^2}{2}\right) - gy + C_1 \qquad \text{(c)}$$

When $\theta = -12° = -\left(\frac{12}{360}\right)(2\pi)$ rad $= -.2094$ rad, $\dot{\theta} = \dot{y} = 0$. We can then solve for the constant of integration using $y = .3\,\theta$.

$$C_1 = (227)\left[\frac{[(.3)(-.2094)]^2}{2}\right] + (9.81)(.3)(-.2094) = -.1683$$

Hence,

$$\dot{y}^2 = 2\left[(-227)\left(\frac{y^2}{2}\right) - gy - .1683\right] \qquad \text{(d)}$$

[5]Note that a positive θ gives negative values for F_1' and F_2' on M and vice versa. It is for this reason that we require the minus signs.

Example 12.7 (Continued)

For the static **equilibrium** configuration of the rod, we require from Fig. 12.12(a)

$$\underline{\sum M_A = 0:}$$

$$-(Mg)(.3) - F_1(.3) - F_2(.1) = 0$$

Substituting values from Eqs. (a) and noting that we are only using the magnitudes of the forces above for the required negative moments we get

$$-(5)(9.81)(.3) - (300\,\theta_{Eq})(.3) - (120\,\theta_{Eq})(.1) = 0$$

Solving for θ_{Eq}

$$\theta_{Eq} = -.1443 \text{ rad}$$

Hence

$$y_{Eq} = (.3)(-.1443) = -.04328 \text{ m}$$

Now go to Eq. (d) and substitute y_{Eq}. We get

$$\dot{y}_{Eq} = \sqrt{2}\left[(-113.5)(-.04328)^2 - (9.81)(-.04328) - .1683\right]^{1/2}$$

The desired result is then

$$\dot{y}_{Eq} = 0.968 \text{ m/s}$$

12.4 A Comment

In Part A, we have considered only rectilinear motions of particles. Actually in Chapter 11, we considered the coplanar motion of particles having a constant acceleration of gravity in the minus y direction and zero acceleration in the x direction. These were the *ballistic* problems. We treated them earlier in Chapter 11 because the considerations were primarily kinematic in nature. In the present chapter, they correspond to the coplanar motion of a particle having a constant force in the minus y direction along with an initial velocity component in this direction, plus a zero force in the x direction, with a possible initial velocity component in this direction. Therefore, in the context of Chapter 12 we would have integrated two scalar equations of Newton's law in rectangular components (Eqs. 12.3) for a single particle. The resulting motion is sometimes called *curvilinear* translation.

PROBLEMS

12.1. A particle of mass 1 slug is moving in a constant force field given as

$$\boldsymbol{F} = 3\boldsymbol{i} + 10\boldsymbol{j} - 5\boldsymbol{k} \text{ lb}$$

The particle starts from rest at position (3, 5, −4). What is the position and velocity of the particle at time $t = 8$ sec? What is the position when the particle is moving at a speed of 20 ft/sec?

12.2. A particle of mass m is moving in a constant force field given as

$$\boldsymbol{F} = 2m\boldsymbol{i} - 12m\boldsymbol{j} \text{ N}$$

Give the vector equation for $\boldsymbol{r}(t)$ of the particle if, at time $t = 0$, it has a velocity $\boldsymbol{V}_0$ given as

$$\boldsymbol{V}_0 = 6\boldsymbol{i} + 12\boldsymbol{j} + 3\boldsymbol{k} \text{ m/sec}$$

Also, at time $t = 0$, it has a position given as

$$\boldsymbol{r}_0 = 3\boldsymbol{i} + 2\boldsymbol{j} + 4\boldsymbol{k} \text{ m}$$

What are coordinates of the body at the instant that the body reaches its maximum height, y_{max}?

12.3. A block is permitted to slide down an inclined surface. The coefficient of friction is .05. If the velocity of the block is 30 ft/sec on reaching the bottom of the incline, how far up was it released and how many seconds has it traveled?

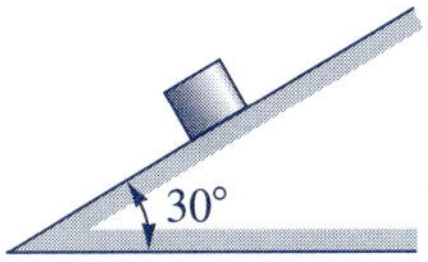

Figure P.12.3.

12.4. An arrow is shot upward with an initial speed of 80 ft/sec. How high up does it go and how long does it take to reach the maximum elevation if we neglect friction?

12.5. A mass D at $t = 0$ is moving to the left at a speed of .6 m/sec relative to the ground on a belt that is moving at constant speed to the right at 1.6 m/sec. If there is coulombic friction present with $\mu_d = .3$, how long does it take before the speed of D relative to the belt is .3 m/sec to the left?

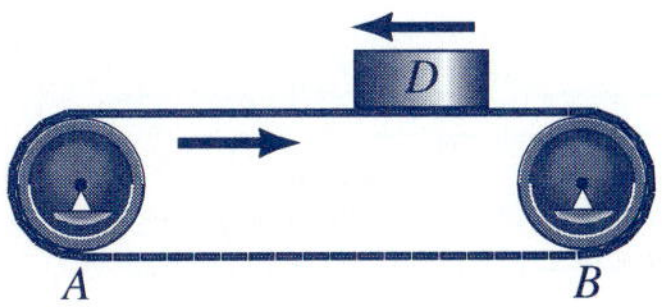

Figure P.12.5.

12.6. Do Problem 12.5 with the belt system inclined 15° with the horizontal so that end B is above end A.

12.7. A drag racer can develop a torque of 200 ft-lb on each of the rear wheels. If we assume that this maximum torque is maintained and that there is no wind friction, what is the time to travel a quarter mile from a standing start? What is the speed of the vehicle at the quarter-mile mark? The weight of the racer and the driver combined is 1,600 lb. For simplicity, neglect the rotational effects of the wheels.

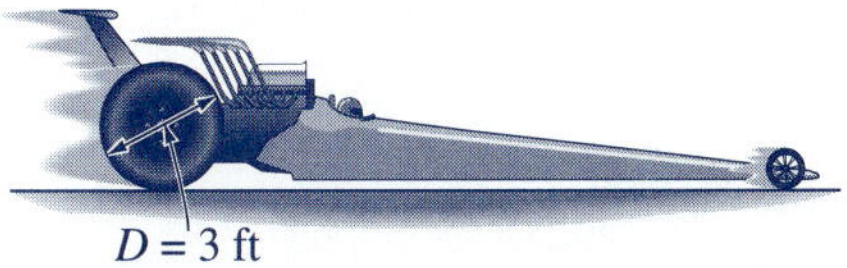

Figure P.12.7.

12.8. A truck is moving down a 10° incline. The driver strongly applies his brakes to avoid a collision and the truck decelerates at the steady rate of 1 m/sec². If the static coefficient of friction μ_s between the load W and the truck trailer is .3, will the load slide or remain stationary relative to the truck trailer? The weight of W is 4,500 N and it is not held to the truck by cables.

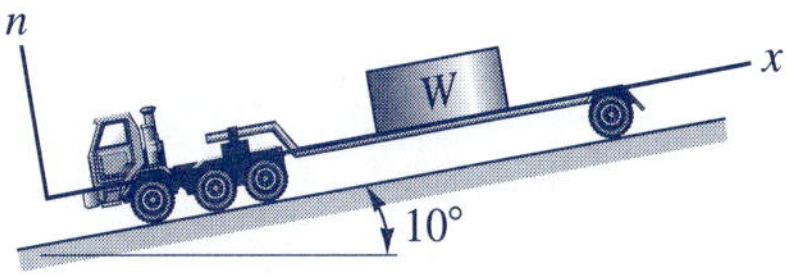

Figure P.12.8.

12.9. A simple device for measuring reasonably uniform accelerations is the pendulum. Calibrate θ of the pendulum for vehicle accelerations of 5 ft/sec², 10 ft/sec², and 20 ft/sec². The bob weighs 1 lb. The bob is connected to a post with a flexible string.

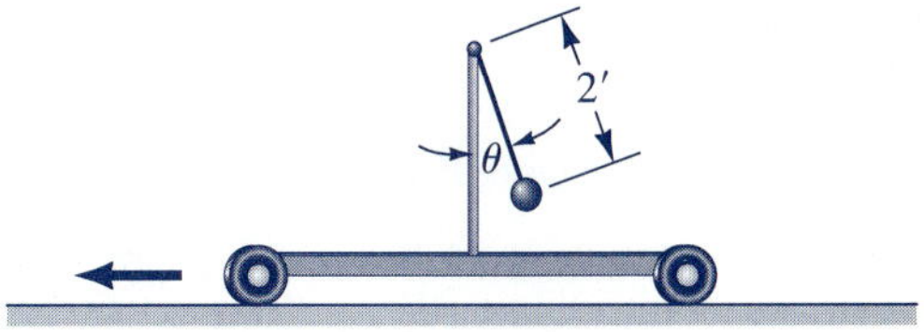

Figure P.12.9.

12.10. A piston is being moved through a cylinder. The piston is moved at a constant speed V_p of .6 m/sec relative to the ground by a force F. The cylinder is free to move along the ground on small wheels. There is a coulombic friction force between the piston and the cylinder such that μ_d = .3. What distance d must the piston move relative to the ground to advance .01 m along the cylinder if the cylinder is stationary at the outset? The piston has a mass of 2.5 kg and the cylinder has a mass 5 kg.

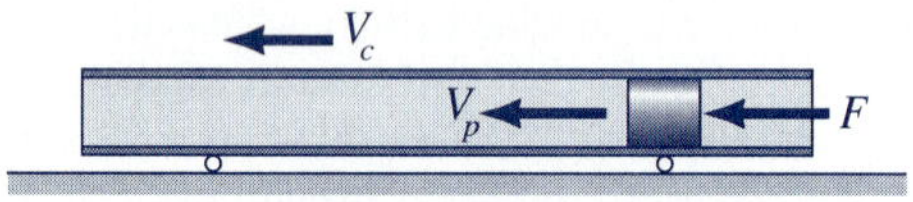

Figure P.12.10.

12.11. A force F of 5,000 N is suddenly applied to mass A. What is the speed after A has moved .1 m? Mass B is a triangular block of uniform thickness.

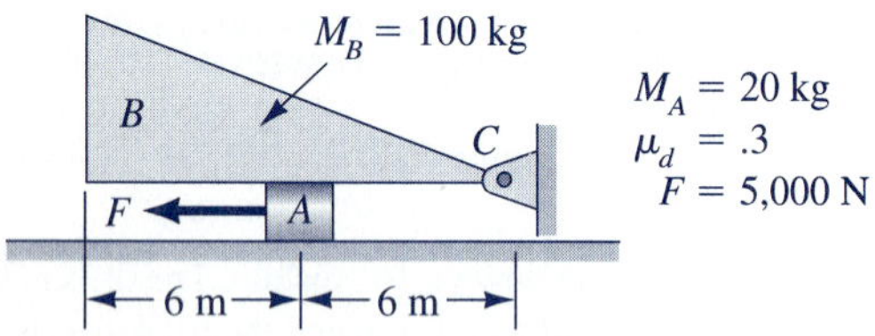

Figure P.12.11.

12.12. A fighter plane is moving on the ground at a speed of 350 km/hr when the pilot deploys the braking parachute. How far does the plane move to get down to a speed of 200 km/hr? The plane has a mass of 8 Mg. The drag is $27.5V^2$ with V in m/s (1 Mg = 10^3 kg).

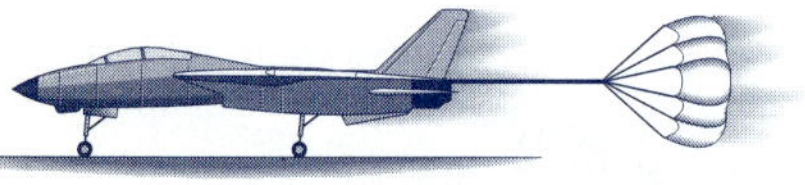

Figure P.12.12.

12.13. Blocks A and B are initially stationary. How far does A move along B if A moves .2 m relative to the ground?

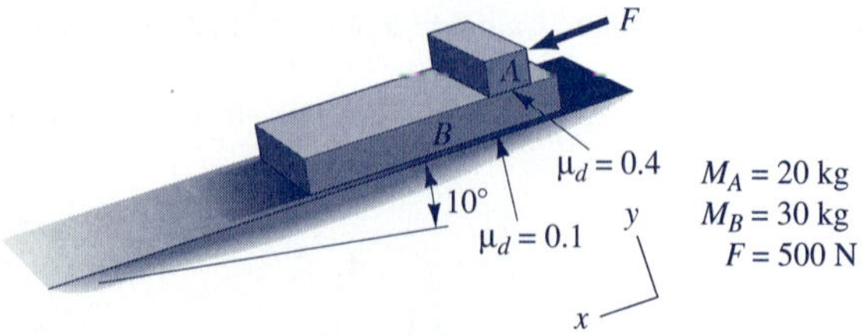

Figure P.12.13.

12.14. A 30-N block at the position shown has a force F = 100 N applied suddenly. What is its velocity after moving 1 m? Also, how far does the block move before stopping? Member AB weighs 200M.

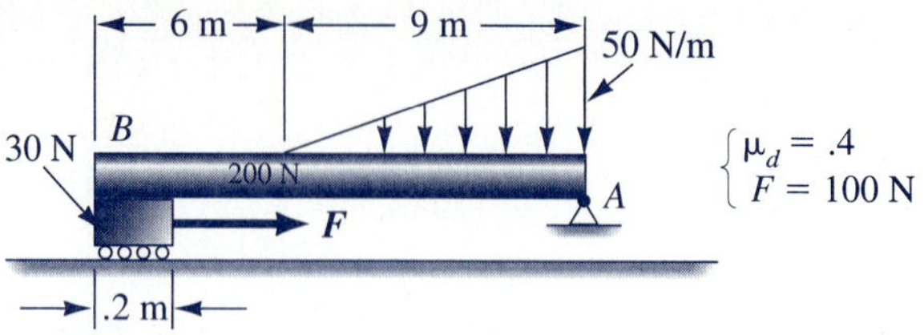

Figure P.12.14.

12.15. A block B of mass M is being pulled up an incline by a force F. If μ_d is .3, at what angle α will the force F cause the maximum steady acceleration?

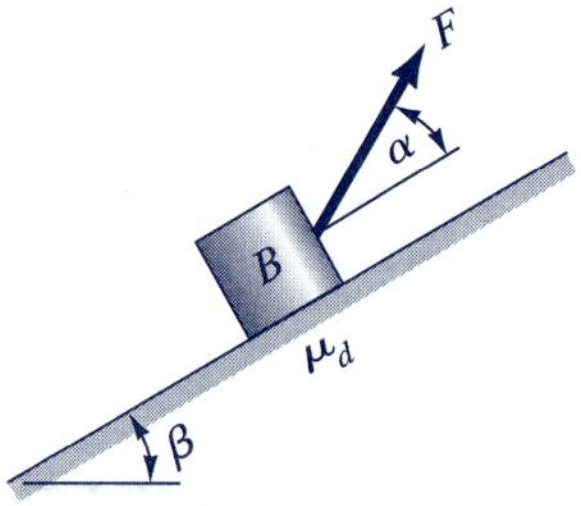

Figure P.12.15.

12.16. A 10-kN force is applied to body B whose mass is 15 kg. Body A has a mass of 20 kg. What is the speed of B after it moves 3 m? Take μ_d = .28. The center of gravity of body A is at its geometric center.

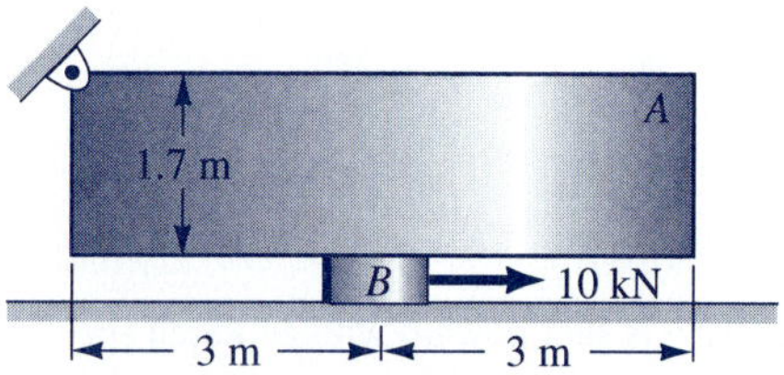

Figure P.12.16.

12.17. A constant force F is applied to the body A when it is in the position shown. What should F be if A is to attain a velocity of 2 m/s after moving 1 m? The spring is unstretched at the position shown.

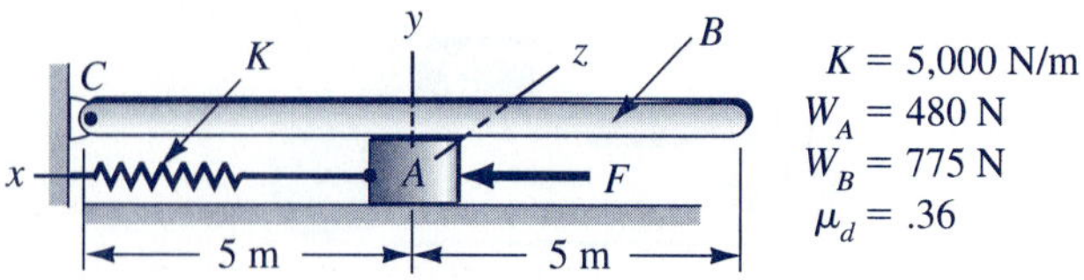

Figure P.12.17.

12.18. Two slow moving steam roller vehicles are moving in opposite directions on a straight path. They start at A and B at the time $t = 0$. How far from point A do they pass each other? What are their speeds when this happens? [*Hint:* Show that the time for this is 1.5 hours.] Note t is in hours.

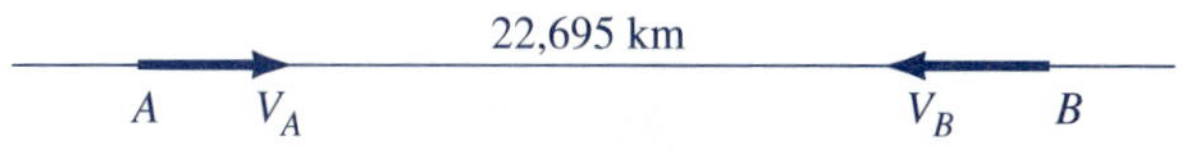

$$V_A = 6t + \sqrt{3t} + 3 \text{ km/hr} \qquad V_B = 5 + t^{2/3} + 0.5t^{1/3} \text{ km/hr}$$

Figure P.12.18.

12.19. As you learned in chemistry, the *coefficient of viscosity* μ is a measure, roughly speaking, of the "stickiness" of a fluid. To measure this property for a highly viscous liquid-like oil, we let a small sphere of metal of radius R descend in a container of the liquid. From fluid mechanics, we know that a drag force will be developed from the oil given by the formula

$$F = 6\pi\mu VR$$

This relation is called *Stoke's law*. The other forces acting on the sphere are its weight (take the density of the sphere as ρ_{Sphere}) and the buoyant force, which is the weight of the oil displaced (take the density of the oil as ρ_{Oil}). The sphere will reach a constant velocity called the *terminal velocity* denoted as $V_{\text{Term.}}$. Show that

$$\mu = \frac{2}{9}\frac{gR^2}{V_{\text{Term.}}}\left(\rho_{\text{Sphere}} - \rho_{\text{Oil}}\right)$$

12.20. A force F is applied to a system of light pulleys to pull body A. If F is 10 kN and A has a mass of 5,000 kg, what is the speed of A after 1 sec starting from rest?

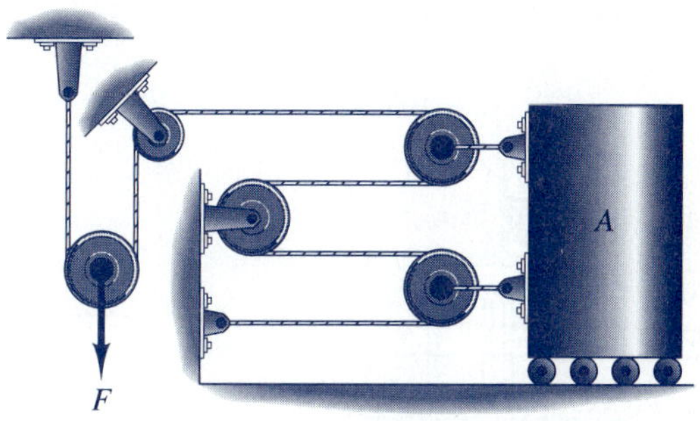

Figure P.12.20.

12.21. A force represented as shown acts on a body having a mass of 1 slug. What is the position and velocity at $t = 30$ sec if the body starts from rest at $t = 0$?

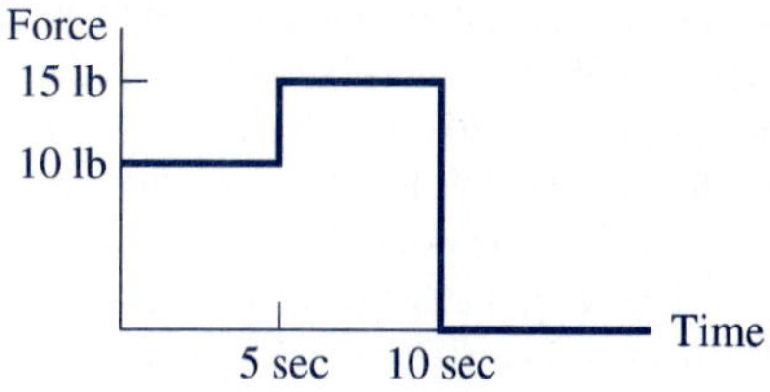

Figure P.12.21.

12.22. A body of mass 1 kg is acted on by a force as shown in the diagram. If the velocity of the body is zero at $t = 0$, what is the velocity and distance traversed when $t = 1$ min? The force acts for only 45 sec.

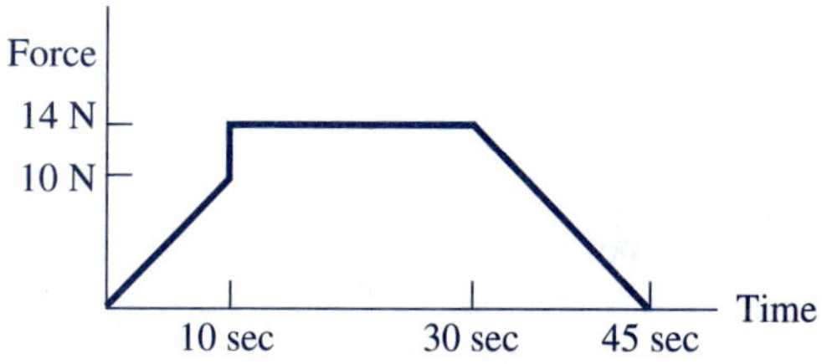

Figure P.12.22.

12.23. Three coupled streetcars are moving down an incline at a speed of 20 km/hr when the brakes are applied for a panic stop. All the wheels lock except for car B, where due to a malfunction all the brakes on the front end of the car do not operate. How far does the system move and what are the forces in the couplings between the cars? Each streetcar weighs 220 kN and the coefficient of dynamic friction μ_d between wheel and rail is .30. Weight is equally distributed on the wheels.

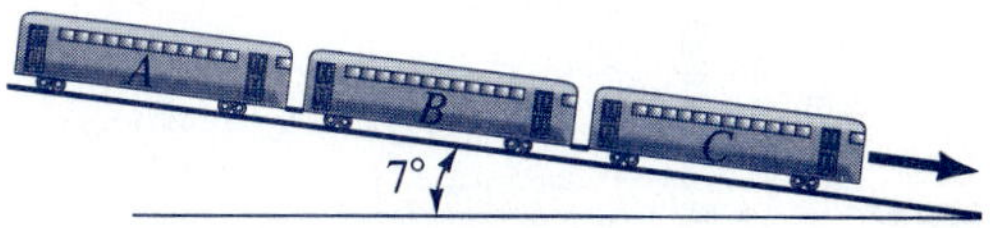

Figure P.12.23.

12.24. A body having a mass of 30 lbm is acted on by a force given by

$$F = 30t^2 + e^{-t} \text{ lb}$$

If the velocity is 10 ft/sec at $t = 0$, what is the body's velocity and the distance traveled when $t = 2$ sec?

12.25. A body of mass 10 kg is acted on by a force in the x direction, given by the relation $F = 10 \sin 6t$ N. If the body has a velocity of 3 m/sec when $t = 0$ and is at position $x = 0$ at that instant, what is the position reached by the body from the origin at $t = 4$ sec? Sketch the displacement-versus-time curve.

12.26. A water skier is shown dangling from a kite that is towed via a light nylon cord by a powerboat at a constant speed of 30 mph. The powerboat with passenger weighs 700 lb and the man and kite together weigh 270 lb. If we neglect the mass of the cable, we can take it as a straight line as shown in the diagram. The horizontal drag from the air on the kite plus man is estimated from fluid mechanics to be 80 lb. What is the tension in the cable? If the cable suddenly snaps, what is the instantaneous horizontal relative acceleration between the kite system and the powerboat?

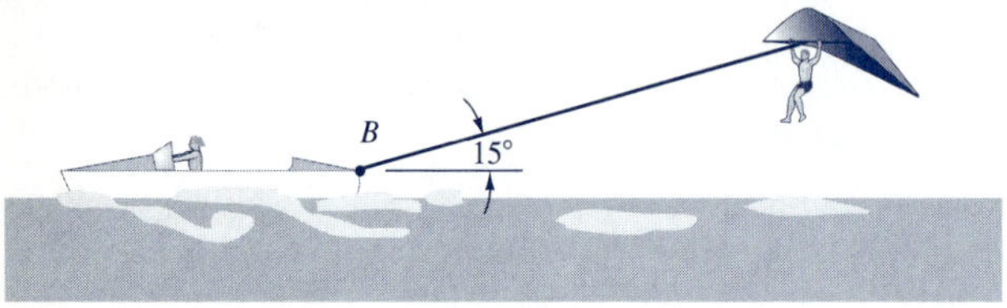

Figure P.12.26.

12.27. A mass M is held by stiff light telescoping rods that can elongate or shorten freely but cannot bend. Each rod is pin connected at the ends A, B, C, and D. The system is on a horizontal, frictionless surface. Two linear springs having spring constants $K_1 = 880$ N/m and $K_2 = 1{,}400$ N/m are connected to the rods as shown in the diagram. If mass $M = 3$ kg is moved .003 m to the right and is released from rest, what is the equation for the velocity in the x direction as a function of x? What is the speed of the mass when it returns to the vertical position of the rods?

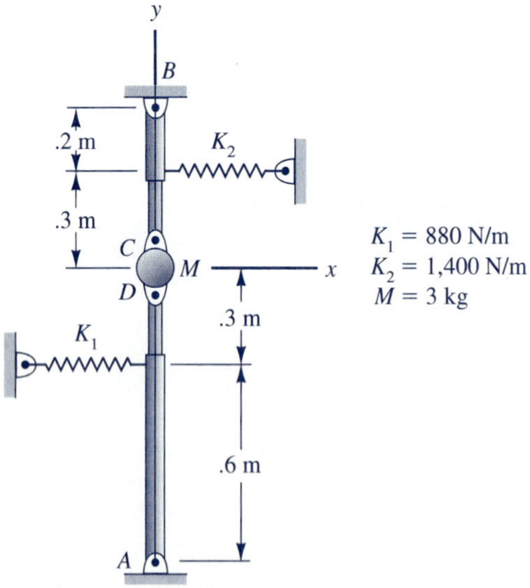

Figure P.12.27.

12.28. A force given as $5 \sin 3t$ lb acts on a mass of 1 slug. What is the position of the mass at $t = 10$ sec? Determine the total distance traveled. Assume the motion started from rest.

12.29. A block A of mass 500 kg is pulled by a force of 10,000 N as shown. A second block B of mass 200 kg rests on small frictionless rollers on top of block A. A wall prevents block B from moving to the left. What is the speed of block A after 1 sec starting from a stationary position? The coefficient of friction μ_d is .4 between A and the horizontal surface.

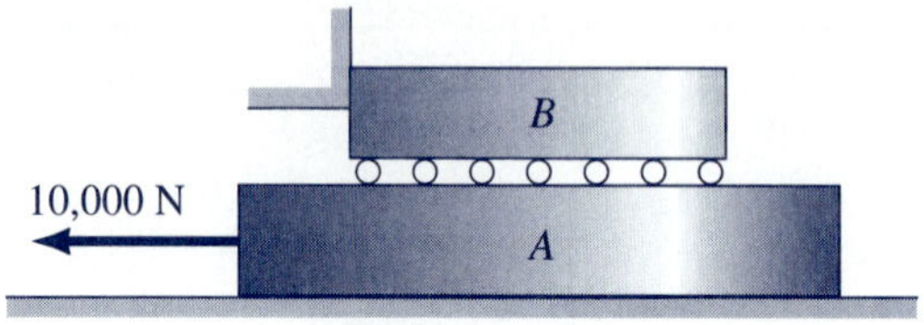

Figure P.12.29.

12.30. Block B weighing 500 N rests on block A, which weighs 300 N. The dynamic coefficient of friction between contact surfaces is .4. At wall C there are rollers whose friction we can neglect. What is the acceleration of body A when a force F of 5,000 N is applied?

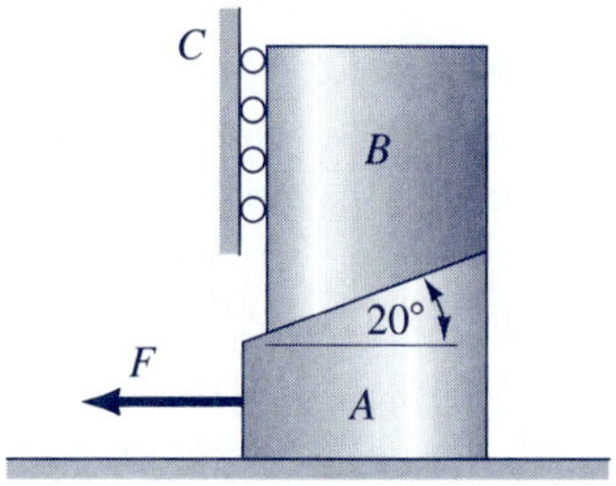

Figure P.12.30.

12.31. A body A of mass 1 lbm is forced to move by the device shown. What total force is exerted on the body at time $t = 6$ sec? What is the maximum total force on the body, and when is the first time this force is developed after $t = 0$?

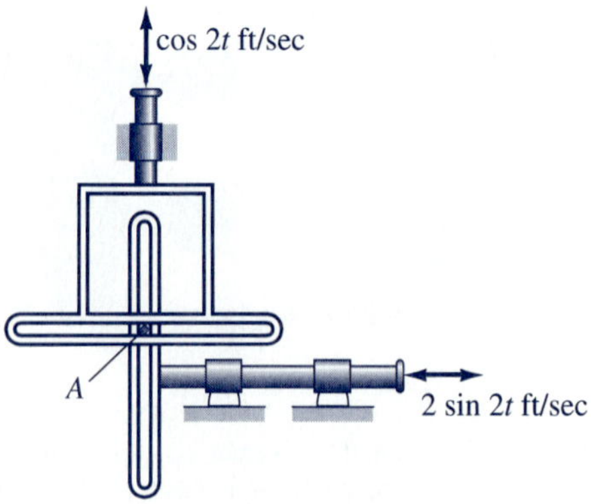

Figure P.12.31.

12.32. Do Problem 12.10 for the case where there is viscous friction between piston and cylinder given as 150 N/m/sec of relative speed. Also, what is the maximum distance l the piston can advance relative to the cylinder?

12.33. The high-speed aerodynamic drag on a car is $.02V^2$ lb with V in ft/sec. If the initial speed is 100 mi/hr, how far will the car move before its speed is reduced to 60 mi/hr? The mass of the car is 2,000 lbm.

12.34. A block slides on a film of oil. The resistance to motion of the block is proportional to the speed of the block relative to the incline at the rate of 7.5 N/m/sec. If the block is released from rest, what is the *terminal speed*? What is the distance moved after 10 sec?

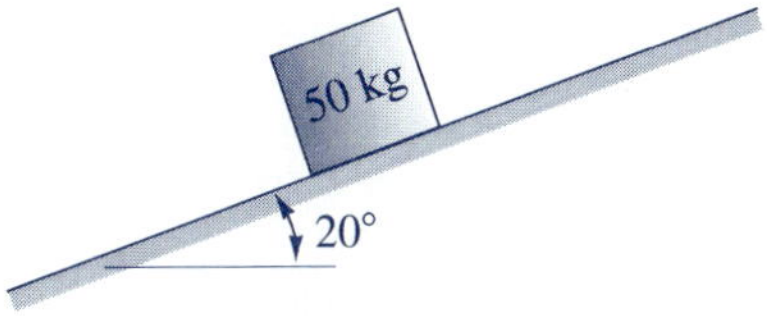

Figure P.12.34.

12.35. When you study fluid mechanics, you will learn that the drag D on a body when moving through a fluid with mass density ρ is given as $\frac{1}{2}C_D\rho V^2 A$ where V is the velocity of the body relative to the fluid; A is the frontal area of the object; and C_D is the so-called *coefficient of drag* usually determined by experiment.

A racing plane on landing is moving at a speed of 350 km/hr when a braking parachute is deployed. This parachute has a frontal area of 30 m² and a $C_D = 1.2$. The plane has a frontal area of 20 m² and a $C_D = 0.4$. If the plane and parachute have a combined mass of 8 Mg, how long does it take to go from 350 km/hr to 200 km/hr by just coasting? Take $\rho = 1.2475$ kg/m³ and neglect rolling resistance from the tires. There is no wind.

Figure P.12.35.

12.36. In the previous problem, what is the largest frontal area of the braking parachute if the maximum deceleration of the plane is to be $5g$'s when at a speed of 350 km/s the parachute is first deployed?

12.37. Mass B is on small rollers and moves down the incline. It is connected to a linear spring, which at the position shown is stretched from its undeformed length of 2 m to a length of 5 m. What is the speed of B after it moves 1 m? Use Newton's law as well as the x coordinate shown in the diagram.

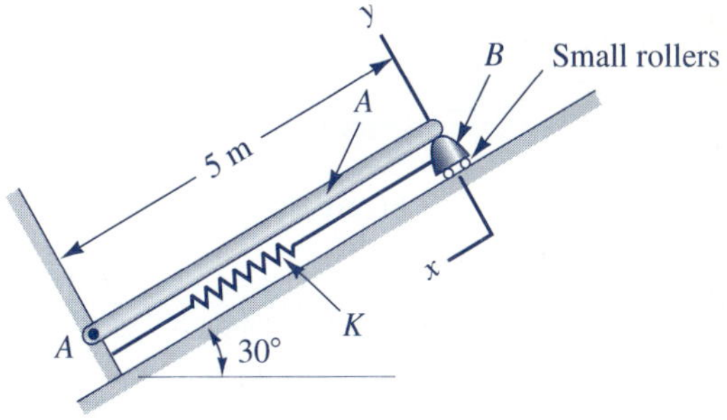

$M_A = 40$ kg
$M_B = 20$ kg
$\mu_d = .2$
$l_0 = 2$ m (unstretched length of spring)
$K = 20$ N/m

Figure P.12.37.

12.38. A wedge of wood having a specific gravity of 0.6 is forced into the water by a 150-lb force. The wedge is 2 ft in width.

(a) What is the depth d?

(b) What is the speed of the wedge when it has moved upward 0.48 ft after releasing the 150-lb force assuming the wedge does not turn as it rises? Recall, a buoyant force equals the weight of the volume displaced (Archimedes).

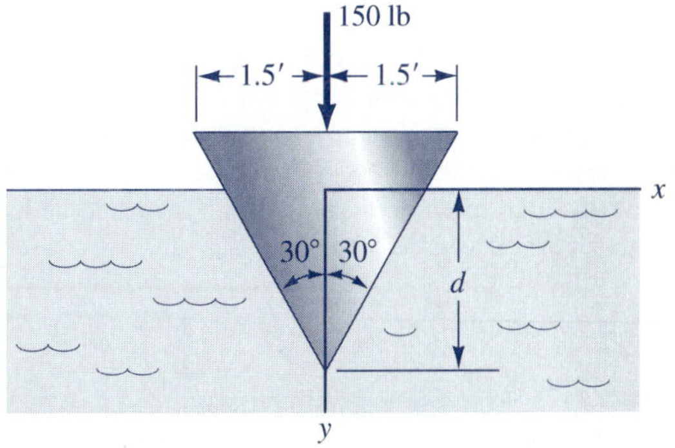

Figure P.12.38.

12.39. A poison dart gun is shown. The cross-sectional area inside the tube is 1 in^2. The dart being blown weighs 3 oz. The dart gun bore has a viscous resistance given as .3 oz per unit velocity in ft/sec. The hunter applies a constant pressure p at the mouth of the gun. Express the relation between p, V (velocity), and t. What constant pressure p is needed to cause the dart to reach a speed of 60 ft/sec in 2 sec? Assume the dart gun is long enough.

Figure P.12.39.

12.40. Using the diagram for Problem 12.5, assume that there is a lubricant between the body D of mass 5 lbm and the belt such that there is a viscous friction force given as .1 lb per unit relative velocity between the body and the belt. The belt moves at a uniform speed of 5 ft/sec to the right and initially the body has a speed to the left of 2 ft/sec relative to ground. At what time later does the body have a zero instantaneous velocity relative to the ground?

12.41. In Problem 12.40 assume that the belt system is inclined 20° from the horizontal with end B above end A. What minimum belt speed is required so that a body of mass M moving downward will come to a permanent halt relative to the ground? For this belt speed, how long does it take for the body to slow down to half of its initial speed of 2 ft/sec relative to the ground?

12.42. One of the largest of the supertankers in the world today is the *S.S. Globtik London*, having a weight when fully loaded of 476,292 tons. The thrust needed to keep this ship moving at 10 knots is 50 kN. If the drag on the ship from the water is proportional to the speed, how long will it take for this ship to slow down from 10 knots to 5 knots after the engines are shut down? (The answer may make you wonder about the safety of such ships.)

12.43. A cantilever beam is shown. It is observed that the vertical deflection of the end A is directly proportional to a vertical tip load F provided that this load is not too excessive. A body B of mass 200 kg, when attached to the end of the beam with F removed, causes a deflection of 5 mm there after all motion has ceased. What is the speed of this body if it is attached suddenly to the beam and has descended 3 mm?

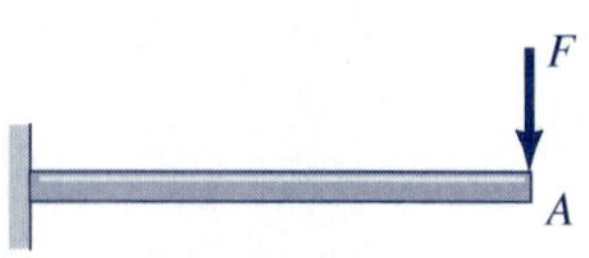

Figure P.12.43.

12.44. The spring shown is nonlinear. That is, K is not a constant, but is a function of the extension of the spring. If $K = 2x + 3$ lb/in. with x measured in inches, what is the speed of the mass when $x = 0$ after it is released from a state of rest at a position 3 in. from the equilibrium position? The mass of the body is 1 slug.

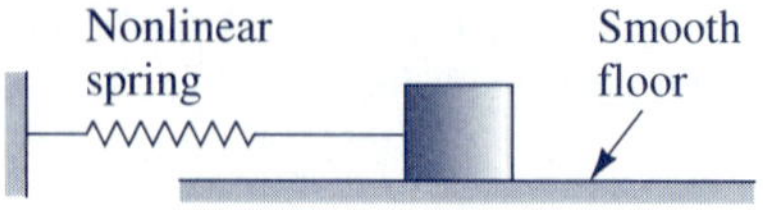

Figure P.12.44.

12.45. A particle of mass m is subject to the following force field:

$$\boldsymbol{F} = m\boldsymbol{i} + 4m\boldsymbol{j} + 16m\boldsymbol{k} \text{ lb}$$

In addition, it is subjected to a frictional force $\boldsymbol{f}$ given as

$$\boldsymbol{f} = -m\dot{x}\boldsymbol{i} - m\dot{y}\boldsymbol{j} + 2m\dot{z}\boldsymbol{k} \text{ lb}$$

The particle is stationary at the origin at time $t = 0$. What is the position of the particle at time $t = 1$ sec?

12.46. A beebee is shot vertically upward with an initial velocity of 120 ft/sec. If the air resistance is $1.4 \times 10^{-5}V^2$ lb, how much time elapses for the projectile to reach its maximum elevation? How high does it go? The beebee weighs .85 oz.

12.47. If in the previous problem, the beebee has reached a maximum height of 92.75 ft, what is the speed when it returns to the ground, assuming it does not reach its terminal velocity? If it has reached the terminal velocity, what is your answer?

12.48. A rocket weighing 5,000 lb is fired vertically from a test stand on the ground. A constant thrust of 20,000 lb is developed for 20 seconds. If just as an exercise, we do not take into account the amount of fuel burned, and if we neglect air resistance, how high up does this hypothetical rocket go? Note that neglecting fuel consumption is a serious error! In the next problem we will investigate the case of the variable mass problem.

***12.49.** Calculate the velocity after 20 seconds for the case where there is a *decrease* of mass of a rocket of 100 lbm/sec as a result of exhaust combustion products leaving the rocket at a speed of 6,000 ft/sec relative to the rocket. At the outset the rocket weighs 5,000 lb. [*Hint:* Start with Newton's law in the form $\boldsymbol{F} = (d/dt)(m\boldsymbol{V})$ where $\boldsymbol{F}$ is the weight, a variable that decreases as fuel is burned. The first term on the right side of this equation is $m(dV/dt)$ where m is the instantaneous mass of the rocket and unburned fuel. Now there is a force on the 100 lbm/sec of combustion products being expelled from the rocket at a speed relative to the rocket of 6,000 ft/sec. The rate of change of linear momentum associated with this force clearly must be $(dm/dt)(6{,}000)$. The *reaction* to this force for this momentum change is on the rocket in the direction of flight of the rocket and must be added to $m(dV/dt)$. The force exerted by the exhaust gases on the rocket is a propulsive force and is called the *thrust* of the rocket. Again, neglect drag of the atmosphere since it will be small at the outset because of low velocity and small later because of the thinness of the atmosphere.]

12.50. We start with a cylindrical tank with diameter 50 ft containing water up to a depth of 10 ft. Initially the solid movable cylindrical piston A having a diameter of 20 ft and a centerline colinear with the centerline of the tank is positioned so that its top is flush with the bottom of the tank. Now the cylinder is moved upward so that the following data apply at the instant of interest assuming the free surface of the water remains flat;

$$h_2 = 2 \text{ ft} \qquad \dot{h}_2 = 5 \text{ ft/sec} \qquad \ddot{h}_2 = 3 \text{ ft/sec}^2$$

What is the external force from the *ground* support on the water needed for this condition not including the force required to support the dead weight of the water?

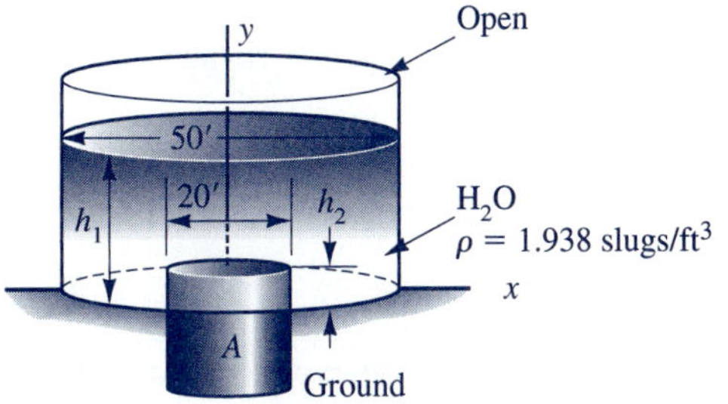

Figure P.12.50.

12.51. A sleeve slides downward along a pipe on which there is dry friction with $\mu_d = .35$. A wire having a constant tension of 80 N is attached to the sleeve and moves with it always retaining the same angle α with the horizontal. If the sleeve weighs 60 N, what should α be for the sleeve to move for 10 seconds before stopping after starting downward with an initial speed of 5 m/s?

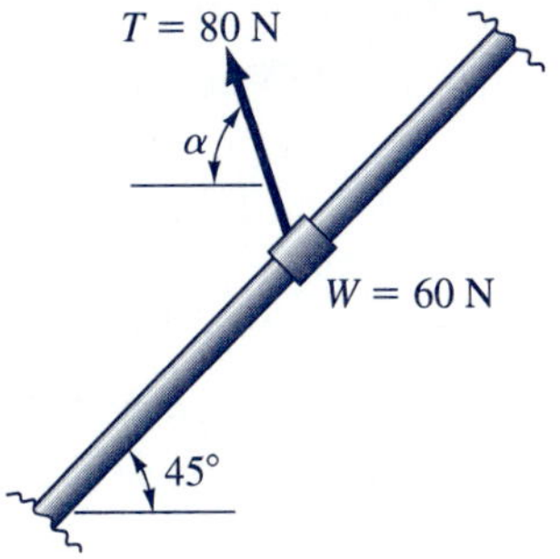

Figure P.12.51.

12.52. An electron having a charge of $-e$ coulombs is moving between two parallel plates in a vacuum with an impressed voltage E. If at $t = 0$, the electron has a velocity V_0 at an angle α_0 with the horizontal in the xy plane, what will be the trajectory equation taking the initial conditions to be at the origin of xy? Show that

$$y = \frac{eE}{2m} + \frac{x^2}{(V_0 \cos \alpha_0)^2} + x \tan \alpha_0$$

where m is the mass of the electron. Note we have neglected gravity here since it is very small compared with the electrostatic force.

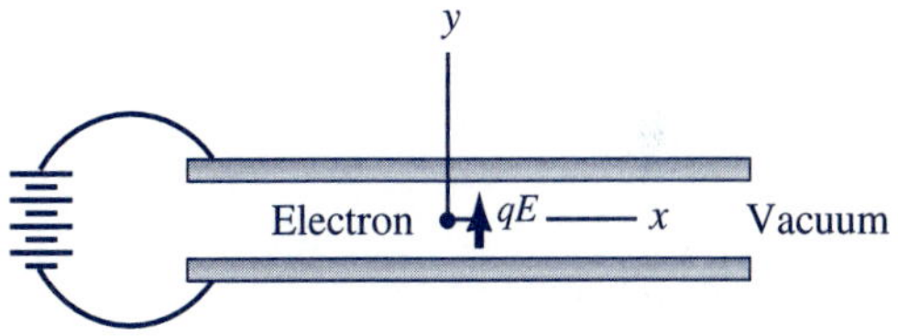

Figure P.12.52.

12.53. A system of light pulleys and inextensible wire connects bodies A, B, and C as shown. If the coefficient of friction between C and the support is .4, what is the acceleration of each body? Take M_A as 100 kg, M_B as 300 kg, and M_C as 80 kg.

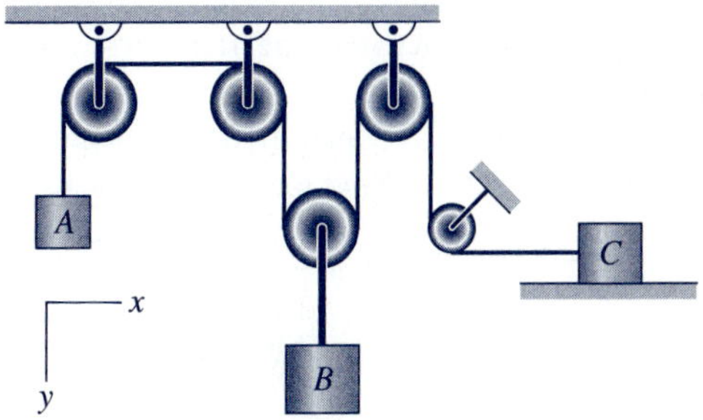

Figure P.12.53.

Part B: Cylindrical Coordinates; Central Force Motion

12.5 Newton's Law for Cylindrical Coordinates

In cylindrical coordinates we can express Newton's law as follows:

$$F_{\bar{r}} = m(\ddot{\bar{r}} - \bar{r}\dot{\theta}^2) \quad (12.15a)$$

$$F_{\theta} = m(\bar{r}\ddot{\theta} - 2\dot{\bar{r}}\dot{\theta}) \quad (12.15b)$$

$$F_z = m\ddot{z} \quad (12.15c)$$

If the motion is known, it is a simple matter to ascertain the force components using Eqs. 12.15. The inverse problem of determining the motion given the forces is particularly difficult in this case. The reason for this difficulty, as you may have already learned in your differential equations course, is that Eqs. 12.15a and 12.15b are *nonlinear*[6] for all force functions. For this reason, we cannot present integration procedures as in Part A of this chapter. The following example will serve to illustrate the kind of problem we are able to solve with the methods thus far presented in this chapter.

[6]A differential equation is nonlinear if the dependent variable and its derivatives form powers greater than unity or form products anywhere in the equation.

Example 12.8

A platform shown in Fig. 12.13 has a constant angular velocity ω equal to 5 rad/sec. A mass B of 2 kg slides in a frictionless chute attached to the platform. The mass is connected via a light inextensible cable to a linear spring having a spring constant K of 20 N/m. A swivel connector at A allows the cable to turn freely relative to the spring. The spring is unstretched when the mass B is at the center C of the platform. If the mass B is released at r = 200 mm from a stationary position relative to the platform, what is its speed relative to the platform when it has moved to position r = 400 mm? What is the transverse force on the body B at this position?

We have here a coplanar motion for which cylindrical coordinates are most useful. Because the motion is coplanar, we can use r instead of $\bar{r}$ with no ambiguity. Applying Eq. 12.15a first, we have

$$-20r = 2(\ddot{r} - 25r)$$

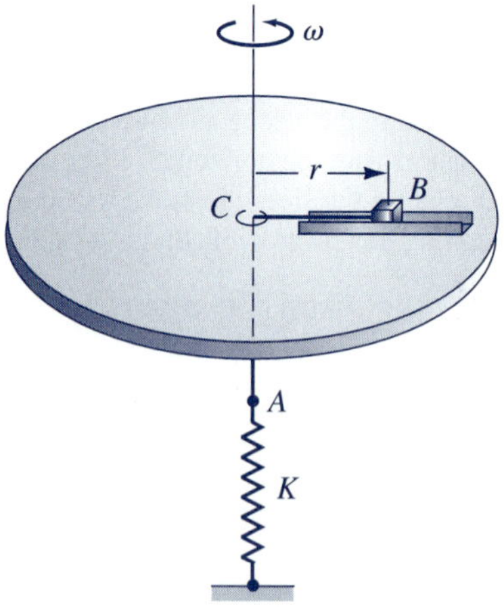

Figure 12.13. Slider on rotating platform.

Example 12.8 (Continued)

Therefore,

$$\ddot{r} = 15r \qquad \text{(a)}$$

As in Example 12.5, we can replace $\ddot{r}$ so as to allow for a separation of variables.

$$\ddot{r} \equiv \frac{dV_r}{dt} \equiv \frac{dV_r}{dr}\frac{dr}{dt} \equiv V_r \frac{dV_r}{dr} = 15r$$

Therefore,

$$V_r \, dV_r = 15r \, dr$$

Integrating, we get

$$\frac{V_r^2}{2} = \frac{15r^2}{2} + C_1 \qquad \text{(b)}$$

To determine C_1, note that, when $r = .20m$, $V_r = 0$. Hence,

$$C_1 = -\frac{.600}{2}$$

Equation (b) then becomes

$$V_r^2 = 15r^2 - .600 \qquad \text{(c)}$$

When $r = .40$ m, we get for V_r from Eq. (c):

$$V_r = 1.342 \text{ m/sec} \qquad \text{(d)}$$

This is the desired velocity relative to the platform.

To get the transverse force F_θ, go to Eq. 12.15b. Substituting the known data into the equation, we have

$$F_\theta = 2[(.40)(0) + (2)(1.342)(5)]$$

$$F_\theta = 26.84 \text{ N}$$

This is the transverse force on the mass B.

Although you will be asked to solve problems similar to the preceding example, the main use of cylindrical coordinates in Part B of this chapter will be for gravitational central force motion. We shall first present the basic physics underlying this motion expressing certain salient characteristics of the motion, and then we shall arrive at a point where we can effectively employ cylindrical coordinates to describe the motion.

12.6 Central Force Motion—An Introduction

At this time, we shall consider the motion of a particle on which the resultant force is always *directed toward some point fixed in inertial space.* Such forces are termed *central forces* and the resulting motion of this particle is called *central force motion.* A simple example of this is the case of a space vehicle moving with its engine off in the vicinity of a large planet (see Fig. 12.14).

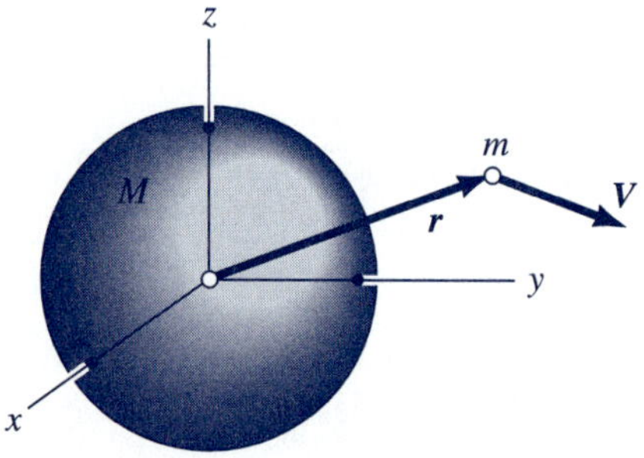

Figure 12.14. Body m moving about a planet.

The space vehicle is very small compared to the planet and may be considered to be a particle. Away from the planet's atmosphere, this vehicle will experience no frictional forces, and, if no other astronautical bodies are reasonably close, the only force acting on the vehicle will be the gravitational attraction of the fixed planet.[7] This force is directed toward the center of the planet and, from the gravitational law, is given as

$$\boldsymbol{F} = -G\frac{M_{\text{planet}}m_{\text{body}}}{r^2}\hat{\boldsymbol{r}} \tag{12.16}$$

In the ensuing problems for this chapter and also for Chapter 14, we shall need to compute the quantity GM in the equation above. For this purpose, note that, for any particle of mass m at the surface of any planet of mass M and radius R, by the law of gravitation:

$$W = mg = \frac{GMm}{R^2}$$

[7]We are neglecting drag developed from collisions of the space vehicle with solar dust particles.

where g is the acceleration of gravity at the surface of the planet. Solving for GM, we get

$$GM = gR^2 \tag{12.17}$$

Thus, knowing g and R for a planet, it is a simple matter to find GM needed for orbit calculations around this planet.

As pointed out earlier, the motion of a space vehicle with power off is an important example of a central force motion—more precisely a *gravitational* central force motion. The vehicle is usually launched from a planet and accelerated to a high speed outside the planet's atmosphere by multistage rockets (see Fig. 12.15). The velocity at the final instant of powered flight is called the *burnout* velocity. After burnout, the vehicle undergoes gravitational central force motion. Depending on the position and velocity at burnout, the vehicle can go into an orbit around the earth (elliptic and circular orbits are possible), or it can depart from the earth's influence on a parabolic or a hyperbolic trajectory. In all cases, the motion must be coplanar.

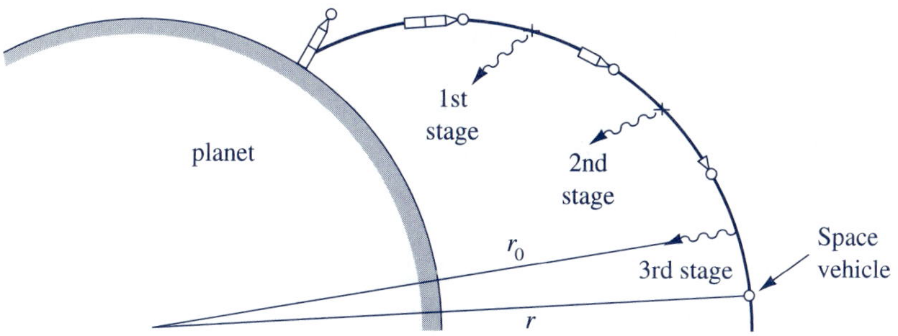

Figure 12.15. Launching a space vehicle.

In the following sections, we shall make a careful detailed study of gravitational central force trajectories. Those who do not have the time for such a detailed study of the trajectories can still make many useful and interesting calculations in Chapter 14 using energy and momentum methods that we shall soon undertake.

*12.7 Gravitational Central Force Motion

For gravitational central force motion, we shall employ an inertial reference xy in the plane of the trajectory with the origin of the reference taken at the point P toward which the central force is directed (see Fig. 12.16). We shall use cylindrical coordinates r and θ for describing the motion. Because $z = 0$ at all times, these coordinates are also called polar coordinates. Since the motion is coplanar in plane xy, we can delete the overbar used previously for r with no danger of ambiguity.

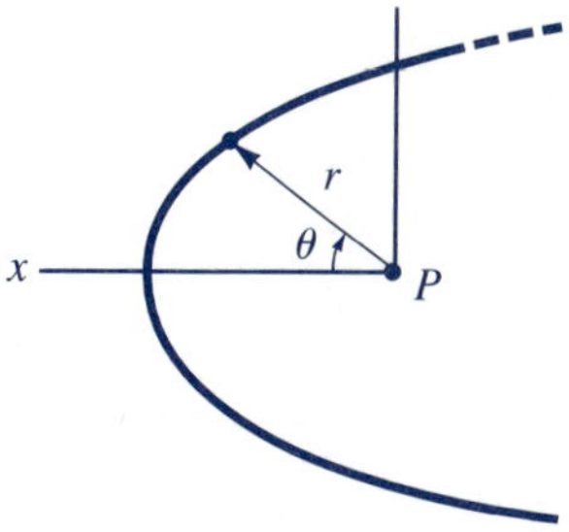

Figure 12.16. xy is inertial reference in plane of the trajectory.

Let us consider *Newton's law* for a body of mass m, which is moving near a star of mass M:

$$m\frac{d\mathbf{V}}{dt} = -G\frac{Mm}{r^2}\hat{\mathbf{r}} \tag{12.18}$$

Canceling m and using cylindrical coordinates and components, we can express the equation above in the following manner:

$$(\ddot{r} - r\dot{\theta}^2)\boldsymbol{\epsilon}_r + (r\ddot{\theta} + 2\dot{r}\dot{\theta})\boldsymbol{\epsilon}_\theta = -\frac{GM}{r^2}\hat{\mathbf{r}} \tag{12.19}$$

Since $\boldsymbol{\epsilon}_r$ and $\hat{\mathbf{r}}$ are identical vectors, the scalar equations of the preceding equation become

$$\ddot{r} - r\dot{\theta}^2 = -GM/r^2 \tag{12.20a}$$

$$r\ddot{\theta} + 2\dot{r}\dot{\theta} = 0 \tag{12.20b}$$

Equation 12.20b can be expressed in the form

$$\frac{1}{r}\frac{d}{dt}(r^2\dot{\theta}) = 0 \tag{12.21}$$

as you can readily verify. We can conclude from Eq. 12.21 that

$$r^2\dot{\theta} = \text{constant} = C \tag{12.22}$$

Equation 12.22 leads to an important conclusion. To establish this, consider the area swept out by r during a time dt, which in Fig. 12.17 is the shaded

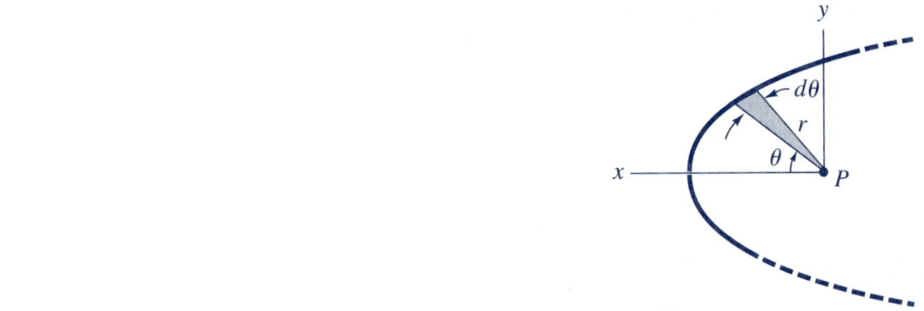

Figure 12.17. Particle sweeps out area.

area. By considering this area to be that of a triangle, we can express it as

$$dA = \frac{r^2\,d\theta}{2}$$

Dividing through by dt, we have

$$\frac{dA}{dt} = \frac{r^2\dot{\theta}}{2}$$

Now dA/dt is the rate at which area is being swept out by r; it is called *areal velocity*. And, since $r^2\dot{\theta}$ is a constant for each gravitational central force motion (see Eq. 12.22), we can conclude that the areal velocity is a constant for each gravitational central force motion. (This is Kepler's second law.) This means that when r is decreased, $\dot{\theta}$ must increase, etc. The constant, understand, will be different for each different trajectory.

In order to determine the general trajectory, we replace the independent variable t of Eq. 12.20a. Consider first the time derivatives of r:

$$\dot{r} = \frac{dr}{dt} = \frac{dr}{d\theta}\frac{d\theta}{dt} = \frac{d\theta}{dt}\frac{dr}{d\theta} = \frac{C}{r^2}\frac{dr}{d\theta} \tag{12.23}$$

where we have used Eq. 12.22 to replace $d\theta/dt$. Next, consider $\ddot{r}$ in a similar manner:

$$\ddot{r} = \frac{d\dot{r}}{dt} = \frac{d}{dt}\left(\frac{C}{r^2}\frac{dr}{d\theta}\right) = \frac{d}{d\theta}\left(\frac{C}{r^2}\frac{dr}{d\theta}\right)\frac{d\theta}{dt} \tag{12.24}$$

Again, using Eq. 12.22 to replace $d\theta/dt$, we get

$$\ddot{r} = \left[\frac{d}{d\theta}\left(\frac{C}{r^2}\frac{dr}{d\theta}\right)\right]\frac{C}{r^2} \tag{12.25}$$

For convenience, we now introduce a new dependent variable, $u = 1/r$, into the right side of this equation

$$\begin{aligned}\ddot{r} &= \left[\frac{d}{d\theta}\left(Cu^2\frac{d(1/u)}{d\theta}\right)\right]Cu^2\\ &= \left\{\frac{d}{d\theta}\left[Cu^2\left(-\frac{1}{u^2}\right)\frac{du}{d\theta}\right]\right\}Cu^2\\ &= -C^2u^2\frac{d^2u}{d\theta^2}\end{aligned}$$

By replacing $\ddot{r}$ in this form in Eq. 12.20a and $\dot{\theta}^2$ in the form C^2u^4 from Eq. 12.22, and finally, r by $1/u$, we get

$$-C^2u^2\frac{d^2u}{d\theta^2} - C^2u^3 = -GMu^2$$

Canceling terms and dividing through by C^2, we have

$$\frac{d^2u}{d\theta^2} + u = \frac{GM}{C^2} \tag{12.26}$$

This is a simple differential equation that you may have already studied in your differential equations course. Specifically, it is a second-order differential equation with constant coefficients and a constant driving function GM/C^2. We want to find the most general function $u(\theta)$, which when substituted into the differential equation satisfies the differential equation—i.e., renders it an identity. The theory of differential equations indicates that this general solution is composed of two parts. They are:

1. The general solution of the differential equation with the right side of the differential equation set equal to zero and hence given as

$$\frac{d^2u}{d\theta^2} + u = 0 \tag{12.27}$$

This solution is called the *complementary* (or *homogeneous*) solution, u_c.

2. *Any* solution u_p that satisfies the full differential equation. This part is called the *particular solution.*

The desired general solution is then the sum of the complementary and particular solutions. It is a simple matter to show by substitution that the function $A \sin \theta$ satisfies Eq. 12.27 for any value of A. This is similarly true for $B \cos \theta$ for any value of B. The theory of differential equations tells us that there are two independent functions for the solution of Eq. 12.27. The general complementary solution is then

$$u_c = A \sin\theta + B\cos\theta \tag{12.28}$$

where A and B are arbitrary constants of integration. Considering the full differential equation (Eq. 12.26), we see by inspection that a particular solution is

$$u_p = \frac{GM}{C^2} \tag{12.29}$$

The general solution to the differential equation (Eq. 12.26) is then

$$u = \frac{GM}{C^2} + A\sin\theta + B\cos\theta \tag{12.30}$$

By simple trigonometric considerations, we can put the complementary solution in the equivalent form, $D \cos(\theta - \beta)$, where D and β are then the constants of integration.[8] We then have as an alternative formulation for u (= $1/r$):

$$u = \frac{1}{r} = \frac{GM}{C^2} + D\cos(\theta - \beta) \tag{12.31}$$

You may possibly recognize this equation as the general *conic equation* in polar coordinates with the focus at the origin. In your analytic geo-

[8]By expanding $[D \cos(\theta - \beta)]$ as $[(D \cos\beta) \cos\theta + (D \sin\beta) \sin\theta]$, we see, since D and β are arbitrary, that $[D \cos(\theta - \beta)]$ is equivalent to $[A \sin\theta + B \cos\theta]$, where A and B are arbitrary.

metry class, you probably saw the following form for the general conic equation.[9]

$$\frac{1}{r} = \frac{1}{\epsilon p} + \frac{1}{p}\cos(\theta - \beta) \qquad (12.37)$$

where ϵ is the *eccentricity*, p is the distance from the *focus to the directrix*, and β is the angle between the x axis and the axis of symmetry of the conic section.

Comparing Eqs. 12.31 and 12.37, we see that

$$p = \frac{1}{D} \qquad (12.38a)$$

$$\epsilon = \frac{DC^2}{GM} \qquad (12.38b)$$

[9]A *conic section* is the locus of all points whose distance from a *fixed point* has a *constant ratio* to the distance from a *fixed line*. The fixed point is called the *focus* (or focal point) and the line is termed the *directrix*. In Fig. 12.18 we have shown point P, a directrix DD, and a focus O. For a conic section to be traced by P, it must move in a manner that keeps the ratio $r/\overline{DP}$, called the *eccentricity*, a fixed number. Clearly, for every acceptable position P, there will be a mirror image position P' (see the diagram) about a line normal to the directrix and going through the focal point O. Thus, the conic section will be *symmetrical* about axis OC.

Using the letter ϵ to represent the eccentricity, we can say:

$$\frac{r}{\overline{DP}} \equiv \epsilon = \frac{r}{p + r\cos\eta} \qquad (12.32)$$

where p is the distance from the focus to the directrix. Replacing $\cos\eta$ by $-\cos(\theta - \beta)$, where β (see Fig. 12.18) is the angle between the x axis and the axis of symmetry, we then get

$$\frac{r}{p - r\cos(\theta - \beta)} = \epsilon \qquad (12.33)$$

Now, rearranging the terms in the equation, we arrive at a standard formulation for conic sections:

$$\frac{1}{r} = \frac{1}{\epsilon p} + \frac{1}{p}\cos(\theta - \beta) \qquad (12.34)$$

To understand the significance of the eccentricity ϵ, let us consider conic sections in terms of a reference xy, where x is the axis of symmetry (i.e., consider $\beta = 0$ in preceding formulations and refer to Fig. 12.19). Equation 12.34 can be expressed for these rectangular coordinates in the following manner:

$$\frac{1}{\sqrt{x^2 + y^2}} = \frac{1}{\epsilon p} + \frac{1}{p}\frac{x}{\sqrt{x^2 + y^2}} \qquad (12.35)$$

Simple algebraic manipulation permits us to put the preceding equation into the following form:

$$(1 - \epsilon^2)x^2 + y^2 + 2p\epsilon^2 x - \epsilon^2 p^2 = 0 \qquad (12.36)$$

If $\epsilon > 1$, the coefficients of x^2 and y^2 are different in sign and unequal in value. The equation then represents a *hyperbola*.

If $\epsilon = 1$, only one of the squared terms remains and we have a *parabola*.

If $\epsilon < 1$, the coefficients of the squared terms are unequal but have the same sign. The curve is that of an *ellipse*.

If $\epsilon = 0$, clearly we have a *circle* since the coefficients of the squared terms are equal in value and sign.

In Appendix III, we discuss in more detail the particular case of the ellipse.

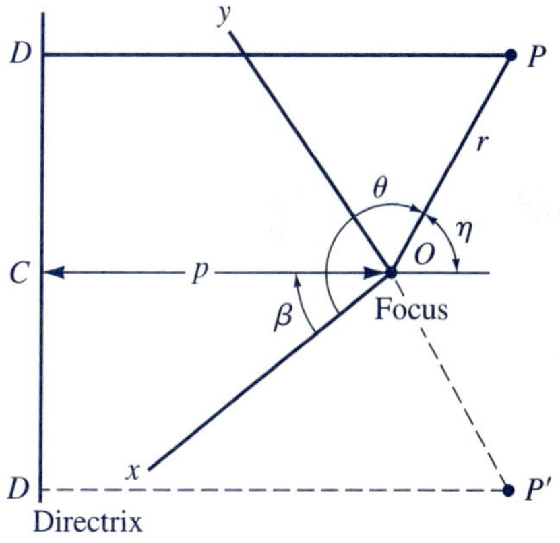

Figure 12.18. $r/\overline{DP} = \epsilon \equiv$ constant for conic section.

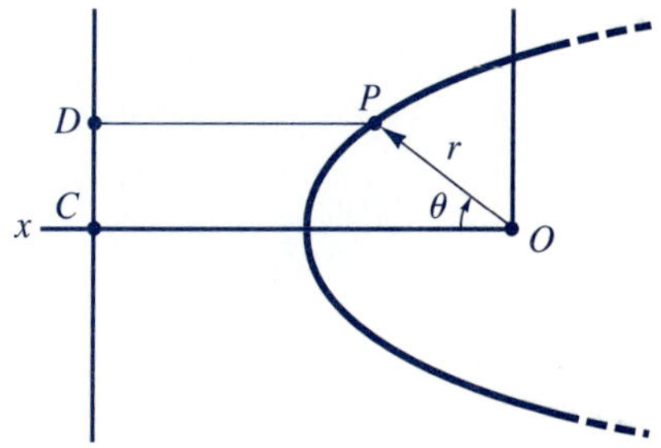

Figure 12.19. Case for $\beta = 0$; x axis is axis of symmetry.

From our knowledge of conic sections, we can then say that if

$$\frac{DC^2}{GM} > 1, \text{ the trajectory is a hyperbola} \tag{12.39a}$$

$$\frac{DC^2}{GM} = 1, \text{ the trajectory is a parabola} \tag{12.39b}$$

$$\frac{DC^2}{GM} < 1, \text{ the trajectory is an ellipse} \tag{12.39c}$$

$$\frac{DC^2}{GM} = 0, \text{ the trajectory is a circle} \tag{12.39d}$$

Clearly, DC^2/GM, the eccentricity, is an extremely important quantity. We shall next look into the practical applications of the preceding general theory to problems in space mechanics.

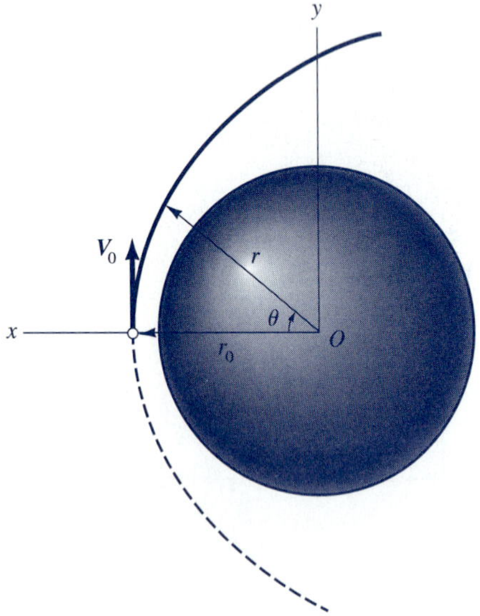

Figure 12.20. Launching at axis of symmetry.

*12.8 Applications to Space Mechanics

We shall now employ the theory set forth in the previous section to study the motion of space vehicles—a problem of great present-day interest. We shall assume that at the end of powered flight the position $\boldsymbol{r}_0$ and velocity $\boldsymbol{V}_0$ of the vehicle are known from rocket calculations. The reference employed will be an inertial reference at the center of the planet and so the reference will translate with the planet relative to the "fixed stars." Accordingly, the earth will rotate one cycle per day for such a reference. We know that the trajectory of the body will form a plane fixed in inertial space and so, for convenience, we take the *xy* plane of the reference to be the plane of the trajectory. It is the usual practice to choose the *x* axis to be the axis of symmetry for the trajectory. If there is a *zero radial velocity* component at "burnout," then the launching clearly occurs at a position along the axis of symmetry of the trajectory (i.e., along the *x* axis). This case has been shown in Fig. 12.20, wherein the subscript 0 denotes launch data. If, on the other hand, a radial component $(V_r)_0$ is present at burnout, then the launch condition occurs at some position θ_0 from the *x* axis, as shown in Fig. 12.21. We generally do not know θ_0 a priori, since its value depends on the equation of the trajectory. Finally, the angle α shown in the diagram will be called the *launching angle* in the ensuing discussion.

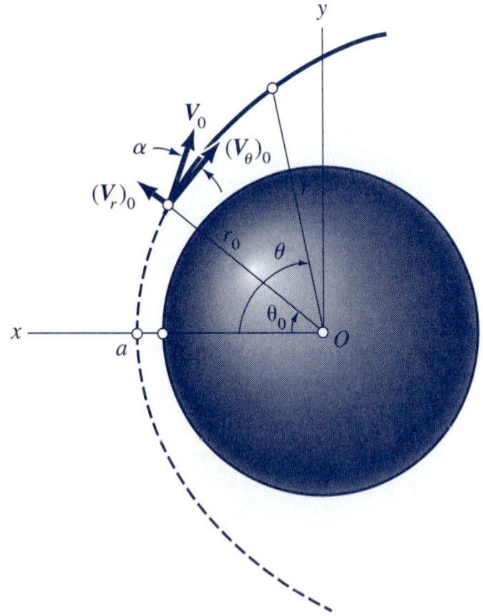

Figure 12.21. Burnout with radial velocity present.

Since the *x* axis has been chosen to be the axis of symmetry, the equation of motion of the vehicle after powered flight is given in terms of arbitrary constants C and D by Eq. 12.31 with the angle β set equal to zero. Thus, we have

$$\frac{1}{r} = \frac{GM}{C^2} + D\cos\theta \tag{12.40}$$

The problem is to find the constants C and D from launching data. We shall illustrate this step in the examples following this section. Note that when these constants are evaluated, the value of the eccentricity $\epsilon = DC^2/GM$ is then available so that we can state immediately the general characteristics of the trajectory.

Furthermore, if the vehicle goes into orbit, we can readily compute the *orbital time* τ for one cycle around a planet. We know from the theory that the aerial velocity is constant and given as

$$\frac{dA}{dt} = \frac{r^2\dot{\theta}}{2} = \text{constant} \tag{12.41}$$

But $r^2\dot{\theta}$ equals the constant C in accordance with Eq. 12.22. Hence,

$$dA = \frac{C}{2}\,dt \tag{12.42}$$

The area swept out for one cycle is the area of an ellipse given as πab, where a and b are the semimajor and semiminor diameters of the ellipse, respectively. Hence, we have on integrating Eq. 12.42:

$$A = \pi ab = \int_0^\tau \frac{C}{2}\,dt = \frac{C}{2}\tau$$

Therefore,

$$\tau = \frac{2\pi ab}{C} \tag{12.43}$$

We have shown in Appendix III that

$$a = \frac{\epsilon p}{1-\epsilon^2} \tag{12.44a}$$

$$b = a(1-\epsilon^2)^{1/2} \tag{12.44b}$$

Replacing p by $1/D$ in accordance with Eq. 12.38a, we then get

$$a = \frac{\epsilon}{D(1-\epsilon^2)} \tag{12.45a}$$

$$b = a(1-\epsilon^2)^{1/2} = \frac{\epsilon}{D(1-\epsilon^2)^{1/2}} \tag{12.45b}$$

Thus, we can get the orbital time τ quite easily once the constants of the trajectory, D and C, are evaluated.

To illustrate many of the previous general remarks in a most simple manner, we now examine the special case where, as shown in Fig. 12.22, various launchings (i.e., burnout conditions) are made from a given point a such that the launching angle $\alpha = 0$. Clearly $(V_r)_0 = 0$ for these cases and the launching axis corresponds to the axis of symmetry of the various trajectories. Only V_0 will be varied in this discussion.

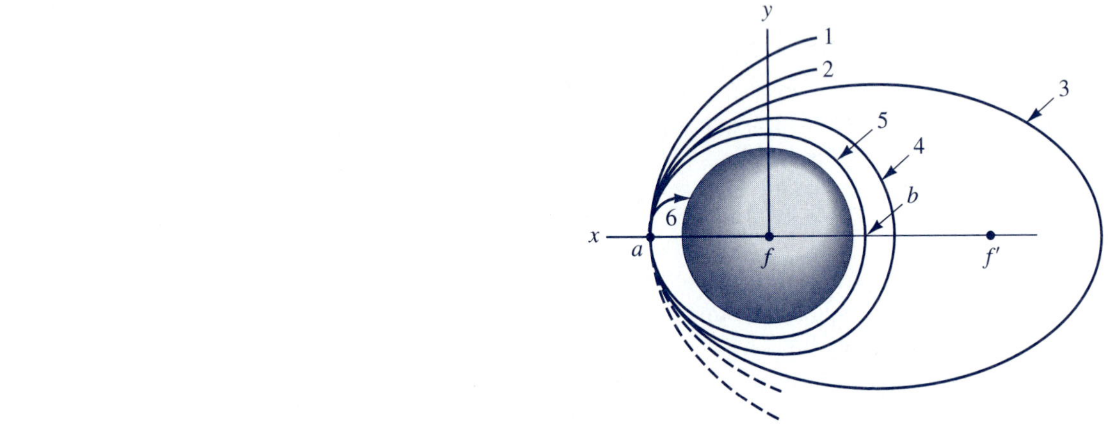

Figure 12.22. Various launchings from the earth or some other planet.

The constants C and D are readily available for these trajectories. Thus, we have from Eq. 12.22:

$$C = r^2\dot{\theta} = rV_\theta = r_0 V_0 \tag{12.46}$$

And from Eq. 12.40, setting $r = r_0$ when $\theta = \theta_0 = 0$, we get, on solving for D:

$$D = \frac{1}{r_0} - \frac{GM}{C^2} = \frac{1}{r_0} - \frac{GM}{r_0^2 V_0^2} \tag{12.47}$$

Since C and D above, for a given r_0, depend only on V_0, we conclude that the eccentricity here is dependent only on V_0 for a given r_0.

If V_0 is so large that DC^2/GM exceeds unity, the vehicle will have the trajectory of a hyperbola (curve 1) and will eventually leave the influence of the earth. If V_0 is decreased to a value such that the eccentricity is unity, the trajectory becomes a parabola (curve 2). Since a further decrease in the value of V_0 will cause the vehicle to orbit, curve 2 is the limiting trajectory with our launching conditions for outer-space flight. The launching velocity for this case is accordingly called the *escape velocity* and is denoted as $(V_0)_E$. We can solve for $(V_0)_E$ for this launching by substituting for C and D from Eqs. 12.46 and 12.47 into the equation $DC^2/GM = 1$. We get

$$(V_0)_E = \sqrt{\frac{2GM}{r_0}} \tag{12.48}$$

a result that is correct for more general launching conditions (i.e., for cases where launching angle $\alpha \neq 0$). Thus, launching a vehicle with a speed equaling or exceeding the value above for a given r_0 will cause the vehicle to leave the earth until such time as the vehicle is influenced by other astronomical bodies or by its own propulsion system. If V_0 is less than the escape velocity, the vehicle will move in the trajectory of an ellipse (curve 3). The closest point to the earth is called *perigee*; the farthest point is called *apogee*. Clearly, these points lie along the axis of symmetry. Such an orbiting vehicle is often called a space satellite. (Kepler, in his famous first law of planetary motion, explained the motion of planets about the sun in this same manner.) One focus for the aforementioned conic curves is at the center of the planet. Another focus f' now moves in from infinity for the satellite trajectories. As the launching speed is decreased, f' moves toward f. When the foci coincide, the trajectory is clearly a circle and, as pointed out earlier (see Eq. 12.39d), the eccentricity ϵ is zero. Accordingly, the constant D must be zero (the constant C clearly will not be zero) and, from Eq. 12.47, the speed for a *circular* orbit $(V_0)_C$ is

$$(V_0)_C = \sqrt{\frac{GM}{r_0}} \tag{12.49}$$

For launching velocities less than the preceding value for a given r_0, the eccentricity becomes negative and the focus f' moves to the left of the earth's center. Again, the trajectory is that of an ellipse (curve 5). However, the satellite will now come closer to the earth at position b, which now becomes the perigee, than at the launching position, which up to now had been the minimum distance from the earth.[10] If friction is encountered, the satellite will slow up, spiral in toward the atmosphere, and either burn up or crash. If V_0 is small enough, the satellite will not go into even a temporary orbit but will plummet to the earth (curve 6). However, for a reasonably accurate description of this trajectory, we must consider friction from the earth's atmosphere. Since this type of force is a function of the velocity of the satellite and is not a central force, we cannot use the results here in such situations for other than approximate calculations.

[10]Note that with the positive x axis going through perigee, r is *minimum* when $\theta = 0$. From Eq. 12.40, we can conclude for this case (θ is measured here from perigee) that, to minimize r, the constant D must be positive. The eccentricity must then be positive for θ measured from perigee. If the positive x axis goes through apogee, then r is *maximum* when $\theta = 0$. From Eq. 12.40 we can conclude that D must be negative for this case (θ is here measured from apogee). Thus, the eccentricity is negative for θ measured from apogee. This is clearly the case for curve 5.

Example 12.9

The first American satellite, the Vanguard, was launched at a velocity of 18,000 mi/hr at an altitude of 400 mi (see Fig. 12.23). If the "burnout" velocity of the last stage is parallel to the earth's surface, compute the maximum altitude from the earth's surface that the Vanguard satellite will reach. Consider the earth to be perfectly spherical with a radius of 3,960 mi (r_0 is therefore 4,360 mi).

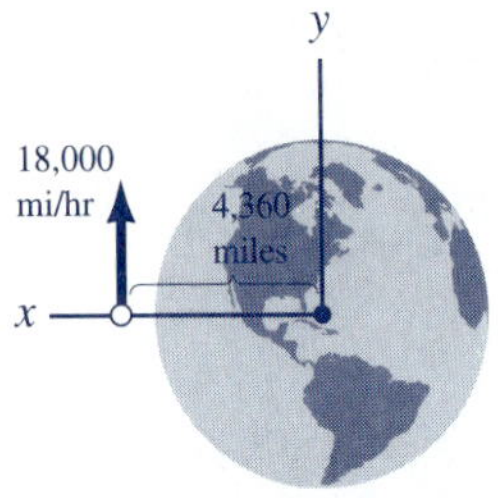

Figure 12.23. Launching of the Vanguard satellite.

We must now compute the quantities GM, C, and D from the initial data and other known data. To determine GM, we employ Eq. 12.17 and in terms of units of miles and hours we get

$$\begin{aligned} GM &= (32.2)\left(\frac{3{,}600^2}{5{,}280}\right)(3{,}960^2) \\ &= 1.239 \times 10^{12} \text{ mi}^3/\text{hr}^2 \end{aligned} \tag{a}$$

The constant C is readily determined directly from initial data as

$$\begin{aligned} C &= r_0 V_0 = (4{,}360)(18{,}000) \\ &= 7.85 \times 10^7 \text{ mi}^2/\text{hr} \end{aligned} \tag{b}$$

Finally, the constant D is available from Eq. 12.47:

$$\begin{aligned} D &= \frac{1}{r_0} - \frac{GM}{C^2} = \frac{1}{(4{,}360)} - \frac{1.239 \times 10^{12}}{(7.85 \times 10^7)^2} \\ &= .283 \times 10^{-4} \text{ mi}^{-1} \end{aligned} \tag{c}$$

The eccentricity DC^2/GM can now be computed as

$$\epsilon = \frac{DC^2}{GM} = \frac{(.283 \times 10^{-4})(7.85 \times 10^7)^2}{1.239 \times 10^{12}} = .1408 \tag{d}$$

The Vanguard will thus definitely not escape into outer space.

The trajectory of this motion is formed from Eq. 12.40:

$$\frac{1}{r} = \frac{1.239 \times 10^{12}}{(7.85 \times 10^7)^2} + .283 \times 10^{-4} \cos\theta$$

Example 12.9 (Continued)

Therefore,

$$\frac{1}{r} = 2.01 \times 10^{-4} + .283 \times 10^{-4} \cos\theta \qquad \text{(e)}$$

We can compute the maximum distance from the earth's surface by setting $\theta = \pi$ in the equation above:

$$\frac{1}{r_{max}} = (2.01 - .283) \times 10^{-4} = 1.727 \times 10^{-4}\ \text{mi}^{-1}$$

Therefore,

$$r_{max} = 5{,}790\ \text{mi} \qquad \text{(f)}$$

By subtracting 3,960 mi from this result, we find that the highest point in the trajectory is 1,830 mi from the earth's surface.

Example 12.10

In Example 12.9, first compute the escape velocity and then the velocity for a circular orbit at burnout.

Using Eq. 12.48, we have for the escape velocity:

$$(V_0)_E = \sqrt{\frac{2GM}{r_0}} = \left[\frac{2(1.239 \times 10^{12})}{4{,}360}\right]^{1/2}$$

$$(V_0)_E = 23{,}840\ \text{mi/hr}$$

For a circular orbit, we have from Eq. 12.49:

$$(V_0)_C = \sqrt{\frac{GM}{r_0}} = 16{,}860\ \text{mi/hr}$$

Thus, the Vanguard is almost in a circular orbit.

Example 12.11

Determine the orbital time in Example 12.9 for the Vanguard satellite.

We employ Eqs. 12.44 for the semimajor and semiminor axes of the elliptic orbit. Thus, recalling that $p = 1/D$ we have

$$a = \frac{\epsilon}{D(1-\epsilon^2)} = \frac{.1408}{(.283\times 10^{-4})(1-.1408^2)}$$

$$= 5{,}080 \text{ mi}$$

$$b = a(1-\epsilon^2)^{1/2} = 5{,}080(1-.1408^2)^{1/2}$$

Therefore, from Eq. 12.43 we have for the orbital time:

$$\tau = \frac{\pi ab}{C/2} = \frac{(\pi)(5{,}080)(5{,}030)}{(7.85\times 10^7)/2}$$

$$\tau = 2.05 \text{ hr} = 122.7 \text{ min}$$

Example 12.12

A space vehicle is in a circular "parking" orbit around the planet Venus, 320 km above the surface of this planet. The radius of Venus is 6,160 km, and the escape velocity at the surface is 1.026×10^4 m/sec. A retro-rocket is fired to slow the vehicle so that it will come within 32 km of the planet. If we consider that the rocket changes the speed of the vehicle over a comparatively short distance of its travel, what is this change of speed? What is the speed of the vehicle at its closest position to the surface of Venus?

We show the vehicle in a circular parking orbit in Fig. 12.24. We shall consider that the retro-rockets are fired at position A so as to establish a new elliptic orbit with apogee at A and perigee at B.

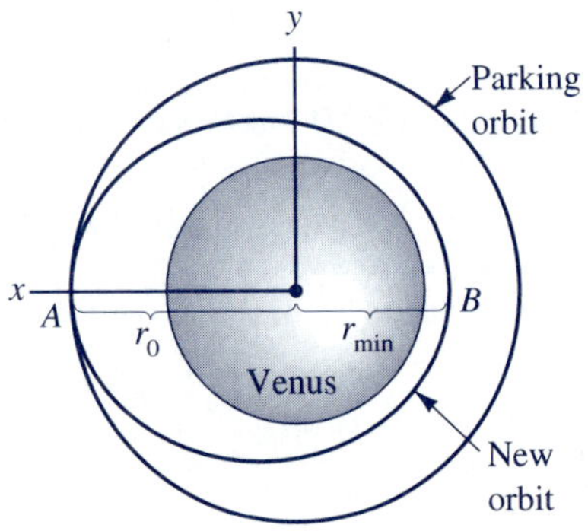

Figure 12.24. Change of orbit.

As a first step, we shall compute GM using the escape-velocity equation 12.48. Thus, we have

$$V_E = \sqrt{\frac{2GM}{R}}$$

Therefore,

$$GM = \frac{V_E^2 R}{2} = \left[\left(\frac{1.026\times 10^4}{1{,}000}\right)(3{,}600)\right]^2 \left(\frac{.6160}{2}\right)$$

$$= 4.20 \times 10^{12} \text{ km}^3/\text{hr}^2$$

Example 12.12 (Continued)

The equation for the *new elliptic orbit* is given as

$$\frac{1}{r} = \frac{GM}{C^2} + D\cos\theta \qquad \text{(a)}$$

Note that when

$$\theta = 0, \qquad r = r_0 = 6{,}480 \text{ km} \qquad \text{(b)}$$

$$\theta = \pi, \qquad r = r_{\text{min}} = 6{,}192 \text{ km} \qquad \text{(c)}$$

To determine the constant C, we subject Eq. (a) to the conditions (b) and (c). Thus,

$$\frac{1}{6{,}480} = \frac{4.20 \times 10^{12}}{C^2} + D \qquad \text{(d)}$$

$$\frac{1}{6{,}192} = \frac{4.20 \times 10^{12}}{C^2} - D \qquad \text{(e)}$$

Adding these equations, we eliminate D and can solve for C. Thus,

$$\frac{8.40 \times 10^{12}}{C^2} = \frac{1}{6{,}480} + \frac{1}{6{,}192}$$

Therefore,

$$C = 1.631 \times 10^8 \text{ km}^2/\text{hr}$$

Accordingly, for the new orbit,

$$r_0 V_0 = 1.631 \times 10^8$$

Therefore,

$$V_0 = 25{,}168 \text{ km/hr}$$

For the *circular* parking orbit the velocity V_c is

$$V_c = \sqrt{\frac{GM}{r_0}} = \sqrt{\frac{4.20 \times 10^{12}}{6{,}480}}$$
$$= 25{,}458 \text{ km/hr}$$

The change in velocity that the retro-rocket must induce is then

$$\Delta V = 25{,}168 - 25{,}458 = \boxed{-290 \text{ km/hr}}$$

The velocity at the perigee at B is easily computed since

$$r_B V_B = C = 1.631 \times 10^8$$

Therefore,

$$V_B = (1.631 \times 10^8)/6{,}192 = \boxed{26{,}300 \text{ km/hr}}$$

Now let us consider more general launching conditions where the launching angle α is not zero (see Fig. 12.25). The constant C is still easily evaluated (see Eq. (12.46)) in terms of launching data as $r_0(V_\theta)_0$. To get D, we write Eq. 12.40 for launching conditions. Thus,

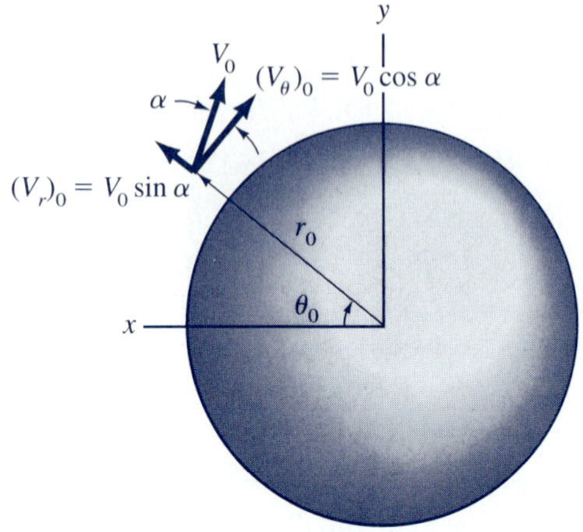

Figure 12.25. Launch with radial velocity.

$$\frac{1}{r_0} = \frac{GM}{C^2} + D\cos\theta_0 \tag{12.50}$$

The value of θ_0 is not yet known. Thus, we have two unknown quantities in this equation, namely D and θ_0. Differentiating Eq. 12.40 with respect to time and solving for $\dot{r}$, we get

$$\dot{r} = Dr^2\dot{\theta}\sin\theta = DC\sin\theta \tag{12.51}$$

Noting that $\dot{r}$ is equal to V_r and submitting the preceding equation to launching conditions, we then form a second equation for the evaluation of the unknown constants D and θ_0. Thus,

$$(V_r)_0 = DC\sin\theta_0 \tag{12.52}$$

Rearranging Eq. 12.50, we have

$$\frac{1}{r_0} - \frac{GM}{C^2} = D\cos\theta_0 \tag{12.53}$$

Divide both sides of Eq. 12.52 by C. Now, squaring Eqs. 12.52 and 12.53, adding terms, and using the fact that $\sin^2\theta_0 + \cos^2\theta_0 = 1$, we get for the constant D the result :[11]

$$D = \left\{\left(\frac{1}{r_0} - \frac{GM}{C^2}\right)^2 + \left[\frac{(V_r)_0}{C}\right]^2\right\}^{1/2} \tag{12.54}$$

[11]The student has the option of formulating Eqs. 12.52 and 12.53 for each problem and finding D from these equations, or he/she can use Eq. 12.54 directly. In some of the homework problems we shall ask you to do both.

Having taken the positive root for D, we note (see footnote #10 on page 545) that θ is to be measured from perigee. The eccentricity is

$$\epsilon = \frac{C^2}{GM}\left\{\left(\frac{1}{r_0} - \frac{GM}{C^2}\right)^2 + \left[\frac{(V_r)_0}{C}\right]^2\right\}^{1/2} \tag{12.55}$$

First, bringing C^2 into the bracket and then replacing C by $r_0(V_\theta)_0$ in the entire equation, we get the eccentricity conveniently in terms of launching data:

$$\epsilon = \frac{r_0(V_\theta)_0}{GM}\left\{(V_r)_0^2 + \left[(V_\theta)_0 - \frac{GM}{r_0(V_\theta)_0}\right]^2\right\}^{1/2} \tag{12.56}$$

One can show, using the preceding formulations, that the equation for the escape velocity developed earlier, namely

$$V_E = \sqrt{\frac{2GM}{r}}$$

is valid for any launching angle α. Remember that V_E in this equation is measured from a reference xyz at the center of the planet translating in inertial space. The velocity attainable by a rocket system relative to the planet's surface does not depend on the position of firing on the earth, but depends primarily on the rocket system and trajectory of flight. However, the velocity attainable by a rocket system relative to the aforementioned reference xyz *does* depend on the position of firing on the planet's surface. This position, accordingly, is important in determining whether an escape velocity can be reached. The extreme situations of a launching at the equator and at the North Pole are shown in Fig. 12.26 and should clarify this point. Note that the motion of the planet's surface adds to the final vehicle velocity at the equator, but that no such gain is achieved at the North Pole.

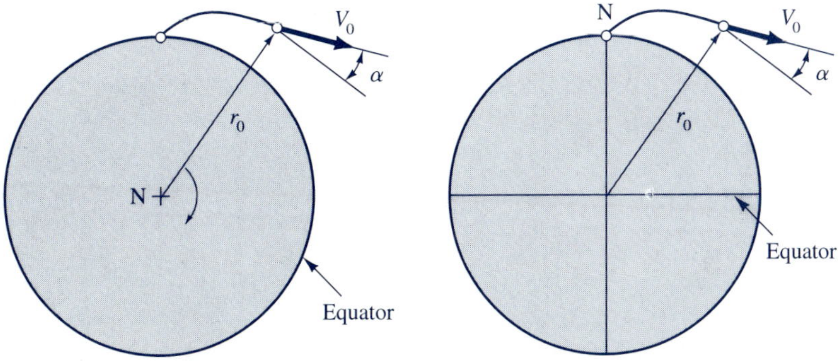

Figure 12.26. Launching at equator and North Pole.

Example 12.13

Suppose that the Vanguard satellite in Example 12.9 is off course by an angle $\alpha = 5°$ at the time of launching but otherwise has the same initial data. Determine whether the satellite goes into orbit. If so, determine the maximum and minimum distances from the earth's surface.

The initial data for the launching are

$$r_0 = 4{,}360 \text{ mi}, \qquad V_0 = 18{,}000 \text{ mi/hr}$$

Hence,

$$\begin{aligned}(V_r)_0 &= (18{,}000)\sin\alpha = (18{,}000)(0.0872)\\ &= 1{,}569 \text{ mi/hr}\\ (V_\theta)_0 &= (18{,}000)\cos\alpha = (18{,}000)(0.996)\\ &= 17{,}930 \text{ mi/hr}\end{aligned}$$

To determine whether we have an orbit, we would have to show first that the eccentricity ϵ is less than unity. This condition would preclude the possibility of an escape from the earth. Furthermore, we must be sure that the perigee of the orbit is far enough from the earth's surface to ensure a reasonably permanent orbit. Actually, for both questions we need only calculate r for $\theta = 0$ and $\theta = \pi$. An infinite value of one of the r's will mean that we have an escape condition, and a value not sufficiently large will mean a crash or a decaying orbit due to atmospheric friction.

Using the value of GM as 1.239×10^{12} mi^3/hr^2 from Example 12.9 and using Eq. 12.54 for the constant D, we can express the trajectory of the satellite (Eq. 12.40) as

$$\begin{aligned}\frac{1}{r} = \frac{1.239 \times 10^{12}}{[(4{,}360)(17{,}930)]^2}\\ +\left\{\left[\frac{1}{4{,}360} - \frac{1.239 \times 10^{12}}{[(4{,}360)(17{,}930)]^2}\right]^2\right.\\ \left.+\left[\frac{1{,}569}{(4{,}360)(17{,}930)}\right]^2\right\}^{1/2} \cos\theta\end{aligned}$$

Example 12.13 (Continued)

Therefore,

$$\frac{1}{r} = 2.03 \times 10^{-4} + 3.33 \times 10^{-5} \cos\theta \text{ mi}^{-1} \qquad \text{(a)}$$

Set $\theta = 0$:

$$\frac{1}{r(0)} = 20.3 \times 10^{-5} + 3.33 \times 10^{-5} \text{ mi}^{-1}$$

Hence,

$$r(0) = 4{,}230 \text{ mi}$$

Thus, after being launched at a position 400 mi above the earth's surface, the satellite comes within 270 mi of the earth as a result of a 5° change in the launching angle. This satellite, therefore, must be launched almost parallel to the earth if it is to attain a reasonably permanent orbit.

Now, setting $\theta = \pi$, we get

$$\frac{1}{r(\pi)} = 20.3 \times 10^{-5} - 3.33 \times 10^{-5}$$

Hence,

$$r_{\text{max}} = 5{,}893 \text{ mi}$$

Obviously, the maximum distance from the earth's surface is 1,933 mi.

PROBLEMS

12.54. A device used at amusement parks consists of a circular room that is made to revolve about its axis of symmetry. People stand up against the wall, as shown in the diagram. After the whole room has been brought up to speed, the floor is lowered. What minimum angular speed is required to ensure that a person will not slip down the wall when the floor is lowered? Take $\mu_s = .3$.

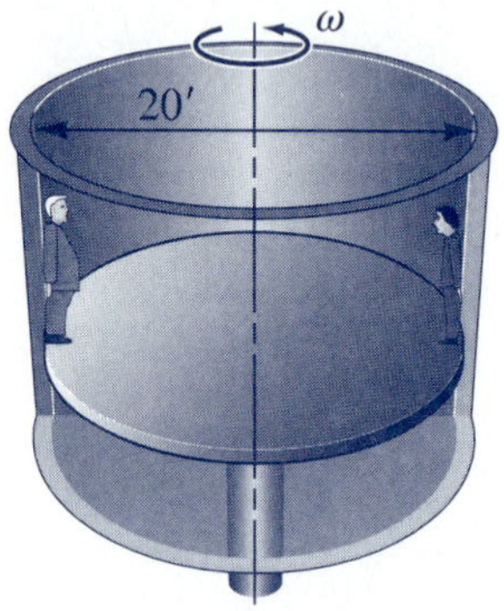

Figure P.12.54.

12.55. A flywheel is rotating at a speed of $\omega = 10$ rad/sec and has at this instant a rate of change of speed $\dot{\omega}$ of 5 rad/sec^2. A solenoid at this instant moves a valve toward the centerline of the flywheel at a speed of 1.5 m/sec and is decelerating at the rate of .6 m/sec^2. The valve has a mass of 1 kg and is .3 m from the axis of rotation at the time of interest. What is the total force on the valve?

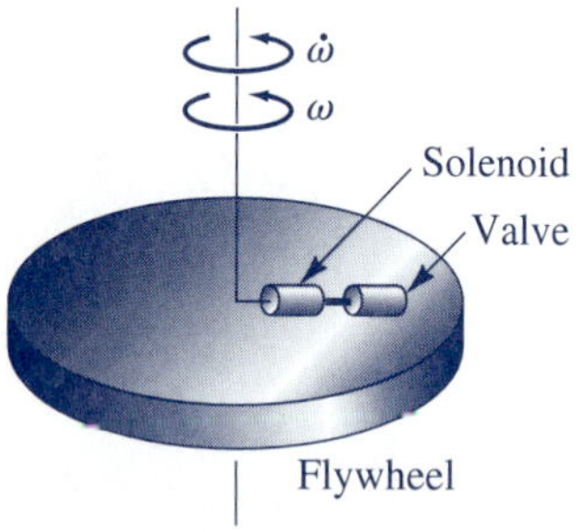

Figure P.12.55.

12.56. A conical pendulum of length l is shown. The pendulum is made to rotate at a constant angular speed of ω about the vertical axis. Compute the tension in the cord if the pendulum bob has weight W. What is the distance of the plane of the trajectory of the bob from the support at O?

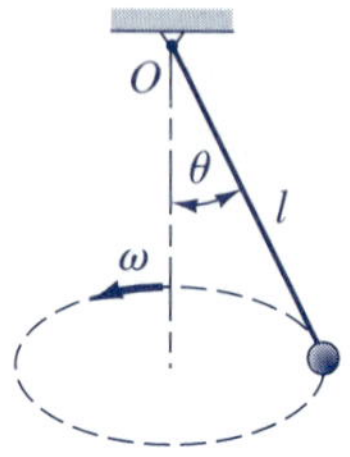

Figure P.12.56.

12.57. A shaft AB rotates at an angular velocity of 100 rpm. A body E of mass 10 kg can move without friction along rod CD fixed to AB. If the body E is to remain stationary relative to CD at any position along CD, how must the spring constant K vary? The distance r_0 from the axis is the unstretched length of the spring.

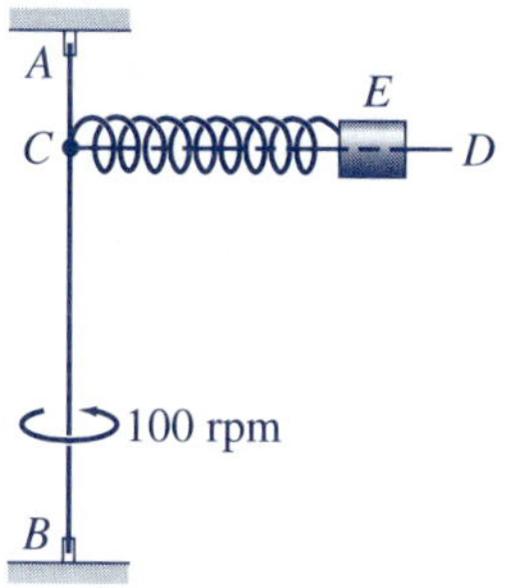

Figure P.12.57.

12.58. A device consists of three small masses, three weightless rods, and a linear spring with $K = 200$ N/m. The system is rotating in the given fixed configuration at a constant speed $\omega = 10$ rad/s in a horizontal plane. The following data apply:

$M_A = 2$ kg $\quad$ $M_B = 3$ kg $\quad$ $M_C = 2$ kg

If the spring is stretched by an amount .025 m, determine the total force components acting on the mass at C and the tensile force in member DA. [*Hint:* Consider a single particle, then a system of particles; DA and DB are pin connected.]

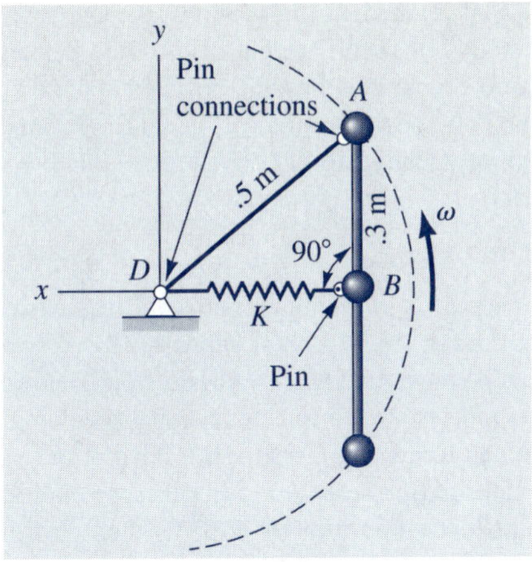

Figure P.12.58.

12.59. In the preceding problem consider that member DA is welded to the sphere at A. Now, at the instant of interest, there is also an angular acceleration of the system having the value of .28 rad/sec^2 counterclockwise. What are the force components acting on particle C, and what are the force components from rod AD acting on particle A? See hint given in the preceding problem.

12.60. A device called a *flyball governor* is used to regulate the speed of such devices as steam engines and turbines. As the governor is made to rotate through a system of gears by the device to be controlled, the balls will attain a configuration given by the angle θ, which is dependent on both the angular speed ω of the governor and the force P acting on the collar bearing at A. The up-and-down motion of the bearing at A in response to a change in ω is then used to open or close a valve to regulate the speed of the device. Find the angular velocity required to maintain the configuration of the flyball governor for $\theta = 30°$. Neglect friction.

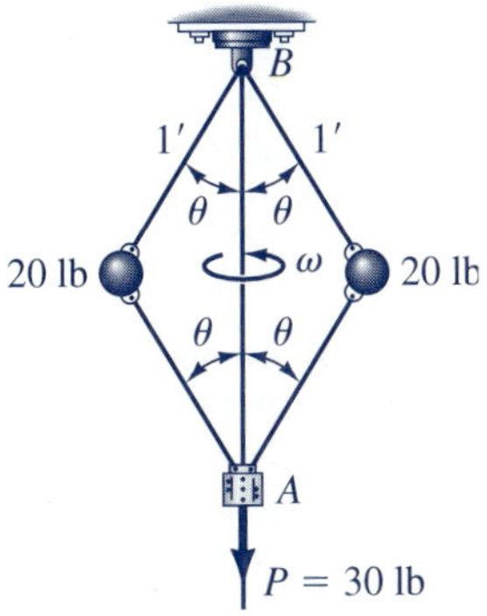

Figure P.12.60.

12.61. A platform rotates at 2 rad/sec. A body C weighing 450 N rests on the platform and is connected by a flexible weightless cord to a mass weighing 225 N, which is prevented from swinging out by part of the platform. For what range of values of x will bodies C and B remain stationary relative to the platform? The static coefficient of friction for all surfaces is .4.

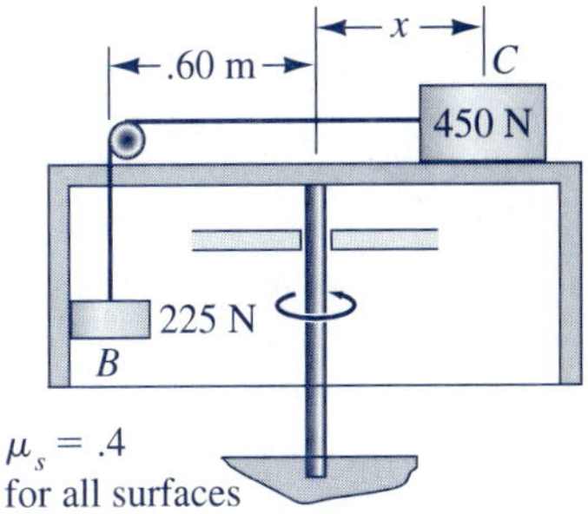

Figure P.12.61.

12.62. A particle moves under gravitational influence about a body M, the center of which can be taken as the origin of an inertial reference. The mass of the particle is 50 slugs. At time t, the particle is at a position 4,500 mi from the center of M with direction cosines $l = .5$, $m = -.5$, $n = .707$. The particle is moving at a speed of 17,000 mi/hr along the direction $\boldsymbol{\epsilon}_t = .8\boldsymbol{i} + .2\boldsymbol{j} + .566\boldsymbol{k}$. What is the direction of the normal to the plane of the trajectory?

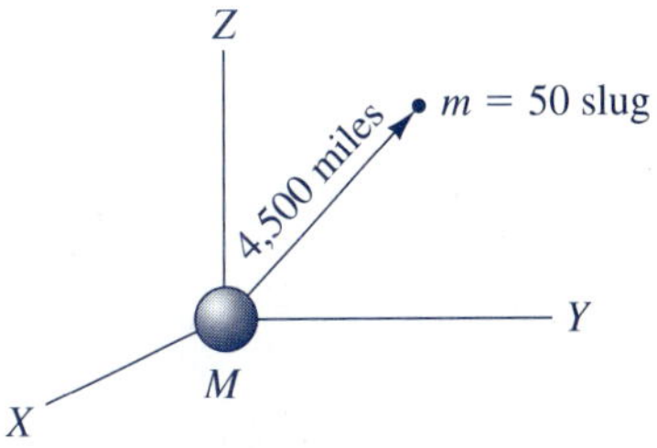

Figure P.12.62.

12.63. If the position of the particle in Problem 12.62 were to reach a distance of 4,300 mi from the center of body M, what would the transverse velocity V_θ of the particle be?

12.64. Use Eqs. 12.38b and 12.40 to show that if the eccentricity is zero, the trajectory must be that of a circle.

12.65. A satellite has at one time during its flight around the earth a radial component of velocity 3,200 km/hr and a transverse component of 26,500 km/hr. If the satellite is at a distance of 7,040 km from the center of the earth, what is its areal velocity?

12.66. Compute the escape velocity at a position 8,000 km from the center of the earth. What speed is needed to maintain a circular orbit at that distance from the earth's center? Derive the equation for the speed needed for a circular orbit directly from Newton's law without using information about eccentricities, etc.

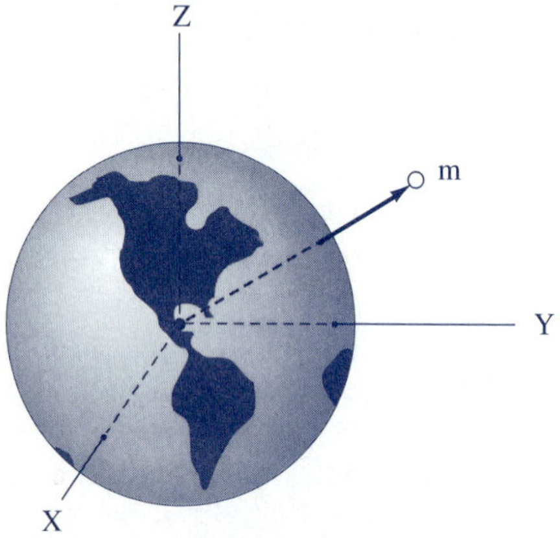

Figure P.12.66.

12.67. A small sphere is swinging in the *xy* plane at the end of a thin light rod while in a tank of water. If we neglect the buoyant force (see next problem) on the sphere and on the rod, determine the angular acceleration $\ddot{\theta}$ and the tensile force T on the rod for the following conditions, which include viscous drag D on the sphere only.

$$M = .02 \text{ kg} \qquad L = 3.3 \text{ m} \qquad \theta = 65°$$
$$\dot{\theta} = 35°/\text{sec} \qquad D = 1.5 \times 10^{-3} V^2 \text{ N}$$

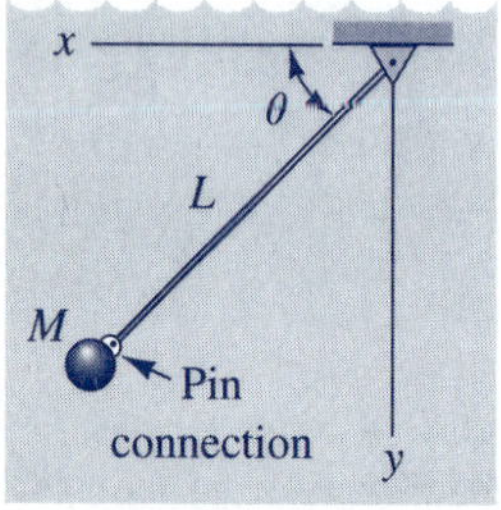

Figure P.12.67.

12.68. As you learned in high school, the buoyant force on a submerged body equals the weight of the fluid displaced. Do the preceding problem but now include the buoyant force on the sphere whose diameter we shall take to be 10 mm. The volume of a sphere is $\frac{4}{3}\pi r^3$ and the specific weight of water is 9,806 N/m^3.

12.69. A mass M is swinging around a vertical axis at the end of a weightless cord of length L. M is supported by a frictionless platform that can be moved vertically upward from its lowest position, where it just touches M. Formulate an equation giving the tension T in the cord in terms of M, L, and ω. What is the value of θ at which the platform first ceases to touch M as the platform is moved down from its highest position ($\theta = 0$) for the following data:

$$\omega = 8 \text{ rad/s} \qquad M = 3.1 \text{ kg} \qquad L = .42 \text{ m}$$

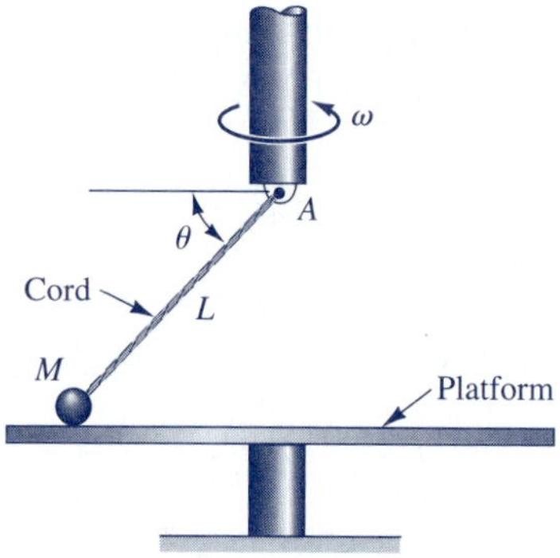

Figure P.12.69.

12.70. A satellite is in a circular (parking) orbit around the earth, whose radius is 6,370 km. If the velocity of the satellite is 25,000 km/hr, how much time is needed for one complete orbit?

12.71. A space vehicle is in a circular orbit around the earth in a plane corresponding to the equator and moving so as to remain above a specific position on the earth's surface. This means that the satellite has the same angular speed as the earth, making it useful as a communications satellite. What should the radius of the orbit be? The radius of the earth is 3,960 mi. Work in units of miles and hours.

12.72. Consider a satellite of mass m in a circular orbit around the earth at a radius R_0 from the center of the earth. Using the universal law of gravitation (Eq. 1.11) with M as the mass of the earth and using *Newton's law* in a direction normal to the path, show that

$$V_{Circ.} = \sqrt{\frac{GM}{R_0}}$$

for a circular orbit. Now at the earth's surface use the universal gravitational law again and the weight of the body, to show that $GM = gR^2_{Earth}$, where g is the acceleration of gravity.

12.73. The acceleration of gravity on the planet Mars is about .385 times the acceleration of gravity on earth, and the radius of Mars is about .532 times that of the earth. What is the escape velocity from Mars at a position 100 mi from the surface of the planet?

12.74. In 1971 Mariner 9 was placed in orbit around Mars with an eccentricity of .5. At the lowest point in the orbit, Mariner 9 is 320 km from the surface of Mars.

(a) Compute the maximum velocity of the space vehicle relative to the center of Mars.

(b) Compute the time of one cycle.

Use the data in Problem 12.73 for Mars.

12.75. A man is in orbit around the earth in a space-shuttle vehicle. At his lowest possible position, he is moving with a speed of 18,500 mi/hr at an altitude of 200 mi. When he wants to come back to earth, he fires a retro-rocket straight ahead when he is at the aforementioned lowest position and slows himself down. If he wishes subsequently to get within 50 mi from the earth's surface during the first cycle after firing his retro-rocket, what must his decrease in velocity be? (Neglect air resistance.)

12.76. The Pioneer 10 space vehicle approaches the planet Jupiter with a trajectory having an eccentricity of 3. The vehicle comes to within 1,000 mi of the surface of Jupiter. What is the speed of the vehicle at this instant? The acceleration of gravity of Jupiter is 90.79 ft/sec^2 at the surface and the radius is 43,400 mi.

12.77. If the moon has a motion about the earth that has an eccentricity of .0549 and a period of 27.3 days, what is the closest distance of the moon to the earth in its trajectory?

12.78. The satellite Hyperion about the planet Saturn has a motion with an eccentricity known to be .1043. At its closest distance from Saturn, Hyperion is 1.485×10^6 km away (measured from center to center). What is the period of Hyperion about Saturn? The acceleration of gravity of Saturn is 13.93 m/sec^2 at its surface. The radius of Saturn is 57,600 km.

12.79. Two satellite stations, each in a circular orbit around the earth, are shown. A small vehicle is shot out of the station at A tangential to the trajectory in order to "hit" station B when it is at a position E 120° from the x axis as shown in the diagram. What is the velocity of the vehicle relative to station A when it leaves? The circular orbits are 200 miles and 400 miles, respectively, from the earth's surface.

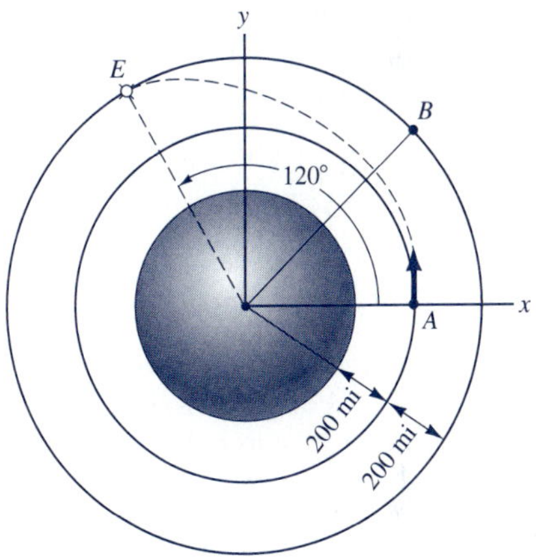

Figure P.12.79.

12.80. In Problem 12.79, determine the total velocity of the vehicle as it arrives at E as seen by an observer in the satellite B. The values of C and D for the vehicle from Problem 12.79 are 7.292×10^7 mi^2/hr and 7.373×10^{-6} mi^{-1}, respectively.

12.81. The Viking I space probe is approaching Mars. When it is 80,650 km from the center of Mars, it has a speed of 16,130 km/hr with a component (V_r) toward the center of Mars of 15,800 km/hr. Does Viking I crash into Mars, go into orbit, or have one pass in the vicinity of Mars? If there is no crash, how close to Mars does it come? The acceleration of gravity on the surface of Mars is 4.13 m/sec^2, and its radius is 3,400 km. Do not use formula for D as given by Eq. 12.54, but work from the trajectory equations.

12.82. A meteor is moving at a speed of 20,000 mi/hr relative to the center of the earth when it is 350 mi from the surface of the earth. At that time, the meteor has a radial velocity component of 4,000 mi/hr toward the center of the earth. How close does it come to the earth's surface? Do this problem without the aid of Eq. 12.54.

12.83. Do Problem 12.82 with the aid of Eq. 12.54.

12.84. The moon's radius is about .272 times that of the earth, and its acceleration of gravity at the surface is .165 times that of the earth at the earth's surface. A space vehicle approaches the moon with a velocity component toward the center of the moon of 3,200 km/hr and a transverse component of 8,000 km/hr relative to the center of the moon. The vehicle is 3,200 km from the center of the moon when it has these velocity components. Will the vehicle go into orbit around the moon if we consider only the gravitational effect of the moon on the vehicle? If it goes into orbit, how close will it come to the surface of the moon? If not, does it collide with the moon? Do this problem without the aid of Eq. 12.54.

12.85. Do Problem 12.84 with the aid of Eq. 12.54.

12.86. Assume that a satellite is placed into orbit about a planet that has the same mass and diameter as the earth but no atmosphere. At the minimum height of its trajectory, the satellite has an elevation of 645 km from the planet's surface and a velocity of 29,800 km/hr. To observe the planet more closely, we send down a smaller satellite from the main body to within 16 km of this planet at perigee. The "subsatellite" is given a velocity component toward the center of the planet when the main satellite is at its lowest position. What is this radial velocity, and what is the eccentricity of the trajectory of the subsatellite? What is a better way to get closer to the planet?

12.87. Suppose that you are on a planet having no atmosphere. This planet rotates once every 6 hr about its axis relative to an inertial reference XYZ at its center. The planet has a radius of 1,600 km, and the acceleration of gravity at the surface is 7 m/sec^2. A bullet is fired by a man at the equator in a direction normal to the surface of the planet as seen by this man. The muzzle velocity of the gun is 1,500 m/sec. What is the eccentricity of the trajectory and the maximum height h of the bullet above the surface of the planet?

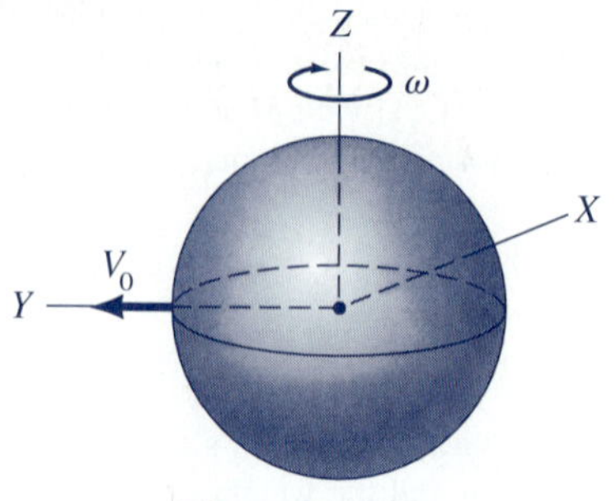

Figure P.12.87.

***12.88.** A satellite is launched at A. We wish to determine the time required, Δt, to get to position B. Show that for this calculation we can employ the formulation

$$\Delta t = \frac{1}{C}\int_{\theta_0}^{\theta_B} r^2 \, d\theta$$

For integration purposes, show that the formulation above becomes

$$\Delta t = \frac{1}{C}\int_{\theta_0}^{\theta_B} \frac{d\theta}{[(GM/C^2) + D\cos\theta]^2}$$

Carry out the integration.

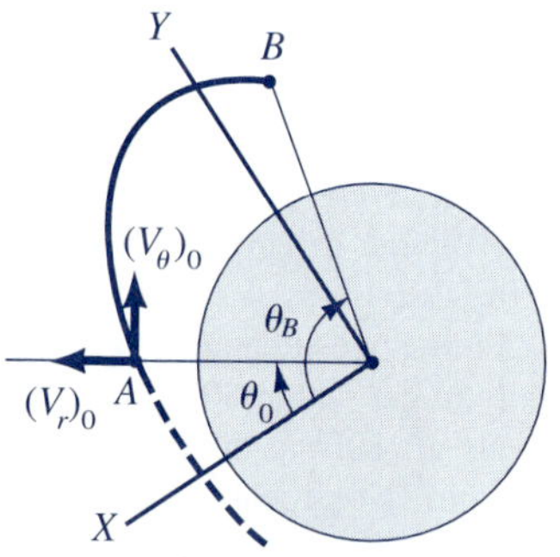

Figure P.12.88.

***12.89.** A satellite is launched at a speed of 20,000 mi/hr relative to the earth's center at an altitude of 340 mi above the earth's surface. The guidance system has malfunctioned, and the satellite has a direction 20° up from the tangent plane to the earth's surface. Will the satellite go into orbit? Give the time required for one cycle if it goes into orbit or the time it takes before it strikes the earth after firing. Neglect friction in both cases. (See Problem 12.88 before doing this problem.)

Part C: Path Variables

12.9 Newton's Law for Path Variables

We can express Newton's law for path variables as follows:

$$F_t = m\frac{d^2s}{dt^2} \quad (12.57a)$$

$$F_n = m\frac{(ds/dt)^2}{R} \quad (12.57b)$$

Notice that the second of these equations is always nonlinear, as discussed in Section 12.5.[12] This condition results from both the squared term and the radius of curvature R. It is therefore difficult to integrate this differential equation. Accordingly, we shall be restricted to reasonably simple cases. We now illustrate the use of the preceding equations.

[12]Equation 12.57a could also be nonlinear, depending on the nature of the function F_t.

Example 12.14

A portion of a roller coaster that one finds in an amusement park is shown in Fig. 12.27(a). The portion of the track shown is coplanar. The curve from A to the right on which the vehicle moves is that of a parabola, given as

$$(y - 100)^2 = 100x \quad \text{(a)}$$

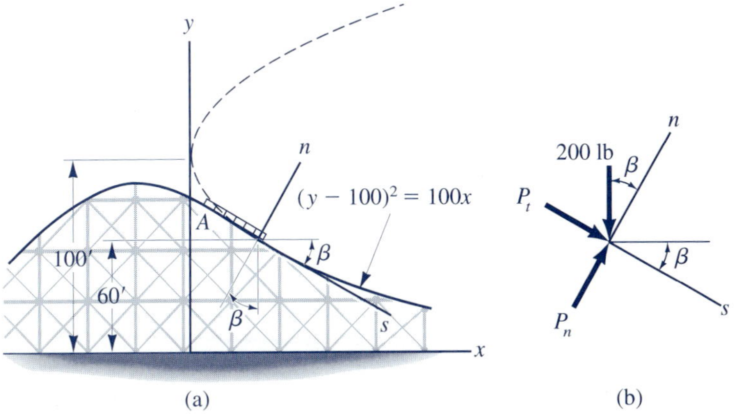

Figure 12.27. Roller coaster trajectory.

Example 12.14 (Continued)

with x and y in feet. If the train of cars is moving at a speed of 40 ft/sec when the front car is 60 ft above the ground, what is the total normal force exerted by a 200-lb occupant of the front car on the seat and floor of the car?

Since we require only the force F normal to the path, we need only be concerned with a_n. Thus, we have

$$a_n = \frac{(ds/dt)^2}{R} = \frac{40^2}{R} \tag{b}$$

We can compute R from analytic geometry as follows:

$$R = \frac{\left[1 + (dy/dx)^2\right]^{3/2}}{\left|d^2y/dx^2\right|} \tag{c}$$

wherein from Eq. (a) we have

$$\frac{dy}{dx} = \frac{50}{y - 100} \tag{d}$$

$$\frac{d^2y}{dx^2} = \frac{d}{dx}\left(\frac{dy}{dx}\right) = \left[\frac{d}{dy}\left(\frac{dy}{dx}\right)\right]\left(\frac{dy}{dx}\right) = -\frac{50}{(y-100)^2}\frac{dy}{dx} = -\frac{2{,}500}{(y-100)^3} \tag{e}$$

Substituting into Eq. (c), we have

$$R = \frac{\left[1 + \left(\frac{50}{y-100}\right)^2\right]^{3/2}}{\left|2{,}500/(y-100)^3\right|}$$

At the position of interest, we get

$$R = \frac{\left[1 + \left(\frac{2{,}500}{1{,}600}\right)\right]^{3/2}}{(2{,}500/64{,}000)} = 105 \text{ ft} \tag{f}$$

Example 12.14 (Continued)

Accordingly, we now have for F_n, as required by **Newton's law**:

$$F_n = \frac{W}{g} a_n = \frac{200}{g} \frac{1{,}600}{105} = 94.6 \text{ lb} \tag{g}$$

Note that F_n is the *total* force component normal to the trajectory needed on the occupant for maintaining his motion on the given trajectory. This force component comes from the action of gravity and the forces from the seat and floor of the car. These forces have been shown in Fig. 12.27(b), where P_n and P_t are the normal and tangential force components from the car acting on the occupant. The resultant of this force system must, accordingly, have a component along n equal to 94.6 lb. Thus,

$$-200 \cos \beta + P_n = 94.6 \tag{h}$$

To get β, note with the help of Eq. (d) that

$$\tan^{-1}\left(\frac{dy}{dx}\right)_{y=60} = \tan^{-1} \frac{50}{-40} = -51.3° \tag{i}$$

Therefore,

$$\beta = 51.3°$$

Substituting into Eq. (h) and solving for P_n, we get

$$P_n = 200 \cos 51.3° + 94.6$$

$$P_n = 220 \text{ lb}$$

This is the force component *from* the vehicle *onto* the passenger. The reaction to this force is the force component *from* the passenger onto the vehicle.

Part D: A System of Particles

12.10 The General Motion of a System of Particles

Let us examine a system of n particles (Fig. 12.28) that has interactions between the particles for which *Newton's third law* of motion (action equals

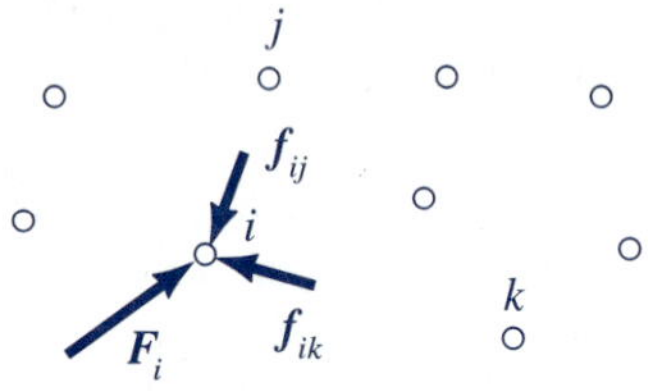

Figure 12.28. Forces on ith particle of the system.

reaction) applies. *Newton's second law* for any particle (let us say the ith particle) is then

$$m_i \frac{d^2 \boldsymbol{r}_i}{dt^2} = \boldsymbol{F}_i + \sum_{\substack{j=1 \\ i \neq j}}^{n} \boldsymbol{f}_{ij} \tag{12.58}$$

where $\boldsymbol{f}_{ij}$ is the force on particle i from particle j and is thus considered an *internal* force for the system of particles. Clearly, the $j = i$ term of the summation must be deleted since the ith particle cannot exert force on itself. The force $\boldsymbol{F}_i$ represents the resultant force on the ith particle from the forces *external* to the system of particles.

If these equations are added for all n particles, we have

$$\sum_{i=1}^{n} m_i \frac{d^2 \boldsymbol{r}_i}{dt^2} = \sum_{i=1}^{n} \boldsymbol{F}_i + \sum_{i=1}^{n} \sum_{j=1}^{n} \boldsymbol{f}_{ij} \tag{12.59}$$

Carrying out the double summation and excluding terms with repeated indexes, such as $\boldsymbol{f}_{11}$, $\boldsymbol{f}_{22}$, etc., we find that for each term with any one set of indexes there will be a term with the reverse of these indexes present. For example, for the force $\boldsymbol{f}_{12}$, a force $\boldsymbol{f}_{21}$ will exist. Considering the meaning of the indexes, we see that $\boldsymbol{f}_{ij}$ and $\boldsymbol{f}_{ji}$ represent action and reaction forces between a pair of particles. Thus, as a result of *Newton's third law*, the double summation in Eq. 12.59 should add up to zero. *Newton's second law* for a system of particles then becomes:

$$\boldsymbol{F} = \sum_{i=1}^{n} m_i \frac{d^2 \boldsymbol{r}_i}{dt^2} = \frac{d^2}{dt^2} \sum_{i=1}^{n} m_i \boldsymbol{r}_i \tag{12.60}$$

where $\boldsymbol{F}$ now represents the vector sum of all the *external* forces acting on *all* the particles of the system.

To make further useful simplifications, we use the first moment of mass of a system of n particles about a fixed point A in inertial space given as

$$\text{first moment vector} \equiv \sum_{i=1}^{n} m_i \boldsymbol{r}_i$$

where $\boldsymbol{r}_i$ represents the position vector from the point A to the ith particle (Fig. 12.29). As explained in Chapter 8, we can find a position, called the

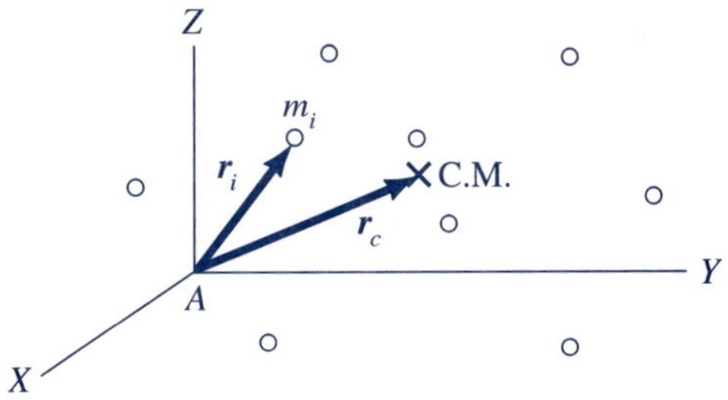

Figure 12.29. Center of mass of system.

center of mass of the system, with position vector $\boldsymbol{r}_c$, where the entire mass of the system of particles can be concentrated to give the correct first moment. Thus,

$$\boldsymbol{r}_c \sum_{i=1}^{n} m_i = \sum_{i=1}^{n} m_i \boldsymbol{r}_i$$

Therefore,

$$\boldsymbol{r}_c = \frac{\sum m_i \boldsymbol{r}_i}{\sum m_i} = \frac{\sum m_i \boldsymbol{r}_i}{M} \tag{12.61}$$

Let us reconsider Newton's law using the center-of-mass concept. To do this, replace $\sum m_i \boldsymbol{r}_i$ by $M\boldsymbol{r}_c$ in Eq. 12.60. Thus,

$$\boldsymbol{F} = \frac{d^2}{dt^2}(M\boldsymbol{r}_c) = M\frac{d^2\boldsymbol{r}_c}{dt^2} \tag{12.62}$$

We see that *the center of mass of any aggregate of particles has a motion that can be computed by methods already set forth, since this is a problem involving a single hypothetical particle of mass M*. You will recall that we have alluded to this important relationship several times earlier to justify the use of the particle concept in the analysis of many dynamics problems. We must realize for such an undertaking that $\boldsymbol{F}$ is the total *external* force acting on *all* the particles.

Example 12.15

Three charged particles in a vacuum are shown in Fig. 12.30. Particle 1 has a mass of 10^{-5} kg and a charge of 4×10^{-3} C (coulombs) and is at the origin at the instant of interest. Particles 2 and 3 each have a mass of 2×10^{-5} kg and a charge of 5×10^{-5} C and are located, respectively, at the

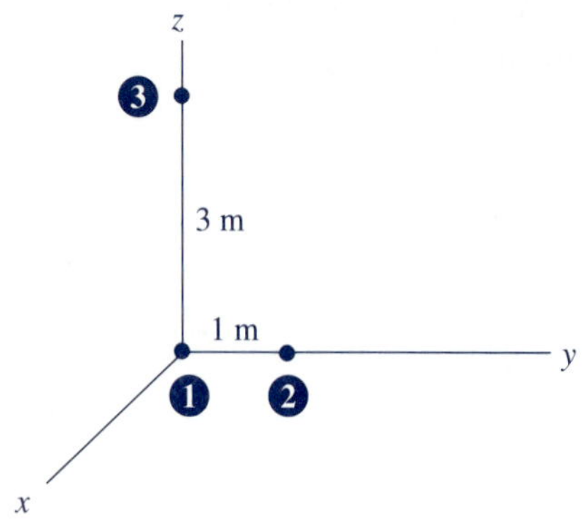

Figure 12.30. Charged particles in field ***E***.

instant of interest 1 m along the y axis and 3 m along the z axis. An electric field $\boldsymbol{E}$ given as

$$\boldsymbol{E} = 2x\boldsymbol{i} + 3z\boldsymbol{j} + 3(y + z^2)\boldsymbol{k} \text{ N/C} \tag{a}$$

is imposed from the outside. Compute: (a) the position of the center of mass for the system, (b) the acceleration of the center of mass, and (c) the acceleration of particle 1.

To get the position of the center of mass, we merely equate moments of the masses about the origin with that of a particle having a mass equal to the sum of masses of the system. Thus,

$$(1 + 2 + 2) \times 10^{-5}\boldsymbol{r}_c = (2 \times 10^{-5})\boldsymbol{j} + (2 \times 10^{-5})3\boldsymbol{k}$$

Therefore,

$$\boldsymbol{r}_c = .4\boldsymbol{j} + 1.2\boldsymbol{k} \text{ m} \tag{b}$$

To get the acceleration of the mass center, we must find the sum of the *external* forces acting on the particles. Two external forces act on each particle: the force of gravity and the electrostatic force from the external field. Recall from physics that this electrostatic force is given as $q\boldsymbol{E}$, where q is the charge on the particle. Hence, the total external force for each particle is given as follows:

$$\boldsymbol{F}_1 = -(9.81)(10^{-5})\boldsymbol{k} + \boldsymbol{0} \text{ N} \tag{c}$$
$$\boldsymbol{F}_2 = -(9.81)(2 \times 10^{-5})\boldsymbol{k} + (5 \times 10^{-5})(3\boldsymbol{k}) \text{ N} \tag{d}$$
$$\boldsymbol{F}_3 = -(9.81)(2 \times 10^{-5})\boldsymbol{k} + (5 \times 10^{-5})(9\boldsymbol{j} + 27\boldsymbol{k}) \text{ N} \tag{e}$$

Example 12.15 (Continued)

The sum of these forces $\boldsymbol{F}_T$ is

$$\boldsymbol{F}_T = 45 \times 10^{-5}\boldsymbol{j} + 100.9 \times 10^{-5}\boldsymbol{k} \text{ N} \tag{f}$$

Accordingly, we have for $\ddot{\boldsymbol{r}}_c$:

$$\ddot{\boldsymbol{r}}_c = \frac{45 \times 10^{-5}\boldsymbol{j} + 100.9 \times 10^{-5}\boldsymbol{k}}{5 \times 10^{-5}}$$

$$\ddot{\boldsymbol{r}}_c = 9\boldsymbol{j} + 20.2\boldsymbol{k} \text{ m/sec}^2 \tag{g}$$

Finally, to get the acceleration of particle 1, we must include the coulombic forces from particles 2 and 3. As you learned in physics, this force is given between two particles a and b with charges q_a and q_b as follows:

$$f_{\text{coul}} = -\frac{q_a q_b}{4\pi\epsilon_0 r^2}\hat{\boldsymbol{r}}$$

where $\hat{\boldsymbol{r}}$ is the unit vector between the particles, and ϵ_0 is the dielectric constant equal to 8.854×10^{-12} F/m (farads per meter) for a vacuum. Note that the coulombic force is repulsive between like charges. The total coulombic force $\boldsymbol{F}_C$ from particles 2 and 3 is

$$\begin{aligned}\boldsymbol{F}_C &= -\frac{(4 \times 10^{-5})(5 \times 10^{-5})}{(4\pi\epsilon_0)(1^2)}\boldsymbol{j} - \frac{(4 \times 10^{-5})(5 \times 10^{-5})}{(4\pi\epsilon_0)(3^2)}\boldsymbol{k} \\ &= -18\boldsymbol{j} - 2\boldsymbol{k} \text{ N}\end{aligned} \tag{h}$$

The total force acting on particle 1 is then

$$(\boldsymbol{F}_1)_T = \underbrace{-(9.81)(10^{-5})\boldsymbol{k}}_{\substack{\text{from}\\\text{weight}}} + \underbrace{\boldsymbol{0}}_{\substack{\text{from}\\\text{external}\\\text{field}}} + \underbrace{(-18\boldsymbol{j} - 2\boldsymbol{k})}_{\substack{\text{from}\\\text{internal}\\\text{field}}} \text{ N} \tag{i}$$

Clearly, the internal field dominates here. **Newton's law** then gives us

$$\ddot{\boldsymbol{r}}_1 = \frac{-18\boldsymbol{j} - 2\boldsymbol{k}}{10^{-5}}$$

$$\ddot{\boldsymbol{r}}_1 = -18 \times 10^5\boldsymbol{j} - 2 \times 10^5\boldsymbol{k} \text{ m/sec}^2 \tag{j}$$

We see here from Eqs. (g) and (j) that although the particles tend to "scramble" away from each other due to very strong internal coulombic forces, the center of mass accelerates slowly by comparison.

Example 12.16

A young man is standing in a canoe awaiting a young lady (Fig. 12.31). The man weighs 150 lb. and, as shown, is positioned near the end of the canoe, which weighs 200 lb. When the young lady appears, he quickly scrambles forward to greet her, but when he has moved 20 ft to the forward end of the canoe, he finds (not having studied mechanics) that he cannot reach her. How far is the tip of the canoe from the dock after our hero has made the 20-ft dash? The canoe is in no way tied to the dock and there are no water currents. Neglect friction from the water on the canoe.

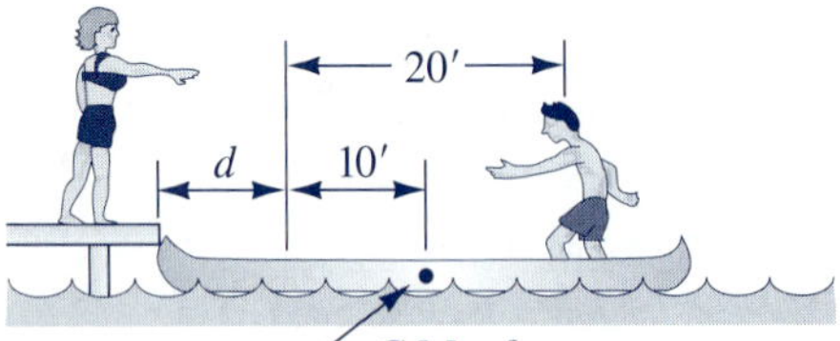

Figure 12.31. Man in canoe awaits his date.

The center of mass of the man plus the canoe cannot change position during this action since there is no net external force acting on this system during this action. Hence the first moment of mass about any fixed position must remain constant during this action. In Fig. 12.32 we have shown the man in the forward position and we choose the position at the tip of the dock to equate moment of mass at the beginning of the action and just when the man has moved the 20 ft. We then can say, noting that we are denoting the unspecified distance between the tip of the canoe and the forward position of the man as d as shown in Figs. 12.31 and 12.32,

$$\frac{200}{g}(d+10)+\frac{150}{g}(d+20)=\frac{150}{g}(x+d)+\frac{200}{g}(x+d+10)$$

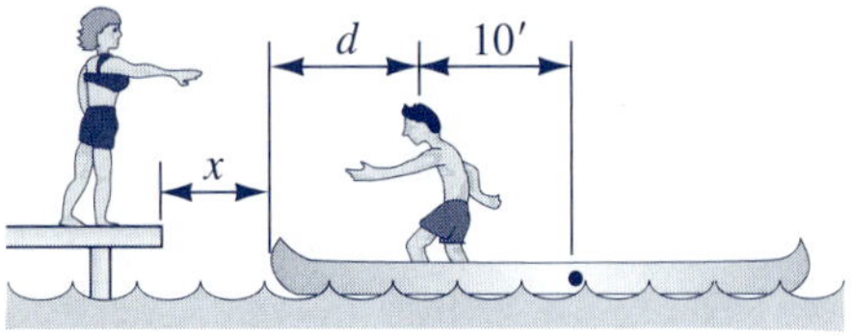

Figure 12.32. Man rushes forward to greet his date.

Canceling terms where possible we then have

$$350x = 3{,}000 \qquad \therefore \qquad \boxed{x = 8.571 \text{ ft.}}$$

PROBLEMS

12.90. A warrior of old is turning a sling in a vertical plane. A rock of mass .3 kg is held in the sling prior to releasing it against an enemy. What is the minimum speed ω to hold the rock in the sling?

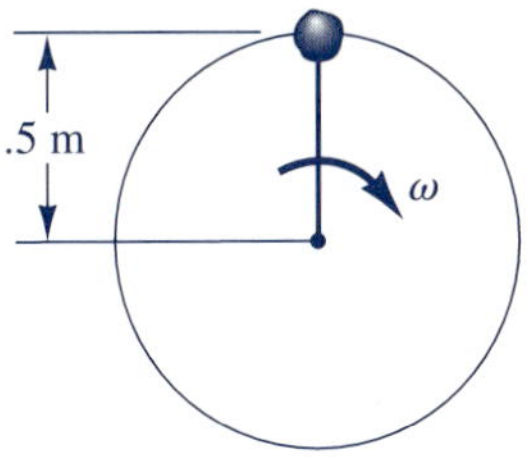

Figure P.12.90.

12.91. A car is traveling at a speed of 55 mi/hr along a banked highway having a radius of curvature of 500 ft. At what angle should the road be banked in order that a zero friction force is needed for the car to go around this curve?

12.92. A car weighing 20 kN is moving at a speed V of 60 km/hr on a road having a vertical radius of curvature of 200 m as shown. At the instant shown, what is the maximum deceleration possible from the brakes along the road for the vehicle if the coefficient of dynamic friction between tires and the road is .55?

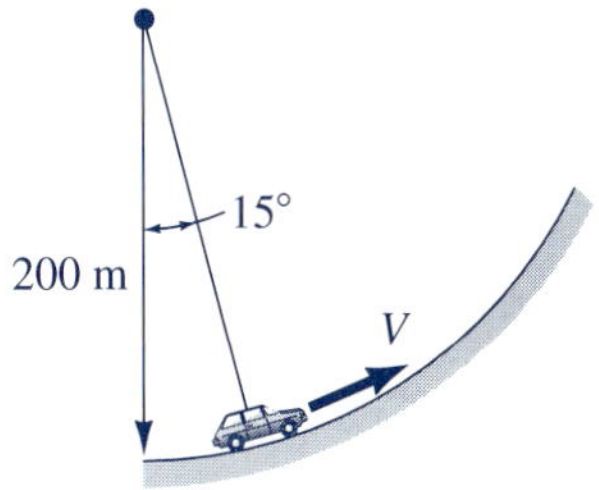

Figure P.12.92.

12.93. A particle moves at uniform speed of 1 m/sec along a plane sinusoidal path given as

$$y = 5 \sin \pi x \text{ m}$$

What is the position between $x = 0$ and $x = 1$ m for the maximum force normal to the curve? What is this force if the mass of the particle is 1 kg?

12.94. A catenary curve is formed by the cable of a suspension bridge. The equation of this curve relative to the axes shown can be given as

$$y = \frac{a}{2}(e^{ax} + e^{-ax}) = a \cosh ax$$

with x and y in feet. A small one-passenger vehicle is designed to move along the catenary to facilitate repair and painting of the bridge. Consider that the vehicle moves at uniform speed of 10 ft/sec along the curve. If the vehicle and passenger have a combined mass of 250 lbm, what is the force normal to the curve as a function of position x?

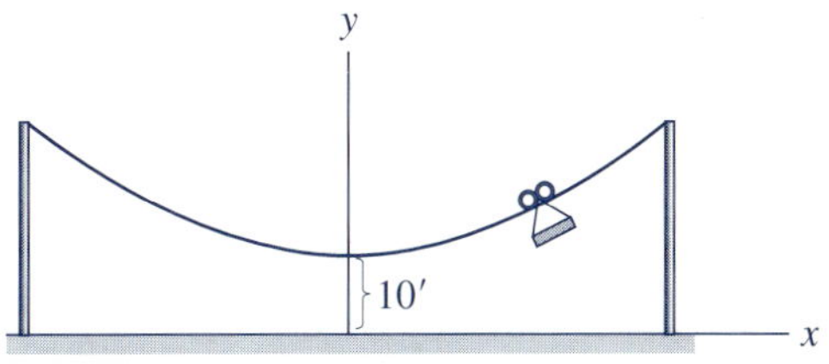

Figure P.12.94.

12.95. A rod CD rotates with shaft G–G at an angular speed ω of 300 rpm. A sleeve A of mass 500 g slides on CD. If no friction is present between A and CD, what is the distance S for no relative motion between A and CD?

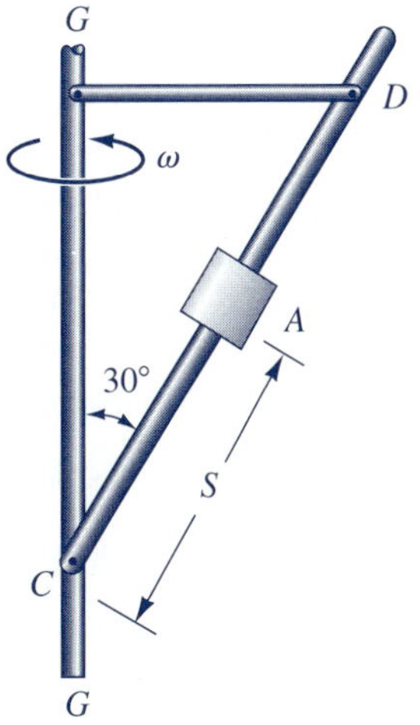

Figure P.12.95.

12.96. In Problem 12.95, what is the range of values for S for which A will remain stationary relative to CD if there is coulombic friction between A and CD such that $\mu_s = .4$?

12.97. A circular rod EB rotates at constant angular speed ω of 50 rpm. A sleeve A of mass 2 lbm slides on the circular rod. At what position θ will sleeve A remain stationary relative to the rod EB if there is no friction?

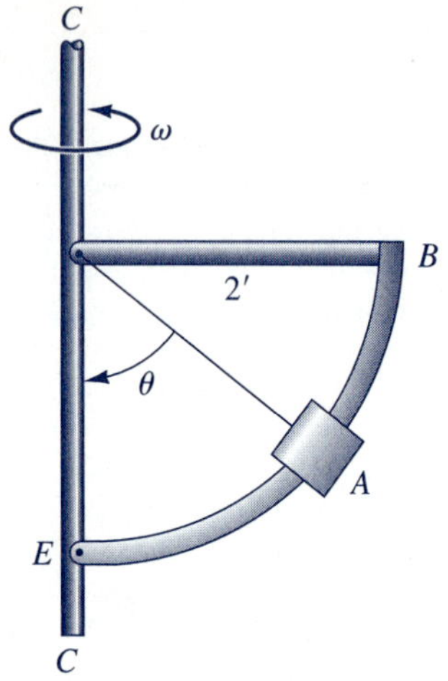

Figure P.12.97.

12.98. In Problem 12.97 assume that there is coulombic friction between A and EB with $\mu_s = .3$. Show that the minimum value of θ for which the sleeve will remain stationary relative to the rod is 75.45°.

12.99. The following data for a system of particles are given at time $t = 0$:

$$M_1 = 50 \text{ kg at position } (1, 1.3, -3) \text{ m}$$

$$M_2 = 25 \text{ kg at position } (-.6, 1.3, -2.6) \text{ m}$$

$$M_3 = 5 \text{ kg at position } (-2.6, 5.3, 1) \text{ m}$$

The particles are acted on by the following respective external forces:

$$\boldsymbol{F}_1 = 50\boldsymbol{j} + 10t\boldsymbol{k} \text{ N (particle 1)}$$

$$\boldsymbol{F}_2 = 50\boldsymbol{k} \text{ N} \qquad \text{(particle 2)}$$

$$\boldsymbol{F}_3 = 5t^2\boldsymbol{i} \text{ N} \qquad \text{(particle 3)}$$

What is the velocity of M_1 relative to the mass center after 5 sec, assuming that at $t = 0$, the particles are at rest?

***12.100.** Given the following force field:

$$\boldsymbol{F} = -2x\boldsymbol{i} + 3\boldsymbol{j} - z\boldsymbol{k} \text{ lb/slug}$$

what is the force on any particle in the field per unit mass of the particle. If we have two particles initially stationary in the field with position vectors

$$\boldsymbol{r}_1 = 3\boldsymbol{i} + 2\boldsymbol{j} \text{ ft}$$

$$\boldsymbol{r}_2 = 4\boldsymbol{i} - 2\boldsymbol{j} + 4\boldsymbol{k} \text{ ft}$$

what is the velocity of each particle relative to the center of mass of the system after 2 sec have elapsed? Each particle has a weight of .1 oz.

12.101. A stationary uniform block of ice is acted on by forces that maintain constant magnitude and direction at all times. If

$$F_1 = (25g) \text{ N}$$

$$F_2 = (10g) \text{ N}$$

$$F_3 = (15g) \text{ N}$$

what is the velocity of the center of mass of the block after 10 sec? Neglect friction. The density of ice is 56 lbm/ft³.

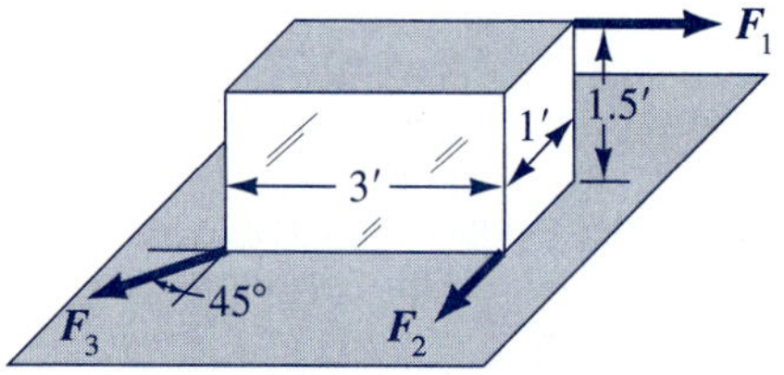

Figure P.12.101.

12.102. A space vehicle decelerates downward (Z direction) at 1,613 km/hr/sec while moving in a translatory manner relative to inertial space. Inside the vehicle is a rod BC rotating in the plane of the paper at a rate of 50 rad/sec relative to the vehicle. Two masses rotate at the rate of 20 rad/sec around BC on rod EF. The masses are each 300 mm from C. Determine the force transmitted at C between BC and EF if the mass of each of the rotating bodies is 5 kg and the mass of rod EF is 1 kg. BC is in the vertical position at the time of interest. Neglect gravity.

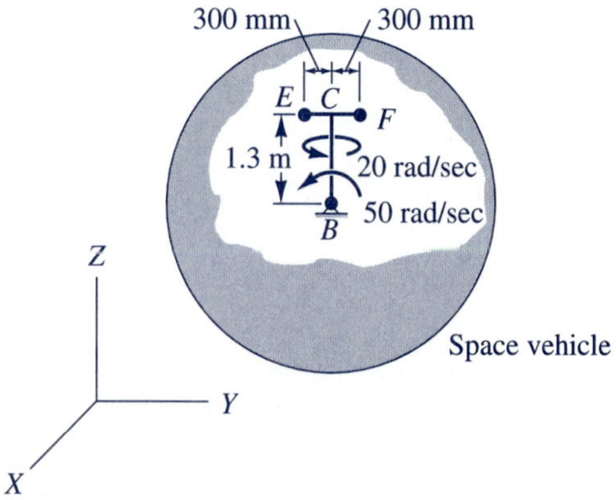

Figure P.12.102.

12.103. Two men climb aboard a barge at A to shift a load with the aid of a fork lift. The barge has a mass of 20,000 kg and is 10 m long. The load consists of four containers each with a mass of 1,300 kg and each having a length of 1 m. The men shift the containers to the opposite end of the barge, put the fork lift where they found it, and prepare to step off the barge at A, where they came on. If the barge has not been constrained and if we neglect water friction, currents, wind, and so on, how far has the barge shifted its position? The fork lift has a mass of 1,000 kg.

Figure P.12.103.

12.104. An astronaut on a space walk pulls a mass A of 100 kg toward him and shortens the distance d by 5 m. If the astronaut weighs 660 N on earth, how far does the mass A move from its original position? Neglect the mass of the cord.

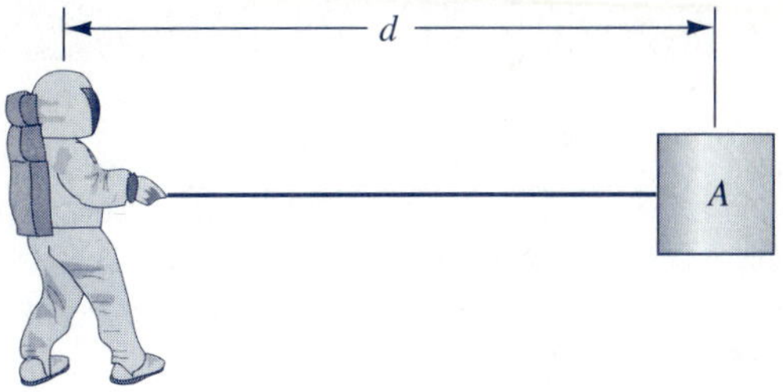

Figure P.12.104.

12.105. Two identical adjacent tanks are each 10 ft long, 5 ft high, and 5 ft wide. Originally, the left tank is completely full of water while the right tank is empty. Water is pumped by an internal pump from the left tank to the right tank. At the instant of interest, the rate of flow Q is 20 ft³/sec, while $\dot{Q}$ is 5 ft³/sec². What horizontal force on the tanks is needed at this instant from the foundation? Assume that the water surface in the tanks remains horizontal. The specific weight of water is 62.4 lb/ft³.

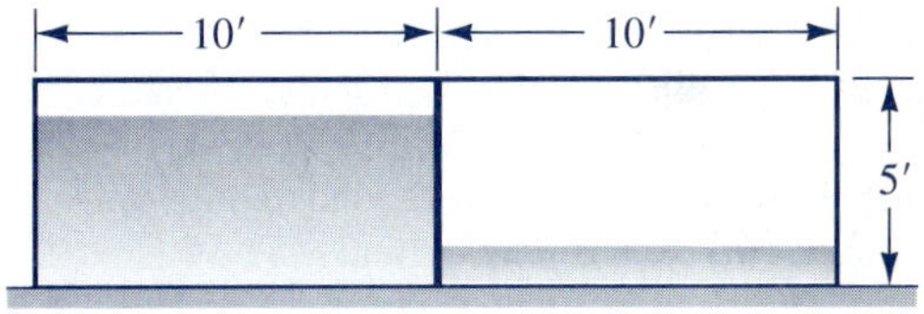

Figure P.12.105.

12.11 Closure

In this chapter, we integrated Newton's law for various coordinate systems. Also, with the aid of the mass center concept, we formulated Newton's law for any aggregate of particles. In the next two chapters, we shall present alternative procedures for more efficient treatment of certain classes of dynamics problems for particles. You will note that, since the new concepts are all derived from Newton's law, whatever problems can be solved by these new methods could also be solved by the methods we have already presented. A separate and thorough study of these topics is warranted by the gain in insight into dynamics and the greater facility in solving problems that can be achieved by examining these alternative methods and their accompanying concepts. As in this chapter, we will make certain generalizations applicable to any aggregate of particles.

PROBLEMS

12.106. A block A of mass 10 kg rests on a second block B of mass 8 kg. A force F equal to 100 N pulls block A. The coefficient of friction between A and B is .5; between B and the ground, .1. What is the speed of block A relative to block B in 0.1 sec if the system starts from rest?

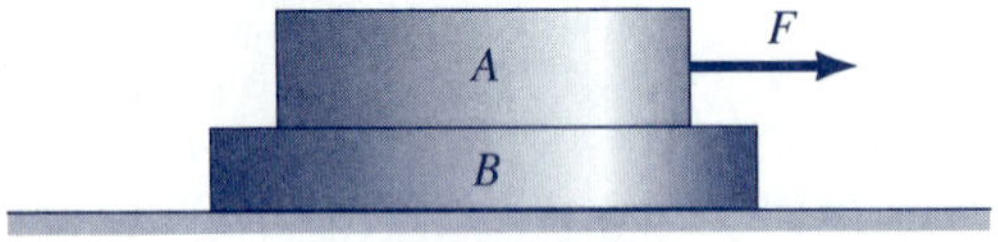

Figure P.12.106.

***12.107.** A block B slides from A to F along a rectangular chute where there is coulombic friction on the faces of the chute. The coefficient of dynamic friction is .4. The bottom face of the chute is parallel to face $EACF$ (a plane surface) and the other two faces are perpendicular to $EACF$. The body weighs 5 lb. How long does it take B to go from A to F starting from rest?

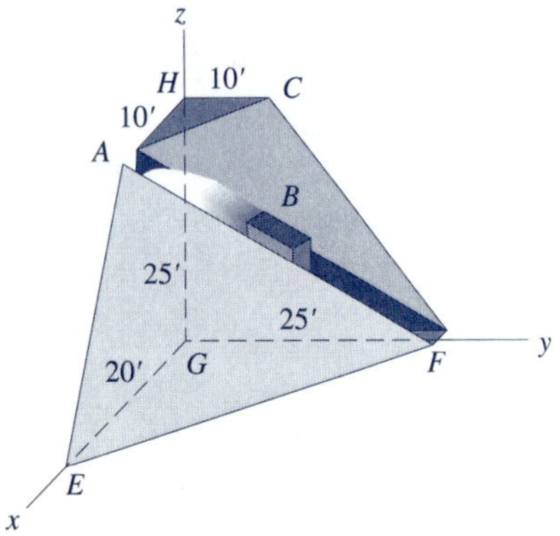

Figure P.12.107.

12.108. A tugboat is pushing a barge at a steady speed of 8 knots. The thrust from the tugboat needed for this motion is 800 lb. The barge with load weighs 100 tons. If the water resistance to the barge is proportional to the speed of the barge, how long will it take the barge to slow to 5 knots after the tugboat ceases to push? (*Note:* 1 knot equals 1.152 mi/hr.)

Figure P.12.108.

12.109. A spring requires a force x^2 N for a deflection of x mm, where x is the deflection of the spring from the undeformed geometry. Because the deflection is not proportional to x to the first power, the spring is called a *nonlinear* spring. If a 100-kg block is suddenly released on the undeformed spring, what is the speed of the block after it has descended 10 mm?

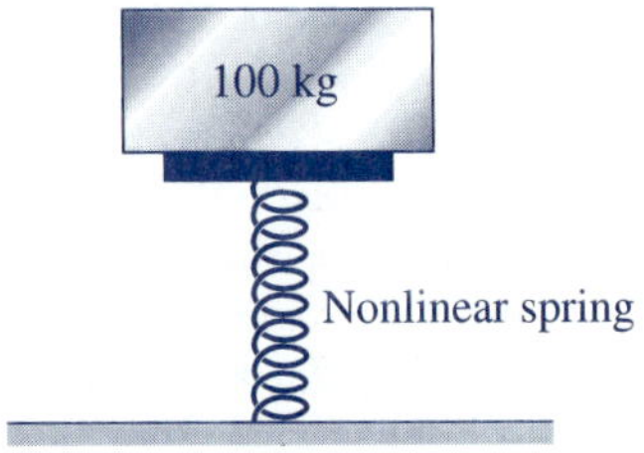

Figure P.12.109.

12.110. A horizontal platform is rotating at a constant angular speed ω of 5 rad/s. Fixed to the platform is a frictionless chute in which two identical masses each of 2 kg are constrained by a pair of linear springs each of spring constant K = 250 N/m. If the unstretched length l_0 of each of the springs is .18 m, show that at steady state the angle θ must have the value 36.87°. Springs are fixed to the platform at A.

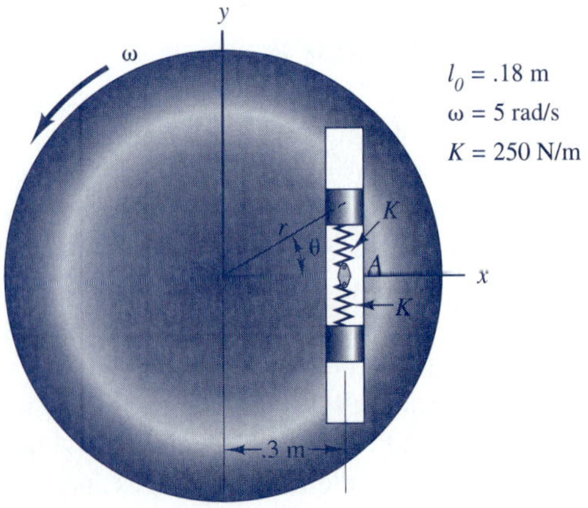

Figure P.12.110.

12.111. What is the velocity and altitude of a communications satellite that remains in the same position above the equator relative to the earth's surface?

12.112. A satellite is launched and attains a velocity of 19,000 mi/hr relative to the center of the earth at a distance of 240 mi from the earth's surface. The satellite has been guided into a path that is parallel to the earth's surface at burnout.

(a) What kind of trajectory will it have?
(b) What is its farthest position from the earth's surface?
(c) If it is in orbit, compute the time it takes to go from the minimum point (perigee) to the maximum point (apogee) from the earth's surface.
(d) What is the minimum escape velocity for this position of launching?

12.113. A rocket system is capable of giving a satellite a velocity of 35,200 km/hr relative to the earth's surface at an elevation of 320 km above the earth's surface. What would be its maximum distance h from the surface of the earth if it were launched (1) from the North Pole region or (2) from the equator, utilizing the spin of the earth as an aid?

12.114. A space vehicle is to change from a circular parking orbit 320 km above the surface of Venus to one that is 1,620 km above this surface. This motion will be accomplished by two firings of the rocket system of the vehicle. The first firing causes the vehicle to attain an apogee that is 1,620 km above the surface of Venus. At this apogee, a second firing is accomplished so as to achieve the desired circular orbit. What is the change in speed demanded for each firing if the thrust is maintained in each instance over a small portion of the trajectory of the vehicle? Neglect friction. The radius of Venus is 6,160 km, and the escape velocity at the surface is 1.026×10^4 m/sec^2.

12.115. Weights A and B are held by light pulleys. If released from rest, what is the speed of each weight after 1 sec? Weight A is 10 lb and weight B is 40 lb.

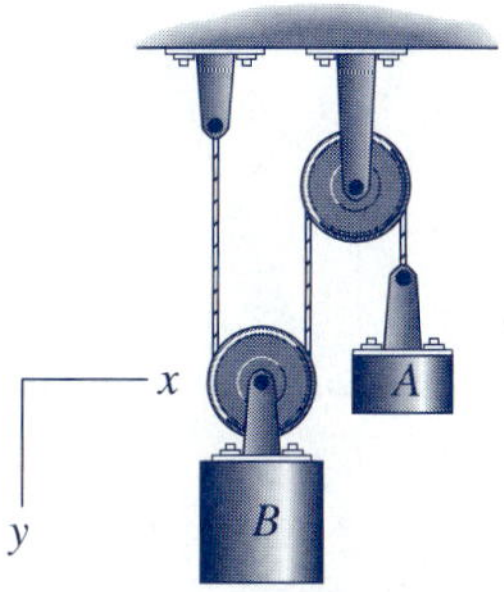

Figure P.12.115.

12.116. The following data are given for the flyball governor (read Problem 12.60 for details on how the governor works):

$$l = .275 \text{ m}$$
$$D = 50 \text{ mm}$$
$$\omega = 300 \text{ rpm}$$
$$\theta = 45°$$

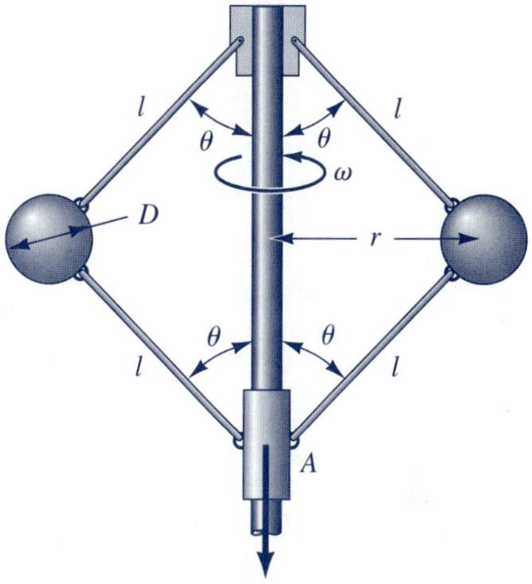

Figure P.12.116.

What is the force P acting on frictionless collar A if each ball has a mass of 1 kg and we neglect the weight of all other moving members of the system?

12.117. A spy satellite to observe the United States is put into a circular orbit about the North and South Poles. The satellite is to make 10 cycles/day (24 hr). What must be the distance from the surface of the earth for this satellite?

Figure P.12.117.

12.118. A skylab is in a circular orbit about the earth at a distance of 500 km above the earth's surface. A space shuttle has rendezvoused with the skylab and now, wishing to depart, decouples and fires its rockets to move more slowly than the skylab. If the rockets are fired over a short time interval, what should the relative speed between the space shuttle and skylab be at the end of rocket fire if the space shuttle is to come as close as 100 km to the earth's surface in subsequent ballistic (rocket motors off) flight?

12.119. A space vehicle is launched at a speed of 19,000 mi/hr relative to the earth's center at a position 250 mi above the earth's surface. If the vehicle has a radial velocity component of 3,000 mi/hr toward the earth's center, what is the eccentricity of the trajectory? What is the maximum elevation above the earth's surface reached by the vehicle? Do not use Eq. 12.54.

12.120. A skier is moving down a hill at a speed of 30 mi/hr when he is at the position shown. If the skier weighs 180 lb, what total force do his skis exert on the snow surface? Assume that the coefficient of friction is .1. The hill can be taken as a parabolic surface.

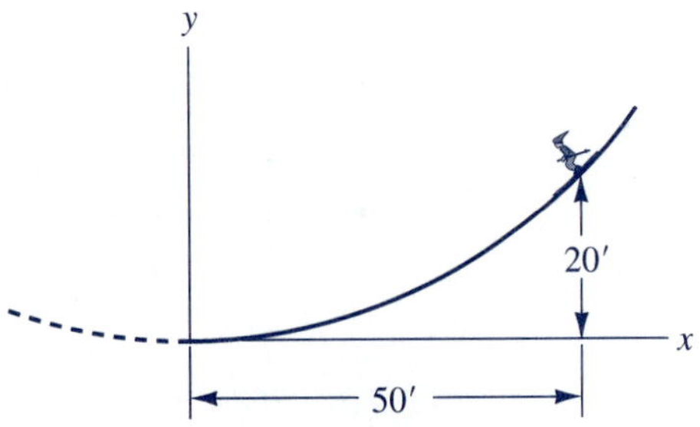

Figure P.12.120.

12.121. A submarine is moving at constant speed of 15 knots below the surface of the ocean. The sub is at the same time descending downward while remaining horizontal with an acceleration of $.023g$. In the submarine a flyball governor operates with weights having a mass each of 500g. The governor is rotating with speed ω of 5 rad/sec. If at time t, $\theta = 30°$, $\dot{\theta} = .2$ rad/sec, and $\ddot{\theta} = 1$ rad/sec^2, what is the force developed on the support of governor system as a result solely of the motion of the weights at this instant?

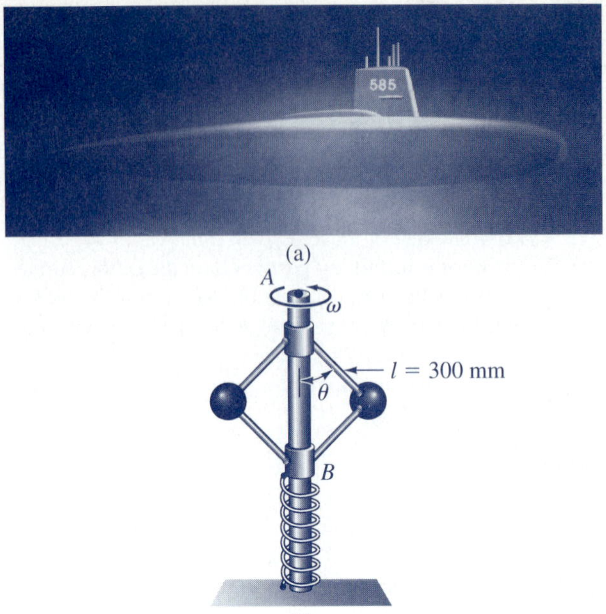

Figure P.12.121.

12.122. A mass spring system is shown. Write two simultaneous differential equations describing the motion of the mass. The spring has an unstretched length r_0. Consider that the spring does not bend and only changes length. Neglect all masses except that of the particle. If you restrict the motion to small rotations, how can you simplify the equations? Consider that the motion is confined to the xy plane.

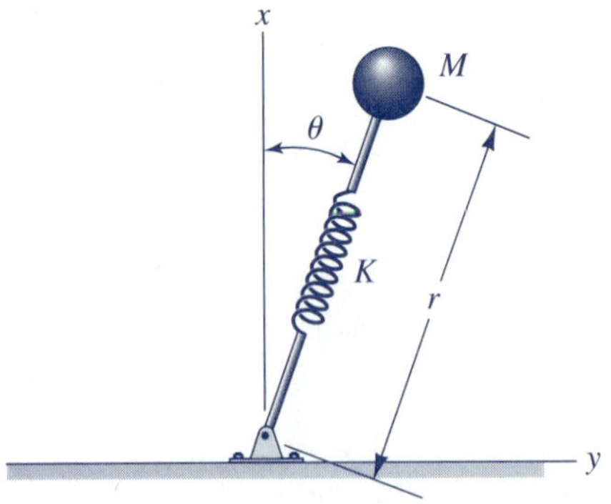

Figure P.12.122.

12.123. Three bodies have the following weights and positions at time t:

$$W_1 = 10 \text{ lb}, \quad x_1 = 6\text{ft}, \quad y_1 = 10 \text{ ft}, \quad z_1 = 10 \text{ ft}$$

$$W_2 = 5 \text{ lb}, \quad x_2 = 5 \text{ ft}, \quad y_2 = 6 \text{ ft}, \quad z_2 = 0$$

$$W_3 = 8 \text{ lb}, \quad x_3 = 0, \quad y_3 = -4 \text{ ft}, \quad z_3 = 0$$

Determine the position vector of the center of mass at time t. Determine the velocity of the center of mass if the bodies have the following velocities:

$$V_1 = 6\boldsymbol{i} + 3\boldsymbol{j} \text{ ft/sec}$$

$$V_2 = 10\boldsymbol{i} - 3\boldsymbol{k} \text{ ft/sec}$$

$$V_3 = 6\boldsymbol{k} \text{ ft/sec}$$

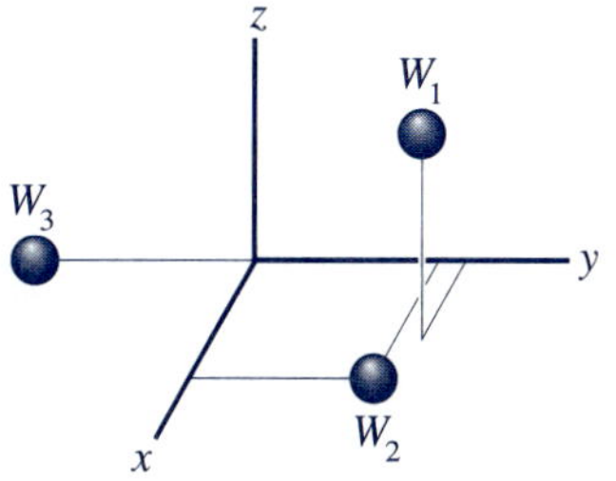

Figure P.12.123.

12.124. In Problem 12.123, the following external forces act on the respective particles:

$$F_1 = 6t\boldsymbol{i} + 3\boldsymbol{j} - 10\boldsymbol{k} \text{ lb} \quad \text{(particle 1)}$$

$$F_2 = 15\boldsymbol{i} - 3\boldsymbol{j} \text{ lb} \quad \text{(particle 2)}$$

$$F_3 = \boldsymbol{0} \text{ lb} \quad \text{(particle 3)}$$

What is the acceleration of the center of mass, and what is its position after 10 sec from that given initially? From Problem 12.123 at $t = 0$:

$$r_C = 3.70\boldsymbol{i} + 4.26\boldsymbol{j} + 4.35\boldsymbol{k} \text{ ft}$$

$$V_C = 4.78\boldsymbol{i} + 1.304\boldsymbol{j} + 1.435\boldsymbol{k} \text{ ft/sec}$$

12.125. A small body M of mass 1 kg slides along a wire from A to B. There is coulombic friction between the mass M and the wire. The dynamic coefficient of friction is .4. How long does it take to go from A to B?

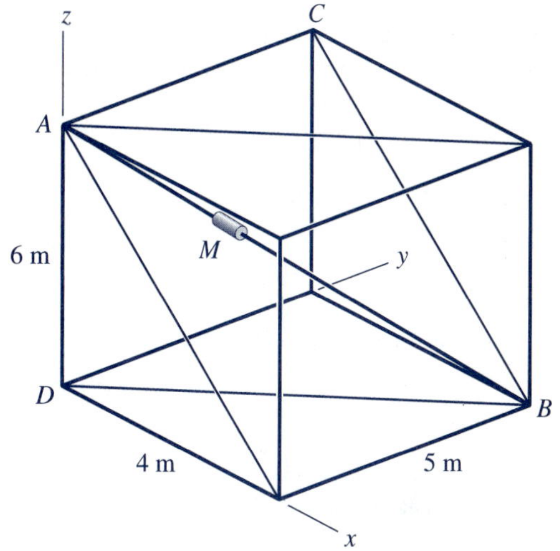

Figure P.12.125.

12.126. For $M = 1$ slug and $K = 10$ lb/in., what is the speed at $x = 1$ in. if a force of 5 lb in the x direction is applied suddenly to the mass–spring system and then maintained constant? Neglect the mass of the spring and friction.

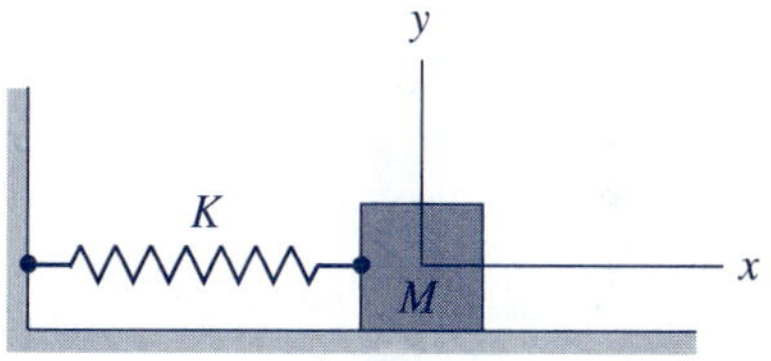

Figure P.12.126.

12.127. A rod B of mass 500 kg rests on a block A of mass 50 kg. A force F of 10,000 N is applied suddenly to block A at the position shown. If the coefficient of friction μ_d is .4 for all contact surfaces, what is the speed of A when it has moved 3 m to the end of the rod?

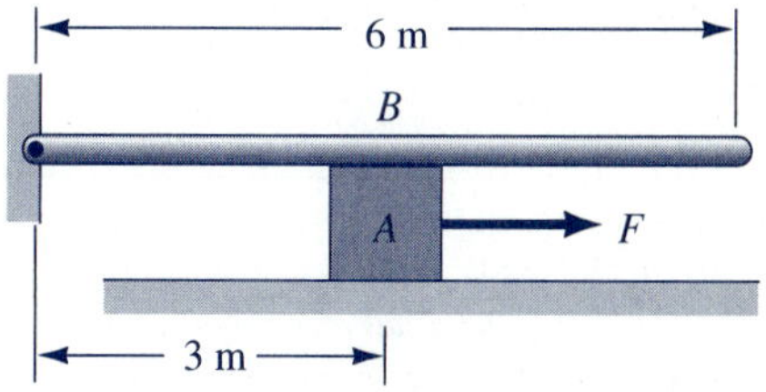

Figure P.12.127.

12.128. A simply supported beam is shown. You will learn in your course on strength of materials that a vertical force F applied at the center causes a deflection δ at the center given as

$$\delta = \frac{1}{48}\frac{FL^3}{EI}$$

If a mass of 200 lbm, fastened to the beam at its midpoint, is suddenly released, what will its speed be when the deflection is $\frac{1}{8}$ in.? Neglect the mass of the beam. The length of the beam, L, is 20 ft. Young's modulus E is 30×10^6 psi, and the moment of inertia of the cross section I is 20 in.^{4}.

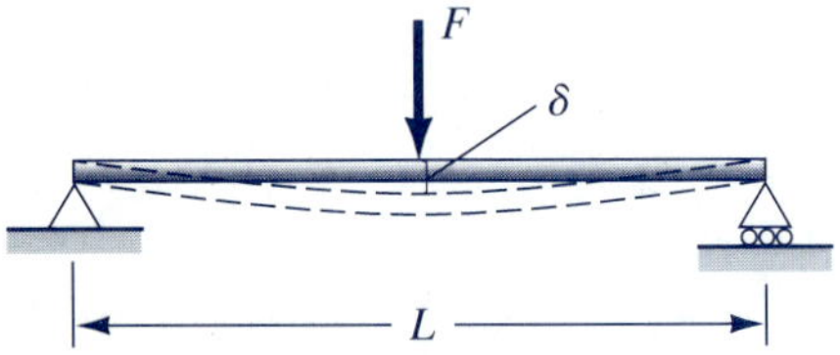

Figure P.12.128.

12.129. A piston is shown maintaining air at a pressure of 8 psi above that of the atmosphere. If the piston is allowed to accelerate to the left, what is the speed of the piston after it moves 3 in.? The piston assembly has a mass of 3 lbm. Assume that the air expands *adiabatically* (i.e., with no heat transfer). This means that at all times pV^k = constant, where V is the volume of the gas and k is a constant which for air equals 1.4. Neglect the inertial effects of the air.

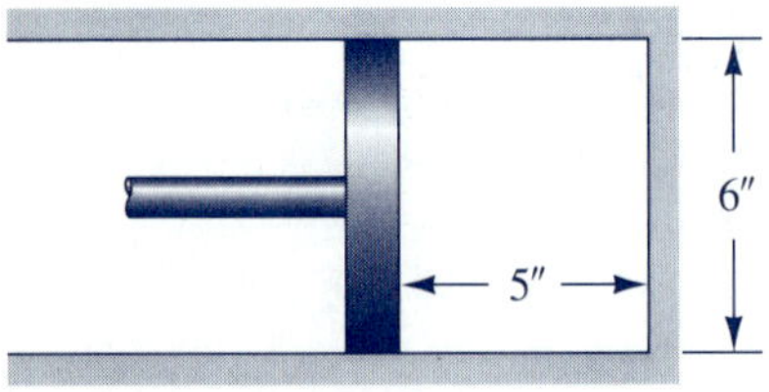

Figure P.12.129.

***12.130.** In Example 12.6 assume that there are adiabatic expansions and compressions of the gases (i.e., that pv^k = constant with $k = 1.4$). Compare the results for the speed of the piston. Explain why your result should be higher or lower than for the isothermal case.

12.131. Body A and body B are connected by an inextensible cord as shown. If both bodies are released simultaneously, what distance do they move in $\frac{1}{2}$ sec? Take M_A = 25 kg and M_B = 35 kg. The coefficient of friction μ_d is .3.

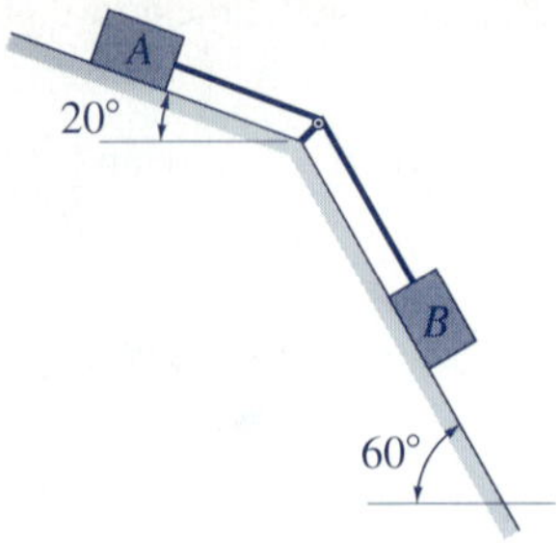

Figure P.12.131.

12.132. A force F of 2 kN is exerted on body C. If μ_d for all surface contacts is .2, what is the speed of C after it moves 1 m? The body C is initially stationary at the position shown, when the force F is applied. Solve using Newton's law. The following are the masses of the three bodies involved.

$$M_A = 100 \text{ kg} \qquad M_B = 80 \text{ kg} \qquad M_C = 50 \text{ kg}$$

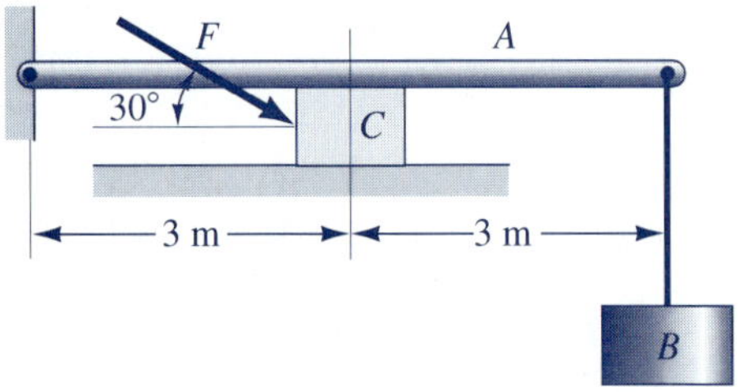

Figure P.12.132.

12.133. A constant force F of 5,000 N acts on block A. If we do not have friction anywhere, what is the acceleration of block A?

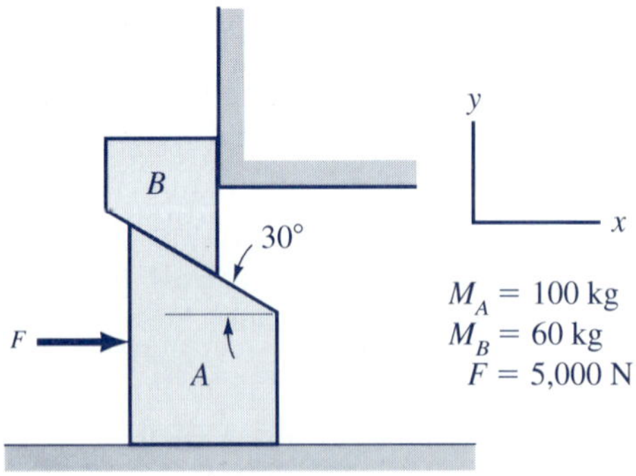

Figure P.12.133.

12.134. The system shown is released from rest. What distance does the body C drop in 2 sec? The cable is inextensible. The coefficient of dynamic friction μ_d is .4 for contact surfaces of bodies A and B.

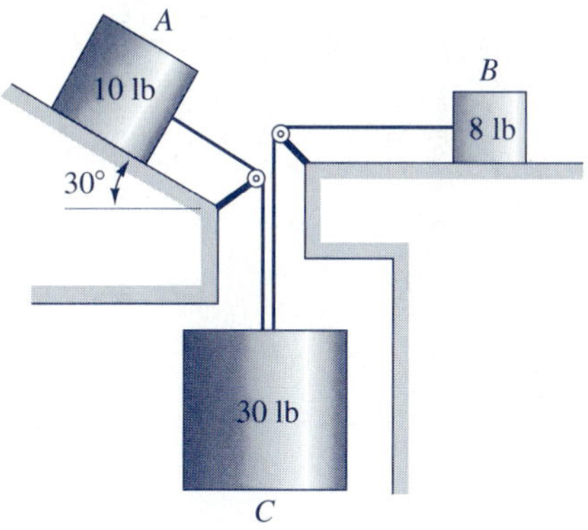

Figure P.12.134.

12.135. Do Problem 12.134 for the case where there is viscous damping for the contact surfaces of bodies A and B given as $.5V$ lb, with V in ft/sec.

12.136. Two bodies A and B are shown having masses of 40 kg and 30 kg, respectively. The cables are inextensible. Neglecting the inertia of the cable and pulleys at C and D, what is the speed of the block B 1 sec after the system has been released from rest? The dynamic coefficient of friction μ_d for the contact surface of body A is .3. [*Hint:* From your earlier work in physics, recall that pulley D is instantaneously rotating about point a and hence point c moves at a speed that is twice that of point b.]

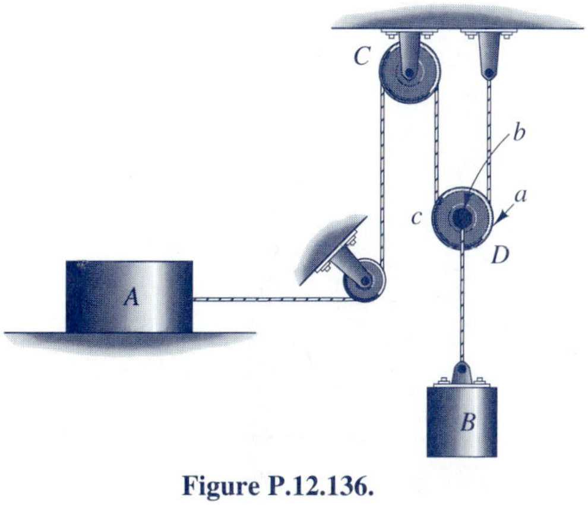

Figure P.12.136.

12.137. Bodies A, B, and C have weights, of 100 lb, 200 lb, and 150 lb, respectively. If released from rest, what are the respective speeds of the bodies after 1 sec? Neglect the weight of pulleys.

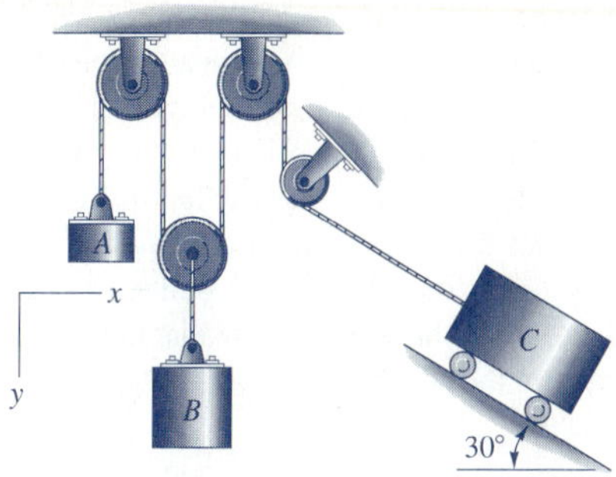

Figure P.12.137.

12.138. A car is moving at a constant speed of 65 km/hr on a road part of which ($A \rightarrow B$) is parabolic and part of which ($C \rightarrow D$) is circular with a radius of 3 km. If the car has an anti-lock braking system and the static coefficient of friction μ_s between the road and the tires is 0.6, what is the maximum deceleration possible at the $x = 2$ km position and at the $x = 10$ km position? The total vehicle weight is 12,000 N.

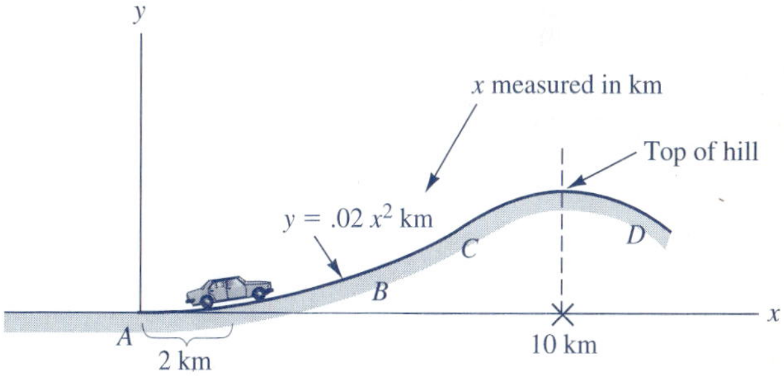

Figure P.12.138.

12.139. A mass of 3 kg is moving along a vertically oriented parabolic rod whose equation is $y = 3.4x^2$. A linear spring with $K = 550$ N/m connects to the mass and is unstretched when the mass is at the bottom of the rod having an unstretched length $l_0 = 1$ m. When the spring centerline is 30° from the vertical, as shown in the diagram, the mass is moving at 2.8 m/s. At this instant, what is the force component on the rod directed normal to the rod?

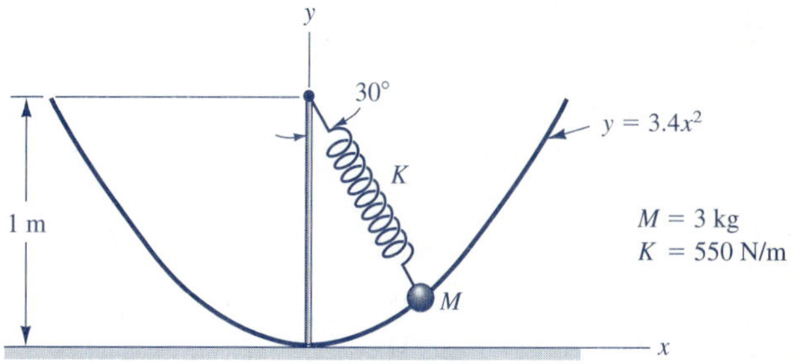

Figure P.12.139.

12.140. A heated cathode gives off electrons which are attracted to the positive anode. Some go through a small hole and enter the parallel plates at an angle with the horizontal of $\alpha_0 = 0$ and a velocity of V_0. Determine the horizontal and vertical motions of the electron inside the plates as a function of time. Letting $x = l$, find the time that the electron is in the parallel plate region and then obtain the exit vertical velocity. Assuming straight-line motion until the electron hits the screen, show that the vertical position of impact, assuming the screen is flat, is

$$y_{\text{Impact}} = \frac{eElL}{mV_0^2} + \frac{eEl^2}{2mV_0^2}$$

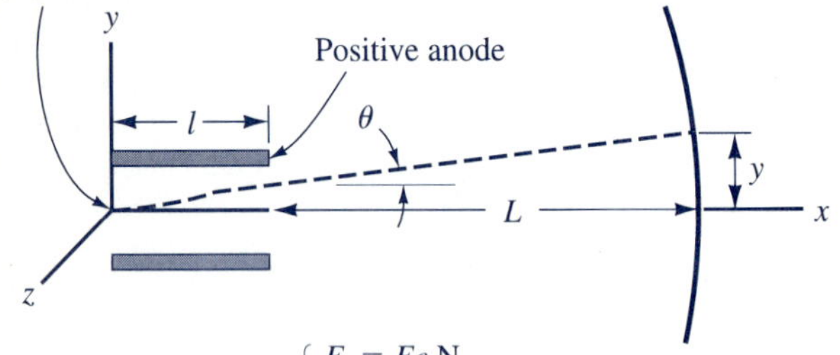

$$\begin{cases} F_y = Ee \text{ N} \\ F_x = 0 \\ F_z = 0 \end{cases}$$

Figure P.12.140.

***12.141.** A weightless cord supports two identical masses each of weight W. The cord is being pulled at a constant speed V_0 by a force F. Formulate an equation for F in terms of V_0, L, l, W, and h. Determine F for the following conditions:

$V_0 = 2.2$ m/s $\quad W = 40$ N

$L = 3.3$ m $\quad h = .16$ m

$l = .26$ m

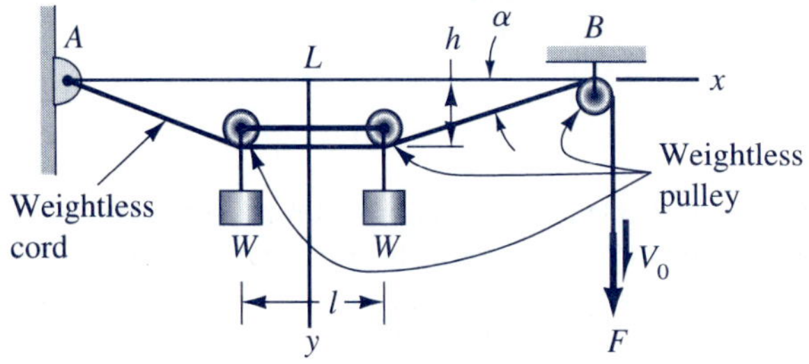

Figure P.12.141.

CHAPTER 13

Energy Methods for Particles

Part A: Analysis for a Single Particle

13.1 Introduction

In Chapter 12, we integrated the differential equation derived from Newton's law to yield velocity and position as functions of time. At this time, we shall present an alternative procedure, that of the method of energy, and we shall see that certain classes of problems can be more easily handled by this method in that we shall not need to integrate a differential equation.

To set forth the basic equation underlying this approach, we start with *Newton's law* for a particle moving relative to an inertial reference, as shown in Fig. 13.1. Thus,

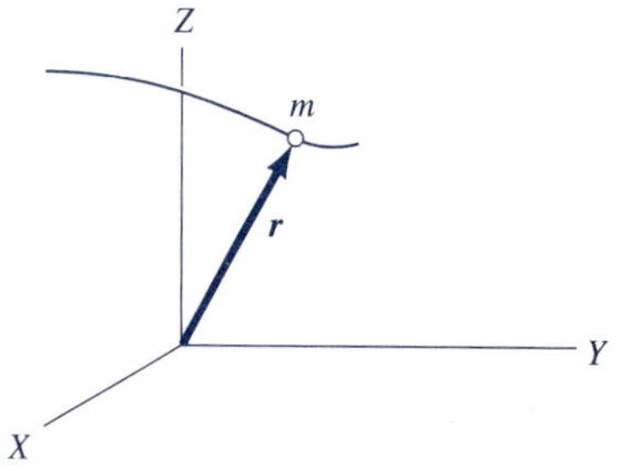

Figure 13.1. Particle moving relative to an inertial reference.

$$\boldsymbol{F} = m\frac{d^2\boldsymbol{r}}{dt^2} = m\frac{d\boldsymbol{V}}{dt} \qquad (13.1)$$

Multiply each side of this equation by $d\boldsymbol{r}$ as a dot product and integrate from r_1 to r_2 along the path of motion:

$$\int_{r_1}^{r_2} \boldsymbol{F} \cdot d\boldsymbol{r} = m\int_{r_1}^{r_2} \frac{d\boldsymbol{V}}{dt} \cdot d\boldsymbol{r} = m\int_{t_1}^{t_2} \frac{d\boldsymbol{V}}{dt} \cdot \frac{d\boldsymbol{r}}{dt}\, dt$$

In the last integral, we multiplied and divided by dt, thus changing the variable of integration to t. Since $d\boldsymbol{r}/dt = \boldsymbol{V}$, we then have

$$\int_{r_1}^{r_2} \mathbf{F} \cdot d\mathbf{r} = m\int_{t_1}^{t_2}\left(\frac{d\mathbf{V}}{dt} \cdot \mathbf{V}\right) dt = \frac{1}{2}\, m\int_{t_1}^{t_2} \frac{d}{dt}(\mathbf{V} \cdot \mathbf{V})\, dt$$

$$= \frac{1}{2}\, m\int_{t_1}^{t_2} \frac{d}{dt} V^2\, dt = \frac{1}{2}\, m\int_{V_1}^{V_2} d(V^2)$$

On carrying out the integration, we arrive at the familiar equation

$$\int_{r_1}^{r_2} \boldsymbol{F} \cdot d\boldsymbol{r} = \tfrac{1}{2}m(V_2^2 - V_1^2) \tag{13.2}$$

where the left side is the well-known expression for *work* (to be denoted at times as $\mathcal{W}_{1-2}$)[1] and the right side is clearly the change in *kinetic energy* as the mass moves from position $\boldsymbol{r}_1$ to position $\boldsymbol{r}_2$.

We shall see in Section 13.7 that for any system of particles, including, of course, rigid bodies, we get a work–energy equation of the form 13.2, where the velocity is that of the mass center, the force is the resultant external force on the system, and the path of integration is that of the mass center. Clearly, then, we can use a single particle model (and consequently Eq. 13.2) for:

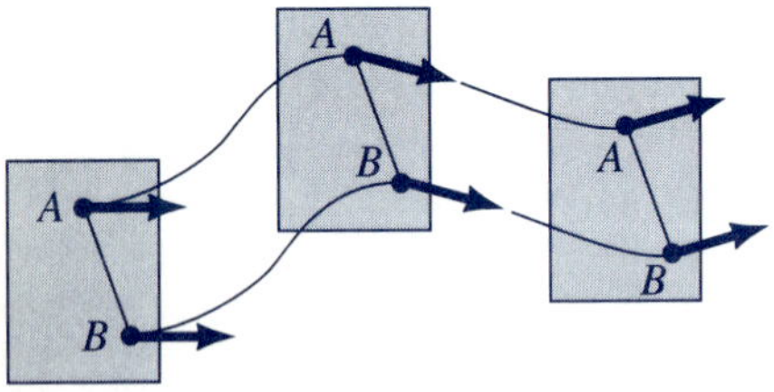

Figure 13.2. Translating body.

1. *A rigid body moving without rotation.* Such a motion was discussed in Chapter 11 and is called translation. Note that lines in a translating body remain parallel to their original directions, and points in the body move over a path which has identically the same form for all points. This condition is illustrated in Fig. 13.2 for two points A and B. Furthermore, each point in the body has at any instant of time t the same velocity as any other point. Clearly the motion of the center of mass fully characterizes the motion of the body and Eq. 13.2 will be used often for this situation.
2. Sometimes for *a body whose size is small compared to its trajectory*. Here the paths of points in the body differ very little from that of the mass center and knowing where the center of mass is tells us with sufficient accuracy all we need to know about the position of the body. However, keep in mind that the *velocity* and *acceleration* relative to the center of mass of a part of the body may be *very large*, irrespective of how small the body may be when compared to the trajectory of its center of mass. Then, information about the velocity and acceleration of this part of the body relative to the center of mass would require a more detailed consideration beyond a simple one-particle model centered around the center of mass.

Thus, as in our considerations of Newton's law in Chapter 12, when the motion of the mass center characterizes with sufficient accuracy what we want to know about the motion of a body, we use a particle at the mass center for energy considerations.

Next, suppose that we have a component of Newton's law in one direction, say the x direction:

$$F_x\boldsymbol{i} = m\frac{dV_x}{dt}\boldsymbol{i} \tag{13.3}$$

[1] It is important to note that the work done by a force system depends on the path over which the forces move, except in the case of conservative forces to be considered in Section 13.3. Thus, $\mathcal{W}_{1-2}$ is called a *path function* in thermodynamics. However, kinetic energy depends only on the instantaneous state of motion of the particle and is independent of the path. Kinetic energy is called, accordingly, a *point function* in thermodynamics.

In the next section, we shall present a more general definition of work.

Taking the dot product of each side of this equation with $dx\boldsymbol{i} + dy\boldsymbol{j} + dz\boldsymbol{k}$ ($= d\boldsymbol{r}$), we get, after integrating in the manner set forth at the outset:

$$\int_{x_1}^{x_2} F_x\, dx = \frac{m}{2}\left[(V_x)_2^2 - (V_x)_1^2\right] \tag{13.3a}$$

Similarly,

$$\int_{y_1}^{y_2} F_y\, dy = \frac{m}{2}\left[(V_y)_2^2 - (V_y)_1^2\right] \tag{13.3b}$$

$$\int_{z_1}^{z_2} F_z\, dz = \frac{m}{2}\left[(V_z)_2^2 - (V_z)_1^2\right] \tag{13.3c}$$

Thus, the foregoing equations demonstrate that the work done on a particle in any direction equals the change in kinetic energy associated with the component of velocity in that direction.

Instead of employing Newton's law, we can now use the energy equations developed in this section for solving certain classes of problems. This energy approach is particularly handy when velocities are desired and forces are functions of position. However, please understand that any problem solvable with the energy equation can be solved from Newton's law; the choice between the two is mainly a question of convenience and the manner in which the information is given.

Example 13.1

An automobile is moving at 60 mi/hr (see Fig. 13.3) when the driver jams on his brakes and goes into a skid in the direction of motion. The car weighs 4,000 lb, and the dynamic coefficient of friction between the rubber tires and the concrete road is .60. How far, l, will the car move before stopping?

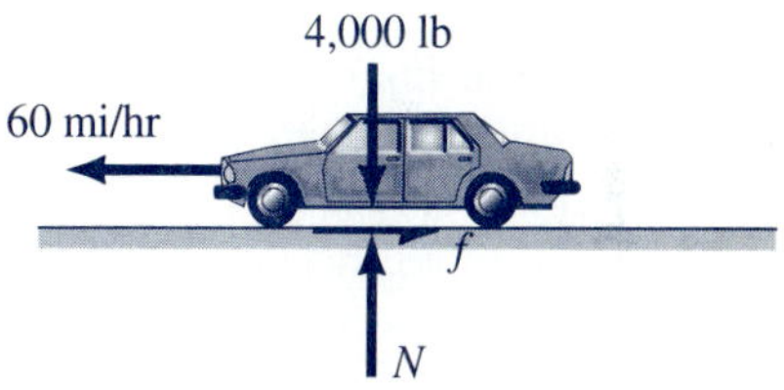

Figure 13.3. Car moving with brakes locked.

A constant friction force acts, which from Coulomb's law is $\mu_d N = (.60)(4{,}000) = 2{,}400$ lb. This force is the only force performing work, and clearly it is changing the kinetic energy of the vehicle from that corresponding to the speed of 60 mi/hr (or 88 ft/sec) to zero. (You will learn in thermodynamics that this work facilitates a transfer of kinetic energy of the vehicle to an increase of internal energy of the vehicle, the road, and the air, as well as the wear of brake parts) From the **work–energy equation** 13.2, we get[2]

$$-2{,}400l = \frac{1}{2}\frac{4{,}000}{g}(0 - 88^2)$$

Hence,

$$l = 200 \text{ ft}$$

(Perhaps every driver should solve this problem periodically.)

[2]Note that the sign of the work done is negative since the friction force is opposite in sense to the motion.

Example 13.2

Shown in Fig. 13.4 is a light platform B guided by vertical rods. The platform is positioned so that the spring has been compressed 10 mm. In this configuration a body A weighing 100 N is placed on the platform and released suddenly. If the guide rods give a total constant resistance force f to downward movement of the platform of 5 N, what is the largest distance that the weight falls? The spring used here is a *nonlinear* spring requiring $.5x^2$ N of force for a deflection of x mm.

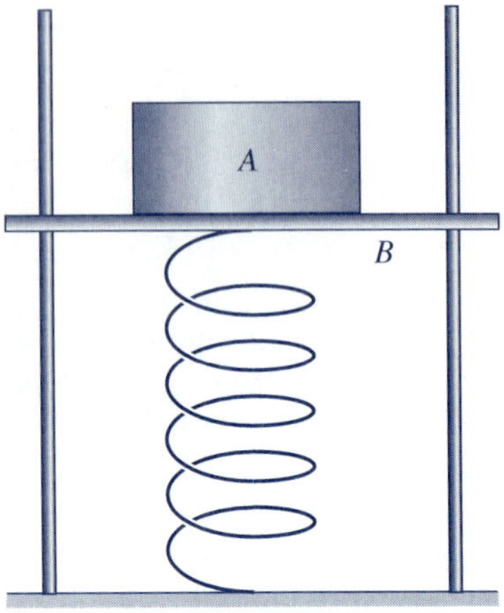

Figure 13.4. Preloaded nonlinear spring.

We take as the position of interest for the body the location δ below the initial configuration at which location the body A reaches zero velocity for the first time after having been released. The change in kinetic energy over the interval is accordingly zero. Thus, zero net work is done by the forces acting on the body A during displacement δ. These forces comprise the force of gravity, the friction force from the guides, and finally the force from the spring. Using as the origin for our measurements the *undeformed* top end position of the spring,[3] we can say:

$$\int_{10}^{(10+\delta)} \boldsymbol{F} \cdot d\boldsymbol{r} = \int_{10}^{(10+\delta)} \left(W_A - f - .5x^2\right) dx$$
$$= \int_{10}^{(10+\delta)} \left(100 - 5 - .5x^2\right) dx = 0 \quad \text{(a)}$$

Integrating, we get

$$95\delta - \frac{.5}{3}\left[(10+\delta)^3 - 10^3\right] = 0 \quad \text{(b)}$$

Therefore,

$$\delta^3 + 30\delta^2 - 270\delta = 0 \quad \text{(c)}$$

One solution to Eq. (c) is $\delta = 0$. Clearly, no work is done if there is no deflection. But this solution has no meaning for this problem since the force in the spring is only $.5x^2 = .5(10)^2 = 50$ N, when the weight of 100 N is released. Therefore, there must be a nonzero positive value of δ that satisfies the equation and has physical meaning. Factoring out one δ from the equation, we then set the resulting quadratic expression equal to zero. Two roots result and the positive root $\delta = 7.25$ mm is the one with physical meaning.

$$\delta = 7.25 \text{ mm}$$

[3]Since the force in the spring is a function of the elongation of the spring from its *undeformed* geometry, we must put the origin of our reference at a position corresponding to the undeformed geometry. At this position, both x and the spring force are zero simultaneously.

In the following example we deal with two bodies which can be considered as particles, rather than with one body as has been the case in the previous examples. We shall deal with these bodies separately in this example. Later in the chapter, we shall consider *systems* of particles, and in that context we will be able to consider this problem as a system of particles with less work needed to reach a solution.

Example 13.3

In Fig. 13.5, we have shown bodies A and B interconnected through a block and pulley system. Body B has a mass of 100 kg, whereas body A has a mass of 900 kg. Initially the system is stationary with B held at rest. What speed will B have when it reaches the ground at a distance $h = 3$ m below after being released? What will be the corresponding speed of A? Neglect the masses of the pulleys and the rope. Consider the rope to be inextensible.

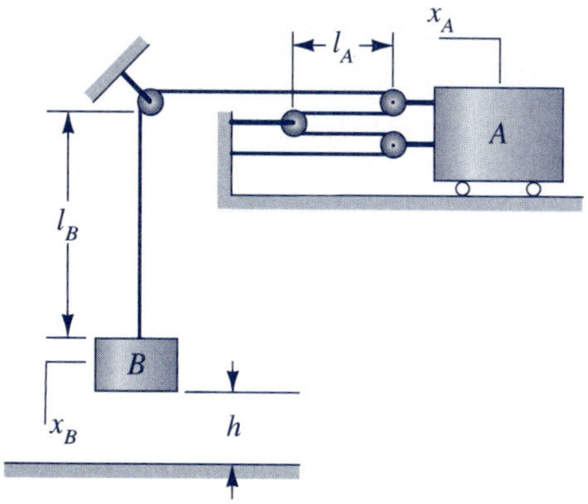

Figure 13.5. System of blocks and pulleys.

You will note from Fig. 13.5 that, as the bodies move, only the distances l_B and l_A change; the other distances involving the ropes do not change. And because the rope is taken as inextensible, we conclude that at all times

$$l_B + 4l_A = \text{constant} \tag{a}$$

Differentiating with respect to time, we can find that

$$\dot{l}_B + 4\dot{l}_A = 0$$

Therefore,

$$\dot{l}_B = -4\dot{l}_A \tag{b}$$

On inspecting Fig. 13.5, you should have no trouble in concluding that $\dot{l}_A = -V_A$ and that $\dot{l}_B = V_B$. Hence, from Eq. (b), we can conclude that

$$V_B = 4V_A \tag{c}$$

Next take the differential of Eq. (a):

$$dl_B + 4dl_A = 0$$

Therefore,

$$dl_B = -4dl_A \tag{d}$$

Example 13.3 (Continued)

Note that $dx_B = dl_B$ and that $dx_A = -dl_A$. Hence we see from Eq. (d) that a movement magnitude Δ_A of body A results in a movement magnitude, $4\Delta_A$, of body B:

$$\Delta_B = 4\Delta_A \tag{e}$$

With these kinematical conclusions as a background, we are now ready to proceed with the work–energy considerations.

For this purpose, we have shown a free-body diagram of body B in Fig. 13.6. The **work–energy equation** for body B can then be given as follows:

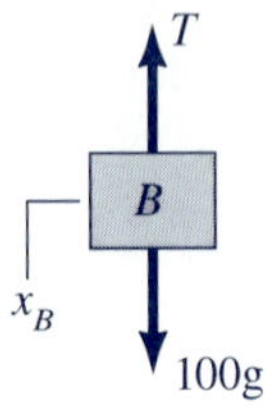

Figure 13.6. Free-body diagram of B.

$$(100g - T)h = \tfrac{1}{2}100V_B^2$$

Therefore,

$$(981 - T)(3) = \tfrac{1}{2}100V_B^2 \tag{f}$$

Now consider the free-body diagram of body A in Fig. 13.7. The **work–energy equation** for body A is then

$$(4T)(\Delta_A) = \tfrac{1}{2}900V_A^2 \tag{g}$$

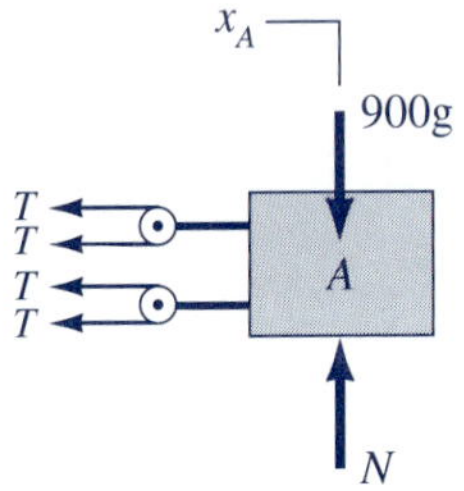

Figure 13.7. Free-body diagram of A.

But according to Eq. (e),

$$\Delta_A = \frac{\Delta_B}{4} = \frac{h}{4} = \frac{3}{4}\text{ m} \tag{h}$$

And according to Eq. (c),

$$V_A = \tfrac{1}{4}V_B \tag{i}$$

Substituting the results from Eqs. (h) and (i) into (g), we get

$$(4T)\left(\frac{3}{4}\right) = \frac{1}{2}900\left(\frac{V_B^2}{16}\right) \tag{j}$$

Example 13.3 (Continued)

Adding Eqs.(f) and (j), we can eliminate T to form the following equation with V_B as the only unknown:

$$(981)(3) = \tfrac{1}{2}(V_B^2)(100 + \tfrac{900}{16})$$

Therefore,

$$V_B = 6.14 \text{ m/sec downward}$$

Hence,

$$V_A = 1.534 \text{ m/sec to the left}$$

13.2 Power Considerations

The rate at which work is performed is called *power* and is a very useful concept for engineering purposes. Employing the notation $\mathcal{W}_k$ to represent work, we have

$$\text{power} = \frac{d\mathcal{W}_k}{dt} \qquad (13.4)$$

Since $d\mathcal{W}_k$ for any given force $\boldsymbol{F}_i$ is $\boldsymbol{F}_i \cdot d\boldsymbol{r}_i$, we can say that the power being developed by a system of n forces at time t is, for a reference xyz,

$$\text{power} = \frac{\sum_{i=1}^{n} \boldsymbol{F}_i \cdot d\boldsymbol{r}_i}{dt} = \sum_{i=1}^{n} \boldsymbol{F}_i \cdot \boldsymbol{V}_i \qquad (13.5)$$

where $\boldsymbol{V}_i$ is the velocity of the point of application of the ith force at time t as seen from reference xyz.[4]

In the following example we shall illustrate the use of the power concept. Note, however, that we shall find use of Newton's law advantageous in certain phases of the computation.

[4]We could have defined work $\mathcal{W}_k$ in terms of power as follows:

$$\mathcal{W}_k = \int_{t_1}^{t_2} (\boldsymbol{F} \cdot \boldsymbol{V})\, dt$$

When the force acts on a particular particle, the result above becomes the familiar $\int_{r_1}^{r_2} \boldsymbol{F} \cdot d\boldsymbol{r}$, where $\boldsymbol{r}$ is the position vector of the particle since $\boldsymbol{V}\, dt = d\boldsymbol{r}$. There are times when the force acts on *continuously changing* particles as time passes (see Section 13.8). The more general formulation above can then be used effectively.

Example 13.4

In hilly terrain, motors of an electric train are sometimes advantageously employed as brakes, particularly on downhill runs. This is accomplished by switching devices that change the electrical connections of the motors so as to correspond to connections for generators. This allows power developed during braking to be returned to the power source. In this way, we save much of the energy lost when employing conventional brakes—a considerable saving in every round trip. Such a train consisting of a single car is shown in Fig. 13.8 moving down a 15° incline at an initial speed of 3 m/sec. This car has a mass of 20,000 kg and has a cogwheel drive. If the conductor maintains an adjustment of the fields in his generators so as to develop a constant power *output* of 50 kW, how long does it take before the car moves at the rate of 5 m/sec? Neglect the wind resistance and rotational effects of the wheels. The efficiency of the generators is 90%.

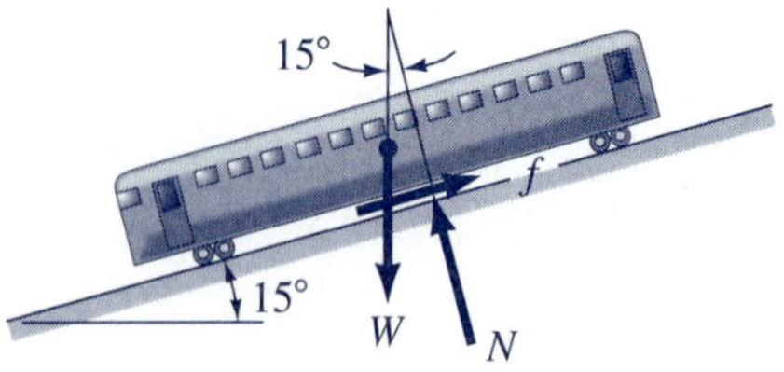

Figure 13.8. Train moving downhill with generators acting as brakes.

We have shown all the forces acting on the car in the diagram. **Newton's law** along the direction of the incline can be given as

$$W \sin 15° - f = M \frac{dV}{dt} \tag{a}$$

where f is the traction force from the rails developed by the generator action. Multiplying by V to get power, we get

$$W \sin 15° \, V - fV = MV \frac{dV}{dt} \tag{b}$$

If the efficiency of the generators (i.e., the power output divided by the power input) is .90, we can compute fV, which is the power input to the generators from the wheels, in the following manner:

$$\frac{\text{generator output}}{.90} = fV \tag{c}$$

Example 13.4 (Continued)

Hence,

$$fV = \frac{(50)(1{,}000)}{.90} = 55{,}560 \text{ W} \qquad \text{(d)}$$

Equation (b) can now be given as[5]

$$(20{,}000)(9.81)(.259)V - 55{,}560 = 20{,}000\, V\frac{dV}{dt}$$

Therefore,

$$2.54V - 2.78 = V\frac{dV}{dt} \qquad \text{(e)}$$

We can separate the variables as follows:

$$dt = \frac{V\,dV}{2.54V - 2.78} \qquad \text{(f)}$$

Integrating, using formula 1 in Appendix I, we get

$$t = \frac{1}{2.54^2}\left[2.54V - 2.78 + 2.78\ln(2.54V - 2.78)\right] + C \qquad \text{(g)}$$

To get the constant of integration C, note that when $t = 0$, $V = 3$ m/sec. Hence,

$$0 = \frac{1}{2.54^2}\left\{(2.54)(3) - 2.78 + 2.78\ln\left[(2.54)(3) - 2.78\right]\right\} + C$$

Therefore,

$$C = -1.430$$

We thus have for Eq. (g):

$$t = \frac{1}{2.54^2}\left[2.54V - 2.78 + 2.78\ln(2.54V - 2.78)\right] - 1.430$$

When $V = 5$ m/sec, we get for the desired value of t:

$$t = \frac{1}{2.54^2}\left\{(2.54)(5) - 2.78 + 2.78\ln\left[(2.54)(5) - 2.78\right]\right\} - 1.430$$

$$t = 1.0963 \text{ sec}$$

[5]One watt (W) is 1 J/sec, where J ≡ joule, which in turn is 1 N-m.

PROBLEMS

13.1. What value of constant force P is required to bring the 100-lb body, which starts from rest, to a velocity of 30 ft/sec in 20 ft? Neglect friction.

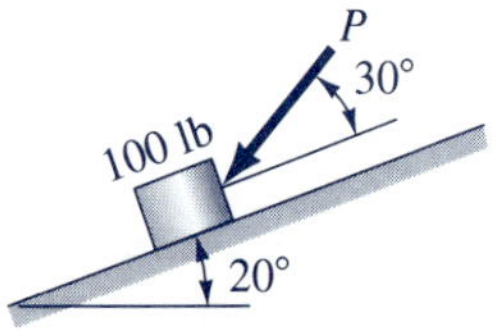

Figure P.13.1.

13.2. A light cable passes over a frictionless pulley. Determine the velocity of the 100-lb block after it has moved 30 ft from rest. Neglect the inertia of the pulley. The dynamic coefficient of friction between block and incline is 0.2

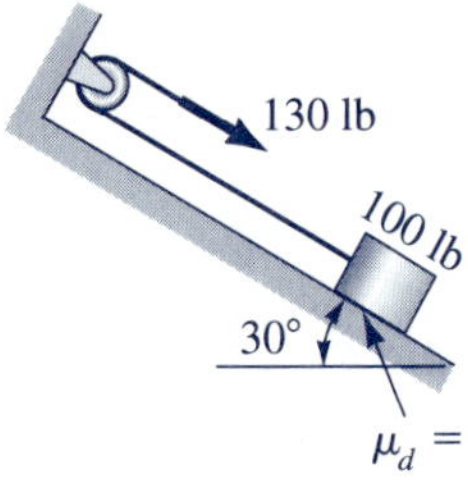

Figure P.13.2.

13.3. In Problem 13.2, the pulley has a radius of 1 ft and has a resisting torque at the bearing of 10 lb-ft. Neglect the inertia of the pulley and the mass of the cable. Compute the kinetic energy of the 100-lb block after it has moved 30 ft from rest.

13.4. A light cable is wrapped around two drums fixed between a pair of blocks. The system has a mass of 50 kg. If a 250-N tension is exerted on the free end of the cable, what is the velocity change of the system after 3 m of travel down the incline? The body starts from rest. Take μ_d for all surfaces as .05.

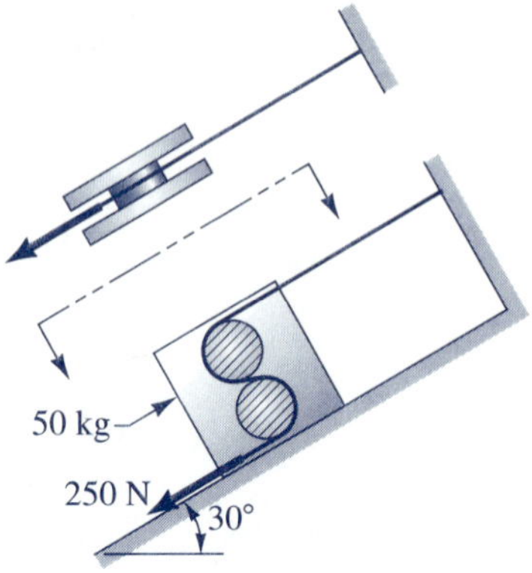

Figure P.13.4.

13.5. A 50-kg mass on a spring is moved so that it extends the spring 50 mm from its unextended position. If the dynamic coefficient of friction between the mass and the supporting surface is .3,

(a) What is the velocity of the mass as it returns to the undeformed configuration of the spring?

(b) How far will the spring be compressed when the mass stops instantaneously before starting to the left?

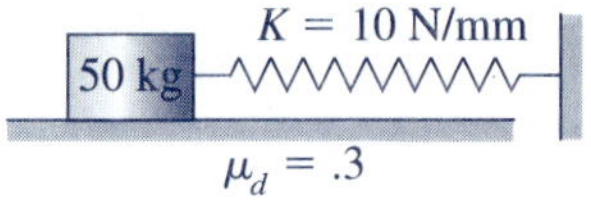

Figure P.13.5.

13.6. A truck–trailer is shown carrying three crushed junk automobile cubes each weighing 2,500 lb. An electromagnet is used to pick up the cubes as the truck moves by. Suppose the truck starts at position 1 by applying a constant 600 in.-lb total torque on the drive wheels. The magnet picks up only one cube C during the process. What will the velocity of the truck be when it has moved a total of 100 ft? The truck unloaded weighs 5,000 lb and has a tire diameter of 18 in. Neglect the rotational effects of the tires and wind friction.

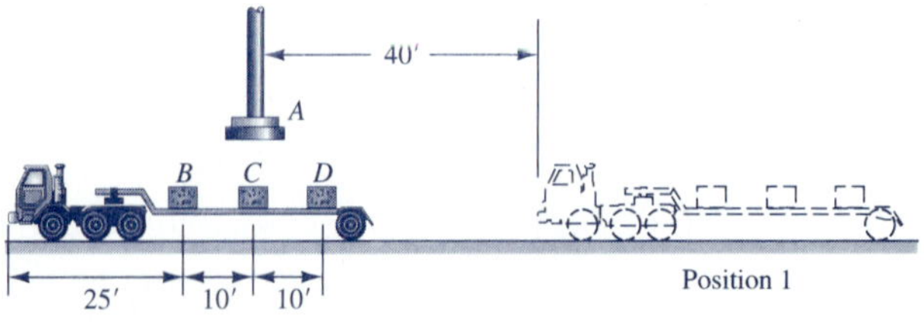

Figure P.13.6.

13.7. Do Problem 13.6 if the first cube B and the last cube D are removed as they go by the magnet.

13.8. A passenger ferry is shown moving into its dock to unload passengers. As it approaches the dock, it has a speed of 3 knots (1 knot = .563 m/sec). If the pilot reverses his engines just as the front of the ferry comes abreast of the first pilings at A, what constant reverse thrust will stop the ferry just as it reaches the ramp B? The ferry weighs 4,450 kN. Assume that the ferry does not hit the side pilings and undergoes no resistance from them. Neglect the drag of the water.

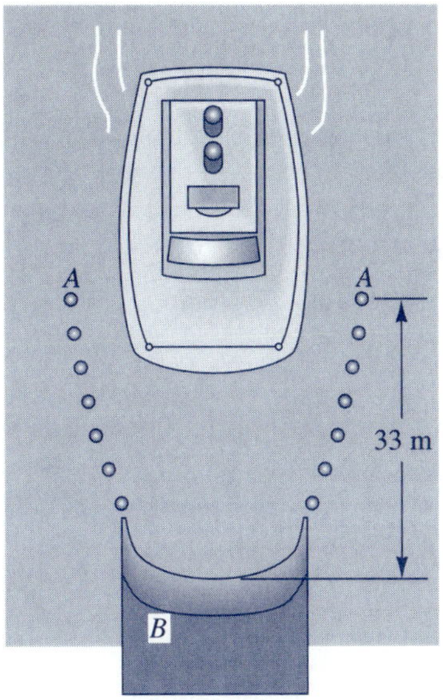

Figure P.13.8.

13.9. Do Problem 13.8 assuming that the ferry rubs against the pilings as a result of a poor entrance and undergoes a resistance against its forward motion given as

$$f = 9(x + 50)\text{ N}$$

where x is measured in meters from the first pilings at A to the front of the ferry.

13.10. A freight car weighing 90 kN is rolling at a speed of 1.7 m/sec toward a spring-stop system. If the spring is nonlinear such that it develops a $.0450x^2$-kN force for a deflection of x mm, what is the maximum deceleration that the car A undergoes?

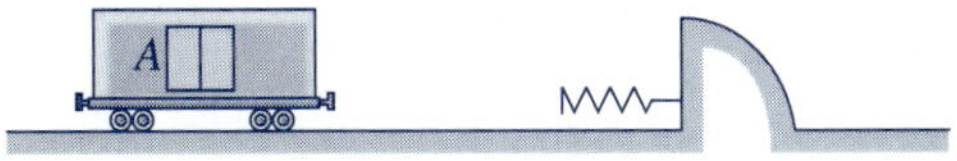

Figure P.13.10.

13.11. A 1,000 N force is applied to a 3,000-N block at the position shown. What is the speed of the block after it moves 2 m? There is Coulomb friction present. Assume at all times that the pressure at the bottom of the block is uniform. Neglect the height of the block in your calculations. Roller at right end moves with the block.

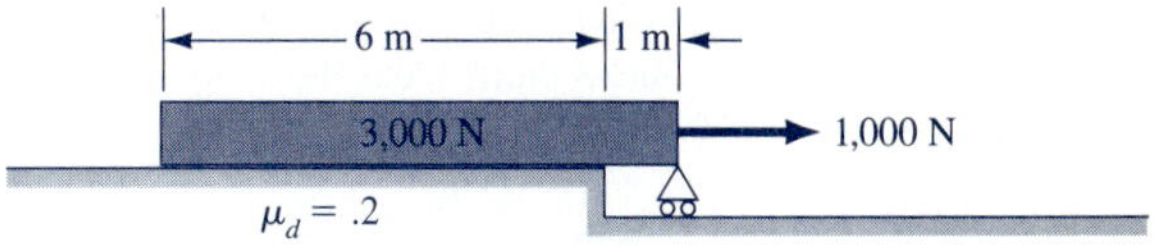

Figure P.13.11.

13.12. Two blocks A and B are connected by an inextensible chord running over a frictionless and massless pulley at E. The system starts from rest. What is the velocity of the system after it has moved 3 ft? The coefficient of dynamic friction μ_d equals .22 for bodies A and B.

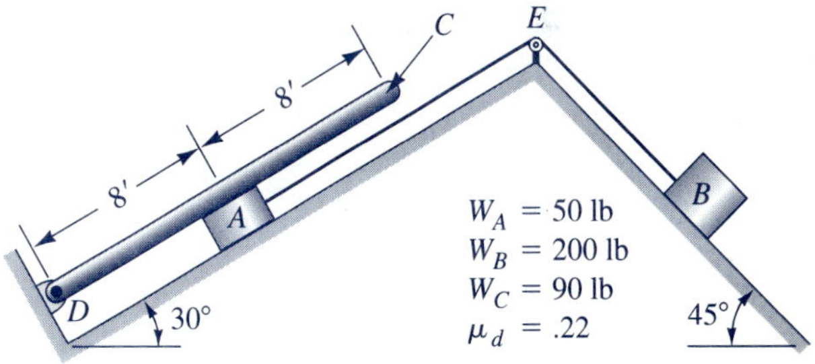

Figure P.13.12.

13.13. What are the velocities of blocks A and B when, after starting from rest, block B moves a distance of .3 ft? The dynamic coefficient of friction is .2 at all surfaces.

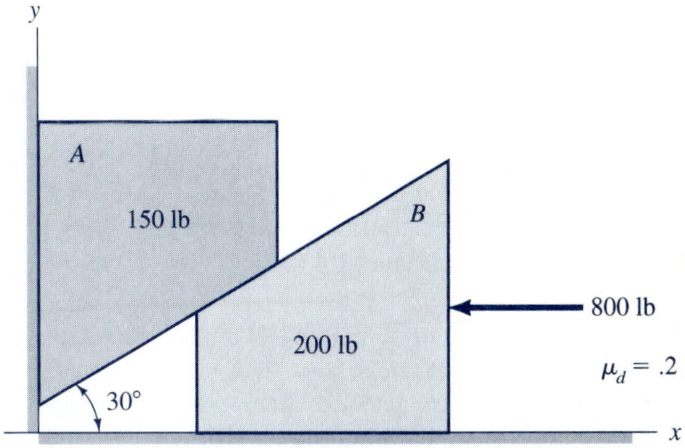

Figure P.13.13.

13.14. A particle of mass 10 lbm is acted on by the following force field:

$$\boldsymbol{F} = 5x\boldsymbol{i} + (16 + 2y)\boldsymbol{j} + 20\boldsymbol{k} \text{ lb}$$

When it is at the origin, the particle has a velocity V_0 given as

$$V_0 = 5\boldsymbol{i} + 10\boldsymbol{j} + 8\boldsymbol{k} \text{ ft/sec}$$

What is its kinetic energy when it reaches position (20, 5, 10) while moving along a frictionless path? Does the shape of the path between the origin and (20, 5, 10) affect the result?

13.15. A plate *AA* is held down by screws *C* and *D* so that a force of 245 N is developed in each spring. Mass *M* of 100 kg is placed on plate *AA* and released suddenly. What is the maximum distance that plate *AA* descends if the plate can slide freely down the vertical guide rods? Take $K = 3{,}600$ N/m.

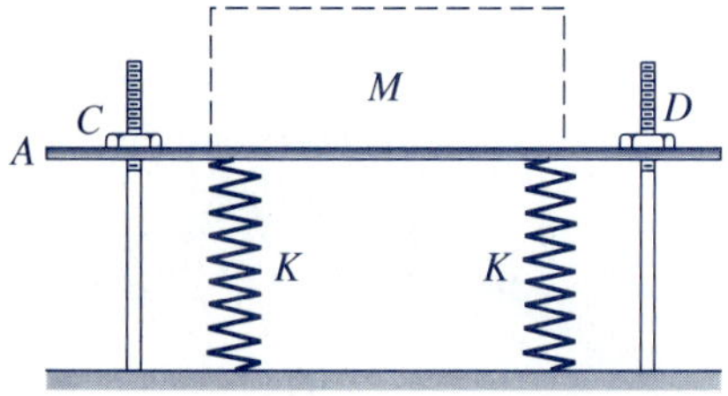

Figure P.13.15.

13.16. A 200-lb block is dropped on the system of springs. If $K_1 = 600$ lb/ft and $K_2 = 200$ lb/ft, what is the maximum force developed on the body?

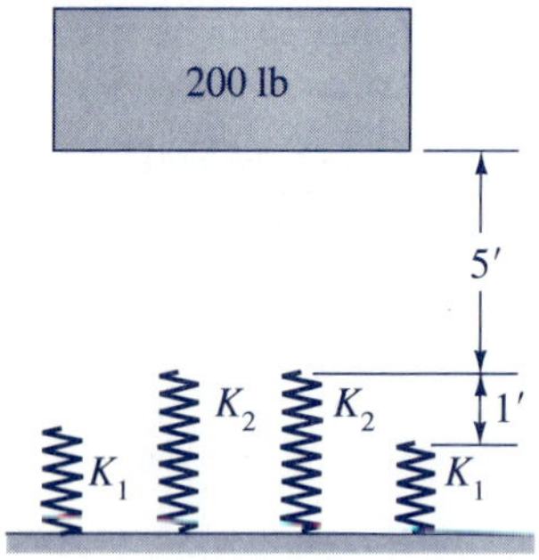

Figure P.13.16.

13.17. A block weighing 50 lb is shown on an inclined surface. The block is released at the position shown at a rest condition. What is the maximum compression of the spring? The spring has a spring constant *K* of 10 lb/in., and the dynamic coefficient of friction between the block and the incline is .3.

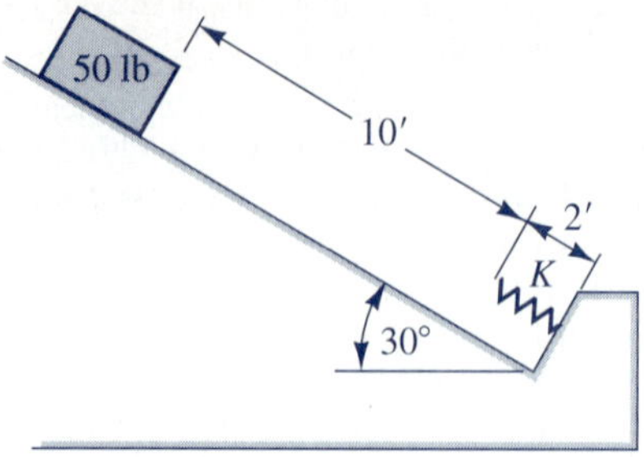

Figure P.13.17.

13.18. A classroom demonstration unit is used to illustrate vibrations and interactions of bodies. Body *A* has a mass of .5 kg and is moving to the left at a speed of 1.6 m/sec at the position indicated. The body rides on a cushion of air supplied from the tube *B* through small openings in the tube. If there is a constant friction force of .1 N, what speed will *A* have when it returns to the position shown in the diagram? There are two springs at *C*, each having a spring constant of 15 N/m.

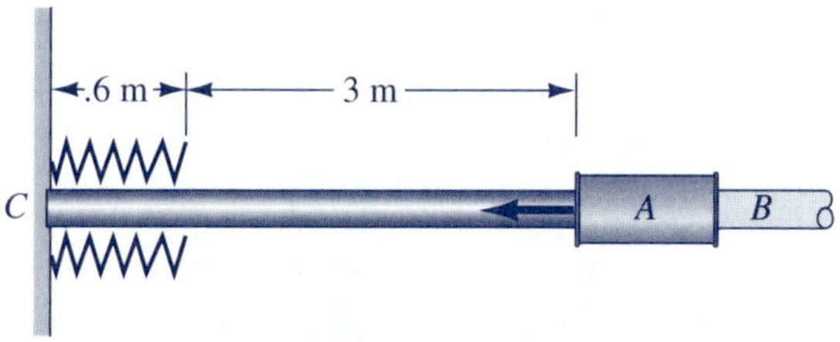

Figure P.13.18.

13.19. An electron moves in a circular orbit in a plane at right angles to the direction of a uniform magnetic field *B*. If the strength of *B* is slowly changed so that the radius of the orbit is halved, what is the ratio of the final to the initial angular speed of the electron? Explain the steps you take. The force $\boldsymbol{F}$ on a charged particle is $q\boldsymbol{V} \times \boldsymbol{B}$, where q is the charge and $\boldsymbol{V}$ is the velocity of the particle.

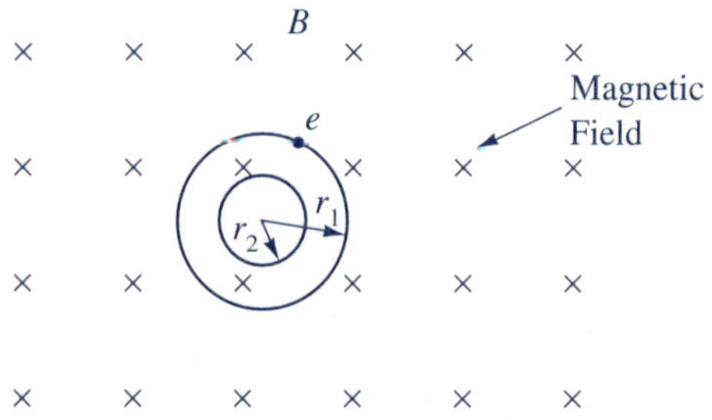

Figure P.13.19.

13.20. A light rod CD rotates about pin C under the action of constant torque T of 1,000 N-m. Body A having a mass of 100 kg slides on the horizontal surface for which the dynamic coefficient of friction is .4. If rod CD starts from rest, what angular speed is attained in one complete revolution? The entire weight of A is borne by the horizontal surface.

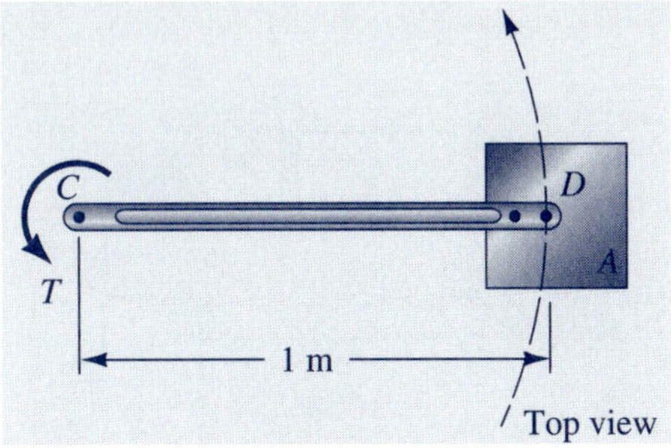

Figure P.13.20.

13.21. An astronaut is attached to his orbiting space laboratory by a light wire. The astronaut is propelled by a small attached compressed air device. The propulsive force is in the direction of the man's height from foot to head. When the wire is extended its full length of 20 ft, the propulsion system is started, giving the astronaut a steady push of 5 lb. If this push is at right angles to the wire at all times, what speed will the astronaut have in one revolution about A? The weight on earth of the astronaut plus equipment is 250 lb. The mass of the laboratory is large compared to that of the man and his equipment.

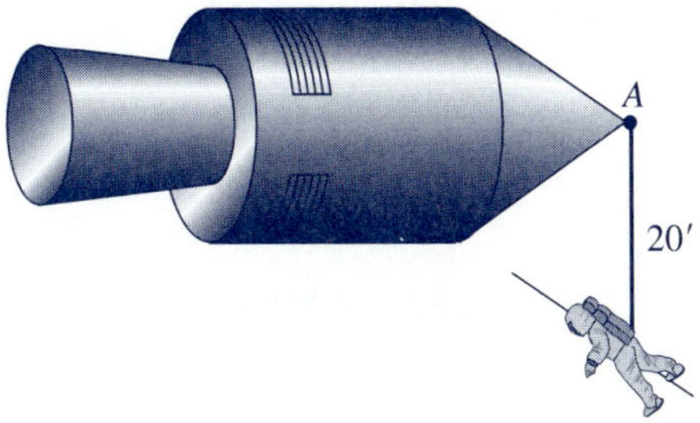

Figure P.13.21.

13.22. Body A, having a mass of 100 kg, is connected to body B by an inextensible light cable. Body B has a mass of 80 kg and is on small wheels. The dynamic coefficient of friction between A and the horizontal surface is .2. If the system is released from rest, how far d must B move along the incline before reaching a speed of 2 m/sec?

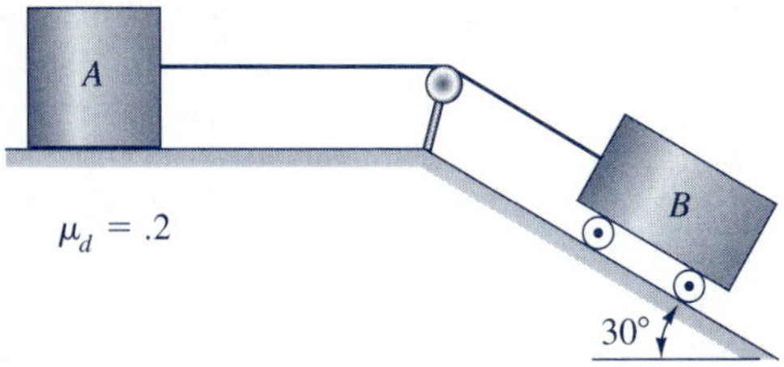

Figure P.13.22.

13.23. A conveyor has drum D driven by a torque of 50 ft-lb. Bodies A and B on the conveyor each weigh 30 lb. The dynamic coefficient of friction between the conveyor belt and the conveyor bed is .2. If the conveyor starts from rest, how fast along the conveyor do A and B move after traveling 2 ft? Drum C rotates freely, and the tension in the belt on the underside of the conveyor is 20 lb. The diameter of both drums is 1 ft. Neglect the mass of drums and belt. A and B do not slip on belt.

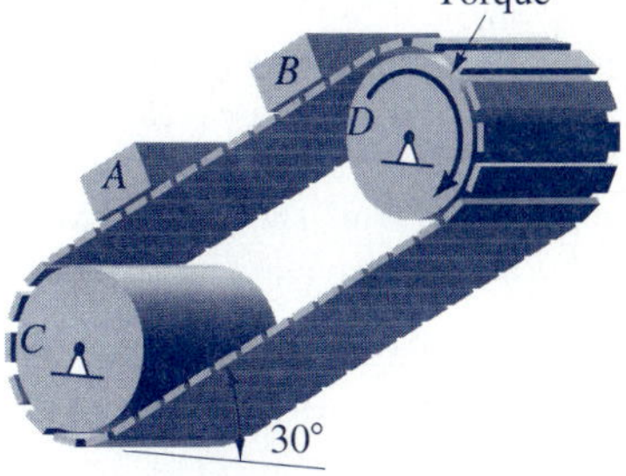

Figure P.13.23.

13.24. Bodies A and B are connected to each other through two light pulleys. Body A has a mass of 500 kg, whereas body B has a mass of 200 kg. A constant force F of value 10,000 N is applied to body A whose surface of contact has a dynamic coefficient of friction equal to .4. If the system starts from rest, what distance d does B ascend before it has a speed of 2 m/sec? [*Hint:* Considering pulley E, we have instantaneous rotation about point e. Hence, $V_b = \frac{1}{2}V_c$.]

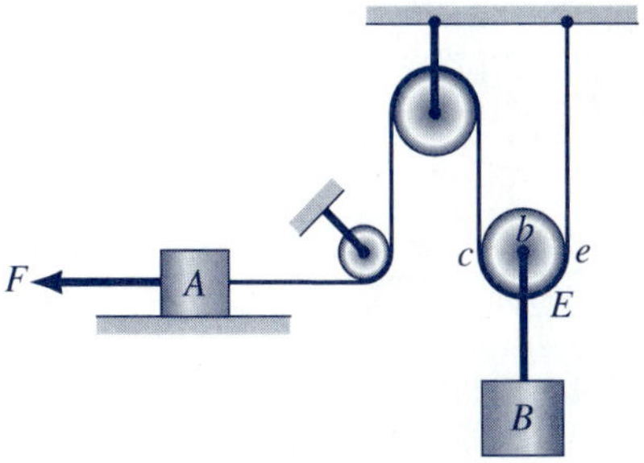

Figure P.13.24.

13.25. A rope tow for skiers is shown pulling 20 skiers up a 20° incline. The driving pulley A has a diameter of 5 ft. The idler pulley B rotates freely. The system has been stopped to allow a fallen skier to untangle himself. The driving pulley starts from rest and is given a torque of 5,000 ft-lb. With this torque, what distance d do skiers move before their speed is 15 ft/sec? The tension on the slack side of the tow can be taken as zero. The coefficient of friction between skis and slope is .15 and the average weight of the skiers is 150 lb. Neglect the mass of the rope and the pulleys.

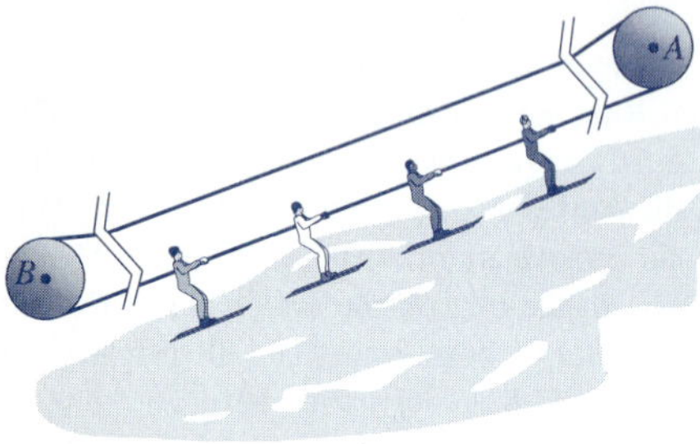

Figure P.13.25.

13.26. A uniform block A has a mass of 25 kg. The block is hinged at C and is supported by a small block B as shown in the diagram. A constant force F of 400 N is applied to block B. What is the speed of B after it moves 1.6 m? The mass of block B is 2.5 kg and the dynamic coefficient of friction for all contact surfaces is .3.

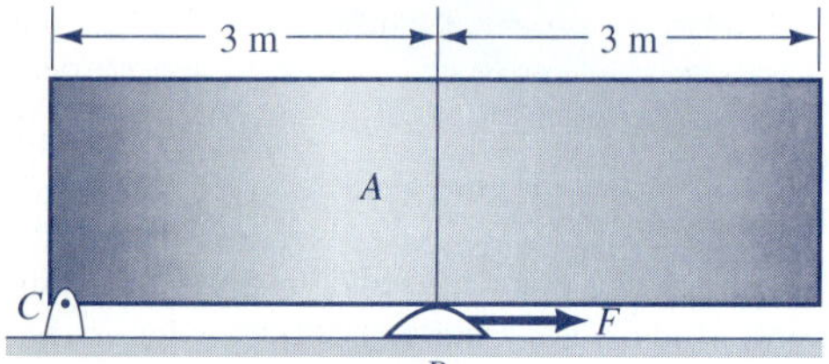

Figure P.13.26.

13.27. Block A weighs 200 lb and block B weighs 150 lb. If the system starts from rest, what is the speed of block B after it moves 1 ft? Neglect the weight of the pulleys.

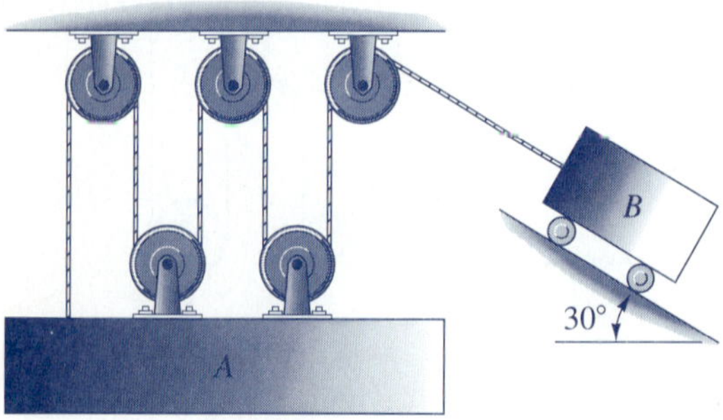

Figure P.13.27.

13.28. A weight W is to be lowered by a man. He lets the rope slip through his hands while maintaining a tension of 130 N on the rope. What is the maximum weight W that he can handle if the weight is not to exceed a speed of 5 m/sec starting from rest and dropping 3 m? Use the coefficients of friction shown in the diagram. Neglect the mass of the rope. There are three wraps of rope around the post.

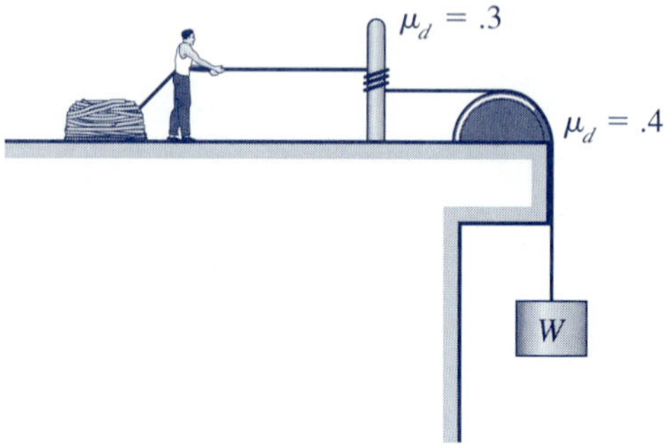

Figure P.13.28.

13.29. A vehicle B is being let down a 30° incline. The vehicle is attached to a weight A that restrains the motion. Vehicle B weighs 2,000 lb. What should the minimum restraining weight A be if, after starting from rest, the system does not exceed 8 ft/sec after moving 10 ft? There are two wraps around the post.

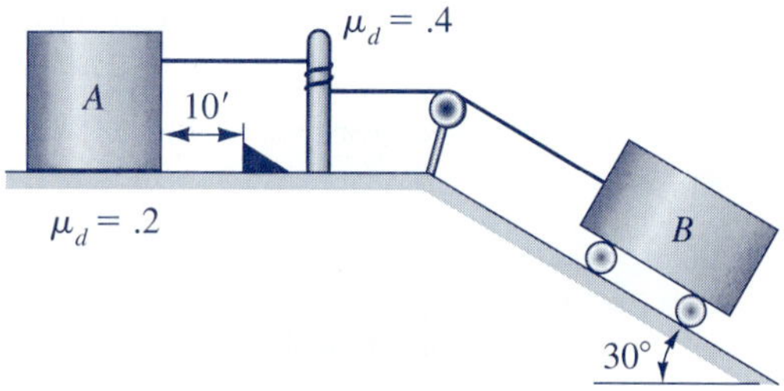

Figure P.13.29.

***13.30.** A spiral path is given parametrically in terms of the parameter τ as follows:

$$x_p = A \sin \eta\tau \text{ ft}$$
$$y_p = A \cos \eta\tau \text{ ft}$$
$$z_p = C\tau \text{ ft}$$

where A, η, and C are known constants. A particle P of mass 1 lbm is released from a position of rest 1 ft above the xy plane. The particle is constrained by a spring ($K = 2$ lb/ft) coiled around the path. The spring is unstretched when P is released. Neglect friction and find how far P drops. Take $\eta = \pi/2$, $A = C = 1$.

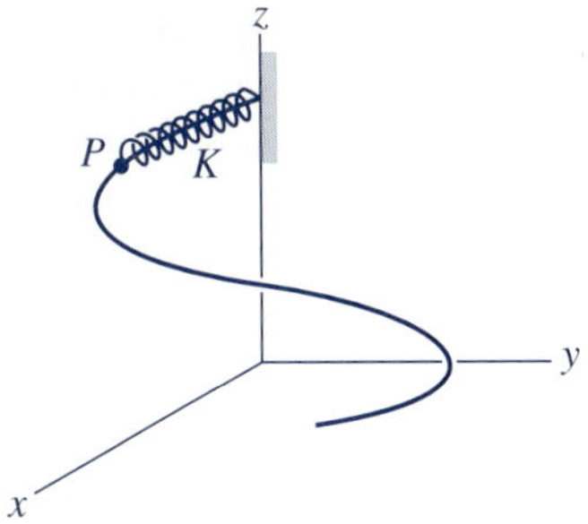

Figure P.13.30.

13.31. A body A of mass 1 lbm is moving at time $t = 0$ with a speed V of 1 ft/sec on a smooth cylinder as shown. What is the speed of the body when it arrives at B? Take $r = 2$ ft.

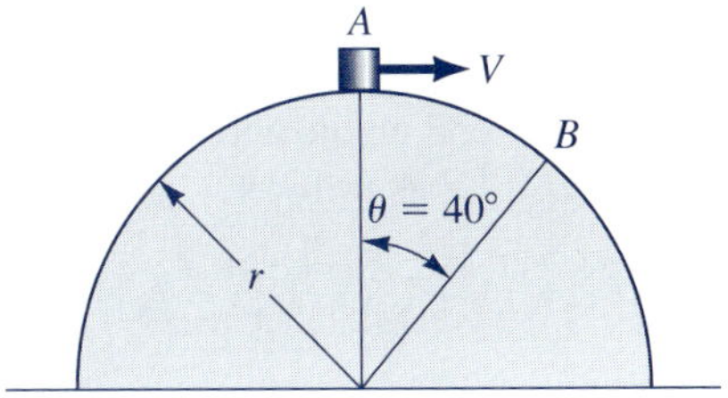

Figure P.13.31.

13.32. An automobile engine under test is rotating at 4,400 rpm and develops a torque of 40 N-m. What is the horsepower developed by the engine? If the system has a mechanical efficiency of .90, what is the kilowatt output of the generator? [*Hint:* The work of a torque equals the torque times the angle of rotation in radians.]

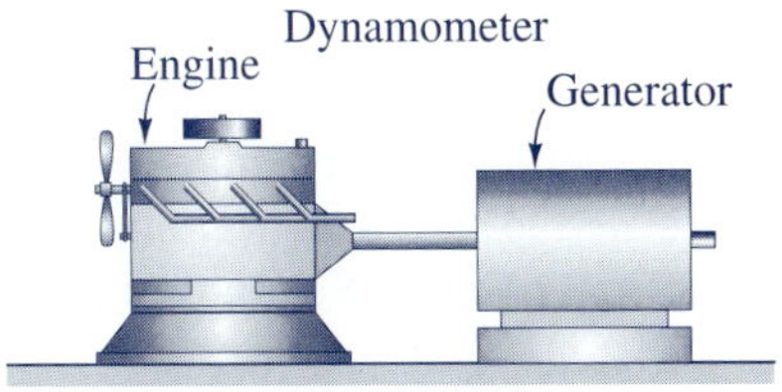

Figure P.13.32.

13.33. A rocket is undergoing static thrust tests in a test stand. A thrust of 300,000 lb is developed while 300 gal of fuel (specific gravity .8) is burned per second. The exhaust products of combustion have a speed of 5,000 ft/sec relative to the rocket. What power is being developed on the rocket? What is the power developed on the exhaust gases? (1 gal = .1337 ft^3.)

13.34. A 15-ton streetcar accelerates from rest at a constant rate a_0 until it reaches a speed V_1, at which time there is zero acceleration. The wind resistance is given as κV^2. Formulate expressions for power developed for the stated ranges of operation.

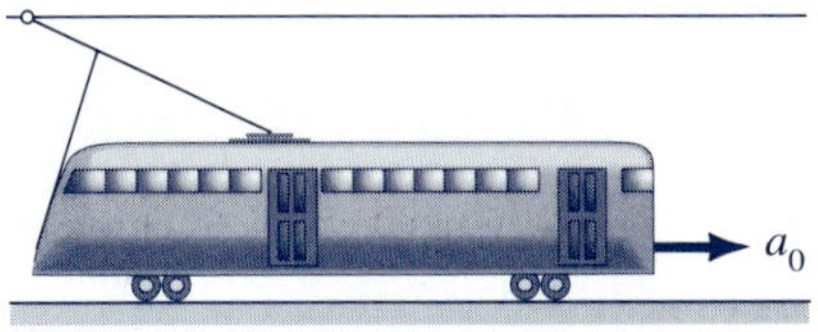

Figure P.13.34.

13.35. What is the maximum horsepower that can be developed on a streetcar weighing 133.5 kN? The car has a coefficient of static friction of .20 between wheels and rail and a drag given as $32V^2$ N, where V is in m/sec. All wheels are drive wheels.

13.36. A 7,500-kg streetcar starts from rest when the conductor draws 5 kW of power from the line. If this input is maintained constant and if the mechanical efficiency of the motors is 90%, how long does the streetcar take to reach a speed of 10 km/hr? Neglect wind resistance. (1 kW = 1.341 hp.)

13.37. A children's boat ride can be found in many amusement parks. Small boats each weighing 100 lb are rotated in a tank of water. If the system is rotating with a speed $\dot{\theta}$ of 10 rpm, what is the kinetic energy of the system? Assume that each boat has two 60-lb children on board and that the kinetic energy of the supporting structure can be accounted for by "lumping" an additional 30 lbm into each boat. If a wattmeter indicates that 4 kW of power is being absorbed by the motor turning the system, what is the drag for each boat? Take the mechanical efficiency of the motor to be 80% (1 kW = 1.341 hp.)

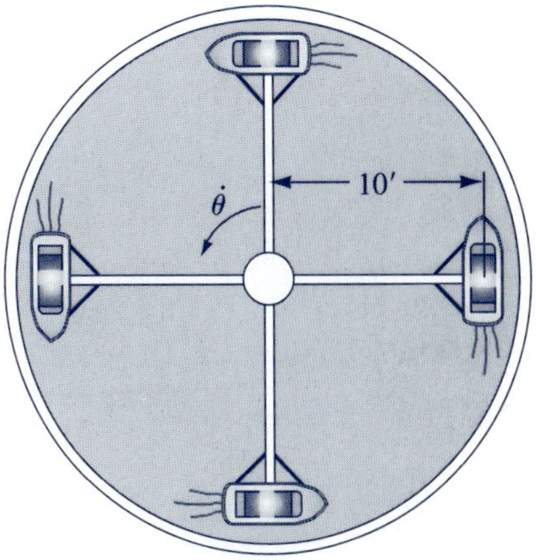

Figure P.13.37.

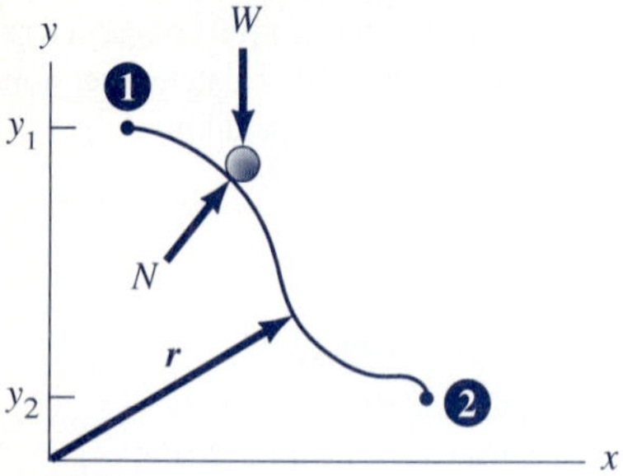

Figure 13.9. Particle moving along frictionless path.

13.3 Conservative Force Fields

In Section 10.6 we discussed an important class of forces called conservative forces. For convenience, we shall now repeat this discussion.

Consider first a body acted on only by gravity W as an active force (i.e., a force that can do work) and moving along a frictionless path from position 1 to position 2, as shown in Fig. 13.9. The work done by gravity $\mathcal{W}_{1-2}$ is then

$$\begin{aligned}\mathcal{W}_{1-2} &= \int_1^2 \boldsymbol{F} \cdot d\boldsymbol{r} = \int_1^2 (-W\boldsymbol{j}) \cdot d\boldsymbol{r} = -W\int_1^2 dy \\ &= -W(y_2 - y_1) = W(y_1 - y_2)\end{aligned} \tag{13.6}$$

Note that the work done *does not depend* on the path, but depends only on the positions of the end points of the path. *Force fields whose work like gravity is independent of the path are called conservative force fields.* In general, we can say for conservative force field $\boldsymbol{F}(x, y, z)$ that, along any path between positions 1 and 2, the work is

$$\mathcal{W}_{1-2} = \int_1^2 \boldsymbol{F} \cdot d\boldsymbol{r} = \mathcal{V}_1(x, y, z) - \mathcal{V}_2(x, y, z) \tag{13.7}$$

where $\mathcal{V}$ is a function of position of the end points and is called the *potential energy function.*[6] We may rewrite Eq. 13.7 as follows:

$$-\int_1^2 \boldsymbol{F} \cdot d\boldsymbol{r} = \mathcal{V}_2(x, y, z) - \mathcal{V}_1(x, y, z) = \Delta\mathcal{V} \tag{13.8}$$

Note that the potential energy, $\mathcal{V}(x, y, z)$, depends on the reference xyz used or, as we shall often say, the *datum* used. However, the *change* in potential energy, $\Delta\mathcal{V}$, is *independent* of the datum used.[7] Since we shall be using the change in potential energy, the datum is arbitrary and is chosen for convenience. From Eq. 13.8, we can say that *the change in potential energy,* $\Delta\mathcal{V}$ $(= \mathcal{V}_2 - \mathcal{V}_1)$, of a conservative force field is *the negative of the work done by this conservative force field on a particle in going from position 1 to position 2 along any path.* For any *closed* path, clearly the work done by a conservative force field $\boldsymbol{F}$ is then

$$\oint \boldsymbol{F} \cdot d\boldsymbol{r} = 0 \tag{13.9}$$

Hence, this is a second way to define a conservative force field. How is the potential energy function $\mathcal{V}$ related to $\boldsymbol{F}$? To answer this query, consider that an infinitesimal path $d\boldsymbol{r}$ starts from point 1. We can then give Eq. 13.8 as

$$\boldsymbol{F} \cdot d\boldsymbol{r} = -d\mathcal{V} \tag{13.10}$$

[6]We shall also use the notation P.E. or simply PE for $\mathcal{V}$. Note that we used V for potential energy in Statics as is common practice. Here in Dynamics we have switched to $\mathcal{V}$ to avoid confusion with V the velocity.

[7]Thus, considering Eq. 13.6, the value of y itself for a particle at any time depends on the position of the origin O of the xyz reference. However, changing the position of O but keeping the same direction of the xyz axes (i.e., *changing the datum*) does not affect the value of $y_2 - y_1$.

Expressing the dot product on the left side in terms of components, and expressing $d\mathcal{V}$ as a total differential, we get

$$F_x\,dx + F_y\,dy + F_z\,dz = -\left(\frac{\partial \mathcal{V}}{\partial x}dx + \frac{\partial \mathcal{V}}{\partial y}dy + \frac{\partial \mathcal{V}}{\partial z}dz\right) \tag{13.11}$$

We can conclude from this equation that

$$\begin{aligned} F_x &= -\frac{\partial \mathcal{V}}{\partial x} \\ F_y &= -\frac{\partial \mathcal{V}}{\partial y} \\ F_z &= -\frac{\partial \mathcal{V}}{\partial z} \end{aligned} \tag{13.12}$$

In other words,

$$\begin{aligned} \boldsymbol{F} &= -\left(\frac{\partial \mathcal{V}}{\partial x}\boldsymbol{i} + \frac{\partial \mathcal{V}}{\partial y}\boldsymbol{j} + \frac{\partial \mathcal{V}}{\partial z}\boldsymbol{k}\right) \\ &= -\left(\frac{\partial}{\partial x}\boldsymbol{i} + \frac{\partial}{\partial y}\boldsymbol{j} + \frac{\partial}{\partial z}\boldsymbol{k}\right)\mathcal{V} \\ &= -\textbf{grad}\ \mathcal{V} = -\boldsymbol{\nabla}\mathcal{V} \end{aligned} \tag{13.13}$$

The operator **grad** or $\boldsymbol{\nabla}$ that we have introduced is called the *gradient* operator[8] and is given as follows for rectangular coordinates:

$$\textbf{grad} \equiv \boldsymbol{\nabla} \equiv \left(\frac{\partial}{\partial x}\boldsymbol{i} + \frac{\partial}{\partial y}\boldsymbol{j} + \frac{\partial}{\partial z}\boldsymbol{k}\right) \tag{13.14}$$

We can now say as a third definition that a *conservative force field must be a function of position and expressible as the gradient of a scalar function.* The *inverse* to this statement is also valid. That is, *if a force field is a function of position and the gradient of a scalar field, it must then be a conservative force field.*

Two examples of conservative force fields will now be presented and discussed.

Constant Force Field. If the force field is constant at all positions, it can always be expressed as the gradient of a scalar function of the form $\mathcal{V} = -(ax + by + cz)$, where a, b, and c are constants. The constant force field, then, is $\boldsymbol{F} = a\boldsymbol{i} + b\boldsymbol{j} + c\boldsymbol{k}$.

In limited changes of position near the earth's surface (a common situation), we can consider the gravitational force on a particle of mass, m, as a

[8]The gradient operator comes up in many situations in engineering and physics. In short, the gradient represents a *driving action.* Thus, in the present case, the gradient is a driving action to cause mass to move. And, the gradient of temperature causes heat to flow. Finally, the gradient of electric potential causes electric charge to flow.

constant force field given by $-mg\boldsymbol{k}$ (or $-W\boldsymbol{k}$). Thus, the constants for the general force field given above are $a = b = 0$ and $c = -mg$. Clearly, $\text{PE} = mgz$ for this case.

Force Proportional to Linear Displacements. Consider a body limited by constraints to move along a straight line. Along this line is developed a force directly proportional to the displacement of the body from some position O at $x = 0$ along the line. Furthermore, this force is always directed toward point O; it is then termed a *restoring* force. We can give this force as

$$\boldsymbol{F} = -Kx\boldsymbol{i} \tag{13.15}$$

where x is the displacement from point O. An example of this force is that of the linear spring (Fig.13.10) discussed in Section 12.3. The potential energy of this force field is given as follows wherein x is measured from the **undeformed** geometry (don't forget this important factor) of the spring:

$$\text{PE} = \frac{Kx^2}{2} \tag{13.16}$$

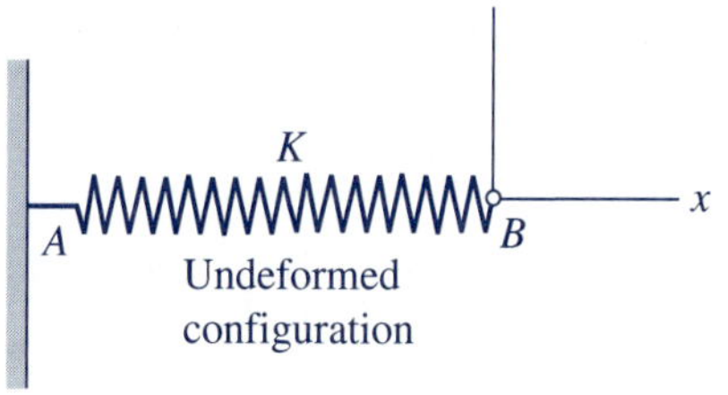

Figure 13.10. Linear spring.

What is the physical meaning of the term PE? Note that the change in potential energy has been defined (see Eq. 13.8) as the *negative* of the work done by a conservative force as the particle on which it acts goes from one position to another. Clearly, the change in the potential energy is then *directly equal* to the work done by the *reaction* to the conservative force during this displacement. In the case of the *spring*, the reaction force would be the force *from* the surroundings acting *on* the spring at point B (Fig. 13.10). During extension or compression of the spring from the undeformed position, this force (from the surroundings) does a *positive* amount of work. This work can be considered as a measure of the energy *stored* in the spring. Why? Because when allowed to return to its original position, the spring will do this amount of positive work on the surroundings at B, provided that the return motion is slow enough to prevent oscillations; and so on. Clearly then, since PE equals work of the surroundings on the spring, then PE is in effect the stored energy in the spring. In a general case, PE is the energy stored in the force field as measured from a given datum.

In previous chapters, several additional force fields were introduced: the gravitational central force field, the electrostatic field, and the magnetic field. Let us see which we can add to our list of conservative force fields.

Consider first the central gravitational force field where particle m, shown in Fig. 13.11, experiences a force given by the equation

$$\boldsymbol{F} = -G\frac{Mm}{r^2}\hat{\boldsymbol{r}} \tag{13.17}$$

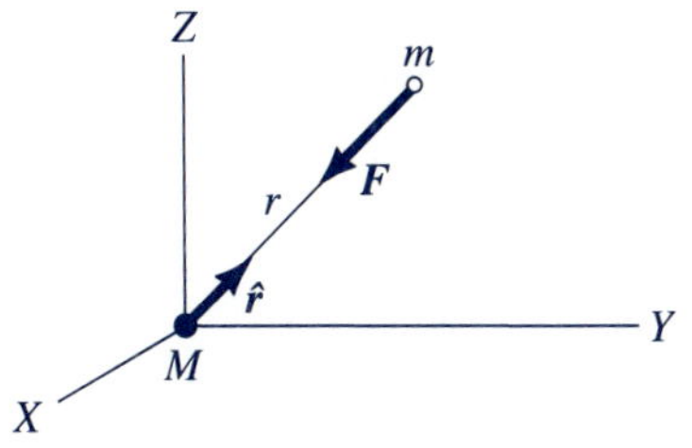

Figure 13.11. Central force on m.

Clearly, this force field is a function of spatial coordinates and can easily be expressed as the gradient of a scalar function in the following manner:

$$\boldsymbol{F} = -\textbf{grad}\left(-\frac{GMm}{r}\right) \tag{13.18}$$

Hence, this is a conservative force field. The potential energy is then

$$\text{PE} = -\frac{GMm}{r} \tag{13.19}$$

Next, the force on a particle of unit positive charge from a particle of charge q_1 is given by Coulomb's law as

$$\boldsymbol{E} = \frac{q_1}{4\pi\epsilon_0 r^2}\hat{\boldsymbol{r}} \tag{13.20}$$

Since this equation has the same form as Eq. 13.17 (i.e., is also a function of $1/r^2$), we see immediately that the force field from q_1 is conservative. The potential energy per unit charge is then

$$\text{PE} = \frac{q_1}{4\pi\epsilon_0 r} \tag{13.21}$$

The remaining field introduced was the magnetic field where $\boldsymbol{F} = qV \times \boldsymbol{B}$. For this field, the force on a charged particle depends on the velocity of the particle. The condition that the force be a function of position is not satisfied, therefore, and the magnetic field does *not* form a conservative force field.

13.4 Conservation of Mechanical Energy

Let us now consider the motion of a particle upon which only a conservative force field does work. We start with Eq. 13.2:

$$\int_{r_1}^{r_2} \boldsymbol{F} \cdot d\boldsymbol{r} = \tfrac{1}{2}mV_2^2 - \tfrac{1}{2}mV_1^2 \tag{13.22}$$

Using the definition of potential energy, we replace the left side of the equation in the following manner:

$$(\text{PE})_1 - (\text{PE})_2 = \tfrac{1}{2}mV_2^2 - \tfrac{1}{2}mV_1^2 \tag{13.23}$$

Rearranging terms, we reach the following useful relation:

$$(\text{PE})_1 + \tfrac{1}{2}mV_1^2 = (\text{PE})_2 + \tfrac{1}{2}mV_2^2 \tag{13.24}$$

Since positions 1 and 2 are arbitrary, obviously *the sum of the potential energy and the kinetic energy for a particle remains constant at all times during the motion of the particle*. This statement is sometimes called the *law of conservation of mechanical energy for conservative systems*. The usefulness of this relation can be demonstrated by the following examples.

Example 13.5

A particle is dropped with zero initial velocity down a frictionless chute (Fig. 13.12). What is the magnitude of its velocity if the vertical drop during the motion is h ft?

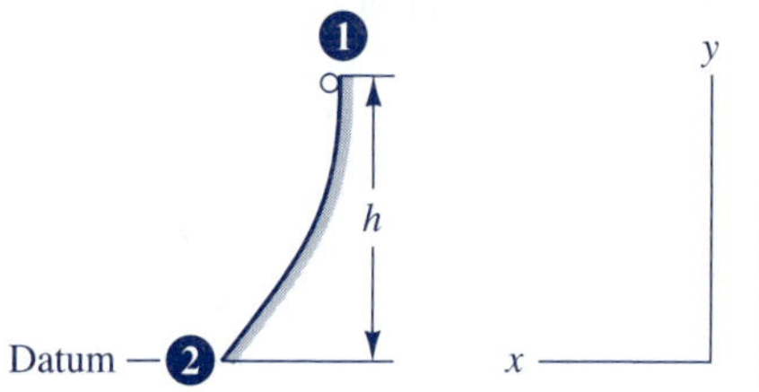

Figure 13.12. Particle on frictionless chute.

For small trajectories, we can assume a uniform force field $-mg\boldsymbol{j}$. Since this is the only force that can perform work on the particle (the normal force from the chute does no work), we can employ the **conservation-of-mechanical-energy** equation. If we take position 2 as a datum, we then have from Eq. 13.24:

$$mgh + 0 = 0 + \frac{1}{2}mV_2^2$$

Solving for V_2, we get

$$V_2 = \sqrt{2gh}$$

The advantages of the energy approach for conservative fields become apparent from this problem. That is, not all the forces need be considered in computing velocities, and the path, however complicated, is of no concern. If friction were present, a nonconservative force would perform work, and we would have to go back to the general relation given by Eq. 13.2 for the analysis.

Example 13.6

A mass is dropped onto a spring that has a spring constant K and a negligible mass (see Fig. 13.13). What is the maximum deflection δ? Neglect the effects of permanent deformation of the mass and any vibration that may occur.

In this problem, only conservative forces act on the body as it falls. Using the lowest position of the body as a datum, we see that the body falls a distance $h + \delta$. We shall equate the *mechanical energies* at the uppermost and lowest positions of the body. Thus,

$$\underbrace{mg(h+\delta)}_{\text{PE gravity}} + \underbrace{0}_{\text{PE spring}} + \underbrace{0}_{\text{KE}} = \underbrace{0}_{\text{PE gravity}} + \underbrace{\tfrac{1}{2}K\delta^2}_{\text{PE spring}} + \underbrace{0}_{\text{KE}} \qquad \text{(a)}$$

Rearranging the terms,

$$\delta^2 - \frac{2mg}{K}\delta - \frac{2mgh}{K} = 0 \qquad \text{(b)}$$

We may solve for a physically meaningful δ from this equation by using the quadratic formula.

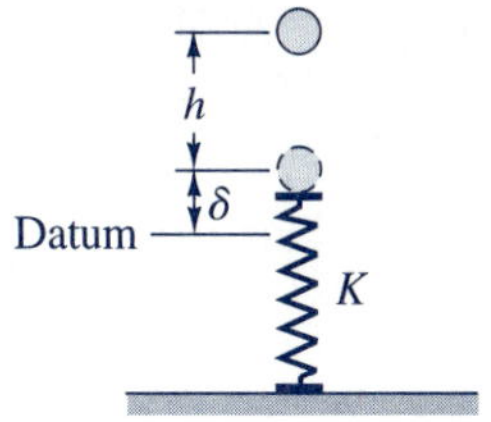

Figure 13.13. Mass dropped on spring.

Example 13.7

A ski jumper moves down the ramp aided only by gravity (Fig. 13.14). If the skier moves 33 m in the horizontal direction and is to land very smoothly at B, what must be the angle θ for the landing incline? Neglect friction. Also determine h.

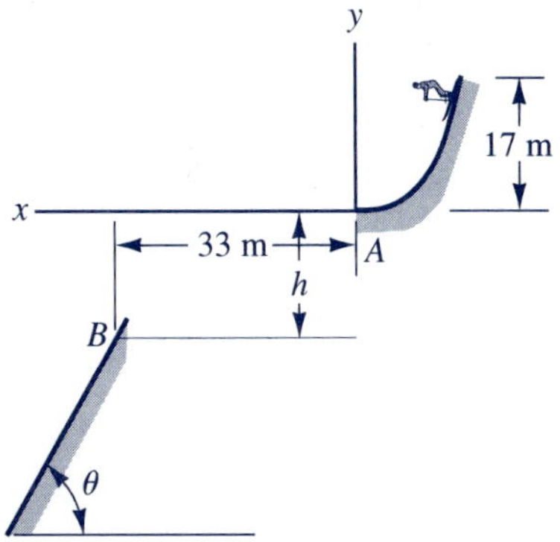

Figure 13.14. A ski jump with a landing ramp at an angle θ to be determined.

We first use **conservation of mechanical energy** along the ramp. Thus

$$(mg)(17) = \tfrac{1}{2}mV^2$$

$$\therefore\ V = \sqrt{(2g)(17)} = 18.26 \text{ m/s}$$

Example 13.7 (Continued)

Using a reference xy at A as shown in Fig. 13.14 and measuring time from the instant that the skier is at the origin, we now use **Newton's law** for the free flight. Thus

$$\ddot{y} = -9.81$$
$$\dot{y} = -9.81t + C_1$$
$$y = -9.81\frac{t^2}{2} + C_1 t + C_2$$

When $t = 0, \dot{y} = 0$, and we take $y = 0$. Hence,

$$C_1 = C_2 = 0$$

Also,

$$\ddot{x} = 0$$
$$\dot{x} = C_3$$
$$x = C_3 t + C_4$$

When $t = 0, \dot{x} = 18.26$, and $x = 0$,

$$\therefore C_3 = 18.26 \qquad C_4 = 0$$

Thus we have

$$\dot{y} = -9.81t \quad \text{(a)} \qquad \dot{x} = 18.26 \quad \text{(c)}$$
$$y = -9.81\frac{t^2}{2} \quad \text{(b)} \qquad x = 18.26t \quad \text{(d)}$$

To get h, set $x = 33$ in Eq. (d) and solve for the time t.

$$\therefore 33 = 18.26t \qquad t = 1.807 \text{ sec}$$

Hence, going to Eq. (b) we get

$$h = \left| -9.81\left(\frac{1.807^2}{2}\right) \right| = \boxed{16.01 \text{ m}}$$

Now get $\dot{y}$ at landing. Using Eq. (a) we have

$$\dot{y} = -(9.81)(1.807) = -17.73 \text{ m/s}$$

Also, we have at all times

$$\dot{x} = 18.26 \text{ m/s}$$

For best landing, ***V*** is parallel to incline

$$\therefore \tan\theta = \frac{-\dot{y}}{\dot{x}} = \frac{17.73}{18.26}$$

$$\boxed{\theta = 44.15°}$$

Example 13.8

A block A of mass .200 kg slides on a frictionless surface as shown in Fig. 13.15. The spring constant K_1 is 25 N/m and initially, at the position shown, it is stretched .40 m. An elastic cord connects the top support to point C on A. It has a spring constant K_2 of 10.26 N/m. Furthermore, the cord disconnects from C at the instant that C reaches point G at the end of the straight portion of the incline. If A is released from rest at the indicated position, what value of θ corresponds to the end position B where A just loses contact with the surface? The elastic cord (at the top) is initially unstretched.

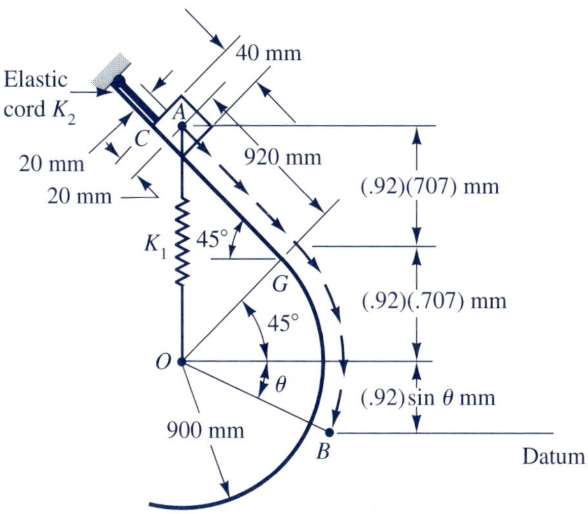

Figure 13.15. Mass A slides along frictionless surface.

We have conservative forces performing work on A so we have **conservation of mechanical energy.** Using the datum at B and using l_0 as the unstretched length of the spring with δ as the elongation of the spring, we then say that

$$mgz_1 + \frac{mV_1^2}{2} + \frac{1}{2}K_1\delta_1^2 = mgz_2 + \frac{mV_2^2}{2} + \frac{1}{2}K_1\delta_2^2 + \frac{1}{2}K_2(\overline{CG})^2$$

where the last term is the energy in the elastic cord when it disconnects at G. Therefore, noting that $\overline{CG}$ = .94 m and that $\overline{OB}$ = .92 m, we have on observing vertical distances in Fig. 13.15:

$$(.200)(9.81)[(.92)(.707) + (.92)(.707) + (.92)\sin\theta] + 0 + \tfrac{1}{2}(25)(.40)^2$$
$$= 0 + \tfrac{1}{2}(.20)V_2^2 + \tfrac{1}{2}(25)(.92 - l_0)^2 + \tfrac{1}{2}(10.26)(.94)^2 \qquad \text{(a)}$$

Example 13.8 (Continued)

To get l_0, examine the initial configuration of the system. With an initial stretch of .40 m for the spring, we can say observing again vertical distances in Fig. 13.15:

$$l_0 = [(.92)(.707) + (.92)(.707)] - .40$$
$$= .901 \text{ m}$$

Equation (a) can then be written as

$$V_2^2 = .1490 + 18.05 \sin\theta \qquad \text{(b)}$$

We now use **Newton's law** at the point of interest B where A just loses contact. This condition is shown in detail in Fig. 13.16, where you will notice that the contact force N has been taken as zero and thus deleted from the free-body diagram. In the radial direction, we have

$$-F_{sp} + (.200)(g)\sin\theta = -.200\left(\frac{V_2^2}{.92}\right)$$

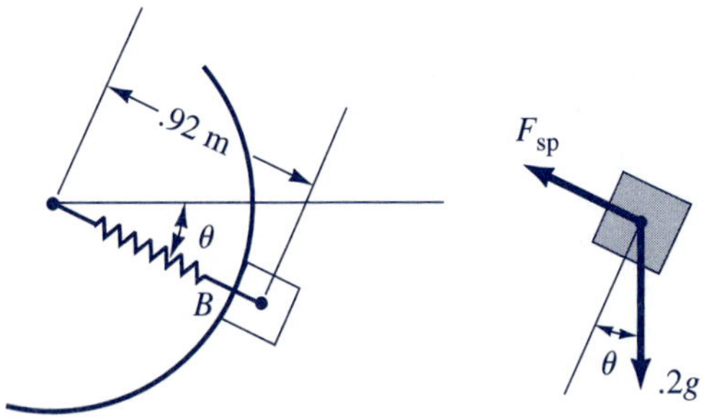

Figure 13.16. Contact is first lost at θ.

Therefore,

$$-(25)(.92 - .901) + (.200)(9.81)\sin\theta = -\left(\frac{V_2^2}{4.60}\right)$$

This equation can be written as

$$V_2^2 = 2.20 - 9.03 \sin\theta \qquad \text{(c)}$$

Solving Eqs. (b) and (c) simultaneously for θ, we get

$$\theta = 4.34°$$

13.5 Alternative Form of Work-Energy Equation

With the aid of the material in Section 13.4, we shall now set forth an alternative energy equation which has much physical appeal and which resembles the *first law of thermodynamics* as used in other courses. Let us take the case where certain of the forces acting on a particle are conservative while others are not. Remember that for conservative forces the negative of the change in potential energy between positions 1 and 2 equals the work done by these forces as the particle goes from position 1 to position 2 along any path. Thus, we can restate Eq. 13.2 in the following way:

$$\int_1^2 \boldsymbol{F} \cdot d\boldsymbol{r} - \Delta(\text{PE})_{1,2} = \Delta(\text{KE})_{1,2} \tag{13.25}$$

where the integral represents the work of *nonconservative* forces and the Δ represents the final state minus the initial state. Calling the integral $\mathcal{W}_{1-2}$, we than have, on rearranging the equation:

$$\Delta(\text{KE} + \text{PE}) = \mathcal{W}_{1-2} \tag{13.26}$$

In this form, we say that the work of *nonconservative* forces goes into changing the kinetic energy plus the potential energy for the particle. Since potential energies of such common forces as linear restoring forces, coulombic forces, and gravitational forces are so well known, the formulation above is useful in solving problems if it is understood thoroughly and applied properly.[9]

[9]Equation 13.26, you may notice, is actually a form of the first law of thermodynamics for the case of no heat transfer.

Example 13.9

Three coupled streetcars (Fig. 13.17) are moving at a speed of 32 km/hr down a 7° incline. Each car has a weight of 198 kN. Specifications from

Figure 13.17 Coupled streetcars.

Example 13.9 (Continued)

the buyer requires that the cars must stop within 50 m beyond the position where the brakes are fully applied so as to cause the wheels to lock. What is the maximum number of brake failures that can be tolerated and still satisfy this specification? We will assume for simplicity that the weight is loaded equally among all the wheels of the system. There are 24 brake systems, one for each wheel. Take $\mu_d = .45$.

The friction force f on any one wheel where the brake has operated is ascertained from **Coulomb's law** as

$$f = \frac{198{,}000 \cos 7^\circ}{8}(.45) = 11{,}050 \text{ N}$$

We now consider the **work–energy relation** 13.26 for the case where a minimum number of good brakes, n, just causes the trains to stop in 50 m. We shall neglect the kinetic energy due to rotation of the rather small wheels. This assumption permits us to use a single particle to represent the three cars, wherein this particle moves a distance of 50 m. Using the end configuration of the train as the datum for potential energy of gravity, we have for Eq. 13.26:

$$\Delta KE + \Delta PE = \mathcal{W}_{1-2}$$

$$\left(0 - 3\left\{\frac{1}{2}\frac{198{,}000}{g}\left[\frac{(32)(1{,}000)}{3{,}600}\right]^2\right\}\right) + [0 - (3)(198{,}000)(50)\sin 7^\circ]$$
$$= -(n)(11{,}050)(50)$$

$$n = 10.89$$

The number of brake failures that can accordingly be tolerated is $24 - 11 = 13$.

Number of brake failures to be tolerated = 13

Another example of conservation of mechanical energy will be in the next section (Example 13.11) for the case of a system of particles.

PROBLEMS

13.38. A railroad car traveling 5 km/hr runs into a stop at a railroad terminal. A vehicle having a mass of 1,800 kg is held by a linear restoring force system that has an equivalent spring constant of 20,000 N/m. If the railroad car is assumed to stop suddenly and if the wheels in the vehicle are free to turn, what is the maximum force developed by the spring system? Neglect rotational inertia of the wheels of the vehicle.

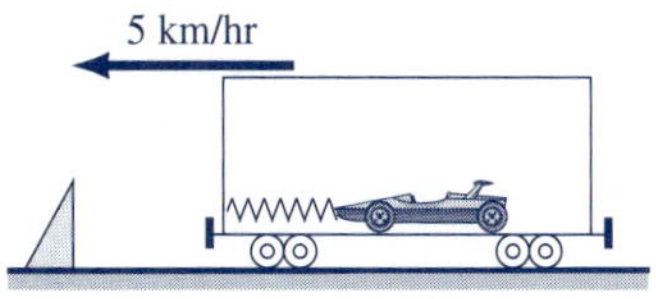

Figure P.13.38.

13.39. A mass of one slug is moving at a speed of 50 ft/sec along a horizontal frictionless surface, which later inclines upward at an angle 45°. A spring of constant $K = 5$ lb/in. is present along the incline. How high does the mass move?

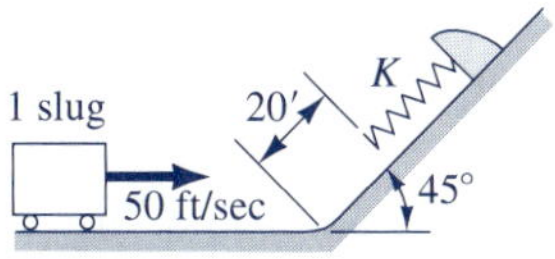

Figure P.13.39.

13.40. A block weighing 10 lb is released from rest where the springs acting on the body are horizontal and have a tension of 10 lb each. What is the velocity of the block after it has descended 4 in. if each spring has a spring constant $K = 5$ lb/in.?

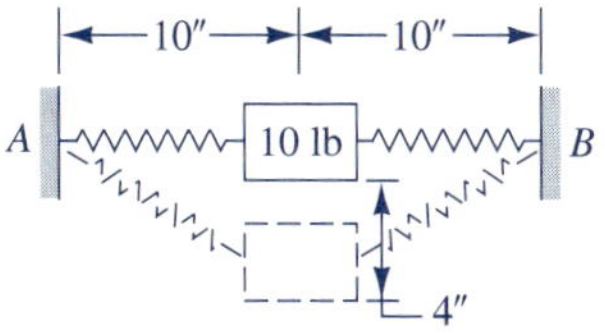

Figure P.13.40.

13.41. A nonlinear spring develops a force given as $.06x^2$ N, where x is the amount of compression of the spring in millimeters. Does such a spring develop a conservative force? If so, what is the potential energy stored in the spring for a deflection of 60 mm?

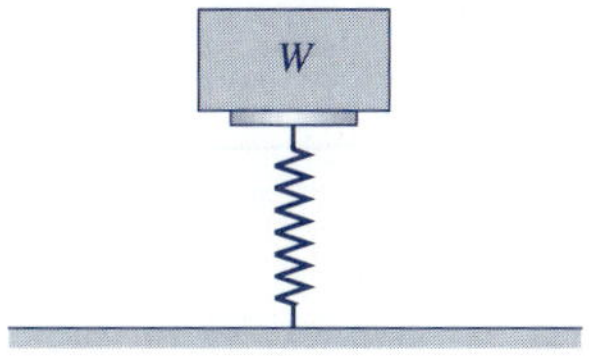

Figure P.13.41.

13.42. In Problem 13.41, a weight W of 225 N is released suddenly from rest on the nonlinear spring. What is the maximum deflection of the spring?

13.43. A vector operator that you will learn more about in fluid mechanics and electromagnetic theory is the *curl* vector operator. This operator is defined for rectangular coordinates in terms of its action on V as follows:

$$\textbf{curl } \boldsymbol{V}(x, y, z) = \left(\frac{\partial V_z}{\partial y} - \frac{\partial V_y}{\partial z}\right)\boldsymbol{i} + \left(\frac{\partial V_x}{\partial z} - \frac{\partial V_z}{\partial x}\right)\boldsymbol{j} + \left(\frac{\partial V_y}{\partial x} - \frac{\partial V_x}{\partial y}\right)\boldsymbol{k}$$

(When the curl is applied to a fluid velocity field V as above, the resulting vector field is twice the angular velocity field of infinitesimal elements in the flow.) Show that if F is expressible as $\nabla\phi(x, y, z)$, then it must follow that **curl** $F = \mathbf{0}$. The converse is also true, namely that *if* **curl** $F = \mathbf{0}$, *then* $F = \nabla\phi(x, y, z)$ *and is thus a conservative force field.*

13.44. Determine whether the following force fields are conservative or not.

(a) $\boldsymbol{F} = (10z + y)\boldsymbol{i} + (15yz + x)\boldsymbol{j} + \left(10x + \frac{15y^2}{2}\right)\boldsymbol{k}$

(b) $\boldsymbol{F} = (z \sin x + y)\boldsymbol{i} + (4yz + x)\boldsymbol{j} + \left(2y^2 - 5\cos x\right)\boldsymbol{k}$

See Problem 13.43 before doing this problem.

13.45. Given the following conservative force field:

$$\boldsymbol{F} = (10z + y)\boldsymbol{i} + (15yz + x)\boldsymbol{j} + \left(10x + \frac{15y^2}{2}\right)\boldsymbol{k}\ N$$

find the force potential to within an arbitrary constant. What work is done by the force field on a particle going from $\boldsymbol{r}_1 = 10\boldsymbol{i} + 2\boldsymbol{j} + 3\boldsymbol{k}$ m to $\boldsymbol{r}_2 = -2\boldsymbol{i} + 4\boldsymbol{j} - 3\boldsymbol{k}$ m? [*Hint:* Note that if $\partial\phi/\partial x$ equals some function $(xy^2 + z)$, then we can say on integrating that

$$\phi = \frac{x^2y^2}{2} + zx + g(y, z)$$

where $g(y, z)$ is an arbitrary function of y and z. Note we have held y and z constant during the integration.]

13.46. If the following force field is conservative,

$$\boldsymbol{F} = (5z \sin x + y)\boldsymbol{i} + (4yz + x)\boldsymbol{j} + (2y^2 - 5\cos x)\boldsymbol{k} \text{ lb}$$

(where x, y, and z are in ft), find the force potential up to an arbitrary constant. What is the work done on a particle starting at the origin and moving in a circular path of radius 2 ft to form a semicircle along the positive x axis? (See the hint in Problem 13.45.)

13.47. A body A can slide in a frictionless manner along a stiff rod CD. At the position shown, the spring along CD has been compressed 6 in. and A is at a distance of 4 ft from D. The spring connecting A to E has been elongated 1 in. What is the speed of A after it moves 1 ft? The spring constants are $K_1 = 1.0$ lb/in. and $K_2 = .5$ lb/in. The mass of A is 30 lbm.

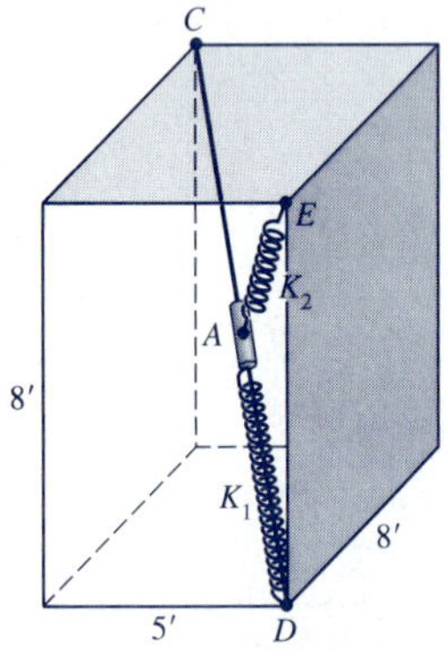

Figure P.13.47.

13.48. A collar A of mass 10 lbm slides on a frictionless tube. The collar is connected to a linear spring whose spring constant K is 5.0 lb/in. If the collar is released from rest at the position shown, what is its speed when the spring is at elevation EF? The spring is stretched 3 in. at the initial position of the collar.

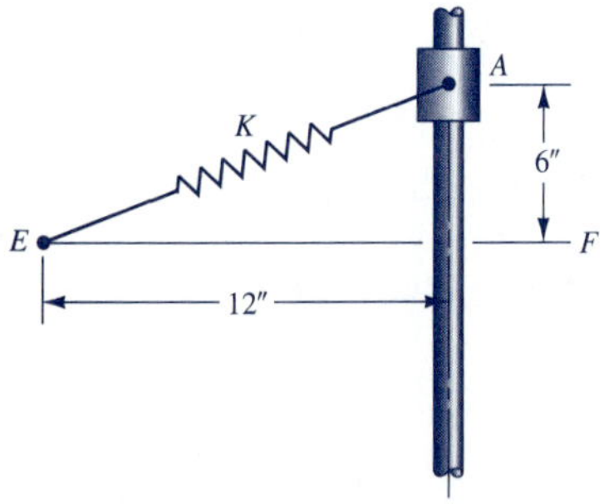

Figure P.13.48.

13.49. A mass M of 20 kg slides with no friction along a vertical rod. Two springs each of spring constant $K_1 = 2$ N/mm and a third spring having a spring constant $K_2 = 3$ N/mm are attached to the mass M. At the starting position when $\theta = 30°$, the springs are unstretched. What is the velocity of M after it descends a distance d of .02 m?

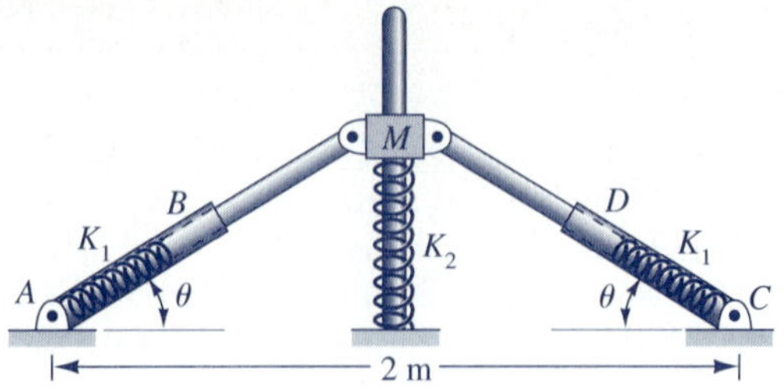

Figure P.13.49.

13.50. A collar A having a mass of 5 kg can slide without friction on a pipe. If released from rest at the position shown, where the spring is unstretched, what speed will the collar have after moving 50 mm? The spring constant is 2,000 N/m.

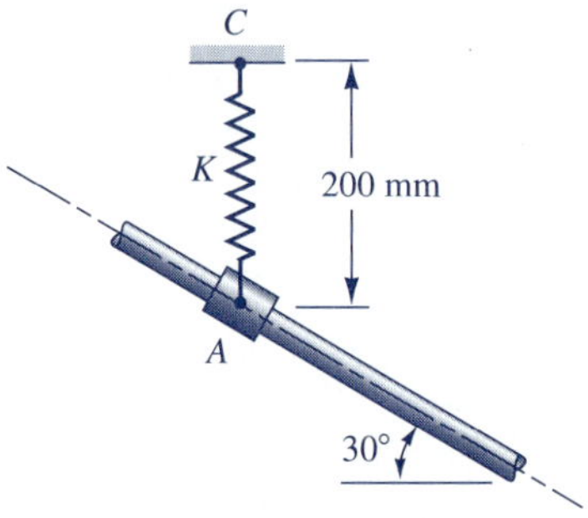

Figure P.13.50.

13.51. A slotted rod A is moving to the left at a speed of 2 m/sec. Pins are moved to the left by this rod. These pins must slide in a slot under the rod as shown in the diagram. The pins are connected by a spring having a spring constant K of 1,500 N/m. The spring is unstretched in the configuration shown. What distance d do the pins reach before stopping instantaneously? The mass of the slotted rod is 10 kg. The spring is held in the slotted rod so as not to buckle outward. Neglect the mass of the pins.

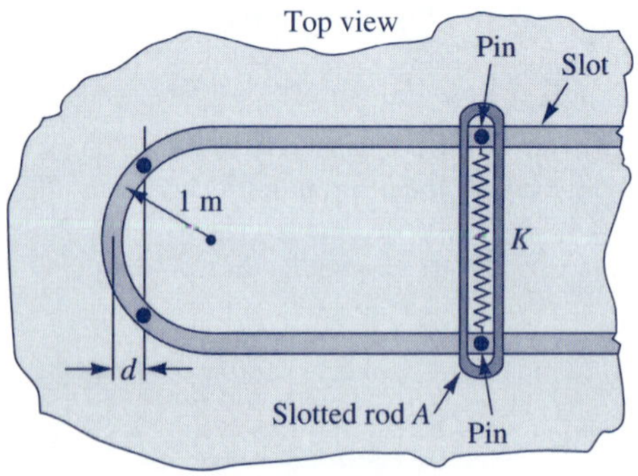

Figure P.13.51.

13.52. The top view of a slotted bar of mass 30 lbm is shown. Two pins guided by the slotted bar ride in slots which have the equation of a hyperbola $xy = 5$, where x and y are in feet. The pins are connected by a linear spring having a spring constant K of 5 lb/in. When the pins are 2 ft from the y axis, the spring is stretched 8 in. and the slotted bar is moving to the right at a speed of 2 ft/sec. What is $\dot{V}$ of the bar? [*Hint:* Differentiate energy equation.]

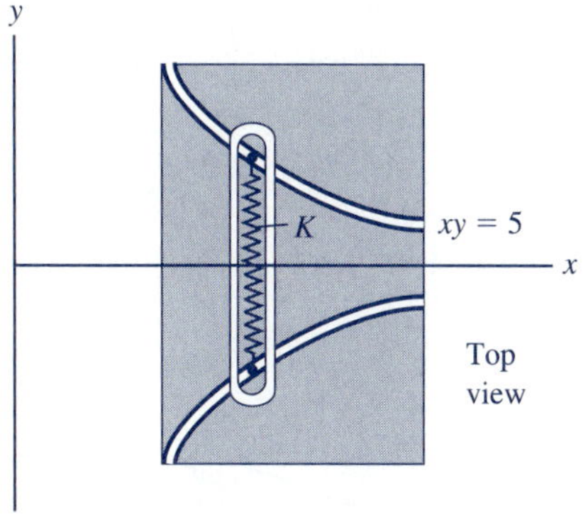

Figure P.13.52.

13.53. In Problem 13.52, what is the speed of the slotted bar when $x = 2.25$ ft?

13.54. Perhaps many of you as children constructed toy guns from half a clothespin, a wooden block, and bands of rubber cut from the inner tube of an automobile tire [see diagram (a)]. Rubber band A holds the half-clothespin to the wooden "gun stock." The "ammunition" is a rubber band B held by the clothespin at C by friction and stretched to go around the block at the other end. The rubber band B when laid flat as in (b) has a length of 7 in. To "load the ammunition" takes a force of 20 lb at C. If the gun is pointed upward, estimate how high the fired rubber band will go when "fired" if it weighs 4 oz. To "fire" the gun you push lowest part of clothespin toward the nail (see diagram) to release at C.

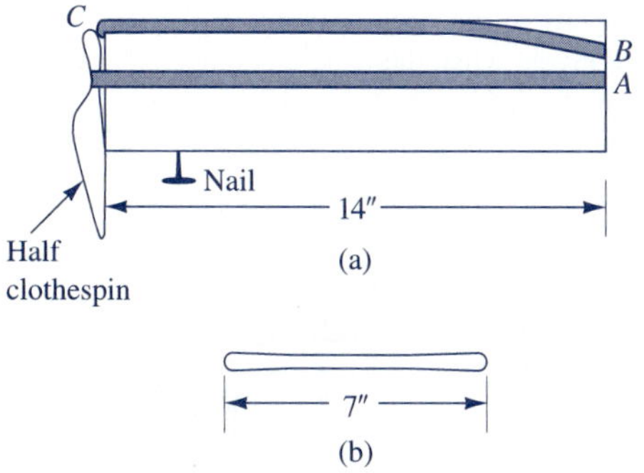

Figure P.13.54.

13.55. A meteor has a speed of 56,000 km/hr when it is 320,000 km from the center of the earth. What will be its speed when it is 160 km from the earth's surface?

13.56 Do Problem 13.2 using the energy equation in the usual form of the first law of thermodynamics.

13.57. Do Problem 13.5 using the energy equation in the usual form of the first law of thermodynamics.

13.58. Do Problem 13.17 using the energy equation in the usual form of the first law of thermodynamics.

13.59. Do Problem 13.18 using the energy equation in the usual form of the first law of thermodynamics.

13.60. A constant-torque electric motor A is hoisting a weight W of 30 lb. An inextensible cable connects the weight W to the motor over a stationary drum of diameter $D = 1$ ft. The diameter d of the motor drive is 6 in., and the delivered torque is 150 lb-ft. The dynamic coefficient of friction between the drum and cable is .2. If the system is started from rest, what is the speed of the weight W after it has been raised 5 ft?

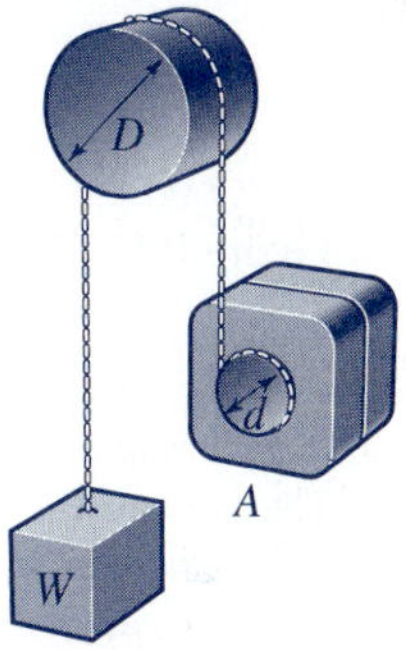

Figure P.13.60.

13.61. A body A weighing 10 lb, can slide along a fixed rod B–B. A spring is connected between fixed point C and the mass. AC is 2 ft in length when the spring is unextended. If the body is released from rest at the configuration shown, what is its speed when it reaches the y axis? Assume that a constant friction force of 6 oz acts on the body A. The spring constant K is 1 lb/in.

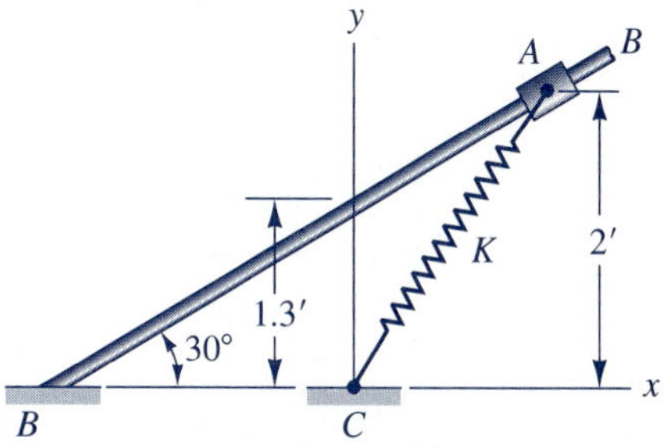

Figure P.13.61.

13.62. A body A is released from rest on a vertical circular path as shown. If a constant resistance force of 1 N acts along the path, what is the speed of the body when it reaches B? The mass of the body is .5 kg and the radius r of the path is 1.6 m.

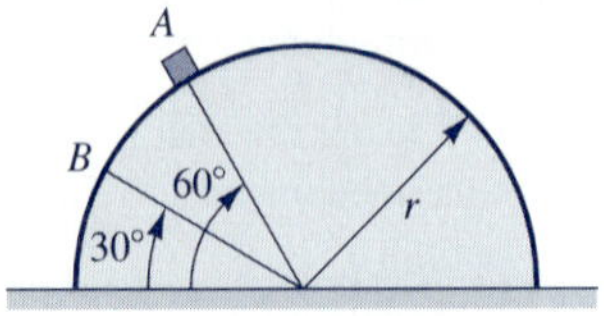

Figure P.13.62.

13.63. A cylinder slides down a rod. What is the distance δ that the spring is deflected at the instant that the disk stops instantaneously? Take $\mu_d = .3$.

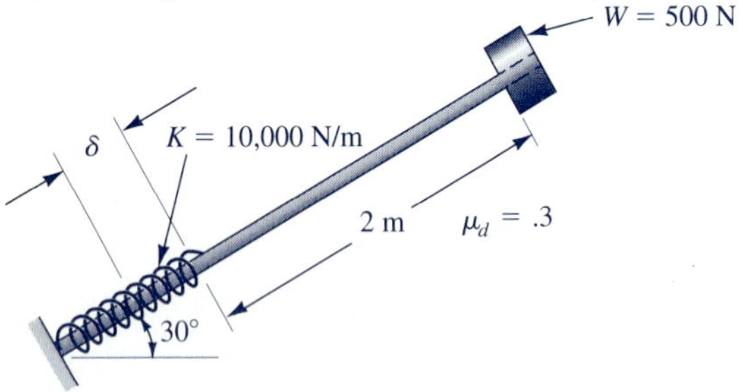

Figure P.13.63.

13.64. In ordnance work a very vital test for equipment is the *shock* test, in which a piece of equipment is subjected to a certain level of acceleration of short duration. A common technique for this test is the *drop test.* The specimen is mounted on a rigid carriage, which upon release is dropped along guide rods onto a set of lead pads resting on a heavy rigid anvil. The pads deform and absorb the energy of the carriage and specimen. We estimate through other tests that the energy E absorbed by a pad versus compression distance δ is given as shown, where the curve can be taken as a parabola. For four such pads, each placed directly on the anvil, and a height h of 3 m, what is the compression of the pads? The carriage and specimen together weigh $50g$ N. Neglect the friction of the guides. (*Note:* 1 J = 1 N-m.)

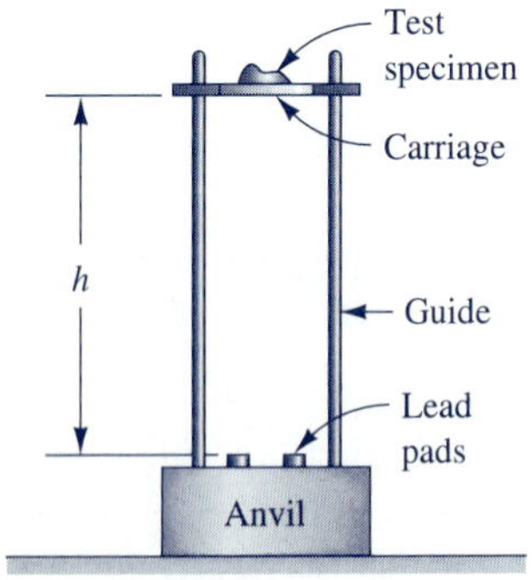

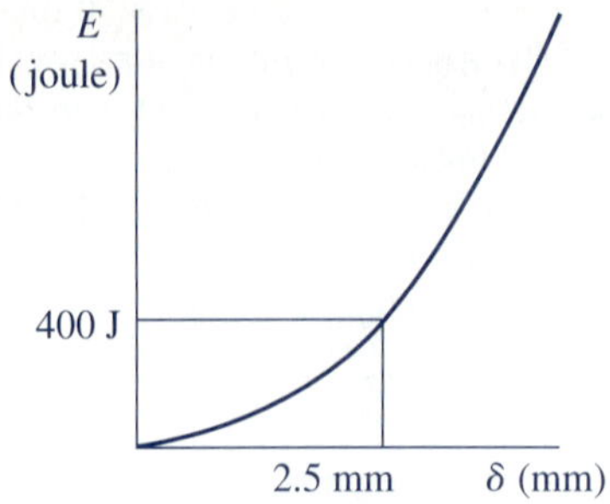

Figure P.13.64.

13.65. Two bodies are connected by an inextensible cord over a frictionless pulley. If released from rest, what velocity will they reach when the 500-lb body has dropped 5 ft?

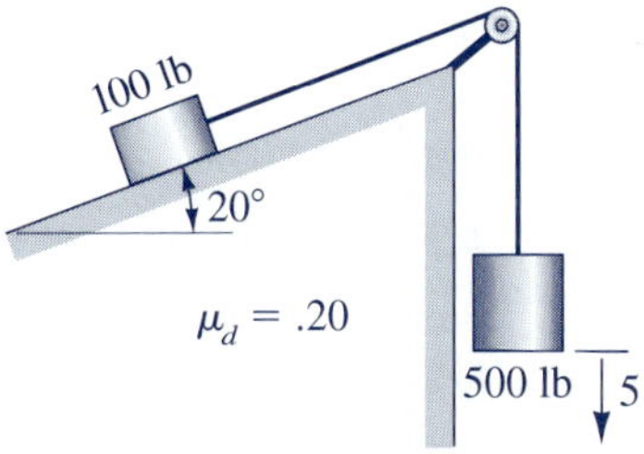

Figure P.13.65.

13.66. Suppose in Example 13.9 that only the brakes on train A operate and lock. What is the distance d before stopping? Also, determine the force in each coupling of the system.

13.67. A large constant force F is applied to a body of weight W resting on an inclined surface for which the coefficient of dynamic friction is μ_d. The body is acted on by a spring having a spring constant K. If initially the spring is compressed a distance δ, compute the velocity of the body in terms of F and the other parameters that are given, when the body has moved from rest a distance up the incline of $\frac{3}{2}\delta$.

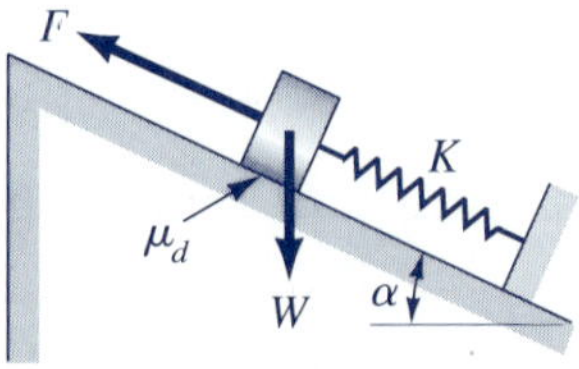

Figure P.13.67.

Part B: Systems of Particles

13.6 Work–Energy Equations

We shall now examine a system of particles from an energy viewpoint. A general aggregate of n particles is shown in Fig. 13.18. Considering the ith particle, we can say, by employing Eq. 13.2:

$$\int_1^2 \boldsymbol{F}_i \cdot d\boldsymbol{r}_i + \int_1^2 \left(\sum_{\substack{j=1 \\ j \neq i}}^{n} \boldsymbol{f}_{ij} \right) \cdot d\boldsymbol{r}_i = \left(\tfrac{1}{2} m_i V_i^2\right)_2 - \left(\tfrac{1}{2} m_i V_i^2\right)_1 \qquad (13.27)$$

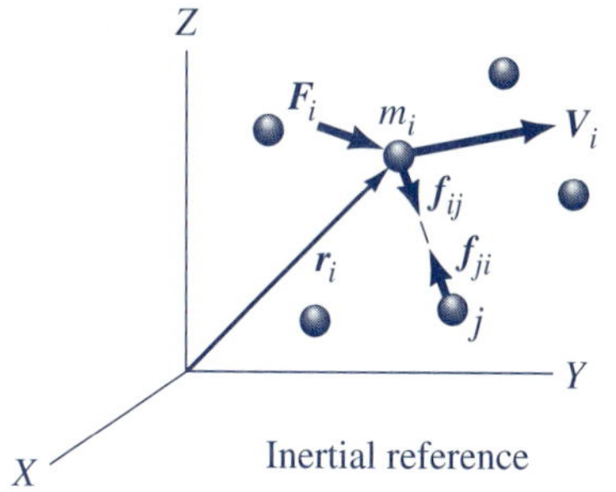

Figure 13.18. System of particles.

where, as in Chapter 12, $\boldsymbol{f}_{ij}$ is the force from the jth particle onto the ith particle, as illustrated in the diagram, and is thus an internal force. In contrast, $\boldsymbol{F}_i$ represents the total *external* force on the ith particle. In words, Eq. 13.27 says that for a displacement between $\boldsymbol{r}_1$ and $\boldsymbol{r}_2$ along some path, the energy relations for the ith particle are:

external work + internal work
= (change in kinetic energy relative to XYZ) (13.28)

Furthermore, we can adopt the point of view set forth in Section 13.5 and identify conservative forces, both external and internal, so as to utilize potential energies for these forces in the energy equation. To qualify as a conservative force, an internal force would have to be a function of only the spatial configuration of the system and expressible as the gradient of a scalar function. Clearly, forces arising from the gravitational attraction between the particles, electrostatic forces from electric charges on the particles, and forces from elastic connectors between the particles (such as springs) are all conservative internal forces.

We now sum Eqs. 13.27 for all the particles in the system to get the energy equation for a *system of particles.* We do *not* necessarily get a cancellation of contributions of the internal forces as we did for Newton's law in Chapter 12 because we are now adding the *work* done by each internal force on each particle. And even though we have pairs of internal forces that are equal and opposite, the *movements* of the corresponding particles in general are *not* equal. The result is that the work done by a pair of equal and opposite internal forces is not always zero. However, in the case of a *rigid body*, the contact forces between pairs of particles making up the body have the same motion, and so in this case the internal work is *zero* from such forces.[10] Also, if there is a system of rigid bodies interconnected by pin or ball joint connections, and if there is no friction at these movable connections, then again there will be no internal work. (Why?) We can then say for the system of particles that

$$\Delta(\text{KE} + \text{PE}) = \mathcal{W}_{1-2} \qquad (13.29)$$

[10]We shall show this more directly in Chapter 17.

where $\mathcal{W}_{1-2}$ represents the net work done by *internal and external* nonconservative forces, and PE represents the total potential energy of the conservative *internal and external* forces. Clearly, if there are no nonconservative forces present then Eq. (13.29) degenerates to the conservation-of-mechanical-energy principle. As pointed out earlier, since we are employing the *change* in potential energy, the datums chosen for measuring PE are of little significance here.[11] For instance, any convenient datum for measuring the potential energy due to gravity of the earth yields the same result for the term ΔPE.

Looking back on Eq. (13.27), which on summation over all the particles gave rise to Eq. (13.29), namely the equation to be used for a system of particles, we wish to make the following point. It is the fact that the work contribution of each force stems from the *movement of each force with its specific point of application.* This should be clear from the use of $d\mathbf{r}_i$, with i identifying each particle. This will be an important consideration later.

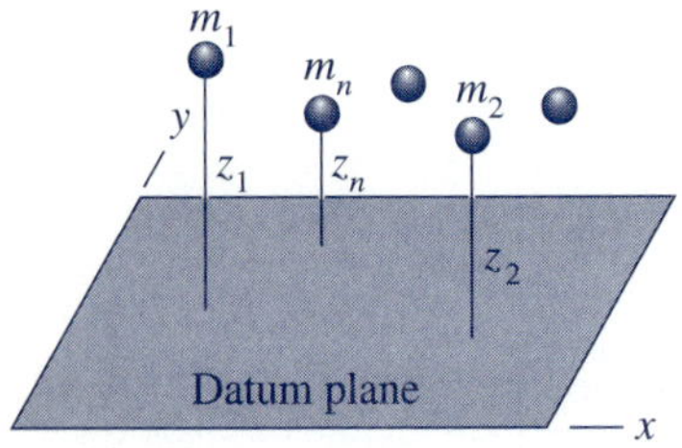

Figure 13.19. Particles above reference plane.

Let us now consider the action of gravity on a system of particles. The potential energy relative to a datum plane, xy, for such a system (see Fig. 13.19) is simply

$$\text{PE} = \sum_i m_i g z_i$$

Note that the right side of this equation represents the first moment of the weight of the system about the xy plane. This quantity can be given in terms of the center of gravity and the entire weight of W as follows:

$$\text{PE} = W z_c$$

where z_c is the vertical distance from the datum plane to the center of gravity. Note that if g is constant, the center of gravity corresponds to the center of mass. And so for any system of particles, the change in potential energy is readily found by concentrating the entire weight at the center of gravity or, as is almost always the case, at the center of mass.

Before proceeding with the problems we wish to emphasize certain salient features governing the work–energy principle for a system of particles.

1. In computing work, we must remember to have the forces move **with their points of application** (see Eq. 13.27).
2. Both **internal** and **external** forces may be present as conservative and as nonconservative forces and must be accounted for.
3. The kinetic energy must be the **total** kinetic energy and not just that of the mass center.

[11]One precaution in this regard must again be brought to your attention. You will remember that in the spring-force formula, $-Kx$, the term x represents the elongation or contraction of the spring from the *undeformed* condition. This condition must not be violated in the potential-energy expression $\frac{1}{2}Kx^2$.

Example 13.10

In Fig. 13.20, two blocks have weights W_1 and W_2, respectively. They are connected by a flexible, *elastic* cable of negligible mass which has an equivalent spring constant of K_1. Body 1 is connected to the wall by a spring having a spring constant K_2 and slides along a horizontal surface for which the dynamic coefficient of friction with the body is μ_d. Body 2 is supported initially by some external agent so that, at the outset of the problem, the spring and cable are unstretched. What is the total kinetic energy of the system when, after release, body 2 has moved a distance d_2 and body 1 has moved a smaller distance d_1?

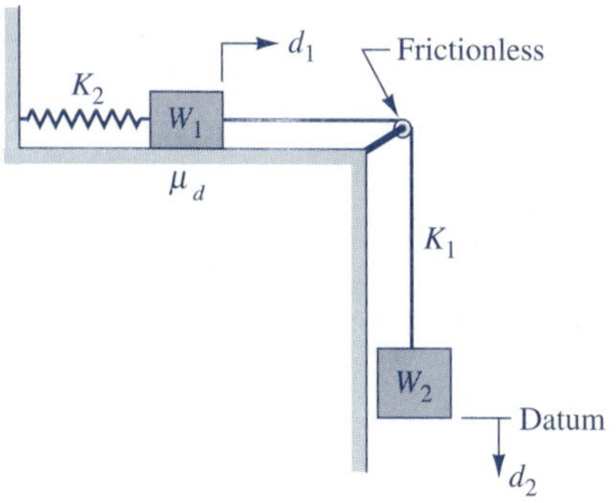

Figure 13.20. Elastically connected bodies.

Use Eq. 13.29. Only one nonconservative force exists in the system, the external friction force on body 1. Therefore, the work term of the equation becomes

$$\mathcal{W}_{1-2} = -W_1\mu_d d_1 \qquad \text{(a)}$$

Three conservative forces are present; the spring force and the gravitational force are *external* and the force from the elastic cable is *internal*. (We neglect mutual gravitational forces between the bodies.) Using the initial position of W_2 as the datum for gravitational potential energy, we have, for the total change in potential energy:

$$\Delta PE = \left[\tfrac{1}{2}K_2 d_1^2 - 0\right] + \left[\tfrac{1}{2}K_1\left(d_2 - d_1\right)^2 - 0\right] + \left[0 - W_2 d_2\right]$$

We can compute the desired change in kinetic energy from Eq. 13.29 as

$$\Delta KE = -W_1\mu_d d_1 - \tfrac{1}{2}K_2 d_1^2 - \tfrac{1}{2}K_1\left(d_2 - d_1\right)^2 + W_2 d_2 \qquad \text{(b)}$$

As an additional exercise, you should arrive at this result by using the basic Eq. 13.28, where you cannot rely on familiar formulas for potential energies.

In the following example, we will see how using a system of particles approach can make for great simplification in a problem over the procedure of dealing with particles individually. Also we will have a case where there is no nonconservative work, which then results in a conservation of mechanical energy.

Example 13.11

Masses A and B, each having a mass of 75 kg, are constrained to move in frictionless slots (see Fig. 13.21). They are connected by a light rod of length l = 300 mm. Mass B is connected to two massless linear springs, each having a spring constant K = 900 N/m. The springs are unstretched when the connecting rod to masses A and B is vertical. What are the velocities of B and A when A descends a distance of 25 mm? There is no friction in the end connections of the rod.[12]

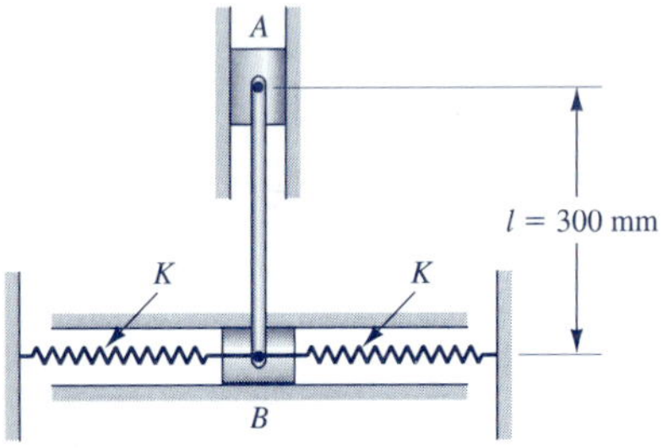

Figure 13.21. Two interconnected masses constrained by linear springs.

We shall use a **system of particles** approach for this case. This will eliminate the need to calculate the work of the rod on each mass that we would need had we elected to deal with each mass separately. For a system of particles approach, this work is internal between rigid bodies, having zero value as a result of **Newton's third law** and having ideal pin-connected joints.

We next note that only conservative forces are present (gravitational force and spring forces) so the first law form of our energy equation degenerates to conservation of mechanical energy. In Fig. 13.22, we show

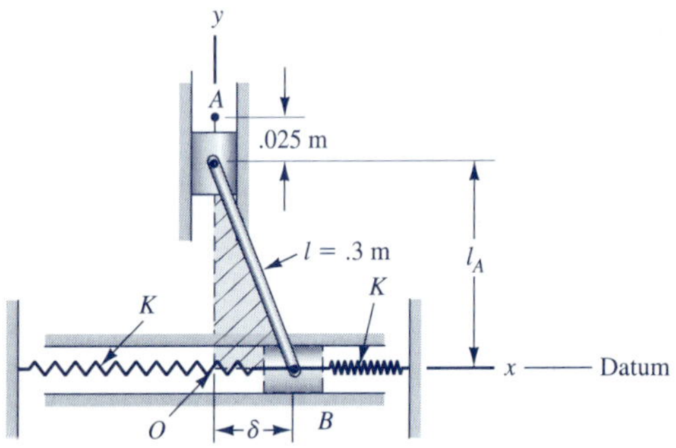

Figure 13.22. System in a configuration wherein mass A has dropped 25 mm.

[12]This is an example of an **unstable equilibrium** (a topic considered in Chapter 10) in that any slight movement of block B from its central position to the right or to the left causes A to start to accelerate downward.

Example 13.11 (Continued)

the system in a configuration where mass A has dropped a distance of .025 m. We can then say for the beginning and end configurations using the datum shown in Fig. 13.22,

$$\Delta[\text{KE} + \text{PE}] = \mathcal{W}_{1-2} = 0$$

$$\left(\tfrac{1}{2}M_A V_A^2 - 0\right) + \left(\tfrac{1}{2}M_B V_B^2 - 0\right) + \left[M_A g(.3 - .025) - M_A g(.3)\right] + \left[2\tfrac{1}{2}(900)(\delta^2) - 0\right] = 0 \quad \text{(a)}$$

We have three unknowns here. They are δ, V_A, and V_B. Observing the shaded triangle in Fig. 13.22 and using the Pythagorean theorem, we have

$$l_A^2 + \delta^2 = .3^2 \quad \text{(b)}$$

Taking the time derivative we get

$$2l_A\dot{l}_A + 2\delta\dot{\delta} = 0$$

We note that $\dot{l}_A = V_A$ and that $\dot{\delta} = V_B$. We then see from the preceding equation that

$$V_B = -\frac{l_A}{\delta}V_A \quad \text{(c)}$$

Now, returning to Fig. 13.22, we can compute δ for the case at hand. Noting that A has descended a distance of .025 m, thus making $l_A = .3 - .025 = .275$ m, we next go to Eq. (b) to get δ. Thus

$$(.275)^2 + \delta^2 = .3^2$$

$$\therefore \delta = .1199 \text{ m} \quad \text{(d)}$$

Substituting data from Eqs. (c) and (d) into Eq. (a) (conserving mechanical energy) we get

$$V_A = -.1524 \text{ m/s} \quad \therefore \text{ from (c)}, \quad V_B = -\frac{.275}{.1199}V_A = .3496 \text{ m/s}$$

Thus,

$V_A = .1524$ m/s downward $\quad V_B = .3496$ m/s to the right or the left

13.7 Kinetic Energy Expression Based on Center of Mass

In this and the next section, we shall introduce the center of mass into our discussion in order to develop useful expressions for the kinetic energy of an aggregate of particles. Also, we shall develop the work–energy equation for the center of mass set forth at the outset of this chapter.

Consider a system of n particles, shown in Fig. 13.23. The total kinetic energy relative to xyz of the system of particles can be given as

$$\text{KE} = \sum_{i=1}^{n} \tfrac{1}{2} m_i V_i^2 \tag{13.30}$$

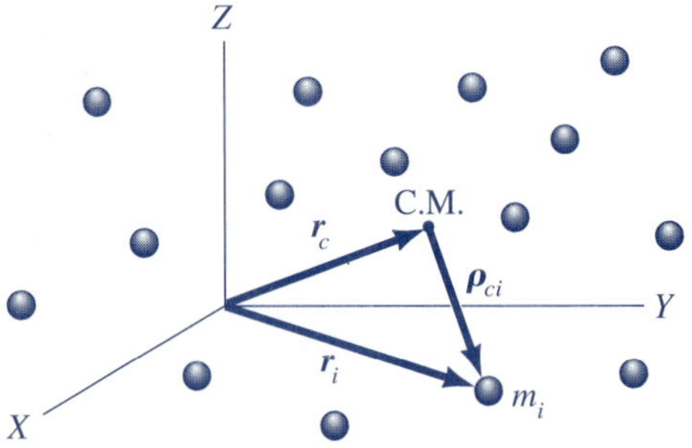

Figure 13.23. System of particles with center of mass.

We shall now express Eq. 13.30 in another way by introducing the mass center. Note in the diagram we have employed the vector $\boldsymbol{\rho}_{ci}$ as the displacement vector from the center of mass to the ith particle. We can accordingly say:

$$\boldsymbol{r}_i = \boldsymbol{r}_c + (\boldsymbol{r}_i - \boldsymbol{r}_c) = \boldsymbol{r}_c + \boldsymbol{\rho}_{ci} \tag{13.31}$$

Differentiating with respect to time, we get

$$\dot{\boldsymbol{r}}_i = \dot{\boldsymbol{r}}_c + (\dot{\boldsymbol{r}}_i - \dot{\boldsymbol{r}}_c) = \dot{\boldsymbol{r}}_c + \dot{\boldsymbol{\rho}}_{ci}$$

Therefore,

$$\boldsymbol{V}_i = \boldsymbol{V}_c + \dot{\boldsymbol{\rho}}_{ci} \tag{13.32}$$

From our earlier discussions on simple relative motion we can say that $\dot{\boldsymbol{\rho}}_{ci}$ is the motion of the ith particle *relative to the mass center*.[13] Substituting

[13]Note that

$$\dot{\boldsymbol{\rho}}_{ci} = \dot{\boldsymbol{r}}_i - \dot{\boldsymbol{r}}_c$$

That is, $\dot{\boldsymbol{\rho}}_{ci}$ is the *difference* between the velocity of the ith particle and that of the mass center. This is then the velocity of the particle *relative* to the center of the mass (i.e., relative to a reference translating with c or to a nonrotating observer moving with c.)

the relation above into the expression for kinetic energy, Eq. 13.30, we get

$$\text{KE} = \sum_{i=1}^{n} \tfrac{1}{2} m_i (\boldsymbol{V}_c + \dot{\boldsymbol{\rho}}_{ci})^2 = \sum_{i=1}^{n} \tfrac{1}{2} m_i (\boldsymbol{V}_c + \dot{\boldsymbol{\rho}}_{ci}) \bullet (\boldsymbol{V}_c + \dot{\boldsymbol{\rho}}_{ci})$$

Carrying out the dot product, we have

$$\text{KE} = \tfrac{1}{2} \sum_{i=1}^{n} m_i V_c^2 + \sum_{i=1}^{n} m_i \boldsymbol{V}_c \bullet \dot{\boldsymbol{\rho}}_{ci} + \tfrac{1}{2} \sum_{i=1}^{n} m_i \dot{\rho}_{ci}^2 \tag{13.33}$$

Since $\boldsymbol{V}_c$ is common for all values of the summation index, we can extract it from the summation operation, and this leaves

$$\text{KE} = \tfrac{1}{2} \left(\sum_{i=1}^{n} m_i \right) V_c^2 + \boldsymbol{V}_c \bullet \left(\sum_{i=1}^{n} m_i \dot{\boldsymbol{\rho}}_{ci} \right) + \tfrac{1}{2} \sum_{i=1}^{n} m_i \dot{\rho}_{ci}^2 \tag{13.34}$$

Perform the following replacements:

$$\sum_{i=1}^{n} m_i \text{ by } M, \qquad \text{and} \qquad \sum_{i=1}^{n} m_i \dot{\boldsymbol{\rho}}_{ci} \text{ by } \frac{d}{dt} \sum_{i=1}^{n} m_i \boldsymbol{\rho}_{ci}$$

We then have

$$\text{KE} = \tfrac{1}{2} M V_c^2 + \boldsymbol{V}_c \bullet \frac{d}{dt} \sum_{i=1}^{n} m_i \boldsymbol{\rho}_{ci} + \tfrac{1}{2} \sum_{i=1}^{n} m_i \dot{\rho}_{ci}^2 \tag{13.34}$$

But the expression

$$\sum_{i=1}^{n} m_i \boldsymbol{\rho}_{ci}$$

represents the first moment of mass of the system about the center of mass for the system. Clearly by definition, this quantity must always be zero. The expression for kinetic energy becomes

$$\text{KE} = \tfrac{1}{2} M V_c^2 + \tfrac{1}{2} \sum_{i=1}^{n} m_i \dot{\rho}_{ci}^2 \tag{13.35}$$

Thus, we see that the *kinetic energy* for some reference *can be considered to be composed of two parts: (1) the kinetic energy of the total mass moving relative to that reference with the velocity of the mass center, plus (2) the kinetic energy of the motion of the particles relative to the mass center.*

Example 13.12

A hypothetical vehicle is moving at speed V_0 in Fig. 13.24. On this vehicle are two bodies each of mass m sliding along a horizontal rod at a speed v relative to the rod. This rod is rotating at an angular speed ω rad/sec relative to the vehicle. What is the kinetic energy of the two bodies relative to the ground (XYZ) when they are at a distance r from point A?

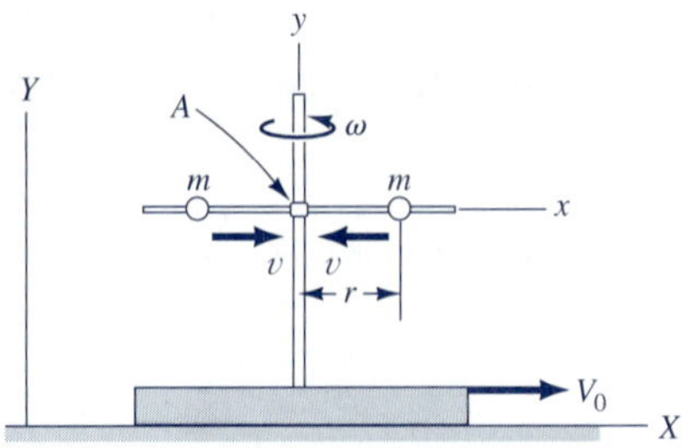

Figure 13.24. Moving device.

Clearly, the center of mass corresponds to point A and is thus moving at a speed V_0 relative to the ground. Hence, we have as part of the kinetic energy the term

$$\tfrac{1}{2}MV_c^2 = mV_0^2 \tag{a}$$

The velocity of each ball relative to the center of mass is easily formed using cylindrical components. Thus, imagining a reference xyz at A translating with the vehicle relative to XYZ, we have for the velocity of each ball relative to xyz:

$$\dot{\rho}^2 = \dot{r}^2 + (\omega r)^2 = v^2 + (\omega r)^2 \tag{b}$$

The total kinetic energy of the two masses relative to the ground is then

$$\text{KE} = mV_0^2 + m\left[v^2 + (\omega r)^2\right] \tag{c}$$

In Example 13.12, we considered a case where the bodies involved constituted a finite number of *discrete* particles. In the next example, we consider a case where we have a *continuum* of particles forming a rigid body. The formulation given by Eq. 13.35 can still be used but now, instead of summing for a finite number of discrete particles, we must integrate to account for the infinite number of infinitesimal particles comprising the system. We are thus taking a glimpse, for simple cases, of rigid-body dynamics to be studied later in the text. Those that do not have time for studying such energy problems in detail will be able to solve simple but useful rigid-body dynamics problems on the basis of these examples as well as later examples in this chapter.

Example 13.13

A thin uniform hoop of radius R is rolling without slipping such that O, the mass center, moves at a speed V (Fig. 13.25). If the hoop weighs W lb, what is the kinetic energy of the hoop relative to the ground?

Clearly, the hoop cannot be considered as a finite number of discrete finite particles as in the previous example, and so we must consider an infinity of infinitesimal contiguous particles. It is simplest to employ here the center-of-mass approach. The main problem then is to find the kinetic energy of the hoop relative to the mass center O, that is, relative to a reference xy translating with the mass center as seen from the ground reference XY (see Fig. 13.26). The motion relative to xy is clearly simple rotation; accordingly, we must find the angular velocity of the hoop for this reference. The no slipping condition means that the point of contact of the hoop with the ground has instantaneously a zero velocity. Observe the motion from a stationary reference XY. As you may have learned in physics, and as will later be shown (Chapter 15), the body has a *pure instantaneous rotational* motion about the point of contact. The angular velocity ω for this motion is then easily evaluated by considering point O rotating about the instantaneous center of rotation A. Thus,

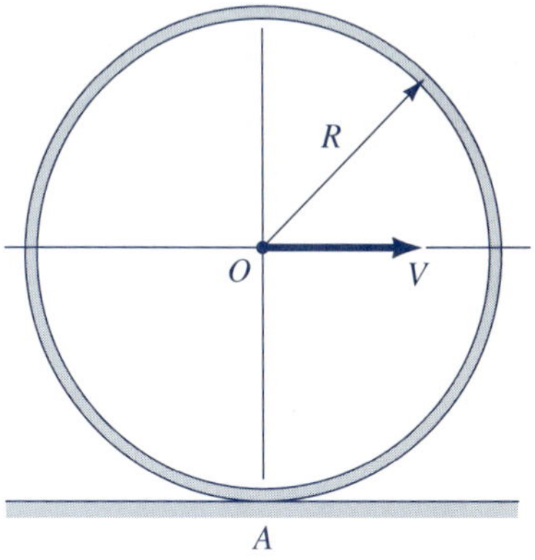

Figure 13.25. Rolling hoop.

$$\omega = \frac{V}{R} \tag{a}$$

Since reference xy *translates* relative to reference XY, an observer on xy sees the *same angular velocity* ω for the hoop as the observer on XY. Accordingly, we can now readily evaluate the second term on the right side of Eq. 13.35. As particles, use elements of the hoop which are $R\,d\theta$ in length, as shown in Fig. 13.26, and which have a mass per unit length of $W/(2\pi Rg)$. We then have, on replacing summation by integration, the result

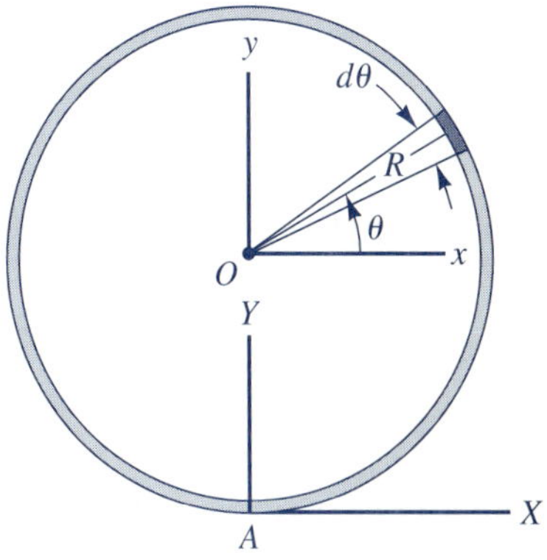

Figure 13.26. xy translates with O relative to XY.

$$\begin{aligned}\frac{1}{2}\sum_{i=1}^{n} m_i\dot{\rho}_{ci}^2 &= \frac{1}{2}\int_0^{2\pi}\left[\left(\frac{W}{2\pi Rg}\right)(R\,d\theta)\right](\omega R)^2 \\ &= \frac{1}{2}\int_0^{2\pi}\left[\frac{W}{2\pi Rg}(R\,d\theta)\right]\left(\frac{V}{R}R\right)^2 \\ &= \frac{1}{2}\frac{W}{g}V^2\end{aligned} \tag{b}$$

The kinetic energy of the hoop is then in accordance with Eq. 13.35:

$$\text{KE} = \underbrace{\frac{1}{2}\frac{W}{g}V^2}_{(\text{KE})_{\text{C.M.}}} + \underbrace{\frac{1}{2}\frac{W}{g}V^2}_{(\text{KE})_{\text{Rel. to C.M.}}} = \boxed{\frac{W}{g}V^2} \tag{c}$$

Example 13.13 (Continued)

Suppose that the body were a generalized cylinder of mass M (see Fig. 13.27) such as a tire of radius R having O as the center of mass with axisymmetrical distribution of mass about the axis at O. Then, we would express Eq. (b) as follows:

$$\frac{1}{2}\sum_{i}^{n} m_i \dot{\rho}_{ci}^2 = \frac{1}{2}\iiint_M (dm)(r\omega)^2 \tag{d}$$

You will recall from Chapter 9 that

$$\iiint_M r^2\, dm$$

is the *second moment of inertia* of the body taken about the z axis at O. That is,

$$I_{zz} = \iiint_M r^2\, dm$$

Thus, we have for the kinetic energy of such a body:

$$\text{KE} = \frac{1}{2}MV^2 + \frac{1}{2}I_{zz}\omega^2 \tag{e}$$

You may also recall from Chapter 9 that we could employ the *radius of gyration k* to express I_{zz} as follows:

$$I_{zz} = k^2 M \tag{f}$$

Hence, Eq. (e) can be given as

$$\text{KE} = \frac{1}{2}MV^2 + \frac{1}{2}k^2 M\omega^2$$

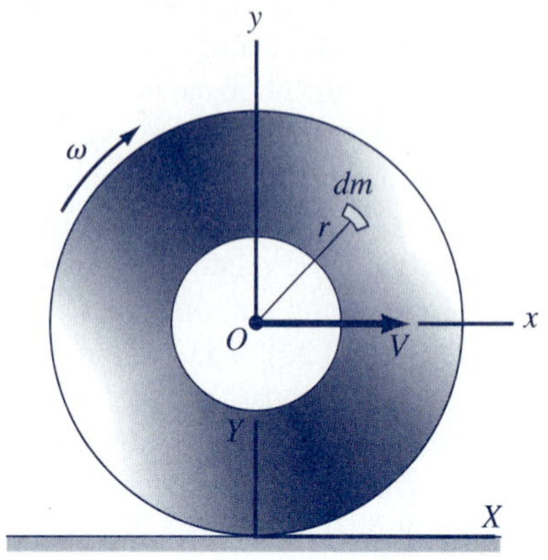

Figure 13.27. Rolling generalized cylinder of mass M.

We shall examine the kinetic energy formulations of rigid bodies carefully in Chapter 17. Here, we have used certain familiar results from physics pertaining to kinematics of plane motion of a nonslipping rolling rigid body. For a more general undertaking, we shall have to carefully consider more general aspects of kinematics of rigid-body motion. This will be done in Chapter 15. Also, in the last example we see one term of the inertia tensor I_{ij} showing up. The vital role of the inertia tensor in the dynamics of rigid bodies will soon be seen.

13.8 Work–Kinetic Energy Expressions Based on Center of Mass

The work–kinetic energy expressions of Section 13.6 were developed for a system of particles without regard to the mass center. We shall now introduce this point into the work–kinetic energy formulations. You will recall from Chapter 12 that *Newton's law* for the mass center of any system of particles is

$$\boldsymbol{F} = M\ddot{\boldsymbol{r}}_c \tag{13.36}$$

where $\boldsymbol{F}$ is the total *external* force on the system of particles. By the same development as presented in Section 13.1, we can readily arrive at the following equation:

$$\int_1^2 \boldsymbol{F} \cdot d\boldsymbol{r}_c = \left(\tfrac{1}{2}MV_c^2\right)_2 - \left(\tfrac{1}{2}MV_c^2\right)_1 \tag{13.37}$$

It is *vital* to understand from the left side of Eq. 13.37, where we note the term $d\boldsymbol{r}_c$, that the *external forces must all move with the center of mass* for the computation of the proper work term in this equation.[14] We wish next to point out that the single particle model represents a special case of the use of Eq. 13.37. Specifically, the single particle model represents the case where the motion of the center of mass of a body sufficiently describes the motion of the body and where the external forces on the body essentially move with the center of mass of the body. Such cases were set forth in Section 13.1.

Before proceeding to the examples, let us consider for a moment the case of the cylinder rolling without slipping down an incline (see Fig. 13.28). We shall consider the cylinder as an *aggregate of particles* which form a rigid body—namely a cylinder. When using such an approach, we require that *all the forces both external and internal must move with their respective points of application.* Let us then consider the external work done on the particles making up the cylinder other than the work done by gravity. Clearly, only particles on the *rim* of the cylinder are acted on by external forces other than gravity. Consider one such particle during one rotation of the cylinder. This particle will have acting on it a friction force f and a normal force N at the *instant* when the particle is in *contact* with the inclined surface. The particle will have *zero* external force (except for gravity) at all other positions during the cycle. Now, at the instant of this contact, the normal force N has zero velocity in its direction because of the rigidity of the bodies. Therefore, N transmits no power and does no work on the particle during the cycle under consideration. Also, the friction

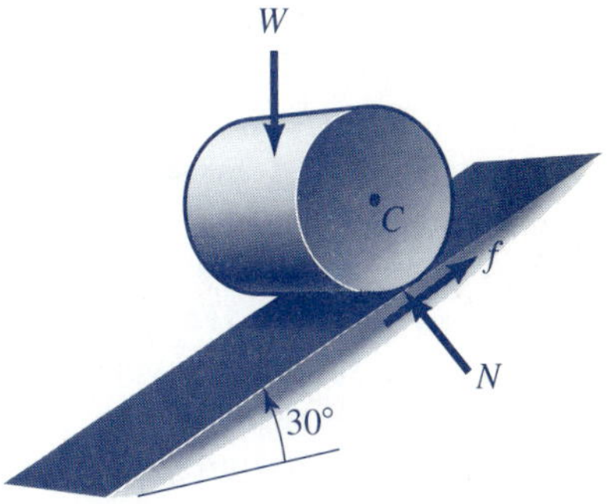

Figure 13.28. Cylinder on incline.

[14]This is in direct contrast to the work–energy equation for a system of particles wherein as was pointed out emphatically earlier, each external force moves with its *actual* point of application. Also, only external forces are involved for the center-of-mass approach, in contrast to the system of particles where internal forces may also be involved. Note that in Examples 13.1, 13.2, and 13.9 we were using a particle approach and thus were really considering the motion of the center of mass. The friction forces then moved with the center of mass.

force f acts on a particle having zero velocity at the instant of contact because of the *no slipping* condition. Accordingly, f transmits no power and does no work on the particle during this cycle.[15] This result must be true for each and every particle on the rim of the cylinder. Thus, clearly, f and N do no work when the cylinder rolls down the incline. Also, because of the rigidity of the body the internal forces do no work as pointed out earlier. Thus, only gravity does work.

However, in considering the motion of the *center of mass* C of the cylinder in Fig. 13.28, we note that force f now *moves* with C and hence *does* work.

At the risk of being repetitive, we now summarize the key features for properly using the center-of-mass approach.

1. Only **external** forces are involved.
2. Forces all move with the **center of mass** when computing work (see Eq. 13.37).
3. Only the kinetic energy of the center of mass is used.

[15]Another way of understanding this is to express work differently as was done in footnote 4. Once again, we multiply and divide the usual expression for work by dt as follows:

$$\int_1^2 \boldsymbol{F} \cdot d\boldsymbol{r} = \int_1^2 \boldsymbol{F} \cdot \frac{d\boldsymbol{r}}{dt}\,dt = \int_1^2 \boldsymbol{F} \cdot \boldsymbol{V}\,dt$$

We can now clearly see with $\boldsymbol{V} = \boldsymbol{0}$ at the point of contact that there will be zero work from the friction force f there.

Example 13.14

A cylinder with a mass of 25 kg is released from rest on an incline, as shown in Fig. 13.29. The diameter of the cylinder is .60 m. If the cylinder rolls without slipping, compute the speed of the centerline C after it has moved 1.6 m along the incline . Also, ascertain the friction force acting on the cylinder. Use the result from Problem 13.76 that the kinetic energy of a cylinder rotating about its own stationary axis is $\frac{1}{4}MR^2\omega^2$, where ω is the angular speed in rad/sec.

In Fig. 13.29 we have shown the free body of the cylinder. We proceed to use the **work–energy equation** for a **system of particles**. Recall that we can concentrate the weight at the center of gravity (Section 13.6). Accordingly, using the lowest position as a datum and noting from our earlier discussion that the friction force f does no work we have

$$\Delta(\text{PE} + \text{KE}) = \mathcal{W}_{1-2}$$

$$\left[0 - (25)(9.81)(1.6)\sin 30°\right] + \left\{\left[\tfrac{1}{2}(25)V_c^2 + \tfrac{1}{4}(25)(.30)^2(\omega^2)\right] - 0\right\} = 0 \quad \text{(a)}$$

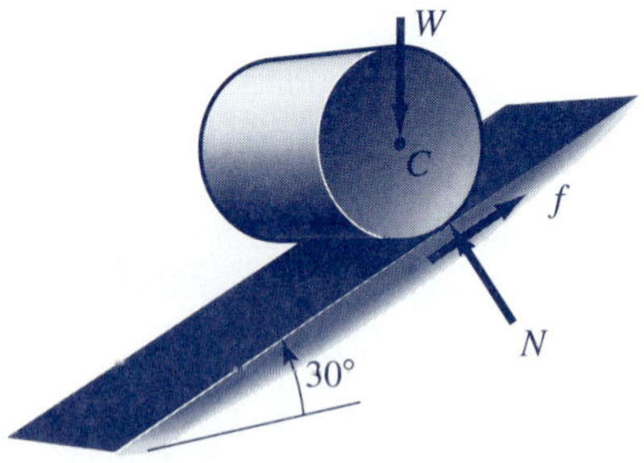

Figure 13.29. Free-body diagram of cylinder.

Example 13.14 (Continued)

where the kinetic energy of the cylinder is given as the kinetic energy of the mass taken at the mass center (straight line motion of C) plus kinetic energy of the cylinder relative to the center of mass (pure rotation about C). Noting from Example 13.13 that

$$\omega = \frac{V}{R} = \frac{V}{.30}$$

we substitute into Eq. (a) and solve for V_c. We get

$$V_c = 3.23 \text{ m/sec} \tag{b}$$

Now to find f, we *consider the motion of the mass center of the cylinder*. This means that we use Eq. 13.37 for the **center of mass**. Now *all external forces must move with the center of mass*; thus, f does work. Since the center of mass moves along a path always at right angles to N, this force still does no work. Accordingly, we can say:

$$-f(1.6) + W(1.6 \sin 30°) = \tfrac{1}{2}MV_c^2$$

$$-f(1.6) + (25)(9.81)(1.6) \sin 30° = \tfrac{1}{2}(25)(3.23^2)$$

$$f = 41.1 \text{ N}$$

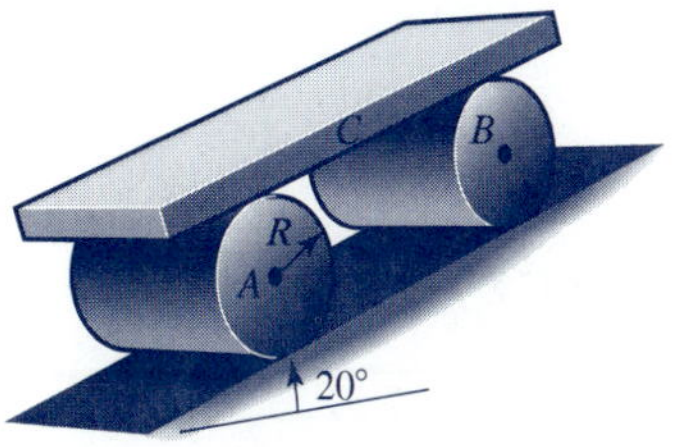

Figure 13.30. Three rigid bodies moving without slipping at any of the contact points.

Before going further, let us consider the two cylinders and the block in Fig. 13.30 as simply a **system of particles**. If there is no slipping between the block and the cylinders, the velocities of the particles on the block and the cylinders at the points of contact between these bodies have the *same* velocity at any time t. Furthermore, the friction force on the cylinder from the block is *equal* and *opposite* to the friction force on the block from the cylinder at the point of contact. We can then conclude that there is zero net work done by the friction forces between block and cylinders when considering them as an aggregate of particles.

Also, in the next problem, we will consider as a system of particles, rigid bodies which are joined by rigid connectors with frictionless interconnections.

Example 13.15

An external torque T of 50 N-m is applied to a solid cylinder B (see Fig. 13.31), which has a mass of 30 kg and a radius of .2 m. The cylinder rolls without slipping. Block A, having a mass of 20 kg, is dragged up the 15° incline. The dynamic coefficient of friction μ_d between block A and the incline is .25. The connections at C and D are frictionless.

(a) What is the velocity of the system after moving a distance d of 2 m?
(b) What is the friction force on the cylinder?

Neglect the mass of the connecting rod.

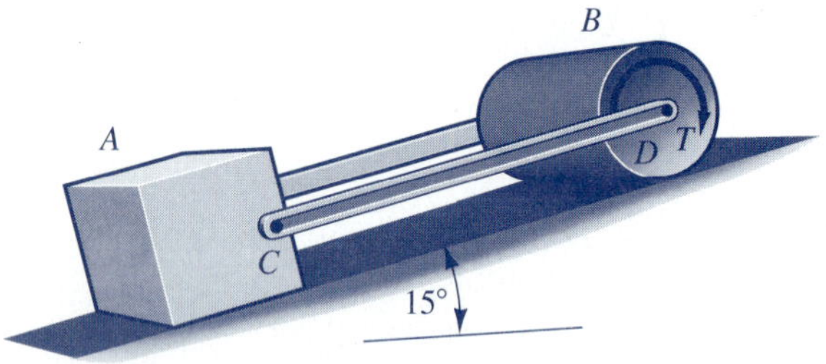

Figure 13.31. Torque-driven cylinder moves without slipping.

We show a free-body diagram of the system in Fig. 13.32. We begin by employing a **system of particles** point of view. Note there are pairs of internal forces present between the rod CD and body A at the contact point

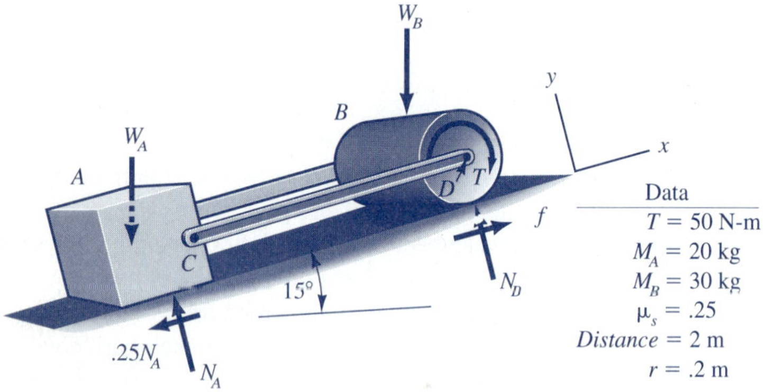

Figure 13.32. Free-body diagram of the system.

Example 13.15 (Continued)

and similarly between CD and cylinder B. These force pairs are equal and opposite because of Newton's third law. And because the forces in each pair move exactly the same distance at the respective points of contact, there will be zero internal work from these force pairs. Hence, using the uppermost configuration as the datum,

$$\mathcal{W}_{1\to 2} = \Delta\text{PE} + \Delta\text{KE}$$

$$T\theta - (\mu_d N_A)(d) = \left[(W_A + W_B)(d)(\sin 15°) - 0\right] + \left[(M_A + M_B)\frac{V^2}{2} + \frac{1}{4}M_B r_B^2 \omega_B^2 - 0\right] \quad \text{(a)}$$

Note that as the cylinder moves without slipping a distance d along the incline, the circumference of the cylinder must come into contact with the incline along the very same distance d. Hence, by dividing d by the radius r, we get the rotation of the cylinder in radians associated with the movement of its center.

$$\theta = \frac{d}{r}$$

We then get for Eq. (a), on substituting data for the problem

$$(50)\left(\frac{2}{.2}\right) - (.25)[(20g)(\cos 15°)](2) = [(50g)(2)(.2588)] + \left[(50)\frac{V^2}{2} + \frac{1}{4}(30)(.2^2)\frac{V^2}{(.2)^2}\right]$$

$$V = 2.158 \text{ m/s}$$

Next, use the **center-of-mass** approach. We have on noting that a couple which is translating does no work. (Why?)

$$\int_1^2 \boldsymbol{F} \cdot d\boldsymbol{r}_C = \tfrac{1}{2}M_{\text{Total}}(V_2^2 - V_1^2)$$

$$-(.25)(N_A)(d) - (W_A + W_B)(\sin 15°)(d) + fd = \tfrac{1}{2}(50)(2.158^2)$$

$$-(.25)[(20g)(\cos 15°)](2) - (50g)(.2588)(2) + f(2) = 116.4$$

$$f = 232.5 \text{ N}$$

Example 13.16

In Example 13.15, suppose that cylinder B is *slipping*. What is the dynamic coefficient of friction $(\mu_d)_B$ between the cylinder and the incline so that the system reaches a speed of 1.5 m/s after moving a distance $d = 2$ m starting from rest?

Using the **center-of-mass** approach, we have

$$\int_1^2 \boldsymbol{F} \cdot d\boldsymbol{r}_C = \left(\tfrac{1}{2}MV_C^2\right)_2 - \left(\tfrac{1}{2}MV_C^2\right)_1$$

$$-(W_A \cos 15°)(.25)(d) + (W_B \cos 15°)(\mu_d)_B(d) - (W_A + W_B)(\sin 15°)(d) = \frac{1}{2}\frac{W_A + W_B}{g}V^2 - 0$$

$$-(20g)(\cos 15°)(.25)(2) + (\mu_d)_B(30g)(\cos 15°)(2) - (50g)(\sin 15°)(2) = \frac{1}{2}(50)(1.5^2) - 0$$

$$(\mu_d)_B = .7122$$

In the next example, we shall consider a case where *internal forces* do work.

Example 13.17

A diesel-powered electric train moves up a 7° grade in Fig. 13.33. If a torque of 750 N-m is developed at each of its six pairs of drive wheels, what is the increase of speed of the train after it moves 100 m? Initially, the train has a speed of 16 km/hr. The train weighs 90 kN. The drive wheels have a diameter of 600 mm. Neglect the rotational energy of the drive wheels.

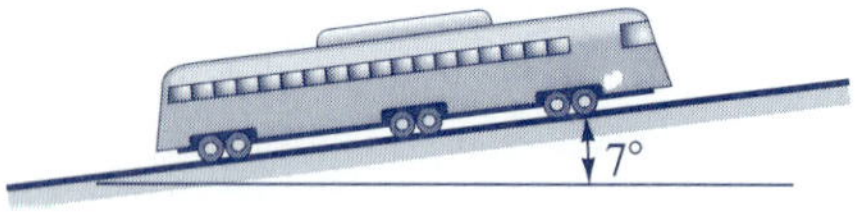

Figure 13.33. Diesel–electric train.

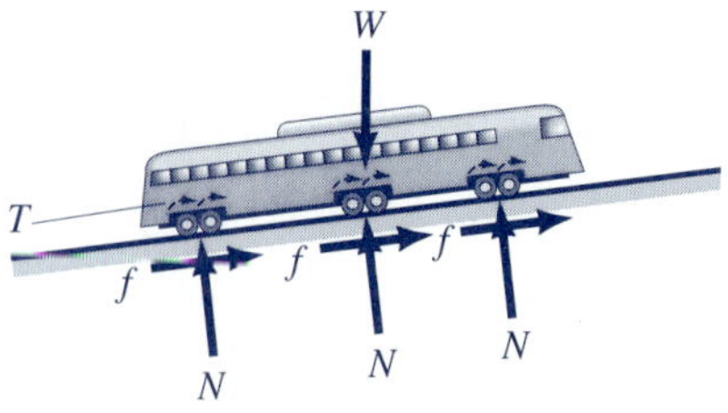

Figure 13.34. External and internal forces and torques.

We shall consider the train as a **system of particles** including the 6 pairs of wheels and the body. We have shown the train in Fig. 13.34 with the external forces, W, N, and f. In addition, we have shown certain internal

Example 13.17 (Continued)

torques *T*.[16] The torques shown act on the *rotors* of the motors, and, as the train moves, these torques rotate and accordingly do work. The *reactions* to these torques are equal and opposite to *T* according to Newton's third law and act on the *stators* of the motors (i.e., the field coils). The stators are stationary, and so the reactions to *T* do *no* work as the train moves. Thus we have an example wherein, using a **system of particles approach**, internal forces perform a nonzero amount of work. We now employ Eq. 13.29. Thus

$$\Delta PE + KE = \mathcal{W}_{1\to 2} \qquad \text{(a)}$$

For the rolling without slipping condition, the friction forces *f* do no work. We then have

$$\left[(90{,}000)(100\sin 7^\circ - 0)\right] + \left\{\frac{1}{2}\frac{90{,}000}{g}V^2 - \frac{1}{2}\frac{90{,}000}{g}\left[\frac{(16)(1{,}000)}{3{,}600}\right]^2\right\}$$
$$= (6)(750)(\theta) \qquad \text{(b)}$$

where θ is the clockwise rotation of the rotor in radians. Assuming direct drive from rotor to wheel, we can compute θ as follows for the 100-m distance *d* over which the train moves:

$$\theta = \frac{d}{r} = \frac{100}{.3} = 333.3 \text{ rad} \qquad \text{(c)}$$

Substituting into Eq. (b) and solving for *V*, we get

$$V = 10.38 \text{ m/sec}$$

Hence, the increase of speed of the train is

$$\Delta V = \frac{(10.38)(3{,}600)}{1{,}000} - 16 = \boxed{21.4 \text{ km/hr}} \qquad \text{(d)}$$

To determine the friction forces *f*, we now adopt a **center-of-mass** approach. Thus all forces now move with the center of mass. And they must be *external forces*. Accordingly we have

$$\left[6f - (90{,}000)(\sin 7^\circ)\right](100)$$
$$= \frac{1}{2}\frac{90{,}000}{9.81}(10.38)^2 - \frac{1}{2}\frac{90{,}000}{9.81}\left(\frac{(16)(1{,}000)}{3{,}600}\right)^2$$

$$\boxed{f = 2{,}500 \text{ N}}$$

[16]Figure 13.34. accordingly, is *not* a free-body diagram.

PROBLEMS

13.68. A chain of total length L is released from rest on a smooth support as shown. Determine the velocity of the chain when the last link moves off the horizontal surface. In this problem, neglect the friction. Also, do not attempt to account for centrifugal effects stemming from the chain links rounding the corner.

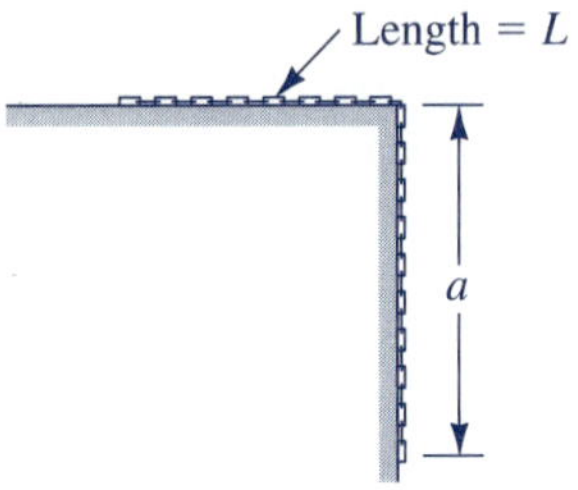

Figure P.13.68.

13.69. A chain is 50 ft long and weighs 100 lb. A force P of 80 lb has been applied at the configuration shown. What is the speed of the chain after force P has moved 10 ft? The dynamic coefficient of friction between the chain and the supporting surface is .3. Utilize an approximate analysis.

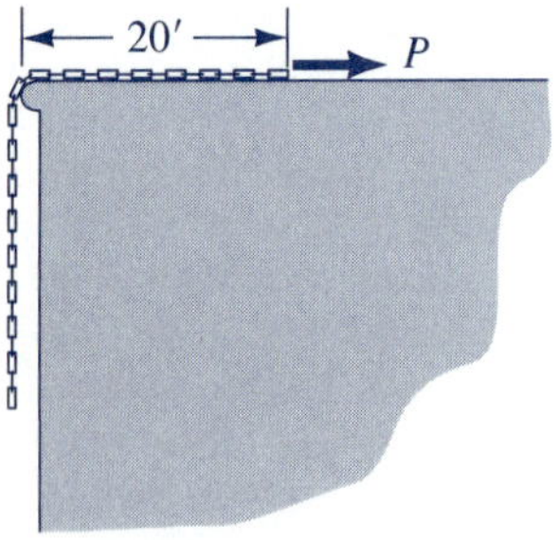

Figure P.13.69.

13.70. A bullet of weight W_1 is fired into a block of wood weighing W_2 lb. The bullet lodges in the wood, and both bodies then move to the dashed position indicated in the diagram before falling back. Compute the amount of internal work done during the action. Discuss the effects of this work. The bullet has a speed V_0 before hitting the block. Neglect the mass of the supporting rod and friction at A.

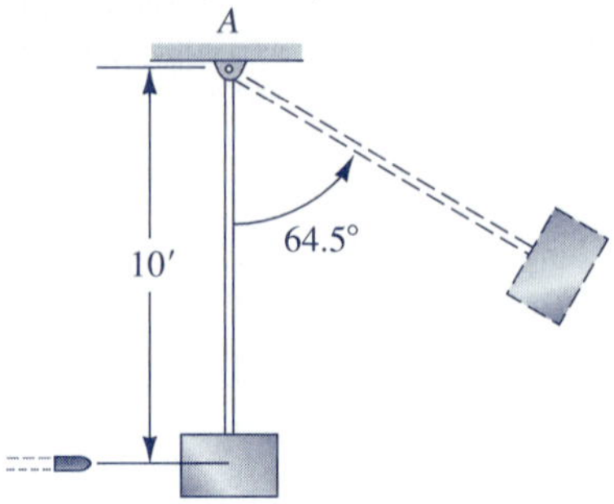

Figure P.13.70.

13.71. A device is mounted on a platform that is rotating with an angular speed of 10 rad/sec. The device consists of two masses (each is .1 slug) rotating on a spindle with an angular speed of 5 rad-sec relative to the platform. The masses are moving radially outward with a speed of 10 ft/sec, and the entire platform is being raised at a speed of 5 ft/sec. Compute the kinetic energy of the system of two particles when they are 1 ft from the spindle.

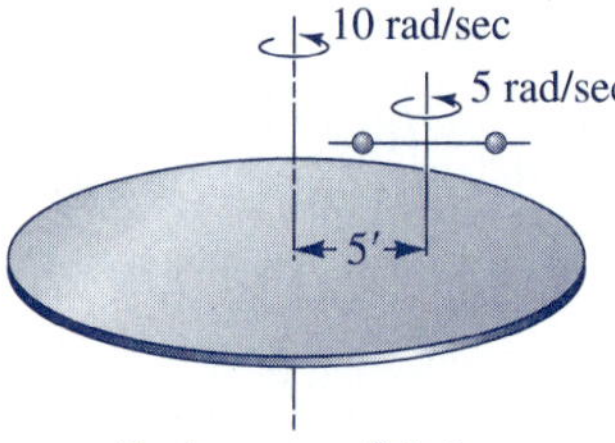

Figure P.13.71.

13.72. A hoop, with four spokes, rolls without slipping such that the center C moves at a speed V of 1.7 m/sec. The diameter of the hoop is 3.3 m and the weight per unit length of the rim is 14 N/m. The spokes are uniform rods also having a weight per unit length of 14 N/m. Assume that rim and spokes are thin. What is the kinetic energy of the body?

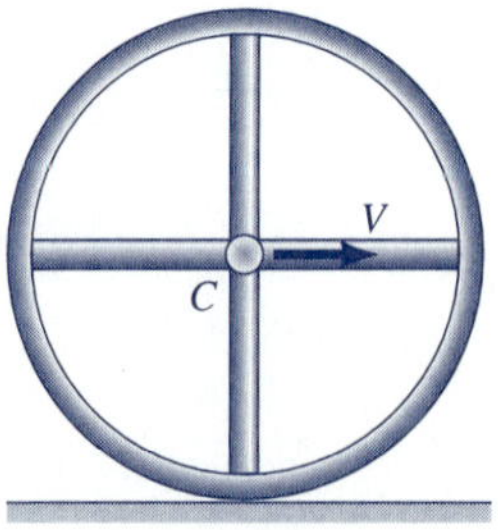

Figure P.13.72.

13.73. Three weights A, B, and C slide frictionlessly along the system of connected rods. The bodies are connected by a light, flexible, inextensible wire that is directed by frictionless small pulleys at E and F. If the system is released from rest, what is its speed after it has moved 300 mm? Employ the following data for the body masses:

Body A: 5 kg

Body B: 4 kg

Body C: 7.5 kg

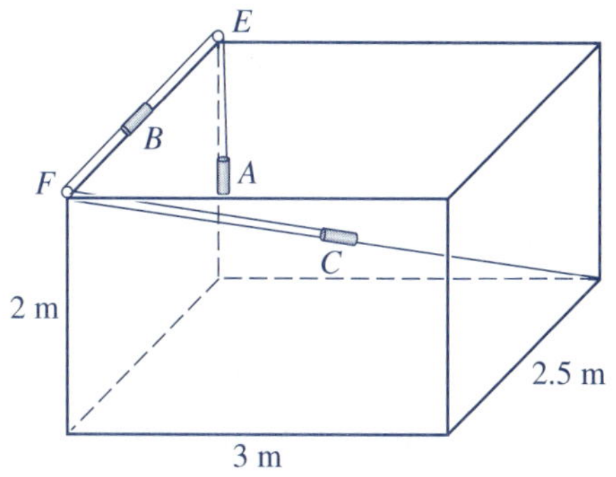

Figure P.13.73.

13.74. Bodies E and F slide in frictionless grooves. They are interconnected by a light, flexible, inextensible cable (not shown). What is the speed of the system after it has moved 2 ft? The weights of bodies E and F are 10 lb and 20 lb, respectively. B is equidistant from A and C. E remains in top groove.

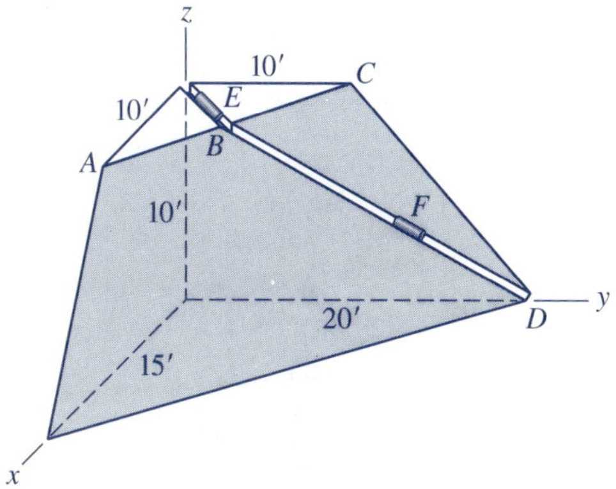

Figure P.13.74.

13.75. A tank is moving at the speed V of 16 km/hr. What is the kinetic energy of each of the treads for this tank if they each have a mass per unit length of 300 kg/m?

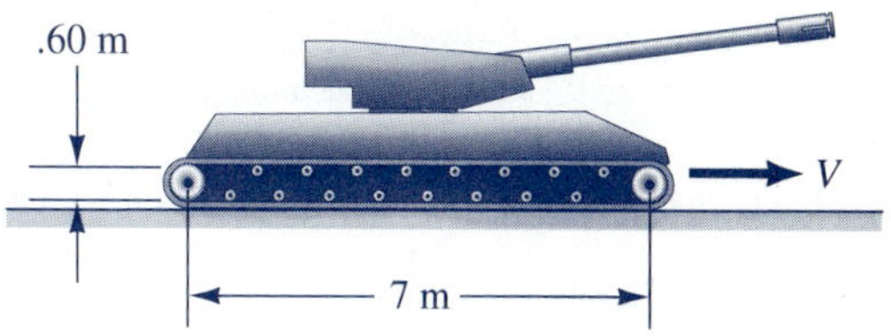

Figure P.13.75.

13.76. A cylinder of radius R rotates about its own axis with an angular speed of ω. If the total mass is M, show that the kinetic energy is $\frac{1}{4}MR^2\omega^2$.

13.77. Cylinders B and C each weigh 100 lb and have a diameter of 2 ft. Body A, weighing 300 lb, rides on these cylinders. If there is no slipping anywhere, what is the kinetic energy of the system when the body A is moving at a speed V of 10 ft/sec? Use result of Problem 13.76.

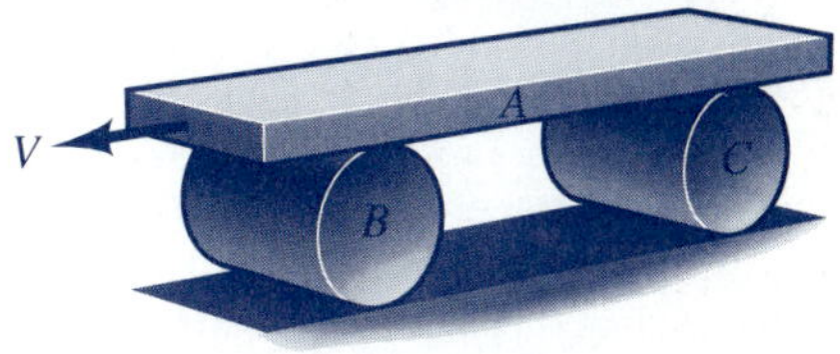

Figure P.13.77.

13.78. A pendulum has a bob with a comparatively large uniform disc of diameter 2 ft and mass M of 3 lbm. At the instant shown, the system has an angular speed $\dot{\theta}$ of .3 rad/sec. If we neglect the mass of the rod, what is the kinetic energy of the pendulum at this instant? What error is incurred if one considers the bob to be a particle as we have done earlier for smaller bobs? Use the result of Problem 13.76.

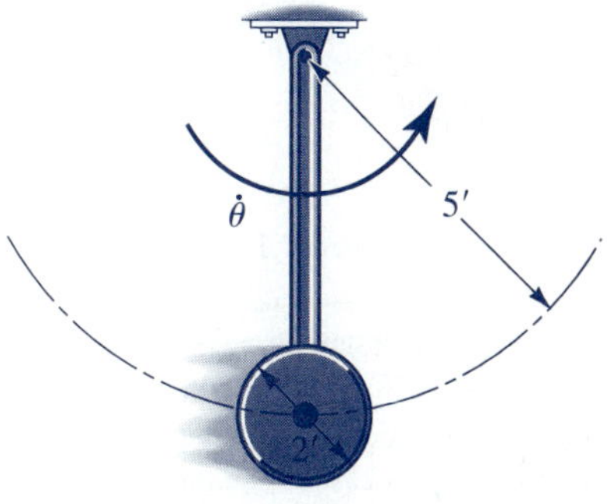

Figure P.13.78.

13.79. In Problem 13.78 compute the maximum angle that the pendulum rises.

13.80. Do Example 13.3 by treating as an aggregate of particles.

13.81. Do Problem 13.27 by treating as an aggregate of particles.

13.82. Do Problem 13.22 by treating as an aggregate of particles.

13.83. Do Problem 13.24 by treating as an aggregate of particles.

13.84. A constant force F is applied to the axis of a cylinder, as shown, causing the axis to increase its speed from 1 ft/sec to 3 ft/sec in 10 ft without slipping. What is the friction force acting on the cylinder? The cylinder weighs 100 lb.

Figure P.13.84.

13.85. A cylinder with a mass of 25 kg is released from rest on an incline, as shown. The inner diameter D of the cylinder is 300 mm. If the cylinder rolls without slipping, compute the speed of the centerline O after the cylinder has moved 1.6 m along the incline. Ascertain the friction force acting on the cylinder. The radius of gyration k at O is $.30/\sqrt{2}$ m.

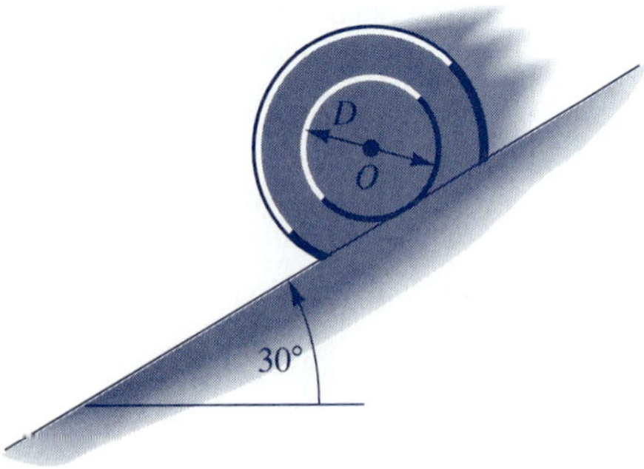

Figure P.13.85.

13.86. A uniform cylinder having a diameter of 2 ft and a weight of 100 lb rolls down a 30° incline without slipping, as shown. What is the speed of the center after it has moved 20 ft? Compare this result with that for the case when there is no friction present. [*Hint:* Use the result of Problem 13.76.]

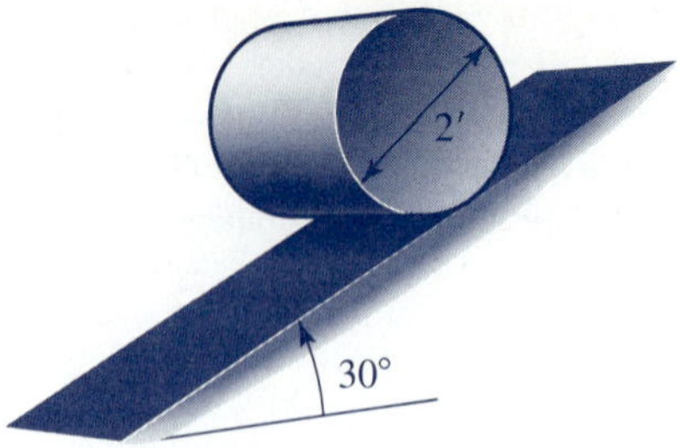

Figure P.13.86.

13.87. Cylinders A and B each have a mass of 25 kg and a diameter of 300 mm. Block C, riding on A and B, has a mass of 100 kg. If the system is released from rest at the configuration shown, what is the speed of C after the cylinders have made half a revolution? Use the result of Problem 13.76.

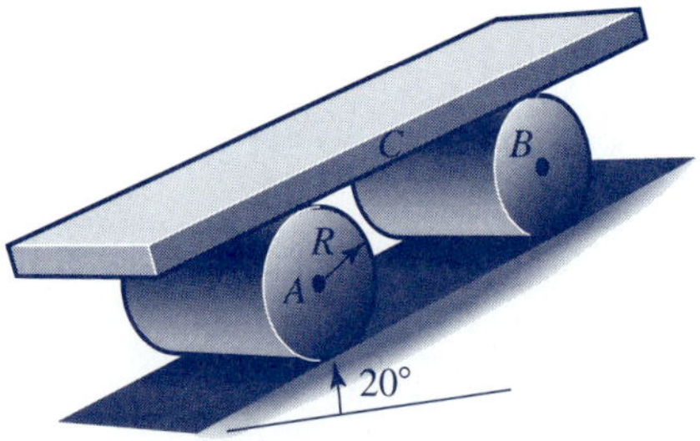

Figure P.13.87.

13.88. Shown are two identical blocks A and B, each weighing 50 lb. A force F of 100 lb is applied to the lower block, causing it to move to the right. Block A, however, is restrained by the wall C. If block B reaches a speed of 10 ft/sec in 2 ft starting from rest at the position shown in the diagram, what is the restraining force from the wall? The dynamic coefficient of friction between B and the ground surface is .3. Do this problem first by using Eq. 13.28. Then check the result by using separate free-body diagrams, and so on.

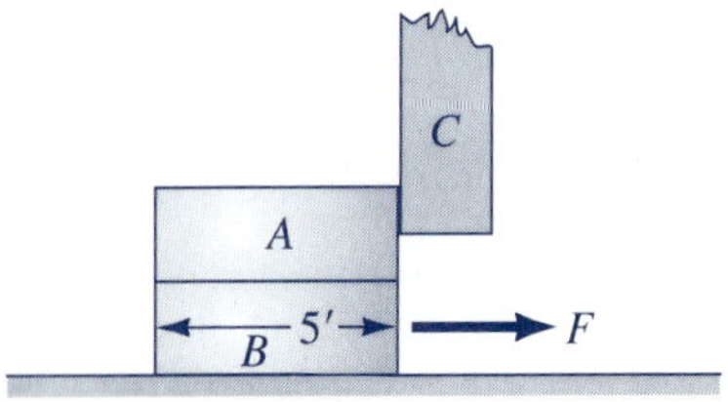

Figure P.13.88.

13.89. What is the tension T to accelerate the end of the cable downward at the rate of 1.5 m/sec^2? From body C, weighing $50g$ N, is lowered a body D weighing $12.5g$ N at the rate of 1.5 m/sec^2 relative to body C. Neglect the inertia of pulleys A and B and the cable. [*Hint:* From earlier courses in physics, recall that pulley B is rotating instantaneously about point e, and hence point b has an acceleration half that of point f. We will consider such relations carefully at a later time.]

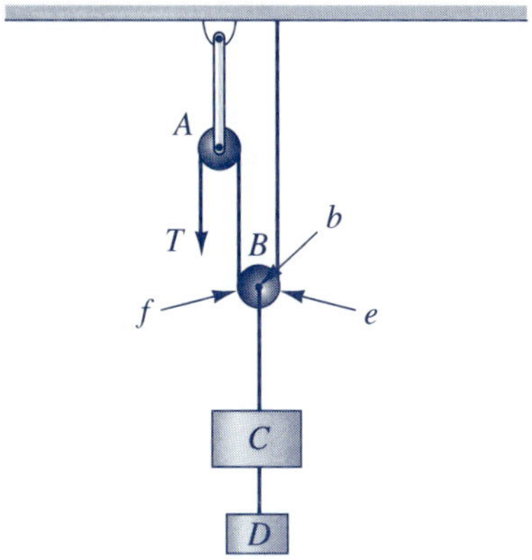

Figure P.13.89.

13.90. Cylinder C is connected by a light rod AB and can roll without slipping along the stationary cylinder D. Cylinder C weighs 30 N. A constant torque T = 20 N-m is applied to AB when it is vertical and stationary. What is the angular speed of AB when it has rotated 90°? The system of bodies is in the vertical plane. Recall from physics that a body which is rolling without slipping has instantaneous rotation about the point of contact.

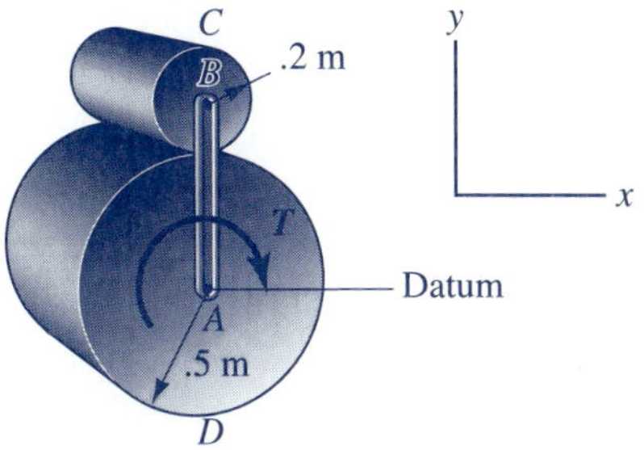

Figure P.13.90.

13.91. An 800-N force F is pulling the vehicle. The cylinders A and B each weigh 1,000 N and roll without slipping. The indicated spring has a spring constant K equal to 50.0 N/mm and is compressed a distance δ of 20.0 mm. The pad slides on the upper guide with a dynamic coefficient of friction μ_d equal to .3. Neglect all masses except the cylinders, whose diameter D is .2 m.

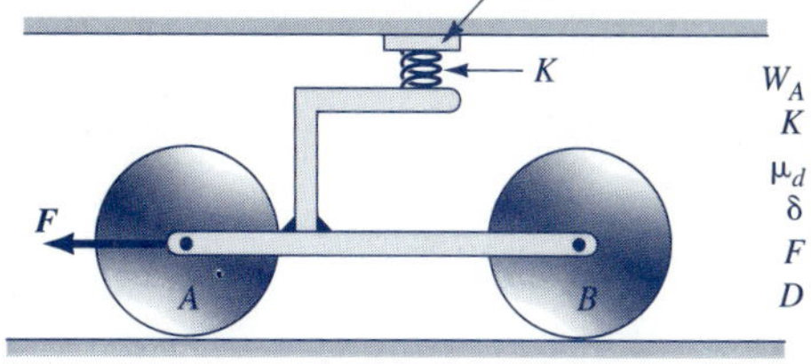

$W_A = W_B$ = 1,000 N
K = 50.0 N/mm
μ_d = .3
δ = 20.0 mm
F = 800 N
D = .2 m

Figure P.13.91.

(a) What is the velocity of the vehicle after it moves a distance of 1.7 m starting from rest?

(b) What is the total friction force f on the cylinders from the ground?

13.92. A cylinder weighing 500 N rolls without slipping, first on a horizontal surface and then along a 30° incline.

(a) How far up the incline does it move?

(b) What are the friction forces on the cylinder along the horizontal surface and along the incline?

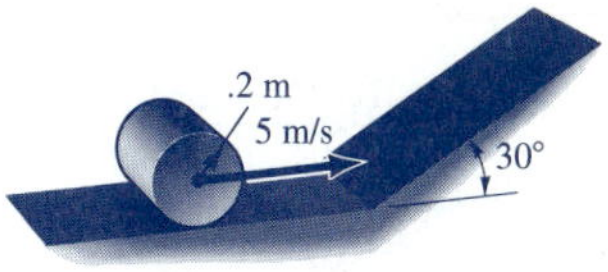

Figure P.13.92.

13.93. A hoop with four spokes is released from rest from a vertical position.

(a) What is the velocity of point C after it moves 1.3 m?

(b) What is the tension in the wire?

The rim and the spokes each have a weight per unit length of 15 N/m and are to be considered as thin. The wire is wrapped around the hoop and is the sole support.

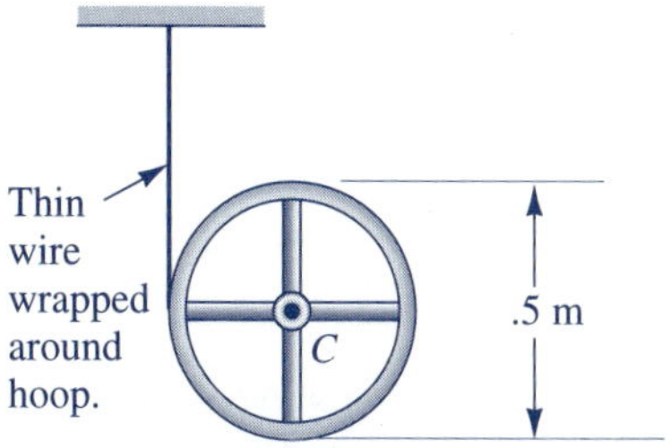

Figure P.13.93.

13.94. Three cylinders roll without slipping starting from rest. What is the speed of the system after moving .3 m? What is the *total* friction from the two walls on the system?

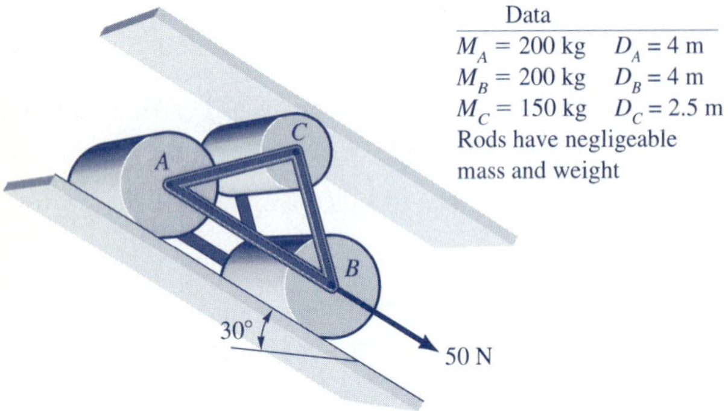

Figure P.13.94.

13.95. Find the velocity V_A after starting from rest and moving 5 m. What is the friction force from the incline on cylinder A? There is only rolling without slipping for the cylinders.

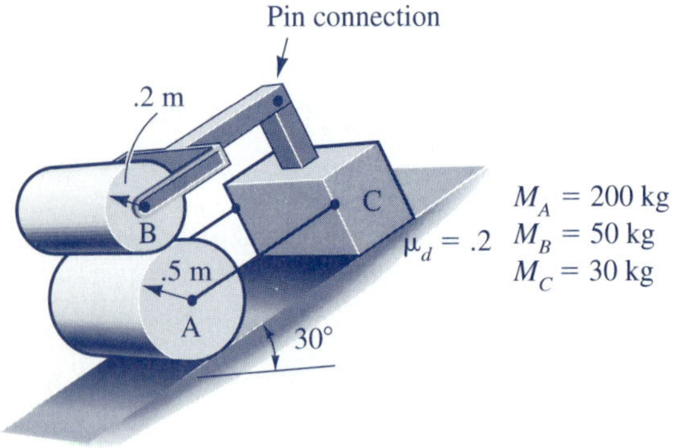

Figure P.13.95.

13.96. A cylinder is about to roll down an incline without slipping. It is connected to a linear spring. What is the angular speed of the cylinder after it rotates 20° starting from rest? The spring is originally unstretched.

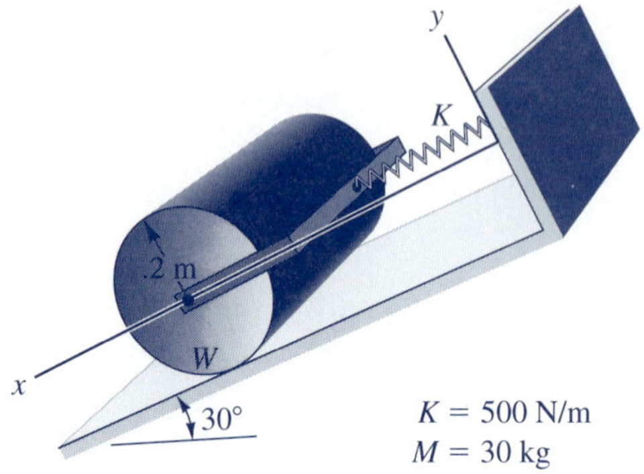

Figure P.13.96.

13.97. Three cylinders are connected together by light rods. Cylinders A have a mass of 5 kg each and cylinder B has a mass of 3 kg. If there is no slipping anywhere,

(a) What is the speed of the system after moving .8 m? The system starts from rest.

(b) What are the friction forces from the ground on each cylinder A?

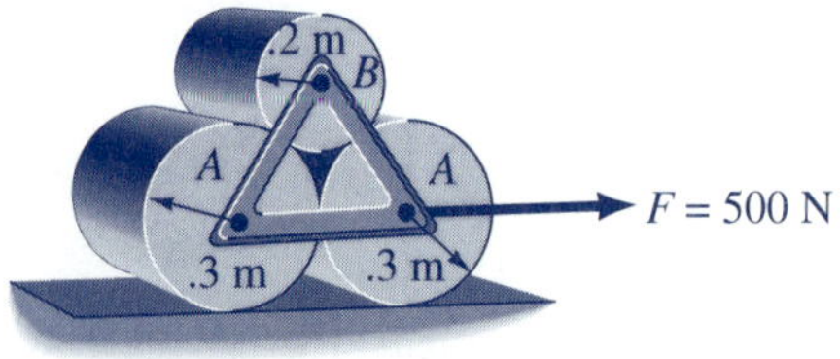

Figure P.13.97.

13.9 Closure

In this chapter, we presented the energy method as applied to particles. In Part A, we presented three forms of the energy equation applied to a *single* particle. The basic equation was

$$\int_1^2 \boldsymbol{F} \cdot d\boldsymbol{r} = \tfrac{1}{2}\left(MV^2\right)_2 - \tfrac{1}{2}\left(MV^2\right)_1 \tag{13.38}$$

For the case of only conservative forces acting, we presented the equation for the *conservation of mechanical energy*:

$$(\text{PE})_1 + (\text{KE})_1 = (\text{PE})_2 + (\text{KE})_2 \tag{13.39}$$

Finally, for both conservative and nonconservative forces, we presented an equation resembling the *first law of thermodynamics* as it is usually employed:

$$\Delta(\text{PE} + \text{KE}) = \mathcal{W}_{1-2} \tag{13.40}$$

In Part B, we considered a *system of particles* and presented the above equation again, but this time the work and potential-energy terms are from both *internal* and *external* force systems.[17] Furthermore, all work and potential-energy terms are evaluated by using the *actual movement* of the points of application of internal and external forces.

Next, we presented the work–energy equation for the *center of mass* of any system of particles:

$$\int_1^2 \boldsymbol{F} \cdot d\boldsymbol{r}_c = \tfrac{1}{2}\left(MV_c^2\right)_2 - \tfrac{1}{2}\left(MV_c^2\right)_1 \tag{13.41}$$

where $\boldsymbol{F}$, the resultant *external force*, *moves with the center of mass* in the computation of the work expression. We pointed out that the *single particle* model is a *special case* of the use of Eq. 13.41 applicable when the motion of the center of mass of a body sufficiently describes the motion of a body and where the external forces on the body move with the center of mass of the body.

To illustrate the use of the work–energy equation for a system of particles, we considered various elementary plane motions of simple rigid bodies. A more extensive treatment of the energy method applied to rigid bodies is found in Chapter 17.

We now turn to yet another useful set of relations derived from Newton's law, namely the methods of linear impulse-momentum and angular impulse-momentum for a particle and systems of particles.

[17]As will be seen in Chapter 14, this equation for a system of particles is the *only one* that involves internal forces. Note, however, that for a *rigid body* the internal forces *do no work*.

PROBLEMS

13.98. A tractor exerts a force of 800 lb on a block A, which has a dynamic coefficient of friction with block B of .7. Block B has a dynamic coefficient of friction of .2 with the ground. If block A weighs 400 lb and block B weighs 600 lb, what is the speed of the block A when, after starting from rest, the tractor has moved 2 ft? What is the acceleration of block B?

Figure P.13.98.

13.99. A body A is released from a condition of rest on a frictionless circular surface. The body then moves on a horizontal surface CD whose dynamic coefficient of friction with the body is .2. A spring having a spring constant $K = 900$ N/m is positioned at C as shown in the diagram. How much will the spring be compressed? The body has a mass of 5 kg.

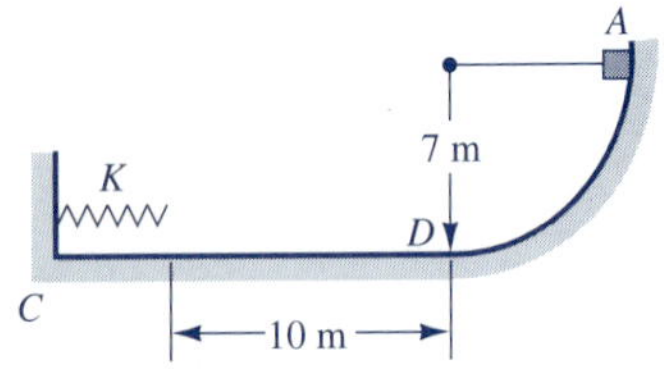

Figure P.13.99.

13.100. A cylinder is about to roll down an incline dragging block B. After starting from rest, what is the angular speed of the cylinder when it has moved .5 m? Use the following data:

$$(R_A)_{OUTSIDE} = 2.5 \text{ m} \qquad (R_A)_{INSIDE} = 1 \text{ m}$$
$$M_A = 100 \text{ kg} \qquad M_B = 30 \text{ kg}$$

The wire is thin and wraps around the inner cylinder of A. The kinetic energy of the compound cylinder due to rotation about its centerline is given as 0.8 times that of a solid cylinder of outside radius $r = 2.5$ m.

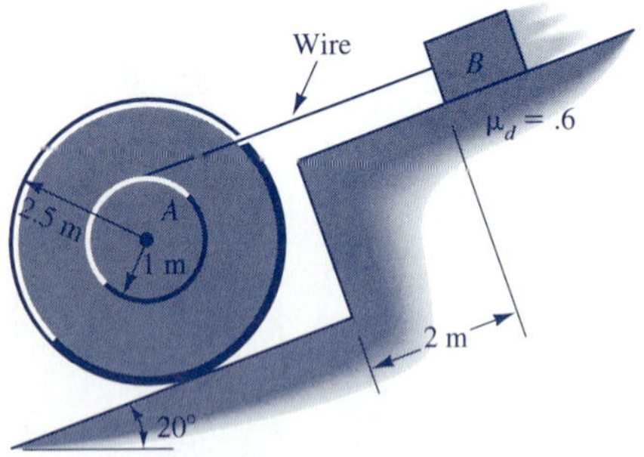

Figure P.13.100.

13.101. The cylinders in the system roll without slipping.

(a) What is the velocity of the system after it moves 1 m starting from rest?

(b) What is the total friction force f_{TOT} for the two cylinders?

(c) What is the acceleration of the system?

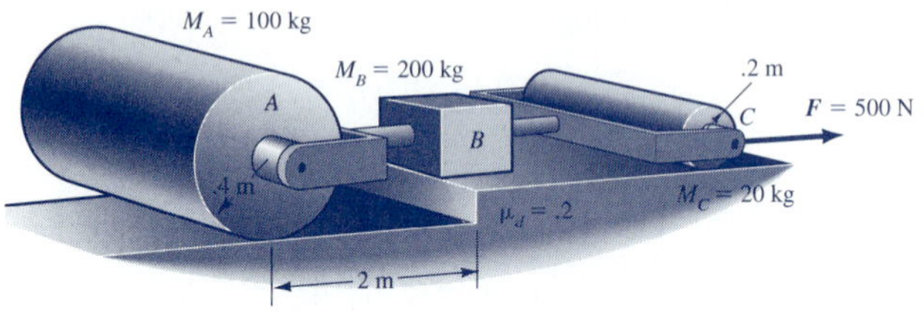

Figure P.13.101.

13.102. A 180-lb man runs up an escalator while it is not in operation in 10 sec. What is the horsepower developed by the man? If the escalator is moving at a speed of 2 ft/sec and carrying, on the average, 2,000 people per hour, what is the power requirement on the driving motor assuming that the average weight of a passenger is 150 lb? Take the mechanical efficiency of the drive system to be 80%. Assume that passengers enter and leave at the same speed of 2 ft/sec and that there are equal numbers of passengers on the escalator at any one time.

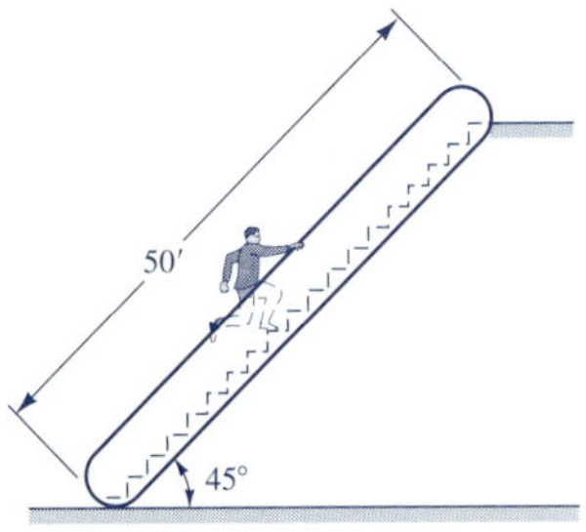

Figure P.13.102.

13.103. Grain is coming out of a hopper at the rate of 7,200 kg/hr and falls onto a conveyor system that takes the grain into a bin. The conveyor belt moves at a steady speed of 2 m/sec. What power in watts is needed to operate the system for an efficiency of .6? What power is needed if we double the belt speed?

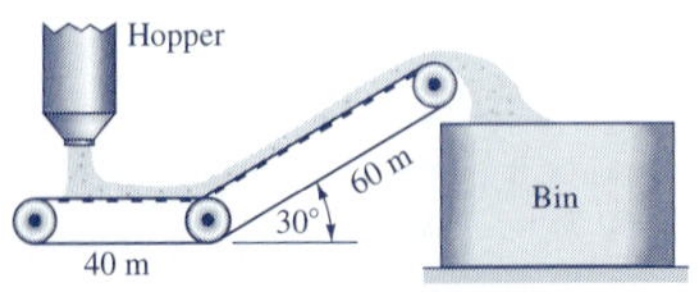

Figure P.13.103.

13.104. A self-propelled vehicle A has a weight of $\frac{1}{4}$ ton. A gasoline engine develops torque on the drive wheels to help move A up the incline. A counterweight B of 300 lb is also shown in the diagram. What horsepower is needed when A is moving up at a speed of 2 ft/sec and has an acceleration of 3 ft/sec^2? Neglect the weight of the pulley. [*Hint:* The pulley rolls along cord dg without slipping. It therefore has an instantaneous center of rotation at d. What does this mean about the relative value of velocity of point b on the pulley and point a?]

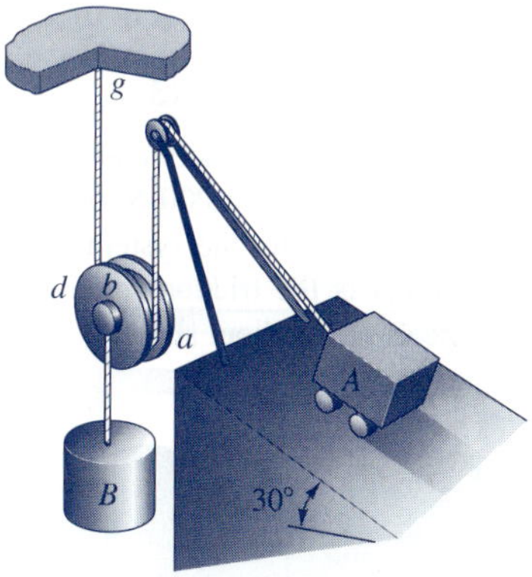

Figure P.13.104.

***13.105.** Set up an integro-differential equation (involving derivatives and integrals) for θ in Problem 13.31 if there is Coulombic friction with $\mu_d = .2$.

13.106. At what angle θ does body A of Problem 13.31 leave the circular surface?

***13.107.** Show that the work–energy equation for a particle can be expressed in the following way:

$$\int_0^x F\,dx = \int_0^V V\,d(mV)$$

Integrating the right side by parts,[19] and using relativistic mass $m_0/\sqrt{1 - V^2/c^2}$, where m_0 is the *rest mass* and c is the speed of light, show that a relativistic form of this equation can be given as

$$\int_0^x F\,dx = \frac{m_0c^2}{\sqrt{1 - V^2/c^2}} - m_0c^2 = mc^2 - m_0c^2$$

so that the *relativistic kinetic energy* is

$$\text{KE} = mc^2 - m_0c^2$$

***13.108.** By combining the kinetic energy as given in Problem 13.107 and m_0c^2 to form E, the total energy, we get the famous formula of Einstein:

$$E = mc^2$$

in which energy is equated with mass. How much energy is equivalent to 6×10^{-8} lbm of matter? How high could a weight of 100 lb be lifted with such energy?

13.109. A 100-lb boy climbs up a rope in gym in 10 sec and slides down in 4 sec after he reaches uniform speed downward. What is the horsepower developed by the boy going up? What is the average horsepower dissipated on the rope by the boy going down after reaching uniform speed? The distance moved before reaching uniform speed downward is 2 ft.

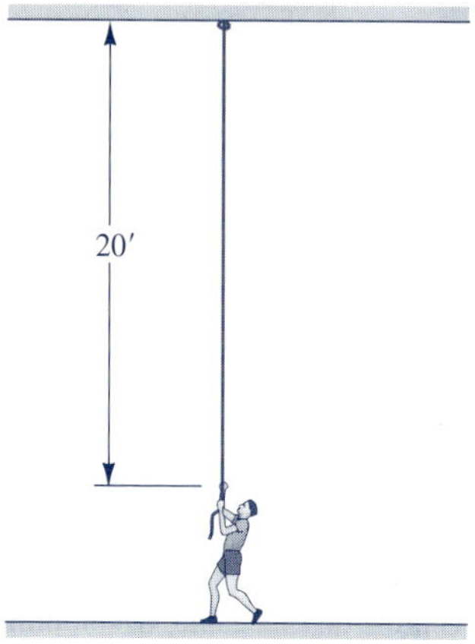

Figure P.13.109.

13.110. An aircraft carrier is shown in the process of launching an airplane via a catapult mechanism. Before leaving the catapult, the plane has a speed of 192 km/hr relative to the ship. If the plane is accelerating at the rate of $1g$ and if it has a mass of 18,000 kg, what horsepower is being developed by the catapult system at the end of launch on the plane if we neglect drag? The thrust from the jet engines of the plane is 100,000 N.

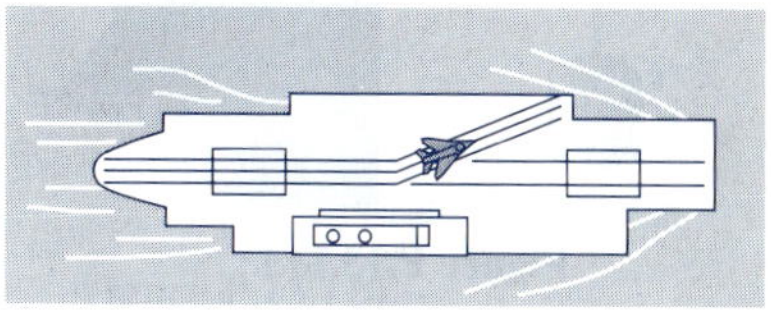

Figure P.13.110.

[19] To integrate by parts, note that

$$d(uv) = u\,dv + v\,du$$

Now integrate these terms:

$$\int_1^2 d(uv) = \int_1^2 u\,dv + \int_1^2 v\,du$$

Therefore,

$$\int_1^2 u\,dv = (uv)\Big|_1^2 - \int_1^2 v\,du$$

The last formulation is called integration by parts.

13.111. Vehicle B, weighing 25 kN, is to go down a 30° incline. The vehicle is connected to body A through light pulleys and a capstan. What should body A weigh if starting from rest it restricts body B to a speed of 5 m/sec when B moves 3 m? There are two wraps of rope around the capstan.

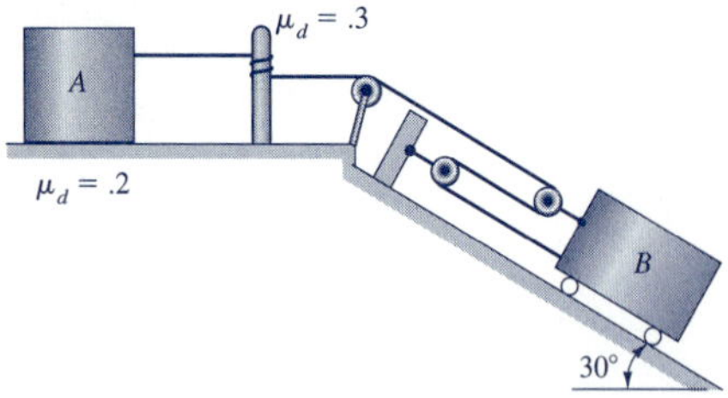

Figure P.13.111.

13.112. A jet passenger plane is moving along the runway for a takeoff. If each of its four engines is developing 44.5 kN of thrust, what is the horsepower developed when the plane is moving at a speed of 240 km/hr?

13.113. Block B, with a mass of 200 kg, is being pulled up an incline. A motor C pulls on one cable, developing 4 hp. The other cable is connected to a counterweight A having a mass of 150 kg. If B is moving at a speed of 2 m/sec, what is its acceleration? [*Hint:* Start with Newton's law for A and B.]

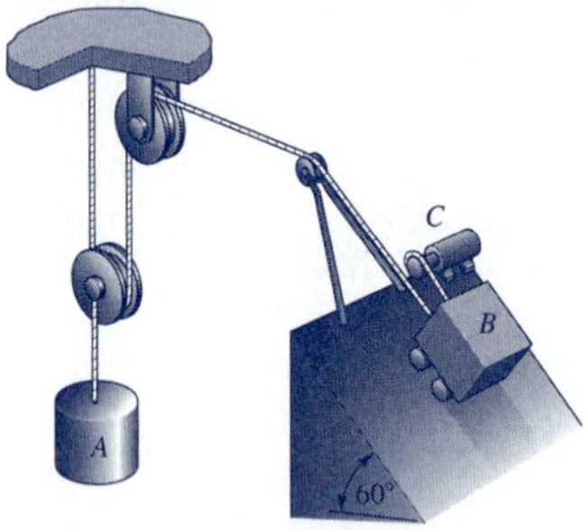

Figure P.13.113.

13.114. A block G slides along a frictionless path as shown. What is the minimum initial speed that G should have along the path if it is to remain in contact when it gets to A, the uppermost position of the path? The block weighs 9 N. What is the normal force on the path when for the condition described the block is at position B?

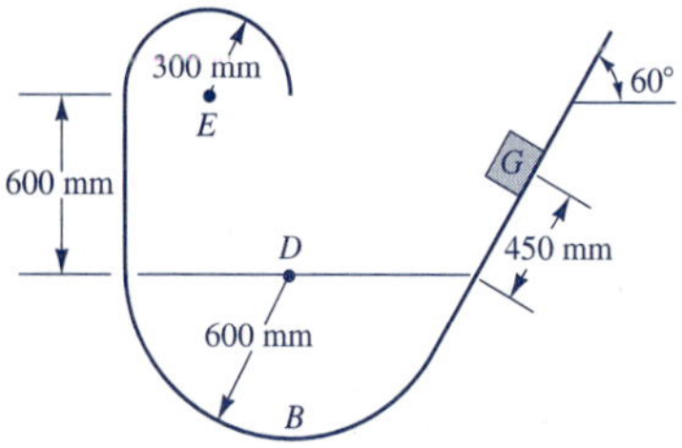

Figure P.13.114.

13.115. Cylinders A and B have masses of 50 kg each. Cylinder A can only rotate about a stationary axis while cylinder B rolls without slipping. Block C has a mass of 100 kg. Starting from rest, what is the speed of C after moving .1 m? Force P is 500 N and the diameter of the cylinders is .2 m.

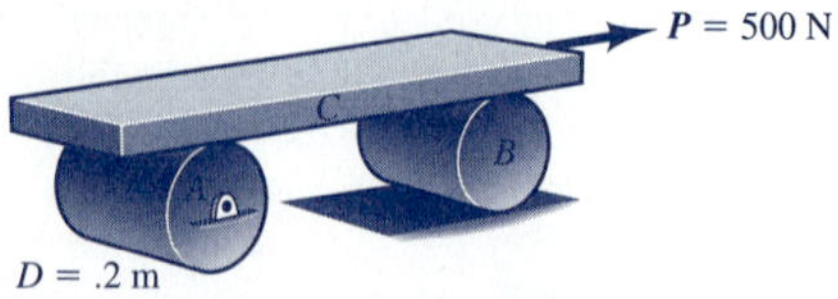

Figure P.13.115.

13.116. A system of 4 solid cylinders and a heavy block move vertically downward aided by a 1,000-N force F. What is the angular speed of the wheels after the system descends .5 m after starting from rest? What is the friction force from the walls on each wheel? The wheels roll without slipping.

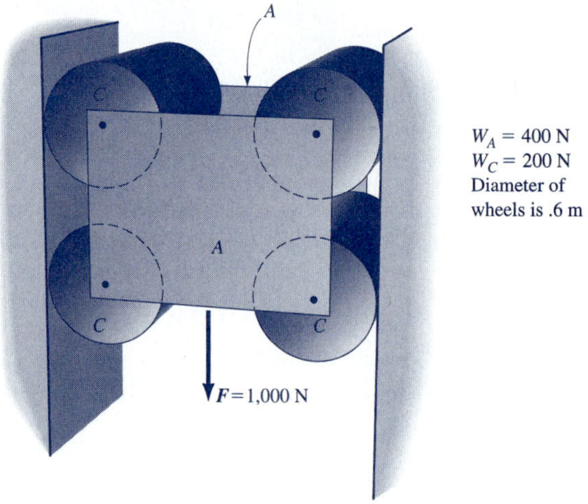

Figure P.13.116.

13.117. A collar B having a mass of 100 g moves along a frictionless curved rod in a vertical plane. A light rubber band connects B to a fixed point A. The rubber band is 250 mm in length when unstretched. A force of 30 N is required to extend the band 50 mm. If the collar is released from rest, what distance must d be so that the downward normal force on the rod at C is 20 N?

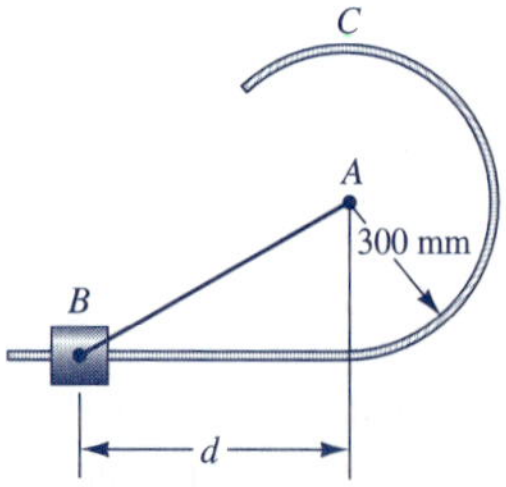

Figure P.13.117.

13.118. When your author was a graduate student he built a system for examining the effects of high-speed moving loads over elastically supported beams (see the diagram). A "vehicle" slides along a slightly lubricated square tube guide. At the base of the vehicle is a spring-loaded light wheel which will run over the beam (not shown). The vehicle is catapulted to a high speed by a stretched elastic cord (shock cord) which is pulled back from position *A–A* to the position *B* shown prior to "firing." At *A–A* the shock cord is elongated 10 in., while at the firing position it is elongated 30 in. A force of 10 lb is required for each inch of elongation of the cord. If the cord weighs a total of 1.5 lb and the vehicle weighs 10 oz, what is the speed of the vehicle when the cord reaches *A–A* after firing? Take into account in some reasonable way the kinetic energy of the cord, but neglect friction.

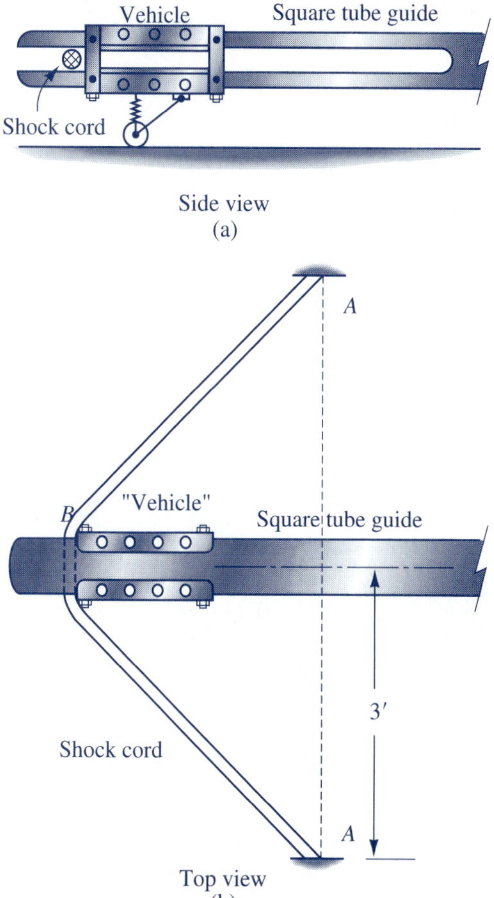

Figure P.13.118.

13.119. A body *B* of mass 60 kg slides in a frictionless slot on an inclined surface as shown. An elastic cord connects *B* to *A*. The cord has a "spring constant" of 360 N/m. If the body *B* is released from rest from a position where the elastic cord is unstretched, what is body *B*'s speed after it moves .3 m?

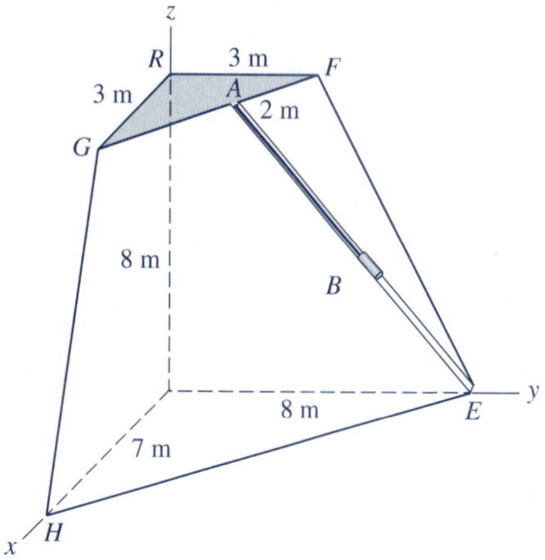

Figure P.13.119.

13.120. A collar slides on a frictionless tube as shown. The spring is unstretched when in the horizontal position and has a spring constant of 1.0 lb/in. What is the minimum weight of *A* to just reach *A*′ when released from rest from the position shown in the diagram? What is the force on the tube when *A* has traveled half the distance to *A*′?

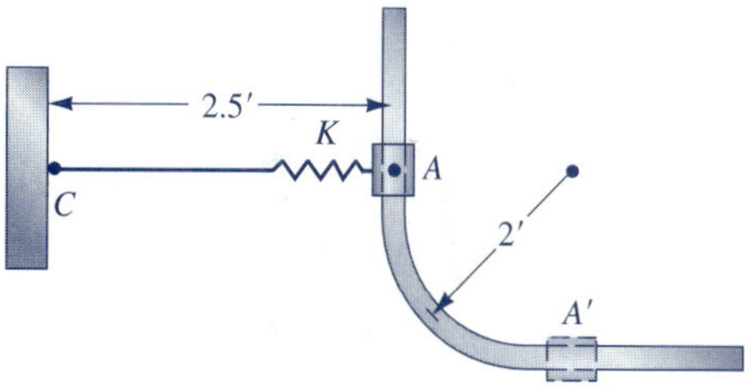

Figure P.13.120.

13.121. A 15-kg vehicle has two bodies (each with mass 1 kg) mounted on it, and these bodies rotate at an angular speed of 50 rad/sec relative to the vehicle. If a 500-N force acts on the vehicle for a distance of 17 m, what is the kinetic energy of the system, assuming that the vehicle starts from rest and the bodies in the vehicle have constant rotational speed? Neglect friction and the inertia of the wheels.

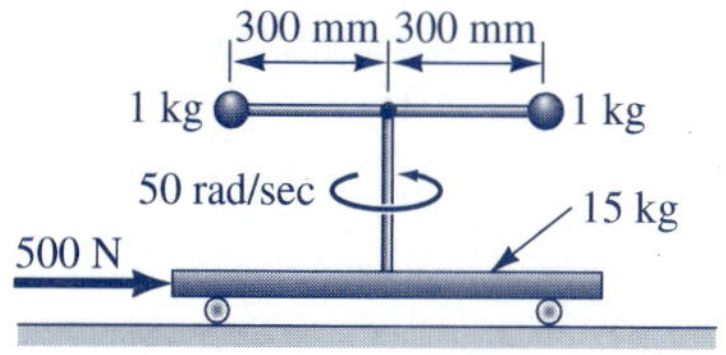

Figure P.13.121.

13.122. Two identical solid cylinders each weighing 100 N support a load *A* weighing 50 N. If a force *F* of 300 N acts as shown, what is the speed of the vehicle after moving 5 m? Also, what is the total friction force on each wheel? Neglect the mass of the supporting system connecting the cylinders. Note that the kinetic energy of the angular motion of a cylinder about its own axis is $\frac{1}{4}MR^2\omega^2$. The system starts from rest.

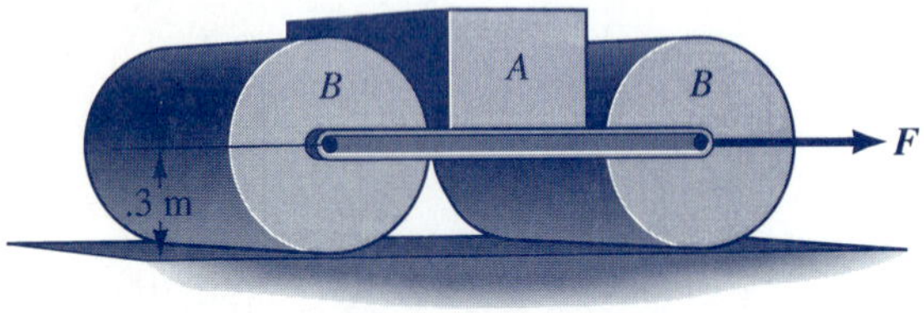

Figure P.13.122.

13.123. A triangular block of uniform density and total weight 100 lb rests on a hinge and on a movable block *B*. If a constant force *F* of 150 lb is exerted on the block *B*, what will be its speed after it moves 10 ft? The mass of block *B* is 10 lbm, and the dynamic coefficient of friction for all contact surfaces is .3.

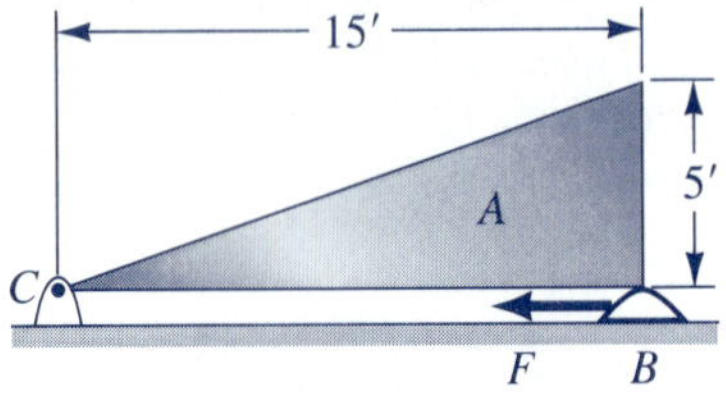

Figure P.13.123.

13.124. Three blocks are connected by an inextensible flexible cable. The blocks are released from a rest configuration with the cable taut. If A can only fall a distance h equal to 2 ft, what is the velocity of bodies C and B after each has moved a distance of 3 ft? Each body weighs 100 lb. The coefficient of dynamic friction for body C is .3 and for body B is .2.

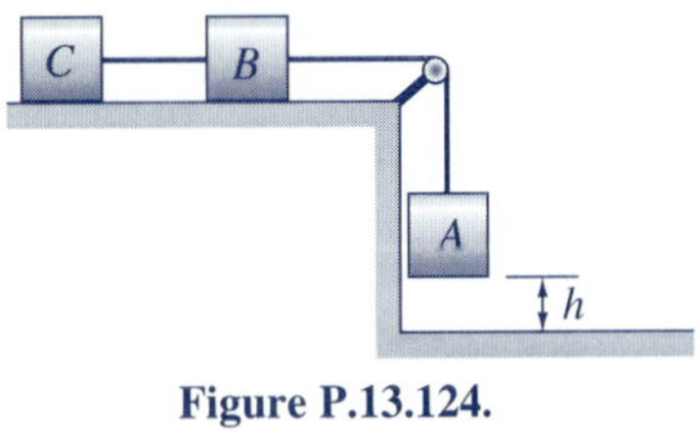

Figure P.13.124.

13.125. Two discs move on a horizontal frictionless surface shown looking down from above. Each disc weighs 20 N. A rectangular member B weighing 50 N is pulled by a force F having a value of 200 N. If there is no slipping anywhere except on the horizontal support surface, what is the speed of B after it moves 18 cm? Determine the friction forces from the walls onto the cylinders.

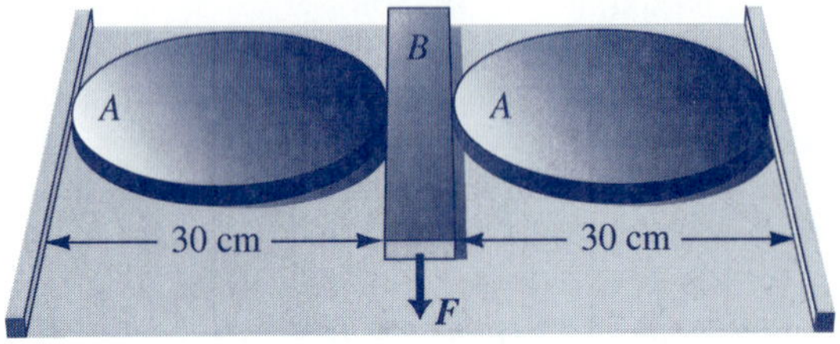

Figure P.13.125.

13.126. Rod *AB* is pinned to block *C* and is welded to cylinder *D*. Cylinder *E* rolls without slipping along the incline and rotates around cylinder *D*, which does not rotate at all. There is a constant friction torque between *D* and *E* of 25 N-m. Starting from rest, what is the speed of the system after moving .1 m along the incline? What is the frictional force between the ground and cylinder *E*? Neglect the mass of rod *AB*. Take the kinetic energy of rotation of *E* as 0.8 times that of the kinetic energy of rotation of a solid cylinder of diameter *D* = 0.3 m. The length of *AB* is .5 m.

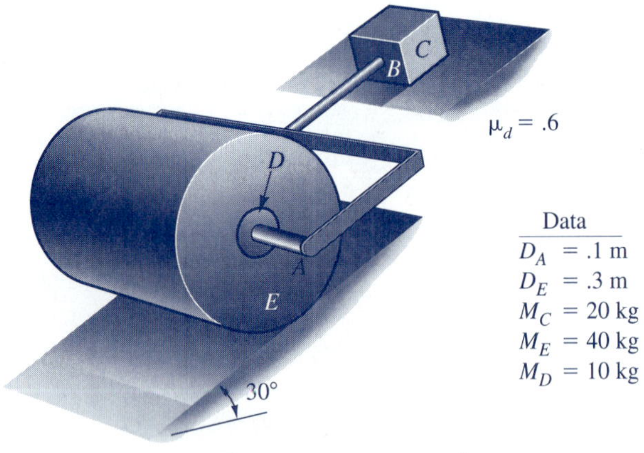

Figure P.13.126.

CHAPTER 14

Methods of Momentum for Particles

Part A: Linear Momentum

14.1 Impulse and Momentum Relations for a Particle

In Section 12.3, we integrated differential equations of motion for particles that are acted upon by forces that are functions of time. In this chapter, we shall again consider such problems and shall present alternative formulations, called *methods of momentum*, for handling certain of these problems in a convenient and straightforward manner. We start by considering Newton's law for a particle:

$$\boldsymbol{F} = m\frac{d\boldsymbol{V}}{dt} \tag{14.1}$$

Multiply both sides by dt and integrate from some initial time t_i to some final time t_f:

$$\int_{t_i}^{t_f} \boldsymbol{F}\,dt = \int_{t_i}^{t_f} m\frac{d\boldsymbol{V}}{dt}\,dt = m\boldsymbol{V}_f - m\boldsymbol{V}_i \tag{14.2}$$

Note first that this is a vector equation, in contrast to the work–kinetic energy equation 13.2. The integral

$$\int_{t_i}^{t_f} \boldsymbol{F}\,dt$$

which we shall denote as $\boldsymbol{I}$, is called the *impulse* of the force $\boldsymbol{F}$ during the time interval $t_f - t_i$, whereas $m\boldsymbol{V}$ is the *linear-momentum vector* of the particle.

Equation 14.2, then, states that *the impulse **I** over a time interval equals the change in linear momentum of a particle during that time interval.* As we shall demonstrate later, the impulse of a force may be known even though the force itself is not known.

Finally, you must remember that to produce an impulse, a force need only exist for a time interval. Sometimes we use the work integral so much that we tend to think—erroneously—that a force acting on a stationary body does not produce an impulse.

We now illustrate the use of the impulse-momentum equation.

Example 14.1

A particle initially at rest is acted on by a force whose variation with time is shown graphically in Fig. 14.1. If the particle has a mass of 1 slug and is constrained to move rectilinearly in the direction of the force, what is the speed after 15 sec?

From the definition of the impulse, the area under the force–time curve will, in the one-dimensional example, equal the impulse magnitude. Thus, we simply compute this area between the times $t = 0$ and $t = 15$ sec:

$$\text{impulse} = \underbrace{\tfrac{1}{2}(10)(10)}_{\text{area 1}} + \underbrace{(5)(15)}_{\text{area 2}} = 125 \text{ lb-sec}$$

The final velocity, then, is given as

$$125 = (1)(V_f) - 0$$

Therefore,

$$V_f = 125 \text{ ft/sec}$$

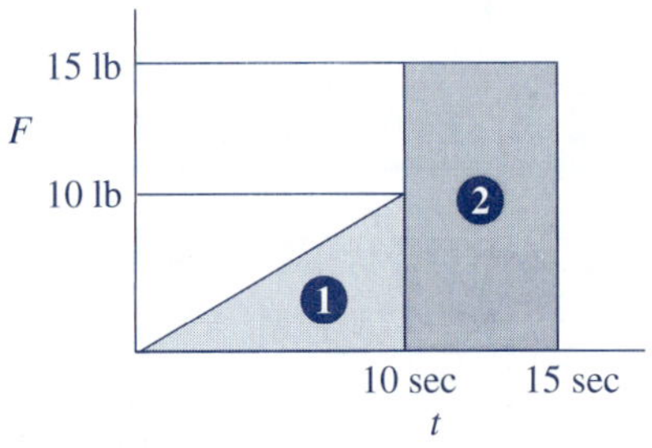

Figure 14.1. Force-versus-time plot.

Note that the impulse-momentum equation is useful when the force variation during a time interval is a curve that cannot be conveniently expressed mathematically. The impulse, which is the area under an F versus t curve, can then be found with the help of a *planimeter*, thus permitting a quick solution of the velocity change during the time interval.[1]

[1]A planimeter is a mechanical device for measuring the area of a plane region bounded by an arbitrary curve.

Example 14.2

A particle A with a mass of 1 kg has an initial velocity $\boldsymbol{V}_0 = 10\boldsymbol{i} + 6\boldsymbol{j}$ m/sec. After particle A strikes particle B, the velocity becomes $\boldsymbol{V} = 16\boldsymbol{i} - 3\boldsymbol{j} + 4\boldsymbol{k}$ m/sec. If the time of encounter is 10 msec, what average force was exerted on the particle A? What is the change of linear momentum of particle B?

The impulse $\boldsymbol{I}$ acting on A is immediately determined by computing the change in linear momentum during the encounter:

$$\begin{aligned}\boldsymbol{I}_A &= (1)(16\boldsymbol{i} - 3\boldsymbol{j} + 4\boldsymbol{k}) - (1)(10\boldsymbol{i} + 6\boldsymbol{j}) \\ &= 6\boldsymbol{i} - 9\boldsymbol{j} + 4\boldsymbol{k} \text{ N-sec}\end{aligned}$$

Since

$$\int_{t_i}^{t_f} \boldsymbol{F}_A \, dt = (\boldsymbol{F}_{av})_A \Delta t$$

the average force $(\boldsymbol{F}_{av})_A$ becomes

$$(\boldsymbol{F}_{av})_A(0.010) = 6\boldsymbol{i} - 9\boldsymbol{j} + 4\boldsymbol{k}$$

Therefore,

$$(\boldsymbol{F}_{av})_A = 600\boldsymbol{i} - 900\boldsymbol{j} + 400\boldsymbol{k} \text{ N}$$

On the basis of the principle that action equals reaction, an equal but opposite average force must act on the object B during the 10-msec time interval. Thus, the impulse on particle B is $-\boldsymbol{I}_A$. Equating this impulse to the change in linear momentum, we get

$$\Delta(m\boldsymbol{V})_B = -\boldsymbol{I}_A = -6\boldsymbol{i} + 9\boldsymbol{j} - 4\boldsymbol{k} \text{ N-sec}$$

During impacts where the exact force variation is unknown, the impulse momentum principle is very useful. We shall examine impacts in more detail in a later section.

Example 14.3

Two bodies, 1 and 2, are connected by an inextensible and weightless cord (Fig. 14.2). Initially, the bodies are at rest. If the dynamic coefficient of friction is μ_d for body 1 on the surface inclined at angle α, compute the velocity of the bodies at any time t before body 1 has reached the end of the incline.

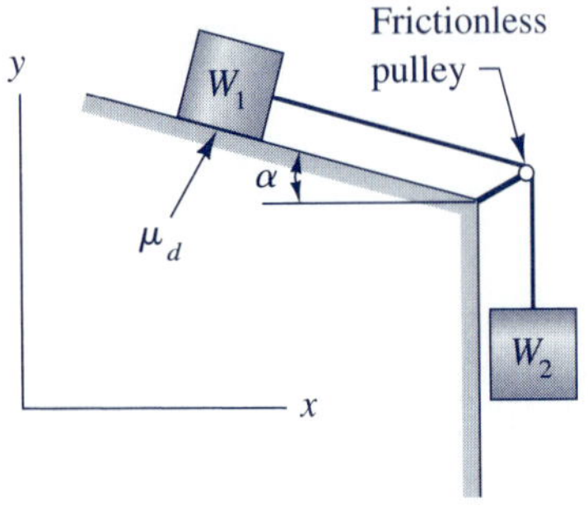

Figure 14.2. Two bodies connected by a cord.

Since only constant forces exist and since a time interval has been specified, we can use momentum considerations advantageously. The free-body diagrams of bodies 1 and 2 are shown in Fig. 14.3. Equilibrium considerations lead to the conclusion that $N_1 = W_1 \cos \alpha$, so the friction force f_1 is

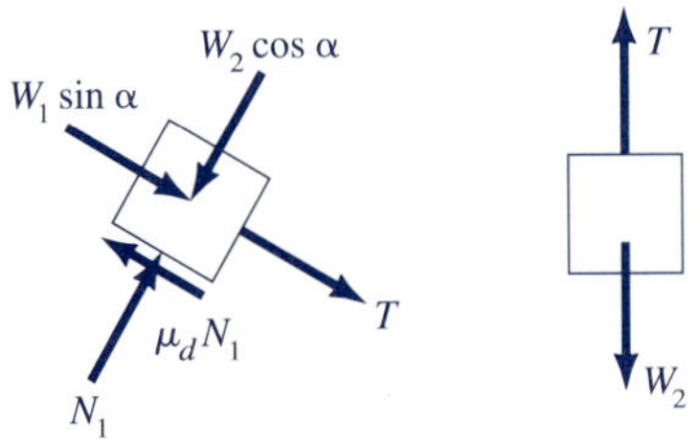

Figure 14.3. Free-body diagrams of W_1 and W_2.

$$f_1 = \mu_d N_1 = \mu_d W_1 \cos \alpha$$

For body 1, take the component of the **linear impulse-momentum** equation along the incline:

$$\int_0^t (-\mu_d W_1 \cos \alpha + W_1 \sin \alpha + T)dt = \frac{W_1}{g}(V - 0)$$

Carrying out the integration, we have

$$(-\mu_d W_1 \cos \alpha + W_1 \sin \alpha + T)t = \frac{W_1}{g} V \tag{a}$$

For body 2, we have for the **momentum equation** in the vertical direction:

$$\int_0^t (W_2 - T)dt = \frac{W_2}{g}(V - 0)$$

where, because of the inextensible property of the cable and the frictionless condition of the pulley, the magnitudes of the velocity V and the force T are the same for bodies 1 and 2. Integrating the equation above, we write:

$$(W_2 - T)t = \frac{W_2}{g} V \tag{b}$$

Example 14.3 (Continued)

By adding Eqs. (a) and (b), we can eliminate T and solve for the desired unknown V. Thus,

$$(-\mu_d W_1 \cos\alpha + W_1 \sin\alpha + W_2)t = \frac{V}{g}(W_1 + W_2)$$

Therefore,

$$V = \frac{gt}{W_1 + W_2}(W_2 + W_1 \sin\alpha - \mu_d W_1 \cos\alpha) \qquad \text{(c)}$$

Note that we have used considerations of linear momentum for a *single* particle each time in solving this problem.

Example 14.4

A conveyor belt is moving from left to right at a constant speed V of 1 ft/sec in Fig. 14.4. Two hoppers drop objects onto the belt at the total rate n of 4 per second. The objects each have a weight W of 2 lb and fall a height h of 1 ft before landing on the conveyor belt. Farther along the belt (not shown) the objects are removed by personnel so that, for steady-state operation, the number N of objects on the belt at any time is 10. If the dynamic coefficient of friction between belt and conveyor bed is .2, estimate the average difference in tension $T_2 - T_1$ of the belt to maintain this operation. The weight of the belt on the conveyor bed is 10 lb.

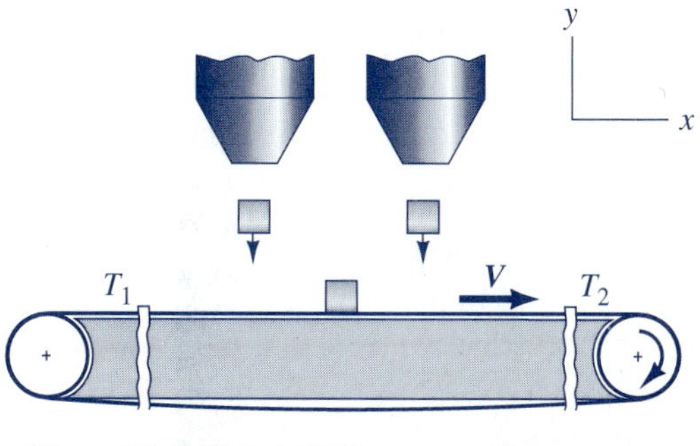

Figure 14.4. Objects falling on moving conveyor.

Example 14.4 (Continued)

We shall superimpose the following effects to get the desired result.

1. A friction force from the bed onto the belt results from the static weight of the ten objects riding on the belt and the weight of the portion of belt on the bed.
2. A friction force from the bed onto the belt results from the force in the y direction needed to change the *vertical* linear momentum of the falling objects from a value corresponding to the free-fall velocity just before impact ($\sqrt{2gh}$) to a value of zero after impact.
3. Finally, the belt must supply a force in the x direction to change the *horizontal* linear momentum of the falling objects from a value of zero to a value corresponding to the speed of the belt.

Thus, we have for the first contribution, which we donate as ΔT_1, the following result:

$$\Delta T_1 = (NW + 10)\mu_d = [(10)(2) + 10](.2) = 6 \text{ lb} \quad \text{(a)}$$

As for the second contribution, we can only compute an average value $(\Delta T_2)_{av}$ by noting that each impacting object is given a vertical change in linear momentum equal to

$$\begin{aligned} \text{vertical change in linear momentum per object} &= \frac{W}{g}(\sqrt{2gh}) \\ &= \frac{2}{g}\sqrt{(2g)(1)} \\ &= .498 \text{ lb-sec} \end{aligned}$$

where we have assumed a free fall starting with zero velocity at the hopper. For four impacts per second, we have as the total vertical change in linear momentum per second the value (4)(.498) = 1.994 lb-sec. The average vertical force during the 1-sec interval to give the impulse needed for this change in linear momentum is clearly 1.994 lb. Since this result is correct for every second, 1.994 lb is the average normal force that the bed of the conveyor must transmit to the belt for arresting the vertical motion of the falling objects. The desired $[(\Delta T_2]_{av}$ for the belt arising from friction is accordingly given as

$$[(\Delta T)_2]_{av} = (\mu_d)(1.994) = .399 \text{ lb} \quad \text{(b)}$$

Finally, for the last contribution $[(\Delta T)_3]_{av}$, we note that the belt must give in the horizontal direction for each impacting object a change in linear momentum having the value

$$\begin{aligned} \text{horizontal change in linear momentum per object} &= \frac{W}{g}(1) \\ &= .0621 \text{ lb-sec} \end{aligned}$$

Example 14.4 (Continued)

For four impacts per second we have as the total horizontal change in linear momentum developed by the belt during 1 sec the value (4)(.0621) = .248 lb-sec. The average horizontal force during 1 sec needed for this change in linear momentum is clearly .248 lb. Thus, we have

$$[(\Delta T)_3]_{av} = .248 \text{ lb} \tag{c}$$

The total average difference in tension is then

$$(\Delta T)_{av} = 6 + .399 + .248 = \boxed{6.65 \text{ lb}} \tag{d}$$

14.2 Linear-Momentum Considerations for a System of Particles

In Section 14.1, we considered impulse-momentum relations for a single particle. Although Examples 14.3 and 14.4 involved more than one particle, nevertheless the impulse-momentum considerations were made on one particle at a time. We now wish to set forth impulse-momentum relations for a *system* of particles.

Let us accordingly consider a system of n particles. We may start with Newton's law as developed previously for a system of particles:

$$\boldsymbol{F} = \sum_{j=1}^{n} m_j \frac{d\boldsymbol{V}_j}{dt} \tag{14.3}$$

Since we know that the internal forces cancel, $\boldsymbol{F}$ must be the *total external* force on the system of n particles. Multiplying by dt, as before, and integrating between t_i and t_f, we write:

$$\boxed{\int_{t_i}^{t_f} \boldsymbol{F}\, dt = \boldsymbol{I}_{\text{ext}} = \left(\sum_{j=1}^{n} m_j \boldsymbol{V}_j\right)_f - \left(\sum_{j=1}^{n} m_j \boldsymbol{V}_j\right)_i} \tag{14.4}$$

Thus, we see that *the impulse of the total external force on the system of particles during a time interval equals the sum of the changes of the linear-momentum vectors of the particles during the time interval.*

We now consider an example.

Example 14.5

A 3-ton truck is moving at a speed of 60 mi/hr. [See Fig. 14.5(a).] The driver suddenly applies his brakes at time $t = 0$ so as to lock his wheels in a panic stop. Load A weighing 1 ton breaks loose from its ropes and at time $t = 4$ sec is sliding *relative to the truck* at a speed of 3 ft/sec. What is the speed of the truck at that time? Take μ_d between the tires and pavement to be .4.

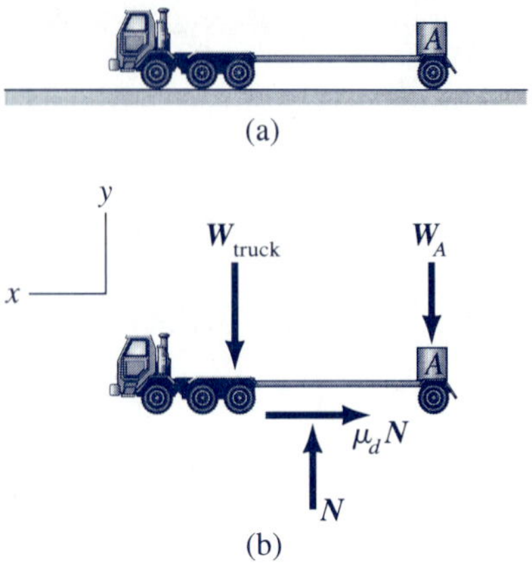

Figure 14.5. Truck undergoing panic stop.

Since we *do not know* the nature of the forces between the truck and load A while the latter is breaking loose, it is easiest to consider the *system* of two particles comprising the truck and the load simultaneously whereby the aforementioned forces become *internal* and are *not* considered. Accordingly, we have shown the system with all the external loads in Fig. 14.5(b). Clearly, $N = (4)(2{,}000) = 8{,}000$ lb and the friction force is $(.4)(8{,}000) = 3{,}200$ lb. We now employ Eq. 14.4 in the x direction as follows:

$$\int_{t_1}^{t_2} F_x \, dt = \left(\sum_j m_j \mathbf{V}_j \right)_2 - \left(\sum_j m_j \mathbf{V}_j \right)_1$$

$$\int_0^4 (-3{,}200)\, dt = \left[\frac{(3)(2{,}000)}{g} V_2 + \frac{(1)(2{,}000)}{g} (V_2 + 3) \right] - \left[\frac{(4)(2{,}000)}{g} \frac{(60)(5{,}280)}{3{,}600} \right] \tag{a}$$

Note that the first quantity inside the first brackets on the right side of Eq. (a) is the momentum of the truck at $t = 4$ sec, and the second quantity inside the same brackets is the momentum of the load at this instant. We may readily solve for V_2:

$$V_2 = 35.7 \text{ ft/sec}$$

Introducing *mass-center* quantities into Eq. 14.4 is easy and sometimes advantageous. You will remember that:

$$M r_c = \sum_{j=1}^{n} m_j r_j \tag{14.5}$$

Differentiating with respect to time, we get

$$M V_c = \sum_{j=1}^{n} m_j V_j \tag{14.6}$$

Thus, we see from this equation that *the total linear momentum of a system of particles equals the linear momentum of a particle that has the total mass of the system and that moves with the velocity of the mass center.* Using Eq. 14.6 to replace the right side of Eq. 14.4, we can say:

$$\int_{t_i}^{t_f} \boldsymbol{F}\, dt = \boldsymbol{I}_{\text{ext}} = M(\boldsymbol{V}_c)_f - M(\boldsymbol{V}_c)_i \qquad (14.7)$$

Thus, *the total external impulse on a system of particles equals the change in linear momentum of a hypothetical particle having the mass of the entire aggregate and moving with the mass center.*

When the separate motions of the individual particles are reasonably simple, as a result of constraints, and the motion of the mass center is not easily available, then Eq. 14.4 can be employed for linear-momentum considerations as was the case for Example 14.5. On the other hand, when the motions of the particles individually are very complex and the motion of the mass center of the system is reasonably simple, then clearly Eq. 14.7 can be of great value for linear-momentum considerations. Also, as in the case of energy considerations, we note that the single-particle model is really a *special case* of the center-of-mass formulation above, wherein the motion of the center of mass of a body describes sufficiently the motion of the body in question.

Example 14.6

A truck in Fig. 14.6 has two rectangular compartments of identical size for the purpose of transporting water. Each compartment has the dimensions 20 ft × 10 ft × 8 ft. Initially, tank *A* is full and tank *B* is empty. A pump in tank *A* begins to pump water from *A* to *B* at the rate Q_1 of 10 cfs (cubic feet per second) and 10 sec later is delivering water at the rate Q_2 of 30 cfs. If the level of the water in the tanks remains horizontal, what is the average horizontal force needed to restrain the truck from moving during this interval?

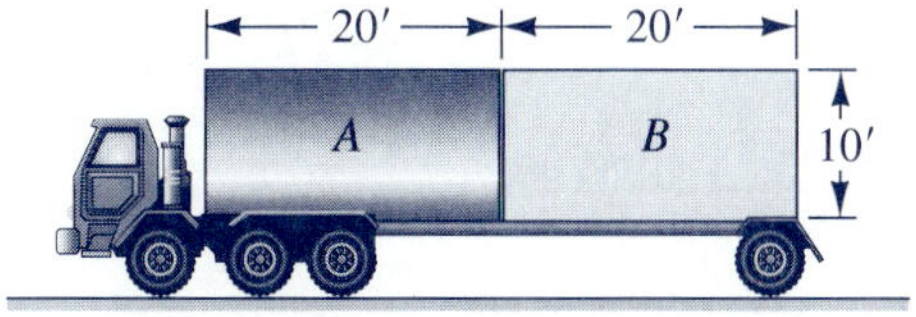

Figure 14.6. Truck with tank compartments.

Example 14.6 (Continued)

In this setup, the mass center of the water in the tanks is moving from left to right and moving *nonuniformly* during the time interval of interest. We show the water in Fig. 14.7 at some time t where the level in

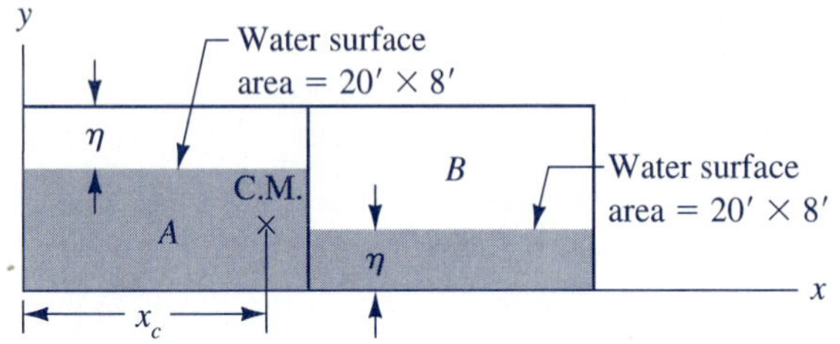

Figure 14.7. Compartments showing flow of water.

tank A has dropped an amount η while, by conservation of mass, the level in tank B has risen exactly the same amount η. The position x_c of the center of mass at this instant can be readily calculated in terms of η. Thus, using the basic definition of the center of mass, we can say:

$$Mx_c = (M_A)(x_A) + (M_B)(x_B)$$

$$[(20)(8)(10)](\rho)(x_c) = [(20)(8)(10 - \eta)](\rho)(10) + [(20)(8)(\eta)](\rho)(30) \quad \text{(a)}$$

Since we are interested in the time rate of change of x_c so that we can profitably employ Eq. 14.7, we next differentiate with respect to time as follows:

$$[(20)(8)(10)](\rho)(\dot{x}_c) = -[(20)(8)\dot{\eta}](\rho)(10) + [(20)(8)(\dot{\eta})](\rho)(30) \quad \text{(b)}$$

But $(20)(8)\dot{\eta}$ is the volume of flow[2] from tank A to tank B at time t. Using Q to represent this volume flow, we get for the equation above:

$$[(20)(8)(10)](\rho)\dot{x}_c = -(\rho)(10)Q + (\rho)(30)Q = (20)(\rho)Q$$

Solving for $\dot{x}_c$, we have

$$\dot{x}_c = \frac{1}{80}Q \quad \text{(c)}$$

[2]Remember that 20 ft × 8 ft is the area of the top water surface in each tank, as shown in Fig. 14.7.

Example 14.6 (Continued)

Now consider the momentum equation in the x direction for the water using the center of mass. We can say from Eq. 14.7:

$$\int_0^{10} F\,dt = \left[(M\dot{x}_c)_2 - (M\dot{x}_c)_1\right]$$

Therefore,

$$(F_{av})(10) = \left[(20)(8)(10)(\rho)\right]\left[(\dot{x}_c)_2 - (\dot{x}_c)_1\right]$$
$$= \left[(20)(8)(10)(\rho)\right]\left[\tfrac{1}{80}(Q_2 - Q_1)\right] \quad \text{(d)}$$

where we have used Eq. (c) in the last step. Putting in $Q_2 = 30$ cfs and $Q_1 = 10$ cfs, we then get for the average force during the 10-sec interval of interest on using $\rho = 62.4/g$ slugs/ft^3:

$$F_{av} = 77.5 \text{ lb} \quad \text{(e)}$$

This is the average horizontal force that the truck exerts on the water. Clearly, this force is also what the ground must exert on the truck in the horizontal direction to prevent motion of the truck during the water transfer operation.

From another viewpoint, this system is not unlike a propulsion system like a jet engine to be studied with the aid of a control volume (see Section 5.4) in your fluids course.

If the total external force on a system of particles is zero, it is clear from the previous discussion that there can be no change in the linear momentum of the system. This is the principle of *conservation of linear momentum*, which means, furthermore, that *with a zero total impulse on an aggregate of particles, there can be no change in the velocity of the mass center*. If at some time t_0 the velocity of the mass center of such a system of particles is zero, then this velocity must remain zero if the impulse on the system of particles is zero. That is, no matter what movements and gyrations the elements of the system may have, they must be such that the center of mass must remain stationary. We reached the same conclusion in Chapter 12, where we found from Newton's law that if the total external force on a system of particles is zero, then the acceleration of the center of mass is zero.[3]

[3]Problems 12.103 and 12.104 are examples of this condition.

14.3 Impulsive Forces

Let us now examine the action involved in the explosion of a bomb that is initially suspended from a wire, as shown in Fig. 14.8. First, consider the situation *directly after* the explosion has been set off. Since very large forces are present from expanding gases, a *fragment* of the bomb receives an appreciable impulse during this short time interval. Also, directly after the explosion, the gravitational forces are no longer counteracted by the supporting wire, so there is an additional impulse acting on the fragment. But since the gravitational force is small compared to forces from the explosion, the gravitational impulse on a fragment can be considered negligibly small for the short period of time under discussion compared to that of the expanding gases acting on the fragment. A plot of the impulsive force (from the explosion) and the force of gravity on a fragment is shown in Fig. 14.9. It is clear from this diagram

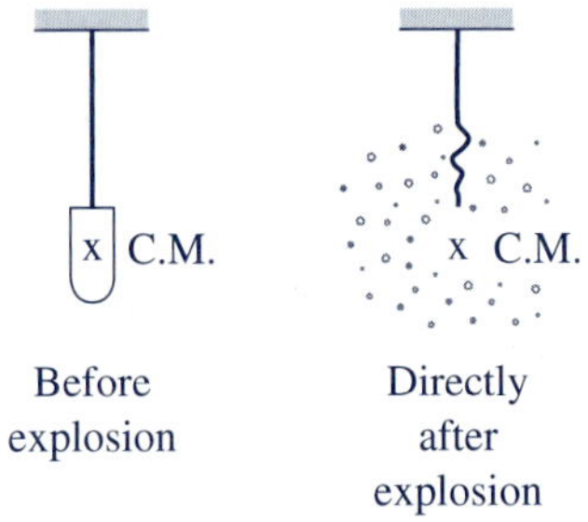

Figure 14.8. Exploding bomb.

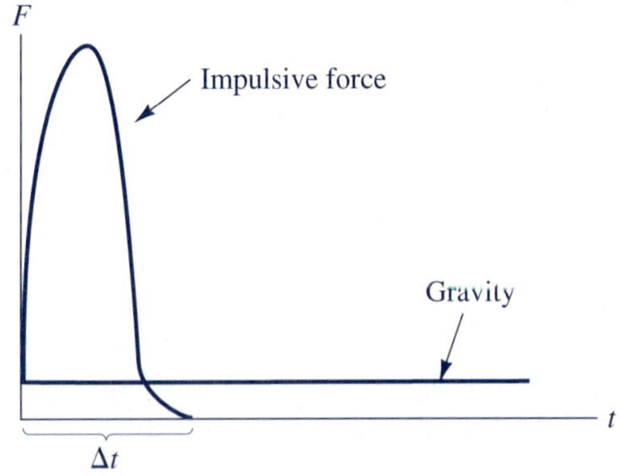

Figure 14.9. Plot of impulsive force and gravity force.

that the impulse from the explosion lasts for a very short time Δt and can be significant, whereas the impulse from gravity during the same short time is by comparison negligible. Forces that act over a very short time but have nevertheless appreciable impulse are called *impulsive forces*. In actions involving very small time intervals, we need only consider impulsive forces. Furthermore, during a very short time Δt an impulsive force acting on a particle can change the velocity of the particle in accordance with the impulse-momentum equation an appreciable amount while the particle undergoes very little change in position during the time Δt.[4] It is simplest in many cases to consider the *change in velocity of a particle from an impulsive force to occur over zero distance*.

Up to now, we have only considered a fragment of the bomb. Now let us consider all the fragments of the bomb taken as a system of particles. Since the explosive action is *internal* to the bomb, the action causes impulses that for any direction have equal and opposite counterparts, and thus *the total impulse on the bomb due to the explosion is zero*. We can thus conclude that *directly after* the explosion *the center of mass of the bomb has not moved appreciably* despite the high velocity of the fragments in all directions, as illustrated in Fig. 14.8. As time progresses beyond the short time interval described above, the gravitational impulse increases and has significant effect. If there were no friction, the center of mass would descend from the position of support as a freely falling particle under this action of gravity.

The following problems will illustrate these ideas.

[4]This idealization can be explained more precisely as follows. For an impulsive force F acting on a body of mass M, we can say from the linear momentum equation

$$\int_0^{\Delta t} F\,dt = F_{AV}\,\Delta t = MV_{\max} \qquad \therefore\ V_{\max} = \left(\frac{F_{AV}}{M}\right)(\Delta t)$$

The maximum movement of the body M during this time interval according to Newton's law on using the above result for V is then

$$x_{\max} = \int_0^{\Delta t} V_{\max}\,dt = \int_0^{\Delta t}\left(\frac{F_{AV}}{M}\,\Delta t\right)dt = \left(\frac{F_{AV}}{M}\right)(\Delta t)^2$$

Note that $V_{\max}$ is proportional to Δt while x is proportional to $(\Delta t)^2$. Clearly for a *very small* interval Δt the value of the movement x of the mass M can be considered *second order* compared to the value of the velocity V. For simplicity, with minimal error, we can say that the *mass M does not move while undergoing a change of velocity in response to an impulsive force*.

Example 14.7

Some top-flight tennis players hit the ball on a service at the instant that the ball is at the top of its trajectory after being released by the free hand. The ball is often given a speed V of 120 mi/hr by the racquet directly after the impact is complete. If the time of duration of the impact process is .005 sec, what is the magnitude of the average force from the racquet on the ball during this time interval? Take the weight of the ball as 1.5 oz.

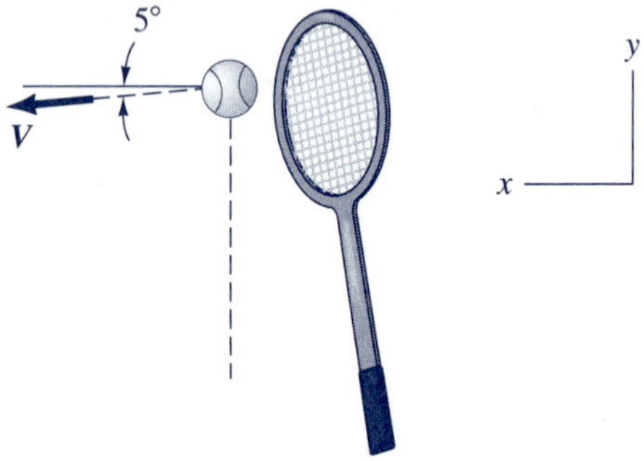

Figure 14.10. Impact of a tennis ball at service.

We have here acting on the ball during a very small time interval an **impulsive** force and the force of gravity. We will ignore the gravity force during the time of impact and we will consider that the ball achieves a post impact velocity while not moving, as explained earlier in the model for impulsive force behavior. As shown in Fig. 14.10, the impulse $\boldsymbol{I}$ generated on the ball by the racquet accordingly is

$$\boldsymbol{I} = \frac{15}{(16)(32.2)}\left[(120)\left(\frac{5{,}280}{3{,}600}\right)\right][\cos 5°\boldsymbol{i} - \sin 5°\boldsymbol{j}]$$

$$= .5124[.996\boldsymbol{i} - .0872\boldsymbol{j}] \text{ lb-sec}$$

Next, we go to the **impulse momentum** equation. Thus

$$(\boldsymbol{F}_{av})(.005) = .5124(.996\boldsymbol{i} - .0872\boldsymbol{j})$$

The magnitude of the average force is finally given as follows:

$$|\boldsymbol{F}_{av}| = 102.6 \text{ lb}$$

After the impact, the ball will have a trajectory determined by gravity, wind forces, and the initial post-impact conditions.

Example 14.8

A 9,000-N idealized cannon with a recoil spring ($K = 4{,}000$ N/m) fires a 45-N projectile with a muzzle velocity of 625 m/sec at an angle of 50° (Fig. 14.11). Determine the maximum compression of the spring.

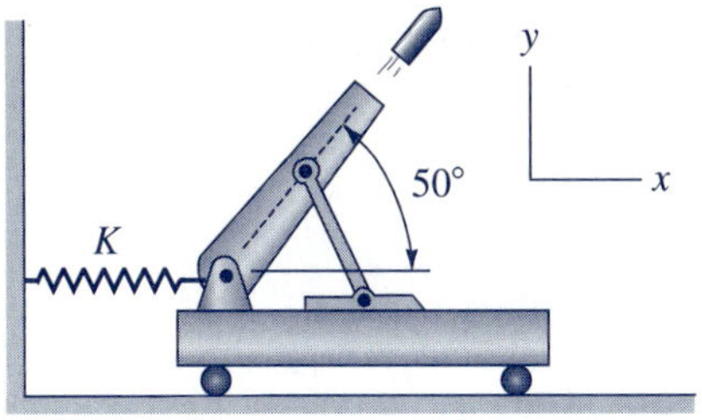

Figure 14.11. Idealized cannon..

The firing of the cannon takes place in a very short time interval. The force on the projectile and the force on the cannon from the explosion are impulsive forces. As a result, the cannon can be considered to achieve a recoil velocity instantaneously without having moved appreciably. Like the exploding bomb, the impulse on the cannon *plus* projectile is zero, as a result of the firing process. Since the linear momentum of the cannon plus projectile is zero just before firing, this linear momentum must be zero directly after firing. Thus, just after firing, we can say for the x direction:

$$(MV_x)_{\text{cannon}} + (MV_x)_{\text{projectile}} = 0 \tag{a}$$

Using V_c for the cannon velocity along the x axis and $V_p = V_c + 625 \cos 50°$ for the projectile velocity along the x axis we get

$$\frac{9{,}000}{g} V_c + \frac{45}{g}\left[(625)(\cos 50°) + V_c\right] = 0$$

Solving for V_c, we get

$$V_c = -2.00 \text{ m/sec} \tag{b}$$

After this initial impulsive action, which results in an instantaneous velocity being imparted to the cannon, the motion of the cannon is then impeded by the spring. We may now use **conservation of mechanical energy** for a particle in this phase of motion of the cannon. Denoting δ as the maximum deflection of the spring, we can say:

$$\frac{1}{2}\frac{9{,}000}{g}(2.00^2) = \frac{1}{2}(4{,}000)(\delta^2)$$

Therefore,

$$\delta = .958 \text{ m}$$

Example 14.9

For target practice, a 9-N rock is thrown into the air and fired on by a pistol. The pistol bullet, of mass 57 g and moving with a speed of 312 m/sec, strikes the rock as it is descending vertically at a speed of 6.25 m/sec. [See Fig. 14.12(a).] Both the velocity of the bullet and the rock are parallel to the *xy* plane. Directly after the bullet hits the rock, the rock breaks up into two pieces, *A* weighing 5.78 N and *B* weighing 3.22 N. What is the velocity of *B* after collision for the given coplanar postcollision velocities of the bullet and the piece *A* shown in Fig. 14.12(b)? The bodies, for clarity, are shown separated in the diagram. Keep in mind, nevertheless, that they are very close to each other at post-impact. In our model of the impact process, they would not even have moved relative to each other during this process. The indicated 219-m/sec and 25-m/sec velocities are in the *xy* plane. If we neglect wind resistance, how high up does the center of mass of the rock and bullet system rise after collision?

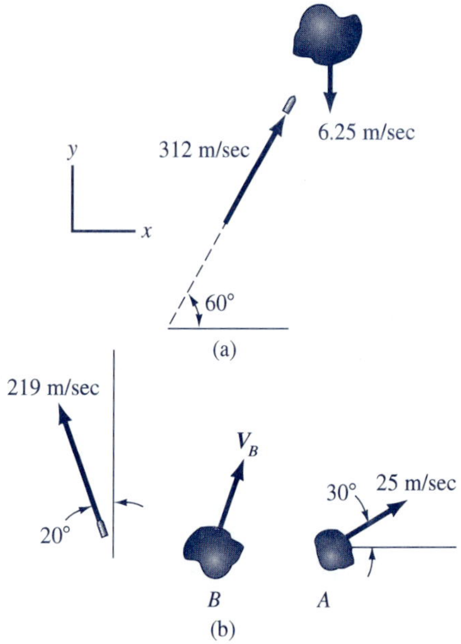

Figure 14.12. Bullet striking a rock.

Linear momentum is conserved during the collision, so we can equate linear momenta directly before and directly after collision. Thus,

$$(.057)(312)(.5\boldsymbol{i} + .866\boldsymbol{j}) + \frac{9}{g}(-6.25\boldsymbol{j})$$
$$= (.057)(219)(-\sin 20°\boldsymbol{i} + \cos 20°\boldsymbol{j})$$
$$+ \frac{5.78}{g}25(.866\boldsymbol{i} + .5\boldsymbol{j}) + \frac{3.22}{g}\left[(V_B)_x\boldsymbol{i} + (V_B)_y\boldsymbol{j}\right]$$

Example 14.9 (Continued)

We may solve for the desired quantities $(V_B)_x$ and $(V_B)_y$ to get

$$(V_B)_x = 1.235 \text{ m/sec}$$
$$(V_B)_y = -28.7 \text{ m/sec}$$

We now compute the velocity of the center of mass just before collision. Thus,

$$M\boldsymbol{V}_c = \left(\frac{9}{g} + .057\right)\boldsymbol{V}_c = \frac{9}{g}(-6.25)\boldsymbol{j} + (.057)(312)(.5\boldsymbol{i} + .866\boldsymbol{j})$$

Therefore,

$$\boldsymbol{V}_c = 9.125\boldsymbol{i} + 9.92\boldsymbol{j} \text{ m/sec}$$

Hence, for the center of mass there is an initial velocity upward of 9.92 m/sec just before collision. Directly after collision, since there has been no appreciable external impulse on the system during collision, the center of mass *still has* this upward speed. But now considering larger time intervals, we must take into account the action of gravity, which gives the center of mass a downward acceleration of 9.81 m/sec.^{2} Thus,

$$\ddot{y}_c = -9.81$$
$$\dot{y}_c = -9.81t + C_1$$
$$y_c = -9.81\frac{t^2}{2} + C_1 t + C_2$$

When $t = 0$, $\dot{y}_c = 9.92$ and we take $y_c = 0$ for convenience. Hence we have

$$\dot{y}_c = -9.81t + 9.92 \tag{a}$$
$$y_c = -9.81\frac{t^2}{2} + 9.92t \tag{b}$$

Set $\dot{y}_c$ in (a) equal to zero and solve for t. We get

$$t = 1.011 \text{ sec}$$

Substitute this value of t in Eq. (b) and solve for y_c, which now gives the desired maximum elevation of the center of mass after collision. Thus,

$$(y_c)_{\text{max}} = 5.01 \text{ m} \tag{c}$$

PROBLEMS

14.1. A body weighing 100 lb reaches an incline of 30° while it is moving at 50 ft/sec. If the dynamic coefficient of friction is .3, how long before the body stops?

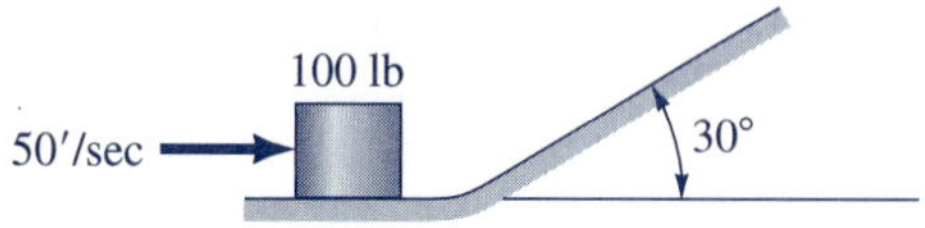

Figure P.14.1.

14.2. A particle of mass 1 kg is initially stationary at the origin of a reference. A force having a known variation with time acts on the particle. That is,

$$\boldsymbol{F}(t) = t^2\boldsymbol{i} + (6t + 10)\boldsymbol{j} + 1.6t^3\boldsymbol{k}\ \text{N}$$

where t is in seconds. After 10 sec, what is the velocity of the body?

14.3. A unidirectional force acting on a particle of mass 16 kg is plotted. What is the velocity of the particle at 40 sec? Initially, the particle is at rest.

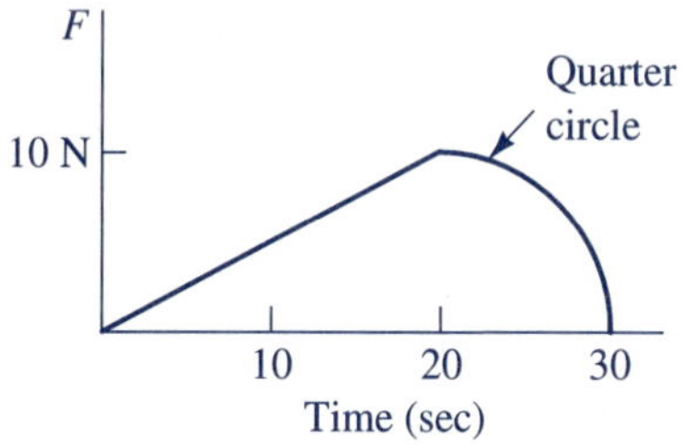

Figure P.14.3.

14.4. A 100-lb block is acted on by a force P, which varies with time as shown. What is the speed of the block after 80 sec? Assume that the block starts from rest and neglect friction. The time axis gives time intervals.

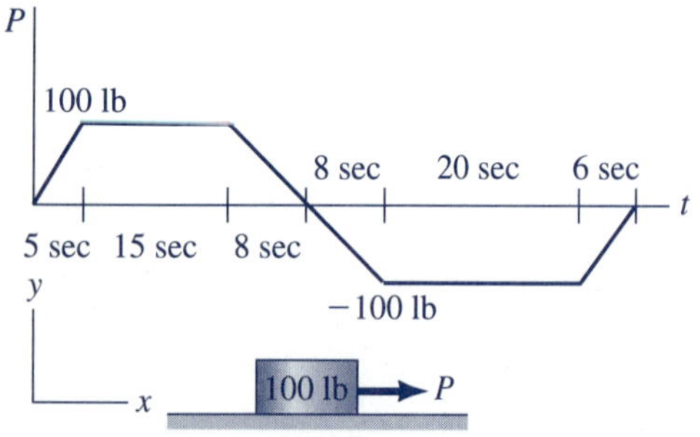

Figure P.14.4.

14.5. If the coefficient of static friction is .5 in Problem 14.4 and the coefficient of dynamic friction is .3, what is the speed of the block after 28 sec?

14.6. A body is dropped from rest. (a) Determine the time required for it to acquire a velocity of 16 m/sec. (b) Determine the time needed to increase its velocity from 16 m/sec to 23 m/sec.

14.7. A body having a mass of 5 lbm is acted on by the following force:

$$\boldsymbol{F} = 8t\boldsymbol{i} + (6 + 3\sqrt{t})\boldsymbol{j} + (16 + 3t^2)\boldsymbol{k}\ \text{lb}$$

where t is in seconds. What is the velocity of the body after 5 sec if the initial velocity is

$$\boldsymbol{V}_1 = 6\boldsymbol{i} + 3\boldsymbol{j} - 10\boldsymbol{k}\ \text{ft/sec?}$$

14.8. A body with a mass of 16 kg is required to change its velocity from $\boldsymbol{V}_1 = 2\boldsymbol{i} + 4\boldsymbol{j} - 10\boldsymbol{k}$ m/sec to a velocity $\boldsymbol{V}_2 = 10\boldsymbol{i} - 5\boldsymbol{j} + 20\boldsymbol{k}$ m/sec in 10 sec. What average force $\boldsymbol{F}_{av}$ over this time interval will do the job?

14.9. In Problem 14.8, determine the force as a function of time for the case where force varies linearly with time starting with a zero value.

14.10. A hockey puck moves at 30 ft/sec from left to right. The puck is intercepted by a player who whisks it at 80 ft/sec toward goal A, as shown. The puck is also rising from the ice at a rate of 10 ft/sec. What is the impulse on the puck, whose weight is 5 oz?

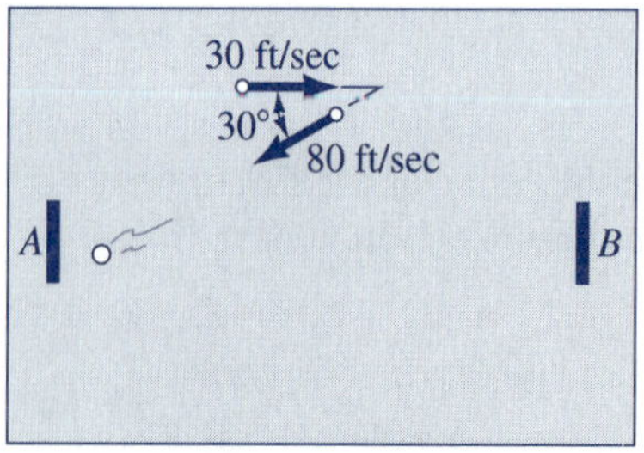

Figure P.14.10.

14.11. Gravel is released from a hopper at the rate of 1 kg/sec. At the exit of the hopper it has a speed of .15 m/s. The belt is moving at a constant speed of 3 m/s. If there is 20 kg of gravel on the conveyor belt at all times and if the belt on the conveyor bed has a weight of 50 N, what is the difference in tension $T_2 - T_1$ for the belt to maintain operation? The dynamic coefficient of friction between bed and belt is 0.4. Assume that the gravel drops 0.2 m from the hopper outlet.

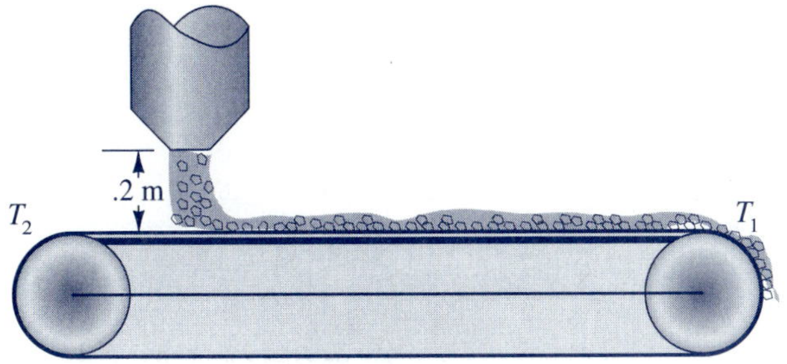

Figure P.14.11.

14.12. Do Problem 12.5 by methods of momentum.

14.13. Do Problem 12.6 by methods of momentum.

14.14. A commuter train made up of two cars is moving at a speed of 80 km/hr. The first car has a mass of 20,000 kg and the second 15,000 kg.

(a) If the brakes are applied simultaneously to both cars, determine the minimum time the cars travel before stopping. The coefficient of static friction between the wheels and rail is .3.

(b) If the brakes on the first car only are applied, determine the time the cars travel before stopping and the force F transmitted between the cars.

14.15. Compute the velocity of the bodies after 10 sec if they start from rest. The cable is inextensible, and the pulleys are frictionless. For the contact surfaces, $\mu_d = .2$.

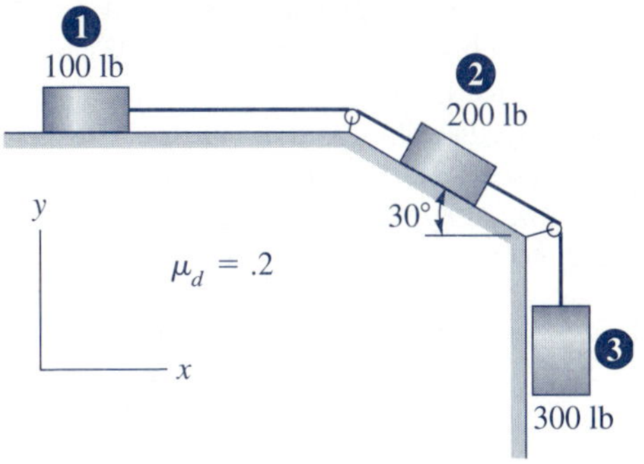

Figure P.14.15.

14.16. Two boxes per second each weighing 100 lb land on a circular conveyor at a speed of 5 ft/sec in the direction of the chute. If there are 6 boxes on the circular belt at any one time, determine the average torque needed to rotate the belt at an angular speed of .2 rad/sec. The dynamic coefficient of friction between the belt and the conveyer bed is .3. What horsepower is needed for operating this belt? Neglect the rotational effect on the boxes themselves as they drop from the chute onto the conveyor. Also, does the radial change in velocity of the boxes affect the torque needed by the conveyor? Neglect any radial slipping of the boxes as they land.

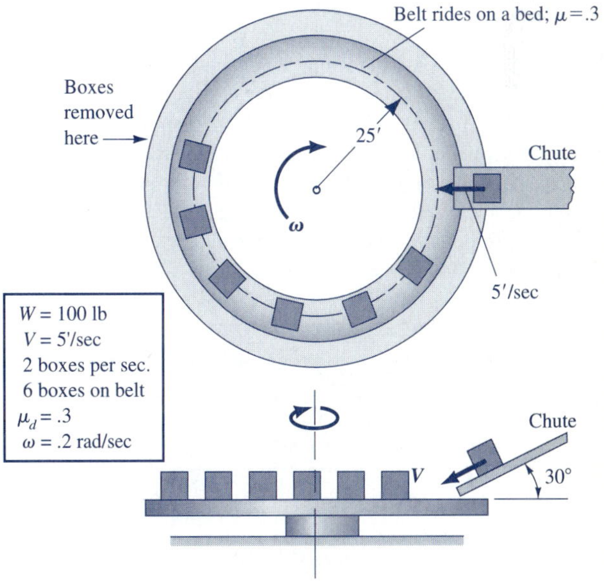

Figure P.14.16.

14.17. A vertical conveyor has sprocket A as the driver, and sprocket B turns freely. The bodies to be lifted are pushed onto the conveyor by a plunger C and are taken off from the conveyor at D as shown in the diagram. If the belt runs at 2,000 mm/sec and the bodies being transported each has a mass of 250 g, what average torque is required by the driving sprocket A? On the average, 40 bodies are on the conveyor at any time.

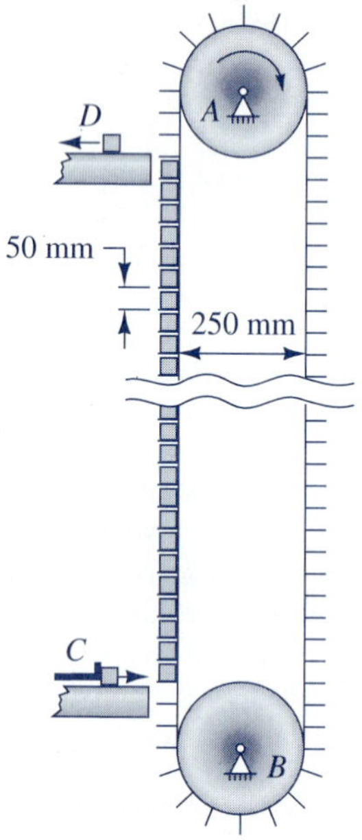

Figure P.14.17.

14.18. A conveyor A is feeding boxes onto a conveyor B. Each box weighs 2 lb and lands on conveyor B with a downward-speed component of 3 ft/sec. Conveyor belt A has a speed of .2 ft/sec. If conveyor B runs at a speed of 5 ft/sec and if five boxes land per second on the average, what net average force T_2 must be exerted on the conveyor belt B to slide it over its bed? At any time, 50 boxes are on belt B. Take $\mu_d = .2$ for all surfaces. Neglect the weight of conveyor belt B.

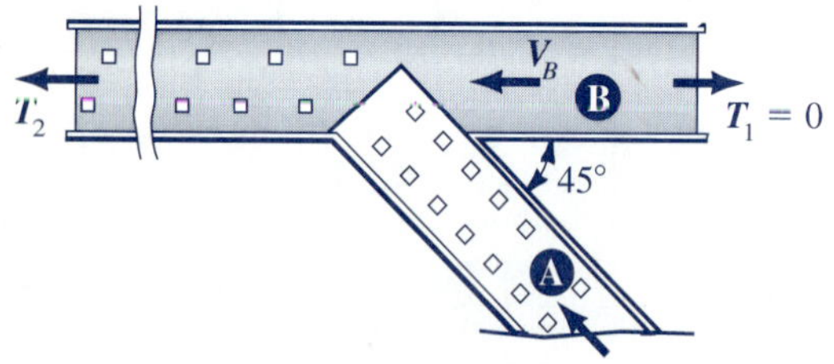

Figure P.14.18.

14.19. An idealized one-dimensional pressure wave (i.e., pressure is a function of one coordinate and time) generated by an explosion travels at a speed V of 1,200 ft/sec, as shown at time $t = 0$. The peak pressure of this wave is 5 psia. What impulse per square foot is delivered to a wall oriented at right angles to the x axis? The wave is reflected from the wall, and the pressure at the wall is double the incoming pressure at all times. Do the problem for two time intervals corresponding to the interval (a) from when the wave front first touches the wall to when the peak reaches the wall and (b) from when the peak hits the wall to when the end of the wave reaches the wall.

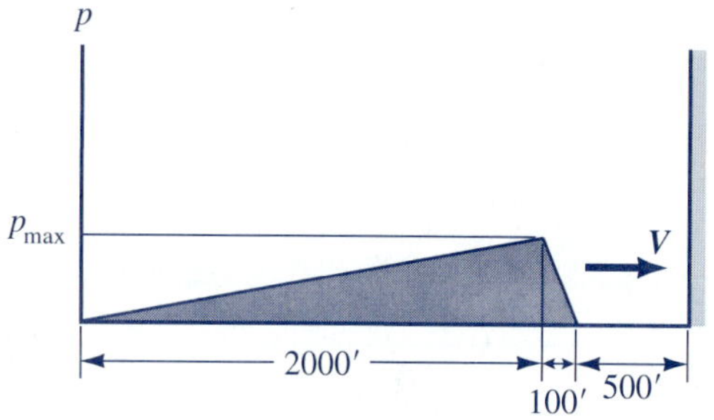

Figure P.14.19.

14.20. Blocks A and B move on frictionless surfaces. The blocks are interconnected with a light bar. Body A weighs 30 lb; the weight of body B is not known. A constant force F of 100 lb is applied at the configuration shown. If a speed of 25 ft/sec is reached by A after 1 sec, what impulse is developed on the vertical wall?

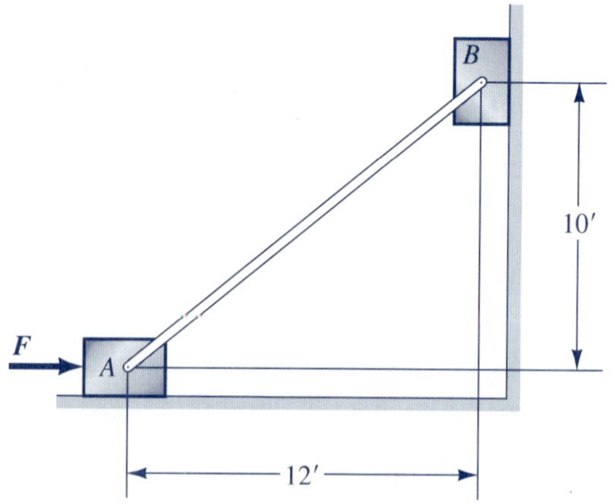

Figure P.14.20.

14.21. In Problem 14.20, compute the impulse on the horizontal surface. A moves 4 ft in 1 sec and $W_B = 20$ lb.

14.22. An antitank airplane fires two 90-N projectiles at a tank at the same time. The muzzle velocity of the guns is 1,000 m/sec relative to the plane. If the plane before firing weighs 65 kN and is moving with a velocity of 320 km/hr, compute the change in its speed when it fires the two projectiles.

14.23. A toboggan has just entered the horizontal part of its run. It carries three people weighing 120 lb, 180 lb, and 150 lb, respectively. Suddenly, a pedestrian weighing 200 lb strays onto the course and is turned end for end by the toboggan, landing safely among the riders. Since the toboggan path is icy, we can neglect friction with the toboggan path for all actions described here. If the toboggan is traveling at a speed of 35 mph just before collision occurs, what is the speed after the collision when the pedestrian has become a rider? The toboggan weighs 30 lb.

Figure P.14.23.

14.24. An 890-N rowboat containing a 668-N man is pushed off the dock by an 800-N man. The speed that is imparted to the boat is .30 m/sec by this push. The man then leaps into the boat from the dock with a speed of .60 m/sec relative to the dock in the direction of motion of the boat. When the two men have settled down in the boat and before rowing commences, what is the speed of the boat? Neglect water resistance.

Figure P.14.24.

14.25. Two vehicles connected with an inextensible cable are rolling along a road. Vehicle B, using a winch, draws A toward it so that the relative speed is 5 ft/sec at $t = 0$ and 10 ft/sec at $t = 20$ sec. Vehicle A weighs 2,000 lb and vehicle B weighs 3,000 lb. Each vehicle has a rolling resistance that is .01 times the vehicle's weight. What is the speed of A relative to the ground at $t = 20$ sec if A is initially moving to the right at a speed of 30 ft/sec?

Figure P.14.25.

14.26. Treat Example 14.3 as a two-particle system in the impulse-momentum considerations. Verify the results of Example 14.3 for V. (Be sure to include *all* external forces for the system.)

14.27. Determine the velocity of body A and body B after 3 sec if the system is released from rest. Neglect friction and the inertia of the pulleys.

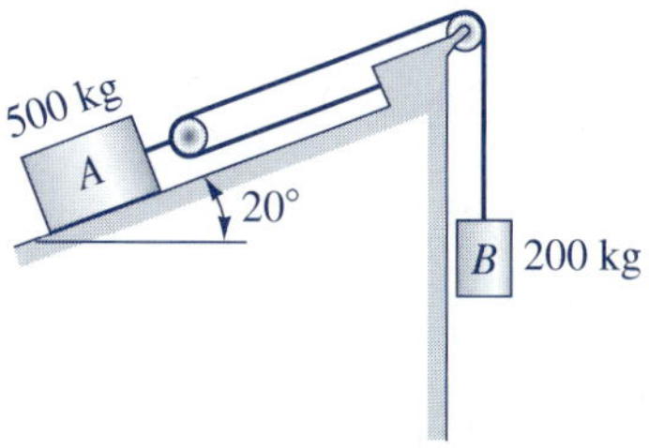

Figure P.14.27.

14.28. Do Problem 14.27 by considering a system of particles. (Be sure to include *all* external forces for the system of bodies A and B.)

14.29. A 40-kN truck is moving at the speed of 40 km/hr carrying a 15-kN load A. The load is restrained only by friction with the floor of the truck where there is a dynamic coefficient of friction of .2 and the static coefficient of friction is .3. The driver suddenly jams his brakes on so as to lock all wheels for 1.5 sec. At the end of this interval, the brakes are released. What is the final speed V of the truck neglecting wind resistance and rotational inertia of the wheels after load A stops slipping? The dynamic coefficient of friction between the tires and the road is .4.

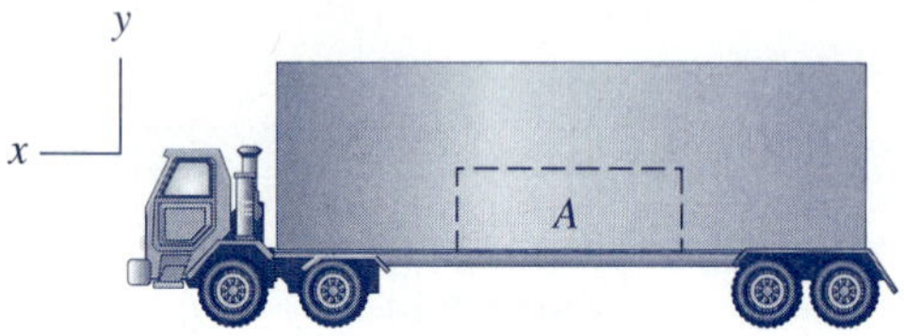

Figure P.14.29.

14.30. A 1,300-kg Jeep is carrying three 100-kg passengers. The Jeep is in four-wheel drive and is under test to see what maximum speed is possible in 5 sec from a start on an icy road surface for which $\mu_s = .1$. Compute V_{max} at $t = 5$ sec.

Figure P.14.30.

14.31. Two adjacent tanks A and B are shown. Both tanks are rectangular with a width of 4 m. Gasoline from tank A is being pumped into tank B. When the level of tank A is .7 m from the top, the rate of flow Q from A to B is 300 liters/sec, and 10 sec later it is 500 liters/sec. What is the average horizontal force from the fluids onto the tank during this 10-sec time interval? The density of the gasoline is $.8 \times 10^3$ kg/m^3. Tank A is originally full and tank B is originally empty.

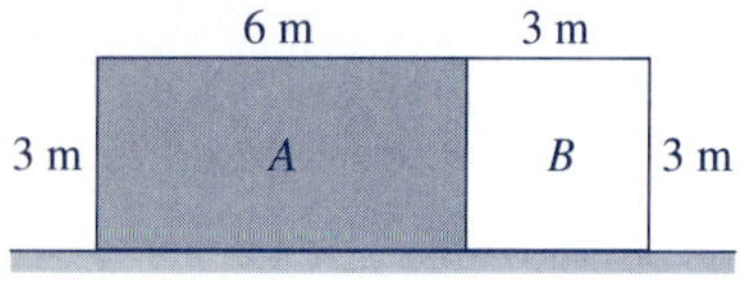

Figure P.14.31.

14.32. Two tanks A and B are shown. Tank A is originally full of water ($\rho = 62.4$ lbm/ft^3), while tank B is empty. Water is pumped from A to B. If initially 100 cfs of water is being pumped and if this flow increases at the rate of 10 cfs/sec^2 for 30 sec thereafter, what is the average vertical force onto the tanks from the water during this time period, aside from the static dead weight of the water?

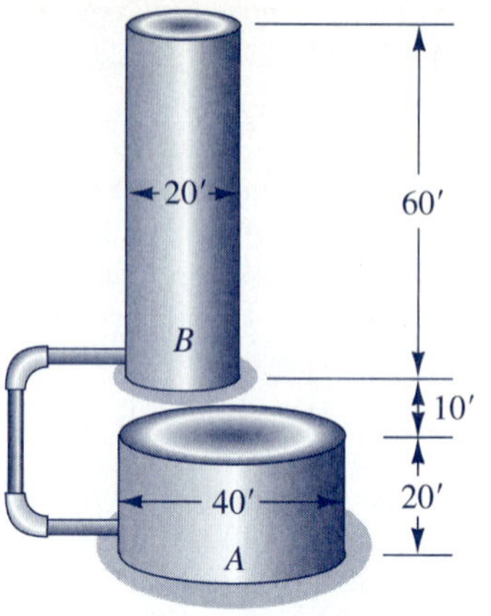

Figure P.14.32

14.33. A device to be detonated is shown in (a) suspended above the ground. Ten seconds after detonation, there are four fragments having the following masses and position vectors relative to reference XYZ:

$$m_1 = 5 \text{ kg}$$
$$\boldsymbol{r}_1 = 1{,}000\boldsymbol{i} + 2{,}000\boldsymbol{j} + 900\boldsymbol{k} \text{ m}$$
$$m_2 = 3 \text{ kg}$$
$$\boldsymbol{r}_2 = 800\boldsymbol{i} + 1{,}800\boldsymbol{j} + 2{,}500\boldsymbol{k} \text{ m}$$
$$m_3 = 4 \text{ kg}$$
$$\boldsymbol{r}_3 = 400\boldsymbol{i} + 1{,}000\boldsymbol{j} + 2{,}000\boldsymbol{k} \text{ m}$$
$$m_4 = 6 \text{ kg}$$
$$\boldsymbol{r}_4 = X_4\boldsymbol{i} + Y_4\boldsymbol{j} + Z_4\boldsymbol{k}$$

Find the position $\boldsymbol{r}_4$ if the center of mass of the device is initially at position $\boldsymbol{r}_0$, where

$$\boldsymbol{r}_0 = 600\boldsymbol{i} + 1200\boldsymbol{j} + 2{,}300\boldsymbol{k} \text{ m}$$

Neglect wind resistance.

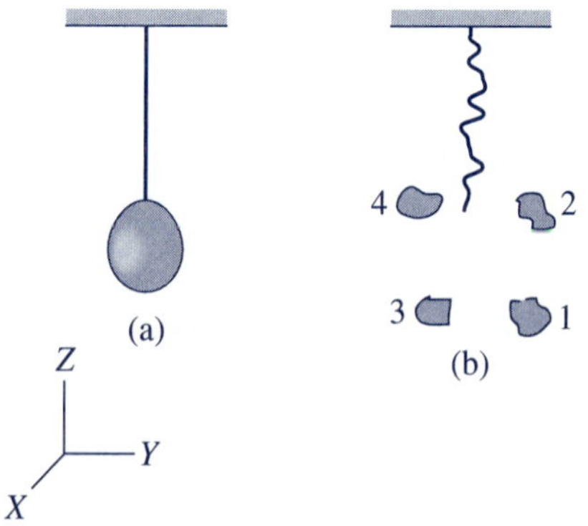

Figure P.14.33.

14.4 Impact

In Section 14.3, we discussed impulsive forces. We shall in this section discuss in detail an action in which impulsive forces are present. This situation occurs when two bodies collide but do not break. The time interval during collision is very small, and comparatively large forces are developed on the bodies during the small time interval. This action is called *impact*. For such actions with such short time intervals, the force of gravity generally causes a negligible impulse. The impact forces on the colliding bodies are always equal and opposite to each other, so the net impulse on the *pair* of bodies during collision is *zero*. This means that the total linear momentum directly after impact (postimpact) equals the total linear momentum directly before impact (preimpact).

We shall consider at this time two types of impact for which certain definitions are needed. We shall call the normal to the *plane of contact* during the collision of two bodies the *line of impact*. If the centers of mass of the two colliding bodies lie along the line of impact, the action is called *central impact* and is shown for the case of two spheres in Fig. 14.13.[5] If, in addition, the velocity vectors of the mass centers approaching the collision are collinear with the line of impact, the action is called *direct central impact*. This action is illustrated by $\boldsymbol{V}_1$ and $\boldsymbol{V}_2$ in Fig 14.13. Should one (or both) of the velocities have a line of action not collinear with the line impact—for example, $\boldsymbol{V}'_1$ and/or $\boldsymbol{V}'_2$—the action is termed *oblique central impact*.

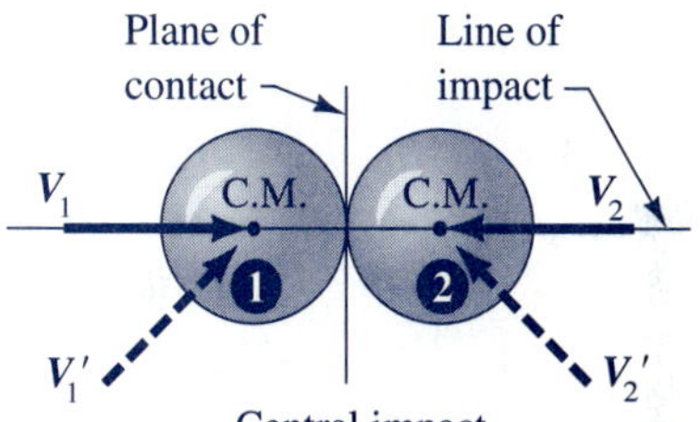

Figure 14.13. Central impact of two spheres.

In either case, linear momentum is conserved during the short time interval from directly before the collision (indicated with the subscript i) to directly after the collision (indicated with subscript f). That is,

$$(m_1\boldsymbol{V}_1)_i + (m_2\boldsymbol{V}_2)_i = (m_1\boldsymbol{V}_1)_f + (m_2\boldsymbol{V}_2)_f \qquad (14.8)$$

In the *direct-central-impact* case for *smooth* bodies (i.e., bodies with no friction), this equation becomes a single scalar equation since $(\boldsymbol{V}_1)_f$ and $(\boldsymbol{V}_2)_f$ are collinear with the line of impact. Usually, the initial velocities are known and the final values are desired, which means that we have for this case one scalar equation involving two unknowns. Clearly, we must know more about the manner of interaction of the bodies, since Eq. 14.8 as it stands is valid for materials of any deformability (e.g., putty or hardened steel) and takes no account of such important considerations. Thus, we cannot consider the bodies undergoing impact only as particles as has been the case thus far, but must, in addition, consider them as deformable bodies of finite size in order to generate enough information to solve the problem at hand.

For the *oblique-impact case*, we can write components of the linear-momentum equation along the line of impact and for smooth (frictionless) bodies, along two other directions at right angles to the line of impact. If we know the initial velocities, then we have six unknown final velocity components and only three equations. Thus, we need even more information to establish fully the final velocities after this more general type of impact. We now consider each of these cases in more detail in order to establish these additional relations.

[5]Noncentral or *eccentric impact* is examined in Chapter 17 for the case of plane motion.

Case 1. Direct Central Impact. Let us first examine the direct-central-impact case. We shall consider the period of collision to be made up of two subintervals of time. The *period of deformation* refers to the duration of the collision, starting from initial contact of the bodies and ending at the instant of maximum deformation. During this period, we shall consider that impulse $\int D\,dt$ acts oppositely on each of the bodies. The second period, covering the time from the maximum deformation condition to the instant at which the bodies just separate,[6] we shall term the *period of restitution*. The impulse acting oppositely on each body during this period we shall indicate as $\int R\,dt$. If the bodies are *perfectly elastic*, they will reestablish their initial shapes during the period of restitution (if we neglect the internal vibrations of the bodies), as shown in Fig. 14.14(a). When the bodies do not reestablish their initial shapes [Fig. 14.14(b)], we say that *plastic deformation* has taken place.

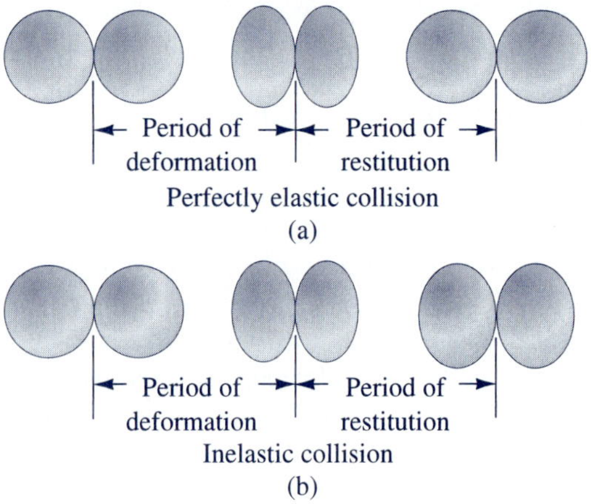

Figure 14.14. Collision process.

The ratio of the impulse during the restitution period $\int R\,dt$ to the impulse during the deformation period $\int D\,dt$ is a number ϵ, which depends mainly on the physical properties of the bodies in collision. We call this number the *coefficient of restitution*. Thus,

$$\epsilon = \frac{\text{impulse during restitution}}{\text{impulse during deformation}} = \frac{\int R\,dt}{\int D\,dt} \tag{14.9}$$

We must strongly point out that the coefficient of restitution depends also on the size, shape, and approach velocities of the bodies before impact. These dependencies result from the fact that plastic deformation is related to the magnitude and nature of the force distributions in the bodies and also to the rate of loading. However, values of ϵ have been established for different materials and can be used for approximate results in the kind of computations

[6]If they don't separate, the end of the second period occurs when the bodies cease to deform. We call such a process a **plastic** impact.

to follow. We shall now formulate the relation between the coefficient of restitution and the initial and final velocities of the bodies undergoing impact.

Let us consider *one* of the bodies during the two phases of the collision. If we call the velocity at the maximum deformation condition $(V)_D$, we can say for mass 1:

$$\int D\,dt = \left[(m_1 V_1)_D - (m_1 V_1)_i\right] = -m_1\left[(V_1)_i - (V_1)_D\right] \qquad (14.10)$$

During the period of restitution, we find that

$$\int R\,dt = -m_1\left[(V_1)_D - (V_1)_f\right] \qquad (14.11)$$

Dividing Eq. 14.11 by Eq. 14.10, canceling out m_1, and noting the definition in Eq. 14.9, we can say:

$$\epsilon = \frac{(V_1)_D - (V_1)_f}{(V_1)_i - (V_1)_D} \qquad (14.12)$$

A similar analysis for the other mass (2) gives

$$\epsilon = \frac{(V_2)_D - (V_2)_f}{(V_2)_i - (V_2)_D} = \frac{(V_2)_f - (V_2)_D}{(V_2)_D - (V_2)_i} \qquad (14.13)$$

In this last expression, we have changed the sign of numerator and denominator. At the intermediate position at the end of deformation and the beginning of restitution the masses have essentially the same velocity. Thus, $(V_1)_D = (V_2)_D$. Since the quotients in Eqs. 14.12 and 14.13 are equal to each other, we can add numerators and denominators to form another equal quotient, as you can demonstrate yourself. Noting the abovementioned equality of the V_D terms, we have the desired result:

$$\epsilon = -\frac{(V_2)_f - (V_1)_f}{(V_2)_i - (V_1)_i} = -\frac{\text{relative velocity of separation}}{\text{relative velocity of approach}} \qquad (14.14)$$

This equation involves the coefficient ϵ, which is presumably known or estimated, and the initial and final velocities of the bodies undergoing impact. Thus, with this equation we can solve for the final velocities of the bodies after collision when we use the linear-momentum equation 14.8 for the case of direct central impact.

During a *perfectly elastic* collision, the impulse for the period of restitution equals the impulse for the period of deformation,[7] so the coefficient of restitution is *unity* for this case. For inelastic collisions, the coefficient of restitution is less than unity since the impulse is diminished on restitution as a

[7]The impulses are equal because during the period of restitution the body can be considered to undergo identically the reverse of the process corresponding to the deformation period. Thus, from a thermodynamics point of view, we are considering the elastic impact to be a *reversible* process.

result of the failure of the bodies to resume their original geometries. For a *perfectly plastic* impact, $\epsilon = 0$ [i.e., $(V_2)_f = (V_1)_f$] and the bodies remain in contact. Thus ϵ ranges from 0 to 1.

Case 2. Oblique Central Impact. Let us now consider the case of oblique central impact. The velocity components along the line of impact can be related by the scalar component of the linear-momentum equation 14.8 in this direction and also by Eq. 14.14, where velocity components along the line of impact are used and where the coefficient of restitution may be considered (for smooth bodies) to be the same as for the direct-central-impact case. If we know the initial conditions, we can accordingly solve for those velocity components after impact in the direction of the line of impact. As for the other rectangular components of velocity, we can say that for smooth bodies, these velocity components are unaffected by the collision, since no impulses act in these directions on either body. That is, the velocity components normal to the line of impact for each body are the same immediately after impact as before. Thus, the final velocity components of both bodies can be established, and the motions of the bodies can be determined within the limits of the discussion. The following examples are used to illustrate the use of the preceding formulations.

Note that the mass and materials of the colliding bodies for both direct or oblique central impact can be different from each other.

Example 14.10

Two billiard balls (of the same size and mass) collide with the velocities of approach shown in Fig. 14.15. For a coefficient of restitution of .90, what are the final velocities of the balls directly after they part? What is the loss in kinetic energy?

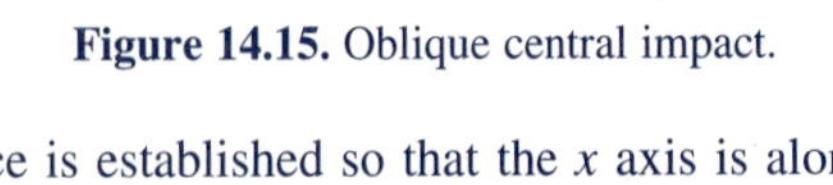

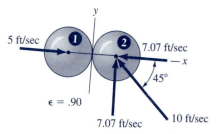

Figure 14.15. Oblique central impact.

A reference is established so that the x axis is along line of impact and the y axis is in the plane of contact such that the reference plane is par-

Example 14.10 (Continued)

allel to the billiard table. The approach velocities have been decomposed into components along these axes. The velocity components $(V_1)_y$ and $(V_2)_y$ are unchanged during the action. Along the line of impact, **linear-momentum** considerations lead to

$$5m - 7.07m = m[(V_1)_x]_f + m[(V_2)_x]_f \qquad \text{(a)}$$

Using the **coefficient-of-restitution** relation (Eq. 14.14), we have

$$\epsilon = .90 = -\frac{[(V_2)_x]_f - [(V_1)_x]_f}{-7.07 - 5} \qquad \text{(b)}$$

We thus have two equations, (a) and (b), for the unknown components in the x direction. Simplifying these equations, we have

$$[(V_1)_x]_f + [(V_2)_x]_f = -2.07 \qquad \text{(c)}$$

$$[(V_1)_x]_f + [(V_2)_x]_f = -10.86 \qquad \text{(d)}$$

Adding, we get

$$[(V_1)_x]_f = -6.47 \text{ ft/sec}$$

Solving for $[(V_2)_x]_f$ in Eq. (c), we write

$$[(V_2)_x]_f - 6.47 = -2.07$$

Therefore,

$$[(V_2)_x]_f = 4.40 \text{ ft/sec}$$

The final velocities after collision are then

$$(\boldsymbol{V}_1)_f = -6.47\boldsymbol{i} \text{ ft/sec}$$

$$(\boldsymbol{V}_2)_f = 4.40\boldsymbol{i} + 7.07\boldsymbol{j} \text{ ft/sec}$$

The loss in kinetic energy is given as

$$(\text{KE})_i - (\text{KE})_f = (\tfrac{1}{2}m5^2 + \tfrac{1}{2}m10^2) - \left[\tfrac{1}{2}m6.47^2 + \tfrac{1}{2}m(7.07^2 + 4.40^2)\right]$$

$$\Delta\text{KE} = \tfrac{1}{2}m[25 + 100 - (41.9 + 50.0 + 19.33)]$$

$$= 6.89m \text{ ft-lb}$$

Please note that mechanical energy is conserved *only* if ϵ is unity (i.e., a perfectly elastic impact). For all other cases, there is always dissipation of mechanical energy into heat and permanent deformation. However, *all* impacts involve conservation of linear momentum for the system.

Example 14.11

A pile driver is used to force a pile A into the ground (Fig. 14.16) as part of a program to properly prepare the foundation for a tall building. The device consists of a piston C on which a pressure p is developed from steam or air.

The piston is connected to a 1,000-lb hammer B. The assembly is suddenly released and accelerates downward a distance h of 2 ft to impact on pile A weighing 400 lb. If the earth develops a constant resisting force to movement of 25,000 lb, what distance d will the pile move for a drop involving no contribution from p (which is then 0 psig). Take the impact as *plastic*. The weight of the piston and the connecting rod is 100 lb.

We begin by using **conservation of mechanical energy** for the freely falling system to a position just before impact (preimpact). Using the initial configuration as the datum we have

$$0 + (1{,}000 + 100)(2) = \frac{1}{2}\left(\frac{1{,}100}{g}\right)V^2 + 0$$

$$\therefore\ V = \sqrt{2gh} = \sqrt{(2)(32.2)(2)} = 11.35 \text{ ft/sec}$$

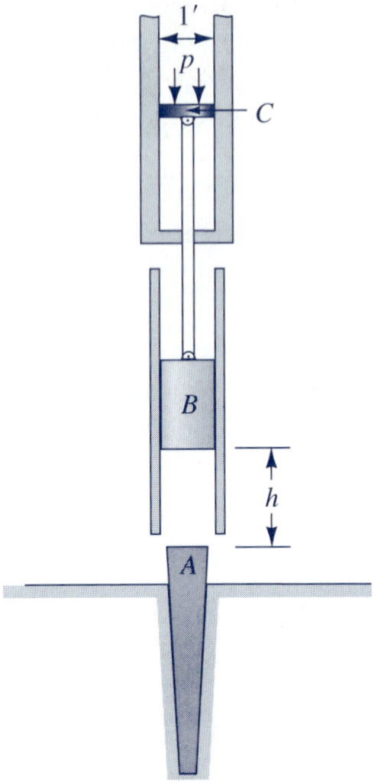

Figure 14.16. Steam-driven pile driver.

Now we get to the impact process. We have **conservation of linear momentum** while the bodies remain hypothetically at the position at which contact is first made. Thus, for plastic impact we can say

$$\frac{1{,}100}{g}(11.35) + 0 = \frac{1{,}500}{g}V \qquad \therefore\ V = 8.32 \text{ ft/sec}$$

Finally, we come to the post-impact process where we shall use the **work energy equation** for the pile driver and the pile.

$$(1{,}500 - 25{,}000)(d) = 0 - \frac{1}{2}\left(\frac{1{,}500}{g}\right)(8.32^2)$$

where the term on the left side must be negative because the net force on the system (23,500 lb) is in the opposite direction to the motion (see Eq. 13.2). Solving for d we get

$$d = .0686 \text{ ft} = .823 \text{ in}$$

*14.5 Collision of a Particle with a Massive Rigid Body

In Section 14.4, we employed conservation-of-momentum considerations and the concept of the coefficient of restitution to examine the impact of two smooth bodies of comparable size. Now we shall extend this approach to include the impact of a spherical body with a much larger and more massive *rigid* body, as shown in Fig. 14.17.

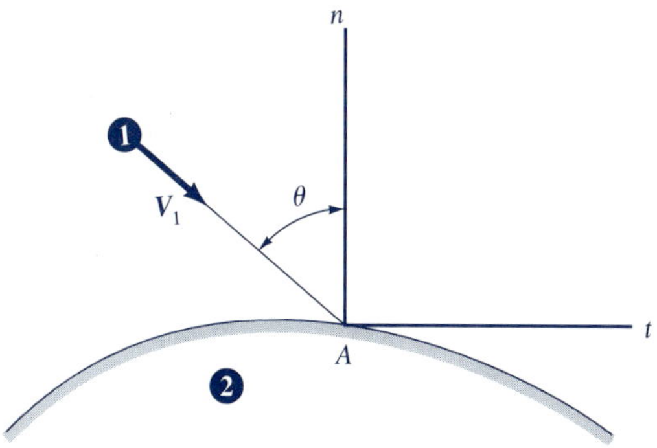

Figure 14.17. Small body collides with large body.

The procedure we shall follow is to consider the massive body to be a spherical body of *infinite* mass with a radius equal to the local radius of curvature of the surface of the massive body at the point of contact A. This condition is shown in Fig. 14.18. The line of impact then becomes identical with the normal n to the surface of the massive body at the point of impact. Note that the case we show in the diagram corresponds to oblique central impact. With no friction, clearly only the components along the line of impact n can change as a result of impact. But in this case, the velocity of the sphere representing the massive body must undergo no change in value after impact because of its infinite mass.[8] We cannot make good use here of the conservation of the linear-momentum equation in the n direction because the infinite mass of the hypothetical body (2) will render the equation indeterminate. However, we can use Eq. 14.14, assuming we have a coefficient of restitution ϵ for the action. Noting that the velocity of the massive body *does not change*, we accordingly get

$$\epsilon = -\frac{\left[(V_1)_n\right]_f - \left[(V_2)_n\right]}{\left[(V_1)_n\right]_i - \left[(V_2)_n\right]} \tag{14.15}$$

Thus, knowing the velocities of the bodies before impact, as well as the quantity ϵ, we are able to compute the velocity of the particle after impact. If the

[8]Otherwise, there would be an infinite change in momentum for this sphere.

collision is perfectly elastic, $\epsilon = 1$, and we see from Eq. 14.15 that for a stationary massive body

$$[(V_1)_n]_i = -[(V_1)_n]_f$$

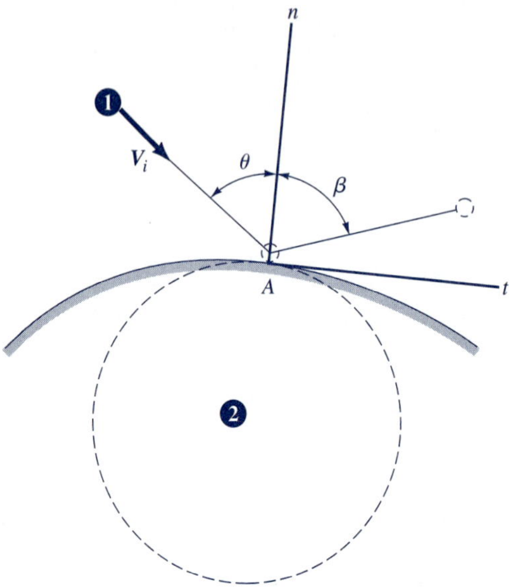

Figure 14.18. Angle of incidence and angle of reflection.

This means that the angle of incidence θ equals the angle of reflection β. For $\epsilon < 1$ (i.e., for an inelastic collision), the angle of reflection β will clearly exceed θ as shown in Fig. 14.18.

We now illustrate the use of these formulations.

Example 14.12

A ball is dropped onto a concrete floor from height h (Fig. 14.19). If the coefficient of restitution is .90 for the action, to what height h' will the ball rise on the rebound?

Here the massive body has an infinite radius at the surface. Furthermore, we have a direct central impact. Accordingly, from Eq. 14.15 we have

$$\epsilon = -\frac{(V)_f - 0}{(V)_i - 0} = \frac{\sqrt{2gh'}}{\sqrt{2gh}}$$

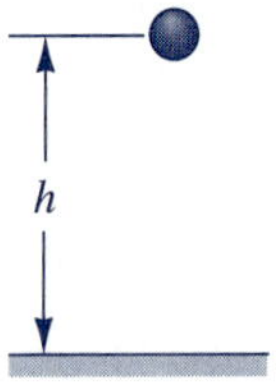

Figure 14.19. Ball dropped on concrete floor.

Solving for h', we get

$$h' = \epsilon^2 h = .81h$$

In the following interesting example as well as in some homework problems, we will have to determine, for a given uniform distribution of stationary particles in space, how many of these particles collide per unit time with a rigid body translating through this cloud of particles at constant speed V_0. To illustrate how this may be accomplished easily, we have shown a cone-cylinder moving through such a cloud of particles at constant speed V_0 in Fig. 14.20.

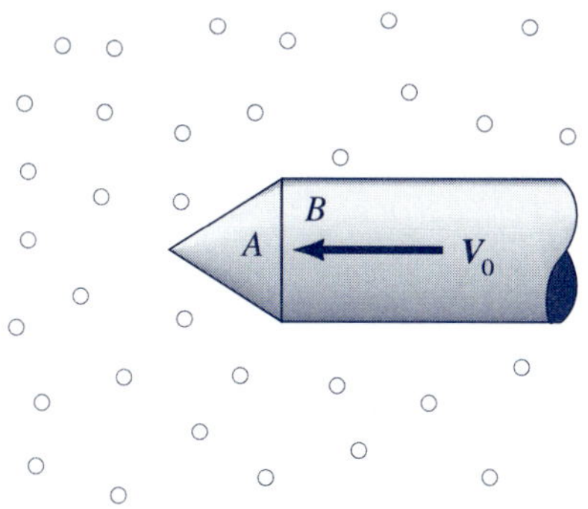

Figure 14.20. A cone–cylinder moving through a cloud of particles.

During a time interval Δt, the cone A moves a distance $V_0\,\Delta t$, colliding with all the particles in the volume swept out by the conical surface during this time interval as shown in Fig. 14.21, where this region is outlined with dashed lines. This volume can easily be calculated. It is that of a right circular cylinder shown in Fig. 14.22 having a cross section corresponding to the *projected* area of the cone taken along the axis parallel to the direction of motion of the moving body. Clearly, by adding the volume of cone A to the right circular cylinder along its axis at the forward end and then deleting the same volume at the rear end, we reproduce the dashed volume in Fig 14.21 during the time interval Δt. In general, the volume swept out by a body during a time interval can readily be found by using the *projected* area of the body in the direction of motion. We then use this area to sweep out a volume during this time interval. This negates having to deal with the actual more complicated three-dimensional end surface itself. We shall make use of this procedure in the following example.

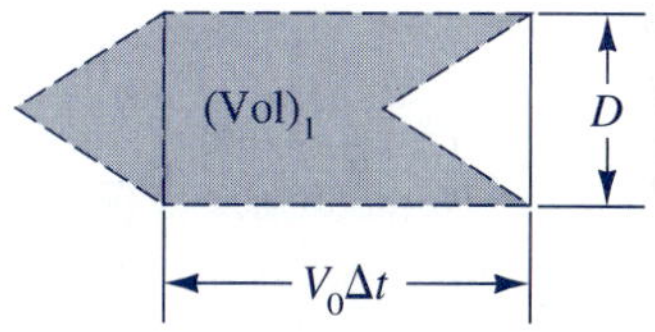

Figure 14.21. Dashed region is volume swept out by the cone A during Δt.

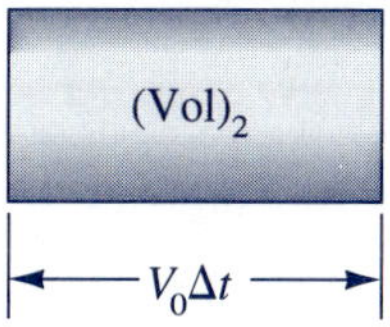

Figure 14.22. Volume swept by cone A.

Example 14.13

A satellite in the form of a sphere with radius R [Fig. 14.23(a)] is moving above the earth's surface in a region of highly rarefied atmosphere. We wish to estimate the drag on the satellite. Neglect the contribution from the antennas.

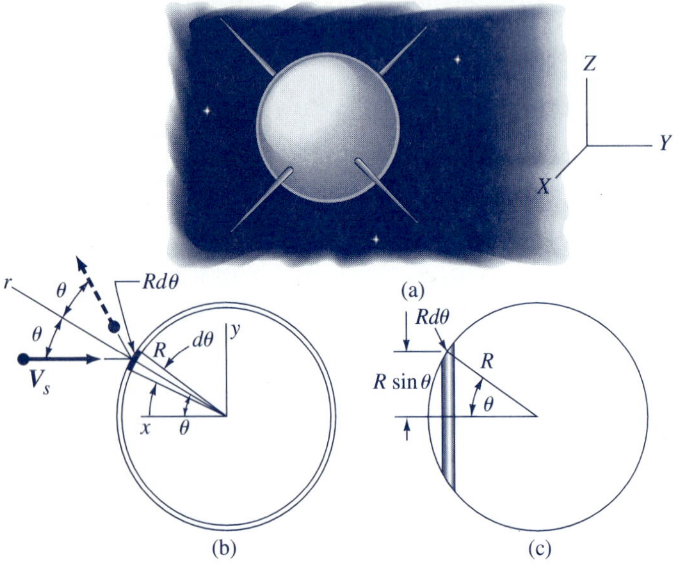

Figure 14.23. Satellite moving at high speed V_s in space.

In this highly rarefied atmosphere, we shall assume that the average spacing of the molecules is large enough relative to the satellite that we cannot use the continuum approach of fluid dynamics, wherein matter is assumed to be continuously distributed. Instead, we must consider collisions of the individual molecules with the satellite, which is a noncontinuum approach, as discussed in Section 1.7. The mass per molecule is m slugs and the number density of the molecules is uniformly n molecules/ft.^{3} Since the satellite is moving with a speed V_s much greater than the speed of the molecules (the molecules move at about the speed of sound), we can assume that the molecules are stationary relative to inertial space reference XYZ and that only the satellite is moving. Furthermore, we assume that when the satellite hits a molecule there is an elastic, frictionless collision.

To study this problem, we have shown a section of the satellite in Fig. 14.23(b). A reference xyz is fixed to the satellite at its center. We shall consider this reference also to be an inertial reference—a step that for small drag will introduce little error for the ensuing calculations. Relative to this reference, the molecules approach the satellite with a horizontal velocity V_s, as shown for one molecule. They then collide with the surface

Example 14.13 (Continued)

with an angle of incidence measured by the polar coordinate θ. Finally, they deflect with an equal angle of reflection of θ. The component of the impulse given to the molecule in the x direction $(I_{mol})_x$ is

$$(I_{mol})_x = (mV_s \cos 2\theta) - (-mV_s) = (mV_s(1 + \cos 2\theta) \qquad \text{(a)}$$

This is the impulse component that would be given to any molecule hitting a strip that is $R\,d\theta$ in width and which is revolved around the x axis as shown in Fig. 14.23(c). The number of such collisions per second for this strip can readily be calculated as follows:[9]

collisions for strip per second

$$= \begin{bmatrix}\text{projected area}\\ \text{of the strip}\\ \text{in } x \text{ direction}\end{bmatrix}\begin{bmatrix}\text{distance the}\\ \text{strip moves}\\ \text{in 1 sec}\end{bmatrix}\begin{bmatrix}\text{number of}\\ \text{molecules per}\\ \text{unit volume}\end{bmatrix} \qquad \text{(b)}$$

$$= [(R\,d\theta \cos\theta)(2\pi R \sin\theta)][V_s][n]$$

$$= 2\pi R^2 n V_s \sin\theta \cos\theta\, d\theta$$

The impulse component dI_x provided by the strip in 1 sec is the product of the right sides of Eqs. (a) and (b). Thus,

$$dI_x = 2\pi m n R^2 V_s^2 (\sin\theta \cos\theta)(1 + \cos 2\theta)\, d\theta \qquad \text{(c)}$$

Noting that $2 \sin\theta \cos\theta = \sin 2\theta$, we have

$$dI_x = \pi m n R^2 V_s^2 (\sin 2\theta + \sin 2\theta \cos 2\theta)\, d\theta$$

$$= \pi m n R^2 V_s^2 \left(\sin 2\theta + \frac{\sin 4\theta}{2}\right) d\theta$$

Integrating from $\theta = 0$ to $\theta = \pi/2$,[10] we get the total impulse for 1 sec by the sphere:

$$I_x = \pi m n R^2 V_s^2 \left(\int_0^{\pi/2} \sin 2\theta\, d\theta + \tfrac{1}{2}\int_0^{\pi/2} \sin 4\theta\, d\theta\right)$$

$$= \pi m n R^2 V_s^2 \left(-\tfrac{1}{2}\cos 2\theta\Big|_0^{\pi/2} - \tfrac{1}{8}\cos 4\theta\Big|_0^{\pi/2}\right) \qquad \text{(d)}$$

$$= \pi m n R^2 V_s^2 (1 + 0) = \pi m n R^2 V_s^2$$

The average force needed to give this impulse by the satellite is clearly $\pi m n R^2 V_s^2$, and so the reaction to this force is the desired drag.

[9]As is shown here the volume swept out by the strip in one second will be a right circular tube of length $V_s\,\Delta t = (V_s)(1)$ and thickness $R\,d\theta\,\cos\theta$ and having a radius equal to $R \sin\theta$.

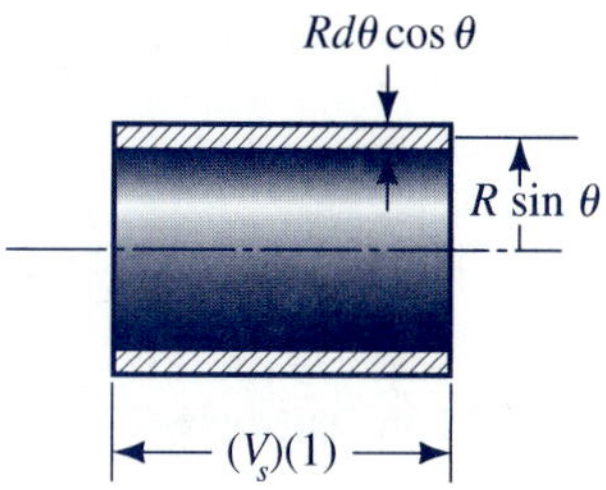

[10]We integrate only up to $\pi/2$ because collisions take place only on the *front* part of the sphere. (Note also, we are already rotating for any θ completely around the axis of the sphere.) This is so since, in our model, the molecules are moving only from left to right toward the sphere with no collisions possible beyond $\theta = \pi/2$.

PROBLEMS

14.34. Two cylinders move along a rod in a frictionless manner. Cylinder A has a mass of 10 kg and moves to the right at a speed of 3 m/sec, while cylinder B has a mass of 5 kg and moves to the left at a speed of 2.5 m/sec. What is the speed of cylinder B after impact for a coefficient of restitution ϵ of .8? What is the loss in kinetic energy?

Figure P.14.34.

14.35. In Problem 14.34, what coefficient of restitution is needed for body A to be stationary after impact?

14.36. Two smooth cylinders of identical radius roll toward each other such that their centerlines are perfectly parallel. Cylinder A has a mass of 10 kg, and cylinder B has a mass of 7.5 kg. What is the speed at which cylinder A moves directly after collision for a coefficient of restitution $\epsilon = .75$?

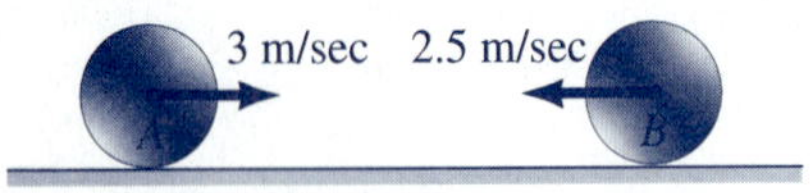

Figure P.14.36.

14.37. Cylinder A, weighing 10 lb, moves toward stationary cylinder B, weighing 40 lb, at the speed of 20 ft/sec. Mass B is attached to a spring having a spring constant K equal to 10 lb/in. If the collision has a coefficient of restitution $\epsilon = .9$, what is the maximum deflection δ of the spring? Assume that there is no friction along the rod and that the spring has negligible mass.

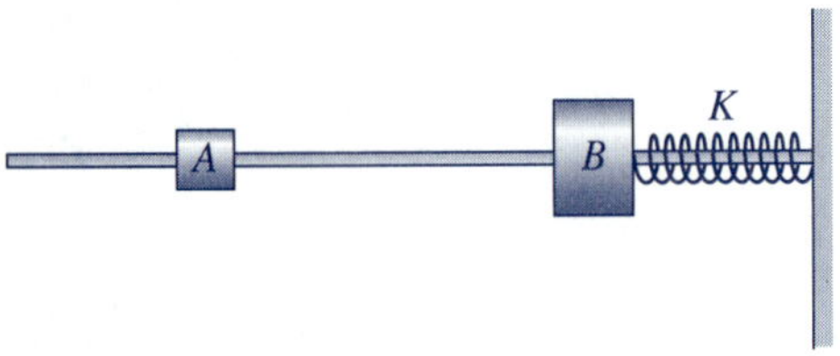

Figure P.14.37.

14.38. Do Problem 14.37 for the case where there is a perfectly plastic impact and the spring is nonlinear such that $5x^{3/2}$ lb of force is required for a deflection of x inches.

14.39. Assume a perfectly plastic impact as the 5-kg body falls from a height of 2.6 m onto a plate of mass 2.5 kg. This plate is mounted on a spring having a spring constant of 1,772 N/m. Neglect the mass of the spring as well as friction, and compute the maximum deflection of the spring after impact.

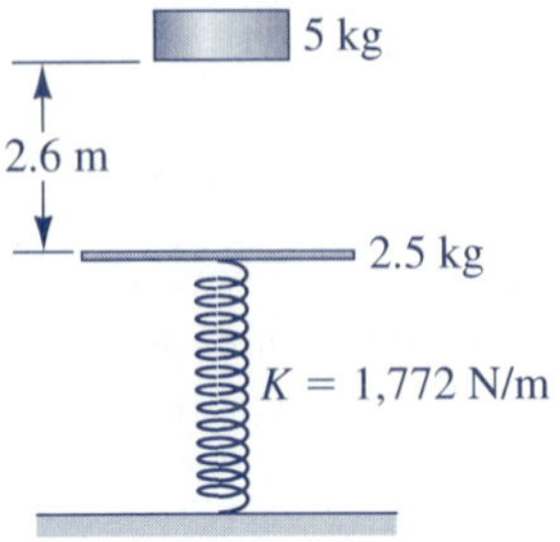

Figure P.14.39.

14.40. Identical spheres B, C, and D lie along a straight line on a frictionless surface. Sphere A, which is identical to the others, moves toward the other spheres at a speed V_A in a direction collinear with the centers of the spheres. For perfectly elastic collisions, what are the final velocities of the bodies?

14.41. In Problem 14.40, (a) What is the final velocity of sphere D if $\epsilon = .80$ for all spheres and $V_A = 50$ ft/sec? (b) Set up a relation for the speed of the $(n + 1)$th sphere in terms of the speed of the nth sphere, again for $\epsilon = .80$ and $V_A = 50$ ft/sec.

14.42. A spherical mass M_1 of 20 lbm is held at an angle θ_1 of 60° before being released. It strikes mass M_2 of 10 lbm with an impact having a coefficient of restitution equal to .75. Mass M_2 is held by a light rod of length 2 ft at the end of which is a torsional spring requiring 500 ft-lb per radian of rotation. The spring has no torque when l_2 is vertical. What is the maximum rotation of l_2 after impact? The length of $l_1 = 18$ in. [*Hint:* The work of a couple C rotating on angle $d\theta$ is $C\,d\theta$. A trial-and-error solution for θ_2 will be necessary.]

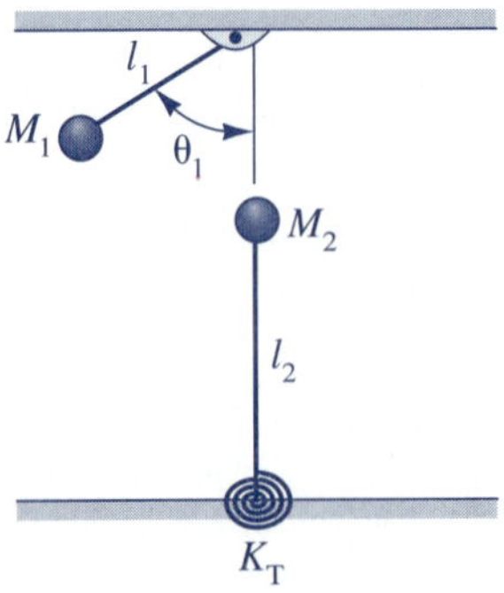

Figure P.14.42.

14.43. Cylinder A, weighing 20 lb, is moving at a speed of 20 ft/sec when it is at a distance 10 ft from cylinder B, which is stationary. Cylinder B weighs 15 lb and has a dynamic coefficient of friction with the rod on which it rides of .3. Cylinder A has a dynamic coefficient of friction of .1 with the rod. What is the coefficient of restitution if cylinder B comes to rest after collision at a distance 12 ft to the right of the initial position?

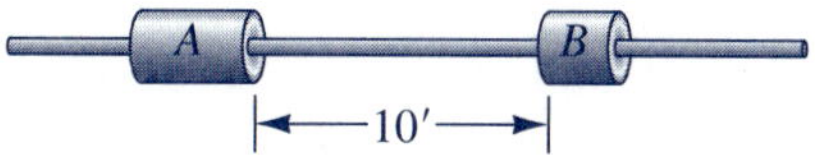

Figure P.14.43.

14.44. A load is being lowered at a speed of 2 m/sec into a barge. The barge weighs 1,000 kN, and the load weighs 100 kN. If the load hits the barge at 2 m/sec and the collision is plastic, what is the maximum depth that the barge is lowered into the water, assuming that the position of loading is such as to maintain the barge in a horizontal position? The width of the barge is 10 m. What are the weaknesses (if any) of your analysis? The density of water is 1,000 kg/m.[3] [Hint: Recall the Archimedes Principle]

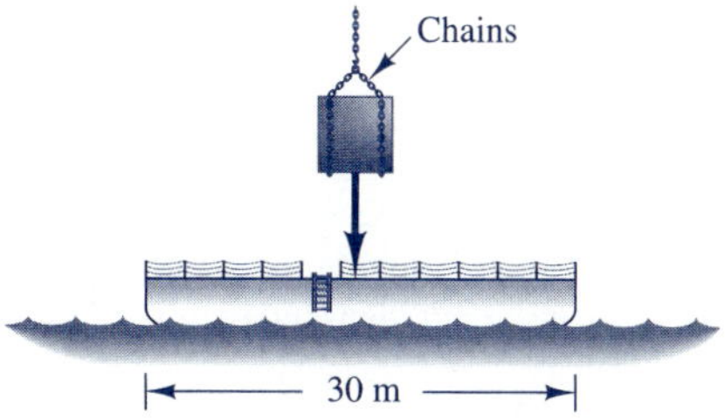

Figure P.14.44.

14.45. A tractor-trailer weighing 50 kN without a load carries a 10-kN load A as shown. The driver jams on his brakes until they lock for a panic stop. The load A breaks loose from its ropes. When the truck has stopped the load is 3 m from the left end of the trailer wall (see diagram) and is moving at a speed of 4 m/sec relative to the truck. The coefficient of dynamic friction between the load A and the trailer is .2 and between the tires and road is .5. If there is a plastic impact between A and the trailer and the driver keeps his brakes locked, how far d does the truck then move?

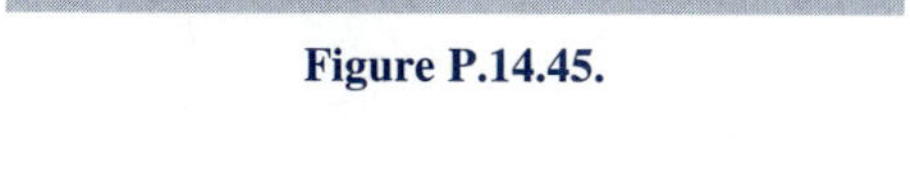

Figure P.14.45.

14.46. Two identical cylinders, each of mass 5 kg, slide on a frictionless rod. Each is fastened to a linear spring (K = 5,000 N/m) whose unstretched length is .65 m. The spring mass is negligible. If the cylinders are released from rest by raising the restraints,

(a) What is their speed just after colliding with a coefficient of restitution of .6?

(b) How close do they come to the walls?

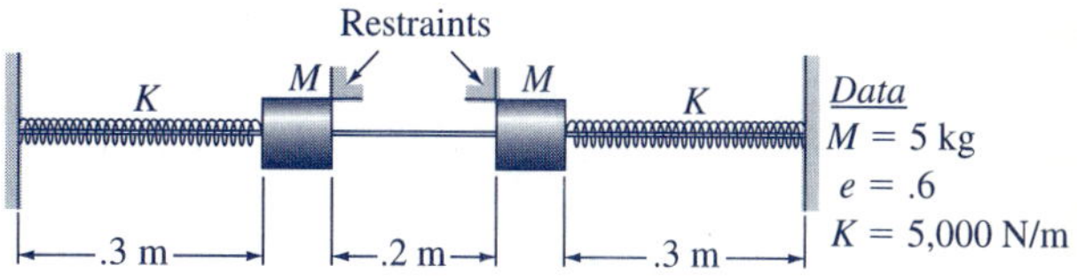

Figure P.14.46.

14.47. A light arm, connected to a mass A, is released from rest at a horizontal orientation. Determine the maximum deflection of the linear spring (K = 3,000 N/m) after A impacts with body B with a coefficient of restitution equal to .8. If body B does not reach the spring, indicate this fact. Note that there is Coulomb friction between the body B and the floor with μ_d = .6. Consider bodies A and B to be small.

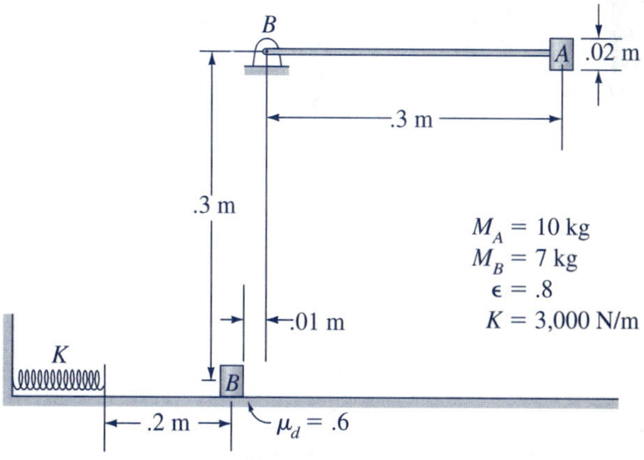

Figure P.14.47.

14.48. Mass M_A slides down the frictionless rod and hits mass M_B, which rests on a linear spring. The coefficient of restitution ϵ for the impact is .8. What is the total maximum deflection δ of the spring?

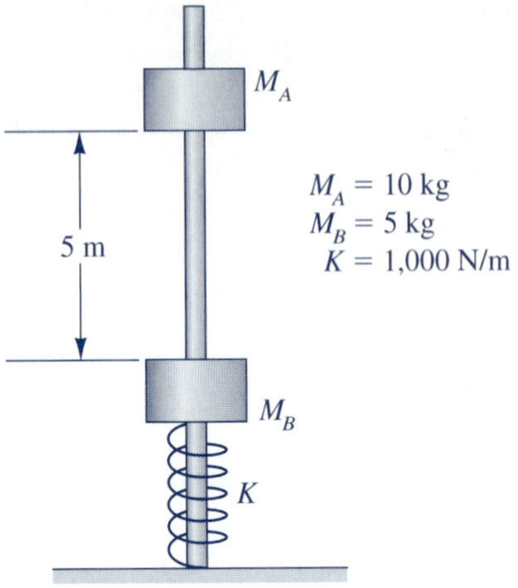

Figure P.14.48.

14.49. A cart A having a mass of 5 kg is released from rest at the position shown. As it rolls along, a constant resisting force of 4 N acts between the wheels and the surface. The cart collides with a block B having a mass of 3 kg. The coefficient of restitution is 0.5. Determine the maximum deflection δ_{max} of the spring having a spring constant of 15 N/m. Also, determine the maximum angle of rotation θ_{max} of the light rod supporting block B. The blocks are small.

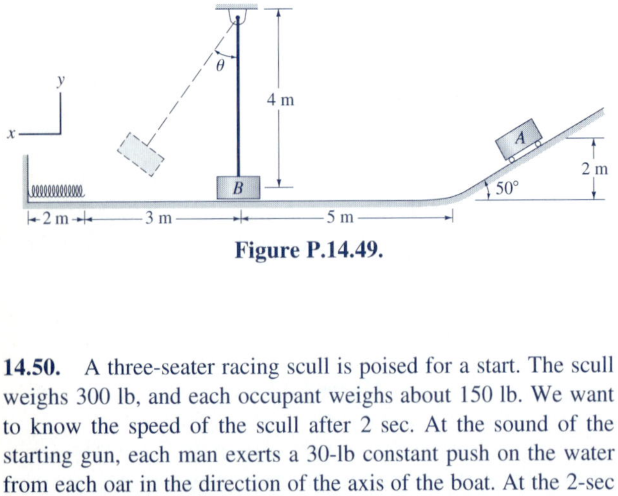

Figure P.14.49.

14.50. A three-seater racing scull is poised for a start. The scull weighs 300 lb, and each occupant weighs about 150 lb. We want to know the speed of the scull after 2 sec. At the sound of the starting gun, each man exerts a 30-lb constant push on the water from each oar in the direction of the axis of the boat. At the 2-sec mark, each man is moving to the left relative to the hull with a speed of 1 ft/sec. Neglect the inertia of the oars as well as water and air friction.

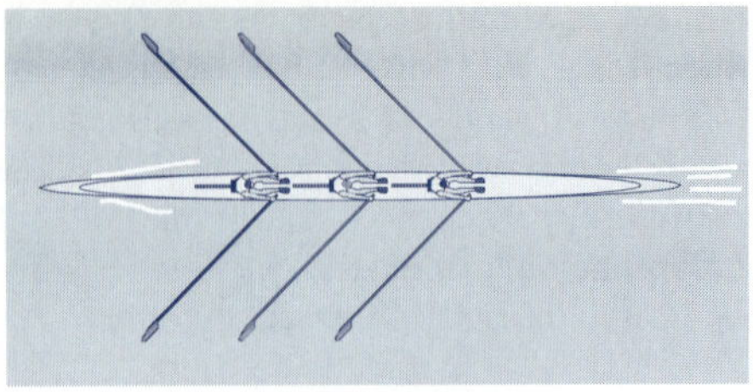

Figure P.14.50.

14.51. Do Example 14.11 for a constant pressure $p = 50$ psig.

14.52. A thin disc A weighing 5 lb translates along a frictionless surface at a speed of 20 ft/sec. The disc strikes a square stationary plate B weighing 10 lb at the center of a side. What are the velocity and direction of motion of the plate and the disc after collision? Assume that the surfaces of the plate and disc are smooth. Take $\epsilon = .7$.

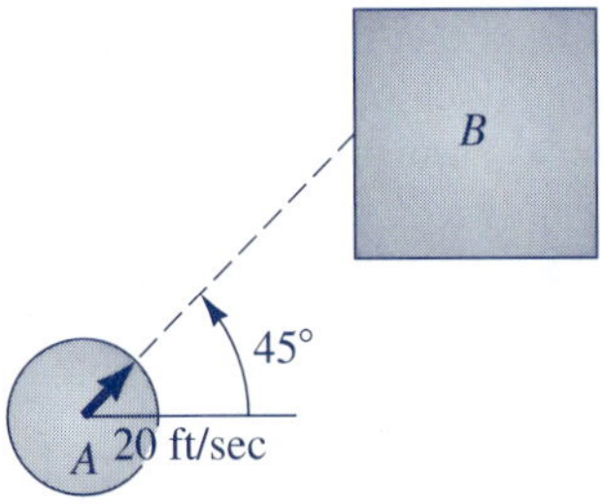

Figure P.14.52.

14.53. In Problem 14.52 at the instant of contact between the bodies a clamping device firmly connects the bodies together so as to form one rigid unit. Find the velocity of the center of mass of the system after impact.

14.54. The theory of collisions of *subatomic* particles is called the theory of *scattering*. The coefficient-of-restitution concept presented for macroscopic bodies in this chapter cannot be used. However, conservation of momentum can be used.

A neutron N shown moving with a speed V_0 strikes a stationary proton P. After collision the velocity of the neutron is V_N and that of the proton is V_P, as shown in the diagram. For an *elastic* collision, prove that $\phi + \theta = \pi/2$. [*Hint:* Use the vector polygon concept and the Pythagorean theorem. Also, take the mass of proton and neutron to be equal.]

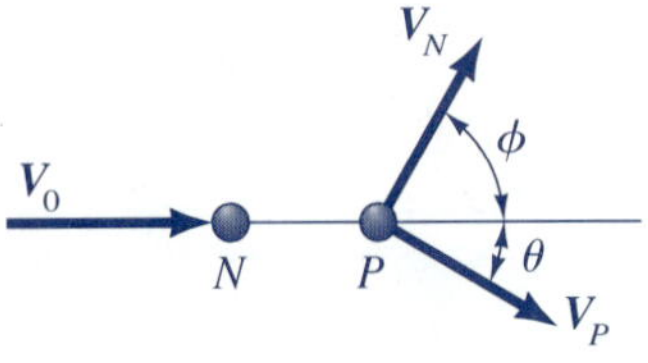

Figure P.14.54.

$*$14.55. A neutron N is moving toward a stationary helium nucleus He (atomic number 2) with kinetic energy 10 MeV. If the collision is inelastic, causing a loss of 20% of the kinetic energy, what is the angle θ after collision? See the first paragraph (only) of Problem 14.54. [*Hint:* There is no need (if one is clever) to have to convert the atomic number to kilograms.]

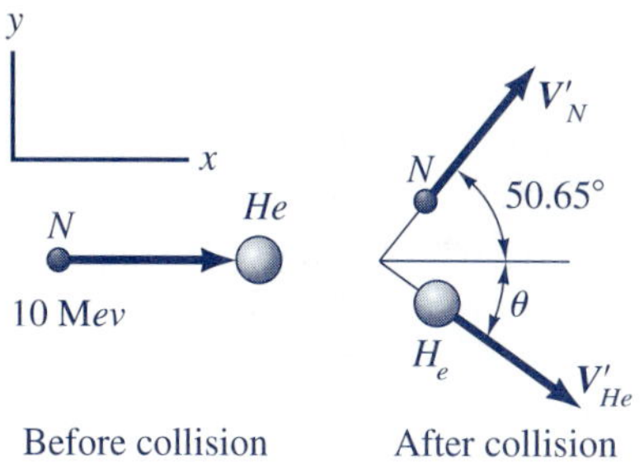

Figure P.14.55.

14.56. Cylinders A and B are free to slide without friction along a rod. Cylinder A is released from rest with spring K_1 to which it is connected initially unstretched. The impact with cylinder B has a coefficient of restitution ϵ equal to .8. Cylinder B is at rest before the impact supported in the position shown by spring K_2. Assume springs are massless.

(a) How much is the lower spring compressed initially?
(b) How much does cylinder B descend after impact before reaching its lowest position?

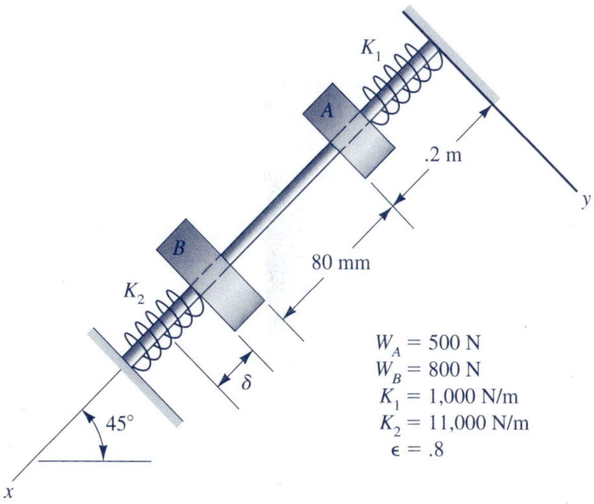

Figure P.14.56.

14.57. Masses A and B slide on a rod which is frictionless. The spring is initially *compressed* from .8 m to the position shown. The system is released from rest. A and B undergo a *plastic* impact. The spring is massless.

(a) What is the speed of the masses after B moves .2 m?
(b) What is the loss in *mechanical energy* for the system?

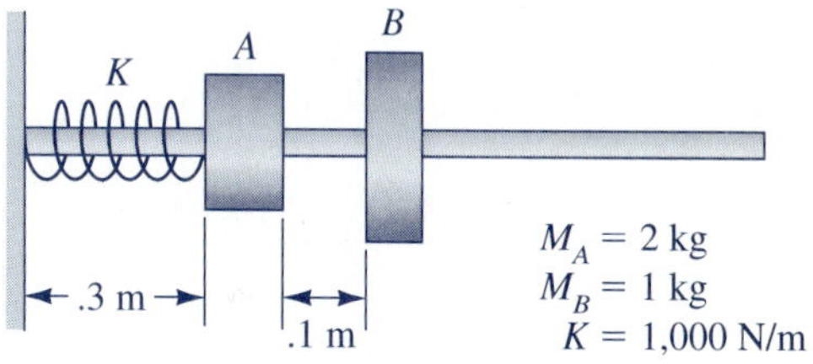

Figure P.14.57.

14.58. A ball is thrown against a floor at an angle of 60° with a speed at impact of 16 m/sec. What is the angle of rebound α if $\epsilon = .7$? Neglect friction.

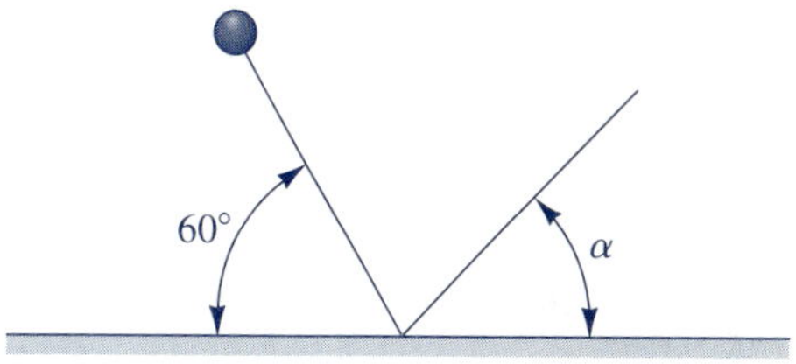

Figure P.14.58.

14.59. A ball strikes the xy plane of a handball court at $\boldsymbol{r} = 3\boldsymbol{i} + 7\boldsymbol{j}$ ft. The ball has initially a velocity $\boldsymbol{V}_1 = -10\boldsymbol{i} - 10\boldsymbol{j} - 15\boldsymbol{k}$ ft/sec. The coefficient of restitution is .8. Determine the final velocity $\boldsymbol{V}_2$ after it bounces off the xy, yz, and xz planes once. Neglect gravity and friction.

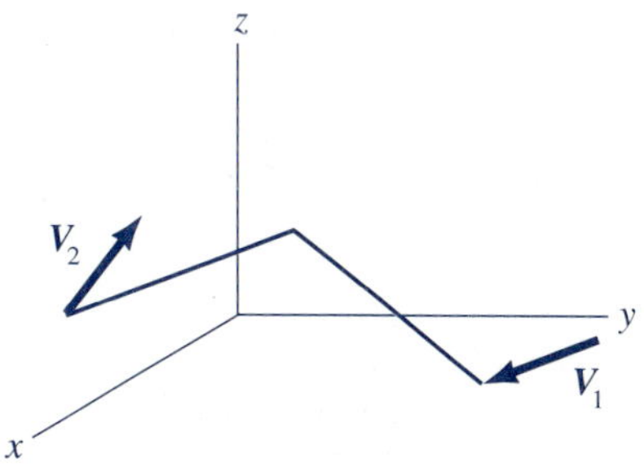

Figure P.14.59.

14.60. A space vehicle in the shape of a cone–cylinder is moving at a speed V m/sec, many times the speed of sound through highly rarefied atmosphere. If each molecule of the gas has a mass m kg and if there are, on the average, n molecules per cubic meter, compute the drag on the cone–cylinder. The cone half-angle is 30°. Take the collision to be perfectly elastic.

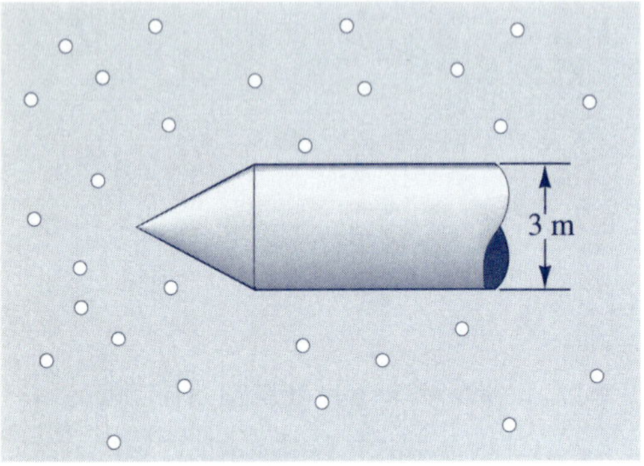

Figure P.14.60.

14.61. Do Problem 14.60 for a case where the collisions are assumed to be inelastic. Assume the coefficient of restitution to be .8.

14.62. A double-wedge airfoil section for a space glider is shown. If the glider moves in highly rarefield atmosphere at a speed V many times greater than the speed of sound, what is the drag per unit length of this airfoil? Assume the collision to be perfectly elastic. There are n molecules per ft^3, each having a mass m in slugs.

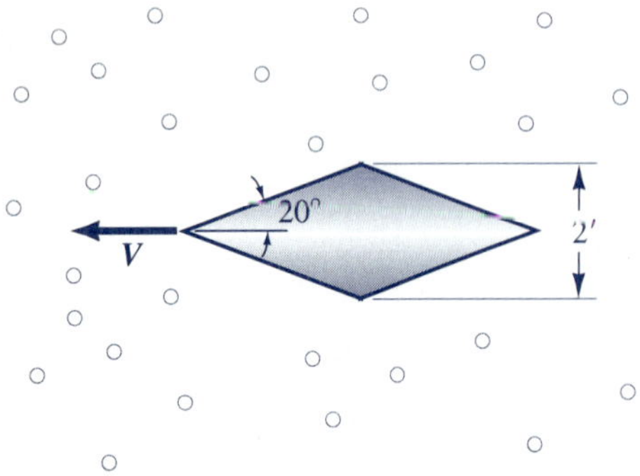

Figure P.14.62.

14.63. Consider a parallel beam of light having an energy flux of S watts/m^2, shining normal to a flat surface that completely absorbs the energy. You learned in physics that an impulse dI is developed on the surface during time dt given by the formula

$$dI = \frac{S}{c}\,dt\,dA$$

where c is the speed of light in vacuo in m/sec. If the surface reflects the light, then we have an impulse dI developed on the surface given as

$$dI = 2\frac{S}{c}\,dt\,dA$$

Compute the force stemming from the reflection of light shining normal to a perfectly reflecting mirror having an area of 1 m^2. The light has an energy flux S of 20 W/m^2. Take the speed $c = 3 \times 10^8$ m/sec. What is the radiation pressure p_{rad} on the mirror?

***14.64.** The Echo satellite when put into orbit is inflated to a 45-m-diameter sphere having a skin made up of a laminate of aluminum over mylar over aluminum. This skin is highly reflectant of light. Because of the small mass of this satellite, it may be affected by small forces such as that stemming from the reflection of light. If a parallel beam of light having an energy density S of .50 W/mm^2 impinges on the Echo satellite, what total force is developed on the satellite from this source? From physics (see Problem 14.63), the radiation pressure, p_{rad}, on a reflecting surface from a beam of light inclined by θ° from the normal to the surface is

$$p_{\text{rad}} = 2\frac{S}{c}\cos^2\theta$$

The pressure is in the direction of the incident radiation.

Part B: Moment of Momentum

14.6 Moment-of-Momentum Equation for a Single Particle

At this time, we shall introduce another auxiliary statement that follows from Newton's law and that will have great value when extended to the case of a rigid body. We start with Newton's law for a particle in the following form:

$$\boldsymbol{F} = \frac{d}{dt}(m\boldsymbol{V}) = \dot{\boldsymbol{P}}$$

where the symbol $\boldsymbol{P}$ represents the linear momentum of the particle. We next take the moment of each side of the equation about a point a in space (see Fig. 14.24):

$$\boldsymbol{\rho}_a \times \boldsymbol{F} = \boldsymbol{\rho}_a \times \dot{\boldsymbol{P}} \tag{14.16}$$

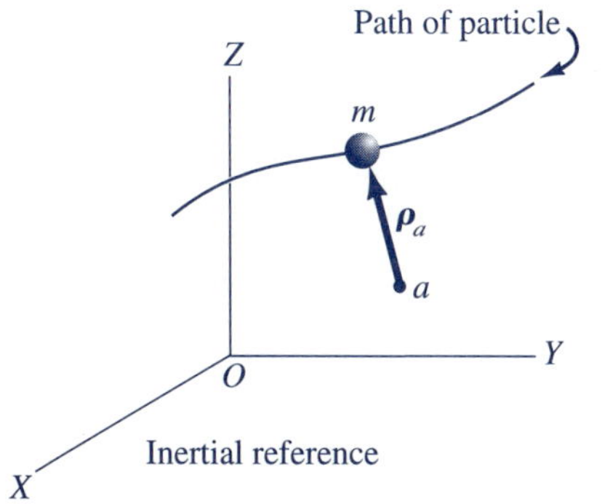

Figure 14.24. Point a fixed in inertial space.

If this point a is positioned at a fixed location in XYZ, we can simplify the right side of Eq. 14.16. Accordingly, examine the expression $(d/dt)(\boldsymbol{\rho}_a \times \boldsymbol{P})$:

$$\frac{d}{dt}(\boldsymbol{\rho}_a \times \boldsymbol{P}) = \boldsymbol{\rho}_a \times \dot{\boldsymbol{P}} + \dot{\boldsymbol{\rho}}_a \times \boldsymbol{P} \tag{14.17}$$

But the expression $\dot{\boldsymbol{\rho}}_a \times \boldsymbol{P}$ can be written as $\dot{\boldsymbol{\rho}}_a \times m\dot{\boldsymbol{r}}$. The vectors $\boldsymbol{\rho}_a$ and $\boldsymbol{r}$ are measured in the same reference from a fixed point a to the particle and from the origin to the particle, respectively (see Fig. 14.25). They are thus different at all times to the extent of a constant vector $\overrightarrow{Oa}$. Note that

$$\boldsymbol{r} = \overrightarrow{Oa} + \boldsymbol{\rho}_a$$

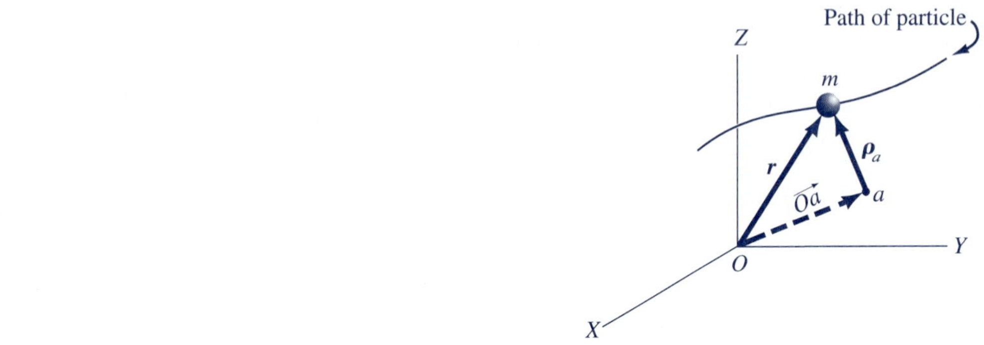

Figure 14.25. Position vectors to m and a.

Therefore,

$$\dot{\boldsymbol{r}} = \dot{\boldsymbol{\rho}}_a$$

Accordingly, the expression $\dot{\boldsymbol{\rho}}_a \times m\dot{\boldsymbol{r}}$ is zero. Thus, Eq. 14.17 becomes

$$\frac{d}{dt}(\boldsymbol{\rho}_a \times \boldsymbol{P}) = \boldsymbol{\rho}_a \times \dot{\boldsymbol{P}} \qquad (14.18)$$

and Eq. 14.16 can be written in the form

$$\boldsymbol{\rho}_a \times \boldsymbol{F} = \boldsymbol{M}_a = \frac{d}{dt}(\boldsymbol{\rho}_a \times \boldsymbol{P}) = \dot{\boldsymbol{H}}_a$$

Therefore,

$$\boldsymbol{M}_a = \dot{\boldsymbol{H}}_a \qquad (14.19)$$

where $\boldsymbol{H}_a$ *is the moment about point a of the linear momentum vector*. Also, $\boldsymbol{H}$ is termed the *angular momentum vector*. Equation 14.19, then, states that *the moment* $\boldsymbol{M}_a$ *of the resultant force on a particle about a point a, fixed in an inertial reference, equals the time rate of change of the moment about point a of the linear momentum of the particle relative to the inertial reference.* This is the desired alternative form of Newton's law.

The scalar component of Eq. 14.19 along some axis, say the z axis, can be useful. Thus,

$$M_z = \dot{H}_z$$

where M_z is the torque of the total external force about the z axis and H_z is the moment of the momentum (or angular momentum) about the z axis.

Example 14.14

A boat containing a man is moving near a dock (see Fig. 14.26). He throws out a light line and lassos a piling on the dock at A. He starts drawing in on the line so that when he is in the position shown in the diagram, the line is taut and has a length of 25 ft. His speed V_1 is 5 ft/sec in a direction normal to the line. If the net horizontal force F on the boat from tension in the line and from water resistance is maintained at 50 lb essentially in the direction of the line, what is the component of his velocity toward piling A (i.e., V_A) after the man has pulled in 3 ft of line? The boat and the man have a combined weight of 350 lb.

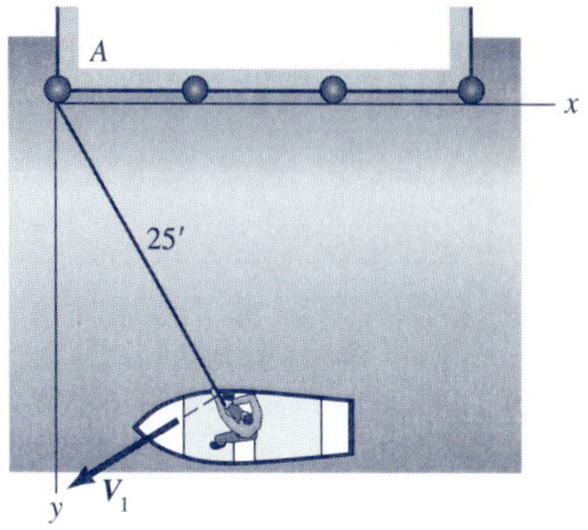

Figure 14.26. Man pulls toward piling.

We may consider the boat and man as a particle for which we can apply the **moment of momentum** equation. Thus,

$$M_A = \dot{H}_z \tag{a}$$

Clearly, here $\boldsymbol{M}_A = \boldsymbol{0}$ since $\boldsymbol{F}$ goes through A at all times. Thus, $\boldsymbol{H}_A$ is a constant—that is, the angular momentum about A must be constant. Observing Fig. 14.27, we can say accordingly

$$\boldsymbol{r}_1 \times m\boldsymbol{V}_1 = \boldsymbol{r}_2 \times m\boldsymbol{V}_2$$

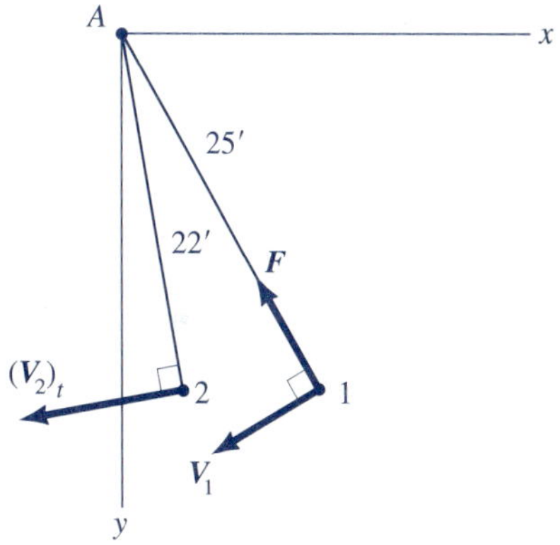

Figure 14.27. Boat at positions 1 and 2.

Since $\boldsymbol{r}_1$ is perpendicular to $\boldsymbol{V}_1$ and $\boldsymbol{r}_2$ is perpendicular to $(\boldsymbol{V}_2)_t$, we get a simple scalar product from above. Thus

$$(25)(m)(5) = (22)(m)(V_2)_t$$

Therefore,

$$(V_2)_t = 5.68 \text{ ft/sec} \tag{b}$$

We need more information to get the desired result V_A toward the piling. We have not yet used the fact that $F = 50$ lb. Accordingly, we now employ the **work–kinetic energy** equation from Chapter 13. Thus,

$$\int_1^2 \boldsymbol{F} \cdot d\boldsymbol{s} = \left(\frac{1}{2}MV^2\right)_2 - \left(\frac{1}{2}MV^2\right)_1$$

$$(50)(3) = \frac{1}{2}\frac{350}{g}(V_2)^2 - \frac{1}{2}\frac{350}{g}(25)$$

Therefore,

$$V_2 = 7.25 \text{ ft/sec} \tag{c}$$

Now V_2 is the *total* velocity of the boat at position 2. To get the desired component V_A toward the piling, we can say, using Eqs. (b) and (c):

$$V_2^2 = (V_2)_t^2 + V_A^2$$

$$(7.25)^2 = (5.68)^2 + V_A^2$$

Therefore,

$$V_A = 4.51 \text{ ft/sec}$$

14.7 More on Space Mechanics

Many problems of space mechanics can be solved by using energy and angular-momentum methods of this and the preceding chapter without considering the detailed trajectory equations of Chapter 12. Let us therefore set forth some salient factors concerning the motion of a space vehicle moving in the vicinity of a planet or star with the engine shut off and with negligible friction from the outside.[11]

After the space vehicle has been propelled at great speed by its rocket engines to a position outside the planet's atmosphere (the final powered velocity is called the *burnout* velocity), the vehicle then undergoes plane, gravitational, *central-force motion* (Section 12.6). If it continues to go around the planet, the vehicle is said to go into *orbit* and the trajectory is that of a circle or that of an ellipse. If, on the other hand, the vehicle escapes from the influence of the planet, then the trajectory will either be a parabola or a hyperbola. In the case of an elliptic orbit, the position closest to the surface of the planet is called *perigee* (see Fig. 14.28) and the position farthest from the surface of the planet is called *apogee*. Notice that at apogee and perigee the velocity vectors $\boldsymbol{V}_a$ and $\boldsymbol{V}_p$ of the vehicle are parallel to the surface of the planet and so at these points (and only at these points)

$$V = V_\theta; \qquad V_r = 0$$

In the case of a *circular* orbit of radius r and velocity V_c, we can use Newton's law and the gravitational law to state

$$\frac{GMm}{r^2} = m(r\omega^2)$$

where M is the mass of the planet and ω is the angular speed of the radius vector to the vehicle. Replacing the acceleration term $r\omega^2$ by V_c^2/r and solving for V_c, we get

$$V_c = \sqrt{\frac{GM}{r}} \tag{14.20}$$

Knowing GM and r, we can readily compute the speed V_c for a particular circular orbit. In Section 12.6 we showed that GM can be easily computed using the relation

$$GM = gR^2 \tag{14.21}$$

[11]Those readers who have studied Sections 12.7 and 12.8 have already gone into these factors in considerable depth.

where g is the acceleration of gravity at the surface of the planet and R is the radius of the planet.

In gravitational central-force motion, only the conservative force of gravity is involved, and so we must have *conservation of mechanical energy*. Furthermore, since this force is directed to O, the center of the planet, at all times (see Fig. 14.28), then the moment about O of the gravitational force must be zero. As a consequence, we must have *conservation of angular momentum* about O.[12]

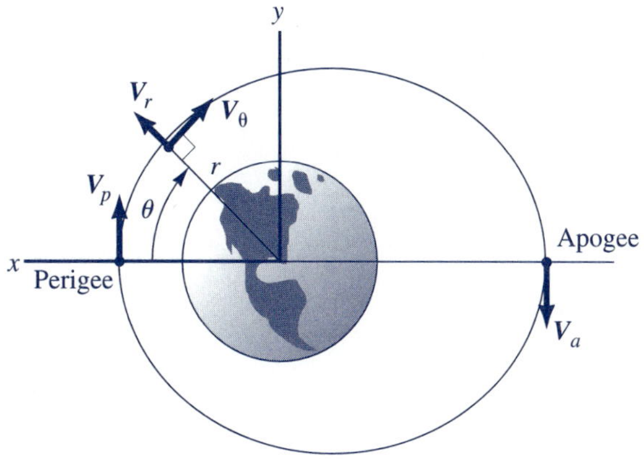

Figure 14.28. Elliptic orbit with perigee and apogee.

We shall illustrate in the next example the dual use of the conservation-of-angular-momentum principle and the conservation-of-mechanical-energy principle for space mechanics problems. In the homework problems you will be asked to solve again some of the space problems of Chapter 12 using the principles above without getting involved with the trajectory equations. Such problems, you will then realize, are sometimes more easily solved by using the two principles discussed above rather than by using the trajectory equations.

[12]Those who have studied the trajectory equations of Chapter 12 might realize that

$$C = rV_\theta = \text{constant}$$

is actually a statement of the conservation of angular momentum since mrV_θ is the moment about O of the linear momentum relative to O.

Example 14.15

A space-shuttle vehicle on a rescue mission (see Fig. 14.29) is sent into a circular orbit at a distance of 1,200 km above the earth's surface. This orbit is inserted so as to be in the same plane as that of a spacecraft whose rocket engines will not start, thus preventing it from initiating a procedure for returning to earth. The goal of the shuttle is to enter a trajectory that will permit docking with the disabled spacecraft and then to rescue the occupants. The timing of insertion of the circular orbit of the space shuttle has so been chosen that the space shuttle by firing its rockets at the position shown can, by the proper change of speed, reach apogee at the same time and same location as does the crippled space vehicle. At this time, docking procedures can be carried out. Considering that the rocket engines of the space-shuttle vehicle operate during a *very short distance* of travel[13] to achieve the proper velocity V_0 for the mission, determine the change in speed that the space shuttle must achieve. The radius of the earth is 6,373 km.

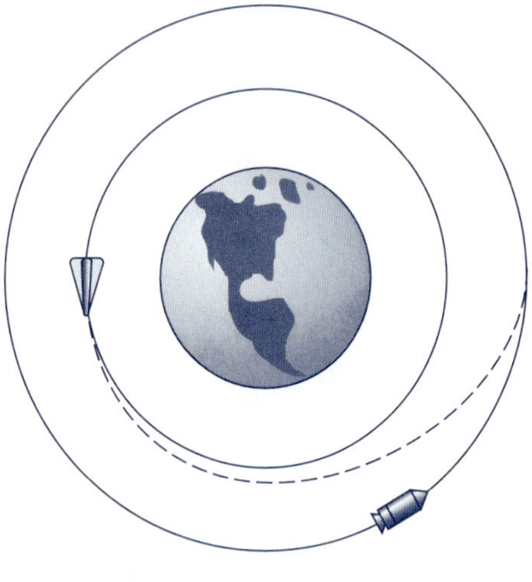

Figure 14.29. Rescue mission for space-shuttle vehicle.

[13]During this part of the flight we do *not* have central-force motion.

Example 14.15 (Continued)

We shall first compute GM. Thus, working with kilometers and hours,

$$GM = gR^2 = \left[(9.81)\left(\frac{3{,}600^2}{1{,}000}\right)\right](6{,}373)^2 = 5.16 \times 10^{12} \text{ km}^3/\text{hr}^2$$

The velocity for the circular orbit for the space shuttle is then

$$V_c = \sqrt{\frac{GM}{r}} = \sqrt{\frac{5.16 \times 10^{12}}{7{,}573}} = 26{,}105 \text{ km/hr} \qquad \text{(a)}$$

From **conservation of angular momentum** for the space-shuttle rescue orbit we can say

$$mr_0V_0 = m(rV)_{\text{apogee}}$$
$$(7{,}573)(V_0) = (10{,}000)(V)_{\text{apogee}}$$

Therefore,

$$V_0 = 1.320V_{\text{apogee}} \qquad \text{(b)}$$

where V_0 is the speed of the space shuttle just *after* firing rockets. Next, we use the principle of **conservation of mechanical energy** for the rescue orbit. Thus,

$$-\frac{GMm}{r_0} + \frac{mV_0^2}{2} = -\frac{GMm}{r} + \frac{mV_{\text{apogee}}^2}{2}$$
$$-\frac{5.16 \times 10^{12}}{7{,}573} + \frac{V_0^2}{2} = -\frac{5.16 \times 10^{12}}{10{,}000} + \frac{V_{\text{apogee}}^2}{2} \qquad \text{(c)}$$

Substitute for V_{apogee} using Eq. (b) and solve for V_0. We get

$$V_0 = 27{,}861 \text{ km/hr} \qquad \text{(d)}$$

Hence, using Eq. (a), we can say:

$$\Delta V = 27{,}861 - 26{,}105 = \boxed{1{,}756 \text{ km/hr}}$$

PROBLEMS

14.65. A particle rotates at 30 rad/sec along a frictionless surface at a distance 2 ft from the center. A flexible cord restrains the particle. If this cord is pulled so that the particle moves inward at a velocity of 5 ft/sec, what is the magnitude of the total velocity when the particle is 1 ft from the center?

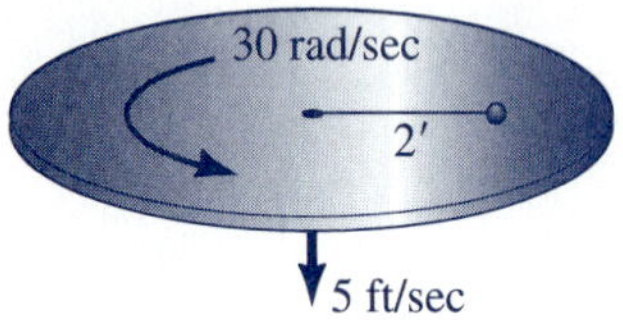

Figure P.14.65.

14.66. A satellite has an apogee of 7,128 km. It is moving at a speed of 36,480 km/hr. What is the transverse velocity of the satellite when $r = 6{,}970$ km?

14.67. A system is shown rotating freely with an angular speed ω of 2 rad/sec. A mass A of 1.5 kg is held against a spring such that the spring is compressed 100 mm. If the device a holding the mass in position is suddenly removed, determine how far toward the vertical axis of the system the mass will move. The spring constant K is .531 N/mm. Neglect all friction and inertia of the bar. The spring is not connected to the mass.

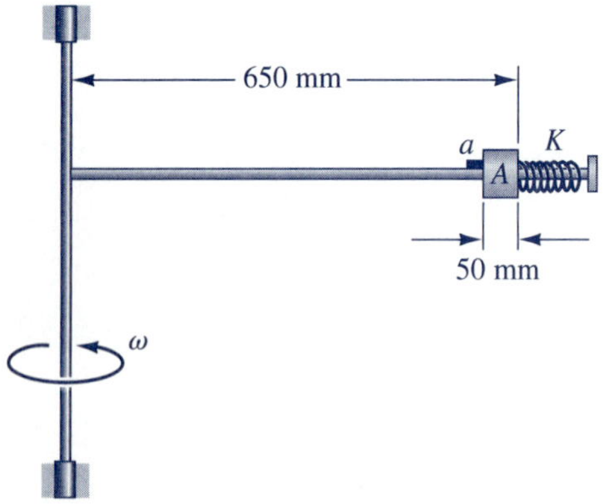

Figure P.14.67.

14.68. Do Problem 14.67 for the case where there is Coulombic friction between the mass A and the horizontal rod with a constant μ_d equal to .4.

14.69. A body A weighing 10 lb is moving initially at a speed of V_1 of 20 ft/sec on a frictionless surface. An elastic cord AO, which has a length l of 20 ft, becomes taut but not stretched at the position shown in the diagram. What is the radial speed toward O of the body when the cord is stretched 2 ft? The cord has an equivalent spring constant of .3 lb/in.

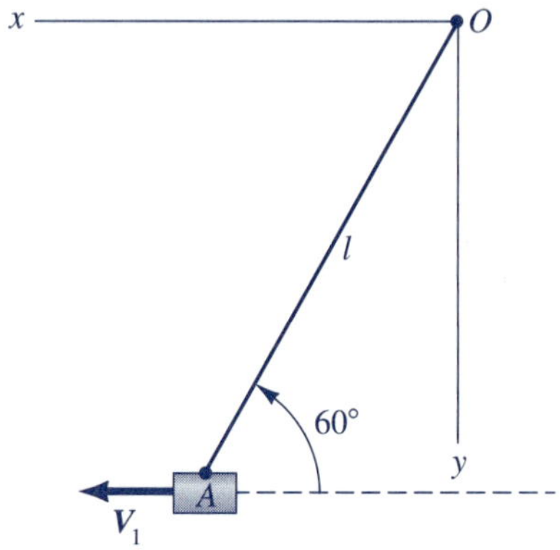

Figure P.14.69.

14.70. A small ball B weighing 2 lb is rotating about a vertical axis at a speed ω_1 of 15 rad/sec. The ball is connected to bearings on the shaft by light inextensible strings having a length l of 2 ft. The angle θ_1 is 30°. What is the angular speed ω_2 of the ball if bearing A is moved up 6 in.?

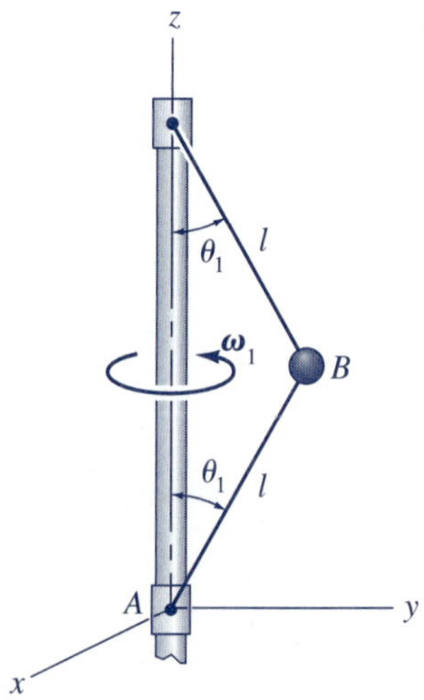

Figure P.14.70.

14.71. A mass m of 1 kg is swinging freely about the z axis at a speed ω_1 of 10 rad/sec. The length l_1 of the string is 250 mm. If the tube A through which the connecting string passes is moved down a distance d of 90 mm, what is ω_2 of the mass? You should get a fourth-order equation for ω_2 which has as the desired root $\omega_2 = 21.05$ rad/sec.

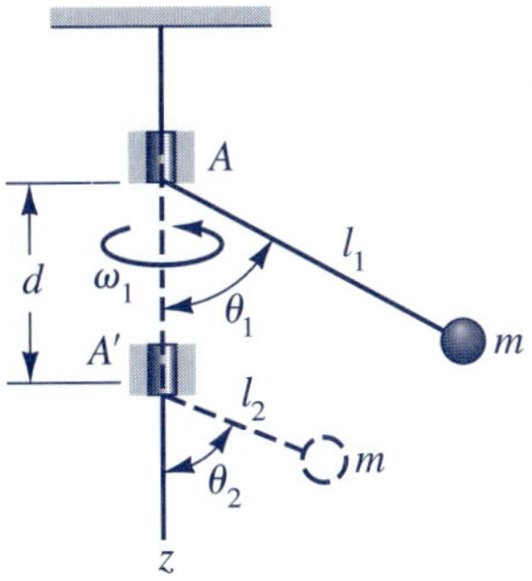

Figure P.14.71.

14.72. A small 2-lb ball B is rotating at angular speed ω_1 of 10 rad/sec about a horizontal shaft. The ball is connected to the bearings with light elastic cords which when unstretched are each 12 in. in length. A force of 15 lb is required to stretch the cord 1 in. The distance d_1 between the bearings is originally 20 in. If bearing A is moved to shorten d by 6 in., what is the angular velocity ω_2 of the ball? Neglect the effects of gravity and the mass of the elastic cords. [*Hint:* You should arrive at a transcendental equation for θ_2 whose solution is 54.49°.]

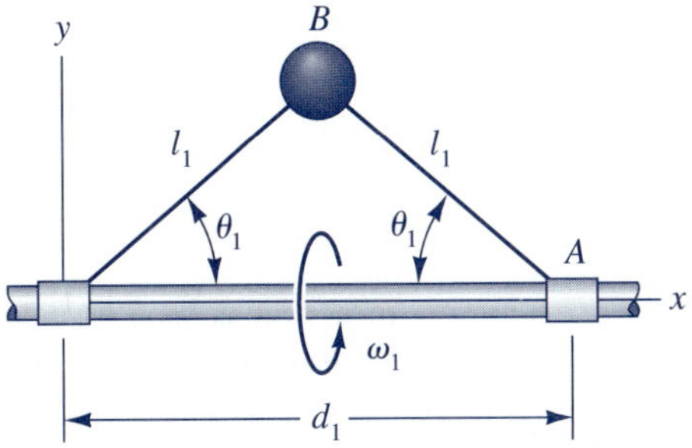

Figure P.14.72.

14.73. A space vehicle is moving at a speed of 37,000 km/hr at position A, which is perigee at a distance of 250 km from the earth's surface. What are the radial and transverse velocity components as well as the distance from the earth's surface at B? The trajectory is in the xy plane.

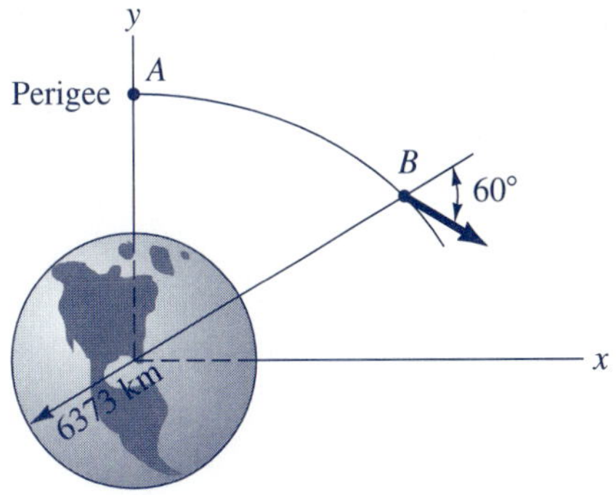

Figure P.14.73.

14.74. A space vehicle is in orbit A around the earth. At position (1) it is 5,000 miles from the center of the earth and has a velocity of 20,000 mi/hr. The transverse velocity at (1) is 15,000 mi/hr. At apogee, it is desired to continue in the circular orbit shown dashed. What change in speed is needed to change orbits when firing at apogee?

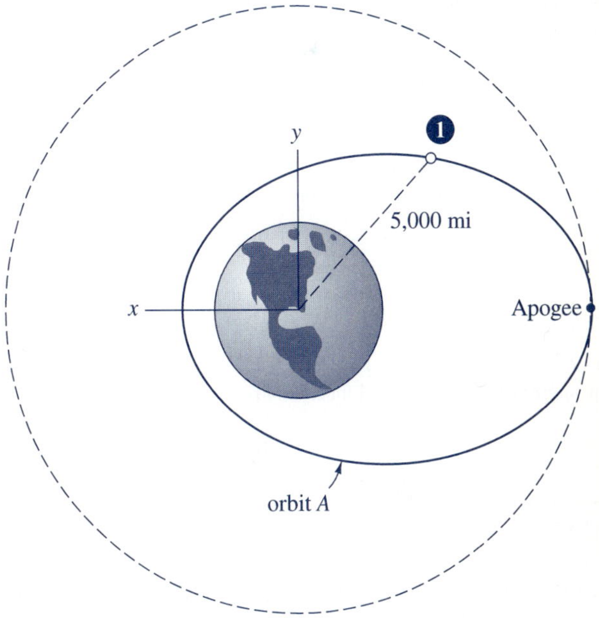

Figure P.14.74.

14.75. Do Problem 12.75 using the principles of conservation of momentum and conservation of mechanical energy.

14.76. In Problem 12.86 find the radial velocity by using the method of conservation of angular momentum and mechanical energy.

14.77. Do Problem 12.82 by the method of conservation of angular momentum and mechanical energy.

14.78. In Problem 12.87, find the height of the bullet above the surface of the planet by the methods of conservation of angular momentum and mechanical energy.

14.79. In Problem 12.119, find the maximum elevation above the earth's surface by the methods of conservation of angular momentum and mechanical energy.

14.80. Do Problem 12.114 by methods of conservation of angular momentum and mechanical energy. [*Hint:* The escape velocity = $\sqrt{2GM/r} = \sqrt{2}\,V_c$.]

14.81. Do Problem 12.113 using the principles of conservation of angular momentum and mechanical energy.

14.82. A space vehicle is in a circular orbit 1,200 km above the surface of the earth. A projectile is shot from this space vehicle at a speed relative to the vehicle of 5,000 km/hr in a radial direction as seen from the vehicle. What are the *apogee* and the *perigee* distances from the center of the earth for the trajectory of the projectile?

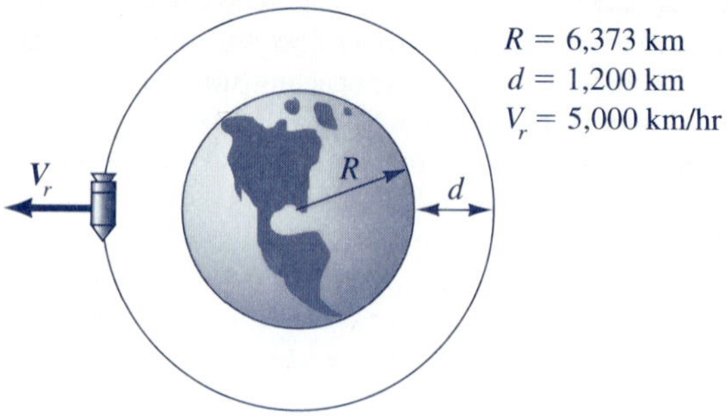

Figure P.14.82.

14.83. A space vehicle is in a circular parking orbit 300 miles above the surface of the earth. If the vehicle is to reach an apogee at location 2 which is 500 miles above the earth's surface, what increase in velocity must the vehicle attain by firing its rockets for a short time at location 1? The radius of the earth is 3,960 miles.

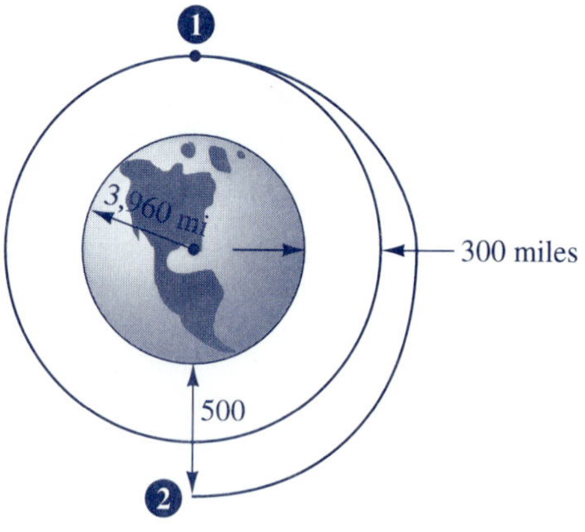

Figure P.14.83.

14.84. A space station is in a circular parking orbit around the earth at a distance of 5,000 mi from the center. A projectile is fired ahead in a direction tangential to the trajectory of the space station with a speed of 5,000 mi/hr relative to the space station. What is the maximum distance from earth reached by the projectile?

14.85. A skylab is in a circular orbit about the earth 500 km above the earth's surface. A space-shuttle vehicle has rendezvoused with the skylab and now, after disengaging from the skylab, its rocket engines are fired so as to move the vehicle with a speed of 800 m/sec relative to the skylab in the opposite direction to that of the skylab. Assume that the firing of the rocket takes place over a short distance and does not affect the skylab. What speed would the space-shuttle vehicle have when it encounters appreciable atmosphere at about 50 km above the earth's surface? What is the radial velocity at this position?

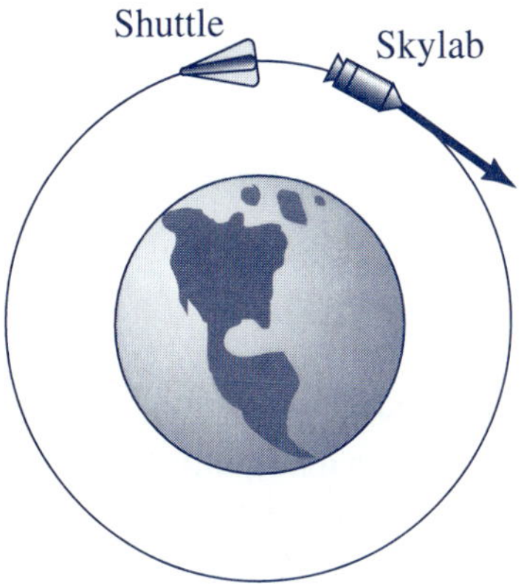

Figure P.14.85.

14.86. A space probe is approaching Mars. When the probe is 50,000 mi from the center of Mars it has a speed V_0 of 10,000 mi/hr with a component $(V_r)_0$ toward the center of Mars of 9,800 mi/hr. How close does the probe come to the surface of Mars? If retro-rockets are fired at this lowest position A, what change in speed is needed to alter the trajectory into a circular orbit as shown? The acceleration of gravity at the surface of Mars is 12.40 ft/sec^2, and the radius R of the planet is 2,107 mi.

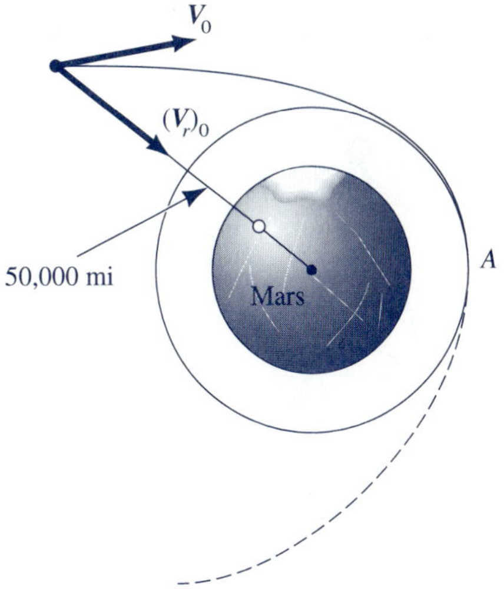

Figure P.14.86.

14.87. In Problem 14.86, a midcourse correction is to be made to get the probe within 1,000 mi from the surface of Mars. If V_0 at r_0 = 50,000 mi is still to be 10,000 mi/hr, what should be the radial velocity component $(V_r)_0$?

14.88. The Apollo command module is in a circular parking orbit about the moon at a distance of 161.0 km above the surface of the moon. The lunar exploratory module is to detach from the command module. The lunar-module rockets are fired briefly to give a velocity V_0 relative to the command module in the opposite direction. If the lunar module is to have a transverse velocity of 1,500 m/sec when it is 80 km from the surface of the moon before rockets are fired again, what must V_0 be? What is the radial velocity at this position? The radius of the moon is 1,733 km, and the acceleration of gravity is 1.700 m/sec^2 at the surface.

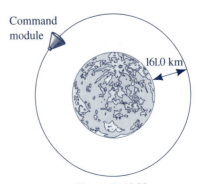

Figure P.14.88.

14.8 Moment-of-Momentum Equations for a System of Particles

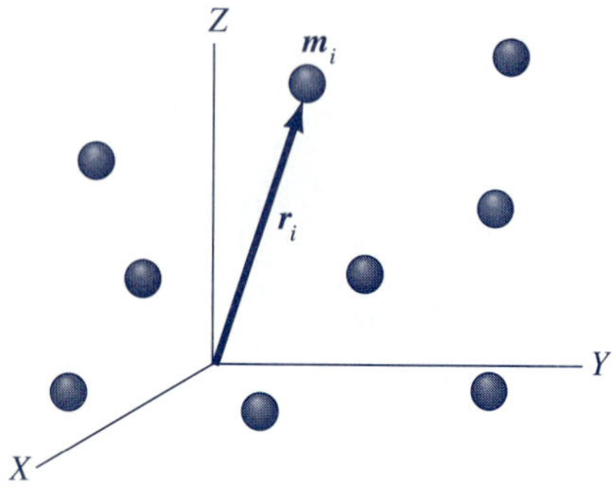

Figure 14.30. System of n particles.

We shall now develop the moment-of-momentum equations for an aggregate of particles. The resulting equations will be of vital importance when we apply them to rigid bodies in later chapters. We shall consider a number of cases.

Case 1. Fixed Reference Point in Inertial Space. An aggregate of n particles and an inertial reference are shown in Fig. 14.30. The moment of momentum equation for the ith particle is now written about the origin of this reference:

$$\boldsymbol{r}_i \times \boldsymbol{F}_i + \boldsymbol{r}_i \times \left(\sum_{\substack{j=1 \\ i \neq j}}^{n} \boldsymbol{f}_{ij} \right) = \frac{d}{dt}(\boldsymbol{r}_i \times \boldsymbol{P}_i) \tag{14.22}$$

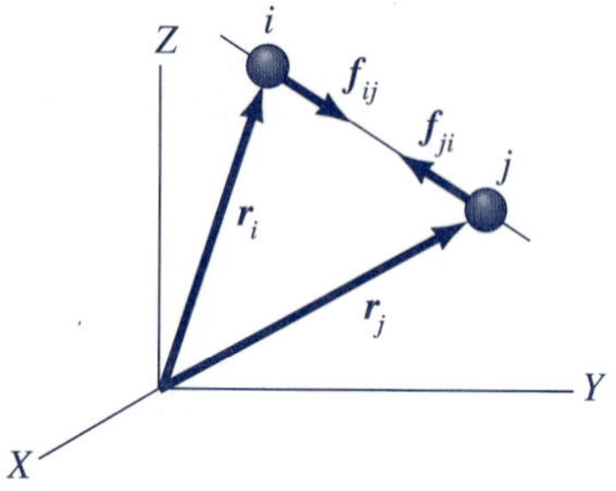

Figure 14.31. Internal equal and opposite forces.

where, as usual, $\boldsymbol{f}_{ij}$ is the internal force from the jth particle on the ith particle. We now sum this equation for all n particles:

$$\sum_{i=1}^{n} \boldsymbol{r}_i \times \boldsymbol{F}_i + \sum_{i=1}^{n}\sum_{j=1}^{n} (\boldsymbol{r}_i \times \boldsymbol{f}_{ij}) = \frac{d}{dt}\left[\sum_{i=1}^{n} (\boldsymbol{r}_i \times \boldsymbol{P}_i)\right] = \dot{\boldsymbol{H}}_{\text{total}} \tag{14.23}$$

where the summation operation has been put after the differentiation on the right side (permissible because of the distributive property of differentiation with respect to addition). For any pair of particles, the internal forces will be equal and opposite and collinear (see Fig. 14.31). Hence, the forces will have a zero moment about the origin. (This result is most easily understood by remembering that, for purposes of taking moments about a point, forces are transmissible.) We can then conclude that the expression

$$\sum_{i=1}^{n}\sum_{j=1}^{n} (\boldsymbol{r}_i \times \boldsymbol{f}_{ij})$$

in this equation is zero. Realizing that $\sum_i \boldsymbol{r}_i \times \boldsymbol{F}_i$ is the total moment of the external forces about the origin, we have as a result for Eq. 14.23:

$$\boldsymbol{M}_a = \dot{\boldsymbol{H}}_a \tag{14.24}$$

Thus, *the total moment* $\boldsymbol{M}$ *of external forces acting on an aggregate of particles about a point a fixed in an inertial reference* (the point in the development was picked as the origin merely for convenience) *equals the time rate of change of the total moment of the linear momentum relative to the inertial reference, where this moment is taken about the aforementioned point a.*[14]

We may express Eq. 14.24 in a different form by considering the *center of mass*. In a manner analogous to kinetic energy of an aggregate of particles, we can first show that the angular momentum of an aggregate of particles about a fixed point can be given as the angular momentum of the center of mass about the fixed point plus the angular momentum of the particles relative to the center of mass.

Accordingly, consider the center of mass c of an aggregate of particles as shown in Fig. 14.32. For the ith particle, we can say:

$$\boldsymbol{r}_i = \boldsymbol{r}_c + \boldsymbol{\rho}_{ci} \tag{14.25}$$

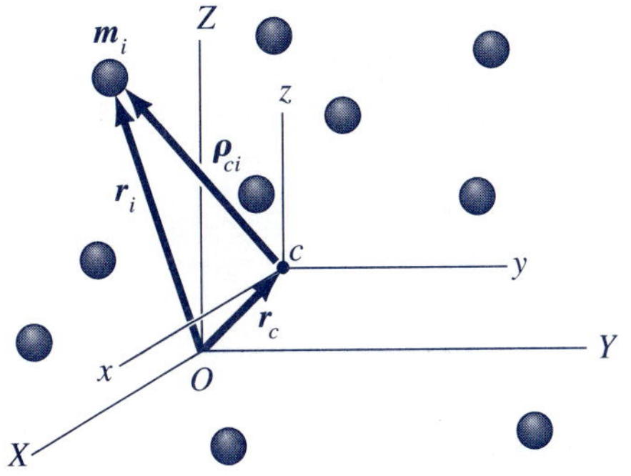

Figure 14.32. c is center of mass of aggregate.

The angular momentum for the aggregate of particles about O is then

$$\begin{aligned} \boldsymbol{H}_0 &= \sum_i (\boldsymbol{r}_c + \boldsymbol{\rho}_{ci}) \times \boldsymbol{P}_i \\ &= \sum_i (\boldsymbol{r}_c + \boldsymbol{\rho}_{ci}) \times \left[(m_i)(\dot{\boldsymbol{r}}_c + \dot{\boldsymbol{\rho}}_{ci})\right] \end{aligned} \tag{14.26}$$

Carry out the cross product and extract $\boldsymbol{r}_c$ from the summations:

$$\boldsymbol{H}_0 = \boldsymbol{r}_c \times M\dot{\boldsymbol{r}}_c + \boldsymbol{r}_c \times \sum_i m_i\dot{\boldsymbol{\rho}}_{ci} + \left(\sum_i m_i\boldsymbol{\rho}_{ci}\right) \times \dot{\boldsymbol{r}}_c + \sum_i \boldsymbol{\rho}_{ci} \times m_i\dot{\boldsymbol{\rho}}_{ci} \tag{14.27}$$

But since c is the center of mass, it follows that

$$\sum_i m_i\boldsymbol{\rho}_{ci} = \boldsymbol{0}$$
$$\sum_i m_i\dot{\boldsymbol{\rho}}_{ci} = \boldsymbol{0}$$

[14]Point a could also be moving with a constant velocity V_0 relative to inertial reference XYZ. However, a would then be fixed in another inertial reference $X'Y'Z'$, which is translating with respect to XYZ at a speed V_0.

Going back to Eq. 14.27, we see that the second and third expressions on the right side are to be deleted and we get then the desired result for $\boldsymbol{H}_0$:

$$\boldsymbol{H}_0 = \boldsymbol{r}_c \times M\dot{\boldsymbol{r}}_c + \sum_i \boldsymbol{\rho}_{ci} \times m_i\dot{\boldsymbol{\rho}}_{ci} = \boldsymbol{r}_c \times M\dot{\boldsymbol{r}}_c + \boldsymbol{H}_c$$

where $\boldsymbol{H}_c$ is the moment about the center of mass of the linear momentum as seen from the center of mass for the aggregate.[15] This may be rewritten and expressed for *any* fixed point a where, using $\boldsymbol{r}_{ac}$ as the position vector from fixed point a to the center of mass c, we have

$$\boldsymbol{H}_a = \boldsymbol{H}_c + \boldsymbol{r}_{ac} \times M\dot{\boldsymbol{r}}_{ac} \tag{14.28}$$

Thus, in a manner analogous to the case of kinetic energy (see Section 13.7), the moment of momentum about point a is the sum of the moment of momentum relative to the center of mass plus the moment of momentum of the center of mass about point a. Note that $\dot{\boldsymbol{r}}_{ac}$ is the velocity of c relative to fixed point a and is thus equal to the velocity $\boldsymbol{V}_c$ of the mass center relative to XYZ. Thus, we can express Eq. (14.28) as

$$\boldsymbol{H}_a = \boldsymbol{H}_c + \boldsymbol{r}_{ac} \times M\boldsymbol{V}_c \tag{14.29}$$

Furthermore, we have for $\dot{\boldsymbol{H}}_a$:

$$\dot{\boldsymbol{H}}_a = \dot{\boldsymbol{H}}_c + \boldsymbol{r}_{ac} \times M\dot{\boldsymbol{V}}_c$$

where we have used the fact that $\dot{\boldsymbol{r}}_{ac} = \boldsymbol{V}_c$ to delete one expression. Note in effect we have put dots over $\boldsymbol{H}_a$, $\boldsymbol{H}_c$, and $\boldsymbol{V}_c$ in Eq (14.29) to reach to above equation. We may now restate Eq. 14.24 for *a fixed point a* as follows on replacing $\dot{\boldsymbol{H}}_a$ using the above equation. Then, using $\boldsymbol{a}_c$ for $\dot{\boldsymbol{V}}_c$ we have the desired result:

$$\boldsymbol{M}_a = \dot{\boldsymbol{H}}_c + \boldsymbol{r}_{ac} \times M\boldsymbol{a}_c \tag{14.30}$$

Case 2. Reference Point at the Center of Mass. We can use Eq. 14.30 for this purpose. First, we will replace $\boldsymbol{M}_a$ using the left side of Eq. 14.23. But in so doing, we will replace $\boldsymbol{r}_i$ in the first expression by $(\boldsymbol{r}_c + \boldsymbol{\rho}_{ci})$. Note next that Eq. 14.30 calls for stationary point a. We will want a to be the origin O of XYZ and so $\boldsymbol{r}_{ac}$ becomes simply $\boldsymbol{r}_c$. Finally, we replace $\boldsymbol{a}_c$ by $\ddot{\boldsymbol{r}}_c$ in Eq. 14.30 and we have after these steps

$$\sum_i (\boldsymbol{r}_c + \boldsymbol{\rho}_{ci}) \times \boldsymbol{F}_i + \sum_j \sum_i \boldsymbol{r}_i \times \boldsymbol{f}_{ij} = \dot{\boldsymbol{H}}_c + \boldsymbol{r}_c \times M\ddot{\boldsymbol{r}}_c$$

The internal forces $\boldsymbol{f}_{ij}$ give zero contribution in this equation as explained earlier and we have on rearranging the remaining terms in the equation

$$\boldsymbol{r}_c \times \sum_i \boldsymbol{F}_i + \sum_i \boldsymbol{\rho}_{ci} \times \boldsymbol{F}_i = \boldsymbol{r}_c \times M\ddot{\boldsymbol{r}}_c + \dot{\boldsymbol{H}}_c$$

[15]That is, as seen from a reference xyz translating with c relative to XYZ—in other words, as seen by a nonrotating observer moving with c.

From Newton's law for the center of mass, we know that $\sum \boldsymbol{F}_i = M\ddot{\boldsymbol{r}}_c$ and so the first terms on the left and right sides of the equation above cancel. The remaining expression on the left side of the equation is the moment about the center of mass of the external forces. We then get

$$\boldsymbol{M}_c = \dot{\boldsymbol{H}}_c \tag{14.31}$$

We thus get the same formulation for the center of mass as for a fixed point in inertial space. Please note that $\boldsymbol{H}_c$ is the moment about the center of mass of the linear momentum as seen from the center of mass but that the time derivative is as seen from inertial reference *XYZ*.

Case 3. Point Accelerating Toward or Away from the Mass Center. There is yet a third point of interest to be considered and that is a point a accelerating toward or away from the mass center of the aggregate (Fig. 14.33).

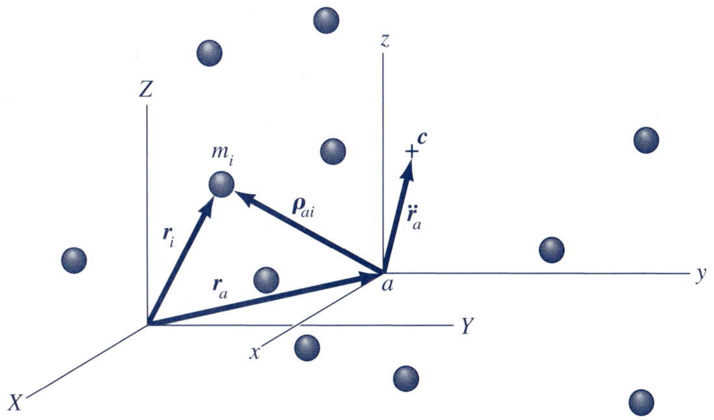

Figure 14.33. Point a accelerates toward or away from c.

For such a point, we can again give the same simple equation presented for cases 1 and 2. Thus,

$$\boldsymbol{M}_a = \dot{\boldsymbol{H}}_a \tag{14.32}$$

where $\boldsymbol{H}$ is taken relative to point a (i.e., relative to axes xyz translating with point a). We have asked for the derivation of this equation in Problem 14.96.

The component of the equation $\boldsymbol{M}_a = \dot{\boldsymbol{H}}_a$ for any one of the three cases in say the x direction,

$$M_x = \dot{H}_x$$

can be very useful. Here, M_x is the torque about the x axis, and H_x is the moment of momentum (angular momentum) about the x axis. We now examine such a problem in the following example.

Example 14.16

A heavy chain of length 20 ft lies on a light plate A which is freely rotating at an angular speed of 1 rad/sec (see Fig. 14.34). A channel C acts as a guide for the chain on the plate, and a stationary pipe acts as a guide for the chain below the plate. What is the speed of the chain after it moves 5 ft starting from rest relative to the platform? Neglect friction, the angular momentum of the plate, and the angular momentum of the vertical section of the chain about its own axis. The chain weight per unit length, w, is 10 lb/ft.

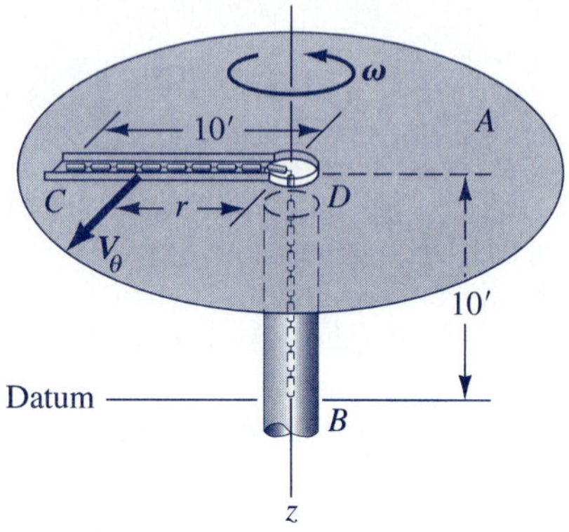

Figure 14.34. Sliding chain.

We shall first apply the **moment-of-momentum** equation about point D for the chain and plate. Taking the component of this equation along the z axis, we can say:

$$M_z = (\dot{H})_z \tag{a}$$

Clearly $M_z = 0$, and so we have conservation of angular momentum. That is,

$$\begin{aligned} H_z &= \text{constant} \\ (H_z)_1 &= (H_z)_2 \end{aligned} \tag{b}$$

where 1 and 2 refer to the initial condition and the condition after the chain moves 5 ft. We can then say:

$$\int_0^{10} r(V_\theta)_1\left(\frac{w}{g}\,dr\right) = \int_0^{5} r(V_\theta)_2\left(\frac{w}{g}\,dr\right)$$

$$\int_0^{10} r(\omega_1 r)\left(\frac{w}{g}\,dr\right) = \int_0^{5} r(\omega_2 r)\left(\frac{w}{g}\,dr\right)$$

$$(1)\left(\frac{w}{g}\right)\int_0^{10} r^2\,dr = (\omega_2)\left(\frac{w}{g}\right)\int_0^{5} r^2\,dr$$

Therefore,

$$\omega_2 = 8 \text{ rad/sec} \tag{c}$$

To find the speed of movement of the chain, we must next go to *energy* considerations. Because only conservative forces are acting here, we may employ the **conservation-of-mechanical-energy** principle. In so doing, we shall use as a datum the end of the chain B at the initial condition (see Fig. 14.34). We can then say:

$$(\text{PE})_1 = (10)(w)(10) + (10)(w)(5) = 1{,}500 \text{ ft-lb}$$

Observing Fig. 14.35, we can say for condition 2:

$$\begin{aligned} (\text{PE})_2 &= (5)(w)(10) + (10)(w)(5) - (5)(w)(2.5) \\ &= 875 \text{ ft-lb} \end{aligned}$$

As for kinetic energy, we have

$$(\text{KE})_1 = \frac{1}{2}\left(10\,\frac{w}{g}\right)\left(V^2_{\text{channel}}\right)_1 + \frac{1}{2}\left(10\,\frac{w}{g}\right)\left(V^2_{\text{pipe}}\right)_1 + \frac{1}{2}\int_0^{10}(r\omega_1)^2\,\frac{w}{g}\,dr$$

Example 14.16 (Continued)

where the first two expressions on the right side give the kinetic energy from the motion relative to the channel and pipe, respectively. The last expression is the kinetic energy due to rotation of that part of the chain that is in the channel. Clearly, $V_{\text{channel}} = V_{\text{pipe}} = 0$ initially, and so we have

$$(\text{KE})_1 = \frac{1}{2}(1)^2\left(\frac{10}{g}\right)\int_0^{10} r^2\,dr = 51.8 \text{ ft-lb}$$

Furthermore, at condition 2, we have (see Fig. 14.35)

$$(\text{KE})_2 = \frac{1}{2}\left(5\frac{w}{g}\right)\left(V^2_{\text{channel}}\right)_2 + \frac{1}{2}\left(15\frac{w}{g}\right)\left(V^2_{\text{pipe}}\right)_2 + \frac{1}{2}\int_0^5 (r\omega_2)^2\frac{w}{g}\,dr$$

Note that $(V_{\text{channel}})_2 = (V_{\text{pipe}})_2$. Simply calling this quantity V_2, we have

$$(\text{KE})_2 = \frac{1}{2}(20)\left(\frac{w}{g}\right)(V_2^2) + \frac{1}{2}(8^2)\left(\frac{w}{g}\right)\int_0^5 r^2\,dr$$
$$= 3.11V_2^2 + 414$$

We can now state

$$(\text{PE})_1 + (\text{KE})_1 = (\text{PE})_2 + (\text{KE})_2$$
$$1{,}500 + 51.8 = 875 + (3.11\,V_2^2 + 414)$$

Therefore,

$$V_2 = 9.19 \text{ ft/sec}$$

We can conclude that the chain is moving at a speed of 9.19 ft/sec along the channel and down the stationary pipe and that the plate *A* is rotating at an angular speed of 8 rad/sec.

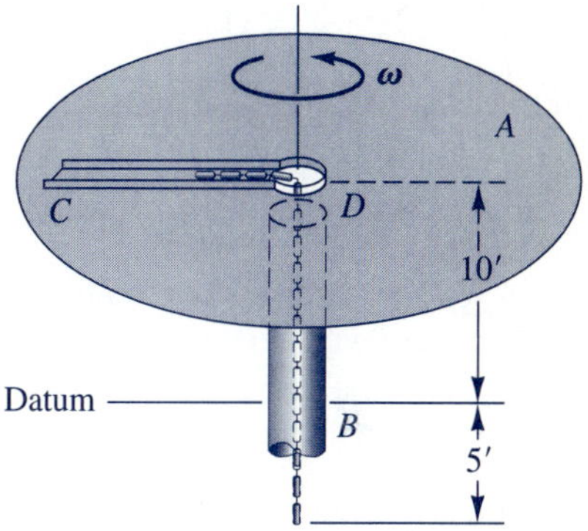

Figure 14.35. Chain after motion of 5 ft.

Much time will be spent later in the text in applying $\boldsymbol{M}_a = \dot{\boldsymbol{H}}_a$ to a rigid body. There, the rigid body is considered to be made up of an infinite number of contiguous elements. Summations then give way to integration, and so on. The final equations of this section accordingly are among the most important in mechanics.

In the homework assignments, we have included, as in Chapter 13, several very simple rigid-body problems to illustrate the use of the equation $\boldsymbol{M}_a = \dot{\boldsymbol{H}}_a$ and to give an early introduction to rigid-body mechanics.[16] We now illustrate such a problem.

[16]The instructor may wish not to get into rigid-body dynamics at this time. This approach presents no loss in continuity.

Example 14.17

A uniform cylinder of radius 400 mm and mass 100 kg is acted on at its center by a force of 500 N (see Fig. 14.36). What is the friction force f? Take $\mu_s = .2$.

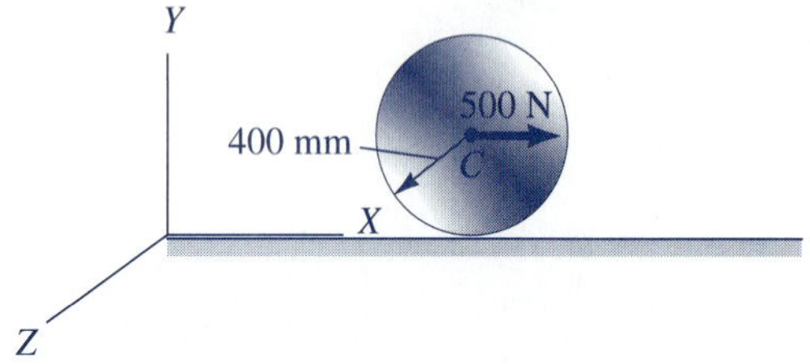

Figure 14.36. Rolling cylinder.

We have shown a free-body diagram of the cylinder in Fig. 14.37. A reference xyz with origin at C translates with the center of mass. We first apply **Newton's law** relative to inertial reference XYZ.[17] Thus, for the X direction we have for the center of mass C:

$$500 - f = 100\ddot{X}_c \tag{a}$$

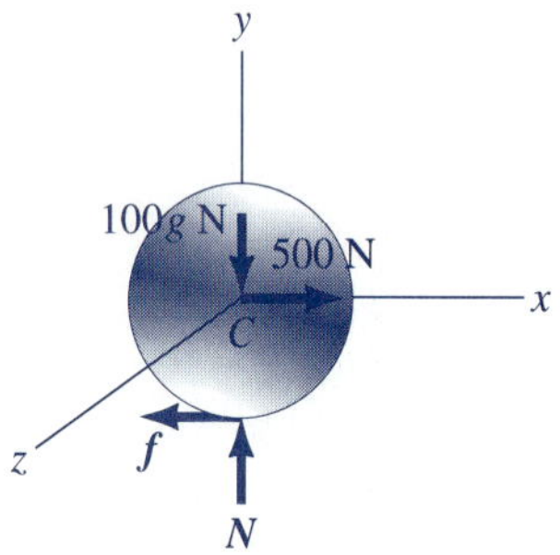

Figure 14.37. Free body.

Next, we write the **moment-of-momentum** equation about the z axis, which goes through the *center of mass*. Thus, noting that we have simple circular motion relative to the z axis for all particles of the cylinder and observing Fig. 14.38:

$$M_z = \frac{d}{dt}(H_z)$$

$$-(f)(.40) = \frac{d}{dt}\left[\int_0^{2\pi}\int_0^{.40}\underbrace{(\rho r\,dr\,d\theta\,l)}_{dm}(r)\underbrace{(r\omega)}_{V_\theta}\right]$$

[17]The reader is cautioned that although the diagram of this problem looks like those solved by energy methods in Section 13.8 of the previous chapter, this is not such a problem since distance is not involved. Instead, we deal with the linear acceleration and the angular acceleration.

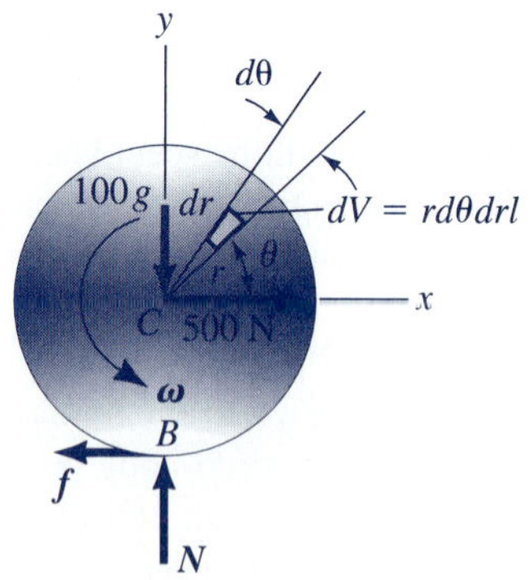

Figure 14.38. Element dV in cylinder. Unknown ω shown as positive.

Example 14.17 (Continued)

where ρ is the mass density of the cylinder and l is the thickness of the cylinder. Evaluating the integral and differentiating with respect to time as seen from *XYZ*, we get

$$.40f = -(\rho l)(2\pi)(\dot{\omega})\left(\frac{.40^4}{4}\right) \qquad \text{(b)}$$
$$f = -.1005(\rho l)\dot{\omega}$$

We can determine ρl as follows from geometry:

$$M = 100 = (\rho l)[\pi(.40)^2]$$
$$\rho l = 198.9 \text{ kg/m}^2 \qquad \text{(c)}$$

We have two equations (a) and (b) with three unknowns, $f, \ddot{X}_c$, and $\dot{\omega}$. We now need another independent equation. This equation can be found from **kinematics**. Thus, assuming a *no-slipping* condition, we have pure instantaneous rotation about point B. From your work in physics (we shall later prove this) we can say for point C of the cylinder:

$$(.40)\omega = -\dot{X}$$

Therefore,

$$(.40)\dot{\omega} = -\ddot{X} \qquad \text{(d)}$$

Substituting for ρl and $\dot{\omega}$ in Eq. (b) using Eqs. (c) and (d), we get

$$f = (-.1005)(198.9)\left(-\frac{\ddot{X}}{.40}\right) \qquad \text{(e)}$$

Now solve for $\ddot{X}$ from Eq. (a) and substitute into Eq. (e):

$$f = (.1005)(198.9)\left(\frac{5 - .01f}{.40}\right)$$

Solving for f, we get

$$f = 166.6 \text{ N}$$

We must now check to see whether our no-slipping assumption is valid. The maximum possible friction force clearly is

$$f_{max} = (100)(9.81)(.2) = 196.2 \text{ N}$$

which is greater than the actual friction force, so that the no-slip assumption is consistent with our results.

*14.9 Looking Ahead— Basic Laws of Continua

In the preceding three chapters, we have presented three alternate approaches. They were, broadly speaking:

1. Direct application of Newton's law.
2. Energy methods.
3. Linear-momentum methods and moment-of-momentum methods

These all come from a *common* source (i.e., Newton's law) and so we can use any one for particle and rigid-body problems.

Later, when you study more complex continua such as a flowing fluid with heat transfer and compression you will have to satisfy four basic laws. These basic laws are:

1. Conservation of mass.
2. Linear momentum and moment of momentum (these are now Newton's law).
3. First law of thermodynamics.
4. Second law of thermodynamics.

For more general continua, the above mentioned four basic laws[18] are *independent* of each other (i.e., they must be separately satisfied) whereas in particle and rigid-body mechanics that we have been studying, 2 and 3 directly above, are equivalent to each other; 1 is satisfied by simply keeping the mass M constant; and 4 is satisfied by making sure that friction impedes the relative motion between two bodies in contact.

Furthermore, we applied the approaches of the preceding three chapters to free bodies. For more general continuum studies, such as fluid flow, we can apply the four basic laws to systems (i.e., free bodies) and also to so-called control volumes (fixed volumes in space) as discussed in the Looking Ahead Section 5.4.

Thus, in this book, we are considering a very simple phase of continuum mechanics whereby, in effect, we need only consider explicitly one of the basic laws. Your view will broaden as you move through the curriculum.

In some mechanics books there is presented an elementary presentation for determining the force developed by a stream of water or other fluid on a

[18]Electrical engineering students will, in addition, spend considerable time studying four other basic laws which are the famous Maxwell equations.

vane or some other object that deflects the stream of fluid. Your author has refrained from including this material. It is felt that the procedure for this computation should be undertaken in a more mature and thorough manner in a fluid mechanics course. There, the **linear momentum equation** is developed around the concept of the control volume and must be executed with care. In essence, the total external force at the control surface from fluids as well as those from solids such as vanes plus external forces such as gravity acting on what is inside the control volume—all equals the net efflux rate of linear momentum of flow through the control surface plus the rate of change of linear momentum inside the control volume. The execution of this principle should be done with care and precision and should not be undertaken lightly in a very limited simple-minded way.

Using a similar approach, the other basic laws are developed in the fluid mechanics course. Thus, for **moment of momentum**, we use the moments about any convenient point in inertial space of external forces acting at the control surface and also of external forces acting on anything inside the control volume and we equate the sum of these moments with the rate of flow of angular momentum through the control surface plus the rate of change of angular momentum inside the control volume.

Similarly, for the **first law of thermodynamics**, we add the rate of heat flow through the control surface, plus the rate of work passing through the control surface from fluids, plus the equivalent rate of work from electric currents in wires passing through the control surface, and finally plus the rate of work transmitted by shafts or any other devices passing through the control surface all at any time t. This is then equated to the flow of mechanical and internal energy through the control surface plus the rate of change of mechanical and internal energy inside the control volume at time t.

For the **conservation of mass**, we equate the net efflux rate of mass through the control surface with the rate of decrease of mass inside the control volume.

Although a similar approach can be made for the **second law of thermodynamics**, it is not as useful in this form and we shall defer this to your thermodynamics course.

Your author believes these laws in the above form should be taken up in *concert* and in *generality* for the greatest understanding and benefit for the student. Elementary treatments found in many mechanics books do not contribute to the understanding of the basic laws needed in fluid mechanics[19] and in later courses and may even present a hindrance for deeper understanding needed later.

[19]See I.H. Shames, *Mechanics of Fluids*, McGraw-Hill, 3rd ed., 1992, Chapters 5 and 6.

14.89. A system of particles is shown at time t moving in the xy plane. The following data apply:

$$m_1 = 1 \text{ kg}, \quad V_1 = 5\boldsymbol{i} + 5\boldsymbol{j} \text{ m/sec}$$
$$m_2 = 0.7 \text{ kg}, \quad V_2 = -4\boldsymbol{i} + 3\boldsymbol{j} \text{ m/sec}$$
$$m_3 = 2 \text{ kg}, \quad V_3 = -4\boldsymbol{j} \text{ m/sec}$$
$$m_4 = 1.5 \text{ kg}, \quad V_4 = 3\boldsymbol{i} - 4\boldsymbol{j} \text{ m/sec}$$

(a) What is the total linear momentum of the system?
(b) What is the linear momentum of the center of mass?
(c) What is the total moment of momentum of the system about the origin and about point (2, 6)?

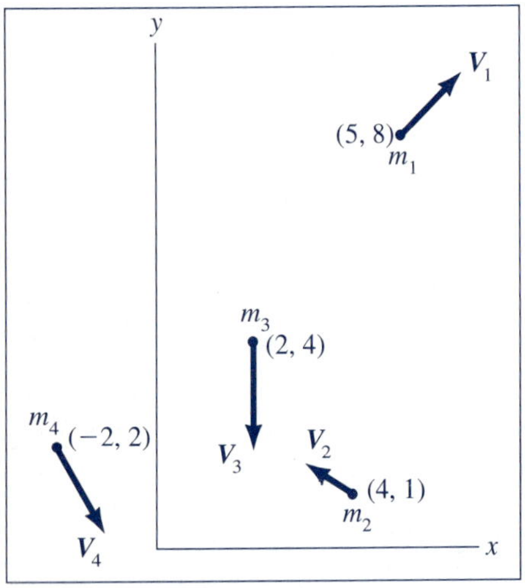

Figure P.14.89.

14.90. A system of particles at time t has the following velocities and masses:

$$V_1 = 20 \text{ ft/sec}, \quad m_1 = 1 \text{ lbm}$$
$$V_2 = 18 \text{ ft/sec}, \quad m_2 = 3 \text{ lbm}$$
$$V_3 = 15 \text{ ft/sec}, \quad m_3 = 2 \text{ lbm}$$
$$V_4 = 5 \text{ ft/sec}, \quad m_4 = 1 \text{ lbm}$$

Determine (a) the total linear momentum of the system, (b) the angular momentum of the system about the origin, and (c) the angular momentum of the system about point a.

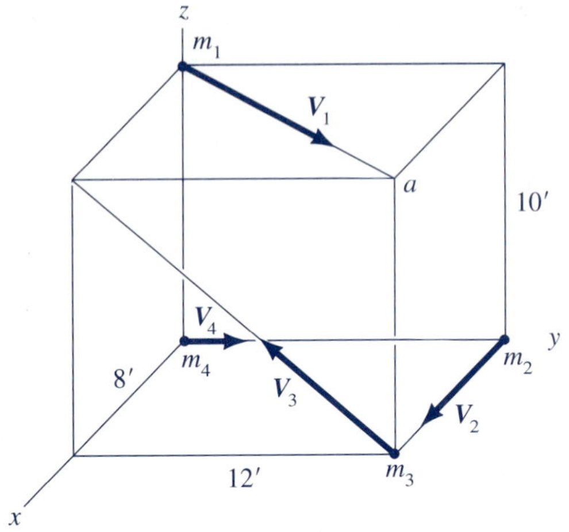

Figure P.14.90.

14.91. A system of particles at time t_1 has masses $m_1 = 2$ lbm, $m_2 = 1$ lbm, $m_3 = 3$ lbm and locations and velocities as shown in (a). The same system of masses is shown in (b) at time t_2. What is the total linear impulse on the system during this time interval? What is the total angular impulse $\int \boldsymbol{M}\,dt$ during this time interval about the origin?

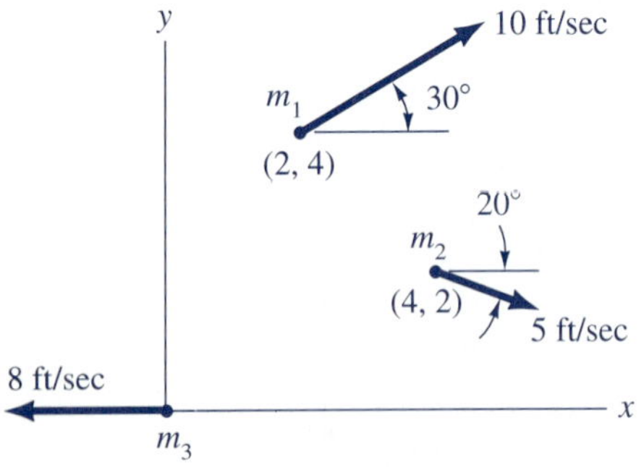

(a) Time t_1

Figure P.14.91-a.

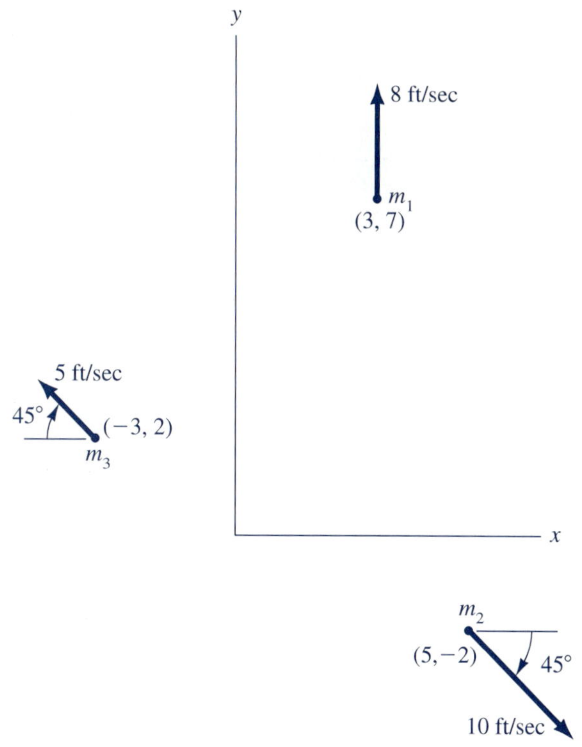

(b) Time t_2

Figure P.14.91-b.

14.92. Two masses slide along bar *AB* at a constant speed of 1.5 m/sec. Bar *AB* rotates freely about axis *CD*. Consider only the mass of the sliding bodies to determine the angular acceleration of *AB* when the bodies are 1.5 m from *CD* if the angular velocity at that instant is 10 rad/sec.

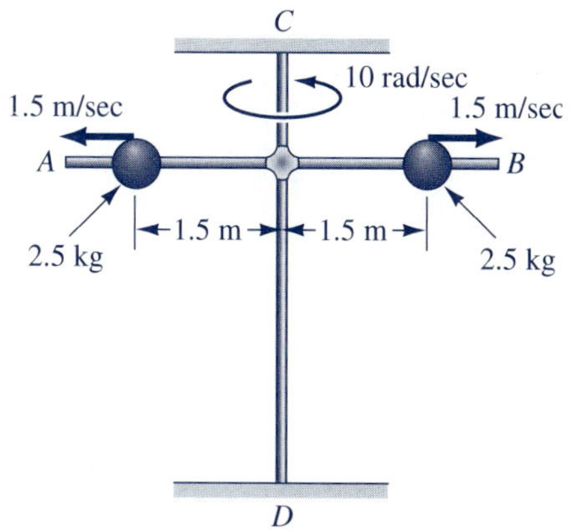

Figure P.14.92.

14.93. A mechanical system is composed of three identical bodies *A*, *B*, and *C* each of mass 3 lbm moving along frictionless rods 120° apart on a wheel. Each of these bodies is connected with an inextensible cord to the freely hanging weight *D*. The connection of the cords to *D* is such that no torque can be transmitted to *D*. Initially, the three masses *A*, *B*, and *C* are held at a distance of 2 ft from the centerline while the wheel rotates at 3 rad/sec. What is the angular speed of the wheel and the velocity of descent of *D* if, after release of the radial bodies, body *D* moves 1 ft? Assume that body *D* is initially stationary (i.e., is not rotating). Body *D* weighs 100 lb.

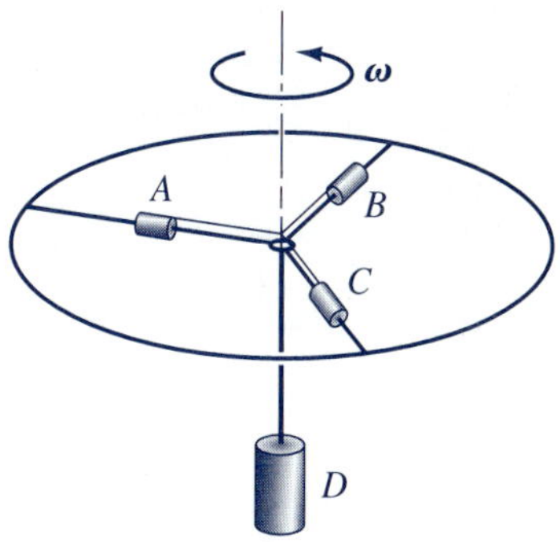

Figure P.14.93.

14.94. Two sets of particles *a*, *b*, and *c*, *d* (each particle of mass *m*) are moving along two shafts *AB* and *CD*, which are, in turn, rigidly attached to a crossbar *EF*. All particles are moving at a constant speed V_1 away from *EF*, and their positions at the moment of interest are as shown. The system is rotating about *G*, and a constant torque of magnitude *T* is acting in the plane of the system. Assume that all masses other than the concentrated masses are negligible and that the angular velocity of the system at the instant of discussion is ω. Determine the instantaneous angular acceleration in terms of m, T, ω, s_1, and s_2.

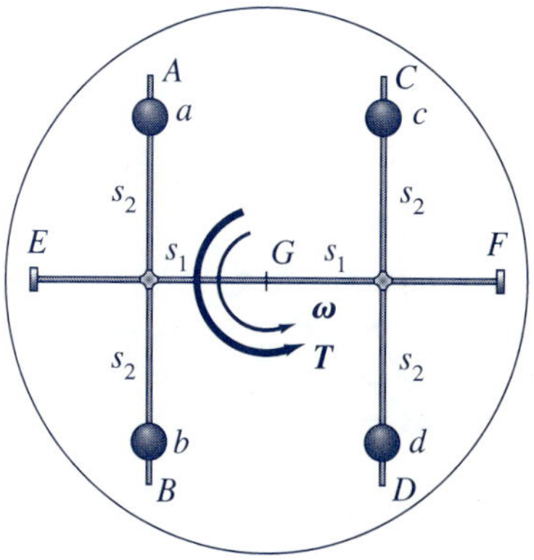

Figure P.14.94.

14.95. A uniform rod with a mass of 7 kg/m lies flat on a frictionless surface. A force of 250 N acts on the rod as shown in the diagram. What is the angular acceleration of the rod? What is the acceleration of the mass center?

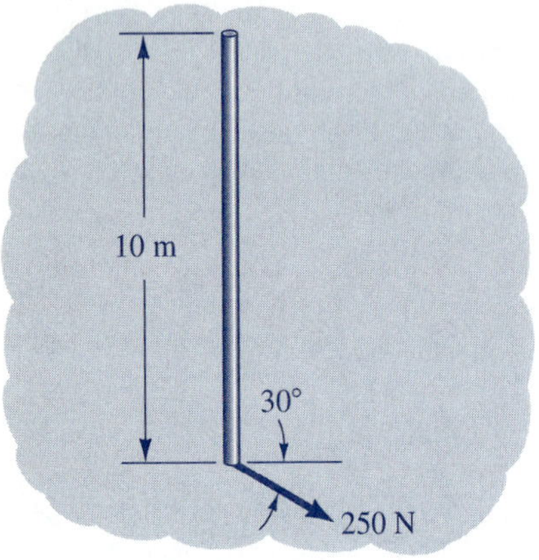

Figure P.14.95

***14.96.** Consider an aggregate of particles with C as the mass center and point A accelerating toward or away from C. Start with the expression for $\dot{\boldsymbol{H}}$ about O given as

$$\boldsymbol{M}_0 = \dot{\boldsymbol{H}}_0 = \frac{d}{dt}\left[\sum_i \boldsymbol{r}_i \times m_i \dot{\boldsymbol{r}}_i\right] = \sum_i \boldsymbol{r}_i \times \dot{\boldsymbol{P}}_i = \sum_i (\boldsymbol{r}_A \times \boldsymbol{\rho}_{Ai}) \times \dot{\boldsymbol{P}}$$

Formulate $\boldsymbol{M}_0$ in terms of $\boldsymbol{F}_i$ and use Newton's law to eliminate terms. Next show from the resulting equation that

$$\boldsymbol{M}_A = \left(\sum_i m_i \boldsymbol{\rho}_{Ai}\right) \times \ddot{\boldsymbol{r}}_A + \sum_i \boldsymbol{\rho}_{Ai} \times m_i \ddot{\boldsymbol{\rho}}_{Ai}$$

Replace $\sum_i m_i \boldsymbol{\rho}_{Ai}$ by $M\boldsymbol{\rho}_{Ac}$ Explain why it follows then that

$$\boldsymbol{M}_A = \dot{\boldsymbol{H}}_A$$

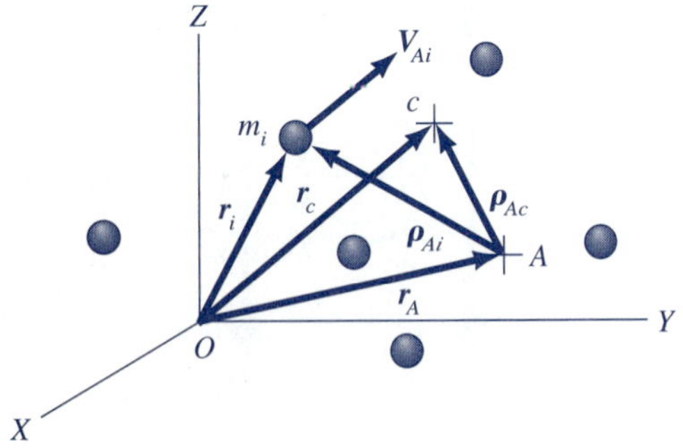

Figure P.14.96.

14.97. A uniform cylinder of radius 1 m rolls without slipping down a 30° incline. What is the angular acceleration of the cylinder if it has a mass of 50 kg?

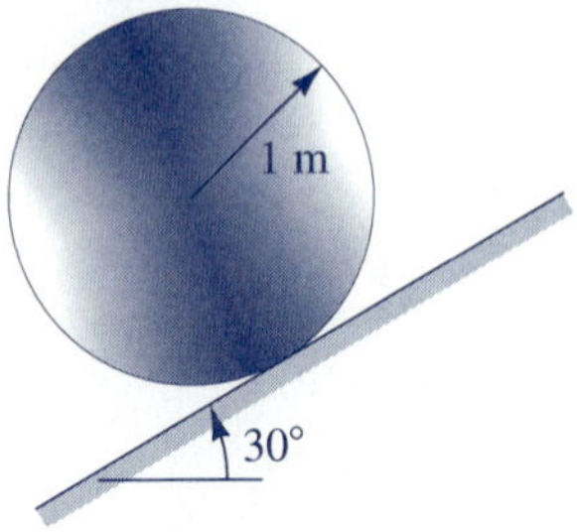

Figure P.14.97.

14.98. A cylinder of length 3 m and mass 45 kg is acted on by a torque $T = (11.25t + 21t^2)$ N-m (where t is in seconds) about its geometric axis. What is the angular speed after 10 sec? The cylinder is at rest when the torque is applied.

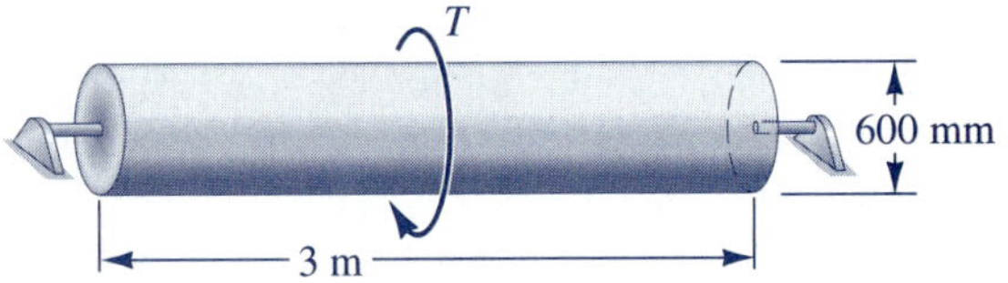

Figure P.14.98.

14.99. A constant torque T of 800 N-m is applied to a uniform cylinder of radius 400 mm and mass 50 kg. A 1.500-kN weight is attached to the cylinder with a light cable. What is the acceleration of W?

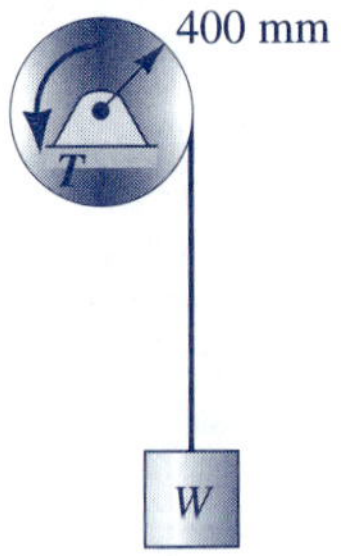

Figure P.14.99.

***14.100.** In Problem 14.99, the torque T is $T = (300 + .2t^2)$ N-m, where t is in seconds. When $t = 0$, the system is at rest. Determine the acceleration of W at the instants when it has zero velocity for $t > 0$.

14.101. A constant torque T of 500 in.-lb is applied to a uniform cylinder of radius 1 ft. A light inextensible cable is wrapped partly around an identical cylinder and is then connected to a block W weighing 100 lb. What is the acceleration of W if the cable does not slip on the cylinders? Take $\mu_d = .3$ for the block. For the cylinders, $W_A = W_B = 100$ lb.

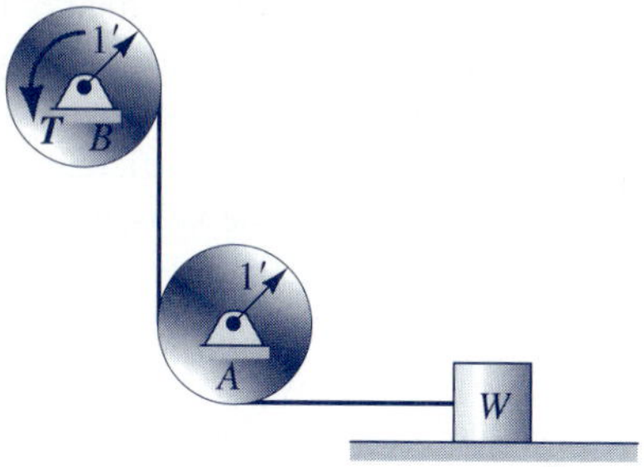

Figure P.14.101.

14.102. A canal with a rectangular cross section is shown having a width of 30 ft and a depth of 5 ft. The velocity of the water is assumed to be zero at the banks and to vary parabolically over the section as shown in the diagram. If δ is the radial distance from the centerline of the channel, the transverse velocity V_θ is given as

$$V_\theta = \frac{1}{20}(225 - \delta^2) \text{ ft/sec}$$

What is the angular momentum H_0 about O at any time t of the water in the circular portion of the canal (i.e., between the x and y axes)? The radial component V_r is zero.

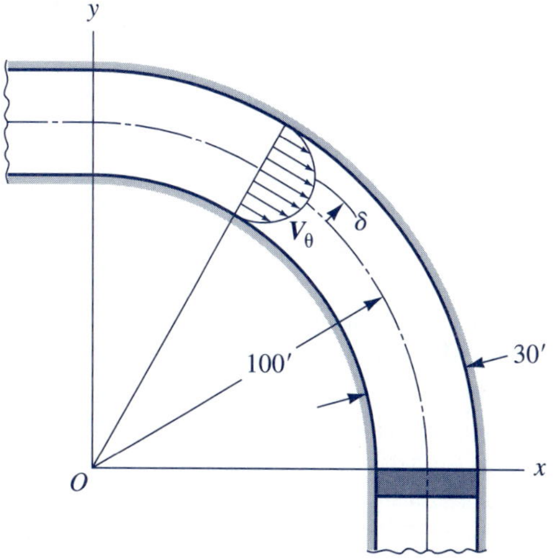

Figure P.14.102.

14.103. A hoop with mass per unit length 6.5 kg/m lies flat on a frictionless surface. A 500-N force is suddenly applied. What is the angular acceleration of the hoop? What is the acceleration of the mass center?

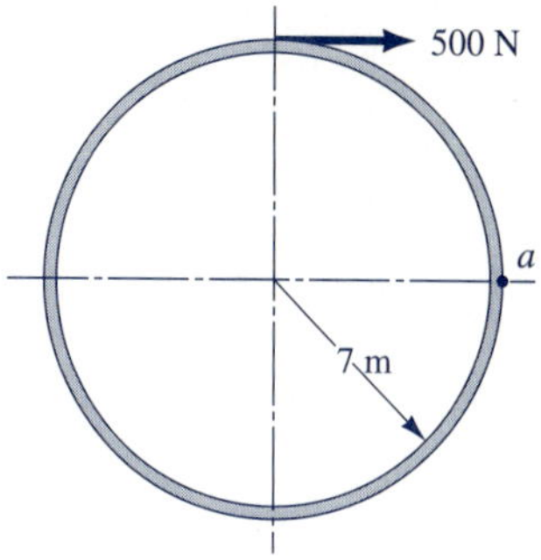

Figure P.14.103.

14.104. Do Problem 14.103 for the case where a force given as:

$$\boldsymbol{F} = 50\boldsymbol{i} + 75\boldsymbol{j} \text{ N}$$

is applied at point a instead of the 500-N force.

14.105. A cylinder weighing 50 lb lies on a frictionless surface. Two forces are applied simultaneously as shown in the diagram. What is the angular acceleration of the cylinder? What is the acceleration of the mass center?

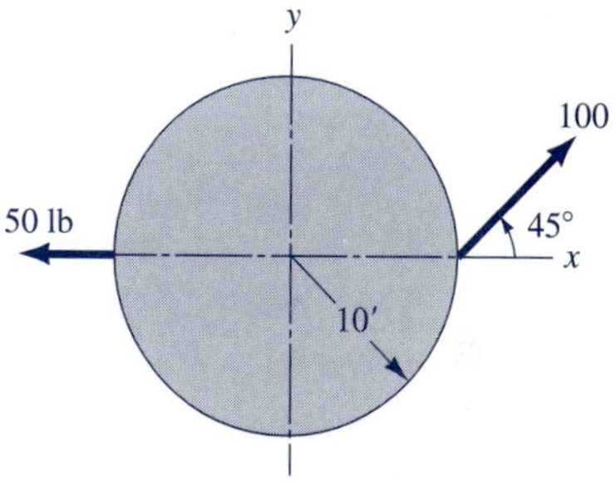

Figure P.14.105.

14.106. A thin uniform hoop rolls without slipping down a 30° incline. The hoop material weighs 5 lb/ft and has a radius R of 4 ft. What is the angular acceleration of the hoop?

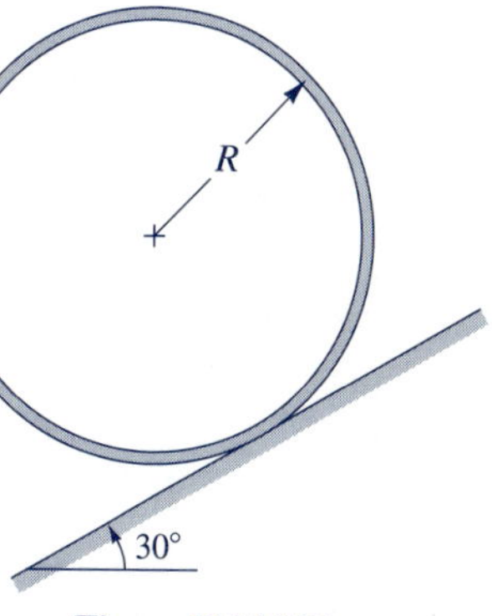

Figure P.14.106.

14.10 Closure

One of the topics studied in this chapter is the impact of bodies under certain restricted conditions. For such problems, we can consider the bodies as particles before and after impact, but during impact the bodies act as deformable media for which a particle model is not meaningful or sufficient. By making an elementary picture of the action, we introduce the coefficient of restitution to yield additional information we need to determine velocities after impact. This is an empirical approach, so our analyses are limited to simple problems. To handle more complex problems or to do the simple ones more precisely, we would have to make a more rational investigation of the deformation actions taking place during impact—that is, a continuum approach to part of the problem would be required. However, we cannot make a careful study of the deformation aspects in this text since the subject of high-speed deformation of solids is a difficult one that is still under careful study by engineers and physicists.

Note in the last two chapters we started with Newton's law $\boldsymbol{F} = M\boldsymbol{a}$ and performed the following operations:

1. Took the dot product of both sides using position vector $\boldsymbol{r}$.
2. Multiplied both sides by dt and integrated.
3. Took the cross product of both sides using position vector $\boldsymbol{r}$.

These steps permitted a surprisingly large number of very useful formulations and concepts that have occupied us for some considerable time. These were the energy methods, the linear-momentum methods, and the moment-of-momentum methods. It should now be clear that Newton's law requires considerable study to fully explore its use.

In our study of moment of momentum for a system of particles, we set forth one of the key equations of mechanics, $\boldsymbol{M}_A = \dot{\boldsymbol{H}}_A$, and we introduced in the examples several considerations whose more careful and complete study will occupy a good portion of the remainder of the text. Thus, in Example 14.17 we have "in miniature," as it were, the major elements involved in the study of much of rigid-body dynamics. Recall that we employed Newton's law for the mass center and the moment-of-momentum equation about the mass center to reach the desired results. In so doing, however, we had to make use of certain elementary kinematical ideas from our earlier work in physics. Accordingly, to prepare ourselves for rigid-body dynamics in Chapters 16 and 17, we shall devote ourselves in Chapter 15 to a rather careful examination of the general kinematics of a rigid body.

Although we shall be much concerned in Chapter 15 with the kinematics of rigid bodies, we shall not cease to consider particles. You will see that an understanding of rigid-body kinematics will permit us to formulate very powerful relations for the general relative motions of a particle involving references that move in any arbitrary manner with respect to each other.

PROBLEMS

14.107. A disc is rotated in the horizontal plane with a constant angular speed ω of 30 rad/sec. A body A with a mass of .4 lbm is moved in a frictionless slot at a uniform speed of 1 ft/sec relative to the platform by a force F as shown. What is the linear momentum of the body relative to the ground reference XY when $r = 2$ ft and $\theta = 45°$? What is the impulse developed on the body as it goes from $r = 2$ ft to $r = 1$ ft? Neglect the mass of the disc.

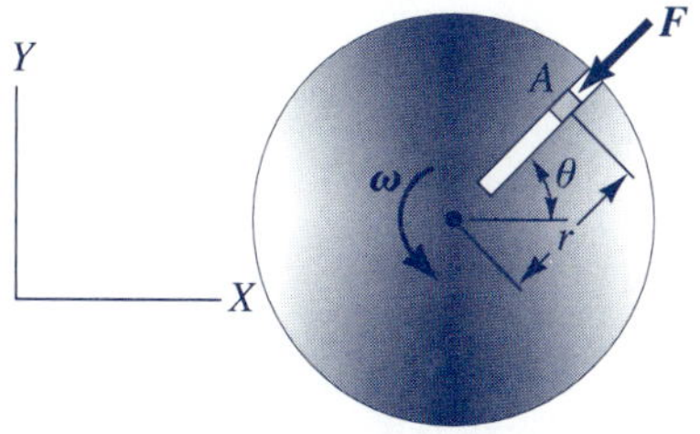

Figure P.14.107.

14.108. Three bodies are towed by a force $F = (100 + 50e^{-t})$ lb as shown. If $W_1 = 30$ lb, $W_2 = 60$ lb, and $W_3 = 50$ lb, what is the speed 5 sec after the application of the given force? The dynamic coefficient of friction is .3 for all surfaces.

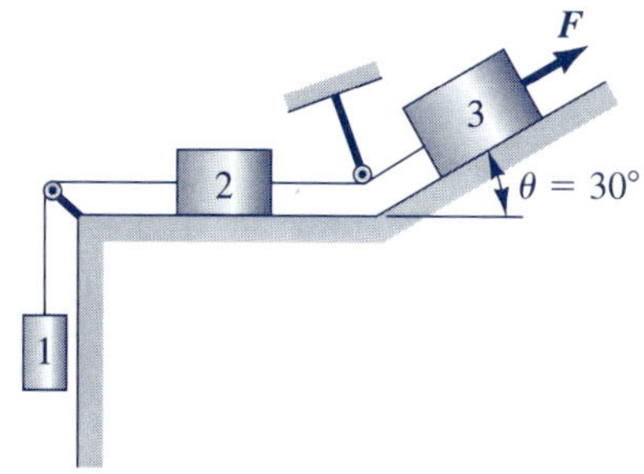

Figure P.14.108.

14.109. A space vehicle is in a circular parking orbit around the earth at a distance of 100 km from the earth's surface. What increase in speed must be given to the vehicle by firing its rockets so as to attain a radial velocity of 2,000 km/hr at an elevation of 200 km?

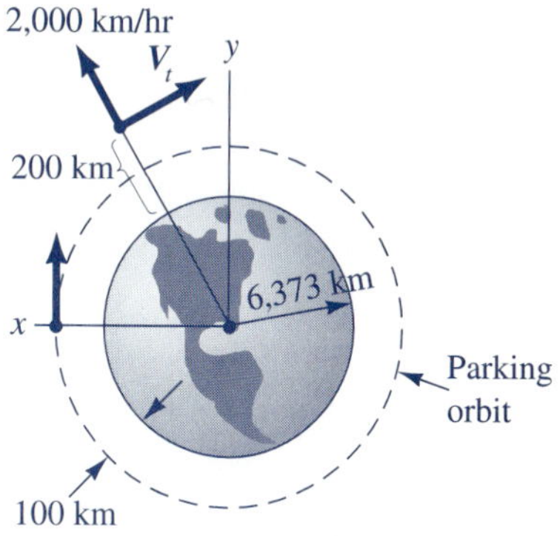

Figure P.14.109.

14.110. A space ship is in a circular parking orbit around the earth at 200 miles above the earth's surface. At space headquarters, they wish to get the vehicle to a position 10,000 miles from the center of the earth with a velocity at this position of 25,000 mi/hr. The command is given to fire rockets directly to the rear for a specified short time interval. What is the change in speed needed for this maneuver? What are the radial and tangential velocity components of the 25,000 mi/hr velocity vector?

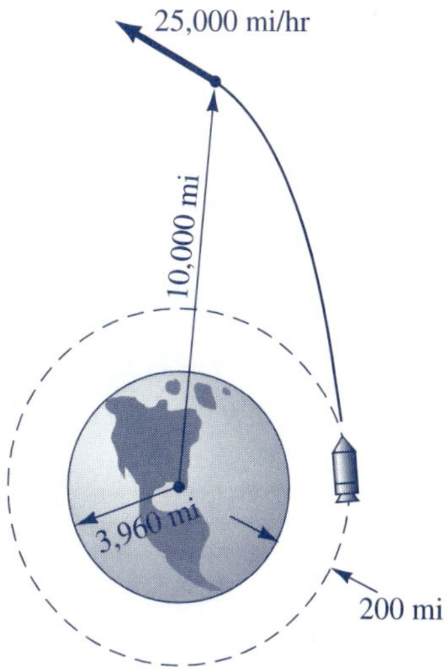

Figure P.14.110.

14.111. A small elastic ball is dropped from a height of 5 m onto a rigid cylindrical body having a radius of 1.5 m. At what position on the x axis does the ball land after the collision with the cylinder?

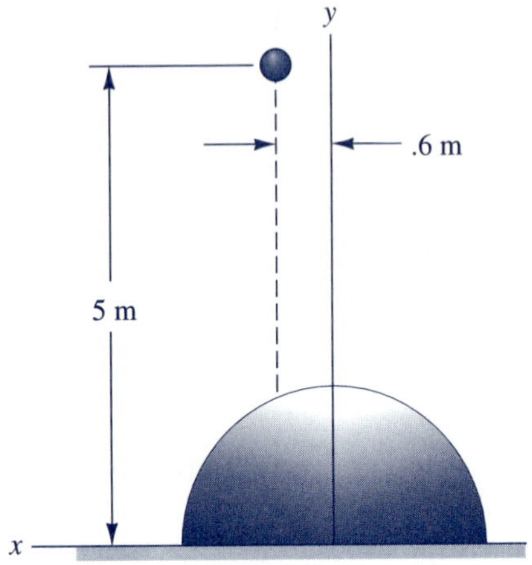

Figure P.14.111.

14.112. Do Problem 14.111 for an inelastic impact with $\epsilon = .6$.

14.113. A small elastic sphere is dropped from position (2, 3, 30) ft onto a hard spherical body having a radius of 5 ft positioned so that the z axis of the reference shown is along a diameter. For a perfectly elastic collision, give the speed of the small sphere directly after impact.

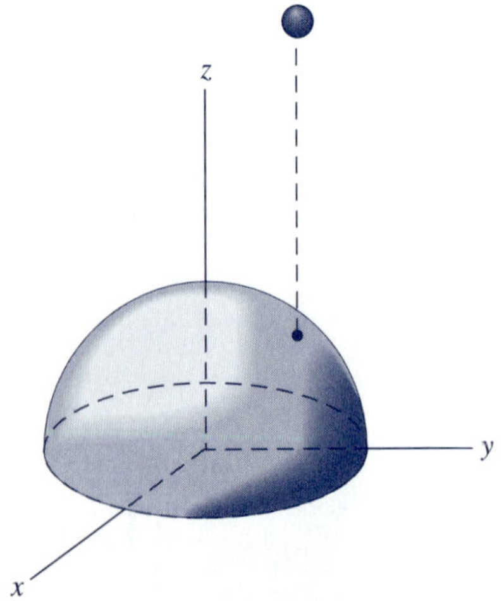

Figure P.14.113.

14.114. Do Problem 14.113 for an inelastic impact with $\epsilon = .6$.

14.115. A bullet hits a smooth, hard, massive two-dimensional body whose boundary has been shown as a parabola. If the bullet strikes 1.5 m above the x axis and if the collision is perfectly elastic, what is the maximum height reached by the bullet as it ricochets? Neglect air resistance and take the velocity of the bullet on impact as 700 m/sec with a direction that is parallel to the x axis.

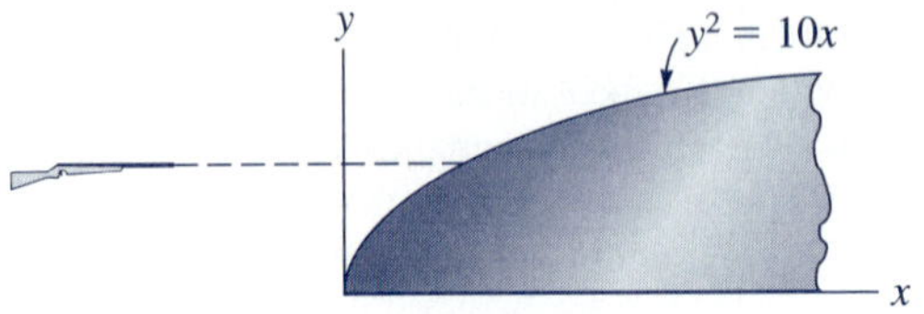

Figure P.14.115.

14.116. In Problem 14.115, assume an inelastic impact with $\epsilon = .6$. At what position along x does the bullet strike the parabola after the impact?

14.117. A space vehicle is in a circular "parking" orbit (1) around the earth 200 km above the earth's surface. It is to transfer to another circular orbit (2) 500 km above the earth's surface. The transfer to the second orbit is done in two stages.

1. Fire rockets so the vehicle has an *apogee* equal to the radius of the second circular orbit. What change of speed is required for this maneuver?
2. At *apogee* rockets are fired again to get into the second circular orbit. What is this second change of speed?

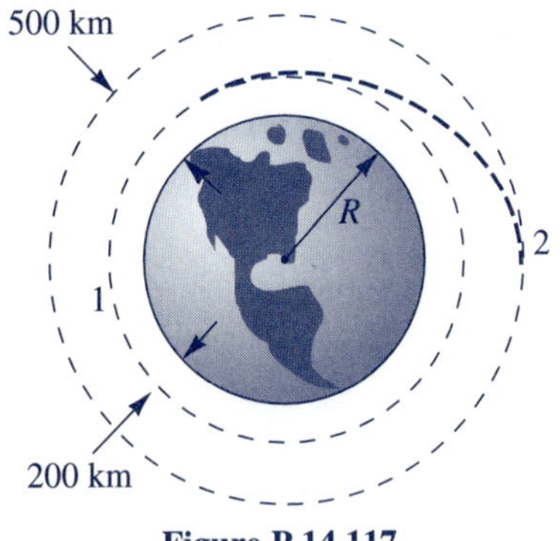

Figure P.14.117.

***14.118.** A tugboat weighing 100 tons is moving toward a stationary barge weighing 200 tons and carrying a load C weighing 50 tons. The tug is moving at 5 knots and its propellers are developing a thrust of 5,000 lb when it contacts the barge. As a result of the soft padding at the nose of the tug, consider that there is plastic impact. If the load C is not tied in any way to the barge and has a dynamic coefficient of friction of .1 with the slippery deck of the barge, what is the speed V of the barge 2 sec after the tug first contacts the barge? The load C slips during a 1-sec interval starting at the beginning of the contact.

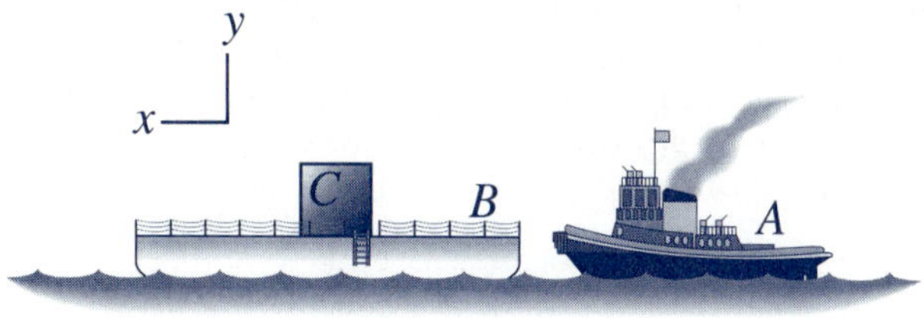

Figure P.14.118.

14.119. A hopper drops small cylinders each weighing 10 N onto a conveyor belt which is moving at a speed of 3 m/sec. At the top, the cylinders are dropped off as shown. If at any time t there are 14 cylinders on the belt and if 10 cylinders are dropped per second from a hopper from a height of 300 mm above the belt, what average torque is needed to operate the conveyor? The weight of the belt that is on the conveyor bed is 100 N. The coefficient of friction μ_d between the belt and the bed is .3. The radius of the driving cylinder is 300 mm. Neglect bearing friction.

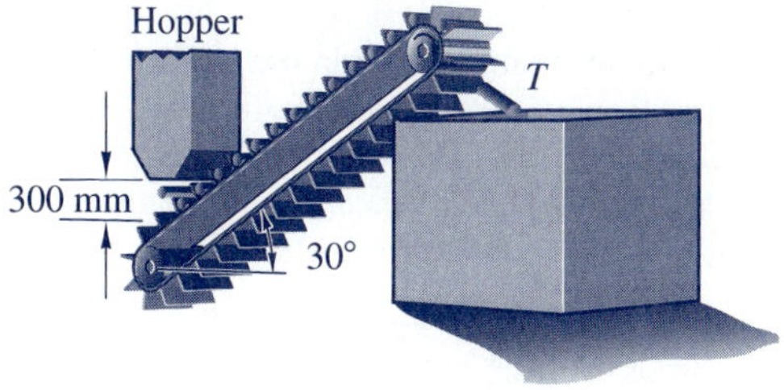

Figure P.14.119.

14.120. A body A weighing 2 tons is allowed to slide down an incline on a barge as shown. Body A moves a distance of 25 ft along the incline before it is stopped at B. If we neglect water resistance, how far does the barge shift in the horizontal direction? If the maximum speed of body A relative to the incline of the barge is 2 ft/sec, what is the maximum speed of the barge relative to the water? The weight of the barge is 20 tons.

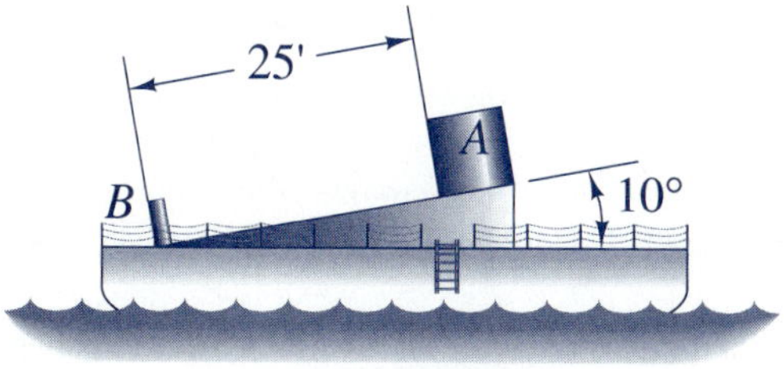

Figure P.14.120.

14.121. A water droplet of diameter 2 mm is falling in the atmosphere at the rate of 2 m/sec. As a result of an updraft, a second water droplet of diameter 1 mm impinges on the aforementioned droplet. The velocity of the second droplet just prior to impingement is $3\boldsymbol{i} + 1\boldsymbol{j}$ m/sec. After impingement three droplets are formed moving parallel to the xy plane. We have the following information:

$$D_1 = .6 \text{ mm}, \quad V_1 = 2 \text{ m/sec}, \quad \theta_1 = 45^\circ$$

$$D_2 = 1.2 \text{ mm}, \quad V_2 = 1 \text{ m/sec}, \quad \theta_2 = 30^\circ$$

Find D_3, V_3, and θ_3.

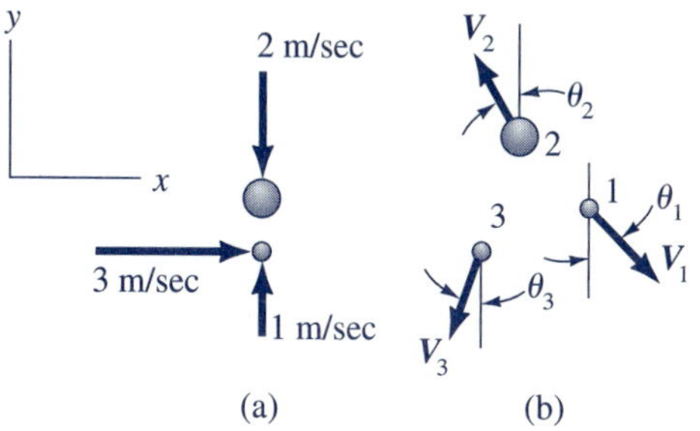

Figure P.14.121.

14.122. If the coefficient of restitution is .8 for the two spheres, what are the maximum angles from the vertical that the spheres will reach after the first impact? Neglect the mass of the cables.

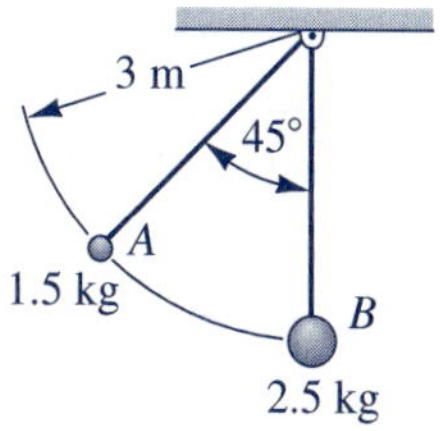

Figure P.14.122.

14.123. Thin discs A and B slide along a frictionless surface. Each disc has a radius of 25 mm. Disc A has a mass of 85 g, whereas disc B has a mass of 227 g. What are the speeds of the discs after collision for $\epsilon = .7$? Assume that the discs slide on a frictionless surface.

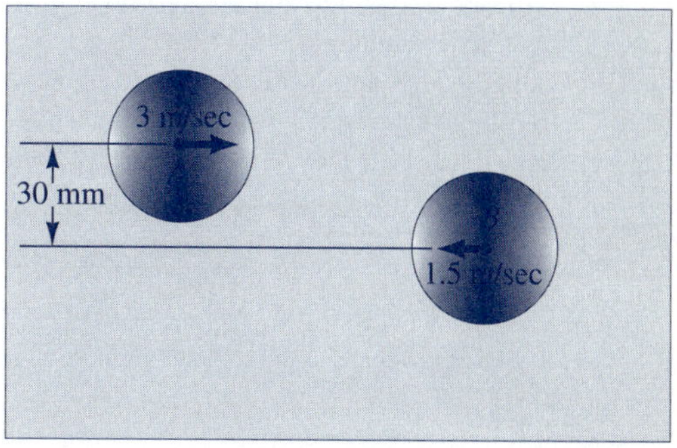

Figure P.14.123.

14.124. A BB is shot at the hard, rigid surface. The speed of the pellet is 300 ft/sec as it strikes the surface. If the direction of the velocity for the pellet is given by the following unit vector:

$$\boldsymbol{\epsilon} = -.6\boldsymbol{i} - .8\boldsymbol{k}$$

what is the final velocity vector of the pellet for a collision having $\epsilon = .7$?

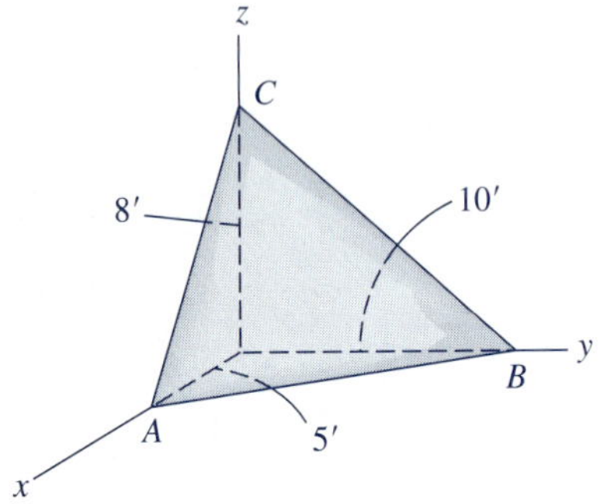

Figure P.14.124.

***14.125.** A chain of wrought iron, with length of 7 m and a mass of 100 kg, is held so that it just touches the support AB. If the chain is released, determine the total impulse during 2 sec in the vertical direction experienced by the support if the impact is plastic (i.e., the chain does not bounce up) and if we move the support so that the links land on the platform and not on each other? [*Hint:* Note that any chain *resting* on AB delivers a vertical impulse. Also check to see if the entire chain lands on AB before 2 sec.]

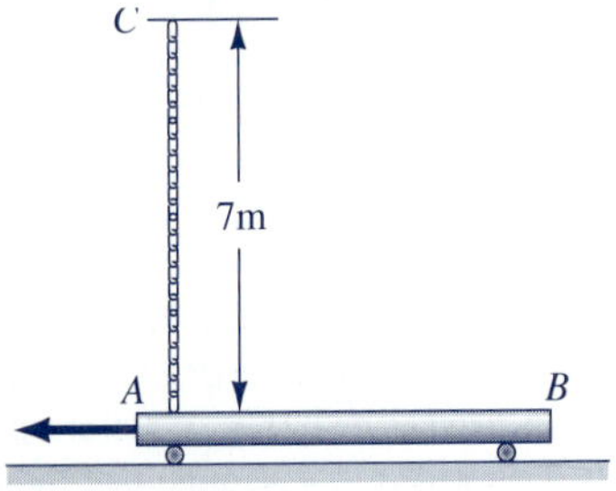

Figure P.14.125.

14.126. Two trucks are shown moving up a 10° incline. Truck A weighs 26.7 kN and is developing a 13.30-kN driving force on the road. Truck B weighs 17.8 kN and is connected with an inextensible cable to truck A. By operating a winch b, truck B approaches truck A with a constant acceleration of .3 m/sec.² If at time $t = 0$ both trucks have a speed of 10 m/sec, what are their speeds at time $t = 15$ sec?

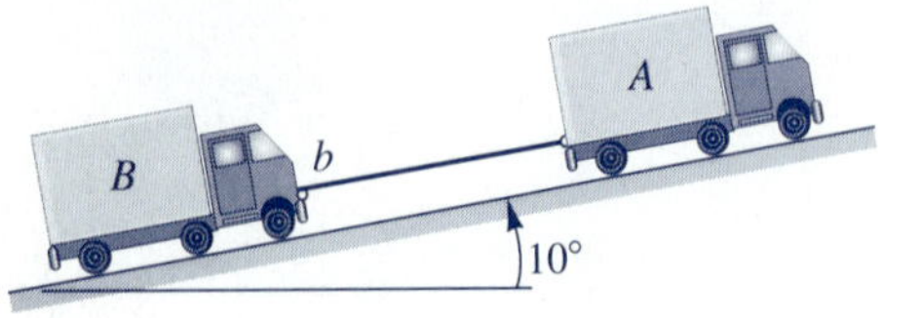

Figure P.14.126.

14.127. Compute the angular momentum about O of a uniform rod, of length $L = 3$ m and mass per unit length m of 7.5 kg/m, at the instant when it is vertical and has an angular speed ω of 3 rad/sec.

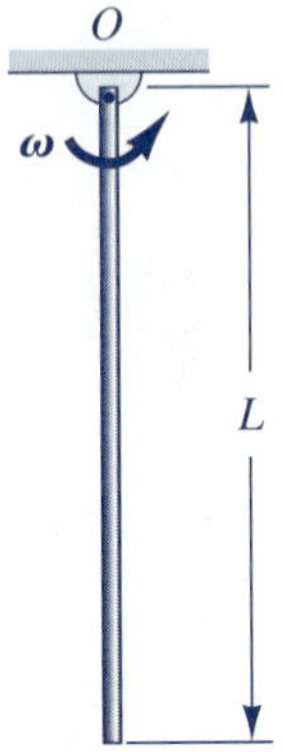

Figure P.14.127.

14.128. A wheel consisting of a thin rim and four thin spokes is shown rotating about its axis at a speed ω of 2 rad/sec. The radius of the wheel R is 2 ft and the weight per unit length of rim and spoke is 2 lb/ft. What is the moment of momentum of the wheel about O? What is the total linear momentum?

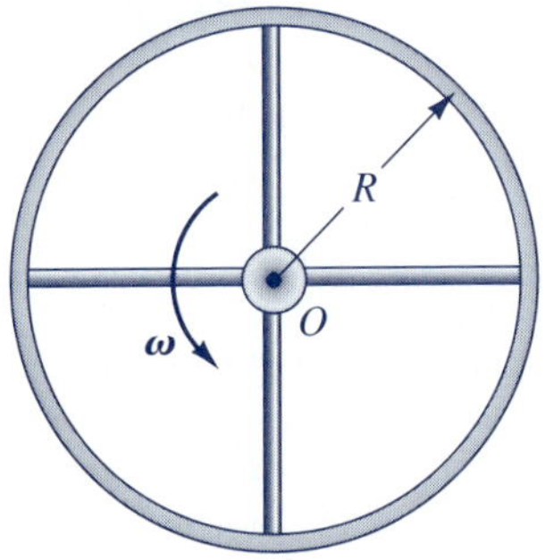

Figure P.14.128.

14.129. Two uniform cylinders A and B are connected as shown. The density of the cylinders is 10,000 kg/m,³ and the system is rotating at a speed ω of 10 rad/sec about its geometric axis. What is the angular momentum of the body?

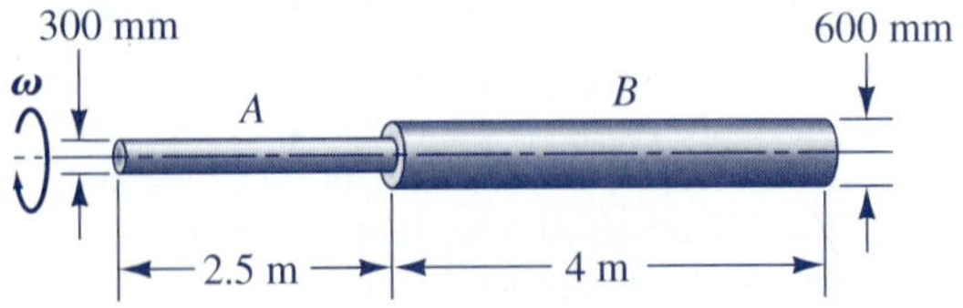

Figure P.14.129.

14.130. A closed container is full of water. By rotating the container for some time and then suddenly holding the container stationary, we develop a rotational motion of the water, which, you will learn in fluid mechanics, resembles a vortex. If the velocity of the fluid elements is zero in the radial direction and is given as $10/r$ ft/sec in the transverse direction, what is the angular momentum of the water?

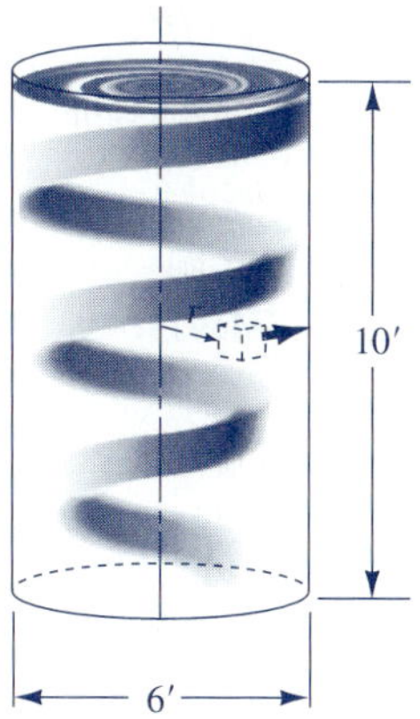

Figure P.14.130.

14.131. Identical thin masses A and B slide on a light horizontal rod that is attached to a freely turning light vertical shaft. When the masses are in the position shown in the diagram, the system rotates at a speed ω of 5 rad/sec. The masses are released suddenly from this position and move out toward the identical springs, which have a spring constant $K = 800$ lb/in. Set up the equation for the compression δ of the spring once all motions of the bodies relative to the rod have damped out. The mass of each body is 10 lbm. Neglect the mass of the rods and coulombic friction. Show that $\delta = .08361$ in. satisfies your equation.

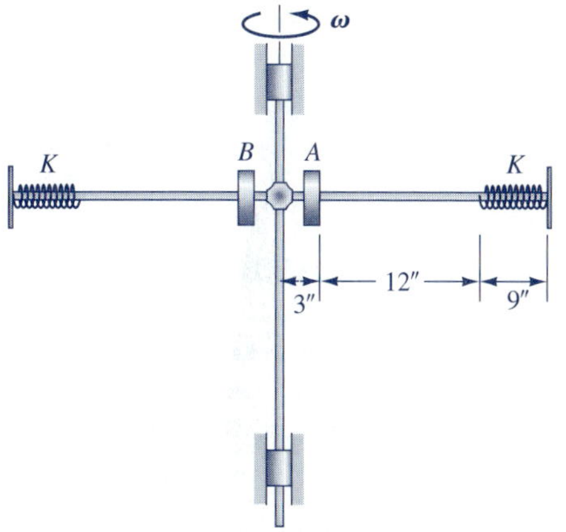

Figure P.14.131.

14.132. A spacecraft has a burnout velocity V_0 of 8,300 m/sec at an elevation of 80 km above the earth's surface. The launch angle α is 15°. What is the maximum elevation h from the earth's surface for the spacecraft?

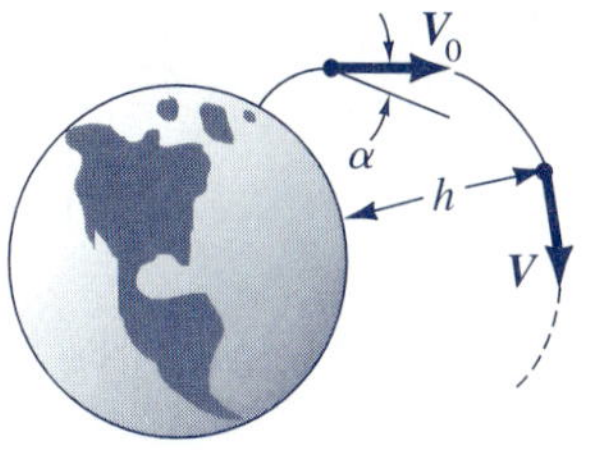

Figure P.14.132.

14.133. A set of particles, each having a mass of 1/2 slug, rotates about axis A–A. The masses are moving out radially at a constant speed of 5 ft/sec at the same time that they are rotating about the A–A, axis. When they are 1 ft from A–A, the angular velocity is 5 rad/sec and at that instant a torque is applied in the direction of motion which varies with time t in seconds as

$$\text{torque} = (6t^2 + 10t) \text{ lb-ft}$$

What is the angular velocity when the masses have moved out radially at constant speed to 2 ft?

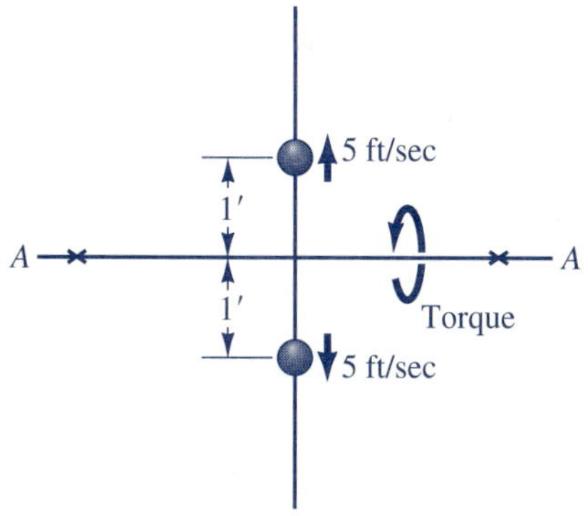

Figure P.14.133.

14.134. A torpedo boat weighing 100,000 lb moves at 40 knots (1 knot = 6,080 ft/hr) away from an engagement. To go even faster, all four 50-caliber machine guns are ordered to fire simultaneously toward the rear. Each weapon fires at a muzzle velocity of 3,000 ft/sec and fires 500 rounds per minute. Each slug weighs 2 oz. How much is the average force on the boat increased by this action? Neglect the rate of change of the total mass of boat.

14.135. A device to be detonated with a small charge is suspended in space [see (a)]. Directly after detonation, four fragments are formed moving away from the point of suspension. The following information is known about these fragments:

$$m_1 = 1 \text{ lbm}$$
$$V_1 = 200\boldsymbol{i} - 100\boldsymbol{j} \text{ ft/sec}$$
$$m_2 = 2 \text{ lbm}$$
$$V_2 = 125\boldsymbol{i} + 180\boldsymbol{j} - 100\boldsymbol{k} \text{ ft/sec}$$
$$m_3 = 1.6 \text{ lbm}$$
$$V_3 = -200\boldsymbol{i} + 150\boldsymbol{j} + 180\boldsymbol{k} \text{ ft/sec}$$
$$m_4 = 3.2 \text{ lbm}$$

What is the velocity V_4?

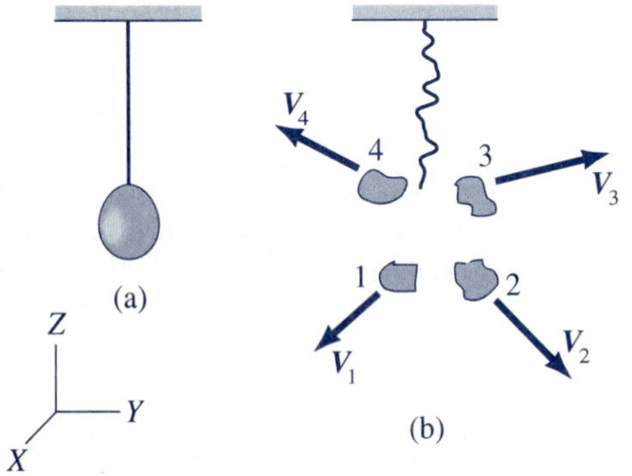

Figure P.14.135.

14.136. A hawk is a predatory bird which often attacks smaller birds in flight. A hawk having a mass of 1.3 kg is swooping down on a sparrow having a mass of 150 g. Just before seizing the sparrow with its claws, the hawk is moving downward with a speed V_H of 20 km/hr. The sparrow is moving horizontally at a speed V_S of 15 km/hr. Directly after seizure, what is the speed of the hawk and its prey? What is the loss in kinetic energy in joules?

14.137. The principal mode of propulsion of an octopus is to take in water through the mouth and then after closing the inlet to eject the water to the rear. If a 5-lb octopus after taking in 1 lb of water is moving at a speed of 3 ft/sec, what is its speed directly after ejecting the water? The water is ejected at an average speed to the rear of 10 ft/sec relative to the initial speed of the octopus. What horsepower is being developed by the octopus in the above action if it occurs in 1 sec?

***14.138.** In the *fission* process in a nuclear reactor, a ^{235}U nucleus first absorbs or captures a neutron [see (a)]. A short time later, the ^{235}U nucleus breaks up into fission products plus neutrons, which may subsequently be captured by other ^{235}U nuclei and maintain a *chain reaction*. Energy is released in each fission. In (b) we have shown the results of a possible fission. The following information is known for this fission:

	Mass No.	Kinetic Energy (MeV)	Direction of $\boldsymbol{V}$
Product *A*	138	*E*	$\boldsymbol{\epsilon}_A = .3\boldsymbol{i} - .2\boldsymbol{j} + .98\boldsymbol{k}$
Product *B*	96	90	$\boldsymbol{\epsilon}_B = l_B\boldsymbol{i} + m_B\boldsymbol{j} + n_B\boldsymbol{k}$
Neutron 1	1	10	$\boldsymbol{\epsilon}_1 = .6\boldsymbol{i} + .8\boldsymbol{j}$
Neutron 2	1	10	$\boldsymbol{\epsilon}_2 = .4\boldsymbol{i} - .6\boldsymbol{j} - .693\boldsymbol{k}$

What is the energy *E* of product *A* in MeV and what is the vector $\boldsymbol{\epsilon}_B$ for the velocity of product *B*? Assume that before fission the nucleus of ^{235}U plus captured neutrons is stationary: [*Hint:* You do not have to actually convert MeV to joules or atomic number to kilograms to carry out the problem.]

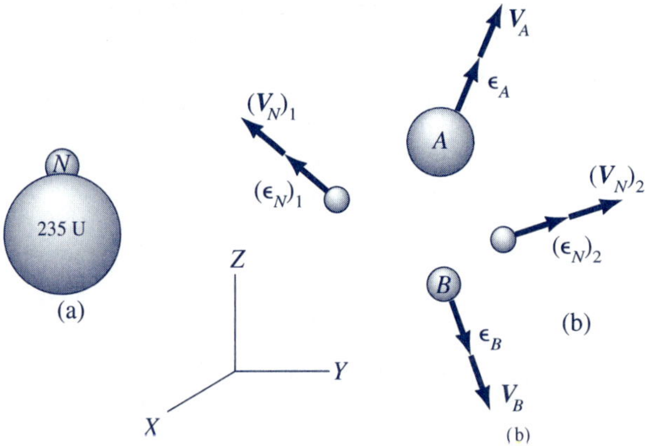

Figure P.14.138.

CHAPTER 15

Kinematics of Rigid Bodies: Relative Motion

15.1 Introduction

In Chapter 11, we studied the kinematics of a particle. During virtually all of this study only a single reference was used. However, at the end of that chapter, we briefly introduced the use of two references—for the case of *simple relative motion* involving two references *translating* with respect to each other.

One of the things we shall do in this chapter is to generalize the formulations for multireference analysis. There are two reasons for doing this. First, we shall be able to analyze complicated motions in a more simple systematic way by using several references. Second, the motion of a particle is often known relative to a moving body (such as an airplane), to which we can fix a reference *xyz*, while the motion of the plane (and hence *xyz*) is known relative to an *inertial reference XYZ* (such as the ground). Now **Newton's law** in the form $\boldsymbol{F} = m\boldsymbol{a}$, is valid *only* for an inertial reference. Hence, to use **Newton's law** for the particle we must express the acceleration of the particle relative to the inertial reference directly. Accordingly, for practical reasons we must become involved in multireference systems.

A reference is a rigid body, and, before we can set forth multireference considerations, we must first study the kinematics of a rigid body. In so doing, we will also set the stage for our main effort in the remaining portion of the text involving the dynamics of rigid bodies.

15.2 Translation and Rotation of Rigid Bodies

For purposes of dynamics, a rigid body is considered to be composed of a continuous distribution of particles having fixed distances between each other. We shall profitably define once again two simple types of motion of a rigid body:

Translation. As pointed out in Chapter 11, if a body moves so that all the particles have at time t the same velocity relative to some reference, the body is said to be in *translation* relative to this reference at this time. The velocity of a translating body can vary with time and so can be represented as $\mathbf{V}(t)$. Accordingly, translational motion does not necessarily mean motion along a straight line. For example, the body shown in Fig. 15.1 is in translation over the interval indicated because at each instant, each particle in the body has a common velocity. A characteristic of translational motion is that a straight line between two points of the body such as ab in Fig. 15.1 always retains an orientation parallel to its *original* direction during the motion.

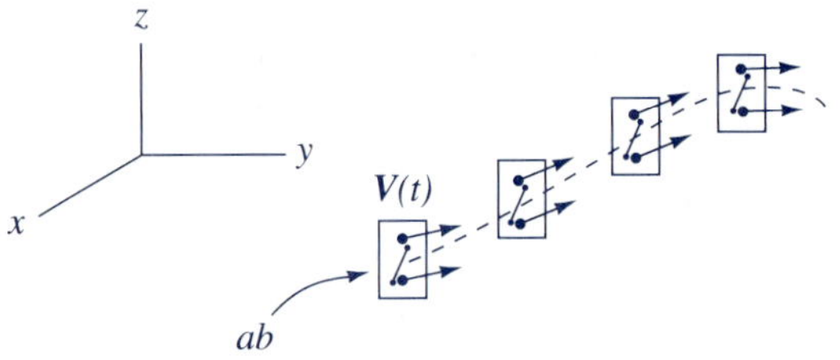

Figure 15.1. Translation of a body.

Rotation. If a rigid body moves so that along some straight line all the particles of the body, or a hypothetical extension of the body, have zero velocity relative to some reference, the body is said to be in *rotation* relative to this reference. The line of stationary particles is called the *axis of rotation*.

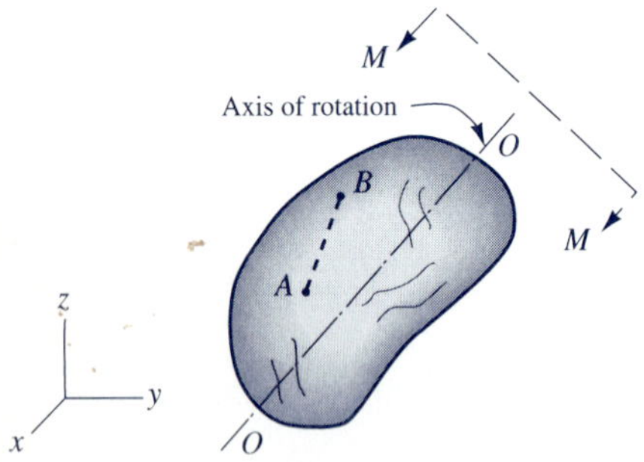

Figure 15.2. Rotation of a body.

We shall now consider how we measure the rotation of a body. A single revolution is defined as the amount of rotation in either a clockwise or a counterclockwise direction about the axis of rotation that brings the body back to its original position. Partial revolutions can conveniently be measured by observing *any* line segment such as AB in the body (Fig. 15.2) from a viewpoint M-M directed along the axis of rotation. In Fig. 15.3, we have shown this view of AB at the beginning of the partial rotation as seen along the axis of rotation, as well as the view $A'B'$ at the end of the partial rotation. The angle β that these lines form will be the same for the initial and final

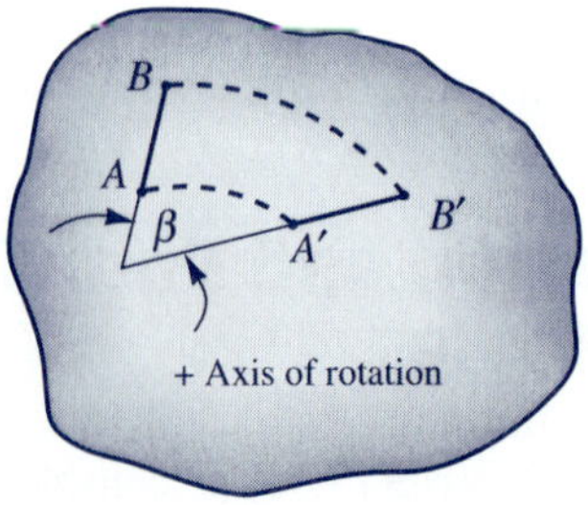

Figure 15.3. Measure of a partial rotation.

projections viewed along the axis of rotation of *any* line segment so examined in the partial rotation of the rigid body. Accordingly, the angle β so formed during a partial rotation is the measure of rotation.

In Chapter 1, we pointed out that finite rotations, although they have a magnitude and a direction along the axis of rotation, are not vectors. The superposition of rotations is not commutative, and therefore rotations do not add according to the parallelogram law, which, you will recall, is a requirement of all vector quantities. However, we can show (see Appendix IV) that as rotations become *infinitesimal*, they satisfy in the limit the commutative law of addition, so that infinitesimal rotations $d\beta$ are vector quantities. Therefore, the *angular velocity* is a vector quantity having a magnitude $d\beta/dt$ with an orientation parallel to the axis of rotation and a sense in accordance with the right-hand-screw rule. We shall employ $\boldsymbol{\omega}$ to represent the angular velocity vector. Note that this definition does not prescribe the line of action of this vector, for the line of action may be considered at positions other than the axis of rotation. The line of action depends on the situation at hand (as will be discussed in later sections).

15.3 Chasles' Theorem

We have just considered two simple motions of a body, translation and rotation. We shall now demonstrate that at each instant, the motion of any rigid body can be thought of as the superposition of both a translational motion and a rotational motion.

Consider for simplicity a body moving in a plane. Positions of the body are shown tinted at times t and $(t + \Delta t)$ in Fig. 15.4. Let us select any point B of the body. Imagine that the body is displaced without rotation from its position at time t to the position at time $(t + \Delta t)$ so that point B reaches its correct final position B'. The displacement vector for this translation is shown at $\Delta \boldsymbol{R}_B$. To reach the correct orientation for $(t + \Delta t)$, we must now rotate the body an angle $\Delta\phi$ about an axis of rotation which is normal to the plane and which passes through point B'.

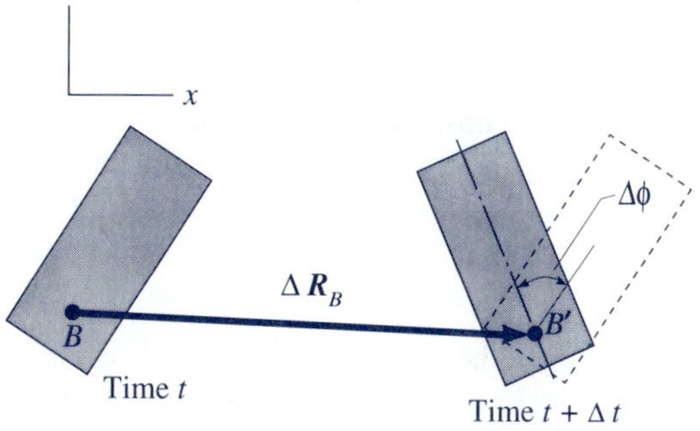

Figure 15.4. Translation and rotation of a rigid body.

What changes would occur had we chosen some other point C for such a procedure? Consider Fig. 15.5, where we have included an alternative procedure by translating the body so that point C reaches the correct final position C'. Next, we must rotate the body an amount $\Delta\phi$ about an axis of rotation which is normal to the plane and which passes through C' in order to get to the final orientation of the body. Thus, we have indicated two routes. We conclude from the diagram that the displacement $\Delta \boldsymbol{R}_C$ differs from $\Delta \boldsymbol{R}_B$, but there is no difference in the amount of rotation $\Delta\phi$. Thus, in general, $\Delta \boldsymbol{R}$ *and the axis of rotation will depend on the point chosen, while the amount of rotation* $\Delta\phi$ *will be the same for all such points.*

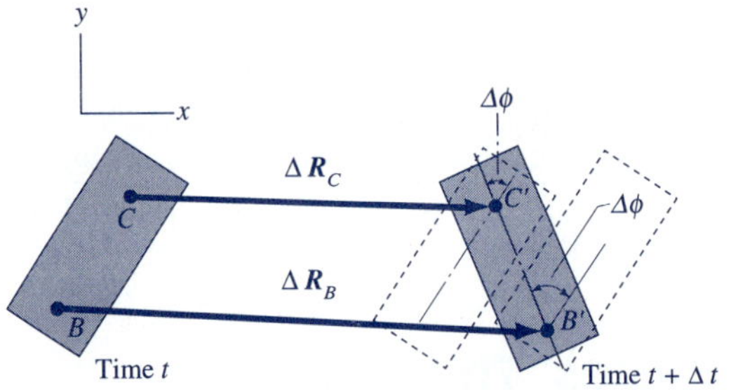

Figure 15.5. Translation and rotation of a rigid body using points B and C.

Consider now the ratios $\Delta \boldsymbol{R}/\Delta t$ and $\Delta\phi/\Delta t$. These quantities can be regarded as an average translational velocity and an average rotational speed, respectively, of the body, which we could superpose to get from the initial position to the final position in the time Δt. Thus, $\Delta \boldsymbol{R}/\Delta t$ and $\Delta\phi/\Delta t$ represent an average measure of the motion during the time interval Δt. *If we go to the limit by letting* $\Delta t \to 0$, *we have instantaneous translational and angular velocities which, when superposed, give the instantaneous motion of the body.* The displacement vector of the chosen point B in the previous discussion represents the translation of the body during the time Δt. Furthermore, the chosen point B undergoes no other motion during Δt other than that occurring during translation. Thus, we can conclude that, in the limit, the *translational velocity* used for the body corresponds to the *actual instantaneous* velocity of the chosen point B at time t. The angular velocity $\boldsymbol{\omega}$ to be used in the movement of the body, as described above, is the same vector for *all* points B chosen. Accordingly, $\boldsymbol{\omega}$ is the *instantaneous angular* velocity of the body.

We have thus far considered the movement of the body along a plane surface. The same conclusions can be reached for the general motion of an arbitrary rigid body in space. We can then make the following statements for the description of the general motion of a rigid body relative to some reference at time t These statements comprise **Chasles' theorem.**

1. Select any point B in the body. Assume that all particles of the body have at the time t a velocity equal to $\boldsymbol{V}_B$, the actual velocity of the point B.
2. Superpose a pure rotational velocity $\boldsymbol{\omega}$ about an axis of rotation going through point B.

With $\boldsymbol{V}_B$ and $\boldsymbol{\omega}$, the actual instantaneous motion of the body is determined, and $\boldsymbol{\omega}$ will be the same for all points B which might be chosen. Thus, only the translational velocity and the axis of rotation change when different points B are chosen. However, clearly understand that the *actual instantaneous axis of rotation* at time t is the one going through those points of the body having zero velocity at time t.

15.4 Derivative of a Vector Fixed in a Moving Reference

Two references XYZ and xyz move arbitrarily relative to each other in Fig. 15.6. Assume we are observing xyz from XYZ. Since a reference is a rigid system, we can apply **Chasles' theorem** to reference xyz. Thus, to fully describe the motion of xyz relative to XYZ, we choose the origin O, and we superpose a translation velocity $\dot{\boldsymbol{R}}$, equal to the velocity of O, onto a rotational velocity $\boldsymbol{\omega}$ with an axis of rotation through O.

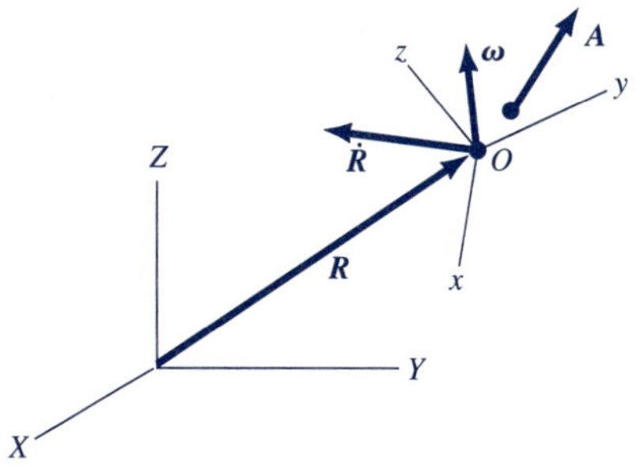

Figure 15.6. Vector $\boldsymbol{A}$ fixed in xyz moving relative to XYZ.

Now suppose that we have a vector $\boldsymbol{A}$ of *fixed length* and of *fixed orientation* as seen from reference xyz. We say that such a vector is "fixed" in reference xyz. Clearly, the time rate of change of $\boldsymbol{A}$ as seen from reference xyz must be zero. We can express this statement mathematically as

$$\left(\frac{d\boldsymbol{A}}{dt}\right)_{xyz} = \boldsymbol{0}$$

However, as seen from XYZ, the time rate of change $\boldsymbol{A}$ will *not* necessarily be zero. To evaluate $(d\boldsymbol{A}/dt)_{XYZ}$, we make use of **Chasles' theorem** in the following manner:

1. Consider the *translational* motion $\dot{\boldsymbol{R}}$. This motion does not alter the direction of $\boldsymbol{A}$ as seen from XYZ. Also, the magnitude of $\boldsymbol{A}$ is fixed; thus, vector $\boldsymbol{A}$ cannot change as a result of this motion.[1]
2. We next consider *solely* a pure rotation about a stationary axis collinear with $\boldsymbol{\omega}$ and passing through point O.

[1]The *line of action* of A, however, will change as seen from XYZ. But a change of line of action does not signify a change in the vector, as pointed out in Chapter 1 on the discussion of equality of vectors.

To best observe this rotation, we shall employ at O a *stationary* reference $X'Y'Z'$ positioned so that Z' coincides with the axis of rotation. This reference is shown in Fig. 15.7. Now the vector $\boldsymbol{A}$ is rotating at this instant about

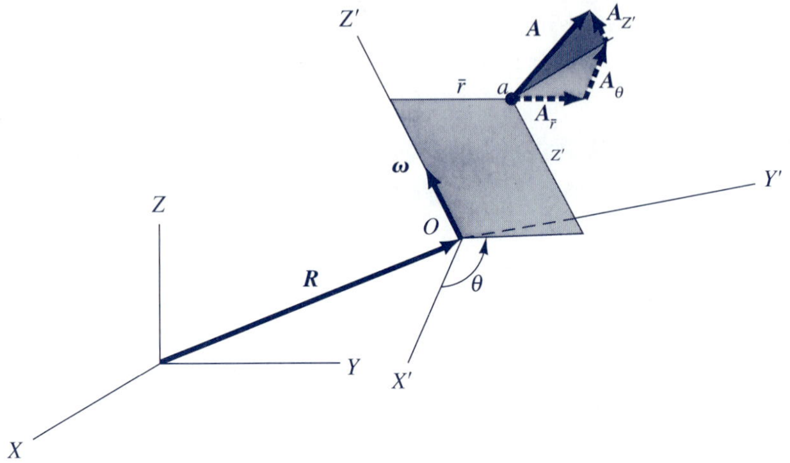

Figure 15.7. Cylindrical components for vector $\boldsymbol{A}$.

the Z' axis. We have shown cylindrical coordinates to the end of $\boldsymbol{A}$ (i.e., at point a); and have shown cylindrical components $A_{\bar{r}}$, A_θ, and $A_{Z'}$. In Fig. 15.8, we have shown point a with unit vectors $\boldsymbol{\epsilon}_{\bar{r}}$, $\boldsymbol{\epsilon}_\theta$, and $\boldsymbol{\epsilon}_{Z'}$, for cylindrical coordinates at this point. We can accordingly express $\boldsymbol{A}$ as

$$\boldsymbol{A} = A_{\bar{r}}\boldsymbol{\epsilon}_{\bar{r}} + A_\theta\boldsymbol{\epsilon}_\theta + A_{Z'}\boldsymbol{\epsilon}_{Z'}$$

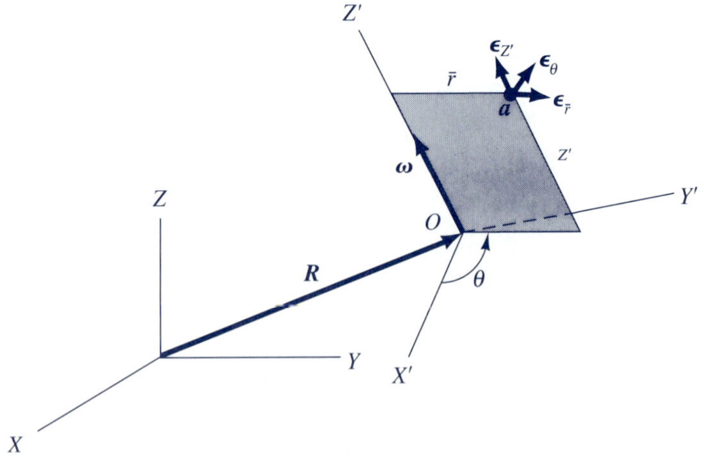

Figure 15.8. Unit vectors for cylindrical coordinates.

Clearly, as $\boldsymbol{A}$ rotates about Z', the values of the cylindrical scalar components of $\boldsymbol{A}$ for $X'Y'Z'$, namely $A_{\bar{r}}$, A_θ, and $A_{Z'}$, do not change. Hence, as seen from

$X'Y'Z'$, $\dot{A}_{\bar{r}} = \dot{A}_\theta = \dot{A}_Z = 0$. Also, noting that $\dot{\boldsymbol{\epsilon}}_{Z'} = \mathbf{0}$, we can say that

$$\left(\frac{dA}{dt}\right)_{X'Y'Z'} = A_{\bar{r}}\left(\frac{d\boldsymbol{\epsilon}_{\bar{r}}}{dt}\right)_{X'Y'Z'} + A_\theta\left(\frac{d\boldsymbol{\epsilon}_\theta}{dt}\right)_{X'Y'Z'}$$

We have already evaluated the time derivatives of the unit vectors for cylindrical coordinates. Hence, using Eqs. 11.28 and 11.32 and noting that $\dot{\theta}$ corresponds to ω, we have

$$\left(\frac{dA}{dt}\right)_{X'Y'Z'} = A_{\bar{r}}\omega\boldsymbol{\epsilon}_\theta - A_\theta\omega\boldsymbol{\epsilon}_{\bar{r}}$$

But the right hand side is simply the cross product of $\boldsymbol{\omega}$ and $\boldsymbol{A}$ as you can see by carrying out the cross product with cylindrical components. Thus,

$$\begin{aligned}\boldsymbol{\omega} \times \boldsymbol{A} &= \omega\boldsymbol{\epsilon}_{Z'} \times \left(A_{\bar{r}}\boldsymbol{\epsilon}_{\bar{r}} + A_\theta\boldsymbol{\epsilon}_\theta + A_{Z'}\boldsymbol{\epsilon}_{Z'}\right)\\ &= \omega A_{\bar{r}}\boldsymbol{\epsilon}_\theta - \omega A_\theta\boldsymbol{\epsilon}_{\bar{r}}\end{aligned}$$

We conclude that

$$\left(\frac{dA}{dt}\right)_{X'Y'Z'} = \boldsymbol{\omega} \times \boldsymbol{A}$$

Since $X'Y'Z'$ is stationary relative to XYZ, we would observe the same time derivative from the latter reference as from the former reference. That is, $(d/dt)_{XYZ} = (d/dt)_{X'Y'Z'}$ and we can conclude that

$$\left(\frac{d\boldsymbol{A}}{dt}\right)_{XYZ} = \boldsymbol{\omega} \times \boldsymbol{A} \qquad (15.1)$$

The foregoing result gives the time rate of change of a vector $\boldsymbol{A}$ fixed in reference xyz moving arbitrarily relative to reference XYZ. From this result, we see that $(d\boldsymbol{A}/dt)_{XYZ}$ depends only on the vectors $\boldsymbol{\omega}$ and $\boldsymbol{A}$ and not on their lines of action. Thus, we can conclude that the time rate of change of $\boldsymbol{A}$ fixed in xyz is not altered when:

1. The vector $\boldsymbol{A}$ is fixed at some other location in xyz provided the vector itself is not changed.
2. The actual axis of rotation of the xyz system is shifted to a new parallel position.

We can differentiate the terms in Eq. 15.1 a second time. We thus get

$$\left(\frac{d^2\boldsymbol{A}}{dt^2}\right)_{XYZ} = \left(\frac{d\boldsymbol{\omega}}{dt}\right)_{XYZ} \times \boldsymbol{A} + \boldsymbol{\omega} \times \left(\frac{d\boldsymbol{A}}{dt}\right)_{XYZ} \qquad (15.2)$$

Using Eq. 15.1 to replace $(d\mathbf{A}/dt)_{XYZ}$ and using $\dot{\boldsymbol{\omega}}$ to replace $(d\boldsymbol{\omega}/dt)_{XYZ}$, since the reference being used for this derivative is clear,[2] we get

$$\left(\frac{d^2\mathbf{A}}{dt^2}\right)_{XYZ} = \dot{\boldsymbol{\omega}} \times \mathbf{A} + \boldsymbol{\omega} \times (\boldsymbol{\omega} \times \mathbf{A}) \tag{15.3}$$

You can compute higher-order derivatives by continuing the process. We suggest that only Eq. 15.1 be remembered and that all subsequent higher-order derivatives be evaluated when needed.

In this discussion thus far, we have considered a vector $\mathbf{A}$ fixed in a reference xyz. But a reference xyz is a rigid system and can be considered a *rigid body*. Thus, the words "*fixed in a reference xyz*" in the previous discussion can be replaced by the words "*fixed in a rigid body*." The angular velocity $\boldsymbol{\omega}$ used in Eq. 15.1 is then the angular velocity of the rigid body in which $\mathbf{A}$ is fixed. We shall illustrate this condition in the following examples, which you are urged to study very carefully. An understanding of these examples is vital for attaining a good working grasp of rigid-body kinematics.

As an aid in carrying out computations involving the triple cross product, we wish to point out that the product

$$\omega_1\mathbf{k} \times (\omega_1\mathbf{k} \times C\mathbf{j}) = -\omega_1^2 C\mathbf{j}$$

That is, the product is minus the product of the scalars and has a direction corresponding to the last unit vector, $\mathbf{j}$. Remembering this will greatly facilitate our computations.[3]

Additionally, consider a situation where the angular velocity of body A relative to body B is given as $\boldsymbol{\omega}_1$, while the angular velocity of body B relative to the ground is $\boldsymbol{\omega}_2$. What is the *total* angular velocity $\boldsymbol{\omega}_T$ of body A relative to the ground? In such a case, we must remember that the angular velocity $\boldsymbol{\omega}_1$ of body A *relative* to body B is actually the *difference* between the total angular velocity $\boldsymbol{\omega}_T$ of body A as seen from the ground and the angular velocity $\boldsymbol{\omega}_2$ of body B as seen from the ground. Thus,

$$\boldsymbol{\omega}_1 = \boldsymbol{\omega}_T - \boldsymbol{\omega}_2$$

Solving for $\boldsymbol{\omega}_T$, we get

$$\boldsymbol{\omega}_T = \boldsymbol{\omega}_1 + \boldsymbol{\omega}_2$$

We see from above that to get the total angular velocity $\boldsymbol{\omega}_T$, we simply add the various relative angular velocities just as we would with any pair of vectors.

[2]When it is clear from the discussion what reference is involved for a time derivative, we shall use the dot to indicate a time derivative.

[3]Of course, if the $\mathbf{j}$ vector were a $\mathbf{k}$ vector, then clearly we would arrive at a null value for the triple vector product.

Example 15.1

A disc C is mounted on a shaft AB in Fig. 15.9. The shaft and disc rotate with a constant angular speed ω_2 of 10 rad/sec relative to the platform to which bearings A and B are attached. Meanwhile, the platform rotates at a constant angular speed ω_1 of 5 rad/sec relative to the ground in a direction parallel to the Z axis of the ground reference XYZ. What is the angular velocity vector $\boldsymbol{\omega}$ for the disc C relative to XYZ? What are $(d\boldsymbol{\omega}/dt)_{XYZ}$ and $(d^2\boldsymbol{\omega}/dt^2)_{XYZ}$?

The total angular velocity $\boldsymbol{\omega}$ of the disc relative to the ground is easily given at all times as follows:

$$\boldsymbol{\omega} = \boldsymbol{\omega}_1 + \boldsymbol{\omega}_2 \text{ rad/sec} \qquad \text{(a)}$$

At the instant of interest as depicted by Fig. 15.9, we have for $\boldsymbol{\omega}$:

$$\boldsymbol{\omega} = 5\boldsymbol{k} + 10\boldsymbol{j} \text{ rad/sec}$$

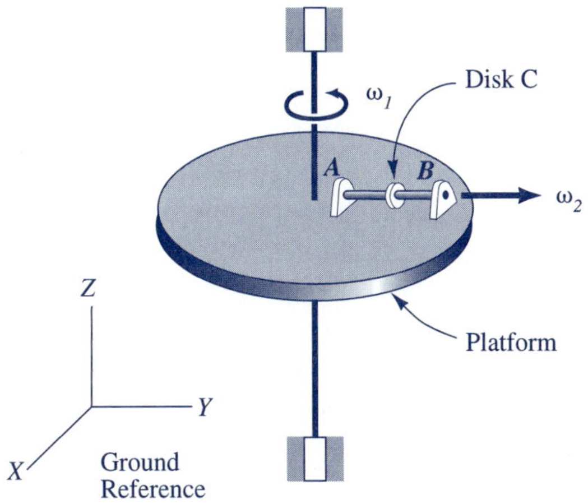

Figure 15.9. Rotating disc on rotating platform.

To get the first time derivative of $\boldsymbol{\omega}$, we go back to Eq. (a), which is always valid and hence can be differentiated with respect to time. Using a dot to represent the time derivative as seen from XYZ, we have

$$\dot{\boldsymbol{\omega}} = \dot{\boldsymbol{\omega}}_1 + \dot{\boldsymbol{\omega}}_2 \qquad \text{(b)}$$

Consider now the vector $\boldsymbol{\omega}_2$. Note that this vector is constrained in direction to be always collinear with the axis AB of the bearings of the shaft. This clearly is a physical requirement. Also, since ω_2 is of constant value, we may think of the vector $\boldsymbol{\omega}_2$ as *fixed* to the platform along AB. Therefore, since the platform has an angular velocity of $\boldsymbol{\omega}_1$ relative to XYZ, we can say:

$$\dot{\boldsymbol{\omega}}_2 = \boldsymbol{\omega}_1 \times \boldsymbol{\omega}_2 \qquad \text{(c)}$$

Example 15.1 (Continued)

As for $\dot{\boldsymbol{\omega}}_1$, namely the other vector in Eq. (b), we note that as seen from *XYZ*, $\boldsymbol{\omega}_1$ is a constant vector and so at all times $\dot{\boldsymbol{\omega}}_1 = \mathbf{0}$. Hence Eq. (b) can be written as follows:

$$\dot{\boldsymbol{\omega}} = \boldsymbol{\omega}_1 \times \boldsymbol{\omega}_2 \tag{d}$$

This equation is valid at all times and so can be differentiated again. At the instant of interest as depicted by Fig. 15.9, we have for $\dot{\boldsymbol{\omega}}$:

$$\dot{\boldsymbol{\omega}} = 5\boldsymbol{k} \times 10\boldsymbol{j} = -50\boldsymbol{i} \text{ rad/sec}^2 \tag{e}$$

To get $\ddot{\boldsymbol{\omega}}$, we now differentiate (d) with respect to time. We have

$$\begin{aligned} \ddot{\boldsymbol{\omega}} &= \dot{\boldsymbol{\omega}}_1 \times \boldsymbol{\omega}_2 + \boldsymbol{\omega}_1 \times \dot{\boldsymbol{\omega}}_2 \\ &= \mathbf{0} + \boldsymbol{\omega}_1 \times (\boldsymbol{\omega}_1 \times \boldsymbol{\omega}_2) \end{aligned} \tag{f}$$

where we have used the fact that $\dot{\boldsymbol{\omega}}_1 = \mathbf{0}$ at all times as well as Eq. (c) for $\dot{\boldsymbol{\omega}}_2$. At the instant of interest, we have

$$\ddot{\boldsymbol{\omega}} = 5\boldsymbol{k} \times (5\boldsymbol{k} \times 10\boldsymbol{j}) = -250\boldsymbol{j} \text{ rad/sec}^3$$

Example 15.2

In Example 15.1, consider a position vector $\boldsymbol{\rho}$ between two points on the rotating disc (see Fig. 15.10). The length of $\boldsymbol{\rho}$ is 100 mm and, at the instant of interest, is in the vertical direction. What are the first and second time derivatives of $\boldsymbol{\rho}$ at this instant as seen from the ground reference?

It should be obvious that the vector $\boldsymbol{\rho}$ is fixed to the disc which has at all times an angular velocity relative to *XYZ* equal to $\boldsymbol{\omega}_1 + \boldsymbol{\omega}_2$. Hence, at all times we can say:

$$\dot{\boldsymbol{\rho}} = (\boldsymbol{\omega}_1 + \boldsymbol{\omega}_2) \times \boldsymbol{\rho} \tag{a}$$

At the instant of interest, we have noting that $\boldsymbol{\rho} = 100\boldsymbol{k}$

$$\dot{\boldsymbol{\rho}} = (5\boldsymbol{k} + 10\boldsymbol{j}) \times 100\boldsymbol{k} = 1{,}000\boldsymbol{i} \text{ mm/sec} \tag{b}$$

To get the second derivative of $\boldsymbol{\rho}$, go back to Eq. (a) and differentiate:

$$\ddot{\boldsymbol{\rho}} = (\dot{\boldsymbol{\omega}}_1 + \dot{\boldsymbol{\omega}}_2) \times \boldsymbol{\rho} + (\boldsymbol{\omega}_1 + \boldsymbol{\omega}_2) \times \dot{\boldsymbol{\rho}}$$

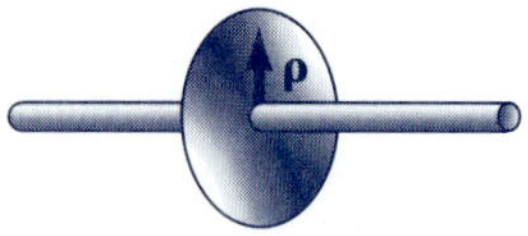

Figure 15.10. Displacement vector $\boldsymbol{\rho}$ in disc.

Example 15.2 (Continued)

Noting that $\dot{\boldsymbol{\omega}}_1 = \mathbf{0}$ at all times and, as discussed in Example 15.1, that $\boldsymbol{\omega}_2$ is fixed in the platform, we can say:

$$\ddot{\boldsymbol{\rho}} = (\mathbf{0} + \boldsymbol{\omega}_1 \times \boldsymbol{\omega}_2) \times \boldsymbol{\rho} + (\boldsymbol{\omega}_1 + \boldsymbol{\omega}_2) \times \dot{\boldsymbol{\rho}} \qquad \text{(c)}$$

At the instant of interest we have, on noting Eq. (b):

$$\ddot{\boldsymbol{\rho}} = (5\boldsymbol{k} \times 10\boldsymbol{j}) \times 100\boldsymbol{k} + (5\boldsymbol{k} + 10\boldsymbol{j}) \times 1{,}000\boldsymbol{i} \text{ mm/sec}^2$$

$$\ddot{\boldsymbol{\rho}} = 10\boldsymbol{j} - 10\boldsymbol{k} \text{ m/sec}^2$$

Although we shall later formally examine the case of the time derivative of vector $\boldsymbol{A}$ as seen from XYZ when $\boldsymbol{A}$ is *not fixed* in a body or a reference xyz, we can handle such cases less formally with what we already know. We illustrate this in the following example.

Example 15.3

For the disc in Fig. 15.9, $\omega_2 = 6$ rad/sec and $\dot{\omega}_2 = 2$ rad/sec^2, both relative to the platform at the instant of interest. At this instant, $\omega_1 = 2$ rad/sec and $\dot{\omega}_1 = -3$ rad/sec^2 for the platform relative to the ground. Find the angular acceleration vector $\dot{\boldsymbol{\omega}}$ for the disc relative to the ground at the instant of interest.

The angular velocity of the disc relative to the ground at all times is

$$\boldsymbol{\omega} = \boldsymbol{\omega}_1 + \boldsymbol{\omega}_2 \qquad \text{(a)}$$

For $\dot{\boldsymbol{\omega}}$, we can then say

$$\dot{\boldsymbol{\omega}} = \dot{\boldsymbol{\omega}}_1 + \dot{\boldsymbol{\omega}}_2 \qquad \text{(b)}$$

It is apparent on inspecting Fig. 15.11 that at all times $\boldsymbol{\omega}_1$ is vertical, and so we can say:

$$\dot{\boldsymbol{\omega}}_1 = \frac{d}{dt}_{XYZ}(\omega_1\boldsymbol{k}) = \dot{\omega}_1\boldsymbol{k} \qquad \text{(c)}$$

Example 15.3 (Continued)

However, $\boldsymbol{\omega}_2$ is changing direction and, most importantly, is changing magnitude. Because of the latter, $\boldsymbol{\omega}_2$ cannot be considered fixed in a reference or a rigid body for purposes of computing $\dot{\boldsymbol{\omega}}_2$. To get around this difficulty, we fix a unit vector $\boldsymbol{j}'$ *onto the platform* to be collinear with the centerline of the shaft *AB* as shown in Fig. 15.11. We know the angular velocity of this unit vector; it is $\boldsymbol{\omega}_1$ at all times. We can then express $\boldsymbol{\omega}_2$ in the following manner, which is valid at all times:

$$\boldsymbol{\omega}_2 = \omega_2 \boldsymbol{j}' \qquad \text{(d)}$$

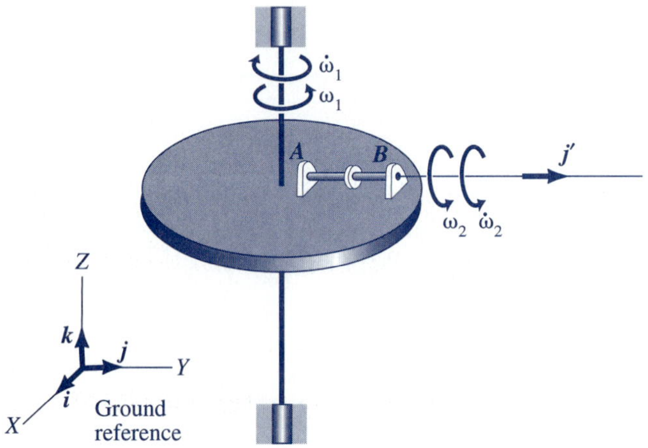

Figure 15.11. Unit vector $\boldsymbol{j}'$ fixed to platform.

We can differentiate the above with respect to time as follows:

$$\dot{\boldsymbol{\omega}}_2 = \dot{\omega}_2 \boldsymbol{j}' + \omega_2 \dot{\boldsymbol{j}}'$$

But $\boldsymbol{j}'$ is *fixed* to the platform which has angular velocity $\boldsymbol{\omega}_1$ relative to *XYZ* at all times. Hence, we have for the above,

$$\dot{\boldsymbol{\omega}}_2 = \dot{\omega}_2 \boldsymbol{j}' + \omega_2 (\boldsymbol{\omega}_1 \times \boldsymbol{j}') \qquad \text{(e)}$$

Thus, Eq. (b) then can be given as

$$\dot{\boldsymbol{\omega}} = \dot{\omega}_1 \boldsymbol{k} + \dot{\omega}_2 \boldsymbol{j}' + \omega_2 (\boldsymbol{\omega}_1 \times \boldsymbol{j}')$$

This expression is valid at all times and could be differentiated again. At the instant of interest, we can say, noting that $\boldsymbol{j}' = \boldsymbol{j}$ at this instant,

$$\dot{\boldsymbol{\omega}} = -3\boldsymbol{k} + 2\boldsymbol{j} + 6(2\boldsymbol{k} \times \boldsymbol{j})$$

$$\dot{\boldsymbol{\omega}} = -12\boldsymbol{i} + 2\boldsymbol{j} - 3\boldsymbol{k} \text{ rad/sec}^2$$

PROBLEMS

15.1. Is the motion of the cabin of a ferris wheel rotational or translational if the wheel moves at uniform speed and the occupants cause no disturbances? Why?

15.2. A cylinder rolls without slipping down an inclined surface. What is the actual axis of rotation at any instant? Why? How is this axis moving?

15.3. A reference xyz is moving such that the origin O has at time t a velocity relative to reference XYZ given as

$$V_0 = 6\boldsymbol{i} + 12\boldsymbol{j} + 13\boldsymbol{k} \text{ ft/sec}$$

The xyz reference has an angular velocity $\boldsymbol{\omega}$ relative to XYZ at time t given as

$$\boldsymbol{\omega} = 10\boldsymbol{i} + 12\boldsymbol{j} + 2\boldsymbol{k} \text{ rad/sec}$$

What is the time rate of change relative to XYZ of a directed line segment $\boldsymbol{\rho}$ going from position (3,2,–5) to (–2,4,6) in xyz? What is the time rate of change relative to XYZ of position vectors $\boldsymbol{i}'$ and $\boldsymbol{k}'$?

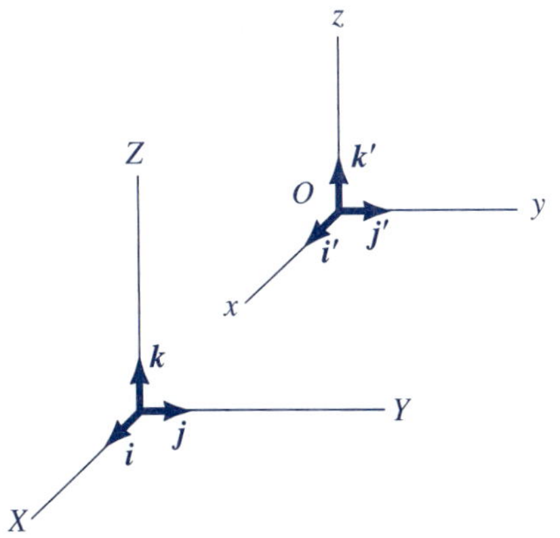

Figure P.15.3.

15.4. A reference xyz is moving relative to XYZ with a velocity of the origin given at time t as

$$V_0 = 6\boldsymbol{i} + 4\boldsymbol{j} + 6\boldsymbol{k} \text{ m/sec}$$

The angular velocity of reference xyz relative to XYZ is

$$\boldsymbol{\omega} = 3\boldsymbol{i} + 14\boldsymbol{j} + 2\boldsymbol{k} \text{ rad/sec}$$

What is the time rate of change as seen from XYZ of a directed line segment $\boldsymbol{\rho}_{1,2}$ in xyz going from position 1 to position 2 where the position vectors in xyz for these points are, respectively,

$$\boldsymbol{\rho}_1 = 2\boldsymbol{i}' + 3\boldsymbol{j}' \text{ m}$$
$$\boldsymbol{\rho}_2 = 3\boldsymbol{i}' - 4\boldsymbol{j}' + 2\boldsymbol{k}' \text{ m}$$

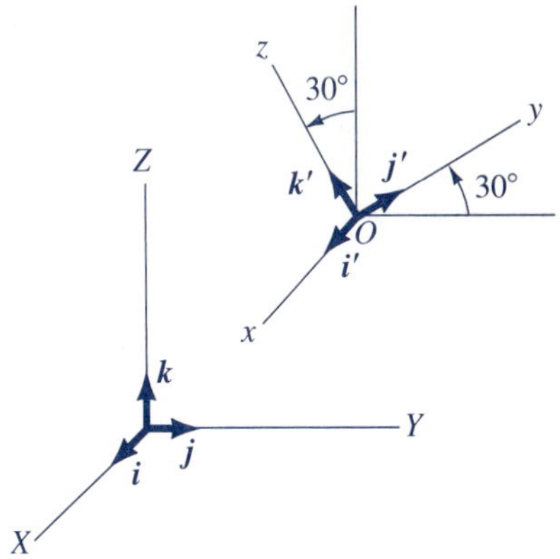

Figure P.15.4.

15.5. Find the second derivatives as seen from XYZ of the vector $\boldsymbol{\rho}$ and the unit vector $\boldsymbol{i}'$ specified in Problem 15.3. The angular acceleration of xyz relative to XYZ at the instant of interest is

$$\dot{\boldsymbol{\omega}} = 5\boldsymbol{i} + 2\boldsymbol{j} + 3\boldsymbol{k} \text{ rad/sec}^2$$

15.6. Find the second derivative as seen from XYZ of the vector $\boldsymbol{\rho}_{1,2}$ specified in Problem 15.4. Take the angular acceleration of xyz relative to XYZ at the instant of interest as

$$\dot{\boldsymbol{\omega}} = 15\boldsymbol{i} - 2\boldsymbol{k} \text{ rad/sec}^2$$

15.7. A platform is rotating with a constant speed ω_1 of 10 rad/sec relative to the ground. A shaft is mounted on the platform and rotates relative to the platform at a speed ω_2 of 5 rad/sec. What is the angular velocity of the shaft relative to the ground? What are the first and second time derivatives of the angular velocity of the shaft relative to the ground?

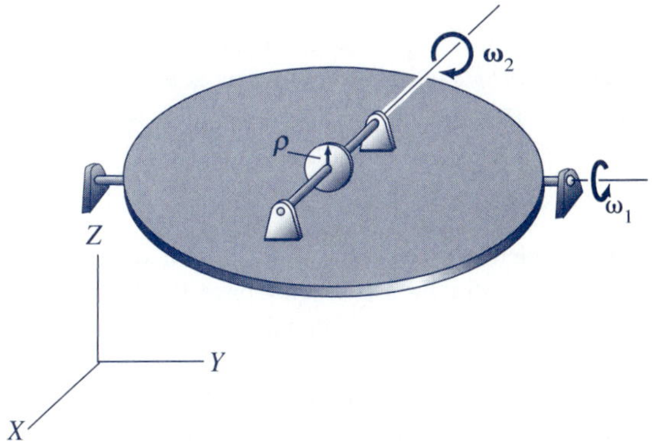

Figure P.15.7.

15.8. In Problem 15.7, what are the first and second time derivatives of a directed line segment $\boldsymbol{\rho}$ in the disc at the instant that the system has the geometry shown? The vector $\boldsymbol{\rho}$ is of length 10 mm.

15.9. A tank is maneuvering its gun into position. At the instant of interest, the turret A is rotating at an angular speed $\dot{\theta}$ of 2 rad/sec relative to the tank and is in position $\theta = 20°$. Also, at this instant, the gun is rotating at an angular speed $\dot{\phi}$ of 1 rad/sec relative to the turret and forms an angle $\phi = 30°$ with the horizontal plane. What are $\boldsymbol{\omega}$, $\dot{\boldsymbol{\omega}}$, and $\ddot{\boldsymbol{\omega}}$ of the gun relative to the ground?

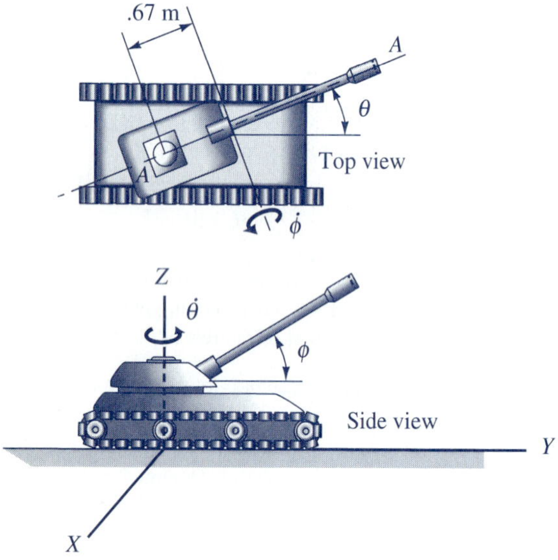

Figure P.15.9.

15.10. In Problem 15.9, determine $\boldsymbol{\omega}$ and $\dot{\boldsymbol{\omega}}$ assuming that the tank is also rotating about the vertical axis at a rate of .2 rad/sec relative to the ground in a clockwise direction as viewed from above.

15.11. A particle is made to move at constant speed V equal to 10 m/sec along a straight groove on a plate B. The plate rotates at a constant angular speed ω_2 equal to 3 rad/sec relative to a platform C while the platform rotates with a constant angular speed ω_1 of 5 rad/sec relative to the ground reference XYZ. Find the first and second derivatives of V as seen from the ground reference.

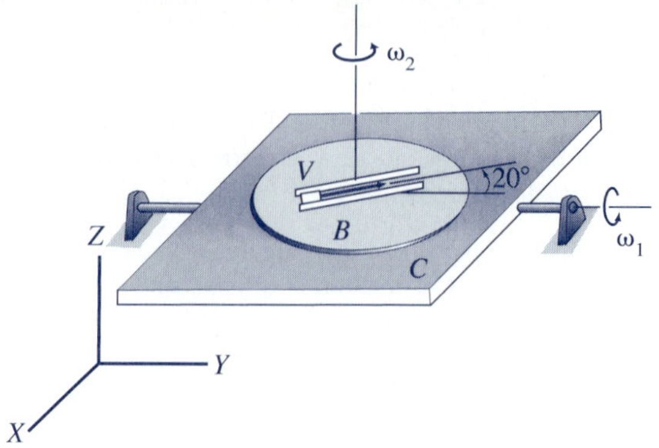

Figure P.15.11.

15.12. A jet fighter plane has just taken off and is retracting its landing gear. At the end of its run on the ground, the plane is moving at a speed of 200 km/hr. If the diameter of the tires is 460 mm and if we neglect the loss of angular speed of the wheels due to wind friction after the plane is in the air, what is the angular speed $\boldsymbol{\omega}$ and the angular acceleration $\dot{\boldsymbol{\omega}}$ of the left wheel (under the wing) at the instant shown in the diagram? Take $\omega_2 = .4$ rad/sec and $\dot{\omega}_2$ is .2 rad/sec^2 at the instant of interest.

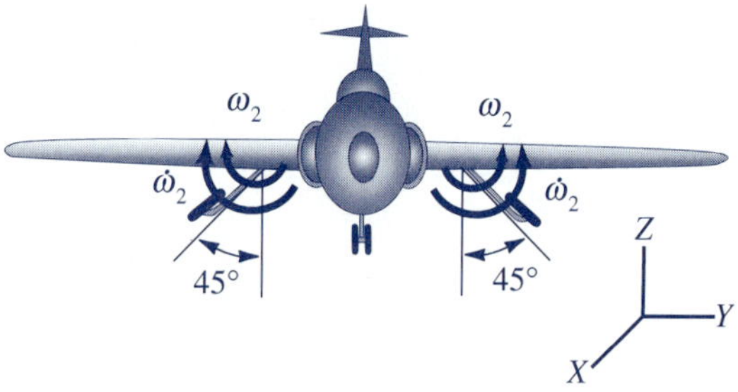

Figure P.15.12.

15.13. A truck is carrying a cockpit for a worker who repairs overhead road fixtures. At the instant shown in the diagram, the base D is rotating with constant speed ω_2 of 1 rad/sec relative to the truck. Arm AB is rotating at constant angular speed ω_1 of 2 rad/sec relative to DA. Cockpit C is rotating relative to AB so as to always keep the man upright. What are $\boldsymbol{\omega}$, $\dot{\boldsymbol{\omega}}$, and $\ddot{\boldsymbol{\omega}}$ of arm AB relative to the ground at the instant of interest? The truck is stationary.

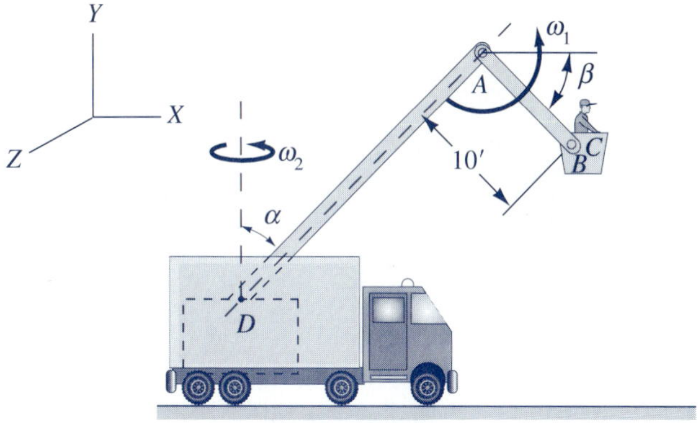

Figure P.15.13.

15.14. An electric motor M is mounted on a plate A which is welded to a shaft D. The motor has a constant angular speed ω_2 relative to plate A of 1,750 rpm. Plate A at the instant of interest is in a vertical position as shown and is rotating with an angular speed ω_1 equal to 100 rpm and a rate of change of angular speed $\dot{\omega}_1$ equal to 30 rpm/sec—all relative to the ground. The normal projection of the centerline of the motor shaft onto the plate A is at an angle of 45° with the edge of the plate FE. Compute the first and second time derivatives of $\boldsymbol{\omega}$, the angular velocity of the motor, as seen from the ground.

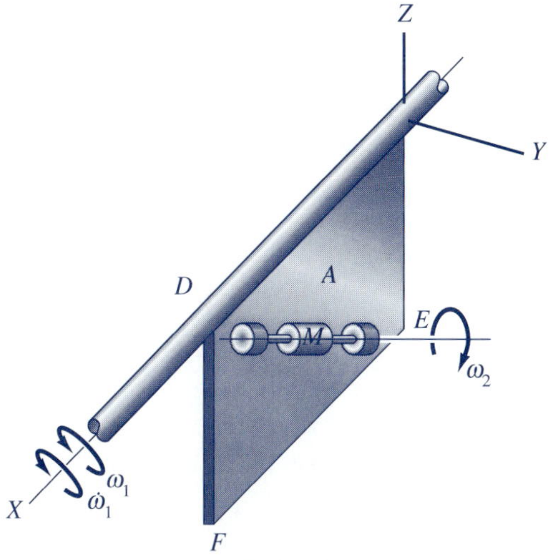

Figure P.15.14.

15.15. A racing car is moving at a constant speed of 200 mi/hr when the driver turns his front wheels at an increasing rate, $\dot{\omega}_1$, of .02 rad/sec^2. If ω_1 = .0168 rad/sec at the instant of interest, what are $\boldsymbol{\omega}$ and $\dot{\boldsymbol{\omega}}$ of the front wheels at this instant? The diameter of the tires is 30 in.

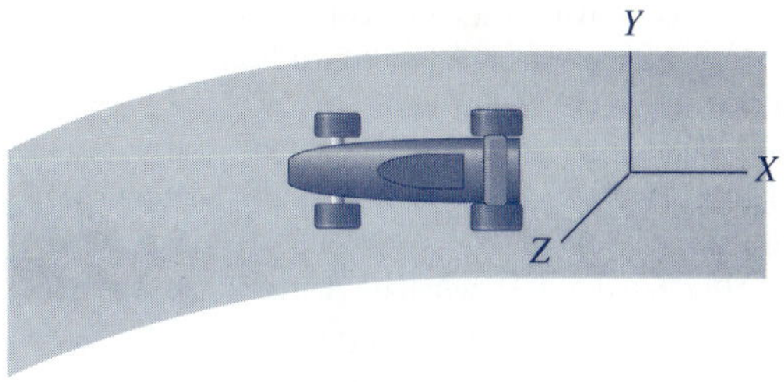

Figure P.15.15.

15.16. A cone is rolling without slipping such that its centerline rotates at the rate ω_1 of 5 revolutions per second about the $\mathbf{Z}$ axis. What is the angular velocity $\boldsymbol{\omega}$ of the body relative to the ground? What is the angular acceleration vector for the body?

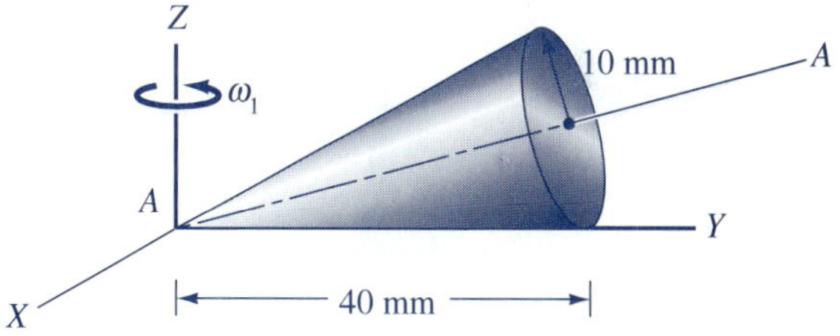

Figure P.15.16.

15.17. A small cone A is rolling without slipping inside a large conical cavity B. What is the angular velocity $\boldsymbol{\omega}$ of cone A relative to the large cone cavity B if the centerline of A undergoes an angular speed ω_1 of 5 rotations per second about the Z axis?

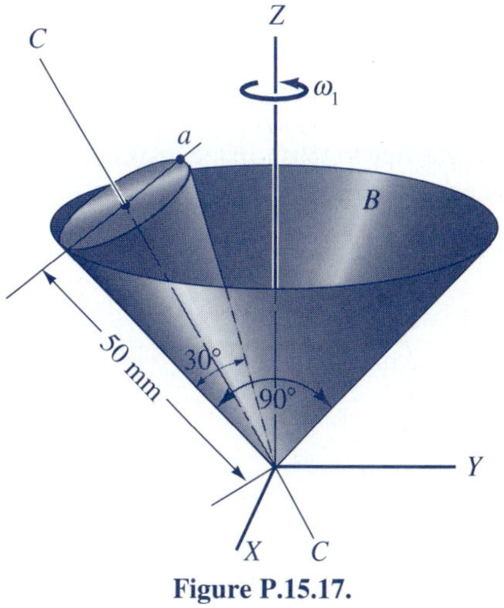

Figure P.15.17.

15.18. An amusement park ride consists of a stationary vertical tower with arms that can swing outward from the tower and at the same time can rotate about the tower. At the ends of the arms, cockpits containing passengers can rotate relative to the arms. Consider the case where cockpit A rotates at angular speed ω_2 relative to arm BC, which rotates at angular speed ω_1 relative to the tower. If θ is fixed at 90°, what are the total angular velocity and the angular acceleration of the cockpit relative to the ground? Use $\omega_1 = .2$ rad/sec and $\omega_2 = .6$ rad/sec.

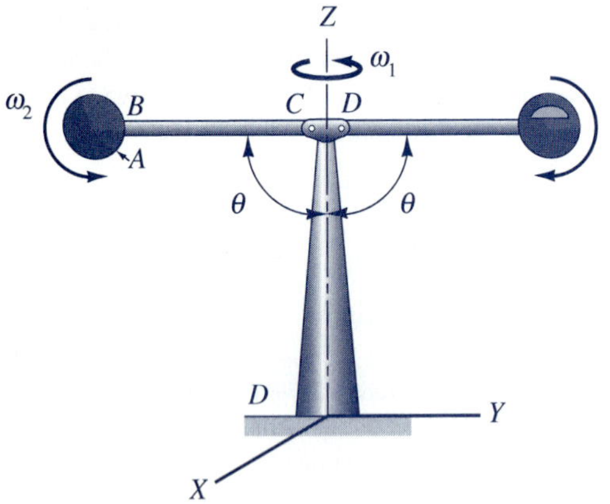

Figure P.15.18.

15.19. In Problem 15.18, find $\dot{\boldsymbol{\omega}}$ of the cockpit for the case where $\dot{\theta} = \omega_3 = .8$ rad/sec at the instant that $\theta = 90°$.

15.20. Mass A is connected to an inextensible wire. Supports C and D are moving as shown.

(a) What is the velocity vector of mass A?

(b) If cylinder G is free to rotate and there is no slipping, what is its angular velocity?

The following data apply:

$h = 2$ m	$(V_x)_2 = .24$ m/s
$L = 3$ m	$(V_y)_2 = .21$ m/s
$l = 2$ m	$R = 1$ m
$(V_x)_1 = .5$ m/s	$\alpha = 45°$
$(V_y)_1 = .6$ m/s	

The last four problems of this set are designed for those students who have studied Example 15.3.

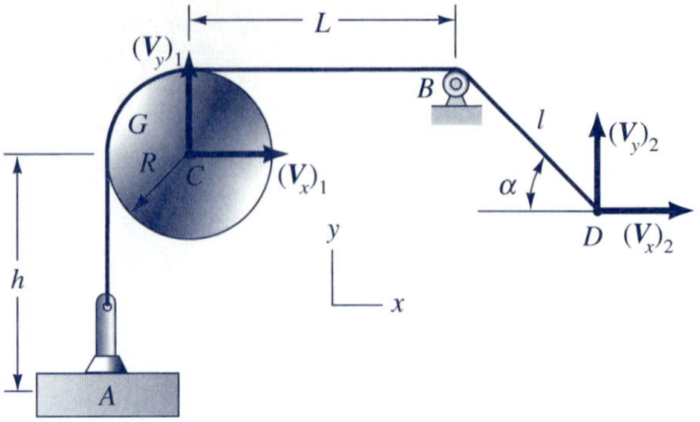

Figure P.15.20.

15.21. In Problem 15.18, find $\dot{\boldsymbol{\omega}}$ of the cockpit A for the case where $\dot{\omega}_1 = .2$ rad/sec² and $\dot{\omega}_2 = .3$ rad/sec².

15.22. In Problem 15.13, find $\dot{\boldsymbol{\omega}}$ of beam AB relative to the ground if at the instant shown the following data apply:

$$\omega_1 = .3 \text{ rad/sec}$$
$$\dot{\omega}_1 = .2 \text{ rad/sec}^2$$
$$\omega_2 = .6 \text{ rad/sec}$$
$$\dot{\omega}_2 = -.1 \text{ rad/sec}^2$$

15.23. In Problem 15.9, find the angular acceleration vector $\dot{\boldsymbol{\omega}}$ for the gun barrel, if, for the instant shown in the diagram, the following data apply:

$\dot{\phi} = .30$ rad/sec,	$\theta = 20°$
$\ddot{\phi} = .26$ rad/sec²,	$\phi = 30°$
$\dot{\theta} = .17$ rad/sec	
$\ddot{\theta} = -.34$ rad/sec²	

15.24. In Problem 15.11, find $\dot{\mathbf{V}}$ if at the instant shown in the diagram:

$$\omega_1 = 5 \text{ rad/sec}$$
$$\dot{\omega}_1 = 10 \text{ rad/sec}^2$$
$$\omega_2 = 2 \text{ rad/sec}$$
$$\dot{\omega}_2 = 3 \text{ rad/sec}^2$$
$$V = 10 \text{ m/sec}$$
$$\dot{V} = 5 \text{ m/sec}^2$$

15.5 Applications of the Fixed-Vector Concept

In Section 15.4, we considered the time derivative, as seen from a reference *XYZ*, of a vector $\boldsymbol{A}$ fixed in a rigid body or fixed in reference *xyz*. The result was a simple formula:

$$\dot{\boldsymbol{A}} = \boldsymbol{\omega} \times \boldsymbol{A}$$

where $\boldsymbol{\omega}$ is the angular velocity relative to *XYZ* of the body or the reference in which $\boldsymbol{A}$ is fixed. In this section, we shall use the preceding formula for a *vector connecting two points a and b in a rigid body* (see Fig. 15.12). This vector, which we denote as $\boldsymbol{\rho}_{ab}$, clearly is fixed in the rigid body. The body in accordance with **Chasles' theorem** has a velocity $\dot{\boldsymbol{R}}$ relative to *XYZ* corresponding to some point *O* in the body plus an angular velocity $\boldsymbol{\omega}$ relative to *XYZ* with the axis of rotation going through *O*. We can then say on observing from *XYZ*:

$$\dot{\boldsymbol{\rho}}_{ab} = \boldsymbol{\omega} \times \boldsymbol{\rho}_{ab} \tag{15.4}$$

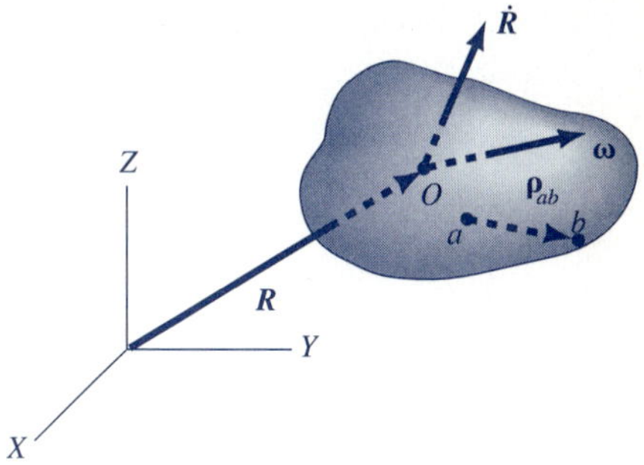

Figure 15.12. $\boldsymbol{\rho}_{ab}$ fixed in rigid body.

Now consider position vectors at *a* and *b* as shown in Fig. 15.13. We can say:

$$\boldsymbol{r}_a + \boldsymbol{\rho}_{ab} = \boldsymbol{r}_b$$

Taking the time derivative as seen from *XYZ*, we have

$$\left(\frac{d\boldsymbol{r}_a}{dt}\right)_{XYZ} + \left(\frac{d\boldsymbol{\rho}_{ab}}{dt}\right)_{XYZ} = \left(\frac{d\boldsymbol{r}_b}{dt}\right)_{XYZ}$$

This equation can be written as

$$\left(\frac{d\boldsymbol{\rho}_{ab}}{dt}\right)_{XYZ} = \boldsymbol{V}_b - \boldsymbol{V}_a \tag{15.5}$$

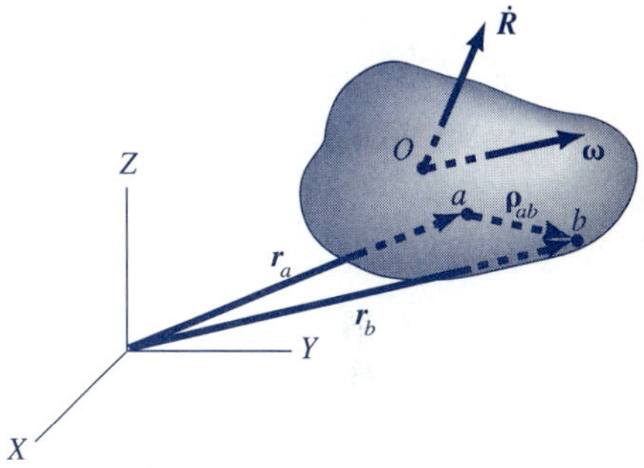

Figure 15.13. Insert position vectors.

Since $(d\boldsymbol{\rho}_{ab}/dt)_{XYZ}$ is the *difference* between the velocity of point *b* and that at point *a* as noted above, we can say that $(d\boldsymbol{\rho}_{ab}/dt)_{XYZ}$ is the velocity of point *b* *relative* to point *a*.[4] Next, using Eq. 15.4 to replace $(d\boldsymbol{\rho}_{ab}/dt)_{XYZ}$, we have, on rearranging terms, a very useful equation:

$$\boldsymbol{V}_b = \boldsymbol{V}_a + \boldsymbol{\omega} \times \boldsymbol{\rho}_{ab} \tag{15.6}$$

In using the foregoing equation, we must be sure that we get the sequence of subscripts correct on $\boldsymbol{\rho}$ since a change in ordering brings about a change in sign (i.e., $\boldsymbol{\rho}_{ab} = -\boldsymbol{\rho}_{ba}$). This equation is a statement of the physically obvious result that *the velocity of particle b of a rigid body as seen from XYZ equals the velocity of any other particle a of this body as seen from XYZ plus the velocity of particle b relative to particle a.*

[4]That is, $(d\boldsymbol{\rho}_{ab}/dt)_{XYZ}$ is the velocity of *b* as seen by an observer translating relative to *XYZ* with point *a*, i.e., as seen by a nonrotating observer moving with *a*.

Differentiating Eq. 15.6 again, we can get a relation involving the acceleration vectors of two points on a rigid body:

$$\boldsymbol{a}_b = \boldsymbol{a}_a + \left(\frac{d\boldsymbol{\omega}}{dt}\right)_{XYZ} \times \boldsymbol{\rho}_{ab} + \boldsymbol{\omega} \times \left(\frac{d\boldsymbol{\rho}_{ab}}{dt}\right)_{XYZ}$$

Hence, we have on using Eq. 15.4 in the last expression

$$\boldsymbol{a}_b = \boldsymbol{a}_a + \dot{\boldsymbol{\omega}} \times \boldsymbol{\rho}_{ab} + \boldsymbol{\omega} \times (\boldsymbol{\omega} \times \boldsymbol{\rho}_{ab}) \tag{15.7}$$

We have thus formulated relations between *the motions of two points of a rigid body as seen from a single reference*. Such relations can be very useful in the study of machine elements.

Before going to the examples, let us now consider the case of a circular cylinder rolling *without slipping* (see Fig. 15.14). The point of contact A of the cylinder with the ground has instantaneously *zero velocity* and hence we have pure instantaneous rotation at any time t about an instantaneous axis of rotation at the line of contact. The velocity of any point B of the cylinder can then easily be found by using Eq. 15.6 for points B and A. Thus:

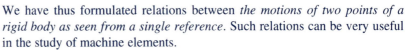

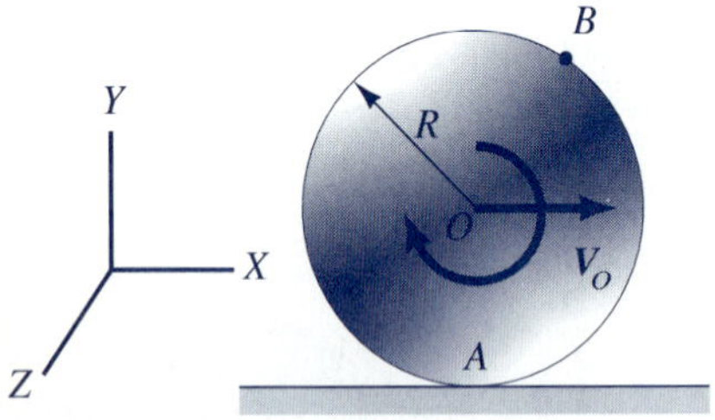

Figure 15.14. Cylinder rolling without slipping on a flat surface.

$$\boldsymbol{V}_B = \boldsymbol{V}_A + \boldsymbol{\omega} \times \boldsymbol{\rho}_{AB}$$

Therefore,

$$\boldsymbol{V}_B = \boldsymbol{0} + \boldsymbol{\omega} \times \boldsymbol{\rho}_{AB} = \boldsymbol{\omega} \times \boldsymbol{\rho}_{AB}$$

From the above equation it is clear that for computing the velocity of any point on the cylinder we can think of the cylinder as *hinged* at the point of contact. In particular for point O, the center of the cylinder, we get from above:

$$\boldsymbol{V}_0 = -\omega R \boldsymbol{i}$$

If the velocity V_0 is known, clearly the angular velocity has a magnitude of V_0/R.

Another way of relating V and ω is to realize that the distance s that O moves must equal the length of circumference coming into contact with the ground. That is, measuring θ from the X axis to the Y axis:

$$s = -R\theta$$

Differentiating we get:

$$V_0 = -R\dot{\theta} = -R\omega$$

thus reproducing the previous result. Differentiating again, we get

$$a_0 = -R\ddot{\theta} = -R\alpha \tag{15.8}$$

relating now the acceleration of O and the angular acceleration α. Clearly, the acceleration vector for O must be parallel to the ground. Again, for computing $\boldsymbol{a}_0$, we have a simple situation.

Next, let us determine the acceleration vector for the *point of contact A* of the cylinder. Thus, we can say for points A and O:

$$\boldsymbol{a}_O = \boldsymbol{a}_A + \dot{\boldsymbol{\omega}} \times \boldsymbol{\rho}_{AO} + \boldsymbol{\omega} \times (\boldsymbol{\omega} \times \boldsymbol{\rho}_{AO})$$

Therefore,

$$-R\ddot{\theta}\boldsymbol{i} = \boldsymbol{a}_A + \ddot{\theta}\boldsymbol{k} \times R\boldsymbol{j} + \dot{\theta}\boldsymbol{k} \times (\dot{\theta}\boldsymbol{k} \times R\boldsymbol{j}) \qquad (15.9)$$

Carrying out the products:

$$-R\ddot{\theta}\boldsymbol{i} = \boldsymbol{a}_A - R\ddot{\theta}\boldsymbol{i} - R\dot{\theta}^2\boldsymbol{j}$$

Therefore, cancelling terms, we get

$$\boldsymbol{a}_A = R\dot{\theta}^2\boldsymbol{j} \qquad (15.10)$$

We see that *point A is accelerating upward toward the center of the cylinder.*[5] This information will be valuable for us in Chapter 16 when we study rigid-body dynamics.

[5]This conclusion must apply also to a sphere rolling without slipping on a flat surface. As for acceleration of other points of the cylinder, we do not have a simple formula but must insert data for these points into the acceleration formula valid for two points of a rigid body.

Example 15.4

Wheel D rotates at an angular speed ω_1 of 2 rad/sec counterclockwise in Fig. 15.15. Find the angular speed ω_E of gear E relative to the ground at the instant shown in the diagram.

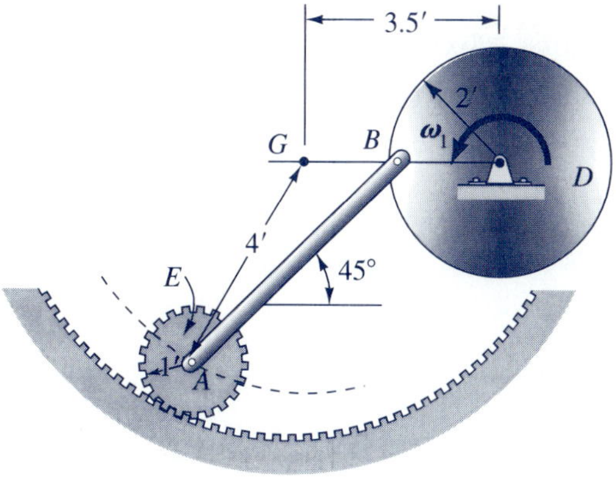

Figure 15.15. Two-dimensional device.

We have information about two points of one of the rigid bodies, namely AB, of the device. At B, the velocity must be downward with the

Example 15.4 (Continued)

value of $(\omega_1)(r_D)$ = 4 ft/sec as shown in Fig. 15.16. Furthermore, since point A must travel a circular path of radius GA we know that A has velocity V_A with a direction at right angles to GA. Accordingly, since the angle between GA and the vertical is $(90° - 45° - \alpha) = (45° - \alpha)$ as can readily be seen on inspecting Fig. 15.16, then the angle between V_A and the horizontal must also be $(45° - \alpha)$ because of the *mutual perpendicularity* of the sides of these angles. If we can determine velocity V_A, we can get the desired angular speed of gear A immediately.

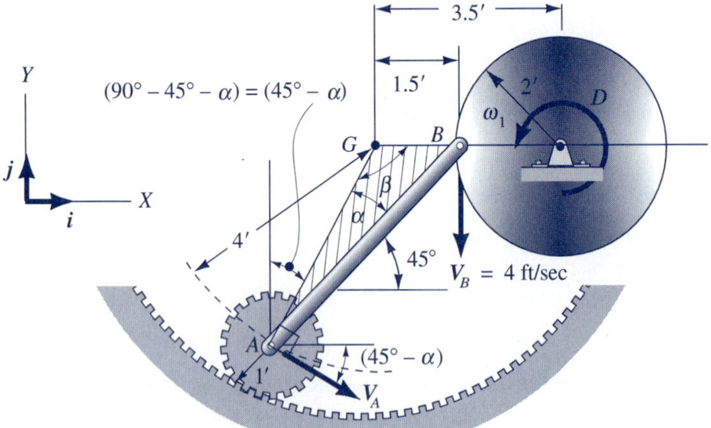

Figure 15.16. Velocity vectors for two points of a rigid body shown.

Before examining rigid body AB, we have some geometrical steps to take. Considering triangle GAB in Fig. 15.16, we can first solve for α using the law of sines as follows:

$$\frac{GA}{\sin(\measuredangle GBA)} = \frac{GB}{\sin \alpha}$$

Therefore, since $\measuredangle GBA = 45°$

$$\frac{4}{\sin 45°} = \frac{1.5}{\sin \alpha} \tag{a}$$

Solving for α, we get

$$\alpha = 15.37° \tag{b}$$

The angle β is then easily evaluated considering the angles in the triangle GBA. Thus,

$$\begin{aligned}\beta &= 180° - \alpha - \measuredangle GBA \\ &= 180° - 15.37° - 45° = 119.6°\end{aligned} \tag{c}$$

Example 15.4 (Continued)

Finally, we can determine AB of the triangle, again using the law of sines. Thus,

$$\frac{AB}{\sin\beta} = \frac{GA}{\sin 45°}$$

$$\frac{AB}{\sin 119.6°} = \frac{4}{.707}$$

Solving for AB, we get

$$AB = 4.92 \text{ ft} \qquad \text{(d)}$$

We now can consider bar AB as our rigid body. For the points A and B on this body, we can say:

$$\boldsymbol{V}_A = \boldsymbol{V}_B + \boldsymbol{\omega}_{AB} \times \boldsymbol{\rho}_{BA}$$

Noting that the motion is coplanar and that $\boldsymbol{\omega}_{AB}$ must then be normal to the plane of motion, we have[6]

$$V_A[\cos(45° - \alpha)\boldsymbol{i} - \sin(45° - \alpha)\boldsymbol{j}]$$
$$= -4\boldsymbol{j} + \omega_{AB}\boldsymbol{k} \times 4.92(-\cos 45°\boldsymbol{i} - \sin 45°\boldsymbol{j})$$

Inserting the value $\alpha = 15.37°$, we then get the following vector equation:

$$V_A(.869)\boldsymbol{i} - V_A(.494)\boldsymbol{j} = -4\boldsymbol{j} - 3.48\omega_{AB}\boldsymbol{j} + 3.48\omega_{AB}\boldsymbol{i} \qquad \text{(e)}$$

The scalar equations are

$$\begin{aligned} .869V_A &= 3.48\omega_{AB} \\ -.494V_A &= -4 - 3.48\omega_{AB} \end{aligned} \qquad \text{(f)}$$

Solving, we get[7]

$$\begin{aligned} V_A &= -10.66 \text{ ft/sec} \\ \omega_{AB} &= -2.66 \text{ rad/sec} \end{aligned} \qquad \text{(g)}$$

Thus, point A moves in a direction *opposite* to that shown in Fig. 15.16. We now can readily evaluate ω_E, which clearly must have a value of

$$\omega_E = \frac{V_A}{r_E} = \frac{10.66}{1} = \boxed{10.66 \text{ rad/sec}}$$

in the counterclockwise direction.

[6]Our practice will be to consider unknown angular velocities as *positive*. The sign for the unknown angular velocity coming out of the computations will then correspond to the *actual convention* sign for the angular velocity.

[7]By having assumed ω_{AB} as positive and thus *counterclockwise* for the reference *xy* employed, we conclude from the presence of the minus sign that the assumption is wrong and that ω_{AB} must be *clockwise* for the reference used. It is significant to note that as a result of the initial positive assumption, the result $\omega_{AB} = -2.66$ rad/sec gives at the same time the *correct convention sign* for the actual angular velocity for the reference used.

Example 15.5

In the device in Fig. 15.17, find the angular velocities and angular accelerations of both bars.

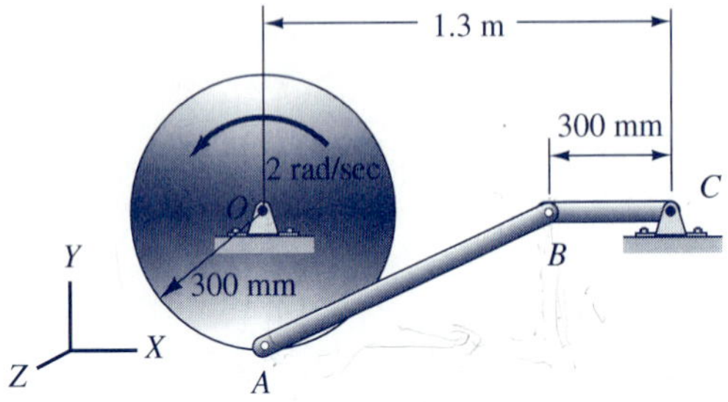

Figure 15.17. Two-dimensional device.

We shall consider points A and B of bar AB. Note first that at the instant shown:

$$\boldsymbol{V}_B = -(.300)(\omega_{BC})\boldsymbol{j} \text{ m/sec} \quad \text{(a)}$$

$$\begin{aligned} \boldsymbol{V}_A &= (2)(.300)\boldsymbol{i} \\ &= .600\boldsymbol{i} \text{ m/sec} \end{aligned} \quad \text{(b)}$$

Noting that $\boldsymbol{\omega}_{AB}$ must be oriented in the Z direction because we have plane motion in the XY plane, we have for Eq. 15.6:

$$\begin{aligned} \boldsymbol{V}_B &= \boldsymbol{V}_A + \boldsymbol{\omega}_{AB} \times \boldsymbol{\rho}_{AB} \\ -.300\omega_{BC}\boldsymbol{j} &= .600\boldsymbol{i} + (\omega_{AB}\boldsymbol{k}) \times (\boldsymbol{i} + .300\boldsymbol{j}) \\ -.300\omega_{BC}\boldsymbol{j} &= .600\boldsymbol{i} + \omega_{AB}\boldsymbol{j} - .300\omega_{AB}\boldsymbol{i} \end{aligned} \quad \text{(c)}$$

Note we have assumed ω_{BC} and ω_{AB} as positive and thus counterclockwise. The scalar equations are:

$$\begin{aligned} .600 &= .300\omega_{AB} \\ -.300\omega_{BC} &= \omega_{AB} \end{aligned} \quad \text{(d)}$$

We then get

$$\begin{aligned} \omega_{AB} &= 2 \text{ rad/sec} \\ \omega_{BC} &= -6.67 \text{ rad/sec} \end{aligned} \quad \text{(e)}$$

Therefore, ω_{AB} is counterclockwise while ω_{BC} must be clockwise.

Let us now turn to the angular acceleration considerations for the bars. We consider separately now points A and B of bar AB. Thus,

$$\begin{aligned} \boldsymbol{a}_A &= (r\omega^2)\boldsymbol{j} = (.300)(2^2)\boldsymbol{j} = 1.200\boldsymbol{j} \text{ m/sec}^2 \\ \boldsymbol{a}_B &= \rho_{BC}\omega_{BC}^2\boldsymbol{i} + \rho_{BC}\dot{\omega}_{BC}(-\boldsymbol{j}) \\ &= (.300)(-6.67^2)\boldsymbol{i} - .300\dot{\omega}_{BC}\boldsymbol{j} \\ &= 13.33\boldsymbol{i} - .300\dot{\omega}_{BC}\boldsymbol{j} \end{aligned}$$

Example 15.5 (Continued)

Again, we have assumed $\dot{\boldsymbol{\omega}}_{BC}$ positive and thus counterclockwise. Considering bar AB, we can say for Eq. 15.7:

$$\boldsymbol{a}_B = \boldsymbol{a}_A + \dot{\boldsymbol{\omega}}_{AB} \times \boldsymbol{\rho}_{AB} + \boldsymbol{\omega}_{AB} \times (\boldsymbol{\omega}_{AB} \times \boldsymbol{\rho}_{AB}) \qquad \text{(f)}$$

Noting that $\dot{\boldsymbol{\omega}}_{AB}$ must be in the Z direction, we have for the foregoing equation:

$$\begin{aligned} &13.33\boldsymbol{i} - .300\dot{\omega}_{BC}\boldsymbol{j} \\ &\quad = 1.200\boldsymbol{j} + \dot{\omega}_{AB}\boldsymbol{k} \times (\boldsymbol{i} + .300\boldsymbol{j}) + (2\boldsymbol{k}) \times [2\boldsymbol{k} \times (\boldsymbol{i} + .300\boldsymbol{j})] \qquad \text{(g)} \end{aligned}$$

The scalar equations are

$$17.33 = -.300\dot{\omega}_{AB}$$
$$-.300\dot{\omega}_{BC} = \dot{\omega}_{AB}$$

We get

$$\dot{\omega}_{AB} = -57.8 \text{ rad/sec}^2$$
$$\dot{\omega}_{BC} = 192.6 \text{ rad/sec}^2$$

Clearly, for the reference used, $\dot{\omega}_{AB}$ must be clockwise and $\dot{\omega}_{BC}$ must be counterclockwise.

Example 15.6

(a) In Example 15.5, find the *instantaneous axis of rotation* for the rod AB.

The intersection of the instantaneous axis of rotation with the xy plane will be a point E in a hypothetical rigid-body extension of bar AB having zero velocity at the instant of interest. We can accordingly say:

$$\boldsymbol{V}_E = \boldsymbol{V}_A + \boldsymbol{\omega}_{AB} \times \boldsymbol{\rho}_{AE}$$

Therefore,

$$\boldsymbol{0} = .60\boldsymbol{i} + (2\boldsymbol{k}) \times (\Delta x\boldsymbol{i} + \Delta y\boldsymbol{j}) \qquad \text{(a)}$$

where Δx and Δy are the components of the directed line segment from point A to the center of rotation E. The scalar equations are:

$$0 = .60 - 2\Delta y$$
$$0 = 2\Delta x$$

Clearly, $\Delta y = .3$ and $\Delta x = 0$. Thus, the center of rotation is point O.

Example 15.6 (Continued)

We could have easily deduced this result by inspection in this case. The velocity of each point of bar AB must be at *right angles* to a line from the center of rotation to the point. The velocity of point A is in the horizontal direction and the velocity of point B is in the vertical direction. Clearly, as seen from Fig. 15.18, point O is the only point from which lines to points A and B are normal to the velocities at these points.

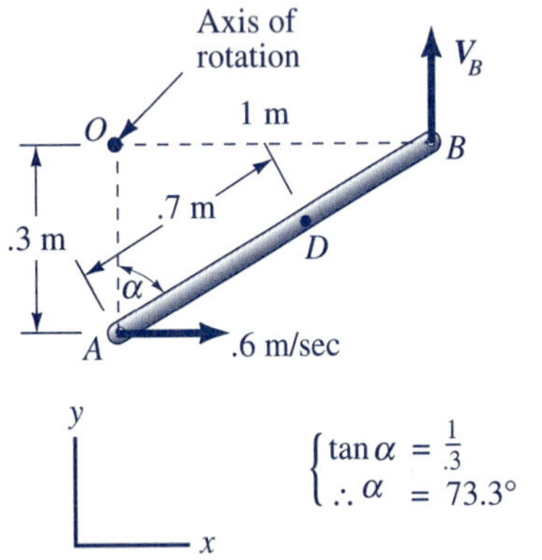

Figure 15.18. Instantaneous axis of rotation of AB.

(b) Now using the instantaneous axis of rotation, find the magnitudes of the velocity and acceleration of point D (Fig. 15.18) using data from the previous example.

In Fig. 15.19, we show the velocity vector normal to line OD. Using the law of cosines for triangle AOD, we can find OD which is a key distance for this example. Thus noting from Fig. 15.18 that $\alpha = 73.3°$, we have

$$\overline{OD} = \left[.7^2 + .3^2 - (2)(.7)(.3)(\cos 73.3°)\right]^{1/2} = .6777 \text{ m}$$

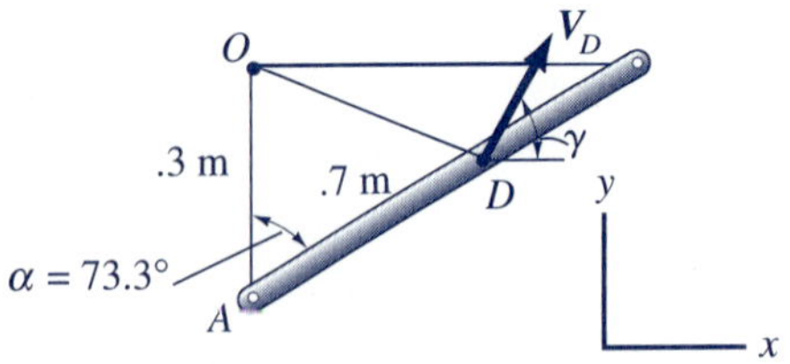

Figure 15.19. Velocity vector for point D.

We then say from rotational motion about the instantaneous center of rotation O,

$$V_D = (.6777)(\omega_{AB}) = (.6777)(2) = 1.355 \text{ m/s}$$

Example 15.6 (Continued)

For the acceleration, we have (see Fig. 15.20)

$$a_D = \left[(a_D)_c^2 + (a_D)_t^2\right]^{1/2}$$

where $(a_D)_c$ and $(a_D)_t$, respectively, are the centripetal and tangential components of acceleration at point D. Noting that r for point D is .6777 m, we get for the above

$$\therefore a_D = \left\{\left(\frac{V_D^2}{r}\right)^2 + \left[(r)(\dot{\omega}_{AB})\right]^2\right\}^{1/2}$$

$$= \left\{\left(\frac{1.355^2}{.6777}\right)^2 + [(.6777)(57.8)]^2\right\}^{1/2} = 39.26 \text{ m/s}^2 \quad \text{(b)}$$

We now get the vectors $\mathbf{V}_D$ and $\boldsymbol{a}_D$. For this purpose we determine the angle β of the tinted triangle in Fig. 15.20 by first using the law of sines for triangle AOD

$$\frac{.7}{\sin(90° - \beta)} = \frac{.6777}{\sin 73.3°}$$

$$\therefore \beta = 8.373°$$

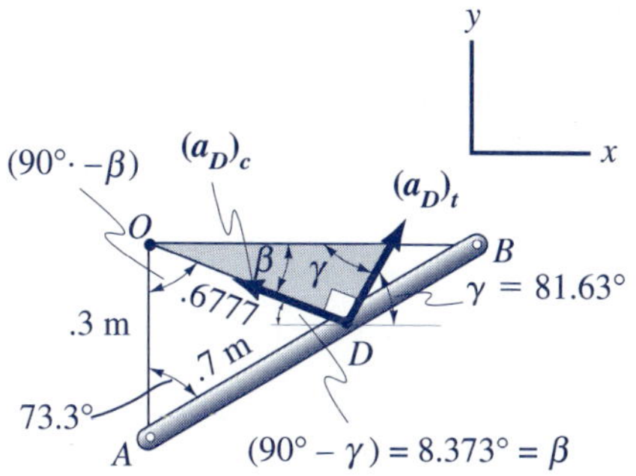

Figure 15.20. Acceleration components of point D.

Hence, looking at the tinted triangle it is clear that $\gamma = 90° - 8.373° = 81.63°$. We can now give V_D (see Fig. 15.19).

$$V_D = V_D(\cos\gamma \boldsymbol{i} + \sin\gamma \boldsymbol{j}) = 1.355(\cos 81.63\boldsymbol{i} + \sin 81.63\boldsymbol{j})$$

$$\boldsymbol{V}_D = .1972\boldsymbol{i} + 1.341\boldsymbol{j} \text{ m/s}$$

Example 15.6 (Continued)

For the acceleration vector, we refer back to Eq. (b) for components of $\boldsymbol{a}_D$. Noting Fig. 15.20, we have

$$\begin{aligned}\boldsymbol{a}_D &= r(\dot{\omega}_{AB})[\cos\gamma \boldsymbol{i} + \sin\gamma \boldsymbol{j}] + \frac{V_D^2}{r}[-\cos\beta\boldsymbol{i} + \sin\beta\boldsymbol{j}) \\ &= (.6777)(-57.8)[\cos 81.63°\boldsymbol{i} + \sin 81.63°\boldsymbol{j}] \\ &\qquad + \frac{1.355^2}{.6777}[-\cos 8.373°\boldsymbol{i} + \sin 8.373°\boldsymbol{j}]\end{aligned}$$

$$\therefore \quad \boldsymbol{a}_D = -8.38\boldsymbol{i} - 38.36\boldsymbol{j} \text{ m/s}^2$$

*Example 15.7

A disk E is rotating about a fixed axis HG at a constant angular speed ω_1 of 5 rad/sec in Fig. 15.21. A bar CD is held by the wheel at D by a ball-joint connection and is guided along a rod AB cantilevered at A and B by a collar at C having a second ball-joint connection with CD, as shown in the diagram. Compute the velocity of C.

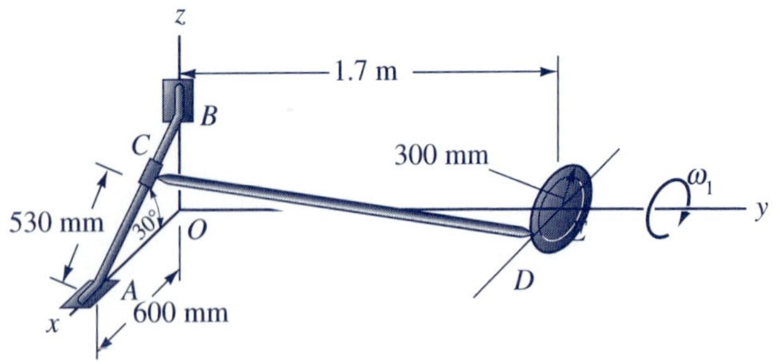

Figure 15.21. Three-dimensional device.

We shall need the vector $\boldsymbol{\rho}_{DC}$. Thus,

$$\begin{aligned}\boldsymbol{\rho}_{DC} &= \boldsymbol{r}_C - \boldsymbol{r}_D \\ &= [(.600 - .530\cos 30°)\boldsymbol{i} + .530\sin 30°\boldsymbol{k}] - (1.7\boldsymbol{j} + .300\boldsymbol{i}) \\ &= -.1590\boldsymbol{i} - 1.7\boldsymbol{j} + .265\boldsymbol{k} \text{ m}\end{aligned}$$

Example 15.7 (Continued)

Now employ Eq. 15.6 for rod CD. Thus,

$$\boldsymbol{V}_C = \boldsymbol{V}_D + \boldsymbol{\omega}_{CD} \times \boldsymbol{\rho}_{DC}$$

Therefore, assuming C is going from B to A

$$V_C(\cos 30°\boldsymbol{i} - \sin 30°\boldsymbol{k})$$
$$= (5)(.30)\boldsymbol{k} + (\omega_x\boldsymbol{i} + \omega_y\boldsymbol{j} + \omega_z\boldsymbol{k}) \times (-.1590\boldsymbol{i} - 1.7\boldsymbol{j} + .265\boldsymbol{k})$$
$$V_C(.866\boldsymbol{i} - .500\boldsymbol{k}) = 1.50\boldsymbol{k} - 1.7\omega_x\boldsymbol{k} - .265\omega_x\boldsymbol{j} + .1590\omega_y\boldsymbol{k}$$
$$+.265\omega_y\boldsymbol{i} - .1590\omega_z\boldsymbol{j} + 1.7\omega_z\boldsymbol{i})$$

The scalar equations are:

$$.866V_C = .265\omega_y + 1.7\omega_z \qquad \text{(a)}$$
$$0 = -.265\omega_x - .1590\omega_z \qquad \text{(b)}$$
$$-.500V_C = 1.50 - 1.7\omega_x + .1590\omega_y \qquad \text{(c)}$$

From these equations, we cannot solve for ω_x, ω_y, and ω_z because the spin of CD about its own axis (allowed by the ball joints) can have *any value* without affecting the velocity of slider C. However, we can determine V_C, as we shall now demonstrate.

In Eq. (b), solve for ω_x in terms of ω_z.

$$\omega_x = -.600\omega_z \qquad \text{(d)}$$

In Eq. (a), solve for ω_y in terms of ω_z:

$$\omega_y = 3.27V_C - 6.415\omega_z \qquad \text{(e)}$$

Substitute for ω_x and ω_y in Eq. (c) using the foregoing results:

$$-.500V_C = 1.50 - (1.7)(-.600\omega_z) + (.1590)(3.27V_C - 6.415\omega_z)$$

Therefore,

$$-1.020V_C = 1.5 + 1.020\omega_z - 1.020\omega_z$$
$$V_C = -1.471 \text{ m/sec}$$

Hence,

$$\boldsymbol{V}_c = -1.471(\cos 30°\boldsymbol{i} - \sin 30°\boldsymbol{k})$$

$$\boldsymbol{V}_c = -1.274\boldsymbol{i} + .7355\boldsymbol{k} \text{ m/sec}$$

Clearly, contrary to our assumption C is going from A to B.

Before going on to the next section, we wish to point out a simple relation that will be of use in the remainder of the chapter. Suppose that you have a moving particle whose position vector $\boldsymbol{r}$ has a magnitude that is constant (see Fig. 15.22). This position vector, however, has an angular velocity $\boldsymbol{\omega}$ relative to xyz. We wish to know the velocity of the particle P relative to xyz.

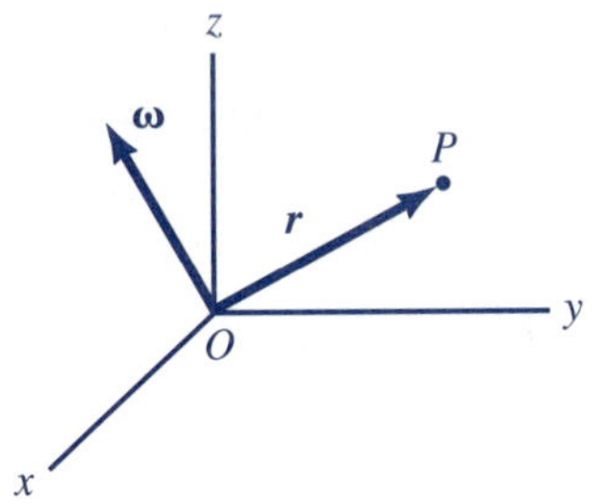

Figure 15.22. Position vector $\boldsymbol{r}$ has constant magnitude but rotates relative to xyz with angular velocity $\boldsymbol{\omega}$.

We could imagine for this purpose that particle P is part of a rigid body attached to xyz at O and rotating with angular velocity $\boldsymbol{\omega}$. This situation is shown in Fig. 15.23. Using Eq. 15.6, we can then say:

$$\boldsymbol{V}_P = \boldsymbol{V}_O + \boldsymbol{\omega} \times \boldsymbol{\rho}_{OP}$$

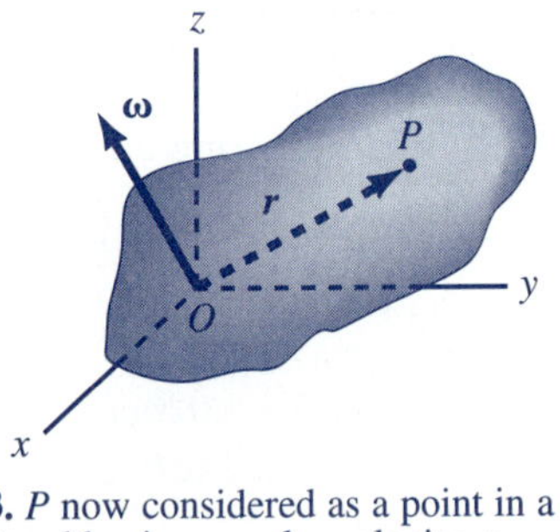

Figure 15.23. P now considered as a point in a rigid body attached at O and having angular velocity $\boldsymbol{\omega}$.

But $\boldsymbol{V}_O = \boldsymbol{0}$ and $\boldsymbol{\rho}_{OP}$ is simply $\boldsymbol{r}$. Hence, we have

$$\boldsymbol{V}_P = \boldsymbol{\omega} \times \boldsymbol{r}$$

We thus have a simple formula for the velocity of a particle moving at a fixed distance from the origin of xyz. This velocity is simply the cross product of the angular velocity $\boldsymbol{\omega}$ of the position vector about xyz and the position vector $\boldsymbol{r}$.

PROBLEMS

15.25. A body is spinning about an axis having direction cosines $l = .5$, $m = .5$, and $n = .707$. The angular speed is 50 rad/sec. What is the velocity of a point in the body having a position vector $\boldsymbol{r} = 6\boldsymbol{i} + 4\boldsymbol{j}$ ft?

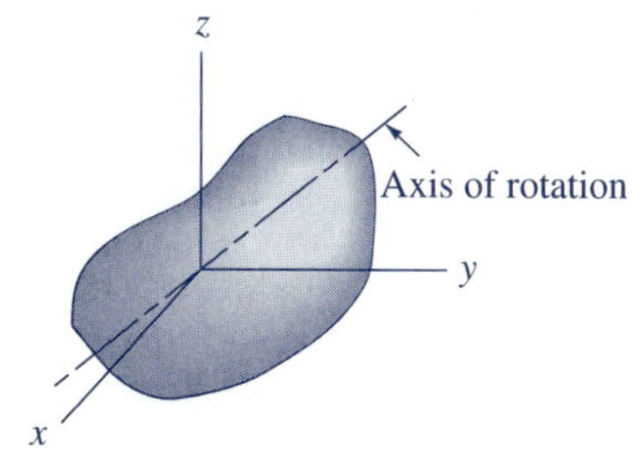

Figure P.15.25.

15.26. In Problem 15.25, what is the relative velocity between a point in the body at position $x = 10$ m, $y = 6$ m, $z = 3$ m and a point in the body at position $x = 2$ m, $y = -3$ m, $z = 0$ m?

15.27. If the body in Problem 15.25 is given an additional angular velocity $\boldsymbol{\omega}_2 = 6\boldsymbol{j} + 10\boldsymbol{k}$ rad/sec, what is the direction of the axis of rotation? Compute the velocity at $\boldsymbol{r} = 10\boldsymbol{j} + 3\boldsymbol{k}$ ft if the actual axis of rotation goes through the origin.

15.28. A wheel is rolling along at 17 m/sec without slipping. What is the angular speed? What is the velocity of point B on the rim of the wheel at the instant shown?

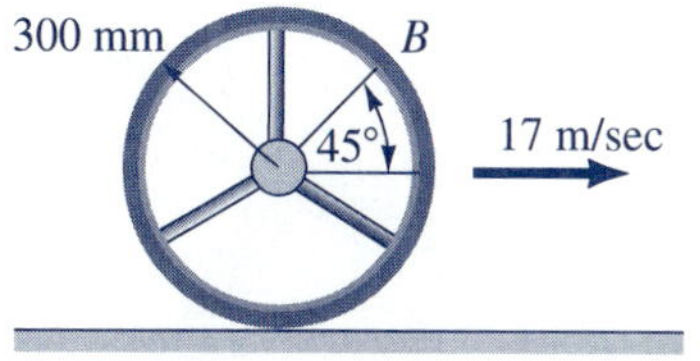

Figure P.15.28.

15.29. A flexible cord is wrapped around a spool and is pulled at a velocity of 10 ft/sec relative to the ground. If there is no slipping at C, what is the velocity of points O and D at the instant shown?

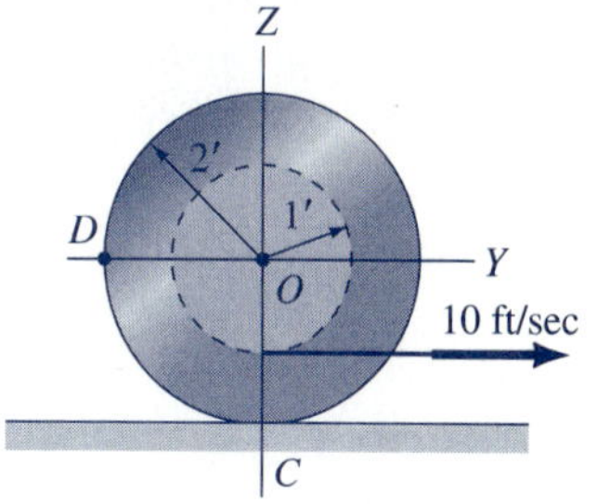

Figure P.15.29.

15.30. A piston P is shown moving downward at the constant speed of 1 ft/sec. What is the speed of slider A at the instant of interest?

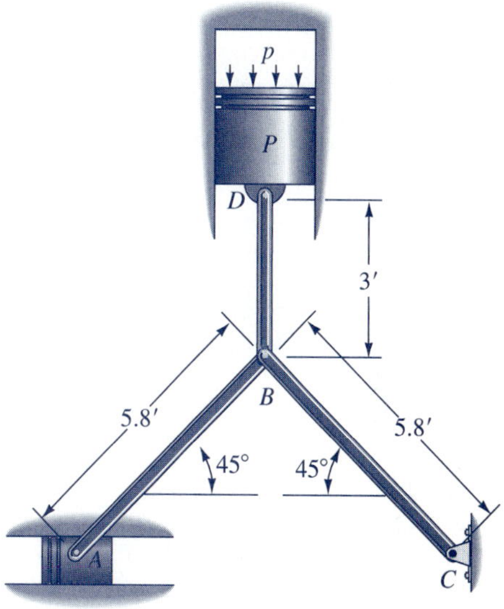

Figure P.15.30.

15.31. A rod AB is 1 m in length. If the end A slides down the surface at a speed V_A of 3 m/sec, what is the angular speed of AB at the instant shown?

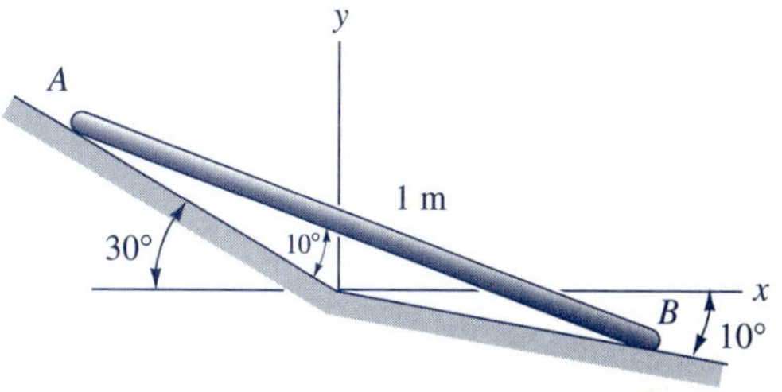

Figure P.15.31.

15.32. A plate moves along a horizontal surface. Components of the velocity for three corners are:

$$(V_A)_x = 2\text{m/sec}$$
$$(V_B)_y = -3\text{m/sec}$$
$$(V_C)_y = 5\text{m/sec}$$

What is the angular speed of the plate and what is the velocity of corner D?

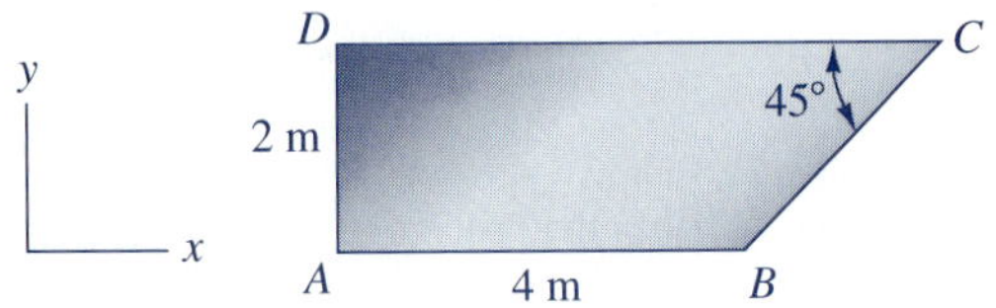

Figure P.15.32.

15.33. Rod DC has an angular speed ω_1 of 5 rad/sec at the configuration shown. What is the angular speed of bar AB?

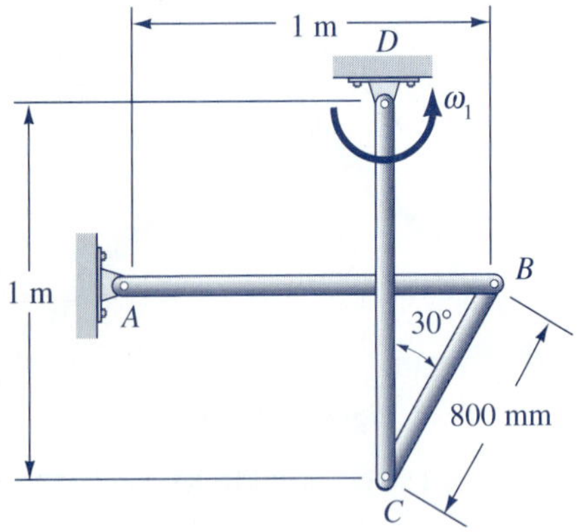

Figure P.15.33.

15.34. A system of meshing gears includes gear A, which is held stationary. Rod $A'C'$ rotates with a speed ω_1 of 5 rad/sec. What is the angular speed of gear C? The gears have the following diameters:

$$D_A = 600 \text{ mm}$$
$$D_B = 350 \text{ mm}$$
$$D_C = 200 \text{ mm}$$

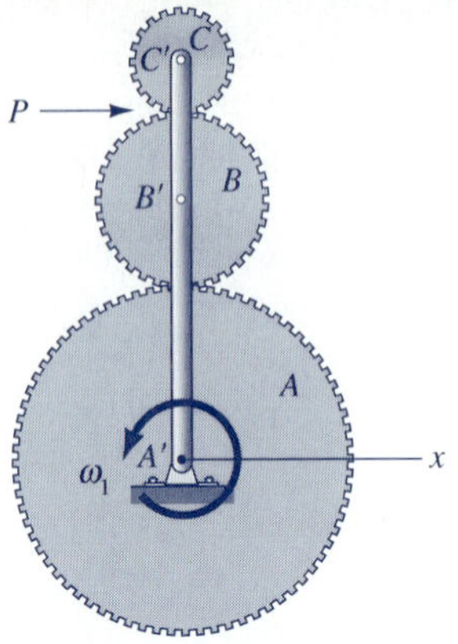

Figure P.15.34.

15.35. In Problem 15.34 take $\omega_1 = 10$ rad/sec. If gear C is to translate, what angular speed should gear A have?

15.36. A bar moves in the plane of the page so that end A has a velocity of 7 m/sec and decelerates at a rate of 3.3 m/sec^2 What are the velocity and acceleration of point C when BA is at 30° to the horizontal?

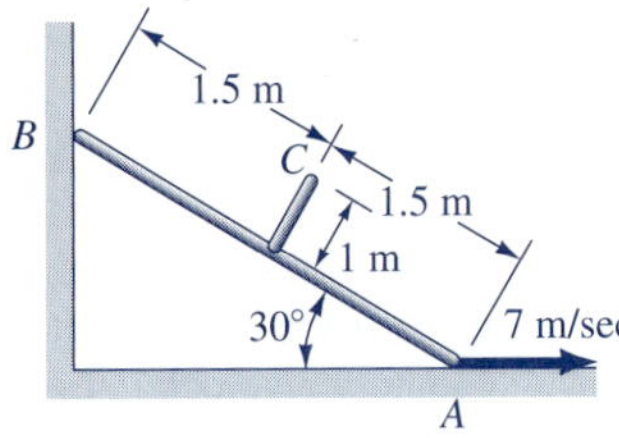

Figure P.15.36.

15.37. Bar AB is rotating at a constant speed of 5 rad/sec clockwise in a device. What is the angular velocity of bar BD and body EFC? Determine the velocity of point D [*Hint:* What is the direction of the velocity of point G?]

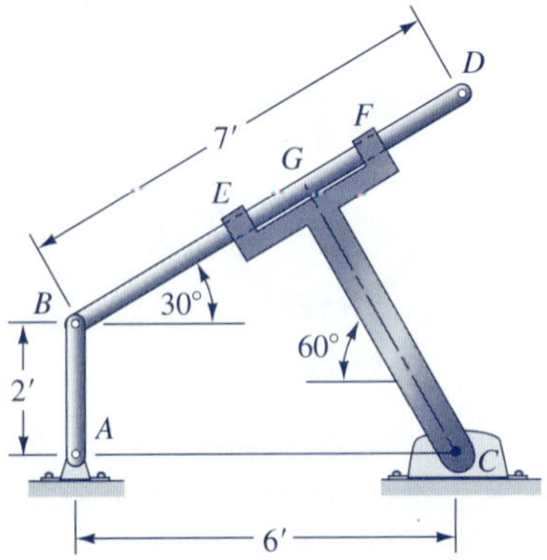

Figure P.15.37.

15.38. A wheel rotates with an angular speed of 20 rad/sec. A connecting rod connects points A on the wheel with a slider at B. Compute the angular velocity of the connecting rod and the velocity of the slider when the apparatus is in the position shown in the diagram.

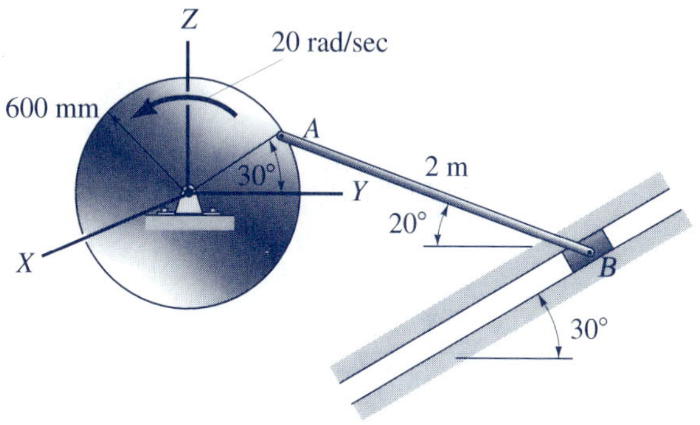

Figure P.15.38.

15.39. In Problem 15.38, if $V_B = 14.30$ m/sec and $\omega_{AB} = -9.33$ rad/sec, where is the instantaneous axis of rotation of connecting rod AB?

15.40. A piston, connecting rod, and crankshaft of an engine are represented schematically. The engine is rotating at 3,000 rpm. At the position shown, what is the velocity of pin A relative to the engine block and what is the angular velocity of the connecting rod AB?

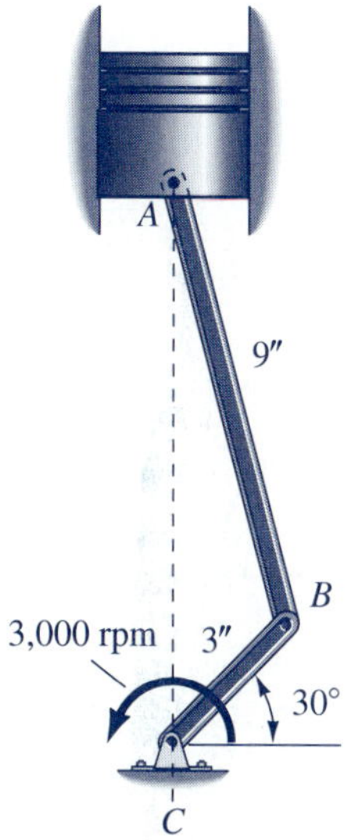

Figure P.15.40.

15.41. Member AB is rotating at a constant speed of 4 rad/sec in a counterclockwise direction. What is the angular velocity of bar BC for the position shown in the diagram? What is the velocity of point D at the center of bar BC? Bar BC is 3 ft in length.

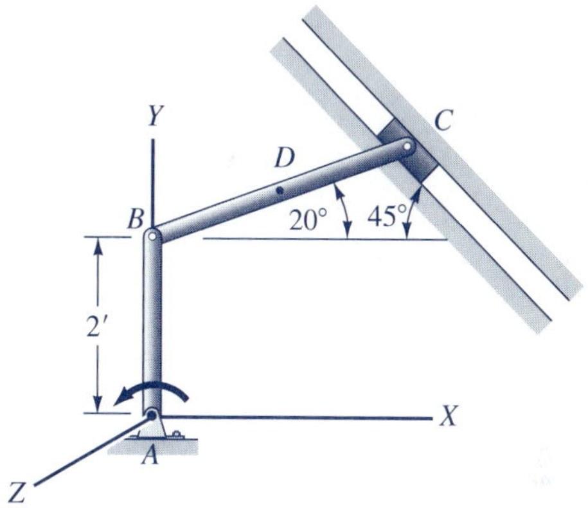

Figure P.15.41.

15.42. In Problem 15.41, determine in the simplest manner the instantaneous axis of rotation for bar BC.

15.43. Suppose that bar AB of Problem 15.41 has an angular velocity of 3 rad/sec counterclockwise and a counterclockwise angular acceleration of 5 rad/sec^2. What is the angular acceleration of bar BC, which is 3 ft in length?

15.44. A rod is moving on a horizontal surface and is shown at time t. What is V_y of end A and ω of the rod at the instant shown? [*Hint:* Use the fact that the rod is inextensible.]

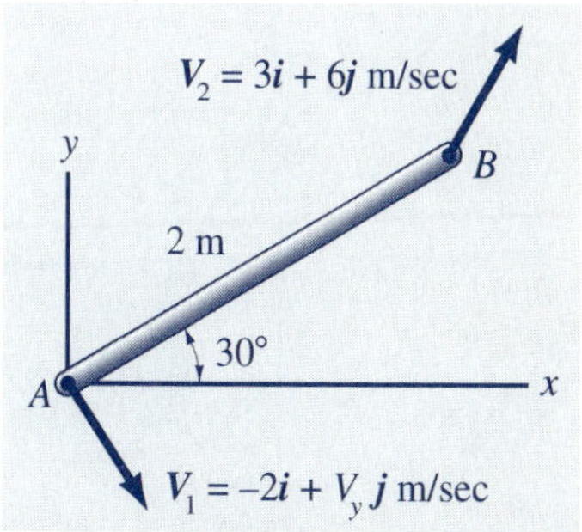

Figure P.15.44.

15.45. A plate $ABCD$ moves on a horizontal surface. At time t corners A and B have the following velocities:

$$V_A = 3\boldsymbol{i} + 2\boldsymbol{j} \text{ m/sec}$$
$$V_B = (V_B)_x\boldsymbol{i} + 5\boldsymbol{j} \text{ m/sec}$$

Find the location of the instantaneous axis of rotation.

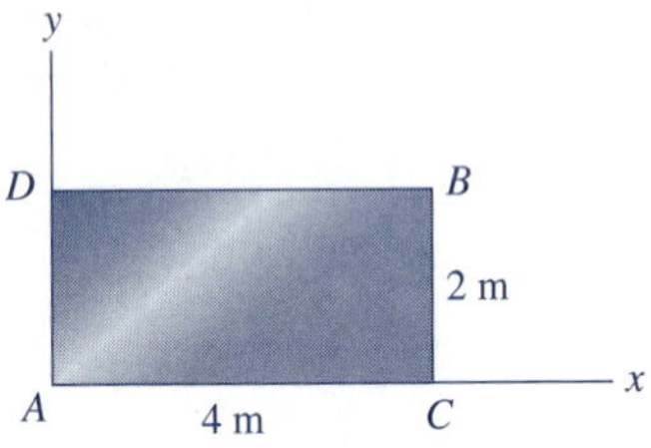

Figure P.15.45.

15.46. Find the velocity and acceleration relative to the ground of pin B on the wheel. The wheel rolls without slipping. Also, find the angular velocity of the slotted bar in which the pin B of the wheel slides when θ of the bar is 30°.

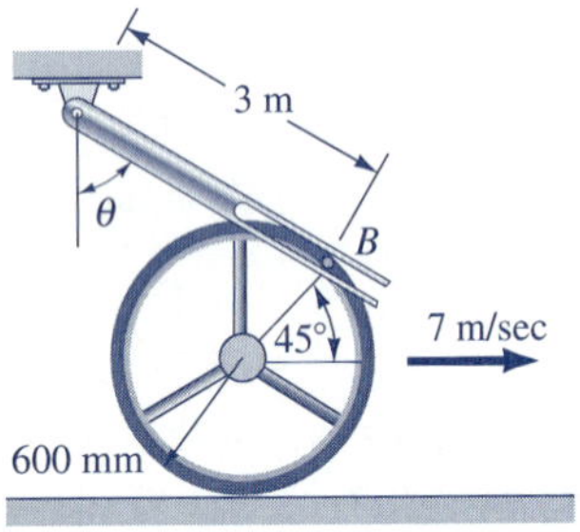

Figure P.15.46.

15.47. If $\omega_1 = 5$ rad/sec and $\dot{\omega}_1 = 3$ rad/sec² for bar CD, compute the angular velocity and angular acceleration of the gear D relative to the ground. Solve the problem using Eqs. 15.6 and 15.7, and then check the result by considering simple circular motion of point D.

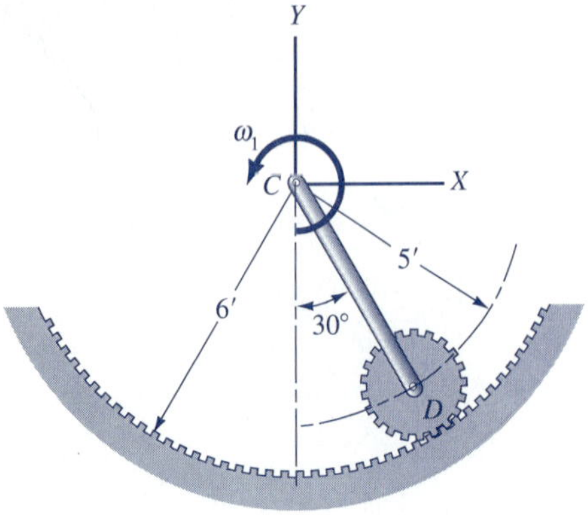

Figure P.15.47.

15.48. A mechanism with two sliders is shown. Slider A at the instant of interest has a speed of 3 m/sec and is accelerating at the rate of 1.7 m/sec². If member AB is 2.5 m in length, what are the angular velocity and angular acceleration for this member?

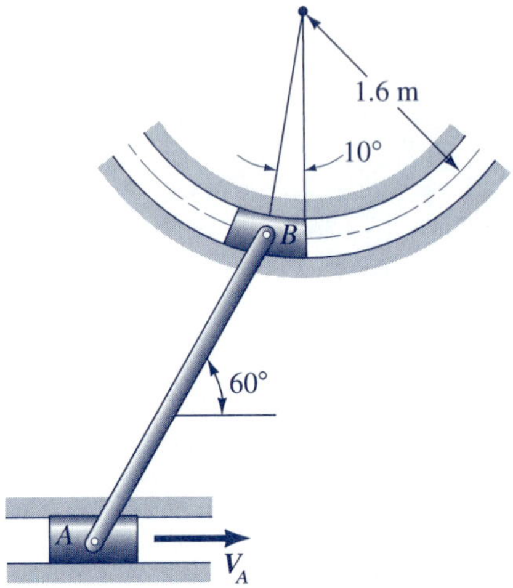

Figure P.15.48.

15.49. In Problem 15.48 find the instantaneous center of rotation of bar AB if V_A is 2.7 m/sec.

15.50. The velocity of corner A of the block is known to be at time t:

$$V_A = 10\boldsymbol{i} + 4\boldsymbol{j} - 3\boldsymbol{k} \text{ m/sec}$$

The angular speed about edge $\overline{AD}$ is 2 rad/sec, and the angular speeds about the diagonals $\overline{AF}$ and $\overline{HE}$ are known to be 3 rad/sec and 6 rad/sec, respectively. What is the velocity of corner B at this instant?

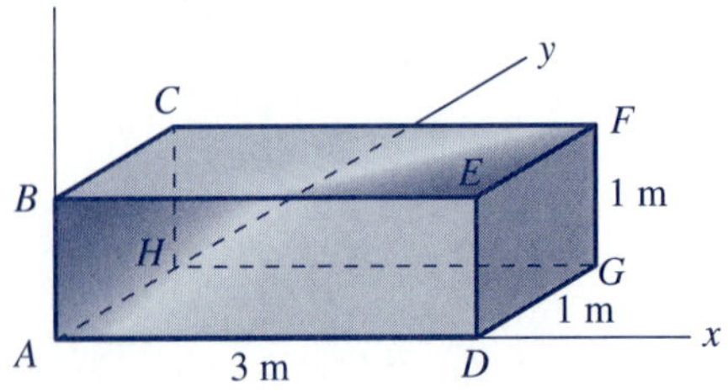

Figure P.15.50.

15.51. A rigid sphere is moving in space. The velocities for two points A and B on the surface have the values at time t:

$$V_A = 6i + 3j + 2k \text{ ft/sec}$$
$$V_B = (V_B)_x i + 6j - 4k \text{ ft/sec}$$

The position vectors for points A and B are at time t:

$$r_A = 10i + 15j + 12k \text{ ft}$$
$$r_B = 7i + 20j + 18k \text{ ft}$$

What is the angular velocity of the sphere? At the instant of interest the sphere has zero spin about axis $\overline{AB}$.

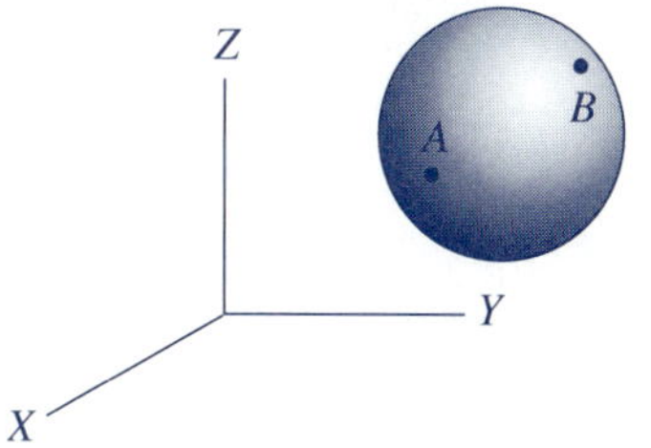

Figure P.15.51.

15.52. A conveyor element moves down the incline at a speed of 5 ft/sec. A shaft and platform move with the conveyor element but have a spin of .5 rad/sec about the centerline AB. Also, the shaft swings in the YZ plane at a speed ω_1 of 1 rad/sec. What is the velocity and acceleration of point D on the platform at the instant it is in the YZ plane, as shown in the diagram? Note that at the instant of interest AB is vertical.

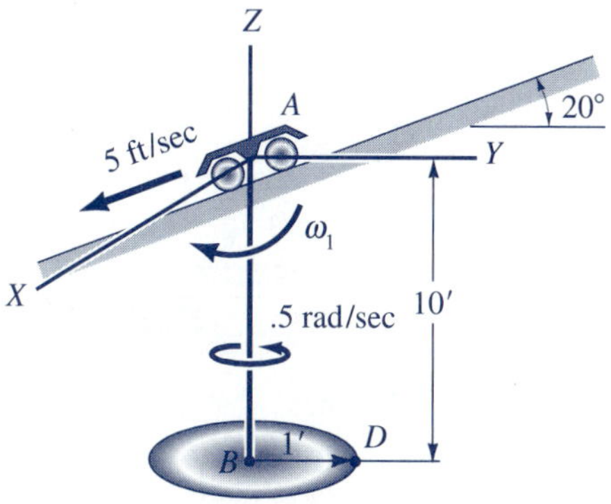

Figure P.15.52

15.53. A conveyor element moves down an incline at a speed of 15 m/sec. A plate hangs down from the conveyor element and, at the instant of interest shown in the diagram, is spinning about AB at the rate of 5 rad/sec. Also, the axis AB swings in the YZ plane at the rate ω_1 of 10 rad/sec and $\dot{\omega}_1 = 3$ rad/sec² at the instant of interest. DB is parallel to the X axis at this instant. Find the velocity and acceleration of point D at the instant shown.

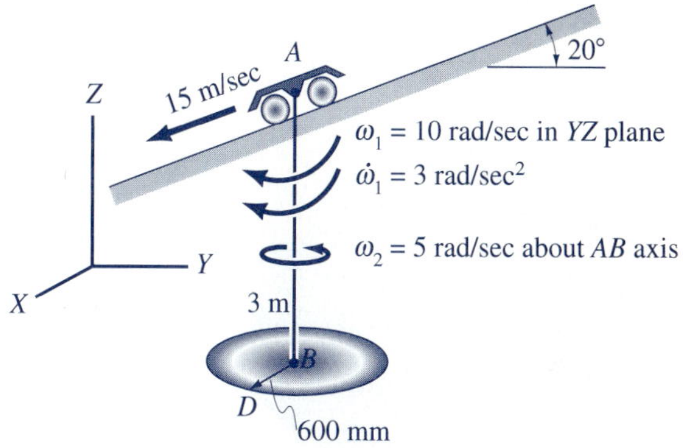

Figure P.15.53.

15.54. A cylinder rolls without slipping. It has an angular velocity $\omega = .3$ rad/sec and an angular acceleration $\dot{\omega} = .014$ rad/sec². What are the angular velocity and angular acceleration of member AB?

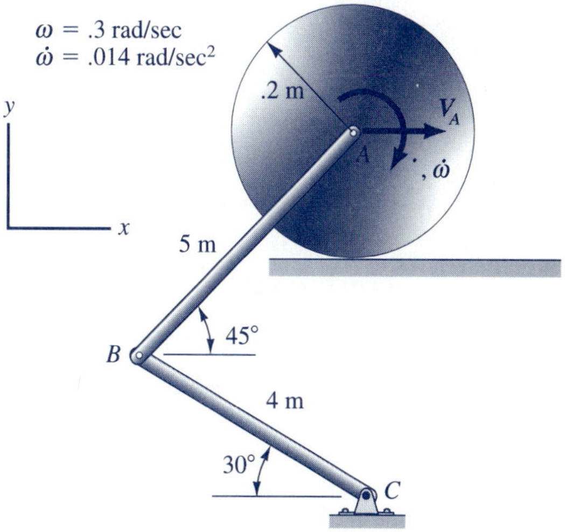

Figure P.15.54.

15.55. Slider A moves in a parabolic slot with speed $\dot{s} = 3$ m/s and $\ddot{s} = 1$ m/s^2 at the instant shown in the diagram. Cylinder E is connected to A by rod AB.

(a) Find the angular velocity of cylinder E at the time of interest.

(b) Also, find the angular acceleration of cylinder E and rod AB at this instant.

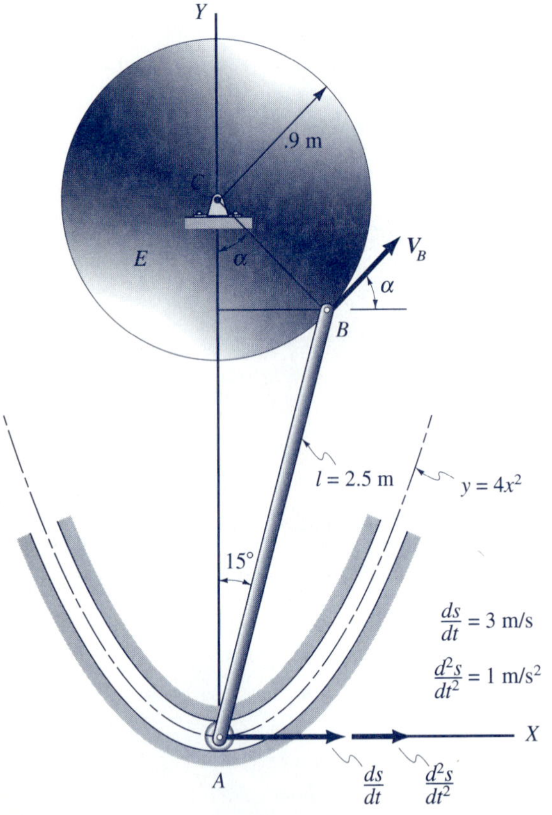

Figure P.15.55.

15.56. Find ω_A and $\dot{\omega}_A$ at the instant shown. The following data apply:

$R_A = .3$ m $\quad R_B = .2$ m $\quad CD = 5$ m $\quad V_B = .2$ m/s

Disc A rolls without slipping.

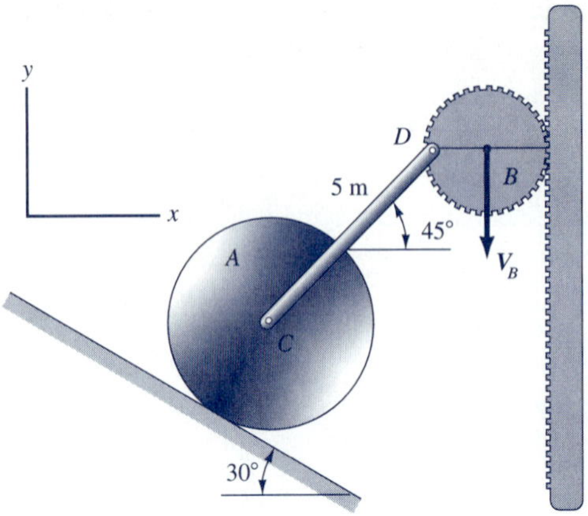

Figure P.15.56.

15.57. Find the velocity and acceleration of the center of A.

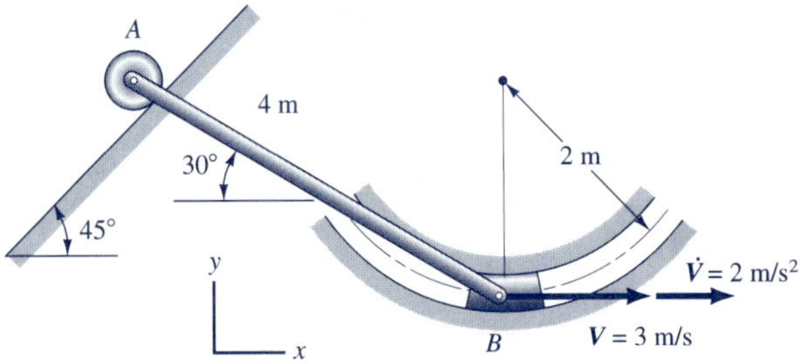

Figure P.15.57.

15.58. What is the angular velocity of rod AD? What is the magnitude of the velocity of point C of rod AD? Rod BC is vertical at the instant of interest.

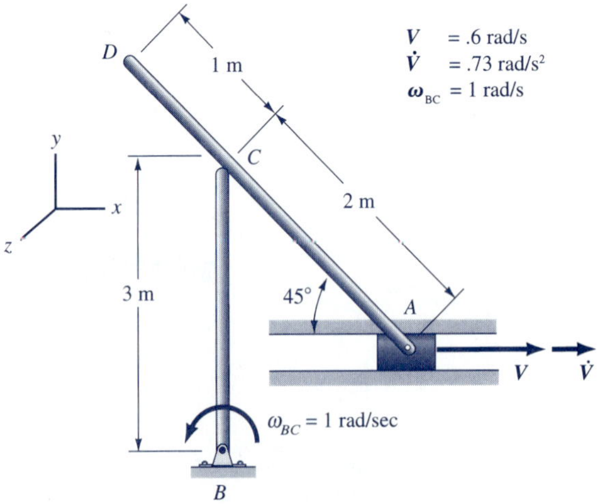

Figure P.15.58.

15.59. What are the angular velocities of the two rods? Slider A has a speed of .4 m/sec, whereas slider C has a speed of 1.2 m/sec.

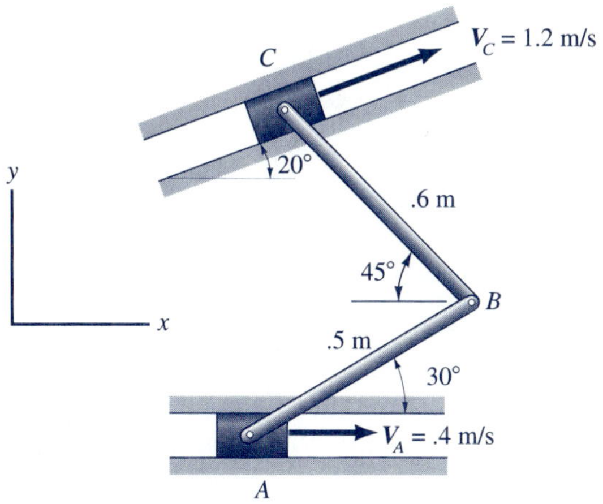

Figure P.15.59.

15.60. In Problem 15.33, find the instantaneous center O of rotation for rod CB in the simplest possible manner. What is the speed of the midpoint of CB found using O? From Problem 15.33, ω_{BC} = 2.89 rad/sec.

15.61. Find ω_E and $\dot{\omega}_E$ at the instant shown.

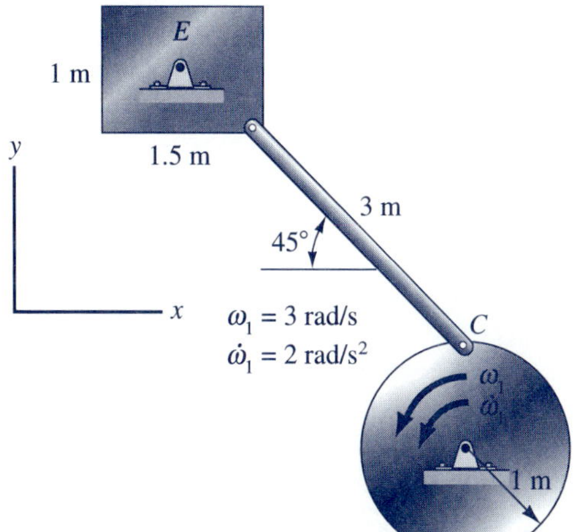

Figure P.15.61.

15.62. A bent rod is pinned to a slider at A and a cylinder at B. Find the velocity and acceleration of the slider at the instant depicted in the diagram.

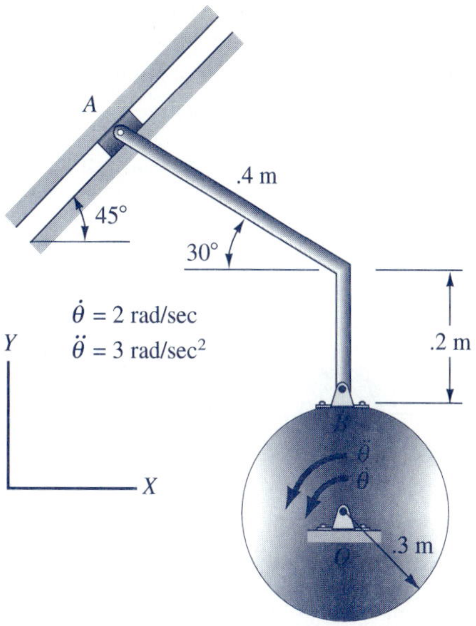

Figure P.15.62.

15.63. A cylinder rolls without slipping. Develop a formula for $\boldsymbol{a}_B$ in terms of V_0, $\dot{V}_0$, and R. Then get a formula for $\boldsymbol{a}_C$ in terms of V_0, $\dot{V}_0$, R, and d.

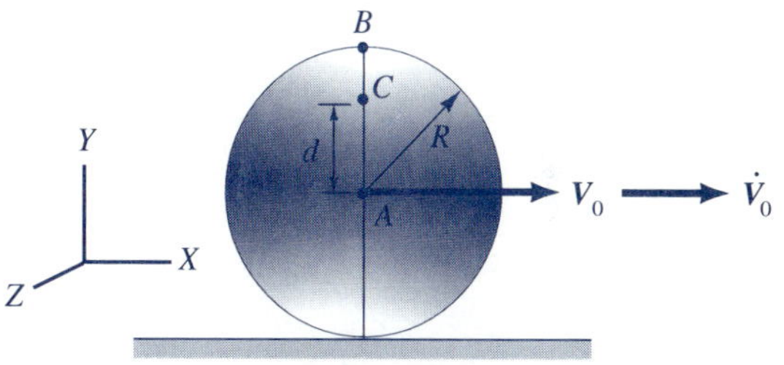

Figure P.15.63.

15.64. Two stationary half-cylinders F and I are shown, on which roll cylinders G and H. If the motion is such that line BA has an angular speed of 2 rad/sec clockwise, what is the angular speed and the angular acceleration of cylinder H relative to the ground? The cylinders roll without slipping.

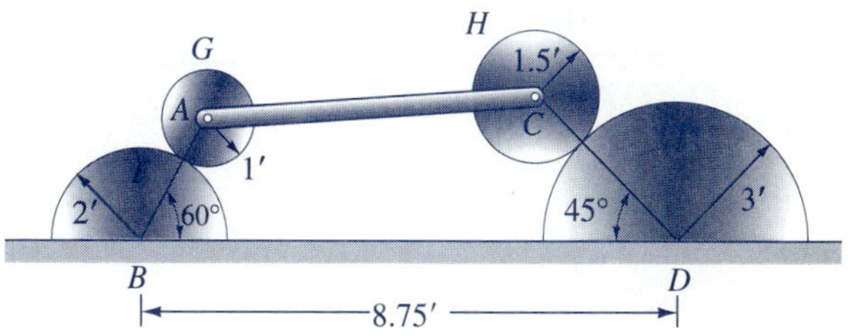

Figure P.15.64.

15.65. In Problem 15.64, assume that cylinder G is rotating at a speed of 5 rad/sec clockwise as seen from the ground. What is the speed and rate of change of speed of point C relative to the ground? Assume that no slipping occurs.

15.66. A wheel D of radius $R_1 = 6$ in. rotates at a speed $\omega_1 = 5$ rad/sec as shown. A second wheel C is connected to wheel D by connecting rod AB. What is the angular speed of wheel C at the instant shown? The radius $R_2 = 12$ in. The wheels are separated by a distance $d = 2$ ft. At A and at B there are ball-and-socket connections.

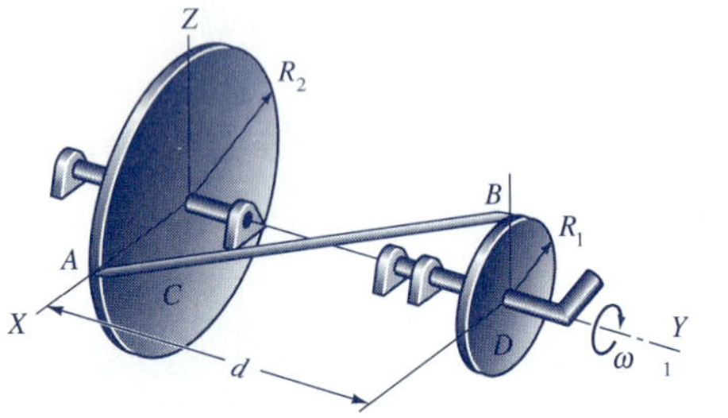

Figure P.15.66.

***15.67.** A bar AB can slide along members CD and FG of a rigid structure. If A is moving at a speed of 300 mm/sec along CD toward D and is at this instant a distance of 300 mm from C, what is the speed of B along FG? At A and B there are ball-and-socket-joint connections.

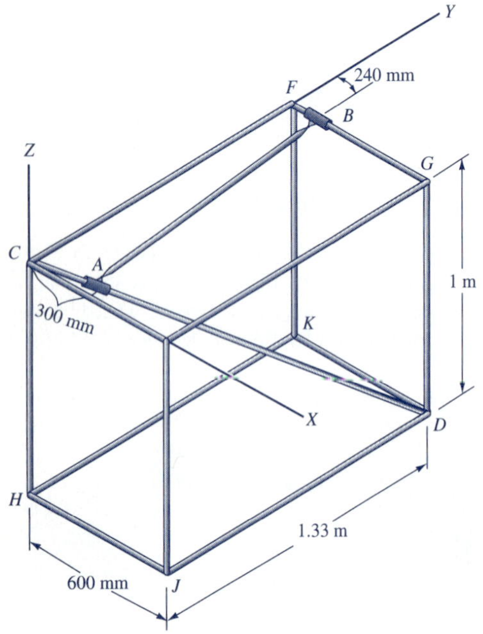

Figure P.15.67.

15.68. Member AB connects two sliders A and B. If $V_B = 5$ m/s and $\dot{V}_B = 3$ m/s^2, what are ω_{AB} and $\dot{\omega}_{AB}$ at the configuration shown?

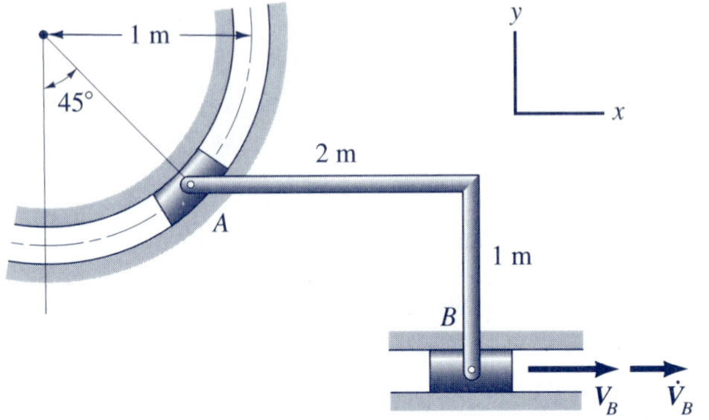

Figure P.15.68.

15.69. Find ω_{AB} and $\dot{\omega}_{AB}$. Cylinder D rolls without slipping with angular motion given as

$$\omega_D = .2 \text{ rad/s and } \dot{\omega}_D = .3 \text{ rad/s}^2$$

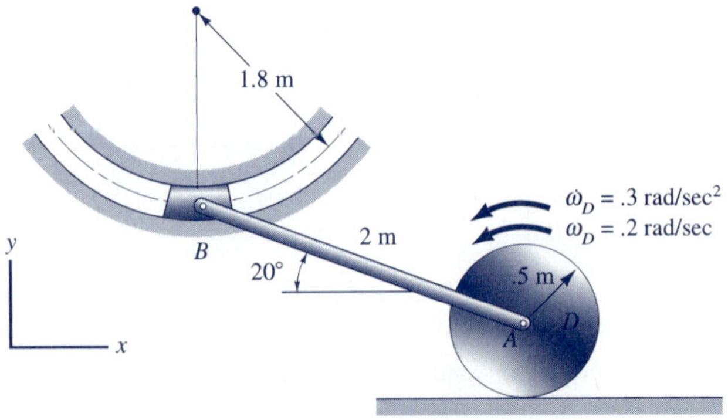

Figure P.15.69.

15.6 General Relationship Between Time Derivatives of a Vector for Different References

In Section 15.4, we considered the time derivatives of a vector $\boldsymbol{A}$ "fixed" in a reference xyz moving arbitrarily relative to XYZ. Our conclusions were:

$$\left(\frac{d\boldsymbol{A}}{dt}\right)_{xyz} = \boldsymbol{0}$$

$$\left(\frac{d\boldsymbol{A}}{dt}\right)_{XYZ} = \boldsymbol{\omega} \times \boldsymbol{A}$$

We now wish to extend these considerations to include time derivatives of a vector $\boldsymbol{A}$ which is not necessarily fixed in reference xyz. Primarily, our intention in this section is to relate time derivatives of such vectors $\boldsymbol{A}$ as seen both from reference xyz and from XYZ, two references moving arbitrarily relative to each other.

For this purpose, consider Fig. 15.24, where we show a moving particle P with a position vector $\boldsymbol{\rho}$ in reference xyz. Reference xyz moves arbitrarily relative to reference XYZ with translational velocity $\dot{\boldsymbol{R}}$ and angular velocity $\boldsymbol{\omega}$ in accordance with **Chasles' theorem.** We shall now form a relation between $(d\boldsymbol{\rho}/dt)_{xyz}$ and $(d\boldsymbol{\rho}/dt)_{XYZ}$. We shall then extend this result so as to relate the time derivative of any vector $\boldsymbol{A}$ as seen from any two references.

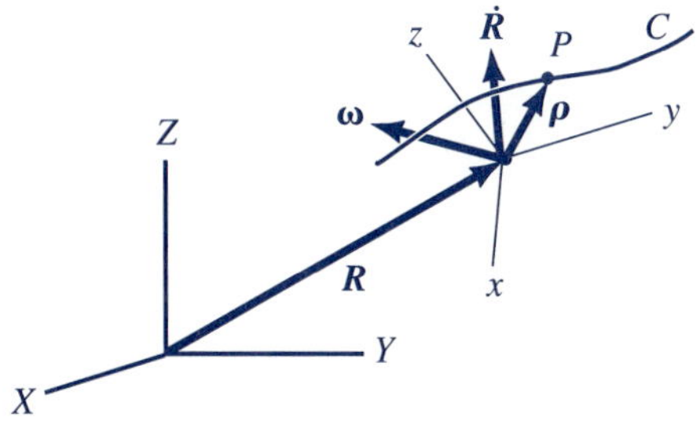

Figure 15.24. xyz moves relative to XYZ.

To reach the desired results effectively, we shall express the vector $\boldsymbol{\rho}$ in terms of components parallel to the xyz reference:

$$\boldsymbol{\rho} = x\boldsymbol{i} + y\boldsymbol{j} + z\boldsymbol{k} \tag{15.11}$$

where $\boldsymbol{i}, \boldsymbol{j},$ and $\boldsymbol{k}$ are unit vectors for reference xyz. Differentiating this equation with respect to time for the xyz reference, we have:[8]

$$\left(\frac{d\boldsymbol{\rho}}{dt}\right)_{xyz} = \dot{x}\boldsymbol{i} + \dot{y}\boldsymbol{j} + \dot{z}\boldsymbol{k} \tag{15.12}$$

[8]Note that $\dot{x}$, $\dot{y}$, and $\dot{z}$ are time derivatives of scalars and accordingly there is no identification with any reference as far as the time derivative operation is concerned.

If we next take the derivative of $\boldsymbol{\rho}$ with respect to time for the XYZ reference, we must remember that $\boldsymbol{i}$, $\boldsymbol{j}$, and $\boldsymbol{k}$ of Eq. 15.11 generally will each be a function of time, since these vectors will generally have some rotational motion relative to the XYZ reference. Thus, if dots are used for the time derivatives:

$$\left(\frac{d\boldsymbol{\rho}}{dt}\right)_{XYZ} = (\dot{x}\boldsymbol{i} + \dot{y}\boldsymbol{j} + \dot{z}\boldsymbol{k}) + (x\dot{\boldsymbol{i}} + y\dot{\boldsymbol{j}} + z\dot{\boldsymbol{k}}) \tag{15.13}$$

The unit vector $\boldsymbol{i}$ is a vector *fixed* in reference xyz, and accordingly $\dot{\boldsymbol{i}}$ equals $\boldsymbol{\omega} \times \boldsymbol{i}$. The same conclusions apply to $\boldsymbol{j}$ and $\boldsymbol{k}$. The last expression in parentheses can then be stated as

$$\begin{aligned}(x\dot{\boldsymbol{i}} + y\dot{\boldsymbol{j}} + z\dot{\boldsymbol{k}}) &= x(\boldsymbol{\omega} \times \boldsymbol{i}) + y(\boldsymbol{\omega} \times \boldsymbol{j}) + z(\boldsymbol{\omega} \times \boldsymbol{k}) \\ &= \boldsymbol{\omega} \times (x\boldsymbol{i}) + \boldsymbol{\omega} \times (y\boldsymbol{j}) + \boldsymbol{\omega} \times (z\boldsymbol{k}) \\ &= \boldsymbol{\omega} \times (x\boldsymbol{i} + y\boldsymbol{j} + z\boldsymbol{k}) = \boldsymbol{\omega} \times \boldsymbol{\rho}\end{aligned} \tag{15.14}$$

In Eq. 15.13 we can replace $(\dot{x}\boldsymbol{i} + \dot{y}\boldsymbol{j} + \dot{z}\boldsymbol{k})$ by $(d\boldsymbol{\rho}/dt)_{xyz}$, in accordance with Eq. 15.12, and $(x\dot{\boldsymbol{i}} + y\dot{\boldsymbol{j}} + z\dot{\boldsymbol{k}})$ by $\boldsymbol{\omega} \times \boldsymbol{\rho}$, in accordance with Eq. 15.14. Hence,

$$\left(\frac{d\boldsymbol{\rho}}{dt}\right)_{XYZ} = \left(\frac{d\boldsymbol{\rho}}{dt}\right)_{xyz} + \boldsymbol{\omega} \times \boldsymbol{\rho} \tag{15.15}$$

We can generalize the preceding result for any vector $\boldsymbol{A}$:

$$\left(\frac{d\boldsymbol{A}}{dt}\right)_{XYZ} = \left(\frac{d\boldsymbol{A}}{dt}\right)_{xyz} + \boldsymbol{\omega} \times \boldsymbol{A} \tag{15.16}$$

where, you must remember, $\boldsymbol{\omega}$ without subscripts will always be the *angular velocity of the xyz reference relative to the XYZ reference.* Note that Eq. 15.1 is a special case of Eq. 15.16 since for $\boldsymbol{A}$ fixed in xyz, $(d\boldsymbol{A}/dt)_{xyz} = \boldsymbol{0}$. We shall have much use for this relationship in succeeding sections.

15.7 Relationship Between Velocities of a Particle for Different References

We shall now define the velocity of a particle again in the presence of several references:

The velocity of a particle relative to a reference is the derivative as seen from this reference of the position vector of the particle in the reference.

In Fig. 15.24, the velocities of the particle P relative to the XYZ and the xyz references are, respectively,[9]

$$\boldsymbol{V}_{XYZ} = \left(\frac{d\boldsymbol{r}}{dt}\right)_{XYZ}, \qquad \boldsymbol{V}_{xyz} = \left(\frac{d\boldsymbol{\rho}}{dt}\right)_{xyz} \tag{15.17}$$

Since a vector can always be decomposed into *any* set of orthogonal components, $\boldsymbol{V}_{XYZ}$ can be expressed in components parallel to the xyz reference at any time t while $\boldsymbol{V}_{xyz}$ may be expressed in components parallel to the XYZ reference at any time t.

Now, we shall relate these velocities by first noting that

$$\boldsymbol{r} = \boldsymbol{R} + \boldsymbol{\rho} \tag{15.18}$$

Differentiating with respect to time for the XYZ reference, we have

$$\left(\frac{d\boldsymbol{r}}{dt}\right)_{XYZ} \equiv \boldsymbol{V}_{XYZ} = \left(\frac{d\boldsymbol{R}}{dt}\right)_{XYZ} + \left(\frac{d\boldsymbol{\rho}}{dt}\right)_{XYZ} \tag{15.19}$$

The term $(d\boldsymbol{R}/dt)_{XYZ}$ is clearly the velocity of the origin of the xyz reference relative to the XYZ reference, according to our definitions, and we denote this velocity as $\dot{\boldsymbol{R}}$. The term $(d\boldsymbol{\rho}/dt)_{XYZ}$ can be replaced, by use of Eq. 15.15, in which $(d\boldsymbol{\rho}/dt)_{xyz}$ is the velocity of the particle relative to the xyz reference. Denoting $(d\boldsymbol{\rho}/dt)_{xyz}$ simply as $\boldsymbol{V}_{xyz}$, we find that the foregoing equation then becomes the desired relation:

$$\boldsymbol{V}_{XYZ} = \boldsymbol{V}_{xyz} + \dot{\boldsymbol{R}} + \boldsymbol{\omega} \times \boldsymbol{\rho} \tag{15.20}$$

We reiterate the understanding that $\boldsymbol{\omega}$ *without* subscripts represents the angular velocity of xyz relative to XYZ. This $\boldsymbol{\omega}$ always goes into the last expression of Eq. 15.20.

Note that in Sections 15.4 and 15.5 we considered the motion of *two* particles in a rigid body as seen from a *single* reference. Now we are considering the motion of a *single* particle as seen from *two* references.

The multireference approach can be very useful. For instance, we could know the motion of a particle relative to some device, such as a rocket, to which we attach a reference xyz. Furthermore, from telemetering devices, we know the translational and rotational motion (**Chasles' theorem**) of the rocket (and hence xyz) relative to an inertial reference XYZ. It is often important to know the motion of the aforementioned particle relative directly to the inertial reference. The multireference approach clearly is invaluable for such problems.

We now illustrate the use of Eq. 15.20. We shall proceed in a particular methodical way which we encourage you to follow in your homework problems. In these problems, we remind you the dot over a vector generally represents a time derviative as seen from XYZ.

[9]Generally, we have employed $\boldsymbol{r}$ as a position vector and $\boldsymbol{\rho}$ as a displacement vector. With two references, we shall often use $\boldsymbol{\rho}$ to denote a position vector for one of the references.

Example 15.8

An airplane moving at 200 ft/sec is undergoing a roll of 2 rad/min (Fig. 15.25). When the plane is horizontal, an antenna is moving out at a speed of 8 ft/sec relative to the plane and is at a position of 10 ft from the centerline of the plane. If we assume that the axis of roll corresponds to the centerline, what is the velocity of the antenna end relative to the ground when the plane is horizontal?

A *stationary reference XYZ on the ground* is shown in the diagram. A moving reference *xyz is fixed to the plane* with the x axis along the axis of roll and the y axis collinear with the antenna. We announce this formally as follows:

Fix *xyz* to plane.
Fix *XYZ* to ground.

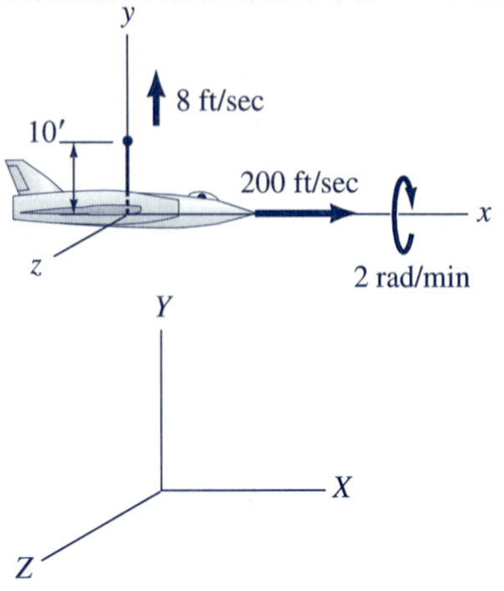

Figure 15.25. *xyz* fixed to plane; *XYZ* fixed to ground.

We then proceed in the following manner:

A. Motion of particle (antenna end) relative to *xyz*[10]

$$\boldsymbol{\rho} = 10\boldsymbol{j} \text{ ft}$$
$$V_{xyz} = 8\boldsymbol{j} \text{ ft/sec}$$

B. Motion of *xyz* (moving reference) relative to *XYZ* (fixed reference)

$$\dot{\boldsymbol{R}} = 200\boldsymbol{i} \text{ ft/sec}$$
$$\boldsymbol{\omega} = -\tfrac{2}{60}\boldsymbol{i} = -\tfrac{1}{30}\boldsymbol{i} \text{ rad/sec}$$

We now employ Eq. 15.20 to get

$$V_{XYZ} = V_{xyz} = \dot{\boldsymbol{R}} + \boldsymbol{\omega} \times \boldsymbol{\rho}$$
$$= 8\boldsymbol{j} + 200\boldsymbol{i} + \left(-\frac{\boldsymbol{i}}{30}\right) \times (10\boldsymbol{j})$$

$$V_{XYZ} = 200\boldsymbol{i} + 8\boldsymbol{j} - \tfrac{1}{3}\boldsymbol{k} \text{ ft/sec}$$

[10]Note that since the corresponding axes of the references are parallel to each other at the instant of interest, the unit vectors $\boldsymbol{i}$, $\boldsymbol{j}$, and $\boldsymbol{k}$ apply to either reference at the instant of interest. We will arrange *xyz* and *XYZ* this way whenever possible.

Note from the preceding example that in Part *A*, we are using the dynamics of a particle as presented in Chapters 11-14, while in Part *B* we are implementing **Chasles' theorem** as presented in this chapter. Your author based on long experience urges the student to work in this methodical manner.

Example 15.9

A tank is moving up an incline with a speed of 10 km/hr in Fig. 15.26. The turret is rotating at a speed ω_1 of 2 rad/sec relative to the tank, and the gun barrel is being lowered (rotating) at a speed ω_2 of .3 rad/sec relative to the turret. What is the velocity of point *A* of the gun barrel relative to the tank and relative to the ground? The gun barrel is 3 m in length. We proceed as follows (see Fig. 15.27).

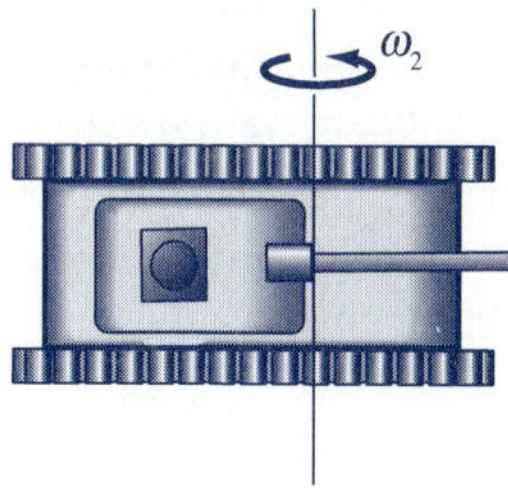

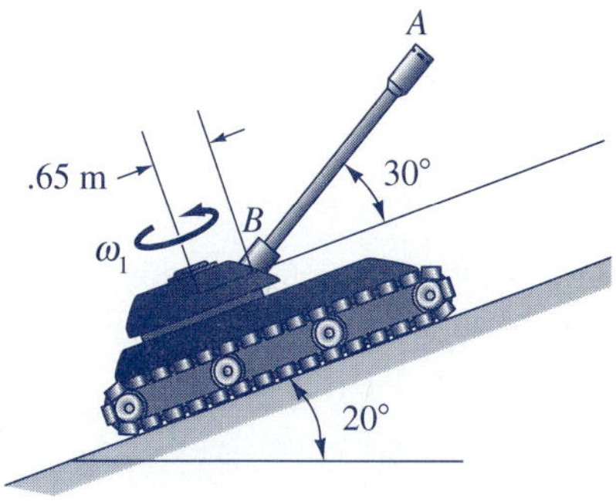

Figure 15.26. Tank with turret and gun barrel in motion.

Fix *xyz* to turret.
Fix *XYZ* to tank.

A. Motion of particle relative to *xyz*

$$\boldsymbol{\rho} = 3(\cos 30°\boldsymbol{j} + \sin 30°\boldsymbol{k}) = 2.60\boldsymbol{j} + 1.50\boldsymbol{k} \text{ m}$$

Since $\boldsymbol{\rho}$ is fixed in the gun barrel, which has an angular velocity $\boldsymbol{\omega}_2$ relative to *xyz*, we have

$$\begin{aligned} \boldsymbol{V}_{xyz} &= \left(\frac{d\boldsymbol{\rho}}{dt}\right)_{xyz} = \boldsymbol{\omega}_2 \times \boldsymbol{\rho} = (-3\boldsymbol{i}) \times (2.60\boldsymbol{j} + 1.5\boldsymbol{k}) \\ &= -.780\boldsymbol{k} + .45\boldsymbol{j} \text{ m/sec} \end{aligned}$$

B. Motion of *xyz* relative to *XYZ*

$$\boldsymbol{R} = .65\boldsymbol{j}$$

Since $\boldsymbol{R}$ is fixed in the turret, which is rotating with angular speed $\boldsymbol{\omega}_1$ relative to *XYZ*, we have

$$\begin{aligned} \dot{\boldsymbol{R}} &= \boldsymbol{\omega}_1 \times \boldsymbol{R} = 2\boldsymbol{k} \times .65\boldsymbol{j} = -1.3\boldsymbol{i} \text{ m/sec} \\ \boldsymbol{\omega} &= \boldsymbol{\omega}_1 = 2\boldsymbol{k} \text{ rad/sec} \end{aligned}$$

We can now substitute into the basic equation relating $\boldsymbol{V}_{xyz}$ to $\boldsymbol{V}_{XYZ}$. That is,

$$\begin{aligned} \boldsymbol{V}_{XYZ} &= \boldsymbol{V}_{xyz} + \dot{\boldsymbol{R}} + \boldsymbol{\omega} \times \boldsymbol{\rho} \\ &= (-.780\boldsymbol{k} + .45\boldsymbol{j}) - 1.3\boldsymbol{i} + (2\boldsymbol{k}) \times (2.60\boldsymbol{j} + 1.50\boldsymbol{k}) \end{aligned}$$

$$\boldsymbol{V}_{XYZ} = -6.5\boldsymbol{i} + .45\boldsymbol{j} - .780\boldsymbol{k} \text{ m/sec}$$

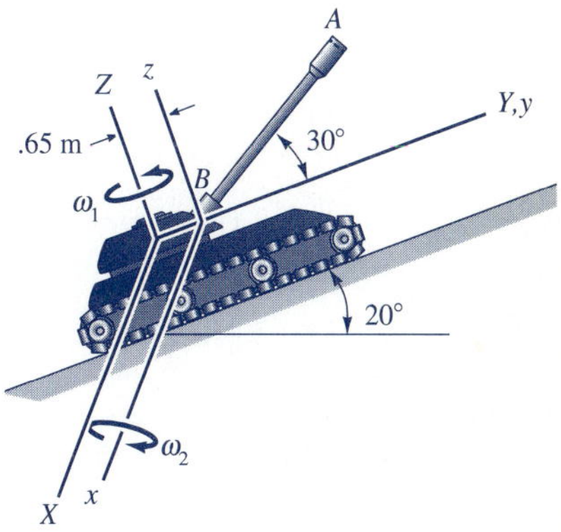

Figure 15.27. *xyz* fixed to turret; *XYZ* fixed to tank.

This result is the desired velocity of *A* relative to the tank. Since the tank is moving with a speed of (10)(1,000)/(3,600) = 2.78 m/sec relative to the ground, we can say that *A* has a velocity relative to the ground given as

$$\boldsymbol{V}_{\text{ground}} = \boldsymbol{V}_{XYZ} + 2.78\boldsymbol{j}$$

$$\boldsymbol{V}_{\text{ground}} = -6.5\boldsymbol{i} + 3.23\boldsymbol{j} - .780\boldsymbol{k} \text{ m/sec}$$

Example 15.10

A gunboat in heavy seas is firing its main battery (see Fig. 15.28). The gun barrel has an angular velocity ω_1 relative to the turret, while the turret has an angular velocity ω_2 relative to the ship. If we wish to have the velocity components of the emerging shell to be zero in the stationary X and Z directions at a certain specific time t, what should ω_1 and ω_2 be at this instant? At this instant, the ship has a translational velocity given as

$$\boldsymbol{V}_{ship} = .02\boldsymbol{i} + .016\boldsymbol{k} \text{ m/s}$$

Take the inclination of the barrel to be $\theta = 30°$. Determine also the velocity of the gun barrel tip A.

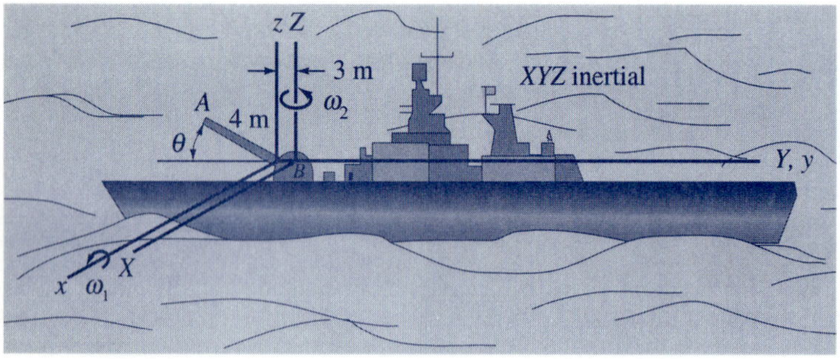

Figure 15.28. A gunboat in heavy seas firing its main battery.

We proceed to solve this problem by the following positioning of axes shown on Fig. 15.28.

Fix xyz to turret.
Fix XYZ to the ground (inertial reference).

We can now proceed with the detailed analysis of the problem.

A. Motion of A relative to xyz

$$\boldsymbol{\rho} = -(4)(.866)\boldsymbol{j} + (4)(.5)\boldsymbol{k} = -3.464\boldsymbol{j} + 2\boldsymbol{k} \text{ m}$$
$$\boldsymbol{V}_{xyz} = \boldsymbol{\omega}_1 \times \boldsymbol{\rho} = \omega_1\boldsymbol{i} \times (-3.464\boldsymbol{j} + 2\boldsymbol{k}) = -3.464\omega_1\boldsymbol{k} - 2\omega_1\boldsymbol{j} \text{ m/s}$$

Example 15.10 (Continued)

B. Motion of *xyz* relative to *XYZ*

$$\boldsymbol{R} = -3\boldsymbol{j} \text{ m}$$
$$\dot{\boldsymbol{R}} = \omega_2\boldsymbol{k} \times (-3\boldsymbol{j}) + (.02\boldsymbol{i} + .016\boldsymbol{k}) = (3\omega_2 + .02)\boldsymbol{i} + .016\boldsymbol{k} \text{ m/s}$$
$$\boldsymbol{\omega} = \omega_2\boldsymbol{k} \text{ rad/s}$$

We can now proceed with the calculations.

$$\begin{aligned} \boldsymbol{V}_{XYZ} &= \boldsymbol{V}_{xyz} + \dot{\boldsymbol{R}} + \boldsymbol{\omega} \times \boldsymbol{\rho} \\ &= (-3.464\omega_1\boldsymbol{k} - 2\omega_1\boldsymbol{j}) + (3\omega_2 + .02)\boldsymbol{i} + .016\boldsymbol{k} + (\omega_2\boldsymbol{k}) \times (-3.464\boldsymbol{j} + 2\boldsymbol{k}) \\ &= -3.464\omega_1\boldsymbol{k} - 2\omega_1\boldsymbol{i} + 3\omega_2\boldsymbol{i} + .02\boldsymbol{i} + .016\boldsymbol{k} + 3.464\omega_2\boldsymbol{i} \end{aligned}$$
$$\therefore \boldsymbol{V}_{XYZ} = (3\omega_2 + 3.464\omega_2 + .02)\boldsymbol{i} + (-2\omega_1)\boldsymbol{j} + (-3.464\omega_1 + .016)\boldsymbol{k} \text{ m/s}$$

Let $(\boldsymbol{V}_{XYZ})_X = \boldsymbol{0}$

$$\therefore 6.464\omega_2 = -.02 \qquad \omega_2 = -.003094 \text{ rad/s}$$

Let $(\boldsymbol{V}_{XYZ})_Z = \boldsymbol{0}$

$$\therefore -3.464\omega_1 = -.016 \qquad \omega_1 = .004619 \text{ rad/s}$$

Finally, we can give $\boldsymbol{V}_{XYZ}$ as $\quad \boldsymbol{V}_{XYZ} = -2\omega_1\boldsymbol{j} = -.009238\boldsymbol{j} \text{ m/s}$

In some of the homework problem diagrams, in the remainder of the chapter, a set of axes *xyz* has been shown as a suggestion for use by the student. This has been done to help clarify the geometry of the diagram. Also, if the student chooses to use these axes he/she will be able to compare more easily his/her solution with that of the author as presented in the instructor's manual. However, (and note this carefully) the student must decide independently as to how to *fix this reference* and to state clearly as we have done in the examples *how this reference has been fixed.*

Also, we strongly urge the student to make careful clear diagrams and to follow the orderly progression of steps (**A. Motion of particle etc., etc.** followed by **B. Motion of *xyz* etc., etc.**).

PROBLEMS

15.70. A space laboratory, in order to simulate gravity, rotates relative to inertial reference XYZ at a rate ω_1. For occupant A to feel comfortable, what should ω_1 be? Clearly, at the center room B, there is close to zero gravity for zero-g experiments. A conveyor along one of the spokes transports items from the living quarters at the periphery to the zero-gravity laboratory at the center. In particular, a particle D has a velocity toward B of 5 m/sec relative to the space station. What is its velocity relative to the inertial reference XYZ?

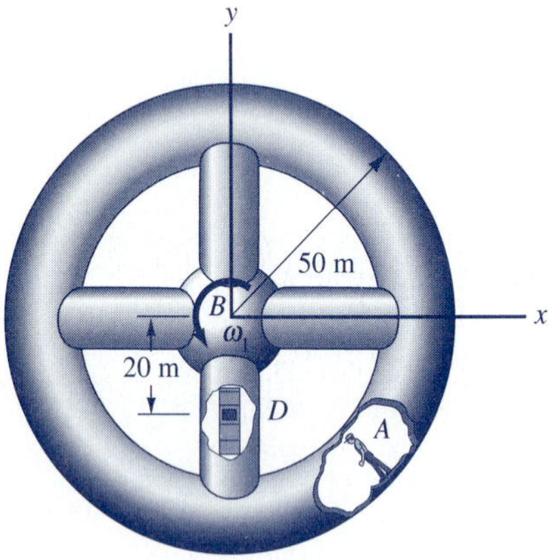

Figure P.15.70.

15.71. Bodies a and b slide away from each other each with a constant velocity of 5 ft/sec along the axis C–C mounted on a platform. The platform rotates relative to the ground reference XYZ at an angular velocity of 10 rad/sec about axis E–E and has an angular acceleration of 5 rad/sec^2 relative to the ground reference XYZ at the time when the bodies are at a distance $r = 3$ ft from E–E. Determine the velocity of particle b relative to the ground reference.

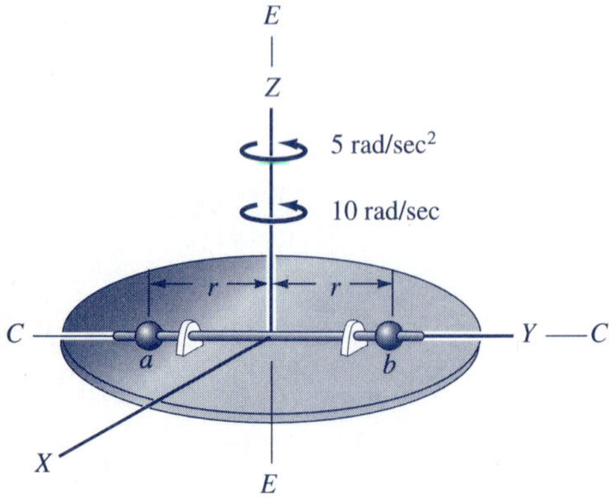

Figure P.15.71.

15.72. A particle rotates at a constant angular speed of 10 rad/sec on a platform, while the platform rotates with a constant angular speed of 50 rad/sec about axis A–A. What is the velocity of the particle P at the instant the platform is in the XY plane and the radius vector to the particle forms an angle of 30° with the Y axis as shown?

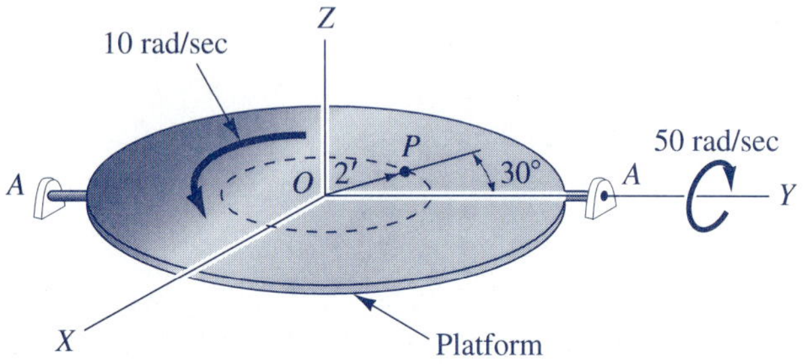

Figure P.15.72.

15.73. A platform A is rotating with constant angular speed ω_1 of 1 rad/sec. A second platform B rides on A, contains a row of test tubes, and has a constant angular speed ω_2 of .2 rad/sec relative to the platform A. A third platform C is in no way connected with platforms A and B. E on platform C is positioned above A and B and carries dispensers of chemicals which are electrically operated at proper times to dispense drops into the test tubes held by B below. What should the angular speed ω_3 be for platform E at instant shown if it is to dispense a drop of chemical having a zero tangential velocity relative to the test tube below?

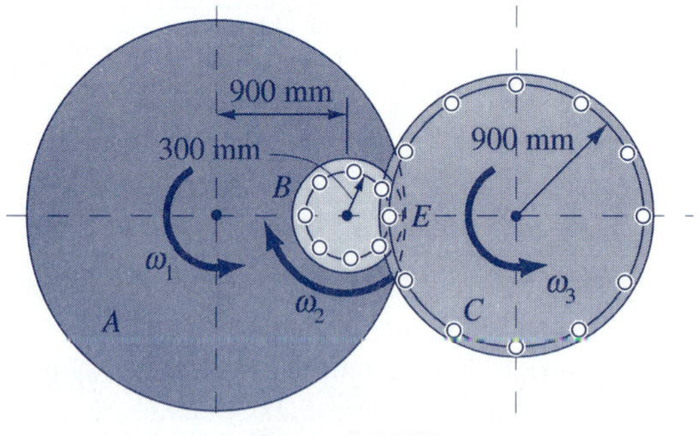

Figure P.15.73.

15.74. In an amusement park ride, the cockpit containing two occupants can rotate at an angular speed ω_1 relative to the main arm OB. The arm can rotate with angular speed ω_2 relative to the ground. For the position shown in the diagram and for $\omega_1 = 2$ rad/sec and $\omega_2 = .2$ rad/sec, find the velocity of point A (corresponding to the position of the eyes of an occupant) relative to the ground.

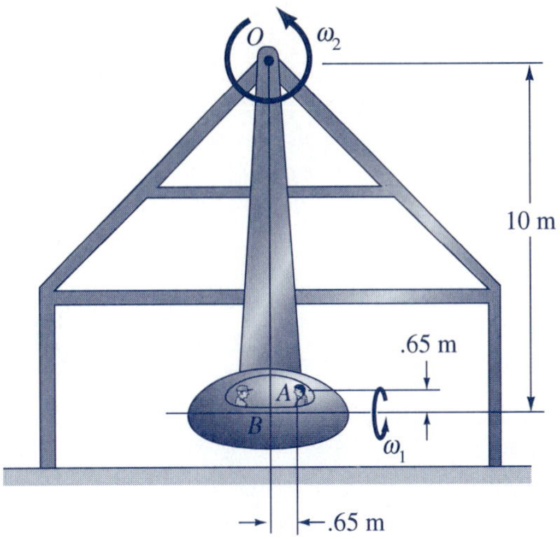

Figure P.15.74.

15.75. A water sprinkler has .4 cfs (cubic ft/sec) of water fed into the base. The sprinkler turns at the rate ω_1 of 1 rad/sec. What is the speed of the jet of water relative to the ground at the exits? The outlet area of the nozzle cross section is .75 in^2. [*Hint:* The volume of flow through a cross section is *VA*, where *V* is the velocity and *A* is the area of the cross section.]

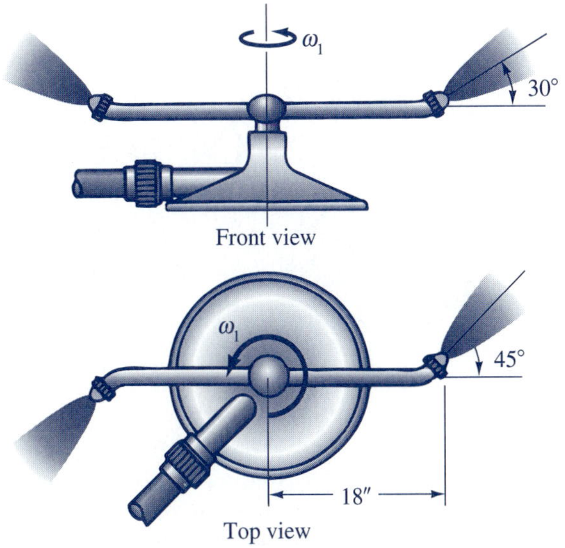

Figure P.15.75.

15.76. A tank is moving over rough terrain while firing its main gun at a fixed target. The barrel and turret of the gun partly compensate for the motion of the tank proper by giving the barrel an angular velocity $\boldsymbol{\omega}_1$ relative to the turret and, simultaneously, by giving the turret an angular velocity $\boldsymbol{\omega}_2$ relative to the tank proper such that any instant the velocity of end *A* of the barrel has zero velocity in the *X* and *Z* directions relative to the ground reference. What should these angular velocities be for the following translational motion of the tank:

$$V_{\text{TANK}} = 10\boldsymbol{i} + 4\boldsymbol{k} \text{ m/s}$$

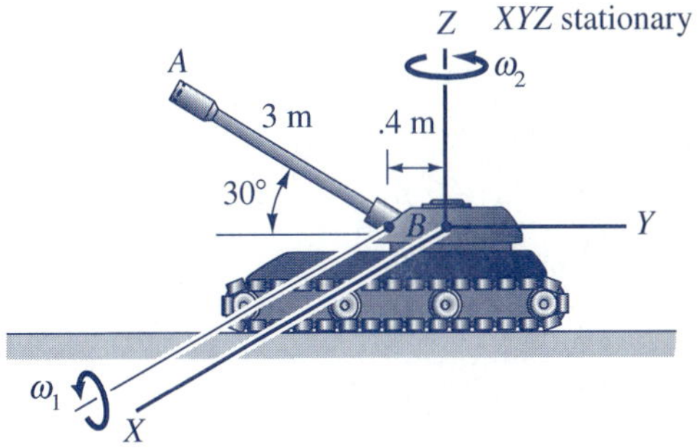

Figure P.15.76.

15.77. We can show that Eq. 15.6 is actually a special case of Eq. 15.20. For this purpose, consider a rigid body moving relative to *XYZ*. Choose two points *a* and *b* in the body. The body has a translational velocity corresponding to the velocity of point *a* and a rotational velocity $\boldsymbol{\omega}$ as shown in the diagram. Now embed a reference *xyz* into the body with origin at point *a*. Next, use this diagram and consider point *b* to show that Eq. 15.20 can be reformulated to be identical to Eq. 15.6.

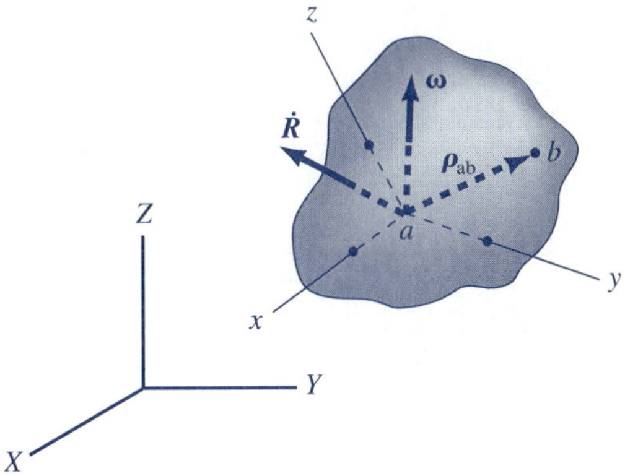

Figure P.15.77.

15.78. A simple-impulse type of turbomachine called a *Pelton* water wheel has a single jet of water issuing out of a nozzle and impinging on the system of buckets attached to a wheel. The runner, which is the assembly of buckets and wheel, has a radius of r to the center of the buckets. The shape of the bucket is also shown where a horizontal midsection of the bucket has been taken. Note that the jet is split in two parts by the bucket and is rotated relative to the bucket in the horizontal plane as measured by β. If we neglect gravity and friction, the speed of the water relative to the bucket is unchanged during the action. Suppose that 8 liters of water per second flow through the nozzle, whose cross-sectional area at the exit is 2,000 mm^2. If r = 1 m, what should ω_1 be (in rpm) for the water on average to have zero velocity relative to the ground in the Y direction when it comes off the bucket? Take β = 10°. (Why is it desirable to have the exit velocity equal to zero in the Y direction?) See the hint of Problem 15.75.

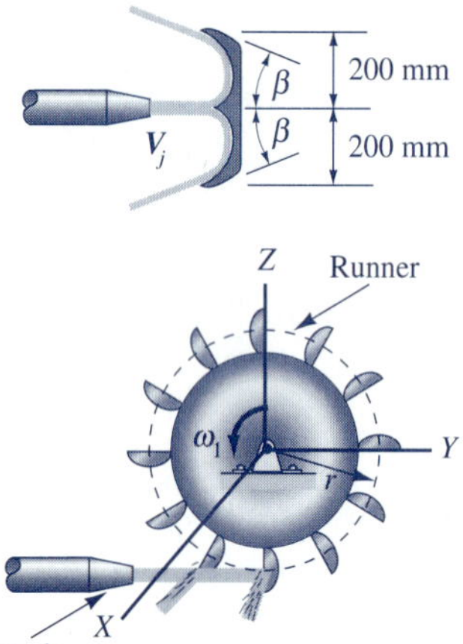

Figure P.15.78.

15.79. A propeller-driven airplane is moving at a speed of 130 km/hr. Also, it is undergoing a yaw rotation of 1/4 rad/sec and is simultaneously undergoing a loop rotation of 1/4 rad/sec. The propeller is rotating at the rate of 100 rpm with a sense in the positive Y direction. What is the velocity of the tip of the propeller a relative to the ground at the instant that the plane is horizontal as shown? The propeller is 3 m in total length and at the instant of interest the blade is in a vertical position.

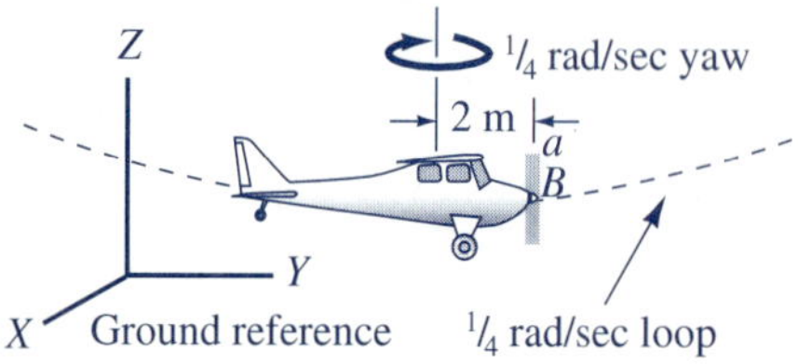

Figure P.15.79.

15.80. A crane moves to the right at a speed of 5 km/hr. The boom OB, which is 15 m long, is being raised at an angular speed ω_2 relative to the cab of .4 rad/sec, while the cab is rotating at an angular speed ω_1 of .2 rad/sec relative to the base. What is the velocity of pin B relative to the ground at the instant when OB is at an angle of 35° with the ground? The axis of rotation O of the boom is 1 m from the axis of rotation A–A of the cab, as shown in the diagram.

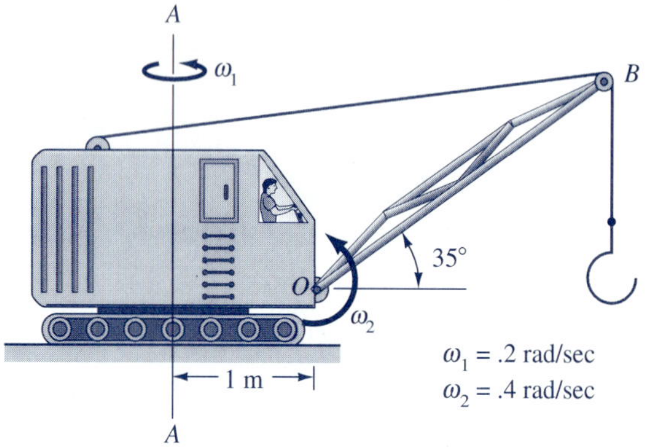

Figure P.15.80.

15.81. A power shovel main arm AC rotates with angular speed ω_1 of .3 rad/sec relative to the cab. Arm ED rotates at a speed ω_2 of .4 rad/sec relative to the main arm AC. The cab rotates about axis A–A at a speed ω_3 of .15 rad/sec relative to the tracks which are stationary. What is the velocity of point D, the center of the shovel, at the instant of interest shown in the diagram? AB has a length of 5 m and BD has a length of 4 m.

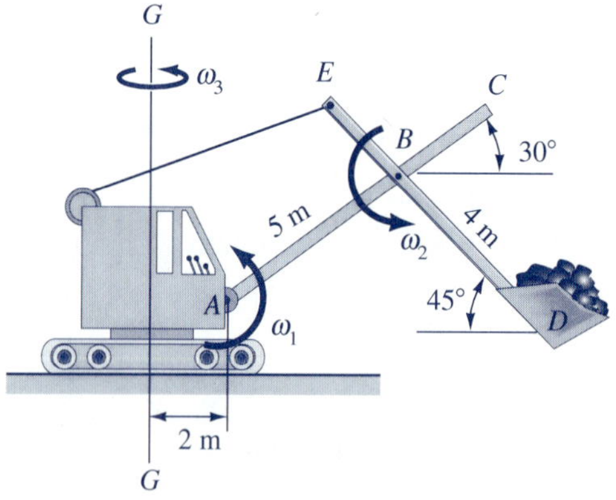

Figure P.15.81.

15.82. An antiaircraft gun is shown in action. The values of ω_1 and ω_2 are .3 rad/sec and .6 rad/sec, respectively. At the instant shown, what is the velocity of a projectile *normal* to the direction of the gun barrel when it just leaves the gun barrel as seen from the ground?

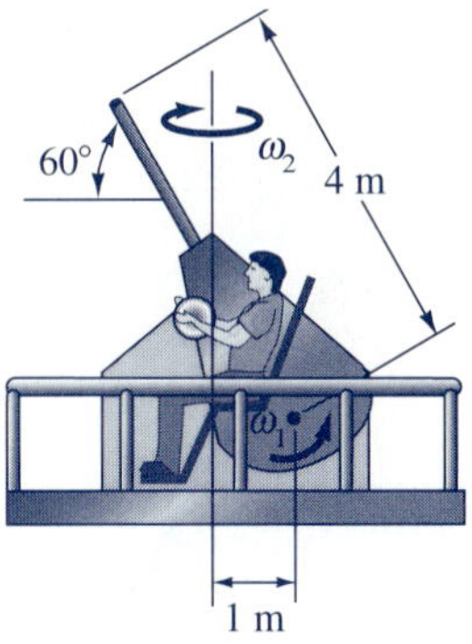

Figure P.15.82.

15.83. A cone is rolling without slipping about the Z axis such that its centerline rotates at the rate ω_1 of 5 rad/sec. Use a multireference approach to determine the total angular velocity of the body relative to the ground.

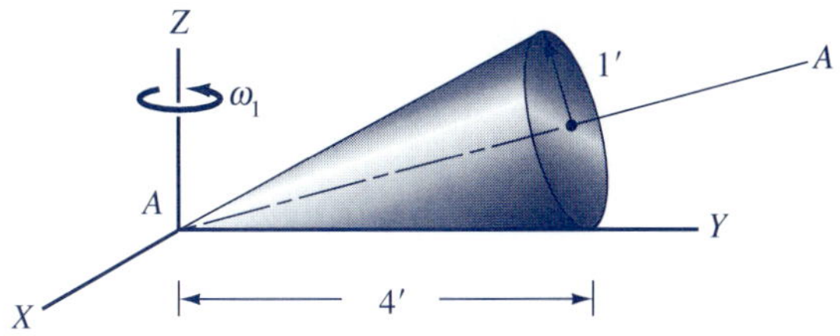

Figure P.15.83.

15.84. Find the velocity of gear tooth A relative to the ground reference XYZ. Note that ω_1 and ω_2 are both relative to the ground. Bevel gear A is free to rotate in the collar at C. Take $\omega_1 = 2$ rad/sec and $\omega_2 = 4$ rad/sec.

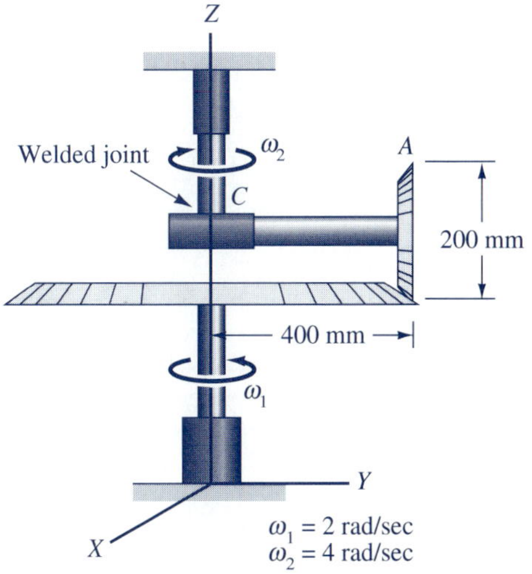

Figure P.15.84.

15.85. In a merry-go-round, the main platform rotates at the rate ω_1 of 10 revolutions per minute. A set of 45° bevel gears causes B to rotate at an angular speed $\dot{\theta}$ relative to the platform. The horse is mounted on AB, which slides in a slot at C and is moved at A by shaft B, as indicated in the diagram, where part of the merry-go-round is shown. If $AB = 1$ ft and $AC = 15$ ft, compute the velocity of point C relative to the platform. Then, compute the velocity of point C relative to the ground. Take $\theta = 45°$ at the instant of interest. What is the angular velocity of the horse relative to the platform and relative to the ground at the instant of interest?

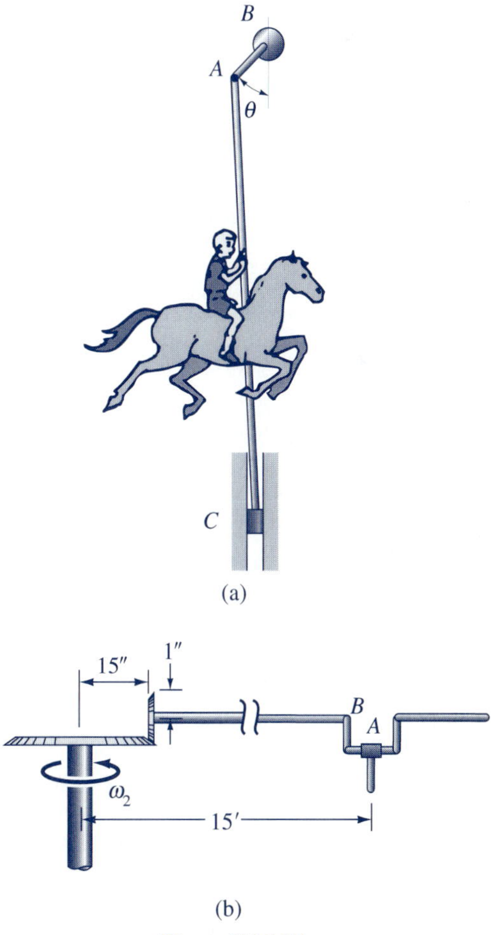

Figure P.15.85.

15.86. Rod BO rotates at a constant angular speed $\dot{\theta}$ of 5 rad/sec clockwise. A collar A on the rod is pinned to a slider C, which moves in the groove shown in the diagram. When $\theta = 60°$, compute the speed of the collar A relative to the ground. What is the speed of collar A relative to the rod?

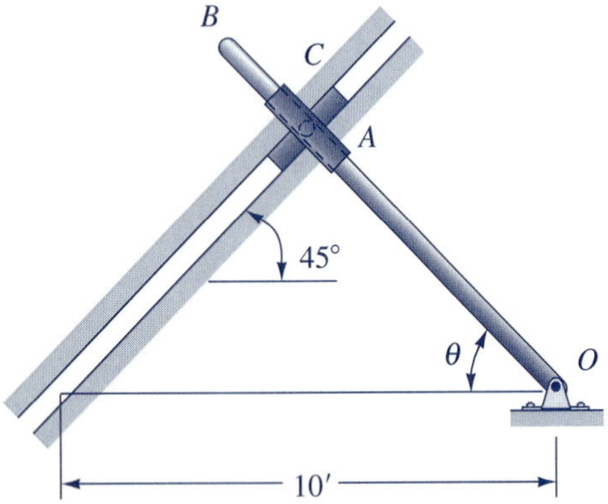

Figure P.15.86.

15.87. Work Problem 15.86 assuming that pin O is on rollers moving to the right at a speed of 3 ft/sec relative to the ground. In addition, OB rotates at a constant angular speed $\dot{\theta}$ of 5 rad/sec clockwise all at the instant of interest.

15.88. Rod AD rotates at a constant speed $\dot{\theta}$ of 2 rad/sec. Collar C on the rod DA is constrained to move in the circular groove shown in the diagram. When the rod is at the position shown, compute the speed of collar C relative to the ground. What is the speed of collar C relative to the rod AD? Point A is stationary.

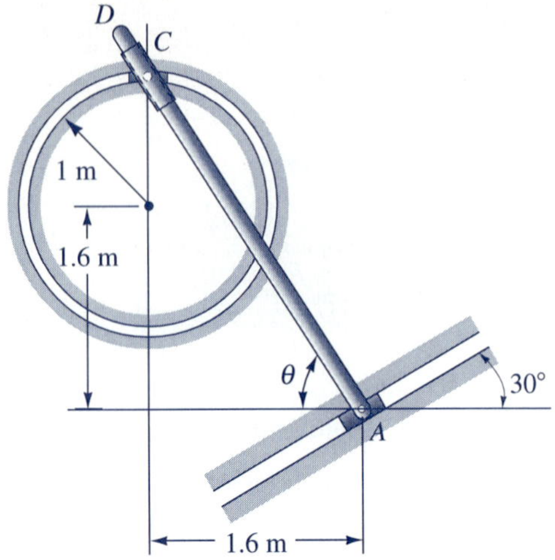

Figure P.15.88.

15.89. In Problem 15.88, assume, in addition to the rotation of bar AD, that pin A is moving at a speed of 1.6 m/sec up the grooved incline.

15.90. Rod AC is connected to a gear D and is guided by a bearing B. Bearing B can rotate only in the plane of the gears. If the angular speed of AC is 5 rad/sec clockwise, what is the angular speed of gear D relative to the ground? The diameter of gear D is 2 ft.

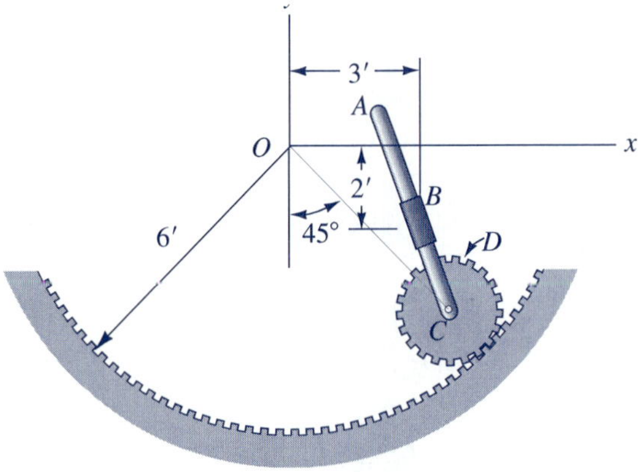

Figure P.15.90.

15.8 Acceleration of a Particle for Different References

The acceleration of a particle relative to a coordinate system is simply the time derivative, as seen from the coordinate system, of the velocity relative to the coordinate system. Thus, observing Fig. 15.29, we can say:

$$\begin{aligned} \boldsymbol{a}_{XYZ} &= \left(\frac{d}{dt}\mathbf{V}_{XYZ}\right)_{XYZ} = \left(\frac{d^2\mathbf{r}}{dt^2}\right)_{XYZ} \\ \boldsymbol{a}_{xyz} &= \left(\frac{d}{dt}\mathbf{V}_{xyz}\right)_{xyz} = \left(\frac{d^2\boldsymbol{\rho}}{dt^2}\right)_{xyz} \end{aligned} \quad (15.21)$$

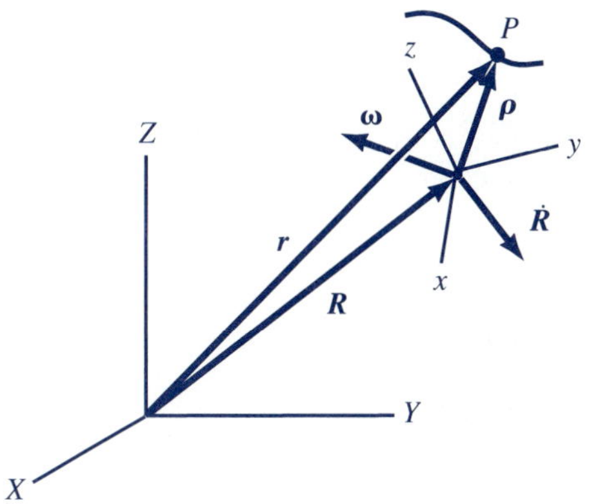

Figure 15.29. *xyz* moves arbitrarily relative to *XYZ*.

This notation may at first seem cumbersome to you, but it will soon be simplified.

Let us now relate the acceleration vectors of a particle for two references moving arbitrarily relative to each other. We do this by differentiating with respect to time the terms in Eq. 15.20 for the *XYZ* reference. Thus,

$$\left(\frac{d\mathbf{V}_{XYZ}}{dt}\right)_{XYZ} \equiv \boldsymbol{a}_{XYZ} = \left(\frac{d\mathbf{V}_{xyz}}{dt}\right)_{XYZ} + \ddot{\boldsymbol{R}} + \left[\frac{d}{dt}(\boldsymbol{\omega} \times \boldsymbol{\rho})\right]_{XYZ} \quad (15.22)$$

Now carry out the derivative of the cross product using the product rule.

$$\boldsymbol{a}_{XYZ} = \left(\frac{d\mathbf{V}_{xyz}}{dt}\right)_{XYZ} + \ddot{\boldsymbol{R}} + \boldsymbol{\omega} \times \left(\frac{d\boldsymbol{\rho}}{dt}\right)_{XYZ} + \left(\frac{d\boldsymbol{\omega}}{dt}\right)_{XYZ} \times \boldsymbol{\rho} \quad (15.23)$$

To introduce more physically meaningful terms, we can replace

$$\left(\frac{d\boldsymbol{V}_{xyz}}{dt}\right)_{XYZ} \quad \text{and} \quad \left(\frac{d\boldsymbol{\rho}}{dt}\right)_{XYZ}$$

using Eq. 15.16 in the following way:

$$\left(\frac{d\boldsymbol{V}_{xyz}}{dt}\right)_{XYZ} = \left(\frac{d\boldsymbol{V}_{xyz}}{dt}\right)_{xyz} + \boldsymbol{\omega} \times \boldsymbol{V}_{xyz}$$
$$\left(\frac{d\boldsymbol{\rho}}{dt}\right)_{XYZ} = \left(\frac{d\boldsymbol{\rho}}{dt}\right)_{xyz} + \boldsymbol{\omega} \times \boldsymbol{\rho}$$

Substituting into Eq. 15.23, we get

$$\boldsymbol{a}_{XYZ} = \left(\frac{d\boldsymbol{V}_{xyz}}{dt}\right)_{xyz} + \boldsymbol{\omega} \times \boldsymbol{V}_{xyz} + \ddot{\boldsymbol{R}} + \boldsymbol{\omega} \times \left(\frac{d\boldsymbol{\rho}}{dt}\right)_{xyz}$$
$$+ \boldsymbol{\omega} \times (\boldsymbol{\omega} \times \boldsymbol{\rho}) + \left(\frac{d\boldsymbol{\omega}}{dt}\right)_{XYZ} \times \boldsymbol{\rho}$$

You will note that $(d\boldsymbol{V}_{xyz}/dt)_{xyz}$ is $\boldsymbol{a}_{xyz}$; that $(d\boldsymbol{\rho}/dt)_{xyz}$ is $\boldsymbol{V}_{xyz}$; and that $(d\boldsymbol{\omega}/dt)_{XYZ}$ is $\dot{\boldsymbol{\omega}}$. Hence, rearranging terms, we have

$$\boldsymbol{a}_{XYZ} = \boldsymbol{a}_{xyz} + \ddot{\boldsymbol{R}} + 2\boldsymbol{\omega} \times \boldsymbol{V}_{xyz} + \dot{\boldsymbol{\omega}} \times \boldsymbol{\rho} + \boldsymbol{\omega} \times (\boldsymbol{\omega} \times \boldsymbol{\rho}) \quad (15.24)$$

where $\boldsymbol{\omega}$ and $\dot{\boldsymbol{\omega}}$ are the angular velocity and acceleration, respectively, of the *xyz* reference relative to the *XYZ* reference. The vector $2(\boldsymbol{\omega} \times \boldsymbol{V}_{xyz})$ is called the *Coriolis acceleration vector*; we shall examine its interesting effects in Section 15.10.

Although Eq. 15.24 may seem somewhat terrifying at first, you will find that, by using it, problems that would otherwise be tremendously difficult can readily be carried out in a systematic manner. *You should keep in mind when solving problems that any of the methods developed in Chapter 11 can be used for determining the motion of the particle relative to the xyz reference or for determining the motion of the origin of xyz relative to the XYZ reference.* We shall now examine several problems, in which we shall use the notation, $\boldsymbol{\omega}_1$, $\boldsymbol{\omega}_2$, etc., to denote the various angular velocities involved. The notation, $\boldsymbol{\omega}$ (i.e., without subscripts), however, will we repeat be reserved to represent the angular velocity of the *xyz* reference relative to the *XYZ* reference.

Example 15.11

A stationary truck is carrying a cockpit for a worker who repairs overhead fixtures. At the instant shown in Fig. 15.30, the base D is rotating at angular speed ω_2 of .1 rad/sec with $\dot{\omega}_2 = .2$ rad/sec^2 relative to the truck. Arm AB is rotating at angular speed ω_1 of .2 rad/sec with $\dot{\omega}_1 = .8$ rad/sec^2 relative to DA. Cockpit C is rotating relative to AB so as to always keep the man upright. What are the velocity and acceleration vectors of the man relative to the ground if $\alpha = 45°$ and $\beta = 30°$ at the instant of interest? Take $DA = 13$ m.

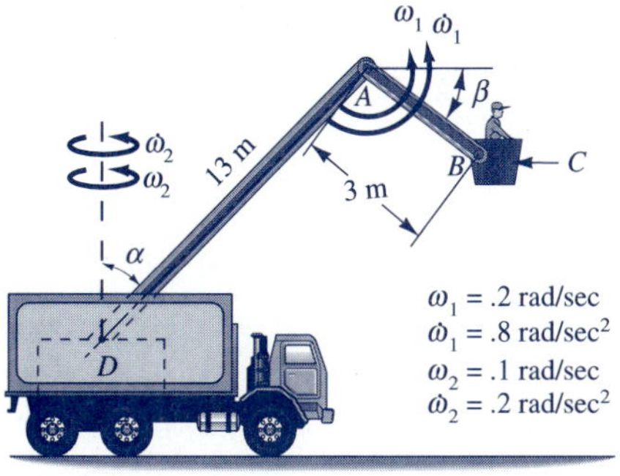

Figure 15.30. Truck with moving cockpit.

Because of the rotation of the cockpit C relative to arm AB to keep the man vertical, clearly, each particle in that body including the man has the same motion as point B of arm AB. Therefore, we shall concentrate our attention on this point.

Fix xyz to arm DA.
Fix XYZ to truck.

This situation is shown in Fig. 15.31.

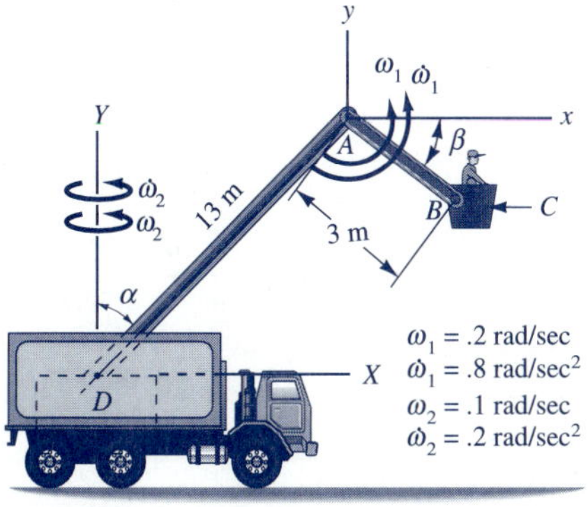

Figure 15.31. *xyz* fixed to *DA*; *XYZ* fixed to truck.

A. Motion of *B* relative to *xyz*

$$\boldsymbol{\rho} = 3(\cos\beta\boldsymbol{i} - \sin\beta\boldsymbol{j}) = 2.60\boldsymbol{i} - 1.5\boldsymbol{j} \text{ m}$$

Example 15.11 (Continued)

Since $\boldsymbol{\rho}$ is fixed in AB, which has angular velocity $\boldsymbol{\omega}_1$ relative to xyz, we have

$$\begin{aligned} \boldsymbol{V}_{xyz} &= \boldsymbol{\omega}_1 \times \boldsymbol{\rho} = (.2\boldsymbol{k}) \times (2.60\boldsymbol{i} - 1.5\boldsymbol{j}) \\ &= .520\boldsymbol{j} + .3\boldsymbol{i} \text{ m/sec} \\ \boldsymbol{a}_{xyz} &= \left(\frac{d\boldsymbol{\omega}_1}{dt}\right)_{xyz} \times \boldsymbol{\rho} + \boldsymbol{\omega}_1 \times \left(\frac{d\boldsymbol{\rho}}{dt}\right)_{xyz} \end{aligned}$$

As seen from xyz, only the value of $\boldsymbol{\omega}_1$ and not its direction is changing. Also note that $(d\boldsymbol{\rho}/dt)_{xyz} = \boldsymbol{V}_{xyz}$. Hence,

$$\begin{aligned} \boldsymbol{a}_{xyz} &= (.8\boldsymbol{k}) \times (2.60\boldsymbol{i} - 1.5\boldsymbol{j}) + (.2\boldsymbol{k}) \times (.520\boldsymbol{j} + .3\boldsymbol{i}) \\ &= 1.09\boldsymbol{i} + 2.14\boldsymbol{j} \text{ m/sec}^2 \end{aligned}$$

B. Motion of *xyz* relative to *XYZ*

$$\boldsymbol{R} = 13(.707\boldsymbol{i} + .707\boldsymbol{j}) = 9.19\boldsymbol{i} + 9.19\boldsymbol{j} \text{ m}$$

Since $\boldsymbol{R}$ is fixed in DA, and since DA rotates with angular velocity $\boldsymbol{\omega}_2$ relative to XYZ, we have

$$\begin{aligned} \dot{\boldsymbol{R}} &= \boldsymbol{\omega}_2 \times \boldsymbol{R} = (.1\boldsymbol{j}) \times (9.19\boldsymbol{i} + 9.19\boldsymbol{j}) \\ &= -.919\boldsymbol{k} \text{ m/sec} \\ \ddot{\boldsymbol{R}} &= \dot{\boldsymbol{\omega}}_2 \times \boldsymbol{R} + \boldsymbol{\omega}_2 \times \dot{\boldsymbol{R}} \\ &= (.2\boldsymbol{j}) \times (9.19\boldsymbol{i} + 9.19\boldsymbol{j}) + (.1\boldsymbol{j}) \times (-.919\boldsymbol{k}) \\ &= -1.838\boldsymbol{k} - .0919\boldsymbol{i} \text{ m/sec}^2 \\ \boldsymbol{\omega} &= \boldsymbol{\omega}_2 = .1\boldsymbol{j} \text{ rad/sec} \\ \dot{\boldsymbol{\omega}} &= \dot{\boldsymbol{\omega}}_2 = .2\boldsymbol{j} \text{ rad/sec}^2 \end{aligned}$$

Hence,

$$\begin{aligned} \boldsymbol{V}_{XYZ} &= \boldsymbol{V}_{xyz} + \dot{\boldsymbol{R}} + \boldsymbol{\omega} \times \boldsymbol{\rho} \\ &= .520\boldsymbol{j} + .3\boldsymbol{i} - .919\boldsymbol{k} + (.1\boldsymbol{j}) \times (2.60\boldsymbol{i} - 1.5\boldsymbol{j}) \end{aligned}$$

$$\boxed{\boldsymbol{V}_{XYZ} = .3\boldsymbol{i} + .520\boldsymbol{j} - 1.179\boldsymbol{k} \text{ m/sec}}$$

$$\begin{aligned} \boldsymbol{a}_{XYZ} &= \boldsymbol{a}_{xyz} + \ddot{\boldsymbol{R}} + 2\boldsymbol{\omega} \times \boldsymbol{V}_{xyz} + \dot{\boldsymbol{\omega}} \times \boldsymbol{\rho} + \boldsymbol{\omega} \times (\boldsymbol{\omega} \times \boldsymbol{\rho}) \\ &= 1.09\boldsymbol{i} + 2.14\boldsymbol{j} - 1.838\boldsymbol{k} - .0919\boldsymbol{i} \\ &\quad + 2(.1\boldsymbol{j}) \times (.520\boldsymbol{j} + .3\boldsymbol{i}) + (.2\boldsymbol{j}) \times (2.60\boldsymbol{i} - 1.5\boldsymbol{j}) \\ &\quad + (.1\boldsymbol{j}) \times [(.1\boldsymbol{j}) \times (2.60\boldsymbol{i} - 1.5\boldsymbol{j})] \end{aligned}$$

$$\boxed{\boldsymbol{a}_{XYZ} = .978\boldsymbol{i} + 2.14\boldsymbol{j} - 2.42\boldsymbol{k} \text{ m/sec}^2}$$

Notice that the essential aspects of the analysis come in the consideration of parts A and B of the problem, while the remaining portion involves direct substitution and vector algebraic operations.

Example 15.12

A wheel rotates with an angular speed ω_2 of 5 rad/sec on a platform which rotates with a speed ω_1 of 10 rad/sec relative to the ground as shown in Fig. 15.32. A valve gate A moves down the spoke of the wheel, and when the spoke is vertical the valve gate has a speed of 20 ft/sec, an acceleration of 10 ft/sec^2 along the spoke, and is 1 ft from the shaft centerline of the wheel. Compute the velocity and acceleration of the valve gate relative to the ground at this instant.

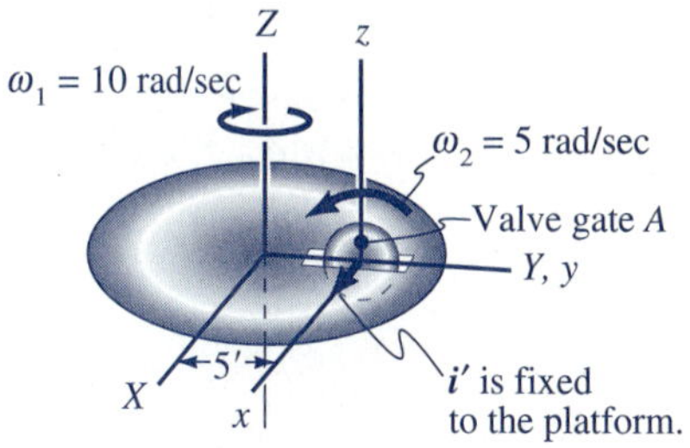

Figure 15.32. *xyz* fixed to wheel; *XYZ* fixed to ground.

Fix xyz to wheel.
Fix XYZ to ground.

A. Motion of particle relative to *xyz*

$$\boldsymbol{\rho} = \boldsymbol{k} \text{ ft}$$
$$\boldsymbol{V}_{xyz} = -20\boldsymbol{k} \text{ ft/sec}$$
$$\boldsymbol{a}_{xyz} = -10\boldsymbol{k} \text{ ft/sec}^2$$

B. Motion of *xyz* relative to *XYZ*

$$\boldsymbol{R} = 5\boldsymbol{j} \text{ ft}$$

Since $\boldsymbol{R}$ is fixed to the platform:

$$\dot{\boldsymbol{R}} = \boldsymbol{\omega}_1 \times \boldsymbol{R} = (-10\boldsymbol{k}) \times (5\boldsymbol{j}) = 50\boldsymbol{i} \text{ ft/sec}$$
$$\ddot{\boldsymbol{R}} = \dot{\boldsymbol{\omega}}_1 \times \boldsymbol{R} + \boldsymbol{\omega}_1 \times \dot{\boldsymbol{R}}$$
$$= \boldsymbol{0} + (-10\boldsymbol{k}) \times (50\boldsymbol{i}) = -500\boldsymbol{j} \text{ ft/sec}^2$$
$$\boldsymbol{\omega} = \boldsymbol{\omega}_2 + \boldsymbol{\omega}_1 = 5\boldsymbol{i} - 10\boldsymbol{k} \text{ rad/sec}$$
$$\dot{\boldsymbol{\omega}} = \dot{\boldsymbol{\omega}}_2 + \dot{\boldsymbol{\omega}}_1$$

Note that $\boldsymbol{\omega}_2$ is of constant magnitude but, because of the bearings of the wheel, $\boldsymbol{\omega}_2$ must rotate with the platform. In short, we can say that $\boldsymbol{\omega}_2$ is *fixed* to the platform and so $\dot{\boldsymbol{\omega}}_2 = \boldsymbol{\omega}_1 \times \boldsymbol{\omega}_2$. Hence,

$$\dot{\boldsymbol{\omega}} = \boldsymbol{\omega}_1 \times \boldsymbol{\omega}_2 + \boldsymbol{0}$$
$$= (-10\boldsymbol{k}) \times (5\boldsymbol{i}) = -50\boldsymbol{j} \text{ rad/sec}^2$$

We then have

$$\boldsymbol{V}_{XYZ} = \boldsymbol{V}_{xyz} + \dot{\boldsymbol{R}} + \boldsymbol{\omega} \times \boldsymbol{\rho}$$
$$= -20\boldsymbol{k} + 50\boldsymbol{i} + (5\boldsymbol{i} - 10\boldsymbol{k}) \times \boldsymbol{k}$$

$$\boldsymbol{V}_{XYZ} = 50\boldsymbol{i} - 5\boldsymbol{j} - 20\boldsymbol{k} \text{ ft/sec}$$

Example 15.12 (Continued)

Also,

$$\begin{aligned} \boldsymbol{a}_{XYZ} &= \boldsymbol{a}_{xyz} + \ddot{\boldsymbol{R}} + 2\boldsymbol{\omega} \times \boldsymbol{V}_{xyz} + \dot{\boldsymbol{\omega}} \times \boldsymbol{\rho} + \boldsymbol{\omega} \times (\boldsymbol{\omega} \times \boldsymbol{\rho}) \\ &= -10\boldsymbol{k} - 500\boldsymbol{j} + 2(5\boldsymbol{i} - 10\boldsymbol{k}) \times (-20\boldsymbol{k}) + (-50\boldsymbol{j}) \times \boldsymbol{k} \\ &\quad + (5\boldsymbol{i} - 10\boldsymbol{k}) \times [(5\boldsymbol{i} - 10\boldsymbol{k}) \times \boldsymbol{k}] \end{aligned}$$

$$\boldsymbol{a}_{XYZ} = -100\boldsymbol{i} - 300\boldsymbol{j} - 35\boldsymbol{k} \text{ ft/sec}^2$$

Example 15.13

In Example 15.12, the wheel accelerates at the instant under discussion with $\dot{\omega}_2 = 5$ rad/sec^2, and the platform accelerates with $\dot{\omega}_1 = 10$ rad/sec^2 (see Fig. 15.32). Find the velocity and acceleration of the valve gate A.

If we review the contents of parts A and B of Example 15.12, it will be clear that only $\ddot{\boldsymbol{R}}$ and $\dot{\boldsymbol{\omega}}$ are affected by the fact that $\dot{\omega}_1 = 10$ rad/sec^2 and $\dot{\omega}_2 = 5$ rad/sec^2. In this regard, consider $\boldsymbol{\omega}_2$. It is no longer of constant value and cannot be considered as *fixed* in the platform. However we can express $\boldsymbol{\omega}_2$ as $\omega_2\boldsymbol{i}'$ *at all times*, wherein $\boldsymbol{i}'$ is *fixed* in the platform as shown in Fig. 15.32. Thus, we can say for $\boldsymbol{\omega}$:

$$\boldsymbol{\omega} = \omega_2\boldsymbol{i}' + \boldsymbol{\omega}_1$$

Therefore,

$$\begin{aligned} \dot{\boldsymbol{\omega}} &= \dot{\omega}_2\boldsymbol{i}' + \omega_2\dot{\boldsymbol{i}}' + \dot{\boldsymbol{\omega}}_1 \\ &= 5\boldsymbol{i}' + 5(\boldsymbol{\omega}_1 \times \boldsymbol{i}') - 10\boldsymbol{k} \\ &= 5\boldsymbol{i}' + 5(-10\boldsymbol{k}) \times \boldsymbol{i}' - 10\boldsymbol{k} \end{aligned}$$

At the instant of interest, $\boldsymbol{i}' = \boldsymbol{i}$. Hence,

$$\dot{\boldsymbol{\omega}} = 5\boldsymbol{i} - 50\boldsymbol{j} - 10\boldsymbol{k} \text{ rad/sec}^2$$

Hence, we use the above $\dot{\boldsymbol{\omega}}$ in part B of Example 15.12 to compute $\boldsymbol{V}_{XYZ}$ and $\boldsymbol{a}_{XYZ}$. The computation of $\ddot{\boldsymbol{R}}$ is straightforward and so we can compute $\boldsymbol{a}_{XYZ}$ accordingly. We leave the details to the reader.

An understanding of Examples 15.11, 15.12, and 15.13, involving two angular velocities of component parts is sufficient for most of the homework problems of this section covering a wide range of applications. In the next example, we have three angular velocities to deal with. We urge you to examine it carefully if time allows. It is an interesting problem, and comprehension of the three different analyses given will ensure a strong grasp of multireference kinematics.

Example 15.14[11]

To simulate the flight conditions of a space vehicle, engineers have developed the *centrifuge*, shown diagrammatically in Fig. 15.33. A main *arm*, 40 ft long, rotates about the *A–A* axis. The pilot sits in a *cockpit*, which can rotate about axis *C–C*. The *seat* for the pilot can rotate inside the cockpit about an axis shown as *B–B*. These rotations are controlled by a computer that is set to simulate certain maneuvers corresponding to the entry and exit from the earth's atmosphere, malfunctions of the control system, and so on. When a pilot sits in the cockpit, his/her head has a position which is 3 ft from the seat as shown in Fig. 15.33. At the instant of interest the main arm is rotating at 10 rpm and accelerating at 5 rpm^2. The cockpit is rotating at a constant speed about *C–C* relative to the main arm at 10 rpm. Finally, the seat is rotating at a constant speed of 5 rpm relative to the cockpit about axis *B–B*. How many *g*'s of acceleration relative to the ground is the pilot's head subject to?[12] Note that the three axes, *A–A, C–C*, and *B–B*, are orthogonal to each other at time *t*.

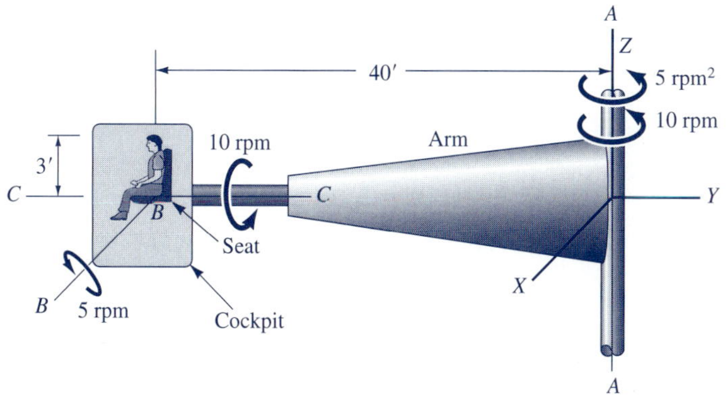

Figure 15.33. Centrifuge for simulating flight conditions.

[11]Example 15.14 was given as two homework problems in both the first and second editions of this text. They were so instructive that for subsequent editions the author decided to move the problems into the main text.

[12]A g of acceleration is an amount of acceleration equal to that of gravity (32.2 ft/sec^2 or 9.81 m/sec^2). Thus, a $4g$ acceleration is equivalent to an acceleration of 128.8 ft/sec^2.

Example 15.14 (Continued)

In Fig. 15.34 the arm of the centrifuge rotates relative to the ground at an angular velocity of ω_1. The cockpit meanwhile rotates relative to the arm with angular speed ω_2. Finally, the seat rotates relative to the cockpit at an angular speed ω_3. For constant ω_2, we see that, because of bearings in the arm, the vector $\boldsymbol{\omega}_2$ is "fixed" in the arm. Also, for constant ω_3, because of bearings in the cockpit, the vector $\boldsymbol{\omega}_3$ is "fixed" in the cockpit. Before we examine the acceleration of the pilot's head, note that at the instant of interest:

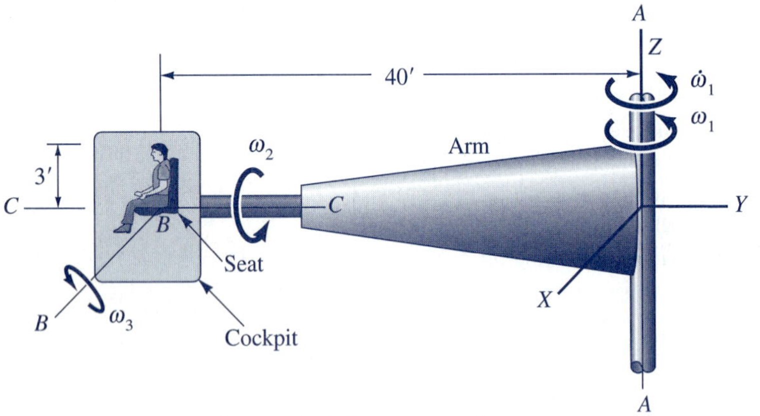

Figure 15.34. Centrifuge listing $\boldsymbol{\omega}$'s.

$$\omega_1 = \omega_2 = 10 \text{ rpm} = 1.048 \text{ rad/sec}$$
$$\dot{\omega}_1 = 5 \text{ rpm}^2 = .00873 \text{ rad/sec}^2$$
$$\omega_3 = 5 \text{ rpm} = .524 \text{ rad/sec}$$

We shall do this problem using three different kinds of moving references xyz.

ANALYSIS I

Fix xyz to arm.
Fix XYZ to ground.

Note in Fig. 15.35 that xyz and the arm to which it is fixed are shown dark. Note also that the axes xyz and XYZ are parallel to each other at the instant of interest.

Example 15.14 (Continued)

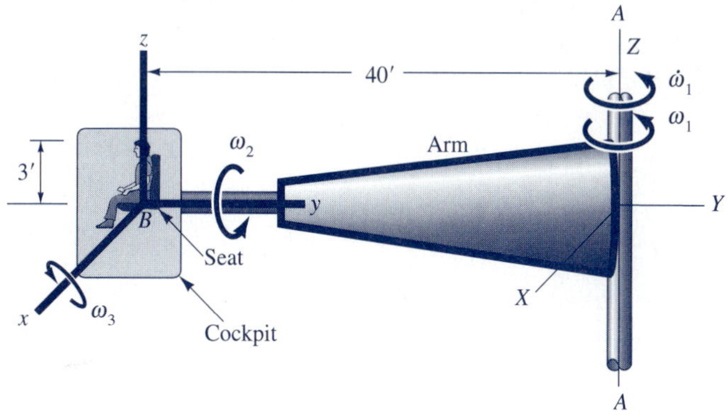

Figure 15.35. Centrifuge with *xyz* fixed to arm.

A. Motion of particle relative to *xyz*

$$\boldsymbol{\rho} = 3\boldsymbol{k} \text{ ft}$$

Note that $\boldsymbol{\rho}$ is "fixed" to the seat and that the seat has an angular velocity of $(\boldsymbol{\omega}_2 + \boldsymbol{\omega}_3)$ relative to the arm and thus to *xyz*. Hence,

$$\begin{aligned} \boldsymbol{V}_{xyz} &= (\boldsymbol{\omega}_2 + \boldsymbol{\omega}_3) \times \boldsymbol{\rho} \\ &= (1.048\boldsymbol{j} + .524\boldsymbol{i}) \times 3\boldsymbol{k} = 3.14\boldsymbol{i} - 1.572\boldsymbol{j} \text{ ft/sec} \end{aligned}$$

$$\boldsymbol{a}_{xyz} = \left(\frac{d\boldsymbol{V}_{xyz}}{dt}\right)_{xyz} = \left[\frac{d}{dt_{xyz}}(\boldsymbol{\omega}_2 + \boldsymbol{\omega}_3)\right] \times \boldsymbol{\rho} + (\boldsymbol{\omega}_2 + \boldsymbol{\omega}_3) \times \left(\frac{d\boldsymbol{\rho}}{dt}\right)_{xyz}$$

Clearly, relative to the arm, and thus to *xyz*, $\boldsymbol{\omega}_2$ is constant. And $\boldsymbol{\omega}_3$ is fixed in the cockpit that has an angular velocity of $\boldsymbol{\omega}_2$ relative to *xyz*. Thus, we have

$$\begin{aligned} \boldsymbol{a}_{xyz} &= (\boldsymbol{0} + \boldsymbol{\omega}_2 \times \boldsymbol{\omega}_3) \times \boldsymbol{\rho} + (\boldsymbol{\omega}_2 + \boldsymbol{\omega}_3) \times \boldsymbol{V}_{xyz} \\ &= (1.048\boldsymbol{j} \times .524\boldsymbol{i}) \times 3\boldsymbol{k} + (1.048\boldsymbol{j} + .524\boldsymbol{i}) \times (3.14\boldsymbol{i} - 1.572\boldsymbol{j}) \\ &= -4.12\boldsymbol{k} \text{ ft/sec}^2 \end{aligned}$$

B. Motion of *xyz* relative to *XYZ*

$$\boldsymbol{R} = -40\boldsymbol{j} \text{ ft}$$

Note that $\boldsymbol{R}$ is fixed in the arm, which has an angular velocity $\boldsymbol{\omega}_1$ relative to *XYZ*. Hence,

$$\begin{aligned} \dot{\boldsymbol{R}} &= \boldsymbol{\omega}_1 \times \boldsymbol{R} = 1.048\boldsymbol{k} \times (-40\boldsymbol{j}) = 41.9\boldsymbol{i} \text{ ft/sec} \\ \ddot{\boldsymbol{R}} &= \boldsymbol{\omega}_1 \times \dot{\boldsymbol{R}} + \dot{\boldsymbol{\omega}}_1 \times \boldsymbol{R} \\ &= 1.048\boldsymbol{k} \times 41.9\boldsymbol{i} + .00873\boldsymbol{k} \times (-40\boldsymbol{j}) \\ &= 43.9\boldsymbol{j} + .349\boldsymbol{i} \text{ ft/sec}^2 \\ \boldsymbol{\omega} &= \boldsymbol{\omega}_1 = 1.048\boldsymbol{k} \text{ rad/sec} \\ \dot{\boldsymbol{\omega}} &= \dot{\boldsymbol{\omega}}_1 = .00873\boldsymbol{k} \text{ rad/sec}^2 \end{aligned}$$

Example 15.14 (Continued)

We can now substitute into the following equation:

$$\boldsymbol{a}_{XYZ} = \boldsymbol{a}_{xyz} + \ddot{\boldsymbol{R}} + 2\boldsymbol{\omega} \times \boldsymbol{V}_{xyz} + \dot{\boldsymbol{\omega}} \times \boldsymbol{\rho} + \boldsymbol{\omega} \times (\boldsymbol{\omega} \times \boldsymbol{\rho})$$

Therefore,

$$\boldsymbol{a}_{XYZ} = 3.64\boldsymbol{i} + 50.5\boldsymbol{j} - 4.12\boldsymbol{k} \text{ ft/sec}^2$$

$$|\boldsymbol{a}_{XYZ}| = \frac{\sqrt{3.64^2 + 50.5^2 + 4.12^2}}{32.2} = \boxed{1.578\ g}$$

ANALYSIS II

Fix *xyz* to cockpit.
Fix *XYZ* to ground.

This situation is shown in Fig. 15.36.

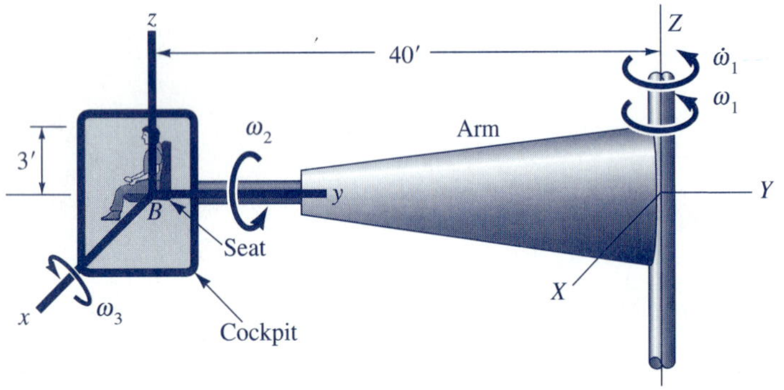

Figure 15.36. Centrifuge with *xyz* fixed to cockpit.

A. Motion of particle relative to *xyz*

$$\boldsymbol{\rho} = 3\boldsymbol{k} \text{ ft}$$

Note that $\boldsymbol{\rho}$ is fixed to the seat, which has an angular velocity of $\boldsymbol{\omega}_3$ relative to the cockpit and thus relative to *xyz*. Hence,

$$\boldsymbol{V}_{xyz} = \boldsymbol{\omega}_3 \times \boldsymbol{\rho} = .524\boldsymbol{i} \times 3\boldsymbol{k} = -1.572\boldsymbol{j} \text{ ft/sec}$$

$$\boldsymbol{a}_{xyz} = \left(\frac{d\boldsymbol{\omega}_3}{dt}\right)_{xyz} \times \boldsymbol{\rho} + \boldsymbol{\omega}_3 \times \left(\frac{d\boldsymbol{\rho}}{dt}\right)_{xyz}$$

But $\boldsymbol{\omega}_3$ is constant as seen from the cockpit and thus from *xyz*. Hence,

$$\boldsymbol{a}_{xyz} = \boldsymbol{0} \times \boldsymbol{\rho} + \boldsymbol{\omega}_3 \times \boldsymbol{V}_{xyz} = .524\boldsymbol{i} \times (-1.572\boldsymbol{j})$$
$$= -.824\boldsymbol{k} \text{ ft/sec}^2$$

Example 15.14 (Continued)

B. Motion of *xyz* relative to *XYZ*. The origin of *xyz* in this analysis has the same motion as the origin of *xyz* in the previous analysis. Thus, we use the results of analysis I for $\boldsymbol{R}$ and its time derivatives.

$$\boldsymbol{R} = -40\boldsymbol{j} \text{ ft}$$
$$\dot{\boldsymbol{R}} = 41.9\boldsymbol{i} \text{ ft/sec}$$
$$\ddot{\boldsymbol{R}} = 43.9\boldsymbol{j} + .349\boldsymbol{i} \text{ ft/sec}^2$$
$$\boldsymbol{\omega} = \boldsymbol{\omega}_1 + \boldsymbol{\omega}_2 = 1.048\boldsymbol{j} + 1.048\boldsymbol{k} \text{ rad/sec}$$
$$\dot{\boldsymbol{\omega}} = \dot{\boldsymbol{\omega}}_1 + \dot{\boldsymbol{\omega}}_2$$

We are given $\dot{\boldsymbol{\omega}}_1$ about the Z axis and $\boldsymbol{\omega}_2$ is fixed in the arm, which is rotating with angular velocity $\boldsymbol{\omega}_1$ relative to the XYZ reference. Hence,

$$\begin{aligned}\dot{\boldsymbol{\omega}} &= \dot{\boldsymbol{\omega}}_1 + \boldsymbol{\omega}_1 \times \boldsymbol{\omega}_2 = .00873\boldsymbol{k} + (1.048\boldsymbol{k} \times 1.048\boldsymbol{j}) \\ &= -1.098\boldsymbol{i} + .00873\boldsymbol{k} \text{ rad/sec}^2\end{aligned}$$

We can now substitute into the key equation, 15.24:

$$\begin{aligned}\boldsymbol{a}_{XYZ} &= \boldsymbol{a}_{xyz} + \ddot{\boldsymbol{R}} + 2\boldsymbol{\omega} \times \boldsymbol{V}_{xyz} + \dot{\boldsymbol{\omega}} \times \boldsymbol{\rho} + \boldsymbol{\omega} \times (\boldsymbol{\omega} \times \boldsymbol{\rho}) \\ &= 3.64\boldsymbol{i} + 50.5\boldsymbol{j} - 4.12\boldsymbol{k} \text{ ft/sec}^2\end{aligned}$$

$$|\boldsymbol{a}_{XYZ}| = \boxed{1.578g}$$

ANALYSIS III

Fix *xyz* to seat.
Fix *XYZ* to ground.

This situation is shown in Fig. 15.37.

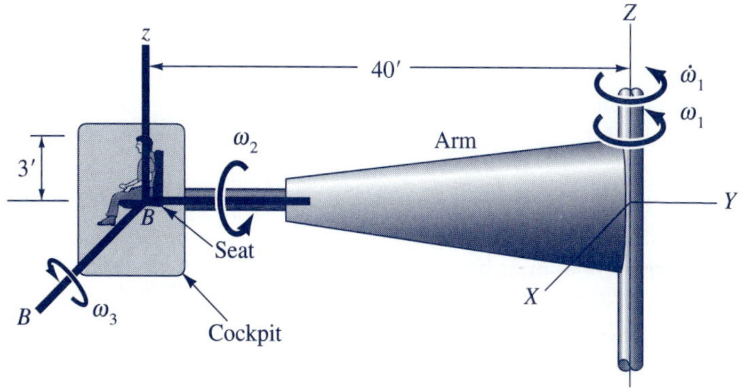

Figure 15.37. Centrifuge with *xyz* fixed to seat.

Example 15.14 (Continued)

A. Motion of particle relative to *xyz*

$$\boldsymbol{\rho} = 3\boldsymbol{k} \text{ ft}$$

Since the particle is fixed to the seat and is thus fixed in *xyz*, we can say:

$$\boldsymbol{V}_{xyz} = \boldsymbol{0}$$
$$\boldsymbol{a}_{xyz} = \boldsymbol{0}$$

B. Motion of *xyz* relative to *XYZ*. Again, the origin of *xyz* has identically the same motion as in the previous analyses. Thus, we have the same results as before for $\boldsymbol{R}$ and its derivatives.

$$\boldsymbol{R} = -40\boldsymbol{j} \text{ ft}$$
$$\dot{\boldsymbol{R}} = 41.9\boldsymbol{i} \text{ ft/sec}$$
$$\ddot{\boldsymbol{R}} = 43.9\boldsymbol{j} + .349\boldsymbol{i} \text{ ft/sec}^2$$
$$\boldsymbol{\omega} = \boldsymbol{\omega}_1 + \boldsymbol{\omega}_2 + \boldsymbol{\omega}_3 = 1.048\boldsymbol{k} + 1.048\boldsymbol{j} + .524\boldsymbol{i}$$
$$\dot{\boldsymbol{\omega}} = \dot{\boldsymbol{\omega}}_1 + \dot{\boldsymbol{\omega}}_2 + \dot{\boldsymbol{\omega}}_3$$

Note that $\dot{\boldsymbol{\omega}}_1$ is given. Also, $\boldsymbol{\omega}_2$ is fixed in the arm, which rotates with angular speed $\boldsymbol{\omega}_1$ relative to *XYZ*. Finally, $\boldsymbol{\omega}_3$ is fixed in the cockpit, which has an angular velocity $\boldsymbol{\omega}_2 + \boldsymbol{\omega}_1$ relative to *XYZ*. Thus,

$$\begin{aligned}\dot{\boldsymbol{\omega}} &= \dot{\boldsymbol{\omega}}_2 + \boldsymbol{\omega}_1 \times \boldsymbol{\omega}_2 + (\boldsymbol{\omega}_1 + \boldsymbol{\omega}_2) \times \boldsymbol{\omega}_3 \\ &= .00873\boldsymbol{k} + (1.048\boldsymbol{k} \times 1.048\boldsymbol{j}) + (1.048\boldsymbol{k} + 1.048\boldsymbol{j}) \times (.524\boldsymbol{i}) \\ &= -1.098\boldsymbol{i} + .549\boldsymbol{j} - .540\boldsymbol{k}\end{aligned}$$

We now go to the basic equation, 15.24.

$$\boldsymbol{a}_{XYZ} = \boldsymbol{a}_{xyz} + \ddot{\boldsymbol{R}} + 2\boldsymbol{\omega} \times \boldsymbol{V}_{xyz} + \dot{\boldsymbol{\omega}} \times \boldsymbol{\rho} + \boldsymbol{\omega} \times (\boldsymbol{\omega} \times \boldsymbol{\rho})$$

Substituting, we get

$$\boldsymbol{a}_{XYZ} = 3.64\boldsymbol{i} + 50.5\boldsymbol{j} - 4.12\boldsymbol{k} \text{ ft/sec}^2$$

$$|\boldsymbol{a}_{XYZ}| = 1.578g$$

In the final example of this series, we have a case where it is advantageous to use cylindrical coordinates in parts of the problem and then later to convert to rectangular coordinates.

Example 15.15

A submersible (see Fig. 15.38) is moving relative to the ground reference XYZ so as to have the following motion at the instant of interest for point A fixed to shaft $\overline{CD}$ which in turn is fixed to the submersible:

$$\boldsymbol{V} = 3\boldsymbol{i} + .6\boldsymbol{j} \text{ m/s}$$
$$\boldsymbol{a} = 2\boldsymbol{i} + 3\boldsymbol{j} - .5\boldsymbol{k} \text{ m/s}^2$$

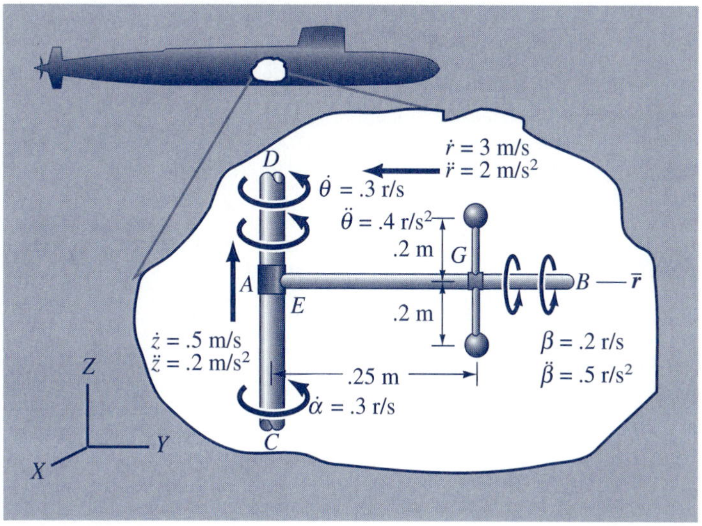

Figure 15.38. Rotating device inside a moving submersible. $\overline{CD}$ is fixed to the submersible.

At the instant of interest, the vessel has an angular speed of rotation $\dot{\alpha}$ = .3 rad/s about the centerline of $\overline{CD}$ as seen from the ground reference. A horizontal rod $\overline{EB}$ has the following angular motion about $\overline{CD}$:

$$\dot{\theta} = .3 \text{ rad/s} \qquad \ddot{\theta} = .4 \text{ rad/s}^2$$

Two spheres, each of mass 1 kg, are mounted on a rod turning about $\overline{EB}$ with the following angular motion

$$\dot{\beta} = .2 \text{ rad/s} \qquad \ddot{\beta} = .5 \text{ rad/s}^2$$

Also, the rod and the attached spherical masses advance toward $\overline{CD}$ at the following rate:

$$\dot{r} = -3 \text{ m/s} \qquad \ddot{r} = -2 \text{ m/s}^2$$

at a time when r = .25 m. Finally, at the instant of interest, the horizontal rod $\overline{EB}$ moves up along vertical rod $\overline{CD}$ with a speed of .5 m/s and a rate of change of speed of .2 m/s². What force must rod $\overline{EB}$ exert at point G at this instant *due only to the motion of the two spheres*?

Example 15.15 (Continued)

We will first consider the motion of the *center of mass* of the rotating spheres which clearly must be G. We now proceed to get the acceleration of G relative to XYZ (see Fig. 15.39).

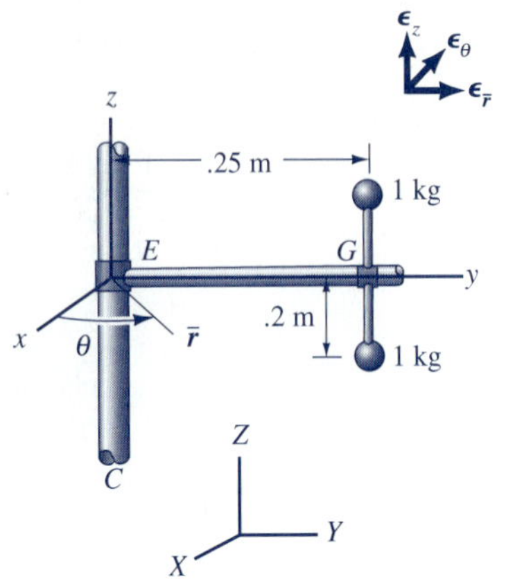

Figure 15.39. Reference xyz fixed to the vessel.

> Fix xyz to the vessel at A.
> Fix XYZ to the ground.

A. Motion of G relative to *xyz* (using cylindrical coordinates). Use Figs. 15.38 and 15.39.

$$\boldsymbol{\rho} = .25\boldsymbol{\epsilon}_{\bar{r}} = .25\boldsymbol{j} \text{ m}$$

$$\begin{aligned}
\boldsymbol{V}_{xyz} &= \dot{\bar{r}}\boldsymbol{\epsilon}_{\bar{r}} + \bar{r}\dot{\theta}\boldsymbol{\epsilon}_\theta + \dot{z}\boldsymbol{\epsilon}_z = -3\boldsymbol{\epsilon}_{\bar{r}} + (.25)(.3)\boldsymbol{\epsilon}_\theta + .5\boldsymbol{\epsilon}_z \\
&= -3\boldsymbol{j} - .075\boldsymbol{i} + .5\boldsymbol{k} = -.075\boldsymbol{i} - 3\boldsymbol{j} + .5\boldsymbol{k} \text{ m/s} \\
\boldsymbol{a}_{xyz} &= (\ddot{\bar{r}} - \bar{r}\dot{\theta}^2)\boldsymbol{\epsilon}_{\bar{r}} + (\bar{r}\ddot{\theta} + 2\dot{\bar{r}}\dot{\theta})\boldsymbol{\epsilon}_\theta + \ddot{z}\boldsymbol{\epsilon}_z \\
&= \left[-2 - (.25)(.3)^2\right]\boldsymbol{\epsilon}_{\bar{r}} + \left[(.25)(.4) + (2)(-3)(.3)\right]\boldsymbol{\epsilon}_\theta + .2\boldsymbol{\epsilon}_z \\
&= -2.023\boldsymbol{\epsilon}_{\bar{r}} - 1.7\boldsymbol{\epsilon}_\theta + .2\boldsymbol{\epsilon}_z = 1.7\boldsymbol{i} - 2.023\boldsymbol{j} + .2\boldsymbol{k} \text{ m/s}^2
\end{aligned}$$

B. Motion of *xyz* relative to *XYZ*

$$\begin{aligned}
\dot{\boldsymbol{R}} &= 3\boldsymbol{i} + .6\boldsymbol{j} \text{ m/s} \\
\ddot{\boldsymbol{R}} &= 2\boldsymbol{i} + 3\boldsymbol{j} - .5\boldsymbol{k} \text{ m/s}^2 \\
\boldsymbol{\omega} &= .3\boldsymbol{k} \text{ rad/s} \\
\dot{\boldsymbol{\omega}} &= \boldsymbol{0} \text{ rad/s}^2
\end{aligned}$$

We may now express $\boldsymbol{a}_{XYZ}$ for point G. Thus

$$\begin{aligned}
\boldsymbol{a}_{XYZ} &= \boldsymbol{a}_{xyz} + \ddot{\boldsymbol{R}} + 2\boldsymbol{\omega} \times \boldsymbol{V}_{xyz} + \dot{\boldsymbol{\omega}} \times \boldsymbol{\rho} + \boldsymbol{\omega} \times (\boldsymbol{\omega} \times \boldsymbol{\rho}) \\
&= (1.7\boldsymbol{i} - 2.023\boldsymbol{j} + .2\boldsymbol{k}) + (2\boldsymbol{i} + 3\boldsymbol{j} - .5\boldsymbol{k}) + 2(.3\boldsymbol{k}) \\
&\quad \times (-.075\boldsymbol{i} - 3\boldsymbol{j} + .5\boldsymbol{k}) + \boldsymbol{0} \times \boldsymbol{\rho} + (.3\boldsymbol{k}) \times (.3\boldsymbol{k} \times .25\boldsymbol{j}) \\
&= 5.5\boldsymbol{i} + .9095\boldsymbol{j} - .3\boldsymbol{k} \text{ m/s}^2
\end{aligned}$$

Now we apply **Newton's law** to the mass center G at the instant of interest. Denoting the force from the rod AB onto G as $\boldsymbol{F}_{\text{ROD}}$, we get

$$\begin{aligned}
\boldsymbol{F}_{\text{ROD}} - 2\text{mg}\boldsymbol{k} &= 5.5\boldsymbol{i} + .9095\boldsymbol{j} - .3\boldsymbol{k} \\
\therefore \boldsymbol{F}_{\text{ROD}} &= (2)(1)(9.81)\boldsymbol{k} + 5.5\boldsymbol{i} + .9095\boldsymbol{j} - .3\boldsymbol{k}
\end{aligned}$$

$$\boldsymbol{F}_{\text{ROD}} = 5.5\boldsymbol{i} + .9095\boldsymbol{j} + 19.32\boldsymbol{k} \text{ N}$$

This is our desired result.

PROBLEMS

15.91. A truck has a speed V of 20 mi/hr and an acceleration $\dot{V}$ of 3 mi/hr/sec at time t. A cylinder of radius equal to 2 ft is rolling without slipping at time t such that relative to the truck it has an angular speed ω_1 and angular acceleration $\dot{\omega}_1$ of 2 rad/sec and 1 rad/sec^2, respectively. Determine the velocity and acceleration of the center of the cylinder relative to the ground.

Figure P.15.91.

15.92. A wheel rotates with an angular speed ω_2 of 5 rad/sec relative to a platform, which rotates with a speed ω_1 of 10 rad/sec relative to the ground as shown. A collar moves down the spoke of the wheel, and, when the spoke is vertical, the collar has a speed of 20 ft/sec, an acceleration of 10 ft/sec^2 along the spoke, and is positioned 1 ft from the shaft centerline of the wheel. Compute the velocity and acceleration of the collar relative to the ground at this instant. Fix xyz to platform and use cylindrical coordinates.

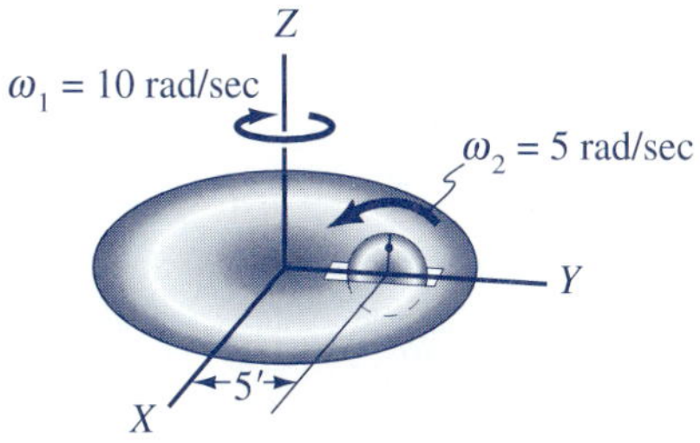

Figure P.15.92.

15.93. In Problem 15.71, determine the acceleration of the particle at the instant of interest.

15.94. In Problem 15.72, find the acceleration of the particle P relative to the ground reference.

15.95. In Problem 15.74, find the acceleration of point A relative to the ground.

15.96. In Problem 15.79, find the acceleration of the tip of the propeller relative to the ground reference. Take the yaw rotation to be zero and the loop rotation radius r to be 500 m.

15.97. In Problem 15.80, find the acceleration of point B relative to the ground.

15.98. In Problem 15.80, find the acceleration of point B relative to the ground for the following data at the instant of interest shown in the diagram.

$$\omega_1 = .2 \text{ rad/sec}$$
$$\dot{\omega}_1 = -.1 \text{ rad/sec}^2$$
$$\omega_2 = .4 \text{ rad/sec}$$
$$\dot{\omega}_2 = .3 \text{ rad/sec}^2$$

15.99. In Problem 15.82, determine the acceleration of the top tip of the gun relative to the ground.

15.100. In Problem 15.74, find the acceleration of point A relative to the ground for the configuration shown. Take $\omega_1 = 2$ rad/sec $\dot{\omega}_1 = 3$ rad/sec^2, $\omega_2 = .1$ rad/sec, and $\dot{\omega}_2 = 2$ rad/sec^2. How many g's of acceleration is this point subject to?

15.101. In Problem 15.81, find the acceleration of D relative to the ground. [*Hint:* Use two position vectors to get $\boldsymbol{\rho}$.]

15.102. Find the acceleration of gear tooth A relative to the ground in Problem 15.84.

15.103. In Problem 15.92, the wheel accelerates at the instant under discussion with 5 rad/sec^2 relative to the platform, and the platform increases its angular speed at 10 rad/sec^2 relative to the ground. Find the velocity and acceleration of the collar relative to the ground.

15.104. As with the velocity equation 15.20, we can easily show that Eq. 15.7, relating accelerations between two points on a rigid body, is actually a special case of Eq. 15.24. Thus, consider the diagram showing a rigid body moving arbitrarily relative to *XYZ*. Choose two points *a* and *b* in the body and embed a reference *xyz* in the body with the origin at *a*. Now express the acceleration of point *b* as seen from the two references. Show how this equation can be reformulated as Eq. 15.7.

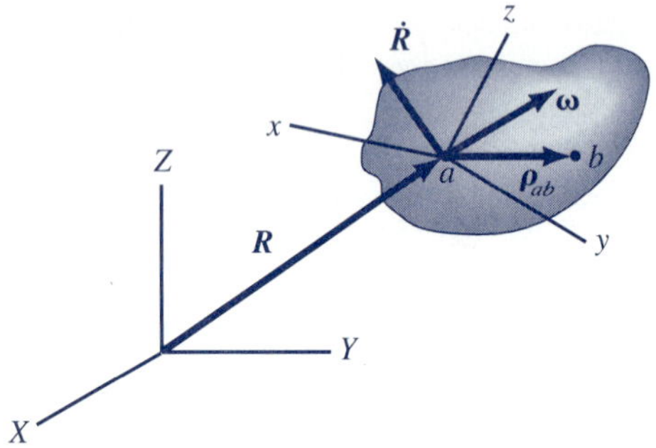

Figure P.15.104.

15.105. Solve Problem 15.81 for the following data:

$$\omega_1 = .3 \text{ rad/sec}$$
$$\dot{\omega}_1 = .2 \text{ rad/sec}^2$$
$$\omega_2 = .40 \text{ rad/sec}$$
$$\dot{\omega}_2 = .10 \text{ rad/sec}^2$$
$$\omega_3 = .15 \text{ rad/sec}$$
$$\dot{\omega}_3 = -.2 \text{ rad/sec}^2$$

15.106. In Problem 15.82, find the component of acceleration of the projectile relative to the ground which is normal to the gun barrel at the instant that the projectile just leaves the barrel. Use the following data:

$$\omega_1 = .3 \text{ rad/sec}$$
$$\dot{\omega}_1 = .2 \text{ rad/sec}^2$$
$$\omega_2 = -.6 \text{ rad/sec}$$
$$\dot{\omega}_2 = -.4 \text{ rad/sec}^2$$

15.107. In Problem 15.88, find the magnitude of the acceleration of collar *C* relative to the ground for the following data at the instant shown:

$$\dot{\theta} = 2 \text{ rad/sec}$$
$$\ddot{\theta} = 4 \text{ rad/sec}^2$$

15.108. A truck is moving at a constant speed $V = 1.7$ m/sec at time *t*. The truck loading compartment has at this instant a constant angular speed $\dot{\theta}$ of .1 rad/sec at an angle $\theta = 45°$. A cylinder of radius 300 mm rolls relative to the compartment at a speed ω_1 of 1 rad/sec, accelerating at a rate $\dot{\omega}_1$ of .5 rad/sec² at time *t*. What are the velocity and acceleration of the center of the cylinder relative to the ground at time *t*? The distance *d* at time *t* is 5 m.

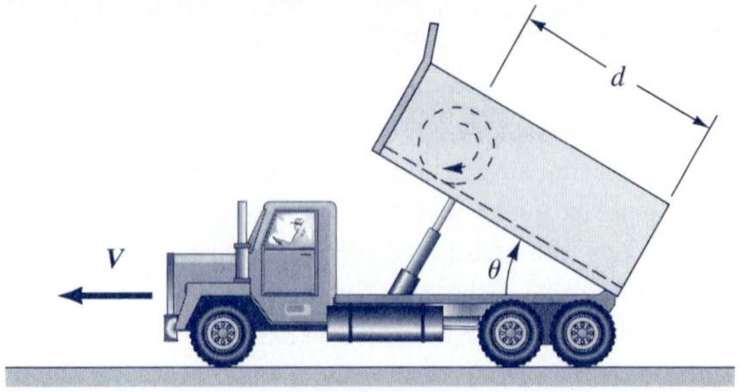

Figure P.15.108.

***15.109.** In Example 15.14, suppose at the instant of interest that there is an angular acceleration $\dot{\omega}_2 = .3$ rad/sec² of the cockpit relative to the arm and that there is an angular acceleration $\dot{\omega}_3 = .2$ rad/sec² of the seat relative to the cockpit. Find the number of *g*'s to which the pilot's head is subjected. Follow analysis I in the example. [*Hint:* The angular velocity $\boldsymbol{\omega}_3$ can always be expressed as $\omega_3\hat{\mathbf{c}}$, where $\hat{\mathbf{c}}$ is a unit vector *fixed to the cockpit* having a direction along the *x* axis at the instant of interest.]

15.110. A ferris wheel is out of control. At the instant shown, it has an angular speed ω_1 equal to .2 rad/sec and a rate of change of angular speed $\dot{\omega}_1$ of .04 rad/sec² relative to the ground. At this instant a "chair" shown in the diagram has an angular speed ω_2 relative to the ferris wheel equal to .25 rad/sec and a rate change of speed $\dot{\omega}_2$, again relative to the ferris wheel, equal to .03 rad/sec². In the figure, we have shown details of the passenger at this instant. Note that the hinge of the seat is at *A*. How many *g*'s of acceleration is the passenger's head subject to?

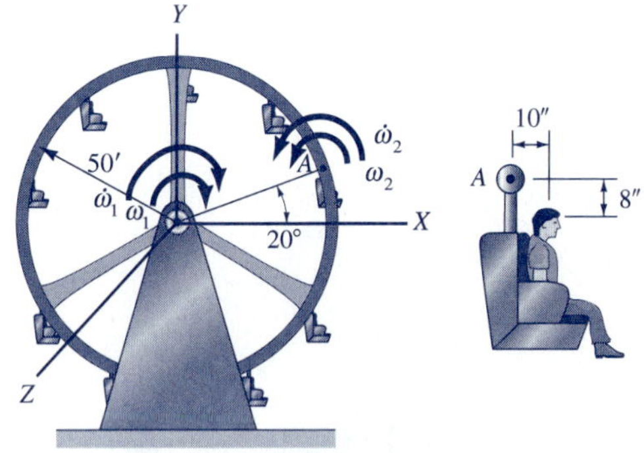

Figure P.15.110.

15.111. A shaft *BC* rotates relative to platform *A* at a speed $\omega_1 = .34$ rad/sec. A rod is welded to *BC* and is vertical at the instant of interest. A tube is fixed to the vertical rod in which a small piston head is moving relative to the tube at a speed *V* of 3 m/sec with a rate of change of speed $\dot{V}$ of .4 m/sec². The platform *A* has an angular velocity relative to the ground given as $\omega_2 = .8$ rad/sec with a rate of change of speed of .5 rad/sec². Find the acceleration vector of the piston head relative to the ground.

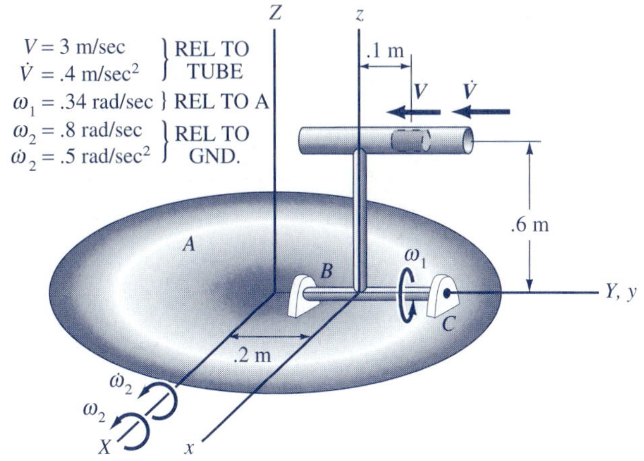

Figure P.15.111.

15.112. A communications satellite has the following motion relative to an inertial reference XYZ.

$$\boldsymbol{\omega}_1 = 3\boldsymbol{i} + 4\boldsymbol{j} + 10\boldsymbol{k} \text{ rad/s} \qquad \dot{\boldsymbol{\omega}}_1 = 2\boldsymbol{i} + 3\boldsymbol{k} \text{ rad/s}^2$$
$$\boldsymbol{V}_0 = \boldsymbol{a}_0 = \boldsymbol{0}$$

A wheel at A is rotating relative to the satellite at a constant speed $\omega_2 = 5$ rad/s. What is the acceleration of point D on the wheel relative to XYZ at the instant shown? The following additional data apply:

$$OA = 1 \text{ m} \quad AD = .2 \text{ m}$$

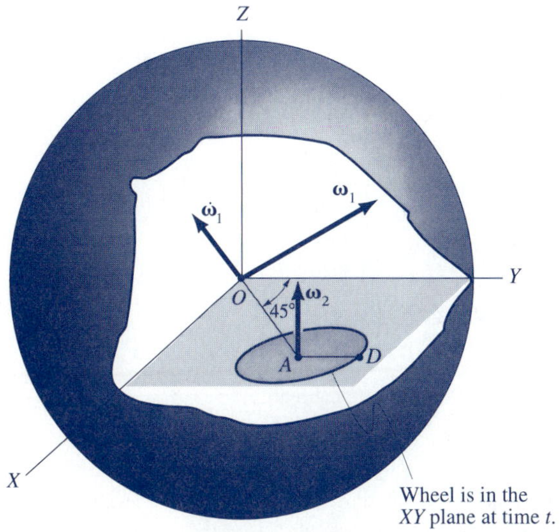

Figure P.15.112.

15.113. A particle moves in a slot of a gear with speed $V = 2$ m/s and a rate of change of speed $\dot{V} = 1.2$ m/s² both relative to the gear. Find the acceleration vector for the particle at the configuration shown relative to the ground reference XYZ.

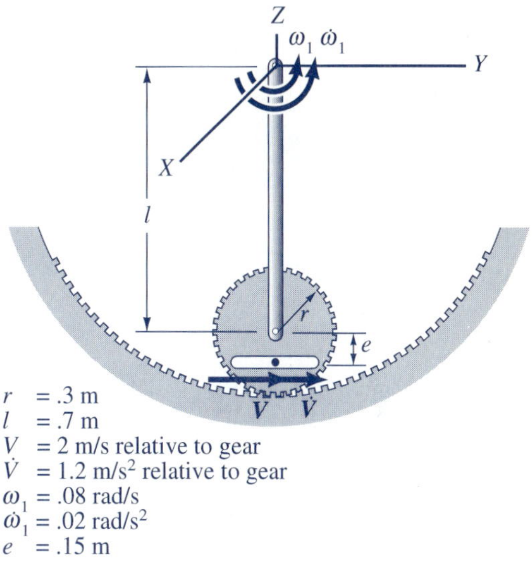

Figure P.15.113.

15.114. A submarine is undergoing an evasive maneuver. At the instant of interest, it has a speed $V_s = 10$ m/s and an acceleration $a_s = 15$ m/s² at its center of mass. It also has an angular velocity about its center of mass C of $\omega_1 = .5$ rad/s and an angular acceleration $\dot{\omega}_1 = .02$ rad/s². Inside is a part of an inertial guidance system that consists of a wheel spinning with speed $\omega_2 = 20$ rad/s about a vertical axis of the ship. Along a spoke shown at the instant of interest, a particle is moving toward the center with r, $\dot{r}$ and $\ddot{r}$ as given in the diagram. What is the acceleration of the particle relative to inertial reference XYZ? Just write out the formulations for $\boldsymbol{a}_{XYZ}$ but do not carry out the cross products.

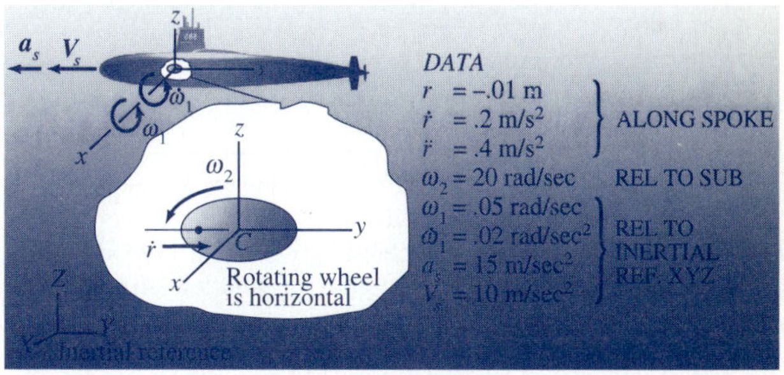

Figure P.15.114.

15.115. Find $\boldsymbol{V}$ and $\boldsymbol{a}$ of B relative to XYZ. The single blade portion AB is rotating as shown relative to the helicopter with speed ω_2 about an axis parallel to the X axis at the instant of interest while the entire blade system is rotating about the vertical axis with speed ω_1.

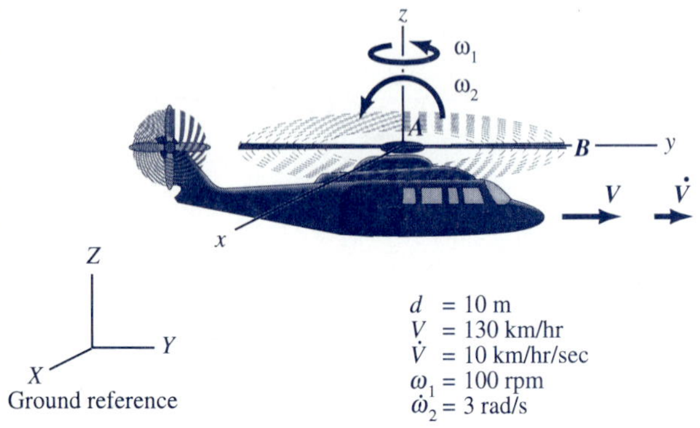

Figure P.15.115.

15.116. An F-16 fighter plane is moving at a constant speed of 800 km/hr while undergoing a loop as shown in the diagram. At the instant of interest, it has an angular roll velocity ω_2 of 5 rad/min relative to the ground. A solenoid is activated at this instant and moves the moving portion of a gate valve downward at a speed of 3 m/s with an acceleration of 5 m/s^2 all relative to the plane. What is the total external force on the moving portion of the gate valve if it is 1 m above the axis of roll at the instant of interest? The moving portion of the valve has a weight of 10 N.

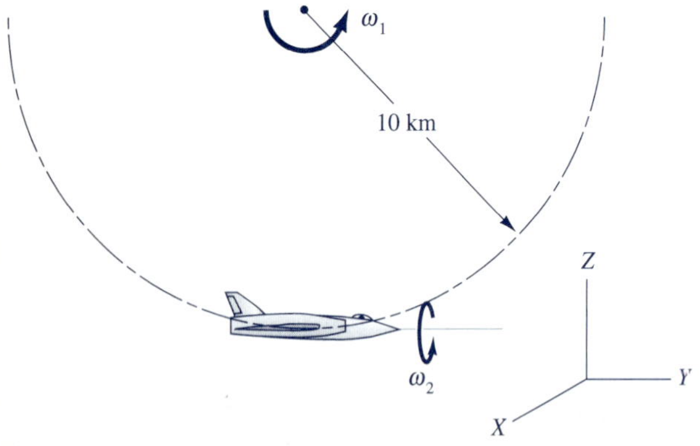

Figure P.15.116.

15.117. A robot moves a body held by its "jaws" G as shown in the diagram. What is the velocity and acceleration of point A at the instant shown relative to the ground? Arm EH is welded to the vertical shaft MN. Arm HKG is one rigid member which rotates about EH. How do you want to fix xyz?

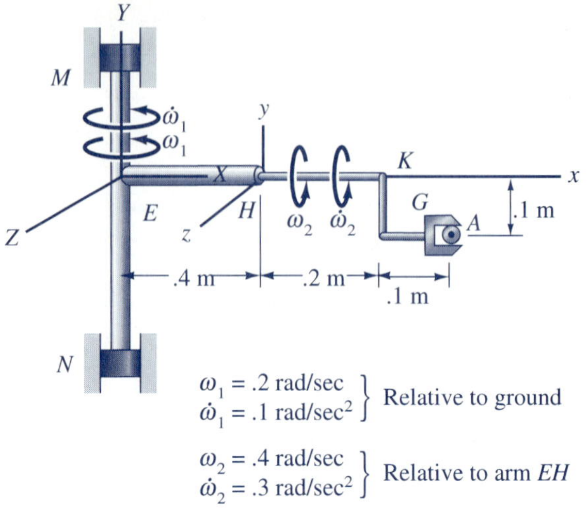

Figure P.15.117.

15.118. The turret of the main gun of a destroyer has at time t an angular velocity $\omega_1 = 2$ rad/s and a rate of change of angular velocity $\dot{\omega}_1 = 3$ rad/s^2 both relative to the ship. The gun barrel has $\omega_2 = .5$ rad/s and $\dot{\omega}_2 = .3$ rad/s^2 relative to the turret.

(a) Find the acceleration of the tip A of the gun at time t relative to the destroyer.

(b) If the destroyer has a translational acceleration relative to land equal to

$$\boldsymbol{a}_{\text{Destroyer}} = .05\boldsymbol{i} + .26\boldsymbol{j} - 2.2\boldsymbol{k} \text{ m/s}^2$$

what is the acceleration of A relative to the land at time t?

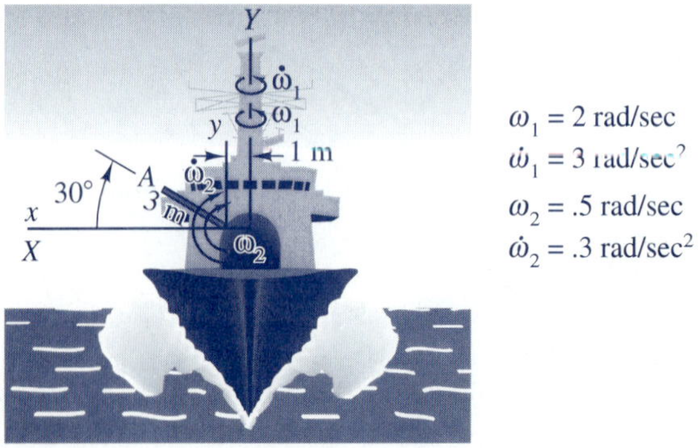

Figure P.15.118.

*15.9 A New Look at Newton's Law

The proper form of Newton's law has been presented as

$$\boldsymbol{F} = m\boldsymbol{a}_{XYZ} \tag{15.25}$$

where the acceleration is measured relative to an inertial reference. There are times when the motion of a particle is known and makes sense only relative to a noninertial reference. Such a case would arise, for example, in an airplane or rocket, where machine elements must move in a certain way relative to the vehicle in order to function properly. Therefore, the motion of the machine element relative to the vehicle is known. If, however, the vehicle is undergoing a severe maneuver relative to inertial space, we cannot use Eq. 15.25 with the acceleration of the machine element measured relative to the vehicle. This is so since the vehicle is not at that instant an inertial reference, and to disregard this fact will lead to erroneous results. In such problems, the motion of the vehicle may be known relative to inertial space, and we can employ to good advantage the multireference analysis of the previous section. Attaching the reference xyz to the vehicle and XYZ to inertial space, we can then use Newton's law in the following way:

$$\boldsymbol{F} = m\left[\boldsymbol{a}_{xyz} + \ddot{\boldsymbol{R}} + 2\boldsymbol{\omega} \times \boldsymbol{V}_{xyz} + \dot{\boldsymbol{\omega}} \times \boldsymbol{\rho} + \boldsymbol{\omega} \times (\boldsymbol{\omega} \times \boldsymbol{\rho})\right] \tag{15.26}$$

Clearly, the bracketed expression is the required quantity $\boldsymbol{a}_{XYZ}$ needed for Newton's law. It is the usual practice to write Eq. 15.26 in the following form:

$$\boldsymbol{F} - m\left[\ddot{\boldsymbol{R}} + 2\boldsymbol{\omega} \times \boldsymbol{V}_{xyz} + \dot{\boldsymbol{\omega}} \times \boldsymbol{\rho} + \boldsymbol{\omega} \times (\boldsymbol{\omega} \times \boldsymbol{\rho})\right] = m\boldsymbol{a}_{xyz} \tag{15.27}$$

This equation may now be considered as Newton's law written for a *noninertial* reference xyz. The terms $-m\ddot{\boldsymbol{R}}$, $-m(2\boldsymbol{\omega} \times \boldsymbol{V}_{xyz})$, and so on, are then considered as forces and are termed *inertial forces*. Thus, we can take the viewpoint that for a noninertial reference, xyz, we can still say force $\boldsymbol{F}$ equals mass times acceleration, $\boldsymbol{a}_{xyz}$, provided that we include with the applied force $\boldsymbol{F}$, all the inertial forces. Indeed, we shall adopt this viewpoint in this text. The inertial force $-2m\boldsymbol{\omega} \times \boldsymbol{V}_{xyz}$ is the very interesting *Coriolis force*, which we shall later discuss in some detail.

The inertial forces result in baffling actions that are sometimes contrary to our intuition. Most of us during our lives have been involved in actions where the reference used (knowingly or not) has been with sufficient accuracy an inertial reference, usually the earth's surface. We have, accordingly, become conditioned to associating an acceleration proportional to, and in the same direction as, the applied force. Occasions do arise when we find ourselves relating our motions to a reference that is highly noninertial. For example, fighter pilots and stunt pilots carry out actions in a cockpit of a plane while the plane is undergoing severe maneuvers. Unexpected results frequently occur for flyers if they use the cockpit interior as a reference for their actions. Thus, to move their hands from one position to another relative to the cockpit sometimes requires an exertion that is not the one anticipated, causing considerable confusion. The next example will illustrate this, and the sections that follow will explore further some of these interesting effects.[13]

[13]At this juncture we should remind ourselves that "physical feel" or "intuition" is really a direct consequence of past experiences. For this reason, many of the things you will later formally learn will initially be at variance with your physical feel and intuition. Thus, certain phenomena occurring in supersonic fluid flow will seem very strange, since our direct experience with fluid flow (faucets, swimming, and so on) has been entirely subsonic. Because you have not moved with speeds approaching the speed of light and because you have not been prowling around the nucleus of an atom, you will find the tenets of relativity theory and quantum mechanics absolutely bizarre. Should you have little feel for the Coriolis force at this time, do not be unduly concerned (unless you have spent a lot of time moving about high-speed merry-go-rounds). We must in such instances rely on the theory. Working with the theory, we can often build up a strong "physical feel" in the new areas.

Example 15.16

The plan view of a rotating platform is shown in Fig. 15.40. A man is seated at the position labeled A and is facing point O of the platform. He is carrying a mass of $\frac{1}{50}$ slug at the rate of 10 ft/sec in a direction straight ahead of him (i.e., toward the center of the platform). If this platform has an angular speed of 10 rad/sec and an angular acceleration of 5 rad/sec^2 relative to the ground at this instant, what force $\boldsymbol{F}$ must he exert to cause the mass to accelerate 5 ft/sec^2 toward the center?

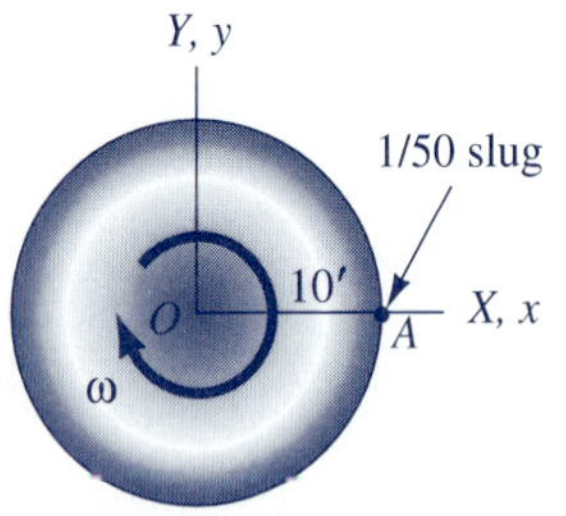

Figure 15.40. Rotating platform.

For purposes of determining inertial forces, we proceed as follows:

Fix xyz to platform.
Fix XYZ to ground.

Example 15.16 (Continued)

A. Motion of mass relative to *xyz* reference

$$\boldsymbol{\rho} = 10\boldsymbol{i} \text{ ft}, \quad \boldsymbol{V}_{xyz} = -10\boldsymbol{i} \text{ ft/sec}, \quad \boldsymbol{a}_{xyz} = -\ 5\boldsymbol{i} \text{ ft/sec}^2$$

B. Motion of xyz relative to *XYZ*

$$\dot{\boldsymbol{R}} = \boldsymbol{0}, \quad \ddot{\boldsymbol{R}} = \boldsymbol{0}, \quad \boldsymbol{\omega} = -10\boldsymbol{k} \text{ rad/sec}, \quad \dot{\boldsymbol{\omega}} = -5\boldsymbol{k} \text{ rad/sec}^2$$

Hence,

$$\boldsymbol{a}_{XYZ} = -5\boldsymbol{i} + 2(-10\boldsymbol{k})\times(-10\boldsymbol{i}) + (-5\boldsymbol{k})\times 10\boldsymbol{i} + (-10\boldsymbol{k})\times(-10\boldsymbol{k}\times 10\boldsymbol{i})$$

Therefore,

$$\boldsymbol{a}_{XYZ} = -5\boldsymbol{i} + (200\boldsymbol{j} - 50\boldsymbol{j} - 1{,}000\boldsymbol{i})$$

Employing **Newton's law** (Eq. 15.27) for the mass, we get

$$\boldsymbol{F} - \tfrac{1}{50}(200\boldsymbol{j} - 50\boldsymbol{j} - 1{,}000\boldsymbol{i}) = \tfrac{1}{50}(-5\boldsymbol{i})$$

Solving for **F**, we get

$$\boldsymbol{F} = 3j - 20.1\boldsymbol{i} \text{ lb}$$

This force $\boldsymbol{F}$ is the *total* external force on the mass. Since the man must exert this force and also withstand the pull of gravity (the weight) in the $-\boldsymbol{k}$ direction, the force exerted by the man on the mass is

$$\boldsymbol{F}_{\text{man}} = 3\boldsymbol{j} - 20.1\boldsymbol{i} + \tfrac{g}{50}\boldsymbol{k} \text{ lb} \qquad \text{(a)}$$

If the platform were *not* rotating at all, it could serve as an inertial reference. Then, we would have for the total external force $\boldsymbol{F}'$:

$$\boldsymbol{F}' = \tfrac{1}{50}(-5\boldsymbol{i}) = -\tfrac{1}{10}\boldsymbol{i} \text{ lb}$$

The force exerted by the man, $\mathbf{F}'_{\text{man}}$, is then

$$\boldsymbol{F}'_{\text{man}} = -\tfrac{1}{10}\boldsymbol{i} + \tfrac{g}{50}\boldsymbol{k} \text{ lb} \qquad \text{(b)}$$

This force is considerably different from that given in Eq. (a).

As a matter of interest, we note that aviators of World War I were required to carry out such maneuvers on a rapidly rotating and accelerating platform so as to introduce them safely to these "peculiar" effects.

*15.10 The Coriolis Force

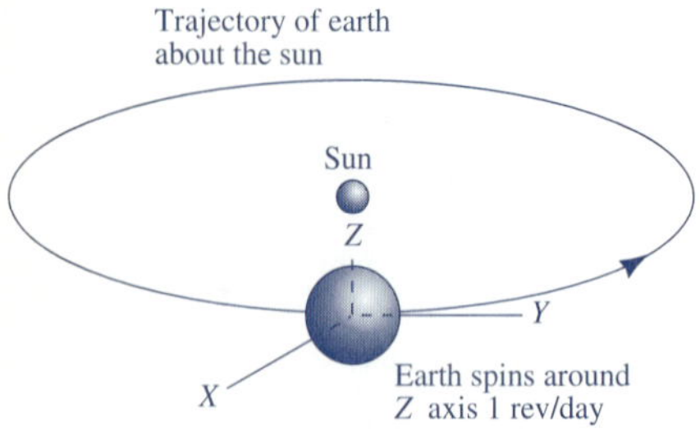

Figure 15.41. Proposed inertial reference.

Of great interest is the Coriolis force, defined in Section 15.9, particularly as it relates to certain terrestrial actions. For many of our problems, the earth's surface serves with sufficient accuracy as an inertial reference. However, where the time interval of interest is large (such as in the flight of rockets, or the flow of rivers, or the movement of winds and ocean currents), we must consider such a reference as noninertial in certain instances and accordingly, when using **Newton's law**, we must include some or all of the inertial forces given in Eq. 15.27. For such problems (as you will recall from Chapter 11, we often use an inertial reference that has an origin at the center of the earth (see Fig. 15.41) with the Z axis collinear with the N-S axis of the earth and moving such that the earth rotates one revolution per 24 hr relative to the reference. Thus, the reference approaches a translatory motion about the sun. To a high degree of accuracy, it is an inertial reference.

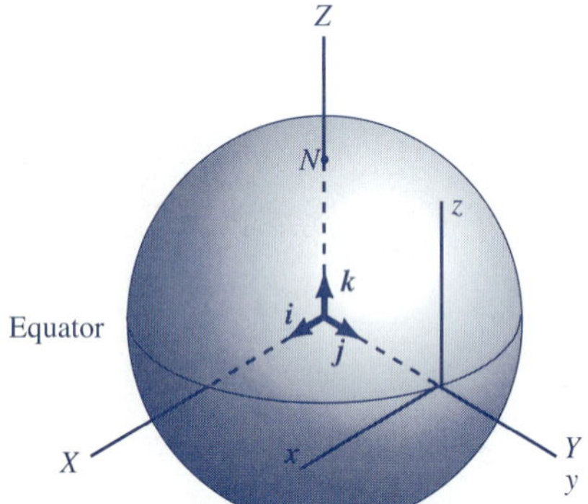

Figure 15.42. xyz fixed to earth.

We start by considering particles that are stationary relative to the earth. We choose a reference xyz fixed to the earth at the equator as shown in Fig. 15.42. The angular velocity of xyz fixed anywhere on the earth's surface can readily be evaluated as follows:

$$\boldsymbol{\omega} = \frac{2\pi}{(24)(3{,}600)}\boldsymbol{k} = 7.27 \times 10^{-5}\boldsymbol{k} \text{ rad/sec}$$

Newton's law, in the form of Eq. 15.27, for a "stationary" particle positioned at the origin of xyz simplifies to

$$\boldsymbol{F} - m\ddot{\boldsymbol{R}} = \boldsymbol{0} \tag{15.28}$$

since $\boldsymbol{\rho}$, $\boldsymbol{V}_{xyz}$, and $\boldsymbol{a}_{xyz}$ are zero vectors. Let us next evaluate the inertial force, $-m\ddot{\boldsymbol{R}}$, for the particle, using $R = 3{,}960$ mi:

$$\begin{aligned} -m\ddot{\boldsymbol{R}} &= -m(-|\boldsymbol{R}|\omega^2\boldsymbol{j}) = m(3{,}960)(5{,}280)(7.27 \times 10^{-5})^2\boldsymbol{j} \\ &= m(.1105)\boldsymbol{j} \text{ lb} \end{aligned}$$

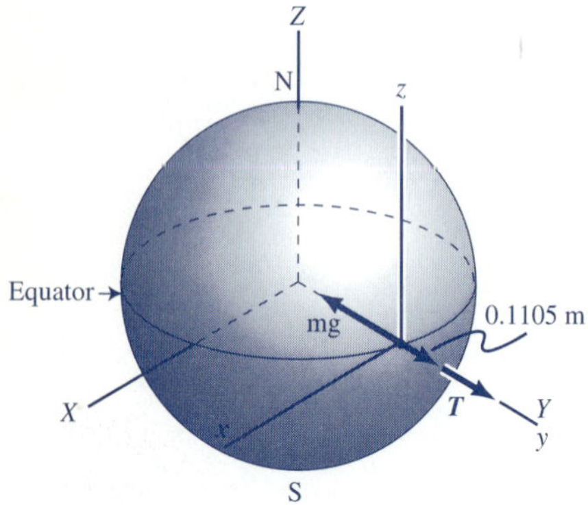

Figure 15.43. Plumb bob at equator.

Clearly, this is a "centrifugal force," as we learned in physics. Note in Fig. 15.43 that the direction of this force is collinear with the gravitational force on a particle, but with opposite sense. Note further that the centrifugal force has a magnitude that is (.1105 m/32.2 m) $\times$ 100 = .34% of the gravitational force at the indicated location. Thus, clearly, in the usual engineering problems, such effects are neglected.

Assume that the particle is restrained from resting on the surface of the earth by a flexible cord. In accordance with Eq. 15.28, the external force $\boldsymbol{F}$ (which includes gravitational attraction and the force from the cord) and the centrifugal force $-m\ddot{\boldsymbol{R}}$ add up to zero, and hence these forces are in equilibrium. They are shown in Fig. 15.43 in which T represents the contribution of the cord. Clearly, a force T radially out from the center of the earth will restrain the particle, and so the direction of the flexible cord will point toward the center of the earth. On the other hand, at a nonequatorial location this will not be true. The gravity force points toward the center of the earth (see Fig. 15.44), but the centrifugal force—now having the value $m[R(\sin\,\theta)\omega^2]$—points radially out from the Z axis, and thus T, the restraining force, must be inclined somewhat from a direction toward the center of the earth. Therefore, except at the equator or at the poles (where the centrifugal force is zero), a *plumb bob* does not point directly toward the center of the earth. This deviation is very small and is negligible for most but not all engineering work.

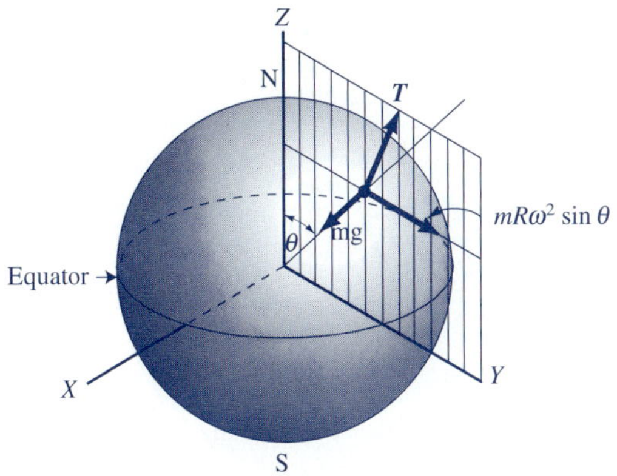

Figure 15.44. Plumb bob does not point to center of earth.

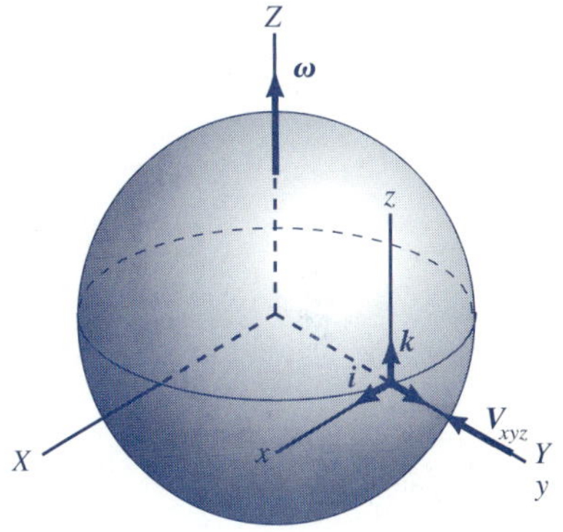

Figure 15.45. Free fall at the equator.

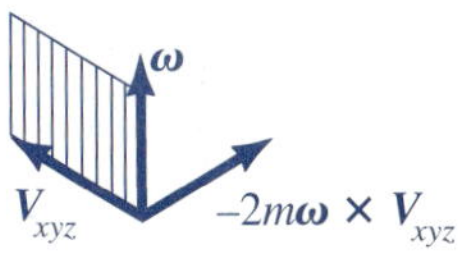

Figure 15.46. Direction of Coriolis force.

Consider now a body that is held above the earth's surface so as to always be above the same point on the earth's surface. (The body thus moves with the earth with the same angular motion.) If the body is released we have what is called a *free fall*. The body will attain initially a downward velocity $\boldsymbol{V}_{xyz}$ relative to the earth's surface (see Fig. 15.45). Now in addition to a centrifugal force described earlier, we have a *Coriolis force* given as

$$\boldsymbol{F}_{\text{Coriolis}} = -2m\boldsymbol{\omega} \times \boldsymbol{V}_{xyz}$$

In Fig. 15.46 we have shown the $\boldsymbol{\omega}$ and $\boldsymbol{V}_{xyz}$ vectors. The Coriolis force must point to the right as you should verify (do not forget the minus sign). If we dropped a mass from a position in xyz above a target, therefore, the mass as a result of the Coriolis force would curve slightly away from the target (see Fig. 15.47) even if there were no friction, wind, etc., to complicate matters. Furthermore, the induced motion in the x direction itself induces Coriolis-force components of a smaller order in the y direction, and so forth. You will surely begin to appreciate how difficult a "free fall" can really become when great precision is attempted.

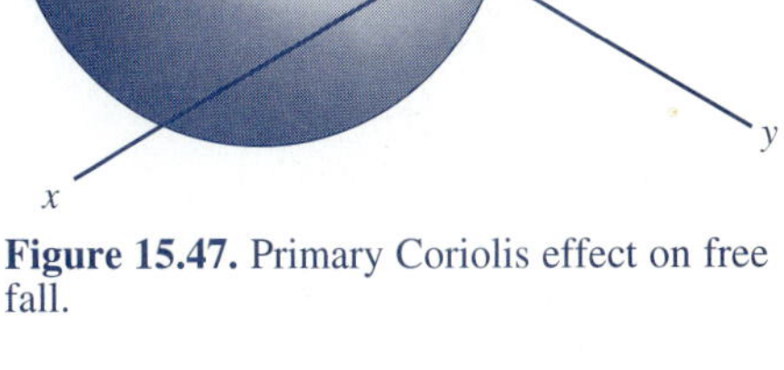

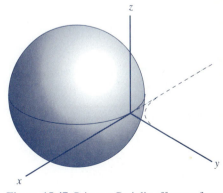

Figure 15.47. Primary Coriolis effect on free fall.

Finally, consider a current of air or a current of water moving in the Northern Hemisphere. In the absence of a Coriolis force, the fluid would move in the direction of the pressure drop. In Fig. 15.48 the pressure drop has been shown for simplicity along a meridian line pointing toward the equator. For fluid motion in this direction, a Coriolis force will be present in the negative y direction and so the fluid will follow the dashed-line path BA. The prime induced motion is to the right of the direction of flow developed by the pressure alone. By similar argument, you can demonstrate that, in the Southern Hemisphere, the Coriolis force induces a motion to the left of the flow that would be present under the action of the pressure drop alone. Such effects are of significance in meteorology and oceanography.[14]

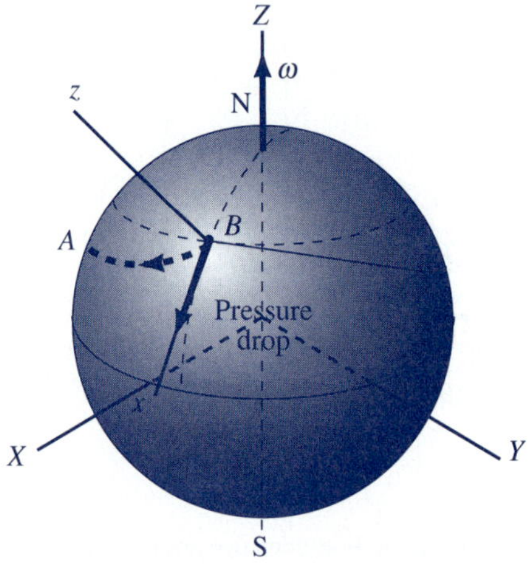

Figure 15.48. Coriolis effect on wind.

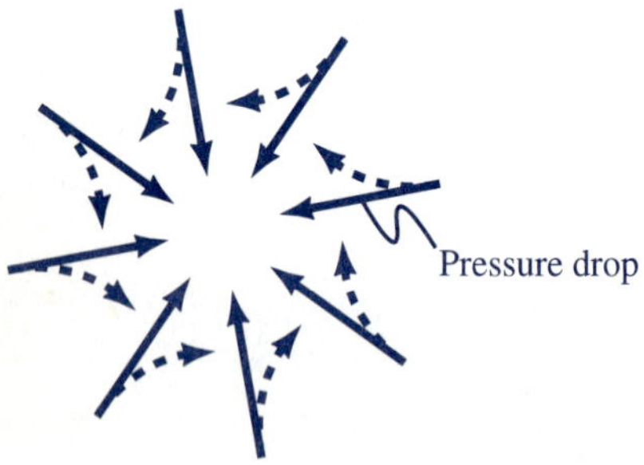

Figure 15.49. Beginning of whirlpool.

The conclusions in the preceding paragraph explain why cyclones and whirlpools rotate in a counterclockwise direction in the Northern Hemisphere and a clockwise direction in the Southern Hemisphere. In order to start, a whirlpool or cyclone needs a low-pressure region with pressure increasing radially outward. The pressure drops are shown as full lines in Fig. 15.49. For such a pressure distribution, the air will begin to move radially inward. As this happens, the Coriolis force causes the fluid in the Northern Hemisphere to swerve to the right of its motion, as indicated by the dashed lines. This result is the beginning of a counterclockwise motion. You can readily demonstrate that in the Southern Hemisphere a clockwise rotation will be induced.

[14]Keep in mind that the Coriolis force in these situations is small but, because it persists during long time intervals and because the resultant of other forces is often also small, this force usually must carefully be taken into account in studies of meteorology and oceanography.

Note that the famous Gulf Stream going north from the Caribbean swings eastward toward the British Isles as a result of the Coriolis force. With the prevailing winds, this results in a more moderate climate for these lands.

PROBLEMS

15.119. A reference xyz is attached to a space probe, which has the following motion relative to an inertial reference XYZ at a time t when the corresponding axes of the references are parallel:

$$\ddot{\boldsymbol{R}} = 100\boldsymbol{j} \text{ m/sec}^2$$
$$\boldsymbol{\omega} = 10\boldsymbol{i} \text{ rad/sec}$$
$$\dot{\boldsymbol{\omega}} = -8\boldsymbol{k} \text{ rad/sec}^2$$

If a force $\boldsymbol{F}$ given as

$$\boldsymbol{F} = 500\boldsymbol{i} + 200\boldsymbol{j} - 300\boldsymbol{k} \text{ N}$$

acts on a particle of mass 1 kg at position

$$\boldsymbol{\rho} = .5\boldsymbol{i} + .6\boldsymbol{j} \text{ m}$$

what is the acceleration vector relative to the probe? The particle has a velocity $\boldsymbol{V}$ relative to xyz of

$$\boldsymbol{V} = 10\boldsymbol{i} + 20\boldsymbol{j} \text{ m/sec}$$

15.120. In the space probe of Problem 15.119, what must the velocity vector $\boldsymbol{V}_{xyz}$ of the particle be to have the acceleration

$$\boldsymbol{a}_{xyz} = 495.2\boldsymbol{i} + 100\boldsymbol{j} \text{ m/sec}^2$$

if all other conditions are the same? Is there a component of $\boldsymbol{V}_{xyz}$ that can have any value for this problem?

15.121. A mass A weighing 4 oz is made to rotate at a constant angular speed of $\omega_2 = 15$ rad/sec relative to a platform. This motion is in the plane of the platform, which, at the instant of interest, is rotating at an angular speed $\omega_1 = 10$ rad/sec and decelerating at a rate of 5 rad/sec^2 relative to the ground. If we neglect the mass of the rod supporting the mass A, what are the axial force and shear force at the base of the rod (i.e., at 0)? The rod at the instant of interest is shown in the diagram. The shear force is the total force acting on a cross-section of the member in a direction *tangent* to the section.

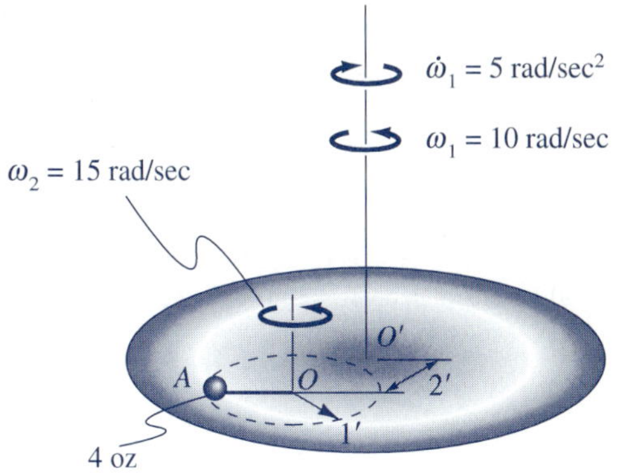

Figure P.15.121.

15.122. In Problem 15.91, what is the total external force acting on the cylinder for the case when

$$V = 5 \text{ ft/sec}$$
$$\dot{V} = -2 \text{ ft/sec}^2$$
$$\omega_1 = 2 \text{ rad/sec}$$
$$\dot{\omega}_1 = 1 \text{ rad/sec}^2?$$

The mass of the cylinder is 100 lbm.

15.123. A truck is moving at constant speed V of 10 mi/hr. A crane AB is at time t at $\theta = 45°$ with $\dot{\theta} = 1$ rad/sec and $\ddot{\theta} = .2$ rad/sec^2. Also at time t, the base of AB rotates with speed $\omega_1 = 1$ rad/sec relative to the truck. If AB is 30 ft in length, what is the axial force along AB as a result of mass M of 100 lbm at B?

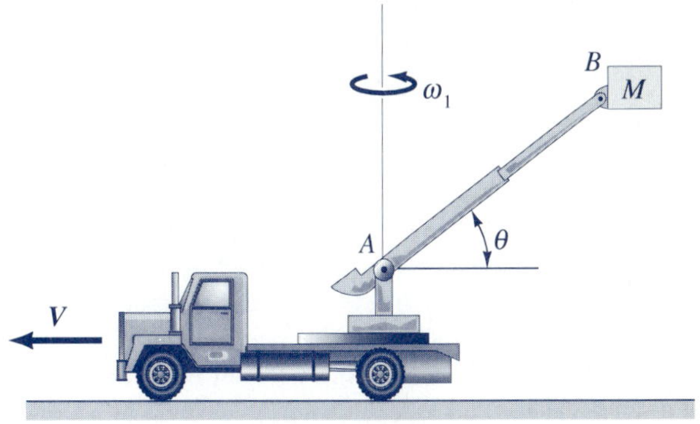

Figure P.15.123.

15.124. An exploratory probe shot from the earth is returning to the earth. On entering the earth's atmosphere, it has a constant angular velocity component ω_1 of 10 rad/sec about an axis normal to the page and a constant component ω_2 of 50 rad/sec about the vertical axis. The velocity of the probe at the time of interest is 1,300 m/sec vertically downward with a deceleration of 160 m/sec^2. A small sphere is rotating at ω_3 = 5 rad/sec inside the probe, as shown. At the time of interest, the probe is oriented so that the trajectory of the sphere in the probe is in the plane of the page and the arm is vertical. What are the axial force in the arm and the bending moment at its base (neglect the mass of the arm) at this instant of time, if the sphere has a mass of 300 g? (The bending moment is the couple moment acting on the cross section of the beam.)

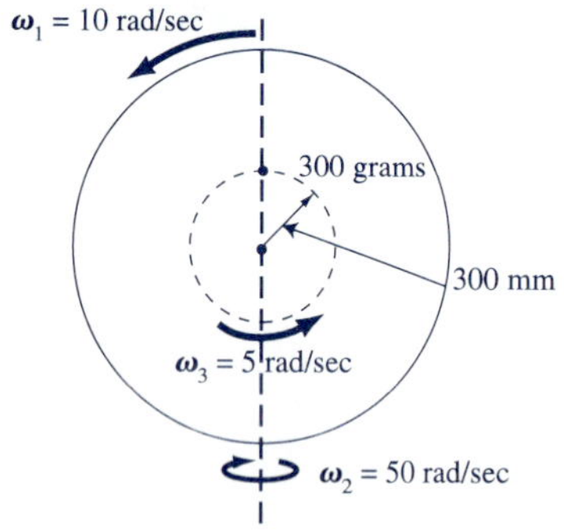

Figure P.15.124.

15.125. A river flows at 2 ft/sec average velocity in the Northern Hemisphere at a latitude of 40° in the north–south direction. What is the Coriolis acceleration of the water relative to the center of the earth? What is the Coriolis force on 1 lbm of water?

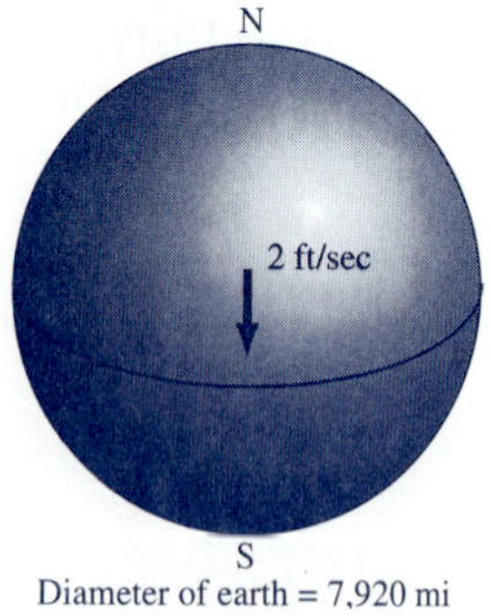

Figure P.15.125.

15.126. A clutch assembly is shown. Rods *AB* are pinned to a disc at *B*, which rotates at an angular speed ω_1 = 1 rad/sec and $\dot{\omega}_1$ = 2 rad/sec^2 at time *t*. These rods extend through a rod *EF*, which rotates with the rods and at the same time is moving to the left with a speed *V* of 1 m/sec. At the instant shown, corresponding to time *t*, what is the axial force on the member *AB* as a result of the motion of particle *A* having a mass of .6 kg?

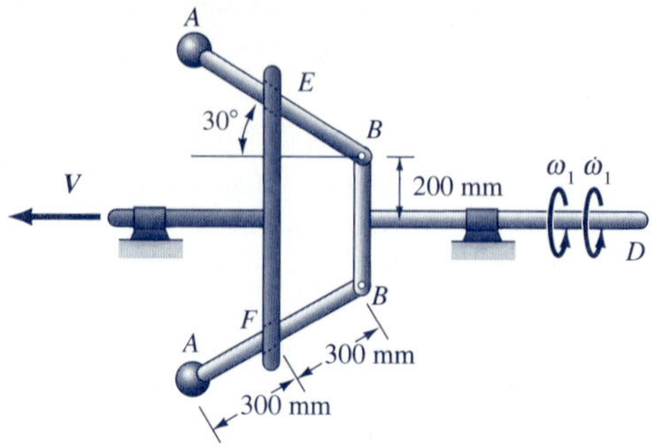

Figure P.15.126.

15.127. A flyball governor is shown. The weights *C* and *D* each have a mass of 200 g. At the instant of interest, θ = 45° and the system is rotating about axis *AB* at a speed ω_1 of 2 rad/sec. At this instant, collar *B* is moving upward at a speed of .5 m/sec. If we neglect the mass of the members, find the axial forces in the members at the instant of interest. What is the total shear force F_s on the members? (The shear force is the force component tangent to the cross section of the member.)

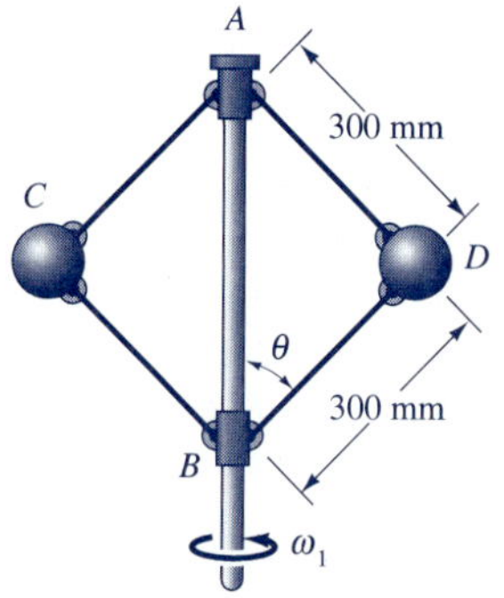

Figure P.15.127.

15.128. A man throws a ball weighing 3 oz from one side of a rotating platform to a man diametrically opposite, as shown. What is the Coriolis acceleration and force on the ball? Relative to the platform, in what direction does the ball tend to go as a result of the Coriolis force?

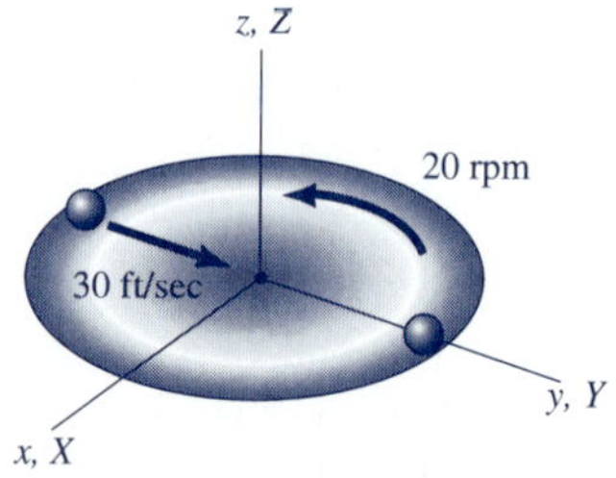

Figure P.15.128.

15.11 Closure

In this chapter, we first presented Chasles' theorem for describing the motion of a rigid body. Making use of Chasles' theorem for describing the motion of a reference *xyz* moving relative to a second reference *XYZ*, we presented next a simple but much used differentiation formula for vectors $\boldsymbol{A}$ *fixed* in the reference *xyz* or a rigid body. Thus,

$$\left(\frac{dA}{dt}\right)_{XYZ} = \boldsymbol{\omega} \times \boldsymbol{A}$$

where $\boldsymbol{\omega}$ is the angular velocity of *xyz* or the rigid body relative to *XYZ*.

We next considered *two points fixed in a rigid body in the presence of a single reference*. We can relate velocities and accelerations of the points relative to the aforementioned reference as follows:

$$\boldsymbol{V}_b = \boldsymbol{V}_a + \boldsymbol{\omega} \times \boldsymbol{\rho}_{ab}$$
$$\boldsymbol{a}_b = \boldsymbol{a}_a + \dot{\boldsymbol{\omega}} \times \boldsymbol{\rho}_{ab} + \boldsymbol{\omega} \times (\boldsymbol{\omega} \times \boldsymbol{\rho}_{ab})$$

where $\boldsymbol{\omega}$ is the angular velocity of the body relative to the single reference. These relations can be valuable in studies of kinematics of machine elements.

We then considered *one particle in the presence of two references xyz and XYZ*. We expressed the velocity and acceleration as seen from the two references as follows:

$$\boldsymbol{V}_{XYZ} = \boldsymbol{V}_{xyz} + \dot{\boldsymbol{R}} + \boldsymbol{\omega} \times \boldsymbol{\rho}$$
$$\boldsymbol{a}_{XYZ} = \boldsymbol{a}_{xyz} + \ddot{\boldsymbol{R}} + 2\boldsymbol{\omega} \times \boldsymbol{V}_{xyz} + \dot{\boldsymbol{\omega}} \times \boldsymbol{\rho} + \boldsymbol{\omega} \times (\boldsymbol{\omega} \times \boldsymbol{\rho})$$

In computing $\boldsymbol{V}_{xyz}$, $\boldsymbol{a}_{xyz}$, $\dot{\boldsymbol{R}}$, and $\ddot{\boldsymbol{R}}$, we use the various techniques presented in Chapter 11 for computing the velocity and acceleration of a particle relative to a given reference. Thus, use can be made of Cartesian components, path components, and cylindrical components as presented in that chapter. We then explored some interesting and often unexpected effects that occur when we use a noninertial reference.

You will have occasion to use these two important formulations in your basic studies of solid and fluid mechanics as well as in your courses in kinematics of machines and machine design.

Now that we can express the motion of a rigid body in terms of a velocity vector $\dot{\boldsymbol{R}}$ and an angular velocity vector $\boldsymbol{\omega}$, our next job will be to relate these quantities with the forces acting on the body. You may recall from your physics course and from the end of Chapter 14 that for a body rotating about a fixed axis in an inertial reference, we could relate the torque T and the angular acceleration α as

$$T = I\alpha$$

where I is the mass moment of inertia of the body about the axis of rotation. In Chapter 16, we shall see that this motion is a special case of plane motion, which itself is a special case of general motion.

PROBLEMS

15.129. A light plane is circling an airport at constant elevation. The radius R of the path = 3 km and the speed of the plane is 120 km/hr. The propeller of the plane is rotating at 100 rpm relative to the plane in a clockwise sense as seen by the pilot. What are $\boldsymbol{\omega}$, $\dot{\boldsymbol{\omega}}$, and $\ddot{\boldsymbol{\omega}}$ of the propeller as seen from the ground at the instant shown in the diagram?

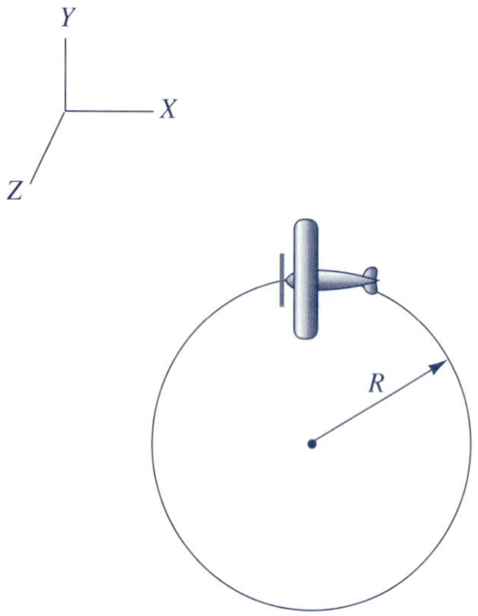

Figure P.15.129.

***15.130.** In Problem 15.7, find the angular acceleration $\dot{\boldsymbol{\omega}}$ of the disc for the configuration shown in the diagram, if, at the instant shown, the following data apply:

$$\omega_1 = 3 \text{ rad/sec}$$
$$\dot{\omega}_1 = 2 \text{ rad/sec}^2$$
$$\omega_2 = -10 \text{ rad/sec}$$
$$\dot{\omega}_2 = -4 \text{ rad/sec}^2$$

15.131. A slider A has at the instant of interest a speed V_A of 3 m/sec with a deceleration of 2 m/sec^2. Compute the angular velocity and angular acceleration of bar AB at the instant of interest. What is the position of the instantaneous axis of rotation of bar AB?

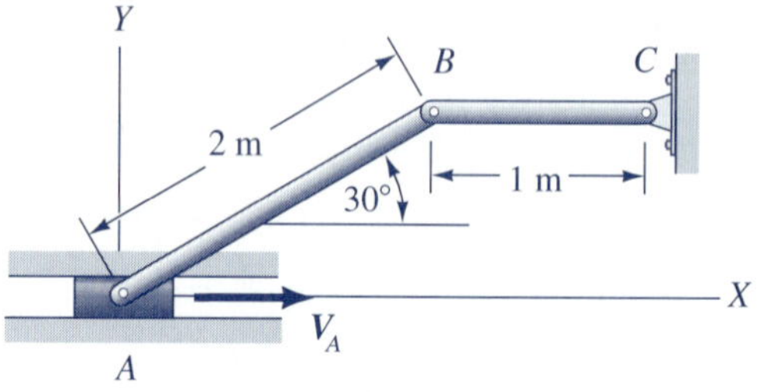

Figure P.15.131.

15.132. A cylinder C rolls without slipping on a half-cylinder D. Rod BA is 7 m long and is connected at A to a slider which at the instant of interest is moving in a groove at the speed V of 3 m/sec and increasing its speed at the rate of 2 m/sec^2. What is the angular speed and the angular acceleration of cylinder C relative to the ground?

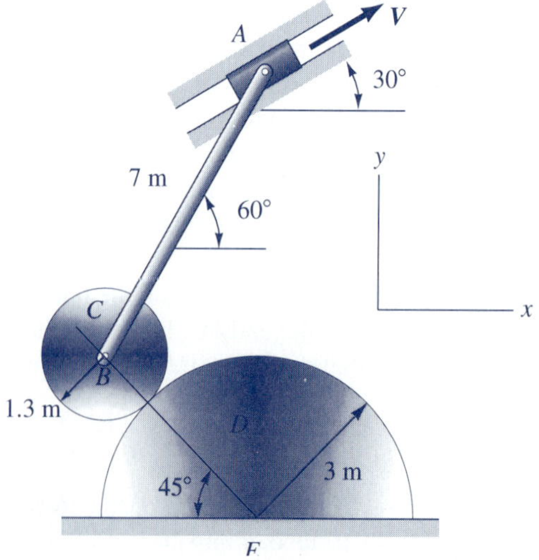

Figure P.15.132.

15.133. A wheel is rotating with a constant angular speed ω_1 of 10 rad/sec relative to a platform, which in turn is rotating with a constant angular speed ω_2 of 5 rad/sec relative to the ground. Find the velocity and acceleration relative to the ground at a point b on the wheel at the instant when it is directly vertically above point a.

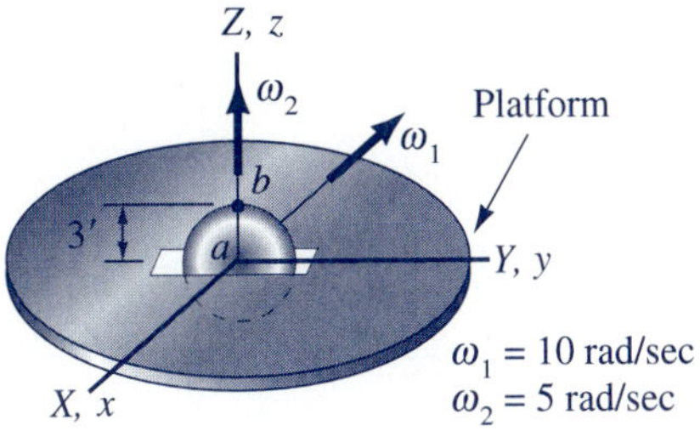

Figure P.15.133.

***15.134.** Solve Problem 15.133 for the case where ω_1 is increasing in value at the rate of 5 rad/sec² and where ω_2 is increasing in value at the rate of 10 rad/sec².

***15.135.** A barge is shown with a derrick arrangement. The main beam AB is 40 ft in length. The whole system at the instant of interest is rotating with a speed ω_1 of 1 rad/sec and an acceleration $\dot{\omega}_1$ of 2 rad/sec² relative to the barge. Also, at this instant $\theta = 45°$, $\dot{\theta} = 2$ rad/sec, and $\ddot{\theta} = 1$ rad/sec². What are the velocity and acceleration of point B relative to the barge?

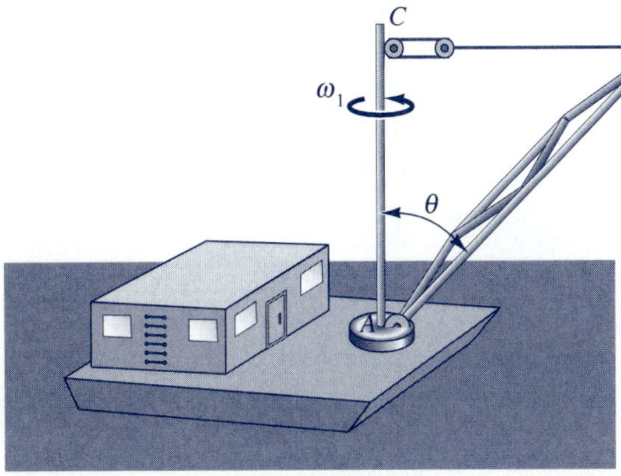

Figure P.15.135.

***15.136.** In Problem 15.86, find the acceleration of the collar C relative to the ground if for the configuration shown:

$$\dot{\theta} = 5 \text{ rad/sec}$$
$$\ddot{\theta} = 8 \text{ rad/sec}^2$$

15.137. In Example 15.11, find axial force for the beam AB at A resulting from cockpit C, which weighs (with occupant) $136g$ N. The following data apply:

$$\beta = 20°$$
$$\alpha = 60°$$
$$\omega_1 = .2 \text{ rad/sec}$$
$$\omega_2 = .1 \text{ rad/sec}$$

15.138. Find ω_B and $\dot{\omega}_B$ if ω_A and $\dot{\omega}_A$ are, respectively, 2 rad/s and 3 rad/s² counterclockwise.

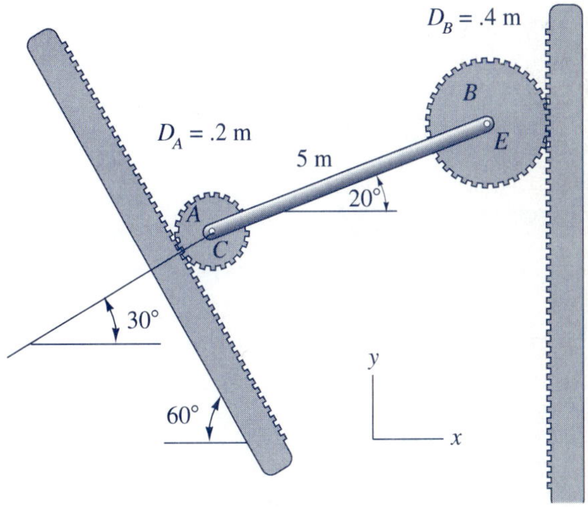

Figure P.15.138.

15.139. Find ω_{AC} and $\dot{\omega}_{AC}$ at the instant shown.

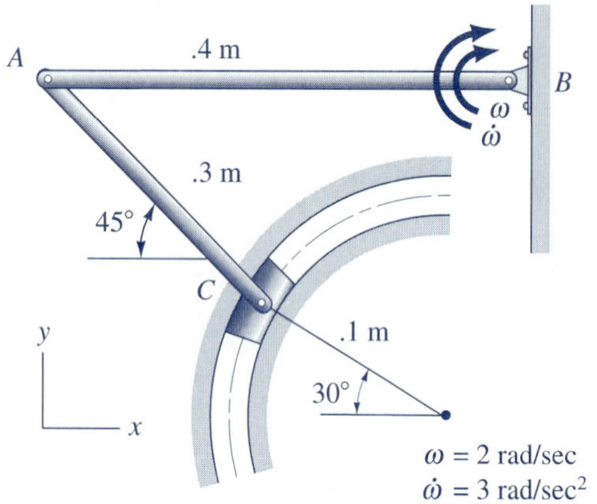

Figure P.15.139.

15.140. A missile travels in a straight line with respect to inertial reference XYZ at speed $V_1 = 10$ ft/sec and change of speed $a_1 = 5$ ft/sec^2. At the same instant the missile rolls about its direction of flight at an angular speed $\omega_1 = 5$ rad/sec and change in angular speed $\dot{\omega}_1 = 5$ rad/sec^2. Inside the missile a rod is rotating at a constant angular speed (relative to the missile) $\omega_2 = 10$ rad/sec about an axis perpendicular to the page. Find the velocity and acceleration of the tip of the rod relative to XYZ at the instant shown.

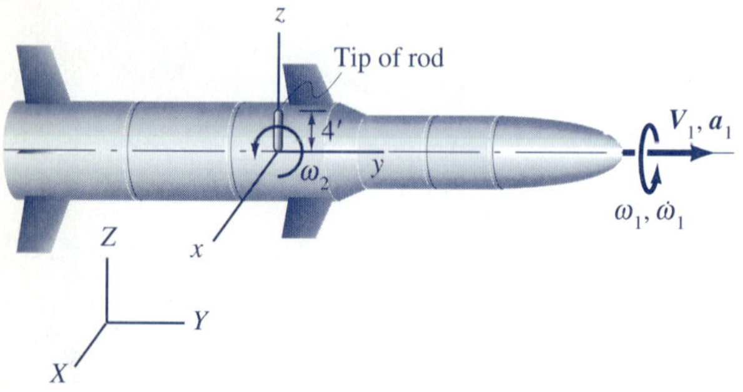

Figure P.15.140.

15.141. A transport plane is undergoing a severe maneuver. As shown, it is moving at a constant speed of 400 km/hr, is rolling at the rate of $\omega_1 = .2$ rad/s, and is in a loop of radius 1,000 m. A solenoid is causing a small machine element to move relative to the plane at a velocity of 10 m/s and an acceleration of 3 m/s^2 both directed downward. If the mass of the machine element is 10 kg, what is the force on it from the plane at this instant? The machine element is at position A at the time of interest.

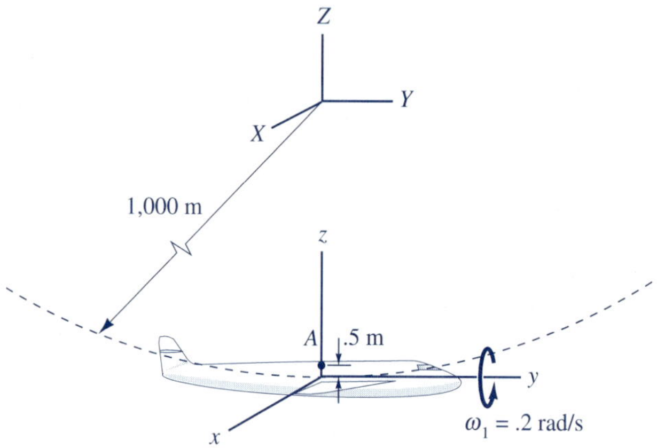

Figure P.15.141.

15.142. A rod moves in the plane of the paper in such a way that end A has a speed of 3 m/sec. What is the velocity of point B of the rod when the rod is inclined at 45° to the horizontal? B is at the upper support.

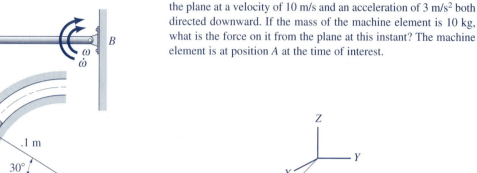

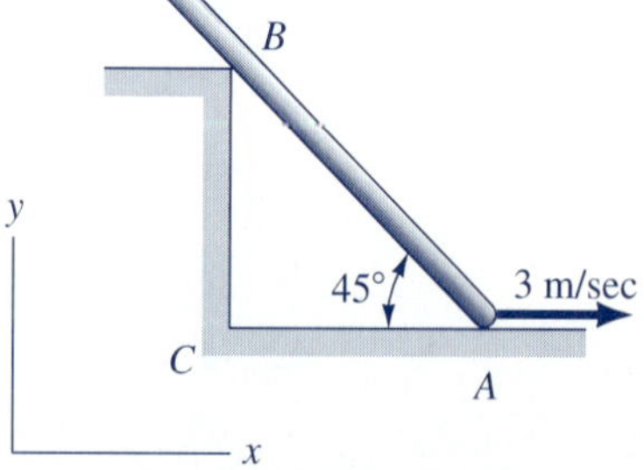

Figure P.15.142.

15.143. A vehicle on a monorail has a speed $\dot{S} = 10$ m/s and an acceleration $\ddot{S} = 4$ m/s^2 relative to the ground reference XYZ when it reaches point A. Inside the vehicle, a 3 kg mass slides along a rod which at the time of interest is parallel to the X axis. This rod rotates about a vertical axis with $\omega = 1$ rad/s and $\dot{\omega} = 2$ rad/s^2 relative to the vehicle at the time of interest. Also at this time, the radial distance d of the mass is .2 m and its radial velocity $v = .4$ m/s inward. What is the dynamic force on the mass at this instant?

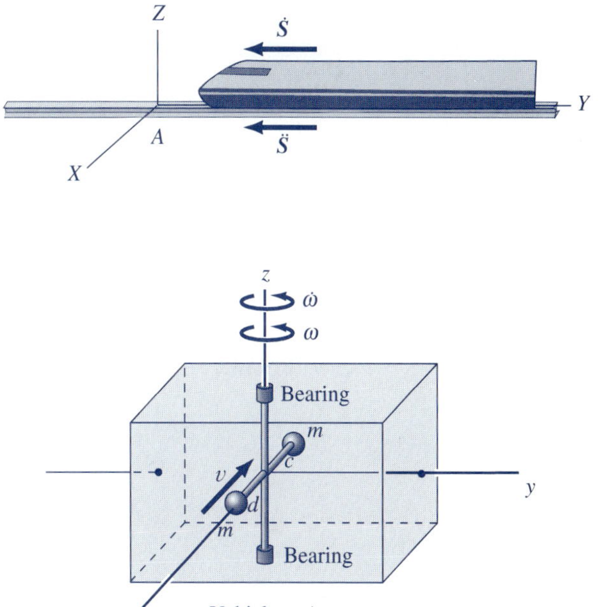

When vehicle is at A:
$\omega = 1$ rad/s $\dot{\omega} = 2$ rad/s^2 $v = .4$ m/s $d = .2$ m Relative to vehicle
$\dot{S} = 10$ m/s $\ddot{S} = 4$ m/s^2 Relative to ground XYZ

Figure P.15.143.

15.144. Cylinder A rolls without slipping. What are ω_{BC}, $\dot{\omega}_{BC}$, and $\dot{\omega}_{CD}$ At the instant shown, $V_A = 5$ m/s and $\dot{V}_A = 3$ m/s^2. Use an intuitive approach only as a check over a formal approach.

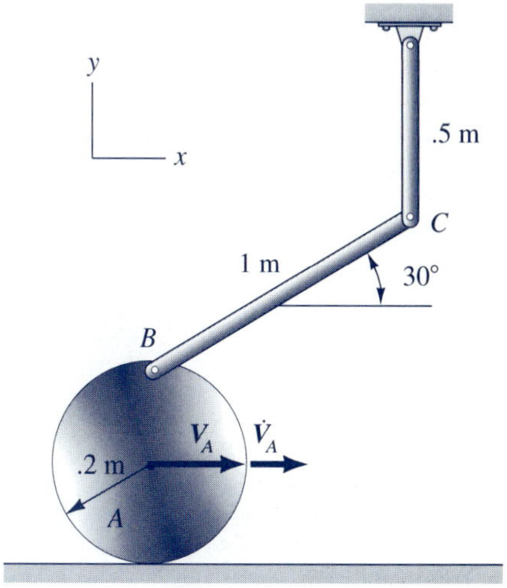

Figure P.15.144.

15.145. What is the magnitude of the velocity of the slider C at the instant shown in the diagram?

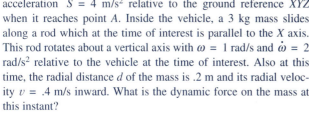

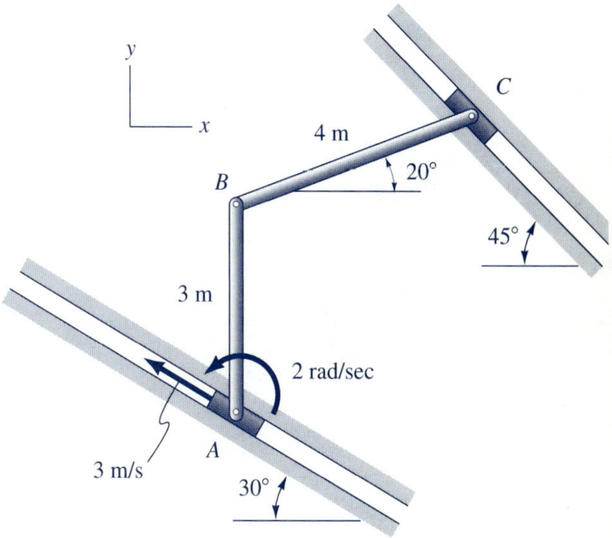

Figure P.15.145.

15.146. Rod AB is mounted on a vertical rod AK *fixed* to a horizontal platform D which rotates with angular speed ω_1 relative to the ground reference XYZ. The shaft AB meanwhile rotates relative to the platform with speed ω_2. Disc G rotates relative to rod AB with speed ω_3 whose value can be determined by a no slipping condition for the disc and platform contact surface. Find the velocity and acceleration vectors for point E on the disc G relative to XYZ. [Suggestion: Fix a second reference to the shaft AB as shown.]

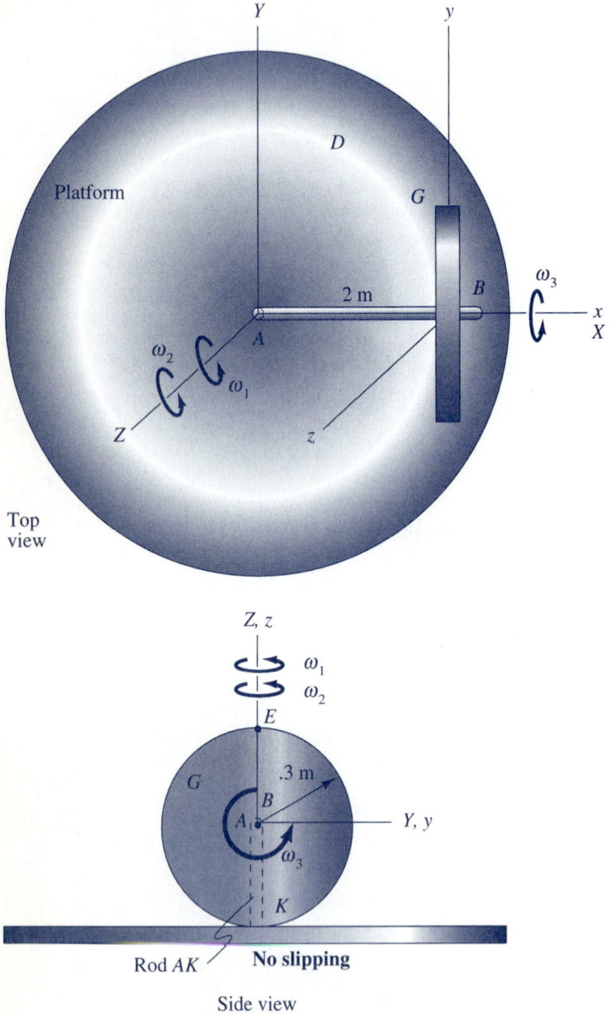

ω_1 = 3 rad/s relative to ground (for platform D)
ω_2 = 2 rad/s 1 rad/s relative to platform (for centerline AB)

Figure P.15.146.

15.147. A conveyor system is shown. Rod AB is welded to plate D. End A is connected to a vehicle which moves with velocity V_2 along a rail. System AB and connected plate D have angular velocities ω_1 and ω_2 relative to the vehicle A as shown in the diagram. On plate D, a particle G has motion given as V_1 and $\dot{V}_1$ along spoke BE which at the instant of interest is parallel to the X axis of the stationary reference XYZ. Determine the acceleration of particle G at the time of interest. Use as a second reference xyz fixed to the plate with the origin at B.

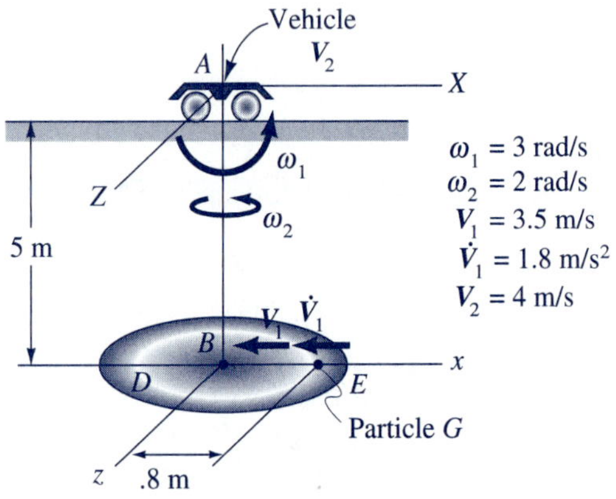

Figure P.15.147.

CHAPTER 16

Kinetics of Plane Motion of Rigid Bodies

16.1 Introduction

In **kinematics** we learned that the motion of a rigid body at any time t can be considered to be a superposition of a translational motion and a rotational motion. The translational motion may have the actual instantaneous velocity of any point of the body, and the angular velocity of the rotation, $\boldsymbol{\omega}$, then has its axis of rotation through the chosen point. A convenient point is, of course, the center of mass of the rigid body. The translatory motion can then be found from particle dynamics. You will recall that the motion of the center of mass of any aggregate of particles (this includes a rigid body) is related to the total external force by the equation

$$\boldsymbol{F} = M\dot{\boldsymbol{V}}_c \tag{16.1}$$

where M is the total mass of the aggregate. Integrating this equation, we get the motion of the center of mass. To ascertain fully the motion of the body, we must next find $\boldsymbol{\omega}$. As we saw in Chapter 14,

$$\boldsymbol{M}_A = \dot{\boldsymbol{H}}_A \tag{16.2}$$

for any system of particles where the point A about which moments of force and linear momentum are to be taken can be (1) the mass center, (2) a point fixed in an inertial reference, or (3) a point accelerating toward or away from the mass center. For these points, we shall later show that the angular velocity vector $\boldsymbol{\omega}$ is involved in the equation above when it is applied to rigid bodies. Also, the inertia tensor will be involved. After we find the motion of the mass center from Eq. 16.1 and the angular velocity $\boldsymbol{\omega}$ from Eq. 16.2, we get the instantaneous motion by letting the entire body have the velocity $\boldsymbol{V}_c$ plus the angular velocity $\boldsymbol{\omega}$, with the axis of rotation going through the center of mass.[1]

[1]Those readers and/or instructors who wish to go to the three-dimensional approach first so as to have plane motion emerge as a special case, should now go to Chapter 18. After the general development and after looking at the solution of three-dimensional problems, one may wish to come back to Chapter 16 to study plane motion dynamics in detail. This approach is entirely optional.

16.2 Moment-of-Momentum Equations

Consider now a rigid body wherein each particle of the body moves parallel to a plane. Such a body is said to be in *plane motion* relative to this plane. We shall consider that axes XY are in the aforementioned plane in the ensuing discussion. The Z axis is then normal to the velocity vector of each point in the body. Furthermore, we consider only the situation where XYZ is an *inertial reference*. A body undergoing plane motion relative to XYZ as described above is shown in Fig. 16.1.

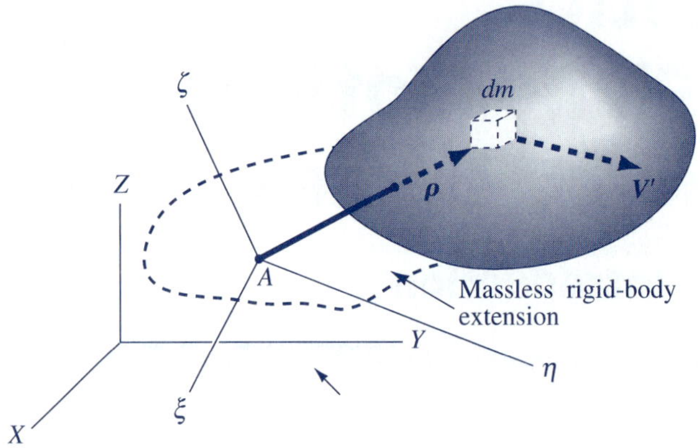

Figure 16.1. Body undergoing plane motion parallel to XY plane. $\xi\eta\zeta$ translates with A.

Choose some point A which is part of this body or a hypothetical massless rigid body extension of this body. An element dm of the body is shown at a position $\boldsymbol{\rho}$ from A. The velocity $\mathbf{V}'$ of dm relative to A is simply the velocity of dm relative to any reference $\xi\eta\zeta$, which *translates* with A relative to XYZ. Similarly, the linear momentum of dm relative to A (i.e., $\mathbf{V}'\,dm$) is the linear momentum of dm relative to $\xi\eta\zeta$ translating with A. We can now give the moment of this momentum (i.e., the angular momentum) $d\mathbf{H}_A$ about A as

$$d\mathbf{H}_A = \boldsymbol{\rho} \times \mathbf{V}'\,dm = \boldsymbol{\rho} \times \left(\frac{d\boldsymbol{\rho}}{dt}\right)_{\xi\eta\zeta} dm$$

But since A is fixed in the body (or in a hypothetical massless extension of the body) and dm is a part of the body having mass, the vector $\boldsymbol{\rho}$ must be *fixed* in the body and, accordingly,

$$\left(\frac{d\boldsymbol{\rho}}{dt}\right)_{\xi\eta\zeta} = \boldsymbol{\omega} \times \boldsymbol{\rho}$$

where $\boldsymbol{\omega}$ is the angular velocity of the body relative to $\xi\eta\zeta$. However, since $\xi\eta\zeta$ translates relative to XYZ, $\boldsymbol{\omega}$ is the angular velocity of the body relative to XYZ as well. Hence, we can say:

$$d\mathbf{H}_A = \boldsymbol{\rho} \times (\boldsymbol{\omega} \times \boldsymbol{\rho})dm \tag{16.3}$$

Note that the angular velocity $\boldsymbol{\omega}$ for the plane motion relative to the XY plane must have a direction *normal* to the XY plane.

Having helped us reach Eq. (16.3), we no longer need reference $\xi\eta\zeta$ and so we now dispense with it. Instead we *fix* reference xyz to the body at point A such that the z axis is *normal* to the plane of motion while the other two axes have arbitrary orientations normal to z (see Fig. 16.2).

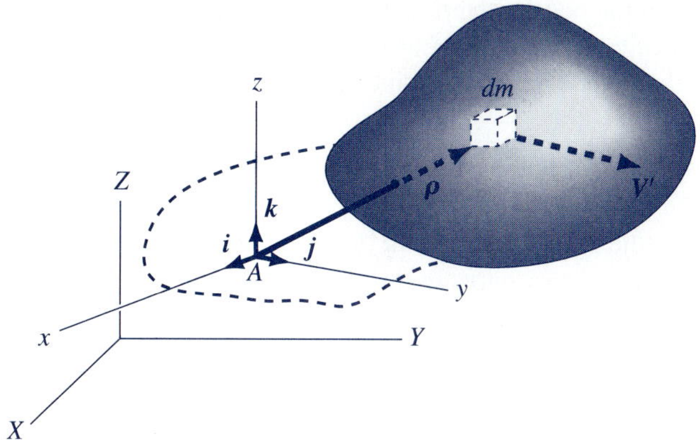

Figure 16.2. Reference xyz fixed to body at A; reference XYZ is inertial.

Note that the z axis will remain normal to XY as the body moves because of the plane motion restriction. Next, we evaluate Eq. 16.3 in terms of components relative to xyz as follows:

$$(dH_A)_x\boldsymbol{i} + (dH_A)_y\boldsymbol{j} + (dH_A)_z\boldsymbol{k}$$
$$= (x\boldsymbol{i} + y\boldsymbol{j} + z\boldsymbol{k}) \times \left[(\omega\boldsymbol{k}) \times (x\boldsymbol{i} + y\boldsymbol{j} + z\boldsymbol{k})\right]dm$$

The scalar equations resulting from the foregoing vector equations are

$$(dH_A)_x = -\omega xz\, dm$$
$$(dH_A)_y = -\omega yz\, dm$$
$$(dH_A)_z = \omega(x^2 + y^2)\, dm$$

Integrating over the entire body, we get[2]

$$(H_A)_x = -\iiint_M \omega xz\, dm = -\omega \iiint_M xz\, dm = -\omega I_{xz}$$
$$(H_A)_y = -\iiint_M \omega yz\, dm = -\omega \iiint_M yz\, dm = -\omega I_{yz} \qquad (16.4)$$
$$(H_A)_z = \iiint_M \omega(x^2 + y^2)\, dm = \omega \iiint_M (x^2 + y^2)\, dm = \omega I_{zz}$$

[2]Note that the massless extension of the rigid body has zero density and hence does not contribute to the integration.

We now have the angular momentum components for reference xyz at A.[3] Note that, because xyz is *fixed* to the body, the inertia terms I_{xz}, I_{yz}, and I_{zz} must be *constants*.

In order to employ the moment-of-momentum equation, $\boldsymbol{M}_A = \dot{\boldsymbol{H}}_A$, at time t, we next restrict point A of the body to be any one of the following three cases.[4]

1. Point A of the body is the *center of mass* of the body.
2. Point A of the body is *fixed* or moving with *constant velocity* at time t in inertial reference XYZ (i.e., point A has zero acceleration at time t relative to XYZ).
3. Point A of the body is *accelerating* toward or away from the mass center at time t.

Using the results of Section 15.6 involving the relation between derivatives of vectors as seen from different references, we next can say, using references XYZ and xyz:

$$\left(\frac{d\boldsymbol{H}_A}{dt}\right)_{XYZ} = \left(\frac{d\boldsymbol{H}_A}{dt}\right)_{xyz} + \boldsymbol{\omega} \times \boldsymbol{H}_A$$

where $\boldsymbol{\omega}$ is the angular velocity of xyz and thus of the body relative to XYZ. Hence, the *moment-of-momentum* equation can be stated as follows:

$$\boldsymbol{M}_A = \left(\frac{d\boldsymbol{H}_A}{dt}\right)_{xyz} + \boldsymbol{\omega} \times \boldsymbol{H}_A \tag{16.5}$$

Using Eqs. 16.4 for the components of $\boldsymbol{H}_A$, we get for this equation:

$$\boldsymbol{M}_A = \frac{d}{dt}_{xyz}(-\omega I_{xz}\boldsymbol{i} - \omega I_{yz}\boldsymbol{j} + \omega I_{zz}\boldsymbol{k}) + \omega\boldsymbol{k} \times (-\omega I_{xz}\boldsymbol{i} - \omega I_{yz}\boldsymbol{j} + \omega I_{zz}\boldsymbol{k})$$

Noting that $\boldsymbol{i}, \boldsymbol{j}$, and $\boldsymbol{k}$ are constant vectors as seen from xyz, as are the inertia terms, we get

$$\boldsymbol{M}_A = -\dot{\omega} I_{xz}\boldsymbol{i} - \dot{\omega} I_{yz}\boldsymbol{j} + \dot{\omega} I_{zz}\boldsymbol{k} - \omega^2 I_{xz}\boldsymbol{j} + \omega^2 I_{yz}\boldsymbol{i}$$

The scalar forms of the equation above are then

$$(M_A)_x = -I_{xz}\dot{\omega} + I_{yz}\omega^2 \tag{16.6a}$$

$$(M_A)_y = -I_{yz}\dot{\omega} - I_{xz}\omega^2 \tag{16.6b}$$

$$(M_A)_z = I_{zz}\dot{\omega} \tag{16.6c}$$

[3]We now see the motivation for presenting earlier the definitions of mass moments and products of inertia. Clearly the inertia tensor enters prominently in the evaluation of the angular motion of a rigid body.

[4]The "body" here includes the hypothetical, massless, rigid-body extension as well as the actual body.

It is important to note emphatically that the angular velocity as given by ω (and later by $\dot{\theta}$) is always taken *relative to the inertial reference XYZ*, whereas the moments of forces (as given by $(M_A)_x$, $(M_A)_y$, and $(M_A)_z$ as well as the inertia tensor components are always taken about the axes *xyz fixed to the body at A* (Eqs. (16.6). Eqs. (16.6) are the *general angular momentum equations for plane motion*. The last equation is probably familiar to you from your work in physics. There you expressed it as

$$T = I\alpha \tag{16.7}$$

or as

$$T = I\ddot{\theta} \tag{16.8}$$

We shall now consider special cases of plane motion, starting with the most simple case and going toward the most general case. However, please remember that for *all* plane motions relative to an inertial reference, the moment of the forces about the z axis at A *always* equals $I_{zz}\dot{\omega}$. The other two equations of 16.6 may get simplified for various special plane motions.

Also, to use Eqs. 16.6, we must remember that point A is *part of the body* (because we took $\boldsymbol{\rho}$ to be fixed in the body so we could use $d\boldsymbol{\rho}/dt = \boldsymbol{\omega} \times \boldsymbol{\rho}$) and is also one of the *three acceptable points* presented in Chapter 14. Furthermore, the xyz axes are *fixed to the body* to render the inertia tensor components constant.

Finally, we note from the derivation that ω, θ, and their derivatives are measured from the inertial reference XYZ.

16.3 Pure Rotation of a Body of Revolution About Its Axis of Revolution

A uniform body of revolution is shown in Fig. 16.3. If the body undergoes pure rotation about the axis of revolution fixed in inertial space reference XYZ, we then have plane motion parallel to any plane for which the axis of revolution is a normal. A reference xyz is *fixed* to the body such that the z axis is collinear with the axis of revolution. Since all points along the axis of revolution are fixed in inertial space XYZ, we can choose for the origin of reference xyz any point A along this axis. The x and y axes forming a right handed triad then have arbitrary orientation. For simplicity, we choose xyz collinear with axes XYZ at time t. Clearly, the plane zy is a plane of symmetry for this body, and the x axis is normal to this plane of symmetry. From our work in Chapter 9, recall[5] that, as a consequence, $I_{xy} = I_{xz} = 0$.

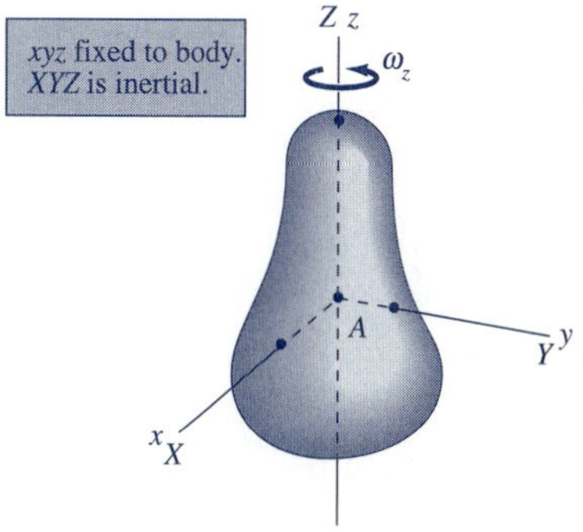

Figure 16.3. Rigid uniform body of revolution at time t.

[5]We pointed out in Chapter 9 that if an axis, such as the x axis, is normal to a plane of symmetry, then the products of inertia with x as a subscript must be zero. This is similarly true for other axes normal to a plane of symmetry.

Similarly, with y normal to a plane of symmetry, xz, we conclude that $I_{yx} = I_{yz} = 0$. Hence, xyz are principal axes. Returning to Eq. 16.6, we find that only one equation of the set has nonzero moment, and that is the familiar equation

$$M_z = I_{zz}\dot{\omega}_z \tag{16.9}$$

The other pair of equations from 16.6 yield

$$\begin{aligned} M_x &= 0 \\ M_y &= 0 \end{aligned} \tag{16.10}$$

Now we turn to *Newton's law*. For this we must use the inertial reference XYZ. Note that at the instant t shown in Fig. 16.3, axes xyz and axes XYZ have been taken as collinear. This means that at this instant the forces on the body needed in Newton's law such as F_X can be denoted as F_x since the directions of X and x are the same at this instant and it is only the direction that is significant here. Since the center of mass of the body is stationary at all times (it is on the axis of rotation), we can accordingly say from *Newton's law*:

$$\begin{aligned} \sum F_x &= 0 \\ \sum F_y &= 0 \\ \sum F_z &= 0 \end{aligned} \tag{16.11}$$

Thus, the applied forces at any time t, the supporting forces, and the weight of the body of revolution satisfy *all* the equations of equilibrium *except* for motion about the axis of revolution where Eq. 16.9 applies.

Notice that the key equation (16.9) has the *same form* as Newton's law for *rectilinear translation* of a particle along an axis, say the x axis. We write both equations together as follows:

$$M_z = I_{zz}\ddot{\theta} \tag{16.12a}$$

$$F_X = M\ddot{X} \tag{16.12b}$$

In Chapter 12 we integrated Eq. 16.12b for various kinds of force functions: time functions, velocity functions, and position functions. The same techniques used then to integrate Eq. 16.12b can now be used to integrate Eq. 16.12a, where the moment functions can also be time functions, angular velocity functions, and angular position functions.

We illustrate these possibilities in the following examples. The first example involves a torque which in part is a function of angular position θ.

Example 16.1

A stepped cylinder having a radius of gyration $k = .40$ m and a mass of 200 kg is shown in Fig. 16.4. The cylinder supports a weight W of mass 100 kg with an inextensible cord and is restrained by a linear spring whose constant K is 2 N/mm. What is the angular acceleration of the stepped cylinder when it has rotated 10° after it is released from a state of rest? The spring is initially unstretched. What are the supporting forces at this time?

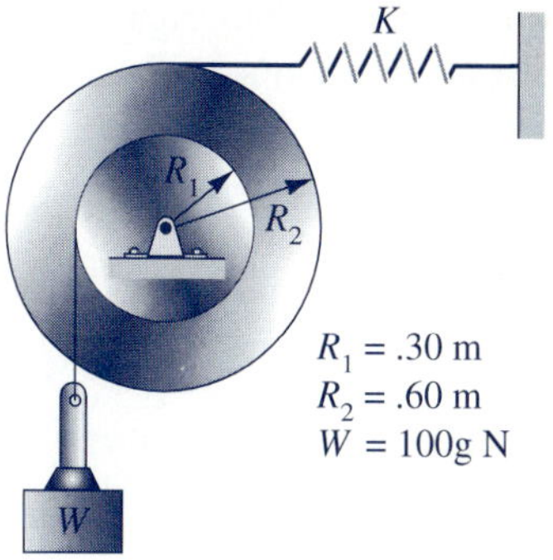

Figure 16.4. Stepped cylinder.

We have shown free-body diagrams of the stepped cylinder and the weight W in Fig. 16.5. A tension T from the cord is shown acting both on the weight W and the stepped cylinder. We have here for the stepped cylinder a body of revolution rotating about its axis of symmetry along which we have chosen point A. Axes xyz are fixed to the body at A with z along the axis of rotation. Furthermore we have shown inertial axes XYZ at A collinear with xyz at the time t.

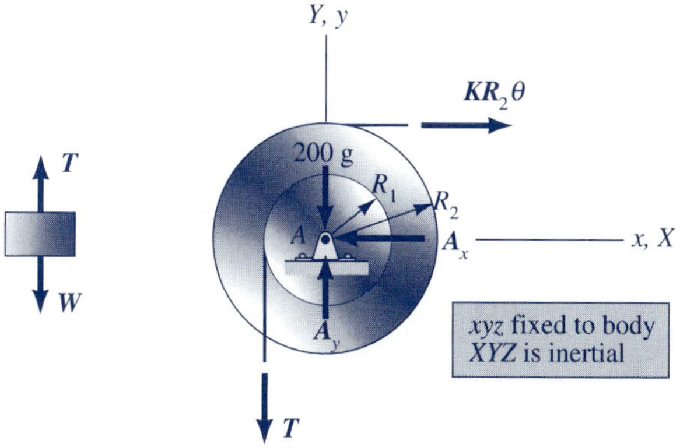

Figure 16.5. Free-body diagrams of components at time t.

We can accordingly apply the **moment-of-momentum** equation about the centerline of the cylinder:

$$TR_1 - KR_2^2\theta = I\ddot{\theta} = (Mk^2)\ddot{\theta}$$

$$T(.30) - [(2)(1{,}000)](.60)^2\theta = (200)(.40)^2\ddot{\theta} \qquad \text{(a)}$$

where as indicated earlier $\dot{\theta}$ is the angular velocity of the body relative to stationary axes XYZ and where θ is the rotation of the cylinder in radians from a position corresponding to the unstretched condition of the spring.

Example 16.1 (Continued)

Now considering the weight W, which is in a translatory motion, we can say, from **Newton's law** using inertial reference XYZ as required by Newton's law

$$T - W = M\ddot{Y}$$

Therefore,

$$T - (100)(9.81) = 100\ddot{Y} \qquad \text{(b)}$$

From **kinematics** we note that

$$R_1\ddot{\theta} = -\ddot{Y}$$

Therefore,

$$.30\ddot{\theta} = -\ddot{Y} \qquad \text{(c)}$$

Substituting for T in Eq. (a) using Eq. (b) and for $\ddot{Y}$ using Eq. (c), we then have

$$\left[(100)(9.81) + (100)(-.30\ddot{\theta})\right](.30)$$
$$-\left[(2)(1{,}000)\right](.60)^2\theta = (200)(.40)^2\ddot{\theta} \qquad \text{(d)}$$

When $\theta = (10°)(2\pi/360°) = .1745$ rad, we get for $\ddot{\theta}$ from Eq. (d) the desired result:

$$\ddot{\theta} = 4.11 \text{ rad/sec}^2$$

From Eqs. (b) and (c), we then have for T:

$$T = 981 - 123.3 = 858 \text{ N}$$

We next use **Newton's law** for the center of mass A of the stepped cylinder. Thus, considering Fig. 16.5, realizing that the center of mass is in equilibrium and assuming collinear orientation of the two sets of axes at time t, we can say $A_X \equiv A_x$ and $A_Y \equiv A_y$ at time t since only direction is involved here. Thus summing forces,

$$-858 - 200g + A_y = 0$$

$$A_y = 2{,}820 \text{ N}$$

$$-A_x + [(2)(1{,}000)](.60)(.1745) = 0$$

$$A_x = 209 \text{ N}$$

It should be clear on examining Fig. 16.4 that the motion of the cylinder, after W is released from rest, will be rotational oscillation. This motion ensues because the spring develops a restoring torque much as the spring in the classic spring–mass system (Fig. 16.6) supplies a restoring force. We shall study torsional oscillation or vibration in Chapter 19 when we consider vibrations. The key concepts and mathematical techniques for both motions you will find to be identical.

The torque in the next example is, in part, a function of time.

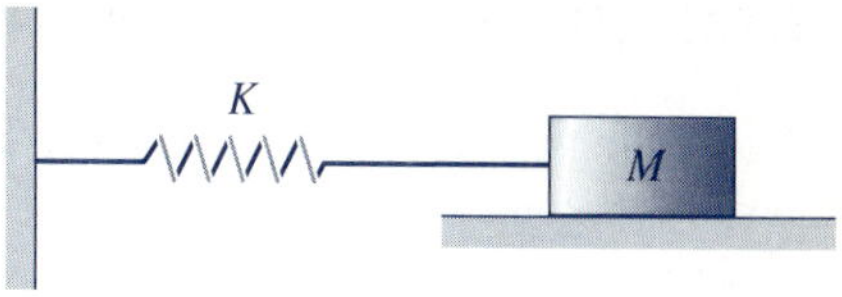

Figure 16.6. Classic spring–mass system.

Example 16.2

A cylinder A is rotating at a speed ω of 1,750 rpm (see Fig. 16.7) when the light handbrake system is applied using force F = $(10t + 300)$ N with t in seconds. If the cylinder has a radius of gyration of 200 mm and a mass of 500 kg, how long a time does it take to halve the speed of the cylinder? The dynamic coefficient of friction between the belt and the cylinder is .3.

We start by showing the free body of the cylinder and of the brake lever in Fig. 16.8. From the belt formula of Chapter 7, we can say for the belt tensions on the cylinder

$$\frac{T_1}{T_2} = e^{\mu_d \beta} = e^{(.3)\left(\frac{3}{4}\right)(2\pi)} = 4.11$$

$$\therefore\ T_1 = 4.11 T_2 \qquad \text{(a)}$$

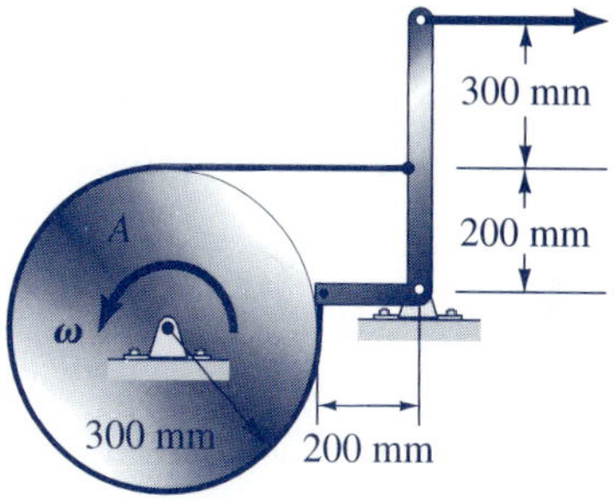

Figure 16.7. Cylinder and handbrake system.

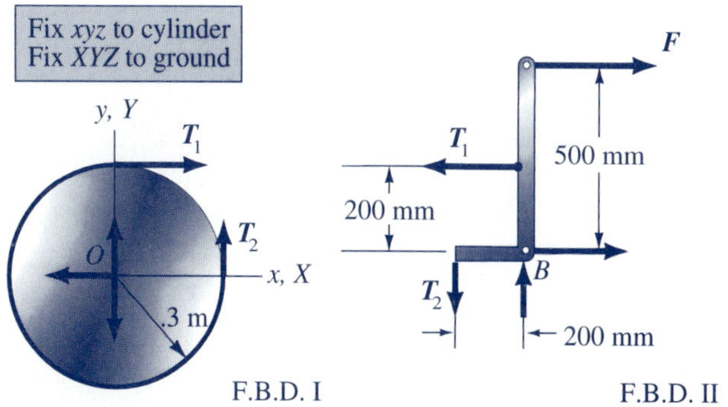

Figure 16.8. Free-body diagrams of cylinder and handbrake lever.

Example 16.2 (Continued)

Now going to the handbrake lever in F.B.D. II and taking moments about point B, we get from **equilibrium**

$$-F(.500) + T_1(.200) + T_2(.200) = 0$$

Inserting $F = 10t + 300$ N, we get for $(T_1 + T_2)$

$$T_1 + T_2 = 2.5(10t + 300) \tag{b}$$

Substitute for T_1 using Eq. (a).

$$4.11T_2 + T_2 = 2.5(10t + 300)$$

$$\therefore\ T_2 = .489(10t + 300) \tag{c}$$

Also from (a)

$$T_1 = (4.11)(.489)(10t + 300) = 2.01(10t + 300) \tag{d}$$

Now going to F.B.D. I in Fig. 16.8 and using axes xyz fixed to the cylinder at O, we next write the **moment-of-momentum** equation.

$$-T_1(.300) + T_2(.300) = (500)(.200)^2\,(\ddot{\theta})$$

Using Eqs. (c) and (d) we then have

$$(.489 - 2.01)(10t + 300)(.300) = (500)(.200)^2\ddot{\theta}$$

Hence

$$\ddot{\theta} = -.02283(10t + 300)$$

Integrating

$$\dot{\theta} = -.02283\left(10\frac{t^2}{2} + 300t\right) + C_1 \tag{e}$$

When $t = 0$,

$$\dot{\theta} = (1{,}750)\left(\frac{2\pi}{60}\right) = 183.3 \text{ rad/s} \qquad \therefore\ C_1 = 183.3$$

Thus

$$\dot{\theta} = -.02283(5t^2 + 300t) + 183.3$$

Set

$$\dot{\theta} = \left(\frac{1}{2}\right)(183.3) = 91.63 \text{ rad/s} \quad \text{and solve for } t$$

$$91.63 = -.02283(5t^2 + 300t) + 183.3$$

Example 16.2 (Continued)

Rearranging, we get

$$t^2 + 60t - 803 = 0$$

Using the quadratic formula, we have

$$t = \frac{-60 \pm \sqrt{60^2 + (4)(803)}}{2}$$

$$t = 11.27 \text{ sec}$$

16.4 Pure Rotation of a Body with Two Orthogonal Planes of Symmetry

Consider next a uniform body having *two* orthogonal planes of symmetry. Such a body is shown in Fig. 16.9, where in (a) we have shown the aforementioned planes of symmetry and in (b) we have shown a view along the intersection of the planes of symmetry. We shall consider pure rotation of such a body about a stationary axis collinear with the intersection of the planes of symmetry, which we take as the z axis. The origin A can be taken anywhere along the axis of rotation, and the x and y axes are fixed in the planes of symmetry, as shown in the diagram. XYZ is taken collinear with xyz at time t. We leave it to the reader to show that the identical equations apply to this case as to the previous case of a body of revolution.

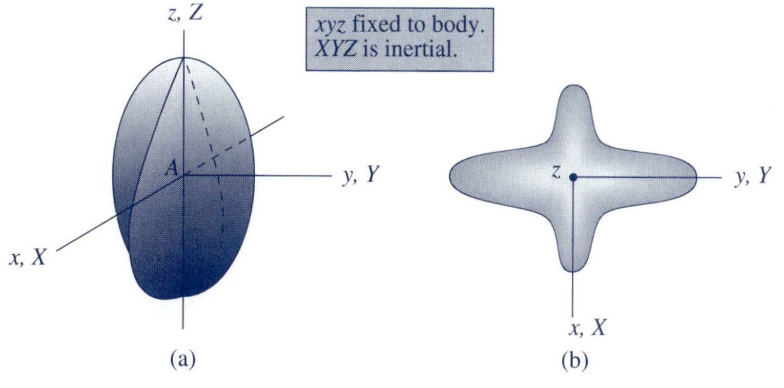

Figure 16.9. Body with two orthogonal planes of symmetry at time t.

The torque in the next example is a function of angular speed.[6]

[6]From now on it will be understood that in the diagrams xyz will be fixed to the body and that XYZ will be fixed to the ground and hence to be an inertial reference. This will avoid cluttering the diagrams unnecessarily.

Example 16.3

A thin-walled shaft is shown in Fig. 16.10. On it are welded identical plates A and B, each having a mass of 10 kg. Also welded onto the shaft at right angles to A and B are two identical plates C and D, each having a mass of 6 kg. The thin-walled shaft is of diameter 100 mm and has a mass of 15 kg. The wind resistance to rotation of this system is given for small angular velocities as $.2\dot{\theta}$ N-m, with $\dot{\theta}$ in rad/sec. Starting from rest, what is the time required for the system to reach 100 rpm if a torque T of 5 N-m is applied? What are the forces on the bearings G and E when this speed is reached?

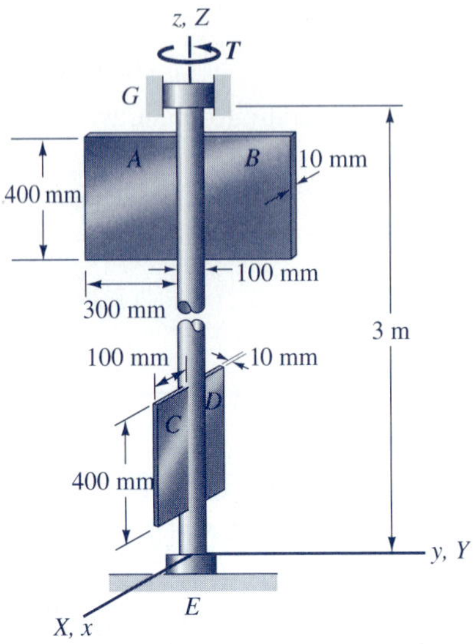

Figure 16.10. Device with rotational resistance.

We have here a body with two orthogonal planes of symmetry. The body is rotating about the axis of symmetry which we take as the z axis for axes xyz fixed to the body at E. As usual we position xyz at time t to be collinear with inertial reference XYZ.

The **moment-of-momentum** equation about the z axis is given as follows using moment of inertia formulas for plates (see inside covers) along with the parallel-axis formula and noting for the thin-walled shaft that we use $I_{zz} = Mr^2$ where, as an approximation, we take the outside radius for r.

$$5 - .2\dot{\theta} = \left\{(15)(.05)^2 + 2\left[\tfrac{1}{12}(10)(.30^2 + .01^2) + 10(.20)^2\right] + 2\left[\tfrac{1}{12}(6)(.10^2 + .01^2) + (6)(.10)^2\right]\right\}\ddot{\theta} \quad \text{(a)}$$

This becomes

$$5 - .2\dot{\theta} = 1.118\frac{d\dot{\theta}}{dt}$$

We can separate the variables as follows:

$$\frac{1.118\,d\dot{\theta}}{5 - .2\dot{\theta}} = dt \quad \text{(b)}$$

Now make the following substitution:

$$5 - .2\dot{\theta} = \eta$$

Therefore, taking the differential

$$-.2d\dot{\theta} = d\eta$$

Hence, we have for Eq. (b):

$$-5.59\frac{d\eta}{\eta} = dt$$

Example 16.3 (Continued)

Integrate to get

$$-5.59 \ln \eta = t + C_1$$

Hence, replacing η

$$-5.59 \ln(5 - .2\dot{\theta}) = t + C_1 \qquad \text{(c)}$$

When $t = 0$, $\dot{\theta} = 0$, and we have for C_1:

$$-5.59 \ln(5) = C_1$$

Therefore,

$$C_1 = -8.99$$

Hence, Eq. (c) becomes

$$-5.59 \ln(5 - .2\dot{\theta}) = t - 8.99$$

Let $\dot{\theta} = (100/60)(2\pi) = 10.47$ rad/sec in the above equation. The desired time t for this speed to be reached then is

$$t = 3.03 \text{ sec}$$

We now consider the supporting forces for the system. For reasons set forth in Section 16.3 we know that

$$M_x = 0$$

$$M_y = 0$$

for the other **moment of momentum** equations. Also from **Newton's law**, while noting that *xyz* and *XYZ* are collinear at time *t*,

$$\sum F_x = 0$$

$$\sum F_y = 0$$

$$\sum F_z = 0$$

for the center of mass. Clearly, the dead weights of bodies (in the z direction) give rise to a constant supporting force of $[2(10 + 6) + 15]g = 461$ N at bearing E. All other forces are zero.

$E_z = 461$ N
All other support forces are zero

16.5 Pure Rotation of Slablike Bodies

We now consider bodies that have a *single* plane of symmetry, such as is shown in Fig. 16.11. Such bodies we shall call *slablike* bodies. We have oriented the body in Fig. 16.8 so that the plane of symmetry is parallel to the XY plane. We shall now consider the pure rotation of such a body about a fixed axis normal to the XY plane and going through a point A in the plane of symmetry of the body. We fix a reference xyz to the body at point A with xy in the plane of symmetry and z along the axis of rotation.

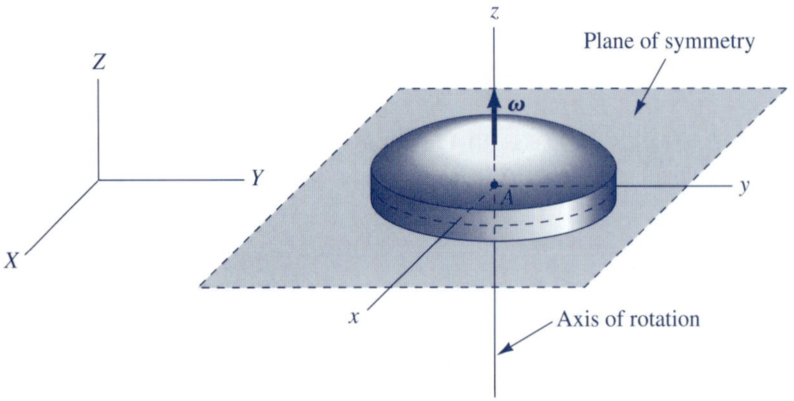

Figure 16.11. Slablike body undergoing pure rotation.

The angular velocity $\boldsymbol{\omega}$ is then along the z axis. Since z is normal to the plane of symmetry, it is clear immediately that $I_{zx} = I_{zy} = 0$. And so the *moment of momentum* equations become for this case:

$$\begin{aligned} M_x &= 0 \\ M_y &= 0 \\ M_z &= I_{zz}\dot{\omega}_z \end{aligned} \tag{16.13}$$

If the center of mass is not at a position along the axis of rotation, then we no longer have equilibrium conditions for the center of mass. It will be undergoing circular motion. However, through *Newton's law* we can relate the external forces on the body to the acceleration of the mass center. We may then have to use the *kinematics* of rigid-body motion to yield enough equations to solve the problem. We now illustrate this case.

Example 16.4

A uniform rod of weight W and length L supported by a pin connection at A and a wire at B is shown in Fig. 16.12. What is the force on pin A at the instant that the wire is released? What is the force at A when the rod has rotated 45°?

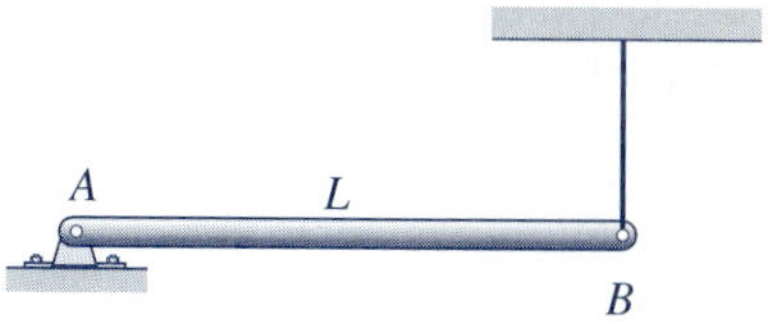

Figure 16.12. Rod supported by wire.

Part A. A free-body diagram of the rod is shown in Fig. 16.13 at the instant that the wire is released at B. We fix xyz to the body at A. XYZ is stationary. The **moment-of-momentum** equation about the axis of rotation at A, on using the formula for I of a rod about a transverse axis at the end, yields

$$\frac{WL}{2} = I\ddot{\theta} = \frac{1}{3}\left(\frac{W}{g}\right)L^2\ddot{\theta}$$

Therefore,

$$\ddot{\theta} = \frac{3}{2}\frac{g}{L} \quad \text{at time } t = 0 \tag{a}$$

Using simple **kinematics** of plane circular motion, we can determine the acceleration of the mass center at $t = 0$. Thus, using the inertial reference

$$\ddot{X} = 0, \qquad \ddot{Y} = \frac{L}{2}\ddot{\theta} = \frac{3}{4}g \tag{b}$$

where we have used Eq. (a) in the last step. Next express **Newton's law** for the mass center using $A_y \equiv A_Y, A_x \equiv A_X$:[7]

$$\frac{W}{g}\ddot{X} = A_x, \qquad \frac{W}{g}\ddot{Y} = W - A_y$$

Accordingly, at time $t = 0$ we have, on noting Eqs. (b):

$$A_x = 0, \qquad A_y = \tfrac{1}{4}W \tag{c}$$

Thus, we see that at the instant of releasing the wire there is an upward force of $\frac{1}{4}W$ on the left support.

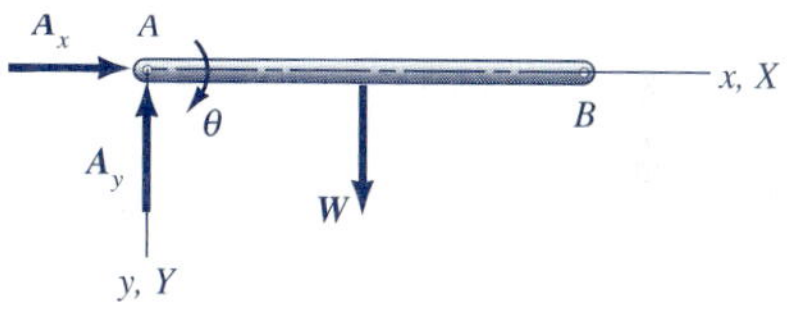

Figure 16.13. Wire suddenly cut.

[7]Note that we can replace A_X by A_x, etc., because of the common direction of X and x as well as the other corresponding axes at time t. However, we cannot replace $\ddot{X}$ by $\ddot{x}$ and $\ddot{Y}$ by $\ddot{y}$. The reason for this is that while the orientations of the respective axes are the same at time t, the fact remains that because of the rotational motion of xyz relative to XYZ, the velocities and accelerations of a particle relative to xyz and XYZ will be different requiring us to use only the XYZ axes when dealing with derivatives of the particle coordinates in Newton's law.

Example 16.4 (Continued)

Part B. We next express the **moment-of-momentum** equation for the rod at any arbitrary position θ. Observing Fig. 16.14, we get

$$\frac{WL}{2}\cos\theta = \frac{1}{3}\frac{W}{g}L^2\ddot{\theta}$$

Therefore,

$$\ddot{\theta} = \frac{3}{2}\frac{g}{L}\cos\theta \qquad \text{(d)}$$

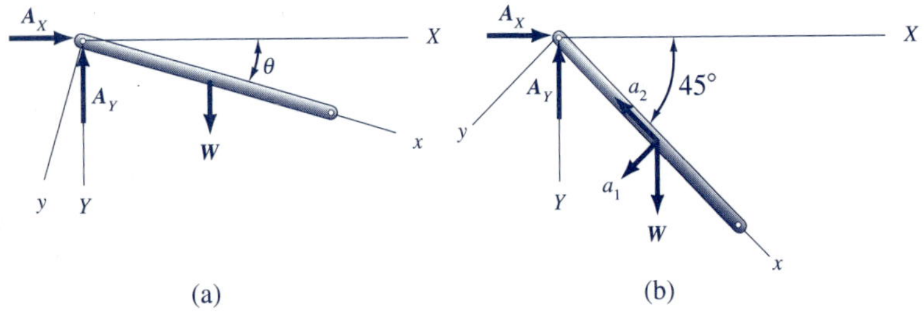

Figure 16.14. (a) Rod at position θ; (b) rod at $\theta = 45°$.

Consequently, at $\theta = 45°$ we have

$$\ddot{\theta} = (1.5)(.707)\frac{g}{L} = 1.060\frac{g}{L} \qquad \text{(e)}$$

We shall also need $\dot{\theta}$, and accordingly we now rewrite Eq. (d) as follows:

$$\ddot{\theta} \equiv \left(\frac{d\dot{\theta}}{d\theta}\right)\left(\frac{d\theta}{dt}\right) \equiv \left(\frac{d\dot{\theta}}{d\theta}\right)(\dot{\theta}) = \frac{3}{2}\frac{g}{L}\cos\theta \qquad \text{(f)}$$

Separating variables, we get

$$\dot{\theta}\,d\dot{\theta} = \frac{3}{2}\frac{g}{L}\cos\theta\,d\theta$$

which we integrate to get

$$\frac{\dot{\theta}^2}{2} = \frac{3}{2}\frac{g}{L}\sin\theta + C$$

When $\theta = 0$, $\dot{\theta} = 0$; accordingly, $C = 0$. We then have

$$\dot{\theta}^2 = 3\frac{g}{L}\sin\theta \qquad \text{(g)}$$

At the instant of interest, $\theta = 45°$ and we get for $\dot{\theta}^2$:

$$\dot{\theta}^2 = 3\frac{g}{L}(.707) = 2.12\frac{g}{L} \qquad \text{(h)}$$

For $\theta = 45°$, we can now give the acceleration component a_1 of the center of mass directed normal to the rod and component a_2 directed along

Example 16.4 (Continued)

the rod [see Fig. 16.14(b)]. From **kinematics** we can say, using Eqs. (e) and (h):

$$a_1 = \frac{L}{2}\ddot{\theta} = \frac{L}{2}\left(1.060\frac{g}{L}\right) = .530g$$

$$a_2 = \frac{L}{2}(\dot{\theta})^2 = \frac{L}{2}\left(2.12\frac{g}{L}\right) = 1.060g \qquad \text{(i)}$$

Now, employing **Newton's law** for the mass center, we have on noting that xy is *no longer collinear* with XY.

$$A_X = \frac{W}{g}(-a_1 \sin 45° - a_2 \cos 45°)$$

Therefore, using Eqs. (i)

$$A_X = -1.124W$$

Also, from **Newton's law**

$$-A_Y + W = \frac{W}{g}(-a_2 \sin 45° + a_1 \cos 45°)$$

Therefore, again using Eq. (i)

$$A_Y = 1.375W \qquad \text{(j)}$$

Consider next the case of a body undergoing pure rotation about an axis which, for some point A in the body (or massless hypothetical extension of the body), is a *principal* axis (see Fig. 16.15). For a reference xyz fixed at A with z collinear with the axis of rotation, it is clear that $I_{zx} = I_{zy} = 0$, and hence the moment of momentum equations simplify to the exact same forms as presented here for the rotation of slablike bodies.

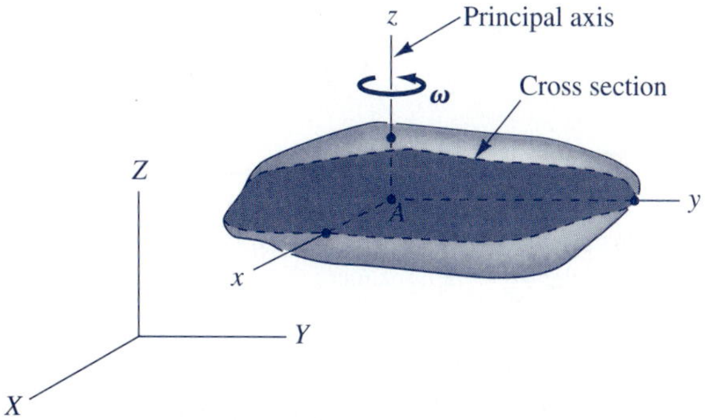

Figure 16.15. Axis z is a principal axis for point A.

PROBLEMS

16.1. A shaft and disc of steel having a density of 7,626 kg/m^3 are subjected to a constant torque T of 67.5 N-m, as shown. After 1 min, what is the angular velocity of the system? How many revolutions have occurred during this interval? Neglect friction of the bearings. Use $\frac{1}{2}Mr^2 = I$ for disc.

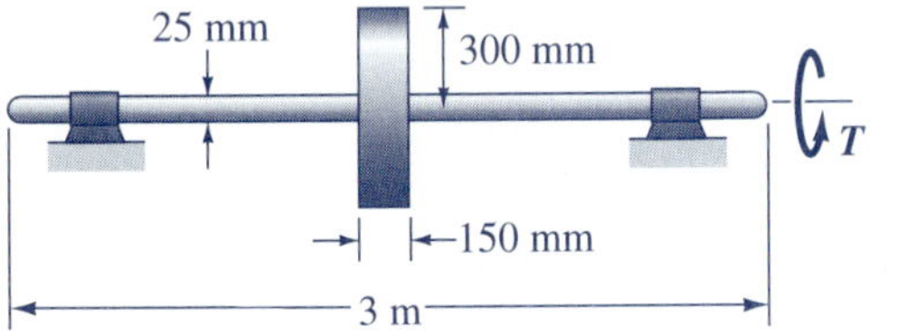

Figure P.16.1.

16.2. In Problem 16.1 include wind and bearing friction losses by assuming that they are proportional to angular speed $\dot{\theta}$. If the disc will halve its speed after 5 min from a speed of 300 rpm when there is no external applied torque, what is the resisting torque at 600 rpm?

16.3. A 400-lb flywheel is shown. A 100-lb block is held by a light cable wrapped around the hub of the flywheel, the diameter of which is 1 ft. If the initially stationary weight descends 3 ft in 5 sec, what is the radius of gyration of the flywheel?

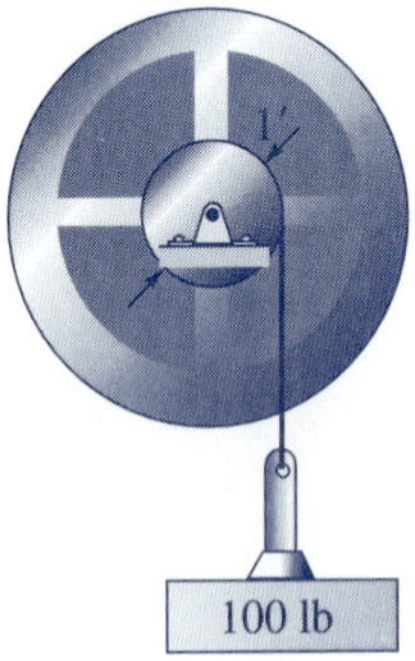

Figure P.16.3.

16.4 A stepped cylinder has the dimensions $R_1 = .30$ m, $R_2 = .65$ m, and the radius of gyration, k, is .35 m. The mass of the stepped cylinder is 100 kg. Weights A and B are connected to the cylinder. If weight B is of mass 80 kg and weight A is of mass 50 kg, how far does A move in 5 sec? In which direction does it move?

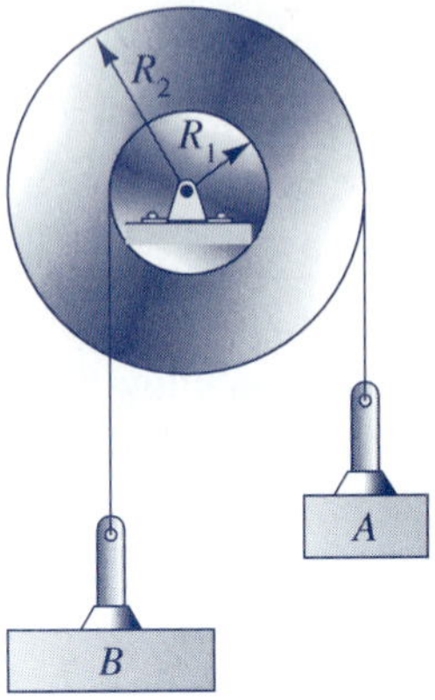

Figure P.16.4.

16.5. Two discs E and F of diameter 1 ft rotate in frictionless bearings. Disc F weighs 100 lb and rotates with angular speed ω_1 of 10 rad/sec, whereas disc E weighs 30 lb and rotates with angular speed ω_2 of 5 rad/sec. Neglecting the angular momentum of the shafts, what is the total angular momentum of the system relative to the ground? Use Eq. 16.4 to compute H from first principles. Consider that the discs are forced together along the axis of rotation. What is the common angular velocity when friction has reduced relative motion between the discs to zero?

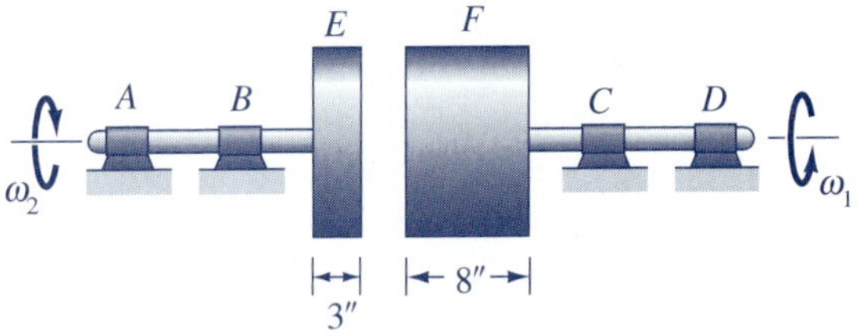

Figure P.16.5.

16.6 In Problem 16.5, if $\mu_s = .2$ between the discs, and it takes 30 sec for them to reach the same angular speed of 6.54 rad/sec, what is the constant normal force required to bring the discs together in such a manner?

16.7. A plunger A is connected to two identical gears B and C, each weighing 10 lb. The plunger weighs 40 lb. How far does the plunger drop in 1 sec if released from rest?

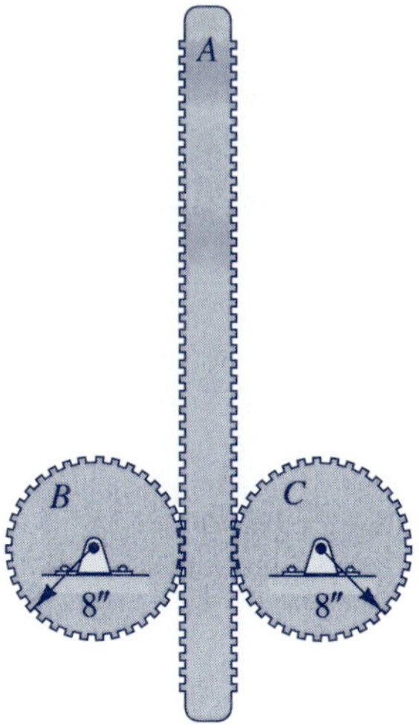

Figure P.16.7.

16.8. A pulley A and its rotating accessories have a mass of 1,000 kg and a radius of gyration of .25 m. A simple hand brake is applied as shown using a force P. If the dynamic coefficient of friction between belt and pulley is .2, what must force P be to change ω from 1,750 rpm to 300 rpm in 60 sec?

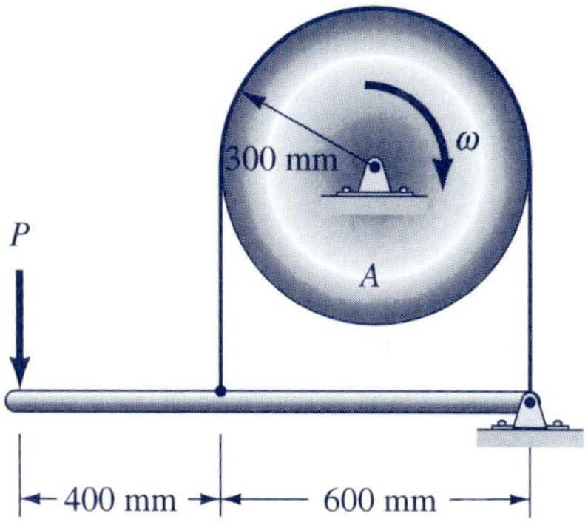

Figure P.16.8.

16.9. A flywheel is shown. There is a viscous damping torque due to wind and bearing friction which is known to be $-.04\omega$ N-m, where ω is in rad/sec. If a torque $T = 100$ N-m is applied, what is the speed in 5 min after starting from rest? The mass of the wheel is 500 kg, and the radius of gyration is .50 m.

Figure P.16.9.

16.10. Two cylinders and a rod are oriented in the vertical plane. The rod is guided by bearings (not shown) to move vertically. The following are the weights of the three bodies:

$$W_A = 1{,}000 \text{ N} \qquad W_B = 300 \text{ N} \qquad W_C = 200 \text{ N}$$

What is the acceleration of the rod? There is rolling without slipping.

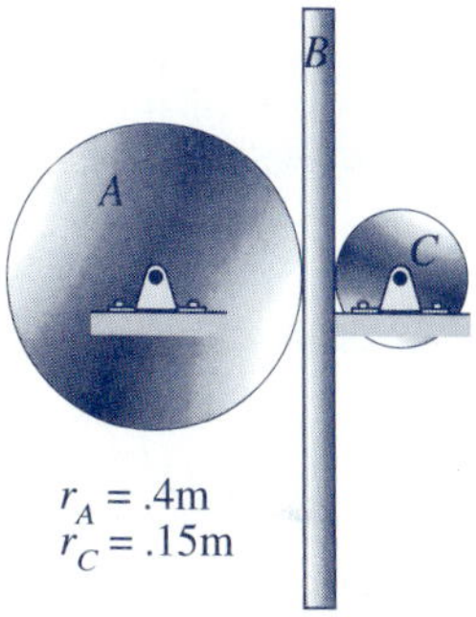

Figure P.16.10.

16.11. A bar A weighing 80 lb is supported at one end by rollers that move with the bar and a stationary cylinder B weighing 68 lb that rotates freely. A 100 lb force is applied to the end of the bar. What is the friction force between the bar and the cylinder as a function of x? Indicate the ranges for non-slipping and slipping conditions. Take $\mu_s = .5$ and $\mu_d = .3$.

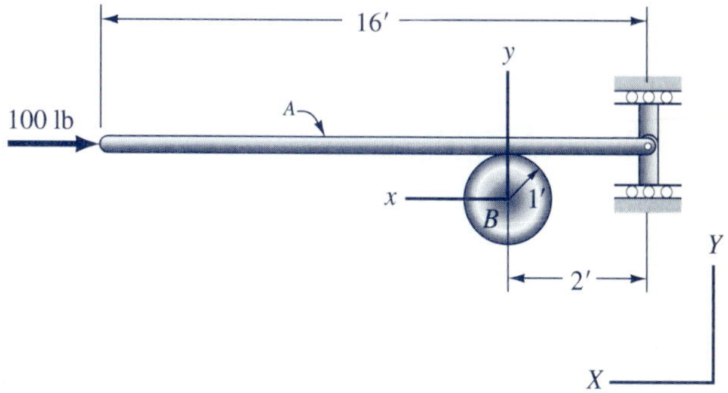

Figure P.16.11.

16.12. Cylinder A has an angular speed ω_1 of 3 rad/sec when it is lowered onto cylinder B, which has an angular speed ω_2 of 5 rad/sec before contact is made. What are the final angular velocities of the cylinders resulting from friction at the surfaces of contact? The mass of A is 500 lbm and of B is 400 lbm. If $\mu_d = .3$ for the contact surface of the cylinders and if the normal force transmitted from A to B is 10 lb, how long does it take for the cylinders to reach a constant speed?

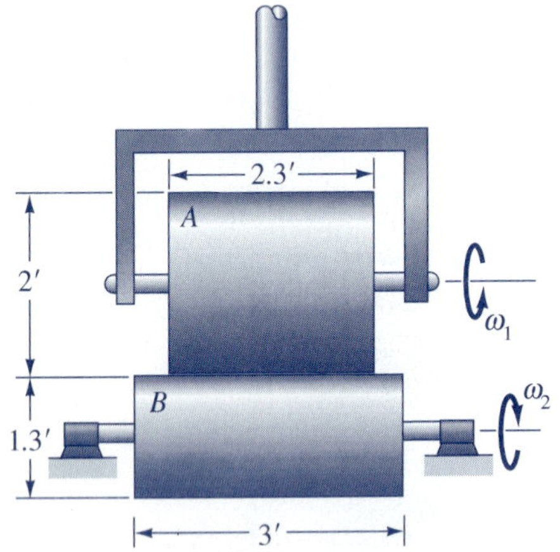

Figure P.16.12.

16.13. A driving cylinder A has a torque T_A of 30 N-m applied to it while the driven cylinder B has a resisting torque T_B of 10 N-m. Cylinder B has a mass of 15 kg, a radius of gyration of 100 mm, and a diameter of 400 mm. Cylinder A has a mass of 50 kg, a radius of gyration of 200 mm, and a diameter of 800 mm. Rod CD is a light rod connecting the cylinders. What is the angular acceleration of cylinder A at the instant shown if the system is stationary at this instant? Rod CD is 1 m long.

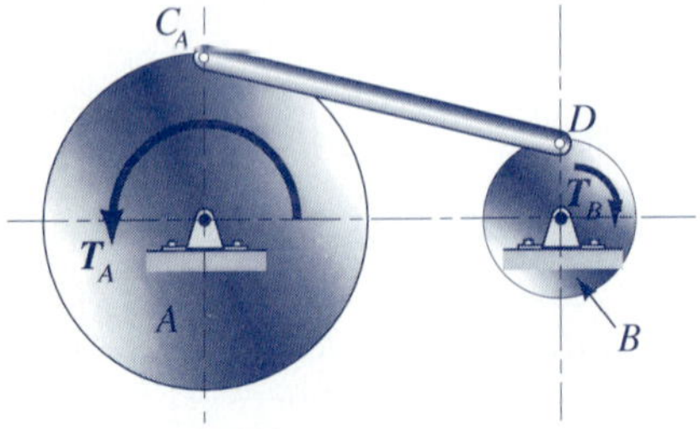

Figure P.16.13.

16.14. Do Problem 16.13 for the case where the angular velocity of B is 20 rad/sec clockwise at the instant of interest.

16.15. A loading vehicle is on a platform that can rotate in order to unload potash into the hold of a ship. The wheels of the vehicle are free to rotate. The vehicle is constrained from moving to the right by a stop at A. If the platform has the following rotational data at time t

$$\theta = .04 \text{ rad} \qquad \dot{\theta} = .05 \text{ rad/sec} \qquad \ddot{\theta} = .012 \text{ rad/sec}^2$$

what are the forces normal to the platform acting on the wheels of the vehicle and what is the force at the stop in a direction parallel to the platform? The total mass of the vehicle with load is 12,000 N. The radius of each wheel is 0.15 m. The radius of gyration at the center of mass of the vehicle is $k = 2.76$ m. Note that the center of mass of the vehicle lies along an axis which passes through the axis of rotation and is perpendicular to the platform. Also, note that θ is measured clockwise here.

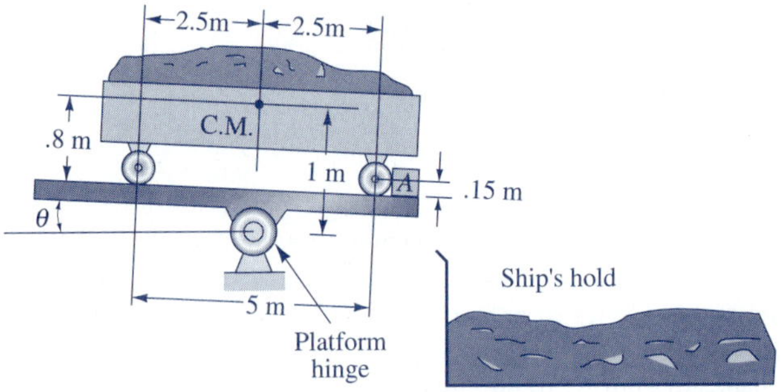

Figure P.16.15.

16.16. A torque T of 100 N-m is applied to a wheel D having a mass of 50 kg, a diameter of 600 mm, and a radius of gyration of 280 mm. The wheel D is attached by a light member AB to a slider C having a mass of 30 kg. If the system is at rest at the instant shown, what is the acceleration of slider C? What is the axial force in member AB? Neglect friction everywhere, and neglect the inertia of member AB.

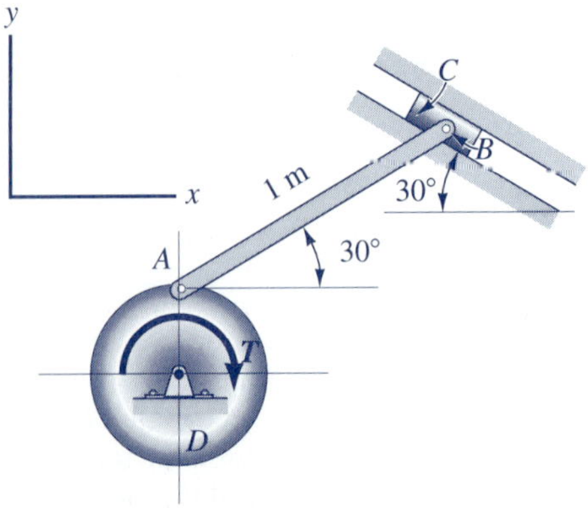

Figure P.16.16.

16.17. Do Problem 16.16 for the case where at the instant of interest $\omega_D = 2$ rad/sec counterclockwise.

16.18. A torque T of 50 N-m is applied to the device shown. The bent rods are of mass per unit length 5 kg/m. Neglecting the inertia of the shaft, how many rotations does the system make in 10 sec? Are there forces coming onto the bearings other than from the dead weights of the system?

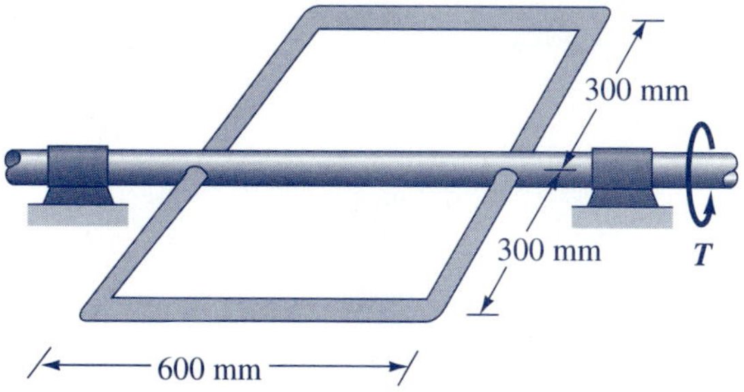

Figure P.16.18.

16.19. An idealized torque-versus-angular-speed curve for a shunt, direct-current motor is shown as curve A. The motor drives a pump which has a resisting torque-versus-speed curve shown in the diagram as curve B. Find the angular speed of the system as a function of time, after starting, over the range of speeds given in the diagram. Take the moment of inertia of motor, connecting shaft, and pump to be I.

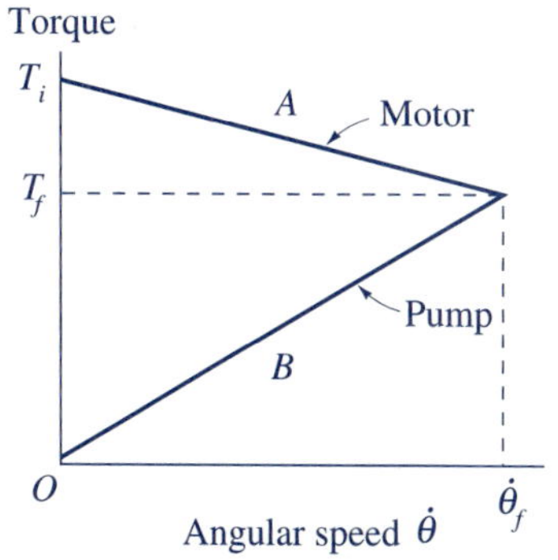

Figure P.16.19.

16.20. Rods of length L have been welded onto a rigid drum A. The system is rotating at a speed ω of 5,000 rpm. By this time, you may have studied stress in a rod in your strength of materials class. In any case, the stress is the normal force per unit area of cross section of the rod. If the cross-sectional area of the rod is 2 in.^{2} and the mass per unit length is 5 lbm/ft, what is the normal stress τ_{rr} on a section at any position r? The length L of the rods is 2 ft. What is τ_{rr} at $r = 1.5$ ft? Consider the upper rod when it is vertical.

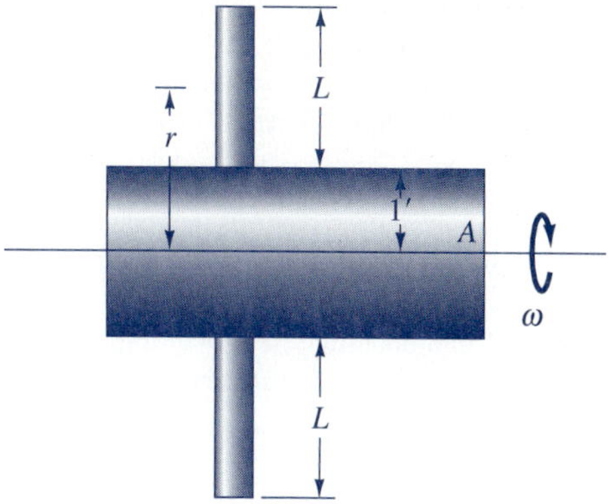

Figure P.16.20.

***16.21.** In Problem 16.20, consider that the mass per unit length varies linearly from 5 lbm/ft at $r = 1$ ft (at the bottom of the rod) to 6 lbm/ft at $r = 3$ ft (at the top of the rod). Find τ_{rr} at any position r and then compute τ_{rr} for $r = 1.5$ ft.

16.22. A plate weighing 3 lb/ft^2 is supported at A and B. What are the force components at B at the instant support A is removed?

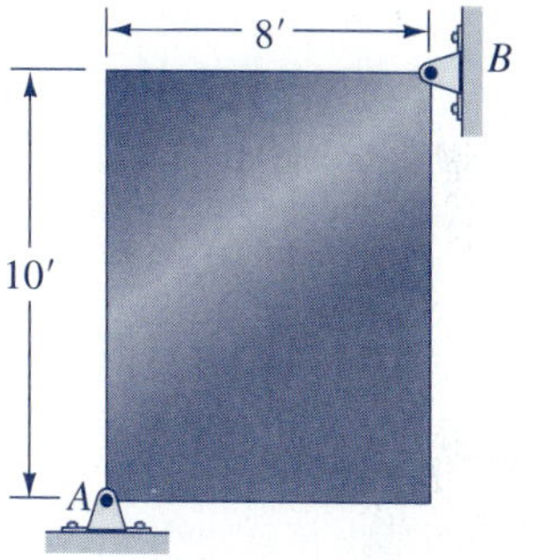

Figure P.16.22.

16.23. When the uniform rigid bar is horizontal, the spring at C is compressed 3 in. If the bar weighs 50 lb, what is the force at B when support A is removed suddenly? The spring constant is 50 lb/in.

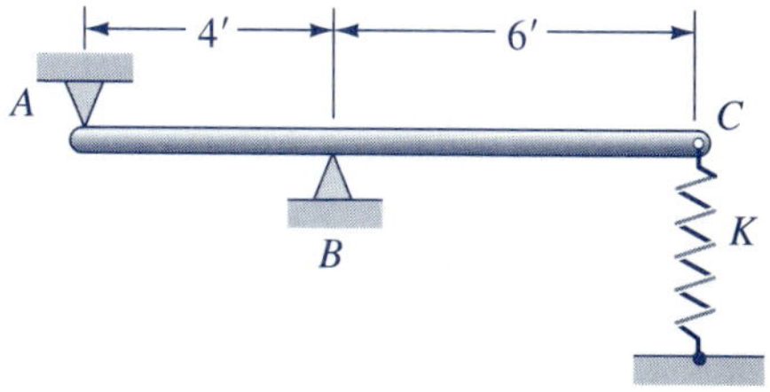

Figure P.16.23.

16.24. An electric motor E drives a light shaft through a coupling D which transmits only torque. A disc A is on the shaft and has its center of gravity 200 mm from the geometric center of the disc as shown in the diagram. A torque T given as

$$T = .005t^2 + .03t \text{ N-m}$$

is applied to the shaft from the motor (t is in seconds measured from when the system is at rest). What are the force components on the bearings when $t = 30$ sec? The disc has a mass of 15 kg and a radius of gyration of 250 mm about an axis going through the center of gravity. Take the disc at the position shown as the instant of interest.

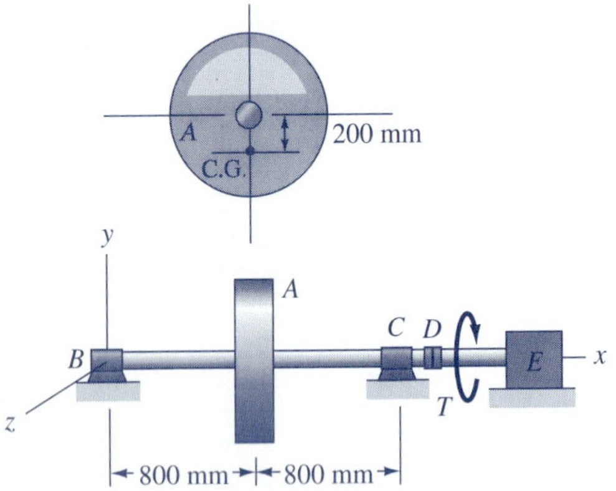

Figure P.16.24.

16.25. A single cam A is mounted on a shaft as shown. The cam has a mass of 10 kg and has a center of mass 300 mm from the centerline of the shaft. Also, the cam has a radius of gyration of 180 mm about an axis through the center of mass. The shaft has a mass per unit length of 10 kg/m and has a diameter of 30 mm. A torque T given as

$$T = .001t^2 + 10 \text{ N-m}$$

is applied at coupling D (t is in seconds). What are the force components in the bearings after 25 sec if the cam has the position shown in the diagram at this instant?

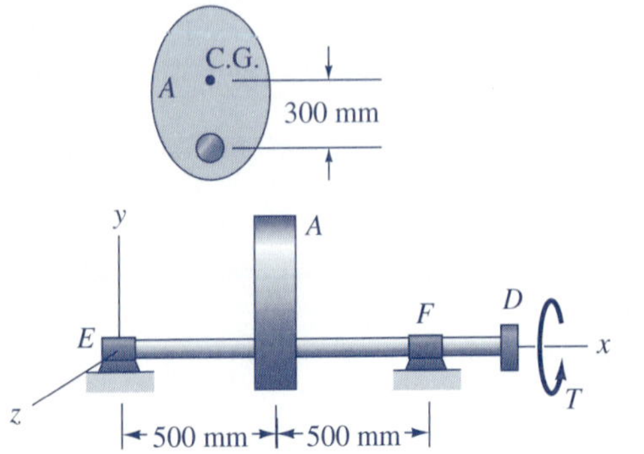

Figure P.16.25.

16.26. A circular plate is rotating at a speed of 10,000 rpm. A hole has been cut out of the plate so that the beam of light is allowed through for very short intervals of time. Such a device is called a *chopper*. If the plate weighed 20 lb originally and the material removed for the hole weighed 3 oz, what are the forces in the bearings A and B from the circular plate for the instant shown?

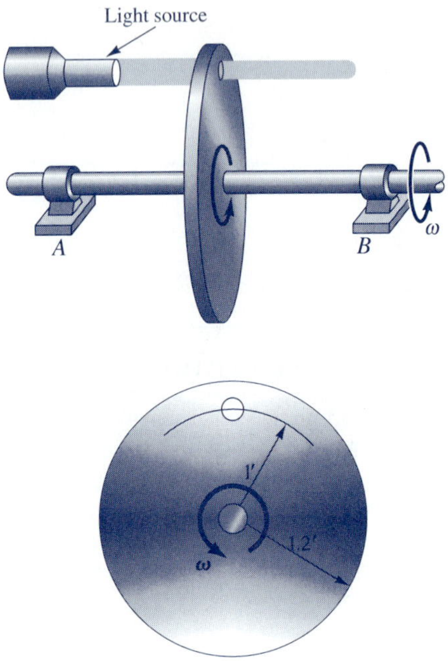

Figure P.16.26.

16.27. Part of a conveyor system is shown. A link belt is meshed around portions of gears A and B. The belt has a mass of 5 kg/m. Furthermore, each gear has a mass of 3 kg and a radius of 300 mm. If a force of 100 N is applied at one end as shown, what is the maximum possible force T that can be transmitted at the other end if $\ddot{\theta}_A = 5 \text{ rad/sec}^2$? The gears turn freely. The system is in a vertical plane.

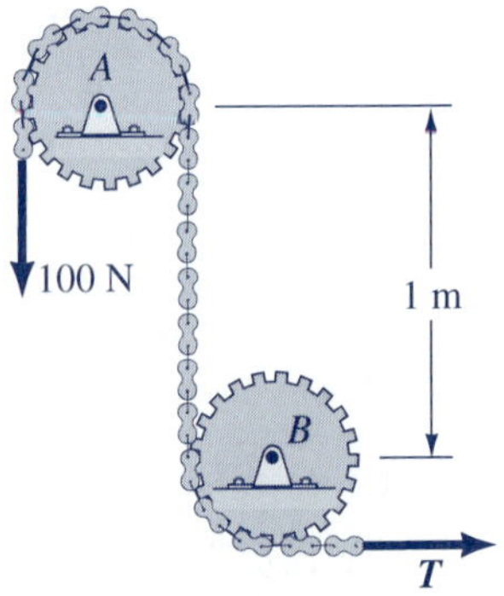

Figure P.16.27.

16.28. A hollow cylinder A of mass 100 kg can rotate over a stationary solid cylinder B having a mass of 70 kg. The surface of contact is lubricated so that there is a resisting torque between the bodies given as $0.2\dot{\theta}_A$ N-m with $\dot{\theta}_A$ in radians per second. The outer cylinder is connected to a device at C which supplies a force equal to $-50\ddot{Y}$ N. Starting from a counter-clockwise angular speed of 1 rad/sec, what is the angular speed of cylinder A after the force at C starts to move downward and moves 0.7 m?

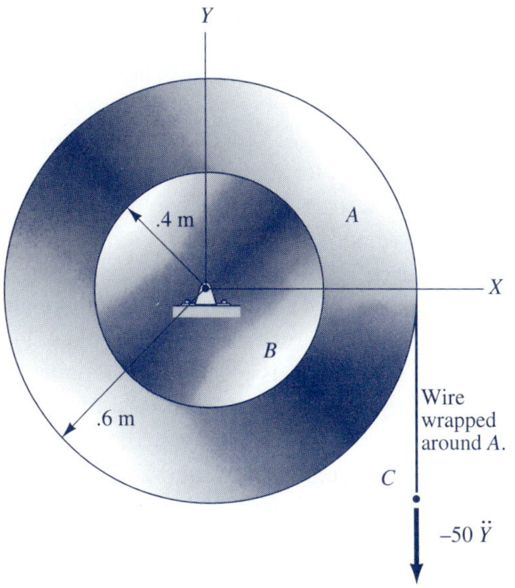

Figure P.16.28.

16.29. A box C weighing 150 lb rests on a conveyor belt. The driving drum B has a mass of 100 lbm and a radius of gyration of 4 in. The driven drum A has a mass of 70 lbm and a radius of gyration of 3 in. The belt weighs 3 lb/ft. Supporting the belt on the top side is a set of 20 rollers each with a mass of 3 lbm, a diameter of 2 in., and a radius of gyration of .8 in. If a torque T of 50 ft-lb is developed on the driving drum, what distance does C travel in 1 sec starting from rest? Assume that no slipping occurs.

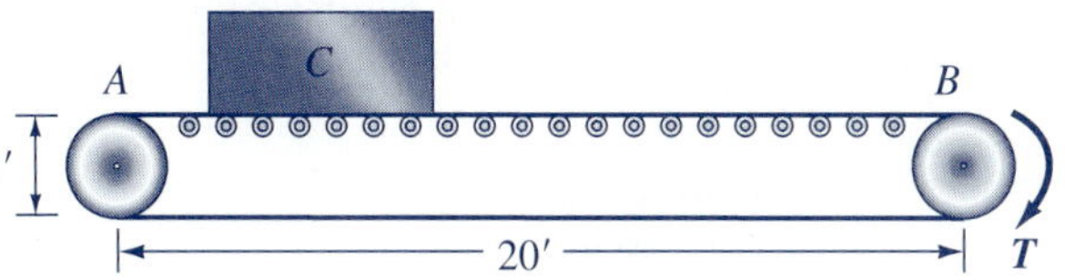

Figure P.16.29.

16.30. A uniform slender member is supported by a hinge at A. A force P is suddenly applied at an angle α with the horizontal. What value should P have and at what distance d should it be applied to result in zero reactive forces at A at the configuration shown if $\alpha = 45°$? The weight of the member AB is W. What is the angular acceleration of the bar for these conditions at the instant of interest?

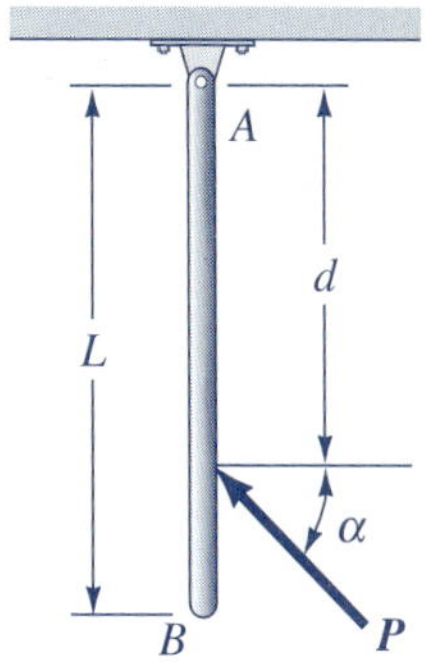

Figure P.16.30.

***16.31.** A rod AB is welded to a rod CD, which in turn is welded to a shaft as shown. The shaft has the following angular motion at time t:

$$\omega = 10 \text{ rad/sec}$$
$$\dot{\omega} = 40 \text{ rad/sec}^2$$

What are the shear force, axial force, and bending moment along CD at time t as a function of r? The rods have a mass per unit length of 5 kg/m. Neglect gravity.

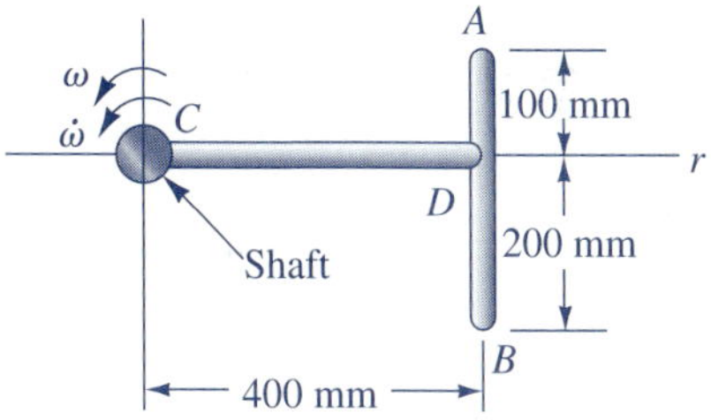

Figure P.16.31.

16.32. A four-bar linkage is shown (the ground is the fourth linkage). Each member is 300 mm long and has a mass per unit length of 10 kg/m. A torque T of 5 N-m is applied to each of bars AB and DC. What is the angular acceleration of bars AB and CD?

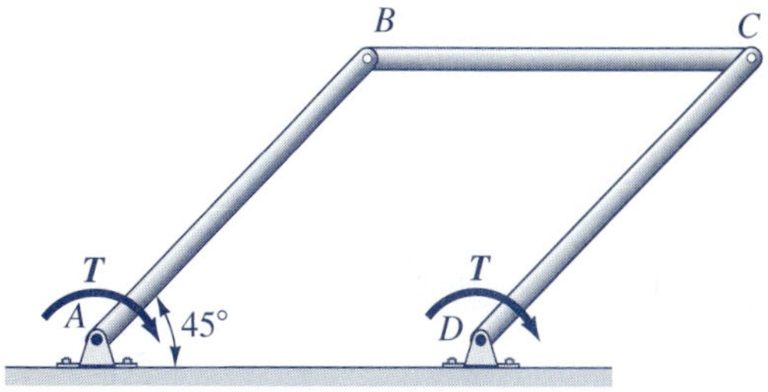

Figure P.16.32.

16.6 Rolling Slablike Bodies

We now consider the rolling without slipping of slablike bodies such as cylinders, spheres, or plane gears. As we have indicated in Chapter 15, the point of contact of the body has instantaneously *zero velocity*, and we have *pure instantaneous rotation about this contact point*. We pointed out that for getting velocities of points on such a rolling body, we could imagine that there is a *hinge* at the point of contact. Also, the acceleration of the *center* of a rolling without slipping sphere or cylinder can be computed using the simple formula—$R\ddot{\theta}$. Finally, you can readily show that if the angular speed is zero, we can compute the acceleration of any point in the cylinder or sphere by again imagining a *hinge* at the point of contact. For other cases, we must use more detailed kinematics, as discussed in Chapter 15.

A very important conclusion we reached in Chapter 15 for cylinders and spheres was that for rolling without slipping the acceleration of the contact point on the cylinder or sphere is *toward the geometric center of the cylinder or sphere*. If the center of mass of the body lies anywhere along the line AO from the contact point A to the geometric center O, then clearly we can use Eq. 16.6 for the point A. This action is justified since point A is then an example of case 3 in Section 16.2 (A accelerates toward the mass center and is part of the cylinder). Thus, for the body in Fig. 16.16 for no slipping we can use $T = I\alpha$ about the point of contact A of the cylinder at the instant shown. However, in Fig. 16.17 we cannot do this because the point of contact A of the cylinder is not accelerating toward the center of mass as in the previous case. We can use $T = I\alpha$ about the *center of mass* in the latter case.

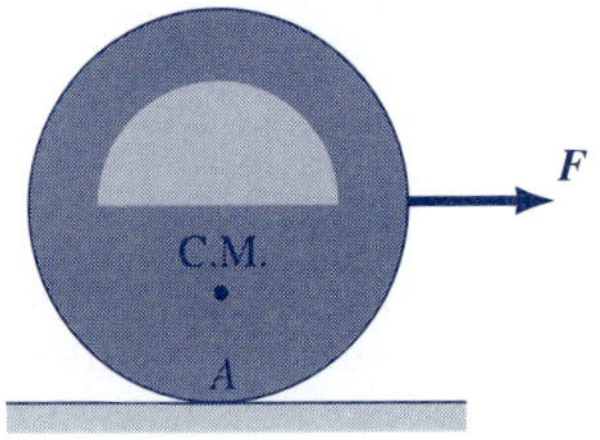

Figure 16.16. Point A accelerates toward center of mass.

We shall now examine a problem involving rolling without slipping. The equations of motion, you can readily deduce, are the same as in the previous section.

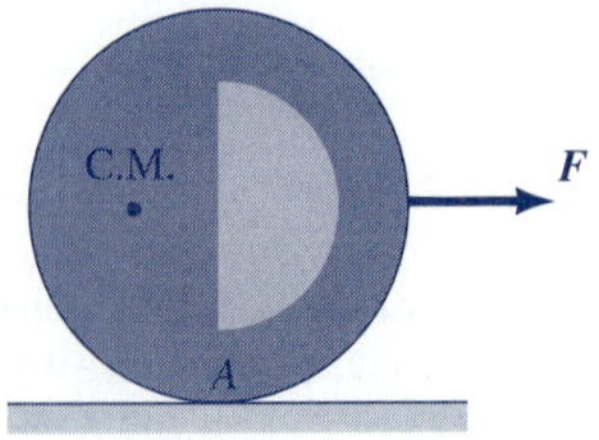

Figure 16.17. Point A does not accelerate toward center of mass.

Example 16.5

A steam roller is shown going up a 5° incline in Fig. 16.18. Wheels A have a radius of gyration of 1.5 ft and a weight each of 500 lb, whereas roller B has a radius of gyration of 1 ft and a weight of 5,000 lb. The vehicle, minus the wheels and roller but including the operator, has a weight of 7,000 lb with a center of mass positioned as shown in the diagram. The steam roller is to accelerate at the rate of 1 ft/sec^2. In part A of the problem, we are to determine the torque T_{eng} from the engine onto the drive wheels.

Figure 16.18. Steam roller moving up incline.

Part A. In Fig. 16.19, we have shown free-body diagrams of the drive wheels and the roller. Note we have combined the two drive wheels into a single 1,000-lb wheel. In each case, the point of contact on the wheel accelerates toward the mass center of the wheel and we can put to good

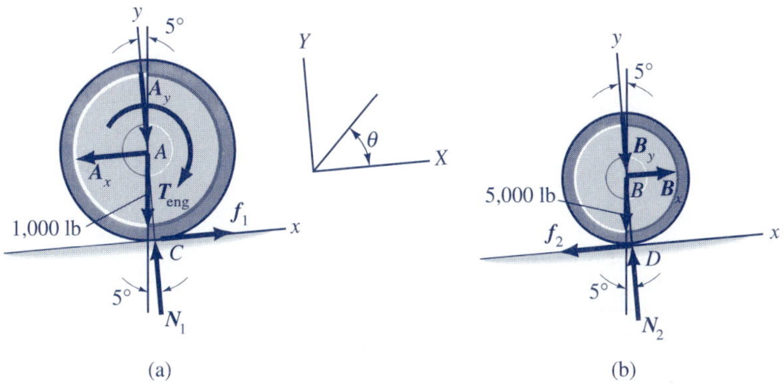

Figure 16.19. Free-body diagrams of driving wheels and roller.

use the **moment-of-momentum** equation (16.9) for the points of contact on the cylinders. Accordingly, we fix xyz to cylinder A and we fix another

Example 16.5 (Continued)

reference xyz to cylinder B at their respective points of contact as has been shown.[8] Hence, for cylinder A we have

$$(A_x + 1{,}000 \sin 5°)(2) - T_{eng} = \frac{1{,}000}{g}(1.5^2 + 2^2)\ddot{\theta}_A \qquad \text{(a)}$$

where we have employed the parallel-axis theorem in computing the moment of inertia about the line of contact at C. Similarly, for the roller, we have

$$(5{,}000 \sin 5° - B_x)(1.5) = \frac{5{,}000}{g}(1^2 + 1.5^2)\ddot{\theta}_B \qquad \text{(b)}$$

We have here two equations and no fewer than five unknowns. By considering the free body of the vehicle minus wheels shown diagrammatically in Fig. 16.20, we can say from **Newton's law** noting once again that $A_X \equiv A_x$, etc., because of the parallel orientation of axes XYZ with axes xyz of Fig. 16.19(a) and Fig. 16.19(b) at time t

$$A_x - B_x - 7{,}000 \sin 5° = \frac{7{,}000}{g}(1) \qquad \text{(c)}$$

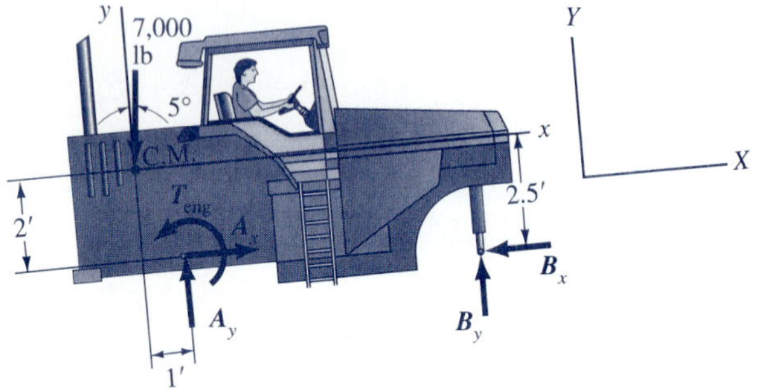

Figure 16.20. Free-body diagram of vehicle without wheels and roller.

Finally, from **kinematics** we can say:

$$\ddot{\theta}_A = -\frac{\ddot{X}}{r_A} = -\frac{1}{2} = -.5 \text{ rad/sec}^2$$
$$\ddot{\theta}_B = -\frac{\ddot{X}}{r_B} = -\frac{1}{1.5} = -.667 \text{ rad/sec}^2 \qquad \text{(d)}$$

where $\ddot{X} = 1 \text{ ft/sec}^2$ is the acceleration of the vehicle up the incline. We can now readily solve the equations. We get B_x directly from Eq. (b) on

[8]We shall use for simplicity axes xyz fixed to different bodies in this and other problems. The directions will thus be the same and this will make for simplicity in the formulations. However, keep in mind that the computation of moments of inertia for any body applies to *the particular reference xyz* fixed to that body. Keeping this in mind, we should not encounter any difficulties and we shall benefit from the simpler notation.

Example 16.5 (Continued)

replacing $\ddot{\theta}_B$ by −.667. Next, we get A_x from Eq. (c). Finally, going back to Eq. (a), we can solve for T_{eng}. The results are:

$$\begin{aligned} T_{eng} &= 3{,}250 \text{ ft-lb} \\ A_x &= 1{,}487 \text{ lb} \\ B_x &= 660 \text{ lb} \end{aligned}$$

Part B. Determine next the normal forces N_1 and N_2 at the wheels and roller, respectively.

We can express **Newton's law** for the wheels and roller in the direction normal to the incline by using the free-body diagrams of Fig. 16.19. Thus,

$$N_1 - A_y - 1{,}000 \cos 5° = 0 \qquad \text{(e)}$$

$$N_2 - B_y - 5{,}000 \cos 5° = 0 \qquad \text{(f)}$$

Next, we consider the free body of the vehicle without the wheels and roller (Fig. 16.20). **Newton's law** in the y direction for the center of mass then becomes

$$A_y + B_y - 7{,}000 \cos 5° = 0 \qquad \text{(g)}$$

The **moment-of-momentum** equation about the center of mass of the vehicle without wheels and roller is

$$A_x(2) - B_x(2.5) + A_y(1) + B_y(11) + T_{eng} = 0 \qquad \text{(h)}$$

We have four equations in four unknowns. Solve for A_y in Eq. (g), and substitute into Eq. (h). Inserting known values for A_x, B_x, and T_{eng}, we have

$$(1{,}487)(2) - (660)(2.5) + 7{,}000 \cos 5° - B_y + B_y(11) + 3{,}250 = 0$$

Therefore,

$$B_y = 1{,}155 \text{ lb}$$

Now from Eq. (g) we get A_y:

$$A_y = 7{,}000 \cos 5° + 1{,}155 = 8{,}128 \text{ lb}$$

Finally, from Eqs. (e) and (f) we get N_1 and N_2.

$$N_1 = 8{,}128 + 1{,}000 \cos 5° = \boxed{9{,}120 \text{ lb}}$$

$$N_2 = -1{,}155 + 5{,}000 \cos 5° = \boxed{3{,}830 \text{ lb}}$$

Hence, on each wheel we have a normal force of 4,560 lb, and for the roller we have a normal force of 3,830 lb.

*Example 16.6

A gear A weighing 100 N is connected to a stepped cylinder B (see Fig. 16.21) by a light rod DC. The stepped cylinder weighs 1 kN and has a radius of gyration of 250 mm along its centerline. The gear A has a radius of gyration of 120 mm along its centerline. A force $F = 1{,}500$ N is applied to the gear at D. What is the compressive force in member DC if, at the instant that F is applied, the system is stationary?

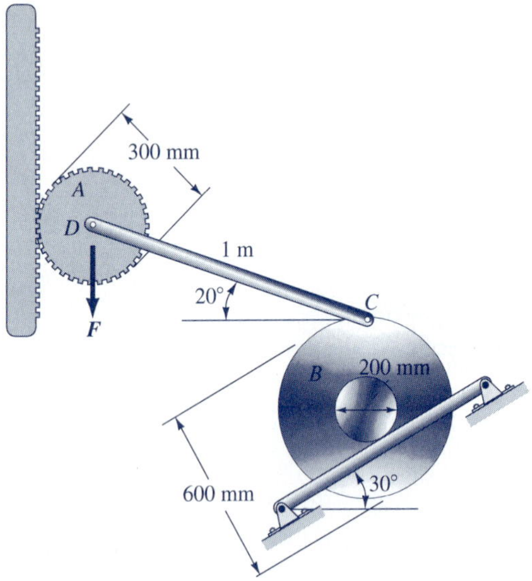

Figure 16.21. Stepped cylinder connected to a gear by a light rod.

Noting that DC is a two-force compressive member, we draw the free-body diagrams for the gear and the stepped cylinder in Fig. 16.22.

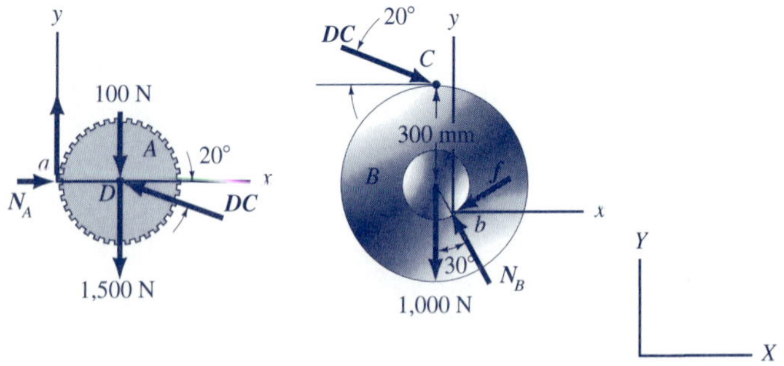

Figure 16.22. Free-body diagram of gear and cylinder.

The **moment-of-momentum** equations about the contact points for both bodies (points a and b, respectively) are

Example 16.6 (Continued)

$$-(100 + 1{,}500)(.15) + DC(\sin 20°)(.15) = \left(\frac{100}{9.81}\right)[(.12)^2 + (.15)^2]\ddot{\theta}_A$$

$$(DC \sin 20° + 1{,}000)(\sin 30°)(.10) - (DC \cos 20°)(.30 + .10 \cos 30°)$$
$$= \frac{1{,}000}{9.81}[(.25)^2 + (.10)^2]\ddot{\theta}_B$$

These equations simplify to the following pair:

$$.0513DC - 240 = .376\ddot{\theta}_A \qquad \text{(a)}$$

$$-.3462DC + 50 = 7.39\ddot{\theta}_B \qquad \text{(b)}$$

Clearly, we need an equation from **kinematics** at this time. Considering rod DC, we can say:[9]

$$\boldsymbol{a}_c = \boldsymbol{a}_D + \dot{\boldsymbol{\omega}}_{DC} \times \boldsymbol{\rho}_{DC} + \boldsymbol{\omega}_{DC} \times (\boldsymbol{\omega}_{DC} \times \boldsymbol{\rho}_{DC})$$

$$\ddot{\theta}_B\boldsymbol{k} \times [(.30 + .10 \cos 30°)\boldsymbol{j} - (.10 \sin 30°)\boldsymbol{i}]$$
$$= \ddot{Y}_D\boldsymbol{j} + \dot{\omega}_{DC}\boldsymbol{k} \times (\cos 20°\boldsymbol{i} - \sin 20°\boldsymbol{j}) + \boldsymbol{0}$$

The scalar equations are

$$-.3866\ddot{\theta}_B = .342\dot{\omega}_{DC} \qquad \text{(c)}$$

$$-.05\ddot{\theta}_B = \ddot{Y}_D + .940\dot{\omega}_{DC} \qquad \text{(d)}$$

Also, from **kinematics** we can say, considering gear A:

$$\ddot{Y}_D = .15\ddot{\theta}_A \qquad \text{(e)}$$

Multiply Eq. (c) by .940/.342 and rewrite Eq. (d) below it with $\ddot{Y}_D$ replaced by using Eq. (e):

$$-1.063\ddot{\theta}_B = .940\dot{\omega}_{DC}$$

$$-.05\ddot{\theta}_B - .15\ddot{\theta}_A = .940\dot{\omega}_{DC}$$

Subtracting, we get

$$-1.013\ddot{\theta}_B + .15\ddot{\theta}_A = 0$$

Therefore,

$$\ddot{\theta}_A = 6.75\ddot{\theta}_B \qquad \text{(f)}$$

Solving Eq. (a), (b), and (f) simultaneously gives us for DC the result

$$DC = 1{,}511 \text{ N (compression)}$$

Also, note that $\ddot{Y}$ comes out negative indicating that D accelerates downward.

[9]Note that because cylinder B has zero angular velocity, we can imagine it to be hinged at b for computing $\boldsymbol{a}_C$. Also, we do not know the sign of $\ddot{Y}_D$ and so we leave it as positive and thus let the mechanics yield the correct sign at the end of the calculations.

16.7 General Plane Motion of a Slablike Body

We now consider *general plane motion* of slablike bodies. The motion to be studied will be parallel to the plane of symmetry. Accordingly, we use the center of mass. The angular velocity vector $\boldsymbol{\omega}$ will be normal to the plane of symmetry, and, in accordance with Chasles' theorem, will be taken to pass through the center of mass. The translational velocity vector $\mathbf{V}_c$ will be parallel to the plane of symmetry. We fix a reference xyz at the center of mass of the body such that the xy plane coincides with the plane of symmetry as shown in Fig. 16.23. As usual, take the inertial reference parallel to xyz at time t. Note that the actual instantaneous axis of rotation is also shown. For the same

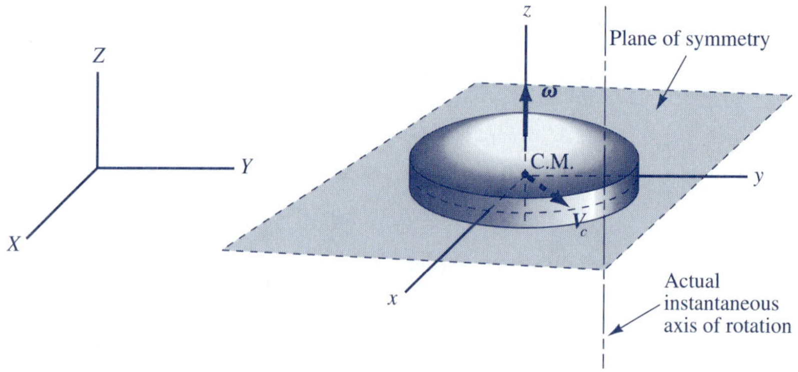

Figure 16.23. Slablike body undergoing general plane motion parallel to XY.

reasons used in Section 16.5 for slablike bodies, the *moment-of-momentum* equations become

$$M_x = 0 \qquad (16.14a)$$

$$M_y = 0 \qquad (16.14b)$$

$$M_z = I_{zz}\dot{\omega} \qquad (16.14c)$$

Furthermore, considering the center of mass, we must have *equilibrium* in the z direction.

$$\sum F_z = 0 \qquad (16.15)$$

while the full form of *Newton's law* holds in the x and y directions.

As in Section 16.5, we can generalize the results of this section to include the plane motion of a body having at the center of mass a *principal* axis z normal to the plane of motion XY. Clearly, for principal axes xyz at A, we get the same equations of motion as for the slablike body.

Example 16.7

Find the acceleration of block B shown in Fig. 16.24. The system is in a vertical plane and is released from rest. The cylinders roll without slipping along the vertical walls and along body B. Neglect friction along the guide rod. The 150 N-m torque M_A is applied to cylinder A.

We first draw free-body diagrams of the three bodies comprising the system as shown in Fig. 16.25 where it will be noticed that we have deleted the horizontal forces since they play no role in this problem. As usual, XYZ is our inertial reference. Points a, b, d, and e in F.B.D. I and F.B.D. III, respectively, are contact points in the respective bodies where, we repeat, there is rolling without slipping. Furthermore, it should be clear that points a and b are accelerating toward respective mass centers. Accordingly we fix xyz to the cylinders at these points.

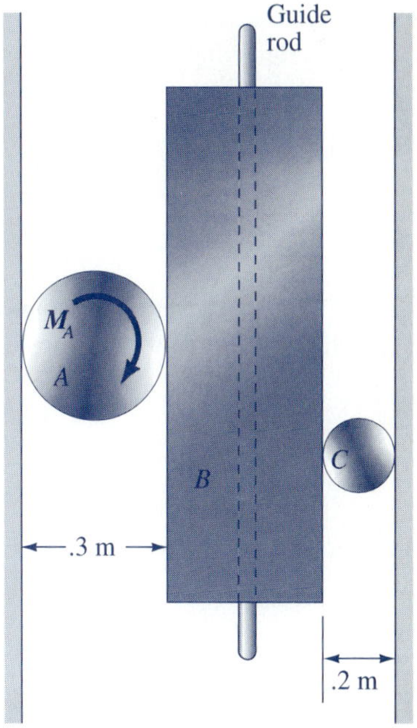

Data
$W_A = 100$ N
$W_B = 300$ N
$W_C = 50$ N
$M_A = 150$ N-m

Figure 16.24. A block and two cylinders in a vertical plane.

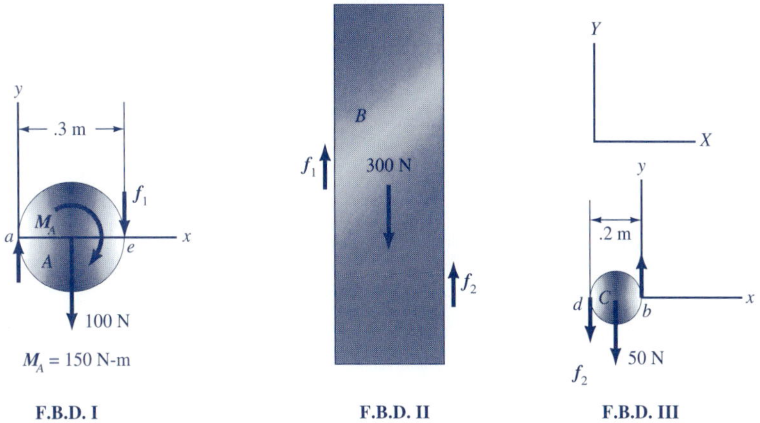

Figure 16.25. Free-body diagrams of the system elements with horizontal forces deleted.

We may immediately write the **moment-of-momentum** equations for the two cylinders about their respective points of contact a and b. Thus

F.B.D. I

$$-(f_1)(.3) - (100)(.15) - 150 = \left[\frac{1}{2}\frac{100}{g}(.15)^2 + \frac{100}{g}(.15)^2\right]\ddot{\theta}_A$$

$$\therefore -.3f_1 - 165 = .344\ddot{\theta}_A \qquad \text{(a)}$$

F.B.D. III

$$(f_2)(.2) + (50)(.1) = \left[\frac{1}{2}\frac{50}{g}(.1)^2 + \frac{50}{g}(.1)^2\right]\ddot{\theta}_C$$

$$.2f_2 + 5 = .07645\ddot{\theta}_C \qquad \text{(b)}$$

Example 16.7 (Continued)

Next going to F.B.D. II we employ **Newton's law** since we have simple translation. Referring now to the inertial reference *XYZ* we have

F.B.D. II

$$-300 + f_1 + f_2 = \frac{300}{g}\ddot{Y}_B \qquad \text{(c)}$$

Since the three bodies are interconnected by nonslip rolling conditions we must next consider the **kinematics** of the system. Thus

$$.3\ddot{\theta}_A = \ddot{Y}_B$$
$$.2\ddot{\theta}_C = -\ddot{Y}_B$$

Using the above results to replace $\ddot{\theta}_A$ and $\ddot{\theta}_C$ in Eqs. (a) and (b) we get

$$-.3f_1 - 165 = 1.1467\ddot{Y}_B \qquad \text{(d)}$$

$$.2f_2 + 5 = -.3823\ddot{Y}_B \qquad \text{(e)}$$

Now solve for f_1 and f_2 in the above equations and substitute into Eq. (c). We get

$$-300 + \frac{1}{.3}(-1.1467\ddot{Y}_B - 165) + \frac{1}{.2}(-.3823\ddot{Y}_B - 5) = \frac{300}{g}\ddot{Y}_B$$
$$36.31\ddot{Y}_B = -875$$

$$\therefore \quad \ddot{Y}_B = -24.10 \text{ m/s}^2$$

Now from Eqs. (d) and (e) we can determine f_1 and f_2.

$$f_1 = -457.9 \text{ N} \qquad f_2 = 21.07 \text{ N}$$

Thus, cylinder *A* forces body *B* downward while cylinder *C* resists this motion.

Notice, unless we want to determine the friction forces at the walls there is no need to use **Newton's law** for the cylinders. Also note that we could not use the **moment-of-momentum** equations for points *c* and *d* of the cylinders even though there is rolling without slipping there. The reason for this, as you must know, is that these points *do not accelerate toward or away from the mass centers of the cylinders.*

Example 16.8

A stepped cylinder having a weight of 450 N and a radius of gyration k of 300 mm is shown in Fig. 16.26(a). The radii R_1 and R_2 are, respectively, 300 mm and 600 mm. A total pull T equal to 180 N is exerted on the ropes attached to the inner cylinder. What is the ensuing motion? The coefficients of static and dynamic friction between the cylinder and the ground are, respectively, .1 and .08.

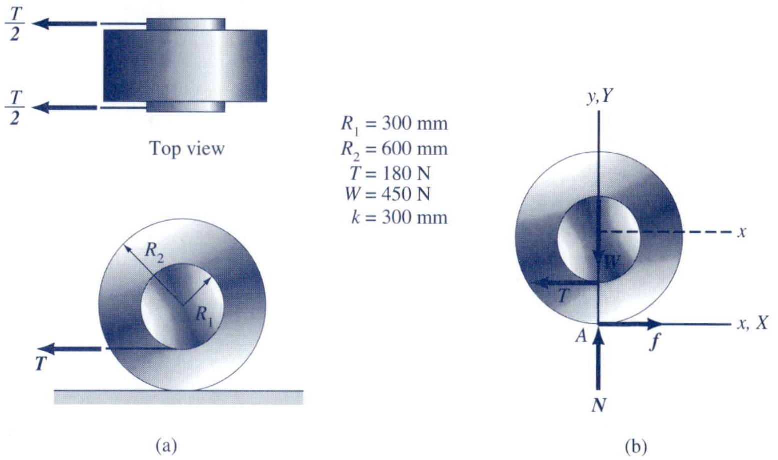

Figure 16.26. (a) Stepped cylinder; (b) free-body diagram of cylinder. *XY* is stationary.

A free-body diagram of the cylinder is shown in Fig. 16.26(b). Let us assume first that there is *no slipping* at the contact surface. Of course, we will have to later check this supposition. We have then pure instantaneous rotation about contact point A. Fix xyz to the body at A. XYZ as usual is stationary. We can then say for the **moment-of-momentum** equation about the axis of contact:

$$T(R_2 - R_1) = \left(\frac{W}{g}k^2 + \frac{W}{g}R_2^2\right)\ddot{\theta} \qquad \text{(a)}$$

wherein we have used the parallel-axis theorem for moment of inertia. Inserting numerical values, we can solve directly for $\ddot{\theta}$ at the instant that the force T is applied. Thus,

$$(180)(.30) = \left[\frac{450}{g}(.30)^2 + \frac{450}{g}(.60)^2\right]\ddot{\theta}$$

Therefore,

$$\ddot{\theta} = 2.62 \text{ rad/sec}^2 \qquad \text{(b)}$$

Example 16.8 (Continued)

We must now check our assumption of no slipping. Employ **Newton's law** for the mass center. In the X direction we get

$$-180 + f = \frac{W}{g}\ddot{X} \tag{c}$$

Using **kinematics** we note that

$$\ddot{X} = -R_2\ddot{\theta} = -.60\ddot{\theta} \tag{d}$$

Substituting into Eq. (c) for $\ddot{X}$ using Eq. (d) and putting in known numerical values, we can solve for f:

$$f = 180 - \frac{450}{9.81}[(.60)(2.62)] = 107.9 \text{ N}$$

Thus, for no slipping, we must be able to develop a friction force of 107.9 N. The maximum friction force that we can have, however, is, according to **Coulomb's law**,

$$f_{\max} = W\mu_s = (450)(.1) = 45 \text{ N} \tag{e}$$

Accordingly, we must conclude that the cylinder *does* slip, and we must re-examine the problem as a *general plane-motion* problem.

Using $\mu_d = .08$, we now take f to be 36 N and employ the **moment-of-momentum** equation for the **center of mass** with xyz now fixed at the **center of mass**. We then have (Fig. 16.26(b))

$$fR_2 - TR_1 = \frac{W}{g}k^2\ddot{\theta} \tag{f}$$

Inserting numerical values, we get for $\ddot{\theta}$:

$$\ddot{\theta} = -7.85 \text{ rad/sec}^2 \tag{g}$$

Now, using **Newton's law** in the X direction for the mass center, we get

$$-T + f = \frac{W}{g}\ddot{X} \tag{h}$$

Inserting numerical values, we get for $\ddot{X}$:

$$\ddot{X} = -3.14 \text{ m/sec}^2 \tag{i}$$

Thus, the cylinder has a linear acceleration of 3.14 m/sec^2 to the left and an angular acceleration of 7.85 rad/sec^2 in the clockwise direction. Equations (g) and (i) are valid at all times, so we can integrate them if we like to get θ and X at any time t.

Example 16.9

A 4.905-kN flywheel rotating at a speed ω of 200 rpm (see Fig. 16.27) breaks away from the steam engine that drives it and falls on the floor. If the coefficient of dynamic friction between the floor and the flywheel surface is .4, at what speed will the flywheel axis move after 2 sec? At what speed will it hit the wall A? The radius of gyration of the flywheel is 1 m and its diameter is 2.30 m. Do not consider effects of bouncing in your analysis. Neglect rolling resistance (Section 7.7) and wind friction losses.

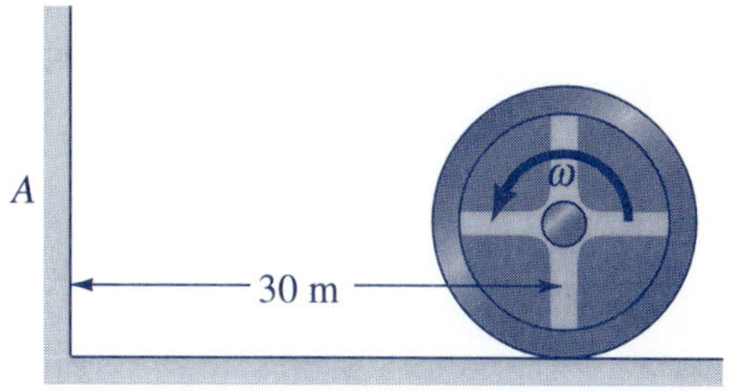

Figure 16.27. Runaway flywheel at initial position.

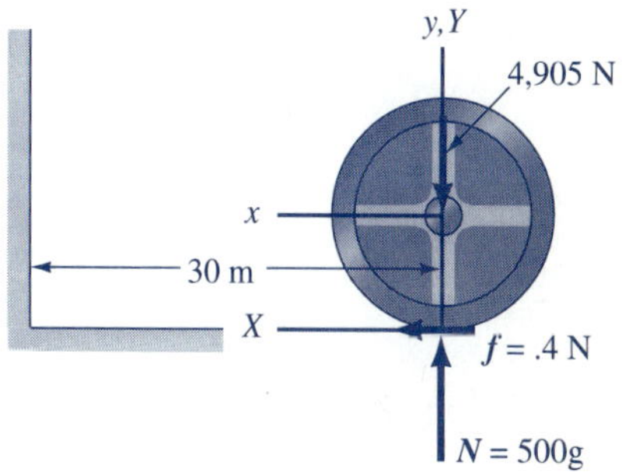

Figure 16.28. xy fixed at initial position.

We assume slipping occurs when the flywheel first touches the floor (see Fig. 16.28). **Newton's law** for the center of mass of the flywheel is

$$(.4)N = \left(\frac{4{,}905}{9.81}\right)\ddot{X}$$

Therefore,

$$\ddot{X} = 3.92 \text{ m/sec}^2$$

Integrate twice:

$$\dot{X} = 3.92t + C_1 \qquad \text{(a)}$$

$$X = 1.962t^2 + C_1t + C_2 \qquad \text{(b)}$$

At $t = 0$, $\dot{X} = 0$ and $X = 0$. Hence, $C_1 = 0$ and $C_2 = 0$. The **moment-of-momentum** equation for axes fixed to the body at the center of mass is next given.

$$(.4)(N)\left(\frac{2.30}{2}\right) = \left(\frac{4{,}905}{9.81}\right)(1)^2\ddot{\theta}$$

Therefore,

$$\ddot{\theta} = 4.51 \text{ rad/sec}^2$$

Integrate twice:

$$\dot{\theta} = 4.51t + C_3 \qquad \text{(c)}$$

$$\theta = 2.26t^2 + C_3t + C_4 \qquad \text{(d)}$$

Example 16.9 (Continued)

When $t = 0$, $\theta = 0$, and $\dot{\theta} = -(200)(2\pi/60) = -20.94$ rad/sec. Hence, $C_3 = -20.94$ and $C_4 = 0$.

We now ask when does the slipping stop? Clearly, it stops when there is *zero velocity* of the point of contact of the cylinder.[10] From **kinematics** we have for this condition:

$$\dot{X} + \left(\frac{2.30}{2}\right)\dot{\theta} = 0 \qquad \text{(e)}$$

Substituting from Eq. (a) and (c) for $\dot{X}$ and $\dot{\theta}$, respectively, we have for Eq. (e):

$$3.92t + \left(\frac{2.30}{2}\right)(4.51t - 20.94) = 0$$

Therefore,

$$t = 2.64 \text{ sec}$$

Since we get a time here greater than zero, we can be assured that the initial slipping assumption is valid. The position $X_{\text{N.S.}}$ at the time of initial no-slipping is deduced from Eq. (b). Thus,

$$X_{\text{N.S.}} = (1.962)(2.64)^2 = 13.67 \text{ m}$$

Accordingly, the flywheel hits the wall *after* it starts rolling without slipping. At $t = 2$ sec, there is still slipping, and we can use Eq. (a) to find $\dot{X}$ at this instant. Thus,

$$(\dot{X})_{2\text{sec}} = (3.92)(2) = 7.85 \text{ m/sec}$$

The speed, once there is no further slipping, is constant, and so the speed at the wall is found by using $t = 2.64$ sec in Eq. (a). Thus,

$$(\dot{X})_{\text{wall}} = (3.92)(2.64) = 10.35 \text{ m/sec}$$

[10]Note that the friction will accelerate the center of mass of the flywheel (which starts out with a zero velocity) while at the same time friction will decrease the angular speed of the flywheel (which starts out at its maximum angular speed). Thus the contact point of the flywheel will be subject to two opposing speeds, one of which is increasing and the other of which is decreasing. When there occurs a cancellation of these speed, we have rolling without slipping and there ceases to be coulombic friction present. And so, neglecting the other resistances to motion there ceases to be any change of speed of the flywheel.

PROBLEMS

16.33. A stepped cylinder is released from a rest configuration where the spring is stretched 200 mm. A constant force F of 360 N acts on the cylinder, as shown. The cylinder has a mass of 146 kg and has a radius of gyration of 1 m. What is the friction force at the instant the stepped cylinder is released? Take $\mu_s = .3$ for the coefficient of friction. The spring constant K is 270 N/m.

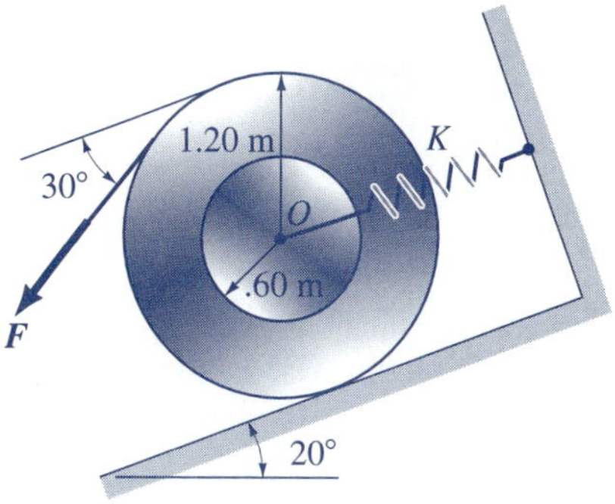

Figure P.16.33.

16.34. A stepped cylinder is held on an incline with an inextensible cord wrapped around the inner cylinder and an outside agent (not shown). If the tension T on the cord at the instant that the cylinder is released by the outside agent from the position shown is 100 lb, what is the initial angular acceleration? What is the acceleration of the mass center? Use the following data:

$$W = 300 \text{ lb}$$
$$k = 3 \text{ ft}$$
$$R_1 = 2 \text{ ft}$$
$$R_2 = 4 \text{ ft}$$
$$\mu_s = .1$$

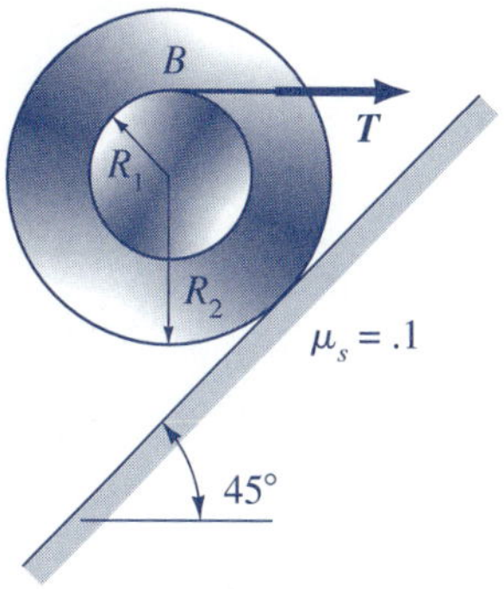

Figure P.16.34.

16.35. The cylinder shown is acted on by a 100-lb force. At the contact point A, there is viscous friction such that the friction force is given as

$$f = .05V_A$$

where V_A is the velocity of the cylinder at the contact point in ft/sec. The weight of the cylinder is 30 lb, and the radius of gyration k is 1 ft. Set up a third-order differential equation for finding the position of O as a function of time.

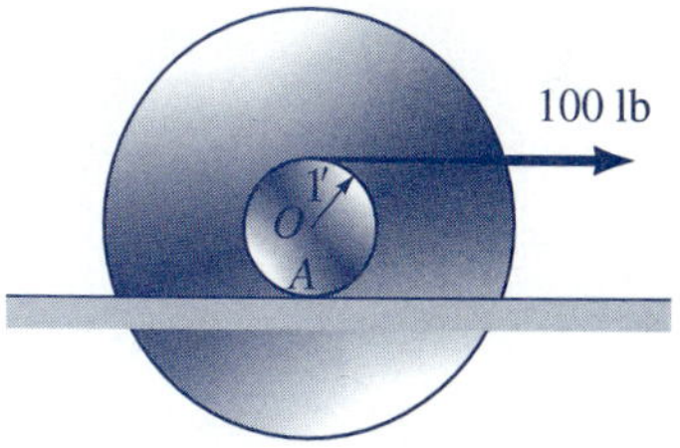

Figure P.16.35.

16.36. The cylinder shown weighs 445 N and has a radius of gyration of .27 m. What is the minimum coefficient of friction at A that will prevent the body from moving? Using half of this coefficient of friction, how far d does point O move in 1.2 sec if the cylinder is released from rest?

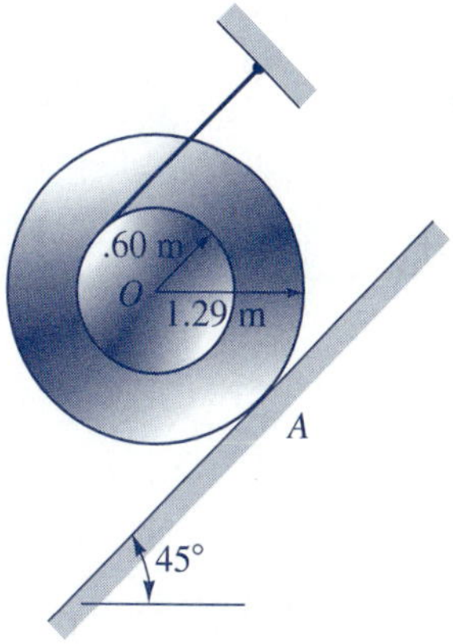

Figure P.16.36.

16.37. The velocities of two points of a cylinder, namely A and B, are

$$V_A = 6 \text{ m/s} \qquad V_B = 2 \text{ m/s}$$

What is the velocity of point D? If the cylinder has a mass of 4.2 kg, what is the angular acceleration for a dynamic coefficient of friction $\mu_d = .35$?

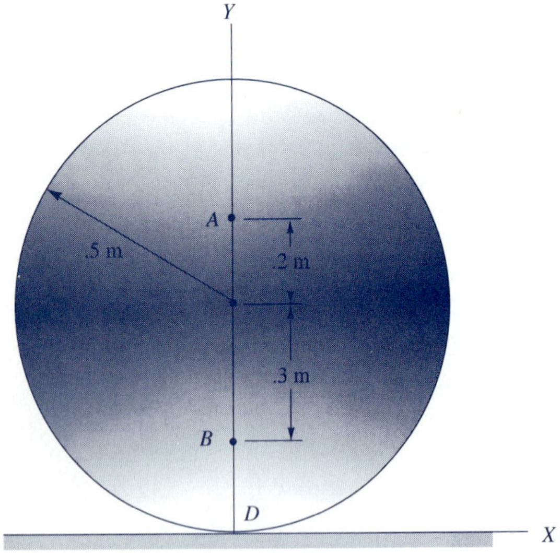

Figure P.16.37.

16.38. A thin ring having a mass of 0.4 kg is released from rest and rolls without slipping under the action of a 10-N force. Two identical metal sectors each of mass 0.83 kg are attached to the ring. What is the angular acceleration of the ring? Each sector has a radius of gyration at its centroid equal to $k = 0.18$ m.

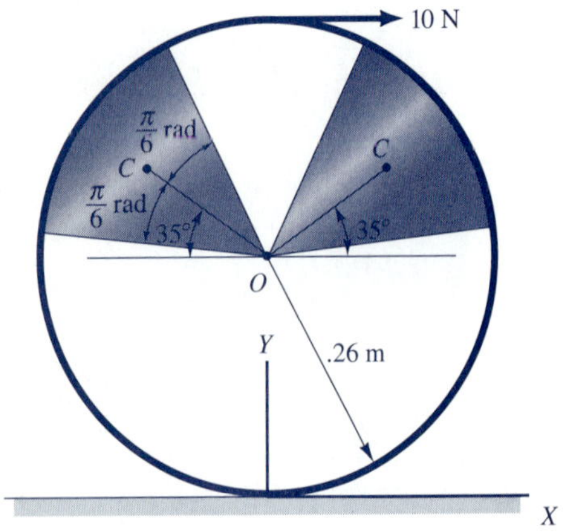

Figure P.16.38.

16.39. A light rod AB connects a plate C with a cylinder D which may roll without slipping. A torque T of value 50 ft-lb is applied to plate C. What is the angular acceleration of cylinder D when the torque is applied? The plate weighs 100 lb and the cylinder weighs 200 lb.

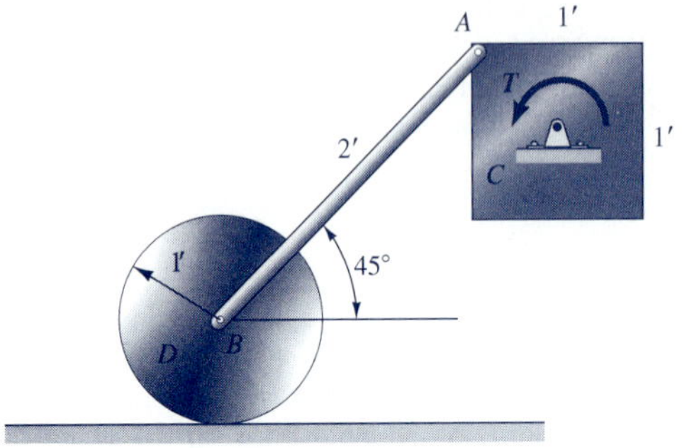

Figure P.16.39.

16.40. A semicircular cylinder A is shown. The diameter of A is 1 ft, and the weight is 100 lb. What is the angular acceleration of A at the position shown if at this instant there is no slipping and the semicylinder is stationary?

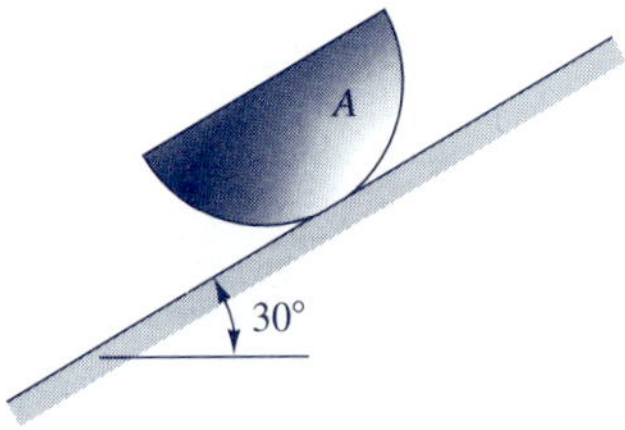

Figure P.16.40.

16.41. A 20 kg bar AB connects two gears G and H. These gears each have a mass of 5 kg and a diameter of 300 mm. A torque T of 5 N-m is applied to gear H. What is the angular speed of H after 20 sec if the system starts from rest? The system is in a horizontal plane. Bar AB is 2 m long.

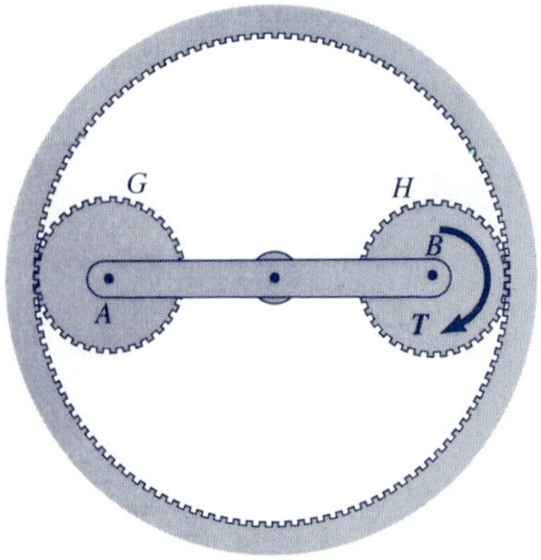

Figure P.16.41.

16.42. A bar C weighing 445 N rolls on cylinders A and B, each weighing 223 N. What is the acceleration of bar C when the 90-N force is applied as shown? There is no slipping.

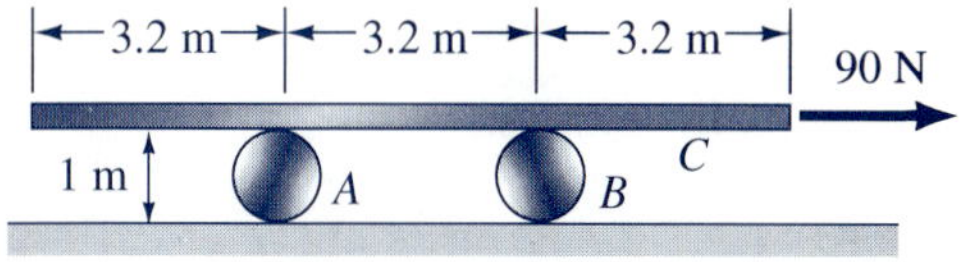

Figure P.16.42.

16.43. In Problem 16.42, at what position of the bar relative to the wheels does slipping first occur after the force is applied? Take $\mu_s = .2$ for the bottom contact surface and $\mu_s = .1$ for the contact surface between bar and cylinders. From Problem 16.42, $\ddot{x}_c = 1.442$ m/sec^2.

16.44. A platform B, of weight 30 lb and carrying block A of weight 100 lb, rides on gears D and E as shown. If each gear weighs 30 lb, what distance will platform B move in .1 sec after the application of a 100-lb force as shown?

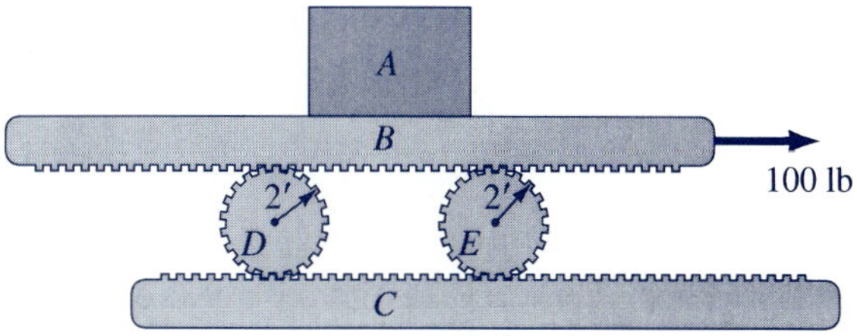

Figure P.16.44.

16.45. A crude cart is shown. A horizontal force P of 100 lb is applied to the cart. The coefficient of static friction between wheels and ground is .6. If D = 3 ft, what is the acceleration of the cart to the right? The wheels weigh 50 lb each. Neglect friction in the axle bearings. The total weight of cart with load is 322 lb. Treat the wheels as simple solid cylinders.

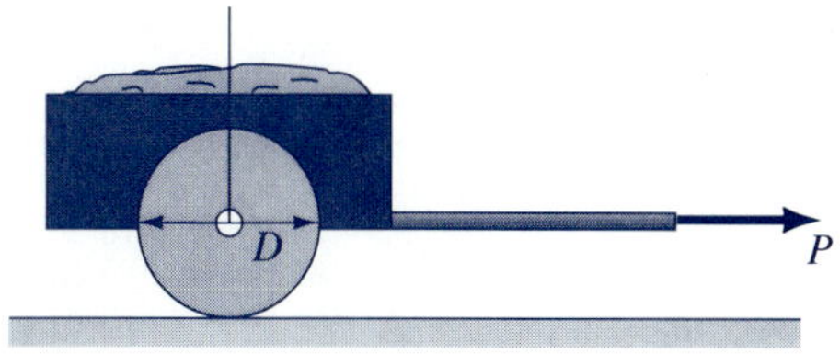

Figure P.16.45.

16.46. What minimum force component P is required to cause the cart in Problem 16.45 to move so that the wheels slip rather than roll without slipping?

16.47. A pulley system is shown. Sheave A has a mass of 25 kg and has a radius of gyration of 250 mm. Sheave B has a mass of 15 kg and has a radius of gyration of 150 mm. If released from rest, what is the acceleration of the 50-kg block? There is no slipping.

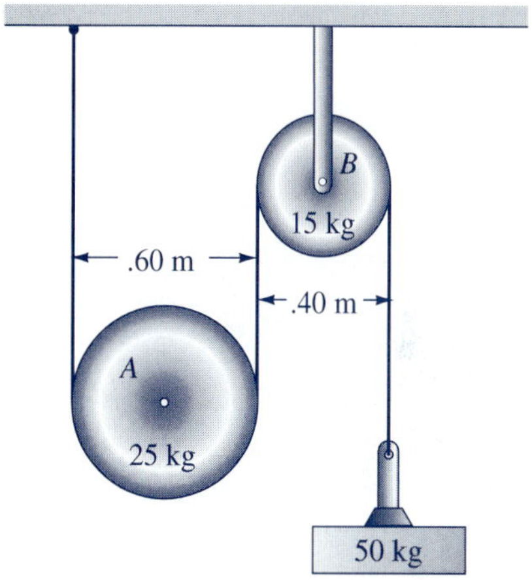

Figure P.16.47.

16.48. A steam locomotive drive system is shown. Each drive wheel weighs 5 kN and has a radius of gyration of 400 mm. At the instant shown, a pressure p = .50 N/mm^2 above atmospheric acts on the piston to drive the train backward. If the train is moving at 1 m/sec backward at the instant shown, what is its acceleration? Members AB and BC are to be considered stiff but light in comparison to other parts of the engine. Also, the piston assembly can be considered light. Only the driving car is in action in this problem. It has one driving system, on each side of the locomotive as shown below. It has two additional wheels of the size and mass described above on each side of the locomotive plus additional small wheels whose rotational inertia we shall neglect. The drive train minus its eight large wheels has a weight of 150 kN. Assume no slipping, and neglect friction in the piston assembly.

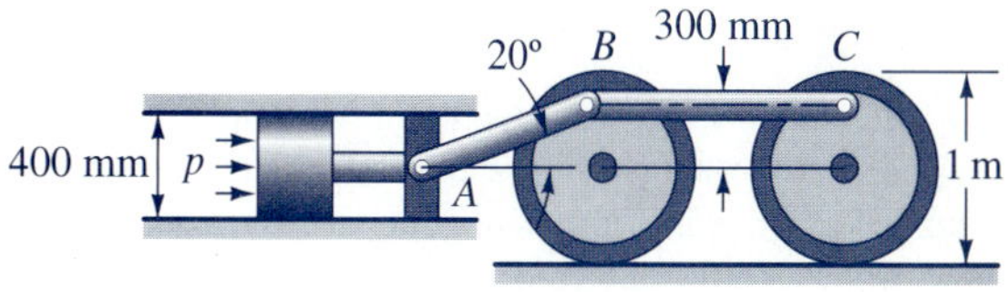

Figure P.16.48.

16.49. A system of interconnected gears is shown. Gear B rotates about a fixed axis, and gear D is stationary. If a torque T of 2.5 N-m is applied to gear B at the configuration shown, what is the angular acceleration of gear A? Gear A has a mass of 1.36 kg while gear B has a mass of 4.55 kg. The system is in a vertical orientation relative to the ground. What vertical force is transmitted to stationary gear D?

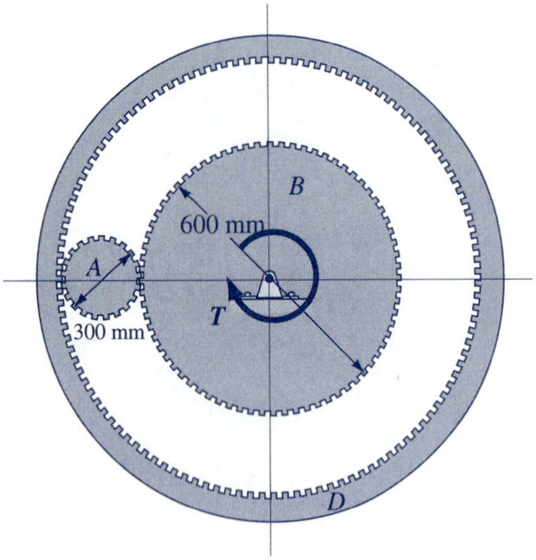

Figure P.16.49.

16.50. A solid semicircular cylinder of weight W and radius R is released from rest from the position shown. What is the friction force at that instant?

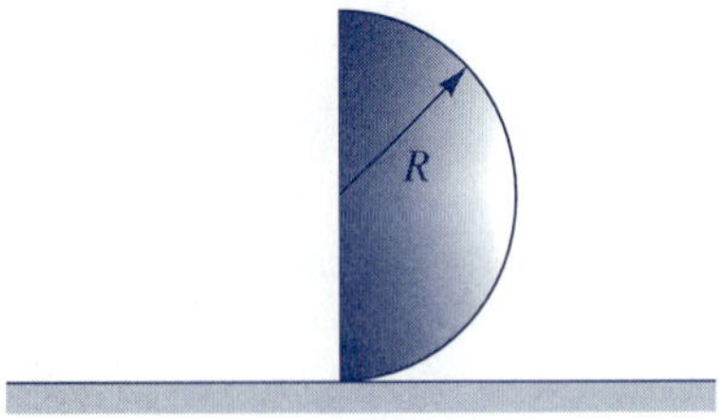

Figure P.16.50.

16.51. A cylinder is shown made up of two semicylinders A and B weighing 15 lb and 30 lb, respectively. If the cylinder has a diameter of 3 in, what is the angular acceleration when it is released from a stationary configuration at the position shown? Assume no slipping.

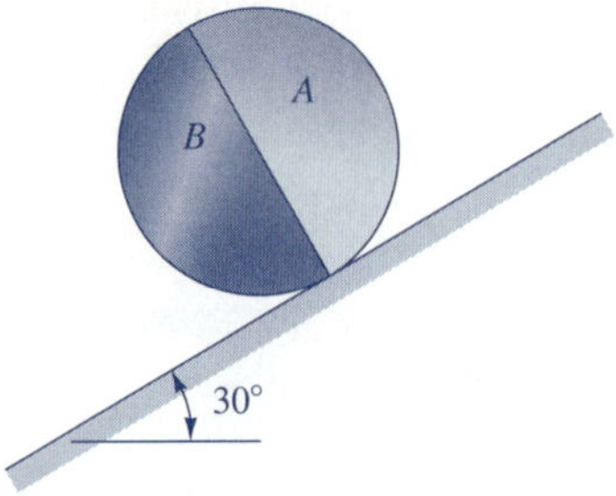

Figure P.16.51.

16.52. A thin-walled cylinder is shown held in position by a cord AB. The cylinder has a mass of 10 kg and has an outside diameter of 600 mm. What are the normal and friction forces at the contact point C at the instant that cord AB is cut? Assume that no slipping occurs.

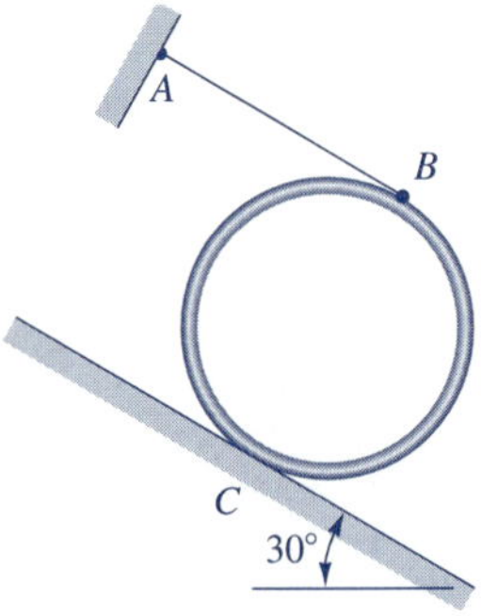

Figure P.16.52.

16.53. A bent rod $CBEF$ is welded to a shaft. At the ends C and F are identical gears G and H, each of mass 3 kg and radius of gyration 70 mm. The gears mesh with a large stationary gear D. A torque T of 50 N-m is applied to the shaft. What is the angular speed of the shaft after 10 sec if the system is initially at rest? The bent rod has a mass per unit length of 5 kg/m. Will there be forces on the bearings of the shaft other than those from gravity? Why?

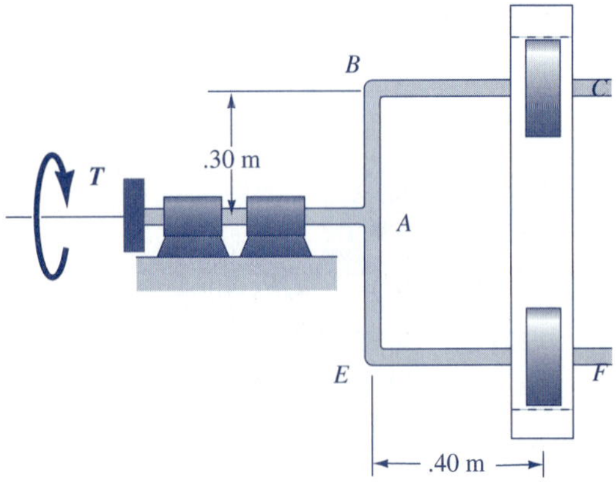

Figure P.16.53. *(Continued on next page)*

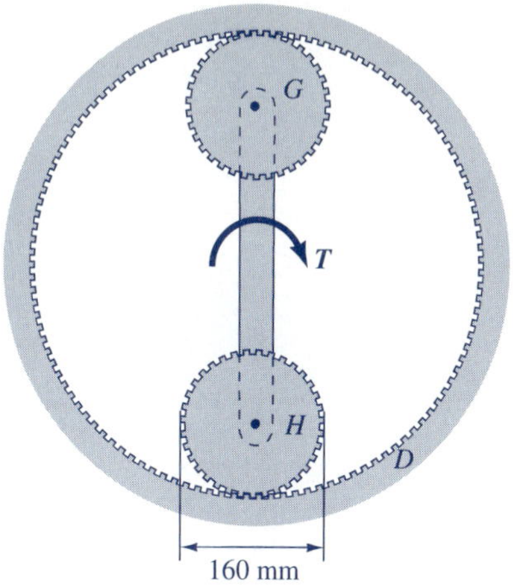

Figure P.16.53.

16.54. A tractor and driver has a mass of 1,350 kg. If a total torque T of 300 N-m is developed on the two drive wheels by the motor, what is the acceleration of the tractor? The large drive wheels each have a mass of 90 kg, a diameter of 1 m, and a radius of gyration of 400 mm. The small wheels each have a mass 20 kg and have a diameter of 300 mm with a radius of gyration of 100 mm.

Figure P.16.54.

16.55. A block B weighing 100 lb rides on two identical cylinders C and D weighing 50 lb each as shown. On top of block B is a block A weighing 100 lb. Block A is prevented from moving to the left by a wall. If we neglect friction between A and B and between A and the wall and we consider no slipping at the contact surfaces of the cylinders, what is the angular speed of the cylinders after 2 sec for $P = 80$ lb?

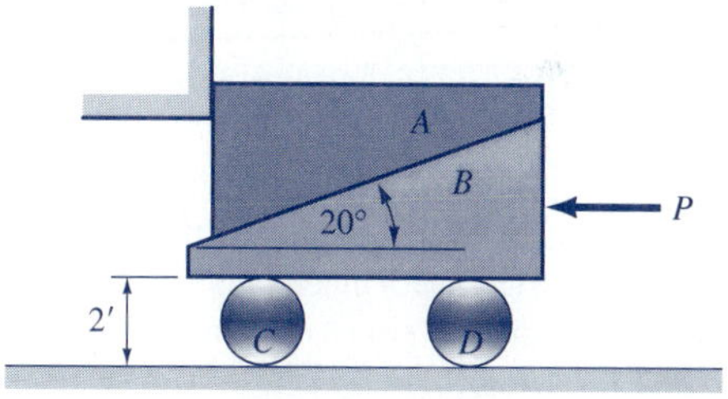

Figure P.16.55.

16.56. A cable is wrapped around two pulleys A and B. A force T is applied to the end of the cables at G. Each pulley weighs 5 lb and has a radius of gyration of 4 in. The diameter of the pulleys is 12 in. A body C weighing 100 lb is supported by pulley B. Suspended from body C is a body D weighing 25 lb. Body D is lowered from body C so as to accelerate at the rate of 5 ft/sec^2 relative to body C. What force T is then needed to pull the cable downward at G at the increasing rate of 5 ft/sec^2?

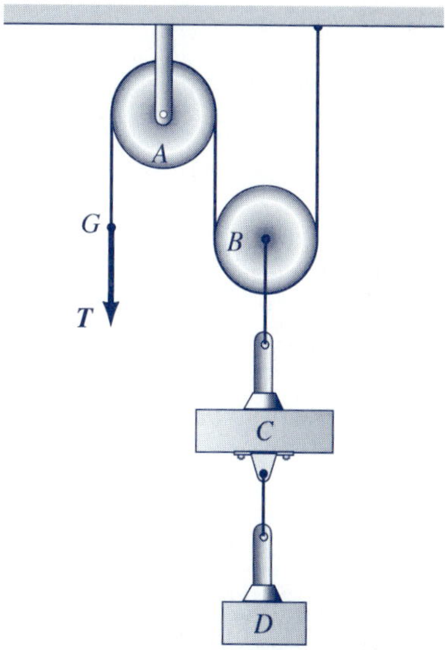

Figure P.16.56.

16.57. A cylinder A is acted on by a torque T of 1,000 N-m. The cylinder has a mass of 75 kg and a radius of gyration of 400 mm. A light rod CD connects cylinder A with a second cylinder B having a mass of 50 kg and a radius of gyration of 200 mm. What is the force in member CD when torque T is applied? The system is stationary at the instant the torque is applied. Assume no slipping of cylinder C along the incline.

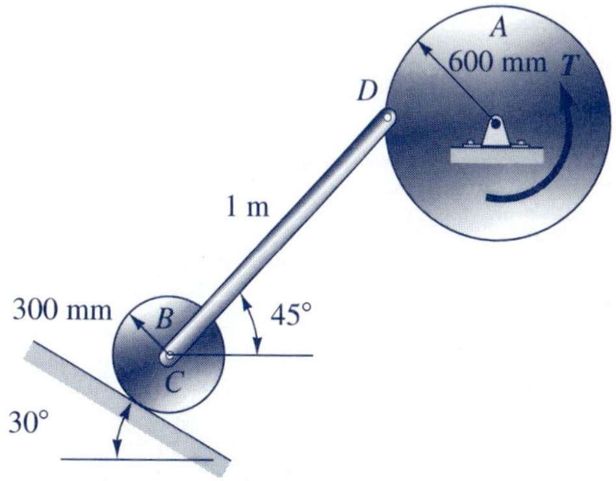

Figure P.16.57.

16.58. A ring rests on a smooth surface as shown from above. The ring has a mean radius of 2 m and a mass of 30 kg. A force of 400 N is applied to the ring at B. What is the acceleration of point A on the ring?

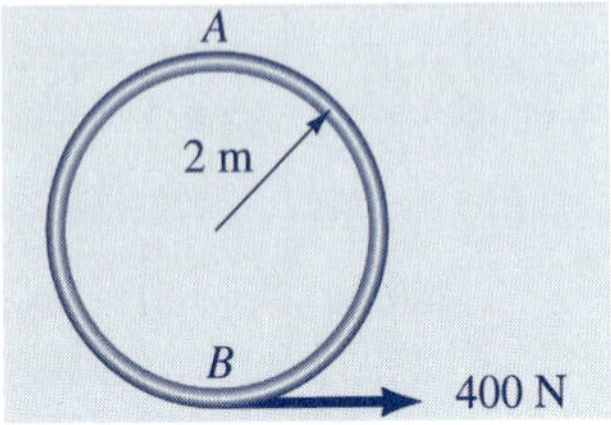

Figure P.16.58.

16.59. A block having a mass of 300 kg rests on a smooth surface as shown from above. A 500-N force is applied at an angle of 45° to the side. What is the acceleration of point B of the block when the force is applied? The center of mass of the block coincides with the geometric center.

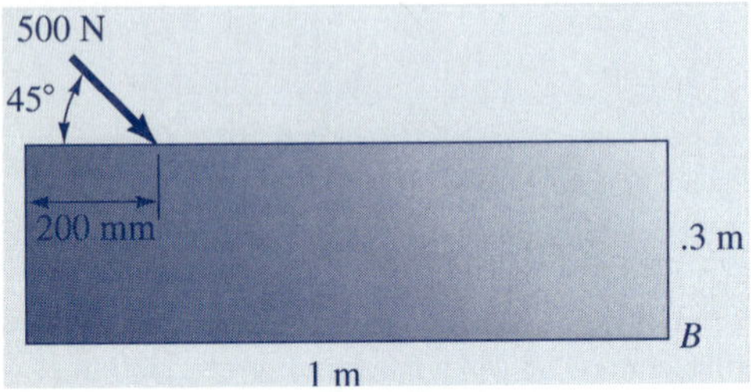

Figure P.16.59.

16.60. A bent rod rests on a smooth surface. The rod has a mass of 20 kg. What is the acceleration of point A when a force $P = 100$ N is applied?

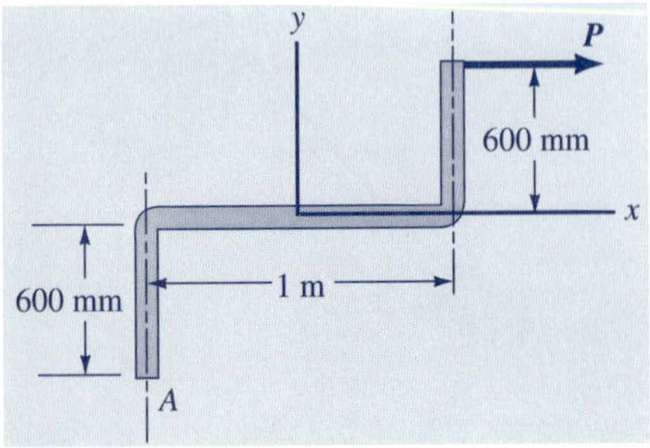

Figure P.16.60.

16.61. A constant force of 100 lb is exerted on a rope wrapped around a 50-lb cylinder. How high does the cylinder rise in 2 sec? How many rotations has the cylinder had at that time? Neglect initial frictional effects by the ground support.

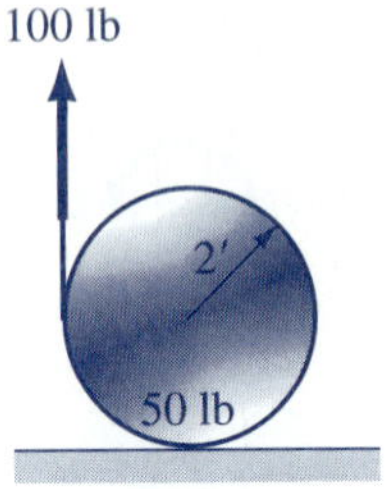

Figure P.16.61.

16.62. A bar of weight W equal to 100 lb is at rest on a horizontal surface S at the instant that a force P equal to 60 lb is applied. Show that the center of rotation at the instant that the force P is applied is 3.27 ft from the left end. The coefficient of friction μ_s equals .2. The length of the bar is 10 ft. Assume that the normal force on the surface is uniform.

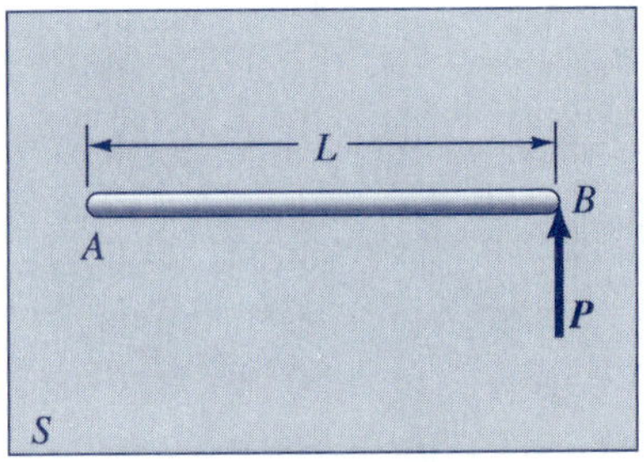

Figure P.16.62.

16.63. A cart B is given a constant acceleration of 5 m/sec^2. On the cart is a cylinder A having a mass of 5 kg and a diameter of 600 mm. If the system is initially stationary, how far does the cylinder move relative to the cart in 1.5 sec? Assume no slipping.

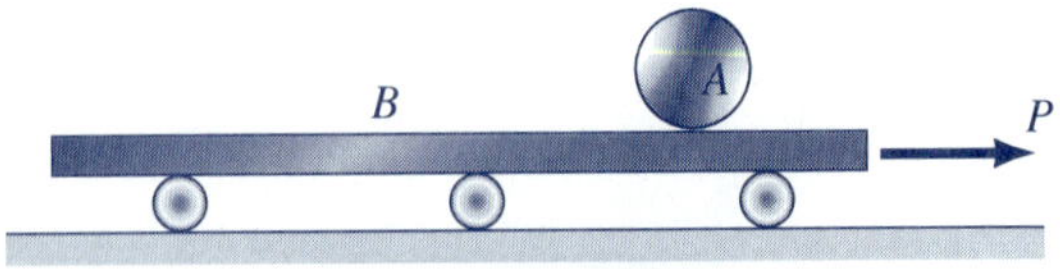

Figure P.16.63.

16.64. A gear A meshes with a stationary pinion B. The hub H of gear A moves along frictionless guide rails DE. The system is in a vertical plane. What are the vertical and angular speeds of the gear after 2 sec if the system is initially at rest? The gear has a mass of 20 kg.

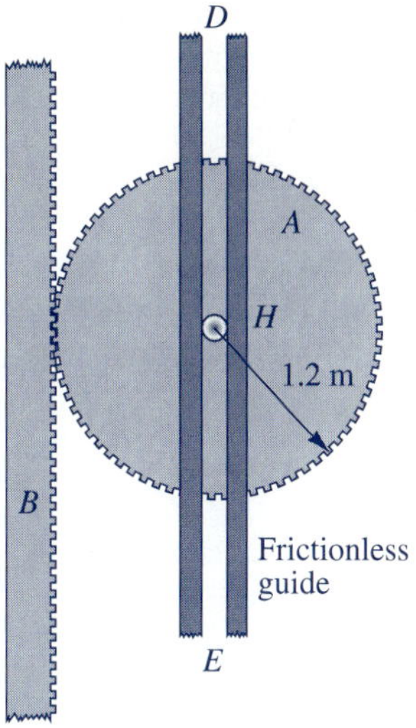

Figure P.16.64.

16.65. In Problem 15.43, compute the forces at pin B and pin C. The mass of rod BC is 25 lbm and the mass of rod AB is 18 lbm. The following data stem from the solution of Problem 15.41:

$$\omega_{BC} = 3.35 \text{ rad/sec} \quad \dot{\omega}_{BC} = 39.7 \text{ rad/sec}^2 \quad a_c = 116.6 \text{ m/sec}^2$$

Neglect the mass of the slider at C, but do not consider it to be frictionless. A strain gauge informs us that there is a torque of 20 ft-lb acting on rod AB at A.

16.66. A circular disc is shown with a circular hole. It rests on a frictionless surface and the view shown is from above. A force F = .04 lb acts on the disc. The thickness of the disc is 2 in and the specific weight is 350 lb/ft³. What is the initial linear acceleration of the center of mass and the angular acceleration of the disc?

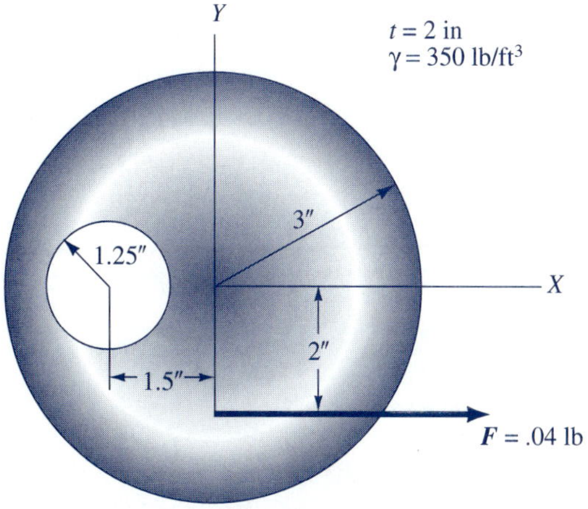

Figure P.16.66.

16.67. In the preceding problem the disc is in the vertical plane and is held up by a horizontal surface where the coefficients of friction are μ_s = .005 and μ_d = .003. What are the initial linear acceleration of the center of mass and the initial angular acceleration of the disc? Start by assuming no slipping.

16.68. A cylinder A slides off the flatbed of a truck (Fig. P.16.68.) onto the road with zero angular velocity. The mass of the cylinder is 100 kg; its radius is 1 m; and its radius of gyration about the axis through the center of mass is 0.75 m. The coefficient of friction μ_d between the cylinder and the pavement is 0.6. If marks on the pavement from the cylinder while it is sliding extend over a distance along the road of 3 m, and if the axis of the cylinder remains perpendicular to the sides of the road during the action, what was the approximate speed of the truck when the cylinder slid off. Neglect the speed of the cylinder relative to the truck when it slides off. [*Hint:* What do the pavement marks signify?]

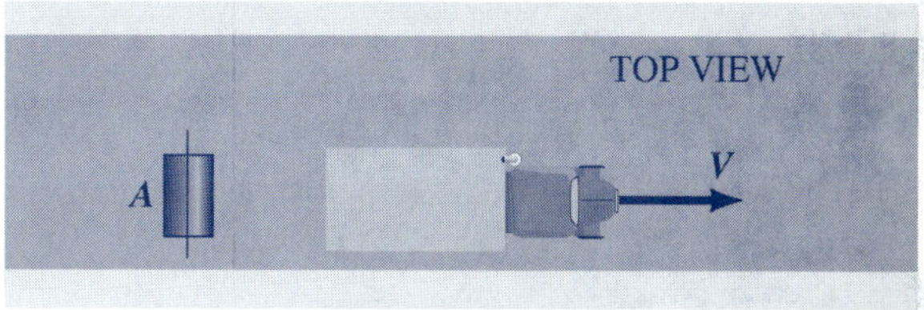

Figure P.16.68.

16.69. Three forces act on a plate resting on a frictionless surface. They are F_1 = 100 lb, F_2 = 200 lb, and a force F_3 = 350 lb whose direction θ is to be determined so that the plate has a counterclockwise angular acceleration of .204 rad/sec². Determine also the acceleration vector for the center of mass of the plate. The mass of the plate is 178 lbm.

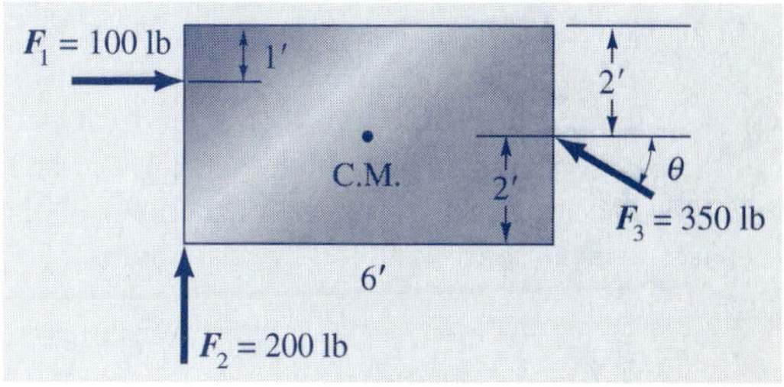

Figure P.16.69.

16.70. In Problem 16.63, what force P is needed to uniformly accelerate the cart so that the cylinder A moves 1 m in 2 sec relative to the cart. Cart B has a mass of 10 kg. Neglect the inertia of the small rollers supporting the cart, and assume there is no slipping.

16.71. A wedge B is shown with a cylinder A of mass 20 kg and diameter 500 mm on the incline. The wedge is given a constant acceleration of 20 m/sec^2 to the right. How far d does the cylinder move in sec relative to the incline if there is no slipping? The system starts from rest.

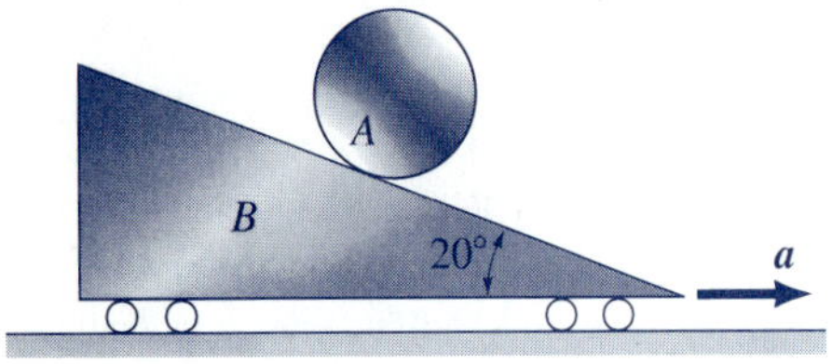

Figure P.16.71.

16.72. A block weighing 100 N is held by three inextensible guy wires. What are the forces in wires AC and BD at the instant that wire EC is cut?

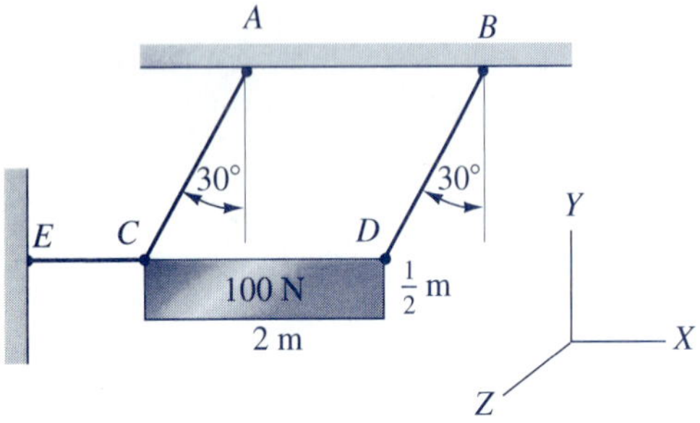

Figure P.16.72.

16.73. A bowler releases his ball at a speed of 3 m/sec. If the ball has a diameter of 250 mm, what spin ω should be put on the ball so there is no slipping? If he puts on only half of this spin ω, keeping the same speed of 3 m/sec, what is the final (terminal) speed of the ball? What is the speed after .3 sec? The ball has a mass of 1.8 kg and a dynamic coefficient of friction with the floor of .1. Neglect wind resistance and rolling resistance (as discussed in Section 7.7).

Figure P.16.73.

16.74. In Problem 16.73, suppose ω is 1.4 times the value ω = 24 rad/sec needed for no slipping. What is the terminal speed of the ball? What is the speed of the ball after .3 sec?

16.75. A tug is pushing on the side of a barge which is loaded with sand and which has a total weight of 50 tons. The tug generates a 3-kN force which is always normal to the barge. If the barge rotates 5° in 20 sec, what is the moment of inertia of the barge at the center of mass which we take at the geometric center of the barge? The distance d for this maneuver is 5 m. What is the acceleration of the center of mass of the barge at t = 35 sec? Neglect the resistance of the water.

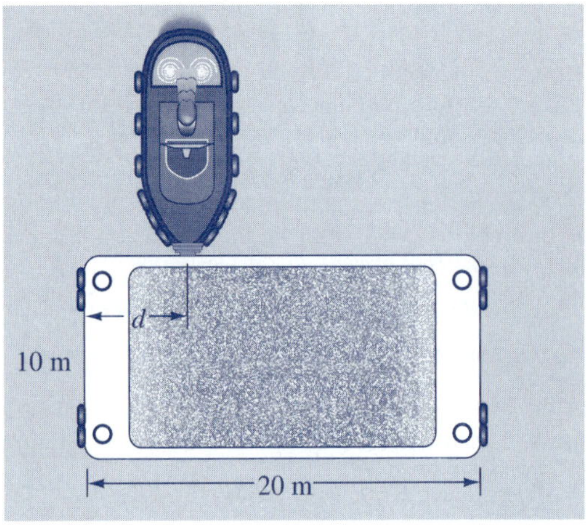

Figure P.16.75.

16.76. A plate A having a mass of 100 lbm is supported by a rod at one end and by a linear spring having a spring constant K = 190 lb/in at the other. If the rod BC is suddenly released at B, what is the angular acceleration of the plate? Also, what is the acceleration of the plate mass center? The plate is oriented as shown at the instant of cutting the left support.

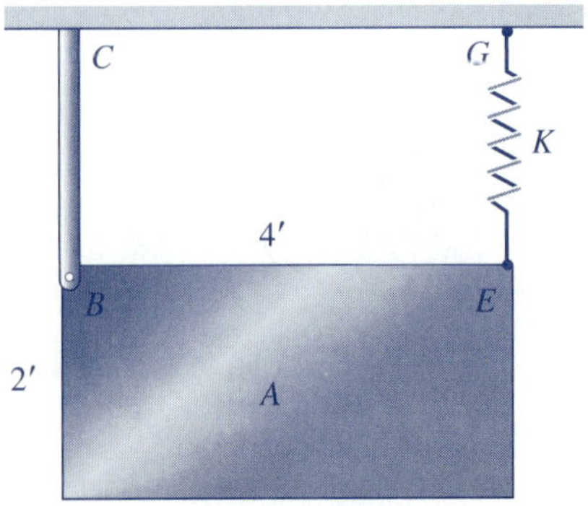

Figure P.16.76.

16.77. The great English liner, the *Queen Elizabeth* (QE II), is the last transatlantic luxury ship left. All the others have been either scrapped or made into pleasure excursion ships. The QE II is 700 ft long and weighs 60,000 tons.

(a) At a top speed of 40 knots, with the engines producing 110,000 horsepower, what is the thrust coming from the propellers?
(b) In a harbor, two tugboats are turning an initially stationary QE II as shown in the diagram. Determine an approximate value for the angular acceleration of the ship. Consider the ship to be a long uniform rod. Include an additional one fourth of the mass of the ship to account for the water which must be moved to accommodate the movement of the ship. Each tug develops a force of 5,000 lb.
(c) If the tugs remain perpendicular to the QE II, and if we assume constant angular acceleration, how many minutes are required to turn the ship 10 degrees?

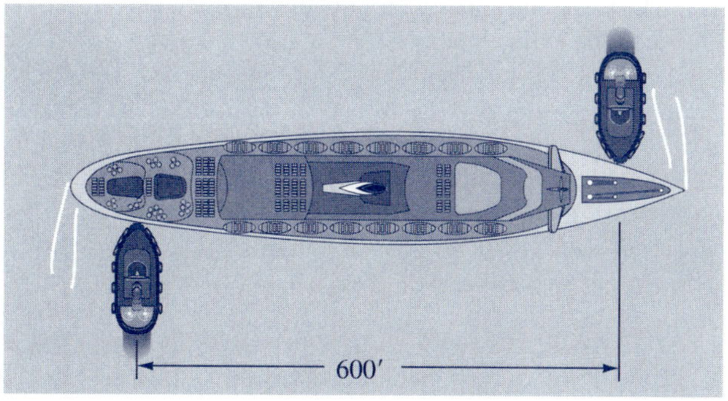

Figure P.16.77.

16.78. A cable supports cylinder *A* of mass 40 kg and then wraps around a light cylinder *B* and finally supports cylinder *C* of mass 20 kg. If the system is released from rest, what are the accelerations of the centers of *A* and *C*? There is no slipping.

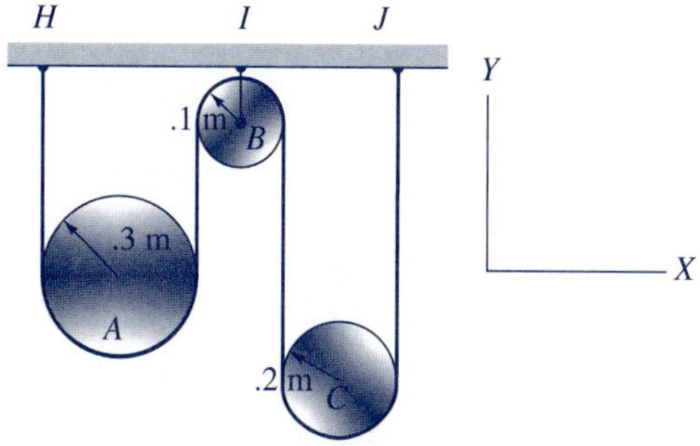

Figure P.16.78.

16.79. A cylinder of mass 20 kg can rotate inside a block *B* whose mass is 35 kg. There is a constant resisting torque for this rotation given as 200 N-m. A horizontal 1,000-N force is applied to a cable firmly wrapped around the cylinder. What is the velocity of the block after moving 0.5 m? What is the angular velocity of the cylinder when the block reaches this position? The coefficient of dynamic friction between block *B* and the floor is 0.3. The system is shown in a vertical orientation.

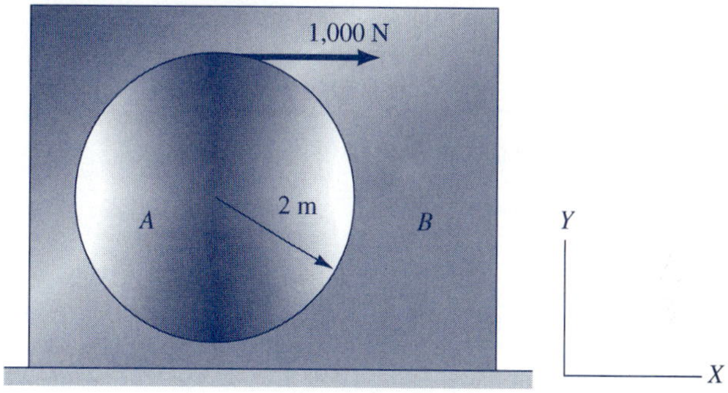

Figure P.16.79.

16.80. A rod *AB* of length 3 m and weight 445 N is shown immediately after it has been released from rest. Compute the tension in wires *EA* and *DB* at this instant.

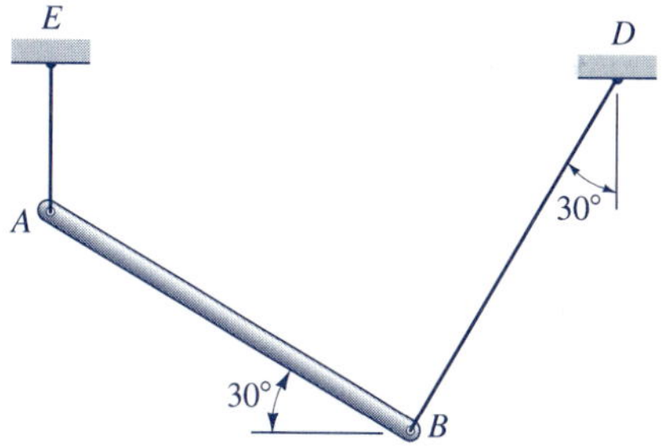

Figure P.16.80.

16.81. Rod *AB* is released from the configuration shown. What are the supporting forces at this instant if we neglect friction? The rod weighs 200 lb and is 20 ft in length.

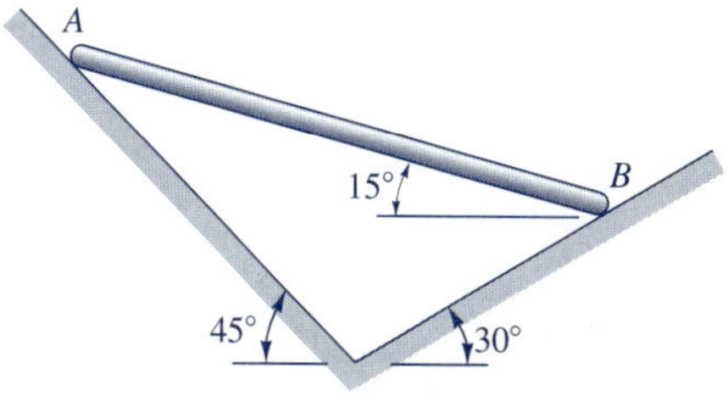

Figure P.16.81.

16.82. A cylinder weighing 100 lb with a radius of 1 ft is held fixed on an incline that is rotating at $\frac{1}{2}$ rad/sec. The cylinder is released when the incline is at position θ equal to 30°. If the cylinder is 20 ft from the bottom A at the instant of release, what is the initial acceleration of the center of the cylinder relative to the incline? There is no slipping.

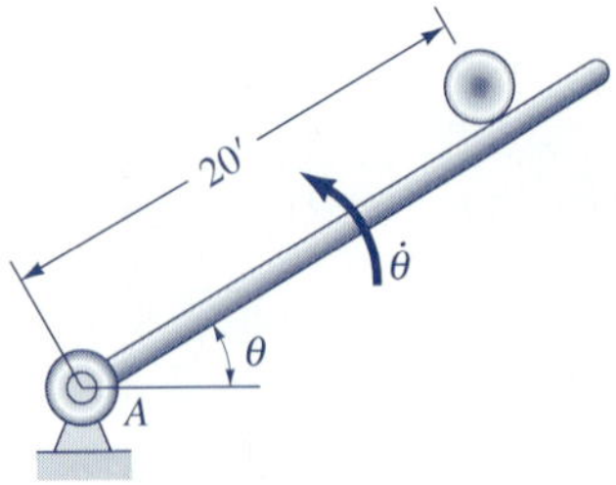

Figure P.16.82.

16.83. In Problem 16.82, $\ddot{\theta} = 2$ rad/sec^2 at the instant of interest and the cylinder is rolling downward at a speed ω_1 of 3 rad/sec relative to the incline. What is the acceleration of the center of the cylinder relative to the incline at the instant of interest? There is no slipping.

16.84. Two identical bars, each having a mass of 9 kg, hang freely from the vertical. A force of 45 N is applied at the center of the upper bar AB. What are the angular accelerations of the bars?

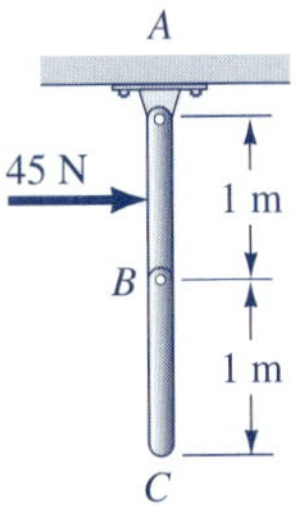

Figure P.16.84.

16.85. A rod BA is made to rotate at a constant speed ω of 100 rpm by a torque not shown. It drives a rod BC, having a mass of 5 kg, which in turn moves a gear D having a mass of 3 kg and a radius of gyration of 200 mm. The diameter of the gear is 450 mm. At the instant shown, what are the forces transmitted by the pins at C and at B?

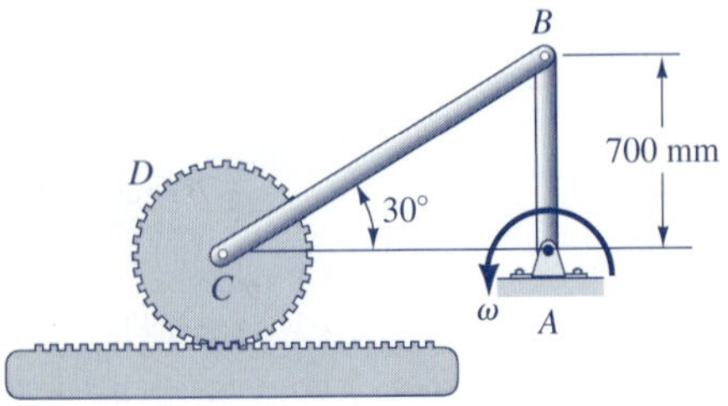

Figure P.16.85.

16.86. A 1-m rod AB weighing 10 kg is suspended at one end by a cord BC and at the other end rides on an inclined surface on small wheels. Initially the wheels are being held at the position shown. At the instant the wheels are released, what is the angular acceleration of rod AB? Neglect friction on the inclined surface.

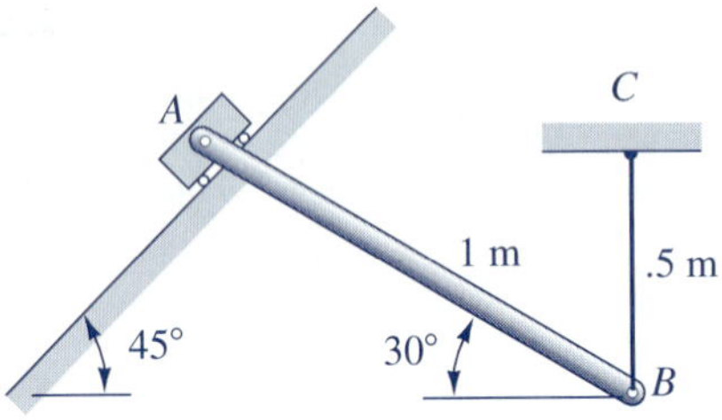

Figure P.16.86.

16.87. A truck is carrying a 10,000 N crate A held by two steel cables each under a tensile force of 800 N. At corner B there is a stop. The truck undergoes a crash with a constant deceleration of 4.6 g's. Cable FG breaks and the crate starts to rotate about corner B where we have the stop. What are the angular acceleration and the forces at the stop at the instant of the break? The center of mass of the crate is at the geometrical center of the crate and the radius of gyration about the center of mass is 2.3 m. Consider that when the rotational acceleration first occurs, the crate has yet to move and that cable DE still has the original tension, whereas cable FG has snapped.

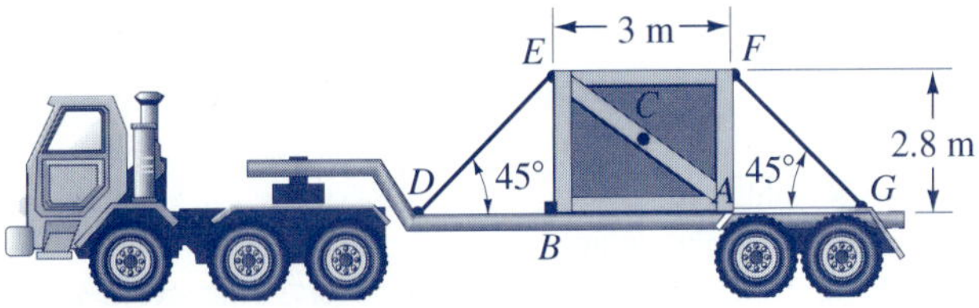

Figure P.16.87.

16.88. An object with a cylindrical hub, thin spokes, and a thin rim rests on a frictionless horizontal surface. The hub weighs 100 N and the spokes and rim each weigh 15 N/m. What is the acceleration of center A when the indicated force is applied? What is the angular acceleration of the system? Finally, what is the acceleration of point B? Use calculus when considering the spokes and the rim. For the hub, the angular momentum about an axis through the center of mass is given as

$$\int_V \boldsymbol{r} \times dm\boldsymbol{V} = \frac{1}{2} MR^2 \omega \boldsymbol{k}$$

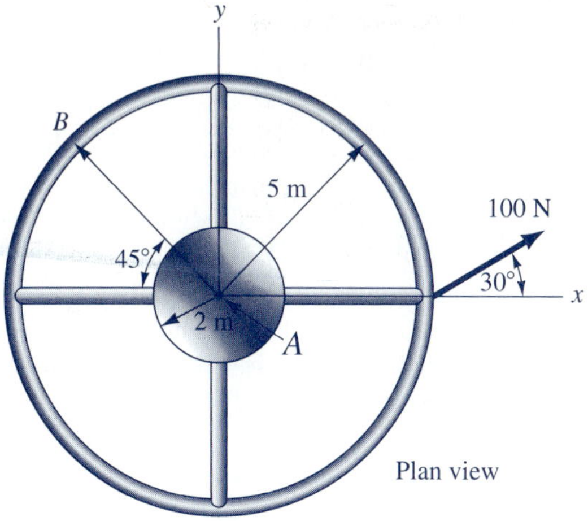

Figure P.16.88.

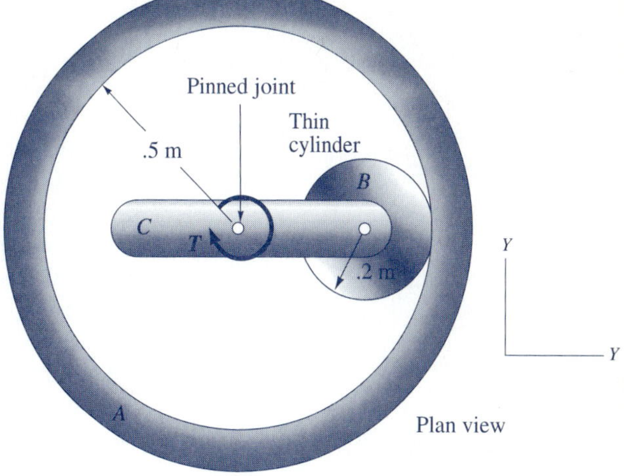

Figure P.16.90.

16.89. We are looking down from above at a baseball player swinging his bat in a horizontal plane in the process of hitting a baseball at point B. The player is holding the bat such that the resultant of the force from his hands is at point A. At what distance d should the ball hit the bat to render as zero the normal force component from the batter's hands onto the centerline of the bat? This point B is called the *center of percussion*. Because this kind of hit feels effortless to the batter it is often called the "sweet spot" by athletes in both baseball and tennis. The radius of gyration about the center of mass is k_z.

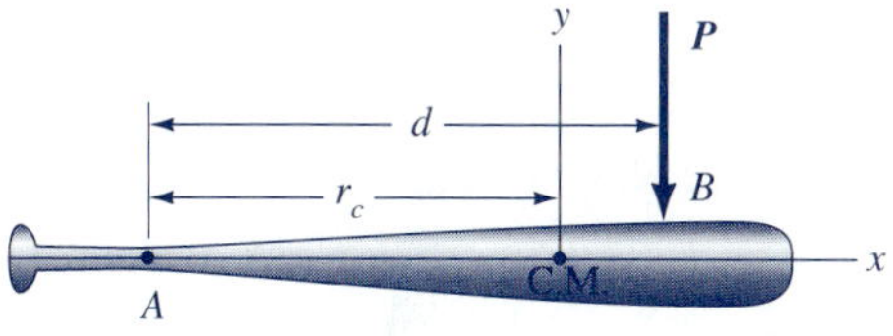

Figure P.16.89.

16.90. A torque $T = 10$ N-m is applied to body C. If there is no slipping, how many rotations does cylinder B make in 1 sec if the system starts from rest? A is stationary at all times. The system starts from rest. We are observing the system from above. The following data apply.

$$M_C = 50 \text{ kg} \qquad M_B = 30 \text{ kg}$$
$$k_C = .2 \text{ m} \qquad k_B = .1 \text{ m}$$

16.91. In Problem 15.48, we determined the following results from kinematics:

$$\omega_{AB} = -.609 \text{ rad/s} \qquad V_B = 4.38 \text{ m/s}$$
$$\dot{\omega}_{AB} = 14.71 \text{ rad/sec}^2 \quad \dot{V}_B = -33.28 \text{ m/s}^2$$

The mass of rod AB is 10 kg. If we neglect the masses of the sliders, what are the forces coming onto the end pins of the rod? The horizontal slot in which slider A is moving is frictionless.

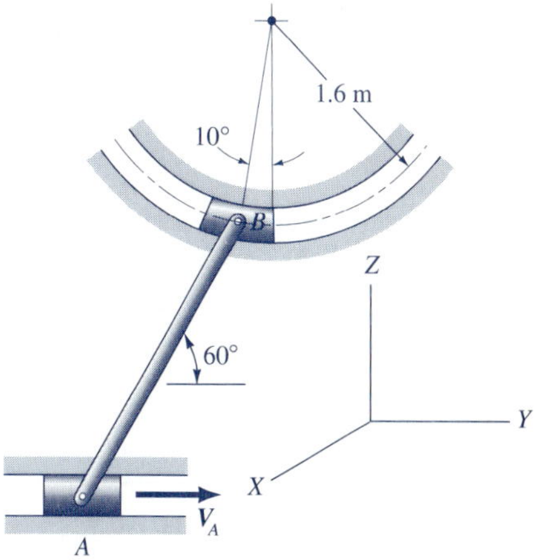

Figure P.16.91.

16.92. In the preceding problem, the slider at A no longer moves in the slot without friction and we do not know the friction force there. However, we have a strain gage mounted on rod AB giving data indicating a 200 N compressive axial force at A. Using the data of the previous problem, compute the force components at the ends of the rod.

16.8 Pure Rotation of an Arbitrary Rigid Body

We now consider a body having an arbitrary distribution of mass rotating about an axis of rotation fixed in inertial space. We consider this axis to be the z axis fixed in the body as well as being an inertial coordinate axis Z. We can take the origin of xyz anywhere along the z axis since all such points are fixed in inertial space. The *moment-of-momentum* equations to be used will now be the general equations 16.6 since I_{zx} and I_{zy} will generally not equal zero. If the center of mass is along the z axis, then it obviously has no acceleration, and so we can then apply the rules of statics to the center of mass. For other cases we shall often need to use *Newton's law* for the center of mass. In this regard it will be helpful to note from the definition of the center of mass that for a system of rigid bodies such as is shown in Fig. 16.29

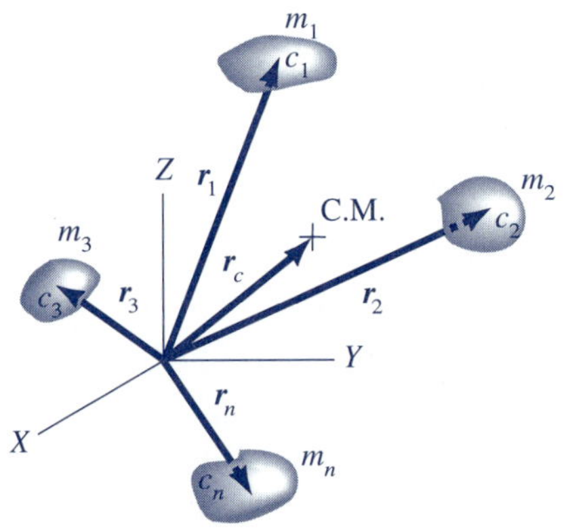

Figure 16.29. n rigid bodies having a total mass M.

$$M\boldsymbol{r}_c = \sum_{i=1}^{n} m_i \boldsymbol{r}_i \tag{16.16}$$

where m_i is the mass of the ith rigid body, $\boldsymbol{r}_i$ is the position vector to the center of mass of the ith rigid body, M is the total mass, and $\boldsymbol{r}_c$ is the position vector to the center of mass of the system. We can then say on differentiating:

$$M\dot{\boldsymbol{r}}_c = \sum_{i=1}^{n} m_i \dot{\boldsymbol{r}}_i \tag{16.17}$$

$$M\ddot{\boldsymbol{r}}_c = \sum_{i=1}^{n} m_i \ddot{\boldsymbol{r}}_i \tag{16.18}$$

In *Newton's law* for the mass center of a system of rigid bodies, we conclude that we can use the centers of mass of the component parts of the system as given on the right side of Eq. 16.18 rather than the center of mass of the total mass.

Example 16.10

A shaft has protruding arms each of which weighs 40 N/m (see Fig. 16.30). A torque T gives the shaft an angular acceleration $\dot{\omega}$ of 2 rad/sec^2. At the instant shown in the diagram, ω is 5 rad/sec. If the shaft without

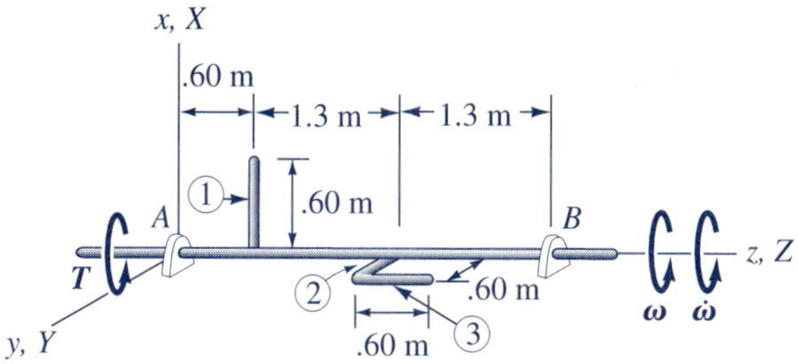

Figure 16.30. Rotating shaft with arms.

arms weighs 180 N, compute the vertical and horizontal forces at bearings *A* and *B* (see Fig. 16.31). Note that we have numbered the various arms for convenient identification.

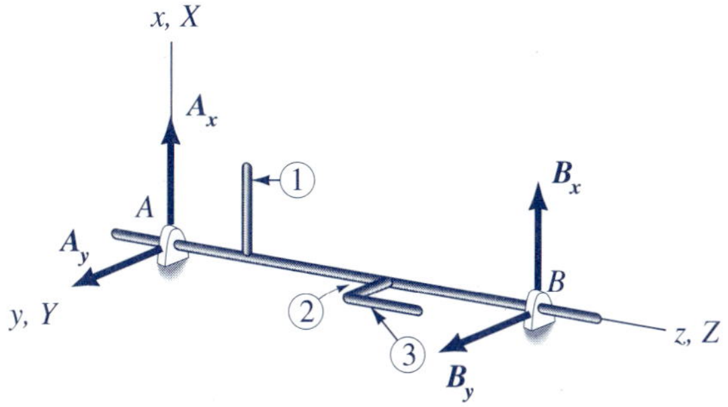

Figure 16.31. Supporting forces.

We first fix a reference *xyz* to the shaft at *A*. Also at *A* we fix an inertial reference *XYZ* to the ground. We can directly use Eqs. 16.6a and 16.6b about point *A*. For this reason, we shall compute the required products of inertia of the shaft system for reference *xyz*. Accordingly, using the parallel-axis theorem, we have:

$$(I_{xz})_{\text{arm(1)}} = 0 + \frac{(40)(.60)}{g}[(.6)(.3)] = .440 \text{ kg-m}^2$$

$$(I_{xz})_{\text{arm(2)}} = 0 + \frac{(40)(.60)}{g}[(1.9)(0)] = 0$$

$$(I_{xz})_{\text{arm(3)}} = 0 + \frac{(40)(.60)}{g}[(2.20)(0)] = 0$$

Hence, for the system, I_{xz} = .440 kg-m^2.

We next consider I_{zy}. Accordingly, we have

Example 16.10 (Continued)

$$(I_{zy})_{\text{arm}(1)} = 0 + \frac{(40)(.60)}{g}[(.60)(0)] = 0$$

$$(I_{zy})_{\text{arm}(2)} = 0 + \frac{(40)(.60)}{g}[(1.9)(0.30)] = 1.394 \text{ kg-m}^2$$

$$(I_{zy})_{\text{arm}(3)} = 0 + \frac{(40)(.60)}{g}[(2.20)(.60)] = 3.23 \text{ kg-m}^2$$

$$(I_{zy})_{\text{shaft}} = 0 + 0 = 0$$

Hence, for the system, $I_{zy} = 4.62$ kg-m^2.

We can now employ the **moment of momentum** equations (Eqs. 16.6) to get the required moments M_x and M_y about point A needed for the motion we are considering. Thus, we have

$$M_x = -(2)(.440) + (5^2)(4.62) = 114.7 \text{ N-m} \quad \text{(a)}$$

$$M_y = -(2)(4.62) - (5^2)(.440) = -20.2 \text{ N-m} \quad \text{(b)}$$

Summing moments of all the forces acting on the system about the y axis at A, we can say (see Fig. 16.31):

$$M_y = -20.2 = -(40)(.60)(.60) - (40)(.60)(1.9) - (40)(.60)(2.2) - (180)(1.6) + (B_x)(3.2)$$

Therefore, we require

$$B_x = 118.9 \text{ N} \quad \text{(c)}$$

Summing moments about the x axis at A, we can say

$$M_x = 114.7 = -B_y(3.2)$$

Therefore, we require

$$B_y = -35.8 \text{ N} \quad \text{(d)}$$

We next use **Newton's law** considering the three arms to be three particles at their mass centers as has been shown in Fig. 16.32. In the x

Example 16.10 (Continued)

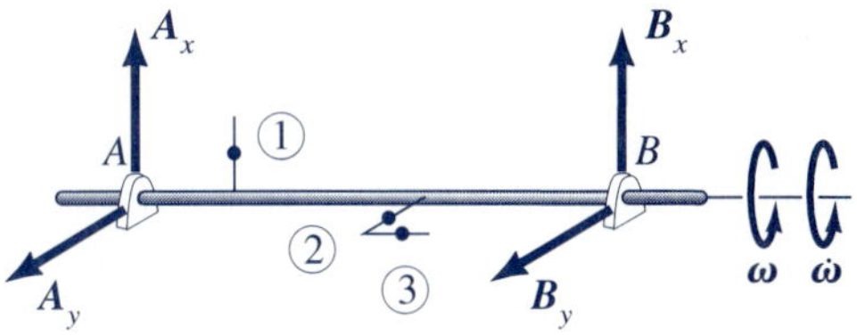

Figure 16.32. Arms replaced by mass centers.

direction at time t we have, using Eq. 16.18 and noting that each of the aforementioned particles has circular motion:

$$118.9 + A_x - 180 - (3)[(40)(.60)] = -\frac{(40)(.60)}{g}(.30)(\omega^2) - \frac{(40)(.60)}{g}(.30)(\dot{\omega}) - \frac{(40)(.60)}{g}(.60)(\dot{\omega})$$

Setting $\omega = 5$ rad/sec and $\dot{\omega} = 2$ rad/sec^2, we get

$$A_x = 110.3 \text{ N} \tag{e}$$

In the y direction, we can say similarly at time t

$$A_y - 35.8 = \frac{(40)(.60)}{g}(.30)(\dot{\omega}) - \frac{(40)(.60)}{g}(.30)(\omega^2) - \frac{(40)(.60)}{g}(.60)(\omega^2)$$

Therefore,

$$A_y = -17.78 \text{ N} \tag{f}$$

The forces acting on the shaft are shown in Fig. 16.33. The reactions to these forces are then the desired forces on the bearings. In the z direction it should be clear that there is no force on the bearings.

Figure 16.33. Forces on shaft.

If, in the last example, we had ignored the constant forces of gravity, we would have determined forces at bearings A and B that are due entirely to the motion of the body. Forces computed in this way are called *dynamic forces*. If the body were rotating with constant speed ω, these forces would clearly have constant values in the x and y directions. Since the xy axes are rotating with the body relative to the ground reference XYZ, such dynamic forces must also rotate relative to the ground about the axis of rotation with the speed ω of the body. This means that, in any *fixed* direction normal to the shaft at a bearing, there will be a *sinusoidal force variation* with a frequency corresponding to the angular rotation of the shaft. Such forces can induce vibrations of large amplitude in the structure or support if a natural frequency or multiple of a natural frequency is reached in these bodies.[11] When a shaft creates rotating forces on the bearings by virtue of its own rotation, the shaft is said to be unbalanced. We shall set up criteria for balancing a rotating body in the next section.

*16.9 Balancing

We shall now set forth the criteria for the condition of dynamic balance in a rotating body. Then, we shall set forth the requirements needed to achieve balance in a rotating body. Consider then some arbitrary rigid body rotating with angular speed ω and a rate of change of angular speed $\dot{\omega}$ about axis AB (Fig. 16.34). We shall set up general equations for determining the supporting forces at the bearings. Consider point a on the axis of rotation at the bearing A and establish a set of axes xyz fixed to the rotating body with the z axis corresponding to the axis of rotation. The x and y axes are chosen for convenience. Axes XYZ are, as usual, inertial axes. Using the *moment-of-momentum* equations (a) and (b) in Eq. 16.6 and including only *dynamic* forces, we get for point a:

$$B_y l = -I_{xz}\dot{\omega} + I_{yz}\omega^2 \tag{16.19a}$$

$$B_x l = -I_{yz}\dot{\omega} - I_{xz}\omega^2 \tag{16.19b}$$

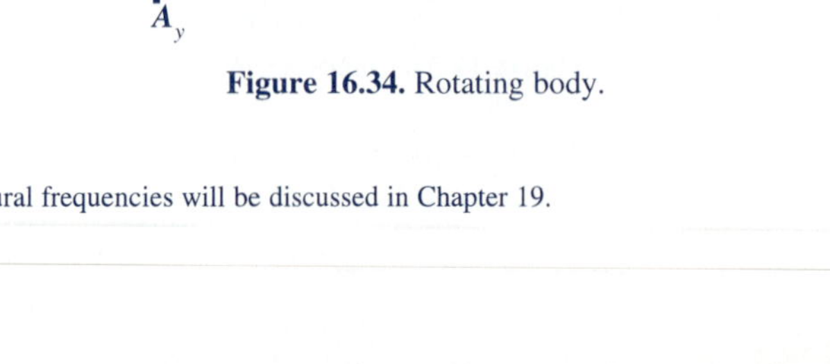

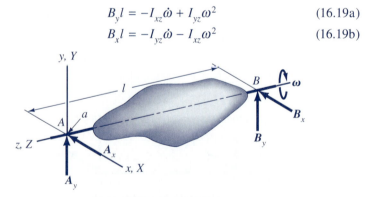

Figure 16.34. Rotating body.

[11]Natural frequencies will be discussed in Chapter 19.

If the axis of rotation is a *principal axis* at bearing A, then $I_{yz} = I_{xz} = 0$ in accordance with the results of Chapter 9. The dynamic forces at bearing B are then zero.

Next, we shall show that if in addition the *center of mass lies along the axis of rotation*, this axis is a principal axis for *all points* on it. In Fig. 16.35 a set of axes $x'y'z'$ fixed to the body and parallel to the xyz axes has been set up at an arbitrary point E along the axis of rotation. We can see from the arrangement of the axes that for any element of the body dm:

$$y' = y, \qquad x' = x, \qquad z' = D + z \tag{16.20}$$

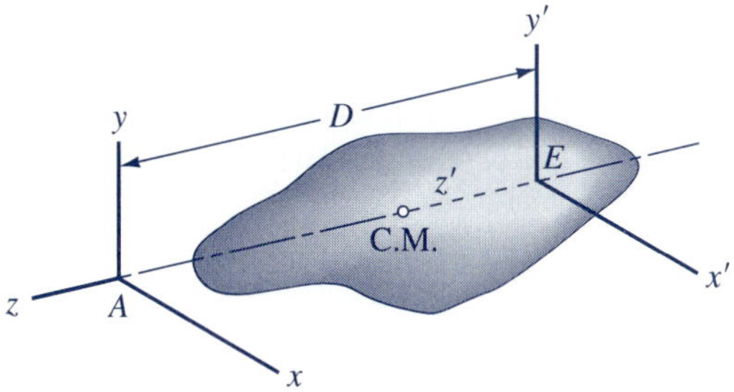

Figure 16.35. Reference $x'y'z'$ fixed at E..

Also, we know for the xyz reference that

$$I_{xz} = \int_M xz\, dm = 0, \qquad I_{yz} = \int_M yz\, dm = 0 \tag{16.21}$$

And if the center of mass is along the centerline, we can say:

$$\int_M y\, dm = \int_M y'\, dm = My_c = 0 \tag{16.22}$$

$$\int_M x\, dm = \int_M x'\, dm = Mx_c = 0$$

We shall now show that all products of inertia involving the z' axis at E are zero under these conditions and, consequently, that the z' axis is a principal axis at E. Substituting from Eqs. 16.20 into 16.21, we get

$$\int_M x'(z' - D)\, dm = 0 \tag{a}$$

$$\int_M y'(z' - D)\, dm = 0 \tag{b}$$

If we carry out the multiplication in the integrand of the above Eqs. (a) and (b), we get

$$\int_M x'z'\, dm - D\int_M x'\, dm = 0 \tag{c}$$

$$\int_M y'z'\, dm - D\int_M y'\, dm = 0 \tag{d}$$

As a result of Eq. 16.22, the second integrals of Eqs. (c) and (d) are zero, and we conclude that the products of inertia $I_{x'z'}$ and $I_{y'z'}$ are zero. Now the xy axes and hence the $x'y'$ axes can have any orientation as long as they are normal to the axis of rotation. This means that at E the z' axis yields a zero product of inertia for all axes normal to it. As a result of our deliberations of Chapter 9, we can conclude that z' is a principal axis for point E. And since E is any point on the axis of rotation, we can say the following:

If the axis of rotation is a principal axis at any point along this axis and if the center of mass is on the axis of rotation, then the axis of rotation is a principal axis at all points on it.

We now consider Fig. 16.36, where reference $x'y'z'$ is set up at bearing B. We can next employ the **moment-of-momentum** equation (16.6) for these axes at B. We get

$$-A_y l = -I_{x'z'}\dot{\omega} + I_{y'z'}\omega^2$$

$$-A_x l = -I_{y'z'}\dot{\omega} - I_{x'z'}\omega^2$$

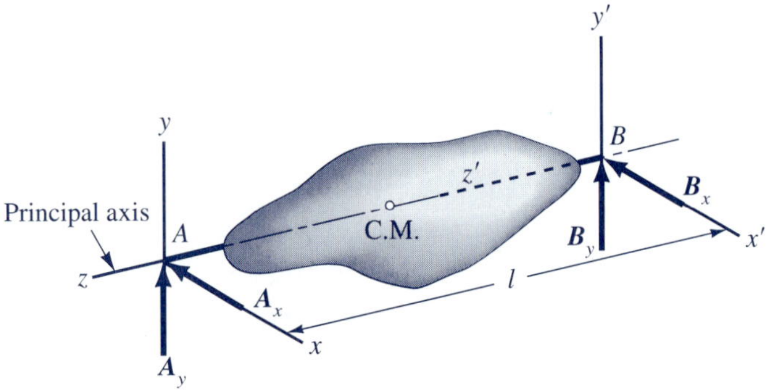

Figure 16.36. Reference $x'y'z'$ fixed at B.

With the z axis a principal axis at A and the center of mass along the axis of rotation, the z' axis at B must be a principal axis, and hence $I_{y'z'} = I_{x'z'} = 0$. The dynamic forces at bearing A, therefore, are zero. The rotating system is thus balanced.

We can now conclude that:

For a rotating system to be dynamically balanced, it is necessary and sufficient (1) that at any point along the axis of rotation this axis is a principal axis and (2) that the center of mass is along the axis of rotation.

We next illustrate how we can make use of these results to balance a rotating body.

Example 16.11

A rotating member carries two particles having weights $W_1 = 5$ lb and $W_2 = 8$ lb at radial distances $r_1 = 1$ ft and $r_2 = 1\frac{1}{2}$ ft, respectively. The weights and a reference xyz fixed to the shaft are shown in Fig. 16.37. They are to be balanced by two other particles having weights W_3 and W_4 (shown dashed) which are to be placed in the balancing planes A and B, respectively. If the weights are placed in these planes at a distance of 1 ft from the axis of rotation, determine the value of these weights and their position relative to the xyz reference.

We have two unknown weights and two unknown angles, that is, four unknowns [see Fig. 16.37(b)], to evaluate in this problem. The condition that the mass center be on the centerline yields the following relations:[12]

$$\int_M y\,dm = 0:$$

$$\frac{W_1}{g} r_1 \cos 20° + \frac{W_2}{g} r_2 \cos 45° - \frac{W_3}{g} r_3 \cos\theta_3 - \frac{W_4}{g} r_4 \cos\theta_4 = 0$$

$$\int_M x\,dm = 0:$$

$$-\frac{W_1}{g} r_1 \sin 20° + \frac{W_2}{g} r_2 \sin 45° + \frac{W_3}{g} r_3 \sin\theta_3 - \frac{W_4}{g} r_4 \sin\theta_4 = 0$$

When the numerical values of r_1, r_2, etc., are inserted, these equations become

$$W_3 \cos\theta_3 + W_4 \cos\theta_4 = 13.18 \qquad \text{(a)}$$

$$W_3 \sin\theta_3 - W_4 \sin\theta_4 = -6.77 \qquad \text{(b)}$$

Now we require that the products of inertia I_{yz} and I_{xz} be zero for the xyz reference positioned so that xy is in the balancing plane B.

$$I_{xz} = 0:$$

$$\frac{W_1}{g}(6)(-r_1 \sin 20°) + \frac{W_2}{g}(2)(r_2 \sin 45°) + \frac{W_3}{g}(9)(r_3 \sin\theta_3) = 0 \qquad \text{(c)}$$

$$I_{yz} = 0:$$

$$\frac{W_1}{g}(6)(r_1 \cos 20°) + \frac{W_2}{g}(2)(r_2 \cos 45°) + \frac{W_3}{g}(9)(-r_3 \cos\theta_3) = 0 \qquad \text{(d)}$$

Equations (c) and (d) can be put in the form

$$9W_3 \sin\theta_3 = -6.71 \qquad \text{(e)}$$

$$9W_3 \cos\theta_3 = 45.2 \qquad \text{(f)}$$

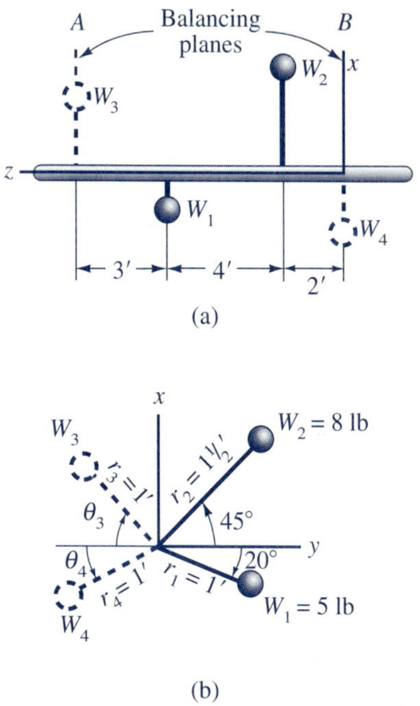

Figure 16.37. Rotating system to be balanced.

[12]We are considering the weights to be particles in this discussion. In some homework problems you will be asked to balance rotating systems for which the particle model will not be proper. You will then have to carry out integrations and/or employ the formulas and transfer theorems for first moments of mass and products of inertia.

Example 16.11 (Continued)

Dividing Eq. (f) into Eq. (e), we get

$$\tan\theta_3 = -.1486$$

$$\theta_3 = 171.5° \text{ or } 351.6°$$

and so, from Eq. (e),

$$W_3 = -\frac{6.71}{9}\frac{1}{\sin\theta_3} = 5.08 \text{ lb}$$

In order to have a positive weight W_3, we chose θ_3 to be 351.6° rather than 171.5°. Now we return to Eqs. (a) and (b). We can then say, on substituting known values of W_3 and θ_3:

$$W_4\cos\theta_4 = 13.18 - 5.01 = 8.16 \quad \text{(g)}$$

$$W_4\sin\theta_4 = 6.77 - .75 = 6.02 \quad \text{(h)}$$

Dividing Eq. (g) into Eq. (h), we get

$$\tan\theta_4 = .738$$

$$\theta_4 = 36.4° \text{ or } 216.4°$$

Hence, from Eq. (g), we have

$$W_4 = \frac{8.16}{\cos\theta_4} = 10.14 \text{ lb}$$

where we use $\theta_4 = 36.4°$ rather than 216.4° to prevent a negative W_4. The final orientation of the balanced system is shown in Fig. 16.38.

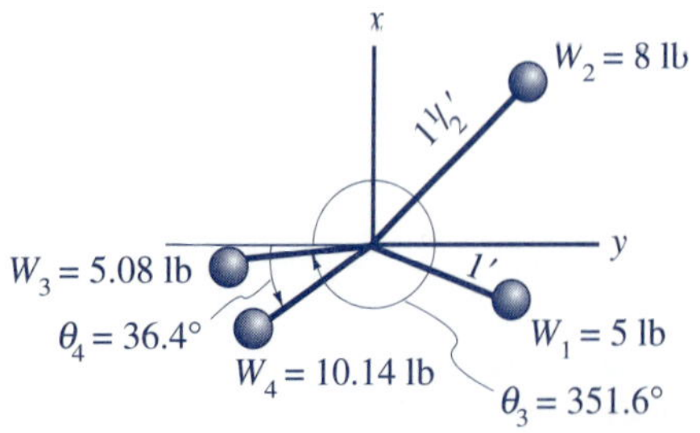

Figure 16.38. Balanced system.

PROBLEMS

16.93. A shaft shown supported by bearings *A* and *B* is rotating at a speed ω of 3 rad/sec. Identical blocks *C* and *D* weighing 30 lb each are attached to the shaft by light structural members. What are the bearing reactions in the *x* and *y* directions if we neglect the weight of the shaft?

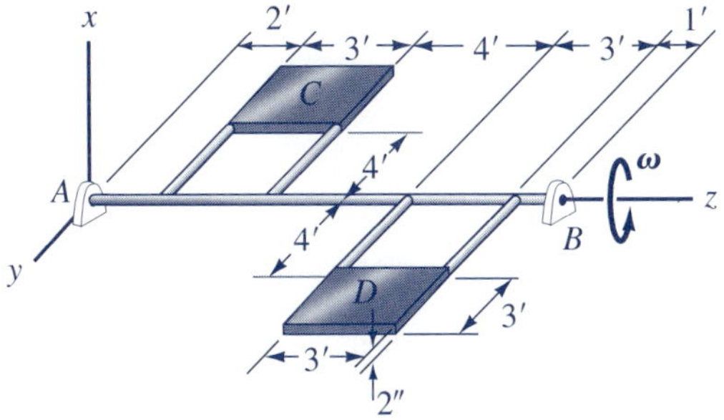

Figure P.16.93.

16.94. Shaft *AB* is rotating at a constant speed ω of 20 rad/sec. Two rods having a weight of 10 N each are welded to the shaft and support a disc *D* weighing 30 N. What are the supporting forces at the instant shown?

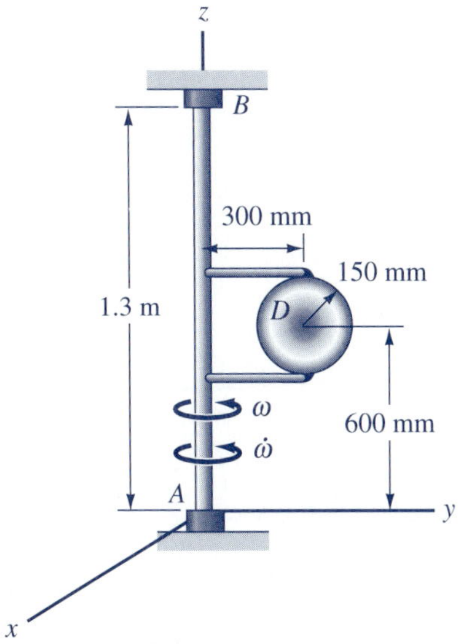

Figure P.16.94.

16.95. Do Problem 16.94 for the case in which ω = 20 rad/sec and $\dot{\omega}$ = 38 rad/sec^2 at the instant of interest as shown.

16.96. A uniform wooden panel is shown supported by bearings *A* and *B*. A 100-lb weight is connected with an inextensible cable to the panel at point *G* over a light pulley *D*. If the system is released from rest at the configuration shown, what is the angular acceleration of the panel, and what are the forces at the bearings? The panel weighs 60 lb.

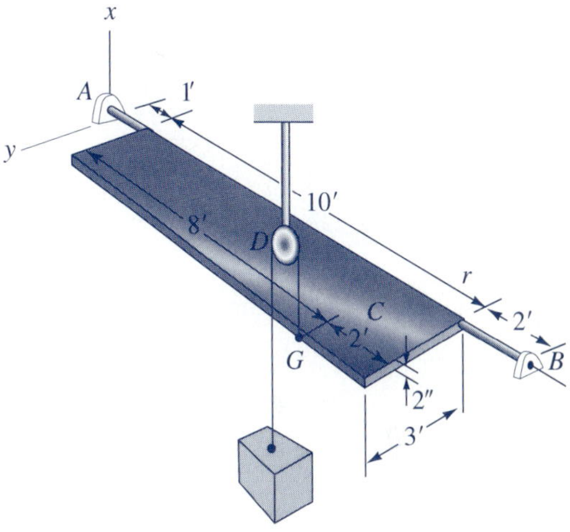

Figure P.16.96.

16.97. Do Problem 16.96 when there is a frictional torque at the bearings of 10 ft-lb and the pulley has a radius of 1 ft and a moment of inertia of 10m-ft^2.

16.98. A thin rectangular plate weighing 50 N is rotating about its diameter at a speed ω of 25 rad/sec. What are the supporting forces in the *x* and *y* directions at the instant shown when the plate is parallel to the *yz* plane?

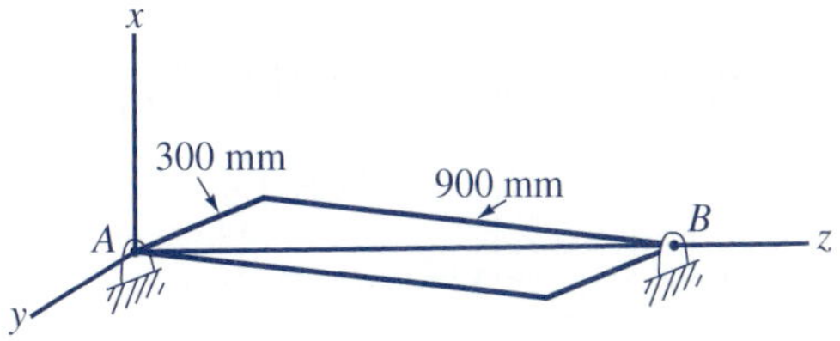

Figure P.16.98.

16.99. A shaft is shown rotating at a speed of 20 rad/sec. What are the supporting forces at the bearings? The rods welded to the shaft weight 40 N/m. The shaft weighs 80 N.

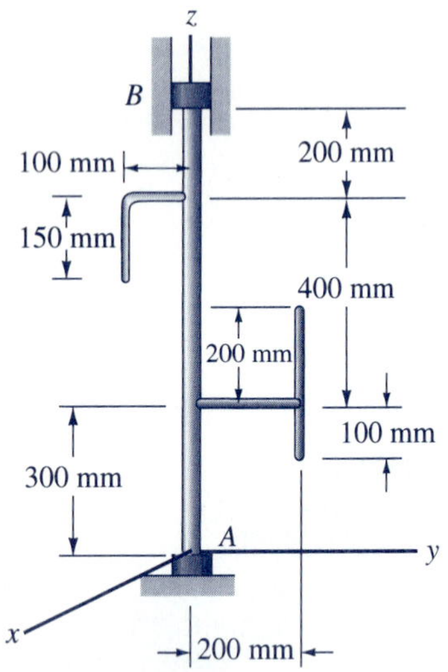

Figure P.16.99.

16.100. A cylinder is shown mounted at an angle of 30° to a shaft. The cylinder weighs 400 N. If a torque T of 20 N-m is applied, what is the angular acceleration of the system? What are the supporting forces in the x and y directions at the configuration shown wherein the system is stationary? Neglect the mass of the shaft. The centerline of the cylinder is in the xz plane at the instant shown.

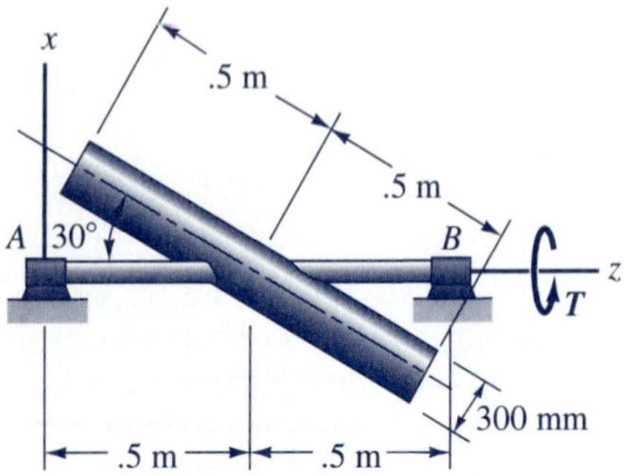

Figure P.16.100.

16.101. A bent shaft has applied to it a torque T including gravity given as

$$T = 10 + 5t \text{ N-m}$$

where t is in seconds. What are the supporting forces at the bearings in the x and y directions when $t = 3$ sec? The shaft is made from a rod 20 mm in diameter and weighing 70 N/m. At $t = 3$ sec, the position of the shaft is as shown.

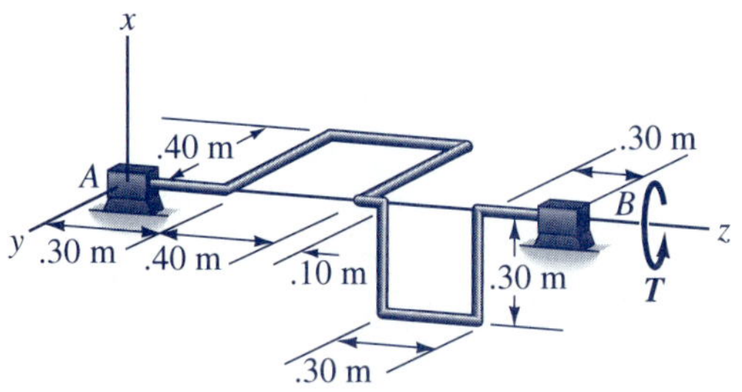

Figure P.16.101.

***16.102.** A shaft has an angular velocity ω of 10 rad/sec and an angular acceleration $\dot{\omega}$ of 5 rad/sec^2 at the instant of interest. What are the bending moments at this instant about the x and y axes just to the right of the bearing at A? Also, what are the twisting moment and shear forces there? The shaft and attached rods have a diameter of 20 mm and a weight per unit length of 50 N/m.

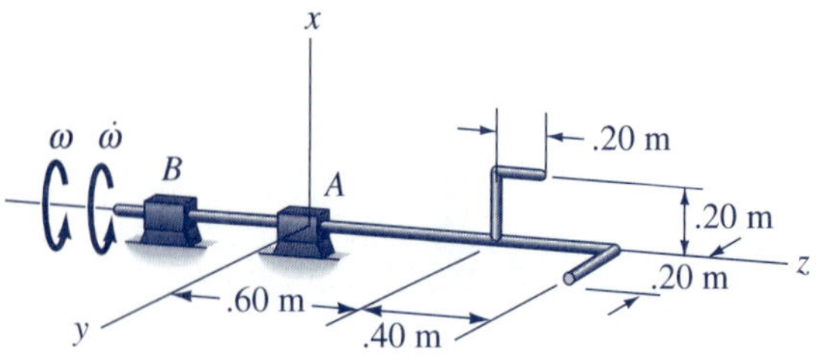

Figure P.16.102.

16.103. Balance the system in planes A and B at a distance 1 ft from centerline. Use two weights.

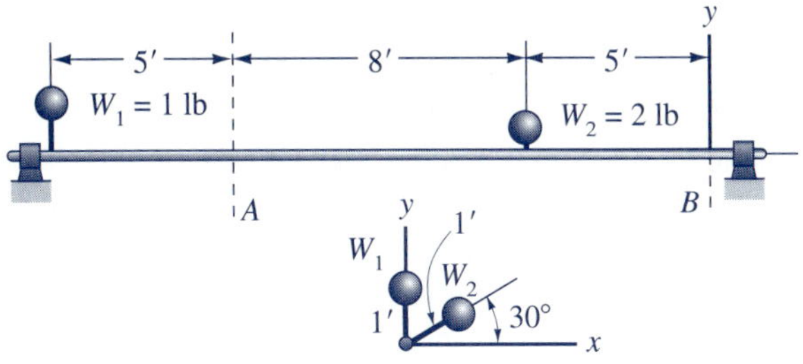

Figure P.16.103.

16.104. Balance the system in Problem 16.103 by using a weight in plane A of $1\frac{1}{2}$ lb and a weight in plane B of 1 lb. You may choose suitable radii in these planes.

16.105. Balance the shaft of Problem 16.94 using rods weighing 50 N/m and welded to the shaft normal to the centerline just next to bearings A and B. Determine the lengths of these rods and their orientations relative to the xy axes.

16.106. A disc and a cylinder are mounted on a shaft. The disc has been mounted eccentrically so that the center of mass is $\frac{1}{2}$ in from the centerline of the shaft. Balance the shaft using balancing planes 5 ft in from bearing A and 3 ft in from bearing B, respectively. The balancing masses each weigh 3 lb and can be regarded as particles. Give the proper position of the balancing masses in these planes.

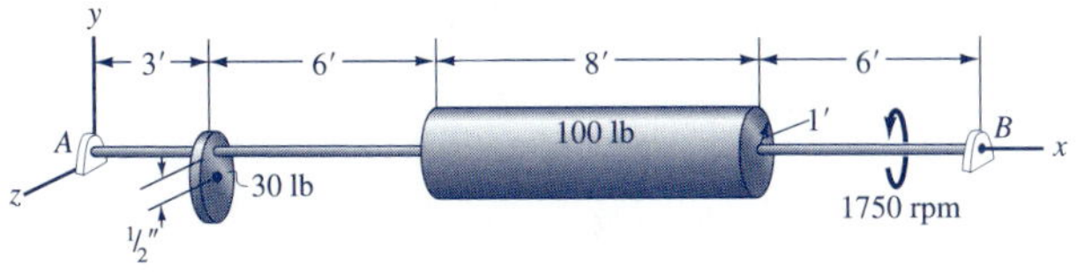

Figure P.16.106.

16.107. Balance the shaft described in Problem 16.106 by removing a small chunk of metal from each of the end faces of the 100-lb cylinder at a position 10 in from the shaft centerline. What are the weights of these chunks and what are their orientations?

16.108. Balance the shaft in Problem 16.99 using balancing planes just next to bearings A and B. At bearing B use a small balancing sphere of weight 30 N and at bearing A use a rod having a weight per unit length of 35 N/m.

16.109. A disc is shown mounted off-center at B on a shaft CD that rotates with angular speed ω. The diameter of the shaft is 2 in. The disc weighs 50 lb and has a diameter of 6 ft. Balance the system using two rods, each weighing 10 lb/ft and having a diameter of 2 in. The rods are to be attached normal to the shaft at position 1 ft in from bearing C and 2 ft. in from bearing D. Determine the lengths of these rods and their inclination.

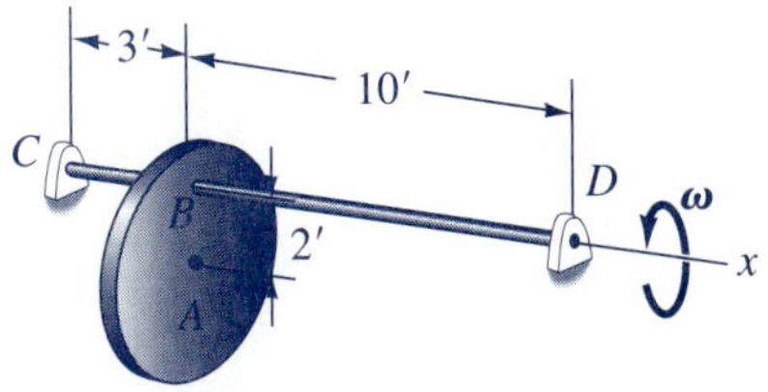

Figure P.16.109.

16.110. Balance the shaft shown for Problem 16.101. Use a balancing plane just next to bearing A and one just next to bearing B. Attach a circular plate normal to the shaft at each bearing, and cut a hole with diameter 60 mm at the proper position in the plate to balance the system. The plates are 30 mm thick and have a specific weight of 8×10^{-5} N/mm^3.

16.10 Closure

In this chapter, we have developed the moment-of-momentum equations for plane motion of a rigid body. We applied this equation to various cases of plane motion starting from the simplest case and going to the most difficult case. Many problems of engineering interest can be taken as plane-motion problems; the results of this chapter are hence quite important. The use of $\boldsymbol{M}_A = \dot{\boldsymbol{H}}_A$ applied to three-dimensional motion of a rigid body is considered in Chapter 18 (starred chapter). Students who cover that chapter will find the development of the key equations (the Euler equations) very similar to the development of Eqs. 16.6, the key equations for plane motion.

Recall next that in Chapter 13 we considered the work–energy equations for the plane motion of simple bodies in the process of rolling without slipping. We did this to help illustrate the use of the work–energy equations for an aggregate of particles. Also, this undertaking served to motivate a more detailed study of kinematics of rigid bodies and to set forth in miniature the more general procedures to come later. We are therefore now ready to examine energy methods as applied to rigid bodies in a more general way. This will be done in Part A of Chapter 17. We shall develop the work–energy equations for three-dimensional motion and apply them to all kinds of motions, including plane motions. The student should not have difficulty in going directly to the general case; indeed, a better understanding of the subject should result.

In Part B of Chapter 17, we shall consider the impulse-momentum equations for rigid bodies. This will be an extension of the useful impulse-momentum methods discussed in Chapter 14 for particles and aggregates of particles. Again, we shall be able to go to the general case and then apply the results to three- and two-dimensional motions (plane motions).

PROBLEMS

16.111. A circular plate A is used in electric meters to damp out rotations of a shaft by rotating in a bath of oil. The plate and its shaft have a mass of 300 g and a radius of gyration of 100 mm. If the shaft and plate very thin down from 30 rpm to 20 rpm in 5 sec, what angular acceleration can be developed by a .005 N-m torque when ω of the shaft is 10 rpm? Assume that the damping torque is proportional to the angular speed.

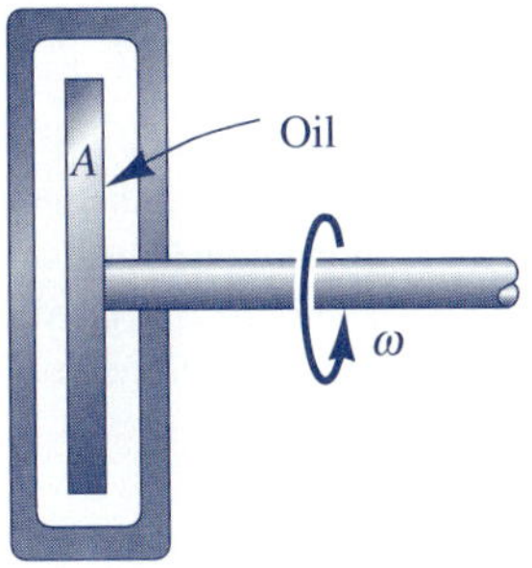

Figure P.16.111.

16.112. The dynamic coefficient of friction for contact surfaces E and G is .2 and for A is .3. If a force P of 250 lb is applied, what will be the tension in the cord HB? Start by assuming no slipping at A. Check your assumption at the end of the calculation.

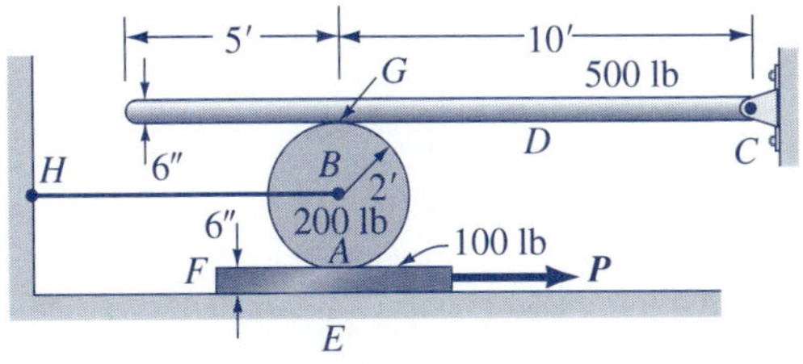

Figure P.16.112.

16.113. A torque T of 15 N-m is applied to a rod AB as shown. At B there is a pin which slides in a frictionless slot in a disc E whose mass is 10 kg and whose radius of gyration is 300 mm. If the system is at rest at the instant shown, what is the angular acceleration of the rod and the disc? The rod has a mass of 18 kg.

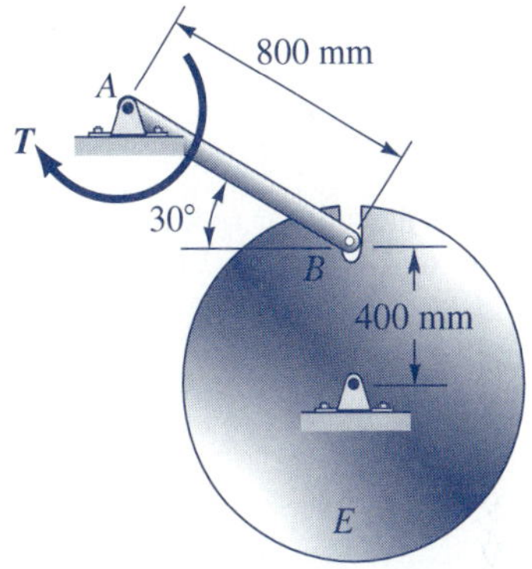

Figure P.16.113.

16.114. A platform A has a torque T applied about its axis of rotation. The platform has a mass of 1,000 kg and a radius of gyration of 2 m. A block B rests on the platform but is prevented from sliding off by very thin stops C and D. The block has a mass of 1 kg and has dimensions 200 mm × 200 mm × 200 mm. The center of mass of the block is at its geometric center. If a torque $T = 20t^2 + 50t$ N-m is applied with t in seconds, when and how does the block first tip? (Because of the small size and mass of B, consider the system to be a slablike body.)

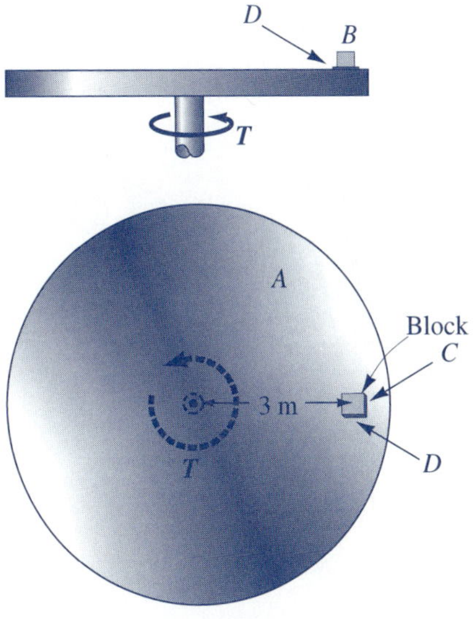

Figure P.16.114.

16.115. A motor B drives a gear C which connects with gear D to driven device A. The top system of shaft and gear has a moment of inertia I_1 about the axis of rotation of 3 lbm-ft^2, whereas the bottom system of device A and gear D has a moment of inertia about its axis of rotation of I_2 equal to 1 lbm-ft^2. If motor B develops a torque given as

$$T = 30 - .02t^2 \text{ in-lb}$$

with t in seconds, what is the angular speed of gear D 6 sec after starting from a stationary configuration? How many revolutions has it undergone during this time interval?

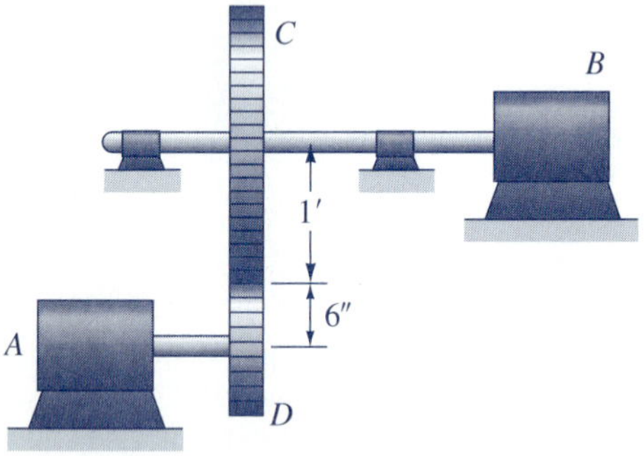

Figure P.16.115.

16.116. A 50-kg container A is being transported by a conveyor as shown. A torque T of 200 N-m is applied to the driving drum. Both driving and driven drums each have a mass of 10 kg and a radius of gyration of 130 mm. The belt has a mass per unit length of 3 kg/m and a dynamic coefficient of friction of .3 with the conveyor bed. What is the acceleration of container A?

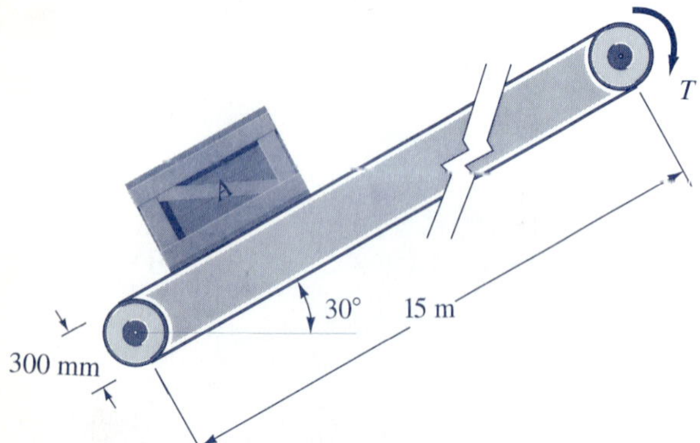

Figure P.16.116.

16.117. A four-bar linkage is shown. A torque T of 10 N-m is applied to member AB, which at the instant shown is rotating clockwise at an angular of speed of 3 rad/sec. Bars AB and CD are 300 mm long. Bar BC is a circular arc of radius 400 mm and length 450 mm. All bars have a mass of 10 kg per meter. What is the angular acceleration of bar AB at the instant shown?

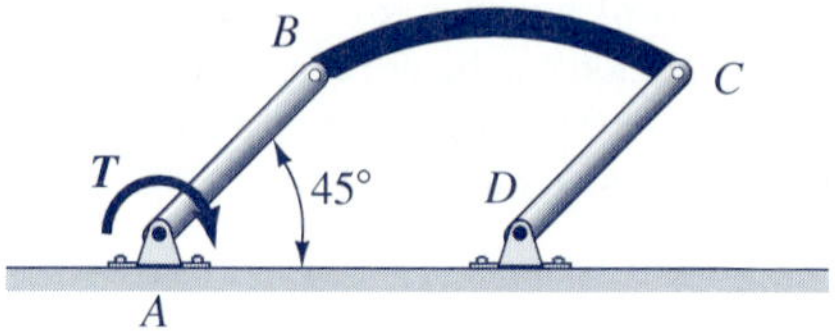

Figure P.16.117.

16.118. Bar AB having a mass of 20 kg is connected to two gears at its ends. Each such gear has a diameter of 300 mm and a mass of 5 kg. The two aforementioned gears mesh with a stationary gear E. If a torque of 100 N-m is applied to the bar AB, what is the angular acceleration of the small gears?

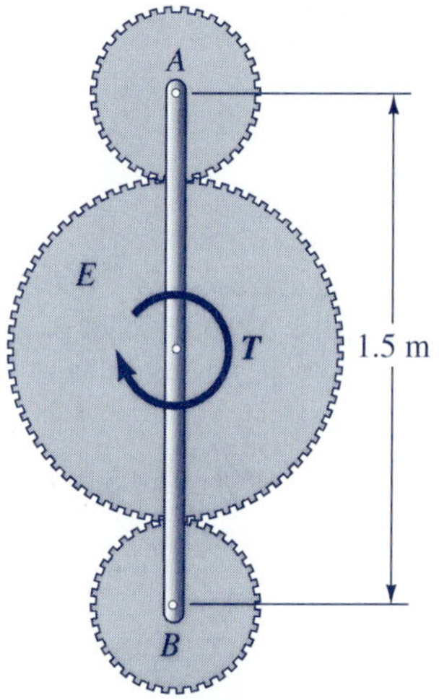

Figure P.16.118.

16.119. An astronaut is assembling a space laboratory in outer space. At the instant shown, he has an H-beam made of composite materials[13] coplanar with two other similar beams. The members are stationary relative to each other. Using a small rocket system that he is wearing, he develops a force F of 200 N always normal to the beam A and in the plane of the beams. At what position d should he exert this force to have the beam A parallel to the tops of beams C and D in 2 sec? What is the acceleration of the center of mass of A at time $t = 1$ sec? Beam A has a mass 200 kg and is 10 m long. Consider beam A to be a long slender rod.

[13]Made up of plastics and various kinds of fibers.

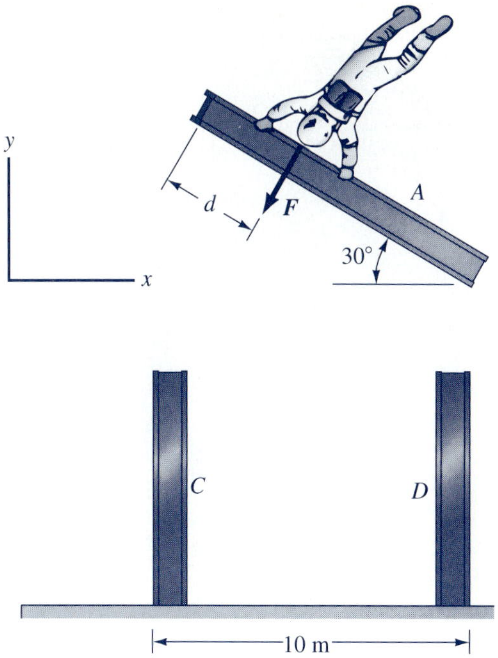

Figure P.16.119.

16.120. Rod *AB* of length 20 ft and weight 200 lb is released from rest at the configuration shown. *AC* is a weightless wire, and the incline at *B* is frictionless. What is the tension in the wire *AC* at this instant?

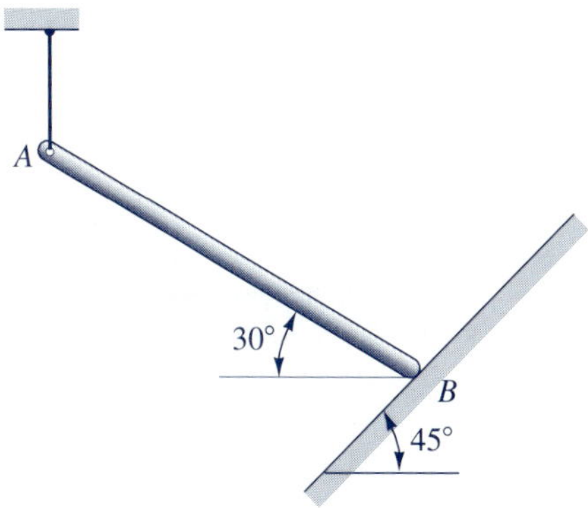

Figure P.16.120.

16.121. Rod *AB* of length 1 m and mass 10 kg is pinned to a disc *D* having a mass of 20 kg and a diameter of .5 m. A torque T = 15 N-m is applied to the disc. What are the angular accelerations of the rod *AB* and disc at this instant?

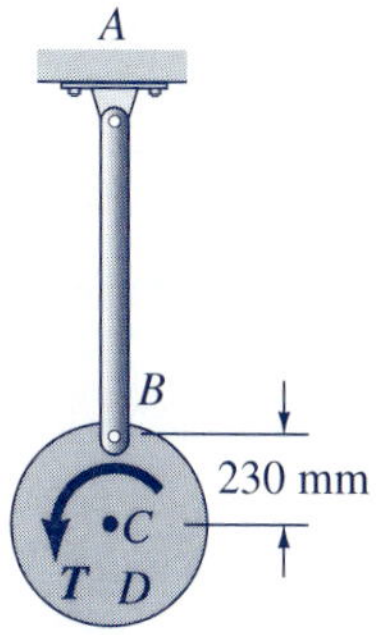

Figure P.16.121.

16.122. A four-bar linkage is shown. Bar *AB* has the following angular motion at the instant shown.

$$\omega_1 = 2 \text{ rad/sec}$$
$$\dot{\omega}_1 = 3 \text{ rad/sec}^2$$

What are the supporting forces at *D* at this instant for the following data?

mass of *AB* = 4 kg
mass of *BC* = 3 kg
mass of *CD* = 6 kg

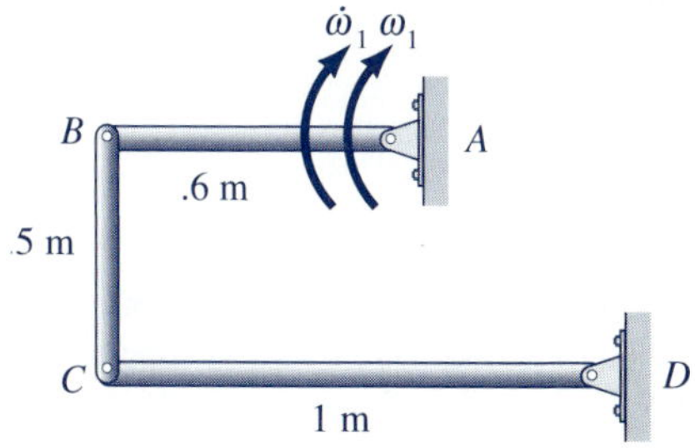

Figure P.16.122.

16.123. Starting from rest, find the acceleration of device A when the 10,000 N force is applied. Proceed as follows:

(a) Draw and label four free-body diagrams.

(b) Write a system of equations whose number equals the number of unknowns.

(c) Do not solve the equations but do put in any numerical data.

Data:

M_J (for 2 wheels) = 50 kg

M_E (for 2 wheels) = 100 kg

M_A = 220 kg

M_C = 40 kg

M_E (for 2 wheels) = 100 kg

k_J = .08 m

k_E = 0.12 m

D_J = 0.2 m

D_E = 0.3 m

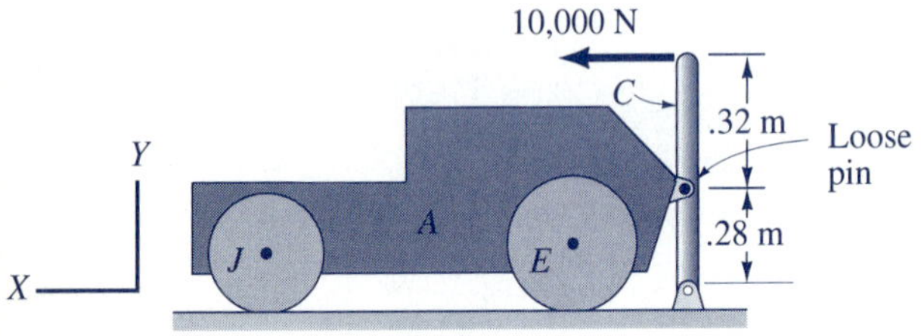

Figure P.16.123.

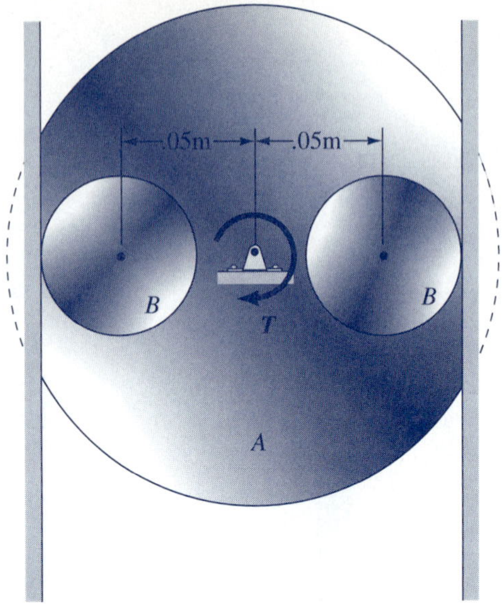

Figure P.16.124.

16.124. A cylinder A can rotate freely about its fixed centerline. Two smaller identical cylinders B have axes of rotation on cylinder A and initially will start to roll without slipping along the indicated walls. What is the initial angular acceleration of cylinder A starting from rest under the action of a torque T = 5 N-m? The system is in a vertical plane. The following data apply:

M_A = 1.8 kg M_B = 1.4 kg r_A = 1.3 m r_B = .04 m

16.125. In Example 15.5 determine the force components at pins A and B. The mass of rod AB is 8 kg and the mass of BC is 5 kg. Use the kinematic results of the example.

16.126. A 10-m I-beam having a mass of 400 kg is being pulled by an astronaut with his space propulsion rig as shown. The force is 40 N and is always in the same direction. Initially, the beam is stationary relative to the astronaut, and the connecting cord is at right angles to the beam. Consider the beam to be a long slender rod. What is the angular acceleration when the beam has rotated 15°? What is the position of the center of mass after 10 sec? (Can you integrate the differential equation for θ to get familiar functions? Explain.)

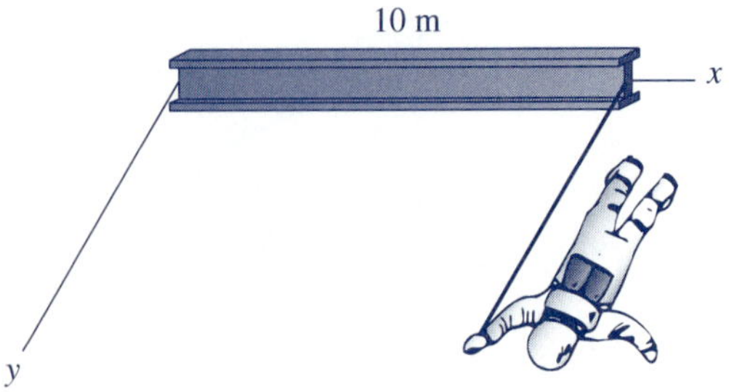

Figure P.16.126.

16.127. A rectangular box having a mass of 20 kg is being transported on a conveyor belt. The center of gravity of the box is 150 mm above the conveyor belt, as shown. What is the maximum starting torque T for which the box will not tip? The belt has a mass per unit length of 2 kg/m, and the driving and driven drums have a mass of 5 kg each and a radius of gyration of 130 mm. The dynamic coefficient of friction between the belt and conveyor bed is .2.

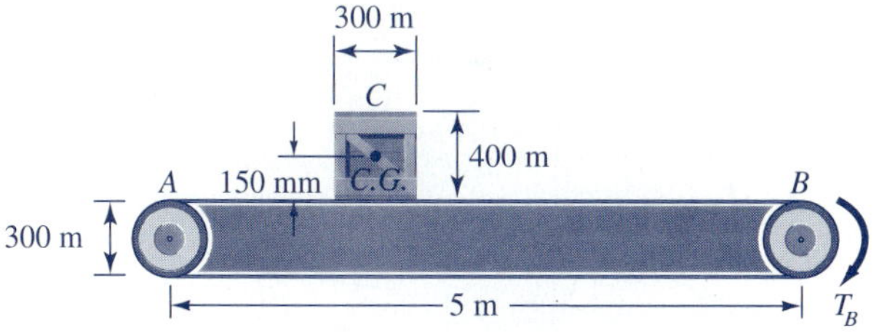

Figure P.16.127.

16.128. A ring is shown supported by wire AB and a smooth surface. The ring has a mass of 10 kg and a mean radius of 2 m. A body D having a mass of 3 kg is fixed to the ring as shown. If the wire is severed, what is the acceleration of body D?

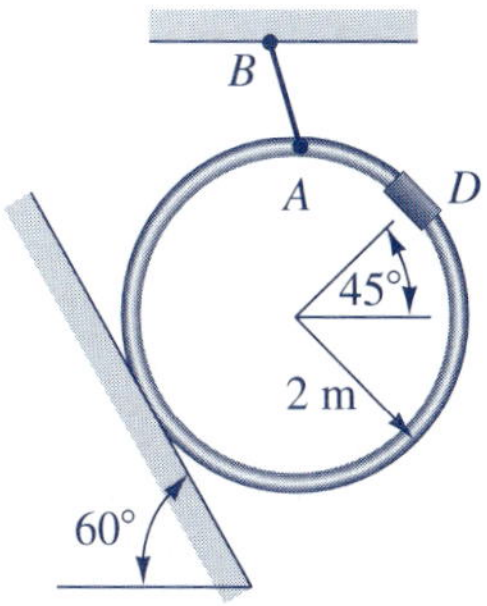

Figure P.16.128.

16.129. If the rod shown is released from rest at the configuration shown, what are the supporting forces at A and B at that instant? The rod weighs 100 lb and is 10 ft long. The static coefficient of friction is .2 for all surface contacts.

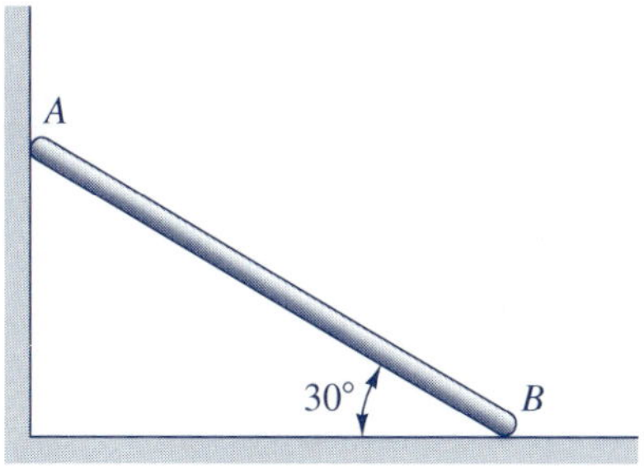

Figure P.16.129.

16.130. Do Problem 16.129 for the case where end A is moving downward at a speed of 10 ft/sec at the instant shown and where $\mu_d = .2$.

16.131. In Problem 16.129, find by inspection the instantaneous axis of rotation for the rod. What are the magnitude and direction of the acceleration vector for the axis of rotation at the instant the rod is released? We know from Problem 16.129 that $\dot{\omega} = 3.107$ rad/sec^2 and $\boldsymbol{a}_c = 7.77\boldsymbol{i} - 13.45\boldsymbol{j}$ ft/sec^2 for the center of mass.

16.132. Identical bars AB and BC are pinned as shown with frictionless pins. Each bar is 2.3 m in length and has a mass of 9 kg. A force of 450 N is exerted at C when the bars are inclined at 60°. What is the angular acceleration of the bars?

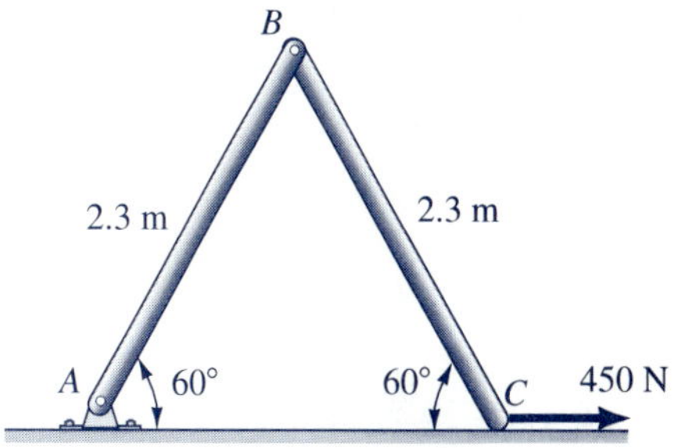

Figure P.16.132.

16.133. A compressor is shown. Member AB is rotating at a constant speed ω_1 of 100 rpm. Member BC has a mass of 2 kg and piston C has a mass of 1 kg. The pressure p on the piston is 10,000 Pa. At the instant shown, what are the forces transmitted by pins B and C?

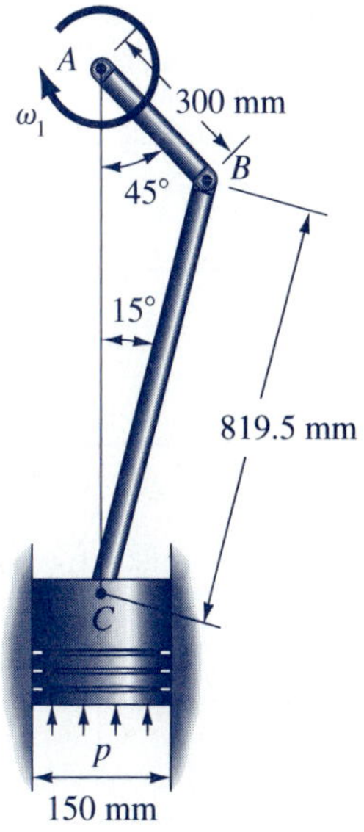

Figure P.16.133.

***16.134.** A thin vertical shaft rotates with angular speed ω of 5 rad/sec in bearings A and D as shown in the diagram. A uniform plate B weighing 50 lb is attached to the shaft as is a disc C weighing 30 lb. What are the bearing reactions at the configuration shown? The shaft weighs 20 lb and the thickness of disc and plate is 2 in.

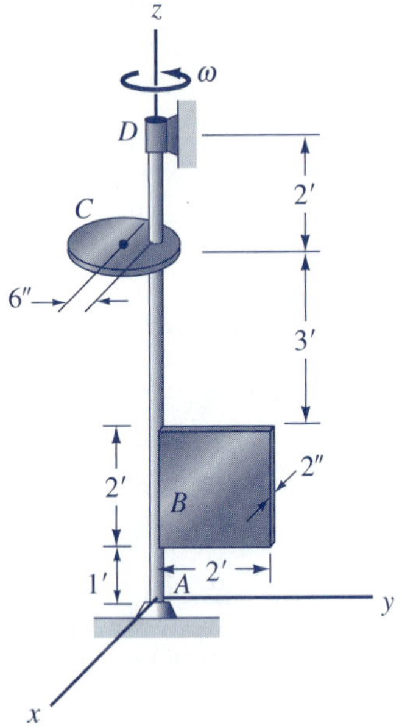

Figure P.16.134.

***16.135.** Do Problem 16.100 for the case where $\omega = 5$ rad/sec at the instant of interest.

***16.136.** In Example 16.10, balance the rotating system by properly placing 36-N spherical masses in balancing planes 300 mm inside from the bearings A and B. Assume that the balancing masses are particles.

16.137. A 25-lb cylinder which is spinning at a rate ω_0 of 500 rpm is placed on an 8 degree incline. The coefficients of friction are $\mu_s = .4$ and $\mu_d = .3$. How far does the cylinder move before there is rolling without slipping? How much time elapses before the cylinder stops moving instantaneously?

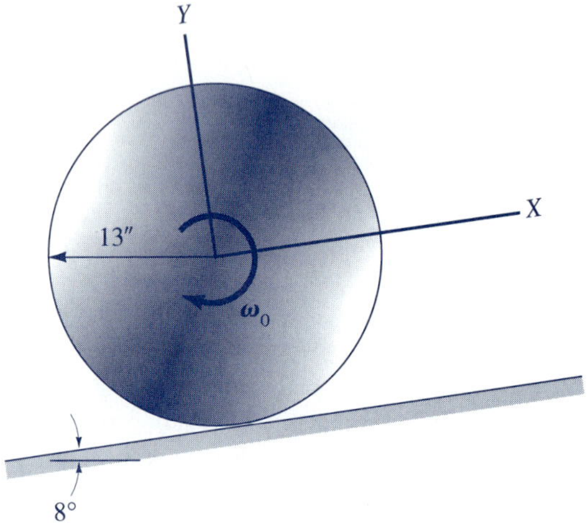

Figure P.16.137.

16.138. In Example 15.11, take ω_2 and $\dot{\omega}_2$ both equal to zero but keep all other data. Determine the force system at A knowing that the following data apply:

$$W_{AB} = 800 \text{ N} \qquad M_{man\text{-}cockpit} = 135 \text{ kg}$$

Note that the man and cockpit are translating and can be considered as a particle of mass 135 kg.

CHAPTER 17

Energy and Impulse–Momentum Methods for Rigid Bodies

17.1 Introduction

Let us pause to reflect on where we have been thus far in dynamics and where we are about to go. In Chapter 12, you will recall, we worked directly with *Newton's law* and integrated it several times to consider the motion of a *particle*. Then, in Chapter 13 and 14, we formulated certain useful integrated forms from *Newton's law* and thereby presented the *energy methods* and the *linear impulse-momentum* methods also for a *particle*. At the end of Chapter 14, we derived the important *angular momentum* equation, $\boldsymbol{M}_A = \dot{\boldsymbol{H}}_A$. In Chapter 16, we returned to Newton's law and along with the angular momentum equation, $\boldsymbol{M}_A = \dot{\boldsymbol{H}}_A$, carried out integrations to solve *plane motion* problems of rigid bodies. In the present chapter, we shall come back to *energy methods* and *linear impulse-momentum methods*—this time for the *general motion* of rigid bodies. In addition, we shall use a certain integrated form of the angular momentum equation $\boldsymbol{M}_A = \dot{\boldsymbol{H}}_A$, namely the *angular impulse-momentum equation*. These equations at times will be applied to a single rigid body. At other times, we shall apply them to several interconnected rigid bodies considered as a whole. When we do the latter, we say we are dealing with a *system* of rigid bodies. We shall consider energy methods first.

Part A: Energy Methods

17.2 Kinetic Energy of a Rigid Body

First, we shall derive a convenient expression for the kinetic energy of a rigid body. We have already found (Section 13.7) that the kinetic energy of an aggregate of particles relative to any reference is the sum of two parts, which we list again as:

1. The kinetic energy of a hypothetical particle that has a mass equal to the total mass of the system and a motion corresponding to that of the mass center of the system, plus
2. The kinetic energy of the particles relative to the mass center.

Mathematically,

$$\text{KE} = \tfrac{1}{2} M |\dot{\boldsymbol{r}}_c|^2 + \tfrac{1}{2} \sum_{i=1}^{n} m_i |\dot{\boldsymbol{\rho}}_i|^2 \tag{17.1}$$

where $\boldsymbol{\rho}_i$ is the position vector from the mass center to the ith particle.

Let us now consider the foregoing equation as applied to a rigid body which is a special "aggregate of particles" (Fig. 17.1). In such a case, the velocity of any particle relative to the mass center becomes

$$\dot{\boldsymbol{\rho}}_i = \boldsymbol{\omega} \times \boldsymbol{\rho}_i \tag{17.2}$$

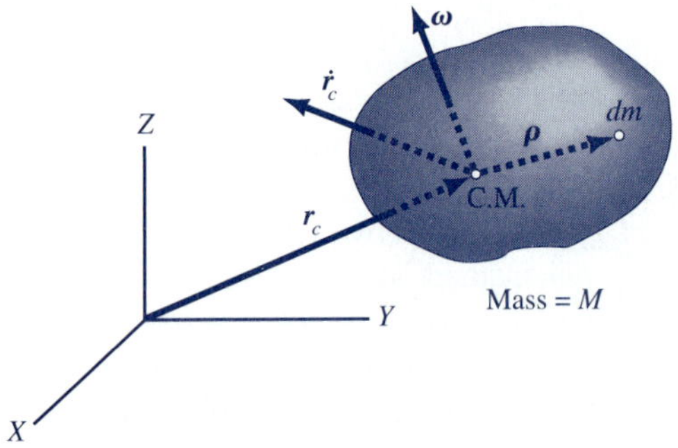

Figure 17.1. Rigid body.

where $\boldsymbol{\omega}$ is the angular velocity of the body relative to reference XYZ in which we are computing the kinetic energy. For the rigid body, the discrete particles of mass m_i become a continuum of infinitesimal particles each of mass dm, and the summation in Eq. 17.1 then becomes an integration. Thus, we can say for the rigid body, replacing $|\dot{\boldsymbol{r}}_c|^2$ by V_c^2.

$$\text{KE} = \tfrac{1}{2} M V_c^2 + \tfrac{1}{2} \iiint_M |\boldsymbol{\omega} \times \boldsymbol{\rho}|^2 \, dm \tag{17.3}$$

where $\boldsymbol{\rho}$ represents the position vector from the center of mass to any element of mass dm. Let us now choose a set of orthogonal directions xyz at the center of mass, so we can carry out the preceding integration in terms of the scalar components of $\boldsymbol{\omega}$ and $\boldsymbol{\rho}$. This step is illustrated in Fig. 17.2. We first express the integral in Eq. 17.3 in the following manner:

$$\iiint_M |\boldsymbol{\omega} \times \boldsymbol{\rho}|^2 \, dm = \iiint_M (\boldsymbol{\omega} \times \boldsymbol{\rho}) \cdot (\boldsymbol{\omega} \times \boldsymbol{\rho}) \, dm \tag{17.4}$$

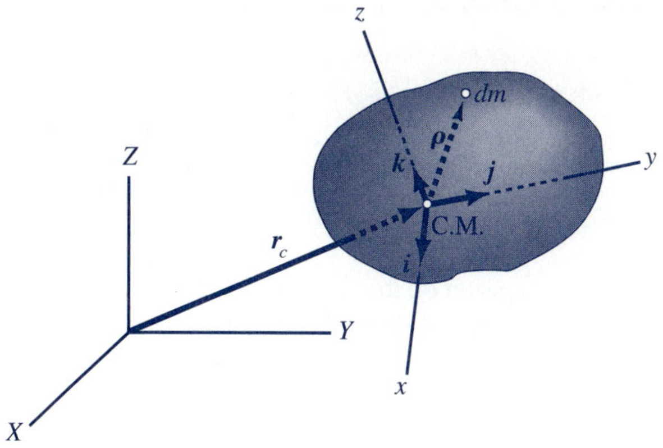

Figure 17.2. Fix xyz at center of mass.

Inserting the scalar components, we get:

$$\iiint_M |\boldsymbol{\omega}\times\boldsymbol{\rho}|^2\,dm = \iiint_M \Big\{\Big[\big(\omega_x\boldsymbol{i}+\omega_y\boldsymbol{j}+\omega_z\boldsymbol{k}\big)\times\big(x\boldsymbol{i}+y\boldsymbol{j}+z\boldsymbol{k}\big)\Big]$$
$$\cdot\Big[\big(\omega_x\boldsymbol{i}+\omega_y\boldsymbol{j}+\omega_z\boldsymbol{k}\big)\times\big(x\boldsymbol{i}+y\boldsymbol{j}+z\boldsymbol{k}\big)\Big]\Big\}\,dm$$

Carrying out first the cross products and then the dot product in the integrand and collecting terms, we form the following relation on extracting the ω's from the integrals.

$$\begin{aligned}\iiint_M |\boldsymbol{\omega}\times\boldsymbol{\rho}|^2\,dm = {} & \left[\iiint_M (z^2+y^2)\,dm\right]\omega_x^2 - \left[\iiint_M xy\,dm\right]\omega_x\omega_y - \left[\iiint_M xz\,dm\right]\omega_x\omega_z - \\ & \left[\iiint_M yx\,dm\right]\omega_y\omega_x + \left[\iiint_M (x^2+z^2)\,dm\right]\omega_y^2 - \left[\iiint_M yz\,dm\right]\omega_y\omega_z - \\ & \left[\iiint_M zx\,dm\right]\omega_z\omega_x - \left[\iiint_M zy\,dm\right]\omega_z\omega_y + \left[\iiint_M (x^2+y^2)\,dm\right]\omega_z^2\end{aligned}$$

You will recognize that the integrals are the moments and products of inertia for the xyz reference. Thus,[1]

$$\begin{aligned}\iiint_M |\boldsymbol{\omega}\times\boldsymbol{\rho}|^2\,dm = {} & I_{xx}\omega_x^2 - I_{xy}\omega_x\omega_y - I_{xz}\omega_x\omega_z \\ & -I_{yx}\omega_y\omega_x + I_{yy}\omega_y^2 - I_{yz}\omega_y\omega_z \\ & -I_{zx}\omega_z\omega_x - I_{zy}\omega_z\omega_y + I_{zz}\omega_z^2\end{aligned}$$

[1]Note that we have deliberately used a matrixlike array for ease in remembering the formulation.

We can now give the kinetic energy of a rigid body in the following form:

$$\begin{aligned}\text{KE} = \tfrac{1}{2}MV_c^2 + \tfrac{1}{2}(&I_{xx}\omega_x^2 - I_{xy}\omega_x\omega_y - I_{xz}\omega_x\omega_z\\ &-I_{yx}\omega_y\omega_x + I_{yy}\omega_y^2 - I_{yz}\omega_y\omega_z\\ &-I_{zx}\omega_z\omega_x - I_{zy}\omega_z\omega_y + I_{zz}\omega_z^2)\end{aligned} \tag{17.5}$$

Note that the first expression on the right side of the preceding equation is the kinetic energy of translation of the rigid body using the center of mass, while the second expression is the kinetic energy of rotation of the rigid body about its center of mass. If principal axes are chosen, Eq. 17.5 becomes

$$\text{KE} = \tfrac{1}{2}MV_c^2 + \tfrac{1}{2}(I_{xx}\omega_x^2 + I_{yy}\omega_y^2 + I_{zz}\omega_z^2) \tag{17.6}$$

Note that for this condition the kinetic energy terms for rotation have the same form as the kinetic energy term that is due to translation, with the moment of inertia corresponding to mass and angular velocity corresponding to linear velocity.

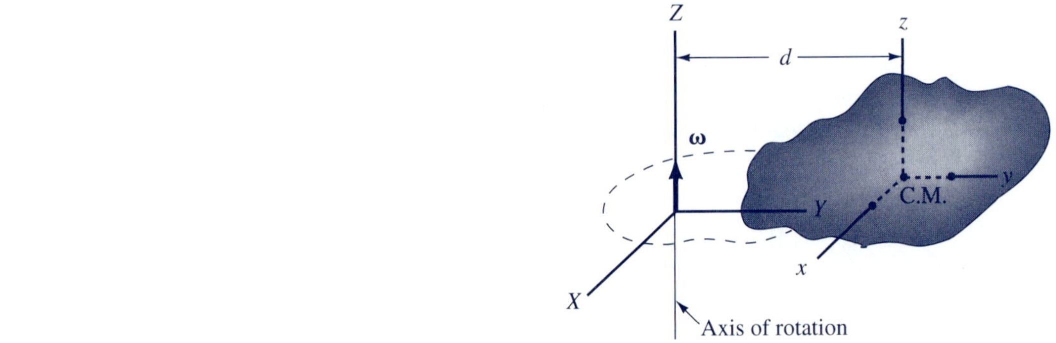

Figure 17.3. Rigid body undergoing pure rotation about Z axis.

As a special case, we shall consider the calculation of kinetic energy of any rigid body undergoing *pure rotation* relative to *XYZ* with angular velocity $\boldsymbol{\omega}$ about an actual axis of rotation[2] going through part of the body or through a rigid hypothetical massless extension of the body. We have shown this situation in Fig. 17.3, where the *Z* axis is chosen to be collinear with the $\boldsymbol{\omega}$ vector and the axis of rotation. The reference *xyz* at the center of mass is chosen parallel to *XYZ*. Clearly, $\omega_x = \omega_y = 0$ and $\omega_z = \omega$ so Eq. 17.5 becomes

$$\text{KE} = \tfrac{1}{2}MV_c^2 + \tfrac{1}{2}I_{zz}\omega^2$$

[2]An actual axis of rotation in *XYZ* is a line along which the velocity relative to *XYZ* is zero.

where I_{zz} is about an axis which goes through the mass center parallel to Z. Note that $V_c = \omega d$, where d is the distance between the axis of rotation Z and the z axis at the center of mass. We then have

$$\begin{aligned} \text{KE} &= \tfrac{1}{2}(Md^2)\omega^2 + \tfrac{1}{2}I_{zz}\omega^2 \\ &= \tfrac{1}{2}(I_{zz} + Md^2)\omega^2 \end{aligned}$$

But the bracketed expression is the moment of inertia of the body about the axis of rotation Z. Denoting this moment of inertia simply as I, we get for the kinetic energy:

$$\text{KE} = \tfrac{1}{2}I\omega^2 \qquad (17.7)$$

This simple expression for pure rotation is completely analogous to the kinetic energy of a body in pure translation.

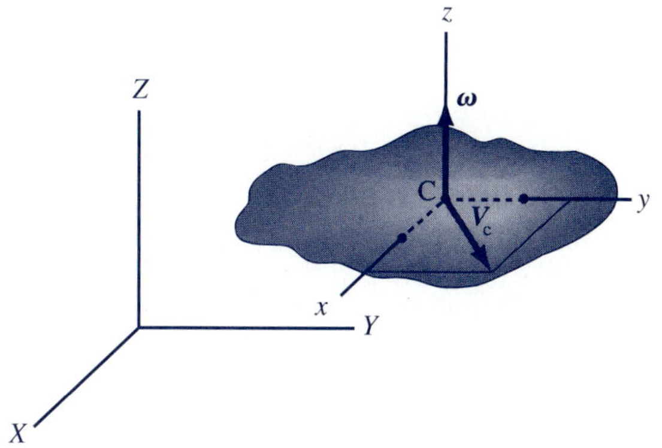

Figure 17.4. Plane motion relative to the *XY* plane.

For a body undergoing *general plane motion* (see Fig. 17.4) parallel to the XY plane, where xyz are taken at the center of mass and oriented parallel to XYZ, we get from Eq. 17.5:

$$\text{KE} = \tfrac{1}{2}MV_c^2 + \tfrac{1}{2}I_{zz}\omega_z^2 \qquad (17.8)$$

We now illustrate the calculation of the kinetic energy in the following example.

Example 17.1

Compute the kinetic energy of the crank system in the configuration shown in Fig. 17.5. Piston A weighs 2 lb, rod AB is 2 ft long and weighs 5 lb, and flywheel D weighs 100 lb with a radius of gyration of 1.2 ft. The radius r is 1 ft. At the instant of interest, piston A is moving to the right at a speed V of 10 ft/sec.

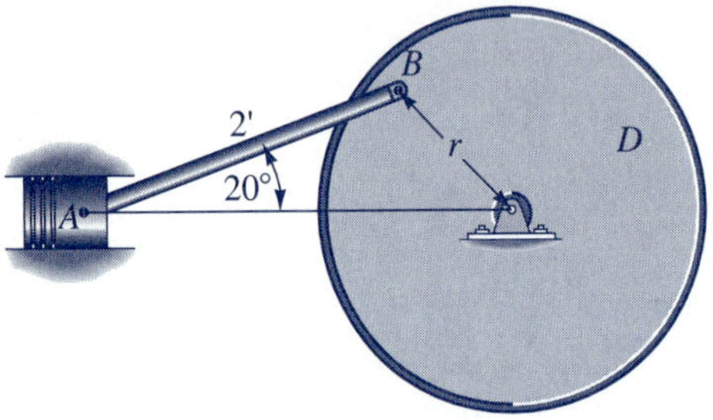

Figure 17.5. Crank system.

We have here a translatory motion (piston A), a plane motion (rod AB), and a pure rotation (flywheel D). Thus, for piston A we have for the kinetic energy:

$$(\text{KE})_A = \frac{1}{2}MV^2 = \frac{1}{2}\left(\frac{2}{32.2}\right)(10^2) = 3.11 \text{ ft-lb} \tag{a}$$

For the rod AB, we must first consider *kinematical* aspects of the motion. For this purpose we have shown rod AB again in Fig. 17.6, where V_A is the known velocity of point A and V_B is the velocity vector for point B oriented at an angle α such that V_B is perpendicular to OB. We can readily find α for the configuration of interest by trigonometric considerations of triangle ABO. To do this, we use the law of sines to first compute the angle β:

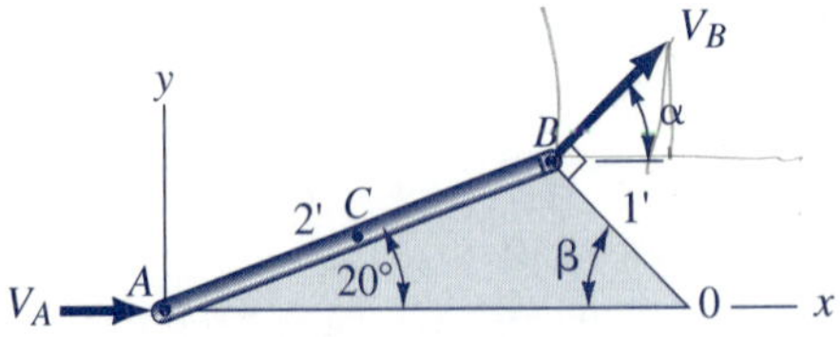

Figure 17.6. Kinematics of rod AB.

$$\frac{2}{\sin\beta} = \frac{1}{\sin 20°}$$

Therefore,

$$\beta = 43.2° \tag{b}$$

Example 17.1 (Continued)

Because V_B is at right angles to OB, we have for the angle α:

$$\alpha = 90^\circ - \beta = 46.8^\circ \qquad \text{(c)}$$

From **kinematics** of a rigid body we can now say:

$$\boldsymbol{V}_B = \boldsymbol{V}_A + (\omega_{AB}\boldsymbol{k}) \times \boldsymbol{\rho}_{AB}$$

Hence,

$$V_B(\cos\alpha\boldsymbol{i} + \sin\alpha\boldsymbol{j}) = 10\boldsymbol{i} + \omega_{AB}\boldsymbol{k} \times (2\cos 20^\circ\boldsymbol{i} + 2\sin 20^\circ\boldsymbol{j})$$

$$\therefore\ V_B(.648\boldsymbol{i} + .729\boldsymbol{j}) = 10\boldsymbol{i} + 1.879\omega_{AB}\boldsymbol{j} - .684\omega_{AB}\boldsymbol{i} \qquad \text{(d)}$$

From this we solve for ω_{AB} and V_B. Thus,

$$\begin{aligned} V_B &= 10.53 \text{ ft/sec} \\ \omega_{AB} &= 4.09 \text{ rad/sec} \end{aligned} \qquad \text{(e)}$$

To get the velocity of the mass center C of AB, we proceed as follows:

$$\begin{aligned} \boldsymbol{V}_C &= \boldsymbol{V}_A + (\omega_{AB}\boldsymbol{k}) \times \boldsymbol{\rho}_{AC} \\ &= 10\boldsymbol{i} + 4.09\boldsymbol{k} \times (.940\boldsymbol{i} + .342\boldsymbol{j}) \\ &= 10\boldsymbol{i} + 3.84\boldsymbol{j} - 1.399\boldsymbol{i} = 8.60\boldsymbol{i} + 3.84\boldsymbol{j} \text{ ft/sec} \end{aligned} \qquad \text{(f)}$$

We can now calculate $(\text{KE})_{AB}$, the kinetic energy of the rod:

$$\begin{aligned} (\text{KE})_{AB} &= \frac{1}{2}M_{AB}V_c^2 + \frac{1}{2}I_{zz}\omega_{AB}^2 \\ &= \frac{1}{2}\left(\frac{5}{32.2}\right)(8.60^2 + 3.84^2) + \frac{1}{2}\left(\frac{1}{12}\frac{5}{32.2}2^2\right)(4.09^2) \\ &= 7.32 \text{ ft-lb} \end{aligned} \qquad \text{(g)}$$

Finally, we consider the flywheel D. The angular speed ω_D can easily be computed using V_B of Eq. (e). Thus,

$$\omega_D = \frac{V_B}{r} = \frac{10.53}{1} = 10.53 \text{ rad/sec} \qquad \text{(h)}$$

Accordingly, we get for $(\text{KE})_D$:

$$(\text{KE})_D = \left[\frac{1}{2}\left(\frac{100}{32.2}\right)(1.2^2)\right](10.53^2) = 248 \text{ ft-lb} \qquad \text{(i)}$$

The total kinetic energy of the system can now be given as

$$\begin{aligned} \text{KE} &= (\text{KE})_A + (\text{KE})_{AB} + (\text{KE})_D \\ &= 3.11 + 7.32 + 248 = \boxed{258 \text{ ft-lb}} \end{aligned} \qquad \text{(j)}$$

17.3 Work–Energy Relations

We presented in Chapter 13 the work–energy relation for a *single* particle m_i in a *system* of n particles (see Fig. 17.7) to reach the following equation:

$$\int_1^2 \boldsymbol{F}_1 \cdot d\boldsymbol{r}_i + \int_1^2 \sum_{\substack{j=1 \\ j \neq i}}^{n} \boldsymbol{f}_{ij} \cdot d\boldsymbol{r}_i = \tfrac{1}{2}(m_i V_i^2)_2 - \tfrac{1}{2}(m_i V_i^2)_1 = (\Delta \mathrm{KE})_i \quad (17.9)$$

where $\boldsymbol{f}_{ij}$ is the force from particle j onto particle i and is an internal force. (Note that since a particle cannot exert a force on itself, $\boldsymbol{f}_{ii} = \boldsymbol{0}$.) Now consider that the particle m_i is part of a rigid body, as shown in Fig. 17.8. From **Newton's third law** we can say that

$$\boldsymbol{f}_{ij} = -\boldsymbol{f}_{ji} \quad (17.10)$$

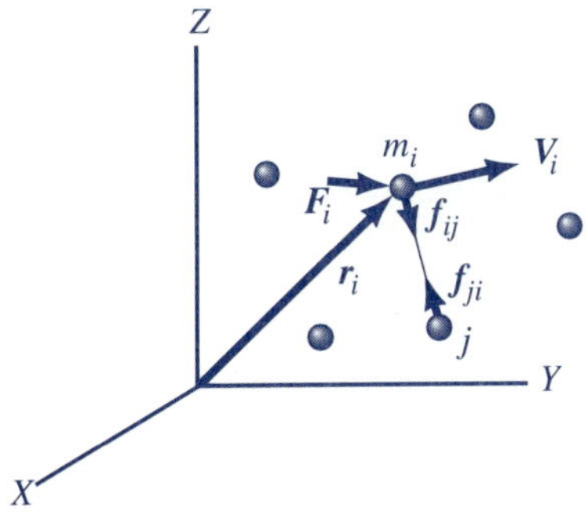

Figure 17.7. System of particles.

It might be intuitively obvious to the reader that for any motion of a rigid body the totality of internal forces $\boldsymbol{f}_{ij}$ can do no work. If not, read the following proof to verify this claim.

Suppose the rigid body moves an infinitesimal amount. We employ *Chasles' theorem*, whereby we give the entire body a displacement $d\boldsymbol{r}$ corresponding to the actual displacement of particle m_i (see Fig. 17.8). The total work done by $\boldsymbol{f}_{ij}$ and $\boldsymbol{f}_{ji}$ is clearly zero for this displacement as a result of

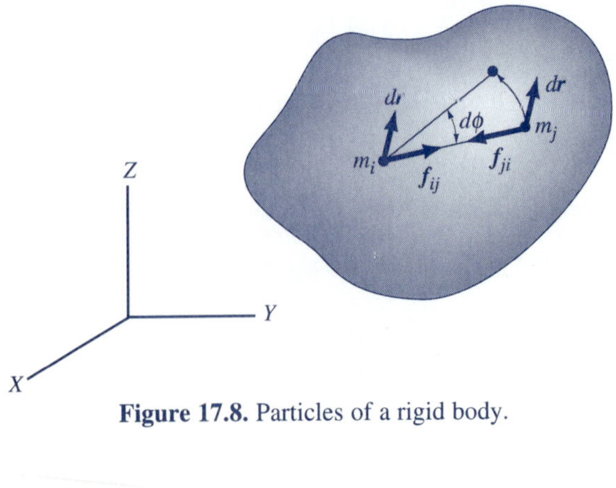

Figure 17.8. Particles of a rigid body.

Eq. 17.10. In addition, we will have a rotation $d\boldsymbol{\phi}$ about an axis of rotation going through m_i. We can decompose $d\boldsymbol{\phi}$ into orthogonal components, such that one component $d\phi_1$ is along the line between m_i and m_j (and thus collinear with $\boldsymbol{f}_{ij}$) and two components are at right angles to this line (see Fig. 17.9). Clearly, the work done by the forces $\boldsymbol{f}_{ij}$ and $\boldsymbol{f}_{ji}$ for $d\boldsymbol{\phi}_1$ is zero. Also, the movement of m_j for the other components of $d\boldsymbol{\phi}$ is at right angles to $\boldsymbol{f}_{ji}$, and again there is no work done. Consequently, the work done by $\boldsymbol{f}_{ij}$ and $\boldsymbol{f}_{ji}$ is zero during the total infinitesimal movement. And since a finite movement is a sum of such infinitesimal movements, the work done for a finite movement of m_i and m_j is zero. But a rigid body consists of *pairs* of interacting particles such as m_i and m_j. Hence, on summing Eq. 17.9 for all particles of a rigid body, we can conclude that the *work done by forces internal to a rigid body for any rigid-body movement is always zero.*

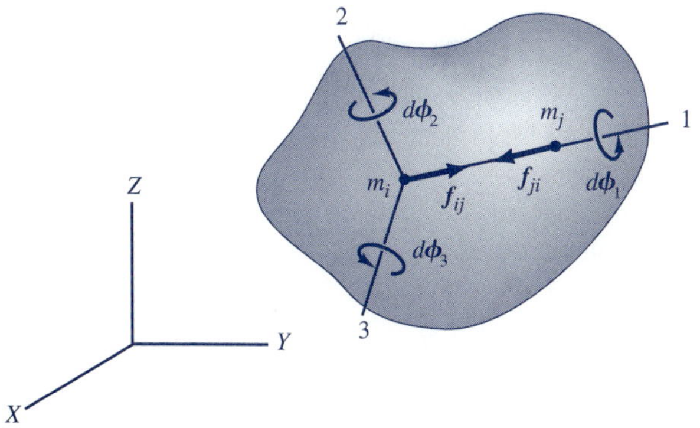

Figure 17.9. Rectangular components of $d\boldsymbol{\phi}$.

We must clearly point out here that although the internal forces *in* a rigid body can do no work, forces *between rigid bodies* of a *system* of rigid bodies *can* do a net amount of work even though Newton's third law applies and even though these forces are *internal to the system.* We shall say more about this later when we discuss systems of rigid bodies.

We accordingly compute the work done on a rigid body in moving from configuration I to configuration II by summing the work terms for all the *external* forces. Thus, for the body shown in Fig. 17.10, we can express the work between I and II in the following manner:

$$(\text{work})_{\text{I,II}} = \underset{\text{path 1}}{\int_{\text{I}}^{\text{II}}} \boldsymbol{F}_1 \cdot d\boldsymbol{s}_1 + \underset{\text{path 2}}{\int_{\text{I}}^{\text{II}}} \boldsymbol{F}_2 \cdot d\boldsymbol{s}_2 + \cdots + \underset{\text{path } n}{\int_{\text{I}}^{\text{II}}} \boldsymbol{F}_n \cdot d\boldsymbol{s}_n \quad (17.11)$$

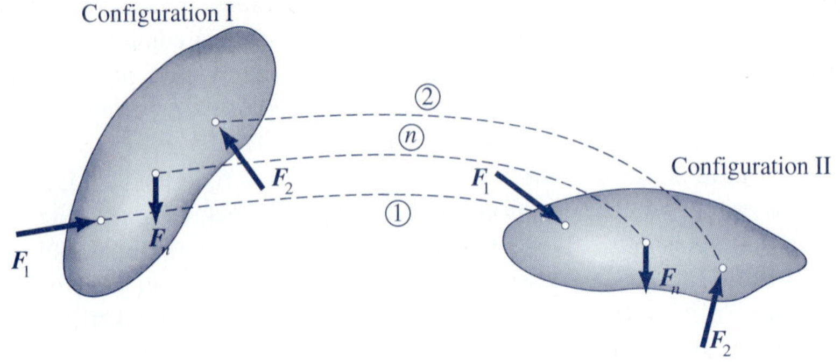

Figure 17.10. Rigid body moves from configuration I to configuration II.

In this equation, we must remember, the dot products of *nonconservative* forces are to be integrated over the *actual paths* along which the *points of application of the forces on the rigid body move*. We must take into account the variations of direction and magnitude of these nonconservative forces along their paths. For conservative forces we can use the concept of potential energy.

Although we can treat *couples* as sets of discrete forces in the foregoing manner, it is often useful to take advantage of the special properties of couples and to treat them separately. It should be a simple matter for you to show (see Fig. 17.11) that a torque T about an axis upon rotating an angle $d\theta$ about the axis does an amount of work $d\mathcal{W}_K$ given as

$$d\mathcal{W}_K = T\,d\theta$$

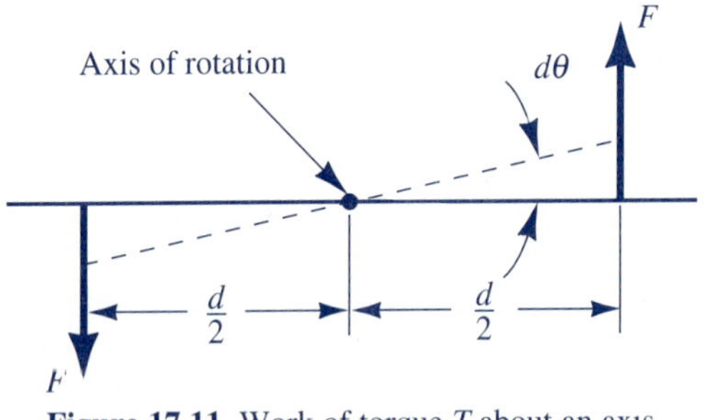

Figure 17.11. Work of torque T about an axis rotating an angle $d\theta$ about the axis.

Dividing and multiplying by dt, we can say further that

$$d\mathcal{W}_K = T\frac{d\theta}{dt}\,dt = T\dot{\theta}\,dt$$

Integrating, we get

$$\mathcal{W}_K = \int_{t_1}^{t_2} T\dot{\theta}\,dt \qquad (17.12)$$

In this case the torque T and angular speed $\dot{\theta}$ are about the same axis. The generalization of Eq. 17.12 for any moment $\boldsymbol{M}$ and any angular velocity $\boldsymbol{\omega}$ (see Fig. 17.12) then is

$$\mathcal{W}_K = \int_{t_1}^{t_2} \boldsymbol{M} \cdot \boldsymbol{\omega}\, dt \qquad (17.13)$$

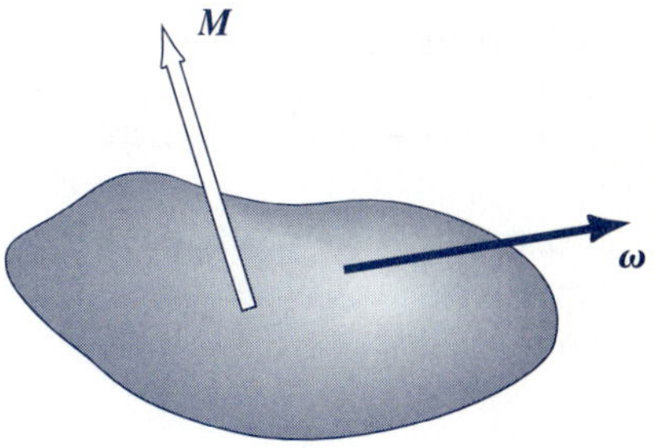

Figure 17.12. $d\mathcal{W}_K = \boldsymbol{M} \cdot \boldsymbol{\omega}\, dt$.

We thus have formulations for finding the work done by external forces and couples on a rigid body. For the conservative forces, we know from Chapter 13 that we can use for work a quantity that is minus the change in potential energy from I to II without having to specify the path taken.

Using this information for computing work, we can then say for any rigid body:

$$\mathcal{W}_K \text{ from I to II} = \Delta\text{KE} \qquad (17.14)$$

where $\mathcal{W}_K$ is the work by *external* forces.

If there are only *conservative* external forces present, we can also say for the rigid body:

$$(\text{PE})_{\text{I}} + (\text{KE})_{\text{I}} = (\text{PE})_{\text{II}} + (\text{KE})_{\text{II}} \qquad (17.15)$$

If both conservative *and* nonconservative external forces are present, we can say:

$$\text{nonconservative } \mathcal{W}_K \text{ from I to II} = \Delta\text{PE} + \Delta\text{KE} \qquad (17.16)$$

These three equations parallel the three we developed for a particle in Chapter 13.

The foregoing equations are expressed for a *single* rigid body. For a *system* of *interconnected rigid* bodies, we distinguish between two types of forces internal to the system. They are

1. Forces internal to any rigid body of the system.
2. Forces *between* rigid bodies of the system.

For a system of bodies, as in the case of a single rigid body, forces of category 1 can do no work. However, if the forces *between two bodies* of 2 system do not move the same distance over the same path, then there may be a net amount of work done on the system by these internal forces. We must include such work contributions when employing Eqs. 17.14–17.16 *for a system of interconnected rigid bodes.*[3] Example 17.4 is an example of this situation.

[3]Recall from Chapter 13, that Eq. 17.16 and hence Eqs. 17.14 and 17.15 are valid for *any* aggregate of particles provided we include the work of internal forces both conservative and nonconservative.

Example 17.2

Neglect the weight of the cable in Fig. 17.13, and find the speed of the 450-N block A after it has moved 1.7 m along the incline from a position of rest. The static coefficient of friction along the incline is .32, and the dynamic coefficient of friction is .30. Consider the pulley B to be a uniform cylinder.

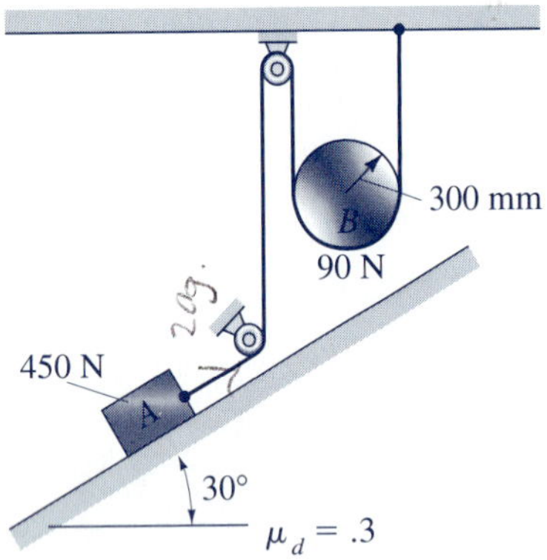

Figure 17.13. Pulley system.

We must first decide which way the block moves along the incline. To overcome friction and move down the incline, the block must create a force in the downward direction of the cable exceeding 90/2 = 45 N. Considering the block A alone (see Fig. 17.14), we can readily decide that the maximum force T_1 to allow A to start sliding downward is

$$\begin{aligned}(T_1)_{max} &= -(.32)\,N + 450 \sin 30° \\ &= -(.32)(450)\cos 30° + 450 \sin 30° = 100.3 \text{ N}\end{aligned}$$

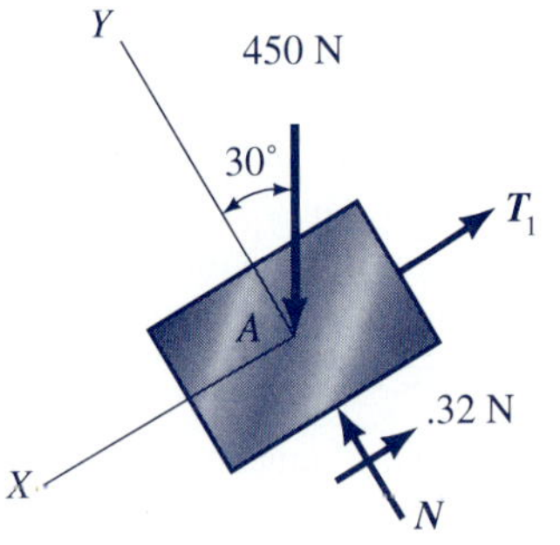

Figure 17.14. Free body of block.

Clearly, the block goes down the incline.

We now use the **work–kinetic energy** equation separately for each body. Thus, for the block we have, using now the dynamic coefficient of friction

$$(450 \sin 30°)(1.7) - (450)(\cos 30°)(.30)(1.7) - T_1(1.7) = \frac{1}{2}\frac{450}{g}V_A^2$$

Therefore,

$$T_1 = 108.1 - 13.49V_A^2 \qquad \text{(a)}$$

Example 17.2 (Continued)

We now consider the cylinder for which the free-body diagram is displayed in Fig. 17.15. Note that the cylinder is in effect rolling without slipping along the right supporting cable. Hence, T_2 does no work as explained in Chapter 13.[4] Thus, the **work–kinetic energy** equation is as follows using the formula $\frac{1}{2}Mr^2$ for I of the cylinder:

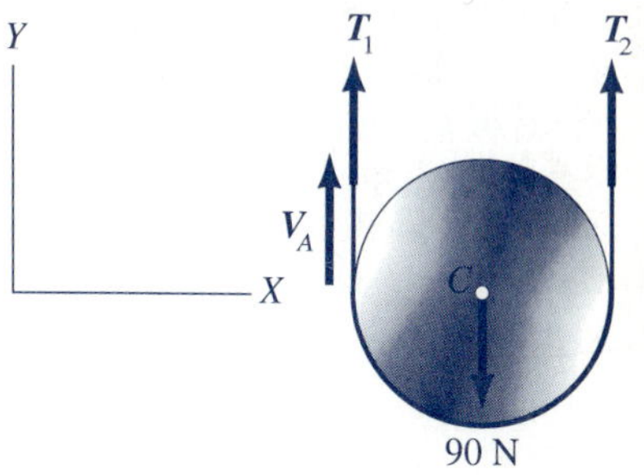

Figure 17.15. Free body of cylinder.

$$T_1(1.7) - 90\left(\frac{1.7}{2}\right) = \frac{1}{2}\frac{90}{g}V_C^2 + \frac{1}{2}\left[\frac{1}{2}\left(\frac{90}{g}\right)(.30)^2\right]\omega^2$$

Therefore,

$$T_1 = 45 + 2.70V_C^2 + .1214\omega^2 \qquad \text{(b)}$$

From **kinematics** we can conclude on inspection that

$$V_C = \frac{1}{2}V_A \qquad \text{(c)}$$

$$\omega = -\frac{V_A}{.60} \qquad \text{(d)}$$

Subtracting Eq. (b) from Eq. (a) to eliminate T_1, and then substituting from Eq. (c) and Eq. (d) for V_C and ω, we then get for V_A:

$$V_A = 2.09 \text{ m/sec} \qquad \text{(e)}$$

This problem can readily be solved as a system, i.e, without disconnecting the bodies. You are asked to do this in Problem 17.25.

[4]Recall that the point of contact of the cylinder has zero velocity, and hence the friction force (in this case, T_2) transmits no power to the cylinder.

In the previous example, we considered the problem to be composed of two *discrete* bodies. We proceeded by expressing equations for each body separately. In the following example, we will consider a *system* of bodies expressing equations for the whole system directly. In this problem, the forces between any two bodies of the system have the *same velocity*; consequently, from Newton's third law, we can conclude that these forces contribute zero net work. We shall illustrate a case where this condition is not so in Example 17.5.

Example 17.3

A conveyor is moving a weight W of 64.4 lb in Fig. 17.16. Cylinders A and B have a diameter of 1 ft and weigh 32.2 lb each. Also, they each have a radius of gyration of .4 ft. Rollers C, D, E, F, and G each have a diameter of 3 in., weigh 10 lb each, and have a radius of gyration of 1 in. What constant torque will increase the speed of W from 1 ft/sec of 3 ft/sec in 5 ft of travel? There is no slipping at any of the rollers and drums. The belt weighs 25 lb.

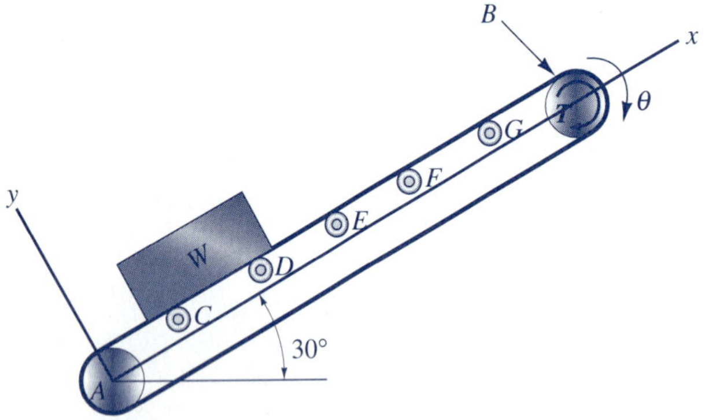

Figure 17.16. Conveyor moving weight W.

We shall use the **work–kinetic energy** relation specified in Eq. 17.14 for this problem. Only external forces and torques do work for the system; the interactive forces between bodies do work in amounts that clearly cancel each other because of the condition of no slipping. Hence,

$$T\theta - W(5)(\sin 30°) = (\text{KE})_2 - (\text{KE})_1 \tag{a}$$

where T is the applied torque. The general expression for the kinetic energy is

$$\text{KE} = 5\left(\frac{1}{2}I_{\text{roll}}\omega_{\text{roll}}^2\right) + 2\left(\frac{1}{2}I_{\text{cyl}}\omega_{\text{cyl}}^2\right) + \frac{1}{2}M_{\text{belt}}V_{\text{belt}}^2 + \frac{1}{2}\frac{W}{g}V_{\text{weight}}^2 \tag{b}$$

From **kinematics** we can say:

$$\omega_{\text{roll}} = -\frac{V_{\text{belt}}}{\left(\frac{1}{2}\right)\left(\frac{3}{12}\right)} = -8V_{\text{belt}}$$

$$\omega_{\text{cyl}} = -\frac{V_{\text{belt}}}{\left(\frac{1}{2}\right)(1)} = -2V_{\text{belt}}$$

$$V_{\text{weight}} = V_{\text{belt}}$$

Example 17.3 (Continued)

Using these results, we can give the kinetic energy at the end and at the beginning of the interval of interest as

$$(KE)_2 = 5\left\{\left(\frac{1}{2}\right)\left(\frac{10}{g}\right)\left(\frac{1}{12}\right)^2[(8)(3)]^2\right\} + 2\left\{\left(\frac{1}{2}\right)\left(\frac{32.2}{g}\right)(.4)^2[(2)(3)]^2\right\}$$
$$+\frac{1}{2}\left(\frac{25}{g}\right)(3)^2 + \frac{1}{2}\left(\frac{64.4}{g}\right)(3^2)$$
$$= 21.4 \text{ ft-lb}$$
$$(KE)_2 = 5\left\{\left(\frac{1}{2}\right)\left(\frac{10}{g}\right)\left(\frac{1}{12}\right)^2[(8)(1)]^2\right\} + 2\left\{\left(\frac{1}{2}\right)\left(\frac{32.2}{g}\right)(.4)^2[(2)(1)]^2\right\}$$
$$+\frac{1}{2}\left(\frac{25}{g}\right)(1^2) + \frac{1}{2}\left(\frac{64.4}{g}\right)(1^2)$$
$$= 2.37 \text{ ft-lb}$$

Substituting these results into Eq. (a), we get

$$T\theta - (64.4)(5)(\sin 30°) = 21.4 - 2.37 \qquad \text{(c)}$$

From **kinematics** again we can say for θ, on considering the rotation of a cylinder and the distance traveled by the belt:

$$(r_{cyl})(\theta) = 5$$

Therefore,

$$\theta = \frac{5}{\frac{1}{2}} = 10 \text{ rad}$$

Substituting back into Eq. (c), we can then solve for the desired torque T:

$$T = \frac{1}{10}[21.4 - 2.37 + (64.4)(5)(\sin 30°)]$$

$$T = 18.00 \text{ ft-lb}$$

In the next example, we have a case of internal forces between bodies that satisfy Newton's third law but do not have identical velocities.

Example 17.4[5]

A diesel-powered electric train moves up a 7° grade in Fig. 17.17. If a torque of 750 N-m is developed at each of its six pairs of drive wheels, what is the increase of speed of the train after it moves 100 m? Initially, the train has a speed of 16 km/hr. The train weighs 90 kN. The drive wheels have a diameter of 600 mm. Neglect the rotational energy of the drive wheels.

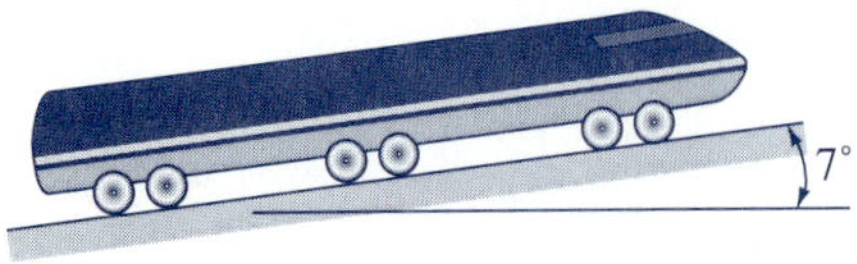

Figure 17.17. Diesel–electric train.

We shall consider the train as a *system of rigid bodies* including the 6 pairs of wheels and the body. We have shown the train in Fig. 17.18 with the external forces, W, N, and f. In addition, we have shown certain internal torques M.[6] The torques shown act on the *rotors* of the motors, and, as the train moves, these torques rotate and accordingly do work. The *reactions* to these torques are equal and opposite to M according to **Newton's third law** and act on the *stators* or the motors (i.e., the field coils). The stators are stationary, and so the reactions to M do *no* work as the train moves. Thus, we have an example of equal and opposite internal forces between bodies of a system performing a nonzero net amount of work. We now employ Eq. 17.16. Thus,

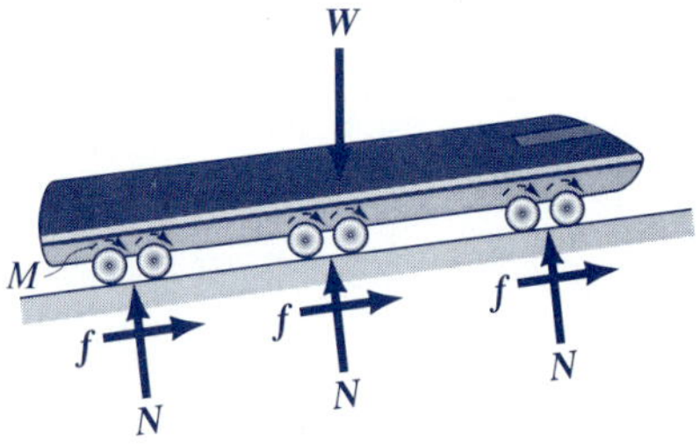

Figure 17.18. External and internal forces and torques.

$$\Delta \text{PE} + \Delta \text{KE} = \mathcal{W}_K \tag{a}$$

Using the initial configuration as the datum, we have[7]

$$\begin{aligned}
&[(90{,}000)(100 \sin 7° - 0)] \\
&\quad + \left\{ \frac{1}{2} \frac{90{,}000}{g} V^2 - \frac{1}{2} \frac{90{,}000}{g} \left[\frac{(16)(1{,}000)}{3,600} \right]^2 \right\} \\
&\quad = (6)(750)(\theta)
\end{aligned} \tag{b}$$

[5]This problem was undertaken in Chapter 13 as a system of particles. Here, we consider it from the viewpoint of a system of interconnected rigid bodies.

[6]Figure 17.18, accordingly, is *not* a free-body diagram.

[7]Recall that for a *rolling* body with *no slipping*, the friction force does *no work*. If we were considering the *center of mass* of the train, then f *would move* with the center of mass and then do work as we shall see in Example 17.5.

Example 17.4 (Continued)

where θ is the clockwise rotation of the rotor in radians. Assuming direct drive from rotor to wheel, we can compute θ as follows for the 100-m distance over which the train moves:

$$\theta = \underbrace{\left(\frac{100}{2\pi r}\right)}_{\text{rev}} \underbrace{(2\pi)}_{\text{rad/rev}} = \frac{100}{.30} \text{ rad} \qquad \text{(c)}$$

Substituting into Eq. (b) and solving for V, we get

$$V = 10.38 \text{ m/sec}$$

Hence,

$$\Delta V = \frac{(10.38)(3{,}600)}{1000} - 16 = \boxed{21.4 \text{ km/hr}}$$

In Chapter 13, we also developed a work–energy equation involving the *mass center* of any system of particles. You will recall that

$$\int_1^2 \boldsymbol{F} \cdot d\boldsymbol{r}_c = \tfrac{1}{2}(MV_c^2)_2 - \tfrac{1}{2}(MV_c^2)_1 \qquad \text{(17.17a)}$$

where $\boldsymbol{F}$ is the *total external force* (only!) which hypothetically *moves with the center of mass*. This equation applies to a rigid body. Note that an external torque makes no work contribution here since equal and opposite forces each having identical motion (that of the mass center) can do no net amount of work. For a system of *interconnected rigid bodies*, we can say:

$$\int_1^2 \boldsymbol{F} \cdot d\boldsymbol{r}_c = \left[\sum_i \tfrac{1}{2} M_i (V_c)_i^2\right]_2 - \left[\sum_i \tfrac{1}{2} M_i (V_c)_i^2\right]_1 \qquad \text{(17.17b)}$$

The force $\boldsymbol{F}$ includes *only external forces* (internal forces between interconnecting bodies are equal and opposite and must move with the mass center of the system; hence they contribute no work to the left side of the foregoing equation). On the other hand, external friction forces on wheels rolling without slipping must move with the mass center of the system in this formulation and thus can *do work*, in contrast to the previous approach, in which the mass center is not used. On the right side, we have summed the kinetic energies of each of the mass centers of the constituent bodies of the system.[8] We now illustrate the use of Eq. 17.17b.

[8]We discussed this topic in Section 16.8.

Example 17.5

A vehicle for traversing swamplands is shown in Fig. 17.19. The vehicle has four-wheel drive and weighs 22.5 kN. Each wheel weighs 2 kN has a diameter of 2.5 m and has a radius of gyration of 180 mm. If each wheel gets a torque of 100 N-m, what is the speed after 20 m of travel starting from rest? Also, determine the friction force from the ground on each wheel. The weight of the vehicle includes that of passengers and baggage. Neglect rolling resistance since the vehicle in this problem is moving on a hard surface. Consider rolling without slipping.

Figure 17.19. A vehicle used in swampland.

We have shown the free-body diagram of the system in Fig. 17.20. We will first use the **system of particles** approach. This includes internal torques from the vehicle frame onto the wheels and the reaction torques from the wheels onto the frame. The former will do internal work because these torques rotate with the wheels. The reaction torques on the frame do not rotate and obviously do no work. Also, because of the no slipping condition, the friction forces from the ground onto the tires do no work as has been explained at length in Chapter 13. Hence, we can say

$$(4)(T)(\theta) = (\text{KE})_2 - (\text{KE})_1$$

Recalling that θ = distance/radius, we get

$$\therefore (4)(100)\left(\frac{20}{1.25}\right) = \left[\left(\frac{4}{2}\right)\left(\frac{2{,}000}{9.81}\right)(.1800)^2\left(\frac{V}{1.25}\right)^2\right] + \frac{1}{2}\left(\frac{22{,}500}{9.81}\right)(V^2)$$

$$\therefore \quad V = 2.354 \text{ m/s}$$

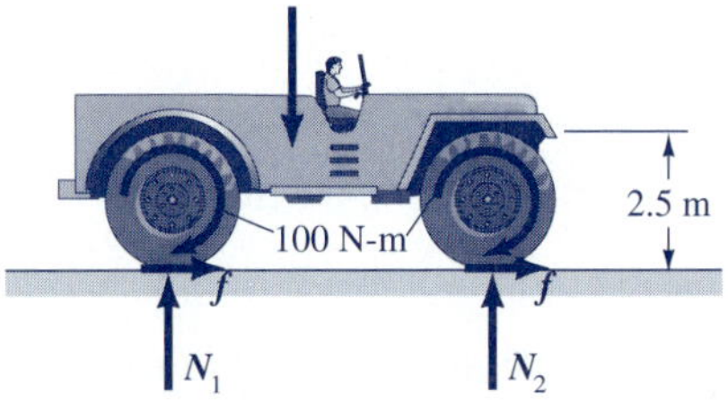

Figure 17.20. External forces and internal torques on swampland vehicle. Query: Is this a freebody diagram?

To get the friction forces f (why are they the same for each wheel?) we use the **center of mass approach**. Thus

$$W_k = (\Delta \text{KE})_{CM}$$

$$\therefore (4)(f)(20) = \frac{1}{2}\left[\frac{22{,}500}{9.81}\right](2.354)^2$$

$$\therefore \quad f = 79.4 \text{ N}$$

We thus have the desired information.

PROBLEMS

In the following problems, neglect friction unless otherwise instructed.

17.1. A uniform solid cylinder of radius 2 ft and weight 200 lb rolls without slipping down a 45° incline and drags the 100-lb block *B* with it. What is the kinetic energy of the system if block *B* is moving at a speed of 10 ft/sec? Neglect the mass of connecting agents between the bodies.

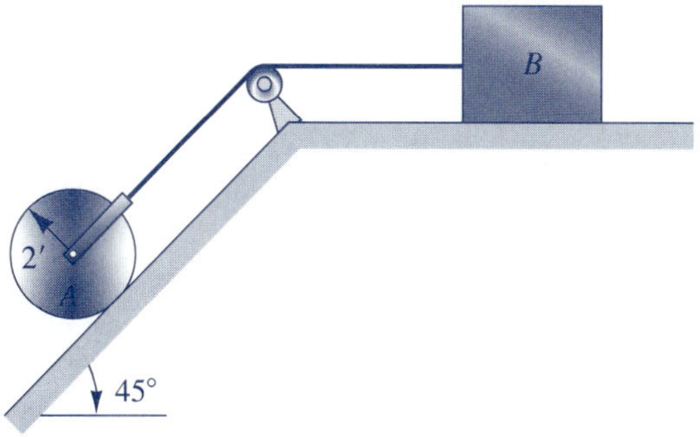

Figure P.17.1.

17.2. A steam roller with driver weighs 5 tons. Wheel A weighs 1 ton and has a radius of gyration of .8 ft. Drive wheels B have a total mass of 1,000 lb and a radius of gyration of 1.6 ft. If the steam roller is coasting at a speed of 5 ft/sec with motor disconnected, what is the total kinetic energy of the system?

Figure P.17.2.

17.3. A thin disc weighing 450 N is suspended from an overhead conveyor moving at a speed of 10 m/sec. If the disc rotates at a speed of 5 rad/sec in the plane of the page (i.e., *ZY* plane), compute the kinetic energy of the disc relative to the ground.

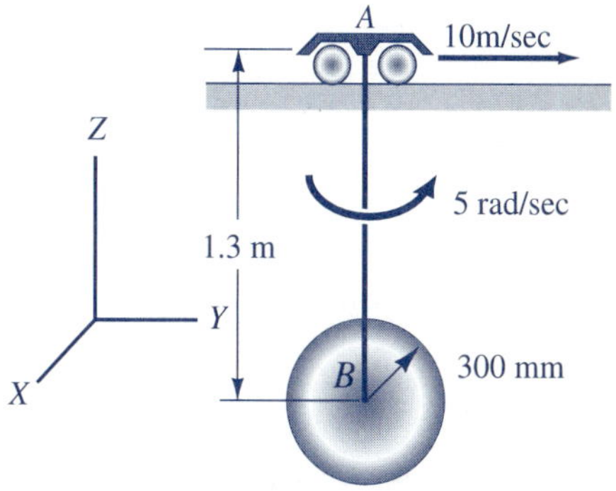

Figure P.17.3.

17.4. Two slender rods *CD* and *EA* are pinned together at *B*. Rod *EA* is rotating at a speed ω equal to 2 rad/sec. Rod *CD* rides in a vertical slot at *D*. For the configuration shown in the diagram, compute the kinetic energy of the rods. Rod *CD* weighs 50 N and rod *EA* weighs 80 N.

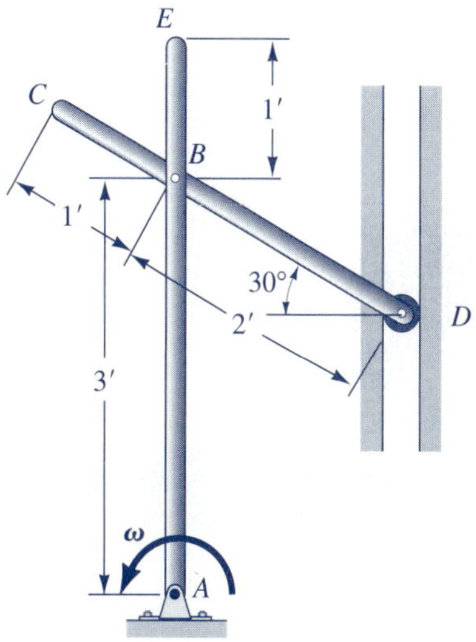

Figure P.17.4.

17.5. Consider the connecting rod AB to be a slender rod weighing 2 lb, and compute its kinetic energy for the data given.

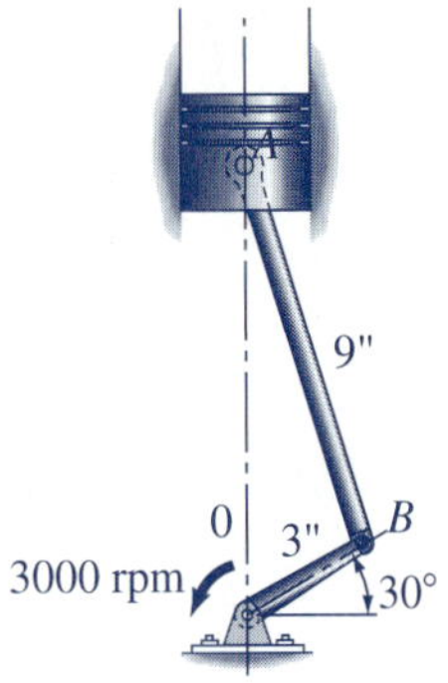

Figure P.17.5.

17.6. Identical rods CB and AB are pinned together at B. Rod BC is pinned to a block D weighing 225 N. Each rod is 600 mm in length and weighs 45 N. Rod BA rotates counterclockwise at a constant speed ω of 3 rad/sec. Compute the kinetic energy of the system when BA is oriented (a) at an angle of 60° with the vertical and (b) at an angle of 90° with the vertical (the latter position is shown dashed in the diagram).

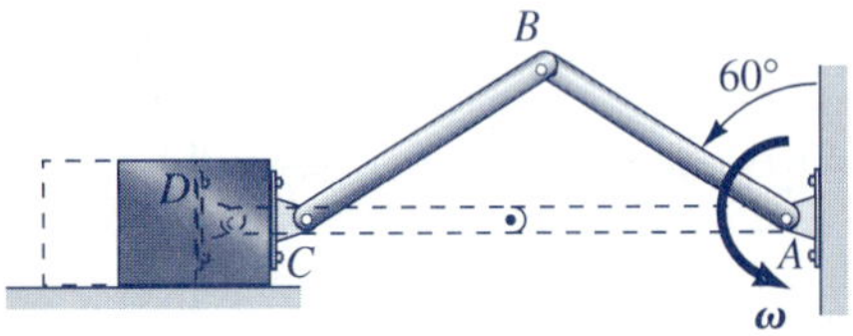

Figure P.17.6.

17.7. Find the kinetic energy of the rotating system described in Example 16.10. The diameter of the shaft is 50 mm.

17.8. The centerline of gear A rotates about axis M–M at an angular speed ω_1 of 3 rad/sec. The mean diameter of gear A is 1 ft. If gear A has a mass of 10 lbm, what is the kinetic energy of the gear? Consider the gear to be a disc.

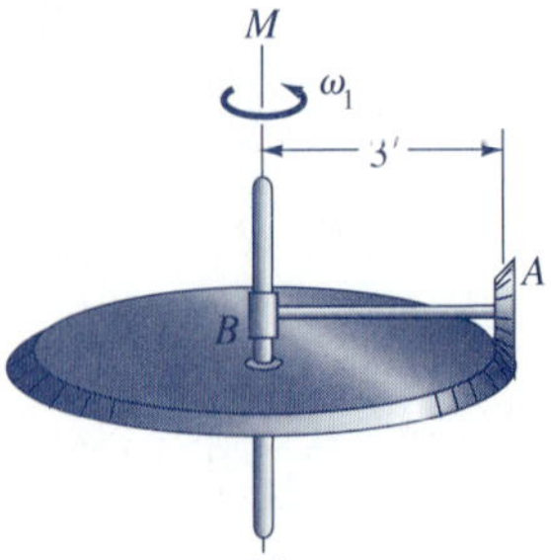

Figure P.17.8.

17.9. A cone B weighing 20 lb rolls without slipping inside a conical cavity C. The cone has a length of 10 ft. The centerline of the cone rotates with an angular speed ω_1 of 5 rad/sec about the Y axis. Compute the kinetic energy of the cone.

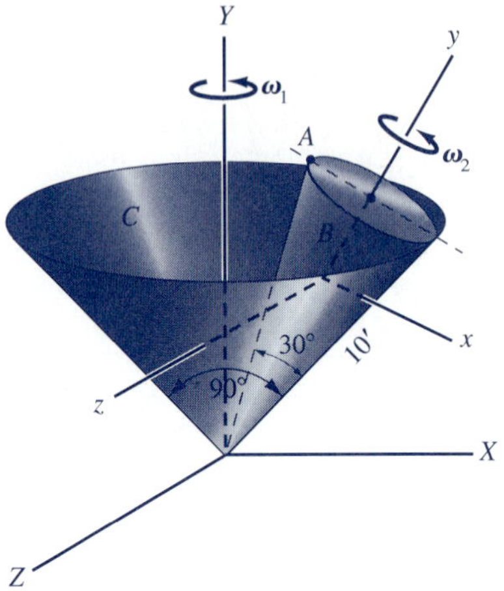

Figure P.17.9.

17.10. A uniform cylinder has a radius r and a weight W_1. A weight W_2, which we shall consider a particle because of its small physical dimensions, is placed at G a distance a from O, the center of the disc, such that OG is vertical. What is the angular velocity of the cylinder when, after it is released from rest, the point G reaches its lowest elevation, as shown at the right? The cylinder rolls without slipping.

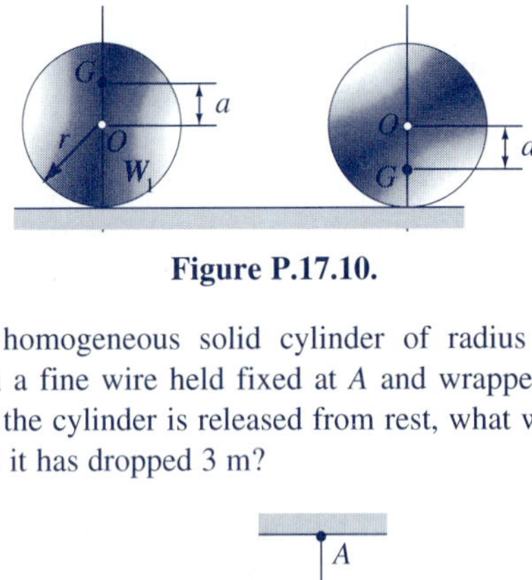

Figure P.17.10.

17.11. A homogeneous solid cylinder of radius 300 mm is shown with a fine wire held fixed at A and wrapped around the cylinder. If the cylinder is released from rest, what will its velocity be when it has dropped 3 m?

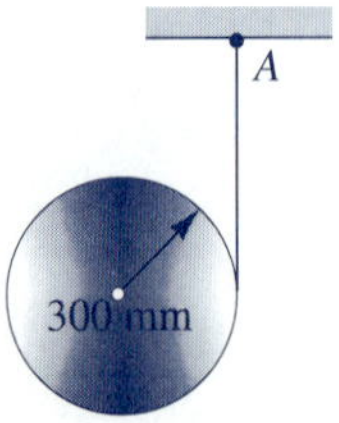

Figure P.17.11.

17.12. Three identical bars, each of length l and weight W, are connected to each other and to a wall with smooth pins at A, B, C, and D. A spring having spring constant K is connected to the center of bar BC at E and to a pin at F, which is free to slide in the slot. Compute the angular speed $\dot{\theta}$ as a function of time if the system is released from rest when AB and DC are at right angles to the wall. The spring is unstretched at the outset of the motion. Neglect friction.

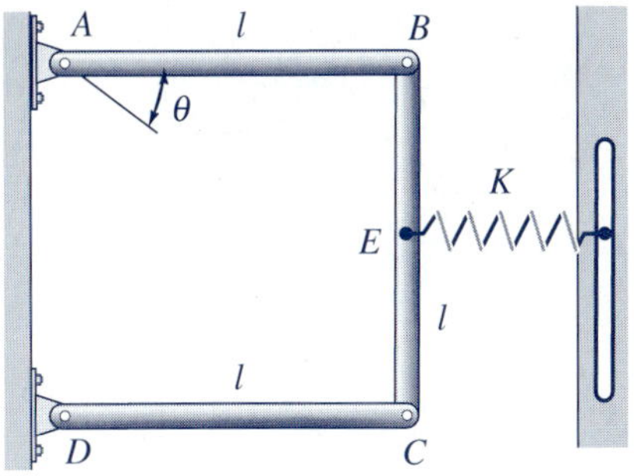

Figure P.17.12.

17.13. A 3-m rod AB weighing 225 N is guided at A by a slot and at B by a smooth horizontal surface. Neglect the mass of the slider at A, and find the speed of B when A has moved 1 m along the slot after starting from a rest configuration shown in the diagram.

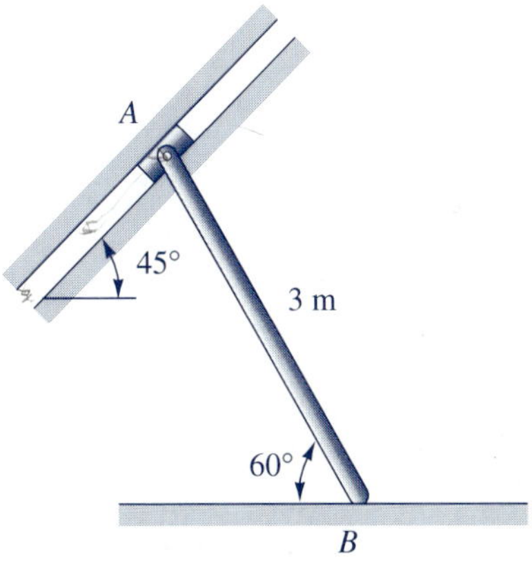

Figure P.17.13.

17.14. A stepped cylinder has radii of 600 mm for the smaller radius and 1.3 m for the larger radius. A rectangular block A weighing 225 N is welded to the cylinder at B. The spring constant K is .18 N/mm. If the system is released from a configuration of rest, what is the angular speed of the cylinder after it has rotated 90°? The radius of gyration for the stepped cylinder is 1 m and its mass is 36 kg. The spring is unstretched in the position shown.

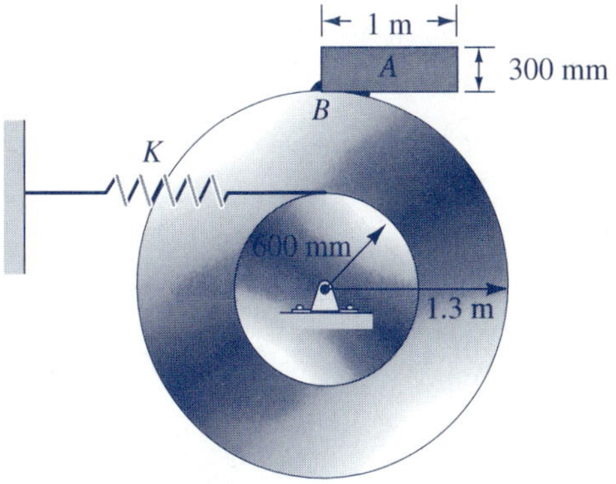

Figure P.17.14.

17.15. A cylinder of diameter 2 ft is composed of two semicylinders C and D weighing 50 lb and 80 lb, respectively. Bodies A and B, weighing 20 lb and 50 lb, respectively, are connected by a light, flexible cable that runs over the cylinder. If the system is released from rest for the configuration shown, what is the speed of B when the cylinder has rotated 90°? Assume no slipping.

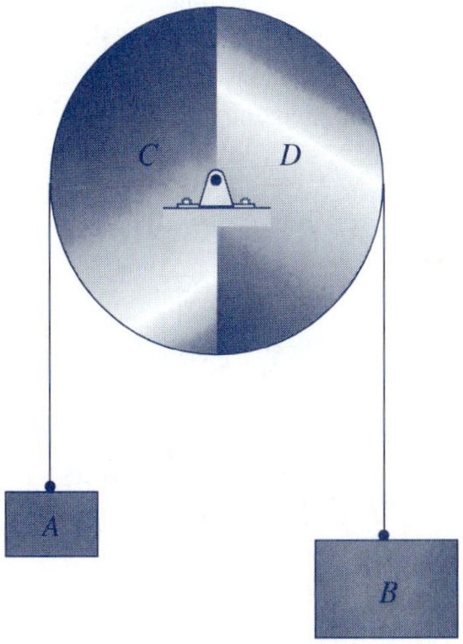

Figure P.17.15.

17.16. Four identical rods, each of length $l = 1.3$ m and weight 90 N, are connected at the frictionless pins A, B, C, and D. A compression spring of spring constant $K = 5.3$ N/mm connects pins B and C, and a weight W_2 of 450 N is supported at pin D. The system is released from a configuration where $\theta = 45°$. If the spring is not compressed at that configuration, show that the maximum deflection of the weight W_2 is .1966 m.

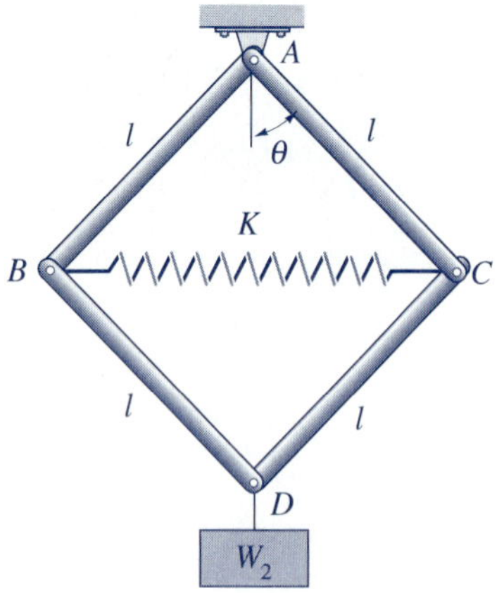

Figure P.17.16.

17.17. A stepped cylinder weighing 30 lb with a radius of gyration of 1 ft is connected to a 50-ft chain weighing 100 lb. The chain hangs down from the horizontal surface a distance of 10 ft when the system is released. Determine the speed of the chain when 30 additional feet of chain have come off the horizontal surface. The coefficient of dynamic friction between the chain and the horizontal surface is .2, and the smaller diameter of the stepped cylinder is 4 in.

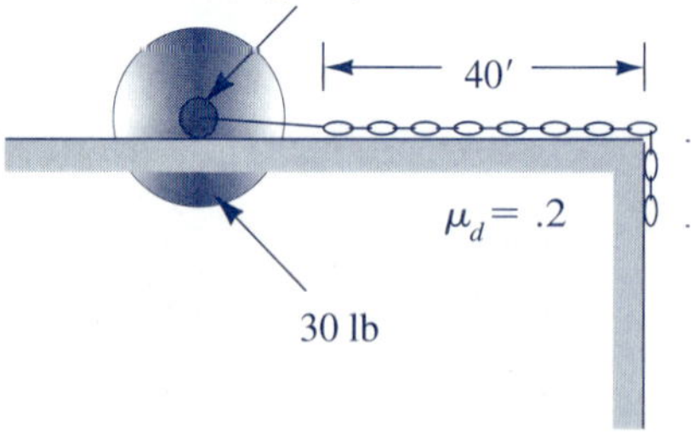

Figure P.17.17.

17.18. The linkage system rests on a frictionless plane. The lengths AB, BF, etc., are each 300 mm, and the bars, all of the same stock, weigh 67.5 N/m. A force F of 450 N is applied at D. What is the speed of D after it moves 300 mm? The system is stationary in the configuration shown. The view of the linkage system is from above.

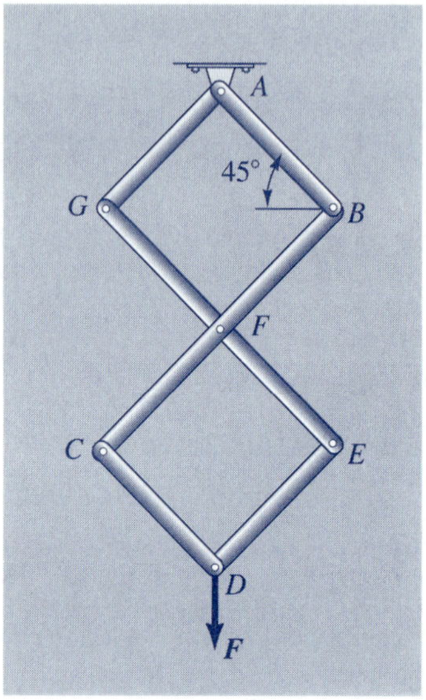

Figure P.17.18.

17.19. Work Problem 17.18 for the case where the system is in a vertical plane.

17.20. A belt weighing 10 lb is mounted over two pulleys of radii 1 ft and 2 ft, respectively. The radius of gyration and weight for pulley A are 6 in. and 50 lb, respectively, and for pulley B are 9 in. and 200 lb, respectively. A constant torque of 20 lb-in. is applied to pulley A. After 30 revolutions of pulley A, what will its angular speed be if the system starts from rest? There is no slipping between belts and pulleys, and pulley B turns freely.

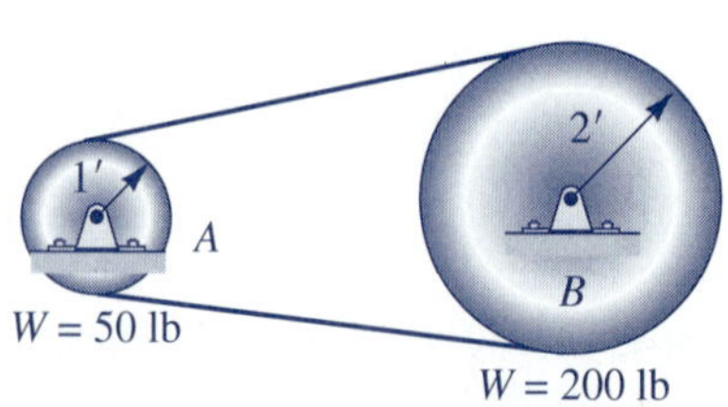

Figure P.17.20.

17.21. Two identical members, AB and BC, are pinned together at B. Also member BC is pinned to the wall at C. Each member weighs 32.2 lb and is 20 ft long. A spring having a spring constant $K = 20$ lb/ft is connected to the centers of the members. A force $P = 100$ lb is applied to member AB at A. If initially the members are inclined 45° to the ground and the spring is unstretched, what is $\dot{\beta}$ after A has moved 2 ft? System is in a vertical plane.

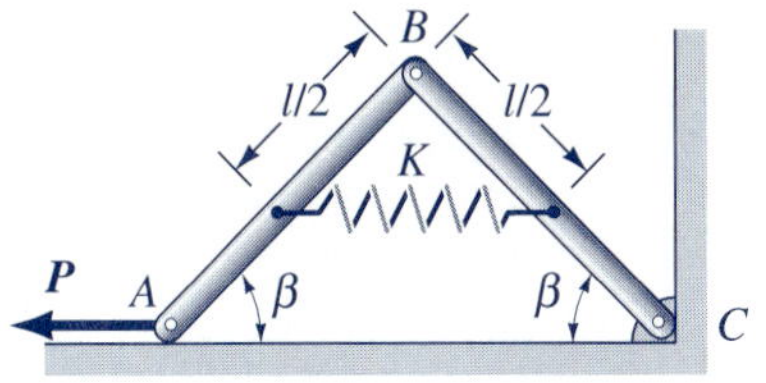

Figure P.17.21.

17.22. A flexible cord of total length 50 ft and weighing 50 lb is pinned to a wall at A and is wrapped around a cylinder having a radius of 4 ft and weighing 30 lb. A 50-lb force is applied to the end of the cord. What is the speed of the cylinder after the end of the cord has moved 10 ft? The system starts from rest in the configuration shown in the diagram. Neglect potential energy considerations arising from the sag of the upper cord.

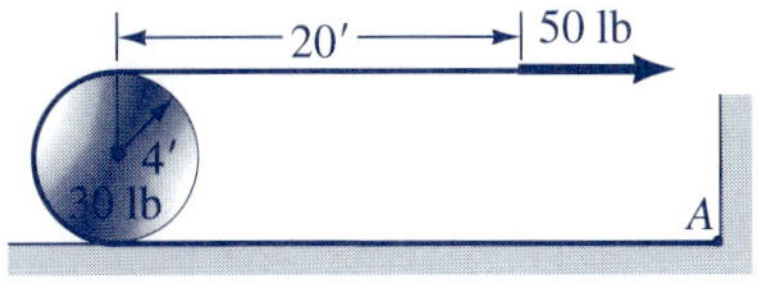

Figure P.17.22.

17.23. In Problem 17.5, suppose that an average pressure of 20 psig (above atmosphere) exists in the cylinder. What is the rpm after the crankshaft has rotated 60° from position shown? The crank rod OB weighs 1 lb and has a radius of gyration about O of 2 in. The diameter of the piston is 4 in., and its weight is 8 oz. The crankshaft is rotating at 3,000 rpm at the position shown. Take the center of mass of the crank rod at the midpoint of OB.

17.24. A right circular cone of weight 32.2 lb, height 4 ft, and cone angle 20° is allowed to roll without slipping on a plane surface inclined at an angle of 30° to the horizontal. The cone is started from rest when the line of contact is parallel to the X axis. What is the angular speed of the centerline of the cone when it has its maximum kinetic energy?

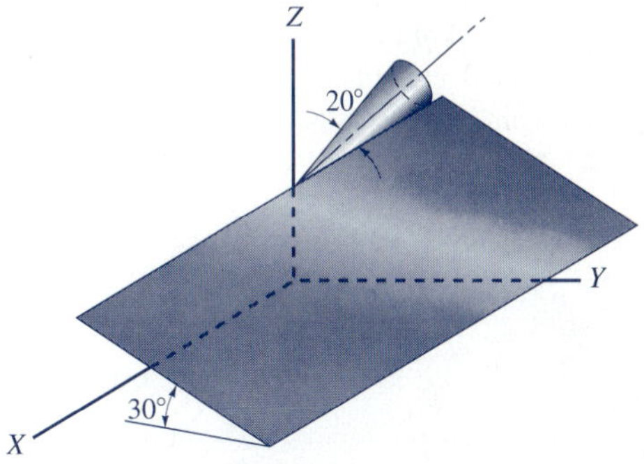

Figure P.17.24.

17.25. Work Example 17.2 by considering the system to be the block, pulley, and cable.

17.26. A weight W_1 is held with alight flexible wire. The wire runs over a stationary semicylinder of radius R equal to 1 ft. A pulley weighing 32.2 lb and having a radius of gyration of unity rides on the wire and supports a weight W_2 of 16.1 lb. If W_1 weighs 128.8 lb and the dynamic coefficient of friction for the semicylinder and wire is .2 what is the drop in the weight W_1 for an increase in speed of 5 ft/sec of weight W_1 starting from rest? The diameter d of the small pulley is 1 ft.

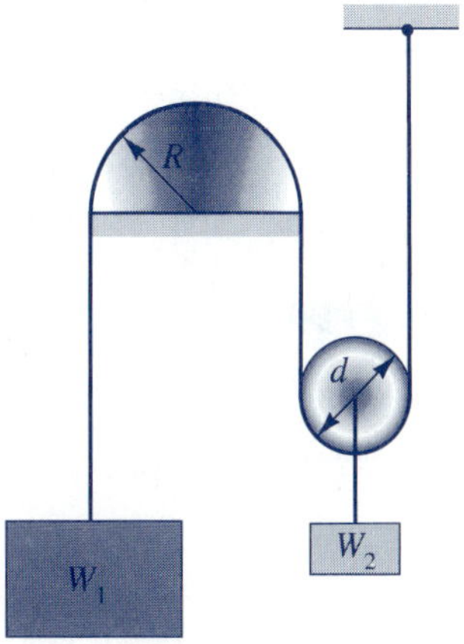

Figure P.17.26.

17.27. A solid uniform block A moves along two frictionless angle-iron supports at a speed of 6 m/sec. One of the supports is inclined at an angle of 20° from the horizontal at B and causes the block to rotate about its front lower edge as it moves to the right of B. What is the speed of the block after it moves 300 mm to the right of B (measured horizontally)? The block weighs 450 N. Consider that no binding occurs between the block and the angle-iron supports.

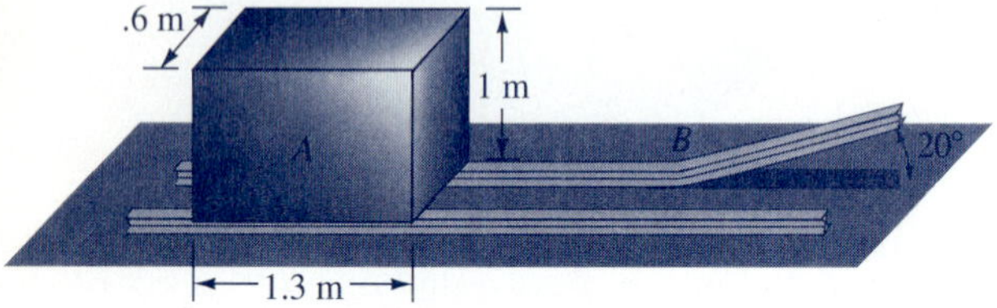

Figure P.17.27.

17.28. In Problem 17.27, will the block reach an instantaneous zero velocity and then slide back or will it tip over onto face A?

17.29. A torque $T = .30$ N-m is applied to a bevel gear B. Bevel gear D meshes with gear B and drives a pump A. Gear B has a radius of gyration of 150 mm and a weight of 50 N, whereas gear D and the impeller of pump A have a combined radius of gyration of 50 mm and a weight of 100 N. Show that the *work of the contact forces between gears B and D is zero*. Next, find how many revolutions of gear B are needed to get the pump up to 200 rpm from rest. Treat the problem as a system of bodies.

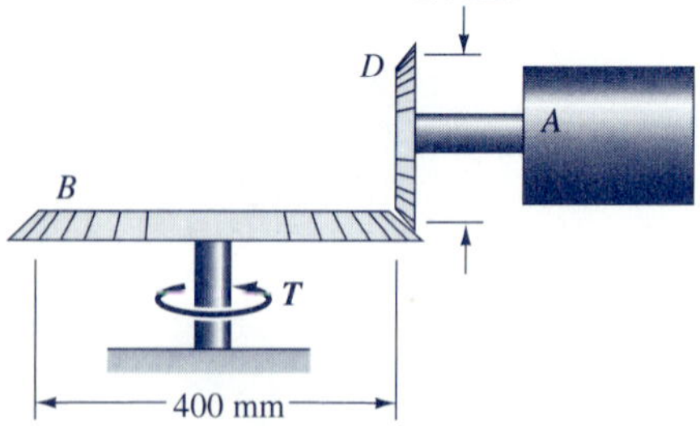

Figure P.17.29.

17.30. A torque T of .5 N-m acts on worm gear E, which meshes with gear A, which drives a gear train. After five revolutions of gear H, what is its angular speed? One revolution of worm gear E corresponds to .2 revolution of gear A. Use the following data:

	k (mm)	W (N)	D (mm)
A	30	10	100
B	30	10	100
C	100	40	300
H	200	100	500

Neglect inertia of the worm gear, and consider an energy loss of 10% of the input due to friction. Note the italicized statement of Problem 17.30, and treat the problem as a system of bodies.

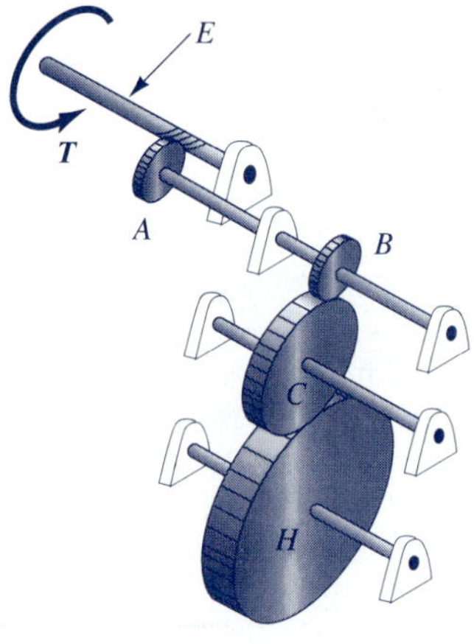

Figure P.17.30.

17.31. A force F of 450 N acts on block A weighing 435 N. Block A rides on identical uniform cylinders B and C, each weighing 290 N and having a radius of 300 mm. If there is no slipping, what is the speed of A after it moves 1 m?

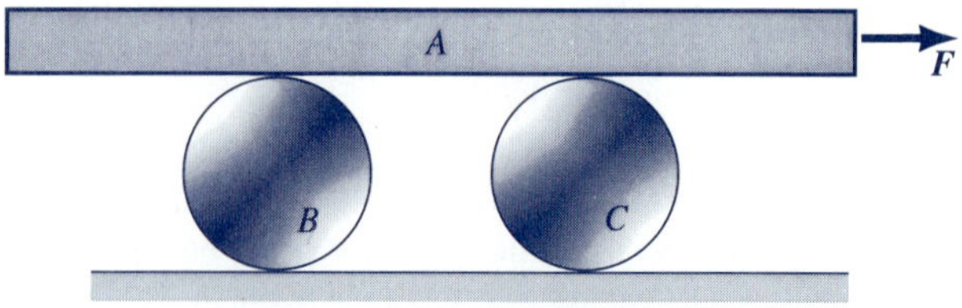

Figure P.17.31.

17.32. Work Example 17.5 using the center-of-mass approach for the whole system. What are the friction forces on the wheels from the ground?

17.33. An electric train (one car) uses its motors as electric generators for braking action. Suppose that this train is moving down a 15° incline at a speed initially of 10 m/sec and, during the next 100 m, the generators develop 1.5 kW-hr of energy. What is the speed of the train at the end of this interval? The train with passengers weighs 200 kN. Each of the eight wheels weighs 900 N and has a radius of gyration of 250 mm and a diameter of 600 mm. Neglect wind resistance, and consider that there is no slipping. The efficiency of the generators for developing power is 90%. [*Hint:* One watt is 1 N-m/sec.] Do not use center of mass approach.

17.34. Work Problem 17.33 using the center of mass approach for the whole train. Also, find the average friction force from the rail onto the wheels. Consider that each wheel is attached to a generator.

17.35. A windlass has a rotating part which weighs 75 lb and has a radius of gyration of 1 ft. When the suspended weight of 20 lb is dropping at a speed of 20 ft/sec, a 100-lb force is applied to the lever at *A*. This action applies the brake shoe at *B*, where there is a coefficient of friction of .5. How far will the 20-lb weight drop before stopping?

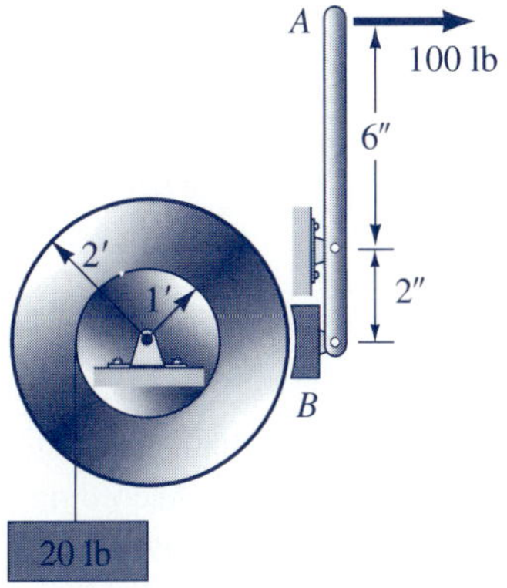

Figure P.17.35.

17.36. A square-threaded screw has a diameter of 50 mm and is inclined 45° to the horizontal. The pitch of the thread is 5 mm, and it is single-threaded. A body *A* weighing 290 N and having a radius of gyration of 300 mm screws onto the shaft. A torque *T* of 45 N-m is applied to *A* as shown. What is the angular speed of *A* after three revolutions starting from a rest configuration? Neglect friction.

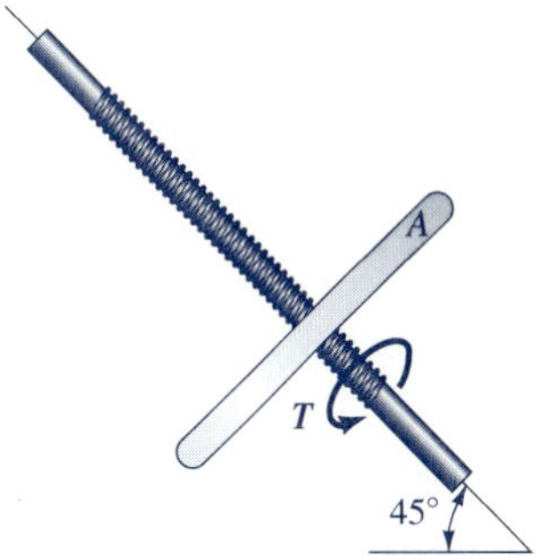

Figure P.17.36.

17.37. A uniform block *A* weighing 64.4 lb is pulled by a force *P* of 50 lb as shown. The block moves along the rails on small, light wheels. One rail descends at an angle of 15° at point *B*. If the force *P* always remains horizontal, what is the speed of the block after it has moved 5 ft in the horizontal direction? The block is stationary at the position shown. Assume that the block does not tilt forward.

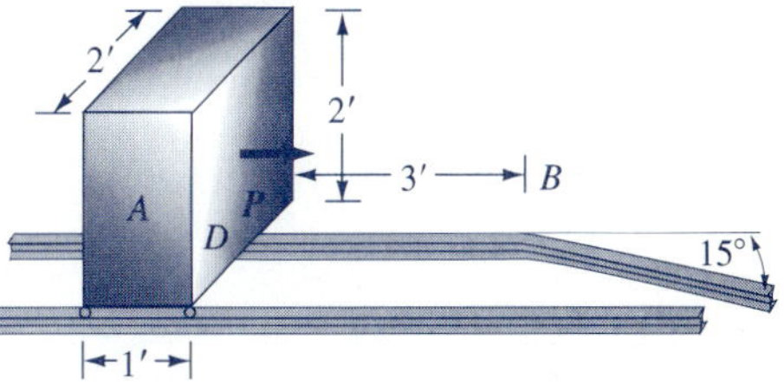

Figure P.17.37.

17.38. A solid uniform rod *AB* connects two light slider bearings *A* and *B*, which move in a frictionless manner along the indicated guide rods. The rod *AB* has a mass of 150 lbm and a diameter of 2 in. Smooth ball-joint connections exist between the rod and the bearings. If the rod is released from rest at the configuration shown, what is the speed of the bearing *A* when it has dropped 2 ft?

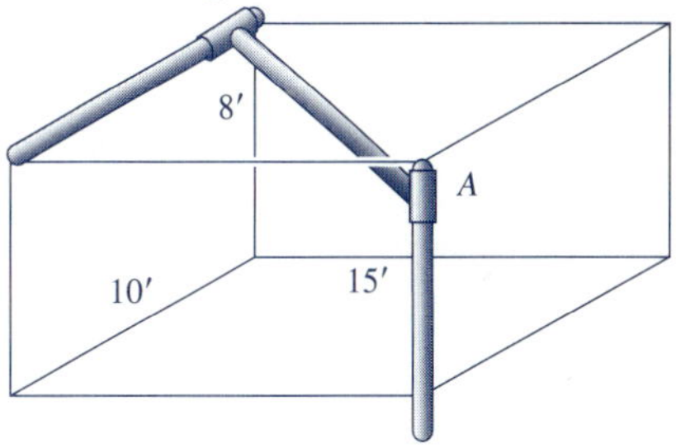

Figure P.17.38.

Part B: Impulse-Momentum Methods

17.4 Angular Momentum of a Rigid Body About Any Point in the Body

As we go to three dimensions, we will need formulations for linear momentum and angular momentum of rigid bodies. The linear momentum is simply $\iiint \boldsymbol{V}\, dm = M\boldsymbol{V}_c$. We shall now formulate an expression for the more complicated angular momentum $\boldsymbol{H}$ of a rigid body about a point. For this purpose, we choose a point A in a rigid body or hypothetical massless extension of the rigid body as shown in Fig. 17.21. An element of mass dm at a position $\boldsymbol{\rho}$ from A is shown. The velocity $\boldsymbol{V}'$ of dm relative to A is simply the velocity of dm relative to reference $\xi\eta\zeta$ which *translates* with A relative to XYZ. Similarly, the linear momentum of dm relative to A is the linear momentum of dm relative to a reference $\xi\eta\zeta$ translating with A. We can now give the angular momentum $d\boldsymbol{H}_A$ for element dm about A as

$$d\boldsymbol{H}_A = \boldsymbol{\rho} \times \boldsymbol{V}'\, dm = \boldsymbol{\rho} \times \left(\frac{d\boldsymbol{\rho}}{dt}\right)_{\xi\eta\zeta} dm \tag{17.18a}$$

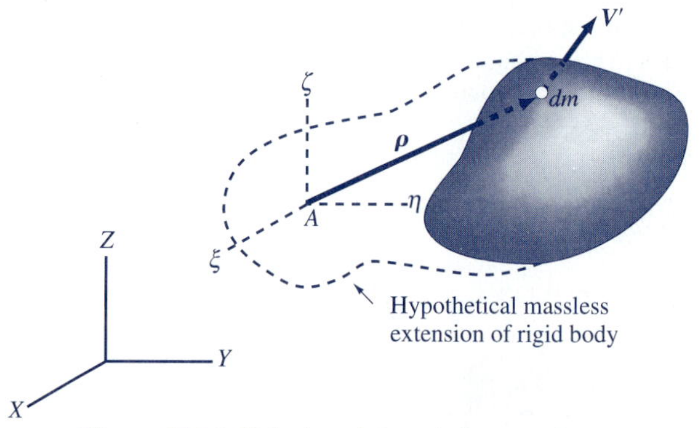

Figure 17.21. Velocity of *dm* relative to point *A*.

But since A is fixed in the body (or in the hypothetical massless extension of the body), the vector $\boldsymbol{\rho}$ must be fixed in the body. Accordingly, $(d\boldsymbol{\rho}/dt)_{\xi\eta\zeta} = \boldsymbol{\omega} \times \boldsymbol{\rho}$, where $\boldsymbol{\omega}$ is the angular velocity of the body relative to $\xi\eta\zeta$. However, since $\xi\eta\zeta$ translates with respect to XYZ, $\boldsymbol{\omega}$ *is also the angular velocity of the body relative to XYZ as well.* Hence, we can say:

$$d\boldsymbol{H}_A = \boldsymbol{\rho} \times (\boldsymbol{\omega} \times \boldsymbol{\rho})\, dm \tag{17.18b}$$

We shall find it convenient to express Eq. 17.18 in terms of orthogonal components. For this purpose, imagine an arbitrary reference xyz fixed to the body or rigid-body extension of the body having the origin at A and any arbitrary

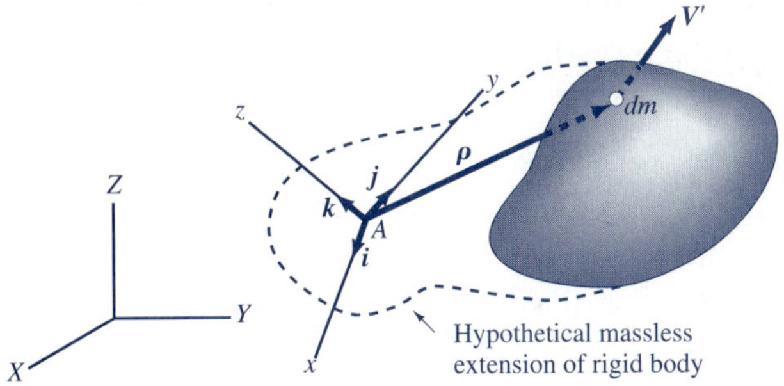

Figure 17.22. Reference *xyz* at *A*.

orientation relative to *XYZ*,[9] as shown in Fig. 17.22. We next decompose each of the vectors in Eq. 17.18b into rectangular components in the $\boldsymbol{i}$, $\boldsymbol{j}$, and $\boldsymbol{k}$ directions associated with the x, y, and z axes, respectively. Thus,

$$d\boldsymbol{H}_A = (dH_A)_x\boldsymbol{i} + (dH_A)_y\boldsymbol{j} + (dH_A)_z\boldsymbol{k} \tag{17.19a}$$

$$\boldsymbol{\rho} = x\boldsymbol{i} + y\boldsymbol{j} + z\boldsymbol{k} \tag{17.19b}$$

$$\boldsymbol{\omega} = \omega_x\boldsymbol{i} + \omega_y\boldsymbol{j} + \omega_z\boldsymbol{k} \tag{17.19c}$$

We then have for Eq. 17.18b:

$$(dH_A)_x\boldsymbol{i} + (dH_A)_y\boldsymbol{j} + (dH_A)_z\boldsymbol{k} = (x\boldsymbol{i} + y\boldsymbol{j} + z\boldsymbol{k}) \times [(\omega_x\boldsymbol{i} + \omega_y\boldsymbol{j} + \omega_z\boldsymbol{k}) \times (x\boldsymbol{i} + y\boldsymbol{j} + z\boldsymbol{k})]\,dm \tag{17.20}$$

Carrying out the cross products and collecting terms, we have

$$(dH_A)_x = \omega_x(y^2 + z^2)\,dm - \omega_y xy\,dm - \omega_z xz\,dm \tag{17.21a}$$

$$(dH_A)_y = -\omega_x yx\,dm + \omega_y(x^2 + z^2)\,dm - \omega_z yz\,dm \tag{17.21b}$$

$$(dH_A)_z = -\omega_x zx\,dm - \omega_y zy\,dm + \omega_z(x^2 + y^2)\,dm \tag{17.21c}$$

If we integrate these relations for all the mass elements dm of the rigid body, we see that the components of the inertia tensor for point A appear:

$$(H_A)_x = I_{xx}\omega_x - I_{xy}\omega_y - I_{xz}\omega_z \tag{17.22a}$$

$$(H_A)_y = -I_{yx}\omega_x + I_{yy}\omega_y - I_{yz}\omega_z \tag{17.22b}$$

$$(H_A)_z = -I_{zx}\omega_x - I_{zy}\omega_y + I_{zz}\omega_z \tag{17.22c}$$

We thus have components of the angular momentum vector $\boldsymbol{H}_A$ for a rigid body about point A in terms of an arbitrary set of directions x, y, and z at point A.

We now illustrate the calculation of $\boldsymbol{H}_A$ in the following example.

[9]At this time we can forget about the axes ξ, η, and ζ. They only become necessary when we ask the question: What is the velocity or linear momentum of a particle relative to point A. To repeat, the velocity or linear momentum of a particle relative to point A is the velocity or momentum relative to a reference $\xi\eta\zeta$ translating with point A as seen from XYZ or, in other words, relative to a nonrotating observer moving with A.

Example 17.6

A disc B has a mass M and is rotating around centerline E–E in Fig. 17.23 at a speed ω_1 relative to E–E. Centerline E–E, meanwhile, has an angular speed ω_2 about the vertical axis. Compute the angular momentum of the disc about point A as seen from ground reference XYZ.

The angular velocity of the disc relative to the ground is

$$\boldsymbol{\omega} = \omega_1 \boldsymbol{i} + \omega_2 \boldsymbol{j} \tag{a}$$

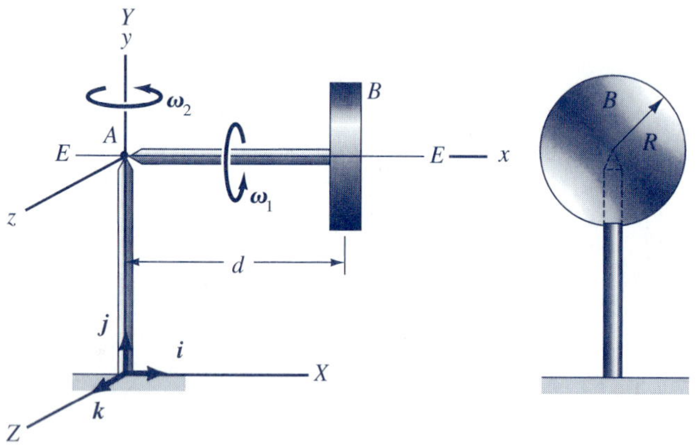

Figure 17.23. Rotating disc.

Consider a set of axes xyz with the origin at A and fixed to the body having cylinder B. At the instant of interest, the xyz axes are parallel to the inertial reference XYZ and we can say (see Fig. 17.24):

$$\omega_x = \omega_1, \qquad \omega_y = \omega_2, \qquad \omega_z = 0 \tag{b}$$

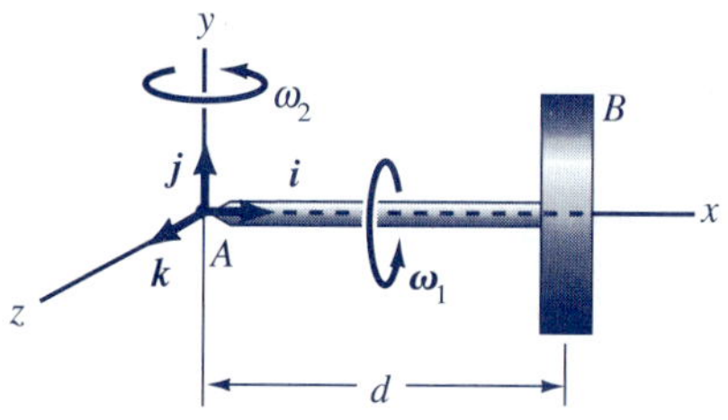

Figure 17.24. xyz axes at A.

The inertia tensor for the disc taken at A is next presented.

$$\begin{aligned} I_{xx} &= \tfrac{1}{2}MR^2 & I_{xy} &= 0 & I_{xz} &= 0 \\ I_{yx} &= 0 & I_{yy} &= \tfrac{1}{4}MR^2 + Md^2 & I_{yz} &= 0 \\ I_{zx} &= 0 & I_{zy} &= 0 & I_{zz} &= \tfrac{1}{4}MR^2 + Md^2 \end{aligned} \tag{c}$$

Note that the product-of-inertia terms are zero because the xy and the xz planes are planes of symmetry. Clearly, moments of inertia for the xyz axes are principal moments of inertia. Now going to Eq. 17.22, we have

$$\begin{aligned} (H_A)_x &= \frac{MR^2}{2}\omega_1 \\ (H_A)_y &= \left(\tfrac{1}{4}MR^2 + Md^2\right)\omega_2 \\ (H_A)_z &= 0 \end{aligned} \tag{d}$$

As seen in Example 17.5, when *xyz* are *principal* axes, $\boldsymbol{H}_A$ simplifies to

$$\boldsymbol{H}_A = I_{xx}\omega_x\boldsymbol{i} + I_{yy}\omega_y\boldsymbol{j} + I_{zz}\omega_z\boldsymbol{k} \tag{17.23}$$

which is analogous to the linear momentum vector $\boldsymbol{P}$. That is,

$$\boldsymbol{P} = MV_x\boldsymbol{i} + MV_y\boldsymbol{j} + MV_z\boldsymbol{k}$$

Note that mass plays the same role as does I, and $\boldsymbol{V}$ plays the same role as does $\boldsymbol{\omega}$.

In Chapter 16, we considered with some care the plane motion of a slablike body, the motion being parallel to the plane of symmetry of the body. We have shown such a case in Fig. 17.25. A reference xyz is shown fixed to the body at A with xy at the midplane of the body and with the z axis oriented normal to the plane of motion. Recall now that for a slablike body the plane xy must be a plane of symmetry or be a principal plane, and consequently that $I_{zx} = I_{zy} = 0$. Also, the only nonzero component of $\boldsymbol{\omega}$ is ω_z. Going back to Eq. 17.22, we see that only $(H_A)_z$ is nonzero, with the result

$$(H_A)_z = (I_{zz})_A\omega_z \tag{17.24}$$

Because of the importance of plane motion of slablike bodies, we shall often use the foregoing simple formula.

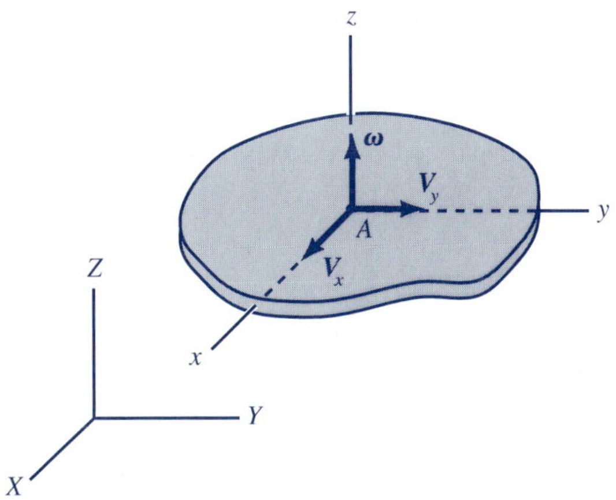

Figure 17.25. Slablike body in plane motion.

We leave it for you to show that the Eq. 17.24 also applies to a body of revolution rotating about its axis of symmetry in inertial space, where z is taken along this axis. Also, Eq. 17.24 is valid for a body having two orthogonal planes of symmetry rotating about an axis corresponding to the intersection of these planes of symmetry in inertial space, where z is taken along this axis. We are now ready to relate linear and angular momenta with force system causing the motion.

17.5 Impulse-Momentum Equations

You will recall that **Newton's law** for the center of mass of any body is

$$\boldsymbol{F} = M\frac{d\boldsymbol{V}_c}{dt} = \frac{d}{dt}(M\boldsymbol{V}_c)$$

where $\boldsymbol{F}$ is the total *external* force on the body. The corresponding *linear impulse-momentum* equation can then be given as

$$\int_{t_1}^{t_2} \boldsymbol{F}\,dt = \boldsymbol{I}_{\text{lin}} = (M\boldsymbol{V}_C)_2 - (M\boldsymbol{V}_C)_1 \tag{17.25}$$

where $\boldsymbol{I}_{\text{lin}}$ is the *linear impulse*. For a system of n rigid bodies we have, for the foregoing equation:

$$\int_{t_1}^{t_2} \boldsymbol{F}\,dt = \boldsymbol{I}_{\text{lin}} = \left[\sum_{i=1}^{n} M_i(\boldsymbol{V}_C)_i\right]_2 - \left[\sum_{i=1}^{n} M_i(\boldsymbol{V}_C)_i\right]_1 \tag{17.26}$$

where $\boldsymbol{F}$ is the total *external* force on the system, M_i is the mass of the ith body, and $(V_C)_i$ is the velocity of the center of mass of the ith body. We are justified in forming the preceding equation as a result of Eq. 16.17.

For the *angular impulse-momentum equation*, we consider points A which are part of the rigid body or massless extension of the rigid body and which, in addition, are either:

1. The center of mass.
2. A point fixed or moving at constant $\boldsymbol{V}$ in inertial space.
3. A point accelerating toward or away from the center of mass.

In such cases we can say:

$$\boldsymbol{M}_A = \dot{\boldsymbol{H}}_A$$

where $\boldsymbol{H}_A$ is given by Eq. 17.22. Integrating with respect to time, we then get the desired *angular impulse-momentum equation*:

$$\int_{t_1}^{t_2} \boldsymbol{M}_A\,dt = \boldsymbol{I}_{\text{ang}} = (\boldsymbol{H}_2)_A - (\boldsymbol{H}_1)_A \tag{17.27}$$

where $\boldsymbol{I}_{\text{ang}}$ is the *angular impulse*. We now illustrate the use of the *linear impulse-* and *angular impulse-momentum equations*.

Example 17.7

A thin bent rod is sliding along a smooth surface (Fig. 17.26). The center of mass has the velocity

$$V_C = 10\boldsymbol{i} + 15\boldsymbol{j} \text{ m/sec}$$

and the angular speed ω is 5 rad/sec counterclockwise. At the configuration shown, the rod is given two simultaneous impacts as a result of a collision. These impacts have the following impulse values:

$$\int_{t_1}^{t_2} F_1\, dt = 5 \text{ N-sec}$$

$$\int_{t_1}^{t_2} F_2\, dt = 3 \text{ N-sec}$$

What is the angular speed of the rod and the linear velocity of the mass center, directly after the impact? The rod weighs 35 N/m.

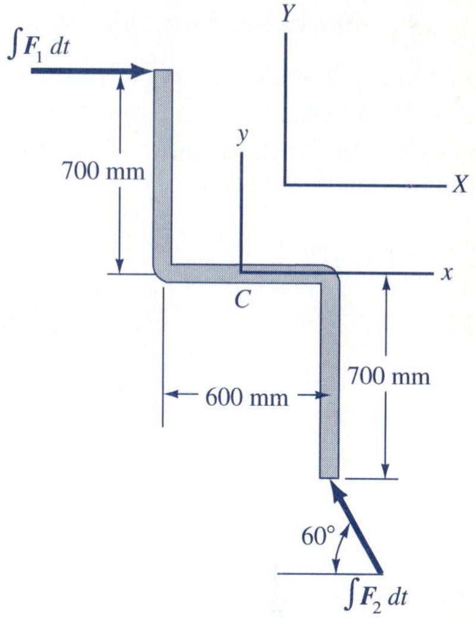

Figure 17.26. Bent rod slides on smooth horizontal surface.

The velocity of the mass center after the impact can easily be determined using the **linear impulse-momentum equation** (Eq. 17.25). Thus, we have

$$5\boldsymbol{i} + 3\sin 60°\boldsymbol{j} - 3\cos 60°\boldsymbol{i} = (.7 + .7 + .6)\left(\frac{35}{g}\right)(V_2 - 10\boldsymbol{i} - 15\boldsymbol{j})$$

Solving for V_2:

$$V_2 = 10.49\boldsymbol{i} + 15.36\boldsymbol{j} \text{ m/sec} \qquad \text{(a)}$$

For the angular velocity, we use the **angular impulse momentum equation** (Eq. 17.27) simplified for the case of plane motion of a slablike body. Again using the center of mass at which we fix xyz, we have for Eq. (17.27):

$$\int_1^2 \boldsymbol{M}\, dt = (I_{zz}\omega_2 - I_{zz}\omega_1)\boldsymbol{k} \qquad \text{(b)}$$

Putting in numerical data and canceling $\boldsymbol{k}$, we get

$$-(5)(.70) + (3)(\sin 60°)(.30) - (3)(\cos 60°)(.70) = I_{zz}(\omega_2 - 5) \qquad \text{(c)}$$

We next compute I_{zz} at C:

$$I_{zz} = \frac{1}{12}\left[\frac{35}{g}(.60)\right](.60)^2$$

$$+ 2\left[\frac{1}{12}\left(\frac{35}{g}\right)(.70)(.70)^2 + \left(\frac{35}{g}\right)(.70)(.30^2 + .35^2)\right] \qquad \text{(d)}$$

$$= 1.330 \text{ kg-m}^2$$

Going back to Eq. (c), we can now give ω_2:

$$\omega_2 = 2.16 \text{ rad/sec}$$

Example 17.8

A solid block weighing 300 N is suspended from a wire (see Fig. 17.27) and is stationary when a horizontal impulse $\int F\,dt$ equal to 100 N-sec is applied to the body as a result of an impact. What is the velocity of corner *A* of the block just after impact: Does the wire remain taut?

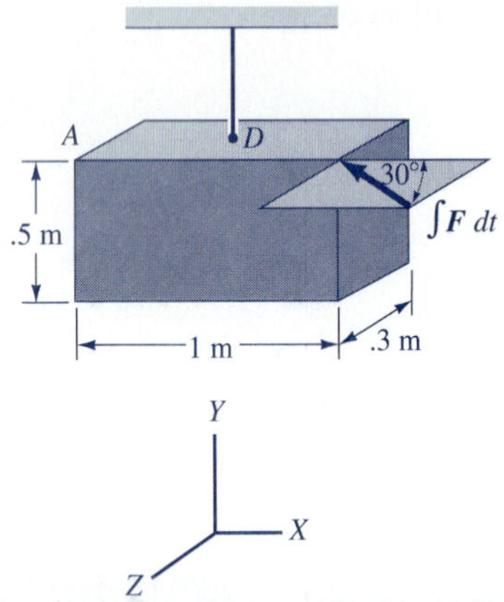

Figure 17.27. Stationary block under impact.

For the **linear momentum equation** we can say for the center of mass (see Fig. 17.28) in the *z*, *x*, and *y* directions:

$$-100 \sin 30° = \frac{300}{g}\left[(V_c)_z - 0\right]$$

$$-100 \cos 30° = \frac{300}{g}\left[(V_c)_x - 0\right] \qquad \text{(a)}$$

$$0 = \frac{300}{g}\left[(V_c)_y - 0\right]$$

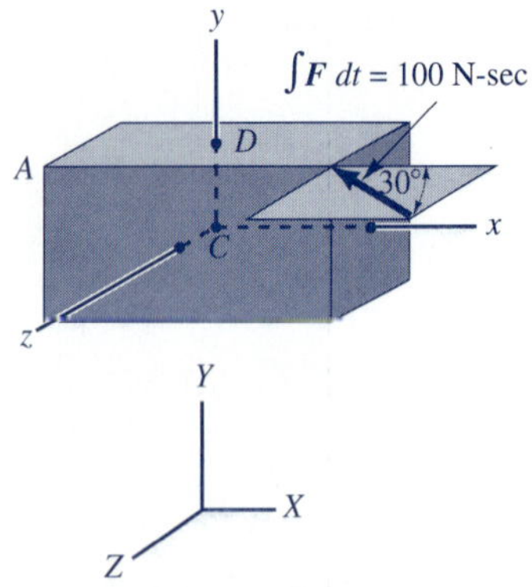

Figure 17.28. *xyz* fixed at center of mass.

Example 17.8 (Continued)

From these equations, we get

$$V_C = -2.83\boldsymbol{i} - 1.635\boldsymbol{k} \text{ m/sec} \tag{b}$$

For the **angular momentum equation** about C, we can say, on noting that xyz are principal axes:

$$\begin{aligned} -(100)(\sin 30°)(.25) &= I_{xx}\omega_x - 0 \\ (100)(\sin 30°)(.5) - 100(\cos 30°)\left(\frac{.3}{2}\right) &= I_{yy}\omega_y - 0 \\ (100)(\cos 30°)(.25) &= I_{zz}\omega_z - 0 \end{aligned} \tag{c}$$

Note that

$$\begin{aligned} I_{xx} &= \frac{1}{12}\left(\frac{300}{g}\right)(.3^2 + .5^2) = .866 \text{ kg-m}^2 \\ I_{yy} &= \frac{1}{12}\left(\frac{300}{g}\right)(1^2 + .3^2) = 2.78 \text{ kg-m}^2 \\ I_{zz} &= \frac{1}{12}\left(\frac{300}{g}\right)(1^2 + .5^2) = 3.19 \text{ kg-m}^2 \end{aligned} \tag{d}$$

We then get for $\boldsymbol{\omega}$ as seen from XYZ from Eq. (c):

$$\boldsymbol{\omega} = -14.43\boldsymbol{i} + 4.32\boldsymbol{j} + 6.79\boldsymbol{k} \text{ rad/sec}$$

Hence, for the velocity of point A, we have

$$\begin{aligned} V_A &= V_C + \boldsymbol{\omega} \times \boldsymbol{\rho}_{CA} \\ &= -2.83\boldsymbol{i} - 1.635\boldsymbol{k} + (-14.43\boldsymbol{i} + 4.32\boldsymbol{j} + 6.79\boldsymbol{k}) \\ &\quad \times (-.5\boldsymbol{i} + .25\boldsymbol{j} + .15\boldsymbol{k}) \end{aligned}$$

$$V_A = -3.88\boldsymbol{i} - 1.230\boldsymbol{j} - 3.08\boldsymbol{k} \text{ m/sec}$$

Finally, to decide if wire remains taut, find the velocity of point D after impact.

$$\begin{aligned} V_D &= V_C + \boldsymbol{\omega} \times \boldsymbol{\rho}_{CD} \\ &= -2.83\boldsymbol{i} - 1.635\boldsymbol{k} + (-14.43\boldsymbol{i} + 4.32\boldsymbol{j} + 6.79\boldsymbol{k}) \times (.25\boldsymbol{j}) \\ &= -4.53\boldsymbol{i} - 5.24\boldsymbol{k} \text{ m/sec} \end{aligned}$$

Since there is zero velocity component in the y direction stemming from the given impulse, we can conclude that the wire remains taut.

In the following example we consider a problem involving a system of interconnected bodies.

Example 17.9

A tractor weighs 2,000 lb, including the driver (Fig. 17.29). The large driver wheels each weigh 200 lb with a radius of 2 ft and a radius of gyration of 1.8 ft. The small wheels weigh 40 lb each, with a radius of 1 ft and a radius of gyration of 10 in. The tractor is pulling a bale of cotton weighing 300 lb. The coefficient of friction between the bale and the ground is .2. What torque is needed on the drive wheels from the motor for the tractor to go from 5 ft/sec to 10 ft/sec in 25 sec? Assume that the tires do not slip.

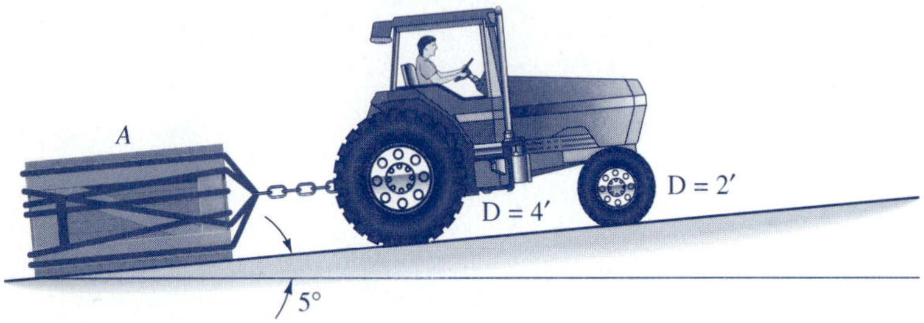

Figure 17.29. Tractor pulling bale of cotton.

We have shown a free-body diagram of the system in Fig. 17.30. Noting on inspection that $N_1 = 300 \cos 5°$, we can give the **linear momentum equation** for the system in the X direction as

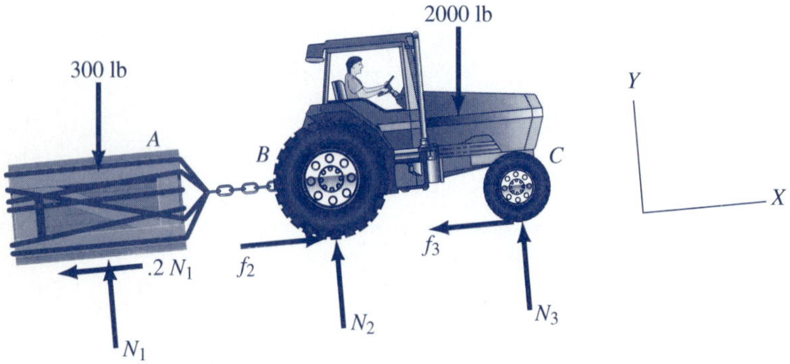

Figure 17.30. Free-body diagram of system.

$$\left[f_2 - f_3 - (.2)(300)\cos 5° - 300 \sin 5° - 2{,}000 \sin 5°\right](25) = \frac{2{,}300}{g}(10 - 5)$$

Therefore,

$$f_2 - f_3 = 275 \qquad \text{(a)}$$

Example 17.9 (Continued)

We next consider free-body diagrams of the wheels in Fig. 17.31. The **impulse-angular momentum equation** for the drive wheels then can be given about the center of mass as

$$\left[-T + f_2(2)\right](25) = \frac{400}{g}(1.8)^2\left[(\omega_B)_2 - (\omega_B)_1\right]$$

Noting from **kinematics** that $\omega_B = -V/2$, we have

$$-T + 2f_2 = -4.025 \qquad \text{(b)}$$

The **impulse-angular momentum equation** about the center of mass for the front wheels is then

$$-(f_3)(1)(25) = \frac{80}{g}\left(\frac{10}{12}\right)^2\left[(\omega_C)_2 - (\omega_C)_1\right]$$

Noting from **kinematics** again that $\omega_C = -V/1$, we get from the equation above:

$$f_3 = .345 \text{ lb} \qquad \text{(c)}$$

From Eq. (a) we may now solve for f_2. Thus,

$$f_2 = .345 + 275 = 275.3 \text{ lb}$$

Finally, from Eq. (b) we get the desired torque T:

$$T = 4.025 + (2)(275.3)$$

$$T = 555 \text{ ft-lb}$$

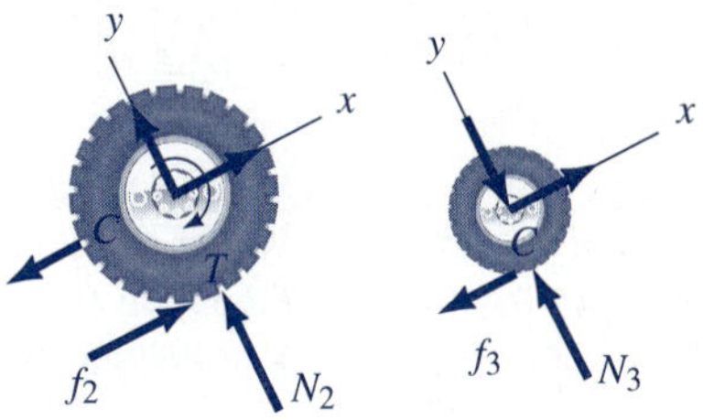

Figure 17.31. Free-body diagrams of wheels. *xy* axes are fixed to wheels.

In Example 17.8, there was no obvious convenient stationary point or stationary axis which could be considered as part of a rigid-body extension of *all* the bodies at any time. Therefore, in order to use the formulas for $\boldsymbol{H}$ given by Eq. 17.22, we considered rigid bodies *separately*. In the following example, we have a case where there is a stationary axis present which can be considered as part of (or a hypothetical rigid-body extension of) all bodies in the system at the instants of interest. And for this reason, we shall consider the angular momentum equation for the entire system using this stationary axis. Also, if the torque about such a common axis for a system of bodies is zero, then the angular momentum of the system about the aforestated axis must be *conserved*. In the example to follow, we shall also illustrate conservation of angular momentum about an axis for such a case.

Example 17.10

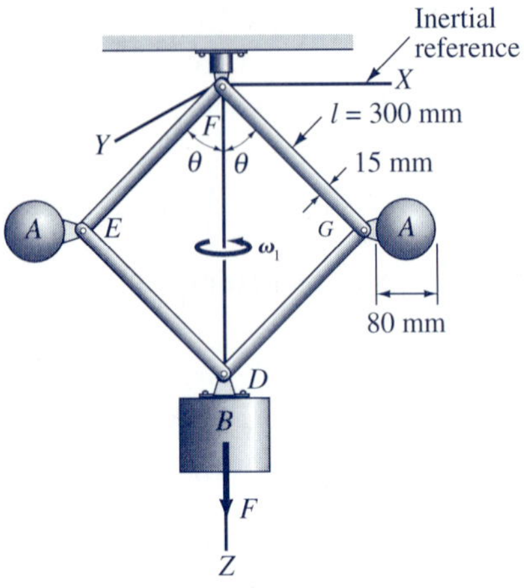

Figure 17.32. Flyball governor apparatus; Y axis is normal to page.

A flyball-governor apparatus (Fig. 17.32) consists of four identical arms (solid rods) each of weight 10 N and two spheres of weight 18 N and radius of gyration 30 mm about a diameter. At the base and rotating with the system is a cylinder B of weight 20 N and radius of gyration along its axis of 50 mm. Initially, the system is rotating at a speed ω_1 of 500 rpm for $\theta = 45°$. A force F at the base B maintains the configuration shown. If the force is changed so as to decrease θ from 45° to 30°, what is the angular velocity of the system?

Clearly, there is zero torque from external forces about the stationary axis FD which we take as a Z axis at all times. Hence, we have conservation of angular momentum about this axis at all times. And, since the axis is an axis of rotation for all bodies of the system,[10] we can use Eq. 17.22 for computing H about FD for all bodies in the system. As a first step we shall need I_{ZZ} for the members of the system.

Consider first member FG, which is shown in Fig. 17.33. The axes $\xi\eta\zeta$ are principal axes of inertia for the rod at F. The η axis is collinear with the Y axis, and these are normal to the page. The axes XYZ are reached by $\xi\eta\zeta$ by rotating $\xi\eta\zeta$ about the η axis an angle θ. Using the transformation equations for I_{ZZ} (see Eq. 9.13), we can say:

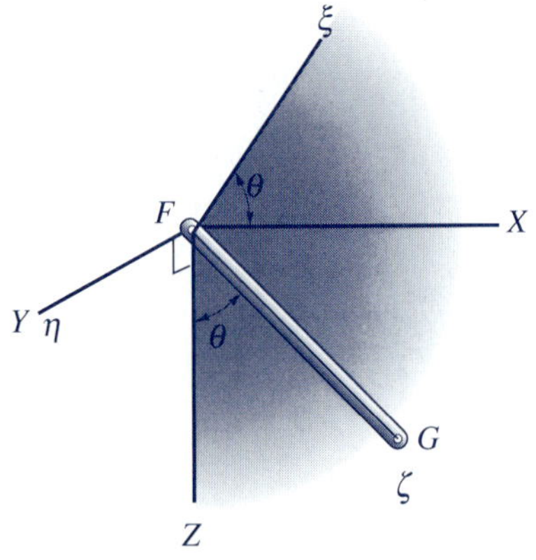

Figure 17.33. $\xi\eta\zeta$ are principal axes of FG at F.

$$\begin{aligned}(I_{ZZ})_{FG} &= I_{\xi\xi}\left[\cos\left(\frac{\pi}{2}+\theta\right)\right]^2 + I_{\eta\eta}\left(\cos\frac{\pi}{2}\right)^2 + I_{\zeta\zeta}(\cos\theta)^2 \\ &= \left[\frac{1}{3}\frac{10}{g}(.30)^2\right]\sin^2\theta + 0 + \left[\frac{1}{2}\frac{10}{g}(.0075)^2\right]\cos^2\theta\end{aligned} \quad \text{(a)}$$

For the sphere we have, using the parallel axis theorem

$$(I_{ZZ})_{\text{sphere}} = \frac{18}{g}(.03)^2 + \frac{18}{g}[(.30)\sin\theta + .04]^2 \quad \text{(b)}$$

Finally, for cylinder B we have

$$(I_{ZZ})_{\text{cyl}} = \frac{20}{g}(.05)^2 \quad \text{(c)}$$

Conservation of angular momentum about the Z axis then prescribes the following:

$$\left[4(I_{ZZ})_{FG} + 2(I_{ZZ})_{\text{sphere}} + (I_{ZZ})_{\text{cyl}}\right]_{\theta=45°}\frac{(500)(2\pi)}{60} = \left[4(I_{ZZ})_{FG} + 2(I_{ZZ})_{\text{sphere}} + (I_{ZZ})_{\text{cyl}}\right]_{\theta=30°}\omega_2$$

[10]That is, at any time t the stationary axis FD either is part of a rigid body directly or is part of a hypothetical extension of a rigid body for all bodies of the system.

Example 17.10 (Continued)

Substituting from Eqs. (a), (b), and (c), we have

$$\left(4\left[\frac{1}{3}\frac{10}{g}(.30)^2(.707)^2 + \frac{1}{2}\frac{10}{g}(.0075)^2(.707)^2\right]\right.$$
$$\left. + 2\left\{\frac{18}{g}(.03)^2 + \frac{18}{g}\left[(.30)(.707) + .04\right]^2\right\} + \frac{20}{g}(.05)^2\right)\frac{(500)(2\pi)}{60}$$
$$= \left(4\left[\frac{1}{3}\frac{10}{g}(.30)^2(.5)^2 + \frac{1}{2}\frac{10}{g}(.0075)^2(.866)^2\right]\right.$$
$$\left. + 2\left\{\frac{18}{g}(.03)^2 + \frac{18}{g}\left[(.30)(.5) + .04\right]^2\right\} + \frac{20}{g}(.05)^2\right)\omega_2$$

Therefore,

$$\omega_2 = 92.4 \text{ rad/sec} = 883 \text{ rpm}$$

Before closing the section, we note that we have worked with *fixed points* or axes in inertial space and with the *mass center*. What about a point *accelerating toward the mass center*? A common example of such a point is the point of contact A of a cylinder rolling without slipping on a circular arc with the center of mass of the cylinder coinciding with the geometric center of the cylinder. We can then say:

$$\boldsymbol{M}_A = \dot{\boldsymbol{H}}_A$$

The question then arises: Can we form the familiar angular momentum equation from above about point A? In other words, is the following equation valid for plane motion?

$$\int_{t_1}^{t_2} M_A \, dt = I_A\omega_2 - I_A\omega_1 \tag{17.28}$$

The reason we might hesitate to do this is that the point of contact *continually changes* during a time interval when the cylinder is rolling. However, we have asked you to prove in Problem 17.60 that for rolling without slipping along a circular or straight path, the equation above is still valid.[11] At times it can be very useful.

[11]The statement is actually valid for point A when there is rolling of the cylinder without slipping on a *general* path.

PROBLEMS

17.39. A uniform cylinder C of radius of 1 ft and thickness 3 in. rolls without slipping at its center plane on the stationary platform B such that the centerline of CD makes 2 revolutions per second relative to the platform. What is the angular momentum vector for the cylinder about the center of mass of the cylinder? The cylinder weighs 64.4 lb.

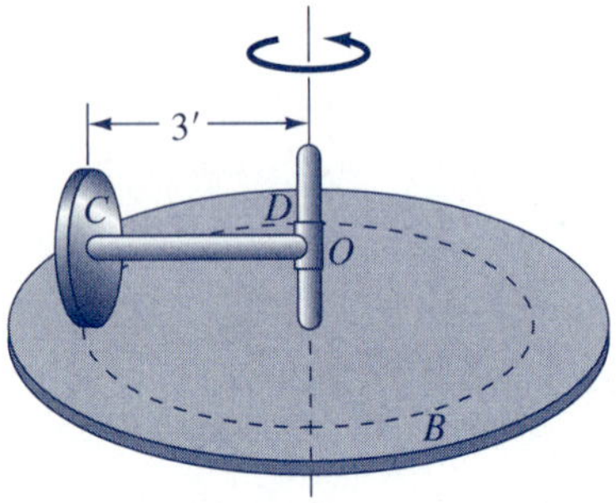

Figure P.17.39.

17.40. In Problem 17.39, find the angular momentum of the disc about the stationary point O along the vertical axis A–A.

17.41. A platform rotates at an angular speed of ω_1, while a cylinder or radius r and length a mounted on the platform rotates relative to the platform at an angular speed of ω_2. When the axis of the cylinder is collinear with the stationary Y axis, what is that angular momentum vector of the cylinder about the center of mass of the cylinder? The mass of the cylinder is M.

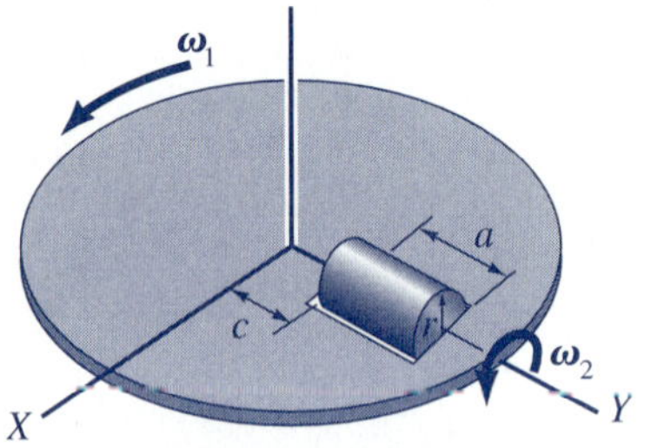

Figure P.17.41.

17.42. A disc A rotates relative to an inclined shaft CD at the ratio ω_2 of 3 rad/sec while shaft CD rotates about vertical axis FE at the rate ω_1 of 4 rad/sec relative to the ground. What is the angular momentum of the disc about its mass center as seen from the shaft CD? What is the angular momentum of the disc about its mass center as seen from the ground? The disc weighs 290 N.

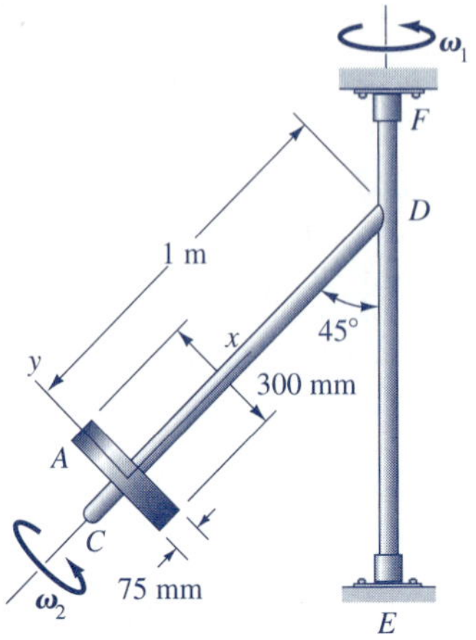

Figure P.17.42.

17.43. Work Problem 16.5 by methods of momentum.

17.44. A flywheel having a mass of 1,000 kg is brought to speed of 200 rpm in 360 sec by an electric motor developing a torque of 60 N-m. What is the radius of gyration of the wheel?

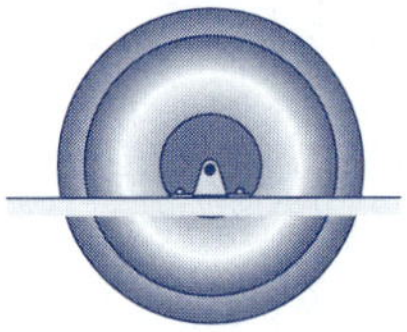

Figure P.17.44.

17.45. Work Problem Example 16.2 by method of angular - momentum.

17.46. Work Problem 16.8 by method of angular momentum.

17.47. A light plane is coming in for a landing at a speed of 100 km/hr. The wheels have zero rotation just before touching the runway. If $\frac{1}{10}$ the weight of the plane is maintained by the upward force of the runway for the first second, what is the approximate length of the skid mark left by the wheel on the runway? The wheels each weigh 100 N and have a radius of gyration of 180 mm and a diameter of 450 mm. The plane weighs with load 8,000 N. The coefficient of friction between the tire and runway is .3.

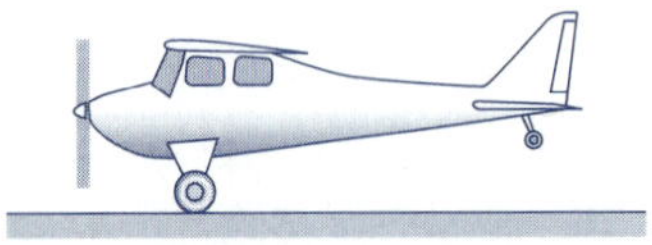

Figure P.17.47.

17.48. Work Problem 17.47 for the case where the upward force from the ground on the plane during the first second after touchdown is

$$N = 8{,}000t^2 \text{ N}$$

where t is in seconds after touchdown.

17.49. A circular conveyor carries cylinders a from position A through a heat treatment furnace. The cylinders are dropped onto the conveyor at A from a stationary position above and picked up at B. The conveyor is to turn at an average speed ω of 2 rpm. The cylinders are dropped onto the conveyor at the rate of 9 per minute. If the resisting torque due to friction is 1 N-m, what average torque T is needed to maintain the prescribed angular motion? Each cylinder weighs 300 N and has a radius of gyration of 150 mm about its axis.

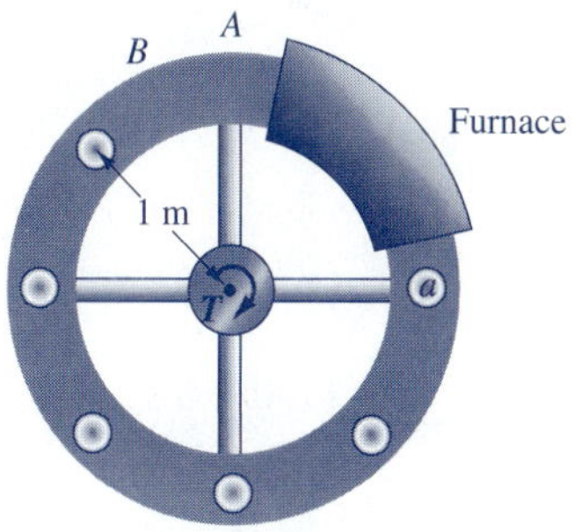

Figure P.17.49.

17.50. A circular *towing tank* has a main arm A which has a mass of 1,000 kg and a radius of gyration of 1 m. On the arm rides the model support B, having a mass of 200 kg and having a radius of gyration about the vertical axis at its mass center of 600 mm. If a torque T of 50 N-m is developed on A when B is at position $r = 1.8$ m, what will be the angular speed 5 sec later if B moves out at a constant radial speed of .1m/sec. The initial angular speed of the arm A is 2 rpm. Neglect the drag of the model.

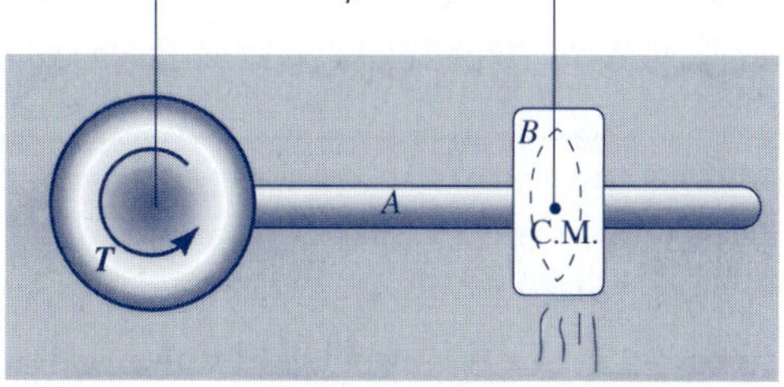

Figure P.17.50.

17.51. A steam roller with driver weighs 5 tons. Wheel A weighs 2 tons and has a radius of gyration of .8 ft. Drive wheels B have a total weight of 1 ton and a radius of gyration of 1.5 ft. If a total torque of 400 ft-lb is developed by the engine on the drive wheels, what is the speed of the steam roller after 10 sec starting from rest? There is no slipping.

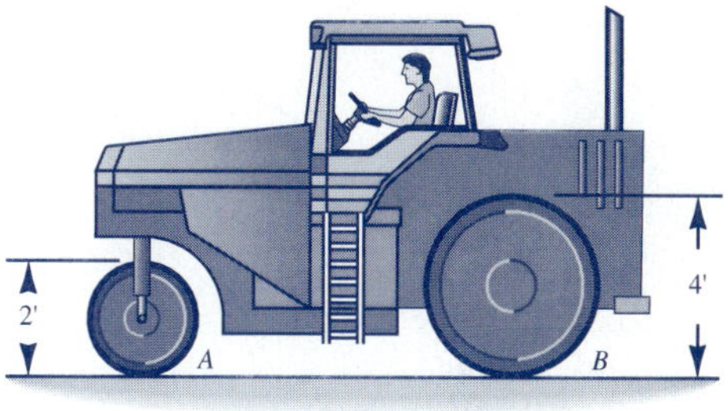

Figure P.17.51.

17.52. An electric motor D drives gears C, B, and device A. The diameters of gears C and B are 6 in. and 16 in., respectively. The mass of A is 200 lbm. The combined mass of the motor armature and gear C is 50 lbm, while the radius of gyration of this combination is 8 in. Also, the mass of B is 20 lbm. If a constant counterclockwise torque of 60 lb-ft is developed on the armature of the motor, what is the speed of A in 2 sec after starting from rest? Neglect the inertia of the small wheels under A.

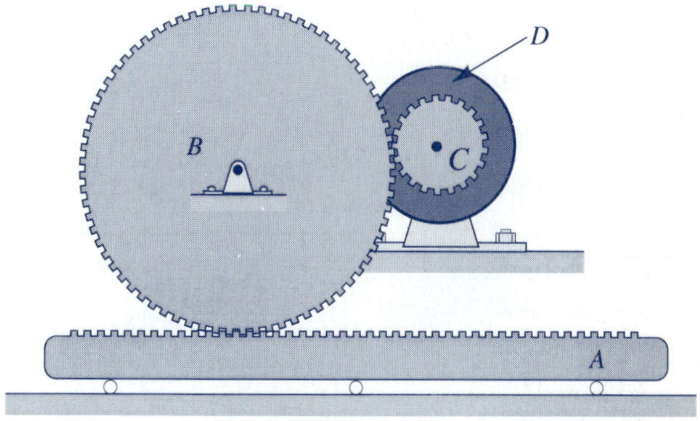

Figure P.17.52.

17.53. A conveyor is moving a weigh W of 64.4 lb. Cylinders A and B have a diameter of 1 ft and weigh 32.2 lb each. Also, they each have a radius of gyration of .8 ft. Rollers C, D, E, F and G each have a diameter of 3 in., weigh 10 lb each, and have a radius of gyration of 2 in. What constant torque T will increase the speed of W from 3 ft/sec to 5 ft/sec in 3 seconds? The belt weighs 50 lb.

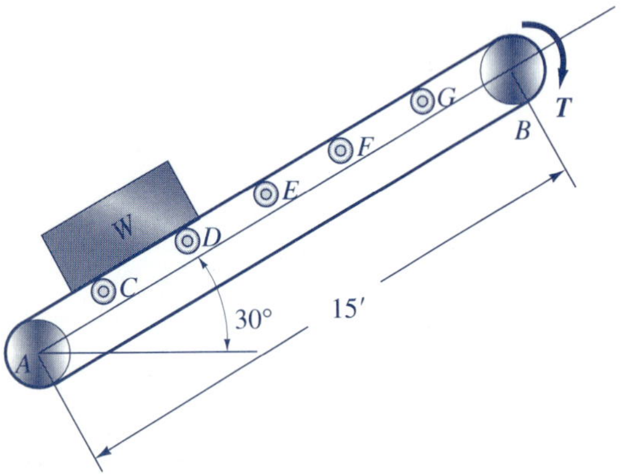

Figure P.17.53.

17.54. A rectangular block A is rotating freely at a speed ω of 200 rpm about a light hollow shaft. Attached to A is a circular rod B which can rotate out from the block A about a hinge at C. This rod weighs 20 N. When the system is rotating at the speed ω of 200 rpm, the rod B is vertical as shown. If the catch at the upper end of B releases so that B falls to a horizontal orientation (shown as dashed in the diagram), what is the new angular velocity? The block A weighs 60 N. Neglect the inertia of the shaft.

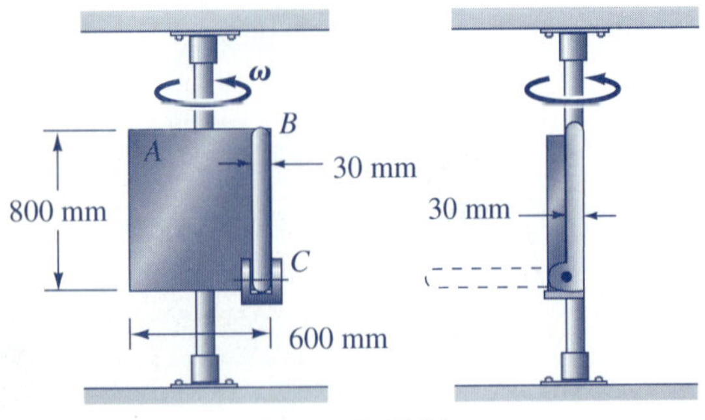

Figure P.17.54.

17.55. A space laboratory is in orbit and has an angular velocity ω of .5 rad/sec relative to inertial space so as to have a partial "gravitational" force for the living quarters on the outside ring. The space lab has a mass of 4,500 kg and a radius of gyration about its axis equal to 20 m. Two space ships C and D, each of mass 1,000 kg, are shown docked so as also to get the benefit of "gravity." the centers of mass of each vehicle is .7 m from the wall of the space lab. The radius of gyration of each vehicle about an axis at the mass center parallel to the axis of the space lab is .5 m. Small rocket engines A and B are turned on to develop a thrust each of 250 N. How long should they be on to increase the angular speed so as to have $1g$ of gravity at the outer radius of the space lab?

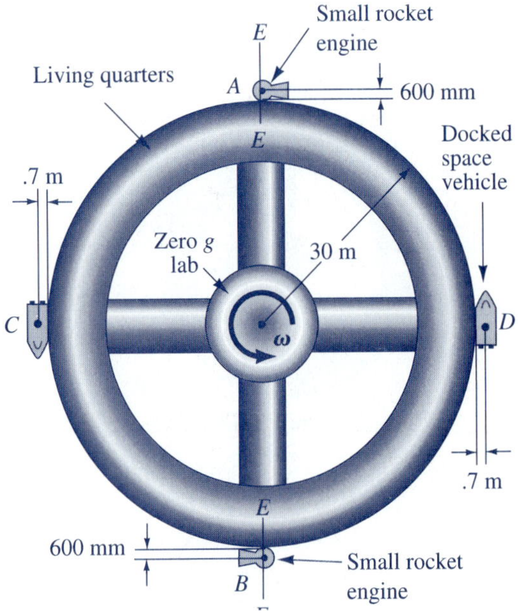

Figure P.17.55.

17.56. In Problem 17.55 the space lab and docked vehicles C and D are rotating at a speed ω for $1g$ gravity at the outer periphery of the space lab. The space vehicles are detached simultaneously. In this detachment process devices on the space lab produces an impulsive torque on each vehicle so that each vehicle ceases to rotate relative to inertial space. For how long and in what directions should the small rockets A and B of the space lab be fired to bring the angular speed ω of the space lab back to normal? The rockets can be rotated about axes E–E and, for this maneuver, they are developing a thrust of 100 N each.

17.57. A turbine is rotating freely with a speed ω of 6,000 rpm. A blade breaks off at its base at the position shown. What is the velocity of the center of mass of the blade just after the fracture? Does the blade have an angular velocity just after fracture assuming that no impulsive torques or forces occur at the fracture? Explain.

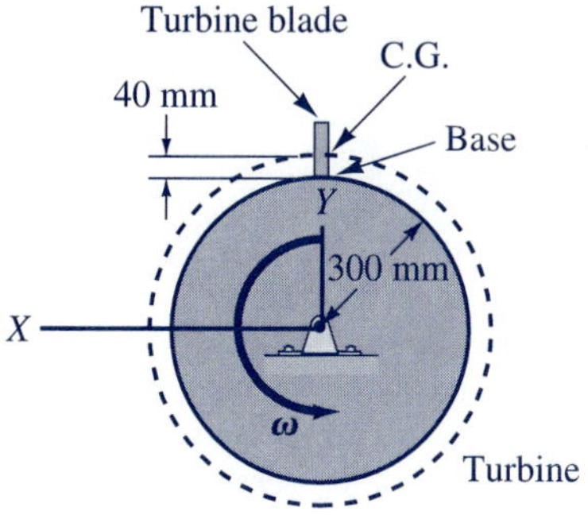

Figure P.17.57.

17.58. Two rods are welded to a drum which has an angular velocity of exactly 2,000 rpm. The rod A breaks at the base at the position shown. If we neglect wind friction, how high up does the center of mass of the rod go? What is the angular orientation of the rod at the instant that the center of mass reaches its apex? Assume that there are no impulsive torques or forces at fracture. The Y axis is vertical. Neglect friction. Use exact value of 2,000 rpm throughout.

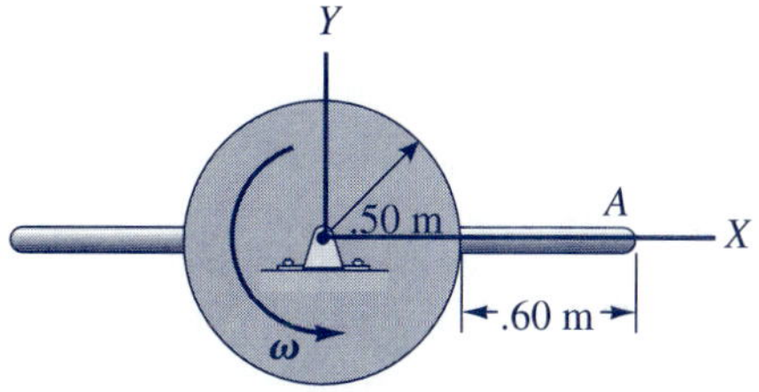

Figure P.17.58.

17.59. A stepped cylinder is released on a 45° incline where the dynamic coefficient of friction at the contact is .2 and the static coefficient of friction is .22. What is the angular speed of the stepped cylinder after 4 sec? The stepped cylinder has a weight of 500 N and a radius of gyration about its axis of 250 mm. Be sure to check to see if the cylinder moves at all!

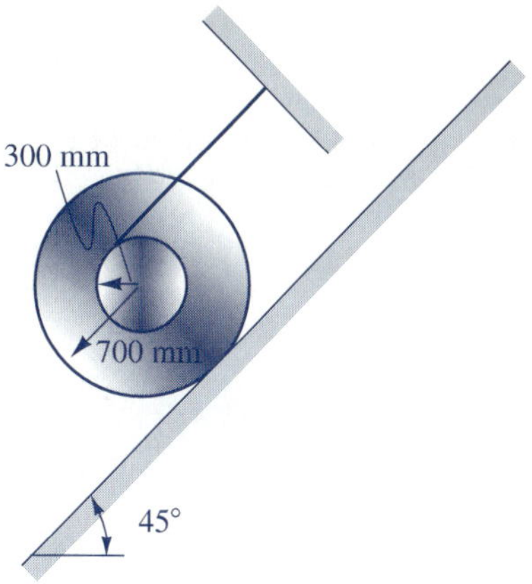

Figure P.17.59.

17.60. Prove that you can apply the angular momentum equation about the contact point A on a cylinder rolling without slipping on a circular (and hence including a straight) path. A force P always normal to OA acts on the cylinder as do a couple moment T and weight W. Specifically, prove that

$$\int_{t_1}^{t_2} (2Pr + W \sin\theta\, r + T)\, dt = M(k^2 + r^2)(\omega_2 - \omega_1) \quad \text{(a}$$

where ω is the total angular speed of the cylinder. [*Hint:* Express the *angular momentum* equation about C and then, from *Newton's law* using the cylindrical component in the transverse direction, show on integrating that

$$\int_{t_1}^{t_2} (f + P + W \sin\theta)\, dt = -M(R - r)(\dot{\theta}_2 - \dot{\theta}_1)$$

where f is the friction force at the point of contact. Now let xy rotate with line OC. From *kinematics* first show that $R\theta = -r\phi$, where ϕ is the rotation of the cylinder relative to xy. Then, show that $\omega = -[(R - r)/r]\dot{\theta}$. From these three considerations, you should readily be able to derive Eq. (a).]

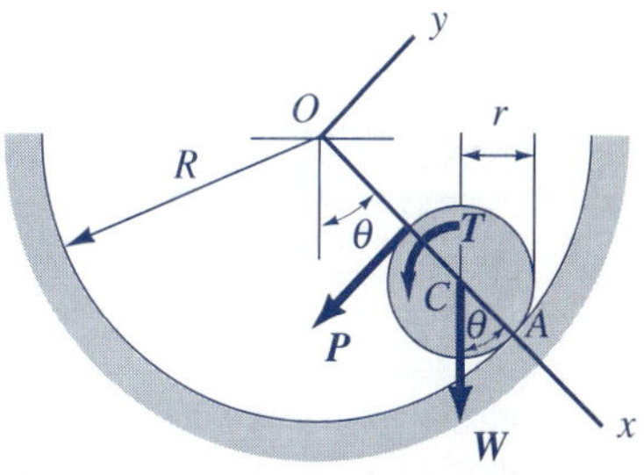

Figure P.17.60.

17.61 A slab A weighing 2 kN rides on two rollers each having a mass of 50 kg and a radius of gyration of 200 mm. If the system starts from rest, what minimum constant force T is needed to prevent the slab from exceeding the speed of 3 m/sec down the incline in 4 sec? There is no slipping.

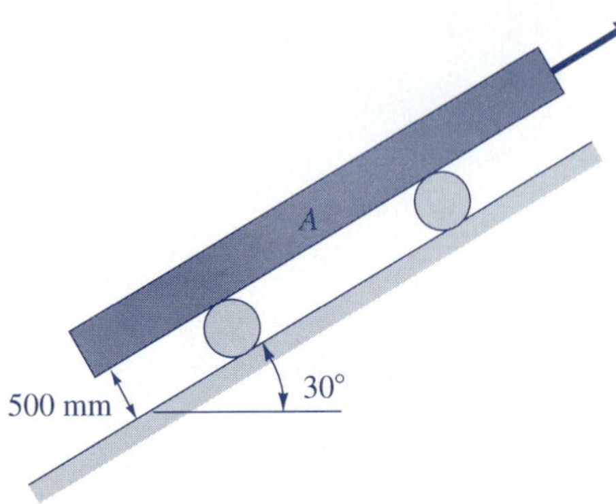

Figure P.17.61.

17.62. A main gear A rotates about a fixed axis and meshes with four identical floating gears B. The floating gears, in turn, mesh with the stationary gear F. If a torque T of 200 N-m is applied to the main gear A, what is its angular speed in 5 sec? The following data apply:

$$M_A = 100 \text{ kg}, \qquad k_A = 250 \text{ mm}$$
$$M_B = 20 \text{ kg}, \qquad k_B = 40 \text{ mm}$$

The system is horizontal. Read the first sentence of Problem 17.60.

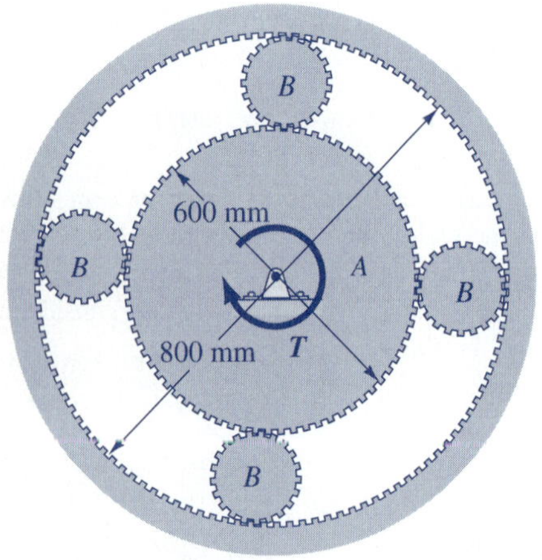

Figure P.17.62.

17.63. Two spheres, each of weight 2 N and diameter 30 mm, slide in smooth troughs inclined at an angle of 30°. A torque T of 2 *N*-m is applied as shown for 3 sec and is then zero. How far d up the inclines do the spheres move? The support system exclusive of the spheres has a weight of 10 N and a radius of gyration for the axis of rotation of 100 mm. Neglect friction and wind-resistance losses. Treat the spheres as particles.

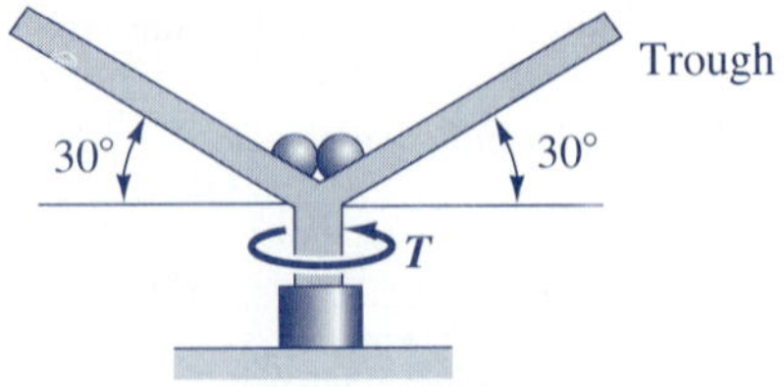

Figure P.17.63.

17.64. Two small spheres, each of weight 3 N, slide on a smooth rod curved in the shape of a parabola as shown. The curved rod is mounted on a platform on which a torque T of 1.5 N-m is applied for 2 sec. What is the angular speed of the system after 2 sec? Neglect friction. The curved rod and the platform have a mass of 5 kg and a radius of gyration of 200 mm.

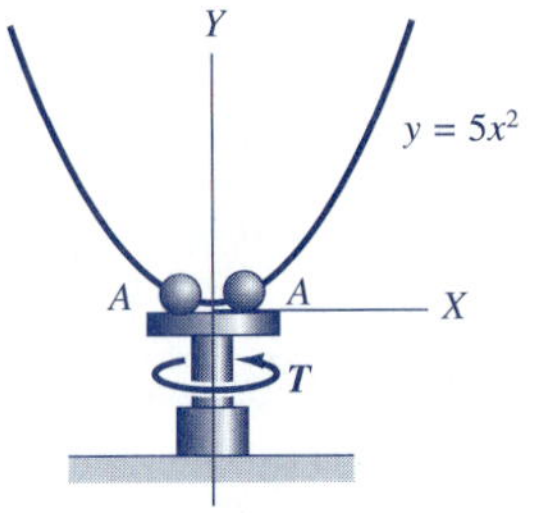

Figure P.17.64.

17.65. A disc of mass 3 kg is suspended between two wires. A bullet is fired at the disc and lodges at point A, for which $r = 100$ mm and $\theta = 45°$. If the bullet is traveling at a speed of 600 m/sec before striking the disc, what is the angular velocity of the system directly after the bullet gets lodged? The bullet weighs 1 N (*Caution:* What point in the disc should you work with? It is not 0!)

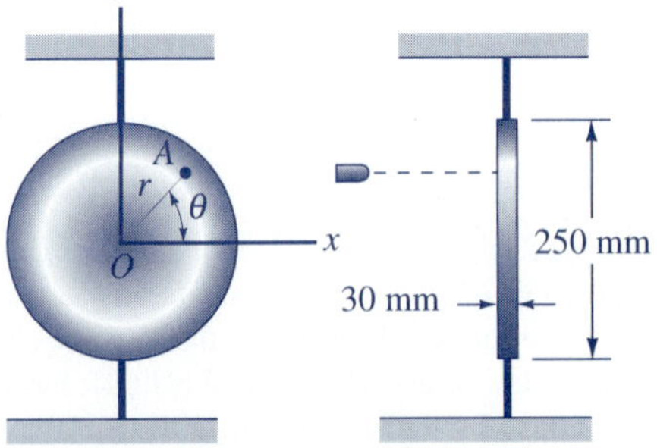

Figure P.17.65.

17.6 Impulsive Forces and Torques: Eccentric Impact

In Chapter 14, we introduced the concept of an *impulsive force*. Recall that an impulsive force F acts over a very short time interval Δt but has a very high value during this interval such that the impulse $\int_0^{\Delta t} F\,dt$ is significant. The impulse of other ordinary forces (not having very high peaks during Δt) is usually neglected for the short interval Δt. The same concept applies to torques, so that we have *impulsive torques*. The impulsive force and impulsive torque concepts are most valuable for the consideration of impact of bodies. Here, the collision forces and torques are impulsive while the other forces, such as gravity forces, have negligible impulse during collision.

In Chapter 14, we considered the case of *central impact* between bodies. Recall that for such problems the mass centers of the colliding bodies lie along the line of impact.[12] At this time, we shall consider the *eccentric impact of slab-like* bodies undergoing plane motion such as shown in Fig. 17.34. For eccentric impact, at *least one of the mass centers does not lie along line of impact*. The bodies in Fig. 17.32 have just begun contact whereby point A of one body has just touched point B of the other body. The velocity of point A just before contact (preimpact) is given as $(V_A)_i$, while the velocity just before contact for point B is $(V_B)_i$. (The i stands for "initial," as in earlier work.) We shall consider only *smooth bodies,* so that the impulsive forces acting on the body at the point of contact are *collinear* with the line of impact. As a result of the impulsive forces, there is a *period of deformation*, as in our earlier studies, and a *period of restitution*. In the period of deformation, the bodies are deforming, while in the period of restitution there is a complete or partial recovery of the original geometries. At the end of the period of deformation, the points A and B have the *same velocity* and we denote this velocity as V_D. Directly after impact (post impact), the velocities of points A and B are denoted as $(V_A)_f$ and $V_B)_f$, respectively, where the subscript f is used to connote the final velocity resulting solely from the impact process. We shall be able to use the *linear impulse-momentum equation* and the *angular impulse-momentum* equation to relate the velocities, both linear and angular, for preimpact and postimpact states. These equations do not take into account the nature of the material of the colliding bodies, and so additional information is needed for solving these problems.

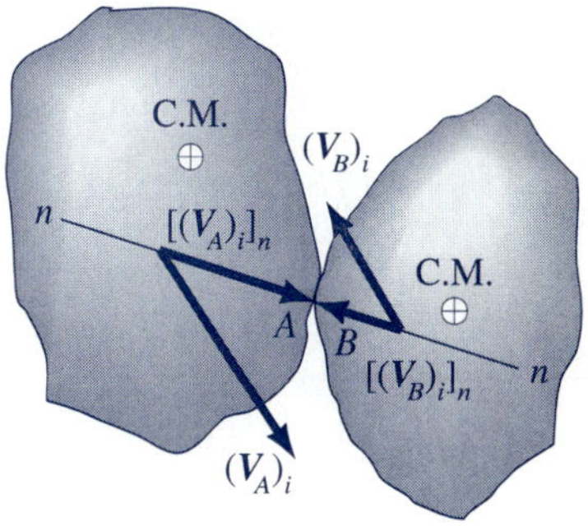

Figure 17.34. Eccentric impact between two bodies.

For this reason, we use the ratio between the impulse on each body during the period of restitution, $\int R\,dt$, and the impulse on each body during the period of deformation, $\int D\,dt$. As in central impact, the ratio is a number ϵ, called the *coefficient of restitution*, which depends primarily on the materials of the bodies in collision. Thus,

$$\epsilon = \frac{\int R\,dt}{\int D\,dt} \tag{17.29}$$

[12]The line of impact is normal to the plane of contact between the bodies.

We shall now show that the components along the line of impact n–n of $\mathbf{V}_A$ and $\mathbf{V}_B$, taken at pre- and postimpact, are related to ϵ by the very same relation that we had for central impact. That is,

$$\epsilon = -\frac{\left[(V_B)_f\right]_n - \left[(V_A)_f\right]_n}{\left[(V_B)_i\right]_n - \left[(V_A)_i\right]_n} \tag{17.30}$$

Recall that the numerator represents the relative velocity of separation along n of the points of contact, whereas the denominator represents the relative velocity of approach along n of these points.

We shall first consider the case where the bodies are in *no way constrained* in their plane of motion; we can then neglect all impulses except that coming from the impact. We now consider the body having contact point A. In Fig. 17.35 we have shown this body with impulse $\int D\,dt$ acting. Using the component of the *linear momentum equation* along line of impact n–n, we can say for the center of mass;

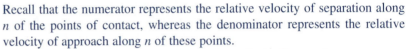

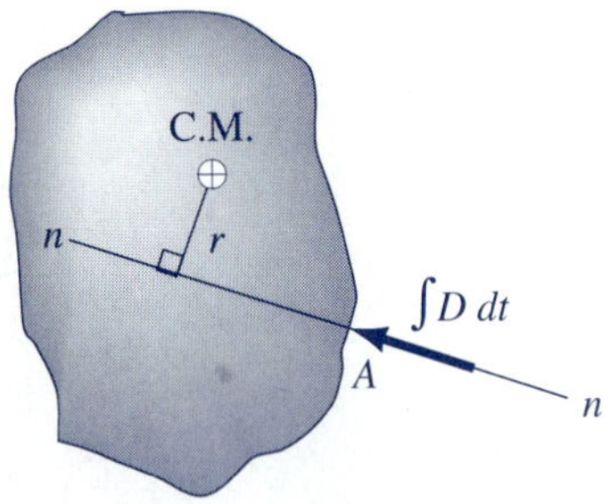

Figure 17.35. Impulse acting on one of the bodies.

$$\int D\,dt = M\left[(V_C)_D\right]_n - M\left[(V_C)_i\right]_n \tag{17.31}$$

where $(V_C)_i$ refers to the preimpact velocity of the center of mass and where $(V_C)_D$ is the velocity of the center of mass at the end of the deformation period. Similarly, for the period of restitution, we have

$$\int R\,dt = M\left[(V_C)_f\right]_n - M\left[(V_C)_D\right]_n \tag{17.32}$$

For angular momentum, we can say for the deformation period using r as the distance from the center of mass to n–n:

$$r\int D\,dt = I\omega_D - I\omega_i \tag{17.33}$$

Similarly, for the period of restitution:

$$r\int R\,dt = I\omega_f - I\omega_D \tag{17.34}$$

Now, substitute the right sides of Eqs. 17.31 and 17.32 into Eq. 17.29. We get on cancellation of M:

$$\epsilon = \frac{\left[(V_C)_f\right]_n - \left[(V_C)_D\right]_n}{\left[(V_C)_D\right]_n - \left[(V_C)_i\right]_n} = \frac{\left[(V_C)_D\right]_n - \left[(V_C)_f\right]_n}{\left[(V_C)_i\right]_n - \left[(V_C)_D\right]_n} \tag{17.35}$$

Next, substitute for the impulses in Eq. 17.29 using Eqs. 17.33 and 17.34. We get on canceling only I:

$$\epsilon = \frac{r\omega_f - r\omega_D}{r\omega_D - r\omega_i} = \frac{r\omega_D - r\omega_f}{r\omega_i - r\omega_D} \tag{17.36}$$

Adding the numerators and denominators of Eqs. 17.35 and 17.36, we can then say on rearranging the terms:

$$\epsilon = \frac{\left\{\left[(V_C)_D\right]_n + r\omega_D\right\} - \left\{\left[(V_C)_f\right]_n + r\omega_f\right\}}{\left\{\left[(V_C)_i\right]_n + r\omega_i\right\} - \left\{\left[(V_C)_D\right]_n + r\omega_D\right\}} \tag{17.37}$$

We pause now to consider the *kinematics* of the motion. We can relate the velocities of points A and C on the body (see Fig. 17.36) as follows:

$$\boldsymbol{V}_A = \boldsymbol{V}_C + \boldsymbol{\omega} \times \boldsymbol{\rho}_{CA} \tag{17.38}$$

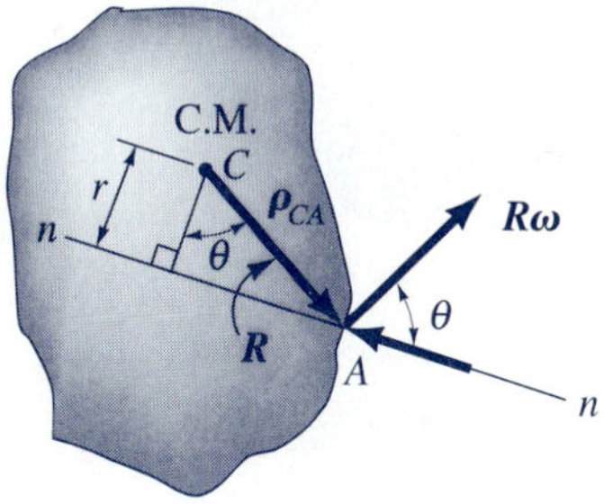

Figure 17.36. Slab with $|\boldsymbol{\rho}_{CA}|$ as R.

Note that the magnitude of $\boldsymbol{\rho}_{CA}$ is R as shown in the diagram. Since $\boldsymbol{\omega}$ is normal to the plane of symmetry of the body and thus to $\boldsymbol{\rho}_{CA}$, the value of the last term in Eq. 17.38 is $R\omega$ with a direction normal to R as has been shown in Fig. 17.36. The components of the vectors in Eq. 17.38 in direction n can then be given as follows:

$$(V_A)_n = (V_C)_n + \omega R \cos\theta \tag{17.39}$$

Since $R \cos \theta = r$ (see Fig. 17.36), we conclude that

$$(V_A)_n = (V_C)_n + r\omega \tag{17.40}$$

With the preceding result applied to the initial condition (i), the final condition (f), and the intermediate condition (D), we can now go back to Eq. 17.37 and replace the expressions inside the braces ({ }) by the left side of Eq. 17.40 as follows:

$$\epsilon = \frac{\left[(V_A)_D\right]_n - \left[(V_A)_f\right]_n}{\left[(V_A)_i\right]_n - \left[(V_A)_D\right]_n} \tag{17.41}$$

A similar process for the body having contact point B will yield the preceding equation with subscript B replacing subscript A:

$$\epsilon = \frac{\left[(V_B)_D\right]_n - \left[(V_B)_f\right]_n}{\left[(V_B)_i\right]_n - \left[(V_B)_D\right]_n} = \frac{\left[(V_B)_f\right]_n - \left[(V_B)_D\right]_n}{\left[(V_B)_D\right]_n - \left[(V_B)_i\right]_n} \tag{17.42}$$

Now add the numerators and denominators of the right side of Eq. 17.41 and the extreme right side of Eq. 17.42. Noting that

$$\left[(V_A)_D\right]_n = \left[(V_B)_D\right]_n \tag{17.43}$$

we get Eq. 17.30, thus demonstrating the validity of that equation.

Let us next consider the case where one or both bodies undergoing impact is constrained to *rotate about a fixed axis*. We have shown such a body in Fig. 17.37 where O is the axis of rotation and point A is the contact point. If an impulse is developed at the point of contact A (we have shown the impulse during the period of deformation), then clearly there will be an

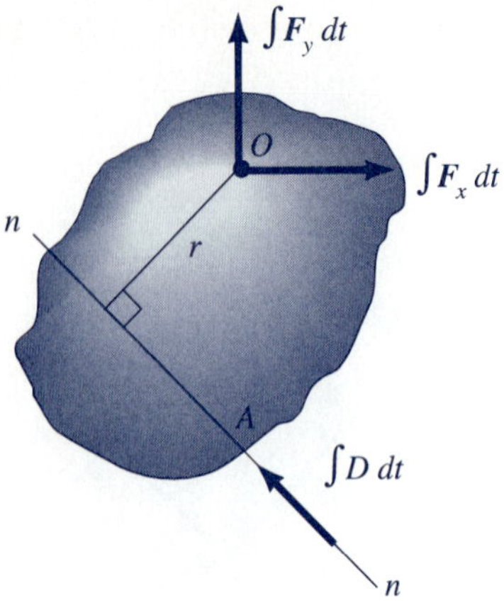

Figure 17.37. Impact for a body under constraint at O.

impulsive force at O, as shown in the diagram. We shall employ the *angular impulse-momentum* equation about the fixed point O. Thus, we have for the period of deformation and the period of restitution:

$$r\int D\,dt = I_0\omega_D - I_0\omega_i$$
$$r\int R\,dt = I_0\omega_f - I_0\omega_D$$

Now solve for the impulses in the equation above, and substitute into Eq. 17.29. Canceling I_0, the moment of inertia about the axis of rotation at O, we get

$$\epsilon = \frac{r\omega_f - r\omega_D}{r\omega_D - r\omega_i} = \frac{r\omega_D - r\omega_f}{r\omega_i - r\omega_D} \tag{17.44}$$

In Fig. 17.38 we see that

$$V_A = R\omega$$

Therefore,

$$(V_A)_n = R\omega\cos\theta = r\omega$$

Using the above result in Eq. 17.44, we get

$$\epsilon = \frac{\left[(V_A)_D\right]_n - \left[(V_A)_f\right]_n}{\left[(V_A)_i\right]_n - \left[(V_A)_D\right]_n} \tag{17.45}$$

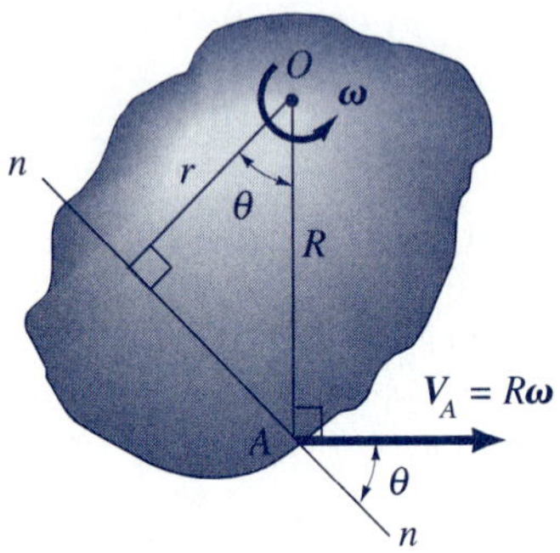

Figure 17.38. Velocity of point A is $R\omega$.

But this expression is identical to Eq. 17.41. And by considering the second body, which is either free or constrained to rotate, we get an equation corresponding to Eq. 17.42. We can then conclude that Eq. 17.30 is valid for impact where one or both bodies are constrained to rotate about a fixed axis.

In a typical impact problem, the motion of the bodies preimpact is given and the motion of the bodies postimpact is desired. Thus, there could be four unknowns—two velocities of the mass centers of the bodies plus two angular velocities. The required equations for solving the problem are formed from linear and angular momentum considerations of the bodies taken separately or taken as a system. Only impulsive forces are taken into consideration during the time interval spanning the impact. If the bodies are considered separately, we simply use the formulations of Section 17.5, remembering to observe Newton's third law at the point of impact between the two bodies. Furthermore, we must use the coefficient of restitution equation 17.30. Generally, kinematic considerations are also needed to solve the problem. When there are no other impulsive forces other than those occurring at the point of impact, it might be profitable to consider the bodies as one system. Then, clearly, as a result of Newton's third law, we must have *conservation of linear momentum* relative to an inertial reference, and also we must have *conservation of angular momentum* about *any one axis* fixed in inertial space.

We now illustrate these remarks in the following series of examples.

Example 17.11

A rectangular plate A weighing 20 N has two identical rods weighing 10 N each attached to it (see Fig. 17.39). The plate moves on a plane smooth surface at a speed of 5 m/sec. Moving oppositely at 10 m/sec is disc B, weighing 10 N. A perfectly elastic collision ($\epsilon = 1$) takes place at G. What is the speed of the center of mass of the plate just after collision (postimpact)? Solve the problem two ways: consider the bodies separately and consider the bodies as a system.

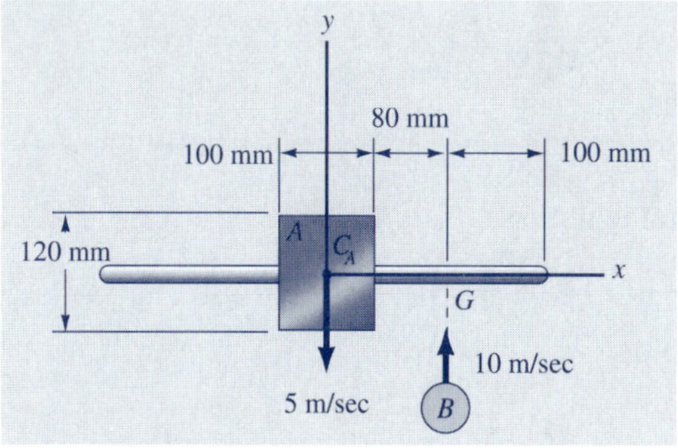

Figure 17.39. Colliding bodies.

Solution 1. We can consider the disc to be a particle since this body will only translate. Let point G be the point of contact on the rod. We then have, for Eq. 17.30:

$$\epsilon = 1 = -\frac{(V_G)_f - (V_B)_f}{-5 - 10}$$

Therefore,

$$(V_G)_f - (V_B)_f = 15 \qquad \text{(a)}$$

Now, consider linear and angular momentum for each of the bodies. For this purpose we have shown the bodies in Fig. 17.40 with only impulsive forces acting. We might call such a diagram an "impulsive free-body diagram." We then see that C_A must move in the plus or minus y direction after impact. We can then say for body A, using **linear impulse-momentum** and **angular impulse-momentum equations** (the latter about the center of mass):

$$\int F\,dt = \frac{40}{g}\left[\left(V_{C_A}\right)_f - (-5)\right] \qquad \text{(b)}$$

$$(.13)\int F\,dt = \left[\frac{1}{12}\left(\frac{20}{g}\right)(.10^2 + .12^2)\right.$$

$$\left. + 2\left(\frac{1}{12}\right)\left(\frac{10}{g}\right)(.18)^2 + 2\left(\frac{10}{g}\right)(.14)^2\right](\omega_A - 0) \qquad \text{(c)}$$

$$= .0496\omega_A$$

Example 17.11 (Continued)

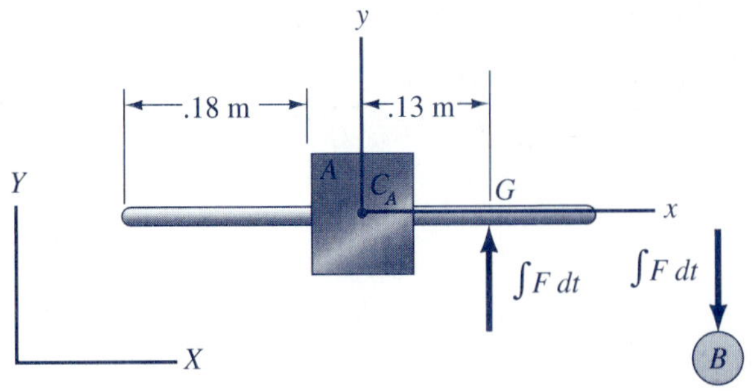

Figure 17.40. Impulsive free-body diagrams.

For body B we have for the **linear impulse-momentum equation**:

$$-\int F\,dt = \frac{10}{g}\left[(V_B)_f - 10\right] \qquad \text{(d)}$$

From **kinematics** we have for the plate with arms:

$$(V_G)_f = (V_{C_A})_f + (\omega_A)(.13) \qquad \text{(e)}$$

We have now a complete set of equations which we can proceed to solve. We get:

$$(V_{C_A})_f = -.305 \text{ m/sec}$$

Solution 2. Equation (a) above from the coefficient of restitution and Eq. (e) above from kinematics also apply to solution 2. Substituting for $(V_G)_f$ in Eq. (a) of solution 1 using Eq. (e) of solution 1, we get for solution 2:

$$(V_{C_A})_f + .13\omega_A - (V_B)_f = 15 \qquad \text{(a)}$$

Conservation of linear momentum for the system leads to the requirement in the y direction that

$$\frac{40}{g}(-5) + \frac{10}{g}(10) = \frac{40}{g}(V_{C_A})_f + \frac{10}{g}(V_B)_f$$

Therefore,

$$4(V_{C_A})_f + (V_B)_f = -10 \qquad \text{(b)}$$

Also **angular momentum is conserved** about any fixed z axis. We choose the axis at the position corresponding to C_A at the time of impact. Noting that I for the plate and arms is .0496 kg-m^2 from solution 1 (see Eq. (c)) and noting that B can be considered as a particle, we have

Example 17.11 (Continued)

$$\underbrace{\frac{10}{g}(10)(.13)}_{\substack{\text{angular}\\\text{momentum}\\\text{preimpact}}} = \underbrace{(.0496)\omega_A + \frac{10}{g}(V_B)_f(.13)}_{\substack{\text{angular}\\\text{momentum}\\\text{postimpact}}}$$

Therefore,

$$\omega_A = -2.67(V_B)_f + 26.7 \qquad \text{(c)}$$

Solving Eqs. (a), (b), and (c) simultaneously we get:

$$\boxed{(V_{C_A})_f = -.305 \text{ m/sec}}$$

We leave it to you to demonstrate there has been *conservation of mechanical energy* during this perfectly elastic impact. We could have used this fact in place of Eq. (a) in solution 1.

Note that there was some saving of time and labor in using the system approach throughout for the preceding problem wherein a rigid body, namely the plate and its arms, collided with a body, the disc, which could be considered as a particle. In problems involving two colliding rigid bodies neither of which can be considered a particle, we must consider the bodies separately since the system approach does not yield a sufficient number of independent equations as you can yourself demonstrate.

In the preceding example, the bodies were not constrained except to move in a plane. If one or both colliding bodies is pinned, the procedure for solving the problem may be a little different than what was shown in Example 17.11. Note that there will be unknown supporting impulsive forces at the pin of any pinned body. If we are not interested in the supporting impulsive force for a pinned body, we only consider *angular momentum* about the pin for that pinned body; in this way the undesired unknown supporting impulsive forces at the pin do not enter the calculations. Other than this one factor, the calculations are the same as in the previous example.

You will recall from momentum considerations of particles that we considered the collision of a comparatively small body with a very massive one. We could not use the conservation of momentum equation for the collision between such bodies since the velocity change of the massive body went to zero as the mass (mathematically speaking) went to infinity, thus producing an indeterminacy in our idealized formulations. We shall next illustrate the procedure for the collision of a very massive body with a much smaller one. You will note that we cannot consider a system approach for linear or angular momentum conservation for the same reasons set forth in Chapter 14.

Example 17.12

A 20-lb rod AB is dropped onto a massive body (Fig. 17.41). What is the angular velocity of the rod postimpact for the following conditions:

A. Smooth floor; elastic impact.
B. Rough floor (no slipping); plastic impact.

In either case, the velocity of end B preimpact is

$$V_B = \sqrt{2gh} = \sqrt{(2)(32.2)(2)} = 11.35 \text{ ft/sec}$$

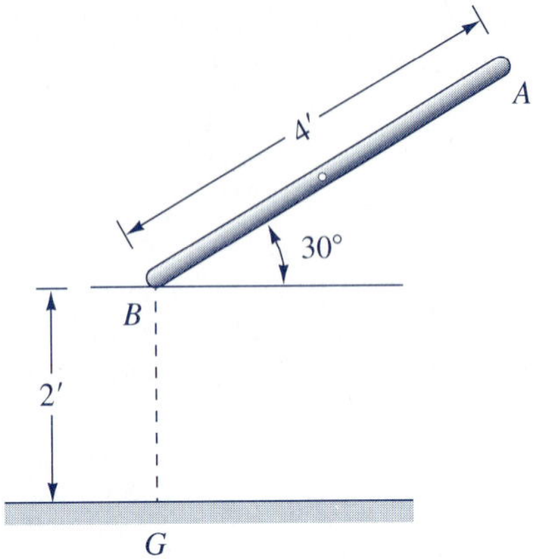

Figure 17.41. Falling rod on a massive body.

We now consider each case separately.

Case A. Equation 17.30 can be used here. Thus,

$$\epsilon = 1 = -\frac{\left[(V_B)_f\right]_n - 0}{-11.35 - 0}$$

Therefore,

$$\left[(V_B)_f\right]_n = 11.35 \text{ ft/sec} \qquad \text{(a)}$$

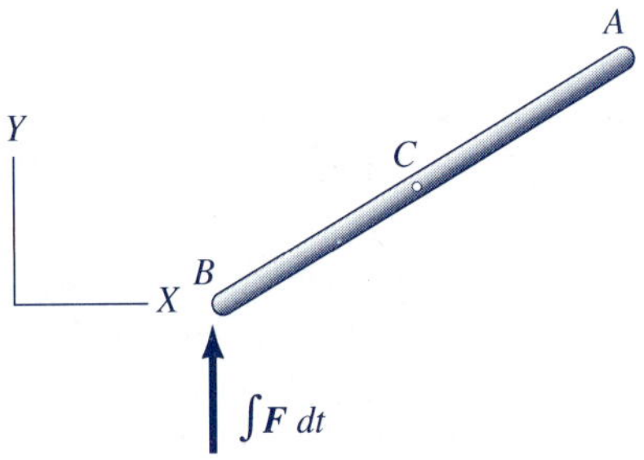

Figure 17.42. Impulsive free-body diagram.

Next, considering rod AB in Fig. 17.42 we have for **linear impulse-** and **angular impulse-momentum** considerations (the latter about an axis at the center of mass).

$$\int F\,dt = \frac{20}{g}\left[(V_C)_f - (-11.35)\right] \qquad \text{(b)}$$

$$-(2)(\cos 30°)\int F\,dt = \frac{1}{12}\left(\frac{20}{g}\right)(4^2)\omega_f \qquad \text{(c)}$$

From **kinematics**, we have[13]

$$(\boldsymbol{V}_B)_f = (\boldsymbol{V}_C)_f + \boldsymbol{\omega}_f \times \boldsymbol{\rho}_{CB}$$

$$\left[(V_B)_x\right]_f \boldsymbol{i} + 11.35\boldsymbol{j} = (V_C)_f\boldsymbol{j} + \omega_f\boldsymbol{k} \times (2)(-.866\boldsymbol{i} - .5\boldsymbol{j})$$

$$\left[(V_B)_x\right]_f \boldsymbol{i} + 11.35\boldsymbol{j} = (V_C)_f\boldsymbol{j} - 1.732\omega_f\boldsymbol{j} + \omega_f\boldsymbol{i}$$

Hence, the scalar equations are

$$11.35 = (V_C)_f - 1.732\omega_f \qquad \text{(d)}$$

$$\left[(V_B)_x\right]_f = \omega_f \qquad \text{(e)}$$

[13]Note that since the initial velocity of C is vertical and since the impulsive force is vertical, the final velocity of C must be vertical. This fact is used in the kinematics.

Example 17.12 (Continued)

We now have a complete set of equations considering $\int F\,dt$ as an unknown.

Solving, we have for the desired unknowns:

$$\omega_f = -9.07 \text{ rad/sec}$$
$$\left[(V_B)_x\right]_f = -9.07 \text{ ft/sec}$$

You can demonstrate that energy has been conserved in this action. We could have used this fact in lieu of Eq. (a) for this problem.

Case B. Here we have no slipping on the rough surface and zero vertical movement of point B. Accordingly, we have shown rod BA with vertical and horizontal impulses in Fig. 17.43. The **linear momentum equations** for the center of mass then are

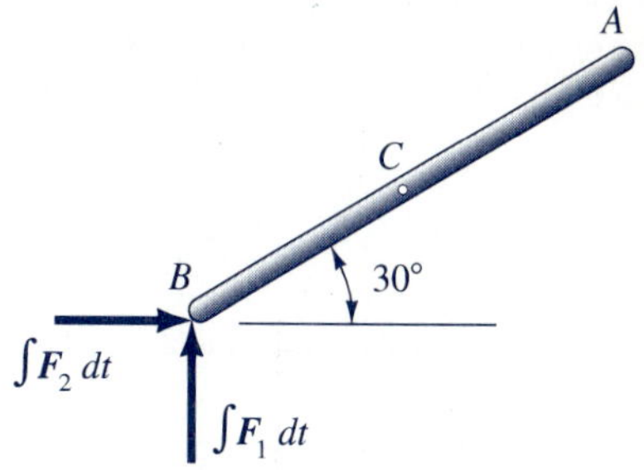

Figure 17.43. Impulsive free-body diagram.

$$\int F_1\,dt = \frac{20}{g}\left\{\left[(V_C)_y\right]_f - (-11.35)\right\} \qquad \text{(f)}$$
$$\int F_2\,dt = \frac{20}{g}\left\{\left[(V_C)_x\right]_f - 0\right\} \qquad \text{(g)}$$

The **angular impulse-momentum equation** about the center of mass is

$$-2(\cos 30°)\int F_1\,dt + 2(\sin 30°)\int F_2\,dt = \frac{1}{12}\left(\frac{20}{g}\right)(4^2)\omega_f \qquad \text{(h)}$$

From **kinematics**, noting that at postimpact there is *pure rotation* about point B, we have

$$[(V_C)_y]_f = 2(\cos 30°)(\omega_f) = 1.732\omega_f \qquad \text{(i)}$$
$$[(V_C)_x]_f = -2(\sin 30°)(\omega_f) = -\omega_f \qquad \text{(j)}$$

Substitute for $\int F_1\,dt$ and $\int F_2\,dt$ from Eqs. (f) and (g) into Eq. (h). We get on then employing Eqs. (i) and (j):

$$-(2)(.866)\left(\frac{20}{g}\right)(1.732\omega_f + 11.35) + (2)(.5)\left(\frac{20}{g}\right)(-\omega_f) = \frac{1}{12}\left(\frac{20}{g}\right)(4^2)\omega_f$$

Therefore,

$$\omega_f = -3.69 \text{ rad/sec}$$

PROBLEMS

17.66. A rod AB slides on a smooth surface at a speed of 10 m/sec and hits a disc D moving at a speed of 5 m/sec. What is the postimpact velocity of point A for a coefficient of restitution $\epsilon = .8$? The rod weighs 30 N and the disc weighs 8 N. Solve by considering AB and D separately.

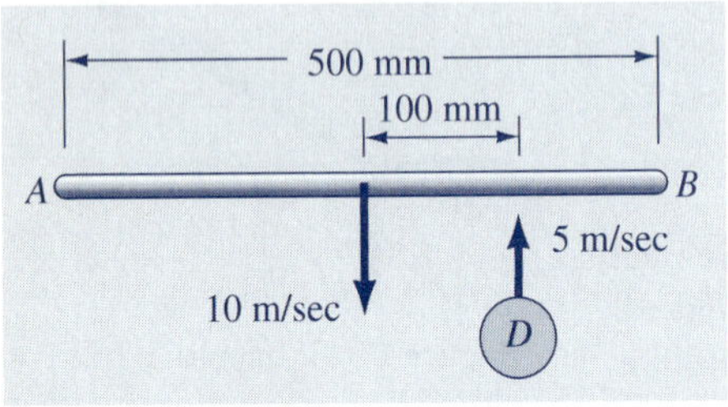

Figure P.17.66.

17.67. Solve Problem 17.66 by considering the two bodies as a system.

17.68. Rods AB and HD translate on a horizontal frictionless surface. When they collide at G we have a coefficient of restitution of .7. Rod HD weighs 70 N and rod AB weighs 40 N. What is the postimpact angular speed of AB?

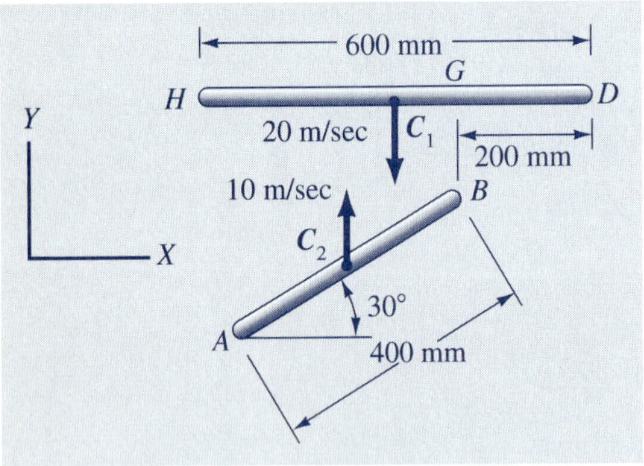

Figure P.17.68.

17.69. Two slender rods 20 lb each with small 45° protuberances are shown on a smooth horizontal surface. The rods are identical except for the position of the protuberances. Rod A moves to the left at a speed of 10 ft/sec while rod B is stationary. If the protuberance surfaces are smooth, and an impact having $\epsilon = .8$ occurs, what should d be in order for the postimpact angular speed of A to be 5 rad/sec? Neglect the protuberance for determination of moments of inertia and centers of mass.

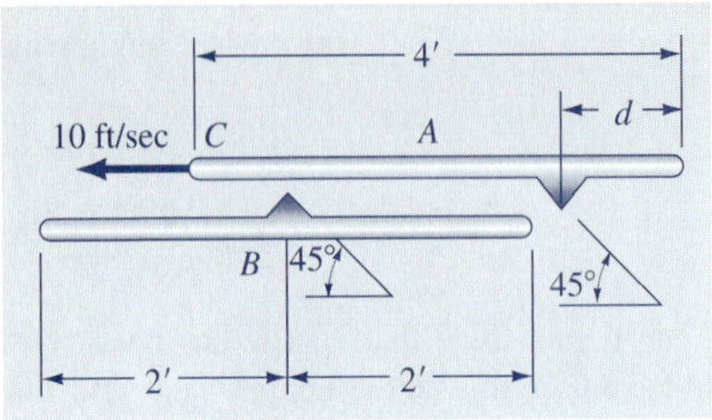

Figure P.17.69.

17.70. A 22-N sphere moving at a speed of 10 m/sec hits the end of a 1-m rod having a mass of 10 kg. The coefficient of restitution for the impact is .9. What is the postimpact angular velocity of the rod if it is stationary just before impact? The rod is pinned at O.

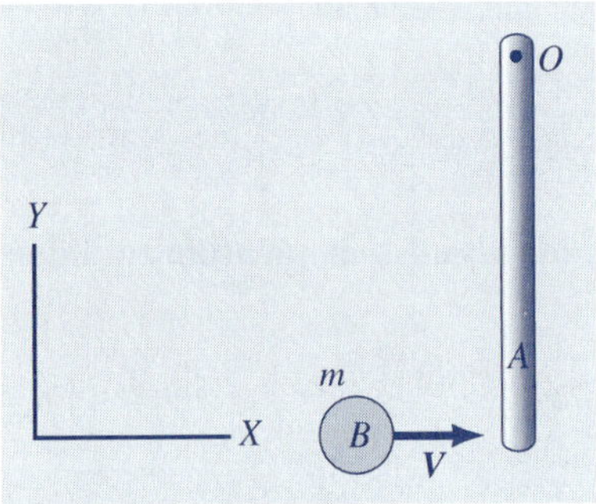

Figure P.17.70.

17.71. A rod A weighing 50 N rotates freely about a hinge at a speed of 10 rad/sec on a frictionless surface just prior to hitting a disc B weighing 20 N and moving at a speed of 5 m/sec. If the coefficient of restitution is .8, what is the postimpact angular speed of A? The contact surface between the rod and the disc is smooth.

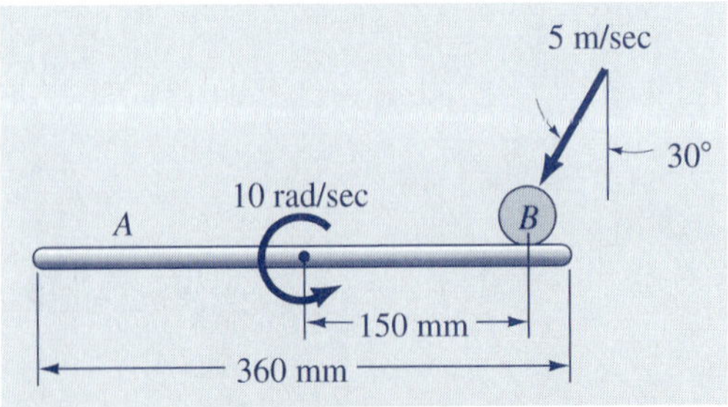

Figure P.17.71.

17.72. A stiff bent rod is dropped so that end A strikes a heavy table D. If the impact is plastic and there is no sliding at A, what is the postimpact speed of end B? The rod weighs per unit length 30 N/m.

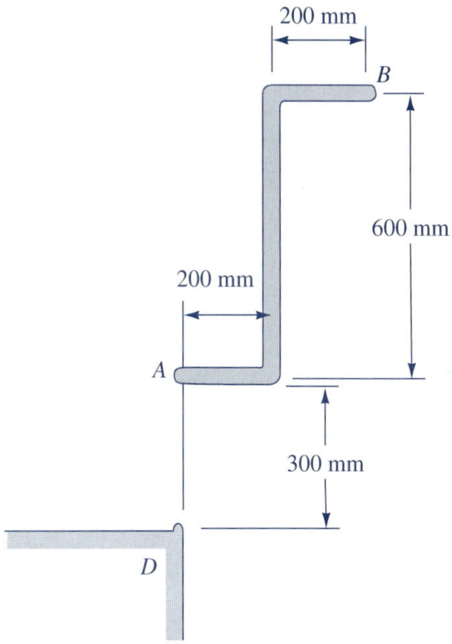

Figure P.17.72.

17.73. Solve Problem 17.72 for an elastic impact at A. Take the surface of contact to be smooth. Demonstrate that energy has been conserved.

17.74. A drumstick and a wooden learner's drum are shown in (a) of the diagram. At the beginning of a drum roll, the drumstick is horizontal. The action of the drummer's hand is simulated by force components F_x and F_y, which make A a stationary axis of rotation. Also, there is a constant couple M of .5 N-m. If the action starts from a stationary position shown, what is the frequency of the drum roll for perfectly elastic collision between the drumstick and the learner's drum? The mass of the drumstick is 200 g. Idealize the drumstick as a uniform slender rod.

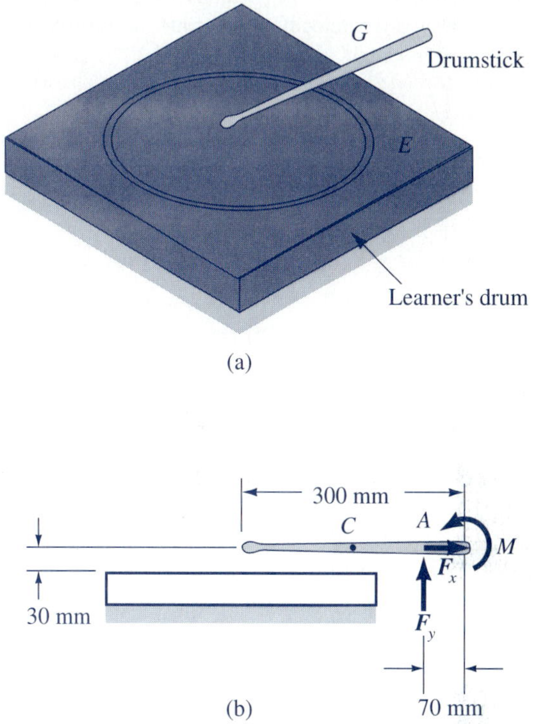

Figure P.17.74.

17.75. A block of ice 1 ft × 1 ft × $\frac{1}{2}$ ft slides along a surface at a speed of 10 ft/sec. The block strikes stop D in a plastic impact. Does the block turn over after the impact? What is the highest angular speed reached? Take $\gamma = 62.4$ lb/ft^2.

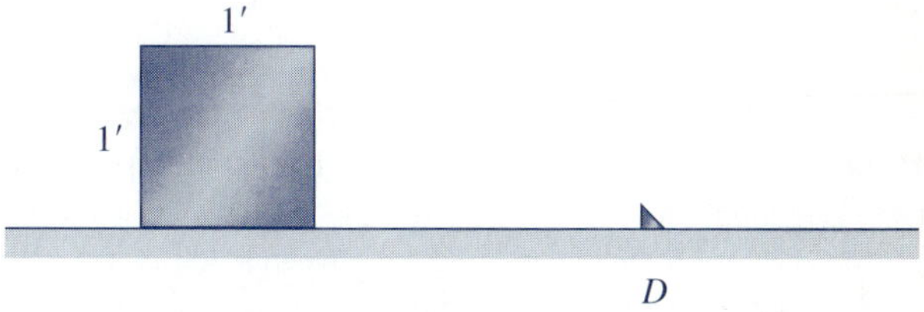

Figure P.17.75.

17.76. A horizontal rigid rod is dropped from a height 10 ft above a heavy table. The end of the rod collides with the table. If the coefficient of impact ϵ between the end of the rod and the corner of the table is .6, what is the postimpact angular velocity of the rod? Also, what is the velocity of the center of mass postimpact: The rod is 1 ft in length and weighs 1.5 lb.

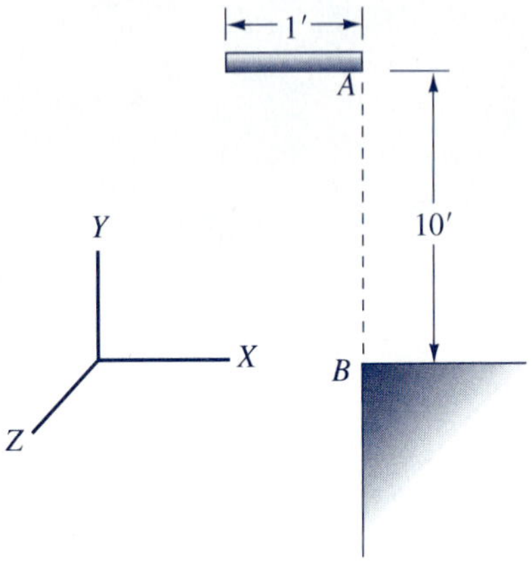

Figure P.17.76.

17.77. A rod A is dropped from a height of 120 mm above B. If an elastic collision takes place at B, at what time Δt later does a second collision with support D take place? The rod weighs 40 N.

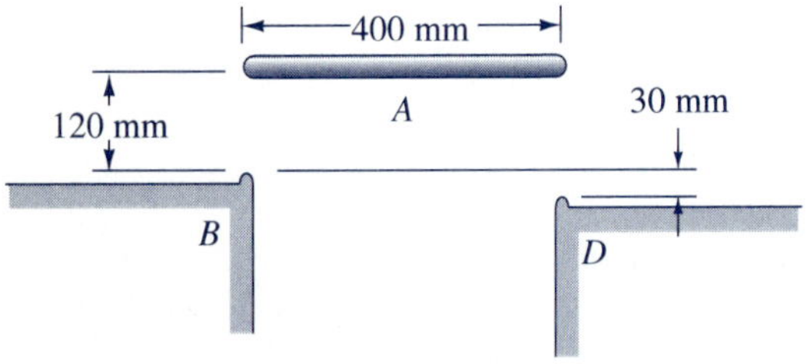

Figure P.17.77.

17.78. A packing crate falls on the side of a hill at a place where there is smooth rock. If $\epsilon = .8$, determine the speed of the center of the crate just after impact. The crate weighs 400 N and has a radius of gyration about an axis through the center and normal to the face in the diagram of $\sqrt{2}$ m.

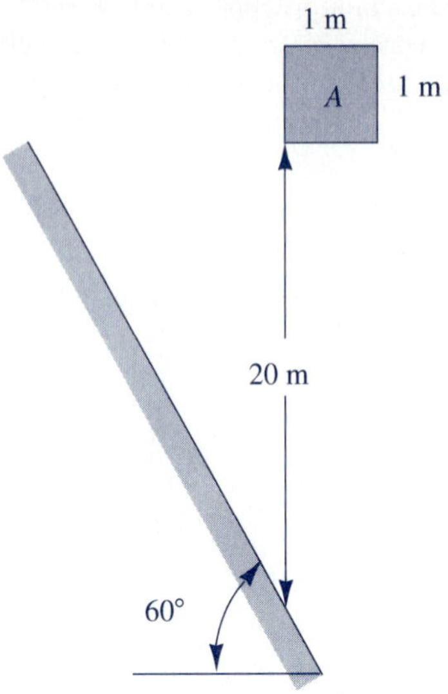

Figure P.17.78.

17.79. An arrow moving essentially horizontally at a speed of 20 m/sec impinges on a stationary wooden block which can rotate freely about light rods DE and GH. The arrowhead weighs 1.5 N, and the shaft, which is 250 mm long, weighs .7 N. If the block weighs 10 N, what is the angular velocity of the block just after the arrowhead becomes stuck in the wood? The arrowhead sinks into the wood at point A such that the shaft sticks out 250 mm from the surface of the wood.

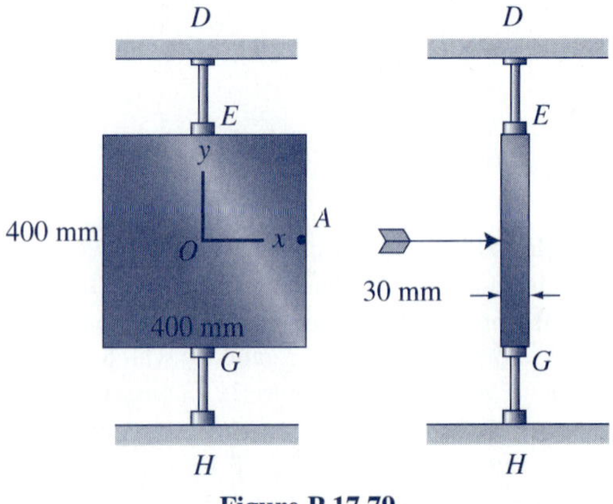

Figure P.17.79.

17.7 Closure

Let us now pause for an overview of the text up to this point. Recall the following:

(a) In Chapter 13, we studied energy methods for single particles and systems of particles with a short introduction to coplanar rigid body motions.
(b) Then in Chapter 14, we presented linear and angular momentum principles for a single particle and systems of particles with again a short introduction to plane motion of rigid bodies.

These methods are derived from Newton's law. In short, they are integrated forms of Newton's law which bring in useful concepts and greater ease in solving many problems. Next, after studying *Chasles' theorem* and kinematics of rigid bodies in Chapter 15, we went to Chapter 16.

(c) In Chapter 16, we studied the dynamics of plane motion for rigid bodies using Newton's law and the equation $\boldsymbol{M}_A = \dot{\boldsymbol{H}}_A$ directly rather than integrated of forms of these equations, namely the energy and momentum equations.

Now in Chapter 17, we went through a partial recycle of the above steps. That is, we went back to Chapters 13 and 14 this time for three-dimensional formulations and focused on rigid bodies and systems of rigid bodies. Naturally, there is an overlap with those earlier chapters plus an expansion of viewpoints to include a general formulation and use of $\boldsymbol{H}$ and a look at eccentric coplanar impact of more complex bodies. Again, with the aforementioned integrated forms of *Newton's law*, we were able to solve some interesting problems.

We are now at a stage comparable to what we were in just preceding Chapter 16. In Chapter 18, we go back again to Newton's law and $\boldsymbol{M}_A = \dot{\boldsymbol{H}}_A$, this time for the dynamics of general three-dimensional motion of rigid bodies. This is considered the province of a second course in Dynamics and accordingly is a starred chapter. Interested students who go ahead will unlock the mysteries of gyroscopic motion and the performance of gyros among other interesting applications and concepts. In the process, those students will meet the famous Euler equations of motion whose simplified, special form we have been using up to this point.

PROBLEMS

17.80. Gear E rotates at an angular speed ω of 5 rad/sec and drives four smaller "floating" gears A, B, C, and D, which roll within stationary gear F. What is the kinetic energy of the system if gear E weighs 50 lb and each of the small gear weighs 10 lb?

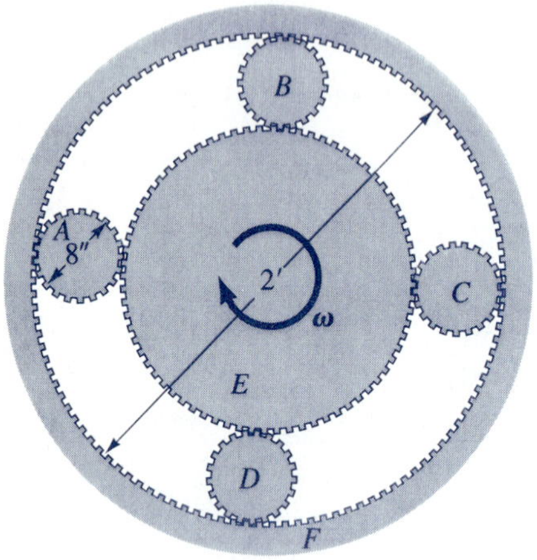

Figure P.17.80.

17.81. A homogeneous rectangular parallelepiped weighing 200 N rotates at 20 rad/sec about a main diagonal held by bearings A and B, which are mounted on a vehicle moving at a speed 20 m/sec. What is the kinetic energy of the rectangular parallelepiped relative to the ground?

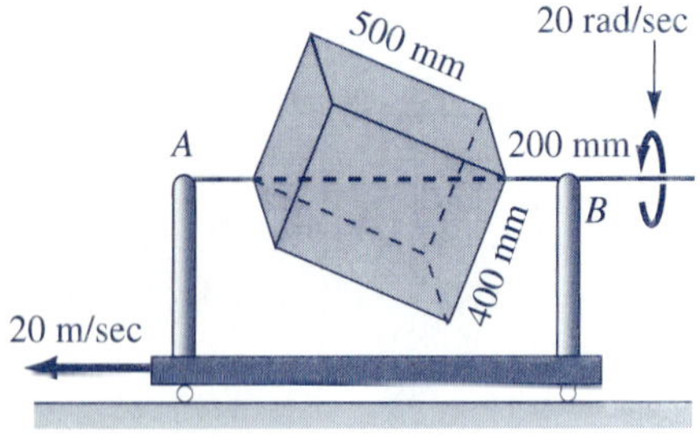

Figure P.17.81.

17.82. A rod AB is held at a position $\theta = 45°$ and released. HA is a light wire to which the rod is attached. When AB is vertical, it strikes a stop E and undergoes an elastic collision. What position d of the stop will result in a zero postimpact velocity of point A? The rod has a mass $M = 10$ kg.

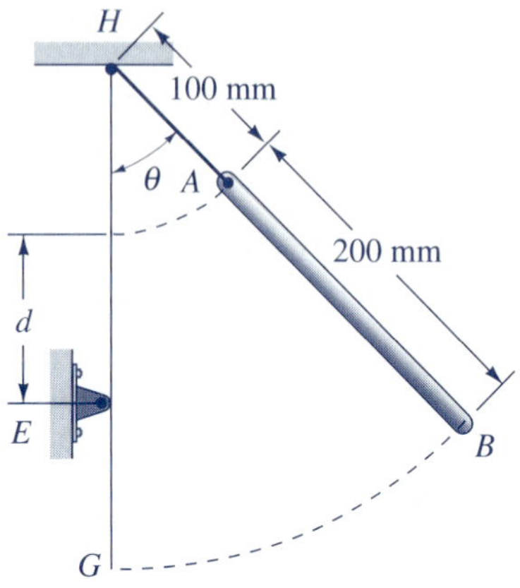

Figure P.17.82.

17.83. A stepped cylinder weighs 100 lb and has a radius of gyration of 4 ft. A 50-lb block A is welded to the cylinder. If the spring is unstretched in the configuration shown and has a spring constant K of .5 lb/in., what is the angular speed of the cylinder after it rotates 90°? Assume that the cylinder rolls without slipping.

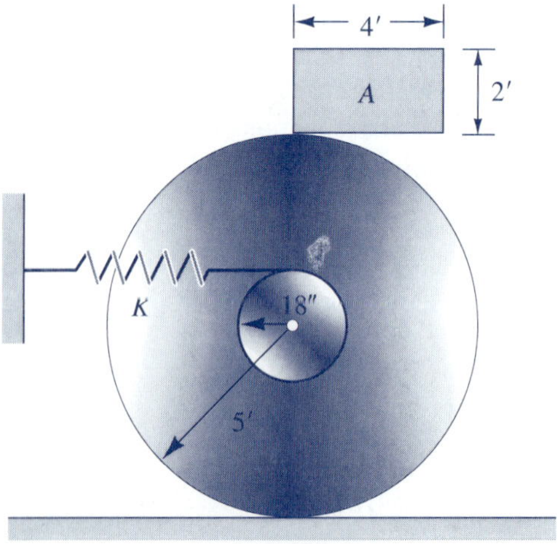

Figure P.17.83.

17.84. A tractor with driver weighs 3,000 lb. If a torque of 200 ft-lb is developed on each of the drive wheels by the motor, what is the speed of the tractor after it moves 10 ft? The large drive wheels each weigh 200 lb and have a diameter of 3 ft and a radius of gyration of 1 ft. The small wheels each weigh 40 lb and have a diameter of 1 ft with a radius of gyration of .4 ft. Do not use the center-of-mass approach for the whole system.

Figure P.17.84.

17.85. Work Problem 17.84 using the center of mass of the whole system. Find the friction forces on each wheel.

17.86. What is the angular momentum vector about the center of mass of a homogeneous rectangular parallelepiped rotating with an angular velocity of 10 rad/sec about a main diagonal? The sides of the rectangular parallelepiped are 1 ft, 2 ft, and 4 ft, as shown, and the weight is 4,000 lb.

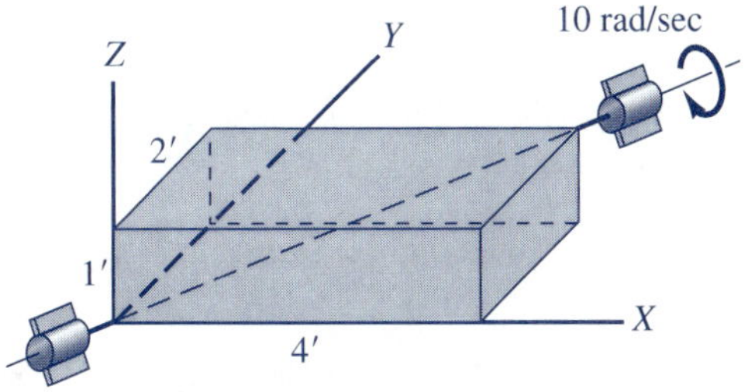

Figure P.17.86.

17.87. A force P of 200 N is applied to a cart. The cart minus the four wheels weighs 150 N. Each wheel has a weight of 50 N, a diameter of 400 mm, and a radius of gyration of 150 mm. The load A weighs 500 N. If the cart starts from rest, what is its speed in 20 sec? The wheels roll without slipping.

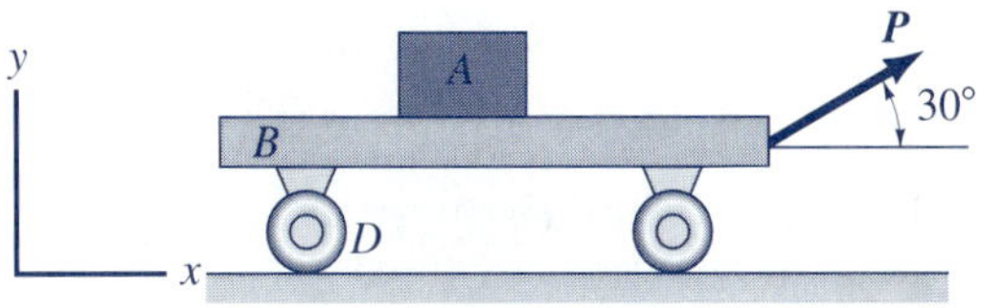

Figure P.17.87.

***17.88.** A rod weighing 90 N is guided by two slider bearings A and B. Smooth ball joints connect the rod to the bearings. A force F of 45 N acts on bearing A. What is the speed of A after it has moved 200 mm? The system is stationary for the configuration shown. Neglect friction.

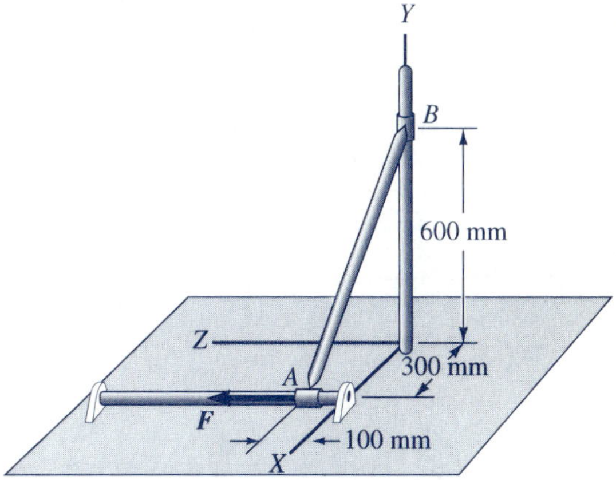

Figure P.17.88.

***17.89.** A device with thin walls contains water. The device is supported on a platform on which a torque T of .5 N-m is applied for 2 sec and is zero thereafter. What is the angular velocity ω of the system at the end of 2 sec assuming that, as a result of low viscosity, the water has no rotation relative to the ground in the vertical tubes. The system of tubes and platform have a weight of 50 N and a radius of gyration of 200 mm. [*Hint:* The pressure in the liquid is equal at all times to the specific weight γ times the distance d below the free surface of the liquid.] Note that for water γ = 9,810 N/m^3. Note: water heights in the tubes change with angular speed.

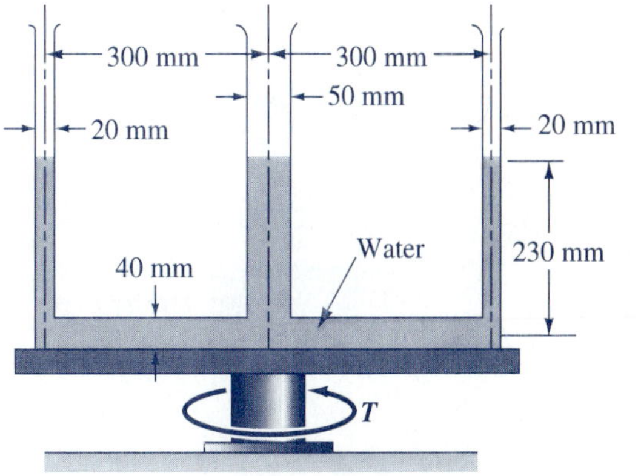

Figure P.17.89.

***17.90.** In Problem 17.89 what is the final angular speed of the system when viscosity has had its full effect and there is no movement of the water relative to the container walls? Disregard other frictional effects.

17.91. A bullet weighing $\frac{1}{2}$ N is fired at a wooden block weighing 60 N. What is the angular speed of the block after the bullet has lodged in the block at the right end? Two light hollow rods support the block at the longitudinal midplane. The bullet has a velocity of 400 m/sec in a direction along the longitudinal midplane of the block. [*Hint:* Where is the instantaneous axis of rotation postimpact?]

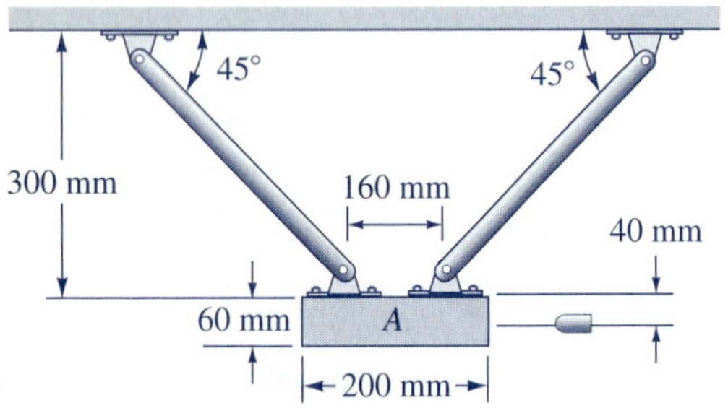

Figure P.17.91.

17.92. A device consists of two identical rectangular plates each weighing 100 N welded to a rod weighing 50 N. The device rests horizontally on a smooth surface. As a result of a collision, a horizontal impulse of 30 N-sec is delivered to point *D*. What is the velocity of corner *E* on plate *A* postimpact?

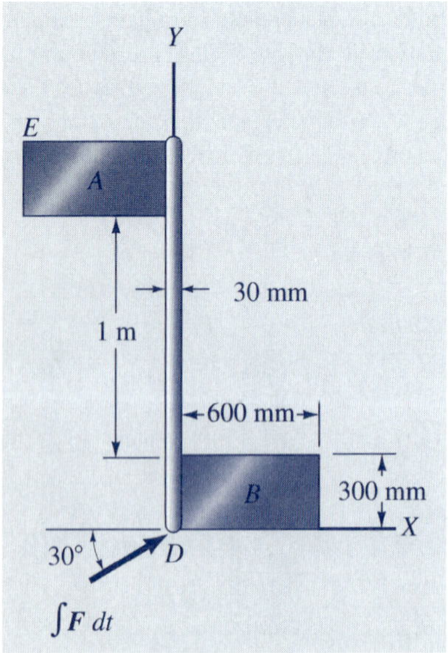

Figure P.17.92.

17.93 A cylinder *A* of weight 150 N and radius of gyration 100 mm is placed onto a conveyor belt which is moving at the constant speed of V_B = 10 m/sec. Give the speed of the axis of the cylinder at time t = 5 sec. The coefficient of friction between the cylinder and the belt is .5.

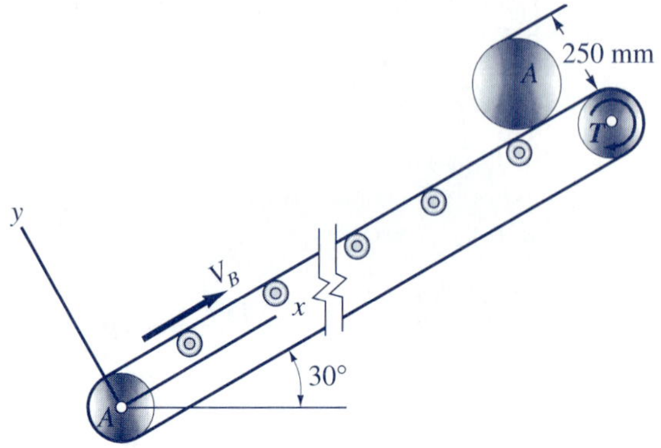

Figure P.17.93.

17.94 A rectangular rod *A* rests on a smooth horizontal surface. A disc *B* moves toward the rod at a speed of 10/m sec. What is the postimpact angular velocity of the rod for a coefficient of restitution of .6? The rod weighs 50 N, and the disc *B* weighs 8 N.

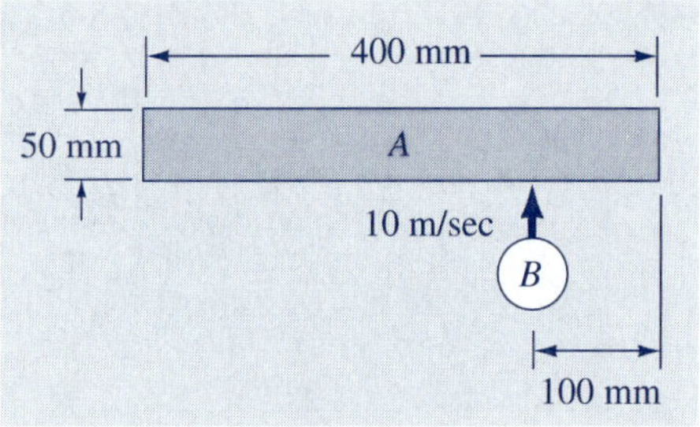

Figure P.17.94.

17.95. A block *B* weighs 10 lb is dropped onto the end of a rectangular rod *A* weighing 20 lb. What is the angular speed of rod *A* postimpact for ϵ = .7? The rod is pinned at its center as shown.

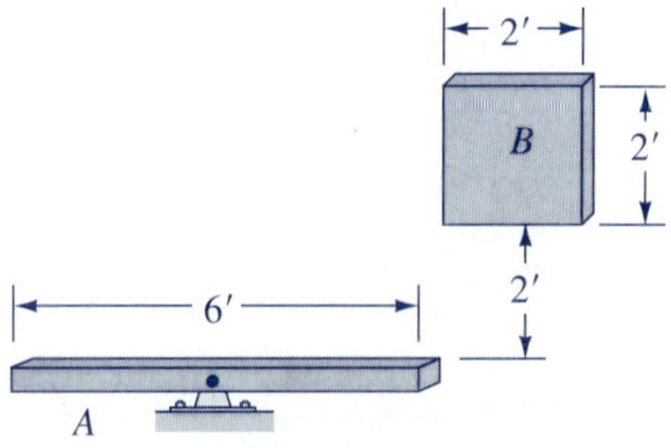

Figure P.17.95.

CHAPTER 18

Dynamics of General Rigid-Body Motion

18.1 Introduction[1]

Consider a rigid body moving arbitrarily relative to an inertial reference XYZ as shown in Fig. 18.1.

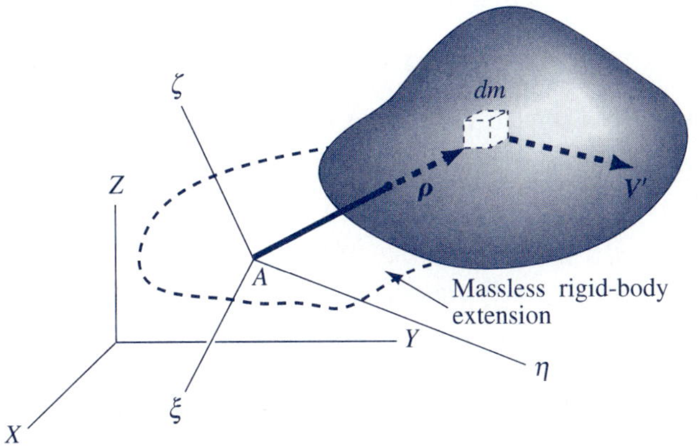

Figure 18.1. A rigid body undergoing arbitrary motion relative to inertial reference XYZ. Reference $\xi\eta\zeta$ translates with A.

Choose some point A in this body or in a hypothetical massless extension of this body. An element dm of the body is shown at a position $\boldsymbol{\rho}$ from A. The velocity $\boldsymbol{V}'$ of dm relative to A is simply the velocity of dm relative to a reference $\xi\eta\zeta$ which *translates* with A relative to XYZ. Similarly, the linear momentum of dm relative to A (i.e., $\boldsymbol{V}'\,dm$) is the linear momentum of dm relative to

[1]Until Eq. 18.1, we will be repeating the development of the formulations of the components of $\boldsymbol{H}_A$ first done in Section 16.2. This will eliminate the inconvenience of having to turn back at various times as we move along in Chapter 18.

$\xi\eta\zeta$ translating with A. We can now give the moment of this momentum (i.e., the angular momentum) $d\boldsymbol{H}_A$ about A as

$$d\boldsymbol{H}_A = \boldsymbol{\rho} \times \boldsymbol{V}'\,dm = \boldsymbol{\rho} \times \left(\frac{d\boldsymbol{\rho}}{dt}\right)_{\xi\eta\zeta} dm$$

but since A is fixed in the body (or in a hypothetical massless extension of the body) the vector $\boldsymbol{\rho}$ must be fixed in the body and, accordingly,

$$\left(\frac{d\boldsymbol{\rho}}{dt}\right)_{\xi\eta\zeta} = \boldsymbol{\omega} \times \boldsymbol{\rho}$$

where $\boldsymbol{\omega}$ is the angular velocity of the body relative to $\xi\eta\zeta$. However, since $\xi\eta\zeta$ translates relative to XYZ, $\boldsymbol{\omega}$ is the angular velocity of the body relative to XYZ as well. Hence, we can say:

$$d\boldsymbol{H}_A = \boldsymbol{\rho} \times (\boldsymbol{\omega} \times \boldsymbol{\rho})\,dm \tag{18.1}$$

Having helped us reach Eq. 18.1, we no longer need reference $\xi\eta\zeta$ translating with point A. Instead, we now insert reference xyz having its origin fixed at A but having at this time an *arbitrary* angular velocity $\boldsymbol{\Omega}$ relative to XYZ. We will have use of $\boldsymbol{\Omega}$ shortly.

Next, we evaluate $d\boldsymbol{H}_A$ in Eq. 18.1 in terms of components relative to xyz as follows:

$$(dH_A)_x\boldsymbol{i} + (dH_A)_y\boldsymbol{j} + (dH_A)_z\boldsymbol{k} = (x\boldsymbol{i} + y\boldsymbol{j} + z\boldsymbol{k}) \times \left[(\boldsymbol{\omega}) \times (x\boldsymbol{i} + y\boldsymbol{j} + z\boldsymbol{k})\right]dm$$

Note that $\boldsymbol{\omega}$ is the angular velocity vector of the *body* relative to XYZ and $\boldsymbol{\Omega}$ is the angular velocity vector of the reference xyz relative to XYZ. The scalar equations resulting from the foregoing vector equations are

$$\begin{aligned}
(dH_A)_x &= (x^2\,dm)\omega_x - (xy\,dm)\omega_y - (xz\,dm)\omega_z \\
(dH_A)_y &= -(yx\,dm)\omega_x + (y^2\,dm)\omega_y - (yz\,dm)\omega_z \\
(dH_A)_z &= -(zx\,dm)\omega_x - (zydm)\omega_y + (z^2\,dm)\omega_z
\end{aligned}$$

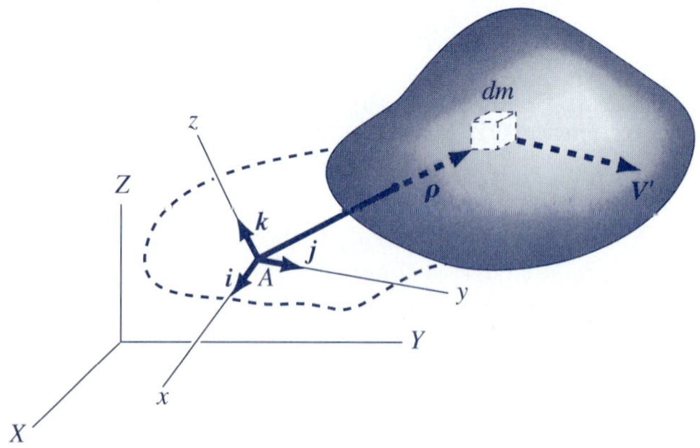

Figure 18.2. xyz fixed to body at A.

We next integrate the above equations over the domain of the rigid body deleting of course the massless hypothetical extension. We see on noting the definitions of the mass moments and products of inertia that we get the components of $\boldsymbol{H}_A$ along an arbitrary set of axes xyz at A. We thus have at any time t

$$\begin{aligned}(H_A)_x &= I_{xx}\omega_x - I_{xy}\omega_y - I_{xz}\omega_z \\ (H_A)_y &= -I_{yx}\omega_x + I_{yy}\omega_y - I_{yz}\omega_z \\ (H_A)_z &= -I_{zx}\omega_x - I_{zy}\omega_y + I_{zz}\omega_z\end{aligned} \tag{18.2}$$

where we repeat $\boldsymbol{\omega}$ is the angular velocity of the body relative to XYZ at time t. Now the axes xyz served *only* to give a set of directions for $\boldsymbol{H}_A$ at time t. The reference xyz remember could have any angular velocity $\boldsymbol{\Omega}$ relative to XYZ.

Note that the angular velocity $\boldsymbol{\Omega}$ did not enter the formulations for $\boldsymbol{H}_A$ at time t. The reason for this result is that the values of the components of $\boldsymbol{H}_A$ along xyz at time t do not in any way depend on angular velocity $\boldsymbol{\Omega}$—they depend only on the instantaneous orientation of xyz at time t. To illustrate this point, suppose that we have two sets of axes xyz and $x'y'z'$ at point A in Fig. 18.3. At time t they coincide as has been shown in the diagram, but xyz has zero angular velocity relative to XYZ, whereas $x'y'z'$ has an angular velocity $\boldsymbol{\Omega}$ relative to XYZ. Clearly, one can say at time t:

$$\begin{aligned}(H_A)_x &= (H_A)_{x'} \\ (H_A)_y &= (H_A)_{y'} \\ (H_A)_z &= (H_A)_{z'}\end{aligned}$$

However, *the time derivatives* of the corresponding components will not be equal to each other at time t. Accordingly, in the next section, where $\dot{\boldsymbol{H}}_A$ is treated, we must properly account for $\boldsymbol{\Omega}$.

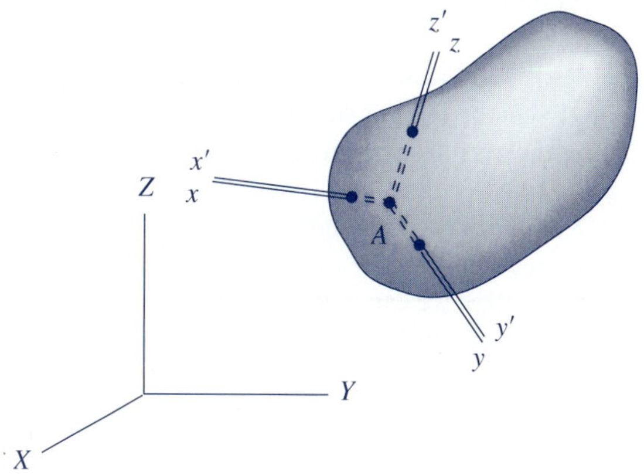

Figure 18.3. xyz and $x'y'z'$ coincide at time t.

18.2 Euler's Equations of Motion

We shall now restrict point A of Section 18.1 further, as we did in Chapter 17, by considering only those points for which the equation $\boldsymbol{M}_A = \dot{\boldsymbol{H}}_A$ is valid:

1. The mass center.
2. Points fixed or moving with constant V at time t in inertial space (i.e., points having zero acceleration at time t relative to inertial reference XYZ).
3. A point accelerating toward or away from the mass center.

We learned in Chapter 15 that derivatives of a vector as seen from different references could be related as follows:

$$\left(\frac{d\boldsymbol{A}}{dt}\right)_{XYZ} = \left(\frac{d\boldsymbol{A}}{dt}\right)_{xyz} + \boldsymbol{\omega} \times \boldsymbol{A}$$

where $\boldsymbol{\omega}$ is the angular velocity of xyz relative to XYZ. We shall employ this equation in the basic *moment-of-momentum equation* to shift the observation reference from XYZ to xyz in the following way where now $\boldsymbol{\Omega}$ represents the angular velocity of xyz. Thus

$$\boldsymbol{M}_A = \left(\frac{d\boldsymbol{H}_A}{dt}\right)_{XYZ} = \left(\frac{d\boldsymbol{H}_A}{dt}\right)_{xyz} + \boldsymbol{\Omega} \times \boldsymbol{H}_A \tag{18.3}$$

The idea now is to choose the angular velocity $\boldsymbol{\Omega}$ of reference xyz at A in such a way that $(d\boldsymbol{H}_A/dt)_{XYZ}$ is most easily evaluated. With this accomplished, the next step is to attempt the integration of the resulting differential equation.

With regard to attempts at integration, we point out at this early stage that Eq. 18.3 is valid only as long as point A is one of the three qualified points just discussed. Clearly, if A is the mass center, then Eq. 18.3 is valid at all times and can be integrated with respect to time provided that the mathematics are not too difficult. However, if for cases (2) and (3) point A qualifies only at time t, then Eq. 18.3 is valid only at time t and accordingly cannot be integrated. If, on the other hand, for case (2), there is an axis of rotation fixed in inertial space, then Eq. 18.3 is valid at all times for any point A along the axis of rotation and accordingly can be integrated. We have already done this in Chapter 16. If, furthermore, the axis of rotation always goes through the fixed point A but does not have a fixed orientation in inertial space (see Fig. 18.4), we can again use Eq. 18.3 at all times and attempt to integrate it with respect to time. The carrying out of such integrations may be quite difficult, however.[2]

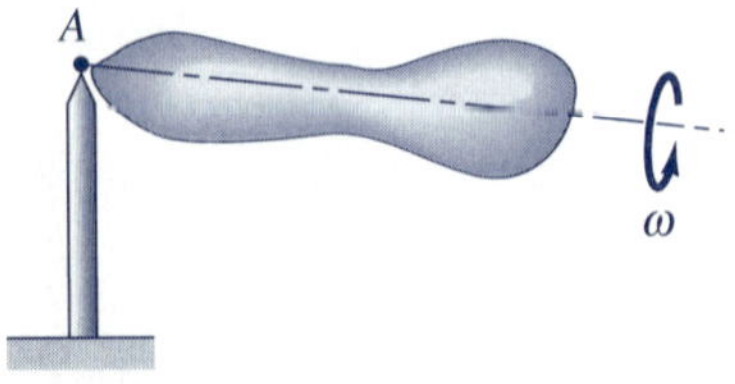

Figure 18.4. Axis of rotation goes through fixed point A.

Returning to Eq. 18.3, we can work directly with this equation selecting a reference xyz for each problem to yield the simplest working equation. On the other hand, we can develop Eq. 18.3 further for certain classes of references xyz. For example, we could have xyz translate relative to XYZ. This would

[2]In a later section we shall examine this case in some detail.

mean that $\boldsymbol{\Omega} = \mathbf{0}$ so that Eq. 18.3 would seem to be more simple for such cases.[3] However, the body will be rotating relative to xyz and the moments and products of inertia measured about xyz will then be time functions. Since the computation of these terms as time functions is generally difficult, such an approach has limited value. On the other hand, the procedure of *fixing xyz* in the body (as we did for the case of plane motion in Chapter 16) does lead to very useful forms of Eq. 18.3, and we shall accordingly examine these equations with great care. Note first that the moments and products of inertia will be constants for this case and that $\boldsymbol{\Omega} = \boldsymbol{\omega}$. Hence, we have

$$\boldsymbol{M}_A = \left(\frac{d\boldsymbol{H}_A}{dt}\right)_{xyz} + \boldsymbol{\omega} \times \boldsymbol{H}_A \tag{18.4}$$

Employing components for all vectors along axes xyz and utilizing Eq. 18.2, we get on dropping the subscript A:

$$\begin{aligned} M_x\boldsymbol{i} + M_y\boldsymbol{j} + M_z\boldsymbol{k} = \frac{d}{dt}_{xyz}&[(\omega_x I_{xx} - \omega_y I_{xy} - \omega_z I_{xz})\boldsymbol{i} \\ &+(-\omega_x I_{yx} + \omega_y I_{yy} - \omega_z I_{yz})\boldsymbol{j} + (-\omega_x I_{zx} - \omega_y I_{zy} + \omega_z I_{zz})\boldsymbol{k}] \\ &+\boldsymbol{\omega} \times [(\omega_x I_{xx} - \omega_y I_{xy} - \omega_z I_{xz})\boldsymbol{i} \\ &+(-\omega_x I_{yx} + \omega_y I_{yy} - \omega_z I_{yz})\boldsymbol{j} + (-\omega_x I_{zx} - \omega_y I_{zy} + \omega_z I_{zz})\boldsymbol{k}] \end{aligned}$$

In the first expression on the right side of the foregoing equation, the vectors $\boldsymbol{i}, \boldsymbol{j}$, and $\boldsymbol{k}$ are constant vectors as seen from xyz. Also, because xyz is fixed in the body, the moments and products of inertia are constant. Only ω_x, ω_y, and ω_z, the angular velocity components of the rigid body, are time functions. We then can say:

$$\begin{aligned} M_x\boldsymbol{i} + M_y\boldsymbol{j} + M_z\boldsymbol{k} &= (\dot{\omega}_x I_{xx} - \dot{\omega}_y I_{xy} - \dot{\omega}_z I_{xz})\boldsymbol{i} + (-\dot{\omega}_x I_{yx} + \dot{\omega}_y I_{yy} - \dot{\omega}_z I_{yz})\boldsymbol{j} \\ &+(-\dot{\omega}_x I_{zx} - \dot{\omega}_y I_{zy} + \dot{\omega}_z I_{zz})\boldsymbol{k} + (\omega_x I_{xx} - \omega_y I_{xy} - \omega_z I_{xz})(\boldsymbol{\omega} \times \boldsymbol{i}) \\ &+(-\omega_x I_{yx} + \omega_y I_{yy} - \omega_z I_{yz})(\boldsymbol{\omega} \times \boldsymbol{j}) + (-\omega_x I_{zx} - \omega_y I_{zy} + \omega_z I_{zz})(\boldsymbol{\omega} \times \boldsymbol{k}) \end{aligned}$$

Carrying out the cross products, collecting terms, and expressing as scalar equations, we get

$$\begin{aligned} M_x = \dot{\omega}_x I_{xx} + \omega_y\omega_z(I_{zz} - I_{yy}) + I_{xy}(\omega_z\omega_x - \dot{\omega}_y)& \\ - I_{xz}(\dot{\omega}_z + \omega_y\omega_x) - I_{yz}(\omega_y^2 - \omega_z^2)& \end{aligned} \tag{18.5a}$$

$$\begin{aligned} M_y = \dot{\omega}_y I_{yy} + \omega_z\omega_x(I_{xx} - I_{zz}) + I_{yz}(\omega_x\omega_y - \dot{\omega}_z)& \\ - I_{yx}(\dot{\omega}_x + \omega_z\omega_y) - I_{zx}(\omega_z^2 - \omega_x^2)& \end{aligned} \tag{18.5b}$$

$$\begin{aligned} M_z = \dot{\omega}_z I_{zz} + \omega_x\omega_y(I_{yy} - I_{xx}) + I_{zx}(\omega_y\omega_z - \dot{\omega}_x)& \\ - I_{zy}(\dot{\omega}_y + \omega_x\omega_z) - I_{xy}(\omega_x^2 - \omega_y^2)& \end{aligned} \tag{18.5c}$$

[3]We shall later find it advantageous not to fix xyz to the body for certain problems.

This is indeed a formidable set of equations. For the important special case of *plane motion* the z axis is always normal to the XY plane which is the plane of motion. Hence $\boldsymbol{\omega}$ must be normal to plane XY and thus collinear with the z axis. Thus replacing ω_z by ω and setting the other components equal to zero, we get the *moment of momentum equations* for *general plane motion*. Thus we have

$$(M_A)_x = -I_{xz}\dot{\omega} + I_{yz}\omega^2$$
$$(M_A)_y = -I_{yz}\dot{\omega} - I_{xz}\omega^2$$
$$(M_A)_z = I_{zz}\dot{\omega}$$

The reader may now or at any time later go back to Chapter 16 for a rather careful study of the use of the above plane motion *moment of momentum* equations. We now continue with the three-dimensional approach.

Note now that if we choose reference xyz to be *principal* axes of the body at point A, then it is clear that the products of inertia are all zero in the system of equations 18.5, and this fact enables us to simplify the equations considerably. The resulting equations given below are the famous *Euler equations* of motion. Note that these equations relate the angular velocity and the angular acceleration to the moment of the external forces about the point A.

$$M_x = I_{xx}\dot{\omega}_x + \omega_y\omega_z(I_{zz} - I_{yy}) \quad (18.6a)$$
$$M_y = I_{yy}\dot{\omega}_y + \omega_z\omega_x(I_{xx} - I_{zz}) \quad (18.6b)$$
$$M_z = I_{zz}\dot{\omega}_z + \omega_x\omega_y(I_{yy} - I_{xx}) \quad (18.6c)$$

In both sets of Eqs. 18.5 and 18.6, we have three simultaneous first-order differential equations. If the motion of the body about point A is known, we can easily compute the required moments about point A. On the other hand, if the moments are known functions of time and the angular velocity is desired, we have the difficult problem of solving simultaneous nonlinear differential equations for the unknowns ω_x, ω_y, and ω_z. However, in practical problems, we often know some of the angular velocity and acceleration components from constraints or given data, so, with the restrictions mentioned earlier, we can sometimes integrate the equations readily as we did in Chapter 16 for plane motion. At other times we use them to solve for certain desired *instantaneous values* of the unknowns.

We shall now discuss the use of Euler's equations.

18.3 Application of Euler's Equations

In this section, we shall apply the **Euler equations** to a number of problems. Before taking up these problems, let us first carefully consider how to express the components $\dot{\omega}_x$, $\dot{\omega}_y$, and $\dot{\omega}_z$ for use in **Euler's equations**. First note that $\dot{\omega}_x$, $\dot{\omega}_y$, and $\dot{\omega}_z$ are time derivatives as seen from XYZ of the components of $\boldsymbol{\omega}$ along reference xyz. A possible procedure then is to express ω_x, ω_y, and ω_z first in a way that ensures that these quantities are correctly stated over a time interval rather than at some instantaneous configuration. Once this is done, we can simply differentiate these scalar quantities with respect to time in this interval to get $\dot{\omega}_x, \dot{\omega}_y$, and $\dot{\omega}_z$.

To illustrate this procedure, consider in Fig. 18.5 the case of a block E rotating about rod AB, which in turn rotates about vertical axis CD. A reference xyz is fixed to the block at the center of mass so as to coincide with the principal axes of the block at the center of mass. When the block is vertical as shown, the angular speed and rate of change of angular speed relative to rod AB have the known values $(\omega_2)_0$ and $(\dot{\omega}_2)_0$, respectively. At that instant, AB has an angular speed and rate of change of angular speed about axis CD of known values $(\omega_1)_0$ and $(\dot{\omega}_1)_0$, respectively. We can immediately give the angular velocity components at the instant shown as follows:

$$\omega_x = 0$$
$$\omega_y = (\omega_2)_0$$
$$\omega_z = (\omega_1)_0$$

But to get the quantities $(\dot{\omega}_x)_0$, $(\dot{\omega}_y)_0$, and $(\dot{\omega}_z)_0$ for the instant of interest[4] we must first express ω_x, ω_y, and ω_z as *general functions of time* in order to permit differentiation with respect to time.

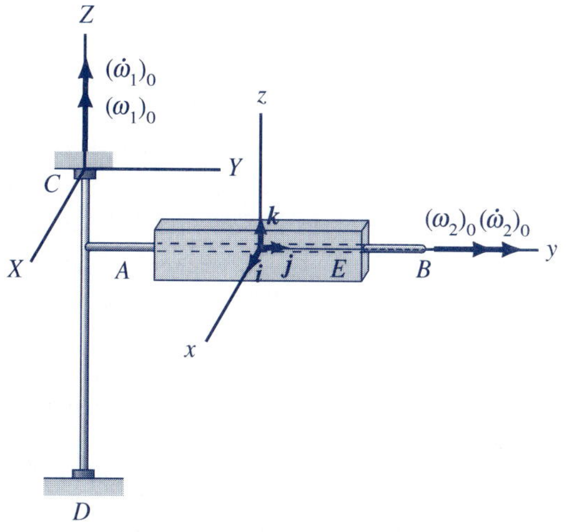

Figure 18.5. Block at time t_0.

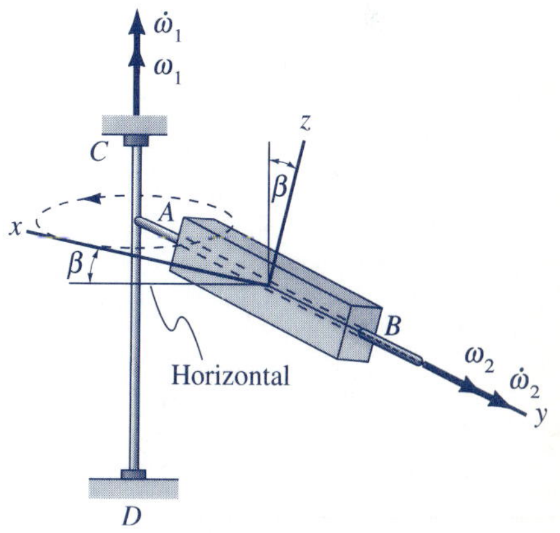

Figure 18.6. Block at time t.

To do this differentiating, we have shown the system at some arbitrary time in Fig. 18.6. Note that the x axis is at some angle β from the horizontal. When β becomes zero, we arrive back at the configuration of interest, and ω_1,

[4]You may be tempted to say $(\dot{\omega}_x)_0 = 0$, $(\dot{\omega}_y)_0 = (\dot{\omega}_2)_0$, and $(\dot{\omega}_z)_0 = (\dot{\omega}_1)_0$ by just inspecting the diagram. You will now learn that this will not be correct.

$\dot{\omega}_1$, ω_2, and $\dot{\omega}_2$ become known values $(\omega_1)_0$, $(\dot{\omega}_1)_0$, $(\omega_2)_0$, and $(\dot{\omega}_2)_0$, respectively. The angular velocity components for this arbitrary situation are:

$$\omega_x = \omega_1 \sin\beta, \qquad \omega_y = \omega_2, \qquad \omega_z = \omega_1 \cos\beta \tag{18.7}$$

Since these relations are valid over the time interval of interest, we can differentiate them with respect to time and get

$$\begin{aligned} \dot{\omega}_x &= \dot{\omega}_1 \sin\beta + \omega_1 \cos\beta\dot{\beta} \\ \dot{\omega}_y &= \dot{\omega}_2 \\ \dot{\omega}_z &= \dot{\omega}_1 \cos\beta - \omega_1 \sin\beta\dot{\beta} \end{aligned} \tag{18.8}$$

It should be clear upon inspecting the diagram that $\dot{\beta} = -\omega_2$, and so the preceding terms become

$$\begin{aligned} \dot{\omega}_x &= \dot{\omega}_1 \sin\beta - \omega_1\omega_2 \cos\beta \\ \dot{\omega}_y &= \dot{\omega}_2 \\ \dot{\omega}_z &= \dot{\omega}_1 \cos\beta + \omega_1\omega_2 \sin\beta \end{aligned} \tag{18.9}$$

If we now let β become zero, we reach the configuration of interest and we get from Eqs. 18.7 and 18.8 the proper values of the angular velocity components and their time derivatives at this configuration:

$$\begin{aligned} \omega_x &= 0, & \dot{\omega}_x &= -(\omega_1)_0(\omega_2)_0 \\ \omega_y &= (\omega_2)_0, & \dot{\omega}_y &= (\dot{\omega}_2)_0 \\ \omega_z &= (\omega_1)_0, & \dot{\omega}_z &= (\dot{\omega}_1)_0 \end{aligned}$$

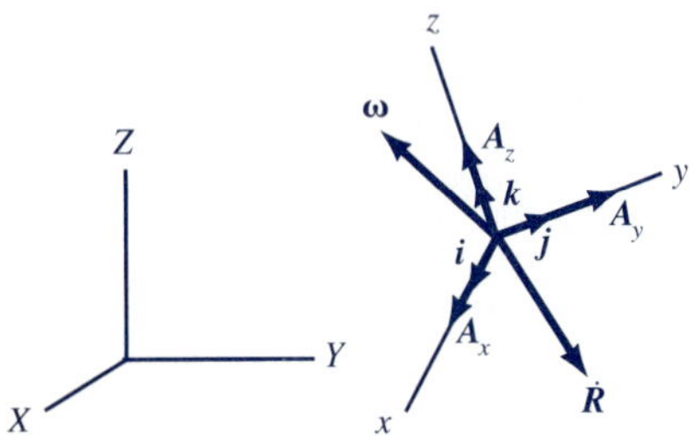

Figure 18.7. Components of A along xyz.

Actually, we do not have to employ such a procedure for the evaluation of these quantities. There is a simple direct approach that can be used, but we must preface the discussion of this method by some general remarks about the time derivative, as seen from the XYZ axes, of a vector $\boldsymbol{A}$. This vector $\boldsymbol{A}$ is expressed in terms of components always parallel to the xyz reference, which moves relative to XYZ (Fig. 18.7). We can then say, considering $\boldsymbol{i}, \boldsymbol{j}$, and $\boldsymbol{k}$ as unit vectors for reference xyz:

$$\begin{aligned} \left(\frac{d\boldsymbol{A}}{dt}\right)_{XYZ} &= \frac{d}{dt}_{XYZ}(A_x\boldsymbol{i} + A_y\boldsymbol{j} + A_z\boldsymbol{k}) \\ &= \dot{A}_x\boldsymbol{i} + \dot{A}_y\boldsymbol{j} + \dot{A}_z\boldsymbol{k} + A_x(\boldsymbol{\omega}\times\boldsymbol{i}) + A_y(\boldsymbol{\omega}\times\boldsymbol{j}) + A_z(\boldsymbol{\omega}\times\boldsymbol{k}) \end{aligned} \tag{18.10}$$

If we decompose the vector $(d\boldsymbol{A}/dt)_{XYZ}$ into components parallel to the xyz axes at time t and carry out the cross products on the right side in terms of xyz components, then we get, after collecting terms and expressing the results as scalar equations:

$$\left[\left(\frac{d\boldsymbol{A}}{dt}\right)_{XYZ}\right]_x = \dot{A}_x + A_z\omega_y - A_y\omega_z \tag{18.11a}$$

$$\left[\left(\frac{d\boldsymbol{A}}{dt}\right)_{XYZ}\right]_y = \dot{A}_y + A_x\omega_z - A_z\omega_x \tag{18.11b}$$

$$\left[\left(\frac{d\boldsymbol{A}}{dt}\right)_{XYZ}\right]_z = \dot{A}_z + A_y\omega_x - A_x\omega_y \tag{18.11c}$$

We can learn an important lesson from these equations. If you take the time derivative of a vector $\mathbf{A}$ with respect to a reference *XYZ* and express the *components* of this vector parallel to the axes of a reference *xyz* rotating relative to *XYZ* (these are the terms on the left side of the above equations), then the results are in general *not the same* as *first* taking the components of the vector $\mathbf{A}$ along the directions *xyz* and *then* taking time derivatives of these scalars. Thus,

$$\left[\left(\frac{d\mathbf{A}}{dt}\right)_{XYZ}\right]_x \neq \frac{d(A_x)}{dt} = \dot{A}_x \qquad \text{etc.} \tag{18.12}$$

How does this result relate to our problem where we are considering $\dot{\omega}_x$, $\dot{\omega}_y$, and $\dot{\omega}_z$? Clearly, these expressions are time derivatives of the components of the vector $\boldsymbol{\omega}$ along the moving *xyz* axes, and so in this respect they correspond to the terms on the right side of inequality 18.12. Let us then consider vector $\mathbf{A}$ to be $\boldsymbol{\omega}$ and examine Eq. 18.11:

$$\begin{aligned}\left[\left(\frac{d\boldsymbol{\omega}}{dt}\right)_{XYZ}\right]_x &= \dot{\omega}_x + \omega_z\omega_y - \omega_y\omega_z\\ \left[\left(\frac{d\boldsymbol{\omega}}{dt}\right)_{XYZ}\right]_y &= \dot{\omega}_y + \omega_x\omega_z - \omega_z\omega_x\\ \left[\left(\frac{d\boldsymbol{\omega}}{dt}\right)_{XYZ}\right]_z &= \dot{\omega}_z + \omega_y\omega_x - \omega_x\omega_y\end{aligned} \tag{18.13}$$

We see that the last two terms on the right side in each equation cancel for this case, leaving us

$$\begin{aligned}\left[\left(\frac{d\boldsymbol{\omega}}{dt}\right)_{XYZ}\right]_x &= \dot{\omega}_x\\ \left[\left(\frac{d\boldsymbol{\omega}}{dt}\right)_{XYZ}\right]_y &= \dot{\omega}_y\\ \left[\left(\frac{d\boldsymbol{\omega}}{dt}\right)_{XYZ}\right]_z &= \dot{\omega}_z\end{aligned} \tag{18.14}$$

We see that for the vector $\boldsymbol{\omega}$ (i.e., the angular velocity of the *xyz* reference relative to the *XYZ* reference), we have an exception to the rule stated earlier (Eq. 18.12). Here is the one case where the derivative of a vector as seen from one set of axes *XYZ* has components along the directions of another set of axes *xyz* rotating relative to *XYZ*, wherein these components are respectively equal to the simple time derivatives of the scalar components of the vector along the *xyz* directions. In other words, you can take the derivative of $\boldsymbol{\omega}$ first from the *XYZ* axes and then take scalar components along *xyz*, or you can take scalar components along *xyz* first and then take simple time derivatives of the scalar components, and the results are the same.

If we fully understand the exceptional nature of Eq. 18.14, we can compute $\dot{\omega}_x$, $\dot{\omega}_y$, *and* $\dot{\omega}_z$ *in a straightforward manner by simply first determining*

$(d\boldsymbol{\omega}/dt)_{XYZ}$ *and then taking the components*. This is a step that we have practiced a great deal in *kinematics*. For instance, for the problem introduced at the outset of this discussion, we see by inspecting Fig. 18.6 that at all times

$$\boldsymbol{\omega} = \omega_2 \boldsymbol{j} + \omega_1 \boldsymbol{k}_1 \tag{18.15}$$

where $\boldsymbol{k}_1$ is the unit vector in the fixed Z direction. Now differentiate with respect to time for the XYZ reference:

$$\dot{\boldsymbol{\omega}} = \dot{\omega}_2 \boldsymbol{j} + \omega_2 \dot{\boldsymbol{j}} + \dot{\omega}_1 \boldsymbol{k}_1 \tag{18.16}$$

But $\boldsymbol{j}$ is fixed in rod AB that is rotating with angular velocity $\omega_1 \boldsymbol{k}_1$ relative to XYZ. We then get

$$\dot{\boldsymbol{\omega}} = \dot{\omega}_2 \boldsymbol{j} + \omega_2 (\omega_1 \boldsymbol{k}_1) \times \boldsymbol{j} + \dot{\omega}_1 \boldsymbol{k}_1 \tag{18.17}$$

When the xyz axes are parallel to the XYZ axes, the unit vector $\boldsymbol{k}$ becomes the same as the unit vector $\boldsymbol{k}_1$, and ω_1, ω_2, etc., become known $(\omega_1)_0$, $(\omega_2)_0$, etc. We then get for that configuration:

$$\dot{\boldsymbol{\omega}}_0 = (\dot{\omega}_2)_0 \boldsymbol{j} - (\omega_1)_0 (\omega_2)_0 \boldsymbol{i} + (\dot{\omega}_1)_0 \boldsymbol{k} \tag{18.18}$$

The components of this equation give the desired values of $\dot{\omega}_x$, $\dot{\omega}_y$, and $\dot{\omega}_z$, at the instant of interest. Thus, we have

$$\begin{aligned} \dot{\omega}_x &= -(\omega_1)_0 (\omega_2)_0 \\ \dot{\omega}_y &= (\dot{\omega}_2)_0 \\ \dot{\omega}_z &= (\dot{\omega}_1)_0 \end{aligned} \tag{18.19}$$

which are the same results developed earlier.

In most of the following examples we shall proceed by the second method discussed here. That is, we shall get $\dot{\omega}_x$, $\dot{\omega}_y$, and $\dot{\omega}_z$, using the following formulations:

$$\dot{\omega}_x = \left[\left(\frac{d\boldsymbol{\omega}}{dt} \right)_{XYZ} \right]_x \tag{18.20a}$$

$$\dot{\omega}_y = \left[\left(\frac{d\boldsymbol{\omega}}{dt} \right)_{XYZ} \right]_y \tag{18.20b}$$

$$\dot{\omega}_z = \left[\left(\frac{d\boldsymbol{\omega}}{dt} \right)_{XYZ} \right]_z \tag{18.20c}$$

Example 18.1

In Fig. 18.8 a thin disc of radius $R = 4$ ft and weight 322 lb rotates at an angular speed ω_2 of 100 rad/sec relative to a platform. The platform rotates with an angular speed ω_1 of 20 rad/sec relative to the ground. Compute the bearing reactions at A and B. Neglect the mass of the shaft and assume that bearing A restrains the system in the radial direction.

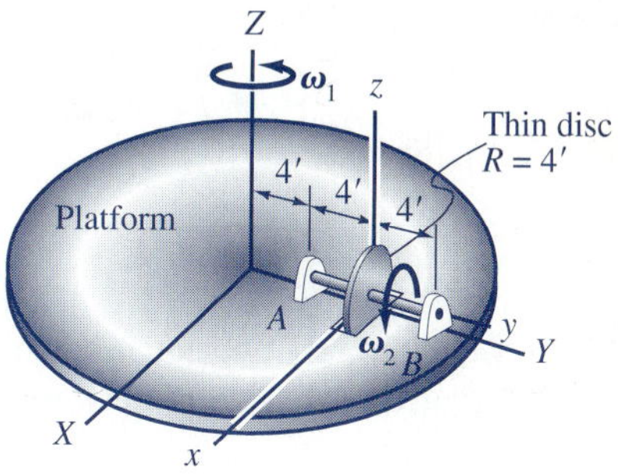

Figure 18.8. Rotating disc on platform.

Clearly, we shall need to use **Euler's equations** as part of the solution to this problem, and so we *fix a reference xyz to the center of mass* of the disc as shown in Fig. 18.8. *XYZ is fixed to the ground.* In using **Euler's equations**, the key step is to get the angular velocity components and their time derivatives for the body as seen from *XYZ*. Accordingly, we have

$$\boldsymbol{\omega} = \boldsymbol{\omega}_1 + \boldsymbol{\omega}_2 = -20\boldsymbol{k} + 100\boldsymbol{j} \text{ rad/sec}$$

Hence, we have for the *xyz* components:

$$\omega_x = 0$$
$$\omega_y = 100 \text{ rad/sec}$$
$$\omega_z = -20 \text{ rad/sec}$$

Next, we have

$$\dot{\boldsymbol{\omega}} = \dot{\boldsymbol{\omega}}_1 + \dot{\boldsymbol{\omega}}_2 = \boldsymbol{0} + \boldsymbol{\omega}_1 \times \boldsymbol{\omega}_2$$
$$= (-20\boldsymbol{k}) \times (100\boldsymbol{j}) = 2{,}000\boldsymbol{i} \text{ rad/sec}^2$$

We thus have for the *xyz* components:

$$\dot{\omega}_x = 2{,}000 \text{ rad/sec}^2$$
$$\dot{\omega}_y = 0$$
$$\dot{\omega}_z = 0$$

Before going to the **Euler's equations**, we shall need the principal moments of inertia of the disc. Using formulas from the front inside covers, we get

$$I_{yy} = \frac{1}{2}\frac{W}{g}R^2 = \frac{1}{2}(10)(16) = 80 \text{ slug-ft}^2$$
$$I_{xx} = I_{zz} = \frac{1}{4}\frac{W}{g}R^2 = 40 \text{ slug-ft}^2$$

We can now substitute into the **Euler's equations**.

$$M_x = (40)(2{,}000) + (100)(-20)(40 - 80) = 160{,}000 \text{ ft-lb}$$
$$M_y = (80)(0) + (0)(-20)(40 - 40) = 0$$
$$M_z = (40)(0) + (0)(100)(80 - 40) = 0$$

Example 18.1 (Continued)

Now the moment components above are generated by the bearing-force components (see Fig. 18.9). Hence, we can say:

$$M_x = 160{,}000 = 4B_z - 4A_z \qquad \text{(a)}$$

$$M_y = 0 \qquad \text{(b)}$$

$$M_z = 0 \qquad = 4A_x - 4B_x \qquad \text{(c)}$$

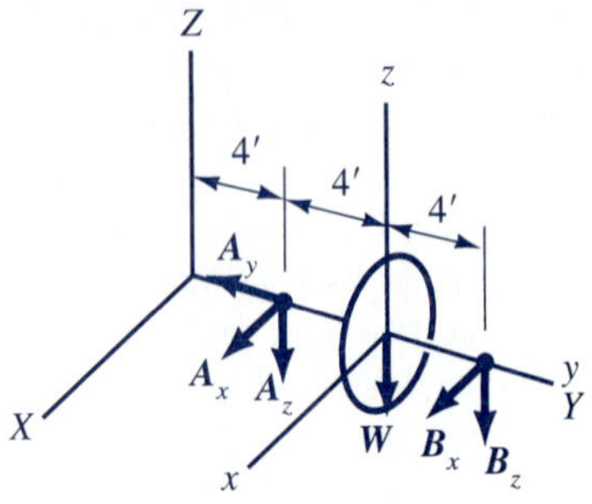

Figure 18.9. Bearing forces.

We have effectively two equations for four unknowns.

We next use **Newton's law** for the mass center:

$$A_z + B_z - 322 = 0$$

$$A_x + B_x = 0 \qquad \text{(d)}$$

$$-A_y = -\left(\frac{322}{g}\right)(8)(20)^2$$

The first two equations are equilibrium equations. The third equation relates the radial force A_y, from the bearing A, and the radial acceleration of the center of mass of the disc which you will notice is in simple circular motion about the Z axis. We now have enough equations for all the unknowns. It is then a simple matter to evaluate the forces from the bearings. They are:

$$A_x = B_x = 0$$
$$A_y = 32{,}000 \text{ lb}$$
$$B_z = 20{,}161 \text{ lb}$$
$$A_z = -19{,}839 \text{ lb}$$

The *reactions* to these forces are the desired forces *onto* the bearings.

In Example 18.1, you may have been surprised at the large value of the bearing forces in the z direction. Actually, if we did not include the weight of the disc, then A_z and B_z would have formed a sizable couple. This couple stems from the fact that a body having a high angular momentum about one axis is made to move such that the aforementioned axis rotates about yet a second axis. Such a couple is called a *gyroscopic couple*. It occurs in no small measure for the front wheels of a car that is steered while moving at high speeds. It occurs in the jet engine of a plane that is changing its direction of flight. You will have opportunity to investigate these effects in the homework problems.

Example 18.2

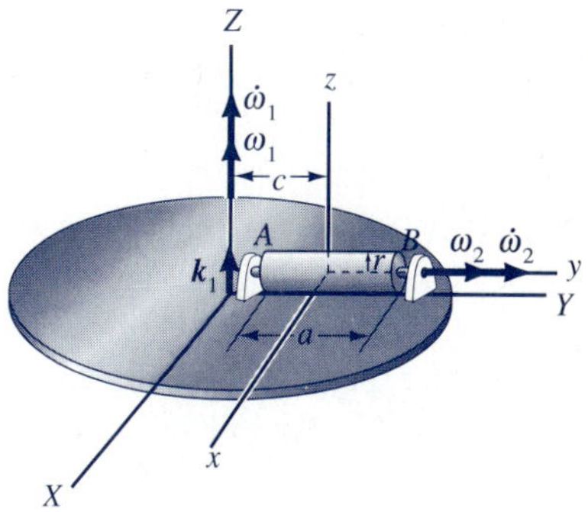

Figure 18.10. Rotating cylinder on platform.

A cylinder *AB* is rotating in bearings mounted on a platform (Fig. 18.10). The cylinder has an angular speed ω_2 and a rate of change of speed $\dot{\omega}_2$, both quantities being relative to the platform. The platform rotates with an angular speed ω_1 and has a rate of change of speed $\dot{\omega}_1$, both quantities being relative to the ground. Compute the moment of the supporting forces of the cylinder *AB* about the center of mass of the cylinder in terms of the aforementioned quantities and the moments of inertia of the cylinder.

We shall do this problem by two methods, one using axes fixed to the body and using **Euler's equations**, and the other using axes fixed to the platform and using Eq. 18.2.

Method 1: Reference fixed to cylinder. In Fig. 18.10 we have fixed axes *xyz* to the cylinder at the mass center. To get components of $\boldsymbol{M}$ parallel to the inertial reference, we consider the problem when the *xyz* reference is parallel to the *XYZ* reference. The angular velocity vector $\boldsymbol{\omega}$ for the body is then

$$\boldsymbol{\omega} = \boldsymbol{\omega}_1 + \boldsymbol{\omega}_2 = \omega_1 \boldsymbol{k} + \omega_2 \boldsymbol{j}$$

Hence,

$$\begin{aligned} \omega_x &= 0 \text{ rad/sec} \\ \omega_y &= \omega_2 \text{ rad/sec} \\ \omega_z &= \omega_1 \text{ rad/sec} \end{aligned} \qquad \text{(a)}$$

Also, we can say noting that $\boldsymbol{j}$ is fixed to the centerline of the cylinder

$$\begin{aligned} \dot{\boldsymbol{\omega}} = \dot{\boldsymbol{\omega}}_1 + \dot{\boldsymbol{\omega}}_2 &= \dot{\omega}_1 \boldsymbol{k} + \left(\frac{d}{dt}\right)_{XYZ} (\omega_2 \boldsymbol{j}) \\ &= \dot{\omega}_1 \boldsymbol{k} + \dot{\omega}_2 \boldsymbol{j} + \omega_2 (\boldsymbol{\omega}_1 \times \boldsymbol{j}) \\ &= \dot{\omega}_1 \boldsymbol{k} + \dot{\omega}_2 \boldsymbol{j} + \omega_2 (\omega_1 \boldsymbol{k} \times \boldsymbol{j}) \\ &= \dot{\omega}_1 \boldsymbol{k} + \dot{\omega}_2 \boldsymbol{j} - \omega_1 \omega_2 \boldsymbol{i} \end{aligned}$$

Accordingly, we have at the instant of interest

$$\begin{aligned} \dot{\omega}_x &= -\omega_1 \omega_2 \text{ rad/sec}^2 \\ \dot{\omega}_y &= \dot{\omega}_2 \text{ rad/sec}^2 \\ \dot{\omega}_z &= \dot{\omega}_1 \text{ rad/sec}^2 \end{aligned} \qquad \text{(b)}$$

The **Euler equations** then become

$$M_x = I_{xx}(-\omega_1 \omega_2) + \omega_1 \omega_2 (I_{zz} - I_{yy}) \qquad \text{(c)}$$

$$M_y = I_{yy} \dot{\omega}_2 + 0 \qquad \text{(d)}$$

$$M_z = I_{zz} \dot{\omega}_1 + 0 \qquad \text{(e)}$$

Since $I_{zz} = I_{xx}$ we see that $I_{xx}(-\omega_1 \omega_2))$ cancels $\omega_1 \omega_2 I_{zz}$ in Eq. (c), and we then have the desired result:

Example 18.2 (Continued)

$$M = -I_{yy}\omega_1\omega_2\mathbf{i} + I_{yy}\dot{\omega}_2\mathbf{j} + I_{zz}\dot{\omega}_1\mathbf{k} \qquad \text{(f)}$$

Method II: Reference fixed to platform. We shall now do this problem by having xyz at the mass center C of the cylinder again, but now fixed to the platform. In other words, the cylinder rotates relative to the xyz reference with angular speed ω_2. Keeping this in mind, we can still refer to Fig. 18.10.

Obviously, we cannot use **Euler's equations** here and must return to Eq. 18.2.

$$\mathbf{M}_c = \left(\frac{d\mathbf{H}_C}{dt}\right)_{xyz} + \mathbf{\Omega} \times \mathbf{H}_C \qquad \text{(a)}$$

Because the cylinder is a body of revolution about the y axis, the products of inertia I_{xy}, I_{xz}, and I_{yz} are always zero, and I_{xx}, I_{yy}, and I_{zz} are *constants* at all times. Were these conditions not present, this method of approach would be very difficult, since we would have to ascertain the time derivatives of these inertia terms. Thus, using Eq. 18.2, remembering that $\boldsymbol{\omega}$, the angular velocity of the body, goes into $\mathbf{H}_C$ while $\mathbf{\Omega}$ is the angular velocity of xyz, we see that

$$\begin{aligned}\left(\frac{d\mathbf{H}_C}{dt}\right)_{xyz} &= \left(\frac{d}{dt}\right)_{xyz}(H_x\mathbf{i} + H_y\mathbf{j} + H_z\mathbf{k})_C \\ &= \left(\frac{d}{dt}\right)_{xyz}(I_{xx}\omega_x\mathbf{i} + I_{yy}\omega_y\mathbf{j} + I_{zz}\omega_z\mathbf{k}) \qquad \text{(b)} \\ &= \left(\frac{d}{dt}\right)_{xyz}(0\mathbf{i} + I_{yy}\omega_2\mathbf{j} + I_{zz}\omega_1\mathbf{k})\end{aligned}$$

Note that $\mathbf{i}, \mathbf{j}$, and $\mathbf{k}$ are constants as seen from xyz. Only ω_1 and ω_2 are time functions and undergo simple time differentiation of scalars. Thus,

$$\left(\frac{d\mathbf{H}_C}{dt}\right)_{xyz} = I_{yy}\dot{\omega}_2\mathbf{j} + I_{zz}\dot{\omega}_1\mathbf{k} \qquad \text{(c)}$$

Noting further that $\mathbf{\Omega} = \omega_1\mathbf{k}$, we have on substituting Eq. (c) into Eq. (a):

$$\begin{aligned}M &= I_{yy}\dot{\omega}_2\mathbf{j} + I_{zz}\dot{\omega}_1\mathbf{k} + \omega_1\mathbf{k} \times (H_x\mathbf{i} + H_y\mathbf{j} + H_z\mathbf{k}) \\ &= I_{yy}\dot{\omega}_2\mathbf{j} + I_{zz}\dot{\omega}_1\mathbf{k} + \omega_1\mathbf{k} \times (0\mathbf{i} + I_{yy}\omega_2\mathbf{j} + I_{zz}\omega_1\mathbf{k}) \qquad \text{(d)}\end{aligned}$$

$$M = -I_{yy}\omega_1\omega_2\mathbf{i} + I_{yy}\dot{\omega}_2\mathbf{j} + I_{yy}\dot{\omega}_1\mathbf{k}$$

This equation is identical to the one obtained using method I.

PROBLEMS

18.1. The moving parts of a jet engine consist of a *compressor* and a *turbine* connected to a common shaft. Suppose that this system is rotating at a speed ω_1 of 10,000 rpm and the plane it is in moves at a speed of 600 mi/hr in a circular loop of radius 2 mi. What is the direction and magnitude of the gyroscopic torque transmitted to the plane from the engine through bearings A and B? The engine has a weight of 200 lb and a radius of gyration about its axis of rotation of 1 ft. The radius of gyration at the center of mass for an axis normal to the centerline is 1.5 ft. What advantage is achieved by using two oppositely turning jet engines instead of one large one?

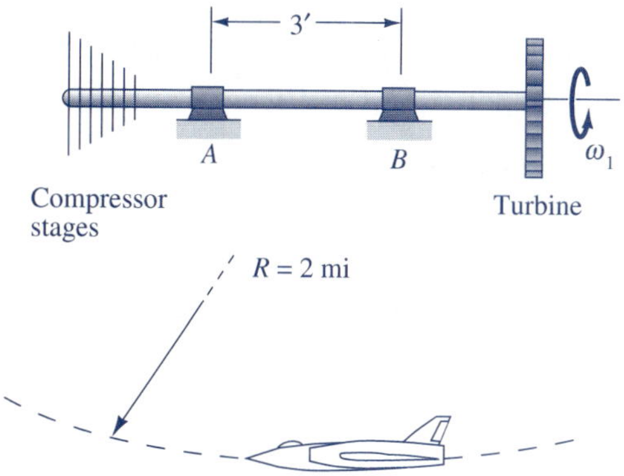

Figure P.18.1.

18.2. A space capsule (unmanned) is tumbling in space due to malfunctioning of its control system such that at time t, $\omega_1 = 3$ rad/sec, $\omega_2 = 5$ rad/sec, and $\omega_3 = 4$ rad/sec. At this instant, small jets are creating a torque T of 30 N-m. What are the angular acceleration components at this instant? The vehicle is a body of revolution with $k_z = 1$ m, $k_y = k_x = 1.6$ m, and has a mass of 1,000 kg.

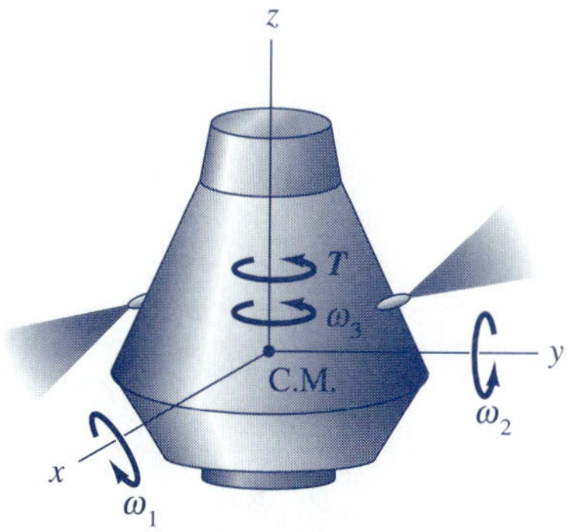

Figure P.18.2.

18.3. The left front tire of a car moving at 55 mi/hr along an unbanked road along a circular path having a mean radius of 150 yd. The tire is 26 in. in diameter. The rim plus tire weighs 30 lb and has a combined radius of gyration of 9 in. about its axis. Normal to the axis, the radius of gyration is 7.5 in. What is the gyroscopic torque on the bearings of this front wheel coming solely from the motion of the front wheel?

18.4. In Problem 18.3, suppose that the driver is turning the front wheel at a rate ω_3 of .2 rad/sec at the instant where the radius of curvature of the path is 150 yd. What is then the torque needed on the wheel solely from the motion of the wheel?

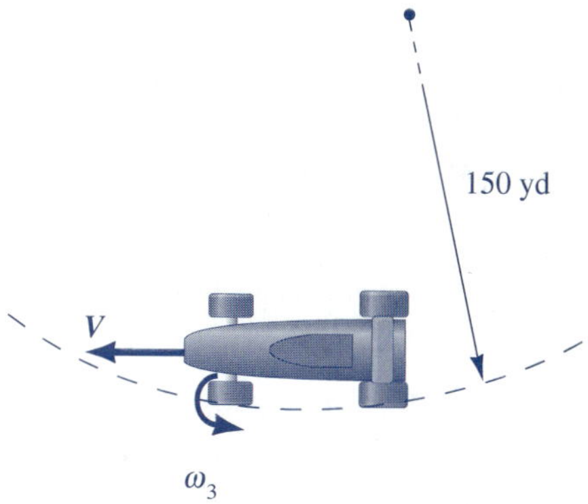

Figure P.18.4.

18.5. A student is holding a rapidly rotating wheel in front of him. He is standing on a platform that can turn freely. If the student exerts a torque M_1 as shown, what begins to happen initially? What happens a little later?

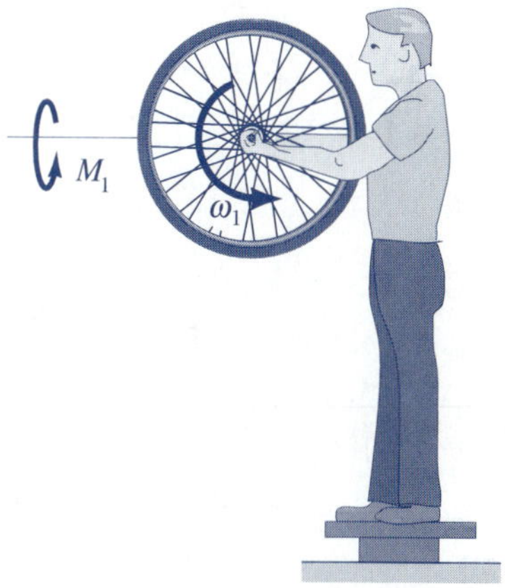

Figure P.18.5.

18.6. An electric motor is mounted on a rotating platform having an angular velocity ω_1 of 2 rad/sec. The motor drives two fans at the rate ω_2 of 1,750 rpm relative to the platform. The fans plus armature of the motor have a total weight of 100 N and a radius of gyration along the axis of 200 mm. About the Z axis, the radius of gyration is 200 mm. What is the torque coming onto the bearings of the motor as a result of the motion?

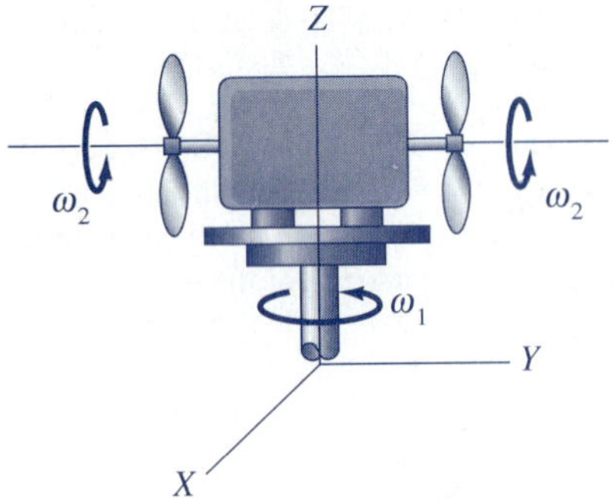

Figure P.18.6.

18.7. A lug wrench is translating in inertial space inside an orbiting space vehicle. A torque $\boldsymbol{T} = 2\boldsymbol{i} + 6\boldsymbol{j} + 5\boldsymbol{k}$ N-m is exerted at the center of the wrench. What is the acceleration of end A at this instant? Approximate the wrench as two slender rods. The wrench weighs 12 N.

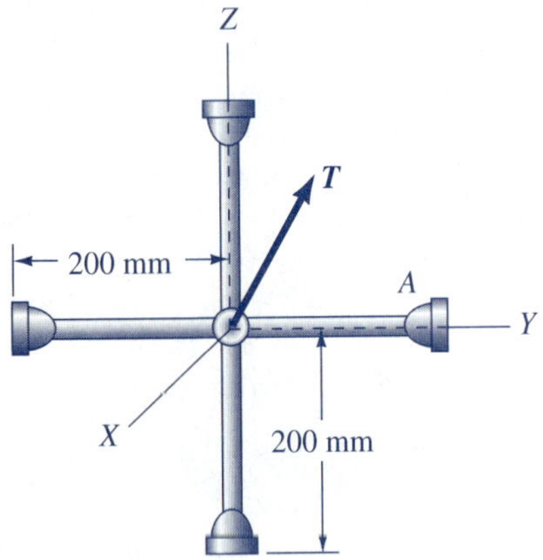

Figure P.18.7.

18.8. Work Problem 18.7 for the case where

$$\boldsymbol{\omega} = 3\boldsymbol{i} - 2\boldsymbol{j} + 4\boldsymbol{k} \text{ rad/sec}$$

about an axis of rotation through the center of mass at the instant when $\boldsymbol{T}$ is applied.

18.9. A propeller-driven airplane is at the bottom of a loop of radius 2,000 ft and traveling at 350 mi/hr. The propeller consists of two identical blades at right angles, weighs 322 lb, has a radius of gyration of 2 ft about its axis of rotation, and is rotating at 1,200 rpm. If the propeller rotates counterclockwise as viewed from the rear of the plane, compute the torques coming onto the propeller at the bearings from the motion if one blade is vertical and the other is horizontal at the time of interest.

***18.10.** A thin disc weighing 32.2 lb rotates on rod AB at a speed ω_2 of 100 rad/sec in a clockwise direction looking from B to A. The radius of the disc is 1 ft, and the disc is located 10 ft from the centerline of the shaft CD, to which rod AB is fixed. Shaft CD rotates at $\omega_1 = 50$ rad/sec in a counterclockwise direction as we look from C to D. Find the tensile force, bending moment, and shear force on rod AB at the end A due to the disc.

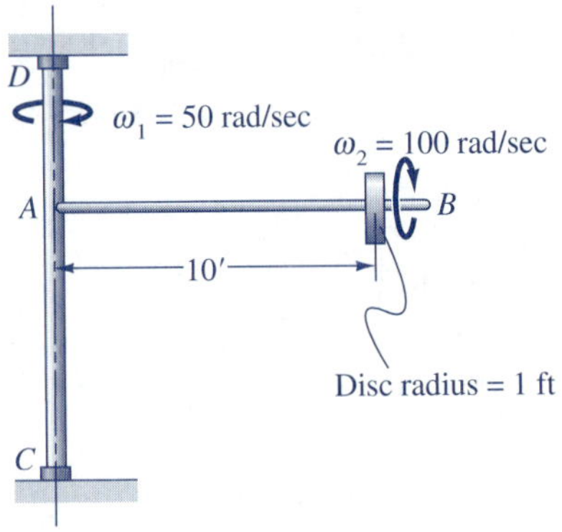

Figure P.18.10.

18.11. The turbine in a ship is parallel to the longitudinal axis of the ship and is rotating at a rate ω_1 of 800 rpm counterclockwise as viewed from stern to bow. The turbine weighs 445 kN and has radii of gyration at the mass center of 1 m about axes normal to the centerline and of 300 mm about the centerline. The ship has a pitching motion, which is approximately sinusoidal, given as

$$\theta = .3 \sin \frac{2\pi}{15} t \text{ rad}$$

The amplitude of the pitching is thus .3 rad and the period is 15 sec. Determine the moment as a function of time about the mass center needed for the motion of the turbine.

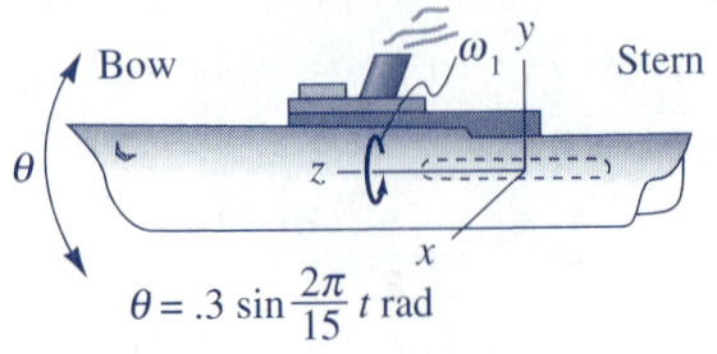

Figure P.18.11.

18.12. Explain how the roll of a ship can be stabilized by the action of a heavy rapidly spinning disc (gyroscope) rotating in a set of bearings in the ship as shown.

Figure P.18.12.

18.13. A 10-kg disc rotates with speed $\omega_1 = 10$ rad/sec relative to rod AB. Rod AB rotates with speed $\omega_2 = 4$ rad/sec relative to the vertical shaft, which rotates with speed $\omega_3 = 2$ rad/sec relative to the ground. What is the torque coming onto the bearings at B due to the motion at a time when $\theta = 60°$? Take $\dot{\omega}_1 = \dot{\omega}_2 = \dot{\omega}_3 = 0$.

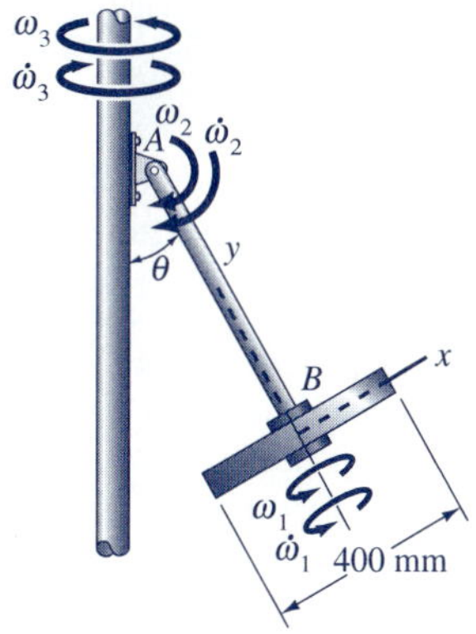

Figure P.18.13.

18.14. Solve Problem 18.13 for the case where $\dot{\omega}_1 = 2$ rad/sec^2, $\dot{\omega}_2 = 3$ rad/sec^2, and $\dot{\omega}_3 = 4$ rad/sec^2 in the directions shown.

18.15. A man is seated in a centrifuge of the type described in Example 15.14. If $\omega_1 = 2$ rad/sec, $\omega_2 = 3$ rad/sec, and $\omega_3 = 4$ rad/sec, what torque must the seat develop about the center of mass of the man as a result of the motion? The man weighs 700 N and has the following radii of gyration as determined by experiment while sitting in the seat:

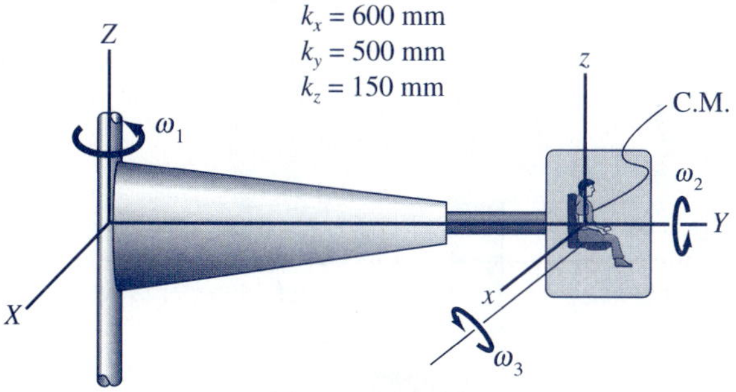

Figure P.18.15.

***18.16.** Work Problem 18.15 for the following data:

$$\dot{\omega}_1 = 3 \text{ rad/sec}^2$$
$$\dot{\omega}_2 = -2 \text{ rad/sec}^2$$
$$\dot{\omega}_3 = 4 \text{ rad/sec}^2$$

The other data are the same.

18.17. A thin disc has its axis inclined to the vertical by an angle θ and rolls without slipping with an angular speed ω_1 about the supporting rod held at B with a ball-and-socket joint. If $l = 10$ ft, $r = 2$ ft, $\theta = 45°$, and $\omega_1 = 10$ rad/sec, compute the angular velocity of the rod BC about axis O-O. If the disc weighs 40 lb, what is the total moment about point B from all forces acting on the system? Neglect the mass of the rod OC. [*Hint:* Use a reference xyz at B when two of the axes are in the plane of O-O and OC.]

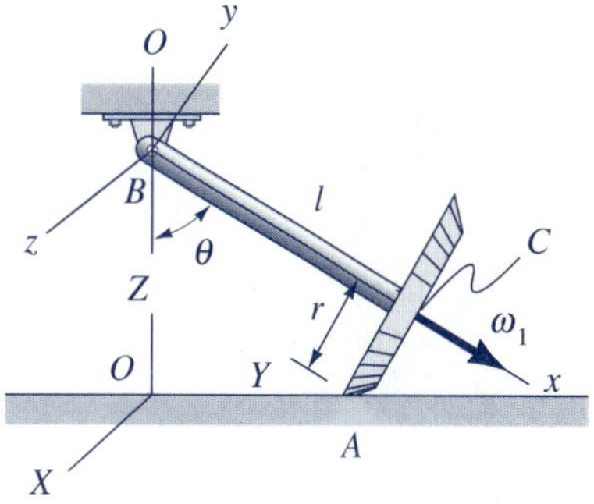

Figure P.18.17.

18.18. A gage indicator CD in an instrument is 20 mm long and is rotating relative to platform A at the rate $\omega_1 = .3$ rad/sec. The platform A Is fixed to a space vehicle which is rotating at speed $\omega_2 = 1$ rad/sec about vertical axis LM. At the instant shown, what are the moment components from the bearings E and G about the center of mass of CD needed for the motion of CD and EG? The indicator weighs .25 N, and the shaft EG weighs .30 N, has a diameter of 1 mm, and a length of 10 mm.

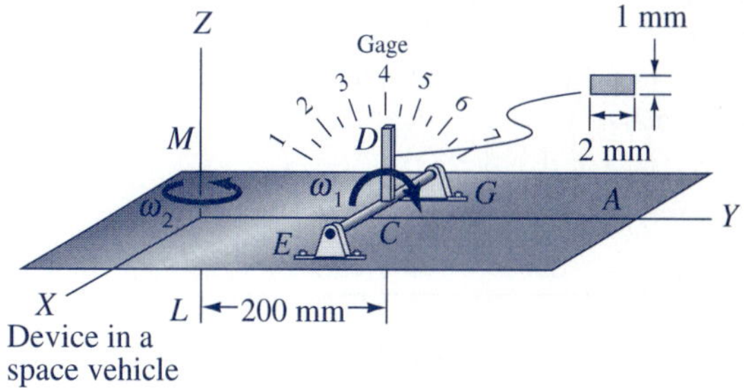

Figure P.18.18.

18.19. An eight-bladed fan is used in a wind tunnel to drive the air. The angular velocity ω_1 of the fan is 120 rpm. At the instant of interest, each blade is rotating about its own axis z (in order to change the angle of attack of the blade) such that $\omega_2 = 1$ rad/sec and $\dot{\omega}_2$ is .5 rad/sec². Each blade weighs 200 N and has the following radii of gyration at the mass center (C.M.):

$$k_x = 600 \text{ mm}$$
$$k_y = 580 \text{ mm}$$
$$k_z = 100 \text{ mm}$$

Consider only the dynamics of the system (and not the aerodynamics) to find the torque required about the z axis of the blade. If a couple moment of 4 N-m is developed in the x direction at the base of the blade, what force component F_y is needed at the base of the blade for the motion described?

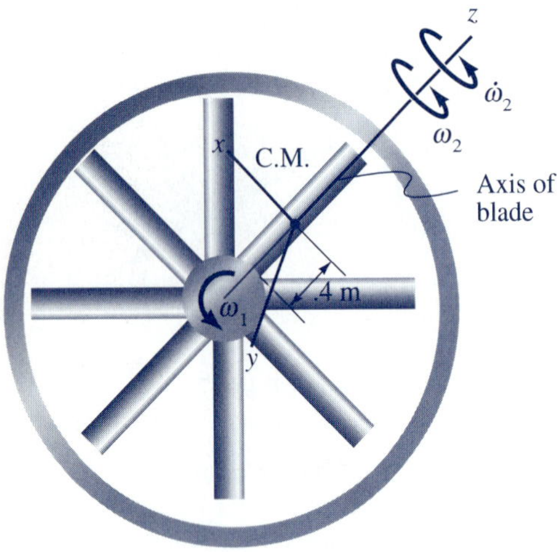

Figure P.18.19.

18.20. A swing-wing fighter plane is moving with a speed of Mach 1.3. (Note that Mach 1 corresponds to a speed of about 1,200 km/hr.) The pilot at the instant shown is swinging his wings back at the rate ω_1 of .3 rad/sec. At the same time he is rolling at a rate ω_2 of .6 rad/sec and is performing a loop as shown. The wing weighs 6.5 kN and has the following radii of gyration at the center of mass:

$$k_x = .8 \text{ m}$$
$$k_y = 4 \text{ m}$$
$$k_z = 6 \text{ m}$$

What is the moment that the fuselage must develop about the center of mass of the wing to accomplish the dynamics of the described motions? Do not consider aerodynamics.

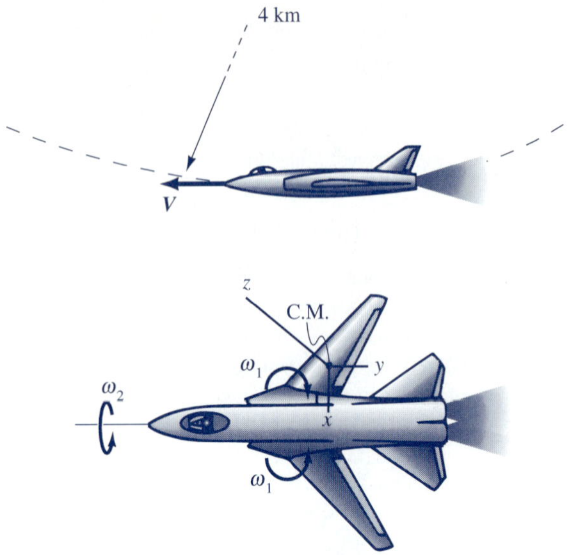

Figure P.18.20.

18.21. An orbiting skylab is rotating at an angular speed ω_1 of .4 rad/sec to give a "gravitational" effect for the living quarters in the outer annulus. A many-bladed fan is mounted as shown on the outer "floor." The fan blades rotate at a speed ω_2 of 200 rpm and the base rotates at a speed ω_3 of 1 rad/sec with $\dot{\omega}_3$ equal to .6 rad/sec² all relative to the skylab. At the instant of interest $\boldsymbol{\omega}_1$, $\boldsymbol{\omega}_2$, and $\boldsymbol{\omega}_3$ are orthogonal to each other. If the blade has a mass of 100 grams and if the radius of gyration about its axis is 200 mm, what is the torque coming onto the fan due solely to the motion? Take the transverse radii of gyration of the fan to be 120 mm.

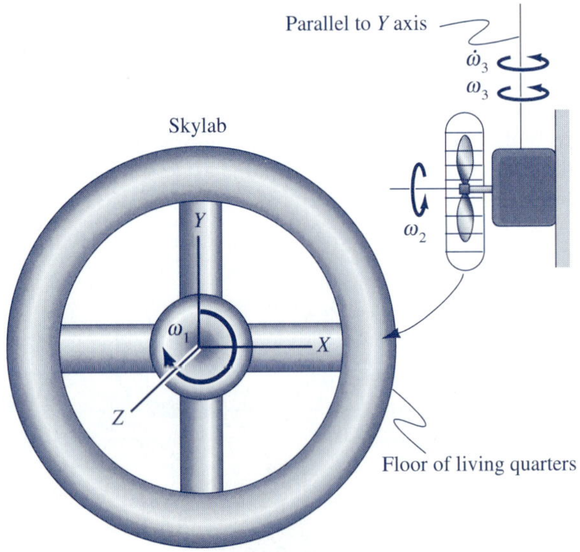

Figure P.18.21.

18.22. You will learn in fluid mechanics that when air moves across a rotating cylinder a force is developed normal to the axis of the cylinder (the *Magnus effect*). In 1926 Flettner used this principle to "sail" a vessel across the Atlantic. Two cylinders were kept at a constant rotational speed by a motor of $\omega_1 = 200$ rpm relative to the ship. Suppose that in rough seas the ship is rolling about the axis of the ship with a speed ω_2 of .8 rad/sec. What couple moment components must the ship transmit to the *base* of the cylinder as a result only of the motion of the ship? Each cylinder weighs 700 lb and has a radius of gyration along the axis of 2 ft and normal to the axis at the center of mass of 10 ft.

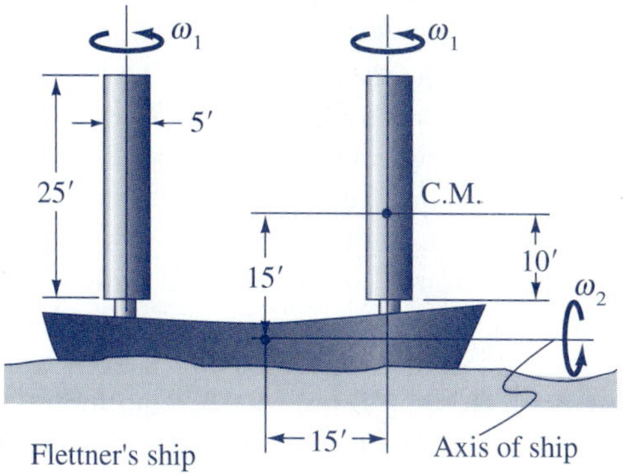

Figure P.18.22.

***18.23.** Part of a clutch system consists of identical rods *AB* and *AC* rotating relative to a shaft at the speed $\omega_2 = 3$ rad/sec while the shaft rotates relative to the ground at a speed $\omega_1 = 40$ rad/sec. As a result of the motion what are the bending moment components at the base of each rod if each rod weighs 10 N?

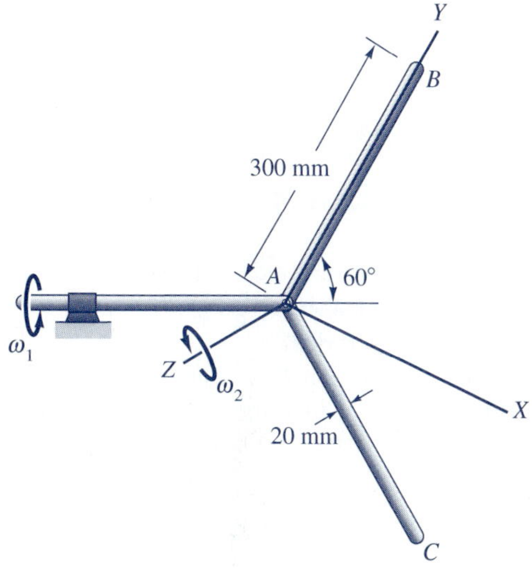

Figure P.18.23.

***18.24.** Solve Problem 18.23 for the case when $\dot{\omega}_1 = 2$ rad/sec^2 and $\dot{\omega}_2 = 6$ rad/sec^2 at the instant of interest.

18.25. A rod *D* weighing 2 N and having a length of 200 mm and a diameter of 10 mm rotates relative to platform *K* at a speed ω_1 of 120 rad/sec. The platform is in a space vehicle and turns at a speed ω_2 of 50 rad/sec relative to the vehicle. The vehicle rotates at a speed ω_3 of 30 rad/sec relative to inertial space about the axis shown. What are the bearing forces at *A* and *B* normal to the axis *AB* resulting from the motion of rod *D*? What torque *T* is needed about *AB* to maintain a constant value of ω_1 at the instant of interest?

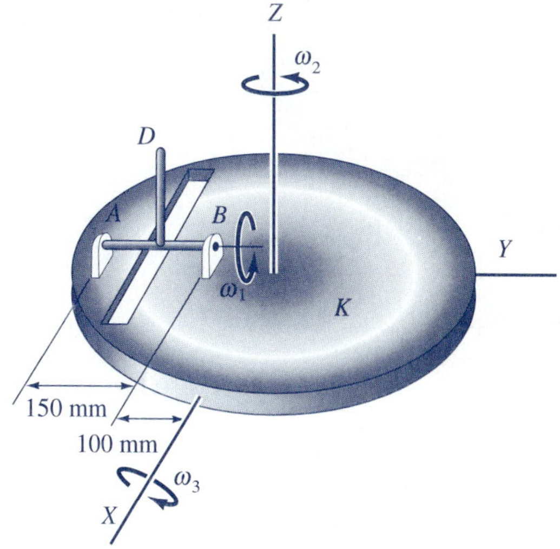

Figure P.18.25.

18.26. Solve Problem 18.6 using a reference at the center of mass of the armature but not fixed to the armature.

18.27. In Problem 18.10, find the moment about the C.M. of the disc using a reference *xyz* fixed to the rod *AB* and not to the disc. Take $\dot{\omega}_1 = 10$ rad/sec^2 and $\dot{\omega}_2 = 30$ rad/sec^2.

18.28. Work Problem 18.11 using reference *xyz* fixed to the ship with the origin at the center of mass of the turbine. Do not use **Euler's equations**.

18.29. Solve Problem 18.13 using a set of axes *xyz* at the center of mass of the disc but fixed to arm *AB*.

18.30. Work Problem 18.13 by using a reference *xyz* fixed to the arm at the center of mass of the disc for the case where $\dot{\omega}_1 = 2$ rad/sec^2, $\dot{\omega}_2 = 3$ rad/sec^2, and $\dot{\omega}_3 = 4$ rad/sec^2 in directions shown.

18.4 Necessary and Sufficient Conditions for Equilibrium of a Rigid Body

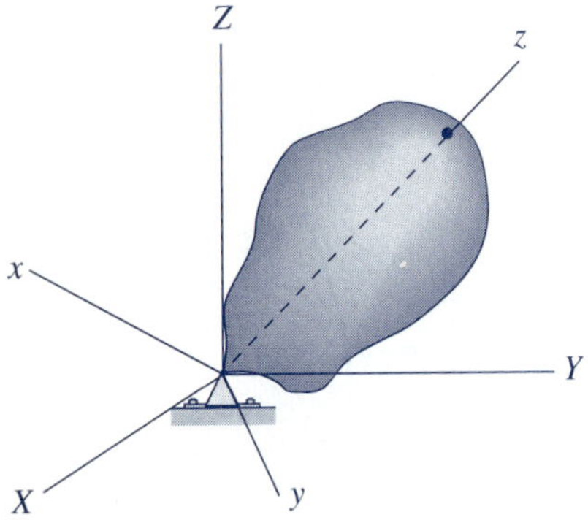

Figure 18.11. Body with a fixed point.

In this chapter, we have employed **Newton's law** at the mass center as well as the equation $\boldsymbol{M}_A = \dot{\boldsymbol{H}}_A$ and from it we derived **Euler's equations** for rigid bodies. We can now go back to our work in Chapter 5 and put on firm ground the fact that $\boldsymbol{M} = \boldsymbol{0}$ and $\boldsymbol{F} = \boldsymbol{0}$ are necessary conditions for equilibrium of a rigid body. (You will recall we accepted these equations for statics at that time by intuition, pending a proof to come later.)

A particle is in equilibrium, you will recall, if it is stationary or moving with constant speed along a straight line in inertial space. To be in a state of equilibrium, every point in a rigid body must accordingly be stationary or be moving at uniform speed along straight lines in inertial space. The rigidity requirement thus limits a rigid body in equilibrium to translational motion along a straight line at constant speed in inertial space. This means that $\dot{\boldsymbol{V}}_C = \boldsymbol{0}$ and $\boldsymbol{\omega} = \boldsymbol{0}$ for equilibrium and so, from *Newton's law* and *Euler's equations*, we see that $\boldsymbol{F} = \boldsymbol{M}_A = \boldsymbol{0}$ are *necessary* conditions for equilibrium.

For a *sufficiency* proof, we go the other way. For a body initially in equilibrium, the condition $\boldsymbol{F} = \boldsymbol{M}_A = \boldsymbol{0}$[5] ensures that equilibrium will be maintained. More specifically, we shall start with a body in equilibrium at time t and apply a force system satisfying the preceding conditions. We address ourselves to the question: Does the body stay in a state of equilibrium? According to *Newton's law* there will be no change in the velocity of the mass center since $\boldsymbol{F} = \boldsymbol{0}$. And, with $\boldsymbol{\omega} = \boldsymbol{0}$ at time t, *Euler's equations* lead to the result for $\boldsymbol{M}_C = \boldsymbol{0}$, that $\dot{\omega}_x = \dot{\omega}_y = \dot{\omega}_z = 0$. Thus, the angular velocity must remain zero. With the velocity of the center of mass constant, and with $\dot{\boldsymbol{\omega}} = \boldsymbol{0}$ in inertial space we know that the body remains in equilibrium. Thus, if a body is *initially in equilibrium*, the condition $\boldsymbol{F} = \boldsymbol{0}$ and $\boldsymbol{M}_A = \boldsymbol{0}$ is *sufficient* for maintaining equilibrium.

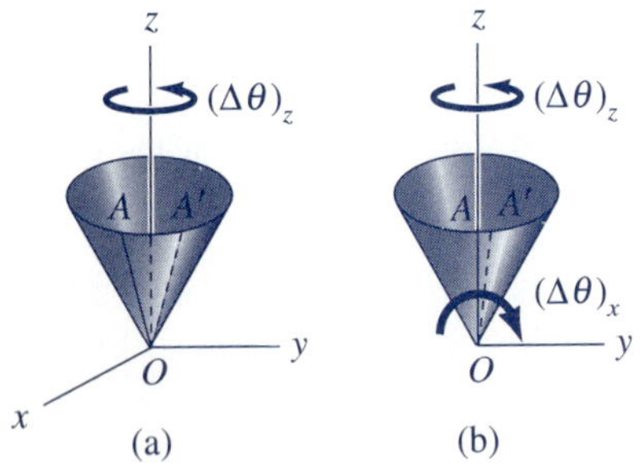

Figure 18.12. $\Delta\theta_z$ causes $\Delta\theta_x$.

18.5 Three-Dimensional Motion About a Fixed Point; Euler Angles

We shall now examine the motion of selected rigid bodies constrained to have a point fixed in an inertial reference (Fig. 18.11). This topic will lead to study of an important device—the gyroscope.

We now show that angles of rotation θ_x, θ_y, and θ_z, along orthogonal axes x, y, and z are not highly suitable for measuring the orientation of a body with a fixed point. Thus, in Fig. 18.12(a) consider a conical surface and observe straight line OA which is on this surface and in the xz plane. Rotate the cone

[5]We have shown in statics that if $\boldsymbol{F} = \boldsymbol{0}$ and $\boldsymbol{M}_A = \boldsymbol{0}$ about some point A in inertial space, then $\boldsymbol{M} = \boldsymbol{0}$ about any point in inertial space.

an angle $(\Delta\theta)_z$, thus causing OA to move to OA' shown as dashed. In Fig. 18.12(b), view line OA along a line of sight corresponding to the x axis. As a result of the rotation $(\Delta\theta)_z$ about the z axis, there will clearly be a rotation $(\Delta\theta)_x$ of this line about the x axis. Thus, we see that θ_x and θ_z are mutually dependent and thus not suitable for our use. This result stems from the fact that we are using directions that have a fixed mutual relative orientation. We now introduce a set of rotations that are *independent.* And, not unexpectedly, the axes for these rotations will not have a fixed relative orientation.

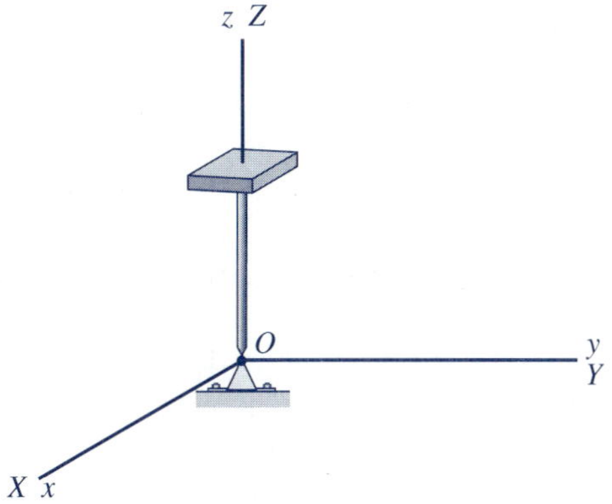

Figure 18.13. Rigid body.

Accordingly, consider the rigid body shown in Fig. 18.13. We shall specify a sequence of three independent rotations in the following manner:

1. Keep a reference xyz fixed in the body, and rotate the body about the Z axis through an angle ψ shown in Fig. 18.14.

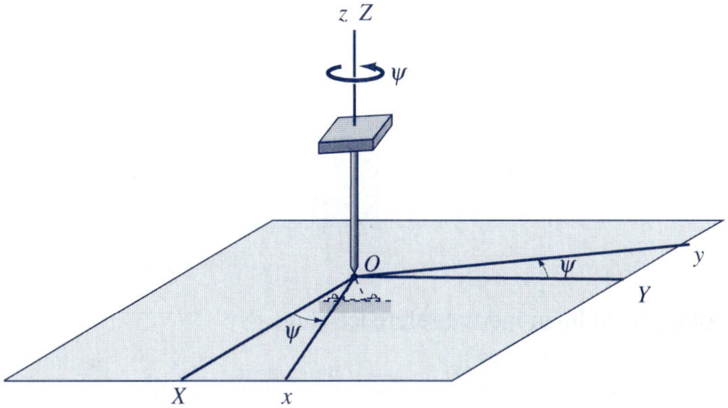

Figure 18.14. First rotation is about Z.

2. Now rotate the body about the x axis through an angle θ to reach the configuration in Fig. 18.15. Note that the z, Z, and y axes form a plane I normal to the XY plane and normal also to the x axis. The axis of rotation for this rotation (x axis) is called the *line of nodes.*

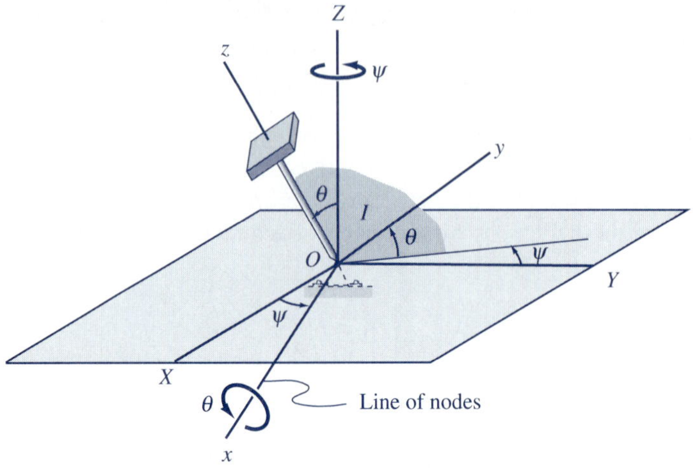

Figure 18.15. Second rotation is about x.

3. Finally, rotate the body an angle ϕ about the z axis. We provide the option here of *detaching* the xyz reference from the body for this movement (see Fig. 18.16), in which case the body rotates an angle ϕ relative to xyz, and the x axis remains collinear with the line of nodes. Or, we can permit the reference xyz to remain fixed in the body (see Fig. 18.17), in which case we can use components of $\boldsymbol{M}$ and $\boldsymbol{\omega}$ along these axes in employing *Euler's equations*. The line of nodes is now identified simply as the normal to plane I containing z and Z and is the same axis as shown in Fig. 18.16.

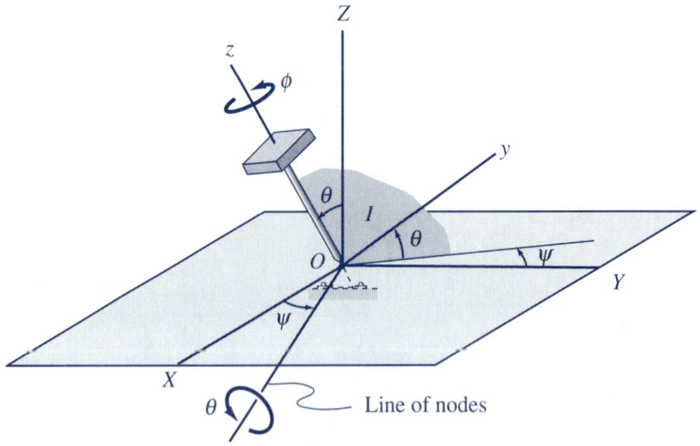

Figure 18.16. Third rotation is about z. xyz is detached.

We thus arrive at the desired orientation. Positive rotations in each case are those taken as counterclockwise as one looks to the origin O along the axis of rotation. (Thus, we have performed three positive rotations here.)

We call these angles the *Euler angles*, and we assign the following names.

$$\psi = \text{angle of precession}$$
$$\theta = \text{angle of nutation}$$
$$\phi = \text{angle of spin}$$

Furthermore, the z axis is usually called the *body axis*, and the Z axis is often called the *axis of precession*. The line of nodes then is normal to the body axis and the precession axis.

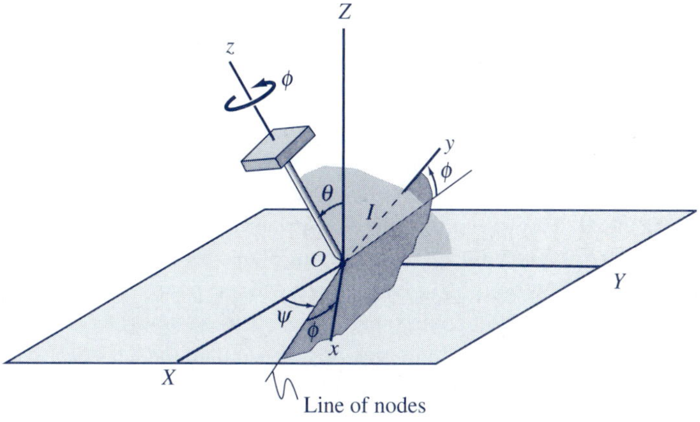

Figure 18.17. Axes xyz are fixed to body.

We have shown that the position of a body moving with one point fixed can be established by three independent rotations given in a certain sequence. For an infinitesimal change in position, this situation would be a rotation $d\psi$ about the Z axis, $d\theta$ about the line of nodes, and $d\phi$ about the body axis z. Because these rotations are infinitesimal, they can be construed as vectors, and the order mentioned above is no longer required. The limiting ratios of these changes in angles with respect to time give rise to three angular velocity vectors (Fig. 18.18), which we express in the following manner:

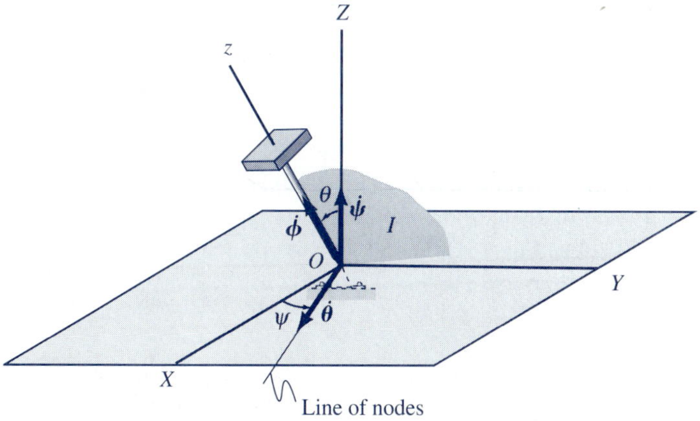

Figure 18.18. Precession, nutation, and spin velocity vectors.

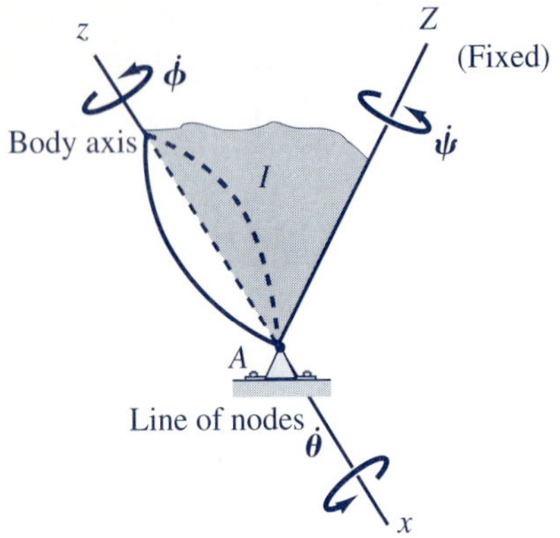

Figure 18.19. Line of nodes always normal to plane I.

$\dot{\boldsymbol{\psi}}$, directed along the Z axis
$\dot{\boldsymbol{\theta}}$, directed along the line of nodes
$\dot{\boldsymbol{\phi}}$, directed along the z body axis

Note that the nutation velocity vector $\dot{\boldsymbol{\theta}}$ is always normal to plane I, and consequently the nutation velocity vector is always normal to the spin velocity vector $\dot{\boldsymbol{\phi}}$ and the precession velocity vector $\dot{\boldsymbol{\psi}}$. However, the spin velocity vector $\dot{\boldsymbol{\phi}}$ will generally *not* be at right angles with the precession velocity $\dot{\boldsymbol{\psi}}$, and so this system of angular velocity vectors generally is *not* an orthogonal system.

Finally, it should be clear that the reference xyz moves with the body during precession and nutation motion of the body, but we can choose that it not move (relative to XYZ) during a spin rotation. Hence for this case, while the body has the angular velocity $\dot{\boldsymbol{\phi}} + \dot{\boldsymbol{\psi}} + \dot{\boldsymbol{\theta}}$ at any time t the reference xyz would have, for the aforestated condition, an angular velocity, denoted as $\boldsymbol{\Omega}$, equal to $\dot{\boldsymbol{\psi}} + \dot{\boldsymbol{\theta}}$. The velocity of the disc relative to xyz is, accordingly, $\dot{\phi}\boldsymbol{k}$.

Consider a body with two orthogonal planes of symmetry forming an axis in the body. The body is moving about a fixed point A on the body axis (Fig. 18.19). How do we decide what axes to use to describe the motion in terms of spin, precession, and nutation? First, we take the axis of the body to be the z axis; the angular speed about this axis is then the spin $\dot{\phi}$. This step is straightforward for the bodies that we shall consider. The next step is not. By inspection find a Z axis in a *fixed direction* so as to form with the aforementioned body axis z a plane I whose angular speed about the Z axis is either known or is sought. Such an axis Z is then the *precession* axis about which we have for the body axis z a precession speed $\dot{\psi}$. The *line of nodes* is then the axis which at all times remains *normal* to plane I containing the body axis z and the precession axis Z. The nutation speed $\dot{\theta}$ finally is the angular speed component of the body axis z about the line of nodes.

18.6 Equations of Motion Using Euler Angles

Consider next a body having a shape such that, at any point along the body axis z, the moments of inertia for all axes normal to the body axis at this point have the same value I'. Such would, of course, be true for the special case of a body of revolution having the z axis as the axis of symmetry.[6] We shall consider the motion of such a body about a fixed point O, which is somewhere along the axis z (see Fig. 18.20). Axes xyz are principal axes. This set of axes has the same nutation and precession motion as the body but will be chosen

[6]You will be asked to show in Problem 18.41 that, if I_{xx}, I_{yy}, and I_{zz} are principal axes and $I_{xx} = I_{yy} = I'$, then $I'_{xx} = I'_{yy} = I'$ for *any* axes x', y' formed by rotating xyz about the z axis. Thus, homogeneous cylinders having regular cross sections such as squares or octagons would meet the requirements of this section.

such that the body rotates with angular speed $\dot{\phi}$ relative to it. Since the reference is not fixed to the body, we cannot use **Euler's equations** but must go back to the equation $\boldsymbol{M}_0 = \dot{\boldsymbol{H}}_0$, which when carried out in terms of components parallel to the *xyz* reference becomes

$$\boldsymbol{M}_0 = \left(\frac{d\boldsymbol{H}_0}{dt}\right)_{xyz} + \boldsymbol{\Omega} \times (H_x\boldsymbol{i} + H_y\boldsymbol{j} + H_z\boldsymbol{k}) \tag{18.21}$$

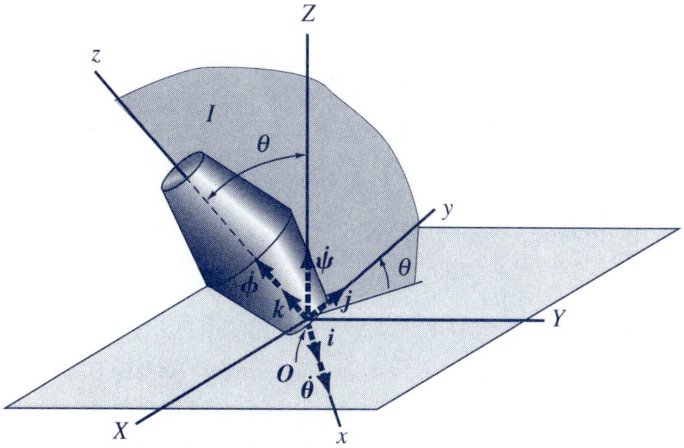

Figure 18.20. Body moving about fixed point *O*.

Since the *xyz* axes remain at *all times* principal axes, we have

$$H_x = I'\omega_x, \qquad H_y = I'\omega_y, \qquad H_z = I\omega_z \tag{18.22}$$

where I is the moment of inertia about the axis of symmetry and I' is the moment of inertia about an axis normal to the z axis at O. Considering Fig. 18.20, we can see by inspection that the angular velocity of the body relative to *XYZ* is at *all times* given by components parallel to *xyz* as follows:

$$\omega_x = \dot{\theta} \tag{18.23a}$$
$$\omega_y = \dot{\psi} \sin\theta \tag{18.23b}$$
$$\omega_z = \dot{\phi} + \dot{\psi}\cos\theta \tag{18.23c}$$

Hence, the components of the angular momentum at all times are:

$$\begin{aligned}(H_x) &= I'\dot{\theta}\\ (H_y) &= I'\dot{\psi}\sin\theta\\ (H_z) &= I(\dot{\phi} + \dot{\psi}\cos\theta)\end{aligned} \tag{18.24}$$

We then have for $\boldsymbol{H}_0$:

$$\boldsymbol{H}_0 = I'\,\dot{\theta}\boldsymbol{i} + I'\,\dot{\psi}\sin\theta\boldsymbol{j} + I(\dot{\phi} + \dot{\psi}\cos\theta)\boldsymbol{k}$$

Remembering that $\boldsymbol{i}, \boldsymbol{j}$ and $\boldsymbol{k}$ are constants as seen from xyz, we can say:

$$\left(\frac{d\boldsymbol{H}_0}{dt}\right)_{xyz} = \left(\frac{d}{dt}\right)_{xyz}\left[I'\dot{\theta}\boldsymbol{i} + I'\dot{\psi}\sin\theta\,\boldsymbol{j} + I(\dot{\phi} + \dot{\psi}\cos\theta)\boldsymbol{k}\right] \tag{18.25}$$
$$= I'\ddot{\theta}\boldsymbol{i} + I'(\ddot{\psi}\sin\theta + \dot{\psi}\dot{\theta}\cos\theta)\boldsymbol{j} + I(\ddot{\phi} + \ddot{\psi}\cos\theta - \dot{\psi}\dot{\theta}\sin\theta)\boldsymbol{k}$$

As for the angular velocity of reference xyz, we have on considering Eq. 18.24 with $\dot{\phi}$ deleted because xyz is not fixed to the body as far as spin is concerned:

$$\boldsymbol{\Omega} = \dot{\theta}\boldsymbol{i} + \dot{\psi}\sin\theta\boldsymbol{j} + \dot{\psi}\cos\theta\boldsymbol{k} \tag{18.26}$$

Consequently, we have

$$\begin{aligned} \boldsymbol{\Omega}\times\boldsymbol{i} &= -\dot{\psi}\sin\theta\boldsymbol{k} + \dot{\psi}\cos\theta\boldsymbol{j} \\ \boldsymbol{\Omega}\times\boldsymbol{j} &= \dot{\theta}\boldsymbol{k} - \dot{\psi}\cos\theta\boldsymbol{i} \\ \boldsymbol{\Omega}\times\boldsymbol{k} &= -\dot{\theta}\boldsymbol{j} + \dot{\psi}\sin\theta\boldsymbol{i} \end{aligned} \tag{18.27}$$

Substituting the results from Eqs. 18.25, 18.24, and 18.27 into Eq. 18.21, we get

$$\begin{aligned} M_x\boldsymbol{i} + M_y\boldsymbol{j} + M_z\boldsymbol{k} = {} & I'\ddot{\theta}\boldsymbol{i} + I'(\ddot{\psi}\sin\theta + \dot{\psi}\dot{\theta}\cos\theta)\boldsymbol{j} \\ & + I(\ddot{\phi} + \ddot{\psi}\cos\theta - \dot{\psi}\dot{\theta}\sin\theta)\boldsymbol{k} \\ & + I'\dot{\theta}(-\dot{\psi}\sin\theta\boldsymbol{k} + \dot{\psi}\cos\theta\boldsymbol{j}) \\ & + I'\dot{\psi}\sin\theta(\dot{\theta}\boldsymbol{k} - \dot{\psi}\cos\theta\boldsymbol{i}) \\ & + I(\dot{\phi} + \dot{\psi}\cos\theta)(-\dot{\theta}\boldsymbol{j} + \dot{\psi}\sin\theta\boldsymbol{i}) \end{aligned} \tag{18.28}$$

The corresponding scalar equations are:

$$M_x = I'\ddot{\theta} + (I - I')(\dot{\psi}^2\sin\theta\cos\theta) + I\dot{\phi}\dot{\psi}\sin\theta \tag{18.29a}$$
$$M_y = I'\ddot{\psi}\sin\theta + 2I'\dot{\theta}\dot{\psi}\cos\theta - I(\dot{\phi} + \dot{\psi}\cos\theta)\dot{\theta} \tag{18.29b}$$
$$M_z = I(\ddot{\phi} + \ddot{\psi}\cos\theta - \dot{\psi}\dot{\theta}\sin\theta) \tag{18.29c}$$

The foregoing equations are valid at all times for the motion of a homogeneous body having $I_{xx} = I_{yy} = I'$ moving about a fixed point on the axis of the body. Clearly, these equations are also applicable for motion about the center of mass for such bodies. Note that the equations are nonlinear and, except for certain special cases, are very difficult to integrate. They are, of course, very useful as they stand when computer methods are to be employed.

As a special case, we shall now consider a motion involving a constant nutation angle θ, a constant spin speed $\dot{\phi}$, and a constant precession speed $\dot{\psi}$. Such a motion is termed *steady precession*. To determine the torque $\boldsymbol{M}$ for a given steady precession, we set $\dot{\theta}$, $\ddot{\theta}$, $\ddot{\phi}$, and $\ddot{\psi}$ equal to zero in Eqs. 18.29. Accordingly, we get the following result:

$$M_x = \{I(\dot{\phi} + \dot{\psi}\cos\theta) - I'\dot{\psi}\cos\theta]\,\dot{\psi}\sin\theta \tag{18.30a}$$
$$M_y = 0 \tag{18.30b}$$
$$M_z = 0 \tag{18.30c}$$

We see that for such a motion, we require a *constant torque about the line of nodes* as given by Eq. 18.30a. Noting that $\dot{\phi} + \dot{\psi}\cos\theta = \omega_z$ from Eq. 18.23c, this torque may also be given as

$$M_x = (I\omega_z - I'\dot{\psi}\cos\theta)\dot{\psi}\sin\theta \tag{18.31}$$

Examining Fig. 18.20, we can conclude that for the body to maintain a constant spin speed $\dot{\phi}$ about its body axis (i.e., relative to xyz) while the body axis (and also xyz) is rotating at constant speed $\dot{\psi}$ about the Z axis at a fixed angle θ, we require a constant torque M_x having a value dependent on the motion of the body as well as the values of the moments of inertia of the body, and having a direction *always normal to the body and precession axes* (i.e., normal to plane I). Intuitively you may feel that such a torque should cause a rotation about its own axis (the *torque axis*) and should thereby change θ. Instead, the torque causes a rotation $\dot{\psi}$ of the body axis about an axis *normal* to the torque axis. As an example, consider the special case where θ has been chosen as 90° for motion of a disc about its center of mass (see Fig. 18.21). In accordance with Eq. 18.31, we have as a required torque for a steady precession the result

$$M_x = I\omega_z\dot{\psi} = I\dot{\phi}\dot{\psi} \tag{18.32}$$

Here for a given spin, the proper torque M_x about the line of nodes maintains a steady rotation $\dot{\psi}$ of the spin axis z about an axis (the Z axis), which is at *right angles* both to the torque and the spin axes and given by Eq. 18.32. Because of this unexpected phenomenon, toy manufacturers have developed various gyroscopic devices to surprise and delight children (as well as their parents). Here is yet another case where relying solely on intuition may lead to highly erroneous conclusions.

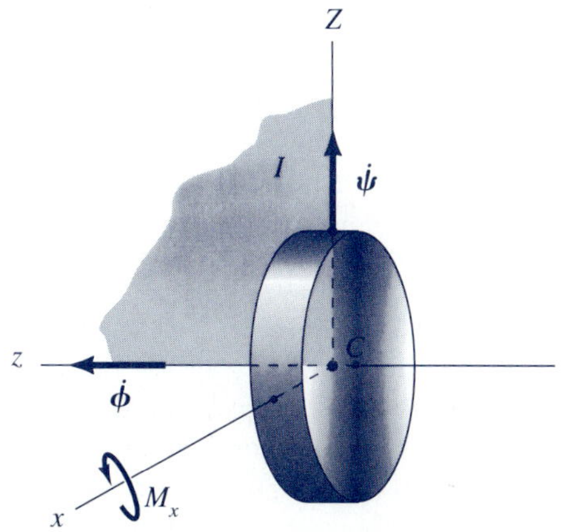

Figure 18.21. Steady precession; $\theta = 90°$.

We should strongly point out that steady precessions are not easily initiated. We must have, at the start, simultaneously the proper precession and spin speeds as well as the proper θ for the given applied torque. If these conditions are not properly met initially, a complicated motion ensues.

Example 18.3

A *single-degree-of-freedom gyro* is shown in Fig. 18.22. The spin axis of disc E is held by a gimbal A which can rotate about bearings C and D. These bearings are supported by the gyro case, which in turn is generally clamped to the vehicle to be guided. If the gyro case rotates about a vertical axis (i.e., normal to its base) while the rotor is spinning, the gimbal A will tend to rotate about CD in an attempt to align with the vertical. When gimbal A is resisted from rotation about CD by a set of torsional springs S with a combined torsional spring constant given as K_t, the gyro is called a *rate gyro*. If the rotation of the gyro case is constant (at speed ω_2), the gimbal A assumes a fixed orientation relative to the vertical as a result of the restraining springs and a damper (not shown). About the body axis z there is a constant angular rotation of the rotor of ω_1 rad/sec maintained by a motor (not shown). This angular rotation is clearly is the spin speed $\dot{\phi}$. Next, note in Fig. 18.23 that the z axis and the fixed vertical axis z form a plane (plane I) which has a known angular speed ω_2 about this fixed vertical axis. Clearly, this fixed vertical axis will be our precession axis, and the precession speed $\dot{\psi}$ equals ω_2. The line of nodes has also been shown; it must at all times be normal to plane I and is thus collinear with axis C-D of gimbal A. With θ fixed, we have a case of steady precession.

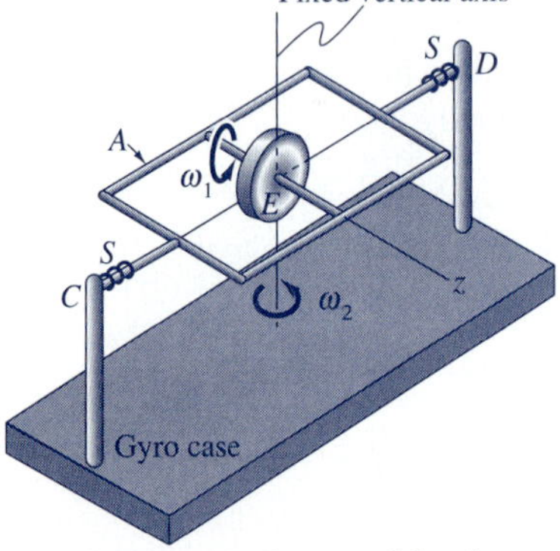

Figure 18.22. Single-degree-of-freedom gyro.

Given the following data:

$$I = 3 \times 10^{-4} \text{ slug-ft}^2$$
$$I' = 1.5 \times 10^{-4} \text{ slug-ft}^2$$
$$\dot{\phi} = 20{,}000 \text{ rad/sec}$$
$$K_t = 4.95 \text{ ft-lb/rad}$$
$$\dot{\psi} = 1 \text{ rad/sec}$$

what is θ for the condition of steady precession? The torsional springs are unstretched when $\theta = 90°$.

We have for Eq. 18.30a:

Example 18.3 (Continued)

$$M_x = K_t\left(\frac{\pi}{2} - \theta\right) = \left[I(\dot{\phi} + \dot{\psi}\cos\theta) - I'\dot{\psi}\cos\theta\right]\dot{\psi}\sin\theta \qquad \text{(a)}$$

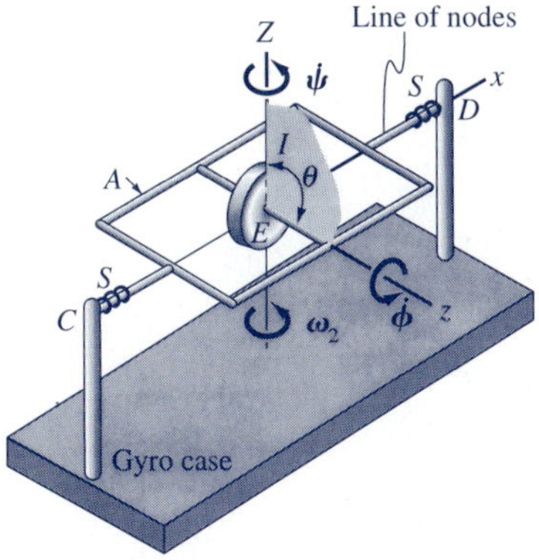

Figure 18.23. Gyro showing line of nodes and precession axis.

Putting in numerical values, we have

$$(4.95)\left(\frac{\pi}{2} - \theta\right)$$
$$= \left[3 \times 10^{-4}(2 \times 10^4 + (1)\cos\theta) - (1.5 \times 10^{-4})(1)\cos\theta\right]\sin\theta$$

Therefore,

$$4.95 \times 10^4\left(\frac{\pi}{2} - \theta\right) = (6 \times 10^4 + 1.5\cos\theta)\sin\theta$$

We can neglect the term (1.5 cos θ), and so we have

$$4.95\left(\frac{\pi}{2} - \theta\right) = 6\sin\theta$$

Therefore,

$$\frac{\pi}{2} - \theta = 1.212\sin\theta \qquad \text{(b)}$$

Solving by trial and error or by computer, we get

$$\theta = 43^\circ \qquad \text{(c)}$$

The way the *rate gyro* is used in practice is to maintain θ close to 90° by a small motor. The torque M_x developed to maintain this angle is measured, and from Eq. 18.30a we have available the proper $\dot{\psi}$, which tells us of the rate of rotation of the gyro case and hence the rate of rotation of the vehicle about an axis normal to the gyro case. Now $\dot{\psi}$ need not be constant as was the case in this problem. If it does not change very rapidly, the results from Eq. 18.30a can be taken as instantaneously valid even though the equation, strictly speaking, stems from steady precession where $\dot{\psi}$ should be constant.

Example 18.4

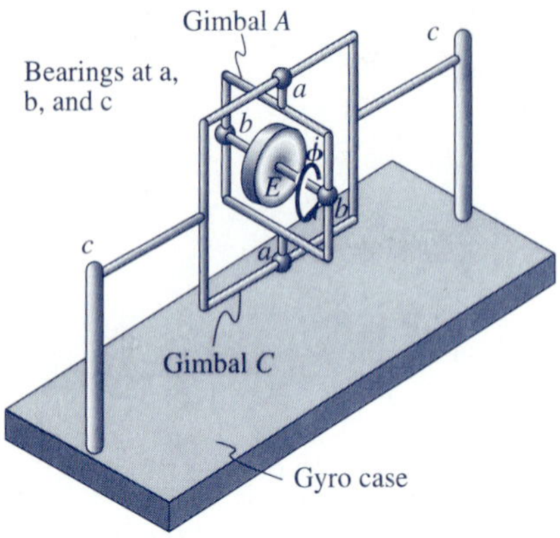

Figure 18.24. Two-degree-of-freedom gyro.

A *two-degree-of-freedom gyroscope* is shown in Fig. 18.24. The rotor *E* rotates in gimbal *A*, which in turn rotates in gimbal *C*. Note that the axes *b–b* of the rotor and *a–a* of the gimbal *C* are always at right angles to each other. Gimbal *C* is held by bearings *c* supported by the gryo case. Axes *c–c* and *a–a* must always be at right angles to each other, as can easily be seen from the diagram. This kind of suspension of the rotor is called a *Cardan suspension*. If the bearings at *a*, *b*, and *c* are frictionless, a torque cannot be transmitted from the gyro case to the rotor.[7] The rotor is said to be *torque-free* for this case.

If the rotor is given a rapid spin velocity in a given direction in inertial space (such as toward the North Star), then for the ideal case of frictionless bearings the rotor will maintain this direction even though the gyro case is given rapid and complicated motions in inertial space. This constancy of direction results since no torque can be transmitted to the rotor to alter the direction of its angular momentum. Thus, the two-dimensional gyro gives a fixed direction in inertial space for purposes of guidance of a vehicle such as a missile. In use, the gyro case is rigidly fixed to the frame of the missile, and measurements of the orientation of the missile are accomplished by having pickoffs mounted between the gyro case and the outer gimbal and between the outer and inner gimbals.

The presence of some friction in the gyro bearings is, of course, inevitable. The counteraction of this friction when possible and, when not, the accounting for its action is of much concern to the gyro engineer. Suppose that the gyro has been given a motion such that the spin axis *b–b* (see Fig. 18.25) has an angular speed ω_1 about axis *c–c* of .1 rev/sec while maintaining a fixed orientation of 85° with axis *c–c*. The gyro case is stationary,

[7]That is, except for the singular situation where the gimbal axes are coplanar.

Example 18.4 (Continued)

and the spin speed $\dot{\phi}$ of the disc relative to gimbal A is 10,000 rpm. What frictional torque must be developed on the rotor for this motion? From what bearings must such a torque arise? The radius of gyration for the disc is 50 mm for the axis of symmetry and 38 mm for the transverse axes at the center of mass. The weight of the disc is 4.5 N.

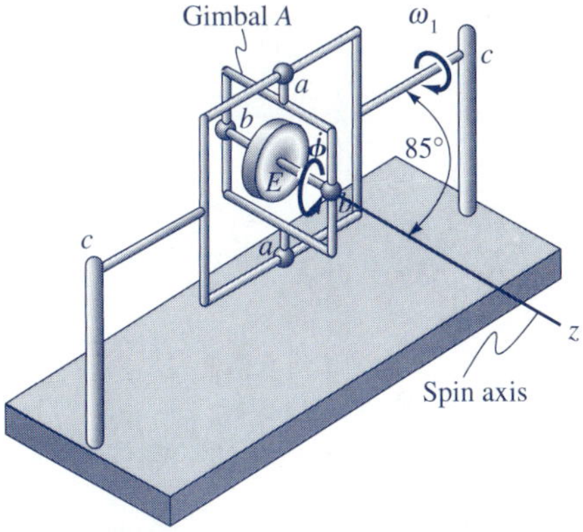

Figure 18.25. Two-degree-of-freedom gyro with body axis z.

Note in Fig. 18.26 that the spin axis z and fixed axis c–c form a plane that has a known angular speed ω_1 about axis c–c. Clearly, c–c then can be taken as the precession axis Z; the precession speed $\dot{\psi} = \omega_1$ is then .10 rev/sec. The line of nodes x is along axis a–a at all times. With $\theta = 85°$ at all times, we have steady precession. A constant torque M_x is required to maintain this motion. We can solve for M_x as follows (see Eq. 18.30(a)):

$$M_x = \left[I(\dot{\phi} + \dot{\psi}\cos\theta) - I'\dot{\psi}\cos\theta\right]\dot{\psi}\sin\theta$$

$$= \left\{\frac{4.5}{9.81}(.05)^2\left[10,000\frac{2\pi}{60} + (.1)(2\pi)\cos 85°\right]\right.$$

$$\left. - \frac{4.5}{9.81}(.038)^2(.1)(2\pi)\cos 85°\right\}(.1)(2\pi)\cos 85°$$

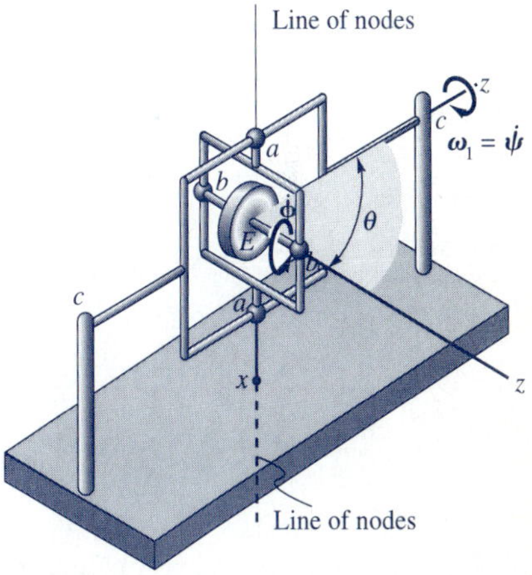

Figure 18.26. Axis c–c is precession axis.

$$M_x = .752 \text{ N-m}$$

Thus, bearings along the a–a axis interconnecting the two gimbals are developing the frictional torque.

PROBLEMS

18.31. The z axis coincides initially with the centerline of the block. The block is given the following rotations in the sequence listed: (a) $\psi = 30°$, (b) $\theta = 45°$, (c) $\phi = 20°$. What are the projections of the centerline OA along the XYZ axes in the final position?

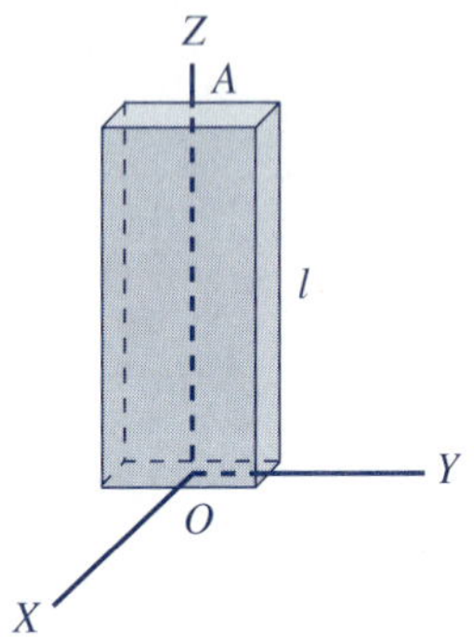

Figure P.18.31.

18.32. A disc A of mean diameter 300 mm rolls without slipping so that its centerline rotates an angular speed ω_1 of 2 rad/sec about the Z axis. What are the precession, nutation, and spin angular velocity components?

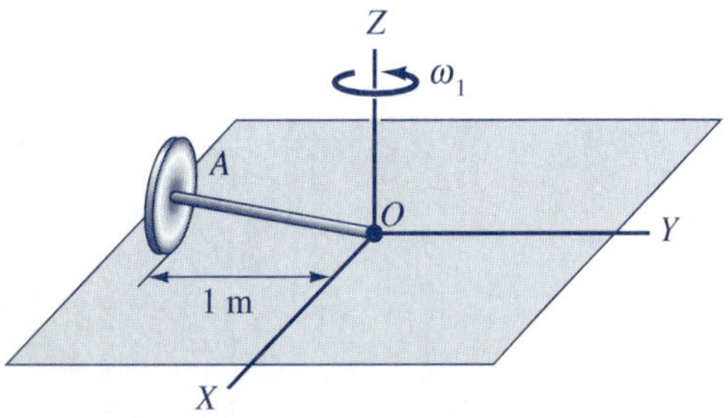

Figure P.18.32.

18.33. A body has the following components of angular velocity:

$$\dot{\phi} = 10 \text{ rad/sec}$$
$$\dot{\theta} = 5 \text{ rad/sec}$$
$$\dot{\psi} = 2 \text{ rad/sec}$$

when the following Euler angles are known to be

$$\psi = 45°, \qquad \theta = 30°$$

What is the magnitude of the total angular velocity?

18.34. If the disc shown were to be undergoing regular precession as shown at the rate of .3 rad/sec, what would have to be the spin velocity $\dot{\phi}$? The disc weighs 90 N. Neglect the mass of the rod.

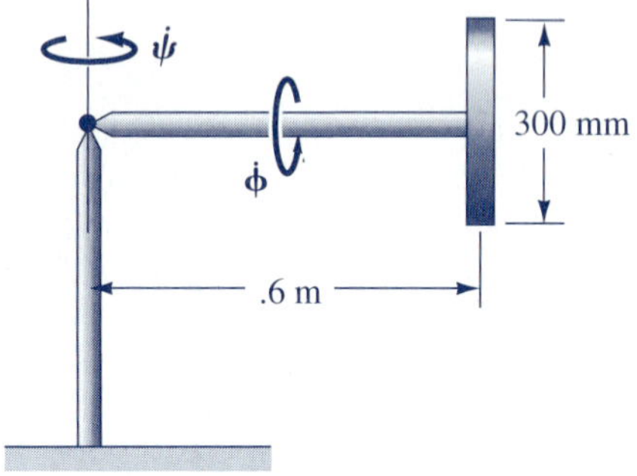

Figure P.18.34.

18.35. In Problem 18.34, explain how you institute such a motion. Would you get the steady precession if for the computed $\dot{\phi}$ you merely released the disc from a horizontal configuration of the disc centerline?

18.36. A 20-lb cylinder having a radius of 1 ft and a length of $\frac{1}{4}$ ft is connected by a 2 ft rod to a fixed point O where there is a ball-joint connector. The cylinder spins about its own centerline at a speed of 50 rad/sec. What external torque about O is required for the cylinder to precess uniformly at a rate of $\frac{1}{2}$ rad/sec about the Z axis at an inclination of 45° to the Z axis? (Compute the torque when the centerline of the cylinder is in the XZ plane.)

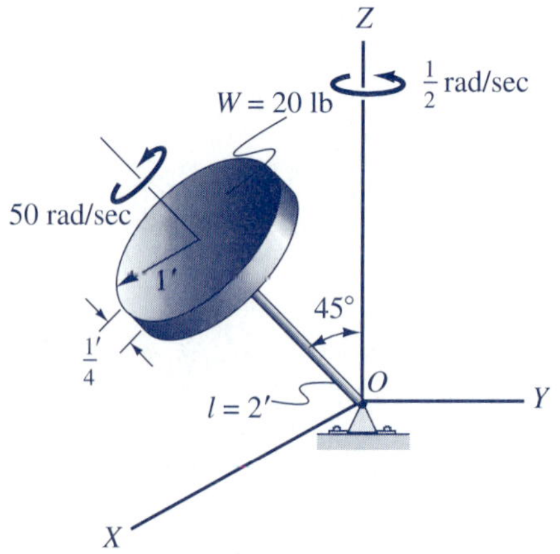

Figure P.18.36.

18.37. The centerline of the rod rotates uniformly in a horizontal plane with a constant torque of 2.29 N-m applied about O. Each cylinder weighs 225 N and has a radius of 300 mm. The discs rotate on a bar AB with a speed ω_1 of 5,000 rpm. Bar AB is held at O by a ball-joint connection. The applied torque is always perpendicular to AB and can only rotate about the vertical axis. What is the precession speed of the system?

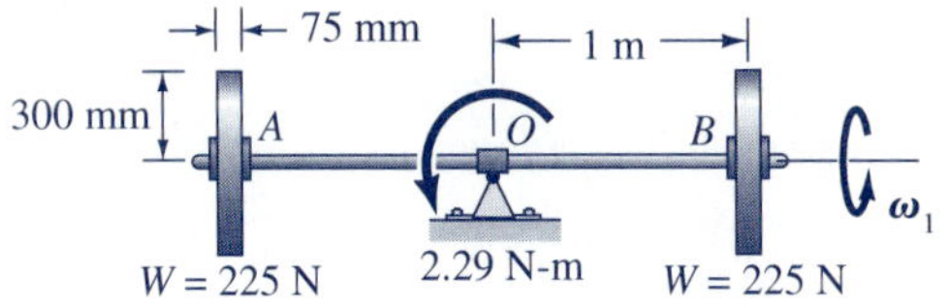

Figure P.18.37.

18.38. (a) In Problem 18.37, consider the disc at B to have an angular speed of 5,000 rpm and the disc at A to have a speed of 2,500 rpm. What is the precession speed for the condition of steady precession?

(b) If the disc at A and the disc at B have angular speeds of 5,000 rpm in opposite directions, what is the initial motion of the system when a torque perpendicular to B is suddenly applied?

18.39. Two discs A and B roll without slipping at their mid-planes. Light shafts cd and ef connect the discs to a centerpost which rotates at an angular speed ω_1 of 2 rad/sec. If each disc weighs 20 lb, what total force downward is developed by the discs on the ground support?

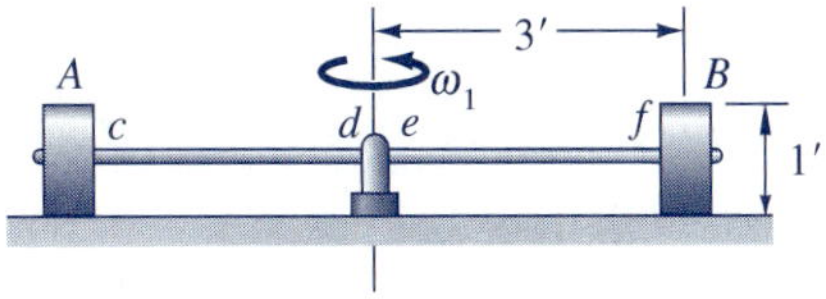

Figure P.18.39.

18.40. A disc is spinning about its centerline with speed $\dot{\phi}$ while the centerline is precessing uniformly at fixed angle θ about the vertical axis. The mass of the disc is M. Consider the evaluation of $\dot{\psi}$, and show that such a state of regular precession is possible if

$$\omega_z^2 > \frac{4I'Mgl}{I^2}$$

Also show that there are, for every θ, two possible precession speeds. In particular, show that as ω_z gets very large, the following precessional speeds are possible:

$$\dot{\psi}_1 = \frac{I\omega_z}{I'\cos\theta}, \qquad \dot{\psi}_2 = \frac{Mgl}{I\omega_z}$$

[*Hint:* Consider Eq. 18.31 for first part of proof. Then use a power expansion of the root when evaluating $\dot{\psi}$.]

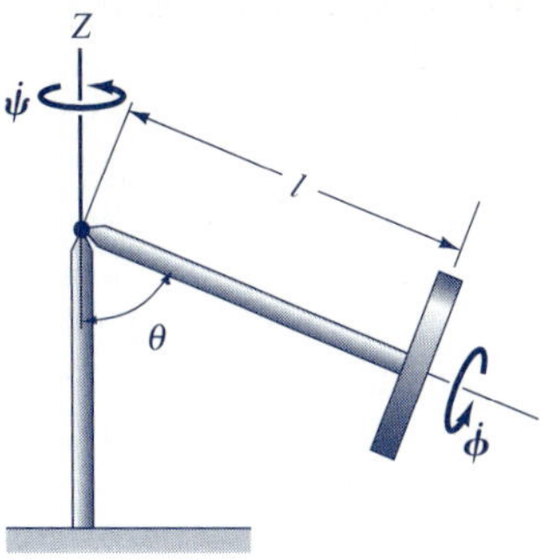

Figure P.18.40.

18.41. A uniform prism has a square cross section. Prove that $I_{\eta\eta}$ for any angle θ equals $I_{xx} = I_{yy}$. Thus, in order to use $I' = I_{xx} = I_{yy}$, as was done in the development in Section 18.6, the body need not be a body of revolution. Show in general that if $I_{xx} = I_{yy}$, and if xyz are principal axes, then $I_{\eta\eta} = I_{xx} = I_{yy}$.

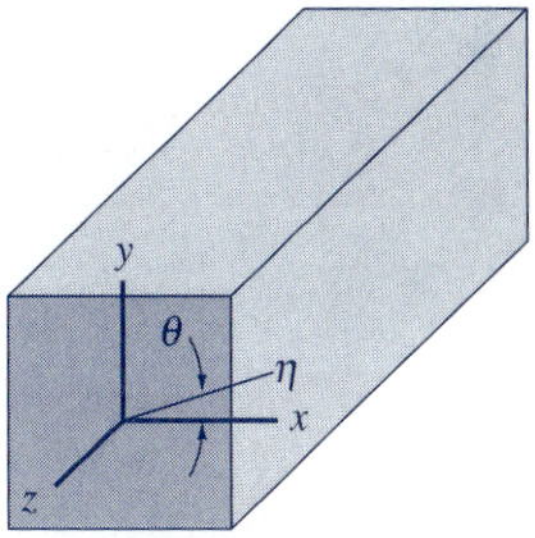

Figure P.18.41.

18.42. A block weighing 50 N and having a square cross section is spinning about its body axis at a rate ω_1 of 100 rad/sec. For an angle $\alpha = 30°$, what is the precession speed $\dot{\psi}$ of the axis of the block? Neglect the weight of rod AB. See Problem 18.41 before proceeding.

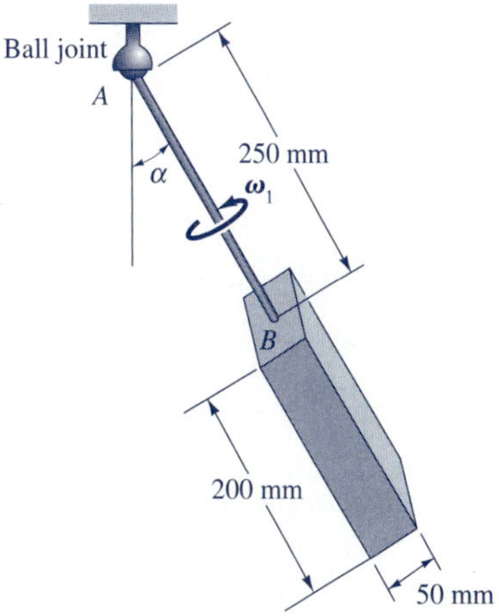

Figure P.18.42.

18.43. In Problem 18.42, at what angle α does a steady rotation of the axis of the block occur about the indicated vertical axis at the rate of 6 rad/sec counterclockwise looking down from above? The angular speed ω_1 is 100 rad/sec.

18.44. A single-degree-of-freedom gyro is mounted on a vehicle moving at constant speed V of 100 ft/sec on a track which is coplanar and is circular, having a mean radius of 200 ft. The disc weighs 1 lb and has a radius of 2 in. It is turning at a speed of 20,000 rpm relative to the gimbal. If the gimbal maintains a rotated position of 15° with the horizontal, what is the equivalent torsional spring constant about axis A–A for the gimbal suspension?

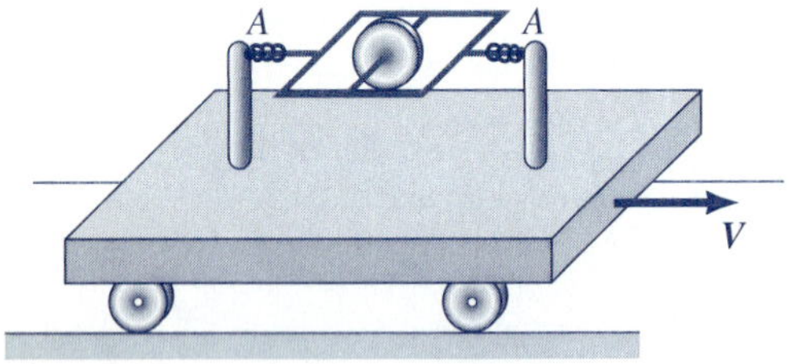

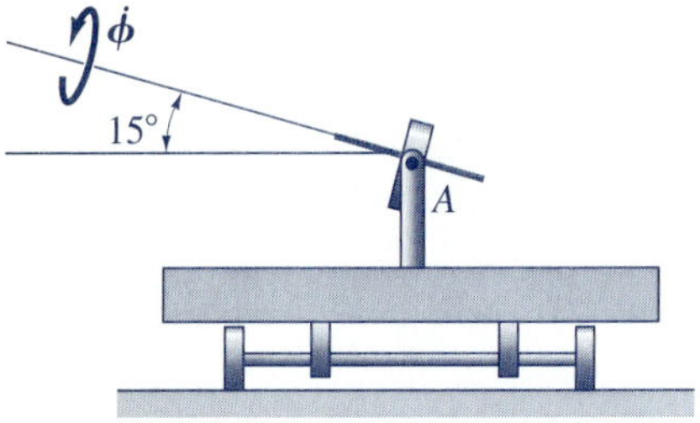

Figure P.18.44.

18.45. In Problem 18.44, where we found that K_t = 1,663 ft-lb/rad, suppose that the speed of the vehicle were adjusted to 50 ft/sec (i.e., half its given speed). What would then be the position of the gimbal for steady-state precession?

18.46. A plate is rotating about shaft CD at a constant speed ω_1 of 2 rad/sec. A single-degree-of-freedom gyro is mounted on the plate. The gyro has mounted on it through a gimbal a disc of weight 3.4 N and radius 50 mm. The disc has a rotational speed ω_2 of 10,000 rpm relative to the gimbal. If the gimbal is to be maintained parallel to the plate, what torque is required? If the bearings are frictionless, explain how this torque is developed. What is the direction of the line of nodes for steady precession?

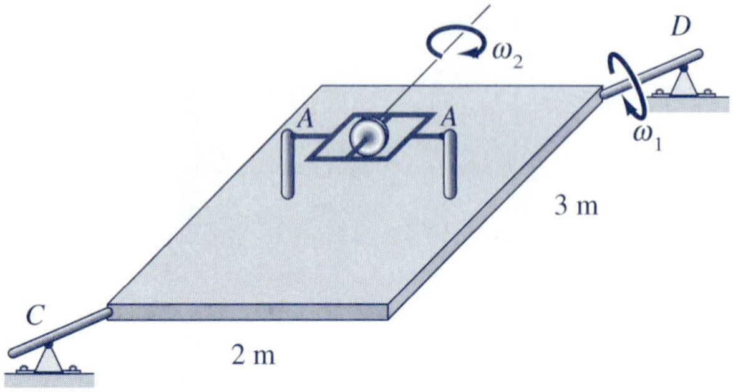

Figure P.18.46.

***18.47.** A solid sphere of diameter 200 mm and weight 50 N is spinning about its body axis at a speed $\dot{\phi}_0$ of 100 rad/sec while its axis is held stationary at an angle θ_0 of 120°. The sphere is released suddenly. What is the precession speed $\dot{\psi}$ when θ has increased by 10°? Use the fact that

$$H_z = \text{const.} = I'\dot{\psi}\sin^2\theta + I\omega_z\cos\theta$$

(This equation can be reached by projecting H_x, H_y, and H_z in the Z direction.)

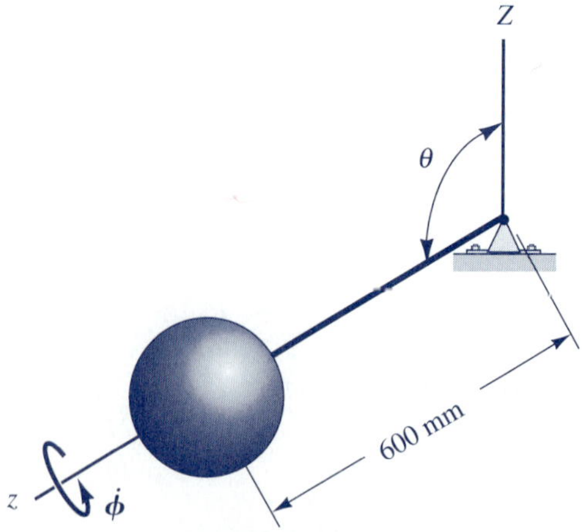

Figure P.18.47.

18.7 Torque-Free Motion

We shall now consider possible *torque-free motion* for a body having $I_{xx} = I_{yy} = I'$ for axes normal to the body axis. An example of a device that can approach such motion is the two-degree-of-freedom gyroscope described in Example 18.4.

Let us now examine the equations of torque-free motion. First, consider the general relation

$$\boldsymbol{M}_C = \dot{\boldsymbol{H}}_C \tag{18.33}$$

Since $\boldsymbol{M}_c$ is zero, $\boldsymbol{H}_c$ must be constant. Thus,

$$\boldsymbol{H}_C = \boldsymbol{H}_0 \tag{18.34}$$

where $\boldsymbol{H}_0$ is the *initial* angular momentum about the mass center. We shall first assume and later justify in this section that all torque-free motions will be *steady precessions* about an axis going through the center of mass and directed *parallel to the vector* $\boldsymbol{H}_0$. Accordingly, we choose Z to pass through the center of mass and to have a direction corresponding to that of $\boldsymbol{H}_0$, as shown in Fig. 18.27. The axis x' normal to axes z and Z forming plane I is then the line of nodes and y' is in plane I. The reference xyz is *fixed* to the body and hence spins about the z axis. Axes xy then rotate in the $x'y'$ plane as shown in the diagram. Using Fig. 18.27, we can then express $\boldsymbol{H}_0$ in terms of its x, y, and z components having unit vectors $\boldsymbol{i}, \boldsymbol{j}$, and $\boldsymbol{k}$ in the following way at all times:

$$\boldsymbol{H}_0 = H_0 \sin\theta \sin\phi \boldsymbol{i} + H_0 \sin\theta \cos\phi \boldsymbol{j} + H_0 \cos\theta \boldsymbol{k} \tag{18.35}$$

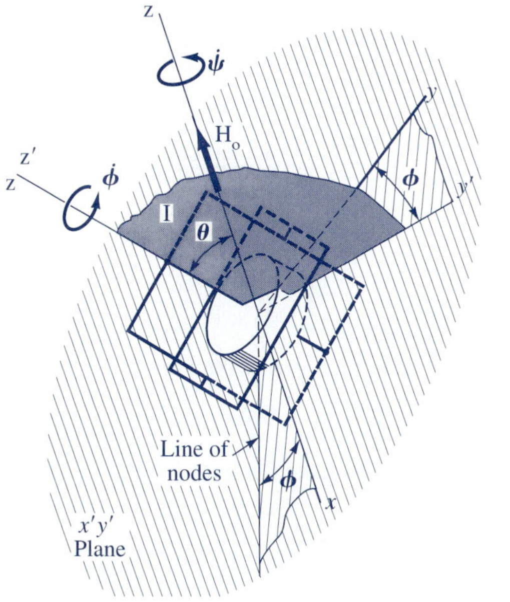

Figure 18.27. Two-degree-of-freedom gyroscope illustrating torque-free motion. Outer gimbal support is not shown.

Since *xyz* are principal axes, we can also state:

$$\boldsymbol{H}_0 = I'\omega_x \boldsymbol{i} + I'\omega_y \boldsymbol{j} + I\omega_z \boldsymbol{k} \tag{18.36}$$

Comparing Eqs. 18.35 and 18.36, we then have

$$\omega_x = \frac{H_0 \sin\theta \sin\phi}{I'} \tag{18.37a}$$

$$\omega_y = \frac{H_0 \sin\theta \cos\phi}{I'} \tag{18.37b}$$

$$\omega_z = \frac{H_0 \cos\theta}{I} \tag{18.37c}$$

By using the preceding formulations for ω_x, ω_y, and ω_z, we can write *Euler's equations* using axes *xyz* fixed to the body in a form that includes the constant H_0;

$$I' \frac{d}{dt}\left(\frac{H_0 \sin\theta \sin\phi}{I'}\right) + \frac{I - I'}{I'I} H_0^2 \sin\theta \cos\theta \cos\phi = 0 \tag{18.38a}$$

$$I' \frac{d}{dt}\left(\frac{H_0 \sin\theta \cos\phi}{I'}\right) + \frac{I' - I}{I'I} H_0^2 \sin\theta \cos\theta \sin\phi = 0 \tag{18.38b}$$

$$I \frac{d}{dt}\left(\frac{H_0 \cos\theta}{I}\right) = 0 \tag{18.38c}$$

From Eq. 18.38c, it is then clear that

$$\left(\frac{H_0 \cos\theta}{I}\right) = \text{constant} \tag{18.39}$$

Thus, since H_0 and I are constant, we can conclude from this equation that *the nutation angle* is a fixed angle θ_0.[8] Now consider Eq. 18.38b, using the fact that $\theta = \theta_0$. Canceling H_0 and carrying out the differentiation, we get

$$-(\sin\theta_0)(\sin\phi)(\dot{\phi}) + \frac{I' - I}{I'I} H_0 \sin\theta_0 \cos\theta_0 \sin\phi = 0$$

Therefore,

$$\dot{\phi} = \frac{I' - I}{I'I} H_0 \cos\theta_0 \tag{18.40}$$

Thus, the *spin speed*, $\dot{\phi}$, is constant.

To get the precession speed $\dot{\psi}$, note from Fig. 18.27 that

$$\omega_z = \dot{\phi} + \dot{\psi} \cos\theta_0$$

Now equate the right side of this equation with the right side of Eq. 18.37c:

$$\dot{\phi} + \dot{\psi} \cos\theta_0 = \frac{H_0 \cos\theta_0}{I} \tag{18.41}$$

[8] We now see that taking Z to be collinear with $\boldsymbol{H}_0$ at the outset is justified.

Substituting for $\dot{\phi}$ from Eq. 18.40 and solving for $\dot{\psi}$, we get

$$\dot{\psi} = \frac{H_0}{I} - H_0 \frac{I' - I}{I'I}$$

Collecting terms, we have

$$\dot{\psi} = \frac{H_0}{I}\left(1 - \frac{I' - I}{I'}\right) = \frac{H_0}{I'} \tag{18.42}$$

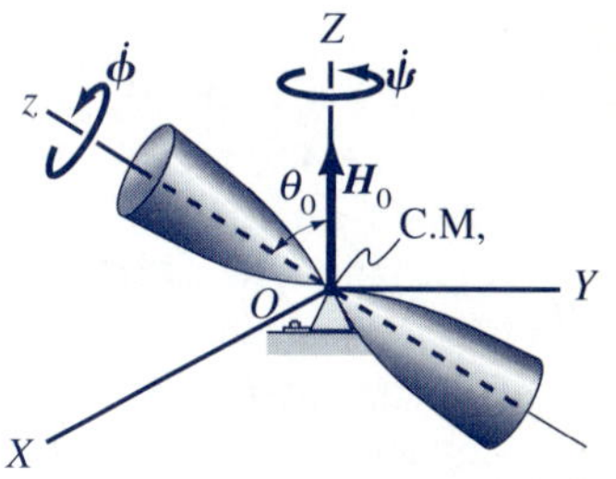

Figure 18.28. Body of revolution is also symmetric about C.M. where it is supported.

The results of the discussion for torque-free motion of the body of revolution can then be given as

$$\theta = \theta_0 \tag{18.43a}$$

$$\dot{\psi} = \frac{H_0}{I'} \tag{18.43b}$$

$$\dot{\phi} = \frac{I' - I}{I'I} H_0 \cos\theta_0 \tag{18.43c}$$

Since $\dot{\theta}$, $\ddot{\theta}$, $\ddot{\psi}$, and $\ddot{\phi}$ are all zero, Eqs. 18.43 depict a case of steady precession, and so the assumption made earlier to this effect is completely consistent with the results emerging from *Euler's equation*. Thus, we can consider the assumption and the ensuing conclusions as correct.

Hence, if a body of revolution is torque-free—as, for example, in the case illustrated in Fig. 18.28, where the center of mass is fixed and where the body has initially any angular momentum vector $\boldsymbol{H}_0$, then at all times the angular momentum $\boldsymbol{H}$ is constant and equals $\boldsymbol{H}_0$. Furthermore, the body will have a regular precession that consists of a constant angular velocity $\dot{\psi}$ of the centerline about a Z axis collinear with $\boldsymbol{H}_0$ at a fixed inclination θ_0 from Z. Finally, there is a constant spin speed $\dot{\phi}$ about the centerline. Thus, two angular velocity vectors $\dot{\boldsymbol{\psi}}$ and $\dot{\boldsymbol{\phi}}$, are present, and the *total* angular velocity $\boldsymbol{\omega}$ is at an inclination of ϵ from the Z axis (see Fig. 18.29) and precesses with angular speed $\dot{\psi}$ about the Z axis. This must be true, since the direction of one component of $\boldsymbol{\omega}$, namely $\dot{\boldsymbol{\phi}}$, precesses in this manner while the other component, $\dot{\boldsymbol{\psi}}$, is fixed in the Z direction. The vector $\boldsymbol{\omega}$ then can be considered to continuously sweep out a cone, as illustrated in Fig. 18.29.

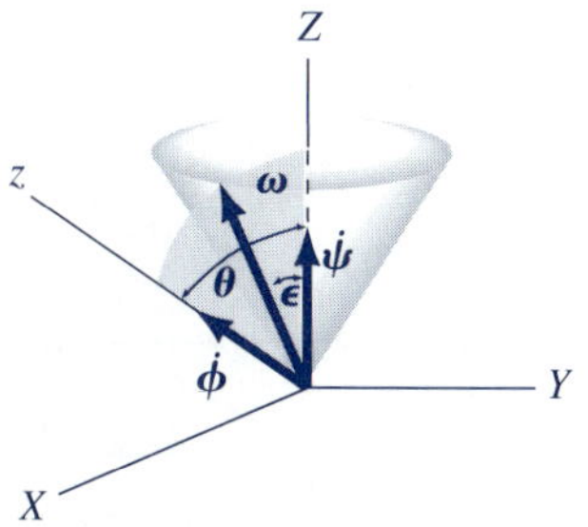

Figure 18.29. Vector $\boldsymbol{\omega}$ sweeps out a conical surface.

We now illustrate the use of the basic formulations for torque-free motion.

Example 18.5

A cylindrical space capsule in orbit is shown in Fig. 18.30. A quarter section of the cylinder can be opened about AB to a test configuration as shown in Fig. 18.31. At the earth's surface, the end plates of the capsule each have a weight of 300 lb and the cylindrical portion weighs 1,800 lb. In the closed configuration, the center of mass of the capsule is at the geometric center.

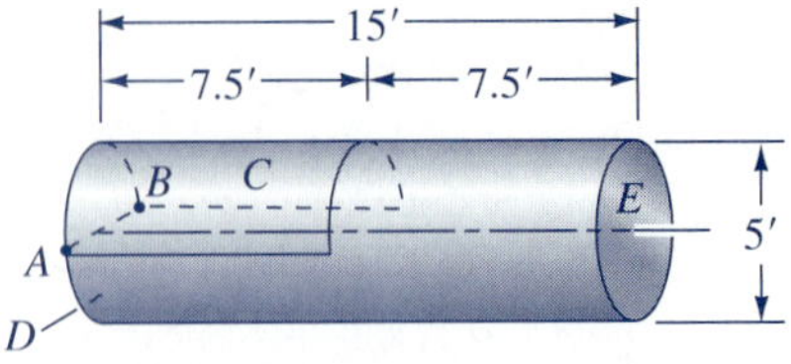

Figure 18.30. Space capsule.

If at time t the capsule is placed in a *test configuration* (Fig. 18.31) with a total instantaneous angular speed ω of 2 rad/sec in the z direction in inertial space,[9] what will be the precession axis for the capsule and the rate of precession of the capsule when door C subsequently is closed by an internal mechanism?

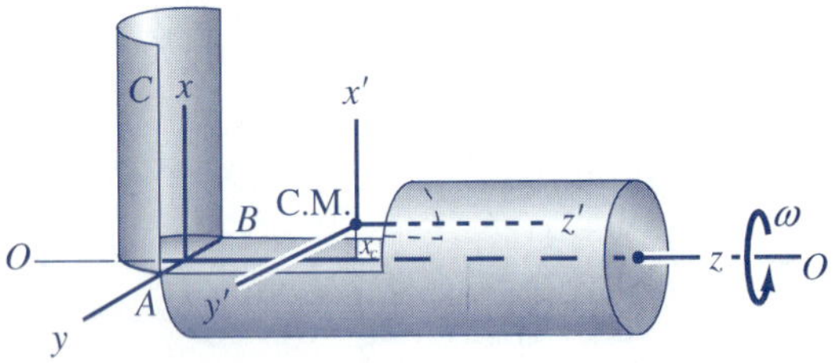

Figure 18.31. Space capsule in initial test configuration.

During a change of configuration, there is a zero net torque on the system so that $\boldsymbol{H}_C$, the angular momentum about the center of mass, is not changed. As a first step we shall compute $\boldsymbol{H}_C$ using data for the instantaneous test configuration. For this calculation we shall need the position of the center of mass.

A reference xyz has been fixed to the system, as shown in Fig. 18.31, and the system has been decomposed into simple portions in Fig. 18.32 for convenience in carrying out ensuing calculations. Employing formulas for positions of centers of mass as given in the front inside covers, we have for moments of mass about the origin of xyz:

$$\frac{2{,}400}{g}\boldsymbol{r}_C = \sum_{i=1}^{6} M_i(\boldsymbol{r}_C)_i = \frac{450}{g}\left(\frac{15}{4}\boldsymbol{i} - \frac{5}{\pi}\boldsymbol{k}\right) + \frac{150}{g}\left[-(.424)\left(\frac{5}{2}\right)(\boldsymbol{k})\right]$$
$$+\frac{150}{g}\left[-(.424)\left(\frac{5}{2}\right)(\boldsymbol{i})\right] + \frac{450}{g}\left(\frac{15}{4}\boldsymbol{k} - \frac{5}{\pi}\boldsymbol{i}\right)$$
$$+\frac{900}{g}\left(\frac{3}{4}\right)(15)\boldsymbol{k} + \frac{300}{g}(15)\boldsymbol{k}$$

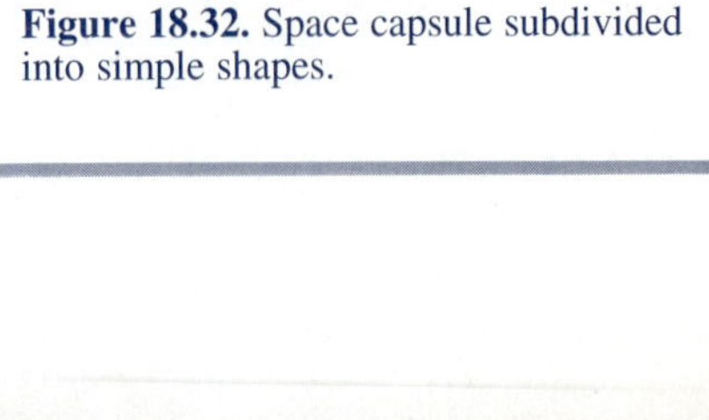

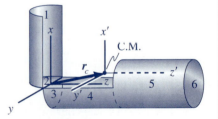

Figure 18.32. Space capsule subdivided into simple shapes.

[9] The initial motion with just rotation about the z axis can be only an *instantaneous* motion at the instant when the device is placed into the shown configuration. At this instant, $\boldsymbol{H}_C$ is at some angle relative to the z axis [as you will soon see in Eq. (d)] and is rotating about z at an angular speed $\boldsymbol{\omega}$. Subsequent motion, being torque-free, requires $\boldsymbol{H}_C$ to be *constant* and thus, in turn, means that the z axis will thereafter have to be rotating about $\boldsymbol{H}_C$.

Example 18.5 (Continued)

Therefore,

$$r_c = 6.44\boldsymbol{k} + .338\boldsymbol{i} \text{ ft} \qquad \text{(a)}$$

To get $\boldsymbol{H}_C$, we next set up a second reference $x'y'z'$ at the center of mass as shown in Fig. 18.31. In accordance with Eq. 18.2, we have for $\boldsymbol{H}_C$, on noting that the only nonzero component of $\boldsymbol{\omega}$ is in the z' direction:

$$\boldsymbol{H}_C = -I_{x'z'}\omega\boldsymbol{i} - I_{y'z'}\omega\boldsymbol{j} + I_{z'z'}\omega\boldsymbol{k} \qquad \text{(b)}$$

To compute $I_{z'z'}$ we proceed as follows, using the decomposed capsule parts of Fig. 18.32 and employing transfer theorems for moments of inertia:

$$(I_{z'z'})_1 = \frac{1}{2}\left(\frac{450}{g}\right)\left(2.5^2 + \frac{7.5^2}{6}\right) + \frac{450}{g}(3.75 - .338)^2 = 272 \text{ slug-ft}^2$$

$$(I_{z'z'})_2 = \frac{1}{4}\left(\frac{150}{g}\right)(2.5^2) + \frac{150}{g}(.338)^2 = 7.81$$

$$(I_{z'z'})_3 = \left\{\frac{1}{2}\left(\frac{150}{g}\right)(2.5)^2 - \frac{150}{g}[(.424)(2.5)]^2\right\} + \frac{150}{g}[.338 + (.424)(2.5)]^2 = 18.43$$

$$(I_{z'z'})_4 = \left[\frac{450}{g}(2.5)^2 - \frac{450}{g}\left(\frac{5}{\pi}\right)^2\right] + \frac{450}{g}\left(.338 + \frac{5}{\pi}\right)^2 = 104.0$$

$$(I_{z'z'})_5 = \frac{900}{g}(2.5)^2 + \frac{900}{g}(.338)^2 = 177.9$$

$$(I_{z'z'})_6 = \frac{1}{2}\left(\frac{300}{g}\right)(2.5)^2 + \frac{300}{g}(.338)^2 = 30.2$$

Accordingly, we have for $I_{z'z'}$:

$$I_{z'z'} = \sum_{i=1}^{6}(I_{zz})_i = 610 \text{ slug-ft}^2 \qquad \text{(c)}$$

We proceed in a similar manner to compute $I_{z'x'}$. We will illustrate this computation for portion 1 of the system and then give the total result. Thus, employing the parallel axis theorem, we have

$$(I_{z'x'})_1 = 0 + \left(\frac{450}{g}\right)\left(-6.44 - \frac{5}{\pi}\right)\left(\frac{7.5}{2} - .338\right) = -383 \text{ slug-ft}^2$$

It is important to remember that the transfer distances (with proper signs) used for computing $(I_{z'x'})_1$ using the parallel-axis theorem are measured from $x'y'z'$, *about which you are making the calculation, to the center of mass of body 1.* For the entire system we have, by similar calculations:

$$I_{z'x'} = -329 \text{ slug-ft}^2$$

Example 18.5 (Continued)

Because of symmetry, furthermore:

$$I_{z'y'} = 0$$

From Eq. (b) we then have for $\boldsymbol{H}_C$:

$$\begin{aligned}\boldsymbol{H}_C &= 329\omega\boldsymbol{i} + 610\omega\boldsymbol{k}\\ &= 659\boldsymbol{i} + 1{,}220\boldsymbol{k} \qquad \text{(d)}\end{aligned}$$

Since the precession axis is collinear with $\boldsymbol{H}_C$, we have thus established this axis (Z axis), as is shown in Fig. 18.33. A reference $\xi\eta\zeta$ has been set up at the center of mass for the closed configuration. The body axis ζ remains at a fixed angle θ with the Z axis and precesses about it with an angular speed $\dot{\psi}$ given in accordance with Eq. 18.43b as

$$\begin{aligned}\dot{\psi} &= \frac{H_C}{I_{\xi\xi}}\\ &= \frac{\sqrt{658^2 + 1{,}220^2}}{\frac{1}{2}\left(\frac{1{,}800}{g}\right)\left(2.5^2 + \frac{15^2}{6}\right) + 2\left(\frac{1}{4}\right)\left(\frac{300}{g}\right)\left(2.5^2\right) + 2\left(\frac{300}{g}\right)(7.5)^2} \qquad \text{(e)}\\ &= \frac{1{,}386}{2{,}300} = \boxed{.603 \text{ rad/sec}}\end{aligned}$$

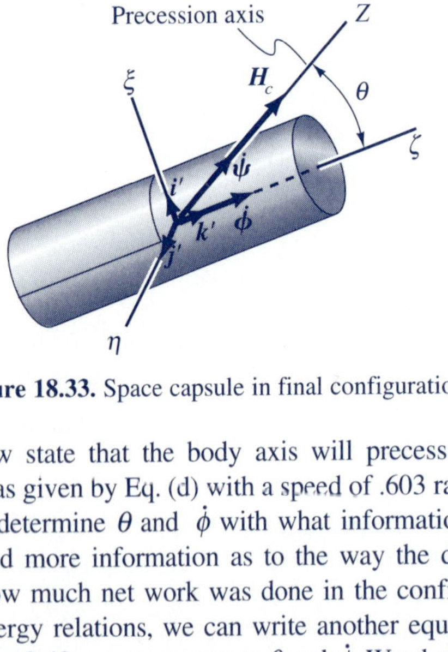

Figure 18.33. Space capsule in final configuration.

We can now state that the body axis will precess around an axis collinear with $\boldsymbol{H}_C$ as given by Eq. (d) with a speed of .603 rad/sec. However, we are unable to determine θ and $\dot{\phi}$ with what information we now have available. We need more information as to the way the door was closed. Thus, knowing how much net work was done in the configuration change from the work energy relations, we can write another equation. And, with Eqs. 18.37 and Eq. 18.40, we can compute θ and $\dot{\phi}$. We shall present several problems with that information available in the homework exercises.

Let us now examine Eqs. 18.43 for the special case where $I = I'$. Here the spin velocity $\dot{\phi}$ must be zero, leaving only *one* angular motion, $\dot{\boldsymbol{\psi}}$, the precession velocity. This rotation is about the Z axis so the direction of angular velocity $\boldsymbol{\omega}$ of the body corresponds to $\boldsymbol{H}_0$. Since this could be a body of revolution, the moment-of-inertia condition for this case ($I = I'$) means that the moments of inertia for principal axes x, y, and z are mutually equal, and we can verify from Eq. 9.13 that all axes inclined to the xyz reference have the same moment of inertia I (and all therefore are principal axes at the point). Thus, the body, if homogeneous, could be a sphere, a cube, any regular polyhedron, or any body that possesses point symmetry. *No matter how we launch this body, the angular momentum* $\boldsymbol{H}$ *will be equal to* $I\boldsymbol{\omega}$ *and will thus always coincide with the direction of angular velocity* $\boldsymbol{\omega}$. This situation can also be shown analytically as follows:

$$\boldsymbol{H} = H_x\boldsymbol{i} + H_y\boldsymbol{j} + H_z\boldsymbol{k} \tag{18.44}$$

For principal axes, we have

$$\boldsymbol{H} = \omega_x I_{xx}\boldsymbol{i} + \omega_y I_{yy}\boldsymbol{j} + \omega_z I_{zz}\boldsymbol{k} \tag{18.45}$$

If $I_{xx} = I_{yy} = I_{zz} = I$, we have for the foregoing

$$\boldsymbol{H} = I(\omega_x\boldsymbol{i} + \omega_y\boldsymbol{j} + \omega_z\boldsymbol{k}) = I\boldsymbol{\omega} \tag{18.46}$$

indicating that $\boldsymbol{H}$ and $\boldsymbol{\omega}$ must be collinear. The situation just described represents the case of a thrown baseball or basketball.

There are *two* situations for the case $I_{xx} = I_{yy}$ in which $\boldsymbol{H}$ and $\boldsymbol{\omega}$ are collinear. Examining Eq. 18.43, we thus see that if θ_0 is 90°, then $\dot{\phi} = \dot{\theta} = 0$, leaving only precession $\dot{\psi}$ along the Z axis (see Fig. 18.27). The Z axis for the analysis corresponds to the direction of $\boldsymbol{H}$. We thus see that since $\boldsymbol{\omega} = \dot{\boldsymbol{\psi}}$ then $\boldsymbol{\omega}$ is collinear with $\boldsymbol{H}$. This case corresponds to a proper "drop kick" or "place kick" of a football [Fig. 18.34(a)] wherein the body axis z is at right angles to the Z axis.

The other case consists of $\theta_0 = 0$. This means that $\dot{\boldsymbol{\phi}}$ and $\dot{\boldsymbol{\psi}}$ have the same direction—that is, along the Z direction (see Fig. 18.27) which then means that $\boldsymbol{\omega}$ and $\boldsymbol{H}$ again are collinear. This case corresponds to a good football pass [Fig. 18.34(b)]. *For all other motions of bodies where* $I_{xx} = I_{yy}$, *the angular velocity vector* $\boldsymbol{\omega}$ *will not have the direction of angular momentum* $\boldsymbol{H}_0$.

Upon further consideration, we can make a simple model of torque-free motion. Start with the fixed cone described earlier (see Fig. 18.29) about the Z axis, where the cone surface is that swept out by the total angular velocity vector $\boldsymbol{\omega}$ of the torque-free body. Now consider a second cone about the spin axis z of the torque-free body (see Fig. 18.35) in direct contact with the initial stationary cone. Rotate the second cone about its axis with a speed and sense corresponding to $\dot{\phi}$ of the torque-free body and impose a no-slipping

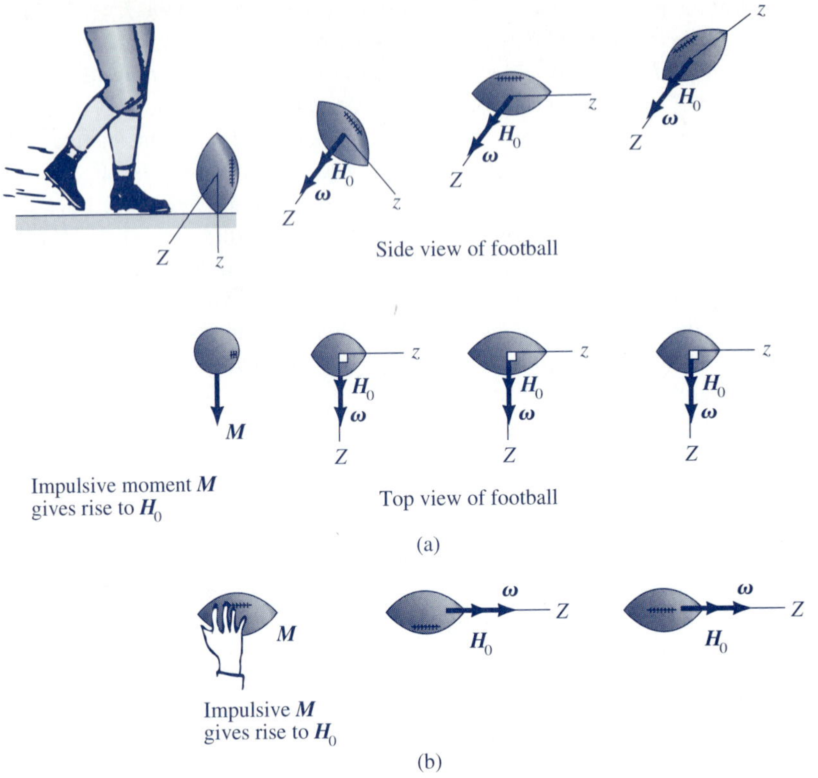

Figure 18.34. Two cases where $\boldsymbol{H}$ and $\boldsymbol{\omega}$ are collinear.

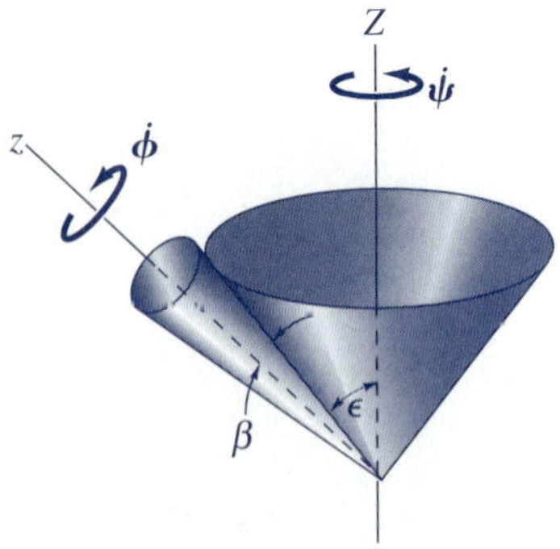

Figure 18.35. Rolling-cone model.

condition between the cones. Clearly, the second cone will precess about the Z axis at some speed $\dot{\psi}'$. Also, the total angular velocity $\boldsymbol{\omega}'$ of the moving cone will lie along the line of contact between cones and is thus collinear with $\boldsymbol{\omega}$. We shall now show that the speed $\dot{\boldsymbol{\psi}}'$ of the cone model equals $\dot{\boldsymbol{\psi}}$ of the torque-free body and, as a consequence, that $\boldsymbol{\omega}'$ for the moving cone equals $\boldsymbol{\omega}$ of the torque-free body. We know now that:

1. $\dot{\boldsymbol{\phi}}$ is the same for both the device and the physical case.
2. The direction of resultant angular velocity is the same for both cases.
3. The direction of the precession velocity must be the same for both cases (i.e., the Z direction).

This situation is shown in Fig. 18.36. Note that $\dot{\boldsymbol{\phi}}$ is the same in both the physical case and the mechanical model and that the directions of $\boldsymbol{\omega}$ and $\boldsymbol{\omega}'$as well as $\dot{\boldsymbol{\psi}}$ and $\dot{\boldsymbol{\psi}}'$ are, respectively, the same for both diagrams. Accordingly, when we consider the construction of the parallelogram of vectors, we see that the vectors $\boldsymbol{\omega}$ and $\boldsymbol{\omega}'$ as well as $\dot{\boldsymbol{\psi}}$ and $\dot{\boldsymbol{\psi}}'$ must necessarily be equal for both the physical case and the model, respectively.

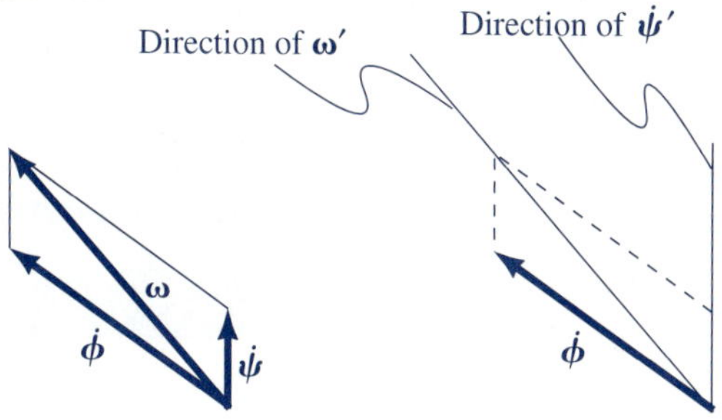

Figure 18.36. Angular vector diagrams.

We shall now investigate more carefully the relation between the sense of rotation for corresponding angular velocities between the model and the physical case for certain classes of geometries of the physical body.

1. $I' > I$. From Eq. 18.43c, we see that when θ_0 is less than $\pi/2$ rad, $\dot{\phi}$ is positive for this case.[10] Thus, the spin must be counterclockwise as we look along the z axis toward the origin. From Eq. 18.43b, we see that $\dot{\psi}$ is positive and thus counterclockwise as we look toward the origin along Z. Clearly, from these stipulations, the rolling-cone model shown in Fig. 18.35 has the proper motion for this case. The motion is termed *regular precession*.
2. $I' < I$. Here, the spin $\dot{\phi}$ will be negative for a nutation angle less than 90° as stipulated by Eq. 18.43c. However, the precession $\dot{\psi}$ must still be positive in accordance with Eq. 18.43b. The rolling-cone model thus far presented clearly cannot give these proper senses, but if the moving cone is *inside* the stationary cone (Fig. 18.37), we have motion that is consistent with the relations in Eq. 18.43. Such motion is called *retrograde precession*.

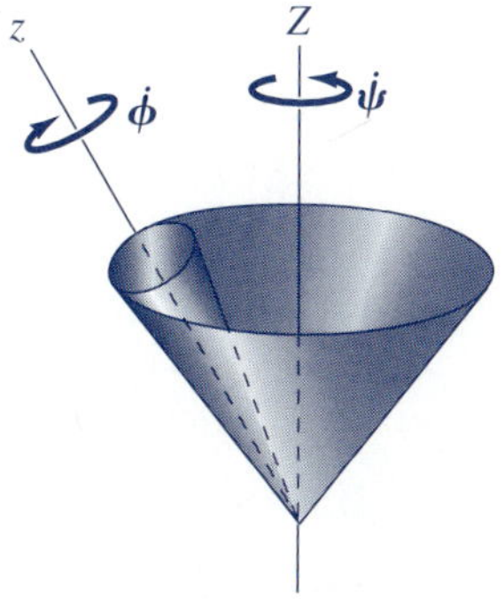

Figure 18.37. Retrograde precession.

[10]Recall from Eq. 18.35 that H_0 is just a magnitude. Also, note that this case corresponds to what has been shown in Fig. 18.29—namely, the case we have just discussed.

Example 18.6

The space capsule of Example 18.5 is shown again in Fig. 18.38 rotating about its axis of symmetry z in inertial space with an angular speed ω_z of 2 rad/sec. As a result of an impact with a meteorite, the capsule is given an impulse $\boldsymbol{I}$ of 20 lb-sec at position A as shown in the diagram. Ascertain the postimpact motion.

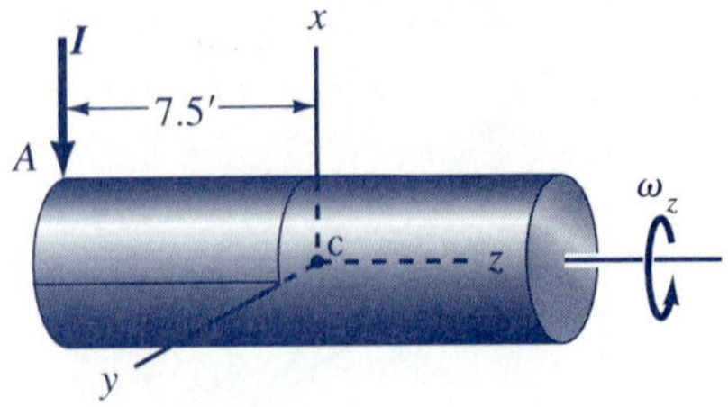

Figure 18.38. Space capsule with impulse.

The impact will give the cylinder an angular impulse:

$$\boldsymbol{I}_{\text{ang}} = (20)(7.5)\boldsymbol{j} = 150\boldsymbol{j} \text{ slug-ft}^2/\text{sec} \tag{a}$$

From the **angular impulse-momentum** equation we can say for the impact:

$$\boldsymbol{I}_{\text{ang}} = \boldsymbol{H}_2 - \boldsymbol{H}_1$$

Therefore,

$$150\boldsymbol{j} = \boldsymbol{H}_2 - I_{zz}\omega_z\boldsymbol{k}$$

The postimpact angular momentum is then

$$\begin{aligned} \boldsymbol{H}_2 &= 150\boldsymbol{j} + I_{zz}\omega_z\boldsymbol{k} \\ &= 150\boldsymbol{j} + \left\{2\left[\frac{1}{2}\left(\frac{300}{g}\right)(2.5)^2\right] + \frac{1{,}800}{g}(2.5)^2\right\}2\boldsymbol{k} \qquad \text{(b)} \\ &= 150\boldsymbol{j} + 815\boldsymbol{k} \text{ slug-ft}^2/\text{sec} \end{aligned}$$

Since the ensuing motion is *torque-free*, we have thus established the direction of the precession axis (Z). This axis has been shown in Fig. 18.39 coinciding with $\boldsymbol{H}_2$ in the yz plane. Furthermore, we can give $\boldsymbol{H}_2$ postimpact as follows remembering that xyz are principal axes:[11]

$$\boldsymbol{H}_2 = 150\boldsymbol{j} + 815\boldsymbol{k} = \omega_x I_{xx}\boldsymbol{i} + \omega_y I_{yy}\boldsymbol{j} + \omega_z I_{zz}\boldsymbol{k} \tag{c}$$

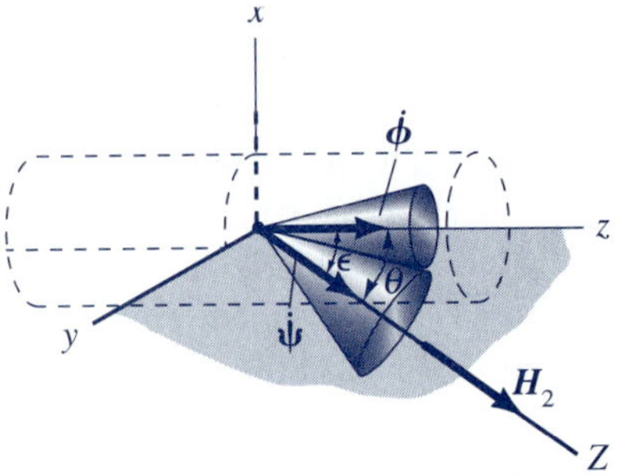

Figure 18.39. Cone model; Z is in yz plane.

Hence, from Eq. (c) we have at postimpact:

$$\begin{aligned} \omega_x &= 0 \\ \omega_y &= \frac{150}{I_{yy}} = \frac{150}{2{,}300} = .0652 \text{ rad/sec} \\ \omega_z &= \frac{815}{I_{zz}} = \frac{815}{407.5} = 2 \text{ rad/sec} \end{aligned}$$

where for I_{yy} we used the value of $I_{\xi\xi}$ as computed in Eq. (e) of Example 18.5. Hence,

$$\boldsymbol{\omega} = .0652\boldsymbol{j} + 2\boldsymbol{k} \text{ rad/sec} \tag{d}$$

[11]Remember that the *position* of a body is considered *not* to change during the action of an impulsive force whereas its linear and angular *momenta do* change. Therefore, the xyz axes postimpact have not moved from the position corresponding to preimpact.

Example 18.6 (Continued)

We can now make good use of the cone model representing the motion. Accordingly, in Fig. 18.39 corresponding to postimpact we have shown two cones, one about the body axis z (this is the moving cone) and one about the Z axis (this is the stationary cone). The line of contact between the cones coincides with the total angular velocity vector $\boldsymbol{\omega}$. The capsule must subsequently have the same motion as the moving cone as it rolls with an angular speed $\dot{\phi} = 2$ rad/sec about its own axis without slipping on the stationary cone having Z as an axis. We can easily compute the angles θ and ϵ using Eqs. (b) and (d). Thus:

$$\tan\theta = \frac{H_y}{H_z} = \frac{150}{815} = 0.1840$$

Therefore,

$$\theta = 10.43°$$

$$\epsilon = \theta - \tan^{-1}\frac{\omega_y}{\omega_z} = 10.43° - \tan^{-1}\frac{0.0652}{2}$$

Therefore,

$$\epsilon = 8.56°$$

In Fig. 18.40 we have shown ω, $\dot{\phi}$, and $\dot{\psi}$ in the yz plane corresponding to postimpact. Knowing $\dot{\phi}$, ω, ϵ, and θ, we can easily compute $\dot{\psi}$. Thus, using the law of sines, we get

$$\frac{\dot{\psi}}{\sin(\theta - \epsilon)} = \frac{\omega}{\sin(\pi - \theta)}$$

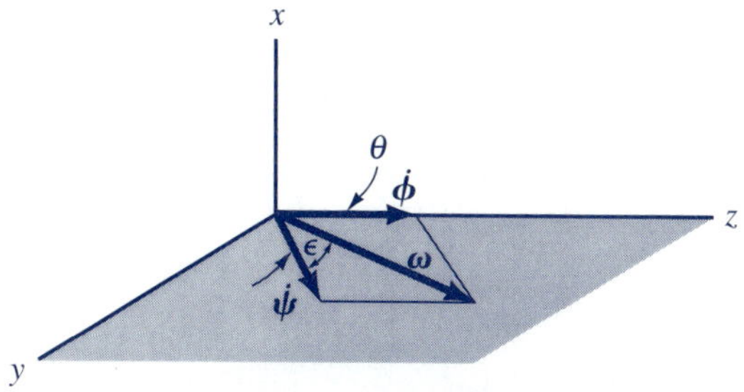

Figure 18.40. Angular-velocity diagram.

Therefore,

$$\dot{\psi} = \frac{\sin(\theta - \epsilon)\omega}{\sin\theta} = \frac{(.0326)(2^2 + .0652^2)^{1/2}}{.1810} = \boxed{.360 \text{ rad/sec}}$$

Thus, we can say that the body continues to spin at 2 rad/sec about its axis, but now the axis precesses about the indicated Z direction at the rate of .360 rad/sec.

PROBLEMS

18.48. A dynamical model of a device in orbit consists of 2,000-lbm cylindrical shell *A* of uniform thickness and a disc *B* rotating relative to the shell at a speed ω_2 of 5,000 rad/min. The disc *B* is 1 ft in diameter and has a mass of 100 lbm. The shell is rotating at a speed ω_1 of 10 rad/min about axis *D–D* in inertial space. If the shaft *FF* about which *B* rotates is made to line up with *D–D* by an internal mechanism, what is the final angular momentum vector for the system? Neglect the mass of all bodies except the disc *B* and the shell.

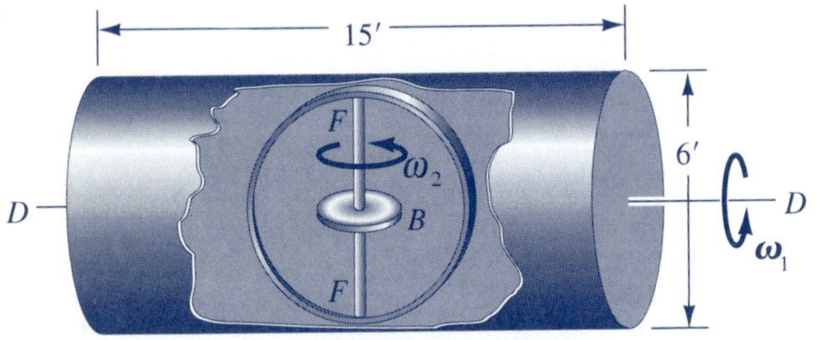

Figure P.18.48.

18.49. A solar energy power unit is in orbit having been given an angular speed ω_1 equal to .2 rad/sec about the *z* axis at time *t*. Vane *B* is identical to vane *A* but is rotated 90° from vane *A*. By an internal mechanism, vane *B* is rotated about its axis to be parallel to vane *A*. What is the new angular speed of the system after this adjustment has taken place? What is the final direction of $\boldsymbol{\omega}$? The vanes on earth each weigh 200 lb and can be considered as uniform blocks. The radii of gyration for the configuration corresponding to vane *A* are as follows at the mass center C.M.:

$$k_x = .5 \text{ ft}$$
$$k_y = 5 \text{ ft}$$
$$k_z = 3.5 \text{ ft}$$

The unit *D* can be considered as equivalent to a uniform sphere of weight on earth of 300 lb and radius 1 ft. (*Advice*: This is a simple problem despite seeming complexity.)

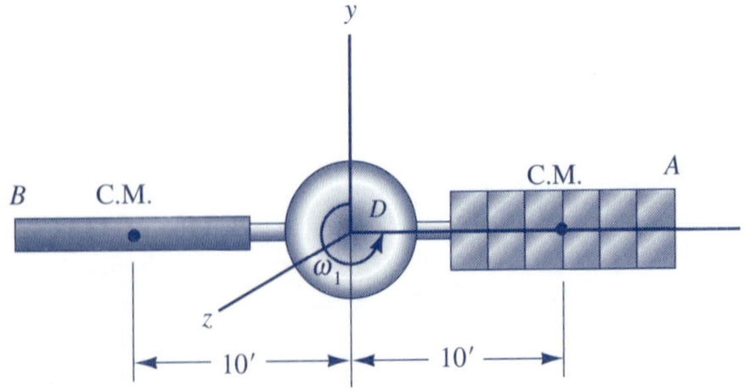

Figure P.18.49.

18.50. A projectile is shot out of a weapon in such a manner that it has an angular velocity $\boldsymbol{\omega}$ at a known angle α from the centerline as it leaves the weapon. Using the cone model, draw a picture depicting the ensuing motion. Denote θ on this diagram, and indicate the direction of $\boldsymbol{H}$. Assume that the spin $\dot{\phi}$ about the axis of symmetry is known, as are the moments of inertia at the C.M. Set up formulations leading to the valuation of he rate of precession of *z* about $\boldsymbol{H}$ and the angle θ between *z* and $\boldsymbol{H}$. [*Hint:* Use trigonometry as well as two of Eqs. 18.43.]

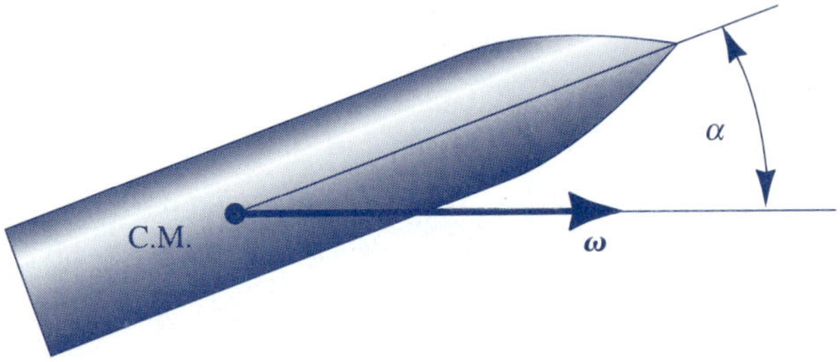

Figure P.18.50.

18.51. A space capsule is rotating about its axis of symmetry in inertial space with an angular speed ω_1 of 2 rad/sec. As a result of an impact with a meteorite at point *A*, an impulse $\boldsymbol{I}$ of 40 lb-sec is developed. Find the axis of precession and the precession velocity for postimpact motion. What are the spin velocity and nutation angle? The mass of the capsule is 3,000 lbm. The radius of gyration for the axis of symmetry is 2 ft, whereas the radius of gyration for transverse axes at the center of mass is 2.5 ft.

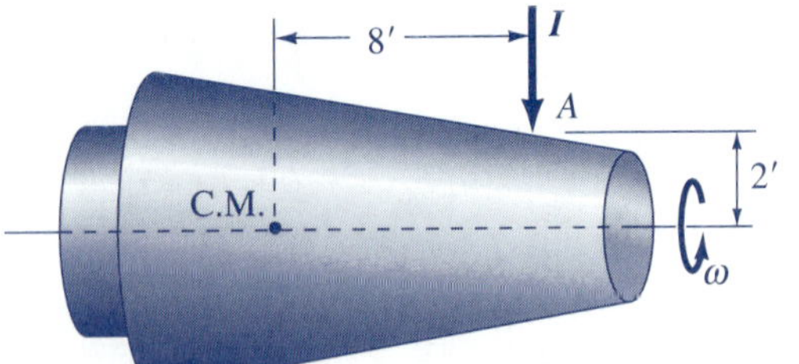

Figure P.18.51.

18.52. Work Problem 18.51 for the case where $\boldsymbol{I}$ is inclined to the right an angle of 45°.

18.53. A rocket casing is in orbit. The casing has a spin of 5 rad/sec about its axis of symmetry. The axis of symmetry is oriented 30° from the precession axis as shown in the diagram. What is the precession speed and the angular momentum of the casing? The casing has a mass of 909 kg, a radius of gyration of .60 m about the axis of symmetry, and a radius of gyration about transverse axes at its center of mass of 1 m.

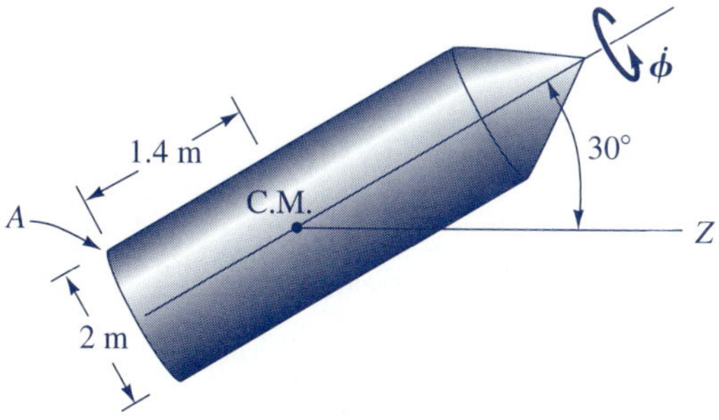

Figure P.18.53.

18.54. In Problem 18.53 assume that an impulse in the vertical direction is developed at point A as a result of an impact with a meteorite. If the impulse from the impact is 133 N-sec, what are the new precession axis and the rate of precession after impact? H_0 from Problem 18.53 is 2,952 kg-m²/sec.

18.55. An object representing dynamically a space device is made of three homogeneous blocks *A*, *B*, and *C* each of specific weight on earth of 6,075 N/m³. Blocks *A* and *C* are identical and are hinged along *aa* and *bb*. At the configuration shown, the system is in orbit and is made to rotate instantaneously about an axis parallel to *RR* at a speed ω_1 of 3 rad/sec. The block *C* is then closed by an internal mechanism. What are the subsequent precession axis and rate of precession?

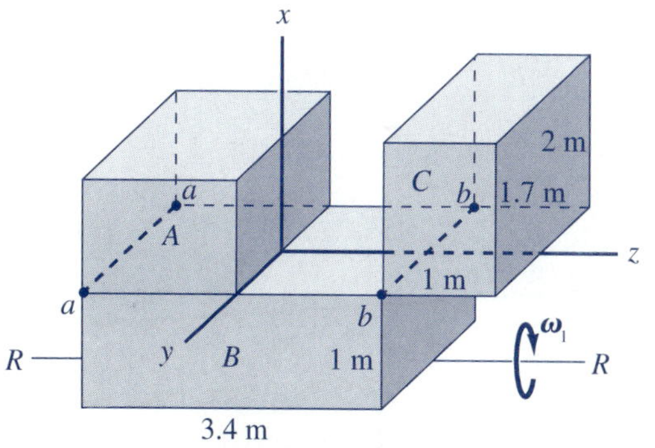

Figure P.18.55.

18.56. A space vehicle has zero rotation relative to inertial space. A jet at *A* is turned on to give a thrust of 50N for .8 sec. Identify the body axis and the subsequent line of nodes. Then, give the nutation angle, the spin speed $\dot{\phi}$, and the precession speed $\dot{\psi}$. The vehicle weighs 10 kN and has a radius of gyration $k_z = 1$ m and, transverse to the *z* axis at the center of mass, $k' = .8$ m. Consider the thrust to be impulsive.

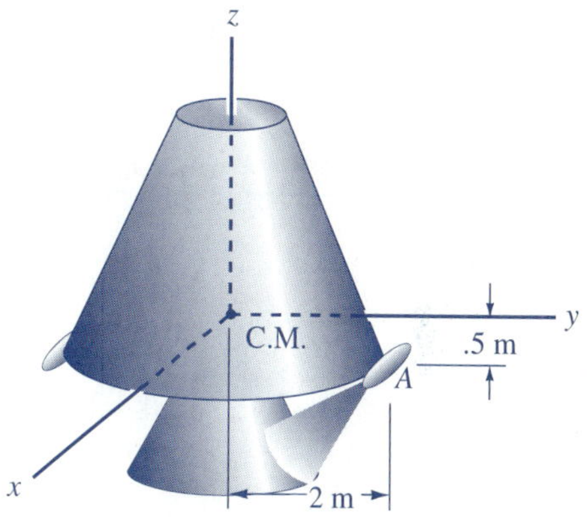

Figure P.18.56.

18.57. An intermediate-stage rocket engine is separated from the first stage by activating exploding bolts. The angular velocity of the spent engine is given as

$$\boldsymbol{\omega} = 2\boldsymbol{i} + 3\boldsymbol{j} + .2\boldsymbol{k} \text{ rad/sec}$$

What is the spin speed $\dot{\phi}$, the precession speed $\dot{\psi}$, and the nutation speed $\dot{\theta}$? Give direction of *Z* axis. Identify the line of nodes. Note that $I_{zz} = 1{,}500$ kg-m² and $I_{xx} = I_{yy} = 2{,}000$ kg-m².

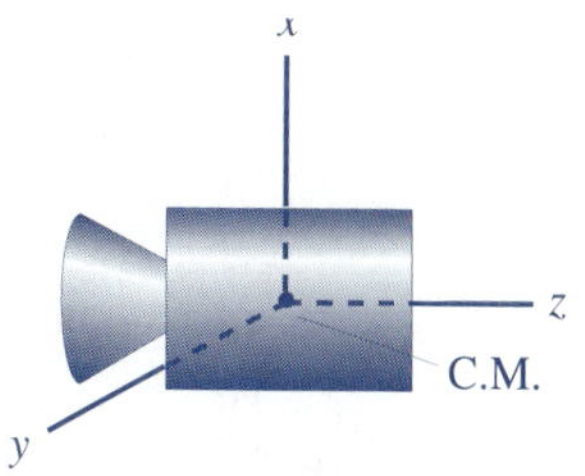

Figure P.18.57.

18.58. In Problem 18.55, if 15 N-m of mechanical energy is added to the bodies from a battery in the closure process, determine the nutation angle θ and spin speed $\dot{\phi}$. The following results are available from Problem 18.55:

$$\left.\begin{aligned} I &= 5{,}615 \text{ kg-m}^2 \\ I' &= 10{,}921 \text{ kg-m}^2 \end{aligned}\right\} \text{closed configuration}$$
$$H_0 = 22{,}270 \text{ kg-m}^2\text{/sec}$$
$$I_{zz} = 6{,}877 \text{ kg-m}^2 \} \text{ open configuration}$$

[*Hint:* Make use of work-energy equation and Eq. 18.37.]

18.59. In Example 18.5, if 20 ft-lb of work is done on the system from an internal power source when going from a test configuration to a closed configuration, determine the nutation angle θ and the spin speed $\dot{\phi}$ for closed configuration. [*Hint:* Make use of work-energy equation and Eq. 18.37.]

18.8 Closure

This chapter brings to a close our study of the motion of rigid bodies. In the final chapter of this text we shall, for the most part, go back to particle mechanics to consider the dynamics of particles constrained to move about a fixed point in a small domain. This is the study of small vibrations (alluded to in Chapter 12) which we have held in abeyance so as to take full advantage of your course work in differential equations.

PROBLEMS

18.60. A plane just after takeoff is flying at a speed V of 200 km/hr and is in the process of retracting its wheels. The back wheels (under wings) are being rotated at a speed ω_1 of 3 rad/sec and at the instant of interest have rotated 30° as shown in the diagram. The plane is rising by following a circular trajectory of radius 1,000 m. If at the instant shown, $\dot{V}$ is 50 km/hr/sec, what is the total moment coming onto the bearings of the wheel from the motion of the wheel? The diameter of the wheel is 600 mm and its weight is 900 N. The radius of gyration along its axis is 250 mm and transverse to its axis is 180 mm. Neglect wind and bearing friction.

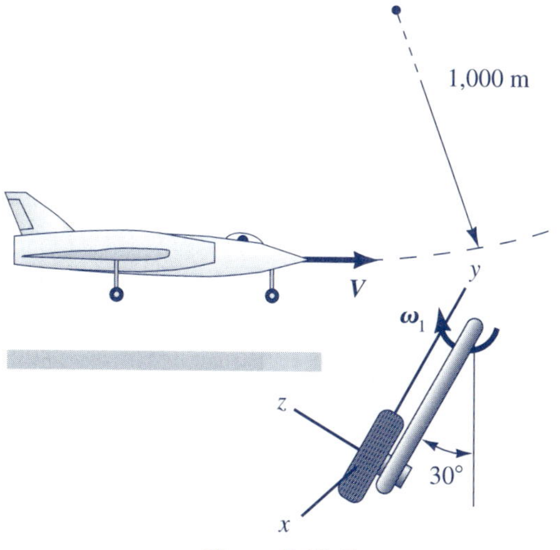

Figure P.18.60.

18.61. A disc A weighing 10 N and of diameter 100 mm rotates with constant speed ω_1 = 15 rad/sec relative to G. (A motor on G, not shown, ensures this constant speed.) The shaft of motor B on C rotates with constant speed ω_2 = 8 rad/sec relative to C and causes platform G to rotate relative to C. Finally, platform C rotates with angular speed ω_3 = 3 rad/sec relative to the ground. What are the supporting forces on bearings H and K of the disc A on platform G? Bearing K alone supports disc A in the axial direction (i.e, it acts as a thrust bearing in addition to being a regular bearing).

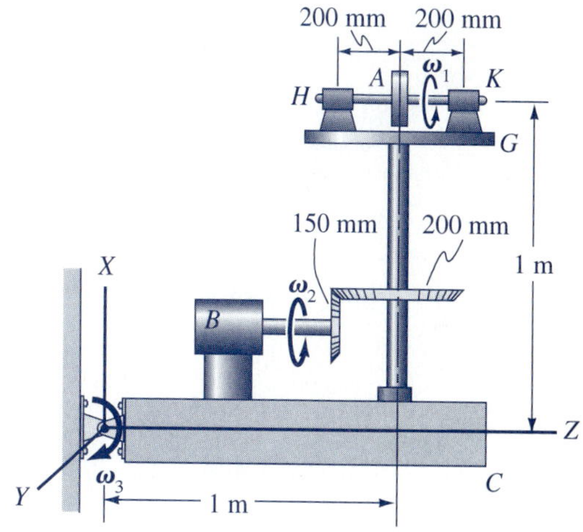

Figure P.18.61.

18.62. Discs A and B are rolling without slipping at their centerlines against an upper surface D. Each disc weighs 40 lb, and each spins about a shaft which connects to a centerpost E rotating at an angular speed ω_1. If a total of 20 lb is developed upward on D, what is ω_1?

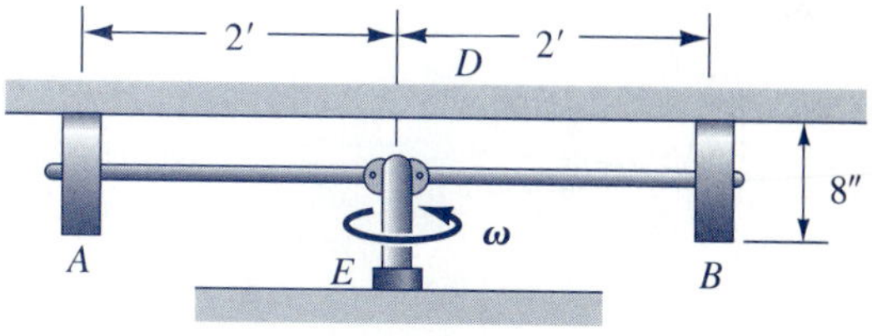

Figure P.18.62.

18.63. A right circular cone weighing 20 N is spinning like a top about a fixed point O at a speed $\dot{\phi}$ of 15,000 rad/sec. What are two possible precession speeds for $\theta = 30°$?

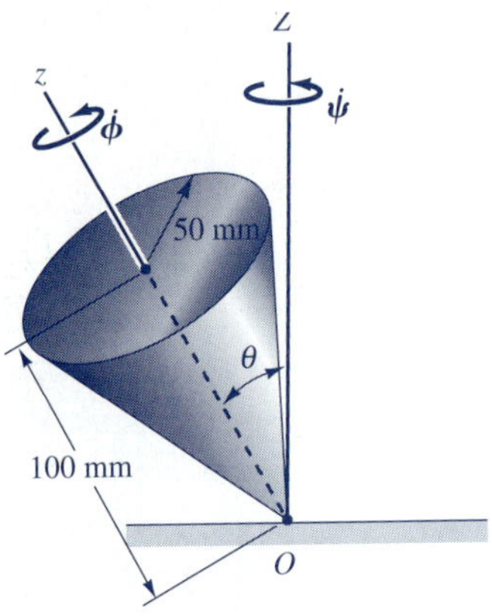

Figure P.18.63.

18.64. A submerged submarine is traveling at 20 knots in a circular path. A single-degree-of-freedom gyroscope (rate gyro) turns 5° against two torsional springs each having a torsional spring constant of 1 N-m/rad. The gyro shown in (b) is viewed from the rear (from stern to bow on the submarine). What is the radius of curvature R of the path of the sub from this reading? This disc weighs 4 N, has a radius of 50 mm, and rotates at 20,000 rpm.

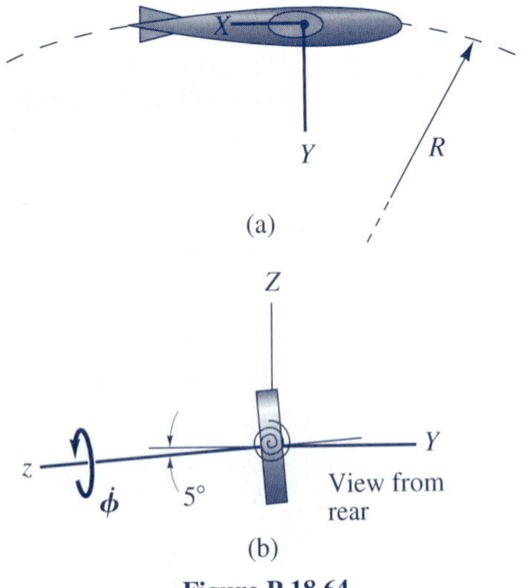

Figure P.18.64.

18.65. Work Problem 18.56 for the case where, before activation of the jet, the vehicle has the following angular velocity:

$$\boldsymbol{\omega} = .20\boldsymbol{i} + .3\boldsymbol{j} + .15\boldsymbol{k} \text{ rad/sec}$$

18.66. In Problem 18.49, the initial angular velocity is:

$$\boldsymbol{\omega} = .3\boldsymbol{i} + .2\boldsymbol{j} + .4\boldsymbol{k} \text{ rad/sec}$$

What are ω_x, ω_y, and ω_z after vane B has been rotated parallel to vane A by an internal mechanism?

18.67. A research space capsule is in orbit having imposed on it an instantaneous angular speed ω of .4 rad/sec. The capsule consists of a spherical unit D which can be considered a uniform sphere of radius .60 m and weight 800 N. Arms A and B extend from the sphere and consist of cylinders which pick up and record dust particle collisions. Each such unit weighs 500 N and has the following radii of gyration at the mass center, C.M.

$$k \text{ (lateral axes)} = .80 \text{ m}$$
$$k \text{ (longitudinal axis)} = .20 \text{ m}$$

If arm A is rotated 90° to position E by an internal mechanism, what is the angular precession speed of the system? Give the direction of Z about which there is precession. All weights are as on earth.

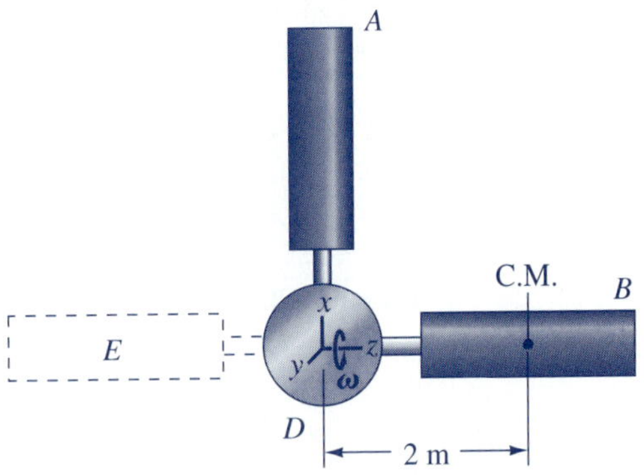

Figure P.18.67.

18.68. In Problem 18.67, 20 N-m of energy is used to cause the change in configuration. What is the spin speed and nutation angle? From a previous solution, $\dot{\psi} = .2064$ rad/sec. [*Hint:* Make use of work-energy equation and Eq. 18.37.]

CHAPTER 19

Vibrations

19.1 Introduction

You will recall that in Chapter 12 we said we would defer a more general examination of particle motion about a fixed point until the very end of the text. We do this to take full advantage of any course in differential equations that you might be taking simultaneously with this course. Accordingly, we shall now continue the work begun in Chapter 12.

19.2 Free Vibration

Let us begin by reiterating what we have done earlier leading to the study of vibrations. Recall that we examined the case of a particle in rectilinear translation acted on either by a constant force, a force given as a function of time, a force that is a function of speed, or, finally, a force that is a function of position. In each case we could separate the variables and effect a quadrature to arrive at the desired algebraic equations, including constants of integration. In particular we considered, as a special case of a force given as a function of position, the linear restoring force resulting from the action (or equivalent action) of a linear spring. Thus, for the spring-mass system shown in Fig. 19.1, the differential equation of motion was shown to be

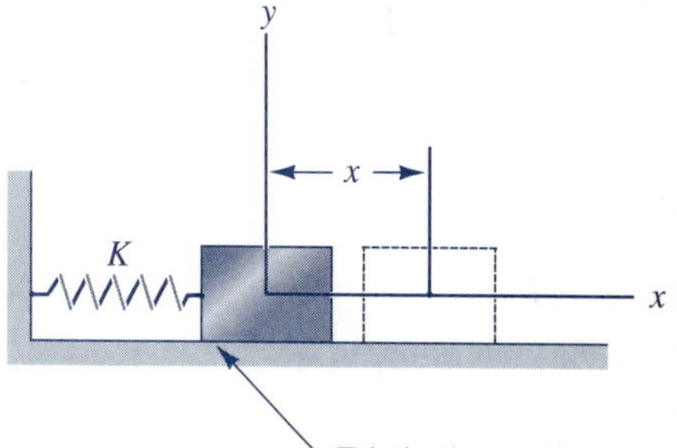

Figure 19.1. Spring–mass system.

$$\frac{d^2x}{dt^2} + \frac{K}{m}x = 0 \tag{19.1}$$

where K is the spring constant and where x is measured from the static equilibrium position of the mass. You will now recognize this equation from your studies in mathematics as a second-order, linear differential equation with constant coefficients.

Instead of rearranging the equation to effect a quadrature, as we did in the previous case,[1] we shall take a more general viewpoint toward the solving of differential equations.

To solve a differential equation, we must find a function of time, $x(t)$, which when substituted into the equation satisfies the equation (i.e., reduces it to an identity $0 = 0$). We can either guess at $x(t)$ or use a formal procedure. You have learned in your differential equations course that the most general solution of the above equation will consist of a linear combination of two functions that cannot be written as multiples of each other (i.e, the functions are linearly independent). There will also be two arbitrary constants of integration. Thus, $C_1 \cos \sqrt{K/m}\, t$ and $C_2 \sin \sqrt{K/m}\, t$ will satisfy the equation, as we can readily demonstrate by substitution, and are independent in the manner described. We can therefore say

$$x = C_1 \cos \sqrt{\frac{K}{m}} t + C_2 \sin \sqrt{\frac{K}{m}} t \qquad (19.2)$$

where C_1 and C_2 are the aforementioned constants of integration to be determined from the initial conditions.

We can conveniently represent each of the above functions by employing rotating vectors of magnitudes that correspond to the coefficients of the functions. This representation is shown in Fig. 19.2, where, if the vector C_1 rotates counterclockwise with an angular velocity of $\sqrt{K/m}$ radians per unit time and if C_1 lies along the x axis at time $t = 0$, then the projection of this vector along the x axis represents one of the functions of Eq. 19.2, namely $C_1 \cos \sqrt{K/m}\, t$. Vectors used in this manner are called *phasors*.

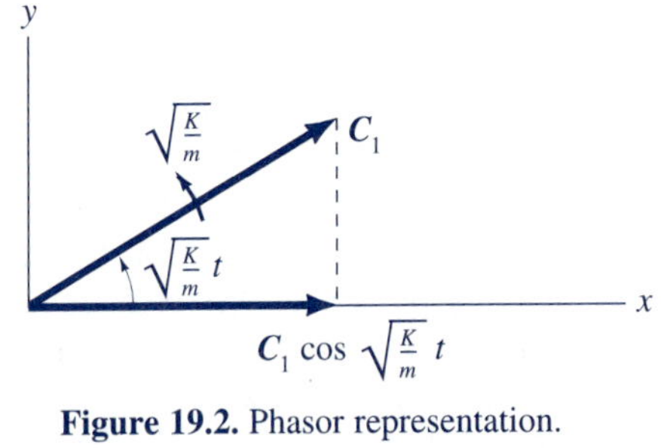

Figure 19.2. Phasor representation.

Consider now the function $C_2 \sin \sqrt{K/m}\, t$, which we can replace by $C_2 \cos (\sqrt{K/m}\, t - \pi/2)$, as we learned in elementary trigonometry. The phasor representation for this function, therefore, would be a vector of magnitude C_2 that rotates with angular velocity $\sqrt{K/m}$ and that is out of phase by $\pi/2$ with

[1]Recall that this can be done by replacing d^2x/dt^2 by $(dV/dx)(dx/dt)$, which is simply $V(dV/dx)$.

the phasor C_1 (Fig. 19.3). Thus, the projection of C_2 on the x axis is the other function of Eq. 19.2. Clearly, because vectors C_1 and C_2 rotate at the same angular speed, we can represent the combined contribution by simply summing the vectors and considering the projection of the resulting single vector

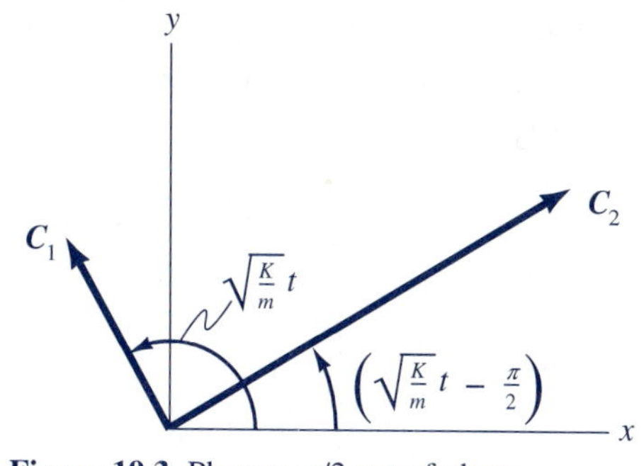

Figure 19.3. Phasors $\pi/2$ out of phase.

along the x axis. This summation is shown in Fig. 19.4 where vector C_3 replaces the vectors C_1 and C_2. Now we can say:

$$C_3 = \sqrt{C_1^2 + C_2^2}, \qquad \beta = \tan^{-1}\frac{C_2}{C_1} \tag{19.3}$$

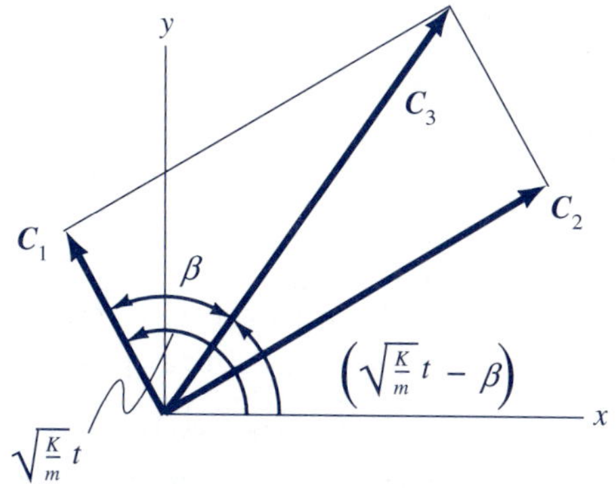

Figure 19.4. Vector sum of phasors.

Because C_1 and C_2 are arbitrary constants, C_3 and β are also arbitrary constants. Consequently, we can replace the solution given by Eq. 19.2 by another equivalent form:

$$x = C_3 \cos\left[\sqrt{\frac{K}{m}}t - \beta\right] \tag{19.4}$$

From this form, you probably recognize that the motion of the body is *harmonic motion*. In studying this type of motion, we shall use the following definitions:

Cycle. The cycle is that portion of a motion (or series of events in the more general usage) which, when repeated, forms the motion. On the phasor diagrams, a cycle would be the motion associated with one revolution of the rotating vector.

Frequency. The number of cycles per unit time is the frequency. The frequency is equal to $\sqrt{K/m}/2\pi$ for the above motion, because $\sqrt{K/m}$ has units of radians per unit time. Often $\sqrt{K/m}$ is termed the *natural frequency* of the system in radians per unit time or, when divided by 2π, in cycles per unit time. The *natural frequency* is denoted generally in the following ways:

$$\omega_n = \sqrt{K/m}\ \text{rad/sec}$$

$$f_n = \frac{1}{2\pi}\sqrt{K/m}\ \text{cycles/sec}$$

Period. The period, T, is the time of one cycle, and is therefore the reciprocal of frequency. That is,

$$T = \frac{2\pi}{\sqrt{K/m}} \tag{19.5}$$

Amplitude. The largest displacement attained by the body during a cycle is the amplitude. In this case, the amplitude corresponds to the coefficient C_3.

Phase angle. The phase angle is the angle between the phasor and the x axis when $t = 0$ (i.e., the angle β).

A plot of the motion as a function of time is presented in Fig. 19.5, where certain of these various quantities are shown graphically.

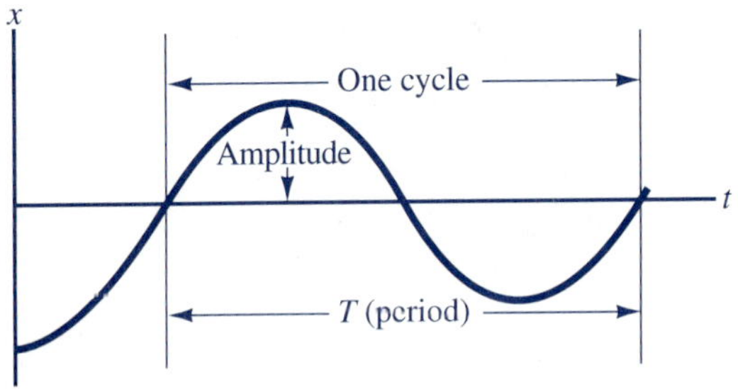

Figure 19.5. Plot of harmonic motion.

It is usually easier to use the earlier form of solution, Eq. 19.2, rather than Eq. 19.4 in satisfying initial conditions. Accordingly, the position and velocity can be given as

$$x = C_1 \cos\sqrt{\frac{K}{m}}t + C_2 \sin\sqrt{\frac{K}{m}}t$$

$$V = -C_1\sqrt{\frac{K}{m}} \sin\sqrt{\frac{K}{m}}t + C_2\sqrt{\frac{K}{m}} \cos\sqrt{\frac{K}{m}}t$$

The initial conditions to be applied to these equations are:

$$\text{when } t = 0 \qquad x = x_0, \; V = V_0$$

Substituting, we get

$$x_0 = C_1, \qquad V_0 = C_2\sqrt{\frac{K}{m}}$$

Therefore, the motion is given as

$$x = x_0 \cos\sqrt{\frac{K}{m}}t + \frac{V_0}{\sqrt{K/m}} \sin\sqrt{\frac{K}{m}}t \tag{19.6a}$$

$$V = -x_0\sqrt{\frac{K}{m}} \sin\sqrt{\frac{K}{m}}t + V_0 \cos\sqrt{\frac{K}{m}}t \tag{19.6b}$$

We can generalize from these results by noting that any agent supplying a linear restoring force for all rectilinear motions of a mass can take the place of the spring in the preceding computations. We must remember, however, that to behave this way the agent must have negligible mass. Thus, we can associate with such agents an *equivalent spring constant* K_e, which we can ascertain if we know the static deflection δ permitted by the agent on application of some known force F. We can then say:

$$K_e = \frac{F}{\delta}$$

Once we determine the equivalent spring constant, we immediately know that the natural frequency of the system is $(1/2\pi)\sqrt{K_e/m}$ cycles per unit time. This natural frequency is the number of cycles the system will repeat in a unit time if some initial disturbance is imposed on the mass. Note that this natural frequency depends only on the "stiffness" of the system and on the mass of the system and is not dependent on the amplitude of the motion.[2]

We shall now consider several problems in which we can apply what we have just learned about harmonic motion.

[2]Actually, when the amplitude gets comparatively large, the spring ceases to be linear, and the motion does depend on the amplitude. Our results do not apply for such a condition.

Example 19.1

A mass weighing 45 N is placed on the spring shown in Fig. 19.6 and is released very slowly, extending the spring a distance of 50 mm. What is the natural frequency of the system? If the mass is given a velocity instantaneously of 1.60 m/sec down from the equilibrium position, what is the equation for displacement as a function of time?

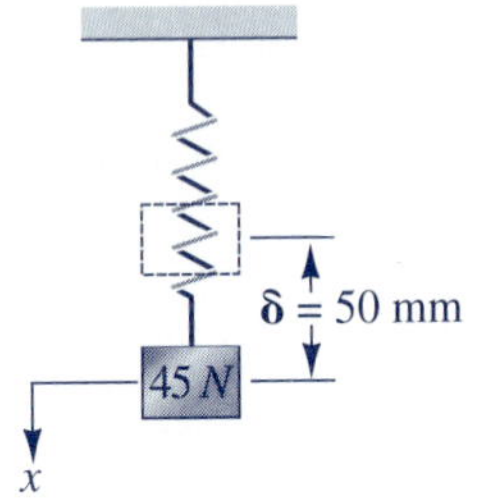

Figure 19.6. x measured from static deflection position.

The spring constant is immediately available by the equation

$$K = \frac{F}{\delta} = \frac{45 \text{ N}}{50 \text{ mm}} = .9 \text{ N/mm}$$

The equation of motion for the mass can be written for a reference whose origin is at the static equilibrium position shown in the diagram. Thus,

$$m\frac{d^2x}{dt^2} = W - K(x + \delta)$$

where δ is the distance from the unextended position of the spring to the origin of the reference. However, from our initial equation, $\delta = F/K = W/K$. Therefore, we have

$$m\frac{d^2x}{dt^2} = W - K(x + \frac{W}{K}) = -Kx$$

and the equation becomes identical to Eq. 19.1:

$$\frac{d^2x}{dt^2} + \frac{K}{m}x = 0 \qquad \text{(a)}$$

Thus, the motion will be an oscillation about the position of static equilibrium, which is an extended position of the spring. Measuring x from the *static equilibrium position* and considering the spring force as $-Kx$, we can thus disregard the weight on the body in writing Newton's law for the body to reach Eq. (a) most directly.

Example 19.1 (Continued)

Accordingly, we can use the results stemming from our main discussion. Employing the notation ω_n as the natural frequency in units of radians per unit time, we have

$$\omega_n = \sqrt{\frac{K}{m}} = \sqrt{\frac{\left(\frac{.9\text{ N}}{\text{mm}}\right)\left(\frac{1{,}000\text{ mm}}{\text{m}}\right)}{\frac{45}{g}\text{ kg}}} = \sqrt{\frac{\left(\frac{.9\text{ N}}{\text{mm}}\right)\left(\frac{1{,}000\text{ mm}}{\text{m}}\right)}{\frac{45}{g}\left(\frac{\text{N}}{\text{m/sec}^2}\right)}} = 14.01\text{ rad/sec}$$

The motion is now given by the equations

$$x = C_1 \sin 14.01t + C_2 \cos 14.01t$$
$$\dot{x} = 14.01C_1 \cos 14.01t - 14.01C_2 \sin 14.01t$$

From the specified initial conditions, we know that when $t = 0$, $x = 0$, and $\dot{x} = 1.6$ m/sec. Therefore, the constants of integration are

$$C_2 = 0, \qquad C_1 = \frac{1.60}{14.01} = .1142$$

The desired equation, then, is

$$x = .1142 \sin 14.01t \text{ m}$$

Example 19.2

A body weighing 22 N is positioned in Fig. 19.7 on the end of a slender cantilever beam whose mass we can neglect in considering the motion of the body at its end.

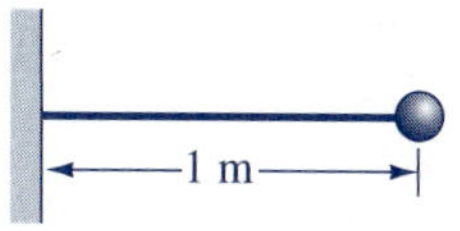

Figure 19.7. Slender cantilever beam with weight at end.

If we know the geometry and the composition of the cantilever beam, and if the deflection involved is small, we can compute from strength of materials the deflection of the end of the beam that results from a vertical load there. This deflection is directly proportional to the load. In

Example 19.2 (Continued)

this case, suppose that we have computed a deflection of 12.5 mm for a force of 4 N (see Fig. 19.8). What would be the natural frequency of the body weighing 22 N for small oscillations in the vertical direction?

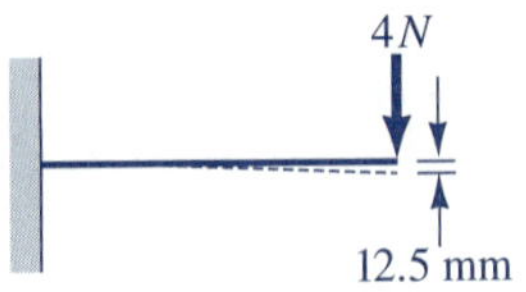

Figure 19.8. Beam acts as linear spring.

Because the motion is restricted to small amplitudes, we can consider the mass to be in rectilinear motion in the vertical direction in the same manner as the mass on the spring in the previous case. The beam now supplies the linear restoring force. The formulations of this section are once again applicable. The equivalent spring constant is found to be

$$K_e = \frac{F}{\delta} = \frac{4}{12.5} = .32 \text{ N/mm}$$

The natural frequency for vibration of the 22-N weight at the end of the cantilever is then

$$\omega_n = \sqrt{\frac{(.32)(1{,}000)}{22/9.81}} = \boxed{11.94 \text{ rad/sec}}$$

Before starting out on the exercises, we wish to point out results of Problem 19.2 that will be of use to you. In that problem, you are asked to show that the equivalent spring constant for springs in *parallel* and subject to the same deflection [see Fig. P.19.2(a)] is simply the sum of the spring constants of the springs. That is,

$$K_e = K_1 + K_2 \tag{19.7}$$

For springs in series [Fig. P.19.2(b)] we have

$$\frac{1}{K_e} = \frac{1}{K_1} + \frac{1}{K_2} \tag{19.8}$$

Also, we wish to point out that, for small values of θ, we can approximate $\sin\theta$ by θ and $\cos\theta$ by unity. To justify this, expand $\sin\theta$ and $\cos\theta$ as power series and retain first terms.

PROBLEMS

19.1. If a 5-kg mass causes an elongation of 50 mm when suspended from the end of a spring, determine the natural frequency of the spring–mass system.

19.2. (a) Show that the spring constant is doubled if the length of the spring is halved.

(b) Show that two springs having spring constants K_1 and K_2 have a combined spring constant of $K_1 + K_2$ when connected in parallel, and have a combined spring constant whose reciprocal is $1/K_1 + 1/K_2$ when combined in series.

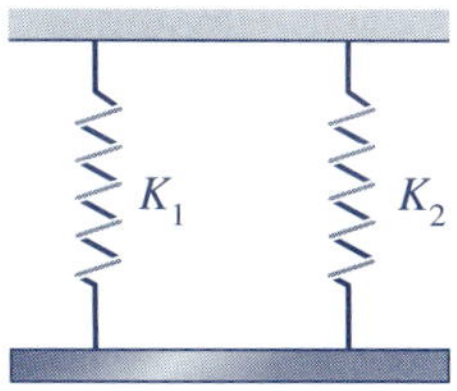

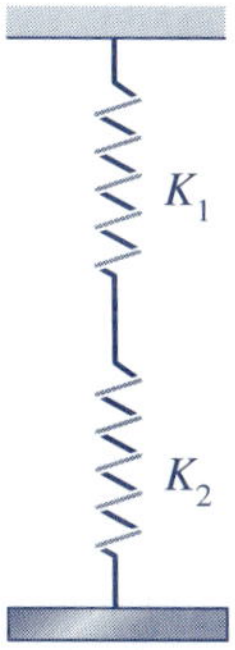

Figure P.19.2.

19.3. A mass M of 2 kg rides on a vertical frictionless guide rod. With only one spring K_1, the natural frequency of the system is 2 rad/sec. If we want to increase the natural frequency threefold, what must the spring constant K_2 of a second spring be?

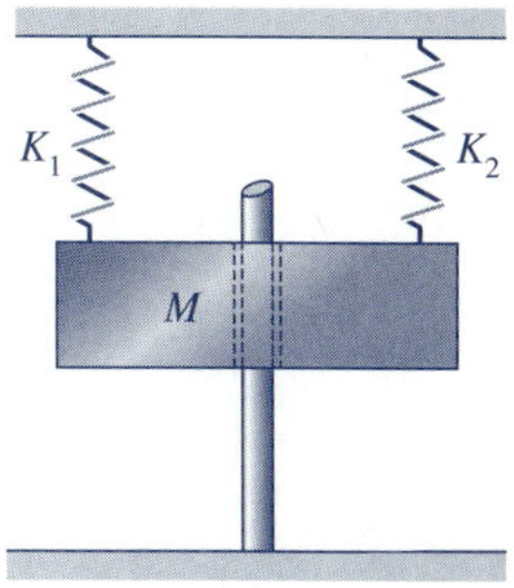

Figure P.19.3.

19.4. A mass M Of 100 g rides on a frictionless guide rod. If the natural frequency with spring K_1 attached is 5 rad/sec, what must K_2 be to increase the natural frequency to 8 rad/sec?

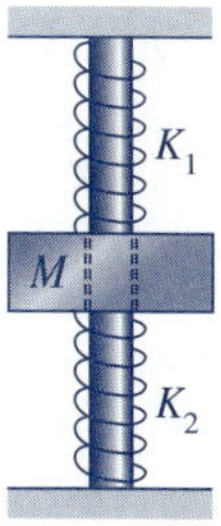

Figure P.19.4.

19.5. For small oscillations, what is the natural frequency of the system in terms of a, b, K, and W? (Neglect the mass of the rod.)

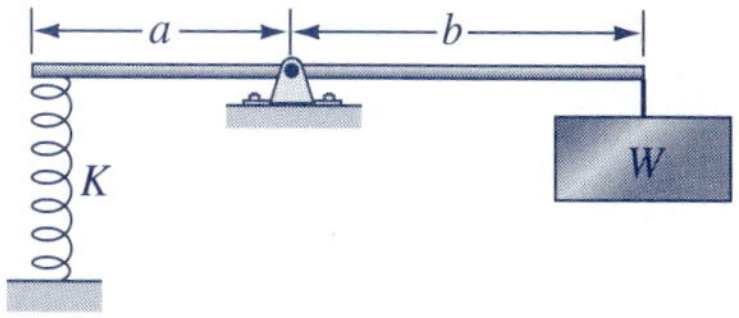

Figure P.19.5.

19.6. A rod is supported on two rotating grooved wheels. The contact surfaces have a coefficient of friction of μ_d. Explain how the rod will oscillate in the horizontal direction if it is disturbed in that direction. Compute the natural frequency of the system.

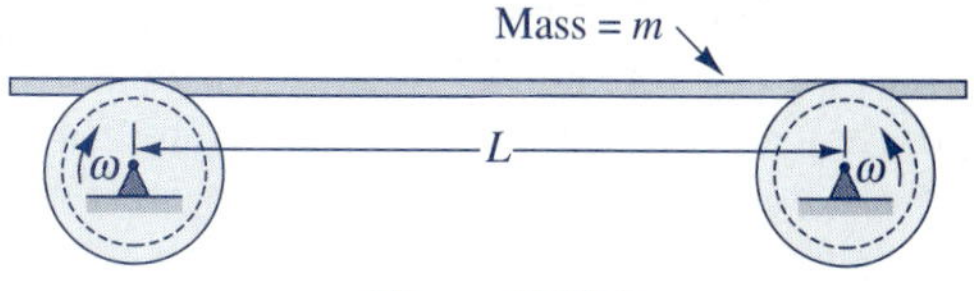

Figure P.19.6.

19.7. A mass is held so it just makes contact with a spring. If the mass is released suddenly from this position, give the amplitude, frequency, and the center position of the motion. First use the *undeformed position* to measure x. Then, do the problem using x' from the static equilibrium position.

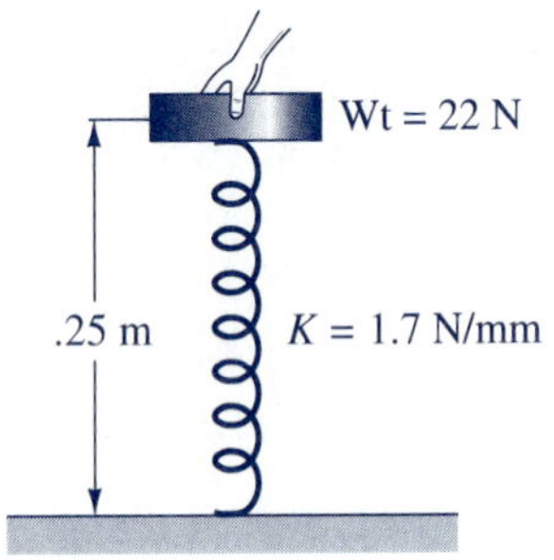

Figure P.19.7.

19.8. A *hydrometer* is a device to measure the *specific gravity* of liquids. The hydrometer weighs .36 N, and the diameter of the cylindrical portion above the base is 6 mm. If the hydrometer is disturbed in the vertical direction, what is the frequency of vibration in cycles/sec as it bobs up and down? Recall from *Archimedes' principle* that the buoyant force equals the weight of the water displaced. Water has a density of 1,000 kg/m^3.

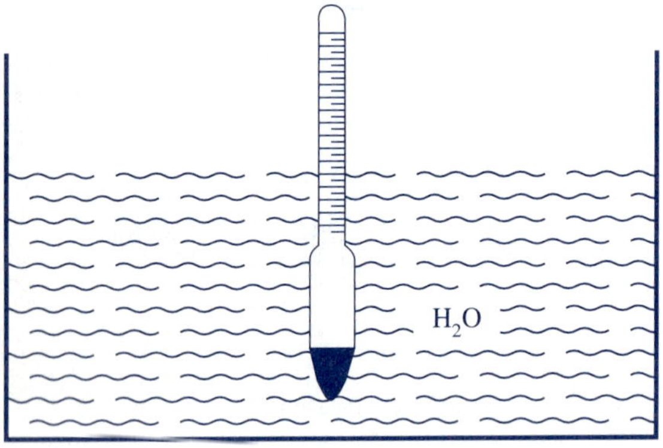

Figure P.19.8.

***19.9.** The hydrometer of Problem 19.8 is used to test the specific gravity of battery acid in a car battery. What is the period of oscillation in this case? [*Hint:* Note if hydrometer goes down, the battery acid surface will have to rise a certain amount simultaneously. The battery acid has a density of 1,100 kg/m^3.]

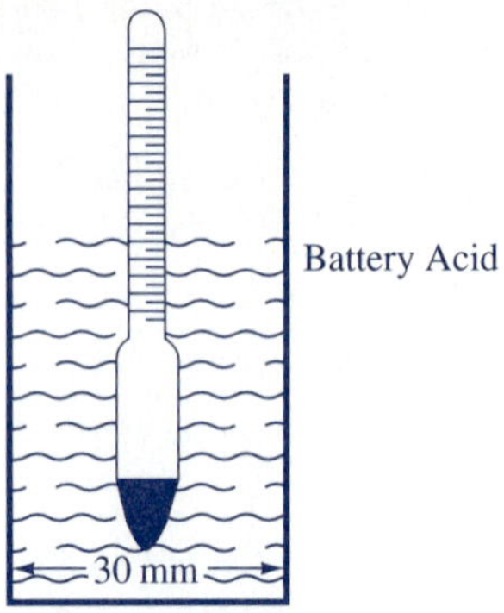

Figure P.19.9.

19.10. A 30-kg block is suspended using two light wires. What is the frequency in cycles/sec at which the block will swing back and forth in the x direction if it is slightly disturbed in this direction? [*Hint:* For small θ, $\sin\theta \approx \theta$ and $\cos\theta \approx 1$.]

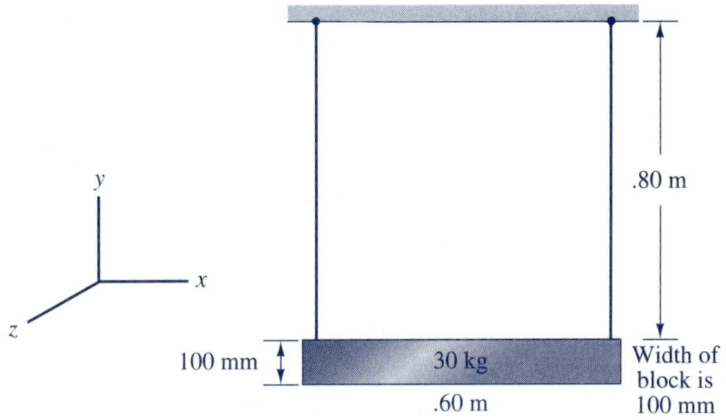

Figure P.19.10.

19.11. In Problem 19.10, what is the period of small oscillations for a small disturbance that causes the block to move in the z direction?

19.12. What is the natural frequency of motion for block A for small oscillation? Consider BC to have negligible mass and body A to be a particle. When body A Is attached to the rod, the static deflection is 25 mm. The spring constant K_1 is 1.75 N/mm. Body A weighs 110 N. What is K_2?

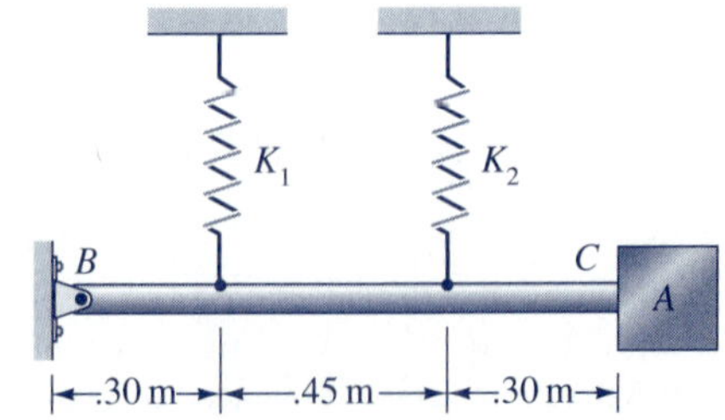

Figure P.19.12.

19.13. If bar ABC is of negligible mass, what is the natural frequency of free oscillation of the block for small amplitude of motion? The springs are identical, each having a spring constant K of 25 lb/in. The weight of the block is 10 lb. The springs are unstretched when AB is oriented vertically as shown in the diagram.

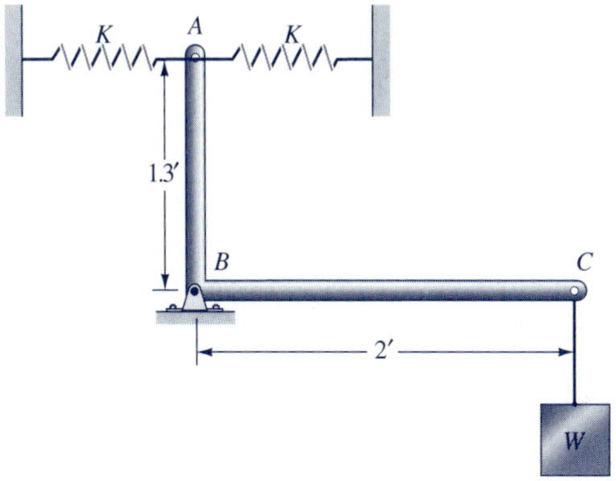

Figure P.19.13.

19.14. Work Problem 19.13 for the case where the springs are both stretched 1 in. when AB is vertical.

19.15. What are the differential equation of motion about the static-equilibrium configuration and the natural frequency of motion of body A for small motion of BC? Neglect inertial effects from BC. The following data apply:

$$K_1 = 15 \text{ lb/in.}$$
$$K_2 = 20 \text{ lb/in.}$$
$$K_3 = 30 \text{ lb/in.}$$
$$W_A = 30 \text{ lb}$$

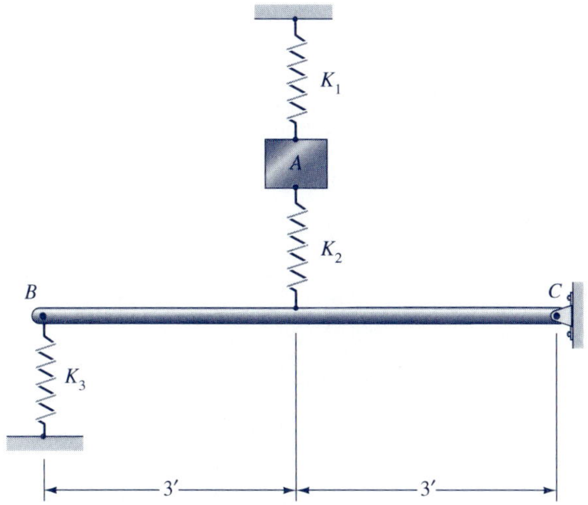

Figure P.19.15.

19.16. A horizontal platform is rotating with a uniform angular speed of ω rad/sec. On the platform is a rod CD on which slides a cylinder A having weight W. The cylinder is connected to C through a linear spring having a spring constant K. What is the equation of motion for A relative to the platform after it has been disturbed? What is the natural frequency of oscillation? Take r_0 as the unstretched length of spring.

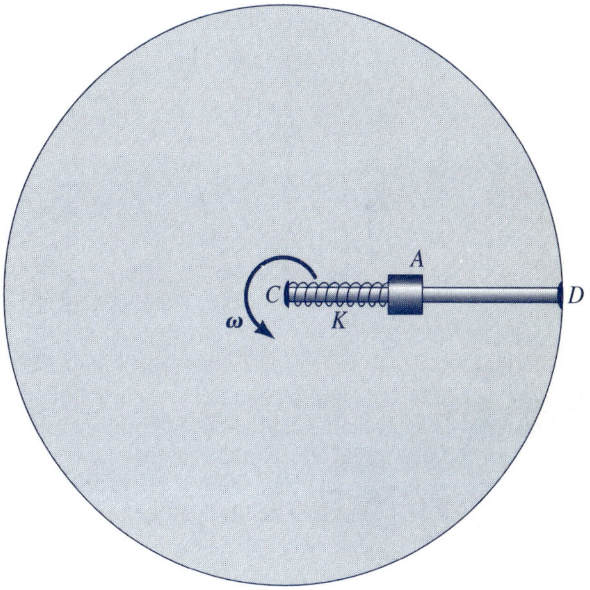

Figure P.19.16.

19.17. A rigid body A rests on a spring with stiffness K equal to 8.80 N/mm. A lead pad B falls onto the block A with a speed on impact of 7 m/sec. If the impact is perfectly plastic, what are the frequency and amplitude of the motion of the system, provided that the lead pad sticks to A at all times? Take W_A = 134 N and W_B = 22 N. What is the distance moved by A in .02 sec? (*Caution:* Be careful about the initial conditions.)

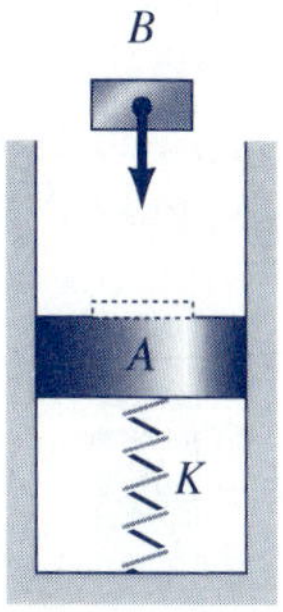

Figure P.19.17.

19.18. A small sphere of weight 5 lb is held by taut elastic cords on a frictionless plane. If 50 lb of force is needed to cause an elongation of 1 in. for each cord, what is the natural frequency of small oscillation of the weight in a transverse direction? Also, determine the natural frequency of the weight in a direction along the cord for small oscillations. Neglect the mass of the cord. The tension in the cord in the configuration shown is 100 lb.

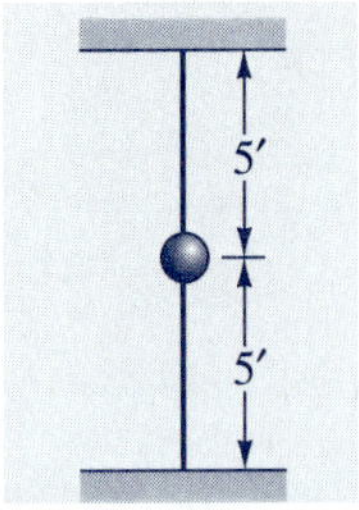

Figure P.19.18.

19.19. Body A weighs 445 N and is connected to a spring having a spring constant K_1 of 3.50 N/mm. At the right of A is a second spring having a spring constant K_2 of 8.80 N/mm. Body A is moved 150 mm to the left from the configuration of static equilibrium shown in the diagram, and it is released from rest. What is the period of oscillation for the body? [*Hint:* Work with half a cycle.]

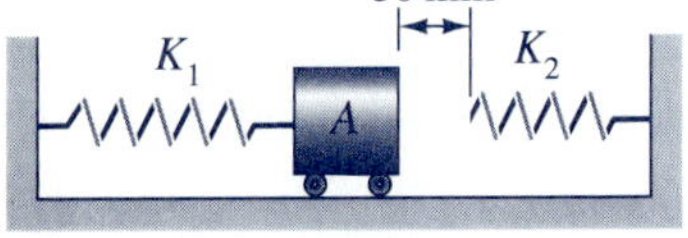

Figure P.19.19.

19.20. Body A, weighing 50 lb, has a speed of 20 ft/sec to the left. If there is no friction, what is the period of oscillation of the body for the following data:

$$K_1 = 20 \text{ lb/in.}$$
$$K_2 = 10 \text{ lb/in.}$$

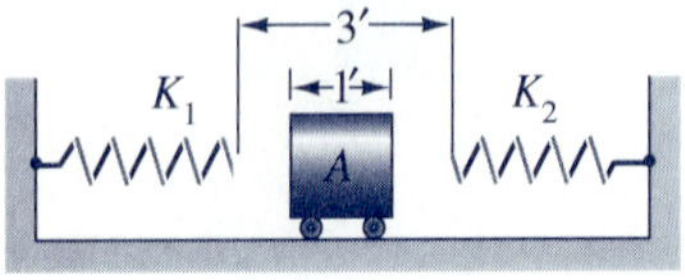

Figure P.19.20.

19.21. A spherical body A of mass 2 kg is attached by a light rod to a shaft BC which is inclined by an angle of 30°. For small, rotational oscillations about BC, what is the natural frequency of the system? [*Hint:* Recall that the moment about an axis n is $(\boldsymbol{r} \times \boldsymbol{F}) \cdot \hat{\boldsymbol{n}}$.]

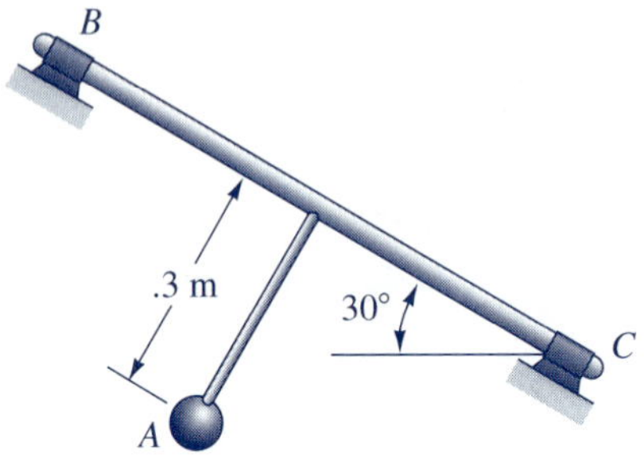

Figure P.19.21.

*__19.22.__ A cube A, .25 m on a side, has a specific gravity of 1.10 and is attached to a cone having a specific gravity of .8. What is the equation for up-and-down motion of the system? Neglect the mass and buoyant force for rod CD. For very small oscillations, what is the approximate natural frequency?

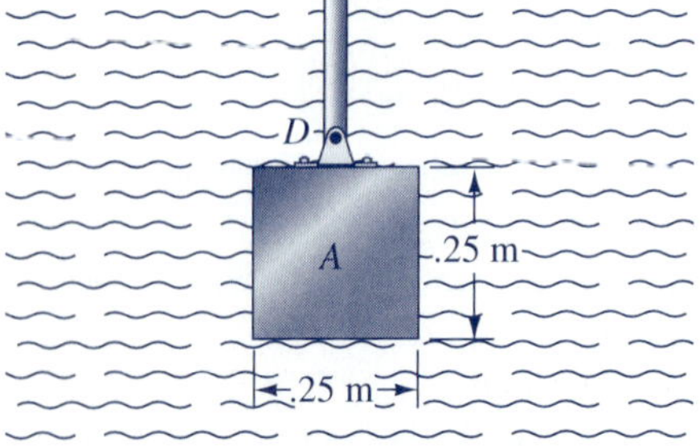

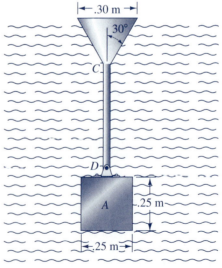

Figure P.19.22.

19.3 Torsional Vibration

We showed in Section 16.2 that, for a body constrained to rotate about an axis fixed in inertial space, the angular momentum equation about the fixed axis is

$$I_{zz}\dot{\omega}_z = I_{zz}\ddot{\theta} = M_z \tag{19.9}$$

Numerous homework problems involved the determination of $\dot{\theta}$ and θ for applied torques which either were constant, varied with time, varied with speed $\dot{\theta}$, or, finally varied with position θ. The analyses paralleled very closely the corresponding cases for rectilinear translation of Chapter 12. Primarily, the approach was that of separation of variables and then that of carrying out one or more quadratures.

Paralleling the case of the linear restoring force in rectilinear translation is the important case where M_z is a *linear restoring torque*. For example, consider a circular disc attached to the end of a light shaft as shown in Fig. 19.9.

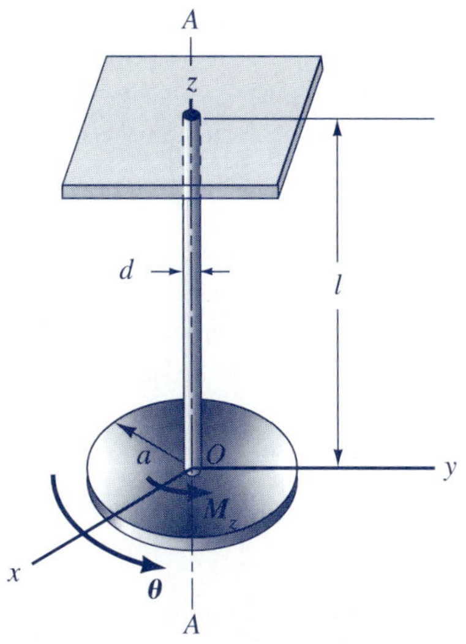

Figure 19.9. Shaft–disc analog of spring–mass system.

Note that the upper end of the shaft is fixed. If the disc is twisted by an external agent about the centerline *A–A* of the shaft, then the disc will rotate essentially as a rigid body, whereas the shaft, since it is so much thinner and longer, will twist and supply a restoring torque on the disc that tries to bring the disc back to its initial position. In considering the possible motions of such a system disturbed in the aforementioned manner, we idealize the problem by *lumping* all elastic action into the shaft and all inertial effects into the disc. We know from strength of materials that for a circular shaft of constant cross section the amount of twist θ induced by torque M_z is, in the elastic range of deformation,

$$\theta = \frac{M_z L}{GJ} \tag{19.10}$$

where G is the shear modulus of the shaft material, J is the polar moment of area of the shaft cross section, and L is the length of the shaft. We can set forth the concept of a torsional spring constant K_t given as

$$K_t = \frac{M_z}{\theta} \tag{19.11}$$

For the case at hand, we have

$$K_t = \frac{GJ}{L} \tag{19.12}$$

Thus, the thin shaft has the same role in this discussion as the light linear spring of Section 19.2. Employing Eq. 19.11 for M_z and using the proper sign to ensure that we have a restoring action, we can express Eq. 19.9 as follows:

$$\ddot{\theta} + \frac{K_t}{I_{zz}}\theta = 0 \tag{19.13}$$

Notice that this equation is identical in form to Eq. 19.1. Accordingly, all the conclusions developed in that discussion apply with the appropriate changes in notation. Thus, the disc, once disturbed by being given an angular motion, will have a *torsional* natural oscillation frequency of $(\omega_n)_t = \sqrt{K_t/I_{zz}}$ rad/sec. The equation of motion for the disc is

$$\theta = C_1 \cos\sqrt{\frac{K_t}{I_{zz}}}t + C_2 \sin\sqrt{\frac{K_t}{I_{zz}}}t \tag{19.14}$$

where C_1 and C_2 are constants of integration to be determined from initial conditions. Thus, for $\theta = \theta_0$ and $\dot{\theta} = \dot{\theta}_0$ at $t = 0$ we have

$$0 = \theta_0 \cos\sqrt{\frac{K_t}{I_{zz}}}t + \frac{\dot{\theta}_0}{\sqrt{K_t/I_{zz}}} \sin\sqrt{\frac{K_t}{I_{zz}}}t \tag{19.15}$$

In the example just presented, the linear restoring torque stemmed from a long thin shaft. There could be other agents that can develop a linear restoring torque on a system otherwise free to rotate about an axis fixed in inertial space. We then talk about an *equivalent* torsional spring constant. We shall illustrate such cases in the following examples.

Example 19.3

What are the equation of motion and the natural frequency of oscillation for small amplitude of a simple plane pendulum shown in Fig. 19.10? The pendulum rod may be considered massless.

Because the pendulum bob is small compared to the radius of curvature of its possible trajectory of motion, we may consider it as a particle. The pendulum has one degree of freedom, and we can use θ as the independent coordinate.[3] Notice from the diagram that there is a restoring torque about point A developed by gravity given as

$$M_x = -WL\sin\theta \tag{a}$$

where W is the weight of the bob. If the amplitude of the motion θ is very small, we can replace $\sin\theta$ by θ and so for this case we have a linear restoring torque given as

$$M_x = -WL\theta \tag{b}$$

We then have an equivalent torsional spring constant for the system

$$K_t = WL \tag{c}$$

The equation of possible *small-amplitude* motions for the pendulum is given as

$$-WL\theta = (ML^2)\ddot{\theta} \tag{d}$$

where we have used the **moment-of-momentum equation** about the fixed point A. Rearranging terms, we get

$$\ddot{\theta} + \frac{WL}{ML^2}\theta = 0 \tag{e}$$

Noting that $W = Mg$, we have

$$\ddot{\theta} + \frac{g}{L}\theta = 0 \tag{f}$$

Accordingly, the natural frequency of oscillation is

$$\omega_n = \sqrt{\frac{g}{L}} \text{ rad/sec} \tag{g}$$

The equation of motion for this system is

$$\theta = C_1 \cos\sqrt{\frac{g}{L}}t + C_2 \sin\sqrt{\frac{g}{L}}t \tag{h}$$

where C_1 and C_2 are computed from known conditions at some time t_0.

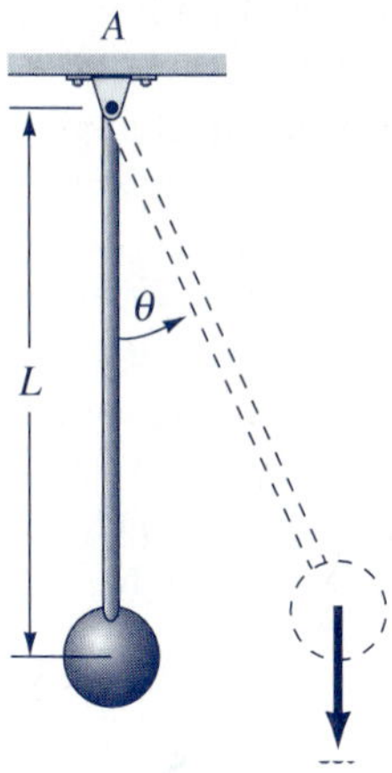

Figure 19.10. Pendulum.

[3]One degree of freedom means that one independent coordinate locates the system.

Example 19.4

A stepped disc is shown in Fig. 19.11 supporting a weight W_1 while being constrained by a linear spring having a spring constant K. The mass of the stepped disc is M and the radius of gyration about its geometric axis is k. What is the equation of motion for the system if the disc is rotated a small angle θ_1 counterclockwise from its static-equilibrium configuration and then suddenly released from rest? Assume the cord holding W_1 is weightless and perfectly flexible.

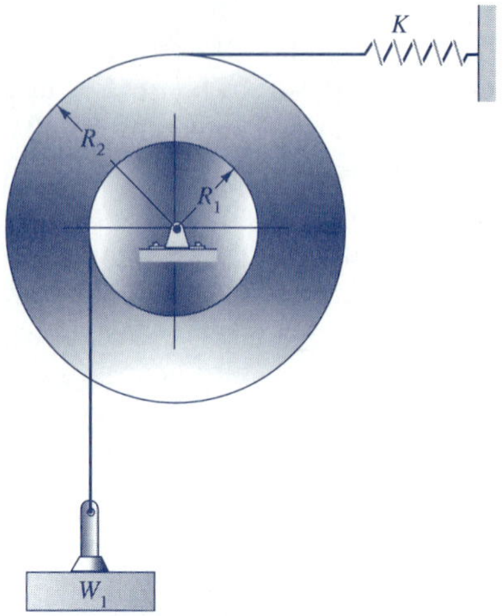

Figure 19.11. Stepped disc.

If we measure θ from the static-equilibrium position as shown in Fig. 19.12(a) the spring is stretched an amount $R_2(\theta + \theta_0)$ wherein θ_0 is the amount of rotation induced by the weight W_1 to reach the static-equilibrium configuration. Consequently, applying the **angular momentum equation** to the stepped disc about the axis of rotation, we get

$$R_1 T - KR_2^2(\theta + \theta_0) = Mk^2\ddot{\theta} \qquad \text{(a)}$$

Next consider the suspended weight W_1. Clearly we have only translation for this body, for which **Newton's law** gives us

$$T - W_1 = -\frac{W_1}{g} R_1\ddot{\theta} \qquad \text{(b)}$$

where we have made the assumption that the **cord** is always taut and is inextensible and have considered the **kinematics** of the motion. We may replace T in Eq. (a) using Eq. (b) as follows:

$$R_1 W_1 - \frac{W_1}{g} R_1^2\ddot{\theta} - KR_2^2(\theta + \theta_0) = Mk^2\ddot{\theta} \qquad \text{(c)}$$

Rearranging terms, we get

$$\left(Mk^2 + \frac{W_1}{g} R_1^2\right)\ddot{\theta} + KR_2^2\theta = R_1 W_1 - KR_2^2\theta_0 \qquad \text{(d)}$$

Considering the **static-equilibrium** configuration of the system, we see on summing moments about the axis of rotation that the right side of the equation above is zero. Accordingly, we have for Eq. (d):

$$\ddot{\theta} + \frac{KR_2^2}{Mk^2 + (W_1/g)R_1^2}\theta = 0 \qquad \text{(e)}$$

We can say immediately that the natural torsional frequency of the system is

$$\omega_n = \sqrt{\frac{KR_2^2}{Mk^2 + (W_1/g)R_1^2}} \text{ rad/sec} \qquad \text{(f)}$$

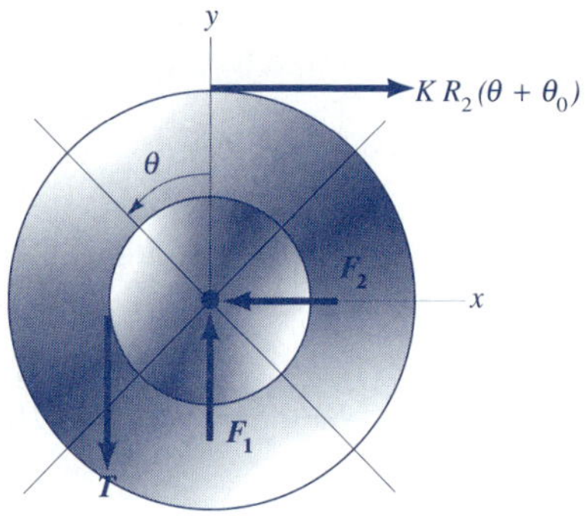

(a)

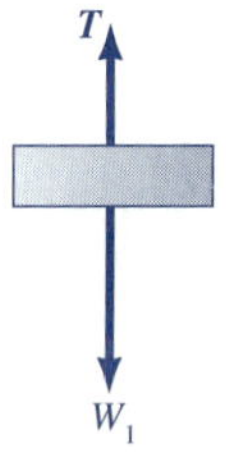

(b)

Figure 19.12. Free-body diagrams.

Example 19.4 (Continued)

The equation of motion is then

$$\theta = C_1 \cos \sqrt{\frac{KR_2^2}{Mk^2 + (W_1/g)R_1^2}}\,t + C_2 \sin \sqrt{\frac{KR_2^2}{Mk^2 + (W_1/g)R_1^2}}\,t \qquad \text{(g)}$$

Submitting Eq. (g) to the initial conditions to determine C_1 and C_2, we get

$$\theta = \theta_1 \cos \sqrt{\frac{KR_2^2}{Mk^2 + (W_1/g)R_1^2}}\,t \qquad \text{(h)}$$

It is important to note that we could have reached Eq. (e) more directly by using θ measured from the *equilibrium configuration*. That is, use the fact that the moment from the weight W_1 is counteracted by the static moment from the stretch $R_2\theta_0$ of the spring. Accordingly, only the moment from the force—$R_2K\theta$ from further stretch of the spring as well as the moment from the inertial force—$(W_1/g)R_1\ddot{\theta}$ of the hanging weight from Eq. (b) need be considered in the angular-momentum equation (a). Thus, we have from this viewpoint:

$$-\frac{W_1}{g} R_1^2\ddot{\theta} - KR_2^2\theta = Mk^2\ddot{\theta} \qquad \text{(i)}$$

Rearranging, we have

$$\ddot{\theta} + \frac{KR_2^2}{Mk^2 + (W_1/g)R_1^2}\theta = 0 \qquad \text{(j)}$$

Accordingly, we arrive at very same differential equation (e) in a more direct manner. We can again conclude as in Example 19.1 that *when the coordinate is measured from an equilibrium configuration we can forget about contributions of torques that are present for the equilibrium configuration and include only new torques developed when there is a departure from the equilibrium configuration.*

Before you start on the problems, we wish to point out that shafts directly connected to each other (see the shafts on the right side of the disc in Fig. P.19.23) are analogous to springs in *series* as far as the equivalent torsional spring constant is concerned. On the other hand, shafts on opposite sides of the disc are analogous to springs in *parallel* as far as the equivalent torsional spring constant is concerned. You should have no trouble justifying these observations.

PROBLEMS

19.23. Compute the equivalent torsional spring constant of the shaft on the disc.

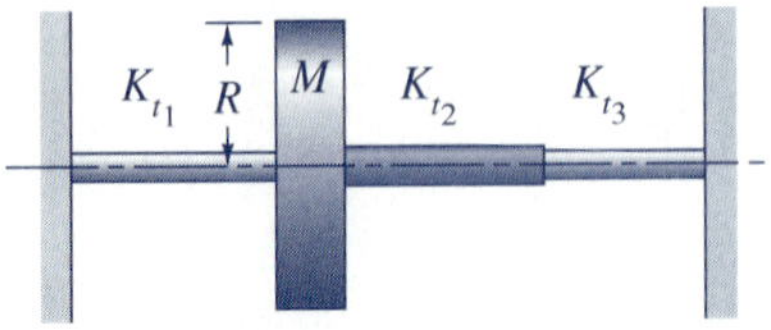

Figure P.19.23.

19.24. What is the equivalent torsional spring constant on the disc from the shafts? The modulus of elasticity G for the shafts is 10×10^{10} N/m^2. What is the natural frequency of the system? If the disc is twisted 10° and then released, what will its angular position be in 1 sec? Neglect the mass of the shafts. The disc weighs 143 N.

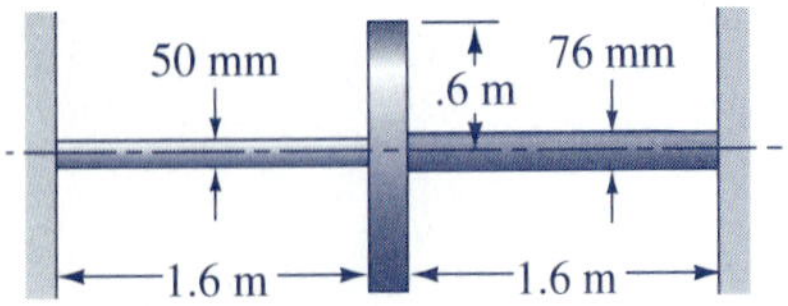

Figure P.19.24.

19.25. A small pendulum is mounted in a rocket that is accelerating upward at the rate of $3g$. What is the natural frequency of rotation of the pendulum if the bob has a mass of $50g$? Neglect the weight of the rod. Consider small oscillations.

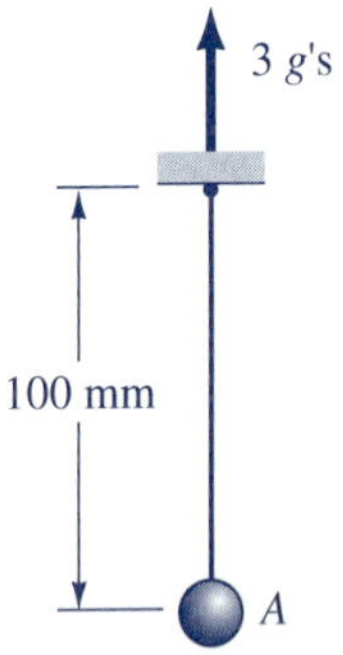

Figure P.19.25.

19.26. Work Problem 19.25 for the case where the rocket is decelerating at $.6g$ in the vertical direction.

19.27. What is the natural frequency for small oscillations of the compound pendulum supported at A?

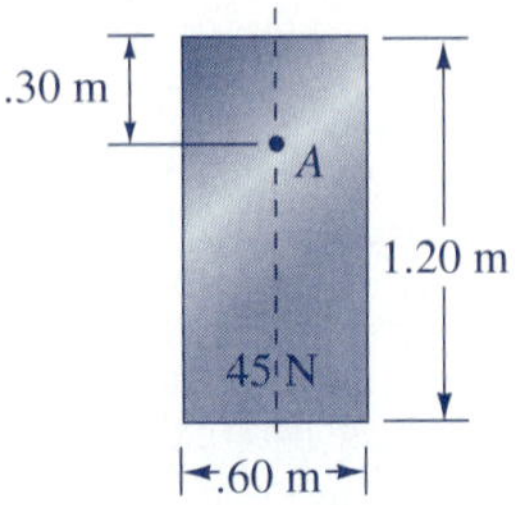

Figure P.19.27.

19.28. A slender rod weighing 140 N is held by a frictionless pin at A and by a spring having a spring constant of 8.80 N/mm at B

(a) What is the natural frequency of oscillation for small vibrations?

(b) If point B of the rod is depressed 25 mm at $t = 0$ from the static-equilibrium position, what will its position be when $t = .02$ sec?

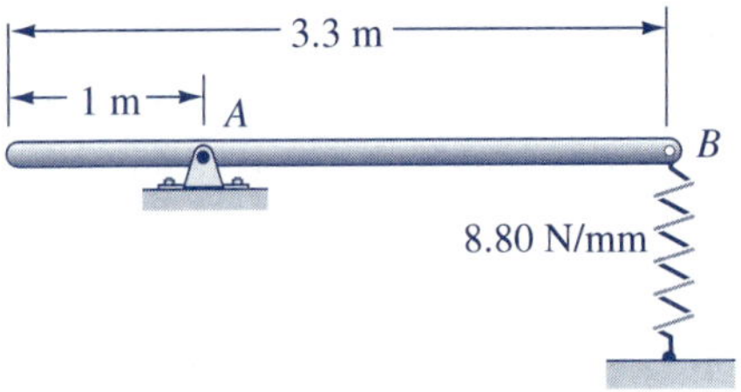

Figure P.19.28.

19.29. What is the natural frequency of the pendulum shown for small oscillations? Take into account the inertia of the rod whose mass is m. Also, consider the bob to be a sphere of diameter D and mass M, rather than a particle. The length of the rod is l.

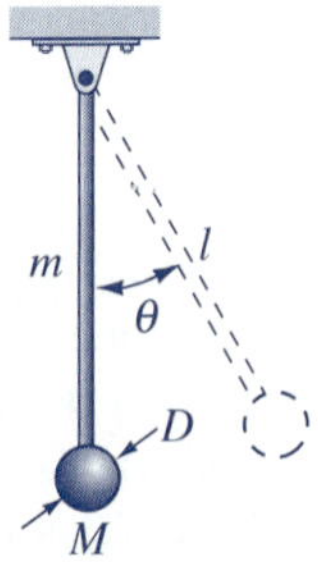

Figure P.19.29.

19.30. A cylinder of mass M and radius R is connected to identical springs and rotates without friction about O. For small oscillations, what is the natural frequency? The cord supporting W_1 is wrapped around the cylinder.

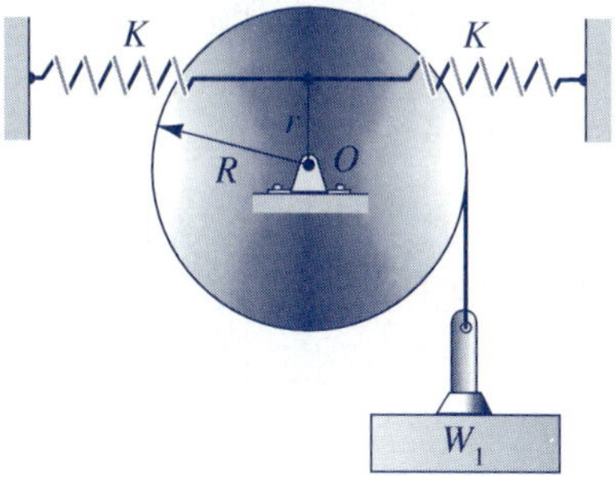

Figure P.19.30.

19.31. The author's 22-ft Columbia sailboat is suspended by straps from a crane. The boat is made to swing freely about support A in the xy plane (the plane of the page). What is the radius of gyration about the z axis at the center of gravity if the period of oscillation is 5 sec? The boat has a mass of 1,000 kg. Neglect the weight of supporting wires and belts.

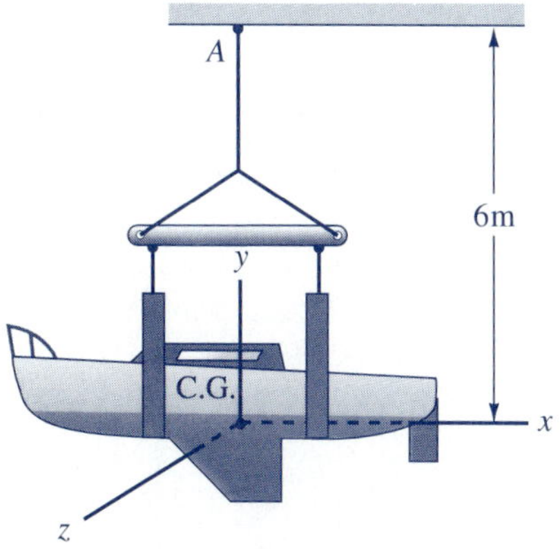

Figure P.19.31.

19.32. A uniform bar of length L and weight W is suspended by strings. What is the differential equation of motion for small torsional oscillation about a vertical axis at the center of mass at C? What is the natural frequency?

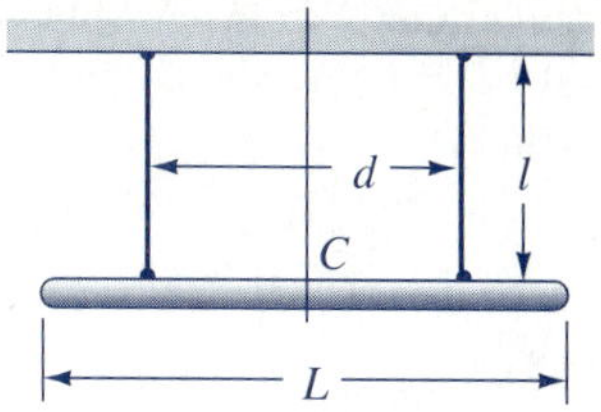

Figure P.19.32.

19.33. In Problem 19.12, do not consider body A to be a particle, and compute the natural frequency of the system for small vibrations. Take the dimension of A to be that of a 150-mm cube. If ω_n for the particle approach is 19.81 rad/sec, what percentage error is incurred using the particle approach?

19.34. Gears A and B weighing 50 lb and 80 lb, respectively, are fixed to supports C and D as shown. If the shear modulus G for the shafts is 15×10^6 psi, what is the natural frequency of oscillation for the system?

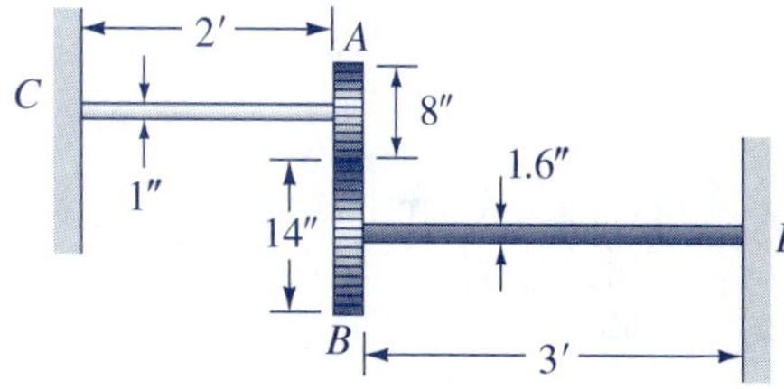

Figure P.19.34.

19.35. A four-bar linkage, $ABCD$, is disturbed slightly so as to oscillate in the xy plane. What is the frequency of oscillation if each bar has a mass of 5.0 g/mm?

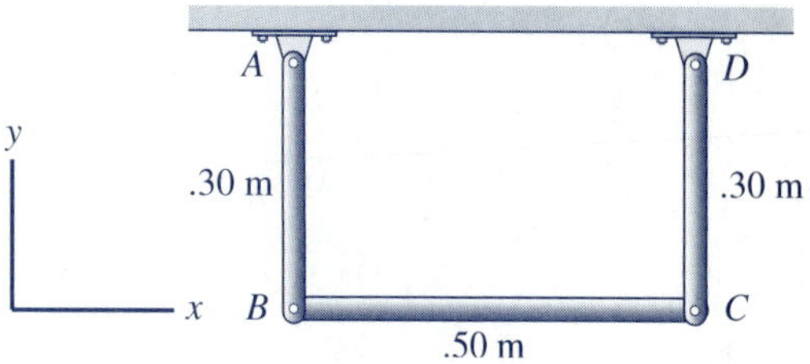

Figure P.19.35.

19.36. A plate A weighing 1 kN is attached to a rod CD. If at the instant that the rod CD is torsionally unstrained, the plate has an angular speed of 2 rad/sec about the centerline of CD, what is the amplitude of twist developed by the rod? Take $G = 6.90 \times 10^{10}$ N/m^2 for the rod.

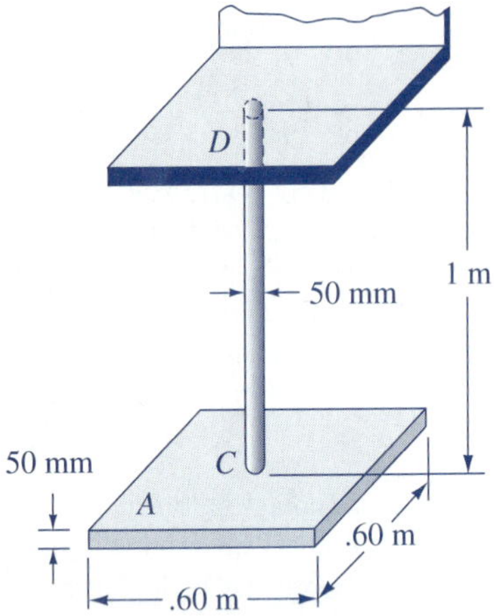

Figure P.19.36.

19.37. A block A having a uniform density of 300 lb/ft^3 is suspended by a fixed shaft of length 3 ft as shown. If the area of the top surface of the block is 5 ft^2, what are the values of a and b for extreme values of natural torsional frequency of the system? The shear modulus G for the shaft is 15×10^6 psi. Compute the natural frequency for the extreme cases.

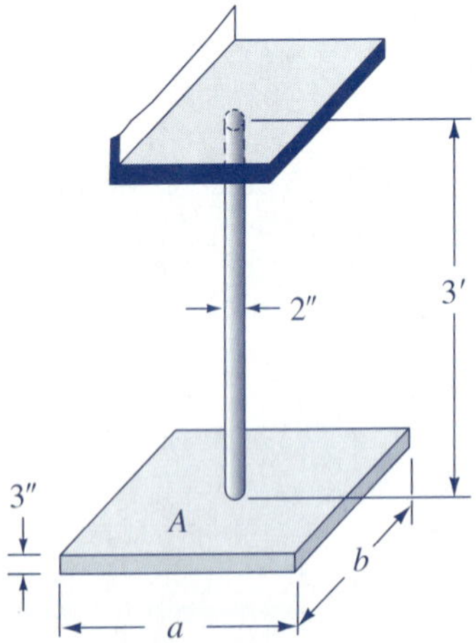

Figure P.19.37.

19.38. A rod of weight W and length L is restrained in the vertical position by two identical springs having spring constant K. A vertical load P acts on top of the rod. What value of P, in terms of W, L, and K, will cause the rod to have a natural frequency of oscillation about A approaching zero for small oscillations? What does this signify physically? [*Hint:* For small θ we may take $\cos \theta = 1$.]

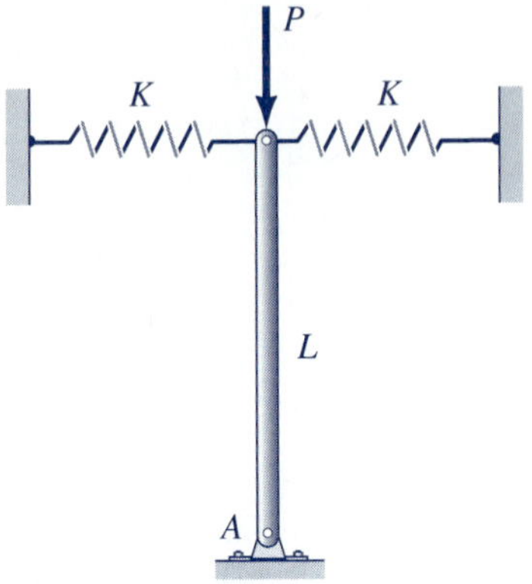

Figure P.19.38.

19.39. A 1-m rod weighing 60 N is maintained in a vertical position by two identical springs having each a spring constant of 50 N/mm. What vertical force P will cause the natural frequency of the rod about A to approach zero value for small oscillations? [*Hint:* For small θ we can say that $\cos \theta = 1$.]

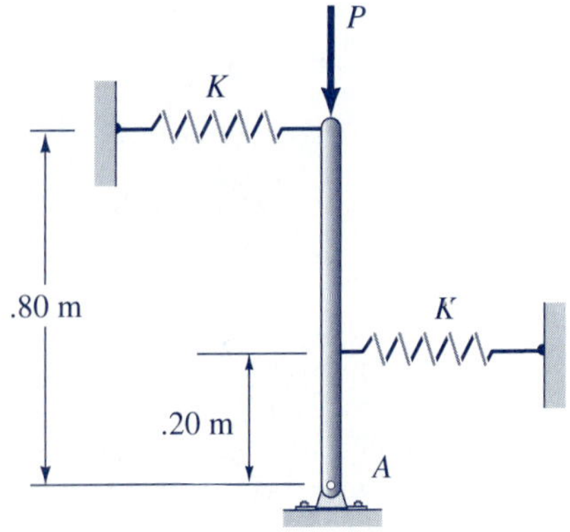

Figure P.19.39.

19.40. What is the natural frequency of torsional vibration for the stepped cylinder? The mass of the cylinder is 45 kg, and the radius of gyration is .46 m. The following data also apply:

$$D_1 = .30 \text{ m}$$
$$D_2 = .60 \text{ m}$$
$$K_1 = .875 \text{ N/mm}$$
$$K_2 = 1.8 \text{ N/mm}$$
$$W_A = 178 \text{ N}$$

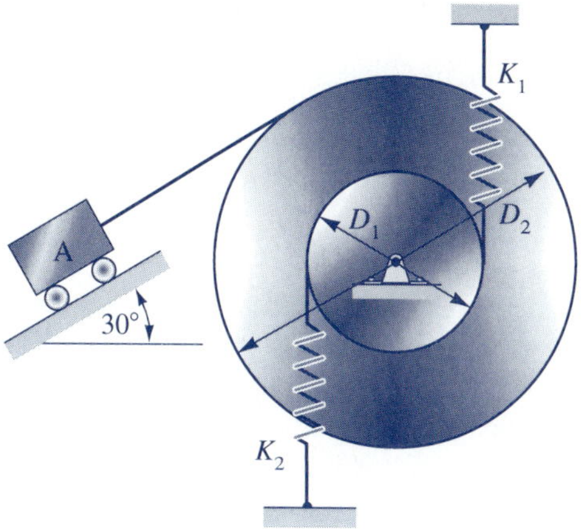

Figure P.19.40.

19.41. A disc A weighs 445 N and has a radius of gyration of .45 m about its axis of symmetry. Note that the center of gravity does not coincide with the geometric center. What are the amplitude of oscillation and frequency of oscillation if, at the instant that the center of gravity is directly below B, the disc is rotating at a speed of .01 rad/sec counterclockwise?

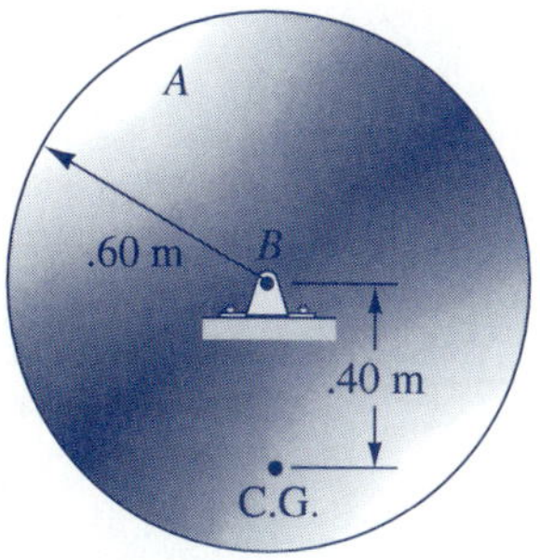

Figure P.19.41.

19.42. A disc B is suspended by a flexible wire. The tension in the top wire is 4,450 N. If the disc is observed to have a period of lateral oscillation of .2 sec for very small amplitude and a period of torsional oscillation of 5 sec, what is the radius of gyration of the disc about its geometric axis? The torsional spring constant for each of the wires is 1,470 N-mm/rad.

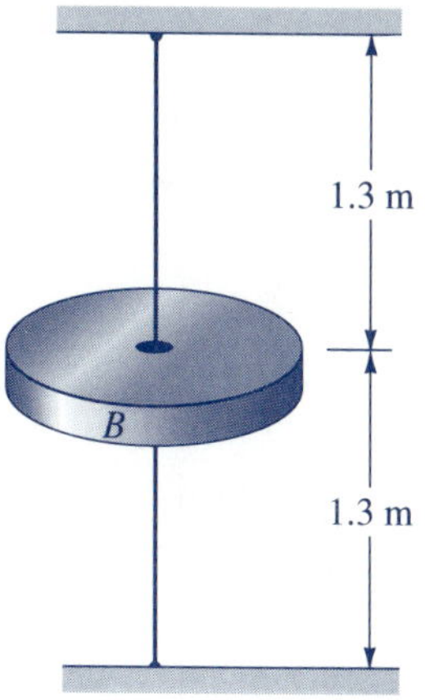

Figure P.19.42.

19.43. Two discs are forced together such that, at the point of contact, a normal force of 50 lb is transmitted from one disc to the other. Disc A weighs 200 lb and has a radius of gyration of 1.4 ft about C, whereas disc B weighs 50 lb and has a radius of gyration about D of 1 ft. What is the natural frequency of oscillation for the system, if disc A is rotated 10° counterclockwise and then released? The center of gravity of B coincides with the geometric center.

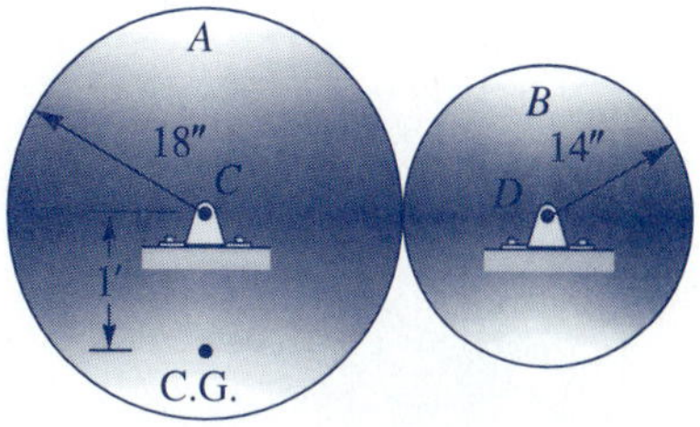

Figure P.19.43.

19.44. In Problem 19.43, find the minimum coefficient of friction for no slipping between the discs. From Problem 19.43, $\omega_n = 3.68$ rad/sec.

*19.4 Examples of Other Free-Oscillating Motions

In the previous sections, we examined the rectilinear translation of a rigid body under the action of a linear restoring force as well as the pure rotation of a rigid body under the action of a linear restoring torque. In this section, we shall first examine a body with one degree of freedom undergoing *plane motion* governed by a differential equation of motion of the form given in the previous section. The dependent variable for such a case varies harmonically with time, and we have a *vibratory plane motion*. Consider the following example.

Example 19.5

Shown in Fig. 19.13(a) on an inclined plane is a uniform cylinder maintained in a position of equilibrium by a linear spring having a spring constant K. If the cylinder rolls without slipping, what is the equation of motion when it is disturbed from its equilibrium position?

We have here a case of plane motion about a configuration of equilibrium. Using xyz as a *stationary* reference, we shall measure the displacement x of the center of mass from the equilibrium position and accordingly shall need to consider only those forces and torques developed as the cylinder departs from this position. Accordingly, we have for **Newton's law** for the mass center [see Fig. 19.13(b)]:

$$-f - Kx = M\ddot{x} \tag{a}$$

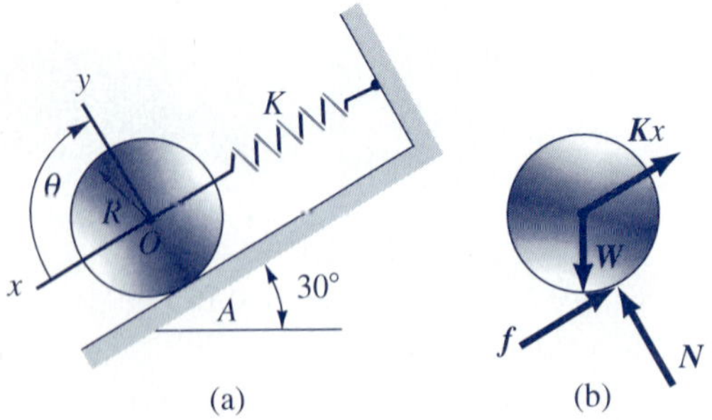

Figure 19.13. Plane-motion vibration.

Example 19.5 (Continued)

Now employ the **angular-momentum** equation about the geometric axis of the cylinder at O. Using θ to measure the rotation of the cylinder about this axis from the equilibrium configuration, we get

$$-fR = \tfrac{1}{2} MR^2\ddot{\theta} \qquad \text{(b)}$$

Noting from **kinematics** that $\ddot{x} = -R\ddot{\theta}$ as a result of the no-slipping condition, we have for Eq. (b):

$$fR = \frac{1}{2} MR^2\left(\frac{\ddot{x}}{R}\right)$$

Therefore,

$$f = \tfrac{1}{2} M\ddot{x} \qquad \text{(c)}$$

Substituting for f in Eq. (a) using this result, we have

$$M\ddot{x} = -\tfrac{1}{2} M\ddot{x} - Kx$$

Therefore,

$$\ddot{x} + \frac{2}{3}\frac{K}{M}x = 0 \qquad \text{(d)}$$

We could also have arrived at the differential equation above by noting that we have instantaneous pure rotation about the line of contact A as a result of the no-slipping condition. Thus, the **angular-momentum** equation can be used as follows about the point of contact on the cylinder:

$$\left(\tfrac{1}{2} MR^2 + MR^2\right)\ddot{\theta} = KxR \qquad \text{(e)}$$

Noting as before that $\ddot{\theta} = -\ddot{x}/R$, we get

$$-\frac{3}{2} MR^2 \frac{\ddot{x}}{R} = KxR$$

Therefore, as before

$$\ddot{x} + \frac{2}{3}\frac{K}{M}x = 0 \qquad \text{(d)}$$

Example 19.5 (Continued)

We may solve the differential equation to give us

$$x = x_0 \cos \sqrt{\frac{2}{3}\frac{K}{M}}t + \frac{\dot{x}_0}{\sqrt{\frac{2}{3}K/M}} \sin \sqrt{\frac{2}{3}\frac{K}{M}}t \qquad \text{(g)}$$

where x_0 and $\dot{x}_0$ are the initial position and speed of the center of mass, respectively. Since $\theta = -x/R$ (we have here only one degree of freedom[4] as a result of the no-slipping condition), we have for θ from Eq. (g):

$$\theta = \frac{-x_0}{R} \cos \sqrt{\frac{2}{3}\frac{K}{M}}t - \frac{\dot{x}_0}{R\sqrt{\frac{2}{3}K/M}} \sin \sqrt{\frac{2}{3}\frac{K}{M}}t \qquad \text{(h)}$$

[4]See footnote 3 on page 973.

*19.5 Energy Methods

Up to now, the procedure has been primarily to work with *Newton's law* or the *angular-momentum equation* in reaching the differential equation of interest. There is an alternative approach to the handling of free vibration problems that may be very useful in dealing with simple systems and in setting up approximate calculations for more complex systems. Suppose we know for a one-degree-of-freedom system that only linear restoring forces and torques do work during possible motions of the system. Then, the agents developing such forces are *conservative* force agents and may be considered to store potential energy. You will recall from Section 13.3 that the *total mechanical energy* for such systems is *conserved*. Thus, we have

$$\text{PE} + \text{KE} = \text{constant} \qquad (19.16)$$

Also, we know from our present study that the system must oscillate harmonically when disturbed and then allowed to move freely with only the linear restoring agents doing work. Thus, if κ is the independent coordinate measured from the static-equilibrium configuration, we have

$$\kappa = A\sin(\omega_n t + \beta) \tag{19.17}$$

Hence,

$$\dot{\kappa} = A\omega_n \cos(\omega_n t + \beta) \tag{19.18}$$

Now at the instant when $\kappa = 0$, we are at the static-equilibrium position and the potential energy of the system is a minimum. Since the total mechanical energy must be conserved at all times once such a motion is under way, it is also clear that the kinetic energy must be at a maximum at that instant. If we take the lowest potential energy as zero, then we have for the total mechanical energy simply the maximum kinetic energy. Also, when the body is undergoing a change in direction of its motion at the outer extreme position, the kinetic energy is zero instantaneously, and accordingly the potential energy must be a maximum and equal to the total mechanical energy of the system. Thus, we can equate the maximum potential energy with the maximum kinetic energy.

$$(\text{KE})_{\text{max}} = (\text{PE})_{\text{max}} \tag{19.19}$$

In computing the $(\text{KE})_{\text{max}}$, we will involve $(\dot{\kappa})_{\text{max}}$ and hence $A\omega_n$, whereas for the $(\text{PE})_{\text{max}}$ we will involve $(\kappa)_{\text{max}}$ and hence A. In this way we can set up quickly an equation for ω_n, the natural frequency of the system. For example, if we have the simple linear spring-mass system of Fig. 19.1, we can say:

$$(\text{PE}) = \tfrac{1}{2}Kx^2$$

Therefore,

$$(\text{PE})_{\text{max}} = \tfrac{1}{2}K(x_{\text{max}})^2 = \tfrac{1}{2}KA^2$$

where we have made use of our knowledge that $x = A\sin(\omega_n t + \beta)$. And, noting that $\dot{x} = A\omega_n\cos(\omega_n t + \beta)$, we have

$$(\text{KE})_{\text{max}} = \tfrac{1}{2}M(\dot{x}_{\text{max}})^2 = \tfrac{1}{2}M(A\omega_n)^2$$

Now, equating these expressions, we get

$$\tfrac{1}{2}KA^2 = \tfrac{1}{2}M(A\omega_n)^2$$

Therefore,

$$\omega_n = \sqrt{\frac{K}{M}}$$

which is the expected result. We next illustrate this approach in a more complex problem.

Example 19.6

A cylinder of radius r and weight W rolls without slipping along a circular path of radius R as shown in Fig. 19.14. Compute the natural frequency of oscillation for small oscillation.

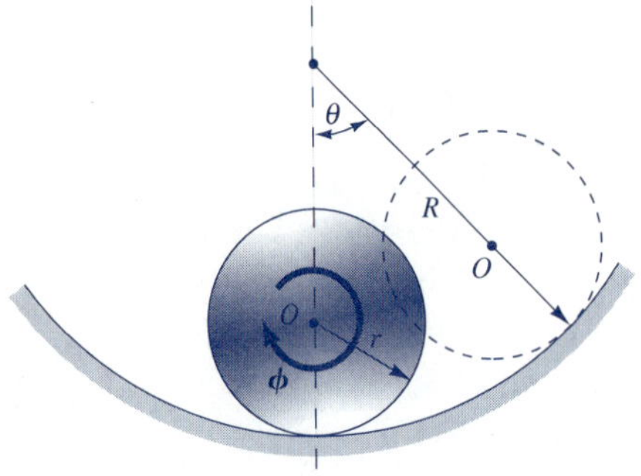

Figure 19.14. Cylinder rolls without slipping.

This system has one degree of freedom. We can use ϕ, the angle of rotation of the cylinder about its axis of symmetry, as the independent coordinate, or we may use θ as shown in the diagram. To relate these variables for no slipping we may conclude, on observing the motion of point O, that for small rotation:

$$(R - r)\theta = r\phi$$

Therefore,

$$\theta = \frac{r}{R - r}\phi \tag{a}$$

The only force that does work during the possible motions of the system is the force of gravity W. The torque developed by W about the point of contact for a given θ is easily determined after examining Fig. 19.15 to be

$$\text{torque} = Wr\sin\theta = Wr\sin\left(\frac{r}{R - r}\phi\right) \tag{b}$$

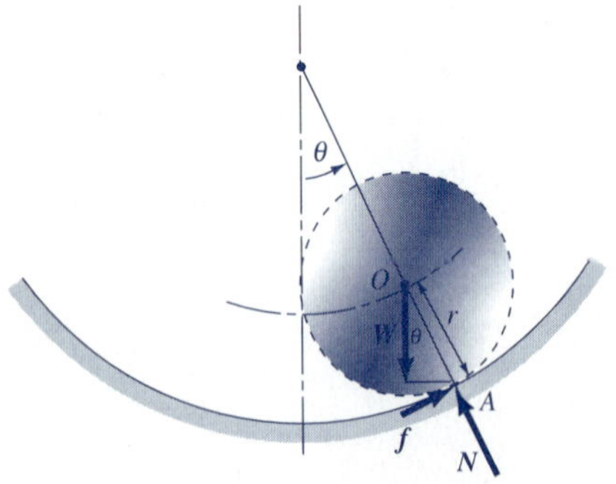

Figure 19.15. Free-body diagram of cylinder.

Example 19.6 (Continued)

This is a restoring torque, and because we limit ourselves to *small oscillations* it becomes $W[r^2\phi/(R-r)]$, which is clearly a linear restoring torque. Because the force doing work on the cylinder is *conservative*, and because it results in a *linear restoring torque*, we can employ the energy formulation of this section.

The motion may be considered to be given as follows:

$$\theta = C\sin(\omega_n t + \beta) \tag{c}$$

or, using Eq. (a),

$$\phi = \frac{R-r}{r} C\sin(\omega_n t + \beta) \tag{d}$$

Expressing the maximum potential and kinetic energies and using C for θ_{max} and the lowest position of O as the datum, we have:

$$\begin{aligned}(\text{PE})_{max} &= W(R-r)(1-\cos\dot{\theta}_{max})\\ &= W(R-r)(1-\cos C)\end{aligned} \tag{e}$$

$$\begin{aligned}(\text{KE})_{max} &= \frac{1}{2}\frac{W}{g}(R-r)^2\dot{\theta}^2_{max} + \frac{1}{4}\frac{W}{g}r^2\dot{\phi}^2_{max}\\ &= \frac{1}{2}\frac{W}{g}(R-r)^2(C\omega_n)^2 + \frac{1}{4}\frac{W}{g}r^2\left(\frac{R-r}{r}C\omega_n\right)^2\end{aligned} \tag{f}$$

We have used Eq. (d) in the last expression of Eq. (f). Expanding cos C in a power series and retaining the first two terms $(1-C^2/2)$, we then get, on equating the right sides of the above equations:

$$W(R-r)\frac{C^2}{2} = \frac{W}{2g}\left[(R-r)^2 + \frac{(R-r)^2}{2}\right]\omega_n^2 C^2$$

Therefore,

$$\omega_n = \sqrt{\frac{g}{\frac{3}{2}(R-r)}} \tag{g}$$

PROBLEMS

19.45. A cylinder of diameter 1 m is shown. The center of gravity of the cylinder is .30 m from the geometric center, and the radius of gyration is .60 m at the center of mass. What is the natural frequency of oscillation for small vibrations without slipping? The cylinder weighs 220 N. Work the problem by two methods.

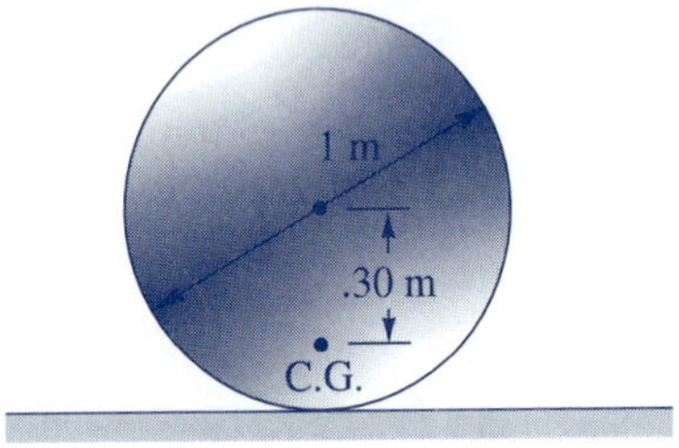

Figure P.19.45.

19.46. A stepped cylinder is maintained along the incline by a spring having a spring constant K. What is the formulation for the natural frequency of oscillation for the system? What is the maximum friction force? Take the weight of the cylinder as W and the radius of gyration about the geometric centerline O as k. The initial conditions are $\theta = \theta_0$ at $t = 0$, and $\dot{\theta} = \dot{\theta}_0$ at $t = 0$. There is no slipping.

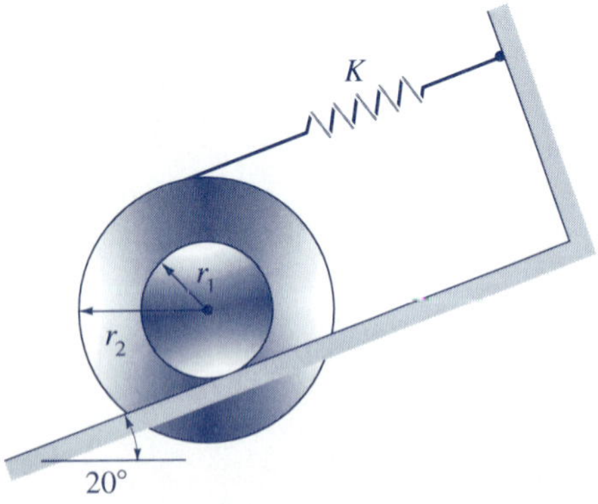

Figure P.19.46.

19.47. Two masses are attached to a light rod. The rod rides on a frictionless horizontal rail. $M_1 = 45$ kg and $M_2 = 14$ kg. What is the natural frequency of oscillation of the system if a small impulsive torque is applied to the system when it is in a rest configuration? Consider the masses as particles. [*Hint:* Consider motion about the center of mass of the system.]

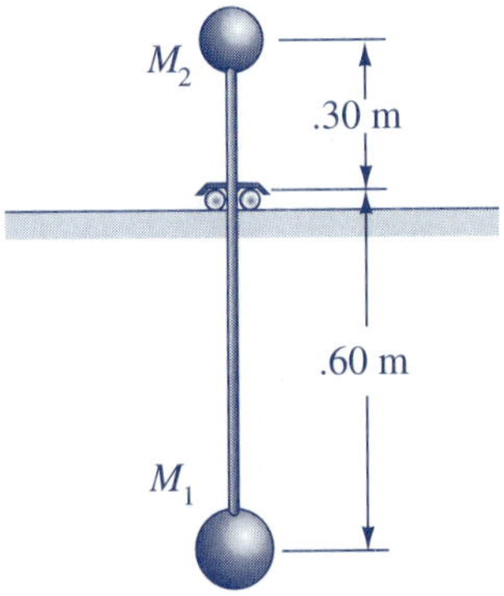

Figure P.19.47.

19.48. Work Problem 19.30 by energy methods.

19.49. Work Problem 19.13 by energy methods.

19.50. Work Problem 19.40 by energy methods.

19.51. A *manometer* used for measuring pressures is shown. If the mercury has a length L in the tube, what is the formulation for the natural frequency of movement of the mercury?

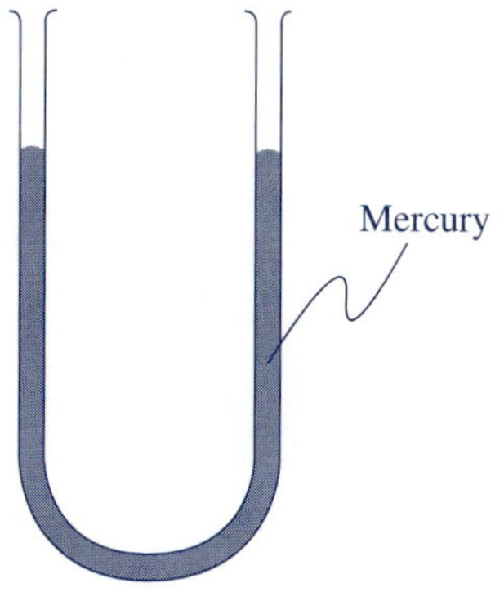

Figure P.19.51.

19.52. An *inclined manometer* is often used for more accurate pressure measurements. If the mercury in the tube has a length L, what is the natural frequency of oscillation of the mercury in the tube?

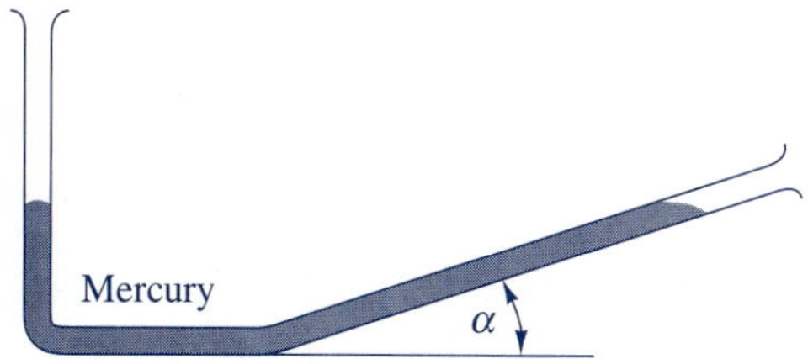

Figure P.19.52.

19.53. A *differential* manometer is used for measuring high pressures. What is the natural frequency of oscillation of the mercury?

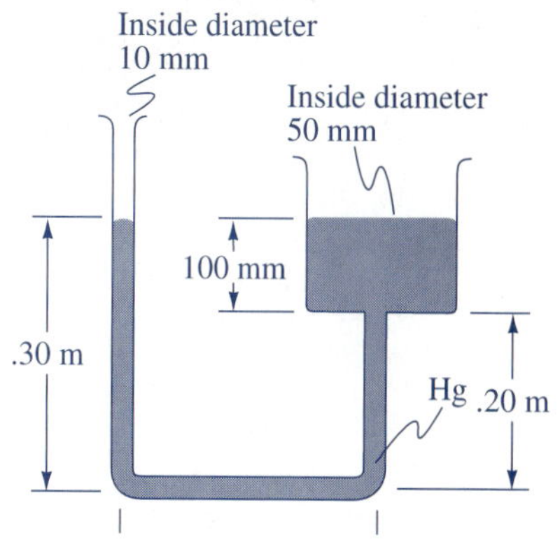

Figure P.19.53.

19.54. A stepped cylinder rides on a circular path. For small oscillations, what is the natural frequency? Take the radius of gyration about the geometric axis O as k and the weight of the cylinder as W.

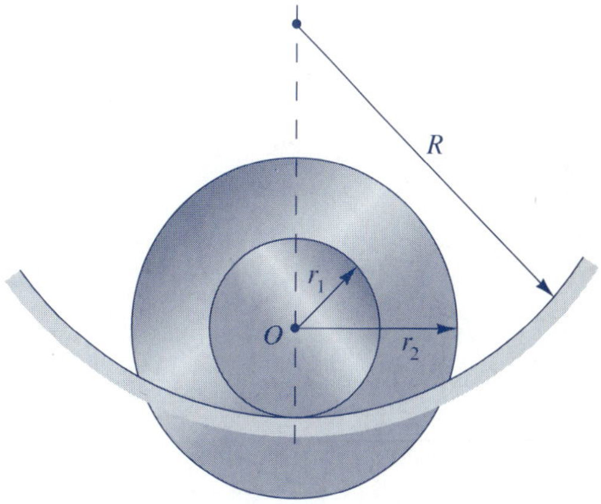

Figure P.19.54.

19.6 Linear Restoring Force and a Force Varying Sinusoidally with Time

We shall now consider the case of a sinusoidal force acting on a spring–mass system (Fig. 19.16) shown with stationary reference xy. The sinusoidal force has a frequency of ω (not to be confused with ω_n, the natural frequency) and an amplitude of F_0. At time $t = 0$, the mass will be assumed to have some known velocity and position, and we shall investigate the ensuing motion.

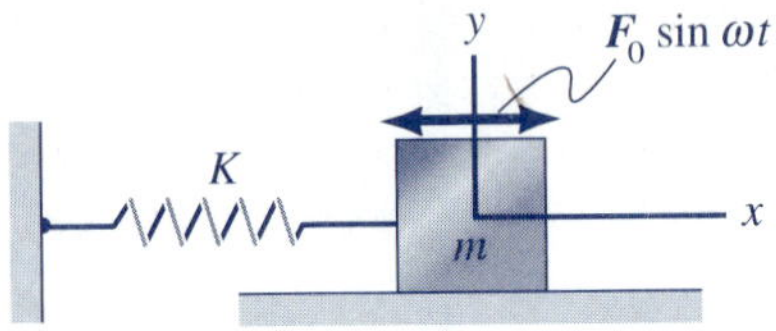

Figure 19.16. Spring–mass system with harmonic disturbance.

Measuring the position x from the unextended position of the spring, we have for *Newton's law*:

$$m\frac{d^2x}{dt^2} = -Kx + F_0 \sin \omega t \qquad (19.20)$$

Rearranging the equation so that the dependent variable and its derivatives are on the left-hand side and dividing through by m, we get the standard form:

$$\frac{d^2x}{dt^2} + \frac{K}{m}x = \frac{F_0}{m}\sin \omega t \qquad (19.21)$$

If the right-hand side is zero the equation is termed *homogeneous*. This was the equation studied in Section 19.5. If any function of t or constant appears on the right side, as in the case above, the equation is *nonhomogeneous*.

The general solution of a nonhomogeneous differential equation of this type is found by getting the general solution of the corresponding homogeneous equation and then finding a *particular solution* that satisfies the full equation. The sum of these solutions, then, is the general solution of the equation. Often, the solution for the homogeneous equation is termed the *complementary solution*.

In this case, we have already ascertained the complementary solution:

$$x_c = C_1 \sin\sqrt{\frac{K}{m}}t + C_2 \cos\sqrt{\frac{K}{m}}t \qquad (19.22)$$

To get a particular solution x_p, we can see by inspection that a function of the form $x_p = C_3 \sin \omega t$ will give a solution if the constant C_3 is chosen properly. Substituting this function into Eq. 19.21, we thus have

$$-C_3\omega^2 \sin \omega t + \frac{K}{m}C_3 \sin \omega t = \frac{F_0}{m}\cos \omega t$$

Clearly, the value of C_3 must be

$$C_3 = \frac{F_0/m}{K/m - \omega^2} \tag{19.23}$$

We can now express the general solution of the differential equation at hand:

$$x = C_1 \sin\sqrt{\frac{K}{m}}t + C_2 \cos\sqrt{\frac{K}{m}}t + \frac{F_0/m}{K/m - \omega^2}\sin\omega t \tag{19.24}$$

Note that there are two arbitrary constants which are determined from the initial conditions of the problem. Do not use the results of Eq. 19.6 for these constants, because we must now include the particular solution in ascertaining the constants. When $t = 0, x = x_0$ and $\dot{x} = \dot{x}_0$. We apply these conditions to Eq. 19.24:

$$\begin{aligned} x_0 &= C_2 \\ \dot{x}_0 &= C_1\sqrt{\frac{K}{m}} + \frac{F_0/m}{K/m - \omega^2}\,\omega \end{aligned} \tag{19.25}$$

Solving for the constants, we get

$$\begin{aligned} C_2 &= x_0 \\ C_1 &= \frac{\dot{x}_0}{\sqrt{K/m}} - \frac{\omega F_0/m}{(K/m - \omega^2)\sqrt{K/m}} \end{aligned} \tag{19.26}$$

Returning to Eq. 19.24, notice that we have the superposition of two harmonic motions—one with a frequency equal to $\sqrt{K/m}$, the natural frequency ω_n of the system, and the other with a frequency ω of the "driving function" (i.e., the nonhomogeneous part of the equation). The frequencies ω and ω_n are not the same in the general case. The phasor representation then leads us to the fact that since the rotating vectors have different angular speeds, the resulting motion cannot be represented by a single phasor, and hence the motion is not harmonic. The two parts of the motion are termed the *transient* part, corresponding to the complementary solution, and the *steady-state* part, corresponding to the particular solution, having frequencies ω_n and ω, respectively. With the introduction of friction (next section), we shall see that the transient part of the motion dies out while the steady state persists as long as there is a disturbance present.

Let us now consider the steady-state part of the motion in Eq. 19.24. Dividing numerator and denominator by K/m, we have for this motion, which we denote as x_p:

$$x_p = \frac{F_0/K}{1-(\omega^2 m/K)}\sin\omega t = \frac{F_0/K}{1-(\omega/\omega_n)^2}\sin\omega t \tag{19.27}$$

It will be useful to study with respect to ω/ω_n the variation of the magnitude of the steady-state amplitude x_p for $F_0/K = 1$, namely

$$\left|\frac{1}{1-(\omega/\omega_n)^2}\right|$$

shown plotted in Fig. 19.17. As the forcing frequency approaches the natural frequency, this term goes to infinity, and thus the amplitude of the forced vibration approaches infinity. This is the condition of *resonance*. Under such circumstances, friction, which we neglect here but which is always present, will limit the amplitude. Also, when very large amplitudes are developed, the properties of the restoring element do not remain linear, so that the theory which predicts infinite amplitudes is inapplicable. Thus, the linear, frictionless formulations cannot yield correct amplitudes at resonance in real problems. The condition of resonance, however, does indicate that large amplitudes are to be expected. Furthermore, these amplitudes can be dangerous, because large force concentrations will be present in parts of the restoring system as well as in the moving body and may result in disastrous failures. It is therefore important in most situations to avoid resonance. If a disturbance corresponding to the natural frequency is present and cannot be eliminated, we may find it necessary to change either the stiffness or the mass of a system in order to avoid resonance.

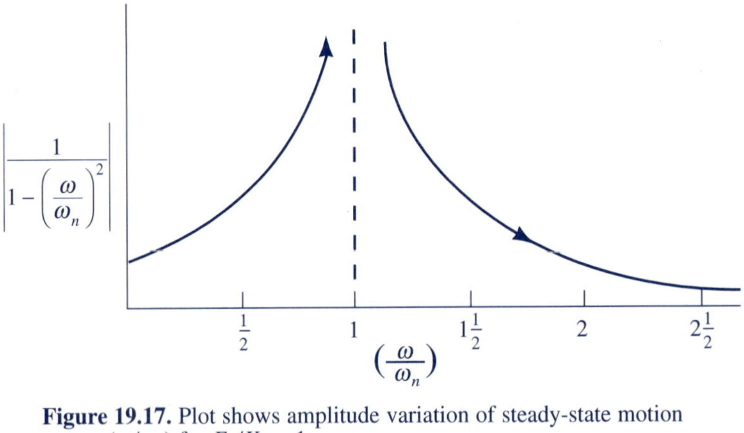

Figure 19.17. Plot shows amplitude variation of steady-state motion versus (ω/ω_n) for $F_0/K = 1$.

From Fig. 19.17 we can conclude that the amplitude will become small as the frequency of the disturbance becomes very high. Also, considering the amplitude C_3 for steady-state motion (Eq. 19.23), we see that below resonance the sign of this expression is positive, and above resonance it is negative, indicating that below resonance the motion is in *phase* with the *disturbance* and above resonance the motion is directly 180° *out of phase* with the *disturbance*.

Example 19.7

A motor mounted on springs is constrained by the rollers to move only in the vertical direction (Fig. 19.18). The assembly weighs 2.6 kN and when placed carefully on the springs causes a deflection of 2.5 mm. Because of an unbalance in the rotor, a disturbance results that is approximately sinusoidal in the vertical direction with a frequency equal to the angular speed of the rotor. The amplitude of this disturbance is 130 N when the motor is rotating at 1,720 rpm. What is the steady-state motion of this system under these circumstances if we neglect the mass of the springs, the friction, and the inertia of the rollers?

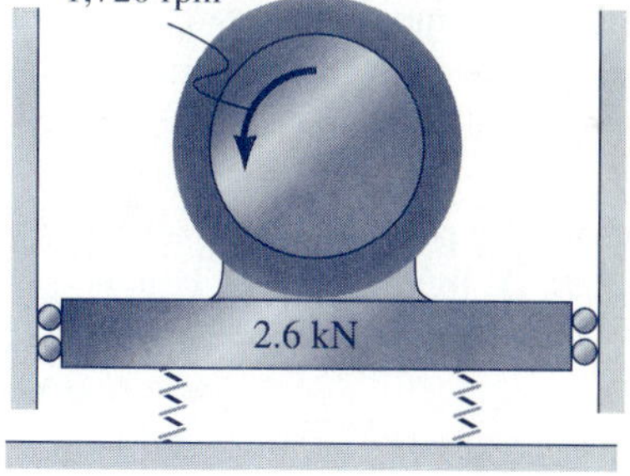

Figure 19.18. Motor with unbalanced rotor.

The spring constant for the system is

$$K = \frac{2{,}600}{2.5} = 1{,}040 \text{ N/mm} = 1.040 \times 10^6 \text{ N/m}$$

and the natural frequency becomes

$$\omega_n = \sqrt{\frac{1.040 \times 10^6}{2{,}600/9.81}}$$
$$= 62.6 \text{ rad/sec} = 9.97 \text{ cycles/sec}$$

The steady-state motion is

$$x_p = \frac{F_0/K}{1-(\omega/\omega_n)^2} \sin \omega t$$
$$= \frac{130/(1.040 \times 10^6)}{1-[1{,}720/(60)(9.97)]^2} \sin \frac{1{,}720}{60}(2\pi)t$$
$$= -1.720 \times 10^{-5} \sin 180.1t \text{ m}$$

$$x_p = -.01720 \sin 180.1t \text{ mm}$$

Note that the driving frequency is above the natural frequency. In starting up motors and turbines, we must sometimes go through a natural frequency of the system, and it is wise to get through this zone as quickly as possible to prevent large amplitudes from building up.

Example 19.8

A mass on a spring is shown in Fig. 19.19. The support of the spring at x' is made to move with harmonic motion in the vertical direction by some external agent. This motion is expressed as $a \sin \omega t$. If at $t = 0$ the mass is displaced in a downward position a distance of 1 in. from the static equilibrium position and if it has at this instant a speed downward of 3 in./sec, what is the position of the mass at $t = 5$ sec? Take $a = 5$ in., $\omega = 10$ rad/sec, $K = 500$ lb/ft, and $m = 1$ slug.

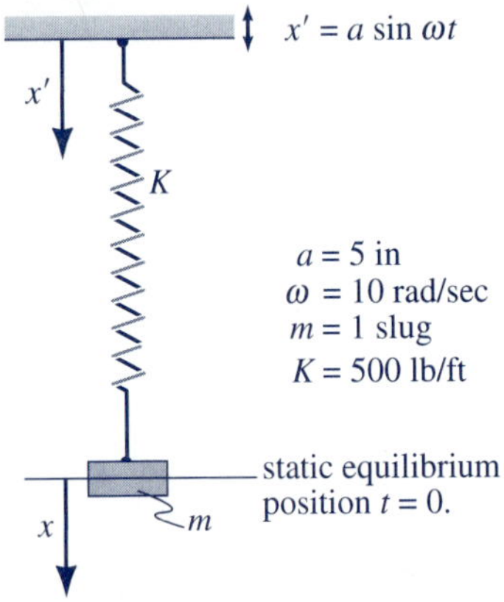

Figure 19.19. Spring–mass system with disturbance.

Let us express **Newton's law** for the mass. Note that the extension of the spring is $x-x'$. Hence,

$$m\frac{d^2x}{dt^2} = -K(x - x')$$

Replacing x' by the known function of time, we get, upon rearranging the terms:

$$\frac{d^2x}{dt^2} + \frac{K}{m}x = \frac{Ka}{m}\sin \omega t$$

This is the same form as Eq. 19.21 for the case where the disturbance is exerted on the mass directly. The solution, then, is

$$x = C_1 \sin \sqrt{\frac{K}{m}}t + C_2 \cos \sqrt{\frac{K}{m}}t + \frac{a}{1 - (\omega/\sqrt{K/m})^2}\sin \omega t$$

Putting in the numerical values of $\sqrt{K/m}$, etc., we have

$$x = C_1 \sin 22.4t + C_2 \cos 22.4t + 6.24 \sin 10t \text{ in.}$$

Example 19.8 (Continued)

Now impose the initial conditions to get

$$1 = C_2$$
$$3 = 22.4C_1 + (6.24)(10)$$

Therefore,

$$C_1 = -2.65$$

The motion, then, is given as

$$x = -2.65 \sin 22.4t + \cos 22.4t + 6.24 \sin 10t \text{ in.}$$

When $t = 5$ sec, the position of the mass relative to the lower datum is given as

$$(x)_5 = -2.65 \sin(22.4)(5) + \cos(22.4)(5) + 6.24 \sin 50 = \boxed{1.177 \text{ in.}}$$

You may approximate the setup of this problem profitably with an elastic band supporting a small body as shown in Fig. 19.20. By oscillating the free end of the band with varying frequency from low frequency to high frequency, you can demonstrate the rapid change of phase between the disturbance and the excited motion as you pass through resonance. Thus, at low frequencies both motions will be in phase and at frequencies well above resonance the motion will be close to being 180° out of phase. Without friction this change, according to the mathematics, is discontinuous, but with the presence of friction (i.e., in a real case) there is actually a smooth, although sometimes rapid, transition between both extremes.

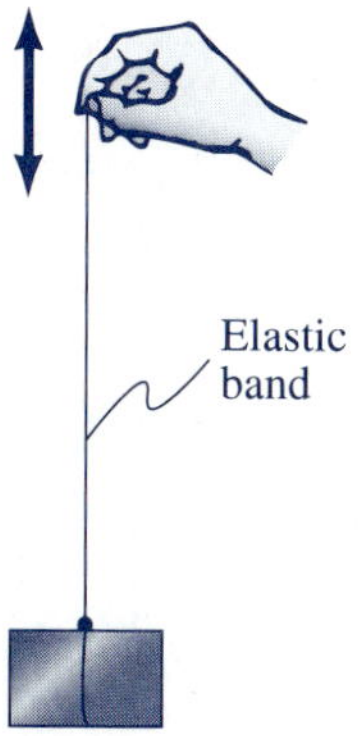

Figure 19.20. Simple resonance and change of phase demonstration.

PROBLEMS

19.55. A mass is held by three springs. Assume that the rolling friction on the floor is negligible, as are the inertial effects of the rollers. The spring constants are:

$$K_1 = 30 \text{ lb/in.}$$

$$K_2 = 20 \text{ lb/in.}$$

$$K_3 = 10 \text{ lb/in.}$$

A sinusoidal force having an amplitude of 5 lb and a frequency of $10/\pi$ cycles/sec acts on the body in the direction of the springs. What is the steady-state amplitude of the motion of the body?

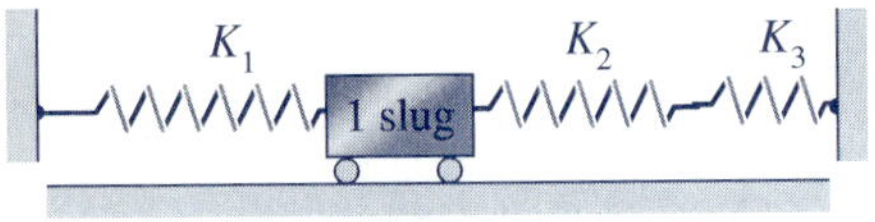

Figure P.19.55.

19.56. In Problem 19.55, the initial conditions are:

(a) The initial position of the body is 3 in. to the right of the static-equilibrium position.

(b) The initial velocity is zero.

(c) At $t = 0$, the sinusoidal disturbing force has a value of 5 lb in the positive direction.

Find the position of the body after 3 sec.

19.57. A sinusoidal force, with amplitude F of 22 N and frequency $1/2\pi$ cycles/sec, acts on a body having a mass of 22 kg. Meanwhile, the wall moves with a motion given as 8 cos t mm. For a spring constant $K = 8.8$ N/mm, what is the amplitude of the steady-state motion? There is no friction.

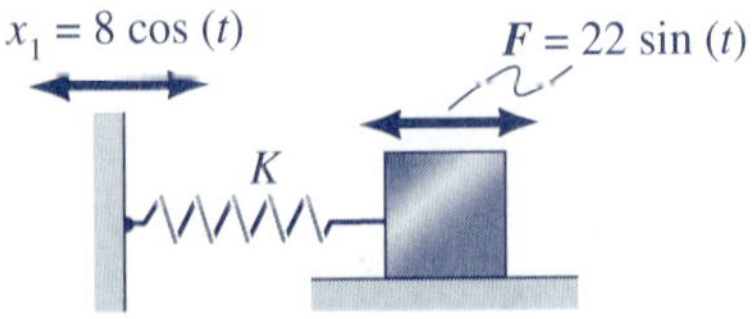

Figure P.19.57.

19.58. In Problem 19.57, suppose that the disturbing force F is 22 sin $(t + \pi/4)$. What is the amplitude of the steady-state motion?

19.59. A torque $T = A \sin \omega t$ is applied to the disc. Express the solution for the transient torsional motion and the steady-state torsional motion in terms of arbitrary constants of integration. Take the shear modulus of elasticity of the shaft as G [*Hint:* Recall that K_t for a shaft is GJ/L.]

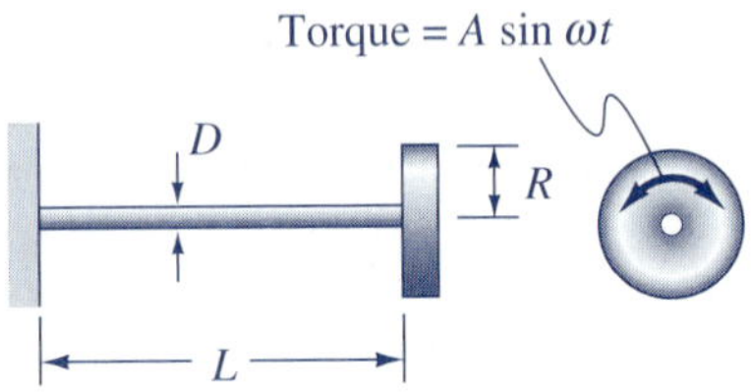

Figure P.19.59.

19.60. A *vibrograph* is a device for measuring the amplitude of vibration in a given direction. The apparatus is bolted to the machine to be tested. A seismic mass M in the vibrograph rides along a rod CD under constraint of a linear spring of spring constant K. If the machine being tested has a harmonic motion $\bar{x}$ of frequency ω in the direction of C–D, then M will have a steady-state oscillatory frequency also of frequency ω. The motion of M relative to the vibrograph is given as x' and is recorded on the rotating drum. Show that the amplitude of motion of the machine is

$$\left| \frac{(\omega/\omega_n)^2 - 1}{(\omega/\omega_n)^2} \right|$$

times the amplitude of the recorded motion x', where $\omega_n = \sqrt{K/M}$.

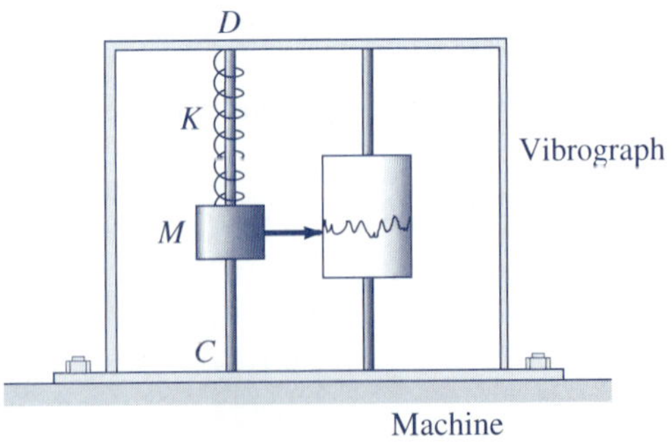

Figure P.19.60.

19.61. A vibrograph is attached rigidly to a diesel engine for which we want to know the vibration amplitude. If the seismic spring-mass system has a natural frequency of 10 cycles/sec, and if the seismic mass vibrates relative to the vibrograph with an amplitude of 1.27 mm when the diesel is turning over at 1,000 rpm, what is the amplitude of vibration of the diesel in the direction of the vibrograph? The seismic mass weighs 4.5 N. See Problem 19.60 before doing this problem.

19.62. Explain how you could devise an instrument to measure torsional vibrations of a shaft in a manner analogous to the way the vibrograph measures linear vibrations of a machine. Such instruments are in wide use and are called *torsiographs*. What would be the relation of the amplitude of oscillations as picked up by your apparatus to that of the shaft being measured? See Problem 19.60 before doing this problem.

19.63. A trailer of weight W moves over a washboard road at a constant speed V to the right. The road is approximated by a sinusoid of amplitude A and wavelength L. If the wheel B is small, the center of the wheel will have a motion x closely resembling the aforementioned sinusoid. If the trailer is connected to the wheel through a linear spring of stiffness K, formulate the steady-state equation of motion x' for the trailer. List all assumptions. What speed causes resonance?

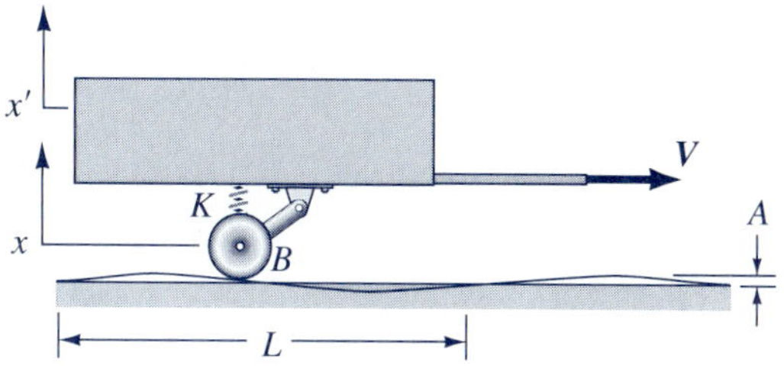

Figure P.19.63.

19.64. In Problem 19.63, compute the amplitude of motion of the trailer for the following data:

$$W = 5.34 \text{ kN}$$

$$V = 16 \text{ km/hr}$$

$$K = 43.8 \text{ N/mm}$$

$$L = 10 \text{ m}$$

$$A = 100 \text{ mm}$$

What is the resonance speed V_{res} for this case? From Problem 19.63, we have

$$x'_p = \frac{A}{\left|1 - (2\pi V/L)^2 (W/gK)\right|} \sin \frac{2\pi Vt}{L}$$

19.65. A cantilever beam of length L has an electric motor A weighing 100 N fastened to the end. The tip of the cantilever beam descends 12 mm when the motor is attached. If the *center of mass* of the armature of the motor is a distance 2 mm from the axis of rotation of the motor, what is the amplitude of vibration of the motor when it is rotating at 1,750 rpm? The armature weighs 40 N. Neglect the mass of the beam.

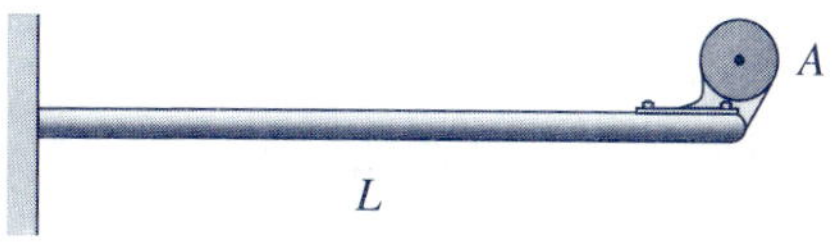

Figure P.19.65.

19.66. Suppose that a 2-N block is glued to the top of the motor in Problem 19.65, where the maximum strength of the bond is ½ N. At what minimum angular speed ω of the motor will the block fly off?

19.67. An important reason for mounting rotating and reciprocating machinery on springs is to decrease the transmission of vibration to the foundation supporting the machine. Show that the amplitude of force transmitted to the ground, F_{TR}, for such cases is

$$F_0 \left| \frac{1}{1 - (\omega/\omega_n)^2} \right|$$

where F_0 is the disturbing force from the machine. The factor $|1/[1 - (\omega/\omega_n)^2]|$ is called the *relative transmission factor*. Show that, unless the springs are soft, $(\omega_n < \omega/\sqrt{2})$, the use of springs actually increases the transmission of vibratory forces to the foundation.

19.68. In Example 19.7, what is the amplitude of the force transmitted to the foundation? What must K of the spring system be to decrease the amplitude by one-half? See Problem 19.67.

19.69. A machine weighing W N contains a reciprocating mass of weight w N having a vertical motion relative to the machine given approximately as $x' = A \sin \omega t$. The machine is mounted on springs having a total spring constant K. This machine is guided so that it can move only in the vertical direction. What is the differential equation of motion for this machine? What is the formulation for the amplitude of the machine for steady-state operation?

19.70. A mass M of .5 kg is suspended from a stiff rod AB via a spring whose spring constant K is 100 N/m. The end of rod AB is given a vertical sinusoidal motion $\delta_A = 2 \sin 14t$ mm, with t in seconds. What is the maximum force on the rod at C long after the motion has started?

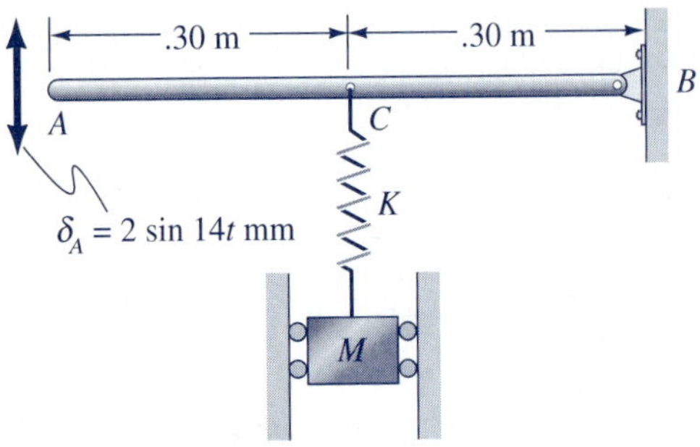

Figure P.19.70.

19.71. In Problem 19.70, what range of frequencies of the motion δ_A must be excluded to keep the maximum force at C less than 7 N? Consider only steady-state motion. [*Hint:* Note that below resonance disturbance and motion are in phase whereas above resonance they are 180° out of phase. Therefore, x_p in Eq. 19.27 will be positive below resonance and negative above resonance.]

19.72. A bob B of weight W is suspended from a vehicle A which is made to have a motion $x_A = \delta \sin \omega t$. If δ is very small, what should ω be so that bob B has an amplitude of motion equal to 1.5δ?

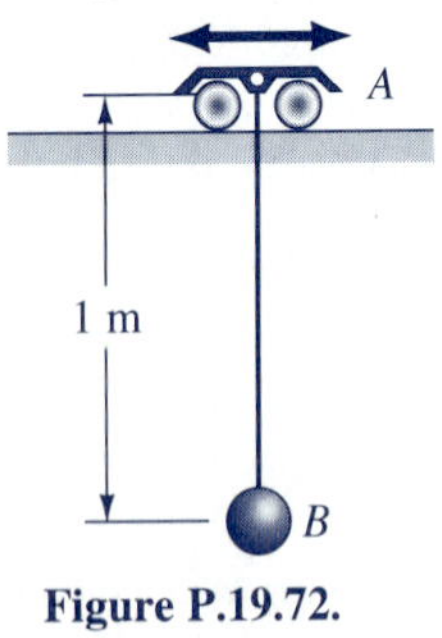

Figure P.19.72.

19.73. wo spheres each of mass $M = 2$ kg are welded to a light rod that is pinned at B. A second light rod AC is welded to the first rod. At A we apply a disturbance $F_o \sin \omega t$. At the other end C, there is a restraining spring which is unstretched when AC is horizontal. If the amplitude of steady-state rotation of the system is to be kept below .02 rad, what ranges of frequencies ω are permitted? The following data apply:

$$l = 300 \text{ mm}$$
$$K = 7.0 \text{ N/mm}$$
$$F_o = 10 \text{ N}$$
$$a = 100 \text{ mm}$$

See the hint in Problem 19.71.

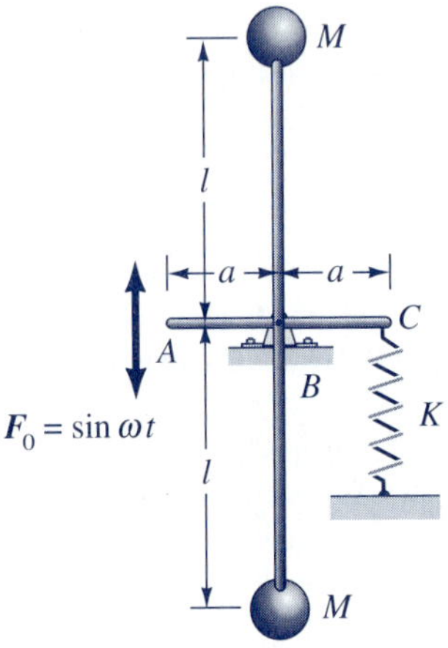

Figure P.19.73.

19.74. In Problem 19.73, what is the angle of rotation of the system 10 sec after the application of the sinusoidal load? The system is stationary at time $t = 0$. Take $\omega = 13$ rad/sec.

19.75 A rod of length L and weight W is suspended from a light support at A. This support is given a movement $x_A = \delta \sin \omega t$, where δ is very small compared to L. At what frequency, ω, should A be moved if the amplitude of motion of tip, B, is to be 1.5δ?

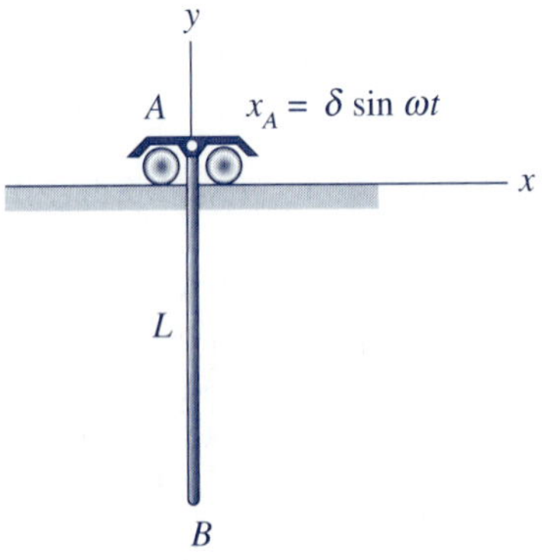

Figure P.19.75.

19.7 Linear Restoring Force with Viscous Damping

We shall now consider the case in which a special type of friction is present. In the chapters on statics, you will recall, we considered coulombic or dry friction for the cases of sliding and impending motion. This force was proportional to the normal force at the interface of contact and dependent on the material of the bodies. At this time, we shall consider the case of bodies separated from each other by a thin film of fluid. The frictional force (called a *damping* force) is independent of the material of the bodies but depends on the nature of the fluid and is proportional for a given fluid to the relative velocity of the two bodies separated by the film. Thus,

$$f = -c\left(\frac{dx}{dt}\right)_{\text{rel}} \tag{19.28}$$

where c is called the *coefficient of damping*. The minus sign indicates that the frictional force opposes the motion (i.e, the friction force must always have a sign opposite to that of the relative velocity).

In Fig. 19.21 is shown the spring-mass model with damping present. We shall investigate possible motions consistent with a set of given initial conditions. The differential equation of motion is

$$m\frac{d^2x}{dt^2} = -Kx - c\frac{dx}{dt}$$

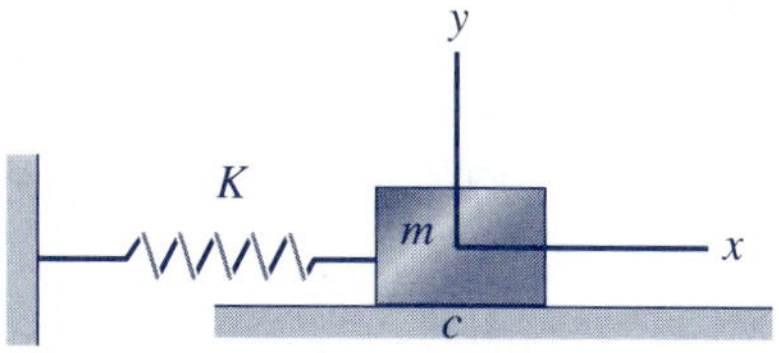

Figure 19.21. Spring–mass system with damping.

In standard form, we get

$$\frac{d^2x}{dt^2} + \frac{c}{m}\frac{dx}{dt} + \frac{K}{m}x = 0 \tag{19.29}$$

This is a homogeneous, second-order, differential equation with constant coefficients. We shall expect two independent functions with two arbitrary constants to form the general solution to this equation. Because of the presence of the first derivative in the equation, we cannot use sines or cosines for trial solutions, since the first derivative changes their form and prevents a cancellation of the time function. Instead, we use e^{pt} where p is determined so as to satisfy the equation. Thus, let

$$x = C_1e^{pt}$$

Substituting, we get

$$C_1 p^2 e^{pt} + \frac{c}{m} C_1 p e^{pt} + \frac{K}{m} C_1 e^{pt} = 0$$

Canceling out $C_1 e^{pt}$, we get

$$p^2 + \frac{c}{m} p + \frac{K}{m} = 0$$

Solving for p, we write

$$p = \frac{-c/m \pm \sqrt{(c/m)^2 - 4K/m}}{2} = -\frac{c}{2m} \pm \sqrt{\left(\frac{c}{2m}\right)^2 - \frac{K}{m}} \qquad (19.30)$$

It will be helpful to consider three cases here.

Case A

$$\frac{c}{2m} > \sqrt{\frac{K}{m}}$$

Here the value p is *real*. Using both possible values of p and employing C_1 and C_2 as arbitrary constants, we get

$$x = C_1 \exp\left\{\left[-c/2m + \sqrt{(c/2m)^2 - K/m}\right]t\right\} + C_2 \exp\left\{\left[-(c/2m) - \sqrt{(c/2m)^2 - K/m}\right]t\right\} \qquad (19.31)$$

Rearranging terms in Eq. 19.31 we get the following standard form of solution:

$$x = \exp[-(c/2m)t]\left\{C_1 \exp\left[\sqrt{(c/2m)^2 - K/m}\, t\right] + C_2 \exp\left[-\sqrt{(c/2m)^2 - K/m}\, t\right]\right\} \qquad (19.32)$$

Since $c/m > \sqrt{(c/2m)^2 - K/m}$, we see from Eq. 19.32 that the first exponential dominates and so as the time t increases, the motion can only be that of an exponential of *decreasing* amplitude. Thus, there can be no oscillation. The motion is illustrated in Fig. 19.22 and is called *overdamped* motion.

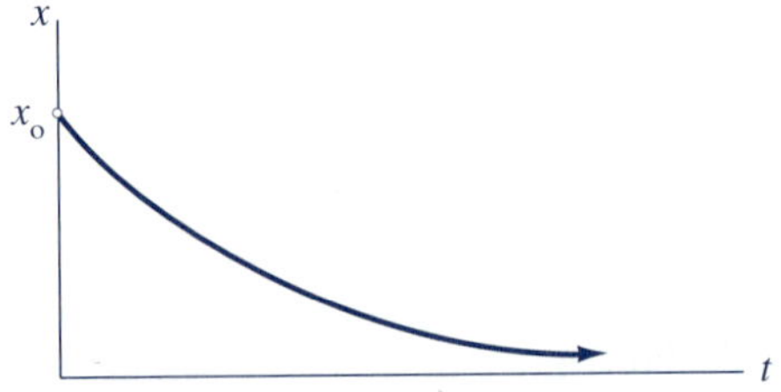

Figure 19.22. Overdamped motion.

Case B

$$\frac{c}{2m} < \sqrt{\frac{K}{m}}$$

This means that we have a negative quantity under the root in Eq. 19.30. Extracting $\sqrt{-1} = i$, we can then write p as follows:

$$p = -\frac{c}{2m} \pm i\sqrt{\frac{K}{m} - \left(\frac{c}{2m}\right)^2}$$

The solution then becomes

$$x = \exp[-(c/2m)t]\Big\{C_1 \exp\Big[i\sqrt{K/m - (c/2m)^2}\, t\Big] + C_2 \exp\Big[-i\sqrt{K/m - (c/2m)^2}\, t\Big]\Big\} \tag{19.33}$$

From complex-number theory, we know that $e^{i\theta}$ may be replaced by $\cos\theta + i\sin\theta$ and thus the equation above can be put in the form

$$x = \exp[-(c/2m)t]\left\{C_1\left[\cos\sqrt{\frac{K}{m} - \left(\frac{c}{2m}\right)^2}\,t + i\sin\sqrt{\frac{K}{m} - \left(\frac{c}{2m}\right)^2}\,t\right] + C_2\left[\cos\sqrt{\frac{K}{m} - \left(\frac{c}{2m}\right)^2}\,t - i\sin\sqrt{\frac{K}{m} - \left(\frac{c}{2m}\right)^2}\,t\right]\right\} \tag{19.34}$$

Collecting terms and replacing sums and differences of arbitrary constants including i by other arbitrary constants, we get the result:

$$x = \exp[-(c/2m)t]\left[C_3\cos\sqrt{\frac{K}{m} - \left(\frac{c}{2m}\right)^2}\,t + C_4\sin\sqrt{\frac{K}{m} - \left(\frac{c}{2m}\right)^2}\,t\right] \tag{19.35}$$

The quantity in brackets represents a harmonic motion which has a frequency less than the free undamped natural frequency of the system. The exponential term to the left of the brackets, then, serves to decrease continually the amplitude of this motion. A plot of the displacement against time for this case is illustrated in Fig. 19.23, where the upper dashed envelope corresponds in form to the exponential function $e^{-(c/2m)t}$. We call this motion *underdamped* motion.

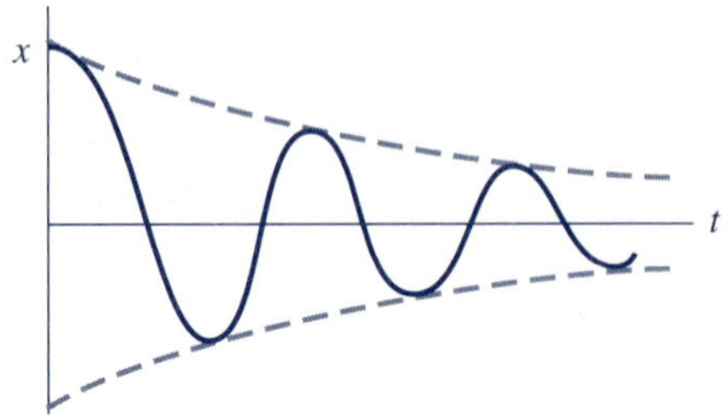

Figure 19.23. Underdamped motion.

Case C

$$\frac{c}{2m} = \sqrt{\frac{K}{m}}$$

Since this is the dividing line between the overdamped case and one in which oscillation is possible, the motion is termed a *critically damped motion*. We have here *identical* roots for p given as

$$p = -\frac{c}{2m} \tag{19.36}$$

and accordingly for such a case the general solution to Eq. 19.29 according to the theory of differential equation is then

$$x = (C_1 + C_2 t)e^{-(c/2m)t} \tag{19.37}$$

First we see from this equation that we do *not* have an oscillatory motion. Also, you will recall from the calculus that as t goes to infinity an exponential of the form e^{-At}, with A a positive constant, goes to zero faster than Ct goes to infinity. Accordingly, Fig. 19.22 can be used to picture the plot of x versus t for this case.

The damping constant for this case is called the *critical* damping constant and is denoted as c_{cr}. The value of c_{cr} clearly is

$$c_{cr} = 2\sqrt{Km} \tag{19.38}$$

It should be clear that, for a damping constant less than c_{cr}, we will have underdamped motion while for a damping constant greater than c_{cr} we will have overdamped motion.

In all the preceding cases for damped free vibration, the remaining step for a complete evaluation of the solution is to compute the arbitrary constants from the initial conditions of the particular problem. Note that in discussing damped motion we shall consider the "natural frequency" of the system to be that of the corresponding *undamped* case and shall refer to the actual frequency of the motion as the frequency of free, damped motion.

Example 19.9

Springs and dashpots are used in packaging delicate equipment in crating so that during transit the equipment will be protected from shocks. In Fig. 19.24, we have shown a piece of equipment whose weight W is 500 N. It is supported in a crate by one spring and two dashpots (or shock absorbers). The value of K for the spring is 30 N/mm and the coefficient of damping, c, is 1 N/mm/sec for each dashpot. The crate is held above a rigid floor at a height h of 150 mm. It is then released and allowed to hit the floor in a plastic impact. What is the maximum deflection of W relative to the crate?

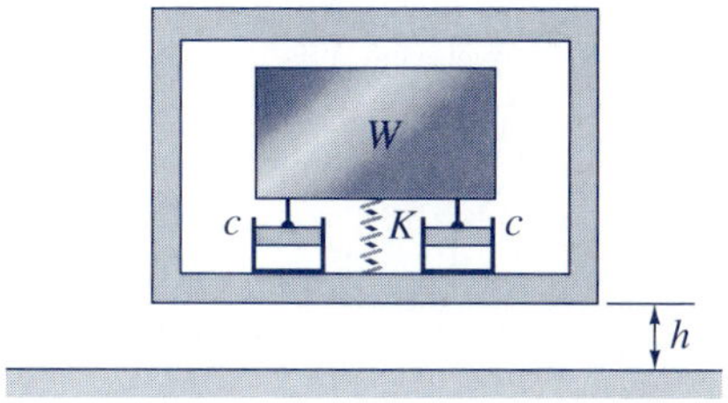

Figure 19.24. Packaging to reduce breakage.

As a first step, we compute the *critical damping* to find what regime we are in.

$$\begin{aligned} c_{cr} &= 2\sqrt{Km} = 2\sqrt{(30)(1{,}000)(500)/g} \\ &= 2{,}473 \text{ N/m/sec} \end{aligned} \tag{a}$$

The total damping coefficient for our case is

$$c_{total} = (2)(1)(1{,}000) = 2{,}000 \text{ N/m/sec}$$

We are therefore *underdamped*. The motion is then given as follows:

$$x = e^{-(c/2m)t}\left[C_3 \cos\sqrt{\frac{K}{m} - \left(\frac{c}{2m}\right)^2}\,t + C_4 \sin\sqrt{\frac{K}{m} - \left(\frac{c}{2m}\right)^2}\,t\right] \tag{b}$$

Note that

$$\frac{c}{2m} = \frac{2{,}000}{(2)(500)/9.81} = 19.62 \text{ sec}$$

$$\frac{K}{m} = \frac{(30)(1{,}000)}{500/9.81} = 589 \text{ sec}^{-2}$$

Example 19.9 (Continued)

Hence,

$$x = e^{-19.62t}(C_3 \cos 14.27t + C_4 \sin 14.27t) \quad \text{(c)}$$

When $t = 0$, at the instant of impact, take

$$x = 0 \quad \text{and} \quad \dot{x} = \sqrt{2gh} = \sqrt{(2)(9.81)(.15)} = 1.716 \text{ m/sec}$$

The first condition renders $C_3 = 0$. For the second condition, note first that

$$\dot{x} = e^{-19.62t}[C_4(14.27)14.27t] - 19.62e^{-19.62t}(C_4 \sin 14.27t)$$

For the second condition ($\dot{x} = 1.716$ at $t = 0$) we get

$$1.716 = C_4(14.27)$$

Therefore,

$$C_4 = .1202$$

Thus, we have for x:

$$x = .1202e^{-19.62t} \sin 14.27t \quad \text{(d)}$$

$$\dot{x} = e^{-19.62t}(1.716 \cos 14.27t - 2.358 \sin 14.27t) \quad \text{(e)}$$

Set $\dot{x} = 0$ and solve for t in order to get the maximum deflection of W.

$$1.716 \cos 14.27t - 2.358 \sin 14.27t = 0$$

Therefore,

$$\tan 14.27t = .7274$$

The smallest t satisfying the equation above is

$$t = .0441 \text{ sec}$$

The value of x for this time is from Eq. (d):

$$x = .1202e^{-(19.62)(.0441)} \sin[14.27(.0441)]$$

$$x = .0298 \text{ m} = 29.8 \text{ mm}$$

Hence, W moves a maximum distance of 29.8 mm downward after impact.

Example 19.10

A block W of 200 N (see Fig. 19.25) moves on a film of oil which is .1 mm in thickness under the block. The area of the bottom surface of the block is 2×10^4 mm^2. The spring constant K is 2 N/m. If the weight is pulled in the x direction and released, what is the nature of the motion?

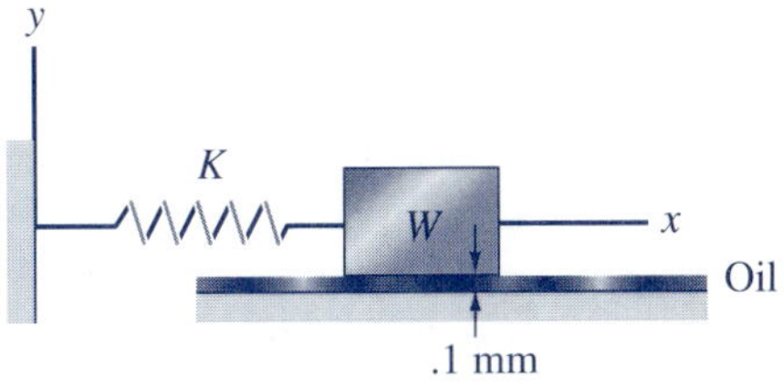

Figure 19.25. Spring–mass on film of oil.

You may have learned in physics that friction force per unit area (i.e., shear stress) on the block W from the oil is given by **Newton's viscosity law** as:

$$\tau = \mu\left(\frac{\partial V}{\partial y}\right)_{\text{block}} \qquad \text{(a)}$$

where τ is the shear stress (force per unit area), μ is the *coefficient of viscosity* (not to be confused with the coefficient of friction), and $\partial V/\partial y$ is the slope of the velocity profile at the block surface (see Fig. 19.26). Now the oil will stick to the surfaces of the block W and the ground surface. And so

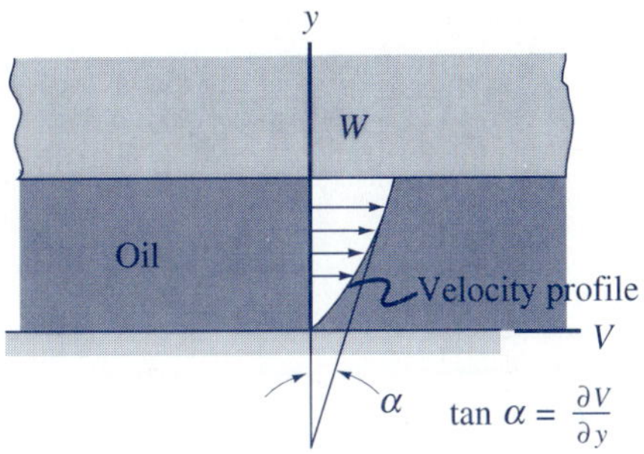

Figure 19.26. Slope of velocity profile at bottom of W.

Example 19.10 (Continued)

we can approximate the velocity profile as shown in Fig. 19.27, where we have used a straight-line profile connecting zero velocity at the bottom and velocity $\dot{x}$ of the block W at the top. Such a procedure gives good results when the film of oil is thin as in the present case. The desired slope $(\partial V/\partial y)_{\text{block}}$ is then approximated as

$$\left(\frac{\partial V}{\partial y}\right)_{\text{block}} = \frac{\dot{x}}{.0001} \tag{b}$$

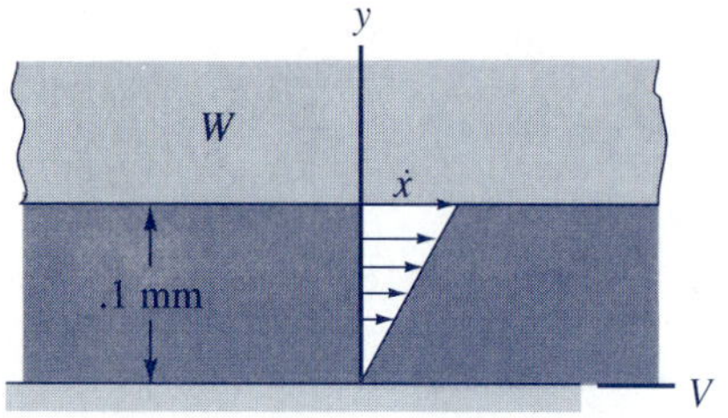

Figure 19.27. Approximate velocity profile.

The coefficient of viscosity can be found in handbooks. For our case, let us say that $\mu = .0080$ N-sec/m^2.

It is now an easy matter to compute the coefficient of damping c. Thus, the friction force is

$$f = \tau A = -\left[(.0080)\left(\frac{\dot{x}}{.0001}\right)\right](2 \times 10^4/10^6) = -1.600\dot{x} \text{ N} \tag{c}$$

Thus, $c = 1.600$. The critical damping for the problem is

$$c_{\text{cr}} = 2\sqrt{Km} = 2\sqrt{(2)\left(\frac{200}{g}\right)} = 12.77$$

Thus, motion clearly will be *underdamped*. The frequency of oscillation is then

$$\omega = \sqrt{\frac{K}{m} - \left(\frac{c}{2m}\right)^2}$$

$$= \sqrt{\frac{2}{200/g} - \left[\frac{1.600}{(2)(200)/g}\right]^2}$$

$$\omega = .311 \text{ rad/sec} = .0495 \text{ cycles/sec}$$

*19.8 Linear Restoring Force, Viscous Damping, and a Harmonic Disturbance

In the spring-mass problem shown in Fig. 19.28 we include driving function $F_0 \cos \omega t$ along with viscous damping. The differential equation in the standard form then becomes

$$\frac{d^2x}{dt^2} + \frac{c}{m}\frac{dx}{dt} + \frac{K}{m}x = \frac{F_0}{m}\cos \omega t \tag{19.39}$$

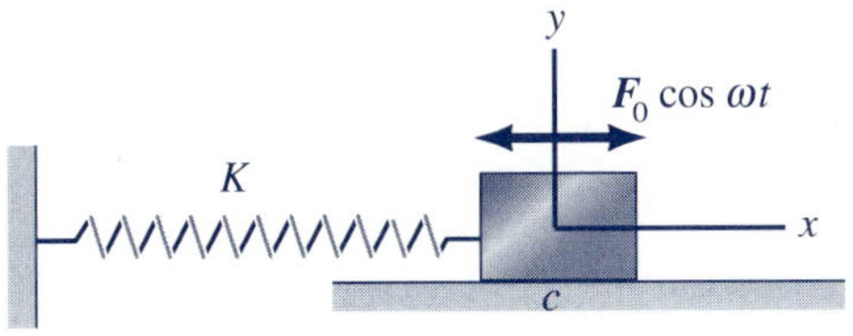

Figure 19.28. Spring–mass system with damping.

Equation 19.39 is a nonhomogeneous equation. The general solution will be the homogeneous solution worked out in Section 19.7, plus any particular solution of Eq. 19.39.

Because there is a first derivative on the left side of the equation, we cannot expect a particular solution of the form $D \cos \omega t$ to satisfy the differential equation. Instead, from the method of *undetermined coefficients* we shall try the following:

$$x_p = D \sin \omega t + E \cos \omega t \tag{19.40}$$

The constants D and E are to be adjusted to facilitate a solution. Substituting into the differential equation, we write

$$-D\omega^2 \sin \omega t - E\omega^2 \cos \omega t + \frac{c}{m}\omega D \cos \omega t - \frac{c}{m}\omega E \sin \omega t$$
$$+ \frac{K}{m} D \sin \omega t + \frac{K}{m} E \cos \omega t = \frac{F_0}{m}\cos \omega t$$

Collecting the terms, we have

$$\left(-D\omega^2 - \frac{c}{m}\omega E + \frac{K}{m}D\right)\sin \omega t + \left(-\frac{F_0}{m} - E\omega^2 + \frac{c}{m}\omega D + \frac{K}{m}E\right)\cos \omega t = 0$$

We set each coefficient of the time functions equal to zero and thus get two simultaneous equations in the unknowns E and D:

$$-D\omega^2 - \frac{\omega c}{m}E + \frac{K}{m}D = 0$$
$$-\frac{F_0}{m} - E\omega^2 + \frac{\omega c}{m}D + \frac{K}{m}E = 0$$

Rearranging and replacing K/m by $\omega_n{}^2$, we get

$$D\left(\omega^2 - \omega_n^2\right) + E\left(\frac{\omega c}{m}\right) = 0$$

$$D\left(-\frac{\omega c}{m}\right) + E\left(\omega^2 - \omega_n^2\right) = -\frac{F_0}{m}$$

Using Cramer's rule, we see that the constants D and E become

$$D = \frac{\begin{vmatrix} 0 & \omega c/m \\ -F_0/m & \omega^2 - \omega_n^2 \end{vmatrix}}{\begin{vmatrix} \omega^2 - \omega_n^2 & \omega c/m \\ -\omega c/m & \omega^2 - \omega_n^2 \end{vmatrix}} = \frac{(F_0/m)(\omega c/m)}{(\omega^2 - \omega_n^2)^2 + (\omega c/m)^2}$$

$$E = \frac{\begin{vmatrix} \omega^2 - \omega_n^2 & 0 \\ -\omega c/m & -F_0/m \end{vmatrix}}{\begin{vmatrix} \omega^2 - \omega_n^2 & \omega c/m \\ -\omega c/m & \omega^2 - \omega_n^2 \end{vmatrix}} = \frac{(F_0/m)(\omega_n^2 - \omega^2)}{(\omega^2 - \omega_n^2)^2 + (\omega c/m)^2}$$

The entire solution can then be given as

$$x = x_c + \frac{(F_0/m)(\omega_n^2 - \omega^2)}{(\omega^2 - \omega_n^2)^2 + (\omega c/m)^2} \cos \omega t + \frac{F_0 \omega c/m^2}{(\omega^2 - \omega_n^2)^2 + (\omega c/m)^2} \sin \omega t \qquad (19.41)$$

The constants of integration are present in the complementary solution x_c and are determined by the initial condition to which the *entire* solution given above is subject.

The complementary solution here is a *transient* in the true sense of the word, because it dies out in the manner explained in Section 19.7. The particular solution is a harmonic motion with the same frequency as the disturbance. Only the amplitude of this motion is affected by the damping present. Note that, mathematically, the amplitude of the steady-state motion cannot become infinite with damping present unless F_0 becomes infinite.

We now write the steady-state solution in the following way:

$$x_p = \frac{(F_0/m)(\omega_n^2 - \omega^2)}{(\omega^2 - \omega_n^2)^2 + (\omega c/m)^2} \cos \omega t + \frac{(F_0/m)(\omega c/m)}{(\omega^2 - \omega_n^2)^2 + (\omega c/m)^2} \sin \omega t \qquad (19.42)$$

We can represent this formulation in a phasor diagram as shown in Fig. 19.29. It should be clear that we can give x_p in the following form:

$$x_p = A \cos(\omega t - \alpha) \qquad (19.43)$$

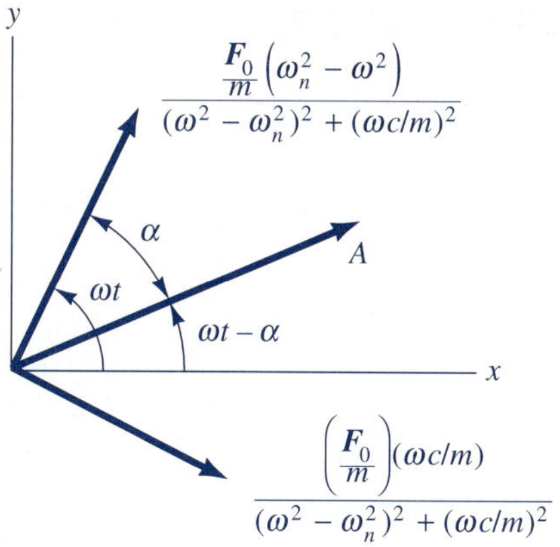

Figure 19.29. Phasor diagram.

where the amplitude A is given as

$$A = \left\{\left[\frac{(F_0/m)(\omega_n^2 - \omega^2)}{(\omega^2 - \omega_n^2)^2 + (\omega c/m)^2}\right]^2 + \left[\frac{(F_0/m)(\omega c/m)}{(\omega^2 - \omega_n^2)^2 + (\omega c/m)^2}\right]^2\right\}^{1/2}$$

$$= \frac{F_0}{m}\frac{\sqrt{(\omega^2 - \omega_n^2)^2 + (\omega c/m)^2}}{(\omega^2 - \omega_n^2)^2 + (\omega c/m)^2}$$

$$= \frac{F_0/m}{\sqrt{(\omega^2 - \omega_n^2)^2 + (\omega c/m)^2}}$$

$$= \frac{F_0}{\sqrt{(m\omega^2 - K)^2 + (\omega c)^2}} \qquad (19.44)$$

and where α, the phase angle, is given as

$$\alpha = \tan^{-1}\left[\frac{(F_0/m)(\omega c/m)}{(\omega^2 - \omega_n^2)^2 + (\omega c/m)^2} \bullet \frac{(\omega^2 - \omega_n^2)^2 + (\omega c/m)^2}{(F_0/m)(\omega_n^2 - \omega^2)}\right]$$

$$= \tan^{-1}\frac{\omega c}{K - m\omega^2} \qquad (19.45)$$

We may express the amplitude A in yet another form by dividing numerator and denominator in Eq. 19.44 by K and by recalling from Eq. 19.38 that the ratio $2\sqrt{Km}/c_{cr}$ is unity. Thus, we get

$$A = \frac{F_0/K}{\sqrt{\left[\left(\frac{\omega}{\omega_n}\right)^2 - 1\right]^2 + \frac{1}{K^2}\left(\frac{2\sqrt{Km}}{c_{cr}}\right)^2(\omega c)^2}}$$

$$= \frac{\delta_{st}}{\sqrt{\left[\left(\frac{\omega}{\omega_n}\right)^2 - 1\right]^2 + \left[2\left(\frac{c}{c_{cr}}\right)\left(\frac{\omega}{\omega_n}\right)\right]^2}} \qquad (19.46)$$

where $F_0/K = \delta_{st}$, is the static deflection. The term

$$= \frac{1}{\sqrt{\left[\left(\frac{\omega}{\omega_n}\right)^2 - 1\right]^2 + \left[2\left(\frac{c}{c_{cr}}\right)\left(\frac{\omega}{\omega_n}\right)\right]^2}}$$

is called the *magnification factor* which is a dimensionless factor giving the amplitude of steady-state motion per unit static deflection. Accordingly, this factor for a given system is useful for examining the effects of frequency changes or damping changes on the steady-state vibration amplitude. A plot of the magnification factor versus ω/ω_n for various values of c/c_{cr} is shown in Fig. 19.30. We see from this plot that small vibrations result when ω is kept far from ω_n. Additionally, note that maximum amplitude does not occur at resonance but actually at frequencies somewhat below resonance. Only when the damping goes to zero does the maximum amplitude occur at resonance. However, for light damping we can usually consider that when $\omega/\omega_n = 1$, we have an amplitude very close to the maximum amplitude possible for the system.

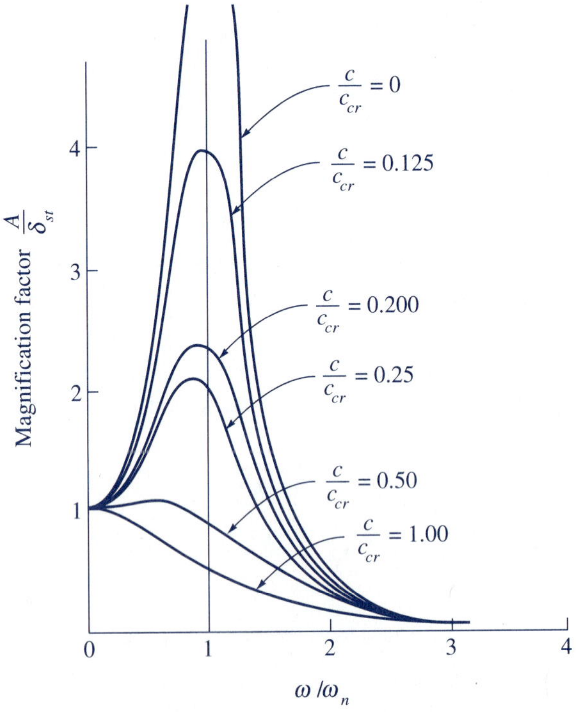

Figure 19.30. Magnification factor plot.

Example 19.11

A *vibrating table* is a machine that can be given harmonic oscillatory motion over a range of amplitudes and frequencies. It is used as a test apparatus for imposing a desired sinusoidal motion on a device.

In Fig. 19.31 is shown a vibrating table with a device bolted to it. The device has in it a body B of mass 16.1 lbm supported by two springs each of stiffness equal to 30 lb/in. and a dashpot having a damping constant c equal to 6 lb/ft/sec. If the table has been adjusted for a vertical motion x' given as sin $40t$ in. with t in seconds, compute:

1. The steady-state amplitude of motion for body B.
2. The maximum number of g's acceleration that body B is subjected to for steady-state motion.
3. The maximum force that body B exerts on the vibrating table during steady-state motion.

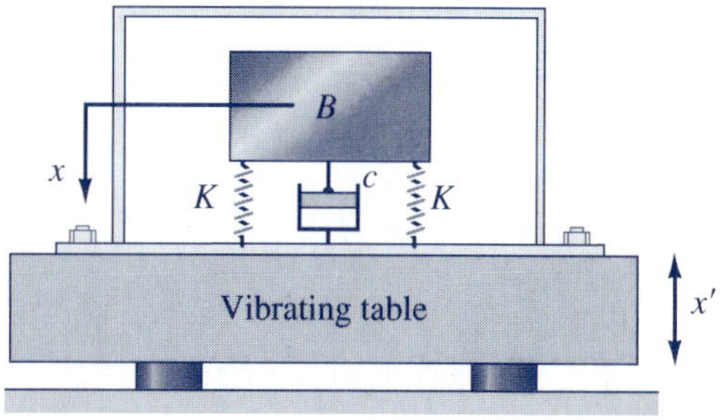

Figure 19.31. A device on a vibrating table.

Measuring the vertical position of body B from the static-equilibrium position with coordinate x, we have from **Newton's law**:

$$M\ddot{x} + c(\dot{x} - \dot{x}') + K(x - x') = 0 \qquad \text{(a)}$$

Using $P \sin \omega t$ to represent x' for now, we have

$$\ddot{x} + \frac{c}{M}\dot{x} + \frac{K}{M}x = \frac{cP\omega}{M}\cos \omega t + \frac{KP}{M}\sin \omega t \qquad \text{(b)}$$

Letting $cP\omega = F_1$ and $KP = F_2$, we have

$$\ddot{x} + \frac{c}{M}\dot{x} + \frac{K}{M}x = \frac{F_1}{M}\cos \omega t + \frac{F_2}{M}\sin \omega t \qquad \text{(c)}$$

Example 19.11 (Continued)

Using a phasor-diagram representation, we can combine the forcing functions into one expression as follows:

$$\frac{F_1}{M}\cos \omega t + \frac{F_2}{M}\sin \omega t = \frac{\sqrt{F_1^2 + F_2^2}}{M}\cos(\omega t - \alpha)$$
$$= \frac{R}{M}\cos(\omega t - \alpha)$$

where $\alpha = \tan^{-1}(F_2/F_1)$ and where $R = \sqrt{F_1^2 + F_2^2}$. Thus, we have

$$\ddot{x} + \frac{c}{M}\dot{x} + \frac{K}{M} = \frac{R}{M}\cos(\omega t - \alpha) \qquad \text{(d)}$$

Except for the phase angle α, Eq. (d) is identical in form to Eq. 19.39. Clearly, if we are interested only in the steady-state amplitude, the phase angle α is of no consequence. Hence setting $\alpha = 0$, we can use the result given by Eq. 19.44 with R taking the place of F_0. Thus, for the amplitude A of mass B, we have

$$A = \frac{R}{\sqrt{(M\omega^2 - K)^2 + (\omega c)^2}} \qquad \text{(e)}$$

The following numerical values apply:

$$M = \tfrac{1}{2}\text{ slug}, \qquad K = (12)(60)\text{ lb/ft}, \qquad \omega = 40\text{ rad/sec},$$
$$c = 6\text{ lb/ft/sec}, \qquad P = \tfrac{1}{12}\text{ ft}$$
$$R = \sqrt{F_1^2 + F_2^2} = \left[(\omega cP)^2 + (KP)^2\right]^{1/2}$$
$$= \left\{\left[(40)(6)(\tfrac{1}{12})\right]^2 + \left[(12)(60)(\tfrac{1}{12})\right]^2\right\}^{1/2} = 63.2$$

Hence, we have for A:

$$A = \frac{63.2}{\sqrt{(800 - 720)^2 + \left[(40)(6)\right]^2}} \qquad \text{(f)}$$
$$= .25\text{ ft.} = 3\text{ in.}$$

To get the maximum steady-state acceleration[5] for body B we compute $|(\ddot{x}_p)|_{\max}$. Thus, we have from Eq. 19.43:

[5]We wish to remind you that the *steady-state* solution corresponds to the *particular* solution $\ddot{x}_p$.

Example 19.11 (Continued)

$$\ddot{x}_p = -A\omega^2 \cos(\omega t - \alpha)$$

$$\left|(\ddot{x}_p)\right|_{max} = \omega^2 A$$

$$= (1{,}600)(.25) = 400 \text{ ft/sec}^2 \qquad \text{(g)}$$

$$= \frac{400}{32.2} g = \boxed{12.41g}$$

The maximum force transmitted to the body by the springs and dashpot during steady-state motion is established clearly when the body B has its greatest acceleration in the upward direction. We have for the maximum force F_B on noting that $\dot{x}_p = 0$ when $\ddot{x}_p$ is maximum:

$$F_B = W_B + \frac{W_B}{g}(\ddot{x}_p)_{max}$$

$$= 16.1 + (\tfrac{1}{2})(400) = 216 \text{ lb} \qquad \text{(h)}$$

If there were no spring-dashpot system between B and the vibratory table, the maximum force transmitted to B would be

$$F_B = W_B + \frac{W_B}{g}(\ddot{x}')_{max}$$

$$= 16.1 + (\tfrac{1}{2})\left[(\tfrac{1}{12})(40)^2\right] = 82.8 \text{ lb} \qquad \text{(i)}$$

We see from Eq. (f) that the amplitude of the induced motion on B is three times what it would be if there were no spring-damping system present to separate B from the table. And from Eqs. (h) and (i) we see that the presence of the spring-damping system has resulted in a considerable *increase* in force acting on body B. Now the use of springs and dashpots for suspending or packaging equipment is generally for the purpose of reducing—not increasing—the amplitude of forces acting on the suspended body. The reason for the increase in these quantities for the disturbing frequency of 40 rad/sec is the fact that the natural frequency of the system is 37.8 rad/sec, thus putting us just above resonance. To protect the body B for disturbances of 40 rad/sec, we must use considerably softer springs.

As an exercise at the end of the section you will be asked in Problem 19.90 to compute K for permitting only a maximum of $\frac{1}{2}$ in. amplitude of vibration for this problem.

*19.9 Oscillatory Systems with Multi-Degrees of Freedom

We shall concern ourselves here with a very simple system that has two degrees of freedom, and we shall be able to generalize from this simple case. In the system of masses shown in Fig. 19.32, the masses are equal, as are the spring constants of the outer springs. We neglect friction, windage, etc. How can we describe the motion of the masses subsequent to any imposed set of initial conditions?

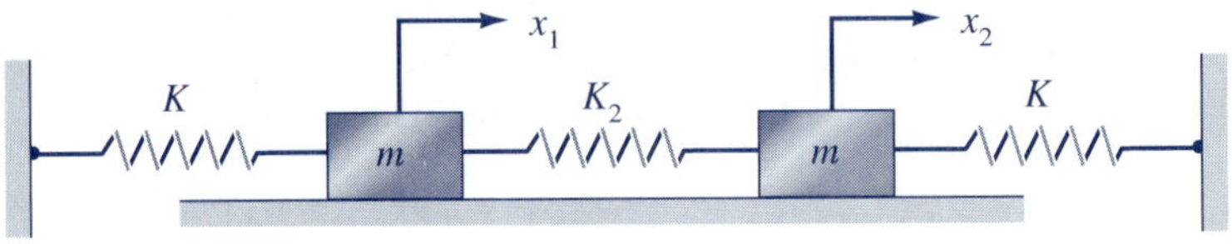

x_1, x_2 measured from equilibrium configuration

Figure 19.32. Two-degree-of-freedom system.

We first express *Newton's law* for each mass. To do this, imagine the masses at any position x_1, x_2 measured from the equilibrium configuration, and then compute the forces. Assume for convenience that $x_1 > x_2$. The spring K_2 is in compression for this supposition, and hence it produces a negative force on the mass at x_1 and a positive force on the mass at x_2. The equations of motion then are:

$$\frac{d^2x_1}{dt^2} = -Kx_1 - K_2(x_1 - x_2) \quad (19.47a)$$

$$\frac{d^2x_2}{dt^2} = -Kx_2 + K_2(x_1 - x_2) \quad (19.47b)$$

If you imagine that the masses are at any other nontrivial position, you will still arrive at the above equations.

Because both dependent variables appear in both differential equations, they are termed *simultaneous* differential equations. We rearrange the equations to the following standard form:

$$\frac{d^2x_1}{dt^2} + \frac{K}{m}x_1 + \frac{K_2}{m}(x_1 - x_2) = 0 \quad (19.48a)$$

$$\frac{d^2x_2}{dt^2} + \frac{K}{m}x_2 - \frac{K_2}{m}(x_1 - x_2) = 0 \quad (19.48b)$$

Finding a solution is equivalent to finding two functions of time $x_1(t)$ and $x_2(t)$, which when substituted into Eqs. 19.48 (a) and (b) reduce each equation to an identity. Only second derivatives and zeroth derivatives appear in these equations, and we would thus expect that sine or cosine functions of time would yield a possible solution. And since both $x_1$and x_2 appear in the same equation, these time functions must be of the same form in order to allow a cancellation of the time function. A trial solution, therefore, might be:

$$x_1 = C_1 \sin(pt + \alpha) \tag{19.49a}$$

$$x_2 = C_2 \sin(pt + \alpha) \tag{19.49b}$$

where C_1, C_2, α, and p are as yet undetermined. Substituting into Eq. 19.48 and canceling out the time function, we get:

$$-C_1 p^2 + \frac{K}{m} C_1 + \frac{K_2}{m}(C_1 - C_2) = 0 \tag{19.50a}$$

$$-C_2 p^2 + \frac{K}{m} C_2 - \frac{K_2}{m}(C_1 - C_2) = 0 \tag{19.50b}$$

Rearranging the above equations, we write:

$$\left(-p^2 + \frac{K}{m} + \frac{K_2}{m}\right)C_1 - \frac{K_2}{m} C_2 = 0 \tag{19.51a}$$

$$-\frac{K_2}{m} C_1 + \left(-p^2 + \frac{K}{m} + \frac{K_2}{m}\right)C_2 = 0 \tag{19.51b}$$

One way of ensuring the satisfaction of this equation is to have $C_1 = 0$ and $C_2 = 0$. This means, from Eqs. 19.49 (a) and (b), that x_1 and x_2 are always zero, which corresponds to the static equilibrium position. While this is a valid solution, since this static equilibrium is a possible motion, the result is trivial. We now ask: Is there a means of satisfying these equations without setting C_1 and C_2 equal to zero?

To answer this, solve for C_1 and C_2 in terms of the coefficients, as if they were unknowns in the above equations. Using Cramer's rule, we then have:

$$C_1 = \frac{\begin{vmatrix} 0 & -K_2/m \\ 0 & -p^2 + K/m + K_2/m \end{vmatrix}}{\begin{vmatrix} -p^2 + K/m + K_2/m & -K_2/m \\ -K_2/m & -p^2 + K/m + K_2/m \end{vmatrix}}$$

$$C_2 = \frac{\begin{vmatrix} -p^2 + K/m + K_2/m & 0 \\ -K_2/m & 0 \end{vmatrix}}{\begin{vmatrix} -p^2 + K/m + K_2/m & -K_2/m \\ -K_2/m & -p^2 + K/m + K_2/m \end{vmatrix}} \tag{19.52}$$

Notice that the determinant in the numerator is in each case zero. If the denominator is other than zero, we must have the trivial solution $C_1 = C_2 = 0$, the significance of which we have just discussed. A *necessary* condition for a *nontrivial* solution is that the denominator also be zero, for then we get the indeterminate form 0/0 for C_1 and C_2. Clearly, C_1 and C_2 can then have possible values other than zero, and so the required condition for a nontrivial solution is:

$$\begin{vmatrix} -p^2 + K/m + K_2/m & -K_2/m \\ -K_2/m & -p^2 + K/m + K_2/m \end{vmatrix} = 0 \tag{19.53}$$

Carrying out this determinant multiplication, we get:

$$\left(-p^2 + \frac{K}{m} + \frac{K_2}{m}\right)^2 = \left(\frac{K_2}{m}\right)^2 \tag{19.54}$$

Taking the roots of both sides, we have:

$$-p^2 + \frac{K}{m} + \frac{K_2}{m} = \pm\frac{K_2}{m} \tag{19.55}$$

Two values of p^2 satisfy the necessary condition we have imposed. If we use the positive roots, the values of p are:

$$p_1 = \sqrt{\frac{K}{m}}$$

$$p_2 = \sqrt{\frac{K}{m} + \frac{2K_2}{m}} \tag{19.56}$$

where p_1 and p_2 are found for the plus and minus cases, respectively, of the right side of Eq. 19.55.

Let us now return to Eqs. 19.51 (a) and (b) to ascertain what further restrictions we may have to impose to ensure a solution, because these equations form the criterion for acceptance of a set of functions as solutions. Employing $\sqrt{K/m}$ for p in Eq. 19.51 (a), we have:

$$\left(-\frac{K}{m} + \frac{K}{m} + \frac{K_2}{m}\right)C_1 - \left(\frac{K_2}{m}\right)C_2 = 0 \tag{19.57}$$

From this equation we see that when we use this value of p it is necessary that $C_1 = C_2$ to satisfy the equation. The same conclusions can be reached by employing Eq. 19.51(b). We can now state a permissible solution to the differential equation. Using A as the amplitude in place of $C_1 = C_2$, we have:

$$x_1 = A\sin\left(\sqrt{\frac{K}{m}}t + \alpha\right) \tag{19.58a}$$

$$x_2 = A\sin\left(\sqrt{\frac{K}{m}}t + \alpha\right) \tag{19.58b}$$

If we examine the second value of p, we find that for this value it is required that $C_1 = -C_2$. Thus if we use B for C_1 and use β as the arbitrary value in the sine function, another possible solution is:

$$x_1 = B\sin\left(\sqrt{\frac{K}{m} + \frac{2K_2}{m}}t + \beta\right) \tag{19.59a}$$

$$x_2 = -B\sin\left(\sqrt{\frac{K}{m} + \frac{2K_2}{m}}t + \beta\right) \tag{19.59b}$$

Let us consider each of these solutions. In the first case, the motions of both masses are in phase with each other, have the same amplitude, and thus move together with simple harmonic motion with a natural frequency $\sqrt{K/m}$. For this motion, the center spring is not extended or compressed, and, since the mass of the spring has been neglected, it has no effect on this motion. This explains why the natural frequency has such a simple formulation.

The second possible independent solution is one in which the amplitudes are equal for both masses but the masses are 180° out of phase. Each mass oscillates harmonically with a natural frequency greater than the preceding motion. Since the masses move in opposite directions in the manner described, the center of the middle spring must be stationary for this motion. It is as if each mass were vibrating under the action of a spring of constant K and the action of half the length of a spring with a spring constant K_2 (Fig. 19.33), which explains why the natural frequency for this motion is $\sqrt{(K + 2K_2)/m}$. (It will be left for you to demonstrate in an exercise that halving the length of the spring doubles the spring constant.)

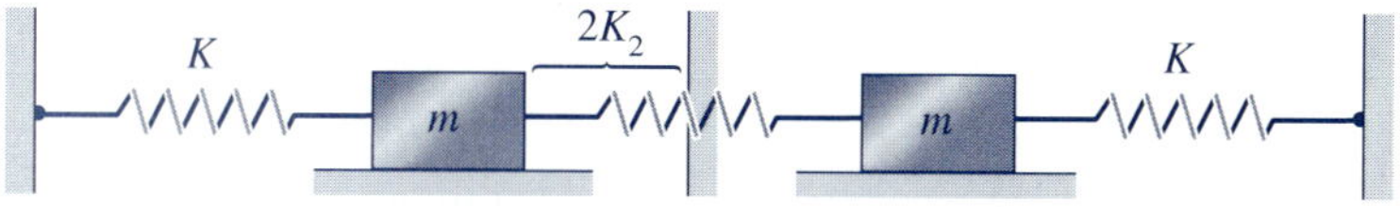

Figure 19.33. Bodies 180° out of phase.

Each of these motions as given by Eqs. 19.58 and 19.59 is called a natural *mode*. The first mode refers to the motion of lower natural frequency, and the second mode identifies the one with the higher natural frequency. It is known from differential equations that the general solution is the sum of the two solutions presented:

$$\begin{aligned} x_1 &= \left[A\sin\left(\sqrt{\frac{K}{m}}t + \alpha\right)\right] + \left[B\sin\left(\sqrt{\frac{K}{m} + \frac{2K_2}{m}}t + \beta\right)\right] \\ x_1 &= \left[A\sin\left(\sqrt{\frac{K}{m}}t + \alpha\right)\right] + \left[-B\sin\left(\sqrt{\frac{K}{m} + \frac{2K_2}{m}}t + \beta\right)\right] \end{aligned} \qquad (19.60)$$

first mode of motion — second mode of motion

Four constants are yet to be determined: A, B, α, and β. These are the constants of integration and are determined by the initial conditions of the motion—that is, the velocity and position of each mass at time $t = 0$.

From this discussion we can make the following conclusions. The general motion of the system under study is the superposition of two modes of motion of harmonic nature that have distinct natural frequencies with amplitudes and phase angles that are evaluated to fit the initial conditions. Thus the basic modes are the "building blocks" of the general free motion.

If the masses, as well as the springs, were unequal, the analysis would still produce two natural frequencies and mode shapes, but these would neither be as simple as the special case we have worked out nor, perhaps, as intuitively obvious.

As we discussed in the first paragraph of this section, two natural frequencies correspond to the two degrees of freedom. In the general case of n degrees of freedom, there will be n natural frequencies, and the general free vibrations will be the superposition of n modes of motion that have proper amplitudes and are phased together in such a way that they satisfy $2n$ initial conditions.

PROBLEMS

19.76. A body of weight W N is suspended between two springs. Two identical dashpots are shown. Each dashpot resists motion of the block at the rate of c N/m/sec. What is the equation of motion for the block? What is c for critical damping?

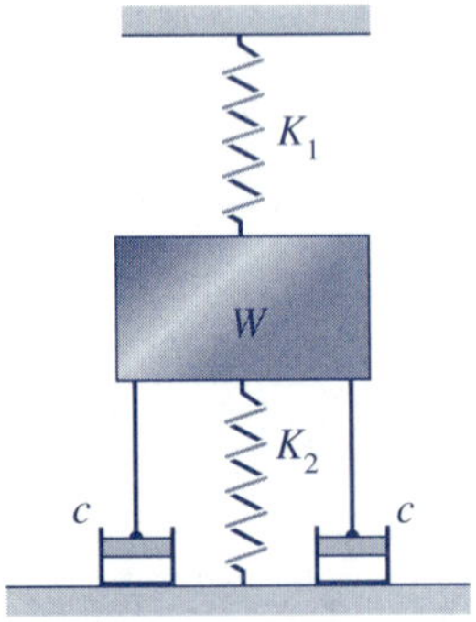

Figure P.19.76.

19.77 In Problem 19.76, the following data apply:

$$W = 445 \text{ N}$$
$$K_1 = 8.8 \text{ N/mm}$$
$$K_2 = 14.0 \text{ N/mm}$$
$$c = 825 \text{ N/m/sec}$$

Is the system underdamped, overdamped, or critically damped? If the weight W is released 150 mm above its static-equilibrium configuration, what are the speed and position of the block after .1 sec? What force is transmitted to the foundation at that instant?

19.78. The damping constant c for the body is $\frac{1}{2}$ lb/ft/sec. If, at its equilibrium position, the body is suddenly given a velocity of 10 ft/sec to the right, what will the frequency of its motion be? What is the position of the mass at t = 5 sec?

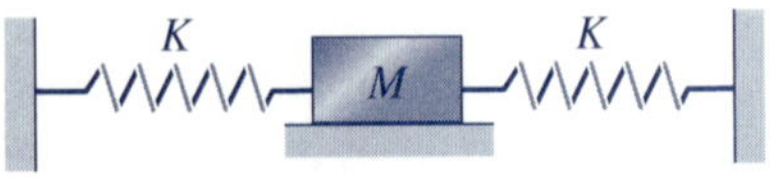

Figure P.19.78.

19.79. The damping in Problem 19.78 is increased so that it is twice the critical damping. If the mass is released from a position 3 in. to the right of equilibrium, how far from the equilibrium position is it in 5 sec? Theoretically, does it ever reach the equilibrium position?

19.80. A plot of a free damped vibration is shown. What should the constant C_3 be in Eq. 19.35 for this motion? Show that ln (x_1/x_2), where x_1 and x_2 are two succeeding peaks, can be given as $(c/4m)\tau$. The expression ln (x_1/x_2) is called the *logarithmic decrement* and is used in vibration work.

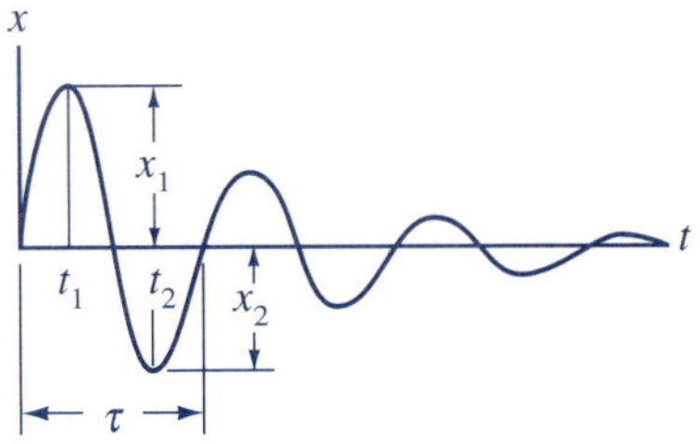

Figure P.19.80.

19.81. A rod of length $2\frac{1}{4}$ m and weight 200 N is shown in the static-equilibrium position supported by a spring of stiffness K = 14 N/mm. The rod is connected to a dashpot having a damping force c of 69 N/m/sec. If an impulsive torque gives the rod an angular speed clockwise of $\frac{1}{2}$ rad/sec at the position shown, what is the position of point A at t = .2 sec?

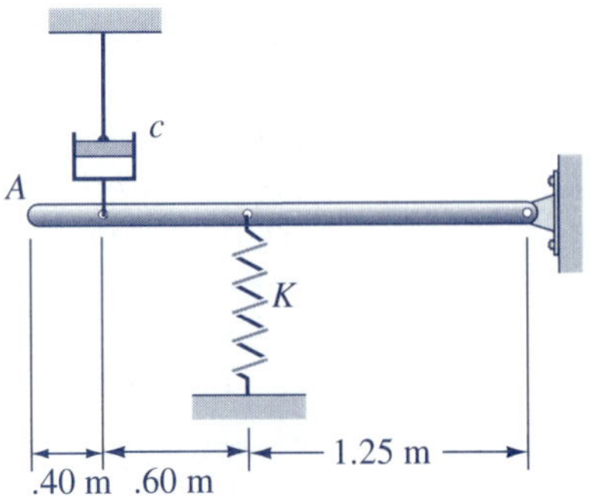

Figure P.19.81.

19.82. A spherical ball of weight 134 N is welded to a vertical light rod which in turn is welded at B to a horizontal rod. A spring of stiffness $K = 8.8$ N/mm and a damper c having a value 179 N/m/sec are connected to the horizontal rod. If A is displaced 75 mm to the right, how long does it take for it to return to its vertical configuration?

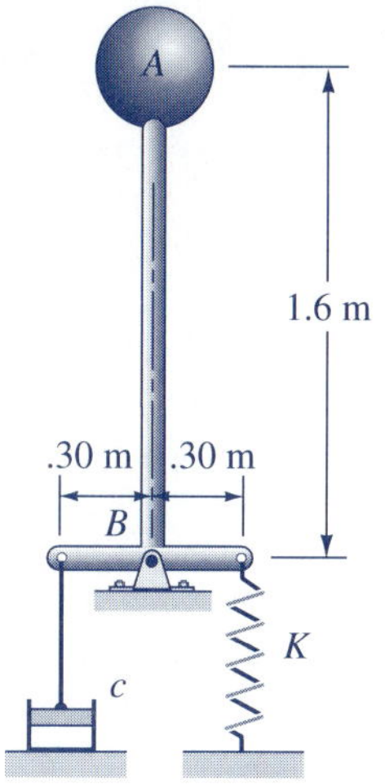

Figure P.19.82.

19.83. Cylinder A of weight 200 N slides down a vertical cylindrical chute. A film of oil of thickness .1 mm separates the cylinder from the chute. If the air pressure before and behind the cylinder is maintained at the same value of 15 psig, what is the maximum velocity that the cylinder can attain by gravity? The coefficient of viscosity of the oil is .00800 N-sec/m^2.

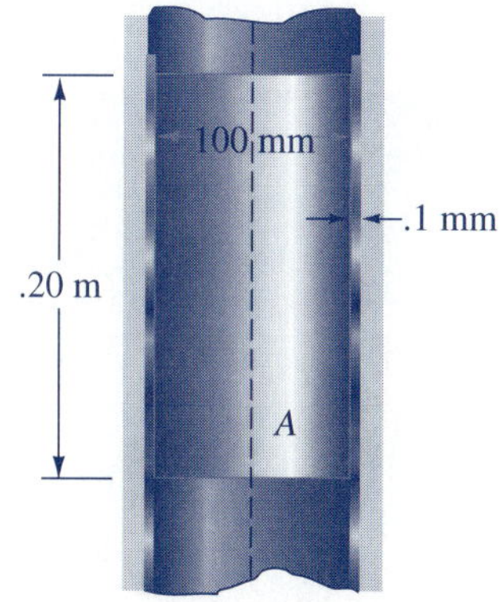

Figure P.19.83.

19.84. A disc A with a mass of 5 kg is constrained during rotation about its axis by a torsional spring having a constant K_T equal to 2×10^{-5} N-m/rad. The disc is in a journal having a diameter 2 mm larger than the disc. Oil having a viscosity .0085 N-sec/m^2 fills the outer space between disc and journal. If we assume a linear profile for the oil film, what is the frequency of oscillation of the disc if it is rotated from its equilibrium position and then released? The diameter of the disc is 40 mm and its length is 30 mm. The oil acts only on the disc's outer periphery.

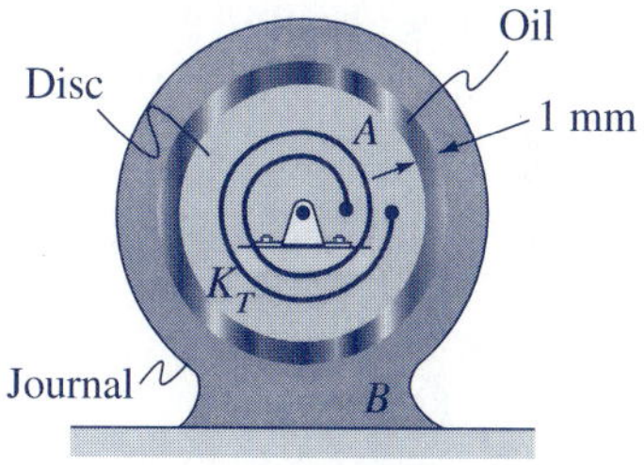

Figure P.19.84.

19.85. A block W weighing 60 N is released from rest at a configuration 100 mm above its equilibrium position. It rides on a film of oil whose thickness is .1 mm and whose coefficient of viscosity is .00950 N-sec/m^2. If K is 50 N/m, how far down the incline will the block move? The block is .20 m on each edge.

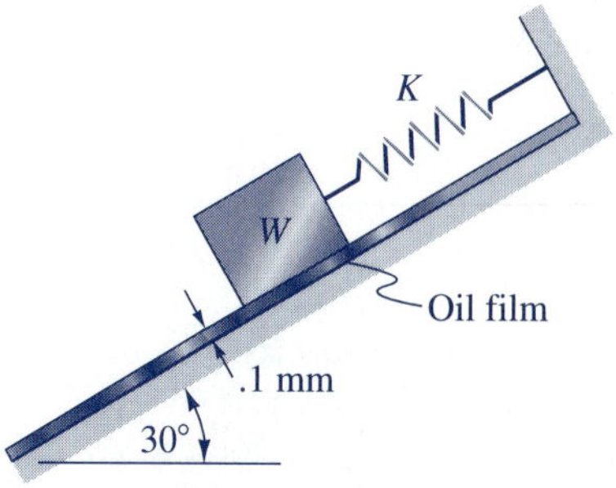

Figure P.19.85.

*19.86. In Problem 19.85, set up two simultaneous equations to determine the spring constant K so that, after W is released, W comes back to its equilibrium position with no oscillation. As a short project, solve for K using a computer.

19.87. A disc B of diameter 100 mm rotates in a stationary housing filled with oil of viscosity .00600 N-sec/m^2. The disc and its shaft have a mass of 30 g and a radius of gyration of 20 mm. The shaft and disc connect to a device that supplies a linear restoring torque of 5 N-mm/rad. Use a linear velocity profile for the oil and find how long each oscillation of the disc about its axis takes.

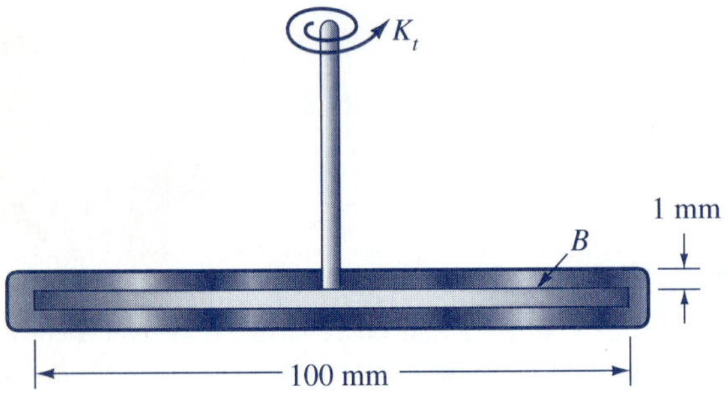

Figure P.19.87.

19.88. Examine the case of the spring-mass system with viscous damping for a sinusoidal forcing function given as $F_0 \sin \omega t$. Go through the steps in the text leading up to Eq. 19.41 for this case.

19.89. A force $F = 35 \sin 2t$ N acts on a block having a weight of 285 N. A spring having stiffness K of 550 N/m and a dashpot having a damping factor c of 68 N-sec/m are connected to the body. What is the amplitude of steady-state motion for the body, and what is the maximum force transmitted to the wall?

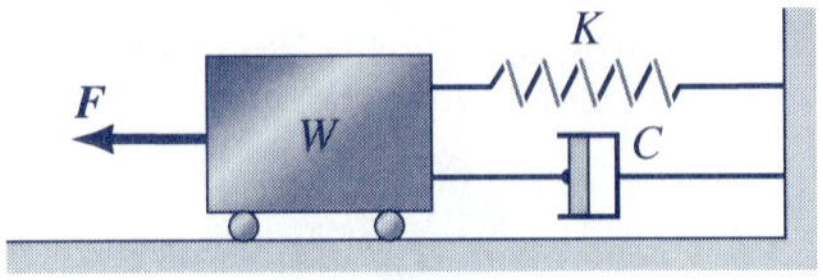

Figure P.19.89.

19.90 In Example 19.11, compute K for an amplitude of steady-state vibration of $\frac{1}{2}$ in.

19.91. A block of mass M rests on two springs, the total spring constant of which is K. Also, there is a dashpot of constant c. A small sphere of mass m is attached to M and is made to rotate at a speed of ω. The distance from the center of rotation to the sphere is r. Derive the equation of motion for the block first by considering the motions of M and m separately as single masses. Show that you could reach the same equation of motion by lumping the masses M and m into one body of mass $(M + m)$ on which a sinusoidal disturbance equal to $mr\omega^2 \sin \omega t$ (from the rotating sphere) is applied.

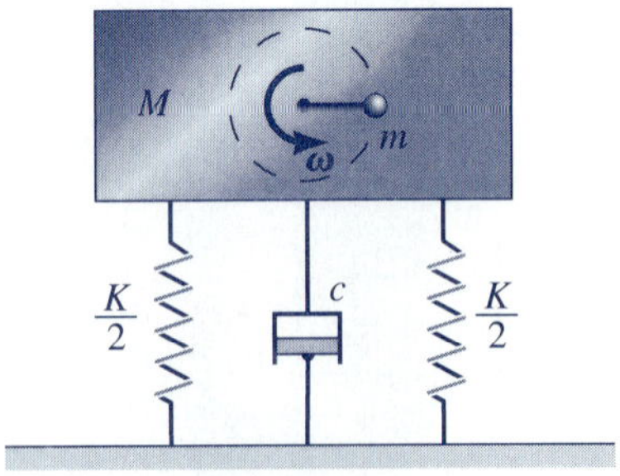

Figure P.19.91.

19.92. A platform weighing 222 N deflects the spring 50 mm when placed carefully on the spring. A motor weighing 22 N is then clamped on top of the platform and rotates an eccentric mass m which weighs 1 N. The mass m is displaced 150 mm from the axis of rotation and rotates at an angular speed of 28 rad/sec. The viscous damping present causes a resistance to the motion of the platform of 275 N-m/sec. What is the steady-state amplitude of the motion of the platform? See Problem 19.91 before doing this problem.

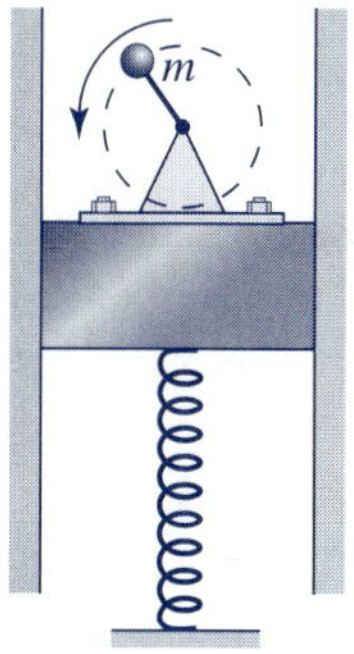

Figure P.19.92.

19.93. A body weighing 143 N is connected by a light rod to a spring of stiffness K equal to 2.6 N/mm and to a dashpot having a damping factor c. Point B has a given motion x' of 30.5 sin t mm with t in seconds. If the center of A is to have an amplitude of steady-state motion of 20 mm, what must c be?

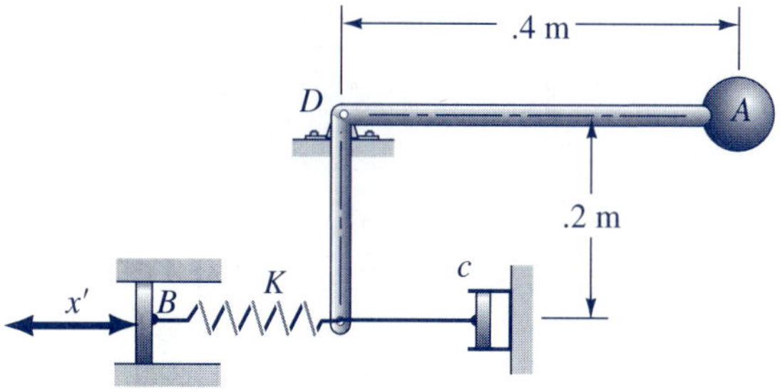

Figure P.19.93.

***19.94.** In Problem 19.15, if we include the inertial effects of rod BC, how many degrees of freedom are there? If rod BC weighs 5 lb, set up the differential equations of motion for the system.

***19.95** Two bodies of equal mass, $M = 1$ slug, are attached to walls by springs having equal spring constants $K_1 = 5$ lb/in. and are connected to each other by a spring having a spring constant $K_2 = 1$ lb/in. If the mass on the left is released from a position $(x_1)_0 = 3$ in. at $t = 0$ with zero velocity and the mass at the right is stationary at $x_2 = 0$ at this instant, what is the position of each mass at the time $t = 5$ sec? The coordinates x_1 and x_2 are measured from the static-equilibrium positions of the body.

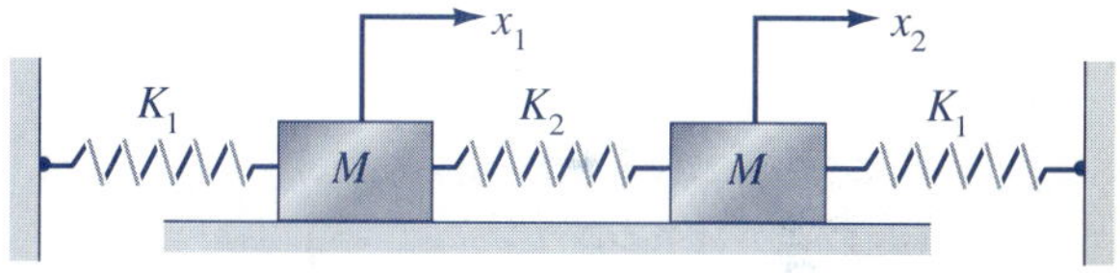

Figure P.19.95.

***19.96.** Let K_2 in Fig. P.19.95 be very small compared to K_1. Assume one mass has been released at $t = 0$ from a position displaced from equilibrium with zero velocity, while the other mass is released from the initial stationary position at that instant with zero velocity. Show that one mass will have a maximum velocity while the other will have a minimum velocity and that there will be a continual transfer of kinetic energy from one mass to the other at a frequency equal to the beat frequency of the natural frequencies of the system.

[*Hint*: Study the phasors $A \cos \sqrt{\frac{K_1}{M}} t$ and $A \cos \sqrt{\frac{K_1}{M} + \frac{2K_2}{M}} t$.]

19.10 Closure

This introductory study of vibration brings to a close the present study of particle and rigid-body mechanics. As you progress to the study of deformable media in your courses in solid and fluid mechanics you will find that particle mechanics and, to a lesser extent rigid-body mechanics, will form cornerstones for these disciplines. And in your studies involving the design of machines and the performance of vehicles you will find rigid-body mechanics indispensable.

It should be realized, however, that we have by no means said the last word on particle and rigid-body mechanics. More advanced studies will emphasize the variational approach introduced in statics. With the use of the calculus of variations, such topics as Hamilton's principle, Lagrange's equation,[6] and Hamilton-Jacobi theory will be presented and you will then see a greater unity between mechanics and other areas of physics such as electromagnetic theory and wave mechanics. Also the special theory of relativity will most surely be considered.

Finally, in your studies of modern physics you will come to more fully understand the limitations of classical mechanics when you are introduced to quantum mechanics.

[6]Some of these topics are covered in the author's text written with C.L. Dym, "Energy and Finite Elements Methods in Structural Mechanics" Taylor and Francis.

PROBLEMS

19.97. If $K_1 = 2K_2 = 1.8K_3$, what should K_3 be for a period of free vibration of .2 sec? The mass M is 3 kg.

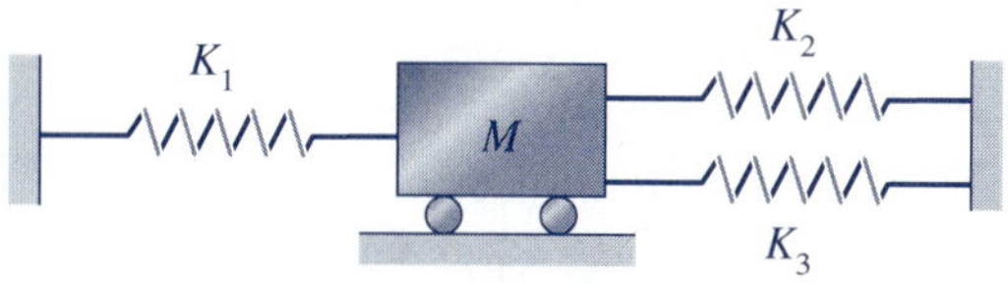

Figure P.19.97.

19.98. In Problem 19.55, determine the natural frequency of the system. If the mass is deflected 2 in. and then released, determine the displacement from equilibrium after 3 sec. Finally, determine the *total* distance traveled during this time.

Figure P.19.98.

19.99. Find the natural frequency of motion of body A for small rotation of rod BD when we neglect the inertial effects of rod BD. The spring constant K_2 is .9 N/mm and the spring constant K_1 is 1.8 N/mm. The weight of block A is 178 N. Neglect friction everywhere. Rod BD weighs 44 N.

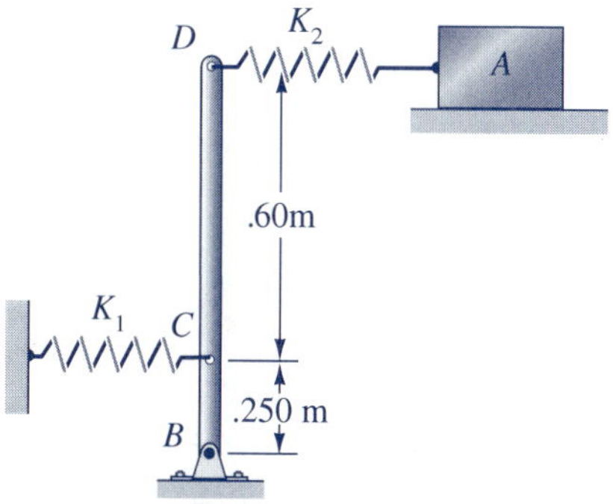

Figure P.19.99.

19.100. What is the equivalent spring constant for small oscillations about the shaft AB? Neglect all mass except the block at B, which weighs 100 lb. The shear modulus of elasticity G for the shaft is 15×10^6 psi. What is the natural frequency of the system for torsional oscillation of small amplitude?

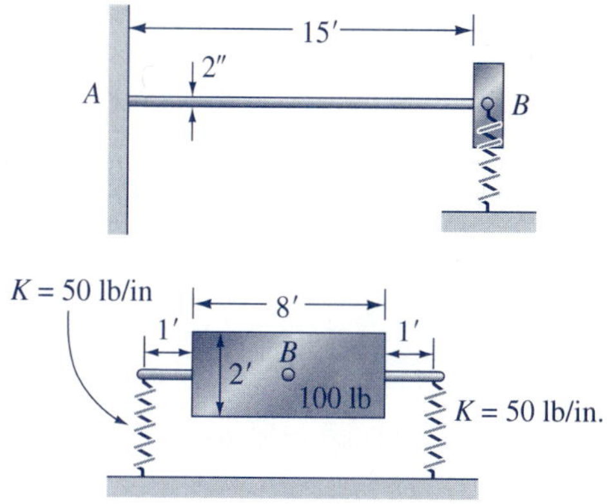

Figure P.19.100.

19.101. What is the radius of gyration of the speedboat about a vertical axis going through the center of gravity, if it is noted that the boat will swing about this vertical axis one time per second? The mass of the boat is 500 kg.

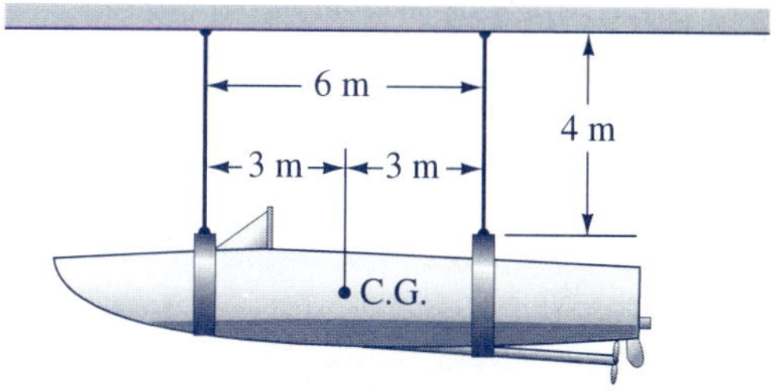

Figure P.19.101.

19.102. A rod of length L and mass M is suspended from a frictionless roller. If a small impulsive torque is applied to the rod when it is in a state of rest, what is the natural frequency of oscillation about this state of rest?

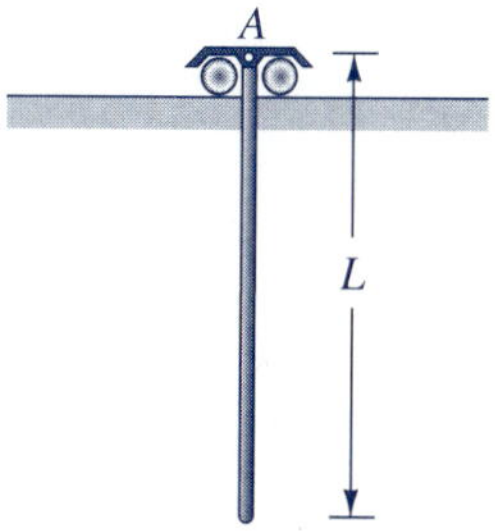

Figure P.19.102.

***19.103.** Solve Problem 19.12 by energy methods.

19.104. A block is acted on by a force F given as

$$F = 90 + 22 \sin 80t \text{ N}$$

and is found to oscillate, after transients have died out, with an amplitude of .5 mm about a position 50 mm to the left of the static-equilibrium position corresponding to the condition when no force is present. What is the weight of the body?

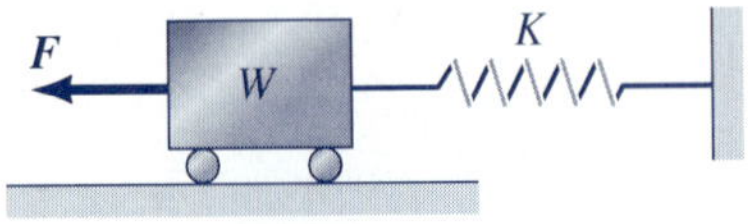

Figure P.19.104.

19.105. A light stiff rod ACB is made to rotate about C such that θ varies sinusoidally with $\omega = 20$ rad/sec. What should the amplitude of rotation θ_0 be to cause a steady-state amplitude of vibration of M to be 20 mm? The following data apply:

$$M = 3 \text{ kg}$$
$$K = 2.5 \text{ N/mm}$$
$$l = 1 \text{ m}$$

What is the one essential difference between the motions of the two masses?

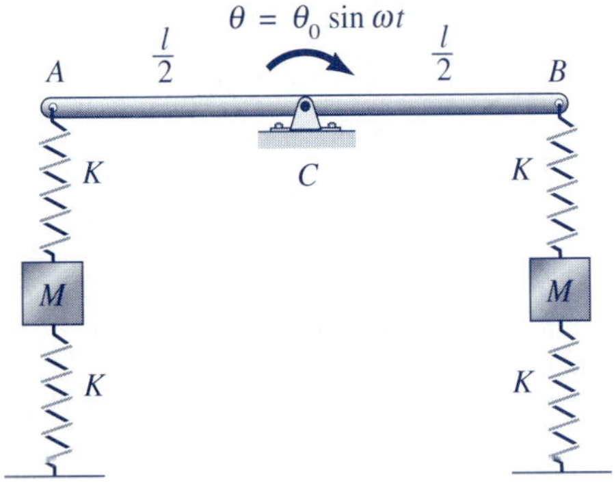

Figure P.19.105.

19.106. In Problem 19.105, what is the angle θ after 5 sec? System is stationary at the outset and AB is horizontal. Take $\omega = 39$ rad/sec and θ_0 as .02 rad.

19.107. A body rests on a conveyor moving with a speed of 5 ft/sec. If the damping constant is 2 lb/ft/sec, determine the equilibrium force in the spring. If the body is displaced 3 in. to the left from the equilibrium position, what is the time for the mass to pass through the equilibrium position again?

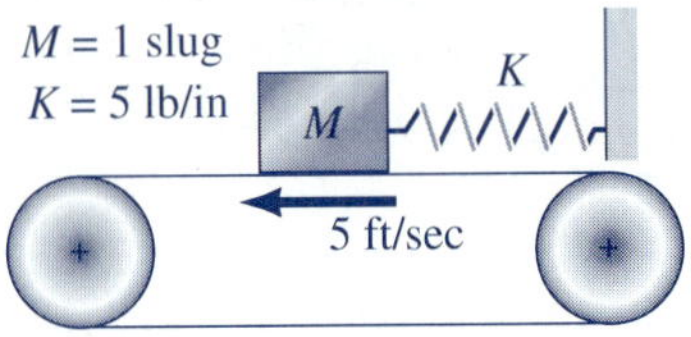

Figure P.19.107.

***19.108.** A motor is mounted on two springs of stiffness 8.8 N/mm each and a dashpot having a coefficient c of 96 N-sec/m. The motor weighs 222 N. The armature of the motor weighs 89 N with a center of mass 5 mm from the geometric centerline. If the machine rotates at 1,750 rpm, what is the amplitude of motion in the vertical direction of the motor? Determine the maximum force transmitted to the ground.

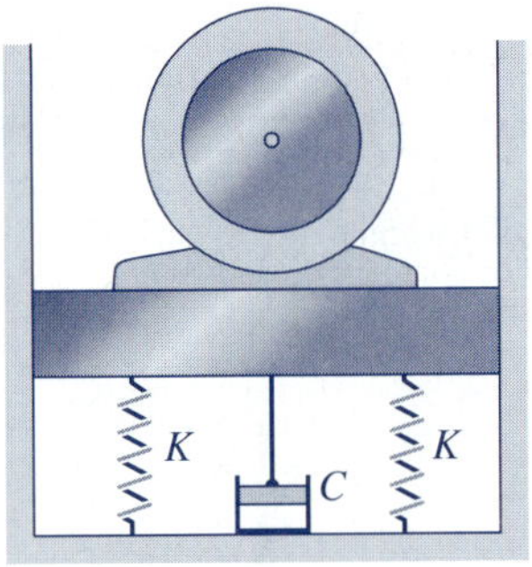

Figure P.19.108.

***19.109.** In Problem 19.108, what is the resonant condition for the system? What is the amplitude of motion for this case? To what value must c be changed if the amplitude at this motor speed is to be halved?

APPENDIX I

Integration Formulas

1. $\int \frac{x\,dx}{a+bx} = \frac{1}{b^2}[a+bx-a\ln(a+bx)]$

2. $\int \frac{dx}{a^2-x^2} = \frac{1}{2a}\ln\left(\frac{a+x}{a-x}\right)$

3. $\int \sqrt{x^2 \pm a^2}\,dx = \frac{1}{2}\left[x\sqrt{x^2 \pm a^2} \pm a^2 \ln\left(x+\sqrt{x^2 \pm a^2}\right)\right]$

4. $\int \sqrt{a^2-x^2}\,dx = \frac{1}{2}\left(x\sqrt{a^2-x^2} + a^2 \sin^{-1}\frac{x}{a}\right)$

5. $\int x\sqrt{a^2-x^2}\,dx = -\frac{1}{3}\sqrt{(a^2-x^2)^3}$

6. $\int x\sqrt{a+bx}\,dx = -\frac{2(2a-3bx)\sqrt{(a+bx)^3}}{15b^2}$

7. $\int x^2\sqrt{a^2-x^2}\,dx = -\frac{x}{4}\sqrt{(a^2-x^2)^3} + \frac{a^2}{8}\left(x\sqrt{a^2-x^2} + a^2 \sin^{-1}\frac{x}{a}\right)$

8. $\int x^2\sqrt{a^2 \pm x^2}\,dx = \frac{x}{4}\sqrt{(x^2 \pm a^2)^3} \mp \frac{a^2}{8}x\sqrt{x^2 \pm a^2} - \frac{a^4}{8}\ln\left(x+\sqrt{x^2 \pm a^2}\right)$

9. $\int \frac{dx}{\sqrt{a^2-x^2}} = \sin^{-1}\frac{x}{a}$

10. $\int \frac{dx}{\sqrt{x^2+a^2}} = \ln\left(x+\sqrt{x^2+a^2}\right) = \sinh^{-1}\frac{x}{a}$

11. $\int x^m e^{ax}\,dx = \frac{x^m e^{ax}}{a} - \frac{m}{a}\int x^{m-1}e^{ax}\,dx$

12. $\int x^m \ln x\,dx = x^{m+1}\left(\frac{\ln x}{m+1} - \frac{1}{(m+1)^2}\right)$

13. $\int \sin^2\theta\,d\theta = \frac{1}{2}\theta - \frac{1}{4}\sin 2\theta$

14. $\int \cos^2 \theta \, d\theta = \frac{1}{2}\theta + \frac{1}{4}\sin 2\theta$

15. $\int \sin^3 \theta \, d\theta = -\frac{1}{3}\cos\theta(\sin^2\theta + 2)$

16. $\int \cos^m \theta \sin\theta \, d\theta = -\dfrac{\cos^{m+1}\theta}{m+1}$

17. $\int \sin^m \theta \cos\theta \, d\theta = \dfrac{\sin^{m+1}\theta}{m+1}$

18. $\int \sin^m \theta \, d\theta = -\dfrac{\sin^{m-1}\theta\cos\theta}{m} + \dfrac{m-1}{m}\int \sin^{m-2}\theta \, d\theta$

19. $\int \theta^2 \sin\theta \, d\theta = 2\theta\sin\theta - (\theta^2 - 2)\cos\theta$

20. $\int \theta^2 \cos\theta \, d\theta = 2\theta\cos\theta + (\theta^2 - 2)\sin\theta$

21. $\int \theta \sin^2\theta \, d\theta = \frac{1}{4}\left[\sin\theta(\sin\theta - 2\theta\cos\theta) + \theta^2\right]$

22. $\int \sin m\theta \cos m\theta \, d\theta = -\dfrac{1}{4m}\cos 2m\theta$

23. $\int \dfrac{d\theta}{(a + b\cos\theta)^2}$

$$= \frac{1}{(a^2 - b^2)}\left(\frac{-b\sin\theta}{a + b\cos\theta} + \frac{2a}{\sqrt{a^2 - b^2}}\tan^{-1}\frac{\sqrt{a^2 - b^2}\tan\frac{\theta}{2}}{a + b}\right)$$

24. $\int \theta\sin\theta \, d\theta = \sin\theta - \theta\cos\theta$

25. $\int \theta\cos\theta \, d\theta = \cos\theta + \theta\sin\theta$

APPENDIX II

Computation of Principal Moments of Inertia

We now turn to the problem of computing the principal moments of inertia and the directions of the principal axes for the case where we do not have planes of symmetry. It is unfortunate that a careful study of this important calculation is beyond the level of this text. However, we shall present enough material to permit the computation of the principal moments of inertia and the directions of their respective axes.

The procedure that we shall outline is that of extremizing the mass moment of inertia at a point where the inertia-tensor components are known for a reference xyz. This will be done by varying the direction cosines l, m, and n of an axis k so as to extremize I_{kk} as given by Eq. 9.13. We accordingly set the differential of I_{kk} equal to zero as follows:

$$\begin{aligned} dI_{kk} = {} & 2lI_{xx}\,dl + 2mI_{yy}\,dm + 2nI_{zz}\,dn \\ & -2lI_{xy}\,dm - 2mI_{xy}\,dl - 2lI_{xz}\,dn \\ & -2nI_{xz}\,dl - 2mI_{yz}\,dn - 2nI_{yz}\,dm = 0 \end{aligned} \tag{II.1}$$

Collecting terms and canceling the factor 2, we get

$$\begin{aligned} (lI_{xx} - mI_{xy} - nI_{xz})dl + (-lI_{xy} + mI_{yy} - nI_{yz})dm \\ +(-lI_{xz} - mI_{yz} + nI_{zz})dn = 0 \end{aligned} \tag{II.2}$$

If the differentials dl, dm, and dn were *independent* we could set their respective coefficients equal to zero to satisfy the equation. However, they are not independent because the equation

$$l^2 + m^2 + n^2 = 1 \tag{II.3}$$

must at all times be satisfied. Accordingly, the differentials of the direction cosines must be related as follows[1]:

$$l\,dl + m\,dm + n\,dn = 0 \tag{II.4}$$

[1]We are thus extremizing I_{kk} in the presence of a constraining equation.

We can of course consider any two differentials as independent. The third is then established in accordance with the equation above.

We shall now introduce the *Lagrange multiplier* λ to facilitate the extremizing process. This constant is an arbitrary constant at this stage of the calculation. Multiplying Eq. II.4 by λ and subtracting Eq. II.4 from Eq. II.2 we get when collecting terms:

$$\left[(I_{xx} - \lambda)l - I_{xy}m - I_{xz}n\right]dl + \left[-I_{xy}l + (I_{yy} - \lambda)m - I_{yz}n\right]dm + \left[-I_{xz}l - I_{yz}m + (I_{zz} - \lambda)n\right]dn = 0 \qquad \text{(II.5)}$$

Let us next consider that m and n are independent variables and consider the value of λ so chosen that the coefficient of dl is zero. That is,

$$(I_{xx} - \lambda)l - I_{xy}m - I_{xz}n = 0 \qquad \text{(II.6)}$$

With the first term Eq. II.5 disposed of in this way, we are left with differentials dm and dn, which are independent. Accordingly, we can set their respective coefficients equal to zero in order to satisfy the equation. Hence, we have in addition to Eq. II.6 the following equations:

$$\begin{aligned} -I_{xy}l + (I_{yy} - \lambda)m - I_{yz}n &= 0 \\ -I_{xz}l - I_{yz}m + (I_{zz} - \lambda)n &= 0 \end{aligned} \qquad \text{(II.7)}$$

A necessary condition for the solution of a set of direction cosines l, m, and n, from Eqs. II.6 and II.7, which does not violate Eq. II.3[2] is that the determinant of the coefficients of these variables be zero. Thus:

$$\begin{vmatrix} (I_{xx} - \lambda) & -I_{xy} & -I_{xz} \\ -I_{xy} & (I_{yy} - \lambda) & -I_{yz} \\ -I_{xz} & -I_{yz} & (I_{zz} - \lambda) \end{vmatrix} = 0 \qquad \text{(II.8)}$$

This results in a cubic equation for which we can show there are three real roots for λ. Substituting these roots into any two of Eqs. II.6 and II.7 plus Eq. II.3, we can determine three direction cosines for each root. These are the direction cosines for the principal axes measured relative to xyz. We could get the principal moments of inertia next by substituting a set of these direction cosines into Eq. 9.13 and solving for I_{kk}. However, that is not necessary, since it can be shown that the three Lagrange multipliers *are* the principal moments of inertia.

[2]This precludes the possibility of a trivial solution $l = m = n = 0$.

APPENDIX III

Additional Data for the Ellipse

If we restrict our attention to the case of an ellipse, as shown in Fig. IV.1, we can compute the length of the major diameter (usually called the major axis) by solving for r from Eq. 12.34 with β set equal to zero, separately for $\theta = 0$ and for $\theta = \pi$, and then adding the results.

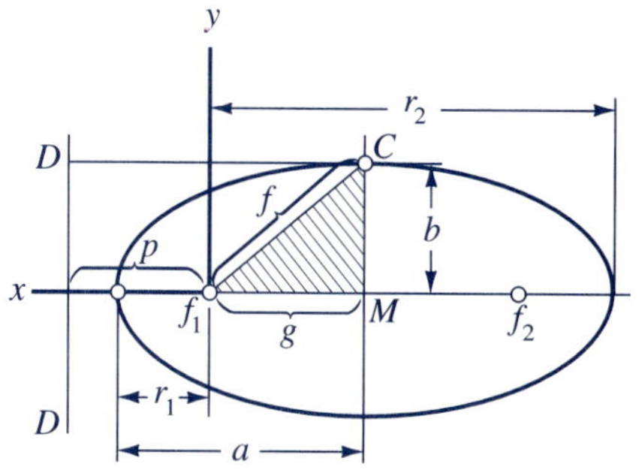

Figure IV.1. Ellipse.

Thus,

$$r_1 = \frac{\epsilon p}{1+\epsilon}, \quad r_2 = \frac{\epsilon p}{1-\epsilon} \tag{IV.1}$$

Therefore,

$$r_1 + r_2 = 2a = \epsilon p\left(\frac{1}{1+\epsilon} + \frac{1}{1-\epsilon}\right)$$

Solving for a, we get

$$a = \frac{\epsilon p}{1-\epsilon^2} \tag{IV.2}$$

The term a is the semimajor diameter. To determine the semiminor diameter, b, we consider point C on the trajectory in Fig. IV.1. Distance r_c is indicated as f in the diagram, and the distance from the focus f_1 to the center at M is g. Using the basic definition of a conic, we can say:

$$\frac{f}{DC} = \frac{f}{p+g} = \epsilon \tag{IV.3}$$

Noting the shaded right triangle in the diagram, we can write

$$f = \sqrt{b^2 + g^2} \tag{IV.4}$$

By substituting Eq. IV.4 into equation IV.3, squaring both sides, and rearranging, we get

$$b^2 + g^2 = \epsilon^2 (p+g)^2 \tag{IV.5}$$

Observing Fig. IV.1 and noting Eq. IV.1, we can express the distance g as follows:

$$g = a - r_1 = a - \frac{\epsilon p}{1+\epsilon} \tag{IV.6}$$

Substituting Eq. IV.6 into Eq. IV.5, we get

$$b^2 + \left(a - \frac{\epsilon p}{1+\epsilon}\right)^2 = \epsilon^2 \left(p + a - \frac{\epsilon p}{1+\epsilon}\right)^2 \tag{IV.7}$$

From Eq. IV.2 we see that

$$p = \frac{a}{\epsilon}(1-\epsilon^2) \tag{IV.8}$$

Substituting Eq. IV.8 into Eq. IV.7, we have

$$b^2 + \left[a - \frac{a(1-\epsilon^2)}{1+\epsilon}\right]^2 = \epsilon^2 \left[\frac{a}{\epsilon}(1-\epsilon^2) + a - \frac{a(1-\epsilon^2)}{1+\epsilon}\right]^2$$

Canceling terms wherever possible, we get the desired result on noting Eq. IV.8:

$$b = a\sqrt{1-\epsilon^2} \tag{IV.9}$$

Finally, we can show by straightforward integration that the area of the ellipse is given as

$$A = \pi ab \tag{IV.10}$$

APPENDIX IV

Proof that Infinitesimal Rotations Are Vectors

You will recall that finite rotations did not qualify as vectors, even though they had magnitude and direction, because they did not combine according to the parallelogram law. Specifically the fact that the combination of finite rotations was not commutative disqualified them as vectors. We shall here show that, in the limit, as rotations become vanishingly small they *do* combine in a commutative manner and accordingly can then be considered as vectors.

Accordingly, consider Fig. V.1 showing a rigid body with point P at position r measured from stationary reference XYZ. If the body undergoes a small but finite rotation $\Delta\phi$ about axis A–A, point P goes to P', as has been in the diagram. We can express the magnitude of Δr between P and P'as follows:

$$|\Delta \boldsymbol{r}| \approx |\boldsymbol{r}| \sin\theta \Delta\phi \qquad \text{(V.1)}$$

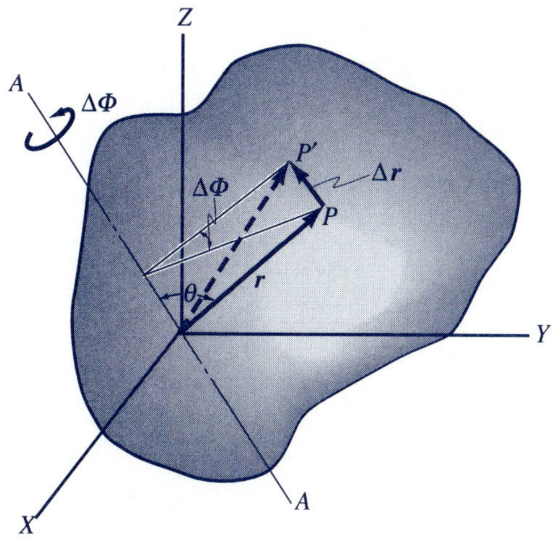

Figure V.1. Rigid body undergoes rotation $\Delta\phi$.

If we assume, for the moment, that $\Delta\phi$ is a vector having a direction along the axis of rotation consistent with the right-hand rule, we may express the equation:

$$\Delta \boldsymbol{r} \approx \Delta \boldsymbol{\phi} \times \boldsymbol{r} \tag{V.2}$$

In the limit as $\Delta\boldsymbol{\phi} \rightarrow 0$ the relation above becomes exact.

Now consider two arbitrary, small, but finite rotations represented by proposed vectors $\Delta\boldsymbol{\phi}_1$ and $\Delta\boldsymbol{\phi}_2$. For the first rotation we get a displacement for point P given as

$$\Delta \boldsymbol{r}_1 \approx \Delta \boldsymbol{\phi}_1 \times \boldsymbol{r} \tag{V.3}$$

And for a second successive rotation we get for point P:

$$\begin{aligned} \Delta \boldsymbol{r}_2 &\approx \Delta \boldsymbol{\phi}_2 \times (\boldsymbol{r} + \Delta \boldsymbol{r}_1) \\ &\approx \Delta \boldsymbol{\phi}_2 \times (\boldsymbol{r} + \Delta \boldsymbol{\phi}_1 \times \boldsymbol{r}) \end{aligned} \tag{V.4}$$

The total displacement for point P is then

$$\begin{aligned} \Delta \boldsymbol{r}_1 + \Delta \boldsymbol{r}_2 &\approx \Delta \boldsymbol{\phi}_1 \times \boldsymbol{r} + \Delta \boldsymbol{\phi}_2 \times (\boldsymbol{r} + \Delta \boldsymbol{\phi}_1 \times \boldsymbol{r}) \\ &\approx \Delta \boldsymbol{\phi}_1 \times \boldsymbol{r} + \Delta \boldsymbol{\phi}_2 \times \boldsymbol{r} + \Delta \boldsymbol{\phi}_2 \times (\Delta \boldsymbol{\phi}_1 \times \boldsymbol{r}) \end{aligned} \tag{V.5}$$

As the rotations become vanishingly small, we can replace the approximate equality sign by an exact equality sign and we can drop the last expression in the equation above as second order. We then have on collecting terms:

$$d\boldsymbol{r}_1 + d\boldsymbol{r}_2 = (d\boldsymbol{\phi}_1 + d\boldsymbol{\phi}_2) \times \boldsymbol{r} \tag{V.6}$$

We see from the above equation that the total displacement of any point P for successive infinitesimal rotations is *independent* of the order of these rotations. Thus, superposition of vanishingly small rotations is commutative and we can now fully accept $d\boldsymbol{\phi}$ as a vector.

APPENDIX V

Computer Projects: Statics & Dynamics

Preface

In this appendix you will find 12 statics projects and 17 dynamics projects specially designed for use on the computer. I have been careful to limit the programming needs for the problems not to go beyond the usual freshman course in Fortran programming. The programs conform completely to the ANSI standard for Fortran 77 and will run on any machine having an ANSI standard compiler.

At SUNY Buffalo and at G.W. we assign one or two projects per semester *on top* of our regular program. No regular class time is used to teach programming or to go over solutions. We give our students literature for logging in, editing, filing, etc. peculiar to the machine we will work on, and the students are supposed to learn to use the machine with the help of our Computing Center "consultants."

I would like to thank my graduate students, Dr. Sun Lei Chang and Dr. Anoop Dhingra, as well as Dr. John Hu; they did the original programming under my direction. Ms. Chashia Tracy Chan also deserves thanks for her help in rewriting the programs to make them totally standard conforming.

Contents

*Note that the **Newton Raphson** method can be profitably employed in Projects 24, 25, 26, 27, and 29. In each of the programs of these projects, will be found a subroutine for this well-known method. More detail is readily available in most mathematics textbooks.

PROJECT 1

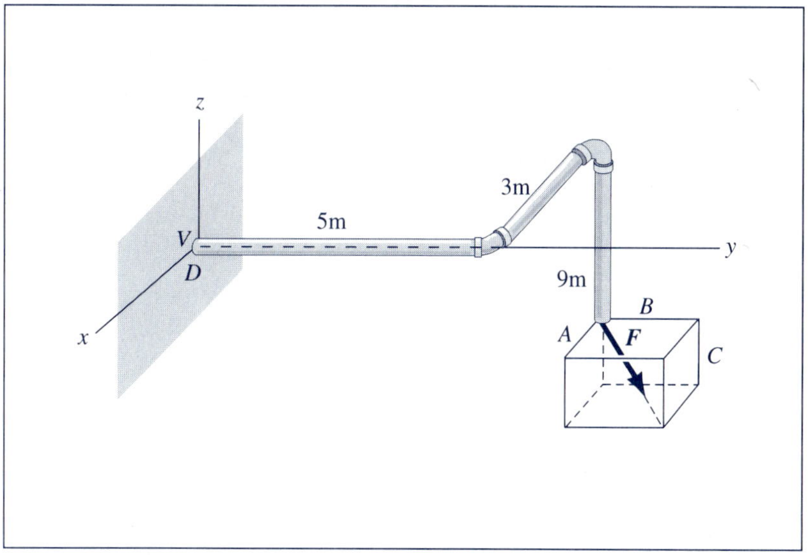

For all possible following sets of values of *A*, *B*, and *C*:

A (1., 2., 3.)
B (1., 2., 3.)
C (1., 2.5, 4.)

find M_x, M_y, and M_z at *D*.

(There are 27 different settings for the direction of force F = 1,000 N.)

Print out results as shown.

*** Project 1 ***

Force = 1,000.0 N

A	B	C	M_x	M_y	M_z
1.0	1.0	1.0	0.2309E + 04	−0.6928E + 04	−0.4619E + 04
			etc.		

PROJECT 2

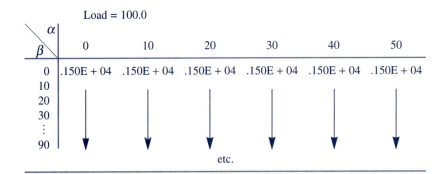

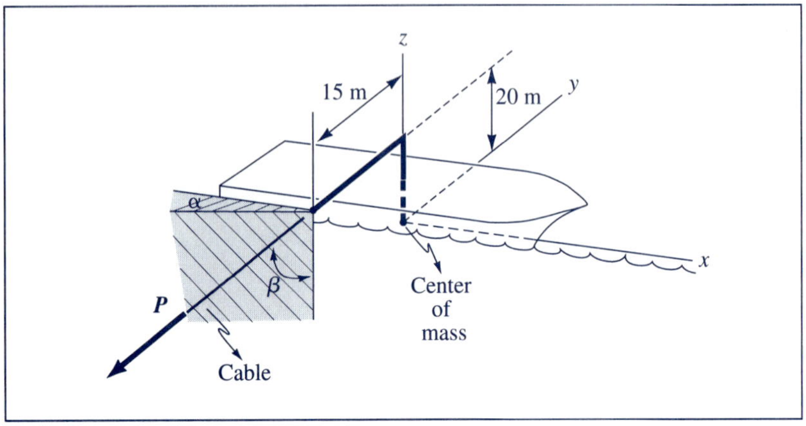

$\begin{cases} \alpha = \text{angle of vertical plane} \\ \beta = \text{angle of cable from vertical axis} \end{cases}$

Find the moment tending to tip the boat about its *x axis* from the cable shown, for the following conditions:

$P = 100$ N, 200 N, 300 N, 400 N
for each α (0°, 10°, 20°, 30°, 40°, 50°)
and for each β (0°, 10°, 20°, 30°, 40°, 50°, 60°, 70°, 80°, 90°)

Print out data as shown.

Load = 100.0

β \ α	0	10	20	30	40	50
0	.150E + 04	.150E + 04	.150E + 04	.150E + 04	.150E + 04	.150E + 04
10	↓	↓	↓	↓	↓	↓
20						
30						
⋮						
90						

etc.

PROJECT 3

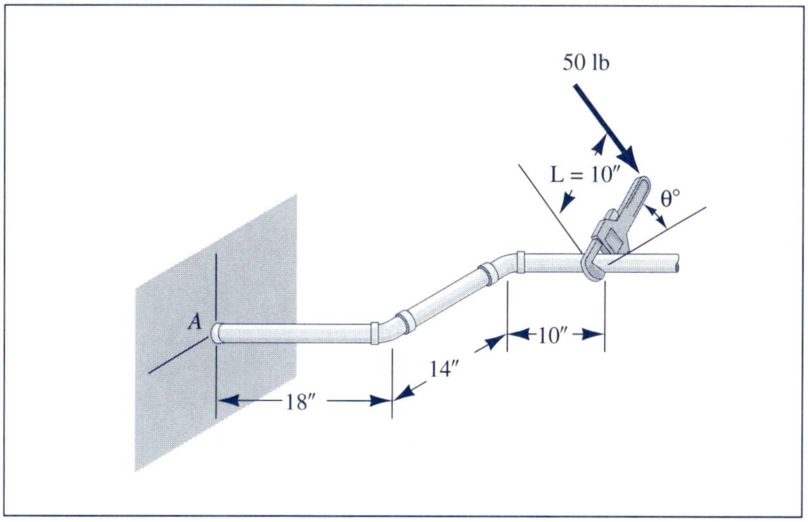

For setting of θ, going from zero to 330° in steps of 30°, compute *components* of *equivalent force system* at "*A*" for the 50-lb force for two distances of *L* being 0 in and 10 in.

Print out data as shown.

Note: I $\rightarrow \hat{\mathbf{i}}$, J $\rightarrow \hat{\mathbf{j}}$, K $\rightarrow \hat{\mathbf{k}}$.

θ \ L	0 in	10 in
0°	F = 0.00I + 0.00J + −50.00K	F = 0.00I + 0.00J + −50.00K
	C = −75.00I + −100.00J + 0.00K	C = −116.67I + −100.00J + 0.00K
30°	F =	F =
	C =	C =
60°		
⋮		
330°	etc.	

PROJECT 4

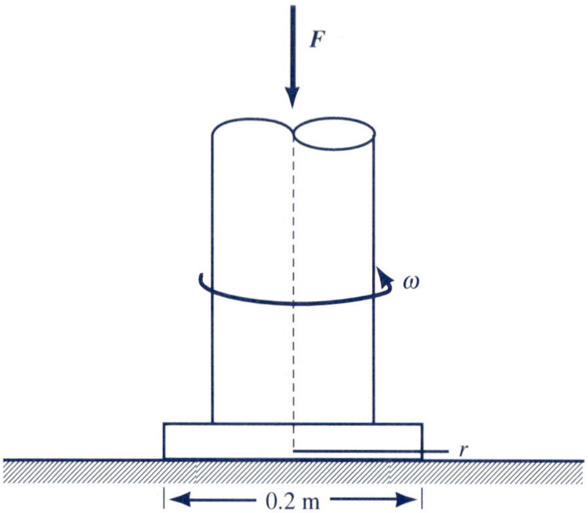

Dry Thrust Bearing

$F = 100, 200, 300$ N

Pressure = $P = K[\log(2 + \sqrt{r})](\cos 2\pi r)\ Pa$

(K is a constant you must determine)

μ varies with r

for	$r = 0.005$ m	$\mu = 0.40$
	$r = 0.015$ m	$\mu = 0.25$
	$r = 0.025$ m	$\mu = 0.15$
	$r = 0.035$ m	$\mu = 0.10$
	$r = 0.045$ m	$\mu = 0.07$
	$r = 0.055$ m	$\mu = 0.05$
	$r = 0.065$ m	$\mu = 0.04$
	$r = 0.075$ m	$\mu = 0.03$
	$r = 0.085$ m	$\mu = 0.02$
	$r = 0.095$ m	$\mu = 0.01$

Find Resisting Torque due to ***Coulomb friction***.

PROJECT 5

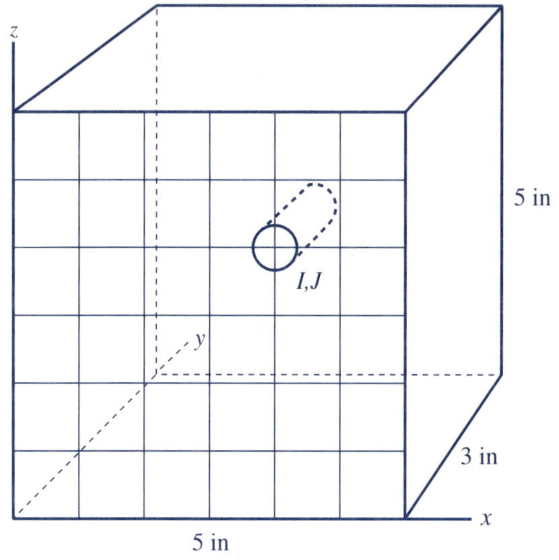

Find Centroidal Coordinates. There are 25 *equally spaced* holes in the block each with its *own diameter* and *length* that will be asked for *interactively* during the problem. Please *echo* the data you use.

$D(I, J)$ Diameter of each hole

$L(I, J)$ Length of each hole

$$\begin{cases} D(I, J) + D(I+1, J) \le \frac{5}{3}'' \\ D(I, J) + D(I, J+1) \le \frac{5}{3}'' \end{cases}$$

Indicate cases where

$D(I, J) + D(I+1, J) > \frac{5}{3}''$ or $D(I, J) + D(I, J+1) > \frac{5}{3}''$

For *your problem*

$$D(I, J) = \begin{bmatrix} .1 & .2 & .3 & .2 & .1 \\ .2 & .1 & .3 & .1 & .2 \\ .3 & .4 & .5 & .4 & .3 \\ .4 & .5 & .4 & .5 & .4 \\ .5 & .3 & .1 & .3 & .5 \end{bmatrix} \text{in.} \qquad L(I, J) = \begin{bmatrix} .1 & .2 & .3 & .2 & .1 \\ .2 & .1 & .3 & .1 & .2 \\ .3 & .4 & .5 & .4 & .3 \\ .4 & .5 & .4 & .5 & .4 \\ .5 & .3 & .1 & .3 & .5 \end{bmatrix} \text{in.}$$

Print out data as shown:

The size of the block:

Length = 5.0 in.
Width = 3.0 in.
Height = 5.0 in.

(D(1,1), L(1,1))   (D(1,2), L(1,2))   ⟶

(D(2,1), L(2,1))   (D(2,2), L(2,2))   ⟶

↓   ↓

(D(5,1), L(5,1))   (D(5,2), L(5,2))   ⟶

The coordinates of center of volume: (2.50000, ______, ______)

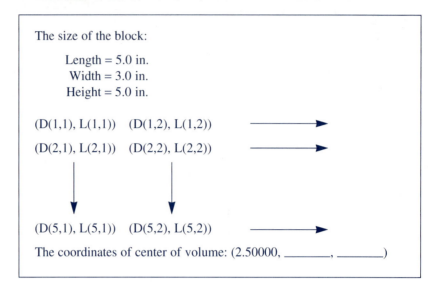

PROJECT 6

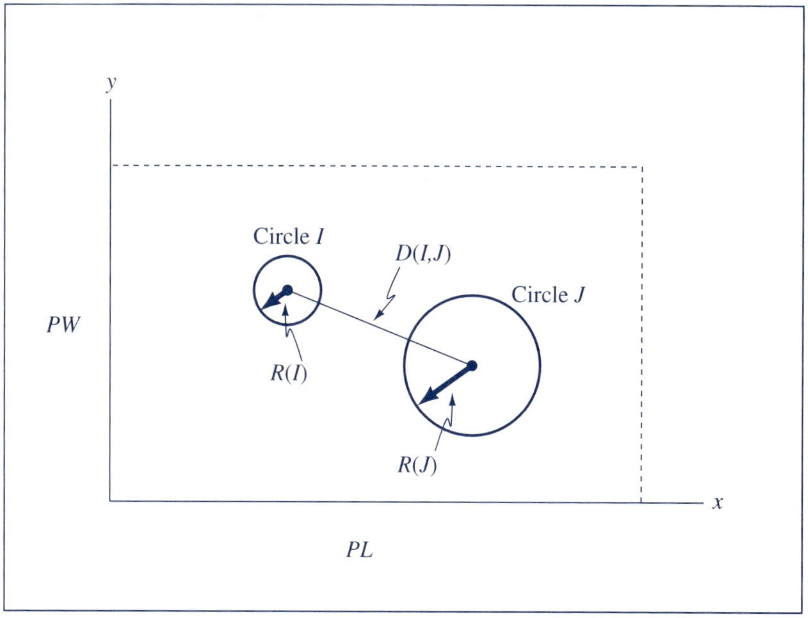

There are up to 100 circular holes randomly distributed in a rectangular plate, each with its own radius and *x*, *y* coordinates that will be asked for interactively during the program. The program will check if *overlaps* occur between holes or hole and boundary. If overlaps occur then the program will print a message indicating kind of overlap. Otherwise, calculate the *centroidal coordinates* of the plate. The plate has *length PL* and *width PW* that will be asked for interactively.

Procedure

a) Input data; Echo
b) Check *overlap* with *boundary*. (Print out which holes have overlap with boundaries.)
 $X(I) + R(I) > X_{max}$ $X(I) - R(I) < 0$
 $Y(I) + R(I) > Y_{max}$ $Y(I) - R(I) < 0$
c) Check *overlay* between *circles*. (Print out which holes overlap with each other.)
 $D(I,J) < R(I) + R(J)$
d) Calculate area and first moments about X and Y axes.
e) Calculate the centroidal coordinates.
f) Print out in the following format:

Length = ________ Width = ________

Hole	XCOOR	YCOOR	RADIUS
1	↓	↓	↓
2			
⋮			

Area of plate is ____________.

The centroidal coordinates are

XCOOR = ____________

YCOOR = ____________

Use your program for the following cases:

Case 1

PL = 50.000
PW = 30.000

X(I)	Y(I)	R(I)
13.00	21.00	4.00
45.00	24.00	2.00
38.00	25.00	4.00
5.00	23.00	3.00
25.00	2.00	1.00

Case 2

PL = 28.00
PW = 14.00

X(I)	Y(I)	R(I)
5.0	12.0	3.0
18.5	2.0	1.0
25.0	13.0	0.5
16.0	10.0	2.0
22.0	12.0	3.0
18.0	3.0	2.0

PROJECT 7

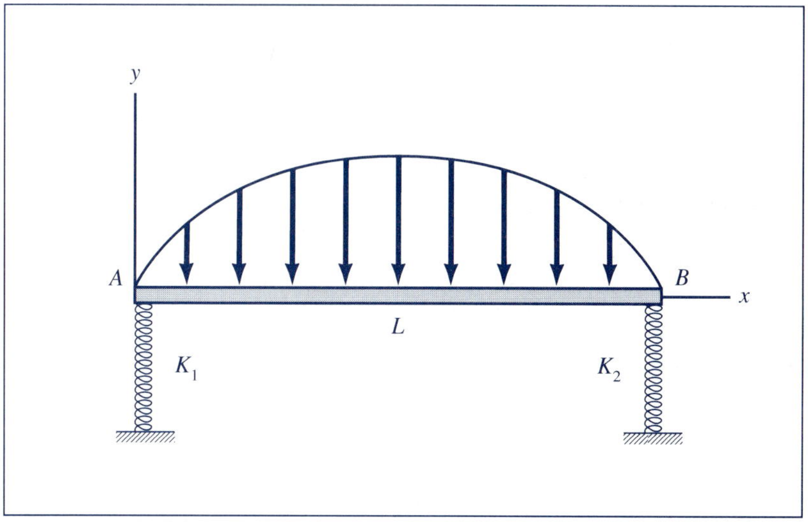

A nonuniform force distribution acts on a rigid beam *AB* supported by two different nonlinear springs. Compute the slope of beam *AB* for the following conditions.

Force: $-\left[10\sin\left(2\pi\frac{X}{L}\right)+15\log_{10}\left(\frac{X}{5}+1\right)\right]e^{-X}\ \frac{\text{N}}{\text{m}}$

Spring 1: $K_1 = |Y|^{3/2}\times 5\times 10^4\ \frac{\text{N}}{\text{mm}}$

Spring 2: $K_2 = |Y|^{4/3}\times 10^4\ \frac{\text{N}}{\text{mm}}$

The length of the beam L will be inputted interactively.

Work out for $L = 2.0$ m and $L = 2.5$ m

In your output give:

Length of beam
Y_1 and Y_2 in mm
Slope of AB in radians and in degrees.

PROJECT 8

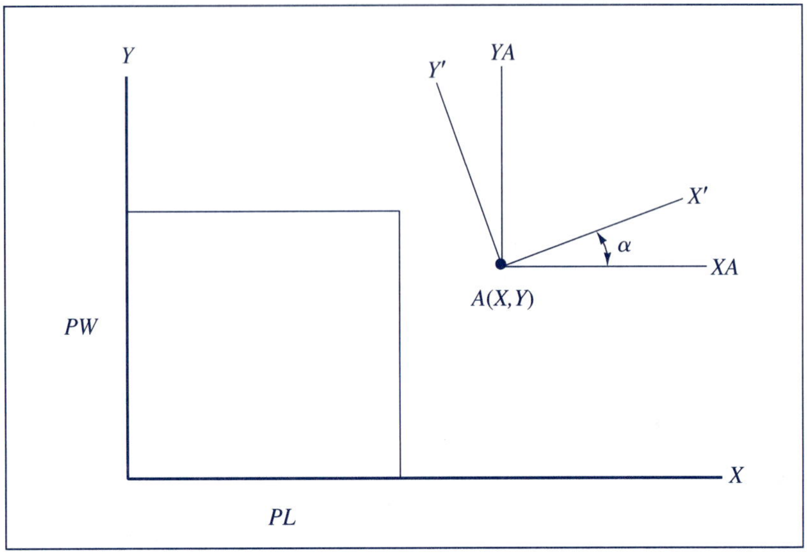

For *any set* of values given interactively.

Length: PL
Width: PW
Position: $A(X,Y)$
Angle: α

Find at A and for the following data

$I_{X'X'}, I_{Y'Y'}, I_{X'Y'}$:	Second moments of area (cross-hatched).
I'_1, I'_2:	Principal second moments of area.

Note: Point A can be inside area.

Work out for the *following data*:

$$PL = 18.00 \text{ mm}$$
$$PW = 12.00 \text{ mm}$$
$$\alpha = 22.5°$$
$$(X,Y)_A = 15.00 \text{ mm}, -8.00 \text{ mm}$$

PROJECT 9

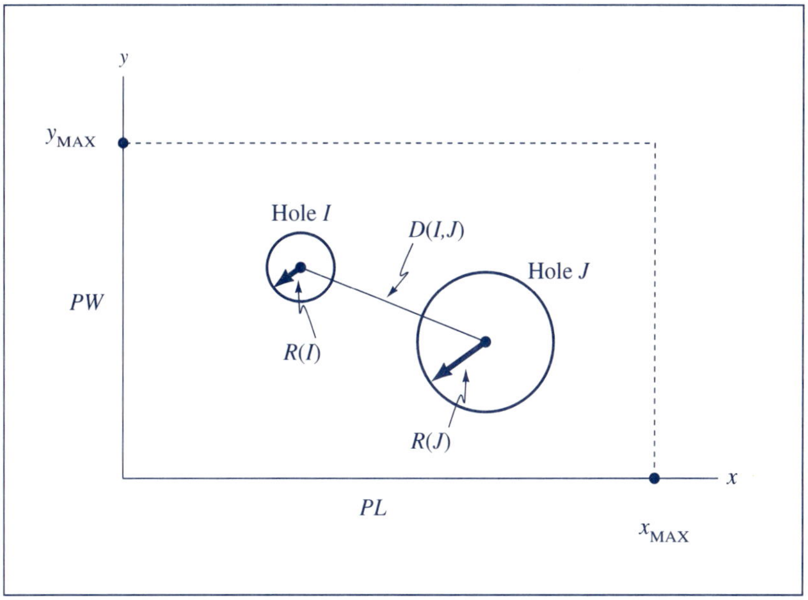

There are up to 100 circular holes randomly distributed in a rectangular plate. Each hose has its own radius and *x*, *y* coordinates that will be asked for interactively during the program. The program will check if *overlaps* occur between *holes* or *hole* and *boundary*. If overlaps occur then the program will print a message. Otherwise, the program calculates I_{XX}, I_{YY}, I_{XY} for area of the plate surface.

Procedure

a) Input. Specify PL, PW, X(I), Y(I), R(I), and N (the number of holes).
b) Check overlap with boundary

For $1 \leq I \leq N$

$$\text{If} \begin{cases} X(I) + R(I) > PL \\ X(I) - R(I) < 0 \\ Y(I) + R(I) > PW \\ Y(I) - R(I) < 0 \end{cases}$$

Then print out: "Circle I has overlap with boundary."

PROJECT 10

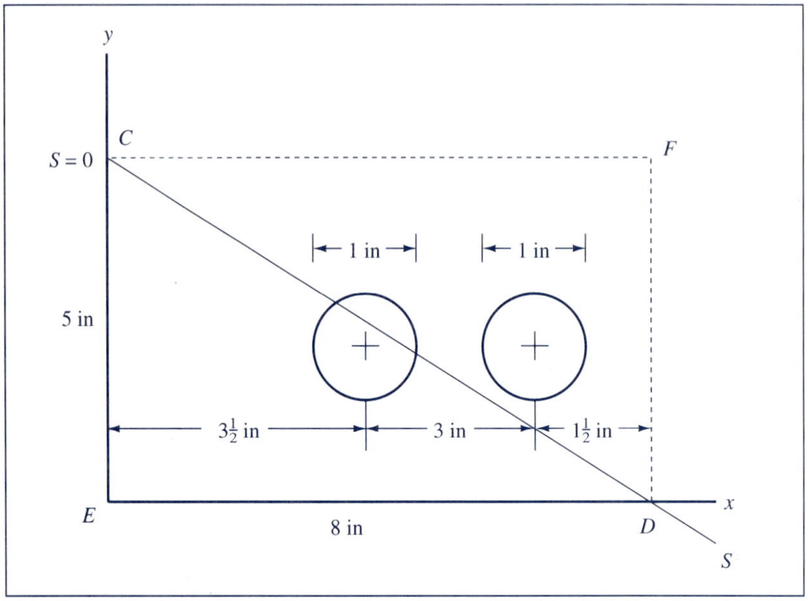

At what point S along CD do you get the maximum second moment of area for area $CEDF$ having 2 holes. What is its value? (Even if you know intuitively where this point is, show this via the computer.)

PROJECT 11

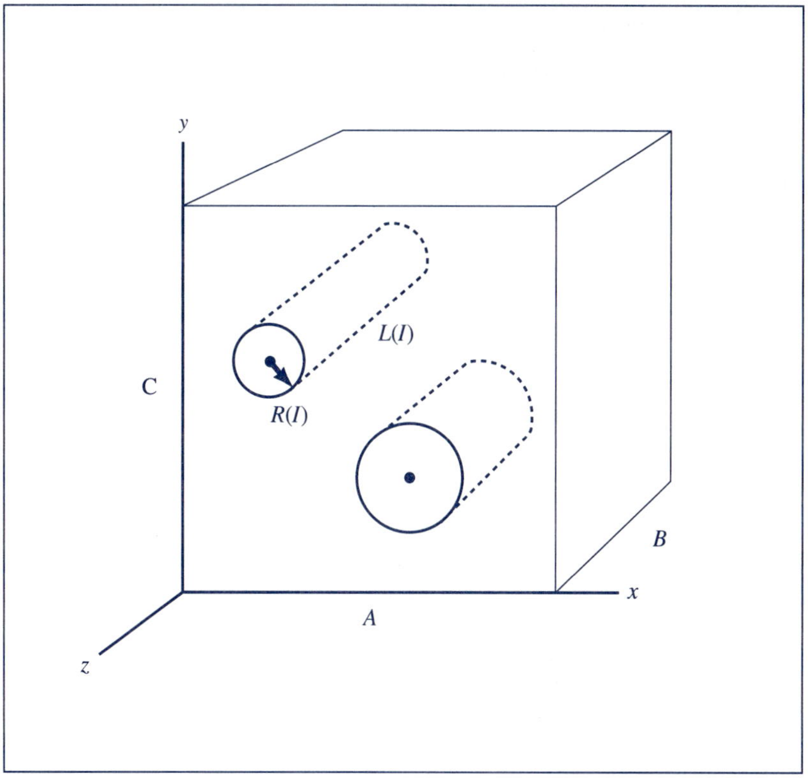

User selects dimensions A, B, C for a block with a random system of holes having

$$X(I)$$
$$Y(I)$$
$$R(I)$$
$$L(I)$$

Check for overlap of holes with boundary. If so print out which holes overlap with boundary. Check for overlap of holes with each other. If so print out which holes overlap with each other. Compute I_{xx}, I_{yy}, and I_{xy} for unit density of block. Run program for the following cases.

Case 1

A = 50 B = 60 C = 70

Hole	X(I)	Y(I)	L(I)	R(I)
1	12.00	18.00	29.00	5.50
2	27.00	32.00	3.00	5.10
3	35.00	41.00	41.00	1.70
4	20.00	20.00	23.00	0.10

Case 2

A = 20 B = 30 C = 40

Hole	X(I)	Y(I)	L(I)	R(I)
1	4.00	4.00	13.00	2.00
2	4.00	15.00	23.00	2.50
3	14.00	3.00	24.00	1.20
4	13.00	19.00	1.00	1.10
5	19.00	25.00	28.00	3.00
6	19.00	26.00	1.00	0.10
7	10.00	15.00	30.00	0.30
8	2.00	15.00	1.00	0.10

PROJECT 12

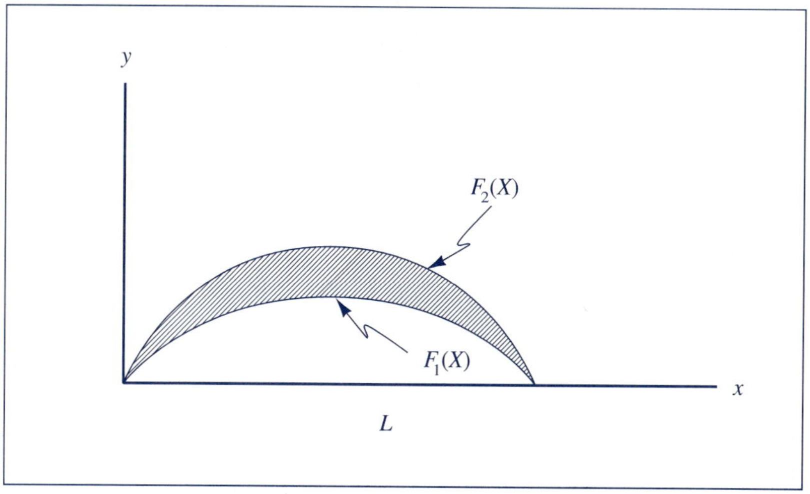

Write a program for computing the second moments and products of area I_{xx}, I_{yy}, I_{xy} for the cross-hatched area. User inputs L.

The functions describing the curves are:

$$F_1(X) = X\left(\frac{X-L}{2}\right)\left(\sinh\frac{X}{L}\right)e^{-X/L}$$

$$F_2(X) = X\left(\frac{L-X}{L^2}\right)\cosh\left(\frac{L-X}{L}\right)$$

Run problem for $L = 1$, $L = 50$.

PROJECT 13

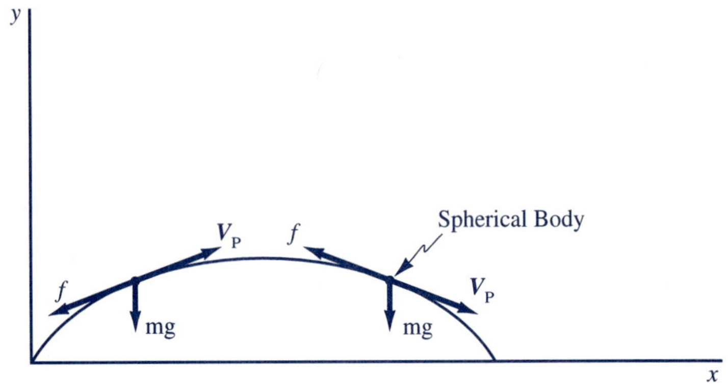

Projectile with Friction

Newton's Law for projectile motion (a spherical body) is given as:

$$m\frac{d\mathbf{V}_p}{dt} = -\frac{1}{2}C_D\rho\left|\mathbf{V}_p\right|^2\frac{(\pi D^2)}{4}\left[\frac{-\mathbf{V}_p}{\left|\mathbf{V}_p\right|}\right] - mg\mathbf{j}$$

where

C_D = drag coeffiecient for air
ρ = density of air
D = diameter of sphere
μ = coefficient of viscosity

Let

$$\frac{m}{(3\pi D\mu)} = \tau \qquad \text{(Dimension of time)}$$

$$\frac{\rho\left|\mathbf{V}_p\right|D}{\mu} = Re \qquad \text{Reynolds number (Dimensionless)}$$

$$\therefore \quad \frac{d\mathbf{V}_p}{dt} = -\frac{C_D Re}{24\tau}\mathbf{V} - g\mathbf{j}$$

The Scalar Equations are:

$$\frac{du}{dt} = \frac{C_D \text{ Re}}{24\tau} u \qquad \rightarrow u = \frac{dx}{dt}$$

$$\frac{dv}{dt} = -\frac{C_D Re}{24\tau} v - g \qquad \rightarrow v = \frac{dy}{dt}$$

I

Problem:

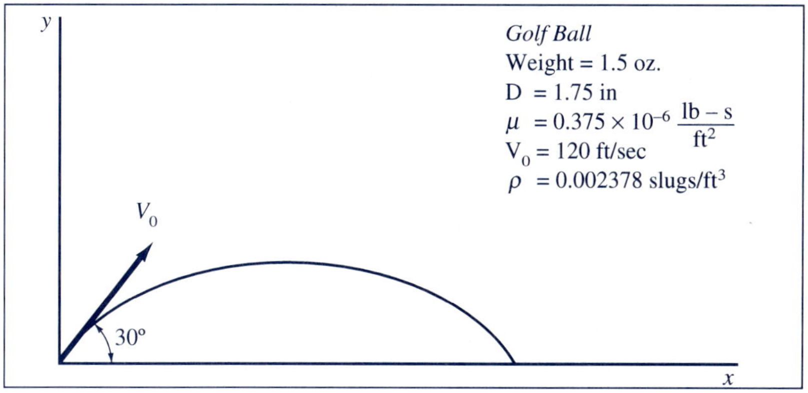

a) Find *trajectory* at *discrete points*.
b) Find time *of flight*.

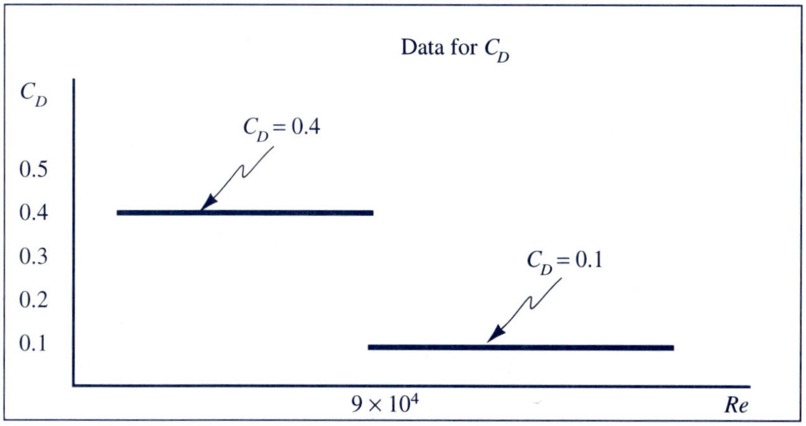

Algorithm—Method of *Central Differences*:

$$u(t) = u(t - \Delta t) - \frac{C_D \,\text{Re}}{24\tau}\left[\frac{u(t) + u(t - \Delta t)}{2}\right]\Delta t$$

$$v(t) = v(t - \Delta t) - \frac{C_D \,\text{Re}}{24\tau}\left[\frac{v(t) + v(t - \Delta t)}{2}\right]\Delta t - g\Delta t$$

$$x(t) = x(t - \Delta t) + \frac{\Delta t}{2}\left[u(t - \Delta t) + u(t)\right]$$

$$y(t) = y(t - \Delta t) + \frac{\Delta t}{2}\left[v(t - \Delta t) + v(t)\right]$$

Use $\Delta t = .04$ sec.

Program should end with $y \leq 0$ (when ball hits ground)

Note: $\tau = \dfrac{m}{3\pi D\mu} = \dfrac{1.5/[(16)(g)]}{3\pi(1.75/12)(0.375 \times 10^{-6})} = 5,650$ sec.

Print out result:

t (sec)	x (ft)	y (ft)
0.04	4.149	2.37

and thereafter every 0.2 seconds

Hints: (1) Solve for $u(t)$ and $v(t)$ from Eqs. I before writing program

(2) Let $U_1 = u(t - \Delta t)$ $\quad V_1 = v(t - \Delta t)$
$U_2 = u(t)$ $\quad V_2 = v(t)$

Starting with initial data for U_1 and V_1 solve for U_2 and V_2. Then *increment* by letting $V_1 = V_2$ and $U_1 = U_2$. This is done with a DO loop needed to determine C_D and to print out.

(3) Use the condition

```
If ((I/5)*5 .Eq. I)
Print . . .
```

to print out every 5*th* term

PROJECT 14

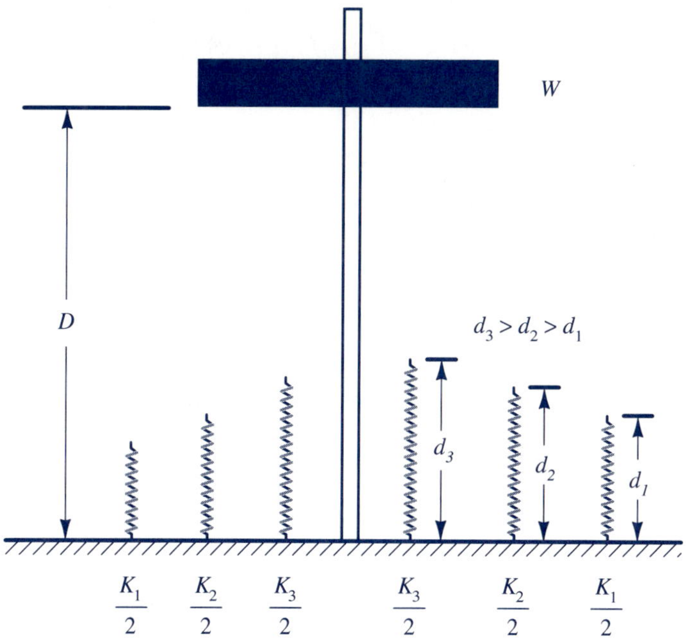

Six Linear Springs

Develop a program to find how close bottom of *W* comes to the base (ground) for the data:

W (weight)	(N)
D	(m)
d_1, d_2, d_3	(m)
k_1, k_2, k_3	(N/m)

that the user will supply interactively. Print out data used and desired distance.

Run program for the following data:

W = 1000N
D = 1.00 m
d_1 = 0.20 m k_1 = 15,000 N/m
d_2 = 0.25 m k_2 = 16,000 N/m
d_3 = 0.30 m k_3 = 18,000 N/m

PROJECT 15

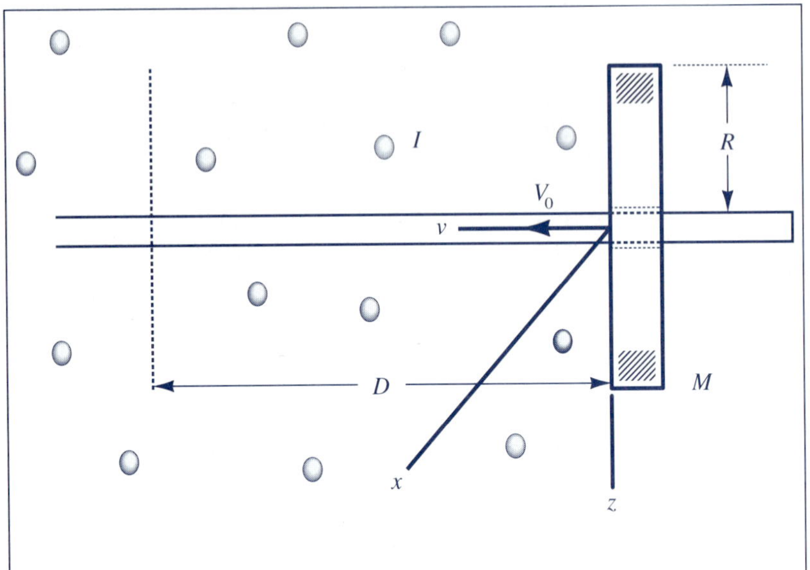

A Circular Plate of M and Radius R

A circular plate moving initially at speed V_0 to left hits a random distribution of particles which are initially stationary and which have the following data:

$M(I)$	mass
$E(I)$	coefficient of restitution
$X(I)$, $Y(I)$, $Z(I)$	position

Check that the $Y(I)$ coordinates are in ascending order. To avoid the possibility of particle collisions make sure that for the particles, $X(I) \neq X(J)$ and $Z(I) \neq Z(J)$ for any $I \neq J$. Write a program for the speed of the disc after it moves a distance D. If plate stops or reverses direction before reaching D, have statement printed that plate does not reach position $Y = D$. User supplies all above data interactively. Use SI units. Consider that the data is such that the particles do not collide with each other after impacting with the plate.

Run program for following data (SI units). Echo this data in your output.

The mass of the plate is 100.00 kg
Radius is 2.00 m
The initial speed of the plate is 60.00 m/s
The distance D is 55 m

No.	Mass (kg)	Restitution Coefficient	*X* Coordinate (m)	*Y* Coordinate (m)	*Z* Coordinate (m)
1	2.500	0.230	1.200	1.200	0.400
2	5.500	0.450	0.890	2.300	0.980
3	3.300	0.890	3.200	5.800	0.440
4	7.500	0.440	4.200	7.600	0.890
5	2.200	0.230	0.440	11.100	6.400
6	5.500	0.210	0.360	13.500	0.870
7	3.100	0.670	0.720	16.600	0.010
8	3.100	0.190	0.540	18.300	9.800
9	2.200	0.450	0.540	21.700	32.700
10	1.700	0.100	0.210	28.600	7.600
11	0.760	0.880	0.760	31.900	0.890
12	0.650	0.560	0.230	36.380	0.650
13	5.800	0.100	0.100	40.100	0.430
14	5.100	0.670	1.400	42.100	1.650
15	3.200	0.230	1.780	48.400	4.200
16	2.100	0.540	5.300	49.100	2.700
17	0.200	0.220	2.300	51.500	1.400
18	0.560	0.550	3.200	54.600	1.000
19	0.320	0.230	1.100	56.400	0.430
20	1.650	0.230	1.430	61.800	3.200

PROJECT 16

In project 16 each particle is to have its own constant velocity component V_y before impact.

1. Assume particles are very small compared to the plate.
2. Insure that $X(I) \neq X(J)$ and $Z(I) \neq Z(J)$ for $I \neq J$.

User will specify the velocity component V_y before impact keeping $V_x = V_z = 0$.

Procedure: Choose small distances of plate movement equal to 0.01 m. At the beginning of the n*th* interval you will have the position of the entire system and the velocities of all the particles as well as the plate velocity $(V_p)_n$. With these velocities compute new positions after the time interval $\frac{0.01}{(V_p)_n}$. Now the plate will have moved from $(Y_p)_m$ to $(Y_p)_{m+1}$, a distance equal to 0.01 m.

If

a) A particle i has a change of position which causes it to cross position $(Y_p)_{n+1}$ during this time interval.

b) Then let impact occur giving the plate a new velocity. As an approximation consider this new velocity to occur at the beginning of the $(n+1)$ time step.

c) If the velocity of the plate should become zero or negative before reaching position D, print out the fact that the plate does not reach position D.

The Y coordinates can be in any order of sequence.

Run program for the same following data:

The mass of the plate is 100.00 kg.
Radius is 2.00 m.
D = 55 m.
The initial speed of the plate is 60.00 (m/s).

PROJECT 17

Determine if the torpedo hits the freighter and if so how far D from the bow of the freighter. The freighter is 20 meters long. Do this for all the following sets of values of V_1, V_2, α:

$$\alpha = (15, 20, 25, 30, 35, 40, 45)^\circ$$
$$V_1 = (15, 20, 25, 30, 35, 40) \text{ m/s}$$
$$V_2 = (20, 25, 30, 35, 40, 45) \text{ m/s}$$

where

V_1 = velocity of the freighter
V_2 = velocity of the torpedo
α = degree as shown

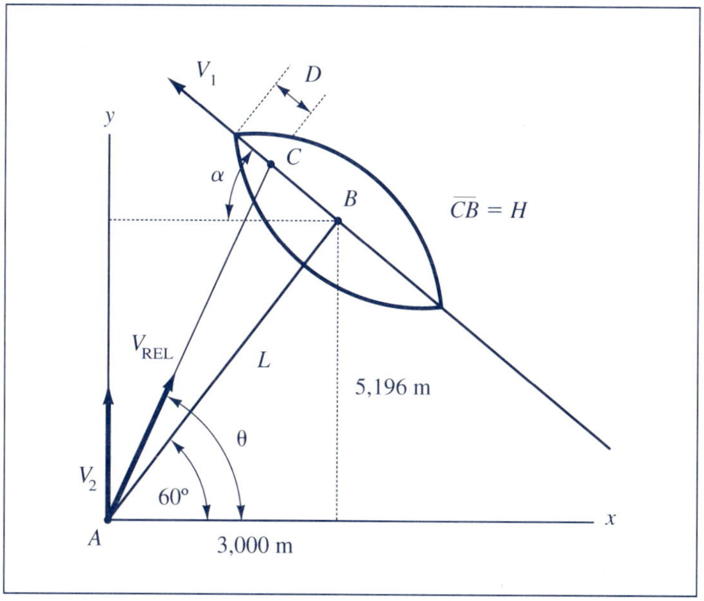

Hint: Use law of sines for triangle ABC.

PROJECT 18

Do project 17 where the velocity of the light freighter at the configuration shown is 10 km/hr and which we take at the time $t = 0$. The velocity varies in the following manner.

$$V_1 = 10 + 1.8\sqrt{te^{-0.1t}}\,\text{km/hr}$$

where t is in seconds.

Procedure: Choose small time intervals of 0.01 seconds. Compute velocity of the torpedo relative to the freighter at each time interval. After each time interval find how much the torpedo has moved along a line *normal* to the freighter and along a direction *parallel* to the freighter. When the normal distance equals or exceeds $\sqrt{(3,000)^2 + (5,196)^2}$ make your conclusions. User enters V_2 km/hr and $\alpha°$ interactively.

Run program for:

$V_2 = 45$ km/hr
$V_2 = 35$ km/hr
$V_2 = 20$ km/hr
$\alpha = 30°$

PROJECT 19

A mass M can slide in a frictionless manner along rod EF. At position shown, spring K_1 is compressed D_1 inches and M is at distance D_2 feet from F. Spring K_2 is elongated D_3 inches. The spring constants are K_1 lb/in and K_2 lb/in. The mass is M lbm. Find the velocity of the mass as a function of the distance it moves, and find the amplitude of the vibration. User specifies M lbm, K_1 lb/in, K_2 lb/in, D_1 in, D_2 ft, D_3 in. Run the program for the following data:

M = 30 lbm
K_1 = 1.0 lb/in
K_2 = 0.5 lb/in
D_1 = 6 in
D_2 = 4 ft
D_3 = 1 in

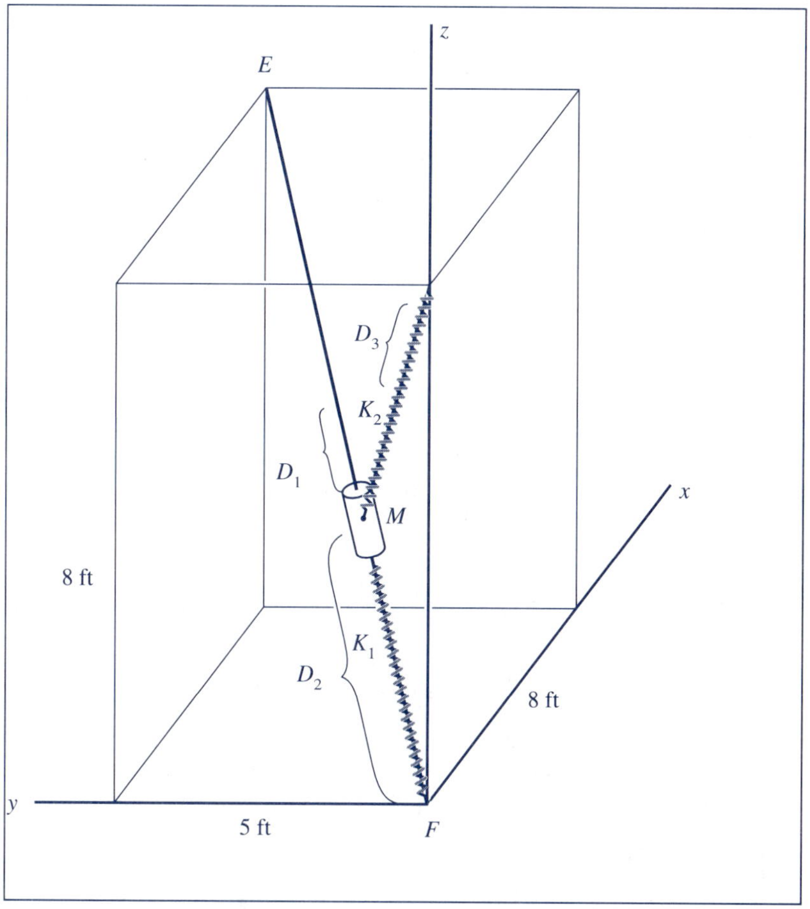

PROJECT 20

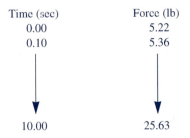

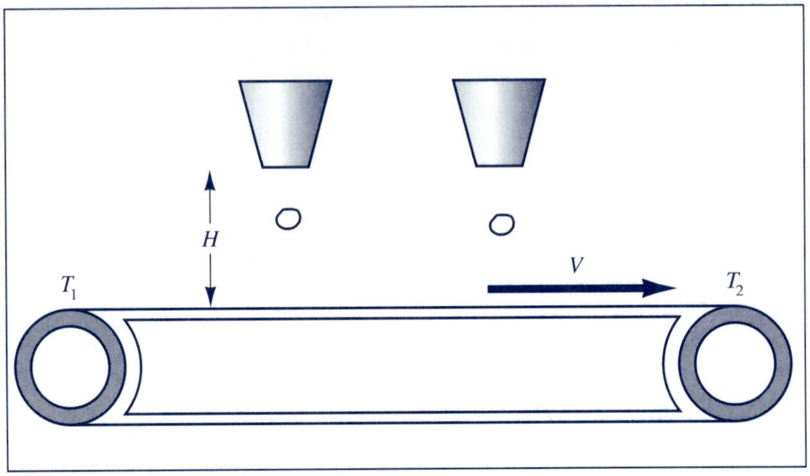

Find $(T_2 - T_1)$ as a function of time as the belt accelerates uniformly from V_1 ft/sec to V_2 ft/sec in T sec. $N(t)$ bodies at any time t, each of mass M lbm, hit the belt from the hoppers after falling a distance H. The weight of the belt resting on the bed is W lb and the coefficient of dynamic friction between belt and bed of the conveyor is U. The number of impacts per second, $N(t)$, is $20e^{-0.1t}\,|\sin t|$. Also at $t(0)$ there are 2 particles on the belt. Work the problem out in 100 time intervals.

Run problem for the following data:

W = 20 lb
V_1 = 1.5 ft/sec
V_2 = 7.5 ft/sec
T = 10 sec
M = 0.5 lbm
H = 2 ft
U = 0.23

Take time intervals of 0.001 sec and print out the result at every tenth of a second as follows:

Time (sec)	Force (lb)
0.00	5.22
0.10	5.36
↓	↓
10.00	25.63

PROJECT 21

Piston P moves downward at a speed of 1 ft/sec, when $\alpha = 45°$ and BP is vertical. Find the velocity and acceleration of A as α goes from 45° to 20° for each degree.

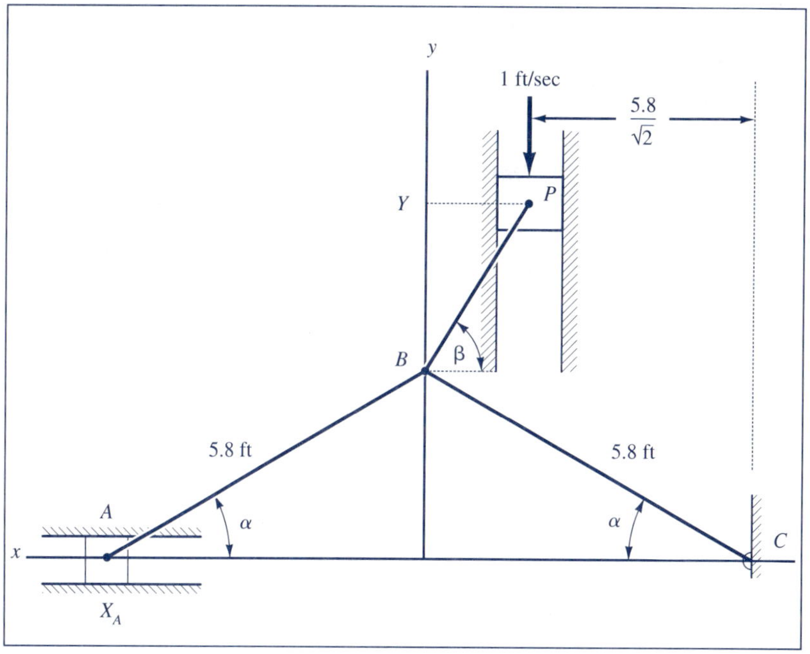

Procedure: Using simple trigonometry, write two equations relating α, β, and Y. Differentiate with respect to time to reach two equations relating $\dot{\alpha}$, $\dot{\beta}$, and $\dot{Y}$. Differentiate again to get two equations relating $\ddot{\alpha}$, $\ddot{\beta}$, and $\ddot{Y}$. (Here $\ddot{Y} = 0$). Now with the computer, using these results and some more trig, get for each α the velocity and acceleration of A. Print out your results.

PROJECT 22

Do project 21 with the velocity of the piston varying with *position* so as to increase as the square of its vertical distance going from 1 ft/sec to 3 ft/sec as α goes from $\alpha = 45°$ to $\alpha = 20°$.

Procedure: Develop equations as instructed in project 21. Write a subroutine giving for any value I, which will be a dummy variable going from 45 to 20 in steps of 1, the values of α, β, and Y. Now get the velocity of the piston to vary as asked for above. Use the subroutine to facilitate this. Next as I goes from 45 to 20, get α, β, $\dot{\alpha}$, $\dot{\beta}$, $\dot{Y}$, and finally $\ddot{Y}$ in a DO loop calling in the subroutine for each I. Now get X_A and $\dot{X}_A$. Print out results.

PROJECT 23

Find the *magnitude* of the velocity and the *magnitude* of the acceleration of the man in the cockpit as arm *DA* rotates 90° in 20 equal increments. Get 20 readings during this part of the motion. Consider 20 successive *stationary* axes *XYZ* at *D* with *XY* axes in the plane of *DAB* for each setting. Take angular accelerations as *constant* and the ω's given as *initial* values.

Procedure: Compute $\boldsymbol{V}_{XYZ}$ and $\boldsymbol{a}_{XYZ}$ with β and $\dot{\beta}$ unspecified. In a DO loop for each rotation of 4.5° of *DA* starting from 0°, determine ω_2 after each interval. Find the time for that interval. Then get β, ω_1, ω_2 at the end of the interval. Now get $|\boldsymbol{V}_{XYZ}|$, $|\boldsymbol{a}_{XYZ}|$ at the end of the interval and print out results for each interval, 0°, 4.5°, 9°, etc.

Take α = 45° and constant DA = 13 m

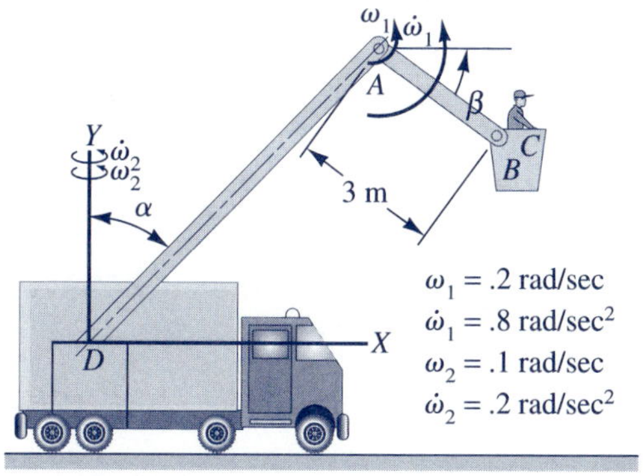

PROJECT 24

Start with Fig. 15.17, find ω_{BC} in 20 steps as the disk rotates 90° from the position shown.

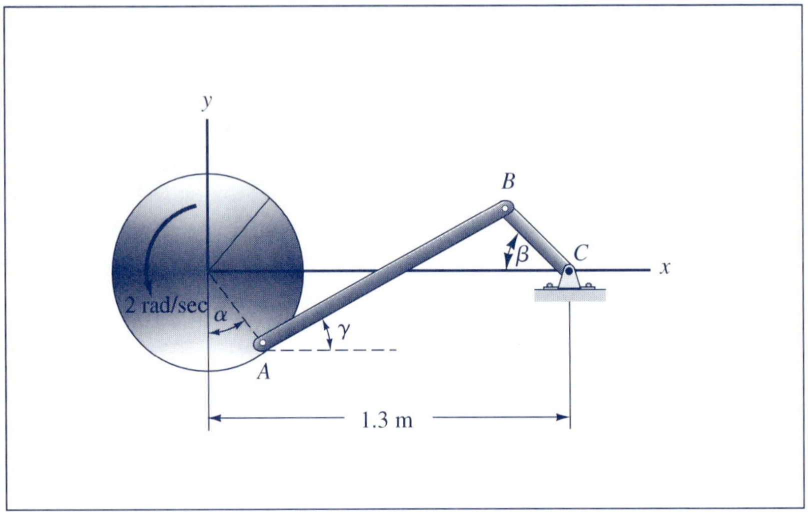

Procedure:

a) For each α, find β and γ.
b) Consider rod AB. Get ω_{AB} and V_B. Also get $\dot{\beta}$. Then get $\dot{\omega}_{AB}$ and $\dot{\omega}_{BC}$.
c) For each α, print out ω_{BC} and $\dot{\omega}_{BC}$.

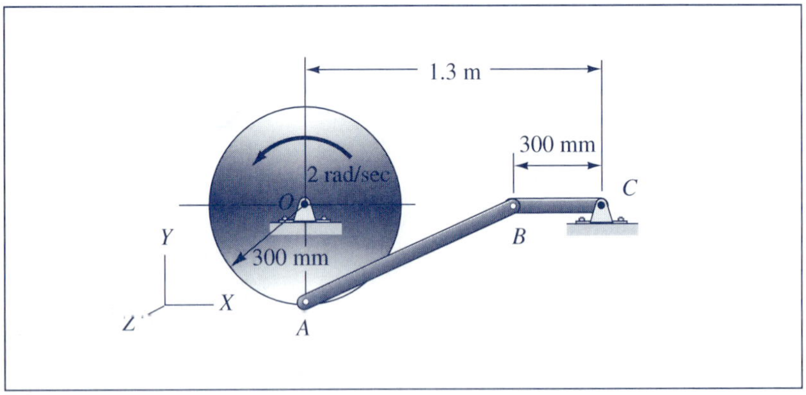

PROJECT 25

Compute the angular velocity and angular acceleration of the four bar linkage in FBARS.FOR. Print the angular acceleration of *BC* and α in 20 steps.

PROJECT 26

Do project 24 for variable angular speed of disc given as:

$$\omega_{DISC} = 2 + 1.3\,|\alpha|^{3/2} \text{ rad/sec}$$

where α is in radians.

PROJECT 27

Compute the angular velocity and angular acceleration in FBAR.FOR. For this case the angular speed of the disk is variable and is given as:

$$\omega = 2 + 1.3\lambda^{3/2} \text{ rad/sec}$$

Print the angular acceleration of *BC* and α in 20 steps.

PROJECT 28

In Example 15.14, we want to chart the performance characteristics of the centrifuge for the configuration shown to give the number of *g*'s acceleration of the astronauts head for the following conditions:

ω_1 2 → 20 rpm in 10 steps
ω_2 2 → 12 rpm in 6 steps
ω_3 = 5 rpm, 10 rpm, and 15 rpm
$\dot{\omega}_1$ = 5 rpm^2, 8 rpm^2, and 10 rpm^2

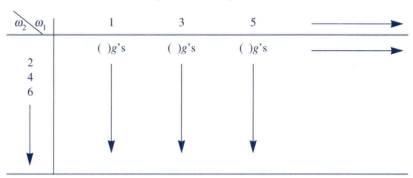

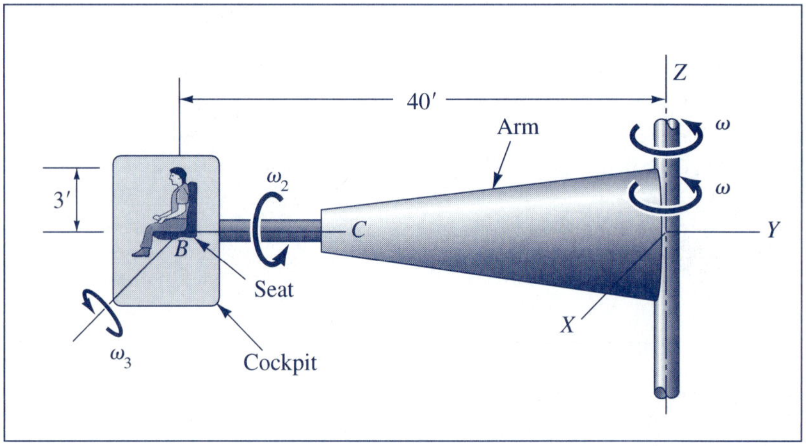

Given the results in the following format:

For ω_3 = 5 rpm, $\dot{\omega}_1$ = 5 rpm^2

ω_2 \ ω_1	1	3	5	→
	( )*g*'s	( )*g*'s	( )*g*'s	→
2	↓	↓	↓	
4				
6				
↓				

For ω_3 = 10 rpm, $\dot{\omega}_1$ = 5 rpm^2 etc.

PROJECT 29

In the centrifuge of example 15.14, find the values of ω_1 and ω_2 to maintain the same magnitude of acceleration, assuming the other data is fixed. Get results for accelerations of 0.5 g, 1.0 g and 1.5 g.

Use the *Newton-Raphson method* to determine the minimum value of ω_1 for any value of ω_2 which ranges from 0 rpm to 20 rpm.

Print out ω_1 in the following format:

ω_2	0.5 g	1.0 g	1.5 g
0.00	$(\omega_1)_{min}$	$(\omega_1)_{min}$	$(\omega_1)_{min}$
0.50	↓	↓	↓
1.00			
↓			
20.00			

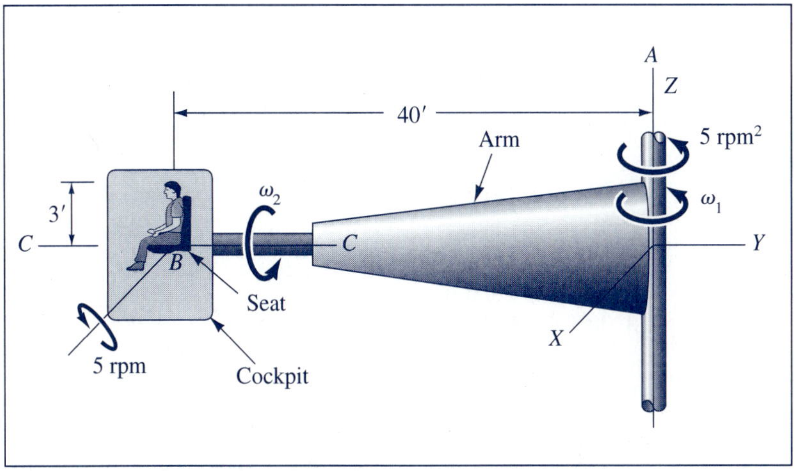

ANSWERS

2.2. $F = 38.5$ N @ 66.6° from x axis.
2.4. $L = 2.75$ km.
2.6. $B = 17.32$ N $\alpha = 60°$
2.8. $F_A = 100$ N @ −120° with horizontal.
$F_B = 76.53$ N @ −67.5° with horizontal.
$F_C = 76.53$ N @ −22.5° with horizontal.
2.10. $F = 846$ N @ 17.68° with horizontal.
2.12. $T_{AC} = 767.2$ N $\alpha = 36.8°$
2.14. $F = 1{,}206$ N.
2.16. $F = 137.5$ N @ 43.34° from x direction.
2.18. $F = 242$ lb @ 3.07° from x direction.
2.22. $F_{slot} = 36.4$ lbf; $F_{vertical} = 81.5$ lbf.
2.24. $F_{BC} = .630F$ $F_{vert} = .590F$.
2.26. 2,690 lb 803.8 lb.
2.28. $F_{AC} = 707$ N $\alpha = 90°$.
2.30. $\boldsymbol{F} = 215.9\boldsymbol{i} + 1968\boldsymbol{j} + 3151\boldsymbol{k}$ N.
2.32. $F = 37.4$ lb l = .267 m = .535 n = −.802
2.34. $\boldsymbol{F}_1 + \boldsymbol{F}_2 = 918.6\boldsymbol{i} - 1581\boldsymbol{j} - 835.8\boldsymbol{k}$ N.
2.36. $F_x = 400$ N $F_y = -1007$ N.
2.40. $\boldsymbol{F} = 25.7\boldsymbol{i} + 24.7\boldsymbol{j} + 16\boldsymbol{k}$ lb.
2.42. $\boldsymbol{A} = \pm 5\sqrt{2}\,\boldsymbol{i} \mp 5\sqrt{2}\,\boldsymbol{k}$.
2.44. $\boldsymbol{f} = .465\boldsymbol{i} + .814\boldsymbol{j} + .349\boldsymbol{k}$.
$\boldsymbol{F} = 46.5\boldsymbol{i} + 81.4\boldsymbol{j} + 34.9\boldsymbol{k}$ N.
2.46. −164 −.465 −10.5.
2.48. $\boldsymbol{D} = 10\boldsymbol{i} - .769\boldsymbol{j} - 3.77\boldsymbol{k}$.
2.52 .418 ft.
2.54. 37.05 N.
2.56. $A = 2.5$ N $\alpha = 45.7°$
2.58. −75 ft^2 95.94°.
2.60. −28.83 N.
2.62. 47.51°.
2.64. $(18\boldsymbol{i} + 20\boldsymbol{j} - 42\boldsymbol{k})$ 47.
2.68. $.804\boldsymbol{i} + .465\boldsymbol{j} + .372\boldsymbol{k}$
2.70. 640 m^2.
2.74. −29.6.
2.76. (a) $-43\boldsymbol{i} + 49\boldsymbol{j} + 2\boldsymbol{k}$.
(b) −136.
(c) −136.
2.78. $L_{DT} = 373$ miles $L_{TC} = 689$ miles
162 miles longer.
2.80. $F_x = 57.1$ N $F_y = 342.8$ N $F_z = 971.4$ N.
2.82. $F = 231.3$ N.
2.84. 32.4 ft-lb.
2.86. 112.4° −190.72 lb.
2.88. 35.7kN.
2.90. 19.87m.
2.92. $\boldsymbol{F} = -80.1 \times 10^{-13}\boldsymbol{k}$ N.
2.94. 251 ft^2.
2.96. 18.21m $(l, m, n) = (.5145, .6860, .5145)$.
2.98. $T_{AB} = 500$ N $T_{AC} = 866$ N $\alpha = 30°$.
2.100 15.90°.

3.2. $4\boldsymbol{i} - 16\boldsymbol{j} - 3\boldsymbol{k}$ ft.
3.4. $6\boldsymbol{i} + 7.16\boldsymbol{j} + 7.598\boldsymbol{k}$ m.
3.6. −1067.4 N-m 1959.3 N-m.
3.8. $\pm 2\sqrt{2z}\,\boldsymbol{j} + z\boldsymbol{k}$.
3.10. −18,026 N-m −6,824.8 N-m.
3.12. 13.8 m.
3.14. $-257.5\boldsymbol{k}$ N-m.
3.16. 8944 ft-lb 4472 ft-lb 0 ft-lb.
3.18. $180\boldsymbol{i} - 50\boldsymbol{k}$ kN-m.
$30\boldsymbol{i} + 75\boldsymbol{j} - 50\boldsymbol{k}$ kN-m.
$-1{,}551.8\boldsymbol{i} + 75\boldsymbol{j} + 389.4\boldsymbol{k}$ kN-m.
3.20. $-84\boldsymbol{i} + 94\boldsymbol{j} - 46\boldsymbol{k}$ N-m.
3.22. $\boldsymbol{M}_A = \frac{10}{\sqrt{3}}a\boldsymbol{k} - \frac{10}{\sqrt{3}}a\boldsymbol{j}$ lb-ft.
$\boldsymbol{M}_D = \boldsymbol{0}$ lb-ft.
$\boldsymbol{M}_I = -\frac{10}{\sqrt{3}}a\boldsymbol{i} + \frac{10}{\sqrt{3}}a\boldsymbol{j}$ lb-ft etc.
3.24. $(7.277F_{BA} + 8.575F_{CD} - 10{,}000)\boldsymbol{i}$ +
$(2.911F_{BA} - 5.145F_{CD})\boldsymbol{j}$ +
$(-2.911F_{BA} + 5.145F_{CD})\boldsymbol{k}$ ft-lb.
3.26. $1.3296F$ ft-lb.
3.28. 22.295 N-m $\boldsymbol{M}_D = -30\boldsymbol{i} + 100\boldsymbol{j} - 36\boldsymbol{k}$ N-m.
3.30. −146.2 lb 77.00 lb-ft.
3.32. 5,769 lb-ft.
3.34. −113.5 kN-m −117.5 kN-m.
3.38. 300 lb-ft 600 lb-ft 1,200 lb-ft.
3.40. 175 N.
3.42. $-7{,}270\boldsymbol{k}$ lb-ft $10{,}405\boldsymbol{k}$ lb-ft.
3.44. $\boldsymbol{M}_A = \boldsymbol{M}_P = -261\boldsymbol{i} - 261\boldsymbol{j}$ N-m.
3.46. 420 ft-lb.
3.48. $\boldsymbol{C} = 100\boldsymbol{i} + 50\boldsymbol{j} - 224\boldsymbol{k}$ lb-ft.
3.50. −1,857 N-m.
3.52 $\boldsymbol{M}_P = 48\boldsymbol{i} - 36\boldsymbol{j} - 225.6\boldsymbol{k}$ N-m.
$M_E = -146.9$ N-m.
3.54. $M = 3{,}635$ lb-in @ 68.2° to horizontal.
3.56. $\boldsymbol{C} = 35.35\boldsymbol{i} + 22.36\boldsymbol{j} + 80.07\boldsymbol{k}$ N-m.
3.58. 120 lb-ft 160 lb-ft 60 lb.
3.60. 1,750 N-m.
3.62. 408.4 N-m.
3.64. 1,179 ft-lb.
3.66. $-452\boldsymbol{k}$ lb-ft $-1{,}202\boldsymbol{k}$ lb-ft.
3.68 $10{,}600\boldsymbol{i} + 4{,}500\boldsymbol{j} - 5{,}000\boldsymbol{k}$ m.
12,554 m.
3.70. −27.2 N-m.
3.72. 277.6 N-m.

4.2. $F = 15$ kN $C = 30$ kN-m C.C.W.

4.4. $F = 150$ N $C = 187.5$ N-m.

4.6. $M_A = 8\boldsymbol{k}$ kN-m $F_A = F_B = -10\boldsymbol{j}$kN.
$\mathbf{M}_B = 22.72\boldsymbol{k}$ kN-m.

4.8. Move 200 lb force 5 ft to left.

4.10. $F_A = -200\boldsymbol{j} - 150\boldsymbol{k}$ N.
$C_A = 34.0\boldsymbol{i} + 26.0\boldsymbol{k}$ N-m.

4.12. $F = 20\boldsymbol{i} - 60\boldsymbol{j} + 30\boldsymbol{k}$ N.
$C_A = 900\boldsymbol{i} + 680\boldsymbol{j} + 760\boldsymbol{k}$ N-m.

4.14. 12.375 m from origin.

4.16. $F = -44.567\boldsymbol{i} - 33.425\boldsymbol{j} - 22.283\boldsymbol{k}$ N.
$C = -31.007\boldsymbol{i} - 160.46\boldsymbol{j} + 302.71\boldsymbol{k}$ kN-m.

4.18. $F_R = -204\boldsymbol{i} + 604\boldsymbol{j} + 408\boldsymbol{k}$ lb.
$C_A = 8{,}160\boldsymbol{i} + 2{,}032\boldsymbol{j} + 3{,}264\boldsymbol{k}$ ft-lb.
$C_B = 2{,}032\boldsymbol{j} - 816\boldsymbol{k}$ ft-lb.

4.20. $F_R = 400\boldsymbol{i} - 1{,}900\boldsymbol{j} + 600\boldsymbol{k}$ N.
$C_R = 24{,}200\boldsymbol{i} + 2{,}000\boldsymbol{j} - 3{,}300\boldsymbol{k}$ N-m.

4.22. $F_R = -50\boldsymbol{k}$ kN $C_R = 7.5\boldsymbol{i} + 50\boldsymbol{j}$ kN-m.

4.24. $F_1 = 26.9$ lb $F_2 = 17.6$ lb $F_3 = 35.5$ lb.

4.26. $F = 2{,}100\boldsymbol{i} - 500\boldsymbol{j}$ lb $\bar{x} = -.05$ ft.

4.28. $F_R = 400\boldsymbol{i} - 1600\boldsymbol{j}$ N
$C_R = -1{,}800\boldsymbol{i} - 2{,}400\boldsymbol{j} - 12{,}600\boldsymbol{k}$ N-m.

4.30. $F_R = 39.44\boldsymbol{i} + 74.7\boldsymbol{j}$ N.
$\bar{x} = .669$ m.

4.32. $F_R = -100\boldsymbol{k}$ N $\bar{x} = 2.5$ m $\bar{y} = 2.2$ m.
$F_R = \boldsymbol{0}$ $C_R = 280\boldsymbol{i} + 450\boldsymbol{j}$ N-m.

4.34. $F_R = \boldsymbol{0}$ $C_k = 860\boldsymbol{i} + 900\boldsymbol{j}$ N-cm.

4.36. $F_R = 353.5\boldsymbol{i} - 653.5\boldsymbol{j}$ N $\bar{x} = 9.2739$ m.

4.38. $F_R = 43{,}000$ lb $\bar{x} = 23.209$ ft.

4.42. $F = 3{,}164\boldsymbol{k}$ lb.

4.44. $\bar{x} = 10.37$ in. $\bar{y} = \bar{z} = 0$.

4.48. $\bar{x} = .289$ $\bar{y} = .400$.

4.50. 10.84 m.

4.52. $\bar{x} = 1.292$ ft $\bar{y} = 7.63$ ft.

4.54. $\bar{x} = .210$ ft $\bar{y} = .0756$ ft.

4.56. $\bar{y} = 3.808$ m.

4.58. $F = -37.5\boldsymbol{k}$ kN $\bar{x} = .844$ m $\bar{y} = 1.067$ m
(origin at front left lower corner of the load).
original weight 90 kN.
lost weight = 52.5 kN.

4.60. $F_R = -111{,}780\boldsymbol{k}$ lb $\bar{x} = -3.78$ ft
(in front of trailer C.G.).
$F_R = -86{,}386\boldsymbol{k}$ lb $\bar{x} = -7.329$ ft.

4.62. $W = .02739\gamma$. $x_c = .2042$ m $y_c = .1$ m
$z_c = -.1968$ m.

4.64. $F_R = 2.315 \times 10^6$ lb $\bar{x} = 20$ ft $\bar{y} = 12.44$ ft.

4.66. $F_R = 262$ N.

4.68. 4,025 N-m 596.3 N-m.

4.70. $p_a = 7.8644 \times 10^4$ Pa.

4.72. $F = 61{,}740$ lb 10.386 ft.

4.74. $F = 8761$ lb 2.615 ft.

4.76. $F = 1.697 \times 10^{10}$ N 24.04 m from base along inclined surface.

4.78. $F = 666 \times 10^8$ N.
@ $\frac{40}{3}$ m from base.

4.80. $\bar{x} = 21.2$ ft $\bar{y} = 4.67$ ft.

4.82. $x_c = .07441$ m.

4.84. $\boldsymbol{F} = -400\boldsymbol{j}$ kN $\boldsymbol{M}_{\text{outside lane}} = -900\boldsymbol{k}$ kN-m
$\boldsymbol{M}_{\text{inside lane}} = -300\boldsymbol{k}$ kN-m.

4.86. 1,415 kN 1.915 m from front of load.

4.88. $\boldsymbol{F}_R = 4.698\boldsymbol{i} - 10.09\boldsymbol{j}$ kN.
$\boldsymbol{M}_R = -3\boldsymbol{i} + 3.2316\boldsymbol{k}$ kN-m.

4.90. $r' = 17.57x^2 - 7.027x + .7026$.

4.92. $l = 3.51$ m.

4.94. $F = 2{,}200$ lb $\bar{x} = 4.136$ ft

4.96. −217.2 N-m.

4.98. $\boldsymbol{F}_R = 500\boldsymbol{i} - 1{,}220\boldsymbol{j}$ N
$\boldsymbol{C}_R = 240\boldsymbol{i} - 2{,}190\boldsymbol{k}$ N-m.

4.100. $\boldsymbol{F}_R = 58{,}900$ lb $\bar{x} = 3.919$ from bottom left corner.

4.102. $\bar{x} = 1.20$ ft $\bar{y} = 1.125$ ft $\bar{z} = \frac{t}{2}$ ft.

4.104. $\bar{y} = 1.299$ ft.

4.106. −1,550 lb $\bar{x} = 20.04$ ft.

4.108. $\bar{x} = 10.94$ ft $\bar{y} = 12.67$ ft.

4.110. 485.397 kN @ 1.636 m below top of gate.
132.381 kN @ 1 m below top of gate.

4.112. $\bar{x} = 4.98$ m $\bar{y} = 2.65$ m.

5.18. $T_{BC} = 26.79$ lb $T_{BA} = 37.9$ lb.

5.20. $T_{AB} = 111.8$ lb $T_{BD} = 109.9$ lb $T_{BC} = 63.7$ lb.

5.22. 27 lb 36.35 lb 4.653 in.

5.24. 671 N, 447 N, 1,000 N.

5.26. 409.8 N-m.

5.28. $A_x = 4{,}233$ N, $A_y = 3{,}140$ N, $B_x = 4{,}233$ N,
$B_y = -1{,}840$ N.

5.30. $A_x = 2{,}000$ N, $A_y = 6{,}970$ N, $M_A = 62{,}360$ N-m
$B = 530.4$ N.

5.32. $A_x = 8.00$ kN $A_y = -12.50$ kN $B_x = -8.00$ kN
$B_y = 22.5$ kN.

5.34. $F_{BD} = 462$ lb $F_{BC} = 215$ lb $F_{AB} = 375$ lb.

5.36. $T_A = 125.0$ N $f = 125$ N.

5.38. $T = 117.4$ N $\alpha = 79.8°$

5.40. $A_x = 433$ N, $A_y = 790$ N $M_A = 1{,}167$ N-m.

5.42. $A_x = 200$ N, $A_y = 3{,}464$ N $M_A = 1{,}192$ N-m.

5.44. $A_x = 9{,}736$ N $A_y = -2{,}670$ N $B_x = -9{,}736$ N
$B_y = 6{,}670$ N.

5.46. $\alpha = 17.46°$.

5.48. 58.7 ft-lb.

5.50. $\beta = \tan^{-1}\left[\dfrac{\dfrac{W_2}{\tan\alpha_1} - \dfrac{W_1}{\tan\alpha_2}}{W_1 + W_2}\right]$.

5.52. $A_x = 408$ N $A_y = -258$N $G_x = -749.5$ N
$G_y = 583$ N.

5.54. $T = 20$ N-m.

5.56. $T_{AB} = 40.5$ kN $T_{BC} = 39.3$ kN.

5.58. 72 lb 447 lb.

5.60. 4 m.

5.62. $F = \frac{W}{2}\frac{r_1 - r_2}{r_2}$

5.64. $R_x = 0$ $R_y = 58{,}900$ lb $M_B = 142{,}500$ ft-lb.

5.66. $R_x = 0$, $R_y = 4{,}953$ lb $M = 61{,}082.5$ ft-lb.

5.68. $R_C = 1{,}006$ lb $M_C = 10{,}108$ ft-lb.
$R_D = 294$ lb $M_D = 2{,}770$ ft-lb.

5.70. 270 lb 253 lb.

5.72. $W_{max} = 2.5$ ton $B_y = 10.8$ ton $A_y = 1.7$ ton
$C_y = 1.7$ ton $M_c = 34$ ft-ton $D_y = 1.7$ ton
$M_D = 85$ ft-ton.

5.74. 17.55 ton (2 supports) 24.9 ton M = 70 ton-ft.

5.76. $F_1 = 293$ N $F_2 = 52.37$ N $F_3 = 254.3$ N.

5.78. $\boldsymbol{A} = -500\boldsymbol{j} + 1{,}500\boldsymbol{k}$ lb
$\boldsymbol{M}_A = 26{,}260\boldsymbol{i} - 9{,}100\boldsymbol{k}$ ft-lb
$\boldsymbol{B} = -500\boldsymbol{j}$ lb
$\boldsymbol{M}_B = -9{,}100\boldsymbol{k}$ ft-lb.

5.80. $F = 57.14$ lb $A_y = 160.1$ lb
$B_y = 93.0$ lb $B_z = 22.6$ lb $A_z = 18.08$ lb.

5.82. $A_x = 0$ $A_y = 50$ N $A_z = 100$ N
$M_x = -200$ N-m.
$M_y = -220$ N-m $M_z = 110$ N-m.

5.84. $B_y = 3{,}000$ lb $B_z = 26{,}500$ lb $C_z = 17{,}000$ lb.

5.86. 3 ft $A_z = 50$ N $B_z = 50$ N.

5.88. $P = 33.7$ lb $A_z = 25$ lb $A_y = -7.50$ lb.

5.92. 11,394 lb.

5.94. 65,300 lb.

5.96. $F_{EC} = 4.36$ kN $A_x = .800$ kN $A_y = 196.7$ kN.

5.98. $B_x = 165.9$ N $B_y = 206.3$ N $F_{CB} = 208.8$ N.

5.100. $C_x = 576$ lb $C_y = 1{,}326$ lb $M_c = 8009.6$ N-m.

5.102. $T_1 = 209$ N $T_2 = 202$ N $F = 286$ N.

5.104. $A = 10{,}640$ lb $C = 6{,}520$ lb $D = 6{,}520$ lb
$G = H = 7{,}500$ lb $F = 10{,}640$ lb.

5.106. 1154 N

5.108. 9.418×10^6 *Pa*.

5.110. $\tau = (6.833 - 6.50z - \frac{z^3}{3}) \times 10^4$ *Pa*.

5.112. $\tau_{zz} = 281.7$ psi

5.114. $G_x = 750$ lb $G_y = 650$ lb.

5.116. $F_x = A_x = 806$ lb $F_y = A_y = 500$ lb.

5.118. $R_1 = 41$ kN $R_2 = 88$ kN $R_3 = 141$ kN.

5.120. $F_{CD} = 1{,}694$ lb $F_{EF} = 4{,}931$ lb.

5.122. $A_x = 13.15$ lb $A_y = 142.6$ lb.

5.124. $T_E = 1{,}688$ N $T_D = 2{,}840$ N.

5.126. $T = 30.67$ lb.

5.128. $C_x = -322.3$ lb $C_y = -161.3$ lb $C_z = -583.6$ lb
$D_x = -322.7$ lb $D_z = -398.9$ lb.

5.130. $T = 2{,}121$ lb $H = 3{,}000$ lb $V = 3{,}000$ lb
$T = 1{,}148$ lb $H = 2{,}121$ lb $V = 5{,}121$ lb.

5.132. $T_{DB} = 353$ lb $T_{AC} = 289$ lb $T_{EC} = 394$ lb.

5.134. $T_R = 1.928$ N $T_P = 709$ N $T_A = 2{,}129$ N
$T_D = 1{,}012$ N $l = .0828$ $m = .728$ $n = .618$.

5.136. $F_{AB} = 8{,}000$ lb $E_x = 5{,}000$ lb $E_y = 6{,}928$ lb
$M_E = 5{,}000$ ft-lb.

5.138. $A_x = -3{,}984$ N $A_y = -7{,}800$ N $B_x = 3{,}984$ N
$B_y = 4{,}800$ N.

5.140. $A_x = -925$ N $A_y = 150$ N.

5.142. 63.75 kN-m.

5.144. $F = 996.7$ N.

5.146. $A_y = B_y = 18{,}170$ N $A_x = 63{,}660$ N.

5.148. $C_x = 600$ lb $C_y = 0$ $C_z = -320$ lb
$F_D = 1{,}033$ lb $F_A = 312.5$ lb.

5.150. $p = 208$ psi gage.

5.152. $\boldsymbol{A} = 433\boldsymbol{i} - 533\boldsymbol{j} - 19.00\boldsymbol{k}$ lb $E = 240$ lb.
$\boldsymbol{H} = -433\boldsymbol{i} + 433\boldsymbol{j} - 520\boldsymbol{k}$ lb $K = 0$.

5.154. $A_x = -28.13$ lb $A_y = -98$ lb $B_x = 70$ lb
$B_y = 0$.

5.156. $f = 15.08$ kN.

5.158. $A_x = 0$ $A_y = 1{,}938$ lb $C_y = B_y = 3{,}062$ lb
$D_y = 1{,}938$ lb. Ram force = 9,798 lb.

5.160. $T_{EF} = 1{,}174$ N.

5.162. $A_x = 1.399 \times 10^4$ N $A_y = 5.549 \times 10^3$ N.
$M_A = 1.355 \times 10^4$ N-m $B = 2{,}887$ N.

6.2. $EF = 2{,}000$ lb T $AF = 4{,}808$ lb T
$BC = 2{,}670$ lb. C etc.

6.4. $DE = 18{,}720$ lb C $DH = 8{,}825$ T
$HG = 18{,}720$ lb T etc.

6.6. $AB = DE = 26.8$ kN C $GC = CF = 3.39$ kN C
$AG = FE = 19$ kN T $BC = CD = 20$ kN C.
$BG = DF = 3.14$ kN T $GF = 21.36$ kN C.

6.8. $AB = 707$ lb C
$AC = CE = 500$ lb T
$EB = 0$
$BD = 500$ lb C
$DF = 707$ lb C.

6.10. $AB = 6{,}950$ lb C
$AC = 4{,}914$ lb T
$BC = 3{,}207$ lb T
$CD = 0$.

6.12. $AB = 353.5$ kN C
$AL = 250$ kN T
$LK = 250$ kN T
$LB = 100$ kN T
$BC = 316.2$ kN T
$BK = 70.8$ kN T.

6.14. $JI = 25$ kN T $BH = 8.64$ kN C
$AJ = 31.25$ kN C $BC = 50$ kN C
$IH = 56.25$ kN T $CD = 50$ kN C
$BJ = 6.25$ kN T $HC = 0$ etc.

6.16. $CD = 583$ lb C
$AC = BC = AD = 0$
$BD = 1{,}158$ lb T
others are zero.

6.18. $AC = 14.14$ kN T
$CD = 14$ kN T
$DE = 2$ kN C
$AD = 24.5$ kN C
others are zero.

6.20. $F_{AB} = 24{,}246$ lb C, $F_{BC} = 32{,}709.5$ lb T
$F_{DC} = 1{,}350$ lb C, $F_{DF} = 22{,}709.5$ lb C.

6.22. $DC = 1{,}202$ lb T $DE = 0$.

6.24. $GF = 21.3$ kN T.

6.26. $BF = 0$ $AB = 258$ kN T.

6.28. $BC = 115.5$ kN T $BK = 57.7$ kN C
$DE = 77.0$ kN T $DI = 38.50$ kN T
$EF = 38.50$ kN T.

6.30. $DG = 90$ kN C $DF = 56.6$ kN C
$AB = 127.3$ kN T $AC = 90$ kN C
$CB = 50$ kN C $CD = 90$ kN C.

6.32. $FH = HE = 4.72$ K T $FE = 2.5$ K C $FC = 0$ K.

6.34. $FI = .558$ K C $EF = .5$ K C $DH = 1.118$ K T.

6.36. $F_{LC} = 41.63$ K C $F_{KL} = 162.5$ K T
$F_{HC} = 83.38$ K T $F_{FG} = 50.03$ K C.

6.38. $M = -500x + 2{,}500$ ft-lb
$M = -15x^2 - 200x + 1{,}000$ ft-lb.

6.40. $V = -737.5$ lb $M = 3{,}690$ ft-lb
$V = 262.5$ lb $M = 6{,}850$ ft-lb
$V = 262.5$ lb $M = 1{,}312.5$ ft-lb.

6.42. $\underline{0 < s < 14.14}$ $V = -37.1$ lb $H = -37.1$ lb
$M = 37.1s$ ft-lb
$\underline{14.14 < s \le 29.14}$ $V = -52.5$ lb $H = 0$
$M = 52.5s - 217$ ft-lb.
etc.

6.44. $\underline{0 \le x < 10}$ $H = 0$ $V_x = 0$ $V_y = -20s$
$M_y = 0$ $M_z = 0$ $M_x = -10s^2$
$\underline{10 < s < 20}$ $H = 0$ $V_y = 200$ N $V_z = 0$
$M_x = 1{,}000$ N-m $M_z = 200(s - 10)$ $M_y = 0$
$\underline{20 < s < 30}$ $H = 200$ N $V_z = -1{,}000$ N
$V_x = 0$ $M_y = 0$ $M_x = -1{,}000s + 21{,}000$ N-m
$M_z = 2{,}000$ N-m.

6.46. $\underline{0 < \theta < \frac{\pi}{4}}$ $V = -70.7 \sin\theta$ N
$H = -70.7 \cos\theta$ N
$M = 424 - 424 \cos\theta$ N-m
$\frac{\pi}{4} < \theta < \frac{\pi}{2}$ $V = 29.3 \sin\theta$ N
$H = 29.3 \cos\theta$ N
$M = 176 \cos\theta$ N-m.

6.48. Section $\underline{AB}$ $H = 0$
$V_x = 0$
$V_z = 11.36s - 262$ lb
$M_y = 410$ ft-lb $M_z = 0$
$M_x = -5.68s^2 + 262s - 2{,}194$ ft-lb
Section $\underline{BC}$ $V = 130.02 + 5.64s$ lb
$H = 227.54 - 9.87s$ lb
$M_{x'} \equiv$ (axial torque) $= -70.47$ ft-lb
$M_{z'} =$ (bending torque) $= -123.33$ ft-lb
Section $\underline{CD}$ $V_z = -262 + 11.36s$ lb
$M_y \equiv$ (axial torque) $= -.477$ ft-lb
$M_x = -3{,}021 + 262s - 5.58s^2$ ft-lb.

6.50. $\underline{0 < x < 15}$
$V = M = 0$
$\underline{5 < x \le 10}$
$V = 500$ lb
$M = -500(x - 5)$ ft-lb
$\underline{10 \le x < 25}$
$M = -500(x - 5) - 30(x - 10)^2/2$.

6.52. $\underline{0 < x < 10}$
$V = -737.5$ lb
$M = 737.5x$ ft-lb
$\underline{10 < x < 25}$
$V = 262.5$ lb
$M = 737.5x - 1{,}000(x - 10)$
$\underline{25 < x < 10}$
$V = 262.5$ lb
$M = -262.5x + 10{,}500$ ft-lb.

6.54. $\underline{0 < x \le 5}$
$V = -1.333$ N
$M = 1.333x$ N-m
$\underline{5 \le x \le 15}$
$V = -20x^2 + 600x - 3{,}833$ N
$M = 1{,}333x - 200(x - 5)^2 + \frac{20}{3}(x - 9)^3$ N-m
$\underline{15 \le x < 25}$
$V = 667$ N
$M = 667x + 16{,}660$ N-m.

6.56. -500 N-m.

6.58. $M_{max} = -5{,}334$ N-m.

6.60. $M_{max} = -6{,}500$ ft-lb.

6.62. $\underline{0 < x < 3}$
$V = -60 + 5x^2$ N
$M = 60x - \frac{5}{3}x^3$ N-m
$\underline{3 < x < 6}$
$V = -60 + 5x^2$ N
$M = 60x - \frac{5}{3}x^3 - 5{,}000$ N-m
$\underline{6 < x < 11}$
$V = -1{,}000$ N
$M = 1{,}000x - 16{,}000$ N-m
$M_{max} = 5{,}000$ N-m.

6.64. $\underline{0 < x < 5}$
$V = .596x^{3/2}$ kN
$M = -.238x^{5/2}$ kN-m
$\underline{5 < x < 10}$
$V = 6.66 - 3(x-5) + \frac{3}{10}(x-5)^2$ kN
$M = -6.66x + 19.99 + \frac{3}{2}(x-5)^2 - \frac{1}{10}(x-5)^3$
$M_{max} = -22.6$ kN-m

6.66. length = 230 ft $T_{max} = 565.8$ lb.

6.68. $T_{max} = 17{,}088$ lb $L = 81.5$ ft.

6.70. $T_{max} = 35{,}200$ N.

6.72. $T_{max} = 109$ lb h = 118.1 ft.

6.74. elevation @ B = 17.84 m
61.68 m dragging.

6.76. $A_x = 675$ N $B_x = 675$ N $A_y = 650$ N
$B_y = 500$ N
$T_{AC} = 937.1$ N $\alpha = 43.92°$.

6.78. $BC = 45.3$ kN C
$DC = 32$ kN C
$DE = 32$ kN C
$BA = 45.3$ kN T
$DB = BE = AE = 0$.

6.80. $AE = 1{,}250$ lb T
$AD = 1{,}250$ lb T
$ED = 1{,}030$ lb C
$CE = 1{,}060$ lb C
$CA = 1{,}060$ lb C
$CD = 1{,}500$ lb T.

6.82. $\underline{0 \le x < 3}$
$V = 10x$ N
$M = -\frac{10x^2}{2}$ N-m
$\underline{3 < x < 9}$
$V = 10x - 19.44$ N
$M = -10\frac{x^2}{2} + 19.44(x-3)$ N-m
$9 \le x < 12$
$V = 70.6$ N
$M = -90(x-4.5) + 19.44(x-3) + 500$ N-m.

6.84. $\underline{0 \le x < 10}$
$V = M = 0$
$\underline{10 < x < 20}$
$V = -650$ lb
$M = 650(x-10)$ ft-lb
$\underline{20 < x < 40}$
$V = 350$ lb
$M = 650(x-10) - 1{,}000(x-20)$ ft-lb
$\underline{40 < x < 65}$
$V = 0$
$M = -500$ ft-lb.

6.86. $y = h(1 - \cos\frac{\pi x}{l})$.

6.88. $DE = 10{,}928$ N T $CE = 8{,}000$ N C
$DC = 0$ $BD = 10{,}928$ N T $BA = 4{,}000$ N T.

6.90. $\underline{3 < x \le 6}$
$V = 1.110$ kN
$M = -1.110x + 50$ kN-m
$\underline{6 \le x \le 14}$
$V = 1.110 + \frac{(x-6)^2}{20}$ kN
$M = 50 - 1.110x - \frac{(x-6)^3}{60}$ kN-m
$\underline{14 \le x < 20}$
$V = 4.31$ kN
$M = 86.27 - 4.31x$ kN-m.

7.4. 600 lb.

7.6. 151.0 lb 139.0 lb.

7.8. $\mu_s = 0.322$.

7.10. $F = 52.76$ N.

7.14. $(\mu_s)_{max} = 0.249$.

7.16. at start $F = 4{,}142$ lb
for movement $F = 4{,}414$.

7.18. $P = 733.6$ N.

7.20. $f = 115.5$ N
$\mu_{min} = .578$.

7.24. C moves 1.5 m to left.

7.26. $T = 123.8$ ft-lb.

7.28. 750 N (clockwise)
50 N (counterclockwise).

7.30. $F = 196.7$ N.

7.34. $32.68 \text{ lb} < W_1 < 67.32$ lb.
$W_1 = 50$ lb (no friction).

7.36. $\mu_{min} = 0.225$.

7.38. $\alpha_{min} = 28.0°$.

7.40. 4.76 ft.

7.40. 1.691 m.

7.44. 251.5 lb.

7.46. $W_2 = 7.245$ N $\mu_{min} = 0.0279$.

7.48. $T = \frac{P\mu}{3}\left[\frac{D_2^3 - D_1^3}{D_2^2 - D_1^2}\right]$.

7.50. $T = \frac{PD\mu_d}{4}$.

7.52. $T = 320$ N.

7.54. $T = 188.6$ N-m.

7.56. 832 N.

7.58. 267 lb.

7.60. 136.8 N.

7.62. $\mu_s = 0.260$.

7.64. $\mu_s = 0.048$.

7.66. $P = 202$ N $\mu_5 = 0.556$.

7.68. $x = 277$ mm.
7.70. $F_x = 256$ N $F_y = 150.4$ N.
7.72. $F_{min} = 2{,}210$ N $\mu_s = 0.4$.
7.78. 133.6 in.-lb 155.6 in.-lb.
7.80. $W = 6{,}100$ lb.
7.84. 0.2387°.
7.86. $\mu_s = .00308$.
7.88. $F = 128.2$ N.
7.90. $\theta = 30.96°$ $T = 292$ lb.
7.92. 7.11 N.
7.94. 3,333 N.
7.96. $P = 13.22$ lb C.W. $P = 163.2$ lb C.C.W.
7.98. 40.7 N-m.
7.100. 94.7 mm.
7.102. 35.55° above horizontal.
7.106. $\theta = 41.9°$.
7.108. 256 N.
7.110. 1.002×10^4 N.
7.112. $W_2 = 429.18$ N.
7.114. $W_c = 810$ N.
7.116. $T = 877$ N-m.

8.4. $M_x = 125$ ft^3 $M_y = 200$ ft^3.
8.8. $\bar{x} = 14.30$ ft $\bar{y} = 5.74$ ft.
8.12. $x_c = 0.1691$ m $y_c = 0.363$ m.
8.14. $x_c = 2.02$ mm $y_c = 83.6$ mm.
8.16. $x_c = 0.1217$ m $y_c = 0.4478$ m.
8.18. $x_c = 7.23$ in. $y_c = 2.55$ in. $M_{z'} = 226.1$ in.^{3}
8.20. $x_c = y_c = 242.22$ mm.
8.22. $x_c = 1.7172$ m $y_c = 0.1722$ m.
8.24. $x_c = 2.889$ m $y_c = 2.667$ m.
8.26. $y_c = 315.7$ mm.
8.28. $x_c = 40.1$ mm $y_c = 19.51$ mm.
8.30. $\bar{x} = 12.92$ ft.
8.32. $x_c = \frac{a}{2}$ $y_c = \frac{2}{3}b$ $z_c = \frac{4}{3}c$.
8.34. $\bar{z} = \frac{3}{8}a$.
8.36. $\boldsymbol{r}_c = 1.179\boldsymbol{i} + .955\boldsymbol{j} + .284\boldsymbol{k}$ m.
8.38. $x_c = 2.571$ m.
8.40. $\bar{x} = 8.22$ m $\bar{y} = \bar{z} = 0$.
8.42. $x_c = y_c = 0$ $z_c = 9.78$ in.
8.44. center of volume $\bar{x} = -9.75$ mm
$\bar{y} = 122.55$ mm $\bar{z} = 0$
center of mass and gravity
$\bar{x} = -32.76$ mm $\bar{y} = 447$ mm $\bar{z} = 0$.
8.46. $\bar{x} = 41.95$ mm $\bar{y} = 493$ mm $\bar{z} = 608$ mm.
8.48. $\boldsymbol{r}_c = .742\boldsymbol{j} - .1720\boldsymbol{k}$ m.
8.50. $y_c = \frac{2}{3}\left(\frac{b}{\pi}\right)$
8.52. $A = 1{,}751$ in.^{2} $V = 5{,}242$ in.^{3}
8.54. $A = .8624$ m^2 $V = .06329$ m^3.
8.56. $\boldsymbol{r}_c = 3.39\boldsymbol{i} + 3.44\boldsymbol{j} - 3\boldsymbol{k}$ in.
8.58. $I_{xx} = \dfrac{ab^3\pi}{4}$.
8.60. $I_{xx} = 1.113$ units^4 $I_{yy} = .535$ units^4.
$I_{xy} = .750$ units^4.
8.62. $I_{yy} = \frac{5}{2}\pi^2 - 8$ ft^4.
8.66. $I_{xx} = 666.7$ ft^4 $I_{yy} = 1{,}257$ ft^4.
$I_{xy} = 791.7$ ft^4.
8.68. $I_{xx} = 4{,}540$ ft^4 $I_{yy} = 11{,}250$ ft^4.
8.70. $I_{xx} = 6.646$ ft^4 $I_{yy} = 15.39$ ft^4.
$I_{xy} = 9.52$ ft^4.
8.76. $I_{xx} = 1{,}512$ ft^4 $I_{xy} = 559$ ft^4.
8.78. $I_{xx} = \frac{5\sqrt{3}}{16}R^4$ $I_{yy} = \sqrt{3}R^4\left(\frac{5}{16}\right)$ $I_{xy} = 0$.
8.80. $I_{x_cx_c} = 8.463 \times 10^7$ mm^4
$I_{y_cy_c} = 1.8869 \times 10^8$ mm^4.
8.82. $I_{x'x'} = 140.6$ ft^4 $I_{y'y'} = 439$ ft^4 $I_{x'y'} = 213$ ft^4.
8.84. $I_{xx} = 91.92$ ft^4 $I_{yy} = 1{,}455$ ft^4 $I_{xy} = -96.52$ ft^4.
$J_p = 1{,}547$ ft^4.
8.88. 109.2 mm^4 2,367 mm^4.
8.90. 1,299 mm^4 79.1 mm^4.
8.94. $I_1 = .003781$ m^4 $I_2 = .0002557$ m^4.
8.96. $\bar{x} = 3.16$ mm $\bar{y} = 1.323$ mm.
$I_1 = 2.11 \times 10^4$ mm^4 $I_2 = 8.0675 \times 10^3$ mm^4.
8.98. $y_c = 1.671$ m.
8.100. $I_{xx} = 3.29 \times 10^7$ mm^4 $I_{x_cx_c} = 9.85 \times 10^6$ mm^4
$I_{yy} = 2.89 \times 10^6$ mm^4 $I_{y_cy_c} = 1.607 \times 10^6$ mm^4
$I_{xy} = 6.90 \times 10^6$ mm^4 $I_{x_cy_c} = 1.457c \times 10^6$ mm^4.
8.102. $x_c = \frac{5}{6}h$ $y_c = \frac{20}{21\pi}a$ $z_c = 0$.
8.104. 6.75° 96.75°.
8.106. $A = 151.24$ m^3 $V = 113.0$ m^3.
8.108. $x_c = 1.500$ in. $I_{x_cx_c} = 83.250$ in^4.
$I_{y_cy_c} = 19.250$ in^4 $I_{x_cy_c} = 0$.
8.110. 12,708 m^4.
8.112. $M_z = 10.616s$ in^3
$M_x = 185.7 - 0.465y^2$
$M_x = (.1886)[316.8 + (4 + 3\eta)\sqrt{(\eta + 2)^3}$.

9.2. 4,333 lbm-ft^2 15,333 lbm-ft^2.
9.4. $I_{yy} = \frac{1}{12}M(a^2 + b^2)$ $I_{zz} = \frac{1}{12}M(b^2 + l^2)$
$I_{xx} = \frac{1}{12}M(a^2 + l^2)$.
9.6. $\frac{1}{2}Mr^2$.
9.8. 2.67×10^7 grams-mm^2
3.95×10^8 grams-mm^2.
9.10. 1.723×10^6 grams-mm^2.
9.12. 3,959 kg-mm^2.

9.14. $I_{xx} = 1.004 \times 10^5$ mm^4.
$I_{yy} = 1{,}875$ mm^4
$I_{xy} = 1.172 \times 10^4$ mm^4
$(I_{xx})_M = 205$ kg-mm^2
$(I_{yy})_M = 3.82$ kg-mm^2
$(I_{xy})_M = 23.9$ kg-mm^2.

9.16. 37.0 kg-mm^2 166.8 kg-mm^2 203.8 kg-mm^2.

9.20. $I_{y'y'} = 6.21$ slug-ft^2 $I_{z'z'} = I_{x'x'} = 29.0$ slug-ft^2
$I_{xx} = 119.1$ slug-ft^2 $I_{yy} = 18.63$ slug-ft^2
$I_{zz} = 106.6$ slug-ft^2.

9.22. $I_{xx} + I_{yy} + I_{zz} = \frac{M}{6}(a^2 + b^2 + c^2) + 2M(x^2 + y^2 + z^2)$

9.24. $I_{x''x''} = 3{,}870$ kg-m^2
$I_{y''y''} = 4{,}615$ kg-m^2.

9.26. 1.258×10^{-2} kg-m^2 1.239×10^{-2} kg-m^2
3.91×10^{-3} kg-m^2.

9.28. 1.650 kg-m^2 1.438 kg-m^2 .513 kg-m^2.

9.30. $k = 2.54$ ft $I = 28{,}400$ lbm-ft^2.

9.32. $I_{xx} = 8{,}093$ lbm-in.^{2} $I_{yy} = 1{,}603$ lbm-in.^{2}
$I_{xy} = 1{,}282$ lbm-in.^{2}

9.34. $I_{cc} = 37.81$ kg-m^2.

9.36. 3,026 lbm-ft^2.

9.38. .524 kg-m^2.

9.40. −.00696 kg-m^2.

9.44. 362 kg-mm^2.

9.46. $(I_{xx})_M = 534$ kg-mm^2
$(I_{yy})_M = 16.59 \times 10^2$ kg-mm^2
$(I_{zz})_M = 21.9 \times 10^2$ kg-mm^2
$(I_{xy})_M = 5.68 \times 10^2$ kg-mm^2
$(I_{xz})_M = (I_{yz})_M = 0$.

9.48. .0493 kg-m^2 .00187 kg-m^2 .0503 kg-m^2.

9.50. 1,075 kg-m^2 92.35 kg-m^2.

9.52. $I_{yy} = 7.58\rho_0$ kg-m^2 $I_{yz} = -1.789\rho_0$ kg-m^2.

10.2. $S = 1{,}250$ N
$S = 750$ N.

10.4. $\theta = 19.48°$.

10.6. $W = .351\,T$.

10.8. $\theta = 8.53°$.

10.10. $P = (W/2)\cot\theta$.

10.12. 2,513 lb.

10.14. $T_{CE} = 7.42$ kN
$T_{DE} = 28.8$ kN.

10.16. $\tan\beta = \frac{1}{\sqrt{3}}[(a - 3b)/(b + a)]$.

10.18. $T' = 40$ N-m.

10.20. $P = .0545$ N.

10.22. $W = 270$ lb.

10.24. $W = 2{,}770$ N.

10.26. $C = 108.6$ N.

10.28. $d = 72.0$ mm.

10.32. $d = .2$ ft.

10.34. 25.9°.

10.36. 77.3°.

10.38. 1,066 N.

10.40. $\theta = 19.22°$.

10.42. 34.5°.

10.44. .440 m.

10.46. $a = .358$ m.

10.48. $a = .1126$ m.

10.52. When $d > 2$, stable equilibrium.
When $d < 2$, unstable equilibrium.

10.56. $W_{max} = 250$ lb.

10.60. $x = 4$ m.

10.61. $Q = 3P$.

10.62. $P = 7{,}540$ lb.

10.63. $\theta = 27.7°$.

10.64. $\cos\theta = \dfrac{\cos\theta_0(aK_1 + aK_2) + W}{aK_1 + aK_2}$.

10.66. $\theta = 0$ (unstable)
$\theta = 28.1°$ (stable).

10.67. $W_{max} = 1{,}000$ N.

10.68. $R > (h/2)$ for stable equilibrium.
$R < (h/2)$ for unstable equilibrium.

11.2. $\dot{x} = 15.30$ ft/sec $\dot{y} = 5.351$ ft/sec.

11.4. $\boldsymbol{a} = .6765\boldsymbol{i} - 1.2075\boldsymbol{j} - .3177\boldsymbol{k}$ ft/sec^2.

11.6. $a(3) = 12$ m/sec^2 $d = 60.94$ m.

11.8. 2.0177 ft/sec 1.522 ft/sec^2.

11.10. $\vec{V} = 2\boldsymbol{i} - 1.296\boldsymbol{j}$ m/sec
$\boldsymbol{a} = .6\boldsymbol{i} + 9.21\boldsymbol{j}$ m/sec^2
$a_n = 8.05$ m/sec^2.

11.12. $v = v_n\boldsymbol{i} + \left[-v_A + v_C\sin\alpha + \dfrac{v_C^2(\cos^2\alpha)(t)}{\{h^2 + [v_c(\cos\alpha)(t)]^2\}^{\frac{1}{2}}}\right]\boldsymbol{j}$.

11.14. $x^4 + 149.9(y - x) = 0$ $d = 5.312$ ft.

11.16. $9.06 < d < 25.16$ ft.

11.18. $\delta = 9.148$ m.

11.20. $d = 89.97$ ft.

11.22. 4.22 ft.

11.24. $\bar{x} = 9.25 \times 10^4$ m $\bar{y} = .856 \times 10^4$ m.

11.26. $d = 280$ m $\Delta\tau = 2.04$ sec.

11.28. $400\cos\alpha\left[\sin\beta - \dfrac{\cos\beta}{4}\right] = -21.72$.

$12{,}000 = [400\cos\alpha\cos\beta + 1.178]\left(\dfrac{400\sin\alpha}{4.905}\right)$.

11.30. $\boldsymbol{a}_1 = 12.5\boldsymbol{j}$ ft/sec^2 $\boldsymbol{a}_2 = 21.65\boldsymbol{i} - 12.5\boldsymbol{j}$ ft/sec^2
$\boldsymbol{a}_3 = \boldsymbol{O}$.

11.32. $a_n = .460$ m/sec^2 $V = 73.63$ km/hr.

11.34. $\omega = 17.13$ rpm.

11.36. $\boldsymbol{\epsilon}_n = .995\boldsymbol{i} - .0995\boldsymbol{j} \quad R = 101.5\text{m}.$

11.38. $|\boldsymbol{a}| = 10.616 \text{ ft/sec}^2.$

11.40. $V = 891.4$ km/hr.

11.42. $7.68 \text{ ft/sec}^2 \quad 49.4 \text{ ft/sec}^2.$

11.44. $x = -8.94 \text{ ft} \quad y = -2.24 \text{ ft}.$

11.46. $\boldsymbol{a} = .02\boldsymbol{\epsilon}_t + .01504\boldsymbol{\epsilon}_n \text{ m/sec}^2.$

11.48. $\dot{\boldsymbol{a}} = 5\boldsymbol{\epsilon}_t + 6\boldsymbol{\epsilon}_n \text{ m/sec}^3.$

11.50. $\dot{\theta} = 1.063$ rad/sec
$\ddot{\theta} = .275 \text{ rad/sec}^2.$

11.52. $\Omega = 53.3 \text{ rad/sec} \quad \dot{\Omega} = 72 \text{ rad/sec}^2.$

11.54. $\boldsymbol{V} = 21.5\boldsymbol{\epsilon}_{\bar{r}} + 358\boldsymbol{\epsilon}_\theta$ mm/sec
$\boldsymbol{a} = -517\boldsymbol{\epsilon}_{\bar{r}} + 127.4\,\boldsymbol{\epsilon}_\theta \text{ mm/sec}^2.$

11.56. $\boldsymbol{V} = -3\boldsymbol{\epsilon}_{\bar{r}} + 3\boldsymbol{\epsilon}_\theta$ m/sec
$\boldsymbol{a} = -16.60\boldsymbol{\epsilon}_{\bar{r}} - 28.8\boldsymbol{\epsilon}_\theta \text{ m/sec}^2.$

11.58. $\boldsymbol{V}(2) = .7524\boldsymbol{\epsilon}_{\bar{r}} + 1.139\boldsymbol{\epsilon}_\theta + 24\boldsymbol{\epsilon}_z$ m/sec
$\boldsymbol{a}(2) = -1.064\boldsymbol{\epsilon}_{\bar{r}} + 2.364\boldsymbol{\epsilon}_\theta + 12\boldsymbol{\epsilon}_z \text{ m/sec}^2.$

11.60. $\boldsymbol{r} = 11.66\boldsymbol{\epsilon}_{\bar{r}} + (t^3 + 10)\,\boldsymbol{\epsilon}_z$ ft
$\boldsymbol{V} = 11.66\boldsymbol{\epsilon}_{\bar{r}} + 3t^2\boldsymbol{\epsilon}_z$ ft/sec
$\boldsymbol{a} = 6t\boldsymbol{\epsilon}_z \text{ ft/sec}^2.$

11.62. $\boldsymbol{V} = 1.061\boldsymbol{\epsilon}_{\bar{r}} + .04242\boldsymbol{\epsilon}_\theta + 1.061\boldsymbol{\epsilon}_z$ m/sec
$\boldsymbol{a} = -5.268\boldsymbol{\epsilon}_{\bar{r}} + .4329\boldsymbol{\epsilon}_\theta + 5.345\boldsymbol{\epsilon}_z$ m/sec.

11.64. $\boldsymbol{a} = -4\boldsymbol{\epsilon}_{\bar{r}} + 3\boldsymbol{\epsilon}_\theta + .01989\boldsymbol{\epsilon}_z \text{ ft/sec}^2.$

11.66. $\boldsymbol{V} = 1.500\boldsymbol{\epsilon}_{\bar{r}} + .600\boldsymbol{\epsilon}_\theta + 2.60\boldsymbol{\epsilon}_z$ m/sec
$\boldsymbol{a} = -1.200\boldsymbol{\epsilon}_{\bar{r}} + 6\boldsymbol{\epsilon}_\theta - 9.81\boldsymbol{\epsilon}_z \text{ m/sec}^2.$

11.68. $\boldsymbol{V} = -.01062\boldsymbol{\epsilon}_{\bar{r}} + 12.27\boldsymbol{\epsilon}_\theta$ ft/sec
$\boldsymbol{a} = -77.28\boldsymbol{\epsilon}_{\bar{r}} + 1.093\boldsymbol{\epsilon}_\theta \text{ ft/sec}^2.$

11.70. $\bar{r} = .382 + 2.48\,z^2$ ft
$\dot{Z} = .00694$ ft/sec
$\dot{Y} = .0239$ ft/sec.

11.72. Particle 1 $2.397\boldsymbol{i} - .397\boldsymbol{j}$ m/sec
Particle 2 $.397\boldsymbol{i} + 2.603\boldsymbol{j}$ m/sec, etc.

11.74. $\boldsymbol{F} = -10{,}680\boldsymbol{i} + 7.36\boldsymbol{j}$ N.

11.76. $\omega = 27.4 \text{ rad/sec} \quad \Omega = 553$ rad/sec.

11.78. $\boldsymbol{V}_{xyz} = -10\boldsymbol{j} - 12\boldsymbol{k}$ ft/sec
$\boldsymbol{a}_{xyz} = 5\boldsymbol{j} - 34.2\boldsymbol{k} \text{ ft/sec}^2.$

11.80. Hit at 3.946 m to right of center.

11.82. Hit at 77 ft from bow.

11.84. $\boldsymbol{F} = -.0652\boldsymbol{k}$ N.

11.86. $\alpha = 18.55°.$

11.88. $6.76 \text{ sec} \quad \beta = 80.53°.$

11.90. $\boldsymbol{F} = -5.73\boldsymbol{i} + 46.1\boldsymbol{j}$ N.

11.92. $\boldsymbol{V}_{xyz} = 36.1\boldsymbol{i} + 19.44\boldsymbol{j} - 99.2\boldsymbol{k}$ m/sec
$\boldsymbol{a}_{xyz} = -1094\boldsymbol{i} + 4.44\boldsymbol{j} - 8.85\boldsymbol{k} \text{ m/sec.}^2$

11.94. $\boldsymbol{F} = 163.1\boldsymbol{i} + 244.6\boldsymbol{j} + 1.009 \times 10^4\boldsymbol{k}$ N.

11.96. $\boldsymbol{V} = 136\boldsymbol{i} + 80\boldsymbol{j} + 5\boldsymbol{k}$ ft/sec
$\boldsymbol{r} = 1{,}523\boldsymbol{i} + 1{,}004\boldsymbol{j} + 106\boldsymbol{k}$ ft.

11.98. Hit at midpoint of freighter.

11.100. $y = 34.19$ km.

11.102. $\boldsymbol{V} = 1.742\boldsymbol{i} + .8360\boldsymbol{j}$ m/sec
$\boldsymbol{a} = 6.338\boldsymbol{i} + 10.322\boldsymbol{j}$ m/sec.

11.104. 128.5 ft/sec.

11.106. $A = 635.8 \text{ m}^2.$

11.108. .00255 g's.

11.110. $\boldsymbol{V} = \boldsymbol{\epsilon}_{\bar{r}} + 10\boldsymbol{\epsilon}_\theta + 2\boldsymbol{\epsilon}_z$ ft/sec
$\boldsymbol{a} = -20\boldsymbol{\epsilon}_{\bar{r}} + 4\boldsymbol{\epsilon}_\theta \text{ ft/sec}^2 \quad \boldsymbol{a} \cdot \boldsymbol{\epsilon} = -15.2 \text{ ft/sec}^2.$

11.112. $a = 7.21 \text{ ft/sec}^2.$

11.114. $\bar{x} = 17.49$ m
$\bar{y} = 15.29$ m
$\dot{x} = 10 \text{ m/sec} \quad \dot{y} = .1623$ m/sec.

11.116. $d = 982.2 \text{ m} \quad \delta = .463$ m.

11.118. $\alpha = 27.62°.$

11.120. $\boldsymbol{F}_{\text{max}} = .01962\boldsymbol{i} - .02943\boldsymbol{j} + .304\boldsymbol{k}$ N.

11.122. $\boldsymbol{V} = 149\boldsymbol{i} + 200\boldsymbol{j} + 60\boldsymbol{k}$ m/sec.
Tensile force on rod is 45 N.

11.124. $\boldsymbol{\epsilon}_0 = .2931\boldsymbol{i} + .1466\boldsymbol{j} + .5863\boldsymbol{k}.$

12.2. $\boldsymbol{r} = 10\boldsymbol{i} + 8\boldsymbol{j} + 7\boldsymbol{k}$ m.

12.4. 99.4 ft 2.485 sec.

12.6. 6.26 sec.

12.10. $d = .01021$ m.

12.12. 162.8 m.

12.14. 10.37 m.

12.16. 62.90 m/sec.

12.18. $V_A = 14.12 \text{ km/hr} \quad V_B = 6.833$ km/hr.

12.20. 4 m/sec.

12.22. 435 m/sec 16,490 m.

12.24. 96.8 ft/sec 64.1 ft.

12.26. 82.82 lb $13.22 \text{ ft/sec}^2.$

12.28. 17.22 ft distance = 17.22 ft.

12.30. $77.53 \text{ m/sec}^2.$

12.32. $d = 13.86 \text{ mm} \quad l = 20$ mm.

12.34. 22.4 m/sec $d = 108.1$ m.

12.36. $A = 48.83 \text{ m}^2.$

12.38. $d = 2.4754 \text{ ft} \quad V = -2.72$ ft/sec.

12.40. $t = .522$ sec.

12.42. $t = 8.58$ hours.

12.44. $V = 1.9365$ ft/sec.

12.46. $t = 2.10 \text{ sec} \quad h = 92.7$ ft.

12.48. $h = 77{,}280$ ft.

12.50. $F = 2411$ lb.

12.54. $\dot{\theta} = 31.29$ rpm.

12.56. $d = g/\omega^2.$

12.58. 350 N.

12.60. $\omega = 9.64$ rad/sec.

12.62. $\boldsymbol{\epsilon}_n = -.594\boldsymbol{i} + .396\boldsymbol{j} + .701\boldsymbol{k}.$

12.66. $V_E = 35{,}921 \text{ km/hour} \quad V_C = 25{,}397$ km/hour.

12.68. $\ddot{\theta} = 1.131 \text{ rad/sec}^2 \quad T = .1978$ N.

12.70. $\Delta t = 2.07$ hours.

12.74. $V_{\text{max}} = 15{,}094 \text{ km/hour} \quad \tau = 5.36$ hours.

12.76. $V = 194{,}500$ mph.

12.78. $\tau = 548$ hours.

12.80. 484 mph.
12.82. $h = 56.1$ miles.
12.86. $V_r = 6210$ km/hour $\epsilon = .326$.
12.90. $\omega = 4.43$ rad/sec.
12.92. $a_t = -8.51$ m/sec^2.
12.94. $$(F_n)_{\text{TOTAL}} = \frac{250}{y}\left[\frac{(1 + a^4 \sin h^2 ax)^{3/2}}{a^3 \cos h\, ax}\right]^{-1}(100) + 250 \cos\left[\tan^{-1}(a^2 \sinh ax)\right].$$
12.96. From S = 15.66 mm to 138.0 mm.
12.100. $(\boldsymbol{V}_1 - \boldsymbol{V}_C)_{at\ t=2} = -487\boldsymbol{i} + 15{,}450\boldsymbol{j} + 84.2\boldsymbol{k}$ ft/sec
$(\boldsymbol{V}_2 - \boldsymbol{V}_C)_{at\ t=2} = -581\boldsymbol{i} + 15{,}450\boldsymbol{j} + 319\boldsymbol{k}$ ft/sec.
12.102. $F = -30.822$ kN.
12.104. 2.01m.
12.106. .1171 m/sec.
12.108. $\Delta t = 48.9$ sec.
12.112. 6620 miles 1.123 hours 24,290 mph.
12.114. $(\Delta V)_1 = 1131$ km/hour $(\Delta V)_2 = 1088$ km/hour.
12.116. $F = 199.5$ N.
12.118. $\Delta V = 408$ km/hour.
12.120. 224 lb.
12.122. $-Mg + K(r_0 - r) = M(\ddot{r} - r\dot{\theta}^2)$
$g\theta = r\ddot{\theta} + 2\dot{r}\dot{\theta}$.
12.124. $\boldsymbol{a}_c = 1.4(6t + 15)\boldsymbol{i} - 14\boldsymbol{k}$ ft/sec^2
$(x_c) - (x_c)_0 = 2498$ ft
$(y_c) - (y_c)_0 = 13.05$ ft.
$(z_c) - (z_c)_0 = -686$ ft.
12.126. $V = 0$.
12.128. $V = .484$ ft/sec.
12.130. 3130 ft/sec.
12.132. $V = 4.706$ m/sec.
12.134. 38.0 ft.
12.136. $\dot{s}_B = .309$ m/sec.
12.138. .5933 g's.

13.2. $V = 34.8$ ft/sec.
13.4. $V = 3.98$ m/sec.
13.6. $V = 6.04$ ft/sec.
13.8. $F = 19.6$ kN.
13.10. -45.2 m/sec^2.
13.12. $V = 6.002$ ft/sec.
13.14. $KE = 1334$ ft-lb.
13.16. $F = 1800$ lb.
13.18. .211 m/sec.
13.20. $\omega = 8.74$ rad/sec.
13.22. $d = 1.835$ m.
13.24. $d = .312$ m.
13.26. $V = 18.75$ m/sec.
13.28. $W = 121.0$ kN.
13.30. .288 ft.
13.32. 24.7 HP 16.57 kW.
13.34. Power $= 932\, a_0 V + \kappa V^3$
for $a_0 = 0$ Power $= \kappa V^3$.
13.36. $\Delta t = 6.44$ sec.
13.38. 8333 N.
13.40. $V = 3.40$ ft/sec.
13.42. $\delta = 106.1$ mm.
13.46. $d = -5z \cos x + xy + 2y^2 z + \text{const.}$
13.48. $V = 6.397$ ft/sec.
13.50. $V = .389$ m/sec.
13.52. $\dot{V} = 107.3$ ft/sec^2.
13.54. $h = 23.33$ ft.
13.56. $V = 34.80$ ft/sec.
13.58. $\delta = 1.518$ ft.
13.60. $V = 55.8$ ft/sec.
13.62. $V = 2.853$ m/sec.
13.64. $\delta = 2.398$ mm.
13.66. $d = 149.12$ m $F_{AB} = 58{,}955$ N $F_{CB} = 29{,}477$ N.
13.68. $V = \left[\frac{q}{L}\left(L^2 - a^2\right)\right]^{\frac{1}{2}}$.
13.70. $(\mathcal{W}_K)_{\text{internal}} = -\frac{1}{2}\frac{\mathcal{W}_1}{g}V_0^2 + 5.7\left(\mathcal{W}_1 + \mathcal{W}_2\right)$.
13.72. $KE = 61.02$ N-m.
13.74. $V = 6.78$ ft/sec.
13.78. $KE = .1069$ ft-lb ERROR = 1.952%.
13.80. $V = 6.138$ m/sec.
13.82. $d = 1.835$ m.
13.84. $F = 1.863$ lb $f = .621$ lb.
13.86. $(V_C)_f = 20.72$ ft/sec $(V_C)_{f=0} = 25.4$ ft/sec.
13.88. $F_C = 31.2$ lb.
13.90. $\omega = 6.83$ rad/sec.
13.92. $d = 3.823$ m $\begin{cases} f = 0 \text{ horizontal surface} \\ f = 83.35 \text{ N on incline} \end{cases}$
13.94. $V = 1.414$ m/sec $f_{\text{total}} = 915$ N.
13.96. $\omega = 3.17$ rad/sec.
13.98. $V_A = 12.94$ ft/sec $a = 4.29$ ft/sec^2.
13.100. $\omega = .499$ rad/sec.
13.102. 1.157 HP Power Input = 6.70 HP.
13.104. .558 HP.
13.106. $\theta = 48.0°$.
13.110. 5471 HP.
13.112. 15,900 HP.
13.114. $V = 1.716$ m/sec 58.5 N.
13.116. $\omega = 11.90$ rad/sec $f = 130.0$ N.
13.118. 114.9 ft/sec.
13.120. $\mathcal{W} = 17.63$ lb $F_n = 36.33$ N.
13.122. $V = 9.17$ m/sec $f = 85.7$ N.
13.124. $V = 2.32$ ft/sec.
13.126. $V = .4937$ m/s $f = 186.1$ N.

14.2. $V = 333i + 400j + 4{,}000k$ m/sec.
14.4. $V = 177.1$ ft/sec to left.
14.6. $t = 1.631$ sec $\Delta t = .7136$ sec.
14.8. $F_{AV} = 12.8i - 14.40j + 48.0k$ N.
14.10. $I = -.964i - .388j + .97k$ lb-sec.
14.12. $t = .646$ sec.
14.14. $t = 7.55$ sec $t = 13.21$ sec $F = 25{,}233$ N.
14.16. 1.961 HP.
14.18. $T_2 = 21.70$ lb.
14.20. $T_x = 76.7$ lb-sec.
14.22. $\Delta V = 10.00$ km/hour.
14.24. $V = .402$ m/sec.
14.28. $V_A = 5.183$ m/sec $V_B = 10.37$ m/sec.
14.30. 4.905 m/sec.
14.32. $F_\omega = 965$ lb.
14.34. $(V_B)_f = 4.10$ m/sec $\Delta KE = 18.15$ N-m.
14.36. $(V_A)_f = -1.130$ m/sec.
14.38. $\delta = 5.610$ in.
14.42. $\theta = 11.81°$.
14.44. $\delta = .750$ m.
14.46. 4.648 m/s $\delta = .36$ m.
14.48. $\delta = .7990$ m.
14.50. 14.86 ft/sec.
14.52. $(V_A)_f = -1.88i + 14.14j$
$(V_B)_f = 8.01j$.
14.56. $\Delta = .05142$ m $\delta = .059$ m.
14.58. 50.5°.
14.60. Drag $= 3.53\ mnV^2$.
14.62. Drag $= .468\ mnV^2$.
14.64. $F_x = \frac{4}{3}\frac{\pi s R^2}{c}$ 3.53N.
14.66. 37,306 km/hour.
14.68. $d = .205$ m.
14.70. $\omega_2 = 8.292$ rad/sec.
14.72. $\omega_2 = 5.107$ rad/sec.
14.74. 4071 mi/hour.
14.76. 6210 km/hour.
14.78. $h = 183$ km.
14.80. $(\Delta V)_1 = 1135$ km/hour
$(\Delta V)_2 = 1085$ km/hour.
14.82. 6354 km 9373 km.
14.84. $r_{max} = 32{,}534$ miles.
14.86. $r_A = 8900$ miles $\Delta V = 7285$ mph.
14.88. $V_0 = 741$ km/hour
$V_r = 826$ km/hour.
14.90. $P = 2.02i - .0435j + .596k$ slug-ft/sec
$H_0 = 1.975i - 1.326j - 25.8k$ slug-ft²/sec
$H_a = -5.61i - 16.76j - 1.212k$ slug-ft²/sec.
14.92. $\dot{\omega} = -20.0$ rad/sec².
14.94. $\dot{\omega} = \dfrac{T - 852Vm\omega}{4m(s_1^2 + s_2^2)}$
14.98. $\omega = 593$ cycles/sec $= 3725$ rad/sec.
14.100. 21.0 m/sec².
14.102. $H = 34.4 \times 10^6$ slug-ft²/sec.
14.104. $\dot{\omega} = .0375$ rad/sec² $\dot{V}_C = .1749i + .262j$ m/sec².
14.106. $\dot{\omega} = 2.01$ rad/sec².
14.108. $V = 27.7$ ft/sec.
14.110. $(V_2)_t = 12{,}975$ mi/hour
$(V_2)_r = 21{,}370$ mi/hour
$\Delta V = 31{,}190 - 17{,}260 = 13{,}930$ mi/hour.
14.112. $x = 4.464$ m.
14.114. $V_f = 34.35$ ft/sec.
14.116. $x = -20{,}566$ m.
14.118. $V = 2.778$ ft/sec $= 1.645$ knots.
14.120. $\delta = 2.238$ ft $V_B = .1791$ ft/sec.
14.122. $\theta_A = 5.47°$ $\theta_B = 29.9°$.
14.124. $V_f = 161i + 170.8j - 26.1k$ ft/sec.
14.126. $(V_A)_f = 26.6$ m/sec. $(V_B)_f = 31.1$ m/sec.
14.128. $H_0 = 7.57$ slug-ft²/sec $P_0 = 0$.
14.130. $H_0 = 5480$ slug-ft²/sec.
14.132. $h = 3000$ km $r_{max} = 9371$ km.
14.134. $F = 2329$ lb.
14.136. $V = 18$ km/hour $\Delta KE = 3.24$ joules.
14.138. $E = 58.96$ Mev $l_B = -.325$ $m_B = .18746$
$n_B = -.97417$.

15.4. $-10.66i + 7.31j - 35.18k$ m/s.
15.6. $-521i + 108.7j + 65.2k$ m/s.
15.8. $\dot{\rho} = 10i + 5j$ mm/sec
$\ddot{\rho} = -1250k$ mm/sec².
15.10. $\omega = .940i + .342j + 1.8k$ rad/sec.
$\dot{\omega} = -.616i + 1.692j$ rad/sec².
15.12. $\omega = -.4i + 170.8j - 170.8k$ rad/sec.
$\dot{\omega} = -.2i - 68.32j - 68.32k$ rad/sec².
15.14. $\dot{\omega} = 3.14i + 1356j$ rad/sec²
$\ddot{\omega} = 407j + 14{,}200k$ rad/sec³.
15.16. $\omega = -121.6j$ rad/sec.
$\dot{\omega} = 3823i$ rad/sec².
15.18. $\dot{\omega} = .12j$ rad/sec²
$\ddot{\omega} = -.024i$ rad/sec³.
15.20. $V_A = .5i + .1212j$ m/s
$\omega = .4788$ rad/sec.
15.22. $\dot{\omega} = .18i - .1j + .2k$ rad/sec².
15.24. $\dot{V} = -20.5i - 2.14j + 17.10k$ m/sec².
15.26. $V = -243i + 207j + 25k$ m/sec.
15.28. $\omega = 56.7$ rad/sec $V_B = 29j - 12.03k$ m/sec.
15.30. $V_A = -2$ ft/sec.
15.32. $\omega = 4$ rad/sec $V_D = -6i - 19j$ m/sec.
15.34. $\omega_C = -10$ rad/sec.
15.36. $V_C = -.548i - .373j$ m/sec
$a_C = -43.4i - 63.7j$ m/sec².

15.38. $\omega_{AB} = -9.33$ rad/sec $\quad V_B = -12.38\boldsymbol{j} - 7.149\boldsymbol{k}$ m/sec.

15.40. $\omega_{BA} = -54.7$ rad/sec $\quad V_A = 79.8$ ft/sec.

15.44. $V_y = 14.66$ m/sec $\quad \omega = -5$ rad/sec.

15.46. $V_B = 11.95\boldsymbol{i} - 4.949\boldsymbol{j}$ m/sec

$\boldsymbol{a}_B = -57.77\boldsymbol{i} - 57.77\boldsymbol{j}$ m/sec^2

$\dot{\theta} = 2.625$ rad/sec.

15.48. $\omega_{AB} = -.609$ rad/sec $\quad \dot{\omega}_{AB} = 14.71$ rad/sec^2.

15.50. $V_B = 5.03\boldsymbol{i} + 2\boldsymbol{j} - 3\boldsymbol{k}$ m/sec.

15.52. $V_D = -.5\boldsymbol{i} - 14.7\boldsymbol{j} - 2.710\boldsymbol{k}$ ft/sec

$\boldsymbol{a}_D = -1.25\boldsymbol{j} + 10\boldsymbol{k}$ ft/sec^2.

15.54. $\boldsymbol{\omega}_{AB} = -0.0176\boldsymbol{k}$ rad/sec

$\dot{\boldsymbol{\omega}} = -4.34 \times 10^{-4}\boldsymbol{k}$ rad/sec^2.

15.56. $\omega_A = 3.643$ rad/sec

$\dot{\omega}_A = -6.45$ rad/sec^2.

15.58. $\omega = 1.273$ rad/sec $\quad V_C = 2.163$ m/sec.

15.60. $V = 1.156$ m/sec.

15.62. $V_A = 5.478$ m/sec $\quad a_A = -929.6$ m/sec^2.

15.64. $\omega_H = 3.93$ rad/sec $\quad \dot{\omega}_H = 20.7$ rad/sec^2.

15.66. $\omega_C = 5.00$ rad/sec.

15.68. $\omega_{AB} = -5$ rad/sec $\quad \dot{\omega}_{AB} = -360.8$ rad/sec^2.

15.70. $\boldsymbol{V}_{XYZ} = 8.86\boldsymbol{i} + 5\boldsymbol{j}$ m/sec.

15.72. $\boldsymbol{V}_{XYZ} = -17.32\boldsymbol{i} - 10\boldsymbol{j} - 50\boldsymbol{k}$ ft/sec.

15.74. $\boldsymbol{V}_{XYZ} = 1.30\boldsymbol{i} + 1.8\boldsymbol{j} + .130\boldsymbol{k}$ m/sec.

15.76. $\omega_1 = 15.40$ rad/sec $\quad \omega_2 = -31.37$ rad/sec.

15.78. $\omega_1 = 1.985$ rad/sec.

15.80. $\boldsymbol{V}_{XYZ} = -2.05\boldsymbol{i} + 4.92\boldsymbol{j} - 2.66\boldsymbol{k}$ m/sec.

15.82. $\boldsymbol{V}_{\perp \text{ barrel}} = -.908\boldsymbol{i} - .5253\boldsymbol{j} - .6\boldsymbol{k}$ m/sec.

15.84. $\boldsymbol{V}_{XYZ} = 4.00\boldsymbol{i}$ m/sec.

15.86. $V_{XYZ} = 37.9$ ft/sec rel. to ground

$V_{xyz} = 9.813$ ft/sec rel. to rod.

15.88. $V_{xyz} = 3.756$ m/sec $\quad V_{XYZ} = 7.165$ m/sec.

15.90. $\omega_D = 9.028$ rad/sec.

15.92. $\boldsymbol{V}_{XYZ} = 50\boldsymbol{i} - 5\boldsymbol{j} - 20\boldsymbol{k}$ ft/sec.

$\boldsymbol{a}_{XYZ} = -100\boldsymbol{i} - 300\boldsymbol{j} - 35\boldsymbol{k}$ ft/sec^2.

15.94. $\boldsymbol{a}_{XYZ} = 2600\boldsymbol{i} - 173.2\boldsymbol{j} - 1732\boldsymbol{k}$ ft/sec^2.

15.96. $\boldsymbol{a}_{XYZ} = -161.9\boldsymbol{k}$ m/sec^2.

15.98. $\boldsymbol{a}_{XYZ} = -5.08\boldsymbol{i} + 2.314\boldsymbol{j} + 2.70\boldsymbol{k}$ m/sec^2.

15.100. $\boldsymbol{a}_{XYZ} = 1.950\boldsymbol{i} - 18.69\boldsymbol{j} - 1.207\boldsymbol{k}$ m/sec^2.

$|\boldsymbol{a}_{XYZ}| = 1.919$ g's.

15.102. $\boldsymbol{a}_{XYZ} = -25.6\boldsymbol{j} - 57.6\boldsymbol{k}$ m/sec^2.

15.106. $\boldsymbol{a}_{\perp\text{gun barrel}} = .403\boldsymbol{i} \quad .233\boldsymbol{j} - 1.647\boldsymbol{k}$.

15.108. $\boldsymbol{V}_{XYZ} = -1.113\boldsymbol{i} + .1202\boldsymbol{j}$ m/sec

$\boldsymbol{a}_{XYZ} = .0969\boldsymbol{i} - .1859\boldsymbol{j}$ m/sec^2.

15.110. $\boldsymbol{a}_{XYZ} = -1.204\boldsymbol{i} - 2.570\boldsymbol{j}$ ft/sec^2.

$|\boldsymbol{a}_{XYZ}| = .08814$ g's.

15.112. $\boldsymbol{a}_{XYZ} = -73.22\boldsymbol{i} - 112.63\boldsymbol{j} + 67.3\boldsymbol{k}$ m/sec^2.

15.114. $\boldsymbol{a}_{XYZ} = -.4\boldsymbol{j} + (-15\boldsymbol{j}) + 2(5\boldsymbol{i} + 20\boldsymbol{k}) \times (.2\boldsymbol{j}) + (.02\boldsymbol{i} - 10\boldsymbol{j}) \times (-.01\boldsymbol{j}) + (.5\boldsymbol{i} + 20\boldsymbol{k}) \times [(.5\boldsymbol{i} + 20\boldsymbol{j}) \times (-.01\boldsymbol{j})]$ m/sec^2.

15.116. $\boldsymbol{F} = -.51\boldsymbol{i} + .1359\boldsymbol{j} - .07176\boldsymbol{k}$ N.

15.118. $\boldsymbol{a}_{XYZ} = -15.50\boldsymbol{i} + .405\boldsymbol{j} - 7.80\boldsymbol{k}$ m/sec^2

$(\boldsymbol{a}_A)_{XYZ} = -1.05\boldsymbol{i} + .665\boldsymbol{j} - 2.2\boldsymbol{k}$ m/sec^2.

15.122. $\boldsymbol{F} = 12.42\boldsymbol{j}$ lb.

15.124. Axial force = 30.7 N compression

Bending moment = 27 N-m.

15.126. $F_{\text{axial}} = 1.791$ N.

15.128. $-125.7\boldsymbol{i}$ ft/sec^2 $\quad$ .732 lb in plus x direction.

15.130. $\dot{\boldsymbol{\omega}} = -4\boldsymbol{i} + 2\boldsymbol{j} + 30\boldsymbol{k}$ rad/sec^2.

15.132. $\omega_C = 2.07$ rad/sec $\quad \dot{\omega}_C = -1.799$ rad/sec^2.

15.134. $\boldsymbol{a}_{XYZ} = -300\boldsymbol{i} + 15\boldsymbol{j} - 300\boldsymbol{k}$ ft/sec^2.

15.136. 162.2 ft/sec^2.

15.138. $\omega_B = -.5077$ rad/sec

$\dot{\omega}_B = -1.0115$ rad/sec^2.

15.140. $\boldsymbol{V}_{XYZ} = 20\boldsymbol{i} - 30\boldsymbol{j}$ ft/sec

$\boldsymbol{a}_{XYZ} = 20\boldsymbol{i} + 5\boldsymbol{j} - 500\boldsymbol{k}$ ft/sec^2.

15.142. $\boldsymbol{V}_B = 1.500\boldsymbol{i} - 1.500\boldsymbol{j}$ m/sec.

15.144. $V_C = 10$ m/sec $\quad \omega_{CD} = 20$ rad/sec $\quad \omega_{BC} = 0$.

15.146. $\boldsymbol{V}_{XYZ} = 2\boldsymbol{j}$ m/sec

$\boldsymbol{a}_{XYZ} = -13.33\boldsymbol{k}$ m/sec^2.

16.2. 2.12 N-m.

16.4. 16.70 m down.

16.6. $F = .672$ lb.

16.8. $P = 678$ N.

16.10. $a_B = -3.27$ m/sec^2.

16.12. $t = .285$ sec.

16.14. $\ddot{\theta}_A = -.8657$ rad/sec^2.

16.16. $F_{AB} = 163.4$ N.

16.18. 552 Rev.

16.20. $\tau_{rr} = 71{,}833$ psi.

16.22. $F_x = 87.7$ lb $\quad F_y = 169.7$ lb.

16.24. $B_y = C_y = 2244$ N $\quad B_z = C_z = 5.27$ N.

16.26. $A_y = B_y = 3200$ lb.

16.28. $\dot{\theta}_A = -.9583$ rad/sec.

16.30. $\ddot{\theta} = \dfrac{2y}{L}$

16.32. $\ddot{\theta} = -49.97$ rad/sec^2.

16.34. $a_0 = -12.13$ ft/sec^2 $\quad \ddot{\theta} = -1.035$ rad/sec^2.

16.36. -2.08 m.

16.38. $\ddot{\theta} = -14.96$ rad/sec^2.

16.40. 28.5 rad/sec^2.

16.42. 1.442 m/sec^2.

16.44. .1056 ft.

16.46. $P = 1437$ lb.

16.48. 3.43 m/sec^2.

16.50. $f = .283\mathcal{W}$.

16.52. $f = 24.53$ N $\quad N = 85.0$ N.

16.54. .405 m/sec^2.

16.56. $T = 68.53$ lb.

16.58. $\boldsymbol{a} = \boldsymbol{0}$.

16.60. $\boldsymbol{a} = -2.512\boldsymbol{i} + 6.26\boldsymbol{j}$ m/sec^2.

16.64. 13.08 m/sec $\dot{\theta} = 10.90$ rad/sec.

16.66. $\ddot{X} = .1361$ ft/sec^2 $\ddot{Y} = 0$ $\ddot{\theta} = .6932$ rad/sec^2.

16.68. $V_0 = 7.732$ m/sec.

16.70. $P = 8.75$ N.

16.72. $BD = 49.5$ N $AC = 37.0$ N.

16.74. $\dot{X} = -3.343$ m/sec
$(\dot{X})_3 = -3.294$ m/sec.

16.76. $\ddot{\theta} = 19.32$ rad/sec^2 $\ddot{Y} = -16.100$ m/sec^2.

16.78. $\ddot{Y}_A = -2.18$ m/sec^2 $\ddot{Y}_C = 2.18$ m/sec^2.

16.80. $T_B = 246$ N $T_A = 201$ N.

16.82. $\dot{\omega} = 7.40$ rad/sec^2 $\ddot{X} = -7.40$ ft/sec^2.

16.84. $\ddot{\theta}_{BC} = -6.43$ rad/sec^2 $\ddot{\theta}_{AB} = 4.29$ rad/sec^2.

16.86. $\ddot{\theta}_{AB} = 6.54$ rad/sec^2.

16.88. $\boldsymbol{a}_A = 1.1308\boldsymbol{i} + .6529\boldsymbol{j}$ m/sec^2
$\dot{\omega} = .17125$ rad/sec^2
$\boldsymbol{a}_B = .52549\boldsymbol{i} + .04752\boldsymbol{j}$ m/sec^2.

16.90. .222 Rev.

16.92. $A_x = -32$ N
$A_y = -212.4$ N
$B_x = -176.6$ N
$B_y = -26.40$ N.

16.94. $B_x = 0$ $A_x = 0$
$B_y = -235$ N $A_y = -254$ N
$A_z = 50$ N.

16.96. $\dot{\omega} = -6.26$ rad/sec^2 $B_x = 6.90$ lb $B_y = 0$
$A_x = 28.9$ lb $A_y = 0$.

16.98. $B_x = 25$N $B_y = 60.2$ N
$A_x = 25$ N $A_y = -60.2$ N

16.100. $B_x = 200$ N $B_y = -21.93$ N
$A_x = 200$ N $A_y = -21.93$ N.

16.102. $M_x = -9.171$ N-m $V_x = -48.9$ N
$M_y = 20.9$ N-m $V_y = 8.66$ N
$M_z = -.3415$ N-m.

16.104. $r_3 = 1.260$ ft $\theta_3 = 249.5°$
$r_4 = 1.098$ ft $\theta_4 = 192.2°$.

16.106. $y_D = -.667$ in. $z_D = 0$
$y_C = 5.67$ in. $z_C = 0$.

16.108. $\theta_A = 270°$ $L_A = .318$ m.

16.110. $\theta_B = 223.1°$ $r_B = 1.727$ m
$\theta_4 = 254.3°$ $r_4 = 2.21$ m.

16.112. $T = 169.6$ lb.

16.114. $t = 9.174$ sec.

16.116. 16.90 m/sec^2.

16.118. –41 rad/sec^2.

16.120. 60.4 lb.

16.122. $D_x = 6.96$ N $D_y = 31.23$ N.

16.124. $\ddot{\theta}_A = -3.26$ rad/sec^2.

16.126. $\ddot{\theta} = .0580$ rad/sec^2
$X = 5$ m $Y = 5$ m.

16.128. $\boldsymbol{a}_D = 4.06\boldsymbol{i} - 7.20\boldsymbol{j}$ m/sec^2.

16.130. $N_A = 17.13$ lb $N_B = 38.9$ lb
$F_A = 3.43$ lb $F_B = 7.78$ lb.

16.132. $\ddot{\theta} = -18.34$ rad/sec^2.

16.134. $A_x = 0$ $A_y = -21.83$ lb
$A_z = 100$ lb.

16.136. $\theta_C = 226.2°$ $r_C = .256$ m
$\theta_D = 266.8°$ $r_D = .416$ m.

16.138. $A_x = -192.7$ N $A_y = 2500$ N
$M_A = 5647.5$ N-m.

17.2. 4627 ft-lb.

17.4. 24.5 N-m.

17.6. 45.8 N-m 4.954 N-m.

17.8. $KE = 18.95$ ft-lb.

17.10. $\omega = \left[\dfrac{8\mathcal{W}_2 a_g}{3\mathcal{W}_1 r^2 + 2\mathcal{W}_2 (r-a)^3}\right.$.

17.12. $V_B = -.575$ m/sec.

17.14. $\omega = 2.79$ rad/sec.

17.18. $V_D = 5.40$ m/sec.

17.20. $\omega_A = 20$ rad/sec $\omega_B = 10.0$ rad/sec.

17.22. $V_C = 11.93$ ft/sec.

17.24. $\omega_z = 2.79$ rad/sec.

17.26. $\Delta = .985$ ft.

17.30. $\dot{\theta}_H = 35.30$ rad/sec.

17.32. $V = 2.354$ m/s $f = 79.4$ N.

17.34. $V = 4.60$ m/sec $f = 7480$ N.

17.36. 25.3 rad/sec.

17.38. $V_A = 13.61$ ft/sec.

17.40. $(H_0)_x = 0$ $(H_0)_y = 12\pi\ \dfrac{\text{slug-ft}^2}{\text{sec}}$
$(H_0)_z = 74\pi\ \dfrac{\text{slug-ft}^2}{\text{sec}}$.

17.42. $(H_c)_x = 1.941$ kg-m^2/sec $(H_c)_y = .510$ kg-m^2/sec
$(H_c)_z = 0$.

17.44. $h = 1.016$ m.

17.46. $T_1 = 1130$ N $P = 678.1$ N.

17.48. $L = 8.47$ m.

17.50. $\omega = 2.732$ RPM.

17.52. $V_A = -27.3$ ft/sec.

17.54. $\omega = 9.09$ rad/sec.

17.56. $t = .0467$ sec.

17.58. $y_{max} = 1431$ m 116.1°.

17.62. $\omega_A = -108.7$ rad/sec.

17.64. $\omega = 9.90$ rad/sec.

17.66. $V_A = -11.04$ m/sec.

17.68. $(\omega_2)_f = -165.2$ rad/sec $(\omega_1)_f = 24.22$ rad/sec.

17.70. $\omega_f = 7.64$ rad/sec.

17.72. $\boldsymbol{V}_B = 1.542\boldsymbol{i} - 1.028\boldsymbol{j}$ m/sec.

17.74. $f = 15.05$ per sec.

17.76. -15.24 ft/sec $\omega_f = 60.9$ rad/sec.
17.78. $[(V_C)_y]_f = -12.39$ m/sec.
$[(V_C)_x]_f = 12.85$ m/sec.
17.80. 15.52 ft-lb.
17.82. $d = .1246$ m.
17.84. $V = 7.29$ ft/sec.
17.86. $(H_C)_x = -14{,}550 \dfrac{\text{lbm-ft}^2}{\text{sec}}$

$(H_C)_y = -24{,}700 \dfrac{\text{lbm-ft}^2}{\text{sec}}$

$(H_C)_z = -14{,}530 \dfrac{\text{lbm-ft}^2}{\text{sec}}$
17.88. 2.32 m/sec.
17.90. $\omega = 4.11$ rad/sec.
17.92. $V_E = -.3117\boldsymbol{i} - .434\boldsymbol{j}$ m/sec.
17.94. $\omega = 14.78$ rad/sec.

18.2. $\dot{\omega}_x = 12.19$ rad/sec^2
$\dot{\omega}_y = 7.31$ rad/sec^2
$\dot{\omega}_z = .030$ rad/sec^2.
18.4. $-.808\boldsymbol{j}$ ft-lb.
18.6. $149.8\boldsymbol{i}$ N-m.
18.8. $\boldsymbol{a} = -122.6\boldsymbol{i} - 5\boldsymbol{j} + 22.9\boldsymbol{k}$ m/sec^2.
18.10. Shear force = 32.2 lb
Tensile force = 25,000 lb
Moment = -2178 ft-lb.
18.14. $\boldsymbol{M} = 8.35\boldsymbol{i} - .586\boldsymbol{j} + 3.59\boldsymbol{k}$ N-m.
18.16. $\boldsymbol{M} = -148.8\boldsymbol{i} + 300\boldsymbol{j} - 108.6\boldsymbol{k}$ N-m.
18.18. Moment about the center of mass of *CD* due to motion of *CD*: $M_{CD} = -3.18 \times 10^{-9}$ N-m
Moment about the center of mass *EG* due to motion of *EG*: $M_{EG} = -1.147 \times 10^{-9}$ N-m.
18.20. $\boldsymbol{M} = -2462\boldsymbol{i} - 1106\boldsymbol{j} - 2212\boldsymbol{k}$ N-m.
18.22. $\boldsymbol{M} = 1474\boldsymbol{i}$.
18.24. $T_x = 3.72$ N-m
$T_y = -.00524$ N-m
$T_z = -20.95$ N-m.
18.26. $\boldsymbol{M} = 149.4\boldsymbol{i}$ N-m.
18.28. $\boldsymbol{M} = -2390 \sin .419t\boldsymbol{i} + 4.29 \times 10^4 \cos .419t\boldsymbol{j}$ N-m.
18.30. $\boldsymbol{M} = 8.35\boldsymbol{i} - .586\boldsymbol{j} + 3.59\boldsymbol{k}$ N-m.
18.32. $\dot{\psi} = 2$ rad/sec
$\dot{\theta} = 0$
$\dot{\phi} = -13.33$ rad/sec.
18.34. 1744 rad/sec.
18.36. $T_x = -24.9$ ft-lb.
18.38. $\dot{\psi} = .00283$ rad/sec
Result is an angular acceleration in the direction of the torque equal to .0488 rad/sec^2.
18.42. $\dot{\psi} = -5.43$ rad/sec;
5.82 rad/sec.
18.44. 1.663 ft-lb/rad.
18.46. .504 N-m
from the posts in a direction normal to the plate.
18.48. $\boldsymbol{H} = 32.4\boldsymbol{i} + 93.2\boldsymbol{k} \dfrac{\text{lbm} - \text{ft}^2}{\text{sec}}$
18.50.
$$\frac{\dot{\psi}}{\sin\alpha} = \frac{\dot{\phi}}{\sin(\phi - \alpha)}$$
$$\omega^2 = \dot{\psi} + \dot{\phi}^2 + 2\dot{\phi}\dot{\psi}\cos\theta$$
$$\dot{\phi} = \frac{I_{xx} - I_{zz}}{I_{zz}}\dot{\psi}\cos\theta$$
18.52. $\dot{\psi} = 1.314$ rad/sec
$\dot{\phi} = 2$ rad/sec
$\theta = 12.9°$.
18.54. $\dot{\psi} = 3.26$ rad/sec.
18.56. $\theta = 13.98°$
$\dot{\phi} = -.0442$ rad/sec.
$\dot{\psi} = .1264$ rad/sec.
18.58. $\theta = 128.3°$
$\dot{\phi} = -1.194$ rad/sec.
18.60. $\boldsymbol{M} = -29.5\boldsymbol{i} + 3186\boldsymbol{j} + .409\boldsymbol{k}$ N-m.
18.61. $\boldsymbol{K} = -.1262\boldsymbol{i} + .1433\boldsymbol{j} + 9.17\boldsymbol{k}$ N
$\boldsymbol{H} = -.700\boldsymbol{i} + .1433\boldsymbol{j}$ N.
18.62. 15.54 rad/sec.
18.63. 2310 rad/sec or .0654 rad/sec.
18.64. $R = 62.7$ m.
18.65. $\theta = 47.3°$
$\dot{\phi} = -.1283$ rad/sec
$\dot{\psi} = .525$ rad/sec.
18.66. $\omega_x = .3$ rad/sec
$\omega_y = .1895$ rad/sec
$\omega_z = .423$ rad/sec.
18.67. $\dot{\psi} = .2064$ rad/sec
Z in direction of z axis.
18.68. $\dot{\phi} = 1.905$ rad/sec
$\theta = 71.87°$.

19.4. $K_2 = 3.90$ N-m.
19.6. $\omega_n = \sqrt{\dfrac{2\mu g}{L}}$ rad/sec
19.8. .438 cycles/sec.
19.10. .557 cycles/sec.
19.12. 19.81 rad/sec; 8.34 N/mm.
19.14. 28.6 rad/sec.

19.16. $\ddot{r} + \left(\frac{K}{m} - \omega^2\right)r = \frac{Kr_0}{m}$

$\omega_n = \sqrt{\frac{K}{M} - \omega^2}$

19.18. 16.05 rad/sec; 87.9 rad/sec.

19.20. 1.420 sec.

19.22. $\ddot{x} + .326x + .01230x^2 + .0001550x^3 = 0$

$\omega = .0909$ cycles/sec.

19.24. $(K_t)_{eq} = 2.43 \times 10^5$ N-m/rad

$\omega_n = 304$ rad/sec

$\theta = -7.42°$.

19.26. $\omega_n = 1$ cycle/sec.

19.28. 7.88 cycles/sec

$\theta = -.342°$.

19.30. $\omega_n = \sqrt{\frac{2Kr^2}{R^2\left[(M/2) - (W_1/g)\right]}}$

19.32. $\frac{1}{12}\frac{W}{g}L^2\ddot{\theta} + \frac{Wd^2}{4l}\theta = 0$

$\omega_n\sqrt{\frac{3d^2g}{lL^2}}$ rad/sec.

19.34. 235 rad/sec.

19.36. 1.377°.

19.38. $P = [(2KL - W/2)]$

19.40. 2.32 rad/sec.

19.42. $k = .518$ m.

19.44. $\mu = 0.809$.

19.46. $\omega_n = \sqrt{\frac{K(r_1 + r_2)^2}{(W/g)(k^2 + r_1^2)}}$

$f_{\max} \frac{\left[I_{00}\omega^2 - K(r_1 + r_2)(r_2)\right]A}{r_1}$

19.48. $\omega_n = \sqrt{\frac{2Kr^2}{\frac{1}{2}MR^2 + (W_1/g)R^1}}$.

19.50. 2.32 rad/sec.

19.52. $\omega_n = \sqrt{\frac{(3 + \sin\alpha)g}{L}}$.

19.54. $\omega_n = \sqrt{\frac{g}{(R - r_1)\left[1 + (k^2/r_1^2)\right]}}$.

19.56. $x = .004185$ ft.

19.58. .00992 m.

19.64. 110.7 m $V = 51.4$ km/hr.

19.66. $\omega = 15.95$ rad/sec.

19.68. 17.89 N $K = 553 \times 10^3$ N/m.

19.70. 9.805 N.

19.72. 1.808 rad/sec.

19.74. −11.28°.

19.76. $m\ddot{x} + 2c\dot{x} + (K_1 + K_2)x = 0$

$c_{cr} = \sqrt{\frac{W}{g}(K_1 + K_2)}$

19.78. $x(5) = -.211$ in. $f \cong 6.92$ rad/sec.

19.82. $t = .321$ sec.

19.84. $\omega = .0225$ cycle/sec.

19.86. $e^{-.311\tau}\left[\left(-.05 - \frac{.0155}{\alpha}\right)e^{\alpha\tau} + \right.$

$\left.\left(-.05 + \frac{0.155}{\alpha}\right)e^{\alpha\tau}\right] = 0$ (I)

$e^{-.311\tau}\left[(-.05\alpha - .01555)e^{\alpha\tau} - \right.$

$\left.(-.05\alpha + .01555)e^{-\alpha\tau}\right]$

$-.311e^{-.311\tau}\left[\left(-.05\frac{.01555}{\alpha}\right)e^{\alpha\tau}\right.$

$\left. + \left(-.05 + \frac{.0155}{\alpha}\right)e^{\alpha\tau}\right] = 0$ (III)

19.90. 8.73 lb/in.

19.92. .000705 m.

19.94. 2 degrees of freedom $\ddot{x} + 451x - 773\theta = 0$

$\ddot{\theta} - 386x + 8120\theta = 0$.

19.97. $K_3 = 799$ N/m.

19.98. 1.972 in.; 80.03 in.

19.99. 2.35 rad/sec.

19.100. 48.2 rad/sec.

19.101. $k = .748$ m.

19.102. $\omega_n\sqrt{\frac{6g}{L}}$

19.103. $\omega = 19.80$ rad/sec.

19.104. $W = 64.6$ N.

19.105. $\theta_0 = .0608$ rad.

19.106. .003014 rad.

19.107. .221 sec.

19.108. $A = .001454$ m

$(F_{tr})_{\max} = 337$ N.

19.109. 23.6 rad/sec

.01115 m

$c = 192.0$ N-sec/m.

Index

SI UNIT PREFIXES

Multiplication Factor	Prefix	Symbol	Pronunciation	Term
1 000 000 000 000 = 10^{12}	tera	T	as in *terra*ce	one trillion
1 000 000 000 = 10^{9}	giga	G	jig ′a (*a* as in *a*bout)	one billion
1 000 000 = 10^{6}	mega	M	as in *mega*phone	one million
1 000 = 10^{3}	kilo	k	as in *kilo*watt	one thousand
100 = 10^{2}	hecto	h	heck ′toe	one hundred
10 = 10	deka	da	deck ′a (*a* as in *a*bout)	ten
0.1 = 10^{-1}	deci	d	as in *deci*mal	one tenth
0.01 = 10^{-2}	centi	c	as in *senti*ment	one hundredth
0.001 = 10^{-3}	milli	m	as in *mili*tary	one thousandth
0.000 001 = 10^{-6}	micro	μ	as in *micro*phone	one millionth
0.000 000 001 = 10^{-9}	nano	n	nan ′oh (*an* as in *an*t)	one billionth
0.000 000 000 001 = 10^{-12}	pico	p	peek ′oh	one trillionth

PROPERTIES OF VARIOUS AREAS

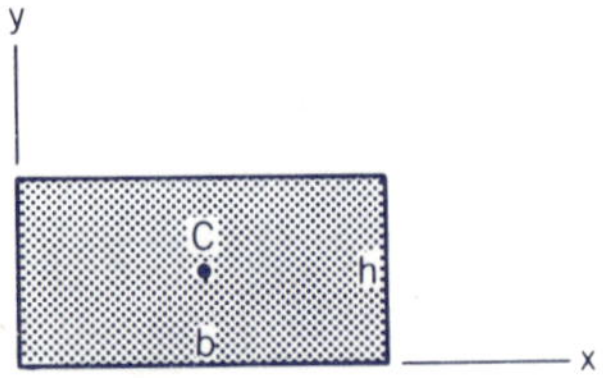

Rectangle

$$A = bh \qquad x_c = \frac{b}{2} \qquad y_c = \frac{h}{2}$$

$$(I_{xx})_c = \frac{1}{12}bh^3$$

$$(I_{yy})_c = \frac{1}{12}hb^3$$

$$(I_{xy})_c = 0$$

$$J_c = \frac{1}{12}bh(b^2 + h^2)$$

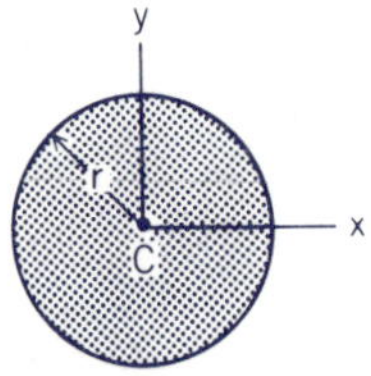

Circle

$$A = \pi r^2 \qquad x_c = 0 \qquad y_c = 0$$

$$(I_{xx})_c = \frac{1}{4}\pi r^4$$

$$(I_{yy})_c = \frac{1}{4}\pi r^4$$

$$J_c = \frac{1}{2}\pi r^4$$

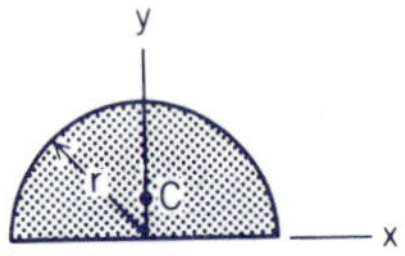

Semi circle

$$A = \frac{\pi r^2}{2} \qquad x_c = 0 \qquad y_c = .424r$$

$$(I_{xx})_c = .00686\,d^4$$

$$(I_{yy})_c = \frac{1}{8}\pi r^4$$

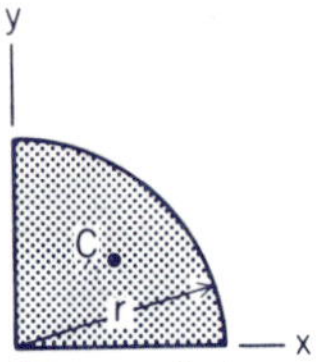

Quarter circle

$$A = \frac{\pi r^2}{4} \qquad x_c = \frac{4r}{3\pi} \qquad y_c = \frac{4r}{3\pi}$$

$$(I_{xx})_c = .0549\,r^4$$

$$(I_{yy})_c = .0549\,r^4$$

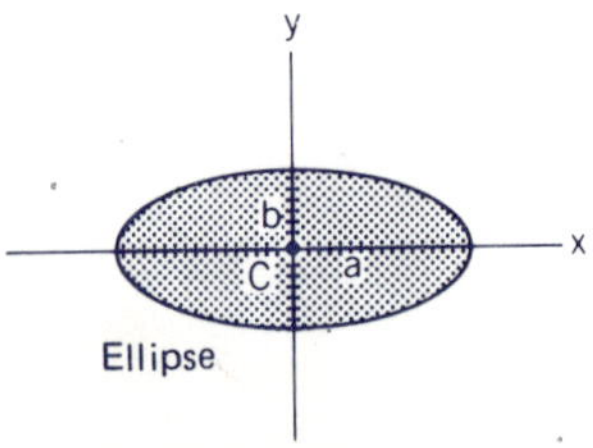

Ellipse

$$A = \pi ab$$

$$(I_{xx})_c = \frac{\pi ab^3}{4}$$

$$(I_{yy})_c = \frac{\pi ba^3}{4}$$